Contemporary Authors

Contemporary Authors

**A Bio-Bibliographical Guide to
Current Writers in Fiction, General Nonfiction,
Poetry, Journalism, Drama, Motion Pictures,
Television, and Other Fields**

FRANCES C. LOCHER
Editor

MARTHA G. CONWAY
B. HAL MAY
DAVID VERSICAL
Associate Editors

volume 105

GALE RESEARCH COMPANY • THE BOOK TOWER • DETROIT, MICHIGAN 48226

EDITORIAL STAFF

Christine Nasso, *General Editor, Contemporary Authors*

Frances C. Locher, *Editor, Original Volumes*

Martha G. Conway, B. Hal May, and David Versical, *Associate Editors*

Anne M. Guerrini and Les Stone, *Senior Assistant Editors*

Tim Connor, Charity Anne Dorgan, Diane L. Dupuis, Susan D. Finley,
Nancy S. Gearhart, Debra G. Jones, Michael L. LaBlanc, Nancy Pear,
Lillian S. Sims, Mary Sullivan, and Susan M. Trosky, *Assistant Editors*

Denise M. Cloutier, Shirley Kuenz, Christine J. May,
Norma Sawaya, and Shirley Seip, *Editorial Assistants*

Linda Metzger, *Index Coordinator*

Adele Sarkissian, *Contributing Editor*

John F. Baker, Trisha Gorman, and Jean W. Ross, *Interviewers*

Andrea Geffner, Arlene True, and Benjamin True, *Sketchwriters*

Eunice Bergin, *Copy Editor*

Special recognition is given to the staff of
Young People's Literature Department, Gale Research Company

Frederick G. Ruffner, *Publisher*   James M. Ethridge, *Editorial Director*

Copyright © 1982 by
GALE RESEARCH COMPANY

Library of Congress Catalog Card Number 62-52046
ISBN 0-8103-1905-5
ISSN 0010-7468

Authors and Media People
Featured in This Volume

Hubert Aquin—Award-winning Canadian novelist, who died in 1977; one of Canada's most popular contemporary writers; *The Antiphonary* and *Hamlet's Twin* are among his best-selling novels.

Uri Avnery—Israeli journalist; editor-in-chief of *Ha'olam Hazeh*, a controversial magazine well known for its opposition to establishment politics and for its exposes of economic and political corruption in Israel.

Jean-Louis Barrault—Internationally acclaimed French actor, director, and mime; director of the official French theatre company; author of many books and play adaptations as well as *Memories for Tomorrow: The Memoirs of Jean-Louis Barrault.*

Maria Isabel Barreno—Portuguese writer; along with her two co-authors, imprisoned and tried for "abuse of press freedom" and "outrage to public decency" for publishing *The Three Marias: New Portuguese Letters.*

Peter Brook—Award-winning British director, playwright, and screenwriter; well known for his 1964 direction of "The Persecution and Assassination of Marat as Performed by the Inmates of the Asylum of Charenton Under the Direction of the Marquis de Sade."

Anatole Broyard—American book reviewer and feature writer for the *New York Times;* also author of two books, *Aroused by Books* and *Men, Women, and Other Anticlimaxes.*

Arthur Bryant—Renowned British historian and biographer; books include *King Charles II, The Medieval Foundation of Britain,* and *The Lion and the Unicorn.*

Harry Chapin—American singer, songwriter, poet, and dramatist, who died in 1981; "WOLD," "Taxi," and "Cat's in the Cradle" are among his well-known songs.

Michael Cimino—American screenwriter and motion picture director; screenplays include "Heaven's Gate" and the Academy Award-winning picture "The Deer Hunter."

Luther Davis—Award-winning playwright and producer of stage plays and motion pictures; author of the popular stage musical "Kismet."

John Wesley Dean III—Disbarred American lawyer; principal witness at the Senate hearings on the Watergate conspiracy; author of *Blind Ambition,* written after serving four months in prison for his role in the conspiracy.

Bernadette Devlin—Civil rights activist in Northern Ireland; author, at age twenty-two, of an autobiography, *The Price of My Soul.*

Christopher Durang—One of the "new American playwrights"; his play "Sister Mary Ignatius Explains It All for You" won an Obie Award, and "A History of the American Film" was nominated for a Tony Award.

Betty Ford—First Lady during the Gerald R. Ford presidency and author of her autobiography, *The Times of My Life.*

Michel Foucault—French scholar and cultural analyst; writer on the history of systems of thought; author of *The History of Sexuality, Madness and Civilization,* and other books.

Celia Gittelson—American publishing executive and first novelist; author of *Saving Grace,* "about a pope who runs away from the Vatican."

Katharine Graham—American newspaper executive; under her leadership the *Washington Post* rose to a position of prominence; currently board chairman of the Washington Post Company.

Mary Hazzard—Award-winning American free-lance writer; author of critically successful novel *Sheltered Lives.*

Jack Heifner—American playwright; author of "Vanities," the longest-running nonmusical in the history of Off-Broadway theatre.

Douglas R. Hofstadter—American computer science professor; author of prize-winning best-seller *Goedel, Escher, Bach: An Eternal Golden Braid.* (Sketch includes interview.)

Howard Kaminsky—American publisher; author of best-selling thriller *The Glow.* (Sketch includes interview.)

Joseph Kessel—Award-winning French author; "one of France's most widely read authors between the two world wars"; well-known books include *L'Equipage* and *The Horsemen.*

Hank Ketcham—American cartoonist; creator of the "Dennis the Menace" cartoon strip.

Osbert Lancaster—British cartoonist, artist, and author; creator of the cartoon character Maudie Littlehampton; also author of autobiographies, including the popular and critically acclaimed *With an Eye to the Future.*

Marghanita Laski—British journalist, broadcaster, critic, and writer; author of novels, including *Love on the Supertax, The Victorian Chaise-Longue,* and *Little Boy Lost,* and biographies, notably *Jane Austen and Her World* and *George Eliot and Her World.*

Stanislaw Lem—Best-selling Polish writer of science fiction, who was dubbed "the Titan of East European science fiction"; *Solaris, The Invincible, Memoirs Found in a Bathtub,* and *The Cyberiad* are among his works.

Mort R. Lewis—Award-winning American comedy writer and amateur historian, specializing in Lincolniana; contributor to books about Lincoln, *Lincoln for the Ages: An Anthology* and *Lincoln: A Contemporary Portrait.*

Herbert R. Lottman—Expatriate American journalist and

authority on international publishing; author of *Camus,* a definitive study of Albert Camus. (Sketch includes interview.)

Julia Markus—American academic and novelist; author of widely acclaimed novels *Uncle* and *American Rose.* (Sketch includes interview.)

Frank McGee—Well-known American broadcast journalist, who died in 1974; former anchorman for NBC News and host of "Today."

James R. Mellow—American writer; his book *Charmed Circle: Gertrude Stein and Company* was nominated for the National Book Award in 1974, and his book *Nathaniel Hawthorne in His Times* was nominated for the American Book Award in 1980.

Stanley Milgram—Noted American social psychologist, recognized for his experiments on human conformity and aggression; his book *Obedience to Authority* was nominated in 1975 for the National Book Award.

Roger Mudd—Award-winning American journalist; long associated with CBS as a congressional correspondent and as Walter Cronkite's substitute on the "CBS Evening News"; now anchoring the "NBC Nightly News."

Martin Mull—American humorist, songwriter, artist, and actor; gained notoriety as a character in the "Mary Hartman, Mary Hartman" television series, and later on "Fernwood 2-Tonight"; well known as lyricist-composer and performer of songs, including "Margie the Midget" and "Ventriloquist Love."

Anthony Newley—British entertainer, playwright, composer, and lyricist; won awards for song "What Kind of Fool Am I?" from his popular musical "Stop the World—I Want to Get Off."

Marsha Norman—Award-winning American playwright; author of Off-Broadway success "Getting Out."

Victoria Ocampo—Grande dame of Argentine letters, who died in 1979; founding editor of *Sur,* which introduced new Latin American writers while offering in Spanish the works of North American and European authors.

Iris Origo—Biographer of Anglo-Irish and American parentage living in Italy, who has been called "the best writer in English about things Italian"; author of well-received biographies, including *Leopardi, The Merchant of Prato,* and *The World of San Bernardino.*

Pa Chin—Pseudonym of Li Fei-kan, mainland Chinese author noted for his rejection of the Confucian family system and his interest in revolution; best-known works in translation include *The Family* and *Cold Nights.*

James Rado—Award-winning American librettist, lyricist, and composer; author of book and lyrics for "Hair," the first pop-rock musical.

Gerome Ragni—Award-winning American actor, librettist, and lyricist; author of book and lyrics for "Hair" and a later pop-rock musical, "Dude, the Highway Life."

Elliott Roosevelt—American businessman and writer; author of several books about his famous parents, Franklin and Eleanor Roosevelt, including *As He Saw It* and a trilogy, *An Untold Story, A Rendezvous With Destiny,* and *Mother R.*

Marcia Rose—American romantic novelist; author of steamy paperbacks, including *Prince of Ice, Music of Love,* and *Second Chances.*

Ken Russell—British screenwriter and director of motion picture and television productions, including critically and commercially acclaimed "Tommy" and "Women in Love."

Al Santoli—American Vietnam veteran and free-lance writer; author of well-received *Everything We Had: An Oral History of the Vietnam War by Thirty-Three American Soldiers Who Fought It.*

George Seaton—Academy Award-winning American screenwriter, producer, and director, who died in 1979; best known as the screenwriter of "The Song of Bernadette," "Miracle on 34th St.," and "Airport." (Sketch includes interview with Seaton's widow, Phyllis Seaton.)

Anne Seifert—American epidemiologist, psychologist, and writer; author of *His, Mine, and Ours: A Guide to Keeping Marriage From Ruining a Perfectly Good Relationship.*

William Shawcross—Award-winning British journalist; author of several books, including *Sideshow: Kissinger, Nixon, and the Destruction of Cambodia.*

Carly Simon—American Singer, composer, and recording artist; among her songs are "You're So Vain."

Frank Snepp—Former CIA chief strategic analyst in Saigon; author of *Decent Interval;* sued by the U.S. Government for violating a secrecy agreement he signed when he joined the CIA. (Sketch includes interview.)

Steve Tesich—Playwright and screenwriter best known for the popular motion picture "Breaking Away," which received an Academy Award for best original screenplay in 1979.

Jack W. Tracy—American writer and publisher; his book *Encyclopaedia Sherlockiana* received a special Edgar Award in 1978.

Margaret Truman—American writer; daughter of President Harry S. Truman; author of mysteries employing her knowledge of the nation's capital, including *Murder in the White House* and *Murder on Capitol Hill.*

Henry A. Wallace—American agronomist, who died in 1965; served as President Franklin D. Roosevelt's secretary of agriculture and later as U.S. vice-president; author of many books, including *America Must Choose* and *New Frontiers.*

C.V. Wedgwood—Distinguished British historian, translator, and biographer, specializing in seventeenth-century Britain; *The Great Rebellion* and *The King's Peace* are among her works.

Linda R. Weltner—American free-lance writer and photographer; author of well-received novels for young adults, *Beginning to Feel the Magic* and *The New Voice.*

Stark Young—Southern American writer, who died in 1963; best known for the Civil War novel *So Red the Rose* and for his theatrical criticism, which appeared in the *New Republic* for twenty-six years.

Preface

This volume of *Contemporary Authors* continues the steps begun with Volume 104 in broadening the series' scope to encompass authors deceased since 1900 whose works are still of interest to today's readers. (Previously, *CA* covered only living writers and authors deceased 1960 or later.) Since the great poets, novelists, short story writers, and playwrights of the early twentieth century are popular writers for study in today's high school and college literature courses, and since their writings continue to be analyzed by today's literary critics, these writers are in many ways as contemporary as the authors *CA* has featured up to this point. Students and others, not recognizing the stated scope of *CA*, have often questioned the absence from the series of major writers of the early twentieth century.

Therefore, future volumes of *CA* will contain full-length sketches on important authors who lived and wrote between 1900 and 1959. To begin providing information on authors from this period, most of whom will receive longer treatment later, we are including in *CA* volumes brief, one-paragraph entries on such authors. These brief entries are further explained in the section of the preface below headed "New Feature: Brief Entries."

The emphasis of *CA* will, of course, continue to be on living and recently deceased authors. A large proportion of the more than 1,400 entries in this volume (which bring to nearly 69,000 the number of authors now represented in the series) cover current, nontechnical writers in all genres—fiction, nonfiction, poetry, drama, etc.—whose books are issued by commercial, risk publishers or by university presses. Authors of books published only by known vanity or author-subsidized firms are ordinarily not included. Since native language and nationality have no bearing on inclusion in *CA*, authors whose writings are in languages other than English are included in *CA* if their works have been published in the United States or translated into English.

Although *CA* focuses primarily on authors of published books, the series also encompasses prominent persons in communications: newspaper and television reporters and correspondents, columnists, newspaper and magazine editors, photojournalists, syndicated cartoonists, screenwriters, television scriptwriters, and other media people.

No charge or obligation is attached to a *CA* listing. Authors are included in the series solely on the basis of the above criteria and their interest to *CA* users.

Compilation Methods

The editors make every effort to secure information directly from living authors through questionnaires and personal correspondence. If authors of special interest to *CA* users are deceased or fail to reply to requests for information, material is gathered from other reliable sources. Biographical dictionaires are checked (a task made easier through the use of Gale's *Biography and Genealogy Master Index* and other volumes in the "Gale Biographical Index Series"), as are bibliographical sources, such as *Cumulative Book Index* and *The National Union Catalog*. Published interviews, feature stories, and book reviews are examined, and often material is supplied by the authors' publishers. Whether prepared from questionnaires or through extensive research, all sketches on living writers are sent to the authors for review prior to publication. Sketches on recently deceased authors are sent to family members, agents, etc., if possible, for a similar review.

New Feature: Brief Entries

CA users have indicated that having some information, however brief, on authors not yet in the series would be preferable to waiting until full-length sketches can be prepared as outlined above under "Compilation Methods." Beginning with Volume 104, therefore, *CA* has introduced one-paragraph entries on authors, including both early twentieth-century and current writers, who presently do not have sketches in *CA*. These short listings, identified by the heading *BRIEF ENTRY*, highlight the author's career and writings and often provide a few sources where additional information can be found.

Brief entries are not intended to replace sketches. Instead, they are designed to increase *CA*'s comprehensiveness and thus better serve *CA* users by providing pertinent information about a large number of authors, many of whom will be the subjects of full sketches in forthcoming volumes.

This volume, for example, includes brief entries on living authors, such as Joel Agee, Thomas Eagleton, and Andrei Sakharov, for whom full-length sketches have not yet been compiled. As noted earlier in the preface, this volume also contains a substantial number of brief entries on authors deceased since 1900 who are still of interest to today's readers. Among the early twentieth-century authors in this volume who are slated for full sketch treatment in the future are Franz Kafka, H.L. Mencken, and Will Rogers.

Informative Sidelights

Numerous *CA* sketches contain Sidelights, which provide a personal dimension to the listing, supply information about the critical reception the authors' works have received, or both. Some authors work closely with *CA*'s editors to develop lengthy, incisive Sidelights, as in the case of Neil Ravin, a physician and novelist, who complains, "People keep asking whether I'm a writer or a doctor, as if the two were mutually exclusive." An inveterate reader of fiction, he admits, "I used to feel guilty reading a novel . . . but now I've got a financial excuse: I made more money this year from [my own novel] *M. D.* than I did from being an endocrine fellow." Ravin claims that *M. D.* "was conceived as the *Catch-22* of medical novels. But I couldn't bring myself to do it. It turned out, as I entered the trance-like sessions of memory in which the book was written, that the hospital experience was not, after all, as absurd as the war experience . . . . Basically the hospital is the polar opposite of war; it is man's last best work. Often it doesn't work, of course, but the whole idea springs from the noble side. So [my novel] changed from a farce, a depiction of absurdity, to a defense."

Publishing professionals find book writing a natural extension of their craft, like Quarto Communications president Tony Meisel, who tells *CA*'s editors: "All my writing is done for the sheer fun of it. Either the subject is one for which no satisfactory book has appeared or, in the case of [my] novel in progress, *The Golden Madonna,* because I have dreamed up such a devilishly obtuse plot as to warrant letting a segment of the public suffer with me." Commenting on the state of the art, Meisel maintains: "Despite all the blather written about the creative process, most inspired by unconscious self-indulgence, the act of writing is essentially a process of organization and intellectual rigor. I used to make my authors, in my editing days, submit detailed, multipaged outlines. They didn't like it, but they wrote better books for it . . . . Any author . . . must remember he or she is writing for an audience, a living, writhing marketplace. If an experience cannot be explained in comprehensible words and metaphors, that act has not been successfully presented to the reader."

CA's editors compile equally incisive Sidelights when authors and media people of particular interest to *CA* readers do not themselves supply Sidelights material or when demand for information about the critical reception their works have received is especially high. For instance, in her Sidelights on playwright Christopher Durang, assistant editor Charity Anne Dorgan reports that the humor of the born satirist "does not step back for comic perspective. It does not really see its target. It leaps onto it, instead, engages it totally and burrows its head into it as if it were a mock target; much in the same way that a mother is a mock target for a not terribly naughty child."

The acclaimed author of *Sheltered Lives* and *Idle and Disorderly Persons,* Mary Hazzard, adds to associate editor B. Hal May's remarks: "When my writing career is summarized it may seem to move in an unbroken line. However, in thinking carefully about it, I find that it has wavered, nearly died at times, and been influenced to a surprising degree by chance."

Iris Origo's Sidelights, by assistant editor Tim Connor, relay the critics' assessment that she is "the best writer in English about things Italian," "a biographer who understands the heart." The author of books on the lives of medieval and nineteenth-century Italians, Origo writes in a manner that brings her historical subjects to life again. She believes that "only by discovering what life 'felt like,' to our subject . . . can we become aware of him as a *person* at all."

Senior assistant editor Les Stone writes about Britain's most eccentric filmmaker, Ken Russell, claiming that throughout his erratic career, Russell has pursued his own vision, rarely compromising to critical expectations. Russell declares: "I follow this code: entertain first, instruct second. I've got lots of films inside me. Some of them will be good, some will be bad. But I'll go on, whatever the critics say about me."

And in her Sidelights on William Shawcross's book *Sideshow: Kissinger, Nixon, and the Destruction of*

Cambodia, assistant editor Mary Sullivan compiles a detailed analysis of America's Cambodian involvement from the late 1960's to the mid-1970's, which Shawcross implies in his book was a "real corruption of democratic processes."

These sketches, as well as others with Sidelights compiled by *CA*'s editors, provide informative and enjoyable reading.

Writers of Special Interest

CA's editors make every effort to include a substantial number of entries in each volume on active authors and media people of special interest to *CA*'s readers. Since *CA* also includes sketches on noteworthy deceased writers, a significant amount of work on the part of *CA*'s editors goes into the compilation of full-length entries on important deceased authors. Some of the prominent writers, both living and deceased, whose sketches are contained in this volume are noted in the list headed "Authors and Media People Featured in This Volume" immediately preceding the preface.

Exclusive Interviews

CA provides exclusive, primary information on certain authors in the form of interviews. Prepared specifically for *CA,* the never-before-published conversations presented in the section of the sketch headed *CA INTERVIEW* give *CA* users the opportunity to learn the authors' thoughts, in depth, about their craft. Subjects chosen for interviews are, the editors feel, authors who hold special interest for *CA*'s readers.

Authors and journalists in this volume whose sketches include interviews are Douglas R. Hofstadter, Howard Kaminsky, Herbert R. Lottman, Julia Markus, George Seaton, and Frank Snepp.

Obituary Notices Make *CA* Timely and Comprehensive

To be as timely and comprehensive as possible, *CA* publishes brief, one-paragraph obituary notices on deceased authors within the scope of the series. These notices provide date and place of birth and death, highlight the author's career and writings, and list other sources where additional biographical information and obituaries may be found. To distinguish them from full-length sketches, obituaries are identified with the heading *OBITUARY NOTICE.*

CA includes obituary notices for authors who already have full-length sketches in earlier *CA* volumes, and 31 percent of the obituary notices in this volume are for such authors. In addition, *CA* provides obituary notices for authors who do not yet have sketches in the series. Deceased authors of special interest presently represented only by obituary notices are scheduled for full-length sketch treatment in forthcoming *CA* volumes.

Contemporary Authors New Revision Series

A major change in the preparation of *CA* revision volumes began with the first volume of the newly titled *Contemporary Authors New Revision Series.* No longer are all of the sketches in a given *CA* volume updated and published together as a revision volume. Instead, sketches from a number of volumes are assessed, and only those sketches requiring *significant change* are revised and published in a *New Revision Series* volume. This change enables us to provide *CA* users with updated information about active writers on a more timely basis and avoids printing sketches from previous volumes in which there has been little or no change. As always, the most recent *CA* cumulative index continues to be the user's guide to the location of an individual author's revised listing.

Retaining *CA* Volumes

As new volumes in the series are published, users often ask which *CA* volumes, if any, can be discarded. Since the *New Revision Series* does not supersede any specific volumes of *CA,* all of the following must be retained in order to have information on all authors in the series:

- all revised volumes
- the two *Contemporary Authors Permanent Series* volumes
- *CA* Volumes 45-48 and subsequent original volumes

The chart following the preface is designed to assist users in keeping their collections as complete as possible.

Cumulative Index Should Always Be Consulted

The key to locating an individual author's listing is the *CA* cumulative index bound into the back of alternate original volumes (and available separately as an offprint). Since the *CA* cumulative index provides access to *all* entries in the *CA* series, the latest cumulative index should always be consulted to find the specific volume containing an author's original or most recently revised sketch.

For the convenience of *CA* users, the *CA* cumulative index also includes references to all entries in three related Gale series—*Contemporary Literary Criticism* (CLC), which is devoted entirely to current criticism of the works of today's novelists, poets, playwrights, short story writers, filmmakers, screenwriters, and other creative writers, *Something About the Author* (SATA), a series of heavily illustrated sketches on authors and illustrators of books for young people, and *Authors in the News* (AITN), a compilation of news stories and feature articles from American newspapers and magazines covering writers and other members of the communications media.

As always, suggestions from users about any aspect of *CA* will be welcomed.

IF YOU HAVE:	YOU MAY DISCARD:
1-4 First Revision (1967)	1 (1962) 2 (1963) 3 (1963) 4 (1963)
5-8 First Revision (1969)	5-6 (1963) 7-8 (1963)

Both 9-12 First Revision (1974)
   AND *Contemporary Authors Permanent Series,*
   Volume 1 (1975)
	9-10 (1964)
	11-12 (1965)

Both 13-16 First Revision (1975)
   AND *Contemporary Authors Permanent Series,*
   Volumes 1 and 2 (1975, 1978)
	13-14 (1965)
	15-16 (1966)

Both 17-20 First Revision (1976)
   AND *Contemporary Authors Permanent Series,*
   Volumes 1 and 2 (1975, 1978)
	17-18 (1967)
	19-20 (1968)

Both 21-24 First Revision (1977)
   AND *Contemporary Authors Permanent Series,*
   Volumes 1 and 2 (1975, 1978)
	21-22 (1969)
	23-24 (1970)

Both 25-28 First Revision (1977)
   AND *Contemporary Authors Permanent Series,*
   Volume 2 (1978)
	25-28 (1971)

Both 29-32 First Revision (1978)
   AND *Contemporary Authors Permanent Series,*
   Volume 2 (1978)
	29-32 (1972)

Both 33-36 First Revision (1978)
   AND *Contemporary Authors Permanent Series,*
   Volume 2 (1978)
	33-36 (1973)

37-40 First Revision (1979)	37-40 (1973)
41-44 First Revision (1979)	41-44 (1974)
45-48 (1974) 49-52 (1975) 53-56 (1975) 57-60 (1976) ↓ ↓ 105 (1982)	NONE: These volumes will not be super-seded by corresponding revised vol-umes. Individual entries from these and all other volumes appearing in the left column of this chart will be revised and included in the *New Revision Series.*
Volumes in the *Contemporary Authors New Revision Series*	NONE: The *New Revision Series* does not replace any single volume of *CA.* All volumes appearing in the left column of this chart must be retained to have in-formation on all authors in the series.

CONTEMPORARY AUTHORS

*Indicates that a listing has been compiled from secondary sources believed to be reliable, but has not been personally verified for this edition by the author sketched.

ABEL, Bob
See ABEL, Robert

*   *   *

ABEL, I(orwith) W(ilbur)   1908-

BRIEF ENTRY: Born August 11, 1908, in Magnolia, Ohio. American labor union official and author. Abel became international president of the United Steelworkers of America in 1965. He began as a steelworker and union organizer in the 1930's, participating in the "Little Steel" strike of 1937. Abel was a member of the pay board of the National Stabilization Program in 1971 and 1972 and a committee member of the President's Cost of Living Council in 1973. His many awards include the Franklin D. Roosevelt Award from the Four Freedoms Foundations, which he won in 1971. He wrote pamphlets on labor and unions, and a book, *Collective Bargaining: Labor Relations in Steel, Then and Now* (Carnegie-Mellon University, 1976). *Address:* 3216 Apache Rd., Pittsburgh, Pa. 15241; and Commonwealth Building, Pittsburg, Pa., 15222. *Biographical/critical sources: Current Biography,* Wilson, 1965; *New York Times,* July 31, 1971; *Biographical Dictionary of American Labor Leaders,* Greenwood Press, 1974; *Biography News,* Gale, November, 1974.

*   *   *

ABEL, Robert   1931-1981
(Bob Abel)

OBITUARY NOTICE—See index for *CA* sketch: Born January 22, 1931, in Middletown, Conn.; died of cancer, December 21, 1981, in New York, N.Y. Editor and author. A senior editor at Dell Publishing Company, Abel was responsible for the publication of Xaviera Hollander's best-seller *The Happy Hooker.* In 1972, after moving to the position of executive editor at Warner Books, Abel gained another notable work, *Sybil* by Flora Rheta Schreiber. He specialized in editing books on wine, food, and travel. After his death a scholarship fund was founded in his name. Abel was a contributor to magazines and newspapers, such as the *New York Times, Realist, Cavalier, Playboy, McCall's,* and *True.* His books include *The Funnies: An American Idiom, The American Cartoon Album, The Book of Beer,* and *The Beer Book.* Obituaries and other sources: *New York Times,* December 30, 1981; *Publishers Weekly,* January 8, 1981.

ABRAMS, Philip   1933(?)-1981

OBITUARY NOTICE: Born c. 1933; died October 31, 1981. Educator, sociologist, and author. Educated at Cambridge University, Abrams played a leading role in establishing and administrating the university's Social and Political Science Tripos. Under his chairmanship, the Department of Sociology and Social Policy at Cambridge became one of the leading centers of postgraduate study and research in Britain. Abrams was a member of the editorial board of *Past and Present* and was the editor of *Sociology,* the journal of the British Sociological Association. He wrote *The Origins of British Society* and co-wrote *Communes, Sociology and Society* with A. McCulloch. Obituaries and other sources: *London Times,* November 10, 1981.

*   *   *

ACHILLES
See LAMB, Charles Bentall

*   *   *

ADAM, Heribert   1936-

PERSONAL: Born July 1, 1936, in Offenbach, Germany (now West Germany). *Office:* Simon Fraser University, Burnaby, British Columbia, Canada.

CAREER: Associated with Institute of Social Research, Frankfurt, West Germany, 1961-65; Simon Fraser University, Burnaby, British Columbia, professor of sociology, 1968—. Formerly associated with University of Natal, Durban, South Africa. Visiting professor at universities in Germany, Egypt, and the United States.

WRITINGS: Suedafrika, Suhrkamp, 1969, 4th edition, 1977; *Modernizing Racial Domination: The Dynamics of South African Politics,* University of California Press, 1971; (editor) *South Africa: Sociological Perspectives,* Oxford University Press, 1971; (with Hermann Giliomee) *Ethnic Power Mobilized: Can South Africa Change?,* Yale University Press, 1979.

BIOGRAPHICAL/CRITICAL SOURCES: New York Review of Books, October 31, 1974.

ADAMS, Frederick C(harles) 1941-

BRIEF ENTRY: Born June 3, 1941, in Montpelier, Vt. American historian, educator, and author. Adams joined the faculty of Drake University in 1973 and has been a professor of history there since 1976. His writings include *Economic Diplomacy: The Export-Import Bank and American Foreign Policy, 1934-1939* (University of Missouri Press, 1976). *Address:* Department of History, Drake University, Des Moines, Iowa 50311. *Biographical/critical sources: Directory of American Scholars,* Volume I: *History,* 7th edition, Bowker, 1978.

*   *   *

ADAMS, Mildred
See KENYON, Mildred Adams

*   *   *

ADAMS, Robert H(ickman) 1937-

PERSONAL: Born May 8, 1937, in Orange, N.J.; son of J. Ross (an actuary) and Lois (Hickman) Adams; married Kerstin Mornestam (a librarian), June 11, 1960. *Education:* University of Redlands, B.A., 1959; University of Southern California, Ph.D., 1965. *Home:* 326 Lincoln St., Longmont, Colo. 80501.

CAREER: Colorado College, Colorado Springs, assistant professor of English, 1962-70; free-lance photographer and writer, 1970—. *Awards, honors:* Photography fellow of National Endowment for the Arts, 1973 and 1978; Guggenheim fellow, 1973 and 1980; award of merit from American Association of State and Local History, 1975; award in the arts from governor of Colorado, 1979.

WRITINGS—Illustrated with own photographs: *White Churches of the Plains,* Colorado Associated University Press, 1970; *The Architecture and Art of Early Hispanic Colorado,* Colorado Associated University Press, 1974; *The New West,* Colorado Associated University Press, 1974; *Denver: A Photographic Survey of the Metropolitan Area,* Colorado Associated University Press, 1977; *Prairie,* Denver Art Museum, 1978; *From the Missouri West,* Aperture, 1980.

Other writings: *Beauty in Photography: Essays in Defense of Traditional Values,* Aperture, 1981.

WORK IN PROGRESS: Where Shall We Be?, a photographic essay about the Rocky Flats Nuclear Weapons Plant.

SIDELIGHTS: Robert Adams commented: "The suburban West (which is the subject of much of my work) is, from a moral perspective, depressing evidence that we have misused our freedom. There is, however, another aspect to the landscape, an unexpected glory. Over the cheap tracts and littered arroyos one sometimes sees a light as clean as that recorded by Timothy O'Sullivan. Since it owes nothing to our care, it is an assurance; beauty is final."

*   *   *

ADAMS, Willi Paul 1940-

PERSONAL: Born January 16, 1940, in Leipzig, Germany (now East Germany); son of Paul (a food store owner) and Elisabeth (a tailoress; maiden name, Junker) Adams; married Angela Meurer (a translator), July 10, 1968; children: Johannes. *Education:* Attended University of Bonn, 1960-62; Free University of Berlin, Ph.D., 1968. *Home:* Beerenstrasse 50, D-1000 Berlin 37, West Germany. *Office:* John F. Kennedy

Institute for North American Studies, Free University of Berlin, Lansstrasse 7, D-1000 Berlin 33, West Germany.

CAREER: Free University of Berlin, Berlin, West Germany, assistant professor of American history, 1971-72; University of Frankfurt, Frankfurt, West Germany, professor of American Studies, 1972-77; Free University of Berlin, professor of North American history, 1977—. Visiting professor at University of Chicago, 1978. Fellow of Charles Warren Center for Studies in American History, Harvard University, 1972, 1975-76, and Woodrow Wilson International Center for Scholars, 1980-81.

MEMBER: American Historical Association, Organization of American Historians, European Association of American Studies, German Association of American Studies, Verband der Historiker Deutschlands, Ranke Gesellschaft, Gesellschaft fuer Kanada-Studien, Immigration History Society, Canadian Historical Association, Berliner Wissenschaftliche Gesellschaft. *Awards, honors:* American Council of Learned Societies fellow, 1972; Bicentennial Prize from American Historical Association, 1976, for *The First American Constitutions.*

WRITINGS: Republikanische Verfassung und buergerliche Freiheit: Die Verfassungen and politischer Ideen der amerikanischen Revolution, Luchterhand Verlag, 1973, revised translation published as *The First American Constitutions: Republican Ideology and the Making of the State Constitutions in the Revolutionary Era,* University of North Carolina Press, 1980; (editor with Wolfgang J. Helbich) *Directory of European Historians of Canada and the United States: Addresses, Publications, Research in Progress,* John F. Kennedy Institute for North American Studies, Free University of Berlin, 1979; (contributor) Bernard Bailyn and John Hench, editors, *The Press and the American Revolution,* American Antiquarian Society, 1980; (contributor) Rob Kroes, editor, *The American Identity: Fusion and Fragmentation,* Amerika Instituut, University of Amsterdam, 1980.

Other writings: (Contributor) Heinrich August Winkler, editor, *Die grosse Krise in Amerika: Vergleichende Studien zur politischen Sozialgeschichte, 1929-1939* (title means "The Great Crisis in Comparative Studies in Political and Social History, 1929-1939"), Goettingen, 1973; (editor with wife, Angela Meurer Adams, and translator) *Die amerikanische Revolution in Augenzeugenberichten* (title means "The American Revolution in Eyewitness Accounts"), Deutscher Taschenbuchverlag, 1976; (editor) *Die deutschsprachige Auswanderung in die Vereinigten Staaten: Berichte ueber Forschungsstand und Quellenbestaende* (title means "The German-speaking Emigration to the United States: Reports on Source Material and the State of the Art"), John F. Kennedy Institute for North American Studies, Free University of Berlin, 1980; (translator with A. M. Adams, and contributor) Richard M. Nixon, *Memoiren,* Ullstein Verlag, 1981. Also contributor to *La Revolution americaine et l'Europe* (title means 'The American Revolution and Europe), edited by Claude Fohlen and Jacques Godechot, 1977. Contributor to history and American studies journals. Member of editorial board of *Amerikastudien/American Studies,* 1980—.

WORK IN PROGRESS: A book on the assimilation of German immigrants in the United States, 1830-1930, publication expected in 1984.

SIDELIGHTS: Adams told *CA:* "Teaching American history in West Germany is a constant challenge to examine some of the presuppositions which many of my American colleagues can afford to let stand unexamined. A prominent example is the 'uniqueness syndrome' in American historiography. The development of American society, it is assumed, is the result of such a unique combination of a natural environment and multi-ethnic population that comparisons with other national histories seem useless. For instance, to consider the Civil War as one of several wars of national unification of the nineteenth century from this point of view is sacrilegious. My European perspective, on the other hand, encourages a synoptic and comparative view of North American and West European history. The rigid division of labor among specialists between U.S. history, Canadian history, and the West European national stories, I think, should be overcome by transnational interpretations, not only in economic and diplomatic history, but also in social, intellectual, and cultural history.''

* * *

ADAMS, William Howard

BRIEF ENTRY: Born in Jackson County, Mo. American art collector and administrator, and author. Adams directed the national program of the National Gallery of Art and served as member of the board of advisers of Dumbarton Oaks. He has also been senior fellow at Harvard Institute and chairman of the Missouri Council on the Arts. His writings include *The Politics of Art: Forming a State Arts Council* (Arts Councils of America, 1966), *Atget's Gardens* (Doubleday, 1979), *The French Garden, 1500-1800* (Braziller, 1979), *The Eye of Thomas Jefferson,* and *Jefferson and the Arts. Address:* 2820 P St. N.W., Washington, D.C. 20007. *Biographical/critical sources: New York Review of Books,* October 14, 1976.

* * *

ADAM-SMITH, Patricia Jean   1926-
(Patsy Adam-Smith)

PERSONAL: Born May 31, 1926, in Gippsland, Victoria, Australia; daughter of Albert (a railway repairman) and Bridget (a railway station mistress) Adam-Smith; children: Cate, and one son. *Education:* Educated through correspondence courses, received A.Mus.A. in piano and violin. *Home:* 47 Hawksburn Rd., South Yarra, Victoria 3141, Australia. *Agent:* Joan Saxton, 11 Nepean St., Glenris, Victoria 3146, Australia. *Office:* State Library of Victoria, Melbourne, Victoria 3000, Australia.

CAREER: A.M.V. *Naracoopa,* radio operator in Tasman Sea and Bass Strait, 1954-60; Adult Education Board, Hobart, Australia, adult education officer, 1960-66; full-time writer, 1966-70; State Library of Victoria, Melbourne, Australia, manuscripts field officer, 1970—. *Military service:* Voluntary Aid Detachment, 1942-44; served in military hospitals; became corporal. *Member:* Australian Society of Authors, Australian Journalists Association, Victorian Fellowship of Australian Writers (state president, 1973-75; federal president, 1974-75). *Awards, honors:* Australia Council literary fellowship, 1965, 1972, 1975, and 1982; book-of-the-year award, 1978, for *The Anzacs;* Officer of the Order of the British Empire, 1980, for service to literature.

WRITINGS—Under name Patsy Adam-Smith: *Rediscovering Tasmania,* Advocate News, 1960; *Moonbird People,* Rigby, 1963; *Hear the Train Blow* (autobiography), Ure Smith, 1962, enlarged and illustrated edition, Thomas Nelson, 1981; *There Was a Ship* (novel), Rigby, 1964; *The Rails Go Westward,* Macmillan, 1964; *Tiger Country,* Rigby, 1965; *The Barcoo Salute* (nonfiction), Rigby, 1966; *No Tribesmen,* Rigby, 1967; *When We Rode the Rails,* Macmillan, 1968; *Folklore of the Australian Railwaymen* (nonfiction), Macmillan, 1969; *Across Australia by Indian Pacific,* Thomas Nelson, 1970; *Romance of Australian Railways,* Rigby, 1973; *Victorian and Edwardian Melbourne in Photographs,* Ferguson, 1974; *The Desert Rail-*

way (nonfiction), Rigby, 1974; *The Anzacs,* Thomas Nelson, 1978; *Outback Heroes,* Landsdowne, 1981; *The Shearers* (social history), Thomas Nelson, 1982; *The Young Irelanders* (nonfiction), Thomas Nelson, 1982; *Australian Women at War,* Kangaroo Press, 1982; *The Railway Family,* Landsdowne, 1983.

Also author of *Tasmania, Port Arthur, Launceston,* and *Hobart* in Rigby's Sketchbook series. Author of radio broadcasts. Contributor of feature articles to periodicals, including *Walkabout, A.M.,* and *People.*

WORK IN PROGRESS: The Troopers, publication by Thomas Nelson expected in 1984.

SIDELIGHTS: Adam-Smith explained in a *Leongatha Star* interview that she began taking herself seriously as a writer while living abroad. In Ireland to research a book, Adam-Smith appeared on a late-night talk show. When she returned to her hotel, she "found the whole pub waiting for me." Her fellow lodgers held a party for her, complete with champagne, exclaiming, "You didn't tell us you were an author." Adam-Smith noted that "I'd have to be a football star to get that sort of publicity in Australia."

When she went back to Australia, she decided to record her country's often neglected history. She wrote about the rise of the railways, the battle of Gallipoli, and the sheep shearer's strikes of the 1890's. Incorporating in her books the testimonies of people who had lived through those times, Adam-Smith endeavors to capture on paper a living social history. "Our historic novels are all bones and no flesh," she disclosed. "I just can't stand to see all this stuff lost."

Adam-Smith told *CA:* "Both my parents were fine raconteurs. Brought up in the bush, before radio and television or movies came to us, we talked around the fire at nights, told and retold stories. 'People are people' was our belief; we didn't judge, didn't think of class (perhaps didn't know of it, we were so isolated), therefore our friends range through all classes and peoples. Later I learned that many do not see people the way we did. So I began to write in my own way, trying to get readers to see the trees as well as the woods."

BIOGRAPHICAL/CRITICAL SOURCES: Melbourne Age, June 23, 1973, January 13, 1979, June 1, 1979, April 23, 1980, July 21, 1980, September 29, 1981; *Melbourne Sun,* December 2, 1978, October 3, 1981; *London Sunday Telegraph,* December 3, 1978; *Grimsby Evening Telegraph,* December 14, 1978; *Southern Evening Echo,* January 26, 1979; *Leongatha Star,* June 23, 1981; *West Australian,* September 15, 1981.

* * *

ADAM-SMITH, Patsy
See ADAM-SMITH, Patricia Jean

* * *

ADASTRA
See MIREPOIX, Camille

* * *

ADDIE, Bob   1911(?)-1982

OBITUARY NOTICE: Born c. 1911; died of cardiorespiratory arrest, January 18, 1982. Journalist and author. A graduate of the University of Alabama journalism school, Addie began his career with the *New York Journal-American,* later moving to the *Washington Times-Herald* as a general reporter and sportswriter. When the *Washington Post* bought the *Times-Herald* in 1954, Addie stayed on as a sportswriter for the *Post*, remaining with the paper until he retired in 1977. He wrote six and seven newspaper columns a week and was a weekly columnist for the *Sporting News*. Addie was well known for his coverage of the Washington Senators baseball team. "He took great pride in being able to say, 'I never missed a day with the Senators in 20 years,'" noted the *Washington Post*. The recipient of several honors, including National Press Club awards, Addie was also president of the Baseball Writers Association and served on the selection committee of the Baseball Hall of Fame. He was the author of *Sports Writer*, a book he wrote after retiring. Obituaries and other sources: *Washington Post*, January 20, 1982.

* * *

ADDIE, Pauline Betz 1919(?)-

BRIEF ENTRY: American professional tennis player and author. Pauline Addie has won Wimbledon and U.S. women's tennis championships. She teaches children and adults and has conducted summer tennis camps. She wrote *Wings on My Tennis Shoes* (Low, 1949) and *Tennis for Everyone: With Official USLTA Rules and Leighton Tennis Tests* (Pond & Co., 1966). *Biographical/critical sources: New York Times Book Review*, June 10, 1973.

* * *

ADDINGTON, Arthur Charles 1939-

PERSONAL: Born May 25, 1939, in St. Albans, England; son of Charles Henry and Valerie (Goodyear) Addington. *Education:* Attended private school in St. Albans, England. *Home:* 6 Fairfield Close, Harpenden, Hertfordshire, England.

CAREER: Banker, 1956—. *Member:* Society of Genealogists, Society of Authors, Royal Stuart Society.

WRITINGS: The Royal House of Stuart: The Descendants of King James VI of Scotland, James I of England, Charles Skilton, Volume I, 1969, Volume II, 1971, Volume III, 1975; (editor) Gerald Paget, *The Lineage and Ancestry of His Royal Highness Prince Charles, Prince of Wales*, two volumes, Charles Skilton, 1977. Contributor to genealogy journals.

WORK IN PROGRESS: Research on the illegitimate descendants of King James VI of Scotland, England's James I; research on the ancestry of the Princess of Wales.

* * *

ADELSON, Sandra 1934-

PERSONAL: Born October 12, 1934, in New York, N.Y.; daughter of Morris (a used-car dealer) and Rose (a secretary; maiden name, Stahl) Herfield; married Melvin Adelson (a high school guidance director), December 18, 1955; children: Bruce, Marcia. *Education:* City College (now of the City University of New York), B.S.Ed., 1955; Hunter College of the City University of New York, M.S., 1968. *Home:* 33 Bradford Blvd., Yonkers, N.Y. 10710. *Agent:* Steve Blackwelder, 128 Second Pl., Brooklyn, N.Y. 11231. *Office:* New Rochelle High School, Clove Rd., New Rochelle, N.Y. 10801.

CAREER: New Rochelle High School, New Rochelle, N.Y., guidance counselor, 1968—.

WRITINGS: Wrap Her in Light (historical novel), Morrow, 1981.

WORK IN PROGRESS: A contemporary novel, completion expected in 1981; a novel set in Renaissance France.

SIDELIGHTS: Sandra Adelson wrote: "The idea for *Wrap Her in Light* began germinating, although I was unaware of it at the time, during two trips to Egypt. To use 'enthralled' as a measure of my response to Egypt's art would actually understate it. Instead of the cold, lifeless passions I had anticipated from a stylized art, I was stunned by the warmth and vitality and familial affection that emanated from even the most pedestrian work. It seemed to me that, separated as we are from that first civilization by time, an unfamiliar language, and strange customs, the early Egyptians have not been depicted as the warm, courageous, spirited, innovative people I believe they were. And so I have attempted to picture the freshness and excitement of a world where everything was new, where possibilities were limitless.

"Everything I've read about Ankhesenamon and her father, Akhenaten, have caused them to spring out of the pages of history with a vitality I found quite compelling. I wanted to picture them as complex, loving, decent people who tried to impress a grand concept—worship of a single God—on their world. Their ultimate failure, caused not so much by their limitations, came about because of the complexities of their society and the self-serving motivations of powerful groups. The predominant issues—conflicting loyalties, ambition, guilt—mirror in the broadest sense those issues we must all work through in accommodating to the realities of our world.

"In a sense I've watched these 'rites of passage' enacted over and over again, as a guidance counselor in a large, suburban high school. *Wrap Her in Light* is not only my first novel—it is the first piece of writing I've ever had published. While it is not at all autobiographical, it does contain elements of those relationships I've observed for almost thirteen years.

"In my own life, there have been certain periods of time when I considered certain involvements to be appropriate—a time when I wanted to be home (when my children were very young), a time when I wanted to return to work (especially since my husband and I were involved in related fields), a time when I wanted to write.

"My contemporary novel is about people living in an affluent suburban community who discover, painfully and shockingly, that the myths they've lived by, the civilized world they fashioned, were quite different from what was intended. They learn their perceptions of themselves and of others, filtered through their own distorted vision, were, in fact, dangerously wrong.

"I've also sketched the outline for a novel set in Renaissance France, where relationships had to be bound by the religious conflicts of the time and by the shifting demands of a capricious court.

"I've traveled abroad quite extensively where my family's collective proficiency in French, German, Russian, and some Arabic has enabled me to gain insights into cultures other than my own."

* * *

ADLER, France-Michele 1942-

PERSONAL: Born May 10, 1942, in Aubenas, Ardeche, France; came to the United States in 1968; daughter of Andre and Suzanne (Dugelay) Parizot; married J. David Adler (in banking). *Education:* Attended University of Nice, 1961-62, and Pitman Institute, 1963. *Home and office:* 333 East 68th St., New York, N.Y. 10021. *Agent:* Robert Cornfield Literary Agency, 145 West 79th St., New York, N.Y. 10024.

CAREER: Contours Travel Agency, Nice, France, reservation agent, 1964-65; Hotel Ducap, Corsica, France, assistant to manager, 1965-68; Clark, Dodge, & Co., New York City, translator, 1968-69; SoGen International Corp. (investment bank), New York City, registered representative, 1971-73; First National City Bank, New York City, marketing representative, 1973-74; free-lance writer, 1974—. *Member:* Authors Guild, Alliance Francaise.

WRITINGS: Sportsfashion, Avon, 1980. Contributing fashion writer to *New York Post,* 1978—; contributor to magazines, including *New York* and *Stores.*

WORK IN PROGRESS: A novel set in the fashion world.

SIDELIGHTS: France-Michele Adler told *CA:* "I enjoy the mix of fashion reporting and novel writing. My work as a fashion writer is fast paced, people oriented, and lively. Fiction writing, on the contrary, is solitary and slow.

"Raised on cowboy and Indian movies, I could live happily in a movie theatre."

AVOCATIONAL INTERESTS: Japanese and Chinese food, travel (including the Orient).

* * *

ADLER, Larry 1939-

PERSONAL: Born July 10, 1939, in White Plains, N.Y.; son of David (a grocer) and Dora (Tomin) Adler. *Education:* University of Wisconsin (now University of Wisconsin—Madison), B.S., 1961; London School of Economics and Political Science, London, Diploma in Business Administration, 1964; Sorbonne, University of Paris, Certificate in French, 1965. *Home:* 324 East 74th St., New York, N.Y. 10021. *Agent:* Writers House, Inc., 21 West 26th St., New York, N.Y. 10010.

CAREER: Advertising copywriter and free-lance writer, 1965—. *Military service:* U.S. Army, 1961-62. Army National Guard, member of 199th Army Band at Camp Smith, N.Y., 1975—; present rank, staff sergeant.

WRITINGS—All juveniles: Man With a Mission: Pele, Raintree Editions, 1976; *Young Women in the World of Race Horses,* McKay, 1978; *Famous Horses in America,* McKay, 1979; *The Texas Rangers,* McKay, 1979; *Heroes of Soccer,* Messner, 1980.

* * *

ADLER, Lucile 1922-

PERSONAL: Born September 9, 1922, in Kansas City, Mo.; daughter of Millard J. and Lucile (Meinrath) Bloch; married Nathan Adler, June 11, 1942 (died September 13, 1980); children: John M., Kathleen. *Education:* Bennington College, B.A., 1943. *Politics:* Liberal Democrat. *Home:* 1239 Canyon Rd., Santa Fe, N.M. 87501.

CAREER: Worked in broadcasting and journalism, 1943-50; writer, 1950—. Gives readings at colleges and universities.

WRITINGS: The Traveling Out (poems), Macmillan, 1967; *The Society of Anna* (poems), Lightning Tree Press, 1974. Also author of *New Poems,* 1981, and two unpublished collections, "On Abeyta Street" and "Winter Wedding at Cristo Rey."

Contributor to anthologies: *New Yorker Book of Poems,* Viking, 1969; L. Lask, editor, *New York Times Book of Verse,* Macmillan, 1970; *Desert Review Anthology,* Desert Review, 1974; Gene Frumlein and Stanley Noyes, editors, *Indian Rio Grande,* San Marcos Press, 1977.

Contributor of poems to magazines, including *Nation, New Yorker, Century, New Mexico Quarterly, Poetry Northwest,* and *New Boston Review.*

WORK IN PROGRESS: A book of poems; *The Juniper Letters,* prose; a novel.

SIDELIGHTS: Adler told *CA:* "My career has been old-fashioned. After some years of odd jobs, I moved to Santa Fe, where I helped bring up children and continued writing, trying to master my craft. Since Nat's death I have tried to complete work he was familiar with, which will be dedicated to him.

"At first my poems were intended simply as a gift to leave my children, an illustrated map of a certain time and place. They have become the best record I can create—the best and most disciplined expression I can offer of a lifetime's response to the world around me and an attempt (beyond the personal) to explore our common landscape with clarity and compassion."

* * *

AGEE, Joel 1940-

BRIEF ENTRY: American author. Agee has written a memoir of his youth entitled *Twelve Years: An American Boyhood in East Germany* (Farrar, Straus, 1981). He was separated as an infant from his father, writer James Agee, and raised in East Germany by his mother. He left East Germany shortly before the construction of the Berlin Wall and began writing in the 1970's. Agee joined the staff of *Harper's* in 1980 and became the magazine's fiction editor in July, 1981. *Address:* 263 Eastern Parkway, Brooklyn, N.Y. 11238. *Biographical/critical sources: New York Times,* April 25, 1981, May 6, 1981; *Publishers Weekly,* May 8, 1981; *Time,* May 11, 1981; *Washington Post,* May 20, 1981, June 29, 1981; *Saturday Review,* July, 1981.

* * *

AGUILA, Pancho 1945-

PERSONAL: Birth-given name, Roberto Ignacio Zelaya, changed in 1968; born September 6, 1945, in Managua, Nicaragua; came to the United States in 1947; son of Ignacio and Esperanza (Solis) Zelaya. *Education:* Studied college courses at Soledad Prison, 1972, and at Folsom Prison College Program, 1975. *Politics:* "Survivor." *Religion:* Unitarian-Universalist. *Home address:* Folsom Prison, P.O. Box B22814A, Represa, Calif. 95671; and 3341 18th St., San Francisco, Calif. 94110.

CAREER: Poet. Read poetry at coffeehouses in San Francisco, Calif., until 1968; sentenced to life in prison, 1969, inmate at Folsom Prison, Represa, Calif., 1969—, escaped from prison and recaptured five months later, 1972. Chairman of writing workshop at Folsom Prison, 1975-77.

WRITINGS—Poems, except as noted: Hi-Jacked, Twin Window, 1975; *Dark Smoke,* Second Coming Press, 1976; *Anti-Gravity,* Aldebaran Review, 1976; *The Beast Has Come* (prose), Cloud House, 1978; *Clash,* Poetry for the People, 1980.

Contributor to literary magazines, including *Ins and Outs Journal, Haight/Ashbury Literary Quarterly, Kite, Prison Literary,* and *Coyote.*

WORK IN PROGRESS: First Passage, fifty poems dedicated to the Sandinista cultural cause; *Latin American Themes,* fifty poems.

SIDELIGHTS: Aguila commented: "My writing has been shaped by the rhythms of street life, by the struggles on the Continent of the Americas, and mostly by the world at large, violently born to a new atomic era in 1945. The poetic spirit in me crystalized into the poem in 1967, when I wrote and read in Haight-Ashbury coffeehouses. Since imprisonment in 1969, a fugitive period in 1972, and seven years of solitary units, I've continued to evolve the poetry and consciousness of this art and our planet. This is why I prophesy that as we enter the end of the century a blackness will engulf us, or a brilliant sun of a new horizon. Survival of the planet, of the global civilization, is the historical task. To write is to further the cause of the continuation of new flowers, new heights, new people, a race to civilize technological, destructive madness—the only poem.''

* * *

ALADJEM, Henrietta H. 1917-

PERSONAL: Born January 21, 1917, in Ramnieu, Romania; married Albert T. Aladjem; children: Albert T., Jr., Ingrid, Martha. *Home:* 25 Gordon Rd., Waban, Mass. 02168.

CAREER: Editor of *Lupus News.* Member of National Institutes of Health Advisory Allergy and Infectious Diseases Council; member of board of directors of Lupus Foundation of America; honorary chairperson of Massachusetts Lupus Foundation. *Member:* League of Women Voters of the United States (past member of board of directors). *Awards, honors:* Named woman of the year by Systemic Lupus Erythematosus Foundation of America, 1976.

WRITINGS: The Sun Is My Enemy, Beacon Press, 1977; *Lupus: Hope Through Understanding,* Lupus Foundation of America, 1981. Also author of *A Patient's Story,* privately printed.

SIDELIGHTS: Lupus is an inflammatory disease whose sufferers, including Henrietta Aladjem, must avoid the sun. Once considered fatal, the disease can now be controlled with appropriate therapy. Aladjem devotes her time (and the proceeds from her writing activities) to educating the public, patients and their families, and the medical community about lupus.

* * *

ALCANTARA, Ruben R(eyes) 1940-

PERSONAL: Born November 19, 1940, in Manila, Philippines; came to the United States in 1963, naturalized citizen, 1976; son of Julio M. (a lawyer) and Febe (a nurse; maiden name, Reyes) Alcantara; married Christina Miessler (a university lecturer), August, 1971. *Education:* University of the Philippines, B.A., 1961; University of Hawaii at Manoa, M.A., 1965, Ph.D., 1974. *Home:* 2825 South King, No. 3502, Honolulu, Hawaii 96826. *Office:* Department of American Studies, University of Hawaii at Manoa, Honolulu, Hawaii 96822.

CAREER: University of Hawaii at Manoa, Honolulu, assistant professor, 1974-81, associate professor of American studies, 1981—.

WRITINGS: Filipinos in Hawaii: Annotated Bibliography, University Press of Hawaii, 1975; *Sakada: Filipino Adaptation in Hawaii,* University Press of America, 1981.

WORK IN PROGRESS: Research on Hawaiian Filipino life, 1900-46.

SIDELIGHTS: Alcantara told *CA:* "Writing about an ethnic experience entails two demands: that one describe general processes and trends and that one capture the reality that an individual participant perceives. Incorporating these two elements in an ethnohistorical account often proves to be the most

difficult task for the writer. Thus we see many works that depersonalize people into large, generalized mass participants in historical events, and we see personalized accounts that leave us with little understanding of general processes and developments.

"I am always aware of a basic question in research and writing: whose perception and interpretation of reality will I describe? I wish to describe, not the perspective of the 'movers of events,' but that of the people experiencing the events, determining the limitations and opportunities in life, and then exercising their options. The view that ethnic groups are victims of circumstance, of limitations imposed by the larger society, or of cultural ideals cannot fully explain all the creative processes that groups undergo in adaptation. It is probably these creative processes that should loom large in significance, whether on the level of the individual, the ethnic group, or the society.''

* * *

ALDEN, Dauril 1926-

PERSONAL: Born January 12, 1926, in San Francisco, Calif.; son of Lawrence C. (a druggist) and Edna (Klimcke) Thompson; married Beata Hambuschen Christ (in real estate); children: Bryson, Grant; stepchildren: Stephen, Michael, Tom. *Education:* University of California, Berkeley, A.B., 1950, M.A., 1952, Ph.D., 1959. *Home:* 5732 17th Ave. N.E., Seattle, Wash. 98105. *Office:* Department of History, DP-20, University of Washington, Seattle, Wash. 98195.

CAREER: University of Washington, Seattle, 1959—, began as assistant professor, became professor of history. Visiting assistant professor at University of California, Berkeley, 1962-63; visiting associate professor at Columbia University, 1967, and University of Michigan, 1969. Research fellow at La Trobe University, 1979, and American Institute of Indian Studies, Goa, India. Chairman of Newberry Library conference on colonial Brazil, 1967-69, and conference on Latin American history, 1980. *Military service:* U.S. Naval Reserve, active duty, 1944-46.

MEMBER: American Historical Association, Economic History Association, Conference on Latin American History (chairman, 1980), Latin American Studies Association, Newberry Library (associate), James Ford Bell Library (associate). *Awards, honors:* Fellow of Henry and Grace Doherty Foundation in Brazil, 1957-58, and Social Science Research Council, 1958-59; grant from American Philosophical Society and Council for Research on Economic History for Portugal, 1968; Gulbenkian fellow in Portugal, 1969; Guggenheim fellow in Brazil, 1976-77; Mellon fellow, 1980.

WRITINGS: Royal Government in Colonial Brazil, University of California Press, 1968; (editor) *Colonial Roots of Modern Brazil,* University of California Press, 1973; (editor with Warren Dean) *Essays Concerning the Socioeconomic History of Brazil and Portuguese India,* University Presses of Florida, 1977. Member of board of editors of *Hispanic American Historical Review,* 1966-70, 1977-83, *Americas,* 1973—, *American Historical Review,* 1978-80, and *Plantation Societies,* 1978—.

WORK IN PROGRESS: For God or Mammon?: The Economic Role and Controversies of the Jesuits in Portugal and Her Empire, 1540-1808.

* * *

ALDRICH, Ruth I(sabelle)

PERSONAL: Born in Milwaukee, Wis.; daughter of Joseph M.

(a wholesale grocer) and Anne (Nelson) Aldrich. *Education:* Milwaukee-Downer College, B.A.; University of Wisconsin (now University of Wisconsin—Madison), M.A., 1948, Ph.D., 1961. *Religion:* Presbyterian. *Home:* 3249 North Summit Ave., Milwaukee, Wis. 53211. *Office:* Department of English, University of Wisconsin—Milwaukee, Milwaukee, Wis. 53201.

CAREER: University of Wisconsin—Milwaukee, instructor, 1949-62, assistant professor, 1962-69, associate professor, 1969-74, professor of English, 1974-80, professor emeritus, 1980—. *Member:* Charles Lamb Society, Sigma Tau Delta, Phi Kappa Phi.

WRITINGS: (Editor) Thomas Holcroft, *The Road to Ruin,* University of Nebraska Press, 1968; *John Galt,* Twayne, 1978. Contributor to literature journals and popular magazines, including *Atlantic Monthly.*

WORK IN PROGRESS: Gothic novels; research on mystery and detective fiction.

SIDELIGHTS: Ruth Aldrich wrote: "I am a detective story buff and enjoy the detective novel in which a detective or detectives are repeated in a series of books; the detectives may be either amateur or professional. Any setting is acceptable. I do not read or enjoy 'psychological' detective fiction (Simenon). There should be more than one murder, and the clues must be fair. The criminal may not escape (unless a sequel is planned). I feel that too much research in this field has stressed the ideas of patterns, formulas, etc. Good writers succeed in adding many twists and creating lifelike characters. To a considerably lesser extent, this is true of the Gothic novel (*Rebecca*)."

* * *

ALEXANDER, Stella Tucker   1912-

PERSONAL: Born June 14, 1912, in Shanghai, China; daughter of George Edwin and Helen (Ferguson) Tucker; children: one son, one daughter. *Education:* St. Hilda's College, Oxford, B.A., 1933, M.A., 1969; attended University of Zagreb (Yugoslavia), 1966. *Religion:* Society of Friends (Quakers). *Home:* 10A Shooters Hill Rd., London SE3 7BD, England.

CAREER: Writer, 1957—. Secretary of East-West Relations Committee of the Society of Friends, 1957-65. Member of East Europe Committee of the British Council, 1963-67, governing body of the Great Britain East Europe Centre, 1967-73, Wyndam Place Trust Commission on International Strategy for Europe, 1974-75, and council of Keston College, 1980—.

WRITINGS: Quaker Testimony Against Slavery and Racial Discrimination, Friends Home Service Committee, 1958; *Church-State Relations in Yugoslavia Since 1945,* Cambridge University Press, 1979; (contributor) Stuart Mews, editor, *Studies in Church History,* Volume XVIII: *Religion and National Identity,* Ecclesiastical History Society, 1982. Contributor of articles and reviews to religious journals and newspapers. Member of editorial board of *Religion in Communist Lands,* 1975—.

WORK IN PROGRESS: Continuing research on religion and churches in Yugoslavia.

SIDELIGHTS: Alexander told *CA:* "I attempt to write in a scholarly manner and as objectively as possible about a period of history in Yugoslavia which is complex, and about which there is very little nonpartisan material: the identification of religion with the various nationalities making up federal Yugoslavia, and the relations of religious bodies—Catholic, Orthodox Moslem—with the communist government of Yugoslavia."

ALEXIS, Katina
See STRAUCH, Katina (Parthemos)

* * *

ALI, Chaudhri Mohamad   1905-1980

OBITUARY NOTICE: Born July 15, 1905, in Jullundur, Punjab, India; died December 1, 1980, in Karachi, Sind, Pakistan. Government official and author. In 1928 Mohamad Ali joined the British colonial civil service in India and held a number of government positions for the next twenty years. In the mid-1940's he joined the partition council that developed the terms for the division of India. In 1947, when Pakistan became independent, Mohamad Ali was appointed secretary-general of the new country. Upon becoming finance minister in 1951, Ali encouraged the growth of industrial production, thus improving the country's financial status. In 1955 Mohamad Ali was named president of the dominant Muslim party in West Pakistan and developed a coalition government in which he held the post of prime minister. He fell from power in late 1956, and except for an unsuccessful attempt at the presidency in 1965, Mohamad Ali remained politically inactive. His book, *The Emergence of Pakistan,* was published in 1967. Obituaries and other sources: *Current Biography,* Wilson, 1956; *The Annual Obituary 1980,* St. Martin's, 1981.

* * *

ALLAN, Norman B.   1921-

BRIEF ENTRY: Born May 31, 1921, in Milwaukee, Wis. American diamond merchant and author. Allan has been a diamond merchant since 1928 and is an active member of Jewish philanthropic organizations. He wrote *Lies My Father Told Me* (New American Library, 1975), based on a screenplay by Ted Allen. *Address:* 18657 George Washington Dr., Southfield, Mich.; and 17540 Wyoming Ave., Detroit, Mich.

* * *

ALLEN, James B(rown)   1927-

PERSONAL: Born June 14, 1927, in Ogden, Utah; son of Harold T. (a mining engineer) and Edna (Brown) Allen; married Renee Jones; children: Kristine Allen Card, J. Michael, Kathleen Allen Bellamy, Nancy, Scott J. *Education:* Attended George Washington University, 1947-48; Utah State University, B.S., 1954; Brigham Young University, M.A., 1956; University of Southern California, Ph.D., 1963. *Office:* Department of History, Brigham Young University, Provo, Utah 84602.

CAREER: Latter-day Saints Seminary, Kaysville, Utah, teacher of religious studies, 1954-55; coordinator of seminaries of the Church of Jesus Christ of Latter-day Saints in Cowley, Wyo., 1955-57, assistant coordinator of seminaries in Los Angeles, Calif., 1957-58; Latter-day Saints Institute of Religion, Los Angeles, associate director, 1959-61, director, 1961-62; Latter-day Saints Institute of Religion, San Bernardino, Calif., director, 1962-63; Brigham Young University, Provo, Utah, assistant professor, 1963-65, associate professor, 1965-71, professor of history, 1971—, chairman of department, 1981—. Instructor at San Bernardino Valley College, 1962-63; visiting associate professor at Utah State University, 1968-69. Assistant church historian of Church of Jesus Christ of Latter-day Saints, 1972-79.

MEMBER: Mormon History Association (member of board of directors, 1966-73; president, 1971-72; chairman of program committee, 1975), Western History Association (chairman of program committee, 1976). *Awards, honors:* Award from Mormon History Association, 1967, for article "The Mormons in the Mountain West: An Annotated Bibliography"; Karl G. Maeser Research and Creative Arts Award from Brigham Young University Alumni Association, 1980; annual award from *Utah Historical Quarterly,* 1980, for article "Good Guys Versus Bad Buys: Rudger Clawson, John Sharp, and Civil Disobedience in Nineteenth-Century Utah."

WRITINGS: (With Richard O. Cowan) *Mormonism in the Twentieth Century,* Brigham Young University Press, 1964, revised edition, 1967; *The Company Town in the American West,* University of Oklahoma Press, 1966; (editor with Marvin S. Hill) *Mormonism and American Culture,* Harper, 1972; (editor with Thomas G. Alexander) *Manchester Mormons: The Journal of William Clayton, 1840-1842,* Peregrine Smith, 1974; (with Glen M. Leonard) *The Story of the Latter-day Saints,* Deseret, 1976; (editor with Dale C. LeCheminant and David J. Whittaker) *Views on Man and Religion: Collected Essays of George T. Boyd,* privately printed, 1976; *The History of Salt Lake City,* Pruett, 1983.

Contributor: John A. Carrol, editor, *Reflections of Western Historians,* University of Arizona Press, 1967; F. Mark McKiernan, Alma R. Blair, and Paul M. Edwards, editors, *The Restoration Movement: Essays in Mormon History,* Coronado Press, 1973; Richard D. Poll and other editors, *Utah's History,* Brigham Young University Press, 1978. Contributor to *Essays on Public Ethics,* edited by Martin B. Hickman, and to *Encyclopedia of American Forest and Conservation History.* Also contributor of more than thirty-five articles and reviews to history and Mormon journals.

Editor of "The Historian's Corner," a column in *Brigham Young University Studies,* 1973—. Editor of "Studies in Mormon History," a series, Brigham Young University Press, 1979—. Editor of *Newsletter* of Mormon History Association, 1970-71; guest editor of *Dialogue: A Journal of Mormon Thought,* spring, 1972; member of editorial board of *Brigham Young University Studies,* 1973—; associate editor of *Journal of Mormon History,* 1974.

WORK IN PROGRESS: The Mormon Community in the Nineteenth Century, as Revealed Through the Life of William Clayton, possible publication by University of Illinois Press, 1982; *A History of the Genealogical Society of the Church of Jesus Christ of Latter-day Saints; A History of the Church of Jesus Christ of Latter-day Saints Since 1950,* for Deseret.

*   *   *

ALLEN, James B(eekman)   1931-

PERSONAL: Born August 7, 1931, in Grand Rapids, Mich.; son of Clarence Dewey and Caroline (Butterfield) Allen; married Rosemary L. Moore (a nurse), February 15, 1964; children: Caroline, Kathleen, Sean, James. *Education:* University of Michigan, A.B., 1954, Ph.D., 1974. *Home:* 550 Avalon S.E., Grand Rapids, Mich. 49503.

CAREER: Fahnestock & Co., Grand Rapids, Mich., office manager, 1957-67; Grand Valley State Colleges, Allendale, Mich., teacher, 1967-68; University of Michigan, Ann Arbor, teacher, 1969-74; Allen's Book Shop, Grand Rapids, bookseller, 1975-80; Grand Rapids Junior College, Grand Rapids, adjunct professor, 1980—. Member of Writers Center at Urban Institute of Grand Rapids; director of Poetry Resource Center

in Southfield, Mich. Director of Recipient Rights for Community Mental Health. *Military service:* U.S. Army, 1954-56. *Awards, honors:* Poetry award from *Writer's Digest,* 1968, for "Necessities"; Jules and Avery Hopwood Awards from University of Michigan, 1973, for poem, and 1974, for essay, "Baudelaire: Martyr to Beauty"; LeFebvre Poetry Award, 1974.

WRITINGS: (Translator) *Rilke's Duino Elegies,* Ann Arbor Publishers, 1974; *See the Lighthouse Burning* (poems), Peter Quince, 1976; *Love Letters From a Lost Son* (poems), Peter Quince, 1976; *Beggars Could Ride* (poems), Seaview, 1981; *Poetry of Lakes in Michigan,* Seaview, in press.

Editor: *New Voices,* Alon, 1975; *All for One,* Peter Quince, 1976; *Midwestern Songs,* Broadsides, 1976.

WORK IN PROGRESS: Great Lakes and Plain Songs (tentative title), prose poems, publication expected in 1984.

SIDELIGHTS: Allen commented: "Poetry is a natural means of expression for me. I use it to make graceful what emerges in pain and requires transformation. It is communication at the most significant feeling level." *Avocational interests:* Tennis, swimming, foreign travel.

*   *   *

ALPERS, Bernard J.   1900-1981

OBITUARY NOTICE: Born March 14, 1900, in Salem, Mass.; died November 2, 1981. Neurologist, educator, and author. Emeritus professor of neurology of the medical college of Thomas Jefferson University, Alpers was also a former president of the American Board of Psychiatry and Neurology, the American Association of Neuropathologists, and the American Neurological Society. His writings include *Clinical Neurology* and *Essentials of the Neurological Examination,* which he co-wrote. Obituaries and other sources: *Who's Who in World Jewry: A Biographical Dictionary of Outstanding Jews,* Pitman, 1972; *New York Times,* November 4, 1981.

*   *   *

ALRED, Gerald J(ames)   1943-

PERSONAL: Born February 24, 1943, in Dayton, Ohio; son of Edgar James (a mechanic) and Leona Jane (a nurse; maiden name, Evans) Alred; married Janice Ruth Moody, August 17, 1974; children: Jeanette Rose, Elaine Ann. *Education:* University of Dayton, B.A., 1965, M.A., 1968; doctoral study at Miami University, Oxford, Ohio. *Religion:* Methodist. *Home:* 4037 North Prospect Ave., Shorewood, Wis. 53211. *Office:* Department of English, University of Wisconsin—Milwaukee, Milwaukee, Wis. 53201.

CAREER: Wells Television, Inc., New York, N.Y., manager and liaison in Dayton, Ohio and manager of Hospital Television Facilities, 1965-68; Sinclair Community College, Dayton, instructor in English, 1968-71; City of Dayton, legislative aide to city commissioner, 1972-74; University of Wisconsin—Milwaukee, instructor, 1974-75, assistant professor, 1975-80, associate professor of English, 1980—. Conference organizer and workshop leader; consultant to business and government. *Member:* American Association for the Advancement of Science, American Business Communication Association (member of board of directors, 1977), Association of Teachers of Technical Writing, Council for Programs in Technical and Scientific Writing, National Council of Teachers of English, Society for Technical Communication.

WRITINGS: (With Charles T. Brusaw) *Practical Writing: Composition for the Business and Technical World,* Allyn &

Bacon, 1973; (with Brusaw and Walter E. Oliu) *NCR Handbook for Effective Writing*, National Cash Register Corp., 1974; (with Brusaw and Oliu) *The Business Writer's Handbook* (alternate selection of Book-of-the-Month Club and selection of Fortune Book Club), St. Martin's, 1976; (with Brusaw and Oliu) *Handbook of Technical Writing*, St. Martin's, 1976; (with Brusaw and Oliu) *Writing That Works: How to Write Effectively on the Job*, St. Martin's, 1980; (editor with D. C. Reep and M. R. Limaye) *Business and Technical Writing: An Annotated Bibliography of Books, 1880-1980*, Scarecrow, 1981. Contributor to business and communication journals.

WORK IN PROGRESS: Business Communication: Theory and Application, with Charles T. Brusaw and Walter E. Oliu, publication by St. Martin's expected in 1985.

SIDELIGHTS: Alred commented: "After graduating from a technical high school, I enrolled as an engineering major at the University of Dayton. I found that I enjoyed writing even more than engineering, and switched my studies to English. When I was hired at Sinclair Community College, I was able to combine my background in engineering with my degrees in English.

"I have continued to study, teach, and write about technical and business writing because, as I have said elsewhere, 'the products of business and technical writing are important to the extent that they enlighten us on the complex and crucial issues of the day and help us conduct our business with some humanity toward our fellow human beings.' "

*   *   *

ALT, Herschel   1897(?)-1981

OBITUARY NOTICE: Born c. 1897 in the Ukraine (now Ukrainian Soviet Socialist Republic); died November 16, 1981, in New York. Mental health and child welfare specialist, educator, and author. A graduate of the University of Toronto, Alt came to the United States in 1923 and worked in child welfare in Los Angeles and St. Louis before he was named to the Jewish Board of Guardians in New York (now the Jewish Board of Family and Children's Services) in the early 1940's. In addition to his association with the board, which ended when he retired in 1965, Alt served as a child welfare adviser to the Israeli Government, as a mental health consultant to the World Health Organization, and as chairman of the welfare advisory board of the U.S. committee of the United Nations International Children's Emergency Fund (UNICEF). He was a member of the New York City Commission for the Foster Care of Children and consultant to the New York City Community Health Board, and he served on the faculties of several universities, including St. Louis University, Columbia University, and the University of Louisville. His writings include *Forging Tools for Mental Health* and *Residential Treatment for Disturbed Children*. With his wife, Edith Seltzer Alt, he wrote a study of the Soviet Union's child-welfare institutions entitled *Russia's Children*. Obituaries and other sources: *New York Times*, November 18, 1981.

*   *   *

ALTFEST, Karen Caplan

PERSONAL: Born in Montreal, Quebec, Canada; daughter of Philip and Betty (Gamer) Caplan; married Lewis J. Altfest (a research director for an investment firm), 1966; children: Ellen Wendy, Andrew Gamer. *Education:* Attended McGill University; Hunter College of the City University of New York, B.A., 1970, M.A., 1973; Graduate School and University Cen-

ter of the City University of New York, Ph.D., 1979. *Religion:* Jewish. *Residence:* New York, N.Y. *Office:* Alumni Association, Graduate Center, City University of New York, 33 West 42nd St., New York, N.Y. 10036.

CAREER: City University of New York, Graduate Center, New York City, member of board of directors of Alumni Association, 1980—; writer. President of Friends of the Children's Center at Graduate Center of the City University of New York, 1973-76, and Yorkville Common Pantry, 1980—. *Member:* Association for Canadian Studies in the United States, American Historical Association, Canadian Historical Association, Association for Canadian Studies, Coordinating Committee for Women in the Historical Profession, Phi Alpha Theta.

WRITINGS: Robert Owen as Educator, Twayne, 1977; (contributor) *Maria Montessori as Educator*, Twayne, 1982. Contributor to history and Canadian studies journals.

WORK IN PROGRESS: A book on Canadian literary nationalism.

SIDELIGHTS: Karen Altfest wrote: "Many people in my family are authors, including my husband, my brother, and my sister and her husband. We encourage and support each other's efforts. I believe in developing my personal and professional interests and forming strong ties to my family and community. I am particularly fortunate to have a husband who shares my interests in scholarship as well as my hobbies."

AVOCATIONAL INTERESTS: Tennis, travel, theatre, reading, community activities.

*   *   *

ALTSCHUL, Aaron Mayer   1914-

PERSONAL: Born March 13, 1914, in Chicago, Ill.; son of Phillip (a jeweler) and Sophie (Fox) Altschul; married Ruth Braude, October 24, 1937; children: Sandra Betty Altschul Norman, Judy Altschul Bonderman. *Education:* University of Chicago, B.S., 1934, Ph.D., 1937. *Religion:* Jewish. *Home:* 700 New Hampshire Ave. N.W., Washington, D.C. 20037. *Office:* Department of Community and Family Medicine, School of Medicine, Georgetown University, Washington, D.C. 20007.

CAREER: University of Chicago, Chicago, Ill., research associate in department of chemistry, 1937-41; U.S. Department of Agriculture, Washington, D.C., member of staff of Southern Regional Research Laboratory, New Orleans, La., 1941-49, head of protein and carbohydrate division, 1949-52, head of oilseed section, 1952-58, chief research chemist at Seed Protein Pioneering Research Laboratory, 1958-66, special assistant to U.S. secretary of agriculture, 1966, special assistant for international nutrition improvement in International Agricultural Development Service, 1967-69, special assistant to U.S. secretary of agriculture for nutrition improvement, 1969-71; Georgetown University, Washington, D.C., professor of nutrition, 1971—, director of division of nutrition, 1975—.

Adjunct professor at Tulane University, 1943-65; visiting lecturer at Massachusetts Institute of Technology, 1960-65, and at Colorado State University, 1968; Underwood-Prescott Memorial Lecturer at Massachusetts Institute of Technology, 1967; Fred W. Tanner Lecturer at Institute of Food Technologists, 1978; Edna W. Park Lecturer at University of Toronto, 1979. Member of agricultural board of National Academy of Sciences and National Research Council; organizer of international agricultural conferences; consultant to industry, United Nations agencies, and National Research and Development Council of Israel. *Member:* American Society of Biological Chemists, American Chemical Society, American Institute of Nutrition,

American Society for Clinical Nutrition, Institute of Food Technologists, Phi Beta Kappa, Sigma Xi, Phi Tau Sigma.

AWARDS, HONORS: Superior service award, 1956, and distinguished service award, 1970, both from U.S. Department of Agriculture; Charles F. Spencer Award from American Chemical Society, 1965; Technion Achievement Award from Chicago chapter of American Society for Technion, Israel Institute of Technology, 1966; D.Sc. from Tulane University, 1968; Rockefeller Public Service Award for the General Welfare of Natural Resources from Princeton University, 1970; international award from Institute of Food Technologists, 1970, named distinguished food scientist of the year by New York section, 1971; named distinguished scientist of the year by District of Columbia section of Society for Experimental Biology and Medicine, 1975; Golden Peanut Award from National Peanut Council, 1975.

WRITINGS: (Editor) *Processed Plant Protein Foodstuffs*, Academic Press, 1958; *Proteins: Their Chemistry and Politics*, Basic Books, 1965; *World Protein Resources*, American Chemical Society, 1966; (editor with Nevin S. Scrimshaw) *Amino Acid Fortification of Protein Foods*, M.I.T. Press, 1971; (editor) *New Protein Foods*, Academic Press, Volume I, 1974, Volume II, 1976, Volume III (with H. L. Wilcke), 1978, Volume IV (with Wilcke), 1981, Volume V, 1983.

WORK IN PROGRESS: Editing *Weight Measurement: A View From a Clinic*, completion expected in 1982.

SIDELIGHTS: Altschul told *CA:* "I have a lifelong professional interest in using vegetable protein foods more efficiently as a way of increasing protein resources and reducing requirements for animal protein. Recently I also became interested in the role of nutrition in preventive medicine. I have organized an obesity clinic and hope to write a book on weight management.

"The problems of famine and scarcity have been with us from the beginnings of history and will probably persist so long as areas exist where social organization and commitment to human dignity are not adequate to meet the needs. I have been concerned with the role of technology as it interfaces with this large social problem. First of all, it must be recognized that the introduction of large-scale public health programs throughout the world has exacerbated the problems of food supply as a result of increased population pressure. This does not negate the role of public health but emphasizes that social organization and social commitment in many areas was not up to dealing with the disturbance in ecology provided by advances in medicine.

"The advances in nutrition and food sciences have now guaranteed that no one need suffer deficiency of micro-nutrients for lack of resources since the vitamins and minerals are easily available; it is only the delivery that has to be worked out. This is not, however, true of the major nutrients, food energy and protein. Clearly these are in short supply in certain parts of the world. The new knowledge of nutrition and the new possibilities introduced by food-production science and food-processing science create a greater flexibility from a technical viewpoint in dealing with problems of making maximum use of available resources to provide sufficient energy and protein for a population. It still puts on the government of any particular place the onus of trying to work out the best solution. This is why I have an interest in the development of alternate sources of protein, and this is the major emphasis of the treatise in which I am now engaged.

"In recent years I have become interested in another aspect of nutrition which is also new in this century. Large numbers of people are overweight because of the abundance of food supply and the tendency towards a more sedentary lifestyle. This has caused personal problems and has exacerbated medical problems. People living in a society like the American society where food is abundant have to become restrained eaters once their growth phase is finished, unless they are engaged in vigorous exercise. And even so they may have to restrain their eating in order to maintain energy balance and not gain weight. The development of restraint in eating is not easy to do. In a sense it is harder to do than restraint in smoking or restraint in alcohol consumption, since neither of the latter are necessary for living, whereas eating is indispensable. This is a complex problem, and it occurs in a society that looks for simple solutions and simplified concepts. We have been engaged in dealing with this problem in a practical way in a clinic and hope that our experience might enable us to write on this subject in a way that would enable more people to approach this problem realistically."

*   *   *

AMACHER, Ryan C(uster) 1945-

PERSONAL: Born November 9, 1945, in Madford, Wis.; son of Armond Edward (in business) and Marcella (Strebig) Amacher; married Susan Smith (a farmer), December 28, 1967. *Education:* Ripon College, A.B., 1967; University of Virginia, Ph.D., 1971. *Home address:* P.O. Box 1203, Clemson, S.C. 29631. *Office:* College of Industrial Management and Textile Science, Clemson University, 165 Sirrine Hall, Clemson, S.C. 29631.

CAREER: University of Virginia, Charlottesville, instructor in economics, 1968-71; University of Oklahoma, Norman, assistant professor, 1972-74, associate professor of economics, 1974; U.S. Treasury, Washington, D.C., senior international economist, 1974-75; Arizona State University, Tempe, associate professor, 1975-79, professor of economics, 1979-81, chairman of department, 1977-81; Clemson University, Clemson, S.C., professor of economics and dean of College of Industrial Management and Textile Science, 1981—. *Member:* American Economic Association, Public Choice Society, Southern Economic Association.

WRITINGS: Yugoslavia's Foreign Trade, Praeger, 1972; (with J. C. Miller, M. V. Pauly, and others) *The Economics of the Military Draft*, General Learning Press, 1973; (editor with R. D. Tollison and T. D. Willett, and contributor) *The Economic Approach to Public Policy: Selected Readings*, Cornell University Press, 1976; (editor with R. J. Sweeney) *The Law of the Sea: U.S. Interests and Alternatives*, American Enterprise Institute for Public Policy Research, 1976; (editor with Willett and Gottfried Haberler) *Challenges to a Liberal International Economic Order*, American Enterprise Institute for Public Policy Research, 1980; (with Sweeney) *Principles of Micro-Economics*, Southwestern, 1980 (also see below); (with Sweeney) *Principles of Macro-Economics*, Southwestern, 1980; (also see below); *Public Managerial Economics*, Southwestern, 1983; *Principles of Economics* (contains 2nd editions of *Principles of Micro-Economics* and *Principles of Macro-Economics*), Southwestern, 1983.

Contributor: Arizona's Economy: Yesterday, Today, and Tomorrow, College of Business Administration, Arizona State University, 1976; Josef Brada, editor, *East-West Business: Theory and Evidence*, Indiana University Press, 1978; William Loehr and Todd Sandler, editors, *Public Goods and Public Policy*, Sage Publications, 1978; A. L. Chickering, editor, *Problems of the International Economy*, Institute for Contemporary Studies (San Francisco, Calif.), 1979; J. R. Clark, editor, *Economics: Strategies for Teaching Principles of Economics in Two-Year Colleges,* Joint Council on Economic Education, 1980; Clark, editor, *Strategies for Teaching Economics,* Joint Council on Economic Education, 1981; Marvin Jackson, editor, *Markets and Marketing: The East-West Nexus,* Indiana University Press, 1982. Contributor of about thirty-five articles and reviews to economic and business journals in the United States and abroad.

SIDELIGHTS: Amacher told *CA:* "I write textbooks for my own recreation as much as anything else. If they successfully meet a market test, so much the better.

"I think we have to make economics straightforward and enjoyable, or it won't be read. Economists loudly condemn the economic illiteracy of the voting public, yet we are, in part, responsible for not writing material that ends this illiteracy."

*   *   *

AMORE, Roy Clayton 1942-

PERSONAL: Born September 10, 1942, in Newark, Ohio; son of Ralph C. (a farmer) and Mary Ellen (Wyckoff) Amore; married Judy Hunt (a teacher), 1962; children: Allison, Justin. *Education:* Ohio University, A.B., 1964; Drew University, B.D., 1967; Columbia University, Ph.D., 1970. *Religion:* Methodist. *Home:* 150 Randolph Pl., Windsor, Ontario, Canada N9B 2T3. *Office:* Department of Religious Studies, University of Windsor, Windsor, Ontario, Canada N9B 3P4.

CAREER: University of Windsor, Windsor, Ontario, assistant professor, 1970-75, associate professor, 1975-81, professor of religious studies, 1981—. Ordained Methodist minister, 1981. Wilson-Craven Professor at Southwestern University, 1978-79. *Member:* Canadian Asian Studies Association, Canadian Society for Studies in Religion, Canadian Council for Southeast Asian Studies (president, 1980-81), American Academy of Religion.

WRITINGS: (Contributor) R. H. Cox, editor, *Religious Systems and Psycholotherapy,* C. C Thomas, 1973; (contributor) F. H. Holck, editor, *Death and Eastern Thought,* Abingdon, 1974; (editor and contributor) *Developments in Buddhist Thought: Canadian Contributions to Buddhist Studies,* Wilfrid Laurier University, 1978; *Two Masters, One Message,* Abingdon, 1978; (with Larry D. Shinn) *Lustful Maidens and Ascetic Kings,* Oxford University Press, 1981. Contributor to *Abingdon Dictionary of Living Religions.* Contributor to theology journals.

WORK IN PROGRESS: Religious Practices of the World, publication expected in 1983; research on the practice of making merit in early Buddhism.

SIDELIGHTS: Amore commented: "I began by studying Christian theology, but became dissatisfied with a one-tradition approach to truth. I took up the study of Eastern religions, especially Buddhism, and now write in the areas of Buddhist ethics and comparative religions. I am also interested in the historical influences of the East upon the West, a subject that is treated in *Two Masters, One Message.* My travels in Buddhist Asia convince me of the oneness of human spirituality."

*   *   *

AMSTUTZ, Mark R(obert) 1944-

PERSONAL: Born January 23, 1944, in Norfolk, Neb.; son of Mahlon Sunday (a minister) and Ruth (Behnke) Amstutz; married Donna Ruth Hustad, June 7, 1967; children: Anne Louise, Caroline Christine. *Education:* Houghton College, B.A., 1965;

American University, M.A., 1967, Ph.D., 1972. *Politics:* Republican. *Religion:* Protestant. *Home:* 205 West Jefferson, Wheaton, Ill. 60187. *Office:* Department of Political Science, Wheaton College, Wheaton, Ill. 60187.

CAREER: American Institute of Certified Public Accountants, New York, N.Y., staff writer, 1967-69; American University, Washington, D.C., instructor in political science, 1970-71; Wheaton College, Wheaton, Ill., assistant professor, 1972-77, associate professor of political science, 1977—, chairman of department, 1980—. Affiliated with U.S. Information Agency, 1971—. *Military service:* U.S. National Guard, 1966-68. U.S. Naval Reserve, 1968—; present rank, lieutenant commander. *Member:* International Studies Association, American Political Science Association.

WRITINGS: (Editor) Lloyd Rodwin, *Nations and Cities,* U.S. Information Agency, 1973; (editor) Michael Kammen, *Peoples of Paradox,* U.S. Information Agency, 1976; *Economics and Foreign Policy,* Gale, 1977; *An Introduction to Political Science,* Goodyear Publishing, 1981.

WORK IN PROGRESS: A book on ethics and foreign policy.

SIDELIGHTS: Amstutz commented: "My introduction to political science was written, in large measure, because of a personal dissatisfaction with current texts on the market. Once I developed a framework (conflict management), I became convinced I had something to say which merited publication."

Amstutz taught in Europe and lived for some fifteen years in South America.

*   *   *

ANBER, Paul
See BAKER, Pauline H(alpern)

*   *   *

ANDERS, Sarah Frances 1927-

PERSONAL: Born January 5, 1927, in Monroe, La.; daughter of Edward Eugene and Malda (Elliott) Anders. *Education:* Louisiana Polytechnic Institute, A.B., 1945; Southern Baptist Theological Seminary, M.R.E., 1948; Florida State University, M.A., 1952, Ph.D., 1955; postdoctoral study at Rensselaer Polytechnic Institute, 1965, and University of New Hampshire, 1968. *Religion:* Baptist. *Office:* Department of Sociology, Louisiana College, Pineville, La. 71360.

CAREER: Director of music education at Baptist churches in Quincy, Fla., 1948-51, and Gadsden, Ala., 1952-53; Florida State University, Tallahassee, assistant director of research laboratory, 1953-55; Mary Hardin-Baylor College (now University of Mary Hardin Baylor), Belton, Tex., professor of sociology, 1955-62, chairman of department, 1962; Louisiana College, Pineville, professor of sociology, 1962—, chairman of department, 1962—, acting dean, 1972-73, Walker Chair of Sociology, 1981—. Guest lecturer at Southern Methodist University, summer, 1961; Staley Lecturer at Averett College, fall, 1973, and Carson-Newman University, winter, 1976; guest lecturer at Southern Baptist Theological Seminary, summer, 1976; Staley Foundation Lecturer. Past president of Texas Council on Family Relations and Southwestern Religious Research Council; past treasurer and research chairperson of Louisiana Council on Family Relations; member of Governor's Committee on Children and Youth, Texas, 1959; and National Council on Family Relations. Chairman of board of Cenla Community Action Program, 1965-66; past member of board of Alexandria-Pineville Young Womens' Christian Association; member of board of Alexandria-Pineville Family Service Agency, Renaissance Children's Receiving Center for Pre-Delinquents, Alexandria-Pineville Mental Health and Child Guidance Clinic, and other civic organizations. Co-chairperson of Arab-Israeli Relief Fund, 1968. *Member:* American Association of University Women, American Sociological Association (fellow), Southwestern Sociological Association, Southwestern Social Science Association, Alpha Chi, Athenians. *Awards, honors:* Award from Chi Omega for outstanding graduate student, 1955; Piper Professor of Texas, 1959; fellowships from National Science Foundation, 1965, 1968, and 1972-73; Alumni Award for excellence in teaching, 1973.

WRITINGS: (With James A. Young) *A Study of Louisiana Pastors: Their Educational Background and the Nature of Their Ministry,* Home Mission Board of SBC, 1973; (with Harry Hollis, David Mace, and others) *Christian Freedom for Women . . . and Other Human Beings,* Broadman, 1975; *Women Alone: Confident and Creative,* Broadman, 1976; (contributor) *Equipping Disciples,* Convention Press, 1977; (contributor) Paul D. Simmons, editor, *Issues in Christian Ethics,* Broadman, 1980; (contributor) Jason Towner, editor, *Solo Flight,* Tyndale, 1980. Contributor to *Sociology: A Pragmatic Approach,* 1981. Contributor to journals, including *Educator, Journal of Educational Sociology, Issues in Christian Ethics,* and *American Journal of Mental Deficiency.*

WORK IN PROGRESS: "A chapter for a book on the aged in certain ethnic groups in the U.S."

SIDELIGHTS: Anders told *CA:* "I have written widely on women in society and religion. I helped develop the concept of the 'single family,' and write to and about single, widowed, and divorced persons in our society. I do workshops and write on these areas and ethical issues. I speak and do lecture series on these areas; mid-life issues, family life conferences, non-marrieds, aging."

*   *   *

ANDERSEN, Juel   1923-

PERSONAL: Birth-given name, Jewell, changed in 1968; born October 12, 1923, in Chicago, Ill.; daughter of Albert L. and Lilian (Levine) Pick; married John Eve Andersen (a computer analyst), December 6, 1957; children: Sigrid A. *Education:* Roosevelt College (now University), B.A., 1951; Boston University, M.A., 1952. *Home and office address:* P.O. Box 235, Arnold, Calif. 95223. *Agent:* Elaine Berman, 445 San Antonio Rd., Los Altos, Calif. 94022.

CAREER: Psychologist at public schools in Beverly, Mass., 1953-56; Juels (maker of handcrafted jewelry), Los Gatos, Calif., owner, 1968-77; writer and lecturer, 1977—.

WRITINGS: (With Cathy Bauer) *The Tofu Cookbook,* Rodale Press, 1979; (with daughter, Sigrid Andersen) *The Tofu Primer,* Creative Arts, 1980; *Juel Andersen's Tofu Kitchen,* Bantam, 1981; *The Tofu Dessert Book,* Creative Arts, 1982.

WORK IN PROGRESS: *Juel Andersen's Tofu Diet.*

SIDELIGHTS: "A fortuitous accident began my career writing cookbooks," Juel Andersen commented. "I have been so intrigued by the incredible versatility and usefulness of this almost miraculous food that after completing three books on tofu I feel I could easily write three more.

"Working with and writing about tofu as an ingredient in American cooking has led me to the conviction that it is the single most valuable contribution to American-style cooking in the last century. Indeed, many far-seeing food processors are recognizing the future of this soybean product.

"The purpose of my forthcoming diet book is to show how weight can be controlled and to show that all the good foods, even desserts, can be enjoyed. One eats lots of tofu and a bare minimum of meat—and that only the best: filet mignon, saddle of lamb, breast of chicken, and duck, lobster, giant prawns and salmon. Is there more to say?

"Writing has become a source of delight, and I promise myself that after the diet book I will certainly write more on other subjects. Having a computer has slain the dragon of typing once and for all, one of the impediments to many a great opus.

"Before I began writing, I spent about twenty years as a goldsmith. I owned my own shop and exhibited gold jewelry and small sculpture. I try to keep up my skills by doing a small amount of commission work.

"Before that was another career as a psychologist for a medium-sized school system in Massachusetts. Short and less than sweet, it was spent giving inadequate tests to impossible children sent to be tested by incompetent teachers. I gave up psychology to become a skilled craftsman and would advise others with a bent toward psychology to do that same or some other useful work.

"I am married to an incomparable Dane and have one daughter, who worked with me on *The Tofu Primer.* I live in California. Part of the time I spend in the flatlands around San Francisco Bay, and the rest of the time at my working address in the Sierra Mountains above Angel's Camp, the home of the famous Mark Twain frog jump."

*   *   *

ANDERSON, Maxwell   1888-1959

BRIEF ENTRY: Born December 15, 1888, in Atlantic, Pa.; died February 28, 1959, in Stamford, Conn. American educator, journalist, and author. Anderson first gained prominence in the early 1920's for his collaborations with playwright Laurence Stallings. Their best known work, *What Price Glory* (1926), captivated audiences with its realistic depiction of war. Anderson later sparked a revival in verse drama with *Elizabeth the Queen* (1930), which became a box office success. He followed it with several other verse dramas, including *Winterset* (1935) and *High Tor* (1937), which strengthened his position as a leading American playwright. Many of Anderson's most successful plays were politically significant: *Winterset* is a *Hamlet*-like retelling of the Sacco-Vanzetti case, and *High Tor* is an allegory in which New England's Dutch traditions are contrasted with criminal ethics. Anderson also adapted some of his plays for motion pictures, but his best-known scripts are probably his adaptation of Erich Maria Remarque's *All Quiet on the Western Front* (1930) and his screenplay for Alfred Hitchcock's "The Wrong Man" (1956). His later plays, including the historical drama *Anne of the Thousand Days* (1948), were considered by many critics to be inferior to his work during the 1930's. *Biographical/critical sources:* *Cyclopedia of World Authors,* Harper, 1958; *Encyclopedia of World Literature in the Twentieth Century,* updated edition, Ungar, 1967; *Twentieth Century Writing: A Reader's Guide to Contemporary Literature,* Transtlantic, 1969; *Twentieth-Century Literary Criticism,* Volume 2, Gale, 1979.

*   *   *

ANDERSON, Walt
See ANDERSON, Walter Truett

ANDERSON, Walter Truett 1933-
(Walt Anderson)

PERSONAL: Born February 27, 1933, in Oakland, Calif.; son of Elbert William (a rancher) and Susan (Martin) Anderson; married Maurica Osborne, February 10, 1968; children: Daniel Griffith. *Education:* University of California, Berkeley, B.A., 1955; California State University, Northridge, M.A., 1967; University of Southern California, Ph.D., 1972. *Home:* 1112 Curtis St., Albany, Calif. 94706. *Agent:* Barbara Lowenstein, 250 West 57th St., New York, N.Y. 10019.

CAREER: TV Guide, Los Angeles, Calif., reporter and author of column "Hollywood Teletype," 1960-64; free-lance writer, 1965—.

WRITINGS—Under name Walt Anderson: (Editor) *The Age of Protest,* Goodyear Publishing, 1969; *Campaigns: Cases in Political Conflict,* Goodyear Publishing, 1970; (editor) *Politics and Environment,* Goodyear Publishing, 1970, revised edition, 1976; *Politics and the New Humanism,* Goodyear Publishing, 1973; (with Joseph Allman) *Evaluating Democracy,* Goodyear Publishing, 1974; *A Place of Power: The American Episode in Human Evolution,* Goodyear Publishing, 1976; (editor) *Therapy and the Arts,* Harper, 1977; *Open Secrets: A Western Introduction to Tibetan Buddhism,* Viking, 1979.

Under name Walter Truett Anderson: *The Upstart Spring: Esalen, Big Sur, and the Human Potential Movement,* Viking, 1982; *The Nation-State: An Introduction to American Government,* Scott, Foresman, 1982.

Contributing editor and author of column "Television," in *Los Angeles,* 1965-69; contributing editor of *Human Behavior,* 1973-79, and Pacific News Service, 1980—; member of board of editors of *Journal of Humanistic Psychology,* 1975—.

WORK IN PROGRESS: Rethinking Liberalism, an anthology, publication expected in 1983; *Further Adventures of the Political Animal,* on politics and evolution, publication expected in 1984.

*   *   *

ANDERSON, Wendell B(ernhard) 1920-

PERSONAL: Born January 10, 1920, in Sandpoint, Ohio; son of Gustav Bernhard (in lumber industry) and Ebba (Reed) Anderson; married Dorothy Dewey (an artist), May 16, 1942 (divorced); married Joan Steers Hightower, September, 1955 (divorced); married Emily Mansfield Ferry (a poet), April 9, 1965. *Education:* Attended University of Oregon, 1939-42, 1945-48, and Reed College, 1943; Franklin Pierce College, B.A., 1969. *Politics:* None. *Religion:* None. *Home:* 1002 La Quinta St., Las Cruces, N.M. 88005.

CAREER: U.S. Fish and Wildlife Service, Washington, D.C., clerk and patrolman at Hart Mountain National Antelope Refuge in Lakeview, Ore., 1942-43; U.S. Forest Service, Washington, D.C., seasonal forest fire lookout, timber faller, laborer, and fire control aide in Oregon, 1942, 1945-47, in New Mexico, 1949-50, 1952, and in Montana, 1951; University of New Mexico, Harwood Foundation Library, Taos, director and operator of county bookmobile program, 1949-51; U.S. National Park Service, Santa Fe, N.M., fire control aide, 1955; New Mexico Department of Public Welfare, Albuquerque, caseworker, 1965-66; creative writing teacher at private school for gifted children with personality disorders in Rindge, N.H., 1966-68; New Mexico Department of Public Welfare, Ala-

mogordo, caseworker, 1969-72; New Mexico Department of Human Services, Alamogordo, child welfare social worker in social services division, 1972-74. Member of Otero County Board for Alcoholism and Alcohol Abuse, 1973-74. *Member:* Rio Grande Writers Association.

WRITINGS—Poems: *The Heart Must Be Half Eagle,* Motive Bookshop, 1950; *Hawk's Hunger,* Motive Bookshop, 1952; (with Judson Crews and Cerise Farallon) *Three on a Match,* Estes Es Press, 1964; *Rocky Mountain Vigil,* privately printed, 1978; *Yes or No,* Windhover Whooping Crane Press, 1978; *Endangered Island,* Terra Alba Moonsong Editions, 1979; *Season of the Crow* (self-illustrated), Namaste Press, 1979.

Work represented in anthologies, including *Poems Southwest,* edited by A. Wilbur Stevens, Prescott College Press, 1968; *Poetry of the Desert Southwest,* edited by James E. Quick, Baleen Press, 1973; *Turquoise Land: Anthology of New Mexican Poetry,* Nortex, 1974; *Poets West,* edited by Lawrence P. Spingarn, Perivale, 1975. Contributor of more than two hundred fifty poems to magazines, including *Yale Review, Western Humanities Review, Wormwood Review, Bitterroot, Spectrum,* and *Cottonwood Review,* and to newspapers.

WORK IN PROGRESS: An autobiography; *Organ Mountain Ouvre,* poems; "Stono," a long poem on the American West.

SIDELIGHTS: "I read Goethe's life and poetry and was much inspired by it," Anderson commented. "I set my goal—to be a poet—very early in life and never varied from it. I published a first poem in a Portland newspaper when I was nineteen and found the 'little magazines' publishing more and more of my poems over the years.

"A singular literary influence on my life was Judson Crews, the poet. I made contact with him in 1941, having submitted some poems to his magazine, *Verse Libre,* and later met him and made a lasting friendship that has evolved over all these years.

"My first marriage to an artist broke up during World War II. I went down to Big Sur to meet Judson, and there I met Henry Miller. We were virtually the first to experience the beauty of that wild coast in those war years, when it was closed to all public traffic and a place called 'Slate Springs' was simply a cottage by the sea and a series of hot baths tucked away in the rock of the shore. It later became the Esalen Institute.

"Judson Crews and Henry Miller changed my life irrevocably. I returned to work in the forests of Oregon. I was a sawmill worker, then went back to college again. I tried for awhile to turn my back on writing and artistic friends, but found myself at a loss, so continued to write poetry over those bitter years from 1945 to 1949.

"I went to Taos to visit with Judson in 1949 and remained there for ten years. I published poetry more and more frequently. I had a love affair that took me to Mexico, to San Miguel de Allende, where I wrote forty poems. This affair broke up, leaving me stranded high and dry. I tried another marriage which ended in divorce.

"The result of all this activity was a nervous breakdown. I emerged run-down physically but made the start all over again, climbing back up out of despair to life. I was a hospital orderly for several years. I took training to become a licensed practical nurse. It was very hard for me to give up the kind of outdoor life in the mountains which I had been used to, but I met a registered nurse during this period. We married within three months and have been married ever since.

"A new phase began in my life. I became a family services caseworker. Then we moved to the East where I taught the writing of poetry to highly endowed children with personality disorders. I returned to college to continue my education and after graduation moved back to the West, where I worked as a social worker in child welfare work. We were compelled by my wife's growing disability, multiple sclerosis, to resign the job. We came to Las Cruces to buy land for our home, 'El Pinar.'

"On April 28, 1980, I began work on a long poem. I had started it tentatively, thinking I would call it 'Yucca Flats.' It was to be a nature poem dealing with the ecology of the small piece of desert land we called 'El Pinar.' It was to be, in minute terms, a celebration of the southwestern cycle of seasons, wildlife, bird life, and the story of the creation of a home. A well was sunk, a mobile home was purchased and placed on an empty flat two miles out of town. One had a fine view of the Mesilla Valley and the Organ Mountains beyond.

"It soon evolved, however, into something more than expected, an exposition in poetic terms of real estate expansion, suburban growth which encroached and is now covering the once solitary and relatively valueless Yucca Flats.

"I began writing about the survival of the wildlife, the ecology of the desert. I began planting desert pines from the Middle East, more popularly known as Mondell or Afghan pines. The poem continued evolving until it became a poetic history of Western expansion, dealing with the American West in terms of the mountain men, the Lewis and Clark expedition, Sacagawea, and all the events leading to the Civil War period in American history. Details of my wife's family background encompassed the prebellum south of Virginia. My own background, the immigrant experience from Europe, Swedish-American, became part of the long poem. It is now a mosaic, a kind of weaving back and forth of this history and the backgrounds, together with the development of the place we named 'El Pinar.'"

AVOCATIONAL INTERESTS: Art (painting, drawing, printmaking, sculpture).

*   *   *

ANDREW, Malcolm (Ross)   1945-

PERSONAL: Born January 27, 1945, in Paddock Wood, England; son of John Malcolm Y. (an academic administrator) and Mary (an academic administrator; maiden name, Faulkner) Andrew; married Lena Bernstroem (a librarian), August 17, 1968; children: Christopher. *Education:* St. Catharine's College, Cambridge, B.A., 1967; Simon Fraser University, M.A., 1969; University of York, D.Phil., 1972. *Home:* 62 Christchurch Rd., Norwich, Norfolk NR2 3NF, England. *Office:* School of English and American Studies, University of East Anglia, Norwich, Norfolk NR4 7TJ, England.

CAREER: English teacher at secondary school in Hertford, England, 1973-74; University of East Anglia, Norwich, England, lecturer in English, 1974—. *Member:* International Arthurian Society, New Chaucer Society, Early English Text Society, Renaissance English Text Society, Mediaeval Academy of America.

WRITINGS: (Editor) *On the Properties of Things*, Book VII, Clarendon Press, 1975; (editor with Ronald Waldron) *The Poems of the Pearl Manuscript: Pearl, Cleanness, Patience, Sir Gawain and the Green Knight*, Edward Arnold, 1978, University of California Press, 1979; *The Gawain-Poet: An Annotated Bibliography, 1839-1977*, Garland Publishing, 1979; (editor) *Two Early Renaissance Bird Poems*, University of South Car-

olina Press, 1982. Contributor of articles and reviews to learned journals.

WORK IN PROGRESS: Editing *Chaucer's General Prologue*, with Charles Moorman, completion expected in 1985; a monograph on the *Gawain* poet, c. 1987.

SIDELIGHTS: Andrew commented: "My consuming interest is literature, especially that of the Middle Ages and the Renaissance. Within this field, I am particularly engaged with editorial theory and practice, narrative technique, and attitudes to love. At work, I am also an active and enthusiastic teacher and administrator."

AVOCATIONAL INTERESTS: Art, music, architecture, motorcycle sport.

*   *   *

ANDREWS, Edgar Harold   1932-

PERSONAL: Born December 16, 1932, in Didcot, England; son of Richard Thomas and Cicely Beatrice Andrews; married Thelma Doris Walker (a company director), September 16, 1961; children: Rachel, Martyn. *Education:* University of London, B.Sc., 1953, Ph.D., 1960, D.Sc., 1968. *Religion:* Evangelical Christian. *Home:* Redcroft, 87 Harmer Green Lane, Welwyn, Hertfordshire, England. *Office:* Department of Materials, Queen Mary College, University of London, Mile End Rd., London E1 4NS, England.

CAREER: Imperial Chemical Industries Ltd., Welwyn Garden City, England, technical officer, 1953-55; Rubber Producers' Research Association, Welwyn Garden City, senior physicist, 1955-63; University of London, Queen Mary College, London, England, reader, 1963-68, professor of materials, 1968—. Chartered engineer. Director of Evangelical Press and QMC-Industrial Research Ltd.; chairman of Clarendon School Trust, 1975-81; consultant to Dow Chemical Co. *Member:* Biblical Creation Society (president, 1978—), Institute of Physics (fellow), Institution of Metallurgists (fellow). *Awards, honors:* A. A. Griffith Silver Medal from Materials Science Club of Great Britain, 1977, for published works on fracture.

WRITINGS: Fracture in Polymers, Oliver & Boyd, 1968; *Is Evolution Scientific?*, Evangelical Press, 1977; *From Nothing to Nature: A Young People's Guide to Evolution and Creation*, Evangelical Press, 1978; (editor and contributor) *Developments in Polymer Fracture*, Applied Science Publishers, 1979; *God, Science, and Evolution*, Evangelical Press, 1980; *The Promise of the Spirit*, Evangelical Press, 1982; *Faith Explained*, Evangelical Press, in press.

Contributor: Leslie Bateman, editor, *Physics and Chemistry of Rubberlike Solids*, Maclaren, 1963; A. C. Strickland, editor, *Physical Basis of Yield and Fracture*, Institute of Physics, 1966; P. L. Pratt, editor, *Fracture 1969*, Chapman & Hall, 1969; William Brown, editor, *Testing of Polymers IV*, Interscience, 1969; H. Stollery, editor, *Shock Tube Research*, Chapman & Hall, 1971; A. D. Jenkins, editor, *Polymer Science: A Materials Science Handbook*, North-Holland Publishing, 1972; A. D. Buckingham and C.E.H. Bawn, editors, *MTP International Review of Science*, Butterworth & Co., 1972; R. N. Howard, editor, *Physics of Glassy Polymers*, Applied Science Publishers, 1973; D. T. Clark and W. J. Feast, editors, *Polymer Surfaces*, Wiley, 1978; J. F. Vincent and J. D. Currey, editors, *The Mechanical Properties of Biological Materials*, Cambridge University Press, 1980. Contributor of more than eighty articles and reviews to scientific journals throughout the world.

SIDELIGHTS: Andrews commented: "Truth is a unity, and this is my basic approach to science and religion. Biblical revelation must be compatible with genuine scientific discovery, but revelation must take precedence since human enquiry is flawed by human nature. The Bible makes it clear that God is sovereign in creation, providence, and the personal salvation of the soul through faith in Jesus Christ.

"In my scientific research I am concerned mainly with understanding the phenomena of interest. Although much of my work is applied (i.e., engineering) science, I am still a physicist at heart, seeking to reveal by research the excellent harmony of nature and its unity as expressed by the laws of science.

"In all my books and papers I try to communicate and explain. I am a teacher. My aim is not to dazzle or impress, not to mystify, but to enable the reader to enter into my own experiences and insights for himself.

"*Is Evolution Scientific?* and *From Nothing to Nature* have been published in Swedish, and the latter book is being translated into Norwegian."

AVOCATIONAL INTERESTS: Music (pianist), travel (Europe, the Far East, the United States).

*   *   *

ANGIOLILLO, Paul F(rancis)   1917-

PERSONAL: Born July 1, 1917, in New York, N.Y.; son of Joseph S. (an importer) and Diletta (Priore) Angiolillo; married Birgitta Brunskog (a librarian), February 28, 1948; children: Carl, Paul F., Jr., Joel, Dea. *Education:* Columbia University, A.B., 1938, M.A., 1939, Ph.D., 1946; postdoctoral study at University of Geneva, 1946-47. *Home:* 70 East Ridae St., Carlisle, Pa. 17013.

CAREER: Teacher at secondary schools, including Great Neck High School, Oratory School in Summit, N.J., and Walden School in New York City, 1939-46; International School of Geneva, Switzerland, teacher, 1947-48; University of Louisville, Louisville, Ky., assistant professor, 1948-51, associate professor, 1951-56, professor of modern languages, 1956-62, director of research, 1952-53; Dickinson College, Carlisle, Pa., professor of French and chairman of department of modern languages, 1962-81; Charles A. Dana professor emeritus of romance languages, 1981——. Visiting professor at Columbia University, summers, 1949-52; Fulbright professor at Lycee de Nantes, 1956-57; visiting professor and chairman of modern language department of American College of Switzerland, 1968-69.

MEMBER: American Association of Teachers of French (past state president), American Association of Teachers of Italian, Alliance Francaise (past president), American Association of University Professors (past president), Modern Language Association of America, Societe des Professeurs Francais en Amerique, Association des Membres de l'Ordre des Palmes Academiques, Italian Culture Council (member of board of directors). *Awards, honors:* Albert Gallatin fellow at University of Geneva, 1946-47; first prize from Geneva-London Press literary contest, 1947, for story "Unseasonable"; officer des Palmes Academiques, 1962; Lindback Award for distinguished teaching, 1964-65; award from government of Italy, for University of Siena, 1967; officer d'academie from government of France, 1967; Ganoe Award for inspirational teaching, 1974-75.

WRITINGS: Armed Forces: Foreign Language Teaching, S. F. Vanni, 1947; *A Criminal as Hero: Angelo Duca*, Regents Press, 1979. Contributor to language and education journals. Editor of newsletter of American Association of Teachers of Italian, 1964-68.

WORK IN PROGRESS: An anthology of Italian literature for American students of Italian; a book (possibly an anthology of translated examples) on comparative literature.

SIDELIGHTS: In June, 1981, the author's colleagues and students established the Paul F. Angiolillo Prize, an annual award given at the commencement ceremony to the outstanding student of Italian or French.

Angiolillo told *CA:* "I am enjoying my retirement hugely, especially the flexibility and freedom from being tied to a fixed schedule. I am amused that my book on Duca has presumably made me a kind of instant authority on the 'heroic bandit,' or 'noble robber,' for I have been asked to write a thirty-five-hundred-word article on the theme for a forthcoming dictionary of literary themes and types."

*   *   *

ANQUILLARE, John   1942-

PERSONAL: Surname is pronounced An-*quill*-ar-ee; born March 31, 1942, in New Haven, Conn.; son of Vincent and Livia (Teadora) Anquillare; married Joyce Walker, August 20, 1966; children: Michael, David. *Education:* University of New Haven, B.S., 1966. *Religion:* Roman Catholic. *Home and office:* 13 Mount Pleasant Rd., West Haven, Conn. 06516.

CAREER: Territory account manager for Best Foods division of CPC International, 1966-75; salesman for Etkind & Solcoff, 1975-77; salesman for Transcon Lines, 1978——; Anquillari D & N Sporting Goods, West Haven, Conn., owner, 1980——. *Awards, honors:* Member of All-American Baseball Team, 1963-64, and All-American Softball Team, 1969-72, 1976, 1978; named most valuable player of National Tournament by American Softball Association, 1970.

WRITINGS: (With Joan Joyce) *Winning Softball*, Contemporary Books, 1975.

SIDELIGHTS: Anquillare told *CA* that, before his book was published, there was no softball instruction book that elaborated on both the mental and physical aspects of the game. His qualifications for writing the book, which is about women's softball as well as men's, are his nine years experience in softball and previous work in baseball. Since 1978 he has conducted ten to fifteen softball clinics a year, throughout the Northeast.

*   *   *

ANTHONY
See TABER, Anthony Scott

*   *   *

ANTONIAK, Helen Elizabeth   1947-

PERSONAL: Born August 10, 1947, in Bethesda, Md.; daughter of Charles (an aeronautical engineer) and Marguarita (a writer; maiden name, Keirnan) Antoniak. *Education:* University of San Diego, A.A., 1967; University of California, Los Angeles, B.A., 1969; San Diego State University, M.S.W., 1972; University of Humanistic Studies, Ph.D., 1980. *Religion:* Roman Catholic. *Home:* 1528 Monitor Rd., San Diego, Calif. 92110.

CAREER: Bayside Settlement House, San Diego, Calif., day care recreation leader, 1967; Vista Associates, teen center youth worker, 1968; Stanford Home for Girls, Sacramento, Calif., house mother, 1969; Service Center Headquarters, Sacramento, government intern, 1969-72; Rancho Pino Mental Health Training Center, Lakeside, Calif., social worker, 1972; City of San Diego Public Employment Program, San Diego, community development specialist, 1973; Home of Guiding Hands, Lakeside, supervisor of foster grandparent program, 1974; Episcopal Community Services, San Diego, community development specialist, 1975-79; Oak Glen School, Ramona, Calif., caseworker, 1981—. Organizer and executive director of Widowed to Widowed Program, 1972-80. Member of local Board of Public Welfare; member of San Diego County Southeast Asian Refugee Coalition; associate member of Stress Management Training Institute; member of Grief Center Task Force. Adult education teacher in San Diego, 1973; designer of creative widowhood/divorce adjustment program. *Member:* Mensa, Academy of Certified Social Workers (life member).

WRITINGS: Alone: Emotional, Legal, and Financial Help for the Widowed or Divorced Woman, Celestial Arts, 1979; *My Most Recent Book,* privately printed, 1980; *Positive Power People* (anthology), Royal C.B.S. Publishers, 1981.

WORK IN PROGRESS: Immaculata Tour Booklet, a tour guide, publication expected in 1981; *Frogstyle,* an adventure novel about an underwater demolition team cruise, 1982; *Funny Is Not Fattening: One Hundred One Ways to Lose Weight,* a humorous look at approaches to losing weight, 1982; *Creative Widowhood Adjustment,* 1983.

SIDELIGHTS: Helen Antoniak commented: "I am a social worker at heart. I have an intense interest in helping people, especially in the areas of grief adjustment and goal setting. I am also a devout Catholic and would like to integrate my spiritual life into my writing career. I love reading as well as writing and feel frustrated that I never seem to find enough time to do either. My favorite authors are John Steinbeck and Erma Bombeck. I love to insert humor into my writing whenever possible. Since my interests are serious, it is surprising how often I can put a comic twist on things."

*   *   *

APEL, Karl-Otto 1922-

PERSONAL: Born March 15, 1922, in Duesseldorf, Germany (now West Germany); son of Otto (a merchant) and Elizabeth (Gerritzen) Apel; married Judith Jahn, December 12, 1953; children: Dorothea, Barbara, Katharina. *Education:* University of Bonn, D.Phil., 1950. *Home:* Am Schillertempel 6, Niedernhausen 6272, West Germany. *Office:* Department of Philosophy, University of Frankfurt, Dantestrasse 4-6, 6 Frankfurt am Main, West Germany.

CAREER: Akademie der Wissenschaften und der Literatur, Mainz, West Germany, research assistant, 1950-52; researched under stipend from German Research Association; University of Mainz, Mainz, West Germany, lecturer in philosophy, 1961-62; University of Kiel, Kiel, West Germany, professor of philosophy, 1962-69; University of Saarbruecken, Saarbruecken, West Germany, professor of philosophy, 1969-72; University of Frankfurt, Frankfurt am Main, West Germany, professor of philosophy, 1972—. Theodor Heuss Visiting Professor at New School for Social Research, 1976-77; Ernst Cassirer Lecturer at Yale University, 1977. *Military service:* German Army, 1940-45. *Member:* Institut International de Philosophie, Allgemeine Gesellschaft fuer Philosophie in Deutschland.

WRITINGS: Die Idee der Sprache in der Tradition des Humanismus von Dante bis Vico (title means "The Idea of Language in the Tradition of Humanism From Dante to Vico"), Bouvier, 1963, third revised edition, 1980; "Die Entfaltung des 'sprachanalytischen' Philosophie und das Problem der Geisteswissenschaften" (essay), published in *Philosophie Jahrbuch,* 1965, translation by Harald Holstelilie published as *Analytic Philosophy of Language and the "Geisteswissenschaften,"* Reidel, 1967; *Transformation der Philosophie,* two volumes, Suhrkamp, 1973, translation by Glyn Adey and David Frisby published as *Toward a Transformation of Philosophy,* Routledge & Kegan Paul, 1980; *Der Denkweg von Charles S. Peirce,* Suhrkamp, 1975, translation by John M. Krois published as *Charles Sanders Peirce: From Pragmatism to Pragmaticism,* University of Massachusetts Press, 1981; *Die Erklaeren: Verstehen Kontroverse in Transzendentalpragmatischer Sicht,* Suhrkamp, 1979, translation by Georgia Warnke to be published as *The Explanation Understanding Controversy in Light of Transcendental Pragmatics,* by M.I.T. Press.

WORK IN PROGRESS: Ethik im Zeitalter der Wissenschaft (title means "Ethics in the Age of Science"), for Suhrkamp; *Transformation der Philosophie,* Volumes III and IV, for Suhrkamp.

SIDELIGHTS: Apel told *CA:* "My *Toward a Transformation of Philosophy* was begun as a rather descriptive account of the development of contemporary philosophy. At the focus of my interest was the so-called 'linguistic turn' of philosophy in its Anglo-Saxon version (Wittgenstein and its aftermath) and its German version (Heidegger and post-Heideggerian 'hermeneutics'). Along with the progress of my work, however, the title took on another meaning. It finally pointed towards a new systematic shape ('Gestalt') of philosophy that appeared to me to be a possible aim of the whole development. I called it sometimes 'transcendental hermeneutics,' sometimes 'transcendental pragmatics,' and recently, in order to comprise these two aspects, 'transcendental semiotics.'

"It is the spirit of these titles that volumes three and four of my work are conceived. The practical (ethical) aspect of this enterprise may be characterized by the normative conception of an 'ideal community of communication.' This conception connects the last essay in *Toward a Transformation of Philosophy* with my work in progress, *Ethics in the Age of Science.* This and my theoretical conception of 'transcendental pragmatics' owe a lot to Charles S. Peirce, who in my opinion is the greatest American philosopher.

"My book *The Explanation: Understanding Controversy* deals in the spirit of transcendental pragmatics with an 'evergreen' of the philosophy of science and the humanities. It was indeed always my conviction that the 'unified science' thesis that denies the essential difference between a communicative understanding of human intentions, reasons, beliefs, etc., and the causal explanation of natural events amounts to a naivety."

*   *   *

APHRODITE, J.
See LIVINGSTON, Carole

*   *   *

APPLETON, Marion Brymner 1906-

PERSONAL: Born March 18, 1906, in Crystal, N.D.; daughter of John Francis (an entrepreneur) and Marion Wallace (Cameron) Appleton. *Education:* University of Washington, Seattle, B.S. in L.S., 1932, B.A., 1933. *Home:* 10752 Durland Ave. N.E., Seattle, Wash. 98125.

CAREER: University of Washington, Seattle, senior librarian in Circulation Division, 1933-35, 1936-43; Seattle Public Library, Seattle, librarian in art department, 1944-63, head of department, 1964-69; writer, 1969—. Assistant librarian at Seattle Art Museum, 1935-39. *Member:* American Association of University Women, United Nations Association, Pacific Northwest Library Association (chairman of picture indexing committee, 1960-69), Henry Gallery Association, Allied Arts of Seattle (chairman of directory committee, 1972-73), Seattle Repertory Organization, Seattle Symphony Women's Association, Friends of the Seattle Public Library. *Awards, honors:* Volunteer in the arts award from University of Washington, Henry Gallery, 1974; awards from Seattle Symphony Women's Association, 1976 and 1977, for *Notable Nourishment.*

WRITINGS: (Editor) *Who's Who in Northwest Art,* Frank McCaffrey, 1941; (editor) *Index of Pacific Northwest Portraits,* University of Washington Press, 1972; *Puget Sound's Eight Lively Arts: A Directory of Arts Organizations,* Allied Arts of Seattle, 1973; (editor) *Notable Nourishment* (cookbook), Madrona, 1975.

WORK IN PROGRESS: A supplement to *Who's Who in Northwest Art,* tentatively entitled *Early Pacific Northwest Art,* publication expected in 1983.

SIDELIGHTS: Marion Appleton wrote: "When I was nine and living in Minneapolis, my favorite place was the Children's Room in the old Minneapolis Public Library. I remember particularly the way the librarian fingered through the cards in the catalog. After entering the University of Washington years later, it was the natural thing to do, when I needed a part-time job, to go to the Seattle Public Library, to the art department, as art history was now an added interest. I'm sure the various indexing projects worked on since that time are directly related to a child's fascination with that old Minneapolis card catalog."

*   *   *

AQUIN, Hubert   1929-1977

PERSONAL: Born October 24, 1929, in Montreal, Quebec, Canada; committed suicide March 15, 1977, in Montreal, Quebec, Canada; son of Jean and Lucille (Leger) Aquin; married Andree Yanacopoulo; children: Stephane, Philippe. *Education:* University of Montreal, L.Ph., 1951; also attended University of Paris. *Religion:* Catholic. *Home:* 126 Les Pins, Laval, Quebec, Canada.

CAREER: Film critic for *L'Autorite,* Montreal, Quebec, and CKAC, 1951-54; director for Radio-Canada, 1954; organizer and supervisor of television programs, 1956; assistant director of Public Affairs Services, 1958; National Film Board of Canada, scenarist, 1959, producer, 1960; screenwriter and producer for l'Office du Film du Quebec, 1964; production adviser for the Pavillon du Quebec and producer of film "Man and Life" for Expo '67, Montreal, 1965; writer. Founder of Association Professionelle des Cineastes et Directeurs, 1963; secretary general of the Centre Culturel du Vieux Montreal, 1967; director of the Centre Culturel de Montreal.

MEMBER: Societe des Auteurs (Montreal; vice-president, 1962-63), Association Professionelle des Cineastes et Directeurs (founder, director, 1963), Rassemblement Pour l'Independance Nationale (vice-president, 1964), Centre Culturel de Montreal (director); Centre Culturel du Vieux Montreal (secretary-general, 1967); Havre des Iles Country Club. *Awards, honors:* Prix David from Ministry of Cultural Affairs of Quebec, 1972, for entire body of work; prize for directing, from Mostra Internazionale del Film d'Autor, San Remo Film Festival, 1962,

for "A Saint-Henri, le 5 septembre"; prix du film Sportif de Cortina for "L'Homme vite"; Prix de la Province de Quebec for *L'Antiphonaire.*

WRITINGS: Prochain Episode (novel), Cercle du Livre de France, 1965, translation by Penny Williams published under same title, McClelland & Stewart, 1967; (translator) Arthur Kopit, "Le Jour ou les p . . . vinrent jouer au tennis" (play), first produced in Montreal at Theatre de L'Egregoire, 1966; "Ne ratez pas l'espion" (musical comedy), first produced in Eastmain, Quebec, at Theatre de la Marjolaine, June 25, 1966; *Trou de memoire* (novel), Cercle du Livre de France, 1968, translation by Alan Brown published as *Blackout,* Anansi, 1974; *L'Antiphonaire* (novel), Cercle du Livre de France, 1969, translation by Brown published as *The Antiphonary,* Anansi, 1973; *Point de fuite* (essays), Cercle du Livre de France, 1971; *Neige noire* (novel), La Presse, 1974, translation by Sheila Fischman published as *Hamlet's Twin,* McClelland & Stewart, 1979; (author of introduction) Charles Auguste Maximilien Globensky, *La Rebellion de 1837 a Saint-Eustache,* Editions du Jour, 1974; *Blocs erratiques,* edited by Rene Lapierre, Quinze, 1977.

Films: "L'Art chinois," 1958; "Quatre Enfants du monde," 1959; "L'Exil en Banlieue," 1960; "Les Grandes Religions," 1961; "Le Temps des amours," 1961; "Le Sport et les hommes," 1961; "Ceux qui parlent francais," 1962; "A Saint-Henri, le 5 septembre," 1962; "Les Bucherons de la Manouane," 1962; "L'Homme vite"; "La Fin des etes"; "Jour apres jour."

Television plays: "Table tournement," Canadian Broadcasting Corp. (CBC-TV) 1968; "Vint-quatre heures de trop," CBC-TV, 1969; "Double Sens," CBC-TV, 1971.

Contributor of articles to *Maclean's* and *Parti Pris.*

Founding editor of *Liberte.*

SIDELIGHTS: The author of four best-selling novels, Aquin became one of Canada's most popular contemporary authors. He also worked as an activist on behalf of the French-Canadian separatist movement. Aquin had already become "a cult figure for members of Quebec's political and artistic avant-garde" at the time of his suicide in 1977, wrote Linda Leith in *Canadian Forum,* and since then he has become "a literary saint and . . . a national hero."

Aquin's first novel, *Prochain Episode,* parallels an episode from the author's early career as a separatist. Suspected of terrorism, Aquin was under observation in a psychiatric hospital when he began writing the critically acclaimed novel. The book is about a young Quebecois who is imprisoned for terrorist activities. Drawing upon his experiences in revolutionary politics, the prisoner begins writing a spy novel. His book, wrote Ofelia Cohn-Sfetcu in *Modern Fiction Studies,* "becomes the embodiment of the creative potentiality of the prisoner, a positive affirmation of human dignity which refuses to be bullied by space and time." In *Essays on Canadian Writing,* Roland Bourneuf observed that Aquin's protagonists are troubled individuals who "attempt to escape inner disintegration through the act of writing; for them . . . writing becomes a question of life or death." Although the prisoner fails to write a satisfactory conclusion for his mystery, Cohn-Sfetcu explained that Aquin expresses "the view that in human life what is of ultimate importance is not the achievement of the goal itself but the groping towards it."

Aquin's novel *Blackout* is also about a revolutionary Quebecois. The book, which is structurally more complex than *Prochain Episode,* consists of a series of narratives pertaining to a murder committed by the revolutionary. His interpretation of the events surrounding the murder—in the form of journal—comprises the first part of the novel. A commentary by the editor of a critical edition of the journal comes next. And last is a version of the murder in which the victim's sister claims that she invented the whole story. Each of these accounts conflicts with the others, obscuring the truth and making it impossible to reach a satisfactory conclusion about what actually occurred. "As in *Prochain episode*," wrote Bourneuf, "nothing is resolved, nothing is freely decided by the narrator."

Aquin's 1969 novel, *The Antiphonary*, is about a woman who begins writing a dissertation on sixteenth-century medicine in an attempt to cope with physical and psychological pressures that are threatening her sanity. Gradually her thesis begins to mirror the events in her life, and it turns into a "highly imaginative tale of smuggled medical treatises, epilepsy and murder," observed *Saturday Night*'s Brian M. Vintcent. In her thesis, said Vintcent, the heroine "allows herself to become what she believes, hopes and fears she is . . . [a] victim of her own and other people's obsessions." According to Bourneuf, the novel "confirms the author's obsession with failure and the constancy of his identity theme."

Hamlet's Twin, Aquin's final novel, is in the form of an autobiographical screenplay written by the book's central character. Typical of Aquin's fiction, the script/novel contains several scenes of emotional and physical violence, including the sadistic murder of the protagonist's wife, Sylvie. The book, said Mark Czarnecki in *Maclean's*, "documents the destruction of human relationships so violently that the reader's emotions are chopped up like Sylvie's body."

Aquin had been criticized in the past for gratuitously including exceptionally brutal scenes in his novels, but Linda Leith argued that "in *Hamlet's Twin* there is . . . aesthetic justification for this element as it provides an extreme contrast to the highly cerebral nature of many of . . . [Aquin's] authorial interjections." Aquin, she continued, was "a writer concerned with ambiguity and coinciding opposites." Bourneuf conjectured that the violent scenes in Aquin's fiction express the author's feeling that "disorder is permanent and widespread." Wayne Grady agreed with both critics, pointing out that in *Hamlet's Twin* Aquin uses the "discontinuity" of his novel's structure to amplify his point that "the course of life is chaotic and unpredictable," while also stressing that "discontinuity presupposes continuity." "The novel," he concluded, "is about opposites . . . that are the same."

Czarnecki claimed that the novel's "superheated intellectual pressure" causes it "to fall apart long before the end." Grady, on the other hand, insisted that even though the book contains flaws, they "are quibbles when stacked up against Aquin's extraordinary energy and insight." *Hamlet's Twin*, he declared, "is unquestionably the master work of a brilliant, complex, and tortured mind, and our first and proper response to it is awe."

BIOGRAPHICAL/CRITICAL SOURCES: Times Literary Supplement, May 19, 1972; *Saturday Night*, September, 1973; *Canadian Forum*, November, 1973, September, 1979; *Maclean's*, May 21, 1979; *Books in Canada*, August, 1979; *Essays on Canadian Writing*, fall-winter, 1979-80; *Contemporary Literary Criticism*, Volume 15, Gale, 1980.*

—*Sketch by Susan M. Trosky*

* * *

ARASTEH, A(bdol) Reza 1927-

PERSONAL: Born September 27, 1927, in Shiraz, Iran; came to the United States in 1957, naturalized citizen, 1976; son of M. Khalil (in business) and Sahra (Bigum) Arasteh; married Josephine Durkatz (a child psychologist), 1957; children: Dariush K., Roya L. *Education:* University of Tehran, B.A., 1948, M.A., 1949; Louisiana State University, Ph.D., 1953; post-doctoral study at University of Chicago, 1953-54. *Politics:* Independent. *Religion:* Humanist ("Loyalty to Life"). *Home and office:* 7905 Custer Rd., Bethesda, Md. 20814. *Agent:* A.P. Watt Ltd., 26/28 Beford Row, London WC1R 4HL, England.

CAREER: University of Tehran, Tehran, Iran, associate professor of psychology, 1955-58; Princeton University, Princeton, N.J., associate professor of Oriental Studies, 1958-60; conducted research on higher consciousness with Erich Fromm, 1960-62; George Washington University, Washington, D.C., senior lecturer in psychiatry and social behavior, 1962-69; University of Tehran, visiting professor of social and analytical psychology, 1969-71; Princeton University, visiting professor, 1971-72; independent consultant and writer, 1972—. Visiting professor at Allahabad University, 1969, 1972, 1981, and Kagawa University and Komazawa University, both 1972-81; participant in international conferences. Director of multi-disciplinary research at Psychiatric Institute of Washington, 1962-67; senior adviser on education and leadership training to the University of Tehran, 1968-69; member of International Development Center at American University; consultant to United Nations and Echotechnic Institute; has worked for Gandhi Peace Foundation, Center for Appropriate Technology, Indian Industrial Development Service, Mustizafan Foundation of New York City, Medical Women's International Association, E. I. du Ponte de Nemours & Co., General Electric Corp., and Control Data Corp.

MEMBER: World Union and Consortium for Rural Technology, International Society for Political Psychology, International Congress of Psychotherapy (affiliate fellow), Congress for Asian Psychology (founding member), American Psychological Association (fellow), American Management Association, American Academy of Political and Social Science, Institute of Advanced Islamic Studies (Peru; honorary member), Royal Society of Medicine (affiliate fellow), Forum for Integrative Studies. *Awards, honors:* Fulbright scholarship, 1951-53; award from UNESCO, 1972, for best publication in social psychology.

WRITINGS: Education and Social Awakening in Iran, E.J. Brill, 1962, 2nd edition, 1968; (with Erich Fromm) *Rumi, the Persian: Rebirth in Creativity and Love*, Ashraf Press (Pakistan), 1963, Routledge & Kegan Paul, 1974; *Final Integration in the Adult Personality: A Measure for Peace*, E. J. Brill, 1964, published in the United States as *Toward Final Personality Integration*, Schenkman, 1973, 2nd edition, Halsted, 1975; *Creativity in the Life Cycle*, E. J. Brill, Volume I, 1968, Volume II, 1969, published in the United States as *Creativity and Human Development*, Schenkman, 1976; *Man and Society in Iran*, E. J. Brill, 1969, 2nd edition, 1970; *Faces of Persian Youth: A Psycho-Social Study*, E. J. Brill, 1970; *Teaching Through Research: A Guide for College Professors in Developing Countries*, E. J. Brill, 1970; *Rediscovering America*, Omen, 1972; (contributor) John White, editor, *Frontiers of Consciousness*, Julian Press, 1973; (contributor) L. F. Rushbrook Williams, editor, *Sufi Studies: East and West*, Dutton, 1974; *Growth to Selfhood*, Routledge & Kegan Paul, 1980; *Revolution of Service: An Analysis of Positive Forces in Man*, Routledge & Kegan Paul, in press.

Other writings: *Cheguneggi roshde adami*, (title means "The Process of Human Growth"), Atashkadeh Press, 1956; *Naghshe* elm o saat dar tajdid hayat melatha, (title means "The Role of Science and Technology in Human Society"), Taban Press, 1968, 3rd edition, 1969; *Sayre ravanshenassi dar gharb* (title means "The Development of Modern Psychology"), Volume I, Dehkhoda, 1970; *Tajdid hayat javanan dar doreh barkhorde tamadonha* (title means "Rebirth of Youth in the Age of Cultural Change"), Elmi Press, 1970. Contributor to *International Encyclopedia of Literature*. Contributor of more than thirty articles and reviews to scholarly journals and popular magazines, including *Tehran Journal, Islamic Review, American Journal of Psychoanalysis,* and *Journal of General Psychology*.

SIDELIGHTS: Arasteh wrote: "The greatest subject, and the most difficult for me, is peace—peace in the individual, the family, the community, and the world. This is not possible without a 'new' kind of man and woman; a new identity must grow out of the ashes of our present civilization. 'Loyalty to Life' must become our new faith, and with productivity, contentment, and service to one another, it can deliver us to universality. My major work, *Final Integration in the Adult Personality: A Measure for Peace,* tries to create such a new image."

BIOGRAPHICAL/CRITICAL SOURCES: Marilyn Ferguson, *The Aquarian Conspiracy,* J. P. Tarcher, 1980.

*   *   *

ARCHER, Stephen M(urphy) 1934-

PERSONAL: Born May 14, 1934, in Winfield, Kan.; son of William A. (a farmer) and Cecelia (Kumbera) Archer; married Paula Karalyn Agrelius (an administrative assistant), August 3, 1959; children: Steven Michael. *Education:* Kansas State Teacher's College (now Emporia State College), B.A., B.S., 1957, M.S., 1958; University of Illinois, Ph.D., 1964. *Politics:* Democrat. *Religion:* None. *Home:* 715 Spring Valley Rd., Columbia, Mo. 65201. *Office:* University Theater, University of Missouri, Columbia, Mo. 65211.

CAREER: High school teacher of drama and speech in Kansas City, Mo., 1958-59; Black Hills Teachers College, Spearfish, S.D., instructor in communications, 1959-62; Kearney State College, Kearney, Neb., assistant professor of theatre and speech, 1964-66; Southern Illinois University, Edwardsville, assistant professor, 1966-70, associate professor of theatre, 1970-71, member of summer extension faculty in England, France, Italy, and Greece, 1970; University of Missouri, Columbia, associate professor, 1971-77, professor of theatre, 1977—, visiting professor, summers, 1969 and 1971, director of theatre, 1972-75.

MEMBER: American Theatre Association (chairman of festival committee, 1972-75), American Society for Theatre Research, University and College Theatre Association, Speech Communication Association, Association for Communication Administration, Theatre Library Association, Players Club.

WRITINGS: (Editor of revision, with Calvin Lee Pritner, and contributor) *A Selected and Annotated Bibliography for the Secondary School Theatre Teacher and Student,* American Educational Theatre Association, 1970; *How Theatre Happens,* Macmillan, 1978; *An Annotated Bibliography of American Actors and Actresses,* Gale, 1982.

Scripts: "TKO" (one-act play), first produced in Hinsdale, Ill., at Hinsdale Community Theatre, March 4, 1973; "The Booth Family" (film strip), Oleson, 1975.

Contributor of more than twenty articles and reviews to speech, theatre, and education journals.

WORK IN PROGRESS: A *Biography of Constant Coquelin,* completion expected in 1985; *A History of the American Theatre,* completion expected in 1986.

SIDELIGHTS: "My primary goal," Archer commented, "is the exploration of the mutual dependency of theatre production and scholarship. My vocational interests are primarily historical, concerning the theatre of America, England, and France. Like most academic writers, I aspire to creating novels and plays. My advice to students is to do that which fulfills you every day; if it's writing, do not let a day go by without exercising your skills."

AVOCATIONAL INTERESTS: Reading, travel, chess.

*   *   *

ARIYOSHI, Sawako 1931-

PERSONAL: Born January 21, 1931, in Wakayama, Japan; daughter of Shinji and Akitsu Ariyoshi; married Akira Jin, March 27, 1962 (divorced May, 1964); children: one daughter. *Education:* Attended Tokyo Women's Christian College, 1949-52. *Home:* 3-16-19 Horinouchi, Suginami-ku, Tokyo 166, Japan. *Agent:* Kurita-Bando Literary Agency, SN Building, 2-5-1 Iidabashi, Chiyoda-ku, Tokyo 102, Japan.

CAREER: Okura Publishing Co., Tokyo, Japan, member of editorial department, 1952-53; correspondent for Azuma Kabuki Committee during U.S. tour, 1954; writer, 1954—. Lecturer at University of Hawaii, Honolulu, 1970-71. Member of Japanese Literary Representatives, 1961, and of Central Board of Education, 1972. *Awards, honors:* Nominated for Akutagawa Literary Prize, 1956, for *Jiuta;* nominated for Naoki Literary Prize, 1957, for *Shiroi tobira;* incentive award from Art Festival, 1957, for "Ishi no niwa"; Ministry of Education award from Art Festival, 1958, for radio adaptation "Homura: A Joruri Song"; fellowship from Rockefeller Foundation, 1959; Literary Award for Women, 1967, for *Hanaoka Sheishu no tsuma;* Ministry of Education award from Art Festival, 1967, for *Aka jishi;* Bunjei Shunjei Readers Award, 1968, for *Umikura;* Fujin Koron Readers Award, 1968, and art incentive award, 1970, both for *Izumo no Okuni.*

WRITINGS—Serialized books: "Rakuyo no fu" (title means "A Song of the Sunset"), published in *Hakuchigun,* March, 1954; "Jiuta" (title means "A Song of Shamisen"), published in *Bungakukai,* January, 1956; "Shiroi tobira" (title means "The White Door"), published in *King,* June, 1957; "Geisha warutsu Itarianio" (title means "Geisha Waltz Italian Style"), published in *Shukan Tokyo,* January-December, 1958, book published under same title, [Japan], 1959; "Kinokawa," published in *Fujin Gahoh,* January, 1959, book published under same title, [Japan], 1964, translation by Mildred Tahara published as *The River Ki,* Kodansha, 1980; "Watashi wa wasurenai" (title means "I Will Never Forget"), published in *The Asahi,* August-December, 1959, book published under same title, Chuo Koron Sha, 1960.

"Tomoshibi" (title means "A Light"), published in *Shukan Bunshun,* January, 1961; "Kohge" (title means "Incense and Flowers"), published in *Fujin Kohron,* January, 1961, book published under same title, Chuo Koron Sha, 1962; "Heiten jikan" (title means "Closing Time"), published in *The Yomiuri,* April-December, 1961, book published under same title, Kodansha, 1962; "Sukezaemon yondai ki" (title means "The Saga of Sukezaemons"), published in *Bungakukai,* January, 1962, book published under same title, Bungei Shunju Sha, 1962; "Arita gawa" (title means "The River Arita"), published in *Nippon,* January-December, 1963, book published under same title, Kodansha, 1963; ''Hishoku,'' published in *Chuo Koron*, April, 1963-June, 1964, book published under same title, Chuo Koron Sha, 1964; ''Ichi no ito'' (title means ''The First String''), published in *Bungei Asahi*, June, 1964-June, 1965, book published under same title, Shinco Sha, 1965; ''Puerto Riko nikki'' (title means ''The Puerto Rico Journals''), published in *Bungei Shunju*, July-December, 1964, book published under same title, Bungei Shunju Sha, 1964.

''Hidaka gawa'' (title means ''The River Hidaka''), published in *Shukan Bunshun*, January-October, 1965, book published under same title, Bungei Shunju Shinsa, 1966; ''Hanoaka Shei-shu no tsuma,'' published in *Shincho*, November, 1966, book published under same title, Shincho Sha, 1967, translation by Wakako Hironaka and Ann Siller Kostant published as *The Doctor's Wife*, Kodansha, 1978; ''Izumo no Okuni'' (title means ''Akoku From Izumo''), published in *Fujin Koron*, January-December, 1966, book published under same title, Chuo Koron Sha, 1969; ''Fushin no toki'' (title means ''The Time of Disbeliefs''), published in *The Nippon Keizai*, January-December, 1966, book published under same title, Shincho Sha, 1968; ''Umikura'' (title means ''The Darkness of the Sea''), published in *Bungei Shunju*, April, 1967-April, 1968, book published under same title, Bungei Shunju, 1968; ''Onna futari Nyuginia'' (title means ''Two Women in New Guinea''; travel), published in *Shukan Asahi*, May-November, 1967, book published under same title, Asahi Shinbun Sha, 1969; ''Mo kyojo ko'' (short stories), published in *Shincho*, January, 1969, book published under same title, Shincho Sha, 1973; ''Owaranu Matsu'' (title means ''The Endless Summer''), published in *Bungakukai*, January-July, 1969; ''Shibazakura'' (title means ''Primrose''), published in *Shukan Shincho*, January, 1969-April, 1970, book published under same title, Shincho Sha, 1970.

''Yuhigaoka Sangokan'' (title means ''The Sunset Building Number Three''), published in *The Mainichi*, April-December, 1970, book published under same title, Shincho Sha, 1971; ''Ariyoshi Sawako shenshu'' (title means ''The Selected Works of Sawako Ariyoshi''), published in *Shincho Sha*, April, 1970-April, 1971, book published under same title, Shincho Sha, 1977; ''Keitonsbiru jiken no kunin'' (title means ''Nine People of . . .''), published in *Sekai*, January, 1972, book published under same title, Shincho Sha, 1972; ''Boke no hana'' (title means ''The Flowers of Japanese Quince''), published in *The Yomiuri*, June, 1972-August, 1974, book published under same title, [Japan], 1973; ''Masagoya Omine'' (title means ''Omine of the Masagoya''), published in *Chou Koron*, January, 1973-August, 1974, book published under same title, Chuo Koron, 1974; ''Boshi Hen'yo,'' published in *Shukan Yomiuri*, January-December, 1973, book published under same title, Kodansha, 1974; ''Ougon densitsu'' (title means ''The Golden Legends''), published in *Shincho*, January, 1974-August, 1975; ''Kinugawa'' (title means ''The River of Kinu''; short stories), published in *Shincho*, January, 1974-August, 1975, book published under same title, Shincho Sha, 1975; ''Fukogo osen'' (title means ''The Complex Contamination''), published in *The Asahi*, October, 1974-June, 1975, book published under same title, Shincho Sha, 1975.

''Aoi tsubo'' (title means ''The Blue Jug''), published in *Bungei Shungei*, January, 1976-February, 1977, book published under same title, Bungei Shunju, 1977; ''Nihonjin banzai'' (title means ''Hail to the Japanese''; play), published in *Chuo Koron*, January-February, 1977; ''Akuyo ni tsuite'' (title means ''A Vicious Woman''), published in *Shukah Asahi*, March, 1978, book published under same title, Shincho Sha, 1978; ''Kazu no Miyasama otome,'' published in *Gunzo*, January, 1977-March, 1978, book published under same title, [Japan],

1978; ''Chugoku repoota'' (title means ''China Reports''; travel), published in *Shukan Shincho*, August, 1978-February, 1979, published as *Ariyoshi Sawako no Chugoku repoto*, [Japan], 1978.

Other books: *Shojorentoh* (title means ''Prayers of Virgins''), Mikasa Shobo, 1957; *Masshiroki no ke* (title means ''Sheer Pure White''), Bungei Shunju Sha, 1957; *Zuihitsu* (title means ''Essays''), Shinsei Sha, 1958; *Ariyoshi Sawako shu* (short stories), [Japan], 1961; *Hina no nikki* (title means ''The Diary of the Dolls''), Bungei Shunju Sha, 1962; *Aka jishi: A gidaya* (title means ''A Red Boar''), Bungei Shunju, 1967; *Midare-mal*, [Japan], 1968; *Watakushi wa wasurenai*, [Japan], 1969; *Kaminaga hime* (title means ''A Princess With Long Hair''), Popular Sha, 1970; *Sarasa Fujin*, [Japan], 1973; *Nidai no ikeri*, [Japan], 1973; *Managoya O-Mine*, [Japan], 1974; *Yu-chi Tso-ho-tzu hsiao shuo hsuan* (short stories), [Japan], 1977; *Fukugo osen sono go* (title means ''The Complex Contamination and Later''; agricultural ecology), Ushio Shuppansha, 1977; *Sojo rento*, [Japan], 1978.

Published by Kodansha: *Dangen* (title means ''Broken String''), 1957; *Kitoh* (title means ''The Prayer''), 1960; *Homura: A Joruri Song* (adaptation of radio script), 1961; *Kyakko* (title means ''The Footlights''), 1962; *Onnayakata* (title means ''The Mansion for Women''), 1965; *Kazunokiya iama otome* (title means ''Princess Kazunokiya''), 1978.

Published by Chuo Koron Sha: *Hano no inochi* (title means ''A Life of a Flower''), 1958; *Eguchi no sato* (title means ''The Country of Eguchi''), 1958; *Shin onna daigaku* (title means ''A New Women's College''), 1960; *Onna deshi* (title means ''A Woman Apprentice''), 1961; *Furi Amerika ni sode wa nurasaje* (plays), 1970.

Published by Shincho Sha: *U-Tsui anjusan* (title means ''The Beautiful Nun''), 1958; *Sanbaba* (title means ''Three Old Women''; short stories), 1961; *Shimmyo* (title means ''A Sewing Woman''), 1971; *Kokotsu no heto* (title means ''The Twilight Years''), 1972.

Published by Shuei Sha: *Sarashina Fujin* (title means ''Madame Sarashina''), 1962; *Wakakusa no uta* (title means ''The Song of Young Grass''), 1963; *Renbu* (title means ''A Series of Dances''), 1963; *Karinui* (title means ''The Bastings''), 1963; *Ranbu* (title means ''The Wild Dances''), 1967; *Nihon no Shimajima, Mukashi to Ima* (title means ''Isolated Islands in Japan''), 1981.

Other: ''Homura: A Joruri Song'' (radio script), first broadcast by NHK Broadcasting, 1958. Also author of television script ''Ishi no niwa'' (title means ''The Stone Garden''), c. 1957. Contributor to anthologies and to magazines.

SIDELIGHTS: Based on historical incidents and cultural facts, Sawako Ariyoshi's writings illustrate the life of the Japanese people, their family traditions, social structure, and domestic proceedings. Her characters range from rich, well-born historical figures to the average Japanese individual, from a crafty princess to typical housewives.

Interested in the domestic life of her country, Ariyoshi explores this topic in two novels. In *Yuhigaoka Sangokan* she investigates the conditions under which housewives in Osaka live. Moving up the social ladder, *The River Ki* looks at the life of the Japanese upper class from the turn of the century to the late 1950's in order to view the effect of social and political changes on traditional Japanese values. With a beautiful aristocratic woman as its protagonist, ''the story is rich in details of Japanese domestic life,'' wrote Brian Weiss of *Best Sellers*. ''The characters are affectionately depicted in bold strokes, there is humor and pathos, and the writing is sound. . . .'' Critically, Ariyoshi's style in *The River Ki* has been compared with that of other social realists, including John Dos Passos, John Steinbeck, and Pearl S. Buck.

Ariyoshi's historical novels not only continue to deal with social and family structures in Japan, but they also explain landmarks in the country's history. *Kazunokiya iama otome,* the novel about a princess who saved herself from a political marriage by switching places with a serving girl, gives an accurate picture of the Meiji Restoration. *The Doctor's Wife* tells the story of Hanaoka Sheishu, the doctor who invented the anesthetic used for surgical procedures in 1805, forty years prior to the anesthetic's discovery in the Western world. Ariyoshi concentrates on the doctor's triumph as well as the devotion of his mother and the plight of his wife's position in her role as an obedient daughter-in-law.

BIOGRAPHICAL/CRITICAL SOURCES: Omoshiru Hambun, July, 1951; *Best Sellers,* July, 1980.

* * *

ARNOLD, Bob 1952-

PERSONAL: Born August 5, 1952, in Adams, Mass.; son of Robert Thomas (in lumber business) and Penny (Scott) Arnold; married Susan Paules, August 28, 1974. *Education:* Attended high school in Wolfeboro, N.H. *Home address:* Green River R.F.D., Guilford, Vt. 05301.

CAREER: Lumberyard worker in Adams, Mass., 1965-70; carpenter and stonemason in Vermont, 1970—. Editor and publisher of Longhouse Press, 1973—. Instructor at Mark Hopkins College, 1977, and at private school in Greenfield, Mass., 1979-82. Worked in nursery school and day care center (as alternative service for a conscientious objector to military duty), 1972-74.

WRITINGS—Books of poems: *Rope of Bells,* Cherry Valley, 1974; (with John Levy and David Giannini) *"3,"* Longhouse Press, 1978; *Along the Way,* Blackberry Press, 1979; *Habitat,* Pentagram Press, 1979; *Thread,* Pentagram Press, 1980; *Love and Landscape,* Coyote Books, 1982.

Editor and publisher of *Longhouse,* 1973—.

WORK IN PROGRESS: A book of essays, journals, poems, and letters about rural life as a manual laborer and builder, publication expected in 1985.

SIDELIGHTS: Arnold told *CA:* "My wife Susan, manual labor, and having plenty of books to read along with writing poems are perhaps the important, or immediate, sidelights of my life. Living on the river here has a lot to do with it, too. My best working performance as a poet comes between September and May, especially during the winter months. The more snow the better. There is something about having to load two wood stoves before the house is warm. Most of the writing is already in my head before I sit at the desk. Saving firewood to split every day brings the first line of a poem. Sometimes a generous letter from a friend will do the same, as I reply in kind. It goes without saying how important a good friend is— I have a few I would not like to live without. Otherwise, my poems tell the rest of my story. Companionship, landscape, and a relationship with wildlife is vital, no matter how timeworn that 'back to nature' request sounds. The seasons of the year elect many of the poems I write, and what jobs are to be done. Winter for woodchopping; spring for pruning and planting; summer for wood and stone building; fall for harvest and travel.

"It was important to my career that I was lucky enough, but didn't know it then, to be the oldest son, in a family of four, of a lumberman who still owns the oldest family lumber business in America—Arnold Lumber, originated in 1788. I learned how to pile lumber, unload boxcars, and work with carpentry crews. On my mother's side I watched and enjoyed the strength and spirit of a large Irish family. I took off for the woods after high school and don't plan ever to come out. I have always avoided cities, yet Seattle is a lovely place, and I have traveled extensively through the northern United States and Canada.''

BIOGRAPHICAL/CRITICAL SOURCES: Maraja One, 1981.

* * *

ARNOLD-FORSTER, Mark 1920-1981

OBITUARY NOTICE—See index for *CA* sketch: Born April 16, 1920, in Swindon, England; died December 25, 1981. Journalist and author. Joining the *Manchester Guardian* in 1946, Arnold-Forster began his career as a German correspondent, holding that post until 1948 when he became a labor correspondent. In 1957 he left the *Guardian* to work for the *Observer* as a chief reporter and a defense correspondent. Shortly afterwards he became the deputy editor of the Independent Television News (ITV). Relying on this television experience, Arnold-Forster wrote the best-selling book for the popular series "The World at War." In 1963 he returned to the *Guardian* staff as a senior specialist writer responsible for editorial policies on defense, Ireland, and European affairs. Besides *The World at War,* Arnold-Forster's other books include *The Seige of Berlin* and a work whose publication is pending. Obituaries and other sources: *London Times,* December 28, 1981.

* * *

ARTHUR, Elizabeth 1953-

PERSONAL: Born November 15, 1953, in New York, N.Y.; daughter of Robert (a writer) and Joan (a writer; maiden name, Vaczek) Arthur; married Robert Gathercole, May 2, 1974 (divorced September, 1980). *Education:* Attended University of Michigan, 1971-73, and Notre Dame University, Nelson, British Columbia, 1976-77; University of Victoria, B.A. (with distinction), 1978, Diploma in Education, 1979. *Residence:* Dorset, Vt. 05251. *Agent:* Jean V. Naggar Literary Agency, 420 East 72nd St., New York, N.Y. 10021.

CAREER: Writer. Member of Ossabaw Island project, 1981. Worked as mountaineering teacher, in construction, and at a recreation vehicle factory, bank, and greenhouse. *Member:* Friends of the Earth, Greenpeace. *Awards, honors:* William Sloane fellowship for Bread Loaf Writers Conference, 1980.

WRITINGS: Island Sojourn, Harper, 1980.

WORK IN PROGRESS: Beyond the Mountain, a novel.

* * *

ARYA, Usharbudh 1934-

PERSONAL: Born March 23, 1934, in Dehradun, India; son of Durgadas and Lakshmi (Devi) Sharma; married Lalita Sharma, August 6, 1961; children: Sushumna, Stomya, Saumya, Angiras. *Education:* University of London, B.A. (with honors), 1965, M.A., 1966; University of Utrecht, D.Litt., 1968. *Office:* Center for Higher Consciousness, 631 University Ave. N.E., Minneapolis, Minn. 55413.

CAREER: Traveling lecturer, 1947-67; University of Minnesota, Minneapolis, assistant professor of Sanskrit and of Indian religions, 1967-73; Center for Higher Consciousness, Minneapolis, founder and director, 1970—. Professor at Himalayan International Institute of Yoga Science and Philosophy. Member of council of religious advisers at University of Minnesota. *Member:* American Oriental Society, Association of Asian Studies, American Academy of Religions, Royal Asiatic Society of Great Britain and Ireland, Association of Humanistic Psychology, Association of Transpersonal Psychology. *Awards, honors:* Grants from State of Minnesota.

WRITINGS: Ritual Songs and Folksongs of the Hindus of Surinam, E. J. Brill, 1968; *Superconscious Meditation,* Himalayan International Institute of Yoga Science and Philosophy, 1974; *Philosophy of Hatha Yoga,* Himalayan International Institute of Yoga Science and Philosophy, 1977; *God,* Himalayan International Institute of Yoga Science and Philosophy, 1979; *Meditation and the Art of Dying,* Himalayan International Institute of Yoga Science and Philosophy, 1979; *Mantra,* Himalayan International Institute of Yoga Science and Philosophy, 1981.

Contributor: Alan Weinstock, editor, *Foundations of Eastern and Western Psychology,* Himalayan International Institute of Yoga Science and Philosophy, 1975; R. M. Ballentine, editor, *The Theory and Practice of Meditation,* Himalayan International Institute of Yoga Science and Philosophy, 1975; S. N. Agnihotri and Justin O'Brien, editors, *Faces of Meditation,* Himalayan International Institute of Yoga Science and Philosophy, 1978. Contributor to *Encyclopedia of Indian Philosophies.* Contributor to scholarly journals.

WORK IN PROGRESS: Yoga Sutras of Patanjali.

SIDELIGHTS: Arya wrote: "I was born into a Sanskrit-speaking family. The early training was strictly traditional and rigorous. I sat with my father for an hour's meditation daily at the age of five. By seven-and-a-half, all four thousand rules (sutras) of Panini's Sanskrit grammar were memorized. By the age of eleven the study of the major philosophical texts, including the Upanishads, was completed. At age thirteen I was examined in public by leading traditional scholars to give threefold interpretation of any of the twenty thousand mantras from the Vedas, and at sixteen I debated with the scholars in the Town Hall of the holy city of Varanasi.

"Throughout those years I also lectured to crowds of up to twenty thousand, as well as in institutions of higher learning, always speaking spontaneously on any topic presented by the audience. Since the age of nineteen I have traveled and lectured widely, living in various parts of the world, including Africa, the Caribbean, South America, many island countries, England, and the United States.

"I have taught deep relaxation methods now widely used by counselors, teachers, nurses, medical doctors, and psychiatrists in their professional practices to deal with problems of stress, tension, anxiety, and psychosomatic symptoms.

"I have tried to create an awakening toward the contemplative heritage of Christianity among the ministers of religion, including Catholic priests and nuns who have learned the ways to deepen the experience of prayer through the art of meditation."

BIOGRAPHICAL/CRITICAL SOURCES: New Age, March, 1977; *St. Paul Pioneer Press,* August 3, 1980.

*   *   *

ASCH, Sholem   1880-1957

BRIEF ENTRY: Born November 1, 1880, in Kutno, Poland; died August 10, 1957, in London, England. Author. Asch was a prolific novelist. Early in his career he wrote in Yiddish to appeal to Jewish readers. Most of his novels celebrate faith in God to redeem humanity from worldly pleasures and pain. Early works such as *The Small Town* (1904) and his play *God of Vengeance* (1918) established Asch as a master of realistic fiction. The world he protrays is so sordid and decaying that belief in a higher being is humanity's only alternative to despair. Asch's most controversial work is probably his biblical trilogy comprised of *The Nazarene* (1939), *The Apostle* (1943), and *Mary* (1949). Although Asch insisted that he sought to improve relations between Jews and Christians through the trilogy, many Jewish readers charged Asch with furthering hatred against them during World War II. Throughout his life, Asch traveled extensively, and his novels portray the plight of Jews in several nations. His works have remained in publication through the continuing interest accorded them by Jewish readers everywhere. *Biographical/critical sources: The Reader's Encyclopedia of American Literature,* Crowell, 1962; *Encyclopedia of World Literature in the Twentieth Century,* updated edition, Ungar, 1967; *Twentieth Century Writing: A Reader's Guide to Contemporary Literature,* Transatlantic, 1969; *Longman Companion to Twentieth Century Literature,* Longman, 1970; *Twentieth-Century Literary Criticism,* Volume 3, Gale 1980.

*   *   *

ASCHER, Carol   1941-
(Carol Lopate)

PERSONAL: Born August 15, 1941, in Cleveland, Ohio; daughter of Paul (a psychoanalyst) and Ellen (Ascher) Bergman; married Phillip Lopate, January 31, 1964 (divorced June, 1970). *Education:* Attended Vassar College, 1959-61; Barnard College, B.A., 1963; attended School of Visual Arts, 1968-69; Columbia University, Ph.D., 1974. *Home:* 158 West 23rd St., New York, N.Y. 10011. *Agent:* Steve Axelrod, Sterling Lord, 660 Madison Ave., New York, N.Y.

CAREER: Anthropologist. Free-lance researcher and writer, 1963-68; U.S. Offices of Education and Economic Opportunity at Teachers College, New York City, writer and researcher, 1969-72; Horace Mann-Lincoln Institute of Teachers College, New York City, researcher on "Social Organization of High Schools Project," 1972-74; Children's Television Workshop, New York, senior researcher on program "The Best of Families," 1975-76; Brooklyn Educational and Cultural Alliance, Brooklyn, N.Y., director of research for Brooklyn Rediscovery, 1976-77, researcher and writer of pamphlet, 1978; Fulton Mall Improvement Association, Brooklyn, writer and editor of newsletter, 1978-80; ERIC Clearinghouse on Urban Education for Teachers College, New York City, research associate and staff writer, 1981—; writer, 1966—.

Researcher for Rockland State Hospital and New York State Hospital, 1963-66; writer and researcher for Josiah Macy, Jr., Foundation, 1967-68; story line researcher for Talent Associates, 1977; legal researcher for Time-Life Television Productions, 1979; consultant and writer on evaluation project for Pratt Institute, 1979-80.

Instructor at Herbert H. Lehman College, 1970-72, York College, 1972, Staten Island Community College, 1974-75, Empire State College, 1977-78; coordinator of women's studies at Sarah Lawrence College, 1977-79; participant in cultural anthropology workshops of Empire State College, 1981. *Member:* PEN, Poets and Writers.

WRITINGS—Under name Carol Lopate: *Six Arguments,* Columbia Review Press, 1966; *Women in Medicine,* Johns Hopkins University Press, 1968; *A Program for Third World Students* (monograph), Teachers College, 1969; (contributor) David Mermelstein, editor, *Economics: Mainstream Readings and Radical Critiques*, Random House, 1976; *Education and Culture in Brooklyn: A History of Ten Institutions* (monograph), Brooklyn Educational and Cultural Alliance, 1979. Contributor of articles and short stories to magazines, including *ERIC-IRCD Bulletin, Liberation Magazine, Edcentric, Feminist Studies, Le Monde Diplomatique, College English, Against the Grain, Resist, Ms., The World,* and *Aphra.*

Under name Carol Ascher: (Contributor) Gaye Tuchman and others, editors, *Hearth and Home: Images of Women in the Mass Media*, Oxford University Press, 1978; (contributor) Edith Hoshimo Altbach, editor, *From Feminism to Liberation*, Schenkman, 1980; *Simone de Beauvoir: A Life of Freedom*, Beacon Press, 1981. Contributor of articles and short stories to magazines, including *ERIC/CUE Fact Sheet, Heresies, Present Tense, Confrontation, Socialist Review, Rooms,* and *Feminist Studies.* Contributor of poetry to periodicals, including *Aphra, The World,* and *Adventures in Poetry.* Contributor of book reviews to magazines, including *Harper's Bookletter, Health-Pac, Liberation Magazine, Social Policy, Teachers College Record, WIN Magazine, In These Times, New Women's Times, New Directions for Women,* and *Parabola.*

WORK IN PROGRESS: Reparations, a novel about two daughters of a refugee from the Holocaust; *The Flood,* a novel about a refugee family in Kansas in the 1950's; "co-editing a book with Sara Ruddick and Louise de Salvo about women writing about women."

SIDELIGHTS: Carol Ascher's *Women in Medicine* focuses on the problem of recruiting women in medical careers as discussed at the 1966 Macy Conference on Women in Medicine. Concentrating on women physicians, Ascher attempts to discover the reason that the number of female doctors in the United States is so far beneath that of other countries. The author, using personal interviews and field research, considers the historical background of women as physicians, the contemporary problems and issues peculiar to women in medicine, and the social and cultural factors influencing women in their career choices. Written for those planning medical careers as well as for career counselors, the book, said a *Choice* reviewer, "presents a comprehensive picture of the possible role of women in American medicine."

Ascher's second book, *Simone de Beauvoir: A Life of Freedom*, is partly the biography, partly literary criticism, and partly the philosophy of the famous French feminist and author. Using careful documentation and research as well as personal commentary, Ascher looks at Simone de Beauvoir as a person in addition to as a writer and philosopher. Ascher zeroes in on her subject as someone with much to give the contemporary women's movement, indicating the significance of Simone de Beauvoir's notion of women as both oppressed and free.

Said a *Best Sellers* reviewer: "Ascher clearly respects her [subject], and equally clearly, describes why she is worthy of that respect. On the other hand, Ascher is no apologist for her subject, and she takes persuasive exception to certain of de Beauvoir's insights."

Ascher told *CA* that the *Los Angeles Times* "called my book 'fascinating.'" "*In Print*," she remarked, "said it was 'the first, and thus far only, major work to give insight into de Beauvoir's 'rich and contradictory character.'""

Ascher continued on her writing in general: "Two themes baffle and concern me in most of what I write: being a woman and being the daughter of refugees from the Nazis. I use what-

ever literary form seems most penetrating at the time to go deeper and deeper into these themes."

BIOGRAPHICAL/CRITICAL SOURCES: Choice, February, 1969; *Science Books and Film*, March, 1969; *Best Sellers*, September, 1981; *Washington Post Book World*, September 27, 1981.

*   *   *

ASCHER, Sheila
(Ascher/Straus, a joint pseudonym)

PERSONAL: Born in New York, N.Y.; daughter of Arnold (a plumber) and Bessie (Eisenberg) Ascher. *Education:* Received B.A. from Brooklyn College and M.A. from Columbia University. *Home:* 176 B. 123rd St., Rockaway Park, N.Y. 11694.

CAREER: Writer, 1973—. *Awards, honors:* Experimental fiction prize from *Panache* magazine, 1973, for story "City/Edge"; Pushcart Prize from Pushcart Press, 1978-79, for excerpt from novel, titled "Even After a Machine Is Dismantled, It Continues to Operate, With or Without Purpose."

WRITINGS—With Dennis Straus, under joint pseudonym Ascher/Straus: *Letter to an Unknown Woman* (story), Treacle Press, 1980; *The Menaced Assassin* (novel), Treacle Press, 1982; *Woman's Nightmare "A"* (novella), Sun & Moon Press, 1982; *Double/Profile* (story collection), Annex Press, 1982.

Space novels; with Straus, under joint pseudonym Ascher/Straus: "As It Returns," first presented in New York at Contemporary Arts Gallery of New York University, May, 1975, presented in Philadelphia, Pa., at Y Poetry Center, October 6-31, 1976, presented in Reno at University of Nevada, April, 1977, presented in Kansas City, Mo., at TELIC Exhibition of Art Research Center, May-July, 1977, published in *Seventh Assembling*, 1977, and in *Intermedia*, forthcoming issue; "The Blue Hangar," first presented in New York at Gateway National Recreation Area, August 2-3, 1975, presented in New York at Twelfth Annual New York Avant Garde Festival, September 27, 1975, published in *Coda*, April/May, 1976, in *Queen Street Magazine*, spring, 1977, and in *Interstate*, 1979; "Twelve Simultaneous Sundays," first presented in New York at Gegenschein Vaudeville Placenter, September 19-December 5, 1976. Also co-publisher with Straus of "Green Inventory," partially published by Ghost Dance Press, winter, 1975-76, and spring, 1977.

Creator of language art gallery installations, including "Language and Structure in North America," Toronto, "Beyond the Page," Philadelphia, "Last Correspondence Show," Sacramento, "First New York Post Card Show," New York, "International Mail Art Exhibition," Northampton, Mass., "TELIC Exhibition," Kansas City, Mo., "Assembling Exhibition," New York.

Contributor to anthologies, including *Pushcart Prize Anthology III*, Pushcart Press, 1978-79; *Likely Stories*, Treacle Press, 1981; *Ariadne's Thread*, Harper, 1982.

Contributor to journals, including *Chicago Review, Interstate, Exile, Chouteau Review, Sun and Moon, Chelsea, Paris Review, Beyond Baroque, Gallimafry, Panache, Aspen Anthology, Aphra, Intermedia, Tamarisk, Zone, Calyx, Annex, Benzene, Fifth Assembling, Ghost Dance, Neoneo Do-Do, Telephone, Sixth Assembling, Gegenschein Quarterly, Source, Eighth Assembling, Margins,* and *Precisely.*

WORK IN PROGRESS: "Two major projects are under way: first, completion of a long novel-in-progress to be published jointly with Dennis Straus, which might be described as an attempt to define the emerging character of the future, the hidden transition of things toward the future already under way. And second, along side all other projects, a certain portion of my time is always set aside for work on *Sheila Ascher's Chronicle,* a long work (described at greater length in Sidelights) which is an artist's notebook, journal and novel, until now appearing in a small trickle in literary journals and serving mainly as a sourcebook for virtually all joint Ascher/Straus works. Time will now be spent seeing the *Chronicle* into print in its own right.''

SIDELIGHTS: ''There is no question when you read what they write, you're in the presence of Genius,'' said Hugh Fox of Sheila Ascher and Dennis Straus, the people behind the Ascher/Straus pseudonym. Though they sign both names on their writings, Ascher and Straus do not work together, and they write for different reasons.

In order to produce a work, the authors avoid collaborating in the conventional manner. They share experiences, material, and observations, but one writes while the other criticizes and edits. ''We're a Collective,'' Ascher told the *Cumberland Journal.* ''We POOL everything. We don't work together. I don't know what he's doing, he doesn't know what I'm doing, then we put it all together. It's very strange.'' According to Straus, Ascher writes to discover life's guiding principles while he identifies writing with dreaming. ''For me reading and writing were like always forms of a dream, a waking dream,'' he explained. Writing, he continued, is ''a matter of finding a way of dreaming—on paper.''

Ascher and Straus produce very experimental literature. Perhaps the most conventional in appearance, *The Menaced Assassin,* their first novel in book form, takes place on the plane of magic and dreams. In the novel, a woman tries to make herself into the person she wants to be, an individual who reflects the cultural obsessions generated by contemporary media.

Unlike *The Menaced Assassin,* Ascher and Straus's other creations are space novels, works that use non-written components like photographs or airfields as well as the written word. Using architecture, ''public spaces,'' or huge edifices to structure these ''environmental narratives,'' the authors bring physical and material elements to the works, so reading the novel becomes an active, public experience instead of a private pastime. For instance, ''Twelve Simultaneous Sundays'' is a space novel written publicly on twelve consecutive Sundays. ''Each week a new element was installed,'' explained Ascher, ''and there was no way to read the whole book at any one time, you had to keep coming back.'' Such an innovation, the authors suggested, could change the style of the novel as a genre. ''The space novel,'' they remarked, ''might at some point signal the end of the novel as a bastion of art privacy, of private consumerism, of product purchase, relaxation, nest building, and interior decoration.''

Ascher told *CA:* ''While the bulk of my published work (narratives, visual language work, book-as-book experiments, 'structural' texts, essays, etc.) is co-published (*not* co-authored—the Ascher/Straus emblem is a sign devised for a collective enterprise including all possible mutually helpful writing procedures *except* writing together) with Dennis Straus, the true, central commitment of my life as a writer is an independent project of vast extension called *Sheila Ascher's Chronicle.* The *Chronicle* is a direct narrative centering on women's lives and unfolding principles of material existence (something as if the procedures of astro-physical observation were applied to daily life). It's neither diary nor autobiography nor so-called realistic fiction, but (perhaps what chronicles have been historically) a sort of ideal novel of vast extension and revealed process, writing as a way of living.''

BIOGRAPHICAL/CRITICAL SOURCES: Cumberland Journal, spring, 1981; *Zone,* spring/summer, 1981; *Library Journal,* October, 1981; *Chelsea #36,* 1977; *Interstate 12,* 1979.

* * *

ASCHER/STRAUS
See ASCHER, Sheila
and STRAUS, Dennis

* * *

ASH, Shalom
See ASCH, Sholem

* * *

ASHER, Maxine 1930-

PERSONAL: Born August 15, 1930, in Chicago, Ill; daughter of Arnold L. Klein (a publisher) and Charlotte Jamison; children: Laurie Broslow, Jan Broslow, Susan Moore. *Education:* University of California, Los Angeles, B.A., 1951; California State University, Northridge, M.A., 1968; Walden University, PH.D., 1975. *Address:* P.O. Box 1984, Palm Springs, Calif. 92263. *Agent:* Heacock Literary Agency, 1121 Lake St., Venice, Calif. 90291.

CAREER: Teacher at public schools in Los Angeles, Calif., 1951-66; coordinator of instructional materials centers at public schools in Las Virgenes Unified School District, Calabasas, Calif. 1966-72; Ancient Mediterranean Research Association, Palm Springs, Calif., director, 1973—. Adjunct professor at University of San Francisco, 1975-76; member of faculty at Pepperdine University, University of California, Los Angeles, Los Angeles Pierce College, California State University, Northridge, and College of the Canyons. Consultant for ''In Search of Atlantis,'' 1977; narrator and director of television documentary ''The Lost City of Atlantis,'' 1979; hostess of radio show ''Outer Reach'' for KGUY-Radio, 1981. *Awards, honors:* Third prize from Columbus Film Festival, c. 1967, for filmstrip ''Who's Running the Show?''; plaque from Adventurer's Club. c. 1974, for work at Las Virgenes Unified Schools.

WRITINGS: Atlantis Conspiracy, Ancient Mediterranean Research Association, 1974; *Ancient Energy: Key to the Universe,* Harper, 1979; *Developing Right Brain Energy,* Ancient Mediterranean Research Association, 1980.

WORK IN PROGRESS: A book on practical aspects of the left and right hemispheres of the brain.

SIDELIGHTS: Maxine Asher wrote: ''In 1973 I led the search for Atlantis off the coast of Spain with Dr. Julian Nava, now U.S. ambassador to Mexico. Since then I have led seven other expeditions worldwide. I give frequent lectures and seminars and may be the only woman explorer who actively searches for lost continents and pre-Genesis civilizations.''

* * *

ASHER, Sandy (Fenichel) 1942-

PERSONAL: Born October 16, 1942, in Philadelphia, Pa.; daughter of Benjamin (a doctor) and Fanny (Weiner) Fenichel; married Harvey Asher (a professor), January 31, 1965; children: Benjamin, Emily. *Education:* Attended University of

Pennsylvania, 1960-62; Indiana University, B.A., 1964; graduate study at University of Connecticut, 1973; Drury College, elementary education certification, 1974. *Residence:* Springfield, Mo. *Agent:* Harold Ober Associates, 40 East 49th St., New York, N.Y. 10017. *Office:* Drury College, 900 North Benton, Springfield, Mo. 65802.

CAREER: WFIU-Radio, Bloomington, Ind., scriptwriter, 1963-64; Ball Associates (advertising agency), Philadelphia, Pa., copywriter, 1964; *Spectator,* Bloomington, drama critic, 1966-67; Drury College, Springfield, Mo., instructor in creative writing, 1978—. *Member:* Phi Beta Kappa.

AWARDS, HONORS: Honorable mention from *Envoi* magazine, 1970, for poem "Emancipation"; award of excellence from Festival of Missouri Women in the Arts, 1974, for "Come Join the Circus"; honorable mention from Unitarian Universalist Religious Arts Guild, 1974, for "Afterthoughts in Eden"; honorable mention from *Bitterroot* magazine, 1975, for poem "Seaweed"; Creative Writing Fellowship grant in playwriting from National Endowment for the Arts, 1978.

WRITINGS—Plays: "Come Join the Circus" (one-act), first produced in Springfield, Mo., at Springfield Little Theatre, December, 1973; "Afterthoughts in Eden" (one-act), first produced in Los Angeles, Calif., at Los Angeles Feminist Theatre, February, 1975; *A Song of Sixpence* (one-act), Performance Publishing, 1976; *The Ballad of Two Who Flew* (one-act), Plays, 1976; "How I Nearly Changed the World but Didn't" (one-act), first produced in Springfield at National Organization for Women Herstory Women's Fair, November, 1977; "The Insulting Princess" (one-act), first produced in Interlochen, Mich., at Interlochen Arts Academy, May, 1979; "Food Is Love" (one-act), first produced in Springfield at Drury College, January, 1979; *The Golden Cow of Chelm* (one-act; first produced in Springfield at United Hebrew Congregation, December, 1980), Plays, 1980; *For Love of Elizabeth* (one-act), Pioneer Drama Service, 1980; "Sunday, Sunday" (two-act), first produced in Lafayette, Ind., at Purdue University, March, 1981; *The Mermaid's Tale* (one-act; first produced in Interlochen at Interlochen Arts Academy, May, 1979), Performance Publishing, 1981.

Other: *The Great American Peanut Book* (nonfiction), Tempo, 1977; *Summer Begins* (novel), Elsevier-Nelson, 1980; *Daughters of the Law* (novel), Beaufort, 1980; *Just Like Jenny* (novel), Delacorte/Dell, 1982. Also author of over seventy poems. Contributor of stories and articles to magazines, including *Highlights for Children, Humpty Dumpty's Magazine, Parents Magazine,* and *Writer's Digest.*

WORK IN PROGRESS: Three young adult novels, *This Mother and Daughter Thing, Things Are Seldom What They Seem,* and *Diamond Street.*

SIDELIGHTS: Asher told *CA:* "I credit my teachers, from elementary school through college and beyond, with instilling in me the confidence needed to write. I write for young people because I know the characters in books are often the only trustworthy friends they have. Peter Pan, Jo March, and the Scarecrow of Oz stuck with me through some hard times."

*   *   *

ASPATURIAN, Vernon V. 1922-

PERSONAL: Born February 16, 1922, in Armavir, U.S.S.R.; came to the United States in 1922, naturalized citizen, 1929; married Suzanne Lee Dohan; children: Heidi Jeanne, Nancy Lee. *Education:* University of California, Los Angeles, B.A., 1947, Ph.D., 1951. *Home:* 1154 William St., State College,

Pa. 16801. *Office:* Slavic and Soviet Language and Area Center, Pennsylvania State University, 306 Burrowes, University Park, Pa. 16802.

CAREER: University of California, Los Angeles, lecturer in political science, 1950-51; Pennsylvania State University, University Park, assistant professor, 1952-56, associate professor, 1956-61, professor of political science, 1961-66, research professor, 1966-74, Evan Pugh Professor, 1974—, director of Slavic and Soviet Language and Area Center, 1965—. Smith-Mundt visiting professor at Graduate Institute of International Affairs, Geneva, Switzerland, 1958-59; visiting professor at Columbia University, 1960, 1967, 1980, Johns Hopkins School of Advanced International Studies, 1961-63, and University of California, Los Angeles, 1964-65; research associate at Washington Center for Foreign Policy Research, 1960-63; visiting scholar at Institute for Advanced Studies, Vienna, Austria, 1971; lecturer for U.S. Information Agency, U.S. International Communications Agency, and U.S. State Department in Eastern and Western Europe; consultant to RAND Corp., Army War College, and Planning Research Corp. *Military service:* U.S. Army, 1943-46, 1951-52; became first lieutenant. U.S. Army Reserve, 1946-56.

MEMBER: American Political Science Association, American Association for the Advancement of Slavic Studies (member of executive council, 1973—). *Awards, honors:* Rockefeller Foundation grant, 1956-57; Smith-Mundt fellowship for Geneva, Switzerland, 1958-59; travel grant from Inter-University Committee for the Soviet Union and Eastern Europe, 1958.

WRITINGS: (With Roy C. Macridis) *Foreign Policy in World Politics,* Prentice-Hall, 1958, 5th edition, 1976; *The Union Republics in Soviet Diplomacy,* Droz, 1960; (with Macridis, Karl Deutsch, and Samuel Finer) *Modern Political Systems: Europe,* Prentice-Hall, 1963, 3rd edition, 1972; *The Soviet Union in the World Communist System,* Hoover Institution, 1966; *Process and Power in Soviet Foreign Policy,* Little, Brown, 1971; *Eurocommunism Between East and West,* Indiana University Press, 1980. Contributor to political science journals.

*   *   *

ASPIZ, Harold 1921-

PERSONAL: Born June 19, 1921, in St. Louis, Mo.; son of Jacob (a writer) and Nellie (Eisenstein) Aspiz; married Sylvia E. Roth (a teacher), April 27, 1952; children: Ira Mayer. *Education:* University of California, Los Angeles, B.A., 1943, M.A., 1944, Ph.D., 1949. *Politics:* Independent. *Home:* 378 Flint Ave., Long Beach, Calif. 90814. *Office:* Department of English, California State University, 1250 Bellflower Blvd., Long Beach, Calif. 90840.

CAREER: Lewis and Clark College, Portland, Ore., assistant professor of English, 1950-51; California State Board of Equalization, Division of Highways, Sacramento, Calif., research technician and statistician, 1952-58; California State University, Long Beach, assistant professor, 1958-62, associate professor, 1962-66, professor of English, 1966—. *Member:* Modern Language Association of America, Melville Society, Philological Association of the Pacific Coast.

WRITINGS: Walt Whitman and the Body Beautiful, University of Illinois Press, 1980. Contributor to literature journals.

WORK IN PROGRESS: Collecting impressions of and reactions to old age; studying Walt Whitman's politics and sexual-creative imagery; research on "science and pseudo-science" in the writings of Herman Melville, and on nineteenth-century sexual theory and naturalistic fiction.

SIDELIGHTS: Aspiz commented: "My Whitman book grew out of diverse interests—eugenics, social theory, history, a fascination with unexamined source materials, a fierce love of poetry, and out of a belief that humanistic studies must interpret life broadly, not limited by lines drawn around disciplines. As a teacher and scholar I want to see life whole, but not view it glumly or without a sense of hope."

BIOGRAPHICAL/CRITICAL SOURCES: Los Angeles Times Book Review, December 28, 1980.

*   *   *

ASPLER, Tony   1939-

PERSONAL: Born May 12, 1939, in London, England; son of Isak (a Queen's Counselor) and Mimi (Young) Aspler; married Brenda Lisle; children: Annabel, Guy Jonas. *Education:* McGill University, B.A., 1959; graduate study at Trinity College, Dublin, 1959-60. *Religion:* Jewish. *Home:* 202 Keewatin Ave., Toronto, Ontario, Canada M4P 1Z8. *Agent:* John Cushman, JCA Literary Agency, Inc., 242 West 27th St., New York, N.Y. 10001. *Office:* Canadian Broadcasting Corp., 354 Jarvis St., Toronto, Ontario, Canada M5W 1E6.

CAREER: Free-lance broadcaster and writer in London, England, 1964-70; Canadian Broadcasting Corp., London, radio producer, 1970-76; Canadian Broadcasting Corp., Toronto, Ontario, executive producer, 1967—.

WRITINGS: The Streets of Askelon (novel), Secker & Warburg, 1971; (editor) Cottie Berland, *Beyond Science,* Roxby Press, 1972; *One of My Marionettes* (novel), Secker & Warburg, 1973; (editor) Lord Energlyn, *Through the Crust of the Earth,* McGraw, 1973; (with Gordon Pape) *Chain Reaction* (novel), Viking, 1978; (with Pape) *The Scorpion Sanction* (novel), Viking, 1980; (with Pape) *The Music Wars* (novel), McClelland & Stewart, 1982. Author of "Wine Guide," a wine column in *FM Guide;* also wine columnist for *Toronto Star.* Contributor to *Punch* and *Listener.*

SIDELIGHTS: "I began writing at university," Tony Aspler commented, "inspired by a particularly fine drama professor. As a result, I started writing short plays. This discipline helped me enormously with dialogue for my novels. Working in radio, too, helped me listen to the way people say things, their rhythms and verbal quirks.

"I wrote two full-length novels before I had my first book published, so I suppose that I have some kind of compulsion to write. It is not a full-time activity with me, much as I would like it to be. I write generally at night when the children are in bed and am very disciplined about it. My last three books have been written with Gordon Pape. How do we write novels in tandem? Well, we begin by working out a detailed plot line and list of characters. This blueprint for a novel runs to sixty or seventy pages and is minute in its record of plot movement and character development. We start in different places and write chapters which we exchange and rewrite, and then I rewrite the final draft to ensure continuity of style. I don't think a reader could tell who wrote what, and when we're asked about who writes the sex scenes we always give credit to the other.

"The three books we have written together are political thrillers with complex plots and a great deal of research. But we do try to introduce a strong psychological element in the interaction of characters. We have been translated into French and Spanish (*Chain Reaction* was no. 3 on the best-seller list in

Argentina!), and my first novel, written alone, *The Streets of Askelon,* is currently being published in Poland."

*   *   *

ASTOR, Susan   1946-

PERSONAL: Born April 2, 1946, in New York, N.Y.; daughter of Irving David (an artist and designer) and Miriam (Plotkin) Miller; married Stuart L. Astor (a printer), December 24, 1967; children: Abigail, Joanna. *Education:* Attended Brandeis University, 1963-64; Adelphi University, B.A. (cum laude), 1967. *Home:* 113 Princeton St., Roslyn Heights, N.Y. 11577.

CAREER: Poet. Gives readings at schools, libraries, and museums; teaches at workshops. *Member:* Poetry Society of America, Poets and Writers, Long Island Poetry Collective. *Awards, honors:* Awards from *Carolina Quarterly,* 1976, Greater Westbury Arts Council, 1978, and Willory Farms, 1980, all for poetry; Triton International Discovery Award, 1979, C. W. Post Poet-in-the-Community Award, 1980, and Nashville County Fine Arts Center Award, 1981, all for poetry.

WRITINGS: Dame (poems), University of Georgia Press, 1980.

Work represented in anthologies, including *Silent Voices,* edited by Paul Feroe, Ally Press, 1978; *A Windflower Almanac,* edited by Ted Kooser, Windflower Press, 1980; *Anthology of Magazine Verse,* edited by Alan Pater, Monitor Book, 1980. Contributor to magazines, including *Partisan Review, Paris Review, Shenandoah, Kansas Quarterly, Poetry Now,* and *Poet Lore.*

WORK IN PROGRESS: A book of poems.

*   *   *

ATKINS, (Arthur) Harold   1910-
(J. P. Jackson)

PERSONAL: Born March 27, 1910, in Nottingham, England; son of Horace George and Grace Adeline (Foweraker) Atkins; married Lily Buxton (in social services), September 17, 1938. *Education:* Balliol College, Oxford, B.A., 1938, M.A., 1942; further graduate study at London School of Economics and Political Science, London. *Politics:* Social Democrat. *Religion:* Church of England. *Home:* 2 Hallgate, Blackheath Park, London S.E.3, England.

CAREER: Nottingham Journal, Nottingham, England, reporter, 1928, scientific and radio correspondent, 1929-35, assistant drama critic, 1931; Reuters, London, England, subeditor at general news desk, 1938-39; *Daily Dispatch,* Manchester, England, sub-editor, 1940-41; *Manchester Guardian,* Manchester, foreign sub-editor, 1941-44; *Evening News,* London, special writer, 1944-49, political correspondent, 1944-45; *Star,* London, news and diary writer, 1949-51; Ministry of National Insurance, London, headquarters press and public relations officer, 1951-53; *Daily Telegraph,* London, foreign sub-editor, 1954-55, features sub-editor, 1955-56, arts and leader page sub-editor and contributor to and sub-editor of "London Day by Day," 1956-76, book reviewer, 1956-81, and assistant theatre critic, 1962-81; free-lance writer, 1976—. Press officer for National Assistance Board, 1951-53; deputy director of Visual Education Research Group, 1956-59. *Member:* National Union of Journalists (life member), National Liberal Club, Oxford Union Club (life member).

WRITINGS: Sinister Smith (novel), Duckworth, 1938; (with Archie Newman) *Beecham Stories,* Robson Books, 1978. Contributor of articles and reviews to magazines, including *So-*

cialist Commentary, Contemporary Review, and *British Weekly,* and newspapers (sometimes under pseudonym J. P. Jackson).

WORK IN PROGRESS: A short life of John Barbirolli, former conductor of Le Halle Orchestra and the New York Philharmonic Orchestra, with Peter Cotes.

AVOCATIONAL INTERESTS: Archaeology, history, English literature, music, theatre, ballet, World War II espionage and resistance movements, science.

*   *   *

ATTRIDGE, Derek   1945-

PERSONAL: Born May 6, 1945, in Dundee, South Africa; son of Henry Lester (a schoolteacher) and Marjorie Julia (Lloyd) Attridge. *Education:* University of Natal, B.A., 1965, B.A., (with honors), 1966; Cambridge University, B.A., 1968, Ph.D., 1972. *Office:* Department of English, University of Southampton, Southampton, Hampshire SO2 3AH, England.

CAREER: Oxford University, Christ Church, Oxford, England, research lecturer in English, 1971-73; University of Southampton, Southampton, England, lecturer in English, 1973—.

WRITINGS: Well-Weighed Syllables: Elizabethan Verse in Classical Metres, Cambridge University Press, 1974; *The Rhythms of English Poetry,* Longman, 1982.

*   *   *

AUDAX
See OAKSEY, John

*   *   *

AUGUET, Roland (Jacques)   1935-

PERSONAL: Born May 16, 1935, in Paris, France; son of Marcel and Marie (Vincent) Auguet; married Francoise Lapeyre, December 22, 1964; children: Milena. *Education:* Attended Institut des Sciences Politiques, Universite de Paris, Sorbonne. *Home:* 30 rue Felicien David, 75016 Paris, France. *Office:* Piece 6257, Radio-France, 116 avenue du President Kennedy, 75016 Paris, France.

CAREER: Professor of letters in Paris, France, 1960-72; Radio-France, Paris, producer, 1970—.

WRITINGS: Cruaute et civilisation: Les Jeux romains, Flammarion, 1970, new edition published as *Les Jeux romains,* Flammarion, 1972, translation of original edition published as *Cruelty and Civilization: The Roman Games,* Allen & Unwin, 1972, new translated edition published as *The Roman Games,* Panther, 1975; *Histoire et legende du cirque,* Flammarion, 1974; *Fetes et spectacles populaires,* Flammarion, 1974, translation published as *Festivals and Celebrations,* F. Watts, 1975; *Caligula; ou, Le Pouvoir a vingt ans,* Payot, 1975; *Le Juif errant: Genese d'une legende,* Payot, 1977. Also author of *Les Empereurs fous.*

WORK IN PROGRESS: A book on nineteenth-century ideologies and the birth of Nazism.

SIDELIGHTS: Auguet told *CA:* "I'm especially interested in the portion of poetry revealed by history, even if this poetry is not exempt from cruelty as was the case in ancient Rome. From there came my interest in the history of celebrations, which constitute the rosy side—at least in general—of civilizations; but this doesn't prevent them from being deeply revelatory. From there also came the interest that I acquired for the mythic character of the wandering Jew which, in tragic or

picaresque forms, summarizes in itself several centuries of our civilization.''

BIOGRAPHICAL/CRITICAL SOURCES: Times Literary Supplement, December 22, 1972.

*   *   *

AUGUSTUS, Albert, Jr.
See NUETZEL, Charles (Alexander)

*   *   *

AULD, Rhoda L(andsman)

PERSONAL: Born in Brooklyn, N.Y.; married Lawrence W. S. Auld (a librarian and educator), 1957; children: two. *Education:* Hunter College (now of the City University of New York), B.A.; Columbia University, M.S.

CAREER: Worked as assistant librarian at American Management Association, New York, N.Y.; cataloger at Brooklyn Public Library, Brooklyn, N.Y.; writer. *Awards, honors:* Awards for tatting and embroidery include blue ribbon from Pacific Northwest Handweavers' Conference, 1971, and prizes from Hawaii's Windward Fair and International Old Lacers.

WRITINGS: Tatting: The Contemporary Art of Knotting With a Shuttle, Van Nostrand, 1974; *Molas: What They Are; How to Make Them; Ideas They Suggest for Creative Applique,* Van Nostrand, 1977. Contributor to magazines, including *McCall's Needlework and Crafts, Good Housekeeping,* and *Woman's Day.*

WORK IN PROGRESS: A book on a little-known aspect of westward expansion; a needlework book with a historical approach, probably limited to the United States; a biography of an early seventeenth-century American.

AVOCATIONAL INTERESTS: Music (including singing with University of Illinois's Oratorio Society).

*   *   *

AVNERY, Uri   1923-

PERSONAL: Birth-given name Uri Ostermann; born September 10, 1923, in Beckum, Westphalia, Germany (now West Germany); son of Alfred Aharon (a banker and financial expert) and Hilde (Englestein) Ostermann; married Rachel Gruenbaum (a teacher), Octover 12, 1958. *Education:* Attended elementary school in Tel-Aviv, Israel. *Politics:* Shelli party. *Religion:* "Agnostic (ex-Jewish)." *Home:* 10 A Rupin St., Tel-Aviv, Israel. *Office:* 3 Gordon St., Tel-Aviv, Israel; and Knesset, Jerusalem, Israel.

CAREER: Bama'avak, editor, 1947-48; *Ha'aretz,* combat correspondent, 1948-49, editorial writer, 1949-50; *Ha'olam Hazeh,* Tel-Aviv, Israel, owner and editor-in-chief, 1950—. Member of Knesset (Israel's parliament), 1965-73 and 1979—. Executive member of the Shelli party. Founding member of Israeli Council for Israeli-Palestinian Peace. *Military service:* Israeli Army, 1948-49.

WRITINGS: Israel Without Zionists: A Plea for Peace in the Middle East, Macmillan, 1968, published as *Israel Without Zionism: A Plan for Peace in the Middle East,* Collier, 1969; (editor with Andrew Mack and Nira Yuval-Davis) *Israel and the Palestinians,* Ithaca Press, 1975.

In Hebrew: *Bisdoth Pleshet* (title means "In the Fields of the Philistines"), [Tel Aviv], 1949; *The Other Side of the Coin,*

[Israel], 1950; *Tselav ha-keres* (title means "The Swastika"), [Israel], 1960.

SIDELIGHTS: Avnery told *CA:* "My father, a member of an old established well-to-do German-Jewish family, was a private banker in Beckum, Westphalia, and later a financial expert in Hannover. As a veteran Zionist from early youth, he took his family to Palestine immediately upon Hitler's rise to power, in 1933. In Palestine he quickly lost the capital he had brought with him, and had to do hard manual work, as did his wife.

"I attended elementary school first in Nahalal, the famous *moshav* in which Moshe Dayan grew up, and later in Tel-Aviv. Because of my family's extreme poverty at that time, I had to leave school after the seventh grade, at the age of fourteen. I then earned my living at many jobs, until 1947, when I turned to journalism as a profession.

"In 1938 I joined the underground *Irgun Tzvai Leumi*, in which I served for three years, before the arrival of Menahem Begin from Poland. I left the *Irgun* because of deepening ideological disagreements, especially concerning its attitude toward the Arabs and social problems.

"After some years of reflection and sporadic political activity, I founded the 'Young Palestine' group in 1946 (commonly known, at the time, as the *Bama'avak* or Struggle group). This group, which argued that the new Jewish community in Palestine constituted a 'new Hebrew nation' within the 'Jewish People,' caused an unprecedented public uproar.

"In 1947, on the eve of war, the group published my first major work, a booklet called 'War and Peace in the Semitic Region,' which called for a radically new approach: an alliance of the Hebrew and Arab national movements in order to purge the common 'Semitic region' from imperialism and colonialism, and create a Semitic confederation, defense alliance, and common market as part of the neutralist Third World. Excerpts from the book were sent to newspapers throughout the Middle East, and published in some Arab journals just before the 1948 war.

"At the outbreak of the war, I joined the *Hagana* army, and later volunteered for 'Samson's Foxes,' the legendary commando outfit fighting on the Egyptian front. I was severely wounded by Egyptian machine guns during the last days of the fighting, and was discharged from the army after several months of convalescence.

"Throughout the war I reported my impressions and experiences as a combat soldier while taking part in nearly all the major battles on the Jerusalem and southern fronts. These reports were published after the war in *Bisdoth Pleshet,* which overnight became the country's biggest best-seller and is still considered the outstanding book of that war. When I wrote a follow-up (*The Other Side of the Coin*), however, which described the atrocities of war, it was boycotted.

"In 1949 the editor of *Ha'aretz* invited me to join his staff as an editorial writer. After a year I quit, protesting that I was not allowed to express my opinions, especially concerning the expulsion of Arab villagers.

"In April, 1950, I bought *Ha'olam Hazeh*, a family magazine established in 1936, and turned it into a uniquely Israeli institution. Nothing like it exists elsewhere.

"*Ha'olam Hazeh* is a combination of a mass-circulation news magazine (like *Time* or *Newsweek*), a general interest illustrated weekly (like *Life, Der Stern,* or *Paris-Match*), and a mouthpiece of aggressive political opposition with exposes of economic and political corruption. It has created a new Hebrew style, now imitated by Israeli papers, and has served as a school of journalism for nearly all the outstanding young writers in the country. Its enemies have denounced it many times as pornographic because it broke, many years ago, the puritanical standards then prevailing in Israel. Today, compared with publications like *Der Stern*, not to mention *Playboy*, *Ha'olam Hazeh* would be considered extremely conservative, much to the disappointment of people who see it for the first time, after hearing about it only from its opponents.

"For more than thirty years, *Ha'olam Hazeh* has attracted large doses of both admiration and hatred because of its untiring dissent from official policies and its hard-hitting attacks on the establishment. It was the first to uncover the facts of the infamous Lavon Affair, as well as scores of corruption episodes, from the illegal archaeological activities of Dayan to the Yadlin and Ofer affairs, which played a major role in bringing down the Rabin cabinet in 1977. Since the early fifties it has advocated the creation of a Palestinian state alongside Israel, and resolutely protested against the treatment of the Arab minority in Israel.

"Attacks against *Ha'olam Hazeh* were often violent. Editorial offices were bombed three times. I was ambushed at night in 1953 and the fingers of both my hands were broken. A prominent reporter was kidnapped in 1957. Our offices were completely burned down in 1972, destroying our invaluable archives. In 1975 an attempt on my life was made by an alleged lunatic, who stabbed me. Menahem Begin recently disclosed that the chief of the Israel security forces asked his support, in the late fifties, for arresting me and detaining me without trial, under emergency regulations, for unspecified security considerations.

"The most resolute attempt to silence the publication came in 1965, when the government enacted a special press law, obviously aimed mainly against 'that certain magazine,' as it was usually called by David Ben-Gurion, who would not utter its name. This provided the final push for starting an operation which had been in my mind for a long time: creation of a new political party to fight for the principles of *Ha'olam Hazeh*—civil rights, government reform, separation of state and religion, equality for the Arab minority, social justice, support for a national Palestinian state, and Israeli-Arab peace and cooperation.

"The new *Ha'olam Hazeh*—New Force Party came into being on the eve of the 1965 elections, as a citizens' volunteer movement, and astounded the country by winning a Knesset seat, unprecedented for a new party at that time. The party repeated that feat in 1969, gaining two seats. However it was defeated in the emotional atmosphere of the 1973 elections, following the Yom-Kippur War, and for five years I was not a member of the cabinet.

"During my first eight years in the Knesset, I was generally considered, by friends and enemies, as Israel's foremost parliamentarian, calling for reforms in practically all spheres of law and administration, and was probably most popular as a thorn in the side of the establishment.

"On the fifth day of the Six-Day War I addressed an open letter to Levi Eshkol, calling upon him to make a dramatic gesture and offer the Palestinian people the opportunity to create an independent Palestinian state in the West Bank and the Gaza Strip. Since then I have campaigned incessantly for peace based on mutual acceptance and recognition, complete withdrawal to the pre-1967 borders, and co-existence of Israel and Palestine as two independent friendly states. For a long time I was alone in the Knesset supporting this line. In 1967 I wrote

Israel Without Zionists, analyzing the conflict and putting forth my ideas. It was translated into seven languages, including Hebrew, and was attacked by another book, published by the Palestine Liberation Organization in Arabic and French.

"However, in 1974, with the beginning of the change in the Palestine Liberation Organization line, I established regular contacts with senior organization officials in Europe, including Sa'id Hamami, who was murdered by extremists because of these contacts, an act which led to the formation, by the end of 1975, of the Israeli Council for Israeli-Palestinian Peace, comprising more than one hundred important personalities. Official contacts between the Council and the PLO were established in mid-1976. I played an active role in these, together with General Mattitiyahu Peled, Lova Eliav, and others. I reported on them to Prime Minister Rabin, with whom I had many conversations on the subject, without winning him over.

"In March, 1977, I took part in creating *Shelli,* an alliance of patriotic peace groups, which includes the *Ha'olem Hazeh* party, *Moked,* Eliav's independent socialists, and others. *Shelli* gained two seats in the May, 1977 elections, and I entered Parliament again in 1979. During the same year *Shelli* constituted itself as a unified party.

"*Shelli* wholeheartedly supported the peace initiative of the late Egyptian president Anwar el-Sadat, and I was one of the first Israelis to enter Egypt with an Israeli passport on the morrow of Sadat's visit in Jerusalem. During long conversations with President Sadat and other leading Egyptian personalities, I stressed my strong support for Palestinian self-determination."

BIOGRAPHICAL/CRITICAL SOURCES: *Uri Avnery and Neo-Zionism,* [Beirut], 1971.

*   *   *

AZBEL, Mark Ya. 1932-

PERSONAL: Born May 12, 1932, in Poltava, U.S.S.R.; naturalized Israeli citizen, 1977; son of Yacov A. (in medicine) and Cecilia (in medicine; maiden name, Slobodkina) Azbel; married Naya Steinman, January 9, 1958 (divorced, October 12, 1966); married Lidia Warshavsky (in biochemistry), November 23, 1967; children: Vadim, Julia. Education: Kharkov University, M.A., 1953, Ph.D., 1955, D.Sc., 1958. Religion: None. Home: 3/7 Yakov Cohen, Ramat-Hasharon, Israel. Office: Department of Physics, Tel Aviv University, Ramat-Aviv, Tel-Aviv, Israel.

CAREER: Kharkov University, Kharkov, U.S.S.R., professor of physics, 1957-64; Moscow University, Moscow, U.S.S.R., professor of physics, 1964-71; Institute for Theoretical Physics, Moscow, department director, 1965-72; Tel-Aviv University, Ramat-Aviv, Tel-Aviv Israel, professor of physics, 1973—; University of Pennsylvania, Philadelphia, adjunct professor, 1980—. Member: American Physicists Society, European Physicists Society. Awards, honors: Lomonosov Prize, 1965 and

1967; Case Western Reserve University Centennial Scholar, 1979.

WRITINGS: (With Ilia Lifshitz and Moisei Kaganov) *Electronnaya Teoriya Metalov,* Nauka, 1967, translation by Albin Tybulewicz published as *Electron Theory of Metals,* Consultants Bureau, 1973; *Refusenik: Trapped in the Soviet Union,* Houghton, 1981.

WORK IN PROGRESS: *The Third Life,* a book on immigrant experiences in Israel and America; *In the Eyes of a Physicist.*

SIDELIGHTS: Azbel's *Refusenik* relates his experiences as a Jewish physicist in the Soviet Union. Despite outstanding credentials, Azbel was harassed by the Soviet secret police and interrogated. He attributed this abuse to totalitarianism. In 1972 Azbel applied for a visa to Israel. The Soviet bureaucracy delayed granting the visa for five years, during which Azbel was considered, according to Jeremy Bernstein, "an enemy of the state." In his appraisal of *Refusenik* in the *New York Times Book Review,* Bernstein wrote, "Soviet jails are full of dissenters no one has ever heard of. It was to call attention to these people that Mr. Azbel wrote this extraordinarily moving book, and it is our responsibility to see that his message is spread as widely as possible."

Azbel told *CA:* "I think Russia's internal policy is more anti-Semitic than an American may imagine. I think racism can be overcome only in a free democratic society which does not need (for internal purposes) any nation as a scapegoat. I am convinced: racism is the sign of an ill society."

BIOGRAPHICAL/CRITICAL SOURCES: *New York Times Book Review,* June 7, 1981.

*   *   *

AZEVEDO, Ross E(ames)

PERSONAL: Born in Sacramento, Calif. Education: University of California, Davis, B.A., c. 1964; Cornell University, M.S., c. 1967, Ph.D., 1972. Office: Industrial Relations Center, University of Minnesota, 271 19th Ave. S., Minneapolis, Minn. 55419.

CAREER: U.S. Pay Board, Washington, D.C., director of macroeconomic studies for Cost of Living Council, 1972-73; University of California, Los Angeles, assistant professor of management, 1973-75; University of Minnesota, Minneapolis, assistant professor of industrial relations, 1975—. Member: American Economic Association, American Institute for Decision Sciences, Industrial Relations Research Association, Western Economic Association.

WRITINGS: (With D.J.B. Mitchell) *Wage-Price Controls and Labor Market Distortions,* Institute of Industrial Relations, University of California, Los Angeles, 1976; *Labor Economics: A Guide to Information Sources,* Gale, 1978.

WORK IN PROGRESS: *Economics of Race and Sex Discrimination; Compensation Practices for Employed Inventors.*

B

BABB, Lawrence, Alan 1941-

BRIEF ENTRY: Born May 2, 1941, in Lansing, Mich. American social anthropologist, educator, and author. Babb has taught anthropology at Amherst College since 1975. His writings include *Walking on Flowers in Singapore: A Hindu Festival Cycle* (Department of Sociology, University of Singapore, 1974) and *The Divine Hierarchy: Popular Hinduism in Central India* (Columbia University Press, 1975). *Address:* Department of Anthropology, Amherst College, Amherst, Mass. 01002. *Biographical/critical sources: Annals of the American Academy of Political and Social Science,* November, 1976.

* * *

BABCOCK, Nicolas
See LEWIS, Tom

* * *

BABULA, William 1943-

PERSONAL: Born May 19, 1943, in Stamford, Conn.: son of Benny F. and Lottie (Zajkowski) Babula; married Karen Gemi, June 19, 1965; children: Jared, Joelle Denise. *Education:* Rutgers University, A.B., 1965; University of California, Berkeley, M.A., 1967, Ph.D., 1969. *Office:* School of Humanities, Sonoma State University, Nichols Hall, Rohnert Park, Calif. 94928.

CAREER: University of Miami, Coral Gables, Fla., assistant professor, 1969-75, associate professor, 1975-77, professor of English, 1977-81, chairman of department, 1976-81; Sonoma State University, Rohnert Park, Calif., professor of English and dean of School of Humanities, 1981—. *Member:* Modern Language Association of America, Shakespeare Association of America, Association of Departments of English, Anglo-American Academy (fellow), South Atlantic Modern Language Association, Southeastern Renaissance Society, Florida Association of Departments of English, Phi Beta Kappa. *Awards, honors:* Grants from Shell, 1974, Institute for the Study of Aging, 1977, and Florida Endowment for the Humanities, 1980-81.

WRITINGS: "Wishes Fall Out as They're Willed": Shakespeare and the Tragicomic Archetype, Elizabethan and Renaissance Studies, University of Salzburg, 1975; (contributor) Kenneth Muir, editor, *Shakespeare Survey Thirty,* Cambridge University Press, 1977; (contributor) G. R. Hibbard, editor, *The Elizabethan Theatre VI,* Macmillan of Canada, 1978; *Shakespeare in Production, 1935-1979: A Reference Catalogue,* Garland Publishing, 1981; (with Louis Marder) *Shakespeare: A Topical Bibliography,* Garland Publishing, 1982. Contributor to *Reader's Encyclopedia of English Literature* and *Peterson's Annual Guide to Graduate Study.* Also contributor to language and literature journals, including *Modern Language Review, Tennessee Studies in Literature, New Spectator, South Atlantic Bulletin, The Carrell, Modern Drama, Dalhousie Review, Oral English,* and *Shakespeare Quarterly.*

SIDELIGHTS: Babula commented: "Scholarship is a business and it has become a very tough one. It is suffering more than any other part of publishing—and that's a lot of suffering."

* * *

BACIK, James Joseph 1936-

PERSONAL: Born October 24, 1936, in Toledo, Ohio; son of George L. and Lillian (Noble) Bacik. *Education:* Athenaeum of Ohio, B.A., 1958, M.A., 1960; Fordham University, M.S., 1969; Oxford University, Ph.D., 1978. *Home and office:* 425 Thurstin, Bowling Green, Ohio 43402.

CAREER: Ordained Roman Catholic priest, 1962; associate pastor of Roman Catholic church in Sandusky, Ohio, 1962-67; St. Thomas More University Parish, Bowling Green, Ohio, associate pastor, 1969—. Assistant professor at Mount St. Mary Seminary, 1969-70; visiting instructor at Marist College, 1970, and Winebrenner Seminary, 1974; instructor at Bowling Green State University, 1971-75, lecturer, 1978-80, visiting assistant professor, 1981—; visiting assistant professor at University of Dayton, 1971-80; adjunct professor at St. John's Provincial Seminary, 1980-81. Host of "Reflections," a weekly program on WLQR-Radio. Member of Toledo Priests' Senate, 1977-79. *Member:* Catholic Theological Society of America, Association of Toledo Priests (president, 1970-72).

WRITINGS: Apologetics and the Eclipse of Mystery: Mystagogy According to Karl Rahner, University of Notre Dame Press, 1980.

Author of a tape cassette series released by St. Anthony Messenger Press, "An American Spirituality for the Eighties," 1980, and "Religious Self-Awareness," 1982. Author of a weekly column in *Catholic Chronicle,* 1971-73, and a column in *National Catholic Reporter,* 1980—. Contributor to religious magazines.

WORK IN PROGRESS: Religious Self-Awareness, a book based on own tape cassette series.

SIDELIGHTS: Bacik feels that one of his most important and necessary tasks is to popularize theology. He believes that there is a strong need for Catholics in the United States to develop a spirituality that is distinctively American. Toward that end he teaches, speaks on radio, writes for national periodicals, and distributes his own newsletter, "Reflections."

Bacik emphasizes the importance of such popular entertainments as art, athletics, and music as catalysts to help people "enrich our self-experience and call attention to particular characteristics of the divine/human relationship," so long as they do not become ends instead of means. He feels that such activities are examples, demonstrations that the human spirit can overcome daily frustration and perceive the possibility of eventual fulfillment.

BIOGRAPHICAL/CRITICAL SOURCES: Catholic Chronicle, January 16, 1981.

* * *

BAILEY, Conrad Charles Maitland 1922-

PERSONAL: Born February 26, 1922, in Parkston, England; son of Albert Edward (a police inspector) and Kathleen (Bunn) Bailey; married Betty Lawrence, April 24, 1943 (divorced, 1974); married second wife, Linda Maria, December 19, 1976; children: Andria, Christopher, Liselle. *Education:* Received M.S.I.A. from Cambridge University. *Politics:* Conservative. *Religion:* Church of England. *Home:* 18 Highlever Rd., Kensington, London W.10, England.

CAREER: Worked in publishing, as graphic artist, and as art editor, 1953-75. Illustrator for British Civil Service. *Military service:* Leading aircraftsman in Royal Air Force. *Member:* Society of Industrial Artists.

WRITINGS: (With Eve Barwell) *How to Make and Fly Kites,* Studio Vista, 1973; *Harrap's Guide to Famous London Graves,* Harrap, 1975. Writer for British Broadcasting Corp. Contributor to *Modern English.*

WORK IN PROGRESS: The Streets of London, a history of street behavior; *From Dickens' Chalet.*

SIDELIGHTS: Bailey commented: "I am interested in all unusual areas of London where little research has been carried out."

* * *

BAKER, Gayle Cunningham 1950-

PERSONAL: Born April 23, 1950, in Elmhurst, Ill.; daughter of David John (a commercial illustrator; also in sales) and Gladys (in merchandising; maiden name, Morrison) Cunningham; married Clifford D. Baker (a professor of special education), August 17, 1974; children: Brian Cunningham. *Education:* Drake University, B.S.E., 1972; University of Northern Colorado, M.S., 1973, graduate study, 1974—. *Home:* 2330 21st Ave., Greeley, Colo. 80631.

CAREER: Teacher of handicapped children at elementary school in Englewood, Colo., 1973-74; Weld Board of Cooperative Educational Services, LaSalle, Colo., designer of remedial reading and mathematics program for middle school in Milliken, Colo., 1974-76, writer for career education project, 1975-77, designer of pre-primary and primary program for severely handicapped and multi-handicapped students, 1979-80; designer of program for mentally handicapped students at ele-

mentary school in Kersey, Colo., 1976-78; Platte Valley Elementary School, Kersey, designer of pre-first grade program, 1980—. Guest lecturer at University of Northern Colorado, 1977—, and Metropolitan State College, Denver, Colo., 1979. Colorado Department of Education, member of career education resource team, 1977, grant reader and evaluator, 1979. Presenter at Colorado Federation Council for Exceptional Children, 1977, and at mainstreaming seminar in Thailand, 1981.

MEMBER: International Reading Association, National Association for Retarded Citizens, National Education Association, Association for the Severely and Profoundly Handicapped, Council for Exceptional Children, Polk County Association for Retarded Citizens (citizen advocate, 1971—), Women's Panhellenic Association of Greeley, Platte Valley School District Education Association (member of executive board, 1981-82), University of Northern Colorado Faculty Dames, Alpha Phi, Gamma Gamma, Kappa Delta, Pi Lambda Theta.

WRITINGS: (With Vivian M. Montey) *Special Delivery: A Book for Kids About Cesarean and Vaginal Birth,* Charles Franklin Press, 1981. Developed book on language for Glenwood State School (Iowa).

SIDELIGHTS: Gayle Baker told *CA:* "I believe that in today's society it is extremely difficult for a woman to blend her family and career together without feeling outside pressure from people and dealing with her own guilt resulting from decisions she's made. Personally I have had to do a great amount of reading and attending classes to educate myself about child rearing, family structure, and women. I also spent a good part of my everyday conversations with people in surveying each about their beliefs, concerns, and feelings pertaining to motherhood and outside-the-home careers. I would strongly recommend every mother-to-be to do the same to assist her in fitting all the pieces of her life together. It's still a struggle, but I'm beginning to feel better about my life because of my ongoing research.

"After having worked outside the home for five years in an established teaching career, I had my first baby. During my year-and-a-half maternity leave I felt it was important to keep myself stimulated so that I wouldn't fall into the trap of a 'stereotyped' housewife and mother. This led to writing *Special Delivery.*

"It's extremely important to me that my son and any future children, and *all* the children of the world, understand their own special delivery. *Special Delivery* is the first complete book on the market to explain to preschool through preteen children about conception, development, nature's way of intending a baby to be born, reasons for a Cesarean, the actual Cesarean birth, and the recovery of the mother after delivery. I believe that my own Cesarean birth experience was a blessing in disguise to trigger the initial idea for this book.

"Now that I have returned to my outside-the-home career I want to comment on my philosophy of education. I have been formally trained and have had a wide variety of teaching experiences, working with numerous handicapping conditions. I believe in assisting every child to reach his/her highest potential during the very short time I know him/her. A teacher should find as many different ways as possible of teaching the same concept to motivate the student. Teaching is similar to the field of entertainment; a good teacher needs to turn the student on to life so that he/she isn't conscious of his/her actual learning. To be able to accomplish this in teaching, a good teacher needs to be re-evaluating his/her life as a person. A teacher needs to experience as much as possible through travel, hobbies, reading, and people so he/she, too, is turned on to life."

BAKER, Jerry

PERSONAL: Born in Detroit, Mich.; married wife, Ilene; children: five. *Education:* Attended public schools in Davison, Mich., Kansas City, Mo., and Detroit, Mich. *Residence:* Troy, Mich.

CAREER: Author, lecturer, and columnist. Police officer in Detroit, Mich., 1956-61; worked as salesman for Strickland Seed Co. and as head of garden centers for S. S. Kresge dime stores in Detroit area; hosted own radio show "Plants Are Like People" in St. Louis, Mo.; guest on television shows, including "The Dinah Shore Show," Los Angeles, Calif., "The Ralph Story Show," Los Angeles, "Regis and Co.," Los Angeles, and "Kennedy and Co.," Chicago, Ill. *Military service:* Served in U.S. Air Force; stationed in England.

WRITINGS: Plants Are Like People (illustrated by Carl Chambers), Nash Publishing, 1971; *Talk to Your Plants, and Other Gardening Know-How I Learned from Grandma Putt*, Nash Publishing, 1973; *I Never Met a House Plant I Didn't Like* (illustrated by Dot Cohn), Simon & Schuster, 1974; *Jerry Baker's Second Back to Nature Almanac*, Pocket Books, 1974; *Jerry Baker's Third Back to Nature Almanac*, Pocket Books, 1975; *Jerry Baker's Bicentennial Gardener's Almanac*, Pocket Books, 1976; *Jerry Baker's Fabulous Everything, Everywhere, Indoor, Outdoor Garden Answer Book*, Grosset, 1976; *Plants Are Like Kids: Indoor and Outdoor Gardening* (illustrated by Robert Pierce), Grosset, 1976; (with Dan Kibbie) *Farm Fever: How to Buy Country Land and Farm It Part Time or Full Time*, Funk, 1977; *One-to-One Plant Problem Solver*, Baronet, 1979.

"Make Friends" series; all published by Simon & Schuster, 1973; all edited by Charles Cook: *Make Friends With Your Annuals; . . . With Your Bulbs; . . . With Your Evergreens and Ground Covers; . . . With Your Flowering Shrubs; . . . With Your Flowering Trees; . . . With Your Fruit Trees; . . . With Your House Plants; . . . With Your Lawn; . . . With Your Perennials and Biennials; . . . With Your Roses; . . . With Your Shade Trees; . . . With Your Vegetable Garden.*

SIDELIGHTS: Jerry Baker likes to refer to himself as "America's Master Gardener," and his extensive knowledge of gardening makes this a fitting appellation. Baker's success lies not as much in his knowledge, however, as in his ability to disseminate it in a direct and humorous way. In 1971 the *Detroit Free Press* called him "probably the most practical and amusing of all the experts around."

Baker first made a mark in the world of gardening when, as a seed salesman, he donned a green derby in order to distinguish himself from his competitors. "Some people laughed," Baker related to the *Detroit News*, "but that was O.K.; I expected them to laugh. It got me attention and made me stand out." Baker was dubbed "the Pied Piper of the Pickle Patch" by his customers.

When Baker took a job with S. S. Kresge, a Detroit-based dime store, his green derby and friendly manner earned him media attention. Going a step further, he began phoning a local radio talk show with answers to listeners' gardening questions, identifying himself as Mr. Grow-It-All. One morning he went to the station dressed in the kelly green suit that was to become Mr. Grow-It-All's trademark. Baker's visits to the radio show led to more media engagements. He began making regular appearances on a Detroit-based morning television show, and invitations from such network programs as "The Dinah Shore Show" followed. Soon, Baker was a frequent guest of radio

and television hosts in Cleveland, St. Louis, Chicago, and Los Angeles. "I sometimes feel like I could write a book about local T.V. shows across the country," Baker told a *Detroit Free Press* interviewer. By 1974 his own radio show, "Plants Are Like People," was nationally syndicated.

"Baker's philosophy about plants is characterized by neat little rules," said a *Free Press* reporter. "He rolls rules off his tongue with the ease that comes from years on the lecture circuit and even more years around green things." Baker credits his grandmother with teaching him everything he knows. "I've read all the scientific books on growing things," he told the *Detroit News*. "A lot of it is stuff she knew and practiced."

BIOGRAPHICAL/CRITICAL SOURCES: Detroit Free Press, April 11, 1971, October 17, 1971, July 29, 1972, December 11, 1972; *Detroit News Sunday Magazine,* January 6, 1974; *Detroit News,* May 21, 1974; *Authors in the News,* Volume II, Gale, 1976.*

*　　　*　　　*

BAKER, Josephine   1906-1975

OBITUARY NOTICE: Born June 3, 1906, in St. Louis, Mo.; died of a stroke, April 12, 1975, in Paris, France. Entertainer and author. Baker started her career in show business while still in elementary school when she began dancing part-time in a chorus line. As a teenager she joined a traveling troupe and wound up in New York City dancing in the chorus line of the musical comedy "Shuffle Along." She performed on Broadway and appeared at the Plantation Club before accepting a dancing part in "La Revue negre," an American production that opened at the Theatre de Champs-Elysee in Paris in 1925. Soon after, she launched her own act at the Folies-Bergere and created a sensation by dancing naked except for a girdle of bananas around her waist. In addition to her music-hall career, Baker was featured in motion pictures, including "Zouzou" and "La Sirene des tropiques," and starred in "La Creole," an operetta about a Jamaican girl. Critical of American racial discrimination, the black entertainer became a French citizen in 1937 and worked for the Resistance during World War II as a lieutenant in the Free French Air Force in North Africa. For her service to France, she was made a chevalier of the French Legion of Honor and was awarded the Croix de Guerre and the Rosette de la Resistance. Baker continued her nightclub career until her death, but she was chiefly involved after the war with raising her adopted children, twelve orphans from various countries. In 1951 she was named the NAACP's Woman of the Year. Her writings include *Voyages et adventures de Josephine Baker* and *Les Memoires de Josephine Baker,* with Marcell Sauvage. Obituaries and other sources: *Current Biography,* Wilson, 1964, June, 1975; *New York Times,* April 13, 1975; *Newsweek,* April 21, 1975.

*　　　*　　　*

BAKER, Pauline H(alpern)   1941-
(Paul Anber)

PERSONAL: Born August 9, 1941, in Jersey City, N.J.; daughter of Michael H. (an attorney) and Dorothy (Dubulier) Halpern; married Raymond Baker (in business), August 29, 1964; children: Deren, Gayle. *Education:* Rutgers University, B.A., 1962; University of California, Los Angeles, M.A., 1963, Ph.D. (with distinction), 1970. *Home:* 7300 Broxburn Court, Bethesda, Md. 20034.

CAREER: University of Lagos, Lagos, Nigeria, lecturer in political science, 1965-72; Rockefeller Foundation, New York,

N.Y., research fellow, 1975-76; U.S. Senate, Washington, D.C., member of professional staff of Foreign Relations Committee, 1977-81; research scientist at Battelle Memorial Institute, 1981—. *Member:* African Studies Association, Council on Foreign Relations.

WRITINGS: *Urbanization and Political Change: The Politics of Lagos, 1917-1967,* University of California Press, 1974. Contributor to African studies journals, including (under pseudonym Paul Anber) *Journal of Modern African Studies.*

SIDELIGHTS: Pauline Baker told *CA:* "As a political scientist, I found Africa fascinating, a land where all the basic theories are being tested. Africa forces us to get back to fundamentals, to examine again many questions we take for granted. It also forces Americans, in particular, to confront how well we as a people are living up to our national ideals about equality, opportunity, and justice."

*   *   *

BAKER, Ronald L(ee)   1937-

PERSONAL: Born June 30, 1937, in Indianapolis, Ind.; married Catherine Anne Neal (a reading specialist), October 21, 1960; children: Susannah Jill, Jonathan Kemp. *Education:* Indiana State University, B.S., 1960, M.A., 1961; further graduate study at University of Illinois, 1963-65; Indiana University, Ph.D., 1969. *Home address:* R.R.1, Box 434, Terre Haute, Ind. 47805. *Office:* Department of English, Indiana State University, Terre Haute, Ind. 47809.

CAREER: Indiana University, Bloomington, folklore library assistant, 1962-63; University of Illinois, Urbana, instructor in English, 1963-65; Indiana University, Fort Wayne, teaching associate in English and folklore, 1965-66; Indiana State University, Terre Haute, instructor, assistant professor, and associate professor, 1966-76, professor of English, 1976—, chairperson of department, 1980—. Visiting lecturer at University of Illinois, autumn, 1972-73; visiting associate professor at Indiana University, summer, 1975, visiting professor, summer, 1978. *Military service:* U.S. Air Force Reserve, personnel specialist, 1960-66.

MEMBER: Modern Language Association of America, American Folklore Society, American Name Society (member of executive committee of place-name survey of the United States; member of board of managers, 1978-80; third vice-president, 1981), Popular Culture Association, Society for the Study of Midwestern Literature, Midwest Modern Language Association, Hoosier Folklore Society (vice-president, 1969-70; president, 1970-79), Indiana Council of Teachers of English, Indiana College English Association.

WRITINGS: *Folklore in the Writings of Rowland E. Robinson,* Bowling Green University Popular Press, 1973; (with Marvin Carmony) *Indiana Place Names,* Indiana University Press, 1975; (contributor) Jackie Mallis, editor, *Ideas for Teaching Gifted Students,* Multi Media Arts, 1979; *Hoosier Folk Legends,* Indiana University Press, in press; (contributor) Fred Tarpley, editor, *Place Names, U.S.A.,* University of Texas Press, in press. Contributor to *Handbook of American Folklore.* Also contributor of about forty articles to professional journals. Editor of *Indiana Names,* 1970-74, *Newsletter of the Indiana Place-Name Survey,* 1971-77, *Midwestern Journal of Language and Folklore,* 1975—, and *Midwestern Language and Folklore Newsletter,* 1978—.

BAKER, Susan (Catherine)   1942-
(Kay Richards)

PERSONAL: Born June 30,1942, in Liverpool, England; daughter of Alexander Robert (a banker and free-lance journalist) and Catherine (Evans) Ellis; married Richard John Baker (a solicitor), June 9, 1973; children: Anthony Lionel, Joanna Lindsay. *Education:* University of Edinburgh, B.Sc., 1963. *Home:* 1 Elm Close, Amersham, Buckinghamshire, England.

CAREER: Macdonald Educational, London, England, children's book editor, 1968—; has worked as a research physicist at metallurgical and electrical laboratories. *Member:* Austrian Alpine Club (United Kingdom section).

WRITINGS—All for young people; all published by Macdonald Educational, except as noted: (Editor, with Valerie Pitt, John Daintith, and Alan Isaacs) *The Hamlyn Junior Science Encyclopedia,* Hamlyn, 1973; (under pseudonym Kay Richards) *Science Magic With Physics,* illustrations by Mike Whittlesea and Brian Edwards, Purnell, 1974; *Answer Book of Science,* Hamlyn, 1975; (with Nora Stein) *Animals,* 1976; (with Stein) *Famous People,* 1976; (with Stein) *Long Ago,* 1976; (with Stein) *Transport,* 1976; (editor) Richard Blythe, *Fabulous Beasts,* illustrations by Fiona French and Joanna Troughton, 1977; *Farms,* 1977; *The Christmas Book,* illustrations by Frank Baber, Kim Blundell, and Sara Cole, 1978, Grosset, 1979; *Looking at Lands: Italy,* 1981; *The First You and Me Book,* BBC Publications, 1981. Editor of "Junior Reference Library" series, 1969.

WORK IN PROGRESS: "At present I am researching and writing books for pre-school children."

SIDELIGHTS: Susan Baker told *CA:* "After receiving a scientific education and training and having enjoyed practical work in laboratories, I discovered that career advancement provided me with a desk job. If that was to be the case, data processing and laboratory management were not going to provide me with the right kind of job satisfaction; so, I moved into the field of scientific publishing. Having learned the basic editorial skills, I found that I was ideally suited to working on the production of color information books for children, which came to the fore in the early 1970's."

*   *   *

BAKER, William D.   1924-

PERSONAL: Born March 5, 1924, in Buffalo, N.Y.; son of William D. (a utilities agent) and Charlotte (Doyle) Baker; married Lois Tukey, June 22, 1946 (divorced March, 1971); married Jane N. Hill (an editor), November 22, 1972; children: (first marriage) Pamela Baker Francke, William B., Priscilla Baker Walker. *Education:* Hobart College, B.A., 1946; University of Chicago, M.A., 1948; Northwestern University, Ph.D., 1950. *Home:* 504 Phillips St., Yellow Springs, Ohio 45387. *Office:* Department of English, Wright State University, Dayton, Ohio 45435.

CAREER: Hobart College (now Hobart and William Smith Colleges), Geneva, N.Y., instructor in English, 1946-47; Foundation for Better Reading, South Bend, Ind., director, 1950; Wayne State University, Detroit, Mich., instructor in English, 1950-51; Michigan State University, East Lansing, assistant professor of English, 1951-56; State University of New York College at Buffalo, professor of English, 1956-63, director of general studies, 1956-62; Center for American Studies, Milan, Italy, director, 1962-63; Rockford College, Rockford, Ill., professor of English, vice-president, and dean, 1963-68; Wright State University, Dayton, Ohio, professor of English, 1968—, dean of Division of Liberal Arts, 1968-70, and University Division, 1970-71. *Military service:* U.S. Naval Reserve, active duty, 1943-46; became lieutenant junior grade. *Member:* Ohio Historical Society, Ohio College English Association, Culture on the Ohio Frontier (founding member).

WRITINGS: Reading Skills, Prentice-Hall, 1953, 2nd edition, 1974; (with Thomas Clark Pollock) *University Spelling Book,* Prentice-Hall, 1955; *The Sound of English,* Prentice-Hall, 1955; *A Guide to Clear Writing,* Michigan State University Press, 1955; (with T. Benson Strandness) *The Experience of Writing,* Prentice-Hall, 1958, revised edition, 1969.

(With Herbert Hackett) *On Assignment,* McGraw, 1960; *Handbook for Communities Serving International Visitors,* National Council for Community Services to International Visitors, 1962; *Of Studies,* McGraw, 1965; *Prose for Effective Composition,* Prentice-Hall, 1964; *Crime and Punishment: A Teacher's Guide With Study Materials,* Washington Square Press, 1966; *Focus on Prose,* Prentice-Hall, 1969.

Reading and Writing Skills, McGraw, 1971; (with T. C. Pollock) *Macmillan Linguistics Laboratory,* Macmillan, 1971; *William Dean Howells: The Ohio Influence on His Life and Works,* Ohio Library Association, 1979.

Contributor: Francis Shoemaker and Louis Foresdale, editors, *Communication in General Education,* W. C. Brown, 1960; Lewis Mayhew, editor, *Social Studies in General Education,* W. C. Brown, 1960; Marion C. Sheridan and others, editors, *The Motion Picture and the Teaching of English,* Appleton, 1965. Contributor of about eighty articles, poems, and reviews to magazines, including *Windless Orchard, American Literary Realism, Mark Twain Journal,* and *Lost Generation Journal.*

Guest editor of *Widening Circle,* autumn, 1973; book review editor of *Antioch Review,* 1974-78, assistant editor, 1975-77; book review editor of *University Times,* 1979—.

WORK IN PROGRESS: Mark Twain in Ohio; Mark Twain's Funniest.

SIDELIGHTS: Baker commented: "If the twentieth century lasts long enough (and if I last with it), I hope to complete studies (mostly newspaper searches) of the reputations of nineteenth-century American authors, especially Mark Twain and William Dean Howells. Retirement is not likely to change this plan, but in the process I hope to discover news stories that can be converted to fiction."

*   *   *

BALDWIN, John W(esley) 1929-

PERSONAL: Born July 13, 1929, in Chicago, Ill.; son of Edward N. (an engineer) and H. Gladys (McDaniel) Baldwin; married Jenny M. Jochens (a professor), December 24, 1954; children: Peter M., Ian T., Birgit, Christopher. *Education:* Wheaton College, Wheaton, Ill., B.A., 1950; Pennsylvania State University, M.A., 1951; Johns Hopkins University, Ph.D., 1956. *Home:* 4828 Roland Ave., Baltimore, Md. 21210. *Office:* Department of History, Johns Hopkins University, Baltimore, Md. 21218.

CAREER: University of Michigan, Ann Arbor, instructor, 1956-58, assistant professor of history, 1958-61; Johns Hopkins University, Baltimore, Md., associate professor, 1961-66, professor of history, 1966—. Member of Commission Internationale de Diplomatique. *Member:* Mediaeval Academy of America (fellow), American Historical Association, Society

for French Historical Studies, Royal Danish Academy of Sciences and Letters (foreign member). *Awards, honors:* Fulbright fellowship, 1953-55; Guggenheim fellowship, 1960; grants and fellowships from Howard Foundation, 1960, American Council of Learned Societies, 1965, National Endowment for the Humanities, 1971, and American Philosophical Society, 1971 and 1982.

WRITINGS: The Medieval Theories of the Just Price, American Philosophical Society, 1959; *Masters, Princes, and Merchants,* two volumes, Princeton University Press, 1970; *Scholastic Culture of the Middle Ages,* Heath, 1971; (editor with Richard Goldthwaite) *Universities in Politics,* Johns Hopkins Press, 1972; *City on the Seine: Paris Under Louis IX,* Macmillan, 1975. Contributor of articles and reviews to scholarly journals.

WORK IN PROGRESS: Editing *The Registers of Philip Augustus,* publication expected by Academie des Inscriptions et Belles-Lettres; a book on the government of Philip Augustus, completion expected in 1982.

*   *   *

BALDWIN, Richard S(heridan) 1910-

PERSONAL: Born May 27, 1910, in Marietta, Ohio; son of Edgar Douglas (a railroad freight agent) and Mahala (Hanes) Baldwin; married Nora Connolly, November 2, 1946 (died March 12, 1977); married Edith Pittman (a graphic artist), December 23, 1978; children: Richard S., John C. *Education:* Ohio State University, B. Sc., 1934; attended Pasadena Playhouse School of Theatre, 1938, and New York University, 1940-41. *Home:* 5 Maryanne Lane, Stamford, Conn. 06905. *Agent:* Frieda Fishbein, 353 North 57th St., New York, N.Y. 10019.

CAREER: Sunday Star, Columbus, Ohio, feature writer and co-author of column "It's a Fine Thing," 1938-39; *Savings Bank Journal,* Mt. Vernon, N.Y., associate editor and staff writer, 1940-43; *Los Angeles Times,* Los Angeles, Calif., television programming consultant, 1945-46; Dudley L. Parsons (public relations firm), partner, 1946-55; Barden Corp., Danbury, Conn., director of public relations and advertising, 1955-63; Research Corp., New York, N.Y., assistant to the president, 1963-78, secretary, 1968-78. Free-lance writer, 1934-40. *Wartime service:* Senior civilian technical representative for Carl L. Norden Co., in European theater during World War II. *Member:* American Civil Liberties Union, Common Cause, League of Women Voters, Chemists Club (New York).

WRITINGS: (Editor) *A Practical Guide to Combatting Malnutrition,* Appleton-Century-Crofts, 1970; (editor) *Science in Liberal Arts Colleges,* Columbia University Press, 1972; *The Fungus Fighters: Two Women Scientists and Their Discovery,* Cornell University Press, 1981. Also author of plays, including "New World," "Love Is Not Enough," "A Triangle Has Two Sides," "A Man of the People" (screenplay), and "Kiss and Run" (screenplay), all as yet unproduced.

WORK IN PROGRESS: A novel; short stories; plays; screenplays.

SIDELIGHTS: The Fungus Fighters chronicles the work of researchers Elizabeth Hazen and Rachel Brown, focusing on their discovery of Nystatin, the first antifungal antibiotic to be safe and effective in the treatment of human disease. Presenting a view of the current state of mycological research, the book also describes the nonmedical uses of Nystatin.

Baldwin told *CA:* "I had an early interest in writing but received my major motivation from English composition courses I took at Ohio State University under Edwin Beck and others.

I was drawn to playwriting by my experience at Pasadena Playhouse and continued with Albert Maltz's courses in playwriting at New York University. I have written three plays: one of which died in rehearsal in Florida, one that got a reading from an Off-Off Broadway group, and another that got nowhere. I have also written two screenplays, one of which reached a story conference at the Selznick studio before being turned down.

"Finding that free-lance writing didn't provide much of a living, I took the first of a series of jobs, all involving writing and editing, and became something of a specialist on annual reports and other corporate literature. This aided my job with a nonprofit science foundation, where I also got into science writing and editing books on human nutrition and science education. After retirement, I researched and wrote the account of the two women scientists who discovered the first antibiotic effective against human fungus diseases. Now, I'm getting back into short stories, plays, and screenplays, as well as the book I'm working on.

AVOCATIONAL INTERESTS: Travel (particularly to Mexico and the Carribbean), photography, cooking, vegetable gardening.

BIOGRAPHICAL/CRITICAL SOURCES: Washington Post Book World, May 24, 1981; *Wall Street Journal,* May 26, 1981.

* * *

BALDWIN, Roger (Nash) 1884-1981

OBITUARY NOTICE: Born January 21, 1884, in Wellesley, Mass.; died of heart failure, August 26, 1981, in Ridgewood, N.J. Sociologist, educator, and author. One of the founders of the American Civil Liberties Union (ACLU), Baldwin served as executive director of the organization from its inception until his retirement in 1950. Under his leadership the ACLU helped abolish the Pennsylvania coal and iron police, defended John T. Scopes in the Tennessee "Monkey Trial" of 1925, took part in the Sacco-Vanzetti case, helped lift the ban on James Joyce's *Ulysses,* and defended the right of free speech for everyone, including the Ku Klux Klan and the American Nazi Party. In addition to his ACLU activities, Baldwin was a trustee of the American Fund for Public Service and was affiliated with several organizations, including the International League for the Rights of Man, the National Conference of Social Welfare, the Inter-American Association for Democracy and Freedom, the American League for Peace and Democracy, and the Friends of the Soviet Union. He also taught civil liberties law at the University of Puerto Rico. In 1981 Baldwin received the Medal of Freedom, the nation's highest civilian honor. He was the co-author of a textbook, *Juvenile Courts and Probation,* written with Bernard Flexner. Obituaries and other sources: *Celebrity Register,* 3rd edition, Simon & Schuster, 1973; *New York Times,* August 27, 1981; *Newsweek,* September 7, 1981; *Time,* September 7, 1981; *New Republic,* September 23, 1981.

* * *

BALLANTRAE, Lord
See FERGUSSON, Bernard Edward

* * *

BALLINGER, (Violet) Margaret (Livingstone) 1894-1980
(Margaret Hodgson)

OBITUARY NOTICE—See index for CA sketch: Born January

11, 1894, in Glasgow, Scotland; died February 7, 1980, in Cape Province, South Africa. Politician and author best known as an authority on South Africa. As a member of South Africa's Parliament for twenty-three years, Ballinger worked to improve living conditions in her country and fought to end racial discrimination. Even before her election, the politician was interested in social, political, and economic reforms, but her appointment as representative of two million Africans magnified her concerns about racial discrimination against blacks in South Africa. Though she lost her seat in 1948 when apartheid policies ended the representation of blacks in Parliament, Ballinger continued to promote anti-racist policies as the first president of the South African Liberal Party, which she helped to found in 1953. The politician was also the founder of the Margaret Ballinger Home for Crippled and Convalescent African Children, and she was a member of the Nursing Council, the South African Council of Women, and the South African Institute of Race Relations. In 1913 she received a Queen Victoria Scholarship, and, in addition to earning the Royal African Society Medal, Ballinger was awarded honorary degrees from the University of Rhodes and the University of Cape Town. Earlier in her career she was a lecturer at the University of the Witwatersrand. Ballinger's books include *Bechuanaland Protectorate, Basutoland, All Union Politics Are Native Affairs, Influence of Holland on Africa, From Union to Apartheid: A Trek to Isolation,* and *Britain in South Africa.* Obituaries and other sources: *The Annual Obituary 1980,* St. Martin's, 1981.

* * *

BANKS, Ann 1943-

PERSONAL: Born November 30, 1943, in Palm Beach, Fla.; daughter of Richard G. (a university administrator) and Isabel (a travel agent; maiden name, Day) Banks. *Education:* University of Florida, Gainesville, B.A., 1966. *Home:* 21 Lee St., Cambridge, Mass. 02139.

CAREER: University of Miami, Miami, Fla., editor and writer in publications office, 1966-68; Brown University, Providence, R.I., associate editor of *Brown Alumni Monthly,* 1968-73; Harvard University, Cambridge, Mass., editor of *Harvard Today,* 1973-74; *Harper's Weekly,* New York, N.Y., associate editor, 1974-75; Boston College, Boston, Mass., instructor in journalism, 1976; research associate for American Studies Center, 1977-81; writer. Associate fellow at Institute for Policy Studies, summer, 1977; executive editor and co-project director of radio series "First Person America: Voices From the Thirties," for National Public Radio, 1979-80. Consultant to Library of Congress American Folklore Center, 1979-80, Nation Institute (planning director for 1981 American Writers' Congress), 1980-81, and WGBH Office of Radio and Television for Learning, 1981. Panelist and participant on radio talk shows and seminars.

AWARDS, HONORS: Award for "excellence in writing" from *Atlantic,* 1972, for articles contributed to *Brown Alumni Monthly;* citations from American Alumni Council, 1972 and 1973, both for articles in *Brown Alumni Monthly;* citation from *Newsweek* for public affairs coverage in *Harvard Today;* Ford Foundation research grant, 1976-77; Rockefeller Foundation research grant, 1977-78; National Science Foundation research grant, 1978; Alicia Patterson Foundation fellowship, 1979-80; award for best arts documentary from Corporation for Public Broadcasting, 1981, for "First Person America."

WRITINGS: Goodbye, House (for children), Harmony Books, 1979; (editor) *First Person America* (nonfiction), Knopf, 1980;

(editor) *Harlem Document* (nonfiction), Matrix, 1981. Contributor to periodicals, including *New York Times Book Review, Mother Jones, Novel, Southern Exposure, Atlantic Monthly,* and *Harper's.*

*   *   *

BANKS, Carolyn

PERSONAL: Born February 9, 1941, in Pittsburgh, Pa.; daughter of Phillip J. and Victoria (Zbel) Dogonka; married Donald Banks (divorced). *Education:* University of Maryland College Park, B.A. (with high honors), 1968, M.A., 1969. *Home:* Morning Glory Farm, Etlan, Va. 22719. *Office:* Piedmont Virginia Community College, 315 Seven and One Half St. S.W., Charlottesville, Va. 22901.

CAREER: Currently an instructor at Piedmont Virginia Community College, Charlottesville; writer. Formerly an instructor of journalism and creative writing at the University of Maryland and Bowie State College. *Member:* Mystery Writers of America, Authors Guild, P.E.N. *Awards, honors:* Calvert Review Prose Award from the University of Maryland, 1968; Maryland fellowship, 1969.

WRITINGS: (Editor with Morris Freedman) *American Mix,* Lippincott, 1972; *Mr. Right* (novel), Viking, 1979; *The Adventures of Runcible Spoon,* Ethos Enterprises, 1979; *The Darkroom* (novel), Viking, 1980; *All in a Row* (novel), Viking, in press. Contributor of book reviews to *Washington Post Book World.* Contributor to numerous periodicals, including *American Education, American Heritage, Family Weekly,* and *Sports Illustrated.*

WORK IN PROGRESS: The Country Gentleman, a mystery.

SIDELIGHTS: Mr. Right, Banks's first novel, is a suspenseful tale about a woman, Lida, and her love affair with Duvivier, an author of sadomasochistic novels who writes under several pseudonyms. As her relationship with the novelist progresses, Lida discovers through her job as a librarian that Duvivier is not her lover's real name, and upon investigation learns his true name and that he was once a college professor. Duvivier has kept his real name hidden, fearing it will link him to the murder of a college coed who was seen with him on the night of her death. Because he cannot recall the events of the evening, Duvivier has led himself to believe he is the killer, though in reality he is not. Afraid that Lida will reveal his identity, Duvivier plots her death.

Mr. Right has been warmly received by critics. Eve Zibart of the *Washington Post Book World* called it "devious and delicious" and recommended "a swift second reading is worthwhile just to admire Banks's wiliness." The *New York Times Book Review* used Banks's description of Duvivier to describe Banks: "She is the sort of writer 'read by certain sophisticated people as one who offered light escape while, at the same time, not harshly insulting their intelligence.'"

Banks's second novel, *The Darkroom,* is based on the U.S. Central Intelligence Agency's (CIA) disclosure that it tested mind-altering drugs on people without informing them of the personality changes they would suffer, and never explaining the devastating alterations (that sometimes led to suicide) to the families of the victims. *The Darkroom* deals with a seemingly mild-mannered, intelligent man who violently murders his mother, wife, and three children after disfiguring photographs of them. Unaware that he is a victim of CIA drug experimentation, the man, William Thomas Holland, flees into the wilderness and after a time is presumed dead. But a CIA agent, aware that Holland was treated with mind-bending

chemicals, continues stalking Holland. When the agent and murderer meet, Holland is found living in a secluded cabin, under a new name, with a divorcee and her two sons. His pastime? Distorting photographs of his new companions.

Commenting on Banks's second book, Stanley Ellin of the *Washington Post Book World* wrote: "All this [CIA drug experimentation] is now a matter of public record, and Carolyn Banks has drawn from that record to set forth a story which is the more effective because it is not accusatory. Those who may feel that paranoia, whatever colors drape it, is no substitute for conscience will find in Carolyn Banks' novel the most dramatically telling argument for their increasingly unpopular position."

BIOGRAPHICAL/CRITICAL SOURCES: Washington Post, February 10, 1979, May 12, 1980, May 3, 1981; *New York Times Book Review,* March 25, 1979.

*   *   *

BANNING, Margaret Culkin   1891-1982

OBITUARY NOTICE—See index for *CA* sketch: Born March 18, 1891, in Buffalo, Minn.; died January 4, 1982, in Tryon, N.C. Author. Banning wrote more than forty books and four hundred short stories, usually exploring changing life-styles. Known primarily as a "woman's novelist," she was an advocate of women's rights who once stated: "Women should get over being afraid of being seen without men. I believe in personal independence for all women." Her novels generally dealt with social issues like relationships between races, birth control, which she discussed in *The Vine and the Olive,* or marriages involving different religious faiths, as *Fallen Away* exemplified. Her one book that did not concern such topics was *Mesabi,* a novel on the mining industry, which she came to know through her second husband LeRoy Salsich, president of Oliver Iron Mining Company. Banning studied the conditions of women in post-World War II England, and she worked in refugee camps in Germany and Austria. Banning was a frequent contributor to magazines such as *Reader's Digest.* Her other books include *This Marrying, Path of True Love, The Case for Chastity, Salud: A South American Journal, Conduct Yourself Accordingly,* and *I Took My Love to the Country* as well as a novel in progress at the time of her death. Obituaries and other sources: *New York Times,* January 6, 1982; *Chicago Tribune,* January 7, 1982; *Time,* January 18, 1982; *Publishers Weekly,* January 22, 1982; *AB Bookman's Weekly,* February 15, 1982.

*   *   *

BARBERA, Henry   1929-

PERSONAL: Born December 21, 1929, in New York, N.Y.; son of John S. (a naval architect) and Rosalie (a dress designer; maiden name, Consigliaro) Barbera; married Penny Jones (a puppeteer), April 1, 1970. *Education:* Hofstra University, B.A., 1953; Columbia University, M.A., 1954, Ph.D., 1971. *Politics:* Independent. *Religion:* None. *Home and office:* 228 West 11th St., New York, N.Y. 10014.

CAREER: Hunter College (now of the City University of New York), New York City, instructor in sociology, 1956-59, 1964-65; National Opinion Research Center, New York City, research analyst, 1959-64; Columbia University, Bureau of Applied Social Research, New York City, project director, 1966-70; City College of the City University of New York, New York City, associate professor of sociology, 1971-77; consultant on international change, 1977-80; State University of New

York College at Purchase, adjunct professor of sociology, 1980—. Vice-president of Early Childhood Puppet Theater, 1977—; member of board of directors of Arba Sicula, Inc., 1981—. *Military service:* U.S. Army, paratrooper, 1946-49. *Member:* American Sociological Association, Sociology of World Conflicts (member of council), Inter-University Seminar on the Armed Forces and Society (fellow).

WRITINGS: Rich Nations and Poor in Peace and War, Heath, 1973; *The Rise of Hope, the Rise of Discontent: Change, Inequality, and Passion in World Society,* University of Wisconsin Press, 1981. Contributor of about a dozen articles to academic journals.

WORK IN PROGRESS: The Military Factor: Effects of War, Advanced Technology, and Combat Organization on Character and Social Structure, Values, and Socioeconomic Development, completion expected in 1984.

SIDELIGHTS: Henry Barbera wrote: "My main professional interest is in applying the concept of social structure to large social facts, like armies, nations, and world society, in historical and comparative perspective. In my book *Rich Nations and Poor in Peace and War* I sought to measure and explain the effect that wars may have had on the course of socioeconomic development. The empirical findings of the work reveal that wars do not affect the wealth of nations, considered individually or collectively. In *The Rise of Hope, the Rise of Discontent* national feelings are conceived of as functions of alteration in the bases of material power. A notable consequence of change in the structures of international stratification, for example, can be seen in the politics of resentment and in the economics of envy.

"At present I am searching for evidence to substantiate or refute my belief that a military, rather than an economic or religious, interpretation of history could help to account for the victory of the principle of achievement over that of ascription, as a value basis of social facts. I am taken by the thought that a combat organization may actually become the enemy of inherited privilege under conditions of war, and only under conditions of peace may it become the benefactor. The idea of doing such a study came to me while preparing an article that traces a variety of social consequences of inventing the gun; the book will be called *The Military Factor.*"

* * *

BARBUSSE, Henri   1873-1935

BRIEF ENTRY: Born May 17, 1873, in Asieres, France; died of pneumonia, August 30, 1935, in Moscow, U.S.S.R. French journalist and novelist. Barbusse began his career as a journalist for *Petit Parisien* and for *Echo de Paris.* Later he became the editor of *Je Sais Tout.* The protege of Catulle Mendes, Barbusse began writing poetry in the symbolist tradition but then concentrated on fiction, particularly naturalistic novels. His most famous work, the realistic novel *Le Feu* (1916; title means "Under Fire"), provided an exact description of trench warfare in World War I and served as a plea to abolish war. *Le Feu,* like Barbusse's other novels, exhibits his ability to communicate powerful emotions. Moving from pacifism to communism, the author began writing propaganda and manifestos. He was a correspondent to *L'Humanite,* a mouthpiece for communism in France, and he served as a delegate to the Seventh Congress of the Third International in Moscow. The organizer of the First World Congress Against War and Fascism, he founded Clarte, a revolutionary group which espoused peace and a better social system. He also formed the Republican Association of Ex-Service Men in France. In 1917 the novelist

received the Prix Goncourt for *Le Feu;* earlier he earned several citations as a private serving in World War I. Barbusse's works include *Pleureuses* (1895; title means "Weeping Women"), *Les Suppliantes* (1903; title means "The Suppliants"), *L'Enfer* (1908; title means "The Inferno"), *Clarte* (1919; title means "Light"), *Les Enchainements* (1925; title means "Chains"), and *Staline* (1935). *Biographical/critical sources: Twentieth Century Authors: A Biographical Dictionary of Modern Literature,* H. W. Wilson, 1942; *The Oxford Companion to French Literature,* corrected edition, Clarendon Press, 1966; *Cassell's Encyclopaedia of World Literature,* revised edition, Morrow, 1973.

* * *

BARFOOT, Joan   1946-

PERSONAL: Born May 17, 1946, in Owen Sound, Ontario, Canada. *Education:* University of Western Ontario, B.A., 1969. *Residence:* London, Ontario.

CAREER: Journalist and writer. Worked as newspaper reporter for *Owen Sound Sun Times, London Free Press, Windsor Star,* Mirror Publications, and *Toronto Sunday Sun. Member:* London (Ontario) City Press Club. *Awards, honors: Books in Canada* award for first novels, 1978, for *Abra.*

WRITINGS: Abra (novel), Ryerson, 1978 (published in England as *Gaining Ground,* Women's Press, 1980).

SIDELIGHTS: Barfoot's *Abra* is about a young matron who deserts her husband and children to live as a recluse in the Canadian wilderness. Writing with "intelligence, sensitivity, and inventiveness," Barfoot was "able to take what has become a hackneyed theme and make it new," according to *Books in Canada* critic Sheila Fischman.

Another *Books in Canada* reviewer, Douglas Hill, described the book as "tough, complex, and convincing in the emotional truth it delivers." *Canadian Literature*'s Miriam Waddington disagreed, observing that the protagonist's "abandonment of her children, her lack of guilt, her rationalization of her problems, are not in the least convincing." Critic David Godfrey concurred, writing in *Books in Canada* that the novel suffers from "psychological unbelievability." *London Tribune*'s Kathryn Buckley reported that although *Abra* "reads as the egotistic and heartless escape of a possessive neurotic from life and responsibility," the book is "written with honesty and sincerity."

BIOGRAPHICAL/CRITICAL SOURCES: Books in Canada, April, 1979, January, 1980; *Canadian Literature,* spring, 1980; *Times Literary Supplement,* April 18, 1980; *London Tribune,* July 18, 1980; *Contemporary Literary Criticism,* Volume 18, Gale, 1981.*

* * *

BARING, Maurice   1874-1945

BRIEF ENTRY: Born April 27, 1874, in London, England; died of a paralytic disease, December 14, 1945, in Beauly, Scotland. British author. As the son of a banker and member of the nobility, Baring confined his writing to the setting he knew best. In novels like *Cat's Cradle* (1925), he depicted high society and the cultured values of his day with practiced insight and a subtle sense of humor, but without the critical tone of the moralist. His themes centered on the conflict between desire and duty. In *Daphne Adeane* (1926), for example, he pitted physical passion against sacred love. Baring's early work included plays, poems, children's books, and travel writing. His turn-of-the-century work as a diplomat and journalist took him to most of the capitals of eastern and western Europe. The time he spent in Moscow prompted several books on the people, lifestyle, and literature of Russia, including *The Russian People* (1911). In his autobiography, *The Puppet Show of Memory* (1922), Baring revealed himself as a humane Christian, refined and aristocratic. Though his style was that of a detached observer, his writing was sensitive and romantic. Baring's reputation among his critics rests upon his integrity as an artist and chronicler of the society in which he lived. *Biographical/critical sources: Twentieth Century Authors: A Biographical Dictionary of Modern Literature,* H. W. Wilson, 1942, 1st supplement, 1955; *Encyclopedia of World Literature in the Twentieth Century,* updated edition, Ungar, 1967.

*   *   *

BARNES, Stephen Emory 1952-
(Steven Barnes)

PERSONAL: Born March 1, 1952, in Los Angeles, Calif.; son of Emory Flake (an employment counselor) and Eva Mae (a real estate broker; maiden name, Reeves) Barnes. *Education:* Attended Pepperdine University, 1970-74. *Religion:* Episcopalian. *Home address:* P.O. Box 70253, Los Angeles, Calif. 90070. *Agent:* Blassingame/Spectrum, 225 West 34th St., New York, N.Y. 10001.

CAREER: Writer. Columbia Broadcasting System, Hollywood, Calif., tour guide, 1974-76; Pepperdine University, Malibu, Calif., manager of audio-visual and multi-media department, 1978-80. Creative consultant to Don Bluth Productions, 1980. *Awards, honors:* Second place in National Korean Karate Championships, 1972; nominated for Hugo Award, 1980, for short story "The Locusts."

WRITINGS—Under name Steven Barnes: *Ki: How to Generate the Dragon Spirit* (nonfiction), Sen-do Publications, 1976; (with Larry Niven) *Dream Park* (novel), Ace Books, 1981; (with Niven) *The Descent of Anansi* (novel), Tor Books, 1982; *Streetlethal* (novel), Ace Books, 1982; "The Secret of NIMH" (animated cartoon), Don Bluth Productions, 1982. Contributor of short stories to *Analog* and *Isaac Asimov's Science Fiction Magazine.*

WORK IN PROGRESS: A sequel to *Dream Park; The Legacy of Heorot,* with Larry Niven and Jerry Pournelle, publication expected in 1984; *Holistic Martial Arts,* 1983; *Human Resources Management Through Science Fiction,* an anthology-textbook, edited with Warren Paul, 1984; "Streetlethal," a screenplay, with Karen Willson; *The Legend of the Ghyss,* a children's book, with Toni Young, 1983; *Cats Melt in the Rain,* a children's book, with Young, 1983; *God Save the King,* a novel and screenplay, 1983.

SIDELIGHTS: Steven Barnes wrote: "My primary area of interest is human mental and physical development. To this end I research psychology, parapsychology, and kinesiology, practice and teach martial arts, and meditate and study comparative religious philosophy. My major viewpoint is that all human beings are perfect, but that we allow ourselves to dwell in our illusions of imperfection, creating fear, hate, and all negativity in human experience. At any moment we are capable of creating perfection in our lives merely by accepting our divinity. Virtually no Western discipline creates a proper balance between Body, Mind, and Spirit. To this end I have attempted to synthesize a belief system which enables me to grow without ceasing, love without reservation, and face life by accepting death. Life is too short to spend in sorrow or regret and too long to live without sober and informed evaluation.

"To say that 'all men are brothers' is to avoid the real point. We are all expressions of the same Life, call it God, Holy Spirit, Ki, ch'i, prana, kundalini, or anything else you please—these are merely words, symbols, and symbols are only shadows of the Truth. If I have any real goal in life it is to strip away the 'knowledge' I have learned and reenter the Void from which came all things and to which all things must inevitably return.''

BIOGRAPHICAL/CRITICAL SOURCES: Isaac Asimov's Science Fiction Magazine, March, 1981; *Analog,* August 17, 1981.

*   *   *

BARNES, Steven
See BARNES, Stephen Emory

*   *   *

BARNETT, Isobel (Morag) 1918-1980

OBITUARY NOTICE: Born June 30, 1918, in Aberdeen, Scotland; committed suicide, October 20, 1980, in Cossington, Leicestershire, England. Physician, media personality, and author. Wife of the lord mayor of Leicester, Barnett was a general medical practitioner during World War II but abandoned her medical career after she was appointed justice of the peace in Leicester County in 1948. A popular public speaker, Barnett became a well-known radio and television personality, appearing regularly on the long-running radio show "Any Questions" and as a panel member of the BBC-TV game show "What's My Line?" After her husband died in 1970 Barnett served as director of a unit shares trust; she was one of the first women in Britain ever to do so. On October 16, 1980, Barnett was convicted for shoplifting a carton of cream and a can of tuna. Four days later she was found electrocuted in her bathtub. Sources agree that Barnett died by her own hand, and some list drug overdose as the cause of death. Among her writings are an autobiography, *My Life Line,* and a recipe book, *Lady Barnett's Cookbook.* Obituaries and other sources: *New York Times,* October 22, 1980; *Time,* November 17, 1980; *The Annual Obituary 1980,* St. Martin's, 1981.

*   *   *

BARNETT, Richard B(aity) 1941-

PERSONAL: Born May 5, 1941, in Kansas City, Mo.; son of Henry Clinton (a minister) and Ruth (Chenoweth) Barnett; married Joan Isaly (a high school teacher), July 10, 1965; children: Jennifer Helene, Melissa Joy. *Education:* Attended University of Ibadan, 1961-62; College of Wooster, B.A., 1965; University of California, Berkeley, M.A., 1966, Ph.D., 1975. *Politics:* Liberal left. *Religion:* "Nondenominational." *Home:* 1614 Meadowbrook Heights Rd., Charlottesville, Va. 22901. *Office:* Department of History, University of Virginia, Charlottesville, Va. 22903.

CAREER: Ewing Christian College, Allahabad, India, visiting lecturer in history, 1963-65; San Francisco State University, San Francisco, Calif., acting instructor in history, 1972-73; University of Virginia, Charlottesville, assistant professor, 1974-78, associate professor of history, 1979—, director of Center for South Asian Studies, 1982—. Consultant to National Endowment for the Humanities.

MEMBER: American Institute of Indian Studies (member of board of trustees), Association for Asian Studies, South Asian Studies Association of Australia and New Zealand, Southern Atlantic States Association of Asian and African Studies. *Awards, honors:* Social Science Research Council junior fellow, 1969-71, senior fellow, 1977-78; University of Virginia W.F. Gee fellow, 1975, 1977, 1980; American Institute of Indian Studies and Hays-Fulbright senior fellow, 1977-78; University of Virginia sesquicentennial associate, 1981.

WRITINGS: North India Between Empires: Awadh, the Mughals, and the British, 1720-1801, University of California Press, 1980. Contributor to Asian studies and Middle East studies journals.

WORK IN PROGRESS: Islamic Civilizations of Hinterland India, 1720-1850 (tentative title), for Cambridge University Press, completion expected in 1984; research on eighteenth-century Hyderabad, India.

SIDELIGHTS: Barnett told *CA:* "Since my footloose student days, I have lived in South Asia for a total of four years, off and on, developing language abilities in Urdu, Hindi, and Persian. The discipline of history seems to provide the most freedom of any to pursue one's fascinations with this rich and rewarding cultural region, so here I am a historian, although I hated and feared history in high school and college."

AVOCATIONAL INTERESTS: Running, bookbinding, photography, making beer, solar energy.

*　　*　　*

BARNSTONE, Aliki   1956-

PERSONAL: Born September 1, 1956, in New Haven, Conn.; daughter of Willis (a professor and writer) and Helle (a painter; maiden name, Tzalopoulou) Barnstone. *Education:* Brown University, BA. (with honors), 1980. *Home:* 64 Preston St., Providence, R.I. 02906.

CAREER: Writer.

WRITINGS: The Real Tin Flower: Poem About the World at Nine (introduction by Anne Sexton), Macmillan, 1968; (editor with father, Willis Barnstone) *A Book of Women Poets From Antiquity to Now,* Schocken, 1980; *Windows in Providence,* Curbstone Press, 1981.

Work represented in anthologies, including *The Arts and Skills of English,* Volume IV, edited by Owen Thomas, Holt, 1972; *Zero Makes Me Hungry: A Collection of Poems for Today,* edited by Edward Lueder and Primus St. John, Lothrop, 1976; *Poets From A to Z,* edited by David Ray, Swallow Press, 1980. Contributor of articles and poems to magazines, including *Chicago Review, New Letters, Ms., Icarus, Teen,* and *Women and Literature,* and newspapers.

WORK IN PROGRESS: The Language of Apples, poems; editing *A Book of World Poetry From Antiquity to Now,* with W. Barnstone.

BIOGRAPHICAL/CRITICAL SOURCES: Time, December 22, 1980; *Los Angeles Times Book Review,* February 1, 1981; *Times Literary Supplement,* May 29, 1981.

*　　*　　*

BARON of REMENHAM
See THOMAS, (William) Miles (Webster)

*　　*　　*

BARR, Alfred H(amilton), Jr.   1902-1981

OBITUARY NOTICE—See index for *CA* sketch: Born January 28, 1902, in Detroit, Mich.; died August 15, 1981, in Salis-bury, Conn. Curator and author. Regarded by some as "possibly the most innovative and influential man of the 20th century," Alfred Barr, the founding director of the Museum of Modern Art in New York, created a multi-departmental museum encompassing both traditional and modern visual arts, such as industrial design, architecture, photography, film, and theatre design. "He made the Museum of Modern Art," said John Russell of the *New York Times,* "into something that has long been the envy of the world." Barr's trip to Germany and Russia in 1927 was a critical influence on the author. In Germany he came into contact with the Bauhaus artists and their publication programs as well as with the international style of architecture. In Russia he saw the makings of Stalin's new regime and was introduced to the Russian avant-garde. After his retirement as director of the Museum of Modern Art, Barr concentrated on writing, producing two major works, *Picasso: Fifty Years of His Art* and *Matisse: His Art and His Public.* A sequence of galleries in the museum were named after Barr, and he received numerous awards, including the Lord and Taylor American Design Award, a Star of Italian Solidarity, an award of merit from the American Institute of Architects, and the Skowhegan Gertrude Vanderbilt Whitney Award. His books include *First Loan Exhibition: Cezanne, Gauguin, Seurat, Van Gogh; American Art of the Twenties and Thirties; A Brief Survey of Modern Painting; Cubism and Abstract Art; Twentieth Century Italian Art;* and *New American Painting as Shown in Eight European Countries, 1958-59.* Obituaries and other sources: *New York Times,* August 23, 1981.

*　　*　　*

BARRAULT, Jean-Louis   1910-

PERSONAL: Born September 8, 1910, in Vesinet, France; son of Jules (a pharmacist) and Marcelle Helene (Valette) Barrault; married Madeleine Renaud (an actress), September 5, 1940. *Education:* Attended painting classes at Ecole du Louvre, 1931; studied acting with Charles Dullin at Theatre de l'Atelier, 1931-35; studied mime with Etienne Decroux. *Home:* 18 Avenue du President Wilson, Paris 16e, France.

CAREER: Actor, director, producer, and mime. Associated with Theatre de l'Atelier, 1931-35, Le Grenier des Augustins (founder), 1935-40, Comedie Francaise, 1940-46, Compagnie Renaud-Barrault (co-founder with wife, Madeleine Renaud), 1946-59, Theatre Marigny, 1946-58, Theatre du Palais-Royal, 1958-59, Theatre de l'Odeon (renamed Theatre de France), 1959-68, Theatre des Nations, 1965-67, 1972-74, and Theatre d'Orsay (founder), 1974—. Actor in stage productions, including "Volpone," 1931, "Autour d'une mere," 1935, "Hamlet," 1936, 1946, "Le Cid," 1940, "Le Proces," 1946, "Les Fourberies de Scapin," 1952, "Batiste," 1952, "Christophe Colomb," 1957, "Intermezzo," 1957, "Tete d'or," 1959, 1968, "Rabelais," 1968, and "Zarathustra," 1974. Actor in more than twenty-five films, including "Les Beaux Jours," 1935, "Helene," 1936, "Drole de drame," 1937, "Les Enfants du Paradis," 1944, "Le Cocu magnifique," 1945, and "The Longest Day," 1962. Director and producer of stage productions, including "Autour d'une mere," 1935, "El Cerco de Numanica," 1937, 1965, "Phedre," 1942, "Le Soulier de satin," 1943, "Hamlet," 1946, "Histoire de Vasco," 1957, "Le Voyage," 1961, "Les Paravents," 1966, "Rabelais," 1968, and "Jarry sur la butte," 1970. Performed as a mime in film and stage productions, including "Les Enfants du Paradis," 1944, "Batiste," 1952, and "Intermezzo," 1957. Director and producer of opera for major companies in France, Germany, Italy, and the United States. *Military service:* French Army, served in World War II.

AWARDS, HONORS: Commander of French Legion of Honor; Catholic Stage Guild of Ireland merit award, 1952, for work in the theatre; Best Dominic prize for play direction, 1965; Syndicate of French Drama Critics award for best show of the season and best French creation, 1969, for "Rabelais."

WRITINGS: A propos de Shakespeare et du theatre (lectures), Parade, 1949; *Reflexions sur le theatre,* J. Vautrain, 1949, translation by Barbara Wall published as *Reflections on the Theatre,* Rockliff, 1951; *Une Troupe et ses auteurs: Extraits et commentaires a propos de Shakespeare, Moliere, Marivaux, P. Claudel, A. Gide, Kafka, Feydeau, M. Archard, et J.P. Sartre,* J. Vautrain, 1950; *Je suis homme de theatre,* Editions du Conquistadore, 1955; *Nouvelles Reflexions sur le theatre,* preface by Armand Salacrou, Flammarion, 1959, translation by Joseph Chiari published as *The Theatre of Jean-Louis Barrault,* Hill & Wang, 1961; *Journal de bord: Japon, Israel, Grece, Yougoslavie,* Julliard, 1961; (with Simone Benmussa) *Oden Theatre de France,* Le Temps, 1965; *Mise en scene de Phedre,* Editions du Seuil, 1972; *Souvenirs pour demain,* Editions du Seuil, 1972, translation by Jonathon Griffin published as *Memories for Tomorrow: The Memoirs of Jean-Louis Barrault,* Dutton, 1974; (and author of preface) *Correspondence: Paul Claudel, Jean-Louis Barrault* (letters), introduction and notes by Michel Lioure, Gallimard, 1974; (with Collin Higgins) *Comme je le pense,* Gallimard, 1975; (co-author) *Moliere,* Hachette Realities, 1976.

Adapter of plays, including: "Autour d'une mere" (based on the novel *As I Lay Dying* by William Faulkner), first produced in Paris at Theatre de l'Atelier, May, 1935; (with Andre Gide) *Le Proces, piece tiree du roman de Kafka* (based on the novel *The Trial* by Franz Kafka; first produced in Paris at Theatre Marigny, 1947), Gallimard, 1947, translation by Jacqueline Sundstrom and Frank Sundstrom published as *The Trial,* Secker & Warburg, 1950, published as *The Trial: A Dramatization Based on Franz Kafka's Novel,* Schocken, 1964; "L'Amerique" (based on the novel *Amerika* by Franz Kafka), first produced in Paris at Theatre Marigny; *Saint-Exupery* (based on the work of Antoine de Saint-Exupery; first produced in 1967), Gallimard, 1975; *Rabelais: A Dramatic Game in Two Parts* (based on *Gargantua* and *Pantagruel* by Francois Rabelais; first produced in Paris at Elysee Montmartre, December 5, 1968; produced on Broadway at the New York City Center, May 19, 1970; produced on the West End at Old Vic Theatre, 1969), translated by Robert Baldick, Hill & Wang, 1971; *Jarry sur la butte* (based on the writings of Alfred Jarry; first produced in Paris, 1970), Gallimard, 1970; *Ainsi parlait Zarathoustra* (based on *Also Sprach Zarathustra* by Friedrich Wilhelm Nietzsche), Gallimard, 1975.

Founding editor and contributor to the *Cahiers de la Compagnie Renaud-Barrault.* Contributor of articles to *Elites Francaises* and *La Revue Theatrale.*

SIDELIGHTS: Barrault's versatile theatrical career has spanned fifty years, earning him international acclaim as an actor, director, producer, and mime. *Time* magazine called him "one of the towering figures of the French stage"; *Listener* named him "France's finest actor and impressario, its Olivier, Gielgud, and Reinhardt rolled into one. . . . France's greatest cultural treasure"; and *Cue* critic Glen Loney dubbed him "a legend in his own time." Barrault's diverse theatrical credits are divided equally between the avant-garde and the classical. As an actor, director, and producer, he has introduced to the public the innovative works of Eugene Ionesco, Samuel Beckett, George Scheharde, Paul Claudel, and Christopher Fry and has collaborated on stage adaptations with Andre Gide, Antonin Artaud, and Jacques Prevert; he has also produced, directed,

and performed in the works of traditional authors such as Shakespeare, Racine, Moliere, and Chekhov. A *Times Literary Supplement* reviewer capsulized Barrault's formula for success: "With contempt for convention but respect for tradition, he has appealed to every spectrum of taste."

Memories for Tomorrow: The Memoirs of Jean-Louis Barrault recounts the successes and failures of the author's career from its beginning at the Theatre de l'Atelier in 1931 through the years of his association with the Comedie Francaise. Barrault includes anecdotes of his professional relationship with his wife, actress Madeleine Renaud, and reminisces about his more than twenty years as the founding director of his own theatrical troupe, the Compagnie Renaud-Barrault. Devoting the final chapter of *Memories* to an account of his nine years as director of the Theatre de France, the actor recalls the events that provoked his controversial dismissal as head of the official French theatre company.

Barrault began his theatrical career as an acting apprentice under the tutelage of Charles Dullin at the Theatre de l'Atelier. Very little in the author's early life foretells of his decision at the age of twenty to write Dullin asking for an audition. In *Memories* "Barrault doesn't really explain, and perhaps doesn't know," noted a *Times Literary Supplement* reviewer, "why a young man with an average French background—peasants on one side, lower middle-class tradesman on the other, should have discovered in his early twenties that he wanted to devote himself to the theatre." Though Barrault's mother had performed in amateur theatrical productions and his uncle had a talent for pastels, the family seemed to have no special proclivities toward the arts. Barrault himself had no stage experience and had only been to the theatre perhaps ten times when he decided to make it his career. "Not exactly ground, there, for the imperatives of a vocation," he admits in his memoirs. "I prefer to give up trying to understand. What is certain, clear, and decisive is that I wanted more and more to go on the stage. I wanted it frantically."

In 1931 Barrault was accepted as a student at the Theatre de l'Atelier. Too poor to pay tuition or even to rent a room, he swept the stage, helped with props, and slept in the wardrobe room and loges of the theatre. Then, on his twenty-first birthday, September 8, 1931, Barrault made his acting debut playing the role of a servant in Ben Johnson's "Volpone." Earning fifteen francs a day as a member of the company, from 1931 to 1935 the actor continued studying the techniques of his master. "It was Dullin who ultimately taught me most," Barrault revealed in an interview in *Cue* many years later. "He had the marvelous quality to be able to be a virgin each morning. He forgot all his knowledge each night. And came into the Theatre each morning like a child—astonished and full of wonder. And I never forgot this quality."

It was also during his four years at the Atelier that Barrault received his first lessons in mime from a fellow student, Etienne Decroux. In *Memories,* Barrault recalls how the two young actors spent countless hours "discovering that limitless world, the muscles of the human body" and establishing "the difference between wordless pantomime and silent mime." Together they spent three weeks learning to "walk without changing places." At this time, comments Barrault in *Reflections on the Theatre,* he discovered that "the whole problem of the theatre is to make *silence* vibrate." Several years later, in 1944, Barrault received international acclaim as a mime when he played the role of Batiste, a clown in love, in the film "Les Enfants du Paradis." Since then, according to *New York Times Magazine* critic Philip Hope-Wallace, Barrault's stature as a mime has been "equaled only by his friend and pupil Marcel Marceau."

Barrault debuted as a producer and director in 1935 when he presented his own adaptation of William Faulkner's novel *As I Lay Dying*. Entitled "Autour d'une mere," the pantomime drama lasted four performances and was "a dismal failure," noted Luce Klein and Arthur Klein in *Theatre Arts*. Nevertheless, the Kleins pointed out, "since that day a long career has been in the making" because the production earned Barrault a movie contract for the film "Les Beaux Jours." Then during the filming the actor made his decision to leave Dullin and to form his own theatrical company, which he called Le Grenier des Augustins.

Barrault's new company was actually a theatrical community housed in a top floor studio on the rue des Grand-Augustins. There for the next few years the author led the life of a bohemian rebel. Surrounded by comrades such as Jacques Prevert, Antonin Artaud, and other surrealists, and inspired by the teachings of Freud, Marx, and the Eastern religions, the author was, he recalls "a libertarian, sowing my wild oats." "What I remember from this period," he recollects in *Memories,* "is the effervescence, freedom from care and complete liberty of my behavior. . . . Anarchy is a kind of nobility. It consists of an entire and absolute responsibility for onself."

Throughout his years at Le Grenier, Barrault continued his film career, and it was during the filming of "Helene" in 1936 that he met and fell in love with his leading lady, the woman who was to become his wife, Madeleine Renaud. "In most people's eyes, Madeleine and I came from two antipodes," commented Barrault. "I was a young anarchist, no doubt a 'Communist,' untidy, dishevelled good-for-nothing with no morality." On the other hand, Renaud was a member of the establishment, an actress in the traditional theatre, and a societaire (life member) of the Comedie Francaise. "She must have provided an important counterbalance to his [Barrault's] more extravagant tendencies," opined a *Times Literary Supplement* critic, "and they seem to have had a perfect working partnership for the past thirty years."

Barrault married Madeleine Renaud in 1940, following the demobilization of France. In the same year he joined the Comedie Francaise. "In the eyes of my comrades, I was ratting," the author said of his decision to join the tradition-oriented company. "Some thought I was really terrified of the liberty I proclaimed in other circumstance." In *Memories* Barrault offers the following explanation for his actions: "When a tree is cut back, it puts more strength into roots. After the Fauvism of the Atelier, after the emancipation brought by Surrealism, I was ready to receive the classical graft, that of the Francais. . . . After the uprooting caused by the world catastrophe, I felt the need to replant myself. Betray? Betray whom or what? Ideas? Politics? Leave them to their own betrayals. Let us work with supplying life."

Barrault was elected a societaire of the Comedie Francaise in 1942. He spent six successful years with the company, highlighting his career with productions such as Moliere's "La Princesse d'Elide," Claudel's "Le Soulier de satin," and Gide's translation of *Hamlet,* in which Barrault played the title role. When he accepted the societariat, the actor felt that he was making a long-term commitment, because, he explains in his memoirs, "to accept membership of the Societe is to engage oneself for life, as in a monastery." However, in September, 1945, the French government formed a commission to update the statutes governing the company. This action was possible because, although technically a private society, the Comedie Francaise was economically dependent on the state. A number of societaires protested the proceedings, seeking the right to elect their own representatives to the commission. Refusing

their request, the government instead presented the societaires with the revised statutes, including the stipulation that those who were not content were no longer bound by their previous commitment to remain with the company. Nine societaires, including Barrault and his wife, took advantage of the open door.

In the fall of 1946 Barrault and Renaud formed their own company at the Theatre Marigny. Originally financed with money the couple earned by continuing their film careers, the Compagnie Renaud-Barrault eventually became the most successful private theatre group ever to exist in France. For thirteen years, Barrault and his repertory company created what Hope-Wallace called "theartrical magic." With Barrault producing, directing, and starring in many of its productions, the company toured the world with a repertoire of fifty plays. After thirteen years, the Barrault entourage acquired "the status of a second national theatre," remarked a *Times Literary Supplement* reviewer. This is perhaps the reason that in 1959 Andre Malraux, the minister of French cultural affairs, offered Barrault official backing and use of the Theatre de l'Odeon.

After Barrault was appointed the director of France's new official theatre, the Compagnie Renaud-Barrault moved into the Theatre de l'Odeon and together they became known as the Theatre de France. The nationalization of Barrault's troupe provided France with an internationally renowned repertory company fully costumed and complete with a repertoire of thirty active plays; the Compagnie Renaud-Barrault, in turn, was provided with a subsidy and a larger theatre. For nine years the arrangement pleased both Barrault and the state.

But in May, 1968, Paris was rocked by social upheavals. "The Sorbonne and other principal universities were occupied by the students. Barricades, tear gas, trees uprooted," Barrault describes in his memoirs. "It was the misfortune of the Odeon to be situated in the centre of the clashes." On May 15, the actor learned from a member of his company that the students were planning to occupy the Odeon. He contacted the Ministry of Cultural Affairs for instructions on how to proceed should such an event occur. "The official reply from the Ministry was," according to Barrault, "'If the students put their plan into practice, *ouvrez-leur les portes et entamez le dialogue!'* (open the doors to them and start discussion)." That evening, as the audience left the theatre, the Odeon was rushed by twenty-five hundred students from the Sorbonne. For the next forty-eight hours Barrault and Madeleine Renaud engaged the students in talks. Confusion followed; Barrault recalls in *Memories* that he was insulted by the students, misquoted by the press, and chastised and then abandoned by his superiors. During the ordeal, he received only one communication from Malraux, in which the minister expressed displeasure with Barrault's handling of the affair.

The students destroyed the theatre and its contents, including the property of the Compagnie Renaud-Barrault, and on August 28, 1968, Barrault was fired. His dismissal came in what *Time* called a "curt letter" from Malraux. A *Listener* critic offered this explanation for the dismissal: "Malraux had realised that by yielding one toy victory at the Odeon to the students, he could distract them from the real theatres of power—the Assembly, Senate and headquarters of Radio-Televion Francaise. To do so, he needed to cast Barrault as student collaborator as pretext for ritual disavowal of him."

"The resilience of Barrault—the courage that confronts his timidity and the steel that sustains his flexibility—was proved by his reaction to this disaster," commented a critic in the *Times Literary Supplement*. Within one month of his dismissal as director of the Theatre de France, Barrault had secured a theatre, contracted actors, and was ready to begin rehearsals of "Rabelais." Written, produced and directed by Barrault, who also starred in the production, "Rabelais" opened in Paris in December, 1968. At the close of the 1968-69 theatre season the production received the French Drama Critics' award for the best show of the year and was named best new French creation.

While awaiting the Broadway opening of "Rabelais" in 1970, Barrault spoke to *New York Times* reporter John Gruen about what the French call "the events of May." He admitted, "Yes, I have suffered deeply, as has my wife. But life goes on and we must live. . . . We had our nine years at the National Theater. Now I believe the gods are watching over us very carefully, and a new period is beginning for us."

AVOCATIONAL INTERESTS: Collecting books on the theatre, swimming.

BIOGRAPHICAL/CRITICAL SOURCES: Theatre Arts, October, 1947; Jean-Louis Barrault, *Reflections on the Theatre,* Rockliff, 1951; *New York Times Magazine,* January 20, 1957; Barrault, *The Theatre of Jean-Louis Barrault,* Hill & Wang, 1961; *Time,* September 13, 1968; *Cue,* October 4, 1969; *Saturday Review,* May 16, 1970; *New York Times,* May 17, 1970; *Christian Science Monitor,* May 25, 1970; *Times Literary Supplement,* June 16, 1972, July 26, 1974; Barrault, *Memories for Tomorrow: The Memoirs of Jean-Louis Barrault,* Dutton, 1974; *New Statesman,* July 5, 1974; *Listener,* July 25, 1974; *Spectator,* September 14, 1974.*

—*Sketch by Lillian S. Sims*

*   *   *

BARRENO, Maria Isabel
See MARTINS, Maria Isabel Barreno de Faria

*   *   *

BARRICELLI, Jean-Pierre 1924-

PERSONAL: Born June 5, 1924, in Cleveland, Ohio; son of Giovanni A. (a surgeon) and Orfea (a professor; maiden name, Malvezzi) Barricelli; married Norma Gaeta (a professor), October 19, 1957; children: Marco A., Laura C., Franca R. *Education:* Harvard University, B.A., 1947, M.A., 1948, Ph.D., 1953. *Home:* 5984 Windemere Way, Riverside, Calif. 92506. *Office:* Department of Literatures and Languages, University of California, Riverside, Calif. 92521.

CAREER: Western Reserve University (now Case Western Reserve University), Cleveland, Ohio, lecturer in Spanish and French, summers, 1946-50; Harvard University, Cambridge, Mass., teaching assistant in French and Italian, 1948-50, 1951-53; Brandeis University, Waltham, Mass., assistant professor of romance languages and comparative literature and director of Wien International Scholarship Program, 1953-62; University of California, Riverside, professor of comparative literature, 1963—, chairman of department of literatures and languages, 1976—. Conductor of Waltham Symphony Orchestra and Cafarelli Opera Association, both 1955-60. Lecturer in music at Cambridge School of Adult Education, Cambridge, 1954-58; visiting professor at Norwegian School of Economics and Business Administration, and University of Bergen, both 1962-63. *Military service:* U.S. Army, in psychological warfare, 1943-46; served in Europe; became major; received five Bronze Stars. U.S. Army Reserve, 1946-50.

MEMBER: International Comparative Literature Association, Modern Language Association of America (member of exec-

utive committee on literature and other arts), American Comparative Literature Association (member of advisory board, 1976-79), Dante Society of America, National Association for the Advancement of the Humanities, Law and Humanities Institute (member of board of governors, 1980—), Phi Beta Kappa, Sigma Delta Pi. *Awards, honors:* Fulbright fellowships, 1950-51, 1962-63; University of California Humanities Institute award, 1972-73; named outstanding educator of America, 1974; distinguished teaching award from University of California, Riverside, 1975.

WRITINGS: (With Leo Weinstein) *Ernest Chausson,* University of Oklahoma Press, 1955; *Dodecahedron* (poems), Vantage, 1956; *Demonic Souls* (on Balzac), Edda, 1964; *The Prince,* Barron's, 1975; *Alessandro Manzoni,* Twayne, 1976.

Editor: Alfred de Vigny, *Chatterton,* Prentice-Hall, 1967; *Chekhov's Great Plays,* New York University Press, 1981; (with Joseph Gibaldi) *Interrelations of Literature,* Modern Language Association of America, 1981.

Translator: Giacomo Leopardi, *Poems,* Las Americas, 1963; Wergeland, *Poems,* The Norseman, 1974; Virgil, *Aeneid I,* University of California, Riverside, 1975. Editor of *Italian Quarterly,* 1969-75, and *Heliconian,* 1975—.

WORK IN PROGRESS: Giacomo Leopardi, publication by Twayne expected in 1983; *Literature and Music,* completion expected in 1983; *Die Englische Komodie,* publication by Carl Winter Verlag expected in 1984; *Literature and Law,* completion expected in 1984.

SIDELIGHTS: Barricelli wrote: "My writing began with a need to publish in order to advance (though I had published creatively with no advancement connected with it), but then came a compulsion to put my ideas in print. I consider vital all that has to do with the humanities, particularly literature, which is the basis of culture.

"Literature is not there to be studied just for itself, but in relation to every other discipline and human endeavor. It has a centrifugal force. There is more of life in literature than in any other form of human expression.

"I have traveled around the world, speak five languages, and work with twelve. Though my primary interdisciplinary interests involve music and law, I also study literature in the context of the visual arts, philosophy, theater, and history. Knowledge is one, and without becoming dilettantes, we should all try to savor as many of its ingredients as energy and inclination permit. What else is culture but a composite? And how else are we to cultivate values and develop judgment but out of a background of solid (but also *broad*) exposure? We must integrate knowledge. Scientists who only isolate and social scientists who only measure, kindly take note."

AVOCATIONAL INTERESTS: Playing piano, composing music, painting.

*   *   *

BARSH, Russel Lawrence 1950-

PERSONAL: Born May 4, 1950, in New York, N.Y.; son of Harold (a dentist) and Jacqueline (an actress and teacher; maiden name, Gross) Barsh; married Elizabeth Tracy (a social worker and counselor), December 22, 1972. *Education:* Harvard University, A.B. (summa cum laude), 1971, J.D., 1974. *Residence:* Seattle, Wash. *Office:* School of Business Administration, DJ-10, University of Washington, Seattle, Wash. 98195.

CAREER: University of Washington, Seattle, assistant professor, 1974-77, associate professor of business administration,

1977—, editor of *Journal of Contemporary Business,* 1977-81. Consultant to Union of Nova Scotia Indians and Oglala Sioux Tribe. *Member:* Washington State Bar Association. *Awards, honors:* Named one of Seattle's one hundred newsmakers of tomorrow by Seattle Chamber of Commerce and *Time,* 1978.

WRITINGS: The Washington Fishing Rights Controversy: An Economic Critique, University of Washington Press, 1977, revised edition, 1979; *Indian Treaties as Law,* Washington State Superintendent of Public Instruction, 1978; (with James Y. Henderson) *The Road: Indian Tribes and Political Liberty,* University of California Press, 1980. Contributor to American Indian and law journals.

WORK IN PROGRESS: The Fire and *The Chain,* sequels to *The Road,* dealing with historical and contemporary tribal political culture and philosophy and with the tribal political nationalism movement in the United States and Canada.

* * *

BARTENIEFF, Irmgard 1900(?)-1981

OBITUARY NOTICE: Born c. 1900 in Germany; died August 27, 1981. Physical therapist, dance theoretician, and author. Bartenieff studied with dance theoretician Rudolf Laban before fleeing Nazi Germany in 1936. After immigrating to the United States, she taught, wrote, and lectured on Labanotation, a system of dance notation developed by her former teacher. In 1943, upon earning a degree in physical therapy from New York University, Bartenieff went to work with polio victims and conducted developmental research on newborn children. Working at the Albert Einstein Medical College Day Hospital as a dance therapist and research assistant in nonverbal behavior from 1957 to 1967, Bartenieff developed a system of notation and observation of patient behavior using Laban movement analysis techniques. In her private practice as a therapist she specialized in dance injuries and back problems. She founded the Laban Institute of Movement Studies in New York in 1978 and was a senior member of the Dance Notation Bureau of New York. Bartenieff wrote *Body Movement: Coping With the Environment.* Obituaries and other sources: *New York Times,* September 2, 1981.

* * *

BARTON, M. Xaveria 1910-

BRIEF ENTRY: Born May 25, 1910, in Detroit, Mich. American geographer, educator, and author. Sister Xaveria was a professor of geography at Marygrove College until her retirement in 1975. Her writings include *Music Readiness Program* (Seraphic Press), *Europe and the Mediterranean World,* revised edition (McGraw, 1963), and *Lands of the Eastern Hemisphere* (McGraw, 1964). *Address:* 8500 Marygrove Dr., Detroit, Mich. 48221. *Biographical/critical sources: American Men and Women of Science,* 13th edition, Bowker, 1976.

* * *

BARTOS, Otomar J(an) 1927-

PERSONAL: Born November 16, 1927, in Prague, Czechoslovakia; son of Joseph and Terezie (Loeffelmannova) Bartos; married wife, Joan, February 1, 1958 (divorced December 21, 1980); children: Joseph, Peter, David, Mary, James. *Education:* Attended Charles University, 1946-50; received B.A. from University of Colorado, M.A., 1954; Yale University, Ph.D., 1956. *Religion:* Roman Catholic. *Home address:* Lee Hill Rd., Boulder, Colo. 80302. *Office:* Department of Sociology, University of Colorado, Boulder, Colo. 80309.

CAREER: University of Hawaii, Honolulu, assistant professor, 1956-58, associate professor of sociology, 1958-67; University of Pittsburgh, Pittsburgh, Pa., professor of sociology, 1967-69; Dartmouth College, Hanover, N.H., professor of sociology, 1969-70; University of Colorado, Boulder, professor of sociology, 1971—. Instructor at Whittier College, summer, 1958; visiting professor at Northwestern University, 1963-64; instructor at University of Colorado, 1966. Investigator with Air Force Office of Scientific Research, 1962-67; consultant to Systems Development Corp., 1958-62. *Member:* American Sociological Association. *Awards, honors:* Fellowship for Salzburg Seminar in American Studies, 1950; Social Science Research Council fellowship, 1959-60.

WRITINGS: Simple Models of Group Behavior, Columbia University Press, 1967; *The Process and Outcome of Negotiations,* Columbia University Press, 1974.

WORK IN PROGRESS: Sociological Theory; research on the process of negotiation.

* * *

BATCHELOR, John Calvin 1948-

PERSONAL: Born April 29, 1948, in Bryn Mawr, Pa.; son of C. R. and J. S. Batchelor. *Education:* Princeton University, A.B., 1970; attended University of Edinburgh, New College, 1973-74; Union Theological Seminary, M.Div., 1976. *Residence:* New York City. *Agent:* The John Schaffner Agency, 425 East 51st St., New York N.Y. 10021. *Office:* c/o Congdon & Lattes, Empire State Bldg., 350 Fifth Ave., Room 7910, New York, N.Y. 10118.

CAREER: SoHo Weekly News, New York City, editor and book reviewer, 1975-77; *Village Voice,* New York City, book reviewer, 1977—.

WRITINGS: The Further Adventures of Halley's Comet, Congdon & Lattes, 1981.

WORK IN PROGRESS: The Birth of the People's Republic of Antarctica.

SIDELIGHTS: Batchelor's novel, *The Further Adventures of Halley's Comet,* is a dystopian satire concerning events surrounding the famous comet's expected passage by the Earth in 1986. Evil industrialists intend to use the comet to aggrandize their hedonistic positivism but are momentarily thwarted by the inept forces of rebellion that are under the leadership of the comet incarnate. "Batchelor's wildly ambitious first novel," said the *New York Times Book Review*'s David Quammen, "is full of mordant humor, lofty ambitions and silliness."

Batchelor told *CA:* "My literary influences are the Gospel of Matthew, Augustine's *Confessions,* Rabelais, Martin Luther, Laurence Sterne, Tom Paine, Thackeray, Cooper, Stevenson, Wells especially, Twain especially; and of those still living, Kurt Vonnegut, Tom Pynchon, John Gardner. I have read too much science fiction, not enough poetry, and cannot abide the novel of manners, class humor, and anything that takes political dogma as truth or Voltaire in vain, especially, 'Crush this infamy!'"

BIOGRAPHICAL/CRITICAL SOURCES: Washington Post Book World, February 1, 1981; *Cleveland Plain Dealer,* March 8, 1981; *New York Times Book Review,* April 5, 1981; *Los Angeles Times Book Review,* March 22, 1981; *Denver Post,* April 12, 1981.

BATTCOCK, Gregory   1938-1980

OBITUARY NOTICE—See index for *CA* sketch: Born July 2, 1938, in New York, N.Y.; died December 25, 1980, in San Juan, Puerto Rico. Critic, educator, artist, and author. An abstract expressionist, Battcock designed costumes and sets for the Greek Royal Theatre and for the Royal Opera in London. With an interest in art education, which his *New Ideas in Art Education* explains, he went on to become a professor of art history at William Patterson College in addition to being an adjunct professor at New York University, from which he received his Ph.D. in 1979. In 1973 he became the editor of *Arts Magazine*, and he frequently contributed to such magazines as *Art and Artist*, *Art in America*, *Domus*, *Art Journal*, *Film Culture*, *Soho News*, and *Projekt*. Earlier in his career, a collection of Battcock's works was exhibited at the Schainen Stern Galleries in New York. The artist was apparently murdered by an intruder in his home in Puerto Rico. His books include *The New Art*, *Minimal Art: A Critical Anthology*, *Why Art*, *New Artist's Video*, *Beyond Appearance*, and *The New Music*. Obituaries and other sources: *The Annual Obituary 1980*, St. Martin's, 1981.

* * *

BEARMAN, Jane (Ruth)   1917-

PERSONAL: Born September 12, 1917, in Minneapolis, Minn.; daughter of Arthur Samuel (a produce broker) and Sarah Ruth (Berman) Bearman; married Saul Frances (a life scientist), November 2, 1941; children: David J., Sally Ann. *Education:* Attended Minneapolis Art Institute, 1932-37, American Academy of Art, 1934-35, and Chicago Institute of Art, 1935-36; University of Minnesota, B.A., 1937; also attended Montclair College. *Home and office:* 30 Spier Dr., Livingston, N.J. 07039.

CAREER: Artist. Dayton Co., Minneapolis, Minn., advertising artist, 1937-41; Department of War Training, New York City, art director, 1941-45; author and illustrator of children's books, 1945—. Lecturer at Seton Hall University, 1969-70. Board member of Friends of Livingston Library, 1958-65. Work has been exhibited in one-woman shows, including Panoras Gallery, New York City, 1966, Hallmark Gallery, Kansas City, Mo., 1966-67, Brandeis University, Waltham, Mass., 1968-69, Carver Museum, Tuskeegee Institute, Ala., 1968-69, Loyola University, Chicago, Ill., 1970-71, Gallery 9, Chatham, N.J., 1976, Jewish Community Center, Minneapolis, Minn., 1978, and Temple B'nai Jeshurun, Short Hills, N.J., 1980; has participated in numerous traveling exhibitions, including Contemporary American Graphics, 1965-66, Impressions in Water Color, 1969-70, New Jersey Printmakers, 1969-70, and U.S. State Department exhibitions in Israel and Egypt, 1980-81.

MEMBER: National Association of Women Artists, Painters and Sculptors Society, Artists Equity Association, American Field Service (local president, 1960-61), New Jersey Watercolor Society. *Awards, honors:* First place in graphics from Montclair Museum Annual State Exhibition, 1962; medal of honor from Painters and Sculptors Society, 1962; first place in oils from Hunterdon Annual State Exhibition, 1965; Mary Yelen Prize, 1970, and medal of honor, 1973, both from National Association of Women Artists; Bainbridge Award, 1974.

WRITINGS—For children; self-illustrated; published by Union of American Hebrew Congregations, except as noted: *Happy Chanuko*, 1943; *Fun on Sukos*, 1946; *Mother Goose ABC*, Saalfield Publishing, 1946; *Passover Party*, 1946; *Purim Pa-*

rade, 1947; *Shovuos Time*, 1947; *Good Shabos*, 1950; (with Mildred Weil) *Shalom!: A Holiday Book for Little Children*, Jonathan David, 1958; *David: A Bible Hero*, Jonathan David, 1965; *Jonathan: A Bible Hero*, Jonathan David, 1965; *The Eight Nights: A Chanukah Counting Book*, edited by Daniel B. Syme, 1978.

Illustrator: Lillian Freehof, *Candle Light Stories*, Bloch, 1951.

Contributor of articles to professional journals, including *National Parent-Teacher*, *Progressive Woman*, and *Prime Time*.

SIDELIGHTS: Bearman told *CA:* "When I was a teenager, I taught Sunday school. I realized then that the books we used were antiquated, dull, and that the illustrations were not at all interesting to the children. I thought then that some day I would try my hand at colorful picture books for preschoolers about the Jewish holidays, books the children would really relate to. It was gratifying when the first of the holiday series was accepted and published. The editor's comment in all six books was, 'This is the first picture book in English about this lovely holiday.'

"I don't believe in talking down to children. If a book doesn't interest me as an adult, regardless of the age of the child for whom it is selected, I would never buy it. That's a pretty good rule to go by, whether one is doing the selecting or the creating. Having small children of my own, being aware of their interests, did help me when I began in this work.

"Because I am primarily an artist, most of my books have been picture books. In the Bible hero books, which are not picture books, but which I wrote and illustrated, I followed as closely as possible the words of the Soncino translation of the David and Jonathan stories."

AVOCATIONAL INTERESTS: Art, music, books.

* * *

BEECHER, John   1904-1980

OBITUARY NOTICE—See index for *CA* sketch: Born January 22, 1904, in New York, N.Y.; died of lung fibrosis, May 11, 1980, in San Francisco, Calif. Poet, educator, rancher, and author. The great-great nephew of Henry Ward Beecher, the famous abolitionist, and of Harriet Beecher Stowe, the author of *Uncle Tom's Cabin*, John Beecher was a champion of unpopular causes who, according to the poet William Carlos Williams, "spoke for the conscience of the people." Though Beecher is often called "the best poet the South has ever produced," some Southerners, he once remarked, thought of him as a "demon with horns and a long tail" because he advocated political liberty for minorities and laborers. The poet himself experienced unfair labor practices when he began working in an Alabama steel mill at the age of sixteen. His poem "Report to the Stockholders" captures the sad conditions of the workers and their need of a union. Another poem, "In Egypt Land," describes the revolt of black farmers and the development of their union which Beecher witnessed as an administrator with the Federal Emergency Relief Administration and with the U.S. Department of Agriculture during President Franklin Roosevelt's New Deal. While an officer on the S. S. *Booker T. Washington*, the first integrated ship in the U.S. Merchant Marine, Beecher produced a journal, *All Brave Sailors*, illustrating the brotherhood between the men. "It was a floating democracy," he recalled over thirty years later, "the kind of world we could have if men were free to develop all their potentialities." In 1950 Beecher was blacklisted when he refused to sign a loyalty oath. He subsequently lost his job as a sociology professor, became a rancher, and opened his own press. Birmingham, Alabama, of which the poet is an honorary citizen, declared May 1, 1973, Beecher Day. Among his other honors are several Western Books Exhibition awards. Beecher's works include *To Live and Die in Dixie, Hear the Wind Blow!, Collected Poems, 1924-1974, Tomorrow Is a Day,* and an incomplete autobiography. Obituaries and other sources: *Philadelphia Bulletin,* June 28, 1974; *Atlanta Journal,* August 22, 1974; *New York Times,* May 15, 1980; *The Annual Obituary 1980,* St. Martin's, 1981.

*   *   *

BEHR, Marion 1939-

PERSONAL: Born September 12, 1939, in Rochester, N.Y.; daughter of Justin Max (a film producer) and Sophie (a translator; maiden name, Koffler) Rosenfeld; married Omri Marc Nathan Behr (a patent attorney), June 24, 1962; children: Dawn Marcy Jael, Darrin Justin Mason, Dana Marisa Jana. *Education:* Syracuse University, B.A., 1961, M.F.A., 1962. *Home:* 24 Fishel Rd., Edison, N. J. 08820. *Office:* Women Working Home, Inc., 24 Fishel Rd., Edison, N.J. 08820.

CAREER: Free-lance illustrator, 1962-76; Women Working Home, Inc., Edison, N.J., founder, 1980, president, 1980—. Art work represented in exhibitions, including Lowe Art Center, Syracuse, N.Y., 1962; Contemporary American Artists Exhibit, Scarsdale, N.Y., 1964; New School for Social Research, New York, N.Y., 1968; Douglass College, New Brunswick, N.J., 1977. *Member:* National Alliance of Homebased Businesswomen (founder, 1980; president, 1980—).

WRITINGS: (Illustrator) Wendy Lazar, *Jewish Holiday Book,* Doubleday, 1977; (with Lazar) *Women Working Home: The Homebased Business Guide and Directory,* WWH Press, 1981, second edition in press.

SIDELIGHTS: Behr told *CA:* "The idea for the book and a survey about women working from their homes began approximately five years ago when I was one of four panelists addressing a group of eager, intelligent women in Princeton. I recall that everyone on the panel worked from their homes. Represented were a caterer, a party planner, and a plant lady. I spoke on my experience as a free-lance artist. Most of the women in the audience were curious and also anxious and dissatisfied because each of them had many abilities, but few of them were able to capitalize on their talents. The town's jobs were all filled, and a commute to New York City was too complicated for most. It seemed to me then that working from home would provide a solution for many.

"That evening an idea was born. I started to research how one could begin a survey to find out what types of jobs women were in fact doing from their homes. I contacted a number of research experts. All of them estimated it would cost approximately fifty thousand dollars to begin to find out what types of jobs women working from their homes had created.

"Then I spoke with a friend who belonged to a number of organizations; the two of us formulated a sample questionnaire designed to find out more about 'The Invisible Work Force,' a phrase we coined in the original questionnaire we printed and circulated.

"At the beginning, a number of New Jersey organizations provided assistance in mailing or reprinting our forms. We asked for name, address, type of work, cost, references, a letter describing work and home environment, and, if possible, a description of personal joys and frustrations.

"We received an abundance of mail. So many of these women had gone unnoticed for too long and suddenly someone wanted to know about them. We read the letters carefully and planned an outline for a book similar to the *Whole Earth Catalogue.* We also formed plans for some type of association because so many women working from home wrote about their need to communicate with others. The isolation experienced by many of these women was a tremendous problem.

"An editor of a new national magazine, *Enterprising Women,* received one of our questionnaires and called me for an interview. After the story appeared, we began to receive mail from women throughout the country. At this point, I was also meeting with a number of individuals from government agencies who either had been referred or offered help.

"My friend had a full-time job and could no longer continue to work on the now-sizable project. I called Wendy Lazar immediately, and we formed Women Working Home, Inc. We proceeded to develop the book *Women Working Home.* Several publishers expressed interest in our manuscript. When Arleen Priest heard about our project and the positive response it had received, her reaction was: let's publish it ourselves.

"The book *Women Working Home: The Homebased Business Guide and Directory* has a number of sections. The first part of the book gives necessary information on how to begin a homebased business. This was written in part by ourselves, both of us having worked from our own homes for a number of years, and in part by individuals who are experts in the field they have written about. For example, 'Advertising Strategy From the Home Office' is written by a woman who runs her own successful homebased advertising agency. Likewise, 'How to Market Yourself' is written by a homebased marketing consultant. A woman who runs a business organizing everything from corporations to individual kitchens gives expert advice on how to get organized.

"Throughout, we included quotations giving all types of homebased business advice or describing women's joys and frustrations with their home/work environment. These were taken from letters written to us by hundreds of homebased businesswomen over the past few years. They give a marvelous insight into the hearts and minds of women at all age levels and from diversified social and economic backgrounds who are determined to build interesting, financially rewarding lives. Discovering the range of these women has been one of our most exciting findings.

"The book also includes a directory of women working from their homes in twenty states in approximately one hundred ten occupations. This reads like a 'who's who' and gives women looking for ideas an abundance of information. We have an occupational listing, an idea section, photographs of women working in their home environments, and, last, but certainly not least, several essays by women who have been in business describing how and why they chose the homebased business solution.

"This is possibly one of the typical American stories—from a dream, our book developed into a reality. It's marvelous to be living in a country, in a day and age, when three women who grew up together can see a dream become an actuality."

AVOCATIONAL INTERESTS: Travel, renovating a farm in the Catskill mountains.

BIOGRAPHICAL/CRITICAL SOURCES: Enterprising Women, September, 1980; *New York Times,* October 12, 1980, May 26, 1981; *Executive Female,* November/December, 1980; *Family Circle,* July 1, 1981; *Ms.,* August, 1981.

BEIT-HALLAHMI, Benjamin 1943-

PERSONAL: Born June 12, 1943, in Tel Aviv, Israel; son of Shlomo and Nehama (Sokolski) Beit-Hallahmi. *Education:* Hebrew University of Jerusalem, B.A., 1966; Michigan State University, M.A., 1968, Ph.D., 1970. *Politics:* Progressive. *Religion:* Atheist. *Office:* Department of Psychology, University of Haifa, Haifa 31999, Israel.

CAREER: University of Michigan, Ann Arbor, clinical psychologist, 1970-73, research associate, 1972-77; University of Haifa, Haifa, Israel, senior lecturer in psychology, 1973—. Visiting associate professor at Michigan State University, 1978-80; member of visiting faculty at University of Pennsylvania, Hebrew University of Jerusalem, Central Michigan University, and University of Tel Aviv. *Military service:* Israel Defense Forces, 1963-66; became lieutenant. *Member:* International Society for Research on Aggression, International Council of Psychologists, American Psychological Association, American Sociological Association, Society for the Scientific Study of Religion. *Awards, honors:* Grant from Israel Interfaith Committee, 1978.

WRITINGS: (Editor) *Research in Religious Behavior,* Brooks/Cole, 1973; (with Michael Argyle) *The Social Psychology of Religion,* Routledge & Kegan Paul, 1975; *Psychoanalysis and Religion: A Bibliography,* Norwood, 1978; (with Albert I. Rabin) *Twenty Years Later: Kibbutz Children Grown,* Springer Publishing Co., 1981; (editor with Joseph R. Blasi, A. I. Rabin, and Simon Shur) *The Kibbutz Bibliography,* Norwood, 1981. Contributor of about fifty articles to professional journals. Member of editorial board of *New Outlook.*

WORK IN PROGRESS: *The Psychological Study of Religion,* completion expected in 1984.

SIDELIGHTS: Beit-Hallahmi told *CA:* "I have always been motivated by a desire to understand human culture in human history. Human culture is a riddle, which can be broken down to smaller riddles, such as religion (or psychology) and then studied. That's what I try to do.

"I see my writings as contributions to enlightenment (my own and others'). I regard both religion and psychology as cultural creations, with religion being closer to art, while psychology is, if not a science, at least a discipline."

*   *   *

BEIZER, Boris 1934-
(Ethan I. Shedley)

PERSONAL: Born June 25, 1934, in Brussels, Belgium; came to the United States in 1941, naturalized citizen, 1943; son of Mechel (a jeweler) and Esther (Koton) Beizer; married Ruth Abraham (a laboratory technician), June 12, 1955; children: Paul, Richard. *Education:* City College (now of the City University of New York), B.S., 1956; University of Pennsylvania, M.S.E.E., 1963, Ph.D., 1966. *Agent:* Hy Cohen Literary Agency Ltd., 111 West 57th St., New York, N.Y. 10019. *Office:* Data Systems Analysts, Inc., North Park Dr., Pennsauken, N.J. 08109.

CAREER: Republic Aviation Corp., Long Island, N.Y., engineer, 1956-57; Airborne Instruments Laboratories, Mellville, N.Y., engineer, 1957-59; Philco Corp., Willow Grove, Pa., senior staff member, 1959-61; Navigation Computer Corp., Valley Forge, Pa., senior staff member, 1961-63; Pennsylvania Research Associates, Philadelphia, Pa., senior staff member,

1963-66; Data Systems Analysts, Inc., Pennsauken, N.J., director of research and development, 1966—. *Member:* Institute of Electrical and Electronic Engineers, Operations Research Society of America, Institute of Management Sciences.

WRITINGS: Architecture of Computer Complexes, Plenum, 1971; *Micro-Analysis of Computer Performance,* Van Nostrand, 1978; (under pseudonym Ethan I. Shedley) *Earth Ship and Star Song* (fiction), Viking, 1979; (under Shedley pseudonym) *The Medusa Conspiracy* (fiction), Viking, 1980; *Software Testing Techniques,* Van Nostrand, 1982. Contributor of about forty poems and technical articles to journals.

SIDELIGHTS: Beizer told *CA:* "I believe that every technologist has a twofold responsibility—to the perfection and enhancement of his craft, and to society for the control and prevention of abuse of that craft. The first responsibility has prompted my nonfiction technical works, and the latter responsibility has made the fiction inevitable. Inevitable because a reader is more moved and affected if he is being entertained than if he is reading a dry, doomsaying essay."

AVOCATIONAL INTERESTS: Sailboat racing, sailing, photography, jewelry crafting, machine work.

*   *   *

BELFRAGE, Sally 1936-

PERSONAL: Born October 4, 1936, in Los Angeles, Calif.; daughter of Cedric (a writer) and Molly (a writer) Belfrage; married Sari Nashashibi, January 27, 1960 (died); married Bernard Pomerance (a playwright), November 21, 1965; children: Eve, Alexander. *Education:* Attended Hunter College, 1954-55, and London School of Economics, 1959-60. *Home:* 51 Randolph Ave., London W9, England. *Agent:* Anthony Sheil, 2 Morwell St., London WC2, England.

CAREER: John Calder (publisher), London, England, office worker, 1955-56; Cassells, London, in design and topography, 1956-57; Foreign Languages Publishing House, Moscow, U.S.S.R., translations editor, 1957-58; New American Library, New York, N.Y., reader, 1963-65; writer.

WRITINGS—Nonfiction: A Room in Moscow, Reynal, 1959; *Freedom Summer,* Viking, 1965; *Flowers of Emptiness: Reflections on an Ashram,* Dial, 1981.

WORK IN PROGRESS: A 1950's memoir.

SIDELIGHTS: Belfrage's first book, *A Room in Moscow,* recounts her experiences living as a Muscovite during the winter of 1957-58, and as an employee of the Foreign Languages Publishing House. The book was praised in most critical quarters as a welcome glimpse of Soviet life. *Manchester Guardian*'s Emanuel Litvinoff wrote, "It is a unique, outrageous, lively, and intelligent account of a winter in Moscow spent among a group of Muscovite bohemians." A reviewer for the *Times Literary Supplement* called it "animated, candid, entertaining, and artlessly instructive" and added, "The colloquial, gossipy ease of her style, too, matches the directness and honesty of her observation." Belfrage told *CA* that "the book was published in nine countries and supported its author at the London School of Economics and for a year of travel in the Middle East."

Freedom Summer is Belfrage's autobiographical account of activities involving the Student Non-Violent Coordinating Committee (SNCC) in Mississippi during racial hostilities in 1964. In the *New York Review of Books* Walker Percy described it as "a low-keyed and all the more effective treatment of the gritty routine of running a Freedom library, of the Negroes, the daily procession of small harassments, the obscene phone calls, the cars that try to run you down in the street, and finally the registration drive and a week-end in the Greenwood jail.'' *Saturday Review*'s Charles Shapiro called Belfrage ''a superb reporter [who] catches the spirit of the workers and conveys a sense of the pressures of a perpetual crisis situation.''

Flowers of Emptiness details Belfrage's experiences in an Indian ashram. Accompanied by two friends, she traveled to Poona, India, to study under the tutelage of Guru Bhagwan Shree Rajneesh. Unlike her two friends, who had already accepted the guru's philosophy before journeying to India, Belfrage is largely skeptical of the guru and his methods. Her conversion is the focus of the book. Anatole Broyard, writing in the *New York Times*, called *Flowers of Emptiness* ''a serious adventure, described with impeccable taste.'' *Newsweek*'s Jim Miller judged it ''an altogether remarkable essay on gurus and disciples.'' He added that *Flowers of Emptiness* is ''an utterly absorbing odyssey.''

Belfrage told *CA:* ''When I began this work, it was generally agreed that the business of a writer was to write. Now it seems that publishers believe the business of a writer is to be a television personality. Faced with this challenge, I feel the same as Ferdinand the Bull did about the bullfights in Madrid, preferring 'to sit just quietly under the cork tree and smell the flowers' (which is rather like writing to me). So far the Banderilleros and Picadors and Matadors have failed to persuade me that they know what I want to do, or that the kind of writing I want to read or write can long survive this treatment. It's not that I can stop doing it, but how to communicate it? Designs for space capsules solicited.''

Belfrage's husband, Bernard Pomerance, is the author of the play ''The Elephant Man.''

BIOGRAPHICAL/CRITICAL SOURCES: Spectator, October 17, 1958; *Manchester Guardian,* October 24, 1958; *Times Literary Supplement,* October 31, 1958; *New Statesman,* December 27, 1958; *Christian Science Monitor,* February 12, 1959; *Chicago Tribune,* February 15, 1959; *Atlantic,* March, 1959; *New York Times,* April 19, 1959, April 17, 1981; *New York Review of Books,* July 1, 1965; *Saturday Review,* August 14, 1965; *Washington Post,* March 16, 1981; *Newsweek,* March 23, 1981; *New York Times Book Review,* May 3, 1981.

* * *

BELL, Whitfield Jenks, Jr. 1914-

PERSONAL: Born December 3, 1914, in Newburgh, N.Y.; son of Whitfield Jenks and Lillian Victoria (Hengstler) Bell. *Education:* Dickinson College, A.B., 1935; University of Pennsylvania, A.M., 1938, Ph.D., 1947. *Office:* American Philosophical Society, 104 South Fifth St., Philadelphia, Pa. 19106.

CAREER: Dickinson College, Carlisle, Pa., instructor, 1937, 1938-39, 1941-43, associate professor, 1945-50, professor of history, 1950-54; American Philosophical Society and Yale University, *Papers of Benjamin Franklin,* assistant editor, 1954-56, associate editor, 1956-61; American Philosophical Society, Philadelphia, Pa., associate librarian, 1961-66, librarian, 1966-80, executive officer, 1977—. Visiting professor at College of William and Mary, 1953-54. *Wartime service:* American Field Service volunteer, 1943-45; served in Italy and Germany. *Member:* American Historical Association, Society of American Studies, American Antiquarian Society, Massachusetts Historical Society, College of Physicians of Philadelphia (honorary fellow), Phi Beta Kappa, Cosmos Club (Washington

D.C.), Franklin Inn Club (Philadelphia). *Awards, honors:* Litt.D., Franklin College, 1960; LL.D., Dickinson College, 1964, Washington College, 1981.

WRITINGS: Early American Science: Needs and Opportunities for Study, Institute of Early American History and Culture, 1955, reprinted, Russell, 1971; (editor, with Leonard W. Labaree) *Mr. Franklin: A Selection From His Personal Letters,* Yale University Press, 1956, reprinted, Ticknor & Fields, 1981; (consultant) Frank R. Donovan, *The Many Worlds of Benjamin Franklin* (juvenile), American Heritage Publishing Co., 1963; *John Morgan, Continental Doctor,* University of Pennsylvania Press, 1965; (compiler with Murphy D. Smith) *Guide to the Archives and Manuscript Collections of the American Philosophical Society,* American Philosophical Society, 1966; (with others) *A Cabinet of Curiosities: Five Episodes in the Evolution of American Museums,* University Press of Virginia, 1967; *The Colonial Physician and Other Essays,* Science History Publications, 1975.

Editor, *Bibliography of the History of Medicine in the U.S. and Canada,* 1948-53; visiting editor, *William and Mary Quarterly,* 1953-54. Contributor of articles to professional journals and other periodicals, including *Life* and *Antiques.*

* * *

BELL-VILLADA, Gene Harold 1941-

PERSONAL: Born December 5, 1941, in Port-au-Prince, Haiti; came to the United States in 1959; son of Gene H. (in business) and Carmen (a journalist; maiden name, Villada) Bell; married Audrey Dobek (a teacher), August 11, 1975. *Education:* University of Arizona, B.A., 1963; University of Paris, Diplome, 1966; University of California, Berkeley, M.A., 1967; Harvard University, Ph.D., 1974. *Office:* Department of Romance Languages, Williams College, Williamstown, Mass. 01267.

CAREER: State University of New York at Binghamton, instructor in Spanish, 1971-73; Yale University, New Haven, Conn., lecturer in Spanish, 1973-74; Williams College, Williamstown, Mass., assistant professor of Spanish, 1975—. *Member:* Modern Language Association of America, Latin American Studies Association, Pacific Coast Council on Latin American Studies.

WRITINGS: Borges and His Fiction, University of North Carolina Press, 1981. Contributor to magazines, including *Nation, Praxis, Commonweal, Science and Society,* and *New Republic.*

WORK IN PROGRESS: Research for *Art for Art's Sake and Literary Life,* on origins and development of doctrine in Europe and America; research for *Gabriel Garcia Marquez: The Man and His Work; Perspectives Industries, Inc.,* a novel.

SIDELIGHTS: Bell-Villada told *CA:* ''I grew up in Latin America and have traveled extensively there, as well as in Europe; I have lived off and on in France and the Netherlands. My interests include international relations, problems of culture, and relations between society and culture.

''Some things that currently fascinate me are the recent emergence of South American writing as a major cultural presence in the world, the increasing rigidification of United States political, social, and intellectual life, the ability of the human mind to believe in all manner of strange and monstrous thoughts, and the modern spectacle of global madness and unreality.''

AVOCATIONAL INTERESTS: Music, good food, street life.

BIOGRAPHICAL/CRITICAL SOURCES: Washington Post Book World, April 26, 1981.

BENCHLEY, Nathaniel (Goddard) 1915-1981

OBITUARY NOTICE—See index for *CA* sketch: Born November 13, 1915, in Newton, Mass.; died of a liver infection, December 14, 1981, in Boston, Mass. Journalist, novelist, and humorist. At the start of his career Benchley worked as a reporter for the *New York Herald Tribune* and as the assistant drama editor of *Newsweek* magazine, a position which he left to devote himself to free-lance endeavors. In his writings, Benchley combined comedy, farce, melodrama, and satire to produce low-key humor. For example, when commenting on the extraordinary energy and cunning required in loafing, the author advised: "If you think you are loafing too much, lie down until the feeling passes." His characters, said a *Washington Post* reporter, "were constantly bemused and bewildered by the encroachments of modern society on good sense and good nature." Benchley wrote in various genres, including plays, biographies, novels, screenplays, articles, short stories, and juveniles such as *Red Fox and His Canoe,* which sold more than one hundred thousand copies, or *Sam the Minute Man,* which sold more than seventy-five thousand. *The Off-Islanders,* probably Benchley's most famous book, was released by United Artists in 1966 as a motion picture titled "The Russians Are Coming, the Russians Are Coming." The next year, Paramount adapted Benchley's *The Visitors* into a film, "The Spirit Is Willing," starring Sid Caesar and Vera Miles. Among his other books are *Side Street, A Firm Word or Two, Humphrey Bogart* (biography), *Oscar Otter, Kilroy and the Gull,* and *All Over Again.* Works to be published posthumously include *Speak Easy* and *Snip.* Benchley's father, Robert, was a well-known humorist, and his son Peter is the author of the best-seller *Jaws.* Obituaries and other sources: *Washington Post,* December 15, 1981; *New York Times,* December 15, 1981; *Newsweek,* December 28, 1981; *Publishers Weekly,* January 1, 1982; *Time,* January 4, 1982, *AB Bookman's Weekly,* February, 1982.

* * *

BENCHLEY, Robert (Charles) 1889-1945
(Guy Fawkes)

BRIEF ENTRY: Born September 15, 1889, in Worcester, Mass.; died of a stroke, November 21, 1945, in New York, N.Y. American actor, humorist, and author. Benchley is best remembered for his books of humorous essays, such as *Twenty Thousand Leagues Under the Sea; or, David Copperfield* (1928) and *My Ten Years in a Quandary, and How It Grew* (1936). He also gained wide popularity as a radio and film star, winning an Academy Award for the short film "How to Sleep." Benchley was an editor of *Life* in the 1920's. His early attacks on the complexity of the modern world were aired in the *Harvard Lampoon* when he served as that magazine's president. Over the years he created and developed the character of the "little man." Humorously beleaguered and often paralyzed by everyday events, the "little man" never conceded the losing battle against the modern order of things and evoked a warm and sympathetic response from both critics and the public. Books published after Benchley's death include *Benchley—Or Else!* (1947) and *Chips Off the Old Benchley* (1949). *Biographical/critical sources: Current Biography,* Wilson, 1941, 1946; *Twentieth Century Authors: A Biographical Dictionary of Modern Literature,* 1st supplement, H. W. Wison, 1955; *Newsweek,* March 30, 1970; *Twentieth-Century Literary Criticism,* Volume 1, Gale, 1978.

BENELL, Julie 1906(?)-1982

OBITUARY NOTICE: Born c. 1906 in Nashville, Ill.; died after a long illness, January 1, 1982. Pianist, actress, journalist, and author. A former concert pianist and Broadway actress, Benell was also a radio and television performer before becoming a reporter and food editor with the *Dallas Morning Star,* her employer for twenty-five years. Her writings include a recipe book, *Let's Eat at Home.* Obituaries and other sources: *Foremost Women in Communications,* Bowker, 1970; *Who's Who of American Women,* 11th edition, Marquis, 1979; *New York Times,* January 4, 1982.

* * *

BENNETT, Margot 1912-1980

OBITUARY NOTICE: Born in 1912 (some sources say 1903), in Lenzi, Scotland; died December 6, 1980. Advertising copywriter and author. Noted for her humor, stylistic originality, and sensitive character development, Bennett was primarily a crime-fiction writer, although some of her best-known work was science fiction. Her writings include *Time to Change Hats, Away Went the Little Fish, The Golden Pebble, The Widow of Bath,* and *The Man Who Didn't Fly.* Obituaries and other sources: *The Encyclopedia of Science Fiction: An Illustrated A to Z,* Grenada, 1979; *Science Fiction and Fantasy Literature,* Volume II: *Contemporary Science Fiction Authors II,* Gale, 1979; *The Annual Obituary 1980,* St. Martin's, 1981.

* * *

BENNETT, Robert Russell 1894-1981

OBITUARY NOTICE: Born June 15, 1894, in Kansas City, Mo.; died August 18, 1981, in New York, N.Y. Composer, conductor, orchestrator, and author. Best known for his orchestrations of more than three hundred Broadway musicals, Bennett began arranging musical scores while serving in the army during World War I. After the war he got a job as an orchestrator for T. B. Harms and Co., and his initial effort, Cole Porter's "An Old Fashioned Garden," was the year's biggest hit. By 1922 he was scoring full-length musicals. During his career as an orchestrator, Bennett seldom scored fewer than five Broadway musicals a season, and he sometimes had as many as twenty-two shows running simultaneously. Noted for his speed and prolific output, Bennett was able to listen to a number two or three times and then score it from memory. Among the musicals he orchestrated were Jerome Kern's "Show Boat," Irving Berlin's "Annie Get Your Gun," George Gershwin's "Porgy and Bess," Cole Porter's "Kiss Me Kate," Burton Lane's "Finian's Rainbow," and Kurt Weill's "Lady in the Dark." For Richard Rodgers, Bennett scored "Oklahoma!," "Carousel," "South Pacific," "The King and I," and "The Sound of Music." In 1955 Bennett won an Academy Award for the scoring of the movie version of "Oklahoma!" Bennett also served as a guest conductor of symphony orchestras and as the musical director of the National Broadcasting Company (NBC). He had his own radio show and composed classical music. His original compositions include six symphonies, a full-length opera, two one-act operas, and several other orchestral works. His writings include a book, *Instrumentally Speaking.* Obituaries and other sources: *Current Biography,* Wilson, 1962; *New York Times,* August 19, 1981.

BENOIST-MECHIN, Jacques 1901-

PERSONAL: Born July 1, 1901, in Paris, France; son of Gabriel (a diplomat) and Marie-Louise (Gatel) Benoist-Mechin. *Education:* Attended Sorbonne, University of Paris; also attended schools in Switzerland, England, and the United States. *Home:* 52 avenue de Clichy, 75018 Paris, France.

CAREER: Editor of *Quotien*, 1923-24; International News Service, Paris, France, 1925-28, began as editor, became director of Paris bureau; editor-in-chief of *Europe nouvelle*, 1928-31; secretary general of *Intransigeant*, 1931-32; writer, 1931—; historian, 1932—. Chief of prisoners of war for diplomatic service of government of France, Berlin, Germany, 1940-41; secretary general to vice-president of council of government of France, 1941; French ambassador to Turkey, 1941; general of administrative services in French negotiations with Hitler, Mussolini, and Franco, 1941; secretary of state, 1942. Professor at Ecole Libre des Sciences Politiques, 1940. *Military service:* French Army, 1921-23 and 1939-40; prisoner of war, 1940. *Awards, honors:* Academie Francaise prize.

WRITINGS—All published by A. Michel, except as noted: (With Georges Blaizot) *Bibliographie des oeuvres de Paul Claudel*, A. Blaizot, 1931; *Histoire de l'armee allemande depuis l'armistice*, Volume I: *De l'armee imperiale a la Reichswehr*, 1936, translation by Eileen R. Taylor published as *History of the Germany Army Since the Armistice: From the Imperial Army to the Reichswehr*, Scientia (Zurich), 1939, reprinted, Fertig, 1979, Volume II: *De la Reichswehr a l'armee nationale*, 1938, revised edition of original volumes published in six volumes as *Histoire de l'armee allemande*, Volume I: *L'Effondrement, 1918-1919*, 1964, Volume II: *La Discorde, 1919-1925*, 1964, Volume III: *L'Essor, 1925-1937*, 1964, Volume IV: *L'Expansion, 1937-1938*, 1964, Volume V: *Les Epreuves de force, 1938*, 1965, Volume VI: *Le Defi, 1939*, 1966; *Eclaircissements sur "Mein Kampf" d'Adolf Hitler*, 1939; *L'Ukraine des origines a Staline*, 1941; *La Moisson de quarante: Journal d'un prisonnier de guerre*, 1941; *Ce qui demeure: Lettres de soldats tombes au champ d'honneur, 1914-1918*, 1942.

Le Loup et le leopard, Volume I: *Mustapha Kemal; ou, La Mort d'un empire*, 1954, Volume II: *Ibn Seoud; ou, La Naissance d'un royaume*, 1955, translation by Dennis Weaver published as *Arabian Destiny*, Elek, 1957, Essential Books, 1958, Volume III: *Le Roi Saud; ou, L'Orient a l'heure des releves*, 1960; *Soixante Jours qui ebranlerent l'occident: 10 mai-10 juillet 1940*, 1955-56, Volume I: *La Bataille du nord, 10 mai-4 juin*, Volume II: *La Bataille de France, 4 juin-24 juin*, Volume III: *La Fin du regime, 25 juin-10 juillet*, translation of all volumes by Peter Wiles published in one volume as *Sixty Days That Shook the West: The Fall of France, 1940*, Putnam, 1963; *Retour a Marcel Proust*, P. Amiot, 1957; *Un Printemps arabe*, 1959.

Arabie: Carrefour des siecles, 1961; *Deux Etes africains: Mai-juin 1967, juillet 1971*, 1972; *A destins rompus*, 1974; *L'Homme et ses jardins; ou, Les Metamorphoses du paradis terrestre*, 1975; *Faycal, roi d'Arabie: L'Homme, le souverain, sa place dans le monde, 1906-1975*, 1975; *Avec Marcel Proust*, 1977.

"*Le Reve le plus long de l'histoire*" series; published by Clairefontaine: *Lawrence d'Arabie; ou, Le Reve fracasse*, 1961; *Alexandre le grand; ou, Le Reve depasse*, 1964, translation by Mary Ilford published as *Alexander the Great: The Meeting of East and West*, Hawthorn, 1966; *Cleopatre; ou, Le Reve evanoui*, 1964; *Bonaparte en Egypte; ou, Le Reve inassouvi*, 1966; *Lyautey l'africain; ou, Le Reve immole*, 1966; *L'Empereur Julien; ou, Le Reve calcine*, 1969.

Translator of English titles into French, including James Joyce's *Fragments d'Ulysses*, D. H. Lawrence's *Defense de Lady Chaterly*, N. F. R.; William Speaeght's *Le Heros egare*, Editions Plon; Michihiko Hachiya's *Le Journal d'Hiroshima;* Vincent Cronin's *L'Ile au rayon de miel*.

Translator of German titles into French, including E. R. Curtis's *Essai sur France*, Grasset, 1932; Goethe's *Lettres a Madame de Stolberg*, Stock; Gustav Droysen's *Alexander le grande*, Grasset; Comte H. Polzer-Hoditz's *L'Empereur Charles et la mission historique de l'Autriche*, Grasset; Andrea Salome's *Frederic Nietzsche*, Grasset, 1932; Kasimir Edschmidt's *Destin allemand*, Editions Plon; Rene Fuelop Miller's *La Victoire sur la douleur;* Adalbert Barwolf's *Il n'y a plus qu'a prier;* Fritz von Unruh's *Nouvel Empire*, 1925.

SIDELIGHTS: Called "a splendid factual summary" by *Best Sellers*, Benoist-Mechin's *Sixty Days That Shook the West* provides a daily chronicle of the events precipitating the fall of France in 1940. According to Gordon Harrison of the *New York Herald Tribune Books*, Benoist-Mechin was a key member of the Vichy government. In September, 1944, he was imprisoned for helping to organize the occupation government of the Nazis in France. On June 6, 1947, he received a death sentence from the French High Court of Justice, a sentence which was later commuted though Benoist-Mechin remained in prison until 1953. *Sixty Days*, said a *Times Literary Supplement* reviewer, "is the raw material of history, and, as is often the case, is much more exciting reading than the sifted results might be."

In subsequent years, Benoist-Mechin traveled extensively in the Mideast to gather material for his books on the Arab world.

BIOGRAPHICAL/CRITICAL SOURCES: Times Literary Supplement, August 2, 1957, March 15, 1963; *New York Times*, June 1, 1958; *Best Sellers*, May 1, 1963; *New York Times Book Review*, May 12, 1963; *New York Times Herald Tribune Books*, May 26, 1963.

*   *   *

BENSKO, John 1949-

PERSONAL: Born November 28, 1949, in Birmingham, Ala.; son of John, Jr. (a geologist) and Patricia (Blanton) Bensko; married Rosemary Collins (a student), May, 1980; children: Thomas. *Education:* Attended St. Louis University, 1967-68, and Auburn University, 1968-69; University of Alabama, B.A., 1973, M.F.A., 1979. *Home:* 7744 Castleton Place, Norfolk, Va. 23505. *Office:* Old Dominion University, Norfolk, Va. 23508.

CAREER: University of Alabama, Tuscaloosa, graduate teaching assistant, 1974-78, teaching and writing fellow, 1979, part-time instructor, 1979-80; Old Dominion University, Norfolk, Va., instructor in English, 1980—; poet, 1981—. Consultant for Center for the Study of Southern Culture at University of Mississippi. *Member:* Modern Language Association, P.E.N., South Atlantic Modern Language Association. *Awards, honors:* Fellowship in poetry from University of Alabama, 1979, for teaching and writing; winner of Yale Series of Younger Poets competition, 1980, for *Green Soldiers*.

WRITINGS: Green Soldiers (poetry), foreword by Richard Hugo, Yale University Press, 1981. Contributor of poetry to periodicals, including *Carolina Quarterly, Black Warrior Review, Critical Quarterly, New Orleans Review, Poetry Northwest, Prairie Schooner, INTRO 10*, and *Shenandoah*.

WORK IN PROGRESS: "Currently working on a book of poems based on travels abroad and on life in suburbia."

SIDELIGHTS: John Bensko's *Green Soldiers* was selected as the best of 625 entries in the Yale Series of Younger Poets competition, and it contains forty-two poems concentrating on people. "Bensko has found his own good way to write poetry and not run away from people," observed Maureen Sullivan-Drury of *Best Sellers.* Some people appear in scenarios from past decades. For example, in the first part of *Green Soldiers* the poet fabricates historical events, such as the world wars, so that they appear to be contemporary happenings. The second half of the book deals with people living imaginary scenes during the twentieth century. "This is a very bright, a brilliant book," wrote Louis Simpson of the *Washington Post Book World.* "John Bensko should go far."

Bensko told *CA:* "I enjoyed several years in the writing program at the University of Alabama, and I have a strong interest in the cultural background which the South offers to writers, even though my subject matter is not particularly regional."

BIOGRAPHICAL/CRITICAL SOURCES: Washington Post Book World, June 7, 1981; *Best Sellers,* July, 1981; *Chicago Sun-Times,* August 23, 1981; *Times Literary Supplement,* January 29, 1982.

*   *   *

BENSON, J(ack) L(eonard) 1920-

PERSONAL: Born June 25, 1920, in Kansas City, Mo.; son of Oliver Wilmer and Jesse (Burnett) Benson; married Linda Melton (a poet), October 7, 1954. *Education:* University of Missouri, B.A., 1941; Indiana University, M.A., 1947; University of Basle, Ph.D., 1952. *Home:* "Mayfield," Montague, Mass. 01351. *Office:* Art History Program, University of Massachusetts, Amherst, Mass. 01003.

CAREER: Yale University, New Haven, Conn., instructor in art history, 1952-53; researcher in Cyprus and Greece, 1953-58; University of Mississippi, Oxford, associate professor of classics, 1958-60; Wellesley College, Wellesley, Mass., associate professor of art history, 1961-64; University of Massachusetts, Amherst, professor of art history, 1965—. Visiting professor at Princeton University, 1960-61; member of Institute for Advanced Study, Princeton, N.J., 1964-65. *Military service:* U.S. Naval Reserve, active duty, 1942-46; became lieutenant senior grade.

MEMBER: Archaeological Institute of America (president of Western Massachusetts branch, 1966—), Vereinigung der Freunde Antiker Kunst, Classical Association of New England, Massachusetts Archaeological Society, Phi Beta Kappa. *Awards, honors:* Fulbright fellowship, 1956; Guggenheim fellowship, 1957; American Council of Learned Societies fellowship, 1964; American Philosophical Society grant, 1965.

WRITINGS: Die Geschichte der Korinthischen Vasen (title means "The History of Corinthian Vases"), Benno Schwabe, 1953; *Ancient Leros* (monograph), Greek, Roman, and Byzantine Studies, 1961; *Horse, Bird, and Man: The Origins of Greek Painting,* University of Massachusetts Press, 1970; *Bamboula at Curium,* University of Pennsylvania Press, 1972; *The Necropolis of Kaloriziki,* Studies in Mediterranean Archeology, 1973; (translator) Ernst Buschor, *On the Meaning of Greek Statues,* University of Massachusetts Press, 1980; (with Agnes N. Stillwell) *Corinth: Results of Excavations Conducted by the American School of Classical Studies at Athens,* Volume XV: *Corinthian Pottery of the Potters' Quarter,* American School of Classical Studies at Athens, 1981. Contributor to professional journals.

WORK IN PROGRESS: Proto-Corinthian Vase Painting; Periodicity in Ancient Art; American Tonalist Painting.

SIDELIGHTS: Benson told *CA:* "My great interest is in the way in which the artistic record of the ancient Greeks, particularly Athenians, in painting and sculpture can be interpreted as a reflection of the spiritual evolution of a new era in human history. The background of my thinking is derived from the writings of Rudolf Steiner and Wilhelm Dilthey."

AVOCATIONAL INTERESTS: Watercolor painting, studying decorative arts and nineteenth-century American art.

*   *   *

BENTHAM, Frederick 1911-

PERSONAL: Born October 23, 1911, in London, England; son of Percy George (a sculptor) and Ellen Celia (Hobbs) Bentham; married Ilse Ruhm (a health visitor). *Education:* Attended Regent Street Polytechnic and Central School of Arts and Crafts. *Home and office:* 29 Shaftesbury Ave., Norwood Green, Middlesex UB2 4HH, England.

CAREER: General Electric Co., London, England, assistant to theatre engineer, 1929-32; Strand Electric, London, in charge of research and development, publicity, and demonstration theatre, 1932-65, director, 1957-70; Rank Strand, Stratford-upon-Avon, England, technical liaison manager, 1970-73; writer, 1932—. *Member:* Chartered Institute of Building Services (fellow), Art Workers Guild (master, 1969), Association of British Theatre Technicians (chairman, 1973-78), Society of Theatre Consultants (chairman, 1971-73), Society of British Theatre Designers (honorary member), Society of Television Lighting Directors (honorary member).

WRITINGS: Stage Lighting, Pitman, 1950; *Fifty Years in Stage Lighting,* Strand Electric, 1964; *The Art of Stage Lighting,* Pitman, 1968, revised edition, 1976, 2nd revised edition, 1980; *New Theatres in Britain,* Strand Electric, 1970. Contributor to technical journals, including *Builder.* Editor of *Tabs Quarterly,* 1956-73, and *Sightline,* 1973—.

WORK IN PROGRESS: Fifty Years of Theatre and Lighting, "an autobiographical history in some technical detail of developments I have encountered during this time."

SIDELIGHTS: Bentham wrote: "The inherited artist in me and a dislike of figures (numbers) would have made life as a pure engineer impossible. Theatrical lighting has proved an ideal field for me as inventor rather than as engineer. In particular, the control or the 'playing' of lighting has fascinated me ever since boyhood when I found it a more fertile form of expression in my model theatres than the pushing on and off of the 'actors.' An early invention of mine (1935) was an organ console to play light instead of music. Developments on this theme followed over the decades and became identified with the Strand Electric or British way of stage lighting. My swan song in this direction was the control installed in 1972 in the Royal Shakespeare Theatre at Stratford-upon-Avon, the first to use a software-program computer.

"As to writing, I have always found this easy to do on my own subject, and over the years this has extended to cover theatre architecture. Long, long ago I wanted to be an architect—I love looking at buildings. I find all sport tedious but have adopted canal cruising as a hobby in recent years. This to some extent makes up for the loss of my former hobby, playing light to music (color music). Extensive lecturing has been a valuable adjunct to my writing, both because of the audience reaction vital to the understanding of theatre itself and as a corrective to the sense of writing in a void. Nevertheless, I have most enjoyed the writing of the 'anon' editorials, or technological parables, in the two journals of which I have been editor.''

* * *

BERG, Joan
See VICTOR, Joan Berg

* * *

BERGER, Suzanne E(lizabeth) 1944-

PERSONAL: Born April 5, 1944, in Texas; daughter of Robert O. and Dorothy (Rogers) Berger; married Michael P. Ripple (in social services), November 11, 1978. *Education:* Northwestern University, B.A. (with honors), 1966; Johns Hopkins University, M.A., 1969; Northeastern University, M.Ed., 1976. *Home and office:* 2 Billingham, Somerville, Mass. 02144.

CAREER: Massachusetts Bay Community College, Wellesley, part-time teacher, 1972-75, Boston University, Boston, Mass., part-time lecturer in English, 1974—. Writer for Education Development Center, 1977-80. Judge for Academy of American Poets, Williams College, 1981. *Member:* American Poets and Writers (member of board of directors). *Awards, honors:* Scholar at Bread Loaf Writers Conference, 1974, fellow, 1980—; fellow of MacDowell Colony, 1979, 1981; resident of Ossabaw Project, 1980—.

WRITINGS: Joan Norris, Michael Peich, editors, *These Rooms* (poems), Penmaen Press, 1979, 2nd edition, 1980. Co-author of *Foster Parenting Adolescents* and *Foster Parenting Retarded Children*, both 1979. Contributor to magazines, including *Massachusetts Review, Ploughshares, Prairie Schooner, Aspen Anthology*, and *Tendril*.

WORK IN PROGRESS: A book of poems, completion expected in 1982.

SIDELIGHTS: Suzanne Berger told *CA:* "I like to explore the human spirit in conflict with itself and the world, and also its brief moments of harmony." *Avocational interests:* Contemporary art, studying social issues.

* * *

BERKE, Joel Sommers 1936-1981

OBITUARY NOTICE: Born January 7, 1936, in Brooklyn, N.Y.; died December 8, 1981, in New York. Political scientist, educator, and author. A specialist in the problems of financing public schools that serve poor children in urban areas, Berke was a senior research scientist at the Education Policy Research Institute of the Educational Testing Service in Washington. Berke worked as a legislative aide to the New York State Senate during the 1950's and was adjunct professor of political science at the Maxwell Graduate School of Syracuse University beginning in 1969. He wrote *Answers to Inequity: An Analysis of the New School Finance Laws* and co-wrote *Federal Aid to Education: Who Benefits? Who Governs?* and *Financing Equal Educational Opportunity: Alternatives for State Finance.* Obituaries and other sources: *Leaders in Education,* 5th edition, Bowker, 1974; *New York Times,* December 10, 1981.

* * *

BERLINER, Don 1930-

PERSONAL: Born July 3, 1930, in Columbus, Ohio; son of Abe H. and Helen (Kolitz) Berliner. *Education:* Ohio State University, B.Sc., 1953; graduate study at Ohio University, 1958. *Office:* 1202 South Washington St., Alexandria, Va. 22314.

CAREER: Painesville Telegraph, Painesville, Ohio, reporter and photographer, 1959-62; *Science Trends,* Washington, D.C., staff writer and editor, 1962-65; National Investigations Committee on Aerial Phenomena, Kensington, Md., staff writer, 1965-68; free-lance aviation writer, 1969—. *Military service:* Ohio Air National Guard, 1948-50. U.S. Air Force, 1950-51; became staff sergeant. *Member:* International Aerobatic Club, International Society of Aviation Historians, Experimental Aircraft Association.

WRITINGS—Published by Lerner, except as noted: *Air Racing,* 1979; *Homebuilt Aircraft,* 1979; *Aerobatics,* 1980; *Yesterday's Airplanes,* 1980; *Scale Model Planes,* 1982; *Flying Model Planes,* 1982; *Personal Planes,* 1982; *Helicopters,* 1982; *Scale Modelers Source Book,* Kalmbach, 1982; *The World Air Speed Record,* Van Nostrand, in press.

Author of ''Competition Scene,'' a monthly column in *Air Progress,* 1965-73.

SIDELIGHTS: Berliner commented that his specialties include ''sporting aviation, historic aviation, aeronautical science from the layman's standpoint, and the serious side of the UFO mystery.'' He added: ''I have covered aviation events in Western and Eastern Europe, for European as well as American magazines. I also think UFO's are the greatest scientific mystery of our time, and thus deserving of far more serious study than has been done to date.''

* * *

BERMAN, Bennett H(erbert) 1927-

PERSONAL: Born July 10, 1927, in Syracuse, N.Y.; son of Mervin (in sales) and Jessie (an occupational therapist; maiden name, Grass) Berman; married Roslyn Ozur, June 5, 1948 (divorced March 20, 1966); married Lynne Brooks-Finn (an educator), July 12, 1967; children: Steven, Sharon, Scott; Geri Finn-Woodburn (stepdaughter). *Education:* Syracuse University, B.S., 1949; Wayne State University, M.Ed., 1970, Ed.D., 1974. *Home and office:* 16215 Buckingham Rd., Birmingham, Mich. 48009.

CAREER: Jam Handy Organization (sales promoters), Detroit, Mich., program planner and writer, 1950-61; Wilding, Inc. (sales promoters and trainers), Southfield, Mich., regional director, 1961-68; independent management and personnel training consultant in Birmingham, Mich., 1970—. Project director at University of Michigan, 1976-79. *Military service:* U.S. Army Air Forces, 1944-47; became technical sergeant. *Member:* American Society for Training and Development, National Society for Performance and Instruction, American Educational Sciences Association, Association for Educational Communication Technology.

WRITINGS: (With Michael Mombeck) *West Point: An Illustrated History,* Quadrangle, 1979; *Evaluation Techniques in Human Services,* University of Michigan Press, 1980; *Eddie's Game* (novel), Tower, 1981; *Turning Off Burning Out in Human Services,* C. C Thomas, 1982; *Instructional Design in Human Services Training,* C.C Thomas, 1982.

Filmscripts: ''Eddie's Game'' (based on own novel), Cinema Productions, 1982. Author of filmscripts for industrial corporations, including General Motors Corp., Ford Motor Co., Sylvania, and Kelvinator.

Radio scripts: ''Murder by Experts,'' Mutual Network, 1949; ''Buckingham Theatre,'' Canadian Broadcasting Corp. (CBC), 1950.

Television scripts: "Blue Goose Cafe," Dumont Network, 1950; "Armstrong Circle Theatre," Columbia Broadcasting System (CBS), 1951; "TV Golf Pro" (syndicated), Weill Productions, 1954; "Route 66," National Broadcasting Co. (NBC), 1958; "TV Billiards With Willie Mosconi," Davis-Daniels, 1959.

Comedy writer. Contributor of articles, stories, and humor to professional journals and popular magazines, including *Adam* and *Esquire.*

SIDELIGHTS: Berman wrote: "The enrichment of human behavior and improvement of human productivity are of special vocational interest to me, as well as improved training and service delivery within the health care field, specifically for those serving the developmentally disabled population.

"Another interest is humor. I have taught college-level courses in humor and have developed a joke-writing formula that I may turn into a book on the psychology of humor. I have a huge collection of books, records, and photographs about humor, and have written for various comedians. I also love a good mystery and look forward to writing in the whodunit field."

* * *

BERNARD, Richard Marion 1948-

PERSONAL: Born January 16, 1948, in Duncan, Okla.; son of Milo M. (a teacher) and Elizabeth (a teacher; maiden name, Cole) Bernard; married Terry Bowman (a statistical analyst), December 27, 1969; children: Benjamin Cole. *Education:* University of Oklahoma, B.A., 1970; Wake Forest University, M.A., 1971; University of Wisconsin—Madison, Ph.D., 1977. *Politics:* Democrat. *Religion:* Christian. *Home:* 603 North 52nd St., Milwaukee, Wis. 53208. *Office:* Department of History, Marquette University, Milwaukee, Wis. 53233.

CAREER: Austin Community College, Austin, Tex., part-time instructor in history, 1973-74; University of Maryland, European Division, Heidelberg, West Germany, lecturer in history and sociology, 1974-75; Marquette University, Milwaukee, Wis., assistant professor of history, 1977—, director of urban affairs, 1978—. *Member:* American Historical Association, Organization of American Historians, Social Science History Association, Southern Historical Association, Wisconsin Historical Society, Milwaukee County Historical Society.

WRITINGS: *The Melting Pot and the Altar,* University of Minnesota Press, 1980; *The Poles in Oklahoma,* University of Oklahoma Press, 1980; (editor with Bradley R. Rice, and contributor) *Sunbelt Cities: Metropolitan Growth and Political Change Since World War II,* University of Texas Press, 1982. Contributor to history journals.

SIDELIGHTS: Bernard told *CA:* "I am not nearly so optimistic as some about the prospect of the downtowns of our major cities reviving and regaining their earlier prominence. The automobile, whether powered by gasoline, electricity, or solar power, is here to stay, and with it is the automobile culture. If transportation costs force a shrinkage of the metropolitan area, that retrenchment will result in clustering around shopping centers and outlying office complexes. If Americans must travel less, they will confine themselves to their suburban neighborhoods. They will not return to downtown—not, at least, in the massive numbers some predict. Houston, not New York, is the future."

AVOCATIONAL INTERESTS: Country music.

BERNIER, Olivier 1941-

PERSONAL: Born August 12, 1941, in Hartford, Conn.; son of Georges and Jessie (Bernheim) Bernier; divorced. *Education:* Lycee Henri IV, Paris, France, baccalaureate, 1958; Harvard University, B.A., 1962; New York University, M.A., 1966. *Home and office address:* 157 East 72nd St., New York, N.Y. 10021. *Agent:* Paul R. Reynolds & Co., 12 East 41st St., New York, N.Y. 10017.

CAREER: Martha Jackson Gallery, New York, director of exhibitions, 1966-68; private art dealer in New York City, 1968-78; writer, 1978—.

WRITINGS: *Pleasure and Privilege: Life in France, Naples, and America, 1770-1790* (nonfiction), foreword by Louis Auchincloss, Doubleday, 1981; *Art and Craft* (novel), Seaview, 1981; *The Eighteenth-Century Woman,* Doubleday, 1982. Contributor of articles to periodicals, including *House and Garden, Vogue,* and *New York Times.*

WORK IN PROGRESS: A biography of Lafayette, publication by Dutton expected in 1982.

SIDELIGHTS: "In a history filled with detail and rich in nuance Olivier Bernier presents a delightful picture of life in the civilized western world of the late eighteenth century," wrote *Best Sellers's* Dennis Linehan in his review of *Pleasure and Privilege.* A social history of France, the book deals with life in the country's major cities, such as Paris and Versailles, as well as discusses the tourist center of Naples and the New World in America from the French perspective. In *Pleasure and Privilege,* Bernier, an American born of French parents, writes on a variety of topics, including food, fashions, art, literature, and medicine, so he illustrates the pageantry and the poverty of pre-revolutionary France.

Bernier offers the level of sophistication of eighteenth-century health care facilities as an example of the penurious nature of French society. He explained: "On the whole, it was safer to be left untreated . . . a TB sufferer went to his grave much faster if attended by a reputable physician." On the aristocratic side of society, *Pleasure and Privilege,* said Anatole Broyard of the *New York Times,* proves that in the eighteenth century "good taste ruled everything. As much art went into the design of a doorknob as into a painting or a tragedy."

Critically acclaimed as a history, *Pleasure and Privilege,* commented the *Quill and Quire's* Paul Stewe, "is both refreshing and a corrective to our habit of equating history with progress." "Just as French nobility found it refreshing to read about America and its homey differences," noted Broyard, "so Americans in their unadorned affluence ought to find it entertaining and instructive to look through the other end of the opera glasses. For a learned and witty excursion through savoir vivre, one could hardly ask for a better companion than Mr. Bernier."

Bernier told *CA:* "I am interested in literature, history, and travel. I speak French and Italian and am familiar with Europe and North Africa. I am also willing and able to give lectures on a variety of subjects."

BIOGRAPHICAL/CRITICAL SOURCES: *New York Times,* April 11, 1981; *Best Sellers,* June, 1981; *New York Times Book Review,* June 7, 1981; *Quill and Quire,* July, 1981.

* * *

BERNSTEIN, Anne C(arolyn) 1944-

PERSONAL: Born April 8, 1944, in New York, N.Y.; daughter

of Alfred J. and Clara (Handelman) Bernstein. *Education:* Brandeis University, B.A. (magna cum laude), 1965; University of California, Berkeley, Ph.D., 1973. *Agent:* Rhoda Weyr, William Morris Agency, 1350 Avenue of the Americas, New York, N.Y. 10017.

CAREER: Family therapist in Berkeley, Calif., 1974—. Director of family therapy training program at University of San Francisco, 1977—; psychologist with Rockridge Health Plan, 1979—. Treasurer of board of directors of Children's Rights Group. *Member:* American Family Therapy Association, American Orthopsychiatric Association, Society for the Psychological Study of Social Issues, American Psychological Association, San Francisco Media Alliance, Phi Beta Kappa.

WRITINGS: The Flight of the Stork (parent education), Delacorte, 1978. Contributor to *Parents' Magazine* and *Psychology Today.*

WORK IN PROGRESS: Books on children's thinking about changes in family structure and about their own bodies and medical care.

SIDELIGHTS: Anne C. Bernstein wrote: "After too many years of writing only academic papers, it has been my joy to resume writing for people, not professors. *The Flight of the Stork* was an opportunity to unlearn the bad habits that were part of my professional education. A filmmaker friend wrote to me: 'As with your article, it's a treat to find social science that's written in English. Maybe you should teach a course in non-obfuscatory writing for social scientists.' I have never accepted the prejudice that good writing and social science are not compatible. Social science has a great deal to contribute to a general audience that insists that information be accessible and attractively packaged.

"I have been a regular contributor to *Parents' Magazine,* writing about child development and family life. I am especially interested in changes in family structure and what that means for the children growing up in today's families. Some years ago, the three-year-old daughter of a divorced friend told me, 'When I grow up, I'm going to get married and live happily ever after, all by myself.' She started me on an investigation of the child's eye view of alternative families that I am now developing into a book on children's experience of shared parenting and multiple parenting (as a parent remarries) households. I am also working on a book for parents and medical practitioners about children's ideas about their bodies, in sickness and in health, and how adults can more effectively inform children about malady and remedy, life and death."

*   *   *

BERNSTEIN, Gerry 1927-
(G.F. Morrison)

PERSONAL: Born May 9, 1927, in Chicago, Ill.; daughter of Irving (in sales) and Dorothy (Polensky) Medow; married Carl Bernstein (a chemist in research and development), December 4, 1948; children: Alan, Richard, Daniel. *Education:* Attended Roosevelt University, 1946-47. *Religion:* Jewish. *Residence:* Deerfield, Ill. *Address:* c/o Chicago Review Press, Inc., 215 W. Ohio St., Chicago, Ill. 60610.

CAREER: Secretary in Chicago, Ill., 1947-51, and Deerfield, Ill., 1973-76; writer. *Member:* League of Women Voters (member of board of directors, 1967-69).

WRITINGS: Freezer Cookery, Chicago Review Press, 1980; (contributor) Charlene Tibbetts and A.M. Tibbetts, editors, *Strategies: A Rhetoric and Reader,* Scott, Foresman, 1980.

WORK IN PROGRESS: Kaleidoscope: A French Journey, under pseudonym G.F. Morrison.

SIDELIGHTS: Bernstein told *CA:* "I love to travel and discover unexpected adventures around corners in strange places. As an observer I find value in the smallest experiences. My travel notes become material for essays and short stories. In them I try to evoke the flavor and essence of an adventure. One who takes the same path every day does not see his surroundings through a stranger's eyes." *Avocational interests:* Cooking, travel.

*   *   *

BERNSTEIN, Richard K. 1934-

PERSONAL: Born June 17, 1934, in New York, N.Y.; son of Milton (a business executive) and Belle (Kussy) Bernstein; married Anne E. Hendon (a physician), December 23, 1956; children: Julie Ann, Laura Ann, Jeffrey K., Lili Ann. *Education:* Columbia University, B.A., 1954, B.S., 1955, graduate study, 1957, 1959-60, and 1978; Albert Einstein College of Medicine, M.D., 1983. *Home:* 1160 Greacen Point Rd., Mamaroneck, N.Y. 10543. *Office:* Albert Einstein College of Medicine, 1300 Morris Park Ave., Bronx, N.Y. 10461.

CAREER: National Silver Co. (now a subsidiary of National Silver Industries, Inc.), New York City, industrial engineer, data processing manager, personnel manager, and purchasing agent, 1955-58; Clay Adams, Inc., New York City, assistant to executive vice-president, 1958-64, director of research, development, and marketing, 1964-67; National Silver Industries, Inc., New York City, corporate secretary and director of corporate planning, 1967-68, vice-president of product development and marketing of National Silver Co., 1975-78, consultant and member of board of directors, 1978—. Guest collaborator in clinical research at Rockefeller University, 1977-79; research associate at Brooklyn Hospital, 1978-79. Consultant in diabetes health care to Becton Dickinson & Co., 1978, to American Foundation for the Blind, 1979, and to Diabetes Research and Training Center of the Albert Einstein College of Medicine and Montefiore Hospital and Medical Center, 1979—. Deliverer of papers at Joslin Clinic, Boston, University of Alabama International Symposium on Nutrition and the Diabetic Child, International Symposium on New Approaches to the Management of Patients with Insulin-Dependent Diabetes Mellitus, International Symposium on Normoglycemia for the Diabetic, International Study Group on Diabetes in Children and Adolescents, and American Diabetes Association postgraduate workshops.

MEMBER: International Society for General Semantics, National Flute Association, American Medical Association, American Association of Diabetes Educators, American Diabetes Association (trustee of New York affiliate), American Society of Mechanical Engineers, American Society for the Advancement of Science, American Institute of Industrial Engineers, Mensa, European Association for the Study of Diabetes, Juvenile Diabetes Foundation (member of national education committee; member of research grant review committee, 1976-79; education chairman of Westchester Chapter, 1977-79), Federation of American Scientists, Astronomical Society of the Pacific, New York Diabetes Association (trustee of Westchester Chapter, 1977-79), New York Society for General Semantics (treasurer and trustee), Amateur Astronomers Association, Astronomical League, Institute of Electrical and Electronics Engineers, Institute of General Semantics, Engineering in Medicine and Biology Society, Society for Advanced Medical Systems, Catboat Association, Alpha Pi Mu.

WRITINGS: (Contributor) Zvi Laron, *Pediatric and Adolescent Endocrinology,* Volume 7, S. Karger AG (Basel, Switzerland), 1979; *Diabetes: The Glucograf Method for Normalizing Blood Sugar,* Crown, 1981. Contributor to journals, including *Diabetes Care, Acta Paediatr* (Belgium), and *Diabetes.*

WORK IN PROGRESS: Studying the feasibility of normalizing blood sugar throughout gestation in pregnant diabetics from a deprived inner-city population.

SIDELIGHTS: As an insulin-dependent diabetic since the age of twelve, Bernstein relied on daily urine tests to determine the amount of insulin needed to control high sugar levels in his blood. Regulation by means of these often inaccurate tests had never been achieved since patients continually experienced erratic swings in their blood sugar. These swings are known to be both life threatening and the cause of physical disabilities and emotional disturbances in millions of diabetics. In 1971 Bernstein acquired a newly marketed colorimeter (a portable electronic instrument) that would accurately determine blood sugar levels in one minute by using a drop of blood obtained from a single finger prick. With the aid of this device, Bernstein, by 1974, had arrived at a method by which patients could achieve continuous blood sugar stability.

Bernstein explained in the preface of his book *Diabetes: The Glucograf Method for Normalizing Blood Sugar* that with "the likelihood of . . . dreaded complications I would somehow have to normalize my blood sugar and keep it normal virtually all the time." He did so my measuring his blood sugar levels six times daily with his colorimeter. Gradually he was able to alter his diet, insulin use, and timing to achieve normal blood sugar levels 90 percent of the time. Although Bernstein's method "bore little relation to what I had been taught or had read regarding the treatment of diabetes," it produced highly favorable results. The problems, common to diabetics, that plagued him began to disappear: "I observed that my chronic acne had cleared up, fatty growths on my eyelids . . . disappeared, and I stopped producing kidney stones. . . . Frequent skin and sinus infections no longer occurred. I no longer felt continually tired. . . . I had reduced my insulin dose [by 80 percent]. . . . The frequency and severity of insulin reactions (hypoglycemia) dropped considerably, and as a result, the emotional stress that diabetes had continually forced on . . . [my] family was eased. . . . My chronic gray pallor vanished, and for the first time in 27 years I started to look healthy." More important was the possibility that the less than twenty minutes spent daily in such monitoring would stave off and in some cases protect against the dangerous and often fatal ailments of advanced diabetes.

Bernstein eventually called his regimen the "Glucograph Method." Dr. John A. Owen, Jr., explained its significance in *Modern Medicine:* It "clearly and for all time, cut the diabetic umbilical cord [to a doctor]. Now it was possible for any diabetic to truly know himself, more immediately and pragmatically than any physician, and to *act* on that knowledge, to take the control of his diabetes entirely into his own hands. The physician had become optional." Bernstein noted in his book: "After contemplating my new life for a few months, I started to think about the millions of insulin-dependent diabetics who were still living in the prison from which I had escaped. I've spent much of the past seven years attempting to familiarize clinicians and researchers around the world with this method for achieving physiologically normal blood sugar. It is now being used successfully by many diabetics." To further establish his regimen, he began studying medicine in 1979 to "be in a position to train physicians in the proper treatment of diabetes."

Prior to his discovery of the Glucograf Method, Bernstein worked as an engineer. In this capacity he directed the development of a number of well-known products for the clinical laboratory, including the "Dynac" centrifuge, "Sedi-Stain" for urine sediment analysis, "Pre-Cal," a microhematocrit tube, and "Sedi-Cal," a semi-micro urinalysis tube. He also holds U.S. and foreign patents in the medical/surgical field.

AVOCATIONAL INTERESTS: Flute, sailing, music (Baroque through 1946), painting, investments, home and boat repairs, landscape architecture, photography, astrophotography.

BIOGRAPHICAL/CRITICAL SOURCES: Richard K. Bernstein, *Diabetes: The Glucograf Method for Normalizing Blood Sugar,* Crown, 1981; *Modern Medicine,* May, 1981; *Journal of the American Association of Diabetes Educators,* summer, 1981; *Journal of the American Medical Association,* October 23, 1981.

BERRY, I. William 1934-

PERSONAL: Born November 29, 1934, in New York, N.Y.; son of Abraham A. (a jurist) and Ruth (Janapoll) Berry; married Deidre Grimes (an educator), February 22, 1964; children: Gregory R., Alexandra G. *Education:* Columbia University, A.B., 1954; Yale University, LL.B., 1959. *Home and office:* 1300 Midland Ave., Yonkers, N.Y. 10704. *Agent:* Claire M. Smith, Harold Ober Associates, Inc., 40 East 49th St., New York, N.Y. 10017.

CAREER: Celina Evening Standard, Celina, Ohio, reporter and sports editor, 1956-58; *New Haven Register,* New Haven, Conn., part-time copy editor, 1958-59; Newhouse Newspapers, Jersey City, N.J., and New York City, copy editor and night news editor, 1959-62, part-time staff writer, editor, and author of ski columns, 1971-76; *New York Herald Tribune,* New York City, copy desk chief, 1962-66; *Troy Daily News,* Troy, Ohio, editor-in-chief, 1966-67; *Education News,* New York City, managing editor, 1967-69; *Ski,* New York City, executive editor, 1969-71; free-lance writer, 1971—. Attorney, with private practice in Yonkers, N.Y., 1961—. Workshop instructor at Colorado Mountain College, summers, 1977—; member of faculty at Antioch College, 1966-67.

MEMBER: International Business Writers (charter member; member of board of directors), U.S. Ski Writers (member of board of directors, 1978-80), Eastern Ski Writers (president, 1978-80), Council of Writers Organizations, New York State Bar Association. *Awards, honors:* Award from *Inland Daily Press,* 1967, Harold Hirsch Award from U.S. Ski Association, 1976.

WRITINGS: Where to Ski, New American Library, 1974; *Skier's Almanac,* Scribner, 1978; *Kids on Skis,* Scribner, 1980; *Complete Guide to North American Skiing,* Scribner, 1982; *Investing in Leisure,* Scribner, 1982.

Eastern correspondent for *Ski Industry Letter.* Author of "Insider," a column in *Skier's Advocate,* and "Liftlines," a column in *Ski Business.* Contributor of several hundred articles to magazines. Equipment editor of *Skier's Advocate;* contributing editor of *Ski.*

WORK IN PROGRESS: "I see some fascinating potential problems the recreation industry will have vis-a-vis energy development, and will probably tackle that fairly soon in book form."

SIDELIGHTS: Berry told *CA:* "Each summer I teach a workshop on how to survive as a writer; it is tough to teach and harder to do, though my books have always gotten excellent reviews. I have zeroed in on the financial side of recreation, with offshoots on the political, environmental, and development aspects as well, and am increasingly less interested in travel.

"*Investing in Leisure* is a serious financial book trying to tie together all elements of this huge (third largest in U.S.) but amorphous industry into a comprehensive unity—a very challenging, interesting, often exciting venture. The underlying question is, can you make money out of your favorite pastime(s)? How?

"I sense that free-lance writers are falling on hard times because of a confluence of unfortunate economic forces; this may not abate for a couple of years. However, I see some interesting new ventures into which writers must commit, beyond the traditional print media. Overall, this is a tough way to make a living, but I don't know of too many that are any easier and and none that are more pleasing."

BIOGRAPHICAL/CRITICAL SOURCES: Ski Area Management, July, 1981.

*   *   *

BESANT, Annie (Wood)   1847-1933

BRIEF ENTRY: Born October 1, 1847, in London, England; died September 20, 1933, in Adyar, India. British social reformer, theosophist, and author. A colorful and outspoken figure, Besant was known for her emotional yet effective propagandist writing. Under the auspices of the National Secular Society, she published a birth control pamphlet that led to her prosecution on obscenity charges. Later she advocated Fabian socialism in her magazine, *Our Corner*. In 1889 Besant converted to theosophy, a philosophy she maintained until her death. As international president of the Theosophical Society from 1907 to 1933, she wrote such influential appeals as *The Ideals of Theosophy* (1912) and *Theosophy and World Problems* (1922). In 1893 she moved to India and adopted Hinduism as her underlying religion. She devoted her skill as a propagandist to India's home rule movement and wrote such works as *Shall India Live or Die?* (1925). Besant's work for the Indian cause led to a brief arrest during World War I, after which she served as president of the Indian National Congress. Her other writings include *On the Nature and Existence of Jesus of Nazareth* (1873), *Four Great Religions* (1897), and *Autobiography* (1893). *Biographical/critical sources: Twentieth Century Writers: A Biographical Dictionary of Modern Literature,* H. W. Wilson, 1942; *The McGraw-Hill Encyclopedia of World Biography,* McGraw, 1973.

*   *   *

BESTERMAN, Theodore (Deocatus Nathaniel)   1904-1976

OBITUARY NOTICE: Born November 18, 1904, in Geneva, Switzerland; died November 10, 1976. Parapsychologist, librarian, editor, bibliographer, and author. A librarian and investigations officer for the Society for Psychical Research, Besterman compiled the Society's library catalogue in 1927, adding three supplements by 1931. He gave up the study of parapsychology in 1935, when he left the society and pursued a career as an editor and bibliographer. Besterman worked as a joint editor of the Oxford Books on Bibliography, as general editor of the Association of Special Libraries and Information Bureaux, and as editor and executive officer of the British Union Catalogue of Periodicals. In 1952, he founded the Institut et Musee Voltaire in Geneva and served as its director until 1973. He was a chevalier of the Legion of Honor. Besterman wrote a wide range of bibliographical works, several books on psychical research, and writings on Voltaire; his numerous publications include *A Bibliography of Annie Besant, Crystal-Gazing, Library Catalogue of the Society for Psychical Research, The Beginnings of Systematic Bibliography, Select Writings of Voltaire,* and *Voltaire.* Obituaries and other sources: *Biographical Dictionary of Parapsychology, With Directory and Glossary, 1964-1966,* Garrett Publications, 1964; *Longman Companion to Twentieth Century Literature,* Longman, 1970; *Who's Who in the World,* 2nd edition, Marquis, 1973; *Library Association Record,* January, 1977; *Eighteenth Century Studies,* winter, 1977-78. (Exact date of death provided by Voltaire Foundation.)

*   *   *

BETTEN, Neil B.   1939-

PERSONAL: Born May 19, 1939, in New York, N.Y.; son of Ben and Adele (Greenblatt) Betten; married Edith Kalnins (a realtor), March 21, 1964; children: Saul, Joshua. *Education:* State University of New York at Binghamton, B.A., 1961; University of Minnesota, Ph.D., 1968. *Politics:* Liberal. *Religion:* Jewish. *Home:* 3131 Ortega Dr., Tallahassee, Fla. 32312. *Office:* Department of History, Florida State University, Tallahassee, Fla. 32306.

CAREER: Indiana University, Northwest Campus, Gary, 1967-70, began as lecturer, became assistant professor of history; Florida State University, Tallahassee, assistant professor, 1970-72, associate professor, 1972-78, professor of history, 1978—. President of Big Bend Central Labor Council, 1978-79; director of union workshops; director of labor history symposium for American Federation of Labor-Congress of Industrial Organizations, (AFL-CIO), 1979. Guest on television and radio programs. *Member:* American Federation of Teachers (state vice-president, 1974-75), Florida Education Association (member of board of directors, 1975-76), United Faculty of Florida (local president, 1972-73; state president, 1973-78). *Awards, honors:* Fellowship from Council on Research in Economic History, 1969; grants from American Philosophical Society, 1970, Florida Citizens' Committee for the Humanities, 1973, Florida Endowment for the Humanities, 1974 and 1975, and American Federation of Teachers, 1974 and 1975.

WRITINGS: (Editor with Raymond A. Mohl) *Urban America in Historical Perspective,* Weybright & Talley, 1970; *Catholic Activism and the Urban Worker, 1920-1940,* University Presses of Florida, 1976. Also co-author of *Ethnicity and the Steel Industry: Newcomers to Steel City,* Twayne.

Contributor: Mohl and J. F. Richardson, editors, *The Urban Experience: Themes in American History,* Wadsworth, 1973; *The Chicano,* American Bibliographical Center-Clio Press, 1975; *Catholics in America, 1776-1976,* Bishops Bicentennial Committee, 1976; Michael Belok, editor, *New History of Education,* Ann Prakashan, 1979; Theodore Kornweibel, editor, *In Search of the Promised Land: Essays in Black Urban History,* Kennikat, 1980.

Contributor to *Encyclopedia of Southern History.* Also contributor of more than thirty articles to scholarly journals. Editor of *United Faculty,* 1975-77; associate editor of *Journal of Urban History,* 1975-77, member of editorial board, 1977-79.

WORK IN PROGRESS: A History of Community Organizing; research on public sector collective bargaining.

SIDELIGHTS: Betten wrote: "I came from a working-class trade union family. I tried my first union organizing at the age of fifteen (and failed), and have remained a union activist. My writing certainly grows out of this commitment."

BETTS, Glynne Robinson 1934-

PERSONAL: Born February 23, 1934, in Virginia; daughter of Frederick H. (an executive) and Jessie M. Robinson; divorced; children: Elizabeth, William, Katherine. *Education:* Wells College, A.B., 1956; received certificate as media specialist from New York City Board of Education, 1974; postgraduate study at Columbia University, 1957, and at New York University, 1975; studied photography with Lisette Model, 1967, Ansel Adams, 1968, Paul Coponigro, 1969-71, and George Tice, 1971. *Politics:* Democrat. *Home and office address:* 116 East 63rd St., New York, N.Y. 10021. *Agent:* Elizabeth Darhansoff, 70 East 91st St., New York, N.Y. 10028.

CAREER: Professional photographer and photojournalist, 1968—. Clients include Children's Television Workshop, Sesame Place, Seatrain, Inc., New York State Bar Association, Martin Jaffe Design, New York Botanical Garden, Northern Manhattan Improvement Corp., Wave Hill Center for Environmental Studies, Center for Population and Family Health, Columbia University, International Women's Art Festival, Morgenthau for District Attorney Campaign, Dillon Gordon, and Hawkey & Shortt. Photographer for television programs, including "Sesame Street," "The Electric Company," "Feeling Good," and "3-2-1 Contact."

Work exhibited at Riverdale Neighborhood House, New York, 1968, Guild Hall, Easthampton, New York, 1970, Soho Photo Gallery, New York, 1973 and 1974, New York Public Library, 1973, Wells College, Aurora, N.Y., 1973 and 1974-75, Cosmopolitan Club, New York, 1976, Community Gallery of Metropolitan Museum of Art, 1976, Carnegie House, New York, 1978.

Conductor of New York Public Library's photography workshop for junior high school students, 1973; conductor of photostudy project for fifth-grade students at P.S. 81 in New York, 1974-75. News and publicity photographer for Riverdale Neighborhood House, New York, 1974-76. Guest lecturer at University of Maine, 1979. *Member:* American Society of Magazine Photographers, Society of Photographers in Communications.

WRITINGS: (And photographer) *Writers in Residence*, introduction by Christopher Lehmann-Haupt, Viking, 1981.

Contributor of photographs and articles to periodicals, including *New York Times, Washington Post, New York Daily News, Christian Science Monitor, Village Voice, San Francisco Chronicle, Los Angeles Times, Westchester Magazine*, and *Opera News*.

WORK IN PROGRESS: "I feel it's bad luck to talk about work in progress, but I have two books in the works and several stories perking."

SIDELIGHTS: According to many literary critics, a sense of place is important to writers and often gives insight to their creations. "A writer's space," said Bruce Cook of the *Detroit News*, "will tell you far more about his work than a lengthy literary essay will." With this in mind, Glynne Robinson Betts photographed the retreats of forty American writers of the nineteenth and twentieth centuries and compiled the pictures in *Writers in Residence*. Organized by the region of the country in which the covered authors lived, the book shows the environments of the writers and how those physical settings are reflected in the works of Herman Melville, Louisa May Alcott, Washington Irving, Edith Wharton, Flannery O'Connor, Ross MacDonald, and others. "Impressed by the honesty and clarity of . . . [Betts's] camera, by the breadth of her field," Art Seidenbaum, book editor of the *Los Angeles Times*, called *Writers in Residence* "a true album, a visual, honorable footnote to a family of America's most gifted citizens."

Betts told *CA:* "I love to make photographs, and I love to write. But I wish there was more time!

"I just returned from a month in China with fantastic photos and an idea for a book. The trip gave me a new appreciation of our country and what we have here, but it also made me aware of those things the Chinese have that we make light of—continuity, a broader sense of time, and communal sharing."

BIOGRAPHICAL/CRITICAL SOURCES: Betty L. English, editor, *Women at Their Work*, Dial, 1977; *Los Angeles Times*, May 27, 1981; *Detroit News*, May 31, 1981.

*   *   *

BEVENOT, Maurice 1897-1980

OBITUARY NOTICE: Born in 1897; died November 19, 1980. Clergyman, theologian, educator, and author. Ordained a priest in the Society of Jesus (Jesuits) in 1930, Bevenot began his study of St. Cyprian, a bishop and martyr of the early church, while a student at the Gregorian University in Rome. Beginning in 1936, Bevenot went to Heythrop Pontifical Athenaeum and continued to teach and write there after its incorporation into the London University as Heythrop College in 1970, at which time he became a senior fellow. His studies of St. Cyprian, which became his life work, established Bevenot as an authority on the hermeneutics of manuscript study and led to the priest's lifelong interest in ecumenism and religious toleration. During the Second World War, Bevenot took part in "The Sword of the Spirit," a religious movement dedicated to combating totalitarianism and bringing together all peoples in order to secure a Christian peace. He also worked with the Council of Christians and Jews. The culmination of Bevenot's service to the cause of ecumenism came with his appointment to the Secretariat for Promoting Christian Unity. An integral part of the Second Vatican Council, the Secretariat drafted proposals on Church unity and on the establishment of cordial relations among Christians of all faiths. Bevenot's writings include *St. Cyprian's De Unitate, Chapter 4, in the Light of the Manuscripts* and *The Tradition of Manuscripts: A Study in the Transmission of St. Cyprian's Treatises*. Obituaries and other sources: *The Annual Obituary 1980*, St. Martin's, 1981.

*   *   *

BINGHAM, Charlotte Mary Therese 1942-

PERSONAL: Born June 29, 1942, in Haywards Heath, Sussex, England; daughter of John Michael Ward (a writer) and Madeleine (Ebel) Bingham; married Terence Joseph Brady (an actor and writer), January 15, 1964; children: Candida, Matthew. *Education:* Attended Sorbonne, University of Paris, 1959-60. *Politics:* Liberal. *Religion:* Roman Catholic. *Home:* 111 East Sheen Ave., London SW14 8AX, England. *Agent:* A. D. Peters & Co. Ltd., 10 Buckingham St., London WC2N 6BU, England.

CAREER: Writer, 1963—. *Member:* Writers Guild of Great Britain.

WRITINGS: Coronet Among the Weeds, Heinemann, 1963; *Lucinda*, Heinemann, 1966; *Coronet Among the Grass*, Heinemann, 1972; (with husband, Terence Brady) *Rose's Story*, Sphere, 1972, Pocket Books, 1975; *No, Honestly!*, Penguin, 1974. Writer with T. Brady for television series "Take Three

Girls,'' ''Boy Meets Girl,'' ''Upstairs, Downstairs,'' ''No, Honestly,'' ''Yes, Honestly,'' ''Thomas and Sarah,'' and ''Pig in the Middle.'' Contributor to magazines, including *Vogue, Harper's, Tattler,* and *Catholic Herald.*

WORK IN PROGRESS: The Upper Class, a novel with husband, T. Brady; ''A Dip Before Breakfast,'' a stage play with T. Brady.

SIDELIGHTS: Charlotte Bingham told *CA:* ''I turned to writing at the age of eighteen because of an inability to master the arts of shorthand and typing. The resultant humorous book, *Coronet Among the Weeds,* has been described as a book about being a debutante, which I no longer bother to deny, having too much regard for my royalties.

''Shortly after its publication I met and married Terence Brady, who put an end to any treasured thoughts of early retirement by lassoing me into partnership with him. Some of our television series have appeared in the United States, most notably our contributions to 'Upstairs, Downstairs' and 'No, Honestly,' which was based loosely upon *Coronet Among the Grass.*''

*   *   *

BISHOP, Donald H(arold) 1920-

PERSONAL: Born September 9, 1920, in Fulton, N.Y.; son of Harold (a contractor) and Vivian (Butts) Bishop; married Lieselotte Osthoff (a secretary), June, 1952; children: Michael, Karen, David. *Education:* Cornell University, B.Sc., 1947; Yale University, M.Div., 1950; University of Edinburgh, Ph.D., 1953. *Home:* 1600 Gaines Rd., Pullman, Wash. *Office:* Department of Philosophy, Washington State University, Pullman, Wash. 99164.

CAREER: Ordained minister of United Methodist Church, 1947; Hampton Institute, Hampton, Va., chaplain, 1953, instructor in sociology, 1953-55; University of California, chaplain to Methodist students, 1955-57; Iowa Wesleyan College, Mount Pleasant, chaplain and instructor in philosophy and religion, 1957-59; Washington State University, Pullman, instructor, 1959-61, assistant professor, 1961-64, associate professor, 1964-70, professor of philosophy, 1970—. *Member:* American Philosophical Association, American Academy of Religion, Society for Asian and Comparative Philosophy. *Awards, honors:* Fulbright fellowship, summer, 1964; sabbatical leave award from the Committee for Religion in Higher Education, 1966-67; grant from Indian Council for Cultural Relations, summer, 1978.

WRITINGS: Indian Thought: An Introduction, Wiley, 1975; *Leaders of the Indian Renaissance,* Wiley Eastern Private, 1981.

WORK IN PROGRESS: Religions of the World, completion expected in 1982; *Chinese Thought: An Introduction.*

SIDELIGHTS: Bishop wrote: ''I have traveled extensively in the Far East—India, Thailand, Japan, Taiwan, mainland China. My vital concern is bringing about understanding and better relations between the United States and the rest of the world. I am interested in the basic philosophies, religions, and motivations of people. I look upon the world as one and all people as brothers and sisters.

''Many people, when they travel, only see the superficial and surface things. This, I think, is unfortunate. I like to go behind the scenes, meet people in the home as well as on the street and in the market place, get to know them as human beings. This requires sympathetic identification and is tremendously rewarding. I see every individual, no matter where or in what

country, first as a person and as a member of the whole human race and only secondarily as a member of a particular portion of it. My writings, I believe, reflect this premise of the universal nature of man.''

*   *   *

BISHOP, John 1935-

PERSONAL: Born May 3, 1935, in Mansfield, Ohio; son of William and Bernice (Dickson) Bishop; divorced; children: Matthew, Christopher. *Education:* Received B.F.A. from Carnegie Institute of Technology (now Carnegie-Mellon University). *Agent:* Flora Roberts, Inc., 65 East 55th St., New York, N.Y. 10022. *Office:* c/o Circle Repertory Theatre, 99 Seventh Ave. S., New York, N.Y. 10014.

CAREER: Playwright.

*WRITINGS—*Plays: ''The Trip Back Down'' (two-act), first produced on Broadway at Longacre Theatre, January 4, 1977; ''Cabin Twelve,'' (one-act), first produced Off-Broadway at Circle Repertory Theatre, January 5, 1978; ''Winter Signs'' (two-act), first produced Off-Broadway at Circle Repertory Theatre, February 28, 1979.

SIDELIGHTS: Bishop's ''The Trip Back Down'' is about a stock car racer who, discouraged about his losses, returns to the security of his home town only to find himself unable to give in to the routine of small-town life. ''What is interesting in the play,'' wrote *Nation*'s Harold Clurman, is its atmosphere, its local speech, its sense of place and character, the people who rarely occupy important roles in recent American drama . . . John Bishop knows these people intimately; he does not write as a tourist among them but as a companion.'' *New Yorker* critic Brendan Gill observed that ''The Trip Back Down'' is a ''well-written and well-constructed play, serious in its intentions and yet often effectively comic in tone.''

Critics were also impressed with Bishop's next play, ''Cabin Twelve.'' In his review of the play Howard Kessel of *Women's Wear Daily* remarked, ''What impresses one about Bishop's writing is how skillful he is at putting the most basic, awkward things . . . on stage.'' The drama focuses on the grief, guilt, and frustration of a man and his son who are making burial arrangements for another son who was killed in a highway accident. *Villager*'s C. Lee Jenner pointed out that the play's ''terse, idiomatic dialogue suits the emotionally inarticulate characters. And while the subject matter is grim, the tone remains brave.''

''Winter Signs'' is quite different from Bishop's first two plays, and it fared less well with critics. It is a suspense drama set in a lonely old house during a thunderstorm and features a Civil War ghost and tales of homosexual murder. Reviewer Debbi Wasserman of *New York Theatre Review* thought the play was ''a confusing conglomerate of symbols, images and events.'' *New York Times* critic Richard Eder described the play as a ''study of tensions, frustrations and jealousies'' and complained that the suspense ''perches on top of it, distractingly, like a hat worn in a parlor.'' *New York Post*'s Marilyn Stasio, however, found some of the suspense elements ''tingling.''

Bishop told *CA:* '' 'The Trip Back Down' meant to examine why someone loses when he is possessed of the skills and desire to be winning. More than that, it is about the 'winners and losers' syndrome that seems to pervade so much thinking in our society. It amused me that some critics thought the play was about a loser (naturally enough, for it is a critic's task to determine what succeeds and what fails) when the play is trying to say that winning and losing are insidious labels that are much too prevalent in our culture.''

BIOGRAPHICAL/CRITICAL SOURCES: New Yorker, November 3, 1975, January 17, 1977, March 20, 1978; *New York Times,* January 5, 1977, January 6, 1978; *New York Post,* January 5, 1977, January 7, 1978; *Village Voice,* January 24, 1977; *Nation,* January 29, 1977; *Women's Wear Daily,* January 10, 1978; *Villager,* January 12, 1978; *Contemporary Literary Criticism,* Volume 10, Gale, 1979; *New York Theatre Review,* April, 1979.

*　　*　　*

BLACK, Susan Adams   1953-

PERSONAL: Born February 17, 1953, in Cincinnati, Ohio; daughter of David Delaine (a planning counselor) and Margaret Stout (a computer programmer; maiden name, Reeve) Black. *Education:* University of California, Berkeley, B.A., 1976. *Agent:* Richard Krawetz & Associates, 337 East 13th St., New York, N.Y. 10013. *Office:* FilmMedia Corp., 260 South Beverly Dr., Beverly Hills, Calif. 90212.

CAREER: KNXT-TV, Los Angeles, Calif., production assistant, 1977-78; Talent & Booking Publishing, Inc., Hollywood, Calif., managing editor, 1978-80; Xiphias Computer Graphics, Santa Monica, Calif., graphics programmer and documentation writer, 1979-80; FilmMedia Corp., Beverly Hills, Calif., production supervisor, 1980—.

WRITINGS: Crash in the Wilderness (juvenile), Raintree, 1980; *Louise LaBiche in Hollywood* (self-illustrated serial), Platinum Jackalopes Publishing, 1980; *This Is Pop* (self-illustrated juvenile), Overleaf Press, 1982. Editor of *Talent and Booking Directory,* 1978-80.

WORK IN PROGRESS: The Louise LaBiche Chronicles: A Study in Tension, a self-illustrated collection of stories, publication by Dirty Dog Cartoons expected in 1982 or 1983; *Lady in a Greenhouse,* a novel; *My Dog Bitman,* a self-illustrated juvenile.

SIDELIGHTS: Susan Black wrote: "The alienation of modern life will get you every time. Keep your sense of humor. When in doubt, shop."

*　　*　　*

BLACKBURNE, Kenneth (William)   1907-1980

OBITUARY NOTICE: Born December 12, 1907, in Bristol, England; died November 4, 1980, in Castletown, Isle of Man. Colonial administrator and author. Blackburne entered the British Colonial Service at the age of twenty-two and became the assistant district officer in Nigeria in 1930. He remained with the service until his retirement in 1963, serving in Africa, the Middle East, and the Carribbean as well as in London. In his last assignment with the service, he assumed the dual office of Captain-General and Governor-in-Chief of Jamaica in 1957, representing the British Government during the difficult period just prior to the island's independence. Once independence was achieved, Blackburne was asked by the new government to remain in Jamaica as the first Governor-General. He agreed to do so for one year, after which he retired. He was named to the Order of the British Empire in 1939 and was knighted in 1952. He wrote *Lasting Legacy: A Story of British Colonialism,* based on his years of field experience. Obituaries and other sources: *The Annual Obituary 1980,* St. Martin's, 1981.

BLACKTON, Peter
See WILSON, Lionel

*　　*　　*

BLACKWOOD, Algernon (Henry)   1869-1951

BRIEF ENTRY: Born in 1869 in Kent, England; died December 10, 1951, in London, England. British novelist and short story writer. Blackwood believed that ordinary mortals possessed secret, psychic powers, and he described his own writing as a quest to extend these human faculties. His speculative fiction, collected in *John Silence* (1908), *Pan's Garden* (1912), and *Tales of the Uncanny and Supernatural* (1949), dealt with psychic ability and the occult. Blackwood gained his early writing experiences as a reporter for New York City newspapers. His other books include a colorful autobiography, *Episodes Before Thirty* (1923), and such children's books as *Sambo and Snitch* (1927). He objected to his writing being passed off superficially as "ghost" or "horror" stories, but late in life Blackwood read his stories on British television, establishing a considerable reputation with the British public. *Biographical/critical sources: Twentieth Century Authors: A Biographical Dictionary of Modern Literature,* H. W. Wilson, 1942.

*　　*　　*

BLAKESLEE, Alton (Lauren)   1913-

PERSONAL: Born June 27, 1913, in Dallas, Tex.; son of Howard Walter (a science editor) and Marguerite (Fortune) Blakeslee; married Virginia Boulden, July 2, 1937; children: Dennis, Carolyn Sandra Blakeslee Stallcup. *Education:* Attended Duke University, 1931-33; Columbia University, A.B., 1935. *Home:* 13 Vista Way, Port Washington, N.Y. 11050. *Agent:* Julian Bach, 747 Third Ave., New York, N.Y. 10017. *Office:* American Cancer Society, 777 Third Ave., New York, N.Y. 10017.

CAREER: Journal Every Evening, Wilmington, Del., reporter, 1935-39; Associated Press, staff member and news editor in Baltimore, Md., 1939-42, foreign news desk staff member in New York City, 1942-46, correspondent to U.S. Navy Antarctic Expedition, 1946-47, science reporter in New York City, 1946-69, science editor in New York City, 1969-78; American Cancer Society, New York City, consultant and writer, 1978—. Visiting professor of science journalism at University of Missouri, 1975, and Syracuse University, 1978-79. Consultant to *Harper Dictionary of Contemporary Usage* and *American Heritage Dictionary. Member:* National Association of Science Writers (president, 1958-59), American Tentative Society (founder and president, 1973—), Sigma Delta Chi.

AWARDS, HONORS: George Westinghouse science writing award from American Association for Advancement of Science, 1952; George Polk Award, 1952; Lasker Foundation Medical Journalism Award, 1954, 1963, and 1964; award of merit from American Heart Association, 1954; James T. Grady Award from American Chemical Society, 1959; Howard Blakeslee Award from American Heart Association, 1963 and 1964; distinguished service award from Sigma Delta Chi, 1965; honor award for distinguished service in journalism from University of Missouri, 1966; science writers award from American Dental Association, 1967; Edward J. Meeman Award from Scripps-Howard Foundation, 1968; Robert T. Morse Award from American Psychiatric Association, 1973; American Academy of Family Physicians award, 1976; Claude Bernard Award from National Society for Medical Research, 1978; First Distinguished Journalism award from American Heart Association, 1978; Carr Van Anda Award from Ohio University School of Journalism, 1978.

WRITINGS: Polio and the Salk Vaccine: What You Should Know About It, Grosset, 1956; (with Jeremiah Stamler) *Your Heart Has Nine Lives: Nine Steps to Heart Health,* Prentice-Hall, 1963; *What You Should Know About Drugs and Narcotics,* Associated Press, 1969; *What You Can Do About Dangerous Drugs,* Associated Press, 1971. Author of pamphlets and booklets on health and science.

WORK IN PROGRESS: A book on how to choose a good nursing home; writing on health care at all ages.

SIDELIGHTS: Blakeslee told *CA:* "It was my good fortune to be an on-scene reporter/writer during the great revolution in science and technology beginning in the 1940's that powerfully affected human lives. There came the A-bomb and the H-bomb and nuclear power plants; antibiotics; heart-lung machines, putting the heart on holiday for better repair, and transplants of hearts and other borrowed organs; Sputnik and the Space Age and men landing on the Moon; the beginnings of conquests over heart diseases and cancers; understanding of the genetic code and gene splicing; solid-state physics and computers; the explosive new knowledge in astronomy helping to explain the Universe we live in—and much, much more. And likely it is only the beginning."

AVOCATIONAL INTERESTS: Tennis.

*   *   *

BLANCO WHITE, Amber 1887-1981
(Amber Reeves)

OBITUARY NOTICE: Born July 1, 1887; died December 26, 1981. Educator and author. As a young woman, Amber Blanco White reportedly served as the inspiration for novelist H. G. Wells's model of the New Woman, whose role in society he described in his book *Ann Veronica.* A 1932 collaboration with Wells resulted in publication of his book *The Work, Wealth, and Happiness of Mankind.* A highly regarded lecturer, Blanco White spoke on economic, social, and psychological issues. As Amber Reeves she wrote several books, including *The Reward of Virtue* and *Give and Take.* Among her books written under the name Amber Blanco White are *The Nationalization of Banking* and *Ethics for Unbelievers.* Obituaries and other sources: *Who's Who,* 126th edition, St. Martin's, 1974; *Who Was Who Among English and European Authors, 1931-1949,* Gale, 1978; *London Times,* January 6, 1982.

*   *   *

BLOCH, Chana Florence 1940-

PERSONAL: Born March 15, 1940, in New York, N.Y.; daughter of Benjamin (a dentist) and Rose (Rosenberg) Faerstein; married Ariel A. Bloch (a professor), October 26, 1969; children: Benjamin Daniel, Jonathan Max. *Education:* Cornell University, B.A., 1961; Brandeis University, M.A., 1963, M.A., 1965; University of California, Berkeley, Ph.D., 1975. *Religion:* Jewish. *Home:* 12 Menlo Pl., Berkeley, Calif. 94707. *Office:* Department of English, Mills College, Oakland, Calif. 94613.

CAREER: Hebrew University of Jerusalem, Jerusalem, Israel, instructor in English literature, 1964-67; Mills College, Oakland, Calif., instructor, 1973-75, assistant professor, 1975-81, associate professor of English literature, 1981—. *Member:* Modern Language Association of America, Poetry Society of America. *Awards, honors:* Discovery Award for poetry, 1974;

Graves Award from Pomona College, 1976-77; translation award from Columbia University's Translation Center, 1978, for *A Dress of Fire;* fellowship from National Endowment for the Humanities, 1980-81.

WRITINGS: A Dress of Fire: Selected Poetry of Dahlia Ravikovitch, Menard, 1976; *The Secrets of the Tribe* (poems), Sheep Meadow Press, 1980.

Work represented in anthologies, including *A Geography of Poets,* 1978; *Voices Within the Ark,* 1980; and *The Pushcart Prize, VI,* 1981.

Contributor of poems and translations (from Yiddish and Hebrew) to literary journals and popular magazines, including *Playboy, Midstream,* and *Judaism.*

WORK IN PROGRESS: George Herbert and the Bible, publication expected in 1983.

*   *   *

BLOCK, Arthur John 1916(?)-1981

OBITUARY NOTICE: Born c. 1916; died of cardiac arrest, October 17, 1981, in Manhattan, N.Y. Publicist, journalist, and author. The first arts critic for the financial newspaper *The American Banker,* Block also was a publicity man for several motion picture companies, including Avco Embassy Pictures, Eagle Lion, and Universal. His writings include two plays, "I Swear by Appollo" and "In Small Print Upside Down," and two books, *Classical Roman Civilization* and *Classical Greek Civilization.* Obituaries and other sources: *New York Times,* October 20, 1981.

*   *   *

BLOOMINGDALE, Teresa 1930-

PERSONAL: Born July 26, 1930, in St. Joseph, Mo.; daughter of Arthur Victor (in newspaper work) and Helen (Cooney) Burrowes; married Arthur Lee Bloomingdale (an attorney), July 2, 1955; children: Lee, John, Michael, James, Mary, Daniel, Peggy, Ann, Timothy, Patrick. *Education:* Received B.A. from Duchesne College, Omaha, Neb. *Politics:* Republican. *Religion:* Roman Catholic. *Home:* 2044 South 86th Ave., Omaha, Neb. 68124.

CAREER: Creighton University, School of Law, Omaha, Neb., legal secretary, 1952-54; Webster School, St. Joseph, Mo., teacher, 1954-55; writer. *Member:* Associated Alumnae of the Sacred Heart.

WRITINGS: I Should Have Seen It Coming When the Rabbit Died, Doubleday, 1979; *Up a Family Tree,* Doubleday, 1981. Author of "A Mother's Meditation," a syndicated humor column, and a weekly column in *Our Sunday Visitor.* Contributor to magazines, including *McCall's, Good Housekeeping,* and *Catholic Digest.*

SIDELIGHTS: Teresa Bloomingdale wrote: "My motivation? The idiotic pranks of ten children prompted me to share the humorous aspects of motherhood. I am vitally interested in children—mine and everybody's. I see them as funny, lovable, loving creatures to be enjoyed fully. Foreign languages in which I have great expertise are babytalk and adolescent slang."

*   *   *

BOBRI, Vladimir V. 1898-

PERSONAL: Original surname, Bobritsky; born May 13, 1898, in Charkov, Ukraine (now Soviet Union); came to the United

States in 1921; son of Vasily K. and Sofia R. Bobritsky; married Margaret Rinaudo. *Education:* Imperial Art School, Charkov, Soviet Union, graduated, 1921. *Home address:* Elting Rd., Rosendale, N.Y. 12472. *Office:* New York Society of the Classic Guitar, 409 East 50th St., New York, N.Y. 10022.

CAREER: Graphic artist, muralist, and stage designer; operated a textile firm and worked in advertising; directed radio programs. *Member:* Society of the Classic Guitar, New York Society of the Classic Guitar (president). *Awards, honors:* Member of Order of Izabela la Catolica; art awards include several from Art Directors Club for advertising design, and numerous awards for children's book illustrations.

WRITINGS: Two Guitars, Macmillan, 1972; *A Musical Voyage With Two Guitars,* Macmillan, 1974; *Segovia Technique,* Macmillan, 1977.

Illustrator: B. Bundy, *A Kiss Is Round* (juvenile), Lothrop, 1954; Esphyr, Slobodkina, *Boris and His Balalaika,* Abelard, 1964; R. Gans, *Icebergs,* Crowell, 1964. Also illustrator of *Taxco* (collection of pastels), text by P. K. Thomaja, Lacca.

Editor and art director of *Guitar.*

WORK IN PROGRESS: Research on the music of Soviet Georgia, Brazil, and Rumania.

SIDELIGHTS: Bobri commented: "Meeting Andres Segovia in 1936 began a continuous friendship and collaboration on behalf of the classic guitar. With the Society of the Classic Guitar I have helped organize more than two hundred fifty concerts, featuring artists of international reputation. I have traveled extensively in Europe, Asia, and South and Central America." *Avocational interests:* Collecting musical instruments, books, and music.

*   *   *

BOEHM, Karl   1894-1981

OBITUARY NOTICE: Born August 28, 1894, in Graz, Austria; died following a stroke, August 14, 1981, in Salzburg, Austria. Conductor and author best known for his preeminence as an operatic conductor in the Mozart-Wagner-Richard Strauss repertory. Boehm conducted in several provincial opera houses throughout Europe, was general director of the Dresden Opera, and served two terms as head of the Vienna State Opera before launching a free-lance career in 1956. He conducted at major musical centers in Europe, including Salzburg, Vienna, Paris, Milan, and Berlin, and in 1957 began a twenty-one year association with the Metropolitan Opera as a principal conductor. On the occasion of his seventieth birthday the Austrian Cabinet voted the conductor the honorary title of General Music Director of Austria. In 1965 a recording of Alban Berg's "Wozzeck," with Boehm conducting the chorus and orchestra of the Berlin German Opera, won a Grammy Award as best opera album of the year. Boehm wrote his memoirs, *Ich errinere mich ganz genau* (title means "I Remember Everything Exactly"). Obituaries and other sources: *Current Biography,* Wilson, 1968; *Who's Who in Opera,* Arno, 1976; *New York Times,* August 15, 1981.

*   *   *

BOISSONEAU, Robert   1937-

PERSONAL: Born September 23, 1937, in Detroit, Mich.; son of S. N. (a timekeeper) and Dorothea (De Lamarter) Boissoneau; married Jo Ellen Fitzgerald, October 15, 1960; children: Mark, Deborah, Keith. *Education:* Eastern Michigan University, B.A., 1960; Medical College of Virginia, M.H.A., 1965;

Ohio State University, Ph.D., 1974. *Home:* 2113 South Paseo Loma, Mesa, Ariz. 85202. *Office:* Center for Health Services Administration, Arizona State University, Tempe, Ariz. 85287.

CAREER: Ohio State University, Columbus, instructor and administrator of Means Hall, 1967-72; University of Missouri, Columbia, assistant professor of health services management, 1972-75; Eastern Michigan University, Ypsilanti, professor of health administration and dean of College of Human Services, 1975-80; Arizona State University, Tempe, professor of health services administration, 1980—. Member of advisory board of Desert Samaritan Hospital and St. Joseph Mercy Hospital, Ann Arbor, Mich.; consultant to Michigan Department of Mental Health and U.S. Department of Health, Education and Welfare's Bureau of Health Manpower. *Military service:* U.S. Army, Medical Service, 1960-62; became captain. *Member:* American College of Hospital Administrators, American Hospital Association, American Public Health Association, Academy of Management. *Awards, honors:* D.Sc. from Indiana Northern Graduate School of Professional Management, 1979.

WRITINGS: Continuing Education in the Health Professions, Aspen Systems Corp., 1980. Contributor to health administration journals.

WORK IN PROGRESS: Health administration research.

*   *   *

BOOKER, Anton S.
See RANDOLPH, Vance

*   *   *

BORICH, Michael   1949-

PERSONAL: Born May 16, 1949, in Waterloo, Iowa; son of Milo A. (an automobile club representative) and Dorothy (Mulholland) Borich; married Lynn McClintock (a television producer), June 6, 1969; children: Aeron Michael. *Education:* University of Northern Iowa, B.A., 1971; University of California, Irvine, M.F.A., 1979. *Home:* 3104 Peeble Dr. S.W., Cedar Rapids, Iowa 52404. *Office:* Department of Communication Arts, Kirkwood Community College, Cedar Rapids, Iowa 52406.

CAREER: High school English teacher in Norway, Iowa, 1971-72, and Waterloo, Iowa, 1974-77; University of California, Irvine, instructor in poetry writing, 1977-79; University of Wisconsin, Green Bay, instructor in fiction writing, 1979-81; Kirkwood Community College, Cedar Rapids, Iowa, instructor in communication arts, 1981—. Producer of "Writer in Performance," first broadcast by SSPN-Television, 1978-79; news editor for "Real to Reel," on WLUK-TV, 1981. *Awards, honors:* Grant from National Endowment for the Arts, 1977.

WRITINGS: The Black Hawk Songs (poetry), University of Illinois Press, 1975; *I Drank Two Hundred Bears* (teachers resource book), Iowa Arts Council, 1977; (editor) *Summer Arts: Glendive* (anthology), Montana Arts Council, 1977. Sportswriter for *Cedar Rapids Gazette,* 1981—. Contributor of poems and stories to magazines, including *New Yorker, Paris Review, North American Review,* and *Kansas Quarterly.*

WORK IN PROGRESS: Sport's Zaniest Heroes, with father, Milo Borich; *Weeble,* a juvenile novel; *Quackers,* a juvenile novel.

SIDELIGHTS: Borich wrote: "My feeling is that a writer should be able to write on any topic, in any style, not become locked into one category. Thus, I have attempted to learn as much as I can about the mechanics of writing—of putting words on paper in sensible constructions—but I do not want to feel limited or pigeonholed by one genre. I want to feel as comfortable writing poetry and fiction as I am writing plays or television news copy.''

* * *

BOSHELL, Buris R(aye) 1923-

PERSONAL: Born October 9, 1923, in Bear Creek, Ala.; son of Harvey M. and Lela (Alexander) Boshell; married Martha Sue Johnson (a teacher); children: Patricia Boshell Wilson, Thomas Eppinger. *Education:* Alabama Polytechnic Institute, B.S., 1947, graduate study, 1949-51; Harvard University, M.D., 1953. *Religion:* Baptist. *Home:* 3017 Old Ivy Rd., Birmingham, Ala. 35210. *Office:* 1808 Seventh Ave. S., Birmingham, Ala. 35294.

CAREER: Peter Bent Brigham Hospital, Boston, Mass., intern, 1953-54, resident, 1954-56, chief medical resident, 1958-59; Harvard University, Cambridge, Mass., research fellow in medicine, 1956-58; University of Alabama, Birmingham, assistant professor, 1959-62, associate professor, 1962-64, professor, 1964—, Ruth Lawson Hanson Professor of Medicine, 1967—, director of division of endocrinology and metabolism, 1970—, medical director of Diabetes Research and Education Hospital, 1973—. Diplomate of American Board of Internal Medicine; clinical investigator, 1959-62, and chief of medicine, 1962-64, for Veterans Administration Hospital; medical director of U.S. Pipe & Foundry, Central Bancshares of the South, and Rust Engineering. Visiting professor at University of Mexico, 1975, and University of the Witwatersrand, 1975. Member of National Commission on Diabetes, 1975—, chairman of subcommittee on scope, 1975—; president of board of directors of Diabetes Trust Fund of Alabama; member of board of directors of Diabetes Research Laboratory. Member of board of directors of Central Bank of Birmingham. *Military service:* U.S. Army, 1946-47.

MEMBER: American College of Physicians (fellow), American College of Clinical Pharmacology and Chemotherapy (fellow), American Medical Association, American Association of University Professors, American Diabetes Association (member of board of directors, 1973—), Endocrine Society, American Federation for Clinical Research, American Society for Clinical Pharmacology and Therapeutics, Southern Society for Clinical Investigation, New England Diabetes Association, Alabama Medical Association, Alabama Academy of Science, Alabama Diabetes Association, New York Diabetes Association, Jefferson County Medical Association, Birmingham Academy of Medicine, Sigma Xi, Omicron Delta Kappa, Phi Kappa Phi, Gamma Sigma Delta, Tau Kappa Alpha, Alpha Omega Alpha. *Awards, honors:* Senior U.S. scientist award from Alexander von Humboldt Foundation, for West Germany, 1975.

WRITINGS: (Contributor) *Treatment of Neuromuscular Disorders,* Heober, 1966; *Your Miniature Pinscher,* Denlingers, 1969; *The Diabetic at Work and Play,* C. C Thomas, 1973, 2nd edition, 1979; *Diabetes Mellitus: Forty Case Studies,* Medical Examination Publishing, 1976, 2nd edition, 1981; *The Diagnosis and Management of Endocrine Disorders in Primary Practice,* Addison-Wesley, 1982. Contributor to medical journals.

WORK IN PROGRESS: A book on the walking horse; a large series of monographs.

SIDELIGHTS: Boshell told *CA:* ''As director of the division of endocrinology and metabolism and as medical director of the Diabetes Hospital, I am in a position that is certainly stimulating every day of the week. We visualize the important things to common diabetes in several categories and are making efforts to have investigations active in each one of these areas.

''Clearly diabetes is a genetic disease; however, considerable controversy still exists in spite of extensive investigation. Most of the misinformation that has appeared in literature is probably because we have been comparing apples with bananas and oranges rather than apples with apples. It will take large numbers of patients in order to totally clarify the heterogeneity of this very important and common disease. Because of this, we are putting one of our major thrusts in the genetic area.'' For example, a team headed by the immuno-geneticist Dr. Ron Acton, explained Boshell, has ''already found that most of the black diabetics with insulin dependent diabetes have caucasian genes, and I am sure that they will add a good deal of additional understanding to the whole problem of heterogeneity in diabetes in the near future.

''Additionally, we are also concerned with the problem of autoimmunity as it relates to diabetes, thyrotoxicosis, and many other endocrine syndromes. Because of this, we have a rather extensive program going on in immunology, largely again under the direction of Dr. Acton.''

Boshell also studies diabetics whose problems are ''receptors rather than insulin deficiency. It is my opinion that the neuroendocrine approach is going to be the most important avenue for productive research in the future in this area.''

He continued: ''From the standpoint of theraputics, of course, we are very interested in the possibility of an implantable artificial pancreas as well as pancreatic transplantation using the beta cells.'' Boshell and his associates are also investigating closed loop systems, ''a method whereby diabetes can be very controlled, and we see it as an important advance in the future.'' And, according to the doctor, researchers ''are devising new media techniques to improve the reproductivity of the islet cells in culture and hopefully will, before too long, have a tissue bank that will be utilizable. They will, of course, need the collaborative efforts of Dr. Acton and others in the immunology field relevant to the problem of tissue rejection, but I sincerely believe that this problem can be overcome in the not-too-distant future.

''At this point, one floor of our hospital remains totally unfinished, and it is hopeful here that we will take three-quarters of the floor and develop it into a very important cellular endocrinology program and then retain one-quarter of the floor for visiting professors. Already one of our patients has given us a condominium in the city for use by visiting faculty, and we are quite hopeful that we will have the visiting professors' laboratory completed on the sixth floor in the not-too-distant future. This will allow us, then, to invite exciting individuals from throughout the world to come six months, a year, or whatever, to provide the stimulation and so forth to our growing, active group of investigators.

''Working with a transplant specialist from Belfast, we are developing a rather extensive clinical program and have more than fifty thousand registered patients in the clinic. We are trying to gear up so that we can handle the demands of at least two hundred patients a day in the outpatient area. Already, we keep forty inpatient beds full at all times in addition to approximately ten adolescent beds in a nearby hospital.

''Our goals, of course, in terms of health delivery are to provide enough patients for teaching and clinical research and to provide consultative resources to other divisions and departments in the university as well as a consultative facility and faculty for utilization of physicians throughout the Southeast. Currently about one-third to one-half are coming from out of state, and it appears that this is going to increase.''

AVOCATIONAL INTERESTS: The walking horse.

* * *

BOTEL, Morton 1925-

PERSONAL: Born April 8, 1925, in Philadelphia, Pa.; son of Harry and Celia (Cherry) Botel; married Rita Lillian Rubin, March 5, 1945; children: Neil Evan, Bonnie Karen Botel-Sheppard, Mikel. *Education:* University of Pennsylvania, B.S., 1945, M.S., 1947, Ed.D., 1951. *Politics:* Democrat. *Religion:* Jewish. *Office:* Graduate School of Education, University of Pennsylvania, 3700 Market St., Room B21, Philadelphia, Pa. 19104.

CAREER: Teacher of mathematics, social studies, and English at public schools in Mount Pleasant, Del., 1947-49; reading and English supervisor at public schools in Bucks County, Pa., 1951-57, assistant superintendent in charge of curriculum and curriculum research, 1957-66; University of Pennsylvania, Philadelphia, associate professor, 1965-70, professor of education, 1970—, coordinator of language in education program. Instructor at Kutztown State College, summer, 1952, Trenton State College, 1953 and 1956, Pennsylvania State University, 1954-60, and University of Pennsylvania, summer, 1960, associate professor, summer, 1965. Chairman of board of directors of Botel/Sheppard Associates; member of board of directors of Curriculum Development Associates. Member of Pennsylvania State Reading Committee, 1957-60, and Pennsylvania State Curriculum Commission, 1958-60. *Military service:* U.S. Navy, 1943-46.

MEMBER: International Reading Association (member of Bucks County council, 1962—; president, 1962-63), American Educational Research Association, National Education Association, National Council of Teachers of English, National Council of Teachers of Mathematics, Association for Supervision and Curriculum Development, Delaware Valley Reading Association (president, 1956-57), Pennsylvania State Education Association, Pennsylvania Association for Supervision and Curriculum Development, Phi Delta Kappa. *Awards, honors:* D.H.L. from Rider College, 1977.

WRITINGS: Predicting Readability Levels, Follett, 1963; *How to Teach Reading,* Follett, 1972; (with Alvin Granowsky) *The Syntactic Complexity Formula,* Graduate School of Education, University of Pennsylvania, 1973; (with Ralph C. Preston) *The Study Habits Checklist,* Science Research Associates, 1974; (with son, Neil E. Botel) *A Critical Analysis of the Taxonomy of Educational Objectives,* Curriculum Development Associates, 1975; *Forming and Re-Forming the Reading/Language Arts Curriculum,* Curriculum Development Associates, 1975; (with JoAnn Seaver) *Literacy Plus,* Curriculum Development Associates, 1977; (with Seaver) *Parent Aid in Reading,* Curriculum Development Associates, 1977; (with Seaver) *Making Friends With Books,* Curriculum Development Associates, 1978; *Botel Reading Inventory: Word Opposites, Word Recognition, Phonics Inventory, Spelling Placement Test,* Follett, 1978; *Botel Milestone Tests,* Botel/Sheppard Associates, 1979.

Juveniles: *Interesting Reading Series,* ten volumes, Penns Valley Publishers, 1959; *Beginning to Read Books,* ten volumes, Follett, 1962; (with John Dawkins) *Communicating: Games for Communicating, Sentences for Communicating,* Heath, 1973; (with Cora Holsclaw, Aileen Brothers, and Gloria Cammarota) *Spelling and Writing Patterns I-VI, 3140 Important Words,*

1120 Power Words, Follett, 1975; *Bantam Bookbins: Levels E-J for Grades Five to Twelve,* Bantam, 1975; (with J. Seaver) *CDA Reading: Syllabary, Groundwork, Patterns, Explorations, Bookshops (A.B.C.), Up Beat Bookshop, Games for Reading and Communication,* Curriculum Development Associates, 1977; *Skylark Collections,* Bantam, 1977; (with Seaver, Paul Rozin, and Lila Gleitman) *The Syllabary,* Curriculum Development Associates, 1977; (with Seaver) *Language Arts Phonics,* Botel/Sheppard Associates, 1980; (with daughter, Bonnie Botel-Sheppard, Robert Botel-Sheppard, and Robert Stokes) *Testwiseness Comprehension,* Botel/Sheppard Associates, 1980; (with R. C. Preston) *Ways to Read, Write, Study: Science,* Botel/Sheppard Associates, 1980; (with Preston, Katherine Connor, and Joan Willens) *Ways to Read, Write, Study: Social Studies,* Botel/Sheppard Associates, 1980; (with Preston) *How to Study,* Science Research Associates, 1981.

Contributor: *Frontiers of Elementary Education,* Syracuse University Press, 1957; *Controversial Issues in Reading,* Bureau of Educational Services, Lehigh University, 1961; *Books in the Schools,* American Book Publishers Council, 1961; *Frontiers of Education,* Educational Records Bureau, 1962; Albert J. Mazurciewicz, editor, *New Perspectives in Reading Instruction,* Pittman Publishing, 1964; *Perspectives on the Instructional Dimensions Study,* National Institute of Education, 1978. Contributor to education journals.

WORK IN PROGRESS: Research on early acquisition of reading ability, holistic evaluation, and adult basic literacy.

* * *

BOTTOMLY, Heath 1919-

PERSONAL: Born September 30, 1919, in Chinook, Mont.; son of Raymond Victor (an attorney) and Mouriel (an artist; maiden name, Heath) Bottomly; married Elizabeth Simpson (a Bible teacher), July 5, 1945; children: Roc, Viki Bottomly McHugh, Kirk, Sheri Bottomly Carlson, Kris Bottomly Hurst. *Education:* University of Montana, B.A., 1941; U.S. Military Academy, B.S., 1944; George Washington University, M.A., 1963. *Religion:* Nondenominational Christian. *Home:* Spring Hill Ranch, 12460 Irwin Way, Boulder Creek, Calif. 95006.

CAREER: U.S. Air Force, career officer, 1944-74, fighter pilot, flight leader, and squadron commander in Pacific theater, 1944-48, curriculum planner at Air University, 1948-52, staff officer of Joint Chiefs of Staff and assistant to chairman of Joint Chiefs of Staff, 1952-56, attended Royal Air Force Staff College, Bracknel, England, 1956-57, director of operations of British Third Air Force, 1957-60, assistant secretary of Joint Chiefs of Staff, 1960-64, deputy commander of Nellis Air Force Base in Nevada, and chief of F-105 combat training, 1964-67, combat wing commander in Vietnam and Thailand, 1967-70, chief of combat readiness inspections and inspector general, 1970-74, special intelligence observer during Arab-Israeli war, operations director of nuclear alert force of 81st Tactical Fighter Wing in Europe and North Africa, retiring as colonel; associated with Campus Crusade for Christ International; currently associate staff member of Military Ministry. Public speaker. *Awards, honors*—Military: Four Legions of Merit, two Distinguished Flying Crosses, seventeen Air Medals. Other: Bronze award, 1974, for film ''A Warlord Meets Christ.''

WRITINGS: Prodigal Father (autobiography), Regal Books, 1975. Author of films ''A Warlord Meets Christ'' and ''The Conversion of Colonel Bottomly.''

WORK IN PROGRESS: Boys, Boys, Boys; Giants; In Pursuit of Excellence.

SIDELIGHTS: Bottomly, "the warlord of Southeast Asia," commented on his works in progress: "*Boys, Boys, Boys* is an experiential development on how to raise boys *right*. It will focus on the importance of raising sons with loving toughness and discipline, drawing on the methods and experiences of my father, who raised seven sons and got seven Eagle Scouts. *Giants* is a discussion of the unique elements that make great men great. *In Pursuit of Excellence* includes observations from my travels (two hundred fifty thousand miles a year), and hopeful evidence that the common people of America are turning this country around and going back to the old traditional standards of excellence in work, service, study, and home discipline."

* * *

BOTTOMS, David 1949-

PERSONAL: Born September 11, 1949, in Canton, Ga.; son of David H. (a funeral director) and Louise (a registered nurse; maiden name, Ashe) Bottoms; married Margaret Lynn Bensel, February 5, 1972. *Education:* Mercer University, B.A., 1971; West Georgia College, M.A., 1973; doctoral study at Florida State University, 1979—. *Home:* 3708 B Rockbrook Rd., Tallahassee, Fla. 32301. *Agent:* Maria Carvainis Agency, 235 West End Ave., New York, N.Y. 10023. *Office:* Florida State University, P.O. Box 5866, Tallahassee, Fla. 32313.

CAREER: High school teacher of English in Douglasville, Ga., 1974-78. *Member:* International P.E.N. *Awards, honors:* Walt Whitman Award from Academy of American Poets, 1979, for *Shooting Rats at the Bibb County Dump*.

WRITINGS: Jamming With the Band at the VFW (poetry chapbook), Burnt Hickory Press, 1978; *Shooting Rats at the Bibb County Dump* (poetry), Morrow, 1980.

Work represented in anthologies, including *Traveling America With Today's Poets,* edited by David Kherdian, Macmillan, 1977; *A Geography of Poets,* edited by Edward Field, Bantam, 1979; *Contemporary Southern Poetry,* edited by Guy Owen and Mary C. Williams, 1979. Contributor to magazines, including *Atlantic Monthly, Harper's, Poetry, American Poetry Review, Paris Review,* and *Antaeus.*

WORK IN PROGRESS: Rest at the Mercy House, poems.

SIDELIGHTS: According to Robert Penn Warren, "David Bottoms is a strong poet, and much of his strength emerges from the fact that he is temperamentally a realist. In his vision the actual world is not transformed but illuminated." Warren was the judge for the 1979 Walt Whitman Award, which was won by Bottoms.

Bottoms commented: "I am interested in many other things besides poetry, especially sports and music. A lot of my time is spent hunting and fishing. I also play a lot of golf, and used to play a lot of baseball. Though I don't play music regularly any more, a whole lot of my life has been spent playing guitar and banjo in bluegrass and country and western bands. Most of my poetry comes from these experiences and other non-academic pursuits. That's the way I believe it should be."

BIOGRAPHICAL/CRITICAL SOURCES: New York Times, April 20, 1979; *Macon Telegraph and News,* September 16, 1979, May 13, 1981; *Atlanta Journal and Constitution,* May 11, 1980; *Florida Flambeau,* June 3, 1980; *St. Petersburg Times,* August 3, 1980; *Chicago Tribune Book World,* August 17, 1980.

BOUTILIER, Mary A(nn) 1943-

PERSONAL: Born November 29, 1943, in Houlton, Maine; daughter of Lloyd George (a plumber) and Mary (McKinnon) Boutilier. *Education:* St. Joseph College, West Hartford, Conn., B.A., 1966; graduate study at University of Michigan, 1969; Georgetown University, Ph.D., 1974. *Home:* 175 Prospect St., Apt. 20A, East Orange, N.J. 07017. *Office:* Department of Political Science, Seton Hall University, South Orange, N.J. 07079.

CAREER: Seton Hall University, South Orange, N.J., instructor, 1970-74, assistant professor, 1974-78, associate professor of political science, 1978—, chairperson of department, 1977—, chairperson of collective bargaining agent of faculty, 1979-80, representative to Harry S Truman Fellowship Foundation, 1979-80. Administrative intern at Kean College, 1977; guest on radio and television programs. *Member:* North American Society for the Sociology of Sport, American Political Science Association, American Association of University Professors (vice-chairperson of local chapter, 1977), Women's Equity Action League, Northeastern Political Science Association, New Jersey Political Science Association (member of executive committee, 1977-79), Pi Sigma Alpha, Kappa Gamma Pi.

WRITINGS: (With Rita Mae Kelly) *The Making of Political Women: A Study of Socialization and Role Conflict,* Nelson-Hall, 1978. Contributor to *Sex Roles: A Journal of Research.* Member of editorial board of *Polity: Journal of the Northeastern Political Science Association,* 1979—.

WORK IN PROGRESS: The Sporting Woman, with Lucinda San Giovanni, publication expected in 1982.

SIDELIGHTS: Mary Boutilier wrote: "I am very concerned about the progress of women and minorities. It was out of interest in the promotion of women into nontraditional roles that I began the study of women and politics. Precisely because women have not traditionally been political, I thought it important to study those women who had been. Instead of studying the typical apolitical women, Rita Kelly and I researched the socialization and background of thirty-six political women. We attempted to get a wide range of political activity; thus, the women range from those for whom the only political act was marrying a political man, for example Yvonne De Gaulle, to women who became involved in politics on their own and reached the heights of political power, e.g. Golda Meir.

"One of the factors that emerged from the study of political women was the high incidence of sporting activity by political women. Sports was also another love of my own. It seemed only appropriate to investigate the position of women in yet another nontraditional area. Along with Lucinda San Giovanni, one of the first women in the country to offer a course in the sociology of sport, I began to review the literature on women and sport and continued my extensive involvement in softball, tennis, golf, basketball, and other sports. From this research and activity, Lucinda and I attempted to apply a feminist framework to understanding the position of women in sports. This framework has helped us become aware of both the good aspects of sports—those that women should emulate—and the bad—those pitfalls of sport as played by men that women should avoid. It is to this distinction that *The Sporting Woman* is addressed."

* * *

BOUVIER, Leon F(rancis) 1922-

PERSONAL: Born February 24, 1922, in Moosup, Conn.; son

of Stanislas (a physician) and Rose (Donais) Bouvier; married Theresa Fallon (a nurse), February 19, 1944; children: Thomas, Lynne Bouvier Graham, Linda Bouvier Finnegan, Kenneth. *Education:* Spring Hill College, B.S. (cum laude), 1961; Brown University, M.A., 1963, Ph.D., 1971. *Politics:* Liberal Democrat. *Home:* 2051 North Woodstock St., Arlington, Va. 22207. *Office:* Population Reference Bureau, 1754 N St., Washington, D.C. 20006.

CAREER: Siena College, Loudonville, N.Y., instructor in sociology and chairman of department, 1963-65; University of Scranton, Scranton, Pa., assistant professor of sociology, 1965-66; University of Rhode Island, Kingston, 1966-76, began as instructor, became associate professor of sociology; Population Reference Bureau, Washington, D.C., vice-president, 1975-76. Visiting assistant professor at Georgetown University, summer, 1966 (professional lecturer, 1972-73), and University of Massachusetts, summer, 1967; research associate at Institute for Cuba and the Caribbean, University of Miami, Coral Gables, Fla., 1971-73; workshop director. Member of board of social science advisers of Center for Information on America, 1975-76; consultant to Oak Ridge National Laboratory, U.S. Committee on Vital and Health Statistics, and Federal Interagency Committee on Education.

MEMBER: World Population Society, International Union for the Scientific Study of Population, American Sociological Association, Population Association of America, American Association of University Professors, Southern Regional Demographic Group, New England Universities Demographic Research Association (member of board of directors).

WRITINGS: An Ethnic Profile of Rhode Island: 1960 (monograph), University of Rhode Island, 1968; *Workbook and Reader in Sociology* (monograph), McCutchan, 1968, 2nd edition, 1971; *The Negro in Rhode Island: A Demographic Analysis* (monograph), University of Rhode Island, 1969; (with Everett S. Lee) *Population Profiles* (monographs), Center for Information on America, 1972-75; (with S.L.N. Rao) *Socio-Religious Factors in Fertility Decline,* Ballinger, 1975. Also author, with R. Weller, of *Introduction to Population Studies* and *Workbook and Reader in Population Studies,* both for Wadsworth.

Contributor: *The Family in Transition: A Round Table Conference,* U.S. Government Printing Office, 1970; W. C. Bier, editor, *Aging: Its Challenge to the Individual and to Society,* Fordham University Press, 1974; A. Richmond and D. Kebat, editors, *Internal Migration: The New World and the Third World,* Sage Publications, 1976. Also contributor to *Hidden Minorities,* edited by Joan Rollins, Ramparts. Contributor of about twenty-five articles to sociology, demography, and political science journals.

* * *

BOWEN, Edmund (John) 1898-1980

OBITUARY NOTICE: Born April 28, 1898, in Worcester, England; died November 19, 1980. Photochemist and author best known for his work in the quantum analysis of photochemical reactions. Attending Balliol College, Oxford, on a Brackenbury Scholarship, Bowen obtained his B.A. and M.A. before transferring to University College, Oxford, in 1922 and earning his D.Sc. there in 1947. During experiments to develop methods for the quantum determination of light yields from the decomposition of phosphorous and chlorine oxides, the photochemist designed the fluorescent quantum counter, a device which made possible the first quantitative measurement of alternative photochemical reaction pathways. Elected to the Royal Society of London in 1935, Bowen served as Aldrichian Prae-

lector in Chemistry at University College from 1952 to 1965, at which time he was elected an honorary fellow of the college. Bowens's other honors include a Davy Medal in 1963 and the Niels Finsen Medal in 1968. Among his writings are *The Chemical Aspects of Light* and *Luminescence in Chemistry.* He also co-wrote *The Fluorescence of Solutions* and edited *Recent Progress in Photobiology.* Obituaries and other sources: *The Annual Obituary 1980,* St. Martin's, 1981.

* * *

BOWEN, (Ivor) Ian 1908-
(Charles Hogarth, a joint pseudonym)

PERSONAL: Born December 3, 1908, in Cardiff, Wales; son of Ivor (a judge) and Edith May (Dummett) Bowen; married Erica Baillie, June 1, 1934 (divorced, 1950); married Isobel Margaret Lindsay Smith (an economic analyst), September 17, 1951; children: Sarah Bowen Mason, Ivor Richard, David Lindsay, Frances Margaret. *Education:* Christ Church, Oxford, B.A., 1930, M.A., 1934. *Politics:* "Uncommitted parliamentary democrat." *Religion:* Agnostic. *Home address:* Xalet Verena, La Massana, Andorra.

CAREER: Oxford University, Oxford, England, fellow of All Souls College, 1930-37, lecturer at Brasenose College, 1931-40; Ministry of Works, chief statistical officer, 1940-45; Oxford University, Hertford College, lecturer, 1946-47; University of Hull, Hull, England, professor of economics and commerce, 1947-58; University of Western Australia, Nedlands, professor of economics, 1958-73; International Bank for Reconstruction and Development, Washington, D.C., economist and editor, 1972-74; associated with International Monetary Fund, 1974-77; writer, 1977—. Visiting professor at University of California, Berkeley, 1955; fellow of All Souls College, Oxford, 1968. Consultant with Fenners Ltd., 1950-79. *Member:* Royal Economic Society, British Institute of Management (founding member), American Economic Association, Australian Academy of Social Sciences (fellow), Reform Club.

WRITINGS: Cobden, Duckworth, 1934; *Britain's Industrial Survival,* Faber, 1947; (contributor) D.N. Chester, editor, *Lessons of the British War Economy,* Cambridge University Press, 1951; *Population,* Cambridge University Press, 1954; *Seven Lectures on Manpower Planning With Special Reference to Thailand,* University of Western Australia, 1967; *Acceptable Inequalities,* Allen & Unwin, 1970; *Economics and Demography,* Allen & Unwin, 1976. Also author of *Largo Island,* with John Creasey under joint pseudonym Charles Hogarth. Editor of *Oxford University Bulletin of Statistics,* 1940-41, and *Finance and Development,* 1974-77.

WORK IN PROGRESS: Research on population and economic development; a survey of current world political and economic trends (especially European).

SIDELIGHTS: Bowen commented: "My main academic interests are the political economy of capital formation, economic development, and population change (especially through internal and external migration), in addition to a special interest in economic and social statistics. I have sought to assess the imponderables that elude statistical measures by sojorns in different Asian, American, and European societies. As an educator, I have sought to simplify difficult arguments. I have not wanted to propound doctrines or even to disseminate facts, but I want people to become intelligently and critically more aware both of facts and doctrines. A lifetime education is valuable for itself and may often contribute to material progress."

BIOGRAPHICAL/CRITICAL SOURCES: K. M. Kohan, *Works and Buildings,* H.M.S.O., 1952; M. C. Fleming, *Construction and the Related Professions,* Pergamon, 1980.

* * *

BOWEN, Joshua David 1930-

PERSONAL—Education: Graduated from Harvard University.

CAREER: Worked as stage actor and director; associated with newspaper in Raleigh, N.C.; served with Foreign Political Association; owner of out-of-print bookstore in San Antonio, Tex., 1972—; Corona Publishing Co., San Antonio, founder and owner, 1977—.

WRITINGS—For children: *The Land and People of Peru,* Lippincott, 1963, revised edition, 1973; *Hello South America,* Norton, 1964; *The Struggle Within,* Norton, 1965, revised edition, Grosset, 1972; *The Land and People of Chile,* Lippincott, 1966, revised edition, 1976; *Hello Brazil,* Norton, 1967; *The Island of Puerto Rico,* Lippincott, 1968. Editor of United Fruit Company's *Middle America.* Contributor to proceedings of the Academy of Political Science, 1970. Contributor of articles to magazines, including *National Observer, New York Times,* and *Reader's Digest.*

SIDELIGHTS: Of Bowen's book *The Struggle Within,* a critic for the *New York Times Book Review* wrote: "As an example of the new view that boys and girls are intellectual beings capable of following and enjoying the direct, uncute discussion of issues, Mr. Bowen's judicious analysis of the present racial crisis and its historical antecedents is good to find. . . . It is written with painstaking lucidity, [and] there is nothing primerish or condescending about it."

Bowen commented: "Although I am no longer writing, I am involved with books in every possible way. Since 1972 I have had an out-of-print bookstore in San Antonio, and in 1977 I established Corona Publishing Co., which produces 'books for use' that are distributed mostly in Texas. One of these books is *Digging Into South Texas Pre-history: A Guide for Amateur Archaeologists,* by Dr. Thomas R. Hester, with a preface by John Graves."

BIOGRAPHICAL/CRITICAL SOURCES: New York Times Book Review, January 23, 1966.

* * *

BOWERS, Mary Beacom 1932-

PERSONAL: Born May 22, 1932, in Hamilton, Ohio; daughter of Howard C. (in manufacturing) and Henrietta (Klenke) Alspaugh; married John Bliss Beacom (died June, 1969); married David Bowers, July 6, 1972 (died March, 1976); children: (first marriage) Susanna. *Education:* University of North Carolina, A.B., 1954; Kent State University, doctoral study, 1971-74, M.A., 1978. *Home:* 409 Fort St., Marietta, Ohio 45750. *Office:* Pardson Corp., 306 Warren St., Marietta, Ohio 45750.

CAREER: Kent State University, Kent, Ohio, lecturer in English, 1970-75; part-time English teacher in Louisville, Ky., 1975-78; Pardson Corp., Marietta, Ohio, editor of *Bird Watcher's Digest,* 1978—. Librarian and registrar at Akron Art Institute. *Member:* American Society of Magazine Editors, National Organization for Women, National Audubon Society, Modern Language Association of America, American Civil Liberties Union.

WRITINGS: (Editor) *Stories About Birds and Bird Watchers,* Atheneum, 1981. Contributor to academic journals.

WORK IN PROGRESS: An ornithological anthology, publication by Atheneum expected in 1983.

SIDELIGHTS: Bowers told *CA:* "I have selected thirty-eight exciting and poignant stories from the pages of the popular *Bird Watcher's Digest,* interspersed with twenty attractive black-and-white illustrations by national wildlife artist Bob Hines. The cover features Robert Bateman's full-color painting of a downy woodpecker, and Roger Tory Peterson has written the foreword.

"The stories range in subject matter from methods of keeping a clean bird list to birding in the Aleutians to reflections on extinction. They are full of humor, adventure, and philosophy. Contributors include Roger Tory Peterson on penguins, Olin Sewall Pettingill, Jr., on birding in the Antarctic, Faith McNulty on raising a baby starling, and Peter Dunne on hawk watching in New Jersey.

"The Birding Book Society called *Stories About Birds and Bird Watchers* 'a zestful, enchanting testamonial to nature's graceful aviators and to the hardy watchers who follow them,'" said Bowers.

AVOCATIONAL INTERESTS: Modern fiction and literature, films, political and social issues, the environment.

* * *

BOWMAN, Clell Edgar 1904-

PERSONAL: Born April 13, 1904, in Aredale, Iowa; son of Heber Charles and Nellie (Barber) Bowman; married Grace Eileen Snapp, June 15, 1935 (deceased); children: Alan Anthony, June Carol Bowman Zufelt, Barry Charles. *Education:* University of California, Berkeley, B.Sc., 1926; attended Harvard University, 1928-29. *Home:* 410 Merritt Ave., No. 9, Oakland, Calif. 94610. *Office:* Aquarius Aquarium, 4200 Park Blvd., Oakland, Calif. 94602.

CAREER: Eastman Kodak Co., Rochester, N.Y., chemist, 1926-27; Shell Development Co., Emeryville, Calif., assistant chemist, 1929-30; Bowman Laboratories, Richmond, Calif., manager, 1930-31; worked for Ford Motor Co., Richmond, and American Chemical Products Co., Rochester, N.Y., 1931-35; Garlock Packing Co., Palmyra, N.Y., chemist, 1935-47; worked for Stanford Research Institute, American Radiator, Chevron Chemical, Griffin Chemical, and Nopco Chemical, 1947-58; Foremost Chemical Products Co., Oakland, Calif., development chemist, 1958-65; Great Western Chemical Co., Richmond, general chemist, 1965-79; Aquarius Aquarium, Oakland, storekeeper, 1979—.

WRITINGS: *A Baptism of Fire* (novel), Arthur H. Stockwell, 1942; *Bold Steer* (novel), Branden Press, 1974; *Male Order* (mystery), Exposition Press, 1976; *Human Equation* (mystery), Exposition Press, 1976; *The Bereaved Husband* (novel), Exposition Press, 1976; *Crossexion* (novel), Exposition Press, 1976; *Saturday's Child* (novel), Exposition Press, 1976; *Hoarse Laughs That Grab You* (jokes), Clelboman Book, 1978.

WORK IN PROGRESS: Pirouette, a novel of age and youth; *Highway Robbery,* a crime novel; *The Avocado,* nonfiction.

AVOCATIONAL INTERESTS: Avocado growing, freshwater tropical fish.

* * *

BOZARTH-CAMPBELL, Alla (Linda Renee) 1947-

PERSONAL: Born May 15, 1947, in Portland, Ore.; daughter of Rene Malcom (a clergyman) and Alvina (a writer; maiden name, Heckel) Bozarth; married Philip Campbell (a clergyman), September 12, 1971. *Education:* Northwestern University, B.S.S., 1971, M.A., 1972, Ph.D., 1974. *Politics:* Democrat. *Residence:* Minneapolis, Minn.

CAREER: Ordained Episcopal priest, 1974; Wisdom House, Inc. (center for feminist and holistic spirituality), Minneapolis, Minn., director and psychotherapist, 1975—. Lecturer in feminist theology, religion, and the arts; teacher of oral interpretation. Member of advisory board of Fellowship of Christian Ministries. *Member:* National Association of Women's Studies, Speech Communication Association. *Awards, honors:* Academy of American Poets award, 1969 and 1971.

WRITINGS: Womanpriest: A Personal Odyssey, Paulist Press, 1978; *Gynergy,* Wisdom House, 1978; *In the Name of the Bee and the Bear and the Butterfly,* Wisdom House, 1978; *The Word's Body: An Incarnational Aesthetic of Interpretation,* University of Alabama Press, 1979. Contributor of articles to journals, including *Contemplative Review, St. Paul's Printer,* and *Sisters Today.* Member of editorial board of *Contemplative Review.*

WORK IN PROGRESS: Life Is Goodbye/Life Is Hello: Grieving Well Through All Kinds of Loss; Love's Prism: A Woman's Perspective, an unpublished manuscript; *My Body's Wood Is Bone: Collected Poems, 1970-1980.*

SIDELIGHTS: In 1974 Bozarth-Campbell was one of eleven women ordained as Episcopal priests. Four bishops who had lost patience with church traditions prohibiting females from rising above the rank of deacon performed the ordination, which was later declared invalid by the Episcopal House of Bishops. Bozarth-Campbell's *Womanpriest: A Personal Odyssey* is an autobiographical account of the controversial events surrounding her ordination and her role in the feminist movement. *Commonweal* critic Francine Cardman appraised the book as "a fascinating document in the growing dossier of the confrontation of feminism and the churches."

Bozarth-Campbell told *CA:* "The most significant experience in my life was my ordination to the priesthood of the Episcopal Church along with ten other women on July 29, 1974, in Philadelphia, a history-making event. From this came my work, *Womanpriest.* My vocation to poetry (since the age of thirteen) led me to my doctorate in oral interpretation, speech, and drama, and to the scholarly book, the *Word's Body. Life Is Goodbye* and *Love's Prism* emerge from my work as a feminist and gestalt therapist. The poetry collections are all of my life, a direct celebration of the unity between life and art."

BIOGRAPHICAL/CRITICAL SOURCES: Newsweek, August 12, 1974, August 26, 1974; *Time,* August 12, 1974, August 26, 1974; *Christian Century,* September 4, 1974, February 20, 1980; *Commonweal,* August 31, 1979.

*   *   *

BRADFORD, Leroy   1922-

PERSONAL: Born November 24, 1922, in Valedon, N.M.; daughter of John W. (a rancher) and Roberta (a teacher; maiden name, Noling) Guess; married William F. Morgan, February 14, 1940 (divorced, 1965); married Kenneth Bradford (a machinist), January 20, 1971; children: Alice May Morgan, David Morgan. *Education:* Attended Eastern Arizona College, 1939-41, and Highline Community College, Midway, Wash., 1979-80. *Politics:* "Not interested." *Religion:* Atheist. *Home:* 3511 South St., Seattle, Wash. 98188.

CAREER: Southern Pacific Railroad, Tucson, Ariz., agent and telegrapher, 1941-50; Missouri Pacific Railroad, Little Rock,

Ark., centralized traffic control operator, 1950-53; Seattle Public Library, Seattle, Wash., library clerk, 1962-64· U.S. Peace Corps, volunteer in Brasilia, Brazil, 1965-68; *Seattle Times,* Seattle, library clerk, 1968-71; State of Washington, Seattle, clerk and typist, 1974-78. *Member:* Mensa, Phi Theta Kappa.

WRITINGS: Staying Awake: More Fun Than Sleeping, Adams Press, 1981, 2nd edition, 1982.

SIDELIGHTS: Leroy Bradford commented: "I presently have a life-style based on being awake twenty-one hours a day. I have been experimenting for several years with ways of cutting down on my sleep requirements. My book, *Staying Awake,* gives full details how anyone can add from three to five hours a day to their 'awake-time.' The method I have developed for teaching the body to compress its sleeping time is based on scientific research into the phases of sleep. I am fully convinced that some day, with the aid of electronic sleep devices, anyone who wants to can spend only ten minutes a day sleeping."

AVOCATIONAL INTERESTS: Oil painting, wine making, writing, plant mutations, reading.

BIOGRAPHICAL/CRITICAL SOURCES: Record Chronicle (Renton, Wash.), October 12, 1981.

*   *   *

BRADLEY, Alfred   1925-

PERSONAL: Born December 15, 1925, in London, England; son of Alfred Watson and Winifred Daisy Bradley; married Judith Tegetmeier, November 7, 1953; children: Jeremy, Simon, Petra, Alison, Jonathan, Rachel. *Education:* Attended University College, Oxford. *Politics:* "Left of center." *Religion:* Agnostic. *Home:* 274 High St., Boston Spa, Yorkshire, England. *Agent:* Harvey Unna, Harvey Unna & Stephen Durbridge Ltd., 14 Beaumont Mews, Marylebone High St., London W1N 4HE, England. *Office:* British Broadcasting Corp., New Broadcasting House, Oxford Rd., Manchester, England.

CAREER: Theatrical producer, 1950-54; County of Leicestershire, England, drama adviser, 1954-59; British Broadcasting Corp., Manchester, England, senior radio producer, 1959—. *Awards, honors:* Gold award for distinguished service from Society of Authors, 1980.

WRITINGS—Editor: Worth a Hearing (radio plays), Blackie & Son, 1967; *You and Me* (plays), Blakie & Son, 1973; *Out of the Air* (radio plays), Longman, 1978; (with Kay Jamison) *Dandelion Clocks: Stories of Childhood,* M. Joseph, 1978; *The Northern Drift* (poems and prose), Blackie & Son, 1980. Also editor of *In a Few Words* (stories).

Published plays: (With Stan Barstow) *Ask Me Tomorrow* (based on novel by Barstow), Samuel French, 1966; *The Tale of the Red Dragon* (for children; see also below) Dobson, 1972; *The Wizard of Oz* (for children; adapted from the novel by L. Frank Baum; see also below), Dobson, 1972; (with Barstow) *Stringer's Last Stand,* Samuel French, 1972; (with Michael Bond) *Paddington on Stage* (collection of seven short plays; adapted from Bond's play "The Adventures of Paddington"), Houghton, c. 1974; *The Scatterbrained Scarecrow of Oz* (for children) Dobson, 1976; (with Alex Glasgow) *The Emperor and the Nightingale* (musical for children; adapted from story by Hans Christian Andersen; see also below), Dobson, 1978.

Other plays: "Quartet for Harps"; "Better Halves"; "A Kind of Loving."

Television scripts: "Jackanory Playhouse" (for children); "Just Good Friends"; "No Experience Necessary"; "The Tale of the Red Dragon"; "The Emperor and the Nightingale."

Radio scripts: (Co-author) "Wish You Were Here"; (co-author) "Come to the Fair"; "The Wizard of Oz"; (with Barstow) "Stringer's Last Stand."

*   *   *

BRADLEY, Matt 1947-

PERSONAL: Born January 16, 1947, in Memphis, Tenn.; son of Don M. (an insurance salesman) and Mildred (Andrews) Bradley; married Susan Cloninger (a telephone company manager), November 27, 1976. *Education:* United States Air Force Academy, B.S., 1969. *Home:* 7920 Harmon Dr., Little Rock, Ark. 72207.

CAREER: Free-lance photojournalist, 1975—. President of Bradley Publishing, Inc., 1981—. *Military service:* U.S. Air Force, 1969-74; became captain. *Member:* National Press Photographers Association.

WRITINGS: Matt Bradley's Arkansas (photography), Rose Publishing (Little Rock, Ark.), 1975; *Arkansas, Its Land and People* (photography), Museum of Science and History (Little Rock), 1980; *The Hogs: Moments Remembered* (photography), Bradley Publishing, 1981. Contributor of photographs to numerous magazines, including *American Illustrated, American Heritage, Boy's Life, Exploring, Flying, Forbes, Newsweek,* and *National Geographic.*

SIDELIGHTS: Matt Bradley told *CA:* "My publishing philosophy is the same as that on my photography—to produce the highest quality work possible."

*   *   *

BRADY, Lillian 1902-

PERSONAL: Born February 5, 1902, in Eagle Grove, Iowa; daughter of Andrew and JoAnna Christensen; married DeLisle Brady (an artist and clothier), June 14, 1923; children: Ruth Anne Bredenberg. *Education:* Graduated from Mankato Business College, 1920. *Politics:* Republican. *Religion:* Methodist. *Home:* 522 Andrews, Nashua, Iowa 50658.

CAREER: Writer. Lindeke, Warner & Sons (wholesalers of dry goods and manufacturers), St. Paul, Minn., assistant advertising manager, 1921-1923; manager and buyer for family-owned clothing store, Nashua, Iowa, 1936-1955. Author-in-residence, St. Paul, Minn., school system, 1973; visiting lecturer in University of Minnesota, summers, 1972 and 1973. *Member:* National League of American Pen Women (president, 1976-77), Order of the Eastern Star (worthy matron, 1940), Isabella Federatis Club. *Awards, honors:* Dorothy Canfield Fisher Award nomination, 1973, and Blue Flame Ecology Award of Minnesota, 1974, both for *Aise-Ce-Bon, a Raccoon.*

WRITINGS: Aise-Ce-Bon, a Raccoon (juvenile; illustrated by Jerome Connolly), Harvey House, 1971; *Saga of a Whitetail Deer* (juvenile), Amber Crest, 1981.

WORK IN PROGRESS: The Clock Who Wanted to Be a Friend; Wilderness Acres, "a book covering thirty years of experience and adventure at our wilderness acres in northern Minnesota"; also doing research on foxes, "one of the most misunderstood animals."

SIDELIGHTS: Lillian Brady cites her hope that "children will have a better understanding of preserving wildlife and conserving its habitat" as her major objective in writing nature stories for young people. According to Brady, Harvard University has commended her books not only for their literary merit, but for their scientific worth as well.

Brady's books grow directly out of her and her husband's concern for and contact with nature. "When the state refuge in Minnesota was opened to hunting," she explained, "we acquired land and created our own refuge for the birds and animals." Brady frequently speaks to young people, illustrating her lectures with wildlife slides and photographs.

*   *   *

BRAHAM, Allan (John Witney) 1937-

PERSONAL: Born August 19, 1937, in Croydon, Surrey, England; son of Dudley and Florence (Mears) Braham; married Helen Clare Butterworth, June 15, 1963; children: Lucy, Sophy. *Education:* Courtauld Institute of Art, London, B.A., 1960, Ph.D., 1967. *Home:* 6c Belsize Park Gardens, London NW3 4LD, England. *Office:* National Gallery, Trafalgar Sq., London WC2N 5DN, England.

CAREER: National Gallery, London, England, assistant keeper, 1962-73, deputy keeper, 1973-78, keeper and deputy director, 1978—, coordinator of exhibitions.

WRITINGS: Durer, Spring Art Books, 1965; *Murillo,* Purnell, 1966; (editor of revision) Neil Maclaren, *The Spanish School,* 2nd edition (Braham was not associated with 1st edition), National Gallery, 1971; *The National Gallery in London: Italian Painting of the Italian Renaissance,* Knorr & Hirth, 1971; *Rubens,* National Gallery, 1974; (with Peter Smith) *Francois Mansart,* two volumes, Zwemmer, 1975; "The Rokeby Venus," *Velazquez,* National Gallery, 1976; (with Hellmut Hager) *Carlo Fontana: The Drawings at Windsor Castle,* Zwemmer, 1978; *The Architecture of the French Enlightenment,* University of California Press, 1980; *The National Gallery Lends Italian Renaissance Portraits: Catalogue of an Exhibition Organised in Conjunction With the Arts Council of Great Britain,* National Gallery, 1980. Also author of *High Renaissance Painting,* National Gallery, *Giovanni Battista Moroni,* 1978, and *Italian Renaissance Portraits,* 1979. Contributor to scholarly journals.

*   *   *

BRANCH, Alan E(dward) 1933-

PERSONAL: Born January 10, 1933, in London, England; son of Leslie (a cashier) and Gertrude (a secretary; maiden name, Bartlett) Branch; married Kathleen Debenham (a district nurse), March 5, 1960; children: David Alan, Anna Louise. *Education:* Attended City of London College, 1952-55. *Home:* 19 The Ridings, Emmer Green, Reading, Berkshire, England.

CAREER: Shipping executive with Sealink Ltd.; consultant on shipping and export matters for British Board of Trade, 1975-1981, and for other organizations. Lecturer at University of London Center for Business Studies, Reading College of Technology, and City and East London College. *Member:* Chartered Institute of Transport (fellow), Institute of Export (fellow).

WRITINGS: The Elements of Shipping, Chapman & Hall, 1964, 5th edition, 1981; *A Dictionary of Shipping/International Trade Terms and Abbreviations,* Witherby, 1976, 2nd edition, 1983; *The Elements of Export Practice,* Methuen, 1979; *The Economics of Shipping Practice and Management,* foreword by T. Bolton, Chapman & Hall, 1982; *The Elements of Export Marketing,* Chapman & Hall, in press.

SIDELIGHTS: Branch commented that *The Elements of Shipping,* on sale in nearly a hundred countries, was "the first book to be published in the United Kingdom embracing the economic, political, commercial, and operating aspects of shipping."

"I believe that education in shipping and international trade is very important to increasing professionalism in this area. Such professionalism is most essential to the provision of well-managed and operated services and the development of world trade and resources."

AVOCATIONAL INTERESTS: Sailing, cricket, walking.

* * *

BRANDES, Georg (Morris Cohen) 1842-1927

BRIEF ENTRY: Born February 4, 1842, in Copenhagen, Denmark; died February 19, 1927, in Copenhagen, Denmark. Danish historian, critic, and philosopher. After traveling in Europe, Brandes acquired a cosmopolitan outlook that made him reject the provincial backwardness of his native Denmark. In *Main Currents in Nineteenth Century Literature* (1872-90), he attacked the Danish educational and cultural establishment. His published demand for the right of free thought aroused much controversy and greatly influenced Danish literary expression. During the 1870's he began to believe that the individual person was more important than an idea or trend. In *Aristocratic Radicalism* (1889), Brandes first presented his theory of the "great personality." His dedication to Nietzsche's views of the hero led to a series of biographies, including the critically well-received *William Shakespeare* (1895-96). Brandes also believed that literature must deal with the problems of one's own time, and he turned his attention to contemporaries, both European and Danish. Through such works as *Men of the Modern Breakthrough* (1883), he introduced a series of emerging Danish writers to the rest of the world and assured Denmark's entry into the twentieth-century literary milieu. *Biographical/critical sources: Twentieth Century Authors: A Biographical Dictionary of Modern Literature,* H. W. Wilson, 1942, 1st supplement, 1955; *Encyclopedia of World Literature in the Twentieth Century,* updated edition, Ungar, 1967; B. Nolin, *Georg Brandes,* Twayne, 1976.

* * *

BRANDON, Johnny
(Francis Edwards, Ed Franks, Ricardo Martinelli, Gerry Rich)

PERSONAL: Born in the 1920's in London, England; permanent resident of United States; son of Edgar (an artist) and Florence (a teacher; maiden name, Brown) Brandon. *Education:* Attended private secondary schools in London, England; studied dance under Buddy Bradley and attended Guildhall School of Drama during 1940's. *Politics:* "Equal-opportunity-multi-racial-democracy." *Religion:* "No formal affiliation, but a believer." *Home:* 200 East 17th St., New York, N.Y. 10003. *Agent:* Robert Youdleman, 424 Madison Ave., New York, N.Y. 10017.

CAREER: Singer and dancer in British Variety since age of eleven; actor in films, including "The Young Mr. Pitt," 1942, and "The Day Will Dawn," and in stage plays, including "Love From Judy," 1952-54; lyricist and composer, 1949—. Recording artist, 1951-62; choreographer of British Broadcasting Corp. (BBC-TV) specials during 1950's; star of television series "Dreamer's Highway," BBC-TV, 1955; writer of special material for National Broadcasting Co. (NBC-TV) series "Hey Jeannie"; creator of nightclub acts. *Military service:* Served in British Army, Royal Signal Corps; in charge of Variety Department, British Forces Network in Germany; became sergeant. *Member:* American Guild of Authors and Composers, Dramatists Guild, Broadcast Music, Inc. *Awards,*

honors: Ivor Novello Award, 1957, for song "Your Love Is My Love"; Antoinette Perry ("Tony") Award nomination, 1979, for "Eubie!"; Audelco Award nominations, 1979, for "Suddenly the Music Starts," and 1980, for "The More You Get the More You Want."

WRITINGS—Lyricist and composer of songs for plays: "Dreams and Dreams Ago," "I Don't Care What They Say," "Oy, Oy, Oy, Oy, Sarah," "Paddling," "Sugar Hill Hattie," "Don't Sing," and "Maid to Measure" for Leigh Stafford's "Maid to Measure," first produced on the West End at Cambridge Theatre, 1950; "Once Upon a Time," "Let's Pretend," "Is There Something to What He Said?," "Papa, Let's Do It Again," "A Genuine Feminine Girl," "Cindy," "Think Mink," "Tonight's the Night," "Who Am I?," "If You've Got It, You've Got It," "The Life That I Planned for Him," "If It's Love," "Got the World in the Palm of My Hand," "Call Me Lucky," "Laugh It Up," and "What a Wedding" for Joe Sauter and Mike Sawyer's *Cindy* (first produced Off-Broadway at Gate Theatre, March 19, 1964; first produced on the West End at Fortune Theatre, 1965), Wemar Music, 1965.

"It Took a Long, Long Time," "Sing Me Sunshine," "Ruined," "Nothing Like a Friend," "Where Is 'Away,'" "Heavens to Betsy," "The Right Kind of People," and "Where Do I Stand" for Robert Emmet's "Peg," first produced in Valley Forge, Pa., 1967; "Island of Happiness," "That'll Be The Day," "Come-Along-a-Me, Babe," "Nothin's Gonna Change," "There Aren't Many Ladies in the Mile End Road," "Syncopatin'," "Voodoo," "How Do You Stop Loving Someone?," "Drums," "Feminine-inity," "That's What's Happening, Baby," "Me," and "Nobody to Cry To" for Guy Bolton and P. G. Wodehouse's *Who's Who, Baby?* (first produced Off-Broadway at Players Theatre, January 29, 1968), published by Tams-Witmark.

"King Joe," "Seduction," "Billy Noname," "Boychild," "A Different Drummer," "Look Through the Window," "It's Our Time Now," "Hello World," "At the End of the Day," "I Want to Live," "Manchild," "Color Me White," "We're Gonna Turn on Freedom," "Mother Earth," "Sit In—Wade In," "Movin'," "The Dream," "Black Boy," "Burn, Baby, Burn," "We Make a Promise," and "Get Your Slice of Cake" for William W. Mackey's "Billy Noname," first produced Off-Broadway at Truck and Warehouse Theatre, March 2, 1970; "Love! Love! Love!," "Power Driven Engine," "Liberal Blues," and others for "Love! Love! Love!" (revue), first produced in New York at Astor Place Theatre, 1977.

"Nothing Ever Happens in Greece," "Come on and Dance," "Somethin's Doin'," "Bring It on Home," "Bite Your Tongue," "There Are Ways of Gettin' Things Done," "Diplomacy," "You've Got It," "Do Us a Favor," "Dance of the Golden Apple," "Helen," "Hold On Tight," "Do What You Must Do," "Somebody Touched Me," "You Never Know the Mind of a Woman," "Good or Bad," and "Finale" from Lucia Victor's "Helen," first produced in New York at AMAS Repertory Theatre, 1977; "Ain't Doin' Nothin' But Singin' My Song," "Somewhere Along the Road," "Reach Out," "Preacher Man," "Law and Order," "Fine Someone to Love," "Streets of Bed-Stuy," "Mother's Day," "Overnight," "Sing Our Song," and "Lovin'" for "Ain't Doin' Nothin' but Singin' My Song" (revue), first produced in New York at Theatre Off Park, 1978.

"Sparrow in Flight" (theme) for Charles Fuller's "Sparrow in Flight," first produced in New York at AMAS Repertory Theatre, November 2, 1978; (contributor and adapter of lyrics) "Eubie" (revue), first produced on Broadway at Ambassador Theatre, September 20, 1978; "Suddenly the Music Starts,"

"My Home Town," "Faces in a Crowd," "Funky People," "Super Bad," "I'll Scratch Your Back," "Goodnight," "Boogie Woogie Ball," "Talk Your Feelings," "Your Love Is My Love," "Dancing Dan," "Dance! Dance! Dance!," "Whole Lotta Real Good Feeling," "Remember Someone," "Everybody's Doing the Disco," "Stuff," "Syncopatin'," "Kansas City Blues," "Manhattan Lullaby," "One Day at a Time," "You," "It's My Turn Now," "Strolling Down Broadway," and "Finale" from "Suddenly the Music Starts" (revue), first produced in New York at AMAS Repertory Theatre, May 3, 1979.

"The More You Get," "Average Man," "Everybody's Got a Hustle," "I'll Get It All Together," "This Must Be My Moment," "Wheel of Fire," "Back Up Singer's Blues," "What Is Life Without a Little Magic?," "Songwriter," "Gonna Give You All My Lovin'," "Nothing's Gonna Change," "Slow Burn," "Somethin' for Nothin'," "This Is the Time of Our Life," "What Is Done Is Done," and "Brazilsalsa" for Dan Owens's "The More You Get the More You Want," first produced in New York at BTA Theatre, 1980; "New York City," "Big Time," "There's a Dream With Your Name Written on It," "New Woman," "When He Smiles at Me," "Circle of Love," "Waiting for the Love to Start," "Why Can't You See With Your Heart?," "What Is There to Say?," "There's Always Another Song to Sing," "Red Gingham Gown," "Excitement," "Click! (It'll All Go Away)," "Stop Running From Each Other," "A Man Is a Wonderful Thing to Be," "Carryin' On," "Vonetta Sweetwater," and "Talk Your Feelings," for own "Vonetta Sweetwater Carries On," first produced in New York at Theatre Off Park, February 3, 1982.

Also composer and lyricist, under own name and pseudonyms Francis Edwards, Ed Franks, Ricardo Martinelli, and Gerry Rich, of numerous songs, including "Once Upon a Wintertime," "Tomorrow," "Don't Worry," "Anyone Can Be a Millionaire," "Let's," "Words That I Whisper," "Puerto Rican Pedlar," "A Screamin' Ball at Dracula Hall," "Rainbow Kisses," "Venetian Sunset," "Who Am I?," "Telephone Song," "Sittin' in the Sun," "A Love to Last a Lifetime," "A Door That Is Open," "The Years Between," "Struttin' Down Jane Street," and "The Happy Heart of Paris." Also composer of title song for television documentary "A Piece of the Action," c. 1975, and theme for a segment of Kraft TV Theatre.

Recordings: "Slow Poke," Columbia, 1952 (released in England as "Slow Coach"). Also recorded songs, including "Tomorrow," "Don't Worry," and "Millionaire," on such labels as Columbia, Pye/Nixa, Decca, London, and King.

Original cast albums: "Cindy," ABC Paramount, 1964; "Billy Noname," Roulette, 1970; "Eubie!," Warner Brothers, 1980.

WORK IN PROGRESS: Lyrics and composition for Eric Blau's "Shim Sham," to be produced on Broadway, 1982; "Sing Me Sunshine," based on the play "Peg O' My Heart" by J. Hartley Manners; "Touch," a revue.

SIDELIGHTS: Brandon entered show business at the age of eleven as a song and dance man in British Variety. While still in his teens, he appeared in several films and on the London stage in a number of revues and plays, including the first British production of William Saroyan's "The Time of Your Life" for the Old Vic Company. Brandon began writing songs at fourteen, and was composer and lyricist for several successful London musicals.

During the 1950's, Brandon was a popular singer, appearing in concerts and nightclubs in England and on the Continent.

He wrote most of his own material, including his top ten hits "Tomorrow" and "Don't Worry." His songs have also been recorded by Sarah Vaughan, Bill Haley and the Comets, Teresa Brewer, and Eydie Gorme.

Brandon settled in New York and returned to the theatre in 1964, writing the songs for the hit musical "Cindy." Since then, he has written lyrics and music for plays and revues, many of them concerning the experiences of black Americans. Brandon believes that a dramatist's primary duty is "to entertain in the broadest sense of the word," but he adds, "I very much feel the writer *should* be socially aware and . . . create a truer picture of our multi-racial society."

Brandon told *CA:* "I am concerned more with the state of the theatre rather than black theatre. To me there should just be an American theatre, and hopefully that is where we are going. Too many talented and productive directors, choreographers, producers, actors, and designers who are black or a member of some other minority group are confined to a kind of parochial theatre and not given the opportunity to develop in summer stock, regional theatres, and in the commercial arenas of Broadway and Off-Broadway. Unless there is a dramatic reason for specific ethnic casting, writers have a responsibility to see that their works are cast multiracially to properly represent that pattern of life in the United States and to see that this multiracialism spills over into all creative areas, back stage and the front of the house, too! We do have a certain amount of power as writers and can't keep passing the buck to producers."

BIOGRAPHICAL/CRITICAL SOURCES: New York Times, March 20, 1964, January 30, 1968, March 3, 1970; Otis L. Guernsey, editor, *Playwrights/Lyricists/Composers on Theater,* Dodd, Mead, 1974.

*   *   *

BRANDON, Robert Joseph   1918-
(Robin Brandon)

PERSONAL: Born July 18, 1918, in Wimbledon, England; son of Robert Joseph (a military officer and accountant) and Margaret Beryl (Browne) Brandon; married Patricia Mary Ashhurst Le Brasseur, October 25, 1947 (divorced, 1970); married Janis Percival Gamon, August 3, 1971; children: Robert Joseph, Christopher John. *Education:* Graduate of Royal Military Academy, Woolwich, England, 1938. *Home:* 4 quai des Fosses, 83360 Port Grimaud, France. *Office:* 12 place du Marche, 83360 Port Grimaud, France.

CAREER: British Army, Royal Artillery, career officer, 1939-62, retiring as lieutenant colonel; South Devon Holdings Ltd., Salcombe, Devonshire, England, managing director, 1978—; Robin Brandon Charters Ltd., Saint Peter Port, Guernsey, Channel Islands, managing director, 1979—; Prestige Yachting (yacht charter and brokerage), Port Grimaud, France, managing director, 1981—. Yachtmaster examiner and official yacht measurer for Royal Yachting Association and Board of Trade, 1979—. *Member:* Cruising Association, Royal Cruising Club, Royal Ocean Racing Club.

WRITINGS—Under name Robin Brandon: *South Biscay Pilot,* Adlard Coles, 1971; *The Good Crewman,* Adlard Coles, 1972; *South France Pilot,* Imrays, 1974; *East Spain Pilot,* Imrays, 1976; *South England Pilot,* Imrays, Chart IV, 1979, Chart V, 1980, Charts I, II, and III, in press.

WORK IN PROGRESS: West Italy Pilot, publication by Imrays expected in 1984; *North France Pilot,* publication by Imrays expected in 1985.

SIDELIGHTS: Robin Brandon told *CA:* "After a twenty-three-year career in the Royal Artillery, I retired to become a company director in a small firm in Salcombe, Devon, producing, facturing, and selling yachting and sports clothing and equipment, when unexpectedly I was offered the opportunity to write a yachting guide to the harbors in northern Spain. Seizing this opportunity, and with only my military training to assist, I wrote my first book. It was an instant success and paved the way for a series of similar works covering other coasts. Unfortunately, as with all specialist books, the remuneration is small, and I therefore have also had to run a yacht charter and brokerage business in the south of France, writing books in any moments that I can snatch from my business."

AVOCATIONAL INTERESTS: Yachting, photography, exploring, history, old buildings.

BIOGRAPHICAL/CRITICAL SOURCES: Sunday Telegraph Magazine, May 25, 1980.

*   *   *

BRANDON, Robin
  See BRANDON, Robert Joseph

*   *   *

BRASSENS, Georges   1921-1981

OBITUARY NOTICE: Born October 22, 1921, in Sete, France; died of intestinal cancer, October 30, 1981, in Sete, France. Composer, singer, and author. A troubadour of traditional French ballads, Brassens wrote more than one hundred thirty-five songs during his career and sold more than twenty million copies of his recordings. In addition to writing songs of love, life, and death, Brassens wrote whimsical ballads ridiculing the police, justice, society, and the establishment. Among his most popular songs are "The Gorilla," "Park Benches," "The Butterfly Chase," and "To Die for One's Ideas." His books include *La Tour des miracles,* a novel, and *Poemes et chansons,* a collection of poems and songs. Obituaries and other sources: *The International Who's Who,* Europa, 1980; *Washington Post,* November 1, 1981; *Newsweek,* November 9, 1981.

*   *   *

BRAY, Howard   1929-

PERSONAL: Born May 28, 1929, in Albany, N.Y. *Education:* Washington University, St. Louis, Mo., B.A., 1952. *Office:* c/o Fund for Investigative Journalism, 1346 Connecticut Ave., N.W., Washington, D.C. 20036.

CAREER: Fund for Investigative Journalism, Washington, D.C., president, 1973—.

WRITINGS: The Pillars of the Post, Norton, 1980.

SIDELIGHTS: The Pillars of the Post traces the ownership of the *Washington Post* from its acquisition in 1933 by financier Eugene Meyer through the ascension in the late 1970's of Meyer's grandson, Donald Graham, to publisher of the *Post.* Howard Bray's account of the intervening years, when the *Post* was transformed from a bankrupt local newspaper into one of the most prestigious news agencies in the world, is told through an examination of the executive officers of the *Post.*

Bray's approach—focusing on personalities, particularly Katharine Graham's—caused mixed feelings among most reviewers. *New York Times Book Review* critic Anthony Smith noted that the book "provides a thoroughly good read without leaving you feeling that you've been turned into a voyeur," but also lamented that it "falls into the trap of personalization: the stories are all about people, not processes." *Washington Post Book World* critic George E. Reedy felt Bray's concentration on Katharine Graham and editor Benjamin Bradlee provided the "often tangled narrative" with a focal point. "But otherwise," Reedy wrote, "it is essential to maintain a chart when reading the book in order to keep the cast of characters straight."

BIOGRAPHICAL/CRITICAL SOURCES: Washington Post Book World, April 13, 1980; *Best Sellers,* June, 1980; *America,* June 21, 1980; *New York Times Book Review,* July 27, 1980; *Journalism Quarterly,* autumn, 1980.

*   *   *

BREITMAN, Richard D(avid)   1947-

PERSONAL: Born March 27, 1947, in Hartford, Conn.; son of Saul Harold and Gloria (Salz) Breitman. *Education:* Yale University, B.A., 1969; Harvard University, M.A., 1971, Ph.D., 1975. *Home:* 3460 39th St. N.W., Washington, D.C. 20016. *Office:* Department of History, American University, Washington, D.C. 20016.

CAREER: American University, Washington, D.C., assistant professor, 1976-81, associate professor of history, 1981—. *Member:* American Historical Association, McLean Gardens Residents Association (vice-chairman, 1980; chairman, 1981). *Awards, honors:* Carnegie fellow, Yale University, 1969-70.

WRITINGS: German Socialism and Weimar Democracy, University of North Carolina Press, 1981. Contributor to history journals.

WORK IN PROGRESS: A book on European Jewish refugees and American refugee policy, 1933-45, with Alan M. Kraut and Thomas Imhoof, publication expected in 1983.

SIDELIGHTS: Breitman told *CA:* "One of the greatest challenges for a scholar, particularly in the field of history, is to achieve competence without becoming overly specialized or intellectually narrow. I have tried to maintain a general interest in subjects such as socialism, fascism, and the Holocaust. I also follow current politics in Europe and the United States."

AVOCATIONAL INTERESTS: Theatre, playing tennis, the Boston Celtics.

*   *   *

BREND, Ruth M(argaret)   1927-

PERSONAL: Born January 8, 1927, in Winnipeg, Manitoba, Canada; came to the United States in 1959, naturalized citizen, 1964; daughter of Willie and Margaret (Hodgson) Brend. *Education:* University of Manitoba, B.A., 1946, diploma in social work, 1947; Multnomah School of the Bible, diploma, 1952; University of Michigan, M.A., 1960, Ph.D., 1964. *Religion:* Christian Reformed. *Home:* 3363 Burbank Dr., Ann Arbor, Mich. 48105. *Office:* Department of Linguistics, Michigan State University, A-615 Wells Hall, East Lansing, Mich. 48824.

CAREER: Social worker in Manitoba, Canada, 1947-50; associated with the Summer Institute of Linguistics and Wycliffe Bible Translators, Mexico, 1952-57; University of Michigan, Ann Arbor, research assistant, 1957-64; Michigan State University, East Lansing, lecturer, 1964-66, assistant professor, 1966-67, associate professor, 1967-76, professor of linguistics, 1976—. Fulbright professor in Norway, 1975-76. Consultant to Summer Institute of Linguistics (Mexico, India, Peru, Colombia), 1962—. *Member:* International Association of Phonetic Sciences, Linguistic Society of America. *Awards, hon-*

ors: Honorary degree from Multnomah School of the Bible, 1972.

WRITINGS: A Tagmemic Analysis of Mexican Spanish Clauses, Mouton, 1968; (editor) *Kenneth L. Pike: Selected Writings,* Mouton, 1972; (editor) *Advances in Tagmemics,* North-Holland Publishing, 1974; (editor) *Studies in Tone and Intonation by Members of the Summer Institute of Linguistics,* S. Karger, 1975; (editor with Pike) *Tagmemics,* Volume I: *Aspects of the Field,* Volume II: *Theoretical Foundations,* Mouton, 1976; (editor with Pike) *The Summer Institute of Linguistics: Its Work and Contributions,* Mouton, 1977. Editor of *Language Learning,* 1963-64.

WORK IN PROGRESS: A book on application of linguistic theory to the language classroom, publication expected in 1982; research on tagmemic theory and applied linguistics.

SIDELIGHTS: Ruth Brend commented: "A major impetus to my linguistic study is my interest in the Summer Institute of Linguistics and the Wycliffe Bible Translators, whose members are analyzing unwritten languages of many countries of the world, with the object of translating the Scriptures into those languages. Occasionally I hold workshops for these groups, assisting them in their language analysis problems and helping prepare manuscripts for publication.

"Within tagmemic theory, I feel the major thrust of my studies is in the area of discourse analysis. Findings at this level are proving to be of immense help in the understanding and analysis of all areas of language structure."

*　　*　　*

BREUER, Georg 1919-

PERSONAL: Born October 24, 1919, in Vienna, Austria; son of Ernst and Dora (Fraenkel) Breuer; married Rosa Grossmann (a journalist), December 10, 1949; children: four. *Education:* Educated in Austria. *Home:* Birnbaumg 4/3, A-1100, Vienna, Austria.

CAREER: Worked as journalist; free-lance writer, 1960—. *Awards, honors:* Austrian State Prize for scientific journalism, 1980.

WRITINGS—In English: Wetter nach Wunsch?, Deutsche Verlags-Anstalt, 1976, translation published as *Weather Modification: Prospects and Problems,* Cambridge University Press, 1980; *Geht uns die Luft aus?,* Deutsche Verlags-Anstalt, 1978, translation published as *Air in Danger: Ecological Perspectives of the Atmosphere,* Cambridge University Press, 1980; *Der Sogenannte Mensch,* Koesel, 1981, translation published as *Sociobiology and the Human Dimension,* Cambridge University Press, 1982.

Other: *Koennte Oesterreich Ueberleben?* (title means "Could Neutral Austria Survive the Consequences of a Nuclear World War?"), Jugend und Volk, 1964; *Triumph der Phantasten* (title means "Ancestors and Beginnings of Space Research"), Schwann, 1967; *Kann der Weltuntegang verhindert werden?* (title means "Political Problems of the Nuclear Age"), Europa-Verlag, 1968; *Interview mit der Zukunft* (title means "Interview With the Future"), Schwann, 1970; *Menschen aus dem Katalog?* (title means "Men to Order?"), Schwann, 1969; *Augen in das All* (title means "Astronomical Technology"), Schwann, 1970; *Selbstmord auf Abruf?* (title means "Suicide on Request?"), Schwann, 1971; *Die Herausforderung* (title means "The Energy Problems"), C. Bertelsmann, 1975; *Energie ohne Angst* (title means "Energy Without Anxiety"), Koesel, 1980; *Wer verhindert das Elektroauto?* (title means "Who's Holding Up the Electrocar?"), Koesel, in press.

Contributor to periodicals and journals, including *Naturwissenschaftliche Rundschau.*

SIDELIGHTS: Breuer told *CA:* "My 'career' was to a large extent shaped by world history. A few weeks after I had enlisted in the Vienna Academy of Music, Hitler invaded Austria and I had to leave my country to avoid political and racial persecution. Several of my relatives were killed in Nazi concentration camps for no other reason than that they were Jews. Others died in France as members of the resistance movement. My wife and her family (whom I did not know at the time) were imprisoned and tortured by Nazis in 1943 for being members of the Austrian resistance; my future father-in-law was sent to a concentration camp for political reasons and survived.

"I myself spent the war years as a refugee in England. I started my journalistic career as an editor of a duplicated paper for young Austrian refugees. I returned to Austria in December, 1945, and worked as a journalist. Later I became a free-lance writer.

"In my work I concentrate on the popular presentation of scientific and technical topics of general relevance for society like nuclear weapons and disarmament, nuclear and alternative energies, environmental problems, etc. I want lay readers to understand complicated problems, avoid oversimplification, and present balanced accounts weighing pro and con in a non-partisan manner.

"In my translations I prefer work on similar lines, sometimes adapting and supplementing them for Central European readers. In a preface for the German edition of his book *Scientific Knowledge and Its Social Problems,* which I translated and adapted, J. Ravetz wrote: 'I recall being told that the great scholars of classical philology believed that a good establishment of a text should not merely reproduce what was the author's original holograph, but should indeed make a better representation of the author's original thoughts. At the time I considered this as a good joke; but after seeing the editorial work done by the translator of this book, I can appreciate that the goal is a necessary part of philological scholarship, and its achievement is feasible in work of the highest class.'

"In the 1960's I was honorary (that means doing a lot of work without being paid for it) secretary of the Austrian March Movement for Nuclear and General Disarmament in East and West. Since 1973 I have been honorary secretary of an Austrian committee of solidarity for victims of repression in Czechoslovakia, that is, people who are persecuted and forbidden further work in their occupations as scientists, writers, artists, physicians, etc., because of their political or religious convictions, their support for the 'Prague Spring' of 1968, or for Charta 1977 and the ideas of human rights."

*　　*　　*

BREWSTER, Townsend 1924-

PERSONAL: Born July 23, 1924, in Glen Cove, N.Y.; son of Townsend (a postal clerk) and Sara (a teacher; maiden name, Tyler) Brewster. *Education:* Queens College (now of the City University of New York), B.A., 1947; Columbia University, M.A., 1962. *Home:* 171-29 103rd Rd., Jamaica, N.Y. 11433. *Agent:* Ronelda Roberts, 1214 Ridge Blvd., Suite 3F, Brooklyn, N.Y. 11209. *Office: Harlem Cultural Review,* 1 West 125th St., New York, N.Y. 10027.

CAREER: Writer, 1947-59; Hicks & Greist (advertising agency), New York City, copywriter, 1959-61; Lennen & Newell (advertising agency), New York City, librarian, 1962-67; writer, 1967-69; City College of the City University of New York,

New York City, lecturer in theatre, 1969-73; *Players*, Los Angeles, Calif., theatre critic, 1974; writer, 1974——. Vice-president of Harlem Performance Center; member of board of directors of Frank Silvera Writers Workshop and Harlem Cultural Council. Playwright-in-residence at University of Denver, 1969. *Military service:* U.S. Army, 1943-45.

MEMBER: International Brecht Society, Outer Critics Circle, Dramatists Guild, Maple Leaf Society, Ragtime Society. *Awards, honors:* Fellow of National Theatre Conference, 1947; Koussevitzky Foundation scholar, 1947; William Morris scholar at American Theatre Wing, 1955; award from *Story*, 1969, for play "Please Don't Cry and Say 'No'"; Louise Bogan Memorial Prize in poetry from New York Poetry Forum, 1975, for "Dos Suenos"; grant from Harlem Cultural Council, 1976; grant from National Endowment for the Arts, 1977; Jonathan Swift Award for satire from Virginia Commonwealth University, 1979, for play "The Ecologists."

WRITINGS: The Tower (libretto for opera; first performed in Santa Fe, N.M., at Santa Fe Opera, August 2, 1957), Boosey & Hawkes, 1958; (translator) Plautus, *Rudens*, Continental Play Service, 1963; *Lady Plum Blossom* (two-act musical play for young people; first produced in Corvallis, Ore., at Oregon State University, April, 1972), Modern Theatre for Youth, 1973; (contributor of translation) Bernard F. Dukore, editor, *Dramatic Theory and Criticism: Greeks to Grotowski*, Holt, 1974.

Unpublished plays: "Little Girl, Big Town" (revue), first produced in New York City at Queens College, May 1, 1953; "Please Don't Cry and Say 'No'" (one-act), first produced off-Broadway at Downtown Circle in the Square, December 6, 1972; "Though It's Been Said Many Times, Many Ways" (one-act), first produced in New York City at Harlem Performance Center, December 22, 1976; "Three by One" (trilogy of one-act plays), first produced in New York City at Harlem Performance Center, December 8, 1977; "The Girl Beneath the Tulip Tree" (one-act), first produced in New York City at Harlem Performance Center, December 8, 1977; "Black-Belt Bertram" (one-act), first produced in New York City at Double Image Theatre, May, 1979; "Arthur Ashe and I" (one-act), first produced in New York City at Riverside Church, June 20, 1979. Also author of "The Ecologists."

Librettos for opera and lyrics for musical plays: "The Choreography of Love" (jazz opera), first broadcast by WNYC-Radio, February 16, 1946; "Revue Sketches," first produced in Akron, Ohio, at Weathervane Theatre, August 8, 1970; "Harlequinades for Mourners" (four-act play), first produced in New York City at New Theatre, September 14, 1970. Also author of libretto for the folk opera "Of Angels and Donkeys."

Work represented in anthologies, including *Today's Negro Voices*, Messner, 1970. Translator, adapter, and continuity writer for "NBC Television Opera," 1950-51. Author of "A Word on Plays," a column in *Big Red*, 1980——. Television critic for *Show Business*; theatre critic for *Amsterdam News, Routes*, and *Harlem Cultural Review*; book critic for *Harlem Cultural Review*. Contributor of stories, poems, and reviews to magazines, including *Players, Pioneer, Oracle, Counterpoint, Classical Outlook, Music Journal*, and *Commonweal*, and newspapers. Editor of *Harlem Cultural Review*.

WORK IN PROGRESS: "Memorials," a trilogy of plays, including "The Jade Funerary Suit," "Praise Song," and "This Is the Gloaming of the Age of Aquarius."

SIDELIGHTS: Brewster told *CA:* "I began writing as a lyric poet. While I was an undergraduate at Queens College, a fellow student, a composer, asked me for a libretto. At first I declined, not considering myself a dramatist, but being a great opera buff, allowed myself to be persuaded. The resulting work, 'The Choreography of Love,' was not only a great hit on campus but was also broadcast, and, then and there, the poet became loyal to the stage.

"Opera has continued to loom large in my writing career. In 1947 I was one of the four writers selected to inaugurate the libretto-writing department at Tanglewood, and I made my professional debut as a translator-adapter and continuity writer for the 'NBC Television Opera.' The initial translation, 'Carmen,' was subsequently repeated as the first opera telecast in color, and the 'Gianni Schicchi' was later sung at the Metropolitan Opera. On a grant from the Harlem Cultural Council, I translated 'L'Amant anonyme,' the only fully-surviving opera of eighteenth-century black composer Joseph Boulogne, the Chevalier de Saint-Georges.

"Though I still turn out an occasional *rondeau* or sonnet, most of my current versifying takes the form of lyrics for musicals and of the songs that are the features of most of my plays, a few of which are in meter. I have turned out little fiction.

"With two or three exceptions, my plays are comedies, though for me comedy means Wilde and Wycherley, Moliere and Marivaux (who, along with Brecht, is one of my favorite playwrights), rather than Neil Simon. For a definition of comedy, I turn to Victor Hugo, who saw it as 'criticism of human nature.' Most of my comedies fall into the category of 'This is a dream of happiness' or 'This is the way of the world.' I sometimes refer to the former as my *L'Elisir d'amore* vein.

"If Joseph Papp is correct in observing that Afro-American playwrights derive from television and films rather than from literature and drama, then I am one of the exceptions. I feel that I have had the chronological advantage of being able to realize when I encountered the works of Bullins and Baraka that they shared the African heritage not only with Wole Soyinka and Aime Cesaire, but also with Terence and Pushkin."

*　　*　　*

BRIDSON, Gavin (Douglas Ruthven) 1936-

PERSONAL: Born December 2, 1936, in Manchester, England; son of Douglas Geoffrey (a writer) and Vera (a textile designer; maiden name, Richardson) Bridson; married Diane Mary Sheppard (a botanist; separated); children: Stella. *Education:* Attended school in Woolhampton, England. *Home:* 34 Highbury Pl., London N.5, England. *Office:* Linnean Society of London, Burlington House, Piccadilly, London W1V 0LQ, England.

CAREER: Writer. *Military service:* British Army, Royal Hampshire Regiment, 1954-56; served in Malaya. *Member:* Linnean Society of London (fellow).

WRITINGS: (With Geoffrey Wakeman) *A Guide to Nineteenth-Century Colour Printers*, Plough Press, 1975; (with V. C. Phillips and A. P. Harvey) *Natural History Manuscript Resources in the British Isles*, Bowker, 1980. Contributor to natural history journals.

WORK IN PROGRESS: Research on the history of graphic arts printing methods, firms, and practitioners in England, 1750-1900.

*　　*　　*

BRIER, Peter A. 1935-

PERSONAL: Born March 5, 1935, in Vienna, Austria; came to the United States in 1940, naturalized citizen, 1945; son of

Francis Simon (a mobile home manufacturer) and Stella (Loewenberg) Brier; married Nurith Goldschmidt (a television journalist), May 29, 1975. *Education:* Yale University, B.A., 1956; Harvard University, M.A., 1958; Occidental College and Claremont Graduate School Intercollegiate Program of Graduate Studies, Ph.D., 1971. *Politics:* Democrat. *Religion:* Jewish. *Home address:* 1847 Craig Ave., Altadena, Calif. 91001. *Office:* Department of English, California State University, Los Angeles, Calif. 90032.

CAREER: California State University, Los Angeles, assistant professor, 1971-76, associate professor, 1976-81, professor of English, 1981—. *Member:* Modern Language Association of America, Philological Association of the Pacific Coast.

WRITINGS: (With Anthony Arthur) *American Prose and Criticism: A Guide to Information Sources,* Gale, 1981. Contributor to literature journals and literary magazines, including *Denver Quarterly.*

SIDELIGHTS: Brier wrote: "The literary researches of Isaac D'Israeli have engaged my interest. They anticipate modern popular literary history. The current gap between literature and critical theory has something to do with the death of literary history. A better understanding of the origins of popular literary history might provide clues to a significant revival of formal literary history."

*   *   *

BRIGHTMAN, Robert   1920-

PERSONAL: Born in 1920 in Montreal, Quebec, Canada; came to the United States in 1920, naturalized citizen, 1923; married wife, Mollie (a high school teacher), 1939; children: one son. *Education:* Polytechnic Institute of Brooklyn, B.S., 1939; New York University, B.A., 1943. *Home:* 5 Sussex Rd., Great Neck, N.Y. 11020.

CAREER: Foreman and general supervisor of heavy construction work for Reiss Construction Co., 1937-39; advertising copywriter with G. M. Basford, 1939-46; home and shop editor for *Mechanix Illustrated,* 1945-70; *Reader's Digest,* Pleasantville, N.Y., general books editor, 1970-72; free-lance writer and editor, 1973—. Worked in graphic arts, amateur sales, motion pictures, editing and titling, photo processing, and as staff photographer for Eastman Kodak, Rochester, N.Y. Teacher in adult programs; guest on more than fifty radio and television programs.

WRITINGS: The Homeowner Handbook of Carpentry and Woodworking, Crown, 1974; *Bernzomatic Torch Tips,* Dorison House, 1977; *Fix-It Duro-Loctite Guide to Home and Auto Care and Repair,* Dorison House, 1978; *One Hundred One Practical Uses for Propane Torches,* TAB Books, 1978. Author of instruction booklets for Stanley Tools. Contributor to magazines, including *Popular Mechanics, Better Homes and Gardens,* and *McCall's,* and to newspapers.

SIDELIGHTS: Brightman's interests include shopwork, home repair and maintenance, building telescopes (including mirror grinding and polishing), automobiles, and hi-fidelity sound systems.

Brightman told *CA:* "I became interested in writing after selling my first short story to *Popular Mechanics* on how to store a wet shaving brush in the medicine cabinet!"

AVOCATIONAL INTERESTS: Photography, music, reading, astronomy, tennis, skating, cycling, travel.

BRINT, Armand Ian   1952-

PERSONAL: Born October 21, 1952, in New Mexico; son of Harold L. (a systems analyst) and Shirly (Markus) Brint. *Education:* Attended San Francisco State University; New College of California, B.A., 1977. *Home:* 1710-A Grant St., Berkeley, Calif. 94703.

CAREER: Berkeley Holistic Health Center, Berkeley, Calif., founder and director, 1975-76, administrator and teacher, 1976-79; writer. Member of executive committee of Natural Healing Defense Council; health consultant.

WRITINGS: (Editor with Edward Bauman, Wright, and Piper, and contributor) *Holistic Health Handbook,* And-Or Press, 1978; (editor with Bauman, Wright, and Piper, and contributor) *Holistic Health Lifebook,* And-Or Press, 1981.

WORK IN PROGRESS: Panoramas, poems.

SIDELIGHTS: Brint told *CA:* "I began writing about preventive health care and maintenance out of my experience at a holistic health center. My writing career has taken me down two very different roads: health care, involving journalistic and technical writing and editing; and fiction, particularly poetry. Much of my inspiration for poetry comes from my travels and life in Greece."

*   *   *

BROADBENT, Donald E(ric)   1926-

PERSONAL: Born May 26, 1926, in Birmingham, England; son of Herbert Arthur (an export sales manager) and Hannah Elizabeth (a secretary) Broadbent; married Margaret Wright, June 28, 1949 (divorced, 1972); married Margaret Hope Pattison Gregory (a psychologist), November 11, 1972; children: (first marriage) Patricia Anne Broadbent Cowell, Judith Elizabeth (deceased). *Education:* Pembroke College, Cambridge, B.A., 1949, Sc.D., 1965. *Office:* Department of Experimental Psychology, Oxford University, South Parks Rd., Oxford OX1 3UD, England.

CAREER: Cambridge University, Cambridge, England, member of staff at Medical Research Council Applied Psychology Unit, 1949-58, director of unit, 1958-74, member of external staff, 1974—. Fellow of Wolfson College, Oxford. Member of board of governors of Technical Change Centre; past member of British Social Science Research Council and Royal Air Force flight personnel research committee; chairman of Scientific Committee of St. Dunstan's. *Military service:* Royal Air Force, pilot, 1944-49; became sergeant. Royal Air Force Reserve, 1949-54. *Member:* British Psychological Society (president, 1965), British Association for the Advancement of Science (president of psychology section, 1967), Royal Society (member of council, 1978-80), Ergonomics Society, Experimental Psychology Society, U.S. Academy of Science (foreign associate). *Awards, honors:* Commander of Order of the British Empire, 1974; distinguished scientific contribution award from American Psychological Association, 1975; honorary doctorates from University of Southampton, 1975, and University of York, 1979.

WRITINGS: Perception and Communication, Pergamon, 1958; *Behaviour,* Eyre & Spottiswoode, 1961; *Proceedings of DSIR Conference on Ergonomics in Industry,* H.M.S.O., 1961; *Decision and Stress,* Academic Press, 1971; *In Defence of Empirical Psychology,* Methuen, 1974. Contributor to psychology journals.

WORK IN PROGRESS: Research on selective and control processes in attention and memory and on mental health in industry.

SIDELIGHTS: In *A History of Psychology in Autobiography,* Broadbent wrote: "My father was, for most of the time the family stayed together, an executive in a British-based, multinational company. He must have been a good one. Class boundaries were stiffer in those days than Americans or the modern British can imagine, and our background was relatively poor. But he rose meteorically, and in the 1930's, we lived briefly at a level of affluence I shall never see again. It did not last, however. At the start of World War II, he parted from the company and from the family, and I never saw him again. My mother's theory was that the rapid shift of role and class had been too great a strain. Whether this is true or not, it colored her attitude toward my own schooling. Hence I became part of an extraordinary paradox: In those days before Social Security, my mother kept herself and me by clerical work in small local offices of the civil service, and for most of the war, we lived in a four-roomed cottage that had no bathroom and required us to make essential periodic trips outside to the end of the yard. Yet, at the same time, she was determined that never, under any circumstances, would I later be handicapped in dealing with people who had a heavier ballast of educational advantage. So instead of getting me the best schooling she could afford, she made up her mind with sublime arrogance as to which she thought was the best school in the country, and that was where I went: Winchester.

"I dwell on this because it has probably made my attitude toward psychology dour and puritan, in a way that has sometimes offended younger colleagues. It is perhaps an attitude that is particularly irritating when expressed in the accent and style of the upper-class British. Nevertheless, I decided then, and still believe, that self-realization and the development of personal experience are neither dignified nor respectable goals in life, that most of the world lives within extremely tight economic margins, and that positions of privilege (such as the conduct of scientific research) demand obligations in return. Hence, for example, the fact that I never held a university job."

BIOGRAPHICAL/CRITICAL SOURCES: David Cohen, editor, *Psychologists on Psychology,* Routledge & Kegan Paul, 1977; G. Linzey, editor, *A History of Psychology in Autobiography,* Volume VIII, W. H. Freeman, 1980.

*　　*　　*

BROCK, Horace   1908(?)-1981

OBITUARY NOTICE: Born c. 1908; died of a stroke, November 16, 1981, in New York, N.Y. Pilot, airline executive, and author. One of the first to pilot the Boeing B-314 flying boat, Brock became Pan American's Atlantic Division manager in the 1940's. He also held executive posts at Panagra, Middle East Airlines, and New York Airways. His writings, which focus on the history of air travel, include *Flying the Oceans: A Pilot's Story of Pan Am* and *More About Pan Am.* Obituaries and other sources: *New York Times,* November 17, 1981.

*　　*　　*

BROCK, Russell Claude   1903-1980

OBITUARY NOTICE: Born October 24, 1903, in London, England; died September 3, 1980, in London, England. Thoracic surgeon and author of books in his field. Brock was a pioneer of heart and lung surgery at London's Brompton Guy's and hospitals. His surgical breakthroughs in the treatment of thoracic disorders are widely credited as the precursors to open heart surgery and heart transplantation. An authority on lung surgery as well, Brock wrote two standard reference texts on the subject, *Anatomy of the Bronchial Tree* and *Lung Abscess.* His other writings include *Life and Work of Sir Astley Cooper* and a prize-winning essay, "New Growths of the Lung." In 1954 Brock was knighted by the queen of England, and in 1965 he was made a life peer and named Baron Brock of Wimbledon. Obituaries and other sources: *Who's Who in the World,* 2nd edition, Marquis, 1973; *The International Who's Who,* Europa, 1980; *Who's Who,* 132nd edition, St. Martin's, 1980; *The Annual Obituary 1980,* St. Martin's, 1981.

*　　*　　*

BRODHEAD, Michael John   1935-

PERSONAL: Born November 20, 1935, in Abilene, Kan.; son of Richard Garrett (in sales) and Elizabeth (a social worker; maiden name, Gaston) Brodhead; married Hwa-di Chang (a cooking instructor), November 3, 1969; children: Lynus J., John M. *Education:* University of Kansas, B.A., 1959, M.A., 1962; University of Minnesota, Ph.D., 1967. *Home:* 1790 West 12th St., Reno, Nev. 89503. *Office:* Department of History, University of Nevada, Reno, Nev. 89557.

CAREER: University of Kansas, Lawrence, curator of Kansas Collection at university library, 1965-67; University of Nevada, Reno, assistant professor, 1967-71, associate professor, 1971-79, professor of history, 1979—. Visiting associate professor at University of Kansas, 1972-73. *Military service:* U.S. Army, 1954-56. *Member:* American Society for Environmental History, Organization of American Historians, Council on Abandoned Military Posts, Western History Association, Kansas State Historical Society, Nevada Historical Society.

WRITINGS: Persevering Populist: The Life of Frank Doster, University of Nevada Press, 1969; *A Soldier-Scientist in the American Southwest: Being a Narrative of the Travels of Brevet Captain Elliott Coues, Assistant Surgeon, U.S.A., Through Kansas and the Territories of Colorado and New Mexico, to Arizona, and Thence to the Coast of California; Together With His Observations Upon the Natural History, Especially the Avifauna, of the Regions Traversed, 1864-1865,* Arizona Historical Society, 1973; (with Paul Russell Cutright) *Elliott Coues: Naturalist and Frontier Historian,* University of Illinois Press, 1981. Contributor to history journals.

WORK IN PROGRESS: Research on contributions to natural history by officers and men of the U.S. Army in the nineteenth century.

SIDELIGHTS: Brodhead told *CA:* "It's comforting for me to realize that I'm now involved in historical studies of a non-political sort—political history is in some respects the least productive approach to understanding the past. Yet I'm bothered by the fact that I've done far too little research and writing on those who do most to build and maintain societies, the so-called common people. We historians talk a good game about 'history from the bottom up' but don't do much about it."

*　　*　　*

BROMMER, Gerald F(rederick)   1927-

PERSONAL: Born January 8, 1927, in Berkeley, Calif.; son of Edgar Carl and Helen Christine (Wall) Brommer; married Georgia Elizabeth Pratt, December 19, 1948. *Education:* Concordia Teachers College, Seward, Neb., B.A., 1948; University of Nebraska, M.A., 1955; further graduate study at Chouinard Art Institute, 1955, University of California, Los Angeles, 1956-57, Otis Art Institute, 1958-59, and University of Southern California, 1959-61. *Religion:* Lutheran. *Home:* 11252 Valley Spring Lane, North Hollywood, Calif. 91602. *Agent:* Challis Galleries, 1390 South Coast Hwy., Laguna Beach, Calif. 92652; and Fireside Gallery, 5-6 Dolores St., Carmel, Calif. 93921.

CAREER: Artist and author. St. Paul's Lutheran School, North Hollywood, Calif., teacher, 1948-55; Lutheran High School, Los Angeles, Calif., chairman of art department, 1955-73; chief designer for Daystar Designs, Inc., 1963-73. Work exhibited in numerous group shows and in more than sixty one-man shows, including exhibitions at Challis Galleries, Laguna Beach, Calif., 1971-82, the Winter Art Gallery, Tucson, Ariz., 1972-82, Fireside Gallery, Carmel, Calif., 1972-82, Spencer Galleries, Pasadena, Calif., 1975-77, Gallery of Fine Arts, Wichita, Kan., 1981-82, and Louis Newman Galleries, Beverly Hills, Calif., 1980-82. Work housed in permanent collections of New York State University, Utah State University, Alan Hancock College, and in State of California collection and Howard Ahmanson collection. Lecturer. *Member:* National Watercolor Society (treasurer, 1963; vice-president, 1965-66 and 1982; president, 1966-67 and 1982-83), West Coast Watercolor Society, Artists for Economic Action, National Art Education Association, Artists Equity, Rocky Mountain National Watercolor Society. *Awards, honors:* Named alumnus of the year by Concordia Teachers College, 1975.

WRITINGS—Published by Davis Publications: *Wire Sculpture and Other Three-Dimensional Construction,* 1968; *Relief Printmaking,* 1970; *Drawing: Ideas, Materials, and Techniques,* 1972, revised edition, 1978; *Transparent Watercolor: Ideas and Techniques,* 1973; *Space:* (juvenile), 1974; *Movement and Rhythm* (juvenile), 1975; (with George F. Horn) *Art in Your World* (juvenile), 1977; (with Horn) *Art: Your Visual Environment* (juvenile), 1977; *Landscapes,* 1977; *The Art of Collage,* edited by Horn and Sarita R. Rainey, 1978; *Discovering Art History,* 1981.

Editor; published by Davis Publications: Jack Selleck, *Faces,* 1977; (with Horn) Albert W. Porter, *The Art of Sketching,* 1977; (with Horn) Joseph A. Gatto, *Cities,* 1977; (with Horn) Gatto and others, *Exploring Visual Design,* 1978; Mary Korstad Mueller, *Murals: Creating an Environment,* 1979; Albert W. Porter, *Creative Watercolor Painting,* 1982; Norman Fullner, *Airbrush Painting,* 1982.

Contributor of articles to periodicals, including *School Arts, Southwestern Art, Today's Art,* and *Art and Activities.*

WORK IN PROGRESS: A book, tentatively titled *Illustrated Guide to Art Career Opportunities,* publication by Davis Publications expected in 1982 or 1983.

SIDELIGHTS: Brommer has employed various media and techniques in his artwork. He has been most recognized for his work in traditional watercolor, but he has also experimented with rice paper collage and has created murals of duco on Masonite. Two of his best-known works are "Tuscany Hilltown" and "Cannery Row."

Brommer told *CA:* "The books I write are an outgrowth of my own three decades of teaching. I really do not write to tell people how to teach or make art in schools. I write because I like to think that I can provide a visual and verbal stimulus to help teachers communicate their own ideas to students. Ideally, I like to provide dozens of ideas and examples and allow teachers and/or students to select the projects, ideas, and examples that best fit their personal situations. There is no such thing as an ideal art curriculum that can satisfy the needs of five thou-

sand art teachers in five thousand different situations. But I can hope to show what has been done and provide a variety of thoughts that can be formulated into a sequential program suited to each individual circumstance.

"Excellence in teaching art is absolutely essential to fostering improved taste and discrimination in all the arts. To provide anything less than excellent examples, excellent teaching, and excellent ideas is to shortchange our young people, leaving them ill-equipped to make qualified and personal aesthetic judgments. It is one of our most important contributions to the lives of our young people—this matter of the pursuit of the excellence in the arts.

"I am not conscious of the fact that my own painting and design have influenced what I say in my books—except that I like to think that I also strive for excellence in what I do for myself. Instead, I write with the idea of providing help and direction to teachers who are looking for assistance. Very fine art teachers do not need much help, but there are many who want to tap into the wide range of art activity going on throughout the country, and that is where my books might help.

"My latest book, *Discovering Art History,* is an attempt to bring the extremely wide range of visual art history into focus for young people to enjoy. I like to stress relationships in art history and hope that young readers will begin to see such relationships in their own environments. After twenty years of teaching art history to high school people and seeing the changes such study has made in hundreds of lives, I hope that the book can make a definite and positive contribution to the teaching of visual arts in our nation's schools."

Brommer added that his work in progress, tentatively titled *Illustrated Guide to Art Career Opportunities,* "deals with careers in art. Although the subject has been handled in various ways before, this book will be highly visual and in contemporary layout design and format. It is hoped that the visual presentation will motivate young people to read further on the several hundred career opportunities presented in the book. Photographs will be contributed by many of the top professionals in their respective fields, who are as enthusiastic about the project as I am."

BIOGRAPHICAL/CRITICAL SOURCES: School Arts, January, 1978, April, 1979.

*　　*　　*

BROOK, Peter (Stephen Paul) 1925-

PERSONAL: Born March 21, 1925, in London, England; son of Simon (a chemist) and Ida (a chemist; maiden name, Jansen) Brook; married Natasha Parry (an actress), November 3, 1951. *Education:* Magdalen College, Oxford, B.A., 1944. *Office:* International Center of Theatre Research, 9 rue du Cirque, Paris 8, France.

CAREER: Writer. Director of stage productions for Birmingham Repertory Theatre, including "Man and Superman," 1945, and "The Lady From the Sea," 1946; Royal Opera House, including "Boris Godunov," 1947, and "Salome," 1950; Metropolitan Opera, including "Faust," 1953, and "Eugene Onegin," 1957; and Royal Shakespeare Co., including "King Lear," 1962, "The Persecution and Assassination of Marat as Performed by the Inmates of the Asylum of Charenton Under the Direction of the Marquis de Sade" (also called "Marat/Sade"), 1964. Director of motion pictures for Crown Film Unit, 1945, and "The Beggar's Opera," 1953, "Marat/Sade," 1967, and "Tell Me Lies," 1968. Director of television productions, including "Box for One," 1949, "King Lear," 1953, and "Heaven and Earth," 1957. Founded International Center of Theatre Research, 1970. *Member:* Association of Cinematographers and Allied Technicians.

AWARDS, HONORS: Named best director by London Critics' Poll, 1964, and New York Drama Critics' Poll, 1965, and received Antoinette Perry ("Tony") Award for best director from League of New York Theatres and Producers, and Outer Circle Award, both 1965, all for "The Persecution and Assassination of Marat as Performed by the Inmates of the Asylum of Charenton Under the Direction of the Marquis de Sade''; Commander of the Order of the British Empire and Chevalier de l'Ordre des Arts et des Lettres, both 1965; Drama Desk Award for best director, Antoinette Perry Award for best director, and named best director by New York Drama Critics' Poll, all 1970, all for "A Midsummer Night's Dream''; Shakespeare Award from Freiherr von Stein Foundation, 1973; and other awards.

WRITINGS: The Empty Space (nonfiction), Atheneum, 1968; *Cosmopolitan Tales,* Mojave Books, 1980.

Plays: (And director) "U.S.," first produced on West End at Aldwych Theatre, October 13, 1966.

Screenplays: (Co-author and director) "Moderato Cantabile," 1960; (and director) "Lord of the Flies" (adapted from the novel by William Golding), 1962; (and director) "King Lear" (adapted from the play by William Shakespeare), 1971; (with Jeanne de Salzmann; and director) "Meetings With Remarkable Men," 1979.

SIDELIGHTS: Many theatre critics rank Brook among the most influential figures of the twentieth-century stage. His revolutionary productions of Shakespearean works such as "A Midsummer Night's Dream" and "King Lear," both of which employed spare settings and offbeat costuming to spark fresh interpretations, revealed Brook's interest in the Absurdist theatre of Samuel Beckett and the political didacticism of Bertolt Brecht. The modern theatre's strength, Brook contended, "lies in making certain little concentrated events in which one can participate—the unique quality of living events that technology makes more and more inaccessible." This twin interest in art and social relevance has endeared Brook to reviewers such as *New York Times*'s Anthony Lewis. "In an increasingly technological world, of huge abstractions, he sees the theater supplying the elements of community and life for which people yearn," wrote Lewis. "It is almost a religious experience."

Brook's initiation to the theatre was fairly auspicious. After graduating from Magdalen College at age twenty, he created brief advertising films for Crown Film Unit. He then involved himself in a production of George Bernard Shaw's "Pygmalion" by the Entertainments National Service Organization. While directing a dress rehearsal, Brook was observed by William Armstrong, a prominent British stage director. Armstrong referred Brook to the Birmingham Repertory Theatre, where the latter debuted in 1945 as director of Shaw's "Man and Superman." The following year, critics raved about his direction of Shakespeare's "Romeo and Juliet," in which his casting of youthful actors was considered a welcome departure from the stodgy productions that had plagued recent presentations of Shakespeare's work.

Brook scored again with his 1953 production of Gounod's opera "Faust" for the Metropolitan Opera. Rejecting the opera's medieval setting, he placed the action in the nineteenth century and emphasized the customs of that period. "Faust" was therefore more subtly unconventional than Brook's previous efforts. He also directed his first film, "The Beggar's Opera," in 1953. His grasp of cinematic technique was deemed sufficient by

most critics, but some complained that scenes were alternately too cinematic and too stage-like. Less successful was Brook's second film, "Moderato Cantabile," an experimental work described by Andrew Sarris as "an exercise in languorous introspection of the Resnais—*Hiroshima Mon Amour* school."

In 1964 Brook implemented improvisation and aspects of Antonin Artaud's "Theatre of Cruelty" in the play "The Persecution and Assassination of Marat as Performed by the Inmates of Charenton Under the Direction of the Marquis de Sade" ("Marat/Sade"). Brook was extremely successful in instilling an obsession with deranged and violent behavior in his actors, and the subsequent performances shocked audiences. "The 'Marat/Sade,'" noted Lewis, "with its unforgettable evocation of the inmates of the Asylum at Charenton, left some in its audience physically ill." Brook repeated his success in 1967 when he directed the film version of the play.

Two other works Brook directed in the 1960's were not as well received. Both the play "U.S." and the motion picture "Tell Me Lies" suffered, according to reviewers, from their contrived attempts at relevance to the Vietnam War. And Sarris complained that "*Tell Me Lies* provides an entirely new set of cinematic conceptions that miscarry in the messiest ways imaginable."

Throughout the 1960's Brook also lectured on drama at universities. In 1968 his comments were collected and published as *The Empty Space.* In the book, Brook divides the theatre into four categories: he calls conventional theatre "deadly," dubs ritualistic works "holy," accessible works "rough," and considers his own style "immediate." The "immediate" approach, according to Gerald Weales, is one "in which the creativity happens at that moment and is shared by performers and audience alike." Weales added that "performers must constantly walk the line between discipline and discovery, avoiding a sealed and finished production, creating the play fresh with each performance."

The Empty Space was generally welcomed by critics as thought-provoking insight into the modern theatre. Weales called it "an exploration." In *Drama,* Edward Argent observed that "it is essential reading for anyone seriously interested in the drama—infuriating to some, baffling maybe, but essential." *New Leader*'s Albert Bermel praised Brook's "tact and eclecticism" and called *The Empty Space* "an absorbing document."

Brook continued directing in the 1970's. His most notable works were the motion pictures "King Lear" and "Meetings With Remarkable Men." *New York Times*'s Vincent Canby called "King Lear" a film "of lovely surprises." He noted, "It's a downhill journey, but one that, by the flash of the lightning that the play provides, illuminates, for a very brief time, the essence of existence without comprehensible moral order, and makes it bearable." John Simon disagreed, contending that "there is almost no poetry at all in the film." He charged that "Brook will do anything for an effect, however nonsensical."

"Meetings With Remarkable Men" was less successful. Brook's biography of Russian mystic G. I. Gurdjieff concentrated on the philosopher's search for enlightenment in the Near East. *Newsweek*'s Jack Kroll complained that Brook's solemn approach overwhelmed the drama. "The ineffable is indeed ineffable," Kroll conceded, "but surely a film on this subject should get under your skin, disrupt your complacency, make you feel the possibility of another kind of inner life." Janet Maslin, in *New York Times,* similarly charged, "Watching this handsome, affectless effort feels a little like receiving a series of postcards in the mail, each one beautiful but missing a message on the back." She added, "Certainly 'Meetings With Remarkable Men' is a film that requires supplementary energy, whether it comes from the curiosity or the prior knowledge that the right audience may provide."

BIOGRAPHICAL/CRITICAL SOURCES: New York Times, October 4, 1955, May 18, 1958, January 15, 1971, December 5, 1971, December 22, 1971, August 5, 1979; Andrew Sarris, *The American Cinema: Directors and Direction, 1929-1968,* Dutton, 1968; *New Statesman,* October 18, 1968; *London,* November, 1968; *Vogue,* November 15, 1968; *New York Times Book Review,* November 17, 1968; *New Leader,* December 2, 1968; *Book World,* December 29, 1968; *Drama,* spring, 1969; *Cue,* February 13, 1971; *Newsweek,* September 3, 1979; *New York,* May 26, 1980.*

—*Sketch by Les Stone*

* * *

BROVKA, Petr (Pyatrus Ustinovich)   1905-1980

OBITUARY NOTICE: Born June 25, 1905, in Putilkovichi, Russia (now Vitebsk Region of Belorussia, U.S.S.R.); died March 24, 1980, in U.S.S.R.; buried in Minsk, U.S.S.R. Poet, novelist, translator, and editor. Honored as the People's Poet of Belorussia, Brovka celebrated the ideals of the Russian Revolution and the heroism of the Russian people. His early poems, published in the 1920's and 1930's, romanticized the heroic struggle of the Revolution and hailed the advent of a new social order. Two major works from this period are *Praz gory i step* (title means "Through Mountains and Steppes") and *1914,* both narrative poems written in a lyrical style. In later years his poems extolled the patriotism, good will, and peaceful aspirations of the Soviet people. Among Brovka's other writings are a novel, *Kalandry* (title means "The Calendars"), philosophical works and librettos, translations of works by Mayakovsky, Prokofiev, and Byron, and several volumes of poetry. He was also editor in chief of the first *Belorussian Soviet Encyclopedia.* Obituaries and other sources: *International Who's Who in Poetry,* 5th edition, Melrose, 1977; *Who's Who in the Socialist Countries,* K. G. Saur, 1978; *The International Who's Who,* Europa, 1980; *The Annual Obituary 1980,* St. Martin's, 1981.

* * *

BROWN, Alan R.   1938-

PERSONAL: Born February 7, 1938, in Detroit, Mich.; married wife, Linda; children: Lisa, Jennifer. *Education:* Attended University of California, Los Angeles, 1955-56 and 1959-60; University of California, Berkeley, A.A., 1958; Los Angeles State College, B.A., 1961, M.A., 1963; University of Texas, Ph.D., 1967. *Home address:* P.O. Box 4010, Scottsdale, Ariz. 85285. *Office:* Teacher Corps Project, College of Education, Arizona State University, Tempe, Ariz. 85287.

CAREER: Vista Del Mar Child Care Center, Los Angeles, Calif., counselor of emotionally disturbed adolescents, 1959-61; Orange County Probation Department, Santa Ana, Calif., deputy probation officer, 1961-62; Los Angeles County Probation Department, Los Angeles, research assistant, 1963-64; Veterans Administration Hospital, clinical psychology trainee in Waco and Temple, Tex., 1964-1967, clinical intern in Dallas, Tex., 1966-67; Consultation Service, Phoenix, Ariz., psychologist, 1967-68; Arizona State University, Tempe, assistant professor, 1968-71, associate professor of special education, 1971-74, director of Teacher Corps Project, 1974—. Director of Camp Roosevelt, Inc., 1962-64; research assistant with Texas

State Department of Mental Health and Mental Retardation, 1966; clinical psychology trainee at Dallas Child Guidance Clinic, 1966-67; clinical child psychologist at Denver Department of Health and Hospitals, 1967. Member of board of directors of South Phoenix Channel One Project (drug prevention program); Teachers Corps Youth Advocacy Loop (national network), member of board of directors, 1975-80, chairperson of board of directors, 1975, member of executive committee, 1975-77 and 1979-80, chairperson of Interagency Task Force, 1976-80; Far West Teacher Corps Network, member of board of directors, 1975-80, member of executive committee, 1978-80; member of board of directors of Adolescent Parenting Project, 1978-80. Teacher at workshops in Guam, summers, 1971-73; developer of workshops and conferences; guest on television programs.

MEMBER: American Psychological Association, National Staff Development Council, American Educational Research Association, Teacher Educators for Children With Behavior Disorders, Council for Exceptional Children, Arizona State Psychological Association (chairperson of public relations committee, 1973-74).

WRITINGS: Prejudice in Children, C. C Thomas, 1972; (with Connie Avery) *Modifying Children's Behavior,* C. C Thomas, 1973; (contributor) *In Service of Youth: New Roles in the Governance of Teacher Education,* Association of Teacher Educators, 1980; *Needs Assessment Approaches for Community Based Education,* Recruitment and Community Technical Resource Center, Howard University, 1980; (with Bonnie Rabe) *Building an Effective Collaborative School Improvement and Staff Development Program,* National Council of States on Inservice Education, 1980; (contributor) *Positive School Learning Climates,* Center for Urban Education, University of Nebraska at Omaha, 1980; (editor with Roland Goddu, and contributor) *Networking for Interagency Collaboration: Integrating Technology and Human Service Delivery,* Teacher Corps Youth Advocacy Loop, University of Vermont, 1981. Member of editorial boards of monographs published by Teacher Corps Youth Advocacy Loop and Far West Teacher Corps Network, both 1975-80.

WORK IN PROGRESS: Unfinished Business: Reforming the American Public Education System.

* * *

BROWN, Barbara W(ood)   1928-

PERSONAL: Born June 10, 1928, in Teaneck, N.J.; daughter of Raymond D. (an attorney) and Mildred (Upson) Wood; married Lloyd W. Brown, October 30, 1953; children: Susan M., Grace E. *Education:* Middlebury College, A.B., 1950; Wesleyan University, Middletown, Conn., M.A.L.S., 1969, C.A.S., 1975. *Home:* 26 South Main St., Colchester, Conn. 06415.

CAREER: Teacher of Latin and French at private schools in St. Albans, Vt., 1950-52, and Colchester, Conn., 1952-53; high school teacher of Latin and French in Glastonbury, Conn., 1956-57; Bacon Academy, Colchester, teacher of Latin, French, and history, 1960—. Town historian of Colchester. *Member:* Association for the Study of Connecticut History, Connecticut Historical Society, Connecticut Society of Genealogists, Vermont Genealogical Society, Colchester Historical Society (historian).

WRITINGS: Flintlocks and Barrels of Beef: Colchester, Connecticut, and the American Revolution (monograph), Bacon Academy, 1976; (with James M. Rose) *Tapestry: A Living*

History of the Black Family in Southeastern Connecticut, New London County Historical Society, 1979; (with Rose) *Black Roots in Southeastern Connecticut, 1650-1900*, Gale, 1980.

WORK IN PROGRESS: Colchester Men in the Revolution; History of Merchants Row, Colchester; continuing research on Connecticut black history.

* * *

BROWN, Christy 1932-1981

PERSONAL: Born in 1932 in Dublin, Ireland; died of asphyxiation, September 6, 1981, in Parbrook, England; son of a bricklayer and Bridget Brown; married Mary Carr (a dental receptionist), October, 1972. *Home:* Longacre, Withial Lane, Parbrook, Glastonbury, Somerset, England.

CAREER: Novelist and poet. *Awards, honors:* Christopher Award from Christopher Society for *My Left Foot.*

WRITINGS: My Left Foot (autobiography), foreword and epilogue by Robert Collis, Secker & Warburg, 1954, Simon & Schuster, 1955, published as *The Childhood Story of Christy Brown*, Pan Books, 1972; *Down All the Days* (novel; Book-of-the-Month Club alternate selection), Stein & Day, 1970; *Come Softly to My Wake: The Poems of Christy Brown*, Stein & Day, 1971; *Background Music* (poetry), Stein & Day, 1973; *A Shadow on Summer* (novel), Stein & Day, 1974; *Wild Grow the Lilies* (novel), Stein & Day, 1976; *Of Snails and Skylarks* (poetry), Secker & Warburg, 1977, Stein & Day, 1978.

WORK IN PROGRESS: A Promising Career, publication expected in 1982.

SIDELIGHTS: Born with cerebral palsy, the tenth of twenty-two children, Brown was so disabled that he could not eat, drink, or dress by himself. He did have, however, the use of his left foot, which he used to paint pictures and to type books and poetry on an electric typewriter. Because Brown was unable to communicate or to move by himself, he was presumed to be totally disabled for his first five years. The first indication of his potential appeared, said *Newsweek*'s S. K. Oberbeck, when "at age five, sitting on the floor watching his sister do sums on a chipped slate, Christy Brown's left foot reached out and snatched the chalk from her hand." Although Brown did not master speech until he was eighteen, he soon learned to write—with his left foot—in chalk on the linoleum floor.

"From very early on I had the urge to write," Brown told *New York Times* reporter Desmond Rushe. "As far back as I can remember I was always writing bits and pieces. . . . I had to compensate for being handicapped and the only way I could do it was to put my thoughts down on paper." Brown's urge to write resulted in *My Left Foot*, an autobiography published when the author was twenty-one years old. The book, a chronicle of Brown's struggle to overcome his staggering handicap, begins with the author's birth in an Irish slum. Brown later dismissed the work as "the kind of book they expected a cripple to write, too sentimental and corny," but Oberbeck appraised it as "an engaging, inspiring autobiography."

Brown's next book, *Down All the Days*, took fifteen years to complete. This fictionalized autobiography was, according to Robert Ostermann of *National Observer*, "an astonishing achievement, for it poured out in a verbal flood the coming to physical, imaginative, and intellectual life of a Dublin slum child born into the same crippling prison as its author."

Brown once described *Down All the Days* as "just a slice of life, a very raw slice of life," and most critics agreed. A *Times Literary Supplement* reviewer observed that "Christy Brown's

Dublin slums are larger than life, dens of roistering blasphemy and fornication." Often focusing on the sexuality of its seedy characters, the book contains "a goodly number of O'Portnoyesque sexual gropings," noted a *Time* reporter, who also pointed out that Brown "too often confuses the artificial throbbing of sex for thematic development."

Eugene A. Dooley of *Best Sellers* praised *Down All the Days* for its "picturesque language and the phrasing of incidents" and commended its literary style. A *Times Literary Supplement* critic thought Brown's style was "too facilely romantic and anecdotal," but admitted that "Brown writes with a breadth of understanding that makes him already one of the most discerning and lively observers of Irish life." Oberbeck concurred, stating that the book is "tender, gritty, immensely warm in its penetration of the hair-trigger tempers and passions that explode, recoil and reverberate in . . . [Brown's] deftly etched episodes."

Down All the Days became a best-seller and was translated into fourteen languages. It was followed by two books of poetry that Ostermann described as "more poetic ore than refined metal." Brown's collection of love lyrics, *Come Softly to My Wake*, fared well. According to Desmond Rushe, the book's "first issue of five thousand copies . . . sold out, which is remarkable for a volume of poetry." Brown's second book of poems, *Background Music*, was followed by a novel, *A Shadow on Summer*. *America*'s Peter LaSalle maintained that the novel "demonstrates again that Brown is a master word-wielder." *New York Times* critic Anatole Broyard, however, criticized Brown's overuse of adjectives and cliches.

Brown's last novel, *Wild Grow the Lilies*, was also faulted for its excessive verbiage. Ostermann pointed out that Brown "has barely stayed the flood of words so fitting for *Down All the Days*, and can't resist muffling every sentence in *Lilies* with five adjectives where one would do." Valentine Cunningham of *New Statesman* agreed that the novel is wordy and filled with "blarneyfied eloquence" but still found delight in Brown's "filthy-minded pun-palace."

BIOGRAPHICAL/CRITICAL SOURCES: Christy Brown, *My Left Foot*, foreword and epilogue by Robert Collis, Secker & Warburg, 1954; *Times Literary Supplement*, May 28, 1970, April 16, 1976, May 19, 1978; *New York Times*, May 30, 1970, October 18, 1971, February 3, 1975; *Newsweek*, June 8, 1970, October 16, 1972; *New York Times Book Review*, June 14, 1970; *Time*, June 15, 1970, October 16, 1972; *Best Sellers*, June 15, 1970; *Booklist*, November 1, 1973, June 15, 1976, October 15, 1978; *Critic*, January, 1974; *New Statesman*, August 2, 1974, April 16, 1976; *America*, March 22, 1975; *Christian Science Monitor*, March 26, 1975; *National Observer*, September 25, 1976.

OBITUARIES: Detroit Free Press, September 8, 1981; *Detroit News*, September 8, 1981; *New York Times*, September 8, 1981; *London Times*, September 8, 1981.*

* * *

BROWN, Jerry Earl 1940-

PERSONAL: Born June 24, 1940, in Palestine, Tex.; son of William Monroe (a builder) and Elvie (Walston) Brown; married Frances Plank (a librarian), April 4, 1971. *Education:* Attended Santa Ana Junior College, 1962, Texas Tech University, 1963-67, and University of Colorado, 1968-70. *Politics:* "Apolitical." *Religion:* None. *Residence:* Boulder, Colo. *Agent:* James Allen, Virginia Kidd, P.O. Box 278, Milford, Pa. 18337. *Office:* National Writers Club, 1450 South Havana, Suite 620, Aurora, Colo. 80012.

CAREER: Aspen Police Force, Aspen, Colo., police patrolman, 1970-71; Aspen Security Patrol, Aspen, security patrolman, 1971-73; National Writers Club, Aurora, Colo., assistant director and member of board of directors, 1977-81. Speaker at writers' workshops and conferences. *Military service:* U.S. Marine Corps, Morse code and radio operator, 1958-62. *Member:* Authors Guild.

WRITINGS: Under the City of Angels (science fiction novel), Bantam, 1981. Contributor of articles, stories, and reviews to magazines, including *Canoe, Runner, Colorado High Country, Snowy Egret, Gent,* and *Dude,* and newspapers. Editor of *National Writers Club Professional Bulletin,* 1977-79, *Authorship,* 1977—, and *Flash Market News,* 1977—.

WORK IN PROGRESS: Roaring Fork, "a mainstream story based on my Aspen cop experience."

SIDELIGHTS: Brown told *CA:* "As far back as I can remember, I was creating stories in one way or another, playing them out with myself, playmates, or a legion of toy characters. This early penchant for creating fiction served well as a means of escape from an environment often tumultuous and, for the most part, culturally arid.

"Born in a farmhouse near Palestine, Texas, in the year before the United States went to war against Hitler and Hirohito, I grew up in eastern Texas and developed a strong love for the hills, fields, and streams. These things sustained me during those years: my imagination, movies, books, and the woods.

"I hated school, was a terrible student, a random and infrequent reader until my teens. Science fiction, war stories, and westerns, from Asimov to Alan Lemay, constituted the bulk of my literary nourishment, and I usually refused on principle to read anything assigned by a teacher. This sort of rebellious hubris did me little good, but one kind and patient English teacher saw through my foolishness and decided I had some writing talent. The writing of 'themes' for her is the only assignment I can remember ever having faced with any energy or enthusiasm.

"By the time I graduated from Palestine High School, I was hot to see the world and committed the brash act of enlisting in the Marine Corps, only to soon discover I'd traded one stifling environment for another. It was in the Marine Corps that I began to read seriously, out of boredom, intellectual hunger, and again as a means to escape my immediate milieu. The haphazard reading this time inclined toward the literary and philosophical. Out of all that I read, I believe Camus, Millay, and Faulkner stirred me the most and deepest.

"I left the Marines with an earnest desire to write, but with little of the discipline or willingness to be still that such an ambition requires. I drifted from job to job, in and out of college, from place to place. I wrote short stories and collected the usual midden of rejection slips. I read and wandered, pondering the country and its ills, and pondering myself. We seemed to be on equally confused courses.

"It was in a geology course at the University of Colorado where the first seeds of *Under the City of Angels* were sown. The professor was talking about tectonic plates and the coast of California, elements of a topic that wrenched me out of my usual classroom woolgathering and pulled my attention to the map he was drawing on the blackboard. The idea that half the West Coast, given enough time on the geological scale, could split or shear off from the rest of the continent was fascinating. Later this alarming possibility grew into various scenarios in my mind and finally served as plot situation and background for my book. In researching the novel, I became well ac-quainted with the history, location, structure, and caprices of the San Andreas Fault and its many branches.

"At first the geologists I consulted scoffed at the notion of a disaster taking place the size of that which occurs in the book. Eventually, though, they too became drawn into the old speculative-fiction game of 'what if,' and given the plot premise of the book, they admitted the West Coast could suffer such a catastrophe.

"Though *Angels* is not, strictly speaking, a story of environmental protest, the pro-environmental theme should be evident to anyone who reads it, and though I am not as a rule a joiner, my sympathies lie strongly with such groups as Friends of the Earth, the Sierra Club, and the numerous organizations for a sensible and vitally needed space program that have sprung to life in recent years.

"Some of the questions and dilemmas I have found that I want to deal with are those that writers have confronted for ages but that have today, I believe, an unprecedented poignancy. Are the so-called eternal verities really eternal? Is there a soul and if there is, is it immutable and also eternal? In a world made constantly unstable by accelerated and sometimes catastrophic change, what, if anything, remains constant? In a world where all the so-called timeless truths seem to be undergoing or seem to have already undergone demolition, in a world where cynicism rules and faith seems dead and love at best seems only temporary and often confused with lust, what, if anything, is of lasting value?

"*Angels* confronts and tries to answer at least some of these questions in a way that is affirmative, not because I set out to write a novel about faith or a novel that said, yes, there is love and it heals, but that is what I found in this particular story after I had written it."

* * *

BROWNE, Joseph William 1914-

PERSONAL: Born August 10, 1914, in Brooklyn, N.Y.; son of James Emmet and Catherine (Daly) Browne. *Education:* St. John's University, Jamaica, N.Y., B.A., 1937; Fordham University, M.A., 1948, Ph.D., 1951. *Office:* Department of Philosophy, St. John's University, Grand Central and Utopia Parkway, Jamaica, N.Y. 11432.

CAREER: Entered Congregatio Missionis Sancti Vicentii a Paulo (Congregation of the Mission; Vincentians), 1937, ordained Roman Catholic priest, 1942; St. John's University, Jamaica, N.Y., assistant professor, 1942-49, associate professor, 1949-51, professor, 1951-54, athletic moderator, 1943-51; Niagara University, Niagara Falls, N.Y., professor of philosophy, 1954-56; St. John's University, professor of philosophy, 1958—, academic vice-president, 1958—. *Member:* International Berkeley Society, American Catholic Scholars, National Catholic Education Association, American Catholic Philosophical Association, American Association of University Professors, American Academy of Political and Social Science, Fellowship of Catholic Scholars.

WRITINGS: Berkeley's Intellectualism, St. John's University Press, 1975. Also author of *The Ethics of Thomistic Personalism.*

WORK IN PROGRESS: Personal Dignity.

* * *

BROYARD, Anatole 1920-

PERSONAL: Born July 16, 1920, in New Orleans, La.; son

of Anatole (a builder and construction worker) and Edna Broyard; married Alexandra Nelson (a dancer); children: Todd, Bliss. *Education:* Attended Brooklyn College and New School for Social Research. *Home:* 1316 Cross Highway, Fairfield, Conn. 06430. *Office:* New York Times, 229 West 43rd St., New York, N.Y. 10036.

CAREER: New School for Social Research, New York City, lecturer in sociology and literature, 1958-79; *New York Times,* New York City, book reviewer and feature writer, 1971—. Lecturer in creative writing at Columbia University, 1978-80. *Military service:* U.S. Army; served in World War II; became captain.

WRITINGS: Aroused by Books (book reviews), Random House, 1974; *Men, Women and Other Anticlimaxes* (essays), Methuen, 1980. Author of short stories. Contributor of articles on popular culture to periodicals, including *New Republic, Publishers Weekly, Mademoiselle, New York Times Magazine,* and *New York Times Book Review.*

WORK IN PROGRESS: A novel.

SIDELIGHTS: Broyard's two books are selections of his writings that have appeared in the *New York Times. Aroused by Books* contains 107 book reviews and essays originally published in the *Times* between 1971 and 1973. *Men, Women and Other Anticlimaxes,* Broyard's second book, features fifty personal essays that appeared in the *Times* from 1977 to 1979.

As the title of *Aroused by Books* suggests, Broyard's book reviews are characteristically energetic, and his writing reflects his enthusiasm. "Broyard has the rare gift that distinguishes the born writer," commented Ernest van den Haag in the *National Review.* "Whatever arouses his passions he can communicate fully; hence his reactions are infectious." Benjamin DeMott echoed van den Haag's opinion. Writing in *Atlantic,* DeMott said: "[Broyard] tends to favor writing that charges him up physically. He speaks out strongly for 'gut truths,' for 'rhetoric that pulled my pulse,' for a novelist whose 'imagination stalks the back fences and overturns the garbage cans of our emotions.'"

A *Sewanee Review* critic, on the other hand, argued that Broyard's writing revealed a "penchant for hyperbole and . . . [a] compulsion to titillate the reader." But, the critic added, "this consideration aside, Broyard writes journalism of high caliber when it comes to writers like Ford Madox Ford, Anthony Powell, John Updike, Eudora Welty, V. S. Pritchett, Alfred Kazin, and Lionel Trilling." Van den Haag also objected to Broyard's writing, but for different reasons: "He cannot write without coining memorable phrases, right, left, and in the middle. A delight to read. But it may also make a tedious book appear less tedious—even when its tediousness is scrupulously remarked on." Still, insisted van den Haag, Broyard's book is a "marvelous performance."

Broyard's "fluid prose" also marked his second book, a collection of essays on life in Connecticut as seen from a former New Yorker's perspective. *Men, Women and Other Anticlimaxes* focuses "with wit, subtlety, and amplitude on the befuddling vicissitudes of private life as we're living it now," commented the *National Review*'s Jane Larkin Crain. His subjects include "such potentially done-to-death matters as the contemporary status of fatherhood, love and marriage, friendship, children, the sexes, [and] domesticity," continued Crain. "Broyard, though caught up in an essentially interior world, manages to convey, in a strong personal voice, a commitment to centers that hold, to a sense of life untainted by the masturbatory brand of introspection in which so much commentary on private life abounds these days."

Critic Joseph McLellan of the *Washington Post Book World* also praised *Men, Women, and Other Anticlimaxes* for its portraits of Connecticut life. "Broyard slowly, cumulatively creates in these pages a hymn to Connecticut-ness, a paean to the leisurely pace and open spaces of a region just beyond suburbia but on the civilized outer fringes of farm country," McLellan said. "In Broyard's compact essays, Connecticut becomes a microcosm. It has a distinctive character of its own, thrown into sharp perspective by the looming shadow of the giant city next door, but he shows it also as a stage for universal human dramas."

BIOGRAPHICAL/CRITICAL SOURCES: Atlantic, February, 1975; *National Review,* February 28, 1975, September 5, 1980; *Sewanee Review,* October, 1975; *Washington Post Book World,* February 19, 1980.

*   *   *

BRUCE, David (Kirkpatrick Este)   1898-1977

OBITUARY NOTICE: Born February 12, 1898, in Baltimore, Md.; died of a heart attack, December 5, 1977, in Washington, D.C. Diplomat, statesman, and author. Awarded the Medal of Freedom upon his retirement, Bruce was one of the most distinguished members of the American diplomatic corps. He held three of the top diplomatic posts in Europe, serving as ambassador to England, France, and Germany. He also headed the American delegation to the Paris peace talks after discussions to end the Vietnam War had stalled and opened the first liaison office in Peking following the U.S. recognition of China. He began his career as a Baltimore lawyer in 1921 and was elected three years later to the Maryland House of Delegates. In the 1930's he lived as a gentleman farmer on his Virginia tobacco plantation and served in the state's House of Delegates for one year. During World War II he helped set up the Office of Strategic Services and later commanded O.S.S. operations in the European theater. After the war he worked as an administrator of the Marshall Plan in Paris and was appointed ambassador to France in 1949. Bruce held other high posts in the American Government, including under secretary of state and assistant secretary of commerce, and ended his career in 1976 as the chief American delegate to the North Atlantic Treaty Organization (NATO). He was the author of *Revolution to Reconstruction* and *Sixteen American Presidents.* Obituaries and other sources: *Current Biography,* Wilson, 1949, 1961, 1978; *International Who's Who,* Europa, 1977; *New York Times,* December 6, 1977; *Newsweek,* December 19, 1977; *Who's Who,* 130th edition, St. Martin's, 1978; *Political Profiles: The Nixon/Ford Years,* Facts on File, 1979.

*   *   *

BRYANT, Arthur (Wynne Morgan)   1899-

PERSONAL: Born February 18, 1899, in Dersingham, Norfolk, England; son of Sir Francis Bryant (a sergeant-at-arms to King George V); married Sylvia Mary Shakerley, 1924 (divorced, 1939); married Anne Elaine Brooke, 1941. *Education:* Received M.A. from Queen's College, Oxford. *Home:* Myles Place, The Close, Salisbury, Wiltshire, England.

CAREER: Cambridge School of Arts, Crafts, and Technology, England, headmaster, 1923-25; Oxford University, Oxford, England, lecturer in history and English literature, 1925-35; editor of *Ashridge Journal,* 1930-39; London University, London, England, Watson Professor of American History, 1935; *Illustrated London News,* London, writer of column "Our Note Book," 1936—. Served as a governor of Ashridge, 1936-49; chairman of council, 1946-49. Lecturer in Europe and the

United States; lecturer to H.M. forces, 1940-46; editor of speeches for Neville Chamberlain. Producer of pageants. Chairman of St. John and Red Cross Hospital Library; trustee of Historic Churches Preservation Council; president of Common Market Safeguards Campaign and Tyneham Action Group. Vice-president of Royal Literary Fund; member of Advisory Talks Council of the British Broadcasting Corp. (BBC); trustee of English Folk Music Fund. *Military service:* Royal Flying Corps and Royal Air Force; served in World War I.

MEMBER: English Association (past president), Royal Historical Society (fellow), Royal Society of Literature (fellow), Society of Authors, Wisbech Society, Friends of the Vale of Aylesbury, Athenaeum Club, Beefsteak Club, Grillion's Club, Pratt's Club, MCC Club. *Awards, honors:* Commander of the Order of the British Empire, 1949; knight of Grace St. John of Jerusalem, 1954; companion of honor, 1967; Chesney Gold Medal from Royal United Service Institute, 1955; gold medal for literature from *London Sunday Times;* gold medal from Royal Institute of Chartered Survivors; honorary member of Southampton Chamber of Commerce; LL.D. from University of Edinburgh, University of St. Andrews, and University of New Brunswick.

WRITINGS: The Spirit of Conservatism, Methuen, 1929; *King Charles II,* Longmans, Green, 1931, revised edition, Collins, 1955; *Macaulay,* P. Davies, 1932, Appleton, 1933, reprinted, Harper, 1979; *The Man in the Making* (part I of "Samuel Pepys" trilogy), Cambridge University Press, 1933; *The England of Charles II,* Longmans, Green, 1934, reprinted, Books for Libraries, 1972, published as *Restoration England,* Collins, 1960; (editor) *The Man and the Hour: Studies of Six Great Men of Our Time,* P. Allan, 1934, Kennikat Press, 1972; *The National Character,* Longmans, Green, 1934.

The Years of Peril (part II of "Samuel Pepys" trilogy), Cambridge University Press, 1935; (editor) King Charles II, *The Letters, Speeches and Declarations of King Charles II,* Cassell, 1935; *The American Ideal,* Longmans, Green, 1936, reprinted, Books for Libraries, 1969; *George V,* P. Davies, 1936; (editor) *Postman's Horn: An Anthology of the Letters of Latter Seventeenth Century England,* Greenwood Press, 1936, reprinted, 1970; *Humanities in Politics,* Hutchinson, 1938; *The Saviour of the Navy* (part III of "Samuel Pepys" trilogy), Cambridge University Press, 1938, reprinted, Collins, 1967; (editor) Arthur Neville Chamberlain, *In Search of Peace,* Hutchinson, 1939.

English Saga (1840-1940), Collins, 1940, published as *Pageant of England,* Harper, 1941, abridged edition published as *Only Yesterday: Aspects of English History, 1840-1940,* Collins, 1965; *Unfinished Victory,* Macmillan, 1940; *The Years of Endurance, 1793-1802,* Harper, 1942, reprinted, Collins, 1975.

Years of Victory, 1802-1812, Collins, 1944, Harper, 1945, reprinted, Collins, 1975; *Historian's Holiday,* Dropmore Press, 1946, revised edition, Collins, 1951; *The Age of Elegance, 1812-1822,* Collins, 1950, Harper, 1951, reprinted, Collins, 1975; *The Story of England: Makers of the Realm,* Collins, 1953, Houghton, 1954, published as *Makers of England: The Atlantic Saga,* Doubleday, 1962 (original volume also published as *Makers of the Realm: The Story of Britain's Beginnings,* Fontana, 1972).

The Turn of the Tide: A History of the War Years Based on the Diaries of Field Marshal Lord Alanbrooke, Doubleday, 1957; *Triumph in the West: A History of the War Years Based on the Diaries of Field Marshal Lord Alanbrooke,* Doubleday, 1959, reprinted, Greenwood Press, 1974; *Jimmy, the Dog in*

My Life, Lutterworth, 1960; *Liquid History: To Commemorate Fifty Years of the Port of London Authority,* [London], 1960; *A Choice for Destiny: Commonwealth and Common Market,* Collins, 1962; (author of introduction) King James II, *The Memoirs of James II,* Chatto & Windus, 1962; *The Age of Chivalry* (volume II of *The Story of England*), Collins, 1963, Doubleday, 1964.

The Fire and the Rose: Dramatic Moments in British History, Collins, 1965, Doubleday, 1966, revised edition, Fontana, 1972; *The Medieval Foundation,* Collins, 1966, published as *The Medieval Foundation of England,* Doubleday, 1967; *Protestant Island,* Collins, 1967, *Set in a Silver Sea,* Doubleday, 1968; *The Lion and the Unicorn: A Historian's Testament,* Collins, 1969, Doubleday, 1970.

Nelson, Collins, 1970; *The Great Duke; or, The Invincible General,* Collins, 1971; *Jackets of Green: A Study of the History, Philosophy, and Character of the Rifle Brigade,* Collins, 1972; *A Thousand Years of British Monarchy,* John Pinches, 1973.

Contributor to periodicals, including *London Sunday Times, Sunday Express,* and *Illustrated London News.*

SIDELIGHTS: Arthur Bryant is a renowned British historian whose ability to make the past come alive for modern readers has gained him both critical acclaim and popular success. His great love for his country permeates his work; one writer said that Bryant's patriotism is "a passion that runs in his blood." Although some critics find him overly sentimental, many consider his work accurate, useful, and informative. He is generally recognized for his skill in condensing large amounts of information into what one critic called "eminently readable" works.

Bryant was one of the original officers to serve in the newly formed Royal Air Force during World War I. After the war, he won a scholarship from Cambridge but decided to attend Oxford instead. Upon leaving Oxford, he ran a children's library in a house that had once belonged to Charles Dickens. He was eventually appointed headmaster of the Cambridge School of Arts, Crafts, and Technology, becoming the youngest headmaster in England. It was shortly after he resigned from that post that he began writing.

The 1931 publication of *King Charles II* won him immediate popular success. His reputation as a historian was quickly established, and since that time he has written more than twenty historical works. *King Charles II* gives "a better understanding of the period in which modern England came into being," wrote Charles Petrie of *Saturday Review. Spectator's* John Buchan called the biography "the best study of the man yet published," but a writer for *Times Literary Supplement* suggested that Bryant portrayed Charles as being more virtuous than he actually was.

Bryant is especially known for his biographical writings. One of his more extensive biographies is his three-volume series on the life of Samuel Pepys, a famous seventeenth-century English diarist. The first volume is taken largely from the diaries; for the later volumes Bryant used official correspondence and naval documents. Graham Greene of *Spectator* felt that Bryant's portrayal of Pepys was "a little too rosy," but he applauded the manner in which Bryant selected and arranged "the vast material of the diary." With W. P. Lipscomb, Bryant later adapted the Pepys story for the stage, and the production ran for one hundred fifty performances.

Ambrose Agius of *Best Sellers* called Bryant's *The Medieval Foundation of England* a "work full of intricate historical lore."

He recommended the book for anyone planning to visit England, as they will find their "pleasure and profit immeasurably enhanced by a previous reading of this account of the people and events that went into her [England's] making." The *New York Times Book Review*'s Charles Ferguson declared *Medieval Foundation* a great book, and he marveled at Bryant's thoroughness in tracing English history through thousands of years. In the book, Bryant tells of the influx and invasions of various peoples, including Romans, Saxons, Vikings, and Normans, and he describes the effect each group had on the growth and development of English agriculture, trade, and law. A writer for the *Economist* suggested that Bryant was guilty of oversimplification, but conceded that this was probably inevitable, given the vast scope of his subject.

In *Set in a Silver Sea,* Bryant takes up the telling of English social history where he left off in *Medieval Foundation.* He traces British life from the Restoration through the reign of Queen Victoria, creating what Agius called a "colorful and engaging . . . portrait" of the English character. Among other things, he describes the sports, food, and farming of the period and discusses both country and city life. Bryant's analysis of the English character caused *Christian Science Monitor*'s Eric Forbes-Boyd to praise his "ability to plumb the deeper currents of thought and emotion underlying the scenes he so brilliantly reconstructs."

The Lion and the Unicorn contains selections from Bryant's weekly column "Our Note Book," which was published in the *Illustrated London News* for thirty-three years. The book, "running as it does dead counter to fashions, attitudes and modes of thought current in these late 'sixties, says much that still needs saying, is unaffected, civilised and deeply pondered," wrote David Williams in *Punch.* Williams went on, however, to call Bryant "square," and asked if he is not "sometimes perhaps deliberately blind to the way things are going?" Williams noted that Bryant, accustomed as he is to "scrutinising the once slow process of historical change," is reluctant to realize that people today must adapt to change much more rapidly than their ancestors had to. "We are going down the rapids fast, and what we should concentrate on is navigation, not nostalgia."

When reviewers find fault with Bryant's work, it is usually to criticize his tendency to be unduly generous when reviewing British history; they suggest that he sometimes allows his fierce patriotism to color his judgment. Others find his deep love for his mother country charming, and most agree that he is a distinguished and able historian.

AVOCATIONAL INTERESTS: Collecting old furniture, pictures, and books.

BIOGRAPHICAL/CRITICAL SOURCES: Spectator, October 10, 1931, November 24, 1933; *Times Literary Supplement,* October 15, 1931, November 2, 1933, December 23, 1944, December 18, 1953; *Saturday Review,* October 24, 1931, May 19, 1962; *Christian Science Monitor,* November 25, 1933, May 11, 1968; *New York Times,* February 12, 1939; *New York Herald Tribune Book Review,* May 27, 1951; *Nation,* May 25, 1957; *Economist,* November 12, 1966; *New York Times Book Review,* September 17, 1967, December 10, 1972; *New Statesman,* October 20, 1967; *Book World,* May 12, 1968; *Best Sellers,* May 15, 1968, July 15, 1976; *Punch,* December 31, 1969.*

—*Sketch by Mary Sullivan*

* * *

BRYDEN, Bill
See BRYDEN, William Campbell Rough

BRYDEN, William Campbell Rough   1942-
(Bill Bryden)

PERSONAL: Born April 12, 1942, in Greenock, Scotland; son of George (an engineer) and Catherine (Rough) Bryden; married Deborah Morris (a potter), July 24, 1970; children: Dillon Michael George, Mary Kate. *Education:* Attended high school in Greenock, Scotland. *Home:* 13 Allfarthing Lane, London SW18, England. *Agent:* Kenneth Ewing, Fraser & Dunlop Scripts, Ltd., 91 Regent St., London W1R 8RU, England. *Office:* National Theatre, South Bank, London SE1 9PX, England.

CAREER: Royal Court Theatre, London, England, assistant to William Gaskill, 1966-68; Royal Lyceum, Edinburgh, Scotland, associate director, 1971—; National Theatre, London, associate director, 1975—; Scottish Television, Glasgow, Scotland, director, 1979—. Director of plays, including "Misalliance," 1965, "Journey of the Fifth Horse," 1967, "Backbone," 1968, "Passion," 1971 and 1977, "Corunna," 1971, "The Baby Elephant," 1971, "Willie Rough," 1972, "The Thrie Estates," 1973, "The Bevellers," 1973, "Benny Lynch," 1974, "Spring Awakening," 1974, "Romeo and Juliet," 1974, "The Iceman Cometh," 1974 and 1980, "The Flouers of Edinburgh," 1975, "How Mad Tulloch Was Taken Away," 1975, "The Playboy of the Western World," 1975, "Watch It Come Down," 1976, "Il Campiello," 1976, "The Plough and the Stars," 1977, "Counting the Ways," 1977, "Old Movies," 1977, "Lark Rise," 1978, "American Buffalo," 1978, "The World Turned Upside Down," 1978, "The Long Voyage Home," 1979, "Dispatches," 1979, "Candleford," 1979, "Hughie," 1979, "The Crucible," 1980, "Don Quixote," 1982, and "Civilians."

WRITINGS—Under name Bill Bryden; plays: (And director) *Willie Rough* (two-act; first produced in Edinburgh, Scotland, at Royal Lyceum, 1972), Southside, 1972; (and director) *Benny Lynch: Scenes From a Short Life* (three-act; first produced in Edinburgh at Royal Lyceum, 1974), Southside, 1975; (librettist) *Hermiston* (two-act opera; first produced in Edinburgh at King's Theatre, 1975), Scottish Opera, 1977; (and director) *Old Movies* (two-act; first produced in London, England, at National Theatre, 1976), Heinemann, 1977; (and director) *Il Campiello: A Venetian Comedy* (five-act; first produced in London at National Theatre, 1976), Heinemann, 1977; "Civilians" (two-act), first produced in Glasgow, Scotland, at Theatre Royal, 1980; (with Steven Phillip Smith, Stacy Keach, and James Keach) *The Long Riders* (screenplay; released by United Artists, 1980), Futura, 1980.

WORK IN PROGRESS: "A Song of Ireland," a screenplay; a stage play.

SIDELIGHTS: "Just when everyone thought the Western was washed up as a movie genre," asserted Gene Siskel in the *Chicago Tribune,* "along comes . . . 'The Long Riders' to remind us that applying such notions as 'dead' or 'alive' to types of movies is just plain silly." The story of the James-Younger gang, "The Long Riders," follows the bandits from their stint in the Confederate Army and their early, popular raids as disgruntled losers of the Civil War, to their calamitous robbery of a Northfield, Minn., bank. Despite the fact that the James-Younger gang has been the subject of numerous Westerns, "The Long Riders," noted Roger Angell in the *New Yorker,* "manages to make it fresh and alive again—in some stretches singing this heroic folk romance as well as it has ever been done before." While *Nation*'s Robert Hatch declared

Bryden's screenplay "sharp and often witty," David Ansen of *Newsweek* appraised it as "basically an assemblage of bits and pieces that doesn't build toward any real emotional pay-off." Ansen added, however, that "'The Long Riders' is still the best Western in many years—it has the laconic elegance of a ritual." Angell pronounced it "an American beauty."

BIOGRAPHICAL/CRITICAL SOURCES: Chicago Tribune, May 16, 1980; *New Yorker,* May 19, 1980; *New York,* May 26, 1980; *New Republic,* May 31, 1980; *Newsweek,* June 2, 1980; *Nation,* June 7, 1980; *Time,* June 16, 1980.

*   *   *

BUCHANAN, Patrick
See CORLEY, Edwin (Raymond)

*   *   *

BUGBEE, Emma   1888(?)-1981

OBITUARY NOTICE: Born c. 1888 in Shippensburg, Pa.; died October 6, 1981, in Warwick, R.I. Journalist with the *New York Herald Tribune* from 1911 to 1966. To her readers, Bugbee was best known for her coverage of Eleanor Roosevelt. In her profession, however, she was a leading activist against the male-dominated environment of the newspaper business. For many decades Bugbee was one of only two female reporters employed by the *New York Herald* (which later became *New York Herald Tribune*), and until the end of World War I she and her colleague Ishbel Ross were excluded from the city room. To alleviate the isolation and unfair working conditions imposed on women in the field, she became a founder of the Newspaper Women's Club of New York and led efforts to expand the role and opportunities for female journalists. She was the author of a children's book, *Peggy Goes Overseas,* published by Dodd in 1945. Obituaries and other sources: *Authors of Books for Young People,* 2nd edition, Scarecrow, 1971; *New York Times,* October 10, 1981; *Time,* October 26, 1981.

*   *   *

BUITRAGO, Ann Mari   1929-

PERSONAL: Surname is pronounced Bwee-trago; born January 12, 1929, in Sharon, Pa.; daughter of Eugenio Maria (an electrical and mechanical engineer) and Helen (Goodall) Buitrago. *Education:* Attended College of Wooster, 1947-49; San Jose State College (now University), B.A., 1951; University of Kansas, M.A., 1955; City University of New York, Ph.D., 1977. *Home:* 383 Pacific St., Brooklyn, N.Y. 11217. *Office:* Fund for Open Information and Accountability, Inc., 339 Lafayette St., New York, N.Y. 10012.

CAREER: Rutgers University, New Brunswick, N.J., 1971-77, began as lecturer, became assistant professor; Fund for Open Information and Accountability, Inc., New York, N.Y., co-director, 1977—.

WRITINGS: (With Leon Andrew Immerman) *Are You Now or Have You Ever Been in the FBI's Files?: How to Secure and Interpret Your FBI Files,* Grove, 1980.

WORK IN PROGRESS: Mississippi Freedom: The Democratic Party Challenge at Atlantic City; Labor and the Cold War; research on civil rights decisions of the Fifth Circuit Court of Appeals.

SIDELIGHTS: Ann Buitrago told *CA:* "I wrote my first book because the demands for help from the Fund for Open Information and Accountability, in the face of the F.B.I.'s deter-mined resistance, outran our personal capacities. With the book's publication our work, educating and assisting individuals and groups and holding the government accountable, has been greatly facilitated."

AVOCATIONAL INTERESTS: Watching a group/family of American eagles in Pembroke, Maine.

*   *   *

BULGAKOV, Mikhail (Afanas'evich)   1891-1940

BRIEF ENTRY: Born in 1891 in Kiev, Russia (now U.S.S.R.); died of sclerosis, March 10, 1940, in Moscow, U.S.S.R. Russian novelist, playwright, and short story writer. In 1921, following the Russian Revolution, Bulgakov left Kiev and his brief career in medicine for a literary life in Moscow. His first major work was *Belaia gvardiia* (1925; translated as *The White Guard,* 1971), a novel unique in Russian literature of the day for its sympathetic treatment of those who had resisted Bolshevism in Kiev. Bulgakov's stage version of the book, produced at the Moscow Art Theatre in 1926 under the title *Dni Turbinykh* (translated as *The Days of the Turbins,* 1934), was enormously popular with theatregoers, many of whom wept openly at its nostalgic evocation of old Russia. Over the next two years Bulgakov wrote a collection of short stories, a novel, and two plays, all of which satirized the Soviet way of life. Such controversial works were not often tolerated by Soviet officials, however, and in 1928 Bulgakov's plays were temporarily banned from the stage. Thereafter he wrote biographical plays about such artists as Cervantes, Moliere, and Pushkin, allowing him to indirectly address the theme of the persecuted artist. Although very much a man of the theatre, Bulgakov is best known in the West for his posthumous novel *Master i Margarita* (1966; translated as *The Master and Margarita,* 1967). Critics hailed the book as a masterpiece of political and social satire, a bizarre, Hoffmannesque fantasy that draws its inspiration from the Faust legend, the crucifixion of Christ, and a visit by the devil to Moscow. *Residence:* Moscow, U.S.S.R. *Biographical/critical sources: Twentieth Century Writing: A Reader's Guide to Contemporary Literature,* Transatlantic, 1969; *World Authors, 1950-1970,* H. W. Wilson, 1975; *Twentieth-Century Literary Criticism,* Volume 2, Gale, 1979.

*   *   *

BULKLEY, Dwight H(atfield)   1919-

PERSONAL: Born May 15, 1919, in Bangkok, Thailand; U.S. citizen born abroad; son of Lucius Constant (a physician and missionary) and Edna (a teacher; maiden name, Bruner) Bulkley; married Virginia Heiss, 1942 (marriage ended, 1951); married Miriam Wilson, 1953 (marriage ended, 1972); children: Brian David. *Education:* Pomona College, B.A., 1941. *Home and office:* BioMagnetics Institute, 6519 40th Ave. N.E., Seattle, Wash. 98115. *Agent:* Morton H. Dorchin, 841 Southeast Fifth Ter., Pompano Beach, Fla. 33060.

CAREER: U.S. Embassy, Bangkok, Thailand, vice-consul and political expert, 1945-48; free-lance writer, 1948-52; Psychological Research Foundation, Phoenix, Ariz., research associate, 1952-53; Institute of Humanics, Colorado Springs, Colo., biologist, 1953-54; National Distillers, Research Division, Cincinnati, Ohio, chemist, 1955-59; North American Aviation Corp., Anaheim, Calif., aerospace chemist and senior engineer in Autonetics Division, 1959-66; owner and operator of Jet Print, Newport, Calif., 1967-70, and Sudden Printing, Medford, Ore., 1970-72; free-lance writer and researcher, 1973—. Founder of BioMagnetics Institute; University of Washington,

Seattle, biologist-observer on Soviet trawler in the Bering Sea, 1977. *Military service:* U.S. Army, Office of Strategic Services, 1943-46; served in Ceylon, Burma, and Thailand.

WRITINGS: Psycles: Using Your Circadian Rhythms to Control Accidents, Illness, and Psychological Problems, Bobbs-Merrill, 1981.

Monographs; all published by BioMagnetics Institute: *The Mechanisms of Life,* 1952; *Psycles,* 1966; *BioMagnetics and Life,* 1972; *An Electromagnetic Model for Dynamic Turnover and the Continuous Self-Replication of Biological Macromolecules,* 1973; *Epilepsy Breakthrough,* 1978; *The Thanatist,* 1978.

Contributor to magazines, including *Intellect* and *Psychological Reports.*

WORK IN PROGRESS: Psycles II, a sequel; a children's book "on the secret of life," completion expected in 1985; continuing research on microphysics of life processes, including enzyme catalysis, biosynthesis, and motility; research "to further new visions of life and its ultimate potentials."

SIDELIGHTS: Bulkley described himself as "an adventurer who sailed the bundar boats of Karachi, hunted sambar in the Kra Isthmus, roamed the ancient ziggurats of Angkor, climbed the Schonnige Platte in Switzerland and Adams Peak in Ceylon, milked cobras of venom, rode elephants and buffaloes, wrestled bear cubs, circled the great pyramid and sphinx on a camel, was zapped by a stingray off the coast of Trincomallee, and brought tears to the eyes of an elephant in the Cincinnati zoo; sipped Pernod in Casablanca, arak in Kandy, tiger's milk in Kanchanaburi, and B & B in the inner sanctum of the Stork Club in New York City; danced native dances in Nakorn Rajasima and Anuradhapura, shouted 'avast ye lubbers' high in the rigging of a Bounty-like schooner off Kawaii, fell into cactus in a midnight brawl between Tijuana and Ensenada, and wore a necklace of nine human skulls from a Tantric yogi in Putthaparthi."

As a philosopher, he "slung dead bodies in a mortuary in Phoenix, meditated in Buddhist monasteries, attended Jesuit retreats, and smoked opium with junketing senators touring the opium dens of Bangkok; fasted thirty days on just water, spent many soul-searching nights alone on a desert mountain top, and journeyed the cosmos in an all-night peyote ritual led by Navajo Indians; led a college symposium on the transformation of consciousness; spent seven months with the incredible Sai Baba, man of miracles in India; forgave Fritz Perls for being too tired, Linus Pauling for being adamant, Ram Dass for retreating to his house when his lecture was busted in Anaheim, Frank Lloyd Wright for biffing off three days later, Timothy Leary for beating on my typewriter, Dr. Albert St. Gyorgyi for being too old, and psychologist Dr. Caster for dying too soon."

As a musician, he "played duo-piano with the famous Spivey in her penthouse nightclub in New York; was sewn into silks and brocades to sing and dance in royal performance before the king of Thailand; played an alto horn in Beethoven's Fifth, sang Danse Macabre in a national champion glee club, and boozed it up with a Neapolitan orchestra in a bistro in Sorrento."

As a scientist, he "saved our national defense by providing the emergency solution to prevent 'imminent catastrophic failure' of the computer brains of all our Minuteman missiles; invented a novel molecular model kit, an artificial fish bait, a Psycles calculator, and an autographic micro parallel plate plastometer, defended my monograph on the secret of life at a university symposium hosted by a professor of biology, studied the length/sex frequency of pollock in Alaskan waters, and brainstormed with a physicist the microphysics of a spinning flagellum."

Bulkley told *CA:* "From the circumstances of my birth in Thailand and schooling in India, I have been privileged with worldwide adventures in many fields and now find myself, past sixty years of age, with a tiger by the tail and not about to let go!

"As a biologist, I stumbled on an exciting, simple, but monumental discovery which will impact both medicine and psychology with a historic opening-up of the specific psychogenesis of scores of health and behavioral mysteries. The secret lies in a predictable set of time lags in stress reactions. They pinpoint—for the first time in history—the specific subconscious reasons for a wide spectrum of acute troubles, from accidental mishaps to many acute diseases and behavioral aberrations.

"My two thousand case histories are what Freud and Jung spent their lives searching for and never found: a precision bridge to the unconscious genesis of much acute suffering. Those stubbed toes, cut fingers, slips, falls, spills, breaks, and even car wrecks and many ills don't 'just happen' by chance. Incredible as it may seem, with Psycles they are shown to be done on purpose, with precision, as intended! The timing is the giveaway on motives.

"During five months in 1981, to promote *Psycles,* I drove an 18,000-mile, 65-city, nationwide talk show tour with over 218 television and radio appearances.

"*Psycles* is not just another 'pop psychology'; it is truly revolutionary; its insights are uniquely healing; it's a whole new breath of fresh air in the health field, showing that many of our acute troubles are actually corrective responses to a prior stress incident. These are predictable and preventable; the knowledge of these reaction time lags is like a precision tool for problem-solving self-insight, and promises freedom from needless suffering.

"I see myself as a knight in shining armor, leading the cognitive self-responsibility troops (who don't recognize me as their leader yet!) against the robot view of the academic behavioral, mindless, linear-particle thinkers who tout a meaningless, statistical, random chance universe. With my revolutionary case histories, I *prove* that we DO our troubles on purpose and can UN-do, unbind, or decondition ourselves for a new, marvelous, exciting life!

"*Psycles* is only one of three revolutions I am generating. The other two have to do with a wrenching shift from obsolescent chemical models in the life sciences to microphysics and electromagnetics—which solves mystery after mystery! What fun!"

BIOGRAPHICAL/CRITICAL SOURCES: New York World Journal Tribune, January 29, 1967; *Seattle Times,* February 7, 1976; *Star,* April 27, 1976; *Seattle Post Intelligencer,* February 27, 1977; *Perspectives on Consciousness and Psi Research,* September, 1979; *Library Journal,* March 1, 1981; *Medford Mail Tribune,* April 8, 1981; *San Jose Mercury News,* April 22, 1981; *Arizona Republic,* May 20, 1981; *Honolulu Star-Bulletin,* June 14, 1981; *San Diego Tribune,* June 24, 1981; *Richmond Times-Dispatch,* June 24, 1981; *Columbia State,* June 25, 1981; *Baltimore Sun,* June 29, 1981; *Salt Lake Tribune,* August 10, 1981; *Globe,* August 11, 1981.

*   *   *

BURKE, David 1927-

PERSONAL: Born May 17, 1927, in Melbourne, Australia;

son of John William (an accountant) and Gertrude Olive (an opera singer; maiden name, Davies) Burke; married Helen Patricia Wane (a journalist), March 5, 1957; children: Mary, Anne, Margaret, Jane, Julia. *Education:* Attended school in South Brisbane, Queensland, Australia. *Residence:* Sydney, Australia. *Agent:* Curtis Brown Ltd., William St., Paddington, New South Wales, Australia. *Office address:* P.O. Box 82, Mosman, New South Wales 2088, Australia.

CAREER: Worked as radio scriptwriter and production assistant, Melbourne, Australia, 1948-50; *Melbourne Herald-Sun*, Melbourne, reporter, feature writer, and sub-editor, 1950-56; *Sydney Morning Sun-Herald*, Sydney, Australia, reporter and feature writer, 1956-62; free-lance author, 1965—; has also worked for Victorian Railways and in public relations. *Member:* Royal Australian Historical Society, Australian Railway Historical Society, Rail Transport Museum.

WRITINGS: (With C. C. Singleton) *Railways of Australia*, Angus & Robertson, 1963; *Monday at McMurdo* (novel), Muller, 1967; *Come Midnight Monday* (juvenile), illustrations by J. Mare, Methuen, 1976; *Great Steam Trains of Australia*, Rigby, 1978; *Darknight* (novel), Methuen, 1979; *Observer's Book of Steam Locomotives of Australia*, Methuen, 1979; *Full Steam Across the Mountains*, illustrations by Phil Belbin, Methuen, 1981.

WORK IN PROGRESS: A history of intercolonial travel between Sydney and Melbourne, publication by Methuen expected in 1982 or 1983.

SIDELIGHTS: David Burke told *CA:* "I regard myself as a general free-lance writer, but my lifelong interest in railroads has led me to study the history of various Australian railways and their impact on the social and economic development of Australia. I tend to alternate between fact and fiction in my writing. I am almost constantly doing research at national and state libraries, archives, etc., and I maintain comprehensive files."

MEDIA ADAPTATIONS: Come Midnight Monday was adapted for television and produced as a seven-episode serial by the Australian Broadcasting Commission, first broadcast in 1982.

*   *   *

BURTON, Jane

PERSONAL—Home: Warren House, Albury Heath, Albury, Guildford, Surrey GU5 9BD, England.

CAREER: Photographer.

WRITINGS—With own photographs: (Editor) *In Praise of Animals: An Anthology for Friends*, Muller, 1956; *Baby Animals*, Longacre Press, 1961; (with Douglas Charles Gohn) *Tropical Fish*, revised edition, Hamlyn, 1971; *Animals of the African Year: The Ecology of East Africa*, Holt, 1972; (with Maurice Burton) *The Colorful World of Animals*, Longmeadow Press, 1975 (published in England as *The Colourful World of Animals*, Sundial Press, 1976); *Wondrous World of Fishes*, Colour Library International, 1976; (with David Gibson) *Wondrous World of Horses*, Colour Library International, 1976; *Aquarium Fishes*, Crescent Books, 1978; (with M. Burton) *The Family of Animals*, Mayflower Books, 1979.

Photographer: M. Burton, *The Sixth Sense of Animals*, Taplinger, 1972; Diane Hughes, *World Encyclopedia of Animals*, Octopus, 1978.

SIDELIGHTS: Jane Burton wrote: "I am only persuaded to write if, by wrapping a text around them, a batch of photographs will be most readily sold."

BURTON, Thomas G(lenn)   1935-

PERSONAL: Born January 7, 1935, in Memphis, Tenn.; son of H. Glen (a restaurant owner) and Rosalie (Medlin) Burton; married Janice Hall, 1954 (divorced, 1970); married Annette Lowder, August 8, 1972; children: David Hall, Michael Thomas, John Paul, Lewis Carlton. *Education:* David Lipscomb College, B.A., 1956; Vanderbilt University, M.A., 1958, Ph.D., 1966. *Home:* 1703 Galen Dr., Johnson City, Tenn. 37601. *Office:* Department of English, East Tennessee State University, Johnson City, Tenn. 37614.

CAREER: High school English teacher in Nashville, Tenn., 1957-58; East Tennessee State University, Johnson City, 1958—, began as instructor, professor of English, 1967—. *Member:* International Arthurian Society, Victorians Institute, Tennyson Society, Appalachian Writers Association, South Atlantic Modern Language Association, Tennessee Folklore Society (president, 1965 and 1966), Tennessee Philological Association (president, 1974).

WRITINGS: (Editor with Ambrose N. Manning) *A Collection of Folklore*, East Tennessee State University, 1966, revised edition, 1970; (editor with Manning) *The East Tennessee State University Collection of Folklore: Folksongs*, East Tennessee State University, 1967; (editor) *Folksongs II*, East Tennessee State University, 1969; (editor) *Essays in Memory of Christine Burleson*, East Tennessee State University, 1969; *Some Ballad Folks*, East Tennessee State University, 1978; (editor) *Tom Ashley, Sam McGee, Bukka White: Tennessee Traditional Singers*, University of Tennessee Press, 1981. Author of "Singing Out," a column in *Johnson City Press Chronicle*, 1966-71. Contributor to folklore journals.

WORK IN PROGRESS: An analysis of voiceprints of Tennyson reading his own verse.

*   *   *

BUSBY, Mabel Janice
See STANFORD, Sally

*   *   *

BUSBY, Roger (Charles)   1941-

PERSONAL: Born July 24, 1941, in Leicester, England; son of Alfred Urban (a printer) and Emma May (Vyse) Busby; married wife, Maureen-Jeanette (a secretary), 1968. *Education:* University of Aston in Birmingham, certificate in journalism, 1963. *Home:* Sunnymoor, Bridford, near Exeter, Devonshire EX6 7HS, England. *Office:* Devon and Cornwall Constabulary, Police Headquarters, Middlemoor, Exeter, Devonshire EX6 7HQ, England.

CAREER: Caters News Agency, Birmingham, England, journalist, 1959-66; *Birmingham Evening Mail*, Birmingham, journalist, 1966-73; Devon and Cornwall Constabulary, Exeter, England, police force information and public relations officer, 1973—. *Member:* Institute of Public Relations, Crime Writers Association, National Union of Journalists.

WRITINGS—Crime novels: (With Gerald Holtham) *Main Line Kill*, Walker & Co., 1968; *Robbery Blue*, Collins, 1969; *The Frighteners*, Collins, 1970; *Deadlock*, Collins, 1971; *A Reasonable Man*, Collins, 1972; *Pattern of Violence*, Collins, 1973; *New Face in Hell*, Collins, 1976; *Garvey's Code*, Collins, 1978.

SIDELIGHTS: Busby told *CA:* "I enjoy writing as a hobby which helps me to relax after a hard day at work. My subject is police fiction, a rich vein in the everyday drama of life, and I have been greatly influenced by the work of such American authors as Richard Dougherty and Joseph Wambaugh. Despite the thousands of words of fact and fiction written about them, the police remain an enigma to the average man in the street, who finds it hard to believe that underneath the uniforms the cops are only human after all."

AVOCATIONAL INTERESTS: Astronomy, walking in Dartmoor.

* * *

BUSH, Patricia J(ahns) 1932-

PERSONAL: Born June 13, 1932, in Saginaw, Mich.; daughter of Edwin Earl (a teacher) and Marcia (a teacher; maiden name, Rozell) Jahns; married James Ter Bush (a stockbroker and naval officer) June 27, 1954; children: Sunley Hamilton, James Ter, Jr. *Education:* University of Michigan, B.S., 1954; University of London, M.Sc., 1972; University of Minnesota, Ph.D., 1978. *Home:* 4749 Reservoir Rd. N.W., Washington, D.C. 20007. *Agent:* Peter Miller Agency, 1021 Avenue of the Americas, Suite 403, New York, N.Y. 10018. *Office:* School of Medicine, Georgetown University, Washington, D.C. 20007.

CAREER: Medical University of South Carolina, Charleston, instructor in pharmacy, 1965-69; Georgetown University, Washington, D.C., assistant professor of community and family medicine, 1972-77; University of Southern California, Los Angeles, assistant professor of pharmacy, 1978; Georgetown University, assistant professor of community and family medicine, 1978—. Assistant professor at Howard University, 1980-81. *Member:* American Public Health Association (chairperson of pharmacy services committee, 1980-81), American Sociological Association, American Pharmaceutical Association, Academy of Pharmaceutical Sciences, Sigma Xi, Rho Chi, Phi Kappa Phi. *Awards, honors:* Bush Foundation fellowship, 1976-77.

WRITINGS: (Editor with A.I. Wertheimer) *Perspectives on Medicines in Society*, Drug Intelligence Publications, 1977; *Drugs, Alcohol, and Sex*, Richard Marek, 1981. Contributor of about thirty articles and reviews to professional journals and newspapers.

WORK IN PROGRESS: With Frances R. Davidson, *Medicines, Abusable Substances, and Children, Grades K-6*, based on a survey of 420 elementary-school children.

SIDELIGHTS: Patricia Bush wrote: "I particularly want to take scientific material on medicines and the results of research and transform them into useful information to help people with their everyday lives.

"People can be helped in two ways. Physicians can learn how to be better prescribers, and other people can learn how to take more responsibility for the medicines they take. This means that people need to have information, and they need to learn how to use it, whether they are physicians or patients.

"Some people take medicines too lightly and some abusable substances too seriously. In terms of the harm done to individuals and society, alcohol and tobacco are clearly way out in front. We need to recognize that many of society's views and laws on drugs are morally based and do not reflect their potential for physical or psychological damage.

"Although my writing has been mainly for the academic press to date, *Drugs, Alcohol, and Sex* has convinced me that it is possible to translate academic gobbledespeak into stuff that ordinary people can use."

* * *

BUTLER, Lionel Harry 1923-1981

OBITUARY NOTICE: Born December 17, 1923, in Dudley, Worchestershire, England; died November 26, 1981, in London, England. Educator and author best known for his expertise on the Order of Knights Hospitallers and his reorganization and display of the museum collection of the Venerable Order of St. John. Appointed the first professor of medieval history at St. Andrews University in 1955, Butler expanded the popularity of medieval studies and was elected dean of arts in 1966 and vice-principal in 1971. His talent as an administrator earned him the appointment of principal of Royal Holloway College in 1973, where he remained until his death. Under his direction the college grew rapidly in enrollment and facilities. Butler's publications include a translation of R. Fawtier's work on the Capetian kings of France and a book, *Medieval Monasteries of Great Britain*, both written in collaboration with others. Obituaries and other sources: *Who's Who*, 126th edition, St. Martin's, 1974; *Who's Who in the World*, 3rd edition, Marquis, 1976; *London Times*, December 2, 1981.

* * *

BUTLER, Sandra (Ada) 1938-

PERSONAL: Born April 19, 1938, in Massachusetts; daughter of Seamon (in sales) and Sayde (Stein) Steen; children: Janice, Alison. *Education:* Goddard College, San Francisco, Calif., B.A., 1976, M.A., 1978. *Politics:* "Feminist." *Religion:* Jewish.

CAREER: Women's Studies Collective (community outreach program), San Francisco, Calif., founder and instructor, 1971-72; KPOO-FM (educational radio), San Francisco, community outreach coordinator and developer, producer, and moderator of program "Sound of Sisters," 1974-75; Sexual Trauma Center, San Francisco, director, 1977-78; independent consultant, 1978—. Public lecturer, 1979—; guest on television and radio shows. *Member:* American Orthopsychiatric Association, Sex Information and Education Council of the United States (SIECUS), Society for the Study of Social Problems, Society for the Psychological Study of Social Issues, San Francisco Women's Center.

WRITINGS: Conspiracy of Silence: The Trauma of Incest, New Glide, 1978.

WORK IN PROGRESS: A nonfiction book about sexual violence against women and children; short stories about women's lives.

SIDELIGHTS: In her first book, *Conspiracy of Silence*, Butler reveals the extent of nonconsensual incest and exposes the myths about the kinds of families in which such things occur. Butler explores the subject of incestuous assault with the intention of creating an atmosphere of openness and understanding in which victims can seek and receive help. "When I first began my research," Butler admits in *Conspiracy*, "I had to dispel my own set of stereotypes about families in which incestuous assault takes place. I had expected to find violent, alcoholic men—men who live in families with too little money and too many children; men who are abusive and uncaring and unfeeling. . . . I never expected to find a sexually abusive father living on my street or attending my house of worship."

Nevertheless, after thousands of hours of interviews with men and women, both victims and agressors, the author says she realized that "such a simplistic, culture-bound analysis cannot hold up in the face of the growing number of aggressors whose singular characteristic in common is that they sexually assault their own children." "By our insistence that it is only 'those people' who assault their children," explains Butler, "we can avoid facing the abuse that has been going on around us." She reports: "The true range of families dealing with incestuous assault has little to do with class, race, economic status or social background. Were it possible to provide a more realistic profile of a typical family in which incestuous abuse occurs, it would more likely be a middle-class family composed of husband, wife and children living together in a nuclear situation." "Incest," notes Butler, "is relentlessly democratic."

Butler told *CA:* "Incestuous assault, rape, and pornography are undersides of our society that must be exposed. It is only by creating a dialogue about these previously silent and verboten issues that we can begin to mend, heal, and move towards lives of greater strength and compassion."

*   *   *

BUTTERWORTH, Emma Macalik   1928-

PERSONAL: Born September 5, 1928, in Vienna, Austria; came to the United States in 1955, naturalized citizen, 1958; daughter of Josef (a designer) and Olga (Pomaisel) Macalik; married William Edmund Butterworth III (a writer), July 12, 1950; children: Patrica Olga (Mrs. Thomas Black), William Edmund IV, John Scholefield II. *Education:* Attended University of Vienna, 1945-50. *Home address:* Creek Dr., P.O. Drawer A-L, Fairhope, Ala. 36532. *Agent:* John Cushman, JCA Literary Agency, Inc., 242 West 27th St., Suite 4A, New York, N.Y. 10001.

CAREER: Vienna State Opera, Vienna, Austria, member of Corps de Ballet, 1936-44; calligrapher, engrosser, and illuminator, 1947—.

WRITINGS: The Complete Book of Calligraphy, Lippincott, 1980, *As the Waltz Ended,* Four Winds, 1982.

WORK IN PROGRESS: A novel about a young woman who comes to the United States as the bride of an American, publication by Four Winds expected in 1983.

C

CABELL, James Branch 1879-1958

BRIEF ENTRY: Born April 14, 1879, in Richmond, Va.; died May 5, 1958, in Richmond, Va. American journalist and author. Though his early books were praised by H. L. Mencken, Burton Rascoe, Sinclair Lewis, and Mark Twain, Cabell's work went largely unnoticed until 1921, when an attempt was made to suppress *Jurgen* (1919) on grounds of obscenity. The novel was vindicated, and the accompanying notoriety made Cabell's name a household word and his books best-sellers. His popularity and his critical reputation declined sharply in the 1930's. Some critics attribute this to a backlash, arguing that no writer could fulfill the expectations reviewers harbored for Cabell. Others have suggested that in a literary climate increasingly dominated by realism there was simply no place for Cabell's complex, mannered, and ironic fantasies. Cabell continued to write novels, short stories, and essays throughout his life, but his most important works are the eighteen books that make up the *Biography of Manuel,* including *Jurgen, The Cream of the Jest* (1917), *Figures of Earth* (1921), and *The High Place* (1923). In the *Biography,* Cabell explores three attitudes toward life—the gallant, the chivalric, and the poetic—as these attitudes are adopted by the descendants of Dom Manuel, count of the imaginary province of Poictesme. The novels are characterized by skepticism and pessimism, and they ridicule human beings' belief in their own importance. Cabell's heroes seek ultimate truth and ideal beauty, but finally abandon their aspirations and find a measure of contentment in ordinary life, as inadequate as it may be. In 1955 Cabell wrote an autobiography, *As I Remember It. Biographical/critical sources: Oxford Companion to American Literature,* 4th edition, Oxford University Press, 1965; *The Reader's Encyclopedia,* 2nd edition, Crowell, 1965; *Concise Dictionary of American Literature,* Greenwood Press, 1969; *The Penguin Companion to American Literature,* McGraw, 1971.

* * *

CAIRNEY, John 1930-

PERSONAL: Born February 16, 1930, in Glasgow, Scotland; son of Thomas (a works foreman) and Mary (Coyle) Cairney; married Sheila Cowan, May 29, 1954 (divorced May 8, 1980); married Alannah O'Sullivan (an actress), September 27, 1981; children: (first marriage) Jennifer, Alison, Lesley, Jane, Jonathan. *Education:* Attended Glasgow School of Art, 1947-48; Glasgow University, B.A., 1953; Royal Scottish Academy of Music and Drama, diploma, 1953. *Politics:* "Left Wing." *Religion:* Roman Catholic. *Home:* 197 Onslow Dr., Dennistoun, Glasgow, Scotland. *Agent:* Keedick Lecture Bureau, 475 Fifth Ave., New York, N.Y. 10017. *Office:* Shanter Productions, 197 Onslow Dr., Glasgow G31 2QE, Scotland.

CAREER: Wilson Barret Company, Edinburgh, Scotland, actor, 1952-53; Glasgow Citizens Theatre, Glasgow, Scotland, actor, 1953-54; Bristol Old Vic, Bristol, England, actor, 1954-56; actor in films for Rank Organization, Associated British Picture Corp., and Columbia Pictures in London, England, 1956-65; British Broadcasting Corp. (BBC-TV), London, and Scottish Television, Glasgow, actor, 1965-70; Shanter Productions, Glasgow, writer, director, and actor, 1970—. Actor in plays, including "Hamlet," 1960, "The Entertainer," 1972, and "Cyrano de Bergerac," 1974; actor in television productions, including "The Robert Burns Story," 1969, "Jackanor," 1970, "Elizabeth R," 1971, "Scotch on the Rocks," 1972, "McGonagall," 1976, "The Ivor Novello Story," 1977, "The Robert Burns Story," 1978, and "Mackintosh," 1979; actor in television series "This Man Craig," 1968, and "Burns," 1978. Founder and director of Shanter Productions Theatre Consultants, Scotland, 1970—, and Robert Burns Festival, Ayr, Scotland, 1975—. *Military service:* Royal Air Force, 1948-50; served as entertainer. *Member:* British Actor's Equity, Associated British Theatre Technicians, New Zealand Actors' Equity, Writers Guild, Songwriters Guild, Scottish Society of Playwrights, Edinburgh Arts Club, Glasgow Art Club, British Broadcasting Corp. Club, Performing Rights Society. *Awards, honors:* Royal Scottish Academy of Music and Drama silver medal, James Bridie Award, and Alec Guiness Award, all 1953; citation from Scottish Tourist Board, 1977, for Burns Festival; Jubilee medal, 1978.

WRITINGS—Plays; produced in Ayr, Scotland, at Robert Burns Festival, except as noted: "An Edinburgh Salon" (revue), first produced in Edinburgh, Scotland, August, 1974; "Holy Fair" (two-act musical), first produced in June, 1975; "Lingering Star" (two-act), first produced in Greenock, Scotland, June, 1976; "Kirk Session Follies" (two-act musical), first produced in June, 1977; "Bard" (two-act musical), first produced in June, 1978; "The Scotland Story" (pageant), first produced in Linlithgow, Scotland, August, 1978; "Knox and Mary" (duologue), first produced in Glasgow, Scotland, April, 1979; "Clarinda Correspondence" (two-act duologue), first produced in Irvine, Scotland, June, 1979; "Drunk Man Looks at Burns" (two-act duologue), first produced in Irvine, June,

1979; "As Others Saw Him" (two-act documentary), first produced in Largs, Scotland, June, 1979; "The Byron Letters" (duologue), first produced in New Zealand, September, 1980; "A Wartime Childhood in Glasgow," first produced in December, 1980; "Black-out," first produced in Toronto, Ontario, May, 1981.

Teleplays, except as noted: "Another School of Thought," first broadcast by British Broadcasting Corp. (BBC-TV), 1968; "New Year Soliloquy" (poem), first broadcast by Scottish Television, 1968; "The Robert Burns Story," first broadcast by Scottish Television, 1969; "McGonagall," first broadcast by Scottish Television, 1970; "Robert Louis Stevenson," first broadcast by CFAC-TV, 1971; "The Ivor Novello Story" (musical), first broadcast by Scottish Television, 1973; "Mackintosh" (lecture), first broadcast by Scottish Television, 1976; "Robert Service" (duologue), CFAC-TV, 1977; "Two for a Show" (duologue), first broadcast by Border Television, 1979; "The Real Dorothy Parker," first broadcast by Radio New Zealand, 1980. Also author of a series of six plays, "Burns," for Scottish Television, 1968.

Author of "An Actor's Life," a series of articles in *Scotsman*, 1962. Contributor of series of poems, "The Women in My Life," to *Annabelle Magazine;* contributor to newspapers and periodicals, including *Drama, People's Journal, Sunday Post,* and *Glasgow Herald.*

WORK IN PROGRESS: Dramas about Oscar Wilde and the Brownings, completion expected in 1982; a book, *The Lecturer,* completion expected in 1983; a book, *My Life With Robert Burns,* completion expected in 1986; an autobiography, *Such Is Life,* completion expected in 1989.

SIDELIGHTS: Cairney told *CA:* "I have the unique experience of being a solo performer who travels around the world performing his own scripts. This allows me to research, write, and perform my own material at my own discretion anywhere I wish, providing people want to hear me. I depend solely on my own whim, industry, daring, imagination, impudence, and dogged professionalism. My wife and I make a back-to-back artistic team capable of dealing with nearly every exigency in the theatrical and literary worlds, both as writers and performers of the spoken word."

*   *   *

CAIRNS, J(ames) F(ord)   1914-

PERSONAL: Born October 4, 1914, in Carlton, Australia; son of James John (a clerk) and Letitia (Ford) Cairns; married wife, Gwendolyne Olga, February 14, 1939; children: Philip James, Barry Tallis (adopted). *Education:* Attended University of Melbourne, 1941-48. *Politics:* Socialist. *Religion:* None. *Home:* 21 Wattle Rd., Hawthorn, Victoria 3122, Australia.

CAREER: Clerk, 1932-35; police officer in Victoria, Australia, 1935-44; University of Melbourne, Parkville, senior tutor, 1946-48, lecturer, 1948-51, senior lecturer in economic history, 1951-55; House of Representatives, Canberra, Australia, representative, 1955-77, treasurer, 1974-75; writer, 1977—. Australian minister for overseas trade and secondary industry, 1972-74, deputy prime minister, 1974-75. *Military service:* Australian Army, 1945-46.

WRITINGS: Living With Asia, Lansdowne, 1965; *The Eagle and the Lotus,* Lansdowne, 1969; *Tariffs or Planning,* Lansdowne, 1970; *Silence Kills,* Vietnam Moratorium Committee, 1971; *The Quiet Revolution,* Gold Star, 1972, Widescope International Publishers, 1975; *Oil in Troubled Waters,* Wide-

scope International Publishers, 1976; *Growth to Freedom,* Down to Earth Foundation, 1979.

WORK IN PROGRESS: Research on repression as the base of civilization, its origins and consequences.

*   *   *

CALDER, Ritchie
See RITCHIE-CALDER, Peter Ritchie

*   *   *

CALKINS, Rodello   1920-
(Rodello Hunter)

BRIEF ENTRY: Born March 23, 1920, in Provo, Utah. American author. Hunter's books evoke the American West and its people. *A House of Many Rooms: A Family Memoir* (Knopf, 1965) contains reminiscenses of Hunter's simple childhood in a Mormon home. *Wyoming Wife* (Knopf, 1969) describes her marriage, in middle years, and subsequent move to rural Wyoming. She also wrote a book about the Mormon faith, *A Daughter of Zion* (Knopf, 1972), and a volume of poems, *The Soul of Jackson Hole* (Grand Teton Printing & Publishing, 1974). *Biographical/critical sources: American Women Writers: A Critical Reference Guide From Colonial Times to the Present,* Ungar, 1979-80.

*   *   *

CALVERT, Patricia   1931-
(Peter J. Freeman)

PERSONAL: Born July 22, 1931, in Great Falls, Mont.; daughter of Edgar C. (a railroad worker) and Helen P. (a children's wear buyer; maiden name, Freeman) Dunlap; married George J. Calvert (in insurance business), January 27, 1951; children: Brianne L. Calvert Elias, Dana J. Calvert Halbert. *Education:* Winona State University, B.A., 1976, graduate study, 1976—. *Politics:* Liberal Democrat. *Religion:* Unitarian-Universalist. *Home:* Foxwood Farm, R.R.2, Chatfield, Minn. 55923. *Office:* Mayo Clinic, 200 Southwest First St., Rochester, Minn. 55901.

CAREER: St. Mary's Hospital, Great Falls, Mont., laboratory clerk, 1948-49; clerk typist at General Motors Acceptance Corp., 1950-51; Mayo Clinic, Rochester, Minn., cardiac laboratory technician, 1961-64, enzyme laboratory technician, 1964-70, senior editorial assistant in section of publications, 1970—. *Member:* American Medical Writers Association, Children's Reading Round Table, Society of Children's Book Writers, Society of Midland Authors. *Awards, honors:* Best book award from American Library Association, juvenile fiction award from Society of Midland Authors, and juvenile award from Friends of American Writers, all 1980, for *The Snowbird;* award for outstanding achievement in the arts from Young Women's Christian Association, 1981, for *The Snowbird.*

WRITINGS: (Contributor) Lyle L. Miller, editor, *Developing Reading Efficiency,* 4th edition, Burgess, 1980; *The Snowbird* (juvenile), Scribner, 1980; *The Money Creek Mare* (juvenile), Scribner, 1981; *The Stone Pony* (juvenile), Scribner, 1982; *The Hour of the Wolf* (juvenile), Scribner, in press. Contributor of more than a hundred articles and stories to children's magazines (sometimes under pseudonym Peter J. Freeman), including *Highlights for Children, Friend, Junior Life,* and *Jack and Jill.*

SIDELIGHTS: Patricia Calvert commented: "I am everlastingly fascinated by that country from which we are all emigrants: the land of childhood—and that is the reason why my fiction is for (and about) children. When an acquaintance recently expressed to me the hope that, since I'd now had a couple of children's books published, I could write 'a real one' (that is, a novel for adults), I had to discourage him quickly. To write for and about children—and to write for and about the child in myself—is really all I intend to do.''

*   *   *

CAMEJO, Peter Miguel 1939-

BRIEF ENTRY: Born December 31, 1939, in New York, N.Y. American political organizer and author. Camejo has worked on the national level for the Socialist Workers party since 1963. Since 1977 he has served as national field organizer for the Southwest. His writings include *Guevara's Guerrilla Strategy: Why It Failed* (Pathfinder Press, 1972), *Racism, Revolution, Reaction, 1861-1877: The Rise and Fall of Reconstruction* (Monad Press, 1976), *The Lesser Evil?: The Left Debates the Democratic Party and Social Change* (Pathfinder Press, 1978), and an edited work, *The Nicaraguan Revolution* (Pathfinder Press, 1979). *Address:* 1250 Wilshire, Los Angeles, Calif. 90017.

*   *   *

CAMPBELL, Albert Angus 1919-1980

OBITUARY NOTICE: Born August 10, 1919, in Leiters, Ind.; died December 15, 1980, in Ann Arbor, Mich. Social psychologist and author best known for pioneering the use of sample surveys for studying the attitudes of various groups. Campbell worked with other social scientists in Washington, D.C., during World War II to provide the government with studies of trends in American social and economic life. In 1970 Campbell became director of the Institute for Social Research, a position he held for five years. Campbell was the author or co-author of seven books based on behavioral studies, including *The Voter Decides, White Attitudes Towards Black People,* and *The Sense of Well Being in America.* Obituaries and other sources: *Who's Who in America,* 40th edition, Marquis, 1978; *The Annual Obituary 1980,* St. Martin's, 1981.

*   *   *

CAMPBELL, Alla (Linda Renee) Bozarth
See BOZARTH-CAMPBELL, Alla (Linda Renee)

*   *   *

CANHAM, Erwin D(ain) 1904-1982

OBITUARY NOTICE—See index for *CA* sketch: Born February 13, 1904, in Auburn, Me.; died after abdominal surgery, January 3, 1982, in Agana, Guam. Editor and author. Canham joined the staff of the *Christian Science Monitor* as a reporter in 1925 and became its editor-in-chief in 1964, serving as a correspondent in Geneva, as chief of the Washington bureau, as a general news editor, and as a managing editor in the interim. Under his editorship, the *Christian Science Monitor* became known for its direct and decisive coverage of national news and for its interpretive writing style. Canham held many civic positions, including deputy chairman of the U.S. delegation to the United Nations Conference on Freedom of Information, chairman of the National Manpower Council, director of the National Bureau of Economic Research, and trustee of the Boston Museum of Fine Arts. He also taught Sunday school. As the last resident commissioner of the Northern Mariana Islands, where he eventually made his home, Canham brought the territory to commonwealth status. The editor re-

ceived many honors in his lifetime, most notably the Julian Yorks Award of the Massachusetts Jewish War Veterans of the U.S.A. and honorary degrees from Bates College, Brigham Young University, Boston University, Yale University, and Temple University. In the 1940's and 1950's Canham was made a chevalier and an officer of the French Legion of Honor as well as a commander of the Order of Orange-Nassau. His works include *Awakening: The World at Mid-Century, Commitment to Freedom: The Story of the Christian Science Monitor, Man's Great Future, The Christian Science Way of Life,* and *The Ethics of United States Foreign Relations.* Obituaries and other sources: *Newsweek,* January 18, 1982; *Time,* January 18, 1982.

*   *   *

CAPLAN, David 1947-

PERSONAL: Born February 4, 1947, in Montreal, Quebec, Canada; came to the United States in 1981; son of Hyman and Sonia (Roskes) Caplan; married Barbara Wexler (a social worker), June 18, 1978. *Education:* Massachusetts Institute of Technology, B.S., 1968, Ph.D., 1971; McGill University, M.D., 1975. *Office:* Department of Neurology, University Hospital, Temple University, 3401 North Broad St., Philadelphia, Pa. 19140.

CAREER: Harvard University, Cambridge, Mass., resident in neurology, 1976-79; University of Ottawa, Ottawa, Ontario, assistant professor of medicine, 1979-81; Temple University, Philadelphia, Pa., associate professor of neurology, 1981. *Member:* American Academy of Neurology, Academy of Aphasia.

WRITINGS: (With Simeon Locke and Lucia Hellar) *A Study in Neurolinguistics,* C. C Thomas, 1972; (editor) *Biological Studies of Mental Processes,* M.I.T. Press, 1980; (editor with Michael Arbib and John Marshall) *Neural Modeled Language Processing,* Academic Press, 1982; (editor) *Biological Perspectives on Language,* M.I.T. Press, 1983.

WORK IN PROGRESS: A textbook on aphasia and neurolinguistics.

SIDELIGHTS: Caplan told *CA:* ''The study of aphasia symptoms and syndromes is being undertaken more and more in a linguistic and language processing perspective. It is as if we think of the aphasic as someone who speaks a foreign language—albeit related to his native tongue—and it is our job to try to describe that language and to understand how to present material for the reeducation that will move the patient from what he knows and can do to a more complete and normative level of function. In looking at the problem the patient's way, applying knowledge and techniques of study developed in normative linguistics and psycholinguistics, we are discovering new aspects of the functional organization of the brain.''

*   *   *

CAREY, Jane Perry (Clark) 1898-1981

OBITUARY NOTICE—See index for *CA* sketch: Born in 1898 in Washington; died October 24, 1981, in Manhattan, N.Y. Political scientist, consultant, educator, and author. A specialist in the study of displaced persons and refugees, Carey was a consultant on those subjects for the U.S. Government during World War II. After the war she continued as an adviser for the military government in Germany, working occasionally for the State Department or for the United Nations High Commissioner for Refugees. Also an expert on international relations, Carey traveled extensively to such areas as the Middle

East and China in addition to writing, with her husband Andrew Carey, articles on Greece, Turkey, Sweden, Iran, Italy, and Libya. Beginning in 1929 the political scientist taught American government and constitutional law, another area of specialization for Carey, for nearly twenty-five years. Carey received several research awards from the Council for Research in the Social Sciences as well as the Star of Solidarity from the government of Italy. Her books include *Deportation of Aliens From the United States to Europe, The Rise of New Federalism: Federal-State Cooperation in the United States, The Role of Uprooted People on European Recovery, Italy: Change and Progress,* and *The Web of Modern Greek Politics.* Obituaries and other sources: *New York Times,* October 27, 1981.

* * *

CARLINE, Richard (Cotton) 1896-1980

OBITUARY NOTICE: Born in 1896 in Oxford, England; died November 18, 1980, in England. Painter, educator, and author. Following his teaching experiences at the Ruskin Drawing School and the University of London, Carline became committed to the improvement of the quality of fine arts instruction in public education. He served the fine arts in his official capacities as art councillor to UNESCO and chairman of the Artists International Association. An active arts sponsor, he organized several exhibitions and founded the Hampstead Artists' Council. Carline promoted the work of his artist brother-in-law, Stanley Spencer, and achieved success with his own Postimpressionist works, some of which are housed in the Tate Gallery and the Bristol Art Gallery. Carline produced four art books: *Pictures in the Post: The Story of the Picture Postcard; The Arts of West Africa,* an early study of native African art; *Draw They Must,* a highly regarded text in the field of art education; and *Stanley Spencer at War.* Obituaries and other sources: *The Annual Obituary 1980,* St. Martin's, 1981.

* * *

CARLSON, Daniel (Bick) 1960-

PERSONAL: Born October 20, 1960, in New York, N.Y.; son of Albert W. D. (a publisher) and Dale (an author; maiden name, Bick) Carlson; married Loraine Ferraiolo, May 16, 1981. *Education:* Attended University of Pennsylvania, 1979—. *Politics:* Democrat. *Religion:* None. *Home:* 4522 Osage Ave., Apt. 1B, Philadelphia, Penn. 19143. *Agent:* Toni Mendez, 140 East 56th St., New York, N.Y. 10021.

CAREER: Writer.

WRITINGS: (With mother, Dale Bick Carlson) *The Shining Pool* (juvenile), Atheneum, 1979.

WORK IN PROGRESS: A science fiction novel for young adults, completion expected in 1982.

SIDELIGHTS: Carlson told *CA:* "While I am majoring in business administration to earn a living, I am now working on a second young-adult novel. *The Shining Pool,* my first novel, was conceived when I was seventeen and published when I was nineteen."

* * *

CARLSON, Edgar M(agnus) 1908-

PERSONAL: Born July 12, 1908, in Amery, Wis.; son of David (a farmer) and Hilda (Swanson) Carlson; married Ebba Edquist, July 11, 1954; children: David J.E., Joanna L. Carlson Swanson, Samuel Edquist. *Education:* Gustavus Adolphus College,

B.A., 1930; Augustana Theological Seminary, Rock Island, Ill., B.D., 1933; University of Chicago, Ph.D., 1944. *Politics:* Independent. *Home:* 5320 Brookview Ave., Minneapolis, Minn. 55424. *Office:* Office of the President, Hamline University, 1536 Hewitt Ave., St. Paul, Minn. 55104.

CAREER: Ordained Lutheran minister, 1933; pastor of Lutheran church in Minneapolis, Minn., 1933-37; Gustavus Adolphus College, St. Peter, Minn., professor of religion, 1937-42; Augustana Theological Seminary, Rock Island, Ill., professor of Bible and church history, 1942-44; Gustavus Adolphus College, president, 1944-68; Minnesota Private College Council, St. Paul, executive director, 1968-75; Luther/Northwestern Theological Seminary, St. Paul, visiting professor of systematic theology, 1976-79; Hamline University, St. Paul, interim president, 1980—.

WRITINGS: The Reinterpretation of Luther, Westminster, 1948; *The Church and the Public Conscience,* Muhlenberg Press, 1956; *The Classic Christian Faith,* Augustana Press, 1959; *Church Sponsored Higher Education,* Lutheran Church in America, 1967; *Public Policy and Church-Related Higher Education,* Lutheran Church in America, 1972; *The Future of Church-Related Higher Education,* Augsburg, 1977; (translator) Gustaf Wingren, *Credo,* Augsburg, 1981.

* * *

CARLSON, Ellsworth C. 1917-

BRIEF ENTRY: Born May 27, 1917, in Bridgeport, Conn. American historian, educator, and author. Carlson joined the faculty at Oberlin College in 1950 and has been a professor of history since 1962. During the 1940's he taught in China and worked as a country specialist for the U.S. Department of State. He wrote *The Kaiping Mines, 1877-1912* (Chinese Economic and Political Studies, Harvard University, 1957) and *The Foochow Missionaries, 1847-1880* (East Asian Research Center, Harvard University, 1974). *Address:* Department of History, Oberlin College, Oberlin, Ohio 44074.

* * *

CARLSON, Ron 1947-

PERSONAL: Born September 15, 1947, in Logan, Utah; son of Edwin and Verna (Mertz) Carlson; married Georgia Elaine Craig (a teacher), June 14, 1969. *Education:* University of Utah, B.A., 1970, M.A., 1972. *Home:* 1272 East Fifth S., Salt Lake City, Utah 84102.

CAREER: Hotchkiss School, Lakeville, Conn., teacher, 1971-81; writer, 1981—. *Awards, honors:* Grant from Connecticut Commission on the Arts, 1978.

WRITINGS: Betrayed by F. Scott Fitzgerald (novel), Norton, 1977; *Truants* (novel), Norton, 1981. Contributor of articles and stories to popular magazines, including *Oui,* and newspapers. Past editor of *Hotchkiss Alumni.*

WORK IN PROGRESS: A series of short stories about three boys growing up in 1961.

SIDELIGHTS: Carlson told *CA:* "After ten years of teaching at a private boarding school in the East, I have come West to write. I like the sky here, the higher weather, and the longer light.

"Private school life, as vigorous as it is, is simply omnivorous: the dorm, the teaching, the sports. It was my first job, and it was a good one, but I decided to write. I will probably teach again, at another level, in a year or two.

''My first two novels were written during time away from school in summers and on one sabbatical, and now it is time to see if I am really as disciplined as the brochures have it. I believe strongly in the special point of view, worldview, and I work at achieving an intriguing and honest narrator's voice. Rarely, thus far, have I written in the third person. My first two books have been about young people—characters, it would seem, who have recently been flung out onto the planet—and the books take their heart from the characters' observations about the ironic space between things the way they are and things the way they should be; that is, between the rude and the ideal, between life and death. Theirs is an artistic distance. As one says: 'I am always the person looking into other cars.'

''Though I wrote it to expunge the feeling, this passage still nags me: 'I have thought for a long time that it was paramount, essential, to be the best or the worst. Partly out of the superlative viewpoints those extremes offer, the amazing vistas, the thrilling false euphorias, roads not taken, roads that, I guess, should not be taken, and especially, because of the distances from crowds. The middleground is so goddamned crowded. To be like everyone else, yikes; that is the cardinal sin. That is what I had thought.'''

BIOGRAPHICAL/CRITICAL SOURCES: Waterbury Republican, June 23, 1977; *Deseret News,* July 23, 1977; *Salt Lake Tribune,* July 24, 1977; *Phoenix Gazette,* August 6, 1977; *Glendale News Herald,* August 18, 1977; *Lakeville Journal,* February, 1981.

*   *   *

CAROE, Olaf Kirkpatrick   1892-1981

OBITUARY NOTICE: Born November 15, 1892, in London, England; died November 23, 1981, in Sussex, England. Government official in British foreign service and author. Caroe joined the Indian civil service in 1919 and served in the northwest region of British India for many years. In 1946, after holding several high political posts, including secretary of the province, Caroe was selected governor of the North-West Frontier Province (now part of Pakistan). During this time the fate of British India was undecided, and after a year of difficult work, Caroe asked to be granted leave. He returned to England, where he became an active churchman, club member, and writer. His books reflect the personal observations and experiences of his official career. Caroe was the author of five books, including *Wells of Power, Soviet Empire,* and *From Nile to Indus.* Obituaries and other sources: *The Author's and Writer's Who's Who,* 6th edition, Burke's Peerage, 1971; *Who's Who,* 126th edition, St. Martin's, 1974; *International Author's and Writer's Who's Who,* 8th edition, Melrose, 1977; *London Times,* November 25, 1981.

*   *   *

CARR, Margaret   1935-
(Martin Carroll, Carole Kerr)

PERSONAL: Born November 25, 1935, in Salford, England; daughter of Richard Taylor (in police work) and Isabel (a librarian; maiden name, Jackson) Carr. *Education:* Attended high school. *Home:* Waverley, Wavering Lane, Gillingham, Dorset, England. *Office:* Council Offices, Wincanton, Somerset, England.

CAREER: Writer. Also worked as a secretary. *Member:* Crime Writers Association.

*WRITINGS—*All novels; all published by R. Hale: *Spring Into Love,* 1967; *Tread Warily at Midnight,* 1971; *Sitting Duck,*

1972; *Who's the Target?,* 1974; *Wait for the Wake,* 1974; *Too Close for Comfort,* 1974; *Blood Will Out,* 1975; *Sharendel,* 1976; *Blindman's Bluff,* 1976; *Out of the Past,* 1976; *Dare the Devil,* 1976; *Twin Tragedy,* 1977; *The Witch of Wykham,* 1978; *Daggers Drawn,* 1981.

Under pseudonym Martin Carroll: *Begotten Murder,* 1967; *Blood Vengeance,* 1968; *Dead Trouble,* 1968; *Goodbye Is Forever,* 1968; *Too Beautiful to Die,* 1969; *Bait,* 1970; *Miranda Said Murder,* 1970; *Hear No Evil,* 1971.

Under pseudonym Carole Kerr: *Not for Sale,* 1975; *Shadow of the Hunted,* 1975; *A Time to Surrender,* 1975; *Love All Start,* 1977; *Lamb to the Slaughter,* 1978; *An Innocent Abroad,* 1979; *When Dreams Come True,* 1980; *Stolen Heart,* 1981.

WORK IN PROGRESS: A novel, tentatively titled *Murder in Mind.*

*   *   *

CARROLL, Jonathan   1949-

PERSONAL: Born January 26, 1949, in New York, N.Y.; son of Sidney (a screenwriter) and June (an actress and lyricist; maiden name, Sillman) Carroll; married Beverly Schreiner (an artist), June 19, 1971; children: Ryder Pierce. *Education:* Rutgers University, B.A. (cum laude), 1971; University of Virginia, M.A., 1973. *Home:* Grinzingerstrasse 99/1, 1190 Vienna, Austria; and 1 West 72nd St., New York, N.Y. 10023. *Agent:* Harold Ober, 40 East 49th St., New York, N.Y. 10017.

CAREER: North State Academy, Hickory, N.C., English teacher, 1971-72; St. Louis Country Day School, St. Louis, Mo., English teacher, 1973-74; American International School, Vienna, Austria, English teacher, 1974—. *Awards, honors:* Emily Clark Balch fellowship in creative writing at University of Virginia, 1972.

WRITINGS: The Land of Laughs (novel), Viking, 1980. Contributor of short stories to periodicals, including *Transatlantic Review, Sport, Cimarron Review, Folio, Christian Science Monitor,* and *Four Quarters,* and of book reviews to *St. Louis Globe-Democrat* and *Cleveland Plain Dealer.*

WORK IN PROGRESS: Mr. Elf, a novel ''set in Vienna and New York about ghosts, families, guilt, and repayed debts, not necessarily in that order,'' completion expected in late 1981.

SIDELIGHTS: Jack Sullivan of the *Washington Post Book World* heralded Jonathan Carroll's first book, *The Land of Laughs,* as a ''beguiling and original novel.'' Elaborating that Carroll ''deftly avoids the cliches of contemporary occult fiction,'' the critic also observed that the author's ''descriptions of his small-town Missouri setting are charming and paradoxically down-to-earth; his characters are engaging, sweet-natured antiquarian oddballs; and his sense of humor is nicely attuned to his fantastic subject matter.'' Sullivan noted, however, that this ''whimsical fantasy'' soon develops into a ''malevolent horror . . . full of startling juxtapositions and surprises.'' Carroll explained his purpose in writing this tale in a *Publishers Weekly* interview. ''I have tried to show,'' he disclosed, ''that in literature as well as in life, the very things that delight us may well turn around and hurt or scare us, unendingly.''

BIOGRAPHICAL/CRITICAL SOURCES: Publishers Weekly, June 15, 1980; *Washington Post Book World,* May 3, 1981.

*   *   *

CARROLL, Martin
See CARR, Margaret

CARROLL, Robert P(eter) 1941-

PERSONAL: Born January 18, 1941, in Dublin, Ireland; son of Thomas Francis (a printer) and Kathleen (Merrick) Carroll; married Mary Anne Stevens (a primary school teacher), March 31, 1968; children: Finn Tomas, Alice Louisa, Saul Steve. *Education:* Trinity College, Dublin, B.A., 1962, M.A., 1967; University of Edinburgh, Ph.D., 1967. *Politics:* "Vaguely anarchistic." *Religion:* None. *Home:* 5 Marchmont Ter., Glasgow G12 9LT, Scotland. *Office:* 3 Southpark Ter., Glasgow G12 8LG, Scotland.

CAREER: Worked as bartender, bookseller, building site worker, bus conductor, and operator of a taxicab company, 1963-67; teacher of English literature and language at secondary school in Bathgate, Scotland, 1968; University of Glasgow, Glasgow, Scotland, lecturer, 1968-81, senior lecturer in Semitic studies, 1981—. *Member:* Society for the Study of the Old Testament, Association of University Teachers.

WRITINGS: When Prophecy Failed (nonfiction), Seabury, 1979; *From Chaos to Covenant* (nonfiction), S.C.M. Press, 1981. Editor of *Transactions of the Glasgow University Oriental Society,* 1974-79.

WORK IN PROGRESS: A collection of poems; a collection of short stories; a novel; a commentary on the book of Jeremiah, completion expected in 1984.

SIDELIGHTS: Carroll told *CA:* "*When Prophecy Failed* is an analysis of the work of Leon Festinger's theory of cognitive dissonance as applied to the failure of biblical prophecy. It is an attempt to develop a hermeneutic of prophecy as clarified by this analysis. It is equally an attempt to look at meaning in relation to social movements. *From Chaos to Covenant* is an introduction to the study of the book of Jeremiah, stressing the creative role of the redactional construction of that book. Again questions about hermeneutic and communal responses to national disasters are to the fore in the analysis. The subtext of the biblical text is treated as a series of reflections of social movement responding to political crises of the period.

"My first books were written to further my academic career, but now I am turning to the more important field of imaginative fiction writing. Academic writing is too objective to be creative in a stimulating way, but imaginative writing requires more space than hitherto has been available. A second career in such writing may be emerging over the next decade. . . . We shall see.

"In fiction the writer creates, from personal observations, experiences, knowledge, and projection, a world in which the tensions between imagination and the everyday world are partially resolved to provide a comprehensive(?) account of some event, life, or story. It is an exploration into possibility and imagination, not necessarily restricted by reality, which attempts to do what cannot be done by nonfiction. The poetic status of fiction is greater than that of nonfiction and allows for statements about the nature of reality which would be too generalized in nonfiction."

*   *   *

CARRON, Malcolm 1917-

BRIEF ENTRY: Born May 15, 1917, in Detroit, Mich. American minister, academic administrator, and author. Carron joined the Society of Jesus (Jesuits) in 1939 and was ordained a Roman Catholic priest in 1951. He joined the faculty of the University of Detroit in 1956 and served as president of the university from 1966 to 1979. In 1980 he became president of University of Detroit High School. His books include *The Contract Colleges of Cornell University: A Cooperative Educational Enterprise* (Cornell University Press, 1958) and an edited work, *Readings in the Philosophy of Education,* (3rd edition, University of Detroit Press, 1963). *Address:* 8400 South Cambridge, Detroit, Mich. 48221. *Biographical/critical sources: Leaders in Education,* 5th edition, Bowker, 1974; *Who's Who in America,* 41st edition, Marquis, 1980.

*   *   *

CARRY, (Benjamin) Peter 1942-

PERSONAL: Born August 25, 1942, in Valley Stream, N.Y.; son of William J. (an engineer) and Eleanor (Murphy) Carry; married Virginia Ellen Sullivan (an editor and publicist), December 11, 1971; children: Jessie V., William J. III. *Education:* Princeton University, A.B., 1964. *Religion:* Roman Catholic. *Home:* 160 Riverside Dr., New York, N.Y. 10024. *Office: Sports Illustrated,* Time and Life Bldg., New York, N.Y. 10020.

CAREER/WRITINGS: Sports Illustrated, New York, N.Y., staff writer, 1970-73, associate editor, 1973-75, senior editor, 1975-79, assistant managing editor, 1979—. Author of about one hundred twenty-five articles for *Sports Illustrated.* Contributor to *New York Times, Harper's Bazaar,* and *Collier's Encyclopedia. Military service:* U.S. Navy, 1965-68; became lieutenant; received Secretary of Navy Commendation Medal.

*   *   *

CARSON, Clayborne 1944-

PERSONAL: Born June 15, 1944, in Buffalo, N.Y.; son of Clayborne and Louise (Lee) Carson; married Susan Ann Beyer (a librarian), 1967; children: David Malcolm, Temera Lea. *Education:* University of California, Los Angeles, B.A., 1967, M.A., 1970, Ph.D., 1975. *Home:* 884 Boyce St., Palo Alto, Calif. 94301. *Office:* Department of History, Stanford University, Stanford, Calif. 94305.

CAREER: Los Alamos Scientific Laboratory, Los Alamos, N.M., laboratory assistant, summers, 1962-64; Audience Studies, Inc., Los Angeles, Calif., editor, 1965-66; *Los Angeles Free Press,* Los Angeles, staff writer, 1966-67; University of California, Los Angeles, computer programmer at Survey Research Center, 1968-71, acting assistant professor of history, 1971-74; Stanford University, Stanford, Calif., assistant professor, 1974-81, associate professor of history, 1981—.

MEMBER: American Historical Association, Organization of American Historians, Social Science History Association, Association for the Study of Afro-American Life and History, Southern Historical Association. *Awards, honors:* Andrew Mellon fellow at Stanford University, 1977; fellow at Center for the Study of Civil Rights and Race Relations, Duke University, 1978-79.

WRITINGS: The Struggle: SNCC and the Black Awakening of the 1960's, Harvard University Press, 1981. Contributor of about one dozen articles and reviews to scholarly journals and popular magazines, including *Nation* and *New West,* and newspapers.

WORK IN PROGRESS: Studying the impact of public school desegregation on American society; a book on the history of Afro-American politics.

BIOGRAPHICAL/CRITICAL SOURCES: Los Angeles Times Book Review, May 31, 1981.

* * *

CARTER, (Bessie) Lillian 1898-

BRIEF ENTRY: Born August 15, 1898, in Richland, Ga. American nurse, civic worker, and author. Lillian Carter, the colorful and outspoken mother of former U.S. president Jimmy Carter, began her career as a nurse, caring for the poor people of Georgia. She ended her official career with the U.S. Peace Corps as a volunteer worker in India from 1966 to 1968, but she has remained active in civic affairs. In 1977 she was the first woman to receive the Covenant of Peace Award from the Synagogue Council of America. She wrote *Miss Lillian and Friends: The Plains, Georgia, Family Philosophy and Recipe Book* (A & W Publishers, 1977) and *Away From Home: Letters to My Family* (Simon & Schuster, 1977). *Address:* Plains, Ga. 31780. *Biographical/critical sources: Current Biography,* Wilson, 1978.

* * *

CARTNAL, Alan 1950-

PERSONAL: Born February 3, 1950, in Santa Monica, Calif.; son of Arthur Leo (a filling station owner) and Blanche (Wallace) Cartnal. *Education:* Received B.A. and M.S. from University of California, Los Angeles. *Politics:* Democrat. *Home:* 7314½ South La Cienega Blvd., Inglewood, Calif. 90302. *Agent:* Maureen Lasher, 1210 Tellem Dr., Pacific Palisades, Calif. 90272.

CAREER: Los Angeles Times, Los Angeles, Calif., feature writer and fashion correspondent, 1972-78; *New West,* Beverly Hills, Calif., lifestyle and fashion editor, 1978-80; gossip coordinator of Hollywood segment of television program "Good Morning, America," 1981—.

WRITINGS: California Crazy (nonfiction), Houghton, 1981. Writer for KABC-TV. Contributor to magazines, including *Esquire* and *Intro.*

WORK IN PROGRESS: Another nonfiction book on Hollywood; "a new look at movieland morality, similar to the Kinsey Report"; a study of Los Angeles culture, completion expected in time for the 1984 Olympic Games.

SIDELIGHTS: Cartnal told *CA:* "I'm one of the first writers of 'nonfiction trash.' Most novelists dream up or invent bizarre, spectacular events—but I believe that the reality of California and Hollywood, in particular, creates a kind of fictional character in the lives of real people—rich and famous or strivers of status recognition. My writing is full of the gay sensibility—wit, sophistication, sexuality, but mainly a humorous look at the comic book characters that inhabit the planet.

"I may also be one of the first writers of body consciousness—which is an obsession with Californians. I work out in a gym with Nautilus equipment every day, jog constantly, and am a 10-K freak.

"I like writing that is like cruising—that lets the eye bask on a spectacle and take it all in—enjoying the sensuousness of the scene and sexual and moral hang-ups of the rich and famous.

"One critic wrote that, before reading Cartnal, one should have a face lift and a frontal lobotomy. I prefer it if my readers are lounging with hardly any clothes on, getting a tan, in a wonderful setting where they feel absolutely glorious and they become turned onto their own magnificence and the fun of living while they read. For me writing is fun. I consider myself a 'fun' writer, a grown-up Dennis the Menace who dishes the new tribal rites of California culture."

BIOGRAPHICAL/CRITICAL SOURCES: Time, May 18, 1981; *People,* June 29, 1981; *After Dark,* July, 1981; *Gentlemen's Quarterly,* August, 1981.

* * *

CARY, Bob 1921-

PERSONAL: Born October 20, 1921, in Joliet, Ill.; son of Rex L. and Cornelia (Heun) Cary; married Lillian Kluge (a photographic laboratory technician), February 1, 1948; children: Marjory Lynn Cary Kaveney, Barbara Kay Cary Hall. *Education:* Joliet Community College, A.A., 1941; attended Chicago Academy of Fine Art, 1946-47. *Home address:* P.O. Box 505, Ely, Minn. 55731. *Office: Ely Echo,* 2 East Sheridan, Ely, Minn. 55731.

CAREER: Joliet Herald News, Joliet, Ill., outdoor writer, 1950-56; *Joliet Spectator,* Joliet, reporter, 1956-57; radio station WJOL, Joliet, outdoor broadcaster, 1957; *Chicago Daily News,* Chicago, Ill., outdoor editor, 1958-66; Canadian Border Outfitters, Ely, Minn., owner, 1966-74; *Ely Echo,* Ely, managing editor, 1974—. Managing editor of *Joliet Spectator,* 1965-66. Instructor in wilderness canoeing, winter camping, and survival techniques. *Military service:* U.S. Marine Corps, 1942-45; served in Asia and Pacific theater; became sergeant; received four battle stars. *Member:* Association of Great Lakes Outdoor Writers.

WRITINGS: Winter Camping, self-illustrated, Stephen Greene Press, 1978; *Big Wilderness Canoe Manual,* self-illustrated, McKay, 1978. Field editor of *Minnesota Sportsman.*

WORK IN PROGRESS: Magazine articles on winter camping and bear hunting.

SIDELIGHTS: Cary told *CA:* "I am interested in environmental studies, conservation and outdoor recreation. I am also a photographer and illustrator of outdoor subjects. I was born and raised in the country, practically grew up outdoors. I started canoeing in my youth, and as a Chicago resident I often went to Minnesota for canoeing, hunting, and fishing. Finally my wife and I decided, 'Why hang around Chicago? Let's get!' So we got; we now live in Minnesota and I can enjoy the outdoors every day, while collecting material for my writing."

* * *

CASADY, Cort (Boon) 1947-

PERSONAL: Born April 22, 1947, in McAllen, Tex.; son of Simon (an editor and publisher) and Virginia Kent (Boon) Casady. *Education:* Harvard University, B.A. (cum laude), 1968. *Residence:* Los Angeles, Calif. *Agent:* International Creative Management, 8899 Beverly Blvd., Los Angeles, Calif. 90048. *Office:* 1543 Sunset Plaza Dr., Los Angeles, Calif. 90069.

CAREER: Writer, composer, and performer. Columbia Broadcasting System (CBS-TV), Los Angeles, Calif., production assistant for "The Smothers Brothers Comedy Hour," 1968; Aquarius Theatre, Hollywood, Calif., associate producer of "Hair," 1968-69; Ken Kragen & Friends, Inc., Beverly Hills, Calif., personal manager for celebrities, 1969-71; Cort Casady Management, Beverly Hills, Calif., personal manager for celebrities, 1971-73; night club performer in San Diego, San Francisco, and Los Angeles, Calif., 1974-76; staff songwriter at Al Gallico Music Corp., 1977-79; musical director of television series "One Night Band," CBS-TV/M.T.M. Productions, 1981-82; scriptwriter for television programs, 1977—; composer of themes and scores for television programs, 1980—. *Member:* Writers Guild of America (West), American Federation of Television and Radio Artists, American Film Society, Broadcast Music Inc. (BMI), Screen Actors Guild.

WRITINGS: (With John Davidson) *The Singing Entertainer: A Contemporary Study of the Art of Being a Professional,* Alfred Publishing, 1979; *The Book of Bad Advice,* Alfred Publishing, 1982.

Scriptwriter for television programs, including "The American Flier," MCA-TV, 1977; "The Jim Nabors Show," syndicated, 1978; "Barbara Mandrell and the Mandrell Sisters," National Broadcasting Co. (NBC), 1980-81; "A Special Kenny Rogers," Columbia Broadcasting System (CBS), 1980; "Kenny Rogers and the American Cowboy," CBS, 1980; "The Eddie Rabbitt Special," NBC, 1980; "John Schneider: Back Home," CBS, 1980.

Composer of themes and scores for television programs, including "First Time, Second Time," CBS, "Nichols and Dymes," NBC, "One Night Band," CBS, "Rick and Bob's America," American Broadcasting Co. (ABC).

Composer of songs, including (with Marshall Chapman) "A Women's Heart (Is a Handy Place to Be)," (with Chapman) "Rode Hard and Put Up Wet," "Only First Love," "Hands," (with Tony McCashen) "Nobody Stays Together Anymore," "Here We Are," "Say You Always Will," "The Country's in the Music."

Author of television screenplay "Kenny Rogers as the Gambler," 1980. Writer of concert and nightclub acts for entertainers, including Dottie West, Johnny Lee, and Mickey Gilley. Contributor to periodicals, including *San Diego Magazine.*

SIDELIGHTS: Casady considers himself "fortunate to be getting an opportunity to create in all the areas I enjoy—television, comedy, music, and live onstage." One recent success was the television series "Barbara Mandrell and the Mandrell Sisters," for which he and a team of seven other writers generated scripts. "I know when I write a television show that *somebody* will watch it," he said. "When people say, 'Hey, I saw the show! What did *you* write?,' I say, 'I wrote all the stuff you thought was *funny.* The rest was written by somebody else.'"

Besides television writing, Casady has written several screenplays, most notably the two-hour made-for-television movie "Kenny Rogers as the Gambler." Popular with audiences, the film, noted its author, "earned an impressive fifty share in the ratings, making it one of the most watched TV movies of the 1980 season." Another screenplay is based on his father's 1979 campaign for mayor of San Diego.

Casady also has written concert and nightclub acts for other performers, and his original songs have been recorded by artists such as Cyrstal Gayle, Jessie Colter, Dennis Roussos, and Marshall Chapman. "Writing for other performers," Casady explained, "helps me as a performer. And I like to think the fact that I perform [with his country-rock band Canyon] makes me a better writer." Casady's first book, *The Singing Entertainer,* which he wrote for television personality John Davidson, is a "handbook for aspiring performers."

His second book, *The Book of Bad Advice,* is "a compendium of the worst advice given and received on subjects such as finance, relationships, health, and careers."

Casady told *CA:* "After learning the business side of show business as a personal manager of a variety of recording artists

(Mason Williams, Kenny Rogers, Pat Paulson, Jennifer Warnes), I turned to songwriting in 1974 and, in mid-1976, to writing for television. Happily, I've been able to pursue both careers with some success. I look forward someday to producing both music and television in addition to writing."

*   *   *

CASSEDY, Sylvia   1930-

PERSONAL: Born January 29, 1930, in Brooklyn, N.Y.; daughter of Jacob (a pharmacist) and Minnie (Singer) Levine; married Leslie Verwiebe, June 19, 1949 (died September 3, 1950); married Edward S. Cassedy, Jr. (a professor), March 28, 1952; children: Ellen (Mrs. Jeffrey Blum), Steven, Amy, Susannah. *Education:* Brooklyn College, B.A., 1950; attended Johns Hopkins University, 1959-60. *Home:* 6 Hampshire Rd., Great Neck, N.Y. 11023.

CAREER: Queens College of the City University of New York, Saturday Enrichment Program, Flushing, N.Y., teacher of creative writing to children, 1973-74; Great Neck Public Library, Great Neck, N.Y., teacher of creative writing to children, 1975—; Manhasset Public Schools Parent-Teacher Association, Saturday Enrichment Program, Long Island, N.Y., teacher of creative writing to children, 1977—. Instructor in teaching creative writing to children for Nassau County Board of Cooperative Education, Nassau County, N.Y., 1978-79.

WRITINGS—All for children: *Little Chameleon* (illustrated by Rainey Bennett), World, 1966; *Pierino and the Bell* (illustrated by Evaline Ness), Doubleday, 1966; (editor and translator with Kunihiro Suetake) *Birds, Frogs, and Moonlight* (verse; illustrated by Vo-Dinh), Doubleday, 1967; *Marzipan Day on Bridget Lane* (illustrated by Margot Tomes), Doubleday, 1967; (editor and translator with Parvathi Thampi) *Moon-Uncle, Moon-Uncle: Rhymes from India* (illustrated by Susanne Suba), Doubleday, 1972; *In Your Own Words: A Beginner's Guide to Writing,* Doubleday, 1979.

WORK IN PROGRESS: A novel for children.

*   *   *

CASSEL, Virginia Cunningham

PERSONAL: Born in Pittsburgh, Pa.; daughter of John Henry (a sales engineer) and Anna Lucretia (Enyeart) Cunningham; married Samuel H. Cassel, Jr. (divorced); children: Gretchen Cassel Eick, David Cunningham. *Education:* Attended Beaver College; Western Reserve University (now Case Western Reserve University), B.A., 1955; University of New Mexico, M.A., 1956. *Residence:* Albuquerque, N.M.

CAREER: Cuyahoga County Welfare Department, Cleveland, Ohio, caseworker, 1952-54; Presbyterian Hospital, Albuquerque, N.M., special teacher of Navajo Indian children under treatment for tuberculosis, 1956-58; administrator of program for the elderly at Bergen County Tuberculosis & Health Association in New Jersey, 1958; Jarvie Commonweal Services (private agency), New York, N.Y., caseworker, 1959-60; teacher of slow learners at public elementary school in Washington, D.C., 1961-64; teacher at a school for talented children in Washington, D.C., 1964-65; program analyst for Office of Economic Opportunity, Head Start program, 1965-66; U.S. Office of Education, Washington, D.C., education specialist (including work with disadvantaged youth, early childhood, institutionalized youth, and innovative programs in public schools), 1967-78; writer, 1978—. Director of bilingual Indian education workshop, 1978. *Member:* Authors Guild.

WRITINGS: Juniata Valley (historical novel), Viking, 1981.

WORK IN PROGRESS: A sequel to *Juniata Valley,* about Pontiac's war in central Pennsylvania; a novel about Harper's Ferry, Virginia, at the time of John Brown's raid, 1859.

SIDELIGHTS: Virginia Cassel told *CA:* "I was editor of our high school literary magazine and on the staff of the Beaver College literary magazine. I have written poems and short stories since childhood but never tackled a novel until I began to do geneological research on my mother's family at the National Archives in Washington, D.C. The material about the Indian depredations in the Juniata Valley, where Mother's ancestors lived, was so fascinating that it called for a novel, so I began writing my first book before retiring. As I got into the story, the research took so much time and energy that I decided to retire from my government job in order to devote my time to writing.

"I deplore the trend that appears to be taking over America: The increasing emphasis on technology, on market place values at the expense of the arts and humanities and the search for truth. It is disturbing that history departments at many universities are cutting staff and courses. Unless we know our past and can evaluate what is worth preserving as opposed to what must be changed or discarded, we cannot be prepared for the future. An inscription at the National Archives reads, 'The past is prologue.'

"I think this is why I have chosen to write historical novels. Many individuals who would never read a history, who have no real interest in following the great historic tides, may read a novel that deals with long-gone times and (eternal optimist that I am) a spark may be lighted that will make them want to know more.

"Because of an overriding interest in the ancient world, I studied modern Greek with a tutor from Athens one year and learned enough to communicate reasonably well on five trips to Greece. I visited the Greek mainland, the Peloponnesus, and sixteen islands. Samos, where Antony and Cleopatra spent their 'honeymoon,' was particularly lovely. Mycenae, Bergama, Ephesus, and ancient Halicarnassus were sites where the past came alive. I have also visited many countries in Europe, learning enough Spanish to be able to use it in Spain, and Mexico."

AVOCATIONAL INTERESTS: Music, theatre, ballet, painting, gardening.

*   *   *

CASSIDY, (Charles) Michael (Ardagh) 1936-

PERSONAL: Born September 24, 1936, in Johannesburg, South Africa; son of Charles Stewart (an engineer) and Mary (Craufurd) Cassidy; married Carol Bam, December 16, 1969; children: Catherine, Deborah, Martyn. *Education:* Cambridge University, M.A., 1958; Fuller Theological Seminary, Pasadena, Calif., B.D., 1963. *Politics:* Progressive Federal party. *Religion:* Anglican. *Home:* Namirembe, Flamingo Dr., Hilton, Natal 3245, South Africa. *Office:* African Enterprise, P.O. Box 647, Pietermaritzburg, Natal, South Africa.

CAREER: African Enterprise, Pietermaritzburg, South Africa, founder, president, and team leader, 1964—. *Member:* Michaelhouse Old Boys' Clubs, St. Catherine's Society.

WRITINGS: Decade of Decisions, Marshall, Morgan & Scott, 1970, published in the United States as *Where Are You Taking the World Anyway?,* Regal Books, 1973; *Prisoners of Hope,* African Enterprise, 1974; *The Relationship Tangle,* African

Enterprise, 1974; (editor) *I Will Heal Their Land,* African Enterprise, 1974; *Together in One Place,* Evangel Publishing House, 1978; (editor) *Facing the New Challenges,* Evangel Publishing House, 1978; *Christianity for the Open-Minded,* Intervarsity Christian Fellowship, 1978. Also author of *Bursting the Wineskins* and *Decide Now.* Author of "Window on the Word," a weekly column. Contributor to theology journals and religious magazines.

WORK IN PROGRESS: Hope for South Africa; revising *The Relationship Tangle.*

SIDELIGHTS: "My basic motivation in life and in writing," Cassidy told *CA,* "is to share the Christian message of hope and new life in Jesus Christ. As a result of a deep spiritual experience during my undergraduate days at Cambridge, I became interested in the communication of the Christian faith, particularly to those who were seekers, doubters, skeptics, or agnostics. I also became deeply concerned for my continent of Africa and my country of South Africa. It seemed to me that in South Africa the intractable and almost insoluble political and racial problems could find no answer unless such answers were born out of spiritual reawakening such as took place in the eighteenth century in England under the Wesleys. That particular phenomenon of the Wesleyan revival has constituted for me a major source of inspiration in my own life and work. The Wesleyan reawakening saved England from catastrophe and bloody revolution and perhaps spiritual reawakening may have the same potential and a similar destiny in South Africa. So it is concerns along these lines which motivate me in my work and in my writing.

"For example, in my newspaper column I am particularly concerned to reach the secular man in the street, who perhaps never even darkens the door of a church. Some of my other writings are focused on Christians in an attempt to build them up in their faith, but always with a view to moving them out in mission and in concern for the world.

"I believe that in the real sense every Christian needs three conversions—the first to Christ, the second to the church, and the third to the world. Another of my great concerns is to see Christians come together in new unity and to that end I have initiated several major conferences on the African continent. First was the Congress on Mission and Evangelism in Durban in 1973, which drew together most of the senior church leaders of our country. That was followed by the Pan African Christian Leadership Assembly held in Nairobi in 1976. Eight hundred leaders attended that from forty-seven out of forty-nine African countries. It was then our privilege to play a major role in the launching of the South African Leadership Assembly, which took place in Pretoria in 1979. This drew together some six thousand South African church leaders of all ages, denominations, races, and backgrounds. I believe that whenever Christians come together there is always an overflow in terms of concern for the world and the society around.

"I have had the privilege of traveling in almost every part of Africa, in a number of parts of Latin America, as well as in Europe and Australia. Somehow Africa still fascinates me more than anywhere else and I feel it is a continent which will perhaps be coming in a special way into its own in the twenty-first century. My somewhat inadequate efforts in Latin and French have paid off in terms of helping me with French as the other major linguafranca of Africa. Unfortunately, I do not find too many Africans talking Latin to each other!"

AVOCATIONAL INTERESTS: "I am a keen photographer and a compulsive tinkler on the piano. I enjoy photography because of its ability to capture and eternalize special moments and memories that would otherwise be forever lost. As to my piano, I adore music but will remain in a state of frustration as I was far too undisciplined as a child ever to master a real basic. So even in music there are judgment days!''

* * *

CASTLE, Sue G(aronzik) 1942-

PERSONAL: Born February 2, 1942, in Harrisburg, Pa.; daughter of Benjamin L. and Sadye (Latt) Garonzik; married Jay S. Castle (a screenwriter), February 27, 1965; children: Jennifer, Bethany. *Education:* Smith College, B.A., 1961; Columbia University, M.S., 1963. *Home:* 23 Stephenson Ter., Briarcliff, N.Y. 10510.

CAREER: Massachusetts Institute of Technology, Cambridge, Mass., research assistant, 1962; Advanced Computer Techniques, New York, N.Y., systems analysts, 1963-71; free-lance writer of books and articles for children and adults, 1971—. Teacher of creative movement to children, 1973—; member of board of directors of Ossining Children's Center, 1976-81.

WRITINGS: The Complete Guide to Preparing Baby Foods at Home, Doubleday, 1973, revised edition published as *The Complete New Guide to Preparing Baby Foods,* 1981; *Face Talk, Hand Talk, Body Talk* (juvenile), illustrated with photographs by Frances McLaughlin-Gill, Doubleday, 1976. Contributor of articles to magazines and newspapers.

WORK IN PROGRESS: Various manuscripts for children's books; travel articles; a book about how and why to delay a child's entry into school.

SIDELIGHTS: ''As long as there aren't books already published on a subject,'' Sue Castle commented, ''an editor is ready to consider a nonfiction book even though you are not a 'professional' writer. My first book, *The Complete Guide to Preparing Baby Food at Home,* came from my asking an editor at Doubleday to have a writer do a book on homemade baby foods. She said, 'Why not you?' I began a career that is growing along with my children.''

While teaching classes in creative movement to children, Castle found that there were no books about body language currently available to young readers. She submitted an outline of her class to a Doubleday editor, who thought it would make an interesting book. Castle then found a photographer, Frances McLaughlin-Gill, who enjoys working with children and whose work has been published and exhibited around the world. With the help of local children, many of whom had participated in creative movement classes, Castle and Gill assembled *Face Talk, Hand Talk, Body Talk,* a collection of captioned photographs showing how children's body language communicates a wide range of emotions and reactions.

Castle told *CA:* ''I find it easy to write about what my children are involved in and to include their ideas. In recent years we have traveled to Egypt and Italy with them, and I hope to use these very successful trips as a take off for further writing. I feel that in writing for children you have to talk and listen to them and to value their concerns and interests.''

* * *

CATTO, Max(well Jeffrey) 1909-
(Max Finkell, Simon Kent)

PERSONAL: Born July 29, 1909, in Manchester, England. *Education:* Attended University of Manchester. *Home:* 32 Denewood Rd., London N.6, England.

CAREER: Playwright and novelist.

WRITINGS—Novels: *River Junk,* Arthur Barker, 1937; *The Hairy Man,* M. Secker, 1939; *Ginger Charley,* M. Secker, 1939; *The Flanagan Boy,* Harrap, 1949; *The Killing Frost,* Heinemann, 1950, published as *Trapeze,* Landsborough, 1959; *The Sickle,* Heinemann, 1952; *The Mummers,* Heinemann, 1953; *A Prize of Gold,* Heinemann, 1953; *Gold in the Sky,* Heinemann, 1956, Morrow, 1958; *The Devil at Four O'Clock,* Heinemann, 1958, Morrow, 1959; *The Melody of Sex,* Heinemann, 1959, Morrow, 1960; *Mister Moses,* Morrow, 1961; *D-Day in Paradise,* Heinemann, 1963, Morrow, 1964; *The Tiger in the Bed,* Morrow, 1963; *I Have Friends in Heaven,* Heinemann, 1965, Little, Brown, 1966; *Love From Venus,* Heinemann, 1965; *Bird on the Wing,* Heinemann, 1966; *The Banana Men,* Simon & Schuster, 1967; *Murphy's War,* Simon & Schuster, 1969; *King Oil,* Simon & Schuster, 1970; *The Fattest Bank in New Orleans,* Heinemann, 1971; *Sam Casanova,* Heinemann, 1973, Signet, 1977; *Mister Midas,* M. Joseph, 1976; *The Empty Tiger,* St. Martin's, 1977.

Under pseudonym Simon Kent: *Fleur-de-Lys Court,* Heinemann, 1950; *The Doctor on Bean Street,* Crowell, 1952 (published in England as *For the Love of Doc,* Heinemann, 1952); *A Hill in Korea,* Hutchinson, 1953; *Fire Down Below,* Hutchinson, 1954; *Ferry to Hongkong,* Hutchinson, 1957; *The Lions at the Kill,* Hutchinson, 1959; *Charlie Gallagher My Love!,* Hutchinson, 1960, Macmillan, 1961.

Plays: *Green Waters* (three-act; produced Off-Broadway at Masque Theater, November 4, 1936), Samuel French, 1937; ''The Bowery Touch,'' first produced in 1937; *They Walk Alone* (three-act; first produced on the West End at Shaftesbury Theatre, January 19, 1939; produced on Broadway at Shubert Theatre, March 12, 1941), M. Secker, 1939; *Punch Without Judy* (three-act; first produced in 1939), Allen & Unwin, 1940; ''Wise Guys,'' first produced in 1940; ''Black Racket,'' first produced in 1942; ''Gather No Moss,'' first produced in 1945; ''Can-Can,'' first produced on Broadway at Shubert Theatre, May 7, 1953; ''The Doctor in Bean Street,'' first produced in 1953.

Unpublished plays; under pseudonym Max Finkell: ''Decor'' (three-act comedy); ''Side-Show in Paris'' (three-act comedy); ''Polka'' (three-act); ''Procession in Purple'' (three-act); ''Venetian Summer'' (three-act comedy); ''French Salad'' (three-act), first produced in 1934.

Screenplays: (With Jack Whittingham) ''West of Zanzibar,'' Universal-J. Arthur Rank, 1955.

SIDELIGHTS: Catto began his literary career as a playwright but soon shifted most of his attention to novels, averaging more than one book a year between 1950 and 1970. Many of his novels are adventure stories set in the American West, Africa, the Pacific, and other exotic locales. Though he often uses the conventions of the western, the crime thriller, the mystery, and the war story, the quality of his writing places his books outside the realm of formulaic genre fiction. Critics have praised Catto's craftsmanship, especially his skillful handling of background, character, and dialogue, as well as his salty and satirical humor.

MEDIA ADAPTATIONS: Nine of Catto's books and one of his plays have been made into films. ''The Devil at Four O'Clock,'' which starred Spencer Tracy and Frank Sinatra, was one of the highest grossing films of 1961. ''Trapeze'' and ''Murphy's War'' were also major box office successes. Other movies based on Catto's works are: ''Daughter of Darkness'' (based on ''They Walk Alone''), ''Bad Blonde'' (based on *The Flanagan Boy*), ''A Prize of Gold,'' ''A Hill in Korea,'' ''Ferry to Hongkong,'' ''Seven Thieves'' (based on *Lions at the Kill*), and ''Mister Moses.''

BIOGRAPHICAL/CRITICAL SOURCES: New York Herald Tribune Book Review, November 2, 1952; *New York Times*, January 26, 1958, June 7, 1959; *Times Literary Supplement*, September 5, 1958; *Catholic World*, June, 1959; *New York Times Book Review*, April 3, 1960, May 14, 1961, March 1, 1964; *Best Sellers*, September 15, 1967, May 1, 1970, March, 1978; *Books and Bookmen*, September, 1967.*

*   *   *

CHAPIN, Harry (Forster)   1942-1981

PERSONAL: Born December 7, 1942, in Greenwich Village, N.Y., died in an automobile accident, July 16, 1981, on Long Island, N.Y.; son of James Forbes (a musician) and Elspeth (Burke) Chapin; married Sandra Campbell Gaston (a poet), November 28, 1968; children: Jaime, Jonothon, Jason, Jennifer, Josh. *Education:* Attended Cornell University, 1960-64. *Office:* 198 New York Ave., Huntington, N.Y. 11743.

CAREER: Singer, songwriter, poet, and dramatist. Founding trustee of World Hunger Year, 1974-81; member of the President's Committee on International, Domestic, and World Hunger, 1978-81; honorary chairman of the Suffolk County Hunger Hearings. Chairman of the board of trustees of the Performing Arts Foundation of Long Island, N.Y.; member of the board of directors of the Eglevsky Ballet, 1979-81, and the Long Island Business Association, 1979-81. President of Story Songs, Inc. *Member:* American Federation of Television and Radio Artists (AFTRA), American Society of Composers, Authors, and Publishers (ASCAP), American Federation of Musicians, National Association of Recording Arts and Sciences, Actors Equity, Screen Guild.

AWARDS, HONORS: First prize for best feature documentary from New York and Atlanta, Ga., film festivals, and Academy Award nomination, all 1969, for ''Legendary Champions''; Grammy Award nomination from the National Academy of Recording Arts and Sciences, 1972, for best new artist, 1975, for best male vocal performance, for ''Cat's in the Cradle''; two Tony Award nominations from the League of New York Theatres and Producers, 1975, for ''The Night That Made America Famous''; Man of the Year award from the Long Island Advertisers, 1977; named One of Ten Outstanding Young Men by the U.S. Jaycees, 1977; Lone Eagle Award from Long Island Public Relations Society, 1978.

WRITINGS: ''The Legendary Champions'' (documentary screenplay), Turn of the Century Fights, 1968; (composer of music and lyrics) ''The Night That Made America Famous'' (two-act musical), first produced on Broadway at the Ethel Barrymore Theatre, February 26, 1975; *Looking . . . Seeing* (poems), Crowell, 1978.

Composer and lyricist of songs, including: ''Taxi,'' ''WOLD,'' (with wife, Sandy Chapin) ''Cat's in the Cradle,'' ''A Better Place to Be,'' ''Sniper,'' ''Mr. Tanner,'' ''What Made America Famous,'' ''Mail Order Annie,'' ''Halfway to Heaven,'' ''30,000 Pounds of Bananas,'' ''Dance Band on the Titanic,'' ''The Mayor of Candor Lied,'' ''If My Mary Were Here,'' ''Fall in Love With Him,'' ''The Parade's Still Passing By,'' ''Roll Down the River,'' ''Why Should People Stay the Same,'' ''Bluesman,'' ''Country Dreams,'' ''Mercenaries,'' ''Manhood,'' ''There Only Was One Choice,'' ''If You Want to Feel,'' ''Poor Damned Fool,'' ''Jenny,'' ''It Seems You Only Love Me When It Rains,'' ''Flowers Are Red,'' and ''Sequel.''

Recordings: ''Heads and Tails,'' Warner Bros., 1972; ''Sniper and Other Love Songs,'' Elektra, 1972; ''Short Stories,'' Elektra, 1973; ''Verities and Balderdash,'' Elektra, 1974; ''Portrait Gallery,'' Elektra, 1975; ''On the Road to Kingdom Come,'' Elektra, 1976; ''Greatest Stories Live,'' Elektra, 1976; ''Dance Band on the Titanic,'' Elektra, 1977; ''Living Room Suite,'' Elektra, 1978; ''Legends of the Lost and Found,'' Elektra, 1980; ''Sequel,'' Boardwalk, 1980.

WORK IN PROGRESS: At the time of his death Chapin was writing a feature film based on the song ''Taxi'' and a documentary about grandfathers; his survivors are expected to complete the projects. Chapin was also planning an album of new songs.

SIDELIGHTS: The son of a big-band drummer, Chapin began his musical career in the late fifties as a trumpeter and songwriter. While still a teenager Chapin began playing guitar in a folk music group formed with his brothers, Tom and Steve. The group performed periodically throughout the sixties, though it essentially disbanded in 1965. Chapin then turned to filmmaking, delving into a two-and-one-half-year project that resulted in the Academy Award-nominated ''Legendary Champions,'' a documentary about boxing. Another documentary, ''Blue Water, White Death,'' featured Chapin's music, inspiring him to rededicate himself to a musical career. By 1971 Chapin had a backing band and a recording contract.

Chapin began performing his own compositions when ''I couldn't find anybody dumb enough to sing these story-songs for me.'' His ''story-songs'' are insightful glimpses into the lives of ordinary people in common situations. ''WOLD,'' for example, is about an aging disc jockey who calls his estranged wife to inform her of his success. But the lyrics reveal that the man is lonely and desperate, as are many of Chapin's subjects, who include truck drivers, tailors, factory workers, handymen, children, and lovers. ''Taxi,'' Chapin's first hit, is a tale of a taxi driver who recognizes his passenger as his former lover, a rich socialite, who, like the cabbie, has many unfulfilled dreams. ''Taxi'' earned Chapin a Grammy nomination in 1972. Commenting on his musical style, Chapin said: ''Nobody during the past decade so consistently has used the extended narrative form. For stories of ordinary people and cosmic moments in their non-cosmic lives, you have to turn back to Harry Chapin.''

In addition to writing songs, Chapin wrote a volume of poetry, *Looking . . . Seeing*. Dedicated to Chapin's wife, Sandy, ''a better poet than I will ever be,'' *Looking . . . Seeing* contains didactic, social poems as well as emotional poems of growth, love, and loss. The book received little critical notice but sold well at Chapin's concerts. Chapin also penned a Broadway musical, ''The Night That Made America Famous,'' combining drama, rock music, and creative film and lighting techniques. Though the revue closed after seventy-five performances, it was nominated for two Tony awards.

Undoubtedly, Chapin's popularity was due in large part to his gregarious personality and his close contact with his fans. During his concerts he often called for volunteers from the audience to join him in songs, and after each performance he signed autographs, posed for photographers, and talked with admirers. At fund-raisers, he was known to greet cars as they arrived, and on his last birthday, he personally served cake to two hundred fans who had organized a pre-concert party for him.

After ''Cat's in the Cradle'' hit the top of the popular music charts in 1974, Chapin felt he should use his place in the limelight for a purpose other than his own glorification. ''I had to face my own '60's bullshit about the social responsibility of successful people,'' Chapin is quoted by William Hammond of the *Flint Voice*. During his brief career, Chapin raised over five million dollars for various charitable organizations. He performed nearly half of his two hundred-plus concerts for charity, accepting neither payment for performing, nor reimbursement for transportation and lodging. At these benefits, Chapin tried to convey his belief that people can make the world a better place by involving themselves in social causes. He told the *Flint Journal:* "An awful lot of people in our society right now are like shipmates on the Titanic. They polish the brass. They clean the linen. They worry about how the table is set. But it doesn't matter. The only thing that matters is who's on the bridge, who's the lookout and who is in the engine room. The thing you have to do is get out there and work, work, work, work, work."

World hunger was Chapin's primary concern, and with friend Bill Ayres he founded World Hunger Year (WHY) and spent a great deal of his time lobbying in Washington for programs to alleviate worldwide starvation. In 1978 Chapin's efforts paid off: President Carter formed the Presidential Commission on World Hunger to study impoverishment and push for reform in the United States and abroad. (The commission was terminated under the Reagan administration.) The singer was also dedicated to Ralph Nader's Public Interest Research Group, a consumer protection agency. Commenting on Chapin's involvement, Nader was quoted by *Rolling Stone*'s Dave Marsh: "I've never seen an example of an entertainer who dedicated so many hours or so much imagination to a civic cause. A lot of them go to soirees, a lot of them give lip service, but the duration of Harry's commitment is unprecedented."

Harry Chapin's life ended tragically one summer afternoon in a fiery car crash on a Long Island freeway. He seemed to foreshadow his manner of death in many of his poems. In "The Great Divide," he referred to being "cradled in my Detroit casket," and in "Plains Crossing" he likened the progression of life to a trip on a highway: "The poles, / the lines, / the miles, / the time, / sagging, sagging / until . . . / the taut shriek / of rubber on the road, / the shattered windshield / and blood." But the grassroots singer was not preoccupied with the thought of his death. Michael Moore of the *Flint Voice* spoke with Chapin about musician John Lennon's murder and asked him if he ever feared it would happen to him. "He [Harry] told me that if he ever spent a second thinking about it that it would do him in," Moore related.

Chapin was eulogized by fans across the country who organized memorial concerts and services on his behalf. He was also honored by fellow musicians and politicians. Dave Marsh reported: "No other singer—not Bing Crosby, nor Elvis Presley, nor John Lennon—has ever been so widely honored by the nation's legislators. Nine senators and thirty congressmen paid tribute to Harry Chapin on the floor." Capturing Chapin's charismatic appeal, Marsh added: "For many who knew him, he was a legitimate hero, not so much for his music as for his consistent and conscientious willingness to fight the battles, to stand up for a just cause, no matter how hopeless." Others honored Chapin with similar words, noting his steadfast and untiring service to society. Chapin himself once explained his professional drive to Moore: "You go when you're ready to go and until then you live life for all it's worth."

BIOGRAPHICAL/CRITICAL SOURCES: Looking . . . Seeing, Crowell, 1978; *Rolling Stone,* April 6, 1978; *Flint Voice,* December, 1980; *Flint Journal,* December 12, 1980; *Food Monitor,* September/October, 1981; *People,* March 15, 1982.

OBITUARIES: Flint Voice, July 17, 1981; *Flint Journal,* July 17, 1981, July 18, 1981; *Detroit Free Press,* July 17, 1981; *New York Times,* July 17, 1981; *Detroit News,* July 18, 1981;

Chicago Tribune, July 18, 1981; *Village Voice,* July 29-August 4, 1981; *Rolling Stone,* September 3, 1981.

[Sketch reviewed by personal friend Michael Moore of the *Flint Voice*.]

—*Sketch by Nancy S. Gearhart*

*   *   *

CHAPMAN, Laura   1935-

PERSONAL: Born October 14, 1935, in New York, N.Y.; daughter of Henry K. (a lawyer) and Katherine (Bab) Chapman; married Alan J. Hruska (a lawyer), September 7, 1958; children: three. *Education:* Cornell University, B.A., 1955; Yale University, LL.B., 1958. *Agent:* Sterling Lord Agency, Inc., 660 Madison Ave., New York, N.Y. 10021.

CAREER: Writer.

WRITINGS: A Change of Heart, Dutton, 1976; *Legal Relations,* Dutton, 1977; *Multiple Choice,* Doubleday, 1978.

WORK IN PROGRESS: A historical novel based on the lives of Maria and Elizabeth Gunning.

*   *   *

CHAPMAN, Richard Arnold   1937-

BRIEF ENTRY: Born August 15, 1937, in Bexleyheath, England. British political scientist, educator, and author. Chapman has been a reader in politics at University of Durham since 1971. He edited *Style in Administration: Readings in British Public Administration* (Allen & Unwin, 1971) and *The Role of Commissions in Policy-Making* (Allen & Unwin, 1973) and wrote *Teaching Public Administration: Current Education, Training, and Research Programmes in the United Kingdom* (Joint University Council for Social and Public Administration, 1973) and *The Dynamics of Administrative Reform* (Croom Helm, 1980). *Address:* 10 The Village, Brancepeth, Durham DH7 8DG, England; and Faculty of Social Sciences, University of Durham, 23-26 Old Olvet, Durham DH1 3HY, England. *Biographical/critical sources: Who's Who in the World,* 4th edition, Marquis, 1978.

*   *   *

CHARD, (Maire) Brigid   1934-

PERSONAL: Born August 24, 1934, in Sevenoaks, Kent, England; daughter of Edward (a teacher) and Marjorie (Potts) Groves; married Peter Chard (a headmaster), April 2, 1960; children: Rebecca, Sarah, Rachel, Abigail. *Education:* St. Anne's College, Oxford, M.A. (with honors), 1956. *Politics:* Labour. *Religion:* Church of England. *Residence:* Gloucester, England.

CAREER: Actress, producer, and author of books for young people; actress with Oxford University Drama Society and Edinburgh Festival, summers, 1953-56; worked in repertory companies in Huddersfield, Oldham, Manchester, and Crewe, England, 1956-59; British Broadcasting Corp. (BBC), London, England, studio manager for drama, 1959-60; justice of the peace in Gloucester County, England, 1977—. *Member:* United Nations Association.

WRITINGS—Juveniles: *Ferret Summer,* Rex Collings, 1975; *Hidden Journey,* Rex Collings, 1976; *A Shepherd's Crook,* Rex Collings, 1977; *Voices on the Wind,* Rex Collings, 1980.

WORK IN PROGRESS: A sequel to *Ferret Summer,* as yet untitled.

SIDELIGHTS: Brigid Chard wrote: "I don't think I'm important. My work has to stand on its own, just as in the theatre the actor isn't important but is the medium for someone else's words.

"Oxford, the theatre, and later, the countryside have been my three most important influences, I think. At Oxford I was taught by Tolkien, Lord David Cecil, and Helen Gardiner. Contact with minds like those marks you forever! In the theatre, I was trained in the Method School, a technique of characterization that adapts superbly to writing. Since my marriage, I've returned to the countryside and believe strongly in its effect on people. It puts a pattern and sense of proportion into human life; it's stability in an unstable world

"I didn't mean to write—I wrote my first book just for my eldest daughter and was surprised when it was accepted for publication. I'm still surprised! I write with difficulty, and only when I feel I've got something to say. It has to come second to the needs of my children and the demands of the small holding which I farm. Most of what I am you will find, I hope, in my books, because if you write for young people, you have to be honest with yourself and with them. If you're not, they'll reject you straight away."

*   *   *

CHARDIN, Pierre Teilhard de
See TEILHARD de CHARDIN, (Marie Joseph) Pierre

*   *   *

CHARTERIS, Hugo (Francis Guy)   1922-1970

PERSONAL: Born December 11, 1922, in London, England; died December 20, 1970; son of Guy Lawrence (an investment registrar); married Virginia Adam, c. 1947; children: four. *Education:* Attended Oxford University. *Residence:* Yorkshire, England.

CAREER: London Daily Mail, Hull and London, England, and Paris, France, journalist, c. 1947-51; writer, 1951-70. *Military service:* Scots Guards, 1941-47; served as public relations officer in Malaya and Java; became major; received Military Cross. *Awards, honors:* Award from Scottish Arts Council, 1969, for *The Indian Summer of Gabriel Murray.*

WRITINGS—Novels, except as noted: *A Share of the World,* Collins, 1953; *Marching With April,* Collins, 1956; *Picnic at Porokorro,* Collins, 1958; *The Lifeline,* Collins, 1961; *Clunie/Hugo Charteris* (juvenile), Heinemann, 1963; *Pictures on the Wall,* Collins, 1963; *The River-Watcher,* Collins, 1965; *The Coat,* Collins, 1966, Harcourt, 1970; *The Indian Summer of Gabriel Murray,* Weidenfeld & Nicolson, 1968, Harcourt, 1970. Also author of *Staying With Aunt Rozzie,* 1964, and several television plays, including "The Connoisseur," and "Asquith in Orbit," 1971. Contributor of short stories to *Cornhill* and feature stories to *London Daily Mail* and *London Sunday Telegraph.*

SIDELIGHTS: Charteris's first novel, *A Share of the World,* was his most successful work. The books that followed failed to match its popularity but garnered critical praise for the author. "He is regarded, not without justification, as one of the most resourceful, interesting and thoroughly professional novelists now writing," assessed Frank McGuinness in *London Magazine* before Charteris's death. "The critics have become almost as one in their praise of the genuine if somewhat idiosyncratic value of his work, the enormous narrative skill he brings to it, and the brilliance with which he is able to create

character, mood and background." "What still eludes him," the reviewer added, "is the sort of popular success that would immediately rank him with those best-selling writers who . . . also enjoy critical acclaim."

For this reason, Charteris's work has not appeared in the United States except for *The Coat* and *The Indian Summer of Gabriel Murray,* both of which came out in the year of his death. *The Coat* is about a corrupt minister of fuel in Britain during World War II. Convinced the Nazis will invade England, he pulls his son out of Eton, intending to transport him to America. The politician, however, wants to save his personal fortune as well and so fills his son's custom-made life jacket with one million dollars worth of diamonds. Entrusting his child and wealth to his unfaithful, much younger second wife, the minister sends them to Liverpool. While waiting in the port for their ship, the wife trysts with her lover, leaving her stepson with a drunken acquaintance. Through a variety of events, the son is exposed to several nefarious characters and the jacket is lost. "By turn comic, tender, disturbing and sad," expressed McGuinness, "*The Coat* offers the most authoritative testament yet to Charteris's outstanding talent." The critic elaborated that the book is "a matchless study of youth—subtle, discerning, compassionate, but with no hint of the mawkish and sentimental." Stephen J. Laut also complimented the effort in *Best Sellers:* "The tale of the loss of illusions moves at a great pace; the characters are fascinating, if somewhat shopworn, and the whole experience of the novel is engrossing."

Malcolm Muggeridge compared *The Indian Summer of Gabriel Murray* to *Lady Chatterley's Lover,* noting that it "has none of the solemnity that D. H. Lawrence would have given it, and much more authentic tragedy." In the novel, middle-aged Gabriel abandons a decadent society and promising military career for life in an isolated area of Scotland. There he hunts with a wolfhound and watches birds. His life runs relatively smoothly until he meets Pandora, the dissolute wife of a politician living nearby. The two have a destructive love affair that results in her death and Gabriel's return to his retiring lifestyle. The character of Gabriel dominates the work, prompting *Spectator* reviewer Peter Vansittart to observe: "In this question-raising novel of loves and death the single personality outweighs the plot. Behind both is poetry of terse distinction, the dooms and frustrations lapped by the lyrical, by momentary tenderness, and with larger, sourer implications." A *Times Literary Supplement* critic commented that "the social observation is extraordinarily penetrating," while David Rees remarked in *Encounter* that "Charteris has written an exemplary parable of a hero of our time." Rees continued that the author successfully chronicled "the disintegration of an exceptional man in a society where old truths can no longer give meaning even to those who believe most devoutely in them."

Addressing the reason why Charteris's novels "have never broken out from the walled garden of hardcover into the lush and littered plains of paperbacks," Muggeridge speculated that the writer "stands apart; the comment on the contemporary scene and situation which occurs in all his books . . . is too dry and detached to please generally." His work is like "a digestive biscuit munched in a Berlin cafe," elucidated the critic, "where everyone else is gorging huge chunks of sweet cake *mit Schlag* [with whipped cream]."

AVOCATIONAL INTERESTS: Photography, gardening, shooting.

BIOGRAPHICAL/CRITICAL SOURCES: New Statesman, November 4, 1966; *London Magazine,* January, 1968, June, 1968, October, 1968; *Punch,* June 5, 1968; *Observer Review,* June 9, 1968; *Times Literary Supplement* June 13, 1968; *Spectator,*

June 14, 1968; *Encounter,* October, 1968; *Best Sellers,* March 1, 1970.*

*   *   *

CHASE, Mary (Coyle)   1907-1981

OBITUARY NOTICE—See index for *CA* sketch: Born February 25, 1907, in Denver, Colo.; died of a heart attack, October 20, 1981, in Denver, Colo. Playwright best known for her Pulitzer Prize-winning play "Harvey," the story of an inebriate and his imaginary, six-foot-tall rabbit. While working at newspaper and public relations jobs, Chase began to write plays. The comedy "Harvey" was her first critical success; it opened in November, 1944, at the Forty-Eighth Street Theatre on Broadway and ran for 1,775 performances. A 1952 film version of the play, starring Jimmy Stewart, and several television performances of the comedy increased its popularity. "Harvey" was translated into many languages and performed in many countries. Other successful plays by Chase include "Bernadine," "Mrs. McThing," and "Loretta Mason Potts." In addition, the author wrote a number of books for children and screenplays for two of her stage plays. Obituaries and other sources: *Washington Post,* October 22, 1981; *New York Times,* October 23, 1981; *Time,* November 2, 1981; *Newsweek,* November 2, 1981.

*   *   *

CHATOV, Robert   1927-

PERSONAL: Born November 6, 1927, in New York, N.Y.; married wife, Sophia F.; children: Justin I., Ethan A. *Education:* New York University, B.E., 1949; Northwestern University, M.A., 1951; Wayne State University, J.D., 1957; University of California, Berkeley, Ph.D., 1973. *Home:* 360 Brantwood Rd., Snyder, N.Y. 14226. *Office:* School of Management, State University of New York at Buffalo, Buffalo, N.Y. 14214.

CAREER: Ford Motor Co., Dearborn, Mich., in middle management, 1951-68; University of California, Berkeley, lecturer in business administration, 1970-71; State University of New York at Buffalo, assistant professor, 1972-75, associate professor of environmental analysis and policy, 1975—. Member of adjunct faculty at Wayne State University, 1957-62; visiting associate professor at University of California, Berkeley, 1977-78. Consultant to business and government. *Military service:* U.S. Army, 1946-47; served in Mediterranean theater. *Member:* International Society for Political Psychology, Academy of Management, Academy of Accounting Historians, American Business Law Association, National Defense Executive Reserve, Amateur Chamber Music Society, Okinawan Karate Association.

WRITINGS: Corporate Financial Reporting: Public or Private Control, Free Press, 1975; *An Analysis of Corporate Statements on Ethics and Behavior* (monograph), California Round Table, 1979.

Contributor: D. Votaw and S. P. Sethi, editors, *The Corporate Dilemma,* Prentice-Hall, 1973; Lee E. Preston, editor, *Research in Corporate Social Performance and Policy,* Volume 1, Jai Press, 1978; Nystrom and Starbuck, editors, *Handbook of Organization Design,* Oxford University Press, 1981. Contributor to periodicals, including, *California Management Review, Business of Society Review, Accounting Journal,* and *American Political Science Review.*

WORK IN PROGRESS: The State of the Art in Corporate Codes of Ethics, publication by Pitman expected in 1985; *Public Policy Process and Consequences in the United States,* completion expected in 1983.

SIDELIGHTS: Chatov commented: "I am interested in public policy matters, especially interaction of public and private sectors. My research interests include corporate behavior and governmental operations. My disciplinary focus is on economics, economic history, sociological processes, Freudian psychology, and law and organization theory."

*   *   *

CHAVIARAS, Strates   1935-
(Stratis Haviaras)

PERSONAL: Born June 28, 1935, in Nea Kios, Greece; came to the United States, 1967, naturalized citizen, 1971; son of Chrestos and Georgia Chaviaras; married second wife, Heather Cole; children: (second marriage) Elektra. *Education:* Goddard College, B.A., 1973, M.F.A., 1978. *Home:* 320 Harvard St., Cambridge, Mass. 02138. *Office:* c/o Poetry Room, Harvard University Library, Cambridge, Mass. 02138.

CAREER: Associated with Harvard University, Cambridge, Mass., 1968—, curator of poetry room of Harvard Library, 1974—. Participant in Poets-in-the-Schools program. *Member:* P.E.N., Modern Greek Studies Association. *Awards, honors:* American Book Award nomination, 1980, for *When the Tree Sings.*

WRITINGS—In English; under name Stratis Haviaras: (Editor) *Thirty-Five Post-War Greek Poets,* privately printed, 1972; *Crossing the River Twice* (poems), Cleveland State University Poetry Center, 1976; *When the Tree Sings* (novel), Simon & Schuster, 1979. Contributor to periodicals, including *Iowa Review, Field,* and *Kayak.*

In Greek; under name Strates Chaviaras; poems: *He kyria me ten pyxida: Poiemata* (title means "Lady With a Compass"), privately printed, 1963; *Verolino* (title means "Berlin"), Ekdot, 1965; *I Nychta tou Zylopodarou* (title means "The Night of the Stiltwalker"), privately printed, 1967; *Nekrophaneia* (title means "Apparent Death"), Kedros, 1972.

Also editor and author of introduction of "The Poet' Voice" (a six-hour recording of the poetry of thirteen twentieth-century American poets), Harvard University, 1978.

WORK IN PROGRESS: A novel, *The Children's War,* completion expected in 1983; more recordings for "The Poet's Voice."

SIDELIGHTS: Stratis Haviaras's *When the Tree Sings* is a child's account of growing up in German-occupied Greece during World War II. The child narrator describes the psychological and physical effects of the German presence on the small Greek town.

The thirty brief episodes of the novel contain graphic descriptions of the tortures the villagers suffer at the hands of their captors. A man is tortured to death while a motorcycle's racing engine drowns out his screams and two children are blown up by a land mine. The narrator loses his parents—one is imprisoned and the other is executed. Starvation and the continual executions further add to the villagers' desolation.

The book concerns survival as much as it does suffering. As a *New Yorker* reviewer noted, "In one way . . . the story is an optimistic one, about the miraculous resilience of the children of a proud and wily people: amid the bitterest grief, they are determined to have fun and make mischief, if only to infuriate their oppressors." Francine du Plessix Gray of the

New York Times Book Review echoed this assessment: "No work I've read in recent years has dealt more eloquently with the subject of heroism and resistance or with a community's attempt to survive the holocaustal forces of the 1940's." The novel, she added, is one "of formidable lyric power, narrative gift and emotional resonance."

BIOGRAPHICAL/CRITICAL SOURCES: Esquire, June 5, 1979; *New Yorker,* June 11, 1979; *New York Times,* June 21, 1979; *New York Times Book Review,* June 24, 1979; *Washington Post Book World,* July 15, 1979.

*   *   *

CHEAPE, Charles Windsor   1945-

PERSONAL: Born October 11, 1945, in Charlottesville, Va.; son of Charles Windsor, Jr. (a telephone company engineer) and Evelyn Florence (a legal secretary) Cheape; married Cheryl Cooper (a physical therapist), August 10, 1974. *Education:* University of Virginia, B.A., 1968; Brandeis University, M.A., 1974, Ph.D., 1976. *Home:* 14 North Park St., No. 2-S, Hanover, N. H. 03755. *Office:* Department of History, Dartmouth College, Reed Hall, Hanover, N.H. 03755.

CAREER: Dartmouth College, Hanover, N.H., assistant professor, 1975-81, associate professor of history, 1981—. *Member:* Organization of American Historians, Economic History Association, Business History Conference, Phi Beta Kappa.

WRITINGS: Moving the Masses: Urban Public Transit in New York, Boston, and Philadelphia, 1880-1912, Harvard University Press, 1980. Contributor to economic history journals.

WORK IN PROGRESS: A history of the Norton Co. of Worcester, Mass., publication expected in 1985.

*   *   *

CHEIN, Isidor   1912-

BRIEF ENTRY: Born March 5, 1912, in New York, N.Y. American psychologist, educator, and author. Chein began teaching psychology in 1937 and has been a professor at New York University since 1972. His writings include *The Reactions of Jewish Boys to Various Aspects of Being Jewish* (Jewish Community Center Division, National Jewish Welfare Board, 1959), *The Road to H: Narcotics, Delinquency, and Social Policy* (Basic Books, 1964), and *The Science of Behavior and the Image of Man* (Basic Books, 1972). *Address:* 66-15 Thornton Pl., Rego Park, N.Y. 11374; and Department of Psychology, New York University, 21 Washington Pl., New York, N.Y. 10001. *Biographical/critical sources: American Men and Women of Science: The Social and Behavioral Sciences,* 13th edition, Bowker, 1978.

*   *   *

CHENNELLS, Roy D.   1912(?)-1981

OBITUARY NOTICE: Born c. 1912; died September 8, 1981, in Cleveland, Ohio. Publishing executive. Chennells's career in the publishing field began with the American News Co. in New York, N.Y. He left to manage Georgia News in Atlanta, then became a sales representative in the East for Harper Brothers. Chennells eventually joined the firm of J. C. Winston and Morrow, where he began as a sales representative, became sales manager, and finally vice-president of sales. In 1958 he joined World Publishing Co. in Cleveland, where he became a senior vice-president. A stroke forced him to retire in 1969. Obituaries and other sources: *Publishers Weekly,* November 27, 1981.

CHERNEV, Irving   1900-1981

OBITUARY NOTICE: Born January 29, 1900, in Priluki, Russia (now U.S.S.R.); died in 1981 in San Francisco, Calif. Chess master and author. Chernev came to the United States in 1904 and was educated and employed in New York City. He began writing about chess during the 1930's and produced eighteen books on the subject, including *Practical Chess Endings, Wonders and Curiosities of Chess,* and *The Golden Dozen: The Twelve Greatest Chess Players of All Time.* Chernev taught and lectured on the game as well. Obituaries and other sources: *Times Literary Supplement,* July 16, 1970; *Who's Who in America,* 40th edition, Marquis, 1978; *AB Bookman's Weekly,* December 7, 1981.

*   *   *

CHERNOFF, John Miller   1947-

PERSONAL: Born April 10, 1947, in Pittsburgh, Pa.; son of Harold I. and Florence (Brasley) Chernoff. *Education:* Yale University, B.A., 1968; attended University of Ghana, 1970-71; Hartford Seminary Foundation, Ph.D., 1974. *Home:* 1832 Murdoch St., Pittsburgh, Pa. 15217.

CAREER: Musician and lecturer, 1976—.

WRITINGS: African Rhythm and African Sensibility: Aesthetics and Social Action in African Musical Idioms, University of Chicago Press, 1979. Contributor to *Natural History* and *African Arts.*

WORK IN PROGRESS: Ibrahim Abdulai's Testament: A Dagbana Drummer Talks About His Culture, on the ethnography of the Dagbamba of northern Ghana; *Memoirs of an African Bar-Girl,* completion expected in 1985.

*   *   *

CHESKIN, Louis   1909-1981

OBITUARY NOTICE—See index for *CA* sketch: Born February 19, 1909, in Russia (now U.S.S.R.); ded of a heart attack, October 3, 1981, in Stanford, Calif. Researcher, artist, and author. Cheskin, who immigrated to the United States in 1921, was known for his advancements in motivation research and marketing techniques. After receiving his master's degree from the Illinois Institute of Technology, he continued his studies at the University of Chicago. An artist, Cheskin investigated the effect of color on the consumer. He developed the "system of consumer attitude research" to test the effects of logos, packaging, design, and styling. Consumers, he contended, are attracted to the image of a product rather than to the actual product. In 1945, he founded the Color Research Institute and, five years later, Cheskin Associates, both now located in California. Prior to establishing his companies, Cheskin taught art at the Lewis Institute in Chicago and for the adult education program of the Chicago Board of Education. He was also a member of several educational and civic committees. Cheskin's books include *Colors: What They Can Do For You, Cheskin Color Wheel, Color Guide for Marketing Media, How to Color Tune Your Home, How to Predict What People Will Buy,* and *Problem-Directed Men.* Obituaries and other sources: *New York Times,* October 10, 1981.

*   *   *

CHLAMYDA, Jehudil
See PESHKOV, Alexei Maximovich

CHO, Yong Hyo 1934-

BRIEF ENTRY: Born December 14, 1934, in Sa-Chun, Korea. Political scientist, educator, and author. Cho began teaching political science and urban studies at University of Akron in 1967. He wrote Local Financing for Criminal Justice in Northeast Ohio: Patterns, Trends, and Projections (Center for Urban Studies, University of Akron, 1972), Determinants of Public Policy in the American States: A Model for Synthesis (Sage Publications, 1973), Public Policy and Urban Crime (Ballinger, 1974), and Measuring the Effects of Reapportionment in the American States (National Municipal League, 1976). Address: Center for Urban Studies, University of Akron, Akron, Ohio 44304. Biographical/critical sources: American Men and Women of Science: The Social and Behavioral Sciences, 12th edition, Bowker, 1973.

*   *   *

CHOATE, Judith (Newkirk) 1940-

PERSONAL: Born January 1, 1940, in La Junta, Colo.; daughter of Garth Galen and Elizabeth Stuart (Gilmour) Newkirk; married Edward A. Choate (died, 1975); children: Michael A., Robert N. (deceased), Christopher G. Education: Attended public schools in Belmont, Calif.; attended Actor's Workshop, New York City, 1957-59. Home and office: 11 West 84th St., New York, N.Y. 10024. Agent: Charlotte Sheedy, 145 West 86th St., New York, N.Y. 10024.

CAREER: Worked as a model in New York City, 1957-61; operated own handicraft business, 1962-64, and catering business, 1966; worked in day care center, 1967-68, and nursery school, 1969; free-lance writer, 1969—; consultant to restaurants, 1969-70; National Sudden Infant Death Foundation, Chicago, Ill., executive administrator, 1970-71, executive director, 1971-75; CPO Inc., New York City, secretary-treasurer, 1976—; Mom's Meals, Inc., New York City, owner-operator, 1976—. Appeared on television shows, including "Today" and "Woman."

WRITINGS: (With Jane Green) The Gift-Giver's Cookbook, Simon & Schuster, 1971; (with Green) Scrapcraft, Doubleday, 1973; (with A. B. Bergman) Why Did My Baby Die?: The Phenomenon of Sudden Infant Death Syndrome and How to Cope With It,, Okpaku Communications, 1975; (with Green) Patchwork for Kids, Doubleday, 1975; Awful Alexander (juvenile), drawings by Stephen Kellogg, Doubleday, 1975. Author of films for National Sudden Infant Death, Inc. (NSID), including "One in Three Hundred and Fifty." Also author of column on food and health in Rags Magazine, 1969, and articles and pamphlets on sudden infant death syndrome.

WORK IN PROGRESS: Two books, The Great American Pie Book, with Jane Green, and Passing Time: Essays on Growing Up.

*   *   *

CHODOROW, Nancy (Julia) 1944-

PERSONAL: Born January 20, 1944, in New York, N.Y.; daughter of Marvin (a professor of applied physics) and Leah Ruth (Turitz) Chodorow; married Michael Reich (a professor of economics), June 19, 1977; children: Rachel. Education: Radcliffe College, A.B., 1966; attended London School of Economics and Political Science, London, 1966-67, and Harvard University, 1967-68; Brandeis University, M.A., 1972,

Ph.D., 1975. Office: c/o Merrill College, University of California, Santa Cruz, Calif. 95064.

CAREER: Wellesley College, Wellesley, Mass., instructor in women's studies, 1973-74; University of California, Santa Cruz, lecturer, 1974-76, assistant professor of sociology, 1976—, faculty research grantee, 1975-78. Member: American Sociological Association, Sociologists for Women in Sociology. Awards, honors: Jessie Bernard Award from the American Sociological Association, 1980, for The Reproduction of Mothering.

WRITINGS: The Reproduction of Mothering: Psychoanalysis and the Sociology of Gender (nonfiction), University of California Press, 1978.

SIDELIGHTS: In The Reproduction of Mothering, Chodorow challenges the traditional view that females are biologically predisposed toward nurturing infants. Mothering, she argues, fulfills a woman's psychological need for reciprocal intimacy that begins during her babyhood when she and her mother perceive each other as extensions of themselves. Mothers are also close to their infant sons, says Chodorow, but they view their male children as different and do not share with them the same sense of "oneness" that they experience with their daughters. The author therefore contends that mature males, unaccustomed to a psychologically intimate relationship are, therefore, content to leave mothering to women.

New Statesman's Helen McNeil observed that Chodorow's book "lends authority to the hope that parental roles can change." In Contemporary Sociology, R. L. Coser speculated that Chodorow's work "may provide some of the underpinnings for a theory of feminism," and he appraised the book as "splendid." Critic Leonard Benson of Social Science Quarterly found The Reproduction of Mothering an "extraordinary book . . . exceptionally well executed—in scholarship, organization and imagination."

BIOGRAPHICAL/CRITICAL SOURCES: North American Review, fall, 1978; Ms., October, 1978; Time, February 26, 1979; Contemporary Sociology, July, 1979; New Statesman, April 4, 1980; Social Science Quarterly, September, 1980.

*   *   *

CHOTHIA, Jean 1944-

PERSONAL: Surname is pronounced Cho-tia; born August 31, 1944, in Manchester, England; daughter of Gordon (a teacher) and Mary (a teacher; maiden name, Malley) Sandham; married Cyrus Chothia (a research scientist), July 24, 1967; children: Lucy, Thomas. Education: University of Durham, B.A., 1967; Cambridge University, Ph.D., 1975. Politics: Socialist. Religion: None. Home: 26 Clarendon St., Cambridge, England. Office: Selwyn College, Cambridge University, Cambridge, England.

CAREER: Teacher at comprehensive school in London, England, 1968-70; Cambridge University, Cambridge, England, lecturer and fellow at Selwyn College, 1976—, assistant lecturer in drama and American literature, 1981—.

WRITINGS: Forging a Language: A Study of the Plays of Eugene O'Neill, Cambridge University Press, 1979.

WORK IN PROGRESS: Artifice and Reality on the English Stage.

SIDELIGHTS: Jean Chothia has lived in the United States, Israel, and France.

CHRISTOPHER, Milbourne

PERSONAL: Born in Baltimore, Md.; married wife, Maurine (a journalist).

CAREER: Magician. *Member:* Society of American Magicians (past president).

WRITINGS—All published by Crowell, except as noted: (Compiler) *The Sphinx Golden Jubilee Book of Magic,* Sphinx Publishing, 1951; *Panorama of Magic,* Dover, 1962; *Houdini: The Untold Story,* 1969; *ESP, Seers, and Psychics,* 1970; *The Illustrated History of Magic,* 1973; *Mediums, Mystics and the Occult,* 1975; *Houdini: A Pictorial Life,* 1976; *Milbourne Christopher's Magic Book,* 1977; *Search for the Soul,* 1979.

SIDELIGHTS: Milbourne Christopher's love of magic blossomed in his early childhood when his father broke a string and taught the youth to rejoin it. Later Christopher established himself as one of the foremost American magicians, performing his act in more than sixty-eight countries. In addition he is the author of books on illusionism, occultism, and mysticism, as well as volumes on the history of magic and the lives of magicians.

Christopher's *Houdini: The Untold Story* chronicles the life and career of the master magician Harry Houdini without disclosing the escapist's techniques. The book was favorably received, though many critics expressed a desire to learn *how* Houdini accomplished his tricks, not just when and where. Maurice Zolotow of the *New York Times Book Review,* commenting on Christopher's effort, wrote: "He has brilliantly captured the egotism of the man, as well as some of his perplexing insecurities. Above all, he has made you feel some of the pity and terror which Houdini aroused in his audiences. [But] we are not told concretely how Houdini contrived to escape from jail cells and from packing cases thrown into rivers and from straightjackets and the Chinese Water Torture Cell. And we want to know." *Book World's* Maurice Dolbier remarked: "Mr. Christopher's book moves as swiftly, and holds as much fascination for an audience, as Houdini slipping out of a set of Scotland Yard's best manacles."

BIOGRAPHICAL/CRITICAL SOURCES: Variety, March 26, 1969, April 9, 1969, August 20, 1969, May 13, 1970; *Book World,* March 30, 1969; *Times Literary Supplement,* October 16, 1969; *Pittsburgh Press,* November 30, 1973; *New York Times Book Review,* December 16, 1973, July 8, 1978; *New York Times,* August 23, 1975; *Village Voice,* December 13, 1976.*

*   *   *

CHURCH, William Farr 1912-

BRIEF ENTRY: Born December 13, 1912, in Monmouth, Ill. American historian, educator, and author. Church joined the faculty at Brown University in 1947 and was named Munroe Goodwin Wilkinson Professor of History in 1959. His books include *The Influence of the Enlightenment on the French Revolution* (Heath, 1964), *The Impact of Absolutism in France* (Wiley, 1969), *Richelieu and Reason of State* (Princeton University Press, 1972), and *Louis XIV in Historical Thought* (Norton, 1976). *Address:* 17 Huntington Dr., Rumford, R.I. 02916; and Department of History, Brown University, Providence, R.I. 02912. *Biographical/critical sources: Who's Who in America,* 40th edition, Marquis, 1978.

CIMINO, Michael 1943-

PERSONAL: Born in 1943 in New York, N.Y. *Education:* Yale University, M.F.A., 1963. *Residence:* Los Angeles, Calif. *Agent:* William Morris Agency, 151 El Camino Dr., Beverly Hills, Calif. 90212.

CAREER: Screenwriter and director of motion pictures. Director of documentaries, industry films, and television commercials, 1963-71. *Military service:* U.S. Army Reserve, 1962; served in medical unit. *Awards, honors:* Award for best director from Directors Guild, and Academy Awards for best director and best motion picture from Academy of Motion Picture Arts and Sciences, all 1978, all for "The Deer Hunter."

WRITINGS—Screenplays: (With Deric Washburn and Steve Bocho) "Silent Running," Universal, 1971; (with John Milius) "Magnum Force," Warner Bros., 1973; (and director) "Thunderbolt and Lightfoot," United Artists, 1974; (screen story only, with Washburn, Louis Garfinkle, and Quinn Redeker; and director) "The Deer Hunter," Universal/EMI, 1978; (and director) "Heaven's Gate," United Artists, 1980, revised edition, 1981, 2nd revised edition released as "The Johnson County Wars," 1981.

WORK IN PROGRESS: Directing the motion picture "Nitty Gritty."

SIDELIGHTS: Cimino broke into filmmaking after directing commercials for several years in New York City. His first screen credit was as a co-author of "Silent Running," a science-fiction drama directed by special-effects expert Douglas Trumbull. The 1971 film concerns an eccentric astronaut aboard a greenhouse spaceship. When orders arrive instructing the crew to destroy the greenhouse and return to earth, the astronaut kills his crewmates and points the ship towards deep space. The *New York Times*'s Vincent Canby was impressed with Trumbull's technical abilities but complained that the film's theme "was more like an editorial policy."

In 1972 Cimino co-wrote the screenplay for "Magnum Force," a sequel to the popular police film "Dirty Harry," which featured actor Clint Eastwood. In "Magnum Force," detective Harry Calahan is forced to rid San Francisco's police force of a squad of vigilante rookies recruited by a corrupt police chief. Critics praised the film's departure from the "fascist" bias of "Dirty Harry." Gary Arnold, writing in the *Washington Post,* attributed the series' improvements to "the contributions of a new screenwriter—Michael Cimino."

After "Magnum Force," Cimino was hired by Eastwood to both write and direct "Thunderbold and Lightfoot," a tale of bank robbers roaming the Montana countryside. *Time's* Jay Cocks was impressed with Cimino's initial directorial effort, noting that he "demonstrates a scrupulously controlled style." Cocks added that "Cimino has an obvious affinity for the work of Sam Peckinpah" and lauded the film's "shellbursts of lunatic comedy."

For the next few years, Cimino tried unsuccessfully to develop two projects. "Pearl," a biography of singer Janis Joplin, was cancelled by Twentieth Century-Fox, then produced later as "The Rose"; "Costello," a gangster film with similarities to F. Scott Fitzgerald's *The Great Gatsby,* was dropped by two studios after they each underwent corporate changes. Cimino later told *Guardian* that he "felt everything was going downhill." In 1976, though, his career was revived when he convinced executives at EMI, a British production company, to finance "The Deer Hunter," a war story he improvised for them during a meeting.

"The Deer Hunter" details the experiences of three steel mill workers—Michael, Nick, and Steve—during the Vietnam War. It begins with Steve's wedding and progresses to a deerhunting expedition in which Michael fulfills his vow to kill a deer with one shot. The story then jumps forward in time to the three men's capture during the war. Michael is forced by the enemy to play Russian roulette against Steve and Nick, and he devises a way of escaping by convincing his captors that he can play the game with three bullets. Michael and Nick then kill the Vietnamese and rescue Steve from a muskrat-filled bamboo cage. They each make their separate ways to freedom. Later, Michael learns that Steve is a multi-amputee living in a military ward. When he visits Steve, Michael discovers that Nick is sending huge sums of money to Steve from Vietnam. Michael returns to Vietnam and finds Nick is a regular competitor in a Russian roulette den. Michael realizes that Nick is a drug addict with amnesia. To jar his friend's memory, Michael arranges to play against Nick. They each survive the first round. Then Nick seems to remember Michael, at which point he fires the pistol again and kills himself. "The Deer Hunter" ends with Nick's funeral and the singing of "God Bless America."

Cimino began writing the story, entitled "The Deer Hunter," while scouting locations in Pennsylvania. "It was a terrible way to work," he told *Esquire*'s Jean Vallely, "but there was no alternative. Here was a shot at doing something of substance and I just accepted the conditions and went forward." Cimino worked on the story with several other writers before hiring Deric Washburn, with whom he'd worked on "Silent Running," to write the screenplay. Then he dashed through the eastern states examining more locations. "I drove people," Cimino recalled. "I drove myself. The thought of not putting this together, of failing, drove me crazy."

After Cimino submitted Washburn's script to EMI, executives there were so impressed that they expanded the budget to pay for top actors, including Robert De Niro, Meryl Streep, and Christopher Walken. With the cast assembled, however, numerous problems arose. Cimino was forced to shoot winter scenes during the summer—grass had to be bleached, trees had to be defoliated. In Pittsburgh, the extreme heat caused the actors to continually perspire through the heavy clothing.

More difficulties plagued the production when the crew began filming war scenes in Thailand. Several members of the cast became sick, and torrential rains delayed filming after the actors had recuperated. Finally, Cimino, cinematographer Vilmos Zsigmond, and members of the cast and crew were almost killed when a helicopter they were filming from snagged a bridge cable. De Niro and John Savage dropped into the river below, and a stunt coordinator scrambled onto the runner and unhooked the cable to prevent the helicopter from plunging into the bridge.

When Cimino finished directing "The Deer Hunter," he'd already surpassed his original shooting schedule and budget. Executives at EMI and Universal, the film's distributor, were anxious to see the film. But when Cimino presented the studios with a 210-minute draft, the moguls were alarmed. They ordered Cimino to edit the film to a more commercial length of two hours. He then cut the film to three hours, whereupon EMI threatened to remove him from the project. "I told them I would do everything I could," Cimino said. "I took things out of the movie and then put them back in. The thought that I would be removed and someone else would take over made me physically ill. . . . I was willing to do anything I could to prevent this picture from being taken away from me and

ruined." Cimino finally convinced EMI and Universal to test the film by previewing it in Chicago and Detroit. The showings were an enormous success for him. Viewers, according to Vallely, were "overwhelmed" by the film, and Universal agreed to release the film in December, 1978.

Reviewers disagreed vehemently on the merits of "The Deer Hunter." *Newsweek* called it "a film of great courage and overwhelming emotional power," and *Time*'s Frank Rich compared the film's impact to that of "Last Tango in Paris" and "The Godfather." "This excruciatingly violent . . . Viet Nam saga demolishes the moral and ideological cliches of an era." Marshall Delaney wrote that "*The Deer Hunter* accomplishes what the best dramatic art does: it takes us somewhere we have never been before and brings us back enlarged and broadened." But other critics objected to the film's cavalier distortion of reality, particularly in the use of Russian roulette as a metaphor for war's suicidal nature. "Michael Cimino may say Russian roulette has only symbolic significance," wrote *Spectator*'s Richard West, "though for the life of me I cannot see what it is." Gloria Emerson observed, "Using Russian roulette as his metaphor, Cimino is not bothered by the fact that this odious form of enforced suicide was not practiced by the Vietnamese. . . . It is a stupid and offensive metaphor in terms of the American infantrymen in Vietnam who did not casually risk their lives." And Tom Buckley, writing in *Harper's*, declared that "Cimino's ignorance of what the war was about, symbolically and actually, as reflected in *The Deer Hunter*, is incomplete and perverse to the point of being megalomaniacal."

Despite some critical disdain, "The Deer Hunter" performed admirably at theatre box offices and eventually earned five Academy Awards, including honors for best film and best director. Armed with this success, Cimino managed to convince United Artists to produce "Heaven's Gate," a screenplay that studios had rejected years earlier. The story tells of James Averill, a Harvard graduate who becomes a marshall in Johnson County, Wyoming, during a period of violence between cattle barons and immigrant settlers. Attempting to thwart further theft of their cattle, the barons recruit Nate Champion, an immigrant and former friend of Averill's, to kill thieving immigrants. Champion, however, proves insufficient, and the barons decide to hire their own army to massacre the destitute settlers.

They first slaughter Champion and rape his fiancee, Ella, a prostitute in love with Averill. The immigrants, meanwhile, learn of the mercenaries' intentions and decide to organize themselves. They attack the army that afternoon and, with Averill's leadership, acquit themselves adequately. The following morning, the immigrants launch a second attack from behind moveable walls—a Roman military strategy Averill studied at Harvard. With victory near for the immigrants, the U.S. cavalry rides in and rescues the mercenaries. The immigrants are then arrested. "Heaven's Gate" concludes with Averill as an old man sailing his yacht off the coast of New England. He recalls the violence of his wedding, in which Ella was gunned down by mercenaries as she stepped from the church, and wanders forlornly through the darkness of his yacht.

"Heaven's Gate" proved even more demanding than "The Deer Hunter" for Cimino. Seeking absolute authenticity, he requisitioned a steam locomotive that, because of its size, required constant, and expensive, rerouting through North America. He also multiplied the number of actors from 200 to 1200 and established classes for them in bull-whipping, wagon-driving, and roller skating. As Cimino expanded his conception of the film, the budget grew from $11 million to $15 million and then to $40 million. Cimino was aware that the extravagances jeopardized his career but contended that his revisions were necessary to compensate for the lack of materials needed for filming a western. "You're gambling with your life," Cimino conceded to a *Newsweek* interviewer. "How can you not have trouble making a film over a period of years? One reason is because you don't have the backup one used to have from the studio system—particularly doing period films. The inventory is no longer there. One starts from scratch now on everything." By the time Cimino finished "Heaven's Gate," word had circulated through the film industry of other indulgences: three horses were killed during filming, the crew had to address Cimino as "sir," and a party was thrown to celebrate the film's excessive footage.

Returning to Los Angeles, Cimino once again logged fifteen-hour days editing his film. He finally completed "Heaven's Gate" just days before its initial showing in New York City. As Vallely noted, "*Heaven's Gate* had consumed Cimino's life. He was obsessed, and not simply with making a movie. He wanted a masterpiece."

Unfortunately for Cimino, the premiere of "Heaven's Gate" was a disaster. During the intermission of the nearly four-hour film, critics and studio executives began complaining about the incoherent soundtrack, the unclear cinematography, and the incomprehensible story. The following morning, an overwhelming critical assault was initiated by the *New York Times*'s Vincent Canby, who deemed "Heaven's Gate" "an unqualified disaster." Reviewers for *Time, New York, Newsweek, New York Daily News, Village Voice,* and *New Yorker* all followed suit. *Time*'s Richard Corliss called the film "a four-hour fiasco," and David Ansen, writing in *Newsweek,* complained that "all the really crucial scenes seem to be missing." *New York*'s David Denby blamed both Cimino and United Artists. "Despite some stunning shots and sequences, the movie is truly awful," he wrote, "and responsibility for it must be divided between Michael Cimino . . . , who has been vain, foolish, and wasteful beyond belief, and an inept leadership at United Artists—a group of men who apparently cannot read a script, who lack the confidence to act on their intuitions and doubts, and who watched Cimino dissipate a fortune on nonsense."

In the wake of such negative criticism, Cimino and United Artists withdrew "Heaven's Gate" from distribution. The distributors then granted Cimino an additional $10 million for re-editing. He removed more than an hour of footage, rearranged some scenes, and added a voice-over narration. But when "Heaven's Gate" was released again in April, 1981, most reviewers still panned it. "Cimino has chosen the wrong story to tell," declared Ansen, though he added that "in its new form it is by no means an ignoble failure." Canby called the new version "a muddled compromise" and asserted that "the money that purchased some exceedingly elaborate production values could not buy true coherence." Arnold charged that "there's never a moment in the film where [Cimino] appears to know what he's doing or where he's going in dramatic terms." He added, "It's a maddening exercise in futility trying to make sense of Cimino's incomprehensible class struggle and phantom characters."

Some observers contended that Cimino was unfairly treated by the press. "Even if *Heaven's Gate* is the 'unqualified disaster' that Canby and the others claim," wrote Jean Vallely, "it doesn't account for the vituperative attacks from the press and the movie industry." Producer Frank Yablans agreed. "You look at someone's best work, not his worst," he said. "They were laying for the guy." Cimino contended that he never read any of the reviews, but did express dismay with the relentlessness of the criticism. "At least in the old days," he related, "when they tied you to a post and whipped you, they stopped once you passed out."

BIOGRAPHICAL/CRITICAL SOURCES: New York Times, April 1, 1972, February 10, 1978, November 19, 1980, April 24, 1981; *Washington Post,* January 1, 1974, September 2, 1979, April 25, 1981; *Newsweek,* December 11, 1978, December 1, 1980, May 4, 1981; *Time,* December 18, 1978, December 1, 1980, May 4, 1981; *Esquire,* January 2, 1979; *Guardian,* February 17, 1979; *Harper's,* April, 1979; *Film Comment,* January/February, 1980; *New York,* December 8, 1980; *Rolling Stone,* February 5, 1981.*

—*Sketch by Les Stone*

*   *   *

CLARK, Ella E(lizabeth)   1896-

PERSONAL: Born January 8, 1896, in Summertown, Tenn.; daughter of Samuel L. (a minister) and Linda (a teacher; maiden name, Shaw) Clark. *Education:* Northwestern University, B.A., 1921, M.A., 1927. *Religion:* Protestant. *Home:* 849 Coast Blvd., La Jolla, Calif. 92037.

CAREER: High school teacher in Dunlap, Ill., 1917-19, Pontiac, Ill., 1921-23, and Abingdon, Ill., 1923-26; Washington State University, Pullman, member of English department faculty, 1927-57, professor of English, 1957-61; writer, 1961—. *Member:* National League of American Pen Women, Phi Beta Kappa, Phi Kappa Phi, Theta Sigma Phi.

WRITINGS: (Editor) *Poetry: An Interpretation of Life,* Farrar & Rinehart, 1935; *Indian Legends of the Pacific Northwest* (juvenile), University of California Press, 1953; *Indian Legends of Canada,* McClelland & Stewart, 1960; *Indian Legends From the Northern Rockies,* University of Oklahoma Press, 1966; *Guardian Spirit Quest* (juvenile), Montana Indian Publication Fund, 1974; (editor) *In the Beginning* (juvenile), Montana Indian Publication Fund, 1977; (with Margot Edmonds) *Sacagawea of the Lewis and Clark Expedition,* University of California Press, 1979.

*   *   *

CLARK, Leonard   1905-1981

OBITUARY NOTICE—See index for *CA* sketch: Born August 1, 1905, in St. Peter Port, Guernsey, Channel Islands; died in 1981 in London, England. Educator, editor, poet, and author. Clark began his career as a teacher in Gloucestershire and in London in 1921. In 1936 he left teaching to become an inspector of schools with the Ministry of Education, a time he preserved in *The Inspector Remembers.* Clark was made knight of St. Sylvester in 1970, and he won first prize in 1972 from the *International Who's Who in Poetry* competition for his poem "The Coin." Clark wrote more than sixty books, including *The Open Door: An Anthology of Verse for Children, The Kingdom of the Mind: Essays and Addresses by Albert Mansbridge, 1903-1937, When They Were Children, Prospect of Highgate and Hampstead, Mr. Pettigrew's Harvest Festival,* and *The Tale of Prince Igor.* Obituaries and other sources: Leonard Clark, *Green Wood: A Gloucestershire Childhood* (autobiography), Parrish, 1962; Clark, *A Fool in the Forest* (autobiography), Dobson, 1965; Clark, *Grateful Caliban* (autobiography), Dobson, 1968; Clark, *The Inspector Remembers: Diary of One of Her Majesty's Inspectors of Schools, 1936-1970* (autobiography), Dobson, 1976; *AB Bookman's Weekly,* November 2, 1981.

CLARK, Lydia Benson
See MEAKER, Eloise

*   *   *

CLEMENT, Charles Baxter 1940-

PERSONAL: Born March 27, 1940, in Memphis, Tenn.; *Education:* Princeton University, B.A., 1962; University of Virginia, U.B., 1965; graduate study at University of Heidelberg (West Germany), 1967. *Religion:* Presbyterian. *Home:* 1353 North Astor St., Chicago, Ill. 60610. *Agent:* Alex Hehmeyer, First National Plaza, Chicago, Ill. *Office:* c/o Chicago Board of Trade, 141 West Jackson Blvd., Chicago, Ill. 60604.

CAREER: Admitted to the Bar of Tennessee, 1966, and Illinois, 1976. Member of Chicago Board of Trade, Chicago, Ill., 1975—, Chicago Board Options Exchange, Chicago, 1978, and Mid-West Stock Exchange, 1980. *Member:* Illinois Bar Association, Tennessee Bar Association.

WRITINGS: The Fairy Godmother (novel), Caroline House, 1981.

WORK IN PROGRESS: Two novels.

*   *   *

CLOUGH, Ralph Nelson 1916-

BRIEF ENTRY: Born November 17, 1916, in Seattle, Wash. American government official, educator, and author. Clough's work as a U.S. diplomat between 1941 and 1966 took him to Canada, China, Switzerland, and England. He served as consul general in Taipei, Taiwan, until 1965, and as a member of the U.S. State Department's planning council from 1966 to 1969. He has been a guest scholar at Brookings Institution and adjunct professor at American University since 1975. Clough's writings include *East Asia and U.S. Security* (Brookings Institution, 1975), *The United States, China, and Arms Control* (Brookings Institution, 1975), *Deterrence and Defense in Korea: The Role of U.S. Forces* (Brookings Institution, 1976), and *Island China* (Harvard University Press, 1978). *Address:* 4540 North 41st St., Arlington, Va. 22207; and Brookings Institution, 1775 Massachusetts Ave., Washington, D.C. 20036. *Biographical/critical sources: Who's Who in America,* 40th edition, Marquis, 1978.

*   *   *

COBB, Nathan 1943-

PERSONAL: Born June 16, 1943, in Newton, Mass.; son of Robert H. (a business executive) and Marian (Bullard) Cobb; married Margery McLaughlin (a teacher), June 26, 1965. *Education:* Pennsylvania State University, B.A., 1965. *Home:* 44 Chestnut St., Boston, Mass. 02108. *Office: Boston Globe,* 135 Morrissey Blvd., Boston, Mass. 02107.

CAREER: Boston Globe, Boston, Mass., staff writer, 1969—.

WRITINGS: (With Stanley Cath and Alvin Kahn) *Love and Hate on the Tennis Court,* Scribner, 1977; (with John Cole) *Cityside/Countryside,* Stephen Greene, 1980. Contributor to magazines, including *Psychology Today, Smithsonian, Tennis,* and *Boston.*

SIDELIGHTS: Cobb told *CA:* "I can't imagine anyone paying me to do anything other than write, although I know in my heart that I would make a fine second baseman for the Boston Red Sox. My 'philosophy of writing' is this: if you give ten nonfiction writers the same ten facts and ask each of them to write a story based on those facts, you will be presented with ten quite different stories. The good ones will differ sharply from the bad ones in the ways in which the facts are presented. Read: *style.* Style—the ability to give the content of a story a personality and to use this personality to pull the reader along—is what separates professionals from amateurs. Besides, amateurs think writing is 'fun.' Writing isn't 'fun.' Writing is hard work. Playing second base is 'fun.'"

BIOGRAPHICAL/CRITICAL SOURCES: Boston, May, 1981.

*   *   *

COCKBURN, (Francis) Claud 1904-1981
(Patrick Cork, Kenneth Drew, James Helvick, Frank Pitcairn)

OBITUARY NOTICE—See index for *CA* sketch: Born April 12, 1904, in Peking, China; died of a lung infection, December 15, 1981, in Cork, Ireland. Journalist and author. As a leftist and an individualist, Cockburn was sympathetic to the British working class but antagonistic to bourgeois society. He began his journalistic career as a foreign correspondent for the *London Times,* working in Washington, New York, Berlin, and Paris. In 1933, Cockburn founded *The Week,* "an extremist left-wing news sheet," which he edited until 1946. Two years after his newspaper's inception, the journalist joined the staff of another communist periodical, *Daily Worker,* writing under the pseudonym Frank Pitcairn. Cockburn also contributed to magazines such as *Punch* and *Private Eye.* Early in his career, he received a traveling fellowship from Queen's College. His books include *The Devil's Decade, Beat the Devil, Overdraft of Glory, Mr. Mintoff Comes to Ireland, Nine Bald Men,* and *Jericho Road.* Obituaries and other sources: Claud Cockburn, *I, Claud: The Autobiography of Claud Cockburn,* Penguin, 1967; *London Times,* December 17, 1981; *New York Times,* December 17, 1981; *Newsweek,* December 28, 1981.

*   *   *

COCKING, Clive 1938-

PERSONAL: Born December 28, 1938, in Vancouver, British Columbia, Canada; son of Thomas Warren (an electrician) and Gertrude Beryl Cocking; married Joyce M. Leeming (a nutritionist), June 8, 1962; children: Peter Eyre, Marie Louise. *Education:* University of British Columbia, B.A., 1962. *Home:* 5103 44th Ave., Ladner, Delta, British Columbia, Canada V4K 1C2.

CAREER: Sun, Vancouver, British Columbia, reporter, 1965-68; University of British Columbia, Vancouver, editor of alumni *Chronicle,* 1968-74; Contemporary Dialogue Ltd. (speakers' bureau), Vancouver, vice-president, 1974-75; free-lance writer, 1974—. Member of Delta Hospital Board, 1973-74. *Member:* Association of Canadian Television and Radio Artists. *Awards, honors:* Award for excellence from American Alumni Council, 1969, for *Chronicle.*

WRITINGS: Following the Leaders, Doubleday, 1980. Correspondent for *Observer,* London, England, and Observer Foreign News Service, 1969-73. Contributor to magazines, including *Saturday Night, Maclean's, Saturday Review,* and *Vancouver,* and to newspapers. Contributing editor of *Weekend,* 1975-77.

WORK IN PROGRESS: A novel.

SIDELIGHTS: Cocking told *CA:* "I am conducting research into the lives of some of my ancestors in the distinguished Eyre family of Britain, including such notable nineteenth-century figures as General Sir Vincent Eyre, who served with distinction as an artillery officer during the Afghani siege of Kabul in 1841 (later writing a book about it) and in the Indian Mutiny of 1857. Also Edward John Eyre (after whom Lake Eyre was named) was the first white man to trek across the Great Australian Bight and later went on to become governor of Jamaica, ending his career in controversy for his manner of putting down a rebellion in 1865.''

* * *

COHEN, Albert 1895(?)-1981

OBITUARY NOTICE: Born c. 1895 in Corfu, Greece; died October 17, 1981, in Geneva, Switzerland. Writer and former United Nations (U.N.) official. In 1931 Cohen settled in Geneva, where he served for many years as a senior officer in the International Labor Organization, a U.N. agency. He then turned to writing full time, producing *Le Livre de ma mere, Solal,* and the acclaimed novel *Belle du seigneur,* which won an award from the Acadamie Francaise. Cohen's books were translated into several languages, including English, German, and Spanish. His name had often been mentioned as a possible candidate for the Nobel Prize in literature. Obituaries and other sources: *Chicago Tribune,* October 19, 1981.

* * *

COHEN, Dorothy H. 1915-

BRIEF ENTRY: Born January 28, 1915, in New York, N.Y. American educator and author. Dorothy Cohen began teaching at elementary schools in 1937 and became a college teacher of education in 1949. Since 1964 she has been a senior staff member at Bank Street College of Education, teaching early childhood education and human growth and development. She wrote *Observing and Recording the Behavior of Young Children* (Teachers College Press, 1968), *The Significance of the Young Child's Motor Development* (National Association for the Education of Young Children, 1971), *The Learning Child* (Vintage, 1972), and *Kindergarten and Early Schooling* (Prentice-Hall, 1977). *Address:* 3835 Bailey Ave., New York, N.Y. 10463.

* * *

COHEN, Ronald Dennis 1940-

PERSONAL: Born August 3, 1940, in Los Angeles, Calif.; son of Herman and Helen Cohen; children: Alysha. *Education:* University of California, Berkeley, A.B., 1962; University of Minnesota, M.A., 1965, Ph.D., 1967. *Home:* 1136 North Warren, Gary, Ind. 46403. *Office:* Department of History, Indiana University, Northwest Campus, Gary, Ind. 46408.

CAREER: Hartwick College, Oneonta, N.Y., assistant professor of history, 1967-69; Macalester College, St. Paul, Minn., assistant professor of history, 1969-70; Indiana University, Northwest Campus, Gary, assistant professor, 1970-74, associate professor, 1974—. *Member:* Organization of American Historians, History of Education Society, American Studies Association, Indiana Civil Liberties Union (chapter president).

WRITINGS: (With Raymond Mohl) *The Paradox of Progressive Education: The Gary Plan and Urban Schooling,* Kennikat, 1979.

WORK IN PROGRESS: A history of schools in Gary, Ind., from 1900 to 1960, completion expected in 1983.

COHN, Marvin L(ester) 1924-

PERSONAL: Born March 18, 1924, in New York, N.Y.; son of Samuel Joseph (a food jobber) and Anna (Shore) Cohen; married Helen Balty (a teacher), May 30, 1946; children: Joel Ralph, Carol Elaine. *Education:* City College (now of City University of New York), B.S.S., 1946; Cornell University, M.A., 1948; New York University, Ph.D., 1968. *Office:* Reading Clinic, Adelphi University, Garden City, N.Y. 11530.

CAREER: Secondary school teacher, 1948-51; elementary and secondary school teacher, 1954-66; Adelphi University, Garden City, N.Y., assistant professor, 1966-70, associate professor, 1970-78, professor of reading and head of Reading Clinic, 1978—. Lecturer at Harvard University, C. W. Post College of Long Island University, Hofstra University, Fordham University, Brooklyn College of the City University of New York, Queens College of the City University of New York, State University of New York at Stony Brook, and University of Southern Illinois. Reading clinician at New York University, Hofstra University, and Adelphi University. Expert witness for Nassau County Legal Aid Society, 1975—; member of Nassau Reading Council (past member of executive committee); consultant to New York Foundling Hospital and Jewish Child Care Association. *Military service:* U.S. Army, 1943-46. *Member:* International Reading Association, American Association of University Professors, Phi Delta Kappa.

WRITINGS: Helping Your Teen-Age Student: A Parents' Guide to Ways to Improve Reading and Study Habits, Dutton, 1979, reprinted as *Helping Your Teen-Age Student: What Parents Can Do to Improve Reading and Study Skills,* New American Library, 1980. Contributor to reading and education journals.

WORK IN PROGRESS: Reversals, Dyslexia, and Your Child, on reversals in reading.

SIDELIGHTS: Cohn told *CA:* "I became a teacher under the optimistic but mistaken impression that it would leave me time to practice the skills of a craft I hoped to enter, comedy writing. However, I quickly became concerned with the academic problems I found working in a Harlem junior high school and later in a residential treatment center for disturbed children. I am particularly interested in reversals in reading and writing and in how people learn to become dyslexics. I have worked extensively in developing a schemata-based method of teaching reading comprehension.'' Cohn noted that his surname differs from his father's because of an error on his birth certificate.

* * *

COLDSMITH, Don(ald Charles) 1926-

PERSONAL: Born February 28, 1926, in Iola, Kan.; son of Charles I. (a Methodist minister) and Sarah (Willett) Coldsmith; married Barbara A. Brown, August, 1949 (divorced, 1960); married Edna E. Howell, November 6, 1960; children: Carol Coldsmith Edwards, April Coldsmith Mann, Glenna, Leslie, Connie. *Education:* Baker University, A.B., 1949; University of Kansas, M.D., 1958. *Politics:* Republican. *Religion:* Methodist, *Home address:* Route 5, Box 150, Emporia, Kan. 66801. *Office:* 1024 West 12th, Emporia, Kan. 66801.

CAREER: Young Men's Christian Association (YMCA), Topeka, Kan., youth director, 1949-54; Bethany Hospital, Kansas City, Kan., intern, 1958-59; private practice of medicine in Emporia, Kan., 1959—. Adjunct professor of English at Emporia State University, Emporia. *Military service:* U.S. Army, 1944-46; served in the Philippines and Japan. *Member:* American Medical Association, Western Writers of America (officer), Appaloosa Horse Club, National Rifle Association, Kansas Medical Society, Flint Hill Medical Society, Kiwanis.

WRITINGS: *Horsin' Around* (articles), Naylor, 1975; *Trail of the Spanish Bit* (historical novel), Doubleday, 1980; *Buffalo Medicine* (historical novel), Doubleday, 1981; *Horsin' Around Again* (articles), Corona, 1981; *The Elk-Dog Heritage* (historical novel), Doubleday, 1982; *Follow the Wind* (historical novel), Doubleday, 1982. Author of "Horsin Around," a self-syndicated weekly newspaper column. Contributor to medical journals and equestrian magazines. Contributing editor of *Horse of Course.*

SIDELIGHTS: Coldsmith wrote: "I started writing in about 1967 as a result of my interest in raising horses. I do some medical writing, but prefer writing westerns about the country and Indians, history and nostalgia; I also do some public speaking on these subjects. I am interested in firearms and have worked as a gunsmith and rifle instructor.

"Now I have a full-time medical practice, raise Appaloosa horses and a few cattle, and write when I can. I've enjoyed nearly everything I ever did."

* * *

COLE, K. C. 1946-

PERSONAL: Born August 22, 1946, in Detroit, Mich.; daughter of Robert (in advertising) and Mary Rose (Dennebaker) Cole; married Peter A. Janssen (a writer and editor), January 20, 1974; children: Peter A., Jr. *Education:* Columbia University, B.A., 1968. *Residence:* Washington, D.C.

CAREER: Merrill Lynch, Pierce, Fenner & Smith, New York City, research assistant, 1967; Free Europe, Inc., New York City, research assistant, 1968-69; free-lance reporter in Czechoslovakia, Hungary, and the Soviet Union, 1969-70; free-lance magazine writer, 1970-71; *Saturday Review,* San Francisco, Calif., associate editor, 1973-74; *Newsday,* Long Island, N.Y., feature editor and staff writer, 1974-78; free-lance writer, 1978—. Writer for Exploratorium (museum), 1974; consultant to Select Panel for the Promotion of Child Health and Robert Wood Johnson Foundation. *Member:* National Organization for Women. *Awards, honors:* All-America Award from Educational Press Association of America, 1972.

WRITINGS: *Vision: In the Eye of the Beholder,* Exploratorium, 1978; *Facets of Light: Colors and Images and Things That Glow in the Dark,* Exploratorium, 1980; *What Only a Mother Can Tell You About Having a Baby,* Anchor Press, 1980; *Order in the Universe,* Exploratorium, 1982. Author of columns in *Newsday, Washington Post,* and *New York Times.* Contributor to magazines, including *Smithsonian, Omni, Glamour, Seventeen,* and *Cosmopolitan,* and to newspapers.

WORK IN PROGRESS: A book of personal essays for women, "between the lines of feminism and the traditional feminine attitudes," publication by Anchor Press expected in 1982.

SIDELIGHTS: K. C. Cole commented: "My writing career has changed gear many times. I began straight out of school with a specialty in Eastern European affairs and wrote first about that; then for several years I was an education specialist; then I stumbled on the Exploratorium in 1972 and have been writing about science ever since, and about health. Lately I've been writing personal columns and essays for newspapers on politics and women's issues."

AVOCATIONAL INTERESTS: Sailing, the flute.

COLEMAN, Emily Holmes 1899-1974

PERSONAL: Born January 22, 1899, in Oakland, Calif.; died June 13, 1974, in Tivoli, N.Y.; married Loyd Ring Coleman (a psychologist) in 1921; children: John. *Education:* Received degree from Wellesley College, 1920. *Religion:* Roman Catholic. *Home:* The Farm, Tivoli, N.Y.

CAREER: Society editor of *Paris Tribune* (European edition of *Chicago Tribune*); writer.

WRITINGS: *The Shutter of Snow* (novel), Viking, 1930. Contributor of articles, stories, and poems to *transition,* and of poems to *New Review.* Also author of an unpublished novel, "The Tygon," and numerous unpublished plays, stories, and poems.

SIDELIGHTS: Coleman, a victim of postpartum psychosis, drew upon her experiences as a patient in a mental hospital for her autobiographical novel, *The Shutter of Snow.* Several critics praised the book, pointing out that Coleman's account was authentic and vivid. A reviewer in *Nation and Atheneum* observed, "Mrs. Coleman has succeeded in conveying the pity and terror of [her] condition in a remarkable manner, without exaggeration and without self-pity or sentimentality. It is a success very rarely achieved in any kind of literature."

BIOGRAPHICAL/CRITICAL SOURCES: *Books,* August 17, 1930; *New York Times,* August 31, 1930; *Nation and Atheneum,* December 6, 1930; *Nation,* December 17, 1930; *Dictionary of Literary Biography,* Volume 4: *American Writers in Paris, 1920-1939,* Gale, 1980.*

* * *

COLLIER, (James) Graham 1937-

PERSONAL: Born February 21, 1937, in Tynemouth, England; son of John and Elizabeth May (Usher) Collier. *Education:* Berklee College of Music, diploma, 1963. *Politics:* Social Democrat. *Home:* 38 Shell Rd., London SE13 7TW, England. *Agent:* Julian Burton, Laurence Pollinger Ltd., 18 Maddox St., London W1R 0EU, England.

CAREER: Composer, musician, bandleader, and writer, 1963—. *Military service:* British Army, musician, 1956-63.

WRITINGS: *Inside Jazz,* Quartet, 1973; *Jazz: A Guide for Teachers and Students,* Cambridge University Press, 1975; *Compositional Devices,* Berklee Press, 1975; *Cleo and John,* Quartet, 1976. Author of "Set to Music," a column in *Gay News.*

WORK IN PROGRESS: *Mad Tyreman,* essays; research on Malcolm Lowry and jazz.

* * *

COLLIN, Richard Oliver 1940-

PERSONAL: Born April 22, 1940, in Buffalo, N.Y.; son of Oliver Bryan (a banker) and Margaret (a school administrator; maiden name, O'Day) Collin; divorced; children: Oliver Reid. *Education:* Canisius College, B.A., 1962; attended Harvard University, 1962-64; doctoral study at Oxford University, 1977—. *Home:* 86 Hugh Allen Cres., Oxford OX3 0HN, England. *Agent:* Albert Zuckerman, Writers House, Inc., 21 West 26th St., New York, N.Y. 10010.

CAREER: Intelligence analyst with Defense Intelligence Agency, 1965-72; Center for Mediterranean Studies, Rome, Italy, dean of students, 1972-74; adviser to Saudi Arabian Defence Forces, 1974-75; Oxford University, Oxford, England, lecturer in political history, 1975—, fellow of Oriel College, 1977—. *Military service:* U.S. Army, 1965-67; became captain. *Awards, honors:* Woodrow Wilson fellow; grant from Danforth Foundation.

WRITINGS: The De Lorenzo Gambit, Sage Publications, 1976; (with E. A. Bayne) *Arms and Advisors,* AVFS, 1977; *Contessa* (novel), St. Martin's, 1982.

* * *

COLLINS, Norman Richard 1907-

PERSONAL: Born October 3, 1907, in Beaconsfield, Buckinghamshire, England; son of Oliver Norman and Lizzie Ethel (Nicholls) Collins; married Sarah Helen Martin (a former actress), December 26, 1931; children: Anthea (Mrs. Zbynek Zeman), Cordelia (Mrs. Andrew McNeil), Roderick Martin. *Education:* Educated in Hampstead and London, England. *Home:* Mulberry House, Church Row, London N.W. 3, England. *Agent:* A. D. Peters & Co., 10 Buckingham St., London W.C. 2, England. *Office:* ACC House, 17 Great Cumberland Pl., London W. 1, England.

CAREER: Oxford University Press, London, England, assistant, 1926-29; *London News Chronicle,* London, assistant literary editor, 1929-33; Victor Gollancz Ltd., London, deputy chairman, 1934-44; British Broadcasting Corp. (BBC), London, director-general of overseas service, 1944-46, controller of light programs, 1946-47, controller of television division, 1947-50; Associated Television Corp., London, director, 1954—. Governor of British Film Institute, 1949-51; chairman of High Definition Films, 1950-54; director of Watergate Productions Ltd., 1952-67; chairman of Independent TV Companies Association Ltd., 1960; director of Independent Television News Ltd., 1971-73. Member of Adoption Committee for Aid to Displaced Persons, 1962-70; president of Lifeline, 1962-70; governor of Atlantic Institute, 1965-69; general commissioner of taxes, 1967; chairman of Central School of Speech and Drama, 1967-81; counselor to English Stage Company; vice-president of English Center of P.E.N., 1976—; vice-president of Dickens Fellowship, 1979—. *Member:* Radio Industries Club (president, 1950), National Book League (member of executive committee, 1965-69), National Playing Fields Association (president of appeals committee, 1967-69), Orchestral Concerts Society (director), Sadler's Wells Foundation (governor), Carlton Club, Marylebone Cricket Club, Turf Club, Beefsteak Club.

WRITINGS: The Facts of Fiction, Gollancz, 1932, Dutton, 1933, reprinted, Books for Libraries, 1970; *Penang Appointment,* Gollancz, 1934, Doubleday, 1935, reprinted, Collins, 1964; *The Three Friends,* Gollancz, 1935, Doubleday, 1936, reprinted, Collins, 1963; *Trinity Town,* Gollancz, 1936, Harper, 1937, reprinted, Collins, 1963; *Flames Coming Out of the Top,* Gollancz, 1937, Harper, 1938, reprinted, Collins, 1961; *Love in Our Time,* Harper, 1939.

Gold for My Bride, Harper, 1940 (published in England as *I Shall Not Want,* Gollancz, 1940); *The Quiet Lady,* Harper, 1942 (published in England as *Anna,* Collins, 1942); *London Belongs to Me,* Collins, 1945, published as *Dulcimer Street,* Duell, Sloan & Pearce, 1947; *Black Ivory,* Duell, Sloan & Pearce, 1948.

Children of the Archbishop, Duell, Sloan & Pearce, 1951; *The Bat That Flits,* Duell, Sloan & Pearce, 1952; *Bond Street Story,* Harper, 1959; *The Governor's Lady,* Collins, 1968, Simon &

Schuster, 1969; *The Husband's Story,* Atheneum, 1978; *Little Nelson,* Collins, 1981.

Also author of a play, "The Captain's Lamp," produced in 1938.

SIDELIGHTS: Collins's first novel, *Penang Appointment,* is an adventure about a quiet schoolmaster's tumultuous voyage on a ship of colorful characters. Olga Martion of *New Statesman and Nation* praised Collins's work: "Mr. Collins writes so well, and visualizes the ship and the sea and the people with such astonishing freshness, that every lap of this odd voyage is entertaining."

Another of Collins's works, *Love in Our Time,* earned similar praise. Critic Olga Owens spoke of the novel as being "beautifully conceived, timed, and executed. Mr. Collins has the nicest sense of humor we have met in a long time, and it is amazing that he can be so pungent without once resorting to malice." And Forrest Reid of the *Times Literary Supplement* added that "in its naturalism, in its economy, in its humanity, this really is an admirable novel."

Some of Collins's works, however, have been criticized for being too long, but they have still impressed critics. The *Manchester Guardian*'s Charles Marriott called *Quiet Lady* "a good solid novel, a bit long-winded but earning its length by liveliness of texture." Similarly, a *New Yorker* reviewer found that *Dulcimer Street* "is nearly twice as long as it should be and is not too incisive, but is nevertheless a pleasing, lively narrative, hard to put down once you get into it."

In 1968 Collins, who has spent much of his career in television, commented on his two professions for Gladys Williams of *Books and Bookmen:* "Television is quite a different sort of activity from novel writing. It's more of a team production for one thing, and the results are not so personal and enduring. I can earn my living by television and still go on, with an altogether different part of me being a novelist."

Collins's earlier career as a publisher, he claimed, was incompatible with his aims as a writer. "I had long ago decided to give up being a publisher, because of the feeling that I wanted to write," he told Williams. "You see I should always, with one part of me, have been in competition with my own authors, wanting to write all the books myself."

BIOGRAPHICAL/CRITICAL SOURCES: Times Literary Supplement, January 28, 1932; *Springfield Republican,* May 6, 1933, April 14, 1935; *New York Times,* July 2, 1933, March 8, 1936, February 21, 1937, May 15, 1938, July 30, 1939, July 28, 1940, December 6, 1942, January 12, 1947, October 28, 1951, October 25, 1959; *Saturday Review of Literature,* July 8, 1933, February 8, 1947, September 11, 1948; *Christian Science Monitor,* August 22, 1933, August 12, 1939; *New York Herald Tribune Books,* March 15, 1936; *New Statesman and Nation,* November 6, 1937; *New York Herald Tribune Book Review,* January 19, 1947; *Punch,* April 10, 1968; *Books and Bookmen,* May, 1968; *Best Sellers,* November 15, 1968; *New York Times Book Review,* October 19, 1969; *Los Angeles Times,* December 29, 1978.

* * *

COLLINS, Will
See CORLEY, Edwin (Raymond)

* * *

COLLISON, David (John) 1937-

PERSONAL: Born August 5, 1937, in Ipswich, England; son

of Douglas Roland and Molly (Hedgcock) Collison; married Annie Dodd (an actress); children: Mark, Dominic, Robin. *Education:* Attended secondary school in Ipswich, England. *Politics:* "Right of center." *Religion:* "Cynic awaiting the blinding flash (eagerly)." *Home:* Rowley House, Headley Fields, Headley, Hampshire, England. *Office:* Theatre Projects Services Ltd., 10 Long Acre, London WC2E 9LN, England.

CAREER: Arts Theatre Club, London, England, stage manager, 1955-57; stage manager for West End theatres in London, 1957-59; independent sound designer, 1959; Theatre Projects Sound Ltd., London, managing director, 1963-75; Theatre Projects Services Ltd., London, deputy managing director, 1975—. Member of board of directors of Theatre Projects Consultants Ltd., 1968—, and Theatre Projects Ltd., 1980—. Lecturer on theater sound and acoustics; sound and communications systems consultant. *Member:* Society of Theatre Consultants (founding member), Association of British Theatre Technicians (founding member; past chairman of sound committee).

WRITINGS: Stage Sound, Cassell, 1976, revised edition, 1982.

Plays: "The Physician's Folly" (two-act operetta), first produced in Ipswich, England, at Tower Theatre, May, 1955; "Drake's Parish" (one-act), first produced in Plymouth, England, at Church of St. Andrew, July 28, 1980.

WORK IN PROGRESS: "When the Girls Came Out to Play" (tentative title), a two-act farce; a two-act musical play for children based on "The Tinder Box" by Hans Christian Andersen, for production in London at Polka Theatre.

SIDELIGHTS: Since becoming the first independent sound designer in British theatre in 1959, Collison has contributed his skills to such stage successes as "Mame," "Fiddler on the Roof," "Cabaret," "Sweet Charity," "The Rocky Horror Show," and "Jesus Christ Superstar." He has worked at England's leading theatres, including the Royal Shakespeare Theatre, the Old Vic, the National Theatre, and the New Shakespeare Open Air Theatre.

Collison wrote: "I have always been fascinated by the 'magic of the theatre,' the scenic effects and illusions and the aura of make-believe. Although I work as a consultant on new theatres in many different countries and many different styles, my type of theatre abounds with red plush and gilt, ornate plasterwork, and chandeliers. I have to admit that I have enjoyed many open-stage productions, but I regret being cheated of the thrill of anticipation before the curtain rises and the sudden glorious revelation of an unfamiliar and living world upon which one is being privileged to eavesdrop.

"Writing has intrigued me since the age of fourteen, when I saw a production of 'H.M.S. Pinafore' and decided, with a musically talented school friend, to write an operetta. 'The Physician's Folly' was performed three years later by an amateur company in my hometown for six consecutive performances. The suspicion that I was the reincarnation of W.S. Gilbert sadly faded around the time of this important premiere, as I had secured my first job in the professional theatre (as a very junior assistant stage manager), nightly being exposed to such authors as Shaw, Gide, Anouilh, O'Neill, and Beckett. Not a bad lineup for starters, especially when one considers it included the English-speaking premiers of 'Waiting for Godot' and 'The Waltz of the Toreadors.'

"Disheartened and dispirited, I gave up the world of operetta and musical comedy after one more brief foray. A few years later, however, being employed as sound operator on a long-running West End musical and bored, I attempted my first book. This I considered my P.G. Wodehouse period. But Wodehouse was still writing at the time, and there was obviously not room for two of us, so I put away the pen and became immersed in my new and totally self-created job theatre sound consultant.

"Apart from a few articles for technical magazines, my literary skills lay dormant until some twelve years later when I was approached by Cassell to write a book on sound in the theatre. I was by now convinced that my nonacademic background and annoyingly deficient . . . what is the word? . . . vocabulary precluded me from literary success. However, having finally completed *Stage Sound,* an anecdotal textbook, parts of which some people apparently find readable, I found the courage to research and write a dramatic script for a Son et Lumiere production in 1980. I am now completing a theatrical farce (my Ben Travers period) before rewriting and updating *Stage Sound.*

"My ambition is to one day make enough money from writing to spend half the year in my favorite country, Greece, and the other half in that most beautiful part of England, the Cotswolds."

AVOCATIONAL INTERESTS: Collecting eighteenth-century glass, "thinking about taking long country walks with our dog, Phoebe."

*   *   *

COLVILLE, Derek Kent 1923-

BRIEF ENTRY: Born February 23, 1923, in Scarborough, England. Educator and author. Colville has been a professor of English at State University of New York at Binghamton since 1969. He edited *The Craft of Writing* (Harper, 1961) and wrote *Mental Journey to America: The Impact of Change* (American Studies Research Program, 1964) and *Victorian Poetry and the Romantic Religion* (State University of New York Press, 1970). *Address:* Department of English, State University of New York at Binghamton, Binghamton, N.Y. 13901. *Biographical/critical sources: Directory of American Scholars,* Volume II: *English, Speech, and Drama,* 7th edition, Bowker, 1978.

*   *   *

COMSTOCK, Mary Bryce 1934-

PERSONAL: Born December 19, 1934, in Boston, Mass. *Education:* Bryn Mawr College, B.A., 1956. *Office:* Museum of Fine Arts, 479 Huntington Ave., Boston, Mass. 02115.

CAREER: Museum of Fine Arts, Boston, Mass., assistant in department of classical art, 1960-65, keeper of coins, 1965—, associate curator, 1971—. *Member:* Archaeological Institute of America, American Numismatic Society (fellow), American Numismatic Association, Royal Numismatic Society (fellow).

WRITINGS: (With Cornelius Vermeule) *Roman Medallions,* Museum of Fine Arts (Boston, Mass.), 1962, 2nd edition, 1974; (with Vermeule) *Greek Coins, 1950 to 1963,* Museum of Fine Arts (Boston, Mass.), 1964; (with Vermeule) *Greek, Etruscan, and Roman Bronzes in the Museum of Fine Arts, Boston,* New York Graphic Society, 1971; (with Vermeule) *Sculpture in Stone: The Greek, Roman, and Etruscan Collections of the Museum of Fine Arts, Boston,* [Boston], 1976.

*   *   *

CONSTANTINE, Mildred 1914-

BRIEF ENTRY: Born June 28, 1914, in Brooklyn, N.Y. American art historian, museum curator, and author. Constantine has worked for the Museum of Modern Art since 1949 and has taught history of graphic design at Parsons School of Design since 1971. She wrote *Beyond Craft: The Art Fabric* (Van Nostrand, 1973), *Soviet Revolutionary Film Posters* (Johns Hopkins Press, 1974), *Tina Modotti: A Fragile Life* (Paddington, 1975), and *The Art Fabric: Mainstream* (Van Nostrand, 1981). *Address:* 41 West 71st St., New York, N.Y. 10023; and Department of Graphic Design, Parsons School of Design, 66 Fifth Ave., New York, N.Y. 10011.

*   *   *

COOK, Ann Jennalie   1934-

PERSONAL: Born October 19, 1934, in Wewoka, Okla.; daughter of Arthur Holly and Bertha Mabelle (Stafford) Cook; married John Donelson Whalley (an attorney), September 10, 1975; children: Lee Ann Harrod, Amy Cecil Harrod. *Education:* University of Oklahoma, B.A., 1956, M.A., 1959; Vanderbilt University, Ph.D., 1972. *Religion:* Episcopalian. *Home:* 91 Valley Forge, Nashville, Tenn. 37205. *Office:* Shakespeare Association of America, 6328 Vanderbilt Station, Nashville, Tenn. 37235.

CAREER: University of Oklahoma, Norman, instructor in English, 1956-57; teacher of English at secondary schools in Raleigh, N.C., 1958-60, and Wallingford and North Haven, Conn., both 1960-61; Southern Connecticut State College, New Haven, instructor in English, 1962-64; University of South Carolina, Columbia, assistant professor of English, 1972-74; Shakespeare Association of America, Nashville, executive secretary, 1975—. Associate professor at Vanderbilt University, 1976—. Member of board of directors of Nashville Symphony Guild, Nashville Ballet Society, Checkwood, and Ensemble Theatre Company; member of board of trustees of Council for Research in the Renaissance; consultant to National Endowment for the Humanities.

MEMBER: International Shakespeare Association (member of executive committee, 1981—), Shakespeare Association of America, Modern Language Association of America, American Association of University Professors, Shakespeare Institute, Society for Values in Higher Education, Renaissance Society of America, National Lawyers Wives (member of executive board, 1979—), Southeastern Renaissance Society, Tennessee Bar Auxiliary (president, 1979-80), Phi Beta Kappa. *Awards, honors:* Folger Shakespeare Library fellowship, 1973; Donelson Foundation fellowship, 1974-75.

WRITINGS: The Privileged Playgoers of Shakespeare's London, 1576-1642, Princeton University Press, 1981. Contributor to literature journals. Associate editor of *Shakespeare Studies,* 1973—; member of editorial board of *International Shakespeare,* 1976—, *Early English and Renaissance Drama,* 1980—, and *Shakespeare Quarterly,* 1981—.

WORK IN PROGRESS: Courtship in Shakespeare and His Society.

SIDELIGHTS: Cook told *CA:* ''I am particularly interested in the relationship between the world in which Shakespeare and his audience lived and the world he created on stage. The playwright variously distorted, caricatured, criticized, and/or conformed to his social milieu. But unless we know as precisely as possible what that social milieu was, we may not see Shakespeare's aesthetic intentions accurately. Worse yet, we may apply modern assumptions about such matters as love and marriage and completely misjudge situations in the plays.''

BIOGRAPHICAL/CRITICAL SOURCES: Times Literary Supplement, January 29, 1982.

COOKE, Barclay   1912-1981

OBITUARY NOTICE—See index for *CA* sketch: Born May 11, 1912, in Paterson, N.J.; died November 29, 1981, in Englewood, N.J. Professional backgammon player, athlete, and author. Cooke was heralded as the world's best backgammon player of the 1970's. He won the World Cup for Backgammon in 1974 and the British-American Backgammon Cup the previous year, and he was often the champion of tournaments sponsored by the Racquet and Tennis Club in New York. The skill he demonstrated while playing in the first international duplicate backgammon tournament earned the gamester much praise. A graduate of Yale University in 1934, Cooke was known for his facility as a student hockey player. He continued playing the sport in New York with the St. Nicholas Hockey Club. Besides backgammon and hockey, Cooke was also interested in baseball as well as bridge and the opera. His works include *The Cruelest Game,* with co-author Jon Bradshaw, *Paradoxes and Probabilities,* written with Rene Orlean, and *Championship Backgammon.* Obituaries and other sources: *New York Times,* December 2, 1981.

*   *   *

COOMBS, Charles Anthony   1918-1981

OBITUARY NOTICE: Born April 9, 1918, in Newton, Mass.; died September 20, 1981, in Green Village, N.J. Banker and author. Coombs's thirty years of service with the Federal Reserve Bank of New York culminated with his directorship of the foreign exchange operations. Upon retiring in 1975, he directed finances for the American Express International Banking Corporation, the American International Group, and the Discount Corporation of New York. He wrote *The Arena of International Finance.* Obituaries and other sources: *The International Year Book and Statesmen's Who's Who,* Kelly's Directories, 1978; *Who's Who in America,* 41st edition, Marquis, 1980; *New York Times,* September 21, 1981.

*   *   *

COONEY, Nancy Evans   1932-

PERSONAL: Born September 9, 1932, in Northfork, W.Va; daughter of Earl B. (a banker) and Grace (Howard) Evans; married John Mason Cooney (a university administrator), June 5, 1955; children: James, Carolyn, Christine, Mark. *Education:* University of North Carolina, B.A., 1954; Marshall University, M.A., 1956. *Home:* 691 Red Lion Way, Bridgewater, N.J. 08807.

CAREER: Junior high school teacher in Northfork, W.Va., 1954-55; West Windsor Elementary School, Dutch Neck, N.J., teacher and guidance counselor, 1956-57; Princeton Seminary, Princeton, N.J., librarian, 1957-58; Philip's Bookstore, Cambridge, Mass., general assistant, 1958-59; writer, 1978—. *Member:* Society of Children's Book Writers, Children's Literature Association.

WRITINGS: The Wobbly Tooth (illustrated by Marylin Hafner), Putnam, 1978; *The Blanket That Had to Go,* Putnam, 1981.

WORK IN PROGRESS: More picture books and short-chapter books for young readers, including *Bad Luck Follows Shrimp* and *Sky High.*

SIDELIGHTS: Cooney told *CA:* ''In writing for young children I like to use a universal experience and make it a very specific and personal event that most children can relate to. I try to make it fun by bringing out the humorous side.''

COONTZ, Otto 1946-

PERSONAL: Born November 29, 1946, in Worcester, Mass.; son of Gustaf (in diplomatic corps) and Clare (McSheehy) Coontz. *Education:* Boston University, B.F.A., 1968. *Residence:* Cambridge, Mass.; and New York, N.Y.

CAREER: Walker Home for Children, Needham, Mass., therapist for emotionally disturbed adolescents, 1965-68; International Boutique, Amsterdam, Holland, buyer, 1968-70; Arbor Cafe, Berkeley, Calif., chef, 1970-71; free-lance commercial artist, 1971-74; Harvard University Medical School and Massachusetts General Hospital, Boston, research assistant in study of skin diseases, 1974-78; writer, illustrator of picture books and medical illustrator, 1978—. *Member:* Graphic Artists' Guild, Greenpeace U.S.A.

WRITINGS—Juvenile novels and picture books; self-illustrated: *The Quiet House*, Little, Brown, 1978; *A Real Class Clown*, Little, Brown, 1979; *Starring Rosa*, Little, Brown, 1980; *Hornswoggle Magic*, Little, Brown, 1981; *Mystery Madness*, Houghton, 1982. Also author of *The Town That Dreaded Sundown*.

Illustrator: Bernie Zubrowski, *Milk Carton Blocks* (children's activity book), Little, Brown, 1979. Free-lance illustrator of medical textbooks, children's picture books, and textbooks.

SIDELIGHTS: Coontz told *CA:* "I began as a picture book author-illustrator and free-lance textbook illustrator, and I am now exclusively writing juvenile novels. I write seven days a week—from as little as two hours a day to twelve hours a day. I am active in Greenpeace U.S.A., and I have an avid interest in cetaceans (whales and dolphins) and preserving our natural environment. My favorite authors are Louise Fitzhugh and Eudora Welty. I am addicted to film and see as many as five movies each week. Because of my work habits I tend to be a reclusive sort.

"In writing, I am concerned first with creating an entertainment. Where contemporary issues appear in my work, they serve foremost to lend an immediate and vivid reality to characters, settings, and situations. Beyond this, any reflection on my own opinions concerning contemporary issues would only be inadvertent. I am simulating real people who voice a diversity of opinions and attitudes. Writing for me is like reading; I explore and listen to my characters as if they exist outside myself, with their own stories to tell and deeds to do. I suppose I write books for children because children's literature has been, for the most part, what I like to read. This genre has always seemed to be more adventuresome, humane, and hopeful than most adult fiction. It would seem near impossible to me to spin an adult tale without a certain measure of cynicism. I am essentially an optimist."

AVOCATIONAL INTERESTS: Film, travel, gardening, volleyball.

BIOGRAPHICAL/CRITICAL SOURCES: Worcester Evening Gazette, November 1, 1978; *Washington Post Book World*, November 12, 1978; *Booklist*, November 15, 1978; *New York Times Book Review*, November 9, 1980; *Los Angeles Times Book Review*, November 16, 1980.

*   *   *

COOPER, Jilly 1937-

PERSONAL: Born February 21, 1937, in Hornchurch, England; daughter of W. B. (an engineer and brigadier) and Elaine (Whincup) Sallitt; married Leo Cooper (a publisher), October 7, 1961; children: Matthew Felix, Emily Maud Lavinia. *Education:* Attended private girls' school in Salisbury, England. *Religion:* Church of England. *Agent:* George Greenfield, John Farquharson Ltd., Bell House, 8 Bell Yard, London WC2A 2JU, England. *Office: Sunday Times*, Grays Inn Rd., London W.C.1, England.

CAREER: Worked in advertising and publishing, 1958-69; *Sunday Times*, London, England, author of column, 1969-81.

WRITINGS: How to Stay Married (nonfiction), illustrations by Timothy Jacques, Methuen, 1969, Taplinger, 1970; *How to Survive From Nine to Five* (nonfiction), illustrations by Jacques, Methuen, 1970; *Jolly Super*, Methuen, 1971; *Men and Super Men*, illustrations by Jacques, Methuen, 1972; *Jolly Super Too*, Methuen, 1973, *Women and Super Women*, illustrations by Jacques, Methuen, 1974; *Super Men and Super Women*, Methuen, 1976; *Jolly Superlative*, Methuen, 1976; *Superjilly*, Methuen, 1978; *Work and Wedlock*, Magnum, 1978; *The British in Love*, Arlington, 1979; *Class: A View From Middle England*, illustrations by Jacques, Methuen, 1980, Knopf, 1981; *Supercooper*, Methuen, 1980; (with Tom Hartman) *Violets and Vinegar: An Anthology of Women's Writings and Sayings*, Allen & Unwin, 1980, Stein & Day, 1981; *Love and Other Heartaches*, Arlington, 1981; *Intelligent and Loyal: A Celebration of the Mongrel*, Methuen, 1981.

Novels: *Emily*, Arlington, 1975; *Bella*, Arlington, 1976; *Harriet*, Arlington, 1976; *Octavia*, Arlington, 1977; *Imogene*, Arlington, 1978; *Prudence*, Arlington, 1978.

Children's books: *Little Mabel*, Granada, 1980; *Little Mabel's Great Escape*, illustrations by Jacques, Granada, 1981; *Little Mable Wins*, Granada, 1982.

WORK IN PROGRESS: A novel about equestrian show jumping, publication expected in 1982; a book, with photographs, about the Commons in London, publication by Methuen expected in 1983.

SIDELIGHTS: Jilly Cooper told *CA:* "My aim as a writer is to cheer people up and occasionally, amid the laughs, to make a serious point. I think I started off a very flip, brittle writer because I was frightened of sentimentality. But gradually, I think, I'm putting more heart into my writing. The *Sunday Times* column, which really made my name, is part domestic comedy and part reporting events like a royal wedding or a vets conference."

*   *   *

COOPER, John Milton, Jr. 1940-

BRIEF ENTRY: Born March 16, 1940, in Washington, D.C. American historian, educator, and author. Cooper began teaching at University of Wisconsin—Madison in 1970 and has been a professor of history since 1976. His writings include *The Vanity of Power: American Isolationism and the First World War, 1914-1917* (Greenwood Press, 1969), *Causes and Consequences of World War I* (Quadrangle, 1972), and *Walter Hines Page: The Southerner as American, 1855-1918* (University of North Carolina Press, 1977). *Address:* Department of History, University of Wisconsin—Madison, Madison, Wis. 53706. *Biographical/critical sources: American Men and Women of Science: The Social and Behavioral Sciences*, 13th edition, Bowker, 1978.

*   *   *

COPELAND, Paul W.

PERSONAL Born in New York. *Education:* Graduated from

Whitman College; received M.A. from University of Washington. *Address:* c/o J. B. Lippincott Co., East Washington Sq., Philadelphia, Pa. 19105.

CAREER: Writer. Teacher of English at American University in Beirut, Lebanon; high school teacher in Seattle, Wash., and Aleppo, Syria, 1952. *Awards, honors;* Smith Mundt grant from the U.S. Department of State, 1952.

WRITINGS—Juveniles; published by Lippincott: *The Land and People of Syria,* 1964, revised edition, 1972; *The Land and People of Jordan,* 1965, revised by Frances Copeland Sickles, 1972; *The Land and People of Libya,* 1967, revised edition, 1972.

SIDELIGHTS: In reviewing *The Land and People of Jordan,* a *Best Sellers'* writer found the book "informative and heavy and boring. . . . Perhaps the editors expect the miraculous of the author when they order the geography, the history, past and present political set-ups, the culture and just about everything of a land and its people to be sandwiched into a mere 160 pages." A *Book Week* reviewer, however, felt that *The Land and People of Syria,* "is simple enough for a child of eleven to get an excellent idea of the nation and its people, yet so comprehensive that we wish we had read it before we visited the country."

BIOGRAPHICAL/CRITICAL SOURCES: Book Week, July 19, 1964; *Best Sellers,* June 15, 1965.

*   *   *

CORBIN, John B(oyd) 1935-

PERSONAL: Born April 7, 1935, in Moody, Tex.; son of John Arthur (a farmer) and Lola Mae (Willis) Corbin. *Education:* North Texas State University, B.A., 1957; University of Texas, M.L.S., 1961; University of Oklahoma, Ph.D., 1973. *Home:* 7950 North Stadium Dr., No. 167, Houston, Tex. 77030. *Office:* 4800 Calhoun, Houston, Tex. 77004.

CAREER: University of Texas, Arlington, acquisitions librarian, 1960-63; Texas State Library, Austin, director of technical services, 1963-67; Tarrant County Junior College District, Fort Worth, Tex., director of automation services, 1967-70; Oklahoma Department of Libraries, Oklahoma City, special projects librarian, 1970-72; Colorado State Library, Denver, planning officer, 1972-73; North Texas State University, Denton, assistant professor of library science, 1973-77; Stephen F. Austin State University, Nacogdoches, Tex., associate director of technical services, 1977-81; University of Houston, Houston, Tex., assistant director for administration and systems, 1981—. Conference director. *Military service:* U.S. Army, 1957-59.

MEMBER: American Library Association, Texas Library Association (chairman of ad hoc committee on networks, 1978-80; chairman of College and University Libraries Division, 1970-71). *Awards, honors:* Esther J. Piercy Award from Resources and Technical Services Division of American Library Association, 1970; named librarian of the year by Texas Library Association, 1981.

WRITINGS: Index of State Geological Survey Publications Issued in Series, Scarecrow, 1965, *Supplement: 1963-1980,* 1982; *A Technical Services Manual for Small Libraries,* Scarecrow, 1971; *Developing Computer-Based Library Systems,* Oryx, 1981. Contributor to library and education journals. Editor of *Texas Libraries,* 1965-66, and newsletter of DataPhase Users Group, 1979-81; member of editorial board of *Choice,* 1971-73.

SIDELIGHTS: Corbin told *CA:* "I enjoy teaching very much and am able to interpret complex subjects such as library au-

tomation and systems for students. I attempt to translate this ability into my writings also. Most people could grasp highly technical subjects if they were explained simply and in detail. I enjoy analyzing topics/systems and breaking them down into more manageable topics. I also like to be involved in librarianship that others find too difficult—I like a challenge, in other words."

AVOCATIONAL INTERESTS: "My outside interests include music (opera and symphony in particular), loafing (doing nothing), and reading."

*   *   *

CORDS, Nicholas J. 1929-

PERSONAL: Born July 11, 1929, in Mankato, Minn.; son of Arthur Oscar (a barber) and Lauretta (Lynch) Cords; married Margaret Helen Hurley, December 28, 1968; children: James, John, Nicholas, Daniel. *Education:* Mankato State University, B.S., 1952; University of Minnesota, M.A., 1960, Ph.D., 1970. *Politics:* Democrat. *Religion:* Roman Catholic. *Home:* 3964 Van Dyke St., White Bear Lake, Minn. 55110. *Office:* Department of History, Lakewood Community College, White Bear Lake, Minn. 55110.

CAREER: High school history teacher at public schools in Minnesota, 1952-66; Lakewood Community College, White Bear Lake, Minn., instructor in history, 1967—. Member of White Bear Lake Charter Commission. *Military service:* U.S. Army, 1947-48. *Member:* American Historical Association, Organization of American Historians, Southern Historical Association, Phi Alpha Theta.

WRITINGS: Myth and Southern History, Rand McNally, 1974; *Myth in American History,* Glencoe, 1977; (editor) *Myth and the American Experience,* Glencoe, 1978.

AVOCATIONAL INTERESTS: Reading, music.

*   *   *

CORFIELD, Conrad Laurence 1893-1980

OBITUARY NOTICE: Born August 15, 1893, in Berkshire, England; died October 3, 1980. Civil servant and author. In 1920 Corfield began his twenty-seven years of service in British-Indian affairs. His initial position as secretary to the viceroy in the Punjab led to posts in India's Rajputana and Malwa regions. During the 1940's Corfield acted as adviser to British negotiators in the establishment of an independent Indian nation. He returned to England in 1947 and pursued his political interests at the local level. In 1975 Corfield wrote a memoir, *The Princely India I Knew.* Obituaries and other sources: *Who's Who,* 131st edition, St. Martin's, 1979; *The Annual Obituary 1980,* St. Martin's, 1981.

*   *   *

CORK, Patrick
See COCKBURN, (Francis) Claud

*   *   *

CORLEY, Edwin (Raymond) 1931-1981
(Patrick Buchanan, Will Collins, Ray Corley, David Harper, William Judson)

OBITUARY NOTICE—See index for *CA* sketch: Born October 22, 1931, in Bayonne, N.J.; died of a heart attack, November 7, 1981, in Gulfport, Miss. Advertising executive, publisher, and author. Before becoming a full-time writer, Corley worked as a stage manager for theatres in New York City. After two years he left that job to become the publisher of a magazine, *Off-Broadway,* in 1954. Four years later, Corley was writing copy for New York ad agencies until he became a vice-president at Dancer-Fitzgerald-Sample in 1969. His syndicated column, "Good Books," was carried by nearly one hundred newspapers, and he was an active filmmaker with two of his works winning Robert Flaherty awards. As a novelist, Corley is best known for *Hijacked,* which was adapted into the Metro-Goldwyn-Mayer motion picture "Skyjacked," a 1972 release starring Charlton Heston and Yvette Mimeiux. His other novels, many of which were written under pseudonyms, include *Seige, The Jesus Factor, A Sounder of Swine, Grizzly, The Patchwork Man,* and *Kilman's Landing.* At the time of his death, the author was completing a novel centering on Hurricane Camille, which assailed the Gulf Coast in 1969. The book may be published either under the title *Camille* or *The Eye of the Devil.* Obituaries and other sources: *New York Times,* November 10, 1981; *Publishers Weekly,* November 20, 1981.

* * *

CORLEY, Ray
See CORLEY, Edwin (Raymond)

* * *

CORNELIUS, Wanda Pyle   1936-

PERSONAL: Born January 26, 1936, in Emporia, Kan.; daughter of Thomas H. (a farmer) and Ethel (a teacher; maiden name, Phillips) Pyle; married Rodger E. Cornelius (a mortician), November 29, 1959; children: R. Kent. *Education:* Kansas State College (now Emporia State College), B.A., 1958. *Politics:* Republican. *Religion:* Christian (Disciples of Christ). *Home:* 3500 Hardy, Apt. 46, Hattiesburg, Miss. 39401.

CAREER: Emporia Gazette, Emporia, Kan., society editor, 1953-54; *Enid News and Eagle,* Enid, Okla., feature editor, 1958-59; Cullen & Boren, Dallas, Tex., director of advertising, 1959-62; *Chickasha Star,* Chickasha, Okla., editor, 1962-63; *Winn Parish Enterprise,* Winnfield, La., editor, 1966-68; freelance writer, 1969—. *Member:* National Writers Club. *Awards, honors:* Best feature award from United Press International, 1973, for "Space Age Cattle Rustling."

WRITINGS: (Contributor) James Sanders, editor, *Hobbies: How Thirty-Seven Fascinating Hobbies Were Started,* Jonathan David, 1980; (with Thayne R. Short) *Ding Hao: America's Air War in China, 1937-45* (Doubleday Military Book Club selection), Pelican, 1980; *A Pictorial History of the China-Burma-India Theater,* Pelican, 1982. Contributor to national magazines, including *American History Illustrated, Mature Living, Homebuilt Aircraft,* and *Living With Children.*

WORK IN PROGRESS: The Last Days, a humorous autobiographical look at terminal illness; *Brownie, the Outlaw Steer,* juvenile nonfiction, publication expected by Pelican.

SIDELIGHTS: Wanda Cornelius told *CA:* "I always knew I wanted to be a writer. My journalism career began at age sixteen, at the *Emporia Gazette,* made famous by William Allen White. In 1969 I became terminally ill and was forced to quit high-pressure editing. I began writing free-lance features and articles for major dailies in Louisiana, then for national magazines.

"*Ding Hao* took six years to research and write. It is ironic that a distant relative of Ernie Pyle would also write about a

forgotten theater of World War II, nearly forty years after he won the Pulitzer Prize in journalism in 1944.

"History has always been an enigma to me, but through exhaustive research one finds written history is often also a comedy of errors. So where does one find the truth? By diligently searching for accounts recorded at the time, oral history handed down from generation to generation, journals, diaries, flight logs, squadron journals, and newspaper accounts. It takes many sources to arrive at an accurate description of an event. Sensationalism in journalism also influences documentation for historical purposes, so one must carefully sort out all facts from the mythical products of literary license.

"I worry about the not-too-distant future when the electronic gadgets will replace the written word. With electronic newspapers, and all sorts of information available on the television screen or computer printouts, will published work become passe? Will history be kept in a computer bank at the Smithsonian, to be punched for reference at will? Or will we still cherish favorite volumes, and will history and other records of civilization be written down and published? I cannot imagine life without books, no matter how electronically oriented the world becomes."

BIOGRAPHICAL/CRITICAL SOURCES: Alexandria Town-Talk, January 28, 1981; *Disciple,* February 15, 1981.

* * *

CORWIN, Cecil
See KORNBLUTH, C(yril) M.

* * *

COSMAN, Madeleine Pelner   1937-

BRIEF ENTRY: Born December 4, 1937, in New York, N.Y. American educator and author. Cosman joined the faculty at City College of City University of New York in 1964. Since 1970 she has been a professor of medieval English and comparative literature. She wrote *The Education of the Hero in Arthurian Romance* (University of North Carolina Press, 1966), *Fabulous Feasts: Medieval Cookery and Ceremony* (Braziller, 1976), *Conference on Machaut's World: Science and Art in the Fourteenth Century* (New York Academy of Sciences, 1977), and *Medieval Holidays and Festivals* (Scribner, 1981). *Address:* Institute of Medieval and Renaissance Studies, City College of the City University of New York, New York, N.Y. 10031. *Biographical/critical sources: Directory of American Scholars,* Volume II: *English, Speech, and Drama,* 7th edition, Bowker, 1978.

* * *

COURTIS, Stuart Appleton   1874-1969

OBITUARY NOTICE: Born May 15, 1874, in Wyandotte, Mich.; died October 19, 1969, in Cupertino, Calif. Educator, consultant on education, and author of works in his field. Courtis served in various educational capacities for Detroit public schools and Detroit Teachers College during the 1920's. He was also professor of education at both the University of Michigan and Wayne University (now Wayne State University). He created the Courtis standardizing tests and used them in school surveys in Indiana and New York City. His writings include *Why Children Succeed, The Measurement of Growth,* and *A Picture Dictionary for Children.* Obituaries and other sources: *Who Was Who in America, With World Notables,* Volume V: *1969-73,* Marquis, 1973; *Who Was Who Among North American*

Authors, 1921-1939, Gale, 1976; *Biographical Dictionary of American Educators,* Greenwood Press, 1978.

*   *   *

COURTNEIDGE, Cicely   1893-1980

OBITUARY NOTICE: Born April 1, 1893, in Sydney, Australia; died April 26, 1980, in London, England. Actress in stage productions. Courtneidge scored successes on the British stage in her father's productions of plays such as "Arcadians." During World War I, the family's plummeting finances compelled her to seek work in music halls. Courtneidge then refined her penchant for comedy. In 1923 she began appearing with her husband, Jack Hulbert, in musical and comedy reviews on the stage. The team later worked in several motion pictures, including "The Ghost Train" and "Jack's the Boy." When England entered World War II, Courtneidge and her husband entertained troops throughout Europe. Among the duo's most popular achievements during the war was the comedy "Under the Counter." They later performed the play on Broadway, where it failed to amuse audiences with its depictions of life during wartime. During the 1950's and 1960's Courtneidge continued to appear on the British stage in musicals and comedies, including "Gay's the Word" and "The Bride and the Bachelor." In 1974 she acted with Hulbert in "Move Over Mrs. Markham." She wrote an autobiography, *Cicely.* Obituaries and other sources: *Encyclopaedia of the Musical Theatre,* Dodd, 1976; *Who's Who in the Theatre: A Biographical Record of the Contemporary Stage,* 16th edition, Pitman, 1977; *Who's Who,* 131st edition, St. Martin's, 1979.

*   *   *

COURTNEY, (John) Richard   1927-

PERSONAL: Born June 4, 1927, in Newmarket, England; son of Arthur John (a teacher) and Celia Annie Courtney; married Rosemary Gale (a writer and editor); children: Anne Courtney Chung, John. *Education:* University of Leeds, B.A., 1951, diploma in education, 1952. *Home:* R. R. No. 1, Newmarket, Ontario, Canada L3Y 4V8. *Office:* Ontario Institute for Studies in Education, 252 Bloor St. W., Toronto, Ontario, Canada M5S 1V6.

CAREER: Teacher at primary school in Dalham, England, 1948; teacher of drama at high schools in Leeds, England, 1952-55, and Colne Valley, England, 1955-59; University of London, Institute of Education, London, England, senior lecturer in drama at Trent Park College, 1959-67, warden of Sir Phillip Sassoon Hall, 1961-64; University of Victoria, Victoria, British Columbia, associate professor of theatre, 1968-71; University of Calgary, Calgary, Alberta, professor of drama, 1971-74, head of Developmental Drama Summer School, 1970-72; Ontario Institute for Studies in Education, Toronto, professor of arts and education, 1974—. Lecturer at Goldsmith's College, London, summers, 1973-74; member of faculty at University of Toronto, 1974—; visiting fellow at Melbourne State College, 1979; visiting instructor at University of Western Ontario, 1980; lecturer at universities in England, Australia, the United States, and Hong Kong. Actor with British Broadcasting Corp. Northern Repertory Company, 1954-64, and English Theatre Guild; performed in repertory, music halls, and amateur productions; director of Proscenium Players, Leeds, and educational theatre productions; founder of Four Valleys Youth Theatre, 1955; co-founder of Enfield Youth Theatre, 1961; life patron of North Hertfordshire Youth Theatre. Artist, with exhibitions of paintings. Chairman of task force on arts and education in Canada, 1975-79, and national inquiry into arts and

education in Canada, 1979; guest on television programs in Canada, United States, Hong Kong, and Australia; consultant to Canada Council, Design Canada, and Ontario Arts Council. *Military service:* Royal Air Force, 1945-48.

MEMBER: Canadian Conference of the Arts (member of board of governors, 1970; member of executive committee, 1971; vice-president, 1972; national president, 1973-76), Canadian Child and Youth Drama Association (member of board of directors, 1968-69; president, 1969-72), Creative Education Foundation, Educational Drama Association, Society for Teachers of Speech and Drama, Folklore Society, Royal Society of Arts (fellow), British Society for Aesthetics, British Children's Theatre Association, British Society of Dramatherapy, American Councils of the Arts (members of board of directors, 1974-77), American Drama Therapy Association (founding member), American Theatre Association (member of Theatre Education Commission, 1979-81), American Society for Aesthetics. *Awards, honors:* Alberta Achievement Award from government of Alberta, 1973, for services to arts and education; Canadian Silver Jubilee Medal from governor-general of Canada, 1977; research awards from Design Canada, Ontario Arts Council, and Ontario Ministry of Education.

WRITINGS: Wild Eyed Girl (poems), Stockwell, 1948; *Drama for Youth,* Pitman, 1964; (editor) *College Drama Space,* Institute of Education, University of London, 1964; *Teaching Drama,* Cassell, 1965; *The School Play,* Cassell, 1966; *The Drama Studio,* Pitman, 1967; *Play, Drama, and Thought: The Intellectual Background to Dramatic Education,* Cassell, 1968, 2nd edition, Drama Book Specialists, 1970, 3rd edition, 1974; *Teaching and the Arts: Arts Education in Australia, With Specific Reference to Drama Education in Victoria,* Melbourne State College, 1979; (editor) *The Face of the Future: The Report of the National Inquiry Into Arts and Education in Canada,* Canadian Conference of the Arts, 1979; *The Dramatic Curriculum,* Drama Book Specialists, 1980; (with Paul Park) *Learning in the Arts,* Ministry of Education, Ontario, 1980; (editor) *Drama in Therapy,* Volume I: *Children,* Volume II: (with Gertrud Schattner) *Adults,* Drama Book Specialists, 1981; *History of British Drama,* Littlefield, Adams, 1982; *Re-Play: Studies of Human Drama in Education,* Ontario Institute for Studies in Education Press, 1982.

Contributor: Lawrence Hayes, editor, *Education and the Arts,* Australian National University, 1971; John Hodgson and Martin Banham, editors, *Drama in Education,* Pitman, Volume I, 1973, Volume II, 1974, Volume III, 1975; Nellie McCaslin, editor, *Theatre for Young Audiences,* Longman, 1978; Leslie J. Kaslof, editor, *Wholistic Dimensions in Healing,* Doubleday, 1978; Martin Engel and Jerome Hausman, editors, *Fourth Yearbook on Research in Arts and Aesthetic Education,* Central Midwest Regional Educational Laboratory, 1981.

Editor of monograph series "Discussions in Developmental Drama," University of Calgary, 1971-74. Contributor of more than one hundred articles, stories, poems, and reviews to scholarly journals, popular magazines, and newspapers, including *Gryphon, Players, Connecticut Review, Queen's Quarterly,* and *Orbit.* Contributing editor to *Curriculum Inquiry,* 1975-78.

WORK IN PROGRESS: Peoples in Performance: Perspectives on Drama and Culture, publication by Drama Book Specialists expected in 1983; a book on ritual performance of Canadian Indians of the Pacific Northwest coast, completion expected in 1982; a book on dramatic rituals of ancient peoples, from Neanderthals to the Greeks, 1983; a study of Goldoni, 1982; a book stating Courtney's theory of theatre, 1983.

SIDELIGHTS: Courtney told *CA:* "I have always been concerned with the drama of existence. Human drama commences in the first months of life—we make sense out of the world by creating a dramatic relationship with it—and theatre is simply the tip of the iceberg of human existence.

"In a recent 'Sunrise Semester' series on CBS-TV, I explained that in order to understand this process, we have to examine it from the inside out and from the outside in. How can we understand ourselves or other people unless we do both things at the same time? Our inner world (the 'me') creates a drama between itself and other people and things. Yet, at the same time, the outer world (our society and culture) is made up of other people who are also creating their own dramas; this opens up some possibilities to us, but closes off others. This accounts for two types of my writing: studies in children's play, maturation, and education (the drama of the inner), and studies of ceremonialism and ritual (the drama of the outer).

"Yet, a play in a theatre provides human beings with models as to how to live their lives—how to relate the inner to the outer—and that is what makes theatre so significant as an art form. This accounts for my third type of writing: studies of plays and the theatre."

BIOGRAPHICAL/CRITICAL SOURCES: Yorkshire Evening Post, December 18, 1953; *Bradford Telegraph and Argus,* June 13, 1959; *Amateur Stage,* April, 1964; *Plays and Players,* April, 1964; *Times Literary Supplement,* November 11, 1964, March 31, 1967, May 31, 1968; *Catholic Teachers' Journal,* March/April, 1966; *Speech Teacher,* summer, 1966; *English Progress,* October, 1967; *Education,* November 24, 1967; *Victoria Daily Times,* January 20, 1968, July 20, 1968, May 23, 1970; *Teachers' World,* February 2, 1968; *Cambridge Daily News,* April 18, 1968; *New Society,* April 25, 1968; *Speech and Drama,* autumn, 1968; *Theatre Design and Technology,* October, 1968; *Daily Colonist,* March 9, 1969; *Journal of Creative Behavior,* spring, 1970; *New Literary History,* spring, 1971; *Calgary Herald,* April, 1973; *Ottawa Journal,* May 2, 1975; *Choice,* July/August, 1975; *Educational Theatre Journal,* March, 1976; *Canberra Times,* February 27, 1979; *Children's Theatre Review,* fall, 1981.

*   *   *

COWDREY, (Michael) Colin   1932-

PERSONAL: Born in 1932; son of Ernest Arthur (a tea planter) and Kathleen Mary Cowdrey; married Penelope Susan Chiesman, September 15, 1956; children: Christopher, Jeremy, Carol, Graham. *Education:* Attended Oxford University, 1951-54. *Religion:* Church of England. *Office:* International Division, Barclays Bank International Ltd., 168 Fenchurch St., London EC3P 3HP, England.

CAREER: Kent Cricket Team, team member, 1950-76, captain, 1957-70; England Cricket Team, team member, 1954-75, became captain; Barclays Bank International Ltd., London, England, currently local director. Local director of Whitbread Co. Ltd. Member of council of Winston Churchill Memorial Trust. *Member:* Britain-Australia Society (member of council). *Awards, honors:* Commander of Order of the British Empire.

WRITINGS: Cricket Today, Arthur Barker, 1961; *Time for Reflection,* Muller, 1962; *Tackle Cricket This Way,* Stanley Paul, 1964, new edition, 1969; *The Incomparable Game,* Hodder & Stoughton, 1970; *Autobiography of a Cricketer,* Hodder & Stoughton, 1976.

SIDELIGHTS: Cowdrey wrote: "I think it is valuable for every youngster to set his or her sights toward goals or aspirations—even if they are not achieved. Without these life can lack spark and motivation. A life of purpose helps to form the mind, makes for self-discipline, and is more satisfying—even if success and achievements prove elusive."

*   *   *

COX, Marie-Therese Henriette   1925-
(Molly Cox)

PERSONAL: Born October 18, 1925, in Istanbul, Turkey; daughter of Arthur Joseph (a journalist and businessman) and Aileen (Turner) Cunningham; married Charles Terence Cox (with British radio), June 28, 1947 (died March 17, 1961); children: Dominic, Oliver. *Education:* Studied at a private school in London, England. *Religion:* Roman Catholic. *Home:* Old Workhouse, 4 Berwick Cottages, Marlow, Buckinghamshire, England. *Office:* British Broadcasting Corp. Television, Wood Lane, London W. 12, England.

CAREER: British Broadcasting Corp. (BBC-TV), London, England, news clerk, 1943-45, sound engineer, 1945-50, producer and director of children's programs, 1957—. *Awards, honors:* Golden Nymph Prize, Monte Carlo International Television Festival, 1970, for "Play School" television series; Silver Dove prize, International Catholic Association for Radio and Television, 1972, for "In the Beginning" television series.

WRITINGS—For children; all under name Molly Cox; all adapted from various BBC-TV series: (Editor) *O Jemima!* (poems adapted from "Play School"), illustrated by Mina Martinez, BBC Publications, 1970; (with David Attenborough) *David Attenborough's Fabulous Animals,* BBC Publications, 1975; *The Creation: A Story From the Bible,* illustrated by Graham McCallum, Collins, 1977; *The Family of Abraham: A Story From the Bible,* illustrated by Paul Birkbeck, Collins, 1977; *The Kings of Israel: A Story From the Bible,* illustrated by Birkbeck, Collins, 1978; *Moses and the Laws of God: A Story From the Bible,* illustrated by McCallum, Collins, 1978; *Breakthrough,* BBC Publications, 1981.

Author of numerous scripts and series for BBC-TV, including "In the Beginning," 1971, "Unsolved Mysteries," 1971, "The New Beginning," 1973, "Story Behind the Story," 1973, "Children of Destiny," 1974, "Fabulous Animals," 1975, "The Discoverers," 1976, "Story Beneath the Sands," 1978, and "Breakthrough," 1981.

WORK IN PROGRESS: A television series on medical breakthroughs.

SIDELIGHTS: "Children need serious subject matter to make them wonder," Cox told *CA.* "History, legends, and myths should be passed on. My own childhood was rich with storytelling: fact and fiction with an international flavor. I wanted to share my enthusiasm with others, although I never thought of myself as an author. I wanted to be a painter or journalist, but once I was in television work I had no more need to paint. Television equals words plus pictures." Cox said she believes children's books should be the product of very careful research related in a clear language. Illustrations, she said, should add emotional depth to a book.

*   *   *

COX, Molly
See COX, Marie-Therese Henriette

*   *   *

CRAWFORD, Bill
See CRAWFORD, William Hulfish

CRAWFORD, William Hulfish   1913-1982
(Bill Crawford)

OBITUARY NOTICE: Born March 18, 1913, in Columbus, Ohio (listed in some sources as Hammond, Ind.); died of pneumonia, January 6, 1982, in Washington, D.C. Syndicated cartoonist for the *Newark News.* Crawford's work appeared in more than seven hundred newspapers and was also featured in magazines such as *Time, Newsweek,* and *Esquire.* He also illustrated books. Obituaries and other sources: *Who's Who in America,* 40th edition, Marquis, 1978; *Chicago Tribune,* January 8, 1982; *Newsweek,* January 18, 1982.

*   *   *

CREIGH, Dorothy (Weyer)   1921-

PERSONAL: Surname is pronounced Cree, maiden name rhymes with "here"; born December 4, 1921, in Hastings, Neb.; daughter of Frank E. (a college dean) and Mabelle (Carey) Weyer; married Thomas Creigh, Jr. (a utilities executive), July 17, 1948; children: Mary Elizabeth (Mrs. Ronald H. Pfeil), Thomas III, John Weyer, James Carey. *Education:* Hastings College, B.A., (summa cum laude), 1942; Columbia University, M.S., 1945. *Home:* 1950 North Elm Ave., Hastings, Neb. 68901.

CAREER: Hastings Daily Tribune, Hastings, Neb., society editor, 1941-42, garden editor, 1960; high school teacher of English and journalism in Central City, Neb., 1942-43; Naval Ammunition Depot, Hastings, editor of *Powder Keg,* 1943-44; Ziff-Davis Publishing Co., New York City, part-time clerical worker, and Columbia Broadcasting System, Inc. (CBS), New York City, part-time writer, 1944-45; Associated Press, Richmond, Va., reporter, 1945-46; United Nations Relief and Rehabilitation Administration, New York City, reports officer and economic analyst in Hankow and Shanghai, China, 1946-47; Hastings College, Hastings, instructor in journalism, 1953, instructor in English, 1960-67; writer, 1965—; free-lance consultant, 1974—. Member of board of directors of Hastings Civic Symphony, 1950-60 and 1965—, Nebraska Heart Association, 1966-69, Nebraska Arts Council, 1967—, Nebraska Historical Foundation,1973—, Nebraska State Board of Education, 1974—, and University Funding Commission, 1974—; member of Governor's Commission on Higher Education, 1962; director for numerous projects for the Adams County Historical Society, and for an oral history project funded in part by the National Endowment for the Humanities; panelist for National Endowment for the Humanities, 1975 and 1978, and for Institute of Museum Services, 1979 and 1981.

MEMBER: American Association for State and Local History, Adams County Historical Society (member of board of directors, 1965—), Round Table Study Club. *Awards, honors:* Award of merit from American Association for State and Local History, 1973, for *Adams County: The People* and *Adams County: A Story of the Great Plains;* service to mankind award from Sertoma International, 1975; named Nebraska Woman of the Year, 1979, by Business and Professional Women's Clubs of Nebraska, 1979; Mari Sandoz Award from Nebraska Library Association, 1981, for significant literary contribution to the state.

WRITINGS: (With Celestine Brock) *Teaching High School Journalism,* Nebraska State Department of Education, 1943; (with father, F. E. Weyer) *Hastings College: Seventy-Five Years in Retrospect,* Hastings College, 1958; *Bellevue College,* Hastings College, 1962; *Tales From the Prairie,* Adams County Historical Society, Volume I, 1970, Volume II, 1973, Volume III, 1976, Volume IV, 1979, Volume V, 1982; *Adams County: The People,* Adams County-Hastings Bicentennial Commission, 1971; *Adams County: A Story of the Great Plains,* Adams County-Hastings Bicentennial Commission, 1972; *Where in the World Have We Been?,* Service Press, 1973; *A Primer for Local Historical Societies,* American Association for State and Local History, 1976; *Nebraska: A History,* Norton, 1977; *The Great Plains: A Handbook for Six Documentary Movies,* Adams County Historical Society, 1979; *Nebraksa, Where Dreams Grow,* Miller & Paine, 1980.

Contributor: Thomas K. Krazean, editor, *Local History Today,* Indiana Historical Society, 1980; Richard A. Bartlett, editor, *Rolling Rivers,* McGraw, 1981.

Author of "How to Be an Effective Elected Official," a tape cassette series, released by Executive Institute in 1973. Contributor of more than two hundred articles to magazines, including *Magazine of the Midlands, National Geographic School Bulletin,* and *China Weekly Review,* and newspapers. Editor of *Hastings College Alumni Quarterly,* 1948-51, *Stringing Along,* 1965-66, and *Adams County Historical News,* 1968—.

WORK IN PROGRESS: Sod-House Frankie, for children; biographies of Alice Yocum, Margaret Winger, and Margaretta Dietrich; research on Lewis and Clark and on women and aging for possible movie scripts; research on post-revolutionary China in comparison to pre-revolutionary days.

SIDELIGHTS: Dorothy Creigh told *CA:* "Although I have written on many subjects, particularly in magazines, there is a common thread running through most of my writing: the people and the land of the prairie country. My roots are deeply set into the Great Plains, with its harsh climate of intense extremes, isolation, and subtle beauty. The people who have overcome its rigors and developed its cultural patterns intrigue me. I have no pretensions of ever being another Willa Cather, but I was a protege of Mari Sandoz in my earlier years. Although I have traveled extensively, I am always drawn back irresistibly to the broad prairie country.

"I have a compulsion to write, and have been doing it ever since I can remember. Whether it's a book, magazine piece, newspaper story, or simply a letter, I must spend a certain amount of time every day in front of the typewriter. I do not write easily, however, but struggle with every word. My children equate 'mother' with 'typewriter,' or maybe it's the other way around. The telephone is my enemy; it rings just when I've found the word or phrase I've been struggling over.

"I am intolerant of laziness and stupidity, and have definite opinions about practically everything. A good writer cannot be wishy-washy. Outside of my writing and my family, my prime interest is in education."

AVOCATIONAL INTERESTS: Reading, traveling, knitting, playing duplicate bridge, cooking.

BIOGRAPHICAL/CRITICAL SOURCES: Writer's Digest, April, 1974.

*   *   *

CREPEAU, Richard C(harles)   1941-

PERSONAL: Born June 14, 1941, in Minneapolis, Minn.; son of Charles E. (in sales) and Margaret (Aretz) Crepeau; married Patricia J. Wissler (a writer), July 9, 1964; children: Mark, Kathleen. *Education:* University of Minnesota, B.S., 1963; Marquette University, M.A., 1967; Florida State University, Ph.D., 1973. *Politics:* Democrat. *Religion:* Roman Catholic.

Home: 1585 Kingston St., Titusville, Fla. 32780. *Office:* Department of History, University of Central Florida, Orlando, Fla. 32816.

CAREER: U.S. Peace Corps, Washington, D.C., volunteer high school teacher of European and African history in Ethiopia, 1963-65; Siena College, Memphis, Tenn., instructor in history, 1967-69; Florida State University, Tallahassee, instructor in history, 1969-72; University of Central Florida, Orlando, visiting assistant professor, 1972-73, assistant professor, 1973-78, associate professor of history, 1978—. Instructor at Memphis State University, summer, 1969. Guest on radio and television programs. *Member:* North American Society for Sport History, Popular Culture Association, Arena: Institute for Sport and Social Issues, Popular Culture Association in the South. *Awards, honors:* National Endowment for the Humanities fellowship, 1976.

WRITINGS: (Contributor) Andrew Yiannakis, Thomas D. McIntyre, and other editors, *Sport Sociology: Contemporary Themes,* 2nd edition (Crepeau was not included in 1st edition), Kendall/Hunt, 1979; *Baseball: America's Diamond Mind, 1919-1941,* University Presses of Florida, 1980. Contributor of about one dozen articles and reviews to sport and popular culture journals.

WORK IN PROGRESS: Research on the history of Melbourne Village, Fla.

SIDELIGHTS: Crepeau wrote: "I have had a lifelong involvement with baseball as a player and umpire, stemming from my father's work as a sporting goods salesman, umpire, and Little League official. I combined this with an interest in history and produced my first book. I am also interested in international affairs, especially African affairs, since my two years as a Peace Corps volunteer in Ethiopia."

* * *

CROSS, Gilbert B.
(Jon Winters)

PERSONAL: Born in Walkden, near Manchester, England; son of Gilbert Edward Cross; married; children: two. *Education:* Manchester University, B.A., 1961; London University, postgraduate certificate in education, 1962; University of Louisville, M.A., 1965; University of Michigan, Ph.D., 1971. *Home:* 1244 Ferdon, Ann Arbor, Mich. 48104.

CAREER: Writer.

WRITINGS: (Co-editor) *Drury Lane Journal: Selections From James Winston's Diaries, 1819-1827,* Society Theatre Research, London, 1974; *Next Week East Lynne: Domestic Drama in Performance,* Bucknell University Press, 1976; (under pseudonym Jon Winters) *The Drakov Memoranda,* Avon, 1979; (co-editor) *World Folktales: A Scribners Resource Collection,* Scribners, 1980.

* * *

CROSS, (Alfred) Rupert (Neale)   1912-1980

PERSONAL: Born June 15, 1912; died September 12, 1980; son of Arthur George (a quantity surveyor) and Mary Elizabeth (Dalton) Cross; married Aline Heather Chadwick (a solicitor), 1937. *Education:* Worcester College, Oxford, D.C.L., 1958.

CAREER: Admitted solicitor, 1939; solicitor in London, England, 1939-45; Law Society's School of Law (now College of Law), tutor, 1945-48; Oxford University, Oxford, England, fellow and tutor at Magdalen College, 1948-64, lecturer, 1956-64, Vinerian Professor of English Law, 1964-79; writer, 1979-80. Visiting professor at University of Adelaide, 1962, and University of Sydney, 1968. Member of Archbishop of Canterbury's committee on legal reform and law of evidence, 1959, and Diplock Committee on terrorist activities in Northern Ireland, 1972. Fellow of British Academy; past member of council of Royal National Institute for the Blind. *Awards, honors:* Honorary master of the bench of Middle Temple, 1972; Knight of the Order of the British Empire, 1973; LL.D. from University of Edinburgh, 1973, and University of Leeds, 1975; honorary fellow of Worcester College, Oxford, 1972, and of Magdalen College, Oxford, 1975.

WRITINGS: The Law of Wills, Stevens & Sons, 1947, 3rd edition, 1953; (with Philip Asterley Jones) *An Introduction to Criminal Law,* Butterworth, 1948, 8th edition published as *Cross and Jones' Introduction to Criminal Law,* 1976; (with Jones) *Cases on Criminal Law,* Butterworth, 1949, 5th edition, 1975; *Evidence,* Butterworth, 1958, 5th edition, 1980.

Precedent in English Law, Clarendon Press, 1961, 3rd edition, 1979; (with Nancy Wilkins) *An Outline of the Law of Evidence,* Butterworth, 1964, 4th edition, 1975; *The English Sentencing System,* Butterworth, 1971, 2nd edition, 1975; *Punishment, Prison, and the Public: An Assessment of Penal Reform in Twentieth-Century England by an Armchair Penologist,* Stevens & Sons, 1972; *On Evidence,* revised edition, Butterworth, 1974; *Statutory Interpretation,* Butterworth, 1976. Contributor to law journals.

OBITUARIES: London Times, September 15, 1980.*

* * *

CROWLEY, Frances G(eyer)   1921-

PERSONAL: Born March 22, 1921, in Merano, Italy; daughter of Oscar (a film technician) and Mathilda (a dress specialist; maiden name, Crastan) Geyer; married Cornelius Joseph Crowley (a professor), September 28, 1948; children: Veronica, Robert. *Education:* Hunter College (now the City University of New York), A.B., 1942; Columbia University, A.M., 1945; Washington University, St. Louis, Mo., Ph.D., 1962. *Politics:* Democrat. *Religion:* Protestant. *Home:* 515 North Sprigg, Cape Girardeau, Mo. 63701. *Office:* Department of Modern Languages, Southeast Missouri State University, Cape Girardeau, Mo. 63701.

CAREER: St. Louis University, Adult Education Center, St. Louis, Mo., instructor in Romance languages, 1950-61; University of Missouri, St. Louis, assistant professor of Romance languages, 1961-66; Lindenwood College, St. Charles, Mo., associate professor of Romance languages, 1966-68; Southeast Missouri State University, Cape Girardeau, associate professor, 1968-78, professor of Spanish, 1978—. *Member:* Modern Language Association of America, Renaissance Society of America, Latin American Studies Association.

WRITINGS: (Contributor) *Comentarios reales de los Incas,* Mouton, 1971; *Domingo Faustino Sarmiento,* Twayne, 1972. Contributor to academic journals. Editor and publisher of *Heartland Journal,* 1960-68; editor of *Breve notiziario italiano,* 1965.

WORK IN PROGRESS: Ambassador's Confidante, correspondence of Mary Mann with Domingo Faustino Sarmiento.

SIDELIGHTS: Frances Crowley told *CA:* "I am very concerned about the continuing breakdown of cultural standards in America, particularly in the humanities. A very telling example of this is the current situation in modern languages. When the study of Latin and Greek suffered a precipitous decline some quarter of a century ago, students on the secondary and higher education levels turned to the modern languages. Today, on the other hand, conditions in all languages are literally chaotic, so much so that there is the distinct possibility of the actual disappearance of language departments in many of our universities. I certainly will do everything in my power to prevent this from ever happening.

"I also feel that there is a palpable neglect of intensive research in Latin and American-United States relations. I try to bring this out in the correspondence of Mary Mann with Ambassador (later President) Sarmiento of Argentina in *Ambassador's Confidante*. These letters are a veritable mine of information on education, religion, sociology, economics, personal relations, and general Americana touching on the period with which they deal. I believe seriously that to neglect history and its handmaiden, languages, is to neglect the whole vast panorama of humanity, and this is true of all periods of history, whether ancient, medieval, or modern."

*   *   *

CURRAN, Charles John   1921-1980

OBITUARY NOTICE: Born October 13, 1921, in Dublin, Ireland; died January 9, 1980, in London, England. Administrator, editor, and writer. Curran began his thirty-year association with the British Broadcasting Corporation (BBC) as a producer in 1947. After three years, he moved to Canada for a brief stint as editor of *Fishing News*. In 1951 he returned to the BBC as a writer. Soon afterward he was promoted to senior administrative assistant. Curran then worked at several administrative levels before accepting the position of director-general in 1967. He was knighted in 1974. He wrote of his experiences with the BBC in *A Seamless Robe*. Obituaries and other sources: *Who's Who in the World*, 4th edition, Marquis, 1978; *The International Who's Who*, Europa, 1979; *The Annual Obituary 1980*, St. Martin's, 1981.

*   *   *

CURTIS, Alan R(obert)   1936-

PERSONAL: Born August 27, 1936, in Westboro, Mass.; son of Dorothy K. (Bailey) Curtis; married Merlene G. Gilks, August 27, 1960; children: Donald A., Deborah L., Linda J. *Education:* Boston University, B.S., 1958, M.Ed., 1964, certificate of advanced graduate study in business education, 1972. *Politics:* Independent Republican. *Religion:* Baptist. *Address:* c/o Houghton Mifflin Co., 2 Park St., Boston, Mass. 02107.

CAREER: Teller at savings and loan association in Worcester, Mass., 1956-58; Salter Secretarial School, Worcester, instructor in accounting and business, 1959-60; high school teacher of business and bookkeeping in Lakeville, Mass., 1960-61; high school teacher of mathematics and typing in Millbury, Mass., 1961-64; Curry College, Milton, Mass., instructor in accounting and business, 1964-65; Burdett College, Boston, Mass., instructor in accounting, 1965-66; Newton Junior College, Newtonville, Mass., assistant professor of accounting and typing, 1966-68; Quinsigamond Community College, Worcester, associate professor of accounting and business mathematics, 1968-79.

MEMBER: American Association of University Professors, Association of Teachers of Quantitative Methods, New England Business Educators Association, Eastern Business Teachers Association, Massachusetts Business Educators Association, Delta Pi Epsilon (Epsilon chapter), Phi Delta Kappa, Beta Gamma Sigma (Alpha chapter of Massachusetts). *Awards, honors:* Award for article "How Can Business Education Be Improved in the Commonwealth?"

WRITINGS: Practical Math for Business, Houghton, 1973, 2nd edition, 1977. Contributor to business education journals. Past editor of *Epsilonia*.

SIDELIGHTS: Curtis told *CA:* "I am very interested in curriculum in business administration, especially as it relates to community colleges. I am also interested in new and better programs to prepare teachers and professors of business in higher education, especially in community colleges. I want to improve the personal financial (consumer economics) knowledge of American citizens, especially young people."

*   *   *

CURTIS, James C.   1938-

BRIEF ENTRY: Born July 12, 1938, in Evanston, Ill. American historian, educator, and author. Curtis has taught at University of Delaware since 1970 and he became a professor of American history in 1976. He wrote *The Fox at Bay: Martin Van Buren and the Presidency, 1837-1841* (University Press of Kentucky, 1970) and *Andrew Jackson and the Search for Vindication* (Little, Brown, 1976), and edited *Black Experience in America: Selected Essays* (University of Texas Press, 1970). *Address:* Department of History, University of Delaware, Newark, Del. 19711. *Biographical/critical sources: Directory of American Scholars*, Volume I: *History*, 7th edition, Bowker, 1978.

D

DABNEY, Dick 1933-1981

OBITUARY NOTICE—See index for *CA* sketch: Born October 26, 1933, in Charlottesville, Va.; died of an apparent heart attack, November 16, 1981, in Arlington, Va. Journalist, educator, and author. Dabney's writings usually revolved around the quiet life in Flint Hill, Virginia, his hometown. As he once wrote: "I think that our sense of things in Flint Hill was this: that ours was the real world and always had been, and that somewhere out there, in the dark, teeming cities full of men who could not quite see the stars, another world was forming whose nature we were still blind to." In the 1950's Dabney worked as the manager of the Coffee 'n' Confusion Club, an establishment for beatniks, and as a technical editor of the John F. Holman Company. After earning his academic degrees, the author taught American literature and American civilization classes. The author of "Side Streets," a monthly column in the *Washingtonian,* Dabney also contributed articles to other periodicals, such as the *Washington Post.* In 1974 his novel about Flint Hill, *The Honor System,* received an award from the National Endowment for the Arts. Dabney's books include a collection of short stories, *Someone to Talk To,* another Flint Hill novel, *Old Man Jim's Book of Knowledge,* and a biography, *A Good Man: The Life of Sam Ervin.* Obituaries and other sources: *Washington Post,* November 18, 1981.

* * *

DAGOVER, Lil 1897-1980

OBITUARY NOTICE: Original married name, Daghofer; born September 30, 1897 (listed in some sources as 1894), in Madiven, Java (now Djawa); died January 30, 1980, in Munich, West Germany. Actress in stage productions and motion pictures. Dagover appeared in several films from Germany's "Golden Age" of cinema, including "The Cabinet of Dr. Caligari," Fritz Lang's "Destiny," and F. W. Murnau's "Tartuffe." Her autobiography, *Ich war die Dame,* was published in 1979. Obituaries and other sources: *The World Encyclopedia of Film,* A. & W. Visual Library, 1972; *The Oxford Companion to Film,* Oxford University Press, 1976; *The Encyclopedia of World Theater,* Scribner, 1977; *The Annual Obituary 1980,* St. Martin's, 1981.

* * *

DAHL, Arlene 1928-

BRIEF ENTRY: Born August 11, 1928, in Minneapolis, Minn. American actress, designer, and author. Dahl began her acting career at the age of eight. She has performed on Broadway and on tour, in nearly thirty feature films, and on television programs. From 1950 to 1971 she wrote an internationally syndicated beauty column. Dahl became president of Arlene Dahl Enterprises in 1967. Her books include *Always Ask a Man,* 6th edition (Pocket Books, 1965), *Your Beauty Scope,* twelve volumes (Pocket Books, 1969—), *Arlene Dahl's Secrets of Hair Care* (1970), and *Beyond Beauty* (Simon & Schuster, 1980). *Address:* P.O. Box 911, Beverly Hills, Calif. 90213; and Arlene Dahl Enterprises, 730 Fifth Ave., New York, N.Y. 10019. *Biographical/critical sources: Who's Who in the World,* 4th edition, Marquis, 1978.

* * *

DALY, (Arthur) Leo 1920-

PERSONAL: Born January 23, 1920, in Dublin, Ireland; son of William (a railway engineer) and Rebecca (Foreman) Daly; married Brigid Mary Murphy (a nurse), November 24, 1943; children: Rosaleen Rebecca, Kathleen Nuala, Louise Elizabeth, William Francis, Eugene Leo, John Kieran, Justine Mary, Bridiane. *Education:* Received second level to leaving certificate from St. Mary's College; received Medio-Psychological Association certificate as psychiatric nurse, 1943; International School of Colour Photography, diploma, 1955. *Religion:* Roman Catholic. *Home and office:* 10 Mary St., Mullingar, County Westmeath, Ireland.

CAREER: Mental Health Authority, Mullingar, Ireland, psychiatric nurse, 1943-66; free-lance photojournalist, 1966-69; Radio-Telefis-Eireann, Dublin, Ireland, broadcaster, 1969-75; writer, photographer, and editor, 1975—. Teacher of photography for adult education classes and in vocational schools. *Member:* National Union of Journalists, Mullingar Archaeological and Historical Society (founder). *Awards, honors:* Premier Award from National Drama Festival, 1947, for one-act play "Death's Echo."

WRITINGS—All published by Albertine Kennedy Publishing, except as noted: *James Joyce and the Mullingar Connection,* Dolmen Press, 1975; *Oileain Arann* (title means "The Aran Islands"), 1975; (contributor) Ronnie Walshe, editor, *Sunday Miscellany,* Gill & Macmillan, 1975; (contributor) *Midland Moments,* Athlone Press, 1976; (contributor) Thomas Kennedy, editor, *The Dublin Handbook,* 1978; (editor with Gearoid

O'Brien, and contributor) *The Midlands*, 1979; *Titles* (essays), 1981; *Give Me Your Hand* (novel), 1982.

Author of "Death's Echo" (one-act play), first produced in Mullingar, Ireland, at Bounty Hall, 1947.

Work represented in anthologies, including *New Irish Writing*, Irish Press. Contributor of articles, stories, photographs, and reviews to magazines, including *Hibernia, Cara, Books Ireland*, and *Ireland of the Welcomes*, and to national and provincial newspapers.

WORK IN PROGRESS: Publication of a broadcast of the Radio-Telefis-Eireann series *Islands and Authors* expected by Gill & Macmillan in 1982.

SIDELIGHTS: Daly commented: "Initially my literary interest was in writing for the theatre. In the early 1940's I had some success with a one-act play, but did not pursue my luck. Having become interested in photography and being freed from my hospital work because of an accident, I accepted an offer to study color photography in Kent, England. My qualification from this course led me into photojournalism, which I still practice occasionally during the infrequent lulls in my present occupation as reviewer, editor, and literary 'handyman.'

"Thanks to an understanding employer and the blessings of my wife and family, I was able to retire from my hospital work in 1966 with a reasonable pension, and this release gave me an opportunity to concentrate on my writings. I undertook a short spell of study with the British Drama League, intending to return to writing for the theatre, but returned instead to writing short stories. And I was rewarded by publications in the late sixties and early seventies in *New Irish Writing* and by Radio-Telefis-Eireann broadcasts.

"During the early 1970's I concentrated on research. Throughout this period I subsidized my precarious existence by radio and television work, magazine and newspaper features, and photographic contributions. My outstanding award was when I was given an opportunity to read my paper *James Joyce in the Cloak of St. Patrick* at the James Joyce International Symposium in Zurich in 1979. An expanded version of this paper was published as one of the essays in *Titles*.

"This schizoid literary occupation has successfully diverted me from my main object, the completion of the novel *Give Me Your Hand*, which is in the process of what might be termed perpetual revision. But as a firm believer in the maxim, 'Talent does what it can and genius what it *must*,' I am encouraged to continue. Generally speaking, what has been said about me as an author and journalist and about my work is, in my own opinion, more important than anything I might offer, and I am content to let others speak for me. My work has been generally well received even in academic circles where I know I am an intruder, but they have been generous. For this I am grateful, and I feel that my late vocation is vindicated.

"The author James Joyce has played an important part in my literary career, but has made things difficult for me because all I write is judged by commentators as being imitative of Joyce's works. I am sure that Joyce would not agree. All Irish writing is said to be *aural*, and I give talks on this quality in Joyce's works. For the Joyce Centenary in 1982, I am presenting an entertainment of readings and songs, 'An Encounter With Music and Song in the Works of James Joyce.'"

Daly is also researching the "traces of the Ice Ages in Ireland and their effect on history." He is interested in "various aspects of youth and old age with special reference to growing old gracefully."

DANIELS, Jonathan 1902-1981

OBITUARY NOTICE—See index for *CA* sketch: Born April 26, 1902, in Raleigh, N.C.; died after a long illness, November 6, 1981, in Hilton Head Island, S.C. Editor, politician, historian, and author. After graduating from law school, Daniels worked as a reporter for the *Louisville Times* before joining the staff of the *Raleigh News and Observer*, a periodical owned and operated by his father. He left his position as a reporter to live abroad and to write novels. Upon his return to this country, he resumed work at the *News and Observer* as an associate editor. In 1942 Daniels became President Franklin D. Roosevelt's assistant director of the Office of Civil Defense, a post which led to his appointments as Roosevelt's administrative assistant and press secretary. When the president died in 1945, Daniels became an adviser for the Truman administration. Often called a "political gadfly," Daniels returned to the *News and Observer*, gaining attention for the liberal views he expressed in his editorials. After he retired from the paper, he continued writing columns for the *Island Packet*, a newspaper he founded in 1970. As an author, Daniels is best known for disclosing the love affair between President Roosevelt and Lucy Page Mercer, Mrs. Roosevelt's social secretary. *The End of Innocence* contains a brief discussion of the relationship, but *The Time Between the Wars* gives a more detailed account of the affair. His other works include *Clash of Angels, Tar Heels: A Portrait of North Carolina, The Man of Independence, Prince of Carpetbaggers, They Will Be Heard*, and *The Randolphs of Virginia*. Obituaries and other sources: *New York Times*, November 7, 1981; *Newsweek*, November 16, 1981; *Time*, November 16, 1981.

* * *

DARBY, John 1940-

PERSONAL: Born in 1940 in Belfast, Northern Ireland; son of Patrick and Sadie Darby; married Marie McMahon (a teacher), April 13, 1966; children: Patrick, Michael. *Education:* Queen's University, Belfast, B.A. (with honors), 1961. *Home:* 17 Lever Rd., Portstewart, Northern Ireland. *Office:* Department of Social Administration, New University of Ulster, Coleraine, Northern Ireland.

CAREER: History teacher and department head at secondary school in Belfast, Northern Ireland, 1963-71; research and publications officer with Northern Ireland Community Relations Commission, 1971-74; New University of Ulster, Coleraine, Northern Ireland, lecturer in social sciences, 1974—. *Awards, honors:* Fellow of North Atlantic Treaty Organization at Harvard University, 1980.

WRITINGS: Conflict in Northern Ireland, Barnes & Noble, 1976; (editor with Arthur Williamson) *Violence and the Social Services in Northern Ireland*, Heinemann, 1978; *Cartoons and Conflict*, Appletree Press, 1982; (editor) *Northern Ireland: Background to the Conflict*, Appletree Press, 1982; *A Regulated Conflict*, Gill & Macmillan, 1983. General editor of "Social Studies in Ireland," a series, Appletree Press.

SIDELIGHTS: Darby commented: "My main current interest is to use the conflict in Northern Ireland as a model for developing a general theory of conflict, based on its regulation and control. This provides me with an excuse to indulge my enjoyment of travel." *Avocational interests:* Cultivating orchids, research on Esperanto.

DARK, Alvin Ralph 1922-

PERSONAL: Born January 7, 1922, in Comanche, Okla.; son of Ralph (an oil well engineer) and Cordia (Stallions) Dark; married second wife, Jacolyn Troy, April 10, 1970; children: Allison, Gene, Eve, Margaret, Laura, Rusty. Education: Attended Louisiana State University, 1941-43. Home: 608 Neptune Ave., Leucadia, Calif. 92024.

CAREER: Professional baseball player with Boston Braves (now Atlanta Braves), 1946-49, New York Giants (now San Francisco Giants), 1949-56, St. Louis Cardinals, 1956-58, Chicago Cubs, 1958-59, Philadelphia Phillies, 1960, and Milwaukee Braves (now Atlanta Braves), 1960; San Francisco Giants, San Francisco, Calif., manager, 1961-64; Chicago Cubs, Chicago, Ill., coach, 1965; Kansas City Athletics (now Oakland Athletics), Kansas City, Mo., manager, 1966-67; Cleveland Indians, Cleveland, Ohio, manager, 1968-71; Oakland Athletics, Oakland, Calif., manager, 1974-75; San Diego Padres, San Diego, Calif., manager, 1977. Military service: U.S. Marine Corps Reserve, 1942-46, active duty, 1943-46; served in the Far East. Awards, honors: Named Rookie of the Year by Baseball Writers Association, 1948; member of National League All-Star teams, 1951, 1952, and 1954.

WRITINGS: (With John Underwood) When in Doubt, Fire the Manager: The Life and Times of a Born-Again Big Leaguer, Dutton, 1980.

SIDELIGHTS: In 1948, his first full season of major league baseball, Alvin Dark batted .322 and helped the Boston Braves win the National League pennant. During his fourteen years as a player, Dark amassed a lifetime batting average of .291, played on three All-Star teams, and earned a reputation as a smart, scrappy competitor. Since 1961 he has managed in both the National and American leagues, leading the San Francisco Giants and the Oakland Athletics to championship seasons. His most successful year as a field manager came in 1974, when his Athletics defeated the Los Angeles Dodgers four games to one, winning the World Series.

BIOGRAPHICAL/CRITICAL SOURCES: Sports Illustrated, July 6, 1964, March 13, 1967; March 4, 1974, May 20, 1974; New York Times, February 24, 1974, October 19, 1974; Time, June 3, 1974.

* * *

DASH, Samuel 1925-

BRIEF ENTRY: Born February 27, 1925, in Camden, N.J. American lawyer, educator, and author. Since 1965, Dash has been a professor of law at Georgetown University and director of its Institute on Criminal Law and Procedure. He served as chief counsel to the U.S. Senate select committee on presidential campaign activities (the Senate Watergate Committee), 1973-74. His books include Readings in Criminal Justice (Lerner Law Book Co., 1967), Law, Mental Disorders, and the Juvenile Process, four volumes (Research Foundation, Bar Association of the District of Columbia, 1971), and Chief Counsel: Inside the Ervin Committee—The Untold Story of Watergate (Random House, 1976). Address: 110 Newlands St., Chevy Chase, Md. 20015; and Law Center, Georgetown University, Washington, D.C. 20057. Biographical/critical sources: Who's Who in America, 40th edition, Marquis, 1978; Political Profiles: The Nixon/Ford Years, Facts on File, 1979.

DAVIDSON, Irwin Delmore 1906-1981

OBITUARY NOTICE: Born January 3, 1906, in New York, N.Y.; died of cancer, August 1, 1981, in New Rochelle, N.Y. Judge, public servant, and author. Davidson served in the New York State Assembly from 1937 to 1948. He later occupied the Court of Special Sessions before his election to the House of Representatives. Davidson left Congress after one term. He later presided in the Court of General Sessions. In 1958 he was involved in the controversial sentencing of four teenagers to prison terms for murdering a handicapped youth. He wrote of the trial in The Jury Is Still Out. Davidson also served in the New York State Supreme Court in the 1960's. Obituaries and other sources: Current Biography, Wilson, 1956; Biographical Directory of the American Congress, 1774-1971, U.S. Government Printing Office, 1971; Who's Who in America, 39th edition, Marquis, 1976; New York Times, August 2, 1981.

* * *

DAVIES, Andrew (Wynford) 1936-

PERSONAL: Born September 20, 1936, in Cardiff, Wales; son of William Wynford and Hilda Davies; married Diana Huntley (a teacher); children: Bill, Anna. Education: University College, London, B.A. (with honors), 1957. Religion: Atheist. Agent: Harvey Unna & Stephen Durbridge Ltd., 14 Beaumont Mews, Marylebone High St., London W1N 4HE, England.

CAREER: Writer, teacher, and lecturer. Member: Writers' Guild of Great Britain. Awards, honors: Guardian Award for Children's Fiction, 1979, and Globe Horn Award, 1980, both for Conrad's War.

WRITINGS—All for children: The Fantastic Feats of Doctor Boox (illustrated by Tony Escott), Collins, 1972, Bradbury, 1973; Conrad's War, Blackie & Son, 1978, Crown, 1980; The Legend of King Arthur (illustrated by Peter Archer), Collins, 1979; Marmalade and Rufus (illustrated by John Laing), Abelard-Schuman, 1979; Rose (play), Samuel French, 1980.

Author of over a dozen television plays produced by British Broadcasting Corp. (BBC-TV), including "Is That Your Body, Boy?," 1971, "Grace," 1974, "The Water Maiden," 1974, "The Imp of the Perverse," 1975, "The Signalman," 1976, "Happy in War," 1977, and "The Eleanor Marx Trilogy," 1977. Author of two BBC-TV series, "The Legend of King Arthur" and "To Serve Them All My Days." Author of numerous stage plays, including "Filthy Fryer," 1974, "Randy Robinson," 1976, "Going Bust," and "Brainwashing With the Boys." Also author of a dozen radio plays.*

* * *

DAVIES, Richard Llewelyn
See LLEWELYN-DAVIES, Richard

* * *

DAVIES, Walter C.
See KORNBLUTH, C(yril) M.

* * *

DAVIS, Douglas F(redell) 1935-

PERSONAL: Born May 30, 1935, in Red Oak, Iowa; son of

John Francis and Maxine (Fredell) Davis; married Sharon Alexander (an editor), October 2, 1963; children: Brian, Stephen. *Education:* San Diego State University, B.S., 1962; University of California, San Diego, M.A., 1971. *Religion:* Christian. *Office address:* P.O. Box 411, Santa Cruz, Calif. 95061.

CAREER: Scripps Institute of Oceanography, La Jolla, Calif., laboratory technician, 1962-66; Salk Institute, La Jolla, laboratory technician, 1967-68; Forest History Society, Santa Cruz, Calif., editor of *Journal of Forest History,* 1971-73; free-lance writer and editor, 1973—. *Military service:* U.S. Navy, 1954-58.

WRITINGS—Juveniles: The Jumpy Humpy Fuzzy Buzzy Animal Book, Western Publishing, 1973; *There's an Elephant in the Garage,* Dutton, 1979; *The Lion's Tail,* Atheneum, 1980.

WORK IN PROGRESS: The Secret in the Bottle and *The Good Samaritan,* both juveniles.

* * *

DAVIS, Genny Wright   1948-

PERSONAL: Born September 16, 1948, in Culver City, Calif.; daughter of Francis Herald (a welder) and Mary Ellen (Dorney) Wright; married Bruce Lee Davis (a writer and therapist), September 10, 1977. *Education:* Antioch College West, B.A., 1977. *Home and office:* 21 Crest Rd., Fairfax, Calif. 94930. *Agent:* Toni Mendez, Inc., 140 East 56th St., New York, N.Y. 10022.

CAREER: Worked as flight attendant for American Airlines, 1968-76; Center for Spiritual Healing, Fairfax, Calif., co-director, therapist, and healer, 1977—.

*WRITINGS—*All with husband, Bruce Lee Davis: *The Magical Child Within You,* Celestial Arts, 1977; *Hugs and Kisses,* Workman Publishing, 1977; *Lover's Book,* Macmillan, 1980; *Love and Money,* Macmillan, 1981.

WORK IN PROGRESS: Research on the role of love in healing serious illnesses, including "doing spiritual counseling and laying on of hands to help people find their own experience and beliefs in God."

SIDELIGHTS: Genny Davis wrote: "I have lived and studied with the Espiritista Healers in the Philippines, learning about spiritual healing. I have integrated these experiences within this culture, and my husband and I are leaders of a spiritual community, helping people of all faiths realize the power of forgiveness and love as agents of healing our relationships and illnesses. We plan to continue writing books about love and giving workshops around the United States and in Europe, sharing inner healing and helping professionals and patients discover inner resources for healing and spiritual growth."

* * *

DAVIS, Luther   1921-

PERSONAL: Born August 29, 1921, in New York, N.Y.; son of Charles T. (a manufacturer of surgical supplies) and Henrietta (Roesler) Davis; married Dorothy de Milhau, November 5, 1943 (divorced December 1, 1960); children: Noelle, Laura. *Education:* Yale University, B.A., 1938. *Office:* Pictures, Inc., 18 West 55th St., New York, N.Y. 10019.

CAREER: Writer and producer of stage plays and motion pictures, 1946—; Pictures, Inc. (motion picture producers), New York, N.Y., president, 1963—. Vice-chairman of Classic Stage Co., 1980—. *Military service:* U.S. Army Air Corps, 1942-

46; became major. *Member:* New York Athletic Club. *Awards, honors:* Clarence Derwent Award, 1945, for best American play, "Kiss Them for Me"; Fame Award, 1946, for screenplay, "The Hucksters," and 1964, for screenplay, "Lady in a Cage"; Antoinette Perry (Tony) Award, 1953, for collaboration book of "Kismet"; Edgar Allan Poe Award from Mystery Writers of America, 1963, for "End of the World, Baby," and 1970, for "Daughter of the Mind."

*WRITINGS—*Plays: "Kiss Them for Me" (three-act), first produced on Broadway at Belasco Theatre, March, 1945; (author of book with Charles Lederer) "Kismet" (two-act musical; based on the play with same title by Edward Knoblock), first produced on Broadway at Ziegfeld Theatre, December 3, 1953, revival produced on Broadway at New York State Theatre, June 22, 1965; (author of book) "Timbuktu" (two-act musical; based on the musical "Kismet"), first produced on Broadway at Mark Hellinger Theatre, March 1, 1978.

Screenplays: "The Hucksters" (adapted from the novel by Frederic Wakeman), Metro-Goldwyn-Mayer (MGM), 1947; "B.F.'s Daughter" (adapted from the novel by John P. Marquand), MGM, 1948; "Black Hand," MGM, 1950; "A Lion Is in the Streets" (adapted from the novel by Adria Locke Langley), Warner Bros., 1953; (contributor) "New Faces," Twentieth Century-Fox, 1954; (with Charles Lederer) "Kismet," MGM, 1955; "The Gift of Love" (adapted from a short story by Nelia Gardner White, "The Little Horse"), Twentieth Century-Fox, 1958; "Holiday for Lovers" (adapted from the play by Ronald Alexander), Twentieth Century-Fox, 1959; "The Wonders of Aladdin," MGM, 1961; "Lady in a Cage," Paramount, 1963; "Across 110th Street," United Artists, 1972.

Teleplays: "End of the World, Baby," Universal TV, 1964; "Daughter of the Mind" (adapted from a novel by Paul Gallico, *The Hand of Mary Constable*), American Broadcasting Co. (ABC-TV), 1966; "Arsenic and Old Lace" (adapted from the play by Joseph Kesselring), ABC-TV, 1969; "The Old Man Who Cried Wolf," ABC-TV, 1970. Also author of teleplays for "Ford Startime," "Bus Stop" (series), "Kraft Suspense Theatre," "Run for Your Life," and "The Silent Force."

WORK IN PROGRESS: "Escape," a screenplay, for Sanford Frank Productions; producing plays on Broadway by Sumner Arthur Long, Stanley Ralph Ross, and Edmund H. North.

SIDELIGHTS: When Luther Davis's musical adaptation of the play "Kismet" premiered on Broadway in 1953, Brook Atkinson of the *New York Times* called it "a spectacle that resembles nothing so much as a supercolossal Hollywood wonderwork." Set in the ancient city of Baghdad, "Kismet" is an Arabian adventure involving an enterprising bazaar poet, his beautiful daughter, an enamoured caliph, a chief of police, and his wandering wife. The production unfolds against an expensive and elaborate backdrop, replete, as Atkinson reported, with "crowds of Oriental princes, dancing girls and beggars; jewels, gold pieces, bags of money, opulent processionals, high romance, low intrigue and some garnishings of Minsky." The music of Russian composer Aleksandr Borodin also supplies a score to which the dancers moved in "vivid, barbaric, and imaginative" choreography.

Such extravagance, however, "is no substitute for creation," asserted Atkinson. The reviewer declared that "Kismet" was not written, but rather "assembled from a storehouse of spare parts." Acknowledging the musical's popularity (it ran 583 performances), he observed that "many theatregoers are completely satisfied with ostentatious productions that are as full of carnival magnificence as a costume ball. . . . ["Kismet"] is a display of wealth, but it is not a work of art.'' ''For the good things that are in it,'' Atkinson added, ''are not artistically related.''

The 1965 revival of ''Kismet'' opened to similar criticism. *New York Times* writer Lewis Funke remarked that the musical ''takes full advantage of its visual possibilities.'' ''The stage is filled with gorgeous colors,'' he disclosed, and the sets ''summon the ambience of absolute splendor and delicacy.'' Funke claimed the ''sumptuous costumes . . . [would] make even a calif wonder over his extravgance. . . . This production . . . reeks of riches.'' The reviewer concluded that ''*'Kismet'* remains a tiresome, mechanical musical. Age has done nothing to improve the assembly-line job that Charles Lederer and Luther Davis fashioned from the old play by Edward Knoblock. . . . Fortunately, no one takes 'Kismet' seriously.''

Nonetheless, ''Kismet'' was resurrected as the musical ''Timbuktu!'' in 1978. Although the basic story remained with few changes, the location was switched from Baghdad to Mali, West Africa. The previous all-white cast became an all-black one, and into Borodin's music were incorporated African folk themes. The alterations did not improve the production's critical reception. The *New York Times*'s Richard Eder pronounced it ''a lackluster show,'' while Clive Barnes of the *New York Post* assessed that ''it has a great visual production, a stupid book, [and] a travesty of a score.'' Despite such complaints, ''Timbuktu!,'' starring Eartha Kitt and Melba Moore, proved popular, and its Broadway run and tour lasted for nearly one year.

BIOGRAPHICAL/CRITICAL SOURCES: New York Times, March 21, 1945, March 25, 1945, July 18, 1947, March 25, 1948, March 13, 1950, September 24, 1953, December 4, 1953, February 20, 1954, May 1, 1955, May 17, 1955, December 9, 1955, February 12, 1958, July 25, 1959, December 23, 1961, June 11, 1964, June 23, 1965, March 2, 1978; *New York Post*, March 2, 1978; *New York Daily News*, March 2, 1978; *New Yorker*, March 13, 1978.

*   *   *

DAWSON, Robert L(ewis) 1943-

PERSONAL: Born July 26, 1943, in Buenos Aires, Argentina. *Education:* Trinity College, B.A., 1965; Yale University, M.Phil., 1968, Ph.D., 1972. *Office:* Department of French and Italian, University of Texas at Austin, Austin, Tex. 78712.

CAREER: University of Santa Clara, Santa Clara, Calif., acting assistant professor of French and Italian, 1970-72; Rollins College, Winter Park, Fla., assistant professor of French and Italian, 1973-75; University of Texas at Austin, began as assistant professor, 1975, currently associate professor of French and Italian. *Member:* International Society for Eighteenth-Century Studies (member of executive board), American Society for Eighteenth-Century Studies. *Awards, honors:* Fellowship from La Fondation Camargo, 1972-73.

WRITINGS: Baculard d'Arnaud: Life and Prose Fiction, Voltaire Foundation, 1976; (editor-in-chief) *International Directory of Eighteenth-Century Studies,* American Society for Eighteenth-Century Studies, 1979; *Additions to the Bibliographies of Seventeenth- and Eighteenth-Century French Prose Fiction,* Voltaire Foundation, 1981.

WORK IN PROGRESS: Bibliography of French Dramatic Literature, 1790-1800.

DAY, Alan J(ohn) 1942-

PERSONAL: Born September 23, 1942, in London, England; son of Thomas Edward (a clerk) and Peggy (a clerk; maiden name, Parkhouse) Day; married Patricia Ann Hopkin (a research officer), July 5, 1967; children: William Rufus. *Education:* Received degree (with honors) from Magdalen College, Oxford, 1963. *Politics:* Labour. *Religion:* None. *Home:* 11 George St., Bath BA1 2EH, England. *Office:* Longman Group Ltd., 5 Mile's Buildings, Bath BA1 2QS, England.

CAREER: Research assistant to Greek historian Philip Argenti, 1963-67; secondary school teacher of history in North London, England, 1967; Socialist International, London, England, editor and research officer, 1968-73; Longman Group Ltd., Bath, England, deputy editor of ''Keesing's Publications,'' 1973—. *Member:* National Union of Journalists.

WRITINGS: The Socialist International: A Short History, Socialist International, 1969.

Keesing's reference publications series: (Editor with Henry W. Degenhardt) *Political Parties of the World,* Gale, 1980; (general editor) *Treaties and Alliances of the World,* Gale, 1981; (general editor) *Border and Territorial Disputes,* Longman, 1982.

Contributor to political science journals and newspapers.

WORK IN PROGRESS: Further titles in the Keesing's reference publication series.

SIDELIGHTS: Day told *CA:* ''The Keesing's reference publications series, on which I have been working for the past three years and will be for some time to come, represents an attempt to utilize the large store of information in *Keesing's Contemporary Archives,* which celebrated its fiftieth year of continuous weekly publication in July, 1981. By extracting information from the *Archives* (and from sources available in the Keesing's office and elsewhere) on particular subjects such as political parties or treaties and alliances, and then reworking the material into a reference format, we aim to produce useful reference books as an ancillary operation to the production of the weekly *Archives.* The series started with the *Political Parties* book subject, which itself derived from my experiences working for the Socialist International. There I found that precise information about political parties in many countries was simply not available. Moreover, when such information was provided it was often biased in one way or another. Although my association with the Socialist International obviously indicated my own political leanings, the *Political Parties* book we produced (as well as the other titles in the series) grinds no particular ax and simply seeks to present basic data in the objective manner for which Keesing's has obtained a considerable reputation over the years.''

BIOGRAPHICAL/CRITICAL SOURCES: Economist, January 31, 1981.

*   *   *

DAYAN, Moshe 1915-1981

OBITUARY NOTICE—See index for *CA* sketch: Born May 20, 1915, in Deganya in Jordan Valley; died of a heart attack, October 16, 1981, in Tel Aviv, Israel. Soldier, diplomat, politician, and author. Called ''the mysterious Cyclops of Israeli politics,'' Moshe Dayan personified Israeli nationalism and became a symbol of that nation. The first child born in the first kibbutz, which is called Deganiah A in present-day Israel, Dayan was both a warrior and an advocate of peace. He began his military career at the age of twelve when he defended his collective against Bedouins. Two years later he joined the Haganah, for which he received a ten-year jail sentence because of his affiliation with the Jewish militia. During World War II, after his sentence was reprieved owing to his technical expertise, he lost an eye when a bullet hit the telescope through which he was looking, irreparably damaging his left eye socket. In the 1948 war which established Israel's independence, Dayan was the victorious commander of the Jerusalem front. In 1967 Dayan's popularity increased as he moved from minister of agriculture to his new role as defense minister, only two days before the Six Days War. His military success that year gained the Sinai Peninsula, the West Bank, the Golan Heights, the Gaza Strip, and Jerusalem for Israel. The statesman's popularity, however, waned with Israel's defeat in the October War of 1973, and it remained low until Dayan, as Israel's foreign minister, was instrumental in negotiating the Camp David Peace Treaty with Egypt in 1978. He was elected to the Knesset, Israel's parliament, in the 1950's and remained there for two decades, resigning in 1979 because of political differences with Prime Minister Menachem Begin. Anticipating his death, Dayan revealed: "I don't mind dying and never have. Not that I want to die—I just don't give a damn." His works include *Sinai Diary, Living With the Bible, Moshe Dayan: Story of My Life,* and *Breakthrough.* Obituaries and other sources: *New York Times,* October 17, 1981; *Washington Post,* October 17, 1981; *London Times,* October 17, 1981; *Time,* October 26, 1981; *Newsweek,* October 26, 1981, January 4, 1982.

* * *

DEAN, Herbert Morris 1938-

PERSONAL: Born February 7, 1938, in New London, Conn.; married Joan B. Podrat, 1963; children: Julie, Jonathan. *Education:* Columbia University, A.B., 1959; Tufts University, M.D., 1963. *Home:* 1 Barry Rd., Worcester, Mass. 01609. *Office:* Fallon Clinic, Inc., 630 Plantation St., Worcester, Mass. 01605.

CAREER: Bellevue Hospital, Columbia Medical Division, New York, N.Y., intern, 1963-64, resident, 1964-65; Cleveland Metropolitan General Hospital, Cleveland, Ohio, resident, 1965-66; Boston City Hospital, Boston, Mass., chief resident, 1967-68; University of Massachusetts, Amherst, associate in medicine, 1973—, assistant professor of medicine, 1978—. Hematologist-oncologist at Fallon Clinic. Senior physician at St. Vincent Hospital, 1970. *Member:* American Society of Hematology, American College of Physicians (fellow), American Society of Oncology, Massachusetts Medical Society, Massachusetts Society of Internal Medicine, Worcester County Medical Society.

WRITINGS: Look to Your Health, Van Nostrand, 1980. Contributor to medical journals.

WORK IN PROGRESS: A novel describing acute leukemia.

AVOCATIONAL INTERESTS: Collecting antiquarian medical books, tennis, art.

* * *

DEAN, John Wesley III 1938-

PERSONAL: Born October 14, 1938, in Akron, Ohio; son of John Wesley (a businessman) and Sara (Magill) Dean; married Karla Ann Hennings, February 4, 1962 (divorced, 1970); married Maureen Biner Kane, October 13, 1972; children: John Wesley IV. *Education:* Attended Colgate University, 1957-59; College of Wooster, B.A., 1961; graduate study at American University, 1961-62; Georgetown University, LL.B., 1965.

CAREER: Admitted to the Bar of the District of Columbia and the Bar of Virginia, 1965, right to practice law revoked by District of Columbia Court of Appeals, 1974; Hollabaugh & Jacobs, Washington, D.C., law clerk, 1964; Welch & Morgan, Washington, D.C., associate, 1965; House of Representatives Judiciary Committee, Washington, D.C., chief minority counsel, 1966-67; National Committee on Reform of Federal Criminal Laws, Washington, D.C., associate director, 1967-69; Department of Justice, Washington, D.C., associate deputy attorney general, 1969-70; White House, Washington, D.C., counsel to the president of the United States, 1970-73; imprisoned September 3, 1974, released January 8, 1975; writer, 1975—. *Awards, honors:* Mallory Medal; Constitutional Law award; Law Week award; American jurisprudence prizes for excellence in administering law and for excellence in legislation.

WRITINGS: Blind Ambition: The White House Years, Simon & Schuster, 1976. Contributor to periodicals, including *Rolling Stone.*

SIDELIGHTS: John Dean was a principal witness at the Watergate hearings, the first to incriminate Richard Nixon in the conspiracy to cover up the break-in at the offices of the Democratic National Committee. Himself a participant in the conspiracy, Dean revealed to the world the intricacies of wrongdoing at the highest reaches of the American Government.

The initial crime took place on June 17, 1972, when agents of the Committee to Re-elect the President (CREEP) broke into the offices of the Democratic National Committee at the Watergate complex. Dean was called in by White House assistants John Ehrlichman and H. R. Haldeman to coordinate the cover-up. He leaked information from the Justice Department to CREEP officials, synchronized denials and alibis, and arranged payment of "hush money" to the arrested burglars. White House officials later tried to pass Dean off as the "mastermind" behind the conspiracy, but Dean, in *Blind Ambition,* described his role differently: "I was not the source of authority for the cover-up, yet I became the lynch pin."

By April, 1973, Dean had decided to extricate himself from the conspiracy. In exchange for a promise of testimonial immunity from Special Prosecutor Archibald Cox, Dean resigned his post as White House counsel and agreed to testify before the Senate Watergate Committee. Dean's testimony, broadcast on national television, began with a 245-page account of the cover-up conspiracy, including his own and his colleagues' involvement as well as his conversations with the president. Although he was vociferously attacked by White House personnel and members of the Senate investigating committee, Dean's credibility was eventually sustained by the White House tapes, which confirmed his story detail for detail.

Only thirty-four when he resigned, Dean had had a career of swift success, taking him from law school to the White House in just five years. Upon graduation from Georgetown University in 1965, he quickly landed a job with Welch & Morgan, a firm specializing in communications law. The job served more as an object lesson than as a boost to his career, for he was fired after six months, charged with unethical conduct. Patrick Anderson described the episode in the *New York Times:* "One of Dean's first assignments had been to do some legal work on a corporation that Welch had set up to begin a UHF television station in St. Louis. Meanwhile, Dean had met Boyd Fellows, a 'television management expert' employed by the law firm who was interested in seeking a license for his own UHF station in St. Louis. Fellows's group was formed, with Dean and his mother-in-law, Mrs. Hennings, among the backers.'' For reasons of propriety, Dean maintains, he had intended to resign from Welch & Morgan but was dismissed before he could do so.

Dean next turned to politics. Beginning with a position as chief minority counsel to the House Judiciary Committee, at $7,800 a year, he moved quickly into a $25,000-a-year position as associate director of the National Commission on the Reform of Federal Criminal Law. In 1968 he worked with the group of lawyers who helped write Richard Nixon's position papers on crime (he had been pro-Nixon as early as 1960), and when Nixon's law-and-order campaign succeeded, Dean was offered a job as assistant in the attorney general's office. Now working closely with John Mitchell, Dean became, as Anderson explained, ''the middleman in the complicated process of putting together new legislation.''

The John Dean of the 1960's has been described as a hard-working, ambitious man who strove always to please his boss. According to Anderson, ''he was known as a perfect staff man, a man who always touched base, who always protected himself, who never, never exceeded his authority.'' Louis B. Schwartz, professor of criminal law at the University of Pennsylvania and staff director of the law-reform commission, called him ''bright, smooth, likable, very ambitious and very flexible. He adapts. He was so perceptive about the legislative process that I urged him to write a book about it. . . . He knew exactly how a bill could be hustled through and what the obstacles were. I'd be glad for John to come to our law school and lecture on the legislative process.''

On the other hand, William McCulloch, a representative from Ohio who was Dean's boss on the Judiciary Committee, said of him: ''He was an able young man, but he was in a hell of a hurry.'' Some time between his job at the Justice Department and his job at the White House, Dean's marriage to Karla Hennings, daughter of Missouri Senator Tom Hennings, came to an end; after a brief period as a Washington-style playboy, Dean met Maureen Kane, a twenty-seven-year-old widow and insurance company employee. When they married in 1972, Dean financed the honeymoon with a $4,850 ''loan'' from campaign funds, again jeopardizing his reputation and calling his ethics into question.

In June, 1970, Dean was offered the job as counsel to the president at $42,500 a year. Anderson described his duties: ''He rarely saw the President. He worked out legal briefs to support the Administration's preordained positions on such things as executive privilege and impoundment of funds.'' In *Blind Ambition*, Dean noted that he ''became the White House collecting point for anti-war intelligence reports, and . . . funneled information directly to the President during emergencies.'' Gradually winning the acceptance of Ehrlichman and Haldeman, he eventually was involved in matters of increasing significance.

With his intelligence-gathering experience at the Justice Department and knowledge of wiretapping, Dean was naturally included in the original meeting to plan the Watergate break-in and bugging. Then, as Garry Wills wrote in the *Saturday Review*, ''he became the center of the first, lower-level cover-up before he knew exactly how much there was to be covered up.'' In a review of *Blind Ambition* for the *New York Times Book Review*, J. Anthony Lukacs wrote: ''Dean was one of

the sleaziest White House operatives, a compulsively ambitious striver who pandered to his superiors' worst impulses, largely engineered the cover-up of their activities, turned informer just in time to plea bargain for himself, got sprung from prison after serving only four months and then signed a contract to write this book.''

Dean was sentenced to prison by Judge John Sirica on August 2, 1974, having pleaded guilty the previous October to conspiring to obstruct justice. While serving his sentence, Dean testified at the trial of John Ehrlichman, H. R. Haldeman, John Mitchell, Robert Mardian, and Kenneth Parkinson; all but Parkinson were convicted as key figures in the Watergate conspiracy. Then, on January 8, 1975, Judge Sirica reduced Dean's sentence to time already served. Barred from practicing law, Dean embarked on a writing career. An article he did for *Rolling Stone* magazine in October, 1976, resulted in the resignation of Secretary of Agriculture Earl Butz by revealing Butz's penchant for ethnic humor.

Lukacs described *Blind Ambition* as ''a lively chronicle of megalomania and deception, spiced with intriguing new tidbits and surprisingly valuable insights.'' Written with the assistance of Taylor Branch, a journalist, the book offers, in Garry Wills's words, ''a lizard's-eye view of the slime,'' candidly detailing Dean's own guilt as well as the guilt of his cohorts. In 1979, CBS broadcast ''Blind Ambition,'' a four-part, eight-hour composite of Dean's book; his wife's memoir, *Mo: A Woman's View of Watergate;* and portions of the White House tapes. For the rights to their books, the Deans were paid $100,000.

BIOGRAPHICAL/CRITICAL SOURCES—Books: R. W. Apple, Jr., editor, *Watergate Hearings: Break-in and Coverup*, Viking, 1973; James W. McCord, Jr., *Piece of Tape: The Watergate Story, Fact and Fiction*, Washington Media Services, 1974; Maureen Dean and Hays Gorey, *Mo: A Woman's View of Watergate*, Simon & Schuster, 1975; John Dean, *Blind Ambition: The White House Years*, Simon & Schuster, 1976.

Periodicals: *Washington Post*, April 19, 1973, May 20, 1979; *New Republic*, July 7, 1973, June 22, 1974; *New York Times*, July 8, 1973, May 18, 1979; *New Yorker*, July 9, 1973; *Time*, July 9, 1973, July 29, 1974, August 11, 1975, October 25, 1976; *Newsweek*, July 16, 1973, April 8, 1974, May 13, 1974, November 4, 1974, October 18, 1976, July 4, 1977, September 12, 1977; *New York Times Book Review*, October 31, 1976; *New York Review of Books*, November 25, 1976; *Saturday Review*, December 11, 1976; *National Review*, January 7, 1977; *New Statesman*, March 22, 1977; *Broadcasting*, November 28, 1977.*

—*Sketch by Andrea Geffner*

*   *   *

DEAN, Leonard Fellows   1909-

BRIEF ENTRY: Born December 24, 1909, in Three Rivers, Mich. American educator and editor. Dean began teaching in 1939. He was a professor of English at New York University from 1967 until his retirement in 1975. His writings include editions of Shakespeare's *Twelfth Night* (Allyn & Bacon, 1965), *Twentieth Century Interpretations of Julius Caesar: A Collection of Critical Essays* (Prentice-Hall, 1968), *Twelve Great Plays* (Harcourt, 1970), and *The Play of Language* (Oxford University Press, 1971). *Address:* P.O. Box 3151, Damariscotta, Maine 04543. *Biographical/critical sources: Who's Who in America*, 40th edition, Marquis, 1978.

DEAN, Malcolm 1948-

PERSONAL: Born April 29, 1948, in Newcastle, England; son of Thomas Craig and Mildred Catharine (Hoggard) Dean. *Education:* Received degree from Sheridan College, Oakville, Ontario, Canada. *Home:* 77 Pembroke, No. 1, Toronto, Ontario, Canada M5A 2N9. *Office address:* P.O. Box 6299, Toronto, Ontario, Canada M5W 1P7.

CAREER: Publisher, writer, composer, poet, and filmmaker, 1967—. Canadian Broadcasting Corp. (CBC), Toronto, Ontario, junior news editor for National Radio News Service, 1975; Canadian Press, Toronto, news editor for "Broadcast News," 1975-76; CBC-Radio, Toronto, free-lance documentarist, 1977-79; Laidler Radio Productions, Toronto, executive producer, 1979-80. *Awards, honors:* Creativity award from North York Board of Education, 1967, for "Concerto for Tuba."

WRITINGS: The Astrology Game, Beaufort Book Co., 1980; *Censored!: Only in Canada,* Virgo Press, 1981; *Diet Strategy,* Bantam, 1982.

Films: "Helen," North York Board of Education, 1967; "Christopher's Movie Matinee," National Film Board, 1968.

Audio documentaries: "The Pyramids" and "The Book of the Dead," CBC-FM Radio, 1978; "Ancient Egypt" (three-part record album), CBC-FM Radio, 1978; "Astrology: The Cosmic Conspiracy" (five-part record album), CBC-FM Radio, 1979; "Astrocartography," Astro-Carto-Graphy, 1980.

Editor of monograph series "Ephemeris of Chiron, 1890-2000," Phenomena Publications, 1979, 2nd revised edition, 1981, and editor of *Phenomena: The Newsjournal of Cosmic Influence Research,* 1977-79.

WORK IN PROGRESS: Several films and books.

SIDELIGHTS: Dean commented: "All creatures seek to end their suffering. The status quo is neither necessary nor desirable. Therefore, I explore areas of forbidden, suppressed, or denied knowledge in order to shed light on the nature of the universe. Too few stones have been turned over; people are tripping over boulders all the time without realizing they have stubbed their toes.

"*The Astrology Game* contains the only published and complete bibliography of thirty years of statistical evidence accumulated in favor of planetary influences by the French psychologists Michel and Francoise Gauquelin. *Censored!: Only in Canada* is the first fully documented history of Canadian film censorship; it includes capsule histories of U.S. and British film censorship as well."

BIOGRAPHICAL/CRITICAL SOURCES: Toronto Globe and Mail, November 22, 1980; *Toronto Star,* November 23, 1980, March 15, 1981; *Vancouver Province,* January 4, 1981; *Vancouver Sun,* February 6, 1981; *Jersey Journal,* May 4, 1981; *NOW,* October 29, 1981.

* * *

DEAN, William F(rishe) 1899-1981

OBITUARY NOTICE: Born August 1, 1899, in Carlyle, Ill.; died August 24, 1981, in Berkeley, Calif. Military officer and author. Dean rose in rank to major general before his capture by North Koreans in 1950. That same year he was awarded the Medal of Honor for his actions in Taejon, South Korea. Dean spent the remainder of the Korean War in captivity. In 1953 he was released to acclaim as a hero, whereupon he contended that he was "just a dog-faced soldier." He documented his experiences as a prisoner of war in *General Dean's Story.* Obituaries and other sources: *Current Biography,* Wilson, 1954; *Webster's American Military Biographies,* Merriam, 1978; *New York Times,* August 26, 1981.

* * *

de CHARDIN, Pierre Teilhard
See TEILHARD de CHARDIN, (Marie Joseph) Pierre

* * *

DeCLEMENTS, Barthe 1920-

PERSONAL: Born October 8, 1920, in Seattle, Wash.; daughter of Ralph and Doris (Hutton) DeClements; married Don Macri (divorced); married Gordon Greimes (separated); children: (second marriage) Nicole Greimes Southard, Mari, Christopher, Roger. *Education:* Attended Western Washington College, 1940-42; University of Washington, Seattle, B.A., 1944, M.Ed., 1970, further graduate study, 1974-75. *Politics:* Independent. *Religion:* "Non-denominational." *Home:* 1511 Russell Rd., Snohomish, Wash. 98290. *Office:* Woodway High School, 232 100th Ave. W., Edmonds, Wash. 98020.

CAREER: Teacher at junior high school in Kirkland, Wash., 1944-46; Medical-Dental Building Psychiatric Clinic, Seattle, Wash., psychologist, 1947-48; part-time psychologist at public schools in Seattle, 1950-55; elementary school teacher in Edmonds, Wash., 1961-63, junior high school teacher of English, 1963-67, and 1974-78, high school teacher of English, creative writing, and psychology, 1967-74; Woodway High School, Edmonds, counselor, 1978—. Administrative intern at elementary school in Mountlake Terrace, Wash., 1974-75. Volunteer counselor at Open Door Clinic, 1969-73, 1977. Member of Snohomish County Law and Justice Planning Committee, 1970-73.

WRITINGS: Nothing's Fair in Fifth Grade (juvenile; junior Literary Guild selection), Viking, 1981.

WORK IN PROGRESS: I Don't Remember Asking You to Understand Me, a novel for young adults.

SIDELIGHTS: Barthe DeClements wrote: "My first university degree was in English composition and my second was in educational psychology. In my work I have mingled my two main interests, writing and counseling. Now that my children are grown, I have the time to write stories for young people, which I hope will give them vicarious experiences that will change their heads."

* * *

de GRAFF, Robert F(air) 1895-1981

OBITUARY NOTICE: Born June 9, 1895, in Plainfield, N.J.; died November 1, 1981, in Long Island, N.Y. Publisher. De Graff was founder and president of Pocket Books, the publishing house that revolutionized the field by presenting softcover editions of books at a considerably lower price than hardbound equivalents. De Graff established the company in 1939 when he introduced ten titles at a price of twenty-five cents each. In 1964, sales for Pocket Books totaled more than 300 million copies. Obituaries and other sources: *Current Biography,* Wilson, 1943; *New York Times,* November 3, 1981; *Chicago Tribune,* November 4, 1981; *Time,* November 16, 1981.

DELACORTE, Peter 1943-

PERSONAL: Born February 10, 1943, in New York, N.Y.; son of Albert P. (an editor and teacher) and Letitia (an editor; maiden name, McNeil) Delacorte; married Bonnie Baron (a teacher), October, 1976. *Education:* Princeton University, A.B., 1967. *Politics:* "Supply-side anarchist." *Residence:* San Francisco, Calif. *Agent:* Martha Millard, 352 West 19th St., New York, N.Y. 10011.

CAREER: Free-lance magazine writer.

WRITINGS: (With Michael C. Witte) *The Book of Terns* (cartoons), Penguin, 1978; *Games of Chance* (novel), Seaview, 1980.

WORK IN PROGRESS: California Girls, a novel.

SIDELIGHTS: Delacorte told *CA:* "I was not pleased by the fate of my first novel, which got good-to-rave reviews in the trades and in one national magazine whose circulation is in the billions, but which was virtually unbuyable three weeks after its publication. I am disheartened by editors who rely on silly formulas ('If you can't describe it in a sentence or two, it's not commercial'). The publishing industry, motivated I think more by fear than by economic necessity, is taking a route already traveled by the movie business and charted by television. It is not so much an ethic of giving the public what it wants as it is an obtuse program aimed at the lowest common denominator. Good books, or good movies, or good TV programs that manage to succeed do so usually because they happen to fit into a popular pigeonhole. Authors who are unwilling to conform must have very forceful agents or considerable outside incomes.

"I decided to be a writer when I was fifteen. Were there a time machine at my disposal right now, I would jump into it, get back there and tell myself to get into computer chips. The problem is that I wouldn't believe me."

*   *   *

DELATTRE, Pierre 1930-

PERSONAL: Born July 2, 1930, in Detroit, Mich.; son of Pierre and Ina (Kanto) Delattre; married Nancy Ortenstone; children: Michele, Marc, Carla, Jenny. *Education:* University of Pennsylvania, B.A. (with honors), 1951; University of Chicago, B.D., 1955; Instituto Allende, M.A., 1968. *Politics:* Left. *Religion:* Buddhist.

CAREER: Worked as Presbyterian and Congregational street minister and as founder of center for poetry, art, and theatre in San Francisco, Calif., all 1958-62; waterfront laborer in San Francisco, 1962-65; Instituto Allende, San Miguel de Allende, Mexico, professor of creative writing, 1965—. Director of arts awareness program at Minnesota Museum of Art, 1977. *Awards, honors:* Fellow of MacDowell Colony.

WRITINGS: Tales of a Dalai Lama (fiction), Houghton, 1971; *Walking on Air* (novel), Houghton, 1981. Editor of *Beatitude.*

*   *   *

DELBRIDGE, Rosemary 1949(?)-1981

OBITUARY NOTICE: Born c. 1949; died of a stroke, December 31, 1981. Consumer advocate and journalist. As a member of the British National Consumer Council, Delbridge helped alter legislation to include statutes such as the Credit Unions Act.

She was an advocate of women's rights. Her writings include co-authorship of *Buy Right.* Obituaries and other sources: *London Times,* January 2, 1982.

*   *   *

Del MAR, Marcia 1950-

PERSONAL: Born May 14, 1950, in Cuba.

CAREER: Currently psychiatric social worker in California.

WRITINGS: A Cuban Story, Blair, 1979.

WORK IN PROGRESS: "A Cuban Story," a screenplay.

SIDELIGHTS: For what she described as "political considerations," Marcia Del Mar does not divulge background information, but she told *CA:* "Being a Cuban exile, I wanted to write about our experiences prior to, during, and after the revolution in order to promote greater understanding of the problems and issues that we, as Cubans, have faced both in the United States and in Cuba."

*   *   *

de los RIOS, Francisco Giner
See GINER de los RIOS, Francisco

*   *   *

DEMENT, William Charles 1928-

BRIEF ENTRY: Born July 29, 1928, in Wenatchee, Wash. American psychiatrist, educator, and author. Dement has been a physician since 1955. He began teaching at Stanford University in 1963 and became a professor of psychiatry in 1967; he was named director of Sleep Research Laboratories in 1963 and Sleep Disorders Clinic and Laboratory in 1970. He has received awards from American Psychiatric Association, New York Academy of Medicine, and American Psychological Association. Dement wrote *Some Must Watch While Some Must Sleep* (Stanford Alumni Association, 1972) and *Sleep and Aging* (Raven Press, 1980), and edited *Narcolepsy* (S. P. Boods Division, Spectrum, 1976) and *Sleep Apnea Syndromes* (Alan R. Liss, 1978). *Address:* 440 Gerona Rd., Stanford, Calif. 94305; and Department of Psychiatry, School of Medicine, Stanford University, Stanford, Calif. 94305. *Biographical/critical sources: American Men and Women of Science: The Physical and Biological Sciences,* 14th edition, Bowker, 1979; *Newsweek,* July 13, 1981.

*   *   *

DENT, Robert William 1917-

PERSONAL: Born September 8, 1917, in Portland, Ore.; son of Vyvyan Henry (in business) and Jean (Harden) Dent; married Ellen Margaret Quinlivan (a manager in technical communications), August 3, 1957; children: Vivian, Paul, Mary, John, Sheila. *Education:* University of Oregon, B.A., 1940, M.A., 1942; University of Chicago, Ph.D., 1951. *Politics:* Democrat. *Home:* 15450 Deerhorn, Sherman Oaks, Calif. 91403. *Office:* Department of English, University of California, Los Angeles, Calif. 90024.

CAREER: University of Chicago, Chicago, Ill., instructor in humanities, 1947-51; University of California, Los Angeles, instructor, 1952-56, assistant professor, 1956-60, associate professor, 1960-65, professor of English, 1966—. *Military service:* U.S. Navy, 1942-46; became lieutenant. *Member:*

Modern Language Association of America, Renaissance Society of America, Malone Society, Shakespeare Society of America (bibliographer, 1959-65).

WRITINGS: John Webster's Borrowing, University of California Press, 1960; *Shakespeare's Proverbial Language: An Index,* University of California Press, 1981.

WORK IN PROGRESS: Proverbial Language in English Drama, Excluding Shakespeare, 1495-1616: An Index, publication expected in 1983.

SIDELIGHTS: Dent commented: "I am scarcely a writer in the *Contemporary Authors* sense. My principal publication to date, *Shakespeare's Proverbial Language: An Index,* is just what its title implies: a tool for editors and critics of Shakespeare. It was the outgrowth of a long-standing interest in proverbs, especially of Shakespeare's age, and an almost as long dissatisfaction with Shakespeare's editors and critics in this respect. The volume is an extensive supplement to a Shakespeare index by M. P. Tilley published in 1950. *Proverbial Language in English Drama, Excluding Shakespeare, 1495-1616: An Index,* an almost completed sequel providing similar information for all extant English drama from Henry Medwall to the year of Shakespeare's death, has no such predecessor; it should therefore be of even greater use to students of Marlowe, Jonson, Chapman, and the like. I have enjoyed the underlying research over the past three decades, and it is now a great satisfaction to see the results reaching the publication stage."

*   *   *

DENTRY, Robert
  See WHITE, Osmar Egmont Dorkin

*   *   *

DENYS, Teresa [a pseudonym]   1947-

PERSONAL: Surname is pronounced Dennis; born April 29, 1947, in London, England; daughter of Joseph George (a police officer) and Marjorie (Bird) Denys. *Education:* Attended girl's secondary school in London, England. *Politics:* "Tory, inclining to liberal." *Religion:* Church of England. *Home:* 192 Odessa Rd., Forest Gate, London E.7, England.

CAREER: Newham Public Library Service, London, England, library assistant, 1965-67, branch librarian, 1967-69; National Farmers' Union Insurance Society, Stratford-on-Avon, England, actuarial clerk, 1969-71; Winn Industries Ltd., London, private secretary, 1971-74; writer, 1974—. *Member:* Romantic Novelists Association.

WRITINGS: The Silver Devil (romantic novel), Futura, 1978, Ballantine, 1979; *The Flesh and the Devil* (romantic novel), Futura, 1979, St. Martin's, 1981.

WORK IN PROGRESS: A historical novel set in seventeenth-century England and France and in modern England, publication by Futura expected in 1982; research on ancient Greek legends and epic poetry.

SIDELIGHTS: Teresa Denys told *CA:* "I began writing eight years before thinking of submitting my first manuscript, which was luckily accepted instantly. The principal problems are finding sufficient time to write and my own perfectionism. Currently I am having to travel much too far and too frequently and have difficulty in balancing the demands of two careers and a private life, plus any home life that is not spent at the typewriter."

AVOCATIONAL INTERESTS: Classical theatre, poetry, music.

*   *   *

de SAUSSURE, Eric   1925-

PERSONAL: Born December 23, 1925, in Geneva, Switzerland; came to the United States in 1978; son of Jean (a minister) and Liliane (de Crousaz) de Saussure. *Education:* Attended Ecole des Beaux Arts, 1946-47, and Accademia delle Belle Arti, 1948-49. *Home:* 413 West 48th St., New York, N.Y. 10036.

CAREER: Brother of (interdenominational) monastic Community of Taize, 1949; painter and stained glass artist in Taize, France, 1949-78, and New York, N.Y., 1978—. Work represented in solo and group shows, including Salon d'Art Sacre and Festival Aix-en-Provence, in private collections, including Musee des Estampes, and churches in the United States, Japan, and Europe.

WRITINGS: (Illustrator) *Taize Picture Bible,* Fortress, 1969; *The Secret of Hell's Kitchen* (self-illustrated juvenile), Seabury, 1980. Also author and illustrator of *La Poule dans le pick up,* 1956.

WORK IN PROGRESS: Big Battle in Central Park, a self-illustrated children's book, for Fortress; a self-illustrated children's book, tentatively titled *Yaphank Yaphank.*

SIDELIGHTS: De Saussure is a monk of the Community of Taize, an international brotherhood of Protestants and Roman Catholics dedicated to reconciliation and communion of Christians of all denominations. In 1978 he and a few other brothers were sent to a small Taize community in the "Hell's Kitchen" area of New York City.

De Saussure told *CA:* "In New York I lived in a poor area of Manhattan. It inspired my writing because of good friendships with the street kids. I am chiefly a painter, but from time to time I like to create something for children. As a monk and a painter I have always been interested in creating a religious art in a very modern language. My paintings are abstract and rather demanding. For this reason, I like to have a time of leisure—then, I draw for children or construct puppets. I write for 'young' people from eight to eighty years old.

"*The Lord of the Rings* was one of my first English readings and had an impact on my American writings. My work received several reviews, some good and some severe. I didn't keep them, because as an artist I have never been interested in the opinions of critics. But, I can say that children have responded very well. I am often invited to speak in schools, and I get letters and telephone calls."

BIOGRAPHICAL/CRITICAL SOURCES: Episcopal Times, November, 1980.

*   *   *

DESPALATOVIC, Elinor Murray   1933-

PERSONAL: Surname is pronounced Des-pa-*la*-to-vitch; born August 10, 1933, in Cleveland, Ohio; daughter of Clyde Eugene (a social worker) and Janet (a social worker; maiden name, Page) Murray; married Marijan Despalatovic (a college teacher), August 18, 1962; children: Pavica Catherine, Mirna Susan. *Education:* Attended Oberlin College, 1951-53; Barnard College, B.A. (cum laude), 1955; attended University of Vienna, 1955-56; Columbia University, M.A., 1959, Ph.D., 1969. *Politics:* Democrat. *Religion:* Society of Friends (Quakers). *Home:*

111 Nameaug Ave., New London, Conn. 06320. *Office:* Department of History, Connecticut College, New London, Conn. 06320.

CAREER: University of Michigan, Ann Arbor, lecturer in history, 1962-63; Yale University, New Haven, Conn., research assistant in southern Slavic history, 1964-65; Connecticut College, New London, instructor, 1965-68, assistant professor, 1968-73, associate professor, 1973-78, professor of history, 1978—, chairman of department, 1980—. Member of East European selection committee of International Research and Exchanges Board, 1973-76.

MEMBER: American Historical Association (member of executive council on Slavic and East European studies, 1981-84), American Association for the Advancement of Slavic Studies, American Association for Southeast European Studies (member of executive board, 1973-76), American Association for Croatian Studies (member of executive council, 1981-84), American Association of University Professors, Conference on Slavic and European Studies (member of executive council, 1979—), Croatian Studies Association (member of executive council, 1979—), Phi Beta Kappa. *Awards, honors:* Fulbright fellow, 1955-56, 1971-72, 1978-79; fellow of American Council of Learned Societies, 1971-72; fellow of International Research and Exchanges Board, 1971-72, 1978-79.

WRITINGS: Ljudevit Gaj and the Illyrian Movement, East European Quarterly Press, 1975; (editor with Joel M. Halpern, and author of preface) Rudolf Bicanic, *How the People Live,* University of Massachusetts Press, 1981. Contributor of about twenty articles and reviews to scholarly journals.

WORK IN PROGRESS: The Origins of the Croatian Peasant Party, Part I: *Croatian Peasant Society to 1900,* Part II: *The Founding of the Croatian Peasant Party.*

SIDELIGHTS: Despalatovic told *CA:* "I've had contact with Eastern Europeans most of my life, so it was almost natural that I would specialize in Slavic studies. My parents were social workers, and we lived in the settlement houses where my parents worked; when I was quite young we lived in Slavic communities near Pittsburgh. Then we moved to New York City, and in those settlement houses I got to know refugees from Eastern and Central Europe who were just emigrating, new workers and residents—this was 1940 to 1949. My contact with them interested me in Eastern Europe. Later, as a music student, I became interested in German and eventually studied in Vienna. There I was engaged in East European studies and traveled extensively in that area.

"Choosing a field is not necessarily an intellectual activity. You have to find something that you know will interest you for a long time, something that draws you. It's like choosing a mate. As it happens, my husband is a Croatian, so I now have family as well as professional ties to Eastern Europe. I'm from old American stock myself—Scots-Irish with a little Native American—so I see in my children a blend of my heritage and my individual interest.

"As for writing, in the first stages it's painful, but it's part of what I do; it grows out of my work."

AVOCATIONAL INTERESTS: Music, languages, travel, hiking, camping.

*   *   *

DETZLER, Wayne Alan   1936-

PERSONAL: Born April 18, 1936, in Pontiac, Mich.; son of

Russell D. (a telephone company supervisor) and Edwina Ruby (a teacher) Detzler; married Margaret Partridge, July, 1957; children: Carol, Mark. *Education:* Wheaton College, Wheaton, Ill., B.A., 1959, M.A., 1961; Victoria University of Manchester, Ph.D., 1974. *Home:* 1 Western Rd., Horfield, Bristol BS7 8UP, England. *Office:* Kensington Baptist Church, 208 Stapleton Rd., Easton, Bristol BS5 0NX, England.

CAREER: Ordained Baptist minister, 1960; teacher at Bible school in Seeheim, West Germany, 1964-70; pastor of evangelical church in Stockport, England, 1970-71; Moorlands Bible College, Sopley, England, teacher, 1971-73; Greater Europe Mission, Wheaton, Ill., associate director and member of board of directors, 1973-79; Kensington Baptist Church, Bristol, England, pastor, 1979—. Member of board of directors of Nordiska Bibelinstitutet, Institut Biblique Belge, Moorlands Bible College, Belfast Bible College, and Havering Christian Bookshop. *Member:* Ecclesiastical History Society (England), Pi Gamma Mu.

WRITINGS: The Changing Church in Europe, Zondervan, 1979; *Living Words in Ephesians,* Evangelical Press, 1981.

Contributor: Derek Baker, editor, *Studies in Church History,* Cambridge University Press, 1974; Helmut Bukhardt and Kurt Heinbucher, editors, *Brockhaus Gemeindelexikon* (title means "Brockhaus Church Dictionary"), Wuppertal, 1978. Contributor to *New International Dictionary of the Christian Church* and *Eerdmans Handbook of Christianity.* Contributor to magazines.

WORK IN PROGRESS: Living Words in 1 Peter.

SIDELIGHTS: Detzler commented: "Since arriving in Europe in 1961, I have taken a lively journalistic interest in European religious life. At first I wrote articles for periodicals on both sides of the Atlantic, then in 1977 I wrote my first book. Inasmuch as I intend to live in Europe indefinitely, I plan to write further on European church life and to present lectures in Europe and the United States, which I visit three times annually."

*   *   *

DEVLIN, Bernadette (Josephine)   1947-

PERSONAL: Born April 23, 1947, in Cookstown, County Tyrone, Northern Ireland; daughter of John James (a carpenter) and Elizabeth Bernadette Devlin; married Michael McAliskey (a teacher and dogbreeder), 1973; children: Roison Elizabeth and two other children. *Education:* Attended Queen's University, 1965-69. *Politics:* Socialist. *Religion:* Catholic. *Home:* Coalisland, near Belfast, Northern Ireland.

CAREER: Civil rights activist in Northern Ireland. British Parliament, member from Mid-Ulster, 1969-74.

WRITINGS: The Price of My Soul (autobiography), Knopf, 1969.

SIDELIGHTS: During a civil rights demonstration in Londonderry, Northern Ireland, in October, 1968, Devlin witnessed police beating a young man who had tried to protect her. She later told *Vogue:* "My reaction to what I saw was sheer horror. I could only stand rooted as the police battered and beat, and eventually I was dragged off by another student who came between me and a police baton. After that I *had* to be committed." The experience gave direction to the anger and activism that had been growing in her, and Devlin went on to speak to the crowds for two hours that day. She has continued her role as movement leader and civil rights activist ever since.

Devlin, who has been called everything from an Irish Joan of Arc to a "miniskirted Fidel Castro," felt compelled at the age of twenty-two to write her autobiography, *The Price of My Soul*. To counteract newspaper reports that focused on her youth, gender, and wardrobe rather than her principles, she drew a self-portrait emphasizing the social problems among which she was raised and her dedication to correcting those problems. Devlin explained the book's title: "[It does] not [refer to] the price for which I would be prepared to sell out, but the price we all must pay in life to preserve our own integrity. To gain that which is worth having, it may be necessary to lose everything." Elizabeth Lee Haselden of *Christian Century* related, "With a strong sense of Irish history, personal experience of both economic and religious prejudice, and a 'Catholic background, more strongly Christian than Catholic,' the author depicts herself and Northern Ireland's people and problems with clarity, wit and a surprising amount of objectivity." William McPherson declared in the *Washington Post* that "Devlin has written a magnificent book, full of Gaelic passion and Gaelic despair, irony, self-mockery, wit and outrage—most of all outrage, and so intense as to be overwhelming were it not for the grace with which it is expressed." Noting "her war, however holy, is not religious but economic," McPherson described *The Price of My Soul* "as a most effective personification of the convulsive worldwide struggle of the powerless against the powerful."

Devlin's working-class background strongly influenced her self-styled Marxist beliefs. As she recounted in her autobiography, she grew up listening to her father's bedtime stories, not of fairies and princesses, "but the whole parade of Irish history . . . the English oppression and risings, the English-Irish Trade Agreement that crippled the country's economy." She felt the effects of that economy personally, for her father, whose work card had been randomly stamped "political suspect," could find no work in Ulster and had to travel to England to earn a living.

She experienced also the class division that kept the Catholic minority of Ulster from uniting. Her father was the son of a road sweeper, but her mother had come from a respected, middle-class family. As a result of "marrying down," she was disowned by her family, and the Devlins were ostracized by the community. Out of these experiences, Devlin concluded that the problems in Northern Ireland are economic rather than religious. She believes the hostility between Catholics and Protestants is being used as a weapon by the capitalists to keep the working class of both religions oppressed.

The early death of Devlin's father and the family's subsequent hand-to-mouth existence reinforced her political philosophy. Devlin's father died when she was nine, and her mother, with six children to care for, was forced to live on welfare, an experience Devlin found humiliating. "We have a welfare state that says everybody must be looked after," she contended in *Ms.* "Yet if you need assistance—say, to clothe your children—the welfare come into your house, and you have to prove, by dragging out all your children's clothes, that they are unfit for wearing. This is, to me, the depths of degradation, which I saw as a matter of course in my own family. It has always angered me, and I refuse to allow other people to go through this in order to get welfare. Nobody should be reduced to producing their underwear for the state."

When Devlin was eighteen, her mother died. Despite her familial responsibilities, she managed to put herself through college. It was at Queen's University that she first became involved in politics. Taking action against the injustice she viewed, she helped found the People's Democracy, which she described

as a "non-partisan, non-political organization based on the simple belief that everyone should have the right to a decent life." The goal of the group was equal opportunity, especially in housing and employment, for all citizens of Ulster. It united members of all backgrounds and religions into a common cause, and Devlin was selected as one of "the ten faceless members of a faceless committee" chosen to reduce the role of well-known student personalities.

Initially, Devlin functioned as an organizer of sit-ins and picket lines. She also helped plan the "long march" from Belfast to Londonderry in January, 1969. Then in February of the same year, when the prime minister of Northern Ireland, Terence O'Neill, called for a general election, the People's Democracy decided to formally enter politics. Eight student candidates joined the race, with Devlin challenging then Minister of Agriculture James Chichester-Clark, who later became prime minister. In the election, the Protestant Unionists lost sizable chunks of their majority. Devlin received over one third of the vote in her district for a seat that had gone uncontested for twenty years. The dramatic election was followed by riots in several parts of the country.

When the minister of Parliament for Mid-Ulster died the following month, his widow, Anna Forrest, was selected as the Unionist candidate for the reelection. Devlin opposed her. Determined to run on policy and not stirred-up prejudice, she campaigned tirelessly, traveling the countryside promoting her socialist platform. In *Vogue* Polly Devlin described Devlin: "Passionately articulate, with a quick wit and ready repartee, Bernadette Devlin can make any number of people listen to her, can sway them, scold them, or encourage them, without a pause, without hesitancy, without pretension, without arrogance, and with total conviction."

The twenty-one-year-old activist won the election, becoming the youngest person elected to the British Parliament since William Pitt in 1781, and the youngest woman ever. With disdain for the established behavior code of Parliament, she immediately became its most controversial member. "The British House of Commons has moved so far away from its original function and conception that it has almost forgotten what it's there for," she asserted. "It's concerned with ritual and protocol, and members forget that the *only* reason they are there is because of their constituents." On her first day at Westminster, disregarding protocol and the tradition that kept maiden speeches short and innocuous, she condemned the Unionist power structure in an impassioned address that earned a standing ovation and made newspaper headlines.

Further flouting convention, Devlin continued to participate in civil rights demonstrations. She was arrested several times, once in the House of Commons for assaulting Reginald Maudling, the British home secretary in charge of Northern Ireland. In August of 1969 she manned the barricades at a violent demonstration in Bogside, a Londonderry slum. For her actions she was tried and convicted of "riotous behavior." Sentenced to Armagh Prison, she served four months of her six-month term from June to October, 1970. Four years later Devlin lost her seat in Parliament to a fellow civil rights activist, but she continued to fight for economic equality in Ireland.

Although accused of advocating violence as a means to achieve her political aims, Devlin was determined to work within the law. Before her conviction she cut short a United States tour to raise founds for Ulster's riot victims when she discovered that the agency sponsoring her trip also supported the Irish Republican Army (IRA). When violence mounted in Northern Ireland in the 1970's and more and more men were imprisoned,

Devlin became one of the principal supporters of the IRA hunger strikers fighting for political prisoner status in Ulster jails. In 1980 she led sympathy marches in both Northern Ireland and the Republic of Ireland, speaking out against the settlement that temporarily ended the strike in December.

On the morning of January 16, 1981, in her cottage near Belfast, Devlin and her husband, Michael McAliskey, were shot by intruders. Apprehended on the scene were three men suspected of being members of the Red Hand Commandos, an illegal Protestant extremist group. Devlin and her husband were shot several times each and upon their release from the hospital went into seclusion. In April, however, Devlin announced she would once again run for a seat in Parliament. Intending to campaign in support of political prisoner status for jailed members of the IRA, she yielded to the candidacy of hunger striker Bobby Sands, who won the seat but later died of self-imposed starvation in prison.

Interviewed by J. Fitzgerald in *Ms.*, Devlin assessed her contribution to the civil rights movement in Northern Ireland: "If I have made any contribution, I hope it is that people in Northern Ireland think of themselves in regard to their *class,* as opposed to their religion or to their sex or whether they are well educated. . . . I hope that what I did was to get rid of the feeling of guilt, of inferiority that the poor have; the feeling that somehow God is or they are responsible for the fact that they are not as rich as Henry Ford." Alvin Shuster in the *New York Times Book Review* described her activism: "Trouble was brewing in Northern Ireland, and much of the credit for waking up London and the world to its explosive problems must go to . . . Bernadette Devlin."

BIOGRAPHICAL/CRITICAL SOURCES—Books: Bernadette Devlin, *The Price of My Soul,* Knopf, 1969; George William Target, *Bernadette: The Story of Bernadette Devlin,* Hodder & Stoughton, 1975; Mary-Ellen Kulkin, *Her Way,* American Library Association, 1976.

Periodicals: *Newsweek,* November 3, 1969, October 6, 1975; *New York Times,* November 5, 1969, January 17, 1981, January 18, 1981, January 19, 1981, January 21, 1981, January 22, 1981, February 27, 1981, March 22, 1981; *Saturday Review,* November 8, 1969; *Commonweal,* November 28, 1969; *Best Sellers,* December 15, 1969; *New York Times Book Review,* December 28, 1969; *Atlantic,* January, 1970; *New Yorker,* January 10, 1970; *Christian Century,* February 4, 1970, September 2, 1970; *Washington Post,* March 5, 1970; *Vogue,* August, 1970; *New York Times Magazine,* August 9, 1970; *Ms.,* January, 1975; *People,* May 28, 1979.*

—Sketch by Andrea Geffner
and Anne M. Guerrini

*   *   *

DEVLIN, Gerard M(ichael)   1933-

PERSONAL: Born August 9, 1933, in Waltham, Mass.; son of Joseph Patrick (a plumber) and Anne Marie Devlin; married Leona Virginia Cormier, July 11, 1954; children: Michael G., Deanna-Lyn M., Patricia M. Devlin Petree. *Education:* Graduated from U.S. Army Command and General Staff College. *Politics:* Independent. *Religion:* Roman Catholic. *Home and office:* 21 Saturn Lane, Nashua, N.H. 03062.

CAREER: U.S. Army, career officer, 1950-70, retiring as major; personnel director at American Microwave Corp., 1970-72, and Data General Corp., 1972-75. *Member:* 82nd Airborne Division Association (chairman of Lieutenant General James M. Gavin chapter). *Awards, honors*—Military: Distinguished Ser-

vice Cross, five Bronze Stars, Purple Heart, two Vietnamese Crosses, Combat Infantryman Badge with Star, Senior Parachutist Badge.

WRITINGS: Paratrooper!: The Saga of U.S. Army and Marine Parachute and Glider Combat Troops During World War II (foreword by W. P. Yarborough), St. Martin's, 1979.

WORK IN PROGRESS: A book on the development and combat employment of the U.S. Army Air Force glider pilots in World War II, publication expected in 1982.

SIDELIGHTS: Devlin commented: "I'm a writer of military history, specializing in World War II. Like most guys who spent twenty years in military service, I've been to nearly all parts of the globe. I saw combat in Korea and Vietnam and can speak, read, and write Vietnamese. I have chosen to write about military history and war, since it is something I know about. Hopefully, my writing will illustrate to readers the ugliness and futility of wars and will, in some way, contribute to peace."

*   *   *

DIXON, Colin J.   1933-

PERSONAL: Born November 3, 1933, in London, England; son of Raymond James (an electrician) and Frances (a draftswoman; maiden name, Griffiths) Dixon; married Helen Gibbons (a writer), July 27, 1958; children: Sorrel, Bryony, Garth. *Education:* Received B.Sc., 1957, and A.R.S.M. from Imperial College of Science and Technology, London. *Politics:* Socialist. *Religion:* "Lapsed Quaker." *Home:* 13 Park Rd., Richmond TW10 6NS, England. *Office:* Imperial College of Science and Technology, University of London, Prince Consort Rd., London SW7 2BP, England.

CAREER: University of London, Imperial College of Science and Technology, London, England, lecturer in geology, 1957-68; Ecole des Mines de Paris, Paris, France, research fellow, 1968-69; University of London, Imperial College of Science and Technology, senior lecturer in geology, 1969—. Consultant in economic geography. *Military service:* British Army, 1952-54. British Army Reserve, 1954-57; became sergeant. *Member:* International Association for Mathematical Geology, Institution of Geologists, Geological Society of London.

WRITINGS: Atlas of Economic Mineral Deposits, Chapman & Hall, 1979. Contributor to scientific journals.

WORK IN PROGRESS: Principles of Mining Geology; research on the mineral potential of central Saudi Arabia.

SIDELIGHTS: Dixon commented: "I have devoted my career to teaching and research in the application of geology to mining and mineral exploration. I have acted as consultant to industry and government, mostly in Europe, Africa, and the Near East. I have also campaigned for better state education and have been involved in local political activities. Much of my time has also been spent rebuilding and maintaining an early nineteenth-century house of some architectural interest in Richmond."

*   *   *

DIXON, Jeanne   1936-
(Mary Wood Harper, Josephine Rector Stone)

PERSONAL: Born July 18, 1936, in Two Medicine, Mont.; daughter of Phil E. (a rancher) and Mary (a baker; maiden name, Whipple) Parker; children: Andrea, James. *Education:* Attended University of Denver and University of Montana.

Religion: Protestant. *Address:* Box 5542, Missoula, Mont. 59806. *Agent:* Wendy Weil, Julian Bach Literary Agency Inc., 747 Third Ave., New York, N.Y. 10017.

CAREER: Visalia School, Visalia, Ky., teacher, 1956-57; Terminous School, Terminous, Calif., teacher, 1959-60; associated with Petersen Publishing, Hollywood, Calif., 1960-61; San Fernando Valley public schools, San Fernando Valley, Calif., janitor, 1962-63. Has also worked as a cemetary plot salesperson, a city directory interviewer, and a cook for the National Park Service.

WRITINGS—Juveniles; all published by Atheneum: (Under pseudonym Josephine Rector Stone) *Those Who Fall From the Sun* (fantasy), illustrated by Mal Luber, 1978; (under Stone pseudonym) *Praise All the Moons of Morning* (fantasy), 1979; (under Stone pseudonym) *Green Is for Galanx* (fantasy), 1980; (under Stone pseudonym) *The Mudhead* (fantasy), 1980; *Lady Cat Lost,* 1981.

WORK IN PROGRESS: Under pseudonym Mary Wood Harper, three contemporary romances for Ballantine; a book about bicycle motocross racing for Atheneum, publication expected in 1983.

SIDELIGHTS: ''I was born in North Central Montana at the edge of the Blackfeet Reservation,'' Dixon told *CA.* ''My father was a trapper, a herder, an old-time mountain man. He became foreman of a large sheep ranch, and my earliest years were spent in the company of sheep, sheepdogs, and herders.

''We had so much land we could not see to the end of it, so much land we could not cover it in two days on horseback. Such space was always a glory to me, and I think to my father, but it was a great trial to my mother, who loved parties and conversation. I will always think of her there in our two-room house teaching me to conjugate Latin verbs and how to dance the Big Apple. This was at the end of the Depression, and there were no libraries, no bookstores. Just the same, my mother managed to find me the complete works of Dickens, and she read aloud to me every night from Dickens and from the Bible.

''Our lives were fairly simple then. We had no electricity, no indoor plumbing, no roads, no neighbors for thirty miles. Old Lady Flat Tail was our nearest neighbor, and she looked after me when my parents went away on business, buying sheep, or selling wool, or looking at tractors. Old Lady Flat Tail was a witch doctor, and always had strange things bubbling in pots. She taught me cures for diseases and taught me charms to make me strong. She was a good person, I'm sure, but I was always very glad when my parents came along to pick me up.

''When it was time for me to enter the first grade, I had to leave the ranch and go into town. This was terrible for me because not only did I have to leave my animals and friends behind, but I did not understand about streets, or streetlights, or other children. My teacher warned me I must never jaywalk or I would go to jail. I thought this meant I was not supposed to walk like a bird, and I was very careful never to hop on the sidewalk.

''Eventually we moved to a larger town. This was a terrible catastrophe for me because I went from an environment of freedom to the stifling atmosphere of a city school where we were praised for conformity and scorned for any show of individuality. I was so bored I was sick. My only escape was through my imagination. When the teacher thought that I was a good girl for following her instructions to the letter, I was actually off in a world of my own making, a world peopled with strange creatures: giant lizards, psychic dogs, and mud heads. It was at this time that I began to write.''

Dixon has since become accustomed to cities, and has seen many of the far-away places that once occupied her daydreams. ''I have traveled extensively through the Soviet Union and Scandinavia,'' she said, ''and lived in England for long periods of time.''

Rural Montana is still Dixon's home. ''I have two children, and sometimes it strikes me how very different their childhood is from my own. Although we still live in Montana, Montana is no longer a frontier, and that makes all the difference.''

AVOCATIONAL INTERESTS: Volunteer work, gardening, photography, reading, travel, teaching classes in writing, supporting bicycle motocross.

*　　*　　*

DOCKERY, Wallene T. 1941-

PERSONAL: Born December 15, 1941, in Lineville, Ala.; daughter of Oscar W. and Helen (Irby) Threadgill; married Rex Dockery (a university football coach), July 10, 1971; children: Trey Wallace, John Dee. *Education:* University of Tennessee, Knoxville, B.S., 1964. *Home:* 2734 Hunter's Forest Dr., Germantown, Tenn.

CAREER: Knoxville News-Sentinel, Knoxville, Tenn., reporter, 1967; WBIR-TV, Knoxville, Tenn., weather reporter, 1968-71, hostess of daily morning show, ''Wallene's World,'' 1969-72; *Memphis Press-Scimitar,* Memphis, Tenn., sports columnist, 1981—. *Member:* South Plains Writers (president, 1978-80).

WRITINGS: Weather or Not (juvenile nonfiction), illustrations by Steve Laughbaum, Abingdon, 1976; *Gabby's Christmas Wish* (juvenile fiction), illustrations by Maurine Zook, Shoal Creek Publishers, 1978.

SIDELIGHTS: Dockery told *CA:* ''My interests are certainly the big motivation in my writing. For example, when I was the WBIR-TV weather reporter, I had to speak to many civic groups and school classes. I noticed that there was little available elementary material explaining weather in simple but interesting terms. *Weather or Not* was my attempt to remedy this situation, and it obviously worked, as my book appears in school and public libraries all over the U.S.

''My second book, *Gabby's Christmas Wish,* is especially dear to me. The theme, an evergreen who longs to grow up, was taken from a story my father used to tell me when I was a child. I expanded the story with fiction-writing techniques and changed the viewpoint character to Gabby the Gadabout, who isn't just any bird—he's a Yellow-Chested Red-Crested Winter-Vested Gadabout not about to take no for an answer. So when he finds out his best friend Tommy, a tiny, wistful evergreen, wants more than anything to be a Christmas tree, Gabby sets out to make it happen. But Gabby and Tommy find out the hard way that everyone grows at his own pace, that trees don't grow as fast as Gadabout birds, and nothing in the world can change that. Finally, Gabby's good-hearted solution makes the Christmas wish come true and in the process the wish becomes greater—not that Tommy would be different, but that others would see how wonderful he is.

''My only disappointment is that my father died of cancer several months before the book was published and never saw the dedication: 'In memory of my father, Oscar W. Threadgill, who taught me that we should not be measured by physical size but by the capacity of our hearts.'

''My present writing is also motivated by a personal interest—sports. Since my husband is head football coach at Memphis

State University and my two sons are also very sports-oriented, I am enjoying a new role—that of a sports columnist. I make *no* attempt whatsoever to be objective. In fact, what has made my column so successful and fun to write is the fact that I try to steer away from straight sports reporting. I'm trying to appeal to all readers, women and children included, showing stories behind the stories, the vulnerability of players, coaches, families—the human side of sports.''

* * *

DOERKSON, Margaret 1921-

PERSONAL: Surname is pronounced Dirkson; born February 10, 1921, in Glen Leslie, Alberta, Canada; daughter of David L. (a trapper) and Margaret (McLennan) Dana; married Isaac Doerkson (a forester), October 12, 1938; children: Douglas, Constance Doerkson Baril, Janet Doerkson Hegland. *Education:* Attended elementary school in Alberta, Canada. *Politics:* Social Democrat. *Religion:* Pantheist. *Home address:* Eagle Boy Rd., Box 103, Blind Bay, British Columbia, Canada V0E 1H0.

CAREER: Writer, 1971—. *Member:* Wolf Defenders, Wild Kokwa. *Awards, honors:* Winner of *Edmonton Journal* short story contest, 1972, for ''The Gravel Pit.''

WRITINGS: Jazzy (novel), Beaufort Book Co., 1980.

WORK IN PROGRESS: A contemporary novel; research on natives of North America, witchcraft, superstitions, metaphysics, and religions.

SIDELIGHTS: Margaret Doerkson told *CA:* ''I suppose my involvement with nature, both by circumstance and by inclination, has influenced me the most, along with an insatiable curiosity and a lifelong affair with reading.''

* * *

DOLDEN, A(lfred) Stuart 1893-

PERSONAL: Born May 4, 1893, in London, England; son of Alfred Edwin (an accountant) and Sophia (Luck) Dolden; married Lilian Sharp, February, 1922 (deceased); children: Kenneth Stuart (deceased), Alan John. *Education:* Gibson and Wheldon Law School, Law Society Certificate, 1914. *Politics:* Conservative. *Religion:* Church of England. *Home:* Oaklands, 49 Knighton Lane, Buckhurst Hill, Essex, England.

CAREER: British Railways, London, England, solicitor, 1914-56. *Military service:* British Army, London Scottish Regiment, 1914-18.

WRITINGS: Cannon Fodder (nonfiction), Blandford, 1980, revised edition, 1981.

SIDELIGHTS: Dolden told *CA:* ''Upon returning to my position with the legal department of the Great Eastern Railway, after my demobilization from the London Scottish Regiment in 1919, I was informed by my chief that, as I had spent an open-air life for over four years, I would find it very hard to settle. Therefore, he advised me to go into the common law-criminal section, to enable me to have a more mobile life. I then represented the company in the county and magistrates' courts, and as the Great Eastern Railway merged into the London and North Eastern Railway (and subsequently all railways were nationalized) my area increased considerably, and I spent my life attending courts from London to the Scottish border. I was engaged in an advisory position with the British Rail Legal Service from its inception until I retired at the age of sixty-two.

''During my four-and-a-half years of Army service, I kept, against King's Regulations, a daily diary in small notebooks and on any scraps of paper available. On demobilization I used these to compile a narrative which made my experiences more readable, which I called 'C'est la guerre.' It was not until 1978 that I lent this to one of my old comrades whose enthusiasm for it urged me to consider putting it into a suitable condition for publication under the category of social history; thus, *Cannon Fodder* was born. The Imperial War Museum has requested that the original diaries and papers be sent to them for preservation in their archives.

''The special feature of my book is that it is based on facts and events that were recorded on the very day or soon afterwards and nothing was left to memory. There are many other incidents that I can vividly remember now, but since I cannot remember places or the time at which they took place, I refrained from mentioning them in the book.''

* * *

DONNACHIE, Ian Lowe 1944-

PERSONAL: Born June 18, 1944, in Lanark, Scotland; son of Henri Alsop and Christina (Macleod) Donnachie; married Norma King Stewart, August 11, 1969. *Education:* University of Glasgow, M.A. (with honors), 1966; University of Strathclyde, M.Litt., 1969, Ph.D., 1976. *Politics:* Socialist. *Home:* 21 Woodburn Ter., Edinburgh EH10 4SS, Lothian, Scotland. *Office:* Department of History, Open University in Scotland, 60 Melville St., Edinburgh EH3 7HF, Scotland.

CAREER: University of Strathclyde, Glasgow, Scotland, research assistant in history, 1967-68; Napier College, Edinburgh, Scotland, lecturer in history, 1968-70; Open University in Scotland, Edinburgh, staff tutor in history, 1970—. Consultant, lecturer, and broadcaster. *Member:* Economic History Society, Association for Industrial Archaeology, Association of University Teachers, Society of Antiquaries of Scotland.

WRITINGS: (With John Butt and J. Hume) *Industrial History: Scotland,* David & Charles, 1968; *Industrial Archaeology of Galloway,* David & Charles, 1971; (with Innes Macleod) *Old Galloway,* David & Charles, 1974; *Roads and Canals, 1700-1900,* Holmes McDougall, 1976; (with Alasdair Hogg) *The Wars of Independence and the Scottish Nation,* Holmes McDougall, 1976; (with others) *Historic Industrial Scenes,* Moorland, 1977; (with Butt) *Industrial Archaeology in the British Isles,* B&N, 1979; *A History of the Brewing Industry in Scotland,* Humanities, 1979; (with Macleod) *Victorian and Edwardian Scottish Lowlands From Historic Photographs,* Batsford, 1979, David & Charles, 1980.

Also author of course material for Open University: *War and Economic Growth in Britain, 1793-1815,* 1973; (editor with A. Marwick) *War and Society: Nineteenth and Twentieth Century Documents,* 1973; *Historical Field Studies and Industrial Archaeology,* 1974; *Popular Politics, 1750-1950: Owenite Radicalism,* 1974; *Poverty and Social Welfare in Britain, 1870-1950,* 1974; *The Revolutions of 1848: Britain and Ireland in the 1840's,* 1976; *Technology, Weaponry, and Collaboration, 1939-1975,* 1980.

Author of television films, including ''Great Britain, 1750-1950: Gatehouse-of-Fleet—A Study in Industrial Archaeology'' and ''The Revolutions of 1848: Urban Poverty and Its Remedies.''

Contributor to history and archaeology journals. Assistant editor of *Industrial Archaeology,* 1968-77.

WORK IN PROGRESS: British Radical Politics Since 1900; a biography of independent Labour party leader James Maxton; research on Australian history and on Scottish economic and social history of the nineteenth century.

* * *

DONNELLEY, Dixon   1915-1982

OBITUARY NOTICE: Born July 29, 1915, in Forest Hills, N.Y.; committed suicide, January 6, 1982, in Bethesda, Md. Journalist and public official. Donnelley worked for the *New York Daily News* in the 1930's before moving to the *Washington Post* and then the *Washington Daily News.* He later edited *Visao,* an American magazine published in Brazil. An expert on Latin America and economics, Donnelley advised President Eisenhower and served President Johnson's administration as assistant secretary of state for public affairs. He wrote *Establishing and Operating a Small Newspaper.* Obituaries and other sources: *Who's Who in Government,* Marquis, 1977; *Washington Post,* January 8, 1982.

* * *

DORSON, Richard M.   1916-1981

OBITUARY NOTICE: Born March 12, 1916, in New York, N.Y.; died September 11, 1981, in Bloomington, Ind. Educator, historian, editor, and author. Dorson taught American folklore at Indiana University. His writings include *Davy Crockett: American Comic Legend, New England Popular Tales and Legends, America Rebels: Narratives of the Patriots,* and *American Folklore.* Obituaries and other sources: *New York Times,* September 23, 1981; *AB Bookman's Weekly,* October 19, 1981.

* * *

DOTSON, John L(ouis), Jr.   1937-

PERSONAL: Born February 5, 1937, in Paterson, N.J.; son of John L. (a postal examiner) and Evelyn (a seamstress, maiden name, Nelson) Dotson; married Peggy Burnette (a real estate agent), April 4, 1959; children: John L. III, Christopher, Brandon, Leslie. *Education:* Temple University, B.S., 1958; graduate study at Wayne State University, 1966-68. *Home:* 14 Side Hill Rd., Westport, Conn. 06880. *Office: Newsweek,* 444 Madison Ave., New York, N.Y. 10022.

CAREER/WRITINGS: Newark Evening News, Newark, N.J., reporter, 1959-64; *Detroit Free Press,* Detroit, Mich., reporter and rewriter, 1965; *Newsweek,* New York, N.Y., reporter in Detroit, 1965-69, deputy chief of Los Angeles bureau, 1969-70, chief of Los Angeles bureau, 1970-75, news editor and senior editor, 1975—. Member of board of directors of Institute for Journalism Education, 1975—, treasurer, 1976-79, chairman, 1980—. Chairman of Tri-W Black Families, 1980. *Military service:* U.S. Army Reserve, 1958-65; became first lieutenant. *Awards, honors:* D. Jour. from Temple University, 1981.

Notable assignments include coverage of the 1963 march on Washington in support of civil rights, urban violence during the 1960's, the 1971 Los Angeles earthquake, the 1972 presidential campaign, and the 1976 and 1980 presidential nominating conventions.

SIDELIGHTS: Dotson told *CA:* "I have always felt that the journalist has a special place in society, for he is the recorder of activity in its every nook and cranny, however small and unimportant. Somewhere, at some level of journalism, virtually everything is recorded. Not all of it gets read by as large an audience as *Newsweek*'s, but that does not diminish its importance; it is being recorded and somewhere it is being read. I like that idea in principle, but it is not enough. More ideas must be brought to a larger audience. That is why I feel a special dedication to major-media journalism. Those of us who are minorities bring a special dimension to journalism that has been missing until recently. We provide access to a segment of society—and a viewpoint—that had been hidden from general view for too long."

* * *

DOTY, Carolyn   1941-

PERSONAL: Born July 28, 1941, in Tooele, Utah; daughter of Oran Earl (an engineer) and Dorothy (a teacher; maiden name, Anderson) House; married William Doty (an analyst), February 2, 1963 (divorced); children: Stuart William, Margaret. *Education:* University of Utah, B.F.A., 1963; University of California, Irvine, M.F.A., 1979. *Home:* 307 East 76th St., #5, New York, N.Y. 10021. *Agent:* Rhoda Weyr, William Morris Agency, 1350 Avenue of the Americas, New York, N.Y. 10022.

CAREER: School Testing Service, Berkeley, Calif., assistant director, 1965-70; San Francisco State University, San Francisco, Calif., lecturer, 1980; writer. Member of Squaw Valley Community of Writers. Personnel director of Camping Unlimited for Retarded Children; member of board of directors of Berkeley Day Care Center for the Retarded. *Awards, honors:* Honorable mention from Joseph Henry Jackson Competition of San Francisco Foundation, 1975, for novel in progress; award for excellence from Santa Barbara Writers Conference, 1978.

WRITINGS: A Day Late (novel), Viking, 1980; *Fly Away Home* (novel), Viking, 1982. Contributor to *Paris Review, Bay Guardian, Berkeley Gazette,* and *Los Angeles Times.*

WORK IN PROGRESS: Two novels, *With No Kisses* and *The Cellophane Man.*

SIDELIGHTS: Doty's novel *A Day Late* concerns two grief-stricken people, Sam and Katy, who meet when the latter is picked up by Sam while hitchhiking. Sam's daughter has recently died of a brain tumor, and Katy's boyfriend abandoned her when he discovered her pregnancy. Rosemarie Stewart wrote in the *Sunday Denver Post* that although "the subject matter sounds grim, it doesn't come off that way." *Los Angeles Times* critic Mary Cross observed that "Doty has stripped away the histrionics, the larger-than-life aspects of that emotion, and dealt with grief in a realistic, almost clinical fashion." But, Cross added, "Essentially, this is a short story. . . . The novel doesn't work because it can't. Carolyn Doty tried to cover a ceiling with a miniature."

A reviewer for *New York Times Book Review,* however, was impressed with *A Day Late.* "Carolyn Doty . . . writes with lovely feeling and kindness about her people," contended the critic, who added, "This may be a first novel, but it is the work of a gifted novelist, a writer of intelligence and style who is not afraid to probe into characters too rich and complex for the easy, labeling adjective." The review ended with the assertion that "it takes a writer of considerable skill to make [the characters] seem so absolutely right together, so believable as companions on a journey."

Doty told *CA:* "My principal area of interest lies in writing fiction set in the small towns of the western United States, undoubtedly because I grew up in one of them. The characters I write about tend to be those who have experienced some human tragedy or trauma out of the ordinary range of things. I like to take a character who has done something inconceivable to most people—a child molester, for example—and see if I can't go backward from the event and find experiences, events, etc., that make the action more comprehensible. Also, because of my training and interest in painting, I like to create as visual an environment as is possible, again dealing primarily with the mountains, deserts, and small towns of Utah, Nevada, and Montana.

"I also enjoy teaching creative writing in spite of those who maintain it can't be done. What can be given, I believe, is as much knowledge about the tools available, and as much information as one has at one's command about what it takes to be a writer."

BIOGRAPHICAL/CRITICAL SOURCES: Los Angeles Times, April 24, 1980; *Boston Sunday Globe,* April 27, 1980; *New York Times Book Review,* May 4, 1980; *Sunday Denver Post,* June 8, 1980; *Washington Post Book World,* June 15, 1980; *Christian Science Monitor,* July 30, 1980; *Times Literary Supplement,* May 31, 1981.

* * *

DOWNES, Edward (Olin Davenport) 1911-

PERSONAL: Born August 12, 1911, in Boston, Mass.; son of Edwin Olin (a music critic) and Marian Amanda (Davenport) Downes; married Mildred Fowler Gignoux, October 23, 1943 (divorced August, 1954). *Education:* Attended Columbia University, 1929-30, Manhattan School of Music, 1930-32, Sorbonne, University of Paris, 1932-33, University of Munich, 1932, and 1934-36, and 1938-39; Harvard University, Ph.D., 1958. *Home:* 1 West 72nd St., New York, N.Y. 10023.

CAREER: New York Post, New York City, assistant music critic, 1936-38; *Boston Evening Transcript,* Boston, Mass., music critic, 1939-41; W67 NY-Radio, New York City, commentator and assistant program manager, 1941-42; Office of Strategic Services, Washington, D.C., intelligence analyst and editor, 1943-46; Boston Museum of Fine Arts, Boston, program annotator and lecturer in music, 1946-50; Longy School of Music, Cambridge, Mass., instructor in music, 1948-49; Wellesley College, Wellesley, Mass., lecturer in music, 1948-49; University of Minnesota, Minneapolis, assistant professor of music history, 1950-55; *New York Times,* New York City, assistant music critic, 1955-58; Metropolitan Opera Broadcasts, New York City, quizmaster, 1958—; New York Philharmonic-Symphony Society, New York City, program annotator, 1960-74, and intermission host of symphony broadcasts, 1964-66; Queens College of the City University of New York, professor of music history, 1966-81; WQXR-Radio, New York City, intermission host for "First Hearing" broadcast series, 1968—. Musicologist in residence at Bayreuth Festival Master Classes, 1959-65; music series lecturer at Metropolitan Museum of Art, 1960-66. *Military service:* U.S. Army, 1942-45. *Member:* International Musicological Society, American Musicological Society, American Institute for Verdi Studies, American Music Library Association, Instituto Italiano, Egypt Exploration Society, The Bohemians.

WRITINGS: (Translator) Franz Werfel and Paul Stefan, editor, *Verdi: The Man in His Letters,* L. B. Fischer, 1942, reprinted, Vienna House, 1973; *Adventures in Symphonic Music,* Farrar & Rinehart, 1943, reprinted, Kennikat, 1972; (editor, with H. C. Robbins Landon) Christian Bach, *Temistocle* (opera),

Universal (Vienna), 1965; (editor, with Barry Brook and Sherman Van Solkema) *Perspectives in Musicology,* Norton, 1972; *New York Philharmonic Guide to the Symphony,* Walker & Co., 1976; *Guide to Symphonic Music,* Walker & Co., 1981. Contributor of book reviews and articles to newspapers and periodicals, including *New York Times, Musical Quarterly, Art News, Journal of the American Musicological Society, Notes,* and *Opera News.*

WORK IN PROGRESS: A book on Mozart, for Dutton.

BIOGRAPHICAL/CRITICAL SOURCES: Opera News, April 18, 1970; Bernard Rosenberg and Deena Rosenberg, *The Music Makers,* Columbia University Press, 1978.

* * *

DOWSEY-MAGOG, Paul 1950-

PERSONAL: Born May 23, 1950, in Tripoli, Libya; son of John Myers (a British soldier) and Winifred (a nurse; maiden name, Harnett) Dowsey-Magog. *Education:* St. Mary's College, London, Certificate in Education, 1971. *Politics:* "There are no parties suitable for allegiance; I would prefer small community bodies." *Religion:* "Agnostic or possibly Pantheistic." *Residence:* Cullen Bullen, New South Wales, Australia. *Office:* Querencia, Cullen Bullen, New South Wales 2790, Australia.

CAREER: Teacher of drama, English, and social studies at a state school in Sydney, Australia, 1972-73; Harnett Constructions (specialists in underground installation of cables and pipelines), Sydney, Australia, field project manager, 1973—. Actor with amateur drama companies. Director of a private trust company. Member of local bush fire brigade. *Member:* Organic Farmers Association.

WRITINGS: Overland Through Asia: An Underground Guide, New Glide, 1974.

WORK IN PROGRESS: A nonfiction guide to modern homesteading in Australia, publication expected in 1983; *Trench* (tentative title), a novel about work in an Irish construction company in Australia, publication expected in 1985; a collection of his poems since 1970; a nonfiction book on prevailing attitudes of the late 1960's and early 1970's.

SIDELIGHTS: Dowsey-Magog told *CA:* "One of my main interests is travel to countries with cultures different from my own. I speak English with a variety of local accents, as well as a European polyglot, a self-made mixture of French, Dutch, Italian, German, Yugoslav, and Spanish, and I speak smatterings of such Asian languages as Turkish, Hindi, Pharsee, and Malay. When arriving in a new country, I make a point of learning the basics of communication and I have never had any problem conversing with anyone. A good grounding in Latin may have helped.

"I have increased my awareness by travel, which I have been doing since I was born. My first book is a travel guide for the impecunious, as I have never had much in the way of finance. My first travels were as part of a soldier's family, throughout the Middle and Far East; later, I went by myself through Europe and North America, and then overland from England to Australia. I still have intentions to wander through South America, Scandinavia, and Africa, but these have taken second place for the moment to the development of my homestead in Australia.

"I love the great outdoors and being at one with nature, even in adversity. I have enjoyed camping in both snow and desert.

I have a great liking for trees. I am building a stone house on one hundred acres of bushland in the Blue Mountains, and preparing for imminent retirement to a life of near-self-sufficiency, traditional crafts, and natural lifestyle. Although I am not in any way qualified, I am designing my home and building it completely by myself. I appreciate the beauty in natural materials and in functional design. Something that is nearly one hundred percent functional in all possible areas is not only artistically creative, but also very rare.

"I enjoy reading, good company, and intelligent conversation, an art which is virtually dead—a most distressing symptom of our progress toward nonindividuality.

"My overriding interest is in enhancing and enriching the quality of life, both my own and that of others. There is a grave possibility that future generations may become stagnant city dwellers trapped in self-propagated norms. Modern education seems to skim the surface of too many subjects, or specialize in too few, without giving people tools that enable the individual to learn in depth by himself. Much has already been learned and lost, but can be found again in the great richness of the older rural tradition. Alternative lifestyles are fine, provided we do not pollute them with our modern incompetence to understand the traditional ways of man and nature or create alternatives that are simply spin-offs of our current civilization.

"My main stumbling block, of course, is the creation of time. Perhaps one lifetime will not suffice to scour the depths or learn the skills in so many different areas—the list is endless! Until we can eliminate the waste of time involved in coping with plain existence and the time wasted in the packaged luxury of entertainment provided merely to alleviate the pain of this coping, we don't stand any chance at all."

AVOCATIONAL INTERESTS: Music (folk, classical, rock), good cooking, theatre (especially experimental theatre).

*   *   *

DOWSON, Ernest Christopher   1867-1900

BRIEF ENTRY: Born August 2, 1867, in Kent, England; died of tuberculosis, February 23, 1900, in London, England. English poet, translator, and author of short stories. Left impoverished after the death of his father and the suicide of his mother, Dowson earned his living by translating the work of such French writers as Voltaire, Balzac, and Zola. The inspiration for his most highly regarded poem, "Non sum qualis eram bonae sub regno Cynarae," commonly referred to as "Cynara," is often attributed to his unrequited love for Adelaide, the young daughter of a London restaurateur. Typical of Dowson's poetry and short stories are themes of unhappiness in love, loss of innocence, and the inevitability of death. The mood of unfulfilled longing that permeates his work, coupled with his recklessly unhealthy lifestyle, made him exemplary of what his contemporary William Butler Yeats termed the "tragic generation." Dowson is frequently associated with the 1890's *fin de siecle* (or decadent) period in literature, and much of his early poetry appeared in *The Yellow Book* and *The Savoy,* magazines considered to be the literary showcases for that period. Included among his works are *Dilemmas: Stories and Studies in Sentiment* (1895), *Verses* (1896), and *The Pierrot of the Minute: A Dramatic Phantasy in One Act* (1897). *Biographical/critical sources: Penguin Companion to English Literature,* McGraw, 1971; *Cassell's Encyclopaedia of World Literature,* revised edition, Morrow, 1973; *Twentieth-Century Literary Criticism,* Volume 4, Gale, 1981.

DREW, Kenneth
See COCKBURN, (Francis) Claud

*   *   *

DRYDEN, Ken(neth Wayne)   1947-

PERSONAL: Born August 8, 1947, in Hamilton, Ontario, Canada; son of David Murray and Margaret Adelia (Campbell) Dryden; married Lynda Leah Curran, May 9, 1970. *Education:* Cornell University, A.B., 1969; McGill University, LL.B., 1973.

CAREER: Montreal Voyagers (professional hockey team), Montreal, Quebec, goaltender, 1970-71; Montreal Canadiens (National Hockey League [NHL] team), Montreal, goaltender, beginning in 1971. Member of Canadian team in Canada-Soviet Union hockey series, 1972. Worked on water pollution project with consumer advocate Ralph Nader, summer, 1971; legal adviser to Society to Overcome Pollution, 1972—; member of board of directors of Mont St. Hilaire Nature Foundation. *Member:* Red Key Society, Quill and Dagger, Sigma Phi. *Awards, honors:* Conn Smythe Trophy for most valuable player in NHL Stanley Cup Playoffs, 1971; Calder Memorial Trophy for NHL rookie of the year, 1972; named athlete of the year, 1972; Vezina Trophy for lowest goals-against average in NHL, 1973, 1976-79.

WRITINGS: (With Mark Mulvoy) *Face-Off at the Summit,* Little, Brown, 1973; (with Cec Eaves and John Macfarlane) *Let's Play Better Hockey* (juvenile), photographs by Brian Pickell, McDonald's Restaurants, 1973; (with Rick Salutin) *Les Canadiens* (play), Talonbooks, 1977.

SIDELIGHTS: While managing a career in hockey and the demands of law school, Dryden found time in 1971 to work for Ralph Nader and his raiders. After studying the problem of water pollution with the consumer advocate, Dryden devoted himself to preventing further pollution of water resources. "I've seen, for example, what a sad, sad thing it is when an oyster bed dies," he once commented. He therefore began promoting the creation of a national organization of fishermen, businessmen, and manufacturers that could do research and lobby for clean water. He also became a legal adviser to the Society to Overcome Pollution.

BIOGRAPHICAL/CRITICAL SOURCES: New York Times, August 8, 1971; Murray Dryden and Jim Hunt, *Playing the Shots at Both Ends: The Story of Ken and Dave Dryden,* McGraw, 1972; Frank Orr, *Great Goalies of Pro Hockey* (juvenile), Random House, 1973; Orr, *Hockey Stars of the Seventies* (juvenile), Putnam, 1973; Stan Fischler, *Kings of the Rink* (juvenile), Dodd, 1978.*

*   *   *

DUCHENE, Louis-Francois   1927-

PERSONAL: Born February 17, 1927, in London, England; son of Louis A. (a hotelier) and Marguerite (Laine) Duchene; married Anne M. Purves (a novel reviewer), March 6, 1952; children: Anne Catherine. *Education:* London School of Economics and Political Science, London, B.Sc., 1947. *Home:* 3 Powis Villas, Brighton, Sussex BN1 3HD, England. *Office:* European Research Centre, University of Sussex, Brighton, England.

CAREER: Manchester Guardian, Manchester, England, leader writer, 1949-52; press attache for European Coal and Steel Community in Luxembourg, 1952-55; *Economist,* Paris, France, leader writer, 1956-58; Documentation Center of Action Committee for the United States of Europe, Paris, chief of cabinet, 1958-63; *Economist,* London, England, leader writer, 1963-67; International Institute for Strategic Studies, London, director, 1969-74; University of Sussex, Brighton, England, director of European Research Centre, 1974—. *Awards, honors:* Ford Foundation research grant on international affairs, 1967-69.

WRITINGS: (Editor) *The Endless Crisis: America in the Seventies,* Simon & Schuster, 1970; *The Case of the Helmeted Airman: A Study of W. H. Auden's Poetry,* Rowman & Littlefield, 1972.

WORK IN PROGRESS: A long poem.

AVOCATIONAL INTERESTS: Poetry, chess, travel, hill walking.

*   *   *

DUCKWORTH, Leslie Blakey   1904-
(Blake Lesley)

PERSONAL: Born November 12, 1904, in Bradford, England; married Sarah Rosalind Phillips, September 5, 1927. *Education:* Attended school in Bradford, England. *Religion:* Church of England. *Home:* Birchfield House, Histons Hill, Codsall, Staffordshire WV8 2HA, England.

CAREER: Worked as reporter for *Yorkshire Evening Argus,* Bradford, England; *Express and Star,* Wolverhampton, England, began as reporter, became news editor, 1927-46; *Birmingham Gazette,* Birmingham, England, editor, 1948-50; *Birmingham Post,* Birmingham, news editor, 1950-65, assistant to editor, 1965-69; free-lance writer, 1969—. Member of executive committee of Staffordshire branch of Council for the Protection of Rural England; member of council of Staffordshire branch of Nature Conservation Trust. *Member:* Royal Society for the Protection of Birds, British Trust for Ornithology, Codsall and District Civic Society. *Awards, honors:* Member of Order of the British Empire, 1970; Jubilee Literary Award from Cricket Society, 1975, for *The History of Warwickshire County Cricket Club.*

WRITINGS: (With M. Bartlett-Hewitt) *Music in Our Town: The Story of a Civic Hall,* Cornish Bros., 1945; *Cricket My Love,* Cornish Bros., 1946; *S. F. Barnes: Master Bowler,* Hutchinson, 1967; *Holmes and Sutcliffe: The Run Stealers,* Hutchinson, 1970; *The History of Warwickshire County Cricket Club,* Stanley Paul, 1974. Also author of *Cricket From the Hearth.* Author of a weekly column in *Birmingham Post.* Contributor to magazines and newspapers (sometimes under pseudonym Blake Lesley).

WORK IN PROGRESS: A collection of countryside essays; continuing research on the game of cricket.

AVOCATIONAL INTERESTS: The environment, the countryside, wildlife, the amenity movement.

*   *   *

DUE, Linnea A.   1948-

PERSONAL: Born April 3, 1948, in Berkeley, Calif.; daughter of Floyd O. (a psychoanalyst) and Ellen (a nurse; maiden name, Anderson) Due. *Education:* Sarah Lawrence College, B.A., 1970; University of California, Berkeley, M.A., 1971. *Home and office:* 5846 Vallejo St., Oakland, Calif. 94608.

CAREER: Educational Development Corp., Menlo Park, Calif., writer, 1973-74; Classified Flea Market, Oakland, Calif., graphic designer, 1974-78; Diana Press, Oakland, in advertising, 1978; Oakland Graphics, Oakland, typesetter, 1978—. Editor for Straight Arrow Press, 1973-75. *Awards, honors: High and Outside* was listed among best books for young adults by American Library Association, 1980.

WRITINGS: High and Outside (young adult novel), Harper, 1980.

WORK IN PROGRESS: The Woman Who Starved Herself to Death, a novel that follows six college women since 1968.

SIDELIGHTS: Due told *CA:* "I began *High and Outside* when I returned from a trip—I had a week off work, and no one knew I was in town—so I locked myself in my study and started writing. I became so involved with my characters I wouldn't have been surprised in the least if they'd rung my doorbell one morning. This is the joy of writing for me—when the characters assume their own identities and run away with the story, leaving my idea of the book behind. Listening to the characters is much more interesting than writing about them, and eventually, I suspect, results in a better book."

BIOGRAPHICAL/CRITICAL SOURCES: Library Journal, June 15, 1980, *Best Sellers,* September, 1980.

*   *   *

DUFRECHOU, Carole
See MONROE, Carole

*   *   *

DURANG, Christopher (Ferdinand)   1949-

PERSONAL: Born January 2, 1949, in Montclair, N.J.; son of Francis Ferdinand and Patricia Elizabeth Durang. *Education:* Harvard University, B.A., 1971; Yale University, M.F.A., 1974. *Religion:* "Raised Roman Catholic." *Home address:* c/o O'Brien, 103 East 86th St., New York, N.Y. 10028. *Agent:* Helen Merrill, 337 West 22nd St., New York, N.Y. 10011.

CAREER: Yale Repertory Theatre, New Haven, Conn., actor, 1974; Southern Connecticut College, New Haven, drama teacher, 1975; Yale University, New Haven, playwriting teacher, 1975-76; playwright, 1976—. Actor in plays, including "The Idiots Karamazov" and "Das Lusitania Songspiel." *Member:* Dramatists Guild, Actors Equity Association. *Awards, honors:* Fellow of Columbia Broadcasting System, 1975-76; Rockefeller Foundation grant, 1976-77; Guggenheim fellow, 1978-79; Antoinette Perry Award (Tony) nomination for best book of a musical from League of New York Theatres and Producers, 1978, for "A History of the American Film"; grant from Lecomte du Nuoy Foundation, 1980-81; Off-Broadway Award (Obie) from *Village Voice,* 1980, for "Sister Mary Ignatius Explains It All for You."

WRITINGS—Plays; all published by Dramatists Play Service, except as noted: *A History of the American Film* (first produced in Waterford, Conn., at Eugene O'Neill Playwrights Conference, summer, 1976), produced on Broadway at American National Theatre, March 30, 1978), Avon, 1978; *The Vietnamization of New Jersey* (first produced in New Haven, Conn., at Yale Repertory Theatre, October 1, 1976), 1978; *The Nature and Purpose of the Universe* (first produced in New York at Wonder Horse Theatre, February, 1979), 1979; (with Albert Innaurato) *The Idiots Karamazov* (first produced in New Haven at Yale Repertory Theatre, October 10, 1974), 1980; *Sister Mary Ignatius Explains It All for You* (first produced in New York at Ensemble Studio Theatre, December, 1979, produced in New York at Playwrights Horizons, October 21, 1981), 1980.

Unpublished plays: "Titanic," first produced Off-Broadway at Van Dam Theatre, May 10, 1976; (with Sigourney Weaver) "Das Lusitania Songspiel," first produced Off-Broadway at Van Dam Theatre, May 10, 1976; "Identity Crisis," first produced in New Haven at Yale Repertory Theatre, September 29, 1978; "Beyond Therapy," first produced Off-Broadway at Phoenix Theatre, January 5, 1981; "The Actor's Nightmare," first produced in New York at Playwrights Horizons, October 21, 1981. Also author of "The Marriage of Bette and Boo," "Baby With the Bath Water," and (with Wendy Wasserstein) "When Dinah Shore Ruled the Earth," first produced in New Haven at Yale Cabaret.

Lyricist of songs for plays.

SIDELIGHTS: According to a *New York Times* reviewer, Christopher Durang is a member of the group known as the "new American playwrights," dramatists such as Michael Cristofer, Albert Innaurato, David Mamet, and Sam Shepard who follow in the footsteps of Tennessee Williams, Arthur Miller, and Edward Albee. Writers like Durang, the reviewer claimed, "are not one-play writers—a home run and back to the dugout—but artists with staying power and growing bodies of work." These new playwrights generally concentrate on productions for Off-Broadway, Off-Off Broadway, regional, and institutional theatres because these stages are more receptive to new works. For example, Durang has written several plays for the Yale Repertory Theatre, and since his selection by the Playwrights Commissioning Program in 1978, he generates plays for the Off-Broadway Phoenix Theatre. His writing for the Phoenix is financed by a grant co-sponsored by the National Endowment for the Arts Literature Program and by a large foundation.

Though all of the new playwrights depend on humor as an integral part of their approaches, "Durang is perhaps the most overtly comic," said another *New York Times* reviewer. "Christopher Durang has the wit, the high, rebellious spirits, and the rage of the born satirist," remarked the *New Yorker*'s Edith Oliver. "He is also one of the funniest most original playwrights at work." Focusing on social conventions and morality, Durang parodies American life. He mimics the most average situation and carries it to the extreme. His characters dare to say whatever they think or do whatever they feel, which often results in children snapping at their parents or maids overseeing the heads of households.

Stylistically, Durang specializes in collegiate humor. He deals in cartoons and stereotypes, employing mechanical dialogue and brand names to exploit cliches. In one play, for instance, a character feels compelled to make small talk with a pharmacist, so he asks, "What's in Tylenol?" "The characteristic of his humor," wrote Richard Eder, "is that it does not step back for comic perspective. It does not really see its target. It leaps onto it, instead, engages it totally, and burrows its head into it as if it were a mock target; much in the same way that a mother is a mock target for a not terribly naughty child."

Thus far, Durang has parodied literature, movies, families, the Catholic church, show business, and society. But his lampoons are not vicious or hostile; they are controlled comedies. He "is a parodist without venom," said Antonio Chemasi of *Horizon* magazine. "At the moment he fixes his pen on a target, he also falls in love with it. His work brims with an unlikely mix of acerbity and affection and at its best spills into a compassionate criticism of life."

Durang's first target as a professional playwright was literature. In 1974 the Yale Repertory Theatre produced "The Idiots Karamazov," a satire of Dostoyevsky's *The Brothers Karamazov*. The play, featuring Durang in a leading role, was applauded by critics for its "moments of comic inspiration." "I was . . . impressed—with their [Durang's and his co-author Albert Innaurato's] wit as well as their scholarship," Mel Gussow wrote in the *New York Times*. The playwright followed "The Idiots Karamazov" with "Das Lusitania Songspiel," a musical travesty that met with critical and popular success. "From the evidence presented [in 'Das Lusitania Songspiel']," said Oliver, "Mr. Durang is a spirited, original fellow . . . , who brings back to the theatre a welcome impudence and irreverence."

Durang's major success of the seventies was "A History of the American Film," for which he was nominated for a Tony Award in 1978. A tribute to movie mania, the play illustrates America's perceptions of Hollywood from 1930 to the present. To Eder, the production is "a circus car driven by clowns, powered by soap bubbles and fitted out with bepers [sic] and exploding wheels . . . [that] wobbles and squeals through 60 years of American movies." Comprised of take-offs from movies, the play, noted Chemasi, is "a chronicle so preposterous yet scholarly that the Marx Brothers and a diligent film historian might have collaborated on it."

"A cartoon commentary," "A History of the American Film" encompasses two hundred motion pictures and observes the evolution of movie stereotypes that have reached epic proportions in American culture. There are five characters: a tough gangster typified by James Cagney, an innocent Loretta Young type, a sincere guy, a temptress, and a girl who never gets the man of her dreams. The production parodies movies such as "The Grapes of Wrath," "Citizen Kane," and "Casablanca." Show girls dressed up like vegetables satirize the razzmatazz of big Hollywood productions by singing "We're in a Salad." And the character portraying Paul Henreid's role in "Now, Voyager" is forced to smoke two cigarettes when Bette Davis's character refuses one because she does not smoke. "In Durang's hands," wrote *Time*'s Gerald Clarke, "the familiar images always take an unexpected turn, however, and he proves that there is nothing so funny as a cliche of a different color."

During the production, actors sit in movie theatre seats facing the audience. Sometimes they play the roles of the movies' stars; for other scenes they make up part of the audience. Until "A History of the American Film" discusses the movies of the 1940's and color film, the stage, sets, and props are black, white, and gray, a clever innovation to simulate black-and-white movies.

According to Chemasi, Durang's play is "a history of ourselves and how large a role the movies have played in that history." Inspired by a 1932 Depression romance, "A Man's Castle," starring Spencer Tracy and Loretta Young, "A History of the American Film" proved to Chemasi that Americans look at themselves when they watch movies. "I thought I would write my own hobo shantytown romance," Durang explained, "and it began to spin off into satire. I suddenly realized the character called Loretta could also be the girl in the Busby Berkeley movie who goes on when the star breaks her leg. Then I realized she could be everyone."

After "A History of the American Film," Durang wrote two satires of suburban families, "The Vietnamization of New Jersey" and "The Nature and Purpose of the Universe," as well as a parody of the Catholic church. Called a "savage cartoon" by Mel Gussow and a "clever and deeply felt work" by Frank Rich, "Sister Mary Ignatius Explains It All for You" uses the character of an elderly nun to communicate the hypocrisies of Catholicism. The leading figure, said Gussow, is "a self-mocking sister [who] flips pictures of hell, purgatory and heaven as if they are stops on a religious package tour." Her list of the damned includes David Bowie, Betty Comden, and Adolph Green, and she lists hijacking planes alongside murder as a mortal sin. "Anyone can write an angry play—all it takes is an active spleen," observed Rich. "But only a writer of real talent can write an angry play that remains funny and controlled even in its most savage moments. 'Sister Mary Ignatius Explains It All for You' confirms that Christopher Durang is just such a writer."

In October, 1981, the Obie-winning "Sister Mary Ignatius" was presented on the same playbill as "The Actor's Nightmare," a satire of show business and the theatre. Using the play-within-a-play technique for "The Actor's Nightmare," Durang illustrates the comedy which ensues when an actor is forced to appear in a production he has never rehearsed. Earlier in 1981, the Phoenix Theatre produced Durang's "Beyond Therapy," a parody of modern society. In this play a traditional woman, Prudence, and a bisexual man, Bruce, meet through a personal ad, and their relationship is confounded by their psychiatrists. Hers is a lecherous, he-man Freudian; his is an absent-minded comforter. "Some of Durang's satire . . . is sidesplitting," commented a *New York* reviewer, "and there are many magisterial digs at our general mores, amores, and immores."

BIOGRAPHICAL/CRITICAL SOURCES: New York Times, November 11, 1974, February 13, 1977, March 17, 1977, May 11, 1977, August 21, 1977, March 31, 1977, June 23, 1978, December 27, 1978, February 24, 1979, December 21, 1979, February 8, 1980, August 6, 1980, January 6, 1981, October 22, 1981; *New Yorker,* May 24, 1976, April 10, 1978, January 19, 1981; *Time,* May 23, 1977; Catharine Hughes, *New York Theatre Annual,* Volume 2, Gale, 1978; *Horizon,* March, 1978; *New York Post,* March 31, 1978; *Daily News,* March 31, 1978; *Newsweek,* April 10, 1978; *Nation,* April 15, 1978; *New York,* April 17, 1978, January 19, 1981; *New Republic,* April 22, 1978; *Saturday Review,* May 27, 1978; Hughes, editor, *American Theatre Annual 1978-1979,* Gale, 1980; Hughes, editor, *American Theatre Annual 1979-1980,* Gale, 1981.

—Sketch by Charity Anne Dorgan

*   *   *

DURANT, Ariel K(aufman) 1898-1981

OBITUARY NOTICE—See index for *CA* sketch: Born May 10, 1898, in Proskurov, Russia (now Khmelnitski, U.S.S.R.); died after a long illness, October 25, 1981, in Hollywood Hills, Calif. Author best known for collaborating with her husband, Will Durant, on the eleven-volume series "The Story of Civilization." Durant researched the historical books, but her work was not officially recognized until she was listed as a co-author on the seventh volume. Together the Durants won the Pulitzer Prize for general nonfiction in 1968 for *Rousseau and Revolution,* the tenth book of the series. An emigrant from Russia, Ariel met Will when he was her schoolteacher in New York City. The two decided to marry in 1913 when she was fifteen years old and he twenty-eight. Ariel related that on her wedding day she "roller-skated all the way down from Harlem to City Hall." The couple worked on "The Story of Civilization" from its inception in 1935 until the publication of its final volume, *The Age of Napoleon,* in 1975. Two years later they published their life stories in *A Dual Autobiography.* The Durants received the Presidential Medal of Freedom in 1977. For-

merly known as Ida, Durant legally changed her name to Ariel, the pet name bestowed upon her by her husband. Explaining the reason for his choice of the name from the character in Shakespeare's *The Tempest,* Will said it was "because she was strong and brave as a boy, and as swift and mischievous as an elf." The Durants would have celebrated their sixty-eighth wedding anniversary the week after Ariel's death. Will, ailing at the time of his wife's death, died less than two weeks later. Ariel's other works include *The Lessons of History* and *Interpretations of Life.* Obituaries and other sources: *New York Times,* October 28, 1981; *Chicago Tribune,* October 28, 1981; *Newsweek,* November 9, 1981; *Time,* November 9, 1981; *Publishers Weekly,* December 6, 1981.

*   *   *

DURANT, Will(iam James) 1885-1981

OBITUARY NOTICE—See index for *CA* sketch: Born November 5, 1885, in North Adams, Mass.; died of heart failure, November 7, 1981, in Los Angeles, Calif. Journalist, educator, historian, and author best known for his eleven-volume series, "The Story of Civilization," much of which was written with his wife, Ariel Durant. All the books in the work were best-sellers, and the tenth volume, *Rousseau and the Revolution,* earned its authors a Pulitzer Prize for general nonfiction in 1968. The Durants worked fourteen hours each day, seven days a week on their "absurd enterprise," as Will described it, which was also "immodest in its very conception." The couple once explained that it "gave unity to our lives, and a meaning to each day." Durant began his career intending to be a Roman Catholic priest. Becoming disaffected with Catholicism upon reading Spinoza's "Ethics," he abandoned his plans and was excommunicated from the church shortly afterwards. Durant moved to New York City where he reported for the *New York Evening Journal* and taught at several schools, including Columbia University. He started writing when he was asked to publish his lectures on classical philosophers for the "Little Blue Books" series of pamphlets. After publishing several pamphlets, Durant compiled the lectures in *The Story of Philosophy,* published by the fledgling company Simon & Schuster. The success of the volume, which sold millions of copies, launched Durant on his writing career. Durant explained that in his popular history books, he endeavored "to tell as much as I can, in as little space as I can, of the contribution that genius and labor have made to the cultural heritage of mankind." Durant was awarded the Presidential Medal of Freedom in 1977, the same year in which his and his wife's life stories were published together in *A Dual Autobiography.* Obituaries and other sources: *Detroit News,* November 9, 1981, November 15, 1981; *London Times,* November 10, 1981; *Chicago Tribune,* November 10, 1981; *New York Times,* November 10, 1981; *Detroit Free Press,* November 10, 1981; *Publishers Weekly,* November 20, 1981; *Newsweek,* November 23, 1981; *Time,* November 23, 1981.

*   *   *

DWIGHT, Olivia
See HAZZARD, Mary

*   *   *

DWYER, T. Ryle 1944-

PERSONAL: Born April 20, 1944, in Medford, Ore.; son of John G. (a chemist) and Margaret (Harrigan) Dwyer. *Education:* Attended St. Ambrose College, 1963-64; North Texas State University, B.A., 1967, M.A., 1968, Ph.D., 1973. *Re-*

ligion: Roman Catholic. *Home:* 49 St. Brendan's Park, Tralee, County Kerry, Ireland.

CAREER: Writer. *Member:* Phi Kappa Sigma, Ballybunnion Golf Club.

WRITINGS: Irish Neutrality and the U.S.A., 1939-47, Rowman & Littlefield, 1977; *Eamon de Valera,* Gill & Macmillan, 1980; *De Valera's Foreign Policy, 1917-1959,* Gill & Macmillan, 1981; *Michael Collins and the Treaty,* Mercier Press, 1981.

Work represented in anthologies, including *The Capuchin Annual,* 1971, 1973, 1974, and 1976. Contributor to magazines, including *Irish Echo, Eire-Ireland, Newsday,* and *Canadian,* and to newspapers.

WORK IN PROGRESS: Ireland's Allied P.O.W.s.

DYER, Lucinda   1947-

PERSONAL: Born May 23, 1947, in Indianapolis, Ind.; daughter of Ben Moss (an executive) and Evelyn (McDermit) Dyer. *Education:* Attended Southern Methodist University, 1965-69. *Religion:* Christian. *Residence:* Los Angeles, Calif. *Office:* J. P. Tarcher, Inc., 9110 Sunset Blvd., Suite 212, Los Angeles, Calif. 90069.

CAREER: Flaherty-Dyer, Dallas, Tex., artist's representative, 1971-73; Dallas Symphony Orchestra, Dallas, publicist, 1975-77; Shakespeare Festival of Dallas, director of publicity, 1977-78; J. P. Tarcher, Inc., Los Angeles, Calif., publicist, 1978—.

WRITINGS: Women Power, J. P. Tarcher, 1981.

WORK IN PROGRESS: A children's book, for the Christian market.

E

EAGLETON, Thomas Francis 1929-

BRIEF ENTRY: Born September 4, 1929, in St. Louis, Mo. American lawyer, politician, and author. Eagleton has been a lawyer since 1953. In 1969, after serving as lieutenant governor of Missouri, he was elected as a Democrat to the U.S. Senate, where he opposed war in Southeast Asia and then went on to support such domestic issues as stiff drug-control legislation, federal aid to the poor, and federally funded research on population control. In 1972, presidential hopeful George McGovern chose him as a vice-presidential running mate on the Democratic ticket, but Eagleton resigned before the election. Though his resignation may have been influenced by media reports about his mental health, Eagleton has continued to offer strong support for freedom of the press under the law. He began his third term as U.S. Senator from Missouri in 1981. Eagleton wrote *War and Presidential Power: A Chronicle of Congressional Surrender* (Liveright, 1974). *Address:* 6235 Senate Office Building, Washington, D.C. 20510. *Biographical/critical sources: Current Biography,* Wilson, 1973; *New Republic,* November 9, 1974; *Biography News,* Gale, December, 1974; *New York Times Book Review,* January 12, 1975; *Annals of the American Academy of Political and Social Science,* May, 1975; *Newsweek,* November 17, 1980.

* * *

EAMES, Alexandra 1942-

PERSONAL: Born December 17, 1942, in New York, N.Y.; daughter of J. Owen (an engineer) and Olive (Dean) Eames. *Education:* Attended Bennington College, 1960-61; Parsons School of Design, Certificate in Interior Design, 1964. *Home address:* P.O. Box 1296, Sag Harbor, N.Y. 11963.

CAREER: American Home (magazine), New York, N.Y., associate decorating editor, 1966-71; free-lance interior designer, photostylist, crafts designer, and writer, 1971—.

WRITINGS: Do It With Denim, Pyramid Communications, 1974; *Mother Nature's Craft Book,* Pyramid Communications, 1975; *Great Creative Crafts,* Pyramid Communications, 1975; *Windows and Walls,* Oxmoor, 1980. Contributor to shelter and home furnishings magazines.

* * *

EASTMAN, Harry Claude MacColl 1923-

BRIEF ENTRY: Born July 29, 1923, in Vancouver, British Columbia, Canada. Canadian political economist, educator, and author. Eastman joined the faculty of University of Toronto in 1953, becoming professor of economics in 1963 and vice-president for research and planning in 1977. He also taught at Duke University and was a senior fellow of the Canada Council in Switzerland, 1969-70. His writings include *The Economic Council's Third Annual Review* (Canadian Trade Committee, Private Planning Association of Canada, 1967), *Tariff and Competition in Canada* (St. Martin's, 1968), and *Canada in a Wider Economic Community* (University of Toronto Press, 1972). *Address:* 41 Hawthorn Ave., Toronto, Ontario, Canada M4W 2Z1; and Department of Political Economy, University of Toronto, Toronto, Ontario, Canada M5S 1A1. *Biographical/critical sources: American Men and Women of Science: The Social and Behavioral Sciences,* 12th edition, Bowker, 1973; *The Canadian Who's Who,* Volume 14, University of Toronto Press, 1979.

* * *

EBERHART, George M(artin) 1950-

PERSONAL: Born June 6, 1950, in Hanover, Pa.; son of Richard C. (a craftsman) and Elizabeth (Lautz) Eberhart. *Education:* Ohio State University, B.A., 1973; University of Chicago, M.L.S., 1976. *Residence:* Chicago, Ill. *Office:* American Library Association, 50 East Huron St., Chicago, Ill. 60611.

CAREER: Journal of Law and Economics, Chicago, Ill., bibliographic assistant, 1976-77; University of Kansas, Lawrence, serials and reference librarian at library of School of Law, 1977-80; American Library Association, Chicago, editor of *College and Research Libraries News* for Association of College and Research Libraries, 1980—. Staff librarian at Center for UFO Studies, Evanston, Ill., 1980—. *Member:* American Library Association, Mutual UFO Network, Society for the Investigation of the Unexplained. *Awards, honors: A Geo-Bibliography of Anomalies* was named outstanding academic book by *Choice,* 1980.

WRITINGS: Eleven Years in Pursuit: A Cumulative Index, 1967-1978, Society for the Investigation of the Unexplained, 1979; *A Geo-Bibliography of Anomalies: Primary Access to Observations of UFOs, Ghosts, and Other Mysterious Phenomena,* Greenwood Press, 1980. Contributor of articles and reviews to magazines.

WORK IN PROGRESS: A book tentatively titled *Strange Beasts, Giant Birds, and Bigfoot: A Bibliography of Monsters,* publication by Garland Publishing expected in 1982.

SIDELIGHTS: Eberhart told *CA:* "I have long had an interest in events, behavior, conditions, or discoveries that do not conform to prevailing world views—this diverse set of scientific and historical mysteries I collectively call anomalies, and their study can be termed 'anomalistic science.'

"Anomalies include everything *from* lake monsters, bigfoot, ball lightning, earthquake luminescence, intra-Mercurial planets, falls of ice from the sky, the Bermuda Triangle, spontaneous human combustion, and cattle mutilations, *through* ESP, out-of-body experiences, dowsing, astrology, poltergeists, alchemy, biofeedback, neo-paganism, apparitions, spirit mediums, and haunted houses, *to* phantom panthers, UFO abductions, possession cases, medieval witchcraft, Atlantis, ancient cataclysms, megalithic paleoastronomy, mysterious artifacts, pre-Columbian discoveries of America, lost treasure, assassination conspiracies, the Bavarian Illuminati, and the identities of Kasper Hauser and Anastasia Romanov.

"And that's merely the beginning!

"One would think that such a vast field of scholarship would require minute specialization. The temptation to specialize certainly exists, although I have managed to avoid it by concentrating on the bibliography of anomalistic literature in general. The literature itself encourages a broad outlook: pick up any ten UFO books and you will find that many of the subjects I have listed above will be mentioned, at least in passing.

"In retrospect, I must say that reading and researching the literature of anomalies for the past twenty years has been a very liberal education, since anomalies can occur in any branch of human knowledge. It certainly has given me a grasp on the inter-connectedness of all things, an outlook that has proven beneficial in my career as librarian, researcher, and journalist."

AVOCATIONAL INTERESTS: Reading European literature, classics, satire, American history, and popular science; writing satirical verse and parodies.

*   *   *

EDOM, Clifton C.   1907-

PERSONAL: Born February 12, 1907, in Baylis, Ill.; son of Harry N. (a railroad station agent) and Myrtle (Hubbs) Edom; married Vilia C. Patefield, June 30, 1928; children: Verna Mae Edom Smith. *Education:* Attended Western Illinois University, 1925-26; University of Missouri, B.J., 1946. *Religion:* Presbyterian. *Home and office address:* P.O. Box 1105, Forsyth, Mo. 65653.

CAREER: University of Missouri, Columbia, began as assistant professor, became professor of journalism, 1943-72, professor emeritus, 1972—, founder and director of photojournalism division of School of Journalism. Founder of Pictures of the Year Competition and Exhibition; founder and director of annual Photo Workshop, 1949—. *Member:* International Museum of Photography, National Press Photographers Association, Kappa Alpha Mu (founder). *Awards, honors:* Fellowship from Truman Library; Sprague Award from National Press Photographers Association.

WRITINGS: (With others) *Picture Editing,* Rinehart, 1951; *Missouri Sketchbook,* Lucas Brothers, 1963; *Photojournalism: Principles and Practices,* W. C. Brown, 1976, revised edition, 1980. Contributor to photography journals.

WORK IN PROGRESS: Taney County Album, a pictorial history of the Missouri Ozarks.

*   *   *

EDWARDS, Betty   1926-

PERSONAL: Born April 19, 1926; daughter of Orson McArthur and Winifred (Lon) Wasden. *Education:* University of California, Los Angeles, Ph.D., 1978. *Address:* c/o J. P. Tarcher, Inc., 9110 Sunset Blvd., Suite 212, Los Angeles, Calif. 90069.

CAREER: Professor of art at California State University, Long Beach. *Member:* Phi Kappa Delta.

WRITINGS: Drawing on the Right Side of the Brain: A Course in Enhancing Creativity and Artistic Confidence, self-illustrated, J. P. Tarcher, 1979.

SIDELIGHTS: Edwards has developed a new method for teaching art based upon her theory that, though the left hemisphere of the brain is dominant, the right side controls the perceptual skills necessary for good drawing. Her theory, supported by the "split-brain" studies of Dr. Roger W. Sperry of the California Institute of Technology, grew from her observation that sketches by her students improved significantly when the objects that they were drawing were turned upside-down. Although at first puzzled by this phenomenon, Edwards, according to *Chicago Tribune*'s Connie Lauermann, came to the conclusion that "because the left hemisphere cannot recognize and name upside-down information, the student is forced to draw what he sees, not what he thinks should be there." This is possible only because the right hemisphere takes over the perceptual function.

Edwards's book, *Drawing on the Right Side of the Brain,* describes techniques that the author teaches her students to enable them to shift into "the right side mode." The book, with sales in excess of one hundred thousand copies, has been purchased by a number of corporations for their technically oriented employees in order that they might learn to think more creatively.

BIOGRAPHICAL/CRITICAL SOURCES: Chicago Tribune, August 1, 1979; *New York Times Book Review,* May 4, 1980; *Ms.,* July, 1980.

*   *   *

EDWARDS, David Vandeusen   1941-

BRIEF ENTRY: Born May 25, 1941, in Chicago, Ill. American political scientist, educator, and author. Edwards has taught government at University of Texas since 1970. He has also worked for the Institute for Defense Analysis. He wrote *Arms Control in International Politics* (Holt, 1969), *Political Power: A Reader in Theory and Research* (Free Press, 1969), *American Government: The Facts Reorganized* (General Learning Press, 1974), and *The American Political Experience: An Introduction to Government* (Prentice-Hall, 1979). *Address:* Department of Government, University of Texas, Austin, Tex. 78712. *Biographical/critical sources: American Men and Women of Science: The Social and Behavioral Sciences,* 13th edition, Bowker, 1978.

*   *   *

EDWARDS, Francis
See BRANDON, Johnny

EDWARDS, Ron(ald George)   1930-

PERSONAL: Born October 10, 1930, in Geelong, Australia. *Education:* Received diploma of art from Swinburne Institute. *Home address:* P.O. Box 274, Kurand, Queensland 4872, Australia.

CAREER: Free-lance writer.

WRITINGS: (Editor) *Overlander Songbook,* Rams Skull Press, 1956, new edition, Rigby, 1981; *Index to Australian Folk Songs, 1857-1970,* Rams Skull Press, 1971; *Australian Folk Songs,* Rams Skull Press, 1972; *Australian Bawdy Ballads,* Rams Skull Press, 1974; *Australian Traditional Bush Crafts,* Lansdowne Press, 1975; *The Big Book of Australian Folk Songs,* Rigby, 1976; *Australian Yarns,* Rigby, 1977; *Skills of the Australian Bushman,* Rigby, 1980; *The Stock Saddle,* Rams Skull Press, 1981; *Bush Yarns and Ballads,* Rigby, 1981.

Co-author of "Bullsh" (play), first produced in Melbourne, Australia.

*   *   *

EISLER, Frieda Goldman
See GOLDMAN-EISLER, Frieda

*   *   *

EISNER, Simon
See KORNBLUTH, C(yril) M.

*   *   *

ELETHEA, Abba
See THOMPSON, James W.

*   *   *

ELLER, John   1935-

PERSONAL: Born October 2, 1935, in New York, N.Y.; son of William A. (a police officer) and Margaret (Grey) Eller; married Marian Touchberry (an insurance executive), February 2, 1957; children: Eugene, Jane, John, James. *Education:* Southwest Texas State University, B.S., 1977. *Politics:* Libertarian. *Religion:* None. *Home and office address:* Route 2, Box 2711, Boerne, Tex. 78006. *Agent:* Patricia Falk Feeley, Inc., 1501 Broadway, New York, N.Y. 10036.

CAREER: U.S. Air Force, career officer, 1954-80, cryptographic operator, 1954-64, instructor, 1965-80; retiring as master sergeant; writer, 1980—. Substitute teacher in the Boerne school district.

WRITINGS: Charlie and the Ice Man (novel), St. Martin's, 1981. Contributor to *San Antonio Light.*

WORK IN PROGRESS: Charlie and Heaven's Rage, a novel.

SIDELIGHTS: Eller told *CA:* "I may have tried to garb 'Charlie' with a Don Quixote guise in some unconscious attempt to transform present-day chaos back to a time of order. An impossible task. To be a semi-deity with only a badge for authority, Charlie cannot rest at being a mere observer as society slowly sinks into an abyss of adolescent idiots and punk-rock punks. He knows he will never achieve this herculean labor, but he'd rather light that one candle.

"This attempt might be the reason I prefer the companionship of animals to people. Animals aren't predictable; rather, they're reliable. A dog will incur the wrath of his owner for not responding in a human manner. Yet, as a dog, a dog is the best he can be. He strives to be what he is and what he is supposed to be. Few humans have the capacity or will to do the same.

"As a skinny youngster, under the tutelage and threatening eyes of the nuns, I once considered spending my life as a priest. There were only two fascinating places in the world where I would spend my life saving souls. One was on horseback through the canyons of Texas. The other was trampling through the green hills of Ireland. I have ridden the canyons and one day I would like to stroll with my wife through the cities and hills of Ireland. There has never been any further thought of saving souls.

"I have another Charlie book and a box of short stories hidden in a drawer in my home. If the gods look with favor, the second Charlie should follow the course of the first. I'd like someday to live in a small Mexican village for about a year, weaving a novel in that setting from threads of a story I already have in my head."

BIOGRAPHICAL/CRITICAL SOURCES: Library Journal, June 15, 1981.

*   *   *

ELLIS, (Mary) Amabel (Nassau Strachey) Williams
See WILLIAMS-ELLIS, (Mary) Amabel (Nassau Strachey)

*   *   *

ELLIS, Charles Drummond   1895-1980

OBITUARY NOTICE: Born August 11, 1895, in London, England; died January 10, 1980, in Berkshire, England. Physicist, educator, and author. Ellis became interested in physics while a prisoner of war in Germany during World War I. In the camp he met James Chadwick, whose discovery of the neutron had revolutionized science. Chadwick exposed Ellis to scientific theory and allowed him to assist in experiments. After the war Ellis studied at Trinity College, Cambridge. He began teaching soon after earning his doctorate. His later collaborations with Chadwick were documented in *Radiations From Radioactive Substances,* which they co-authored. During World War II Ellis counseled the British military on atomic weapons. He later advised several industries on the use of science as a means of improvement. Obituaries and other sources: *The Annual Obituary 1980,* St. Martin's, 1981.

*   *   *

ELLIS, Herbert
See WILSON, Lionel

*   *   *

ELLIS, Leigh   1959-

PERSONAL: Born June 21, 1959; daughter of Courtenay Courtenay (a painter) and Emma (a singer; maiden name, Lustgarten) Ellis; married Trasher Manning, June 21, 1979 (divorced). *Education:* Educated privately.

CAREER: Writer.

WRITINGS: Tessa of Destiny, Avon, 1980.

WORK IN PROGRESS: The Quick, a novel about Satanism in Ohio, for Avon.

SIDELIGHTS: Leigh Ellis wrote: "The strangeness of life is my interest."

* * *

ELLISTON, Frederick Allen 1944-

PERSONAL: Born May 22, 1944, in Toronto, Ontario, Canada; son of John Smith (in police work) and Edna Robina (Young) Elliston; married Diane Elizabeth Fowler, March 21, 1970 (divorced); children: Deborah Ann, David Edmund. *Education:* Trinity College, Toronto, Ontario, B.A., 1967; University of Toronto, M.A., 1968, Ph.D., 1974. *Home:* 2005 Eastern Parkway, Schenectady, N.Y. 12309. *Office:* Criminal Justice Research Center, Inc., 1 Alton Rd., Albany, N.Y. 12203.

CAREER: York University, Downsview, Ontario, adjunct instructor in humanities and social science, 1971-72; Union College, Schenectady, N.Y., assistant professor of philosophy, 1972-78; State University of New York at Albany, research fellow at School of Criminal Justice, 1978-80; Criminal Justice Research Center, Inc., Albany, project director, 1980-82. Visiting professor at Bishops' University, 1980-81. *Member:* American Philosophical Association, American Society of Criminologists, Husserl Circle, Heidegger Circle, Society of Phenomenology and Existential Philosophy. *Awards, honors:* Grants from National Endowment for the Humanities, 1976 and 1981-83, National Institute of Mental Health, 1980, National Institute of Law Enforcement and Criminal Justice, 1980, Ethical Values in Science and Technology, 1980-82.

WRITINGS: (Editor with Robert Baker, and contributor) *Philosophy and Sex,* Prometheus Books, 1975; (editor with Peter McCormick, and contributor) *Husserl: Expositions and Appraisals,* University of Notre Dame Press, 1977; (editor with Mary Braggin and Jane English) *Feminism and Philosophy,* Littlefield, Adams, 1977; (editor and contributor) *Heidegger's Existential Analytic,* Mouton, 1978.

(Editor with Hugh J. Silverman, and contributor) *Jean-Paul Sartre: Contemporary Approaches to His Philosophy,* Duquesne University Press, 1980; (editor with McCormick) *Husserl: Shorter Works,* University of Notre Dame Press, 1981; (editor with Norman Bowie) *Ethics, Public Policy, and Criminal Justice,* Oelgeschlager, Gunn & Hain, 1982; (with Lawrence Sherman) *Police Ethics,* Prentice-Hall, 1982; (editor) *Ethics and the Legal Profession,* Prometheus Books, 1982; (with Michael Feldberg) *Moral Issues in Policing,* Pilgrimage Press, 1982; *Professional Dissent: An Ethical Analysis,* Precedent Publishing, 1983; *Teaching Police Ethics,* The Police Foundation, 1983; *Ethics and Professional Responsibility,* Prometheus Books, 1983.

WORK IN PROGRESS: Sentencing and the Public, with Leslie T. Wilkins; *Police Homicides: An Ethical Analysis; Between Solitude and Solace,* a book of poems; editing *Whistleblowing: Conflicting Loyalties in the Workplace,* publication expected by Prentice-Hall; *Legal Ethics: A Guide to the Literature; Ten Case Studies of Whistleblowing: Technical Dissent in the Workplace; Professional Dissent: An Annotated Bibliography.* Contributor to philosophy journals.

SIDELIGHTS: Elliston told *CA:* "My career has completed a circle—perhaps more accurately, a spiral. My father was a policeman and urged me to become a lawyer. I resisted, smitten wit a love of wisdom, and pursued philosophy instead. Ironically, I now find myself working in the criminal justice field." *Avocational interests:* Tennis, chess, music, poetry.

ENGLEFIELD, Ronald 1891-1975

OBITUARY NOTICE: Born February 5, 1891, in London, England; died in January, 1975. Educator and author of *Language: Its Origin and Its Relation to Thought.* Englefield taught at Bowden College. (Date of death provided by sister, M. Englefield.)

* * *

ENGLISH, Charles
See NUETZEL, Charles (Alexander)

* * *

ENGLISH, Thomas Saunders 1928-

BRIEF ENTRY: Born August 6, 1928, in Washington, D.C. American biologist, oceanographer, educator, and editor. English has taught oceanography at University of Washington, Seattle, since 1959. He edited *Ocean Resources and Public Policy* (University of Washington Press, 1973). *Address:* Department of Oceanography, University of Washington, Seattle, Wash. 98195. *Biographical/critical sources: American Men and Women of Science: The Physical and Biological Sciences,* 14th edition, Bowker, 1979.

* * *

ENTWISTLE, Florence Vivienne 1889(?)-1982
(Vivienne)

OBITUARY NOTICE: Born c. 1889; died January 1, 1982. Artist and photographer. Vivienne was best known for her photographs of British politicians and international celebrities. Two hundred of her photographs were collected in *They Came to My Studio.* Obituaries and other sources: *London Times,* January 1, 1982.

* * *

ERWIN, John Seymour 1911-

PERSONAL: Born August 2, 1911, in Vicksburg, Miss.; son of Victor Flournoy (a planter) and Margaret Preston (McNeily) Erwin. *Education:* Attended School of Contemporary Arts, New York, N.Y., 1929-31, Columbia University, 1939-40, and University of Toronto, 1942-43; studied musical composition and orchestration with Alexander Siloti and Serge Rachmaninoff, and piano with Frank Sheriden. *Religion:* Episcopalian. *Home and office:* Erwin Associates, Inc., 10 Waterside Plaza, New York, N.Y. 10010.

CAREER: Professional photographer in New York City, 1936-41; assistant to photographer Marcus Blechman, 1937-40; Vandamm Studio, New York City, assistant to Florence Vandamm, 1947-49; Erwin Associates, Inc., New York City, photographer, 1949-77, president, 1978—. *Military service:* Royal Canadian Air Force, medical researcher, 1941-44; became sergeant. *Member:* Authors Guild. *Awards, honors:* Fellowships from Tiffany Foundation, 1934-35, and Gloucester School, 1935.

WRITINGS: (Music editor) Oliver Bell, Harvey Greene, Joseph P. King, Helen Lecar, and others, editors, *The World and Its People,* twenty-seven volumes, Greystone, 1959-61; *Like Some Green Laurel* (biography based on the letters of Margaret Johnson Erwin, 1821-1863), Louisiana State University Press, 1981. Contributor to *Collier's Encyclopedia* and *Encyclopedia Amer-*

icana. Feature editor and music editor of *American,* 1954-56; television and radio editor of *Show,* 1961-63; senior editor of *Natural History,* 1965-66; editor of *Media Medica,* 1968-70.

WORK IN PROGRESS: A novel tentatively entitled *The Castle of Time,* completion expected in 1983; *Nearing Port,* nonfiction, 1983; *The Shadows We Pursue,* a novel, publication expected in 1984; *Played From Memory,* nonfiction vignettes, 1984; *Quest Unending,* poems.

SIDELIGHTS: Erwin wrote: "I am a nonbeliever in signs, portents, and prognostications of most agents—and many writers—of today; one of the most illogical ones at hand being that 'nostalgia does not pay.' The past has substance, the present is a bad dream, and the future seems to be nebulous lunacy. I do adhere to the belief that many and diverse interests in no way inhibit any writer, provided he lives long enough to make use of them, and without boring his readers into a coma by a repetition of theme—be it racial, religious, a melange of sex, or abstract and restless flights onto the upper roosts of a writer's brain.

"Having a varied background has resulted in an equally varied creative output. My music has been played, but I have rarely heard it; the first warm tremors of published verse did not last beyond the first days of World War II; the same goes for short stories. Content with the completion of any work, I never care about hearing it, or hearing *of* it, again, be it a flop or a best-seller. The sudden, midstream death of a collaborator, Wallace Brockway, brought two major disappointments: an incomplete encyclopedia of King Arthur, including fact and legend, and an incomplete encyclopedia of music and musicians.

"I deplore censorship, considering it to be the beginning of the end of any civilization. Wiser people have said it better and history has proven it true. A panoramic glance at the present clash of cults and minorities and laughable Moral Majorities *should* be telling us something."

AVOCATIONAL INTERESTS: "Landscape painting and cartoons of cats are challenges that are more than mere amusement. The same might be said of the biological sciences and botany (including tropical and sub-tropical plants)."

*   *   *

ESCHMEYER, R(einhart) E(rnst)   1898-
(R. E. Eshmeyer)

PERSONAL: Born May 2, 1898, in New Knoxville, Ohio; son of Ernst (a salesman) and Fredericka (Harlamert) Eschmeyer; married Aurelia Dickman, August, 1919 (died, 1968); married Elba May Butts, 1971 (died, 1975); children: Ruth, Donna, Nancy. *Education:* Heidelberg College, B.A., 1922; also attended Central Theological Seminary (now Eden Theological Seminary), 1919-21. *Politics:* "I vote for the man." *Religion:* United Church of Christ. *Home:* 224 Elizabeth St., East Lansing, Mich. 48823.

CAREER: Ordained to United Church of Christ ministry, 1924; rural school teacher, New Bremen, Ohio, 1916-17; minister in Fremont, Ohio, 1924-30, Bascom, Bettsville, and Fort Seneca, Ohio, 1930-34, Bloomville, Ohio, 1934-41, and Cleveland, Ohio, 1941-46; St. Paul's United Church of Christ, Lansing, Mich., minister, 1954-63, pastor emeritus, 1963—. Member of board of trustees of Heidelberg College, 1946-1954; teacher of oil painting at American Youth Foundation, Camp Miniwanca, for thirty-one summers; has served on various civic and church council committees.

WRITINGS—Under name R. E. Eshmeyer: Ask Any Vegetable (juvenile nonfiction), self-illustrated, Prentice-Hall, 1975; *It*

Crossed My Mind (poems), Adams Press. Contributor of articles on nature to newspapers in Cleveland, Ohio, Akron, Ohio, and Lansing, Mich., and a column, "Junior Sermons," to Sunday edition of *Lansing State Journal.*

WORK IN PROGRESS: An enlarged edition of *It Crossed My Mind.*

AVOCATIONAL INTERESTS: Painting, plaster-of-Paris modeling, photography.

*   *   *

ESHMEYER, R. E.
See ESCHMEYER, R(einhart) E(rnst)

*   *   *

ESKOW, John   1949-

PERSONAL: Born November 11, 1949, in Utica, N.Y.; married wife, Alison (a writer and editor). *Education:* State University of New York, B.A., 1970; Columbia University, M.F.A., 1974. *Home:* 225 West 106th Ave., New York, N.Y. 10025. *Agent:* Erica Spellman, William Morris Agency, 1350 Avenue of the Americas, New York, N.Y. 10019.

CAREER: Writer.

WRITINGS: Smokestack Lightning (novel), Delacorte, 1980. Contributor to periodicals, including *Rolling Stone, New York, Playboy,* and *Penthouse.*

WORK IN PROGRESS: A novel, *The Warning Track;* a screenplay for Alan Pakula.

SIDELIGHTS: Eskow told *CA:* "I was a poet for a number of years but was drummed out of the corps for trying to make poetry cost efficient: I wanted to get paid *x* dollars per metaphor. I harbored a secret desire to write fiction but was terrified by the length. I'm now terrified by the intricacies. Writing screenplays is a wonderful diversion from the bone-crushing work of fiction, but it ups the Maalox consumption to intolerable levels. I'm relieved to be writing another book."

*   *   *

ESPY, Richard   1952-

PERSONAL: Born September 4, 1952, in Denver, Colo.; son of J. Bruce (in business) and Marian (Honan) Espy; married Monica Friedman (a teacher), July 8, 1978. *Education:* University of the Pacific, B.A., 1974; Claremont Graduate School, M.I.S., 1978. *Residence:* Redondo Beach, Calif. *Address:* c/o University of California Press, 2223 Fulton St., Berkeley, Calif. 94720.

CAREER: Palos Verdes Peninsula News, Palos Verdes Peninsula, Calif., reporter and editorial writer, 1978-80; writer, 1980—.

WRITINGS: Politics of the Olympic Games, University of California Press, 1979, revised edition, 1981.

WORK IN PROGRESS: A novel with a courtroom setting; research on "some of the more obscure, but fascinating, areas of South America"; an update of *Politics of the Olympic Games.*

SIDELIGHTS: Espy told *CA:* "Man's ability to organize for some higher purpose, be it for reasons of procreation, protection, or whatever, has been a continuing source of fascination to me. In the past, this organizational aptitude was essential to man's very survival in an extremely hostile environment, and it enabled him to progress—if one can call it that—to his present state. With technological advances now seemingly approaching a geometric, even exponential progression, I wonder if man's organizational ability can sufficiently protect him from himself. I believe it is this thought more than any other which directs my writing.''

*   *   *

ESTERMANN, Carlos   ?-1976

OBITUARY NOTICE: Died June 21, 1976. Clergyman and author of *The Ethnography of Southwestern Angola: The Non-Bantu Peoples, the Ambo Ethnic Group,* Volume I. (Date of death provided by Gordon D. Gibson, curator of African Ethnology, Smithsonian Institution.)

*   *   *

ESTROFF, Sue E.   1950-

PERSONAL: Born July 31, 1950, in Syracuse, N.Y.; daughter of Melvin B. (a merchant) and Elsie (an educational consultant; maiden name, Haft) Estroff. *Education:* Duke University, B.A. (magna cum laude), 1972; University of Wisconsin—Madison, Ph.D., 1978. *Religion:* Jewish. *Home:* 2626 Park Pl., Madison, Wis. *Agent:* Ned Brown, Inc., 407 North Maple Dr., Beverly Hills, Calif. 90210. *Office:* Department of Psychiatry, University of Wisconsin—Madison, Madison, Wis. 53792.

CAREER: University of Wisconsin—Madison, postdoctoral fellow in psychiatry, 1978—. Community mental health consultant. *Member:* American Anthropological Association, Society for Medical Anthropology, Society for Psychological Anthropology, Phi Kappa Phi, Kappa Kappa Gamma. *Awards, honors:* National Science Foundation fellow, 1973-76.

WRITINGS: Making It Crazy, University of California Press, 1981. Contributor to journals in the social and behavioral sciences.

WORK IN PROGRESS: Research on social factors that affect prognosis in chronic illness, staff burn-out, and social relationships between staff and patients on a psychiatric inpatient unit.

SIDELIGHTS: Sue Estroff told *CA:* ''Writing represents more than a medium for conveying facts, even though I am a social scientist. I attempt in my works to convey a sense of whole humanness as well as structure, pattern, and predictability. This often means telling individual stories which encompass the whole—and this is what lures and feeds me.

''My book is a descriptive analysis of what life is like for some de-institutionalized psychiatric patients. It details how enmeshing and paradoxical the mental health system can be for patients, and how the system can perpetuate deviance and not alter it. This is not a collection of happy stories, but the people in the book have important lessons to teach us all.''

BIOGRAPHICAL/CRITICAL SOURCES: Los Angeles Times Book Review, November 1, 1981.

*   *   *

EUWE, Machgielis   1901-1981
(Max Euwe)

OBITUARY NOTICE: Born May 20, 1901, in Watergrafsmeer (listed in some sources as Amsterdam), Netherlands; died November 26, 1981, in Amsterdam, Netherlands. Educator, chess player, and author. Euwe was champion of the chess world from 1935 to 1937. He held the championship of the Neth-

erlands twelve times, and dignified himself in numerous matches with other chess greats, including Paul Keres and Alexander Alekhine. It was the Russian, Alekhine, who lost the world championship to Euwe by upset in 1935. Two years later Euwe agreed to a rematch with Alekhine and was beaten ten victories to four. Euwe was renowned for his analysis of chess. His numerous writings include *Judgement and Planning in Chess, The Logical Approach to Chess,* and *Strategy and Tactics in Chess Play.* Obituaries and other sources: *Who's Who in the World,* 3rd edition, Marquis, 1976; *Who's Who,* 131st edition, St. Martin's, 1979; *London Times,* November 28, 1981; *New York Times,* November 28, 1981.

*   *   *

EUWE, Max
See EUWE, Machgielis

*   *   *

EVANS, David Beecher   1928-

BRIEF ENTRY: Born March 6, 1928, in Peru, Ill. American theologian, historian, educator, and author. Evans has taught theology at St. John's University, Jamaica, N.Y., since 1969. His writings include *Leontius of Byzantium: An Origenist Christology* (Dumbarton Oaks, 1970). *Address:* Department of Theology, St. John's University, Grand Central and Utopia, Jamaica, N.Y. 11432. *Biographical/critical sources: Directory of American Scholars,* Volume IV: *Philosophy, Religion, and Law,* 7th edition, Bowker, 1978.

*   *   *

EVANS, William R.   1938-

PERSONAL: Born September 20, 1938, in Union, N.J.; son of William S. (an executive) and Mary (Cranston) Evans; married Eileen Kennedy (a professor), June 3, 1972. *Education:* Dartmouth College, B.A., 1960; Columbia University, M.A. (with honors), 1961, Ph.D. (with honors), 1970. *Politics:* Democrat. *Religion:* Roman Catholic. *Home:* 591 Duquesne Ter., Union, N.J. 07083. *Office:* Department of English, Kean College of New Jersey, Morris Ave., Union, N.J. 07083.

CAREER: New York Times, New York City, editorial assistant, 1962; Lebanon Valley College, Annville, Pa., instructor in English, 1962-63; Columbia University, New York City, preceptor, 1966-68; Kean College of New Jersey, Union, N.J., instructor, 1970-72, assistant professor, 1972-79, associate professor of English, 1979—; writer, 1981—. Associated with the Strollers, a community theatre group in Maplewood, N.J., 1968—. *Member:* Modern Language Association of America, Shakespeare Association of America, College English Association, Phi Kappa Phi.

WRITINGS: Robert Frost and Sidney Cox: Forty Years of Friendship, University Press of New England, 1981. Contributor of articles to periodicals, including *American Literature, Carolina Quarterly, Robert Frost; Centennial Essays,* and *Dartmouth College Library Bulletin.* Contributor of book reviews to *Eire-Ireland* and *Painted Bride Quarterly.*

WORK IN PROGRESS: Robert Frost and Edward Thomas: Their Poetry and Friendship.

SIDELIGHTS: William Evans's *Robert Frost and Sidney Cox: Forty Years of Friendship* collects one hundred forty-six correspondences of the poet and the professor, who met in 1911 when Frost was in his thirties and Cox only twenty-two. Explaining that neither party was overwhelmed with the other at their first meeting, Evans shows how the men's friendship and mutual admiration alternately blossomed and waned but never failed. The most poignant communications in the book, critics noted, are the letters, written after Cox's death in 1952, persuading Frost to write the foreword to Cox's portrait of the poet. As Peter Davison of the *Washington Post Book World* observed, "Nothing in the William R. Evans' book is more touching or revealing of Frost's weakness and the ambiguity of his literary friendships than the posthumous correspondence in which Cox's publisher, Wilson Follett, entreated Frost to write an introduction to Cox's life work, an appreciative book called *A Swinger of Birches.* Their correspondence displays the Frost fox trot at its most syncopated."

The reviewer continued to praise *Robert Frost and Sidney Cox,* stating: "This exchange is both fascinating and melancholy, matching a heavyweight with a Golden Glove fighter in a match only one of them recognized as a contest." "Professor Evans," commended *Best Sellers*'s John S. Phillipson, "has given us an absorbing account of two intelligent and able men whose friendship, recorded in this volume, is well worth reading about. . . . Never dull, it's truly readable." And Charles Guenther of the *St. Louis Post-Dispatch* added: "The Frost-Cox letters show an important new facet, if not a new dimension to the lives of both men. Frost put it best perhaps: 'Our intimacy was a curious blend of differences that if properly handled might prove an almost literary curiosity.'"

Evans told *CA* that his scholarly interests include Robert Frost, William Shakespeare, and William Bronk. He travels extensively to England, Europe, and New England and sums up his attitude toward writing as follows: "Make it clear, truthful, and interesting."

BIOGRAPHICAL/CRITICAL SOURCES: Best Sellers, July, 1981, *St. Louis Post-Dispatch,* July 5, 1981; *Washington Post Book World,* July 5, 1981, *Union Leader* (New Jersey), August 27, 1981; *Choice,* October, 1981; *Listener,* November 26, 1981.

*   *   *

EWERT, David   1922-

PERSONAL: Born December 5, 1922, in Alexanderhof, U.S.S.R.; came to Canada in 1926, naturalized citizen, 1933; son of David (a farmer) and Margaret (Wiebe) Ewert; married Lena Hamm (a dietician), October 12, 1944; children: Eleanor, Marianne, Ernest, Grace, Doreen. *Education:* University of British Columbia, B.A., 1951; Wheaton College, Wheaton, Ill., M.A., 1957; Central Baptist Seminary, Toronto, Ontario, B.D., 1953; attended Luther Seminary, M.Th., 1960; McGill University, Ph.D., 1969. *Religion:* Mennonite. *Home:* 1515 South Garden, Fresno, Calif. 93727. *Office:* Department of New Testament, Mennonite Brethren Biblical Seminary, 4824 Butler, Fresno, Calif. 93727.

CAREER: Professor of Biblical literature at Mennonite Brethern College in Winnipeg, Manitoba; professor of New Testament at Eastern Mennonite Seminary, Harrisonburg, Va.; currently professor of New Testament at Mennonite Brethren Bible Seminary, Fresno, Calif. Visiting professor at Union Biblical Seminary, Yeotmal, India; Regent College, Vancouver, British Columbia; and Freie Evangelische Theologische Akademie, Basel, Switzerland.

WRITINGS: Stalwart for the Truth, Christian Press, 1975; *Die Wunderwege Gottes mit der Gemlinde Jesu Christi* (title means "The Mysterious Ways of God With the Church of Jesus Christ"), Christian Press, 1978; (editor) *Called to Teach,* Christian Press, 1980; *And Then Comes the End,* Herald Press, 1980; *The Holy Spirit in the New Testament,* Herald Press, 1982. Contributor to magazines.

SIDELIGHTS: Ewert told *CA:* "My writings are all motivated by my call to teach the Scriptures and a concern to provide the church with solid reading material.

"In a sense I was forced into writing when I was on the faculty at the Mennonite College in Winnepeg, Manitoba. This college published a theological journal and every faculty member was required to contribute an item to this periodical six times a year. It was an excellent opportunity for developing writing skills."

*   *   *

EWING, John Alexander   1923-

BRIEF ENTRY: Born March 17, 1923, in Fife, Scotland. American psychiatrist, educator, and author. Ewing has been a physician since 1954. He has been a professor of psychiatry at University of North Carolina since 1963 and director of the Center for Alcohol Studies since about 1970. Ewing's writings include *Law and Drinking Behavior* (Center for Alcohol Studies, University of North Carolina, 1971), *Drinking: Alcohol in American Society—Issues and Current Research* (Nelson-Hall, 1978), and *Drinking: Everything You Want to Know* (Reston, 1981). *Address:* 623 East Franklin St., Chapel Hill, N.C. 27514; and Department of Psychiatry, School of Medicine, University of North Carolina, Box 1020, Chapel Hill, N.C. 27514. *Biographical/critical sources: American Men and Women of Science: The Physical and Biological Sciences,* 14th edition, Bowker, 1979.

F

FABBRI, Diego 1911-1980

OBITUARY NOTICE: Born July 2, 1911, in Forli, Italy; died August 14, 1980, in Riccione, Italy. Editor and author. Fabbri wrote numerous plays and screenplays in which he explored the plight of the faithful Christian in a world of despair. Although he began writing plays in the 1930's, it wasn't until 1950, with the production of "Inquisizione," that Fabbri's fame spread outside the writing community. In "Inquisizione," Fabbri documented a young priest's selfish interests in his efforts to reunite a married couple. Through the guidance of an elderly priest, the young clergyman gradually practices compassion and successfully helps the couple. "Inquisizione" received the National Prize. Fabbri's later plays, including "Processo a Gesu," "Vegli d'armi," and "La bugiarda," continued to dwell on aspects of Christianity, but in an increasingly humorous manner. His screenplays, like his plays, concentrated on the often ambiguous behavior among Christians. Fabbri briefly served as editor of both *La fiera litteraria* and *Il dramma* after World War II. Obituaries and other sources: *The Concise Encyclopedia of Modern Drama,* Horizon Press, 1964; *Cassell's Encyclopaedia of World Literature,* revised edition, Morrow, 1973; *A Concise Encyclopedia of the Theatre,* Osprey, 1974; *The Annual Obituary 1980,* St. Martin's, 1981.

* * *

FAIRCHILD, Louis W. 1901-1981

OBITUARY NOTICE: Born March 3, 1901, in Glen Ridge, N.J.; died October 16, 1981, in Hanover, N.H. Reporter and publisher. Fairchild presided over Fairchild Publications from 1948 to 1963. Prior to his work as a publisher, he wrote for *Paterson Evening News* and *Women's Wear Daily.* Obituaries and other sources: *American Authors and Books, 1640 to the Present Day,* 3rd revised edition, Crown, 1972; *New York Times,* October 17, 1981; *Time,* October 26, 1981.

* * *

FAIRLESS, Caroline S. 1947-

PERSONAL: Born May 1, 1947, in Pittsburgh, Pa.; daughter of Blaine F. and Caroline Sproul (Berner) Fairless. *Education:* Columbia University, B.A. (cum laude), 1971. *Agent:* Elizabeth Ness & Associates, 3024 Wisconsin Ave. N.W., B12, Washington, D.C. 20016. *Office:* St. Charles Hotel Building, Suite 314, Seattle, Wash. 98104.

CAREER: City of Seattle, Seattle, Wash., part-time city transit driver, 1978—; writer. *Awards, honors:* Washington State Governor's Award, 1981, for *Hambone.*

WRITINGS: Hambone (juvenile), Tundra, 1980; *The Dance of the Caterpillars,* Tundra, 1982.

WORK IN PROGRESS: Mercedes, with Woodson Williams; *Ain't No Such Thing as a Round Trip Ticket,* "a book for adults based on my experiences as a busdriver."

SIDELIGHTS: Hambone, Fairless's first book, tells of Jeremy, a farm boy, and his struggles to overcome the loss of his best friend, a pig named Hambone, who has been slaughtered. In memoriam, Jeremy buries some of Hambone's favorite things: mud, their neighbor's rhubarb, a ribbon he won at a fair, and other items close to Hambone's heart. Above the grave Jeremy places a tomato plant, which he calls "Hambone." The new Hambone becomes famous in the community because of the plant's stupendous growth and yield.

Throughout the book, Jeremy grows along with his tomato plant, but his growth is emotional. He confronts his father, who feels that tending a garden is a girl's job, and he deals with his bitter feelings about his mother, who has abandoned the family to pursue a singing career in New York.

Fairless's book has been warmly received by critics. George A. Woods of the *New York Times Book Review* called it "a book of some depth and substance." And the *Seattle Times*'s Don Duncan noted: "Although 'Hambone' is aimed at children, ages six to ten, it is a surprisingly good read for adults—full of compassion for a farm boy whose love of a pig clashes with marketplace realities."

Fairless told *CA:* "In writing for children and adults alike, I offer the opportunity to reestablish contact with the passions of our childhood . . . the loves and hates, joys, fears, sorrows, and dreams.

"I tend to develop my work from what I actually observe: people's behavior both alone and in interaction with others. At this point I only write fiction. I always write what I like to read."

BIOGRAPHICAL/CRITICAL SOURCES: Burlington Free Press, October 29, 1980; *Seattle Times,* November 2, 1980; *New York Times Book Review,* November 9, 1980.

FALASSI, Alessandro   1945-

PERSONAL: Born October 3, 1945, in Siena, Italy; son of Giovanni (in business) and Jolanda (a pianist; maiden name, Mazzuoli) Falassi. *Education:* Gonzaga University, B.A., 1968; University of Florence, doctorate, 1970; University of California, Berkeley, M.A., 1973, Ph.D., 1975. *Religion:* Roman Catholic. *Home:* Via Ferruccio 15, Castellina in Chianti, Siena 53011, Italy. *Office:* University of Siena, Caduti di Vicobello 16, Siena 53100, Italy.

CAREER: University of Colorado, Boulder, professor of anthropology, 1975-79; Semester at Sea program of University of Pittsburgh, Pittsburgh, Pa., "Around the World" professor of anthropology, 1979 and 1981; University of California, Berkeley, professor of anthropology, 1980; currently associated with University of Siena, Siena, Italy. Foreign program director of Italian Program, 1975-79. Deputato della Festa, Siena, 1976—. Local election officer (section president, 1978—). *Member:* International Society for Folk Narrative Research, American Anthropological Association, American Folklore Society, Lions Club. *Awards, honors:* Chicago International Folklore Prize, 1975; prize from Rotary Club, 1976.

WRITINGS: La Terra in Piazza: An Interpretation of the Palio of Siena, University of California Press, 1975; *Folklore by the Fireside: Text and Context of the Tuscan Veglio,* University of Texas Press, 1980.

In Italian: *La santa dell'oca Milano,* Mondadori, 1980; *Per fozza e per amore,* Bompiani, 1980; *Folklore Toscano articoli e saggi analitici Siena,* NCS, 1981.

WORK IN PROGRESS: S.S. Universe, a suspense novel; *Festae: A Reader,* a book on festivals in anthropology.

SIDELIGHTS: Falassi commented: "My interest in people and cultures of the world is both personal and professional. As a traveler twice around the world and as a writer, I have investigated people's varied customs and ways. Anthropology can be one of the best ways to self-understanding and tolerance, a task that, if nothing else, avoids alienation, arrogance, and authoritarian prejudice."

*   *   *

FALCONER, Kenneth
See KORNBLUTH, C(yril) M.

*   *   *

FARR, Finis (King)   1904-1982

OBITUARY NOTICE—See index for *CA* sketch: Born December 31, 1904, in Lebanon, Tenn.; died January 3, 1982, in Portland, Me. Journalist and author. Farr wrote for the radio shows "Mr. District Attorney" and "The March of Time" in addition to working for *Time* magazine and the National Broadcasting Company (NBC). After serving in the armed forces during World War II, he was employed by the Central Intelligence Agency (CIA) for several years. Farr contributed articles to periodicals, including *Sports Illustrated, American Heritage,* and *Saturday Evening Post.* He also wrote many biographies which have been translated throughout the world. Among them number *Frank Lloyd Wright: A Biography, FDR: A Political Biography,* and *Rickenbacker's Luck: An American Life.* Obituaries and other sources: *New York Times,* January 6, 1982.

FAWKES, Guy
See BENCHLEY, Robert (Charles)

*   *   *

FEDER, Jose   1917-

PERSONAL: Born July 8, 1917, in Rigny St. Martin, France; son of Jules (a businessman) and Marblie (Schirmer) Feder. *Education:* Institut Catholique, maitrise en philosophie, 1943, maitrise en theologie, 1949. *Religion:* Roman Catholic. *Home and office:* 35 cours Leopold, 54000 Nancy, France.

CAREER: Entered Order of Society of Jesus (Jesuits), 1936, ordained Roman Catholic priest, 1948; College St. Joseph, Lille, France, professor of letters and religion, 1950-53; College de la Providence, Amiens, France, professor of French, Latin, and religion, 1953-58; Groupe des Etudiants Catholiques, Nancy, France, medical chaplain, 1958—.

WRITINGS: (Editor) *Missel quotidien des fideles,* Mame, 1954, 15th edition, 1969, translation published as *The Layman's Missal: Prayer Book and Ritual,* Helicon, 1962; (with Jean Vermeersch) *Missel pour celebrer l'eucharistie* (children's missal), Mame, 1957; (with Vermeersch) *Pour celebrer l'eucharistie: Livret du catechiste,* Mame, 1959; *Missel de St. Pierre aux Liens,* Secours Catholique, 1962; (with Francois Coudreau) *Le Bapteme des adultes,* Mame, 1964; (editor with Robert Claude) *Prie dans le secret,* Casterman, 1965; *Vivre le mystere: Livre du Chretien,* Mame, 1968; *Comme un feu: Prieres du jour,* Centurion, 1970, second enlarged edition, 1980, translation published as *Prayer for Each Day,* Paulist Press, 1974; *Pour la celebration de l'Eucharistie: Dossier de l'equipe liturgique,* Mame, 1972, second edition, 1978; (with others) *Vivre le mystere Pascal: Missel pour la Semaine Sainte et pour la semaine de Paques,* Mame, 1972; (with others) *Companions of Jesus,* introduction by Paolo Molinari, English Province of the Society of Jesus, 1974; (with others) *Ecouter La Bible: Commentaire Biblique,* 28 volumes, Desclee De Brouwer, 1977—.

WORK IN PROGRESS: Theological study of the word of God; research on Christian anthropology and medicine.

SIDELIGHTS: Feder told *CA:* "My writings were undertaken on a private basis; however, they occupy a place in the current trend of the Church that has marked the twentieth century. Catholics from the preceding generations had only a remote contact with the riches of the Liturgy and of the Holy Scripture. They whispered their prayers; they would listen to some readings in Latin and sing together or listen to others sing, letting themselves be carried away by the melody rather than by the words. Our century has shown an increasing amount of concern in presenting to everybody the Christian message still unrevealed. Such preoccupation appears through scholarly studies, new translations, and numerous publications. We see it as a fundamental effort, crowned by Vatican II.

"What is at stake is most important. In order to keep the believers on the right path, the function of authority is no longer taken into consideration. The surrender of the mind is not accepted any more. For those who are somewhat hesitant to believe, only the Voice speaking through the Scripture will stop the flock from breaking into a rout. Each one of us has to confront some operational doctrines leading to confusion. Some of those doctrines are presented as being incompatible with the Christian tradition, others deny freedom. Only a faith which is personally rooted deep in the Gospel will emerge alive and stronger from this universal turmoil."

"Thus we have to back freedom, and in so doing, we back the Spirit. There is a pseudo-freedom that many worship unknowingly; we call it ignorance. It is a hesitation to go back to the source itself, searching for light, sustenance, and strength. The pastor's role is to help others discover those many gifts through a contact with the Living Christ.

"Aware of that concern we have written, translated, and tried to provide a better understanding of these texts. We are deeply convinced that today's enthusiasm for the Word of God will be for the Church the harbinger of a new era filled with a surprising vitality."

*   *   *

FEDER, Paula (Kurzband)   1935-

PERSONAL: Born November 5, 1935, in New York, N.Y.; daughter of Toby Karl (a pre-retirement counselor and school principal) and Diana (a child guidance supervisor; maiden name, Wollins) Kurzband; married Yves A. Feder, January 31, 1965 (divorced July, 1980); children: Sarah Eleanore. *Education:* Syracuse University, B.A., 1957; Bank Street School of Education, M.A., 1958. *Address:* Box 68, Centerbrook, Conn. 06409.

CAREER: Elementary school teacher at public schools in New York, N.Y., 1958-68; substitute teacher at elementary schools in Clinton and Old Saybrook, Conn., 1974-79; planter in green house in Madison, Conn., 1978-79; writer, 1978—.

WRITINGS: Rhubarb Cookbook, privately printed, 1977; *Where Does the Teacher Live?* (Junior Literary Guild selection; illustrated by Lillian Hoban), Dutton, 1978.

WORK IN PROGRESS: Stringbeans for George, a children's book about school classroom situations; research for children's stories revolving around New York City.

SIDELIGHTS: Feder finds her experiences as a New Yorker and an elementary school teacher an important influence in her writing. She told *CA:* "My classroom story must be set in the city in order for me to work out situations and dialogue, which seem to flow so easily once the story idea has been formed. My whole life centered around the city, and although I moved to Connecticut twelve years ago, my heart is still in New York. My goal is to write several children's stories where the city, past and present, plays an integral role. I have a large collection of books, old and new, on New York City, and I am using them for research on future stories."

*   *   *

FEELEY, Malcolm McCollum   1942-

BRIEF ENTRY: Born November 28, 1942, in North Conway, N.H. American political scientist, educator, and author. Feeley taught political science at New York University until 1972. In 1973 he became Russell Sage fellow at Yale University's School of Law. He wrote *Affirmative School Integration: Efforts to Overcome de Facto Segregation in Urban Schools* (Sage Publications, 1968), *The Impact of Supreme Court Decisions: Empirical Studies* (Oxford University Press, 1973), and *The Process Is the Punishment: Handling Cases in a Lower Criminal Court* (Russell Sage Foundation, 1979). *Address:* School of Law, Yale University, New Haven, Conn. 06520. *Biographical/critical sources: American Men and Women of Science: The Social and Behavioral Sciences,* 12th edition, Bowker, 1973.

FEI-KAN, Li
    See LI Fei-kan

*   *   *

FELD, Rose Caroline   1895-1981

OBITUARY NOTICE: Born May 12, 1895, in Romania; died December 17, 1981, in Newton, Conn. Author of *My Aunt Lucienne* and *Sophie Halenczik, American.* Feld's writing was also featured in the *New York Times,* the *New York Herald Tribune,* and *New Yorker.* Obituaries and other sources: *American Authors and Books, 1640 to the Present Day,* 3rd revised edition, Crown, 1972; *New York Times,* December 19, 1981.

*   *   *

FELDKAMP, Fred   1915(?)-1981

OBITUARY NOTICE: Born c. 1915; died December 7, 1981, in Bryn Mawr, Pa. Producer of motion pictures, editor, and author. Feldkamp worked as an editor for *Life.* He also contributed to the newsreel "The March of Time" and to *New Yorker, Vogue,* and *Harper's.* Feldkamp produced the motion pictures "Operation Manhunt," "The Silken Affair," and "Triple Cross." He edited two posthumous books by Will Cuppy, *The Decline and Fall of Practically Everybody* and *How to Get From January to December.* Obituaries and other sources: *New York Times,* December 8, 1981.

*   *   *

FERGUSSON, Bernard Edward   1911-1980

PERSONAL: Born May 6, 1911, in London, England; died November 28, 1980, in London, England; married Laura Margaret Grenfell, 1950; children: one son. *Education:* Attended Royal Military Academy, Sandhurst.

CAREER: British Army, career officer in Black Watch, 1931-58, served in Palestine, 1937-38, the Middle East, 1941, and India, 1942, commander of 16th Infantry Brigade in Burma, 1943-44, director of combined operations, 1945-46, member of Palestine Police, 1947, retiring as brigadier; writer, 1958-62; governor-general and commander-in-chief of New Zealand, 1962-67; writer, 1967-80. Member of team of international observers in Nigeria, 1968-69; colonel of Black Watch, 1969-76; chairman of British Council, 1972-76; chancellor of University of St. Andrews.

AWARDS, HONORS—Military: Distinguished Service Order. Other: Knight Grand Cross of St. Michael and St. George; Knight Grand Cross of the Royal Victorian Order; officer of the Order of the British Empire; knighted; became Lord Ballantrae, 1972; honorary degrees include D.C.L., D.Litt., and LL.D.

WRITINGS: (Author of introduction) Ladislaus Moholy-Nagy, *Eton Portrait,* photographs by Moholy-Nagy, John Miles, 1937, reprint published as *Portrait of Eton,* Muller, 1949; *Essential French Military Terms: English-French,* Gale & Polden, 1939.

Beyond the Chindwin: Being an Account of the Adventures of Number Five Column of the Wingate Expedition Into Burma, 1943, Collins, 1945, new edition, 1951; *Lowland Soldier* (poems), Collins, 1945; *The Wild Green Earth: An Account of the 16th Brigade in General Wingate's Second Expedition Into Burma, 1944,* Collins, 1946.

The Black Watch and the King's Enemies: A History of the Black Watch During the Second World War, Collins, 1950; *The Watery Maze: The Story of Combined Operations,* Collins,

1951, Holt, 1961; *Rupert of the Rhine,* Collins, 1952; *The Rare Adventure,* Collins, 1954; (editor and author of preface) John N. Kennedy, *The Business of War,* Hutchinson, 1957.

Wavell: Portrait of a Soldier, Collins, 1961; *Look at the Army* (juvenile), Hamish Hamilton, 1962; *Return to Burma,* Collins, 1962.

The Trumpet in the Hall, 1930-1958, Collins, 1970; *Captain John Niven,* Collins, 1972; *Balloon Tytler,* Faber, 1972; (with John C. Stewart) *The Black Watch: A Brief Story of the Regiment From 1725 to the Present Day,* Pilgrim Press, 1975; *Hubble-Bubble* (poems), Collins, 1978; *Travel Warrant,* Collins, 1979.

BIOGRAPHICAL/CRITICAL SOURCES: AB Bookman's Weekly, January 19, 1981.*

* * *

FEUERSTEIN, Phyllis A. 1930-

PERSONAL: Surname is pronounced *Foy*-er-stine; born November 18, 1930, in Brooklyn, N.Y.; daughter of Irving (an eggman) and Rebecca (Shagaloff) Uslan; married Seymour Feuerstein (a sales representative), January 20, 1950; children: Stephanie Feuerstein Brounstein, Jay, Amy. *Education:* Attended Brooklyn College (now of the City University of New York), 1947-51. *Home:* 20330 Ithaca Rd., Olympia Fields, Ill. 60461. *Agent:* Porter, Dierks & Porter-Lent, 215 West Ohio St., Chicago, Ill. 60610.

CAREER: Worked as reporter and feature writer for Star Publications, 1964-74; owner of Joy-Phyl (public relations firm), 1975; feature writer and columnist for *Suburban Tribune,* 1974-78; writer, 1979—. *Member:* Authors Guild, Authors League of America, National Federation of Press Women, Society of Midland Authors, Illinois Press Women. *Awards, honors:* Prizes from National Federation of Press Women, 1972, for articles on health, food, social trends, education, and her column, "Sketches," and 1979, for a story on a young man undergoing a sex change.

WRITINGS: The Not-So-Empty Nest, New Century, 1980. Writer for television series "Magic Door." Author of "Sketches," a column in *Suburban Tribune.* Contributor to national magazines, including children's periodicals.

WORK IN PROGRESS: Chips Off the Same Block, covering reasons why the adult sibling relationship doesn't always work.

SIDELIGHTS: Phyllis Feuerstein wrote: "The area of family relationships is familiar territory to me and I have an uncanny perception of people. I use both, plus a sense of humor, to show how family members get along. When I write I feel I am sharing my thoughts and feelings with other people who will be a little less lonely knowing others feel and experience what they do."

* * *

FEULNER, Patricia N(ancy) 1946-

PERSONAL: Born July 9, 1946, in Queens, N.Y.; daughter of George John and Laura (Sablynski) Feulner; married James J. Lyons, July 6, 1968 (divorced, 1972); married David R. Schlegel (an artist), October 20, 1979. *Education:* Fordham University, B.A., 1968; Ohio State University, M.A., 1969, Ph.D., 1973. *Home:* 4915 Foothill Blvd., San Diego, Calif. 92109. *Office:* Department of Anthropology and Sociology, University of San Diego, Alcala Park, San Diego, Calif. 92110.

CAREER: Northeast Missouri State University, Kirksville, assistant professor of sociology, 1971-72; Ohio State University,

Lima, assistant professor of sociology, 1973-75; University of San Diego, Alcala Park, San Diego, Calif., associate professor of sociology, 1975—, chairman of department of anthropology and sociology, 1980—. Academic director of University of the Third Age, 1978—. Member of board of directors of Senior Adult Services and San Diego Regional Educational Consortium on Aging. *Member:* Western Gerontological Society.

WRITINGS: Women in the Professions: A Social Psychological Study, R & E Research Associates, 1979.

WORK IN PROGRESS: A book, tentatively titled *Sociology of Death and Dying,* publication expected in 1983.

SIDELIGHTS: Patricia Feulner wrote: "My work on women in male professions (such as law, medicine, and university teaching) was a result of my own graduate school and teaching experience, which took place during the very early stages of the women's movement. My research, which indicated that women in these professions are remarkable in so many respects, was a boost to my own career motivation.

"My current interests revolve around gerontology, and I feel that we are now on the brink of a new social movement—dedication to the aim of eliminating ageism."

* * *

FIERING, Norman Sanford 1935-

PERSONAL: Surname is pronounced *Fire*-ring; born January 8, 1935, in New York, N.Y.; son of Benjamin (a textile converter) and Dora (Karp) Fiering; married Renee Dashiell, May 29, 1958; children: Benjamin, Jason, Cassandre. *Education:* Dartmouth College, A.B., 1956; Columbia University, M.A., 1961, Ph.D., 1969. *Religion:* "Jewish secular." *Office:* Institute of Early American History and Culture, P.O. Box 220, Williamsburg, Va. 23185.

CAREER: Stanford University, Stanford, Calif., instructor in history, 1964-69; College of William and Mary, Williamsburg, Va., assistant professor of American history, 1969-72; Institute of Early American History and Culture, Williamsburg, editor of publications, 1972—. *Member:* American Antiquarian Society, American Historical Association, Organization of American Historians. *Awards, honors:* Fellowships from National Endowment for the Humanities, 1975-76, and National Humanities Center, 1978-79.

WRITINGS: Moral Philosophy at Seventeenth-Century Harvard, University of North Carolina Press, 1981; *Jonathan Edwards's Moral Thought and Its British Context,* University of North Carolina Press, 1981. Contributor to history and philosophy journals.

* * *

FINE, Anne 1947-

PERSONAL: Born December 7, 1947, in Leicester, England; married Kit Fine (a university professor), 1968; children: two daughters. *Education:* University of Warwick, B.A. (with honors), 1968. *Residence:* Edinburgh, Scotland. *Agent:* Gina Pollinger, 4 Garrick St., London WC2E 9BH, England.

CAREER: English teacher at Cardinal Wiseman Girls' Secondary School, 1968-70; Oxford Committee for Famine Relief, Oxford, England, assistant information officer, 1970-71; Saughton Jail, Edinburgh, Scotland, teacher, 1971-72; freelance writer, 1973—. Volunteer for Amnesty International. *Awards, honors:* Runner-up in *Guardian/Kestrel* Award competition for children's literature, 1978, for *The Summer-House Loon.*

WRITINGS: *The Summer-House Loon* (juvenile), Crowell, 1978; *The Other, Darker Ned,* Methuen, 1979; *The Stone Menagerie,* Methuen, 1980; *Round Behind the Ice-House,* Methuen, 1981. Contributor of short stories to periodicals.

SIDELIGHTS: Anne Fine told *CA:* "I always write with pencil and eraser. I rewrite each book sentence by sentence and paragraph by paragraph over and over again, and now I use very soft-leaded pencils so that I don't get blisters on my fingers so soon. I must go through dozens of pencils for each piece of work. I don't go near a typewriter until I'm quite finished. I don't think I could ever write anything worth reading on a typewriter, so awkward is it to make the endless alterations."

*　　*　　*

FINKEL, LeRoy 1939-

PERSONAL: Born August 12, 1939, in Berkeley, Calif.; son of Manfred and Vera (Giuant) Finkel; married Mary Ellis (a jewelry store manager), 1963; children: Mimi, Danny. *Education:* University of California, Berkeley, B.S., 1961; San Francisco State University, M.A., 1968. *Home:* 1815 Altschul Ave., Menlo Park, Calif. 94025. *Office:* San Mateo County Office of Education, 333 Main St., Redwood City, Calif. 94063.

CAREER: High school business education teacher in Redwood City, Calif., 1963-81, budget coordinator, 1972-75; San Mateo County Office of Education, Redwood City, computer education curriculum coordinator, 1981—. Member of extension faculty at University of California, Berkeley, 1969—, and faculty of DeAnza College, 1975-80. *Member:* Computer-Using Educators (member of executive board), California Business Education Association. *Awards, honors:* Grant from Apple Education Foundation, 1980.

WRITINGS: (With Robert Albrecht and Jerald Brown) *Basic,* Wiley, 1973, 2nd edition, 1977; (with Albrecht and Brown) *Basic for Home Computers,* Wiley, 1978; (with Albrecht and Brown) *Atari Basic,* Wiley, 1979; (with Brown) *Programming Data Files in Basic,* Wiley, 1981; (with Brown) *Apple II: Data File Programming,* Wiley, 1981; (with Brown and Albrecht) *Basic for the Apple Computer,* Wiley, 1982; (with Howard Franklin and JoAnne Koltnow) *Golden Delicious Games for the Apple Computer,* Wiley, 1982; (with Tony Bove) *TRS-80 Model III User Guide,* Wiley, 1982.

SIDELIGHTS: Finkel wrote: "It is exciting to be part of the leading edge of the technology revolution of the eighties."

*　　*　　*

FINKELL, Max
See CATTO, Max(well Jeffrey)

*　　*　　*

FINKELMAN, Paul 1949-

PERSONAL: Born November 15, 1949, in Brooklyn, N.Y.; son of Simon and Ella (Dobbis) Finkelman. *Education:* Syracuse University, A.B., 1971; University of Chicago, M.A., 1972, Ph.D., 1976. *Home:* 807 Garner Ave., Austin, Tex. 78704. *Office:* Department of History, University of Texas, Austin, Tex. 78712.

CAREER: University of California, Irvine, visiting lecturer in history, 1976-77; Washington University, St. Louis, Mo., Mellon faculty fellow, 1977-78; University of Texas, Austin, assistant professor of U.S. history, 1978—. Delegate to Texas Democratic Convention, 1980. Consultant to Library of Congress.

Member: American Historical Association, Organization of American Historians, American Society for Legal History, Phi Beta Kappa. *Awards, honors:* Grant from National Endowment for the Humanities, 1977; J. Franklin Jameson fellow at Library of Congress, 1978.

WRITINGS: *An Imperfect Union: Slavery, Federalism, and Comity,* University of North Carolina Press, 1981. Contributor to history journals and law reviews.

WORK IN PROGRESS: Research on the history of the problem of fugitive slaves in the nineteenth century.

*　　*　　*

FINLEY, Gerald Eric 1931-

PERSONAL: Born July 17, 1931, in Munich, Germany (now West Germany); son of Frederick James (an artist and teacher) and Winifred M. (a weaver; maiden name, Barker) Finley; married Helen V. Steele (a conciliator), April 21, 1961; children: Christopher, Heath. *Education:* University of Toronto, B.A., 1955, M.A., 1957; Johns Hopkins University, Ph.D., 1965. *Home:* 53 Earl St., Kingston, Ontario, Canada K7L 2G5. *Office:* Department of Art, Queen's University, Kingston, Ontario, Canada K7L 3N6.

CAREER: University of Toronto, Toronto, Ontario, lecturer in art and archaeology, 1959-60; University of Saskatchewan, Saskatoon, lecturer in art and acting director of Norman MacKenzie Art Gallery, 1962-63; Queen's University, Kingston, Ontario, assistant professor, 1963-67, associate professor, 1967-72, professor of art history, 1972, head of department, 1963-73. *Member:* Royal Canadian Academy of Arts, Humanities Association of Canada, Turner Society of Great Britain (vice-president), Toronto Arts and Letters Club. *Awards, honors:* British Council grants, 1967-68, 1972; fellowships from Canada Council, 1968-69, 1975, 1976, 1977, 1978, 1979, from Institute of Advanced Studies in the Humanities at University of Edinburgh, 1979-80, and from Social Sciences and Humanities Research Council of Canada, 1980-81. Guest lecturer at Neuere Fremdsprachliche Philologien, Frei Universitaet, Berlin, 1981.

WRITINGS: *George Heriot,* National Gallery of Canada, 1979; *Landscapes of Memory: Turner as Illustrator to Scott,* University of California Press, 1980; *Turner and George IV in Edinburgh, 1822,* Tate Gallery/University of Edinburgh Press, 1981; *George Heriot: Postmaster Painter of the Canadas,* University of Toronto Press, 1982. Contributor to art and art history journals, including *Connoisseur* and *Burlington.*

WORK IN PROGRESS: A study of Turner as a painter of history.

*　　*　　*

FISHBEIN, Harold Dennis 1938-

BRIEF ENTRY: Born May 13, 1938, in Milwaukee, Wis. American psychologist, educator, and author. Fishbein has taught psychology at University of Cincinnati since 1964; in 1971 he became associate dean of McMicken College of Arts and Sciences. He wrote the text for three sound recordings, *Channel Capacity: Absolute Judgment* (Jeffrey Norton, 1974), *Difference Threshold: Method of Constant Stimuli* (Jeffrey Norton, 1974), and *Scaling: Magnitude Estimation* (Jeffrey Norton, 1974), and a book, *Evolution, Development, and Children's Learning* (Goodyear Publishing, 1976). *Address:* Department of Psychology, McMicken College of Arts and Sciences, University of Cincinnati, Cincinnati, Ohio 45221. *Biographical/*

critical sources: American Men and Women of Science: The Social and Behavioral Sciences, 13th edition, Bowker, 1978.

* * *

FISHER, Charles Alfred 1916-1982(?)

OBITUARY NOTICE: Born April 23, 1916; died c. January, 1982, in St. Albans, England. Educator, geographer, and author. Fisher specialized in the geography of Southeast Asia. He became interested in that region during World War II when, as a prisoner of the Japanese, he was forced to work on the Burma railway. He taught at the University of London from 1964 to 1981. His numerous writings include *South East Asia: A Social, Economic and Political Geography* and *Three Times a Guest.* Obituaries and other sources: *The Author's and Writer's Who's Who,* 6th edition, Burke's Peerage, 1971; *Who's Who,* 131st edition, St. Martin's, 1979; *London Times,* January 11, 1982.

* * *

FISHER, Eugene J(oseph) 1943-

PERSONAL: Born September 10, 1943, in Detroit, Mich.; son of Eugene J. (an attorney) and Caroline M. (Damm) Fisher; married Catherine Ambrosiano (an attorney), December 31, 1970. *Education:* Sacred Heart Seminary, Detroit, Mich., B.A. (magna cum laude), 1965; University of Detroit, M.A. (Catholic theology), 1968; New York University, M.A. (Hebrew studies), 1971, Ph.D., 1976. *Religion:* Roman Catholic. *Home:* 2216 Cocquina Dr., Reston, Va. 22091. *Office:* Secretariat for Catholic-Jewish Relations, National Conference of Catholic Bishops, 1312 Massachusetts Ave. N.W., Washington, D.C. 20005.

CAREER: St. Francis School of Christian Education, New York City, lecturer in Christian education, 1969-71; Archdiocese of Detroit, Office of Religious Education, Detroit, Mich., director of catechist formation, 1971-77; National Conference of Catholic Bishops, Washington, D.C., executive director of Secretariat for Catholic-Jewish Relations, 1977—. Adjunct professor at University of Detroit, 1969-77, and at St. John's Seminary, Plymouth, Mich., 1973-75. Member of national program committee of National Conference of Christians and Jews, 1979—; chairperson of Israel Study Group, 1981-83. Consultant to Vatican Commission for Religious Relations with the Jews; film consultant for "The Day Christ Died."

MEMBER: Service Internationale de Documentation Judeo-Chretienne, Society of Biblical Literature (vice-president of Chesapeake Bay region, 1979-80; president of region, 1980-81), Catholic Biblical Assocation (vice-president of Chesapeake Bay region, 1979-80; president of region, 1980-81), National Association of Professors of Hebrew (member of executive council, 1978—), Biblical Archaeology Society, Fellowship of Reconciliation, National Institute on the Holocaust, Center for Holocaust Studies, Michigan Academy of Arts, Sciences, and Letters.

WRITINGS: Faith Without Prejudice: Rebuilding Christian Attitudes Toward Jews and Judaism, Paulist/Newman, 1977; (with Leon Klenicki) *Understanding the Jewish Experience: A Joint Educational Program,* Department of Education, Anti-Defamation League of B'nai B'rith and U.S. Catholic Conference, 1978; (editor with Daniel Polish) *Formation of Social Policy in the Catholic and Jewish Traditions,* University of Notre Dame Press, 1980; *Priestly Formation and Catholic-Jewish Relations: A Curriculum and Resource Handbook for Seminaries,* National Catholic Education Association, 1981; *Home-*

work for Christians, National Conference of Christians and Jews, 1981.

Contributor to *The Religious Roots of Anti-Semitism: A Handbook for Congregations,* edited by Sr. Noel Boggs, Yolanda Chainey, and others, [Tulsa, Okla.], 1981. Contributor to *New Catholic Encyclopedia.* Contributor of more than fifty articles and reviews to scholarly journals.

WORK IN PROGRESS: A major study of the Church's mission to the Jews, historically and in the present, for Paulist Press's "Stimulus" series, publication expected in 1982.

SIDELIGHTS: Eugene Fisher's book *Faith Without Prejudice* attempts to reestablish a Christian attitude toward Judaism. In 1960, after meeting with Jules Isaac, the Jewish historian who exposed the hostility of Christians toward Jews, Pope John XXIII and the Second Vatican Council began a campaign to smooth Jewish-Christian relations. *Faith Without Prejudice* discusses the historical roots of the religions' attitudes, Jesus as a Jew, and anti-Semitism in the gospels as well as shared aspects of Christianity and Judaism, ecumenical activities, and the portrayal of Jews in religious literature. Fisher also explores the atmosphere for future relations between Christians and Jews, and he proves what Vatican II espoused: that the Romans and their politics were responsible for Jesus's death, not the Jews as many Christians believed. "In place of the Jews as the tormentors and killers of Jesus," said Rabbi Daniel E. Polish, "Fisher presents the passion in the context of the political background of the times: as part of the intercommunal conflicts, and as the exercise of Roman political sovereignty over its beleaguered colony."

Praised for its "conversational style," the book is "guaranteed to sustain the reader's interest," remarked Monika K. Hellwig. Written by a Roman Catholic, *Faith Without Prejudice,* according to Daniel Polish, teaches modern tenets of the church, "strengthening . . . the Christian's own faith by coming to terms with its Jewish roots, and with the evils perpetrated in the name of that faith."

Fisher wrote: "I believe that, after two thousand years of Christian violence against Jews, the renewal of Christian attitudes toward the Jewish people and Judaism is one of the most critical challenges facing the church today. After the Holocaust, Christian treatment of Jews is the litmus test for the viability and credibility both of Western religion and Western civilization. If I can help improve Christian-Jewish relations by even a tiny fraction in my lifetime, my life will have achieved some meaning.

"I have organized an ongoing (and quite unique) trilateral dialogue among Jewish, Christian, and Muslim scholars, located at the Kennedy Institute at Georgetown University."

BIOGRAPHICAL/CRITICAL SOURCES: Liturgy, March, 1978; *NC News Service,* June 30, 1978; *Directions,* September, 1978.

* * *

FISHMAN, Ken 1950-

PERSONAL: Born April 27, 1950, in Syracuse, N.Y.; son of Howard (in business) and Naomi (in business; maiden name, Harris) Fishman. *Education:* New York University, B.F.A., 1972. *Residence:* Santa Monica, Calif.

CAREER: New York University, New York, N.Y., instructor in screenwriting, 1974-80; writer, 1980—.

WRITINGS: "Law and Disorder" (screenplay), Columbia, 1974; "The Mall" (screenplay), Filmways, 1980; *Paradise* (novel), Dell, 1980.

FitzGERALD, Brian Seymour Vesey
See VESEY-FitzGERALD, Brian Seymour

*   *   *

FLORINSKY, Michael T. 1894-1981

OBITUARY NOTICE—See index for *CA* sketch: Born December 27, 1894, in Kiev, Russia (now U.S.S.R.); died October 10, 1981, in Switzerland. Educator, historian, editor, and author known for his two-volume study *Russia: A History and an Interpretation*. Florinsky took ten years of researching and writing to complete the book, which was published in 1963, the year of his retirement. The work covered the years from Lenin's rise to power through World War II. Florinsky lived in Russia until the onset of the Bolshevik Revolution, at which time he immigrated to the West. He had served in the Russian Imperial Army during World War I as an artillery officer. Wounded in combat, Florinsky received four military decorations before 1918. Beginning in 1921, he worked in London and then in New York City as an associate editor on the Carnegie Foundation publication *Economic and Social History of the War*. Florinsky edited twelve volumes about his native Russia for the project. He then joined the faculty of Columbia University in 1931, teaching economics there for more than thirty years. Florinsky wrote several other books on Russia and also a number on Europe. His body of work includes *End of the Russian Empire*, *Fascism and National Socialism*, and *Contemporary Europe*. Obituaries and other sources: *New York Times*, October 14, 1981; *AB Bookman's Weekly*, November 2, 1981.

*   *   *

FONTANET, Joseph 1921-1980

OBITUARY NOTICE: Born February 9, 1921, in Savoy, France; murdered February 2, 1980. Public official and author. Fontanet entered French politics after World War II as a director for the secretary of state. In 1958 he became secretary of state for industry and commerce. The next year, affairs of domestic trade came under his authority. Fontanet served in several capacities during the 1960's. In 1974 Fontanet supported the losing candidate in elections for the French presidency. Soon afterward he was defeated in a bid for a seat in Parliament. He retired from politics and founded the short-lived newspaper *J'informe*. He wrote *Le Social et le vivant*. His murderer is not believed to have known Fontanet's identity. Obituaries and other sources: *Who's Who in the World*, 4th edition, Marquis, 1978; *The International Who's Who*, Europa, 1979; *The Annual Obituary 1980*, St. Martin's, 1981.

*   *   *

FORBERG, Ati
See FORBERG, Beate Gropius

*   *   *

FORBERG, Beate Gropius 1925-
(Ati Forberg)

PERSONAL: Born December 19, 1925, in Germany; daughter of Walter Gropius (an architect); married Charles Forberg (an architect); children: Sarina, Erika. *Education:* Attended Black Mountain College and Chicago Institute of Design. *Residence:* Brooklyn Heights, N.Y.

CAREER: Illustrator and graphic designer. Designed typography and window displays; also worked on magazine and in advertising agencies in Chicago, Ill. Children's book illustrator in New York, N.Y.

WRITINGS—Under name Ati Forberg: *The Very Special Baby: A Christmas Story*, illustrations by Carol Woodard, Fortress, 1969.

Illustrator: Edwin O'Connor, *Benjy*, Little, Brown, 1957; George Mendoza, *And Amadeo Asked, How Does One Become a Man?*, Braziller, 1959; Phyllis McGinley, *Boys Are Awful*, F. Watts, 1962; Charlotte Bronte, *Jane Eyre*, Macmillan, 1962; Wendy Sanford and Mendoza, *The Puma and the Pearl*, Walker, 1962; (and editor) *On a Grass-Green Horn: Old Scotch and English Ballads*, Atheneum, 1965; Edgar Allan Poe, *Tales*, Whitman, 1965; Doris H. Lund, *Attic of the Wind*, Parents Magazine Press, 1967; Helen Cresswell, *Where the Wind Blows*, Funk, 1968; Frances Brailsford, *In the Space of a Wink*, Follett, 1969; Mendoza, *The Starfish Trilogy*, Funk, 1969; Lawrence F. Lowery and Albert B. Carr, *Quiet as a Butterfly*, Holt, 1969.

Ruth J. Adams, *Fidelia*, Lothrop, 1970; Aileen L. Fisher, *Jeanne d'Arc*, Crowell, 1970; Barbara Schiller, *Erec and Enid*, Dutton, 1970; Florence P. Heide, *The Key*, Atheneum, 1971; Chloe Lederer, *Down the Hill of the Sea*, Lothrop, 1971; Sarah F. Tomaino, *Persephone, Bringer of Spring*, Crowell, 1971; Pauline P. Meek, *God Speaks to Me*, John Knox, 1972; Doris Van Liew Foster, *Feather in the Wind: The Story of a Hurricane*, Lothrop, 1972; Yoshiko Uchida, *Samurai of Gold Hill*, Scribner, 1972; Mendoza, *Poem for Putting to Sea*, Hawthorne, 1972; Barbara K. Walker, *The Ifrit and the Magic Gifts*, Follett, 1972; Ann McGovern, *If You Lived With the Circus*, Four Winds, 1972; Fisher, *"You Don't Look Like Your Mother," Said the Robin to the Fawn*, Bowmar, 1973; Lyon S. DeCamp, editor, *Tales Beyond Time: From Fantasy to Science Fiction*, Lothrop, 1973; Anne N. Baldwin, *A Friend in the Park*, Four Winds, 1973; Nancy C. Smith, *Josie's Handful of Quietness*, Abingdon, 1975; Edna Barth, *Cupid and Psyche: A Love Story Retold*, Seabury Press, 1976; Cresswell, *A Game of Catch*, Macmillan, 1977; Robbin Fleisher, *Quilts in the Attic*, Macmillan, 1978; Carol Fenner, *The Skates of the Uncle Richard*, Random, 1978; Barbara S. Hazen, *The Me I See*, Abingdon, 1978.

SIDELIGHTS: As a student at Black Mountain College, Ati Forberg studied art under abstractionist painter Josef Albers. Forberg's works are included in the Kerlan Collection at the University of Minnesota.*

*   *   *

FORD, Betty
See FORD, Elizabeth (Anne) Bloomer

*   *   *

FORD, Cathy Diane 1952-

PERSONAL: Born April 11, 1952, in Lloydminster, Saskatchewan, Canada; daughter of Gerald James and Mary Magdalene (White) Ford; married Dwain Anton Ruckle, May 23, 1974. *Education:* University of British Columbia, B.F.A., 1976, M.F.A., 1978. *Home and office address:* R.R.1, Mayne Island, British Columbia, Canada V0N 2J0.

CAREER: Intermedia Press, Vancouver, British Columbia, editor, 1973-78; Caitlin Press, Vancouver, editor, 1979—. *Member:* League of Canadian Poets. *Awards, honors:* Canada Council grants, 1977, 1980.

WRITINGS: Stray Zale (poetry), Blewointment Press, 1975; *Blood Uttering* (poetry), Intermedia Press, 1976; (editor) *Canadian Short Fiction Anthology,* Volume I, Intermedia Press, 1976; *Tall Trees* (poetry and photographs), Blewointment Press, 1977; *The Murdered Dreams Awake* (poetry), Caitlin Press, 1979; *the womb rattles its pod poems,* Vehicule Press, 1981.

WORK IN PROGRESS: Moon in My Belly, a novel; *Saffron, Rose, and Flame,* a book on one hundred poems based on the life and works of Joan of Arc; *The Desiring Heart,* a book of long poems.

SIDELIGHTS: Cathy Ford wrote: "I support my own belief in new writers and writing by the labors of love entailed in the works of a small literary press, in partnership with two other women, Ingrid Klassen and Carolyn Zonailo. We are now publishing four titles a year at Caitlin.

"I am most interested in growth in terms of language and subject or content; and in moving forward in writing, even in terms of rewriting the past, so that, in the medieval sense, there is no distinction between the past and the present, so that linear progression isn't used."

*   *   *

FORD, Elizabeth (Anne) Bloomer   1918-
(Betty Ford)

PERSONAL: Born April 8, 1918, in Chicago, Ill.; daughter of William Stephenson (a salesman) and Hortense (Neahr) Bloomer; married William C. Warren, 1942 (divorced, 1947); married Gerald R. Ford (a former congressman and the thirty-eighth president of United States), October 15, 1948; children: Michael Gerald, John Garner, Steven Meigs, Susan Elizabeth. *Education:* Attended Bennington College, 1936 and 1937. *Politics:* Republican. *Religion:* Episcopalian. *Home address:* Box 927, Rancho Mirage, Calif. 92270.

CAREER: Dance instructor in Grand Rapids, Mich., 1932-39; Martha Graham Concert Group, New York City, dancer, 1939-41; Herpolscheimer's Department Store, Grand Rapids, fashion director, 1943-48; writer, 1978. Model at John Powers Agency, New York City, 1939-41; Sunday school teacher at Emmanuel on the Hill Episcopal Church, Alexandria, Va., 1961-64. Member of board of directors of League of Republican Women and of The Lambs; member of advisory board of Rosalind Russell Medical Research Fund. Program chairman of Alexandria Cancer Fund; honorary chairman of Palm Springs Desert Museum; chairman of Washington Heart Association's Heart Sunday. Trustee of Eisenhower Medical Center and of Nursing Home Advisory and Research Council, Inc.; national trustee of Nation Symphony Orchestra. Member of national committee on observance of International Women's Year, 1977, and of Golden Circle Patrons Center Theatre for Performing Arts; patron of Salvation Army Auxilary annual fashion show luncheon; supporter of National Endowment for the Arts. Association with Childrens Hospital, Washington, D.C.; formerly associated with Cub Scouts of America. *Member:* American Red Cross Senate Wives Club (president).

AWARDS, HONORS: Silver Anniversary Humanitarian Award, 1975, from Philadelphia Association of Retarded Children; Rita V. Tishman Human Relations Award, 1975, from Women's Division of the Anti-Defamation League of B'nai B'rith; named distinguished woman of the year, 1975, by National Art Association; Silver Spirit of Life Award, 1976, from Los Angeles City of Hope National Medical Center; Centennial Award, 1976, from *McCall's;* Media Award for Communication of Hope, 1976, from American Cancer Society; Spirit

of Independence Award, 1976, from Golden Supper Club; Parson's Award, 1976, from New York Parsons School of Design; named woman of the year, 1976, by *Ladies' Home Journal;* Alfred P. Sloan, Jr., Memorial Award, 1977.

WRITINGS: (Under name Betty Ford; with Chris Chase) *The Times of My Life* (Book-of-the-Month Club selection), Harper, 1978.

SIDELIGHTS: "The point is, I am an ordinary woman who was called onstage at an extraordinary time. I was no different once I became First Lady than I had been before. But through an accident of history, I became interesting to people." Such is the reasoning of Betty Ford, wife of the thirty-eighth president of the United States and author of *The Times of My Life,* an autobiography that, according to A. H. Cain of the *Library Journal,* "reveals why she is one of America's most admired women."

Born in Chicago, Illinois, but raised in Grand Rapids, Michigan, Betty Ford spent her childhood as a tomboy tagging after her older brothers. Like many girls, she took dancing lessons, and she delighted in the surprises her salesman father brought home for her after his trips. By the time she was seventeen, her father had died of accidental carbon monoxide poisoning, and Ford had embarked on a life of her own as a model and a dance instructor.

When she was twenty, Ford met Martha Graham, the renowned dancer and choreographer, at a concert in Ann Arbor, Michigan. "I ran around backstage," Ford recalled, "grabbed Martha's hand and blurted out, 'If I come to New York, can I be at your school?'" Graham agreed and Ford became a member of the dance company's entourage. "[Graham] shaped my whole life. She gave me the ability to stand up to all the things I had to go through, with much more courage than I would have had without her," Ford revealed to *Newsweek.*

In 1941, Ford left Graham's troupe and returned home at her mother's request. She continued to teach dance classes and worked as the fashion coordinator of a department store in Grand Rapids. She dated Bill Warren, whom she remembered as a "blond with curly hair, . . . a good dancer, a good tennis player, he drank and flirted and, unlike some of the men I dated, he wasn't a bit stuffy." Her mother and stepfather, though, "were not enthusiastic about Bill Warren," so he became "all the more alluring" to their child. Ford married Warren in 1942, a union that went "from bloom to bust in five years." "The things that made our dating so amusing," Ford assessed, "were the things that made the marriage difficult. . . . Here I was, ready for a home and children, and Bill was by no means ready to settle down. There was nothing I could do to change him."

Within a year of her divorce, Ford met and married Gerald Ford. She thought she was "marrying a lawyer, and he would practice law until it was time for him to retire, and we would live a quiet life in Grand Rapids." Instead, she became the bride of a politician who arrived "so late for the wedding [because he was campaigning] I almost married the best man." Ford's matron of honor warned her that as a politician's wife she would never "have to worry about other women. Jerry's work will be the other woman." "But I didn't care," Ford insisted, "I was crazy about the man."

As the wife of a congressman, Ford did compete with her husband's work. "My brother and sister-in-law had been right," she reflected. "Work *was* Jerry's mistress. Weekends, when he didn't have any staff in the office, he'd go there anyway, and I'd go, too, and spend the day helping with the filing. I'd putter around, do what simple jobs I could, just to be with him.'' The congressman worked through vacations, campaigned in Grand Rapids instead of celebrating their wedding anniversaries together, and when he became minority leader of the House of Representatives, Ford's husband spent 258 days per year away from home. By then her children had arrived, and they became her "whole life."

Then problems began for Ford. She suffered a pinched nerve plus spinal arthritis, and she fell into a long-term dependency on medication and alcohol to alleviate the pain. Though she felt neglected and resentful, she refused to admit it to herself. "One night," she remembered, "I rolled over in bed, saw Jerry lying beside me and said, 'What are *you* doing here?'— but mostly I bottled up my misery." Feeling as though she were being taken for granted, Ford needed some of the attention that she was doling out as a wife and mother. "I was so hurt," she wrote, "that I'd think: I'm going to get in the car, and I'm going to drive to the beach, and nobody's going to know where I am. I wanted them to worry about me. I wanted them to say, 'Well, my gosh, Mother is gone, what are we going to do?'"

In 1973, Ford's husband was appointed vice-president of the United States to replace Spiro Agnew, who had resigned the position. Eight months later, when Richard Nixon resigned from the presidency, Ford became the First Lady, a job she did not expect or want. "Jerry did not want this [the presidency]," she recalled. "I certainly did not want it, and neither did our children. But the main point was, it was best for the country." Though she was "scared to death" of her new position, she was committed to it from the beginning, and when her husband took his oath of office, Ford "felt like I was taking that oath, too."

Ford adapted to the role of First Lady well. Though the job entailed many responsibilities and pressures, she reveled in them. "It's her turn now, bless her heart," a friend told the *New York Times,* "and now that she doesn't have to worry about things like whether the beds are made, she's loving it." Friends and family felt that Ford's position as the First Lady was where she belonged. "She's a celebrity in her own right," said her son Michael. "I see *her* on TV and in the newspapers now. All those years Mom did all the dirty work, cleaning up after the four of us, taking us to appointments and fixing our meals, and then when Dad got home we'd be so excited to see him we'd just crawl all over him, ignoring her. I know I was at fault for assuming that's the way things were, and not showing my appreciation for all the love and care she had for us." A friend of the Fords added: "After 26 years in his [President Ford's] shadow, she's in the limelight now." Ford, according to a *New York Times* article, saw even more of her husband once they settled in the White House.

She was expected to be, as her friend maintained in a *Ladies' Home Journal* article, "a lovely First Lady, somewhat shy, but thoroughly nice and totally honest," which she was. With a reputation for candor, Ford won "approval for her charm, honesty, and good humor," reported Laura Berman of the *Miami Herald. Newsweek*'s woman of the year in 1975, Ford was the most outspoken First Lady since Eleanor Roosevelt. At her first official public speaking engagement while she was still the vice-president's wife, Ford destroyed her prepared speech because she would "rather say what I want," and she did not hesitate to speak on a variety of sensitive subjects. For example, Ford told a *McCall's* interviewer that reporters had asked her about "everything but how often I sleep with my husband, and if they'd asked me that, I would have told them." When asked, she responded "as often as possible."

In a now famous "60 Minutes" interview, a segment that generated the most mail in the show's history, the First Lady discussed marijuana, equal rights for women, abortion, and the possibility of a premarital affair for her daughter, Susan. Though some individuals, such as W. A. Criswell, the pastor of the world's largest Southern Baptist congregation, and Gordon B. Hinckley, a Mormon elder, were offended by Ford's remarks, most people, including feminist Betty Friedan, were pleased with them. Mary McGrory praised Ford for "getting her information from the real world," and *Newsweek* cited that a 1975 Harris survey "showed overwhelming approval for Betty's plain speaking." Even the president agreed, saying "I'm proud of what Betty had to say." In fact, as *Time* noted, Ford's "husband gives every indication of pride in her enterprise. Hearing about the anti-Betty pickets outside the White House, he responded with a good natured display of liberated gallantry: 'Fine,' he declared. 'Let them demonstrate against you. It takes the heat off me.'"

Ford's appeal, observed Nancy Hawks, chairperson of the National Endowment of the Arts, is that "she's never for a moment pretentious. What she thinks, she says." The household columnist Heloise remarked: "The gals love the way she comes out and says what she thinks. They feel as if she's their next door neighbor, just one of the bunch. She doesn't seem a *bit* stuck up." Ford's priority is honesty. She is willing to say what she perceives to be true, whether it upsets people or not, and this is what people find engaging. "You're foolish if you try to beat around the bush," the First Lady explained. "You just meet yourself coming around the bush the other way." She's "not afraid to say what's on her mind and she's willing to admit some faults, some personal imperfections," wrote Berman.

Shortly after becoming First Lady, Ford discovered that she had breast cancer and underwent a radical mastectomy and chemotherapy. Because of her frankness in facing cancer, she is credited with encouraging and saving other women from the disease. "I got a lot of credit for having gone public with my mastectomy," wrote Ford, "but if I hadn't been the wife of the President of the United States, the press would not have come racing after my story, so in a way it was fate."

Several years after her cancer ordeal, Ford once again showed great courage when facing personal trauma. Ford's dependency on painkillers became more pronounced after her husband lost the 1976 presidential election and her family returned to private life. An alcoholic, she began overmedicating herself. "At first, I was bitter toward the medical profession," she revealed. "Fourteen years of being advised to take pills, rather than wait for the pain to hit. I had never been without my drugs. I took pills for pain, I took pills to sleep, I took mild tranquilizers. Today things are changing. Doctors are being educated right along with the rest of us, but some of them used to be all too eager to write prescriptions. It was easier to give a woman tranquilizers and get rid of her than sit and listen to her." Ford's stay at the U.S. Naval Hospital in Long Beach, a center for alcohol and drug rehabilitation therapy, was actively covered by the press, and Ford herself was vocal about her addiction and rescue since she was eager to help others in similar states. "I'm not out to rescue anybody who doesn't want to be rescued," she commented. "I just think it's important to say how easy it is to slip into a dependency on pills or alcohol. And how hard it is to admit that dependency."

In her autobiography, Ford narrated her life in detail, and her story, suggested Priscilla Johnson McMullan of the *Chicago Tribune,* is one "for the rest of us to emulate." Although the book was well received, Ford worried about it. She "wasn't so sure she'd done the right thing,'' stated *Newsweek* reporters. Ford told them: ''When I saw my name used at the beginning of an article with a picture of a woman smashed out of sight, I thought, 'Why in the world did I ever open my mouth?' Since then, I've had telegrams and phone calls from people all over the world saying 'Please *don't* stop talking.'''

Admired for her willingness to admit just how human she is, Ford shows that she's just an ''average'' American woman with quirks like anybody else. For instance, one of Ford's favorite pranks, which she revealed in *The Times of My Life*, was wedging a cigarette between the fingers of the statue of a Greek goddess in the Yellow Oval Room. After reading the book, Anne Tyler of the *Washington Post Book World* observed that ''you can't help liking her.''

There is no trace of arrogance in the autobiography, and it rings of Ford, who, according to Christopher Lehmann-Haupt of the *New York Times,* ''never stopped being plain Elizabeth Ann Bloomer from Grand Rapids.'' ''It's to both authors' credit,'' remarked Jane Howard in the *New York Times Book Review,* ''that these memoirs sound just like Betty Ford herself: as American as a suburban shopping mall.'' Yet all Ford ever wanted was to leave her ''mark as a very human person interested in America as a country and in its people particularly. I don't feel that because . . . [I was] First Lady I'm any different from what I was before. It can happen to anyone. After all, it *has* happened to anyone.''

AVOCATIONAL INTERESTS: Gardening.

BIOGRAPHICAL/CRITICAL SOURCES—Books: Myra McPherson, *Power Lovers,* Putnam, 1975; Jeffrey Feinman, *Betty Ford,* Award Books, 1976; Betty Ford and Chris Chase, *The Times of My Life,* Harper, 1978; Sheila Rabb Weidenfeld, *First Lady's Lady: With the Fords at the White House,* Putnam, 1979.

Periodicals: *New York Times,* October 15, 1973, August 5, 1975, January 25, 1977, November 8, 1978, November 10, 1978; *New York Post,* December 15, 1973, August 17, 1974; *Time,* December 17, 1973, May 13, 1974, August 12, 1974, August 26, 1974, September 16, 1974, October 7, 1974, December 30, 1974, March 3, 1975, June 23, 1975, July 28, 1975, August 25, 1975, September 1, 1975, December 1, 1975, January 5, 1976, March 22, 1976, May 3, 1976, July 5, 1976, August 16, 1976, August 30, 1976, January 24, 1977, March 21, 1977, April 24, 1978, October 23, 1978; *McCall's,* May, 1974, October, 1974, December, 1974, February, 1975, September, 1975, May, 1976, January, 1977, July, 1978; *Good Housekeeping,* May, 1974, August, 1976, September, 1978; *Newsweek,* June 2, 1974, June 23, 1974, August 19, 1974, October 7, 1974, October 28, 1974, January 27, 1975, August 18, 1975, December 1, 1975, December 29, 1975, July 4, 1976, August 23, 1976, March 21, 1977, August 1, 1977, December 25, 1978, January 15, 1979; *Washington Post Magazine,* July 21, 1974; *Miami Herald,* August 9, 1974; *U.S. News and World Report,* August 19, 1974, October 7, 1974, December 30, 1974, August 25, 1975, December 15, 1975, December 29, 1975, March 8, 1976, October 18, 1976, June 20, 1977; *People,* August 26, 1974, October 23, 1978; *Vogue,* September, 1974, April, 1975; *Biography News,* September, 1974; *Ladies' Home Journal,* October, 1974, May, 1976, July, 1978, October, 1978, November, 1978; *New York Times Magazine,* December 8, 1974.

National Review, August 29, 1975; *Senior Scholastic,* October 7, 1975; *Saturday Evening Post,* September, 1976; *Christian Century,* October 13, 1976, January 17, 1979; *Redbook,* January, 1977; *Human Events,* October 21, 1978; *Washington Post*

Book World, October 29, 1978; *Chicago Tribune,* November 6, 1978; *Washington Post,* November 9, 1978; *New York Times Book Review,* November 26, 1978, September 9, 1979; *Village Voice,* November 27, 1978; *Library Journal,* December 15, 1978; *Book List,* December 15, 1978; *Esquire,* December 19, 1978; *Progressive,* January, 1979; *West Coast Review of Books,* January, 1979; *Best Sellers,* February, 1979; *Reader's Digest,* February, 1979; *New Republic,* May 26, 1979; *Detroit News,* September 15, 1981.*

—*Sketch by Charity Anne Dorgan*

*   *   *

FORD, Paul F(rancis X.)   1947-

PERSONAL: Born April 8, 1947, in Springfield, Mass.; son of Bernard William (an engineer) and Therese Marie (a registered nurse; maiden name, Bourcier) Ford. *Education:* St. John's Seminary College, Camarillo, Calif., B.A., 1969; St. John's Major Seminary, Camarillo, Calif., M.A., 1973; doctoral study at Fuller Theological Seminary, 1975—. *Home:* 9644 Camino Real, Arcadia, Calif. 91006.

CAREER: Entered St. Andrew's Priory, Valyermo, Calif., 1973, oblate of St. Benedict, 1978—; Fuller Theological Seminary, Pasadena, Calif., lecturer in theology, 1978—. Lecturer at Loyola Marymount University, 1981. Theology editor and music consultant for Franciscan Communications Center, 1979-81. Member of Liturgical Commission and Religious Education Congress of Archdiocese of Los Angeles, 1978—. *Member:* International Chesterton Society, Conference on Christianity and Literature, Ecumenical Society of the Blessed Virgin Mary, Church Music Association, National Association of Pastoral Musicians, American Academy of Religion, New York C. S. Lewis Society, Southern California C. S. Lewis Society (founding director, 1974). *Awards, honors:* Award from Christian Workers Foundation, 1978.

WRITINGS: (Author of preface) C. S. Lewis, *The Weight of Glory,* Unicorn Press, 1977; *Companion to Narnia,* Harper, 1980. Contributor to theology journals and *New Oxford Review.* Editorial assistant for *Good News,* 1978-79; editor of *the good word,* 1980-81.

WORK IN PROGRESS: C. S. Lewis: Ecumenical Spiritual Director (tentative title), publication by Harper expected in 1984; an annotated edition of *The Screwtape Letters,* by C. S. Lewis, Harper, 1985; *The Human Experience of Promise,* Harper, 1986.

SIDELIGHTS: Ford told *CA:* ''I am a young, active theologian-in-the-making with a curiousity about many things and a not-so-secret desire to be a contemplative. I most identify with Shasta, the boy of *The Horse and His Boy,* a person longing to be in on the delightful secret that lies 'to the north,' led along to that freedom by an unseen but inexorably loving presence walking at his side through life.

''I was born in the French Canadian 'ghetto' of Ludlow, Massachusetts, and have memories of the softwood forests in spring and fall splendor; but I was raised in the California desert and grew to love the severe seasons even there. I studied for the Roman Catholic priesthood for twelve years (I wanted to become a priest ever since first grade and years of friendly priest-visitors to my home). But toward the end of my course of studies, I thought I had a monastic calling, which led me to spend five years as a Benedictine monk in the California desert with Belgian monks who had been missionaries in China. With their ecumenical foresight, they sent me to Fuller Seminary to get my Ph.D. in theology: I am Fuller's first Roman Catholic graduate student in systematic theology. Through Fuller, I have become aware of the American evangelical world and sense that one of my tasks in life will be to enable dialogue between Protestants and Roman Catholics. One of my major interests is in ecumenical spirituality, and I have been involved in teaching this subject and making myself available as a spiritual director. When the senior monks discerned that I had a more active calling, they asked me to leave monastic life; but I continue to visit the monastery frequently.

"I am founder and first director of the Southern California C. S. Lewis Society, which began as a week-long workshop at the monastery by me and my friend, a Baptist minister. I continue to serve on the council of the society. I am the literary administrator of my late spiritual director and mentor, Monsignor James D. O'Reilly, physicist, philosopher, and theologian; my hope in his regard is to publish at least one collection of his writings—he was a C. S. Lewis to me. I was choral music director at the seminary and assistant choir master at the monastery; music continues to be one of my chief interests. But I get the greatest joy in life from my friends near and far: any spare time I have is devoted to correspondences. It should be no surprise, then, that my favorite literary interest is biography.

"I have been reading C. S. Lewis and G. K. Chesterton since I was sixteen, when I was introduced to both writers by my Jesuit schoolmasters, who gave me one of the last classical educations available in this country (Latin, Greek, English, and rhetoric until they were coming out of my ears). Both men continue to impress me with their joy of life, their clear thinking, and the depth of their spirituality. I dream of completing an idea-index to Lewis (a la Joseph Sprug's *Index to Chesterton*) and a critical edition of Lewis's complete works."

*   *   *

FORSBERG, Roberta Jean   1914-

BRIEF ENTRY: Born April 18, 1914, in Everett, Mass. American educator and author. Forsberg joined the faculty at Whittier College in 1942, and in 1943 she became a professor of English. Her writings include *Chief Mountain: The Story of Canon Middleton* (1964), *Madame de Stael and the English* (Astra Books, 1967), *The World of David Beaty: The Place of the Images* (Astra Books, 1971), and *Antoine de Saint-Exupery and David Beaty: Poets of a New Dimension* (Astra Books, 1974). *Address:* 13620 East Bailey St., Whittier, Calif. 90601; and Department of English, Whittier College, Whittier, Calif. 90608. *Biographical/critical sources: Directory of American Scholars,* Volume II: *English, Speech, and Drama,* 7th edition, Bowker, 1978.

*   *   *

FORSTER, Mark Arnold
   See ARNOLD-FORSTER, Mark

*   *   *

FOUCAULT, Michel   1926-

PERSONAL: Born October 15, 1926, in Poitiers, France; son of Paul (a doctor) and Anne (Malapert) Foucault. *Education:* Attended Ecole Normale Superieure; Sorbonne, University of Paris, licence, 1948 and 1950, diploma, 1952. *Home:* 285 rue de Vaugirard, 75015 Paris, France. *Office:* c/o Gallimard, 5 rue Sebastian-Bottin, 75007, Paris, France.

CAREER: Writer. Worked as teacher of philosophy and French literature at University of Lille, University of Uppsala, Uni-

versity of Warsaw, University of Hamburg, University of Clermont-Ferrand, University of Sao Paulo, and University of Tunis, 1960-68; University of Paris, Vincennes, France, professor, 1968-70; chairman of history of systems of thought at College de France, 1970—. *Awards, honors:* Medal from Center of Scientific Research (France), 1961, for *Madness and Civilization.*

WRITINGS—In English: *Folie et deraison: Histoire de la folie a l'age classique,* Plon, 1961, abridged edition, Union Generale, 1964, translation by Richard Howard published as *Madness and Civilization: A History of Insanity in the Age of Reason,* Pantheon, 1965; *Maladie mentale et psychologie,* Presses Universitaires de France, 1962, translation by Alan Sheridan published as *Mental Illness and Psychology,* Harper, 1976; *Naissance de la clinique: Une Archeologie du regard medical,* Presses Universitaires de France, 1963, translation by A. M. Sheridan Smith published as *The Birth of the Clinic: An Archaeology of Medical Perception,* Pantheon, 1973.

Les Mots el les choses: Une Archeologie des sciences humanes, Gallimard, 1966, translation published as *The Order of Things: An Archaeology of the Human Sciences,* Pantheon, 1971; *L'Archeologie du savoir,* Gallimard, 1969, translation by Smith published as *The Archaeology of Knowledge* (includes "The Discourse on Language"; also see below), Pantheon, 1972; *L'Ordre du discours,* Gallimard, 1971 (translation by Smith published in *The Archaeology of Knowledge* as "The Discourse on Language"; also see above); (editor) *Moi, Pierre Riviere, ayant egorge ma mere, ma soeur et mon frere* [France], 1973, translation by Frank Jellinek published as *I, Pierre Riviere, Having Slaughtered My Mother, My Sister, and My Brother . . . : A Case of Parricide in the 19th Century,* Pantheon, 1975; *Surveiller et punir: Naissance de la prison,* Gallimard, 1975, translation by Sheridan published as *Discipline and Punish: The Birth of the Prison,* Pantheon, 1977.

Histoire de la sexualite, Gallimard, 1976, translation by Robert Hurley published as *The History of Sexuality,* Volume 1, Pantheon, 1978; *Language, Counter-Memory, Practice: Selected Essays and Interviews,* edited by Donald F. Bouchard, translated by Bouchard and Sherry Simon, Cornell University Press, 1977; *Power-Knowledge: Selected Interviews and Other Writings, 1972-1977,* Pantheon, 1981.

Other writings: *Raymond Roussel,* Gallimard, 1963; *Ceci n'est pas une pipe: Deux Lettres et quatre dessins de Rene Magritte* (title means "This Is Not a Pipe: Two Letters and Four Drawings by Rene Magritte"), Fata Morgana, 1973.

Director of *Zone des tempetes,* 1973—. Contributor to periodicals, including *Critique.*

WORK IN PROGRESS: Five more volumes of *The History of Sexuality.*

SIDELIGHTS: In the *New York Times Book Review,* Peter Cawes wrote, "Michel Foucault is one of a handful of French thinkers who have . . . given an entirely new direction to theoretical work in the so-called 'human sciences,' the study of language, literature, psychiatry, intellectual history and the like." But according to Frank Kermode, Foucault is not "writing history of ideas, or indeed history of anything. Unlike historians, he seeks not origin, continuities, and explanations which will fill in documentary breaches of continuity, but rather 'an epistemological space specific to a particular period.' He attempts to uncover the *unconscious* of knowledge."

D. W. Harding explained Foucault's disdain for the history of knowledge: "Foucault believes that our own current intellectual life and systems of scientific thought are built on assumptions profoundly taken for granted and normally not exposed to conscious inspection, and yet likely in time . . . to be discarded.'' *Nation*'s Bruce Jackson agreed. ''Foucault is one of the few social analysts whose work regularly unfits readers to continue looking at things or ideas or institutions in the same way,'' he wrote. ''His archaeologies uncover architectures that make sensible order of what previously seemed sloppiness or incompetence or foolishness or malevolence.''

Sherry Turkle characterized Foucault's method as ''constructive,'' though a more apt definition might be ''reconstructive.'' As Jackson noted, ''Foucault works to uncover, to unearth.'' Similarly, Cawes wrote in *New Republic*, ''The archaeologist, finding a coin here, a pot there, reconstructs cities and civilizations. Foucault, turning over words with immense scholarship and erudition, reconstructs a group of intellectual activities collectively called in French the *sciences humaines*. . . .''

Foucault introduced his archaeological method in *The Order of Things*, in which he presents the idea that ''in any given culture and at any given moment there is only one *episteme* [a system of instinctual knowledge] that defines the conditions of possibility of all knowledge.'' Foucault then attempts ''to dig up and display the 'archaeological' form or forms which would be common to all mental activity,'' and he traces these forms throughout historic cultures.

In *The Order of Things*, Foucault also presented his concept of ''the disappearance of man.'' He explains that ''there was no epistomological consciousness of man'' before the eighteenth century. According to Foucault, only upon the advent of biology, economics, and philology did man appear ''as an object of knowledge and as a subject that knows.'' He then describes the twentieth century as the ''death of man.'' Foucault attributes man's decline to objectivity, which eliminates the necessity of making man the focus of history.

Foucault addressed his archaeological methods in *The Archaeology of Knowledge*. Cawes described the book as ''an attempt to decide just what it is about certain utterances or inscriptions—real objects in a real world which leave traces behind to be discovered, classified and related to one another—that qualifies them as 'statements' . . . belonging to various bodies of knowledge.'' The English-language edition of *The Archaeology of Knowledge* included ''The Discourse on Language,'' an investigation into the ways in which society manipulates language for purposes of politics and power. Cawes described Foucault's perception of language as ''a net *thrown over* the world: it criticized, classified, analyzed. . . .''

The archaeological method has been applied by Foucault to such topics as insanity, sexuality, history, and imprisonment. Even when focusing on a subject such as insanity in the Middle Ages, his studies have had vast implications. In *New Republic*, Frank McConnell noted that *Discipline and Punish*, rather than merely tracing the evolution of penal institutions, presents the argument ''that the invention of the prison is the crucial, inclusive image for all those modes of brutalization, in industry, in education, in the very fabric of citizenship, which defines the modern era of humanistic tyranny, the totalitarianism of the norm.'' And Sherry Turkle wrote that *The History of Sexuality* ''challenges standard interpretations of modern sexual history as a history of repression.''

Resistance to Foucault's work stems largely from his manner of presentation. He has been accused of writing ''obliquely'' and ''rhetorically,'' and Paul Robinson called him ''one of those authors who write with their ears, not with their heads.'' Christopher Lasch declared, ''His writing is difficult, the argument hard to follow, the arrangement of chapters seemingly

arbitrary and the whole very difficult to summarize.'' Cawes described Foucault as ''never a man to use one word where five will do, or to say straightforwardly what can be said obliquely.'' Similarly, Robinson contended, ''What he tries to create, above all else, is a certain tone—highfalutin, patronizing . . . , and, whenever the argument threatens to run thin, opaque.''

Turkle defended Foucault's style as the French method of putting ''poetry into science.'' She declared, ''In order to put into question assumptions deeply embedded in our ordinary language, one has to use language in extraordinary ways.'' Harding summarized: ''Foucault has the dreadful gift . . . of diffusing his meaning very thinly throughout an immense verbal spate, no part of which is quite empty of meaning, redundant, or merely repetitive. But behind all the abstract jargon and intimidating erudition there is undoubtedly an alert and sensitive mind which can ignore the familiar surfaces of established intellectual codes and ask new questions.''

BIOGRAPHICAL/CRITICAL SOURCES: Horizon, autumn, 1969; *New Republic*, March 27, 1971, November 10, 1973, April 1, 1978, October 28, 1978; *Nation*, July 5, 1971, January 26, 1974, March 4, 1978, January 27, 1979; *New York Review of Books*, August 12, 1971, May 17, 1973, January 22, 1976, June 12, 1980; *Spectator*, October 9, 1971; *Times Literary Supplement*, June 9, 1972, February 1, 1974, June 16, 1978; *New York Times Book Review*, October 22, 1972, February 24, 1974, December 7, 1975, February 19, 1978, February 25, 1979, January 14, 1979, November 25, 1979, January 27, 1980; *Esquire*, July, 1975; *Washington Post Book World*, January 7, 1979, March 15, 1981; *New Yorker*, January 29, 1979, July 16, 1979; *Commonweal*, May 12, 1978; Alan Sheridan, *Michel Foucault: The Will to Truth*, Tavistock, 1980.*

—*Sketch by Les Stone*

*　　　*　　　*

FOX, Marcia R(ose) 1942-

PERSONAL: Born May 29, 1942, in Dover, N.H.; daughter of Robert L. (in business) and Leah (Rosenberg) Fox; married Robert Rosenberg (an attorney), October, 1972; children: Lauren Fox Rosenberg. *Education:* Boston University, B.A., 1963; University of Pennsylvania, M.A., 1964; City University of New York, Ph.D., 1975. *Office:* Mobil Oil Corp., 150 East 42nd St., New York, N.Y. 10017.

CAREER: Hunter College of the City University of New York, New York City, lecturer in English, 1967-73; Ohio State University, Columbus, special assistant to dean of College of Law, 1974-75; New York University, New York City, assistant dean of Graduate School of Public Administration, 1975-80; currently associated with Mobil Oil Corp., New York City.

WRITINGS: (Author of introduction) George Gissing, *The Odd Women*, Norton, 1977; *Put Your Degree to Work*, Norton, 1979. Contributor to magazines and newspapers, including *Mademoiselle*.

*　　　*　　　*

FRAIBERG, Selma 1918-1981

OBITUARY NOTICE—See index for *CA* sketch: Born March 8, 1918, in Detroit, Mich.; died of cancer, December 19, 1981, in San Francisco, Calif. Educator, psychoanalyst, and author. Fraiberg specialized in child psychoanalysis, studying child development, the bonding between mothers and their infants, and the adjustments made by children born blind. Her work is often compared to that of Anna Freud, who researched similar topics. Fraiberg taught at the Tulane Medical School in New Orleans, Louisiana, before joining the University of Michigan and later the University of California at San Francisco. She wrote a number of books in her field, the best known being *The Magic Years.* A study of the early years of childhood, the book has been translated into more than ten languages. Fraiberg's other works include *Insights From the Blind: Developmental Studies of Blind Children* and *Every Child's Birthright: In Defense of Mothering.* Obituaries and other sources: *New York Times,* December 22, 1981.

* * *

FRAMPTON, Kenneth Brian 1930-

PERSONAL: Born November 20, 1930, in Woking, England; came to the United States in 1965; son of William Henry (a builder) and Nora Elisabeth Frampton. *Education:* Architectural Association School of Architecture, A.A., 1956. *Home:* 561 Broadway, New York, N.Y. 10013. *Office:* Department of Architecture, Columbia University, New York, N.Y. 10027; and Institute for Architecture and Urban Studies, 8 West 40th St., New York, N.Y. 10018.

CAREER: Douglas Stephen & Partners, London, England, associate, 1959-65; Princeton University, Princeton, N.J., Hodder fellow and visiting professor, 1965-66, associate professor of architecture, 1967-72; Columbia University, New York, N.Y., assistant professor, 1972-74, professor of architecture, 1974—. Senior tutor at Royal College of Art, 1972-76, visiting lecturer, 1977—. Co-founder and editor of Opposition Books. *Military service:* British Army, Royal Engineers, 1956-58. *Member:* Institute for Architecture and Urban Studies (fellow), Royal Institute of British Architects (associate member), Architectural Association. *Awards, honors:* Guggenheim fellowship, 1972-73; Ex Acqueo Award from Comite Internationale des Critiques de'Architecture, 1981, for article in *L'Architecture d'aujourd'hui.*

WRITINGS: (With Douglas Stephen and Michael Carapetian) *British Buildings,* A. & C. Black, 1964; *Modern Architecture: A Critical History,* Oxford University Press, 1980; *Maison de Verre* (title means "House of Glass"), L'Equerre, 1982; *History of Modern Architecture,* ADA Edita, 1982. Technical editor of *Architectural Design,* 1962-65.

WORK IN PROGRESS: Research on the cultural theory of purism.

SIDELIGHTS: Frampton wrote: "I am a teacher, historian, and critic of late nineteenth- and twentieth-century architecture. I am particularly interested in the relations between political and cultural institutions and the realization of architectural form. I am of the opinion that modern urban development is a kind of Pandora's Box, and the place of architecture in the vast expanse of the megalopolis is still difficult to determine. This would account for my interest in urban 'models' which will enable men to maintain some kind of definition of place in a psychological, institutional, and cultural sense against the quality of space-endlessness generally evident in the environment."

AVOCATIONAL INTERESTS: Travel (Germany, Spain, Japan, France), avant-garde film.

* * *

FRANK, Bernhard 1931-

PERSONAL: Born January 30, 1931, in Wuerzburg, Germany (now West Germany); came to the United States in 1948, naturalized citizen, 1953; son of Leo and Elizabeth (Freudenberger) Frank. *Education:* City College (now of the City University of New York), B.S., 1956; New York University, M.A., 1961; University of Pittsburgh, Ph.D., 1965. *Religion:* Jewish. *Home:* 260 Lexington Ave., Buffalo, N.Y. 14222. *Office:* Department of English, Buffalo State College, Buffalo, N.Y. 14222.

CAREER: Buffalo State College, Buffalo, N.Y., professor of comparative literature, 1965—. *Member:* Phi Beta Kappa.

WRITINGS: (Editor and translator) *Modern Hebrew Poetry,* University of Iowa Press, 1980. Editor of *Buckle,* 1977—.

SIDELIGHTS: Frank commented: "English is my third language (German and Hebrew came first). Poetry is my chief love and vocation. I have published in scores of magazines but have yet to have a book of my poems see the light. On my shelf sit five volumes of my poems, a volume of short stories, and six plays. They are the mirrors of my life."

* * *

FRANKEL, Flo 1923-

PERSONAL: Born October 4, 1923, in Evanston, Ill.; daughter of Abel (a business executive and legislator) and Marjorie (Mayer) Davis; married James R. Frankel (an attorney), April 19, 1947; children: Mark, Wendy, Terry, Julie. *Education:* Vassar College, B.A., 1944; National College of Education, M.Ed., 1974. *Home:* 630 Calais Circle, Highland Park, Ill. 60035.

CAREER: Elementary school teacher in Chicago, Ill., 1946-47; Jewish Children's Bureau, Chicago, special education teacher, 1968-75; writer.

WRITINGS: Whatever Happened to Cinderella? (nonfiction), St. Martin's, 1980.

WORK IN PROGRESS: Feminism After Fifty.

* * *

FRANKLIN, Linda Campbell 1941-

PERSONAL: Born February 4, 1941, in Memphis, Tenn.; daughter of Robert Dumont (a writer and librarian) and Mary Mac (a writer and librarian; maiden name, Wilson) Franklin. *Education:* Attended University of Colorado, 1958-60; University of Toledo, B.A., 1962. *Home:* 438 Third Ave., New York, N.Y. 10016. *Office:* Tree Communications, 250 Park Ave. S., New York, N.Y. 10003.

CAREER: Worked as waitress and museum librarian in Memphis, Tenn., as bookstore manager at Jewish Museum, as manager of bicycle shop, and as bookkeeper of a film company, all in New York City, 1965-70; free-lance writer, editor, and illustrator, 1970-76; Tree Communications, Inc., New York City, editor, 1976-81, senior editor, 1981—. Illustrator for filmstrip "A Turn of the Phrase" for Westinghouse Learning Corp., New York City, 1973. Resident at Ossabaw Island Project, an artists' colony in Ossabaw, Ga., 1981. *Member:* Ephemera Society of America, American Printing History Association.

WRITINGS: From Hearth to Cookstove: An American Domestic History of Gadgets and Utensils Made or Used in America From 1700 to 1930, House of Collectibles, 1976, 2nd edition, 1979; *Antiques and Collectibles: A Bibliography of Works in English, Sixteenth Century to 1976,* Scarecrow, 1978; *Library Display Ideas,* McFarland & Co., 1980; *Three Hundred Years of Kitchen Collectibles,* Books Americana, 1981, 2nd edition, 1983; *Breads and Biscuits,* Tree Communications, 1981;

Our Christmas Book, Tree Communications, 1981; (editor) *Birthday Book,* Tree Communications, 1981; *Classroom Display Ideas,* McFarland & Co., 1982. Editor of *Ephemera News* and of *Our Old Fashioned Country Dairy,* Tree Communications, 1980—.

WORK IN PROGRESS: A novel, *Balanced Rocks,* completion expected in 1983; "White Ben," a screenplay adaptation, completion expected in 1983.

SIDELIGHTS: Linda Campbell Franklin's *From Hearth to Cookstove* is a history, and *Three Hundred Years of Kitchen Collectibles* is an identification and price guide to antique kitchen implements and utensils. Franklin gathers information from her experience as a collector and from antique cookbooks and trade catalogues. The books, critics noted, contain many engravings, drawings, and photographs as well as some recipes and anecdotes.

Antiques and Collectibles is an annotated list of 10,000 books located in the major public and private libraries of English-speaking countries. This bibliography contains a coding system to aid the reader in his search for books. Called "very worthwhile" by the *Wilson Library Bulletin, Antiques and Collectibles* covers over two hundred subjects, including bottle tickets, fire fighting equipment, barbed wire, games and toys, shaving mugs, baskets, and Wedgwood pottery. Critically acclaimed, the book, said a *RQ* reviewer, "offers surprises in the serendipitous sense for both browser and peruser."

Unlike the above-mentioned books, *Library Display Ideas* does not deal with antiques or collecting. Rather, it is a handbook mainly for school librarians who require new and innovative ideas for display case and bulletin board designs. This book provides librarians with themes, samples, instructions and manufacturers.

Franklin told *CA:* "Both of my parents are librarians, writers, and lovers of books. So I was born in the right cradle of civilization. If I had a librarian's memory, I could list more titles of childhood books which must have set me on my way, but all I can remember specifically are *Water Babies* (I have an image of ominous, sooty buildings and a ragged chimney sweep as strong today as it was thirty-six years ago); all of Lewis Carroll; all of Mother Goose; many fairy tales—especially the one about Baba Yaga's chicken-leg hut and the Rumpelstiltskin story; my grandmother's singing 'My Darling Clementine' to me when I was about two—that left another strong image of a drowning girl, a swirling river, long feet (her 'number nines'), and, oddly, shoeboxes! It seems possible—and this is the first time I've attempted such a look back—that I could detail many *tableau vivant* scenes, gotten in my mind before I was eight by hearing and reading stories: The cold underwater langour of Kingsley's babies before they moved to the warm seas . . . the furious intensity of Rumpelstiltskin, which almost set the straw on fire . . . Alice's rushing fall through the huge rabbit's hole, which I always associated with the beautiful, round mirror over *our* fireplace . . . the tiny black swan shut out by his fellows for being different . . . the thrashing, pounding legs of the witch's hut, with things—do I remember a comb?—flying out behind to land in the woods. On and on.

"It all seems dark and moody, doesn't it? It sounds as if my childhood, at least my reading, was full of dismal, morbid things. But I was far from morbid; I was rather gleeful. I wrote a 'book,' called *Little Liza Lizard,* in 1947 or 1948, and it certainly wasn't morbid. It was a quite cheerful romance of a self-reliant lizard in a polka dot dress.

"I never saw television until my formative years had already been well spent. I think my usefully 'vivid imagination,' and that of my publisher brother, Robbie, must have come from our rich reading background, although now, like anyone, I absorb many sights and sounds from the TV.

"Most of the themes going through my fiction writing for the last twenty years don't immediately, if at all, relate to my early reading. So I don't know where the themes came from. Variable perception of the duration and passage of time; records of time passing and times past; evidence, tracks, spoor, remains; appearances as clues to past, present, and future; the accumulation of evidence by design and accident; collecting—these are the themes. Some, maybe all, are the stuff of detection and archaeology. I wanted, as I put it then, a 'mystery to solve' as early as age eight. I was always digging in the ground or looking at things close up. I don't know where I got the idea about there being such a thing as a mystery, unless it's just something I grabbed out of the Jungian swamp.

"Living on a farm during my early childhood added another ingredient to the mix: animals and all living and natural things. Great love for, interest in, and peer respect for all creatures influence me as I look at life and as I write. A close study of a pet—be it cat, dog, bird, even tarantula—teaches you so very much about your own soul.

"Influences of another sort are dreams. I use them as a source of experience and viewpoint. Often a dream image, by its nature, refines and sharpens an action. All peripheral activity is vague, and the focus is perfect. I've had long, vivid dreams—perhaps seventy-five percent involving animals—all my life, and I kept a dream journal for fourteen months in the late 1960's. My first remembered dream, which is still a great mystery to me, dates to about 1944. I was on a sandy plain, at the center of the scene. I was trapped in quicksand, like a golden morning glory hole, and as I slowly sank in it, not struggling at all, the light became brilliantly yellow, then orange, deep reddish brown; and then it was gone.

"Nothing has effected my style as much as seventeen years of near-daily letter writing: narratives, three hundred fifty to one thousand words, many sent to my parents as a sort of journal of life in New York City. What a place to live! Material for essays and observations and descriptions and dialogues everywhere. I am in the habit of looking for the stories in things, maybe the 'mystery' I can solve by writing. Somehow it seems to be a form of protection, writing, like armor. Stories can be found in the most deceptively pale, thin, and simple sights and happenings."

BIOGRAPHICAL/CRITICAL SOURCES: Hobbies, December, 1976; *Washington Post Book World,* December 5, 1976; *Christian Science Monitor,* April 28, 1977; *Wilson Library Bulletin,* December, 1978, June, 1981; *American Reference Books Annual,* 1979; *RQ,* spring, 1979; *Museum News,* November, 1979.

*   *   *

FRANKLIN, S(amuel) Harvey 1928-

PERSONAL: Born in 1928, in Birmingham, England; son of Samuel (a molder) and Isabel (a clerk; maiden name, Latimer) Franklin; married Sonya Coleman (a legal executive), November 28, 1953; children: Michael, Margot, Robert. *Education:* University of Birmingham, B.Com. (with honors) and M.A. *Home:* 74 Chaytor St., Wellington, New Zealand. *Office:* Department of Geography, Victoria University of Wellington, Private Bag, Wellington, New Zealand.

CAREER: Victoria University of Wellington, Wellington, New Zealand, member of faculty, 1951-67, professor of geography,

1967—. Consultant to government and business. *Awards, honors:* New Zealand Book Award from Arts Council and Literary Fund, 1979, for *Trade, Growth, and Anxiety.*

WRITINGS: The European Peasantry, Methuen, 1969; *Rural Societies,* Macmillan, 1971; *Trade, Growth, and Anxiety: New Zealand Beyond the Welfare State,* Methuen, 1978. Contributor to academic journals and local magazines. Founding editor of *Pacific Viewpoint,* 1960—.

WORK IN PROGRESS: Research on the future of egalitarian societies and on peasant societies.

AVOCATIONAL INTERESTS: Skiing.

* * *

FRANKS, Ed
  See BRANDON, Johnny

* * *

FRASER, G(eorge) S(utherland) 1915-1980

OBITUARY NOTICE—See index for *CA* sketch: Born November 8, 1915, in Glasgow, Scotland; died January 3, 1980, in Leicester, England. Journalist, educator, poet, critic, translator, editor, and author. Fraser reported for the *Aberdeen Press and Journal* before being inducted into the army in 1939. While in the service in the Middle East, he wrote for military periodicals and worked for the Ministry of Information. A published poet by the age of sixteen, Fraser produced his first major volume of verse, *Home Town Elegy,* in 1944. After the war he returned to journalism and wrote criticism for the publications *New Statesman, Times Literary Supplement, Poetry, Commentary, Listener,* and *Partisan Review.* Along with his reviews, Fraser wrote several books of literary criticism such as *The Modern Writer and His World: Continuity and Innovation in Twentieth Century English Literature* and *Metre, Rhythm, and Free Verse.* In 1959 he began teaching literature at the University of Leicester and continued working there until a year before his death. In addition to publishing other volumes of poetry, including *Leaves Without a Tree* and *Conditions: Selected Recent Poetry,* Fraser edited many books, among which number *The Collected Poems of Keith Douglas, Springtime: An Anthology of Young Poets and Writers,* and *Selections From the Sacred Writings of the Sikhs.* Fraser also translated French works by Patrice de la Tour du Pin, Gabriel Marcel, and Jean Mesnard into English. Obituaries and other sources: *The Annual Obituary 1980,* St. Martin's, 1981.

* * *

FREEMAN, Peter J.
  See CALVERT, Patricia

* * *

FREER, Coburn 1939-

BRIEF ENTRY: Born November 5, 1939, in New Orleans, La. American educator and author. Freer began teaching at University of Montana in 1967 and has been a professor of English since 1976. He wrote *Music for a King: George Herbert's Style and the Metrical Psalms* (Johns Hopkins Press, 1972) and *The Poetics of Jacobean Drama* (Johns Hopkins Press, 1982). *Address:* Department of English, University of Montana, Missoula, Mont. 59801. *Biographical/critical sources: Directory of American Scholars,* Volume II: *English, Speech, and Drama,* 7th edition, Bowker, 1978.

FREMONT-SMITH, Eliot 1929-

PERSONAL: Born April 16, 1929, in Cambridge, Mass.; son of Frank and Frances (Eliot) Fremont-Smith; married Leda C. Schwartz, June, 1963; children: Andrew Eliot. *Education:* Antioch College, B.A., 1953; graduate study at Yale University. *Politics:* "Hopeful." *Religion:* None. *Home:* 42 Olmsted Rd., Scarsdale, N.Y. 10583. *Agent:* Lynn Nesbit, International Creative Management, 410 West 57th St., New York, N.Y. 10019. *Office: Village Voice,* 842 Broadway, New York, N.Y. 10003.

CAREER/WRITINGS: New York Times, New York City, book critic, 1961-68; Little, Brown & Co., Boston, Mass., editor-in-chief, 1968-71; *Saturday Review,* New York City, senior editor, 1972-73; *New York,* New York City, book critic, 1973-75; *Village Voice,* New York City, senior editor and author of weekly column, "Making Book," 1975—. Contributor to magazines and newspapers. *Member:* National Book Critics Circle (chairman and president, 1976—).

SIDELIGHTS: When it was rumored in 1975 that the National Book Award would be discontinued, the newly formed National Book Critics Circle responded with an awards program of its own. Eliot Fremont-Smith, president and chairman of the NBCC, recalled for *Publishers Weekly* how the program came about: "What had happened was that it had been announced that the NBA was going to be revamped or killed, and there were dire predictions throughout the industry that it was going to die. The NBCC offered to help in any way it could by becoming part of the committee, or whatever. We felt strongly that the award shouldn't die, but our participation in its reshaping was not invited, so we said, 'What the hell, we'll have our own awards,'" The NBCC made its first awards presentation in the spring of 1976, when E. L. Doctorow's *Ragtime* won for best novel.

When the NBA was revived as The American Book Award in 1979, many in the publishing industry remained skeptical of its aims and procedures. One charge made against TABA was that a book might be nominated on the basis of sales rather than literary merit. Speaking for the NBCC, Fremont-Smith added: "We all felt TABA doesn't really replace the NBA as an industry award. The latter was organized so that there was a buffer between the industry and the awards process. And TABA, partly due to the way it is organized, seems to have erased that buffer zone." As a result of the controversy surrounding TABA, the National Book Critics Circle Award has received wider publicity and industry support each year.

Apart from his work in the NBCC, Fremont-Smith is a writer and editor for the *Village Voice.* He describes his weekly column, "Making Book," as "a straight review—though I do much more social commentary than straight reviewing these days—and quite often as a column about issues facing the publishing industry or facing criticism." The audience he writes for "is basically me and my conscience," he says, although "I certainly gear the subject matter to the *Voice*'s concerns and review a lot more books on, say, the feminist movement or on gay liberation than I would if I were at *The New York Times.* And I review fewer best sellers and other books that the *Times* has to cover. We don't *have* to, possibly by virtue of the *Times*'s existence."

BIOGRAPHICAL/CRITICAL SOURCES: Publishers Weekly, January 25, 1980.

FRENCH, Simon 1957-

PERSONAL: Born November 26, 1957, in Sydney, Australia; son of Reginald (an electronics design draftsman) and Janette (a school librarian; maiden name, Frederick) French. *Education:* Mitchell College, Teacher's Diploma, 1979. *Home:* 11 Davis Rd., Blacktown, New South Wales 2148, Australia.

CAREER: Infants' teacher at schools in New South Wales, Australia, 1980—. Has also worked as a library clerical assistant, a fruit picker, and in preschool child care. *Awards, honors:* Special mention from the Australian Children's Book of the Year Awards, 1976, for *Hey, Phantom Singlet.*

WRITINGS—Juveniles: *Hey, Phantom Singlet* (illustrated by Alex Nicholas), Angus & Robertson, 1975; *Cannily, Cannily,* Angus & Robertson, 1981.

WORK IN PROGRESS: A first-person novel with a suburban school setting, tentatively titled *Kerbs and Gutters,* for Angus & Robertson.

SIDELIGHTS: French told *CA:* "The suggestion to write a book came rather jokingly from my sixth-grade teacher. As I was someone who enjoyed reading books anyway, the suggestion didn't seem all that ludicrous; and so I set to work. After a few false starts, I became enthused about recording my day-to-day school life and so began putting together a no-holds-barred account of the high school I was attending. All the kids in my class found themselves depicted as characters in their own type of environment—rough and ready, merciless but honest. Almost the entire book was written at school—in notepads concealed inside textbooks, scribbled paragraphs at the back of exercise books. These devious methods worked incredibly well, except for the day my math teacher confiscated two whole chapters and I had to try to remember later what it was I had written.

"Thus, daily classroom humor and drama provided much live footage for the story that evolved. My suburban origins lent me a new cast of characters in addition to those at school, and chapter by chapter I pieced together the story of Matthew, whose dad is in jail, and whose mum has to work to support the family. Trying for publication was really an afterthought and of course did not prove easy. After quite a few rejections, I was lucky, and *Hey, Phantom Singlet* was published just before my seventeenth birthday. Shortly afterwards I finished high school. Being able to write away from the audience who had inspired me so much seemed very difficult for a while. With these sorts of upheavals, a second book was not an easy task.

"The politics in *Cannily, Cannily* are those of adult and peer pressure. The options open to Trevor—the child of two seasonal workers always on the move—are whether to bend to these attendant pressures and 'belong,' or to remain aloof and different, and so endure isolation and torment from the children of a conservative country town. Having been on the receiving end of peer politics, I looked at it as a significant set of experiences and ideas to put across.

"All it seems to take is a single strand of fiction to hold my ideas together, concerned as I am with reporting on real life. The challenge to me, of course, is to translate the realism and honesty to an audience, balancing the language and structure between the economical and the descriptive. My actual method of writing is not altogether studious or methodical; I do not sit down and write for an appointed time each day. Rather it is a single character or situation encountered at any time that causes me to sit with typewriter and paper, and write. I cannot offer any stunning or academic rationale as to how or why I write. My books have been written because I find it enjoyable and because I perceive a need for the type of story that children can relate to their everyday existence. My writing is about coping, interacting, and sometimes personal hardship; but it is more so about succeeding and surviving—that is the essence of growing."

BIOGRAPHICAL/CRITICAL SOURCES: Times Literary Supplement, November 20, 1981.

*　*　*

FRIAR TUCK
See TUCKER, Irwin St. John

*　*　*

FRIEDLANDER, Howard 1941-

PERSONAL: Born March 21, 1941, in Brooklyn, N.Y.; son of Morris (a salesman) and Frieda (Rosenbaum) Friedlander; married Elaine Rosenberger, September 24, 1972; children: Randi, Jeffrey, Eric. *Education:* New York University, B.S., 1964. *Home:* Heritage Hill Rd., Norwalk, Conn. 06851. *Agent:* Shapiro-Lichtman, 2049 Century Park E., Los Angeles, Calif. 90067. *Office:* "Captain Kangaroo Show," c/o CBS-TV, 555 West 57th St., New York, N.Y. 10019.

CAREER: Columbia Broadcasting System, Inc. (CBS-TV), New York City, supervisor of audience services, 1964-65, assistant manager of scenic construction shops, 1966-67; Bob Stewart Productions, New York City, assistant to the producer, 1968; CBS-TV, New York City, head writer and creative consultant for "Captain Kangaroo Show," 1976—; writer. *Member:* National Academy of Television Arts and Sciences, American Film Institute, Writers Guild of America, West.

WRITINGS: "Iceman" (screenplay), Warner Bros., 1971; "Kung Fu" (teleplay), American Broadcasting Co. (ABC-TV), 1972; (with Ed Spielman) "Gordon's War" (screenplay), Twentieth Century-Fox, 1973; "The Return of Charlie Chan" (screenplay), Leisure Concepts, 1975; "The Moonbeam Rider" (screenplay), Universal, 1979. Also author of teleplay "Alive," National Broadcasting Co. (NBC-TV). Writer for television series, including "Just Billy" and "The Joan Rivers Show." Writer of material for comedians, including Phyllis Diller, Joan Rivers, Nipsey Russell, and Fanny Flagg.

WORK IN PROGRESS: Three screenplays, "Judy Judy Judy," "A Romantic Comedy," and "Dazzle"; a teleplay, "The Great Danes"; a musical, "The Eighth Voyage of Sinbad."

SIDELIGHTS: Friedlander told *CA:* "For as long as I can remember my prime ambition has been the same—to be a storyteller, to entertain. And since my interests and moods vary, I am equally at home writing mystery, action, adventure, comedy, or children's stories. I only write what I like. In effect, I tell myself stories. If I like them, why shouldn't others? I follow the basic rule of good dramatic writing: character and conflict. I like to create interesting characters and put them in interesting situations."

BIOGRAPHICAL/CRITICAL SOURCES: Variety, February 23, 1972, June 13, 1977, October 3, 1978; *Esquire,* August, 1973; *New York Times,* February 25, 1973; *New York,* August 20, 1973; *Los Angeles Times,* October 20, 1973; *Hollywood Reporter,* July 22, 1977, January 15, 1981.

FRITCHMAN, Stephen Hole 1902-

BRIEF ENTRY: Born May 12, 1902, in Cleveland, Ohio. American minister and author. Fritchman was pastor of Unitarian Fellowship of the Desert from 1970 to 1976. He has taught English and Bible at universities and has edited religious news for the New York Herald Tribune. His books include Beyond Dogma: A Unitarian Story of Man's Faith in Man (Hodgin Press, 1956) and Heretic: A Partisan Autobiography (Beacon Press, 1977). Address: 604 Cavanagh Rd., Glendale, Calif. 91207. Biographical/critical sources: Who's Who in America, 40th edition, Marquis, 1978.

* * *

FRYM, Gloria 1947-

PERSONAL: Born February 28, 1947, in New York, N.Y.; daughter of Bernard (a store owner) and Claire (Perlstein) Frym; married David T. Benedetti III, October 31, 1975 (divorced). Education: University of New Mexico, B.A., 1968, M.A., 1973. Residence: Berkeley, Calif. Agent: Carol Murray, 2427 10th St., Berkeley, Calif. 94710.

CAREER: University of Albuquerque, Albuquerque, N.M., instructor in English and the humanities, 1970-72; cook, 1972-74; technical writer, 1974-75; writer and editor, 1975—. Visiting poet at Evergreen College, 1977. Member: Poets and Writers.

WRITINGS: Impossible Affection (poems), Christopher's Books, 1979; Second Stories (nonfiction), Chronicle Books, 1979; Back to Forth (poems), Figures, 1981.

Work represented in anthologies, including Dear Gentle Persons: A Collection of Bay Area Poets, edited by Catherine H. Moreno, Hartmus Press, 1978. Contributor to little magazines. Editor of Best Friends, 1971-75; contributing editor of San Francisco Review of Books.

WORK IN PROGRESS: Double Oceans, prose; research on the erotic in the novel; research on new forms of narrative, especially if written by women.

AVOCATIONAL INTERESTS: Travel (Latin America), ornithology, physics, contemporary art.

* * *

FUCHS, Elinor 1933-

PERSONAL: Born January 23, 1933, in Cleveland, Ohio; daughter of Joseph (a violinist) and Lillian (a president of an export company; maiden name, Kessler) Fuchs; married Michael O. Finkelstein (an attorney), May 3, 1962; children: Claire Oakes, Katherine Eban. Education: Radcliffe College, B.A. (summa cum laude), 1955; Hunter College of the City University of New York, M.A., 1975; City University of New York, M.Phil., 1976. Residence: Brooklyn, N.Y. Agent: Lois Berman, 250 West 57th St., New York, N.Y. 10019.

CAREER: Worked as producer and writer in New York, research director for documentary series on President Franklin D. Roosevelt for ABC-TV, script editor of "Dupont Show of the Month," and professional actress; Brooklyn Heights Press, Brooklyn Heights, N.Y., theatre critic, 1974-77; Chelsea Theatre Center, New York, N.Y., literary manager, 1978-79, literary adviser, 1979-80; CBC-Radio, theatre critic, 1980—. Dramaturge with Open Space Theatre Experiment, 1981. Member: Dramatists Guild, Authors League of America, American

Theatre Association, Phi Beta Kappa. Awards, honors: Distinguished achievement award from Los Angeles Drama-Logue, 1980.

WRITINGS: (With Joyce Antler) Year One of the Empire: A Play of American Politics, War, and Protest (first produced in Los Angeles, Calif., 1980), Houghton, 1973.

Unpublished plays: "A. Philip Randolph: Long March to Freedom," first broadcast on television, 1968; "A Dream Play" (adaptation of work by August Strindberg), first produced in New York, N.Y., 1981.

Contributor to theatre journals and Vogue. Editor of American issue of Alternatives theatrales; theatre critic for Soho News, 1978-79.

WORK IN PROGRESS: Waking Up, an account of a personal journey; a modern drama genre study on the mystical dramas of August Strindberg; a play on Simone Weil.

SIDELIGHTS: Elinor Fuchs commented: "My interest in eastern religion, awakened within the past eight years, gives color to much of my work in theatre (and in life). The essential task of life is the interweaving of two perceptions: one, the fundamental energy of existence is love; two, the fundamental nature of physical existence is impermanence. Developing the courage or wisdom to keep both alive, without extinguishing one for the other, is a life's work."

* * *

FUJIWARA, Yoichi 1909-

PERSONAL: Born January 6, 1909, in Omishima, Japan; son of Tomizo (a government official) and Kiwa (Kurose) Fujiwara; married Sada Tsuji, March 20, 1937; children: Shigeko Fujiwara Yoshiya, Tomiko Fujiwara Aono, Kiyoko Fujiwara Murakami. Education: Hiroshima Bunri-ka University, D.Litt., 1950. Politics: None. Religion: Buddhist. Home: 2-5-9 Suminohama, Itsukaichi-machi, Hiroshima-ken 738, Japan.

CAREER: Hiroshima University, Hiroshima, Japan, lecturer, 1942-45, assistant professor, 1945-63, professor, 1963-72; writer, 1972—. Member: Linguistic Society of Japan, Linguistic Society of America.

WRITINGS: Hogengaku (title means "Dialectology"), Sanseido, 1962; A Dialect Grammar of Japanese, Sophia University Press, 1965; Linguistic Atlas of Seto Inland Sea, Tokyo University Press, 1974; A Study of Honorific Expression in Japanese Dialects, Shunyodo, Volume I, 1978, Volume II, 1979.

WORK IN PROGRESS: A comprehensive twelve-volume study of modern Japanese dialects, for Shunyodo.

SIDELIGHTS: Fujiwara told CA: "Linguistic research delves deep into every particular language until it reaches the eventual dialectal reality and there attains the universality sought as science of man. Hence, dialectology, to my conviction, is the most human of linguistic sciences."

BIOGRAPHICAL/CRITICAL SOURCES: Noah S. Brannen and Scott J. Baird, The Sentence Structure of Japanese, University of Tokyo Press, 1972.

* * *

FULTON, Robert Lester 1926-

BRIEF ENTRY: Born November 30, 1926, in Toronto, Ontario, Canada. Sociologist, educator, and author. Fulton has been a professor of sociology at University of Minnesota since 1966 and director of its Center for Death Education and Research since 1969. His books include *Death and Identity* (Wiley, 1965) and *Death, Grief, and Bereavement: A Chronological Bibliography* (Center for Thanatological Studies, University of Minnesota, 1970). He also edited *Education and Social Crisis: Perspectives on Teaching Disadvantaged Youth* (Wiley, 1967) and *Death and Dying: Challenge and Change* (Addison-Wesley, 1978). *Address:* 25 East Monnehaha Parkway, Minneapolis, Minn. 55419. *Biographical/critical sources: Who's Who in America,* 40th edition, Marquis, 1978.

*   *   *

FURCHGOTT, Terry   1948-

PERSONAL: Born July 29, 1948, in New York, N.Y.; daughter of Robert Francis (a pharmacologist) and Lenore (a social service worker; maiden name, Mandelbaum); companion: Glenn Leichman (a psychologist); children: Damon Leo Leichman. *Education:* Radcliffe College, B.A. (with honors), 1970; further study at Camden Arts Centre, London, England, 1972-75. *Residence:* Seattle, Wash. *Address:* c/o Andre Deutsch Ltd., 105 Great Russell St., London WC1B 3LJ, England.

CAREER: Author, illustrator, painter. *Member:* Fremont Artist-Mothers' Cooperative (founding member).

WRITINGS—Juveniles; self-illustrated: (With Linda Dawson) *Phoebe and the Hot-Water Bottles,* Deutsch, 1977; *The Great Garden Adventure,* Deutsch, 1979; *Nanda in India,* Deutsch, 1982.

SIDELIGHTS: Terry Furchgott wrote: "I started doing magazine illustration and posters in high school and continued in college while studying art history. Following graduation, I studied painting in London and turned to children's book illustration as a way to earn money. I wrote my first book with the help of a kindergarten teacher-friend. The story was inspired by the cozy qualities of hot-water bottles and by the corner chemist's shop. *The Great Garden Adventure* was a more conscious attempt to write a feminist-oriented picture book about the joys of gardening. *Nanda* is based on my two years of travel in Asia, which ended with the birth of my son. Today I live in Seattle and have at last started working again, thanks to the childcare and support of my communal housemates and my artist-mothers' cooperative."

G

GALE, Zona 1874-1938

BRIEF ENTRY: Born August 26, 1874, in Portage, Wis.; died of pneumonia, December 27, 1938, in Chicago, Ill.; buried at Silver Lake Cemetery in Portage, Wis. American novelist, playwright, and essayist. Zona Gale won a Pulitzer Prize for drama in 1921 for her adaptation of her 1920 novel, *Miss Lulu Bett.* Through Lulu's revolt against banality this comedy presented a realistic view of small-town, middle-class America while ranking Gale with such realist writers of the era as Sinclair Lewis and Theodore Dreiser. Gale's earlier writing was far more sentimental and sympathetic to small-town life. With her knowledge of colloquial speech and the manners of town-folk, she achieved her first wide success with the local-color stories collected in *Friendship Village* (1908) and three sequels. After 1910 Gale became politically and socially active, particularly with the pacifist cause, which she promoted in *Heart's Kindred* (1915). In *Birth* (1919), Gale showed a growing awareness of the limitations and drawbacks of provincial life, and *Miss Lulu Bett* revealed a tendency toward impressionistic realism. Later novels, like *Preface to a Life* (1926), indicated her growing interest in mysticism. Gale's support of a wide variety of liberal causes, including women's suffrage, pacifism, prohibition of alcohol, and abolition of capital punishment and censorship, were reflected in her writings and in her unusually active civic life, for which she was much admired during her lifetime. *Biographical/critical sources: Twentieth Century Authors: A Biographical Dictionary of Modern Literature,* H. W. Wilson, 1942; *American Literary Realism,* summer, 1968; *Notable American Women, 1607-1950: A Biographical Dictionary,* Belknap Press, 1971.

* * *

GALILEA, Segundo 1928-

PERSONAL: Born April 3, 1928, in Santiago, Chile; son of Manuel and Francisca (Diez) Galilea. *Education:* Catholic University of Chile, S.T.L., 1955. *Home and office:* Cascilla 17003, Santiago 8, Chile.

CAREER: Ordained Roman Catholic priest, 1956; *Pastoral Popular,* Santiago, Chile, editor, 1958-62; Intercultural Center, Cuernavaca, Mexico, member of staff, 1963-67; Latin American Pastoral Institute, Quito, Ecuador, 1968-75; Latin American Religious Conference, Bogota, Columbia, member of theology staff, 1976—.

WRITINGS: Para una pastoral latinaamericana (title means "Toward a Latin American Pastoral Activity"), Paulinos, 1968; *Evangelizacion en America Latina* (title means "Evangelization in Latin America"), Salisianos, 1970; *El siguiente de Cristo,* Paulinos, 1978, translation published as *Following Christ,* Orbis, 1980; *El mensaje de Puebla* (title means "The Message of Puebla"), Paulinos, 1979; *Religiosidad popular y pastoral* (title means "Folk Religions and Pastoral Activity"), Christiandad, 1979; *La espiritualidad de la evangelizacion seguia las bienaventuranzas,* CLAR, 1980, translation published as *Mission and the Beautitudes,* Orbis, in press.

WORK IN PROGRESS: Research on Christian mission in Africa and Asia, from a Latin American perspective.

SIDELIGHTS: Galilea told *CA:* "In my writings, lectures, and ministry as a priest, I've been chiefly preoccupied with the renewal of the church mission in Latin America, the theological background of this renewal, and the methodology (e.g. the 'basic Christian communities'). Lately I've discovered that the Latin American churches cannot fully renew themselves if there is not an offering to foreign missions (Africa, Asia). My concern now is a missiology that is rooted in Latin America. This missiology ought to renew the traditional missiology of the churches. A missiology should be able to relate to old cultures and religions, as Latin Americans are not fully Western-cultured. It should be a missiology within the Third World (countries that are not rich), thus avoiding the classical approach of rich countries evangelizing the poor."

* * *

GALWAY, James 1939-

BRIEF ENTRY: Born December 8, 1939, in Belfast, Northern Ireland. Irish musician and author. Galway and his flute have entertained enthusiastic audiences from England and Ireland to Carnegie Hall in New York City. He began his career with the Berlin Philharmonic Orchestra. Although his repertoire is largely classical, Galway has achieved popular success with concert tours and record albums. He wrote *An Autobiography* (Chappell, 1978). *Biographical/critical sources: New York Times Biographical Service,* April, 1977, January, 1979; *Baker's Biographical Dictionary of Musicians,* 6th edition, Schirmer Books, 1978.

* * *

GAMBACCINI, Peter 1950-

PERSONAL: Surname is pronounced Gam-ba-chee-nee; born

180

June 15, 1950, in New York, N.Y.; son of Mario Matthew (a business executive) and Dorothy (Kiebrick) Gambaccini. *Education:* Attended University of London, 1970, and University of California, Santa Barbara, 1972; Dartmouth College, B.A., 1972. *Home:* 42 West 76th St., New York, N.Y. 10023.

CAREER: Fairpress (newspaper), Westport, Conn., managing editor and reporter, 1973-75; National Broadcasting Company, Inc., New York, N.Y., reporter and researcher, 1976; freelance writer.

WRITINGS: Billy Joel, Quick Fox, 1979; *Bruce Springsteen,* Quick Fox, 1979; *Photographer's Assistant,* Quick Fox, 1981. Contributing editor to *American Photographer, Oui,* and *Avenue.* Contributor of articles to *Horizon, Playboy, Crawdaddy,* and *New York Times.*

AVOCATIONAL INTERESTS: Travel, running, playing the saxophone and flute.

*   *   *

GANDOLFO, Joe M. 1936-

PERSONAL: Born March 13, 1936, in Richmond, Ky.; married Carol Lorentz; children: Mike, Diane, Donna. *Education:* Attended Vanderbilt University, Miami University (Oxford, Ohio), and Wharton School of Finance and Commerce. *Religion:* Roman Catholic. *Home:* 5304 Wood Haven Dr., Lakeland, Fla. 33803. *Office:* Joe Gandolfo & Associates, 2018 South Florida Ave., Lakeland, Fla. 33803.

CAREER: Professional baseball player with the Los Angeles Dodgers, Los Angeles, Calif., 1958; coach and mathematics teacher at junior high school in Fort Lauderdale, Fla., 1959; worked as a lifeguard in Fort Lauderdale; worked as an insurance salesman for Kennesaw Life Insurance Co. in Baton Rouge, La.; independent insurance agent in Lakeland, Fla. Certified Life Underwriter, 1965. Consultant to insurance companies, including American National Insurance Co., Trans World Life Insurance Company of New York, and Kennesaw Life and Accident Insurance Co. Partner in Tampa and Orlando Racquet Clubs. Public speaker in United States, Canada, and Europe. *Awards, honors:* National Quality Award, 1962-81; life and qualifying member of the Million Dollar Round Table, 1965; American Salesmaster Award.

WRITINGS: Ideas Are a Dime a Dozen . . . But the Man Who Puts Them Into Practice Is Priceless, National Underwriter Co., 1967; *On to a Hundred Million,* National Underwriter Co., 1972. Also author of *Selling Is 98 Percent Understanding Human Beings and 2 Percent Product Knowledge* and *God, I'll Give You All the Credit, and I'll Take All the Commissions.*

SIDELIGHTS: Believing that "anything the mind can conceive and believe, it can achieve," Gandolfo doggedly works at becoming America's highest-selling insurance salesman. Writing insurance for more than thirty-five different companies, he has labored as many as nineteen hours a day in his effort. Gandolfo claims he sold $114 million worth of insurance in 1971, $170 million in 1972, and $252 million in 1973. His goal is to turn over one billion dollars of insurance in a single year. The insurance agent also tries to help other salesmen in his field through his books and numerous speaking engagements. Gandolfo asserts that he feels compelled to let his colleagues know how to be successful selling insurance. "I don't want to be egotistical," he once remarked, "but I'm probably the finest salesman in the country and if I don't help other insurance salesmen, who will?"

BIOGRAPHICAL/CRITICAL SOURCES: Florida Trend, September, 1974; *Biography News,* Volume II, Gale, 1975.

*   *   *

GANZ, David L(awrence) 1951-

PERSONAL: Born July 28, 1951, in New York, N.Y.; son of Daniel M. and Beverly Ganz. *Education:* Georgetown University, B.S., 1973; St. John's University, J.D., 1976; further graduate study at New York University, 1977—. *Office:* 170 East 61st St., New York, N.Y. 10021.

CAREER: Ganz, Hollinger & Towe, New York, N.Y., attorney at law, 1977—. Special counsel to United Nations Food and Agriculture Organization in Rome, Italy. *Member:* American Bar Association, American Numismatic Association, American Society of International Law, New York State Bar Association, Flushing Lawyers Club (vice-president, 1980-81). *Awards, honors:* Best writer award from Numismatic Literary Guild, 1972, 1973, and 1975.

WRITINGS: A Critical Guide to Anthologies of African Literature, African Studies Association, 1973; *Fourteen Bits: A Story of America's Bicentennial Coinage,* Three Continents Press, 1976; *The World of Coins and Coin Collecting,* Scribner, 1980; (contributor) Robert Friedberg, *Gold Coins of the World: An Illustrated Standard Catalogue with Valuations,* 5th edition, Coin & Currency Institute, 1980; (contributor) Friedberg, *Paper Money of the United States: A Complete Illustrated Guide with Valuations,* 10th edition, Coin & Currency Institute, 1981; (contributor) R. S. Yeoman, editor, *Guidebook of United States Coins,* 35th edition (Ganz was not associated with earlier editions), Western Publishing, 1981; *Plain Language Guide to Legal Forms,* Prentice-Hall, 1982; (with George Mallis and LeRoy Van Allen) *Silver Dollar Encyclopedia,* First Coinvestors Press, 1982.

Washington correspondent for *Numismatic News Weekly,* 1969-73; special correspondent for *Coin World.* Author of "Under the Glass," a column in *Numismatic News Weekly,* 1969-74; also author of "Coin Market Insiders Report," a monthly column in *COINage,* "Coin Market Perspective," a monthly column in *Coins,* and "Backgrounder," a weekly column in *Coin World,* all 1974—. Editor of *Young Numismatist,* 1971-74; assistant editor of *Numismatic News Weekly,* 1973; contributing editor of *COINage,* 1974—.

SIDELIGHTS: Ganz told *CA:* "Writing, like law, is a very jealous mistress; it is sometimes hard to balance both interests, and yet in my career as a very active practitioner I have found that each satisfies a very different need within me. I enjoy each, work hard at each, and believe that both law and writing, as aspects of my personality, and the abilities that flow from them, have benefited."

*   *   *

GARFINKEL, Alan 1941-

PERSONAL: Born September 6, 1941, in Chicago, Ill.; son of Bernard D. (a tobacconist) and Tillie (Schaffner) Garfinkel; married Sonya Pickus (an editor), July 10, 1965; children: two. *Education:* University of Illinois, B.A., 1963, M.A., 1964; Ohio State University, Ph.D., 1969. *Religion:* Jewish. *Office:* Division of Sponsored Programs, Purdue University, Horde Hall, West Lafayette, Ind. 47907.

CAREER: High school Spanish teacher in Waukegan, Ill., 1964-66; Oklahoma State University, Stillwater, assistant professor of foreign language education, 1969-72; Purdue University,

West Lafayette, Ind., assistant professor, 1972-74, associate professor of foreign language education, 1974—, coordinator of Educational Professions Extension, 1978-80, assistant director of Division of Sponsored Programs, of Purdue Research Foundation, 1981—. Fulbright lecturer in Bogota, Columbia, at University of Los Andes, 1978.

MEMBER: Teachers of English to Speakers of Other Languages International (executive secretary, 1979-81), International Reading Association, American Council on the Teaching of Foreign Languages (bibliographer, 1973—), Modern Language Association of America, National Society for Studies in Education, American Association of Teachers of Spanish and Portuguese, Indiana Foreign Language Teachers Association, Association for Teacher Education in Indiana, Phi Delta Kappa (president).

WRITINGS: (Contributor) Dale L. Lange, editor, *The Britannica Review of Foreign Language Education,* Volume III, Encyclopaedia Britannica, 1971; (with Stanley Hamilton) *Designs for Foreign Language Teacher Education,* Newbury House, 1976; *Modismos al Momento* (title means "Idioms at Your Fingertips"), Newbury House, 1977; *Trabajo y Vida* (title means "Work and Life"), Newbury House, 1982. Contributor to language journals. Editor of "Notes and News," in *Modern Language Journal,* 1974—.

WORK IN PROGRESS: Text for pre-vocational English as a second language (ESL); text for second year Spanish course, publication expected c. 1984.

SIDELIGHTS: Garfinkel told *CA:* "I believe in the power of asking questions, for the questions may be more important than the answers. I am often asked by teachers what level of achievement I expect of their students. It seems to me that I only have the right to ask that these teachers send me people who have a desire to learn in their classes. I should not and do not ask that the work of teaching be done for me.

"It is an economic decision alone that allows us to mix people of all native-language backgrounds into an all English ESL class. People learning here need English instructors to achieve at first and similarly need at least procedural instructions in their native languages. Hiring monolingual English-as-a-second-language teachers aggravates the problem. ESL teachers should know what it means to learn a language from their own experience.

"People often produce what they *know* you expect them to produce. High levels of expectancy are vital to success. I started to write textbooks because I thought I had something novel to say about teaching. Since teachers tend to follow the textbooks they choose, I feel the most direct route to influencing teaching is through writing texts."

* * *

GARRETT, (Ruth) Jane 1914-

PERSONAL: Born November 10, 1914, in Stalham, Norfolk, England; daughter of Christopher E. (an artist) and Berry (an actress; maiden name, Shaw) Perkins; married Stephen Denis Garrett (a professor of mycology), December 17, 1934; children: Rachel Garrett Ratsey, Lucy Garrett Hornsby, Catherine Garrett Sweeney. *Education:* Cambridgeshire Technical College, diploma in social studies (with distinction), 1954. *Religion:* Church of England. *Home:* 179 Hills Rd., Cambridge CB2 2RN, England.

CAREER: Cambridgeshire Mental Welfare Association, Cambridge, England, assistant social worker, 1954-56; Cambridgeshire County Council, Cambridge, England, officer, 1956-62;

United Cambridge Hospitals, Cambridge, social worker in department of psychiatry, 1962-69, head social worker, 1969-73; writer, 1973—. *Member:* Historical Association, Family History Society.

WRITINGS: The Triumphs of Providence: The Assassination Plot, 1696, Cambridge University Press, 1980.

WORK IN PROGRESS: A biography of her father, Christopher Perkins, with special reference to his paintings, 1929-33, publication expected in 1984; *Early Jacobite Activities in England, 1688-92,* completion expected in 1984 or 1985.

SIDELIGHTS: Jane Garrett commented: "I took to writing after retirement from twenty years in psychiatry because I always enjoyed writing case histories and finding out about people. The great advantage of historical research is that the subjects are *dead* and do not demand that one solve their problems—impossible anyway. My first book was the product of five years research and arose from a family legend about ancestral Jacobite activities. The second is a work of filial piety, as my father's work influenced New Zealand painting for twenty years, and little is known about him there now. I'll go back to history when that project is done.

"Very little research has been done on the early history of the Jacobite movement. I am looking forward to further explorations in this comparatively unfrequented field."

* * *

GAVIN, Amanda
See GIBSON-JARVIE, Clodagh

* * *

GAYLORD, Sherwood Boyd 1914-

BRIEF ENTRY: Born June 6, 1914, in Kansas City, Mo. American manufacturing executive and author. Gaylord has worked for General Electric Co. since 1937. He has been manager of the company's market analysis in Fairfield, Conn., since 1974. He wrote *Sensible Speculating With Put and Call Options* (Simon & Schuster, 1976). *Address:* 1 Strawberry Hill Court, Regency Towers, Apt. 10A, Stamford, Conn. 06902. *Biographical/critical sources: Who's Who in the Midwest,* 16th edition, Marquis, 1978.

* * *

GAYN, Mark J. 1909-1981

OBITUARY NOTICE: Born in 1909 in Manchuria, China; died of cancer, December 17, 1981, in Toronto, Ontario, Canada. Journalist and author. A specialist on foreign, especially Asian, affairs, Gayn was one of the first Western journalists admitted to China in the 1960's. He covered China and Japan during the 1930's and 1940's, writing accounts of the firebombing of Tokyo and of the American occupation of Japan. He incurred the wrath of the United States government by writing in 1945 that Chinese leader Chiang Kai-shek was corrupt and unpopular. He was also critical of post-revolutionary China, writing harshly of the political and intellectual regimentation he found there. Gayn's account of occupied Japan was published in a book, *Japan Diary;* a sequel, *New Japan Diary,* was completed shortly before his death. Obituaries and other sources: *Who's Who in America,* 40th edition, Marquis, 1978; *New York Times,* December 24, 1981.

* * *

GELDERMAN, Carol Wettlaufer 1935-

PERSONAL: Born December 2, 1935, in Detroit, Mich.;

daughter of A. J. (an automotive executive) and Irene (Kelly) Wettlaufer; married G. A. Gelderman, Jr., September 26, 1959 (divorced, 1971); children: Gregory III, Margot, Irene. *Education:* Manhattanville College, B.A., 1956; Northwestern University, M.A., 1966, Ph.D., 1972. *Religion:* Catholic. *Home:* 2622 Camp St., New Orleans, La. 70130. *Agent:* Elaine Markson, 44 Greenwich Ave., New York, N.Y. *Office:* Department of English, University of New Orleans, New Orleans, La. 70122.

CAREER: Louisiana State University, New Orleans, assistant professor of English, 1972-77; University of New Orleans, New Orleans, associate professor, 1977-81, professor of English, 1981—. *Member:* Modern Language Association of America, Authors Guild.

WRITINGS: George Fitzmaurice (literary criticism), G. K. Hall, 1979; *Henry Ford: The Wayward Capitalist* (biography), Dial, 1981; *Writing for Professionals,* Scott-Foresman, in press. Publisher of menu book, *New Orleans a la Carte.* Contributor to journals and magazines, including *Eire-Ireland, Prairie Schooner,* and *Lost Generation.*

WORK IN PROGRESS: A biography of Mary McCarthy, for McGraw.

BIOGRAPHICAL/CRITICAL SOURCES: Los Angeles Times Book Review, March 22, 1981; *Detroit News,* April 12, 1981.

*　　*　　*

GEORGE, Sally 1945-

PERSONAL: Born August 24, 1945, in New York, N.Y.; children: Justine Lambert. *Education:* Attended Barnard College, 1962-64; Goddard College, B.A., 1974. *Residence:* Brooklyn, N.Y. *Agent:* McIntosh & Otis, 475 Fifth Ave., New York, N.Y. 10017.

CAREER: Novelist. *Awards, honors:* CAPS award from New York State Council on the Arts, 1977-78, for fiction.

WRITINGS: Frog Salad (novel), Scribner, 1981.

WORK IN PROGRESS: A novel.

SIDELIGHTS: Sally George's first novel, *Frog Salad,* is about a group of ''victim/survivors of the 60's, wistful about the communal purpose of the past, apologetic for their present lives, and more likely to be mistaken for C.I.A. agents than radicals,'' wrote Janet Burroway in the *New York Times Book Review.* The title is derived from the efforts of one character, an artist, to get frogs to pose atop a salad so they can be painted. Burroway called *Frog Salad* ''a breezy cartoon of a novel that has all the virtues of a cartoon: clean line, wit, and the power to send tremors, if not shocks, of recognition.'' The book was also praised by other reviewers, including Elizabeth Duvall of *Atlantic,* who observed that beneath its wit, *''Frog Salad* is really a very dark tale. . . . [It] practically crackles with an original, if nutty viewpoint, and it is consistently and joyfully funny. . . . It offers a lot and promises more.''

BIOGRAPHICAL/CRITICAL SOURCES: Atlantic Monthly, April, 1981; *New York Times Book Review,* June 7, 1981.

*　　*　　*

GERBER, Rudolph Joseph 1938-

PERSONAL: Born October 25, 1938, in St. Louis, Mo.; son of Rudolph V. (an advertiser) and Isabel (Bauer) Gerber; children: Jennifer, Kristin. *Education:* St. Louis University, B.A., 1961, M.A., 1962; Columbia University, M.A., 1964; Uni-

versity of Louvain, Ph.D., 1966; The Hague Academy of International Law, Certificate in International Law, 1970; University of Notre Dame, J.D., 1971. *Religion:* Roman Catholic. *Office:* 101 West Jefferson St., Phoenix, Ariz. 85003.

CAREER: University of Notre Dame, Notre Dame, Ind., assistant professor of philosophy, 1968-71; County of Maricopa, Phoenix, Ariz., deputy public defender, 1972, appeals, trials, and motions attorney, 1972-75, deputy county attorney, 1975-77, training and research deputy attorney, 1977-79; writer. Legal editor for Kennikat Press, 1976—. Adjunct professor at Arizona State University, 1974-79. Associate director of Arizona Criminal Code Commission, 1972-75; member of board of governors of State Bar of Arizona, 1977-79, treasurer, 1978-79; member of World Affairs Council of Phoenix and Arizona Academy. *Awards, honors:* Woodrow Wilson fellow, 1963-64; Fulbright scholar in Belgium, 1964-66.

WRITINGS: Contemporary Punishment: Views, Explanations, and Justifications, University of Notre Dame Press, 1972; *Contemporary Issues in Criminal Justice,* Kennikat, 1976; *The Criminal Law of Arizona,* State Bar of Arizona, 1979. Contributor to law journals.

WORK IN PROGRESS: The Insanity Defense, publication expected in 1983.

SIDELIGHTS: Gerber commented: ''My writing is motivated by my interest in law and philosophy. Money and fame are of little importance compared to the pleasure of communicating in print. While my earlier interests were mostly centered in poetry and fiction, the pressing legal and moral concerns which prompted my legal career are more prominent in my later writings, particularly with respect to the role of law in shaping behavior, the purpose of punishment, and the mental state requirement for criminal liability.''

AVOCATIONAL INTERESTS: Travel, tennis, hiking, camping.

*　　*　　*

GERSTAD, John (Leif) 1924-1981

OBITUARY NOTICE—See index for *CA* sketch: Born September 3, 1924, in Boston, Mass.; died of emphysema, December 1, 1981, in New York, N.Y. Actor, director, producer, educator, and playwright. Gerstad began his lifelong career in the theatre selling lemonade and renting binoculars to patrons of the Shubert Theatre in Boston. By the age of sixteen he had written the play ''Sun at Midnight'' and had seen it produced. Within three years he was acting in a Broadway production of ''Othello'' that starred Jose Ferrer and Paul Robeson. Gerstad appeared on Broadway many times since in such plays as ''The Male Animal,'' ''The Trial of Lee Harvey Oswald,'' ''Come Summer,'' and ''Oklahoma!'' He directed several plays on Broadway, the best-known being ''The Seven-Year Itch.'' Others include ''Debut,'' ''Play That on Your Old Piano,'' and ''Double in Hearts.'' In addition, Gerstad acted in motion pictures and on television. He was featured in the films ''Up the Down Staircase,'' ''A Lovely Way to Die,'' and ''The Swimmer'' and starred in the television programs ''Certain Honorable Men,'' ''The Dillinger Story,'' ''Galileo,'' and ''Give Us Barrabas.'' He also produced and directed ''The Shari Lewis Show'' for television. Gerstad served as dean of the drama department of the New England Conservatory and as head of the drama department of the Hunter Lenox Day Center. Among his writings for the stage are ''The Monday Man,'' ''When the Bough Breaks,'' ''The Fig Leaf,'' and ''The Bouncing Lover.'' Obituaries and other sources: *New York Times,* December 3, 1981.

GIANNESTRAS, Nicholas James   1909-1978

OBITUARY NOTICE: Born May 19, 1909, in Macedonia, Greece; died in June, 1978, in Cincinnati, Ohio. Orthopedic surgeon, educator, and author of *Foot Disorders: Medical and Surgical Management.* Obituaries and other sources: *Who's Who in the Midwest,* 16th edition, Marquis, 1978; *The Writers Directory, 1980-82,* St. Martin's, 1979. (Date of death provided by Pamela Beyer, office manager of Cincinnati Orthopedic Institute.)

*   *   *

GIBSON, Evan K(eith)   1909-

PERSONAL: Born July 4, 1909, in Everett, Wash.; son of Clayton Edgar (an educator) and Jean (Sherwood) Gibson; married Mary Burns, October 7, 1932; children: Keith, Jean Gibson Gildersleeve, Judy Gibson Chase, Joanne Gibson Wallace. *Education:* Seattle Pacific College, A.B., 1933; University of Washington, Seattle, M.A., 1935, Ph.D., 1947. *Religion:* Free Methodist. *Home:* 1216 Ninth Ave. W., Seattle, Wash. 98119.

CAREER: High school teacher of English in Chimacum, Wash., 1934-35; Washington Technical Institute, Seattle, teacher of English, 1935-41; Seattle Pacific College (now University), Seattle, associate professor of English and head of department, 1941-43; Oregon State University, Corvallis, 1947-64, began as assistant professor, became professor of English; Seattle Pacific University, professor of English, 1964-75. Writer, 1940—.

WRITINGS: C. S. Lewis, Spinner of Tales, Eerdmans, 1980. Contributor of about forty articles, stories, and poems to scholarly journals and religious magazines.

WORK IN PROGRESS: A book on C. S. Lewis and some aspects of his Christian doctrine.

SIDELIGHTS: Gibson told *CA:* "I have a continuing interest in the impact that C. S. Lewis is still making upon the reading public. His stature as a belletristic writer and his force as an interpreter of Christianity to the common reader have not yet been adequately evaluated. In addition to the analysis of his fiction which I have already done, I hope to show something of the relation of his writings to the British countryside, the place of creation in both his fiction and nonfiction, and the scope of his view of extraterrestrial reality.

"My interest in the geography of his writings is related to my conviction that an author's locale or environment often contributes more than we realize to the world of his imagination. I believe that if the reader could see what the writer saw, could travel to the places where the writer lived or to which he traveled, his understanding and appreciation of the work would be greatly enhanced. A writer, of necessity, must make tacit assumptions of knowledge on the reader's part which only a few of them will have. Only a fraction of the multitude of details which entered into the writer's consciousness can be anchored in print. The more of these details which the reader can experience directly, the richer will be his reading experience. For this reason my travels in Europe have always been a photography journey to places significant in British literature. The employment of slides and movies in my classes has always been aimed at bringing the student closer to the mental images upon which the writer drew for his literary productions. For instance, I have made a movie, 'With Byron From England to the Alps,' of places mentioned by Byron in Canto III of his *Childe Harold's Pilgrimage.* I hope to do more of this sort of visual research for the writings of C. S. Lewis."

*   *   *

GIBSON, Karon Rose (White)   1946-

PERSONAL: Born October 31, 1946, in Chicago, Ill.; daughter of Ronald Dugald (an insurance claims executive) and Vilma (Sada) White; married Ralph M. Gibson (a policeman), May 22, 1971. *Education:* Mount Sinai Hospital Medical Center School of Nursing, Chicago, Ill., R.N., 1967. *Religion:* Episcopalian. *Home:* 5524 West 54th St., Chicago, Ill. 60638. *Office:* Registered Professional Nurses, 5796 South Archer Ave., Chicago, Ill. 60638.

CAREER: Mount Sinai Hospital, Chicago, Ill., charge nurse in emergency services and psychiatry, 1967-68; Christ Community Hospital, Oak Lawn, Ill., charge nurse in Division of Psychiatric Services, 1968-74; Registered Professional Nurses, Chicago, president and director of nursing and patient services, 1973—. Old Chicago First Aid Towne, manager, 1975—, occupational health nurse and safety co-chairperson, 1980—. Consultant to National Joint Commission on Medicine and Nursing Practice; health consultant to Senior Citizens and Boy Scouts of America. Instructor in cardiopulmonary resuscitation (CPR) at Illinois Heart Association, 1975—. *Member:* National Association of Women Business Owners, Registered Nurses Association, Chicago Police Wives Association.

WRITINGS: On Our Own, St. Martin's, 1981. Contributor to nursing journals, including *RN.* Member of advisory board of *American Nursing News Midwest.*

WORK IN PROGRESS: A study of business and medicine in the world's only indoor amusement park.

SIDELIGHTS: Karon Gibson wrote: "I consider myself a leader in the field of independent nursing practice. My motivation in compiling the contents of my book, *On Our Own,* was a combination of determination to implement progress and to inform the public of the truth 'behind the scenes.' I am 'trenditional.' Due to all the various positions I have held I am now a businesswoman and entrepreneur and a first lady of the nursing profession."

BIOGRAPHICAL/CRITICAL SOURCES: Chicago Tribune, November 15, 1973; *Suburban Week,* March 13, 1974; *McCall's,* August, 1975; *Congressional Record,* August 1, 1975; *Bolingbrook Herald,* April 12, 1978; *Los Angeles Times,* February 12, 1981; *Milwaukee Journal,* February 20, 1981; *St. Paul Dispatch,* February 22, 1981; *Parade,* May 17, 1981.

*   *   *

GIBSON-JARVIE, Clodagh   1923-
(Amanda Gavin)

PERSONAL: Born in September, 1923, in London, England; daughter of John (a banker and farmer) and Ethel (a singer; maiden name, Rowland) Gibson-Jarvie; married John Fry, April, 1949 (divorced, 1957); married David Chapman (a political theorist), December, 1972; children: (first marriage) Amanda, Gavin. *Education:* Open University, B.A. (with honors), 1979. *Politics:* Ecology party. *Religion:* Agnostic. *Home:* Coles Farm, Buxhall, Suffolk IP14 3EB, England.

CAREER: Farm worker in Sussex, England, 1939-41; Ministry of Information, London, England, writer, 1941-46; school secretary in Suffolk, England, 1946-51; teacher at primary school, 1967-70; worked as art teacher, 1971-76; writer, 1976—. Member of Morris Dance Side.

WRITINGS: Variations on a Theme of Murder, Thanet, 1947; *Vicious Circuit,* Boardman, 1956; *He Would Provoke Death,* Boardman, 1957; *Amore Senza Domani,* Frassinelli, 1959; *The Web,* Weidenfeld & Nicolson, 1979.

Juveniles; under pseudonym Amanda Gavin: *To Find a Golden Pony,* Dent, 1959; *The Luck at Lonely Hall,* Dent, 1960; *Ponycare,* Arthur Barker, 1976.

Author of play "Not Quite Cricket."

WORK IN PROGRESS: The Night Before Dark, a novel; a feminist novel; a television play.

AVOCATIONAL INTERESTS: Local history, the countryside, literature, art, music, playing flute, piccolo, and vielle, travel, gardening, breeding lurcher dogs and golden Guernsey goats.

* * *

GIFFIN, James Manning 1935-

PERSONAL: Born October 4, 1935, in New York, N.Y.; son of Lewis A. (a surgeon) and Katherine R. (a sculptress) Giffin; married Elizabeth Curvish (a medical receptionist), June 7, 1959; children: James A., Peter C., Katherine D. *Education:* Amherst College, B.A., 1957; Yale University, M.D., 1961. *Home:* 184 1600 Rd., Delta, Colo. 81416. *Office:* 70 Stafford Lane, Delta, Colo. 81416.

CAREER: Barnes Hospital, St. Louis, Mo., intern and resident in surgery, 1961-66; private practice of general surgery in Springfield, Mo., 1968-78, and Delta, Colo., 1978—. *Military service:* U.S. Army, Medical Corps, 1967-68; chief of surgery at Beach Army Hospital in Mineral Wells, Tex., 1966-67, and 45th Surgical Hospital, Vietnam, 1967-68; became captain; received Bronze Star. *Member:* American College of Surgeons, Great Pyrenees Club of America (member of board of directors, 1975-81). *Awards, honors:* Best medical book award from Dog Writers Association of America, 1981, for *The Dog Owner's Home Veterinary Handbook.*

WRITINGS: The Complete Great Pyrenees, Howell Book, 1977; *The Dog Owner's Home Veterinary Handbook,* Howell Book, 1980; *The Cat Owner's Home Veterinary Handbook,* Howell Book, 1982. Contributor to medical journals and *International Great Pyrenees Review.*

SIDELIGHTS: Giffin commented: "I enjoy writing as a hobby and a relaxation from the pace of medical practice. I hope to be able in the future to devote time to a work of fiction. At present I am engaged in an active medical practice and a number of outdoor sports and recreational pursuits, and my wife and I keep several horses and raise Great Pyrenees dogs.

"Medical writing often can be rather sober and dry. I have been blessed by a publisher who insists that the complex paragraph be struck from the pages and replaced by language which sits more agreeably upon the reader's mental digestive system."

* * *

GILBERT, Bill 1931-

PERSONAL: Born April 9, 1931, in Washington, D.C.; son of Raymond L. (an illustrator) and Marguerite (a writer; maiden name, Hampson) Gilbert; married Lillian Muir (a secretary), November 14, 1959; children: David W. *Education:* Attended University of Maryland, 1950, 1955. *Home:* 1 Miller Fall Court, Derwood, Md. 20855. *Agent:* Art Aveilhe, 1211 Horn Ave., Hollywood, Calif. 90069.

CAREER: Washington Post, Washington, D.C., reporter, 1947-57; Montgomery County Government, Rockville, Md., information director, 1957-61; Washington Senators Baseball Team, Washington, D.C., promotion director, 1961-62; public information officer for departments of labor and defense, Washington, D.C., 1962-65; Metropolitan Washington Council of Governments, Washington, D.C., public affairs director, 1965—. Guest lecturer at colleges and universities; public speaker; public relations consultant. *Military service:* U.S. Air Force, 1951-55. *Awards, honors:* National awards include award of excellence from National Association of Regional Councils, 1981.

WRITINGS: (With Shirley Povich) *All These Mornings,* Prentice-Hall, 1969; (with Mike Curtis) *Keep Off My Turf,* Lippincott, 1972; *Public Relations in Local Government,* International City Management Association, 1975; (with Joe Gallagher) *High School Basketball,* privately printed, 1978; (with Elvin Hayes) *They Call Me the Big E,* Prentice-Hall, 1978; *This City, This Man,* International City Management Association, 1978; (with Morgan Wootten) *From Orphans to Champions,* Atheneum, 1979.

WORK IN PROGRESS: Two baseball novels.

SIDELIGHTS: Gilbert wrote: "As a reporter and author I have written on a wide range of subjects, including urban problems, national and international affairs, sports, police and fire stories, and current political issues. I began my career as a sportswriter for the *Washington Post* at the age of sixteen, hired by the nationally famous columnist Shirley Povich. I retained an interest in athletics after transferring to the newsroom, and I continue that interest today as a baseball coach and Washington's most prolific sportswriter."

* * *

GINER de los RIOS, Francisco 1839-1915

BRIEF ENTRY: Born November 10, 1839, in Ronda, Spain; died February 17, 1915, in Madrid, Spain. Spanish educational reformer and author. Giner de los Rios played a vital role in guiding Spain into a modern system of education and intellectual development. His views on education were based on the philosophy of Karl Krause. As a professor at the University of Madrid, Giner de los Rios was arrested in 1875 for protesting restrictions on academic freedom. After his release he established the nonpolitical, nonreligious Institucion Libre de Ensenanza, which eventually taught students of all ages. Giner de los Rios believed that the rebirth of Spain could be achieved through a gradual process of education, but his approach was revolutionary. He abandoned traditional schoolbooks and tests and encouraged independent study and free thinking, for girls as well as boys. He conducted field trips to museums and the countryside and insisted that physical and moral education were necessary corollaries to intellectual growth. Giner de los Rios was an important influence on some of the great writers of modern Spain. His essays and books were collected posthumously in the eighteen-volume *Obras completas* (1916-27). *Biographical/critical sources: Columbia Dictionary of Modern European Literature,* Columbia University Press, 1947.

* * *

GINSBERG, Leon H(erman) 1936-

PERSONAL: Born January 15, 1936, in San Antonio, Tex.; son of Sam (in business) and Lillian (Gindler) Ginsberg; married Elaine Kaner (a professor of English), July 29, 1956; children: Robert, Michael, Meryl. *Education:* Trinity University, San Antonio, Tex., B.A., 1957; Tulane University, M.S.W., 1959; University of Oklahoma, Ph.D., 1966. *Home:* 1417 Anderson Ave., Morgantown, W.Va. 26505. *Office:* School of Social Work, West Virginia University, Morgantown, W.Va. 26506.

CAREER: West Virginia University, Morgantown, professor of social work, 1968—, dean of social work. Professor at Universidad Pontificia Bolivariana, 1974. Consultant to veterans hospitals and child development programs. *Military service:* U.S. Army Reserve, active duty in Artillery, 1957-58; became captain. *Member:* Council on Social Work Education, National Association of Social Workers, Association of Jewish Center Workers, American Public Welfare Association. *Awards, honors:* Citation of merit from southwestern region of B'nai B'rith's Anti-Defamation League, 1968; distinguished service award from West Virginia Welfare Conference, 1970.

WRITINGS: Life-Span Developmental Psychology: Normative Life Crises, Academic Press, 1975; *Social Work in Rural Communities: A Book of Readings,* Council on Social Work Education, 1976; (with Anita S. Harbert) *Human Services for Older Adults,* Wadsworth, 1979. Contributor of articles and reviews to professional journals, popular magazines, including *Nation,* and newspapers.

SIDELIGHTS: Ginsberg told *CA:* "I have had the good fortune in recent years of serving as a social work practitioner and government official in public welfare as commissioner of the West Virginia Department of Welfare. I was appointed to that position by Governor John D. Rockefeller IV, and my work in it has brought me in touch with many elements of the social welfare industry. My professional work in administering a program that spends several hundred million dollars each year on services to disadvantaged people has given me many understandings of the breadth of social welfare in this country and should make me a more effective educator, when I return to higher education responsibilities.

"I have been on leave from my position as professor at West Virginia University since 1977. The state legislature has authorized the higher education system to provide leaves of absence of up to eight years for those who are involved in state government, which has been particularly advantageous for me.

"I learned how little my colleagues and I thought about the realities of public welfare practice and that has led me to develop the book on *The Practice of Social Work in Public Welfare,* which I am writing under the direction of distinguished Professor Herbert Strean of Rutgers University and Dean Francis Turner of the Laurentian University School of Social Work. This will be the first book on the practice of social work in public welfare to have been published in many years.

"I have often thought too few social work practitioners understand very much about social work theory and education and, similarly, that too few social work educators understand the roles that social work practitioners play. I hope that I, as well as many others, will bridge that chasm, therefore improving both the practice and teaching of social work in this nation."

* * *

GINTER, Maria 1922-

PERSONAL: Born November 23, 1922, in Smolice, Poland; came to United States, 1964; naturalized U.S. citizen, 1974; daughter of Karol (an estate owner) and Jozefine (Skrzynski) Zieleniewski; married Yan Korzybski, March 9, 1943 (killed in action, 1944); married Wadaw Ginter (divorced); married

Walter Kornecki (divorced); married George Ruszczynski (a lawyer), January 14, 1981; children: (first marriage) Zdzislaw Yan Korzybski. *Education:* Attended Sorbonne, University of Paris, 1962-64; C.W. Post Center, Long Island University, B.A., 1970, M.A., 1974. *Religion:* Catholic. *Home:* 555 Jericho Turnpike, Jericho, N.Y. 11753.

CAREER: Art designer, film consultant, journalist, and decorator in Warsaw, Poland, 1943-62; artist in London, England, and Paris, France, 1962-64; writer, artist, and teacher in United States, 1964—. Teacher of French and tennis, 1970-74. Art work has been exhibited all over the world. *Military service:* Polish Underground Army, 1939-44; prisoner of war; received Bravery Cross, Home Army Cross, and Polish Army Cross. *Member:* Polish American Raleigh Club (president), Auto-Valley Club. *Awards, honors:* Nearly fifty athletic awards.

WRITINGS: Life in Both Hands, self-illustrated, translated from Polish by P.C. Blauth-Muszkowski, Hodder & Stoughton, 1964; *Wspomnienia wiezniow pawiaka,* [Poland], 1968; *Poems and Visual Images,* privately printed, 1974; *Galopem na Przelaj,* Iskry [Poland], 1982. Contributor to periodicals, including *German Shepherd Dog Review.*

WORK IN PROGRESS: Moulin d'amour (title means "Windmill of Love"), a novel about Paris; *Zwiatrem pod wiatr* (title means "With Guts Against the Wind"), a book of memoirs.

SIDELIGHTS: Maria Ginter commented: "I write and paint in order to be absolutely free. It's most essential to me—I would hate to work at a regular job. I started writing because of hard war experiences, including prison."

* * *

GISSING, George (Robert) 1857-1903

BRIEF ENTRY: Born November 22, 1857, in Wakefield, England; died of pneumonia, December 28, 1903, in Saint-Jean-de-Luz, France. English educator, novelist, short story writer, essayist, and critic. In his numerous novels Gissing bitterly but realistically portrayed the misery and deprivation suffered by the lower class in Victorian society. A victim of poverty himself, Gissing often included autobiographical elements in his works. As a young man he had a promising academic future. A brilliant classical scholar, he won a scholarship to Owens College, but his career was ruined when he was caught stealing in order to support and reform a prostitute with whom he was associated. After being imprisoned for a short time, he moved to Chicago where he survived by selling short stories to the *Chicago Tribune.* On his return to England, he supported himself as a tutor. Gissing was also forced by economic necessity to produce at least one book each year. Despite his efforts, the author never attained financial security or popularity as a novelist. Although he was strongly influenced by the work of Charles Dickens, Gissing created visions of the underprivileged that lacked humor and were too realistic and grim to appeal to the majority of Victorian readers. His works include *Demos: A Story of English Socialism* (1886), *The Nether World* (1889), *The Emancipated* (1890), *New Grub Street* (1891), and *Charles Dickens: A Critical Study* (1898). *Biographical/critical sources: Twentieth Century Authors: A Biographical Dictionary of Modern Literature,* H. W. Wilson, 1942; *Cyclopedia of World Authors,* Harper, 1958; *The Oxford Companion to English Literature,* 4th edition, Oxford University Press, 1967; *The Penguin Companion to English Literature,* McGraw, 1971; *Cassell's Encyclopaedia of World Literature,* revised edition, Morrow, 1973; *Twentieth-Century Literary Criticism,* Volume 3, Gale, 1980.

GITTELSON, Celia

PERSONAL: Born in New York, N.Y.; daughter of Mark Robert (in real estate) and Natalie (a writer and editor; maiden name, Leavy) Gittelson. *Education:* Sarah Lawrence College, B.A. *Religion:* Jewish. *Residence:* New York, N.Y. *Agent:* Candida Donadio, 111 West 57th St., New York, N.Y. 10019.

CAREER: Farrar, Straus & Giroux (publisher), New York City, associate director of publicity, 1975-77, director of publicity, 1977-79; marketing and promotion director of Congdon & Lattes (publisher), New York City. *Awards, honors:* American Book Award nomination for best first novel from the association of American Publishers, 1981, for *Saving Grace.*

WRITINGS: Saving Grace (novel), Knopf, 1981.

WORK IN PROGRESS: A novel about the atomic bomb.

SIDELIGHTS: Celia Gittelson describes her first novel simply: "It's about a pope who runs away from the Vatican." *Saving Grace,* published in September, 1981, is "a bit of a dream come true" for the young publishing executive (she will say only that she is in her mid-twenties) who had originally set out to write "an amusing short story." On the other hand, she finds it somewhat "embarrassing" and would prefer to "keep it all quiet." As marketing and promotion director for Congdon & Lattes, she knows well the attention and publication parties that come to a new author. "I'm not sure how I'd handle it," she says in a *Publishers Weekly* interview. "In the back of my mind I'm certain I'd be hit by a milk truck the minute I walked out of the party. It must be my Jewish guilt."

The hero of *Saving Grace,* Giuseppe Bellini, ascends reluctantly to the Chair of St. Peter, where the isolation, protocols, and bureaucracy of the Vatican overwhelm his days, and troubling, erotic dreams overtake his nights. Feigning illness, he decamps for the south of Italy and a vacation at his sister's farm. From there he makes his way as a traveling salesman to a tiny village hideout. Meanwhile, a search party comprised of two monsignors, a bishop, and the pope's brother-in-law sets off in quest of the errant pontiff. Trailing close behind are the paparazzi, and after a helicopter crash, all the principals converge on the tiny village. The pope, recovered from his personal crisis, journeys back to Rome of his own accord and resumes his papal duties.

Publishers Weekly notes that there is nothing in Gittelson's New York, Jewish background that prepared her for writing *Saving Grace,* yet the story is plausible, the details convincing. She explains in *Library Journal:* "All I know is that one day a fiery question popped into my brain: What would happen if a pope ran away from the Vatican? On the heels of that, I remembered the words of a writer far more experienced than I, who once remarked to me, 'It's amazing how little you have to know about something to write about it.' And so I began to write. What I hope I have done is to invent a series of very convincing lies. I hope also that I have written a compelling, entertaining narrative that always makes the reader ask, 'What happens next?'"

In his review for the *New York Times,* Christopher Lehmann-Haupt comments: "[Gittelson] so obviously enjoys her inventiveness that the making up of the story is as engaging as the story itself. One ends up rooting for her plausibility. . . . The wonder remains that Miss Gittelson seems to have defied all that advice about sticking to one's own experience, especially in writing a first novel, and to have brought off her rebellion triumphantly. Can it be that in the self-preoccupied Me Era it

is simply a relief to see a young female writer take up a subject apparently remote from herself, her marriage and her career, and to handle it so confidently and expertly? That is certainly part of the pleasure of 'Saving Grace.'"

In September, 1981, Sherwood Productions purchased the film rights to *Saving Grace* for $150,000 plus 5 percent of the picture's profits.

BIOGRAPHICAL/CRITICAL SOURCES: Library Journal, June 15, 1981; *Publishers Weekly,* September 4, 1981; *New York Times,* September 15, 1981, February 3, 1982; *Washington Post Book World,* October 10, 1981; *New York Times Book Review,* October 11, 1981; *Chicago Tribune Book World,* November 15, 1981.

*   *   *

GLASER, Eva Schocken   1918-1982

OBITUARY NOTICE: Born in 1918, in Zwickau, Germany (now East Germany); died January 12, 1982, in White Plains, N.Y. Publisher and editor. Glaser was the daughter of Salman Schocken, founder of the German publishing firm Schocken Verlag. When Schocken Verlag was closed by the Gestapo in 1938, the family, which had already left Germany, revived the company in Tel Aviv and New York and continued to publish the works of such Jewish authors as Franz Kafka, as well as many scholarly titles. Glaser became president of the New York company Schocken Books in 1975, after the death of her brother. As publisher and editor, she expanded her company's list of titles, taking a special interest in the area of women's studies. Obituaries and other sources: *New York Times,* January 13, 1982; *Chicago Tribune,* January 15, 1982; *Publishers Weekly,* January 29, 1982; *AB Bookman's Weekly,* February 22, 1982.

*   *   *

GLUCKSBERG, Harold   1939-

PERSONAL: Born October 18, 1939, in Montreal, Quebec, Canada; naturalized U.S. citizen, 1957; son of Murry and Sonia (Afrin) Glucksberg; married Karen T. Lind (a nurse), December 31, 1970; children: Ari, Mordecai. *Education:* Attended City College (now of the City University of New York), 1956-57, and Queens College (now of the City University of New York), 1957-60; Buffalo Medical School, M.D., 1964. *Politics:* "Liberal humanist." *Religion:* Jewish. *Residence:* Zimbabwe. *Agent:* Writers Alliance, New York, N.Y.

CAREER: King County Hospital, New York, N.Y., intern, 1964-65, resident in medicine, 1965-66; University of Washington, Seattle, fellow in hematology and oncology, 1969-70, senior fellow in oncology, 1970-71, and medicine, 1971-73, instructor, 1971-73, assistant professor of medicine, 1973-75; University of Dar es Salaam, Dar es Salaam, Tanzania, senior lecturer in medicine, 1975-76; University of Washington, assistant professor of medicine, 1976-79; Tulane University, New Orleans, La., assistant professor of medicine, 1980; Maimonides Medical Center, Brooklyn, N.Y., attending physician at emergency center, 1980; doctor and health care planner in Zimbabwe, 1981—. Diplomate of National Board of Medical Examiners; assistant member of Fred Hutchinson Cancer Research Center, 1976-79; co-director of National Nutrition Center of Zaire, 1980. *Military service:* U.S. Army, Medical Corps, 1966-69; became captain. *Member:* American Association of Clinical Oncology, Gibson Honor Society. *Awards, honors:* Mosby Book Award.

WRITINGS: (With J. Singer) *Cancer Care: A Personal Guide,* Johns Hopkins Press, 1980; (contributor) S. Jones and S. Salmon, editors, *Adjuvant Therapy of Cancer,* Volume III, Grune, 1981. Contributor of about thirty articles to medical journals.

WORK IN PROGRESS: Research on the involvement of multinational drug companies in Third World health care.

SIDELIGHTS: Glucksberg wrote: "*Cancer Care* was written to help cancer patients find good care and have as much control over their care as possible. My present interests center on Africa, where I work in Zimbabwe as a doctor and health care planner."

* * *

GLYN, Richard Hamilton 1907-1980

PERSONAL: Born October 12, 1907, in Dorsetshire, England; died October 24, 1980, in London, England; son of Sir Richard FitzGerald Glyn; married Lyndsay Mary Baker (marriage ended, 1969); married Barbara Henwood, 1970; children: (first marriage) two sons, one daughter. *Education:* Attended Worcester College, Oxford.

CAREER: Called to the Bar at Lincoln's Inn, 1935; British Army, Territorial Army, Queen's Own Dorset Yeomanry, commissioned to Field Regiment, 1930, became commander of 141st Field Regiment, 1944-45, and 294th Field Regiment, 1952-55, aide-de-camp of the Territorial Army to the Queen, 1958-62, retiring as colonel; British Parliament, London, England, Conservative member of Parliament for North Dorsetshire, 1957-70, Parliamentary private secretary to president of Board of Trade, 1958, vice-chairman of Conservative Agriculture Committee, 1959-65, and Conservative Defence Committee, 1961-68, chairman of Conservative Army Committee, 1961-68, member of select committee on estimates for defense and overseas, 1964-70, member of Commonwealth War Graves Commission, 1965-70; writer, 1970-80. Justice of the peace of Dorsetshire; member of Chelsea Borough Council and vice-chairman of its housing committee, 1948-50; deputy chairman of Dorset Quarter Sessions, 1952-57; member of Shaftesbury Rural District Council, 1957; made deputy lieutenant of Dorsetshire, 1960. Chairman of Cruft's Dog Show, 1963-73. *Awards, honors*—Military: Territorial Decoration, 1941; named honorary colonel of Queen's Own Dorset and Somerset Yeomanry, 1961. Other: Officer of the Order of the British Empire, 1955.

WRITINGS: Bull Terriers and How to Breed Them: Dealing Fully With White, Coloured and Miniature Bull Terriers, Hall, 1937, 6th edition, 1951; *A Short Account of the Queen's Own Dorset Yeomanry,* 1943; (editor) *Champion Dogs of the World,* Doubleday, 1967; (editor) *The World's Finest Horses and Ponies,* Doubleday, 1971.

SIDELIGHTS: In 1960 Sir Richard succeeded his father as Ninth Baronet of Ewell and Fifth Baronet of Gaunts. In addition to his military and political career, he was actively involved in breeding bull terriers and directing dog clubs and shows.

OBITUARIES: London Times, October 29, 1980.*

* * *

GOBBI, Tito 1915-

BRIEF ENTRY: Born October 24, 1915, in Bassano del Grappa, Italy. Italian baritone opera singer and author. Since the late 1930's, Gobbi has performed in major theatres all over the world, including the Metropolitan Opera in New York City in 1956. He wrote *My Life* (Macdonald & Jane's, 1979). *Address:* Via Valle della Molletta 47, 00 123 La Storta, Rome, Italy.

Biographical/critical sources: Who's Who in Opera, Arno, 1976; *New York Times Book Review,* December 28, 1980.

* * *

GOLDBERG, Robert Alan 1949-

PERSONAL: Born August 16, 1949, in New York, N.Y.; son of Philip J. (in business) and Ruth (Dickler) Goldberg; married Susan Kralick (a clinical specialist), August 8, 1976; children: David, Joshua. *Education:* Arizona State University, B.A., 1971; University of Wisconsin—Madison, M.A., 1972, Ph.D., 1977. *Religion:* Jewish. *Home:* 1703 Herbert Ave., Salt Lake City, Utah 84108. *Office:* Department of History, University of Utah, Salt Lake City, Utah 84112.

CAREER: University of Texas, San Antonio, assistant professor of history, 1977-80; University of Utah, Salt Lake City, assistant professor of history, 1980—. *Member:* Organization of American Historians, Western History Association, Utah Historical Association, Colorado State Historical Society.

WRITINGS: Hooded Empire: The Ku Klux Klan in Colorado, 1921-32, University of Illinois Press, 1981. Contributor to history journals.

WORK IN PROGRESS: The Mobilization of Protest, a study of the civil rights movement, 1960-65; research on Jewish agricultural colonies in the West, 1900-1920.

* * *

GOLDIE, Frederick 1914-1980

OBITUARY NOTICE: Born September 1, 1914, in Glasgow, Scotland; died October 23, 1980, in Glasgow, Scotland. Clergyman, educator, and author. Bishop of Glasgow and Galloway from 1974 until his death, Goldie was the author of the highly regarded *A History of the Episcopal Church in Scotland,* which he wrote during his tenure as a lecturer at Edinburgh Theological College. Obituaries and other sources: *The Annual Obituary 1980,* St. Martin's, 1981.

* * *

GOLDMAN-EISLER, Frieda 1909(?)-1982

OBITUARY NOTICE: Born c. 1909; died after a long illness, January 19, 1982, in London, England. Psycholinguist, educator, and author. After taking her doctorate at the University of Vienna in 1931, Eisler went to England in 1934 for postdoctoral study and research. Her investigations into quantitative measures of psychoanalytic theory and practice led to her interest in the cognitive processes by which speech is produced. She is recognized as a pioneer of the science of psycholinguistics and is especially noted for her study of hesitation pauses in speech. Eisler was the first person in Great Britain to hold the title of Professor of Psycholinguistics. Her book *Psycholinguistics: Studies in Spontaneous Speech* contains summaries of her most important findings. Obituaries and other sources: *London Times,* January 27, 1982.

* * *

GONZALES, Pancho
See GONZALES, Richard Alonzo

* * *

GONZALES, Richard Alonzo 1928-
(Pancho Gonzales)

BRIEF ENTRY: Born May 9, 1928, in Los Angeles, Calif.

American professional tennis player and author. In 1949 Gonzales became one of the youngest winners of the U.S. national singles tennis championship. He retired from the professional circuit in 1961 and began work as a coach, notably of the Davis Cup team. His books include *Man With a Racket: The Autobiography of Pancho Gonzales* (A. S. Barnes, 1959), *Tennis* (Fleet Publishing, 1962), *Winning Tactics for Weekend Singles,* (Holt, 1974), and *Tennis Begins at Forty: A Guide for All Players Who Don't Have Wrists of Steel or a Cannonball Serve, Don't Always Rush the Net or Have a Devastating Overhead, but Want to Win* (Dial, 1976). *Biographical/critical sources: Current Biography,* Wilson, 1949; *Celebrity Register,* 3rd edition, Simon & Schuster, 1973.

* * *

GOODE, Stephen   1943-

PERSONAL: Born March 5, 1943, in Elkins, W.Va.; son of Ersel Ray (in lumber business) and Dorothy (a licensed practical nurse; maiden name, Vanscoy) Goode. *Education:* Davidson College, B.A., 1965; University of Virginia, M.A., 1968; Rutgers University, Ph.D., 1978; studied in Vienna, Austria and Budapest, Hungary. *Home:* 5860 North 14th St., Arlington, Va. 22205.

CAREER: Rutgers University, New Brunswick, N.J., lecturer in history, 1971-72; writer, 1972—.

WRITINGS—For young adults; all published by F. Watts, except as noted: *Affluent Revolutionaries: A Portrait of the New Left,* 1974; *The Prophet and the Revolutionary: Arab Socialism in the Modern Middle East,* 1975; *Guerrilla Warfare and Terrorism,* 1977; *The National Defense System,* 1977; *Assassination!: Kennedy, King, Kennedy,* 1978; *Eurocommunism,* 1980; *The Nuclear Energy Controversy,* 1980; *The New Congress,* Messner, 1980; *The End of Detente?: U.S.-Soviet Relations,* 1981; *The Supreme Court,* Messner, 1982; *The CIA,* 1982; *Reaganomics: Reagan's Economic Program,* 1982; *The Right to Privacy,* 1983; *Foreign Policy in the 1980's,* 1983; *Violence in America,* Messner, 1983; *States Rights Versus the Federal Government,* 1983.

SIDELIGHTS: Goode told *CA:* "I hope that my best characteristics as a writer are clarity and the ability to distill a great deal of information into a readable and interesting book. When I write on politics, I try to present a balanced and complete picture of the issues without advocating one position or another. My training as a historian has given me the historian's bias that nothing can be understood except from a long-range, historic point of view. In my books I stress the origins of present-day political conflicts as well as their significance for today.

"Modern politics, especially in the United States and Europe, is my chief interest. An excellent high school teacher encouraged me to write. I've traveled extensively in Europe and the United States and studied for extended periods of time in Vienna and Budapest."

AVOCATIONAL INTERESTS: Jazz, Mozart, most films, cooking.

* * *

GOODIN, Robert Edward   1950-

PERSONAL: Born November 30, 1950, in Indianapolis, Ind.; son of Walter Burton (a telephone company employee) and Audrey Cecelia (Morton) Goodin; married Margo Hilary Doyne (an editor), May 26, 1972. *Education:* Indiana University, B.A., 1972; University and Nuffield Colleges, Oxford, D.Phil.,

1974. *Office:* Department of Government, University of Essex, Wivenhoe Park, Colchester, England.

CAREER: University of Strathclyde, Glasgow, Scotland, tutor in politics, 1974-75; University of Maryland, College Park, assistant professor of government and politics, 1975-78; University of Essex, Colchester, England, lecturer in government, 1978—. Visiting lecturer at University of Oslo, 1977; U.S. State Department lecturer in Indonesia and the Philippines, 1978; visiting research scholar at Australian National University, 1982-83. *Member:* American Political Science Association, American Society for Political and Legal Philosophy, Political Studies Association (England).

WRITINGS: The Politics of Rational Man, Wiley, 1976; *Manipulatory Politics,* Yale University Press, 1980; *Political Theory and Public Policy,* University of Chicago Press, 1982. Contributor to philosophy and political science journals. Associate editor of *Ethics.*

WORK IN PROGRESS: Research on ethics of social risks and nuclear power and on problems of public choice and social justice (with special reference to Australia, 1982-83).

SIDELIGHTS: Goodin told *CA:* "Some say that public policy can be made without the benefit of theory, emerging instead through trial and error. Others see genuine philosophical issues in public affairs but try to resolve them through fanciful examples. I think both are wrong. The continuing theme that unifies my work on various substantive issues is that both ethical and empirical theory should be used to guide the design and deliberations of political institutions. To be useful, however, philosophical discussions of public affairs must draw upon actual policy experiences rather than on contrived 'desert island' examples; and they must reflect the broader social consequences of policies, rather than just the dilemmas of personal conscience. This forces us to come to grips with what philosophers shun as 'empirical questions.' But, while it is true that philosophers have no particular expertise on such questions, it is equally true that they suffer no special disabilities, except those that they impose on themselves. Intelligent laymen can get enough of a grip on the technical literature even in nuclear power debates to make some morally significant points.

"Methodologically, my starting point is usually with the economic theory of rational egoists attempting to pursue efficiently their perceived interests. But that is only a starting point. The really interesting cases arise when people, though trying to be rational, fail—where they are manipulated, where they make seemingly nonsensical distinctions or pursue nonegoistic goals, etc. It is too easy just to rewrite the utility function of actors who are behaving strangely, as do economists. Likewise, it is too easy just to say that people are irrational (crazy, superstitious, stupid, etc.), as do sociologists and psychologists. The challenge lies in explaining their irrationalities in terms of their underlying rationality. And therein, too, often lies the solution to real policy puzzles emerging from these irrationalities."

* * *

GOODMAN, Herman   1894-1971

OBITUARY NOTICE: Born May 5, 1894, in New York, N.Y.; died after a long illness, February 9, 1971, in New York, N.Y. Physician, educator, and author. A specialist in dermatology and syphilology, Goodman served as a consultant to numerous government bodies and cosmetics companies, in addition to teaching at New York University Medical School. He wrote several books on technical subjects as well as popular works such as *Cosmetics and Your Skin, Your Hair: Its Health, Beauty and Growth,* and, with Carlton Fredericks, *Low Blood Sugar and You.* Obituaries and other sources: *New York Times,* February 12, 1971; *Who's Who in World Jewry: A Biographical Dictionary of Outstanding Jews,* Pitman, 1972.

* * *

GORALSKI, Robert 1928-

PERSONAL: Born January 2, 1928, in Chicago, Ill.; son of Stanley (a commercial artist) and Caroline (Bielas) Goralski; married Margaret Anne Walton, August 22, 1948; children: Douglas, Dorothy Wawner, Katherine. *Education:* University of Illinois, B.S., 1949; graduate study at Johns Hopkins University, 1960-61; William Jewell College, Litt. D., 1969. *Home:* 1399 Wendy Lane, McLean, Va. 22101.

CAREER: WDWS-Radio, Champaign, Ill., news director, 1948-51; Asia Foundation, San Francisco, Calif., assistant representative in Pakistan and Tokyo, Japan, 1952-56; Voice of America, Washington, D.C., editor and desk supervisor, 1956-61; NBC News, New York City, correspondent in Washington, D.C., 1961-75; Gulf Oil Corp., Washington, D.C., director of information, 1975—. U.S. Naval Reserve, 1945-46 and 1951-52. *Member:* International Club, Sigma Alpha Epsilon. *Awards, honors:* Fellowship from Ford Foundation Fund for Adult Education, 1960-61; national security fellow from Hoover Institution, 1972-73.

WRITINGS: (Contributor) *Studies in Asia,* University of Nebraska Press, 1961; *World War II Almanac, 1931-45: A Political and Military Record* (alternate selection of History Book Club), Putnam, 1981. Contributor to *Encyclopaedia Britannica Book of the Year,* 1966-75, and to periodicals, including *New Republic, Washington Post, American Heritage,* and *Journal of National Defense.*

WORK IN PROGRESS: A history of energy's role in World War II, publication expected in 1982.

SIDELIGHTS: In the *Times Literary Supplement,* Philip Warner deemed Goralski's *World War II Almanac* "valuable to students of military history and fascinating to the general reader." Warner added that "factual routine narrative is occasionally enlivened by information about unusual or bizarre accidents" and noted that the book "is completed by a full bibliography, excellent statistical tables and good, if simple, maps."

Goralski told *CA:* "Writing provided me with a creative outlet beyond the narrow and shallow bounds of television news when I was an NBC News correspondent. It continues to provide creative fulfillment beyond the routine of business affairs today. Time expands to meet one's interests, and there is ample opportunity to research, write, and edit copy as an avocation. History is endlessly fascinating, but its main appeal may be its ability to humble anyone; the reader, writer, or researcher comes to appreciate how little is known or understood and how complex even the simplest events of the past were in actuality."

BIOGRAPHICAL/CRITICAL SOURCES: Times Literary Supplement, May 22, 1981.

* * *

GORDON, David J. 1929-

BRIEF ENTRY: Born December 23, 1929, in St. Louis, Mo. American educator and author. Gordon began teaching at Hunter College of the City University of New York in 1960 and became a professor of English in 1977. He wrote *D. H. Lawrence as a Literary Critic* (Yale University Press, 1966) and *Literary Art and the Unconscious* (Louisiana State University Press,

1976). *Address:* Department of English, Hunter College of the City University of New York, 695 Park Ave., New York, N.Y. 10021. *Biographical/critical sources: Directory of American Scholars,* Volume II: *English, Speech, and Drama,* 7th edition, Bowker, 1978.

* * *

GORDON, John Fraser 1916-

PERSONAL: Born February 18, 1916, in London, England; son of Fraser (a sea-going chief engineer) and Dora (Muellerhausen) Gordon. *Education:* Attended City of London College. *Religion:* Church of England. *Home:* 72 Clyde Way, Romford, Essex RM1 4UT, England. *Office:* 85 Queen Victoria St., London E.C.4, England.

CAREER: Dongora Mill Co. Ltd., London, England, managing director, 1963—. Managing director of J. F. Gordon (London) Ltd., 1963—. Freeman of City of London. Cruft's and international judge of dogs until 1974. *Military service:* British Army, 1939-44. *Member:* Wig and Pen, Society of Authors, British Institute of Management.

WRITINGS: The Staffordshire Bull Terrier Handbook, Nicholson & Watson, 1951; *The Bull Terrier Handbook,* Nicholson & Watson, 1957; *The Bulldog Handbook,* Nicholson & Watson, 1957; *The Bulldog,* Nicholson & Watson, 1957; *The Dandie Dinmont Terrier,* Nicholson & Watson, 1959; *The Dandie Dinmont Terrier Handbook,* Nicholson & Watson, 1959.

Staffordshire Bull Terriers, W. & G. Foyle, 1964; *Miniature Schnauzers,* W. & G. Foyle, 1966; *The Staffordshire Bull Terrier Owners Encyclopaedia,* Pelham Books, 1967; *The Spaniel Owners Encyclopaedia,* Pelham Books, 1967; *The Beagle Guide,* Pet Library, 1968; *The Miniature Schnauzer Guide,* Pet Library, 1969; *All About the Boxer,* Pelham Books, 1970; *All About the Cocker Spaniel,* Pelham Books, 1971; *Staffordshire Bull Terriers,* Hutchinson, 1971; *The Bulldog,* Gifford, 1973; *The Pug,* Gifford, 1973.

Published by John Bartholomew & Son, except as noted: *The Irish Wolfhound,* 1973; *The Borzoi,* 1973; *The Bull Terrier,* Gifford, 1973; *Rare and Unusual Dog Breeds,* 1974; *Dogs,* 1976; *The German Shepherd,* 1978; *The Pyrenean Mountain Dog,* 1978; *The Alaskan Malamute,* 1979; *Map of the World's Dogs,* 1979.

Contributor to *Dog World.*

AVOCATIONAL INTERESTS: Horticulture hybrids, philately, antiquarian books, horology.

* * *

GORKY, Maxim
See PESHKOV, Alexei Maximovich

* * *

GOTTESMAN, S. D.
See KORNBLUTH, C(yril) M.

* * *

GOTTSEGEN, Abby J. 1956-

PERSONAL: Born January 8, 1956, in New York, N.Y.; daughter of Monroe (a psychologist) and Gloria (a psychologist) Gottsegen. *Education:* Attended Sorbonne, University of Paris, 1976; Skidmore College, B.A.; Yeshiva University, M.A., 1979, Ph.D.

CAREER: Board of Education, New York, N.Y., psychologist, 1980—. *Member:* New York State Psychological Association (member of executive board of school psychology division).

WRITINGS: Humanistic Psychology, Gale, 1980. Contributor to *Sex Roles.*

WORK IN PROGRESS: Research on the effect of role modeling on the achievement behaviors of children.

*   *   *

GOYDER, George Armin   1908-

PERSONAL: Born June 22, 1908, in London, England; son of William and Lili Julia (Kellersberger) Goyder; married Rosemary Bosanquet, 1937; children: Daniel George, Ellen Rosemary, William Andrew, Lucy Jane, Henry Peter Giles, Hugh Thomas, Mary Julia, Edward Mark. *Education:* Attended London School of Economics and Political Science, London, 1925-27. *Religion:* Church of England. *Home:* Mansel Hall, Long Melford, Suffolk, England.

CAREER: International Paper Co., New York, N.Y., sales representative, 1930-32, overseas sales representative, 1932, world representative, 1932-35; British International Paper Ltd., London, England, chairman and managing director, 1935-72. Appointed to procure, ration, and distribute all paper for British wartime press as general manager of Newsprint Supply Co., 1940-47. *Geographical* magazine, director, 1935-58, chairman, 1958; chairman of Liberal Party Standing Committee on Industrial Partnership, 1966; chairman of Centre for International Briefing, 1967-79. Member of National Assembly of the Church of England, 1948-76. Founding member of board of trustees of William Blake Trust; member of board of governers of Mill Hill School and Monkton Combe School; trustee and fellow of St. Peter's College, Oxford; member of council of Wycliffe Hall; founding member and secretary of British-North American Committee, 1969. *Member:* Reform Club. *Awards, honors:* Best management book and author of the year award from John Player/British Institute of Management, 1975, for *The Responsible Worker;* Commander of Order of the British Empire, 1976.

WRITINGS: The Future of Private Enterprise, Basil Blackwell, 1951, second edition, 1954; *The Responsible Company,* Basil Blackwell, 1961; *The People's Church,* Hodder & Stoughton, 1966; *The Responsible Worker,* Hutchinson, 1975.

WORK IN PROGRESS: Natural Law and the Company, publication expected in 1982.

SIDELIGHTS: Goyder told *CA:* "Everything I write, I write as a Christian who is convinced that we need to return to a social order based on moral law. The acceptance by business of its social responsibility is the condition necessary for the survival of capitalism and the free society of the West. A lifetime spent in business has only served to confirm this conviction."

BIOGRAPHICAL/CRITICAL SOURCES: New International Realities, March, 1981.

*   *   *

GRABOIS, Aryeh   1930-

PERSONAL: Born July 9, 1930, in Odessa, U.S.S.R.; son of Eliezer (a health worker) and Judith (a confection designer; maiden name, Lorberblatt) Grabois; married Carmela Langleben (a teacher), April 20, 1966; children: Shirli. *Education:* Hebrew University of Jerusalem, B.A., 1958, M.A., 1961;

University of Dijon, Ph.D., 1963; postdoctoral study at University of Paris, 1963. *Religion:* Jewish. *Home:* 48 Hantke St., Haifa, Israel 34608. *Office:* Faculty of Humanities, University of Haifa, Mount Carmel, Haifa, Israel 31999.

CAREER: University of Haifa, Haifa, Israel, lecturer, 1963-67, senior lecturer, 1967-71, associate professor, 1971-73, professor of medieval history, 1973—, chairman of department of history, 1968-71, dean of faculty of humanities, 1979—, member of executive committee of university, 1973-79. Visiting professor at University of California, Berkeley, 1979-80. Member of academic council of Ben-Zwi Memorial, 1977—; consultant to Israel Education and Culture Ministry. *Military service:* Israel Defense Forces, 1948-51; became sergeant; received Independence Award and Aleh Award.

MEMBER: Historical Association of Israel (member of executive committee, 1978), Israel Exploration Society, Historical Association (England), Societe d'Etudes Medievales, Society for the Study of the Crusades and the Latin East, B'nai B'rith. *Awards, honors:* Palmes Academiques from French Government, 1980.

WRITINGS: The Illustrated Encyclopedia of Medieval Civilization, Mayflower, 1980. Contributor of more than fifty articles to scholarly journals in Israel, Europe, and the United States.

WORK IN PROGRESS: Research on aspects of social and intellectual history of western Europe in the Middle Ages, on Jewish-Christian relations in western Europe in the Middle Ages, and on medieval pilgrimage to the Holy Land.

SIDELIGHTS: Grabois commented: "I am interested in the human aspect of historical evolution, as part of a civilization which includes the various activities of common people, such as politics, beliefs, thought, literature, and art. This syncretism of the various fields, generally dealt with by specialized scholars, makes it possible to explain the emergence and development of medieval civilization, where particularism and corporate bodies managed to reach a unity, despite their differences."

*   *   *

GRAHAM, Katharine (Meyer)   1917-

PERSONAL: Born June 16, 1917, in New York, N.Y.; daughter of Eugene (a banker and owner of the *Washington Post*) and Agnes (Ernst) Meyer; married Philip Leslie Graham (a publisher of the *Washington Post*), June 5, 1940 (died August 3, 1963); children: Elizabeth Morris Graham Weymouth, Donald Edward, William Welsh, Stephen Meyer. *Education:* Attended Vassar College, 1934-36; University of Chicago, A.B., 1938. *Home:* 2920 R St. N.W., Washington, D.C. 20007. *Office:* 1150 15th St. N.W., Washington, D.C. 20071.

CAREER/WRITINGS: San Francisco News, San Francisco, Calif., reporter, 1938-39; Washington Post Co., Washington, D.C., member of editorial staff of *Washington Post,* 1939-45, president of company, 1963-73, chairman of the board, 1973—, publisher of *Washington Post,* 1969-79. Director of Bowaters Mersey Paper Co. Ltd. and Allied Chemical Corp. Member of the board of directors of the National Center for Resource Recovery, Associated Press, and Newspaper Advertising Bureau; member of advisory committee of John F. Kennedy School of Government for Harvard University Institute of Politics; member of Independent Committee on International Development Issues; member of public policy committee of the Advertising Council; member of governing board of the Business Committee for the Arts; trustee of Federal City Council, George

Washington University, University of Chicago, Urban Institute, and St. Albans School.

MEMBER: National Council of Foreign Policy Association, Women's National Press Club, American Society of Newspaper Editors, Inter-American Press Association (director of executive committee), Washington Press Club, 1925 F Street Club (Washington, D.C.), Cosmopolitan Club (New York City), Sigma Delta Chi, Theta Sigma Phi. *Awards, honors:* Honorary degree from Dartmouth University, 1968; American Newspaper Woman's Club award, 1969, for outstanding personal achievement; gold medal from National Institute of Social Sciences, 1970, for distinguished services to humanity; John Peter Zenger Award, 1973.

SIDELIGHTS: Katherine Graham became president of the Washington Post Company following the death of her husband, Philip, in 1963. Although she had been a reporter in the past and had worked in various departments of the *Washington Post,* Graham considered herself unprepared to head a newspaper. "Any problems I encountered in the beginning did not stem so much from being a woman," she explained. "They stemmed from inexperience. I had the guiding principles from both my father and husband. I had always listened to them discuss their decisions and problems. But there are certain aspects of management that come only with experience."

Under Graham the *Post* was built into a competitor of the *New York Times.* She named Benjamin C. Bradlee as managing editor in 1965, and he was instrumental in luring talented journalists away from other papers. The *Post* was also aided in its rise to prominence by its role in two events of the early 1970's, the publication of the Pentagon Papers and the Watergate affair.

In 1971, two years after Graham took over as the paper's publisher, the *Post* became involved in the fight to publish the Pentagon Papers. Earlier that year the *New York Times* had been ordered by the U.S. Government to refrain from publishing any more of the documents. Risking a restraining order on themselves as well as a violation of the injunction that had restricted the *Times,* Graham and the *Post* decided to publish the papers. "The decision had to be made quickly," Graham later pointed out. "There had never before been prior restraint of the press. Weighing all factors, it seemed like the right thing to do. And I still feel the same." The *Post* did go to court for its action, but the Supreme Court eventually ruled in favor of the two newspapers and their right to publish.

With its coverage of the Watergate scandal, the *Post* again became the focus of national attention. *Post* reporters Carl Bernstein and Bob Woodward were the foremost investigators of the crimes of the Nixon administration, and, despite threats from the White House and warnings from her friend Henry Kissinger, Graham supported the reporters throughout. "Obviously I was full of concerns and high emotions and the need to be careful to check out everything," Graham recalled. "It just happened that our reporters got the story and we backed them because we were sure they were right." In 1973 the *Post* received a Pulitzer Prize for public service in uncovering the Watergate conspiracy.

Graham stepped down as publisher of the *Post* in 1979, but she continues to serve as chairman of the board of the Washington Post Company. The company includes *Newsweek* magazine, the Los Angeles Times-Washington Post News Service, and radio and television stations.

BIOGRAPHICAL/CRITICAL SOURCES: Washington Post, September 21, 1963; *Vogue,* January 1, 1967; *Business World,* May 27, 1967; *Harper's,* December, 1968; *New York Post,* November 29, 1969; *Wall Street Journal,* August 18, 1970;

Detroit News, April 19, 1974; *Biography News,* May, 1974; *Miami Herald,* September 8, 1974; *Authors in the News,* Volume 1, Gale, 1976.*

*   *   *

GRAWOIG, Sheila
   See RAESCHILD, Sheila

*   *   *

GREENBERG, James B(rian) 1945-

PERSONAL: Born March 9, 1945, in Salt Lake City, Utah; son of G. Robert (a biochemist) and Cora (a bookkeeper; maiden name, Silver) Greenberg; married Eva Zavaleta Rios, March 1, 1974; children: Henry Z. *Education:* University of Michigan, B.A., 1969, M.A., 1971, Ph.D., 1978. *Home:* 819 A Ave., Douglas, Ariz. 85607. *Office:* Department of Anthropology, Indiana University, Bloomington, Ind. 47401.

CAREER: University of Denver, Denver, Colo., visiting associate professor of anthropology, 1975-76; Mankato State University, Mankato, Minn., instructor in anthropology, 1977-79; Arizona State University, Tempe, visiting associate professor of anthropology, 1979-80; Indiana University, Bloomington, visiting associate professor of anthropology, 1980—. *Member:* American Anthropological Association, American Ethnological Society, Latin American Studies Association, Latin American Studies Group, Society for Anthropological Economics, Southwestern Anthropological Association, Central States Anthropological Society. *Awards, honors:* Grant from Social Science Research Council, 1981.

WRITINGS: Santiago's Sword: Chatino Peasant Religion and Economics, University of California Press, 1981.

WORK IN PROGRESS: An autobiography of a Chatino man, to show social change and ethnography from a native perspective; research on proletarian household economics and social networks in Agua Prieta, Sonora, and Douglas, Ariz.

SIDELIGHTS: Greenberg told *CA:* "My interest in proletarian household economics and social networks has evolved quite naturally out of my research in this vein in peasant communities in Mexico. Early on in my career it became clear to me that neither the various macro-economic approaches nor the variety of micro-economic analyses were quite adequate as the scale of the former missed many important features of peasant economy, whereas the latter tended to ignore the effects that the wider economy have at the local level. Hence, when I went to Chiapas in the summer of 1972 to conduct comparative research on economic functions of cargo systems and compadrazco, I attempted to use a middle range approach to these problems.

"On the basis of this short study, I concluded that as the relations and means of production have become increasingly capitalistic in order to free surpluses for participation in the wider economy that the cargo system's economic impact on wealth differences in Indian communities have been progressively weakened. I also found evidence of a trend in the choice of compadres from horizontal ties within the community to vertical ties with Ladinos outside the community has been a response over the last several decades to these same economic processes. This research led to a NIMH grant and fellowship to study the economic and social functions of cargo systems and ceremonial expenditures in a closed corporate Chatino community in Oaxaca, Santiago Yaitepec.

"The problematique of this study was in many respects similar to the research proposed here in that it depended on the analysis of household production, consumption, and exchange. The choice of Santiago Yaitepec was fortuitous as the village was in the process of a major change in the mode of production from subsistence production to cash cropping coffee: a process which not only spelled the reorganization of the domestic economy by the market-generated conflict, but gave rise to a rural proletariat—villagers without land or with little land.

"This work was conducted between January 1973 and April 1974. During this period I married my wife, who comes from a neighboring village. Since then I have returned to Oaxaca in 1976 and 1979. Out of my work have come a dissertation, University of Michigan, 1978, and a book, *Santiago's Sword: Chatino Peasant Religion and Economy.* These works demonstrate that investments in ceremonial systems are determined in a complex dialectic between the demands on the local community by the wider society and the local system's ecological, demographic, and economic resources. In particular, the state of economic variables such as leveling, stratification, expropriation, and redistribution of wealth through the cargo system is determined both by interactive processes within the local community and between it and the wider society. These studies also show the relationships that exist between access to the means of production, type of production (e.g., corn versus coffee) and the strategy of participation in cargo systems.

"It was the process of proletarianization of the rural economy I observed in Oaxaca that has led me to rethink peasant household economics; peasant models are not fully satisfactory when applied to proletarian households. It is thus that I have come to an interest in proletarian household economics and social networks as subject matter which deserves a theoretical elaboration in its own right. In terms of my overall career plans I see this research as a means of extending my practical and theoretical skills as an economic anthropologist by applying them to important socio-economic problems. Lastly, I speak Spanish fluently."

*   *   *

GREET, Brian Aubrey 1922-

PERSONAL: Born June 12, 1922, in Bristol, England; son of Walter Henry (a dentist) and Renee (Muir) Greet; married Jill Margaret Edwards (a social worker), July 3, 1954; children: David Michael, Helen Margaret. *Education:* Handsworth Theological College, B.A., 1951; Drew University, S.T.M., 1952; Victoria University of Manchester, B.D., 1958. *Home and office:* 37 Sutton Passeys Cres., Wollaton Park, Nottingham NG8 1BX, England.

CAREER: Ordained Methodist minister, 1951; pastor of Methodist church in South Devon, England, 1945-47; circuit minister at Methodist churches in Mansfield, England, 1952-54; pastor of Methodist churches in Manchester, England, 1954-58, Moreton, England, 1958-63, and Solihull, England, 1963-69; superintendent minister at Methodist church in Guildford, England, 1969-73; Nottingham and Derby District of the Methodist Church, Nottingham, England, district chairman, 1973—. Chaplain at University of Surrey and headquarters of Women's Royal Army Corps, 1969-73; exchange pastor at Methodist church in Mentor, Ohio, 1972. Member of court at University of Nottingham, 1973—; member of Central Religious Advisory Committee; broadcaster of television and radio.

WRITINGS: (Contributor) John Stacey, editor, *The Preachers' Handbook, Number Eleven,* Epworth, 1969; *Broken Bread in a Broken World,* Judson, 1970 (published in England as *To Communion With Confidence,* Marshall, Morgan & Scott, 1970); (contributor) Stacey, editor, *In Church,* Local Preacher's De-

partment, Methodist Church, 1971; *What Makes a Minister?,* Epworth, 1981. Contributor to religious journals.

SIDELIGHTS: "After a fellowship at Drew University in New Jersey," Greet commented, "I returned to circuit work in Mansfield, the heart of Robin Hood country in Sherwood Forest. I took up graduate study at Victoria University of Manchester and served concurrently as a minister on the staff of the Manchester and Salford Mission, having oversight of the branch on the Platt Lane Housing estate. Thereafter I served for five years at Moreton on Merseyside (an extensive housing estate newly established on the site of an old village) which had a large concentration of youth work, and for six years in Solihull, (West Midlands), an affluent and pleasant suburb of Birmingham. In 1973 I was appointed chairman of the Nottingham and Derby District, which includes a wide variety of industry and some beautiful countryside—the Peak National Park, the Vale of Belvoir, and Sherwood Forest.

"I am convinced that 'what makes a minister' is primarily the call of Christ, and that the marks of genuine ministry are derived from Christ's ministry. Unless those authentic marks are manifest, no ecclesiastical ordinance can impart them; and if they are manifest, no ecclesiastical ordinance can take them away.

"I am fully committed to the World Disarmament Campaign and am involved locally in gaining support for the petition which will encourage the United Nations' session on disarmament planned for 1982.

"I have just been appointed chairman of a working party whose task is to examine, and probably revise, the arrangement for the invitation and stationing of ordained ministers in the Methodist Church in Great Britain."

AVOCATIONAL INTERESTS: Travel (Middle East, Europe, Canada, India), art history (especially impressionism and seventeenth-century Dutch work), playing the piano, walking, gardening.

*   *   *

GRIFFITH, Helen V(irginia) 1934-

PERSONAL: Born October 31, 1934, in Wilmington, Del.; daughter of John (a railroad machinist) and Helen (a wholesale building materials company president; maiden name, Williams) Griffith; divorced. *Education:* Attended high school in Woodcrest, Del. *Politics:* Republican. *Religion:* Christian. *Home:* 2200 West 18th St., Wilmington, Del. 19806. *Office:* S. G. Williams & Bros. Co., 301 Tatnall St., Wilmington, Del. 19801.

CAREER: S. G. Williams & Bros. Co. (building products distributors), Wilmington, Del., secretary, 1976—. *Member:* Authors Guild, Society of Children's Book Writers, Delmarva Ornithological Society.

WRITINGS: Mine Will, Said John (juvenile), Greenwillow, 1980; *Alex and the Cat* (juvenile; Junior Literary Guild selection), Greenwillow, 1982; *Alex Remembers* (juvenile), Greenwillow, 1982.

WORK IN PROGRESS: Foxy, "a book for early teens about a mistreated boy and an abandoned dog."

SIDELIGHTS: Griffith told *CA:* "I started writing about seven years ago. A late start, but maybe it's just as well because I haven't had a peaceful moment since. When I'm writing I worry (it's junk; it's unimportant; it's all been said before). When I'm not writing (which is all too often) I worry because

I'm not writing. After each story I'm sure I'll never write again. The only time I believe in myself for a few minutes is when the check comes. But having written—that's fun. It means somebody took me seriously. There is the book: solid, real proof that I've done something in this world. I love having written. That's what makes me write.''

* * *

GRIFFITHS, Kitty Anna (Mrs. G.)

PERSONAL: Born in Kelvedon, Essex, England; daughter of Percy George (a farmer) and Annie Grey (a preacher; maiden name, Arnot) Coe; married Gerald B. Griffiths (a minister), December 29, 1943; children: Ian B., Myfanwy H. (Mrs. Michael Bentley-Taylor), Jonathan G. *Education:* Attended London University, 1940-42. *Religion:* Protestant. *Home:* 14 Taylor Dr., Toronto, Ontario, Canada M4C 3B3. *Office:* 746 Pape Ave., Toronto, Ontario, Canada M4K 3S7.

CAREER: High school teacher, 1942-43; broadcaster, under the name Mrs. G., of a weekly children's radio program, "A Visit With Mrs. G.,'' 1973—. *Member:* National Religious Broadcasters.

WRITINGS—"Come, Meet'' series; published by Zondervan, except as noted: *Come, Meet Abraham, God's Friend,* 1977; *. . . Abraham, the Pioneer,* 1977; *. . . Adam and Eve,* 1977; *. . . Isaac,* 1977; *. . . Joseph, God's Dreamer,* 1977; *. . . Joseph, the Grand Vizier,* 1977; *. . . Noah,* 1977; *. . . Jacob, God's Prince,* 1978; *. . . Jacob, the Grabbing Twin,* 1978; *. . . Jesus, the Baby,* 1978, revised edition, Bible Stories Alive, 1981; *. . . Jesus, the Boy,* 1978, revised edition, Bible Stories Alive, 1981; *. . . Ruth,* 1978.

Other writings; published by Bible Stories Alive: *Moses and the Great Escape,* 1980; *Moses, the Rescued Baby,* 1980; *Moses and the Desert Encounter,* 1981; *Moses and the House for God,* 1981; *Moses and the Journey's End,* 1981; *Jesus, the Carpenter,* 1981; *Jesus and the Temple Thieves,* 1981; *Jesus and the Secret Guest,* 1981; *Jesus and the Frustrated Fisherman,* 1981; *Jesus and the Customs Crew,* 1981; *Jesus and the Kingdom Kids,* 1981; *Jesus and the Dreadful Foe,* 1981; *Jesus and the Trip Abroad,* 1981.

Author of teleplay "The Christmas Story,'' produced by Monarch Productions, 1978.

SIDELIGHTS: Kitty Griffiths's roles as a minister's wife and as a writer and broadcaster of religious stories for children have carried her to many corners of the world. She told *CA* that, due to her husband's career, she has lived in Cardiff, Wales; London, England; Edinburgh, Scotland; Johannesburg, South Africa; and Toronto, Ontario. She has also traveled extensively in Europe, Africa, and South America. Her own work has demanded travel, too. In order to ensure authenticity in her books, Griffiths has taken five trips to the Holy Land to do research and compile material. On two such trips she was the guest of the Israeli Government. Written first for her weekly radio program, her stories are later published in books.

* * *

GRIFFITHS, Ralph A(lan)   1937-

PERSONAL: Born November 4, 1937, in Aberbargoed, Wales; son of Thomas Rowland (an innkeeper) and Marion Lovin (Jones) Griffiths. *Education:* University of Bristol, B.A. (with honors), 1959, Ph.D., 1962. *Home:* 36 Withy Park, Bishopston, Swansea, Wales. *Office:* University College, University of Wales, Singleton Park, Swansea SA2 8PP, Wales.

CAREER: University of Wales, University College, Swansea, lecturer, 1964-71, senior lecturer, 1971-78, reader in medieval history, 1978—. Visiting lecturer at Haverford College and Ohio University; visiting professor at Dalhousie University, 1967. Member of Glamorgan County History Trust and Board of Celtic Studies. *Member:* Royal Historical Society (fellow), Association of University Teachers, Historical Association, United Nations Association, Mediaeval Academy of America. *Awards, honors:* Leverhulme Trust grant, 1976; British Academy grant, 1976.

WRITINGS: (Editor with S. B. Chrimes and C. D. Ross) *Fifteenth-Century England, 1399-1509,* Barnes & Noble, 1972; *The Principality of Wales in the Later Middle Ages,* Volume I: *South Wales, 1277-1536,* University of Wales Press, 1972; *Clyne Castle,* University College, University of Wales (Swansea), 1977; (editor and contributor) *Boroughs of Medieval Wales,* University of Wales Press, 1978; *The Reign of King Henry VI,* University of California Press, 1981; (editor) *Patronage, the Crown, and the Provinces in Later Medieval England,* Humanities, 1981.

Contributor: T. B. Pugh, editor, *The Glamorgan County History,* Volume III, University of Wales Press, 1971; Harry Hearder and H. R. Loyn, editors, *British Government and Administration,* University of Wales Press, 1974; John Cule, editor, *Wales and Medicine,* Conference on the History of Medicine, 1975; C. D. Ross, editor, *Patronage, Pedigree, and Power in Later Medieval England,* Rowman & Littlefield, 1979.

Co-editor of series "Studies in Welsh History,'' University of Wales Press, and "A New History of Wales,'' Christopher Davies; editor of series "Later Medieval British History,'' Harvester Press. Contributor to history, library, and law journals. Associate editor of *Welsh History Review,* 1966—.

WORK IN PROGRESS: Medieval Wales, for Longman, completion expected in 1983; a contribution to the *Oxford Illustrated History of Britain,* 1983; *Pembrokeshire County History: The Middle Ages,* 1985; *Humphrey, Duke of Gloucester,* 1986; research on England and Wales in the fourteenth and fifteenth centuries.

SIDELIGHTS: Griffiths commented: "I am deeply conscious of my debt in teaching, research, and writing, both to my teachers and the tradition of historical investigation in which they worked, and also to generations of students whom I have taught and from whom I have learned much. I am convinced of the importance of continuing research and writing to the truly effective and influential teacher.

"I am concerned that potentially able students from disadvantaged (in terms of wealth or education) backgrounds should benefit to the full from higher education, and I am correspondingly highly delighted when such men and women can be helped toward a realization of their full potential.

"The study of history is a constantly unfolding adventure into the minds of men and women, made all the more compelling because they lived in significantly different ages; and the study of the middle ages in particular because it provides the broadest avenue to an understanding of the foundations of western civilization.''

AVOCATIONAL INTERESTS: Travel (including western Europe, "and with an especially warm attachment to the United States and its academic community'').

* * *

GRINSTEAD, David   1939-

PERSONAL: Born July 20, 1939, in Chicago, Ill.; son of

M. Wayde (a business executive) and Ann (a poet; maiden name, Phipps) Grinstead; married Karen G. Berman, July 27, 1968 (divorced July 1, 1973); married Laura McCallum (a sculptor), August 4, 1979. *Education:* Yale University, B.A., 1961; attended Claremont Graduate School, 1972-74. *Residence:* Brooklyn, N.Y.

CAREER: Santa Monica Evening Outlook, Santa Monica, Calif., news writer, 1967-68; news writer for KABC-TV, 1968, and City News Service, 1968-69. *Military service:* U.S. Marine Corps, Infantry, 1962-66; served in Vietnam; became captain. *Member:* Authors Guild.

WRITINGS: The Earth Movers (novel), Little, Brown, 1980.

Work represented in anthologies, including *1970 O. Henry Prize Stories,* Doubleday.

WORK IN PROGRESS: Other Heroes, a novel about social changes of the 1960's, publication expected in 1983; dramatic pieces.

SIDELIGHTS: Grinstead wrote: "I lived in Madrid and England in 1970, and have traveled extensively in Europe, as well as in Asia and North Africa. I am fascinated with the ways different peoples handle problems of living and express joy and sorrow at stages of life. I have seen some of the horrors and follies of the past twenty years and want to catch these in stories."

* * *

GROTOWSKI, Jerzy 1933-

BRIEF ENTRY: Born August 11, 1933, in Rzeszow, Poland. Polish theatre director, acting coach, and author. Grotowski has managed theatre laboratories in Poland and lectured at Cracow's National Theatrical Academy since 1959. The experimental nature of his work has caused controversy, especially in Eastern Europe, but he has received awards from the government of Poland and institutions in the United States. He wrote *Towards a Poor Theatre* (Simon & Schuster, 1978). *Address:* Teatr Laboratorium, 50-101 Wroclaw, Rynek Ratuaz 27, Poland. *Biographical/critical sources: The International Who's Who,* Europa, 1979.

* * *

GRUITS, Patricia Beall 1923-

PERSONAL: Born February 22, 1923, in Detroit, Mich.; daughter of Harry Lee (a millwright) and Myrtle (a minister; maiden name, Monville) Beall; married J. Peter Gruits (an architectural designer), June 15, 1946; children: Peter, Harry, Patrick, William. *Education:* Attended Central Bible College, Springfield, Mo., 1943-45; National Bible College, B.Th., 1951. *Home:* 1220 Three Mile Dr., Grosse Pointe Park, Mich. 48230. *Office:* Rhema International, 17910 Van Dyke, Detroit, Mich. 48234.

CAREER: Bethesda Missionary Temple, Detroit, Mich., minister of education, 1955—. Founder and president of Rhema International, 1974—, and Rhema, Inc., 1978—.

WRITINGS: Understanding God, Whitaker House, 1972.

WORK IN PROGRESS: Mama Is a Preacher; a book about women in the ministry, using her mother as an example.

SIDELIGHTS: Patricia Gruits commented: "*Understanding God* is a textbook on Christian doctrine designed to satisfy hunger for knowledge of God by teaching how to experience the doctrines and sacraments which were once only tradition. The book uses the oldest and most rewarding technique of religious instruction . . . a systematic question-and-answer method. It presents Biblical truth in logical organization and progressive steps. I have taught this course successfully for more than twenty years and am delighted to see others enjoying the same success as they use this proven course of instruction.

"RHEMA (restoring hope through education and medical aid) International has joined forces with International Child Care in Haiti to build and administer a much-needed hospital and health center in Marigot, Haiti. These facilities will provide health care for the villagers, training for mothers in nutrition and hygiene, and adult education and training centers for medical personnel and directors in nutrition and hygiene, all at the invitation of the Haitian Government.''

* * *

GUARAGNA, Salvatore 1893-1981
(Harry Warren)

OBITUARY NOTICE: Born December 24, 1893, in Brooklyn, N.Y.; died September 22, 1981, in Los Angeles, Calif. Composer and lyricist. Harry Warren, who composed hundreds of hit songs for movies produced by Warner Brothers, Twentieth Century-Fox, and Metro-Goldwyn-Mayer, received three Academy Awards during his fifty-nine-year career. Included among his more memorable tunes are "Lullaby of Broadway," "Chattanooga Choo-Choo," "I Only Have Eyes for You," and "Jeepers Creepers." He collaborated with numerous well-known lyricists, including Johnny Mercer and Ira Gershwin, but is best remembered for his collaboration with Al Dubin on a series of Depression-era movie musicals. The most popular of these, "42nd Street," was adapted for the stage, opening on Broadway in August of 1980. In the final decade of his career, Warren also wrote the lyrics for his own compositions. Shortly before his death, he had written the music and lyrics for eleven new songs, which writer and director James Bridges planned to use for a movie musical entitled "Manhattan Melody." In 1973 Warren was elected into the Songwriter's Hall of Fame. Obituaries and other sources: *Current Biography,* Wilson, 1943; *Who's Who in America,* 39th edition, Marquis, 1976; *International Motion Picture Almanac,* Quigley, 1979; *New York Times,* September 23, 1981.

* * *

GUARESCHI, Giovanni 1908-1968

PERSONAL: Surname is pronounced Gwa-*res*-key; born May 1, 1908, in Fontanelle di Rocca Bianca, Parma, Italy; died July 22, 1968, in Cervia, Italy; son of Augusto (a landowner and merchant) and Lina (a teacher; maiden name, Maghenzani) Guareschi; married Ennia Pallini, February 12, 1940; children: Alberto, Carlotta. *Education:* University of Parma, Licenta Maturita Classica, 1927. *Religion:* Roman Catholic. *Residence:* Parma, Italy.

CAREER: Caricaturist, journalist, and commercial artist in Parma, Italy, 1929-36; *Bertoldo* (humor magazine), Milan, Italy, editor, 1936-42; free-lance writer, 1940-68. *Candido* (humor magazine), Milan, founder and editorial director, 1945-68. *Military service:* Italian Army, 1942-45, became lieutenant; prisoner of war at German concentration camp in Poland, 1943-45.

WRITINGS—In English translation: Il destino si chiama Clotilde: Romanzo d'amore e di avventura, con una importante digressione, [Italy], 1942, Rizzoli, 1971, translation by L. K. Conrad published as *Duncan and Clotilda: An Extravaganza With a Long Digression,* Farrar, Straus, 1968; *Il marito in collegio: Romanzo ameno,* [Italy], 1944, Rizzoli, 1956, translation published as *A Husband in Boarding School,* Farrar, Straus, 1967 (published in England as *School for Husbands,* Macdonald & Co., 1968); *Mondo piccolo "Don Camillo,"* self-illustrated, [Italy], 1948, Rizzoli, 1970, translation by Una Vincenzo Troubridge published as *The Little World of Don Camillo* (Book-of-the-Month Club selection), Pellegrini & Cudahy, 1950; *Diario clandestino, 1943-1945,* [Italy], 1949, Rizzoli, 1970, translation by Frances Frenaye published as *My Secret Diary, 1943-1945,* Farrar, Straus, 1958.

Don Camillo and His Flock, self-illustrated, translation by Frenaye, Pellegrini & Cudahy, 1952 (published in England as *Don Camillo and the Prodigal Son,* Gollancz, 1952), original Italian edition published as *Mondo piccolo "Don Camillo e il suo gregge,"* [Italy], 1953, Rizzoli, 1971; *The House That Nino Built,* translation by Frenaye, Farrar, Straus, 1953; *Il dilemma di Don Camillo,* [Italy], 1953, translation by Franaye published as *Don Camillo's Dilemma,* Farrar, Straus, 1954; *Corrierino delle famiglie* (autobiography), [Italy], 1954, 9th edition, Rizzoli, 1970, translation by Joseph Green published as *My Home Sweet Home,* Farrar, Straus, 1966; *Don Camillo: His Little World and His Dilemma* (contains *Don Camillo's Dilemma* and *The Little World of Don Camillo*), Farrar, Straus, 1954; *Don Camillo prende il diavolo per la coda,* [Italy], 1956, translation by Frenaye published as *Don Camillo Takes the Devil by the Tail,* Farrar, Straus, 1957 (published in England as *Don Camillo and the Devil,* Gollancz, 1957).

Mondo piccolo: "Il compagno Don Camillo," self-illustrated, Rizzoli, 1963, translation by Frenaye published as *Comrade Don Camillo,* Farrar, Straus, 1964; *Vita in Famiglia* (autobiography), [Italy], 1968, translation published as *Family Life,* 1969, translation by L. K. Conrad published as *The Family Guareschi: Chronicles of the Past and Present,* Farrar, Straus, 1970; *Don Camillo e i giovani d'oggi,* self-illustrated, Rizzoli, 1969, translation by Conrad published as *Don Camillo Meets the Flower Children,* Farrar, Straus, 1969 (published in England as *Don Camillo Meets Hell's Angels,* Gollancz, 1970); *The Don Camillo Omnibus* (contains *The Little World of Don Camillo, Don Camillo and the Prodigal Son,* and *Comrade Don Camillo*), Gollancz, 1974.

In Italian: *La scoperta di Milano,* [Italy], 1941, Rizzoli, 1970; *La favola di Natale,* self-illustrated, [Italy], 1945, Rizzoli, 1971; *Italia provvisoria: Album del dopoguerra,* Rizzoli, 1947; *Lo zibaldino: Storie assortite vecchie e nuove,* [Italy], 1948, Rizzoli, 1970; *Una notte nel Cremlino,* [Italy], 1955; *L'Italia in graticola,* Edizioni del Borghese, 1968.

SIDELIGHTS: "The gentleness, the wry fantasy, the perpetual wonder at what God has wrought, good and bad together, and over it all the echo of irrepressible laughter—these are the trademarks of [Guareschi], who is so much more than a professional humorist," said Ned Calmer of *Saturday Review.* An Italian journalist who aired his anti-Communist views in his humorous essays, drawings, and works of fiction, Giovanni Guareschi became world renowned for his political satire.

Guareschi's career as a professional humorist began in 1936 when he became editor of *Bertoldo,* a humorous weekly featuring political satire. In 1945 he founded *Candido,* a similar magazine, and served as its editor-in-chief for several years. In these magazines, as well as in the novels he wrote from the 1940's through the 1960's, Guareschi voiced his controversial political views.

His series of Don Camillo novels, for example, humorously detail the perpetual competition between a village priest, Don Camillo, and the village's Communist mayor, Peppone, as they vie for the villagers' favor. Although Guareschi satirizes both factions in these stories, his political leanings are evident in the ultimate defeat of the Communist mayor.

Guareschi did not, however, escape the consequences of so freely publicizing his political convictions. He was jailed in 1942 for publicly insulting the government but escaped trial after his release by joining the Italian Army. That year Italy broke its alliance with Germany, and Lieutenant Guareschi was captured by the Germans as an enemy and sent to a concentration camp in Poland for two years. In 1954, as editor-in-chief of *Candido,* Guareschi again clashed with political officials, this time for publicizing criticism of Italy's postwar government. As a result, Guareschi was imprisoned once more, serving a one-year sentence as a political dissident. He nonetheless continued to publish political satire in books and articles until his death in 1968, with some works appearing posthumously. Humorous yet humanistic, Guareschi's writings possess what *Saturday Review*'s Harrison Smith defined as "a quality that must come from the soil and some changeless and harmonious human relationship with nature, with God, and the people whom the earth nourishes."

Guareschi's books have been translated into German, Swedish, French, Spanish, Polish, and Lithuanian, as well as into English. Several of the Don Camillo stories have been adapted as motion pictures.

BIOGRAPHICAL/CRITICAL SOURCES: New York Times Book Review, December 17, 1950, January 4, 1970; *Life,* June 14, 1954; *Saturday Review,* February 17, 1951, July 12, 1958, October 3, 1970; Giovanni Guareschi, *My Home Sweet Home* (autobiography), Farrar, Straus, 1966; *Times Literary Supplement,* August 7, 1969, March 12, 1970; Guareschi, *The Family Guareschi: Chronicles of the Past and Present* (autobiography), Farrar, Straus, 1970; *New Yorker,* January 9, 1971.

OBITUARIES: London Times, July 23, 1968; *New York Times,* July 23, 1968; *Washington Post,* July 23, 1968; *Time,* August 2, 1968; *Newsweek,* August 5, 1968; *Publisher's Weekly,* August 5, 1968; *Antiquarian Bookman,* August 5-12, 1968; *Books Abroad,* Spring, 1969.*

* * *

GUGGENHEIM, Marguerite 1898-1979
(Peggy Guggenheim)

OBITUARY NOTICE: Born August 26, 1898, in New York, N.Y.; died after a stroke, December 23, 1979, in Camposampiero, Italy. Art collector and author. Born into a wealthy New York family, Peggy Guggenheim rebelled against her bourgeois Jewish upbringing and embraced the bohemian life of Paris in the 1920's. Through her first husband, painter Laurence Vail, she became acquainted with many writers and artists of the time. When she decided to open an art gallery in England in 1938 she knew nothing about modern art, but with the encouragement of Samuel Beckett, who was then her lover, and the advice of her friend Marcel Duchamp, she began to patronize and exhibit the works of contemporary artists such as Picasso, Kandinsky, Calder, and Arp. After the outbreak of World War II she moved her collection, including many paintings she rescued at the last minute from the German invasion of France, to New York. There she opened her second gallery, which she named Art of This Century. After the war she moved to an eighteenth-century palazzo in Venice, where her collection was on display to the public three days a week. She added little to her collection in her last years, since she found most developments in art "horrible and imitative." Her memoirs, *Out of This Century: Confessions of an Art Addict,* were considered scandalous when first published in 1946 because of her frank discussion of her husbands (she married painter Max Ernst in 1941 and divorced him five years later) and her lovers, who included painter Yves Tanguy and writer John Holms. She also wrote of the artists whose careers she aided, including Jackson Pollock, whom she supported for two years. Obituaries and other sources: *Current Biography*, Wilson, 1962; *New York Times*, July 14, 1974, April 17, 1979, December 24, 1979; *London Times*, April 10, 1980.

*　　　*　　　*

GUGGENHEIM, Peggy
See GUGGENHEIM, Marguerite

*　　　*　　　*

GUMP, Sally
See STANFORD, Sally

*　　　*　　　*

GUTMANN, Myron P. 1949-

BRIEF ENTRY: Born November 4, 1949, in Chicago, Ill. American historian, demographer, educator, and author. Gutmann has taught history at University of Texas since 1976. He wrote *War and Rural Life in the Early Modern Low Countries* (Princeton University Press, 1980). *Address:* Deparment of History, University of Texas, Austin, Tex. 78712. *Biographical/critical sources: Directory of American Scholars,* Volume I: *History,* 7th edition, Bowker, 1978.

*　　　*　　　*

GUY, David 1948-

PERSONAL: Born August 19, 1948, in Pittsburgh, Pa.; son of William Barker (a physician) and Mary Jane (McCutcheon) Guy; married Elizabeth Heard (an electronics technician), June, 1970; children: William Barker II. *Education:* Duke University, A.B., 1970. *Home:* 813 Onslow St., Durham, N.C. 27705. *Agent:* Virginia Barber, 353 West 21st St., New York, N.Y.

CAREER: English teacher and department head at private day school in Winston-Salem, N.C., 1970-76; Duke University, Durham, N.C., library clerk-assistant at Chemistry Library, 1977—. *Member:* Phi Beta Kappa.

WRITINGS: Football Dreams (novel), Seaview, 1980. Contributor to newspapers.

WORK IN PROGRESS: A novel.

SIDELIGHTS: David Guy's *Football Dreams* is the story of Dan Keith, an adolescent who wants to prove something to himself and the rest of the world. Following in the footsteps of his father, Keith feels that he can find his place in the world by being a football player. Through the sport, he expects to gain the respect of his peers, to become irresistible to the opposite sex, and to make his parents proud of him. It is important to the athlete that his parents watch him play the game. But his mother does not understand football, and his father, who is dying of cancer, is blinded after eye surgery and never actually sees his son play. In the end, Keith achieves what he wants: He becomes a good football player. But he does not find happiness, though he learns that relationships do not depend on material success, that some things (love and admiration, for instance) must be earned, not won, while other things can only be given.

Calling the book a touching and amusing first novel, critics commended Guy for illustrating the pain and pleasure of youth so accurately. "The plot, the tone and especially the dialogue make the book more true than interesting and, ultimately, interesting because it rings so true," said Elizabeth Wheeler of the *Los Angeles Times.* Keith's "hard battle for maturity," observed the *Washington Post*'s Joseph McLellan, is told "with a wealth of finely chosen detail." When commenting on *Football Dreams* in a *Library Journal* interview, Guy explained that he wrote a book about adolescents for adults "because the dream of finally proving ourselves survives far beyond adolescence."

BIOGRAPHICAL/CRITICAL SOURCES: Library Journal, October, 1980; *New York Times,* December 23, 1980; *Washington Post,* January 9, 1981; *Chicago Tribune Book World,* February 1, 1981; *Los Angeles Times,* February 6, 1981.

*　　　*　　　*

GUYER, Paul 1948-

PERSONAL: Born January 13, 1948, in New York, N.Y.; son of Irving Henry (an artist) and Betty (an administrator; maiden name, Rubenstein) Guyer; married Pamela Foa (an attorney), May 21, 1978. *Education:* Harvard University, A.B. (summa cum laude), 1969, A.M., 1971, Ph.D., 1974. *Residence:* Chicago, Ill. *Office:* Department of Philosophy, University of Illinois at Chicago Circle, Box 4348, Chicago, Ill. 60680.

CAREER: University of Pittsburgh, Pittsburgh, Pa., assistant professor of philosophy, 1973-78; University of Illinois at Chicago Circle, Chicago, associate professor of philosophy, 1978—. Lecturer at Ohio University and Tufts University, 1975-76, McGill University, 1976-77, University of Edinburgh and University of London, 1978-79, and Northwestern University, University of Chicago, and University of California, San Diego, all 1979-80; lecturer and session chair at Moscow Colloquium on Hegel's Logic. *Member:* American Philosophical Association, American Society for Aesthetics.

WRITINGS: (Contributor) Rolf-Peter Horstmann, editor, *Seminar: Dialektik in der Philosophie Hegels,* Suhrkamp Verlag, 1978; *Kant and the Claims of Taste,* Harvard University Press, 1979; (editor with Ted Cohen, and contributor) *Essays in Kant's Aesthetics,* University of Chicago Press, 1981. Contributor of articles and reviews to philosophy and aesthetics journals.

WORK IN PROGRESS: Research for a book on Kant's theory of knowledge, completion expected in 1984; research on Kant's intentions in the refutation of idealism, his strategies in the transcendental deduction, and his distinction between the beautiful and the sublime.

H

HABERLY, Loyd   1896-1981

PERSONAL: Born December 9, 1896, in Ellsworth, Iowa; died March 27, 1981, in Vero Beach, Fla.; son of Lewis Benote (a farmer) and Nora (Galligan) Haberly; married Virginia Dean in 1942; children: David Tristram. Education: Reed College, A.B., 1918; attended Harvard University, 1919-20; Oxford University, M.A., 1924; Fairleigh Dickinson University, LL.D., 1954. Home: 102 Village Spires, Vero Beach, Fla. 32960.

CAREER: Worked as a mason and carpenter; Seven Acres Press, Long Crendon, England, owner, 1927-35; Gregynog Press, Northern Wales, director, 1936-38; Harvard University, Cambridge, Mass., lecturer in monastic arts, 1939; Washington University, St. Louis, Mo., assistant professor, 1942-46; University of Massachusetts, associate professor, 1946-49; Fairleigh Dickinson University, Rutherford, N.J., professor of English and chairman of department, 1949-59, dean of liberal arts, 1959-66; Wroxton College, Banbury, England, distinguished professor of humanities and dean, 1966-72, distinguished emeritus professor of English, 1972-81. Member of staff of writers conferences at University of New Hampshire, 1940-60. Military service: U.S. Army, infantry, 1918-19; Missouri National Guard, 1942-44. Member: Poetry Society of America (president, 1963-68). Awards, honors: Rhodes scholar, 1921-24.

WRITINGS: Poems, Oxford University Press, 1931; Mediaeval English Pavingtiles (nonfiction), self-illustrated, Basil Blackwell, 1937; The City of the Sainted King, and Other Poems, self-illustrated, Widener Library, Harvard University, 1939; Silent Fame, and Other Poems, Macmillan, 1945; Pursuit of the Horizon: A Life of George Catlin, Painter and Recorder of the American Indian, Macmillan, 1948; (editor) Gaius Plinius Secundus, Pliny's Natural History: An Account by a Roman of What Romans Knew, and Did, and Valued, compact edition, Ungar, 1957; Highlights (poems), Fairleigh Dickinson University Press, 1960; An American Bookbuilder in England and Wales: Reminiscences of the Seven Acres and Gregynog Presses, Bertram Rota, 1979.

Privately printed: Cymberina: An Unnatural History in Woodcuts and Verse, 1926; John Apostate: An Idyll of the Quays, 1927; The Sacrifice of Spring: A Masque of Queens, 1927; When Cupid Wins, None Lose; or, A True Report of Fairy Sport, 1927; Daneway: A Fairy Play, self-illustrated, 1929; Poems, 1930; The Copper Coloured Cupid; or, The Cutting of the Cake (poems), self illustrated, 1931; The Boy and the Bird: An Oregon Idyll, self illustrated, 1932; The Keeper of the Doves: A Tale of Notley Abbey, 1932; The Antiquary, (poem), 1933; Anne Boleyn, and Other Poems, 1934; The Crowning Year, and Other Poems, 1937; Almost a Minister: A Romance of the Oregon Hopyards (poem), self-illustrated, 1942; Artemis: A Forest Tale, self-illustrated, 1942; The Fourth of July: or, An Oregon Orator (poem), self-illustrated, 1942; Midgetina and the Scapegoat (poem), self-illustrated, 1943; Neecha (poem), 1943; Maskerade (poem), 1957; Again, and Other Poems, 1958; Sun Chant, and Other Poems, 1959.

SIDELIGHTS: Haberly told CA: "After finishing my legal studies at Harvard I worked for a year as a mason and a carpenter in the English village of Long Crendon, where I began a career in bookbuilding. I gradually became convinced that mediaeval makers of floortiles printed designs on these from moveable wooden type long before the days of Gutenberg. Mediaeval English Pavingtiles was written as a result of my excavation of the tile-rich site of a nearby Augustinian abbey.

"Along with my verse-volumes issued from the Seven Acres Press at Long Crendon, I had, by 1931, directed the endowed Gregynog Press in Northern Wales in its production of such classic works as Xenophon's Cyropaedia and a verse translation by Poet Laureate Robert Bridges of the Eros and Psyche of the Roman Apuleius, which was printed with a type revived from that used for the first edition of Dante's Paradiso.

"I returned to the United States in 1939 to lecture on monastic life and arts at the Harvard Summer School. I joined the faculty of Fairleigh Dickinson University in 1949 when it was small and new and served as liberal arts dean under the able administration of President Sammartino. In 1963 the board of trustees authorized the purchase of an overseas campus on the historic property known as Wroxton Abbey, located between Shakespeare's Stratford-on-Avon and Banbury, England. It was from this ancestral home of the ennobled North family that an unlucky Lord North mismanaged for George III our American Revolution, making the Abbey somewhat the opposite number to George Washington's Mount Vernon.

"Interest in our Indian and colonial past led me to write a biography of George Catlin and to write articles on early New York and Boston museums."

Serving on the staffs of writers conferences for twenty-one years, Haberly was closely associated with many writers, including Robert Coffin, Margaret Coit, Esther Forbes, and Rolfe

Humphreys, and was a close neighbor and friend of William Carlos Williams.

BIOGRAPHICAL/CRITICAL SOURCES: San Francisco Chronicle, December 10, 1948; *New York Herald Tribune Weekly Book Review,* December 19, 1948; *New York Times,* December 26, 1948; *Saturday Review of Literature,* January 29, 1949.

OBITUARIES: New York Times, March 28, 1981.

*   *   *

HABSBURG-LOTHRINGEN, Geza Louis Eusebius Gebhard Ralphael Albert Maria von
See von HABSBURG-LOTHRINGEN, Geza Louis Eusebius Gebhard Ralphael Albert Maria

*   *   *

HACKADY, Hal

BRIEF ENTRY: Lyricist. Hackady has received awards from the Venice and Cannes Film Festivals and was nominated for the Best Written American Screen Musical Awards in 1962. His lyrics have been performed by leading vocalists and used for more than one hundred feature films and television programs. Some of his best-known works are "Play It Again, Sam" "Shake Me I Rattle," "Pretty Pretty," "Mama a Rainbow," and "I Capricorn." *Address:* 3 East 75th St., New York, N.Y., 10021.

*   *   *

HACKETT, Jan Michele   1952-
(Jan Kerouac)

PERSONAL: Maiden name is pronounced "Care-oh-ack"; born February 16, 1952, in Albany, N.Y.; daughter of Jack (a writer) and Joan V. (a writer and VISTA worker; maiden name, Haverty) Kerouac; married John Lamb Lash (a writer), December 3, 1968 (divorced February, 1972); married Stephen Bernard Hackett, November 3, 1975; children: Natasha (deceased). *Education:* Central Washington University, student, 1979—. *Residence:* Ellensburg, Wash. *Agent:* Joyce K. Cole, Box 5139, Berkeley, Calif.

CAREER: Writer. Employed at a variety of odd jobs in Arizona, Washington, New York, and New Mexico, 1972-77; Mark Hines Creations, Burbank, Calif., ceramic sculptor, 1978.

*WRITINGS—*Under name Jan Kerouac: *Baby Driver: A Story About Myself* (autobiographical novel), St. Martin's, 1981.

WORK IN PROGRESS: A novel.

SIDELIGHTS: Hackett is the daughter of Jack Kerouac, who was the leading spokesman for the "beat" generation.

Hackett told *CA:* "As far back as I can remember I have written poems, which in adolescence were influenced by LSD. Then in 1973 I traveled to South America and had so many odd experiences and adventures that on returning to the States four months later, I realized it was all worth recording. When combined with a tumultuous childhood it was enough for a book. So, in the winter of 1975, on a Yugoslavian freighter bound for Morocco, I began work on the book in earnest, after having the first thirteen pages rejected by the literary agent who had handled a great deal of my father's work. There was a cold rainy spell in Morocco in December, so my husband and I fled north to London, where I wrote the first half of the novel on an English typewriter without an asterisk.

"At twenty-three I found I had high blood pressure—not surprising in view of heavy drug-taking in youth. I continued writing in Seattle University Hospital, then in Hollywood where I also modeled clay faces on pots for a year. Finally in 1978 I found some connections, and by 1980 the manuscript was accepted.

"I speak Spanish and hope that *Baby Driver* will be translated into that language since it already has a good amount of it appearing in the text and the settings are largely in Spanish-speaking countries.

"Unlike *Baby Driver,* which is autobiographical in nature, my next work will be more purely fiction. There will be five main characters—three men and two women. It will span the years 1975-90, and end in India. There will be lots of travel, introspection, some love affairs, and a theme of reincarnation, all tied together perhaps by an accidental contamination by radioactive waste. In 1982 I plan to travel to Europe and Asia while gathering material and spirit for this work. I also love to cook, and will publish a Kerouac cookbook sooner or later."

BIOGRAPHICAL/CRITICAL SOURCES: Washington Post Book World, October 24, 1981; *Los Angeles Times,* December 16, 1981; *People,* December 21, 1981.

*   *   *

HACKETT, Pat

PERSONAL: Born in New Haven, Conn.; daughter of John Christopher (a railroad clerk) and Patricia (Koran) Hackett. *Education:* Barnard College, B.A., 1969. *Agent:* c/o Harcourt Brace Jovanovich, 757 Third Ave., New York, N.Y. 10017.

WRITINGS: (Co-author) "Bad" (screenplay), New World, 1977; (with Andy Warhol) *POPism: The Warhol Sixties,* Harcourt, 1980.

WORK IN PROGRESS: Two screenplays.

*   *   *

HAGGERTY, P(atrick) E(ugene)   1914-1980

OBITUARY NOTICE: Born March 17, 1914, in Harvey, N.D.; died October 1, 1980, in Dallas, Tex. Industrialist, engineer, and author. As an executive with Texas Instruments, Haggerty moved that company into the production of transistors shortly after they were invented and presided over many important developments in electronics. He wrote many articles for scientific and business journals; his best-known book was *The Productive Society.* Obituaries and other sources: *American Men and Women of Science: The Physical and Biological Sciences,* 14th edition, Bowker, 1979; *The International Year Book and Statesmen's Who's Who,* Kelly's Directories, 1979; *New York Times,* October 2, 1980; *The Annual Obituary 1980,* St. Martin's, 1981.

*   *   *

HALE, Irina   1932-

PERSONAL: Born August 2, 1932, in London, England; daughter of Patrick Beauchamp (a Royal British Naval Commander) and Marina (a painter and sculptress; maiden name, Soukovkine) Heard; married John Hale-White (a sculptor), June 26, 1959 (divorced, 1979); married Spartaio Zianna (a painter), November 4, 1979. *Education:* Graduated from Bath Academy of Art, 1954. *Politics:* "Socialist tendencies." *Religion:* Russian Orthodox. *Home:* Casello 132, Chiarone (Borgo Carige), 58010

Prov. Grosetto, Italy. *Agent:* Laura Cecil, 17 Alwyne Villas, London N1, England.

CAREER: Skellfield School, Yorkshire, England, art teacher, 1954-56; Badminton School, Bristol, England, teacher of arts and crafts, 1958-59; free-lance writer and artist, 1959—. Work has appeared in exhibits in London, Cambridge, Rome, Paris, and other European cities. *Awards, honors:* First prize from City of Salzburg, Austria, 1965, for water-color paintings.

WRITINGS: Diciotto l'orsacchiotto (juvenile), Einaudi, Torino, 1974; *Chocolate Mouse and Sugar Pig* (juvenile; self-illustrated), Atheneum, 1978.

WORK IN PROGRESS: Several books for young children; research into thirteenth-century Asia for a young-adult novel; travel diaries; poems; *Donkey's Dreadful Day,* a circus story for young readers, for Atheneum.

SIDELIGHTS: Irina Hale told *CA:* "In the last ten years, my dedication to organic agriculture, medicinal herbs, related animal keeping, and ecology led me to an antinuclear standpoint which spurred my concern for Third World problems and disarmament. Strangely enough, this led to my interest in central Asia, the setting for my forthcoming book for young adults, which is to be historical fantasy." *Avocational interests:* Theatrical animation, pottery, sculpture, dancing, cooking.

* * *

HALL, Jean R(ogers) 1941-

PERSONAL: Born June 4, 1941, in Long Beach, Calif.; daughter of Raymond A. (a chemical engineer) and Dorothy (Conroe) Rogers; married James E. Hall (a biophysicist), September 28, 1964. *Education:* Pomona College, B.A., 1963; University of California, Riverside, M.A., 1966, Ph.D., 1970. *Office:* Department of English, California State University, Fullerton, Calif. 92634.

CAREER: California State University, Fullerton, assistant professor, 1970-74, associate professor, 1974-79, professor of English, 1980—. *Member:* Modern Language Association of America.

WRITINGS: The Transforming Image: A Study of Shelley's Major Poetry, University of Illinois Press, 1980.

WORK IN PROGRESS: A book of essays on six major English Romantic poets.

* * *

HALL, Wayne E(dward) 1947-

PERSONAL: Born May 14, 1947, in Langdon, N.D.; son of Lloyd E. (a tavern manager) and Mary Ann (Wirt) Hall; married Arlene Sorenson, September 17, 1968 (divorced, 1979); married Heather Gaines (a typist), January 19, 1980; children: Benjamin Gaines Taylor, Andrew Sorenson, Adrian Edward. *Education:* University of North Dakota, B.A. (summa cum laude), 1969; attended University of Tuebingen, 1969-70; Indiana University, M.A., 1971, Ph.D., 1978. *Home:* 2359 Victor St., Cincinnati, Ohio 45219. *Office:* Department of English, University of Cincinnati, Cincinnati, Ohio 45221.

CAREER: English teacher at college preparatory school in Delmenhorst, West Germany, 1971-73; University of Cincinnati, Cincinnati, Ohio, Charles Phelps Taft postdoctoral fellow, 1979-80, instructor in English, 1980—. *Member:* Modern Language Association of America, American Committee for Irish Studies, Phi Beta Kappa. *Awards, honors:* Fulbright fellowship for West Germany, 1969-70; Indiana University grant for Ireland,

1977; American Council of Learned Societies grant for Ireland, 1979.

WRITINGS: Shadowy Heroes: Irish Literature of the 1890's, Syracuse University Press, 1980.

Work represented in anthologies, including *Irish Renaissance Annual I,* edited by Zack Bowen, University of Delaware Press, 1980. Contributor of articles and reviews to *Eire-Ireland* and *ACIS Newsletter.*

SIDELIGHTS: Hall wrote: "The kind of literary criticism I do takes a loosely historicist approach and tries to relate the social experience of the Irish writers to the aesthetic experience of their work. Irish literature is so thoroughly entangled in its own history that separating the two seems to me to falsify the writing. And even though my work is 'specialized,' I think that, in a larger context, literary criticism makes the most sense to the most people when it takes up the question of what art has to do with the rest of life."

* * *

HALLAHMI, Benjamin Beit
See BEIT-HALLAHMI, Benjamin

* * *

HAMER, Frank 1929-

PERSONAL: Born February 1, 1929, in England; married wife, Janet (a potter), 1952; children: one daughter. *Home:* Terracotta, 10 The Orchard, Ponthir, Gwent, South Wales.

CAREER: Currently lecturer in ceramics, pottery, and child art at Gwent College of Higher Education, Gwent, Wales.

WRITINGS: Pottery Glazes, Society for Education Through Art, 1974; *The Potter's Dictionary of Materials and Techniques,* Watson-Guptill, 1975; (with wife, Janet Hamer) *Clays: A Ceramic Skillbook,* Watson-Guptill, 1977. Contributor to ceramic and pottery journals.

SIDELIGHTS: Hamer commented: "I see myself primarily as a teacher, and my writing and lecturing are to this end. However, no one can lecture, write, or teach pottery successfully without actually making pots; this must be a deep involvement both technically and artistically. Research of some sort is always in progress, and may result in better pots, magazine articles, or books."

* * *

HAMILTON, W(illis) D(avid) 1936-

PERSONAL: Born March 19, 1936, in Boom Road, New Brunswick, Canada; son of Herman J. and Minnie R. (Mullin) Hamilton; married M. Viola Burke (a teacher), 1956; children: James, Alice, David, Robert, John, Patrick. *Education:* University of New Brunswick, B.A. (with honors), 1957, M.A., 1958, B.Ed., 1961. *Home:* 220 Surrey Cres., Fredericton, New Brunswick, Canada E3B 4L3. *Office:* 351 d'Avery Hall, University of New Brunswick, Fredericton, New Brunswick, Canada E3B 6E3.

CAREER: Worked as teacher, principal, and supervising principal at public schools in New Brunswick and Quebec, Canada, 1958-71; New Brunswick Teachers College, instructor, 1971-73; University of New Brunswick, Fredericton, assistant professor, 1973-75, associate professor, 1975-80, professor of education, 1980—, assistant dean, 1976-80. Co-director of Micmac-Maliseet Educational Development Institute, 1981—.

Member: Canadian Education Association, Canadian Association of University Teachers, Association for Canadian and Quebec Literature.

WRITINGS: Charles Sangster, Twayne, 1971; (editor with W. A. Spray) *Source Materials Relating to the New Brunswick Indian,* Hamray, 1976, revised edition, 1977; *Old North Esk,* Princess, 1979. Contributor to history and genealogy journals.

WORK IN PROGRESS: A revised edition of *Old North Esk;* a critical essay for *Canadian Writers and Their Times: Studies in Form, Context, and Development,* publication by E.C.W. Press expected in 1983; a case study of the Little South West (New Brunswick) Indian Reserve, 1779-1979.

SIDELIGHTS: Hamilton commented: "Without abandoning the field of literary history and criticism, I have, in recent years, directed my attention more and more to research and publications having to do with the native Indians of the Maritime Provinces of Canada and to the initiation of university programs and projects pertaining to the native people and the rural communities of the region. Much of my later writing, therefore, is part of a broader program of activity which I have created for myself in order to feel moderately useful to society in an immediate way."

* * *

HAMLIN, Marjorie (Day) 1921-

PERSONAL: Born April 11, 1921, in Long Beach, Calif.; daughter of Clark Bronson (a businessman) and Charlotte (a pianist; maiden name, Gooding) Day; married Henry Streight Hamlin (a director of publications); children: Priscilla, Jennifer, Lisbeth. *Education:* University of California, Berkeley, B.A., 1943; also attended Washington University, St. Louis, Mo. *Home:* 759 Country Meadow Lane, St. Louis, Mo. 63141. *Office:* Department of Education, Principia College, Elsah, Ill. 62028.

CAREER: Worked as lower and middle school librarian, 1960-73; Principia College, Elsah, Ill., lecturer in education, 1975—. *Member:* National Association of Foreign Students, National Association for the Advancement of Colored People, National Library Association.

WRITINGS: (With Nancy Polette) *Reading Guidance in a Media Age,* Scarecrow, 1975; (author of introduction) Polette, *E Is for Everybody: A Manual for Bringing Fine Picture Books Into the Hands and Hearts of Children,* Scarecrow, 1976; (with Polette) *Celebrating With Books* (juvenile), Scarecrow, 1977; (with Polette) *Exploring Books With Gifted Children,* Libraries Unlimited, 1980.

WORK IN PROGRESS: African essays.

SIDELIGHTS: Marjorie Hamlin wrote: "Parents, teachers, and librarians need all the help they can find to get the best books into the hands of gifted children, the problem solvers of the future. I write to encourage all of us to dim the TV and let the great minds of all ages illumine the way for today's children through their words captured in print. Vision is not limited by national boundaries or ideologies. Great folk and fairy tales, legends and myths, will help children, and ultimately all mankind, to see and acknowledge that there is more which unites us than there is to separate us. We are one species. A child's unprejudiced mind can accept that fact effortlessly when reinforced continuously through contact with inspired authors."

* * *

HANDLER, Philip 1917-1981

OBITUARY NOTICE—See index for *CA* sketch: Born August 13, 1917, in New York, N.Y.; died of cancer, December 29, 1981, in Boston, Mass. Biochemist, educator, administrator, editor, and author. Handler served as president of the National Academy of Sciences for more than ten years. In that position he supervised investigations on enzymes and on the role of nutrition in preventing disease. His discovery of a relationship between Vitamin B deficiencies and pellegra was instrumental in eradicating that disease in the rural South. As eighteenth president of the academy, Handler also concerned himself with the plight of harrassed scientists in repressive regimes. He particularly tried to protect the Soviet dissident Andrei Sakharov. Previous to his association with the National Academy of Sciences, Handler worked as a chemist with the U.S. Department of Agriculture and taught at Duke University. At the school he taught physiology and nutrition before becoming a professor of biochemistry. Handler wrote numerous scientific papers and helped to write *Principles of Biochemistry,* a widely used textbook in medical schools. He also edited *Biology and the Future of Man.* Obituaries and other sources: *New York Times,* December 30, 1981; *Time,* January 11, 1982; *Newsweek,* January 11, 1982.

* * *

HANDLEY, Graham Roderick 1926-

PERSONAL: Born January 8, 1926, in Hampstead, England; son of Vernon Douglas (a paper maker) and Claudia Lillian (George) Handley; married Ruth Barbara Tunnicliffe, September 26, 1951; children: Roland John, Rosamund Kathleen (deceased), Elaine Melissa. *Education:* Received B.A. (with honors) and M.A. from University of Sheffield; Bedford College, London, Ph.D., 1962. *Home:* Glasgow Stud Farmhouse, Crews Hill, Enfield, Middlesex EN2 9DY, England.

CAREER: Assistant master at school in London, England, 1953-57; English teacher and department head at grammar schools in Borehamwood, England, 1957-62, and Hatfield, England, 1962-67; College of All Saints, London, senior lecturer, 1967-76, principal lecturer in English, 1976-80; writer, 1980—. Extramural lecturer at University of London, 1980—. *Military service:* British Army, Intelligence Corps, 1945-48; served in the Far East; became sergeant.

WRITINGS—All published by Pan Books, except as noted: *Brodie's Notes on William Golding's "Lord of the Flies,"* 1965; *Brodie's Notes on D.H. Lawrence's "Sons and Lovers,"* 1967; *Mrs. Gaskell's "Sylvia's Lovers,"* Basil Blackwell, 1967; *Notes on This Day and Age,* 1968; *Dickens's "Hard Times,"* Basil Blackwell, 1968.

Self-Test English, Seymour Press, 1970; (with Eric Newton) *A Guide to Teaching Poetry,* University of London Press, 1971; *Brodie's Notes on Aldous Huxley's "Brave New World,"* 1977; *Steinbeck's "The Grapes of Wrath" and "Of Mice and Men" and "The Pearl,"* 1977; *Brodie's Notes on Ernest Hemingway's "For Whom the Bell Tolls,"* 1977; *Greene's "The Power and the Glory,"* 1977; *Brodie's Notes on Joseph Heller's "Catch-22,"* 1977; *Brodie's Notes on Barry Hines's "A Kestrel for a Knave,"* 1977; *Brodie's Notes on James Joyce's "A Portrait of the Artist as a Young Man,"* 1977; (with Stanley King) *Brodie's Notes on Ken Kesey's "One Flew Over the Cuckoo's Nest,"* 1977; *Brodie's Notes on Keith Waterhouse's "Billy Liar,"* 1977; *Brodie's Notes on Charles Dickens's "Oliver Twist,"* 1977.

George Eliot's "The Mill on the Floss," 1978; *Brodie's Notes on F. Scott Fitzgerald's "The Great Gatsby,"* 1978; *Brodie's Notes on Selected Poems and Letters of John Keats,* 1978; *Brodie's Notes on "Selected Poems" by W. H. Auden,* 1978;

Brodie's Notes on "Chosen Poems of Thomas Hardy," 1978; *Brodie's Notes on Thomas Mann's "Death in Venice" and "Tonio Kroger,"* 1978; (with King) *Brodie's Notes on Charles Dickens's "Bleak House,"* 1978; (with Paul Harris) *Selected Tales of D. H. Lawrence,* 1978; *Brodie's Notes on William Blake's "Songs of Innocence and Experience,"* 1978; *Brodie's Notes on Oscar Wilde's "The Importance of Being Earnest,"* 1978; *Brodie's Notes on William Congreve's "The Way of the World,"* 1978; (with W. T. Currie) *Brodie's Notes on W. B. Yeats Selected Poetry,* 1978; *Shakespeare's "Sonnets,"* 1978; *Brodie's Notes on Ten Twentieth-Century Poets,* 1978; *Dickens's "Dombey and Son,"* 1978; *The College of All Saints, 1964-1978: An Informal History of One Hundred Years, 1878-1978,* John Roberts Press, 1978; *Brodie's Notes on Charles Dickens's "Our Mutual Friend,"* 1979.

Brodie's Notes on Charles Dickens's "Little Dorrit," 1980; *Brodie's Notes on Graham Greene's "Brighton Rock,"* 1980; (with King) *Brodie's Notes on Sean O'Casey's "Shadow of a Gunman" and "The Plough and the Stars,"* 1980; (with wife, Barbara Handley) *Brodie's Notes on Wilkie Collins's "The Woman in White,"* 1980; (editor) *Sport* (stories), J. Murray, 1980; *Brodie's Notes on Evelyn Waugh's "Scoop,"* 1980; (with King) *Brodie's Notes on Graham Greene's "The Quiet American,"* 1981; *The Metaphysical Poets,* 1981; (editor) Emily Bronte, *Wuthering Heights,* Macmillan, 1982.

WORK IN PROGRESS: Editing *Daniel Deronda,* by George Eliot, for Oxford University Press.

*   *   *

HANNEY, Peter 1930-1976

OBITUARY NOTICE: Born in 1930 in Great Britain; died in October, 1976. Museum administrator and author of *Rodents: Their Lives and Habits.* Obituaries and other sources: *The Writers Directory, 1976-78,* St. Martin's, 1976. (Date of death provided by wife, M. C. Hanney.)

*   *   *

HANNULA, Reino 1918-

PERSONAL: Born June 7, 1918, in Hubbardston, Mass.; son of John Henry (in business) and Karoliina (Hannula) Hannula; married Alice Beatrice McIntyre. *Education:* University of California, Los Angeles, B.A., 1960, M.A., 1964. *Politics:* Conservative. *Religion:* "I believe in the Finnish god Vaainaamooinen." *Home:* 674 Church St., San Luis Obispo, Calif. 93401. *Office:* Department of Computer Science, California Polytechnic State University, San Luis Obispo, Calif. 93407.

CAREER: California Polytechnic State University, San Luis Obispo, Calif., lecturer, 1962-65, assistant professor, 1965-74, associate professor, 1974-79, professor of computer science, 1979—. *Member:* Association of Computing Machinery.

WRITINGS: Computer Programming: A System 360/370 Assembly Language Approach (Computer and Information Sciences Book Club selection), Houghton, 1974; *Job Control Language and the Access Methods,* Addison-Wesley, 1979; *Blueberry God: The Education of a Finnish-American,* Quality Hill Books, 1981.

WORK IN PROGRESS: The Finn Halls.

SIDELIGHTS: Hannula commented: "Self-published, *Blueberry God* has sold over eight hundred copies by direct mail in a little over ten weeks. I expect it to be the best selling book about American Finns ever to be printed!"

HANSEN, Joyce 1942-

PERSONAL: Born October 18, 1942, in New York, N.Y.; daughter of Austin Victor (a photographer) and Lillian (Dancy) Hansen. *Education:* Pace University, B.A., 1972; New York University, M.A., 1978. *Religion:* Protestant. *Home:* 19 Dongan Pl., New York, N.Y. 10040.

CAREER: Board of Education, New York, N.Y., teacher of reading and English, 1973—. *Member:* Harlem Writers Guild.

WRITINGS: The Gift-Giver (juvenile), Houghton, 1980; *Home Boy* (young-adult novel), Houghton, 1982.

SIDELIGHTS: Joyce Hansen wrote: "Writing *The Gift-Giver* grew out of several things. Even before I'd thought of the book I sat down one day and read over everything I'd ever written. While doing this it was as if every good piece of literature I'd ever read, every article about writing I'd studied, and every writer's workshop I'd attended suddenly made sense. I could see the flaws in my writing. Not that I didn't know they were there before, but now I could see them clearly.

"When I began writing *The Gift-Giver* it was with a sense of operating with a kind of instinct—of having internalized some of the writer's craft. The most important thing, I think, that came out of the experience of analyzing what I'd been writing was that I knew I had to find my own 'voice.' In the process of learning your craft you study other writers. Finally you have to develop your own style."

*   *   *

HANSEN, Roger D(ennis) 1935-

PERSONAL: Born September 12, 1935, in Honolulu, Hawaii; son of Clarence Edward and Hilda May Hansen. *Education:* Yale University, B.A., 1957; Magdalen College, Oxford, B.A., 1959, M.A., 1959; Princeton University, M.P.A., 1961; Johns Hopkins University, Ph.D., 1970. *Home:* 1312 29th St. N.W., Washington, D.C. 20007. *Office:* School of Advanced International Studies, Johns Hopkins University, 1740 Massachusetts Ave. N.W., Washington, D.C. 20036.

CAREER: National Broadcasting Co. (NBC), Washington, D.C., administrative writer/reporter, 1962-64; National Planning Association, Washington, D.C., international economist, 1964-67, project director, 1967-70; Potomac Association (research firm), Washington, D.C., senior associate, 1971-72; Office of the Special Trade Representative, Washington, D.C., deputy assistant, 1972-73; National Security Council, Washington, D.C., senior member of staff, 1977; Johns Hopkins University, School of Advanced International Studies, Washington, D.C., Jacob Blaustein Professor of International Relations, 1978—. Senior fellow of Overseas Development Council, 1973-77, and Council on Foreign Relations, 1974-77; consultant to U.S. Department of State, 1978-80; Tom Slick Guest Professor at the Lyndon B. Johnson School of Public Affairs, University of Texas, Austin, 1980-81. *Member:* Council on Foreign Relations, Cosmos Club. *Awards, honors:* Rhodes scholar at Oxford University, 1957-59.

WRITINGS: Central America: Regional Integration and Economic Development, National Planning Association, 1967; *The Politics of Mexican Development,* Johns Hopkins Press, 1971; (with Albert Fishlow, Carlos Diaz-Alejandro, and Richard Fagan) *Rich and Poor Nations in the World Economy,* McGraw, 1978; *Beyond the North-South Stalemate,* McGraw, 1979. Contributor to international studies journals, including *Foreign Affairs, World Politics,* and *International Organization.*

HANSEN, Rosanna 1947-

PERSONAL: Born July 11, 1947, in Huron, S.D.; daughter of Walter N. (an agronomist) and Leanna G. (a pianist; maiden name, Dickinson) Parmeter; married Corwith R. Hansen (a teacher of mathematics), May 30, 1970. Education: Oberlin College, B.A., 1969; Johns Hopkins University, M.A., 1970. Home: 1470 Midland Ave., Bronxville, N.Y. 10708. Office: Macmillan Educational Co., 866 Third Ave., New York, N.Y. 10022.

CAREER: U.S. Peace Corps, Washington, D.C., volunteer English teacher at St. Peters College, Iligan, Philippines, 1970-73; Electronic Purchasing, New York City, editorial assistant, 1973; Boating Industry, New York City, production editor and staff writer, 1973-75; Queens College of the City University of New York, Flushing, N.Y., writer in Office of Publications and editor of Campus and Community, 1975-76; Public Affairs Committee, Inc., New York City, managing editor of "Public Affairs Pamphlets," 1976-81; Grosset & Dunlap, Inc., New York City, senior editor of Juvenile Division, 1981-82; Macmillan Educational Co., New York City, senior editor, 1982—. First violinist with Westchester Symphony Orchestra. Member: Authors Guild.

WRITINGS—For children: Gymnastics: The New Era, Grosset, 1980; The Fairy Tale Book of Ballet, photographs by Martha Swope, Grosset, 1980; Wolves and Coyotes, Platt, 1981. Contributor to magazines, including Cosmopolitan, Administrative Management, and Zip.

WORK IN PROGRESS: Research on performing arts and on such endangered animals as pandas and gorillas; writing the entry on mammals and birds for a forthcoming children's encyclopedia.

SIDELIGHTS: Hansen told CA: "When I write for children, my goal is to express ideas both simply and elegantly. Writers John McPhee and Mary Elting have been major influences on my work."

BIOGRAPHICAL/CRITICAL SOURCES: Los Angeles Times Book Review, November 30, 1980.

* * *

HANSER, Richard (Frederick) 1909-1981

OBITUARY NOTICE—See index for CA sketch: Born December 15, 1909, in Buffalo, N.Y.; died December 7, 1981, in Port Chester, N.Y. Journalist, editor, translator, and author best known for his television documentaries. His series "Victory at Sea," a naval history of World War II, won him several honors, including the George Foster Peabody Award. He joined the National Broadcasting Company (NBC-TV) in 1952, writing for the programs "Project 20," "Meet Mr. Lincoln," "Life in the Thirties," and "Mark Twain's America." Before his career in television, Hanser reported for the Buffalo Times and the Cleveland Press. He then worked as an editor with Fawcett Publications and PM. The author also contributed articles to many periodicals such as Saturday Review, Esquire, New York Times Magazine, and Theatre Arts. Among his books number The Coming of Christ, A Noble Treason: The Revolt of the Munich Students Against Hitler, and Putsch: How Hitler Made Revolution. In addition, Hanser translated German works by Hans Habe and H. M. Mons into English. Obituaries and other sources: New York Times, December 10, 1981.

HARDACH, Gerd 1941-

PERSONAL: Born September 29, 1941, in Essen, Germany (now West Germany); son of F. W. (a manager) and Bernardine Hardach; married Irene Pinke (a sociologist), September 27, 1968; children: Felix, Mathis, Sophie-Maria. Education: University of Muenster, degree in sociology, 1965; attended Ecole Pratique des Hautes Etudes, 1965-66; Free University of Berlin, Ph.D., 1968. Politics: Social Democrat. Home: Gruener Weg 19, D-3550 Marburg, West Germany. Office: Krummbogen 28, D-3550 Marburg, West Germany.

CAREER: Technological University of Berlin, Berlin, West Germany, assistant in economics, 1966-69; University of Regensburg, Regensburg, West Germany, assistant in economics, 1969-71; University of Marburg, Marburg, West Germany, professor of social and economic history, 1972—.

WRITINGS: Der soziale Status des Arbeiters in der Fruehindustrialisierung (title means "French Iron Workers in the Industrial Revolution"), Duncker & Humblot, 1969; Waehrungspolitik in Deutschland, 1924-1931 ("Monetary Policy in Germany, 1924-1931"), Duncker & Humblot, 1976; The First World War, University of California Press, 1977, new edition, 1981; A Short History of Socialist Economic Thought, Edward Arnold, 1978; Deutsche Kindheiten (title means "German Childhood"), Athenaeum, 1978, second edition published as Kinder alltag, Rowohlt, 1981; Das Buch vom Markt (title means "History of the Market"), Bucher, 1980.

Contributor to economic and social history journals.

WORK IN PROGRESS: A history of the world economy; a history of the family.

SIDELIGHTS: Hardach wrote: "The essence of history is curiosity: curiosity about human beings in their time, about their individual and collective aspirations, actions, and beliefs. This curiosity has led me to research and write on war and peace, on families and international financial transactions. In my view, the craft of the historian is to reconstruct human experiences from those scraps of information that come to us through archives and libraries, through written and oral tradition."

* * *

HARMAN, David 1944-

PERSONAL: Born July 6, 1944, in Jerusalem, Palestine (now Israel); son of Avraham (a university president) and Zena (Stern) Harman; married Dorothy Gitter (a university lecturer), January 25, 1969; children: Danna, Oren. Education: Hebrew University of Jerusalem, B.A., 1965; Harvard University, Ed.M., 1969, Ph.D., 1971. Religion: Jewish. Home: 53 Shmaryahu-Levin St., Jerusalem, Israel. Office: School of Education, Hebrew University of Jerusalem, Mount Scopus, Jerusalem, Israel.

CAREER: Hebrew University of Jerusalem, Jerusalem, Israel, lecturer, 1971-77, senior lecturer in education, 1977—, director of Center for Pre-Academic Studies, 1971-74. Assistant professor at Harvard University, 1974-77. Chief scientist with Jerusalem Joint Distribution Committee, 1977—; chairman of Israel's national advisory council on youth, 1981-83; consultant to World Bank, Thailand's Ministry of Education, and Foundation for Child Development. Military service: Israel Defense Forces, 1962-65; became captain. Member: Israel Association for Families (chairman, 1979-82), Israel Early Childhood Association (chairman, 1981). Awards, honors: Arco young leader fellow, 1976, and presidential fellow, 1977-79, both of Aspen Institute for Humanistic Studies.

WRITINGS: Program Design, World Education, 1973; *Community Fundamental Education,* Lexington Books, 1974; (editor with David Kline) *Issues in Population Education,* Lexington Books, 1976; (editor) *Recurrent and Nonformal Education,* Jossey-Bass, 1976; *Early Childhood: A New Look at Policymaking,* Aspen Institute for Humanistic Studies, 1978; (with C. St. John Hunter) *Adult Illiteracy in the United States,* McGraw, 1979; (with O. G. Brim) *Learning to Be Parents,* Sage Publications, 1980.

WORK IN PROGRESS: Research on public policies regarding children, families, and communities, on parent education, and on adult learning.

SIDELIGHTS: Harman told *CA:* "Learning is a lifelong process which until recently received little attention in academic literature. My research and writing have been largely focused upon adults as learners, looking at issues such as how adult illiterates learn how to read and write, and how adults learn the skills and knowledge necessary for parenting. There are obvious policy implications in such investigations, implications which form another closely related area of study. It is within this framework that I envision my work."

* * *

HARMON, Lily 1912-

PERSONAL: Born November 19, 1912, in New Haven, Conn.; daughter of Benjamin and Bessie (Horowitz) Perelmutter; married Peter Harnden (marriage ended); married Sidney Harmon (a stage and movie producer; marriage ended); married Joseph H. Hirshhorn (a financier and art collector), 1945 (divorced, 1956); married Henry Rothman (a photographer and frame maker; marriage ended); married Milton Schachter (an industrialist), October, 1972; children: Amy, JoAnn. *Education:* Attended Yale University, 1929-31, Academie Colarossi Paris, 1931-32, and Art Students League, 1932-33. *Home:* 151 Central Park W., New York, N.Y. 10023; and 629 Commercial St., Provincetown, Mass. 02657. *Agent:* Max Gartenberg, 331 Madison Ave., New York, N.Y. 10017.

CAREER: Professional artist and illustrator. Work represented in solo shows in the United States and abroad, including Association of American Artists Galleries, Yamada Gallery, Krasner Gallery, International Salon Palace of Fine Arts (Mexico City), and George M. Modlin Fine Arts Center, and in permanent collections, including those at Whitney Museum of American Art, Tel Aviv Museum, and Smithsonian Institution. *Member:* National Academy of Design (first vice-president, 1981), Artists Equity Association, Provincetown Art Association, Provincetown Fine Arts Work Center (trustee).

WRITINGS: Freehand (autobiography) Simon & Schuster, 1981.

Illustrator: Jane Austen, *Pride and Prejudice,* Books, 1950; Bill Martin, Jr., *Sounds of a Distant Drum,* Holt, 1967; Edith Wharton, *House of Mirth* (Japanese translation), Limited Editions Club, 1975; Guy de Maupassant, *Short Stories of Guy de Maupassant,* Franklin Library, 1976. Also illustrator of Japanese publications, including Thomas Mann, *Buddenbrooks,* Andre Gide, *Symphonie Pastorale* and *Counterfeiters,* Jean-Paul Sartre, *Dirty Hands,* Franz Kafka, *The Castle* and *The Metamorphosis,* all 1965; illustrator of Gide's *Lafcadio's Adventure* and Francois Mauriac's *Therese,* both 1972.

BIOGRAPHICAL/CRITICAL SOURCES: Sunday Star-Ledger (Newark, N.J.), April 26, 1981; *Provincetown Advocate Summer Guide* (Mass.), July 30, 1981.

HARPER, David
See CORLEY, Edwin (Raymond)

* * *

HARPER, Mary Wood
See DIXON, Jeanne

* * *

HARPER, Paula (Hays) 1938-

PERSONAL: Born November 17, 1938, in Boston, Mass.; daughter of Clarence E. (a customs inspector and ragtime pianist) and Maura (an Irish step dancer; maiden name, Lee) Fish; married Lee Hays (an actor and television director; divorced); married Alan Harper (a television writer and producer; divorced). *Education:* Hunter College of the City University of New York, B.A. (magna cum laude), 1966, M.A., 1968; further graduate study at University of New Mexico, 1968-69; Stanford University, Ph.D., 1976. *Politics:* "Feminist." *Residence:* Coral Gables, Fla. *Office:* University of Miami, Art Department, Coral Gables, Fla. 33124.

CAREER: California Institute of the Arts, Valencia, assistant professor of history of art and photography, 1971-72; Hunter College of the City University of New York, New York, N.Y., director of Hunter Arts Gallery, 1977-78; Stanford University, Stanford, Calif., visiting assistant professor of art history, 1979-80; Mills College, Oakland, Calif., visiting assistant professor of art history, 1980-81; University of Miami, Coral Gables, Fla., assistant professor of art history, 1982—. Visiting assistant professor at Mills College, spring, 1979. Curator of museum exhibits; public lecturer. Off-Broadway producer and press agent; dancer with Munt-Brooks Modern Dance Company, 1964-65. Member of board of directors of Lower Manhattan Neighborhood Centers, 1977-78. *Member:* College Art Association (founding member of Women's Caucus for Art, 1972; president of New York chapter of caucus, 1977-78; member of national advisory board of caucus, 1977-80).

WRITINGS: (Contributor) Linda Nochlin and Henry Millon, editors, *Art in the Service of Politics,* M.I.T. Press, 1979; (with Ralph E. Shikes) *Pissarro: His Life and Work,* Horizon Press, 1980; *Daumier's Clowns: New Biographical and Political Functions for a Nineteenth-Century Myth,* Garland Publishing, 1981. Also author of *War, Revolution and Peace: Posters From the Hoover Institution Archives* (exhibition catalog).

Author of "Seachanges" (dance film), Film Institute, City College of the City University of New York, 1965. Contributor to art journals.

WORK IN PROGRESS: Moments of Pleasure, the "autobiography of a long friendship between two women who like men, including conversations, letters, and narratives," with Josephine Stuart; *The Women of Impressionism,* "an account of how Mary Cassatt, Berthe Morisot, and Marie Bracquemond joined the movement, what their relationships were with its men, and how it affected their lives as painters and as women."

SIDELIGHTS: Paula Harper wrote: "I'm interested in posters, prints, and paintings that have political content, ranging from subtle to blatant. This aspect of visual imagery benefits from verbal explication. By analyzing and demonstrating how propaganda works in overtly political posters and commercial advertising, for example, one can possibly immunize people against visual manipulation. Detecting subtle political content is more difficult and requires experience of images and knowledge of the historical context. But a great deal of art wants to persuade you that something is true by showing you a picture of it.

"I am firmly committed to the hope that humane scholarship and good writing can make the ideas and events of art history accessible to a broad audience. We all need art, although some of us don't know it yet."

AVOCATIONAL INTERESTS: Singing and dancing, telling jokes, horseback riding on the beach, "sitting on sunny terraces, sipping good wine, and talking about art."

* * *

HARRELL, Sara (Jeanne) Gordon   1940-

PERSONAL: Born November 7, 1940, in Tuscaloosa, Ala.; daughter of Preston Brooks Harrell (a purchasing agent) and Anne (Frierson) Harrell Cooper; married Caleb Burch Banks (employed with New Orleans Steamship Association), 1964; children: Mark Gordon. *Education:* Attended Georgia Southern College, 1955, University of North Carolina at Chapel Hill, 1966, University of Georgia, 1972, Emory University, 1973. *Politics:* Democrat ("rabid"). *Residence:* Savannah, Ga.

CAREER: Free-lance writer. Has been employed with newspapers and as a secretary. *Member:* Authors Guild, Greenpeace USA. *Awards, honors:* Best in Poetry and Best Short Story awards from Georgia Writer's Association, 1973, for "The Dolphin" (poetry) and "The Colors of Hyacinths" (short story).

WRITINGS—All for young readers: *Semo: A Dolphin's Search for Christ,* illustrations by Jim Cummins, Concordia, 1977; *Tomo-chi-chi,* Dillon, 1977; *Cottage by the Sea,* illustrations by Gordon Willman, Concordia, 1978; *John Ross,* Dillon, 1979; *Willowcat and the Chimney Sweep,* illustrations by Bill Drath, Peachtree Publications, 1980; *Grove of Night,* Avon, 1981. Contributor of poems to *Sahara* and *Dekalb Literary Journal;* contributor of articles to *The Marion, Environmental Quality Magazine,* and *Georgia Conservancy Magazine.*

WORK IN PROGRESS: Annie Rising Fawn; Raven Mocker; Mulberry Silk; another mystery novel; a children's picture book.

SIDELIGHTS: An interest in dolphins started Sara Banks on her writing career. "I am superstitious about dolphins," she told *CA.* "They have always brought me luck. My first poem was about dolphins. My first magazine article was about dolphins, and my first children's book was about dolphins.

"I have always wanted to write but didn't take myself seriously until I was older. I returned to school and began creative writing classes. I became interested and involved in the passage of the Marine Mammal Protection Act and in so doing wrote my first article for publication and my first science articles. From there I went into serious research and wrote my first children's book, *Semo.*"

Another interest important to Banks's writing is the Southeastern American Indian. "I was raised in Savannah," she said, "and stories about Tomo-chi-chi and other Creek Indians were a part of my life."

* * *

HARRIS, Charlaine   1951-

PERSONAL: Born November 25, 1951, in Tunica, Mississippi; daughter of Robert Ashley (a principal) and Jean (a librarian; maiden name, Balentine) Harris; married Hal Schulz (a chemical engineer), August 5, 1978. *Education:* Southwestern at Memphis, B.A., 1973. *Home:* 1185 Sheppard Rd., N.E., Orangeburg, S.C. 29115.

CAREER: Bolivar Commercial, Cleveland, Miss., offset darkroom operator, 1973-74; Clarksdale Press Register, Clarksdale, Miss., typesetter, 1974-76; Delta Design Group, Greenville, Miss., typesetter, 1975-77; Federal Express Corp., Memphis, Tenn., typesetter, 1977-78; writer. *Member:* Mystery Writers of America, Mensa.

WRITINGS: Sweet and Deadly (novel), Houghton, 1980.

WORK IN PROGRESS: Prepared for Rage (tentative title), a novel about rape.

SIDELIGHTS: Harris's novel *Sweet and Deadly* concerns the efforts of a journalist to solve the murder of her parents in a small Southern town. "In this small, self-contained world, everyone seems to know everything about the neighbors," declared a *Washington Post* reviewer. The critic also praised Harris's handling of racial issues and summed up *Sweet and Deadly* as "more than a well-plotted mystery."

Harris told *CA:* "I have always identified myself as a writer internally, though the evidence didn't appear until last year. I have never wanted to do anything else in my life. I have written at least since I was nine years old. The necessity of earning a bare living kept me from writing full time until I was twenty-seven, which was probably a very good thing. I read about eight books per week, both in and out of my genre.

"I chose to write in the mystery genre because I have always enjoyed mysteries myself. It is a multi-level genre, providing not only an intellectual puzzle, but also a study of life and death, however lightly treated. The mystery is also one of the few truly American art forms."

AVOCATIONAL INTERESTS: Animals, gardening, cooking, unsolved murder cases.

BIOGRAPHICAL/CRITICAL SOURCES: Washington Post Book World, July 19, 1981.

* * *

HARRIS, Jana   1947-

PERSONAL: Born September 21, 1947, in San Francisco, Calif.; daughter of Richard H. (a meat packer) and Cicely Ann (Herman) Harris; married Mark Allen Bothwell (a biochemist), August 19, 1977. *Education:* University of Oregon, Eugene, B.S. (with honors), 1969; San Francisco State University, M.A., 1972. *Address:* P.O. Box 331, Route Two, Ringoes, N.J. 08551. *Agent:* Charlotte Sheedy Literary Agency, 145 West 86th St., New York, N.Y. 10024. *Office:* Manhattan Theatre Club, 321 East 73rd St., New York, N.Y. 10021.

CAREER: San Francisco State University, San Francisco, Calif., instructor in poetry in the schools, 1972-78; Modesto Junior College, Modesto, Calif., instructor in creative writing, 1975-78; City University of New York, New York City, instructor in creative writing, 1980—; Manhattan Theatre Club, New York City, acting director for writers-in-performance series, 1980—. Co-coordinator of women-in-poetry program for Intersection, Inc., 1972-73; coordinator for Cody's Books "Poetry Reading" series, 1975-78; poet-in-residence for Alameda County Neighborhood Arts program, 1977-78. Co-producer of "Planet on the Table," a literary program broadcast on KPFA-Radio, 1975-78, and "The Unheard of Hour," a literary interview program broadcast on KSAN-Radio, 1977. Educational mathematics consultant for Project SEED, Inc., at Lawrence Hall of Science at the University of California, Berkeley, 1970-

76. *Member:* Poets and Writers, Inc., Associated Writing Programs, Feminist Writers' Guild, Poets and Writers of New Jersey, Pi Mu Epsilon. *Awards, honors:* Berkeley Civic Arts Commission grant, 1974; New Jersey State Council on the Arts poetry fellowship, 1981.

WRITINGS: *Alaska* (fiction; Book-of-the-Month Club, English-Speaking Union, and Books-Across-the-Sea Program selection), Harper, 1980.

Poetry: *This House That Rocks With Every Truck on the Road,* Jungle Garden, 1976; *Pin Money,* Jungle Garden, 1977; *The Clackamas,* The Smith, 1980; *Who's That Pushy Bitch?,* Jungle Garden, 1981; *Manhattan as a Second Language,* Harper, 1982. Also author of *Running Scared: Early Poems,* Spring Valley.

Contributor: Susan Efros, editor, *This Is Women's Work,* Panjandrum, 1974; Noni Noward, editor, *Anthology of the First Annual Women's Poetry Festival of San Francisco,* New World Press, 1977; John Oliver Simon, editor, *City of Buds and Flowers: A Poet's Eye View of Berkeley,* Aldebaran Review, 1977; A. D. Winans, editor, *Nineteen Plus One: An Anthology of San Francisco Poetry,* Second Coming Press, 1978; Ishmael Reed, editor, *Calafia: The California Poetry,* Yardbird Publishing, 1979; Carol Simone, editor, *Networks: An Anthology of Women Poets,* Vortex, 1979; Barry Wallenstein, editor, *Anthology of the City College of New York Poetry Festival,* City College of the City University of New York, 1979.

Contributor of numerous poems, essays, short stories, and articles to periodicals, including *Nation, Poetry Flash, Ms., Fiction West, Berkeley Poetry Review,* and *New Women's Times Feminist Review.* Associate editor and co-founder, *Poetry Flash,* 1972-78; guest editor, *Libera,* 1973; co-editor, *Feminist Writer's Guild National Newsletter,* 1978.

WORK IN PROGRESS: *The 79ers,* a series of three novels about the 1980's, including *Gold, The Apostates,* and *Night Classes; The Sourlands,* a book of poems about the 1980's.

SIDELIGHTS: Harris, a prolific writer whose works have been published in more than forty periodicals, has made numerous appearances on radio and television programs and has given readings, lectures, and performances throughout the country. She also appeared in the 1978 motion picture "Festival of the Bards."

Harris's first novel, *Alaska,* is based on a collection of first-person interviews she obtained from longtime Alaska residents while she hitchhiked through the state in 1971. The book is a history of Alaska from 1867 to the present told from the perspective of succeeding generations of its women characters. *Best Sellers* critic Lucille Crane pronounced the novel "a fine study of a little known subject and uniquely organized to tell a wonderful story."

Harris told *CA:* "I write to document my own reality. I sit at a desk eight to twelve hours a day writing. Because writing is often an isolating experience and an arduous task, I have several desks in different cities: Ringoes, N.J., New York City, and Berkeley, Calif. I find that changing my surroundings often changes the light on my subjects. When the area around one desk gets too dirty, I move to another desk, hoping that someone will clean up in my absence. I have never been afflicted with writer's block; I think that writer's block is a male affliction. I have never not been able to write. I have, however, been afraid; afraid that everything I write will be bad, afraid that I'll keep writing the same boring story or poem over and over, and afraid that some critic will call my characters trite."

BIOGRAPHICAL/CRITICAL SOURCES: *Booklist,* October 15, 1977; *Best Sellers,* January, 1981.

**HARRIS, Lavinia
See JOHNSTON, Norma**

*   *   *

HARRIS, Madalene   1925-

PERSONAL: Born October 6, 1925, in Oregon; daughter of Arnold E. (an engineer) and Madalene M. (Anderson) Krafft; married Harlan L. Harris (a minister and evangelist), June 7, 1946; children: Lenee Harris Schroeder, Harlan L., Jr., Christine Harris Pinello, David. *Education:* Attended Wheaton College, Wheaton, Ill., 1943-45, and University of Colorado, 1968-69. *Politics:* Republican. *Religion:* Southern Baptist. *Home and office:* 810 Crystal Park Rd., Manitou Springs, Colo. 80829.

CAREER: Writer. Guest on television programs.

WRITINGS: (With Mary Irwin) *The Moon Is Not Enough* (autobiography of Irwin), Zondervan, 1978; (with Nicky Cruz) *Lonely, But Never Alone* (nonfiction), Zondervan, 1981. Contributing editor of *Apogee,* newsletter of High Flight Foundation.

WORK IN PROGRESS: A book on overcoming ineffectiveness in one's personal life; a biography of a European evangelist.

SIDELIGHTS: Madalene Harris told *CA:* "My goal since my high school days has been to write. Long postponement of this desire was necessary in my busy life as a minister's wife and mother of four children. When finally the opportunity came, in a totally different fashion than I had anticipated or planned, I seized the occasion and have made writing the focus of my life.

"I do not write for entertainment. Instead, I try to leave my reader with the motivation and tools for living a richer, more fulfilled life on this earth. I would say that personal discipline is the chief ingredient of a writer's ability to produce. I don't wait for inspiration or spare time. I pray for both, but meanwhile I get my body to the machine and write whether I feel like it or not."

BIOGRAPHICAL/CRITICAL SOURCES: *Ladies' Home Journal,* December, 1979.

*   *   *

HARTLEY, Dorothy   1893-

PERSONAL: Born in October, 1893, in Skipton in Cravens, England; daughter of Edward Thompson (a headmaster) and Amy (Eddy) Hartley. *Education:* Attended secondary school in Loughborough, Leicestershire, England. *Politics:* None. *Religion:* Church of England. *Home:* Fron House, Froncysyllte, near Llangollen, Clwyd, North Wales.

CAREER: Art teacher and writer, 1911—. *Member:* Society of Authors.

WRITINGS: *Life and Work of the People of England,* Batsford, 1925; (editor) *Thomas Tusser,* Country Life Books, 1931; *The Countryman's England,* Batsford, 1935, reprinted, Jill Norman, 1980; *Made in England,* Methuen, 1939; *Irish Holiday,* Lindsay Drummond, 1939; *Food in England,* MacDonald & Co., 1954; *Water in England,* MacDonald & Co., new edition, Macdonald & Jane's, 1978; *Lost Country Life,* Pantheon, 1980. Contributor to magazines and newspapers, including *Harper's* and *The Guardian.*

WORK IN PROGRESS: A cookbook.

SIDELIGHTS: Hartley told *CA:* "Two recent reviews catch much of what I hope readers find in my writings. Of the seventh edition of *Food in England,* the *London Sunday Times* said: 'For food scholarship at its best see Dorothy Hartley's robust, idiosyncratic, irresistable Food in England. . . . As packed with diverse and fascinating information as a Scotch bun with fruit, this untidy bundle of erudition is held together by the writer's huge enjoyment of her subject, her immense curiosity about everything to do with the growth, preparation, preservation and eating of food in this country since the Middle Ages.' And on my last book, published in the United States with the title *Lost Country Life,* a reviewer on the *New Yorker* commented: '[Her] prose is lucid, demure and unemphatic. Her wit is dry and subtle. She never nudges or buttonholes the reader, but trusts to her material which is almost bewilderingly rich. . . . She does not suggest that these were the good old days, or that mediaeval society was better than ours is. Instead, she modestly and accurately explains the ingenuity—the genius—that the humblest human beings have applied to survival.'"

BIOGRAPHICAL/CRITICAL SOURCES: London Sunday Times, December 9, 1979; *New Yorker,* July 28, 1980.

*   *   *

HARTMAN, Jane E(vangeline) 1928-

PERSONAL: Born February 17, 1928, in Long Branch, N.J.; daughter of Frank Cecil (in sales) and Edna (in politics; maiden name, Salisbury) Hartman. *Education:* Attended University of Wisconsin (now University of Wisconsin—Madison), 1945-47; New York University, B.S., 1949; California State University, Los Angeles, M.A., 1957; Brantridge Forest School, Sussex, England, N.D., 1979. *Residence:* Medomak, Me. *Agent:* Sallie Gouveneur, N. Sobel Associates, 128 West 56th St., New York, N.Y. 10022.

CAREER: Winthrop College, Rock Hill, S.C., instructor in health education, 1951-52; worked at YWCA in Plainfield, N.J., 1952-54; Polytechnic School, Pasadena, Calif., director of physical education, 1954-57; Glendale College, Glendale, Calif., instructor in physical education, 1957-58; Pine Manor Junior College, Brookline, Mass., member of health education faculty, chairman of department, and tennis coach, 1959-61; Maryland State College, Towson, assistant professor of health education, 1961-62; Pine Manor Junior College, member of health education faculty, chairman of department, and tennis coach, 1962-71; writer, 1971—. *Member:* Spiritual Frontiers Fellowship, Weimaraner Club of America. *Awards, honors:* Children's Book Council of National Science Teachers Association named as outstanding science books for children *Living Together in Nature,* 1977, *Looking at Lizards,* 1977, *Animals That Live in Groups,* 1978, and *How Animals Care for Their Young,* 1980.

*WRITINGS—*For young adults: *The Original Americans,* J. Weston Walch, 1974; *The Consumer and the Environment,* J. Weston Walch, 1975; *Things About American Indians* (facsimile materials), J. Weston Walch, 1975; *One Hundred Photographs With Text About American Indians* (textbook), J. Weston Walch, 1975; *Living Together in Nature,* Holiday House, 1977; *Looking at Lizards,* Holiday House, 1977; *Animals That Live in Groups,* Holiday House, 1978; *Armadillos, Anteaters, and Sloths,* Holiday House, 1979; *How Animals Care for Their Young,* Holiday House, 1980.

Contributor of more than twenty articles and reviews to magazines, including *Survival, Arizona, National Wildlife, Spiritual Frontiers, Chevron USA, Defenders, American West,* and *Horses, of Course.*

WORK IN PROGRESS: Research on psychic phenomena and holistic health, "particularly where they are related and relative to human well-being."

SIDELIGHTS: Jane Hartman commented: "I am very excited about the possibilities of my current research, as well as my recent studies in homeopathy and radiesthesia, which is the science of the pendulum. This technique is used by many practitioners in Europe and often gives remarkable results. We seem to be teetering on the brink of a revolution in consciousness and in the application of new expanded approaches to timeworn things like conventional medicine. It always amazes me that we are so hesitant about these things in this country, the AMA notwithstanding. Perhaps we are afraid of the 'unknown,' although more likely certain power groups prefer to keep their 'cushy' positions.

"In my own work, I am presently interested in study and research. This may take me abroad in the near future where the psychic approach to healing is openly allowed and encouraged. Hopefully, all this will lead to a publication for adults. I feel I have done enough in the children's line for the time being."

*   *   *

HARTMANN, Helmut Henry 1931-
(Henry Seymour)

PERSONAL: Born September 14, 1931, in Stuttgart, Germany (now West Germany); son of Henry August and Sophie (Porzelt) Hartmann; married Sheila Yvonne Furneaux, December 23, 1955; children: Jeanette Hartmann Ong, Lester. *Education:* Attended school in Munich, Germany. *Religion:* Roman Catholic. *Home:* Godwins, Stalisfield Green, Faversham, Kent ME13 0HY, England. *Agent:* Mark Paterson, Mark Paterson & Associates, 11 and 12 West Stockwell St., Colchester CO1 1HN, England.

CAREER: London Star, London, England, staff member, 1948-50; National Coal Board, Dover, England, budget officer, 1952-58; writer, 1958—. *Military service:* British Army, Royal Medical Corps, 1950-52. *Member:* Crime Writers Association.

*WRITINGS—*Under pseudonym Henry Seymour; novels; published by Gifford, except as noted: *Intrigue in Tangier,* 1958; *Run for Your Money,* 1959; *The Bristol Affair,* 1960; *The Paperchase Murder,* 1961; *Appointment With Murder,* 1962; *Hot Ice,* 1966; *In the Still of the Night,* 1966; *Infernal Idol,* 1967; *The Big Steal,* R. Hale, 1972; *Cold Wind of Death,* R. Hale, 1972.

Author of nearly four hundred books in German, including thrillers, romances, and westerns. Author of numerous books for children, including *Inspektor Dixon und die Tower-Hill-Detektive* (series), Tosa-Verlag; *Alles fuer Bianca,* Weichert; *Harald's geheimnisvolles Abenteuer,* Hirundo; *Was Peter erlebte,* Hirundo; *Drei Herzen fuer Lissy;* and *Armer kleiner Zeitungsboy.*

SIDELIGHTS: Hartmann wrote: "From the age of nineteen, with the publication of my first detective novel, I desired to become a professional writer. I achieved this in 1958 after writing in my spare time in both English and German. Since then, more than four hundred titles of mine have been published in both languages, but mainly in German. My advice to would-be writers is stick to your aim, listen to qualified critics, and write without waiting for inspiration."

HARVEY, Frank 1912-1981

OBITUARY NOTICE: Born August 11, 1912, in Manchester, England; died November 6, 1981, in Ottery St. Mary, Devonshire, England. Actor, playwright, and screenwriter. Harvey achieved success as a dramatist with "Saloon Bar," which had a long run on the West End in 1939. He wrote a number of other successful plays, including an adaptation of Graham Greene's novel *Brighton Rock,* as well as such screenplays as the Oscar-winning "Seven Days to Noon" and "I'm All Right, Jack." Obituaries and other sources: *The Author's and Writer's Who's Who,* 6th edition, Burke's Peerage, 1971; *Who's Who in the Theatre: A Biographical Record of the Contemporary Stage,* 16th edition, Pitman, 1977; *London Times,* November 14, 1981.

*   *   *

HARWIT, Martin Otto 1931-

PERSONAL: Born March 9, 1931, in Prague, Czechoslovakia; came to the United States in 1946, naturalized citizen, 1953; son of Felix Michael (a biochemist) and Regina Hedwig (Perutz) Haurowitz; married Marianne Mark, February 1, 1957; children: Alex, Eric, Emily. *Education:* Oberlin College, B.A., 1951; University of Michigan, M.A., 1953; Massachusetts Institute of Technology, Ph.D., 1960. *Home:* 1105 Taughannock Blvd., Ithaca, N.Y. 14850. *Office:* Department of Astronomy, Cornell University, Space Science Building, Ithaca, N.Y. 14853.

CAREER: University of Michigan, Ann Arbor, physicist, 1954-55; Cornell University, Ithaca, N.Y., assistant professor, 1962-64, associate professor, 1964-68, professor of astronomy, 1968—, chairman of department, 1971-76, acting dean of College of Arts and Sciences, spring, 1976. Vice-president and member of board of directors of Spectral Imaging, Inc., 1971-77. E. O. Hulbert fellow at Naval Research Laboratory and visiting research associate at E. O. Hulbert Space Center, 1963-64; National Academy of Sciences exchange visitor at Czechoslovak Academy of Science, 1969-70; external member of Max Planck Institute for Radioastronomy, 1979—; consultant to National Aeronautics and Space Administration. *Military service:* U.S. Army, 1955-57.

MEMBER: American Astronomical Society, American Physical Society, American Association for the Advancement of Science, Royal Astronomical Society. *Awards, honors:* Fellow of North Atlantic Treaty Organization at Cambridge University, 1960-61; National Science Foundation fellow, 1961-62, grant, 1963-68; grants from National Aeronautics and Space Administration, 1965—, Air Force Cambridge Research Laboratories, 1969—, and Research Corp., 1970-75; senior U.S. scientist award from Alexander von Humboldt Foundation for Max Planck Institute for Radioastronomy, 1976-77.

WRITINGS: Astrophysical Concepts, Wiley, 1973; (with Neil J.A. Sloane) *Hadamard Transform Optics,* Academic Press, 1979; *Cosmic Discovery,* Basic Books, 1981. Contributor of more than a hundred articles to scientific journals.

*   *   *

HASKELL, Edward Froehlich 1906-

BRIEF ENTRY: Born August 24, 1906, in Plevdiv, Bulgaria. Educator and author. Haskell was an instructor at Columbia University's Teachers College until 1975. He has been chairman of the Council for Unified Research in Education since 1948. His writings include *Lance: A Novel About Multicultural*

Men (John Day, 1941), *Plain Truth and Redirection of the Cold War* (1961), *Full Circle: The Moral Force of Unified Science* (Gordon & Breach, 1972), and *Coping With Increasing Complexity: Implications of General Semantics and General Systems Theory* (Gordon & Breach, 1974). *Address:* 509 West 121st St., New York, N.Y. 10027; and Council for Unified Research in Education, 617 West 113th St., New York, N.Y. 10025. *Biographical/critical sources: Who's Who in the East,* 17th edition, Marquis, 1979.

*   *   *

HASTON, Dougal 1940-1977

OBITUARY NOTICE: Born in 1940 in London, England; killed in an avalanche, January 17, 1977, in Leysin, Switzerland. Mountaineering teacher and author of books on mountaineering, including *In High Places* and *Eiger Direct.* Obituaries and other sources: *The Writers Directory, 1976-78,* St. Martin's, 1976. (Date of death provided by Peter D. Boardman, director of the International School of Mountaineering.)

*   *   *

HAUGHTON-JAMES, Jean Rosemary 1924-1981

OBITUARY NOTICE: Born in 1924 in Islington, London, England; died November 1, 1981. Editor and author. As the wife of a Czech diplomat who was imprisoned by his government during the 1950's, Haughton-James became involved with the Czechoslovakian dissident movement. During the liberalization of the 1960's she became editor of the English-language magazine *Czechoslovak Life,* transforming it from a propaganda organ to a forum for intellectual discussion. After the Soviet invasion of 1968, she lost her job and in 1971 she fled to England to avoid arrest. She continued to translate and publish the writings of Czech dissidents and also wrote a novel and an autobiography, *The Price of Freedom.* Obituaries and other sources: *London Times,* November 6, 1981.

*   *   *

HAVIARAS, Stratis
See CHAVIARAS, Strates

*   *   *

HAWKES, (Charles Francis) Christopher 1905-

BRIEF ENTRY: Born June 5, 1905, in London, England. British archaeologist and author. Until 1946 Hawkes worked at the British Museum, where he was in charge of prehistoric and Romano-British antiquities. He was a professor of European archaeology at Oxford University from 1946 to 1972, and has been professor emeritus and honorary fellow of Keble College since 1972. His books include *Greeks, Celts, and Roman: Studies in Venture and Resistance* (Rowman & Littlefield, 1973), *Archaeology Into History* (Dent, 1973), *Celtic Art in Ancient Europe* (Seminar Press, 1976), and *Pytheas: Europe and the Greek Explorers* (Basil Blackwell, 1977). *Address:* Keble College, Oxford University, 19 Walton St., Oxford, England.

*   *   *

HAWKINS, Frances P(ockman) 1913-

PERSONAL: Born May 6, 1913, in San Francisco, Calif.; daughter of Leonard Thomas and Julie (Mehrtens) Pockman; married David Hawkins, 1937; children: Julie Hawkins Fisher. *Education:* Stanford University, B.A., 1935; San Francisco

State University, Kindergarten-Primary Certificate, 1936; graduate study at University of California, 1939. *Office:* Mountain View Center for Environmental Education, University of Colorado, Campus Box 328, Boulder, Colo. 80309.

CAREER: Teacher at public schools in San Francisco, Calif., 1936-41; director of nursery school in Los Alamos, N.M., 1943-44; Los Alamos Scientific Laboratory, Los Alamos, bookbinder, 1944-45; worked as substitute teacher, 1945-53; teacher at and director of private nursery schools in Boulder, Colo., 1953-57; writer, 1957-62; Education Development Center, Newton, Mass., consultant to elementary science study, 1962-64, and to president's scientific advisory committee, 1962-63; University of Colorado, Boulder, associated with Science Advisory Center, 1965-68, co-director of Mountain View Center for Environmental Education, 1970-74, consultant, 1974-79, consultant and giver of workshops for Child Language Center, 1979—. Teacher and director of kindergarten in Boston, Mass., 1963. Lecturer at Hungarian Academy of Science, 1977; public speaker; observer and advisor in English primary schools; consultant to African Primary Science Program (Nigeria and Uganda).

WRITINGS: The Logic of Action: From a Teacher's Notebook, Mountain View Center for Environmental Education, University of Colorado, 1969, 2nd edition, Pantheon, 1974; (contributor) Samuel Meisels, editor, *Open Education and Young Children With Special Needs,* University Park Press, 1979. Co-author of "Northumberland Children," a film released by Thorne Films, Inc., 1971. Contributor of articles and reviews to periodicals, including *Urban Review, Harvard Educational Review,* and *Outlook.*

WORK IN PROGRESS: A professional autobiography, covering the years from 1933 through 1965.

SIDELIGHTS: Hawkins told *CA:* "I am a lifelong student of early learning and an occasional teacher; writing itself has come late in my life and is secondary. To speak briefly about the central concern of my life—early learning—is almost impossible. I have worked in the tradition of, and I hope have added my own insights to, people like John Dewey, Frederick Allen, Anna Freud, and Sibylle Escalona.

"Another continuing interest has been in American Indians. Within the last decade this has focused on fabrics used in their everyday lives and in ceremonies. I am finishing a second Hopi wedding or rain belt, braided in the traditional way that has remained unchanged for close to two thousand years. Hopi men are the traditional weavers, so I am an interloper, if a reverent one.

"Reading fiction remains a delight, as does my preference for a few—Henry James and Virginia Woolf in the past, Graham Greene in the present, to name three favorites."

*   *   *

HAWORTH, Mary
See YOUNG, Mary Elizabeth Reardon

*   *   *

HAY, Dennis   1952-

PERSONAL: Born January 7, 1952, in Liverpool, England; son of Alan White (a bank clerk) and Brenda (Klapka) Hay. *Education:* University of Nottingham, B.A. (with honors), 1973. *Agent:* A. D. Peters & Co. Ltd., 10 Buckingham St., London SC2N 6BU, England.

CAREER: University of Reading, Reading, England, research officer in geography, 1975-79, writer, 1979—. Research assistant at International Institute for Applied Systems Analysis, Laxenburg, Austria, summer, 1977. Member of Anglo-Scottish expedition to Lobouje Peak in the eastern Himalayas, Nepal, 1979-80; leader of British expedition to Kwangde Ri, eastern Himalayas, 1981.

WRITINGS: (With Peter Hall) *Growth Centers in the European Urban System,* University of California Press, 1980.

WORK IN PROGRESS: A contributing article to *Urbanization Processes: Experiences of Western and Eastern Countries,* edited by Tatsuhiko Kawashima.

SIDELIGHTS: Hay's research interests include the urban/spatial structure of Western Europe, the achievement of a standard statistical framework for comparative socio-economic/demographic analysis within Western Europe, and the implications for recreation resources of continuing urban growth.

Hay told *CA:* "As a geographer, I am mainly interested in travel, and after two expeditions to Nepal, the emphasis of my interest has shifted towards Third World geographical studies. Unfortunately few employers in the industrialized regions care enough about these areas to help solve the enormous problems to be found there. Britain is now learning that immediate maximization of profits has been its own downfall—had reinvestment and research been the order of the day, then I, and three million others in Britain, might now be gainfully employed and contributing to the economy. I hope the Third World takes note."

*   *   *

HAYES, Mary Anne   1956-

PERSONAL: Born September 4, 1956; daughter of Joseph P. (an accountant) and Frances (a teacher; maiden name, Gregory) Calabria; married James Hayes (a publisher); children: James, Tracy. *Education:* Attended Brookdale Community College. *Office: Dollars Daily,* P.O. Box 348, Lakehurst, N.J. 08733.

CAREER: Editor of *Dollars Daily* (monthly newspaper), Lakehurst, N.J.

WRITINGS: Ask the Coupon Queen: How to Buy Seventy-one Dollars and Seventy-one Cents Worth of Groceries for Seven Dollars and Nineteen Cents, Simon & Schuster, 1979.

WORK IN PROGRESS: Coupon information.

SIDELIGHTS: Hayes told *CA:* "I became known after the Columbia Broadcasting Co. (CBS) news telecast a supermarket shopping trip at which I purchased seventy-one dollars of groceries for seven dollars. I was named the 'Coupon Queen' after repeating my shopping expertise on Walter Cronkite's national news show.

"I am editor of *Dollars Daily,* a newspaper with a circulation of fifty thousand subscribers. In the paper I share my refunding and coupon information, which shows readers how to cash in on two hundred or more refunds each month and over three thousand annually. The publication also gives specific information on how to receive cash, coupons, and free gifts for grocery products of all national brands."

*   *   *

HAYS, (Lawrence) Brooks   1898-1981

OBITUARY NOTICE—See index for *CA* sketch: Born August 9, 1898, in London, Ark.; died of a stroke, October 11, 1981, in Chevy Chase, Md. Attorney, politician, administrator, educator, and author. As one of Arkansas's Democratic representatives in Congress for sixteen years, Hays was noted for his moderate stance on volatile racial issues. In 1957 he was instrumental in the attempt to alleviate the school desegregation crisis in Little Rock, Arkansas. When Arkansas governor Orval Faubus refused to order school busing, Hays engineered a meeting between the governor and President Eisenhower. Hays later commented that he "felt like the sparrow that flew into the badminton game." His role as mediator in the conflict cost him his Congressional seat the following year when segregationists successfully launched a write-in vote for the candidate of their choice. Hays went on to become a director of the Tennessee Valley Authority (TVA) and a special assistant to Presidents Kennedy and Johnson. The politician also taught at Rutgers University and the University of Massachusetts. Hays began his career as a lawyer and assistant attorney general in his native state before joining the U.S. Department of Agriculture in 1935. He left the governmental department when he was elected to the House in 1942. Hays wrote several books, including *This World: A Christian's Workshop, Hotbed of Tranquility: My Life in Five Worlds,* and *Politics Is My Parish.* Obituaries and other sources: *New York Times,* October 13, 1981; *Newsweek,* October 26, 1981; *Time,* October 26, 1981.

*   *   *

HAYS, H(offman) R(eynolds)   1904-1980

OBITUARY NOTICE—See index for *CA* sketch: Born March 25, 1904, in New York, N.Y.; died of a heart attack, October 10, 1980, in Southampton, N.Y. Educator, poet, playwright, translator, anthropologist, critic, and author. Hays was best known for his translations of Latin American poets such as Pablo Neruda and Cesar Vallejo, and especially for his highly praised anthology *Twelve Spanish American Poets.* He also translated poems and plays by Bertholt Brecht and poems by Juan Ramon Jimenez. Hays's own writing embraced many genres: poetry, fiction, criticism, popular anthropology, and drama, including his best-known play, "The Ballad of Davy Crockett," for which Kurt Weill wrote the music. Hays's artistic attitudes were formed in the socially conscious literary milieu of New York in the Depression, and though his work was not harshly polemical it was informed by a deep concern for social justice. His novel *The Envoys* was sympathetic toward revolutionary movements in Peru and critical of U.S. foreign policy in Latin America; *The Dangerous Sex,* an anthropological and literary study of attitudes toward women, drew praise from feminists in the 1960's. Hays's verse, which developed out of the imagism of William Carlos Williams and Ezra Pound, remains largely uncollected, though four volumes of poems have been published. Hays also wrote several scripts for television in the early years of that medium. In addition, the author taught English at several schools, including University of Minnesota, Wagner College, Fairleigh Dickinson University, and Southampton College. Obituaries and other sources: *New York Times,* October 18, 1980; *The Annual Obituary 1980,* St. Martin's, 1981.

*   *   *

HAYWOOD, Dixie   1933-

PERSONAL: Born May 6, 1933, in Seattle, Wash.; daughter of Lewis Norman (a trucking manager) and Rosalie (Revie) Hamer; married Robert Clarence Haywood (a meteorologist), June 14, 1952; children: Brent Dennis, Todd Robert, Dana Claire. *Education:* Attended Florida State University, 1960-

63, and University of Puget Sound, 1963-64. *Home and office:* 3536 Overholser Dr., Bethany, Okla. 73008.

CAREER: Free-lance teacher of quiltmaking in Tacoma, Wash., 1974-75, Lancaster, Calif., 1975-78, and Oklahoma City, Okla., 1978—. Director of handicapped swimming program in Tacoma, 1970-73. *Member:* International Guild of Craft Journalists, Authors, and Photographers, North American Quilt Guild, National Quilt Association, Oklahoma Designer Craftsmen.

WRITINGS: The Contemporary Crazy Quilt Project Book, Crown, 1977; *Crazy Quilting With a Difference,* Scissortail Publications, 1981. Contributor to *Quiltmaking Teacher's Workbook.*

SIDELIGHTS: Dixie Haywood commented: "Scissortail Publications is a small company I have started in order to publish books in the fabric arts. I hope to add at least one title a year by other craftsmen.

"Both of my books are the result of my own work as a quilt craftsman, designer, and teacher, so my childhood desire to be a writer came from the other interest I have had since childhood—working with fabric."

BIOGRAPHICAL/CRITICAL SOURCES: Quilt, spring, 1980; *Quilt Almanac,* 1981.

*   *   *

HAZEN, Barbara Shook   1930-

PERSONAL: Born February 4, 1930, in Dayton, Ohio; daughter of Charles Harmon (a contractor and engineer) and Elizabeth (Foster) Shook; married Freeman Brackett Hazen, December 27, 1956 (divorced, 1960); children: Freeman Brackett, Jr. *Education:* Smith College, B.A., 1951; Columbia University, M.A., 1952. *Politics:* "Varying." *Religion:* "Presbyterian and/ or eclectic." *Home and office:* 108 East 82nd St., New York, N.Y. 10028; and Otis, Mass. 01253 (summer).

CAREER: Ladies' Home Journal, New York City, editorial assistant in fiction/article department and poetry editor, 1952-56; Western Publishing Co., New York City, children's book editor, 1956-60; free-lance writer, 1960—. Board member of Drama League of City of New York, 1976—. Consultant to Columbia Broadcasting System (CBS) children's records, 1968-74, and *Sesame Street* (magazine), 1973-75. *Member:* American Society of Journalists and Authors, Authors Guild, Bank Street Writers Lab.

WRITINGS: You and Your Lucky Stars: A Zodiac Guide to Dating, Compatibility, and Personal Characteristics, Golden Press, 1970; (with others) *Baby's First Six Years,* Golden Press, 1972; *Your Wedding Your Way,* Western, 1973; *The Dell Encyclopedia of Cats* (illustrated by Roy Wiltshire and Paul Singer), Delacorte, 1974, also published as *The Concise Encyclopedia of Cats,* Octopus Books, 1974; (editor) *Mothers Are Marvelous,* C. R. Gibson, 1977; (editor) *To Be a Friend,* C. R. Gibson, 1977; (editor) *A Cat Lover's Cat Book: The Many Delights of Kittens and Cats* (illustrated by Roland Rodegast), C. R. Gibson, 1978; (editor) *You Can't Have Sunbeams Without Little Specks of Dust: Household Hints, Quotes, and Humorous Anecdotes,* C. R. Gibson, 1980; *Have Yourself a Merry Little Christmas: Hints and Homilies for Happy Holidays,* C. R. Gibson, 1980; *Pets, Pets: Hints, Tips, and Fascinating Facts,* C. R. Gibson, 1980.

Juveniles: *Animal Alphabet from A to Z* (illustrated by Adele Werber), Golden Press, 1958, reprinted, 1976; *Rudolph, the Red-Nosed Reindeer* (adapted from the story by Robert L. May;

illustrated by Richard Scarry), Golden Press, 1958; *Mister Ed, the Talking Horse,* Western, 1958; *The Lion's Nap,* Western, 1958; *Animal Daddies and My Daddy,* Western, 1962; *A Visit to the Children's Zoo* (illustrated by Mel Crawford), Golden Press, 1963; *Playful Puppy* (illustrated by Jan Pfloog), Golden Press, 1967; *Please Pass the P's and Q's: The Barbara Hazen Book of Manners* (illustrated by Mell Lazarus), World Publishing, 1967; *Please Protect the Porcupine: The Barbara Hazen Book of Conservation* (illustrated by Lazarus), World Publishing, 1967; *David and Goliath* (illustrated by Robert J. Lee), Golden Press, 1968; *Ookpik in the City* (illustrated by Irma Wilde), Golden Press, 1968; *What's Inside?* (illustrated by Richard Erdoes), Lion Press, 1968; *City Cats, Country Cats* (illustrated by Ilse-Margret Vogel), Golden Press, 1969; *The Sorcerer's Apprentice* (illustrated by Tomi Ungerer), Lancelot Press, 1969; *The Tiny, Tawny Kitten,* Golden Press, 1969, new edition (illustrated by Pfloog), 1975.

Danny Dougal, the Wanting Boy (illustrated by Ken Longtemps), Lion Press, 1970; *If I Were* (illustrated by Lee Ames), Golden Press, 1970; *Where Do Bears Sleep?* (illustrated by Ian E. Staunton), Addison-Wesley, 1970; *Girls and Boys Book of Etiquette* (illustrated by Nancy Sears), Grosset, 1971; *Happy, Sad, Silly, Mad: A Beginning Book About Emotions* (illustrated by Elizabeth Dauber), Wonder-Treasure Books, 1971; *Raggedy Ann and the Cookie Snatcher* (illustrated by June Goldsborough), Golden Press, 1972; *Frere Jacques* (illustrated by Lilian Obligado), Lippincott, 1973; *A Nose for Trouble* (illustrated by Tim Hildebrandt and Greg Hildebrandt), Golden Press, 1973; *Raggedy Ann and Andy and the Rainy Day Circus,* Golden Press, 1973; *Animal Manners* (illustrated by Leonard Shortall), Golden Press, 1974; *The Gorilla Did It* (illustrated by Ray Cruz), Atheneum, 1974.

Davy Crockett, Indian Fighter (adapted from the Walt Disney Production film based on the story by Tom Blackburn; illustrated by Joseph Guarino), Pyramid Communications, 1975; *Me and the Yellow-Eyed Monster* (illustrated by Tony De Luna), Me-Books, 1975; *Noah's Ark,* Golden Press, 1975; *To Be Me* (illustrated by Frances Hook), Child's World (Elgin, Ill.), 1975, revised edition published as *I'm Glad to Be Me,* 1979; *Why Couldn't I Be an Only Kid Like You, Wigger* (illustrated by Leigh Grant), Atheneum, 1975; (editor) *The Golden Happy Birthday Book: Poems, Riddles, Giggles, Games, Magic, Stories, Presents, and Prizes to Make Your Special Day the Happiest Birthday Ever* (illustrated by Rosalyn Schanzer), Golden Press, 1976; *The Ups and Downs of Marvin* (illustrated by Richard Cuffari), Atheneum, 1976; *World, World, What Can I Do?* (illustrated by Margaret Leibold), Abingdon, 1976; *Amelia's Flying Machine* (illustrated by Charles Robinson), Doubleday, 1977; (adapter) *Wonderful Wizard of Oz* (illustrated by Eleanor Mill), Golden Press, 1977; *Gorilla Wants to Be the Baby* (illustrated by Jacqueline B. Smith), Atheneum, 1978; *The Me I See* (illustrated by Ati Forberg), Abingdon, 1978; *Two Homes to Live In: A Child's-Eye View of Divorce* (illustrated by Peggy Luks), Human Sciences, 1978; *If It Weren't for Benjamin, I'd Always Get to Lick the Icing Spoon* (illustrated by Laura Hartman), Human Sciences, 1979; *Last, First, Middle, and Nick: All About Names,* Prentice-Hall, 1979; *Tight Times* (illustrated by Trina S. Hyman), Viking, 1979; *Step on It, Andrew,* Atheneum, 1980; *Even If I Did Something Awful* (illustrated by Nancy Kincade), Atheneum, 1981; *Very Shy,* Human Sciences, 1981; *It's a Shame About the Rain* (illustrated by Bernadette Simmons), Human Sciences, 1981.

WORK IN PROGRESS: A humorous diet book for adults; a new-viewpoint pet book; and "always a children's book or two on the back burner."

SIDELIGHTS: Hazen told *CA:* "I always wanted to write as a way to find my voice, and also as a way of being heard when no one seemed to listen. My first sale was a soulful four-line poem to *True Confessions* in the third grade, about 'After the sun the rain.' I kept at it. And I'm glad, in spite of parental warnings that this was no way to make a living and that I was becoming more and more like Aunt Union Forever Shook (her real name) who never did. And I'm glad. Words are friends, and writing gives second chances. It's also like traveling: a wonderful way to explore, learn things, and get to know people—including oneself."

AVOCATIONAL INTERESTS: "I am a passionate swimmer, traveler, pizza addict, and also a cat-aholic who is, alas, allergic to cats. Other favorite forms of fun include biking in the city, hiking in the country, any kind of live theatre, and being a vigneron who has two vinerights in Benmarl Vineyard, Marlboro, N.Y. The tasting is terrific."

BIOGRAPHICAL/CRITICAL SOURCES: Chicago Tribune Book World, February 7, 1982.

* * *

HAZZARD, Mary 1928-
(Olivia Dwight)

PERSONAL: Born May 3, 1928, in Ithaca, N.Y.; daughter of Albert S. (a fisheries biologist) and Florence (a historian; maiden name, Woolsey) Hazzard; married Peter Swiggart, August 11, 1952 (divorced June 17, 1981); children: William Field, Katherine Anne. *Education:* Skidmore College, B.S., 1949; Yale University, M.F.A., 1982. *Religion:* Unitarian. *Home:* 452 Woodward St., Waban, Mass. 02168.

CAREER: Writer and free-lance editor, 1952—. *Member:* Authors Guild, Dramatists Guild. *Awards, honors:* Scroll from Mystery Writers of America, 1962, for *Close His Eyes;* fellowship in fiction from Massachusetts Arts and Humanities Foundation, 1977, for *Sheltered Lives;* Molly Kazan Award in Playwriting from Yale Drama School, 1981, for "Diary of the Seducer."

WRITINGS: (Under pseudonym Olivia Dwight) *Close His Eyes* (mystery), Harper, 1961; *The Cat With Five Names* (children's book), Attic Press, 1970; *Sheltered Lives* (novel), Madrona, 1980; *Idle and Disorderly Persons* (novel), Madrona, 1981.

Plays: "Diary of the Seducer" (two-act), first produced in New Haven, Conn., at Yale Drama School Annex Theatre, December 15, 1980; "Gull Feather" (one-act), first produced in New Haven at Yale Drama School Annex Theatre, March 3, 1981; "Little Girls," first produced in New Haven at Yale Drama School Annex Theatre, March, 1982.

Contributor of poems to periodicals, including *Dark Horse* and *Grit.*

WORK IN PROGRESS: Screenplay adaptation of *Close His Eyes,* completion expected in 1982; a one-act play, tentatively entitled "Birthday."

SIDELIGHTS: Mary Hazzard's first novel was a murder mystery with a satirical twist. *Close His Eyes,* published under the pseudonym Olivia Dwight, begins with the apparent suicide of Andrew McNeill, a prominent author who has come to lecture at a midwestern university. A graduate student, hired to catalog the papers of the late author, learns that many in the English department faculty had long wished McNeill dead, including one ambitious scholar who had written a work of criticism based on McNeill's whole career. It turns out that McNeill did not leap from the tower window, as everyone had assumed, but was pushed to his death by the critic. With McNeill out of the way, the murderer had schemed, publishers would eagerly bid for his book and the university would be sure to grant him tenure.

After writing two more mysteries and a children's book, Hazzard began a fourth mystery. In *Lost Lucy* a student of the romantic poets marries a girl whose submissive love recalls the Lucy of William Wordsworth's poems. In time, the husband tires of his wife and plots her murder. He hopes to persuade her to clean the bathroom with a deadly mixture of cleanser and ammonia, but Hazzard decided to spare her heroine. In the end, Lucy breaks free of her passive dependence on her husband and comes to see how dangerously selfish he really is. *Lost Lucy* was never published, but in the book Hazzard found herself describing a feminist viewpoint that would reemerge in her first serious novel, *Sheltered Lives*.

Against the larger background of social unrest in the 1960's and '70's, a woman reevaluates her life in terms of her marriage, her career, and her self-image in *Sheltered Lives*. The central character in the story is an insecure, introspective writer, Anne Craig, whose view of the world has been shaped by her father (a New England minister) and the novels of Jane Austen. When her husband, Nat, a professor of English, becomes involved in antiwar protests at the expense of his career and marriage, Anne departs for Taos, New Mexico, to confer with the sister she has always envied and admired, Harriet, and her artist husband. There she discovers that, contrary to the public mask her sister wears, Harriet is miserably trapped in her role as mother and neglected wife. Anne also learns, from friends back East, that her husband is having an affair. How she contends with failed expectations and a changing world, the conflicting influences of her conservative, New England past and the new freedoms won by the women's movement, comprises the balance of the book.

Drawing parallels between *Sheltered Lives* and Jane Austen's *Sense and Sensibility,* feature writer Kathy Huffhines observed that Hazzard "intends to show what 'sense' and 'sensibility' look like in today's world. . . . The novel is written as if it were Anne's journal for May-October of 1969 and its clear, observant style is an expression of the book's argument for reason. . . . In the end, the emotionalism that initially makes [Harriet] seem more independent traps her in a life of greater conventionality. Anne, who uses her journal to think things out, is more able to act independently and see herself objectively. By the end of the novel, Anne's 'sense' seems to have given her the better chance for a new future, though Hazzard also implies that these changes will make her a bit more like Harriet, opening her life to certain emotional risks."

In his review for the *Washington Post,* Joseph McLellan commented: "The writing is good, sometimes exquisite, the observations sharp and convincing. . . . 'Sheltered Lives' occasionally has the overtones of a feminist novel. . . . Besides women who seek expression in the arts (thick as flies at Taos), the book is stocked with women who join committees, march in demonstrations, ask people to sign petitions—and one earthmother whose child suffers malnutrition because she insists on breast-feeding it. But Mary Hazzard's view is too panoramic, her sympathies and interests too diverse, for her book to be reduced to a simple thesis. This is more than an ordinarily good novel. . . . It illuminates the subjects it touches and it will reward the serious reader richly."

Another who strongly recommended the book was Gail Godwin. "If I were an interested observer from the future," she said, "I think I would have understood more about what was going on in the 1960s and '70s from this novel than from a variety of so-called feminist blockbusters. Ms. Hazzard understands the first thing about good fiction: the character has to be as worthy of interest as we readers think we ourselves are."

Though it proved to be a critical success, *Sheltered Lives* was not easily published. Hazzard recalls that between 1973, when she completed the book, and 1978, thirteen publishers turned down her manuscript. Then, in 1979, a small publishing company in Seattle, Madrona Publishers, announced plans to publish their first novel as soon as they could find a manuscript they liked. Hazzard sent the book off one more time, and Madrona accepted it enthusiastically, pleading with the author not to allow anyone else to publish it. In 1981 she returned to Madrona with her next book, *Idle and Disorderly Persons.*

The new book dealt with issues and circumstances similar to those in *Sheltered Lives*. The settled and orderly lives of Daniel and Phoebe Wyatt have been disrupted by the Vietnam War. Phoebe, a homemaker, joins with her Boston suburban neighbors in demonstrations against the war. Daniel, a university professor, sees less and less of his wife and begins an affair. According to Madrona Publishers, "Mary Hazzard paints a convincing picture of the late-60's, early-70's radical chic that treated the antiwar movement as a social event. Phoebe Wyatt puts herself in the vanguard of this middle-class activism and finds herself doing things she never thought possible. . . . [The Wyatts'] world has been irrevocably changed. In *Idle and Disorderly Persons*, Mary Hazzard portrays the disorder wrought on people by the Vietnam War, a disorder heightened by a lingering sense of futility."

Hazzard told *CA:* "When my writing career is summarized it may seem to move in an unbroken line. However, in thinking carefully about it, I find that it has wavered, nearly died at times, and been influenced to a surprising degree by chance.

"I think I became a writer by default. At the age of eleven I wrote a melodrama called 'The Rich Woman's Daughter,' which my sisters and brother and I performed with great success in the front hall of our home in Ann Arbor, Michigan. I wrote the play simply because nobody else in the family would do it; all of us wanted to act and make posters, but nobody wanted to write. Until I finished high school, I provided the scripts and even the musical scores for one or two increasingly elaborate family productions each year.

"In college, where I majored in drama and spent much of my time acting and building scenery, I was once more persuaded to write. Skidmore at that time was a women's college, and it was hard to find plays that could be produced convincingly with student casts. I wrote the book and lyrics for two musical fantasies in which all the roles (male and female) were played by women.

"In 1950, hoping eventually to find work in the theatre, I entered the M.F.A. directing program at the Yale Drama School. When I found that the courses duplicated the ones I had taken as an undergraduate, I switched to playwriting. At the end of two years, however, I was married and left school.

"After leaving Yale I wrote several more plays, but playwriting without production was frustrating, and I began to wonder whether I might be capable of writing something that didn't depend so much on collaboration. In 1960, in response to a contest calling for mystery novels with an academic background, I wrote *Close His Eyes*. The mystery form seemed similar enough to the dramatic one to keep the project from being overwhelming. Also, I realized that by using the first person, I could write the whole book in dialogue. It didn't win the contest, but it was published by Harper and received good reviews.

"A few years later I wrote a children's book and printed it myself on a hand press in our attic. Since then I have published two more novels (not mysteries and not, thank goodness, hand printed) and several poems. However, in the last few years I have begun to have ideas once more for plays. In 1980 I returned to Yale and to playwriting.

"One of the most unexpected lessons I have learned from these wanderings is that no form of writing is automatically forbidden to me. Before I left Yale (the first time) I was convinced that I was incapable of writing fiction. Yet somehow I found myself attempting it. The same thing was true of poetry, and when I went back to playwriting I was prepared to discover that I had forgotten how. I am finally coming to realize that each new form not only imposes its own rules but offers new opportunities and new freedoms.

"Themes I find myself returning to: (1) other people's ideas of us: how those ideas influence us and make us into what we are or what we appear to be; (2) life seen as raw material for art: what an artist does with experience, and how the fact of being an artist changes that experience; (3) the loss of innocence: a necessary loss but a painful one. Innocence can make us blind, can cause us to hold up impossible ideals for ourselves and for everyone else. It can make us cruel.''

AVOCATIONAL INTERESTS: Reading, bicycling, baking, typesetting, growing green beans and morning glories, "and playing Mozart on the piano when no one else is in the house."

BIOGRAPHICAL/CRITICAL SOURCES: Washington Post, May 15, 1980; *Sojourner,* October, 1980; *Ontario Review,* spring-summer, 1981; *Madrona Publishers Catalog,* summer-fall, 1981.

—*Sketch by B. Hal May*

*   *   *

HEAD, Edith 1898(?)-1981

OBITUARY NOTICE: Born c. 1898 in Los Angeles, Calif.; died of myelobibrosis myeloid, a bone marrow disease, October 24, 1981, in Hollywood, Calif. Costume designer and author. Edith Head, Hollywood's most famous costume designer, was nominated for thirty-five Oscars during her long career and won eight. She entered the movie business in 1923 by answering a want ad for a sketch artist at Paramount Studios and earned her first solo credit as a designer in 1933 for "She Done Him Wrong." She won her first Oscar in 1949 for "The Heiress," and her last in 1973 for "The Sting." In between, she worked on many famous films, including "All About Eve," "A Place in the Sun," "The Ten Commandments," "Butch Cassidy and the Sundance Kid," and "Airport." Some of her costumes started fashion trends, most notably the sarongs she designed for Dorothy Lamour in the 1936 film "Jungle Princess." Head wrote an autobiography, *The Dress Doctor,* and another book, *How to Dress for Success.* Obituaries and other sources: *Current Biography,* Wilson, 1945; *Who's Who in America,* 40th edition, Marquis, 1978; *New York Times,* October 27, 1981; *Time,* November 9, 1981; *Newsweek,* November 9, 1981.

*   *   *

HEARN, (Patricio) Lafcadio (Tessima Carlos) 1850-1904
(Yakumo Koizumi)

BRIEF ENTRY: Born June 27, 1850, in Leukas, Greece; died

of a heart attack, September 26, 1904, in Okubo, Japan; ashes buried at Buddhist cemetery in Japan. Naturalized Japanese professor and author. Hearn is best known for books such as *Japan: An Attempt at Interpretation* (1904), which explained the Japanese land and people to the western world. Hearn was born in Greece and educated with relatives in England. In 1869 he attempted a journalistic career in the United States, where his progress was hampered by poverty and a scandalous and illegal marriage to a black woman. His first successful writing was based on his experiences in New Orleans. His colorful descriptions of Creole life won him critical attention, and later writing from the West Indies added to his reputation. In 1890 he made what was intended to be a brief trip to Japan for *Harper's New Monthly.* He remained there for the rest of his life, married a samurai woman, became a Japanese subject, and adopted the name Yakumo Koizumi. Hearn achieved his best writing and earned lasting acclaim for books written during those years. In such work as *Gleanings in Buddha-Fields* (1897) and *A Japanese Miscellany* (1901) he exhibited his flair for description and style, his love of the exquisite, and his penchant for folk tales. In his book *In Ghostly Japan* (1899), he revealed his taste for the exotic, strange, and supernatural. Hearn's last views of Japan were more disillusioned, as he observed the old traditions fading away, and he began to see Japan as a military threat to the West. *Biographical/critical sources: Cyclopedia of World Authors,* Harper, 1958; *The Reader's Encyclopedia of American Literature,* Crowell, 1962; Beong-cheon Yu, *An Ape of Gods: The Art and Thought of Lafcadio Hearn,* Wayne State University Press, 1964.

*   *   *

HEIFNER, Jack 1946-

PERSONAL: Born March 31, 1946, in Corsicana, Tex.; son of Lee (a car dealer) and Naomi (a salesperson; maiden name, Norris) Heifner. *Education:* Southern Methodist University, B.F.A., 1968. *Address:* 77 West 85th St., 5A, New York, N.Y. 10024. *Agent:* Bret Adams Ltd., 36 East 61st St., New York, N.Y. 10021.

CAREER: Worked in costume shops, as room clerk, and as market researcher; worked in technical and design jobs for American Shakespeare Festival, Julliard School, and American Opera Theatre. Actor with American Shakespeare Festival, in summer stock, and in Off-Broadway productions; actor in plays, including "Othello" and "Twelfth Night." Playwright, 1975—. Co-producer of play "Das Lusitania Songspiel," 1979; Cofounder of Lion Theatre Company. *Member:* American Society of Composers, Authors, and Publishers, Actor's Equity, Dramatists Guild, Screenwriters Guild. *Awards, honors:* Grant from Creative Artists Public Service Program, 1977, for "Tornado"; grant from National Endowment for the Arts, 1978, for "Music-Hall Sidelights"; American Society of Composers, Authors, and Publishers (ASCAP) Award, 1978, for lyrics of "Music-Hall Sidelights"; "Vanities" was nominated as best play of the year by New York Drama Critics Poll.

WRITINGS:—Plays: "Casserole," first produced in New York at Playwrights Horizons, April 18, 1975; *Vanities* (three-act; first produced in New York at Playwrights Horizons, January 15, 1976, produced Off-Broadway at Chelsea Westside Theatre, March 22, 1976, produced in Washington, D.C., at Ford's Theatre Society, October 19, 1976, produced in Los Angeles, Calif., at Mark Taper Forum, November 4, 1976, produced in Buffalo, N.Y., at Studio Arena Theatre, 1976, produced in Seattle Wash., at Seattle Repertory Theatre, 1976), Samuel French, 1976; "Music-Hall Sidelights," first produced in New York at Lion Theatre, October 26, 1978; "Star Treatment," first produced in New York at Lion Theatre, March 6, 1980. Also author of *Patio/Porch* (two one-acts; first produced in New York at Century Theatre, April 13, 1978), Dramatists Play Service. Author of "Tornado" and "America Was."

Other: "Porch" (radio play), National Public Radio, 1977-78 (also see below); "Porch" (sound recording), Public Radio, 1977; "Loveland" (teleplay, situation comedy), Columbia Broadcasting System (CBS-TV), 1979. Also author of "A Wide Place in the Road," a screenplay.

Work included in anthologies, including *The Best Short Plays of 1980,* edited by Stanley Richards, Chilton, 1980, and *Contemporary Scenes for Student Actors,* edited by Michael Schulman and Eve Mekler, Penguin, 1980.

WORK IN PROGRESS: The book for "Smile," a musical based on the film of the same title, with music by Marvin Hamlisch and lyrics by Carolyn Leigh.

SIDELIGHTS: Jack Heifner came from "the fruitcake capital of the world" (Corsicana, Texas, which is where the internationally famous Corsicana fruitcakes are made). In high school, one of his goals was to be popular, though he was "an honor roll student, the vice-president of the student council, and in almost every case, overly involved in high school." "I do admit I was interested in popularity," he revealed, "[but] it was not my full-time profession."

After graduation, he was a self-proclaimed "party boy," attending Southern Methodist University for its country club atmosphere. Yet when "the brothers wanted me to sleep in a dog bed," he left his fraternity and became more concerned with social issues like Vietnam than with parties. Heifner changed his major from business to theatre arts, and he ultimately became the successful playwright who wrote the longest running play in Off-Broadway history. "I'd done every kind of work in the theater," the dramatist said. "I didn't like stage managing and I wasn't particularly good as an actor and I figured they would always need someone to hang a light or sew a hem so I sat down and wrote a play. There wasn't anything left to do."

Heifner began writing seriously when his father died. Amazed by American funerals and fascinated by the amount of food consumed at wakes, the playwright wrote a black comedy about the subjects in 1975. "The first play ['Casserole'] was real hard," he revealed, "but I did the draft of 'Vanities' in a couple of days."

In two days in May, 1975, Heifner wrote a somewhat autobiographical play that Margo Jefferson of *Newsweek* called "an astute, snapshot-sharp chronicle" for three rites of passage. "Vanities" traces the lives of three girls from their high school days to their adult lives. In high school the girls are clones of each other: They look alike, talk alike, and think alike. Kathy, Joanne, and Mary are preoccupied with the opposite sex, football, and popularity. While in college, the girls become sorority sisters, undaunted by significant political events such as assassinations and wars. After graduation, Joanne marries her high school sweetheart; Kathy becomes a physical education teacher; and Mary tours Europe. When the women are reunited in 1974, Joanne remains the happy wife and mother while Mary is the curator of a pornographic artifacts gallery. Kathy, the organizer in high school, has given up teaching and questions what she is to do with her future.

The characters, said Heifner, are "three sides of my head fighting it out," though they are similar to girls he went to school with. "I knew three cheerleaders at the high school," Heifner told the *New York Times.* "I kept their names—Kathy,

Mary and Joanne— in 'Vanities' but they aren't the same girls. They were disappointed when I told my mother in Corsicana to tell them that." Even so, and ironically enough, a *New York Times* reporter noticed that the flesh-and-blood Kathy is a physical education teacher, and Joanne is happily married and has children. The "real" Mary's husband, the reporter claimed, prefers that his wife be left out of the playwright's future creations.

Still, as Heifner explained to *CA:* "The women I used as models for the three women in 'Vanities' included more than just three girls in my high school. I chose another three girls from college and from my later years in New York. The characters are composites. It is not a piece of fact . . . but of fiction. The only relation to the three women I grew up with are the names. I did not know what happened to these women until after the play had been written. In fact, I've never seen or heard from them since high school."

Likened to Mary McCarthy's *The Group* and to Dorothy Parker's *The Big Blonde,* "Vanities," said Jules Aaron of the *Educational Theatre Journal,* is "a penetrating examination of contemporary mores." Thematically, the play criticizes the dream world of college life. More importantly, "Vanities" is a comment on the way society molds people. "What this play is about," Heifner explained, "is three little golden girls who are talking about nothing." As Aaron noted: "The play deals with the *facades* of the American Dream and asks if it is enough to be 'popular' and 'accepted.'"

Popularity and acceptance was enough for "Vanities." After four years and 1,785 performances, it became the longest running non-musical in the history of Off-Broadway theatre. The play, whose original production costs totaled only $200, enjoyed more professional productions (280 by 1980) than any other play in America, including two hundred productions by repertory companies. Home Box Office (HBO), a pay television network, offered a $400,000 production of "Vanities" as the first theatrical program for its subscribers, and the American Broadcasting Company (ABC-TV) did a pilot for a television series based on the play.

Critically, the play has been described as "an amusing and unpretentious comedy." "Mr. Heifner," commented a reviewer for *New Yorker* magazine, "makes his ironic points gently, never scoring off his characters." "Watching *Vanities. . .* is unnervingly funny—like flipping through an old yearbook," wrote Jefferson. Heifner's cliches, praised Clive Barnes of the *New York Times,* "have the tinkle of truth and a giggle of merriment. He makes much of the shrill cries of femininity and powder-room gossip translated through the absent ears of a man." It "constantly holds the interest," the reviewer concluded.

For his part, Heifner looks at the success of "Vanities" as "some sort of wonderful joke. There's no way to figure it out. It's a fluke." "I can't tell anybody why it works, because I don't know why it works," the playwright confessed. "Maybe it's just the total innocence behind how it was written. I'm still amazed so many people like it."

Heifner told *CA:* "If there's any common thread in my works, it would be my interest in the kind of society that creates the type of people shown in 'Vanities' or 'Patio/Porch.' I don't think the plays are judgmental. . . . The characters are judging each other, but the play really just presents the argument.

"If anything, I love the characters . . . feel sympathy for them. I do not love the 'world' that creates such people. The girls in 'Vanities' are upper-middle class . . . but there is one issue never mentioned in the play: Money. It is exactly the Miss

America syndrome that I am exploring in my new work, 'Smile' (about teenage beauty contests).

"I believe all my plays have been about social issues. 'Patio/ Porch' examines the same small town that created the women in 'Vanities,' but 'Patio/Porch' concerns another class structure. 'Vanities' is a play about friendship. It is not a play about women since the same events could happen to three football players or fraternity brothers. 'Patio/Porch' is a study of family relationships. The people in both plays are small town creations. 'Star Treatment' examines a love relationship between a woman and three men. 'Tornado' is about the way such an event can suddenly change beliefs and alter lives. 'America Was' takes place in a United States that has run out of the essentials . . . food, gasoline, water, everything.

"The people in all the plays are ordinary. I don't write about great, gifted artists or 'thinkers.' My concern is with the world of the ordinary person, and I mean 'ordinary' as a compliment—those who are trying to figure out how to get through this life. Even the girls in 'Vanities' are ordinary. If one of them was a great ballerina or a concert violinist, she couldn't have the problems she has in that play."

BIOGRAPHICAL/CRITICAL SOURCES: *New York Times*, March 23, 1976, June 4, 1976, August 15, 1976, August 27, 1976, April 14, 1978, September 9, 1979, February 8, 1980, March 7, 1980, July 30, 1980, August 17, 1980, November 5, 1980; *Newsweek* April 5, 1976; *New Yorker*, April 19, 1976; *Nation*, November 13, 1976; *Educational Theatre Journal*, May, 1977; Catharine Hughes, editor, *New York Theatre Annual*, Gale, Volume 1, 1978, Volume 2, 1978; *New York Post*, April 14, 1978, *New York*, May 1, 1978, March 24, 1980; *New York Theatre Review*, June, 1978; *Contemporary Literary Criticism*, Volume 11, Gale, 1979; Catharine Hughes, editor, *American Theatre Annual 1978-1979*, Gale, 1980; Catharine Hughes, editor, *American Theatre Annual 1979-1980*, Gale, 1981.

—*Sketch by Charity Anne Dorgan*

*   *   *

HEINEMAN, Benjamin Walter, Jr.   1944-

PERSONAL: Born January 25, 1944, in Chicago, Ill.; son of Benjamin Walter (in business) and Natalie (a civic leader; maiden name, Goldstein) Heineman; married Jeanne Cristine Russell (a journalist), June 7, 1975. *Education:* Harvard University, B.A. (magna cum laude), 1965; Balliol College, Oxford, B.Letters, 1967; Yale University, J.D., 1971. *Home:* 4914 30th Pl. N.W., Washington, D.C. 20008. *Agent:* Rafael Sagalyn, 1120 19th St. N.W., Washington, D.C. 20036. *Office:* Califano, Ross & Heineman, 200 Independence Ave. S.W., Washington, D.C. 20201.

CAREER: Admitted to the Bar of District of Columbia, 1973, and U.S. Supreme Court, 1973; *Chicago Sun Times*, Chicago, Ill., reporter, 1968; U.S. Supreme Court, Washington, D.C., law clerk to associate justice Potter Stewart, 1971-72; Center for Law and Social Policy, Washington, D.C., staff attorney, 1973-75; Williams, Connolly & Califano, Washington, D.C., lawyer, 1975-76; U.S. Department of Health, Education and Welfare, Washington, D.C., executive assistant to Secretary of Health, Education and Welfare, 1977-78, assistant secretary for planning and evaluation, 1978-79; Califano, Ross & Heineman, Washington, D.C., partner, 1979—. *Member:* Phi Beta Kappa. *Awards, honors:* Rhodes scholar at Oxford University, 1965-67.

WRITINGS: *The Politics of the Powerless: A Study of the Campaign Against Racial Discrimination*, Oxford University Press,

1972; (with Curtis A. Hessler) *Memorandum for the President: A Strategic Approach to Domestic Affairs in the Eighties*, Random House, 1980. Editor-in-chief of *Yale Law Journal*, 1970-71.

WORK IN PROGRESS: A book on economic and social policy in an era of atomized and changing politics.

*   *   *

HELLMANN, John   1948-

PERSONAL: Born February 14, 1948, in Louisville, Ky.; son of John Michael (a production manager) and Louise (Stickel) Hellmann; married Marilyn McKinley (an arts council director), September 14, 1968. *Education:* University of Louisville, B.A., 1970, M.A., 1973; Kent State University, Ph.D., 1977. *Office:* Department of English, Ohio State University, Lima, Ohio 45804.

CAREER: Ohio State University, Lima, assistant professor of English, 1977—. *Member:* Modern Language Association of America.

WRITINGS: *Fables of Fact: The New Journalism as New Fiction*, University of Illinois Press, 1981. Contributor to literature journals and literary magazines, including *South Atlantic Quarterly, Genre, Critique, Centennial Review*, and *Journal of American Folklore*.

WORK IN PROGRESS: A book on American literature and film of the Vietnam War.

SIDELIGHTS: Hellmann commented: "The 'new journalism' of Norman Mailer and Tom Wolfe, and now the literature and film of the Vietnam War, interest me because they embody a direct confrontation of art with our contemporary world. Popular genres, and especially their use by serious artists, also hold a special interest for me since the continuing power of their formulas reveals them as mirror images of the compulsions, anxieties, and longings of a culture. I am most drawn to studying works that have a profound and mysterious power for me, so that revealing new dimensions of meaning in a novel or film has the added 'edge' of self-discovery. For me criticism, like any worthwhile adventure, combines passionate involvement with detached curiosity."

*   *   *

HELMREICH, Jonathan Ernst   1936-

BRIEF ENTRY: Born December 21, 1936, in Brunswick, Me. American educator, academic administrator, and author. Helmreich has been teaching at Allegheny College since 1962. He became a professor in 1972 and has been dean of instruction since 1966. He wrote *Belgium and Europe: A Study in Small Power Diplomacy* (Mouton, 1976). *Address:* 370 Jefferson St., Meadville, Pa. 16335. *Biographical/critical sources: Who's Who in America*, 40th edition, Marquis, 1978.

*   *   *

HELMREICH, William B.   1945-

PERSONAL: Born August 25, 1945, in Zurich, Switzerland; came to the United States in 1946, naturalized citizen, 1951; son of Leo and Sally (Finklestein) Helmreich; married Helaine Gewirtz (a speech pathologist), June 28, 1970. *Education:* Yeshiva College (now University), B.A., 1967; Washington University, St. Louis, Mo., M.A., 1970, Ph.D., 1971. *Home:* 69-22 266th St., Floral Park, N.Y. 11004. *Agent:* Arthur P. Schwartz, 435 Riverside Dr., New York, N.Y. 10025. *Office:*

Department of Sociology, City College of the City University of New York, 133rd St. and Convent Ave., New York, N.Y. 10031.

CAREER: Georgia State University, Atlanta, assistant professor of sociology, 1970-71; Yale University, New Haven, Conn., lecturer in sociology, 1971-72; City College of the City University of New York, New York, N.Y., professor of sociology and Judaic studies, 1973—. Consultant to American Jewish Committee. *Member:* American Sociological Association. *Awards, honors:* Woodrow Wilson fellowship, 1971; National Endowment for the Humanities fellowship, 1972 and 1975.

WRITINGS: The Black Crusaders, Harper, 1973; *Wake Up Wake Up to Do the Work of the Creator* (alternate Book-of-the-Month Club selection), Harper, 1976; *Afro-Americans and Africa,* Greenwood Press, 1977; *The Things They Say Behind Your Back,* Doubleday, 1982; *The Yeshiva in America,* Free Press, 1982.

AVOCATIONAL INTERESTS: Travel, tennis.

*   *   *

HELVICK, James
See COCKBURN, (Francis) Claud

*   *   *

HENLEY, William Ernest   1849-1903

BRIEF ENTRY: Born August 23, 1849, in Gloucester, England; died July 11, 1903, in Woking, England. British editor, critic, and poet. Henley edited such periodicals as *New Review* and *Scots Observer,* in which he published some of Rudyard Kipling's early work. After having a foot amputated, Henley was hospitalized at Edinburgh Infirmary, where he met and became friends with Robert Louis Stevenson. Later the two collaborated on such plays as "Deacon Brodie" (1892) and "Macaire" (1892). It was said that Henley served as the model for Stevenson's famous pirate, Long John Silver. Henley wrote some of his best poems, including "Evictus" (1875), as a hospital patient. These were later collected in *A Book of Verses* (1888) and *In Hospital* (1903). *Biographical/critical sources: The Penguin Companion to English Literature,* McGraw, 1971; *Webster's New World Companion to English and American Literature,* World Publishing, 1973.

*   *   *

HENRY, Jeanne Heffernan   1940-

PERSONAL: Born November 4, 1940, in Troy, N.Y.; daughter of James Joseph (an accountant) and Emma (an artist; maiden name, Guido) Heffernan; married Frederick Insull Henry (an engineer), December 30, 1967; children: Anne, Nicholas. *Education:* St. Lawrence University, B.A., 1962; Columbia University, M.S., 1963. *Politics:* Democrat. *Religion:* Roman Catholic. *Residence:* Palos Verdes Estates, Calif. *Office:* 2725 Via La Selva, Palos Verdes Estates, Calif.

CAREER: McGraw-Hill Publishing Co., New York, N.Y., editorial trainee, 1963-64; *Business Week,* Los Angeles, Calif., assistant editor, 1964-68; high school teacher of English and journalism in Lakeland, Fla., 1969-70, and Page, Ariz., 1970-73; writer, 1973—.

WRITINGS: (With Barbara Sills) *The Mother to Mother Baby Care Book,* Avon, 1981. Contributor to magazines and newspapers, including *West, Los Angeles Times,* and *New York Times.*

WORK IN PROGRESS: Continuing research on child care subjects; research on mid-coast Maine, its residents, lifestyle, and natural history.

SIDELIGHTS: Realizing that "no pediatrician or other expert tells us how to get gum out of hair," co-authors Jeanne Henry and Barbara Sills concluded that very often the best source of practical help for mothers is other mothers. Their book, *The Mother to Mother Baby Care Book,* an encyclopedic guide to raising children from birth to age three, is a compilation of the advice of more than two hundred parents who were queried by the authors. Four years in the writing, the work begins with descriptions of early symptoms of pregnancy and progresses through a multitude of other subjects, including guidelines for choosing baby equipment, suggestions on discipline, and advice on basic medical problems. Also included is a section entitled "Mothers' Sourcebook," which provides growth and development charts and information as well as resource lists of services, books, and baby-care materials. A *Los Angeles Times* review called the book "a delight to read and a real help."

Henry told *CA:* "I have a growing concern for children raised in households where parents each have full-time careers. Babies and young people do not cope well with overly stressed caretakers. Would you want to be a baby in a house with two deadline-driven parents? Because of this concern, I have chosen to be a full-time caretaker of our two young children and a part-time writer. It is a period of great frustration and occasional exhilaration for me and for my many women friends who are in the same boat—maintaining a toehold in a profession while struggling to raise complete human beings. Where's the exhilaration? My book, yes. My intact marriage, yes. But even more: Last week my daughter's teacher said our girl was one of the two best readers in her second-grade class. Part of this is luck, but a larger factor I know is that there is time for weekly trips to the library, time to work in the library at her school and thus learn what books are exciting to young readers, time to monitor the TV set, and time to have read to her, and now with her, a couple of times a day since she was eighteen months old. Perhaps a competent babysitter-housekeeper could do the same, but in my heart I am not willing to take the risk. For me, putting our children first and my career second is worth it."

AVOCATIONAL INTERESTS: Maine.

BIOGRAPHICAL/CRITICAL SOURCES: Los Angeles Times, May 1, 1981; *Torrance Daily Breeze* (Calif.), May 22, 1981; *Troy Times Record* (N.Y.), August 10, 1981; *Parents,* October, 1981; *Woman's Day,* October 13, 1981.

*   *   *

HERDT, Gilbert H(enry)   1949-

PERSONAL: Born February 24, 1949, in Oakley, Kan.; son of G.W. (in business) and Delores L. (in business; maiden name, Beckman) Herdt. *Education:* University of Washington, Seattle, M.A., 1974; Australian National University, Ph.D., 1977; postdoctoral study at University of California, Los Angeles, 1978-79. *Residence:* Stanford, Calif. *Office:* Department of Anthropology, Stanford University, Stanford, Calif. 94305.

CAREER: Stanford University, Stanford, Calif., assistant professor of anthropology, 1978—. Member of Gender Identity Clinic at University of California, Los Angeles. *Member:* American Anthropological Association (fellow), American Psychological Association, Association for Social Anthropology in Oceania, RAIGBNI.

WRITINGS: Guardians of the Flutes (nonfiction), McGraw, 1981; *Rituals of Manhood* (nonfiction), University of California Press, 1982.

WORK IN PROGRESS: Guardians of the Flutes, Volume II: *Secret Initiation,* publication expected in 1983; research on gender identity theory.

*   *   *

HERGET, Paul 1908(?)-1981

OBITUARY NOTICE: Born c. 1908; died August 27, 1981, in Cincinnati, Ohio. Astronomer, educator, and author. During World War II Herget served as a consultant to the Manhattan Project, which developed the atomic bomb. As an expert on the computation of orbits, he had an important role in the early stages of the United States space program. He was named to the National Academy of Sciences in 1962, and in 1965 he won the James Craig Medal for research. His book *The Computation of Orbits* is considered one of the essential texts on celestial mechanics. Obituaries and other sources: *New York Times,* August 29, 1981.

*   *   *

HERRING, Hubert Clinton 1889-1967

OBITUARY NOTICE: Born December 29, 1889, in Winterset, Iowa; died of a heart attack, September 29, 1967, in Claremont, Calif. Clergyman, educator, and author. Herring was a minister of Congregational churches in the Midwest for several years, but his interest in Latin America eventually became his full-time vocation. A professor of Latin American civilization at Claremont College for over twenty years, he wrote several important books on Latin American culture and history, including *A History of Latin America, America and the Americas,* and *Good Neighbors.* Obituaries and other sources: *The Reader's Encyclopedia of American Literature,* Crowell, 1962; *New York Times,* October 3, 1967; *Who Was Who in America, With World Notables,* Volume V: *1969-1973,* Marquis, 1973.

*   *   *

HERRING, Robert H(erschel) 1938-

PERSONAL: Born March 26, 1938, in Charleston, Miss.; son of Percy Floyd (a minister) and Maureen (Davidson) Herring; married Joan Burns (a personnel director), February 8, 1958; children: Lisa Lynn, Geoffrey. *Education:* Attended Baylor University, 1955-56, and Memphis State University, 1958-59; Mississippi College, B.A., 1960, M.A., 1961; attended University of Tennessee, 1964-66. *Home:* 909 East Burton, Murfreesboro, Tenn. 37130. *Agent:* Theron Raines, Raines & Raines, 475 Fifth Ave., New York, N.Y. 10017. *Office:* Department of English, Middle Tennessee State University, Murfreesboro, Tenn. 37130.

CAREER: Mississippi State University, Starkville, instructor in English, 1962-63; University of Tennessee, Knoxville, instructor in English, 1964-66; Middle Tennessee State University, Murfreesboro, assistant professor of English, 1966—.

WRITINGS: Hub (novel), Viking, 1981. Contributor of stories to magazines, including *Colorado Quarterly, Laurel Review, Mountain Review,* and *Epoch.*

WORK IN PROGRESS: Two novels.

SIDELIGHTS: Herring commented: "*Hub* was a way of letting go of my childhood, of giving a point and place in time a kind of permanence. I suppose every writer is, in his first novel, listening for his own voice, searching for his own unique way of viewing the human condition. In *Hub,* through the eyes of essential innocence—children—I think I've found a satisfactory beginning as a writer."

BIOGRAPHICAL/CRITICAL SOURCES: Houston Post, July 12, 1981; *Pensacola News Journal,* July 16, 1981; *Tennessean,* July 19, 1981; *New Yorker,* August 24, 1981; *New York Times Book Review,* September 13, 1981.

*   *   *

HESS, Alexander 1898(?)-1981

OBITUARY NOTICE: Born c. 1898; died August 10, 1981, in Florida. Air force officer and author. As an officer in the Czechoslovak Air Force, Hess won the Croix de Guerre during the battle for France in 1939-40. Evacuated to England along with other Czech airmen, he served with the Royal Air Force in the Battle of Britain, an experience he described in his book *We Were in the Battle of Britain.* Obituaries and other sources: *London Times,* August 17, 1981.

*   *   *

HESS, Karen 1918-

PERSONAL: Born November 11, 1918, in Blair, Neb.; daughter of Stinus Sorensen and Martha (Hansen) Loft; married John L. Hess (a writer); children: Peter, Michael, Martha. *Home:* 285 Riverside Dr., New York, N.Y. 10025. *Agent:* Timothy Seldes, Russell & Volkening, Inc., 551 Fifth Ave., New York, N.Y. 10017.

CAREER: Writer and editor. *Member:* Authors Guild.

WRITINGS: (With husband, John L. Hess) *Taste of America,* Viking, 1977; (editor of American edition) Elizabeth David, *English Bread and Yeast Cookery,* Viking, 1980; (editor) *Martha Washington's Booke of Cookery,* Columbia University Press, 1981. Author of a syndicated column. Contributor of articles and reviews to magazines, including *Atlantic Monthly, Harper's, Vogue, Prime Time, House and Garden,* and *Organic Gardening,* and newspapers.

SIDELIGHTS: Karen Hess commented: "My primary interest has been in French regional cuisine and French culinary bibliography, but when my husband and I returned to the States (after he was a correspondent in France for ten years), the lamentable state of produce and cookery in my homeland made it clear that my work was here, at least for the present. I have a special interest in bread, and believe that the debasement of flour to lifeless, chalky dust in the nineteenth century was nearly mortal. I believe that American cookery is best suited to our soil, our produce, our very history, and that as long as it is moribund, as it is, we are in no position to understand the cuisine of other peoples. I have a horror of the 'Me Tarzan, you Jane' format of American recipes; I consider that it aggravates the general mindlessness in the kitchen.

"My interest in the roots of American cookery led me to the study of English cookery, still the warp of our cookery in spite of the enrichment of succeeding waves of immigrants and the unique contributions of the blacks and the American Indian. *Martha Washington's Booke of Cookery* contains about five hundred of her recipes, dating from about 1575 to 1625. The book itself is a historical analysis of the seventeenth-century cookery brought to America by early colonists and of the relationship of that cookery to early American cooking in general and that of Virginia in particular.

"Aside from the writers of the past, the one contemporary writer/scholar in my own field who has influenced me is Elizabeth David, to whom I am indebted more than I can say."

*   *   *

HEWER, Humphrey Robert 1903-1974

OBITUARY NOTICE: Born August 16, 1903; died in February, 1974. Zoologist, educator, and author of *British Seals*. Obituaries and other sources: *Who's Who*, 126th edition, St. Martin's, 1974. (Date of death provided by daughter, Gilhain E. Griffiths.)

*   *   *

HEWES, Laurence (Ilsley) 1902-

PERSONAL: Born April 17, 1902, in Kingston, R.I.; son of Laurence Ilsley, Sr. (an engineer) and Agnes (a writer; maiden name, Danforth) Hewes; married Patricia Jackson, January 29, 1932 (died June 6, 1976); married Martha Odle Overholser (a teacher), August 1, 1979; children: Laurence Ilsley III. *Education:* Dartmouth College, B.Sc., 1924; George Washington University, Ph.D., 1946; Harvard University, M.P.A., 1956. *Politics:* Democrat. *Religion:* Presbyterian. *Home:* 1937 Rosewood Valley Dr., Brentwood, Tenn. 37027.

CAREER: Investment banker in San Francisco, Calif., 1925-33; associated with Federal Land Bank, Berkeley, Calif., and State Relief Administration, San Francisco, Calif., 1933-35; Farm Security Administration, Washington, D.C., assistant to undersecretary of agriculture, 1935, assistant to administrator, 1935-39, regional director in San Francisco, 1939-44; American Council on Race Relations, San Francisco, West Coast director, 1944-47; Headquarters of Supreme Commander of Allied Powers, Tokyo, Japan, land reform adviser, 1947-49; U.S. Department of Interior, Washington, D.C., chief land settlement and agricultural economist for Bureau of Reclamation in Denver, Colo., 1950-59; U.S. Outdoor Recreation Resources Review Commission, chief of forecasts and economics, 1959-62; U.S. Department of Agriculture, Washington, D.C., assistant to administrator of Office of Rural Areas Development, 1962-63; U.S. Agency for International Development, Washington, D.C., rural development adviser to mission to India, in New Delhi, 1963-65; U.S. Department of Agriculture, chief of natural resources conservation for Rural Community Development Service, 1965-68; United Nations Food and Agriculture Organization, senior consultant to United Nations development programs in Ethiopia, Tanzania, Panama, India, Pakistan, Sri Lanka, South Vietnam, Mexico, British Honduras, and Nicaragua, 1968-73; writer, 1973—.

Visiting fellow at Center for the Study of Democratic Institutions, Santa Barbara, Calif., 1972, 1973, associate, 1976—. Member of U.S. Department of Agriculture's U.S. Interagency Committee for Post Defense Planning, 1939-41, and of state war boards in California and Arizona, 1941-43; U.S. Department of Agriculture's representative in Mexican labor transportation negotiations, 1942-43, and executive secretary of land and water policy committee, 1965-68; consultant to World Bank. *Member:* American Association for the Advancement of Science, Cheekwood Botanical Gardens and Fine Arts Center, Artus, Cosmos Club. *Awards, honors:* Distinguished service award from U.S. Department of Agriculture, 1968.

WRITINGS: Japanese Land Reform Program, Headquarters of General MacArthur, 1950; *Japan: Land and Men,* Iowa State College Press, 1955; *Boxcar in the Sand* (biography), Knopf, 1957; *Rural Development: World Frontiers,* Iowa State University Press, 1974.

WORK IN PROGRESS: Education of a Bureaucrat, memoirs; *The Highwayman,* a biography of his father, Laurence I. Hewes; a collection of short stories.

SIDELIGHTS: Hewes wrote: "I have been interested in the rural poor around the world, their problems, and efforts to deal with them, particularly government efforts in the field of public administration."

*   *   *

HEYDENREICH, Ludwig Heinrich 1903-

BRIEF ENTRY: Born March 23, 1903, in Leipzig, Germany (now East Germany). German art historian, educator, and author. Heydenreich was director of the Central Institute for the History of Art from 1946 to 1969. Since 1948 he has been an honorary professor at University of Munich. His writings include *Italienische Renaissance* (Beck, 1972), *Leonardo: The Last Supper* (Viking, 1974), *Architecture in Italy, 1400-1600* (Viking, 1974), and *Leonardo the Inventor* (McGraw, 1980). *Address:* 12 Bauer St., Munich 8000, West Germany. *Biographical/critical sources: Who's Who in the World,* 4th edition, Marquis, 1978.

*   *   *

HIAASEN, Carl 1953-

PERSONAL: Born March 12, 1953, in Fort Lauderdale, Fla.; son of K. Odel (a lawyer) and Patricia (Moran) Hiaasen; married Constance Lyford (a registered nurse), November 12, 1970; children: Scott Andrew. *Education:* Attended Emory University, 1970-72; University of Florida, B.S., 1974. *Residence:* Plantation, Fla. *Agent:* Esther Newburg, International Creative Management, 40 West 57th St., New York, N.Y. 10019. *Office: Miami Herald,* 1 Herald Plaza, Miami, Fla. 33101.

CAREER: Cocoa Today, Cocoa, Fla., reporter, 1974-76; *Miami Herald,* Miami, Fla., reporter, 1976—. Professor at Barry College, 1978-79. *Member:* Society of Professional Journalists, Investigative Reporters and Editors, Sigma Delta Chi.

AWARDS, HONORS: 1980 awards include National Headliners Award, distinguished service medallion from Sigma Delta Chi, public service first place award from Florida Society of Newspaper Editors, Clarion Award from Women in Communications, Heywood Broun Award from Newspaper Guild, and finalist for Pulitzer Prize in public service reporting, all for an investigative newspaper series about dangerous doctors; 1981 awards include Green Eyeshade Award from Sigma Delta Chi, first place award in depth reporting from Florida Society of Newspaper Editors, grand prize for investigative reporting from Investigative Reporters and Editors, and finalist for Pulitzer Prize in special local reporting, all for a newspaper series on the drug smuggling industry in Key West.

WRITINGS: (With William Montalbano) *Powder Burn* (novel), Atheneum, 1981. Contributor to magazines and newspapers, including *Rolling Stone, Penthouse, Us,* and *Tropic.*

WORK IN PROGRESS: Bluelight, a novel about alien smuggling in South Florida, with William Montalbano.

SIDELIGHTS: Hiaasen told *CA:* "In *Powder Burn,* our first novel, Bill Montalbano and I tried to use our backgrounds and experiences as newspaper journalists to create an exciting fictional story line based on actual events. Although we invented the characters, the episodes of drug dealing, of violence, of police and judicial frustration described in the novel come directly from our daily reporting."

HIGGINBOTHAM, Sanford Wilson 1913-

BRIEF ENTRY: Born April 19, 1913, in Fordyce, Ark. American historian, editor, and educator. Higginbotham has been a professor of history at Rice University since 1961. He wrote *The Keystone in the Democratic Arch: Pennsylvania Politics, 1800-1816* (Pennsylvania Historical and Museum Commission, 1952), *Pennsylvania and the Civil War* (Pennsylvania Historical and Museum Commission, 1961), and *Man, Science, Learning, and Education* (Rice University, 1963). *Address:* 2415 Dryden Rd., Houston, Tex. 77030; and Department of History, Rice University, Houston, Tex. 77001. *Biographical/critical sources: Who's Who in America,* 40th edition, Marquis, 1978.

*   *   *

HIGGINSON, Margaret V(alliant) 1923-

PERSONAL: Born August 16, 1923, in Georgetown, Del.; daughter of William E. (a business entrepreneur) and Emma (Friedel) Valliant; married William J. Higginson (a marketing executive), June 15, 1960. *Education:* University of New Mexico, B.S., 1947, M.A., 1949; graduate study at Syracuse University, 1950, and New School for Social Research, 1954-59; also attended New York University, 1979-81. *Home:* 85 Viscount Dr. Apt. B42, Milford, Conn. 06460. *Office:* 2 Tudor Pl., Apt. 10CN, New York, N.Y. 10017.

CAREER: Glover Associates, Inc. (management consultants), New York City, manager, corporate secretary, and director, 1953-61; Collier Books, New York City, research manager, 1962; Girl Scouts of the U.S.A., organization specialist, 1963-64; American Management Association, New York City, research program director and research associate, 1964-71; *Research Institute of America,* New York City, editor, 1971-75; free-lance writer, editor, and researcher, 1976—. *Member:* Authors Guild, Academy of Management, Lighting Forum.

WRITINGS: Managing With EDP, American Management Association, 1965; *Management Policies,* Volumes I and II, American Management Association, 1966; (with Thomas L. Quick) *Ambitious Women's Guide to a Successful Career,* American Management Association, 1975, revised edition, 1980; (with Patrick Montana) *Career Life Planning for Americans,* American Management Association, 1976. Contributor to management journals and other periodicals.

WORK IN PROGRESS: A study of succession by chief executive officers, with Robert Fulmer, publication by American Management Association expected in 1982; a book on contemporary executives, with Thomas L. Quick, publication by American Management Association expected in 1983.

SIDELIGHTS: Margaret Higginson told *CA:* "I became a business writer and editor, after almost ten years in management consulting, at a time when the field offered few opportunities for women. I made the move because I wanted to acquire more portable skills and more contact with business people than I had been able to obtain in consulting. Also, the change enabled me to utilize the research experience and skills acquired in consulting. However, most of my education and outside activities have been in other fields—psychology, sociology, literature, art, and interior design.

"My involvement in numerous projects relating to women's careers during the past eight years has reinforced my conviction that women who want to succeed as peers and partners of men need not only substantial technical and technological expertise and superior interpersonal skills, but fortitude and tenacity to deal with the ambivalence of their many roles. Most women still have not come to terms with differences between what they are and actually do, and what they want or need to be and do. (Neither have men, but they seem better able to rationalize the differences.)''

AVOCATIONAL INTERESTS: Boating, design, painting, photography, land, nature.

*   *   *

HIGGS, Gertrude Monro
See MONRO-HIGGS, Gertrude

*   *   *

HILDERBRAND, Robert Clinton 1947-

PERSONAL: Born August 24, 1947, in Marshalltown, Iowa; son of Robert Clinton (a clothier) and Iris (Smith) Hilderbrand; married Darlene Hatch (a college administrator), September 6, 1968. *Education:* University of Iowa, B.A., 1969, M.A., 1974, Ph.D., 1977. *Home:* 403 East Main, Vermillion, S.D. 57069. *Office:* Department of History, University of South Dakota, Vermillion, S.D. 57069.

CAREER: University of South Dakota, Vermillion, assistant professor of history, 1977-78; University of North Carolina, Chapel Hill, visiting assistant professor of history, 1978-79; University of Missouri, Columbia, visiting assistant professor of history, 1979-80; University of South Dakota, assistant professor of history, 1980—. *Member:* American Historical Association, Organization of American Historians, Society of Historians of American Foreign Relations.

WRITINGS: Power and the People, University of North Carolina Press, 1981; (editor) *The Press Conferences of Woodrow Wilson,* Princeton University Press, 1982.

*   *   *

HILTON, Howard H(oyt, Jr.) 1926-

PERSONAL: Born July 8, 1926, in Chicago, Ill.; son of Howard Hoyt (a mortgage banker) and Carolyn (Purviance) Hilton; married Dorothy Watson, January 17, 1948; children: Howard Hoyt III, Rodney Watson, Leslie Elizabeth Ogilvie. *Education:* Attended Dartmouth College, 1944-47. *Politics:* Conservative. *Religion:* Episcopalian. *Home:* 2223 Bendelow Trail, Tampa, Fla. 33609. *Agent:* H. N. Swanson, 8523 Sunset Blvd., Los Angeles, Calif. 90069. *Office:* Hilton Advertising Agency, Inc., 3315 Memorial, Tampa, Fla. 33623.

CAREER: Universal Form Clamp, Chicago, Ill., assistant advertising manager, 1948-49; Mass Brothers Department Stores, Tampa, Fla., advertising director, 1949-58; Hilton Advertising Agency, Inc., Tampa, chairman and owner, 1958—; writer, 1979—. Member of Public Relations Association, 1958—, and Business/Professional Advertising Association, 1977—. Vice-president of Gulf Coast Symphony, 1956; director of Red Cross, 1960-62, Cancer Association, 1964-66, Heart Association, 1968-70, and Lighthouse for the Blind, 1979-81. *Military service:* U.S. Naval Reserve, active duty, 1944-46; became quartermaster; received Star of Nanking. *Member:* Mutual Advertising Agency Network (president, 1975), Tampa Advertising Club (president, 1956-57), Clearwater Advertising Club, Palma Ceia Golf and Country Club, Alpha Delta Sigma. *Awards, honors:* Named Tampa Advertising Man of the Year by Tampa Advertising Club, 1956.

WRITINGS: The Endless Tunnel (novel), Tower, 1980. Also author of an unpublished novel, *Out of the Forest, Thunder.* Contributor of numerous articles to trade and professional journals.

WORK IN PROGRESS: Black Waters, a novel, publication expected in 1982.

SIDELIGHTS: Howard Hilton's first novel, *The Endless Tunnel,* was thirty years in the making, a casual project the author returned to in his free moments away from the advertising world. "I always wanted to write a book, just to see if I could do it," he says. "I was always too busy, though, until my son shamed me into it. He completed his first book, and I decided I'd better finish mine." In the summer of 1979 Hilton reserved a month for himself in the Smoky Mountains and finished his book, a suspense story about people trapped in a tunnel under Boston Harbor.

Hilton comments that he has been writing almost every day of his life. But as head of advertising for Mass Brothers and then president of his own award-winning advertising firm, his writing was largely of a technical or industrial nature and tailored to the needs of the client. When writing a book, though, he is "absolutely unfettered," and the freedom to write whatever he wants has spurred him on to his second and third novels.

Now that he's a published author, Hilton receives calls from other would-be writers asking for his advice and guidance. It's part of the new-found celebrity he says he enjoys. With his agent negotiating with Hollywood producers, he may also see *The Endless Tunnel* developed as a motion picture. In the meantime his hope is that one of his books will be published in hardback: "I want a hardback book in my library with my name on it."

Hilton told *CA:* "In selling my first novel without an agent, my biggest surprise was the interest shown by the publishing houses. In thirty-some contacts, twelve separate publishers requested complete manuscript readings from my query letter. Prior to this, I had imagined I would be fortunate to get even a few requests. Letters which subsequently rejected the complete manuscript for various reasons were very helpful and informative. Hopefully my agent relationship will provide even more direction."

BIOGRAPHICAL/CRITICAL SOURCES: Tampa, January, 1981.

*   *   *

HIMBER, Jacob 1907-

PERSONAL: Born February 20, 1907, in New York, N.Y.; son of Abraham (a tailor) and Sarah (Goldberg) Himber; married Bertha Meyer (a musician and teacher), July 29, 1934; children: Jane Arlene, Victor Roy. *Education:* Attended City College (now of the City University of New York), 1924-28; Columbia University, D.D.S., 1931; attended Dewey School of Orthodontia, 1961-62. *Religion:* Jewish. *Home and office:* 3649D Southwest Natura Ave., Deerfield Beach, Fla. 33441. *Agent:* Writers House, Inc., 132 West 31st St., New York, N.Y. 10001.

CAREER: Private practice of general dentistry in New York, N.Y., 1931-50, and Westchester, N.Y., 1950-73; writer, 1973—. Instructor at Dewey School of Orthodontia, 1962-73. Public school dentist in Eastchester, N.Y. *Military service:* U.S. Army, 1943-45; became first lieutenant. *Member:* American Dental Society (life member), New York State Dental Society (life member), Ninth District Dental Society (life member), Masons, Rotary International, American Legion.

WRITINGS: The Complete Family Guide to Dental Health, McGraw, 1978.

SIDELIGHTS: Himber wrote: "Enforced retirement is repugnant, so, after lecturing and teaching, it seemed natural to put my thinking on paper. My thoughts grew into a book." *Avocational interests:* Bridge, golf, long walks, designing and casting original pieces of jewelry in silver and gold, reading.

*   *   *

HINDUS, Michael S(tephen) 1946-

PERSONAL: Born September 9, 1946, in New York, N.Y.; son of Jack and Theresa Hindus; married Lynne Withey (a writer), July 30, 1974. *Education:* Columbia University, A.B. (cum laude), 1968; University of California, Berkeley, M.A., 1969, Ph.D., 1975; Harvard University, J.D. (cum laude), 1979. *Residence:* Berkeley, Calif. *Office:* 3 Embarcadero Center, Suite 2800, San Francisco, Calif. 94111.

CAREER: University of Minnesota, Minneapolis, assistant professor of history, 1975-77; project director for Massachusetts Supreme Judicial Court, 1977-79; attorney in San Francisco, Calif., 1979—. Lecturer in law at Stanford University, 1982. *Member:* American Society for Legal History, San Francisco Bar Association. *Awards, honors:* Fellow of National Endowment for the Humanities, 1976, Russell Sage Foundation, 1976-78, American Bar Foundation, 1977, and American Philosophical Society, 1977.

WRITINGS: The Records of the Massachusetts Superior Court and Its Predecessors: An Inventory and Guide, State of Massachusetts, 1977; *Prison and Plantation: Crime, Justice, and Authority in Massachusetts and South Carolina, 1767-1878,* University of North Carolina Press, 1980; (with Theodore M. Hammett and Barbara Hobson) *The Files of the Massachusetts Superior Court, 1858-1959: An Analysis and a Plan for Action,* G. K. Hall, 1980; (contributor) Kelly Weisberg, editor, *Women and the Law,* Schenkman, 1981. Contributor of articles and reviews to history journals.

AVOCATIONAL INTERESTS: Travel, hiking.

*   *   *

HIRSCH, Charles S. 1942-

PERSONAL: Born December 18, 1942, in New York, N.Y.; son of Joseph (an artist) and Ruth (a dancer; maiden name, Schindler) Hirsch; married Tina Kugel (a film editor), December 15, 1968 (divorced). *Education:* University of Pennsylvania, B.A., 1964. *Office:* School of Visual Arts, 209 East 23rd St., New York, N.Y. 10010.

CAREER: Film Centre, New York City, founder and co-director, 1964; Garrick Theatre, New York City, program manager, 1965-66; Universal Pictures, New York City, director of new talent, 1966-68; *Millimeter* (magazine), New York City, film critic, 1974; School of Visual Arts, New York City, film chairman, 1977—. Producer, director, and author, 1968—. President of board of directors of Learning Through an Expanded Arts Program. *Member:* American Film Institute, National Academy of Television Arts and Sciences, Writers Guild of America, Association of Independent Video and Filmmakers, Film Forum, Society of Motion Picture and Television Engineers, Film Society of Lincoln Center, Channel Thirteen, Museum of Modern Art. *Awards, honors:* Silver Bear from Berlin Film Festival, 1969, for "Greetings"; MacDowell Colony fellowship, 1975.

WRITINGS—Screenplays: "Greetings," Sigma III, 1968; "Hi, Mom," Sigma III, 1970; "Does Size Really Count?," Distribpix, 1971. Also author of "Citizen Cohen," 1972, "Dead Bodies Don't Dance," 1973, "The Lady Was a Cop," 1976, "Summer Snow," 1978, and "The Weatherman," 1980, all as yet unproduced.

Author of a stageplay, "Call Waiting," as yet unproduced.

WORK IN PROGRESS: A screenplay, "False Start"; a novel, *Clear Breeze.*

SIDELIGHTS: Hirsch told *CA:* "In 1964 a friend got a job for eighty-five dollars a week as an assistant editor for WNYC-TV, and I realized that people paid you to make and write movies. This sent my law school applications into the 'circular file.'

"Early successes were followed by several years of 'line producing,' which I rate slightly higher than cab driving. I finally found my present academic niche, which permits me to write screenplays and stories until one of them gets made as a motion picture, preferably with myself as director and/or producer.

"Students: Don't go into film unless you are prepared to have many disappointments and have the courage of your convictions."

* * *

HIRSCH, Karen 1941-

PERSONAL: Born April 16, 1941, in Ashland, Wis.; daughter of Oscar Clarence (a mechanic) and Demrise (Gaudreau) Hagstrom; married Timothy Hirsch (a university professor), April 16, 1966; children: David, Stephanie. *Education:* Northland College, B.A., 1963; Wisconsin State University—Eau Claire (now University of Wisconsin—Eau Claire), M.A., 1969. *Politics:* Democrat. *Religion:* Unitarian-Universalist. *Home:* 483 Garfield Ave., Eau Claire, Wis. 54701. *Office:* Eau Claire Board of Education, 1222 Mappa St., Eau Claire, Wis. 54701.

CAREER: Teacher at public elementary schools in Wausau, Wis., 1963-67; Wisconsin State University—Eau Claire (now University of Wisconsin—Eau Claire), teacher at campus school, 1969-71; Eau Claire Academy, Eau Claire, teacher, summers, 1971-73; University of Wisconsin—Eau Claire, part-time teacher of remedial reading, 1973-76; high school English teacher at American school in Leysin, Switzerland, 1977-78; Eau Claire Board of Education, Eau Claire, elementary school teacher, 1976-77 and 1978-81, resource teacher for high achieving students, 1981—. Active in civic and religious groups. *Member:* Association for the Gifted, League of Women Voters, Wisconsin Council of Teachers of English, Wisconsin Council of Writers.

WRITINGS—Juvenile novels: *My Sister,* Carolrhoda, 1977; *Becky,* Carolrhoda, 1981; *Before Esther,* Carolrhoda, 1982; *A Girl With Diabetes,* Carolrhoda, 1983.

Contributor to magazines, including *Jack and Jill,* and newspapers.

WORK IN PROGRESS: A juvenile novel; "The Birthday Party," a musical play for children.

SIDELIGHTS: "I both love and fear new experiences," Karen Hirsch told *CA.* "Challenge sits on my shoulder like a little conscience and niggles me to notice the world.

"'Apply for that interesting new teaching position you saw posted!' Challenge urges.

"'Good idea!' I say. A spark lights in me, but then I groan, 'But am I qualified? Can I do that job?'

"Challenge pokes me and whispers, 'How about a year teaching in Europe? Wouldn't that be exciting?'

"'Oh, would it!' I agree. Shivers run through me. I'm thrilled. But then I think of a problem. 'What about the kids? They'll have to go to a French school!'

"After I've sharpened my pencil ten times, Challenge murmurs, 'Who says you only have to write for children? Try writing for adults!'

"'Hmmm,' I answer. 'But what could I write about? Where would I send a manuscript?'

"I've said both yes and no to Challenge. A couple of years ago he argued down all reservations and our family had a wonderful year living in Switzerland. Yes, the French school *was* hard for the kids!

"I've known Challenge a long time. In college he offered me a chance to be an on-stage helper to a mime who had come to present a program to our student body. I argued and argued. I reminded Challenge that I was shy. I told him that I was too skinny. I won the argument. But both Challenge and I were chagrined when we sat in the audience that day and watched another girl working with Marcel Marceau.

"Sometimes Challenge is silent for awhile, afraid, I suppose, of overloading the circuits. I expect he'll give me a breather this fall since I agreed with him to apply for that new job. It starts in September. He also convinced me to teach a short course in writing in October. Yes, he'll be mute this fall.

"But now he's here shrieking, 'Get going! Write! Do that article on teaching composition skills. Write about your mother's girlhood on Lake Superior. Revise that folktale!'

"And I mutter awhile, wondering why he doesn't suggest that I clean a cupboard.

"But it's Challenge that keeps my life fresh and renewed. It's the learning that I'm willing to undertake that keeps me young. The things I steadfastly refuse to tackle, such as learning French, are my loss, and I'm sorry about them.

"I'm happiest when I go ahead and try whatever available opportunities appeal to me. I've even learned—but not until recently—to forgive myself if my efforts produce little. That was a big step for me.

"What is wonderful is that sometimes I do okay, or even well. But either way, Challenge applauds my effort so loudly that I'm nearly always glad that I tried."

* * *

HIRSCH, Linda 1949-

PERSONAL: Born October 11, 1949, in New York, N.Y.; daughter of Sigmund (a plastics manufacturer) and Rose (Schweid) Hirsch; married Warren Lieberman (an art director), May 18, 1980. *Education:* City College of the City University of New York, B.A., 1971; State University of New York at Stony Brook, M.A., 1972. *Residence:* New York, N.Y. *Office:* Hostos Community College, 475 Grand Concourse, Bronx, N.Y. 10451.

CAREER: Hostos Community College, Bronx, N.Y., lecturer in English and instructor of English as a second language, 1975—. Director of the Hostos Writing Laboratory. *Member:* National Council of Teachers of English, American Film Institute, Teachers of English to Speakers of Other Languages, Society of Children's Book Writers, City University of New York Women's Coalition. *Awards, honors:* Leaders of the 80's award from American Association of Women in Community and Junior Colleges, 1980.

WRITINGS: The Sick Story, Hastings House, 1977; (contributor) *Critical Issues in Tutoring*, Networks Publication, 1978; (contributor) *Critical Issues in Writing*, Networks Publication, 1979; *You're Going Out There a Kid, But You're Coming Back a Star* (novel), Hastings House, 1982.

SIDELIGHTS: Linda Hirsch commented to *CA:* "It is my belief that adults frequently underestimate the pains of childhood. Children have far fewer coping mechanisms than adults for dealing with the barrage of difficulties they are confronted with everyday. In my writing, I attempt to humorously explore these difficult situations and some possible solutions."

*   *   *

HIRSCHFELD, Charles   1913-

BRIEF ENTRY: Born February 9, 1913, in Brooklyn, N.Y. American historian, educator, and author. Hirschfeld has been a professor of American history at Richmond College of the City University of New York since 1967 and director of American studies since 1970. He wrote *Baltimore, 1870-1900: Studies in Social History* (Johns Hopkins Press, 1941), *The Great Railroad Conspiracy* (Michigan State College Press, 1953), and *Degradation of Democratic Dogma* (Harper, 1969), and he edited *The Modern World*, 3rd edition (Harcourt, 1980). *Address:* Department of American Studies, Richmond College of the City University of New York, Staten Island, N.Y. 10301. *Biographical/critical sources: Director of American Scholars*, Volume IV: *Philosophy, Religion, and Law*, 6th edition, Bowker, 1974.

*   *   *

HIRSCHMAN, Jack   1933-

PERSONAL: Born December 13, 1933, in New York, N.Y.; son of Stephen Dannemark (a radio programmer) and Nellie (Keller) Hirschman; married Ruth Epstein, December 25, 1954; children: David, Celia. *Education:* City College (now City College of the City University of New York), B.A., 1955; Indiana University, A.M., 1957, Ph.D., 1961. *Home:* 1314 Kearny St., San Francisco, Calif. 94108.

CAREER: Poet, 1952—; Dartmouth College, Hanover, N.H., instructor, 1959-61; University of California, Los Angeles, assistant professor of English, 1961-66. Painter and collage-maker, with exhibitions in Los Angeles and Venice, Calif., 1972. *Member:* Union of Street Poets, Union of Left Writers, Roque Dalton Cultural Brigade.

WRITINGS—Poems: Fragments, privately printed, 1952; *A Correspondence of Americans*, introduction by Karl Shapiro, Indiana University Press, 1960; *Two*, Zora Gallery (Los Angeles), 1963; *Interchange*, Zora Gallery, 1964; *Yod*, Trigram Press (London), 1966; *London Seen Directly*, Cape Golliard (London), 1967; *Wasn't It Like This in the Woodcut*, Cape Golliard, 1967; *Ltd. Interchangeable in Eternity: Poems of Jackruthdavidcelia Hirschman*, privately printed, 1967; *William Blake*, Love Press, 1967; (with Asa Benveniste) *A Word in Your Season*, Trigram Press, 1967; *Jerusalem: A Three-Part Poem*, Love Press, 1968; *Aleph, Benoni and Zaddik*, Tenfingers Press, 1968; *Jerusalem, Ltd.*, Trigram Press, 1968; *Shekinah*, Maya, 1969; *Broadside Golem*, Box Zero, 1969; *Black Alephs: Poems, 1960-1968*, Phoenix Book Shop, 1969.

NHR, Christopher's Books, 1970; *Scintilla*, Tree Books, 1970; *Soledeth*, Q Press, 1971; *DT*, Yes Press, 1971; *The Burning*

of Los Angeles, J'Ose Press, 1971; *HNYC*, Skyline Press, 1971; *Les Vidanges*, Beyond Baroque, 1972; *The R of the Ari's Raziel*, Press of the Pegacycle Lady, 1972; *Adamnan*, Christopher's Books, 1972; *Aur Sea*, Tree Books, 1973; *Cantillations*, Capra, 1973; *Djackson*, Rainbow Resin, 1974; *Cockroach Street*, Street, 1975; *The Cool Boyetz Cycle*, Golden Mountain, 1975; *Kashtaninyah Segodnyah*, Beatitude, 1976; *Lyripol*, City Lights, 1976; *The Arcanes of Le Compte de St. Germain*, Amerus, 1977; *The Jonestown Arcane*, Poetry for the People, 1979; *The Cagliostro Arcane*, Michael Hargraves, 1981.

Editor: Antonin Artaud, *Artaud Anthology*, City Lights, 1965.

Translator: (With Victor Erlich), Vladimir Mayakovsky, *Electric Iron*, Maya, 1970; Artaud, *Love Is a Tree*, Red Hill, 1972; Rene Depestre, *A Rainbow for the Christian West*, Red Hill, 1972; Luisa Pasamanik, *The Exiled Angel*, Red Hill, 1973; Stephane Mallarme, *Igitur*, Press of the Pegacycle Lady, 1973; Ait Djafer, *Wail for the Arab Beggars of the Casbah*, Papa Bach Bookstore, 1973; Jean Cocteau, *The Crucifixion*, Quarter Press, 1975; Johann Maier, *The Book of Noah*, Tree Books, 1975; (with Alexander Altmann), Eleazer of Worms, *Three Tracts*, Beatitude, 1976; Alexander Kohav, *Orange Voice*, Beatitude, 1976; Kohav, *Four Angels in Profile, Four Bears in Fullface*, Beatitude, 1976; Robert Rodzhdestvensky, *Requiem*, Beatitude, 1977; Natasha Belyaeva, *Hunger*, D'Aurora Press, 1977; Alexander Kohav, *Emigroarium*, Amerus, 1977; Santo Cali, *Yossiph Shyryn*, Antigruppo (Sicily, Italy), 1981.

WORK IN PROGRESS: "The Arcanes are a continual work in progress."

SIDELIGHTS: Jack Hirschman lives in the North Beach district of San Francisco, where he is a member of the Union of Street Poets, a group that distributes leaflets of poems to people on the streets of the bay city. He has also been instrumental in the formation of the Union of Left Writers of San Francisco. Hirschman's poems, which have been compared to those of Hart Crane and Dylan Thomas, often reflect the poet's leftist political views and are noted for their novel treatment of language.

Hirschman told *CA:* "It is vitally important at this time that all poets and artists collectivize and form strong left cadres in relation to working class cultural internationalism."

BIOGRAPHICAL/CRITICAL SOURCES: New York Review of Books, February 29, 1968.

*   *   *

HODGSON, Margaret
See BALLINGER, (Violet) Margaret (Livingstone)

*   *   *

HOFSTADTER, Douglas R(ichard)   1945-

PERSONAL: Born February 15, 1945, in New York, N.Y.; son of Robert (a professor) and Nancy (Givan) Hofstadter. *Education:* Stanford University, B.S. (with distinction), 1965; University of Oregon, M.S., 1972, Ph.D., 1975. *Home:* 712 South Henderson St., Bloomington, Ind. 47401. *Office:* Department of Computer Science, Indiana University, Bloomington, Ind. 47405.

CAREER: Indiana University, Bloomington, assistant professor, 1977-80, associate professor of computer science, 1980—. *Member:* American Association for Artificial Intelligence, Association for Computing Machinery, Cognitive Science Society. *Awards, honors:* Nomination for National Book Critics Circle award for nonfiction, 1979, Pulitzer Prize for general nonfiction, 1980, and American Book Award, 1980, all for *Goedel, Escher, Bach: an Eternal Golden Braid;* Guggenheim fellowship, 1980-81, for study of computer perception of style in letter forms.

WRITINGS: Goedel, Escher, Bach: an Eternal Golden Braid (nonfiction), Basic Books, 1979; (with Daniel C. Dennett) *The Mind's I* (nonfiction), Basic Books, 1981. Also author of a column, "Metamagical Themas," in *Scientific American*.

WORK IN PROGRESS: Research on artificial intelligence.

SIDELIGHTS: Hofstadter told *CA* that he is "split by a combination of scientific and artistic interests." In addition to his work as a computer scientist, Hofstadter plays the piano, writes musical compositions, and studies languages. He speaks "French fluently, also German, Italian, Spanish, and Swedish to a lesser extent." The eclectic range of Hofstadter's interests is reflected in his Pulitzer Prize-winning book about consciousness and the abstractions underlying its explanation, *Goedel, Escher, Bach: an Eternal Golden Braid.* In it, Hofstadter uses ideas from many fields of human activity, including art and music, to illustrate, metaphorically, the subtle mechanisms that allow the human psyche to emerge from mere matter.

"The originality of the book, which is considerable," said *Observer*'s Anthony Burgess, "consists in its attempt to relate various fields of human enterprise in which the basic principle of paradox may be observed." The book is centered on a discussion of Kurt Goedel's Incompleteness Theorem which reveals that a related, near-paradoxical phenomenon occurs in mathematics by demonstrating that in any sufficiently complex axiomatic system true but unprovable mathematical statements exist. Hofstadter calls the structures giving rise to such incompleteness "strange loops" and gives examples of them in several areas of human knowledge and endeavor. For example, loops can be seen in the art of Maurits Cornelis Escher, whose drawing "Print Gallery" depicts a man looking at a picture in an art gallery; at the same time, however, the man and the gallery are a part of the picture. A loop can also be found in the music of Johann Sebastian Bach. His "modulating canon" from the "Musical Offering" begins in the key of C and "modulates upward in whole tones to end where it began—in C, only this time an octave higher"; but it can be played on a computer in such a way that "the return to C is made at the original pitch. Thus movement ever farther and farther away from home succeeds only in bringing you home," said Burgess.

Hofstadter goes on to argue that these loops and their relationship to one another form patterns that suggest ways to think about how human consciousness and intelligence are organized and how models of them can perhaps someday be artificially created. *Commonweal* reporter James Gips wrote, "The idea is this: If we truly understand some process . . . that requires intelligence, then we can write a computer program that embodies that process."

Hofstadter's ideas are complex, and his book, said Burgess, "assumes an ability to follow mathematical arguments, hold symbols in the mind, and read complicated music." But, according to the *New York Times Book Review*'s Brian Hayes, Hofstadter's "presentation of [his] ideas is not rigorous." Harry Sumrall of *New Republic* described Hofstadter's technique: "Each chapter is prefaced by a dialogue. These dialogues . . . are witty, playful exchanges that metaphorically describe the subjects treated in the chapters. The chapters then go on to elaborate the dialogues with historical and scientific concepts. These in turn are reinforced by a series of mind games, prints, and musical examples."

Gips hailed *Goedel, Escher, Bach* as "a wondrous book that unites and explains, in a very entertaining way, many of the important ideas of recent intellectual history."

The book sold over one hundred thousand copies during the year following its publication and "has become something of a classic," according to *Psychology Today*'s Howard Gardner.

CA INTERVIEW

CA interviewed Douglas Hofstadter by phone on September 29, 1980.

CA: You said in the preface to Goedel, Escher, Bach: an Eternal Golden Braid *that you wrote the book twice. What were your major dissatisfactions with the first writing?*

HOFSTADTER: Actually, I didn't write it just twice, I wrote it three times. I first did a handwritten version when I was still a graduate student in physics, and I did that in one burst. It took only about two months and was about two hundred and fifty handwritten pages. Then I started to type it up and create the next version. I was dissatisfied with the handwritten version because it didn't explain things clearly enough. With the second version, it took me eight months or more to type up the equivalent of what I had done in pen.

At that point I had to leave it because I hadn't finished my Ph.D. and I needed some time to work on that, so there was a period of about a year and a half that was just a sort of hiatus, although I thought about the ideas quite often. I never did much writing; I was really concentrating on other things. When I came back to it, I had to consider what I had as a finished product in some sense, and as I looked at it, I was really dissatisfied with it that time. What I perceived was a problem in addressing my readers—an inconsistent level. Sometimes, I sounded like I was addressing them as if they were very sophisticated and as if I knew I was talking with an "in" group—certain kinds of phrases that I would use and certain references that I would drop implied that they were members of a very literate group of people who knew all sorts of things. But other times, I would be slightly condescending and would say things in a way that implied they probably weren't familiar with some very elementary ideas.

It was interesting. Friends of mine and other people who read the book would comment on it. They would rarely use really insulting words—although one friend of mine did say, "I think this sounds condescending," which is a word that bothers me a lot. Most of the time they would say that it seemed a little "strange" or a little "stilted" or a little "awkward" or a little "funny" or something like that. I had that sense too, even when I was writing it, but I didn't know how to put it in words and I wasn't even sure what was wrong with it—and sometimes I thought the way I was phrasing things was good. Finally, I started to become sensitive to exactly what was wrong with it. When I began to pin labels on it, saying, "This sounds condescending," or "this is too much of an 'in' remark," I began to hit a medium between those extremes, where I wasn't taking too much for granted—where I was still explaining things, but not in a condescending way.

That was the third version, in doing which, incidentally, I very seldom referred back to the previous writing. I simply started again and rewrote it totally, but this third time I typed it into a computer and had the enormous sort of revolutionary ability to move around my text and copy things, delete things, alter things, and see it in a flash on the screen. That made a fantastic difference to my writing—it speeded the process up enormously, and also it changed my writing style.

CA: Does this have to do with the typesetting process?

HOFSTADTER: No, just the creating of the text. The typesetting came when the text was completely done. In computer science, *text editing* doesn't mean just editing something that already exists, it means text creation and editing, but the shorthand term covers the whole process.

CA: Were you greatly surprised at the book's success?

HOFSTADTER: Not really. It's very hard to know what my expectations were—they varied. Sometimes, at the extreme edges of expectation, I expected what happened. Other times I didn't think that it would do very well. In general, I guess I was fairly confident. I didn't have the confidence that it would go as far as it has gone; I couldn't have predicted that—or if I had predicted it, I wouldn't have done it publicly!

CA: Have you had any personal response that's been particularly satisfying?

HOFSTADTER: Yes. A number of people have written me letters that have been extremely thoughtful. There have been people who have written me the craziest letters—I really can't figure out why they've read my book at all, or *whether* they've read it. Sometimes I get the impression that they don't know anything, they're just absolutely confused and mixed up. It's upsetting when you get correspondence or phone calls from the strangest places and the strangest people. You feel like, "My God, is this what my book represents; it's reaching these real crazies?" I would say the crazies, so to speak, are around 10 percent of the correspondence I get. Another 10 percent of the people who write have something of real interest to say about the book. The most common type of letter is not very exciting; usually it just says, "I liked the book, here's a typographical error, would you answer one question?" or something like that. Once in a while there's a thoughtful, interesting letter from somebody who it obviously resonated with very much.

I find that almost always the people who send really interesting letters are people who have a very good sense of humor. That's important. The sense of humor doesn't necessarily manifest itself directly in what they write—it may be a very serious letter. They often say something about Lewis Carroll and how they love him, so that one can feel that they have a sense of humor. That's a really interesting thing. A lot of the crackpot letters I get don't seem to show that much of a sense of humor—the writers take themselves dead seriously. I didn't mean to concentrate on distinguishing crackpots from noncrackpots. It's just that it comes up because I'm inundated with a barrage of mail of one sort or another and I want to answer it, even though it's a time-consuming thing.

CA: What are the newest concerns in artificial intelligence?

HOFSTADTER: It would be hard to explain the technical issues, but they have to do with the problem that most programs are not flexible enough right now; they can do things within a certain domain but cannot generalize their performance. They are incapable of responding to situations that are slightly different from the ones that they were tailored for. In fact, just the slightest difference can cause the whole program to go completely haywire.

When humans encounter something slightly different than before, very often we hardly even notice the difference at all. If I drink one glass of tomato juice and then another glass of tomato juice, I can't tell the difference between the two glasses.

My perceptive mechanisms filter out every detail—I don't look at the patterns that are made on the glass as I pour the tomato juice toward me. I don't memorize them and compare them with the next glass of tomato juice, which, on a detailed level, won't leave anything like the same patterns. I filter that out completely; I don't even think about it. It's the same thing when I look at a person—in order for me to recognize him the next time, not every hair on his head has to be in exactly the same spot. The funny thing is that very often when somebody has shaved off his beard since we saw him last, we say, "Did you get a haircut?" or "What happened to your mustache?" We look so far beyond those surface-level things that we see something much more essential.

Computers at this point are not very good at anything like that at all. A computer program could be thrown off by a single strand of hair that had moved, not to mention different angles of view, facial expressions, lighting conditions, and so on. In a sense we are thrown off too, but not at the conscious level. Cells in our eyes pick up the positions of all those hairs and send signals back to the visual cortex, and different signals are sent when the hairs are in a different position. But the processing that takes place in the visual cortex is so complex and has so many layers that by the time it reaches the conscious level where we can sense that this is a person to be recognized, we've all but completely ignored the positions of hairs and things like that. We have to learn how to write computer programs that can layer the processing of information in such a way that, as it goes further and further, a higher and higher level of abstraction is reached, so that a lot of irrelevancies are filtered out and the computer can see beyond the surface to grasp more of what the essence is.

This is talking about computer vision, but the same kind of problem exists with flexibility in any place in artificial intelligence—it's really figuring out some way of making programs more flexible. Probably it's best not to discuss it in more technical terms, but simply to say that there are programs that *seem* intelligent, that give a good performance in certain domains—like chess programs, manipulations of mathematical formulas, or something like that—but they're not flexible in that they can't go beyond the domain that they're cut out for. It's that incredible flexibility of real intelligence that we still have to strive to create, and that's a long, long ways away.

CA: Would you comment on the belief that religion and science are incompatible?

HOFSTADTER: Certainly in a very limited sense, a standard sense, they are not very compatible. There are religious scientists, but to my mind that's because they are capable of compartmentalizing their minds. When I say religious scientists, I mean scientists who are very strict believers in standard, orthodox religion that says certain things about the world which simply are incompatible with science. Religious precepts, religious teachings, the ideas of religion that are abstract and have to do with morals are perfectly compatible with science. But if you take religion as trying to tell the story of the universe, you can forget it if you want to be a scientist and want to have an integrated world view. Now that doesn't mean one can't have feelings of awe and mystery and wonder at the universe, and have some sense of there being an incomprehensible order behind all things, but that is not anything remotely resembling the personal god that many religions have.

CA: Many people become disillusioned with math in the beginning stages and thereby close the door to future learning in many areas. Why do you think this happens?

HOFSTADTER: I really don't know. I've always been puzzled by it. It's hard to know whether to blame it on teachers or to say that it's a natural inclination of people. I hope that as microcomputers and personal computers get cheaper, kids in school will be able to use them to learn number concepts and to learn mathematics in a different way. Computers can be programmed to do all sorts of marvelous things, and kids can learn to program in elementary languages that are only now being developed specifically for their use. There are projects now that would teach kids the concept of programming, which is another form of mathematical ideas. It seems to me that has a tremendous potential, that kids can come into the idea of mathematical, or formal, models of the world through computers rather than through math. There's work going on in which kids can program a computer to make designs on a screen, or to play games, or to do various kinds of things that take considerable understanding of what computers can do and how they do it, but it's sort of effortless for many kids. Maybe it will turn out to be a new way for kids to approach mathematical concepts, a less traditional one—and perhaps it's one that fits our society better. It may be there's some sort of mismatch between our society and the teaching methods it uses, and it may turn out that computers will change that.

CA: In addition to your scientific interests, you have very strong artistic ones, such as music. Most of us have grown up with the notion that we could do something in the arts or something in the sciences, but not both. Do you think this is generally true?

HOFSTADTER: I think it's best to do something in both—not necessarily to be a professional, but to be an amateur. That's the nicest thing of all—to be a professional in one and an amateur in the other. I have friends in the humanities who read *Scientific American* with great interest or who buy a book once in a while on a scientific subject and go all the way through it. On the other side, there are scientists who paint or play a musical instrument. They don't necessarily integrate these activities—they may be just several aspects of the person. In my case, there's been a sort of natural integration for some reason; I've always tried to mix the two.

CA: After listing the people who had influenced you musically, you said, "Definitely not Beethoven." Why so specifically not Beethoven?

HOFSTADTER: That reminds me of how, in my Words of Thanks in the book, I sometimes felt tempted to include a paragraph that said, "No thanks to so-and-so." I singled Beethoven out because he's an enigma to me. For some reason I just do not respond to Beethoven. My friends and I even have this long-standing joke about it. But more seriously, it also raises questions such as to what extent one can talk about objective values in music, and what the difference is between objectivity and subjectivity in general, in music or science or anything else. I guess what's most interesting of all is my own attempt to probe what's going on with my dislike of Beethoven and my own willingness to admit—it hasn't come easily—that there are certain pieces by Beethoven that I *do* like, which is all the more puzzling to me. At least I'm willing to be honest about it and say, "Well, actually I kind of like this one." There are other things that get to me—ESP and parapsychology especially—that are much more important dislikes of mine than Beethoven is.

CA: What are your objections to ESP and parapsychology?

HOFSTADTER: I think they have zero foundation and that people who believe in things like that have not informed themselves as to the arguments against them. They haven't read even the most elementary debunking arguments that reveal all sorts of psychological mechanisms going on in the people who claim to manifest ESP or parapsychological phenomena. Then again, there are so many possible mechanisms in the believer that contribute to belief, and there are so many weird phenomena in the world. Finally, it's a question of understanding statistics and probabilities and understanding the relation of physics to the everyday world.

I think that most people could learn to see beyond the delusions of ESP and parapsychology if they were willing to devote the time to thinking about it. Most people aren't. Most people are lazy in that regard. They're not really interested in thinking hard about all the scientific issues that one would have to think about in order to confront these things—psychology, perception, physics, some things having to do with the brain; one has to deal with a lot of the philosophy of science and how it is structured; mathematics and statistics; one has to deal with the fuzzy psychology of willingness to believe and the desire to believe and the desire to trick. It becomes a very complex thing. It's not by any means a trivial thing to try and explain why such things are wrong and why they're not real. But most people are simply not willing to invest that effort. They make up their minds pretty early. They don't read a book. Even one book might make the entire difference, like Martin Gardner's *Fads and Fallacies* made with me. It flipped me around completely.

I think that about certain things, people simply need to be informed. There will always be people who read the *National Enquirer* and swallow everything. But there are more sophisticated people who will believe what they read in the daily newspaper about some strangler, for example, who's been discovered by psychic methods. Almost always such events have actually much more interesting explanations than the supposed ones that are given in the newspapers. Most of the time the reporters have distorted the facts to make sensational articles. When you actually look and see what really happened, it often doesn't even bear any resemblance to what the reporters say. But I have to give credit to some reporters. Occasionally there are articles featuring people who can reproduce all the techniques of the psychics on demand, and who also explain that they're just doing magic, and that there's nothing really psychic there at all. But people are willing to be fooled, *want* to be fooled, and want to believe in something kind of magical. Magic is the most important force on some ultimate level of human belief. You just have to choose your brand of magic. In my case, I guess it's a pretty abstract one that doesn't seem to argue against science, but rather, sees science itself as magical.

CA: One has the feeling that while you're doing the very serious things you do—teaching, writing about math and logic, composing for the piano, studying languages—you're really having a good time. Is this true?

HOFSTADTER: It's true in that it's all part of a fairly integrated life-style. Not in a simplistic sense, but in that the parts enrich each other. I wouldn't praise it above any other life-style. I do enjoy learning about various new aspects of science, doing research, and so forth. I suppose in that sense it's all having fun. It's hard to say.

CA: One detects a certain joy in your book.

HOFSTADTER: Maybe when I can look at it from a perspective of not two years but ten years or more, I'll be able to say that there was a special sense of joy in it. Actually, the two years that I wrote the final version were in some aspects of my life very unhappy. So when I look at that period as a whole, I can't say that I was particularly happy, but that doesn't mean that there were not certain facets of me that were absolutely filled with delight and joy. I would agree with you. There is a lot of joy in the book; there's no question about that. But my personality is one that has to mix its major and minor in a very intimate way, which, by the way, is something that I think my favorite composers excel in—particularly Chopin.

BIOGRAPHICAL/CRITICAL SOURCES: New York Times Book Review, April 29, 1979, November 25, 1979, December 30, 1979; *Scientific American,* July, 1979; *New Republic,* July 21, 1979; *Observer,* September 23, 1979; *Village Voice,* November 19, 1979; *New York Review of Books,* December 6, 1979; *Psychology Today,* December, 1979, March, 1980; *Yale Review,* winter, 1980; *Ethics,* January, 1980; *New York Times,* January 8, 1980, April 15, 1980; *Music Educators Journal,* February, 1980; *Byte,* February, 1980.

—*Interview by Jean W. Ross*

*   *   *

HOGARTH, Charles
See BOWEN, (Ivor) Ian

*   *   *

HOGUE, Charles Leonard   1935-

PERSONAL: Born February 4, 1935, in Caruthersville, Mo.; son of Leonard Guy (an engineer) and Muriel (Morgan) Hogue; married Barbara Jean Mitchell, August 25, 1956; children: James Norman, Brian Thomas, Carolyn Lee. *Education:* University of California, Berkeley, B.S., 1957; University of California, Los Angeles, Ph.D., 1962. *Home:* 1316 Saginaw St., Los Angeles, Calif. 90041. *Office:* Natural History Museum of Los Angeles County, 900 Exposition Blvd., Los Angeles, Calif. 90007.

CAREER: University of California, Los Angeles, scientific illustrator in entomology, 1957-61, junior research entomologist, 1962; Natural History Museum of Los Angeles County, Los Angeles, curator of entomology, 1962-67, senior curator of entomology, 1967—. Adjunct professor at University of Southern California, 1972—; member of Lepidopterists' Foundation, 1963—. *Member:* Society of Systematic Zoology, Entomological Society of America, American Lepidopterists' Society, Association for Tropical Biological Research. *Awards, honors:* Fellow at International Congress of Entomologists, 1964.

WRITINGS: The Armies of the Ant (self-illustrated), World Publishing, 1972; *Insects of the Los Angeles Basin* (self-illustrated), Natural History Museum of Los Angeles County, 1974; *California Insects* (self-illustrated), University of California Press, 1979. Contributor of more than fifty articles to scientific journals.

WORK IN PROGRESS: Insects of the New World Tropics.

*   *   *

HOLLAND, Jack   1947-

PERSONAL: Born June 4, 1947, in Belfast, Northern Ireland; son of Richard (a truck driver) and Elizabeth (Rodgers) Holland; married Mary Regina Hudson, October 5, 1974; children:

Jenny Elizabeth. *Education:* Trinity College, Dublin, B.A. (with honors), 1970; Essex University, M.A., 1972. *Residence:* Brooklyn, N.Y. *Agent:* Amanda Urban, International Creative Management, 40 West 57th St., New York, N.Y. 11222.

CAREER: National Railways of Ireland, Dublin, railway worker, 1970-71; free-lance writer and reviewer, 1972-73; Language Center of Ireland, Dublin, teacher, 1972-73; *Hibernia Fortnightly Review,* Dublin, assistant editor, 1974-76; British Broadcasting Corp. (BBC), Belfast, Northern Ireland, researcher, 1976-77; Rockland Community College, Suffern, N.Y., lecturer, 1977-78; free-lance writer, 1978—.

WRITINGS: Imperium Romanum (history), Volume 3 of "Great Empire" series, Harcourt, 1980; *Too Long a Sacrifice: Life and Death in Northern Ireland Since 1969* (history), Dodd, 1981; *The Prisoner's Wife* (novel), Dodd, 1981; *The Assassins: A History of the Ulster Defence Association,* Mercer Press, 1981. Contributor of articles to newspapers and magazines, including *Village Voice, New York Times Magazine, Nation,* and *New York Daily News.* Author of "Analysis," a column in *Irish Echo,* 1979—.

WORK IN PROGRESS: Druid Time, "a novel combining a history of the Bodecian Rebellion against Nero in A.D. 61 and a modern story of a treasure-hunting archaeologist and his difficulties with his women."

SIDELIGHTS: Jack Holland commented: "I write because I enjoy writing and getting paid for it. It is always rewarding to gain the praise of people one respects, and at the same time to give some pleasure in the process." In remarks published by the *Library Journal,* Holland talked about one of his novels: "*The Prisoner's Wife,* set in contemporary Belfast, is mainly about the moral dilemma of a working-class Catholic woman whose private life becomes inextricably entangled in 'the troubles. . . .' Writing *The Prisoner's Wife* has reminded me that as depraved as they often are, the violent acts which have made the slums of Belfast known throughout the world are resonant with historical meaning. In the end this historical dimension adds a poignant, lyrical quality to the Irish experience which *The Prisoner's Wife* could not but reflect."

BIOGRAPHICAL/CRITICAL SOURCES: Library Journal, June 15, 1981.

*   *   *

HOLLENDER, Edward A.   1899-

PERSONAL: Born January 21, 1899, in New York, N.Y.; son of Frederick and Anna (Cook) Hollender; married Emmy C. Freeberg, August 22, 1931 (died, 1966). *Education:* Received degrees from Massachusetts Institute of Technology, 1922, and Harvard University, 1924. *Politics:* "Independent-Conservative." *Religion:* Christian. *Home:* 91-15 196th St., Hollis, N.Y. 11423.

CAREER: Economic writer, business analyst, and industrial engineer with Bank of Manhattan (now Chase-Manhattan Bank), New York City, 1929-33, National Industrial Conference Board, New York City, 1936-43, U.S. Steel Corp., Pittsburgh, Pa., 1943-45, and U.S. Army, Office of Chief of Engineers, Washington, D.C., 1951-53; Voorhees Technical Institute, New York, teacher of chemistry, physics, and mathematics, 1958-60; teacher of chemistry, earth science, and mathematics at private school in Forest Hills, N.Y., 1960-62; teacher of chemistry at private schools in New York City, 1962-66; Barnard School, New York City, teacher of chemistry and metaphysics, 1967-71; writer and part-time high school chemistry teacher, 1972—.

Military service: U.S. Marine Corps, 1917-19; served in England and Scotland.

WRITINGS: Humanity at the Crossroads, Philosophical Library, 1972.

SIDELIGHTS: Hollender wrote: "At the base of a sound social structure for the future lies the factor of proper education—demonstrating how young people may grow into new areas of living in the most meaningful way: politically, economically, and spiritually free.

"Much instruction at present is still modeled after patterns designed for a previous cultural age—the Greco-Latin—when the desired objectives were primarily training the intellect, and expanding knowledge of the physical world by utilizing an ancient accumulated heritage of basically spiritual wisdom. Now the situation is different, if not actually reversed. We must utilize our vast reservoir of physical data to aid in becoming reacquainted with a total ecological realm, universal as well as global, that must be lived with rather than conquered, and that must be understood and intelligently used instead of exploited. For this purpose our present educational concepts and teaching methods are, in the main, definitely outmoded and generally unsuitable. It is not surprising that young people today find much of their instruction irrelevant and immaterial.

"According to Rene Dubos, the science of biology as it is now taught has little or no significance for understanding man as a thinking, feeling, and willing individual. Psychology, originally a science of the soul, has degenerated into a study of mere human behavior. Modern astronomy extends ideas and methods, useful on earth, into space, with the result that we have accumulated a tremendous amount of information about an inanimate universe devoid of any 'rhyme or reason' for existence. Similar considerations prevail in many other areas of learning, and in the meantime rational answers to the fundamental questions of human origins, significance of current chaos and confusion, and sound programs for future living recede farther and farther into the fog and mist.

"Teachers who are entranced by the idea that learning must be made as easy as possible—a sheer joy, in fact—by using all the latest devices for making the absorption of knowledge painless (and pointless) are following an educational principle that ensures that little or nothing of permanent value will be learned by the students. Three stages in the development of the young person must definitely be recognized wherein the educational approach must be different. It still holds good that if a worthwhile subject is to be mastered it must be wrestled with intellectually, for by so doing a strengthening and expansion of the imagination, inspiration, and intuition becomes immediately possible, and ultimately invaluable to him for future use in all areas of human activity.

"I am an activist, but to date progress has been slow in view of the intense mental fixation of most people upon our materialistic culture. I pin my hopes on the young people—they are way ahead of the generally reactionary faculties."

BIOGRAPHICAL/CRITICAL SOURCES: London, December, 1973.

*   *   *

HOLT, Will 1929-

PERSONAL: Born April 30, 1929, in Portland, Maine; son of William (a doctor) and Marjorie (Scribner) Holt; married Dolly Jonah (an actress). *Education:* Attended Williams College, 1947-48; and Richard Dyer-Bennet School of Minstrelsy, 1948-50. *Politics:* Liberal Democrat. *Home:* 45 East 66th St., New York,

N.Y. 10021. *Agent:* Jay Garon-Brooke Associates, 415 Central Park W., New York, N.Y. 10025.

CAREER: Folksinger, 1947-65; writer, 1955—. Professional actor, 1957-70. *Member:* American Society of Composers, National Academy of Recording Arts and Sciences, American Guild of Authors and Composers, Authors and Publishers, Dramatists Guild. *Awards, honors:* Obie award from *Village Voice,* award from Drama Desk, and award from Outer Critics, all 1970, all for "The Me Nobody Knows."

WRITINGS: Savage Snow (novel), New American Library, 1980; *A Woman of Fortune* (novel), New American Library, 1981.

Musical plays: "Signs Along the Cynic Route" (two-act), first produced Off-Broadway at Actors Playhouse, October 13, 1961; "That Five A.M. Jazz" (two one-act plays), first produced Off-Broadway at Astor Place Theatre, October 20, 1964; "Leonard Bernstein Theatre Songs" (two-act), first produced Off-Broadway at Theatre De Lys, June 6, 1965; "Come Summer" (two-act), first produced on Broadway at Lunt-Fontanne Theatre, March 21, 1969; "The Me Nobody Knows" (two-act), first produced Off-Broadway at Orpheum Theatre, May 17, 1970, produced on Broadway at Helen Hayes Theatre, December, 1970; "Over Here!" (two-act), first produced on Broadway at Shubert Theatre, March 15, 1974; (with Linda Hopkins) "Me and Bessie" (two-act), first produced in Los Angeles, Calif., at Mark Taper Forum, May 7, 1974, produced on Broadway at Ambassador Theatre, October 22, 1975; "A Kurt Weill Cabaret" (two-act), first produced Off-Broadway at Edison Theatre, May 4, 1976; "Music Is" (two-act), first produced in Seattle, Wash., at Seattle Repertory Theatre, October 1, 1976, produced on Broadway at St. James Theatre, December 20, 1976; (with Bruce Vilanch) "Platinum" (two-act), first produced on Broadway at Mark Hellinger Theatre, November 12, 1978; "Turns" (two-act), first produced in New York City at Theatre Workshop, June 5, 1980. Also author of "Ah, Men!" (one-act), first produced in New York City at South Street Theatre.

Also lyricist and composer of songs, including "Lemon Tree," and "Sinner Man."

WORK IN PROGRESS: "Pieces," a novel about four couples.

SIDELIGHTS: Holt told *CA:* "I started out as a folksinger in the fifties, at the Crystal Palace in St. Louis, Missouri. I came to New York and the Village Vanguard, played the Blue Angel supper club circuit, toured with Columbia Concerts, and began writing my own songs, like 'Lemon Tree' and 'Sinner Man.' I took to working on Brecht-Weill material, culminating in a theatre piece, 'A Kurt Weill Cabaret,' for which I was performer, director, writer, and translator. Then I began to write for the theatre.

"Influences on my work included Dyer-Bennet, and hearing the classic guitar used as an accompanying instrument. 'Threepenny Opera' and 'Gypsy,' along with circuses, side shows, and nightclub performing, showed me the economy of style and depth of material possible in musical theatre. I began writing novels when I realized I was giving too many stage directions, and decided to put the descriptions to work."

BIOGRAPHICAL/CRITICAL SOURCES: New York Times, December 15, 1961, May 13, 1964, March 19, 1969, January 1, 1971.

*   *   *

HOLTZ, Herman R(alph) 1919-

PERSONAL: Born June 26, 1919, in Philadelphia, Pa.; son of

David L. (in business) and Anna M. (a dressmaker) Holtz; married Reba Gerson, 1946 (divorced February, 1974); married Sharon Ann Goldberg, March 5, 1974; children: Arlene Marilyn, Donna L., Debbie Holtz Burleson, Alan. *Education:* Capitol Radio Engineering Institute, A.A.S., 1961. *Politics:* Conservative. *Religion:* Jewish. *Home and office:* 13609 Grenoble Dr., Rockville, Md. 20853. *Agent:* Bonita K. Nelson, B. K. Nelson Literary Agency, 10 East 39th St., New York, N.Y. 10016.

CAREER: Vitro Laboratories, Silver Spring, Md., senior engineering writer, 1963-64; U.S. Industries, Educational Sciences Division, Silver Spring, editorial director, 1964-66; Volt Information Sciences, Lanham, Md., general manager, 1967-72; Applied Science Associates, McLean, Va., general manager, 1973-74; *Government Marketing News,* Washington, D.C., president, 1974-78; free-lance writer, 1978—. *Military service:* U.S. Army, Infantry, 1941-45; served in Europe; became sergeant; received Purple Heart.

WRITINGS: Government Contracts: Proposalmanship and Winning Strategies, Plenum, 1979; *The One-Hundred-Billion-Dollar Market: How to Do Business With the U.S. Government,* American Management Association, 1980; *Profit From Your Money-Making Ideas,* American Management Association, 1980; (with Terry Schmidt) *The Winning Proposal: How to Write It,* McGraw, 1981; *Directory of Federal Purchasing Offices,* Wiley, 1981; *Profit-Line Management,* American Management Association, 1981; *Secrets of Practical Marketing for Small Business,* Prentice-Hall, 1982; *How to Be a Successful, Independent Consultant,* Wiley, 1982; *One Thousand and One Little-Known Sources of Financing,* Arco, 1982. Editor of *Citizen's Law Advisor, Government Marketing News,* and *Consulting Opportunities Journal.*

WORK IN PROGRESS: Directory of State- and Local-Government Purchasing, publication expected in 1983.

SIDELIGHTS: Holtz told *CA:* "My writing career is the only work that did not happen to me by chance. In over forty-five working years (beginning when I was orphaned at age fifteen), I have worked at many things, including as a waiter in mediocre and fine restaurants during the Depression years and as an Internal Revenue officer after World War II. I also worked in a television service business of my own, in electronics engineering, in technical writing on space and missile programs and computers, and in my own enterprise as an independent government contractor (primarily on writing projects). But I was always writing, in my spare time at first, later incorporating it into my daily work wherever and however it would fit. Yet, despite this checkered background of experience that would have served me well as a writer of fiction, the fiction genre never attracted me. My drive to write was satisfied most effectively by nonfiction, and my efforts were apparently most appreciated and most rewarded when I wrote on specialized business subjects. That has led me to discover what I should have known much earlier: that style or elegance of expression and fluency are of far less importance in a writer's work than insight—the ability to brush aside the distracting trivia and perceive the essence. It is equally important to be able to bring readers aboard, to share the insights, to enable others to share, and *that* is the essence of my writing.

"Analysis is not a new thing to me. As an engineer, and especially as one schooled in the discipline known as 'value engineering,' I am both trained and experienced in analysis, in logical introspection, in relating cause and effect, in discriminating between essentials and trivia. But unlike many of my fellow engineers, I have a drive to share this insight with others and an ability to do so with written words.

"My present career combines writing (which I cherish most) with consulting and lecturing. The bulk of my consulting consists of assisting companies in writing proposals for government contracts and delivering seminars to their staffs on the subjects of government marketing and proposal writing, but I also write and edit newsletters and handle a miscellany of writing jobs.

"In my writing I do things that either have not been done before or have not been done well enough, in my opinion. I write only on those subjects where I believe that I have something new to say or a better insight than has been revealed by anyone else. There is always a basic theme and purpose for each book. *Government Contracts* tells exactly what the government is and why it's a market; it is a primer, especially for those relatively untrained in proposal writing. *The One-Hundred-Billion-Dollar Market* explains that anyone can win government contracts. *The Winning Proposal* is a graduate course in proposal writing.

"I am an almost total pragmatist. Anything that does not have what I consider to be a practical application is waste, and I detest waste (probably a legacy from a Depression-days, never-quite-enough-of-anything existence). Ergo, I am probably attracted instinctively to writing from a how-to point of view, rather than a gee-whiz philosophy. Too, I am filled with enthusiasm when I analyze a process and uncover the essential mechanism, and whatever fuels my interest for any reason instantly becomes a subject for analysis."

*   *   *

HOOK, Frances 1912-

PERSONAL: Born December 24, 1912, in Ambler, Pa.; daughter of George Herman (a butcher) and Elsie (Campman) Arnold; married Richard Hook (deceased), June, 1937; children: Barbara. *Education:* Pennsylvania Museum School of Art, 1931-35. *Politics:* Democrat. *Religion:* Episcopalian. *Home and office:* Ocean Point Rd., East Boothbay, Me. 04544.

CAREER: Free-lance artist and illustrator. Work exhibited at Philadelphia Galleries, in Chestnut Hill, Pa., at Brick House Gallery, Boothbay Harbor, Me., in Wiscasset, Me., and at Maine Art Gallery. *Awards, honors:* Award of merit from Mead Paper, 1967, for *Train Up a Child;* award for outdoor advertising and magazine ads from Young & Rubicam, 1962, for Northern Tissue.

WRITINGS: (With husband, Richard Hook) *Jesus, the Friend of Children,* edited by D. C. Cook, Standard Publishing, 1977.

Illustrator; all published by Standard Publishing, except as noted: Allan H. Jahsmann and Martin P. Simon, *Little Visits With God,* Concordia, 1957; Jahsmann and Simon, *More Little Visits With God,* Concordia, 1961; *Frances Hook Picture Book,* 1963; Wanda Hayes, *My Jesus Book,* 1963; (stories by Hayes) *My Thank You Book: A Frances Hook Picture Book,* 1964; (stories by Hayes) *My Book of Bible Stories: A Frances Hook Picture Book,* 1964; *Train Up a Child,* Light and Life Press, 1965; *My Book of Friends,* 1968; Marian Bennett, *My Book of Special Days,* 1977; (with R. Hook) Jahsmann and Simon, *Bible Story Book,* 1978; Hayes, *Bible Stories Make Me Happy,* 1979; Richard Baynes, *Jesus Loves Me,* 1979; Hayes, *Jesus Makes Me Happy,* 1979; Hayes, *My Friends Make Me Happy,* 1979.

All published by Child's World, except as noted: (With R. Hook) *Taylor's Bible Story Book,* edited by Kenneth N. Taylor, Tyndale House, 1970, Doubleday, 1976; *Life's Greatest Treasure,* Hallmark, 1971; (written by editors of *Child's World*) *How Do You Feel?,* 1973, revised edition published as *Glad or Sad—How Do You Feel?,* 1979; Barbara Shook Hazen, *To*

Be Me, 1975, revised edition published as *I'm Glad to Be Me,* 1979; Ruth Shannon Odor, *My Quiet Book,* 1977, revised and expanded edition published as *Thank You, God, for Quiet Things,* 1980; Odor, *My Wonder Book,* 1977; Sylvia Root Tester, *Sometimes I'm Afraid,* 1979; Tester, *We Laughed a Lot, My First Day of School,* 1979; Tester, *A Day of Surprises,* 1979; Jane C. Buerger, *Growing as Jesus Grew,* 1980.

Written by Jane Belk Moncure; published by Child's World: *Spring Is Here!,* 1975, revised edition published as *Thank You, God, for Spring,* 1979; *Summer Is Here!,* 1975, revised edition published as *Thank You, God, for Summer,* 1979; *Fall Is Here!,* 1975, revised edition published as *Thank You, God, for Fall,* 1979; *Winter Is Here!,* 1975, revised edition published as *Thank You, God, for Winter,* 1979; *All by Myself,* 1976; *I Never Say I'm Thankful, But I Am,* 1979, special revised edition published as *But I'm Thankful, I Really Am,* 1979; *My Baby Brother Needs a Friend,* 1979; *Wishes, Whispers and Secrets,* 1979; *How Beautiful God's Gifts,* 1980.

Also illustrator of *Little Sleepyheads,* revised edition, Ideals.

WORK IN PROGRESS: The Children; a plate of Jesus; eighteen figurines of children for Roman, Inc., Chicago, Ill.; four plates featuring children.

SIDELIGHTS: Hook told *CA:* "I do the bulk of my work in pastels. I live on the coast of Maine where I also do watercolors of the area. When I'm doing a child's picture and getting exactly the feeling I want, I wouldn't change places with anyone. I get such great satisfaction from my talent. I was strongly influenced by the French impressionists and by the American Mary Cassatt."

BIOGRAPHICAL/CRITICAL SOURCES: Boothbay Register (Maine), August 14, 1981.

* * *

HOOK, Martha 1936-

PERSONAL: Born February 15, 1936, in Dallas, Tex.; daughter of Ben N. (an attorney) and Martha (Moore) Boren; married H. Phillip Hook (a camping executive), December 27, 1957; children: Brenda, Barbara, Mary. *Education:* Attended Austin College, 1953-54; North Texas State University, B.A., 1957; Southern Methodist University, M.A., 1959. *Politics:* Republican. *Religion:* Baptist. *Home and office address:* Pine Cove, Route 8, Box 443, Tyler, Tex. 75703.

CAREER: Philadelphia College of Bible, Philadelphia, Pa., professor of literature, 1957-59; free-lance writer, 1971—. *Member:* Symphony League of Tyler, Texas.

WRITINGS: Little Ones Listen to God (juvenile), Zondervan, 1971; *Women's Workshop on Faith,* Zondervan, 1977.

WORK IN PROGRESS: Imagine That, a collection of children's stories about the Bible.

SIDELIGHTS: Martha Hook commented to *CA:* "My writing grows out of our family's experiences in Christian camping and small-group Bible studies. I am also involved with seminars for women and couples in a public-speaking capacity."

* * *

HOOKER, Richard
See HORNBERGER, H. Richard

* * *

HOOVER, H(elen) M(ary) 1935-

PERSONAL: Born April 5, 1935, in Stark County, Ohio; daughter of Edward Lehr (a teacher) and Sadie (a teacher; maiden name, Schandel) Hoover. *Education:* Attended Mount Union College. *Residence:* Alexandria, Va. *Agent:* Harriet Wasserman, Russell & Volkening, Inc., 551 Fifth Ave., New York, N.Y. 10017.

CAREER: Writer. *Member:* Authors Guild, Smithsonian Institution, New York Museum of Natural History.

WRITINGS—For young people: *Children of Morrow,* Four Winds Press, 1973; *The Lion's Cub,* Four Winds Press, 1974; *Treasures of Morrow,* Four Winds Press, 1976; *The Delikon,* Viking, 1977; *The Rains of Eridan,* Viking, 1977; *The Lost Star,* Viking, 1979; *Return to Earth,* Viking, 1980; *This Time of Darkness,* Viking, 1980; *Another Heaven, Another Earth,* Viking, 1981.

Contributor to *Language Arts.*

WORK IN PROGRESS: A book for young adults.

SIDELIGHTS: In *Language Arts,* Hoover wrote: "I began writing the sort of stories I write for the simple reason that they are the type of stories I liked best when I was a child—that I still like best.

"My parents were both amateur naturalists. They could identify most plants, birds, and animals. Their books reflected their interest in human history and natural history. . . . My parents were good teachers. They gave my imagination something to work on. They gave me a sense of time and wonder. . . .

"There is currently a great deal called science fiction that includes no science. Chemistry, biology, and the most elementary physics are ignored. I like some science in my science fiction. I also like it tempered with characters one cares about. Technology, like slang, ages very quickly. What seems smart today will be *passe* tomorrow. The story that relies strictly on state-of-the-art technology is doomed to a very short shelf life—and to boring the bulk of its readers."

BIOGRAPHICAL/CRITICAL SOURCES: Language Arts, April, 1980.

* * *

HORAN, James David 1914-1981

OBITUARY NOTICE—See index for *CA* sketch: Born July 27, 1914, in New York, N.Y.; died after open-heart surgery, October 13, 1981, in Manhattan, N.Y. Journalist, historian, editor, producer, commentator, and author. Horan worked as a reporter and editor with the *New York Journal-American* for more than thirty years. While employed by the newspaper he won a Pulitzer Prize for public service after helping to write an article about a sick two-year-old girl in need of penicillin. The article was instrumental in obtaining the antibiotic for the child. A historian specializing in the Old West, Horan also wrote several books in that field. They include a trilogy, *The Authentic Wild West, Face and Voice of America's Wild, Wild, West,* and *Mathew Brady: Historian With a Camera,* which revealed previously undiscovered Civil War photographs. Horan also worked in television in a variety of capacities. He produced the series "Turnpike" and served as an editor and scriptwriter for the program "The D.A.'s Man." In addition, he was a commentator on the shows "Armstrong-Circle Theatre Hour" and "Assignment, Teenage Junkie." Obituaries and other sources: *New York Times,* October 14, 1981; *Chicago Tribune,* October 14, 1981; *Publishers Weekly,* October 30, 1981; *AB Bookman's Weekly,* December 21, 1981.

HORN, Richard 1954-

PERSONAL: Born October 23, 1954, in Brooklyn, N.Y.; son of Jerry (a certified public accountant) and Annette (a teacher; maiden name, Werner) Horn. *Education:* Columbia University, B.A., 1975; attended Clare College, Cambridge, 1975-76. *Agent:* Harvey Klinger, Inc., 250 West 57th St., New York, N.Y. 10019.

CAREER: Urban Academy (municipal planning research and development firm), New York, N.Y., editor, 1977-78; freelance writer, 1978—.

WRITINGS: Designs (novel), M. Evans, 1980. Contributor to magazines, including *Architectural Digest, New York,* and *Metropolitan Home,* and newspapers, including *New York Times.*

WORK IN PROGRESS: A novel.

SIDELIGHTS: Horn told *CA:* "My first novel was written as a commercial venture. I do not intend to continue in this direction. At present, I am reading a great deal, as well as writing. The authors who most interest me are Raymond Roussel, Henry Green, Marcel Proust, Robert Musil, Gustave Flaubert, James Joyce (especially *Finnegan's Wake*), and Philippe Sollers. I feel fiction should be a collaboration between writer and reader. Fiction should be complex, perhaps without seeming so. In fiction, words must be revealed as *at once* concrete and hopelessly inadequate, if that fiction is to breathe, to glow."

*   *   *

HORNBERGER, H. Richard
(Richard Hooker)

PERSONAL—Children: five. *Politics:* Republican. *Agent:* c/o Dodd, Mead & Co., 79 Madison Ave., New York, N.Y. 10016.

CAREER: Physician at Thayer Hospital, Waterville, Me. *Military service:* U.S. Army; member of 8055th Mobile Army Surgical Hospital in Korea.

WRITINGS—Under pseudonym Richard Hooker; with William E. Butterworth, except as noted; published by Pocket Books, except as noted: (Sole author) *MASH,* Morrow, 1968; (sole author) *M*A*S*H Goes to Maine,* Morrow, 1971; *M*A*S*H Goes to Paris,* 1974; *M*A*S*H Goes to London,* 1975; *M*A*S*H Goes to New Orleans,* 1975; *M*A*S*H Goes to Hollywood,* 1976; *M*A*S*H Goes to Las Vegas,* 1976; *M*A*S*H Goes to Miami,* 1976; *M*A*S*H Goes to Morocco,* 1976; *M*A*S*H Goes to Vienna,* 1976; *M*A*S*H Goes to Montreal,* 1977; *M*A*S*H Goes to Moscow,* 1977; (sole author) *M*A*S*H Mania,* Dodd, 1977.

SIDELIGHTS: Hornberger served as a U.S. Army doctor with the 8055th Mobile Army Surgical Hospital (MASH) in Korea. Out of this experience he created his 1968 best-selling novel, *MASH.* The novel's witty, irreverent surgeons generate humor amid the horrors of battle casualties and "get away with everything because they can repair wounded troops better than anyone else around," as Richard Rhodes explained in *Washington Post Book World.* Stanley Kauffman of the *New Republic* observed that Hornberger's *MASH* characters "still believe in the life on which their world is spitting, and they spit right back by saving life, if they can, light-heartedly." "The general hysteria in *MASH,*" Rhodes added, "and the brutal turns of surgical duty under battle conditions ring true."

A film version of *MASH* appeared in 1970. Directed by Robert Altman with a screenplay by Ring Lardner, Jr., the film won top prize at the Cannes Film Festival and brought Hornberger's work to international attention. In the fall of 1981, the top-rated television series "M*A*S*H," starring Alan Alda, began its tenth season, demonstrating the continued popularity of Hornberger's characters, now familiar to millions of Americans.

MASH's popular appeal is due in part to Hornberger's quick, original wit. But audiences also responded to the commentary on war that both the novel and the film presented. "It could be Vietnam as well as Korea," Kauffman declared, "and of course it really is Vietnam as well." Hornberger explained to William Joyce: "The film was released in 1970, when much of the country was growing weary of the Vietnam War. Reviewers never got tired of pointing out its anti-war theme. But when you think of it, who is pro-war? The movie wasn't anti-war, it was anti-foolishness of the regular army."

Hornberger spends sixty to seventy hours per week practicing medicine in Waterville, Maine. This demanding schedule would seem to leave Hornberger little time for writing. In fact, the author admitted that writing is "tough when you have a bad patient hanging over your head." Nevertheless, Hornberger created a dozen *MASH* sequels in the decade following the first novel's appearance. When asked about his pseudonym, Richard Hooker, Hornberger revealed, "I got the name from my golf game."

BIOGRAPHICAL/CRITICAL SOURCES: Washington Post Book World, November 17, 1968; *New Republic,* January 31, 1970; *Today's Health,* December, 1970, September, 1974; *New York Times Book Review,* March 5, 1972; *Saturday Review,* April 22, 1972; *Cincinnati Enquirer,* December 2, 1973.*

*   *   *

HORNSBY, Ken 1934-

PERSONAL: Born November 20, 1934, in London, England; son of John Francis and Elsie Louise Hornsby; married Anne Smith (a teacher), January 24, 1957; children: Jill Frances, Ruth Anne. *Education:* Attended New College, Oxford, 1955-56. *Religion:* Church of England. *Home:* 38 Elm Park, Stanmore, Middlesex HA7 4BJ, England. *Office:* Harrison McCann, 2-4 Fitzroy St., London W.1, England.

CAREER: Eastwoods Ltd., London, England, trainee company secretary, 1956-57; Willoden Central Library, London, library assistant, 1957-59; London Press Exchange, London, advertising copywriter, 1959-65; Lintas, London, senior copywriter, 1965-68; Charles Barker, London, deputy creative director, 1968-73; Rupert Chetwynd, London, creative director, 1973-75; Harrison McCann, London, creative director, 1975—. *Military service:* Royal Air Force, 1953-55.

WRITINGS: Is That the Library Speaking? (autobiography), St. Martin's, 1978; *The Padded Sell* (autobiography), St. Martin's, 1980; *Wet Behind the Ears* (comic novel), Dobson, 1980; *The Bitter Harvest* (supernatural mystery), Dobson, 1982.

WORK IN PROGRESS: A Little Learning, a sequel to *Wet Behind the Ears,* publication expected by Dobson; *Maddy,* a novel.

SIDELIGHTS: Hornsby commented: "Until 1978 I had not written a word other than for my business—as an advertising television and press copywriter. Suddenly I thought I would—and have now produced four whole and two half-books in rapid succession. They're all different; you could argue that I'm still searching for what I'm good at. Two are autobiographical; one is a comic novel, one a supernatural mystery. The new ones are a second comic novel and a 'straight' novel. Anything could happen next!''

*   *   *

HOUPT, Katherine Albro   1939-

PERSONAL: Born January 11, 1939, in Buffalo, N.Y.; daughter of John Nelson (an army officer) and Mary (Wilcox) Albro; married T. Richard Houpt (a physiologist), June 30, 1962; children: Thomas Albro, Charles Edward. *Education:* Attended University of Maryland, overseas branch, Munich, West Germany, 1956-57; Pennsylvania State University, B.S., 1960; University of Pennsylvania, V.M.D., 1963, Ph.D., 1972. *Politics:* Democrat. *Religion:* Unitarian-Universalist. *Home:* 1515 Trumansburg Rd., Ithaca, N.Y. 14850. *Office:* Department of Physiology, New York State College of Veterinary Medicine, Cornell University, Ithaca, N.Y. 14853.

CAREER: University of Pennsylvania, Philadelphia, research instructor in physiology, 1963-64; West Park Animal Medical Center, Philadelphia, veterinary clinician, 1964-65; Schneider's Veterinary Clinic, Philadelphia, veterinary clinician, 1965-67; University of Pennsylvania, veterinary clinican at veterinary hospital, 1965, research investigator in biology, 1966-67, member of Neurological Institute, 1970-72; Cornell University, Ithaca, N.Y., lecturer in women's studies program, spring, 1973, research associate, 1973-75, assistant professor of physiology and member of veterinary hospital, 1975—. Private practice of veterinary medicine, 1964-69. Visiting scientist at Council Institute of Animal Physiology, Cambridge, England, 1978-79.

MEMBER: American Physiological Society, Animal Behavior Society, American Society of Animal Science, American Veterinary Ethology Society, American Society of Veterinary Physiologists and Pharmacologists, American Veterinary Medical Association, Women's Veterinary Medical Association, Association for Women in Science, Graduate Women in Science, Eastern Psychological Society, Sigma Xi, Phi Zeta. *Awards, honors:* Grants from Morris Foundation, 1975-77, from National Institutes of Health, 1975-78, from General Foods Corp., 1976-77, and from National Science Foundation, 1977-80.

WRITINGS: (With W. G. Pond) *The Biology of the Pig,* Cornell University Press, 1978; (with T. R. Wolski) *Animal Behavior for Veterinarians and Animal Scientists,* Iowa State University Press, 1981.

Contributor: James Wieffenbach, editor, *The Development of Sweet Preferences,* U.S. Government Printing Office, 1977; L. M. Barker, M. R. Best, and Michael Domjan, editors, *Learning Mechanisms in Food Selection,* Baylor University Press, 1977; Alan Kamil and Theodore Sargent, editors, *Foraging Behavior,* Garland Publishing, 1981; R. R. Kersey, editor, *Veterinary Clinics: Small Animal Practice Symposium on Canine and Feline Geriatric Medicine,* Saunders, 1981; Kersey, editor, *Veterinary Clinics: Small Animal Practices,* Saunders, 1982. Contributor of more than sixty articles and reviews to veterinary and medical journals. Member of editorial board of *Applied Animal Ethology* and *Equine Practice.*

WORK IN PROGRESS: Research on horse behavior and other farm animal behavior, especially on formation and dissolution of the mare-foal bond.

SIDELIGHTS: Katherine Houpt wrote: "In the process of teaching animal behavior to veterinary students, I realized how little is known about the behavior of some of the animals that have been domesticated the longest. This led both to the prep-aration of a book specifically for veterinarians and others interested in domestic animals and also to research on specific aspects of domestic animal behavior, including feeding behavior of pigs and dogs, the social behavior of cats, learning in cows, sheep, goats, and ponies, and equine behavior in general. Originally I became a veterinarian because of my interest in horses, and now I can carry a 'horse crazy' childhood to its logical conclusion.''

*   *   *

HOWARD, Robert Ervin   1906-1936

BRIEF ENTRY: Born January 22, 1906, in Peaster, Tex.; committed suicide June 11, 1936; buried in Greenleaf Memorial Cemetery, Brownwood, Tex. American author. Howard is best known as creator of the character Conan, a barbarian king who lived twelve thousand years ago in the mythical Hyborian Age. Conan was the star of many of Howard's books, including *King Conan* (Gnome Press, 1953), *Conan the Barbarian* (Gnome Press, 1954), and *Conan of Cimmeria* (Lancer Books, 1969), and is still featured in comic books. Howard began writing professionally at the age of fifteen, contributing his adventure stories to *Weird Tales, Oriental Stories, Fight Stories,* and other pulp magazines. He also created a detective character, Steve Harrison, and several other barbarians such as Solomon Kane, Kull, and Bran Mak Morn, but dropped most of them when Conan gained popularity. In addition to his mythical tales, Howard also wrote poetry, Westerns, sports stories, and confessions. Many of his writings remained unpublished until after his death. *Biographical/critical sources: Savage Tales Featuring Conan the Barbarian,* October, 1973; Glenn Lord, editor, *The Last Celt: A Bio-Bibliography of Robert Ervin Howard,* Berkley, 1977.

*   *   *

HOWE, Deborah   1946-1978

PERSONAL: Born August 12, 1946, in Boston, Mass.; died June 3, 1978, in New York, N.Y.; daughter of Lester (a radio announcer) and Mildred Smith; married James Howe (a writer), September 28, 1969. *Education:* Boston University, B.F.A., 1968.

CAREER: Actress in New York, N.Y., 1969-78. *Awards, honors:* Dorothy Canfield Fisher Award, Golden Sower Award, and North Carolina Children's Book Award, all 1981, all for *Bunnicula: A Rabbit-Tale of Mystery.*

WRITINGS—For children: (With husband, James Howe) *Bunnicula: A Rabbit-Tale of Mystery* (illustrated by Alan Daniel), Atheneum, 1979; (with J. Howe) *Teddy Bear's Scrapbook,* Atheneum, 1980.

[Information provided by husband, James Howe]

*   *   *

HOWE, James   1946-

PERSONAL: Born August 2, 1946, in Oneida, N.Y.; son of Lee Arthur (a clergyman) and Lonnelle (a teacher; maiden name, Crossley) Howe; married Deborah Smith (a writer and actress), September 28, 1969 (died June 3, 1978); married Betsy Imershein (a theater producer), April 5, 1981. *Education:* Boston University, B.F.A., 1968; Hunter College, M.A., 1977. *Residence:* New York, N.Y. *Agent:* Lucy Kroll Agency, 390 West End Ave., New York, N.Y. 10024.

CAREER: Free-lance actor and director, 1971-75; Lucy Kroll Agency, New York, N.Y., literary agent, 1976-81; member of advisory boards of Hospice of St. Vincent's Hospital, 1979-81, and Ethnic Heritage Program, Henry Street Settlement, 1980—; member of board of trustees of Village Temple, 1980—. *Wartime service:* Civilian public service, 1968-70. *Member:* Authors Guild.

AWARDS, HONORS: Dorothy Canfield Fisher Award, 1981, Golden Sower Award from department of elementary education at University of Nebraska, 1981, and South Carolina Children's Book Award from South Carolina Association of School Librarians, 1981, all for *Bunnicula: A Rabbit-Tale of Mystery; Boston Globe-Horn Book* honor book award in nonfiction, 1981, for *The Hospital Book; The Hospital Book* was named one of the best books of the year by *School Library Journal,* 1981.

WRITINGS—Juveniles: (With wife, Deborah Howe) *Bunnicula: A Rabbit-Tale of Mystery* (illustrated by Alan Daniel), Atheneum, 1979; (with D. Howe) *Teddy Bear's Scrapbook* (illustrated by David S. Rose), Atheneum, 1980; *The Hospital Book* (illustrated by Mal Warshaw), Crown, 1981; *Howliday Inn* (illustrated by Lynn Munsinger), Atheneum, 1982.

WORK IN PROGRESS: A Night Without Stars, a young adult novel.

* * *

HUANG, Philip Chung-Chih 1940-

BRIEF ENTRY: Born October 1, 1940, in Hong Kong. Historian, educator, and author. Huang has taught modern Chinese history at University of California, Los Angeles, since 1966. His books include *Liang Ch'i-ch'ao and Modern Chinese Liberalism* (University of Washington Press, 1972), *Chinese Communists and Rural Society, 1927-1934* (Center for Chinese Studies, University of California, Berkeley, 1978), and *The Development of Underdevelopment in China: A Symposium* (M. E. Sharpe, 1980). *Address:* Department of History, University of California, 405 Hilgard Ave., Los Angleles, Calif. 90024. *Biographical/critical sources: Directory of American Scholars,* Volume I: *History,* 7th edition, Bowker, 1978.

* * *

HUDD, Roy 1936-

PERSONAL: Born May 16, 1936, in Croydon, England; son of Harold Charles (a carpenter) and Evelyn (Bahram) Hudd; married Ann Vera Lambert (a photographer); children: Maxwell Roy. *Education:* Attended school in Croydon, England. *Residence:* Nettlebed, England. *Agent:* Morris Aza, 652 Finchley Rd., London NW11 7NT, England. *Office:* 52 Queen Anne St., London W.1, England.

CAREER: Actor and comedian, 1958—. Director of Roy Hudd Enterprises Ltd.; chairman of Entertainment Artists Benevolent Fund; member of Haymarket Theatre Leicester Trust. Has worked as commercial artist and window dresser. *Military service:* Royal Air Force, 1955-57. *Member:* Green Room Club.

WRITINGS: Roy Hudd Joke Book, Wolfe Publishing, 1970; *Music Hall,* Eyre Methuen, 1977.

Plays: "Victorian Christmas" (two-act), first produced in Leicester, England, at Haymarket Theatre, December 22, 1978; "Roy Hudd's Very Own Music Hall" (two-act; for one performer), first produced in Henley-on-Thames, England, at Kenton Theatre, January 21, 1979; "Just a Verse and Chorus" (two-act), first produced in Leicester, at Haymarket Theatre, December 19, 1979; "Beautiful Dreamer" (two-act; about Stephen Foster), first produced in Leicester, at Haymarket Theatre, December 18, 1980; (co-author) "Underneath the Arches"

(two-act), first produced in Chichester, England, at Chichester Festival Theatre, July 29, 1981.

WORK IN PROGRESS: A definitive biographical dictionary of British Music Hall; a musical play.

SIDELIGHTS: Hudd began his career at Metropolitan Music Hall in London in 1958. He has played Shakespearean and contemporary roles at the Palace, the Garrick, and other British theatres, including the role of Fagin in the musical "Oliver!" He has given solo shows and appeared in variety shows at British music halls, and has performed in films and on television, including his own series.

Hudd commented: "I am mostly engaged in devising, writing, and acting in theatre shows. I am a compulsive performer. I began writing at the Haymarket Theatre in Leicester, purely to entertain. I use the very popular entertainments of the past to tell the story: music hall, melodrama, minstrel shows, lantern slides, and popular songs. As an actor I like the idea of having an income when I'm not actually acting!

"I find writing a very hard slog. I can only sit down and go from start to finish, concentrating solely on the job at hand. I cannot 'pick' at the subject, that is, work in the theatre as a performer and write during the free time. It is very rewarding to see the thing come to life but cannot compare with 'doing it yourself.' I love performing best of all. I've always written about things close to my heart, performers, and composers. I am about to try the adaptation of a famous novel into a musical, for the first time working with a composer. You can bet I'm writing a great part for myself!"

* * *

HULL, Marion A(da) 1911-

PERSONAL: Born July 23, 1911, in Fairwater, Wis.; daughter of Henry H. (a farmer) and Catherine (Bruhn) Hull. *Education:* Attended Fond du Lac County Rural Normal School, 1928-29; Oshkosh Teachers College (now University of Wisconsin—Oshkosh), B.S., 1940; Columbia University, M.A., 1945; Northwestern University, Ph.D., 1959. *Religion:* Presbyterian. *Home:* 10739 Tropicana Circle, Sun City, Ariz. 85351.

CAREER: Teacher at rural schools in Fond du Lac County, Wis., 1929-38, and elementary school in Neenah, Wis., 1940-41; supervising teacher at public schools in Fond du Lac County, 1941-47; Reformed Church in America, New York, N.Y., executive secretary of Women's Mission Work, 1947-50; Northwestern College, Orange City, Iowa, instructor in education, 1950-55; Northwestern University, Evanston, Ill., instructor in education, 1955-57; Northern Illinois University, DeKalb, assistant professor, 1957-60, associate professor, 1960-70, professor of education, 1970-73. *Member:* Phi Beta Sigma, Pi Lambda Theta, Delta Kappa Gamma, Pi Kappa Delta.

WRITINGS: Phonics for the Teacher of Reading, C. E. Merrill, 1969, 3rd edition, 1981; (editor with Joan H. Kuipers and Christopher D. Lozier) *A Handbook for Evaluation and Measurement,* Associated Educational Services, 1970.

BIOGRAPHICAL/CRITICAL SOURCES: Elementary English Review, December, 1945; *Wisconsin Journal of Education,* May, 1954; Shirley E. Greene, *The Education of Migrant Children,* National Council on Agricultural Life and Labor, 1954.

* * *

HUNTER, Joan
See YARDE, Jeanne Betty Frances Treasure

HUNTER, Richard 1923-1981

OBITUARY NOTICE: Born in 1923 in Germany; died November 25, 1981, in England. Psychiatrist, historian, and author. As a psychiatrist, Hunter was primarily interested in the psychological manifestations of organic neurological disease. He is best known for his historical writing, especially *Three Hundred Years of Psychiatry, 1535-1860,* which he wrote in collaboration with his mother, Ida Macalpine, also a psychiatrist. Obituaries and other sources: *London Times,* December 1, 1981; *AB Bookman's Weekly,* January 18, 1982.

*　　*　　*

HUNTER, Rodello
See CALKINS, Rodello

*　　*　　*

HUNTER, Valancy
See MEAKER, Eloise

*　　*　　*

HYDER, O(liver) Quentin 1930-

BRIEF ENTRY: Born February 3, 1930, in London, England. Psychiatrist and author. Hyder has been a physician since 1955 and a research assistant at New York State Psychiatric Institute since 1968. He wrote *The Christian's Handbook of Psychiatry* (Revell, 1971), *The People You Live With* (Revell, 1975), and *Shape Up* (Revell, 1979). *Address:* 342 Madison Ave., New York, N.Y. 10017. *Biographical/critical sources: Biographical Directory of the Fellows and Members of the American Psychiatric Association,* Bowker, 1977.

*　　*　　*

HYMAN, Helen Kandel 1920-

PERSONAL: Born November 10, 1920, in New York, N.Y.; daughter of Isaac L. (a professor) and Jessie (Davis) Kandel; married Herbert H. Hyman (a college professor), September 30, 1945; children: Lisa, David, Alex. *Education:* Barnard College, B.A., (cum laude), 1942. *Home:* 38 Woodside Ave., Westport, Conn. 06880. *Agent:* Georges Borchardt, 136 East 57th St., New York, N.Y. 10022.

CAREER: Columbia Broadcasting System, Inc., New York, N.Y., writer, 1942-49; free-lance writer, researcher, and editor, 1950—; Institute of Children's Literature, West Redding, Conn., instructor and editor, 1971—. *Member:* Phi Beta Kappa.

WRITINGS: (Adapter) *A Treasury of the World's Greatest Fairy Tales* (juvenile), Danbury Press, 1972; (adapter) James Fenimore Cooper, *The Last of the Mohicans* (juvenile), Danbury Press, 1973; (with Barbara Silverstone) *You and Your Aging Parent: The Modern Family's Guide to Emotional, Physical, and Financial Problems,* Pantheon, 1976.

WORK IN PROGRESS: A nonfiction book and a fantasy.

SIDELIGHTS: Helen Hyman told *CA:* "I have had over twenty years experience as a professional writer of radio dramas and documentaries, interview programs, pamphlets and brochures, fund-raising materials, and benefit programs to name a few. My assignments have come from a number of places, including radio and TV networks, schools, advertising agencies, welfare agencies, health organizations, life insurance companies, universities, hospitals, and publishing houses.

"As a writer-researcher, I have always researched my own assignments and know how to go about tackling new and unfamiliar fields, whether through personal interview, library research or on-the-spot observation. Over the years, I have had to burrow for material in a wide variety of fields, from medicine and social work to fashion and travel.

"I have always been interested in children's literature and was lucky enough to be assigned adaptations to write when I was at CBS. I am more interested now in writing books myself than in adapting them.

"My interest in writing *You and Your Aging Parent* was also a long-standing one, as I've been interested in old people from childhood. I tried to place documentaries and pamphlets on the subject for years but with no success. No one was interested in old age for popular readership until the 1970's."

*　　*　　*

HYNES, Samuel (Lynn) 1924-

PERSONAL: Born August 29, 1924, in Chicago, Ill.; son of Samuel Lynn and Margaret (Turner) Hynes; married Elizabeth Igleheart, July 28, 1944; children: Miranda, Joanna. *Education:* University of Minnesota, B.A., 1947; Columbia University, M.A., 1948, Ph.D., 1956. *Office:* Department of English, Princeton University, Princeton, N.J. 08540.

CAREER: Swarthmore College, Swarthmore, Pa., 1949-68, began as instructor, professor of English literature, 1965-68; Northwestern University, Evanston, Ill., professor of English, 1968-76; Princeton University, Princeton, N.J., professor of English, 1976—. *Military service:* U.S. Marine Corps Reserve, active duty, 1943-46 and 1952-53; became major; received Air Medal and Distinguished Flying Cross. *Member:* English Institute, Phi Beta Kappa. *Awards, honors:* Fulbright fellow, 1953-54; Guggenheim fellow, 1959-60; Explicator Award from the Explicator Literary Foundation, 1962, for *The Pattern of Hardy's Poetry;* Bollingen Foundation fellow, 1964-65; American Council of Learned Societies fellow, 1969; National Endowment for the Humanities senior fellow, 1973-74.

WRITINGS: The Pattern of Hardy's Poetry, University of North Carolina Press, 1961; *William Golding,* Columbia University Press, 1964; *The Edwardian Turn of Mind,* Princeton University Press, 1968; *Edwardian Occasions: Essays on English Writing in the Early Twentieth Century,* Oxford University Press, 1972; *The Auden Generation: Literature and Politics in England in the 1930's,* Bodley Head, 1976, Viking, 1977; (author of introduction) *Rebecca West, A Celebration: A Selection of Her Writings Chosen by Her Publisher and Rebecca West,* Viking, 1977.

Editor: *Further Speculations by T.E. Hulme,* University of Minnesota Press, 1955; *English Literary Criticism: Restoration and Eighteenth Century,* Appleton, 1963; (with Daniel G. Hoffman) *English Literary Criticism: Romantic and Victorian,* Appleton, 1963; *Great Short Works of Thomas Hardy,* Harper, 1967; Arnold Bennett, *The Author's Craft and Other Critical Writings of Arnold Bennett,* University of Nebraska Press, 1968; Christopher Caudwell, *Romance and Realism: A Study in English Bourgeois Literature by Christopher Caudwell,* Princeton University Press, 1970; (and author of introduction) *Twentieth-Century Interpretations of 1984: A Collection of Critical Essays,* Prentice-Hall, 1971; *Graham Greene: A Collection of Critical Essays,* Prentice-Hall, 1973.

WORK IN PROGRESS: Editing *Complete Poetical Works of Thomas Hardy* to be published by Oxford University Press.

I

IAN, Janis 1951-

BRIEF ENTRY: Born April 7, 1951, in New York, N.Y. American singer, composer, and songwriter. Janis Ian has been a recording artist since she was sixteen, but she was only thirteen when she wrote her first song, "Society's Child," which became a million-seller. She has won a platinum and two gold records and a Grammy Award. In addition to such popular songs as "Jesse" and "At Seventeen," Ian wrote a book of poems, *Who Really Cares* (1969). *Address:* 850 Seventh Ave., New York, N.Y. 10019. *Biographical/critical sources: Time,* October 24, 1969; *New York Times Book Review,* February 15, 1970; *New York Times,* February 9, 1977; *Who's Who in America,* 40th edition, Marquis, 1978.

*   *   *

INGRAM, Helen Moyer 1937-

PERSONAL: Born July 12, 1937, in Denver, Colo.; daughter of Oliver Weldon (in sales) and Hazel Margaret (a teacher; maiden name, Wickard) Hill; married in 1960 (divorced); children: Mrill, Maia, Seth. *Education:* Oberlin College, B.A., 1959; Columbia University, Ph.D., 1967. *Home:* 3244 East Waverly, Tucson, Ariz. 85716. *Office:* Department of Political Science, University of Arizona, Tucson, Ariz. 85721.

CAREER: University of New Mexico, Albuquerque, assistant professor of political science, 1963-69; National Water Commission, Arlington, Va., member of political science staff, 1970-71; University of Arizona, Tucson, associate professor, 1972-77, professor of political science, 1977—. Milton R. Merrill Professor at University of Utah, 1981. *Member:* American Political Science Association, Western Political Science Association (president, 1982), Policy Studies Organization. *Awards, honors:* Grants from New Mexico Water Resources Research Center, 1968-69, Arizona Water Resources Research Center, 1973-74, and Water Resources Council, 1973.

WRITINGS: (With Nancy Laney and John R. McCain) *A Policy Approach to Political Representation,* Johns Hopkins Press, 1980; (editor with Dean Mann) *Why Policies Succeed or Fail,* Sage Publications, 1980. Contributor to political science and natural resources journals. Associate editor of *Natural Resources Journal,* 1973—.

WORK IN PROGRESS: Research in water conservation in the West and Indian water rights.

SIDELIGHTS: Helen Ingram told *CA:* "Water in arid environments is a precious commodity, and the way water is allocated is a tracer element that often indicates how wealth, political power, social status and opportunity are distributed. Early in my research and writing I was concerned with describing and explaining the pattern of politics through which water resources projects were authorized and funded by the federal government. As demands for water in the West press close upon supplies, and opportunities for new supply projects dim, I have shifted forces to the reallocation of existing supplies. Currently, my particular interests are water conservation and the disposition of Indian water rights."

*   *   *

IRELAND, Patrick
See O'DOHERTY, Brian

*   *   *

IRON, Ralph
See SCHREINER, Olive (Emilie Albertina)

*   *   *

IRWIN, Francis William 1905-

BRIEF ENTRY: Born February 11, 1905, in Philadelphia, Pa. American psychologist, educator, and author. Irwin taught at University of Pennsylvania from 1926 to 1974. He was a professor of psychology from 1952 to 1974 and was named professor emeritus in 1974. He edited *Journal of Experimental Psychology* from 1947 to 1951 and wrote *Intentional Behavior and Motivation: A Cognitive Theory* (Harper, 1971). *Address:* 2215 Delancey Pl., Philadelphia, Pa. 19103. *Biographical/critical sources: Who's Who in America,* 40th edition, Marquis, 1978.

*   *   *

IVENS, Virginia R(uth) 1922-

PERSONAL: Born July 27, 1922, in Decatur, Ill.; daughter of John Raymond (a pharmacist) and Dessie Lenora (an apprentice pharmacist; maiden name, Underwood) Ivens. *Education:* University of Illinois, B.S., 1950. *Home:* 608 South Edwin St., Champaign, Ill. 61820. *Office:* College of Veterinary Medicine, University of Illinois, 303 Veterinary Medicine Annex, 1101 West Peabody Dr., Urbana, Ill. 61801.

CAREER: Caterpillar Military Engine Co., Decatur, Ill., tracer of blueprints, 1941-45; University of Illinois, Urbana, research assistant, 1950-56, instructor, 1956-71, assistant professor, 1971-79, associate professor of veterinary parasitology, 1979—. Member of board of directors of University of Illinois Employees Credit Union. *Member:* American Society of Parasitologists, Entomological Society of America, American Institute of Biological Sciences, Society of Protozoologists, League of Women Voters, Young Women's Christian Association, Women's Network, Sigma Xi, Phi Zeta. *Awards, honors:* Grants from National Science Foundation, 1966-76, National Institutes of Health, 1977—, and U.S. Department of Agriculture, 1979-81.

WRITINGS: (With Norman D. Levine) *The Coccidian Parasites (Protozoa: Sporozoa) of Rodents* (monograph), University of Illinois Press, 1965; (with Levine) *The Coccidian Parasites (Protozoa, Apicomplexa) of Ruminants* (monograph), University of Illinois Press, 1970; (with Levine and Daniel L. Mark) *Principal Parasites of Domestic Animals in the United States: Biological and Diagnostic Information,* Colleges of Agriculture and Veterinary Medicine, University of Illinois, 1978; (with Levine) *The Coccidian Parasites (Protozoa, Apicomplexa) of Carnivores* (monograph), University of Illinois Press, 1981. Contributor of articles and translations (from Russian) to scientific journals.

WORK IN PROGRESS: *The Coccidian Parasites (Protozoa, Apicomplexa) of Artiodactyla,* a monograph, with Levine; revising *The Coccidian Parasites (Protozoa: Sporozoa) of Rodents,* with Levine.

SIDELIGHTS: Virginia Ivens wrote: "In the late fifties, we started our studies of the coccidia. We examined fecal material from rodents of the Grand Canyon and found them to contain coccidian oocysts.

"In the process of our study of the world literature, we found that the articles on coccidia were widely scattered and difficult to obtain. It was at this time that I began to study Russian in order to translate Russian articles. We found that the taxonomic articles on coccidia did not follow the rules of nomenclature precisely, causing both confusion and error. So, we decided to correct the errors and include the information in world literature with our own articles.

"The rodent coccidia work took eight years to complete. Then, since we found the taxonomic confusion to be widespread, we extended our work to include coccidia of other hosts.

"*Principal Parasites of Domestic Animals in the United States* was to have been nothing more than a rather large pamphlet based on another out-of-print pamphlet, *Microscopic Diagnosis of Parasitism in Domestic Animals.* As senior author, I prepared the manuscript with one specific goal in mind: I wished to make the subject matter understandable both to students who had no previous training in parasitology, and to clients who wished to understand the biology of the parasites in their animals that were under treatment by veterinarians."

BIOGRAPHICAL/CRITICAL SOURCES: Journal of Parasitology, August, 1966, June, 1971; American Veterinary Medical Association Journal, January 15, 1979; Quarterly Review of Biology, June, 1979.

IVERSON, Jeffrey (James) 1934-

PERSONAL: Born January 18, 1934, in Newport, England; married Ann Farrall (a speech therapist), 1962; children: Stephen, Sarah, James. *Education:* Attended high school in Newport, England. *Religion:* Agnostic. *Home:* 54 Britway Rd., Dinas Powis, Glamorganshire, Wales. *Agent:* Sheri Safran Associates Ltd., 4 Princes Mews, Hereford Rd., London W.2, England. *Office:* British Broadcasting Corp., Broadcasting House, Cardiff, Wales.

CAREER: Reporter for *Stockport Advertiser,* 1953-60; *Western Mail,* Cardiff, Wales, deputy news editor, 1960-65; British Broadcasting Corp. (BBC), Cardiff, Wales, industrial correspondent for Wales, 1965-70, staff television producer and editor of "Kane on Friday," 1970-77, editor of "Week In, Week Out," 1977—.

WRITINGS: More Lives Than One? (nonfiction), Souvenir Press, 1976.

WORK IN PROGRESS: The Man Who Was Mesmer, a book on reincarnation which is based on research with tape recordings collected by hypnotist Arnall Bloxham.

MEDIA ADAPTATIONS: More Than One? was produced on television under the title "The Bloxham Tapes."

*   *   *

IZENBERG, Gerald N(athan) 1939-

PERSONAL: Born June 30, 1939, in Toronto, Ontario, Canada; married, 1963; children: two. *Education:* University of Toronto, B.A., 1961; Harvard University, A.M., 1962, Ph.D., 1968; attended University of Zurich, 1965-66; postdoctoral study at Boston Psychoanalytic Institute, 1970-76, and Boston University, 1975-76. *Office:* Department of History, Washington University, St. Louis, Mo. 63130.

CAREER: Brandeis University, Waltham, Mass., assistant professor of history, 1968-75; Washington University, St. Louis, Mo., associate professor of history, 1976—, co-director of program in literature and history. Assistant professor at Harvard University, summer, 1971; member of Cambridge Humanities Seminar, 1975-76. *Member:* American Historical Association, Boston Psychoanalytic Society (associate member), St. Louis Psychoanalytic Society (associate member). *Awards, honors:* Woodrow Wilson fellowship, 1961-62; Foreign Area Foundation fellowship for western Europe, 1965-66; American Council of Learned Societies fellowship, 1975-76.

WRITINGS: The Existentialist Critique of Freud: The Crisis of Autonomy, Princeton University Press, 1976; (contributor) Hoendahl, editor, *The Nobility in German Literature,* Metzler Verlag, 1979. Contributor to "The Psychiatric Foundations of Medicine" series, edited by G.U. Balis, 1978. Contributor to history journals.

WORK IN PROGRESS: Durkheim's Theories of Motivation; a monograph on European Romanticism, 1789-1848; a comparative study of Pirandello and Hesse as exemplars of the problem of value disintegration and reintegration in the 1920's.

J

JACKSON, J. P.
See ATKINS, (Arthur) Harold

*   *   *

JACKSON, Stephanie
See WERNER, Vivian

*   *   *

JACOB, Fred E. 1899-

PERSONAL: Born May 20, 1899, in St. Johns, Mich.; son of John L. (a rancher and horse importer) and Mary C. (Swagart) Jacob; married Evelyn Austin (treasurer and office manager of Jacob Equipment, Inc.), June 13, 1923; children: Arthur Paul (deceased), Frederick A., Lois Anne Jacob Heath. *Education:* University of Michigan, A.B., 1921, journalism certificate, 1921. *Politics:* "Hard-boiled Republican." *Religion:* Episcopalian. *Home:* 3190 Vista Del Mar Dr., Glendale, Calif. 91208. *Office:* Jacob Equipment, Inc. 1901 Riverside Dr., Glendale, Calif. 91201.

CAREER: Denver Express, Denver, Colo., reporter, 1921-22; Colorado-Wyoming sales manager for American Laundry Machinery Co.; Western sales manager for Steven Davis Co. (commercial refrigeration manufacturer); Jacob Equipment, Inc. (designers and installers of commercial wood and steel fixtures), Glendale, Calif., chairman of board of directors, 1930—. Served as vestryman at St. Mark's Church, Glendale, 1948-54. *Military service:* U.S. Air Force, 1942-45; served in three theaters of World War II; became major; received five awards, including Soldiers Medal. *Member:* American Legion Post 127 (member of board of directors of luncheon club; historian), Sky Roamers Flying Club (life member; past director), Aircraft Owners and Pilots Association of Washington, D.C. (charter member, 1939—), Al Malaika Shrine and other Masonic bodies, Young Men's Christian Association (YMCA); also active in Episcopal Diocese affairs and various Republican organizations.

WRITINGS: Takeoffs and Touchdowns: My Sixty Years of Flying (autobiography), introductory comments by James H. Doolittle, A. S. Barnes, 1981. Contributor of articles to technical and trade magazines.

WORK IN PROGRESS: "I am being pressured by two publishers to do an up-to-date book on longtime friend General Jim Doolittle. I may do so along with free-lance writer Bill Wilson doing the leg work, as at eighty-two I don't quite feel up to it alone. I will include hundreds of pictures and much new material. I am also considering writing a book on the illustrious life of the late Jacqueline Cochran, a wonderful pilot whom I first met in 1934. General Eisenhower's books credit her with convincing him it was his duty in 1951 to accept the Republican nomination for the presidency."

SIDELIGHTS: An octogenarian, Fred Jacob is one of the oldest licensed pilots in the United States. His autobiography, *Takeoffs and Touchdowns,* offers hundreds of anecdotes and remembrances of Jacob's career as a pilot, from his first flight in 1918 and barnstorming days in the twenties, to his heroic World War II flights and experiences as a private pilot.

An aviator who has been flying for more than sixty years undoubtedly has numerous stories to tell about close calls and near-misses in the sky. Among the more frightening flights Jacob recalls took place in 1921 when he was still a novice flyer. He agreed to participate in a Colorado National Guard service for his college friend Lieutenant Francis Brown Lowry, the first Denver pilot killed during World War I. Jacob and another pilot were to fly low and drop flowers over the funeral procession route. Jacob tossed blossoms for awhile as the other pilot guided the plane. When they switched duties, Jacob imitated the pilot, easing back the throttle and letting the plane down to three hundred feet. But when he went to ascend, Jacob could not budge the control stick, and the plane continued downward. It dropped to just one hundred feet above the mourners before Jacob, pulling back on the stick, finally got the plane into a slow climb. After they attained a safe altitude, the pair discovered that their near-accident was not the fault of the inexperienced Jacob, but occurred because the other pilot's flower basket had lodged between his body and the control stick in his cockpit, making it virtually impossible for Jacob to maneuver the stick in his own section of the biplane. Jacob also vividly remembers his flight over Niagara Falls when the force of the rushing water and air currents nearly pulled him down. "Scared the pants off me," he told JoAnn Blake of the *Glendale News-Press.*

Much of Jacob's volume deals with his military service. He was rejected for World War I duty because of an injured ankle, but was accepted at age forty-three to be a non-combat flyer ferrying bombers in World War II. He later piloted B-26's in bombing raids with the 387th bomb group. He flew in all three theaters of the war, survived the crash of a Nazi-sabatoged B-

24 bomber, and received the Soldiers Medal for saving three men from a burning plane. He also met many notable figures during his stint, including King George VI, Dwight Eisenhower, Winston Churchill, Charles Lindbergh, James Doolittle, and Glenn Miller, whose band Jacob flew to France just days before the musician was lost while crossing the English Channel in a single-engine plane.

Although now accompanied by a licensed pilot because his hearing is failing, Jacob and his wife of more than fifty years still fly occasionally. Jacob told Blake: "In the old days you had no thought of other airplanes. Now you have to keep your eyes moving, your neck twisting—this takes away the so-called glamour of flying." Nevertheless, he feels safer "above a thousand feet than down here hoping some drunk won't cross the double yellow line and pick me off."

Active in many civic affairs, Jacob is particularly proud of his involvement in Republican politics. In 1966 he was one of fifty people who met with Ronald and Nancy Reagan to help convince the actor to run for governor of California. Reagan was hesitant, but agreed when, according to Jacob, "we fifty anted up the seed money that convinced him he should give it a try."

Jacob told *CA:* "I feel a great need to help our younger generations to understand what a wonderful country we live in. Having traveled the world both in World War II and as a private pilot, I can see how little education they have received from our modern school systems. Maybe that's a sign of old age, but it is the biggest hazard our country has today—the ignorance of our youth as to our past history and their heritage.

"My insurance company thought it a bit unusual for their policy holder Jacob to be gadding about the sky in his eighties, so they came out and took a picture of me and my wife for the front cover of their annual report. It shows you what a pair of old folks can do rather than sit in a rocking chair. Might add that my wife drives her own car, goes to the office every day, is treasurer of Jacob Equipment, runs the books, and is the Queen Bee. But we gotta slow down pretty soon. Folks tell us we are getting too old for this gay life."

BIOGRAPHICAL/CRITICAL SOURCES: Glendale News-Press, October 6, 1981; *General Aviation News,* November, 1981; *Sunday Press,* December 20, 1981.

*   *   *

JACOBSEN, Thorkild   1904-

BRIEF ENTRY: Born June 7, 1904, in Copenhagen, Denmark. American educator and author. Jacobsen was a professor of Assyriology at Harvard University from 1963 to 1974, when he was named professor emeritus. His writings include *Toward the Image of Tommuz and Other Essays on Mesopotamian History and Culture* (Harvard University Press, 1970), *The Treasures of Darkness: A History of the Mesopotamian Religion* (Yale University Press, 1976), *Mesopotamiske urtidssagn* (Gad, 1978), and *Oekolgi* (Aalborg Universitetscenter, 1978). *Address:* East Washington Rd., Bradford, N.H. 03221; and Department of Near Eastern Languages and Civilizations, Harvard University, 6 Divinity Ave., Cambridge, Mass. 02114. *Biographical/critical sources: Who's Who in the World,* 4th edition, Marquis, 1978.

*   *   *

JACOBUS, Mary   1944-

PERSONAL: Born May 4, 1944, in Cheltenham, Gloucestershire, England; came to the United States, 1980. *Education:*

Oxford University, B.A. (with first class honors), 1965, M.A. and D.Phil., both 1970. *Politics:* "Feminist." *Office:* Department of English, Cornell University, Ithaca, N.Y. 14853.

CAREER: Oxford University, Oxford, England, Randall McIver research fellow, 1968-70; Victoria University of Manchester, Manchester, England, lecturer in English, 1970-71; Oxford University, fellow and tutor at Lady Margaret Hall, 1971-80, lecturer in English, 1972-80; Cornell University, Ithaca, N.Y., associate professor of English and women's studies, 1980—. Visiting professor at Georgetown University, 1976.

WRITINGS: Tradition and Experiment in Wordsworth's Lyrical Ballads, Oxford University Press, 1978; (editor and contributor) *Women Writing and Writing About Women,* Croom Helm, 1979.

WORK IN PROGRESS: Research on Wordsworth, Hardy, and feminist literary criticism.

*   *   *

JAFFE, Hilde   1927-

PERSONAL: Born May 21, 1927, in Germany; came to the United States in 1938; daughter of Sol (a butcher) and Fanny (Baer) Wolf; married Melvin Jaffe (an insurance agent), November 25, 1948; children: Barbara Jaffe-Rose, Robert. *Education:* Fashion Institute of Technology, A.A.S., 1963; Queens College of the City University of New York, B.A., 1969. *Residence:* Flushing, N.Y. *Office:* Fashion Institute of Technology, 227 West 27th St., New York, N.Y. 10001.

CAREER: Jack Borgenicht, New York City, designer of children's dresses, 1945-46; designer of children's dresses for Perlberg & Tannenbaum, 1946-49, F. Silverman, 1949-51, and Richling, Ade & Richman, 1953-55; high school teacher of clothing and textiles in Jamaica, N.Y., 1957-59; Fashion Institute of Technology, New York City, professor of fashion design, 1959—, chairperson of department, 1975-78, dean of Art and Design Division, 1980—. *Member:* American Society for Testing and Materials, Fashion Group.

WRITINGS: Children's Wear Design, Fairchild Publications, 1972; (with Nurlie Relis) *Draping for Fashion Design,* Reston, 1973; (contributor) *Apparel Design and Production: A Suggested Program Guide,* U.S. Office of Education, 1973.

SIDELIGHTS: Jaffe told *CA:* "Both *Children's Wear Design* and *Draping for Fashion Design* evolved from notes for classes that I was teaching. There were no appropriate textbooks available in these areas for students preparing for careers in fashion design. My purpose was to give clear and precise instructions to help students express their creative ideas for apparel. Writing these books was necessary for more effective communication with my students. I am delighted that other teachers also have found them useful and that many aspiring fashion designers have used them independently."

*   *   *

JAMES, Anne Eleanor Scott
See SCOTT-JAMES, Anne Eleanor

*   *   *

JAMES, Clive   1939-

BRIEF ENTRY: Born October 7, 1939, in Sydney, Australia. Author. James wrote *Unreliable Memoirs* (J. Cape, 1980), *First Reactions: Critical Essays, 1968-1979* (Knopf, 1980), *The Crystal Bucket* (Chatto-Bodley-Jonathan, 1981), and *Charles*

Charming's Challenges on the Pathway to the Throne (New York Review of Books, 1981). *Address:* 10 Buckingham St., London, England; and *Observer,* 160 Queen Victoria St., London E.C.4, England. *Biographical/critical sources: New York Times,* February 14, 1981.

*   *   *

JAMES, Jean Rosemary Haughton
    See HAUGHTON-JAMES, Jean Rosemary

*   *   *

JAMES, Wilma Roberts   1905-

PERSONAL: Born October 15, 1905, in Sonoma, Calif.; daughter of William K. (a newspaper editor and publisher) and Ethel (Hunter) Roberts; married Alfred R. Lutz, July 15, 1929 (died July 12, 1953); married Edward W. James, December 24, 1956 (deceased); children: William A., Linda Lutz Morgan. *Education:* University of California, San Jose, B.A., 1939. *Politics:* Republican. *Religion:* Protestant. *Home and office:* 2402 Via Camino, Carmichael, Calif. 95608.

CAREER: Teacher in various elementary schools in California, 1939-53; free-lance writer, 1942—; elementary school teacher in North Sacramento, Calif., 1953-66; David C. Cook Publishing Co., Elgin, Ill., staff writer, 1961-77. *Member:* American Association of University Women (chairman of creative writers), National League of American Pen Women, California Writers Club, California Native Plant Society, Carmichael Cactus and Succulent Society. *Awards, honors:* Literary achievement award from Sacramento Regional Arts Council, 1974.

WRITINGS: Know Your Poisonous Plants, Naturegraph, 1973; *Propagate Your Own Plants,* Naturegraph, 1978. Contributor of about three hundred articles and stories to adult and juvenile magazines.

WORK IN PROGRESS: Gardening With Biblical Plants, for Nelson-Hall, to be completed in 1982.

SIDELIGHTS: Wilma James reported that her interest in foods in their natural forms led to *Know Your Poisonous Plants,* which includes information on preventing and dealing with plant poisoning. *Avocational interests:* Travel (including Asia and Europe), gardening, hiking, camping.

BIOGRAPHICAL/CRITICAL SOURCES: Sacramento Bee, January 27, 1979.

*   *   *

JAQUETTE, Jane Stallmann   1942-

BRIEF ENTRY: Born November 10, 1942, in Chicago, Ill. American political scientist, educator, and author. Jaquette has taught political science at Occidental College since 1969. Her books are *The Politics of Development in Peru* (Cornell University, 1971) and *Women in Politics* (Wiley, 1974). *Address:* Department of Political Science, Occidental College, Los Angeles, Calif. 90041. *Biographical/critical sources: American Men and Women of Science: The Social and Behavioral Sciences,* 13th edition, Bowker, 1978.

*   *   *

JARRETT, Marjorie   1923-

PERSONAL: Born June 20, 1923, in Salt Lake City, Utah; daughter of Henry Cardwell (an environmentalist) and Marion (a writer; maiden name, Davis) Clegg; married Lavern Adix,

April 5, 1946 (divorced, 1955); married James Louis Jarrett (a professor), January 3, 1956; children: Russell Devin, James Timothy, Gregory Cardwell, Justin Malcolm. *Education:* University of Utah, B.S., 1946; graduate study at Oxford University and Colorado College. *Home:* 534 Arlington Ave., Berkeley, Calif. 94707. *Agent:* Elaine Markson Literary Agency, Inc., 44 Greenwich Ave., New York, N.Y. 10011.

CAREER: St. George Homes, Inc., Berkeley, Calif., therapist for schizophrenic-autistic adolescents, 1975—.

WRITINGS: Wives of the Wind (novel), Seaview, 1980. Contributor of articles and a story to magazines, including *Encounter, Western Humanities Review,* and *Antioch Review.*

WORK IN PROGRESS: Research on left/right brain activity in schizophrenic adolescents; a novel, *Blue Scherzo.*

*   *   *

JARVIE, Clodagh Gibson
    See GIBSON-JARVIE, Clodagh

*   *   *

JARVIS, Martin   1941-

PERSONAL: Born August 4, 1941, in Cheltenham, England; son of Denys Harry and Margot Lillian (Scottney) Jarvis; married second wife, Rosalind Ayres (an actress), November 23, 1974; children: (first marriage) Toby, Oliver. *Education:* Royal Academy of Dramatic Art, diploma (with honors), 1962. *Home:* 64 Grafton Road, London W3, England. *Agent:* Jean Diamond, c/o London Management, 235 Regent St., London W1A 2JT, England.

CAREER: Actor in England, 1962—. Appeared in plays, including "Twelfth Night," 1962, "Poor Bitos," 1964, "Man and Superman," 1966; "The Spoils of Poynton," 1969, "The Bandwagon," 1969, "The Rivals," 1972, "Hamlet," 1973, "The Prodigal Daughter," 1974, "Paradise Lost," 1975, "The Circle," 1976, "The Woman I Love," 1978, "She Stoops to Conquer," 1978, "The Country Wife," "The Merchant of Venice," and "Caught in the Act"; appeared in motion pictures, including "The Last Escape," 1969, and "IKE—The War Years"; starred in television productions, including "The Forsyte Saga," "Nicholas Nickleby," "Rings on Their Fingers," and "Breakaway"; performed in more than one thousand radio productions, including adaptations of *War and Peace* and *Great Expectations.* Writer, 1967—. Poetry reader. *Member:* British Broadcasting Corporation (BBC) Club. *Awards, honors:* Silver medal for performance in "The Country Wife," and Vanbrugh Award for performance in "The Merchant of Venice," both from Royal Academy of Dramatic Art, 1960.

WRITINGS: Bright Boy, Samuel French, 1977. Author of short stories "Name Out of a Hat," 1967, "Alphonse," 1972, and "Late Burst," 1976. Adapter of twenty "Just William" stories, by Richmal Crompton, for BBC-Radio, 1972-76. Adapter of *Goodbye, Mr. Chips,* by James Hilton, for BBC-Radio and BBC-TV, 1973. Columnist for *Radio Times.*

WORK IN PROGRESS: A play, "Holiday Boy"; a short story, "Woman in Half"; a semi-autobiographical novel set in London.

SIDELIGHTS: Jarvis told *CA:* "I am presently involved in recording an anthology of World War II poems on cassette. These poems are part of a compilation called 'Return to Oasis,' all written in the Western Desert in Egypt in the 1940's. I believe it's important to put my weight behind such a worthy project, as these poems deal with the horror and heroism of war, the futility and absurdity. If we can show people, particularly young people, what it was like we might have a tiny chance of preventing ever going to war again."

AVOCATIONAL INTERESTS: Music, cooking.

* * *

JENKINS, William Marshall, Jr. 1918-

BRIEF ENTRY: Born September 12, 1918, in Guthrie, Ky. American educator, academic administrator, and author. Jenkins has taught history and political science at Western Kentucky State University since 1959; he has been dean of College of Commerce since 1964. His writings include *Nepal: A Cultural and Physical Geography* (University Press of Kentucky, 1960), *The Himalayan Kingdoms: Bhutan, Sikkim and Nepal* (Van Nostrand, 1963), *Kentucky Law and the Cities* (Kentucky Legislative Research Commission, 1966), and *Revenue of Cities* (Western Kentucky University, 1970). *Address:* 1723 Karen Circle, Bowling Green, Ky. 42101; and College of Business and Public Affairs, Western Kentucky University, Bowling Green, Ky. 42101. *Biographical/critical sources: Who's Who in America*, 40th edition, Marquis, 1978.

* * *

JOHNSON, Willard R(aymond) 1935-

PERSONAL: Born November 22, 1935, in St. Louis, Mo.; son of Willard (a bacteriologist) and Dorothy N. (a cook; maiden name, Stovall) Johnson; married Vivian Robinson (a university administrator), December 15, 1957; children: Karen, Kimberly. *Education:* University of California, Los Angeles, B.A., 1957; Johns Hopkins School of Advanced International Studies, M.A., 1961; Harvard University, Ph.D., 1965. *Politics:* Democrat. *Residence:* Newton, Mass. *Office:* Department of Political Science, Massachusetts Institute of Technology, 50 Wadsworth St., Cambridge, Mass. 02138.

CAREER: Massachusetts Institute of Technology, Cambridge, assistant professor, 1964-69, associate professor, 1969-73, professor of political science, 1973—. Adjunct professor at Fletcher School of Law and Diplomacy. Member of U.S. Commission for UNESCO, 1958-63; member of board of directors of Boston Urban League, 1967-72, National Center of Afro-American Artists, 1969-70, and Interfaith Housing Corp., 1970; executive director of Circle, Inc. (community-level development corporation), 1968-70, chairman of board of directors, 1970-72; member of board of directors and chairman of policy committee of TransAfrica, Inc., 1977—.

MEMBER: American Political Science Association, National Conference of Black Political Scientists, African Heritage Studies Association (vice-president, 1978), Council on Foreign Relations, Association of Concerned African Scholars (member of board of directors, 1977—). *Awards, honors:* Ford Foundation grants, 1972 and 1980; Social Science Research Council grant, 1975-76; Rockefeller Foundation fellowship, 1977.

WRITINGS: The Cameroon Federation: Political Integration in a Fragmentary Society, Princeton University Press, 1970; *The Financial Character and Performance of the Commonwealth Development Corporation* (monograph), Center for International Studies, Massachusetts Institute of Technology, 1975; *The Commonwealth Development Corporation's Contribution to Housing Development: A Study From Nairobi* (monograph), Center for International Studies, Massachusetts Institute of Technology, 1975.

Contributor: W. H. Lewis, editor, *French-Speaking Africa: Search for Identity,* Walker & Co., 1965; R. I. Rotberg, editor, *Protest and Power in Black Africa,* Oxford University Press, 1969; M. L. Kilson, editor, *New States in the Modern World,* Harvard University Press, 1975; (author of foreword) Ndiva Kofele-Kale, *An African Experiment in Nation-Building: The United Republic of Cameroon,* Westview, 1979. Contributor to political science journals, including *International Journal.*

WORK IN PROGRESS: Research on African-Arab relations, especially the Arab financial assistance and investment activities in Africa, and U.S. policy toward and relations with Africa, especially South Africa.

SIDELIGHTS: Johnson wrote: "My ongoing research and teaching interests include the work of community-level economic development corporations, African politics, U.S. policy toward Africa, and African-Arab cooperation. I want to promote a broader public understanding of the need to disengage American power (especially corporate interests) from involvement in the South African racist system."

* * *

JOHNSTON, Norma
(Lavinia Harris, Nicole St. John)

PERSONAL: Born in Ridgewood, N.J.; daughter of Eugene Chambers (an engineer) and Marjorie (a teacher; maiden name, Pierce) Johnston. *Education:* Montclair College, B.A. *Politics:* None. *Religion:* Reformed Church in America. *Residence:* Wyckoff, N.J. *Agent:* McIntosh & Otis, Inc. 475 Fifth Ave., New York, N.Y. 10017. *Office address:* St. John Enterprises, Box 67, Wyckoff, N.J. 07481.

CAREER: Writer and editor, 1961—; Glen Rock, N.J., public schools, teacher of English, 1970-72; St. John Enterprises (editorial services), Wyckoff, N.J., president, editor, 1980—. Has also worked in fashion publishing and retailing, religious publishing, and has done free-lance editing for Prentice-Hall and others. Founder, president, and director of Geneva Players, Inc. (religious drama group). *Member:* Authors League of America.

WRITINGS—Under pseudonym Nicole St. John; gothic novels: *The Medici Ring,* Random House, 1975; *Wychwood,* Random House, 1976; *Guinevere's Gift,* Random House, 1977.

For young people; historical novels, except as noted: *The Wishing Star,* Funk, 1963; *The Wider Heart,* Funk 1964; *Ready or Not,* Funk, 1965; *The Bridge Between,* Funk, 1966; *The Keeping Days,* Atheneum, 1973; *Glory in the Flower,* Atheneum, 1974; *Of Time and of Seasons,* Atheneum, 1975; *Strangers Dark and Gold,* Atheneum, 1975; *A Striving After Wind* (sequel to *Of Time and of Seasons*), Atheneum, 1976; *A Mustard Seed of Magic,* Atheneum, 1977; *The Sanctuary Tree,* Atheneum, 1977; *If You Love Me, Let Me Go,* Atheneum, 1978; *The Swallow's Song,* Atheneum, 1978; *The Crucible Year,* Atheneum, 1979; *Pride of Lions: The Story of the House of Atreus* (myth), Atheneum, 1979; *A Nice Girl Like You,* Atheneum, 1980; *Myself and I,* Atheneum, 1981; *The Days of the Dragon's Seed,* Atheneum, 1982; *Timewarp Summer,* Atheneum, 1982.

WORK IN PROGRESS: Change of Heart; under pseudonym Lavinia Harris, *Castle of the Swans.*

SIDELIGHTS: Norma Johnston said she writes "because all my life I have learned through vicarious empathy of literature, and I believe, with Tennessee Williams, that as a writer of fiction 'I give you truth in the pleasant disguise of illusion.'" Johnston said she wanted to be a writer since she was very young. "I have things that I must say, and I can no more hold back from saying them than I can cease to breathe."

Johnston's books are concerned with the "verities I believe to be unchanging in a changing world." Her books are set in the past because "the future can learn of the past. Because people in the past have gone through the same inner and outer struggles that we do now. There are lessons to be learned in the things that they did wrong, and messages for us in the truths they found." Most importantly, said Johnston, she writes "to disturb the status quo and draw people into a closer understanding of themselves, their neighbors, and their God."

Johnston has traveled extensively in the Caribbean, Europe, and the Mediterranean, and has spent summers in England doing historical research.

BIOGRAPHICAL/CRITICAL SOURCES: New York Times Book Review, May 11, 1975.

*   *   *

JONAS, Ann   1919-

PERSONAL: Born July 15, 1919, in Joplin, Mo.; daughter of Morris (a merchant) and Leah (Marov) Moskovitz; married Walter H. Jonas (a business executive), March 30, 1944; children: Wendy Jonas Bischof. *Education:* Attended classes at Goodman Theatre, Chicago, 1936-39, received diploma. *Home and office:* 2425 Ashwood Dr., Louisville, Ky. 40205.

CAREER: WMBH-Radio, Joplin, Mo., commentator, writer, and actress, 1939-40; WJJD-Radio, Chicago, Ill., writer and actress, 1940-41; WHAS-Radio, Louisville, Ky., commentator, writer, actress, and producer, 1942-47; WAVE-Radio and -TV, Louisville, interviewer, actress, and writer, 1947-54; writer, 1960—. *Member:* International Poetry Society (fellow), Poetry Society of America, Haiku Society of America. *Awards, honors:* Yaddo Fellowship, 1968; six awards from *Haiku West,* 1968-72 and 1975; award from *Modern Haiku* for "Haiku Sequence," 1972; Cecil Hemley Memorial Award from Poetry Society of America and Henry Rago Memorial Award from New York Poetry Forum, both for "Dear Deba," 1972; Edwin Markham Poetry Prize from Eugene V. Debs Foundation for "Recovery," 1977.

WRITINGS—Poetry; published in anthologies: Albert Stewart, editor, Dark Unsleeping Land, Morehead University Press, 1960; Stewart, editor, *Deep Summer,* Morehead University Press, 1963; Joy Bale, editor, *Kentucky Contemporary Poetry,* Kentucky Libraries, 1964, 2nd edition, 1967; David Brandenburg and Phyllis Brandenburg, editors, *Kentucky Harvest,* Harvest Press, 1968; Charles Angoff, Gustav Davidson, Hyacinthe Hill, and A.M. Sullivan, editors, *The Diamond Anthology,* Poetry Society of America, 1971; Mabel Ferrett, Pamela Beattie, and John Waddington-Feather, editors, *Ipso Facto,* International Poetry Society, 1975; Louise Louis, editor, *Peopled Parables,* New York Poetry Forum, 1975; Bob Millard, editor, *Sampler: Contemporary Poets of the New South,* Project House Foundation, 1977; Amal Ghose and Sandra Fowler, editors, *Friendship Bridge: Anthology of World Poetry,* Ocarina International, 1979; Wade Hall, editor, *The Kentucky Book,* Courier Data Press, 1979; Deba P. Patnaik, editor, *Concelebration: Merton Poetic Tribute,* Ave Maria Press, 1981.

Contributor to literary and haiku journals, including *Adena, Bitterroot, Carolina Quarterly, Colorado Quarterly, Kentucky Poetry Review, Monk's Pond, Latitudes, Midwest Quarterly, Quest, Orbis, Prism International, Review of General Semantics, Southern Humanities Review, Modern Haiku,* and *Southern Review.*

WORK IN PROGRESS: To Be in Our Bones (poems); a volume of haiku.

SIDELIGHTS: Jonas told *CA* "When a poem comes into being (I can't will it to happen), it runs wild on the page. I write down whatever comes (though much will be discarded later) until it finds its own rough form. Then I clamp down on it with critical judgment and, over a period of time, revise and polish. My poems lean heavily on images, and I have great respect for craft."

AVOCATIONAL INTERESTS: The arts, travel.

*   *   *

JONES, Helen   1917-

PERSONAL: Born January 17, 1917, in Los Angeles, Calif.; daughter of Clyde W. (a rancher) and Carrie (Morrish) Cook; married Hardin B. Jones (a professor), March 17, 1940 (died February, 1978); children: Carolyn Jones Kenter, Hardin, Nancy Jones Snowden, Mark. *Education:* University of California, Los Angeles, B.A., 1938; graduate study at University of California, Berkeley, 1938, and University of Southern California, 1939. *Home:* 1519 Oxford St., Berkeley, Calif. 94709.

CAREER: High school teacher of home economics in Hollywood, Calif., 1939-42; Pleasant Hill Intermediate School, Pleasant Hill, Calif., teacher of home economics, 1953-54; writer, 1954—. *Member:* American Home Economics Association, American Council on Marijuana and Other Psychoactive Drugs (member of board of directors, 1978—), Parents Who Care (member of advisory board), Committees of Correspondence, Berkeley City Club (member of executive board), Marijuana and Health (chairman, 1979—), Omicron Nu.

WRITINGS: (With Beth Bond, Virginia Dobbin, Helen Gofman, Helen Jones, and Lenore Lyon) *The Low-Fat, Low-Cholesterol Diet Book,* Doubleday, 1951, revised edition, 1971; (with husband, Hardin B. Jones) *Sensual Drugs: Deprivation and Rehabilitation of the Mind,* Cambridge University Press, 1977.

WORK IN PROGRESS: A book on marijuana, with P.W. Lovinger, publication by Everest House expected in 1982.

SIDELIGHTS: Helen Jones told *CA:* "I became an author in both the drug and diet fields because of my involvement in my late husband's work. Professor Hardin B. Jones was a professor of medical physics and physiology and a senior scientist at the Donner Laboratory of Medical Physics.

"In the early fifties he and a team of collaborators did the original research on the effects of diet on blood cholesterol and fat in relation to atherosclerosis. A representative from Doubleday approached the laboratory inquiring about the possibility of having a diet book written, based on the laboratory's research. Since I was a trained nutritionist, I wrote the book with two dieticians, a physician, and the wife of a physician. It proved to be a very successful book (on the best-seller list for nonfiction when it first came out) and remains the authoritative book on the subject.

"In 1963 the Lawrence Radiation Laboratory asked me to write a booklet directed towards recently transferred laboratory staff and their families, to help orient them to the Berkeley community. This also proved popular and went through a revision and many printings.

"Professor Jones and I became active in drug abuse education in the mid-sixties when drug use mushroomed on the Berkeley campus and then spread across the country in epidemic proportions. We had three children on the Berkeley campus and observed the effects of drugs on their classmates. Professor Jones counseled students on drug abuse in his office and we had night sessions in our home. The students were eager for information, particularly about marijuana, as they were told constantly in the student newspaper and from the student plaza that marijuana was a harmless drug. As a health scientist, Professor Jones gave the first university class on drug abuse. We traveled extensively in the United States and to more than twenty-five foreign countries studying the drug problem. We wrote *Sensual Drugs* for use in his class as well as for laymen and professionals. It has recently been translated into Swedish.

"In 1973 we traveled under army orders to Germany and Thailand, studying and helping with the drug problems in the army. The study had been requested by the Office of Alcohol and Drug Abuse and the report was made to that office in August, 1973. It has been photoreproduced and distributed within the armed forces.

"Since Professor Jones's death in 1978 I have continued working on the drug problem, mainly on marijuana and health, lecturing and writing on the subject and attending local, national, and international symposiums."

*　　*　　*

JONES, Jeanie Schmit Kayser
See KAYSER-JONES, Jeanie Schmit

*　　*　　*

JONES, Landon Y(oung) 1943-

PERSONAL: Born November 4, 1943, in Rome, Ga.; son of Landon Y. (a business executive) and Ellen E. (Edmondson) Jones; married Sarah Brown, June 20, 1970; children: Rebecca, Landon III, Catherine. *Education:* Princeton University, A.B. (with high honors), 1966. *Agent:* Maxine Groffsky, 2 Fifth Ave., New York, N.Y. 10011. *Office:* Time-Life Bldg., Rockefeller Center, New York, N.Y. 10020.

CAREER: Time, New York City, contributing editor, 1966-69; *Princeton Alumni Weekly,* Princeton, N.J., editor, 1969-74; *People Weekly,* New York City, senior editor, 1974—. *Military service:* U.S. Army Reserve, 1966-72.

WRITINGS: Great Expectations: America and the Baby Boom Generation, Coward, 1980. Contributor of articles to *Atlantic Monthly* and *Esquire.*

SIDELIGHTS: Jones's *Great Expectations* both humorously and seriously examines American social and economic issues with regard to the baby boom between 1946 and 1964, when more than seventy-six million babies were born. This generation grew up in a period that Jones calls, according to the *Washington Post Book World*'s David Burns, the "'Big Barbecue,'" "'a feast spread out for an entire nation, and everyone scrambling for it.'" As a result of the opportunities and riches offered to them, the boom babies comprise America's best-educated, wealthiest generation.

Commenting on the economic consequences of the baby boom, Jones told Sally A. Lodge of *Publishers Weekly:* "Every generation has its common denominators, but the baby boom was the first one to be bound together by the media, and the first to be identified by advertisers as a generational market." Jones notes that the subjects of his study were the first television generation, thus commercials were aimed at them and their seemingly inherent thirst for material goods. "Baby boomers created the notion of fads; the generation will continue to erupt into one fad after another. They begin buying fast and stop all at once, so that poor manufacturers are left with warehouses filled with Davy Crockett hats."

On a serious note, Jones discusses some of the potential troubles that face the baby boomers in the future. With reference to Social Security, the author told Lodge: "Things just aren't being planned. Everyone knows there's going to be an enormous problem ahead, but no one wants to bite the bullet. There are predictions of generational warfare."

Jones's book has been favorably received by critics. In his *Washington Post Book World* review, Burns opined: "This is first-rate social history—journalism with data, sociology minus the jargon. Jones assumes straight-line conclusions based on aggregate statistics, and his technique is anecdotal rather than scientific. Nonetheless, this is a full-length portrait of America 1946-1980." E. J. Dionne of the *New York Times Book Review* remarked that "there is much fun to be had here."

Jones told *CA:* "I wrote *Great Expectations* because I realized, somewhat to my astonishment, that a single group of people—the baby boom generation—was decisively influencing our history. They made us a child-oriented society in the fifties, an adolescent society of turbulence in the sixties, and a me-generation society of young adults in the seventies. Now they are making us a slightly older and, I trust, more stable society as they enter midlife. Yet their biggest crisis—how shall we support them in retirement?—lies ahead."

BIOGRAPHICAL/CRITICAL SOURCES: New York Times, October 20, 1980; *New York Times Book Review,* November 9, 1980; *Publishers Weekly,* November 14, 1980; *Washington Post Book World,* December 15, 1980; *Chicago Tribune Book World,* December 25, 1981.

*　　*　　*

JONES, Tim(othy) Wynne
See WYNNE-JONES, Tim(othy)

*　　*　　*

JONES, Trevor Arthur 1936-

PERSONAL: Born September 5, 1936, in Manchester, England; son of Arthur William (a police officer) and Nora (Berry) Jones; married Marion Jenkinson (a teacher), July 12, 1974 (divorced, 1981); children: Jessica Fay. *Education:* St. Catharine's College, Cambridge, B.A. (with first class honors), 1958; attended London School of Economics and Political Science, London, 1960. *Politics:* "No formal party links/conservative pessimist." *Religion:* Anglican. *Agent:* Curtis Brown Academic Ltd., 1 Craven Hill, London W2 3EP, England. *Office:* Department of History, University of Keele, Keele, Staffordshire ST5 5BC, England.

CAREER: Commonwealth Relations Office, London, England, assistant principal, 1960-62; University of Ghana, Legon, lecturer in history, 1962-64; University of Keele, Keele, England, senior lecturer in history, 1964—. *Member:* Institute of Commonwealth Studies, Sneyd Arms Club (chairman, 1979-80). *Awards, honors:* Fulbright scholarship for University of Washington, Seattle, 1958-59.

WRITINGS: Ghana's First Republic, 1960-1966, Barnes & Noble, 1976. Contributor to *Times Literary Supplement.*

WORK IN PROGRESS: A study of Jeremy Bentham and his family, completion expected in 1984; research on Sir Robert Hart, "the Ulsterman who controlled the Chinese Imperial Customs Service for most of the latter half of the nineteenth century."

SIDELIGHTS: Jones wrote: "I prefer a biographical approach to history, avoiding things like 'psycho-history' or 'Marxist' history. I also prefer to work alone in my field, keeping aloof from other specialists and, in particular, their controversies.

"I have traveled considerably—must be one of the few who have visited Timbuktu the hard way—but I prefer the countryside and coasts of the British Isles."

AVOCATIONAL INTERESTS: Gardening, winemaking, painting, "all things connected with the sea."

*   *   *

JUDD, Cyril
 See KORNBLUTH, C(yril) M.

*   *   *

JUDSON, William
 See CORLEY, Edwin (Raymond)

*   *   *

JURNAK, Sheila
 See RAESCHILD, Sheila

K

KAFKA, Franz   1883-1924

BRIEF ENTRY: Born July 3, 1883, in Prague, Bohemia (now Czechoslovakia); died of tuberculosis, June 3, 1924, in Klosterneuburg, Austria; buried in the Jewish cemetery in Prag-Straschnitz (now Prag-Straznice), Czechoslovakia. European novelist and short story writer. During Kafka's childhood his personality was eclipsed by that of his extrovert father, causing self-doubt and feelings of inadequacy that were to haunt him throughout his short, troubled life. This autobiographical theme recurs in Kafka's stories and forms the basis for his philosophical approach to the dilemma of the individual's relationship to an incomprehensible world. Struggling by day to fit into the mundane life of a civil servant, and that of a Jew in German-speaking Prague, Kafka filled his nights by writing about alienation and exile, fear, and failure. *The Metamorphosis* (1915), for example, is the nightmarish story of a young man who turned into a monstrous insect. Self-doubt prevented Kafka from publishing or even finishing his only three novels, *Amerika* (1927), *The Trial* (1925), and *The Castle* (1930). He was so dissatisfied with his work that he instructed that the manuscripts be destroyed upon his death. Most of his books were published after his death by his friend and executor Max Brod. Although Kafka has been labeled an expressionist and an existentialist, his writing defies classification in any one literary or philosophical school. Some critics felt Kafka's writing was not meant to be, and never would be, fully understood. *Biographical/critical sources: Quarterly Review of Literature,* special Kafka issue, 1945; Max Brod, *Franz Kafka: A Biography,* Schocken, 1947; Heinz Politzer, *Franz Kafka: Parable and Paradox,* Cornell University Press, 1962; Charles Osborne, *Kafka,* Barnes & Noble, 1967; *Twentieth Century Writing: A Reader's Guide to Contemporary Literature,* Transatlantic, 1969; *Twentieth-Century Literary Criticism,* Volume 2, Gale, 1979.

*   *   *

KAHRL, George M(orrow)   1904-

PERSONAL: Born February 17, 1904, in Fairmont, W.Va.; son of Fred W. (in real estate and insurance) and Margaret (Allin) Kahrl; married Faith Jadwin Jessup (a teacher), June 19, 1929; children: Stanley Jadwin, Thomas Allin, Frederick Jessup. *Education:* Attended College of Wooster, 1922-24; Wesleyan University, Middletown, Conn., B.A., 1926; Princeton University, M.A., 1950; Harvard University, Ph.D., 1936.

Politics: Liberal. *Religion:* Presbyterian. *Home:* 401 Gaskin Ave., Gambier, Ohio 43022.

CAREER: American University of Beirut, Beirut, Lebanon, instructor in English, 1926-28; Kenyon College, Gambier, Ohio, instructor in English language and literature, 1930-31; Harvard University, Cambridge, Mass., curator of poetry room of Widener Library, 1933-36, instructor and tutor, 1936; Kenyon College, assistant professor of English literature, 1936-37; Elmira College, Elmira, N.Y., professor of English literature, 1938-69, chairman of Division of Languages and Literature, 1944-64; Kenyon College, visiting professor of English literature, 1972-76; writer, 1946—. Research associate at Harvard University, 1953-54 and 1968-69; visiting professor at Bowdoin College, 1955, and Wesleyan University, Middletown, Conn., 1957.

MEMBER: American Society for Eighteenth Century Studies, Modern Language Association of America, Modern Humanities Research Association, College English Association, Johnsonians (president), Bibliographical Society (England), Johnson Society of London, Garrick Club.

AWARDS, HONORS: Dexter fellow at Harvard University, 1936; grants from Modern Language Association, 1947, American Philosophical Society, 1947-48, 1954, and 1968, Ford Foundation, 1953-54, Pathfinder Fund, 1966, American Council of Learned Societies, 1968 and 1969, and National Endowment for the Humanities, 1973-75; Guggenheim fellowship, 1964-65; Folger Library fellowship, 1968; Huntington Library fellowship, 1969; D.H.L. from Kenyon College, 1974; Doctor of Letters from Elmira College, 1976; George Freedley Memorial Award from Theatre Library Association, 1979, and Barnard Hewitt Award from American Theatre Association, 1980, both for *David Garrick: A Critical Biography.*

WRITINGS: (Contributor) H. Craig, editor, *Essays in Dramatic Literature: The Parrott Presentation Volume,* Princeton University Press, 1935; *Tobias Smollett, Traveler-Novelist,* University of Chicago Press, 1945; (editor with David Mason Little) *The Letters of David Garrick,* three volumes, Harvard University Press, 1963; (contributor) G. S. Rousseau and P.G. Bouce, editors, *Tobias Smollett,* Oxford University Press, 1971; (with George Winchester Stone, Jr.) *David Garrick: A Critical Biography,* Southern Illinois University Press, 1979; *The Garrick Collection of Early English Drama in the British Museum,* British Library Press, 1982; (contributor) Thomas W. Copeland, Edmund Malone, and James M. Osborn, editors,

Boswell's Correspondence With Edmund Burke, Yale University Press, 1982. Contributor to professional journals, including *Harvard Studies and Notes* and *Virginia Magazine of History and Biography.*

SIDELIGHTS: Kahrl told *CA:* "My career as a writer has been based primarily on literary research on the eighteenth century. I have occasionally lectured in England and the United States, and have studied in libraries and collections at major U.S. and British universities and, through the years, the British Museum and the Victoria and Albert Museum. I have always been persuaded that vital teaching must be founded on primary research and publication and in association with international scholars. By choice I have taught in the smaller colleges in direct personal relations with students."

*   *   *

KAMIEN, Marcia   1933-
(Marcia Rose, a joint pseudonym)

PERSONAL: Born February 6, 1933, in Mechanicville, N.Y.; daughter of Joseph Silverman and Anna Pitkin; divorced; children: Sarah Hechtman, Julia Hechtman. *Education:* Syracuse University, A.B., 1953. *Politics:* Liberal. *Home:* 161 Henry St., Brooklyn Heights, N.Y. 11201. *Agent:* Goodman Associates, 500 West End Ave., New York, N.Y. 10024. *Office:* Public Affairs Office, Downstate Medical Center, 450 Clarkson Ave., Brooklyn, N.Y. 11203.

CAREER: Free-lance writer, beginning in the 1960's. Also worked as advertising copywriter for Baton, Barton, Durstine & Osborn and for Holt, Reinhart & Winston. *Awards, honors:* Received five awards for nonfiction.

WRITINGS—With Rose Novak, under joint pseudonym Marcia Rose: *Prince of Ice,* Avon, 1979; *Music of Love,* Ballantine, 1980; *Second Chances,* Ballantine, 1981; *Choices,* Ballantine, 1982.

Also contributor of nonfiction articles to magazines, including *Woman's Day, Cosmopolitan, Glamour,* and *Family Circle.*

WORK IN PROGRESS: Connections, a contemporary novel written under the Marcia Rose pseudonym, completion expected in 1982.

SIDELIGHTS: Marcia Kamien and Rose Novak told *CA:* "Marcia Rose has one husband, four daughters, two cats, two parakeets, three thousand plants, a house in Brooklyn Heights, an apartment in Brooklyn Heights, a house in Mohegan Lake, New York, a house in Lakeville, Connecticut, a part-time job, a volunteer job, four pierced ears, four big brown eyes, and two minds of her own.

"Marcia Rose is not schizoid. She is not Siamese twins. She is two people—Marcia Kamien and Rose Novak—two housewives, two mothers who, ten years ago, met on a Brooklyn Heights playground and talked of diapers, dirty laundry, and dishes, never dreaming that in a few short years they would be together writing steamy sex and delving into the deepest concerns of modern women everywhere: love, independence, love, identity, and love.

"Sitting side by side at a large, white Parsons table, Rose and I always work together, talking each book aloud, usually typing as we talk, and often coming out with identical phrases at the same time—a touch of the occult to which we have finally become accustomed.

"Fantasy, of course, figures large in our stories of men and women, love and romance, connections and separations . . .

but everything is based on real life and real people. We are both adept at listening and encouraging others to tell all, and between us, we have amassed a wealth of untold stories.

"Of course we always alter everything. The story we write is always very different from the original tale. You have to realize that once a character is set in motion, he or she begins to make decisions. We may start out thinking a character is a particular kind of person only to discover as we go along that we were *wrong.*

"In one of our books, *Second Chances,* for instance, we knew that one married couple was miserable, and we knew he was cold and overbearing. But we didn't know he was beating his wife until his wife told one of the other characters. Honestly! It just occurred to us as we were typing, and then we discovered that we had prepared for it in a dozen different ways chapters earlier!

"Many of our friends become very nervous, saying, 'You two must tell each other everything.' That's not quite true; but I think that anyone who wants to can tell what's been happening in our lives by the subject matter we choose.

"Book number five, now in the works, will deal with separation and divorce. I am a recent divorcee. It will also focus on the feelings of friends who remain married. Rose is married and intends to remain that way forever. Called *Connections,* this novel will take place, for the most part, in a small resort town during the course of one summer. Is this town a reflection of Lakeville, where the Novaks have a house, or of Mohegan Lake, where my daughters and I spend our spare time? Or of Fire Island, where both Rose and I spent many happy summers? Probably all of the above.

"Since we specialize in large-scale, multi-character, multi-level books, it is vital for us to be able to see at a glance what each character is doing, when, and—especially—with whom. So the first thing we do when embarking on our latest project is to create a time line which traces the action over the course of the book. Each major character is given a pocket and into this pocket goes all their statistics: age, education, family background, looks, how many children . . . even the number of siblings and first date. Once *we* understand what makes our characters tick, *they* seem to catch on, too. That's when they began to develop a life of their own.

"Did we ever expect to be writing romantic novels for fun and profit? Never! But nothing can be more fun. The next door neighbor is always asking, 'What is it you two do that makes you laugh so much, so often?' "

Feature stories about Marcia Rose have appeared in the *Easton Star-Democrat* (Ill.), *Longview Journal* (Tex.), *Chicago Defender* (Ill.), and *Clovis News Journal* (N.M.). Both Marcia Kamien and Rose Novak were interviewed by NBC-TV News on September 16, 1981.

BIOGRAPHICAL/CRITICAL SOURCES: West Coast Review of Books, September, 1979; *Pittsburgh Courier,* August 29, 1981; *Chicago Tribune,* August 30, 1981; *Willoughby News-Herald* (Ohio), August 30, 1981; *Bradenton Herald* (Fla.), September, 1981; *Kingsport Times-News* (Tenn.), September 6, 1981; *Warren Tribune Chronicle* (Ohio), September 6, 1981.

*   *   *

KAMINS, Robert Martin   1918-

BRIEF ENTRY: Born March 10, 1918, in Chicago, Ill. American economist, educator, and author. Kamins has taught at the University of Hawaii since 1947, becoming a professor of economics in 1963. He directed the Legislative Reference Bureau at the university from 1947 to 1953 and served as dean of academic development from 1963 to 1971. He wrote *Hawaii's Major Taxes: A Time for Examination* (1973), *Who Pays Hawaii's Taxes?: A Study of the Incidence of State and Local Taxes in Hawaii for 1970* (Social Sciences and Linguistics Institute, University of Hawaii at Manoa, 1975), and *Legal and Public Policy Setting for Geothermal Resource Development in Hawaii* (Hawaii Geothermal Project, University of Hawaii, 1976). *Address:* 2400 Parker Pl., Honolulu, Hawaii 96822; and Department of Economics, University of Hawaii, Spalding 252, Honolulu, Hawaii 96822. *Biographical/critical sources:* Who's Who in America, 40th edition, Marquis, 1978.

* * *

KAMINSKY, Howard 1940-
(Brooks Stanwood, a joint pseudonym)

PERSONAL: Born January 24, 1940, in Brooklyn, N.Y.; son of Arthur William (a furrier) and May (Kaminsky) Kaminsky; married Susan Stanwood (an editor and author), January 31, 1970; children: Jessica May. *Education:* Brooklyn College of the City University of New York, B.A., 1961; graduate study at San Francisco State College, 1962. *Home:* 390 West End Ave., New York, N.Y. 10024. *Agent:* John Hawkins, c/o Paul Reynolds Agency, 12 East 41st St., New York, N.Y. 10017. *Office:* Warner Books, Inc., 75 Rockefeller Plaza, New York, N.Y. 10019.

CAREER: Random House, Inc., New York City, director of subsidiary rights, 1965-71; Warner Books, Inc., New York City, executive vice-president and editorial director, 1972-73, president and publisher, 1973—. Independent film producer in New York City, 1971-72.

WRITINGS: (With Larry Yust and Bennett Sims) "Homebodies" (screenplay), Avco Embassy Pictures, 1974.

Novels; with wife, Susan Stanwood Kaminsky, under joint pseudonym Brooks Stanwood: *The Glow*, McGraw, 1979; *The Seventh Child*, Linden Press, 1982.

WORK IN PROGRESS: A novel, *The Wisdom*, with S. Kaminsky under joint pseudonym Brooks Stanwood.

SIDELIGHTS: Howard Kaminsky and his wife, Susan, wrote *The Glow*, a thriller that sold more than one million paperback copies. Set in posh Manhattan, the story revolves around a troupe of aged joggers who at first appear friendly and harmless but turn out to be a sadistic cult that craves the "glow" it receives by consuming the blood of young victims. The group's prime targets are Pete and Jackie Lawrence, a vital, intelligent, up-and-coming couple that befriends the geriatric joggers, later to find themselves locked in a secret laboratory where their blood is extracted for the pleasure of their captors. Jack Sullivan of the *New York Times Book Review* called *The Glow* "an ingeniously topical horror novel," but felt that the author "is sidetracked by the aggressive chic of his heroes and allows them to drop too many names."

Kaminsky also pitted old against young in "Homebodies," which he wrote with Larry Yust and Bennett Sims. This film concerns a band of elderly men and women who are trying to save their apartment building from a wrecking ball, in the process eliminating several young, ambitious people who want to replace the home with skyscrapers. Eventually, the group's hostility is internalized and its members turn on each other.

CA INTERVIEW

CA interviewed Howard Kaminsky by phone on September 15, 1980, at his office in New York City.

CA: The working relationship of the Kaminskys—you and your wife—on the novel The Glow *seems to have been not only successful, but also a very happy one.*

KAMINSKY: Yes. Actually, the only arguments we ever had came when the money came in. Creatively, we didn't have any. The way we work is pretty simple. I am the one who gets the idea, and I basically do the plotting for the book in a very detailed way. I don't proceed with an idea until I have the ending; I have to have a beginning and an end. Then we put the whole book together before we start writing. Our new book, *The Seventh Child*, is made up of about seventy chapters. We generally put most every scene on a card and attach these cards to boards so that we can always follow with our eyes the progression of the plot. When it comes down to the writing, we basically divide the book up fifty-fifty. It's not that I'll write one chapter and my wife will write the following—I might write the first three and she might write the next four, then I'll write one and she'll write two—it's uneven. But the final product is about fifty-fifty. The consistent tone of the book comes basically from a very ruthless rewriting we do of each other's material.

CA: Have you found in this process that each of you has specific strengths? You seem to be very good at plotting, for example, from what you've just said.

KAMINSKY: My strength is there, but in the actual writing of the book, there are certain scenes one of us can do better than the other. Once the book develops to the point where we see the ingredients of certain scenes, then we realize that a given scene is, in terms of subject matter, something that either my wife or myself would handle better. For instance, if we have a scene that involves cooking: my wife is an excellent cook and she would be able to handle that better. There's a scene in our new book which involves a marketing meeting at this company. That's something that I know a little better, so I did that scene. But aside from that, we more or less arbitrarily divide them up, just what we feel we'd like to work on.

CA: Do you ever get to a scene that neither of you wants to do?

KAMINSKY: Yes, frequently. Some of the scenes are more difficult, obviously. The beginning of a book, for example, is a little more difficult to do, or a scene that has a lot of logistics. There's a scene in *The Seventh Child* where there's a party, and a lot of characters are introduced. A scene like that is one that we were both reluctant to do because it's not as much fun and it's sort of hard in a way—introducing the characters, keeping them around, and trying to present them in such a way that the audience becomes familiar with them very quickly. That involves a little more technique than fun-writing. In that sense, yes, there are certain things that you'd rather not do.

CA: Do you change the approach any for the second novel?

KAMINSKY: No. The second book, which we are now about two-thirds finished with, is called *The Seventh Child*, and we did it the same way. It's an idea that I had. The idea always comes from one image. Basically, I can tell it in one line. I get an image and then the story starts coming together, then I talk together with Sue and she takes notes, and she also criticizes the plot as I spin it out, and tells me, "That doesn't work, that's inconsistent, that's illogical, that's dull"—that kind of thing, until we come up with something good.

CA: Is she doing any other work besides the writing now?

KAMINSKY: No. She had been in publishing. She worked with a couple of hardcover companies here in New York, then went on to be a senior fiction editor at the *Saturday Evening Post* and then a senior editor with E. P. Dutton. She's had a lot of experience in editing. She's very good in the process when we both sit down to edit each other's material.

CA: You really seem to enjoy writing together.

KAMINSKY: I have always liked collaborating—collaborating takes some of the terrible isolation and desolation out of writing. Of course, in writing a novel, you still have to write a lot. I've done screenplays before, and basically that's a short form. You can almost dictate them. In writing a novel together, we still have to go off to our respective rooms and just write, so that part is the same as writing alone. But it's also leavened with being together and sharing things and encouraging each other. One of the nice things is that when your energies are flagging or your faith in the book is rapidly going downhill, you have someone else to shout a few words of encouragement to you.

CA: Have you gotten mail from joggers who are horrified by what happens to the joggers in The Glow?

KAMINSKY: Not from joggers. The response we got from that book is interesting. A lot of people who jog told me that they liked the book, but a lot of people who don't jog and who hate jogging complimented us on finally giving joggers what they deserve. So it was viewed differently by the two groups. We got into jogging as a result of writing the book. I had always been a sort of physical fitness nut—I've always worked out, all my life—but I never did any real running, and to get a sense of what this was all about, we started running. We never really got terribly serious; we would run a couple of miles. We still do—we ran yesterday.

CA: Did it bother you that some of the critics commented unfavorably about all the place-names you mentioned in the book?

KAMINSKY: No. First of all, part of the book was about the life-style of a particular couple living in New York very fully. We were not just trying to drop names, but they live in that kind of world. I thought it was an accurate description of this kind of couple—very upwardly mobile, very much involved in two of the areas that are unique to New York—that is, fashion and publishing. We got other criticisms of the book. I didn't get a lot about the place-names; only one or two reviews picked that up.

CA: The screenplay for Homebodies, *like* The Glow, *involved older people in an apartment building.*

KAMINSKY: Yes, that's right. I've always been fascinated by older people. There is always some stuff about older people in things that I've written. My feeling for older people is very strong and I like them. Of course I keep casting them as sort of evil, but I don't mean it that way. I've always had older people on my mind, going back many years. Actually, the head villain in our new book is a very elderly man, but he's got his whole family in it, too.

CA: You were a stand-up comedian at one time.

KAMINSKY: Yes, unsuccessfully; I've been in a lot of other fields unsuccessfully. I did stand-up comedy temporarily while I was in graduate school, and I had a little success playing

clubs in California. But I got out of it—I didn't like doing the same thing over and over again. I never made much money from it.

CA: Where did the ambition come from to go into publishing?

KAMINSKY: Like a lot of other people, I really couldn't get a decent job for quite a while. I had a job here, lost it, and then got another job there, and then was on unemployment for a while and was trying to write. And out of the blue, an opportunity to go to work for Alfred A. Knopf happened, and I loved it because I just loved to read. I knew their list very well—I had been reading some of the top writers on their list for many, many years. They had some good, quality commercial people there too, like Ross MacDonald, Hammett, Chandler, and all the Europeans—Gide, Camus, Mann—they published and the South American writers. So that was my start—I got a job there handling subsidiary rights, and aside from a little time off producing some films, I've been in publishing since 1965.

CA: At the time that you dropped out to do those films, were you bored with publishing?

KAMINSKY: Yes, I was. I wanted to try my hand at something else. But no sooner had I gotten out than this opportunity here at Warner came up. I had some time before *The Friends of Eddie Coyle* was scheduled to start production. I was supposed to co-produce it with Paul Monash. So I took the offer, and I just became fascinated with the business. I'm still fascinated by the business.

CA: You commented in a recent Publishers Weekly *article on the question of whether a publisher's acquisitions should be determined largely from an editorial point of view or from a marketing point of view.*

KAMINSKY: I was diametrically opposite from my good friend Michael Korda at Simon & Schuster, who considers it the editorial department's job to decide what should be published. But there's a difference in hardcover publishing and paperback publishing. In hardcover publishing, a large part of the success is in subsidiary rights. In paperback publishing, we don't rely on rights income, although we like to get it when we *have* rights. Our success comes from having people buy our books. There are different ways to view a book.

CA: Warner has a relatively small management staff, in proportion to the company's size, doesn't it?

KAMINSKY: I think we do. We're a fair-sized company. The final decisions here are made by me in all things, but we have a core group of six or seven people, and in ideal situations I like for all of them to be involved because I value their opinions and they represent different facets of any one thing. I hear a lot of different points of view and learn a lot from them. Of course, there are decisions that I make without consulting with anyone, if I have to, moving very fast, but I like the ability to consult with my colleagues and to get their opinions.

CA: Is the marketing approach very different in a paperback house?

KAMINSKY: Well, there are a lot of areas where it overlaps in terms of promoting authors—doing author tours, certain media advertising, and so on. But we sell into so many different areas that they don't touch in hardcover publishing. A great deal of our books are sold through independent distributors, also called wholesalers, people who also deal with magazines.

That requires a whole different marketing approach to reach those people, sort of a broader net. I really believe that the marketing of a book is absolutely paramount. Three hundred and fifty paperbacks come out every month. The business has gotten a lot of publicity, which has made people more aware of it, and of course it's gotten into this realm of megabucks, which everybody loves. Everybody loves to hear about big sums of money. I think that big sums of money have now passed sex in popularity. (I've always been more interested in sex, myself.)

CA: What do you look for in considering what to publish?

KAMINSKY: Well, a word that may have lost some of its meaning—*freshness,* an idea that is fresh. Also, a book that you can't stop telling other people about. I think the enthusiasm for a book starts with the enthusiasm of the people who are publishing it. If you can get a book and take it to someone and say, "Hey, you've got to read this," that's the start of the process that sometimes yields best-sellers.

CA: Do you have any plans beyond the second novel?

KAMINSKY: I want to do another one. Writing takes a while because I'm busy with this, but I got a lot done this summer when we rented a house on an island off of Maine. There were no cars or phones, so we could get a lot done. I have an idea for another book, and I think eventually I'd like to write a play, which I did when I was in graduate school—I wanted to be a playwright but I gave that up and I think I'd like to try it again sometime. I would probably do that on my own. But aside from that, I just want to continue collaborating with my wife.

BIOGRAPHICAL/CRITICAL SOURCES: New York Times, October 6, 1979; *Washington Post Book World,* October 7, 1979; *New York Times Book Review,* November 4, 1979; *Times Literary Supplement,* February 1, 1980.

—*Interview by Jean W. Ross*

*   *   *

KANN, Robert A. 1906-1981

OBITUARY NOTICE: Born February 11, 1906, in Vienna, Austria; died August 30, 1981, in Vienna, Austria. Historian, educator, and author. A native of Austria and an authority on its history, Kann lived and taught in the United States for nearly forty years. He practiced law in Vienna before coming to the United States in 1938 to study history at Columbia University. He joined the faculty of Rutgers University in 1947. Kann wrote several books, including *The Hapsburg Empire: A Study in Integration and Disintegration* and *The Multinational Empire.* Obituaries and other sources: *Directory of American Scholars,* Volume I: *History,* 7th edition, Bowker, 1978; *New York Times,* September 2, 1981.

*   *   *

KAPROW, Allan 1927-

PERSONAL: Born August 23, 1927, in Atlantic City, N.J.; son of Barnet and Evelyn (Lecomowitz) Kaprow; married Vaughan Peters, March 24, 1955; children: Anton, Amy, Marisa. *Education:* Attended Hans Hofmann School of Fine Arts, New York City, 1947-48; New York University, B.A., 1949, graduate study, 1949-50; Columbia University, M.A., 1952; further study under John Cage at New School for Social Research, 1956-58.

CAREER: Rutgers University, New Brunswick, N.J., instructor, 1953-56, assistant professor of fine arts, 1956-61; Pratt Institute, Brooklyn, N.Y., lecturer in aesthetics, 1960-61; State University of New York at Stony Brook, associate professor, 1961-66, professor of fine arts, 1966-69; California Institute of Arts, Valencia, associate dean, 1969-73, faculty member, 1973-74; University of California, San Diego, professor of visual arts, 1974—. Artist, with numerous one-man shows, including those at Urban Gallery, New York City, 1955-56, Sun Gallery, Provincetown, Mass., 1957, John Gibson Gallery, New York City, 1969, Galerie Gerald Piltzer, Paris, 1974, and Galeria Vandres, Madrid, 1975; numerous group shows in museums in United States and Europe, including Guggenheim Museum, New York City, 1965, Centro de Arte y Communicacion, Buenos Aires, 1972, and Museum of Fine Arts, Dallas, Tex., 1974. Co-founder, Hansa Gallery, New York City, 1952, and Reuben Gallery, New York City, 1959; Judson Gallery, New York City, director, 1960, co-director, 1961; composer of music, Living Theatre, New York City, 1960. Director of experiental education, Institute of Contemporary Art, Boston, Mass., 1965-66; co-director of Project Other Ways, Berkeley Public Schools, Berkeley, Calif., 1968-69; founding member of advanced placement committee on art and art history, Education Testing Service and College Entrance Examination Board, Princeton, N.J., 1969-73; member and chairman of board of trustees, education committee, Museum of Modern Art, Pasadena, Calif., 1973; consultant panelist, visual arts program, National Endowment for the Arts, Washington, D.C., 1975.

AWARDS, HONORS: Katherine White Foundation grant, 1951; research grant from Rutgers University, 1957, and State University of New York at Stony Brook, 1963; Copley Foundation award, c. 1960; Guggenheim fellowship, 1967; gold medal from cultural office of Milan, Italy, 1971; National Endowment for the Arts award, 1974; University of California, San Diego, video grant, 1975, Skowhegan School of Painting and Sculpture annual award and gold medal for "non-categorical art," 1975; Deutscher Akademischer Austauschdienst Kunstlerprogram grant to live and work in Berlin, 1975.

WRITINGS: Assemblage, Environments, and Happenings, Abrams, 1966; *Some Recent Happenings* (pamphlet), Ultramarine, 1966; *Untitled Essay and Other Works* (pamphlet), Ultramarine, 1967; *Standards,* University of Northern Iowa, Department of Art, 1979. Contributor of numerous articles on art, artists, and the theatre to periodicals, including *Art News, City Lights Journal, Art et Architecture, Anthologist, Village Voice,* and *Drama Review.*

SIDELIGHTS: Although primarily a painter and sculptor, Kaprow gained much attention and notoriety in the late fifties and early sixties by his contribution of a theatrical art form called a "happening." Basically, a happening is a nonverbal theatrical presentation that is unrehearsed and acted out by any willing participants. Kaprow's happenings take place in real-life settings, never auditoriums, and they lack a conventional audience. The people who view his happenings are simply those who by chance are at the scene of the production when it takes place. David Bourdon of the *Village Voice* described a typical Kaprow happening: "Watchers stand around Times Square waiting for a signal from a window. When it comes, it tells them to walk to a place on the sidewalk and fall down. A truck comes along and they are loaded up and driven away."

Kaprow's view of modern art helps explain his unusual theatrics. In an essay on Jackson Pollack, Kaprow wrote: "Not satisfied with the *suggestion* through paint of our other senses, we shall utilize the specific substances of sight, sound, movement, people, odors, touch. Objects of every sort are materials for the new art: paint, chairs, food, electric and neon lights, smoke, water, old socks, a dog, movies, a thousand other things which will be discovered by the present generation of artists. Not only will these bold creators show us, as if for the first time, the world we have always had about us but ignored, but they will disclose entirely unheard-of happenings and events, found in garbage cans, police files, hotel lobbies, seen in store windows and on the streets, and sensed in dreams and horrible accidents.''

Happenings are further discussed in Kaprow's book *Assemblages, Environments, and Happenings.* Considered by Richard Kostelanetz of *Kenyon Review* to be ''the most substantial exposition we have of the aesthetic aspirations and critical ideas that inform much of the recent scene,'' *Assemblages* was written during a six-year period and is the definitive source on happenings. Bourdon said of *Assemblages:* ''Whatever its shortcomings, the book is as close to being Kaprow's summa as we are likely to get. In any event, Kaprow's book is a landmark in 20th century art theory.''

BIOGRAPHICAL/CRITICAL SOURCES: Village Voice, August 3, 1967; *Kenyon Review,* Vol. XXX, issue 3, 1968.*

*   *   *

KARAS, Phyllis 1944-

PERSONAL: Born April 7, 1944, in Malden, Mass.; daughter of Maurice (a steel broker) and Belle (Blumenthal) Klasky; married Jacob R. Karas (a physician), August 15, 1965; children: Adam, Joshua. *Education:* George Washington University, B.A., 1965; attended Boston University, 1974-76. *Residence:* Marblehead, Mass. *Agent:* H. Michael Snell, Inc., 7 Meadowview Rd., Wayland, Mass. 01778.

CAREER: Takoma Park Junior High School, Silver Spring, Md., English teacher, 1965-67; writer. *Awards, honors:* Best feature story award from New England Press Association, 1979, for a series on teenage pregnancy.

WRITINGS: A Life Worth Living (novel), St. Martin's, 1981. Contributor to Boston newspapers.

WORK IN PROGRESS: Worlds Apart, a novel about ''a Jewish-American princess'' and a Roman Catholic priest.

SIDELIGHTS: Phyllis Karas told *CA:* ''I write about contemporary women caught in circumstances that force them to rethink their life goals. These women were raised in the fifties to believe that if they were to obey all the rules, the comforts and joys of marriage and motherhood would rightfully be theirs. Things do not work out that way for my women, however. Watching them cope and make the necessary adjustments amid exciting life situations makes, I believe, for fascinating stories.''

BIOGRAPHICAL/CRITICAL SOURCES: Library Journal, June 15, 1981.

*   *   *

KARASU, Toksoz B(yram) 1935-

PERSONAL: Born February 11, 1935, in Erzurum, Turkey; came to the United States in 1966, naturalized citizen, 1971; son of Cemil (a lawyer and writer) and Sabina (a musician; maiden name, Nayir) Karasu; married Sylvia Rabson (a child psychiatrist), May 30, 1976. *Education:* Istanbul School of Medicine, M.D., 1959. *Office:* Department of Psychiatry, Albert Einstein College of Medicine, Bronx Municipal Hospital Center, Bronx, N.Y.

CAREER: St. Jeanne D'Arc Hospital, Montreal, Quebec, junior intern in surgery, 1963-64; St. John General Hospital, New Brunswick, senior rotating intern, 1964-65; Fairfield Hill Hospital, New Haven, Conn., resident, 1966-67; Yale-New Haven Medical Center, New Haven, resident, 1967-68; Connecticut Mental Health Center, New Haven, chief resident, 1968-69; Bronx Municipal Hospital Center, Albert Einstein College of Medicine, Bronx, N.Y., instructor, 1969-71, assistant professor, 1971-76, associate professor, 1976-81, professor of psychiatry, 1981—, director of department, 1975—.

MEMBER: American Psychiatric Association (fellow), American Medical Association, American Psychosomatic Society, American Orthopsychiatric Association (fellow), American Psychopathological Association, American Association for the Advancement of Science, Association for the Advancement of Psychotherapy, Association for Academic Psychiatry, Directors of Psychiatry, Society for Psychotherapy Research, Societe Medico-Psychologique. *Awards/honors:* Fellow of Yale University, 1969.

WRITINGS: (Editor with R. I. Steinmuller) *Psychotherapeutics in Medicine,* Grune, 1978; (editor with Leopold Bellak, and contributor) *Specialized Techniques in Individual Psychotherapy,* Brunner, 1980. Contributor to psychiatry journals.

WORK IN PROGRESS: On Effectiveness of Psychotherapy, a review and critique of methodological issues and outcome research in psychotherapy, publication expected in 1982.

SIDELIGHTS: Karasu wrote: ''I am interested in different conceptualizations of the fundamental nature of man and his ills, therapeutic processes or change agents, the basic nature of the therapeutic relationship and ethics of psychotherapy in terms of the interface between science and art, and the basic principles of therapeutic communication.''

*   *   *

KASHNER, Rita 1942-

PERSONAL: Born March 10, 1942, in Mount Vernon, N.Y.; daughter of Ludwig (in business) and Mildred (a teacher; maiden name, Saretsky) Danziger; married Howard Kashner (an attorney), August 19, 1962; children: Elizabeth Anne, Megan Rachel. *Education:* Smith College, B.A., 1963; Brandeis University, M.A., 1965. *Religion:* Jewish. *Residence:* Scarsdale, N.Y. *Agent:* Jonathan Dolger, 49 East 96th St., New York, N.Y. 10028.

CAREER: Mamaroneck High School, Mamaroneck, N.Y., English teacher, 1976-77; Sunburst Communications, Pleasantville, N.Y., filmstrip writer, 1977-78; writer, 1979—. Teacher at Women's Institute, 1974-75, and Scarsdale Alternative School, 1975-76; member of executive boards of parent teacher associations in Scarsdale, N.Y.; member of school board nominating committee of Scarsdale, 1977-79; Temple Israel Center, member of board of trustees, 1979-82, and chairman of school board, 1980-82. *Member:* Authors Guild.

WRITINGS: Bed Rest (novel), Macmillan, 1981. Author of filmstrip series on grammar, ''How to Write a Really Good Paragraph,'' Sunburst Communications. Contributor of short stories to *Hadassah.*

WORK IN PROGRESS: A novel about a man born illegitimate in Israel.

SIDELIGHTS: In remarks published by the *Library Journal,* Rita Kashner described how her book evolved: ''*Bed Rest* started with the image I had of someone who made her bed so comfortable that she became increasingly reluctant to leave it.'' As

Beth, a wife and mother in her early thirties, retreats deeper and deeper under the covers, cutting herself off from family and friends, fear and guilt begin to exert a debilitating effect on her life. "Trying to re-create the feeling of safety she remembers from her childhood, she begins putting herself to bed—eventually for whole days," Kashner explained. "And with gathering desperation she seeks her mother (whom she has never laid to rest) in her friends, her husband, her children, a potential lover and, finally, in herself."

Brigitte Weeks, editor of the *Washington Post Book World,* commented: "We spend only a few weeks with Beth, luxuriating in the fresh talcum powder and the line-dried sheets. We meet her array of friends, her children—portrayed with fiendish accuracy, her almost-but-not-quite lover, her teachers. Her humor, guts and willingness to love won me over."

BIOGRAPHICAL/CRITICAL SOURCES: Library Journal, June 15, 1981; *Washington Post Book World,* September 27, 1981.

* * *

KASTEIN, Shulamith 1903-

PERSONAL: Born March 1, 1903, in Vienna, Austria; came to the United States in 1940, naturalized citizen, 1949; daughter of Adolf (an engineer) and Camilla (Berdach) Marek; married Alfred Vogl (a physician), August 8, 1926 (divorced July 19, 1932); married Joseph Kastein (a historian and writer), March 26, 1936 (deceased); children: (first marriage) Thomas P. *Education:* University of Vienna, diploma, 1929. *Home and office:* 150 West End Ave., New York, N.Y. 10023.

CAREER: Private practice in speech pathology in New York, N.Y., 1946—; Columbia Presbyterian Medical Center, 1948-68, began as speech pathologist, became director of Speech and Hearing Clinic; co-director of Mount St. Ursula Speech Center, 1968-75. Lecturer in Otolaryngology at College of Physicians and Surgeons, Columbia University, 1952-75; consultant in language and speech pathology to New York Association for the Blind, 1966—. *Member:* American Speech-Language-Hearing Association (fellow), Academy of Aphasia. *Awards, honors:* Humanitarian award from College of New Rochelle, 1979, for work with children; professional achievement award from New York City Speech, Hearing, and Language Association, 1981.

WRITINGS: (Contributor) E. Froeschals, editor, *Twentieth-Century Speech and Voice Correction,* Philosophical Library, 1948; *Speech Hygiene Guidance for Parents of Children With Cerebral Palsy,* Cerebral Palsy Society of New York, 1949; (with Harold Michal-Smith) *The Special Child: Diagnosis, Treatment, Habilitation,* New School for the Special Child (Seattle, Wash.), 1961; (contributor) *Mental Retardation,* Williams & Wilkins, 1962; (with Barbara Trace) *The Birth of Language,* C. C Thomas, 1966; (with Isabelle Spaulding and Battia Scharf) *Raising the Young Blind Child,* Human Sciences, 1980. Also author of *New Trends in Differential Diagnosis: The Child With Communication Disorders,* 1957. Contributor of about twenty-five articles to medical, communication, and speech and hearing journals.

WORK IN PROGRESS: Language and Learning Impaired Children Grow Up, longitudinal studies of former child patients, comprising childhood, adolescence, and adulthood.

SIDELIGHTS: Kastein told *CA:* "Since my school years, when I tutored students in lower grades, I have loved to teach. Since teaching and writing are both means to sharing thoughts, knowledge, and feelings, writing became the tool in my professional life that enabled me to share clinical experience not only with professional audiences but also with readers interested in human development.

"I have been emphasizing the importance of early diagnosis and intervention in children with communication disorders; the importance of studying each development step, each dysfunction, and how—if at all—it affects other functions. Test results do not yield this information. Diagnosis and remediation must be based on the analysis of the quality of the child's response and the behavioral and emotional circumstances in which it is given, as well as on the type of intervention that helps the child arrive at the appropriate answer.

"Verbal language—that is, communication not only with others but with ourselves—is the tool for thinking, learning, and problem-solving. The present staggering number of children with school failures is due to a wide range of causes, such as emotional, psycho-social, cultural as well as environmental (including television viewing), and organic malfunctions (mainly with the brain). They are found in all strata of society, the disadvantaged as well as the advantaged. Since they are all causing or contributing to restrictions or deviations in the development and use of language, the acquisition of academic skills—literacy—is in jeopardy."

* * *

KASZUBSKI, Marek 1951-

PERSONAL: Surname is pronounced Ka-*shoob*-ski; born May 23, 1951, in Lodz, Poland; came to the United States in 1976; son of Artur and Eugenia (Morawska) Kaszubski; married Elzbieta Danecka (a printing engineer), August 16, 1975. *Education:* University of Lodz. LL.M., 1973; University of Maryland, M.L.S., 1978; George Washington University, M.C.L., 1981. *Home:* 8504 Bradford Rd., Silver Spring, Md. 20901. *Office address:* P. W. Associates, P.O. Box 428, College Park, Md. 20740.

CAREER: Judge in Lowicz, Poland, 1975-76; attorney in Lowicz, 1976; P. W. Associates, College Park, Md., editorial assistant, 1977-79, associate editor, 1979—.

WRITINGS: (Editor with Paul Wasserman) *Law and Legal Information Directory,* Gale, 1980, revised edition, 1982.

SIDELIGHTS: Kaszubski told *CA:* "*Law and Legal Information Directory* is a guide to national and international organizations, bar associations, the federal court system, federal regulatory agencies, law schools, continuing legal education, paralegal education, scholarships and grants, awards and prizes, special libraries, information systems and services, research centers, legal periodical publications, and book and media publishers. Working on this directory was a valuable experience for me, and I can only hope that the users will find it helpful now that the vast network of legal institutions and information sources are readily available with the publication of the second edition."

* * *

KATI
See REKAI, Kati

* * *

KAUMEYER, Dorothy 1914-
(Dorothy Lamour, Dorothy Stanton)

BRIEF ENTRY: Born December 10, 1914, in New Orleans, La. American film actress and author. Dorothy Lamour's first film was "Jungle Princess" (1937). She starred in dozens of feature films during the next twenty years, including "High, Wide and Handsome," "St. Louis Blues," "The Road to Singapore," and "Wild Harvest." She also sang in nightclubs and performed on radio programs. In 1967 she starred in the touring company of "Hello, Dolly!" She wrote *Dorothy Lamour: My Side of the Road* (Prentice-Hall, 1980). *Address:* c/o Ben Pearson Agency, 6399 Wilshire Blvd., Suite 505, Los Angeles, Calif. 90048. *Biographical/critical sources: The Complete Encyclopedia of Popular Music and Jazz, 1900-1950,* Arlington House, 1974; *Christian Science Monitor,* December 11, 1974.

*   *   *

KAYSER-JONES, Jeanie Schmit   1935-

PERSONAL: Born November 20, 1935, in Rising City, Neb.; daughter of Nick Cornelius (a farmer) and Loretta (Fohl) Schmit; married H. William Kayser, May 18, 1963 (died June 19, 1963); married Theodore H.D. Jones (a professor of biochemistry), August 22, 1976. *Education:* St. Elizabeth's School of Nursing, Lincoln, Neb., Diploma in Nursing, 1956; University of Colorado, B.S. (cum laude), 1967; University of California, San Francisco, M.S., 1968; University of California, Berkeley, Ph.D., 1978. *Home:* 2665 El Camino Del Mar, San Francisco, Calif. 94121. *Office:* Family Health Care Nursing, University of California, San Francisco, Calif. 94143.

CAREER: Associated with Baylor Hospital, Dallas, Tex., 1960-61; associated with Blue Cross-Blue Shield, 1962-63; Creighton Memorial St. Joseph Hospital, Omaha, Neb., head nurse, 1963-65; University of San Francisco, School of Nursing, San Francisco, Calif., associate professor, 1967-76; University of California, San Francisco, assistant professor of family health care nursing, 1978—. Associate professor at University of San Francisco. Adviser to White House Conference on Aging, 1981. *Member:* Gerontological Society, American Anthropological Association, American Association for the Advancement of Science, Society for Medical Anthropology, American Nurses Association, Western Society for Research in Nursing, California Nurses Association, Sigma Theta Tau. *Awards, honors:* Gold medal in master's women's mile race at Examiner Games (San Francisco, Calif.), 1977, 1978.

WRITINGS: Old, Alone, and Neglected, University of California Press, 1981. Contributor to nursing journals.

WORK IN PROGRESS: Research on the incidence and prevalence of institutionalization; research on quality of care in long-term institutions for the aged; comparison of quality of care and patients' views of care on open wards versus semi-private rooms in a twelve hundred-bed long-term care hospital.

SIDELIGHTS: Jeanie Kayser-Jones commented: "I participated in a nurse exchange program in Denmark in 1959. My husband is British, so we travel to the United Kingdom and the continent about every two years.

"I am frequently invited to professional and community groups on the care of the institutionalized aged. I feel that the care of the aged is an important issue and one that must not be neglected; as people live longer, even more of the aged population will require some type of institutional care. The United States is a country that prides itself on excellence in acute care yet tolerates very low standards in the care of the chronically ill aged. In Scotland the National Health Service, the specialty of geriatrics, and the Geriatric Service serve as catalysts to quality care of the aged, while in the United States the lack of adequate financing of health care, the absence of geriatrics as

a specialty, and the abdication of responsibility for the care of the aged by health professionals act as barriers to quality care. In Scotland, institutions for the aged are government owned and managed by professionals, whereas in the United States most nursing homes are private and the main objective is profit. Without formal institutional structures and without concerned professionals to take responsibility for the implementation of an organized plan of care, the chronically disabled elderly will not receive quality care and conditions in nursing homes will deteriorate further."

AVOCATIONAL INTERESTS: Track, long-distance running.

*   *   *

KAZANTZAKIS, Nikos   1883-1957

BRIEF ENTRY: Born February 18, 1883, in Herakleion, Crete; died of leukemia, October 26, 1957, in Freiburg, Germany; buried on Crete. Greek novelist, poet, playwright, and essayist. Kazantzakis held various government posts in Greece in addition to being a writer and world traveler. Best known for *Bios kai politeia tou Alexe Zormpa* (1946; translated as *Zorba the Greek,* 1952) and *Anaphora ston Gkreko: Mythistorema* (1961; translated as *Report to Greco,* 1965), Kazantzakis also wrote the epic *Odyseia* (1938; translated as *The Odyssey: A Modern Sequel,* 1958), a 33,333-line poem which picks up the tale of Odysseus where Homer left off and chronicles the hero's search for God. As a student, Kazantzakis studied Nietzsche and Bergson and their influence remained, leading him to believe that the quest for freedom was more important than freedom itself, which could never be attained. This served as the theme for *Ho teleutaios peirasmos* (1955; translated as *The Last Temptation of Christ,* 1960), a surrealistic biography of Christ that the Greek Orthodox Church denounced as heresy. He also was condemned by the secular community for his portrayal of Greek heroism in *Ho Kapetan Michales* (1954; translated as *Freedom or Death,* 1956) and criticized by Greek intellectuals for his use of demotic Greek rather than pure Greek. He died while returning from a trip to China, and his remains were taken to Athens to lie in state. The archbishop of Athens, however, refused to permit this honor or to celebrate a funeral Mass for him. *Residence:* Antibes, France. *Biographical/critical sources: The Reader's Encyclopedia,* 2nd edition, Crowell, 1965; *Encyclopedia of World Literature in the Twentieth Century,* updated edition, 1967; *Twentieth Century Writing: A Reader's Guide to Contemporary Literature,* Transatlantic, 1969; *Who's Who in Twentieth Century Literature,* Holt, 1976; *Twentieth-Century Literary Criticism,* Volume 2, Gale, 1979.

*   *   *

KEETON, William Tinsley   1933-1980

OBITUARY NOTICE: Born February 3, 1933, in Roanoke, Va.; died of heart failure, August 17, 1980, in Ithaca, N.Y. Biologist, educator, and author. Keeton specialized in the study of animal behavior, especially bird migration and navigation. In an experiment in which he fastened magnets to the heads of homing pigeons, he demonstrated that birds are able to sense the Earth's magnetic field and use it to find their way. Keeton also investigated birds' perception of smell, sound, light, and barometric pressure, and suggested that these too may be used for orientation and navigation. Keeton was the author of *Biological Science,* an introductory textbook that is widely used in colleges. Obituaries and other sources: *Who's Who in America,* 40th edition, Marquis, 1978; *American Men and Women of Science: The Physical and Biological Sciences,* 14th edition,

Bowker, 1979; *New York Times,* August 21, 1980; *The Annual Obituary 1980,* St. Martin's, 1981.

* * *

KELLEY, True Adelaide 1946-

PERSONAL: Born February 25, 1946, in Cambridge, Mass.; daughter of Mark E. (an illustrator) and Adelaide (an artist; maiden name, True) Kelley; married Steven Lindblom (a writer and illustrator of children's books). *Education:* University of New Hampshire, B.A., 1968; attended Rhode Island School of Design, 1968-71. *Home and office address:* Kensington Rd., Hampton Falls, N.H. 03844.

CAREER: Free-lance illustrator, 1971—; writer, 1978—. *Member:* Seacoast Anti-Pollution League, Boston Graphic Artists Guild (member of board of directors, 1980-81).

WRITINGS—Children's books; self-illustrated: (With husband, Steven Lindblom) *The Mouses' Terrible Christmas,* Lothrop, 1978; (with Lindblom) *The Mouses' Terrible Halloween,* Lothrop, 1980; *A Valentine for Fuzzboom,* Houghton, 1981; *Buggly Bear's Hiccup Cure,* Parents' Magazine Press, 1982; (with Lindblom) *Let's Give Kitty a Bath,* Addison-Wesley, 1982.

SIDELIGHTS: Kelley's *Let's Give Kitty a Bath* is a wordless book.

* * *

KELLY, Alison 1913-

PERSONAL: Born October 17, 1913, in Liverpool, England; daughter of Sir Robert (a surgeon) and A.E. Irma (McDougall) Kelly. *Education:* Lady Margaret Hall, Oxford, M.A. (with honors), 1936; attended Liverpool City College of Art, 1937-39. *Home:* 34 Phillimore Gardens, Flat 8, London W8 7QF, England. *Agent:* Campbell Thomson & McLaughlan Ltd., 31 Newington Green, London N16 9PU, England.

CAREER: Lecturer for Workers Educational Association, 1949-56, and Design Centre, 1956-70; University of London, London, England, extramural lecturer in English architecture and decoration, 1966—. Lecturer at City Literary Institute, London, 1959-81. *Wartime service:* Ministry of Home Security, camouflage officer, 1939-45. *Member:* International Society for the Study of Church Monuments, Society of Architectural Historians, English Ceramic Circle, Wedgwood Society (member of council), Furniture History Society.

WRITINGS: Pottery, Educational Supply Association, 1961; *The Story of Wedgwood,* Faber, 1962, Viking, 1963, revised edition, Faber, 1975; *Decorative Wedgwood in Architecture and Furniture,* Country Life Books, 1965; *The Book of English Fireplaces,* Country Life Books, 1968; *Wedgwood Ware,* Ward, Lock, 1970. Contributor to magazines, including *Country Life, Burlington,* and *Connoisseur.*

WORK IN PROGRESS: Coade Stone.

AVOCATIONAL INTERESTS: Travel (Italy).

* * *

KEMP, Anthony 1939-

PERSONAL: Born January 31, 1939, in London, England; son of Herbert (an oil company executive) and Vera (Jiminez) Kemp; married Ute Klingenschmidt, July 29, 1967; children: Oliver, Fiona. *Education:* Pembroke College, Oxford, M.A., 1976. *Home:* 38 Bullar Rd., Southampton SO2 4GS, England. *Agent:*

A. M. Heath & Co. Ltd., 40-42 William IV St., London WC2N 4DD, England.

CAREER: Teacher of English at private schools in Wuerzburg and Nuremberg, West Germany, 1962-66; U.S. Army, C.D.M.Z., Kaiserslautern, West Germany, civilian quality control official, 1966-70; free-lance writer and translator, 1970—. Consultant to Fort Ltd., Newhaven, Sussex, England. *Military service:* Royal Air Force, 1959-62. *Member:* Fortress Study Group (founder; chairman, 1975-79).

WRITINGS: Castles in Color, Arco, 1977; (translator) G. Schomaekers, *The American Civil War,* Blandford, 1978; *Weapons and Equipment of the Marlborough Wars,* Blandford, 1980; *Maginot Line: The Myth and Reality,* Stein & Day, 1981; *The Unknown Battle: Metz, 1944,* Stein & Day, 1981; (with Richard Holmes) *Singapore: The Bitter End,* Anthony Bird, 1982; *The German Commanders of World War II,* Osprey, 1982. Contributor to journals.

Scripts: "Comrades in Arms?," first broadcast by Southern Television on I.T.V. network, June 1, 1980.

WORK IN PROGRESS: Research on the Reichswald Forest Battles, January to March, 1945.

SIDELIGHTS: Kemp commented: "My interests include historic building restoration, development of fortification, coast artillery, and military history in general."

* * *

KENNECOTT, G. J.
See VIKSNINS, George J(uris)

* * *

KENNEDY, Carol

PERSONAL: Born in London, England; daughter of Alan F. (a physician) and Grace (a broadcasting executive; maiden name, Morley) Kennedy. *Education:* Attended Lycee Francais, London, England. *Home:* 31 Wimbledon Close, The Downs, London S.W.20, England. *Agent:* Anthony Sheil Associates Ltd., 2/3 Morwell St., London WC1B 3AR, England. *Office:* The Director, 116 Pall Mall, London SW1Y 5ED, England.

CAREER: Canadian Press, London, England, staff correspondent, 1965-74; *Director,* London, associate editor, 1974-78, deputy editor, 1979—. London correspondent for *Maclean's,* Toronto, Ontario, 1975—.

WRITINGS: Eccentric Soldiers, Mowbray, 1975; *Buying Antiques in Europe,* Bowker, 1976; *The Entrepreneurs,* Volume II (Kennedy was not associated with Volume I), Scope Books, 1980; *Harewood: The Life and Times of an English Country House,* Hutchinson, 1982.

SIDELIGHTS: Part of Mowbray's "Eccentric" series, *Eccentric Soldiers,* explained Kennedy, is "a collection of biographical sketches of eccentric military commanders from the eighteenth to the twentieth century."

* * *

KENNEDY, Theodore Reginald 1936-

PERSONAL: Born January 4, 1936, in Florida; son of Albert L. and Vera B. (Allen) Kennedy. *Education:* University of Washington, Seattle, B.A., 1970; Princeton University, M.A., 1972, Ph.D., 1974. *Politics:* Democrat. *Religion:* Methodist. *Home:* 22 Brookhaven Blvd., Point Jefferson Station, N.Y. 11776.

Office: Department of Anthropology, State University of New York at Stony Brook, Stony Brook, N.Y. 11794.

CAREER: State University of New York at Stony Brook, associate professor of anthropology, 1974—. Associated with Boeing Co. *Military service:* U.S. Army, 1959-60. *Member:* American Anthropological Association, National Association for the Advancement of Colored People, National Historical Society. *Awards, honors:* Rockefeller Foundation fellow; grants from U.S. Department of Health, Education and Welfare, Ford Foundation, Center for Urban Ethnography at University of Pennsylvania, and New York Foundation.

WRITINGS: You Gotta Deal With It: Black Family Relations in a Southern Community, Oxford University Press, 1980; *Let's Get Down: A Socio-Linguistic Analysis of Black Lifestyle Through a Study of Black Argot—With a Complete Dictionary of Words, Terms, and Expressions,* Oxford University Press, 1982.

WORK IN PROGRESS: Where Is My Father?: A Study of Five White Middle-Class Families; research on death and dying in the black family.

* * *

KENT, Allegra 1938-

BRIEF ENTRY: Born August 11, 1938, in California. American ballet dancer and author. Kent has been a member of the New York City Ballet Company since 1953. She wrote *Allegra Kent's Water Beauty Book* (St. Martin's, 1976). *Address:* 200 East 62nd St., New York, N.Y. 10021. *Biographical/critical sources: Current Biography,* Wilson, 1970.

* * *

KENT, Simon
See CATTO, Max(well Jeffrey)

* * *

KENYON, Mildred Adams 1894-1980
(Mildred Adams)

OBITUARY NOTICE: Born in 1894 in Illinois; died of a heart attack, November 5, 1980, in New York, N.Y. Journalist, translator, critic, and author. An expert on literary and political life in Spain and Latin America, Kenyon lived in Spain during the 1920's, working as a free-lance journalist for the *New York Times.* At the outbreak of the Spanish civil war in 1936, Kenyon returned to the United States and ran an emergency rescue mission in New York City to aid loyalist refugees. Writing exclusively under her maiden name, Mildred Adams, she was a part-time correspondent for the *London Economist* from 1946 to 1975 and a regular contributor to the *New York Times Magazine* and *Book Review* for forty years. In addition to hundreds of articles and essays on subjects ranging from feminism to urban planning, she wrote five books and translated eight volumes of philosophy by the Spanish writer Jose Ortega y Gasset. Kenyon also served as adviser to two literary journals, *Revista de Occidente* in Madrid and *Sur* in Argentina. She was a director and executive committee member of the Foreign Policy Association and served as a director of the Near East Foundation and the Americas Foundation. Her best-known books include *Garcia Lorca: Playwright and Poet, The Right to Be People,* and *Latin America: Evolution or Explosion.* Among her translations of Ortega y Gasset's work are *Man and Crisis, Invertebrate Spain,* and *An Interpretation of Universal History.* Obituaries and other sources: *New York Times,* November 10, 1980; *The Annual Obituary 1980,* St. Martin's, 1981.

KEROUAC, Jan
See HACKETT, Jan Michele

* * *

KERR, Carole
See CARR, Margaret

* * *

KESSEL, Joseph (Elie) 1898-1979

PERSONAL: Surname is accented on second syllable; born February 10, 1898, in Clara, Argentina; died July 23, 1979, in Avernes, France; son of Samuel (a physician) and Raissa (Lesik) Kessel; married Michele O'Brien, March 10, 1949. *Education:* Received licence and M.Lit. from University of Paris; also attended National Conservatory for Dramatic Art. *Religion:* Jewish. *Residence:* Avernes, France.

CAREER: Journalist and foreign correspondent in Afghanistan, Burma, East Africa, Germany, Hong Kong, India, Ireland, Palestine (now Israel), Russia (now U.S.S.R.), and Spain, 1915-79; author, 1922-75. *Military service:* French Air Force, World War I, aviator in Europe, the United States, and Siberia; commander of Legion of Honor, received Croix de Guerre with palms; French Resistance Movement, World War II, aide to General Charles de Gaulle; received Croix de Guerre with palms. *Member:* Academie Francaise. *Awards, honors:* Grand Prix du Roman, 1927, for *Les Captifs,* and Prix des Ambassadeurs, 1958, both from the Academie Francaise; Prix Rainier III de Monaco, 1959, for collected works; Grande Medaille d'Or des Arts, Sciences, et Lettres, 1965; grand officer of Legion of Honor, 1977.

WRITINGS—Novels: *L'Equipage,* Nouvelle Revue Francaise, 1923, reprinted, Gallimard, 1972, translation published as "Pilot and Observer" in *The Pure in Heart* (see below); (with Helene Iswolsky) *Les Rois aveugles,* Editions de France, 1925, reprinted, Plon, 1970, translation by G. & K. De Teissier published as *Blinded Kings,* Doubleday, 1926; *Les Captifs,* Nouvelle Revue Francaise, 1926; *Nuits de princes,* Editions de France, 1927, reprinted, Plon, 1966, translation by Jack Kahane published as *Princes of the Night,* Macaulay, 1928; *Belle de jour,* Nouvelle Revue Francaise, 1929, translation by Geoffrey Wagner, published under same title, St. Martin's, 1962.

Le Coup de grace, Editions de France, 1931, reprinted, Editions Rombaldi, 1969, translation by Katherine Woods published as *Sirocco,* Random House, 1947; *Fortune carree,* Editions de France, 1932, translation by William Almon Wolff published as *Crossroads,* Putnam, 1932; *Les Enfants de la chance,* Gallimard, 1934, reprinted, 1968; *La Passante du Sans-Souci,* Gallimard, 1936, reprinted, 1968; *La Rose de Java,* Gallimard, 1937, reprinted, 1972; *Le Bataillon du ciel,* Julliard, 1947.

Le Tour du malheur, Gallimard, 1950, reprinted, 1976, Volume I: *La Fontaine Medicis,* translation by Herma Briffault published as *The Medici Fountain,* St. Martin's, 1963, Volume II: *L'Affaire Bernan,* translation by Charles Lam Markmann published as *The Bernan Affair,* St. Martin's, 1965, Volume III: *Les Lauriers roses,* Volume IV: *L'Homme de platre.*

Au Grand Socco, Gallimard, 1952; *Les Amants du tage,* Editions du Milieu du Monde, 1954; *Le Lion,* illustrations by Leone Plard, Gallimard, 1958, new edition with illustrations by Tibor Czernus, 1966, translation by Peter Green published as *The Lion* (Book-of-the-Month Club selection), Knopf, 1959; *Les Cavaliers*, Gallimard, 1967, translation by Patrick O'Brian published as *The Horsemen*, Farrar, Straus, 1968.

Short stories: *La Steppe rouge* (contains "Le Chant de Fedka le Boiteux," "Le Poupee," "L'Enfant qui revint," "Au Marche," "Les Deux Fous," "La Croix," and "Le Caveau n"), Nouvelle Revue Francaise, 1922; *Les Coeurs purs*, Gallimard, 1927, translation published in *The Pure in Heart* (see below); *La Nagaika* (contains "La Nagaika," "La Femme du desert," and "La Coupe felee"), Julliard, 1951; *Tous n'etaient pas des anges*, Plon, 1963, translation by Humphrey Hare published as *They Weren't All Angels*, McKay, 1965.

Biography: *Stavisky, l'homme que j'ai connu* (title means "Stavisky, the Man Whom I Have Known"), Gallimard, 1934, published with *Historique de l'affaire Stavisky* by Raymond Thevenin, Gallimard, 1974; *Mermoz*, Gallimard, 1938, reprinted with illustrations by Roger Parry, 1963; *Les Mains du miracle*, preface by Hugh Redwald Trevor-Roper, Gallimard, 1960, translation by Helen Weaver and Leo Raditsa published as *The Man With the Miraculous Hands*, Farrar, Straus, 1961 (translation by Denise Folliot published in England as *The Magic Touch*, Hart-Davis, 1961); *Kisling, 1891-1953*, edited by Jean Kisling, Abrams, 1971; (with Jean Cocteau and Armand Gatti) *Moretti*, Clefs du Temps, 1973.

Travel: *Terre d'amour*, Flammarion, 1927, revised edition published as *Terre d'amour et de feu: Israel, 1925-1961*, Plon, 1965; *Reine et Serre*, Editions de France, 1929; *La Piste fauve*, Gallimard, 1954; *La Vallee des rubis*, Gallimard, 1955, translation by Stella Rodway published as *The Valley of Rubies*, McKay, 1960 (published in England as *Mogok: The Valley of Rubies*, MacGibbon & Kee, 1960); *Hong-Kong et Macao*, Gallimard, 1957; *Afghanistan*, translation by Bernadette Folliot, photographs by Karl Flinker and Max Klimburg, Thames & Hudson, 1959; *Inde: Peninsule des dieux*, photographs by Arnaud de Monbrison, Hachette, 1960; *Les Fils de l'impossible*, Plon, 1970.

Nonfiction: (With G. Suarez) *Le Onze mai*, preface by Francois Le Grix, Nouvelle Revue Francaise, 1924; *Au camp des vaincus; ou, La Critique du onze mai*, illustrations by H.-P. Gassier, Nouvelle Revue Francaise, 1924; *Memoires d'un commissaire du peuple*, photographs by Daniel Jacomet, Champion, 1925; *Les Nuits de Siberie*, Flammarion, 1928; *Vent de sable*, Editions de France, 1929, reprinted, Gallimard, 1966; *Basfonds*, Editions des Portiques, 1932; *Hollywood, ville mirage*, Gallimard, 1937; *L'Armee des ombres: Chronique de la resistance*, Charlot, 1943, translation by Haakon Chevalier published as *Army of Shadows*, Knopf, 1944.

Temoin parmi les hommes, Volume I: *Les Temps de l'esperance*, Del Duca, 1956, Volume II: *Les Jours de l'aventure*, Del Duca, 1956, Volume III; *L'Heure des chatiments*, Del Duca, 1956, Volume IV: *La Nouvelle Saison*, Plon, 1968, Volume V: *Le Jeu du roi*, Plon, 1969, Volume VI: *Les Instants de verite*, Plon, 1969.

Avec les alcooliques anonymes, Gallimard, 1960, translation by Frances Partridge published as *The Enemy in the Mouth: An Account of Alcoholics Anonymous*, Hart-Davis, 1961, published as *The Road Back: A Report on Alcoholics Anonymous*, Knopf, 1962; *En Tanger, zona internacional*, Editorial del Pacifico, 1962; (with Andre Chamson) *Discours de reception de Monsieur Joseph Kessel a l'Academie Francaise et response de Monsieur Andre Chamson*, Gallimard, 1964; *Album: Images, reportage, aventures*, Plon, 1969; *Des Hommes*, Gallimard, 1972.

Other books: *Mary de Cork*, [Paris], 1925; *Makhno et sa juive*, Editions Eos, 1926; *Dames de Californie*, Gallimard, 1929; *La Rage au Ventre*, Nouvelle Societe d'Edition, 1930; *Nuits de Montmartre*, Editions de France, 1932, reprinted, Plon, 1971; *Wagon-lit*, Gallimard, 1932; *Marches d'esclaves*, Editions de France, 1933; *Une Balle perdue*, Editions de France, 1935; *Le Repos de l'equipage*, Gallimard, 1935; *Les Maudru*, Julliard, 1945.

Le Proces des enfants perdus, Julliard, 1951; *Un Mur a Jerusalem* (adapted from film of the same title [see below]), Editions et Publications Premeirs, 1968; *Le Proletariat francais*, Plon, 1968; *La Petit Ane blanc*, Gallimard, 1973; *Les Temps sauvages*, Gallimard, 1975.

Omnibus volumes: *The Pure in Heart* (contains "Pilot and Observer" [translation of *L'Equipage*] and translation of the three stories in *Les Coeurs purs*), Dodd, 1928; *Oeuvres romansque*, twelve volumes, edited by Noel Schumann and Henri Jadoux, Editions Lidis, 1964; *Pour l'honneur* (contains *Une Balle perdue* and *Les Maudru*), Le Cercle du Livre de France, 1964, published with illustrations by Rene Peron, Editions G.P., 1969; *Oeuvres completes*, fifteen volumes, Presses d'Aujourd' Hui, 1975.

Other writings: (With Maurice Druon) "Chant des partisans" (song), 1942; *Le Coup de grace* (three-act drama; adapted from novel of the same title [see above]), Gallimard, 1953; (author of foreword) Henry Torres, *Accuses hors serie*, [Paris], 1957; "The Night of the Generals" (screenplay), Columbia, 1967; 'Un Mur a Jerusalem" (documentary film), Para-France Films, 1967, released in U.S. as "A Wall in Jerusalem," 1972; (author of preface) Claude Levy and Paul Tillard, *Betrayal at the Vel d'Hiv*, translation by Inea Brushnaq, Hill & Wang, 1969; "Au grand balcon" (screenplay); "Le Grand Cirque" (screenplay). Also author of *L'Embarquement pour Gibraltar*, [Paris], 1945, and *Le Premier Amour de l'aspirant Dalleau*, [Paris], 1949. Contributor of articles to journals, including *Le Matin*, *Figaro*, *Paris Soir*, *Journal des debats*, and *Scholar*, and to French newspapers.

SIDELIGHTS: Kessel spent most of his life as a world traveler. His roving began when, as a child, he moved from Argentina to Russia, where he lived until forced by anti-Jewish pogroms to flee to France. Later, as an aviator in the French Air Force, Kessel traveled over much of the world, setting a pattern that was to continue throughout his life. Kessel wrote numerous best-selling books based upon his travel experiences and became according to the *New York Times*, "one of France's most widely read authors between the two world wars."

Critics praised Kessel's books for their highly personal narrative style and for their vivid portrayal of foreign lands. "Kessel writes like a man who unselfconsciously catalogues the beauties of the beloved," observed *New York Times Book Review*'s Robert Payne in his review of *The Valley of the Rubies*. The book, an account of Kessel's trip to Mogok, "is thronged with colorful characters and is surprisingly full of information about modern day Burma," said a *New York Herald Tribune Lively Arts* critic. A *Booklist* reviewer commented that, although *Valley of the Rubies* is a "factual reminiscence," it "reads like fictional adventure."

Kessel was best known for his dramatic, and often violent, tales of fiction. His first novel, *L'Equipage*, for example, mingles "brutality with sentiment," said a *London Times* critic, as it describes the hazards of life on a World War I aviation base. The book sold extremely well and went into one hundred editions within three years of its original publication.

Another of Kessel's novels, *Le Lion* ("The Lion"), a book about life on an African game reserve, was a best-seller in both France and the United States and was a Book-of-the-Month Club selection. Although *Atlantic Monthly*'s Edward Weeks called the story "theatrical" and several other critics found the book's ten-year-old heroine too precocious to be believable. James Stern of the *New York Times* likened the novel to "a piece of perfectly constructed music" because of its swift pace and dramatic climax. A *Wisconsin Library Bulletin* reviewer pronounced the book "a masterpiece of fiction."

Some critics consider *The Horsemen* to be Kessel's masterpiece. The story, set in contemporary Afghanistan, depicts a man's struggle against nature, treachery, and excruciating pain during a tortuous journey through the Afghan wilderness. Bernard Bergonzi of the *New York Times Book Review* observed that the expedition is described in "vivid and often horrifying detail," citing an episode in which the hero's leg is "crudely but effectively amputated" as an example of a "calulatedly tough scene." *Book World*'s Cecelia Holland found *The Horsemen* "gripping" and "worth the reading" but complained that the book contains several technical errors—primarily related to equestrian techniques—that detract from its story. Judson LaHaye of *Best Sellers*, however, proclaimed the book "a brilliant novel of epic grandeur" and stated that "it should rank with many of the more durable classics." *Life* critic Webster Schott commented that *The Horsemen* "is more than a novel. It is an experience."

Kessel's experiences as a member of the Free French during World War II provided him with material for his *Army of Shadows*. The book, a collection of true stories based upon the adventures of Kessel's fellow resistance members, was admired by critics for its power and honesty. Kay Boyles of *Weekly Book Review* praised the book for its "brilliance, intensity, and distinction" and said it "must take its place among the most powerful and stirring stories of our time."

Kessel also wrote several biographies, including two that were about personal acquaintances of his. The first, *Stavisky, l'homme que j'ai connu*, is about Alexandre Stavisky, the notorious swindler who disrupted the French economy and nearly toppled the government before committing suicide in 1934. The next, Kessel's *Man With the Miraculous Hands*, is the story of manual therapist Felix Kersten, personal physician to the infamous Nazi leader Heinrich Himmler. Kersten was able to save the lives of thousands of persecuted individuals by influencing Himmler on their behalf. *New York Times Book Review* critic Telford Taylor found the Kersten biography to be "a fantastic story, authenticated by various disclosures at the Nuremburg trials." Kessel "was himself one of Kersten's patients," wrote G. A. Craig in *New York Herald Tribune Lively Arts*, "and is thus able to describe his powers more convincingly than earlier writers."

MEDIA ADAPTATIONS: Several of Kessel's books have been adapted as films, including *L'Equipage*, released as "The Woman I Love," starring Paul Muni, by RKO in 1937; "Sirocco," starring Humphrey Bogart, released by Columbia Pictures in 1951; "The Lion," starring William Holden, released by Twentieth Century-Fox in 1962; "Belle de Jour," written and directed by Luis Bunuel and starring Catherine Deneuve, released by Allied Artists in 1968; "L'Armee des ombres," written and directed by Jean-Pierre Melville and starring Simone Signoret, released by Valoria Films in 1969; "The Horsemen," directed by John Frankenheimer and starring Omar Sharif, released by Columbia Pictures in 1971; and *Stavisky: The Man Whom I Have Known*, released as "Stavisky," directed by Alain Resnais and starring Jean Paul Belmondo, by Cinemation Industries in 1974.

BIOGRAPHICAL/CRITICAL SOURCES: Times Literary Supplement, August 16, 1928, September 18, 1959, October 11, 1963; *New York Herald Tribune Books*, August 26, 1928; *Saturday Review of Literature*, September 8, 1928, July 1, 1944, May 24, 1947; *New York Times*, September 18, 1932, June 25, 1944, May 4, 1947, June 21, 1959; *Revue des Deux Mondes*, October 15, 1938, February 1, 1941, March 7, 1964; *Weekly Book Review*, June 18, 1944; *Christian Science Monitor*, June 20, 1944, July 9, 1959; *Nation*, July 22, 1944; *New Statesman*, January 6, 1945, August 9, 1963, July 23, 1971; *New York Herald Tribune Weekly Book Review*, April 27, 1947; *New York Herald Tribune Book Review*, June 21, 1959, February 24, 1979; *Time*, June 22, 1959, August 16, 1971; *Saturday Review*, June 27, 1959, June 1, 1968; *Wisconsin Library Bulletin*, July, 1959; *Commonweal*, July 31, 1959; *Atlantic Monthly*, August, 1959; *New York Times Book Review*, April 2, 1961, April 23, 1961, August 18, 1963, February 3, 1967, June 16, 1968, October 19, 1969; *Revue de Paris*, Volume LXXI, 1964; *Best Sellers*, May 15, 1965, June 15, 1968; Henri Peyre, *French Novelists of Today*, Oxford University Press, 1967; *Life*, May 31, 1968; *Book World*, June 16, 1968; *Books Abroad*, autumn, 1968, autumn, 1970; *Books and Bookmen*, August, 1969; *World Literature Today*, winter, 1977.

OBITUARIES: New York Times, July 25, 1979; *Chicago Tribune*, July 25, 1979; *Time*, August 6, 1979.*

—*Sketch by Susan M. Trosky*

*   *   *

KESSEL, Joyce Karen 1937-

PERSONAL: Born January 27, 1937, in Kulm, N.D.; daughter of Theodore F. (a lawyer) and Esther (Stephens) Kessel. *Education:* University of Minnesota, B.S., 1960, M.A., 1966. *Politics:* Democrat. *Home:* 6405 Colony Way, Unit C, Edina, Minn. 55435. *Office:* Lerner Publications Co., 241 First Ave. N., Minneapolis, Minn. 55401.

CAREER: Ramey Air Force Base, Aguadilla, P.R., civilian speech therapist and special reading teacher, 1966-68; special reading teacher at public schools in San Juan, P.R., 1968-70, director of admissions and assistant to superintendent, 1971-78; Lerner Publications Co., Minneapolis, Minn., writer and sales representative, 1978—. *Awards, honors:* Children's Choice Award from Children's Book Council and International Reading Association, 1981, for *Halloween*.

WRITINGS—For children; all published by Carolrhoda: *Halloween*, 1980; *St. Valentine's Day*, 1981; *St. Patrick's Day*, 1981; *Thanksgiving*, 1981.

Co-author of "Archy and Mehitabel" (two-act play; adaptation), first produced in Minneapolis, Minn., at Hennepin Performing Arts Center, June 20, 1981.

WORK IN PROGRESS: Two more holiday books.

SIDELIGHTS: Joyce Kessel commented: "I began selling books for Lerner Publications after having written two books for them. These books were purchased but never published. As I had the opportunity to speak with many librarians and school personnel, I began to recognize areas that were requested with great frequency. One of these was factual information concerning popular holidays. This suggestion was taken by the editor of Carolrhoda Books, a subsidiary of Lerner Publications, and thus began the research and writing of this series of books.

"I am also interested in writing adult material, and have written many short stories, plays, and poems, none of which have been published, with the exception of 'Archy and Mehitabel.' I would also like to write a novel of the Caribbean and the people, if time ever permits.''

AVOCATIONAL INTERESTS: Classical music, painting, theatre, reading, biking, travel, judo, writing poetry, short stories, and plays.

* * *

KETCHAM, Hank
See KETCHAM, Henry King

* * *

KETCHAM, Henry King 1920-
(Hank Ketcham)

PERSONAL: Born March 14, 1920, in Seattle, Wash.; son of Weaver Vinson and Virginia Emma (King) Ketcham; married Alice Louise Mahar (a secretary), June 13, 1942 (deceased); married Jo Anne Stevens, July 1, 1959 (divorced); married Rolande Praeprost, June 9, 1970; children: (first marriage) Dennis L.; (third marriage) Dania, Scott Henry. *Education:* Attended University of Washington, 1938. *Address:* P.O. Box 800, Pebble Beach, Calif. 93953. *Agent:* c/o International Management Group, 1 Erieview Plaza, Cleveland, Ohio 44114.

CAREER: Walter Lantz Productions, Hollywood, Calif., animator, 1938-39; Walt Disney Productions, Burbank, Calif., animator, 1939-42; creator and designer of ''Half-Hitch'' comic strip, c. 1943 and 1970-75; free-lance cartoonist, 1945-51; creator of syndicated comic strip ''Dennis the Menace,'' 1951. Co-designer, Dennis the Menace playground, Monterey, Calif.; founder, Playart Foundation. Appeared in two segments of program ''Curiosity Shop'' for American Broadcasting Co. (ABC-TV), 1970. Work represented in the permanent collections of the William Allen White Foundation, Achenbach Foundation for Graphic Arts, Boston University Library, and Albert T. Reid Collection. *Military service:* U.S. Naval Reserve, 1941-45, chief photographic specialist; Naval War Bond training film program, 1942-45. *Member:* National Cartoonists Society, Phi Delta Theta, Royal and Ancient Golf Club (St. Andrews, Scotland), Cypress Point Golf Club (Pebble Beach, Fla.), Mill Reef Club (Antigua), Golf Club de Geneva, Old Baldy Club (Saratoga, Wyo.), Old Capital Club. *Awards, honors:* Billy De Beck Award from National Cartoonists Society, 1953; certificate for best comic magazine from Boys' Club of America, 1956.

*WRITINGS—*All under name Hank Ketcham; ''Dennis the Menace'' cartoon books; published by Fawcett, except as noted: *Dennis the Menace,* Holt, 1952; *More Dennis the Menace,* Holt, 1953; *Baby Sitter's Guide,* Holt, 1954; *Dennis the Menace Rides Again,* Holt, 1955; *Dennis the Menace Versus Everybody,* Holt, 1956; *Wanted: Dennis the Menace,* Holt, 1956; *Dennis the Menace: Household Hurricane,* Pocket Books, 1958; *In This Corner, Dennis the Menace,* Holt, 1958; *Dennis the Menace: Teacher's Threat,* Holt, 1959; *Dennis the Menace: A.M., Ambassador of Mischief,* Holt, 1960; *Dennis the Menace: Happy Half-Pint,* Random House, 1961; *Dennis the Menace: Who Me?,* Random House, 1962; *Dennis the Menace: Make-Believe Angel,* 1964; *Dennis the Menace and His Pal Joey,* 1968; *Dennis the Menace: All-American Kid,* 1969, revised edition, 1973; *Dennis the Menace and Poor Ol' Mr. Wilson,* 1969; *Dennis the Menace: Here Comes Trouble,* 1969; *Dennis the Menace: Short and Snappy,* 1969; *Dennis the Menace, Your Friendly Neighborhood Kid,* 1969.

Dennis the Menace: Non-Stop Nuisance, 1970; *Dennis the Menace: Where the Action Is,* 1971; *Dennis the Menace: Busy Body,* 1973; *Dennis the Menace, Everybody's Little Helper,* 1973; *Dennis the Menace: Just for Fun,* 1973; *Dennis the Menace: Perpetual Motion,* 1973; *Dennis the Menace: Surprise Package,* 1973; *Dennis the Menace: Voted Most Likely,* 1973; *Dennis Power,* 1973; *Dennis the Menace: The Kid Next Door,* 1974; *Dennis the Menace: Little Pip-Squeak,* 1974; *Dennis the Menace to the Core,* 1975; *Play It Again, Dennis,* 1975; *Dennis the Menace: Little Man in a Big Hurry,* 1976; *Dennis the Menace: The Short Swinger,* 1976; *Dennis the Menace and the Bible Kids,* Word Books, 1977, Volume I: *Jesus,* Volume II: *Moses,* Volume III: *David,* Volume IV: *Joseph,* Volume V: *Women of the Bible,* Volume VI: *More About Jesus,* Volume VII: *The Lord's Prayer,* Volume VIII: *Stories Jesus Told,* Volume IX: *Paul,* Volume X: *In the Beginning; Dennis the Menace and His Girls,* 1978; *Dennis the Menace: Ol' Droopy Drawers,* 1978; *Dennis the Menace Talks About Love Stuff,* Character Imprints, 1978; *Dennis the Menace: Your Mother's Calling,* 1978; *Someone's in the Kitchen With Dennis* (cookbook), F. Watts, 1978; *Dennis the Menace: Short in the Saddle,* 1979; *Dennis the Menace: Ain't Misbehavin',* 1980; *Dennis the Menace: Good Intenshuns,* 1981; *Dennis the Menace: One More Time,* 1981; *Dennis the Menace: The Way I Look at It,* 1981.

Other: *I Wanna Go Home!* (travel), McGraw, 1965; *Riddles, Riddles, Riddles,* Fawcett, 1967; *Half-Hitch* (cartoons), 1972; *Well God, I Goofed Again* (cartoons), Determined Productions, 1975.

Also author of two segments of television series ''Curiosity Shop'' for American Broadcasting Co. (ABC-TV), 1970, and of animated television special ''Mayday for Mother'' for National Broadcasting Co. (NBC-TV), 1980. Contributor of various cartoons to magazines, including *Saturday Evening Post* and *Collier's.*

SIDELIGHTS: Ketcham began his ''Dennis the Menace'' cartoon strip in 1951, when his own son Dennis was four years old. The innocent antics of Dennis Mitchell and the baffled reactions of his parents caught the fancy of a nation teeming with children during the post-World War II baby boom. By 1953 ''Dennis the Menace'' appeared in nearly two hundred newspapers.

Books, records, and the ''Dennis the Menace'' television series followed the strip's success, as did the appearance of Dennis in coloring books and the promotional materials for companies as diverse as Sears, Dairy Queen, and Parke-Davis. As a result, Ketcham continually expanded his staff to include a larger group of professionals—artists, writers, and promoters stationed throughout Europe and America.

Despite the size of the ''Dennis the Menace'' enterprise, the comic strip itself has always been drawn from start to finish by Ketcham, as Jack Markow pointed out in a *Writer's Digest* article. Ketcham's devotion to the strip was also demonstrated in 1976, when he left Geneva, Switzerland, his home of seventeen years, partly out of concern that the All-American Mitchell family might become continental in behavior.

Ketcham has also drawn ''Half-Hitch,'' a spoof of Navy life. The comic first appeared while Ketcham was in the Navy, and it was revived in 1970 when he converted it from its single-panel format to a strip. ''Half-Hitch'' is now used by the U.S. Navy in recruiting, re-enlistment, and instructional materials.

Ketcham told *CA:* ''One ancedote illustrates the widespread appeal of 'Dennis the Menace': Once I was in Stockholm and wanted to cash some travelers checks but didn't have my wallet or any identification. I finally asked for a piece of paper and pencil and quickly drew a picture of Dennis. It was positive ID, and my checks were cashed without question.''

''Dennis the Menace'' cartoons were made into a television series of the same name by Screen Gems Productions, 1959-63.

BIOGRAPHICAL/CRITICAL SOURCES: Newsweek, May 4, 1953; *Americas,* June, 1953; *Look,* October 6, 1953; *Publishers Weekly,* January 9, 1961; *Writer's Digest,* March, 1972; *Time,* December 13, 1976.

* * *

KEYSER, Lester Joseph 1943-

PERSONAL: Born April 7, 1943, in Philadelphia, Pa.; son of Lester (a diesel mechanic) and Catherine (a secretary; maiden name, Luecke) Keyser; married Barbara Yarbrough (a college professor), December 21, 1968; children: Catherine. *Education:* La Salle College, B.A. (magna cum laude), 1965; Tulane University, Ph.D., 1970; New York University, M.A., 1972. *Home:* 9114 Ridge Blvd., Brooklyn, N.Y. 11209. *Office:* College of Staten Island, Staten Island, N.Y. 10301.

CAREER: College of Staten Island, Staten Island, N.Y., associate professor of English, 1970—. Consultant to Division of Communications of United States Catholic Conference. *Member:* Modern Language Association, American Film Institute, Society for Cinema Studies.

WRITINGS: (With Andrew Ruszkowski) *The Cinema of Sidney Poitier,* A. S. Barnes, 1980; *Hollywood in the Seventies,* A. S. Barnes, 1980. Contributor to *Free Speech Yearbook, Literature-Film Quarterly,* and *Journal of Popular Film.*

WORK IN PROGRESS: A book-length study of the films of Martin Scorcese.

* * *

KIBLER, James Everett, Jr. 1944-

PERSONAL: Born June 24, 1944, in Prosperity, S.C.; son of James Everett and Juanita (Connelly) Kibler. *Education:* University of South Carolina, B.A., 1966, Ph.D., 1970. *Politics:* Republican. *Religion:* Lutheran. *Home:* 255 Bloomfield, Athens, Ga. 30605. *Office:* Department of English, University of Georgia, Park Hall, Athens, Ga. 30602.

CAREER: University of South Carolina, Columbia, instructor in English, 1966-70; University of Georgia, Athens, assistant professor, 1970-75, associate professor of English, 1976—. Curator of Athens Museum, 1980-81. *Member:* Society of Southern Literature (chairman of bibliography committee, 1973-80), South Atlantic Modern Language Association (chairman of textual section, 1977), South Caroliniana Society, Athens-Clarke Heritage Foundation, Phi Beta Kappa, Mid-Town Neighborhood Association.

WRITINGS: The Pseudonymous Publications of William Gilmore Simms, University of Georgia Press, 1976; *The Poetry of William Gilmore Simms: An Introduction and Bibliography,* Southern Studies Program, University of South Carolina, 1978; *William Gilmore Simms: An Annotated Checklist of Criticism, 1825-1979,* G. K. Hall, 1979; (editor) *The Dictionary of Literary Biography,* Volume 6: *American Novelists Since World War II, Second Series,* Gale, 1980; (editor) O. B. Mayer, *John Punterick: A Novel of the Old Dutch Fork,* Reprint Co., 1981. Member of editorial board of *Georgia Biography.*

WORK IN PROGRESS: Collecting *Poems of William Gilmore Simms;* editing *Carolina Sports: By Land and Water,* by William Elliott, for Louisiana State University Press.

SIDELIGHTS: Kibler's specialties are antebellum southern literature, twentieth-century southern literature, traditional southern culture, and editorial practices and philosophy.

Kibler told *CA:* ''The literature of antebellum Southerners has much to teach the man of our time, particularly those people from regions outside the South. The Southerner was less materialistic; his view of time was far more wholesome. The traditional Southerner has always known that without a knowledge of the past, there can be no meaningful future. We today are too often concerned only with the present and fail to realize that there is a provincialism of time that is more serious than a provincialism of place. My study of Southern literature and my interests in history, museum curatorship, and historic environmental preservation have reinforced my feelings that the American of today needs to free himself from the provincialism of time.

''My editorial philosophy is that the best editor of earlier texts is actually a 'de-editor,' that is, a preserver and restorer of the author's original intentions against all the corruptions that have likely accrued from edition to edition.''

AVOCATIONAL INTERESTS: Preservation of historic structures, collecting rare books, gardening, travel (England, Germany, Italy).

* * *

KIERAN, John Francis 1892-1981

OBITUARY NOTICE—See index for *CA* sketch: Born August 2, 1892, in New York, N.Y.; died December 10, 1981, in Rockport, Mass. Kieran began his career in 1915 as a part-time sportswriter for the *New York Times.* He was hired full time, however, after writing a story on a golf match that impressed one of his editors who was a golf enthusiast. Kieran had progressed to covering major league baseball when he moved to the *New York Herald Tribune* and then to the Hearst newspapers for ''more money and less prestige.'' He returned to the *New York Times* in 1926 and at the beginning of the next year became the first journalist with the *Times* ever to have a by-lined column. Kieran related that in his long-running column, ''Sports of the Times,'' he ''rambled scandalously.'' Albin Krebs explained in the *Times* that the columnist often tossed ''in quotations from Virgil, Plato or St. Augustine in a discussion of a baseball player's pitching style.'' In addition to the reputation he gained as a sportswriter, Kieran became known as a ''walking encyclopedia'' because of his participation on the radio show ''Information Please.'' As a regular panelist, he surprised listeners with ''his impressive hoard of knowledge . . . on virtually every subject from the sex life of the aardvark to the process of zymosis,'' noted Krebs. It was once said that Kieran possessed ''the thought of a college professor and the accent of a 10th Avenue taxi driver.'' He wrote several books, many of which reflected his interest in ornithology and nature. His works include *The American Sporting Scene, Footnotes on Nature,* and *An Introduction to Birds.* A later volume, *A Natural History of New York City,* won Kieren the highest natural history award given by the John Burroughs Society. Obituaries and other sources: *New York Times,* December 11, 1981; *Time,* December 21, 1981; *Newsweek,* December 21, 1981.

* * *

KILGOUR, John Graham 1937-

PERSONAL: Born July 26, 1937, in Hartford, Conn.; son of John Graham (a janitor) and Mary (Fraser) Kilgour; married

Janet Robertson (a medical technologist), August 7, 1967; children: John Graham, Laura Cameron. *Education:* University of Connecticut, B.A., 1966; Cornell University, M.I.L.R., 1968, Ph.D., 1972. *Politics:* Republican. *Religion:* Protestant. *Residence:* Castro Valley, Calif. *Office:* School of Business and Economics, California State University, 25800 Hillary St., Hayward, Calif. 94542.

CAREER: U.S. Merchant Marine, merchant seaman with marine engineering license, 1959-68; Container Corporation of America, Santa Clara, Calif., assistant industrial relations manager, 1968-69; California State University, Hayward, assistant professor, 1972-76, associate professor, 1977-80, professor of business administration, 1981—, associate dean of School of Business and Economics, 1980—. *Military service:* U.S. Navy, machinist's mate, 1955-58. U.S. Naval Reserve, 1958-67. *Member:* American Society for Personnel Administration, Academy of Management, Industrial Relations Research Association, Castro Valley Rotary Club.

WRITINGS: The United States Merchant Marine: National Maritime Policy and Industrial Relations, Praeger, 1975; *Preventive Labor Relations,* American Management Association, 1981. Contributor of more than a dozen articles and reviews to academic journals.

WORK IN PROGRESS: Research on labor-management relations in the banking industry; research on the impact of word processing and other aspects of the "office of the future" on labor-management relations.

SIDELIGHTS: Kilgour told *CA:* "I am increasingly convinced of the need for teachers to be scholars and scholars to be teachers at the university level. The two are inseparable. In business education this is especially so at the nontraditional, nonresidential schools in which the students often have extensive industrial and commercial experience. Not only does the research and writing strengthen one's command of the subject being taught, but the classroom interaction in such a setting tests and refines it in a way that would be hard to duplicate. The result is better instruction, better writing, and a better understanding of the management process."

* * *

KILIAN, Crawford 1941-

PERSONAL: Born February 7, 1941, in New York, N.Y.; naturalized Canadian citizen, May, 1973; son of Victor William Cosgrove (a writer and engineer) and Verne (a teacher; maiden name Debney) Kilian; married Alice Hayes Fairfax (a teacher), April 8, 1966; children: Anna Catherine, Margaret Cathleen. *Education:* Columbia University, B.A., 1962; Simon Fraser University, M.A., 1972. *Politics:* New Democratic Party. *Home:* 4635 Cove Cliff Rd., North Vancouver, British Columbia V7G 1H7, Canada. *Agent:* Harold Greene, 760 La Cienaga Blvd., Los Angeles, Calif. 90069. *Office:* Capilano College, 2055 Purcell Way, North Vancouver, British Columbia V7J 3H5, Canada.

CAREER: Free-lance writer, 1962-63; Lawrence Radiation Laboratory, Berkeley, Calif., library clerk, 1965-66, technical writer-editor, 1966-67; Vancouver City College, Vancouver, British Columbia, instructor, 1967-68; Capilano College, North Vancouver, British Columbia, instructor, 1968—, coordinator of Communications Department, 1975—. School trustee, North Vancouver, 1980—. *Military service:* U.S. Army, 1963-65.

WRITINGS: Wonders, Inc. (juvenile), illustrations by John Larrecq, Parnassus, 1968; *The Last Vikings* (juvenile), illustrations by David Simpson, Clarke, Irwin, 1975; *Go Do Some*

Great Thing: The Black Pioneers of British Columbia (nonfiction), University of Washington Press, 1978; *The Empire of Time* (novel), Del Rey, 1978; *Icequake* (novel), Douglas & McIntyre, 1979, Bantam, 1980; *Eyas* (novel), Bantam, 1982.

Radio plays; first broadcast by Canadian Broadcasting Corporation, CBC-Radio: "A Strange Manuscript Found in a Copper Cylinder" (adaptation of the novel by James De Mille), 1972; "Little Legion," 1972; "Generals Die in Bed" (adaptation of the novel by Charles Yale Harrison), 1973; "Wonders, Inc." (adaptation of own book), 1973; "Senator Connor's Big Comeback," 1974; "The Mob Has Got the Bomb," 1976.

Contributor of articles and book reviews to literature journals and Vancouver area newspapers.

WORK IN PROGRESS: A sequel to *Icequake,* publication by Douglas & McIntyre expected in 1982.

SIDELIGHTS: Kilian told *CA:* "I write fiction because it's fun, a grown-up form of 'Let's Pretend.' 'Serious fiction' to me is a contradiction in terms no matter how grim the subject matter or earnest the author. A novelist who thinks that writing a story will heal a social evil, or improve its readers, is self-deceiving. A better use of the time and effort would be to call the cops, or run for political office, or to write nonfiction.

"This issue began to clarify for me when I started planning a book about the black pioneers who came to British Columbia in the 1858 gold rush. It seemed at first like a great topic for a slam-bang historical epic, a black western. But the more I learned about the pioneers, the more clearly I saw that forcing their experience into a fictional straitjacket would demean and trivialize that experience. These were real people struggling to make a new life, not puppets pretending to live and die just to amuse someone for a few hours.

"My fiction has, of course, plenty of political and social comment explicit and implicit. People in the world around me are influenced by social pressures and political events; I could hardly tell a plausible lie about the twenty-first century if my characters weren't similarly influenced. Inevitably the concerns and anxieties of the moment turn up in my work: *Empire of Time* is about a super CIA, and was written in the early seventies when Chile and Watergate and Operation Chaos were in the news. *Eyas* is in a sense a novel of parental anxiety and hope, and was planned and written as my wife and I raised our two daughters. But my work reflects general experience rather than particular incident; autobiographical fiction bores and embarrasses me.

"Perhaps the most disastrous thing to happen to a writer in North America is to be able to make a living from writing. In India and Latin America writing is something done as a sideline by chemical engineers, civil servants, and businessmen—people very much involved in their world. Our writers scrape along on academic welfare schemes, or crank out formula work, or make some huge score in best-sellerdom. None of these fates is attractive, because all of them tend to exclude the writer from the surrounding community.

"Even worse, such fates rob the writer of much of the pleasure of writing. Judging by what our serious writers say, writing for them is torture, and life after hours isn't much fun either. The industrious hacks tend to write the same story over and over, changing the color of the heroine's eyes. The blockbuster novelists know they're only one book away from being has-beens.

"So an apprentice writer would be wise to stay away from graduate programs as well as Harlequin and Hollywood. Better to get married, settle down in a community, raise kids, and write exactly what you want to write, what you enjoy writing. If it sells, great. If it doesn't, so what? You and your spouse and the kids won't starve because you've got some kind of productive job. Better to be bored selling insurance than bored writing for money. If that happens, somebody will own your inner life and dictate your dreams. It won't be you.

"By the way, forget about the literary celebrity stuff. Most of the people in your own neighborhood will never have heard of you, and won't read your work even if they learn by chance that you're a writer. The same is true of the talk-show hosts on whose programs you'll appear to tout your latest book. Librarians will be nice to you, which is something. The money is nice for buying snow tires or a new vacuum cleaner, but payday is usually only twice a year. Too often, your royalty statement just tells you that your book hasn't yet earned back its advance, let alone made anything on top. Literary success is most enjoyed by writers with a well-developed taste for anticlimax.

"This brings me back to my original point: write for the fun of it. Not for fame, not for the million-dollar advance. Writing won't make you rich (at least not rich enough); it won't make you immortal. Nothing you write will change anyone's life, which is just as well. So please yourself. Tell the kinds of stories you love to read, the stories you have to read because they address you and your concerns. Maybe no one will read them. Even if millions do, their response to your work will be largely unknown and unknowable. But if you have enjoyed your own work, in the writing of it and the reading of it, you have become a successful writer."

BIOGRAPHICAL/CRITICAL SOURCES: Books in Canada, January, 1979, August-September, 1979.

*   *   *

KING, Leila Pier   1882-1981

OBITUARY NOTICE: Born in 1882 in Dakota Territory; died October 30, 1981, in Chevy Chase, Md. Poet. King was the author of a book of poems on American historical subjects, *The Hunter's Horn.* Two of her poems were collected in the anthology *Our American Heritage.* Obituaries and other sources: *Washington Post,* November 3, 1981.

*   *   *

KING, Tabitha   1949-

PERSONAL: Born March 24, 1949, in Old Town, Me.; daughter of Raymond Geo (a social worker) and Sarah Jane (an administrative assistant; maiden name, White) Spruce; married Stephen E. King (a writer), January 2, 1971; children: Naomi Rachel, Joe Hill, Owen Phillip. *Education:* Attended University of Maine at Orono, 1967-71. *Residence:* Bangor, Me. *Agent:* Kirby McCauley, 60 East 42nd St., New York, N.Y. 10017.

CAREER: Writer. Worked as waitress, 1972-73. *Member:* Writers Guild.

WRITINGS: (Contributor) Dilys Winn, editor, *Murderess Ink,* Workman Publishing, 1979; *Small World* (novel), Macmillan, 1981.

SIDELIGHTS: King's novel *Small World* concerns Dolly Douglas, daughter of an American president of the 1950's. Douglas's scandalous behavior, including posing for a nude portrait during her father's term as president, is detailed in the novel's initial chapters. Later, Dolly marries the inventor of a miniaturizing machine. They begin shrinking buildings and

progress rapidly to people. Eventually Dolly and her husband shrink a journalist and imprison her in a miniature White House. Lynne Cheney wrote, "Dollhouses and tiny people permit Dolly Hardesty . . . to have the kind of control that eludes her in real life." Cheney also noted that King possessed "imaginative power."

As the wife of popular horror novelist Stephen King, Tabitha King is frequently quizzed about the nature of her novel. She told *Library Journal* that "I am asked what sort of book it is, meaning is it a horror story, like some of my husband's. There are parts of *Small World* that are fantastic, even grotesque, and there are parts that I wanted to be suspenseful, but no, it's not a horror story."

BIOGRAPHICAL/CRITICAL SOURCES: Rolling Stone College Papers, winter, 1980; *People,* December 29, 1980; *Library Journal,* February 1, 1981; *Washington Post,* April 21, 1981; *New York Times Book Review,* May 17, 1981.

*   *   *

KING-SMITH, Dick   1922-

PERSONAL: Born March 27, 1922, in Bitton, Gloucestershire, England; son of Ronald (a paper mill director) and Grace (Boucher) King-Smith; married Myrle England, June 2, 1943; children: Juliet (Mrs. Jeremy Hurst), Elizabeth (Mrs. Brian Fisher), Giles. *Education:* Attended Marlborough College, 1936-40; Bristol University, B.Ed., 1975. *Home:* Diamond's Cottage, Queen Charlton, Avon, England. *Agent:* Michael Horniman, A. P. Watt & Son, 26/28 Bedford Row, London WC1R 4HL, England.

CAREER: Farmer, 1947-67; Farmborough Primary School, near Bath, Avon, England, teacher, 1975—. *Military service:* Grenadier Guards, 1941-46; became lieutenant; mentioned in dispatches.

WRITINGS: The Fox Busters, Gollancz, 1978; *Daggie Dogfoot,* Gollancz, 1980; *The Mouse Butcher,* Gollancz, 1981. Contributor of poems and light verse to periodicals, including *Punch, Blackwood's Magazine,* and *Field.*

WORK IN PROGRESS: The Queen's Nose; Mugnus Powermouse, publication expected in 1982.

SIDELIGHTS: King-Smith commented: "I write for the simplest and best of reasons—because I enjoy it. I write for children for a number of reasons: my level of humor is pretty childish (both my grandfathers were punsters of the worst kind, which is the best kind); I think I know what children like to read (teaching helps here); I like to write about animals (farming helps here), whereas adults on the whole prefer to read novels about people; I think an ounce of fantasy is worth a pound of reality; and anyway I couldn't possibly write a modern sort of novel for grown people—I should get the giggles.

"If there is a philosophical point behind what I write, I'm not especially conscious of it; maybe I do stress the need for courage, something we all wish we had more of, and I also do feel strongly for underdogs.

"As for trying to fill a need in children's literature, if I am, it is to produce books that can afford adults some pleasure when they read to their children. I write for fun."

*   *   *

KIPLING, (Joseph) Rudyard   1865-1936

BRIEF ENTRY: Born December 30, 1865, in Bombay, India; died January 18, 1936, in London, England; buried in Poet's

Corner at Westminster Abbey, London, England. British author. When Kipling won the Nobel Prize for literature in 1907, he was at the height of his popularity. One of his earliest successes was *Barrack-Room Ballads* (1892), a collection of poems. He was considered a master storyteller, whether writing for adults, as in *Life's Handicap* (1891), or concocting the immortal children's tales for his *Jungle Books* (1894-95) and *Just So Stories* (1902). Kipling's most appealing works were set in India, where he had lived for many years. His love and understanding for that country was expressed most poignantly in the novel *Kim* (1901). Kipling's popularity stemmed, in part, from his ability to wake man's deepest emotions, such as passion, revenge, and terror, then temper their power with compassion. His strongly imperialist views also contributed to his success, for they matched popular British opinion of the time. With the emergence of democratic liberalism following the Boer War, the main body of Kipling's work came to be regarded as outdated, though his tales of India and his children's books remained popular. *Biographical/critical sources:* Rudyard Kipling, *Something of Myself,* Macmillan, 1937; *Cyclopedia of World Authors,* Harper, 1958; *The McGraw-Hill Encyclopedia of World Biography,* McGraw, 1973.

*   *   *

KIRBY, John B(yron)   1938-

PERSONAL: Born July 27, 1938, in Evanston, Ill.; son of John B. and Margaret E. (Lenehan) Kirby; married Sara M. Smith, November 28, 1964; children: Julie Lyn, Lissa, Tia, Peter. *Education:* University of Wisconsin (now University of Wisconsin—Madison), B.A., 1962; University of Michigan, M.A., 1963; attended University of Denver; University of Illinois, Ph.D., 1971. *Politics:* "Democratic Socialist." *Home:* 107 Chapin Pl., Granville, Ohio 43023. *Office:* Department of History, Denison University, Granville, Ohio 43023.

CAREER: Cook County Public Aid Department, Chicago, Ill., caseworker, 1963-64; Denison University, Granville, Ohio, assistant professor, 1971-76, associate professor of history, 1976—. *Military service:* U.S. Marine Corps. *Member:* Organization of American Historians, American Civil Liberties Union, Democratic Socialist Organizing Committee, Southern Historical Association.

WRITINGS: Black Americans in the Roosevelt Era: Liberalism and Race, University of Tennessee Press, 1980. Contributor to political science, social science, and history journals.

WORK IN PROGRESS: A book on black and white life after 1945; research on Joseph Heller and his vision of contemporary American life.

SIDELIGHTS: Kirby told *CA:* "My writing and teaching grow out of my personal and political concerns. *Black Americans in the Roosevelt Era* derives from my concern with the historical nature of liberalism and with the status of black protest in American life. Other writing, past and future, is linked to my own sense of change in American life, both on a personal and collective level.

"Writing and research, while being a teacher in a liberal arts college, a father of four children, and a husband, do not always come easily. I suspect my view of history has been as much influenced by my personal life, my teaching of undergraduates, and my political concerns as has my previous formal education. For years my primary focus has been on the manner in which social and political change have been affected by the decline of common cultural and social values in this society and the increasing dependency of people upon concentrated private and public institutions. The decline of liberal values and beliefs (which is related to my book on Roosevelt and blacks) has left an enormous void in contemporary American life. How that came about, what its implications are for various interests in our society and especially minority people, and where that leaves us for the future occupies much of my thought and time. That becomes linked both to my personal life and my writing and research interests."

*   *   *

KISSLING, Dorothy (Hight)   1904-1969
(Dorothy Langley)

OBITUARY NOTICE: Born February 14, 1904, in Brownville, Tex.; died in 1969. Poet and novelist. Early in her career she wrote poetry under the name Dorothy Kissling for contributions to the *Chicago Tribune, Saturday Evening Post,* and other publications. With the 1944 publication of her first novel, *Wait for Mrs. Willard,* she permanently adopted the pen name Langley. Her other novels include *Dark Medallion* and *Mr. Bremble's Buttons.* Obituaries and other sources: *American Authors and Books, 1640 to the Present Day,* 3rd revised edition, Crown, 1972. (Date of death provided by Helen Bugbee of Traumwald Press.)

*   *   *

KITCHEL, Denison   1908-

PERSONAL: Born March 1, 1908, in Bronxville, N.Y.; son of William Lloyd (a lawyer) and Grace (Wheeler) Kitchel; married Naomi Douglas, April 22, 1941; children: James Douglas, Harvey Denison. *Education:* Yale University, B.A., 1930; Harvard University, J.D., 1933. *Politics:* Republican. *Religion:* Protestant. *Home:* 2912 East Sherran Lane, Phoenix, Ariz. 85016.

CAREER: Evans, Kitchel & Jenckes (law firm), Phoenix, Ariz., associate, 1934-38, partner, 1938-69, of counsel, 1969—. *Military service:* U.S. Army Air Forces, 1942-45; became lieutenant colonel.

WRITINGS: Too Grave a Risk: The Connally Amendment Issue, Morrow, 1963; *The Truth About the Panama Canal,* Arlington House, 1978.

WORK IN PROGRESS: Research for a biographical novel on the life of Daniel Webster.

*   *   *

KITTO, H(umphrey) D(avy) F(indley)   1897-1982

OBITUARY NOTICE—See index for *CA* sketch: Born February 6, 1897, in Stroud, Gloucestershire, England; died January 21, 1982. Educator and author. Kitto taught Greek at the University of Glasgow before joining the faculty of the University of Bristol. He was a professor of Greek at Bristol for more than fifteen years. An authority in his field, Kitto wrote numerous books on Greek literature and history. His 1951 volume, *The Greeks* was regarded by the *London Times* as a "remarkable introduction to Classical Greece." It has been reprinted more than thirty times. Other works by Kitto include *Greek Tragedy: A Literary Study, Form and Meaning in Drama: A Study of Six Greek Plays and of "Hamlet,"* and *Poiesis: Structure and Thought.* The professor also taught at such schools in the United States as Cornell University, Brandeis University, and the University of California. Obituaries and other sources: *London Times,* January 25, 1982.

KLAUBER, Laurence M(onroe)   1883-1968

OBITUARY NOTICE: Born December 21, 1883, in San Diego, Calif.; died May 8, 1968, in San Diego, Calif. Electrical engineer, inventor, herpetologist, and author. Klauber's forty-three-year career with the San Diego Gas & Electric Co. saw him rise from salesman to chief executive officer, with stints as president and chairman of the board along the way. Under his hand the utility grew dramatically, doubling its operating revenues and its natural gas supply before Klauber retired in 1953. Klauber's outside interests embraced a myriad of civic and para-professional concerns, from the library commission to pollution control. But his abiding passion was for herpetology, a branch of zoology that involves the study of reptiles and amphibians. He was a tireless innovator and scholar in this field, advancing the methods of taxonomy and amassing a personal collection of thirty-six thousand preserved specimens. The rattlesnake was his special province, with an emphasis on venom collection and antivenin studies. Thirty-five years of research and eleven years of writing went into his definitive two-volume study, *Rattlesnakes: Their Habits, Life Histories and Influence on Mankind.* Obituaries and other sources: *National Cyclopaedia of American Biography,* Volume 54, James T. White, 1973; *Who Was Who in America, With World Notables,* Volume V: *1969-1973,* Marquis, 1973.

*   *   *

KLEINBERG, Seymour   1933-

PERSONAL: Born January 5, 1933, in New York, N.Y.; son of Eli and Rose (Dickstein) Kleinberg. *Education:* City College (now of the City University of New York), B.A., 1953; University of Connecticut, M.A., 1955; University of Michigan, Ph.D., 1963. *Religion:* Jewish. *Home:* 310 West 55th St., New York, N.Y. 10019. *Agent:* Ron Bernstein, 200 West 58th St., New York, N.Y. 10019. Department of English, Long Island University, Brooklyn, N.Y. 11201.

CAREER: Flint Junior College (now Charles Stewart Mott Community College), Flint, Mich., instructor in English, 1959-62; Long Island University, Brooklyn, N.Y., assistant professor, 1962-67, associate professor, 1967-72, professor of English, 1972—.

WRITINGS: The Other Persuasion (fiction), Random House, 1977; *Alienated Affections: Being Gay in America,* St. Martin's, 1981.

SIDELIGHTS: As its title implies, *Alienated Affections: Being Gay in America* deals with homosexual life in the United States. In this semi-autobiographical volume, Kleinberg discusses relationships involving gay men and straight women, homosexual relationships, transvestism, and transsexuality. In addition, he surveys gay bars, the arts and homosexuality, homosexuals in prison, and homosexuality and old age.

Throughout *Alienated Affections,* Kleinberg relates personal experiences concerning his own homosexuality, such as his first homosexual encounter at age eleven and a period of psychoanalysis during his twenties. "The book is intensely thoughtful," commented Richard P. Brickner of the *New York Times Book Review,* "but a lot of the thinking evaporates in indecisiveness. To its credit, 'Alienated Affections' does not push a point; but I wish it had been more pointed, its reasoning more purposeful. It has very little passion in it."

BIOGRAPHICAL/CRITICAL SOURCES: New York Times Book Review, January 25, 1981; *Los Angeles Times Book Review,* March 1, 1981.

KLEINMAN, Arthur   1941-

PERSONAL: Born March 11, 1941, in New York, N.Y.; son of Peter W. (an attorney) and Marcia (Kaplan) Kleinman; married Joan Andrea Ryman, March 20, 1965; children: Peter-John, Cici. *Education:* Stanford University, A.B., 1962, M.D., 1967; Harvard University, M.A., 1974. *Home:* 3527 46th N.E., Seattle, Wash. 98105. *Office:* Department of Psychiatry and Behavioral Sciences, University of Washington, Seattle, Wash. 98195.

CAREER: Yale-New Haven Hospital, New Haven, Conn., intern, 1967-68; National Institutes of Health, National Institute of Allergy and Infectious Diseases, and National Institute of Child Health and Development, Bethesda, Md., research fellow in geographic medicine, 1968-70; Harvard University, Cambridge, Mass., research fellow in comparative study of medicine, 1970-72; Massachusetts General Hospital, Boston, resident in psychiatry, 1972-75, clinical instructor in psychiatry, 1975-76; University of Washington, Seattle, associate professor, 1976-79, professor of psychiatry, behavioral sciences, and anthropology, 1979—, member of faculty at School of International Studies, 1976—, head of Division of Cultural Psychiatry, 1976—, and Division of Consultation-Liaison Psychiatry, 1978—, acting head of Psychiatric Consultation-Liaison Service at university hospital, 1977. Diplomate of National Board of Medical Examiners and American Board of Psychiatry and Neurology; research fellow at U.S. Naval Medical Research Unit in Taipei, Taiwan, 1969-70; research associate at Harvard University's East Asian Research Center, 1973-75, research fellow at Peabody Museum of Ethnology, 1974, lecturer, 1974-76. Visiting lecturer at National Taiwan University, 1975; visiting professor at University of Hawaii, 1979; Sandoz Visiting Professor at University of California, San Diego, 1980; lecturer at colleges in the United States and abroad, including University of Michigan, New York University, University of Alaska, Case Western Reserve University, University of Puget Sound, Australian National University, and Hunan Medical College. Member of World Congress of Psychiatry, 1977—, and World Health Organization's Global Advisory Committee on Medical Research, 1980—. World Health Organization consultant to government of Indonesia, 1979.

MEMBER: World Federation for Mental Health, International Association for the Study of Traditional Asian Medicine, American Psychiatric Association, American Anthropological Association (fellow), American Association for the Advancement of Science, American Psychosomatic Society, Society for Medical Anthropology, Society for Psychological Anthropology, Society for Liaison Psychiatry, Society for Applied Anthropology (fellow), Royal Anthropological Institute of Great Britain and Ireland (fellow), Washington State Psychiatric Association, King County Medical Society, Phi Beta Kappa. *Awards, honors:* Grants from National Science Foundation, 1970-72, Foundations' Fund for Research in Psychiatry, 1973-75, Livingston Fund, 1973, Social Science Research Council, 1974-75, Harvard-Yenching Institute, 1975-76, Milton Fund, 1975-76, Wellington Fund, 1975-76, Paul Dudley White Fund, 1975-76, National Institute of Mental Health, 1977-79, 1979-81, and National Academy of Sciences, 1980; Wellcome Medal for Medical Anthropology from Royal Anthropological Institute of Great Britain and Ireland, 1980, for *Patients and Healers in the Context of Culture.*

WRITINGS: (Editor with Peter Kunstadter, E. R. Alexander, and J. L. Gale, and contributor) *Medicine in Chinese Cultures: Comparative Perspectives,* U.S. Government Printing Office,

1975; (editor with T. C. Manschreck, and contributor) *Renewal in Psychiatry,*Hemisphere Publishing-Halsted, 1977; (editor with Kunstadter, Alexander, and Gale, and contributor) *Culture and Healing in Asian Societies: Anthropological, Psychiatric, and Public Health Studies,* Schenkman, 1978; *Patients and Healers in the Context of Culture: An Exploration of the Borderland Between Anthropology, Medicine, and Psychiatry,* University of California Press, 1980; (editor with Carl Eisdorfer, Donna Cohen, and Peter Maxim) *Conceptual Models for Psychopathology,* Spectrum, 1981; (editor with T. Y. Lin, and contributor) *Normal and Abnormal Behavior in Chinese Culture,* D. Reidel, 1981; (editor with Leon Eisenberg, and contributor) *The Relevance of Social Science for Medicine,* D. Reidel, 1981; *Comparison of Outcomes of Patients Treated by Indigenous Healers and Western-Style Doctors in Taiwan,* D. Reidel, 1982.

Contributor: M. E. Wegman, T. Y. Lin, and E. F. Purcell, editors, *Public Health in the People's Republic of China,* Josiah Macy, Jr. Foundation, 1973; *National Council for International Health: Health of the Family,* National Council for International Health, 1975; Paul Ahmed and George Coelho, editors, *Toward New Definitions of Health: Psychosocial Dimensions,* Plenum, 1979; Arthur C. Hastings, James Fadiman, and J. S. Gordon, editors, *Health for the Whole Person,* Westview, 1980; G. M. Rosen, J. P. Geyman, and R. H. Layton, editors, *Behavioral Science in Family Practice,* Appleton, 1980; Everett Mendelsohn and Yehuda Elkana, editors, *Science and Cultures: Sociology of the Sciences,* Volume V, D. Reidel, 1981; Hastings and Fadiman, editors, *Holistic Medicine,* National Institute of Mental Health, 1981; Eisdorfer and other editors, *Conceptual Models for Psychopathology,* Spectrum, 1981; Julio Ruffini, editor, *Advances in Medical Social Science,* Gordon & Breach, 1981; David Mechanic, editor, *Handbook of Health, Health Care, and Health Professions,* Free Press, 1982.

Chairman of editorial board of series "Culture, Illness, and Healing," D. Reidel, 1977—. Contributor to *Harvard Encyclopedia of American Ethnic Groups.* Contributor of more than fifty articles and reviews to medical journals and periodicals in the social sciences. Editor-in-chief of *Culture, Medicine, and Psychiatry: An International Journal of Comparative Cross-Cultural Studies,* 1976—; guest editor of *Hospital Physician,* 1979-80.

WORK IN PROGRESS: Meaning and Medicine: An Introduction to Medical Anthropology, with Byron Good; research on the Chinese model for health care systems, sociocultural determinants of the help-seeking behavior of patients with mental illness, depression and somatization, and the biopsychosocial approach to somatization in family practice.

SIDELIGHTS: Kleinman told *CA:* "I have studied health care in Taiwan and China. Most recently I have been interested in the enormous problem of the somatic presentation of psychological and social distress in those societies and in the United States. My research has tried to determine the psychopathology and social problems that contribute to this behavior. For example, I have assessed the tendency of depressed patients to be misdiagnosed and mistreated as suffering from medical conditions. Comparisons across Chinese and American cultures clarify the role of culture in influencing this behavior and the coping patterns and idioms of distress that undergrid and contribute to it. In this work I have drawn upon my background as an anthropologist and psychiatrist to chart meanings that adhere to illness behavior and their social significances in manipulating personal, family, community, and larger sociopolitical relations. All illness is made meaningful as a function of the attempts to organize it as a part of everyday life. And

these meanings, on the one hand, illumine personal and interpersonal concerns, and on the other, disclose the impact of cultural norms and social situations on individual behavior. There is, moreover, a practical reason for studying this subject, because interpretation of illness meanings is a core clinical activity which can be effectively taught to health professionals so as to improve patient care and facilitate humanistic treatment. I have been working on these questions for the past thirteen years, and have developed both general concepts and practical patient-care strategies as part of my clinical teaching, research, and consultation engagements with this fascinating and still poorly understood subject."

*   *   *

KLONSKY, Milton   1921(?)-1981

OBITUARY NOTICE: Born c. 1921; died of cancer, November 29, 1981, in New York, N.Y. Educator and author of literary nonfiction. Klonsky, who made numerous contributions to literary journals, is credited with reviving the belles lettres essay. His major works include *The Fabulous Ego,* a study of power and corruption in monarchy, and studies on Blake, including *William Blake: The Seer and His Visions.* Obituaries and other sources: *New York Times,* December 5, 1981.

*   *   *

KNAPP, Herbert W.   1931-

PERSONAL: Born February 28, 1931, in Kansas City, Mo. son of Herbert Harry (a lumberman) and Mary Ellen (Coleman) Knapp; married Mary L. Gillham (a teacher, media specialist, and writer), January 29, 1955; children: Eleanor, Sarah. *Education:* University of Missouri, B.A., 1952; University of Kansas City, M.A., 1957. *Residence:* South Egremont, Mass.

CAREER: Pembroke Country-Day School, Kansas City, Mo., teacher, 1959-62; Panama Canal Zone College, Balboa, Republic of Panama, instructor in English, 1963-79. *Military service:* U.S. Army, 1952-54; became sergeant.

WRITINGS—With wife, Mary Knapp: *One Potato, Two Potato: The Secret Education of American Children,* Norton, 1976, published as *One Potato, Two Potato: The Folklore of American Children,* 1978.

WORK IN PROGRESS: Vocabulary Words (with M. Knapp), a novel; *An Ambiguous Utopia,* a nonfiction work about the Panama Canal Zone.

SIDELIGHTS: Knapp told *CA:* "The Panama Canal treaties gave those of us who worked for the Canal Company the option of retiring early on a reduced annuity—an option Mary and I are gratefully exercising. After nineteen years in the tropics, we've chosen to make up for all those winters, springs, and falls we missed by moving to the Berkshire Mountains.

"The two books we have in progress grew out of our experiences as teachers and Zonians. In both books we are describing problems that arise when social engineers take charge of other people's lives 'for their own good.'

"We noticed when we wrote *One Potato* how physical education and recreation specialists disliked children's self-organized play. The experts called it 'disorganized' and imposed their own kind of order wherever they could without regard for the benefits of traditional play. It never occurred to the experts that traditional play could have any benefits.

"We believe we have seen a similar arrogance on the part of education experts in the schools and paternalistic bureaucrats on the Canal Zone—which was a kind of schoolroom society. The Zone, of course, has disturbing implications. It was a very American version of the bureaucratic welfare state, established while Russia was still ruled by a czar and may yet prove to be a portent of things to come in the States.''

* * *

KNAPP, Mary L. 1931-

PERSONAL: Born October 10, 1931, in Leavenworth, Kan.; daughter of Samuel P. (an accountant) and Grace E. (Landis) Gillham; married Herbert W. Knapp (a teacher and writer), January 29, 1955; children: Eleanor, Sarah. *Education:* University of Missouri, B.J., 1952, M.A., 1963. *Residence:* South Egremont, Mass.

CAREER: Balboa High School, Balboa, Republic of Panama, teacher, 1963-79; Panama Canal College, Balboa, media specialist, 1979-82.

WRITINGS—With husband, Herbert Knapp: *One Potato, Two Potato: The Secret Education of American Children,* Norton, 1976, published as *One Potato, Two Potato: The Folklore of American Children,* 1978.

WORK IN PROGRESS: Vocabulary Words, a novel, with H. Knapp.

SIDELIGHTS: Mary Knapp told *CA:* ''*One Potato* was a joy to write for several reasons. We talked to hundreds of ten- and eleven-year-olds about their games and traditions. These children were delightful to know, and the subject of our conversations was fun and often funny. We laughed a lot while writing this book.

''Also, it's always exciting to see something ordinary and commonplace in a new light. Children's folklore is something most people consider trivial in the extreme; we hope that we've shown it is anything but that.

''As parents and teachers Herb and I have a deep interest in children. Making a contribution to the understanding of childhood has been very rewarding for me.

''One of the biggest mistakes I think we make is not letting children work things through on their own. Teachers talk too much; parents push too hard. Kids need time to do things their own way, to dream, to be bored. This is essentially the message of *One Potato.*''

* * *

KNAUS, William A. 1946-

PERSONAL: ''K'' in surname is pronounced; born August 13, 1946, in Pittsburgh, Pa.; son of William A. (a businessman) and Vidal (in retail sales; maiden name, Uidic) Knaus; married Janet L. Garber (a nurse practitioner), February 29, 1980. *Education:* Widener College (now University), B.S., 1968; West Virginia University School of Medicine, M.D., 1972. *Home:* 5320 37th St. N., Arlington, Va. 22207. *Agent:* John Schaffner Literary Agency, 425 East 51st St., New York, N.Y. 10022. *Office:* 2300 K St. N.W., Washington, D.C. 20037.

CAREER: George Washington University, Washington, D.C., intern at medical center, 1972-73, assistant resident, 1974-75, clinical instructor in health care sciences at school of medicine, 1975-77, fellow of critical care medicine at medical center, 1977-78, founder, 1978, and director of intensive care research unit at medical center, 1978—, co-director of intensive care unit at medical center, 1978—, assistant professor of anesthesiology and clinical engineering at medical center, 1978-81,

associate professor, 1981—. Foreign service medical officer in U.S.S.R. for United States Information Agency, 1973-74; professional staff member with Office of the Assistant Secretary for Planning and Evaluation of Department of Health, Education, and Welfare (HEW; now Department of Health and Human Services), 1975-76.

Member of executive committee of U.S.-U.S.S.R. Health Exchange, 1976-78; member of board of overseers of Widener College (now University), 1980—; member of program committee and academic subcommittee of Critical Issues in Medical Technology seminar, 1980. Consultant to National Council for International Health, 1975-77, Health Care Financing Administration of Department of Health and Human Services, 1977—, and Urban Institute, 1978—. Giver of presentations at American Public Health Association national meeting, Washington Journalism Center Conference on Health Care Costs, International Conference on Attitudinal and Behavioral Changes in Rural Life at University of Nebraska, American Federation for Clinical Research, Northern Virginia Health Systems Agency Conference on Medical Care, National Conference on Referral Criteria for X-ray Examinations at Department of Health, Education, and Welfare, Chesapeake Bay Anesthesia Conference, Critical Issues in Medical Technology Conference, Society of Critical Care Medicine Annual Meeting, Hospital Henri Mondor in Creteil, France, Society for Medical Decision Making, Robert Wood Johnson Foundation Clinical Scholars Program annual meeting, Third World Congress on Intensive and Critical Care Medicine, and Second World Congress on Emergency and Disaster Medicine.

MEMBER: American College of Physicians, American Federation of Clinical Research, American Medical Writers Association, Association for the Advancement of Science, Association for the Advancement of Slavic Studies, Society of Critical Care Medicine, District of Columbia Medical Association, Alpha Omega Alpha. *Awards, honors:* Robert Wood Johnson Foundation clinical scholarship at George Washington University, 1975-78; research grant from Health Care Financing Administration, 1978-81; science writing award from American Association of Medical Writers, 1979, for article ''Cholesterol, Diet, and Heart Disease''; outstanding alumnus award from Widener University, 1981; research grant from National Center for Health Care Technology, 1981-83.

WRITINGS: (Contributor) Richard H. Egdahl and Paul M. Gertman, *Quality Assurance in Health Care,* Aspen Systems Corp., 1976; *Inside Russian Medicine: An American Doctor's First-Hand Report,* Everest House, 1981; (contributor) Barbara J. McNeil and Ernest G. Cravalho, *Critical Issues in Medical Technology,* Auburn House, 1981. Contributor of articles to periodicals, including *Clinical Pediatrics, New England Journal of Medicine, Journal of Medical Education, Prism, Medical Care, Archives of Internal Medicine, Journal of Computer Assisted Tomography, Current Reviews in Respiratory Therapy, Annals of Internal Medicine, American Journal Neuroradiology, Neurosurgery, Critical Care Medicine, Journal of the American Medical Association, Health Care Financing Review, Impact: American Medical Association News, New York Times Magazine, Chemistry, Washington Post, New York Times, Esquire, Saturday Evening Post,* and *Reader's Digest.*

WORK IN PROGRESS: A book ''describing a modern intensive care unit and what it is like for doctors, nurses, and patients.''

SIDELIGHTS: As a staff member with the Office of the Assistant Secretary of Planning and Evaluation of the Department of Health, Education, and Welfare (HEW), Knaus told *CA* that he ''participated in the first national survey of physician fees under the Medicare program.'' Committed to improving the quality of health care, he researches "the efficacy of medical technology." In 1978 Knaus founded the intensive care research unit at the George Washington University medical center, "which," explained Knaus, "aims at investigating the utilization of intensive care units and developing a severity of illness index for intensive care patients." He added, "The unit's research also forms the basis of an ongoing comparison of intensive care patients within the U.S. and between the U.S. and France."

In his book, *Inside Russian Medicine: An American Doctor's First-Hand Report,* Knaus presents, according to Robert C. Toth of the *Washington Post Book World,* "the most comprehensive and best-documented general survey of Soviet medicine and its failings yet available." Knaus points out such problems in the Russian system as the inadequate training of doctors, the unsanitary conditions in hospitals, and the lack of antibiotics and other drugs. Soviet doctors earn less money than taxi drivers, and hospitals are referred to as "houses of suffering." Pharmacists still sell hundreds of kinds of teas to cure a bevy of diseases. Knaus noted that while one of the better Moscow hospitals offers eight types of antibiotics, only four are regularly obtainable. George Washington University Hospital, in contrast, stocks sixty-seven different antibiotics.

Knaus also disclosed that while Soviet health care is intended to be free of charge, it is not so in reality. The system is fraught with corruption. Toth explained: "Surgeons are bribed to insure that they, rather than their apprentices, perform operations. Narcotics nurses are bribed to insure injections are given on time. Druggists are bribed to get commonly prescribed but unavailable drugs." As an indicator of the pronounced inadequacy of the Soviet medical establishment, Knaus cited infant mortality rates. When the Russians discontinued publishing such figures in 1974, twenty-two newborns died for every one thousand live births. Knaus assessed that "Soviet health indices resemble those of a developing rather than a developed country."

While Toth commended Knaus on the thoroughness of *Inside Russian Medicine,* the reviewer felt the author was "too reluctant to criticize the political system that pervades and corrupts Soviet medicine." Toth concluded: "By shunning politics, Knaus diagnoses the illness, as it were, but shies away from prescribing the cure. Soviet medicine obviously needs the same kind of fundamental overhaul that American medicine underwent almost a century ago. Knaus' views on reform would have made a valuable final chapter."

BIOGRAPHICAL/CRITICAL SOURCES: Washington Post Book World, June 28, 1981.

*   *   *

KNIGHT, Michael E(mery) 1935-

PERSONAL: Born September 29, 1935, in Roselle Park, N.J.; son of Charles Emery and Emma (Klein) Knight; married Jean Geisler (a teacher), June 13, 1959; children: Michael, Kevin, Christopher, Lee Anne. *Education:* Kean College of New Jersey, B.A., 1966, M.A., 1968; Fordham University, Ph.D., 1973. *Home:* 510 Orange Ave., Cranford, N.J. 07016. *Office:* Department of Early Childhood and Family Studies, Kean College of New Jersey, Union, N.J. 07083.

CAREER: Kean College of New Jersey, Union, adjunct assistant professor, 1968-69, associate professor of early childhood education, 1969—. Member of adjunct faculty at Fordham University, 1972-73, St. Peter's College, 1974-75, and Rutgers University, 1979-81; developer of Training and Development Program at Kean College of New Jersey, 1980-81; workshop

leader; consultant to Fordham Institute for Research and Evaluation. *Member:* International Reading Association, American Society for Training and Development, National Association for the Education of Young Children, New Jersey Association for Teacher Educators (in-service chairperson), New Jersey Association for the Education of Young Children, Kean College Federation of Teachers, Phi Delta Kappa.

WRITINGS: Teaching Children to Love Themselves, Prentice-Hall, 1981.

WORK IN PROGRESS: Applying Piagetian Concepts to Training Programs in Business and Industry; Active Learning Through Children's Literature.

SIDELIGHTS: Knight wrote: "My principal interests are in applying Piagetian theory and self-concept theories to distinctly different learning populations in order to assess their transferability. The application of these theories in learning situations outside of the normal classroom has created some interesting and consistent results. Observations made by Piaget have been duplicated by numerous individuals well beyond the age span usually associated with the particular stage of development. The reaction to new learning situations seems to be the same in industrial or business training settings as in most elementary school classrooms. The time spent in diagnosing the training needs of an organization is clearly a wise investment of its resources."

*   *   *

KNOPF, Edwin H. 1899-1982(?)

OBITUARY NOTICE: Born November 11, 1899, in New York, N.Y.; died c. January, 1982, in Brentwood, Calif. Screenwriter, producer, director, and songwriter. Knopf entered the motion picture business in 1928, following eight years in legitimate theatre and a position with his brother Alfred's publishing house. His credits as director date from the late 1920's and include "Slightly Scarlet" and "The Santa Fe Trail." Knopf is perhaps best known for the highly regarded "Lili," one of many films he produced in the forties and fifties. His screenplays include "Piccadilly Jim" and "Mr. Imperium." Obituaries and other sources: *The ASCAP Biographical Dictionary of Composers, Authors, and Publishers,* 3rd edition, American Society of Composers, Authors, and Publishers, 1966; *International Motion Picture Almanac,* Quigley, 1979; *New York Times,* December 29, 1981, December 31, 1981; *Time,* January 11, 1982.

*   *   *

KOCHAN, Lionel 1922-

PERSONAL: Born in 1922, in Hampstead, England; married Miriam Louise Buchler (a writer), December 23, 1951; children: Nicholas, Anna, Benjamin. *Education:* Cambridge University, B.A.; University of London, B.A. and Ph.D. *Home:* 237 Woodstock Rd., Oxford, England.

CAREER: University of London, London School of Economics and Political Science, London, England, research fellow, 1957-59; instructor in history at Old College, Edinburgh, Scotland.

WRITINGS: Acton on History, Deutsch, 1954; *Russia and the Weimar Republic,* Bowes, 1954; *Pogrom: November 10, 1938,* Deutsch, 1957; *The Making of Modern Russia,* J. Cape, 1962; *The Struggle for Germany, 1914-45,* Aldine, 1963; *Russia in Revolution, 1890-1918,* New American Library, 1967; (editor with wife, Miriam Kochan) *Russian Themes: A Selection of Articles From History Today,* Oliver & Boyd, 1967; (editor)

The Jews in Soviet Russia Since 1917, Oxford University Press, 1970; (author of text, with M. Kochan) *The Jewish Family Album: The Life of a People in Photographs,* photographs by Franz Hubmann, Little, Brown, 1975; *The Jew and His History,* Macmillan, 1977. Contributor of articles to history journals.

SIDELIGHTS: Kochan's books, which deal primarily with European history and Judaism, offer historical facts along with the author's personal commentary and explanation.

In *The Struggle for Germany, 1914-45,* Kochan explains that the division between East and West Germany occurred because Germany was sought as an ally by communist and democratic countries. As a result of the conflicting ideologies, East Germany became a Russian-controlled communist country, while West Germany became a democracy ruled by the Americans, British, and French. Kochan suggests that Germans continue to be torn between the two doctrines and discusses the social and political implications of the division. The *Times Literary Supplement* noted: "Dr. Kochan's essay, as he all too modestly entitles it, is as timely in its appearance as it is rewarding in its clarity. . . . The varying turns of the tug-of-war are familiar enough to historians and diplomatists but are currently relevant and enduringly disturbing."

Kochan's *Russia in Revolution, 1890-1918* is a history of the socialization of Russia with special regard to the policies of Sergei Yulievich Witte, the Russian minister of finance. Under Witte, Russia's economy flourished—the exchange value of the ruble stabilized, protective tariffs were enforced, foreign investments were prompted, and industry advanced substantially. With the advancement of industry came the growth of the proletariat. The Bolsheviks felt the expanding proletariat was in a revolutionary spirit, but constrained by its capitalistic leaders. In order to save the Soviet state from returning to capitalism, the Bolsheviks, according to Kochan, took advantage of the revolutionary mood of the proletariat, acted on Witte's doctrine of centralizing and industrializing, and seized power in Russia.

Critical opinions on *Russia in Revolution* varied. Walter Laqueur of the *New York Review of Books* commented: "Mr. Kochan's survey is a well-written account of the social, political, and economic factors which created a revolutionary situation in Russia." J. P. Nettl of the *New Statesman* wrote: "Kochan's use of sources is substantial, his style competent." Others, however, felt Kochan omitted some pertinent details. *Russia in Revolution* "contains a large number of just and excellent ideas, distinguished in this way from many more detailed and more pretentious works. But few of them are followed up or worked out," the *Times Literary Supplement* noted. "He writes intelligently. But some of the omissions are startling, and seem to have been determined by accident rather than by the necessity, inevitable in a book of these dimensions, to use space with the maximum economy." The *Economist,* too, felt Kochan left out vital information: "[This book is] as incomplete as an account of the French revolution that stopped before the Jacobin terror."

The author of several books on Judaism, such as *The Jew and His History* and *The Jewish Family Album: The Life of a People in Photographs,* Kochan is also the editor of *The Jews in Soviet Russia Since 1917,* a collection of expositions that analyze the problems of post-revolutionary Jews. Included in the volume are writings on anti-Semitism and Jewish literature, religious practices, and demography. "The volume shows signs of excellent editing by Lionel Kochan," said the *Times Literary Supplement.* "It cannot have been an easy job to marshal this galaxy of writers, to avoid overlapping, and to give an air of cohesion and unity to the book." The *Economist* called *The Jews in Soviet Russia* "an unemotional, balanced, and valuable study," while *Observer Review's* Edward Crankshaw, commenting on anti-Semitism, hailed the book as "an indispensable handbook for those who need to penetrate the official smokescreen and arm themselves with the relevant facts and figures of a continuing national disgrace."

BIOGRAPHICAL/CRITICAL SOURCES: Times Literary Supplement, March 1, 1963, February 2, 1967, August 14, 1970, August 21, 1970; *Economist,* December 10, 1966, May 23, 1970, May 21, 1977; *New Statesman,* March 24, 1967; *New York Review of Books,* June 15, 1967; *Observer Review,* May 24, 1970; *Bookseller,* January 30, 1971.*

* * *

KOHUT, Heinz 1913-1981

OBITUARY NOTICE—See index for *CA* sketch: Born May 3, 1913, in Vienna, Austria; died of congestive heart failure, October 8, 1981, in Chicago, Ill. Psychoanalyst, neurologist, educator, and author. Best known for his "self-psychology," Kohut upset his fellow psychoanalysts with the 1971 publication of his theories in *The Analysis of the Self: A Systematic Approach to the Psychoanalytic Treatment of Narcissistic Personality Disorders.* He challenged Freudian theory by proposing that it was a child's early relationship with his parents that affected his later development, rather than the sexual aggression of the Oedipus Complex. Kohut described the change of his colleagues' attitude towards him. "I was Mr. Psychoanalysis. In every room I entered there were smiles. Now, everybody looks away. I've rocked the boat." Gradually, however, his theories gained support. Kohut began his career in 1941 as a neurologist and instructor at the University of Chicago Hospitals. He then joined the University of Chicago as a lecturer in psychiatry, a position he held for more than twenty-five years. Kohut wrote several other books, including *The Psychology of the Self, The Restoration of the Self,* and *The Search for the Self: Selected Essays on Heinz Kohut,* a two-volume work. Obituaries and other sources: *New York Times,* October 10, 1981; *Time,* October 19, 1981.

* * *

KOIZUMI, Yakumo
See HEARN, (Patricio) Lafcadio (Tessima Carlos)

* * *

KOLESAR, Paul 1927-

PERSONAL: Born January 10, 1927, in Pittsburgh, Pa.; married Florence Lesko. *Education:* Graduate of Art Movement Institute, 1950; attended Ringling School of Art and Design, Sarasota, Fla., 1951-52. *Residence:* Hampton, Va. 23666. *Address:* c/o Manyland Books, Inc., 84-39 90th St., Woodhaven, N.Y. 11421.

CAREER: Free-lance writer and artist, 1953—. Artwork represented in private and public collections in the United States and England, including Hampton, Va., Bicentennial Collection, Pittsburgh, Pa., Board of Education, and Butler Institute of American Art. *Awards, honors:* Latham Foundation scholarship, 1950; several plays reached finals in national competitions.

WRITINGS: Two Hearts in a Melting Pot (novel), Manyland Books, 1981.

WORK IN PROGRESS: A play that reflects through triangular characterization the religious and secular aspects in the world of art.

SIDELIGHTS: Two Hearts in a Melting Pot is the story of John Chelovick and his wife, Annah, immigrants from the mountain region of Austria-Hungary who come to the United States in search of freedom and a better life. The dream of America that has motivated and sustained them, however, comes into conflict with the realities of life in their new homeland, including ethnic inequality. Paul Kolesar commented in the *Library Journal:* "Notably, it is a drama of struggle and pain, of laughter and triumph; the heroic exploits of an early steelworker who deserves a high place on any roster of America's builders who turned this country into a powerful nation. . . . From its rich cultural treasure every ethnic group made a sizeable contribution to American culture just as Annah and John who migrated to America made to the small world of *Two Hearts in a Melting Pot.*"

Kolesar told *CA:* "Today, as in days of old, we have walls of racial discrimination, of prejudice, of indifference, a wall between the Israelite and the Arab, the Berlin Wall, the Iron Curtain, the Bamboo Curtain, etc. It seems to be today's favorite pursuit and objective: to build walls. History has given us evidence that an external wall, in time, can be torn down or will crumble with age; it's the internal wall that continues to defy time and age.

"I'm sure we all agree that there is nothing more beautiful in life than life itself; therefore it is our responsibility to pass to one another, beyond the wall, this impression, be it in words, on canvas, carved, in song or dance, or by daily good deeds. The medium of expression need not be masterful but simple and plain for all to understand and to appreciate in order that life may move on peacefully. It was inevitable that I, too, in time, would build a wall—of self-expression.

"I try to build my wall by combining the harmony of color (painting) or words (writing) into a moment of truth. During this period of writing or painting I try not to be influenced by current trends or change of taste. I try to avoid every line or every stroke that does not give something, that does not add weight, knowing that a piece of art should be concrete and meaningful. While in this state of creation, I try to be myself and use that gift as best I can. Above all, my belief should be my courage and my guide. Also, a work of art should be independent of the artist and hopefully continue to live. Unfortunately, this is not always so. Moreover, writing or painting alone will not solve the majority of our problems, but creating can be a challenge, an enchanting experience, a feeling of triumph inside. And that's exactly the sensation I experience when I begin to paint or write on my 'wall,' with love and understanding.

"In my first novel, *Two Hearts in a Melting Pot,* I stress that America's strength is derived from her hybrid character as the greatest melting pot of races, colors, creeds, and ideals that has ever existed. Since no two Americans are alike, perhaps that is why there is no other country in the world like it. Yet in many respects one of the greatest untold stories of American history is that of the laborer. Working people seldom write their personal histories, yet theirs are some of the more dramatic stories of the past two centuries—the commitment, the courage, and the concern of working people who were pitted against great odds in America. And lest we forget, one of the real heroes of the past is the steelworker, the man who is no longer with us, whose name has no place on the scroll of American heritage, and, even more sadly, in a way was never missed.

"Although America has changed, in the novel I tried to go back to some of the values our country used to have. But as we enter a new decade and are on the threshold of a new millennium, I don't think it's asking too much to read and ponder about our origins. Certainly, such reading will make our lives a bit fuller, and, who knows, it may provide some insight on just where we are heading. There is a bankruptcy in ethnicity; it should come out of the closet. Young adults are suffering cultural amnesia; they know very little of the past; a sense of vacuum created by such a loss without regard to who we are and where we have come from. Let's reawaken ethnic values, remake the image, and rediscover values in America. We need more laughter than bitterness in reading about them!

"Thus the personal drama of the steelworker, which has been neglected so long, instilled in me a desire to throw light on his saga of hardship and adventure, and to understand his heritage. The result of this desire to write on my wall of love and understanding was *Two Hearts in a Melting Pot.*"

BIOGRAPHICAL/CRITICAL SOURCES: Library Journal, October 1, 1981.

* * *

KOPERWAS, Sam 1948-

PERSONAL: Born June 11, 1948, in Brooklyn, N.Y.; son of Julius and Barbara (Wolrauch) Koperwas; married Evelyn Brodsky (a teacher), June 25, 1972; children: Michael. *Education:* Brooklyn College of the City University of New York, B.A., 1970; Bowling Green State University, M.F.A., 1973. *Agent:* Russell & Volkening, Inc., 551 Fifth Ave., New York, N.Y. 10017.

CAREER: Writer-in-residence at Arizona State University, 1978. *Awards, honors:* Guggenheim fellowship, 1979-80.

WRITINGS: Westchester Bull (novel), Simon & Schuster, 1976; *Hot Stuff* (novel), Dutton, 1978.

WORK IN PROGRESS: A novel.

BIOGRAPHICAL/CRITICAL SOURCES: New York Times, May 3, 1976; *New Republic,* September 30, 1978.

* * *

KORNBLUTH, C(yril) M. 1923-1958
(Cecil Corwin, Walter C. Davies, Simon Eisner, Kenneth Falconer, S. D. Gottesman, Paul Dennis Lavond, Jordan Park, Ivar Towers; Cyril Judd, a joint pseudonym)

BRIEF ENTRY: Born in 1923 in New York, N.Y.; died of heart failure, March 21, 1958, in Waverly, N.Y. American science fiction writer. Kornbluth's most lasting successes include a novel, *The Space Merchants* (1953), and the stories "The Little Black Bag" (1950) and "The Marching Morons" (1951). Another story, "The Meeting," earned him a posthumous Hugo Award. Kornbluth was a pioneer in the renaissance of science fiction writing that occurred in the 1950's. He contributed heavily to many of the science fiction magazines published at the time, using as many as ten pseudonyms. Kornbluth was critical of the orthodox science fiction that had preceded his own, and he placed more emphasis on social concerns, using satire and cynicism to underscore his point of view. He often wrote of a future wherein big business held evil sway over people's lives, or a future in which technology had surpassed its usefulness and begun to do more harm than good. His perceptiveness was revealed most sharply in his single critical article, "The Failure of the Science Fiction Novel as Social Criticism" (1959). *Biographical/critical sources: Who's Who in Science Fiction,* Elm Tree Books, 1976.

*   *   *

KOTARBINSKI, Tadeusz (Marian)   1886-1981

OBITUARY NOTICE: Born March 31, 1886, in Warsaw, Poland; died October 3, 1981, in Warsaw, Poland. Philosopher, educator, and author. Kotarbinski was a co-founder of the methodology known as praxiology, which involves the study of human action and conduct. Chief among his numerous honors was his chairmanship in philosophy and logic at the University of Warsaw from 1919 to 1961. Two of his approximately three hundred scholarly works were translated into English: *Praxiology: An Introduction to the Science of Efficient Action,* and *Gnosiology: The Scientific Approach to the Theory of Knowledge.* Obituaries and other sources: *Who's Who in the Socialist Countries,* K. G. Saur, 1978; *Who's Who in the World,* 4th edition, Marquis, 1978; *London Times,* October 20, 1981.

*   *   *

KRAFT, Stephanie (Barlett)   1944-

PERSONAL: Born February 18, 1944, in Birmingham, Ala.; daughter of John Raymond and Jeanette (Murphy) Barlett; married David Peterson Kraft (a psychiatrist), June 11, 1966; children: Claire Elizabeth, Paul David. *Education:* Wheaton College, Wheaton, Ill., B.A., 1966; University of Chicago, M.A., 1967; University of Rochester, Ph.D., 1973. *Politics:* "In general, liberal." *Religion:* "Episcopalian become agnostic." *Home:* 35 Mount Pleasant, Amherst, Mass. 01002. *Office: Valley Advocate,* 90 Prospect St., Hatfield, Mass. 01038.

CAREER: Rosary College, River Forest, Ill., part-time instructor in English, 1967-68; Trinity College, Burlington, Vt., instructor in English, 1968-69; Northern Virginia Community College, Annandale, part-time instructor in English, 1973-74; *Valley Advocate,* Hatfield, Mass., staff writer, 1974—. *Member:* National Association of American Pen Women. *Awards, honors:* Woodrow Wilson fellowship, 1966-67.

WRITINGS: No Castles on Main Street: American Authors and Their Homes, Rand McNally, 1979. Contributor to *Antiques World* and *Historic Preservation.*

WORK IN PROGRESS: Research on oil exploration off the Massachusetts coast.

SIDELIGHTS: Kraft told *CA:* "I became aware that I enjoyed writing when I was in graduate school, which is in many respects a strange place to make that discovery. But when I sat down at the typewriter to work on my dissertation each day, I realized that I was happy. That feeling was encouraged by my advisers, who discussed the dissertation at our periodic meetings with such a zest that I began to believe that what I enjoyed writing, they enjoyed reading. It was this positive reinforcement that confirmed my addiction, and I don't hesitate to place all the blame for my present and future productions squarely on their shoulders.

"I was taught very text-centered methods of reading works of literature, methods which de-emphasized biography. I approved of them entirely. But several years after completing my doctoral work, when I was commissioned by the National Trust for Historic Preservation to write an article about the authors' homes that still exist around the country, I found that this opportunity to come in contact with physical evidence about the people who had written the books that had nourished me was something I was starving for.

"I wrote *No Castles on Main Street* partly out of the conviction that, amid energy shortages, economic reverses, and controversies over the roles of women, our literature is full of resources that can help to shockproof us spiritually. I believe that our country gives its best writers, present as well as past, too much facile applause and too little real attention, which includes not only reading but rereading as one historical or personal epoch gives way to another."

*   *   *

KRETZMER, Herbert   1925-

PERSONAL: Born October 5, 1925, in Kroonstad, South Africa; son of William and Tilly Kretzmer; married Elisabeth Margaret Wilson, December 20, 1960; children: Danielle, Matthew. *Education:* Attended Rhodes University. *Home:* 55 Lincoln House, Basil St., London S.W.3, England. *Agent:* London Management, Regent House, 25 Regent St., London W1A 2JT, England. *Office: Daily Mail,* Tudor St., London E.C.4, England.

CAREER: Sunday Express, Johannesburg, South Africa, journalist, 1951-54; *Daily Sketch,* London, England, feature writer and columnist, 1954-59; *Sunday Dispatch,* London, columnist, 1959-61; *Daily Express,* London, drama critic, 1962-78; *Daily Mail,* London, television critic, 1979—. *Awards, honors:* Ivor Novello Award, 1960, for song "Goodness Gracious Me"; award from American Society of Composers, Authors and Publishers, 1969, for song "Yesterday When I Was Young"; television critic of the year award from Phillips Industries, 1980; gold record for song "She."

WRITINGS: Our Man Crichton (play; first produced on the West End at Shaftesbury Theatre, December, 1964), Hodder & Stoughton, 1965; (with Milton Shulman) *Every Home Should Have One* (novel), Hodder & Stoughton, 1980.

Author of song lyrics for plays, including "The Four Musketeers," and films, including "Hieronymus Merkin." Writer for television programs, including "That Was the Week That Was."

*   *   *

KREWER, Semyon E(fimovich)   1915-

PERSONAL: Born March 10, 1915, in Moscow, Russia (now U.S.S.R.); came to United States, 1938; naturalized U.S. citizen, 1943; son of Efim A. (a pharmacist) and Anna (Turgel) Krewer; married Elsa Silberstein (a photographer), July 27, 1939; children: Julie Ann. *Education:* Technische Hochschule, Berlin, diploma, 1937. *Office:* Krewer Research Laboratories, P.O. Box 111, Point Lookout, N.Y. 11569.

CAREER: Columbia University, New York City, research assistant, 1938-40; Photovolt Corp., New York City, director of research, 1940-65, vice-president, 1959-65; Krewer Research Laboratories, Point Lookout, N.Y., owner, 1965—. *Member:* Optical Society of America, American Congress of Rehabilitation Medicine, Arthritis Foundation, New York Academy of Sciences.

WRITINGS: (With Ann Edgar) *The Arthritis Exercise Book,* Simon & Schuster, 1981; *New Hope for Your Arthritic Hand,* Simon & Schuster, 1982.

WORK IN PROGRESS: The Breathing and Relaxation Book.

SIDELIGHTS: Krewer wrote: "I started my career as an atomic physicist as the research assistant to Professors Fermi and Szilard from 1938 to 1939. I carried out the original fusion experiments that led to the letter from Albert Einstein to President Roosevelt in 1939 that resulted in the formation of the Manhattan Project. After 1940, I created radiation monitoring devices for army and civilian uses.''

Krewer, who holds a patent on a hand gym for arthritics, explained that in 1965 he ''was striken by severe rheumatoid arthritis and shifted gears completely to do research and write on rehabilitation and health.'' Physical fitness, which includes endurance training, ''is the same for arthritics as it is for everybody else,'' concluded the author.

*　　*　　*

KRLEZA, Miroslav   1893-1981

OBITUARY NOTICE—See index for *CA* sketch: Born July 7, 1893, in Zagreb, Yugoslavia; died December 29, 1981, in Zagreb, Yugoslavia. Poet, playwright, editor, and novelist. Although one of the major literary figures of Yugoslavia, Krleza was little known outside his native country. So little of Krleza's work was translated and published that when fellow Yugoslavian and Nobel Prize winner Ivo Andric was asked by his Swedish publisher what he could do for him, Andric said, ''Publish Krleza.'' As a Marxist, Krleza worked to establish socialism in Yugoslavia. He founded a political literary periodical, *Plamen* (title means ''Flame''), in 1919 as a part of the effort. Marshall Tito rewarded Krleza for his support by appointing him to the Yugoslav Lexicographical Institute in 1950. At the institute the author edited Yugoslavia's first encyclopedia. Krleza, however, did not hold totally orthodox political beliefs. His views on artistic freedom differed from those of the government. Krleza adamantly fought for a liberal environment in which artists could create, rejecting the party's school of social realism. His activism in this respect drew criticism from conservative Yugoslavian politicians, but Krleza's literary position remained secure. He won several of his country's major literary awards and many international honors, including the Heder Prize and a nomination for the Nobel Prize for literature. Within Krleza's large body of work number the books *The Return of Philip Latinovicz, On the Edge of Reason, The Gold and Silver of Zadar and Nin,* and *The Cricket Beneath the Waterfall and Other Stories.* Obituaries and other sources: *London Times,* December 30, 1981.

*　　*　　*

KRUPP, E(dwin) C(harles)   1944-

PERSONAL: Born November 18, 1944, in Chicago, Ill.; son of Edwin F. (an engineer) and Florence (Olander) Krupp; married Robin Rector (an artist and teacher), December 31, 1968; children: Ethan Hembree. *Education:* Pomona College, B.A., 1966; University of California, Los Angeles, M.A., 1968, Ph.D., 1972. *Agent:* Jane Jordan Browne Multimedia Product Development, Inc., 410 South Michigan Ave., No. 410, Chicago, Ill. 60605. *Office:* Griffith Observatory, 2300 East Observatory Rd., Los Angeles, Calif. 90027.

CAREER: Griffith Observatory, Los Angeles, Calif., curator, 1972-74, director, 1974—. Member of faculty at University of California, El Camino College, and University of Southern California. Host of ''Project: Universe,'' a television series of Public Broadcasting Service. *Member:* American Astronomical Society, Astronomical Society of the Pacific (board member), Sigma Xi, Explorers Club (fellow). *Awards, honors:* Science writing award from American Institute of Physics and U.S. Steel Foundation, 1978, for *In Search of Ancient Astronomies.*

WRITINGS: (Editor and contributor) *In Search of Ancient Astronomies,* Doubleday, 1978; (contributor) Joe Goodwin and others, editors, *Fire of Life: Smithsonian Book of the Sun,* Smithsonian Exposition Books, 1981; (contributor) George O. Abell and Barry Singer, editors, *Science and the Paranormal,* Scribner, 1981; *The Interaction Between Brain and Sky,* Crowell, 1982.

SIDELIGHTS: Krupp wrote: ''I have traveled to, photographed, and studied more than three hundred ancient and prehistoric sites throughout the world, including England, Scotland, Wales, Ireland, Brittany, Malta, Egypt, Central America, Mexico, Peru, and the People's Republic of China.

''I am interested in science as one route to entertainment, and entertainment is for me a vehicle for sharing the experience of science. Rational thought and imaginative thought are tools for survival. Anyone with a Darwinian outlook will recognize that misleading oneself with pseudoscientific notions is a misuse of a valuable tool. It could cost us plenty.

''The interaction of the brain with the sky is a universal and fundamental human experience. What we make of the sky determines how we think of ourselves and how we behave. Traveling to faraway places with strange-sounding names in pursuit of this experience puts one at the heart of human nature. Of course, it's also present back in your own backyard—provided the sky is dark.''

BIOGRAPHICAL/CRITICAL SOURCES: New Scientist, September 13, 1979; *New West,* October 8, 1979.

*　　*　　*

KRYSL, Marilyn   1943-

PERSONAL: Born February 26, 1943, in Kansas; children: Riva Thompson. *Education:* University of Oregon, M.F.A., 1967. *Office:* Department of English, University of Colorado, Boulder, Colo. 80309.

CAREER: Associate professor of English at University of Colorado, Boulder.

WRITINGS: Saying Things, Abbatoir, 1975; *Honey, You've Been Dealt a Winning Hand* (long story), Capra, 1980; *More Palamino, Please, More Fuchsia* (poems), Cleveland State Poetry Center, 1980. Contributor to magazines, including *Atlantic, Nation, Field, Conditions,* and *Seneca Review.*

*　　*　　*

KUFFLER, Stephen   1913-1980

OBITUARY NOTICE: Born August 24, 1913, in Tap, Hungary; died October 10, 1980, in Woods Hole, Mass. Neurobiologist, educator, and author. Kuffler studied in Hungary and Australia before immigrating to the United States in 1945, where he subsequently accepted posts at the University of Chicago, Johns Hopkins University, and Harvard University. Kuffler helped develop a multibeam ophthalmoscope and is especially noted for his work in establishing the chemical basis of neuro-muscular signal transmission. He was awarded a Guggenheim fellowship and numerous other scholastic honors. Kuffler coauthored *From Neuron to Brain.* Obituaries and other sources: *The International Who's Who,* Europa, 1978; *Who's Who in America,* 40th edition, Marquis, 1978; *American Men and Women of Science: The Physical and Biological Sciences,* 14th edition, Bowker, 1979; *The Annual Obituary 1980,* St. Martin's, 1981.

L

LACHENMEYER, Charles W(illiam) 1943-

PERSONAL: Born August 3, 1943, in Brooklyn, N.Y.; son of William (in business) and Dorothea (in business; maiden name, Kapps) Lachenmeyer; children: Nathaniel. *Education:* College of William and Mary, B.A., 1965; University of North Carolina, Ph.D., 1969. *Home and office:* 225 13th St., Brooklyn, N.Y. 11215.

CAREER: Hunter College of the City University of New York, New York, N.Y., associate professor, 1970-74; associate professor of sociology, 1974-75; St. John's University, Jamaica, N.Y., associate professor of sociology, 1975-77; Rutgers University, Newark, N.J., associate professor of management, 1977-78; Hofstra University, Hempstead, N.Y., associate professor of management, 1978-80; writer and consultant, 1980—.

WRITINGS: The Language of Sociology, Columbia University Press, 1971; *The Essence of Social Research,* Free Press, 1973; *Organizational Politicking,* Institute for the Analysis, Evaluation, and Design of Human Action, 1979; *Limits of Planning,* Institute for the Analysis, Evaluation, and Design of Human Action, 1980; *Productive Performance,* Institute for the Analysis, Evaluation, and Design of Human Action, 1980; *Democracy as a Planning System,* Institute for the Analysis, Evaluation, and Design of Human Action, 1981.

WORK IN PROGRESS: Preparation of additional volumes for his series of books on planning and analysis.

SIDELIGHTS: Lachenmeyer told *CA:* "I have developed an analytical system of wide applicability. Its dissemination and continuing development has occupied me full time. Each spinoff publication is self-produced and published, and we have attracted a relatively large audience from diverse backgrounds to date. This analytical system is logico/mathematical in form. To my knowledge it is the most complete problem-solving and planning system in existence. It is the closest approximation to a logic of discovery ever developed in the history of human thought."

*　　*　　*

LACY, Donald Charles 1933-

PERSONAL: Born January 4, 1933, in Henry County, Ind.; son of Charles William (a clergyman and plasterer) and Marian Marcille (Walradth) Lacy; married Dorothy Marie Thomas, November 6, 1959; children: Anne Marie, Donna Jean, Sharon Elizabeth, Martha Elaine. *Education:* Ball State University, B.S., 1954, M.A., 1958; Christian Theological Seminary, Indianapolis, Ind., M.Div., 1961, D.Min., 1976. *Home:* 6417 Columbine Dr., Indianapolis, Ind. 46224. *Office:* Meadowdale Church, 5701 West 34th St., Indianapolis, Ind. 46224.

CAREER: Ordained United Methodist minister, 1960 and 1962; teacher at public schools in Jay County, Ind., 1954-58; pastor of Methodist churches in North Indiana Conference, 1959-68, and South Indiana Conference, including Seymour, Ind., 1968-79; Meadowdale Church, Indianapolis, Ind., minister, 1981—. Associate pastor of United Methodist church in Muncie, Ind., 1962-64. Member of Methodist Commission on Christian Unity and Interreligious Concerns (past chairperson); member of board of directors of Indiana Council of Churches. *Military service:* U.S. Navy, 1955-56. *Member:* International Platform Association, National Association of Evangelicals, Disciples of Christ Historical Society, Phi Delta Kappa, Pi Gamma Mu, Rotary International, Masons (Scottish Rite), Columbia Club.

WRITINGS: (Contributor) Cynthia Pearl Maus and Ronald E. Osborn, editors, *The Church and the Fine Arts,* Harper, 1960; *Gems From James,* Dorrance, 1974; *Called to Be,* C.S.S. Publishing, 1978, second edition, 1980; *Mary and Jesus,* C.S.S. Publishing, 1979. Author of "Lacy's Logic," a column in *Rushville Republican,* 1980-81. Contributor to theology journals and religious magazines, including *Pulpit Digest, Good News, Science of Mind,* and *Interpreter,* and newspapers.

WORK IN PROGRESS: Manuscripts for laity and clergy on the Epistles of John, Book of Acts, and the seventeenth chapter of the Gospel of John.

SIDELIGHTS: Lacy told *CA:* "Writing has been a very strong driving force in my life as far back as high school. For the most part, in terms of published material, it has been an extension of the professional ministry. It is something I have to do in order to feel whole in the total sense of my being.

"My first published article, 'Queen of All Hearts,' was in a Roman Catholic magazine in 1969. It was an interpretation of the Blessed Mother's feelings shortly after the birth of Jesus. The unusual aspect was that it had been turned down by two publications in my own denomination. This experience along with working briefly for a Roman Catholic priest in the Navy and preparing a unique contemporary worship service entitled "Methodist Mass" really provided the background for *Mary and Jesus. Mary and Jesus* received strong endorsements from both Roman Catholics and Protestants. *The Priest* magazine called it 'a "full gospel treatment" of the traditional Christmas topics.' Sister Lois Bannon, the archivist for the Roman Catholic Diocese of Dallas, Texas, said: 'This book can easily serve as a bridge between Non-Catholic and Catholic concerning Mary and her place in the Church and in our lives. I recommend the book to all groups.' Best-selling author and clergyman of the year Dr. Charles L. Allen said: 'I have read this through and really, I think it truly beautiful. You capture the spirit of Christmas in a magnificent manner. This book should have wide circulation and I am sure it will.' The *Indianapolis News* called the book 'an ecumenical breakthrough.'

"*Called to Be* is really the finest piece of published homiletical work that I have done. It is based on the Sermon on the Mount as found in the Gospel of Matthew. William D. Thompson, editor of Abingdon Preacher's Library, said, 'Your sermons in *Called to Be* have been very helpful to me personally, and also as excellent models of good, contemporary, biblical preaching.' Earl Massey, one of the great preachers and teachers of preachers of our time, said, 'The sermons in *Called to Be* are *excellent* and I heartily commend you on your excellent craftmanship and focus. I will also commend them to my students.'

"*Gems From James* was written more for the general reading public than either *Called to Be* or *Mary and James*. While lighter in approach, it has its supporters, including the *North Carolina Christian Advocate* which said, 'This book is an excellent study of the great truths in the Book of James and could be used most profitably by Church Groups.'

"Overall, my writing has provided homiletical expertise for clergy as well as serious spiritual growth for laity. I want to do some quality writing in the near future in the area of ecumenical and interreligious concerns. My greatest concern, as far as the contemporary scene is observed, is that really serious writing that deserves to be published will be sidetracked in favor of that which can sell for a profit, regardless of the moral and literary quality."

BIOGRAPHICAL/CRITICAL SOURCES: North Carolina Christian Advocate, October 26, 1978; *Indianapolis News,* December 6, 1980.

*   *   *

LAING, Frederick

PERSONAL: Born in Baltimore, Md.; son of Marie Theresa Laing (a composer); married Blanche Gilbert, January 3, 1953. *Education:* Educated at a military academy. *Home:* 525 West End Ave., Apt. 10E, New York, N.Y. 10024.

CAREER: Writer. Traveling salesman at age twenty for a clock factory; advertising manager at twenty-three for a maker of clocks and watches; sales promotion manager at twenty-four for a large grocery chain; account executive and writer for Batten, Barton, Durstine & Osborne advertising agency. *Member:* P.E.N., Authors Guild.

WRITINGS:—Novels, except as noted: *Six Seconds a Year,* Crowell, 1948; *The Giant's House,* Dial, 1955; *His Neighbor's Wife,* Redbook, 1957; *A Question of Pride,* Four Winds Press, 1967; *The Bride Wore Braids,* Four Winds Press, 1968, published as *Ask Me If I Love You Now,* Campus Book Club, 1970; *Why Heimdall Blew His Horn: Tales of the Norse Gods* (mythology), Silver Burdette, 1969, revised edition published as *Tales From Scandinavia,* 1979. Also author of two other novels, one for adults and one for all ages, as yet unpublished.

Short stories represented in anthologies, including *The Short Story Reader,* World Publishing Co., 1946; *Literature of Ad-*

venture, Ginn, 1961; *Voices in Literature,* Ginn, 1961; *The Best Short Shorts,* Scholastic Book Services, 1966; *Hit Parade of Short Stories,* Scholastic Book Services, 1967; *Mirrors,* Scholastic Book Services, 1967; *Jobs in Your Future,* Scholastic Book Services, 1968; *Stories for Teenagers,* Globe Book Co., 1969; *Look for Tomorrow,* Scholastic Book Services, 1970; *The Fallen Angel,* Scholastic Book Services, 1970; *The Distant Promise,* Scholastic Book Services, 1970; *Learning From Literature,* Dade County (Fla.) Public Schools, 1977; *Be a Better Reader,* Prentice-Hall, 1978; *Stories of Surprise and Wonder,* Globe Book Co., 1979; *The American Anthology,* Globe Book Co., 1982.

Contributor of about one hundred fifty short stories to magazines, including *Collier's, Cosmopolitan, Redbook, Woman's Home Companion, Good Housekeeping, This Week, American, Seventeen, Co-ed, Literary Cavalcade,* and numerous small publications and foreign periodicals. Staff writer of articles for magazines and news syndicates.

Author of English subtitles for foreign films, including "Gate of Hell," "Magnificent Seven," "Utamaro," "Odd Obsession," "Devi," "Girl in Black," "Rue de Prairies," "Maire Octobre," "Le Rouge est mis," "Mefiez vous fillettes," "The Roof," "The Third Sex," "Love Is My Profession," "Crime and Punishment," "Dreams in a Drawer," "Spring Fragrance," and "Golden Demon," and dubbed English dialogue for "Anna," "Tomorrow Is Too Late," and "Dr. Laurent." Also author of scripts for television and adapter of screen shooting scripts into short stories or short novels.

WORK IN PROGRESS: A number of fiction projects.

SIDELIGHTS: "As a free-lance pro I've done many types of writing," Laing told *CA.* "Some is the best I can do, and the best is never quite good enough. Some is calculated for a wide audience, but even this type of writing insists that I have for it a measure of respect as a good job with decent intentions. I always hope, too, that something I write will contribute, if only in a tiny, granular way, toward a kinder understanding of human needs.

"*Six Seconds a Year,* a first novel I really wanted to write, is about the selfish interests behind the crash of 1929. The publishers, Thomas Y. Crowell, sent out, in advance of publication, a large mailing to writers and critics. Because of the response, the Crowell company decided to feature it as their major book of the season.

"*The Giant's House* is a character study of an immigrant who built a chain of stores similar to the A & P. It is concerned with the effects of success on himself, on the lives of others, and on the national scene. This novel, too, was handled as a major book by another publisher, Dial Press.

"*The Bride Wore Braids,* about the trials of a teenage marriage, has an offbeat history. When it was about to be issued as a paperback, the book club editor at Scholastic asked permission to change the title to *Ask Me If I Love You Now.* This was based on a scene in the novel. Meanwhile, *The Bride Wore Braids* had come to the attention of its present French publishers, Presses de la Cite. They felt the title wouldn't translate well and asked permission to change it to *Face a la vie.* Due, I was told, to the quality of the French reviews, the book moved from the young-adult toward the general market. One result of this was that the writer, who has never before been published in France, began selling by the handful stories which had first been issued in U.S. magazines. *Elle,* which had been the first to publish any of them, displayed three in one issue. *Face a la vie* was serialized in a Italian magazine for women. The Japanese publisher bought it because he had seen the French reviews. Another sale was to Spain and Mexico, with publication by Ediciones Martinez Roca in 1982.''

Reviews of *Six Seconds a Year,* Laing's book about a slick, ambitious salesman who pursues success at the expense of his integrity and ideals, included comments from the *Philadelphia Inquirer* and the *New York Times.* Frank Brookhouser, of the *Inquirer,* remarked: ''The fine art of high-pressure selling gets a going-over in *Six Seconds a Year,* one of the fastest paced novels that has come along since *I Can Get It for You Wholesale* and the earlier James M. Cain books. . . . Laing has made an impressive debut in the novel field with this revealing, amusing, and often tragic picture of a clock company's men and women at work and play.'' *New York Times* critic Mary Sutphen Hurst observed: ''Out of his own varied business background, Mr. Laing paints a realistic picture of the compulsive go-getting of the Twenties—the purposeless, ever increasing crescendo of competition, salesmanship and speculation which ended in the crash. . . . This is an intelligent, soundly constructed, effective first novel.''

In his next book, *The Giant's House,* Laing returned to the subject of success and failure in American business. Loosely based on the history of a large supermarket chain, the story tells of an Irish immigrant who rises from dishwasher to founder of a nationwide chain of grocery stores. John Horgan, the central character, ''emerges as a ruthless, despotic tycoon whose guiding principle in all relationships was to 'plumb for bottom,''' wrote Carol Field of the *New York Herald Tribune.* ''Friendships, promises, loyalties counted for nothing in his forceful drive to expand his empire.'' Also prominent in the story, noted Field, are Paul Marrow, a newspaperman groomed by Horgan to serve as his sales promotion manager, Prudence Boyden, as Marrow's romantic lead, and Ella Evans, ''who calculatingly used her physical charms to climb to social eminence.''

In other reviews, the *Chicago Tribune* called *The Giant's House* ''a readable and powerful novel about big and little affairs. . . . The portrait of Horgan himself, with his cruelty, his bullying, his strength, his irresistible charm and his tragedy, is a real accomplishment.'' John McManis, writing in the *Detroit News,* commented: ''The author . . . served a period as sales promotion manager for a big grocery chain, so he can write with the authority of intimate knowledge. His novel is fast-moving and there isn't a word that is dull or out of place. 'The Giant's House' is a first class story of big business getting bigger.''

The book that brought Laing to the attention of foreign publishers, *The Bride Wore Braids,* opens with the teenage romance of Ken and Judy, a relationship that grows stronger as loneliness and misunderstandings at home increase. When Judy learns that she is pregnant, the young couple consider an abortion but decide instead to leave school, family, and friends, get married, and move to New York City. Once settled in a one-room, roach-infested apartment, their efforts to begin a new life are met with the dismal, financial realities encountered by other high school dropouts. Ken is unqualified for anything but boring, dead-end jobs as a stock clerk and messenger boy, and Judy must supplement their income with the money she earns as a part-time typist. Though conditions worsen for them, they manage to reconcile with their families, save their marriage, and remain independent. There is even hope that life for Ken and Judy will improve; he enrolls in night school, and she continues with her typing to help meet expenses.

A writer for the *Young Reader's Review* observed: ''This hard-hitting, wide-open look at the pitfall of teen-age marriage has a happy ending. Most teen-age marriages do not; few kids are as adult as Judy or as intelligent and hardworking as Ken. But

even the 'happy ending' is realistic. Their marriage is no picnic, but it is a happy marriage. Incident, atmosphere, characterization, and plot are well-integrated to make a readable and memorable book.'' French reviews of the book included these remarks from *L'Ecole et la nation:* ''This American novel of Frederick Laing's speaks to young people without flattering or boring them. The parent-child relationships are rendered with great fidelity of tone. . . . Let's wish it [*Face a la vie*] the success it merits.'' The periodical *Christiene* called the book, ''A very beautiful novel with the ring of truth.''

BIOGRAPHICAL/CRITICAL SOURCES: Philadelphia Inquirer, April 17, 1948; *New York Times,* May 2, 1948, December 18, 1955; *Saturday Review of Literature,* May 8, 1948; *New York Herald Tribune,* October 23, 1955; *Detroit News,* November 6, 1955; *Chicago Tribune,* November 6, 1955; *Time,* November 7, 1955; *Printers' Ink,* December 23, 1955; *Young Reader's Review,* November, 1968; *L'Ecole et la nation,* December, 1970; *Christiene,* December, 1970.

*   *   *

LaMARSH, Judy
See LaMARSH, Julia Verlyn

*   *   *

LaMARSH, Julia Verlyn   1924-1980
(Judy LaMarsh)

OBITUARY NOTICE—See index for *CA* sketch: Born December 20, 1924, in Chatham, Ontario, Canada; died October 27, 1980, in Toronto, Ontario, Canada. Politician, attorney, administrator, television and radio show host, and author. In 1960 LaMarsh became a member of the Canadian Parliament and the only woman in the Liberal party to hold such a seat. She quickly distinguished herself with her outspokenness, giving almost one hundred speeches during her first session of Parliament. Three years later, LaMarsh was appointed by Liberal Prime Minister Lester B. Pearson to the cabinet as the minister of health and welfare. She served in that capacity until she was made secretary of state in 1965. LaMarsh's career in politics, however, was ruined in 1968 when she called Prime Minister Pierre Trudeau a ''bastard'' on public television. The incident resulted in her resignation as secretary of state and the loss of her seat in Parliament. LaMarsh returned to her work in law, which she had practiced before entering politics. She also hosted the radio show ''Person to Person'' and the television program ''LaMarsh Show.'' LaMarsh wrote one book, *The Memoirs of a Bird in a Gilded Cage.* Obituaries and other sources: *The Annual Obituary 1980,* St. Martin's, 1981.

*   *   *

LAMB, Charles Bentall   1914-1981
(Achilles)

OBITUARY NOTICE—See index for *CA* sketch: Born April 11, 1914, in Bolton, Lancashire, England; died May 28, 1981. Military man, educator, administrator, and author. Lamb worked as an apprentice sailor before joining the Royal Air Force in 1934. He served in that branch of the armed forces for twenty years. Afterwards, he was an assistant commandant at the Joint School of Warfare and a lecturer at the Royal Naval College. In 1958 Lamb founded and then managed, until 1973, the White Ensign Association, which provides financial advice to men in the military. Lamb wrote one book, entitled *War in a Stringbag.* (Date of death provided by Pye-Smiths, executors of Lamb's estate.)

LAMOUR, Dorothy
See KAUMEYER, Dorothy

* * *

LAMPO, Hubert 1920-

BRIEF ENTRY: Born September 1, 1920, in Antwerp, Belgium. Belgian author. Lampo writes novels and short stories that critics describe as both realistic and magical. The books, several of which have been translated into English, include *De zwanen van Stonehenge: Een leesboek over magisch-realisme en fantastische literatur* (Meulenhoff, 1972), *Zoomlens op Lampo: Een aforistische bloemlezing uit het werk van Hubert Lampo* (De Arbeiderspers, 1976), *De verzoeking: Een radiospel* (Manteau, 1977), and *Verhalen uit nomansland* (Beckers, 1979). *Address:* c/o Beckers Groep, Brasschaatsteenweg 200, B-2180 Kalmthout, Belgium.

* * *

LANCASTER, Lydia
See MEAKER, Eloise

* * *

LANCASTER, Osbert 1908-

PERSONAL: Born August 4, 1908, in London, England; son of Robert (a publisher) and Clare Bracebridge (Manger) Lancaster; married Karen Elizabeth Harris, July 4, 1933 (died, 1964); married Anne Scott-Janes, 1967; children: (first marriage) Carasophia, William Osbert. *Education:* Lincoln College, Oxford, B.A. (with fourth-class honors), 1930; received certificate for stage design from Slade School of Art, London. *Religion:* Church of England. *Address:* 78 Cheyne Court, Royal Hospital Rd., London S.W.3, England.

CAREER: Cartoonist, artist, and author. Associated with *Architectural Review*, London, England, c. 1936; *London Daily Express*, London, cartoonist, 1939-40, 1946—. Set designer for plays, including "Pineapple Poll," 1951, "Bonne Bouche," 1952, "Love in a Village," 1952, "High Spirits," 1953, "The Rake's Progress," 1953, "All's Well That Ends Well," 1953, "Don Pasquale," 1954, "Coppelia," 1954, "Napoli," 1954, "Falstaff," 1955, "Hotel Paradiso," 1956, "Zuleika," 1957, "L'Italiana in Algeri," 1957, "Tiresias," 1958, "Candide," 1959, "La Fillee mal gardee," 1960, "She Stoops to Conquer," 1960, "La Pietra del Paragone," 1964, "Peter Grimes," 1964, "L'Heure espagnole," 1966, "The Rising Moon," 1970, and "The Sorcerer," 1971.

Art critic for *London Observer*, 1942-44. Member of editorial board of *Architectual Review*, 1946. Sydney Jones Lecturer in Art at Liverpool University, Liverpool, England, 1947. Adviser to Greater London Council Historic Building Board, 1969—. Governor of King Edward VII School, Kings Lynn, Norfolk; served on governing bodies of Royal College of Art and of Council of Industrial Design. Council member of Royal Literary Fund. Designer of book jackets, posters for London transport system, and murals for a hotel in Blanford, England. *Wartime service:* Worked at Press Censorship Bureau, London, c. 1940, and Foreign Office news department, London, 1940; British Embassy, Athens, Greece, first secretary, 1944-46.

MEMBER: Piscatorial Society, Brook's Club, Beefsteak Club, Pratt's Club, Garrick Club. *Awards, honors:* D.Litt. from Birmingham University, 1946, University of Newcastle Upon Tyne, 1970, St. Andrews University, 1974, and Oxford University, 1975; Commander of Order of British Empire, 1953; fellow of University College, London, 1967, and of Royal Institute of British Architects; knighthood conferred in 1975.

WRITINGS—Cartoon collections; all published by J. Murray, except as noted: *Pocket Cartoons*, 1940; *New Pocket Cartoons*, 1941; *Further Pocket Cartoons*, 1942; *More Pocket Cartoons*, 1943; *Assorted Sizes*, 1944; *Cartoons*, Penguin, 1945; *More and More Productions*, Gryphon Press, 1948; *A Pocketful of Cartoons*, Gryphon Press, 1949; *The Alarms and Excursions of Lady Littlehampton*, Houghton, 1952; *Lady Littlehampton and Friends*, Gryphon Press, 1952; *Studies From the Life: New Pocket Cartoons*, Gryphon Press, 1954; *Tableaux vivants: New Pocket Cartoons*, Gryphon Press, 1955.

Private Views: New Pocket Cartoons, Gryphon Press, 1956; *The Year of the Comet: New Pocket Cartoons*, Gryphon Press, 1957; *Etudes: New Pocket Cartoons*, 1958; *Signs of the Times*, Houghton, 1961; *Mixed Notices: New Pocket Cartoons*, 1963; *Graffiti: New Pocket Cartoons*, 1964; *A Few Quick Tricks: New Pocket Cartoons*, 1965; *Fasten Your Safety Belts: New Pocket Cartoons*, 1966; *Temporary Diversions: New Pocket Cartoons*, 1968; *Recorded Live: New Pocket Cartoons*, 1970; *Meaningful Confrontations*, 1971; *Theatre in the Flat*, 1972; *The Littlehampton Bequest*, 1973; *Liquid Assets: New Pocket Cartoons*, 1975; *The Social Contract: New Pocket Cartoons*, 1977.

On architecture; all self-illustrated; all published by J. Murray, except as noted: *Progress at Pelvis Bay*, 1936; *Pillar to Post: The Pocket Lamp of Architecture*, 1939, published as *Pillar to Post: English Architecture Without Tears*, Scribner, 1939 (also see below); *Homes, Sweet Homes*, 1940 (also see below); *Facades and Faces*, 1950; *Here of All Places*, Houghton, 1958, published as *Here, of All Places: A Pocket Lamp of Architecture*, J. Murray, 1959, Readers Union, 1960; *A Cartoon History of Architecture* (contains portions of *Pillar to Post* and *Homes, Sweet Homes*), Houghton, 1964, J. Murray, 1975; *Sailing to Byzantium: An Architectural Companion*, Gamit, 1969.

Other; all published by J. Murray, except as noted: *Our Sovereigns from Alfred to George VI, 871-1937*, 1936; (author of introduction) G. B. Tiepolo, *Twenty-Five Caricatures*, De La More Press, 1943; *Classical Landscape With Figures*, 1947, reprinted, 1975; *The Saracen's Head; or, The Reluctant Crusader* (juvenile), 1948, Houghton, 1949; *Drayneflete Revealed*, 1949, published as *There'll Always Be a Drayneflete*, Houghton, 1950; *All Done From Memory* (autobiography), Houghton, 1953; *Loan Exhibition of Water-Colours, Drawings and Stage Designs by Osbert Lancaster at Norwich Museum* (exhibit catalogue), Norwich, 1955; *The Penguin Osbert Lancaster*, Penguin, 1964; *With an Eye to the Future* (autobiography), Houghton, 1967; *Nobless Oblige: An Enquiry Into the Identifiable Characteristics of the English Aristocracy*, Hamish Hamilton, 1973; (with wife, Anne Scott-James) *The Pleasure Garden: An Illustrated History of British Gardening*, 1977; *Scene Changes*, 1978.

Illustrator: Cyril Northcotte Parkinson, *Parkinson's Law; or, The Pursuit of Progress*, J. Murray, 1958; Parkinson, *The Law and the Profits*, J. Murray, 1960; Parkinson, *In-Laws and Outlaws*, J. Murray, 1961; Nancy Freeman, *The Water Beetle*, Hamish Hamilton, 1962; (and author of introduction) William Shakespeare, *All's Well That Ends Well*, Folio, 1963; Anne Scott-James, *Down to Earth*, Joseph, 1971; Parkinson, *The Law of Delay*, J. Murray, 1971; Charles Hepburn, *Mo and Other Originals*, Hamish Hamilton, 1971; John Betjemin, *An Oxford University Chest*, S. R. Publishers, 1971; Anthony

Powell, *Two Plays,* Heinemann, 1971; Nigel Dennis, *An Essay on Malta,* J. Murray, 1972; Max Beerbohm, *Zuleika Dobson; or, An Oxford Love Story,* Shakespeare Head Press, 1975; Saki, *Short Stories,* Folio, 1976.

Works also appeared in serial form in *Atlantic Monthly* magazine.

SIDELIGHTS: "The Master of the Glazed and Popping Eye," Osbert Lancaster created the cartoon character Maudie Littlehampton, who, said Alan Pryce-Jones, "has become a national figure to be matched with our own Charlie Brown and L'il Abner." Maudie Littlehampton was born in 1939 when Lancaster, after asking the features editor of the *London Daily Express* why British newspapers lacked cartoons, was commissioned to draw daily pocket cartoons for the *Express*'s front page. Since then the cartoonist has been recording the exploits of Maudie, her husband, Will, and her somewhat eccentric family.

"The Littlehamptons have had a . . . versatile history," noted Peter Conrad of *New Statesman,* "sending a converted younger son to Rome to sit with Bernini, another hedge-preaching enthusiast to Massachusetts to be painted with his wife Abigail in all the prickly uprightness of American Gothic, and yet another younger son to distinguish himself in the capture of Shittipore, where he was in turn captured with a sword brandished by J. S. Copley." The family motto, "Mon Deiu Mon Soif," suggested Conrad, indicates an occasional family member's lapse into immorality; for example, *The Littlehampton Bequest,* which chronicles the family history and catalogues family portraits, recorded, among other suspicious moral behavior, that the Viscount Drayneflete had been accused of heterosexual and homosexual indiscretions.

A *Times Literary Supplement* reviewer observed that "by a discreet, often positively witty, husbandry of the rich as-it-were compost heap of the eccentric manners and modes of the English aristocracy, as exemplified in the Littlehamptons, he [Lancaster] has preserved the rich savor of life as it was, and is, lived." Through the Littlehampton cartoons, Lancaster reacts to social and political revolutions that affect the establishment, of which he is a part. A *Christian Science Monitor* critic commented: "Mr. Lancaster's roots spring from Littlehampton soil. His mother-in-law came straight out of his cartoon land: 'She was a woman of quite remarkable, though totally unfashionable beauty, who at first glance gave the impression of having slipped into something loose on coming back from George V's Coronation and had remained in it ever since.'"

Although Lancaster satirizes his social strata, the middle class, many have labeled him a snob, which he is, with a qualification. "At Oxford," wrote Brian Inglis of *Punch,* "Lancaster became a snob—in the most estimable sense of that term: an enjoyer of civilized company."

With an Eye to the Future, the second volume of Lancaster's autobiography, picks up where *All Done From Memory* left off. Since *Memory* recorded the cartoonist's childhood, *With an Eye to the Future* captures his boarding school days, his life at Oxford, and his marriage. Alan Pryce-Jones, a *New York Times Book Review* critic and a contemporary of Lancaster, stated: "Osbert Lancaster is not only funny, he is also an acute observer who has enjoyed the luck of having much to observe."

At home, there was his mother, a grand character who perused *Occult Review* in search of hidden wisdom. "His spiritually-minded mamma," said a reviewer in the *Times Literary Supplement,* "had warned Master Lancaster that 'we are not put into this world to be happy.'" Nonetheless, the reviewer went on to say that the cartoonist "seems to have squeezed happiness

from unpropitious experiences, as when a haemorhage saved him from cramming for the Bar and enabled him to pursue his natural bent at Slade."

At school Lancaster observed a wide array of eccentric individuals which he immortalized in *With an Eye to the Future.* At Charterhouse, an ancient public school, the young cartoonist met many bullies and a headmaster who, according to the *Yale Review,* chalked "the rod in order to inflict a more perfect punishment on the upturned behind of a young fag caught out in some utterly mysterious misdemeanor." Lancaster also pictured the dons he encountered at Oxford, such as Professor Dawkins, whom the cartoonist once found sitting in a chestnut tree "hooting like a macaw."

And Lancaster observed society. He experienced the social milieu of the twenties and early thirties at a ball given for Unity Mitford by her sister, the future Lady Mosely. As the cartoonist prepared to ascend the stairs, he recalled, "the queue came to an abrupt halt and drew to one side to make way for two descending footmen carrying between them the inanimate form of Augustus John who, it appeared had been overcome by the heat rather early in the proceedings; and as I watched that defiantly noble, if temporarily horizontal, figure, beard pointing heavenwards, but still with an expression of quiet pride stamped on the unconscious features, being carried out into the night, I felt more strongly than ever that one epoch was ending and another, markedly less carefree, beginning."

With an Eye to the Future, like the Littlehampton cartoons, has received popular and critical acclaim. "It certainly has many virtues of its own," wrote a critic in the *Yale Review.* "Always there is present the illustrator's eye, highlighting in sharp detail some costume, some decoration of the period, even perhaps as they might be picked up by archaeologists among the ruins of London. If his drawings of character are not very deep, they are sharp and the heart behind the hand is always kindly."

AVOCATIONAL INTERESTS: Trout fishing, architecture, topography.

BIOGRAPHICAL/CRITICAL SOURCES: Osbert Lancaster, *All Done From Memory,* Houghton, 1952; Lancaster, *With an Eye to the Future,* Houghton, 1967; *Punch,* May 31, 1967; *Times Literary Supplement,* June 9, 1967, December 25, 1969, December 28, 1973; *New Statesman,* June 16, 1967, December 14, 1973; *New York Times Book Review,* October 29, 1967; *Christian Science Monitor,* November 16, 1967; *Yale Review,* spring, 1968; *Gambit, Inc.,* August-December, 1969; *Spectator,* November 29, 1969; *Observer Review,* January 4, 1970; *Los Angeles Times,* February 22, 1981; *Washington Post Book World,* May 17, 1981.*

—*Sketch by Charity Anne Dorgan*

*   *   *

LANCOUR, (Adlore) Harold   1908-1981

OBITUARY NOTICE—See index for *CA* sketch: Born June 27, 1908, in Duluth, Minn.; died October 23, 1981. Librarian, educator, editor, consultant, bookseller, and author. Lancour ran a bookstore before working for the New York Public Library as a reference assistant and then for Cooper Union as a librarian and professor. In 1947 he became a professor of library science and the associate director of the Graduate Library at the University of Illinois. After nearly fifteen years, he moved to the University of Pittsburgh as dean of the Graduate School of Library and Information Sciences and professor of library science. During his career, Lancour also served as a consultant to the countries of Mali and Guatemala. He conducted numerous surveys that resulted in such publiations as *Libraries in British West Africa, The University of Liberia Library,* and *Educating the Librarian for 2001.* The works he edited include *Heraldry: A Guide to Reference Books, A Bibliography of Ship Passenger Lists, 1538-1825: Being a Guide to Published Lists of Early Immigrants to North America,* and *Encyclopedia of Library and Information Science.* Obituaries and other sources: *Library Journal,* January 15, 1981.

* * *

LANDE, Lawrence (Montague) 1906-
(Alain Verval, a joint pseudonym)

PERSONAL: Born in 1906 in Ottawa, Ontario, Canada; son of Nathan Lande (in business) and Rachel (Freiman) Lande; married Helen Vera Prentis (deceased); married Helen Ackerman; children: Denise Farber, Nelson. *Education:* McGill University, B.A., 1928; University of Grenoble, Diploma in Philosophy, 1928; University of Montreal, LL.B., 1931. *Home:* 4870 Cedar Cres., Montreal, Quebec, Canada. *Office:* 2045 Peet St., Suite 304, Montreal, Quebec, Canada.

CAREER: Writer and musical composer. Director of Canadian Writer's Foundation; created Lawrence Lande Foundation for Canadian Historical Research at McGill University, 1965; member of board of governors of Montreal Children's Hospital. *Member:* International P.E.N. (past president of Canada Centre), Intercontinental Biographical Association (fellow), Royal Society of Arts (honorary corresponding member), Montefiore Club, Elm Ridge Country Club, University Club, Beaver Club, Grolier Club. *Awards, honors:* Officer of Order of Canada (first listing), 1967; centennial medal from McGill University, 1968, D.Litt., 1969.

WRITINGS—Privately printed, except as noted: *Psalms Intimate and Familiar* (poems), Mussons, 1945; *The Story of Stones,* 1946; *Sackcloth and Light* (essay), 1948; *Credo,* 1950; *Babbling and Random Verse,* 1952; *Toward the Quiet Mind,* McLennan & Stewart, 1954; *The Third Duke of Richmond* (history), distributed by McGill University, 1956; *Old Lamps Aglow* (poems), distributed by McGill University, 1957; *The Ladder* (essays), 1958; *Response* (poems), 1960; (with Thomas Greenwood, under joint pseudonym Alain Verval) *Experience* (poems), 1963; *The Lawrence Lande Collection of Canadiana* (bibliography), McGill University Press, 1965; *Beethoven and Quebec,* McGill University Press, 1966; *L'Accent* (essay and poems), 1970; *A Life From the Sun and More* (music and poems), 1971; *Rare and Unusual Canadiana: First Supplement to the Lande Bibliography,* McGill University Press, 1971; *The Compleat Moralist* (music and poems), 1972; *Adventures in Collecting Books and Blake and Buber,* McLennan Library, McGill University, 1975, 2nd edition, 1976; *Canadian Historical Documents and Manuscripts* (bibliography), Volumes I-V, 1977-81.

WORK IN PROGRESS: Working to activate Canadian documents and manuscripts throughout the principal archives and libraries in Canada.

SIDELIGHTS: Lande's musical compositions for piano appear on more than thirty-five record albums.

Lande told *CA:* "In the rare books department of McGill University there is a Lande Room for a collection of William Blake, the third floor of the McLennan Library at McGill University houses the Lande Room of Canadiana, and the Public Archives and the National Library of Canada also house Lande collections. So, I'm kept busy both as a collector and activator of

Canadian history, and I hope to continue (God willing) this glorious avocation for the rest of my life, with poems and music of course.''

* * *

LANE, Carl D(aniel) 1899-

PERSONAL: Born October 10, 1899, in Portland, Me.; son of Daniel (a designer) and Katherine (Zimmerman) Lane; married Marie Gerlach, July 30, 1924; children: Robert, Alice Louise. *Education:* Attended New York School of Fine and Applied Art. *Politics:* Republican. *Residence:* Rockport, Me. *Home address:* Cranberry Island, Friendship, Me., 04547. *Agent:* Curtis Brown, Ltd., 575 Madison Ave., New York, N.Y. 10022.

CAREER: Self-employed interior decorator, 1923-29; resort operator in Connecticut, beginning 1930; Penobscot Boat Works, Penobscot, Me., naval architect and partner. Free-lance writer, 1925—. *Awards, honors:* Recipient of art awards for acrylic painting.

WRITINGS: (Editor) *The Sea Scout Manual,* 6th edition (Lane was not associated with earlier editions), Boy Scouts of America, 1939; *Boatowner's Sheet Anchor* (self-illustrated), Norton, 1941, revised edition, Funk, 1969; *Chevron and Pipe: Handbook for Crew Leaders,* Boy Scouts of America, 1941; *What the Citizen Should Know About the Merchant Marine* (self-illustrated), Norton, 1941, published as *What You Should Know About the Merchant Marine,* 1943; *The Boatman's Manual,* Norton, 1942, 3rd edition, 1962; *American Paddle Steamboats,* Coward, 1943; *The Fleet in the Forest* (novel), Coward, 1943; *How to Sail* (self-illustrated), Norton, 1947; *River Dragon* (juvenile; illustrated by Charles B. Wilson), Little, Brown, 1948; *The Cruiser's Manual* (self-illustrated), Norton, 1949, 2nd edition, Funk, 1970; *Treasure Cave* (juvenile; self-illustrated), Little, Brown 1950; *The Fire Raft* (juvenile), Little, Brown, 1951; *Mystery Trail* (juvenile; self-illustrated), Little, Brown, 1951; *Black Tide* (juvenile; self-illustrated), Little, Brown, 1952; *Steam Against Steam,* Pequot Press, 1973; *Go South Inside: Cruising the Inland Waterway,* International Marine Publishing, 1977.

Contributor of numerous articles and stories to periodicals, including *American, Argosy, Holiday, Saturday Evening Post,* and *Yachting.*

* * *

LANE, Frederic C(hapin) 1900-

PERSONAL: Born November 23, 1900, in Lansing, Mich.; son of Alfred Church (a geologist) and Susanne (Lauriat) Lane; married Harriet Mirick, June 7, 1927; children: George Mirick, Jonathan Page, Aldreda Lane Altobelli. *Education:* Cornell University, A.B., 1921; Tufts University, M.A., 1922; Harvard University, Ph.D., 1930. *Home and office address:* Whitney Hill, Lanes Rd., Westminster, Mass. 01473.

CAREER: University of Minnesota, instructor, 1926; Johns Hopkins University, Baltimore, Md., instructor, 1928-31, assistant professor, 1931-35, associate professor, 1935-46, professor of history, 1946-66; writer, 1972—. Visiting professor at Harvard University, 1971-72, and at Brandeis University. Historian for U.S. Maritime Commission, 1946-47; assistant director of Social Science Division of Rockefeller Foundation, 1951-54.

MEMBER: International Economic History Association (president, 1965-68), American Academy of Arts and Sciences,

American Philosophical Society, American Historical Association (president, 1965), Economic History Association (president, 1956-58). *Awards, honors:* Guggenheim fellowship, 1958-59; D.H.L. from Michigan State University, 1970; LL.D. from Johns Hopkins University, 1974; Ralph Waldo Emerson Prize from Phi Beta Kappa, 1974, for *Venice, a Maritime Republic;* Premio Internazionale Galileo Galilei from Rotary Italiani, 1980, for contributions to Italian economic history.

WRITINGS: Venetian Ships and Shipbuilders of the Renaissance, Johns Hopkins University Press, 1934; *Andrea Barbarigo, Merchant of Venice,* Johns Hopkins University Press, 1944; (with Eric F. Goldman and Erling Hunt) *The World's History,* Harcourt, 1946, revised edition, 1953; *Ships for Victory: A History of Shipbuilding Under the U.S. Maritime Commission,* Johns Hopkins University Press, 1951; (editor with Jelle Riemersma) *Enterprise and Secular Change,* Richard D. Irwin, Inc. (Homewood, Ill.), 1953; *Venice and History: Collected Papers,* Johns Hopkins University Press, 1966; *Venice, a Maritime Republic,* Johns Hopkins University Press, 1973; *Profits From Power,* State University of New York Press, 1979. Editor of *Journal of Economic History,* 1941-51.

WORK IN PROGRESS: Money and Banking in Medieval Venice, with R. C. Mueller, publication expected in 1983; research on Venetian seamen and finances.

* * *

LANE, Marc J(ay) 1946-

PERSONAL: Born August 30, 1946, in Chicago, Ill.; son of Sam and Evelyn (Light) Lane; married Rochelle Nudelman (an educator), December 21, 1971; children: Allison, Amanda, Jennifer. *Education:* University of Illinois, B.A. (with honors), 1967; Northwestern University, J.D., 1971. *Home:* 6715 North Longmeadow, Lincolnwood, Ill. 60646. *Office:* Law Offices of Marc J. Lane, 180 North LaSalle St., Chicago, Ill. 60601.

CAREER: Law Offices of Marc J. Lane, Chicago, Ill., president, 1971—. President of Medico-Legal Institute, 1976—. *Member:* American Bar Association, Illinois State Bar Association, Chicago Bar Association, Chicago Council of Lawyers (past chairperson of committee on corporate responsibility). *Awards, honors:* Lincoln Award from Illinois State Bar Association, 1973, for "Discrimination in Corporate Pensions and Profit-Sharing Plans," and 1977, for "Foreign Transfers Under the Tax Reform Act of 1976."

WRITINGS: The Doctor's Lawyer: A Legal Handbook for Doctors, C. C Thomas, 1974; *Legal Handbook for Small Business,* American Management Association, 1978; *Corporations: Pre-Organization Planning,* Bureau of National Affairs, 1980; *The Doctor's Law Guide: Essentials of Practice Management,* Saunders, 1980; *Taxation for the Computer Industry,* Wiley, 1980; *Taxation for Small Business,* Wiley, 1980, second edition, 1982; *Taxation for Engineering and Technical Consultants,* Wiley, 1980; *Taxation for Small Manufacturers,* Wiley, 1980; (with Alvin Becker) *Twenty-third Annual Federal Tax Course,* Illinois Institute for Continuing Legal Education, 1980; *Legal Handbook for Nonprofit Organizations,* American Management Association, 1981; *Legal Handbook for Managers,* American Management Association, 1982. Contributor to law journals.

WORK IN PROGRESS: A business law cassette series for the American Management Association.

SIDELIGHTS: Lane told *CA:* "Writing is a healthy discipline for the practicing attorney. Not only does it insist on a grueling awareness of the substantive interrelationships among legal theories, structures, and perspectives, it also fosters the very skills that successful lawyers are made of—precision, compromise, sensitivity, logic, and even self-analysis."

* * *

LANE, Roger 1934-

PERSONAL: Born January 17, 1934, in Providence, R.I.; son of Alfred Baker and Eileen Brenda (O'Connor) Lewis; married Patricia A. Mills, June 26, 1955 (divorced, 1972); married Marjorie Gail Merklin (a school principal), June 30, 1974; children: Margaret Mary, James Michael. *Education:* Yale University, B.A. (summa cum laude), 1955; Harvard University, Ph.D., 1963. *Home:* 707 College Ave., Haverford, Pa. 19041. *Office:* Department of History, Haverford College, Haverford, Pa. 19041.

CAREER: Haverford College, Haverford, Pa., assistant professor, 1963-67, associate professor, 1967-72, professor of history, 1972—.

WRITINGS: Policing the City: Boston 1822-1885, Harvard University Press, 1967; (editor with John Turner) *Riot, Rout, and Tumult: Readings in American Political and Social Violence,* Greenwood Press, 1978; *Violent Death in the City: Suicide, Accident, and Murder in Nineteenth-Century Philadelphia,* Harvard University Press, 1979.

* * *

LANG, Daniel 1915-1981

OBITUARY NOTICE—See index for *CA* sketch: Born May 30, 1915, in New York, N.Y.; died of leukemia, November 17, 1981, in New York, N.Y. Journalist and author best known for his examination of the moral dilemmas faced by nuclear scientists and for his efforts to inform the public of the nuclear threat. Lang began his writing career as a reporter with the *New York Post* in 1939. In 1941 he began a forty-year association with *New Yorker* magazine, serving as a war correspondent in the Mediterranean Theater during World War II and as a contributor of articles about social, scientific, and moral issues following the war. Nearly a third of Lang's one hundred "Reporter-at-Large" articles dealt with the increasing threat of nuclear warfare. His books, all based on his *New Yorker* articles, include *Early Tales of the Atomic Age, The Man in the Thick Lead Suit, From Hiroshima to the Moon,* and *An Inquiry Into Enoughness: Of Bombs and Men and Staying Alive.* Lang received a Sidney Hillman Foundation Award for *Casualties of War,* an account of a rape-murder of a Vietnamese girl by American soldiers, and earned a George Polk Award for *A Backwards Look: Germans Remember.* Lang's last work, the libretto for the opera "Minutes to Midnight," was completed just prior to his death. Obituaries and other sources: *New York Times,* November 17, 1981; *Time,* November 30, 1981; *Publishers Weekly,* December 4, 1981; *AB Bookman's Weekly,* December 21-28, 1981.

* * *

LANGER, Marshall J. 1928-

PERSONAL: Born May 30, 1928, in New York, N.Y.; son of Samuel and Edna (Klein) Langer; married Sally Blass, April 3, 1955 (divorced, 1967); married Barbara Slatko, February 15, 1970; children: Andrew H., Jeffrey S. *Education:* University of Pennsylvania, B.S., 1948; University of Miami, J.D. (summa cum laude), 1951. *Home:* 444 Ave Rovino, Coral Gables, Fla. 33156. *Office:* First National Bank Building, Tenth Floor Southeast, Miami, Fla. 33131.

CAREER: Admitted to the Bar of Florida, 1951; private practice as attorney, 1951—; Bettel, Langer & Blass (law firm), Miami, Fla., partner, 1965—; Schutts & Bowen (law firm), Miami, partner, 1975—. President and managing director of Grand Cayman Trust Corp., Grand Cayman, British West Indies; director of Multibanking Corp. Ltd., Grand Cayman, and of Florida Title Co. Chairman of programs for Practising Law Institute, 1972—. Lecturer and acting director of the Inter-American Bar Association law program, 1955-65, and adjunct professor at University of Miami, 1965—; exchange professor of law at University of Havana, Cuba, 1956; lecturer in the United States, Europe, and Japan. *Member:* Inter-American Bar Association (assistant secretary general, 1956-61), American Bar Association, American Foreign Law Association (chapter president, 1955), Greater Miami Tax Institute (president, 1967), Dade County Bar Association, Zeta Beta Tau (national historian, 1959-60), Omicron Delta Kappa, Phi Kappa Phi, Iron Arrow.

WRITINGS—All published by Practising Law Institute, except as noted: *Doing Business in the Caribbean*, 1972; *1973 Survey of Foreign Tax Havens*, Manacon Services, 1972; (with Roy Albert Povell) *Foreign Tax Havens*, 1973, 2nd edition (sole author), 1973, 3rd edition (with Povell), 1974; (with Povell) *Foreign Tax Havens: Choosing the Right One*, 1973; *Tax and Estate Planning for the Multinational Individual*, 1974; *How to Use Foreign Tax Havens*, 1975, published as *Practical International Tax Planning*, 1979; (with Povell) *Foreign Tax and Business Planning*, 1980.

"Foreign Tax Planning" series; with Povell: *Foreign Tax Planning*, 1976; . . . *1977*, 1977; . . . *1978*, 1978; . . . *1979*, 1979.

SIDELIGHTS: Langer has chaired programs for the Practising Law Institute on business enterprises in the Caribbean and on foreign tax havens. He has also testified before congressional subcommittees on matters concerning tax havens and foreign investments in American real estate.

* * *

LANGLEY, Dorothy
See KISSLING, Dorothy (Hight)

* * *

LARSON, E. Richard   1944-

PERSONAL: Born June 21, 1944, in St. Paul, Minn.; son of Earl Richard (a judge) and Cecill (Carlgren) Larson. *Education:* Dartmouth College, B.A., 1966; University of Minnesota, J.D., 1969. *Home:* 125 Riverside Dr., Apt. 4A, New York, N.Y. 10024. *Office:* American Civil Liberties Union, 132 West 43rd St., New York, N.Y. 10036.

CAREER: National Employment Law Project, New York City, senior attorney, 1970-74; American Civil Liberties Union, New York City, national staff counsel, 1974—.

WRITINGS: (With Laughlin McDonald) *The Rights of Racial Minorities*, Avon, 1980; *Sue Your Boss*, Farrar, Straus, 1981; *Federal Court Awards of Attorney's Fees*, Law & Business, 1981. Contributor to civil rights journals.

* * *

LARSON, Norita D(ittberner)   1944-

PERSONAL: Born April 26, 1944, in St. Paul, Minn.; daughter of Otto L. (a salesman) and Doris (Fischer) Dittberner; married Leland L. Larson (a hospital planner), August 13, 1966; chil-

dren: Eric, Jessica, Emily. *Education:* College of St. Catherine, B.A., 1966. *Politics:* Democrat. *Home:* 955 Lombard Ave., St. Paul, Minn. 55105.

CAREER: Writer, poet, teacher. Montessori pre-school teacher, 1972-73; tutor in public schools in St. Paul, Minn., 1979-80; Environment for Learning (Montessori school), St. Paul, teacher, 1980—. Board member, The Loft ("a place for literature and the arts"). *Member:* Onionskin.

WRITINGS: *Walt Disney: An American Original* (juvenile), Creative Education, 1974; (with Paula Taylor) *Walter Cronkite* (juvenile), Creative Education, 1975. Contributor of poetry to journals, including *Lake Street Review, Studio One,* and *Great River Review.*

WORK IN PROGRESS: *Langston Hughes, Poet of Harlem*, publication by Creative Education expected in 1981 or 1982; a collection of poems, tentatively entitled *Unholy Music.*

SIDELIGHTS: Norita Larson told *CA:* "For the last few years I have combined teaching part time with writing partly for financial reasons. I was surprised to discover the combination quite satisfying in that it expresses both sides of my personality—the social and the solitary. At the present time I am teaching Montessori to preschoolers. Teaching is helpful to any writing for children, because it provides the laboratory, the hands-on experience. Sometime in the future I would like to write fiction for children.

"Right now I am working on a manuscript of poems tentatively entitled *Unholy Music,* which is concerned with the working-class background from which I came. I have been writing and publishing poems for the last five years, and I find this genre has almost nothing to do with what I teach or the biographies I have written. I don't know how to explain such splits, except to say that I seem to operate on a multiplicity of levels. Writing is the way I make sense of it all."

* * *

LASBY, Clarence G(eorge)   1933-

PERSONAL: Born March 23, 1933, in Caroline, N.Y.; son of George S. (a civil servant) and Lois Rose (Shevilar) Lasby; married Geraldine Lorenz, June 27, 1953; children: Kristen A., John C. *Education:* University of Redlands, B.A., 1953; University of California, Los Angeles, M.A., 1959, Ph.D., 1963. *Home:* 6308 Forest Hills Dr., Austin, Tex. 78746. *Office:* Department of History, University of Texas at Austin, Austin, Tex. 78712.

CAREER: University of Texas at Austin, instructor, 1962-65, assistant professor, 1965-68, associate professor, 1968-72, professor of history and chairman of department, 1973—. *Military service:* U.S. Army, 1953-55; became sergeant. *Member:* American Historical Association, Organization of American Historians. *Awards, honors:* Social Science Research Council fellow, 1960-61; Mershon fellow of national security from Ohio State University, 1963-64.

WRITINGS: (Contributor) Michael G. Hall and David D. Van Tassel, editors, *Science and Society in the United States*, Dorsey, 1966; *Project Paperclip: German Scientists and the Cold War*, Atheneum, 1971. Contributor to *Virginia Quarterly Review.*

WORK IN PROGRESS: *Coronary Heart Disease in Twentieth-Century America.*

SIDELIGHTS: Clarence Lasby's *Project Paperclip* is an account of the efforts of the United States and the Soviet Union to obtain foreign scientists during and after World War II. U.S. intelligence forces infiltrated Germany and other European countries in search of the German masterminds behind the Nazi invasions and the innovators of their weaponry. From 1945 to 1952, Lasby revealed, the United States enlisted more than six hundred "alien specialists" for the secret project "Paperclip."

Many German scientists, Lasby reported, willingly joined the U.S. military establishment, often in order to take "a stand against the Bolshevist hordes." According to Lasby, the United States was successful in recruiting superior scientists, but most Americans believed otherwise. "Millions of Americans accepted the thesis that the Russians obtained not only better scientists but more of them," said Lasby. "The Russians did obtain more *technicians* than the United States but fewer and inferior scientists."

In a review of *Project Paperclip,* Sigrid Schultz of *Saturday Review* wrote: "Professor Lasby credits Paperclip with having achieved considerable success in terms of both financial savings and technological advance." The U.S. Navy also believed in the program's success, reporting in its 1949 evaluation: "It is probable that no program has ever paid such rich dividends. It is not only the direct savings in time and money . . . it is also the acquisition for this country of some of the finest technical brains in the world—invaluable additions to the nation's resources."

BIOGRAPHICAL/CRITICAL SOURCES: Saturday Review, December 11, 1971.

* * *

LASKI, Marghanita 1915-
(Sarah Russell)

PERSONAL: Born October 24, 1915, in London, England; daughter of Neville J. (a King's counsel) and Phina (Gaster) Laski; married John Eldred Howard (a publisher), 1937; children: Rebecca, Jonathan. *Education:* Sommerville College, Oxford, B.A., 1936. *Agent:* David Higham Associates, 5-8 Lower John St., London W1R 3PE, England.

CAREER: Journalist, broadcaster, critic, and author. Member of Annan Committee of Inquiry in Future of Broadcasting, 1974-77. *Member:* P.E.N., Women's Press Club of London. *Awards, honors:* Honorary fellow of Manchester Polytechnic, 1971.

*WRITINGS—*Novels: *Love on the Supertax,* illustrations by W. Stein, Cresset, 1944; (under pseudonym Sarah Russell) *To Bed With Grand Music,* Pilot Press, 1946; *Tory Heaven; or, Thunder on the Right,* Cresset, 1948, published as *Toasted English,* Houghton, 1949; *Little Boy Lost,* Houghton, 1949; *The Village,* Houghton, 1952; *The Victorian Chaise-Longue,* Cresset, 1953, Houghton, 1954.

Other: *Mrs. Ewing, Mrs. Molesworth, and Mrs. Hodgson Burnett* (criticism), Arthur Barker, 1950, Oxford University Press (New York), 1961, reprinted, Folcroft, 1976, Norwood, 1977; *Apologies,* illustrations by Anton, Harvill, 1955; *The Offshore Island* (three-act play), Cresset, 1959; (contributor) Antoinette Pirie, editor, *Survivors: Fiction Based on Scientific Fact,* Campaign for Nuclear Disarmament (London), 1960; *Ecstasy: A Study of Some Secular and Religious Experiences,* Cresset, 1961, Indiana University Press, 1962; (contributor) R. M. Wilson, editor, *English Association: Essays and Studies,* Humanities Press, 1966; *Jane Austen and Her World,* Viking, 1969, revised edition, Scribner, 1975; *God and Man,* edited by Anthony Bloom, Darton, Longman, & Todd, 1971; *George Eliot*

and Her World, Thames & Hudson, 1973, Scribner, 1978; *Everyday Ecstasy,* Thames & Hudson, 1980.

Editor: *The Patchwork Book* (juvenile anthology), Pilot Press, 1946; *Stories of Adventure* (juvenile), Pilot Press, 1946; (with Georgina Battiscombe) *A Chaplet for Charlotte Yonge,* Cresset, 1965; *Kipling's English History,* BBC Publications, 1974.

Also author of *Victorian Tales, Domestic Life in Edwardian England,* and *The Secular Responsibility: Conway Memorial Lecture.* Contributor of articles and reviews to newspapers and periodicals, including the *London Times* and *Vogue,* and to *Oxford English Dictionary* supplements.

SIDELIGHTS: Laski's background is as varied as her writings. She grew up influenced by the religious views of her grandfather, Dr. Moses Gaster, the chief rabbi of the Portuguese and Spanish Jews in England, and by the political views of her uncle, Harold Laski, the renowned English liberal. Later she studied fashion design and philological research before deciding on a career in journalism. Laski also held jobs in publishing, dairy farming, nursing, and intelligence, and has worked in radio and television broadcasting. She turned to writing books only after the birth of her second child.

Several of Laski's early novels were set in the realm of fantasy. *Love on the Supertax,* for example, is a science fiction account of an England transformed by war. In *Toasted English,* Laski created a mock utopia in which the caste system is revived in England. The *Atlantic Monthly*'s C. J. Rolo praised the book as "a scorching indictment of a hierarchical society" and observed that the "blandly devastating satire will especially regale those well versed in the mores of Miss Laski's natives." Emmet Dedmon of the *Chicago Sun* added that the satire Laski achieved in *Toasted English* is "in the tradition of Jonathan Swift, that is to say literate, enjoyable and with a purpose."

Laski moved from satire to terror in *The Victorian Chaise-Longue,* a suspense novel about a nightmare in which a woman falls asleep on an antique chaise and finds herself metamorphosed into the longue's original owner, a Victorian lady dying of consumption. *Saturday Review*'s Robert Minton said, "Despite shaky foundations Miss Laski's story holds up to the end because she has succeeded in creating a mood of somber despair." J. H. Jackson of the *San Francisco Chronicle* concurred, stating, "If ever there was a tour-de-force of its kind, this is one. It's a little jewel of horror, and not to be missed."

Laski again explored the difficulties of class consciousness in *The Village,* a humorous novel in which two young lovers from different social strata contend with the snobbery of their parents. *Catholic World* critic Riley Hughes judged the book "a most perceptive comedy of manners in the English tradition" and said that "it delineates . . . the quiet but implacable social revolution which is now taking place within that tradition."

Laski's first serious novel, *Little Boy Lost,* set against the bleak background of post-World War II France, tells about a father's search for his missing son. "*Little Boy Lost,*" said *Spectator*'s Sylvia Norman, "has a simplicity like that of the Blake poem—less naive than ultimate. . . . Character, action and atmosphere are as one here." Critic Mary Ross of the *New York Herald Tribune Book Review* pronounced the novel "a distinguished as well as an extremely appealing book." In 1953 a motion picture adaption of the novel, starring Bing Crosby, was released by Paramount.

Laski also writes books of biographical criticism. Her first, *Mrs. Ewing, Mrs. Molesworth and Mrs. Hodgson Burnett,* is a study of three Victorian writers of children's books. The volume traces the lives and careers of the authors as well as the tradition of children's literature. Although Laski was known primarily as a writer of fiction, the publication of *Jane Austen and Her World* led critics to regard her as a capable biographer as well as a skillful novelist. A *Christian Science Monitor* critic judged the book "a worth-while addition to Janeite literature" and a "valuable introduction" to the novelist. And a reviewer in *New Yorker* commented that, in view of the little that is known about Austen, Laski's book "brings the first fully enduring English novelist into a reasonably satisfactory focus." Laski also wrote *George Eliot and Her World,* a biography of the nineteenth-century novelist Mary Ann Evans, better known as George Eliot.

In her most recent book, *Everyday Ecstasy,* Laski explores ways in which intense human experiences are triggered, how they affect society, and how they can be used to "maximize happiness." Critic Mary Warnock of the *Times Literary Supplement* complained that Laski's arguments are "sometimes hard to follow" and that her literary style lacks the "gentleness and subtlety" that the subject deserves.

BIOGRAPHICAL/CRITICAL SOURCES: San Francisco Chronicle, April 26, 1949, June 16, 1954; *Chicago Sun,* April 27, 1949; *New Yorker,* April 30, 1949, December 24, 1949, August 1, 1977; *New York Herald Tribune Book Review,* May 1, 1949, December 18, 1949, January 20, 1952, June 15, 1952, June 13, 1954; *New York Times Book Review,* May 1, 1949, June 1, 1952; *Christian Science Monitor,* May 5, 1949, December 21, 1949, November 28, 1969; *Atlantic Monthly,* May, 1949, July, 1952; *Saturday Review,* June 4, 1949, December 31, 1949, March 29, 1952, July 19, 1952, August 14, 1954, August 4, 1962, November 8, 1969.

Times Literary Supplement, September 23, 1949, February 1, 1952, November 6, 1953, November 24, 1961, August 28, 1969, June 29, 1973; June 6, 1980; *Spectator,* September 30, 1949, February 1, 1952, November 17, 1961; *New York Times,* December 11, 1949, June 13, 1954, April 26, 1978; *Catholic World,* September, 1952; *Manchester Guardian,* October 23, 1953; *New Statesman and Nation,* December 5, 1953, November 17, 1961; Anthony Bloom, *God and Man,* Darton, Longman & Todd, 1971.*

*   *   *

LAVOND, Paul Dennis
See KORNBLUTH, C(yril) M.

*   *   *

LAW, Richard   1901-1980

OBITUARY NOTICE: Born February 27, 1901, in Helensburgh, Scotland; died November 15, 1980, in London, England. Politician and author. In 1931 Law began his political career as a member of British Parliament, establishing a reputation as one of the new leaders of the Conservative party. His opposition to Chamberlain's appeasement policy in dealing with German militancy helped precipitate the ousting of the Chamberlain government and the formation of an all-party coalition headed by Winston Churchill, in which Law held several posts. In late 1943 he was appointed minister of state. After the war Law also served as minister of education under Churchill until 1945. In 1954 he was made the first Baron Coleraine of Haltemprice and seated in the House of Lords. There he served on a number of committees and councils. Law wrote three books, including *For Conservatives Only,* a discussion of his conservative beliefs. Obituaries and other sources: *Who's Who,* 126th edition, St. Martin's, 1974; *The Annual Obituary 1980,* St. Martin's, 1981.

LAWLER, Donald L(ester)   1935-

PERSONAL: Born March 19, 1935, in New York, N.Y.; son of Lester V. (an engineer) and Anne (a teacher; maiden name, Baumann) Lawler; married Therese Polard (a professor of nursing), August 24, 1957; children: John Michael, Stephen Jude, Amy Christine, James Vincent. *Education:* Georgetown University, B.S., 1956; Columbia University, A.M., 1957; University of Chicago, Ph.D., 1969. *Politics:* Democrat. *Religion:* Roman Catholic. *Home:* 109 Cheshire Dr., Greenville, N.C. 27834. *Office:* Department of English, East Carolina University, Greenville, N.C. 27834.

CAREER: St. Procopius College, Lisle, Ill., instructor in English, 1960-64; Loyola University, Chicago, Ill., instructor in English, 1964-68; East Carolina University, Greenville, N.C., assistant professor, 1968-72, associate professor, 1972-78, professor of English, 1978—. Amateur Athletic Union swim official, 1974—. *Military service:* U.S. Army, 1957-58. *Member:* Modern Language Association of America, Science Fiction Research Association, Victorians Institute (vice-president, 1980—), Society for the Preservation and Encouragement of Barber Shop Quartet Singing in America (local president, 1978-81), South Atlantic Modern Language Association, Greenville Swim Club (president, 1974-75), Brook Valley Home Owners Association (president, 1972-74).

WRITINGS: (With Jerome Klinkowitz) *Vonnegut in America,* Delacorte, 1977; *Approaches to Science Fiction,* Houghton, 1978; (consulting and contributing editor) *Survey of Science Fiction,* five volumes, edited by Frank Magill, Salem Press, 1979; (editor) *Oscar Wilde: The Picture of Dorian Gray* (critical edition), Norton, 1982; (consulting and contributing editor) *Survey of Modern Fantasy,* four volumes, Salem Press, in press.

WORK IN PROGRESS: The Alfred Handbook, publication by Alfred Publishing expected in 1984; research on Wilde, Darwinism, fantasy theory and criticism, and brain physiology.

SIDELIGHTS: Lawler commented: "The need to pay for my children's education has been motivation enough for my writing. The Vonnegut book grew out of a delightful Modern Language Association of America seminar on science fiction in 1975. *Approaches to Science Fiction* evolved from a science fiction course, but the inspiration came from an editor I met at a 1976 meeting of the South Atlantic Modern Language Association. The book on *Dorian Gray* is purely scholarly, done for love of the subject.

"Most of my inspiration develops out of thinking and reading in many areas. Application of the subconscious to problems always brings results, but not always on demand."

AVOCATIONAL INTERESTS: Running, singing, game design.

*   *   *

LAWRENCE, Robert   1912(?)-1981

OBITUARY NOTICE: Born c. 1912, in New York, N.Y.; died of a brain tumor August 9, 1981, in New York, N.Y. Conductor, musicologist, and author. Lawrence's career encompassed many aspects of the music world, from intermission broadcasts at the Metropolitan Opera to wartime troop entertainment in Italy. An indefatigable champion of French opera, especially the works of Massenet, Lawrence realized a major ambition with the 1962 formation of the Friends of French Opera. *Rage for Opera: Its Anatomy as Drawn From Life* is noted among his several books. He also contributed to publications, including *Saturday Review* and the *New York Times,* and was working on *The Great French Operas—and the Famous* at the time of his death. Obituaries and other sources: *New York Times,* August 11, 1981.

*   *   *

LAY, Nancy Duke S. 1938-

PERSONAL: Born January 26, 1938, in the Philippines; daughter of Duke S. (in business) and Cheong Choy (Ping) Lay. *Education:* Columbia University, Ed.D., 1971. *Religion:* Roman Catholic. *Home:* 100 La Salle St., No. 12 B, New York, N.Y. 10027. *Office:* Department of English, City College of the City University of New York, Convent Ave. & 138th St., New York, N.Y. 10031.

CAREER: New School for Social Research, New York City, instructor in foreign languages, 1967; Japan-America Institute, New York City, instructor in English as a foreign language, 1967-70; City College of the City University of New York, New York City, assistant professor of English, 1970—, coordinator of English as a second language, 1973-78. Coordinator of English as a second language at Cooperative College Center of the State University of New York and initiator of Chinatown Planning Council's English Language Center, both 1970; member of national advisory council of Asian American Assembly for Policy Research, 1978; delegate to World Congress on Reading, Singapore, 1976.

MEMBER: Teachers of English to Speakers of Other Languages, Modern Language Association of America, National Association of Foreign Student Affairs, Chinese Language Teachers Association, National Council of Teachers of English, New York Academy of Science, New York State English to Speakers of Other Languages and Bilingual Educators Association (chairperson of special interest group on English as a second language in higher education, 1979-80), City University of New York English as a Second Language Coordinators (president of council, 1979-80). *Awards, honors:* Scholar of Altrusa International Foundation, 1968.

WRITINGS: (With Doris Fassler) *Encounter With a New World,* Prentice-Hall, 1979; *Say It in Chinese,* Dover, 1980; *Vocabulary-Structure Network,* Holt, 1982. Contributor to academic journals. Member of editorial board of *Journal of Basic Writing,* 1972—.

SIDELIGHTS: Nancy Lay's languages include Chinese (Cantonese, Mandarin, and Fookien), Spanish, and Filipino.

*   *   *

LAZERE, Donald 1935-

PERSONAL: Born December 2, 1935, in Sioux City, Iowa. *Education:* Attended Brown University, 1954-55; Northwestern University, B.A., 1958; University of Paris, Diplome des Etudes Francaises Litteraires, 1963; Columbia University, M.A., 1964; University of California, Berkeley, Ph.D., 1973. *Office:* Department of English, California Polytechnic State University, San Luis Obispo, Calif. 93407.

CAREER: New York Times, New York City, editorial assistant for Sunday edition, 1958-59; *New York Post,* New York City, reporter (covering theatre) and editorial assistant, 1959-61; University of California, Berkeley, instructor in English, 1965-74, chairman of California Conference on Public Doublespeak, 1974; San Jose State University, San Jose, Calif., lecturer in English, 1974-76; California Polytechnic State University, San

Luis Obispo, associate professor of English, 1977—. Instructor at Hayward State University, 1965-74; research associate at Center for the Humanities, University of Southern California, 1980-81. Editor for Center for the Study of Democratic Institutions, 1967-68. Public speaker; conducts workshops. *Member:* National Council of Teachers of English. *Awards, honors:* Fellow of National Endowment for the Humanities, 1980-81.

WRITINGS: The Unique Creation of Albert Camus, Yale University Press, 1973. Contributor to *Sartre,* 1981, and editor of *Mass Media and Political Consciousness,* University of California Press. Contributor of articles and reviews to literature and language journals, popular magazines, including *Nation,* and newspapers. Advisory editor of *Praxis.*

WORK IN PROGRESS: Critical Reading, Writing, and Thinking, a textbook; *Composition, the Humanities, and Civic Literacy,* a monograph.

SIDELIGHTS: Lazere commented: "The single principle underlying virtually all of my writing and teaching is the need for literary intellectuals and scholars today to direct their efforts to fostering critical public consciousness toward the rhetoric and semantics of political propaganda and ideology, mass news and entertainment media. My two main literary mentors in developing this position have been Albert Camus and George Orwell."

*   *   *

LECHLITNER, Ruth N. 1901-

PERSONAL: Born March 27, 1901, in Elkhart, Ind.; daughter of Martin (a builder) and Jessie (Wier) James; children: Anne Margaret. *Education:* University of Michigan, A.B., 1923; University of Iowa, M.A., 1926. *Politics:* Democrat. *Religion:* None.

CAREER: Writer.

WRITINGS: A Changing Season: Selections and New Poems, 1962-1972, Branden Press, 1973.

*   *   *

LEE, Virginia 1905(?)-1981

OBITUARY NOTICE: Born c. 1905, in Shanghai, China; died October 16, 1981, in New York, N.Y. Culinary expert, teacher, and author. Despite having had no formal training in the field, Lee was recognized as a master of Chinese cooking soon after immigrating to the United States in 1967. Attention to authenticity and discipline marked her style, and among her devoted students was Craig Claiborne, with whom she collaborated on *The Chinese Cookbook.* Obituaries and other sources: *New York Times,* October 19, 1981.

*   *   *

LEESON, R. A.
See LEESON, Robert (Arthur)

*   *   *

LEESON, Robert (Arthur) 1928-
(R. A. Leeson)

PERSONAL: Born March 31, 1928, in Barnton, Cheshire, England; son of William George (a chemical worker) and Nellie Louisa (a domestic servant; maiden name, Tester) Leeson; married Gunvor Hagen (a teacher, biologist, and geologist), May 25, 1954; children: Frederick Alan, Christine Ann. *Education:*

University of London, B.A. (with honors), 1972. *Home:* 18 McKenzie Rd., Broxbourne, Hertfordshire, England.

CAREER: Worked on local newspapers and magazines in England and Europe, 1944-56; *Morning Star,* London, England, reporter, 1956-58, Parliamentary correspondent, 1958-61, feature writer, 1961-69, literary editor, 1961-80, children's editor, 1969—; free-lance writer and editor, 1969—. Founding member of Other Award Panel, 1975—. Member of British section of the International Board on Books for Young People (treasurer, 1979—). *Military service:* British Army, 1946-48; served in Egypt. *Member:* National Union of Journalists, Writers Guild.

WRITINGS: (Under name R. A. Leeson) *United We Stand: An Illustrated Account of Trade Union Emblems,* Adams & Dart, 1971; (under name R. A. Leeson) *Strike: A Live History, 1887-1971,* Allen & Unwin, 1973; *Children's Books and Class Society: Past and Present,* edited by Children's Rights Workshop, Writers and Readers Publishing Cooperative, 1977; (under name R. A. Leeson) *Travelling Brothers: The Six Centuries Road From Craft Fellowship to Trade Unionism,* Allen & Unwin, 1978.

For children; fiction, except as noted: *Beyond the Dragon Prow* (illustrated by Ian Ribbons), Collins, 1973; *Maroon Boy* (illustrated by Michael Jackson), Collins, 1974; *Bess* (illustrated by Christine Nolan), Collins, 1975; *The Third Class Genie,* Collins, 1975; *The Demon Bike Rider* (illustrated by Jim Russell), Collins, 1976; *The White Horse,* Collins, 1977; *Challenge in the Dark* (illustrated by Russell), Collins, 1978; *The Cimaroons* (nonfiction), Collins, 1978; *Silver's Revenge,* Collins, 1978, Philomel, 1979; *Grange Hill Rules, O.K.?,* BBC Publications, 1980; *Harold and Bella, Jammy and Me* (short stories), Fontana Books, 1980; *It's My Life,* Collins, 1980; *Grange Hill Goes Wild,* Fontana Books, 1980; *Grange Hill for Sale,* Fontana Books, 1981.

WORK IN PROGRESS: A volume of essays on the world of children's literature; a novel for teenage readers.

SIDELIGHTS: "My main concern in all fields of writing, both for adults and children," Leeson told *CA,* "is the relative failure of all branches of literature to reflect the vitality, variety, and importance of working class life. Thus, my books for adults deal with so far unexplored aspects of the history of working people, such as traveling craftsmen. My historical novels for children explore such areas as the Puritan side of Elizabethan and Stuart history, or the exploits of groups like the Cimaroons or escaped slaves. My children's books with a contemporary setting center on the lives of those at day school rather than the traditional boarding school of most school literature.

"Along with concern about the alienation of literature from the potential reader goes a concern with the isolation of the writer. I do a good deal of work in schools, helping children develop their own creative writing style and conducting storytelling sessions for children and adults in libraries, schools, and community centers.

"My method of writing falls into three stages. The first is a long period, perhaps months or years, in which an original idea matures and takes shape. This is followed by a shorter period of perhaps two or three months in which the plot structure is developed. The final writing period is as short as possible, sometimes no more than ten days. The writing begins when the story is so fully formed it *demands* to be told. A good deal of the writing, in fact, has been tried out orally through storytelling before it is set down in its final form."

AVOCATIONAL INTERESTS: Music, walking, gardening.

LEFF, Arthur A(llen) 1935-1981

OBITUARY NOTICE: Born January 6, 1935, in New York, N.Y.; died of cancer, November 2, 1981, in New Haven, Conn. Educator and author. Quoting Shakespeare and drawing analogies from Homer and the Bible, Neff brought an element of dynamism to his teaching that delighted students and drew praise from his superiors. Following graduation from Harvard Law School and five years in the private sector, he taught first at Washington University and then at the Yale Law School, where Dean Harry H. Wellington described him as "one of the best law teachers in America." Leff wrote *Swindling and Selling* in addition to numerous articles, and was working on a legal dictionary at the time of his death. Obituaries and other sources: *Directory of American Scholars,* 7th edition, Bowker, 1978; *Who's Who in American Law,* 2nd edition, Marquis, 1979; *New York Times,* November 4, 1981.

* * *

LEGH, Kathleen Louise Wood
See WOOD-LEGH, Kathleen Louise

* * *

LEHNING, James R(obert) 1947-

PERSONAL: Born August 2, 1947, in Washington, D.C.; son of Thomas Christopher (an electrical engineer) and Eileen (a teacher; maiden name, Sullivan) Lehning; married Joan Mower (a mortgage banker), March 18, 1972; children: Amanda, Charles. *Education:* La Salle College, B.A. (cum laude), 1969; Northwestern University, M.A., 1970, Ph.D., 1977. *Residence:* Salt Lake City, Utah. *Office:* Department of History, University of Utah, Salt Lake City, Utah 84112.

CAREER: Philadelphia Housing Development Corp., Philadelphia, Pa., administrative assistant, 1970-72; University of Pennsylvania, Philadelphia, research associate at Population Studies Center, 1977; University of Utah, Salt Lake City, assistant professor of history, 1978—, fellow of Center for Historical Population Studies. Managing editor of *Peasant Studies.* Member of board of directors of Germantown Homes, Inc., 1971-72. *Member:* American Historical Association, Social Science History Association, Centre d'Histoire Economique et Sociale de la Region Lyonnaise. *Awards, honors:* Woodrow Wilson fellow, 1969; fellow of National Institutes of Health Research and Training, 1977; grant from American Council of Learned Societies, 1981.

WRITINGS: The Peasants of Marlhes, University of North Carolina Press, 1980.

WORK IN PROGRESS: Popular Mentality and Economic Development in Nineteenth-Century France: A Regional Study, completion expected in 1984.

SIDELIGHTS: Lehning described his research emphasis as "an interdisciplinary approach to historical studies, especially utilizing the insights gained from demographic and anthropological studies."

* * *

LEM, Stanislaw 1921-

PERSONAL: Born September 12, 1921, in Lvov, Poland; son of a physician; married wife, Barbara (a roentgenologist), August, 1953; children: Tomek (son). *Education:* Studied medicine in Lvov, Poland, 1939-41, 1944-46, and in Krakow, Poland, 1946-48. *Home:* Ul. Narwik 21, 30-436, Krakow, Poland. *Agent:* Franz Rottensteiner, Marchettigasse 9/17, A-1060 Vienna, Austria.

CAREER: Worked as garage mechanic during World War II; Jagellonian University, Krakow, Poland, assistant in "Science Circle," 1947-49; *Zycie Nauki* (monthly magazine; title means "The Life of Science"), editor, 1947-49; writer, 1949—. Teacher at University of Krakow. *Member:* Polish Astronautical Society (co-founder), Polish Cybernetics Association. *Awards, honors:* Received recognition from Polish Ministry of Culutre, 1965 and 1973; Polish State Prize for literature, 1976.

WRITINGS—In English translation; all science fiction, except as noted: *Dzienniki gwiazdowe,* Iskry, 1957, translation by Michael Kandel published as *The Star Diaries,* illustrated by author, Seabury, 1976; *Sledztwo* (detective novel), Ministerstwa Obrony Narodowej, 1959, translation by Adele Milch published as *The Investigation,* Seabury, 1974; *Solaris,* Ministerstwa Obrony Narodowej, 1961, French translation by Jean-Michel Jasiensko published as *Solaris,* Denoel, 1966, translation from the French edition by Joanna Kilmartin and Steve Cox published as *Solaris,* Walker & Co., 1970; *Pamietnik znaleziony w wannie,* Literackie, 1961, translation by Kandel and Christine Rose published as *Memoirs Found in a Bathtub,* Seabury, 1973; *Powrot z gwiazd,* Czytelnik, 1961, translation by Barbara Marszal and Frank Simpson published as *Return From the Stars,* Harcourt, 1980.

Neizwyciezony i inne opowiadania, Ministerstwa Obrony Narodowej, 1964, German translation by Roswitha Dietrich published as *Der Unbesiegbare,* Verlag Volk und Welt, 1967, translation from the German edition by Wendayne Ackerman published as *The Invincible,* Seabury, 1973; *Bajki robotw* (title means "Fables for Robots"), Literackie, 1964, translation by Kandel published in *Mortal Engines* (a compilation containing portions of *Dzienniki gwiazdowe* [see above] and *Maska* [see below]), Seabury, 1977; *Cyberiada,* Literackie, 1965, translation by Kandel published as *The Cyberiad: Fables for the Cybernetic Age,* Seabury, 1974; *Opowiesci o pilocie Pirxie,* Literackie, 1968, translation by Louis Iribarne published as *Tales of Pirx the Pilot,* Harcourt, 1979; *Bezsennosc* (title means "Insomnia"), Literackie, 1971, portions translated by Kandel and published as *The Futurological Congress (From the Memoirs of Ijon Tichy),* Seabury, 1974; *Doskonala proznia,* Czytelnik, 1971, translation by Kandel published as *A Perfect Vacuum,* Harcourt, 1979; *Katar,* Wydawnictwo Literackie, 1976, translation by Iribarne published as *The Chain of Chance,* Harcourt, 1978; *The Cosmic Carnival of Stanislaw Lem* (reader), edited by Kandel, Continuum, 1981; *More Tales of Pirx the Pilot,* translated by Iribarne, Harcourt, 1981.

In Polish: *Astronauci* (title means "The Astronauts"), Czytelnik, 1951; *Sezam i inne opowiadania* (title means "Sesame and Other Stories"), Iskry, 1954; *Oblok Magellana* (title means "The Magellan Nebula"), Iskry, 1955; *Dialogi* (nonfiction; title means "Dialogues"), Literackie, 1957; *Czas nieutracony* (novel; title means "Time Not Lost"), Volume I: *Szpital przemienienia* (title means "Hospital of the Blessed"), Volume II: *Wsrod umarlych* (title means "Among the Dead"), Volume III: *Powrot* (title means "Return"), Literackie, 1957; *Eden,* Iskry, 1959; *Inwazja z Aldebarana* (title means "Invasion From Aldebaran"), Literackie, 1959.

All published by Literackie, except as noted: *Ksiega robotow* (title means "Book of Robots"), Iskry, 1961; *Wejscie na orbite* (nonfiction; title means "Getting Into Orbit"), 1962; *Noc ksiezycowa* (title means "Lunar Night"), 1963; *Summa technologiae* (nonfiction), 1964; *Polowanie* (title means "The Hunt"), 1965; *Wysoki zamek* (title means "The High Castle"), Ministerstwa Obrony Narodowej, 1966; *Ratujmy kosmos i inne opowiadania* (title means "Let Us Save the Cosmos and Other Stories"), 1966; *Glos pana* (title means "His Master's Voice"), Czytelnik, 1968; *Filozofia przypadku: Literatura w swietle smpirii* (nonfiction; title means "The Philosophy of Chance: Literature Considered Empirically"), 1968; *Opowiadania* (title means "Stories"), 1969; *Fantastyka i futurologia* (nonfiction; title means "Science Fiction and Futurology"), 1970; *Wielkosc urojona* (title means "Imaginary Magnitude"), Czytelnik, 1973; *Opowiadania wybrane* (title means "Selected Stories"), 1973; *Rozprawy i szkice* (title means "Essays and Sketches"), 1975; *Maska* (title means "The Mask"), Wydawnictwo Literackie, 1976; *Suplement* (title means "Supplement"), Wydawnictwo Literackie, 1976; *Powtorka* (title means "Repetition"), Iskry, 1979; *Golem XIV,* Wydawnictwo Literackie, 1981.

Plays: (With Roman Hussarski) *Jacht Paradise,* Czytelnik, 1951. Also author of teleplay "Maska," and screenplay "Przekledaniec" (title means "Roly Poly"), released by Film Polski.

Work represented in *Science Fiction: A Collection of Critical Essays,* edited by Mark Rose, Prentice-Hall, 1976, and *The Mind's Eye: Fantasies and Reflections on Self and Soul,* edited by Douglas C. Hoftstadter and Daniel C. Dennett, Basic Books, 1981.

Contributor to magazines, including *New Yorker.*

WORK IN PROGRESS: A novel, *Wizja Lokalna* (title means "Local Conditions"), publication expected in 1982; another Ijon Tichy novel; another Pirx story.

SIDELIGHTS: While Lem is considered by critics to be "the Titan of East European science fiction," Darko Suvin, the author of the afterword of *Solaris,* more elaborately named him "the fourth great pillar of global [science fiction] since World War II," the other such pillars being American, Russian, and English science fiction. Worldwide, Lem is a best-selling author with works translated into more than thirty languages, the sale of which tops the ten million mark. In the United States, however, Lem remains relatively little known and read. Although the author has been writing since the early 1950's, his numerous books only began to appear in English translation in the early 1970's. Thus, works finished several years prior to publication in English are often mistaken as newly written. George Zebrowski explained in the *Magazine of Fantasy and Science Fiction* that "the cultural-language lag makes him seem a new writer."

Lem, however, has been working long enough to establish himself, noted Suvin, as a "cultural phenomenon unto himself." "He is a man of vast and pyrotechnic intellect who has read everything and forgotten nothing," added Bud Foote in the *Detroit News.* As such, Lem's versatility and style have generated much comment. "Lem transcends the hackneyed conventions of sf," Reuel K. Wilson of *World Literature Today* maintained. "He felicitously combines erudition with suspense, verbal inventiveness with narrative skills, social conscience with a satiric wit and a marvelous gift for grotesque parody." Foote quipped that Lem "is Harpo Marx and Franz Kafka and Isaac Asimov rolled up into one and down the white rabbit's hole."

His sense of humor has elicited the adjectives "zany," "tremendously amusing," and "fantastically humorous," and yet Lem colors his writing with a strong cynicism. "I myself find him a master of utterly terminal pessimism, appalled by all that an insane humanity may yet survive to do," confessed

Kurt Vonnegut in *Nation*. Comparing Lem to Mark Twain, the reviewer postulated "that most of our finest humorists . . . may have been not especially funny people who painstakingly learned their clowning only in order to seem insincere when speaking dismally of the future of mankind." "So I will guess," continued Vonnegut, "that [Lem] . . . is at his funniest when he has looked so hard and long at hopelessness that he is at last exhausted, and is seized by convulsions of laughter that threaten to tear him to pieces." Theodore Solotaroff agreed in the *New York Times Book Review:* "If there is any dominant emotional coloring to Lem's vision it is the dark surreal comedy that has flourished in this century in Eastern Europe, the principal charnel house and social laboratory of the modern age."

Consequently, Lem commonly examines such subjects as the relationship between man and machine and the inability of man to cope with the runaway technology he has created. Wilson clarified that while Lem "believes that modern technology is important and necessary . . . he manifests a humanist's preoccupation with ethical questions. He portrays with irony man's stubborn and arrogant compulsion to subjugate his fellows and the infinite universe around him, yet he clearly admires the very qualities—inventiveness, will and determination—which impel men to compete with each other and with the forces of nature." Solotaroff similarly noted that Lem often raises the questions of whether "a perversion of humanity [would be] produced by the further evolution of computer technology. Or is this evolution being perverted by the uses to which human folly put it?" "And beyond this," continued Solotaroff, "lies the further problem that humanity and technology are locked into a symbiotic relationship that progressively amplifies its consequences of good and evil." Lem confronts "his heroes with the absurd, the grotesque, and the unknown," noted Wilson, in order to stress "human limitations and fallibility."

Lem's novel *Solaris* illustrates man's inadequacies in a totally alien environment. The account of a scientific expedition sent to study a huge, thinking ocean on the planet Solaris, the novel intricately describes the paranoia and fear of the unknown to which the researchers succumb. In a man-made station hovering above the sea, the men try to understand the intelligent but inscrutable liquid mass. Composed of an unknown element, the ocean spews into the atmosphere complicated patterns that rapidly dissolve. Like their predecessors, the scientists are unable to communicate with the being, and one frustrated man bombards the sea with nuclear radiation in violation of international law. The ocean responds by materializing a woman for one of the researchers. Drawn from the man's memory, the creature is an image of the woman towards whom he feels most guilty. Hence, the novel becomes a study of man's inability to comprehend the nature of vastly different worlds and beings. "Lem's talent is for the sensitive and sensuously precise rendering of the mind's struggle to understand an unimaginably alien reality," expounded Donald Marshall in the *Partisan Review*. "His spacemen remain men; their equipment finally matters less than the emotions, imaginings, ideas, commitments they can muster." James Blish summarized one of Lem's contentions in the *Magazine of Fantasy and Science Fiction:* man's "knowledge does not dispell [*sic*] mystery, but increases it."

Expanding on a similar theme, *The Invincible* deals with the mission of the *Invincible* and its crew to determine what became of a previous spaceship on a strange planet. When it arrives, the ship is attacked by unthinking "cybernetic insects and war machines." The reason for the hostile reception escapes the understanding of the crew members. Zebrowski appraised that "Lem realistically shows us what it would be like to come face to face with genuine 'differentness'—an alien non-human

system or being which is beyond our understanding." Realizing that these creatures destroyed the earlier ship, the *Invincible*'s crew determines to combat the strange form of life. However, one officer discovers that "there was nothing to gain through fighting, except the stimulation of an absurdly mindless force." Zebrowski concluded that "the crew of the *Invincible* could do no more than systematically destroy the planet's animations, and to no purpose except the self-satisfaction of revenge and the meaningless exercise of power. We go out into the universe only to meet ourselves and fight with ourselves."

In another work, *Memoirs Found in a Bathtub,* Lem concerns himself with the twisted workings of an espionage system in the future. A mixture of genres, the book, conceded Solotaroff, could be read several ways: "as a spy novel that takes its conventional involutions to absurdity, as a cold war satire, or as another Lemian experiment with his mobius strip of randomness and design." *Memoirs* chronicles the efforts of a nameless spy to discover his mission in Pentagon III, a building housing a vast security system. Pentagon III "is controlled," explained Solotaroff, "by a supremely complicated 'brain,' but one whose conduits of control—orders, tactics, codes, chains of command, etc.—are riddled with paranoid subterfuges to guard its secrets from an enemy that may, in fact, no longer exist." Wilson regarded "this absurdist tragicomedy" as "a timely satire on militarism."

A later book, *The Cyberiad,* is a collection of space-age fables in which robots are refined to the point that they seem human. Machines, robots, and their creators are the heroes of these stories, "with feats of engineering and computer science as their plots," stated Marshall. Written, Wilson noted, with "fantastic wit," *The Cyberiad* displays Lem's impressive command of language. Wilson observed that the author "coins hundreds of grotesque neologisms and nonsense words" while Lem's English translator Michael Kandel reflected that "a thorough study of Lem's wordplay could easily provide material enough for a dissertation or full-length book." Kandel elaborated: "Macaronisms, archaisms, alliteration, rhythm, and stylizations—including scientific lingo, legal jargon, philosophical terminology, bureaucratese, Biblical prose, nursery rhymes and Slavic fairy-tales, underworld slang and dialects, and proper names, and the subtle degrees of nonsense—these might be some of the topics." Dealing with the book's thematic content, George J. Maciuszko of *Books Abroad* assessed that "the author is deeply concerned with things human such as human happiness or the purpose of life, and he skillfully and discreetly points out that a strictly technical progress leads our humanity ad absurdum. The flight of Lem's imagination is breathtaking. At times a reader may become frightened at the realization that whatever is within the limits of our human imagination may also be within the limits of probability."

In *Mortal Engines* Lem advances a view that "humanity [is] not . . . a matter of organic life or biological development," explained Michael Wood in the *New York Review of Books*. Robots and machines are portrayed in many ways as superior to human beings. Apart from their mechanical substantiality, which prompts one machine to describe a human as "a curd that moves for a time—a thinking cheese—the tragic product of a dairy accident, a walking slop," robots possess a humanity humans often lack. *Mortal Engines* contains "several stories," Wood maintained, "which insist on the shiftiness, vengefulness, and general nastiness of human beings." Lem contends that while robots have a "natural decency, only man can be a bastard."

Leaving the subjects of men, robots, and technology, Lem turned to literary criticism in *A Perfect Vacuum*. A collection of reviews of sixteen imaginary books, *A Perfect Vacuum* is an effort to create an art capable of existing independently of anything external, including its maker. Joyce Carol Oates clarified Lem's intention in the *New York Times Book Review:* "The artist is willfully and ingeniously refined out of existence, as [James] Joyce never was, so that the perfect art would be art in a vacuum—a *perfect* vacuum—not only self-referential but lacking a self to which to refer." The nonexistent stories with titles such as "Pericalypsis," "Gigamesh," "Sexplosion," "Odysseus of Ithaca," and "Toi," are reviewed from "the various demented perspectives," observed John Leonard in the *New York Times,* "of the New Critic, the structuralist, the terrorist, the metaphysician, the assistant professor of gerunds and the twit." Many reviewers found the book flawed. "A dull brilliance flickers occasionally within these pages," remarked Peter S. Prescott in *Newsweek,* "but on the whole this is a punishingly tedious exercise, in part because the books Lem 'reviews' truly deserve not to be published, and in part because the reviewer's voice he has assumed is so dusty: he has failed to establish an effective distance between the nonsense of his subjects and the nonsense of his 'critical approach.'" Oates reflected that "Lem draws out each of his jokes laboriously, so that the reader, forced to read synopses of fatuous books, wonders (as readers of reviews assuredly should not) whether it might be easier to read the books themselves."

Critics agree, though, that whatever subject Lem chooses to write about, he does so with a thoroughness of description and knowledge. Gerald Jonas of the *New York Times Book Review* ventured that the author "lays on the technological details so heavily that one is tempted to call the result not science fiction but 'engineering fiction.'" Solotaroff agreed that Lem's "situations come across with a rigor and complexity of description and conjecture that make them seem as if they were developed at Princeton's Institute for Advanced Studies." The reviewer continued: "The clarity and richness of detail pervades Lem's accounts of . . . [his] far-fetched worlds, so that they become in time just as credible and coherent in their strangeness as, say, Thomas Mann's biblical Egypt or Nabokov's Terra."

MEDIA ADAPTATIONS: Solaris was made into the motion picture "Solaris," which was released by Mosfilm in 1972.

BIOGRAPHICAL/CRITICAL SOURCES: Magazine of Fantasy and Science Fiction, May, 1971, July, 1974, July, 1979; *Books Abroad,* spring, 1975; *New York Times Book Review,* August 29, 1976, February 11, 1979, February 17, 1980; *Partisan Review,* summer, 1976; *New York Review of Books,* May 12, 1977; *World Literature Today,* autumn, 1977, summer, 1978, winter, 1980; *New Republic,* November 26, 1977; *Contemporary Literary Criticism,* Gale, Volume 8, 1978, Volume 15, 1980; *Nation,* May 13, 1978; *Time,* January 29, 1979; *New York Times,* February 9, 1979; *New Yorker,* February 26, 1979; *Newsweek,* February 26, 1979, June 30, 1980; *Detroit News,* April 8, 1979; *New Statesman,* June 1, 1979; *Science Fiction and Fantasy Book Review,* June 5, 1979; *Times Literary Supplement,* November 7, 1980.

[Sketch verified by agent, Franz Rottensteiner]

—*Sketch by Anne M. Guerrini*

*   *   *

LEMBECK, Ruth (Louise) 1919-

PERSONAL: Born March 29, 1919, in Philadelphia, Pa.; daughter of Max E. (a businessman and writer) and Emma K. (an artist; maiden name, Cerf) Berkowitz; married John J. Lembeck, February 26, 1950 (died April 12, 1976); children:

James Martin, Peter William. *Education:* Attended Milo School of Fashion, 1938-39, New School for Social Research, 1942, and School of Visual Arts, 1979. *Home and office:* 16 Burkewood Rd., Mount Vernon, N.Y. 10552.

CAREER: Gimbels (department store), New York City, production manager, 1942; Bloomingdale's (department store), New York City, advertising copywriter, 1943-45; Macy's (department store), New York City, advertising copywriter, 1945-47; television, radio, and print writer for advertising agencies in New York City, including Doyle Dane Bernbach, Grey, McCann-Erickson, Compton, and Batten Barton Durstine & Osborn, 1947-62; free-lance writer, 1962—. *Member:* Authors Guild, Advertising Club of Westchester. *Awards, honors:* Honored by city of Mt. Vernon, N.Y., 1979, for contribution to its cultural image.

WRITINGS: "Call Me Mother" (musical comedy), first produced in Westchester at Pennington Theatre, 1964; *Three Hundred Eighty Part-Time Jobs for Women,* Dell, 1968; *Teenage Jobs,* McKay, 1971; *Job Ideas for Today's Woman* (Woman Today Book Club selection), Prentice-Hall, 1973. Author of column "Women at Work" in *Guide to Earning Extra Income,* for Ziff-Davis. Writer of educational filmstrips for Newsweek, Harcourt, and Current Affairs. Contributor of articles and poems to periodicals, including *Vista USA, National Four-H News, Scholastic News Explorer, Directions Eighty, Humpty Dumpty.*

WORK IN PROGRESS: A syndicated radio program.

SIDELIGHTS: "I segued into book writing through one of those chance and fortuitous meetings. Long a staff copywriter at the big advertising agencies, I had tired of their collective neurosis and had struck out on my own. It was while looking for free-lance copy assignments that I met a young man at an obscure little ad agency on Long Island who steered me to an editor friend at a huge publishing/printing company. That editor was on the lookout for new book ideas to keep his presses busy. I submitted a list of likely subjects, he chose one, and my first book was launched. It all seemed natural enough; both my father and grandfather were published authors. The book-writing itself has been relatively quick and easy. It's the research on such fact-based books that takes time: letters to write, telephone calls, notes to collate, waiting, often many weeks, for answers by mail. But researching also has been the fun part, meeting literally hundreds of people in dozens of different spheres of work. Many of those people are written up in the books. Nor is the subject of jobs a dull one. Far from it! Every field has its fascinations, its color. I've made a point of trying to show this, and coming up with fresh ideas for each. Yes, the books have been personally rewarding in many ways, but my poetry for children has provided the greatest thrill. Poetry is a piece of self, and having it published is an act of sharing."

BIOGRAPHICAL/CRITICAL SOURCES: Philadelphia Bulletin, March 25, 1968; *Good Housekeeping,* March, 1969; *Suffern Record* (N.Y.), May 16, 1968; *Newsday,* June 30, 1971; *New Haven Register,* April 12, 1971.

*   *   *

LEMBOURN, Hans Joergen 1923-

PERSONAL: Born March 26, 1923, in Copenhagen, Denmark; son of Edgar Collin (a government official) and Lilly (Holm) Lembourn; married Ellen Winther (an opera singer and actress), July 7, 1973; children: Maria, Thomas. *Education:* Received degree from Copenhagen School of Economics and Business Administration, 1943; University of Copenhagen, M.A., 1951. *Home:* Frederiksgade 12, 1265 Copenhagen K, Denmark. *Office:* Folketinget Christiansborg, Copenhagen, Denmark.

CAREER: Journalist and writer, 1945—; war reporter in Greece during civil war, 1947; reviewer for *Perspektiv* (magazine), 1953-63; editor at Schoenbergske Forlag (publishing company), 1954—. Teacher of economics at the evening high school and Workers' Educational Association, 1955-60. Member of Denmark Parliament, 1964-77, member of School and Education Committee, 1964-71, member of Ombudsman's Committee, Assistance to Developing Countries Committee, and Research Committee, 1968-71, member of Milieu and Culture Committee, 1972-77, delegate to United Nations General Assembly, 1969 and 1970, supervisor of Parliament Library, 1968-77. *Member:* Danish Writers' Union (acting chairman, 1971). *Awards, honors:* Henri Nathansen Birth-day Foundation Award, 1953; Fremads Jubilee Foundation Award, 1961.

WRITINGS—In English translation: *Grev Frederik; eller, Den bedste af alle verdener* (novel), Schoenbergske Forlag, 1958, translation by Evelyn Ramsden published as *The Best of All Worlds; or, What Voltaire Never Knew,* Cape, 1960, Putnam, 1961; *Fyrre dage med Marilyn* (title means "Forty Days With Marilyn"), Schoenbergske Forlag, 1977, translation published as *Diary of a Lover of Marilyn Monroe,* edited by Don Fine, Arbor House, 1979.

Other writings; published by Schoenbergske Forlag, except as noted: *Samtale om natten* (short stories and poems; title means "Dialogue at Night"), [Copenhagen], 1951, Schoenbergske Forlag, 1964; *Der kommer en dag* (novel; title means "Some Day Will Come"), Westerman, 1952; *Se dig ikke tilbage* (novel; title means "Don't Look Behind You"), Westerman, 1953; *Hvide mand: Hvad nu?* (novel; title means "White Man: What Now?"), 1955; *De intellektuelles forraederi* (essays; title means "The Treason of the Intellectuals"), 1956; *Ved daggry* (novel; title means "At Dawn"), 1956; *Enerens oproer* (title means "The Revolt of the Individualist"), 1958.

Naeste station er paradis (short stories; title means "Next Station Is Paradise"), 1960; (editor) *Gaa til modstand* (title means "Join the Resistance"), 1961; (contributor) *The Denmark Book,* Groenlunds, 1962; *For menneskets skyld* (essays; title means "For the Sake of Man"), 1962; *Hold fastere om mig* (novel; title means "Hold Me Tighter"), 1962; *Nu er det foraar* (novel; title means "Now It Is Spring"), 1963; *Umaadelige menneske* (title means "Immense Man"), 1964; (editor) *Danske forfattere om besaettelsen* (title means "Danish Writers About the Occupation"), 1966; *Een/Mange* (essays; title means "One/Many"), 1967; (editor) *Sommer* (title means "Summer"), 1967; *Aaret i nordsjaelland* (essays; title means "The Year in North Sealand"), 1968; *Balladen om Frederik, Johannes go mig* (novel; title means "The Ballad About Frederik, Johannes, and Me"), 1969.

Det korte liv, den lange doed (novel; title means "The Short Life, the Long Death"), 1970; *De afmaegtige* (novel; title means "The Powerless"), 1970; *Hvad laver du egentlig i min seng?* (novel; title means "What Are You Doing in My Bed?"), 1971; *Plant et aebletrae* (political essays; title means "Plant an Apple Tree"), 1973.

Also author of *Sandhedens forbandelse* (novel; title means "The Course of Truth"), 1950, and *Hotel Styx* (novel), 1954, [Copenhagen], 1964. Contributor to *Rapport fra Athen* (title means "Report From Athens"), 1967. Contributor to anthologies.

SIDELIGHTS: Lembourn's *Diary of a Lover of Marilyn Monroe* is the author's account of a forty-day love affair he claims to have had with the actress. One of several books written about Monroe since her suicide in 1962, *Diary of a Lover of Marilyn Monroe* examines Monroe's life as an exploited sex symbol, her addictions to alcohol and pills, and her troubled past. Raised by a schizophrenic mother, Monroe had a speech impediment, was deaf in one ear, was deserted by her father at birth, and was raped at age nine. Later, when a celebrated actress, Monroe was haunted by her childhood. She increasingly feared that she had inherited her mother's mental afflictions. She asked Lembourn, "Could I have an insanity in me that grows with age?"

Lembourn does not believe Monroe was insane. He portrays her as a sensitive, vulnerable woman searching for love but unable to handle the emotional responsibilities of love relationships. According to Lembourn, after their forty-day romance he and Monroe never met again.

The *New York Times Book Review*'s Seymour Peck felt *Diary of a Lover of Marilyn Monroe* is "clearly meant to capitalize on Mr. Lembourn's claim to intimacy with Miss Monroe. . . . Mr. Lembourn acknowledges he wrote down nothing of his conversations with the actress and then proceeds to churn up long passages of dialogue with her, all of which have the fake-sounding stiltedness of dime-novel romance. . . . The most extraordinary thing about it is that he has succeeded in making Miss Monroe . . . boring." Colman McCarthy of the *Washington Post,* on the other hand, described Lembourn's book as "worthwhile reading" that "underscores the timeless truth that a successful union between a man and woman has to do with much more than heart-felt feelings. This diary is a poignant and necessary dispiriting piece of writing."

BIOGRAPHICAL/CRITICAL SOURCES: Washington Post, April 3, 1979; *New York Times Book Review,* April 8, 1979.

*   *   *

LENBURG, Greg 1956-

PERSONAL: Born March 5, 1956, in Gary, Ind.; son of John LeRoy and Catherine (Galich) Lenburg. *Education:* Attended Fullerton College, 1974-79; California State University, Fullerton, B.A., 1981. *Residence:* Anaheim, Calif. *Agent:* Dominick Abel Literary Agency, 498 West End Ave., No. 12-C, New York, N.Y. 10024.

CAREER: Writer, 1975—. Press agent for comic Joe Besser, 1975—.

WRITINGS: (Contributor) Danny Peary, editor, *Close Ups: The Movie Star Book,* Workman Publishing, 1978; (with Jeff Lenburg and Randy Skretvedt) *Steve Martin: The Unauthorized Biography,* St. Martin's, 1980; (with J. Lenburg and Joan Howard Maurer) *The Three Stooges Scrapbook,* Citadel, 1982. Contributor to film periodicals.

SIDELIGHTS: Lenburg commented: "A successful writer must abide by three important guidelines—confidence in himself, hard work, and listening to others."

*   *   *

LENIHAN, John (Howard) 1941-

PERSONAL: Born March 11, 1941, in Seattle, Wash.; son of Howard John and Gladys (Verbrugge) Lenihan; married Ginger Vallery (a vice-president in banking), March 6, 1976; children: Erik Molvar. *Education:* Seattle University, B.A., 1963; University of Washington, Seattle, M.A., 1966; University of Maryland, Ph.D., 1976. *Office:* Department of History, Texas A & M University, College Station, Tex. 77843.

CAREER: Texas A & M University, College Station, assistant professor of history, 1977—. *Military service:* U.S. Army, 1966-68; became captain.

WRITINGS: Showdown: Confronting Modern America in the Western Film, University of Illinois Press, 1980. Contributor to *Performance.*

WORK IN PROGRESS: A book on motion pictures of the McCarthy period; research on society and culture of the 1950's.

SIDELIGHTS: Lenihan told *CA:* "Aside from the professional satisfaction of exploring a relatively uncharted field of social-cultural history, being a film historian affords the opportunity to immerse oneself in what has always been a favorite entertainment. Unfortunately, the fact that motion pictures have been principally a commercial entertainment has, until recent years, discouraged professional historians from considering them relevant to American life and thought and thus worthy of serious analysis. Yet it is precisely because of their function as entertainment that movies invariably connect with (and in turn reveal) the values and interests of the society for which they were fashioned. Westerns, for example, may distort America's frontier heritage, but they do so in accordance with beliefs and concerns of the twentieth century."

*   *   *

LEPPZER, Robert 1958-

PERSONAL: Born July 30, 1958, in Cambridge, Mass.; son of Tony (an electronics engineer) and Elizabeth (O'Neill) Leppzer. *Education:* Attended Hampshire College, 1976-78. *Home address:* P.O. Box 1008, Amherst, Mass. 01004.

CAREER: Producer of independent television and radio documentaries, 1973—, including "Wounded Knee: Roots of the Earth," National Public Radio (NPR), 1976; "The Lessons of the Vietnam War," WHSR-Radio, 1976; "Seabrook: The Environmental Movement and Nuclear Power," WMUA-Radio, 1977; "The Community Examines Nuclear Power," Center for Community Access Television, 1978; "Seabrook 1977," WGBY-TV, 1979; "A Question of Survival," Pacifica Program Service, 1979; "Solar Energy Comes Home," Energy Training and Education Center, 1980; "Early Warnings: Voices From Three Mile Island," NPR, 1980; "Rural Lives," Public Radio Cooperative, 1980; "Crisis in El Salvador: America's Next Vietnam?," Pacifica Program Service, 1981; "From This Day Forward," CollectaVision, 1981. Producer and host of "American Pie," on WHSR-FM Radio, 1973-76; co-producer and co-host of "Undercurrents," on WMUA-FM Radio, 1978-81; video editor. *Member:* Association of Independent Video and Filmmakers. *Awards, honors:* National first prize from National Public Radio's Young People's Radio Festival, 1976, for "Wounded Knee: Roots of the Earth."

WRITINGS: Voices From Three Mile Island: The People Speak Out, Crossing Press, 1980. Contributor to magazines and newspapers, including *New Roots* and *Journal for Exploratory Radio.*

WORK IN PROGRESS: Rural Lives, an oral history of rural New Englanders, publication expected in 1982.

SIDELIGHTS: Leppzer wrote: "I believe that media can be used to transform people's lives for the benefit of society. As a social documentarian, I have dedicated my life to exposing injustice wherever I see it. I want to give a louder voice to people who aren't normally heard—the victims of oppression who struggle for their own freedom and work toward building a more just society. I want to spread a message of hope that people can indeed change things by working together and having the determination to never give up."

BIOGRAPHICAL/CRITICAL SOURCES: Amherst Morning Record, March 24, 1980; *Valley Advocate,* July 15, 1981.

LESLEY, Blake
See DUCKWORTH, Leslie Blakey

*   *   *

LESTER, John
See WERNER, Vivian

*   *   *

LEVIN, William C. 1946-

PERSONAL: Born January 23, 1946, in Brooklyn, N.Y.; son of Jess L. (a manufacturer) and Ruth (a designer; maiden name, Bushel) Levin. *Education:* Boston University, B.S., 1968, M.S., 1970; Northeastern University, Ph.D., 1974. *Home:* 67 Independence St., Canton, Mass. 02021. *Office:* Bridgewater State College, Bridgewater, Mass. 02324.

CAREER: Associated with Bridgewater State College, Bridgewater, Mass. *Member:* American Sociological Association, Eastern Sociological Society, Massachusetts Sociological Society.

*WRITINGS—*With Jack Levin: *Elementary Statistics in Social Research,* Harper, 1972, 2nd edition, 1977; *Ageism: Prejudice and Discrimination Against the Elderly,* Wadsworth, 1980; *The Functions of Discrimination and Prejudice,* Harper, 1982.

WORK IN PROGRESS: A textbook on sociology concepts.

*   *   *

LEVY, Stephen 1947-

PERSONAL: Born May 11, 1947, in Brooklyn, N.Y.; son of Morris (a salesman) and Bess (Barouch) Levy; married Ellen Eichel (a dancer), March 16, 1975. *Education:* Attended Queens College of the City University of New York, 1964-67, and New School College of New School for Social Research, 1967-68. *Politics:* "Anarchist/Neolithic Conservative." *Religion:* Jewish (Sephardic). *Home:* 106 West 13th St., No. 11, New York, N.Y. 10011.

CAREER: New York City Community College, Institute of Study for Older Adults, New York City, teacher of writing and basic English, 1975—; Hospital Audiences, Inc., New York City, leader of poetry writing workshops, 1977—; 92nd Street Young Men's-Young Women's Hebrew Association, New York City, teacher of English as second language, 1978—; New York State Poets-in-the-Schools, New York City, teacher, 1978—; Jewish Welfare Board Lecture Bureau, New York City, lecturer, 1980—; writer. *Member:* Adelantre!, the Judezino Society (co-founder). *Awards, honors:* Grants from Change, Inc., 1975, and Memorial Foundation for Jewish Culture, 1978.

WRITINGS: Some Sephardic Poems (chapbook), Adelantre!, 1975; *Many Hands* (poetry chapbook), Firefly Press/Adelantre!, 1981. Work represented in anthologies, including *Voices Within the Ark: The Modern Jewish Poets,* Avon, 1980; *Gates to the New City: A Treasury of Modern Jewish Tales,* Avon, 1982. Co-editor of *Working Papers in Sephardic and Oriental Jewish Studies* and *Words of the Sephardim.* Contributor to newsletter *Ke xaber?*

WORK IN PROGRESS: Translations; research on Sephardic culture.

SIDELIGHTS: Levy told *CA:* "For years I have been trying, somewhat fitfully, to allow myself to become a better poet and a better Jew."

*   *   *

LEWIS, J. R.
See LEWIS, (John) Roy(ston)

*   *   *

LEWIS, Mort(imer) R(eis)   1908-

PERSONAL: Born June 14, 1908, in New York, N.Y.; son of Fred Mark (a salesman) and Rose (Liebermuth) Lewis; married Isabelle Buckner (in business), February 12, 1955. *Education:* Attended City College of New York (now of the City University of New York), 1925-26. *Politics:* Democrat. *Religion:* Jewish. *Home and office:* 14016 Bora Bora Way, Marina del Rey, Calif. 90291.

CAREER: Writer and lecturer. *Liberty* (magazine), New York, N.Y., in sales promotion, 1930-32; volunteer worker at Los Angeles County General Hospital, Los Angeles, Calif., 1948-51, and Shriners Hospital for Crippled Children, Los Angeles, 1967-69; instructor in basic cardiac life support for American Heart Association, 1978—, and Los Angeles Consortium, 1981—. Member of advisory council of U.S. Civil War Centennial Commission, and member of California Civil War Centennial Commission, 1960-65. *Military service:* Member of Writers and Material Committee of United Service Organizations (USO), 1942, and Writers War Board of Soldier and Sailor Shows Script Committee, 1942-45; expert consultant to Secretary of War on entertainment in armed forces, 1944-45. *Member:* Writers Guild of America, (West; chairman of "CPR Save-a-Life" Committee, 1978—), Dramatists Guild, American Civil Liberties Union (member of Radio and Television Committee, 1951-54), Lincoln Sesquicentennial Association of California (vice-president, 1959), Civil War Round Table of Southern California (president, 1957-58). *Awards, honors:* Citation from California State Senate, 1960, for contributions to Civil War Centennial; American Television Anthology Drama Award from Writers Guild of America, 1963, for "A Pair of Boots" segment of "The Lloyd Bridges Show"; Award of Distinction from United States Civil War Centennial Commission, 1965; citation from California State Senate, 1965, for contributions to Civil War Centennial; Exceptional Service Award from American Heart Association, 1980; Commendation Scroll from Los Angeles County Board of Supervisors, 1980, for cardio-pulmonary resuscitation activities; script grant from National Endowment for the Humanities, 1980; Valentine Davies Award from Writers Guild of America (West), 1982, for "distinguished contribution to the community at large."

WRITINGS: Freddie the De-lighted Firefly (juvenile), Richards Rosen Associates, 1954; (contributor) Ralph Newman, editor, *Lincoln for the Ages: An Anthology,* Doubleday, 1960; (contributor) Allan Nevins and Irving Stone, editors, *Lincoln: A Contemporary Portrait,* Doubleday, 1962.

Revues; all as contributor of sketches: "New Faces of 1936" (two-act), produced on Broadway at Vanderbilt Theatre, May 19, 1936; "Who's Who?" (two-act), first produced Off-Broadway at Hudson Theatre, March 1, 1938; "Keep Off the Grass" (two-act), first produced in Boston, Mass., at Shubert Theatre, April 30, 1940, first produced on Broadway at Broadhurst Theatre, June 24, 1940; "Haw Haw" (two-act), first produced in London, c. 1940.

Contributor of scripts to radio programs, including "Ivory Tent Show," 1933, "Maxwell House Showboat," 1933, "Kate Smith Hour," 1934, "Molasses 'n January," 1935, "Pick an' Pat," 1935-38, "If I Had the Chance," 1938-39, "Behind the Mike," 1940-42, "Are You a Walrus," 1942, "This Is the Truth," 1942, "The Telephone Hour," 1942, "Fun With the Famous," 1943, "Celebrity Theatre," 1943, "Horror, Incorporated," 1943, "The Johnny Morgan Show," 1943, "Philco Radio Hall of Fame" (author of adaptations, including "Showboat," "The Two Mrs. Carrolls," "Experiment Perilous," and "A Bell for Adano"), 1944-45, "The Gay Mrs. Featherstone," 1945, "Jonathan Trimble, Esquire," 1946, "Hollywood Star Theatre," 1948, "Truth or Consequences" (author of stunts), 1947-50; "This Is Your Life," 1951, "Big Town," 1951, "Stroke of Fate" (creator), 1953, and "Sparring Partners," 1953. Also author of material for radio performers, including George Burns, Gracie Allen, Willie Howard, Eugene Howard, Ben Bernie, Ken Murray, Ed Wynn, Olsen and Johnson, Bebe Daniels and Ben Lyon, Stuart Erwin, and Buck an' Bubbles.

Contributor of scripts to television programs, including "Hollywood Screen Test," 1951-53, "Penthouse Party," 1953, "This Is Your Life," 1954-59, "Secret File, U.S.A.," 1954, "Public Defender," 1954-55, "Chevrolet Mystery Theatre" (co-creator; screen stories only) 1960, "How Tall Is a Giant," 1960, "King of Diamonds," 1961, "The Lloyd Bridges Show," 1962, "Our Man Higgins," 1962, "The Untouchables," 1962, "Combat," 1963, "Bonanza," 1964-65, "Bewitched," 1965, "Rawhide," 1965, "Jesse James," 1966, "The Iron Horse," 1966, "Maya," 1967, "The Governor and J.J.," 1970, and "Room 222" (screen story only), 1971.

Author of material for military productions. Contributor to periodicals, including *Reader's Digest, American History Illustrated, West, Wine, Lincoln Herald, Second Spring,* and *Westways.*

WORK IN PROGRESS: A suspense novel, *The Voice Collector;* a one-man play, "Lincoln, the Genu-ine Article"; a documentary-drama for television, "Johnny Reb and Billy Yank."

SIDELIGHTS: Lewis told *CA:* "My interest in Abraham Lincoln began at New York City's Stuyvesant High School, when my English Three teacher, Pauline Lechler, awarded me a small book of Lincoln's speeches (which I still treasure) as a prize for defending the virtues of Warren G. Harding in a classroom debate! I devoured its contents. Later, influenced no doubt by the nature of my professional work as a comedy writer (preceding my work in the dramatic field), I developed an escalating interest in the importance of humor in the life of our most talented storyteller ever to grace the White House, Mr. Lincoln. I have specialized in tracing where he found the stories he didn't invent, and in separating the apocrypha from the authentic Lincoln yarns and quips. I have not only written on Lincoln's humor but have lectured extensively and spoken on television about this delightful subject.

"My involvement in Lincolniana indirectly led to my being responsible for the first public exposure of the idea of televised presidential debates, that, and my having been at one time a consultant for the radio debate program 'America's Town Meeting of the Air.' I was aware that Adlai Stevenson II, the Democratic candidate for president in 1952, was a descendant of Jesse W. Fell and that this maternal great-grandfather of Stevenson had proposed to Lincoln that he debate Stephen Douglas. Therefore, several days after Stevenson's nomination, on July 30, 1952, I wrote him, his campaign manager Wilson Wyatt, chairman of the Democratic National Committee Frank McKinney, and—as it turned out—most importantly, national columnist and radio commentator Drew Pearson, urging that General Eisenhower be challenged to a series of debates a la Lincoln-Douglas, on television and radio. In a letter to me, Pearson wrote that he had gone on the air Sunday evening, August 3, with my suggestion, thanked me for it, and enclosed an excerpt from that portion of his program dealing with the debate idea. A day or two after the Pearson broadcast, Democratic Senator Blair Moody, a strong Stevenson supporter, lofted a trial balloon in the press, suggesting Stevenson-Eisenhower television debates. However, not until Kennedy-Nixon in 1960 did presidential debates become a reality.

"As an amateur historian, who has numbered among his closest friends major professionals such as the late Allan Nevins and Bell I. Wiley, as well as the still very active Stefan Lorant, I have found myself using history in radio and television scripts, not only in historical programs per se, but in disparate areas. The Civil War provided some background for a 'Dennis the Menace' comedy script when little Dennis found a five hundred-dollar Confederate bill in the uniform of his long-dead great-grandfather who had fought for the South. The story revolved around Dennis's efforts to make purchases with the Confederate money. A 'Bonanza' western script entitled 'A Man to Admire' had as a protagonist a former discredited law partner of Lincoln's—and Lincoln, in absentia, was important to the plot structure. These are just two of many examples, including the radio series 'Stroke of Fate,' based on the idea of what might have happened *if*—if by accident, or decision, made differently, history could have been changed. Consultants were members of the Society of American Historians.

"In June, 1969, at Dr. Allan Nevin's invitation, I had the privilege of delivering a lecture at Claremont College (California) on the use of history in radio, television, and films in the very last graduate seminar ever conducted by this distinguished historian, called 'the father of oral history.' I had, previously to this, in 1968, interviewed many of Dr. Nevins's California colleagues, when I initiated an oral history project on him for the Columbia University Oral History Office (which he founded).''

BIOGRAPHICAL/CRITICAL SOURCES: New York Post, November 17, 1936; *New York World Telegram*, October 29, 1943; *TV Guide*, September 29, 1962; *Time*, October 12, 1962.

*   *   *

LEWIS, (John) Roy(ston)   1933-
(J. R. Lewis, David Springfield)

PERSONAL: Born January 17, 1933, in Rhondda, Wales; son of John Harold (a miner) and Ellen (Power) Lewis; married Gwendoline Hutchings (a teacher), February, 1955; children: Mark, Yvette, Sarah. *Education:* University of Bristol, LL.B., 1954; University of Exeter, diploma in education, 1957; University of Durham, M.A., 1978. *Home:* 207 Western Way, Darras Hall, Newcastle upon Tyne, Northumberland, England.

CAREER: Called to the Bar at Inner Temple, 1965; teacher of law at Plymouth College of Technology, 1957-67; Her Majesty's inspector of schools, 1967-75; New College, Durham, England, vice-principal, 1975-81; Wigan College of Technology, Wigan, England, principal, 1981—. Director of Felton Press Ltd.

*WRITINGS—*Novels; published by Collins, except as noted: *A Lover Too Many*, Collins & World, 1969; *A Wolf by the Ears*, Collins & World, 1970; *Error of Judgment*, 1971; *Fenokee Project*, 1971; *A Secret Singing*, 1972; *A Fool for a Client*, 1972; *Blood Money*, 1973; *Of Singular Purpose*, 1973; *A Question of Degree*, 1974; *Double Take*, 1975; *A Part of Virtue*, 1975; *Witness My Death*, 1976; *A Distant Banner*, 1976; *Noth-*

ing But Foxes, 1977; *An Uncertain Sound*, 1978; *An Inevitable Fatality*, 1978; *A Certain Blindness*, 1979.

Law books; under name J. R. Lewis, except as noted: *Cases for Discussion*, Pergamon, 1963; *Law for the Retailer*, Allman & Son, 1964; *Business Law*, Allman & Son, 1965; *Law in Action*, Allman & Son, 1965; *Building Law*, Allman & Son, 1966; *Managing Within the Law*, Allman & Son, 1967; (with J. Anthony Holland) *Registered Land Conveyancing*, Butterworth, 1967; *Landlord and Tenant*, Sweet & Maxwell, 1968; *Outlines of Equity*, Butterworth, 1968; *Civil and Criminal Procedure*, Sweet & Maxwell, 1968, 2nd edition, 1976; (with Holland) *Mercantile Law*, Heinemann, 1969; (under pseudonym David Springfield), *The Company Executive and the Law*, Heinemann, 1970; *Law for the Distributor*, Jordan & Sons, 1975; *Law for the Construction Industry*, Macmillan, 1975; *Administrative Law*, Macmillan, 1976; (editor) *Teaching the Law*, Association of Law Teachers, 1980; *Teaching Public Administration*, Joint University Council for Social and Public Administration, 1980; *Certain Private Incidents*, Templar North, 1980; *The Victorian Bar*, Templar North, in press.

Nonfiction: (Under name J. R. Lewis) *The Struggle for Swinfen*, Templar North, in press.

Writer for radio program "Brought to Justice." Contributor to *Legal Executive*.

SIDELIGHTS: Lewis commented: "I maintain an interest in law and now write articles on legal history. Many of these are concerned with scandals in Victorian society. I have also read pieces on law and life in Victorian Northumberland on the radio program 'Brought to Justice.' Fiction remains an escape, but Victorian studies now take up more of my time.

"My fiction background material often comes from real-life cases, in that I use the law reports as resource material. I intend to continue to write two novels each year but also intend to pursue studies of Victorian society more deeply, to look at the attitudes to law, the essential paradox of moral behavior and public image, and the criminal underworld and its contacts both local and national with the upper echelons. I also intend to research 'scandals of law' and the Victorian private detective.''

AVOCATIONAL INTERESTS: Watching rugby on television.

*   *   *

LEWIS, Tom   1940-
(Nicolas Babcock)

PERSONAL: Born December 3, 1940, in New York, N.Y.; son of Grant Nieman and Judith (Babcock) Lewis; married Madeline Gallo, September 4, 1965; children: Nicholas, Jennifer. *Education:* Columbia University, B.A., 1967. *Religion:* Roman Catholic. *Home address:* P.O. Box 444, Kinderhook, N.Y. 12106. *Agent:* Timothy Seldes, Russell & Volkening, Inc., 551 Fifth Ave., New York, N.Y. 10017.

CAREER: City of New York, N.Y., engineering aide in department of bridges, 1967; Harcourt Brace Jovanovich, Inc., New York City, in college textbook sales, 1967-69, editor of political science, psychology, sociology, and anthropology in college department, 1969-72; Hill & Wang, Inc., New York City, editor, 1972-73; Farrar, Straus & Giroux, Inc., New York City, editor and academic sales manager, 1973-74; free-lance writer, 1974-77; Press Office of the Executive Chamber of the State of New York, Albany, assistant press secretary to the governor and principal speechwriter, 1977-78; *New York Post*, New York City, political reporter, 1978; Madison North Marketing Communications Agency Ltd., Schenectady, N.Y., special consultant, 1978-79; writer, 1979—. Guest lecturer at State University of New York College at Purchase, 1974. Member of New York County Democratic Committee, 1975-77. *Military service:* U.S. Army, Intelligence Corps, 1963-66; became staff sergeant.

WRITINGS: Rooftops (novel; Book-of-the-Month Club alternate), M. Evans, 1981; (under pseudonym Nicolas Babcock) *Billy's Army* (novel), Atheneum, 1982. Contributor of articles, poems, and reviews to periodicals, including *Harper's Weekly, New York, Mother Jones, Westsider, Shantih, Harper's, Mountain Gazette, Columbia Forum,* and *Albany Times-Union.*

WORK IN PROGRESS: A novel; poems.

SIDELIGHTS: Rooftops is a crime novel set in Manhattan's upper west side, an area Lewis knows well. Lewis commented: "Having written my first novel at the approximate midpoint of my adult life, following twenty years as a poet, book editor, and journalist, I expect to go on writing novels—as well as political and historical nonfiction—as long as I am able."

BIOGRAPHICAL/CRITICAL SOURCES: Library Journal, June 15, 1981.

*   *   *

LIBBY, Violet K(elway)   1892(?)-1981

OBITUARY NOTICE: Born c. 1892 in England; died October 24, 1981, in Bridgeport, Conn. Social worker, editor, and author. Following her early career as a social worker and news reporter, Libby wrote and edited for the American Red Cross from 1940 until her transfer to the United States Information Agency in 1956. Her Red Cross affiliation spawned *Henri Dunant: Prophet of Peace,* a biography of the organization's founder. She also wrote *How to Care for the Baby* and contributed extensively to magazines and newspapers. Obituaries and other sources: *Washington Post,* October 26, 1981.

*   *   *

LIEB, Irwin Chester   1925-

BRIEF ENTRY: Born November 9, 1925, in Newark, N.J. American educator and author. Lieb has been a professor of philosophy at the University of Texas since 1963 and a vice-president and graduate dean since 1975. He edited *Charles Pierce's Letters to Lady Welby* (Whitlock, 1953) and wrote *Experience, Existence, and the Good* (Southern Illinois University Press, 1961) and *The Four Faces of Man* (University of Pennsylvania Press, 1971). *Address:* 4612 Shoal Creek Blvd., Austin, Tex. 78756; and Office of the Dean of Graduate Studies, University of Texas, Austin, Tex. 78712. *Biographical/critical sources: Directory of American Scholars,* Volume IV: *Philosophy, Religion, and Law,* 7th edition, Bowker, 1978.

*   *   *

LIEBERSTEIN, Stanley H.   1934-

PERSONAL: Born December 27, 1934, in New York, N.Y.; son of Nathan (in wholesale cake and bakery business) and Pauline (Reisman) Lieberstein; married Judy Levitt (a psychologist), January 24, 1959; children: Susanne, Paul, Warren. *Education:* Brooklyn College (now of the City University of New York), B.A., 1958; Brooklyn Law School, J.D., 1960; graduate study at George Washington University, 1961-63. *Politics:* "Jeffersonian democrat." *Home:* 34 Pequot Trail, Westport, Conn. 06880. *Agent:* Keith Korman, Raines & Raines,

475 Fifth Ave., New York, N.Y. 10017. *Office:* 260 Madison Ave., New York, N.Y. 10016.

CAREER: U.S. Patent and Trademarks Office, Washington, D.C., examiner, 1960-63; law assistant and technical adviser for U.S. Court of Customs and Patent Appeals, 1963-64; patent attorney with Hoffman La-Roche, Inc., in New Jersey, 1964-66; vice-president and general counsel of Oxy Metal Industries, 1966-75; Ostrolenk, Faber, Gerb, & Soffen (law firm), New York, N.Y., partner, 1975—. Member of advisory board of Bureau of National Affairs. Member of Westport Representative Town Meeting, 1977-79. *Member:* American Bar Association, American Chemical Society, New York Patent Law Association (member of board of directors), New Jersey Patent Law Association (president, 1976), Sigma Xi. *Awards, honors: Who Owns What Is in Your Head* was named among best business books of 1979 by *Library Journal.*

WRITINGS: Who Owns What Is in Your Head: How to Protect Your Ideas, Dutton, 1979. Contributor to business and law journals.

WORK IN PROGRESS: "How to Protect and Profit From Your Ideas," an audio course, for American Chemical Society.

SIDELIGHTS: Lieberstein told *CA:* "My book is a result of representing many clients who asked many questions about their rights and how to protect their ideas. It was written on weekends, primarily, over a period of about two years.

"Publishing this book brought home the vulnerability of most 'unknown' writers. Apparently the desire to get into print, coupled with the ignorance of the law and a fear of offending the publisher, puts many a new author at the publisher's mercy. Since new authors rarely have qualified literary agents and may not be able to afford the services of an attorney, there is a need for some means to protect the new author. Just as laws have been enacted to protect workers who cannot negotiate as individuals, there is a need for legislation to invalidate unreasonable terms in contracts that many new writers cannot or will not, whether out of fear or ignorance, negotiate with the publisher."

*   *   *

LIEBERT, Doris   1934-

PERSONAL: Born June 8, 1934, in Olds, Alberta, Canada; came to United States, 1953, naturalized citizen, 1976; daughter of Emanuel (a farmer) and Louise (Kohls) Krause; married Donald Hans Liebert (a professor), June 25, 1961; children: Kurt, Lynn, Suzanne. *Education:* Seattle Pacific University, B.A., 1956; Whitworth College, M.A., 1976. *Religion:* Presbyterian. *Home:* West 1416 Crestwood Court, Spokane, Wash. 99218.

CAREER: Young Life, Pasadena, Calif., counselor, 1959-61; teacher at public schools in Trenton, N.J., 1962-66; Whitworth College, Spokane, Wash., supervisor of student teaching, 1977—. Associated with Washington State University, Pullman. *Member:* American Home Economics Association.

WRITINGS: Loaves and Fishes (nonfiction), Herald Press, 1980.

SIDELIGHTS: Liebert told *CA:* "Concern for world hunger and my own children's understanding and responses to it prompted my interest in writing the book."

*   *   *

LI Fei-kan   1904-
(Pa Chin)

PERSONAL: Born November 25, 1904 (some sources say 1905),

in Chengtu, Szechwan, China (now People's Republic of China); son of a magistrate; married Ch'en Yun-chen (an editor and translator), May 8, 1944; children: Hsiao-lin (daughter), Hsiao-t'ang (son). *Education:* Graduate of Southeastern University (Nanking), 1925; graduate study in France, 1927-28. *Residence:* Shanghai, People's Republic of China.

CAREER: Author, 1928—; editor-in-chief, Wen-hua sheng-huo (Cultural Life Publishing House), 1935-38 and 1946. Member of editorial board, *Feng-huo* (title means "Beacon"), 1937-38, *Na-han* (title means "Outcry"), 1937-38, *Ching ch'un* (title means "Warning the People"), and *P'ing-min chih sheng* (title means "Voice of the Proletariat"). Founder of Chinese Writers Anti-Aggression Association, 1938; committee member of China Association of Literary Workers, 1949, and Cultural and Educational Commission 1949-54; vice-chairman of All-China Federation of Literary and Art Circles, 1953; deputy chief of Afro-Asian Writers' Congress, 1958; chairman of China Peoples Union of Chinese Writers (Shanghai), 1958-68. Delegate to national and international political congresses, including the National People's Congress, 1949, and the Eighth Conference on the Banning of Nuclear Weapons (Japan), 1962; vice-president of the Sino-Soviet Friendship Association, 1959-68. *Awards, honors:* Nominated for a Nobel Prize in literature, 1975.

WRITINGS—All under pseudonym Pa Chin, except as noted; in English: *Chia* (novel), 1931, K'ai-ming, 1936, Harvard University Chinese-Japanese Library, 1959, translation by Sidney Shapiro published as *The Family*, Foreign Languages Press, 1958, new edition with introduction by Olga Lang, Anchor Books, 1972; "Kou" (short story), published in *Kuang-ming*, 1931 (see below), translation published as "Dog" in *Living China: Modern Chinese Short Stories*, edited by Edgar Snow, Harrap, 1936; "Ch'u-lien" (short story), published in *Fu-ch'ou*, 1931 (see below), translation by Richard L. Jen published as "First Love" in *Modern Chinese Literature: Bilingual Series*, Volume III, Ta-lu, 1941; "Hsing" (short story), published in *Fa ti ku-shih*, 1937 (see below), translation by Richard L. Jen published as "Star" in *T'ien-hsia Monthly*, 1937, and in *Modern Chinese Literature: Bilingual Series*, Volume III, Ta-lu, 1941; *Short Stories by Pa Chin*, edited by Wen I (contains "Fu-ch'ou," "Ch'u-lien," and "Kou"), translation by Mo Chin-yi, Chung-ying ch'u-pan she, 1941, published with title *Short Stories by Pa Chin, With English Translations*, Hui-t'ung shu-tien, 1963; "The Puppet" (an extract from *Chia*, 1931 [see above]), translation by Wang Chi-chen, Columbia University Press, 1944; *Han-yeh*, 1947, Ch'en-kuang, 1948, translation by Nathan K. Mao and Liu Ts'un-yan published as *Cold Nights*, University of Washington Press, 1979; *Ying-hsiung ti ku-shih*, P'ing-ming ch'u-pan she, 1953, translation published as *Living Amongst Heroes*, Foreign Languages Press of Peking, 1954; (with others) *I-ch'ang wan'chiu sheng ming ti chan tou*, translation by Cheng Chi-yi and Shen Tzu-kao published as *A Battle for Life: A Full Record of How the Life of Steel Worker Chiu Tsai-kang Was Saved in the Shanghai Kwangtze Hospital*, Foreign Languages Press, 1959.

Novels: *Mieh wang* (title means "Destruction"), 1929, K'ai-ming, 1950; *Ssu-ch'u-ti t'ai-yang* (title means "The Setting Sun"), 1930, K'ai-ming, 1940; *Hai-ti meng* (title means "Dream on the Sea"), K'ai-ming, 1932; *Ch'un t'ien li ti ch'iu-t'ien* (title means "Autumn Day Comes in the Spring"), 1932, K'ai-ming, 1933, Harvard University Chinese-Japanese Library, 1949; *Hsin sheng* (title means "New Life"), 1933, K'ai-ming, 1949; *Meng-ya* (title means "Germs"), Hsien-tai, 1933, revised edition published as *Hsueh* (title means "Snow"), Wen-hua sheng-huo, 1946; *Sha-ting* (title means "Sand-hogs"), 1932, Wen-hua sheng-huo, 1937, Harvard University Chinese-Japanese

Library, 1949; *Ch'un* (title means "Spring"), 1938, K'ai-ming, 1940, Harvard University Chinese-Japanese Library, 1961; *Ch'iu* (title means "Autumn"), 1940, Jen-min wen-hsueh, 1955, Harvard University Chinese-Japanese Library, 1961; *Huo* (title means "Fire"), K'ai-ming, Volume I, 1941, Volume II, 1942, Volume III, 1945; *Ch'i yuan* (title means "Garden of Rest"), 1944, Wen-hua sheng-huo, 1945; *Ti-ssu ping-shih* (title means "Ward Number Four"), 1946, Ch'en-kuang, 1947. Also author of *Wu* (title means "Fog"), 1931, published in *Ai-ch'ing ti san-pu-ch'u*, 1939 (see below), and in *Wu, yu, tien*, 1955 (see below); *Yu* (title means "Rain"), 1932, published in *Ai-ch'ing ti san-pu-ch'u*, 1939 (see below), and in *Wu, yu, tien*, 1955 (see below); *Lei* (title means "Thunder"), 1933, published in *Ai-ch'ing ti san-pu-ch'u*, 1939 (see below); *Tien* (title means "Lightning"), 1934, published in *Ai-ch'ing ti san pu ch'u*, 1939 (see below), and in *Wu, yu, tien*, 1955 (see below); *Li-na* (title means "Lena"), 1934; *Fu yu tzu*, 1953.

Short stories: *Fu-ch'ou* (title means "Revenge"; includes "Fu-ch'ou" and "Ch'u-lien" [title means "First Love"]), 1931, K'ai-ming, 1940; *Kuang-ming* (title means "Glory"; includes "Kou" [title means "Dog"]), 1931, K'ai-ming, 1940; *Tien-Yi* (title means "Electric Chair"), 1932, K'ai-ming, 1940; *Chiang-chun* (title means "The General"; includes "Mei-kuei hua ti hsiang" [title means "The Fragrance of Roses"]), 1933, Sheng-huo, 1934; *Shen, kuei, jen* (title means "Gods, Spirits, Men"; contains "Shen," "Kuei," and "Jen"), Wen-hua sheng-huo, 1935; *Ch'en lo* (title means "Sinking Down"), 1935, Shang-wu yin-shu kuan, 1936; *Fa ti ku-shih* (title means "Story of Hair"; includes "Hsing"), 1936, Wen-hua sheng-huo, 1939; *Ch'ang-sheng t'a* (title means "Pagoda of Long Life"; contains "Ch'ang sheng t'a," "T'a ti pi-mi" [title means "Secret of the Pagoda"], "Yin-shen chu" [title means "The Invisible Pearl"], and "Neng-yen shu" [title means "The Talking Tree"]), 1937, Wen-hua sheng-huo, 1940; *Hei t'u* (title means "Black Earth"), 1939, Wen-hua sheng-huo, 1941; *Lung, hu, kou* (title means "Dragon, Tiger, Dog"), 1941, Wen-hua sheng-huo, 1947; *Fei-yuan wai* (title means "Behind a Desolate Garden"), Nan fang, 1942; *Huan hun ts'ao* (title means "The Grass of Resurrection"; contains "Huan hun ts'ao," "Meng-na li-so" [title means "Mona Lisa"], and "Mou fu-fu" [title means "A Certain Couple"]), Wen-hua sheng-huo, 1945, reprint, 1975; *Hsiao-jen hsiao-shih* (title means "Little Men, Little Things"; contains "Chu yu chi" [title means "Piglet and Chichkens"], "Hsiang yu ti" [title means "Brothers"], "Fu yu ch'i" [title means "Husband and Wife"], "Nu-hai yu mao" [title means "A Girl and Her Cat"], and "Sheng yu ssu" [title means "Life and Death"]), Wen-hua sheng-huo, 1947; *Ching-yeh ti pei-chu* (title means "Tragedy in a Quiet Night"), Wen-hua sheng-huo, 1948; *Wo-men hui-shen liao P'eng Te-huai ssu-ling yuan* (title means "Our Meeting With Commander P'eng Te-huai"), Wen-hsueh ch'u-pan she, 1953; *Pao-wei ho-p'ing ti jen-men* (title means "People Guarding Peace"), Chung ch'ing, 1955; *Ming-chu ho Yu-chi* (title means "Ming-chu and Yu-chi"), Chung-ko shao-nien erh-tung ch'u-pan she, 1957; *Lo ch'e shang* (title means "On the Mule Cart"), Hsin yueh, 1959; *Li Ta-hai*, Tso-chia sh'u-pan she, 1961. Also author of *Mo-pu* (title means "A Duster"), 1932; *Ch'en-mo* (title means "Deep Silence"), two volumes, 1934; *Lun lo*, 1936; *Ya-li-an-no*, 1945; *Pai niao chih ko*, 1947; *Pa Chin hsiao shuo hsuan*, 195(?); *P'iap po*, 195(?).

Essays; under name Li Fei-kan: *Chih-chiao-ko ti ts'an-chu* (title means "The Chicago Tragedy"), P'ing-she, 1926; (with Wu and Hui-lin) *Wu-cheng-fu-chu-i yu shi-chi wen-ti* (title means "Anarchism and Reality: A Problem"), Min-chung, 1927; *Tuan-t'ou-t'ai shang* (title means "On the Scaffold"), Tzu-yu, 1929; *Ts'ung tzu-pen-chu-i tao an-na-ch'i-chu-i* (title means "From

Capitalism to Anarchism''), P'ing-she, 1930; *Tzu-yu hsueh: Wu-i hsun tao che ti wu-shu chou-nien* (title means ''Blood of Freedom: On the Fiftieth Anniversary of the Martyrdom of Five Comrades''), Tzu-yu, 1937.

Essays; under pseudonym Pa Chin: *Tien-ti* (title means ''Fragments''), 1935, Kai-ming, 1949; *Sheng chih ch'an-hui* (title means ''Confessions of a Life''), Shang-wu yin-shu kuan, 1936; *O-kuo hsu-wu-chu-i yun-tung shih-hua* (title means ''History of the Russian Nihilist Movement''), Wen-hua sheng-huo, 1936; *O-kuo she-hui yun-tung shih-hua* (title means ''History of the Russian Socialist Movement''), Wen-hua sheng-huo, 1936; *Tuan-chien* (title means ''Short Conversations''), two volumes, 1937, Liang Yu, 1943; *Meng yu tsui* (title means ''Dreams and Inebriation''), K'ai-ming, 1938; *Hsi-pan-ya ti shu kuang,* P'ing ming ch'u-pan she, 1939; *Wu t'i* (title means ''Unnamed''), 1941, Feng-huo she, 1942; *K'ung-su,* Wen-hua sheng-huo, 1941; *T'an Chieh-ho-fu* (title means ''Chekhov''), P'ing-ming, 1955; *Ta huan-lo ti jih-tzu* (title means ''Days of Great Joy''), Tso-chia ch'u-pan she, 1957; *Hsin sheng chi* (title means ''New Voices Collection''), Jen-min wen-hsueh, 1959; *Yu-i chi* (title means ''Friendship Collection''), Tso-chia ch'u-pan she, 1959; *Ch'ing t'u pu chin ti kan-ch'ing* (title means ''Inexhaustible Friendship''), Pai-hua wen-i ch'u-pan she, 1963; *Hsien-liang ch'iao p'an* (title means ''At the Hsien-liang Bridge''), Tso-chia ch'u-pan she, 1964; (with others) *Shou: Shou i tuan shou ts'ai chih ti ku-shih* (title means ''The Hand: The Story of the Hand Cut Off and the Hand Put on Again''), Shao-nien erh-t'ung ch'u-pan she, 1964.

Travel: *Hai hsing tsa-chi* (title means ''Sea Voyage Notebook''), 1932, K'ai-ming, 1949; *Lu-t'u sui-pi* (title means ''Random Notes of a Voyage''), 1934, P'ing-ming, 1953; *Lu-t'u t'ung hsun* (title means ''Letters From the Road''), two volumes, Wen-hua sheng-huo, 1940; *Lu-t'u tsa-chi* (title means ''Travel Notebook''), Wen yeh pan, 1946; *Hua-sha ch'eng ti chieh-jih* (title means ''Warsaw Diary''), Jen-min wen-hsueh, 1951.

Autobiography: *Pa Chin tzu-chuan* (title means ''Pa Chin's Autobiography''), 1934, Tzu-li shu-tien, 1956, enlarged edition published as *I* (title means ''Memoirs''), Wen-hua sheng-huo, 1936; *Huai-nien* (title means ''Reminiscences''), K'ai-ming, 1947; *Sheng-huo ti hui L,* 1953.

Omnibus volumes: *Men-chien* (collected translations; title means ''The Threshold''), Wen-hua sheng-huo, 1935; *Pa Chin hsuan-chi* (title means ''Pa Chin's Selected Works''), Chung-yang shu-tien, 1936; *Ai-ch'ing ti san-pu-ch'u* (title means ''Love: A Trilogy''; contains *Wu, Yu, Lei,* and *Tien*), K'ai-ming, 1939; *Pa Chin tuan p'ien hsiao shuo hsuan chi* (title means ''Collection of Pa Chin's Short Stories''; contains *Fu-ch'ou, Kuang-ming,* and *Tien-yi*), K'ai-ming, 1940; *Pa Chin hsuan-chi* (title means ''Pa Chin's Selected Works''), K'ai-ming, 1951; *Pa Chin tai-piao tso hsuan* (title means ''Selection of Representative Works of Pa Chin''), Ch'uan ch'ui, 1951; *Pa Chin san-wen hsuan* (title means ''Pa Chin's Selected Essays''), Hsin-hua, 1955; *Pa Chin wen-chi* (title means ''Pa Chin's Collected Works''), fourteen volumes, Jen-min wen-hsueh, 1958-62, Volume I (contains *Mieh-wang, Hsin-sheng, Ssu-ch'u ti t'ai-yang,* and *Hai ti meng*), Volume II (contains *Ch'un-t'ien li ti ch'ui-t'ien, Sha-ting, Hsueh,* and *Li-na*), Volume III (contains *Wu, Yu, Lei,* and *Tien*), Volume IV (contains *Chia*), Volume V (contains *Ch'un*), Volume VI (contains *Ch'iu*), Volume VII (contains *Fu-ch'ou, Kuang-ming,* and *Tien-yi*), Volume VIII (contains *Mo-pu, Chiang-chun, Ch'en-mo, Ch'en-lo,* and *Shen, kuei, jen*), Volume IX (contains *Ch'en-mo II, Fa ti ku-shih, Ch'ang-sheng t'a, Huan-hun ts'ao,* and *Hsiao-jen, hsiao-shih*), Volume X (contains *Yi, Tuan-chien I, Sheng chih ch'an-hui,*

Tien-ti, Meng yu tsui, K'ung-su, Wu-t'i, Hei-t'u, Lung, hu, kou, Fei-yuan wai, Huai-nien, and *Ching-yeh ti pei-chu*), Volume XI (contains *Hai-hsing tsa-chi, Lu-t'u sui-pi, Lu-t'u t'ung-hsun, Lu-t'u tsa-chi,* and *Tuan-chien II*), Volume XII (contains *Huo*), Volume XIII (contains *Ch'i-yuan* and *Ti-ssu ping-shih*), Volume XIV (contains *Han-yeh* and *T'an tzu-chi ch'ung-tso*), revised edition, Nan-kuo ch'u-pan she, 1970; *Wu, yu, tien* (contains *Wu, Yu,* and *Tien*), 1955.

Other: *Tsan ko chi,* Harvard University Chinese-Japanese Library, 1960; *Chan cheng yu ching chi* (economics), 1937; *Ai ti shih tsu chia,* 1949; *Yuki,* 1949; *Yueh yeh,* 1949; *Ch'uang wai,* 195(?); *Pa Chin ming tso hsuan chi,* 195(?); *Sheng huo tsai ying hsiung men ti chung chien,* 1953.

Contributor to *Li-shih hsiao-p'in chin* (title means ''Small Historical Tales''), Ch'en-chung, 1936. (Under name Li Fei-kan) Also contributor to *Ma-k'o-ssu-chu-i ti p'o-ch'an, Ko-ming ti hsien-ch'u,* and *Su-o ko'ming ts'an-shih.*

SIDELIGHTS: Li Fei-kan was born into an aristocratic family whose special privileges and rigid adherence to traditional values alienated the author, eventually leading him to reject the Confucian family system and the existing social order. Seeking to change society, Li began to write essays, novels, and stories that were directed toward the young intellectual activists who were becoming disenchanted with the corrupt and repressive nationalist government of General Chiang Kai-shek. Though Li later became an ardent supporter of the communist revolution, he was at first attracted to Western-style anarchism, and most of his work reflects this interest. Writing under the pseudonym Pa Chin, a *nom de plum* derived from the transliteration of syllables from the names of the well-known anarchists Mikhail Bakunin and Piotr Kropotkin, Li became one of China's best read contemporary authors.

While living in France during the 1920's Li wrote *Mieh wang,* a novel about the anarchist movement in contemporary Shanghai. The book became a favorite with the youthful intelligentsia of China, and thus established Li's reputation as a significant novelist. Li's most popular work, which some critics regard as his masterpiece, is his semi-autobiographical novel, *The Family.* The work was written in response to the suicide of Li's older brother whom the author perceived as a victim of the traditional family system. Though primarily an indictment of that system, the book, said Olga Lang in *Pa Chin and His Writings,* ''provides a rich source of information on the mores and inner relationships which characterized the upper-class Chinese family'' and it contains ''many poetic and warm descriptions of the traditional life, with its family gatherings, festivities, literary games and discussions, walks in the park, and boat rides on the lake.'' Critic Paul Binding of *Books and Bookmen* reported that ''the novel makes exciting, even exhilarating reading,'' and he ''strongly'' recommended it to readers. An English translation of *The Family* is available in the United States.

Cold Nights, which Li's biographer Nathan K. Mao considers to be the author's best work, is also available in English translation. Set in Chungking during the Sino-Japanese war, the novel describes the dismal relationship between a dying man, his wife, his mother, and his child. The wife's desire to escape from responsibility for the others and from the danger of living in a city about to fall to the enemy is forestalled by her husband's mortal illness. Applauding Li's ''deft usage of imagery, symbols, description and dialogue,'' Howard Goldblatt pointed out in *World Literature Today* that the author ''effectively captured the bleakness of life in the deteriorating household of the story's protagonists.'' Li, Mao agreed, ''has successfully illuminated the atmosphere, the moving scenes, the interpersonal conflicts, and the inner thoughts of his characters. . . . To read such a novel is to enlarge the reader's knowledge of humanity." "It is impossible," he concluded, "to imagine a time when, to a Chinese reader, . . . *Family* . . . or *Cold Nights* will cease to be among his most cherished literary pleasures."

Li retained his popularity following the establishment of the People's Republic of China in 1949, and he held several prestigious posts within the newly organized state. In an interview with reporter Chen Tan-chen, published in *Chinese Literature* in 1963, Li claimed that he was dissatisfied with his early anarchist writings because they "simply exposed the iniquities and injustice of the old system . . . without prescribing a remedy." Not until he had "linked [himself] with the people's revolutionary struggle," he said, were his "ideas," "reason," and "ideal" in harmony with his "action," his "emotion," and "reality." Li's assessment of his work conflicts with that of a number of critics, including Lang, who said that the purpose of Li's fiction is "to show its readers how to live, to give them models for emulation," for Li "was not only a creative writer who described society but a revolutionary who wanted to change it." What is more, Lang argued, "[Li] made an important contribution to the victory of Communism in China [for] he helped to create among the intellectuals an emotional climate that induced them to accept the Communist revolution."

Li's career as a novelist declined sharply after 1949 when news reports on the wars in Korea and Vietnam comprised most of his writings. According to Jonathan Mirsky of *New Statesman*, following the revolution Li "never again wrote anything worth reading."

Though Li had disavowed his earlier politics and had revised all of his works to rid them of any traces of anarchism, he fell into disfavor during the cultural revolution of the 1960's. "He really deserves to die ten thousand deaths," urged one newspaper. Later Li was forced to kneel on broken glass before thousands of spectators in a televised exhibition at the People's Stadium. In response to this ordeal, Li shouted, "You have your thoughts, and I have mine! This is a fact and you can't change it even if you kill me."

Little is known about Li's present life, though it is believed that he was "rehabilitated" in 1977.

BIOGRAPHICAL/CRITICAL SOURCES: C. T. Hsia, *A History of Modern Chinese Fiction, 1917-1957*, Yale University Press, 1961; Jaroslav Prusek, editor, *Studies in Modern Chinese Literature*, Akademie-Verlag, 1964; O. Lang, *Pa Chin and His Writings: Chinese Youth Between the Two Revolutions*, Harvard Universtiy East Asian Research Center, 1967; Nathan K. Mao, *Pa Chin*, Twayne Publishers, 1978; *Contemporary Literary Criticism*, Volume 18, Gale, 1981.*

—*Sketch by Susan M. Trosky*

*   *   *

LILLICH, Meredith Parsons   1932-

BRIEF ENTRY: Born February 9, 1932, in Chicago, Ill. American art historian, educator, and author. Lillich has taught art history at Syracuse University since 1968. Writings include *A Redating of the Thirteenth-Century Grisaille Windows of Chartres Cathedral* (Gesta, 1972), *The Stained Glass of St. Pere De Chartres* (Wesleyan University Press, 1974), and *Studies in Cistercian Art and Architecture* (Cistercian Publications, 1981). *Address:* 1247 Comstock Ave., Syracuse, N.Y. 13210; and Department of Fine Arts, Syracuse University, Syracuse, N.Y. 13210. *Biographical/critical sources:* Directory of American Scholars, Volume I: History, 7th edition, Bowker, 1978.

LINCOLN, Bruce   1948-

PERSONAL: Born March 5, 1948, in Philadelphia, Pa.; son of William D. (a realtor) and Geraldine (a clinical psychologist; maiden name, Kovsky) Lincoln; married Louise Gibson Hassett (a curator and art historian), April 17, 1971; children: Rebecca and Martha (twins). *Education:* Haverford College, B.A. (with high honors), 1970; University of Chicago, Ph.D. (with distinction), 1976. *Politics:* "Unaffiliated Marxist, leaning to anarcho-syndicalism." *Religion:* None. *Home:* 3232 South Bryant Ave., Minneapolis, Minn. 55408. *Office:* Humanities Program, University of Minnesota, Minneapolis, Minn. 55455.

CAREER: History of Religions, Chicago, Ill., editorial assistant, 1973-75; University of Minnesota, Minneapolis, assistant professor, 1976-79, associate professor of humanities, religious studies, and South Asian studies, and chairman of religious studies program, 1979—. *Member:* Phi Beta Kappa. *Awards, honors:* Grants from American Council of Learned Societies, 1979, and Rockefeller Foundation, 1981.

WRITINGS: Priests, Warriors, and Cattle: A Study in the Ecology of Religions, University of California Press, 1981; *Emerging From the Chrysalis: Studies in Rituals of Women's Initiation*, Harvard University Press, 1981; (contributor) Ugo Bianchi, editor, *Soteriology of the Oriental Cults in the Roman Empire*, E. J. Brill, 1982; (contributor) Hans-Peter Duerr, editor, *Critical Essays on Mircea Eliade*, Syndikat, 1983. Contributor to encyclopedias, including *Woerterbuch der Mythologie: Iranisches Band* and *Encyclopedia of Religion*. Contributor to scholarly journals.

WORK IN PROGRESS: A study of Indo-European beliefs about death, the otherworld, and the fate of body and soul, publication expected in 1984; editing a study of how religious institutions and ideologies affect and are affected by revolutionary change in the socio-political sphere, 1983.

SIDELIGHTS: Lincoln wrote: "I tend to view religion as the desperate attempt to invest an otherwise meaningless existence with some sense of purpose and worth. It thus has its origins in the human imagination, not in some divine sphere, and proper study of religion begins with the external factors which condition the exercise of the imagination within any given culture, including such factors as geography, climate, and patterns of social, political, and economic organization. In some measure, religion is a valorization and legitimation of those givens, being an attempt to endow the world in which one must live with a sense of transcendent meaning. On the other hand, religion can become a reaction against those same givens and an attempt to flee them for another level of existence beyond this life and world.

"I find myself simultaneously fascinated and utterly repelled by religious phenomena—myths, rituals, cosmologies, soteriologies, and the like. I suppose this is part of my family legacy, my great-grandfather having been a Russian anarchist and atheist, my great-grandmother (his wife) an orthodox Jew."

Lincoln is competent in Sanskrit, Aventan, Greek, Latin, Old Norse, Pahlavi, French, German, Italian, and Spanish, and has some knowledge of Old Persian, Hittite, Russian, Old Irish, Anglo-Saxon, Welsh, Dutch, and Portuguese.

*   *   *

LINDER, Staffan B(urenstam)   1931-

BRIEF ENTRY: Born September 13, 1931, in Norberg, Sweden. Swedish government official and author. Linder has been a professor of economics at Stockholm School of Economics since 1961 and a member of Sweden's Parliament since 1969. He became deputy chairman of the Conservative party in 1970 and Swedish minister of commerce in 1976. He wrote *An Essay on Trade and Transformation* (Wiley, 1961), *Trade and Trade Policy for Development* (Praeger, 1967), and *The Harried Leisure Class* (Columbia University Press, 1970). *Address:* Bravallavagen 41/182, 64 Djursholm, Sweden. *Biographical/critical sources: New York Times,* January 12, 1970; *Washington Post,* January 24, 1970; *New York Times Book Review,* May 17, 1970; *New Republic,* January, 1976.

* * *

LING, Hung-hsun 1894(?)-1981

OBITUARY NOTICE: Born c. 1894 in Canton, China; died August 15, 1981, in Taipei, Taiwan. Engineer, educator, and author. Ling was instrumental in the planning, construction, and administration of China's major railways, working in transportation from 1929 to 1945. After serving as deputy minister of communications for the Chiang Kai-shek government from 1945 until 1949, Ling was named chairman of the Chinese Petroleum Corporation's board of directors, a post he held for twenty years. He also served as chancellor of Chiaotung University, Shanghai's noted school of engineering. Among Ling's writings are *A Comprehensive Survey of Railway Development in China* and *Railway Engineering.* Obituaries and other sources: *New York Times,* August 22, 1981.

* * *

LINK, (Eugene) Perry (Jr.) 1944-

PERSONAL: Born August 6, 1944, in Gaffney, S.C.; son of Eugene (a professor) and Beulah M. (a teacher; maiden name, Meyer) Link; married Sue Jean Wong, August 24, 1978; children: Monica. *Education:* Harvard University, B.A., 1966, M.A., 1969, Ph.D., 1976. *Home:* 1205 Grant St., Santa Monica, Calif. 90405. *Office:* Department of Oriental Languages, University of California, Los Angeles, Calif. 90024.

CAREER: Princeton University, Princeton, N.J., assistant professor/lecturer, 1973-76, assistant professor of East Asian studies, 1976-77; University of California, Los Angeles, assistant professor, 1977-80, associate professor of Oriental languages, 1980—, organizer and chairman of interdisciplinary workshop on modern China, 1977-78. Instructor at Middlebury College, 1971, lecturer-in-charge, 1972, 1978, and 1979. Chair of Harvard University's East Asian Colloquium, 1970-71; co-chair of Columbia University's workshop on writers and publics in modern China, 1974-76; chair of program committee of Southern California China Colloquium, 1979. Visiting scholar at East Asian Institute, 1975-76; visiting associate research linguist at Center for Chinese Studies, 1981. Member of board of trustees of Princeton-in-Asia Foundation, 1976-78; member of advisory committee of Hong Kong's Universities Service Center, 1977—. *Member:* Phi Beta Kappa.

AWARDS, HONORS: Michael C. Rockefeller memorial traveling fellowship from Harvard University, 1966-67; Fulbright fellowship, 1972-73; grant from American Council of Learned Societies, 1977; National Academy of Sciences fellowship for China, 1979-80; grant from American Council of Learned Societies and Social Science Research Council, 1980.

WRITINGS: Mandarin Ducks and Butterflies: Popular Urban Fiction in Early Twentieth-Century Chinese Cities, University of California Press, 1981; (editor) *Chinese Literature, 1979-80,* Indiana University Press, 1982.

Contributor: *The Indochina Story,* Bantam, 1971; Merle Goldman, editor, *Modern Chinese Literature in the May Fourth Era,* Harvard University Press, 1977; George Kao, editor, *Two Writers and the Cultural Revolution,* University of Washington Press, 1980; K. Y. Hsu, editor, *Literature on the People's Republic of China,* Indiana University Press, 1980; Joseph Lau and Leo Lee, editors, *Modern Chinese Stories,* Columbia University Press, 1981. Contributor of about twenty articles, translations, and reviews to scholarly journals in the United States and abroad.

Co-editor of *Bulletin of Concerned Asian Scholars,* 1971-72.

* * *

LINS, Osman 1924-

BRIEF ENTRY: Born July 5, 1924, in Pernambuco, Brazil. Brazilian author. Lins's awards include Brazil's national prize for comedy. Among his writings are *Avalovara* (Edicoes Malhoramentos, 1973), *La Paz existe?* (Summus Editorial, 1977), *Do ideal da gloria* (Summus Editorial, 1977), and *Casos especials de Osman Lins* (Summus Editorial, 1978). *Address:* Alameda Lorena 289 01424, Sao Paulo SP, Brazil. *Biographical/critical sources: Who's Who in the World,* 4th edition, Marquis, 1978.

* * *

LIPSYTE, Marjorie (Rubin) 1932-

PERSONAL: Born April 10, 1932, in Pittsburgh, Pa.; daughter of Henry and Ruby (Price) Rubin; married Robert Lipsyte (a writer), April 6, 1966; children: Sam, Susannah. *Education:* University of Pittsburgh, B.A., 1953. *Agent:* Wendy Lipkind Agency, 225 East 57th St., New York, N.Y. 10022.

CAREER: Associated with *New York Times,* New York, N.Y., 1956-64; associated with New Directions for Women, 1974—. *Member:* Authors Guild, Feminist Writers Guild, Women's Institute for Freedom of the Press.

WRITINGS: Hot Type (novel), Doubleday, 1980.

* * *

LITTLE, Mary E. 1912-

PERSONAL: Born July 29, 1912, in Englewood, Kan.; daughter of Elbert Warfield (a veterinarian) and Pauline Antoinette (a singer; maiden name, Meyer) Little. *Education:* Attended Los Angeles Art Center, 1940-42; Pratt Institute, librarian certificate, 1945. *Politics:* Independent. *Religion:* Anglican Episcopalian. *Residence:* Tucson, Ariz.

CAREER: Writer. New York Public Library, New York, N.Y., clerk and librarian, 1946-50, senior librarian, 1950-74. *Military service:* Women's Army Corps, 1943-45. *Member:* Common Cause, Animal Protection Institute of America, Humane Society of the United States, Arizona Sonora Desert Museum, Humane Society of Arizona. *Awards, honors:* Citation of merit from Society of Illustrators, 1959.

WRITINGS—Juveniles; self-illustrated: Ricardo and the Puppets, Scribner, 1958; *Fidele, the Legend of a Good Dog,* Scribner, 1960; *One, Two, Three for the Library,* Atheneum, 1974; *ABC for the Library,* Atheneum, 1975; *Old Cat and the Kitten,* Atheneum, 1979.

Illustrator: Hugh McCandless, *The Christmas Manger,* Scribner, 1962.

Contributor to periodicals, including *Young Dancer.*

WORK IN PROGRESS: A story for older children; a cat story; the biography of a dog.

SIDELIGHTS: "I emphasize the beauty, glory, and holiness of the ordinary," Little told *CA*, "and humor is the most memorable instrument to convey this. In illustration, I use the simplest, straightest lines, sparest composition, with areas of texture for interest. For the most part, the children of the southeast Bronx, Harlem, and East Harlem are the models for the drawings in my books (from memory, of course).

"I am interested in animal protection, and am especially concerned with the problem of domestic pet overpopulation. I am for humane solutions to the problem, including free spay-neuter clinics, and am against vivisection and the decompression chamber method of euthanasia.

"I studied ballet as a child and young adult. My working career began with a position as head of the dance department in a conservatory of music in a small city. At the same time, I contributed some illustrated, wretchedly rhymed verses about Julia and Anthony, young ballet students, to a magazine. I am drawing on these memories (updated to the present day) in my current work."

AVOCATIONAL INTERESTS: Music, ballet, drama, New York City.

* * *

LIVINGSTON, Carole 1941-
(J. Aphrodite)

PERSONAL: Born February 22, 1941, in New York, N.Y.; daughter of Frank and Sally (Rainer) Rose; married Hyman Livingston, June 14, 1959 (divorced, 1972); children: Jennifer Susan. *Education:* Brooklyn College of the City University of New York, B.A., (magna cum laude), 1968. *Residence:* Fort Lee, N.J. *Office:* Lyle Stuart, Inc., 120 Enterprise Ave., Secaucus, N.J. 07094.

CAREER: Lyle Stuart, Inc. (publisher), Secaucus, N.J., 1960—, currently vice-president in subsidiary rights and publicity. *Member:* Publishers Publicity Association, Confrerie de la Chaine des Rotisseurs, Les Amis du Vin, Wine and Food Society of New York, Women's Party.

WRITINGS: (Under pseudonym J. Aphrodite) *To Turn You On: Thrity-Nine Sex Fantasies for Women*, Lyle Stuart, 1975; *Why Was I Adopted?* (juvenile), Lyle Stuart, 1978; *I'll Never Be Fat Again*, Lyle Stuart, 1980; (with Claire Ciliotta) *Why Am I Going to the Hospital?* (juvenile), Lyle Stuart, 1981.

WORK IN PROGRESS: Another book for children.

SIDELIGHTS: Livingston told *CA:* "My work brings me in contact with authors, regarding the development of book projects, and with other publishers, both domestic and foreign, regarding the sale of publishing rights. My books grew out of a general publishing experience and from specific publicity writing. *To Turn You On* has been published in French, Spanish, Dutch, and German, as well as in English."

AVOCATIONAL INTERESTS: Food, wine, travel.

* * *

LIVINGSTON, M. Jay
See LIVINGSTON, Myran Jabez, Jr.

* * *

LIVINGSTON, Myran Jabez, Jr. 1934-
(M. Jay Livingston)

PERSONAL: Born March 19, 1934, in New York, N.Y.; son of Myran Jabez (an oil company executive) and Josephine (a writer; maiden name, White) Livingston; married Elizabeth Rasmussen, July 28, 1956 (died August 5, 1971); married Bernice Beck (a photographer), November 8, 1971; children: (first marriage) Lisa Browning; (second marriage) Simon Jabez, Sarah Gustine. *Education:* Attended Kenyon College, 1952-56. *Politics:* Independent. *Religion:* Episcopal. *Home:* 10 Main St., Noank, Conn. 06340. *Agent:* Jane Jordan Browne, Multimedia Product Development, Inc., 410 South Michigan Ave., Room 828, Chicago, Ill. 60605.

CAREER: Columbia Broadcasting System, Inc. (CBS-TV), Los Angeles, Calif., writer, director, and producer, 1956-64; McCann-Erickson, Inc. (advertising agency), San Francisco, Calif., writer, director, and producer, 1964-69; Promethean Productions, Los Angeles, writer, director, and producer, 1970-79; writer, 1979-81; Eastman Kodak Co., Rochester, N.Y., writer, director, and producer of documentary and educational films, 1981—. *Member:* Authors Guild, Writers Guild of America (West).

AWARDS, HONORS: Twenty-seven advertising awards for commercials and short films, including Christopher Award from the Columbus Film Festival, and Silver Medal from the New York Film Festival, both 1971; Clio Award for "Most Beautiful Spot"; three awards from American Advertising Federation; two awards from Art Directors Club of Los Angeles; two awards from Art Directors and Artists Club of San Francisco; two Communications Art Awards; two awards from the Atlanta International Film Festival.

WRITINGS: (Under name M. Jay Livingston) *The Prodigy* (novel), Coward, 1978.

WORK IN PROGRESS: The Synapse Function, a suspense novel; *Nightshade*, a mystery novel; *The Adam Encounter*, a novel; work on screenplay adaptation of his own novel, *The Prodigy*.

SIDELIGHTS: Livingston commented: "*The Prodigy* is about child abuse; *The Synapse Function* is about chemical compound poisoning of the environment. To me a passionate involvement with one's subject matter is essential to good writing, and fiction allows projections. Each book is a warning. How far will we let something exist and grow unhindered before we take action? Each book attempts to define that limit and that moment, and each is 'a grotesque' in that the ultimate and most horrifying result is projected as a reality. In this way I hope, without being polemical, to awaken or raise consciousness before 'the bomb' drops.

"As E. M. Forster said in *Howards End,* 'Connect the prose and the passion, and both will be exalted, and human love will be seen at its height.' A good aim and a high aim. I am enjoying my whack at it."

BIOGRAPHICAL/CRITICAL SOURCES: Beverly Hills Times, August 7, 1964; *Back Stage,* June 23, 1978; *Cleveland Plain Dealer,* April 13, 1979; *News-Press of Glendale,* May 4, 1979.

* * *

LIYONG, Taban lo 1938-

PERSONAL: Born in 1938 in Uganda. *Education:* Attended Government Teacher Training College, Kyambogo, Uganda, Knoxville College, University of North Carolina, and Georgetown University; National Teachers College, Kampala, Uganda, B.A.; Howard University, B.A., 1966; University of Iowa, M.F.A., 1968. *Office:* Department of English, University of Nairobi, P.O. Box 30197, Nairobi, Kenya.

CAREER: University of Nairobi, Nairobi, Kenya, member of Institute for Development Studies Cultural Division, 1968—, lecturer in English, 1968—.

WRITINGS: Fixions and Other Stories by a Ugandan Writer, Humanities, 1968 (published in England as *Fixions and Other Stories,* Heinemann, 1969); *The Last Word: Cultural Synthesism,* East African Publishing House, 1969; *Meditations in Limbo* (novel), Equatorial Publishers, 1970, revised edition published as *Meditations,* 1977; (editor) *Eating Chiefs: Lwo Culture From Lolwe to Malkal* (poems), Humanities, 1970; *The Uniformed Man* (stories), East African Literature Bureau, 1971; *Frantz Fanon's Uneven Ribs, With Poems, More and More,* Humanities, 1971; *Another Nigger Dead: Poems,* Humanities, 1972; *Popular Culture of East Africa: Oral Literature,* Longman, 1972; *Thirteen Offensives Against Our Enemies,* East African Literature Bureau, 1973; (editor of reprint) Ham Mukasa, *Sir Apolo Kagwa Discovers Britain,* Heinemann, 1975; *Ballads of Underdevelopment: Poems and Thoughts,* East African Literature Bureau, 1976. Also author of *To Still a Passion* (poems), 1977. Editor of *Mila.*

WORK IN PROGRESS: A Calendar of Wisdom, proverbs in verse; *The African Tourist,* culture criticism; *The American Education of Taban lo Liyong; The Lubumbashi Lectures;* editing *East African Anthology,* literature from Zinjanthropus to Extelcom.*

* * *

LLEWELYN-DAVIES, Richard   1912-1981

OBITUARY NOTICE—See index for *CA* sketch: Born December 24, 1912; died October 26, 1981, in London, England. Architect, urban planner, and author best known for designing the research headquarters of the Atlantic Richfield Company in Philadelphia and the annex to the Tate Gallery in London, England. Llewelyn-Davies believed that architecture should be in harmony with its environment. He was the author of books on architecture, including *Studies in the Functions and Designs of Hospitals, Building Elements, Psychiatric Services and Architecture, Design of Research Laboratories,* and *Children in Hospital.* Obituaries and other sources: *Newsweek,* November 9, 1981.

* * *

LOCHTE, Richard S(amuel)   1944-

PERSONAL: Born October 19, 1944, in New Orleans, La.; son of Richard Samuel (an insurance investigator) and Eileen (a flutist; maiden name, Carbine) Lochte. *Education:* Tulane University, B.A., 1966. *Residence:* Santa Monica, Calif. *Office address:* P.O. Box 5413, Santa Monica, Calif. 90405.

CAREER: Playboy, Chicago, Ill., publicist and writer, 1966-73; free-lance writer, 1973—. *Military service:* U.S. Coast Guard Reserve, 1962-69; became lieutenant commander. *Member:* Writers Guild of America, Mystery Writers of America, National Book Critics Circle.

WRITINGS: The Playboy Writer (nonfiction), HMH Publications, 1968; *Death Mask* (mystery novel), Sherbourne, 1971.

Co-author of "Escape to Athena" (screenplay), ITC/Associated Film Distribution, 1979. Theatre critic for *Los Angeles,* 1974—.

WORK IN PROGRESS: Top Dog, a mystery novel, publication expected in 1982; *The Neon Smile,* a mystery novel, publication expected in 1983; "Ms. Otis Regrets," a screenplay; "The Late News," a screenplay.

SIDELIGHTS: Lochte commented: "It has been said that young writers today are interested in writing The Great American Film instead of The Great American Novel. If true, it is because they are unfamiliar with the differences—make that perils—the two media hold for the writer. As a novelist, the writer is in total control of the material and as such is responsible for research, accuracy, clarity of thought, and so on. As a screenwriter, he or she prepares a blueprint and thereafter is responsible only for cashing the check for services rendered.

"Writing pulled me through schools and college. If I hadn't been interested in it, I'd probably still be stuck back there trying to figure out why $E=mc^2$. When I didn't know an answer, which was often, I made one up. I did some of my most creative writing in college. Later, it was a way of getting away from a nine to five job. What I got away to, of course, was a nine to nine job. Still, work that you like is easy work. The only easier work I can think of is owning a parking lot, because there you can read on the job and you don't have to change typewriter ribbons."

* * *

LOFTUS, Elizabeth F.   1944-

PERSONAL: Born October 16, 1944, in Los Angeles, Calif.; daughter of Sidney (a physician) and Rebecca (a librarian; maiden name, Breskin) Fishman; married Geoffrey R. Loftus (a professor), June 30, 1968. *Education:* University of California, Los Angeles, B.A., 1966; Stanford University, M.A., 1967, Ph.D., 1970. *Office:* Department of Psychology, University of Washington, Seattle, Wash. 98195.

CAREER: New School for Social Research, New York, N.Y., assistant professor of psychology, 1970-73; University of Washington, Seattle, assistant professor, 1973-75, associate professor, 1975-79, professor of psychology, 1979—. Consultant to U.S. Department of Justice and Federal Trade Commission. *Member:* American Psychological Association, American Psychology-Law Society (member of board of directors), Western Psychological Association, Psychonomic Society, Mortar Board, Phi Beta Kappa, Sigma Xi, Psi Chi, Pi Mu Epsilon. *Awards, honors:* Grants from National Institute of Mental Health, 1971-72, 1973-74, 1976—, U.S. Department of Transportation, 1974-76, General Services Administration, 1974-75, and National Science Foundation, 1977—. Fellow of American Council on Education, 1975-76; fellow of Center for Advanced Study in the Behavioral Sciences, Stanford University, 1978-79.

WRITINGS: Learning, Prentice-Hall, 1973; *Human Memory,* Erlbaum, 1976; (with Bourne and Dominowski) *Cognitive Processes,* Prentice-Hall, 1979; *Eyewitness Testimony,* Harvard University Press, 1979; *Memory: Surprising New Insights Into How We Remember and Why We Forget,* Addison-Wesley, 1980; (with C. Wortman) *Psychology,* Random House, 1981. Contributor to psychology journals. Member of editorial boards of *Journal of Experimental Psychology,* 1974—, and *Law and Human Behavior,* 1980—.

SIDELIGHTS: Loftus told *CA* that she believes that memory is highly malleable.

BIOGRAPHICAL/CRITICAL SOURCES: New York Times Book Review, March 9, 1980, April 19, 1981.

* * *

LOGUE, Cal(vin McLeod)   1935-

BRIEF ENTRY: Born July 14, 1935, in Bay Minette, Ala.

American educator and author. Logue began teaching at the University of Georgia in 1967 and became a professor of speech in 1978. His writings include *Readings in Interpersonal and Organizational Communications* (Holbrook, 1969), *Ralph McGill, Editor and Publisher,* three volumes (Moore Publishing, 1969-80), *Speaking: Back to Fundamentals* (Allyn & Bacon, 1976), and *Oratory of Southern Demagogues* (Louisiana State University Press, 1981). *Address:* Department of Speech, University of Georgia, Athens, Ga. 20601. *Biographical/critical sources: Directory of American Scholars,* Volume II: *English, Speech, and Drama,* 7th edition, Bowker, 1978.

* * *

LONDRE, Felicia Hardison   1941-

PERSONAL: Born April 1, 1941, in Fort Lewis, Wash.; daughter of Felix M. (an air force colonel) and Priscilla (Graham) Hardison; married Venne-Richard Londre (an instructor in French), December 16, 1967; children: Tristan Graham, Georgianna Rose. *Education:* University of Montana, B.A. (with high honors), 1962; attended University of Caen, 1962-63; University of Washington, Seattle, M.A., 1964; University of Wisconsin—Madison, Ph.D., 1969. *Religion:* Roman Catholic. *Home:* 528 East 56th St., Kansas City, Mo. 64110. *Office:* Department of Theatre, University of Missouri, 5100 Rockhill Rd., Kansas City, Mo. 64110.

CAREER: University of Wisconsin (now University of Wisconsin—Madison), publicity director for Wisconsin Players, 1964-69; University of Wisconsin, Rock County Campus, Janesville, assistant professor, 1969-75, associate professor of drama and film, 1975; University of Texas, Dallas, assistant professor of theatre and head of theatre program, 1975-78; University of Missouri, Kansas City, associate professor of theatre, and dramaturge with Missouri Repertory Theatre, 1978—. Actress; set designer and technical director; costume and lighting designer; director of drama workshops. Member of Wisconsin Arts Board theatre and film advisory panel, 1974-75; member of advisory board of Bookmark Press, 1981; consultant to Dallas Children's Theatre. *Member:* American Theatre Association. *Awards, honors:* Fulbright grant for France, 1962-63; younger humanist grant from National Endowment for the Humanities, 1971, grant, 1979, senior humanist grant, 1980.

WRITINGS: Tennessee Williams, Ungar, 1979; (contributor) Lina Mainiero and Langdon Lynne Faust, editors, *American Women Writers,* four volumes, Ungar, 1979-81; *Tom Stoppard,* Ungar, 1981; *Federico Garcia Lorca,* Ungar, 1982.

Plays: "Worth a Thousand Words" (one-act), first produced in Missoula, Mont., at Masquer Theatre, May 10, 1962 (published in *Venture,* spring, 1962); "Belonging" (two-act), first produced in Kansas City, Mo., at Unicorn Theatre, May 24, 1981. Contributor of articles and reviews to theatre journals. Member of editorial board of *Theatre History Studies,* 1981.

WORK IN PROGRESS: Research on American themes in plays by women dramatists on the New York stage, 1895-1920; plays.

SIDELIGHTS: Felicia Londre wrote: "I have sought, in my teaching, writing, and directing, to communicate to audiences my enthusiasm and fascination for neglected and controversial masterpieces of dramatic literature. Among the thirty-five stage productions I have directed, for example, are such plays as Vladimir Mayakovsky's 'The Championship of the Universal Class Struggle' and 'The Bedbug,' Yukio Mishima's 'Madame de Sade,' a stage adaptation of the Marx Brothers' 'A Night at the Opera,' Jean Cocteau's 'Eiffel Tower Wedding Party,'

John Ford's ''Tis a Pity She's a Whore,' and Peter Handke's 'Offending the Audience.' I have directed plays by Moliere, Musset, and Labiche in French, and two plays by Federico Garcia Lorca in Spanish. My trips to the U.S.S.R. and my own translations and productions of several Russian folk/fantasy plays have given me a special interest in Russian and Soviet theatre. At present, I am devoting most of my time to dramaturgy and critical writing.''

* * *

LONGYEAR, Christopher R(udston)   1929-

PERSONAL: Born May 8, 1929, in Washington, D.C.,; son of Robert Dudley (a diplomat) and Isabel (Rudston-Reed) Longyear; married N. Jeanne Gaines (a teacher), June 30, 1954; children: Andrew Robert. *Education:* Lehigh University, B.S., 1952; University of Michigan, M.A., 1955, Ph.D., 1961. *Home:* 1208 East Newton St., Seattle, Wash. 98102. *Office:* Department of English, University of Washington, GN-30, Seattle, Wash. 98195.

CAREER: University of Chicago, Chicago, Ill., assistant physicist, 1952-54; Ford Foundation, New York, N.Y., adviser in Lahore, Pakistan, 1961-63; General Electric Co., TEMPO Center for Advanced Studies, Santa Barbara, Calif., member of professionsal staff, 1964-69; University of Connecticut, Storrs, research associate, 1969-71; University of Washington, Seattle, associate professor of English, 1972—. Postdoctoral fellow at Harvard University, 1967-69. *Member:* Modern Language Association of America, American Cybernetics Society, Association for Computational Linguistics, John Barton Wolgamot Society. *Awards, honors:* Fulbright grant for West Germany, 1957-58; American Council of Learned Societies grant, 1971.

WRITINGS: A Manual for Secondary School Teachers of English in West Pakistan, Educational Extension Centre (Lahore, Pakistan), 1963; *Linguistically Determined Categories of Meanings,* Mouton, 1971; (contributor) Klaus Krippendorff, editor, *Communication and Control in Society,* Gordon & Breach, 1979. Contributor of articles and reviews to scholarly journals. Editor of *Language Learning,* 1963-64; associate editor of *American Society for Cybernetics Forum,* 1975—.

WORK IN PROGRESS: Nature's Grammar: A Representational Theory of Language; translating *Le Surmale* (title means "The Super Male"), by Alfred Jarry; *Grace Notes,* poems; a book on the scientific bases for literary language.

SIDELIGHTS: Longyear told *CA:* "I am especially interested in experimental epistemology and formal representations of knowledge structures. The ability of the inventive human mind to combine productively little-understood flashes of intuition with formal, disciplined thought endlessly fascinates me. We can simulate some of the latter on computers, but we have not yet succeeded with much of the former. I now believe intuitive abilities to be related to how representations of any given world of discourse are structured in memory. In humans, much of the structuring occurs under control of the language used, hence my interest in natural languages and in computational linguistics. My research is directed toward exploring how various formal representational structures enable or discourage even the most rudimentary insights. As a polyglot, I can sometimes catch a minor insight happening in the process of translation. I dabble in poetry for similar reasons, but perhaps even more for recreation.''

LOPATE, Carol
See ASCHER, Carol

*   *   *

LOPEZ, Manuel Dennis 1934-

PERSONAL: Born January 25, 1934, in Westfield, Mass.; son of Manuel and Marcel (Bedard) Lopez. *Education:* Clark University, B.A., 1956; Drexel University, M.S.L.S., 1961; also attended New School for Social Research, American International College, Rensselaer Polytechnic Institute, and State University of New York at Buffalo. *Home:* 225 Princeton Court, Eggertsville, N.Y. 14226. *Office:* Lockwood Memorial Library, State University of New York at Buffalo, Amherst, N.Y. 14260.

CAREER: Delaware Valley Council, Philadelphia, Pa., Librarian, 1960-61; State University of New York at Albany, asistant to head of circulation at Hawley Library, 1961-64; State University of New York at Buffalo, reference librarian and bibliographer at Lockwood Memorial Library, 1964—, chairman of social science bibliographers, 1969-71, acting head of reference, 1970-71, guest lecturer in library science, 1971-73 and 1975. *Member:* Society of Indexers, Association of College and Research Libraries, New York Library Association, State University of New York Librarians Association, Association of Librarians of the State University of New York at Buffalo (president, 1967-69), Beta Phi Mu. *Awards, honors:* Grant from *Journal of Library History,* 1969.

WRITINGS: (With Caroline Zalewski) *Serials in Language, Literature, Psychology, Sociology, and Social Work: A Union List of Serials in Selected Libraries in Western New York,* State University of New York at Buffalo, 1965; *Serials in Selected Academic Libraries in the Albany, New York Area: A Union List,* State University of New York at Buffalo, 1966; (with Wallace D. Mohn) *Selected Serials in Western New York,* State University of New York at Buffalo, 1966; *Bibliography of the History of Libraries in New York State,* School of Library Science, Florida State University, 1971, *Supplement: 1968-1972,* State Education Department, State University of New York at Albany, 1976; *New York: A Guide to Information and Reference Sources,* Scarecrow, 1980.

Contributor: Bill Katz and Robert Burgess, editors, *Library Literature: The Best of 1974,* Scarecrow, 1975; Lloyd DeMause, editor, *A Bibliography of Psychohistory,* Garland Publishing, 1975. Also contributor of about twenty articles and reviews to library journals.

WORK IN PROGRESS: Research on history of libraries and books, printing, history in general, and science fiction.

SIDELIGHTS: Lopez told *CA:* "I agree with Thoreau that one should be 'well-travelled' wherever one finds oneself, thus my research on New York and on libraries. I also lived in Greenland for a year." *Avocational interests:* Collecting antique inkwells, "all things Oriental."

*   *   *

LORD THOMAS
See THOMAS, (William) Miles (Webster)

*   *   *

los RIOS, Francisco Giner de
See GINER de los RIOS, Francisco

LOTHRINGEN, Geza Louis Eusebius Gebhard Ralphael Albert Maria von Habsburg
See von HABSBURG-LOTHRINGEN, Geza Louis Eusebius Gebhard Ralphael Albert Maria

*   *   *

LOTTINVILLE, Savoie 1906-

PERSONAL: Born November 17, 1906, in Hagerman, Idaho; son of Walter Jacob and Mary E. (Igoe) Lottinville; married Rita Higgins, June 15, 1933 (died May 22, 1955); married Helene Collins, December 18, 1957; children: Marie Lottinville Livesay, Elinor Lottinville Jones. *Education:* University of Oklahoma, B.A., 1929; Oxford University, B.A., 1932, M.A., 1939. *Politics:* Republican. *Religion:* Roman Catholic. *Home:* 503 Shawnee, Norman, Okla. 73071.

CAREER: Oklahoma City Times, Oklahoma City, Okla., reporter, 1932-33; University of Oklahoma Press, Norman, assistant editor, 1933-35, business manager, 1935-38, director, 1938-67; University of Oklahoma, Norman, Regents Professor of History, 1967-73; writer, 1973—. Vice-president of Doric Corp., 1967. Chairman of Oklahoma Advisory Commission of National Commission on Civil Rights; juror for National Endowment for the Humanities, 1968-73; consultant to National Park Service.

MEMBER: Association of American University Presses (president, 1949-51), Society of American Historians, Western Historical Association, Economic Club of Oklahoma, Phi Beta Kappa, Sigma Delta Chi, Delta Tau Delta, Oklahoma City Men's Dinner Club, St. Catherine's Society. *Awards, honors:* Rhodes scholar at Oxford University, 1932; distinguished service citation from University of Oklahoma, 1966; member of Oklahoma Journalism Hall of Fame; Litt.D. from Southern Methodist University, 1952; D.Hum. from Coe College, 1972.

WRITINGS: (Editor with George E. Hyde) *The Life of George Bent,* University of Oklahoma Press, 1968; (editor) Paul Wilhelm, *Travels in North America, 1822-24,* University of Oklahoma Press, 1973; (editor with Robert V. Hine) *Soldier in the West,* University of Oklahoma Press, 1974; *The Rhetoric of History,* University of Oklahoma Press, 1976; (with Kenneth W. Thompson and others) *Herbert Butterfield: The Ethics of History and Politics,* University Press of America, 1980; (editor) Thomas Nuttall, *A Journal of Travels Into the Arkansas Territory During the Year 1819,* University of Oklahoma Press, 1980.

Contributor: *Probing the American West,* Museum of New Mexico Press, 1962; R. Dugger, *Three Men in Texas,* University of Texas Press, 1967.

WORK IN PROGRESS: Spain in the Mississippi Valley, 1795-1804, with A. P. Nasatir.

SIDELIGHTS: Lottinville told *CA:* "Thirty-five years as a publisher, thirty of them as director of operations, convinced me that I too should have the opportunity to practice what I had been preaching to authors; that is, write books of my own. Believe it or not, I found the task far more exacting than copy-editorship. Daniel Boorstin, Librarian of Congress, has made the discerning distinction between knowledge and information in the nonfiction field. The former, I believe, must precede the latter, for the former has to be right or it is nothing. My modest application of this principle may show in the three large humanistic series I founded and edited for many years at University of Oklahoma Press—'American Exploration and Travel,' 'The Centers of Civilization,' and 'The Western Frontier Library.'"

LOTTMAN, Herbert R.   1927-

PERSONAL: Born August 16, 1927, in New York, N.Y.; son of George D. (a Broadway press agent and a public relations representative) and Betty (Brackman) Lottman. *Education:* New York University, B.A., 1948; Columbia University, M.A., 1951. *Home:* BP 214 75264 Paris Cedex 06, France. *Agent:* Lois Wallace, Wallace & Sheil Agency, Inc., 177 East 70th St., New York, N.Y. 10021.

CAREER: Farrar, Straus & Giroux, New York City, Paris editor, agent, and representative, 1956-69; *Publishers Weekly,* New York City, contributing editor, 1972-79, international correspondent, 1979—; free-lance writer, 1960—.

WRITINGS: Detours From the Grand Tour (travel), Prentice-Hall, 1970; *How Cities Are Saved,* Universe Books, 1976; *Albert Camus: A Biography,* Doubleday, 1979; *The Left Bank,* Houghton, 1982. Contributor to magazines and to newspapers, including *New York Times Magazine, Harper's, Saturday Review, Signature, Travel and Leisure,* and *New York Times.*

SIDELIGHTS: Praising the biography *Camus,* John Sturrock of the *New York Times* marveled at Herbert Lottman's use of indiscriminate detail as well as his ability to portray Camus as an artist and a man. He put forth that "Herbert Lottman's life [of Camus] is the first to be written, either in French or in English, and it is exhaustive, a labor of love and of wonderful industry."

According to Diane Johnson of the *Chicago Tribune, Camus* chronicles its subject's daily actions in addition to being a collection of facts and dates. Though some critics, such as Deidre Bair of the *Washington Post,* found the biographer's use of detail disconcerting, many felt that the exhaustive display of exact facts was, as Harold Clurman of *Nation* put it, the work of "a perceptive and conscientious reporter." Critics claim that these details, gathered through Lottman's original research and from his access to Camus's family members and private letters, provided new and necessary information to the study of the artist. "Lottman has written a brilliant and absorbing book, which supplies new insight simply by including all the light and shade," wrote the *New Statesman*'s Christopher Hitchens. "The detail and care is extraordinary; further slipshod generalisations about Camus will simply not be tolerable from now on."

Some critics also felt that Lottman was able to demystify Camus, presenting the realities surrounding the artist and communicating his total person. The book, Sturrock suggested, is the gallant and necessary work that brings the "lay saint," as Camus was once called, back to the realm of mortals. The biography "allows us to look at and listen to the writer as he works," explained John Leonard of the *New York Times,* "without the blinkers and the earmuffs, the periscopes and the headphones, of the Zeitgeist to mess up our minds." The book is credited with clarifying squabbles concerning Camus and with giving its readers "a clearer look at Camus' real importance," maintained Hitchens. "What emerges from Mr. Lottman's tireless devotions," Leonard observed, "is a portrait of the artist, the outsider, the humanist and skeptic, simultaneously sensuous and austere, righteous and guilty, that breaks the heart." "Lottman's achievement," concluded Johnson, "is considerable."

CA INTERVIEW

This interview was conducted by mail, with Herbert Lottman

writing his replies on December 8, 1980, while he was in an express train traveling from Paris to Rome, where he was journeying to write a story on a huge Vatican publishing project.

Lottman is a contemporary version of that literary figure that was far more common a generation or two ago—the American expatriate who makes a living by extensive journalism. He is a widely published world traveler, the author of a definitive study of Albert Camus, and the world's leading authority on the international publishing scene. Lottman can even turn his hand to humor; for example, the writer published an account of how he discovered a pay phone in Paris from which he could make free calls to anywhere in the world and of how he came to bitterly regret revealing its existence.

CA began by asking why and how Lottman originally went to Paris and how he was able to remain there. "I was one of many in my college generation who dreamed of not just visiting but *living* in Paris," he said. "Elliot Paul's *The Last Time I Saw Paris,* a nostalgic diary published during the Second World War, contributed to that." Lottman was at school when the Fulbright program of scholarships for study abroad was introduced, and he immediately drafted a project. "It was supposed to be done in London, but in those early freewheeling days the Fulbright people actually came back to say that London was full up and what about Paris? So I revised my itinerary and found a friendly teacher of beginner's French who was willing to say I was a good learner, and off I went to Paris in the 1949-50 school year."

As soon as he could find a way to return to Paris after his first visit, he did—this time as the Paris editor, agent, and all-around representative of the publisher Farrar, Straus & Giroux, which was "looking for ways to be more active on the international scene, although they already published Francois Mauriac and Colette at the time."

At first, said Lottman, he wanted to travel as much and as far as he could: "For example, on a vacation I'd fly to Naples or Istanbul rather than visit places close to home in France, and soon I found I knew Italy better than any region of France." Lottman began recording his jaunts to capture "the things I was exploring—often just for fun—or to meet travel expenses." He insisted, however, that he never saw himself as a professional travel writer, "and I wouldn't want to become one or to be considered one: the subject matter lacks the depth and the intellectual standards I need, or think I need, even when combined with literary interests, as in my book *Detours From the Grand Tour.*"

Has Lottman ever been tempted toward fiction? 'In college and soon after that, armed with aesthetic theory and badly assembled lessons in style from some of my favorite writers—Joyce, Yeats, Eliot, Evelyn Waugh, and a number of early twentieth-century English-language writers—I tried writing short stories and even novels. But they were so obviously derivative and so removed from my own experience that I was as dissatisfied as my readers were, and they included a friendly literary agent and a teacher or two." Lottman added reflectively: "Perhaps it's a sour-grapes attitude, but I felt our postwar world was too matter-of-fact for fiction; and I felt silly writing it. So I became a slave to facts."

The facts to which he placed himself in bondage were primarily those connected with the publishing scene. How did this specialty develop? "While exploring the European publishing world for Farrar, Straus & Giroux, I sometimes found myself in a relatively inaccessible place such as Belgrade or Warsaw—inaccessible, that is, for booklovers. The late Roger Smith, at that time executive editor of *Publishers Weekly (PW)*, heard about these trips and asked me to report about any interesting book event wherever I happened to be. Later, when I was ready to concentrate on writing, *PW* offered me the possibility of a regular outlet without restricting my freedom to write for other publications as well.''

Lottman's major work to date, his monumental study of Camus, also grew indirectly out of his publishing contacts. ''The idea was developed with Doubleday's European-based senior editor, Beverly Gordey; she was interested in the life of Camus, I in Camus's times. It was something that could be done—most of it, at least—in Paris, where I happened to be, and in my free time. The sources were often available evenings and weekends, as I was, or at the other end of a phone line, or by mail. Since there were no useful books available on Camus, I had to start from scratch, and that was my good fortune. It was a matter of digging—finding the right people, getting them to talk, always phoning back to check facts or to cross-examine after getting different versions of an incident. These are all things a newspaper or a magazine writer must do all the time.''

Lottman's following project, *The Left Bank,* has recently been completed. He described it as ''a book about the politically engaged writers and artists of Paris—foreigners as well as natives—who happened to love and work and fight in Paris from the 1930's to the Cold War.'' He said he would have liked to go on from his biography of Camus to a similar study of Jean-Paul Sarte, but he explained sadly: ''I found I couldn't get close to him, although he was living only a few blocks away from me at the time. He had surrounded himself with 'authorized' biographers who were busy producing Sartre's version of Sartre and keeping the rest of us away. My ideal subject would be a modern biography of Flaubert, making use of newly discovered materials, but I haven't been able to find an American publisher willing to back the project.''

Lottman's output for *PW* is prodigious, averaging a major report or article a month, plus many shorter pieces. *CA* wondered how he still managed to find time to do any other work, particularly full-scale books, with all the demands of time and concentration. ''My work for *PW* is usually concentrated,'' Lottman replied. ''When I'm on a tour of Yugoslavia, or Brazil, or China, or wherever it is, I'm working nights and breakfasts and weekends—and holidays, too. But between these seven-days-a-week stints I have more free time than I'd have in an office job. By sacrificing weekends and vacations (I travel and/or work while others are on holidays just as I'm sometimes free from nine to five while others are at work), I manage to produce nearly as much as a full-time writer does.''

Lottman is phenomenally fast as a notetaker and as a writer. ''Yes, speed is the answer. I organize my material—years of journalism showed me how—so that when I sit down to the actual writing I can really dash. I write just as well (or as badly) whether I go fast or slow, and many whole chapters of *Albert Camus,* up to eight thousand words in length, were written in a single twelve-hour day, starting at 7 or 8 A.M.—and that included referring to notes or checking references on nearly every line.'' As to his methods: ''I work in longhand, often standing up, revise as I go along, and then type, making more changes. I use no mechanical aids, not even a tape recorder for interviews.''

The secret of his productivity is the planning. ''In the kind of expository writing I do, I plot out everything in advance. I have devised rather complex systems of note-taking and especially information retrieval—too complicated to explain in an interview. And once I have all of this apparatus in hand, the rest is easy. The note-taking often goes on under conditions

just like those of a newspaper city room, but while I can write a news story in a crowd, or in a car, or in a train, or in a plane, the cumbersome notes required for the kind of nonfiction I do makes it necessary for me to have a lot of room and a lot of quiet while writing a book. And I'm stingy—I use nearly every scrap of material I gather, sometimes to the dismay of my editors.''

What is Lottman's favorite reading—if he has time for any? ''I used not to read for relaxation at all—only to learn. Then, when I began writing books that required large amounts of preparatory reading—I'm a very slow reader—I simply didn't have the time or energy for leisure reading. But lately I find myself returning to distraction and turning to my college favorites like Graham Greene or Evelyn Waugh or to sophisticated mystery stories —sophisticated so that I don't feel that I'm *totally* wasting my time.''

Lottman is multilingual, speaking French fluently. ''I can read Italian and even interview—and be interviewed—in it, but that's an Italian I dare not commit to paper. I read Spanish.''

Has he never wanted to be anything other than a writer? ''Being a writer allows you to be so many things because you participate in them. I've stood in kitchens with great chefs preparing meals, flown in an open cockpit with a photographer, stood by as Jean-Luc Godard made a movie, talked books with Simone de Beauvoir, sailed dangerous waters with a crew bringing supplies to a lonely Brittany lighthouse. . . .''

As to what makes him proudest of his profession, Lottman's reply may well serve as a good reporter's credo: ''To think that I'm discovering and putting into useful form some essential knowledge; feeling that I'm correcting errors, not making new ones; making an effort to observe a standard of excellence; eliminating some of the nonsense that often passes for fact; writing the best I can; and hoping that an editor will double-check to save me from nonsense and bad writing.''

BIOGRAPHICAL/CRITICAL SOURCES: Times Educational Supplement, October 28, 1977; *New York Times Book Review,* March 18, 1979, November 25, 1979, April 5, 1981; *New York Times,* March 19, 1979; *Time,* March 19, 1979; *Washington Post Book World,* March 25, 1979, March 15, 1981; *Chicago Tribune,* April 8, 1979; *Nation,* April 14, 1979; *Newsweek,* April 16, 1979; *Chronicle of Higher Education,* April 30, 1979; *Commonweal,* May 11, 1979; *Observer,* June 17, 1979; *New Leader,* June 18, 1979; *MacLean's Magazine,* June 25, 1979; *Economist,* July 7, 1979; *New Statesman,* July 20, 1979; *Best Sellers,* August, 1979; *Books and Bookmen,* August, 1979; *New Catholic World,* November, 1979; *Times Literary Supplement,* December 14, 1979; *American Scholar,* winter, 1979-80; *Modern Age,* winter, 1980.

—*Interview by John F. Baker*

*   *   *

LOUIS, J(ack) C(harles), Jr.   1949-

PERSONAL: Born January 21, 1949, in New York, N.Y.; son of Jack Charles (a securities broker) and Gloria (Trope) Louis. *Education:* Wesleyan University, Middletown, Conn., B.A., 1971. *Home:* 410 East 57th St., New York, N.Y. 10022. *Agent:* Bret Adams Ltd., 36 East 61st St., New York, N.Y. 10021.

CAREER: Orpheus College, San Francisco, Calif., associate instructor in history, 1974-75; *City,* San Francisco, researcher, 1975-76; WNET-TV, New York, N.Y., researcher, 1976-77; writer, 1977—.

WRITINGS: (With Harvey Yazijian) *The Cola Wars* (nonfiction), Everest House, 1980.

Author of "A Die-Hard for Dallas" (two-act play about Jack Ruby), first produced in San Francisco, Calif., at DNA Theatre Company, September 7, 1975. Author of "Tennis Life," a column in *Boston Phoenix.* Also contributor to magazines and newspapers, including *Oui, Advertising Age,* and *In These Times.*

WORK IN PROGRESS: How Do You Spell Belief?, nonfiction on contemporary Christianity; "The Chairman of the Damned," a film script.

SIDELIGHTS: Louis told *CA:* "A wise man once said, 'Study as if you would live forever, live as if you would die tomorrow.' Whether expository, narrative, or poetic, writing embraces both halves of that imperative. It demands the clarity and understanding born of study, even as it depends for its vibrance and depth on a quickened spirit.

"My own nonfiction writing is interdisciplinary, blending investigative reporting with sociology, anthropology, and history. Origins and process are vital, especially as they illuminate something powerful and dramatic in the present. In this sense, nonfiction is also an important wellspring and, indeed, rehearsal for the fictional form."

BIOGRAPHICAL/CRITICAL SOURCES: Atlanta Constitution, December 7, 1980; *Washington Post,* January 21, 1981.

*　　*　　*

LOUIS, Pierre(-Felix) 1870-1925
(Pierre Louÿs)

BRIEF ENTRY: Born December 10, 1870, in Ghent, Belgium; died June 4, 1925, in Paris, France. French novelist and poet. One of Louis's best-known works was *Chansons de Bilitis* (1894), a collection of prose poems so perfectly classical in style, feminine in point of view, and accurately researched that many scholars took them for translations of works by a poetess from ancient Greece. Louis's reverence for physical beauty was revealed in *Aphrodite: Amours antiques* (1896), a novel about a courtesan in old Alexandria. Its eroticism made the novel a best-seller, and Louis's passion for art and form made it a critical success. *La Femme et le pantin* (1898), a psychological novel, was as erotic as his earlier work, but Louis claimed it to be a moral tale, illustrating the ultimate price of passionate excess. His rhythmic sensuality and respect for stylistic precision was carried on by such admirers as musician Claude Debussy. *Biographical/critical sources: Twentieth Century Authors: A Biographical Dictionary of Modern Literature,* H. W. Wilson, 1942; *Columbia Dictionary of Modern European Literature,* Columbia University Press, 1967; *Encyclopedia of World Literature in the Twentieth Century,* updated edition, Ungar, 1967.

*　　*　　*

LOUYS, Pierre
See LOUIS, Pierre(-Felix)

*　　*　　*

LOWRY, (Clarence) Malcolm 1909-1957

BRIEF ENTRY: Born July 28, 1909, near Liverpool, England; died June 27, 1957, in London, England. British poet and novelist. Lowry began writing after he abandoned his studies at Cambridge University for a stint at sea. Mining his experiences he wrote *Ultramarine* (1933), a symbolic stream of consciousness novel concerning a remorseful seafaring youth. After the novel's ambivalent reception, Lowry migrated to Mexico and indulged his alcoholism. He divorced his first wife in 1939, remarried soon afterward, and moved to British Columbia. There Lowry and his wife lived in a handmade shack. For the next fourteen years Lowry continued drinking heavily while he wrote. In 1947 he produced *Under the Volcano,* a novel about an alcoholic British consul in Mexico. Lowry's reputation rests largely on this symbolic and semi-hallucinatory work, which some critics rank with James Joyce's *Ulysses* as a twentieth-century masterpiece. His posthumous publications include *Selected Poems* (1962); a collection of short stories, *Hear Us O Lord From Heaven Thy Dwelling Place* (1961); and three novels, *Lunar Caustic* (1963), *Dark as the Grave Wherein My Friend Is Laid* (1968), and *October Ferry to Gabriola* (1970). *Biographical/critical sources: The Reader's Encyclopedia,* 2nd edition, Crowell, 1965; *Longman Companion to Twentieth Century Literature,* Longman, 1970; *Cassell's Encyclopaedia of World Literature,* revised edition, Morrow, 1973.

*　　*　　*

LUGG, George Wilson 1902-

PERSONAL: Born February 15, 1902, in Coudersport, Pa.; son of Charles H. (a banker) and Minnie J. (a teacher; maiden name, Wilson) Lugg; married Marjorie G. Newman, March 1, 1973; children: Gerald N., Linda A. Lugg Thomas. *Education:* Syracuse University, B.S. in C.E., 1925. *Home:* 907 Northeast 15th Ave., Apt. 4-H, Fort Lauderdale, Fla. 33304. *Agent:* Betty Wright, P.O. Box 1069, Moore Haven, Fla. 33471.

CAREER: New York Telephone Co., Albany, engineer, 1925-61; writer, 1980—. Worked in a tannery, a glass factory, a steel mill, an insulator factory, and on a vegetable farm. Associated with Goodwill Industries, Haven School for the Retarded, and Dade County Council on Aging. *Member:* National Audubon Society, New York Telephone Company Telephone Pioneers.

WRITINGS: The Interest Game, Rainbow Books, 1980; *Religion? No! Good Living? Yes!,* Rainbow Books, 1980.

SIDELIGHTS: The Interest Game, dealing with interest paid on loans by borrowers, tackles the problem of uneven distribution of wealth and offers a solution to the current situation, which allows entrenched wealth to compound itself in the face of surrounding abject poverty.

Lugg's second book asks: "What kind of philosophy do we need to (graciously) accept life as we find it in this confusing world of ours?" Lugg, who describes himself as a "happy agnostic," put the question to many people and compiled a book from fifty of the answers.

*　　*　　*

LUKE, Thomas
See MASTERTON, Graham

*　　*　　*

LUONGO, C. Paul 1930-

PERSONAL: Born December 31, 1930, in Winchester, Mass.; son of Carmine and Carmela (Gilberti) Luongo. *Education:* Bentley College, Diploma, 1951; Cambridge School of Radio and Television, graduated, 1955; Suffolk University, B.S./B.A., 1955; Babson College, M.B.A., 1956. *Residence:* Boston, Mass. *Office:* 441 Stuart St., Boston, Mass. 02116.

CAREER: Raytheon Co., Lexington, Mass., junior executive, 1956-59; account executive with Young & Rubicam, Inc., 1959-62; Copley Advertising Agency, Boston, Mass., vice-president, 1962-64; C. Paul Luongo Co., Boston, president, 1964—. Guest on television and radio programs in Canada and the United States, including "Tomorrow Show" and "Merv Griffin Show." *Military service:* U.S. Army, 1952-54. *Member:* Bostonian Society, New York Athletic Club. *Awards, honors:* A.A.S. from Graham Junior College, 1970.

WRITINGS: America's Best! 100, Sterling, 1980. Author of two syndicated columns, "Public Relations Today," 1974—, and "Communications Today," 1976—.

SIDELIGHTS: Luongo commented: "Of all the things I've done in my life, the writing, editing, and research for *America's Best! 100* was at once the most exciting and frustrating, and more importantly, the most costly decision I've ever made.

"I advise future authors that it is better not to be published at all than to deal with disreputable publishers; forget dealing with literary agents unless you're a big name; don't write a book with the sole intention of making money; don't spend any money you can't afford to lose; don't think that one book on the best-seller list will make you a household name; don't think that many publishers are offering exotic sums to authors—there aren't more than a dozen or so who can demand superstar publishing contracts."

*   *   *

LYDON, James Gavin 1927-

BRIEF ENTRY: Born September 23, 1927, in Boston, Mass. American historian, educator, and author. Lydon began teaching colonial American history at Duquesne University in 1960 and became a professor in 1965. He wrote *Privates, Privateers and Profits* (Parnassus, 1970). *Address:* Department of History, Duquesne University, Pittsburgh, Pa. 15219. *Biographical/critical sources: Directory of American Scholars,* Volume I: *History,* 7th edition, Bowker, 1978.

*   *   *

LYFICK, Warren
See REEVES, Lawrence F.

*   *   *

LYKKEN, David Thoreson 1928-

PERSONAL: Surname is pronounced *Lick*-en; born June 18, 1928, in Minneapolis, Minn.; son of Henry Gilman (an engineer) and Frances (Hamilton) Lykken; married Harriet Betts (a wildlife lobbyist), May 11, 1952; children: Jesse H., Joseph D., Matthew A. *Education:* University of Minnesota, B.A., 1949, M.A., 1952, Ph.D., 1955. *Home:* 4600 Emerson S., Minneapolis, Minn. 55409. *Office:* Department of Psychiatry, University of Minnesota, Minneapolis, Minn. 55455.

CAREER: Minneapolis General Hospital, Minneapolis, Minn., clinical psychologist, 1953; University of Minnesota, Minneapolis, assistant professor, 1957-59, associate professor, 1959-65, professor of psychiatry and psychology, 1965—. Fellow of Center for Advanced Studies in the Behavioral Sciences, Palo Alto, Calif., 1959-60. Member of board of trustees of Personnel Decisions Research Institute; director of Minnesota Twin Study, 1970—; member of Minnesota governor's Commission on Nuclear Safety, 1978—.

MEMBER: International Twin Society, American Psychological Association (fellow), American Association for the Advancement of Science (fellow), Society for Psychophysiological Research (president, 1980-81), Behavior Genetics Society, New York Academy of Sciences. *Awards, honors:* National Science Foundation fellow at University of London, 1954-55; National Institutes of Health fellow, 1955-57; National Institute of Mental Health fellow, 1968-69.

WRITINGS: A Tremor in the Blood: Uses and Abuses of the Lie Detector, McGraw, 1981. Editor of series, "Personality and Psychopathology," Academic Press. Contributor of about seventy articles to psychology journals. Associate editor of *Physiological Psychology.*

WORK IN PROGRESS: A monograph on the psychopathic personality, publication by Academic Press expected in 1984; psychological and psychophysiological studies of twins reared apart.

SIDELIGHTS: Lykken told *CA:* "Too many scientists are reluctant to 'get involved' in public or controversial issues. I am one of a mere handful of scientifically trained people ever to look critically at the mushrooming lie detector industry. I think those with special knowledge or training have an obligation to contribute what they can. I also believe that writing clearly for a general audience is an exciting and respectable challenge.

"Our current work on twins reared apart and reunited as adults is the most exciting research that I have been engaged in. It, too, is controversial but for what I think are confused, mistaken reasons. I hope we shall be able to present our findings in a way that will clarify these issues."

*   *   *

LYNCH, Edith M. 1912-

PERSONAL: Born July 26, 1912, in Toledo, Ohio; daughter of Hans Peter (an engineer) and Anna (Nossen) Carstensen; married Peter J. Lynch, May 15, 1950; children: Carolyn Eileen Lynch Wohlfahrlstaetter. *Education:* Attended Bowling Green State University, 1930-32, and Ohio State University, 1934-42. *Religion:* Lutheran. *Home and office:* 20 Murray Pl., Staten Island, N.Y. 10304.

CAREER: Teacher of math and English at junior high school in Oregon, Ohio, 1930-41; U.S. Department of Labor, Washington, D.C., economist in wage analysis division, 1941-47; National Foremens Institute, labor reporter, 1947-51; National Industrial Conference Board (now The Conference Board), New York City, information specialist, 1951-54; American Management Association, New York City, assistant division manager, 1954-60; National Metal Trades Association, (now American Association of Industrial Management), Willow Grove, Pa., vice-president, 1960-67; National Retail Merchants Association, vice-president of personnel, 1967-78; writer, 1976—. Adjunct professor of economics and management at Wagner College, St. John's University, St. Vincent's College, and Pratt University, 1978-81. Past chairman of Silver Bay Association; member of board of trustees of Staten Island Hospital. *Member:* Personnel Club. *Awards, honors:* Award of merit from the New York Personnel Management Association, 1977.

WRITINGS: (With James M. Black) *How to Move in Management,* McGraw, 1967; *Executive Suite: Female Style,* American Management Association, 1973; *The Woman's Guide to Management,* Cornerstone, 1978; *Decades: Lifestyle Changes in Career Expectations,* American Management Association, 1980; *People Productivity in Retailing,* Lebhar-Friedman, 1980.

SIDELIGHTS: Lynch told *CA:* "I have been very much interested in management—especially personnel management—for the last thirty years. I believe that women and young people have made great progress over these years but that we still have a long way to go.

"My second career, teaching at the universities, has kept me in touch with young people aspiring to be managers. I end my career with great confidence that our future is in good hands because of the caliber of the young people I meet who come from all over the world.

"As for women, here, too, I have great hopes that their progress up the management ladder will be steady and rewarding."

*   *   *

LYND, Helen Merrell 1896-1982

OBITUARY NOTICE: Born March 17, 1896, in LaGrange, Ill.; died January 30, 1982, in Warren, Ohio. Educator, sociologist, and author. An instructor of social philosophy at Sarah Lawrence College from 1928 until 1965, Lynd is best remembered for her book *Middletown: A Study in American Contemporary Culture*, which she wrote with her husband, Robert, a sociology professor at Columbia University. *Middletown*, a study of Muncie, Ind., was the first in-depth sociological study of a small American community. Published in 1929, *Middletown* was followed by *Middletown in Transition* in 1937. Among Lynd's other books are *On Shame and the Search for Identity, England in the Eighteen-Eighties,* and *Towards Discovery.* Obituaries and other sources: *Chicago Tribune,* February 2, 1982; *Newsweek,* February 15, 1982; *Time,* February 15, 1982; *AB Bookman's Weekly,* February 15, 1982.

*   *   *

LYNN, Laurence Edwin, Jr. 1937-

PERSONAL: Born June 10, 1937, in Long Beach, Calif.; son of Laurence Edwin (in U.S. Army Corps of Engineers) and Marjorie Louise (a librarian; maiden name, Hart) Lynn; married second wife, Patricia Ramsey, 1972; children: (first marriage) Stephen Louis, Daniel Laurence, Diana Jane, Julia Suzanne. *Education:* University of California, Berkeley, A.B., 1959; Yale University, Ph.D., 1966. *Religion:* Protestant. *Home:* 38 Witches Spring Rd., R.F.D. 3, Milford, N.H. 03055. *Office:* John Fitzgerald Kennedy School of Government, Harvard University, 79 Boylston St., Cambridge, Mass. 02138.

CAREER: U.S. Department of Defense, Washington, D.C., weapon systems analyst in office of the assistant secretary of state, 1965-66, director of Strategic Mobility and Transportation Division and of economics and mobility forces, 1966-68, deputy assistant secretary of defense for economic and resource analysis, 1968-69; National Security Council, Washington, D.C., assistant for program analysis, 1969-70; Stanford University, Stanford, Calif., associate professor of business economics, 1970-71; U.S. Department of Health, Education and Welfare, Washington, D.C., assistant secretary for planning and evaluation, 1971-73; U.S. Department of the Interior, Washington, D.C., assistant secretary for program development and budget, 1973-74; Brookings Institution, Washington, D.C., senior fellow, 1974-75; Harvard University, Cambridge, Mass., professor of public policy, 1975—. Member of National Academy of Sciences/National Research Council committee on child development research and public policy (past chairman); member of board of overseers of Rand Corp. Institute for Civil Justice. *Military service:* U.S. Army, served in infantry, 1963-65; became first lieutenant.

MEMBER: National Academy of Public Administration, American Economic Association, Council on Foreign Rela-

tions, Nature Conservancy, Society for the Preservation of New England Antiquities, Society for the Protection of New Hampshire Forests, University of California Alumni Association, Phi Beta Kappa, Sigma Chi. *Awards, honors:* Meritorious civilian service medal from U.S. Secretary of Defense, 1969; Presidential Citation of Distinguished Achievement, 1970.

WRITINGS: (Editor) *Knowledge and Policy: The Uncertain Connection,* National Academy of Sciences, 1978; (editor) *Studies in the Management of Social Research and Development: Selected Policy Areas,* National Academy of Sciences, 1979; *The State and Human Services: Organizational Change in a Political Context,* M.I.T. Press, 1980; *Designing Public Policy: A Casebook on the Role of Policy Analysis,* Goodyear Publishing, 1980; (with David Whitman) *The President as Policymaker: Jimmy Carter and Welfare Reform,* Temple University Press, 1981; *Managing the Public's Business,* Basic Books, 1981; (with Steven Smith) *Public Policy Toward the Mentally Ill: Its Past and Future,* Basic Books, 1982; *Managing Public Policy,* Winthrop Publishing, 1983.

Contributor: D. I. Cleland and W. R. King, editors, *Systems, Organizations, Analysis, Management: A Book of Readings,* McGraw, 1969; Robert H. Haveman, Jr., editor, *A Decade of Federal Anti-Poverty Programs: Achievements, Failures, and Lessons,* Academic Press, 1977; Marcia Guttentag, editor, *Evaluation Studies Review Annual,* Volume II, Sage Publications, 1977; Frederick S. Lane, editor, *Managing State and Local Government: Cases and Readings,* St. Martin's, 1980; Joan Aldous, editor, *The Politics and Programs of Family Policy: United States and European Perspectives,* University of Notre Dame Press, 1980; Giandomenico Majone and E. S. Quade, editors, *Pitfalls of Analysis,* International Institute for Applied Systems Analysis, 1980; John T. Dunlop, editor, *Business and Government,* Harvard University Press, 1980. Also contributor of articles and reviews to academic journals.

SIDELIGHTS: Lynn told *CA:* "My professional career has had two phases. The first, from 1965 through 1973, was largely devoted to public service with the federal government. The second, from 1974 to the present, has been devoted primarily to teaching, research, and writing at Harvard University's John F. Kennedy School of Government.

"During my years in government service, I worked with mentors who were gifted public servants—Robert S. McNamara, Henry A. Kissinger, and Elliot L. Richardson—and with colleagues who inspired their associates by their intelligence, resourcefulness, sensitivity, and dedication to the public interest. From this experience I developed the convictions that have motivated much of my writing: (1) That managing the public's business is a high calling, (2) that top governmental positions are the most difficult jobs to do well in our society, (3) that, despite the difficulties, government is manageable, and (4) that it is important for students, scholars of politics and public administration, and a wider public to deepen their understanding of the problems of public management.

"The study of Jimmy Carter and welfare reform teaches valuable lessons. A president who would lead his administration, the Congress, and the country must figure out what he wants and be able to communicate his vision and a sense of urgency to others, including his subordinates in the executive branch, legislators, and the public. He must, moreover, be able to sustain momentum and direct it by his continued interest and involvement in an issue, by the questions he asks and the way he reacts to what he sees and hears, and by his instructions, signals, and cues. He must also check, of course, to see that his advisers are responsive to his interests.

"Above all, the president must be an effective political leader, both inside and outside his administration. That is, he must be able to anticipate the sources and strength of opposition to his proposals and the potential gains and costs to him and his administration of attempting to overcome it, and thus employ a strategic sense to gauge how much to propose and how much to settle for."

BIOGRAPHICAL/CRITICAL SOURCES: Evaluation, Volume IV, 1977; *Educational Evaluation and Policy Analysis,* May-June, 1980.

M

MAAS, Virginia H(argrave) 1913-

PERSONAL: Born August 14, 1913, in Plainfield, N.J.; daughter of Albert Hargrave (a teacher) and Louise (a teacher; maiden name, Stowell) Reynolds; married John William Maas (a civil servant), August 3, 1935; children: Gary Fred. Education: Attended University of Southern California. Home: 15515 Maas Lane S.W., Tacoma, Wash. 98498.

CAREER: Assistant landlord of rental units, 1959—. Member: National League of American Pen Women, Mystery Writers of America, Pacific Northwest Writers Conference, Tacoma Writers Club, Free Lance Club.

AWARDS, HONORS—All from biennial contests of National League of American Pen Women, except as noted: Five awards,1974, for "The Parrot Who Didn't Like Smoke," "Niddy Noddy, The Noodle Maker," "Queen Bess and Lancelot," "Timothy Toolittle," and a newspaper article, "The Apple Bonanza"; two awards, 1976; three awards, 1977, for "Scardust," "The Cowboy Hat," and "Benjie Beaver Gives Up"; three awards, 1978; first prize for novels, 1979, for sample chapters and synopsis of Tethered Rebel; first prize in confessions from Pacific Northwest Writers Conference, 1979; two awards, 1980.

WRITINGS: Castle Craggs (gothic novel), Manor, 1979. Contributor of more than one hundred fifty articles and stories to magazines for children and adults.

WORK IN PROGRESS: Tethered Rebel, a novel about three generations; Now, What Happened B.J.?, a book for children; more juvenile short stories.

SIDELIGHTS: Virginia Maas commented: "I love the sound and feel of words and what you can do with them. I want my reader to laugh and cry with me, because that is what I do when I write humor and pathos. I want to entertain the reader, take him out of his humdrum world (if it is), because that is what writing does for me. My greatest happiness comes from seeing my work in print, and maybe receiving a fan letter from someone who liked it.

"I think that persistence has been the important word in my life. Without it I don't believe I would be a writer today. I kept writing and sending, in spite of rejects, and that is the only reason I have finally been able to call myself a professional writer. The desire to be somebody besides a housewife has goaded me on when I experienced discouragement. Once the well of creativity has been tapped, there is no stopping the juices, and a writer must drink fully and continuously or drown in its depths.

"Becoming and being an author is parallel to becoming and being a parent. You experience life's greatest joys and sorrows through your creation, be it child or book. I have been on panels at the Pacific Writers Conferences, and one thing I usually say to would-be writers is: 'If you are sure you want to write, more than anything else in life, then go ahead, but if you are lukewarm about it, forget it, because it will only bring you frustration and disappointment.' You've got to have an overwhelming desire in order to be successful, at least in my way of thinking. An acceptance letter from an editor is still the greatest thrill I have experienced. Having them call me by my first name, and treating me like a friend is all the reward I need for my hard work.

"I wrote my gothic novel, Castle Craggs, because I love to read gothics, and I thought it would be fun to do one. It was. I appreciated the fact that this genre did not resort to sex or violence to sell the book. Gothics, at least during the seventies, were clean escape reading, good storytelling that was suspenseful, and books you could give to anyone without blushing. I would be ashamed to have my name appear on the jacket of the majority of the books that are selling so heavily. All I expect from a good book is pleasure and a certain amount of information or slant that offers a wider horizon to the reader."

* * *

MAASS, Arthur 1917-

BRIEF ENTRY: Born July 24, 1917, in Baltimore, Md. American educator and author. Maass began his career as a U.S. Government budget analyst. He joined the faculty of Harvard University and has been Frank G. Thomson Professor of Government since 1967. His writings include Muddy Waters: The Army Engineers and the Nation's Rivers (Harvard University Press, 1951), Area and Power: A Theory of Local Government (Free Press, 1959), Design of Water-Resource Systems: New Techniques for Relating Economic Objectives, Engineering Analysis, and Governmental Planning (Harvard University Press, 1962), and . . . And the Desert Shall Rejoice: Conflict, Growth, and Justice in Arid Environments (M.I.T. Press, 1978). Address: Department of Government, Littauer Center, Harvard University, Cambridge, Mass. 02138. Biographical/critical sources: Journal of Political Economy, October, 1962; Amer-

ican Economic Review, December, 1962; *American Political Science Review,* December, 1962, September, 1979; *Who's Who in America,* 39th edition, Marquis, 1976.

*   *   *

MABLEY, Jack 1915-

PERSONAL: Born October 26, 1915, in Binghamton, N.Y.; son of Clarence Ware (an inventor) and Mabelle (a musician; maiden name, Howe) Mabley; married Frances Habeck (a hospital volunteer), August 29, 1940; children: Jill, Ann, Pat, Robert. *Education:* University of Illinois, B.S., 1938. *Politics:* Independent. *Religion:* "Mixed." *Home:* 2275 Winnetka Rd., Glenview, Ill. 60025. *Office:* Chicago Tribune, 435 North Michigan Ave., Chicago, Ill. 60611.

CAREER/WRITINGS: Associated Press, Champaign, Ill., stringer, 1937-38; *Chicago Daily News,* Chicago, Ill., reporter, writer, columnist, 1938-61; *Glenview Post,* Glenview, Ill., publisher, 1948-50; *Chicago American,* Chicago, columnist, 1961-69, assistant managing editor, 1966-69; *Chicago Today,* Chicago, associate editor, 1969-73, columnist, 1973-74; *Chicago Tribune,* Chicago, columnist, 1973—. Contributor of articles on sports, preventive medicine, and general topics to magazines, including *Playboy, Saturday Review,* and *Sports Illustrated.* Lecturer in journalism at Northwestern University, Evanston, Ill., 1949-50. Member of Glenview, Ill., Park Board, 1955-57, president of Village of Glenview, 1957-61, chairman of Glenview police and fire commission, 1962; trustee and president, Skokie Valley Community Hospital, 1971-80; member of the National Council on Hospital Governing Boards of the American Hospital Association; founder of the "Forgotten Children's Fund," 1959. *Military service:* U.S. Naval Reserve, 1941-45; became lieutenant. *Member:* Seven tennis clubs. *Awards, honors:* Citizen fellowship from the Institute of Medicine of Chicago, 1979.

SIDELIGHTS: Mabley told *CA:* "I have been writing daily newspaper columns since 1948, approximately 9,216 columns, or 6,451,200 words. I do not aspire to literary immortality, but always have tried to convey ideas clearly and stimulate thought and discussion among readers. As a writer for a mass circulation periodical, I regard the greatest challenge as communicating simultaneously with the trucker, University of Chicago professor, and high school student. Sometimes I do, sometimes I don't."

*   *   *

MacAVOY, Paul W(ebster) 1934-

BRIEF ENTRY: Born April 21, 1934, in Haverhill, Mass. American economist, educator, and author. MacAvoy has been a professor of economics and management at Yale University since 1976. He edited *Bell Journal of Economics and Management Science,* 1970-75. His writings include *Economic Perspective on the Politics of International Commodity Agreements* (University of Arizona Press, 1977), *Federal Energy Administration Agreements* (American Enterprise Institute for Public Policy Research, 1977), and *The Regulated Industries* (Norton, 1979). *Address:* 652 Nut Plains Rd., Guilford, Conn. 06437; and School of Organization and Management, Yale University, New Haven, Conn. 06520. *Biographical/critical sources: Who's Who in America,* 40th edition, Marquis, 1978.

*   *   *

MacCARTHY, Fiona 1940-

PERSONAL: Born January 23, 1940, in London, England; daughter of Gerald (an army officer) and Yolande (de Belabre) MacCarthy; married David Mellor (a designer), August 19, 1966; children: Corin, Clare. *Education:* Oxford University, M.A., 1961. *Home and office:* Broom Hall, Broom Hall Rd., Sheffield, Yorkshire S10 2DU, England.

CAREER: Guardian, London, England, features writer, 1963-69; *Evening Standard,* London, features writer, 1969-72; free-lance writer, 1972—.

WRITINGS: All Things Bright and Beautiful: Design in Britain, University of California Press, 1972; *A History of British Design: 1830 to Today,* Allen & Unwin, 1979; *The Simple Life: C. R. Ashbee in the Cotswolds,* University of California Press, 1981; *The British Tradition in Design: From 1880,* Lund Humphries, 1981.

WORK IN PROGRESS: "A major study of the arts and crafts movement in Britain, allied to an exhibition on the same theme, with Alan Crawford, for mid-1980's."

SIDELIGHTS: MacCarthy told *CA* that in *The British Tradition in Design* she wrote: "For a century or more, from William Morris onwards, there has been an easily identifiable strain in society in Britain concerned with the improvement of the objects which we use and live with. This movement for reform has, through the years, developed certain ideas on the designer's social role as well as recognizable criteria on aesthetics. From the arts and crafts movement of the late nineteenth century, the Design and Industries Association campaigns between the wars, through to the postwar Council of Industrial Design (now the Design Council), a tradition has evolved which is, I would claim, particularly British: a tradition in the approach to designing and a tradition in reaching the solutions, amounting to a long succession of products, both handmade and mass-produced, with a common visual character. Indeed, the idea that consistent standards are both practically possible and morally desirable, that design solutions can be measured against a sense of ideal rightness, both functional and aesthetic, has dominated much of British design thinking over the past century. It is a concept in which, from the 1930's onwards, the British Government has been investing ever-increasing resources, especially in the education of designers, and since the war it has been at the very center of activities in government-approved design.

"The design movement of the past hundred years has created its own *species humaniores,* the genus which in the early days was known as 'art adviser' but which we are more likely now to designate 'designer.' The designer's professional status has become increasingly sophisticated, but the basic role remains that of problem solver, reconciler of conflicting demands and outside pressures. When it comes down to it, it is the designer who makes the creative leap, the visual synthesis. Designers finally decide how things shall *be.*"

MacCarthy added that this "explains much of what has preoccupied me recently in my writing and its allied occupation, organizing exhibitions. The elite design tradition is, to me, an infinitely interesting aspect of modern British culture.

"The intensely idealistic early twentieth-century phase of British design history especially fascinates me. This was the background to my recent book on C. R. Ashbee, arts and crafts architect and designer, and friend of Frank Lloyd Wright. It was a subject which aroused great public interest: the search for the simple life is very much still with us. And this is a theme I hope I shall develop in several books to come: a large book (and exhibition) on the arts and crafts movement, and perhaps then a study of the life of Eric Gill."

MacCOLLAM, Joel A(llan) 1946-

PERSONAL: Born December 19, 1946, in Albany, N.Y.; son of Allan (a physician) and Jacqueline (Jones) MacCollam; married Jann Scherer, May 3, 1975; children: Jessica, Jordan. *Education:* Hamilton College, B.A., 1968; attended Columbia University, 1968-69; General Theological Seminary, New York, N.Y., M.Div., 1972. *Politics:* Republican. *Residence:* Glendale, Calif. *Office address:* P.O. Box 977, Glendale, Calif. 91209.

CAREER: Ordained Episcopal priest, 1972; pastor of Episcopal churches in Schuylerville, N.Y., 1974-78, and Glendale, Calif., 1978-79. Director of public relations for Door of Hope International, 1980—. President of local volunteer fire department, 1975-78. Management consultant. *Member:* National Society of Fund-Raising Executives, Public Relations Society of America.

WRITINGS: The Weekend That Never Ends, Seabury, 1976; *The Way Doctrine,* Inter-Varsity Press, 1978; *Carnival of Souls,* Seabury, 1979; (editor) *Pharaoh: Let Our People Go,* Door of Hope, 1981. Contributor to magazines, including *Christianity Today, Eternity,* and *Living Church,* and newspapers.

WORK IN PROGRESS: A book on radical restructuring of the local church, publication expected in 1982; a book on religious life in Communist countries, publication by Door of Hope expected in 1982.

*   *   *

MACKAY, Claire 1930-

PERSONAL: Born December 21, 1930, in Toronto, Ontario, Canada; daughter of Grant McLaren (an accountant) and Bernice (a secretary and bereavement counselor; maiden name, Arland) Bacchus; married Jackson Mackay (an economist, engineer, and jazz musician), September 12, 1952; children: Ian, Scott, Grant. *Education:* University of Toronto, B.A. (with honors), 1952; University of British Columbia, M.S.W., 1969; University of Manitoba, Certificate in Rehabilitation Counseling, 1971. *Home and office:* 6 Frank Cres., Toronto, Ontario, Canada M6G 3K5.

CAREER: Polysar Corp., Sarnia, Ontario, library assistant in research department, 1952-55; Plains Hospital, Regina, Saskatchewan, medical social worker, 1969-71; Steelworkers' Union, Toronto, Ontario, research librarian, 1972-78; freelance researcher and writer, 1978—. *Member:* Canadian Authors Association, Writers Union of Canada, Canadian Society of Children's Authors, Illustrators, and Performers (secretary, 1977-78; president, 1979-81), British North American Philatelic Society, Ontario Federation of Naturalists. *Awards, honors:* Grant from Ontario Arts Council, 1980; second prize from *Toronto Star* short story contest, 1980, for "Important Message: Please Read."

WRITINGS—Juveniles: Mini-Bike Hero, Scholastic Book Services, 1974, revised edition, 1978; *Mini-Bike Racer,* Scholastic Book Services, 1976, revised edition, 1979; *Exit Barney McGee,* Scholastic Book Services, 1979; *One Proud Summer* (historical novel), Women's Educational Press, 1981; *Mini-Bike Rescue,* Scholastic Book Services, 1982.

Author of "Women's Words," a monthly feminist column in *Steel Labour,* 1975-78. Contributor to *Canadian Writers Guide.* Contributor of poems and articles to magazines, including *Branching Out, Canadian Women's Studies, Chatelaine, On-*

tario New Democrat, Poetry Toronto, and *Our Family.* Editor of *Canadian Society of Children's Authors, Illustrators, and Performers News,* 1978—.

WORK IN PROGRESS: An adult comic novel; stories and essays.

SIDELIGHTS: Publication of a French translation of Claire Mackay's book *Mini-Bike Hero,* by Editions Heritage, is expected in 1982.

She told *CA:* "My entry into the field of writing (though a secret dream for years) came about largely by fluke. My youngest son nagged me into writing the book, *Mini-Bike Hero.* It altered my life profoundly. I'm still in a bemused state, but now thoroughly hooked on writing.

"One of the great—and occasionally the only—rewards in writing for children is the fan mail from kids to whom you're the best writer who ever lived. I've accumulated many letters, answered all, and find them a powerful antidote to a bad review! I regard each letter as an honor greater than any prize awarded by adult peers and judges—a circumstance that has not yet transpired—and as a gift of confidence when my own has wavered badly. Someday I hope to write that one excellent book that will merit that honor and that gift."

AVOCATIONAL INTERESTS: Birdwatching, collecting dictionaries, philately.

*   *   *

MacLEOD, Celeste (Lipow) 1931-

PERSONAL: Born November 27, 1931, in Phoenix, Ariz.; daughter of Louis (a citrus merchant) and Dorothy (Newman) Lipow; married Ian MacLeod (an architect), December 30, 1956 (divorced, 1965); children: David N., Peter S. *Education:* University of California, Berkeley, B.A., 1953, M.L.S., 1967; attended Columbia University, 1953-54, and Texas Western College, 1957-58. *Home and office:* 2838 Woolsey St., Berkeley, Calif. 94705. *Agent:* Jet Literary Associates, Inc., 124 East 84th St., Suite 4a, New York, N.Y. 10028.

CAREER: Writer. Judah Magnes Museum, Berkeley, Calif., archivist for Western Jewish History Center, 1967-70; Meiklejohn Civil Liberties Institute, Berkeley, archives project director, 1979-80. Worked as camp counselor in the 1950's. Member of Prison Libraries Task Force, 1971-73; member of board of directors of Berkeley Support Services, 1972—, chairman, 1980-81. *Member:* Women's National Book Association, National Women's Political Caucus, American Civil Liberties Union, Sierra Club.

WRITINGS: Horatio Alger, Farewell: The End of the American Dream, Seaview, 1980. Contributor to magazines and newspapers, including *Nation, California Living, Intellectual Digest,* and *American Jewish Historical Quarterly.*

WORK IN PROGRESS: A comic novel about American life, publication expected in 1983.

SIDELIGHTS: Celeste MacLeod wrote: "Travel outside the United States helped shape my perspective as a writer. From 1954 to 1956 I lived in Europe and traveled around the world by freighter, staying in India and Japan with friends I had made at the International Houses in Berkeley and New York. From 1961 to 1963 I lived in Copenhagen and Rome, and from 1974 to 1975 I did research in London. Living abroad increased my appreciation of different ways of life and gave me a fuller view of my own country.

"People—their lives, organizations, institutions, and governments (including their political and economic systems)—interest me most. My major focus is contemporary American society. I aim to depict, analyze, and interpret the United States, through both nonfiction and fiction, and hopefully to help encourage needed changes.

"For instance, I am writing an article about the frustration of working-class Americans who find they can never become affluent, no matter how hard they work, and their vulnerability to such groups as the Ku Klux Klan and the Nazi party that offer clear-cut scapegoats."

BIOGRAPHICAL/CRITICAL SOURCES: Los Angeles Times, October 23, 1980; *New York Times Book Review,* October 26, 1980; *Library Journal,* December 15, 1980; *Berkeley Monthly,* January 1, 1981; *Los Angeles Herald-Examiner,* January 4, 1981; *San Francisco Chronicle,* January 18, 1981; *San Francisco Examiner,* February 8, 1981.

*   *   *

MAGNUSSON, Magnus   1929-

PERSONAL: Born October 12, 1929, in Reykjavik, Iceland; son of Sigursteinn (Icelandic Counsul-General for Scotland) and Ingibjorg (Sigurdardottir) Magnusson; married Mamie Baird (a journalist), June 30, 1954; children: Sally, Margaret, Anna, Siggy (died, 1973), Jon. *Education:* Jesus College, Oxford, B.A. (with honors), 1951. *Home:* Blairskaith House, Balmore-Torrance, Glasgow G64 4AX, Scotland. *Agent:* Deborah Rogers, 5-11 Mortimer St., London W1N 7RH, England.

CAREER: Scottish Daily Express, Glasgow, Scotland, reporter and assistant editor, 1953-61; *Scotsman,* Edinburgh, Scotland, chief feature writer and assistant editor, 1961-68; free-lance writer and broadcaster, 1968—; translator; host of British Broadcasting Corp. (BBC) programs, including "Mastermind," "China," "B.C.: The Archaeology of the Bible Lands," "Chronicle," "Vikings!," and "Living Legends." Lord Rector, Edinburgh University, 1975-78. Stewards chairman of York Archaeological Trust, 1975—; chairman of Scottish Youth Theatre, 1977-78, Scottish Churches Architectural Heritage Trust, 1978—, and Ancient Monuments Board for Scotland, 1981—. *Member:* Royal Society of Edinburgh (fellow), Royal Society of Antiquaries of Scotland (fellow). *Awards, honors: Times Educational Supplement* Information Book Award, 1972, for *Introducing Archaeology;* named Scottish television personality of the year, 1974; Knight of Order of the Falcon (Iceland), 1975; Queen's Silver Jubilee Medal, 1977; honorary doctorate from Edinburgh University, 1978, and York University, 1981.

WRITINGS: Introducing Archaeology, Walck, 1972; *Viking Expansion Westwards,* Walck, 1973; *The Clacken and the Slate: The Story of the Edinburgh Academy, 1824-1874,* Collins, 1974; *Hammer of the North,* Orbis, 1976; *B.C.: The Archaeology of the Bible Lands,* Bodley Head, 1977, published as *Archaeology of the Bible,* Simon & Schuster, 1978; *Landlord or Tenant?: A View of Irish History,* Bodley Head, 1978; *Iceland* (photographs by John Chang McCurdy), Almenna Bokafelagid, 1979; *Vikings!,* Dutton, 1980; *Magnus on the Move,* Macdonald, 1980; *Treasure of Scotland,* Weidenfeld & Nicolson, 1981.

Author of introduction: William Watson, *Ancient China,* BBC Publications, 1974; William L. McKinlay, *Karluk: The Great Untold Story of Arctic Exploration,* Weidenfeld & Nicolson, 1976; Jeffrey Iverson, *More Lives Than One?: Evidence of the Remarkable Bloxham Tapes,* Souvenir, 1976; Emrys Jones,

editor, *The Atlas of World Geography,* Sundial, 1977; Peter Jennings, *Face to Face With the Turin Shroud,* Mowbray, 1978; Yohanan Aharoni and Michael Avi-Yonah, editors, *Modern Bible Atlas,* Allen & Unwin, 1979; Richard Barber, *Living Legends,* BBC Publications, 1980; *Great Books for Today,* Reader's Digest, 1981; Michael S. Rohan and Allan J. Scott, *The Hammer and the Cross,* Alder, 1981; James Kennaway, *Household Ghosts,* Mainstream, 1981.

Contributor: *The Glorious Privilege: The History of the "Scotsman,"* Thomas Nelson, 1967; Ian Grimble and Derick S. Thomson, *The Future of the Highlands,* Routledge & Kegan Paul, 1968; *The "Reader's Digest" Book of Strange Stories, Amazing Facts,* Reader's Digest Press, 1975; Robin Prentice, editor, *The National Trust for Scotland Guide,* J. Cape, 1976; Ray Sutcliffe, editor, *Chronicle,* BBC Publications, 1978; Brian Walker, editor, *Pass the Port,* Christian Brann, 1978; Joseph J. Thorndyke, Jr., editor, *Discovery of Lost Worlds,* American Heritage, 1979.

Translator: (With Hermann Palsson) *Njal's Saga,* Penguin, 1960; Halldor Laxness, *The Atom Station,* Methuen, 1961; Laxness, *Paradise Reclaimed,* Methuen, 1962; (with Palsson) *The Vinland Sagas: The Norse Discovery of America,* Penguin, 1965; Laxness, *The Fish Can Sing,* Methuen, 1966; (with Palsson) Snorri Sturluson, *King Harald's Saga: Harald Hardradi of Norway,* Penguin, 1966; Samivel, *Golden Iceland,* Almenna Bokafelagid, 1967; Laxness, *World Light,* University of Wisconsin Press, 1969; (with Palsson) *Laxdaela Saga,* Penguin, 1969; Laxness, *Christianity under Glacier,* Helgafell, 1973.

Editor of "The Bodley Head Archaeologies," 1970-80; founder and editor of *Popular Archaeology,* 1979-80.

WORK IN PROGRESS: Research for a book and televison series on Scottish Islands and Homer's *Odyssey.*

SIDELIGHTS: Magnus Magnusson lists his recreations as "digging and delving," which result from his work as a reporter—not only of the current scene but also of the world of archaeology. Says Magnusson, "Archaeological reports are the news stories of the past—and luckily, you can't libel the dead!"

Magnusson commented that he considers man-made artifacts unearthed by excavators to be time machines to transport a person into the past. Much of his recent work has been concerned with bringing the past to life again thorough history and archaeology.

*   *   *

MAGOG, Paul Dowsey
See DOWSEY-MAGOG, Paul

*   *   *

MAHMOOD, Mamdani   1946-

PERSONAL: Born April 23, 1946, in Bombay, India; son of Yusuf Karmali and Kulsum (Yusuf) Alibhai. *Education:* University of Pittsburgh, B.A., 1967; Fletcher School of Law and Diplomacy, Tufts University, M.A., 1968, M.A.L.D., 1969; Harvard University, Ph.D., 1974. *Home address:* P.O. Box 8399, Kampala, Uganda. *Office:* Department of Political Science, Makerere University, Kampala, Uganda.

CAREER: University of Dar-es-Salaam, Dar-es-Salaam, Tanzania, lecturer in economics, 1973-76, senior lecturer in political science, 1973-79; Makerere University, Kampala, Uganda, senior lecturer in political science, 1980—.

WRITINGS: The Myth of Population Control, Monthly Review Press, 1972; *From Citizen to Refugee,* Francis Pinter, 1973; *Politics and Class Formation in Uganda,* Monthly Review Press, 1976; *Imperialism and the Amin Regime,* Monthly Review Press, in press. Editor of *Review of African Political Economy, African Development,* and *African Review.*

WORK IN PROGRESS: Imperialism and the Disintegration of the East African Community; The Agrarian Question in Uganda.

* * *

MAIER, Ernest L(ouis) 1938-

PERSONAL: Born August 1, 1938, in Detroit, Mich.; son of Stanley G. and Mildred (a teacher; maiden name, St. Aubin) Maier; married V. Jean McManus; children: Karen, Michael, David. *Education:* University of Detroit, B.S., 1960, M.B.A., 1961; doctoral study at University of Illinois, 1961-64. *Home:* 10095 Burgess Court, Union Lake, Mich. 48085. *Office:* Department of Management, Lawrence Institute of Technology, Southfield, Mich. 48075.

CAREER: Wayne State University, Detroit, Mich., assistant professor of marketing, 1964-67; marketing representative for IBM, 1967-72; Lawrence Institute of Technology, Southfield, Mich., professor of marketing, 1971—. President of Aqua-Weed Control of Oakland County, Inc., 1975—, and Lake Lawns, Inc., 1978—; vice-president of Protection II, 1980—. *Member:* American Marketing Association, Association for Business Simulation and Experiential Learning, Engineering Society of Detroit.

WRITINGS: (With R. Bruce McAfee) *Cases in Selling,* McGraw, 1979. Contributor to magazine of Engineering Society of Detroit.

WORK IN PROGRESS: How to Use the Business Library and Sources of Business Information, 5th edition (Maier was not associated with earlier editions), with H. W. Johnson and E. Anthony Faria, for South-Western.

SIDELIGHTS: Maier wrote: "I am interested in the free enterprise system and education of college youth. I conduct yearly summer tours to Europe."

* * *

MAINGOT, Rodney 1893-1982

OBITUARY NOTICE: Born February 27, 1893, in Trinidad; died January 3, 1982. Surgeon and author. A specialist in abdominal surgery, Maingot wrote numerous books in his field, including *The Management of Abdominal Operations, The Relationship of Art and Medicine,* and *Technique of Gastric Operations.* Obituaries and other sources: *London Times,* January 6, 1982.

* * *

MAIS, Roger 1905-1955

BRIEF ENTRY: Born August 11, 1905, in Kingston, Jamaica; died June 21, 1955, in Kingston, Jamaica. Jamaican writer. Mais's literary output included stories, poems, and plays, but he is better remembered for his novels, *The Hills Were Joyful Together* (1953), *Brother Man* (1954), and *Black Lightning* (1955). While working during the 1940's as a journalist, painter, and photographer, Mais became associated with the Jamaican nationalist movement. When he protested colonial rule in *Now We Know,* he was imprisoned. His novels portrayed his hu-

manism and sympathy for the oppressed, as well as his own prison experiences. His work led to changes in the penal system and social reforms that were felt throughout Jamaica. *Biographical/critical sources: Public Opinion,* June, 1966; *Journal of Commonwealth Literature,* December, 1966.

* * *

MALLORY, Enid Lorraine 1938-

PERSONAL: Born August 22, 1938, in Ottawa, Ontario, Canada; daughter of Milton Robert (a storekeeper) and Mildred (a storekeeper; maiden name, Allison) Swerdfeger; married Gordon Mallory (an engineer), May 14, 1960; children: Peter, Jonathan, Allison, Laurie. *Education:* Attended Queen's University, 1955-58. *Residence:* Peterborough, Ontario, Canada.

CAREER: Children's Aid Society, Belleville, Ontario, child care worker, 1958-59; Peterborough Public Library, Peterborough, Ontario, reference librarian, 1960-63; writer. Co-organizer of Kawartha Heritage Conference. *Member:* Peterborough Historical Society, University Women's Club.

WRITINGS: Ontario Calls You Camping, Macmillan, 1969; *The Green Tiger, James FitzGibbon: A Hero of the War of 1812* (juvenile), McClelland & Stewart, 1976. Contributor of articles to periodicals, including the *Canadian Geographical Journal, The Beaver,* and *Canadian Weekend.*

WORK IN PROGRESS: The Country Stores of Canada: Yesterday and Today, photographs and stories about country stores; a biography of George M. Douglas, an arctic explorer.

SIDELIGHTS: Mallory told *CA:* "I have been writing since I was twelve, so I am probably addicted to it now. Canadian history, especially recent history, is of particular interest to me. My country store research has been great fun. I grew up in a country store, and I also have the stories my eighty-five-year-old father tells me. I would like to record and help people remember the very special role played by country stores in Ontario.

"My next project—along with *Country Stores*—is likely to be a history-folklore book on the Kawartha Lakes area. I believe history at the grass-roots level to be the most significant kind of history. I am intrigued by the way lives have been shaped by the land and the lakes and rivers on which they have been lived.

"The past eighty years are a unique period of Canadian history; they give us our last look at rural isolation, at a strongly individual way of doing things which could differ greatly in communities only a few miles apart. Older rural people remember a rich background of experience, some of it good, some bad, some of it more dramatic and exciting than the manufactured thrillers our children watch on TV. They have a deep, ingrained streak of humour. They even use a language which varies from one township to another, producing a diversity of storytelling styles which will disappear within twenty years.

"It is this inevitable disappearance of a way of life, often harsh, rugged and lonely, but in many ways rich and wonderful, which makes the recording of the recent rural past so important just now."

* * *

MALVEAUX, Julianne M(arie) 1953-

PERSONAL: Born September 22, 1953, in San Francisco, Calif.;

daughter of Proteone Alexandria Malveaux (a social worker). *Education:* Boston College, A.B., 1974, M.A., 1975; Massachusetts Institute of Technology, Ph.D., 1980. *Home:* 563 Ellsworth St., San Francisco, Calif. 94110. *Office:* Department of Economics, San Francisco State University, San Francisco, Calif. 94132.

CAREER: WFAA-TV, Dallas, Tex., media intern, summer, 1975; White House Council of Economic Advisers, Washington, D.C., junior staff economist, 1977-78; Rockefeller Foundation, New York City, research fellow, 1978-80; New School for Social Research, New York City, assistant professor of economics, 1980-81; San Francisco State University, San Francisco, Calif., assistant professor of economics, 1981—. Instructor at Northeastern University and University of Massachusetts. Member of board of directors of National Child Labor Committee. *Member:* American Economic Association, National Economic Association, Feminist Writer's Guild, Delta Sigma Theta, Coalition of One Hundred Black Women.

WRITINGS: (With Phyllis A. Wallace and Linda P. Datcher) *Black Women in the Labor Force,* M.I.T. Press, 1980. Contributor of more than twenty articles and poems to magazines, including *Essence, Black Scholar, Heresies,* and *Journal of Black Poetry.*

WORK IN PROGRESS: The Revolt of Common Folk, publication expected in 1982; *Tales of Uppity Times,* a novel set in the 1970's; continuing research on women in the workplace.

SIDELIGHTS: Julianne Malveaux commented: "I like to describe myself as a poet/writer/economist. My academic training has been in economics, and I have written about my research both for fellow academics and for broader audiences. But I have also been writing poetry since I was sixteen, and have written for a variety of magazines about subjects that include, but are not limited to, money issues. Because I consider myself a 'renaissance person' and have a variety of interests, I finish projects by immersing myself in them for two- or three-day periods at a time. I also maintain the writing habit by keeping a journal, though this is difficult on long vacations. On a recent trip to Jamaica, my first day's notes were more than six pages, but by the last day, I was down to a paragraph.

"My research has often been infuriating—only by viewing detailed occupational data can the extent of occupational segregation be understood. While many of the overt barriers against women's mobility in the workplace have been removed, the more subtle barriers that remain are difficult to act on. So even though women have made some headway, more than half of all women still work in clerical and service jobs, and another quarter work in other female-stratified jobs. This situation does not change considerably for young (twenty-five to thirty-four years old) women.

"Social change is a painstakingly slow process. The image of the woman who has 'come a long way, baby' is belied by the fact that the median age for first marriage is *still* under twenty-two for women. And once people think change has taken place, they're ready for the backlash. So while ERA is as desperately needed as it was in 1973, the perception of change in women's roles has dampened any catalytic movement toward ratification.

"The notion of change is also important when black women in the workplace are viewed. These women are often perceived as 'twofers,' doubly advantaged because of their minority and female status. But I can say both from my research and from personal experience that the myth of the twofer is just that— a myth perpetuated by everyone *except* black women."

MANCHEE, Fred B.   1903(?)-1981

OBITUARY NOTICE: Born c. 1903; died in 1981 in Hyannis, Mass. Advertising executive and author. Formerly a vice-president of Batten, Barton, Durstine, & Osborn, Inc., Manchee was the author of several books, including *The Huckster's Revenge.* Obituaries and other sources: *AB Bookman's Weekly,* December 7, 1981.

*   *   *

MANDEL, Ruth Blumenstock   1938-

PERSONAL: Born August 29, 1938, in Vienna, Austria; came to the United States in 1947, naturalized citizen, 1953; daughter of Michael (a self-employed retailer) and Lea (a self-employed retailer; maiden name, Schmelzer) Blumenstock; married Barrett Mandel, June 18, 1961 (divorced, 1976); children: Maud Strum. *Education:* Brooklyn College (now of the City University of New York), B.A., 1960; University of Connecticut, M.A., 1962, Ph.D., 1969. *Home:* 46 Cameron Court, Princeton, N.J. 08540. *Agent:* Patricia Berens, Sterling Lord Agency, Inc., 660 Madison Ave., New York, N.Y. 10021. *Office:* Center for the American Woman and Politics, Eagleton Institute of Politics, Rutgers University, New Brunswick, N.J. 08901.

CAREER: University of Connecticut, Storrs, assistant instructor in English, 1960-66; University of Pittsburgh, Pittsburgh, Pa., instructor in English, 1968-70; Rider College, Lawrenceville, N.J., assistant professor of English, 1970-71; Rutgers University, New Brunswick, N.J., 1971—, began as assistant professor, became associate professor of politics, director of Center for the American Woman and Politics, 1971—. Member of Mercer County Commission on the Status of Women; member of New Jersey coordinating committee for International Women's Year; public speaker. *Member:* American Association of University Professors, Modern Language Association of America, Women's Caucus for Modern Languages, American Political Science Association, Women's Caucus for Political Science, National Women's Political Caucus.

WRITINGS: In the Running: The New Woman Candidate, Ticknor and Fields, 1981. Member of editorial board of *Signs: Journal of Women in Culture and Society,* 1974—.

WORK IN PROGRESS: Editing a series of academic books on women in politics, with Rita Mae Kelly, publication by Praeger expected in 1983; research on autobiographies of women of achievement in the United States.

BIOGRAPHICAL/CRITICAL SOURCES: Washington Post Book World, July 5, 1981.

*   *   *

MANLEY, Deborah   1932-

PERSONAL: Born February 11, 1932, in Aldershot, Hampshire, England; daughter of Osmond Luxmoore (an army officer) and Petronella (a social worker; maiden name, Snowball) Jones; married Roy Manley (a social administrator), December 12, 1953; children: Brett (daughter), Adam. *Education:* Attended London School of Economics and Political Science, University of London, 1951-53. *Politics:* Labour. *Home:* 28½ Lansdowne Crescent, London W. 11, England.

CAREER: Writer. African Universities Press, Lagos, Nigeria, editor, 1962-68; Ginn & Co. Ltd., London, England, senior editor, 1968-73; Grisewood & Dempsey Ltd., London, senior editor, 1974-80; associated with Schools Council, London, 1981—. Chairman of Local Oxford Committee on Famine Relief, 1964-66; governor of Holland Park School, 1972-76; member of Transport Users Consultative Committee for London, 1975—.

WRITINGS—Juveniles: (With husband, Roy Manley) *Working in Nigeria: A Guide to Careers*, African Universities Press, 1964; *Growing Up: An Anthology of African Childhood* (illustrated by Prue Theobalds), African Universities Press, 1966; (with sister, Peta Ree) *Games for Journeys*, Pan Books, 1972; (with Ebun Clark) *Poetry: An Anthology*, African Universities Press, 1972; (with Ree) *Piccolo Book of Parties and Party Games*, Pan Books, 1973; (with Jenny Williams and Diane James) *On Holiday* (picture book), Dent, 1975; *Piccolo All the Year Round Book*, Pan Books, 1975; (with Moira Maclean, Colin Maclean, and James) *What We Do* (picture book), Dent, 1975; (with M. Maclean, C. Maclean, and James) *At Home* (picture book), Dent, 1976; (with Pamela Cotterill) *Maps and Map Games*, Pan Books, 1976; (with Ree and Margaret Murphy) *The Piccolo Holiday Book* (illustrated by Carol Lawson), Pan Books, 1976, published as *The Holiday Fun Book*, Severn House, 1978; *Piccolo Picnic Book*, Pan Books, 1976; (with M. Maclean, C. Maclean, and James) *The World* (picture book), Dent, 1976.

Let's Look at Insects (illustrated by Annabel Milne and Peter Stebbing), Ward, Lock, 1977; *The Name It Know It Book* (illustrated by M. Maclean and others), Rand McNally, 1977; (with R. Manley) *Piccolo Book of Cartoons*, Pan Books, 1977; (with James) *The Piccolo Craft Book*, Pan Books, 1977; *All About Me* (illustrated by Joanne Cole), Raintree Publishers, 1978; *Around Our House* (illustrated by M. Maclean and C. Maclean), Raintree Publishers, 1978; *Cooking Around the World*, Pan Books, 1978; *The Dragon Seaside Book*, Granada Dragon Books, 1978; (with Ree) *Finding Out: The Young Reader's Guide to Facts and Where to Find Them*, Pan Books, 1978; *Front and Back*, Raintree Publishers, 1978; *Let's Grow Things* (illustrated by M. Maclean and C. Maclean), Raintree Publishers, 1978; *Our New House* (illustrated by Julie Simpson), Raintree Publishers, 1978; *What's Red?*, Raintree Publishers, 1978; *Where Are We Going?* (illustrated by M. Maclean and C. Maclean), Raintree Publishers, 1978.

Animals All (illustrated by George Thompson), Raintree Publishers, 1979; *Animals One to Ten* (illustrated by Michele Noble), Raintree Publishers, 1979; *Bigger and Smaller*, Ray Rourke, 1979; *Captain Jolly and His Boat*, (illustrated by M. Maclean and C. Maclean), Pan Books, 1979; *Farmer Joe's Farm* (illustrated by M. Maclean and C. Maclean), Pan Books, 1979; *Fred's Travelling Fair* (illustrated by M. Maclean and C. Maclean), Pan Books, 1979; *From A to Z* (illustrated by Kailer and Lowndes), Raintree Publishers, 1979; *Fun for One*, Granada Dragon Books, 1979; *My Work*, Longman (London), 1979; *The Other Side* (illustrated by John Astrop), Raintree Publishers, 1979; *Our Baby*, Ray Rourke, 1979; *Penny's Helicopter*, Pan Books, 1979; *What Color Is It?* (illustrated by Cole), Raintree Publishers, 1979; *Finding Out About Bible Times*, David Cook, 1980; *Here Comes Christmas*, Granada Dragon Books, 1980; *It's Fun Finding Out*, Derrydale Books, 1980; *It's Fun Finding Out About Animals*, Derrydale Books, 1980; *It's Fun Finding Out About Long Ago*, Derrydale Books, 1980; *It's Fun Finding Out About People and Places*, Derrydale Books, 1980; *Going Out*, Ray Rourke, 1981; *Me and My Friend*, Ray Rourke, 1981; *My Colours*, Ray Rourke, 1981; *My House*, Ray Rourke, 1981; *Comic, Curious, and Crazy Verse*, Granada Dragon Books, 1982.

Editor; published by Angus & Robertson: Christopher Maynard, *The Amazing World of Dinosaurs*, 1976; Jennifer Cochrane, *The Amazing World of the Sea*, 1976; Neil Ardley, *The Amazing World of Machines*, 1977; Maynard, *The Amazing World of Money*, 1977.

For adults: (With Pamela Royds and Nancy Tuft) *Using London: A Guide for Londoners*, Deutsch, 1971.

WORK IN PROGRESS: Cooking From Long Ago, a children's history of food preparation, with recipes included; *Tracking Down London*, a children's guide.

SIDELIGHTS: Deborah Manley told *CA:* "I've always written and told stories. When we lived in India my sister (now Peta Ree) and I had complete imaginary worlds that we talked about and wrote about. There were long, involved adventure stories, but there were also illustrated guides to flora and fauna and the traditional customs of these worlds."

It was not, however, until she became an editor that Manley wrote anything for publication. She stated: "I began my career in publishing when my children were small, and I then began to write for my various employers. My main output has been paperback books of things for children to do. These are really anthologies of ideas gathered from hundreds of sources, including my own children and now a new generation of children in the family."

* * *

MANSBRIDGE, John   1901(?)-1981

OBITUARY NOTICE: Born c. 1901; died December 5, 1981. Artist, lecturer, and author. A popular English portrait painter, Mansbridge wrote *Graphic History of Architecture*, which he researched for ten years. At his death the artist was writing *Ways of Seeing: The Recreation of Man*, an illustrated, philosophical look at man's creative and scientific progress from the beginning of recorded history to the present. Obituaries and other sources: *London Times*, December 14, 1981.

* * *

MANSERGH, (Philip) Nicholas (Seton)   1910-

PERSONAL: Surname is pronounced *Man*-zer; born June 27, 1910, in Tipperary, Ireland; son of Philip St. George (a civil engineer) and Ethel Mansergh; married Diana Mary Keeton (a historical researcher), December 12, 1939; children: Philip, Daphne Mansergh Gilbert, Martin, Nicholas, Jane. *Education:* Pembroke College, Oxford, M.A., 1936, D.Phil., 1936. *Office:* St. John's College, Cambridge University, Cambridge, England.

CAREER: Oxford University, Oxford, England, tutor in politics, 1937-40; Ministry of Information, London, England, member of staff of Empire Division, 1941-46, director, 1944-46; Dominions Office, London, assistant secretary, 1946-47; Royal Institute of International Affairs, London, Abe Bailey Research Professor of British Commonwealth Relations, 1947-53; Cambridge University, Cambridge, England, Smuts Professor of History of the British Commonwealth, 1953-70, fellow of St. John's College, 1955-69 and 1979—, master of St. John's College, 1969-79. Visiting professor at Australian National University, 1951, University of Toronto, 1953, Duke University, 1957, 1965, Indian School of International Studies, 1958, 1966, and Jawaharlal Nehru University, 1980. *Member:* British Academy (fellow), Royal Commonwealth Society, University Club, Dublin. *Awards, honors:* Member of Order of the British Empire, 1945; fellow of Pembroke College, Oxford,

1954, D.Litt., 1960; Litt.D., Cambridge University, 1970; fellow of Trinity College, Dublin, 1970.

WRITINGS: The Irish Free State: Its Government and Politics, Allen & Unwin, 1934; *The Government of Northern Ireland: A Study in Devolution,* Allen & Unwin, 1936.

Ireland in the Age of Reform and Revolution: A Commentary on Anglo-Irish Relations and on Political Forces in Ireland, 1840-1921, Allen & Unwin, 1940, revised edition published as *The Irish Question, 1840-1921,* 1965, 3rd edition published as *The Irish Question, 1840-1921: A Commentary on Anglo-Irish Relations and on Social and Political Forces in Ireland in the Age of Reform and Revolution,* 1975; *Britain and Ireland,* Longmans, Green, 1942, revised edition, 1946; *The Commonwealth and the Nations: Studies in British Commonwealth Relations,* Royal Institute of International Affairs, 1948, reprinted, Dawsons, 1969; *The Coming of the First World War: A Study in the European Balance, 1878-1914,* Longmans, Green, 1949.

(Editor) *Documents and Speeches on British Commonwealth Affairs,* Oxford University Press, Volumes I-II: *1931-52,* 1953, Volume III: *1952-62,* 1963; *Problems of External Policy, 1931-1939,* Oxford University Press, 1952; *The Multi-Racial Commonwealth,* Royal Institute of International Affairs, 1955; *Commonwealth Perspectives,* Cambridge University Press, 1958; *Survey of British Commonwealth Affairs,* Oxford University Press, Volume I: *1931-39,* 1962, Volume II: *Problems of Wartime Co-Operation and Post-War Change, 1929-1952,* 1958; (editor with E. A. Benians) *The Cambridge History of the British Empire,* Volume III, Cambridge University Press, 1959.

South Africa, 1906-1961: The Price of Magnanimity, Praeger, 1962; *The Commonwealth Experience,* Weidenfeld & Nicolson, 1969, revised edition, 1982.

(Editor with E.W.R. Lumby on Volumes I-V, with Penderel Moon on Volumes V-X) *India: The Transfer of Power, 1942-1947,* H.M.S.O., Volume I: *The Cripps Mission, January-April, 1942,* 1970, Volume II: *"Quit India," 30 April-21 September 1942,* 1971, Volume III: *Reassertion of Authority, Gandhi's Fast and the Succession to the Vice-Royalty, 21 September 1942-12 June 1943,* 1972, Volume IV: *The Bengal Famine and the New Viceroyalty, 15 June 1943-31 August 1944,* 1973, Volume V: *The Simla Conference: Background and Proceedings, 1 September 1944-28 July 1945,* 1975, Volume VI: *The Post-War Phase: New Moves by the Labour Government, 1 August 1945-22 March 1946,* 1976, Volume VII: *The Cabinet Mission, 23 March-29 June 1946,* 1977; Volume VIII: *The Interim Government, 3 July-1 November 1946,* Volume IX: *The Fixing of a Time Limit, 4 November 1946-22 March 1947,* 1980, Volume X: *The Mountbatten Vice-Royalty.*

The Prelude to Partition: Concepts and Aims in Ireland and India, Cambridge University Press, 1978.

SIDELIGHTS: Mansergh told *CA:* "In the Ireland of the 1920's the dominant and divisive issue was the challenge of the unreconciled Republicans to the supporters of the Irish Free State established under the 1921 Anglo-Irish Treaty. As a schoolboy at that time, I could hardly fail to be aware of its local manifestations. Later at Oxford, after graduating in the School of Modern History, I became, under the influence of the Gladstone professor, W.G.S. Adams, absorbed in the problems of Irish Government and by natural progression in those of Anglo-Irish and Commonwealth relations. Though discounting the long-term usefulness of dominion status as a solvent for Anglo-Irish tensions, my interest in its nature and working had been stirred. As a wartime civil servant in the Ministry of Infor-

mation and the Dominions Office in London with responsibilities in the Commonwealth field, that interest was deepened, while after the war the whole perspective widened as I was brought into contact with Indian and Asian nationalism, first through attendance as an Observer at the historic inter-Asian Conference called by Pandit Nehru in Delhi in the spring of 1947 and then at other conferences and as a visiting professor. So it was by way of Ireland, the old Dominions, and India that I was drawn to a study of the history of the Commonwealth. My research interests now are in more specialized Indian and Irish fields."

BIOGRAPHICAL/CRITICAL SOURCES: Norman Hillmer and Philip Wigley, editors, *The First British Commonwealth: Essays in Honor of Nicholas Mansergh,* Cass, 1979.

* * *

MARCUS, Morton 1936-

PERSONAL: Born September 10, 1936, in Manhattan, N.Y.; son of Max Pincus (a garment manufacturer) and Rachel (a dress shop owner; maiden name, Babchek) Marcus; married Wilma Kantrowich, 1958 (divorced, 1971); children: Jana Lin, Valerie Anna. *Education:* Attended Washington University, St. Louis, Mo., 1956-58; Iowa State University, B.A., 1961; Stanford University, M.A., 1968. *Agent:* George Diskant, Zigler, Diskant, Inc., 9255 Sunset Blvd., No. 1122, Los Angeles, Calif. 90069. *Office:* Department of English, Cabrillo College, 6500 Soquel Dr., Aptos, Calif. 95003.

CAREER: Teacher at elementary school in Point Arena, Calif., 1962-63; high school English and history teacher in San Francisco, Calif., 1965-68; high school basketball coach, 1965-66; Cabrillo College, Aptos, Calif., instructor in English, 1968—. Director of county poetry-in-the-schools program in Monterey and Santa Cruz, Calif., 1972-75; gives readings at colleges and universities across the United States; guest on television and radio programs. *Military service:* U.S. Air Force, 1954-58. *Member:* International P.E.N., Poets and Writers. *Awards, honors:* Woodrow Wilson fellowship, 1961-62; fellow of MacDowell Colony, 1975.

WRITINGS: Origins (poetry), Kayak, 1969, 3rd edition, 1974; *The Santa Cruz Mountain Poems,* Capra, 1972; *Where the Oceans Cover Us* (poetry), Capra, 1972; *The Armies Encamped in the Fields Beyond the Unfinished Avenues: Prose Poems,* Jazz Productions, 1977; *The Brezhnev Memo* (suspense novel), Dell, 1980; *Big Winds, Glass Mornings, Shadows Cast by Stars: Poems, 1972-1980,* Jazz Press, 1981.

Work represented in more than forty anthologies, including *California Poets: A Centennial Anthology,* 1976; *Best Poems of 1975: Borestone Mountain Awards,* 1976; *A Geography of Poets,* Bantam, 1979. Contributor to magazines, including *Poetry Northwest, Nation, Choice, Mademoiselle, Chicago Review,* and *Perspective.*

WORK IN PROGRESS: A suspense novel set in Vienna, Austria, during the signing of the "Salt II" treaty in June, 1972, publication by Delacorte expected in 1983; a book of poems based on his grandparents' pre-World War I emigration from Russia, tentatively titled *Ancestors' Child.*

SIDELIGHTS: In a statement prepared to accompany *Big Winds, Glass Mornings, Shadows Cast by Stars,* Marcus told an interviewer: "The history of one civilization after another is of the gradual corruption and eventual betrayal of the primordial human dream of physical and spiritual fulfillment that percolates in man's chromosomes. But the dream remains glittering like star-specks in our cells. It is the alternative to the many kinds of death we suffer each day, and the hopefully healing evocation of the dream's world-vision is my intention in all my writings."

Marcus told *CA:* "Although I am primarily a poet, I find my authorship of thrillers to be perfectly natural. In effect, I am digging under the surface of daily life in both areas, a spy in the dreams of us all. My trips to Greece, Germany, Italy, the Netherlands, and England have inspired both poems and prose. In all my work, I feel I am rediscovering the lost dreams, the forgotten goals of the race. As a poet, I am the one who reminds us where it is we are meant to go both biologically and spiritually."

BIOGRAPHICAL/CRITICAL SOURCES: Poetry: A Magazine of Verse, October, 1969; *Minnesota Review,* Volume IX, numbers 3-4, 1969; *West Coast Poetry Review,* autumn-winter, 1972-73; *Shocks III-IV,* March, 1974; *Dryad XIII,* 1975; *Kayak,* summer, 1981.

*   *   *

MARDER, Arthur (Jacob)   1910-1980

PERSONAL: Born March 8, 1910, in Boston, Mass.; died of cancer, December 25, 1980, in Santa Barbara, Calif.; son of Maxwell J. and Ida (Greenstein) Marder; married Jan North, September 13, 1955; children: Toni Anne, Ted Allen, Kevin North. *Education:* Harvard University, A.B., 1931, A.M., 1934, Ph.D., 1936.

CAREER: University of Oregon, Eugene, assistant professor of history, 1936-38; Harvard University, Cambridge, Mass., research associate at Bureau of International Research and Radcliffe College, 1939-41; Office of Strategic Services, research analyst, 1941-42; Hamilton College, Clinton, N.Y., associate professor of history, 1943-44; University of Hawaii, Honolulu, associate professor, 1944-51, professor, 1951-58, senior professor of history, 1958-64; University of California, Irvine, professor of history, 1964-77, professor emeritus, 1977-80. Visiting lecturer at Harvard University, 1949-50; George Eastman Professor at Oxford University and fellow of Balliol College, 1969-70.

AWARDS, HONORS: Guggenheim fellow, 1941, 1945-46, and 1958; George Louis Beer Prize from American Historical Association, 1941, for *Anatomy of British Sea Power;* Rockefeller Foundation fellow, 1942-43; American Philosophical Society fellow, 1956, 1958, 1963, and 1966; Chesney Memorial Gold Medal from Royal United Service Institute for Defence Studies, 1968; M.A. from Oxford University, 1969, D.Litt., 1971; citation from Board of Admiralty, 1970; honorary commander of Order of the British Empire, 1970; Japan Foundation fellow, 1976; fellow of Royal United Service Institute for Defence Studies, 1977; fellow of National Endowment for the Humanities, 1978-79; distinguished visitor award from Australian-American Education Foundation, 1979.

WRITINGS: The Anatomy of British Sea Power: A History of British Naval Policy in the Pre-Dreadnought Era, 1880-1905, Knopf, 1940 (published in England as *British Naval Policy, 1880-1905: The Anatomy of British Sea Power,* Putnam, 1941); (editor) *Fear God and Dread Nought: The Correspondence of Admiral of the Fleet Lord Fisher of Kilverstone,* Volume I: *The Making of an Admiral, 1854-1904,* Volume II: *Years of Power, 1904-1914,* Volume III: *Restoration, Abdication, and Last Years, 1914-1920,* Harvard University Press, 1952; *Portrait of an Admiral: The Life and Papers of Sir Herbert Richmond,* Harvard University Press, 1952; *From the Dreadnought*

to the Scapa Flow: The Royal Navy in the Fisher Era, 1904-1914, Oxford University Press, Volume I: *The Road to War, 1904-1914,* 1961, Volume II: *The War Years: To the Eve of Jutland,* 1965, Volume III: *Jutland and After: May, 1916-December, 1916,* 1966, Volume IV: *1917: The Year of Crisis,* 1969, Volume V: *Victory and Aftermath: January, 1918-June, 1919,* 1970, 2nd edition, 1978.

Winston Is Back: Churchill at the Admiralty, 1939-40, 1972; *From the Dardanelles to Oran: Studies of the Royal Navy in War and Peace, 1915-1940,* Oxford University Press, 1974; *Operation "Menace": The Dakar Expedition and the Dudley North Affair,* Oxford University Press, 1976; *Old Friends, New Enemies: The Royal Navy and the Imperial Japanese Navy: Strategic Illusions,* Clarendon Press, 1981. Contributor to history journals in England and the United States.

BIOGRAPHICAL/CRITICAL SOURCES: Gerald Jordan, editor, *Naval Warfare in the Twentieth Century, 1900-1945: Essays in Honour of Arthur Marder,* Croom Helm, 1977; *Times Literary Supplement,* December 4, 1981.

OBITUARIES: London Times, December 29, 1980.*

*   *   *

MARE, W(illiam) Harold   1918-

PERSONAL: Born July 23, 1918, in Portland, Ore.; son of Scott Creighton and Gertrude (Knight) Mare; married Clara Elizabeth Potter (a secretary); children: Myra Ann, Sally Elizabeth Mare Walke, Nancy Lee Mare Heyward, William Harold, Judith E. Mare Linton. *Education:* Wheaton College, Wheaton, Ill., B.A., 1941, M.A., 1964; Faith Theological Seminary, B.D., 1945; University of Pennsylvania, Ph.D., 1961. *Home:* 978 Orchard Lakes Dr., Creve Coeur, Mo. 63141. *Office:* 12330 Conway Rd., Creve Coeur, Mo. 63141.

CAREER: Ordained Reformed Presbyterian minister, 1945; Wheaton College, Wheaton, Ill., instructor in Greek, 1942; Faith Theological Seminary, Philadelphia, Pa., instructor in New Testament, 1946-53; pastor of Presbyterian churches in Denver, Colo., 1953-60, and Charlotte, N.C., 1960-63; Covenant College, Lookout Mountain, Tenn., professor of classics and chairman of department, 1963-65; Covenant Theological Seminary, St. Louis, Mo., professor of New Testament, 1965—. Professor at Near East School of Archaeology, 1962, 1964, 1970 (director of school, 1962, 1964), Archaeological School and Excavation at Raddana, Ramallah, Israel, summer, 1972, and excavation at Heshbon, Jordan, summers, 1974, 1976. Public lecturer. Vice-president of Dothan II Publications. Member of Central Moab Survey Team, summer, 1979; director of Decapolis Survey Project in Abila, Jordan, summer, 1980. Member of board of directors of National Presbyterian Missions, vice-president, 1965-67, president, 1967-69.

MEMBER: Association Internationale de Papyrologues, American Classical League, Archaeological Institute of America (vice-president, 1977-78; president, 1978-80), American Society of Papyrologists, American Schools of Oriental Research, Evangelical Theological Society, Near East Archaeological Society (president, 1971—), Society of Biblical Literature, St. Louis Biblical Studies Society, Classical Club of St. Louis.

WRITINGS: Mastering New Testament Greek: For Beginners, Intermediate, and Advanced Students, Baker Book, 1975, revised edition, 1979; *Commentary on I Corinthians,* Zondervan, 1976; (contributor of translation) Edwin Palmer and others, editors, *New International Bible,* New York Bible Society, 1978; *The Archaeology of the Jerusalem Area,* Baker Book, 1982.

Contributor to *Dictionary of Biblical Literature, Pictorial Encyclopedia of the Bible, Wycliffe Bible Encyclopedia, Zondervan Dictionary of Biblical Archeology, Tyndale Family Bible Encyclopedia,* and *International Standard Bible Encyclopedia.* Contributor of about forty articles and reviews to theology journals and denominational magazines, including *Reformed Presbyterian Reporter.* Member of staff of *Religious and Theological Abstracts.*

WORK IN PROGRESS: Commentary on the Epistles to the Hebrews, publication by Moody expected in 1984.

SIDELIGHTS: Mare told *CA:* "My main interests are in New Testament studies and Old and New Testament archaeology. Thus, my writing, past, present and future, centers in these areas. Our Abila of the Decapolis project in north Jordan, which started with a survey in 1980, is expanding into excavation work and a regional survey in 1982 and beyond. We have important and fascinating work to accomplish at Abila, a site that represents ancient archaeological periods, including the Early Bronze, Iron I-II, Roman, Byzantine and Umayyad, and also to some extent the Middle Bronze I, Late Bronze and Hellenistic periods."

*   *   *

MARER, Paul 1936-

PERSONAL: Born June 17, 1936, in Budapest, Hungary; came to the United States in 1956, naturalized citizen, 1961; son of Lajos and Edith Marer; married Erika M. Schwaier (a nurse), August 16, 1963; children: Elizabeth, Heidi, Leah, Eva. *Education:* Florida Southern College, B.A., 1961; University of Pennsylvania, M.A., 1962, Ph.D., 1968. *Home:* 415 Sheffield Dr., Bloomington, Ind. 47401. *Office:* Department of International Business, Graduate School of Business, Indiana University, Bloomington, Ind. 47401.

CAREER: Florida Southern College, Lakeland, instructor in business, summers, 1961-63; *Philadelphia Bulletin,* Philadelphia, Pa., assistant to financial editor, 1964-65; Herbert H. Lehman College of the City University of New York, Bronx, N.Y., lecturer, 1965-68, assistant professor of business, 1968-71; Indiana University, Bloomington, visiting associate professor, 1971-75, associate professor, 1975-77, professor of business, 1977—, coordinator of exchange program with University of Ljubljana, 1977—, research scholar at International Development Institute, 1969—. Research economist at Columbia University's Institute of International Affairs, 1965-70; member of East-West trade advisory committee of U.S. Department of Commerce, 1974-75; expert witness before Congressional committees. *Member:* American Economic Association, Omicron Delta Kappa, Beta Gamma Sigma. *Awards, honors:* Danforth fellow, 1961-65; grants from American Council of Learned Societies, 1971-72, 1979.

WRITINGS: Postwar Pricing and Price Patterns in Socialist Foreign Trade, 1946-1971, International Development Research Center, Indiana University, 1972; *Soviet and East European Foreign Trade, 1946-1969: Statistical Compendium and Guide,* Indiana University Press, 1972; (editor with Robert W. Campbell) *East-West Trade and Technology Transfer,* International Development Research Center, Indiana University, 1974; (editor) *U.S. Financing of East-West Trade: The Political Economy of Government Credits and the National Interest,* Indiana University Press, 1975; *Annotated and Cross-Referenced Bibliography of East-West Commerce,* International Development Institute, Indiana University, 1977.

Contributor: *A Foreign Economic Policy for the 1970's,* Part VI, U.S. Government Printing Office, 1970; Morris Bornstein,

editor, *From Planning Toward the Market,* Yale University Press, 1973; *Reorientation and Commercial Relations of the Economies of Eastern Europe,* U.S. Government Printing Office, 1974; Steve Rosen, and J. R. Kurth, editors, *Contemporary Economic Imperialism,* Heath, 1974; C. H. McMillan, editor, *Changing Perspectives in East-West Commerce,* Heath, 1974; *United States-Romanian Trade Agreement: Hearings,* U.S. Government Printing Office, 1975; C. Mesa-Lago and C. Beck, editors, *Comparative Socialist Systems: Essays on Politics and Economics,* University of Pittsburgh Press, 1975; J. C. Brada, editor, *Quantitative and Analytical Studies in East-West Economic Relations,* International Development Research Institute, Indiana University, 1976; Charles Gati, editor, *The International Politics of Eastern Europe,* Praeger, 1976.

American Role in East-West Trade, U.S. Government Printing Office, 1977; C. T. Saunders, editor, *East-West Cooperation in Business: Interfirm Studies,* Springer-Verlag, 1977; J. F. Triska and P. M. Cocks, editors, *Political Development in Eastern Europe,* Praeger, 1977; *East European Economies Post-Helsinki,* U.S. Government Printing Office, 1977; Brada and V. S. Somanoth, editors, *East-West Trade: Theory and Evidence,* International Development Institute, Indiana University, 1978; Friedrich Levcik, editor, *International Economics: Comparisons and Interdependence,* Springer-Verlag, 1978; *Winning Business in the USSR,* Graham & Trotman, 1978; M. A. Martin and L. F. Dunn, editors, *The Competitive Threat From Abroad: Fact or Fiction,* Purdue University, 1978; Theresa Rakowska-Harmstone and Andrew Gyorgy, editors, *The Governments, Economics, and Politics of Eastern Europe,* Indiana University Press, 1979. Also contributor to *Choice of Partners in East-West Economic Relations,* edited by McMillan and Zbigniew Fallenbuchl, and *International Economic Development and Resource Transfer,* edited by Herbert Giersch.

Editor of "International Trade Information Management Systems," Indiana University, 1969-75, and "Studies in East European and Soviet Planning, Development, and Trade," a book series, International Development Institute, Indiana University, 1974—. Contributor of articles and reviews to scholarly journals and popular magazines, including *Newsweek* and *Business Week.*

*   *   *

MARGHIERI, Clotilde 1901(?)-1981

OBITUARY NOTICE: Born c. 1901; died in 1981 in Rome, Italy. Author, best known for her novel *The Mark on the Arm.* Shortly before her death, Marghieri published *The Double Mirror,* a collection of correspondence with art critic Bernhard Berenson. Obituaries and other sources: *AB Bookman's Weekly,* November 2, 1981.

*   *   *

MARKUS, Julia 1939-

PERSONAL: Born November 19, 1939, in Jersey City, N.J.; daughter of Morris and Ruth (Selman) Markus; divorced. *Education:* Boston University, A.B., 1961, M.A., 1962; University of Maryland, College Park, Ph.D., 1976. *Residence:* Bethel, Conn. *Agent:* Harriet Wasserman, Harriet Wasserman Literary Agency, 230 East 48th St., New York, N.Y. 10017. *Address:* c/o Houghton Mifflin Co., 666 Third Ave., New York, N.Y. 10017.

CAREER: Concordia College, Bronxville, N.Y., instructor in English, 1961-63; Southern Connecticut State College, New Haven, Conn., instructor in English, 1966-71; University of

Maryland, Extension School, instructor in English, 1973-75; Bay College of Baltimore, Baltimore, Md., instructor in English, 1976-77; Decatur House Press, Washington, D.C., cofounder, 1976, vice-president and editor, 1976-80; Hofstra University, Hempstead, Long Island, N.Y., adjunct star professor, 1981—. Member of board of directors of Browning Institute, New York, N.Y., 1973-82. *Member:* P.E.N., Authors Guild. *Awards, honors:* Houghton Mifflin Literary Fellowship award, 1978, for *Uncle;* National Endowment for the Arts grant, 1980.

WRITINGS: La Mora (novel), Decatur House, 1976; *A Patron of the Arts* (novella), Apple-Wood, 1977; (editor) Elizabeth Barrett Browning, *Casa Guidi Windows,* Browning Institute, 1977; *Uncle* (novel), Houghton, 1978; *American Rose* (novel), Houghton, 1981. Editor of Browning Institute Series, 1973-77. Film critic for *Maryland Sentinal,* 1975-76.

WORK IN PROGRESS: The Best of Friends, a novel, for Houghton.

SIDELIGHTS: Markus's novels *Uncle* and *American Rose* have been widely reviewed by critics. Her first work to receive recognition, *Uncle* won for Markus the Houghton Mifflin Literary Fellowship award. Describing the book as "her interpretation of the American Dream," Markus chose as her subject Irving Bender and his family. The story begins with Irv's decision at the age of sixteen to sacrifice his goals in life for those of his brother. He becomes a bootlegger and then the owner of Camp Rose Lake, a summer camp for children. Irv amasses a fortune, helps his brother through college, secures him a job, and continues to care for him when he marries and has a daughter. Irv acts as a benevolent uncle to all the characters in the story. "Surrounded by unpleasant, thwarted people—his troubled niece, his grasping, self-pitying mother—Bender ministers to their emotional demands and grows old alone," noted James Atlas of *Time.* Ultimately Irv realizes, as Christopher Lehmann-Haupt surmised in the *New York Times,* that "charity is next to selfishness." At one point, Irv admits, "I am not what I started out to be."

What critics frequently observed about *Uncle* was its author's economy of words. Irv's life, from his "revelation" at sixteen to his death in a Florida condominium, is covered in only one hundred seventy pages. A *New York Times* writer called the book "taut" and "stripped-down" while a *Newsweek* reviewer asserted, "this short novel portrays a lifetime in the sparest of needlepoints, wrought with economy and precision."

Others commented on her ability in telling a story. Susan Wood, speaking for many readers, proclaimed that "when we find a novel as beautifully written and perceptive as *Uncle,* we cry, like Archimedes in his bath, 'Eureka!'" *Newsweek*'s critic hailed Markus as "a remarkable storyteller, cool but not dispassionate, sharply observant but fair" while Atlas expressed that the author "has a painterly sense of detail, building up scenes with a deliberate eye for the nuances of her characters' gestures and speech."

Markus's next work, *American Rose,* prompted some reviewers, such as Doris Grumbach in the *Chicago Tribune Book World,* to conjecture that "if the Houghton Mifflin fellowship is a mark of literary promise, it was properly awarded to Julia Markus." Grumbach added, "This new book more than justifies her publisher's faith." Calling *American Rose* an "unswerving look at a small group of characters," Linda Barrett Osborne of the *Washington Post Book World* compared the book to *Uncle.* It "has a wider scope, portraying three generations," she noted. The story of the Addis family, *American*

Rose depicts "their daily lives, the decisions and actions connected to jobs, household arrangements, illness, family relations." Osborne continued that "the drama is the drama of ordinary living—marriages, heart attacks, conflicts between parents and children." Grumbach praised Markus's effort as "touching yet cutting, a graphic, almost tactile series of portraits of . . . well-to-do Jews living . . . in Jersey City during this century." "In 'American Rose,'" remarked Anne Tyler of the *New York Times Book Review,* "Julia Markus has once again shown her particular sensitivity to the stoics, to the trudgers, to those who simply hope to make it through the day."

CA INTERVIEW

CA interviewed Julia Markus in the offices of Houghton Mifflin in New York, N.Y., on March 6, 1981.

It took Julia Markus twelve years to get her fiction published, but she was sustained throughout those years by a belief that she had something important to say. Her first published novel, *La Mora,* came out under the imprint of Decatur House Press. When the book elicited respectable reviews, she was encouraged. But she set up her next novel as a test for herself. She decided that if *Uncle* didn't meet her self-imposed standards of quality and acceptance, she would give up trying to be a novelist and "go out and enjoy life." Not only was *Uncle* accepted by Houghton Mifflin as an unsolicited manuscript, but it also won for its author the Houghton Mifflin Literary Fellowship award and an honorarium of ten thousand dollars. It was the first time in four years that the award had been granted.

During the years she wrote fiction without being published, Markus taught, earned her doctorate from the University of Maryland in English literature, and began researching scholarly works. As an expatriate writer living in Italy, Markus was particularly drawn to Robert Browning and Elizabeth Barrett Browning, who had also spent many years in Italy. Her critical edition of Elizabeth Barrett Browning's *Casa Guidi Windows* took two years of hard work comparing manuscripts, writing a preface, and compiling a thorough annotation. "I enjoyed the scholarly work," she says, "but I was disappointed by its inevitably small audience. During all the time I worked in academia, fiction still came first. When you have something you want to say, you want more people to listen."

In writing novels, Markus is drawn more to character than to plot, and her purpose is to show how various characters work out their private destinies. "It sounds hokey, I know, but I'm really fascinated by how people live their lives and how they relate to the people they love. I'm particularly interested in American history and how characters change with the times." She cites the character of Raymond in *American Rose* as a personality of whom she is particularly fond in this sense: He grapples with his boyhood in the 1950's and twenty years later tries to relate to his daughter in a much different time.

Markus seeks the same combination of personal history within the context of social history in other writers. She also likes biography, poetry, history, and contemporary fiction, particularly novels that deal with historical themes and settings. Examples she lists include Italian novelist Elsa Morante's book about World War II, titled *History: A Novel,* and *A Man* by Oriana Fallaci. Markus also reads "a lot of the British," naming C. P. Snow, Graham Greene, E. M. Forster, and George Eliot. "I look for a book that is alive, a book that is almost a pounding heart," she explains. She believes a novel can give the reader a dimension of life that cannot be gained elsewhere.

She declares, "I don't at all believe this talk we hear that the novel is dead."

She became a writer, Markus says, through her love affair with literature. "I always knew as a kid that I'd be an author, but I didn't start writing seriously until I was in my twenties. I figured that to write a novel you had to experience something of life. I started writing when I felt I had something to say." As a young writer, she would bolster her confidence by reading the first novels of writers she admired: Henry James, D. H. Lawrence, and E. M. Forster. Seeing their flaws, she gained the courage to go on. "You don't start out comparing yourself to *Passage to India,* or you can get very discouraged."

In an age of electric typewriters and word processors, Markus writes by hand, with a pencil, in a spiral-bound notebook. Her manuscript goes on the right-hand page, and corrections are written on the page to the left. Unable to complete a manuscript without correction, she prefers to painstakingly read over every word and phrase as she composes. Then she goes through many handwritten drafts before typing up the near-final version. She never writes from an outline. "I find I'm a process writer. What interests me in writing is that I get completely involved in the story. If I have an outline, I know what will happen in the plot, and I get bored to death." Markus reveals that she can write anywhere, such as in buses and trains. In Rome she worked in sidewalk cafes. "Unlike some authors, I generally write wherever I am, and it doesn't bother me."

Though Rome was the setting for *La Mora, Uncle* and *American Rose* were both set in her childhood home of Jersey City, New Jersey. Markus emphasizes that her books are not autobiographical or based on actual people. For the Yiddish sprinkled throughout *American Rose,* she says she had to refer to Leo Rosten's *The Joys of Yiddish.* The schizophrenic sister Helen in *American Rose* was born from library research on mental illness and from a sense of the author's that every family closet has a skeleton or two. "Some of my characters are composites, but others are completely imagined," she disclosed. "Quite frankly, I don't feel that anyone can distinguish between the two." She notes that she used the city where she was born and raised as a setting because it seemed more of a "non-environment" than any place in particular. "After setting *La Mora* in Rome, I chose Jersey City because I thought it would give me the opportunity to find the exotic in the common, to discover what I had missed growing up." After using her hometown in both novels, she took to calling *American Rose* her "good-bye to Jersey City."

Markus bristles at the suggestion by some reviewers that her handling of contemporary life lacks the texture of her descriptions of earlier times. "I find this criticism strange," she comments, "because I consider the endings of my books, which represent the modern period, the most original parts. Some people don't see that because when we look in the past, we enrich it. It looks rich just the way a legend looks rich." She adds, "The more original elements of a work gain the most controversy."

A novelist who writes from the heart, not the head, Markus feels uncomfortable analyzing her works, balancing her strengths and weaknesses. "I look at my work as something alive. I don't evaluate books once I've completed them. If I did, maybe I wouldn't write."

She will probably never suffer through twelve dry years again, though not everything she has written has been published. Her first novel still rests with her agent, "safe and sound," as she describes it. Starting out as *Born on the Fourth of July,* it was

renamed *Nancy Blue* after another book appeared under her original title. It is about a young woman who marries a politician. Markus says the book "got nice rejection letters," but she does not plan to revise it with an eye towards publishing it one day. "No, I don't think so," she asserts. "I don't like to rewrite when I'm finished with a book. I always believe in going on to the next thing, not looking back."

BIOGRAPHICAL/CRITICAL SOURCES: Time, September 18, 1978; *Washington Post,* September 24, 1978; *New Republic,* October 7, 1978; *Newsweek,* October 9, 1978; *New York Times Book Review,* November 12, 1978, March 8, 1981; *New York Times,* November 24, 1978, March 16, 1979; *Times Literary Supplement,* January 25, 1980; *Washington Post Book World,* March 22, 1981; *Los Angeles Times Book Review,* April 19, 1981; *Chicago Tribune Book World,* May 3, 1981.

—*Interview by Trisha Gorman*

*   *   *

MARLBOROUGH
See OAKSEY, John

*   *   *

MARSHALL, Thomas Humphrey   1893-1981

OBITUARY NOTICE: Born December 19, 1893, in London, England; died after a short illness, November 29, 1981, in Cambridge, England. Sociologist, educator, and author. Considered one of the pioneers of modern British sociology, Marshall, with Morris Ginsberg and John Hicks, published a series of writings in 1930 on the application of sociology to the study of social conflicts. His subsequent works, including *Sociology at the Crossroads* and *Social Policy in the Twentieth Century,* became classics in the study of British society. Obituaries and other sources: *Who's Who,* 126th edition, Marquis, 1974; *London Times,* December 3, 1981.

*   *   *

MARTIN, Samuel Elmo   1924-

BRIEF ENTRY: Born January 29, 1924, in Pittsburg, Kan. American educator and author. Martin began teaching at Yale University in 1950 and became professor of Far Eastern linguistics and chairman of the department of linguistics in 1966. He wrote *Beginning Korean* (Yale University Press, 1969), *A Reference Grammar of Japanese* (Yale University Press, 1975), and *Advanced Japanese Conversation* (Far Eastern Publications, Yale University, 1976). *Address:* Department of Linguistics, Yale University, New Haven, Conn. 06520. *Biographical/critical sources: Directory of American Scholars,* Volume III; *Foreign Languages, Linguistics, and Philosophy,* 7th edition, Bowker, 1978.

*   *   *

MARTINELLI, Ricardo
See BRANDON, Johnny

*   *   *

MARTINS, Maria Isabel Barreno de Faria   1939-
(Maria Isabel Barreno)

PERSONAL: Born July 10, 1939, in Lisbon, Portugal; daughter of Joaquim Hipolito Faria and Isabel da Conceicao (Barreno de Faria) Martins; married Pedro M.C. Valente Pereira, 1962 (divorced, 1971); children: Cristovao de Faria Martins Valente,

Marcos de Faria Martins Valente. *Education:* Received B.A. from University of Lisbon, License in Letters, 1962. *Politics:* "Feminist, waiting for the party, or anything, that will articulate feminism and new men." *Religion:* None. *Home:* R. Presidente Wilson, 4-R/c-D, 1000 Lisbon, Portugal. *Agent:* Gloria Safier, Inc., 667 Madison Ave., New York, N.Y. 10021. *Office:* Av. D. Sebastiao, 46 Costa da Caparica, Portugal.

CAREER: Writer. Researcher in human relations and industrial sociology at Institute of Industrial Research in Portugal, 1962-75; dealer in books and handcrafts in Casta da Caparica, Portugal.

WRITINGS—All under name Maria Isabel Barreno; in English translation: (With Maria Fatima Velho da Costa and Maria Teresa Horta) *Novas cartas portuguesas* (nonfiction), Ecor, 1972, translation by Helen R. Lane published as *The Three Marias: New Portuguese Letters,* Doubleday, 1975.

In Portuguese: *De noite as arnores sao negras* (novel), Europa-America, 1968; *Os outros legitimos superiores* (novel), Europa-America, 1970; *A Imagem da mulher na imprensa,* (title means "Images of Women in the Press'), Comissao da condicao feminina, 1976; *A morte de Mae* (novel and essay), Moraes, 1979. Co-author of play adapted from her own book *Novas cartas portuguesas.*

Contributor to *Ms.*

WORK IN PROGRESS: Isaventario de Ana, a novel; "Women's Functions, Women's Jobs, Women's Culture," an essay; "Mulher a mulher," a television series (title means "Woman to Woman").

SIDELIGHTS: Three weeks after the publication of *The Three Marias: New Portuguese Letters,* the Portuguese Government ordered the book withdrawn from bookstores. The authors, Maria Isabel Barreno, Maria Teresa Horta, and Maria Velho da Costa (the "three Marias"), were arrested and charged with "abuse of press freedom" and "outrage to public decency." Their trial, which began in October, 1972, dragged on until April, 1974. During that time, the authors gained international notoriety, and groups of women in other countries, including Holland, France, Germany, and the United States, organized protests to demonstrate their support for the Marias. The trial ended, but before the judge could deliver his verdict, the Fascist Portuguese Government was overthrown by the army, the three were acquitted, and their book was released.

The book evolved from the relationship of the women—all convent-educated, all published writers in their early thirties, all married and mothers of sons. In 1971 they began meeting twice weekly to share their ideas on women's issues. Describing those meetings to Jorjanna Price of the *Houston Post,* Maria Barreno recalled, "We talked together a lot about when we were children, the meaning of writing, of being a woman, the oppression of women not only in Portugal but everywhere." They wrote letters to one another and exchanged essays and poems on such subjects as sexuality, pregnancy, abortion, passion, isolation, fear, and religion. "These brief, unsigned pieces," explained Peter S. Prescott in *Newsweek,* "became a book that draws its unifying metaphor from the celebrated seventeenth-century "Portuguese Letters"—letters allegedly written from a convent near Lisbon by a nun, Mariana, to her lover, a French soldier who abandoned her. . . . The convent serves easily as a metaphor for all marriages, for society, for roles defined for women by men."

Prescott found *The Three Marias: New Portuguese Letters* "sensuous and intelligent, anguished and self-assured," and

he declared it "the best book on the feminine condition that I have read." Christopher Hitchens, writing for the *New Statesman,* agreed. "This is a brilliantly intense book, born out of experience not introspection, and one which gives a better explanation of women's ambivalence towards men than any other tortured effort of that genre."

Other critics, like Jane Kramer of the *New York Times Book Review,* were less enthusiastic. Kramer was "bored silly by too many hymns to the womb." She felt that the authors' "collective lamentations on passion never really penetrate love's tyrannies or its embittering social and familiar uses as much as they detail some morbid and inescapable pathology." Reflecting on the Portuguese Government's charges of obscenity and indecency following the book's original publication, the *New Republic*'s Doris Grumbach doubted that readers would be shocked by the "adolescent, groping, overheated displays of narcissism, [or the] fantasies that are often dull." A *New Yorker* critic thought the book "not particularly indecent and not particularly praiseworthy, either."

Commenting on the wide disagreement among reviewers, Grumbach declared: "Almost every judgment, no matter how diverse, made on the book is true. It is extravagant, overheated, badly written in some parts, finely written in others, often very touching." Echoing Grumbach's mixed reaction, Neal Ascherson of the *New York Review of Books* found the book "maddeningly imprecise" and "self-indulgent." "Where it is precise, however, the book still bites. Where it is erotic, it is neither exhibitionist nor coy but well calculated to touch the mind through emotion."

Critics also differed on whether the book is successful as a feminist piece. Some immediately categorized it as an important feminist work, while others felt that the authors lacked a firm feminist orientation. "There is no doubt that 'The Three Marias' was a political event in Portugal. As a feminist book, though," warned Kramer, it is "in trouble, and part of the trouble is that these three modern Marias are . . . obsessed with love." Still other critics, while agreeing that there is a strong feminist tone to the book, concluded that its message is outdated, because the authors, although successful in demonstrating that women are oppressed, failed to offer any solutions. Barreno herself believes that writing *The Three Marias* strengthened her ideas on feminism. Prior to beginning work on the book, she told Price, she was "interested in feminism but only intellectually. I had the concept, but for the first time I could express what we can call sisterhood, the feeling when people are together. We really can do wonderful things."

Barreno told *CA:* "Almost all subjects are vital—everything adds to the whole. My career is my life and vice-versa. My circumstances are middle-class; there was enough money to go to university and to be part of Lisbon's intellectual milieu. I like to interview people."

AVOCATIONAL INTERESTS: Handcrafts, including crochet.

BIOGRAPHICAL/CRITICAL SOURCES: Houston Post, January 28, 1975; *New York Times Book Review,* February 2, 1975; *New Republic,* February 15, 1975; *New Yorker,* February 24, 1975; *Newsweek,* February 27, 1975; *New York Review of Books,* March 20, 1975; *New Statesman,* November 7, 1975; *Authors in the News,* Volume 1, Gale, 1976.

—*Sketch by Mary Sullivan*

*   *   *

MARTOS, Joseph (John)   1943-

PERSONAL: Born June 11, 1943, in New York, N.Y.; son of

Joseph F. (a warehouse supervisor) and Johanna (a file clerk; maiden name, Gondar) Martos; married Linda Gay Forbes (a teacher), 1968; children: Justin, Ambrose. *Education:* Cathedral College, B.A., 1964; Gregorian University, S.T.B., 1966; attended Boston College, 1968; DePaul University, Ph.D., 1973. *Religion:* Roman Catholic. *Home:* 2617 McFaul St., Sioux City, Iowa 51104. *Office:* Department of Theology and Philosophy, Briar Cliff College, 3303 Rebecca St., Sioux City, Iowa 51104.

CAREER: High school teacher of religion and ethics in Chicago, Ill., 1971-72; religious education coordinator at Roman Catholic parish in Barrington, Ill., 1972-74; high school teacher of religious studies in Woodstock, Ill., 1974-76; Briar Cliff College, Sioux City, Iowa, assistant professor of theology and philosophy, 1976—. *Member:* American Catholic Philosophical Association, American Academy of Religion, College Theological Society, Religious Education Association, Catholic Theological Society of America, Institute for Advanced Philosophic Research.

WRITINGS: Doors to the Sacred: A Historical Introduction to Sacraments in the Catholic Church, Doubleday, 1981.

WORK IN PROGRESS: An introductory volume for a series of books on the sacraments, publication by Thomas Glazier expected in 1982; a set of recorded lectures on the ministry of spiritual care, release by NCR Cassettes expected in 1982; research on history, theology, and catechesis of the Roman Catholic sacraments.

SIDELIGHTS: Martos commented: "As a writer and teacher I see myself as someone who is trying to help my church to weather the transition from the modern to the post-modern world. To do this well we have to know our history, for knowing the complexity of the past helps us to face the uncertainty of the future. I feel somewhat equipped to do this, having been raised in pre-Vatican II Catholicism and pre-Vietnam America, but realizing, regretfully, that those worlds are gone forever."

*   *   *

MARTYN, James Louis 1925-

BRIEF ENTRY: Born October 11, 1925, in Dallas, Tex. American educator and author. Martyn joined the faculty at Union Theological Seminary in 1959 and was named Edward Robinson Professor of Biblical Theology in 1967. He wrote *Easter* (Fortress, 1975), *The Gospel of St. John in Christian History* (Paulist Press, 1978), and *Studies in Luke-Acts* (Fortress, 1980). *Address:* 606 West 122nd St., New York, N.Y. 10027; and Department of Biblical Theology, Union Theological Seminary, 3041 Broadway, New York, N.Y. 10027. *Biographical/critical sources: Directory of American Scholars,* Volume IV: *Philosophy, Religion, and Law,* 7th edition, Bowker, 1978.

*   *   *

MASHECK, Joseph (Daniel) 1942-

PERSONAL: Born January 19, 1942, in New York, N.Y.; son of Joseph Anthony (a mechanical engineer) and Dorothy Anna (Cahill) Masheck. *Education:* Columbia University, A.B., 1963, M.A., 1965, Ph.D., 1973. *Politics:* "Social-democratic." *Religion:* Roman Catholic. *Residence:* New York, N.Y. *Office:* Department of Art History, Barnard College, Columbia University, 606 West 120th St., New York, N.Y. 10027.

CAREER: Columbia University, New York, N.Y., associate curator of photograph collection in department of art history and archaeology, 1965-67; editorial researcher in London, En-

gland, 1967-69; Columbia University, Barnard College, instructor, 1971-73, assistant professor of art history, 1973—. Lecturer at Maidstone College of Art, 1968-69, and at museums and art schools. Member of art panels and competition juries. *Member:* International Association of Art Critics, American Association of University Professors, Columbia University Society of Fellows. *Awards, honors:* National Endowment for the Arts fellow, 1975-76; Guggenheim fellow, 1977-78; Edward Albee Foundation fellow at William C. Flanagan Memorial Creative Persons Center, 1980, 1981.

WRITINGS: (Editor and author of introduction) *Marcel Duchamp in Perspective,* Prentice-Hall, 1975; *The Carpet Paradigm: Critical Prolegomena to a Theory of Flatness,* Out of London Press, 1982. Contributor of more than one hundred fifty articles and reviews to art journals. Contributing editor of *Artforum,* 1973-77, 1980—, editor, 1977-80.

WORK IN PROGRESS: A book on "recent abstract art seen in the light of pre-Renaissance art."

SIDELIGHTS: Masheck wrote: "I see the issue of representation more or less from the viewpoint of Moses; by the same token, the notion (and the theology) of incarnation has much to offer in the contemplation of abstract painting."

*   *   *

MASON, Pamela 1918-

BRIEF ENTRY: Born March 10, 1918, in Westgate, England. British actress and author. Mason made her stage debut in 1936. She wrote *Favorite Cat Stories of Pamela and James Mason* (Messner, 1976), *Marriage Is the First Step Towards Divorce* (Paul Eriksson, 1968), and *The Female Pleasure Hunt* (Prentice-Hall, 1972). *Biographical/critical sources: International Motion Picture Almanac,* Quigley, 1980.

*   *   *

MASTERTON, Graham 1946-
(Thomas Luke)

PERSONAL: Born January 16, 1946, in Uxbridge, England; son of J. (a major in the British Army) and Mary (Bristow-Jones) Masterton; married Wiescka Walach (a literary agent), December, 1976; children: Roland, Luke, Daniel. *Education:* Attended private boys' school in Croydon, England. *Agent:* Wiescka Masterton, Chapter House, Longdown Lane S., Epsom Downs, Surrey, England.

CAREER: Free-lance writer, 1974—. Also worked as newspaper reporter and magazine editor. *Awards, honors:* Edgar Allan Poe Award from Mystery Writers of America, 1979, for *Charnel House.*

WRITINGS—Novels, except as noted: How to Be the Perfect Lover (nonfiction), New American Library, 1975; *How to Drive Your Man Wild in Bed* (nonfiction), New American Library, 1976; *The Djinn,* Pinnacle Books, 1977; *The Manitou,* Neville Spearman, 1977; *Fireflash Five,* Star Books, 1977, reprinted as *Mile Before Morning,* 1979; *Plague,* Star Books, 1977; *The Sphinx,* Pinnacle Books, 1978; *The Devils of D-Day,* Pinnacle Books, 1978; *Rich,* Simon & Schuster, 1979; *The Revenge of the Manitou,* Pinnacle Books, 1979; *The Sweetman Curve,* Ace Books, 1979; *Charnel House,* Bailey & Swinfen, 1979; *The Wells of Hell,* Pocket Books, 1980; *Famine,* Ace Books, 1981; *A Man of Destiny,* Simon & Schuster, 1981 (published in England as *Railroad,* Hamish Hamilton, 1981).

Suspense novels under pseudonym Thomas Luke: *The Hell Candidate,* Pocket Books, 1980; *Phobia,* Pocket Books, 1981.

WORK IN PROGRESS: Unholy Bonds, a novel about international banking.

SIDELIGHTS: Masterton commented: "I write to entertain myself, my family, and my readers and to fill the empty spaces on my library shelves."

BIOGRAPHICAL/CRITICAL SOURCES: Washington Post, May 21, 1981, *Los Angeles Times,* July 19, 1981.

*   *   *

MATHEWS, Louise
See TOOKE, Louise Mathews

*   *   *

MATHIS, James L.   1925-

PERSONAL: Born January 30, 1925, in Dayton, Tenn.; son of Luther L. (a farmer) and Anna (Clarke) Mathis; married Kim Weber (a merchant), June 2, 1948; children: Jeffrey, Mark, Leslie, Lynn. *Education:* Attended Citadel, 1943-44, and University of Missouri, 1944-45; St. Louis University, M.D., 1949. *Home address:* P.O. Box 220, Grimesland, N.C. 27837. *Office:* Department of Psychiatry, School of Medicine, East Carolina University, Greenville, N.C. 27834.

CAREER: Fitzsimons General Hospital, Denver, Colo., intern, 1949-50; Community Hospital-Clinic, Elk City, Okla., resident in general medicine, 1950-51; Crossett Health Center, Crossett, Ark., staff physician, 1951-52; Community Hospital-Clinic, Elk City, surgical assistant, 1952-55; private practice of general medicine in Dayton, Tenn., 1955-60; University of Oklahoma, Oklahoma City, resident in psychiatry at Medical Center, 1960-62, chief resident, 1962-63, instructor, 1963-64, assistant professor of psychiatry, 1964-68, chief of Division of Post-Graduate Education in Psychiatry for the Non-Psychiatrist, 1964-68; Rutgers University, New Brunswick, N.J., associate professor of psychiatry, 1968-70; Medical College of Virginia, Richmond, professor of psychiatry and chairman of department, 1970-76, member of executive committee of college hospital, 1970-76; East Carolina University, Greenville, N.C., professor of psychiatry and chairman of department, 1976—.

Assistant chief of psychiatry at Veterans Administration Hospital, Oklahoma City, 1963-64; acting director of Virginia Treatment Center for Children, 1971-72, and Memorial Guidance Clinic, Richmond, 1971-72 (member of board of directors, 1971-76); acting medical director of Pitt County Mental Health Center, 1976-77; member of board of directors of Jump Street, Inc. (methadone clinic), 1973-76. Member of Virginia governor's committee on mental, indigent, and geriatric patients and chairman of subcommittee of Governor's Commission on Needs of Emotionally Disturbed Children in Virginia, 1971-73; member of advisory committee of Richmond Area Community Council, 1972-76; consultant to Peace Corps, Oklahoma City Police Department, and Office of Economic Opportunity. *Military service:* U.S. Army, Medical Corps, 1943-46, 1949-50; became first lieutenant.

MEMBER: American Medical Association, American Psychiatric Association (fellow), American College of Psychiatrists (fellow), American Board of Psychiatry and Neurology (associate examiner in psychiatry, 1971—), American Psychosomatic Society, American Academy of Psychoanalysis (scientific associate), North Carolina Neuropsychiatric Society, North Carolina State Medical Society, East Carolina Psychiatric Association (president, 1979—), Alpha Omega Alpha.

WRITINGS: (With C. M. Pierce and V. Pishkin) *Basic Psychiatry: A Primer of Concepts and Terminology,* Appleton, 1968, 2nd edition, 1972; *Sexual Deviations,* Nelson-Hall, 1972.

Contributor: J. P. Lysaught, editor, *Programmed Instruction in Medical Evaluation,* Rochester Clearinghouse, 1965; *Proceedings of Biological, Psychological, and Social Aspects of Aging,* Southwestern Center for Gerontological Studies, University of Oklahoma, 1966; Lysaught, editor, *Individualized Instruction in Medical Education,* Rochester Clearinghouse, 1968; *Proceedings of the Second Annual Short Course on Aging,* Southwestern Center for Gerontological Studies, University of Oklahoma, 1968; Claude Frazier, editor, *Is It Moral to Modify Man?,* C. C Thomas, 1973; *Primary Care,* Volume I, Saunders, 1974; D. W. Abse, E. M. Nash, and L.M.R. Louden, editors, *Marital and Sexual Counseling,* 2nd edition (Mathis was not included in 1st edition), Harper, 1974; E. L. Gullick and S. F. Peed, editors, *The Role of the Health Practitioner in Family Relationships: Sexual and Marital Issues,* Technomic Publishing, 1978; D. J. Cox and R. J. Daitzman, editors, *Exhibitionism,* Garland Publishing, 1980.

Tapes; for *Practical Reviews in Pediatrics:* "Treating the Disturbed Adolescent," 1976; "Adolescent Sexuality," 1976; "Chronic Disease in Adolescents," 1977; "The Parents of the Chronically Ill Adolescent," 1977.

Contributor of more than fifty articles to medical journals. Member of editorial board of *Sexual Behavior,* 1972-74; editorial adviser to *World Journal of Psychosynthesis,* 1977—.

WORK IN PROGRESS: Stress: Psychophysiological Aspects; Affective Disorders; "Roots" in Rural East Carolina Medicine.

SIDELIGHTS: Mathis wrote: "My experience is only in scientific writing. The beginner must say what is to be said as briefly and clearly as possible, then eliminate 10 percent of the words. A week or so later, another 10 percent or so can be extracted without harm."

*   *   *

MATTINGLY, George E.   1950-

PERSONAL: Born September 4, 1950, in Missouri; son of William Anthony (in business) and Joan (Pollock) Mattingly; married Lucy Ann Farber (a novelist), May 5, 1979. *Education:* Attended University of Iowa, 1968-70. *Office:* Blue Wind Press, P.O. Box 7175, Berkeley, Calif. 94707.

CAREER: Blue Wind Press, Berkeley, Calif., publisher, 1970—. Designer for Pegasus, Inc. (advertising agency), 1969-72; book designer for Something Else Press, 1972-73; graphic designer with George Mattingly Design, 1973—. Director of West Coast Print Center, 1979-80. Member of National Endowment for the Humanities literature panel, 1981. *Member:* Coordinating Council of Literary Magazines, American Institute for the Graphic Arts, Committee of Small Magazine Editors and Publishers (member of board of directors, 1971-73), Pacific Center for the Book Arts, Artists in Print. *Awards, honors:* Sibley Prize for fiction, 1967.

WRITINGS: Darling Bender (poems), Blue Wind Press, 1970; (with Darrell Gray) *Before It Was Light* (science fiction), Stasis Press, 1972; (editor) *Production Design,* Committee of Small Magazine Editors and Publishers, 1974; *Breathing Space* (poems), Blue Wind Press, 1975; *Sweet Dreams,* Seamark Press, 1981.

Work represented in anthologies, including *None of the Above,* edited by Michael Lally, Crossing Press, 1976; *The Actualist*

Anthology, Spirit Press, 1977. Contributor to more than forty literary magazines. Editor of *Search for Tomorrow,* 1969-75.

WORK IN PROGRESS: Deplaning, poems; *Hot Night,* a science fiction novel; *Design Design,* on graphics.

SIDELIGHTS: Mattingly wrote: "I am a former classical and jazz (fusion) musician, a professional photographer (on assignment most recently to cover the Rio Jazz Festival), and photo-collagist. The major influences on my life and work are Frank O'Hara, surrealism, science fiction, John McLaughlin, Raymond Chandler, Alfred North Whitehead, snorkeling, Miles Davis, Chassagne-Montrachet, John Ashbery, Harry Duncan, the *Times Atlas of the World,* Carey McWilliams, Anselm Hollo, Larry Coryell, Egberto Gismonti, Gevrey-Chambertin, Lewis Thomas, the films of Michael Ritchie, Wim Wenders, and Jean Cocteau."

*   *   *

MAXWELL, A. E.
See MAXWELL, Ann (Elizabeth)

*   *   *

MAXWELL, Ann (Elizabeth)   1944-
(A. E. Maxwell, a joint pseudonym)

PERSONAL: Born April 5, 1944, in Milwaukee, Wis.; daughter of David William and Shirley Jane (Lybrook) Charters; married Evan Lowell Maxwell (a journalist), September 4, 1966; children: Matthew, Heather. *Education:* Attended University of California, Davis, 1962-63; University of California, Riverside, B.A., 1966. *Agent:* James and Elizabeth Trupin, JET Literary Associates, Inc., 124 East 84th St., Suite 4A, New York, N.Y. 10028.

CAREER: Writer. *Member:* Science Fiction Writers of America, Authors Guild.

WRITINGS—Science fiction novels: *Change,* Popular Library, 1975; *The Singer Enigma,* Popular Library, 1976; *A Dead God Dancing,* Avon, 1979; *Name of a Shadow,* Avon, 1980; *The Jaws of Menx,* New American Library, 1981.

With husband, Evan Maxwell; under joint pseudonym A. E. Maxwell: (With Ivar Ruud) *The Year-Long Day* (nonfiction), Lippincott, 1976; *Golden Empire* (historical novel), Fawcett, 1979; *Steal the Sun* (novel), Richard Marek, 1981.

WORK IN PROGRESS: A science fiction novel, *Fire Dancer.*

SIDELIGHTS: Ann Maxwell commented: "I write because it is better than the alternative."

*   *   *

MAYER, Albert   1897-1981

OBITUARY NOTICE—See index for *CA* sketch: Born December 29, 1897, in New York, N.Y.; died of a heart attack, October 14, 1981, in New York, N.Y. Architect, structural engineer, housing planner, and author best known for co-organizing (with Lewis Mumford and Henry Wright) the Housing Study Guild during the 1930's. Mayer designed housing projects in the United States and abroad, including the "new town" of Chandigarh, India. He proposed strict control of urban growth. Mayer was the author of books on architecture and urban planning, including *The Urgent Future: People, Housing, City, and Region,* and *Follow the River.* Obituaries and other sources: *Newsweek,* October 26, 1981.

MAYES, Herbert R(aymond)   1900-

PERSONAL: Born August 11, 1900, in New York, N.Y.; son of Herman and Matilda (Hutter); married Grace Taub, December 6, 1930; children: Victoria, Alexandra. *Home:* 910 Fifth Ave., New York, N.Y. 10021. *Office:* 1345 Avenue of the Americas, New York, N.Y. 10019.

CAREER: Inland Merchant (magazine), editor, 1920-24; Western Newspaper Union, editor of business paper division, 1924-26; Hearst Magazines (now Hearst Corp.), New York City, *American Druggist,* editor, 1926-34, *Pictorial Review,* editor, 1934-37, *Good Housekeeping,* managing editor, 1937-38, editor, 1938-58, *Cosmopolitan,* editor, 1948-51; McCall's Corp. (publishers), New York City, editor of *McCall's,* 1959-62, president of corporation, 1961-65; Oxbridge Communications, Inc., New York City, 1976—. Consultant for Norton Simon, Inc., 1966—. *Member:* Book Table, Illustrators Society, Dutch Treat. *Awards, honors:* Editor of year award from Magazine Editors Council, distinguished achievement award in field of periodicals from University of Southern California, and New York Art Directors Club medal, all 1960.

WRITINGS: Alger, A Biography Without a Hero, Macy-Masius, 1928; (editor) *Editor's Choice* (short stories), Random House, 1956; (editor) *An Editor's Treasury: A Continuing Anthology of Prose, Verse, and Literary Curiosa,* two volumes, Atheneum, 1968; (author of critique) Leo Burnett, editor, *Best Read Ads, 1969: General Interest Magazine Ads,* Daniel Starch & Staff, 1970; (author of critique) George Gribbon, editor, *Best Read Ads, 1969: Special Interest Magazine Ads,* Daniel Starch & Staff, 1970; *The Magazine Maze: A Prejudiced Perspective* (memoir), Doubleday, 1980.

SIDELIGHTS: During Mayes's long and distinguished career as a magazine editor he published stories and articles by numerous well-known writers and other personalities, including Lucille Ball, Willa Cather, Maurice Chevalier, Agatha Christie, Edna Ferber, F. Scott Fitzgerald, Ernest Hemingway, Hubert Humphrey, Jacqueline Kennedy, Sinclair Lewis, Art Linkletter, Clare Boothe Luce, Somerset Maugham, Ogden Nash, John O'Hara, Katherine Anne Porter, J. D. Salinger, William Saroyan, Evelyn Waugh, and Herman Wouk. "Those authors live again in a series of anecdotes" contained in Mayes's book *The Magazine Maze,* disclosed *Time* critic Donald Morrison. In describing his fifty years as an editor, Mayes also provides a historical account of the magazine industry during the twentieth century.

Mayes's first book, *Alger: A Biography Without a Hero,* was widely praised by critics during the 1920's, and it came to be regarded as the definitive account of the life of Horatio Alger, the famous author of 109 rags-to-riches novels. In 1974 Mayes confessed that the book was a hoax. He said that he wrote the book as a satire and admitted that it "literally swarms" with erroneous information. Surprised that historians took the book seriously, Mayes "kept his deception a secret in order to avoid embarrassing his publisher, George Macy, and one of the book's original reviewers, Harry Hansen," according to a report in *Time.*

Mayes also edited an eclectic collection of prose, poetry, lyrics, and jingles entitled *An Editor's Treasury.* Some of these "literary tidbits," wrote Edwin Fadiman, Jr., in *Saturday Review,* "may not be to one's taste, but all are worth sampling."

BIOGRAPHICAL/CRITICAL SOURCES: New Republic, April 18, 1928; *New York Times,* April 22, 1928; *Newsweek,* September 6, 1948; *Saturday Review*, May 5, 1928, October 8, 1960, December 7, 1968; *Atlantic Monthly*, January, 1969; *Time*, June 10, 1974, January 12, 1981; Herbert P.. Mayes, *The Magazine Maze: A Prejudiced Perspective*, Doubleday, 1980.*

*   *   *

MAYS, Willie (Howard, Jr.)   1931-

PERSONAL: Born May 6, 1931, in Westfield, Ala.; son of William Howard (a semiprofessional baseball player and steel plant employee) and Ann Mays; married second wife, Mae Louise Allen, November 27, 1971; children: (first marriage) Michael. *Education:* Educated in Fairfield, Ala. *Residence:* New York, N.Y.; and, Atherton, Calif. *Office:* 51 Mount Vernon Lane, Atherton, Calif. 94025.

CAREER: Professional baseball player. Played with Birmingham Black Barons, Birmingham, Ala., 1948-50; joined New York Giants farm system, 1950; assigned to Class B Interstate League farm team, Trenton, N.J., 1950-51; played with Minneapolis Millers, Triple A American Association, Minneapolis, Minn., 1951; played major league ball with New York Giants, New York City, 1951-57, San Francisco Giants, San Francisco, Calif., 1958-72, and New York Mets, New York City, 1972-73; coach and good-will ambassador for New York Mets, 1973-79. Lecturer for Federal Job Corps program; public relations worker for "Help Young America" campaign, Colgate Palmolive Co.; makes public appearances on behalf of several companies, including Ogden Corp., Bache Inc., and Bally Manufacturing Corp. *Military service:* U.S. Army, 1952-54; served in physical training department.

AWARDS, HONORS: Named National League Rookie of the Year by Baseball Writers' Association, 1951; won National League batting championship, named player of the year by *Sporting News,* received Hickok Belt as athlete of the year, and named Male Athlete of the Year by Associated Press, all 1954; named National League Most Valuable Player by Baseball Writers' Association, 1954 and 1965; named Baseball Player of the Decade (1960-69), by *Sporting News,* 1970; Commissioner's Award, 1970; Golden Plate Award from American Academy of Achievement, 1975; inducted into Black Hall of Fame, 1974, Baseball Hall of Fame, 1979, and San Francisco Bay Area Hall of Fame.

WRITINGS: (With Charles Einstein) *Born to Play Ball* (autobiography), Putnam, 1955; (with Jeff Harris) *Danger in Center Field,* Argonaut, 1963; (with Einstein) *Willie Mays: My Life In and Out of Baseball* (autobiography), Dutton, 1966, revised edition, 1972; (with Howard Liss) *My Secrets of Playing Baseball* (illustrated by David Sutton), Viking, 1967; (with Maxine Berger) *Play Ball,* Wanderer Books, 1980.

SIDELIGHTS: Mays began his major league career with one of the most remarkable teams in baseball history, the 1951 New York Giants. Trailing the Brooklyn Dodgers by thirteen-and-a-half games with six weeks left in the season, the Giants climbed to the top of the standings and won the National League crown in a dramatic playoff. Manager Leo Durocher credited Mays with providing the spark the Giants needed to make their surge, and Mays earned the Rookie of the Year award for his performance.

Mays's value to the Giants was demonstrated again in 1954 when he returned to baseball after serving two years in the Army. The team won its first pennant since the 1951 season, with Mays gaining a National League batting title and Most Valuable Player honors along the way. In the World Series

that year, which the Giants swept from the Cleveland Indians in four games, Mays made his famous over-the-head catch of a drive by Indian Vic Wertz. A *Sporting News* poll judged that play the most thrilling of any in all of sport that year.

Mays continued his career when the Giants moved to San Francisco in 1958. With the aid of his forty-nine home runs and .304 batting average, the Giants won the league pennant in 1962, only to lose the World Series to the New York Yankees. The 1965 season marked another peak for Mays, when he hit a career-high fifty-two home runs and was named the league's Most Valuable Player for the second time. After closing out his career with the New York Mets in 1972 and 1973, Mays boasted a .302 lifetime batting average with 660 home runs, second only to Hank Aaron and Babe Ruth. Mays played in every All-Star game from 1954 to 1973.

Known as "Say-Hey" Willie for his enthusiastic approach to the game, Mays played center field with flair. In a *Saturday Review* cover story, Peter Schrag described Mays's fielding technique: "Mays always moved differently from other players, started instinctively toward the place where the ball was hit—moving from his center field position almost, it seemed, before the batter swung—and he caught fly balls against his belt with the palm of his glove turned up, playing with a casual defiance of error, a disdain for security, and with an emphasis on style that repudiated mere professional competence."

"I think I've given every bit of energy to baseball," Mays said after his retirement, but in 1979 he was ordered to cut all ties to the game when Commissioner Bowie Kuhn objected to Mays's public relations work for an Atlantic City gambling casino. That same year Mays was elected to baseball's Hall of Fame, receiving more votes than any other player in history.

BIOGRAPHICAL/CRITICAL SOURCES: Andrew S. N. Young, *Great Negro Baseball Stars and How They Made the Major Leagues,* Barnes, 1953; *Time,* July 26, 1954, November 12, 1979; Ken Smith, *The Willie Mays Story,* Greenberg, 1954; *New York Times Magazine,* July 11, 1954; Bruce Jacobs, editor, *Baseball Stars of 1955,* Lion Books, 1955; Willie Mays and Charles Einstein, *Born to Play Ball,* Putnam, 1955; *Famous American Athletes of Today,* Page, 1956; Thomas Meany, *Mostly Baseball,* Barnes, 1958; Edward E. Fitzgerald, editor, *Heroes of Sport,* Bartholomew House, 1960.

Arnold Hano, *Willie Mays, the Say-Hey Kid,* Bartholomew House, 1961; Thomas Meany and Tommy Holmes, *Baseball's Best,* Watts, 1964; Joseph Gies and R. H. Shoemaker, *Stars of the Series,* Crowell, 1964; Zander Hollander, editor, *Great American Athletes of the Twentieth Century,* Random House, 1966; Mays and Einstein, *Willie Mays: My Life In and Out of Baseball,* Dutton, 1966; Steve Gelman, *Young Baseball Champions,* Norton, 1966; *Saturday Review,* May 8, 1971; *Associated Press Sports Immortals,* Prentice-Hall, 1974; *Philadelphia Bulletin,* October 6, 1974; *Biography News,* Gale, November, 1974; Ben Richardson and W. A. Fahey, *Great Black Americans,* Crowell, 1976; Einstein, *Willie's Time,* Lippincott, 1979; *Newsweek,* February 5, 1979.

*   *   *

MAZUR, Allan Carl   1939-

PERSONAL: Born March 20, 1939, in Chicago, Ill.; son of Joseph (a merchant) and Esther (Markowitz) Mazur; married Polly Albrecht (a teacher), January 21, 1968; children: Julie, Rachel. *Education:* Illinois Institute of Technology, B.S., 1961; University of California, Los Angeles, M.S., 1964; Johns Hopkins University, Ph.D., 1969. *Religion:* Jewish. *Home:* 246

Scottholm Ter., Syracuse, N.Y. 13224. *Office:* Department of Sociology, Syracuse University, Syracuse, N.Y. 13210.

CAREER: North American Aviation, Downey, Calif., engineer, 1961-64; Massachusetts Institute of Technology, Cambridge, instructor in political science, 1966-67; Lockheed Corp., Sunnyvale, Calif., engineer, 1967-68; Stanford University, Stanford, Calif., assistant professor of sociology, 1968-71; Syracuse University, Syracuse, N.Y., associate professor, 1971-75, professor of sociology, 1975—.

WRITINGS: (With Leon Robertson) *Biology and Social Behavior,* Free Press, 1972; *The Dynamics of Technical Controversy,* Communications Press, 1981. Contributor to academic journals.

WORK IN PROGRESS: Research on sociology of science and technology and on biosociology.

*   *   *

McALLISTER, Amanda
See MEAKER, Eloise

*   *   *

McANALLY, Mary E. 1939-

PERSONAL: Born January 21, 1939, in Illinois; daughter of Virgil Pafford (in oil business) and Mary Frances (Handy) McAnally; married Etheridge Knight (a poet), June 11, 1973; children: Mary Tandiwe, Etheridge Bambata. *Education:* University of Tulsa, B.A. (cum laude), 1962; Princeton Theological Seminary, B.D., 1965; Columbia University, M.A. and doctoral study. *Politics:* "Anarchist—feminist." *Religion:* "Witchcraft." *Home:* 76 North Yorktown, Tulsa, Okla. 74110.

CAREER: Spelman College, Atlanta, Ga., instructor, 1962; Trenton State Hospital for the Criminally Insane, Trenton, N.J., assistant chaplain, 1963; Rutgers University, New Brunswick, N.J., assistant to the chaplain, 1963-64; Christian education director at church in Bartlesville, Okla., 1964; assistant pastor at church in New York City, 1964-65; United Presbyterian Church in the U.S.A., New York City, administrative assistant in office of student world relations, 1965-69; Staten Island Community College, Staten Island, N.Y., instructor in college discovery program, 1969; *American Report,* New York City, associate editor, 1969-71; instructor in Upward Bound Program, Jefferson City, Mo., 1972-73; University of Missouri, Jefferson City, instructor in extension program at federal prison, 1972-73; Indianapolis Settlements, Inc., Indianapolis, Ind., senior citizens supervisor, 1973-74; Legal Services Organization, Indianapolis, supervisor of Volunteers in Service to America (VISTA), 1974-75; Associated Migrant Opportunity Services, Indianapolis, director of education, 1975; Young Women's Christian Association (YWCA), Bloomington, Minn., director, 1975-77; Oklahoma Arts and Humanities Council, Oklahoma City, writer-in-residence in prison arts program, 1977-79; Women's Center, Tulsa, Okla., director, 1977-79; Tulsa Arts and Humanities Council, Tulsa, poet-in-residence, 1978-79; National Indian Child Abuse and Neglect Resource Center, Tulsa, assistant director, 1979-80; Head Start Program, Claremore, Okla., state coordinator, 1980-81; Shelter for Battered Women, Tulsa, director, 1981—. *Member:* Individual Artists of Oklahoma. *Awards, honors:* Beaudoin Gem Stone Award for poetry; Carl Sandburg Award for poetry.

WRITINGS: Poems of Direct Address, Harold House, 1979; *We Will Make a River* (poems), West End Press, 1979; (editor) *Warning: Hitchhikers May Be Escaping Convicts* (poems by

prisoners), Moonlight, 1980; *"The Absence of the Father"* and *"The Dance of the Zygotes"* (poems), Shadow Press, 1981; *Animal Heart Poems,* Full Count Press, 1981; (editor) *Family Violence: Poems on the Pathology,* Moonlight, 1982. Contributor of poems, articles, and reviews to magazines, including *New Letters, Women: A Journal of Liberation, Womanspirit, Dark Horse, Chrysalis,* and *South and West.* Poetry editor of *Nimrod* and *Sister Advocate;* contributing editor of *Sez.*

WORK IN PROGRESS: Editing a tribute to Meridel LeSueur.

*   *   *

McCAIN, Murray (David, Jr.) 1926-1981

OBITUARY NOTICE—See index for *CA* sketch: Born December 28, 1926, in Newport, N.C.; died of cancer, November 19, 1981, in New York, N.Y. Editor and author best known for writing books for children, including *Books!* and *Writing.* In his later years, McCain co-authored books, including *If I Made It, So Can You,* with Virginia Graham. Obituaries and other sources: *Publishers Weekly,* January 1, 1982.

*   *   *

McCARTER, P(ete) Kyle (Jr.) 1945-

PERSONAL: Born July 9, 1945, in Oxford, Miss.; son of Pete Kyle (an educator) and Mary Ann McCarter; married Sherry Ann Martin (a social worker), June 5, 1971; children: Robert K., David K. *Education:* University of Oklahoma, B.A., 1967; McCormick Theological Seminary, M.Div., 1970; Harvard University, Ph.D., 1974. *Politics:* Democrat. *Religion:* Presbyterian. *Home:* 108 Carrsbrook Court, Charlottesville, Va. 22901. *Office:* Department of Religious Studies, University of Virginia, Charlottesville, Va. 22903.

CAREER: University of Virginia, Charlottesville, assistant professor, 1974-79, associate professor of religious studies, 1979—. Visiting lecturer at Harvard University, 1978-79; visiting associate professor at Dartmouth College, 1979.

WRITINGS: The Antiquity of the Greek Alphabet, Scholars Press (Missoula, Mont.), 1975; *Anchor Bible,* Volume VIII: *I Samuel,* Doubleday, 1980.

WORK IN PROGRESS: Anchor Bible, Volume IX: *II Samuel,* for Doubleday; a monograph on the advent of monotheism in Israel.

SIDELIGHTS: McCarter commented: "I plan to write fiction for at least a few years."

*   *   *

McCARTHY, (Daniel) Todd 1950-

PERSONAL: Born February 16, 1950, in Evanston, Ill.; son of Daniel Francis and Barbara Jean (Koenig) McCarthy. *Education:* Stanford University, B.A., 1972. *Agent:* Michael Hamilburg, Mitchell J. Hamilburg Agency, 292 South La Cienega Blvd., Suite 212, Beverly Hills, Calif. 90211. *Office: Daily Variety,* 1400 North Cahuenga Blvd., Los Angeles, Calif. 90028.

CAREER: Paramount Pictures, Los Angeles, Calif., assistant to Elaine May, 1974-75; New World Pictures, Los Angeles, director of advertising and publicity, 1975-77; *Le Film francais,* manager of English-language editions in Paris, France, 1977, and Cannes, France, 1978; *Daily Variety,* Los Angeles, reporter and critic, 1979—. Film critic for *Hollywood Reporter*, 1975-76.

WRITINGS: (Editor with Charles Flynn) *Kings of the Bs: Working Within the Hollywood System*, Dutton, 1975. Contributor to magazines and newspapers, including *American Film* and *Take One*. Hollywood editor of *Film Comment*, 1978-79.

WORK IN PROGRESS: A biography of film director Howard Hawks, for Holt.

* * *

McCLATCHY, J(oseph) D(onald, Jr.) 1945-

PERSONAL: Born August 12, 1945, in Bryn Mawr, Pa.; son of J. Donald (in business) and Mary Jane (Hayden) McClatchy. *Education:* Georgetown University, A.B. (summa cum laude), 1967; Yale University, Ph.D., 1974. *Home address:* Wallace Hill Rd., Wells River, Vt. 05081.

CAREER: LaSalle College, Philadelphia, Pa., instructor in English, 1968-71; Yale University, New Haven, Conn., assistant professor of English, 1974-81; Princeton University, Princeton, N.J., lecturer in creative writing, 1981—. *Member:* International P.E.N., Modern Language Association of America, Phi Beta Kappa, Alpha Sigma Nu. *Awards, honors:* Woodrow Wilson fellowship, 1967-68; O. Henry Award from Doubleday & Co., 1972, for short story "Allonym"; prize from Academy of American Poets, 1972, for "Sea Island Poems"; Chase Going Woodhouse Poetry Prize, 1976, for "Games for Children"; grant from Ingram Merrill Foundation, 1979.

WRITINGS: Anne Sexton: The Artist and Her Critics, Indiana University Press, 1978; *Scenes From Another Life* (poems), Braziller, 1981.

Work represented in anthologies, including *The Poetry Anthology, 1912-1977,* Houghton, 1978; *Anthology of Magazine Verse and Yearbook of American Poetry,* Monitor, 1980. Contributor of articles, poems, translations, and reviews to magazines, including *Nation, New Republic, Film Heritage, Christopher Street, Canto,* and *Shenandoah.* Associate editor of *Four Quarters,* 1968-72; contributing editor of *American Poetry Review;* poetry editor of *Yale Review,* 1980—.

WORK IN PROGRESS: Editing *Contemporary American Poetry: An Anthology; Lost Paradises: The Poetry of James Merrill;* translating *Prince of Aquitaine: Poems of Gerard de Nerval.*

SIDELIGHTS: "I had written all along," McClatchy told *CA.* "What rhyme-dazed child, what 'sensitive' adolescent, what literary college student does not? The real question is, when did I truly begin to read? That was not until my mid-twenties, in the late sixties: I'd been forced out of graduate school by the threat of the military draft, ducked into college teaching, and in off-hours began reading contemporary poetry for the first time—after years of studying only the classics (that is, classical literature and the English canon). I was hooked. What my contemporaries wrote seemed ragged, dumb; no, 'my' contemporaries were Shakespeare, Milton, Pope, Browning—those who knew both the heart's line and the line's resources. Still, my contemporaries—their ages varied, within the limits of the family romance—were *doing* it, given a modern accent to the traditional voices. They were a spur, if not a model. I looked—then, and later—for models elsewhere: Donne, Milton, and Keats; Verlaine, Mallarme, and Valery; Emerson, Whitman, and Stevens; and James Merrill, Robert Lowell, John Ashbery, and John Hollander.

"I should add that I have learned as much about writing a poem—that is to say, about the sort of poem I want to write—from listening closely to certain pieces of music as from reading other poems. This song by Faure (I have it playing now!), that etude by Schumann, those vacant heaves of Mahler, the sweet-and-sour fantasias of Purcell, the slippery stones of a Bach *courante,* the dramatic build of a Verdi aria—these have taught me what I know about rhythm, enjambments, and emotional transitions, the signifying strengths of the line and of pure sound, and how 'meaning' forms and reforms itself in subsequent readings of the poem. If a poem does not *sound,* if it cannot 'carry' itself on modulating, harmonic strophes, then it risks the dry pleasures of merely rational discourse, or the plain dull whimsies of the unconscious.

"I am perceptibly—perhaps self-consciously—at odds with most poetry that is favored by journalistic fashion in America today. It seems to me hearty, vapid, loose: make-it-news broadcasts from the workshop. I have wanted to write poems with shape and a rich sound, with ideas and a good deal of 'speech,' and with epigrammatic surfaces and resounding depths. It takes me a long time to write a poem that pleases me. I begin, usually, with a subject, an urgent abstraction; phrases accrete; rhythms pronounce themselves; a title intrudes; a form suggests itself; the subject is clarified or changed or, often, both; the poem grows enigmatic, greedy for my changes and indifferent to them; there are dozens of drafts: notebook, yellow pad, typed sheets, fair copies, proofs, afterthoughts.

"What interests me in a poem? Its natural energies of voice and subject matter; its capacities to *depart* from itself into formal surprises or layered meanings or into a new topography of images. Its intellectual precision, its sympathies, its details—always its details, *things* observed in their apparent spikiness and obscured lusters. (Could anyone do this better than Elizabeth Bishop?) I often admire what is least valued by the criticasters nowadays. That is, I enjoy the poem that cares to have a mind of its own, instead of joining in a chorus of 'The Land of the Free Association and the Home of the Bravado'; or is formally ingenious; or braises the common tongue in spices both exotic and homegrown. My own poems have occasionally been thought to be 'old-fashioned' by those who forget (if they knew) how Whitman and Hoelderlin and Apollinaire long ago anticipated—indeed, perfected—styles suddenly discovered to be *a la page.* Sadly, too many poets, even some good ones (the Beats, Sylvia Plath, James Wright, Merwin, and Ashbery) have been, poor souls, stuffed and set up as false idols. Those only are saved who are stronger than their gods.

"When I am not writing poems, I write about poetry—reviews, essays, books. I find this enjoyable, useful, and profitable. Everything I have mentioned—my life, my likes—has a common denominator, I suppose: a sense of tradition that is the shadow of one's own silhouette."

AVOCATIONAL INTERESTS: Gardening, travel (especially in Mexico), listening to music, cooking.

BIOGRAPHICAL/CRITICAL SOURCES: New York Times Book Review, September 13, 1981.

* * *

McCLELLAND, Diane Margaret 1931-
(Diane Pearson)

PERSONAL: Born November 5, 1931, in Croyden, England; daughter of William Holker and Miriam Harriet Youde; married Richard Leeper McClelland (an actor and physician), 1975.

Education: Attended secondary school in Croyden, England. *Agent:* Curtis Brown Ltd., 1 Craven Hill, London W2 3EP, England.

CAREER: Jonathan Cape Ltd., London, England, book production assistant, 1948-52; associated with local government, 1952-64; Corgi Books Ltd., London, editor, 1964—.

WRITINGS—Under pseudonym Diane Pearson: *Bride of Tancred* (gothic novel), R. Hale, 1967, Bantam, 1968; *The Marigold Field* (period novel), Lippincott, 1969; *Sarah Whitman* (period novel), Lippincott, 1971; *Csardas* (novel), Lippincott, 1975.

SIDELIGHTS: Diane McClelland told *CA:* "I have never actively thought about why I write or what I am trying to say. I firmly believe that too much dissection of motive destroys the instinct to write. I suppose, however, if I look at what I have written, my intention has unwittingly been to represent the 'little' people of the world, those who are unlauded and unknown but who frequently have just as much courage and sensitivity as the world's giants."

*   *   *

McCORMACK, Gavan Patrick   1937-

PERSONAL: Born October 21, 1937, in Australia; married Fusako Yoshinaga (a potter), 1971; children: Daniel, Noah. *Education:* University of Melbourne, received B.A. and LL.B., M.A., 1962; University of London, received B.A. (with honors) and M.A., Ph.D., 1974; attended University of Tokyo, 1969-70. *Office:* Department of History, La Trobe University, Bundoora, Victoria 3083, Australia.

CAREER: University of Leeds, Leeds, England, lecturer in history, 1971-77; University of Melbourne, Parkville, Australia, lecturer in history, 1977—.

WRITINGS: (With Jon Halliday) *Japanese Imperialism Today: "Co-Prosperity in Greater East Asia,"* Monthly Review Press, 1973; *Chang Tso-lin in Northeast China, 1911-28: China, Japan, and the Manchurian Idea,* Stanford University Press, 1977; (editor) *Crisis in Korea,* Spokesman Books, 1977; (editor with Mark Selden) *Korea, North and South: The Deepening Crisis,* Monthly Review Press, 1978.

*   *   *

McCORMICK, Richard Arthur   1922-

PERSONAL: Born October 3, 1922, in Toledo, Ohio; son of Edward J. (a physician) and Josephine B. McCormick. *Education:* Loyola University, Chicago, Ill., A.B., 1945, M.A., 1950; Gregorian University, S.T.D., 1957. *Home:* 1419 35th St. N.W., Washington, D.C. 20007. *Office:* Kennedy Institute of Ethics, Georgetown University, Washington, D.C. 20057.

CAREER: Entered Society of Jesus (Jesuits, S.J.), 1940, ordained Roman Catholic priest, 1953; Jesuit School of Theology, Chicago, Ill., professor of moral theology, 1957-73; Georgetown University, Washington, D.C., Rose F. Kennedy Professor of Christian Ethics, 1973—. Member of board of directors of Churches' Center for Theology and Public Policy, 1976—; member of ethical advisory board of U.S. Department of Health, Education and Welfare, 1977—. *Member:* American Society of Christian Ethics, American Catholic Theological Society of America (president, 1970). *Awards, honors:* D.Lett. from University of Scranton, 1975; D.H. from Wheeling College, 1976.

WRITINGS: Ambiguity in Moral Choice, Marquette University Press, 1973; (editor with Paul Ramsey) *Doing Evil to Achieve Good: Moral Choice in Conflict Situations,* Loyola University Press, 1978; (editor with Charles E. Curran, and contributor) *Readings in Moral Theology,* Volume I: *Moral Norms and Catholic Tradition,* Paulist Press, 1979, Volume II: *The Distinctiveness of Christian Ethics,* 1980, Volume III: *Readings in Moral Theology,* 1981, Volume IV, 1981; *Persons, Patients, and Problems,* Louisiana State University Press, 1980; *Notes on Moral Theology: 1965 Through 1980,* University Press of America, 1980; *How Brave a New World?: Dilemmas in Bioethics,* Doubleday, 1981.

Contributor: Martin E. Marty and Dean G. Peerman, editors, *New Theology,* number ten, Macmillan, 1973; Robert M. Veatch, Willard Gaylin, and Councilman Morgan, editors, *The Teaching of Medical Ethics,* Institute of Society, Ethics, and the Life Sciences, 1973; James T. Johnson and David H. Smith, editors, *Love and Society: Essays in the Ethics of Paul Ramsey,* Scholars Press (Missoula, Mont.), 1974; George J. Dyer, editor, *An American Catholic Catechism,* Seabury, 1975; Eugene C. Kennedy, editor, *Human Rights and Psychological Research: A Debate on Psychology and Ethics,* Crowell, 1975; Thomas A. Shannon, editor, *Bioethics,* Paulist Press, 1976; Gerald H. Anderson and Thomas F. Stransky, editors, *Mission Trends,* Volume IV: *Liberation Theologies in North America and Europe,* Paulist Press, 1979; John C. Haughey, editor, *Personal Values in Public Policy,* Paulist Press, 1979.

Contributor to theology and medical journals. Associate editor of *America,* 1964-76.

*   *   *

McDERMOTT, Walsh   1909-1981

OBITUARY NOTICE: Born October 24, 1909, in New Haven, Conn.; died of a heart attack, October 17, 1981, in Pawling, N.Y. Physician, educator, and author, best known for his development of drugs to combat infectious diseases. In 1955 he was awarded the Albert Lasker Award for his work in creating the drug isoniazid, used in the treatment of tuberculosis. From 1934 until his death, McDermott was a professor of public health and medicine at the Cornell University Medical College. He also served on the New York City Board of Health for seven years and was the first chairman of the New York Health Research Council. Active in American Indian affairs, McDermott headed an anti-tuberculosis project on an Arizona Navaho reservation and served as chairman of a task force on American Indians under Lyndon Johnson. His published works include *The Cecil-Loeb Textbook of Medicine,* which he edited with P. B. Beeson. Obituaries and other sources: *Who's Who in the World,* 2nd edition, Marquis, 1973; *American Men and Women of Science: The Physical and Biological Sciences,* 14th edition, Bowker, 1979; *New York Times,* October 19, 1981.

*   *   *

McDONALD, Angus W(illiam), Jr.   1941-

PERSONAL: Born December 7, 1941, in Lexington, Ky.; son of Angus W. (a lawyer) and Elizabeth (a social worker; maiden name, Quincy) McDonald; married Susan Stronge (an artist), 1965; children: Louise G., Angus W. III, Elizabeth D. *Education:* Amherst College, B.A. (cum laude), 1965; University of California, Berkeley, M.A., 1969, Ph.D., 1975. *Religion:* Protestant. *Home:* 1056 13th Ave. S.E., Minneapolis, Minn. 55414. *Office:* Control Data Corp., 7600 France Ave., Minneapolis, Minn. 55435.

CAREER: Keio University, Tokyo, Japan, visiting assistant professor of law and research associate, 1971-74; Multimedia Multinational, Minneapolis, Minn., president, 1974-79; Control Data Corp., Minneapolis, senior consultant of international business development, 1979—. Visiting assistant professor at Sophia University, 1973-74, University of Minnesota, 1974-77, University of Wisconsin, 1977, and Stanford University, 1978-79. National coordinator of Committee of Concerned Asian Scholars, 1975-76.

WRITINGS: (Contributor) Maurice Meisner and W. Rhoads Murphey, editors, *The Mozartian Historian: Joseph R. Levenson on China and the World,* University of California Press, 1976; (editor and translator from Chinese) Fang Xiu, *Notes on the History of Malayan Chinese New Literature, 1920-1942,* Center for East Asian Cultural Studies (Tokyo), 1977; *The Urban Origins of Rural Revolution: Elites and the Masses in Hunan Province, China, 1911-1927,* University of California Press, 1978. Contributor to Chinese studies journals. English-language editor (and translator) of *Ampo: Japan-East Asia Quarterly Review,* 1971-74.

WORK IN PROGRESS: The Backwardness of China: Wang Fuzhi, and the Decline of Free Speculation, publication expected "before the author's death, maybe."

SIDELIGHTS: McDonald told *CA:* "I was a PFC in the literary army: a one-book author. I have retired from the army with the pension I deserve, going on into the ranks of those who hope to have an effect on the world directly rather than through the uncertain medium of 'typewriter to paper to publisher to bookstall to shelf to reader to mind to disposition to action.' Interested rather than disinterested, this non-com (with no military experience) flaked out of the academic battles and the continual struggle with one job after another, flaked out to higher paying industry and the chance to be involved with computer-assisted education and other natural language-oriented applications of computers.

"It was the opposite with Wang Fuzhi. At twenty-eight he was a high official in the court of the Ming pretender, fighting against the Manchu barbarians who had captured Beijing and established the Qing dynasty (1644-1911). Outflanked in remnant court politics, Wang went into retirement. He became the hermit of the Hunan mountain, living in bamboo groves and writing prolifically on Chinese philosophy, history, philology, poetry (a good poet, Wang), statecraft, nationhood, and art. He was forgotten by all but a tiny group of Hunanese scholars. Generation after generation kept his name and work alive, assisted by the imperial rule which allowed teachers (but not political officials) to reside and work in their native province. His life and worldly career in ruins, Wang Fuzhi lived in the (woodblock printed) 'publisher to bookstall to shelf to reader to mind to disposition to action cycle' of two hundred years. His most famous student, perhaps, was Mao Zedong.

"Wang wrote in a very dense style of classical Chinese. Unpunctuated. No periods or semicolons interrupted the flow of words or provided landmarks for the curious. You could break his ideas where you would. Seven late Qing (late nineteenth century) scholars punctuated some of his most famous passages—in seven different ways. Seven different ideas. Five star generals in the literary army, like those multi-faceted, glittering balls that used to revolve about a dance-room floor in middle-class America, throw random gleams into all corners of the darkened world. Wang the hermit; Mao the unifier. Prurient scholars poke at the connections, marvel at the melody that is sung (beheld and made sensible by each hearer separately, differently), and try to make their particular sense of

the whole (their punctuation) understandable to others through the uncertain medium of 'typewriter to paper,' etc. It is great fun, although the loneliness of the empty room and the ever-demanding typewriter may offset the sense of accomplishment at making heretofore never-made connections. Both Milton and Wever wrote elegantly about the contradictory tendencies: reflection and action.

"Another book? Probably not. Publisher's schedules are solar, not soul-bound."

AVOCATIONAL INTERESTS: National and international politics, tennis, squash, music, gardening.

* * *

McDONALD, Jerry N(ealon) 1944-

PERSONAL: Born August 15, 1944, in Newark, Ohio; son of Oscar Matthew (an electrician) and Elma Grayce (Powell) McDonald; married Beverly Childers Kerger, June 7, 1965 (marriage ended, January 30, 1978); children: Christian Herendon, Jay Ian. *Education:* Muskingum College, B.A., 1970; University of Texas, M.A., 1972; University of California, Los Angeles, Ph.D., 1978. *Home:* 603 Clement St., No. 1, Radford, Va. 24141. *Office:* Department of Geography, Radford University, Radford, Va. 24142.

CAREER: University of Texas, El Paso, visiting assistant professor of geography, 1978-79; Radford University, Radford, Va., assistant professor of geography, 1979—. Environmental consultant, 1978-79; contract paleontologist, 1979. *Military service:* U.S. Marine Corps, 1965-67. *Member:* Association of American Geographers (chairman of biogeography specialty group), American Association for the Advancement of Science, American Society of Mammalogists, Society of Vertebrate Paleontology, Society of Systematic Zoology.

WRITINGS: North American Bison: Their Classification and Evolution, University of California Press, 1981; (contributor) P. S. Martin and R. G. Klein, editors, *Pleistocene Extinctions,* University of Arizona Press, 1982. Contributor to scientific journals.

WORK IN PROGRESS: A study of biological systematics of North American ovibovines (musk and shrub oxen).

SIDELIGHTS: McDonald told *CA:* "I am currently organizing a major excavation of a paleontological site at Saltville, Virginia. This area has yielded important fossil mammals since at least 1782. This will be the first large-scale systematic excavation at the site.

"I find the most challenging part of my long-term work to be the reconstruction of past ecological relations among now-extinct large mammals, and inferring the evolutionary responses that led to their differential evolution (adaptation) and extinction. Systeses of this type are becoming possible because of the generation of great volumes of geological, paleontological, paleobotanical, ecological, and zoological information in various fields. I also believe that paleoecological work such as I am doing has application to modern conservation problems, another area in which I am quite interested.

"The problems I enjoy doing research on are, for the most part, broad, detailed, and complex. The simple ones do not provide the challenge or satisfaction, but neither do they create the delays or require long periods of research before some product is in hand.

"I try to balance my heavy teaching load at Radford and my research by developing a farm in Ohio, but being three hundred miles from it and with limited available time, work on this task is going much slower than I would like.''

BIOGRAPHICAL/CRITICAL SOURCES: Radford University, winter, 1981.

* * *

McDONALD, Jill (Masefield) 1927-1982

OBITUARY NOTICE—See index for *CA* sketch: Born October 30, 1927, in Wellington, New Zealand; died January 2, 1982, in London, England. Architect, illustrator, and author of children's books. McDonald was trained as an architect but she became interested in illustration during the early 1960's and was later named art director of the *New Zealand School Journal*. She moved to England in 1965 and was enlisted by Penguin Books to help revamp their children's book division, Puffin Books. McDonald created the ''Puffin Club,'' a feature in the children's magazine *Puffin Post* in which a character named Odway the Dog posed philosophical questions for the young readers to answer. At the time of her death McDonald was preparing a book featuring the dialogue between Odway and his readers. She was the author of a dozen children's books, including *Maggy Scraggle, The Pirate's Tale,* and *The Happy Helper Engine.* Obituaries and other sources: *London Times,* January 8, 1982.

* * *

McGEE, (Doctor) Frank 1921-1974

PERSONAL: Born September 12, 1921, in Monroe, La.; died of pneumonia, April 17, 1974, in Manhattan, N.Y.; son of Robert Albert (a farmer and sawmill owner) and Calla (Brown) McGee; married Nialta Sue Beaird, January 25, 1941 (some sources say February 25, 1941); children: Sharon Dian (Mrs. Peter Churchill Labovitz), Michael. *Education:* Attended University of California, Berkeley, 1945-46, and University of Oklahoma, Norman, 1947-48. *Politics:* Democrat. *Home:* 912 Brewster Rd., Scarsdale, N.Y. 10583.

CAREER: KGFF-Radio, Shawnee, Okla., announcer, advertising salesman, disc jockey, commercial copy writer, newsman, and music librarian, 1947-50; WKY-TV, Oklahoma City, Okla., news reporter, 1950-55; WSAF-TV, Montgomery, Ala., news director, 1955-57; National Broadcasting Co., Inc. (NBC-TV), news commentator in Washington, D.C., 1957, and in New York, N.Y., 1958-74, anchorman for ''Monitor,'' 1958-74, and for WNBC-TV's ''Sixth Hour News,'' 1960-64, and ''Eleventh Hour News,'' 1965-74, host for ''World Wide '60,'' 1960, and ''Here and Now,'' 1961-62, co-anchorman with David Brinkley and John Chancellor for the ''NBC Evening News,'' 1970-74, and co-host for ''Today,'' 1971-74. *Military service:* U.S. Army, 1940-45.

AWARDS, HONORS: Headliners Award, 1958, for television and radio news; Robert E. Sherwood Award, 1959; *TV Guide* award, 1960; George Foster Peabody Awards from the University of Georgia, 1964, for television documentary ''The American Revolution of '63,'' and 1966, for coverage of Pope Paul VI's visit to New York; Brotherhood Award from National Conference of Christians and Jews, 1967, for television documentary ''Same Mud, Same Blood''; Emmy Award from National Academy of Television Arts and Sciences, 1968, for satellite coverage of Konrad Adenauer's funeral.

WRITINGS: Author of *They Don't Make Depressions Like That Any More,* a collection of short stories. Also author of his own scripts for the ''Eleventh Hour News'' and the ''Frank McGee Report,'' both on NBC-TV.

SIDELIGHTS: McGee spent most of his broadcasting career at NBC-TV where he became one of television's highest paid and most respected newsmen. McGee joined the network in 1957 and was soon covering major news events, including the federally enforced integration of Central High School in Little Rock, Arkansas, in 1957, President Dwight D. Eisenhower's trip to Europe in 1959, and the assassination of President John F. Kennedy in 1963. He also covered the 1960 presidential election and participated in two of the Kennedy-Nixon debates, serving once as moderator and once as a panelist.

McGee reported on most of the important space stories of the 1960's, becoming a lay expert on the U.S. space program. According to McGee, he became ''established as NBC's rocket man'' following his coverage of the first attempt by the United States to place a satellite in orbit in 1958. He later covered the world's first manned orbital flight, by John Glenn, in 1962 and Edward H. White's walk in space during the Gemini mission in 1965.

McGee, who was known for his perceptive news commentaries, wrote many of his own scripts. During an interview with *New York Times* reporter John P. Shanley, McGee explained that he preferred to write his own scripts because ''you can ad lib your way far more smoothly, when it's necessary, than if you're bound to someone else's material and [are] not familiar with it.''

McGee's role as commentator for a series of ''instant specials'' best demonstrated his ''quick mastery of the medium,'' wrote Farnsworth Fowle in the *New York Times.* The special broadcasts interrupted regularly scheduled programs in order to provide up-to-the-minute information about late-breaking news events. Featured on the program were reports on the Khrushchev-Eisenhower summit conference in Paris in 1960, the trial of Adolph Eichmann in 1961, and the Supreme Court ruling on prayer in public schools in 1963. In commenting upon McGee's instant coverage of President Kennedy's trip to Europe in 1963, John Horn of the *New York Herald Tribune* said: ''The challenge was met by an excellent narrative, written and read by Frank McGee. . . . It had the depth and perceptive comment generally missing in TV's earlier on-the-fly coverage.''

McGee was also associated with several lengthy documentary specials, including ''The American Revolution of '63'' and ''Same Mud, Same Blood.'' ''American Revolution,'' a three-hour program focusing on the civil rights movement, received a Peabody Award in 1964. ''Same Mud,'' an account of racial conflict between American soldiers during the war in Vietnam, was honored with a Brotherhood award from the National Conference of Christians and Jews.

McGee made his last television appearance on the ''Today'' show on April 11, 1974, only a few days before his death.

BIOGRAPHICAL/CRITICAL SOURCES: New York Times, February 5, 1961; *Variety,* September 20, 1961, April 4, 1962; *New York Herald Tribune,* July 8, 1963.

OBITUARIES: Current Biography, Wilson, 1974; *New York Times,* April 18, 1974.*

* * *

McGOUGH, Roger 1937-

PERSONAL: Born November 9, 1937, in Liverpool, England; son of Roger Francis (a docker) and Mary (McGarry) McGough; married Thelma Monaghan (divorced); children: Finn, Tom Tara. *Education:* University of Hull, B.A., 1957,

Certificate in Education, 1960. *Religion:* Roman Catholic. *Home:* 307 Fulham Rd., London S.W.10, England. *Agent:* Hope Leresche & Steele, 11 Jubilee Pl., London SW3 3TE, England.

CAREER: Teacher in Liverpool, England, 1960-62; assistant lecturer at secondary school in Liverpool, 1962-64; Liverpool College of Art, Liverpool, lecturer in liberal studies, 1969-70; Loughborough University of Technology, Loughborough, Leicestershire, England, fellow in poetry, 1973-75. *Member:* Songwriters Guild, Equity, Chelsea Arts Club, Scaffold.

WRITINGS: (With Adrian Henry and Brian Patten) *The Mersey Sound: Penguin Modern Poets Ten,* Penguin, 1967; *"Frinck," "A Life in the Day Of,"* and *"Summer With Monika": Poems* (novel and poems), Ballantine, 1967; *Watchwords* (poems), J. Cape, 1969, new edition, 1972, Merrimack Book Service, 1979; *After the Merrymaking* (poems), J. Cape, 1971, Merrimack Book Service, 1979; *Out of Sequence* (poems), Turret Books, 1973; *Gig* (poems), J. Cape, 1973, Merrimack Book Service, 1979; *Sporting Relations* (poems), Eyre Methuen, 1974; *In the Glassroom* (poems), J. Cape, 1976, Merrimack Book Service, 1979; *Mr. Noselighter* (juvenile), Deutsch, 1976; *Summer With Monika* (poems), Deutsch, 1978, also published with *"Frinck," "A Life in the Day Of"* (see above); *Holiday on Death Row,* J. Cape, 1979; *Unlucky for Some,* Turret Books, 1981; *The Oxford Book of Twentieth Century Verse,* Oxford University Press, 1981; *You Tell Me,* Puffin, 1981; (editor) *Strictly Private,* Kestrel, 1981.

Plays: "Birds, Marriages, and Deaths," first produced in London, England, in 1964; "The Chauffeur-Driven Rolls," first produced in Liverpool, England, in 1966; "The Commission," first produced in Liverpool in 1967; *The Puny Little Life Show* (first produced in London in 1969), Penguin, 1973; "Stuff," first produced in London in 1970; "Word Play," first produced in Edinburgh, Scotland, in 1978; "Golden Nights and Golden Days," first produced in Nottingham, England, at Nottingham Playhouse, 1979; "Summer With Monika," first produced in Hammersmith, England, at Lyric Theatre, 1979; "Lifeswappers," first produced in Edinburgh in 1980; "Watchwords," first produced in Nottingham at Nottingham Playhouse, 1980; "All the Trimmings," first produced in Hammersmith at Lyric Theatre, 1980.

MEDIA ADAPTATIONS: McGough's sound recordings include "The Incredible New Liverpool Scene," released by Columbia Broadcasting System in 1967; "Fresh Liver," released by Island in 1972; "Grimms," released by Island in 1973; "Rockin' Duck," released by Island in 1974; "Sold Out," released by Warner Brothers in 1974; "Sleepers," released by D.J.M. in 1975; "Summer With Monika," released by Island in 1978; and "McGough McGear," "'Scaffold' L. the P.," and "'Scaffold' Live at Queen Elizabeth Hall," all released by Parlophone.

*   *   *

McGREGOR, Iona   1929-

PERSONAL: Born February 7, 1929, in Aldershot, England; daughter of Michael J. (an army education officer) and Clarice (Watkins) McGregor. *Education:* University of Bristol, B.A. (with honors), 1950. *Address:* 30 Howe St., Edinburgh EH3 6TG, Scotland.

CAREER: Edinburgh University Press, Edinburgh, Scotland, sub-editor, 1951-57; teacher of classics at schools in Canterbury, England, 1958-62, and in Cheslehurst, Kent, England, 1962-69; St. George's School for Girls, Edinburgh, teacher of Latin, 1969—. *Member:* P.E.N.

WRITINGS—Juveniles; published by Faber: *An Edinburgh Reel,* 1968; *The Popinjay,* 1969; *The Burning Hill,* 1970; *The Tree of Liberty,* 1972; *The Snake and the Olive,* 1974; *Edinburgh and the Eastern Lowlands,* 1979.

Sub-editor of *Dictionary of the Older Scottish Tongue,* Edinburgh, University Press. Author of "A Kind of Glory" (radio play), first broadcast on August 18, 1971.

WORK IN PROGRESS: "Research for a juvenile novel set in the early nineteenth century and centered round the notorious murderers Burke and Hare."

SIDELIGHTS: McGregor's novels are usually set in Scotland, but *The Snake and the Olive* is an exception. Set in ancient Greece, this book relies on the author's background as a classicist to relate the story of Hippocrates, the father of medicine. According to a *Junior Bookshelf* reviewer, "the Greek historical situation and way of life takes its place naturally in the book."

The story of Hippocrates "is told," said Marcus Crouch of the *Times Literary Supplement,* "sympathetically and with neat character sketches." It illustrates the future physician's struggle to decide whether he should espouse inspiration or science. As a youngster born on the island of Cos, Hippocrates watches sick pilgrims flock to the temple of Ascelpios, the god of healing. He has two role models, each representative of one polarity, from which to learn: his father, the scientific doctor devoted to Ascelpios, and Antigenes, the political, superstitious high priest. By the end of his apprenticeship, Hippocrates comes to know that he must transcend superstition and temple rituals to create more scientific methods of healing.

McGregor told *CA:* "I would describe myself as a 'period' rather than a 'historical' novelist since the setting is a focusing lens for the quirks and clashes of my (very private) characters. It is not an excuse for dramatizing the great public events in which they sometimes find themselves involved. For whatever reasons, the distancing effect of a remoter period helps me pick out the pattern of circumstance and personality I wish to use. An additional bonus is the wider social and technical details I can use in such a setting. Sixteenth-century gunnery and medicine are within my scope. I doubt if I could say the same about their modern equivalents.

"The minute detail found in research, boosted by an interest in the stone building of Scotland, generates character and incident for me. Call it pump priming if you like. Anyway, what is a historical novel? *All* novels are historical fiction since they all modify and interpret past experience."

BIOGRAPHICAL/CRITICAL SOURCES: Times Literary Supplement, April 3, 1969, December 8, 1972, December 6, 1974; *Books and Bookmen,* May, 1969; *Christian Science Monitor,* May 1, 1969; *New Statesman,* May 16, 1969; *History Today,* December, 1969; *Observer,* December 8, 1974; *Junior Bookshelf,* February, 1975.

*   *   *

McKENZIE, Robert T(relford)   1917-1981

OBITUARY NOTICE—See index for *CA* sketch: Born September 11, 1917, in Vancouver, British Columbia, Canada; died October 12, 1981. Educator, political commentator, and author. McKenzie developed his interest in British politics while stationed in London as a current affairs instructor for the Canadian Army during World War II. He stayed in England after the war's end to do doctoral study at the London School of Economics and Political Science. McKenzie's doctoral thesis served as the basis for his first book, *British Political Parties: The Distribution of Power Within the Conservative and Labour Parties,* which caused an uproar during the 1950's and is now regarded as the most influential academic work on British politics since World War II. He became a political commentator for the British Broadcasting Corp. (BBC) in 1955 and thereafter reported on the constitutional implications of each election. McKenzie was considered an excellent interviewer, and he conducted probing interviews with many of England's top political figures. He had been on the faculty of the sociology department of the London School of Economics and Political Science since 1949, beginning as a lecturer and becoming a professor of sociology in 1964. McKenzie retained his Canadian citizenship despite his thirty-seven-year residency in London. He also wrote *Angels in Marble,* a look at the Conservative British working class. Obituaries and other sources: *London Times,* October 14, 1981.

* * *

McLEAVY, Gus 1951-

PERSONAL: Born May 27, 1951, in Boston, Mass.; son of Francis Howland and Rosamond (Helgren) McLeavy. *Education:* Swarthmore College, B.A., 1973. *Residence:* Seattle, Wash.

CAREER: U.S. Postal Service, Concord, N.H., postal clerk, 1973; teacher in Fairbanks, Alaska, and New Ipswich, N.H., 1973-74; *Horse, of Course!* (magazine), Temple, N.H., editorial assistant, 1974-75; worked as vacuum cleaner salesman, recreation director, apple picker, physics equipment technician, administrative officer, grocery clerk, and free-lance writer, 1975-80; Maine Maritime Museum, Bath, Me., archivist, 1979-80; W. B. Saunders (publishers), Philadelphia, Pa., advertising copywriter, 1980-81; free-lance writer, 1981—.

WRITINGS: The Bathroom Almanac: The Ultimate Trivia Book, Fell, 1981. Contributor to magazines.

WORK IN PROGRESS: The Word Thieves, a children's book, with Laura Kelsey; a nonfiction book; a second *Bathroom Almanac; Cargo,* "a novel of man/god/need/greed set in the South Seas"; *The Initiation,* "a novella about a strange men's club entrance rite"; "a science fiction novel about the 'trickle-down' effects of the Reagan administration one hundred years from now."

SIDELIGHTS: McLeavy told *CA:* "The rationale of *The Bathroom Almanac* was essentially pragmatic. About four years ago I was facing my 'late-twenties crisis' of life goals and realities. I knew I would never have the time or independence I craved by working forty hours per week for ten grand a year. I considered panning for gold, but a weekend in February (in Maine!) with a metal detector cured that notion.

"I've always liked 'trivia'—which at least for the purposes of *The Bathroom Almanac*'s subtitle, *The Ultimate Trivia Book,* I'd rather define as 'miscellany'—and, looking around, I noticed that most people had some kind of bathroom reading fare in their homes. These books are all composed of material that is quick, light, and can be read and enjoyed in five-minute batches. And I also saw that none of these books had taken advantage of what I considered the obvious hook, alliteration and all, of bathroom book. I took stock of the trivia and miscellany books available and found them wanting. I decided to gamble that I could take the best of the available trivia, find new stuff, and put it all together in a unique format to create the ultimate bathroom book.

"I quit my job as a grocery clerk, rented out my small home, and took a room back where I went to college. My money ran out after nine months, and I completed *The Bathroom Almanac* during 1979 and 1980 while I was working as an archivist at the Maine Maritime Museum. My research began with the granddaddy of miscellany, the Victorian *Chambers' Book of Days,* and after that it was mostly a one-thing-leads-to-another proposition. Most of the research was conducted in the Swarthmore College and Bowdoin College libraries. I also borrowed books from friends and amassed a sizable collection of my own. In total, I used over two hundred books and one thousand magazines and was supplying new information to my publisher into February, 1981.

"I hope with *The Bathroom Almanac* to make enough money to be freed from the absolute necessity of having to work full time to eat and to devote that work-time to other creative projects. I have some wonderful bar songs that are going begging at the moment. . . . It would be nice if *The Bathroom Almanac* really took off (a gay YMCA camp counselor did my tarot when I was twelve, and if all goes according to plan, it will), but otherwise, if it would just provide another small bankroll so that I could feel secure enough about writing full time, then it will have served its purpose, and will have been a helluva lotta fun to do."

* * *

McMANUS, Patrick (Francis) 1933-

PERSONAL: Born August 26, 1933, in Sandpoint, Idaho; son of Francis Edward and Mabel (an elementary school teacher; maiden name, Klaus) McManus; married Darlene Keough (a business manager), February 3, 1954; children: Kelly McManus Walkup, Shannon McManus Bayfield, Peggy, Erin. *Education:* Washington State University, B.A., 1956, M.A., 1962, further study, 1965-67. *Home:* East 7917 Valley Way, Spokane, Wash. 99206. *Agent:* Oliver Swan, Collier Associates, 280 Madison Ave., New York, N.Y. 10016. *Office:* Department of English and Journalism, Eastern Washington University, Cheney, Wash. 99004.

CAREER: Daily Olympian, Olympia, Wash., news reporter, 1956; Washington State University, Pullman, editor, 1956-59; Eastern Washington University, Cheney, instructor, 1959-67, assistant professor, 1967-71, associate professor, 1971-74, co-director of journalism and English, 1973—, professor of journalism and English, 1974—. News reporter for KREM-TV, 1960-62. *Member:* Authors Guild, Outdoor Writers of America, Sigma Delta Chi.

WRITINGS: A Fine and Pleasant Misery (humor; edited by Jack Samson), Holt, 1978; *Kid Camping From AAAAIIII! to Zip* (juvenile, humor), Lothrop, 1979; *They Shoot Canoes, Don't They?* (humor), Holt, 1981. Associate editor of *Field and Stream,* 1976-81; contributing editor of *Spokane,* 1979—; editor-at-large of *Outdoor Life,* 1981—.

WORK IN PROGRESS: Research for a novel set in the early inland Pacific Northwest.

SIDELIGHTS: McManus told *CA:* "James Thurber once wrote that the writer of short humor pieces sits on the edge of the chair of literature. I suspect the short-humor writer roosts on one of the lower rungs, if he is allowed near the chair at all. Critics do not regard humor writing as serious literary work, which is good. As soon as the humor writer starts thinking of himself as a person of letters, as soon as he perceives his purpose as something other than seeking the ultimate, base, vulgar, gut-busting, psyche-wrenching laugh, he is done for.

I have been chided by some reviewers for not possessing a more serious comic purpose. To provoke the uniquely human phenomenon of laughter is, it seems to me, a serious comic purpose, provided, of course, there is such a thing as a serious comic purpose.''

*　　*　　*

McNAUGHT, Brian Robert 1948-

PERSONAL: Born January 28, 1948, in Detroit, Mich.; son of Waldo E. (a public relations director) and Mary Virginia (Day) McNaught. *Education:* Marquette University, B.A., 1970. *Politics:* Democrat. *Religion:* Roman Catholic. *Home and office:* 1035 Beacon St., Brookline, Mass. 02146. *Agent:* John A. Ware Literary Agency, 392 Central Park W., New York, N.Y. 10025.

CAREER: Birmingham Eccentric, Birmingham, Mich., staff writer and religion editor, 1967; *Michigan Catholic,* Detroit, staff writer and columnist, 1970-74; free-lance columnist, 1974—; free-lance writer, 1975—; *Esplanade,* Boston, Mass., staff writer and editor, 1976; *Metro Gay News,* Detroit, staff writer and editor, 1976-78; Exodus Center, Inc., Boston, co-executive director, 1980. Host of "Church Alive," an educational television talk show, 1973-74; lecturer, 1974—; wrote public relations policy statement for American Institute of Architects, 1976; consultant to Guidance Associates for filmstrip "The Hidden Minority: Homosexuality in Our Society," 1979; sex counselor certified by the American Association of Sex Educators, Counselors, and Therapists, 1980—; appeared on more than twenty-five radio and television talk shows. National director of Social Action for Dignity, 1974-77; founder and member of Dignity/Detroit, 1974; member of National Gay Task Force, 1974—, Catholics for Gay Rights, 1975—, Gay Rights National Lobby, 1977—, Bread for the World, 1978—, Fellowship of Reconciliation, 1978—, and Women's Ordination Conference, 1979—.

MEMBER: American Association of Sex Educators, Counselors, and Therapists, American Civil Liberties Union. *Awards, honors:* John G. Stewart Christian Leadership Award from Christian Brothers of Ireland, 1966; citation for regular column and series of articles about charismatic renewal movement, 1974, and award for best magazine article of the year for "The Sad Dilemma of the Gay Catholic," 1976, both from Catholic Press Association; Margaret Sanger Award from the Institute for Family Research and Education of Syracuse University, 1979, for contributing to the public's understanding of homosexuality.

WRITINGS: (Editor) *Christian Commitment for the 1980's,* Inter-Religious Task Force for Social Analysis, Volume I, *Must We Choose Sides?,* 1979, Volume II, *Which Side Are We On?,* 1980; *A Disturbed Peace: Selected Writings of an Irish-Catholic Homosexual,* Dignity, 1981.

Contributor: Celeste Torniero, editor, *Readings in Human Sexuality,* Dushkin, 1978; I. David Welch, George A. Tate, and Fred Richards, editors, *Positively Gay,* Celestial Artis, 1979; Polly Kellogg, editor, *Teaching and Learning About Lesbians and Gays,* Education Exploration Center, 1981.

Columnist: "Right On," published in *Michigan Catholic,* 1970-74; "A Disturbed Peace," syndicated in a variety of gay-oriented publications, 1974—; "Brian's Column," published in *Insight,* 1978—.

Also contributor of articles and reviews to *U.S. Catholic, Witness, Impact, Humanist,* and *Advocate.*

WORK IN PROGRESS: A children's story, *A Frog Is a Frog,* publication expected in 1982; an autobiography, *When Irish Eyes Are Gay,* publication expected in 1982.

SIDELIGHTS: In 1974 McNaught was dropped as a columnist for the *Michigan Catholic* when, according to *Commonweal*'s Michael Novak, "he publicly admitted that he was a homosexual." Since then McNaught has become an activist in behalf of gay rights.

McNaught told *CA:* "While I write primarily about gay people and our struggle to grow to our full potential in a frequently hostile environment, I am intimately concerned with the quality of each person's life. I am a humanist who believes in a power greater than myself. I believe that ignorance is the enemy of all oppressed people and that all people are oppressed. Writing is a means of gently eliminating ignorance.''

BIOGRAPHICAL/CRITICAL SOURCES: Commonweal, October 18, 1974.

*　　*　　*

MEAKER, Eloise 1915-
(Lydia Benson Clark, Valancy Hunter, Lydia Lancaster, Amanda McAllister)

PERSONAL: Born July 13, 1915, in Auburn, N.Y.; daughter of James S. (a merchant) and Elizabeth (Smith) Case; married Charles Meaker, April 2, 1935; children: Cynthia A. *Education:* Attended high school in Auburn, N.Y. *Residence:* Glendale, Ariz. *Agent:* Shirley Burke, 370 East 76th St., Suite B-704, New York, N.Y. 10021.

CAREER: Writer, 1972—. Worked as grocery clerk and in print shop bindery.

WRITINGS—Novels under pseudonym Valancy Hunter: *Devil's Double,* Dell, 1973; *The Namesake,* Dell, 1974; *The Rebel Heart,* Dell, 1976.

Novels under pseudonym Lydia Benson Clark: *Yesterday's Evil,* Ace Books, 1974; *Demon Cat,* Zebra Books, 1975.

Novels under pseudonym Amanda McAllister: *Waiting for Caroline,* Playboy Press, 1976; *Look Over Your Shoulder,* Playboy Press, 1976.

Novels under pseudonym Lydia Lancaster: *Passion and Proud Hearts,* Warner Books, 1978; *Stolen Rapture,* Warner Books, 1978; *Desire and Dreams of Glory,* Warner Books, 1979; *The Temptation,* Warner Books, 1979; *Her Heart's Honor,* Warner Books, 1980; *To Those Who Dare,* Warner Books, 1982.

Author of weekly newspaper column during the 1950's for the *Phoenix Sun Valley Sun.*

WORK IN PROGRESS: The Chameleons, a novel, publication by Warner Books expected in 1983; *Bitter Seeds of Storm,* publication expected in 1984.

AVOCATIONAL INTERESTS: Squaredancing, swimming, needlepoint, oil painting, horseback riding.

*　　*　　*

MECHIN, Jacques Benoist
See BENOIST-MECHIN, Jacques

*　　*　　*

MEEK, Margaret
See SPENCER MEEK, Margaret (Diston)

MEHRING, Walter 1896-1981

OBITUARY NOTICE: Born April 29, 1896, in Berlin, Germany; died after a long illness, October 3, 1981, in Zurich, Switzerland. Writer best known for his anti-Nazi songs, poems, and novels. Associated with German left-wing intellectuals during World War I, Mehring and others, such as Bertolt Brecht and Erich Kaestner, developed the cabaret as a means of reflecting their artistic and political views. In 1929 Mehring's *Der Kaufmann von Berlin* was performed, but quickly banned by authorities because of its blatant attack on Nazism. When Hitler rose to power in Germany, Mehring's books were burned, and Mehring fled, spending the next few years in Austria and France writing anti-Nazi poetry and novels. In 1940 he was captured by German security police and imprisoned, but in 1941 he escaped to the United States, where he became an American citizen. He worked as a translator in Los Angeles and as a reviewer for periodicals, including the *New York Times.* Among Mehring's most popular writings are *Die verlorene Bibliothek, In Menschenhaut, Arche Noah S.O.S.,* and *Berlin-Dada.* Obituaries and other sources: *Encyclopedia of World Literature in the Twentieth Century,* updated edition, Ungar, 1967; *World Authors, 1950-1970,* H. W. Wilson, 1975; *The Oxford Companion to German Literature,* Clarendon Press, 1976; *Chicago Tribune,* October 6, 1981.

* * *

MEISCH, Lynn A. 1945-

PERSONAL: Surname is pronounced with a long "i"; born February 17, 1945, in Minneapolis, Minn.; daughter of Francis Roman (an artist and architect) and Elaine (an architect; maiden name, Hanson) Meisch. *Education:* Reed College, B.A., 1968; San Francisco State University, M.A., 1973, further graduate study. *Politics:* "Pacifist/Human Rights/Feminist." *Religion:* "Raised Roman Catholic; disagree with many official positions." *Residence:* San Francisco, Calif.

CAREER: Mexican Museum, San Francisco, Calif., teacher of textiles course, 1976; high school history teacher in San Francisco, 1979; Mountain Travel, San Francisco, tour leader to South America, 1979—. Teacher at San Francisco Fibers and Fiberworks, 1980-81. Vice-president of Fundacion Jatari: Andean Education and Research Foundation; adviser to museums and curator of exhibits in California and Ecuador. *Member:* Handweavers Guild of America. *Awards, honors:* Fulbright fellowship, 1977-79; fellowships from Institute for Intercultural Studies, 1977-79, and Inter-American Foundation (for Bolivia), 1981.

WRITINGS—Self-illustrated: *A Traveler's Guide to El Dorado and the Inca Empire: Colombia, Ecuador, Peru, and Bolivia,* Penguin, 1977, revised edition, 1980; *Weaving, Costume, and the Market in Otavalo,* Libri Mundi, 1981. Contributor to magazines and newspapers, including *Co-Evolution Quarterly, New Age Journal, Spin-Off, Pacific Discovery, Super-8 Filmmaker,* and *Textile Museum Journal.* Founder and editor of *On Our Own: Women Travelers Abroad.*

WORK IN PROGRESS: A book on weaving and costume in southern Ecuador.

SIDELIGHTS: Lynn Meisch wrote: "I have traveled extensively in the United States, Mexico, and Central and South America. I give a certain percentage of what I earn from my writings to Fundacion Jatari as a way of sharing with the communities where my work was done (the foundation gives scholarships to Ecuadorian *indigenas*). I also contribute to the schooling of my four Ecuadorian godchildren, partly in return for the amazing hospitality and kindness their families have shown me."

BIOGRAPHICAL/CRITICAL SOURCES: San Francisco Examiner, February 19, 1979.

* * *

MEISEL, Anthony C(lark) 1943-
(Tony Meisel)

PERSONAL: Born February 8, 1943, in New York, N.Y.; son of Herman J. (a surgeon) and Kathleen (a teacher; maiden name, Friedberg) Meisel. *Education:* Columbia University, B.A., 1963; University of Vienna, Ph.D., 1965. *Home:* 255 West End Ave., New York, N.Y. 10023. *Office:* Quarto Communications, Inc., 212 Fifth Ave., New York, N.Y. 10010.

CAREER: J. B. Lippincott Co., Philadelphia, Pa., editor, 1966-68; Hawthorn Books, Inc., New York City, editor, 1968-69; New York Univeristy Press, New York City, editor, 1969-72; Brooklyn College of the City University of New York, Brooklyn, N.Y., assistant professor of art history, 1972-77; Ziff-Davis Publishing Co., New York City, editor, 1977-80; Quarto Communications, Inc., New York City, president, 1981—. Adjunct professor of art at Hunter College of the City University of New York, 1973-75.

WRITINGS—Under name Tony Meisel: (With M. L. del Mastro) *The Rule of St. Benedict,* Doubleday, 1975; *A Manual of Singlehanded Sailing,* Arco, 1981; *Under Sail,* Macmillan, 1982; *The Sailor's Emergency Handbook,* Hodder & Stoughton, 1983. Contributor to magazines, including *Hadassah, Yachting, Women's World, Millions,* and *Motor Boating and Sailing.*

WORK IN PROGRESS: The Golden Madonna, a novel.

SIDELIGHTS: Meisel told CA: "All my writing is done for the sheer fun of it. Either the subject is one for which no satisfactory book has appeared or, in the case of the novel in progress, *The Golden Madonna,* because I have dreamed up such a devilishly obtuse plot as to warrant letting a segment of the public suffer with me. The sailing books spring from a lifelong passion and my major avocation. Most of my other energies go into the production of informational video programming (quite literate programming, I might add), trying to find places for a disastrously large library, and strenuously attacking the poetic excesses of assorted screenwriters.

"Despite all the blather written about the creative process, most inspired by unconscionable self-indulgence, the act of writing is essentially a process of organization and intellectual rigor. I used to make my authors, in my editing days, submit detailed, multipaged outlines. They didn't like it, but they wrote better books for it. Secondly, any author, except perhaps the poet manque, must remember he or she is writing for an audience, a living, writhing marketplace. If an experience cannot be explained in comprehensible words and metaphors, it has not been successfully presented to the reader.

"The person most responsible for getting me to write well is Oliver Moore, currently editor of *Town and Country.* More than anyone else, he showed me how to pluck the essentials from the pile and organize them to make sense and engage the reader. In fact, I've got to a point where I can polish off the first draft of a nonfiction work in about a month of uninterrupted working time. Of course, other work, love, and sporting pursuits always seem to get in the way.

"If I could give any advice to a young author it would be: don't talk about your work, write it! More time is wasted in saloons than at a typewriter. Also, get an agent if possible. Publishers are swamped, and a very few bother with over-the-transom manuscripts. An agent can open doors and absorb some of the anxieties peculiar to the literary profession."

*　　*　　*

MEISEL, Tony
See MEISEL, Anthony C(lark)

*　　*　　*

MELLARD, James Milton   1938-

PERSONAL: Born January 30, 1938, in West Monroe, La.; son of Connie M. (a carpenter) and Pauline (Watts) Mellard; married Sue Gilbert (a secretary), May 28, 1958; children: Tandy Alice, Cynthia Kathleen, Catherine Sue. *Education:* Lamar University, B.A., 1960; University of Oklahoma, M.A., 1961; University of Texas, Ph.D., 1964. *Home:* 107 Forsythe, DeKalb, Ill. 60115. *Office:* Department of English, Northern Illinois University, DeKalb, Ill. 60115.

CAREER: University of Texas, Austin, special instructor in English, 1963-64; University of Southern California, Los Angeles, assistant professor of English, 1964-67; Northern Illinois University, DeKalb, assistant professor, 1967-70, associate professor, 1970-73, professor of English, 1973—, chairman of department, 1978—. *Member:* Modern Language Association of America, Society for the Study of Southern Literature (member of board of directors), Midwest Modern Language Association, South Central Modern Language Association.

WRITINGS: Four Modes: A Rhetoric of Modern Fiction, Macmillan, 1973; (with James Wilcox) *The Authentic Writer: English Rhetoric and Composition,* Heath, 1977; *Quaternion: Stories, Poems, Plays, Essays,* Scott, Foresman, 1978; *The Exploded Form: The Modernist Novel in America,* University of Illinois Press, 1980. Contributor to language journals.

WORK IN PROGRESS: A study of epistemology and history in the modernist American novel; a study of the modes of fiction.

SIDELIGHTS: Mellard wrote: "I started my academic career with a dissertation on humor in Faulkner's novels, but the several articles published from the dissertation had more to do with the formal structures of Faulkner's novels than with humor. My interests turned very soon to myth criticism and the relationship between genres and modes of presentation in fiction. The book, *Four Modes,* though primarily a textbook anthology, contains considerable original criticism on the modes of the 'popular,' the pictorial, the dramatic, and the lyrical. I still plan a book-length study of these modalities in major novels. My feeling is that 'modernist fiction' represents an exploding of the traditional mode (the pictorial) in fiction, a view presented in the critical/historical study *The Exploded Form.*

"My recent interest has been in the application of the same thesis to a set of modernist novels in which theory of history or the epistemological status of history is a major concern (Faulkner's *Absalom!,* Bellow's *Herzog,* Ellison's *Invisible Man,* for example). 'History' is one of the epistemological authorities of modernist literature, but history itself has been seriously questioned in this century, just as all bases for our knowledge have. All my interests, it turns out—genre theory, theory of fictional modes, myth criticism, history—end up focusing upon

the question of the validity of knowledge and the search for reliable or valid epistemological authorities."

BIOGRAPHICAL/CRITICAL SOURCES: Times Literary Supplement, May 1, 1981.

*　　*　　*

MELLOW, James R(obert)   1926-

PERSONAL: Born February 28, 1926, in Gloucester, Mass.; son of James R. (a mechanic/engineer) and Cecilia Margaret (Sawyer) Mellow. *Education:* Northwestern University, B.S., 1950. *Agent:* Georges Borchardt, Inc., 136 East 57th St., New York, N.Y. 10022. *Office address:* P.O. Box 297, Clinton, Conn. 06413.

CAREER: Arts (magazine), New York City, reviewer and production manager, 1955-61, editor in chief, 1961-65; *Industrial Design,* New York City, editor, 1965-69; *Art International,* Lugano, Switzerland, art critic, 1965-69; *New Leader,* New York City, art critic, 1969-72; *New York Times,* New York City, art critic, 1968-74; writer, 1974—. *Military service:* U.S. Army Air Force, 1944-46. *Member:* National Book Critics Circle, Authors Guild. *Awards, honors:* Nominated for National Book Award, 1974, for biography, *Charmed Circle: Gertrude Stein and Company;* nominated for American Book Award, 1980, for biography, *Nathaniel Hawthorne in His Times.*

WRITINGS: (Editor) *The Best in Arts,* Art Digest, Inc., 1962; (editor) *New York: The Art World,* Art Digest, Inc., 1964; *Charmed Circle: Gertrude Stein and Company* (biography), Praeger, 1974; *Nathaniel Hawthorne in His Times* (biography), Houghton, 1980. Contributor of articles to magazines and newspapers, including *Saturday Review, Art News, Gourmet, Horizon,* and *New York Times.*

WORK IN PROGRESS: Loose Ends, a biographical study of the marital and literary lives of F. Scott and Zelda Fitzgerald, publication by Houghton expected in 1984; a biography of Margaret Fuller; a sequence of interlocking biographies of nineteenth-century American literary and cultural figures, including volumes on Henry David Thoreau and Ralph Waldo Emerson.

SIDELIGHTS: James Mellow's biography of Gertrude Stein, *Charmed Circle,* drew wide critical praise and received a nomination for the National Book Award. Susan Heath, writing in *Saturday Review/ World,* commented: "Mellow's study of the outrageous Miss Stein crackles with wit and precision, a fresh, welcome reminder of the Stein that was. . . . It is a busy, ambitious book packed with tangy anecdotes and self-dramatization recalled both by and about Stein and her famous coterie. . . . Mellow revives Stein brilliantly, illuminating the connections between her daily life . . . and the themes and characters of her fiction. . . . It is the wonder and the delight of this critical biographical portrait that the vitality of Gertrude Stein throbs on every page, bound to fascinate her detractors as surely as it will her advocates."

Mellow's next book, *Nathaniel Hawthorne in His Times,* is the first in a series of four biographies, with volumes on Margaret Fuller, Henry David Thoreau, and Ralph Waldo Emerson to come. This book, too, earned nomination for the American Book Award (successor to the defunct National Book Award) and collected many excellent reviews. Charles Nicol of the *Saturday Review* wrote: "Both the scholar and the general reader should welcome James Mellow's thorough, highly illuminating study, a full biography that never lapses into either trivia or sweeping irrelevance. Mellow has recreated Hawthorne's milieu and nicely sketched his acquaintances. . . . The careful shaping of this biography to reveal the experiences on which Hawthorne drew is masterful indeed." *Newsweek* critic Walter Clemons added that "Melville's unsuccessful attempt to break through Hawthorne's defenses leads Mellow into the most searching and pertinent discussion I've yet seen on the puzzling phenomenon of nineteenth-century friendships in which homoerotic ardor was hotly avowed but totally, innocently unrecognized. Mellow is good, too, on the Hawthornes' marriage, one of the happiest in the history of literature, and of the harrowing end of Hawthorne's career."

Mellow told *CA:* "Context is of vital importance to the series of nineteenth-century biographical studies that I regard as my principal long-term project. My theory is that even in dealing with a supposedly reclusive literary figure like Hawthorne, if one follows through on all of the important personal and professional relationships, one will inevitably be drawn into the major social or political issues of the period. The four-volume approach allows me to extend that network of personal relationships, personal rivalries, etc., in much more detailed fashion than is possible in the one-volume biography. Also, since all four major figures knew each other personally and professionally, they will appear and reappear through each of the four volumes (that is one of the more interesting challenges for the biographer), providing an opportunity to explore their characters from a variety of angles. (Having glimpsed Margaret Fuller through Hawthorne's eyes in the first volume, it will now be possible to explore Hawthorne's character through Margaret Fuller's eyes in the second volume.) Furthermore, a large group of subsidiary characters—Elizabeth Palmer Peabody, Charles Sumner, Daniel Webster, Horace Greeley, Franklin Pierce, etc.—will also appear and reappear in the course of the four volumes at different stages of their careers, and therefore in the course of the series will be given substantial biographical attention."

AVOCATIONAL INTERESTS: Art, architecture, design, food, travel, gardening.

BIOGRAPHICAL/CRITICAL SOURCES: New York Times, January 30, 1974; *Washington Post Book World,* February 3, 1974, October 5, 1980; *New York Times Book Review,* February 3, 1974, September 21, 1980; *Newsweek,* February 11, 1974, October 6, 1980; *New Yorker,* February 25, 1974; *Time,* March 4, 1974; *Saturday Review/World,* March 9, 1974; *National Observer,* March 16, 1974; *New York Review of Books,* May 30, 1974; *New Leader,* September 16, 1974; *Saturday Review,* September, 1980.

* * *

MENCKEN, H(enry) L(ouis) 1880-1956

BRIEF ENTRY: Born September 12, 1880, in Baltimore, Md.; died January 29, 1956, in Baltimore, Md. American journalist. As editor and critic for *American Mercury,* Mencken established a reputation for outrageous invective and cynical commentary against American life. His favorite topics included organized religion, politics, middle-class values, American business, and the newspaper trade. His best pieces were collected in *Prejudices* (1919-27). He was widely read and quoted before the Depression, but after 1929 hard times preoccupied many who had been his faithful readers. He entertained a new generation of readers with his autobiographies, *Happy Days* (1940), *Newspaper Days* (1941), and *Heathen Days* (1943). Mencken also produced a scholarly work, *The American Language* (1919), which contrasted the richness of American speech with "English English." The project occupied much of his life, going through several revisions, and at the time of his

death he was considered a leading expert on the subject. Mencken is also noted for his promotion of such writers as Theodore Dreiser, Sherwood Anderson, and Sinclair Lewis, and for adding a vigorous impetus to the growth and development of American literary criticism. *Biographical/critical sources: Twentieth Century Authors: A Biographical Dictionary of Modern Literature,* H. W. Wilson, 1942; *Encyclopedia of World Literature in the Twentieth Century,* updated edition, Ungar, 1967; *The McGraw-Hill Encyclopedia of World Biography,* McGraw, 1973.

* * *

MENDELSSOHN, Kurt (Alfred Georg) 1906-1980

OBITUARY NOTICE—See index for *CA* sketch: Born January 7, 1906, in Berlin, Germany; died September 18, 1980, in Oxford, England. Physicist, science historian, editor, and author best known for his research into liquid helium's properties of superfluidity and superconductivity at extremely low temperatures. Early in 1933, while on a working visit to Oxford, Mendelssohn became the first person in Britain to cool helium gas into a liquid. After the German Reichstag granted Hitler dictatorial powers in March, 1933, Mendelssohn, a Jew, fled with his wife to England, where he became director of a research group at Clarenden Laboratory, Oxford. His work with the low-temperature properties of helium has been significant in the practical application of nuclear physics. Mendelssohn's early writings, *What Is Atomic Energy?, Cryophysics,* and *The Quest for Absolute Zero,* explain his work in physics. His later works dealt with aspects of the interaction between science, technology, sociology, and politics. *In China Now* relates Mendelssohn's observations of the People's Republic of China while he was there as a visiting professor. *The World of Walther Nernst* examines the sociological impact of Germany's prewar scientific and technological growth. In *The Riddle of the Pyramids* Mendelssohn refuted the contention that the ancient Egyptians built pyramids to be used as tombs and theorized that the pharoahs used the projects to build political unity. *The Secret of Western Domination* attacks the notion that Europeans and their descendants have been able to dominate the world because of an innate tendency to be aggressive and exploitive, and offers the Europeans' knowledge of science and technology as an explanation for their world dominance. Mendelssohn was the founder, in 1960, of *Cryophysics* and served as its editor until his death. Obituaries and other sources: *The Annual Obituary 1980,* St. Martin's, 1981.

* * *

MERKLE, Judith A(stria) 1942-

PERSONAL: Born January 14, 1942, in Brunswick, Maine; daughter of Theodore Charles, Jr. (a physicist) and Helene Raphaela Antonia (a pianist; maiden name, Suarez) Merkle; married W. Parkes Riley II (a professor), June 19, 1971; children: Elizabeth Antonia, Marlow Francis Parkes. *Education:* University of California, Berkeley, B.A., 1962, Ph.D., 1974; Harvard University, A.M., 1964. *Residence:* Eugene, Ore. *Office:* Department of Political Science, University of Oregon, Eugene, Ore. 97403.

CAREER: U.S. Navy Department, Washington, D.C., management intern and research analyst, 1964-66; University of California, Berkeley, 1969-71, began as acting instructor, became lecturer in political science; University of Oregon, Eugene, assistant professor of political science, 1971—, director of Russian and East European Studies Center, 1981-82. *Member:* American Political Science Association, American Society for Public Administration, American Association for the Advancement of Slavic Studies, American Diabetes Association, Asian Studies Association, National Organization for Women, Oregon State Employees Association (vice-president, 1980-81).

WRITINGS: Management and Ideology, University of California Press, 1980. Contributor to academic journals.

WORK IN PROGRESS: Research on work restructuring, organizational behavior and organizational justice, and grievance systems.

* * *

MERY, Fernand 1897-

PERSONAL: Born February 11, 1897, in Clermont l'Herault, France; son of Fernand (an industrialist) and Berthe (Berquet) Mery; married Wilhelmine Massonneau, July 2, 1934. *Education:* Attended Faculte des Lettres de Montpelier, Ecole Veterinaire de Lyon, and Ecole Veterinaire d'Alfort. *Politics:* "Apolitical." *Religion:* Roman Catholic. *Home:* 22 bis avenue de Suffren, 75015 Paris, France. *Office:* c/o *Point-de-Vue-Images du Monde,* 116 bis Champs Elysee, 75008 Paris, France.

CAREER: Veterinarian and free-lance writer. President of Academie Veterinaire de France, 1962, and Conseil National de la Protection Animale. Free-lance lecturer and radio broadcaster. *Military service:* French Cavalry, 1914-18; French Army, 1940, director of army canine service and creator of the training code for army dogs; became captain. *Member:* International Society for the Protection of Animals (ISPA), World Wildlife Federation, P.E.N. Club, Association des Ecrivains Combattants, Medecins Ecrivains, Societe des Gens de Lettres, Societe des Auteurs, Association des Amis des Betes (founder and president), Academie Grammont. *Awards, honors:* Grand Prix of the Societe des Gens de Lettres, 1966; Prix litteraire of the Academie Francaise; honorary president of Assistance aux Animaux; Officier des Palmes Academiques; officer of French Legion of Honor.

WRITINGS: Betes et gens devant l'amour, Flammarion, 1933; *Les Chiens de chasse,* photographs by Dim, Payot, 1951; *Ames de betes,* Denoel, 1952; *Avoir un chien,* illustrated by O'Klein, Denoel, 1953; *Ici: Les Betes,* Denoel, 1954; *Les Coulisses du monde animal,* Prisma, 1956, Hachette, 1973; *Sa Majeste le chat,* Denoel, 1956, translation by Elizabeth King and John Rosenberg published as *Her Majesty the Cat,* Criterion, 1957 (published in England as *Just Cats,* Quartet Books, 1973); *Notre Ami le chien,* illustrated by Colyann, Denoel, 1957; (editor with P. C. Blin and others) *Le Chien,* illustrated by Lucy Dawson and Roger Reboussin, Librairie Larousse, 1959.

Medecin des betes, Laffont, 1961; *Les Animaux celebres,* illustrated by Daniel Colin, Denoel, 1964; *Entre chiens,* illustrated by Albert Debout, Editions du Livre, 1964; *Le Chat: Sa vie, son histoire, sa magie,* Pont Royal, 1966, translation by Emma Street published as *The Life, History, and Magic of the Cat,* Hamlyn, 1967, Madison Square Press, 1968; *Chiens d'utilite et de compagnie,* Marguerat, 1966; *Le Chien: Son mystere,* Pont Royal, 1968, translation published as *The Life, History, and Magic of the Dog,* Grosset & Dunlap, 1970 (published in England as *The Dog,* Cassell, 1970).

Le Chow-chow, Crepin-Leblond, 1970; *Les Betes aussi ont leurs languages,* Editions France-Empire, 1971, translation by Michael Ross published as *Animal Languages,* Saxon House, 1975; (editor with R.-P. Audras and others) *Le Chat,* Larousse, 1973; *Les Mysteres du monde animal,* Hachette, 1975.

Also author of *Les Joies du chien,* Realites; *Entre chats,* illustrated by Dubout, Editions Solar; *Moumour le panthere;* and *Les Chiens de compagnie: Bichons, chihuahuas, chows-chows.*

Contributor of articles to *Point-de-Vue-Images du Monde, France-Soir, Le Parisien Libere,* and other magazines.

SIDELIGHTS: As a veterinarian and animal behaviorist, Mery has devoted his life to the study of animals and is recognized as an authority on animal habits. Although active in the study and protection of wild species, Mery is particularly interested in man's domesticated animal companions. Many of Mery's books, generously illustrated, reveal his delight in dogs and cats. Mery's other books reflect his fascination for and wide knowledge of the animal world.

One of Mery's books, *Animal Languages,* discusses communication among birds, insects, amphibians, fish, and mammals and between man and these animals. The book met with mixed reception. While some critics considered it to be well-documented, others found the book's sources unreliable or outdated. Margery C. Coombs of the University of Massachusetts department of zoology speculated that "students and more sophisticated readers are more likely to profit" from *Animal Languages* than the general reader. On the other hand, Maurice Burton noted in *Books and Bookmen* that some readers will "enjoy [Mery's] racy style."

BIOGRAPHICAL/CRITICAL SOURCES: Books and Bookmen, May, 1975; *Library Journal,* August, 1975.

* * *

MEW, Charlotte (Mary) 1870-1928

BRIEF ENTRY: Born November 15, 1870, in London, England; committed suicide, March 24, 1928. British poet. Charlotte Mew spent her whole life in poverty, beset by ill health and the insanity and death of family members in her care. She wrote poems only when she could no longer contain her feelings, and the work she then produced was evidence of her intensity and self-control. The few poems she did not destroy are collected in *The Farmer's Bride* (1916) and *The Rambling Sailor* (1929); some of her short stories also appeared in *Yellow Book.* Through deliberately interrupted meter and ever-changing rhythms, Mew shared the poignant, secret passions that were normally hidden by her reserved behavior. Her work exhibited an attention to detail that attracted Thomas Hardy, who encouraged her writing and secured her financial support from the British Government. This was not enough to overshadow the tragedy in her personal life, however, and at the age of fifty-seven she poisoned herself, leaving behind only small fragments of what many critics regarded as her creative genius. *Biographical/critical sources: Twentieth Century Authors: A Biographical Dictionary of Modern Literature,* H. W. Wilson, 1942.

* * *

MIETHE, Terry Lee 1948-

PERSONAL: Surname is pronounced *Mee*-the; born August 26, 1948, in Clinton, Ind.; son of Billy (a factory foreman) and Rosemary (Procarione) Miethe; married Beverly Jo Deck (a teacher in special education), June 1, 1969; children: John Hayden. *Education:* Lincoln Christian College, A.B. (with honors), 1970; Trinity Evangelical Divinity School, M.A. (with honors; philosophy), 1973; McCormick Theological Seminary, M.Div., 1973; Saint Louis University, Ph.D., 1976; University of Southern California, M.A. (social ethics), 1981. *Home:*

3178 Florinda St., Pomona, Calif. 91767. *Office:* First Christian Church, 1751 North Park Ave., Pomona, Calif. 91768.

CAREER: Ordained minister of Christian church, 1970; assistant minister of Christian church in Lockport, Ill., 1968-69; senior minister of United Church of Christ in Mellott, Ind., 1969-71; minister of Congregational church in Woodburn, Ill., 1973-74; Saint Louis University, St. Louis, Mo., lecturer in philosophy, 1975-78, assistant professor of theological studies, 1976-77; Burroughs Corp., Mission Viejo, Calif., senior engineering project analyst, 1978-79; First Christian Church, Pomona, Calif., associate minister, 1979—. Visiting professor at Fuller Theological Seminary, Azusa Pacific College, and Regent College; member of board of directors of Family Service of Pomona Valley, 1979-81.

MEMBER: American Philosophical Association, American Academy of Religion, Society of Biblical Literature, Evangelical Theological Society, Phi Beta Kappa, Phi Alpha Theta, Psi Chi, Eta Sigma Phi, Alpha Sigma Nu. *Awards, honors:* Babcock fellow at University of Southern California, 1980-81.

WRITINGS: Thomistic Bibliography, 1940-1978, Greenwood Press, 1980; *Reflections,* Claremont Press, 1980; (contributor) Norman L. Geisler, editor, *Biblical Errancy: An Analysis of Its Philosophical Roots,* Zondervan, 1981; *Augustinian Bibliography (1970-1980) and Thought,* Greenwood Press, 1982. Contributor of about forty articles to theology, philosophy, and education journals.

WORK IN PROGRESS: The Philosophy of God: Metaphysicians and Their Thoughts.

SIDELIGHTS: Miethe commented in *Reflections:* "My life is dedicated to learning as much about Ultimate Reality as is possible and sharing this in meaningful ways with as many people as possible."

* * *

MIHAJLOV, Mihajlo 1934-

BRIEF ENTRY: Born September 26, 1934, in Pancevo, Yugoslavia. Yugoslav author. Mihajlov began teaching Russian literature at University of Zagreb in 1963, but has spent many of the years since 1966 in prison, regarded as a dissident by government authorities. He was not able to visit the United States until 1978. He wrote *A Historical Proposal* (Freedom House, 1966), *Russian Themes* (Farrar, Straus, 1968), and *Underground Notes* (Sheed Andrews, 1976). *Address:* c/o Mrs. Marija Ivusie, 3921 Fifth St. N., Apt. 2, Arlington, Va. 22203. *Biographical/critical sources: Current Biography,* Wilson, 1979.

* * *

MILES, Joyce C(rudgington) 1927-

PERSONAL: Born November 15, 1927, in Stafford, England; daughter of Thomas C. and Constance M. (Harris) Buckle; married John C. Miles (a college principal), September 22, 1956. *Education:* Dudley College of Education, Teacher's Certificate, 1965; University of Bristol, M.Litt., 1979; doctoral study at University of Leicester, 1980—. *Home:* The Borie, Middle Rd., Cossington, Bridgwater, Somerset TA7 8LH, England.

CAREER: Shell-Mex and B.P. Ltd., London, England, in public relations, 1952-56; Town and Country Planning Association, London, in public relations, 1958-61; Kitson College of Engineering and Science, Leeds, England, lecturer in English and general studies, 1965-69; North Oxfordshire Technical College, Banbury, England, lecturer in English and general studies, 1971-72; Somerset College of Arts and Technology, Taunton, England, lecturer in general and communication studies, 1973—. Broadcaster on radio and television; visiting lecturer at clubs; public speaker. *Member:* Soroptimist International.

WRITINGS: House Names Around the World, David & Charles, 1972; (with husband, John C. Miles) *Communicating,* Harrap, 1974; *The House Names Book,* Allen & Unwin, 1982. Writer of children's stories for airlines and British Broadcasting Corp., 1958-75. Contributor to magazines and newspapers.

SIDELIGHTS: Joyce Miles commented: "What leads people to call their houses Smockfarthings, Kwitchurbelyakin, Shaupaudra, or Owzitiz? The practice of naming houses dates back many thousands of years, but very little was written about this fascinating subject. My book was one of the first to investigate it; I looked at fashions and tastes in house names in many parts of the world. It proved to be such an intriguing and absorbing subject that I have since devoted much time and research to it. My new book deals with some of the more outrageous names that appear on gateposts all over the United Kingdom.

"Apart from annual visits to Europe, which usually result in a wealth of new house names to add to my enormous collection, I have in recent years traveled to more remote parts of the world."

* * *

MILES, Peter
See MILES, Richard

* * *

MILES, Richard 1938-
(Peter Miles)

PERSONAL: Birth-given name, Gerald Perreau-Saussine; born April 1, 1938, in Tokyo, Japan; son of Robert (a stockbroker) and Eleanor (Child) Perreau-Saussine. *Education:* University of California, Los Angeles, B.A., 1972; University of California, Northridge, Reading Specialist Credential, 1974. *Home:* 268 North Bowling Green Way, Los Angeles, Calif. 90049. *Agent:* Molson-Stanton Associates Agency, 10889 Wilshire Blvd., Westwood, Calif. 90049.

CAREER: Actor, under pseudonym Peter Miles, in motion pictures, including "Passage to Marseille," 1944, "The Red Pony," 1948, and "Quo Vadis," 1951; Gallery Perreau-Saussine, Los Angeles, Calif., art dealer, 1959—; Burbank Unified School District, Burbank, Calif., reading specialist, 1972—. Director of Balcom Trading of Tokyo (importers), 1976—; president of Burbank Teachers Association, 1973-75. *Member:* Writers Guild of America, Academy of American Poets, Ukiyo-e Society of America, National Education Association, Burbank Teachers Association. *Awards, honors:* Federal Poets Award from Georgetown University, 1959, for "Swimmer Emerging"; Prix Jeune Americain from Les Amis du Cercle, 1965, for *That Cold Day in the Park;* Samuel Goldwyn Award from University of California and Samuel Goldwyn Foundation, 1973, for *The Moonbathers,* and 1974, for *Crooked Children* (published as *Angel Loves Nobody*).

WRITINGS—Under pseudonym Richard Miles; novels: *That Cold Day in the Park,* Delacorte, 1965 (also see below); *Angel Loves Nobody,* Prentice-Hall, 1967; *The Moonbathers,* Pyramid Press, 1974; *Paul Jacoulet: Printmaker,* Pacific-Asia Museum, 1982.

Screenplays: "Madmen of Mandoras," Crown International, 1964 (also released as "They Saved Hitler's Brain"); (with Gillian Freeman) "That Cold Day in the Park" (adapted from own novel), Commonwealth United, 1969.

WORK IN PROGRESS: A critical biography of French-Japanese artist Paul Jacoulet (1902-1960).

BIOGRAPHICAL/CRITICAL SOURCES: Best Sellers, July 1, 1967; *Times Literary Supplement* September 19, 1968; *New York,* June 9, 1969; *New York Times,* June 9, 1969; *Washington Post,* July 19, 1969.

*   *   *

MILGRAM, Stanley   1933-

PERSONAL: Born August 15, 1933, in New York, N.Y.; son of Samuel (a cake baker and shop owner) and Adele (Israel) Milgram; married Alexandra Menkin (a psychiatric social worker), December 10, 1961; children: Michele Sara, Marc Daniel. *Education:* Queens College (now Queens College of the City University of New York), A.B., 1954; Harvard University, Ph.D., 1960. *Office:* Graduate Center of the City University of New York, 33 West 42nd St., New York, N.Y. 10036.

CAREER: Yale University, New Haven, Conn., assistant professor of psychology, 1960-63; Harvard University, Cambridge, Mass., assistant professor of social psychology, 1963-67, executive director of comparative international program for department of social relations, 1966-67; City University of New York, New York City, professor of psychology, 1967-79, Distinguished Professor of Psychology, 1980—. Consultant, Polaroid Corp., Cambridge, 1977. *Member:* American Association for the Advancement of Science (fellow, 1971), American Psychological Association, Association of Independent Film and Television Producers.

AWARDS, HONORS: Ford Foundation fellowship, 1954-55; Harvard University fellowship, 1955-57; Social Science Research Council fellowship, 1957-59; American Association for the Advancement of Science socio-psychological prize, 1964, for experiments examining obedience to authority; grant from CBS, Inc., 1969-72, to study effects of television violence; Guggenheim fellowship, 1972-73, to study psychological maps of Paris; New York International Film and Television Festival silver medal, 1974, for *The City and Self;* National Book Award nomination, 1975, for *Obedience to Authority.*

WRITINGS: (With R. Lance Shotland) *Television and Anti-Social Behavior,* Academy Press, 1973; *Obedience to Authority: An Experimental View,* Harper, 1974; (editor) *Psychology in Today's World,* Little, 1975; *The Individual in a Social World: Essays and Experiments,* Addison-Wesley, 1977.

Films: "Obedience," 1968; "The City and the Self," 1974; "Conformity and Independence," 1974; "Invitation to Social Psychology," 1974; "Human Aggression," 1976; "Nonverbal Communication," 1976.

WORK IN PROGRESS: A study of social influence among siblings, with brother, Dr. Joel Milgram; "experimental studies of 'cyranoids'—persons who repeat word-for-word the messages transmitted to them by another individual by means of a radio transmitter."

SIDELIGHTS: Milgram is recognized as one of the foremost social psychologists for his experiments on human conformity and aggression, and is undoubtedly best known for his exper-

iments on obedience, the results of which are documented in his book *Obedience to Authority.*

In the first chapter of his book, Milgram discusses obedience, noting: "Obedience is as basic an element in the structure of social life as one can point to. Some system of authority is a requirement of all communal living, and it is only the man dwelling in isolation who is not forced to respond, through defiance or submission, to the commands of others." Using Hitler and the Nazi Party to exemplify submission to authority, Milgram reminds us that the mass slaughter of millions of people was the idea of just one man, Hitler, and that the killings would not have happened if people had not obeyed Hitler's orders. Milgram concludes: "Facts of recent history and observation in daily life suggest that for many people obedience may be a deeply ingrained behavior tendency, indeed a prepotent impulse overriding training in ethics, sympathy, and moral conduct."

In Milgram's famous test to determine if obedience supersedes moral and ethical consciousness, a laboratory technician instructed a subject to give a verbal test to a learner and to punish incorrect answers by administering electric shocks of increasing voltage to the learner. The learner, actually an actor, received no shocks at all, but simulated responses to the shocks supposedly administered by the test subject. The learner responded to low-voltage shocks with a groan and begged for release as the shocks worsened. If the subject hesitated to continue, the technician ordered him or her to proceed, assuring the subject that the technician himself would assume full responsibility for any harm done. Despite the screams of the learner and the hesitancy of the subjects, two-thirds of those tested obeyed the technician's command to continue, all the while believing the learner was being harmed. Some of the subjects nearly broke down from the strain of the test, but even they persisted.

Milgram concluded that the "most fundamental lesson" of his study is that "ordinary people, simply doing their jobs, and without any particular hostility on their part, can become agents in a terrible destructive process. Moreover, even when the destructive effects of their work become patently clear, and they are asked to carry out actions incompatible with fundamental standards of morality, relatively few people have the resources needed to resist authority."

Milgram was both praised and criticized for this study of human behavior. The American Association for the Advancement of Science applauded the psychologist's work, but some critics claimed his experiment was immoral and unethical because it placed people in extremely stressful situations that could be psychologically harming. Nevertheless, few reviewers denied the test's impact. P. S. Prescott of *Newsweek* commented: "We can argue that the experiments were cruel and should not have been undertaken. We can question whether much truth can be abstracted from . . . deception. . . . But the results of the experiment remain: they are real, they have been repeated, their implications are appalling, and they must not be dismissed." A *Times Literary Supplement* reviewer wrote: "If it is immoral to find out about ourselves in a way we do not like, these experiments are certainly immoral. But then, as the experiments show, morality—at least in its public form—may have quite a lot to answer for."

Milgram told *CA:* "Social psychologists are part of the very social matrix they have chosen to analyze, and thus they can use their experience as a source of insight. The difficulty is to do this in a way that does not drain life of its spontaneity and pleasure. A further aim is to try to find within the particularity of human experience, laws that are general and enduring."

BIOGRAPHICAL/CRITICAL SOURCES: Stanley Milgram, *Obedience to Authority: An Experimental View,* Harper, 1974; *New York Times Book Review,* January 13, 1974; *Newsweek,* January 28, 1974; *Washington Post Book World,* February 3, 1974; *Times Literary Supplement,* June 7, 1974; *Spectator,* July 20, 1974; *Virginia Quarterly Review,* summer, 1974.

*   *   *

MILLER, J. Dale 1923-

PERSONAL: Born February 25, 1923, in Penrose, Utah; son of J. H. and Amanda S. Miller; married wife, Ramona S., June 5, 1947 (marriage ended, 1979); married wife, Geraldine A., July 6, 1979; children: (first marriage) Stephen S., Mary Ann Miller Pearson, Paul W., Dalynn Miller Herd. *Education:* Brigham Young University, A.B., 1947; University of Utah, M.A., 1951, Ph.D., 1964; also attended University of Michigan, Yale University, and Sorbonne, University of Paris. *Politics:* Republican. *Religion:* Church of Jesus Christ of Latter-day Saints (Mormons). *Home:* 2996 Cherokee Lane, Provo, Utah 84601. *Office:* Weidner Communications, 1673 West 820 N., Provo, Utah 84601.

CAREER: State Department of Public Instruction, Salt Lake City, Utah, foreign language specialist, 1959-64; U.S. Department of State, Washington, D.C., regional language supervisor at U.S. embassy in Mexico City, Mexico, 1964-68; Brigham Young University, Provo, Utah, associate professor of modern languages, 1968-76; Weidner Communications, Provo, terminologist, 1977—. Mormon missionary in France; high school teacher; certified language tester, field interviewer, and trainer for Foreign Service Institute; director of Spanish tutors at U.S. embassies and consulates in Latin America; director of Institute of Languages, Port-of-Spain, Trinidad. *Military service:* U.S. Army, 1943-46. *Member:* American Translators Association, National Education Association, National Association of State Foreign Language Supervisors (executive secretary), Utah Foreign Language Teachers Association (president).

WRITINGS: The Visual Adjunct in Foreign Language Teaching, Chilton, 1965; *One Thousand Spanish Idioms,* Brigham Young University Press, 1970, 2nd edition, 1972; *Color Contrasted French and English Sounds,* Brigham Young University Press, 1971; *Multiculture Capsules,* Culture Contrasts Co., 1974; (with Maurice Loiseau) *U.S.A.-France Culture Capsules,* Culture Contrasts Co., 1974; (co-author) *Anglo-Navajo Culture Capsules,* Culture Contrasts Co., 1974; (with Russell H. Bishop) *U.S.A.-Mexico Culture Capsules,* Culture Contrasts Co., 1974, Newbury House, 1977; (with Kaylinda B. Essig) *Seven Hundred French Idioms,* Brigham Young University Press, 1976; (co-author) *U.S.A.-Hispanic South America Culture Capsules,* Newbury House, 1979. Also author of *French Teaching Aids,* 1972, and *Foreign Language Idea File,* 1973.

WORK IN PROGRESS: Research on a comprehensive indexing system for a two-million-word list of technical terminology.

*   *   *

MILLER, Jerome K. 1931-

PERSONAL: Born April 18, 1931, in Great Bend, Kan.; son of Walter J. and Kathleen M. (Kliesen) Miller. *Education:* Emporia State University, B.A., 1965; University of Michigan, A.M.L.S., 1966; University of Kansas, M.A., 1973; University of Colorado, Ed.D., 1976. *Home:* 2111 Galen Dr., Champaign, Ill. 61820. *Office:* Graduate School of Library and In-

formation Science, University of Illinois, 410 David Kinley Hall, 1407 West Gregory Dr., Urbana, Ill. 61801.

CAREER: Bouillon Library, Central Washington University, Ellensburg, bibliographic searcher, 1967-68, cataloger, 1968-70, coordinator of audiovisual library services, 1970-74; University of Illinois, Urbana, lecturer, 1975-76, supervisor of Learning Resources Laboratory, 1975-79, assistant professor of library science, 1976—, member of Graduate School of Library and Information Science executive committee, 1976-77, chairman of doctoral committee, 1977-81, chairman of remodeling committee, 1978-79, chairman of curriculum committee, 1980-81, member of search committee for the selection of the Director of Visual Aids Service, 1978. Member of advisory board of Center for Ecumenical Campus Ministry, Ellensburg, Washington, 1971-73, chairman, 1972-73; member of lay advisory board of Ellensburg Public Schools, 1973-74.

MEMBER: American Association of University Professors, American Library Association (member of board of directors of Library and Information Technology Association, Video and Cable Communications Technical Standards Committee, 1976-77, Statistics for Nonprint Media committee, 1976-77, Audiovisual Section nominating committee, 1977, Ad hoc Copyright Advisory subcommittee, 1978, School Media Quarterly Editorial Committee), Consortium of University Film Centers (archivist, 1971-1978, member of data bank committee, 1971-75, chairman of copyright committee, 1974-76), Washington Association for Educational Communications and Technology (member of planning committee, 1971, membership committee, 1971-73, Nonprint Purchase Specifications committee, 1972-75), Washington Library Association (member of continuing education committee, 1973-74), Educational Film Library Association, Illinois Library Association, Kiwanis Club of Ellensburg (member of board of directors, 1970-74, second vice-president, 1973, first vice-president, 1974), Phi Alpha Theta, Phi Delta Kappa.

AWARDS, HONORS: Okoboji fellowship from Association for Educational Communications and Technology, 1975; Educational Press Association of America distinguished achievement award, 1976, for "Copyright Today."

WRITINGS: Applying the New Copyright Law: A Guide for Educators and Librarians, American Library Association, 1979; *U.S. Copyright Documents: Selected, Annotated, and Indexed for Use by Educators and Librarians,* Libraries Unlimited, 1981. Author of "Copyright Today," a column in *Audiovisual Instruction.* Contributor to library journals.

WORK IN PROGRESS: A book and several articles on school district copyright policies.

SIDELIGHTS: Miller told *CA:* "My interest in copyright began by accident in 1972 when Gerald R. Brong asked me to chair a new committee of the Washington (State) Association for Educational Communications and Technology that was to work on copyright matters. I knew very little about copyright, so I began reading everything I could find on the topic and found it fascinating. Two years later, I was asked to chair the Copyright Task Force for the Association for Educational Communications and Technology. That prompted me to write the 'Copyright Today' column in *Audiovisual Instruction.* Additional study and a dissertation on copyright followed. Since I completed my dissertation in 1976, I have written three books and several articles. Additional books and articles are in the writing or planning stages.

"My purpose in writing and speaking about copyright is to assist educators and librarians in understanding the copyright law and its implications for schools, colleges, and libraries. I am particularly anxious to help educators and librarians understand their rights and use them to the fullest.''

AVOCATIONAL INTERESTS: Gardening, walking.

* * *

MILLER, Marc S(cott) 1947-

PERSONAL: Born December 27, 1947, in Mount Vernon, N.Y.; son of Ben and Ruth (Ash) Miller. *Education:* Attended Lehigh University, 1965-66; Massachusetts Institute of Technology, B.S., 1969; Boston University, M.A., 1973, Ph.D., 1978. *Politics:* Anarchist. *Home:* 51 Davie Circle, Chapel Hill, N.C. 27514. *Office:* Institute for Southern Studies, 604 West Chapel Hill St., Durham, N.C. 27701.

CAREER: Citywide Coordinating Committee, Boston, Mass., desegregation monitor, 1975-76; Institute for Southern Studies, Durham, N.C., research director, 1977—. Assistant director of oral history program of Massachusetts Institute of Technology, 1975-77, and Boston University and Boston Center for Adult Education, both 1977. Member of North Carolina Committee on Occupational Safety and Health. *Member:* Organization of American Historians, Oral History Association, Science for the People.

WRITINGS: (Editor and contributor) *Working Live,* Pantheon, 1981; (co-editor with Pat Bryant) *Militarism and Human Needs,* Institute for Southern Studies, 1982; *The Irony of Victory,* University of Illinois Press, in press. Contributor of articles and reviews to magazines and newspapers, including *Radical Teacher, Boston After Dark,* and *New England Quarterly.* Member of editorial staff of *Southern Exposure,* 1977—.

SIDELIGHTS: Miller told *CA:* ''Writing is no excuse for doing; thinking is no excuse for acting; sidelights do not make a life.''

* * *

MILLER, Robert Moats 1924-

BRIEF ENTRY: Born November 16, 1924, in Evanston, Ill. American historian, educator, and author. Miller began teaching at University of North Carolina in 1956 and became a professor of U.S. history in 1966. His writings include *American Protestantism and Social Issues, 1919-1939* (University of North Carolina Press, 1958) and *How Shall They Hear Without a Preacher?: The Life of Ernest Fremont Tittle* (University of North Carolina Press, 1971). *Address:* Department of History, University of North Carolina, Chapel Hill, N.C. 27514. *Biographical/critical sources: Directory of American Scholars,* Volume I: *History,* 7th edition, Bowker, 1978.

* * *

MILLER, Teresa 1952-

PERSONAL: Born November 23, 1952, in Tahlequah, Okla.; daughter of William Wesley (a lawyer) and Jean (Crane) Miller. *Education:* Northeastern Oklahoma State University, B.A., 1973, M.Ed., 1975. *Politics:* Democrat. *Religion:* Protestant. *Home address:* P.O. Box 395, Tahlequah, Okla. 74464. *Agent:* Virginia Barber and Mary Evans, 353 West 21st St., New York, N.Y. 10011.

CAREER: Writer. *Member:* Authors Guild.

WRITINGS: Remnants of Glory (novel), Seaview, 1981.

WORK IN PROGRESS: Alone Upon the Housetop, a novel.

SIDELIGHTS: Miller told *CA:* ''A fourth generation Oklahoman, I've always been surrounded by supreme storytellers. As a child, I enjoyed nothing more than listening to my grandparents' tales of early Oklahoma. Words like 'character' and 'backbone' were particular favorites, and I find them popping up in my own stories. This is particularly true of my first novel, *Remnants of Glory,* the memory book of ninety-year-old Kate Dexter. Kate's character and backbone are tested by circumstances unknown to my grandparents, but like them, she confronts everyday challenges with extraordinary grace. Whether battling racial prejudice, upholding the rights of her retarded child, or coming to terms with her own passions, Kate steadfastly adheres to a standard of human dignity.

''In recalling stories I've heard, I'm most interested in recapturing the way they were told. My grandmother's accounts of her early hardships are moving, but it's her active stance as a storyteller that brings them to life. When I write, the lesson from the past is not detail, but method. I disagree with those who would limit writers to cleverly disguised case histories of their own lives. More and more, I've come to rely on my imagination and am grateful for the freedom it allows. As long as I know my characters inside and out, I feel equipped to handle any event that befalls them. The wonderful aspect of fiction is the 'what if' factor, and I love the openness, the endless possibilities inherent in a novel.

''About the only thing I can't imagine is not writing at all. I began writing as a child, and my early writings focused on Tahlequah, my hometown. With stories such as 'Gidget Goes to Tahlequah,' 'Godzilla vs. Tahlequah,' 'The Road to Tahlequah,' I ran the gamut. It wasn't until I was in college that I tried writing seriously, too seriously. Mimicking the style of literary greats, I submitted my work to literary and professional magazines. I'd collected a stack of rejection slips before my first novel was accepted. I was totally unprepared for my publishing debut and had to rely on the patience of my editor. 'Be natural,' she'd tell me when I'd attempt to impress her with my loftiness. 'Relax and tell your story.' Without realizing it, she was directing me back to the free-flowing, simple style handed down to me by my grandparents. It was excellent advice.''

* * *

MILLICAN, Arthenia Jackson Bates 1920-

PERSONAL: Born June 1, 1920, in Sumter, S.C.; daughter of Calvin Shepard (an educator) and Susan Emma (a craftswoman; maiden name, David) Jackson; married Noah Bates, June 11, 1950 (divorced, 1956); married Wilbert Millican. *Education:* Morris College, B.A. (magna cum laude), 1941; Atlanta University, M.A., 1948; Louisiana State University, Ph.D., 1972. *Politics:* Democrat. *Religion:* Roman Catholic. *Home and office address:* Route 3, Box 286 G, Baker, La. 70714.

CAREER: High school English teacher in Kershaw, S.C., 1942-45; high school teacher of English and civics in Hartsville, S.C., 1945-46; Morris College, Sumter, S.C., head of department of English, 1947-49; high school English teacher in Halifax, Va., 1949-55; Mississippi Valley State University, Itta Bena, instructor in English, 1955-56; Southern University, Baton Rouge, La., instructor, 1956-59, assistant professor, 1959-63, associate professor, 1963-72, professor of English, 1972-74; Norfolk State University, Norfolk, Va., professor of English, 1974-77; Southern University, professor of English and creative writing, 1977-80. Writer. Instructor at American Youth Foundation's Camp Miniwanca, 1962, 1963. Member of board of directors of Community Advancement Incorporation for East Baton Rouge Parish, 1967-70.

MEMBER: National Council of Teachers of English, Conference on College Composition and Communication, College Language Association (life member; chairman of creative writing committee, 1974-75), Society for the Study of Southern Literature, Conference on Black South Literature and Arts, Louisiana Folklore Society, Gamma Sigma Sigma (chairman of advisory committee, 1959-64).

AWARDS, HONORS: First prize from College Language Association's creative writing contest, 1960, for "The Entertainers"; award of merit from McKendree Writers Association, 1962, for poem "Wishes"; certificate of merit from *Writer's Digest* and bronze medal from American Youth Foundation, both 1963; fiction award from National Endowment for the Arts, 1976, for story "Where You Belong"; award and presidential citation from National Association for Equal Opportunity in Higher Education, 1981.

WRITINGS: The Deity Nodded (novel), Harlo, 1973; *Seeds Beneath the Snow* (short stories), Greenwich Book Publishers, 1969; *Such Things From the Valley* (short stories), H. C. Young Press, 1977; (contributor) Therman B. O'Daniel, editor, *James Baldwin: A Critical Evaluation,* Howard University Press, 1977.

Work represented in anthologies, including *Poetry Broadcast,* 1946; *National Poetry Anthology,* 1958, 1962, 1963, 1973; *Poems by Blacks,* Volume III, edited by Pinkie Gordan Lane, South and West, 1975. Contributor of more than thirty-five articles, poems, stories, and reviews to magazines and newspapers, including *Negro Digest, Black World, Le Monde, Essence, Scriptiana,* and *Mahogany.* Contributing editor of *Obsidian: Black Literature in Review,* 1974-76, and *Callaloo,* 1976—.

WORK IN PROGRESS: Research for a sequel to *The Deity Nodded;* collecting humorous material "peculiar to a local area in southern Louisiana."

SIDELIGHTS: Arthenia Millican told *CA:* "One of the most difficult lessons for me to learn as a student of creative writing is the advice about slanting.

"An essay delivered as a speech eulogizing Langston Hughes soon after his death, entitled 'The Sun Legend: A Tribute to Langston Hughes,' seemed to me to be a masterpiece of slanting. It would be of interest to blacks because Hughes is the subject, and of interest to scholars because it is a research article with the rich allusions to Greek mythology, and of interest to everyone else because the theme is death.

"You know the audacity of young blacks during the sixties. A young black poet said, 'Your idea of finding what you call sun-sense in Hughes is alright. You try to explain his warmth in terms of the folk quality, the African ethos and the humane factor in general; but you messed it up by alluding to Greek mythology. Hughes would have appreciated your using Egyptian mythology.'

"What he did not understand, from my point of view, was that I was a student (anthology-read) of Greek literature. I had the right to allude to Phaeton, the son of Apollo, and the nymph Clymene. Had he asked me, 'What does Africa mean to you?,' I would have said 'nothing' because I had not come to know the joy of riding on the communal wave of the mother spirit that matured with the 'Roots' phenomenon.

"Almost twenty years have passed and I am just coming into the knowledge of what I hope he also understands.

"The oil rigs are being constructed here and there in the Baker community of East Baton Rouge Parish where I used to live.

A court case of slant-drilling against a driller seeking to cash in on this Tuscaloosa Trend opened my eyes. How rich are your unmined resources? Mine? How will you know unless you drill?

"Slant-drilling is illegally mining the resources of another. You may have the rig on your territory but the gold, that black splatter, comes from the other man's territory.

"I know what the young poet was trying to tell me about tradition and the individual talent."

BIOGRAPHICAL/CRITICAL SOURCES: Chantaqua Daily, July 24, 1962; *Baton Rouge News Leader,* February 9, 1969, March 15, 1970, June 14, 1970, August 13, 1972, December 23, 1973, January 13, 1974, May 19, 1974; *Baton Rouge Morning Advocate,* March 13, 1970; *Washington Afro-American,* June 2, 1970; *College Language Association Journal,* June, 1970, December, 1973; *Washington Post,* June 11, 1970; *Delta,* summer, 1970; *Norfolk Journal and Guide,* November 9, 1974; *Norfolk-Portsmouth Ledger Star,* November 18, 1974; *Freedom Ways,* November 11, 1975; *Virginian Pilot,* July 4, 1976, July 10, 1976, August 12, 1976; *Obsidian,* spring, 1977; *Essence,* July, 1980.

*   *   *

MINDELL, Earl L(awrence)   1940-

PERSONAL: Born January 20, 1940, in St. Boniface, Manitoba, Canada; came to United States, 1965; naturalized U.S. citizen, 1972; son of William (an executive) and Minerva Sybil (Galsky) Mindell; married Gail Andrea Jaffe, May 16, 1971; children: Alanna Dayan, Evan Louis-Ashley. *Education:* North Dakota State University, B.S., 1964; University of Beverly Hills, Ph.D., 1980. *Home:* 709 North Hillcrest Rd., Beverly Hills, Calif. 90210. *Agent:* Richard Curtis Associates, Inc., 156 East 52nd St., New York, N.Y. 10022. *Office:* Natural Organics Inc., 15010 Keswick St., Van Nuys, Calif. 91405.

CAREER: Kis-Min Inc. (retail pharmacy), Los Angeles, Calif., president, 1965-70; Natural Organics Inc. (vitamin chain), Los Angeles, secretary/treasurer, 1970—; Adanac Management Inc., Beverly Hills, Calif., president, 1979—. Instructor for Dale Carnegie courses, 1974—; lecturer. Member of board of directors of Western Los Angeles Chamber of Commerce, 1979—. Consultant to Great Earth International in Irvine, Calif. *Member:* International Nutritional Consultants Association, International College of Applied Nutrition, American Pharmaceutical Association, American Academy of General Pharmaceutical Practice, American Institute of the History of Pharmacy, American Nutrition Society, American Dieticians Association, National Health Federation, Orthomolecular Medical Association, California Pharmacists Association, Nutrition Foundation, City of Hope, Almaliakah Shrine, Scottishrine, Masons, Sportsmen's Club.

WRITINGS: Earl Mindell's Vitamin Bible, Rawson-Wade, 1979; *Earl Mindell's Vitamin Bible for Your Kids,* Rawson-Wade, 1981. Author of syndicated column "Know Your Vitamins," 1980—. Contributor of articles to journals.

SIDELIGHTS: Mindell told *CA:* "Dale Carnegie's course 'How to Win Friends and Influence People' was a very big influence in my life. Other positive thinking authors such as Napoleon Hill, Zig Zigler, Norman Vincent Peale, and Earl Nightingale have also been major influences."

BIOGRAPHICAL/CRITICAL SOURCES: Family Circle, April, 1981.

MIREPOIX, Camille   1926-
(Adastra)

PERSONAL: Surname is pronounced Meer-*pwa;* born March 24, 1926, in Manchester, England; married Robert Mirepoix (an artist; deceased); married August George Stegmuller (a schoolmaster) in 1973; children: (first marriage) Fanchon Camille (Mrs. George Canfield). *Education:* Received B.A. *Politics:* Democrat. *Religion:* "Non-sectarian."

CAREER: Journalist, author, and photographer. Advertising manager for *Mexican Life;* in public relations in Cozumel, Mexico; travel and tourism editor for *Intercontinental Horizons,* Beirut, Lebanon; has also worked abroad as a receptionist.

WRITINGS—For children; published by Sterling: *Lebanon in Pictures,* 1969; *Kuwait in Pictures,* 1970; *Afghanistan in Pictures,* 1971; *Liberia in Pictures,* 1971; *Egypt in Pictures,* 1973.

Contributor of vignettes, occasionally under pseudonym Adastra, and numerous articles to periodicals, including *Saturday Evening Post, Herald Tribune, London Times,* and *Cosmopolitan.*

WORK IN PROGRESS: A book set in Mexico in 1943, *Glory for Fanchon,* about a child who wanted to be a diplomat; *Round the World Adventures of a Grandmother,* a pictorial autobiography.

SIDELIGHTS: Mirepoix told *CA:* "I always wanted to write, and I sold my first story to a magazine called the *Gem* when I was seven years old. The guinea I received as a prize was worth five-and-a-half dollars in those days. The story was a good, small, historical story relating to the railway stations in England. When I was nine my second story won a prize from the late Arthur Mee's children's newspaper.

"I became a successful writer through my world travels. I went around the world on a shoestring, writing articles for peanuts to pay for the next freighter reaching Japan, Russia, and all of Europe. In Thailand I made friends with the great James Michener. I traveled all through Africa and loved every minute of it. I knew French and I also picked up Spanish, Portuguese, and Swahili. When I acquired the art of hiring myself out as a receptionist in swank hotels catering to rich American tourists, I traveled on a silver-plated shoestring. It was fun in such countries as Spain and Portugal hearing the Smiths and Joneses from New York say, 'Isn't that young receptionist friendly, and did you hear her good English?' I was invited to the homes of the other employees and learned to love the people of those lands. I'd write articles daily for the local press and got a kick out of being called a 'famous journalist from England.'

"Eventually I reached the Middle East and discovered the quality of both Christian-Arabs and Moslems. They were all wonderful and still are my friends. I traveled to Lebanon, Egypt, Kuwait, and Jordan. I met King Hussein several times and became a family friend. For my book *Kuwait in Pictures,* I received a personal gift from the Sheikh of Kuwait—a fabulous sapphire and pearl necklace, ring, earring, and bracelet set. I was so scared about having them, I asked the American ambassador in Kuwait whether it was right to accept them. He told me it would be insulting not to. Who am I to insult a sheikh?

"I have been an honorary citizen in Jordan, Kuwait, and Lebanon, and I have been a welcome friend in all the lands I lived in and wrote about. I have recorded my experiences in countless articles, and I have just finished research on a giant book of the Middle East, contributing material on Yemen, Oman, Bahrain, and the United Arab Emirates. It will incorporate all my other Middle East books."

BIOGRAPHICAL/CRITICAL SOURCES: Mexico City News, August 24, 1969.

* * *

MITCHELL, Curtis Cornelius, Jr.   1927-

PERSONAL: Born November 26, 1927, in St. Louis, Mo.; son of Curtis Cornelius and Cora Adlenine (Craddock) Mitchell; married Patricia Ann Sterrenburg; children: Susan Marie (Mrs. David Coleman), Richard James, Debra Jean. *Education:* Biola College, B.A. (magna cum laude), 1957; Talbot Theological Seminary, B.D., 1962; Western Baptist Seminary, Th.M., 1963; Grace Theological Seminary, Th.D., 1968. *Home:* 14818 Mansa Dr., La Mirada, Calif. 90638. *Office:* Department of Biblical Studies, Biola College, 13800 Biola Ave., La Mirada, Calif. 90638.

CAREER: Ordained minister of Progressive Brethren, 1957; pastor of Progressive Brethren church in Bellflower, Calif., 1953-55, associate pastor in North Long Beach, Calif., 1956-62; pastor of Baptist churches in Gladstone, Ore., 1963, and Warsaw, Ind., 1964-65; Biola College, La Mirada, Calif., professor of biblical studies, 1966—. *Military service:* U.S. Navy, 1946-48. *Member:* Evangelical Theological Society, Delta Epsilon, Kiwanis.

WRITINGS: God in the Garden: The Story of the Billy Graham New York Crusade, Doubleday, 1957; *Billy Graham: The Making of a Crusader,* Chilton, 1966; *Those Who Came Forward: An Account of Those Whose Lives Were Changed by the Ministry of Billy Graham,* Chilton, 1966; *Let's Live!: Christ in Everyday Life,* Revell, 1975; *Praying Jesus' Way: A New Approach to Personal Prayer,* Revell, 1977; *Billy Graham: Saint or Sinner?,* Revell, 1979. Also author of *The Billy Graham London Crusade,* 1966.

Children's books: *The Early Miracles of Jesus,* Doubleday, 1958; *The Crucifixion,* Doubleday, 1959; *Jesus Spreads His Gospel,* Doubleday, 1961; *The Birth of Christ,* Doubleday, 1963. Contributor to religious journals.*

* * *

MITCHELL, John D(avid) B(awden)   1917-1980

OBITUARY NOTICE: Born May 28, 1917, in England; died December 19, 1980, in Edinburgh, Scotland. Lawyer, educator, and author. A noted British attorney, Mitchell was long associated with the University of Edinburgh, serving as Professor to the Chair of Constitutional Law, and heading the university's Centre of European Governmental Studies and Salvesen Chair of European Institutions from the late 1960's until his death. Mitchell's numerous writings include *The Contracts of Public Authorities,* in which he compared the laws of government contracts in England, France, and the United States, and *Constitutional Law,* a study of the laws of Scotland. Obituaries and other sources: *Who's Who,* 126th edition, St. Martin's, 1974; *Who's Who in the World,* 3rd edition, Marquis, 1976; *The Annual Obituary 1980,* St. Martin's, 1981.

* * *

MOERMAN, Daniel E(llis)   1941-

PERSONAL: Born July 21, 1941, in Paterson, N.J.; son of

H. Ellis (an engineer) and Doris (Marti) Moerman; married Marquisa LaVelle Smith (a college professor), December 31, 1969; children: Jennifer Theresa. *Education:* University of Michigan, A.B., 1963, M.A., 1965, Ph.D., 1974. *Politics:* "Secular humanist." *Home:* 1316 Culver Rd., Ann Arbor, Mich. 48103. *Office:* Department of Behavioral Sciences, University of Michigan—Dearborn, 4901 Evergreen, Dearborn, Mich. 48128.

CAREER: Antioch College, Yellow Springs, Ohio, instructor in anthropology, 1967-70; University of Michigan—Dearborn, instructor, 1972-73, assistant professor, 1973-78, associate professor of anthropology, 1978—. *Member:* American Anthropological Association (fellow), Society for Medical Anthropology, Ethnopharmacological Society, Central States Anthropological Association.

WRITINGS: American Medical Ethnobotany: A Reference Dictionary, Garland Publishing, 1977; *Geraniums for the Iroquois: A Field Guide to American Indian Medicinal Plants,* Reference Publications, 1981; (with Lola Romanucci-Rose and Lawrence Tancredi) *The Anthropology of Medicine,* Bergin, 1982. Contributor to scholarly journals.

SIDELIGHTS: Moerman commented: "My attraction to medicine came quite by accident, while I was pursuing anthropological research in South Carolina (the Sea Islands) in 1970. Since then, I have pursued native American herbalism and the process of healing in more general terms.

"I have been deliberately interested in writing for only a few years. Most of my earlier work was concerned much more with substance than with style; *American Medical Ethnobotany,* for instance, is unreadable—it is a dictionary, and a very useful one at that. But such utility is really only appropriate for specialists or true aficionados. Lately I have been trying to reach a broader audience with material that is still solid and informative, but more accessible. It is very hard to take complicated ideas and make them understandable without trivializing them. The only technique I have been able to develop is to set particular goals with deadlines, and then use the pressure this causes as motivation to do it until it works.

"I am now considering a book on the nature of the whole healing process—again, a very complicated subject easily trivialized. At the moment, I haven't set any goals or deadlines!"

* * *

MOFFATT, Doris 1919-

PERSONAL: Born May 18, 1919, in Pittsburgh, Pa.; daughter of Walter H. (a carpenter) and Elsie (Trainer) Armerbaugh; married George E. Moffatt (a valve service engineer), November 24, 1938; children: Joanne Moffatt Gill. *Education:* Attended Rider College and Mercer County Community College. *Religion:* Presbyterian. *Residence:* Lawrenceville, N.J.

CAREER: H. J. Heinz Co., Pittsburgh, Pa., secretary, 1937-38; General Motors Corp., Pittsburgh, secretary, 1952; G. Norman Burke Agency, Pittsburgh, secretary and copywriter for radio commercials, 1954-55; St. Paul United Methodist Church, Trenton, N.J., secretary, 1960-62. Bible teacher. Member of Lawrence Township Human Relations Advisory Council and Cable Television Origination Advisory Board (secretary, 1981). *Member:* Christian Writers Guild, Philadelphia Writers Conference (associate member).

WRITINGS: Christian Meditation the Better Way, Christian Herald, 1979. Author of "A Woman's Day" (play), first pro-

duced by local church group. Songwriter. Contributor to local newspapers.

WORK IN PROGRESS: As a Butterfly . . . , poems; a children's book, lessons in life drawn from incidents in the lives of birds.

SIDELIGHTS: Doris Moffatt wrote: "Having been a Christian meditator for fourteen years now, I felt compelled to write on the subject for our time. I am interested in bettering the quality of life for mankind. We are products of what we see and hear; therefore, good literature helps develop good people and circumstances. I am both an enthusiastic and intense personality, appreciating the world around me."

AVOCATIONAL INTERESTS: Exercise, natural foods cookery, amateur dramatics.

* * *

MOGULOF, Melvin B(ernard) 1926-

PERSONAL: Born June 17, 1926, in New York, N.Y.; son of Nathan and Ida (Platkin) Mogulof; married Mildred Goldfarb (a social worker), June 3, 1956; children: Daniel, Dena. *Education:* University of Denver, B.S., 1949; Syracuse University, M.A., 1950; University of Connecticut, M.A., 1956; Brandeis University, Ph.D., 1963. *Religion:* Jewish. *Home:* 105 Mt. Lassen Dr., San Rafael, Calif. 94903.

CAREER: Assistant director of Springfield Jewish Community Center, 1956-61; U.S. Department of Health, Education, and Welfare, Washington, D.C., community organization and training center specialist, 1963-64; Office of Economic Opportunity, San Francisco, Calif., regional director of community action, 1964-66; U.S. Department of Housing and Urban Development, San Francisco, regional director of model cities, 1966-68; San Francisco State College, San Francisco, associate professor of social work, 1968-69; Urban Institute, Washington, D.C., senior researcher, 1969-74; Federation of Jewish Philanthropies, New York, N.Y., executive director for community services, 1974-76; free-lance consultant on social program development and evaluation. Senior Fulbright lecturer in England, 1971, and Israel, 1976. Director of President's Advisory Council on Executive Organization, and Social Services Task Force, both 1970; member of advisory committee of New York City Department of Social Services and distribution committee of Greater New York Fund. *Military service:* U.S. Army, 1944-46; became sergeant.

WRITINGS: Citizen Participation: A Review and Commentary on Federal Policies and Practices, Urban Institute (Washington, D.C.), 1969; *Citizen Participation: The Local Perspective,* Urban Institute (Washington, D.C.), 1970; *Interagency Coordination in Federal Regional Councils,* Urban Institute (Washington, D.C.), 1971; *Governing Metropolitan Areas,* Urban Institute (Washington, D.C.), 1971; *Five Metropolitan Governments,* Urban Institute (Washington, D.C.), 1972; *Saving the Coast: California's Experiment in Inter-Government Land Use Regulation,* Lexington Books, 1975.

Contributor: Lee Burchinal, editor, *Rural Youth in Crisis,* U.S. Department of Health, Education, and Welfare, 1964; W. E. Amos and C. F. Welford, editors, *Delinquency Prevention,* Prentice-Hall, 1966; Roland Warren, editor, *Politics in the Ghettos,* Atherton Press, 1969; *Proceedings,* Columbia University Press, 1969; Loewenberg and Dolgoff, editors, *The Practice of Social Intervention,* Peacock, 1972; Richard W. Saxe, editor, *Opening the Schools,* McCutchan, 1972; Melvin Urofsky, editor, *Perspectives on Urban America,* Doubleday,

1973; *Sub-State Regionalism,* U.S. Advisory Commission on Inter-Governmental Relations, 1973; Kent Mathewson, editor, *The Regionalist Papers,* Metropolitan Fund, 1974. Also contributor to *Encyclopedia of Social Work,* 1971.

Contributor to *Urban Institute Publications* (Washington, D.C.), 1969-73, and to *Jerusalem Post,* 1977-78. Contributor of articles to professional journals, including *Social Service Review, Social Work, American Behavioral Scientist, Urban Affairs Quarterly, Urban and Social Change Review,* and *Community Mental Health Journal.*

* * *

MONRO, Gavin
See MONRO-HIGGS, Gertrude

* * *

MONROE, Carole 1944-
(Carole Dufrechou)

PERSONAL: Born May 18, 1944, in New Orleans, La.; daughter of Vivian Kussman; divorced, 1976. *Education:* Louisiana State University, New Orleans, B.A., 1966. *Residence:* New York, N.Y. *Agent:* Maria Carvainis Agency, 235 West End Ave., New York, N.Y. 10023. *Office:* United Media Enterprises, 200 Park Ave., New York, N.Y. 10166.

CAREER: Random House, Inc., New York City, publicity associate, 1971-74; Quick Fox/Music Sales (book publishers), New York City, director of publicity, promotion, and advertising, 1974-77; United Media Enterprises (United Feature Syndicate/Newspaper Enterprise Association), New York City, public relations manager, 1978—. *Member:* Publishers Publicity Association, Publishers Advertising Club, National Cable Television Association.

WRITINGS: (Under name Carole Dufrechou) *Neil Young,* Quick Fox, 1978; (with Lazar Cedeno and Olinda Cedeno) *The Exercise Plus Pregnancy Program,* Morrow, 1980.

WORK IN PROGRESS: A biography of dancer and choreographer Carol Haney.

* * *

MONRO-HIGGS, Gertrude 1905-
(Gavin Monro)

PERSONAL: Born April 25, 1905, in Wimbledon, England; daughter of Walter (in military) and Jessie E. (Coles) Monro-Higgs. *Education:* Attended Bedford College, London. *Politics:* Conservative. *Home:* Holmleigh, Kentwyns Dr., Kerves Lane, Horsham, Sussex RH13 6EU, England.

CAREER: Teacher in Brondesbury, England, 1930-38; Causeway School, Horsham, England, teacher, 1938-57, principal, 1938-57; writer, 1957—. *Member:* Crime Writers Association, West Sussex Writers Club (chairman, 1972-74).

*WRITINGS—*Crime novels; under pseudonym Gavin Monro: *Who Killed Amanda?,* R. Hale, 1967; *A Bent for Blackmail,* R. Hale, 1967; *Marked With a Cross,* R. Hale, 1968; *Trip to Eternity,* R. Hale, 1970.

Also author of *Annabel and the Others* (children's poems). Work represented in anthologies, including *Christian Poetry,* 1976; *Twenty Poems,* West Sussex Federation of Women's Institutes; *The Fireside Book for 1979.* Contributor of poems and stories to adult and juvenile magazines, including *Good Housekeeping, Field, Sussex Life,* and *Woman's Own.*

WORK IN PROGRESS: Fifth crime novel.

BIOGRAPHICAL/CRITICAL SOURCES: West Sussex Gazette, November 8, 1979.

* * *

MONTAGUE, Jeanne
See YARDE, Jeanne Betty Frances Treasure

* * *

MONTALBANO, William Daniel 1940-

PERSONAL: Born September 20, 1940, in New York, N.Y.; son of Vincent Francis (an executive) and Gertrude Mary (a teacher; maiden name, Reilly) Montalbano; married first wife, Kathleen, June 19, 1965 (divorced July, 1977); married Rosanna Mary Bell Thomson (a writer), December 3, 1977; children: (first marriage) Dennis, Andrea; (second marriage) Tiva, Theresa. *Education:* Rutgers University, B.A., 1960; Columbia University, M.S., 1962; graduate study at Universidad Nacional de Buenos Aires, 1964-65, and Harvard University, 1969-70. *Home:* 721 Catalonia, Coral Gables, Fla. 33134. *Agent:* Esther Newberg, c/o International Creative Management, 40 West 57th St., New York, N.Y. 10019. *Office: Miami Herald,* 1 Herald Pl., Miami, Fla. 33101.

CAREER: Star-Ledger, Newark, N.J., reporter, 1960-62; *Patriot Ledger,* Quincy, Mass., deskman, 1962-63; *Buenos Aires Herald,* Buenos Aires, Argentina, reporter, 1964-65; United Press International (UPI), New York City, worked on cables desk, 1965-67; *Miami Herald,* Miami, Fla., correspondent in Latin America, 1967-76, senior correspondent, 1977—, projects editor, 1978-79, chief of correspondents, 1981—; Knight-Ridder Newspapers, Beijing, People's Republic of China, bureau chief, 1979-81.

AWARDS, HONORS: Overseas Press Club citation, 1969 and 1971, for foreign reporting excellence, and 1973, for best interpretation of foreign news; Tom Wallace Award from International-American Press Association, 1971; Maria Moors Cabot prize from Columbia University, 1974; Ernie Pyle Award, 1975; Heywood Brown prize from the Newspaper Guild, 1980; public service awards from the National Headliner's Club and Sigma Delta Chi, both 1980.

WRITINGS: (With Carl Hiaasen) *Powder Burn* (novel), Atheneum, 1981.

WORK IN PROGRESS: Bluelight, a psychological novel about a Key West crawfisherman, with Carl Hiaasen, completion expected in early 1982.

SIDELIGHTS: Powder Burn, Montalbano's first novel, is set in Miami, Fla., and is based on actual episodes that have occurred there during the Cuban-Columbian cocaine wars of recent years. The story concerns an architect, Christopher Meadows, who witnesses a shoot-out between rival drug dealers, during which Meadows's ex-girlfriend and her daughter are accidentally killed. Frightened, but ultimately enraged, Meadows plots revenge based on intellect, while he himself is stalked by the murderers and the Miami police.

Commenting on *Powder Burn,* Sloan Wilson of the *Orlando Sentinel Star* wrote: "This first effort by two fine reporters is . . . successful in entertaining and educating the reader simultaneously."

BIOGRAPHICAL/CRITICAL SOURCES: Orlando Sentinel Star, September 20, 1981; *New York Times Book Review,* January 10, 1982.

MONTEY, Vivian M(arie) 1956-

PERSONAL: Born May 7, 1956, in St. Joseph, Mo.; daughter of James Walter, Sr. and Jacqueline (in real estate; maiden name, Hurley) Williams; married Keith D. Montey, Jr. (a roofing contractor), November 29, 1974; children: Blake David, Hannah Marie. *Education:* Attended high school in Greeley, Colo. *Home:* 26445 Road 25, Milliken, Colo. 80543.

CAREER: Teacher's aide at elementary school in Greeley, Colo., 1974-77; Bonnie Brown Dean, Inc., Greeley, secretary, 1977-78; writer, 1978—. Member of Cesarean Support Group of Greeley.

WRITINGS: (With Gayle Cunningham Baker) *Special Delivery: A Book for Kids About Cesarean and Vaginal Birth,* Charles Franklin Press, 1981.

SIDELIGHTS: Vivian Montey commented: "Gayle Baker and I were roommates in the hospital following the Cesarean deliveries of our sons in 1978. Neither of us could find much information to help Cesarean parents and *nothing* to explain Cesarean delivery to our children. We decided to do something about it, and worked on our book in our spare time for over two years, finally coming up with a text we felt happy with."

*   *   *

MONTGOMERIE, Norah (Mary) 1913-

PERSONAL: Born April 6, 1913, in London, England; married William Montgomerie (a poet and authority on Scottish folk-songs), 1934; children: one son, one daughter. *Education:* Attended Putney School of Art.

CAREER: Free-lance artist in London, England; illustrator at publishing company in Scotland. Worked in evacuation camp school.

WRITINGS—Juvenile; all published by Abelard, except as noted: (With husband, William Montgomerie) *The Will at the World's End,* Hogarth Press, 1956; *Twenty-Five Fables,* self-illustrated, 1961; *Other Brother,* illustrated by Laura N. Baker, 1962; *The Merry Little Fox, and Other Animal Stories,* self-illustrated, 1964; *One, Two, Three: A Little Book of Counting Rhymes,* self-illustrated, 1968.

Editor: (With W. Montgomerie) *Scottish Nursery Rhymes,* illustrated by T. Ritchie, Hogarth Press, 1946, published as *A Book of Scottish Nursery Rhymes,* Oxford University Press, 1966 (also see below); *Sandy Candy, and Other Scottish Nursery Rhymes,* self-illustrated, Hogarth Press, 1948 (also see below); (with Kathleen Lines) *Poems and Pictures,* self-illustrated, Abelard, 1959; *To Read and to Tell,* illustrated by Margery Gill, Bodley Head, 1962, published as *To Read and To Tell: An Anthology of Stories for Children,* Arco, 1964; (with W. Montgomerie) *The Hogarth Book of Scottish Nursery Rhymes* (illustrated by T. Ritchie; contains *Scottish Nursery Rhymes* and *Sandy Candy, and Other Scottish Nursery Rhymes*), Hogarth Press, 1964; *This Little Pig Went to Market: Play Rhymes for Infants and Young Children,* illustrated by M. Gill, Bodley Head, 1966, F. Watts, 1967.

BIOGRAPHICAL/CRITICAL SOURCES: Times Literary Supplement, May 29, 1959, November 23, 1962, September 12, 1975; *Observer,* July 13, 1975; *Growing Point,* October, 1975.*

*   *   *

MOON, G(eoff) J. H. 1915-

PERSONAL: Born April 2, 1915, in Hankow, China; son of Reginald J. (an engineer) and Ethel (May) Moon; married wife, Ruth Mary, September 17, 1941; children: Christopher H., Jennifer, Nicholas J. D. *Education:* Royal Veterinary College, M.R.C.V.S., 1939, M.A.C.V.Sc., 1971. *Religion:* Anglican. *Address:* Box 60175, Titirangi, Auckland 7, New Zealand. *Agent:* Ray Richards, Richards Literary Agency, Box 31240, Milford, Auckland 9, New Zealand.

CAREER: In private veterinary practice in Ryde, Isle of Wight, England, 1939-74; Warkworth Veterinary Club, Warkworth, New Zealand, senior veterinarian, 1957-74. *Member:* New Zealand Veterinary Surgeons Board, New Zealand Veterinary Association (honorary life member). *Awards, honors:* Associateship of the Royal Photographic Society of London and the Photographic Society of New Zealand. *Military service:* Observer Corps, home guard coast defense battery, 1941-45; became lieutenant.

WRITINGS: Focus on New Zealand Birds, A. H. & A. W. Reed, 1960; *Refocus on New Zealand Birds,* A. H. & A. W. Reed, 1967; *Photographing Nature,* Tuttle, 1970; *The Birds Around Us,* Heinemann, 1979, revised edition, 1980; *Everyone's Guide to New Zealand Birds,* Heinemann, 1982.

WORK IN PROGRESS: Two books of color illustrations, *The Waikato River* and *The Natural World of the Maori,* publication of both expected in 1983.

SIDELIGHTS: Moon told *CA:* "Although I photograph and study wild birds, birds are not an important part of my veterinary practice. I am motivated to photograph and study them because there is still much research to be done on New Zealand birds and because much of their behavior and life histories are not adequately documented." *Avocational interests:* Ornithology, overseas travel, photography, boating, the outdoors, fishing.

*   *   *

MOORE, James R(ichard) 1947-

PERSONAL: Born March 13, 1947, in Oak Park, Ill.; son of Richard Albert (in business) and Ruth (Probert) Moore; married Susan Ann Sheldon, June 28, 1970 (divorced, 1980). *Education:* University of Illinois, B.S. (with high honors), 1968; Trinity Evangelical Divinity School, M.Div. (summa cum laude), 1972; Victoria University of Manchester, Ph.D., 1975. *Politics:* Marxist. *Religion:* Christian. *Home:* 83 Shrubland Rd., London E.8, England. *Office:* Faculty of Arts, Open University, Milton Keynes, Buckinghamshire, England.

CAREER: Open University, Milton Keynes, Buckinghamshire, England, lecturer in history of science and technology, 1975—. Editorial consultant for *The Collected Letters of Charles Darwin,* 1977—. Member of the Conference on Faith and History. *Member:* British Society for Social Responsibility in Science, British Society for the History of Science, American Scientific Affiliation, Phi Eta Sigma, Sigma Tau, Eta Kappa Nu, Tau Beta Pi, Phi Kappa Phi. *Awards, honors:* Marshall scholar in England, 1972-75.

WRITINGS: The Post-Darwinian Controversies: A Study of the Protestant Struggle to Come to Terms With Darwin in Great Britain and America, 1870-1900, Cambridge University Press, 1979; *Beliefs in Science: An Introduction,* Open University Press, 1981; *The Future of Science and Belief: Theological Views in the Twentieth Century,* Open University Press, 1981.

Scripts: "The X Club in Belfast, 1874," first broadcast by BBC-Radio, February 17, 1981; "Reflections on the Meaning of Evolution: A View Towards the Future," first broadcast by

BBC-Radio, September 29, 1981; "The Tennessee Evolution Trial," first broadcast by BBC-TV, September 9, 1981.

Correspondent for *Sojourners,* 1976-78. Contributor of more than forty articles and reviews to history and theology journals. Co-editor of *Trinity Studies,* 1970-72; contributing editor of *Post-American,* 1973-76.

WORK IN PROGRESS: Research on religion and society in the life and times of Charles Darwin, "with special reference to the cultural meaning of his death and obsequies"; research on the history of natural theology in science and society, "with special reference to the naturalization of value and belief systems in the biological and human sciences since 1800."

SIDELIGHTS: "From a maelstrom of fundamentalist religion and conservative politics I emerged in the early 1970's full of scholarly ambition and increasingly alienated from the values and beliefs of my youth. My first book (which Philip Toynbee found 'weighty yet provocative' in the *Observer* and another scholar said 'substantially alters the Victorian intellectual landscape' in *Victorian Studies*) was first conceived as an attempt to scotch the obscurantist approach to modern science by showing the historical affinities of Darwinism and orthodox Christian theology. Subsequently, however, I realized that the moral seriousness implicit in this undertaking might call into question the ideological foundations common to Christian beliefs and the scientific enterprise. Thus in recent years I have reaffirmed, as it were, my heritage of discussing moral questions in their own right, of politicizing religious and scientific debate, but from a perspective that can only be said to threaten radically the now-ascendant tradition in which I was raised."

*   *   *

MOORE, Marna
   See REYNOLDS, (Marjorie) Moira Davison

*   *   *

MOORE, Richard R.   1934-

PERSONAL: Born March 22, 1934, in McCamey, Tex.; son of Leon and Lucille (a journalist; maiden name, Gamble) Moore; married Karen Frack (a real estate broker), December 19, 1960; children: Eric Tracy, Patrick Cory, Kelley Sullivan. *Education:* Attended Texas A & M University, 1952-54; Texas Tech University, B.A., 1956, M.A., Ph.D., 1964. *Politics:* Republican. *Religion:* Methodist. *Home:* 144 Sinclair, Corpus Christi, Tex. 78411. *Office:* Department of History, Del Mar College, P.O. Box 273, Corpus Christi, Tex. 78404.

CAREER: Del Mar College, Corpus Christi, Tex., professor of history, 1964—. *Military service:* U.S. Army, 1956-58. *Member:* Coastal Bend Archeological Society (vice-president), South Texas Historical Society.

WRITINGS: West Texas Since the Discovery of Oil: A Modern Frontier, Pemberton Press, 1968. Contributor to *The Heritage of Texas,* Forum Press, 1980. Editor of *Journal of South Texas.*

WORK IN PROGRESS: Reconstruction History of Texas.

*   *   *

MOORHEAD, Diana   1940-

PERSONAL: Born May 28, 1940, in Horsell, Surrey, England; daughter of Arthur Frederick (a farmer and orchardist) and Maisie (a private secretary; maiden name, Allwork) Kinns; married Raymond John Moorhead (a high school teacher), April 22, 1961; children: Geoffrey Philip, Judith Diane. *Education:* Auckland University, B.A., 1961; New Zealand Library School, NZLA certificate, 1978. *Home:* 58 Yeovil Rd., Te Atatu, Auckland 8, New Zealand. *Office:* Massey High School, Private Bag, Massey, Auckland 8, New Zealand.

CAREER: Whitcombe and Tombs (booksellers), Auckland, New Zealand, sales assistant, 1961-62; Te Atatu Play Centre, Auckland, superviser, 1968; Massey High School, Auckland, librarian, 1969—. *Member:* New Zealand Library Association, Children's Literature Association (president, West Auckland branch, 1976-77), Book People, Auckland Secondary Schools Library Association, Wine and Food Society. *Awards, honors:* International Youth Library grant, 1978.

WRITINGS—Juveniles: *In Search of Magic,* Brockhampton Press, 1971; *The Green and the White,* Brockhampton Press, 1974; *Gull Man's Glory,* Hodder & Stoughton, 1976. Regular contributor to *Jabberwocky.*

WORK IN PROGRESS: The Harper, a juvenile fantasy; a reference book on fantasy books for children; more fantasy books for children.

SIDELIGHTS: Moorhead told *CA:* "Reading is my great love; I much prefer it to writing! But every now and then I become pregnant with a story, and nature has to take its course.

"I write fantasy partly because it's the best medium for what I want to say, and partly because I am fascinated by the process of building another world: the landscape, the customs, the history, and the people."

AVOCATIONAL INTERESTS: Traveling, history, good wine, cats.

*   *   *

MOOS, Malcolm C(harles)   1916-1982

OBITUARY NOTICE—See index for *CA* sketch: Born April 19, 1916, in St. Paul, Minn.; died of an apparent heart attack, January 28, 1982, at Ten Mile Lake, Minn. Educator, presidential adviser, and author best known as chief presidential speechwriter during Dwight D. Eisenhower's second presidential term. Moos taught political science at Johns Hopkins University from 1942 to 1956. In 1957 he went to Washington, D.C., as a White House consultant and became an administrative assistant to the president the following year. Moos helped Eisenhower write the president's 1961 farewell address, in which Eisenhower warned the nation of the dangers of the "military-industrial complex," a phrase attributed to Moos. After leaving Washington, Moos served as an adviser to the Rockefeller family, taught public law and government at Columbia University, was planning director of the Ford Foundation, and from 1967 to 1974 was president of the University of Minnesota. He was an unsuccessful Republican candidate in Minnesota's senatorial primary election in 1978. Moos was the author of books on government and public policy, including *Politics, Presidents, and Coattails* and *The Republicans: A History of Their Party,* and a children's book, *Dwight D. Eisenhower.* He also edited and co-authored books and was associate editor of the *Baltimore Evening Sun* from 1945 to 1948. Obituaries and other sources: *Washington Post,* January 30, 1982; *Time,* February 8, 1982.

*   *   *

MORASKY, Robert Louis   1940-

PERSONAL: Born August 7, 1940; married; children: two.

Education: University of Michigan, B.S., 1962, M.A., 1965, Ph.D., 1968. *Home:* 2303 South Third, Bozeman, Mont. 59715. *Office:* Department of Psychology, Montana State University, Bozeman, Mont. 59717.

CAREER: Teacher at public schools in Ann Arbor, Mich., 1962-64; University of Michigan, Ann Arbor, assistant psychologist at Institute for Human Adjustment and director of adult basic education program, 1966-68; State University of New York College at Plattsburgh, began as assistant professor, became associate professor of psychology, 1968-75, chairman of department, 1974-75; Montana State University, Bozeman, associate professor, 1975-79, professor of psychology, 1979—, head of department, 1975-79. Consultant to Center for Programmed Learning for Business, Eastern Airlines, and Ford Motor Co. *Awards, honors:* Grants from National Institute of Mental Health, 1972-72, and Sperry & Hutchinson Foundation, 1976-77.

WRITINGS: Learning Experiences in Educational Psychology, with instructor's manual, W. C. Brown, 1973; (with S. W. Johnson) *Learning Disabilities,* Allyn & Bacon, 1977, 2nd edition, 1980; *Self-Esteem: An Orientation for Parents and Volunteers,* Big Brothers, Big Sisters, 1978. Contributor to education, psychology, and medical journals.

*   *   *

MORGAN, Christopher 1952-

PERSONAL: Born September 30, 1952, in Perth Amboy, N.J.; son of George Leon and Helen (Gecek) Morgan; married Patricia Roehrich, August 7, 1971 (divorced); married Margaret Corlett, December 24, 1978 (divorced). *Education:* Rutgers University, B.A., 1974; also attended San Francisco State University, 1979-80. *Residence:* Seaside, Calif. *Agent:* Michael Larsen/Elizabeth Pomada, 1029 Jones St., San Francisco, Calif. 94109.

CAREER: Free-lance writer, 1978—. *Military service:* U.S. Army, Infantry, 1974-75, in public affairs, 1975-78. U.S. Army Reserve, 1978—; present rank, captain. *Member:* Authors Guild. *Awards, honors:* Keith L. Ware Award for excellence in military journalism from U.S. Army, 1977, for a series on prostitution in Monterey County, Calif.

WRITINGS: The Rich and the Lonely (novel), Beaufort Book Co., 1981. Contributor to newspapers and magazines. Editor of *Fort Ord Panorama;* associate editor of *Army Reserve;* editor of newsletters.

SIDELIGHTS: Morgan told *CA:* "I have been writing professionally since 1975 and have never really wanted to be anything other than a good storyteller. However, the writing impulse was born much earlier for less than artistic reasons. In high school all the guys getting the girls were varsity athletes, except for this one guy who wrote a column for the school newspaper. The athletes had to go through grueling practices every day. All the columnist had to do was write five hundred words once a month. Was there really any choice? Unfortunately, before I learned that most girls weren't crazy about writers, I was hooked. I've been paying the price ever since. If only I'd gone out for the varsity."

BIOGRAPHICAL/CRITICAL SOURCES: Army Reserve, spring, 1981.

*   *   *

MORGENSTERN, Christian 1871-1914

BRIEF ENTRY: Born May 6, 1871, in Munich, Germany (now West Germany); died of tuberculosis, March 31, 1914, in Merano, Austria (now Italy). German poet. Morgenstern was a master of word play. Though he saw himself as a mystic poet, he is admired most for his nonsense verse. He delighted readers with *Galgenlieder* (1905) and *Palmstroem* (1910), in which he peopled an imaginary world with his unique inventions and brought everyday objects to life, injecting them with human feelings. Critics praised his remarkable versatility in rhyme, meter, and style. Morgenstern's expertise in manipulating words, reversing concepts, and making literal interpretations of idioms was comic and appealing; but he saw his effort as a serious attempt to clarify the world around him and to relate it to the mystical reality of his imagination. He was strongly influenced by anthroposophist Rudolf Steiner. Throughout his brief adult life, he also wrote lyric love poems, collected in *Ein Sommer* (1899) and *Ich und Du* (1911), which some critics consider among the most beautiful in the German language. *Biographical/critical sources: Columbia Dictionary of Modern European Literature,* Columbia University Press, 1947; *The Concise Encyclopedia of Modern World Literature,* Hutchinson, 1963; *Encyclopedia of World Literature in the Twentieth Century,* updated edition, Ungar, 1967.

*   *   *

MORLEY, Frank V(igor) 1899-1980

PERSONAL: Born January 4, 1899, in Haverford, Pa.; died October 8, 1980, in Buckinghamshire, England.

CAREER: Century Co. (publisher), New York City, member of staff, 1924-29; Harcourt, Brace & Co. (publisher; now Harcourt Brace Jovanovich, Inc.), New York City, director, editor, and vice-president. Co-founder of publisher, Faber & Faber.

WRITINGS: Travels in East Anglia, Methuen, 1923; *Dora Wordsworth: Her Book,* Selwyn & Blount, 1924; *River Thames,* Methuen, 1926; (with J. S. Hodgson) *Whaling North and South* (with own photographs), Century Co., 1926; *East South East,* Harcourt, 1929; (editor) *Everybody's Boswell,* 1930; *Lamb Before Elia,* J. Cape, 1932, reprinted, Folcroft, 1973; *War Paint: A Story of Adventure,* Faber, 1935, published in the United States as *The Wreck of the Active: A Story of Adventure,* Houghton, 1936; *My One Contribution to Chess,* B. W. Huebsch, 1945.

Death in Dwelly Lane, Harper, 1952; *The Great North Road,* Macmillan, 1961; *The Long Road West: A Journey in History,* Dial, 1971; *Literary Britain,* Harper, 1980.

BIOGRAPHICAL/CRITICAL SOURCES: Publishers Weekly, June 22, 1946, October 31, 1980; *Nature,* September 7, 1957.*

*   *   *

MORRA, Umberto ?-1981

OBITUARY NOTICE: Died in 1981 in Italy. Translator and author. Formerly a director of the Italian Institute in London, Morra translated many writings from the English. Among his publications is *Colloqui con Berenson,* a collection of quotes from the renowned art critic Bernhard Berenson. In 1960 Morra was named a Commander of the Order of the British Empire by Sir Ashley Clarke, England's ambassador to Italy. Obituaries and other sources: *London Times,* November 21, 1981.

*   *   *

MORRIS, David Brown 1942-

PERSONAL: Born August 11, 1942, in New York, N.Y.; married, 1966; children: one. *Education:* Hamilton College, B.A., 1964; University of Minnesota, Ph.D., 1968. *Office:* Department of English, University of Iowa, Iowa City, Iowa 52242.

CAREER: University of Virginia, Charlottesville, assistant professor of English, 1968-72; American University, Washington, D.C., associate professor of literature, 1972-74; University of Iowa, Iowa City, professor of English, 1974—. *Member:* Modern Language Association of America, American Society for Eighteenth Century Studies. *Awards, honors:* Younger humanist fellow of National Endowment for the Humanities, 1972-73.

WRITINGS: The Religious Sublime: Christian Poetry and Critical Tradition in Eighteenth-Century England, University Press of Kentucky, 1972; (editor with Donald Askins) *New Ground,* Southern Appalachian Writers Cooperative, 1977. Contributor to language and literature journals.*

* * *

MORRISON, G.F.
See BERNSTEIN, Gerry

* * *

MORRISON, Jack 1912-

PERSONAL: Born December 17, 1912, in Santa Barbara, Calif.; son of Charles Pacific and Anna Marie Morrison; married Martha Godfrey (marriage ended); married Jeanne Cagney (marriage ended). *Education:* University of California, Los Angeles, B.A., 1934, M.A., 1951; University of Southern California, Ed.D., 1962. *Home:* 15 Eighth Ave. S.E., Washington, D.C. 20003. *Office:* American Theatre Association, 1000 Vermont Ave. N.W., Suite 902, Washington, D.C. 20005.

CAREER: University of California, Los Angeles, director of theatre activities, 1938-47, associate professor of theatre arts, 1957-66; Ohio University, Athens, professor of theatre and dean of College of Fine Arts, 1966-71; associate director of arts in education for JDR 3rd fund, 1971-76; American Theatre Association, Washington, D.C., executive director, 1976—. Member of board of directors of Acting Company and American National Theatre and Academy; convenor of Commonwealth Fund Theatre Awards. *Member:* American Theatre Association (fellow), Phi Kappa Psi, Players Club.

WRITINGS: The Rise of the Arts on the American Campus, McGraw, 1973; (contributor) Jerome Hausman, editor, *Arts and the Schools,* McGraw, 1980. Author of "Washington Routine," a monthly column in *Theatre News.* Contributor to scholarly journals. Executive editor of *Design.*

* * *

MORRISON, James (Ryan) 1924-

PERSONAL: Born November 13, 1924, in Pawling, N.Y.; son of Milnor Bowdoin and Eva (Ryan) Morrison; married Anne Sloan (a school board president), September 8, 1955; children: Anne, George, James, Lucy, Emily. *Education:* Bowdoin College, B.A., 1950. *Home:* 1514 Mesa Ave., Colorado Springs, Colo. 80906. *Agent:* Curtis Brown Ltd., 575 Madison Ave., New York, N.Y. 10022. *Office:* James Morrison Producing Co., Inc., 7 East Bijou, Colorado Springs, Colo. 80903.

CAREER: James Morrison Producing Co., Inc. (producer of films for industrial corporations), Colorado Springs, Colo., president, 1950—. *Military service:* U.S. Army, 1943-46.

WRITINGS: Treehouse (novel), Dial, 1972. Contributor to *Treehouse* and *Wildfire.*

* * *

MORSBERGER, Katharine M. 1931-

PERSONAL: Born May 6, 1931, in Wilkinsburg, Pa.; daughter of Stephen J. (an insurance agent) and Eleanor (Loomis) Miller; married Robert E. Morsberger (a writer and professor of English), June 17, 1955; children: Grace Anne. *Education:* University of North Carolina, Greensboro, B.A., 1952; graduate study at University of Chicago, 1952-53, and University of Iowa, 1954-56; Claremont Graduate School, M.A., 1972, doctoral study, 1974-76. *Politics:* Democrat. *Home:* 1530 Berea Court, Claremont, Calif. 91711. *Agent:* Michael Hamilburg, Mitchell J. Hamilburg Agency, 202 La Cienega Blvd., Suite 212, Beverly Hills, Calif. 90211. *Office:* Pitzer College, Mills Ave., Claremont, Calif. 91711.

CAREER: Miami University, Oxford, Ohio, psychometrist and secretary at Counseling Service, 1956-58; organizer and teacher at cooperative nursery school in Nsukka, Nigeria, 1964-65; New Mexico State University, Agricultural Information Service, Las Cruces, editor, writer, and researcher, 1967-68; Pitzer College, Claremont, Calif., feature writer, 1977—, publications editor, 1980—. Member of faculty at California State Polytechnic University, Pomona, 1973, 1978, and Mount San Antonio College, 1978-79. *Member:* International P.E.N., Western Literature Association, Rocky Mountain Modern Language Association (co-chairperson of popular culture section, 1974), Press Club of Southern California, Claremont Institute for Antiquity and Christianity, Phi Beta Kappa.

WRITINGS: (Contributor) Tetsumaro Hayashi, editor, *A Study Guide to Steinbeck's The Long Valley,* Pierian, 1977; (contributor) Frank N. Magill, editor, *Survey of Science Fiction Literature,* Volume I: *A Clockwork Orange,* Volume II: *1984,* Volume III: *Slaughterhouse-Five,* Volume IV: *The Strange Case of Dr. Jekyll and Mr. Hyde,* Salem Press, 1979; (with husband, Robert E. Morsberger) *Lew Wallace, Militant Romantic,* McGraw, 1980. Contributor to *McGill's Survey of the Cinema.* Contributor of articles and reviews to journals and magazines, including *Civil War Times Illustrated, Journal of Popular Culture, Literature/Film Quarterly,* and *Science Fiction and Fantasy Book Review.* Editor of *Pitzer Participant* and *Pitzer Parent.*

BIOGRAPHICAL/CRITICAL SOURCES: Los Angeles Times Book Review, May 24, 1981.

* * *

MORSE, Donald R(oy) 1931-

PERSONAL: Born June 5, 1931, in New York, N.Y.; son of Abraham (a frozen food distributor) and Leah (a secretary; maiden name, Laznicky) Morse; married Diane Frances Urove (a physical education teacher), December 23, 1956; children: Andrew Keith, Brian Scott, Caryn Beth. *Education:* City College (now of the City University of New York), B.S., 1955; New York University, D.D.S., 1959; Hofstra University, M.A. in biology, 1969; graduate study in psychology at Westchester State College and Temple University. *Agent:* Diana Price, Frommer-Price Literary Agency, 185 East 85th St., New York, N.Y. 10028. *Office:* Temple University School of Dentistry, 3223 North Broad St., Philadelphia, Pa. 19140.

CAREER: New York University, New York, N.Y., instructor in microbiology, 1968-70; Temple University, Philadelphia,

Pa., associate professor of endodontics, 1970—. Part-time private practice in endodontics. Philadelphia Society of Clinical Hypnosis, public relations director, 1976—, secretary, 1978—. *Military service:* U.S. Army, 1959-61; became captain. *Member:* International Hypnosis Society, American Dental Association, American Association of Endodontics, American Board of Endodontics, American Society for Microbiology, American Association for the Advancement of Science, American Society of Clinical Hypnosis, American Society of Psychosomatic Dentistry and Medicine, National Dental Honor Society, Society for Clinical and Experimental Hypnosis, Omicron Kappu Upsilon. *Awards, honors:* Founder's Day Award from New York University, 1959; named outstanding graduate male scholar by Hofstra University, 1969.

WRITINGS: Clinical Endodontology: A Comprehensive Guide to Diagnosis, Treatment and Prevention, C. C Thomas, 1974; (contributor) Stephen Cohen and Richard C. Burns, editors, *Pathways to the Pulp,* Mosby, 1976, second edition, 1980, third edition, 1983; (with Merrick Lawrence Furst) *Stress and Relaxation: Application to Dentistry,* C. C Thomas, 1978; (with Furst) *Stress for Success: A Holistic Approach to Stress and Its Management,* Van Nostrand, 1979; (with Furst) *Women Under Stress,* Van Nostrand, 1982. Author of nearly seventy articles on dentistry, endodontics, microbiology, immunology, pathology, biochemistry, pharmacology, physiology, pain control, hypnosis, meditation, acupuncture, stress management, relaxation therapy, stress changes, career counselling, and course planning.

WORK IN PROGRESS: In Complete Control, with Furst.

SIDELIGHTS: Morse's 1979 book, *Stress for Success: A Holistic Approach to Stress and Its Management,* discusses the nature of stress, its physiological and psychological effects, and methods of controlling and avoiding stress reactions. With co-author M. Lawrence Furst, Morse outlines various methods of coping with stress, including meditation, biofeedback, and hypnosis. The book describes a three-way approach to stress reduction that involves physical exercise, diet, and relaxation. Morse uses the techniques discussed in his book to aid his dental patients undergoing painful procedures.

Morse told *CA:* "I'm interested in holistic health. I try to eat a low-fat, low-sugar, moderate-protein, high-complex carbohydrate diet. I meditate regularly and exercise five to six days a week.

"I have a wonderful wife, family, and diversified career. I teach, practice endodontics part-time, lecture, write, and consult. I have an excellent supporting staff. Although I have occasional 'downs,' I try to keep an even keel. I cherish moments of happiness and try to reflect on the good times. I constantly set attainable goals, and if I fail to meet them, I change my course."

AVOCATIONAL INTERESTS: Tennis, travel, meeting people, theatre, classical music, film, white-water rafting, canoeing, cross-country skiing.

BIOGRAPHICAL/CRITICAL SOURCES: Philadelphia Inquirer, November 8, 1979, December 6, 1979, June 26, 1980, February 5, 1981.

*   *   *

MORTON, A(ndrew) Q(ueen)   1919-

PERSONAL: Born June 4, 1919; son of Alexander and Janet (Queen) Morton; married Jean Singleton, 1948; children: one son, two daughters. *Education:* University of Glasgow, M.A.,

1942, B.D., 1947, B.Sc., 1948. *Home:* Abbey Manse, Culross, Dunfermline, Fife KY12 8JD, Scotland.

CAREER: Ordained minister; minister of St. Andrews Church, Fraserburgh, Scotland, 1949-59; Culross Abbey, Culross, Scotland, minister, 1959—. Member of faculty at University of Edinburgh, 1965—. *Member:* Royal Society of Edinburgh (fellow).

WRITINGS: (With George Hogarth Carnaby Macgregor) *The Structure of the Fourth Gospel,* Oliver & Boyd, 1961; (with James MacLeman) *Christianity and the Computer,* Hodder & Stoughton, 1964, published in the United States as *Christianity in the Computer Age,* Harper, 1965; (with Macgregor) *The Structure of Luke and Acts,* Harper, 1964; (with MacLeman) *Paul, the Man and the Myth: A Study in the Authorship of Greek Prose,* Harper, 1966.

(With Alban D. Winspear and others) *It's Greek to the Computer,* Harvest House, 1971; *The Johannine Epistles: A Critical Concordance,* University of Edinburgh, 1971; (editor with S. Michaelson) *A Critical Concordance to the Gospel of John,* Biblical Research Associates, 1974; (editor with Michaelson) *A Critical Concordance to the Acts of the Apostles,* Biblical Research Associates, 1976; (with Michaelson and J. David Thompson) *A Critical Concordance to the Letter of Paul to the Romans* (edited by J. Arthur Baird and David Noel Freedman), Biblical Research Associates, 1977; *Literary Detection: How to Prove Authorship and Fraud in Literature and Documents,* Scribner, 1978; *A Critical Concordance to I and II Corinthians,* Biblical Research Associates, 1979.

(With Michaelson and Thompson) *A Critical Concordance to the Epistle of Paul to the Galatians,* Biblical Research Associates, 1980; *A Critical Concordance to the Epistle to the Ephesians,* Biblical Research Associates, 1980. Also author of *Authorship and Integrity in the New Testament,* 1963. Contributor to learned journals.

BIOGRAPHICAL/CRITICAL SOURCES: Scientific American, November, 1979.*

*   *   *

MOSTERT, Noel   1929-

PERSONAL: Born December 25, 1929, in Capetown, South Africa; son of Marthinus Johannes (a farmer) and Susanne Magdalene Mostert. *Politics:* None. *Religion:* None. *Agent:* Roberta Pryor, International Creative Management, 40 West 57th St., New York, N.Y. 10019.

CAREER: Cape Times, Capetown, South Africa, shipping correspondent, 1946-47; foreign war correspondent for United Press, 1947-53; *Montreal Star,* Montreal, Quebec, worked as Broadway columnist, drama critic, and special foreign correspondent, 1953-62; currently free-lance writer. *Military service:* Royal Canadian Navy Reserve, 1948—.

WRITINGS: Supership (nonfiction), Macmillan, 1975. Contributor of articles and stories to magazines, including *Holiday, Reporter, Harper's, New Yorker,* and *Reader's Digest.*

WORK IN PROGRESS: The Honeybird, a history of South Africa.

*   *   *

MRS. G.
See GRIFFITHS, Kitty Anna

MUDD, Roger H(arrison) 1928-

PERSONAL: Born February 9, 1928, in Washington, D.C.; son of Kostka (a cartographer) and Irma Iris (Harrison) Mudd; married Emma Jeanne Spears, October 28, 1957; children: Daniel H., Maria M., Jonathan, Matthew M. *Education:* Washington and Lee University, A.B., 1950; University of North Carolina, M.A., 1953. *Home:* 7167 Old Dominion Dr., McLean, Va. 22101. *Office:* NBC News, Room 159, 4001 Nebraska Ave. N.W., Washington, D.C. 20016.

CAREER/WRITINGS: Darlington School, Rome, Ga., teacher of history and English, 1951-52; *Richmond News Leader,* Richmond, Va., news reporter, 1953; WRNL-Radio, Richmond, news director, 1953-56; WTOP-Radio and Television, Washington, D.C., news reporter, 1956-61; Columbia Broadcasting System (CBS), Washington, D.C., correspondent, 1961-80; National Broadcasting Co. (NBC), Washington, D.C., chief Washington correspondent, 1981, co-anchor of "NBC Nightly News," 1982—. Member of board of Citizens Scholarship Foundation of America. Trustee of Randolph-Macon Women's College, 1971-78, Robert F. Kennedy Journalism Awards Committee, 1971-78, and Blue Ridge School, 1978—. *Military service:* U.S. Army, 1945-47. *Member:* Radio-Television Correspondents Association (chairman of executive committee, 1969-70), National Press Club (Washington, D.C.). *Awards, honors:* George Foster Peabody Broadcasting Award from University of Georgia, 1971 and 1979; Emmy award from National Academy of Television Arts and Sciences, 1973 and 1974.

SIDELIGHTS: Mudd's journalism career began in 1953 after he completed work on his master's degree in history. Although he had originally planned to teach contemporary history, Mudd took a job on the *Richmond News Leader* in order to learn more about the relationship between the press and government than was available in textbooks. Soon he was assigned to set up the newspaper's radio news station, WRNL, and function as its news director. At this point, Mudd abandoned his teaching plans for a career in broadcast journalism. After several years with WRNL, he joined radio and television station WTOP in Washington, D.C., as a reporter, and in 1961 he moved to CBS News, where he was assigned to Capitol Hill as a Congressional correspondent.

At CBS Mudd quickly established a reputation for clear, concise writing and reporting of the often confusing Congressional beat. In 1964 Mudd won praise for his coverage of the Civil Rights Bill debate and was selected, along with Robert Trout, to anchor the Democratic National Convention. The Mudd-Trout team replaced Walter Cronkite, stalwart of CBS convention coverage, in an unsuccessful attempt to capture ratings from NBC's popular Chet Huntley and David Brinkley. After that brief experiment ended, Mudd resumed his Congressional coverage and became Cronkite's subrogate, filling in when Cronkite was ill or on vacation. From 1966 to 1973 Mudd chaired the Saturday edition of "The CBS Evening News" in addition to his regular duties, and he hosted the Sunday edition of the newscast in 1970 and 1971.

In 1971 Mudd reported and narrated "CBS Reports: The Selling of the Pentagon," the highly controversial documentary that won a special Peabody Award. Mudd's television report implied that the Pentagon was guilty of impropriety in allocating federal funds to display military hardware at state fairs and other community events in order to promote the concept of American military might. Government officials, however, raised the counter-charge that the program had been deceptively edited in an attempt to undermine public confidence in the Pentagon.

In the storm that followed, Vice-President Spiro Agnew called Mudd's report "a clever propaganda attempt to discredit the Defense establishment," and a House Congressional committee attempted to formally investigate the editing process employed in making the program. Frank Stanton, president of CBS, refused to turn over scripts and notes from the program, claiming that they were privileged material, and was nearly charged with contempt of Congress. The House eventually dropped its investigation plans, and CBS re-aired the program less than a month after its original telecast for the sake of viewers who had missed it.

Mudd continued with "CBS Reports" and, in the hectic period from 1973 to 1974, did special reports and updates on the developing Watergate scandal, the resignation of Vice-President Agnew, the appointment and confirmation hearings of Gerald Ford to the vice-presidency, the Senate Watergate hearings, and the resignation of President Richard M. Nixon.

Mudd took a moment from reporting world problems to include a lighter personal note in the news in 1979, when he announced that President Jimmy Carter had issued a statement expressing regret over the guilty verdict a military commission had handed down against Dr. Samuel A. Mudd in 1865. Dr. Mudd, a distant relative of newscaster Roger, was the Maryland physician who treated John Wilkes Booth's fractured leg only hours after Booth shot President Abraham Lincoln. Convicted of conspiring with Booth, Dr. Mudd became the target of such hostility that the epithet "your name is mud" arose. Newscaster Mudd was happy to report that President Carter had reaffirmed a full pardon issued by President Andrew Johnson in 1869. Mudd observed that Carter's endorsement of the pardon would "sure help back home."

Perhaps Mudd's most controversial broadcast was a 1979 interview with Senator Edward M. Kennedy at the outset of Kennedy's unsuccessful campaign to challenge President Carter for the 1980 Democratic presidential nomination. Under Mudd's probing, Kennedy appeared almost confused, responding to questions about his personal life with rambling answers that shocked most political observers. "In Roger Mudd's celebrated documentary on Senator Kennedy," William F. Buckley wrote in *National Review,* "Mudd asked personal questions he shouldn't have asked, and Kennedy bravely volunteered to answer any questions about Chappaquiddick, which he proceeded not to answer." *Time* magazine later observed that Mudd's "interview with Senator Edward Kennedy . . . caught the candidate at his inarticulate worst and [was] possibly the most important work of political journalism of the entire campaign."

Despite Mudd's respected reputation as a journlist and the fact that he had served as Walter Cronkite's understudy for sixteen years, CBS News announced in February, 1980, that Dan Rather would anchor "The CBS Evening News" when Cronkite stepped down from that post in March, 1981. Mudd was aggrieved by the decision and angry that he had not been informed until hours before it was announced publicly. In July, 1981, Mudd signed with NBC News as chief Washington correspondent, and in April, 1982, began co-anchoring the "NBC Nightly News" with Tom Brokaw.

BIOGRAPHICAL/CRITICAL SOURCES: New York Times, July 27, 1979; *National Review,* December 7, 1979; *Newsweek,* July 14, 1980; *Time,* July 14, 1980; *People,* July 13, 1981.

—Sketch by Michael L. LaBlanc

MULDOON, Roland W. 1941-

PERSONAL: Born April 12, 1941, in Weybridge, England; son of William Edmund and Mary (Clifford) Muldoon; married Claire Burnley (an actress), December 27, 1976; children: L. Jane, Alison C. *Education:* Studied at Bristol Old Vic School, 1961-63. *Politics* Socialist. *Religion:* "Lost." *Home and office address:* P.O. Box 294, London NW1 5BH, England.

CAREER: Cartoon Archetypical Slogan Theatre (CAST), London, England, actor, writer, and director for CAST Presentations Ltd., 1965—. Also worked as photo-researcher, in photographic sales, and as a confidence man. *Awards, honors:* Off-Broadway Award from *Village Voice,* 1980, for solo show, "Full Confessions of a Socialist."

WRITINGS: (With others) *Confessions of a Socialist* (one-act play), Pluto Press, 1979.

Unpublished plays: "John D. Muggins Is Dead" (one-act), first produced in London at Peanuts Club, 1965; "Mr. Oligarchy's Circus" (ten-act), first produced in London at London School of Economics, 1966; "The Trials of Horatio Muggins" (one-act), first produced in London at Young Men's Christian Association (YMCA), 1967; "Auntie Maude Is the Happening Thing" (two-act), first produced on the West End at Royal Court Theatre, 1968; (co-author) "Harold Muggins Is a Martyr" (two-act), first produced in London at Unity Theatre, 1968; "Hilda Muggins" (one-act), first produced in Glasgow, Scotland, at The IONA Community Centre, 1970; "Sam the Man (Labour M.P.)" (one-act), first produced in Cornwall, England, at Canbourne Labour Club, 1972; "Three for the Road" (three one-act plays; contains "The Right to Work," "The Prevention of Terrorism Act—Northern Ireland," and "CUTS"), first produced in London at Institute for Contemporary Arts, The Mall, 1974; "Goodbye Union Jack" (one-act), first produced in Coventry, England, 1976; "What Happens Next?" (two-act), first produced in Exeter, England, at Barnfield Theatre, 1978; "Killer on the Loose" (one-act), first produced in London at North London Polytechnic, 1979; "From One Strike to Another" (one-act), first produced in Coventry at St. Peter's Hall, 1980; "Full Confessions of a Socialist" (one-act), first produced in New York at Labor Theatre, 1980; "Further Confessions of a Socialist" (one-act), first produced in San Francisco at Marina Theatre, 1980; "Sedition 81" (two-act), first produced in Colchester, Essex, England, at University Theatre, 1981.

Screenplays: "Planet of the Mugs," Union Circuit, 1971.

WORK IN PROGRESS: "Hotel Sunshine," a play; "The Return of Sam the Man," a play; "Cocaine," a film script, completion expected in 1983; "Battle for a Power Station," a film script, completion expected in 1984.

SIDELIGHTS: "I have been credited," Muldoon commented, "along with my theatre group Cartoon Archetypical Slogan Theatre (CAST), with having started, or at least having been the first of, a whole generation of political theatre groups in Britain. But while I revel in that accolade, our theatre, in truth, comes out of all the traditions of popular theatre that 'admits that it is present in front of an audience.' We were considered avant-garde in the sixties because in small theatres and non-theatrical environments we presented all our material *to* the audience—a style we called 'presentationism.' But we had really learned it from music hall/variety shows, from rock and roll/pop music, from new-wave American comedians of the time, and traditional pantomime. What we did do that was

unique was to combine our art with our commitment to politics—without either suffering—and it is that which passionately interests me, and I accept the credit for having achieved it. Though I would love to work in any form (I would like to be a character in a Clint Eastwood cowboy movie), I think I would always want to return to play to a sweaty, packed working-class audience where I was changing the material on the spot—in order to maximize the effect of the show.

"After many years of protesting outside the American embassy in Britain, I finally went to the United States and have fallen for the 'cultural melting pot' and all its contradictions. But that could well be a case of 'the grass is greener. . . .' What we, as a theatre group, worry about now is that we do not have a play which suits the summer of 1981—the mood of the rioters in Liverpool; the last time we played Liverpool Eight with our anti-Nazi play 'What Happens Next?,' the people we would have liked to attract to our shows were too alienated from us, and our truck was broken into.

"To sum it up, we go for the laughs—which is a serious business."

BIOGRAPHICAL/CRITICAL SOURCES: Charles Marowitz, *Confessions of a Counterfeit Critic,* Eyre, 1973; David Widgery, *Left in Britain,* Penguin, 1976; *Plays and Players,* January, 1976; *Leveller,* April, 1978; Sandy Craig, *Dreams and Deconstructions,* Amber Lane Press, 1980; Cathy Itzin, *Stages of the Revolution,* Eyre, 1980; *Time Out,* March 21-27, 1980; *Performance,* September/October, 1981.

* * *

MULL, Martin 1943-

PERSONAL: Born in 1943 in Chicago, Ill.; married first wife, Kristin (an artist; divorced); married Sandra Baker. *Education:* Received M.F.A. from Rhode Island School of Design. *Address:* c/o Capricorn Records, 535 Cotton Ave., Macon, Ga. 31201.

CAREER: Instructor in painting at Rhode Island School of Design, Providence; songwriter for Warner Bros.; artist, with several one-man shows at Boston Museum of Fine Arts, at Boston Museum of Contemporary Arts, and at Red Piano Gallery, Hilton Head, S.C.; actor in television series, including "Mary Hartman, Mary Hartman," "Fernwood 2-Night," and "America 2-Night," and in motion pictures, including "FM" and "My Bodyguard"; comedian.

WRITINGS—Recordings: "Martin Mull," Capricorn, 1972; "Martin Mull and His Fabulous Furniture in Your Living Room," Capricorn, 1973; "Normal," Capricorn, 1974; "Days of Wine and Neuroses," Capricorn, 1975; "Sex and Violins"; and "I'm Everyone I've Ever Loved."

Composer of numerous songs, including: "A Girl Named Johnny Cash"; "Margie the Midget"; "Ah, France"; "Martin, Leon, Elton, and John"; "Dancing in the Nude"; "Normal"; "Partly Marion"; "Eggs"; "A Girl Your Size (How Could You Not Miss)"; "Billy One-Eye"; "My Wife"; "In the Eyes of My Dog I'm a Man"; "Straight Talk About the Blues"; "Blacks Keep Giving Me the Blues"; "Noses Run in My Family"; "Dialing for Dollars"; "I'm Everyone I've Ever Loved"; "Humming Song"; "Livin' Above My Station"; "Ventriloquist Love."

Also author of scripts for television shows, including "The Great American Dream Machine" and "The Fifty-first State."

SIDELIGHTS: In a *Rolling Stone* article about Martin Mull, Ralph J. Gleason wrote: "Being funny is the most serious kind of occupation there is and one of the hardest. It's remarkable when anybody is funny at all these days and more remarkable when, as [Martin Mull], the comic can be funny a good part of the time.'' Recognized as one of America's foremost contemporary comedians, Mull first gained nationwide attention as Garth Gimble, a wife beater on the television series ''Mary Hartman, Mary Hartman,'' produced by Norman Lear. When the character was impaled on an aluminum Christmas tree, Lear created a new vehicle for Mull, ''Fernwood 2-Night,'' a mock talk show set in Mary Hartman's hometown, Fernwood, Ohio. As Garth Gimble's twin brother Barth, Mull parodied middle-class American values and deliberately personified tastelessness.

After thirteen weeks, ''Fernwood 2-Night'' became ''America 2-Night,'' and Barth moved from Fernwood to Hollywood. This change in format allowed Barth to interview genuine celebrities in his tactless manner. But even popular guests could not salvage ''America 2-Night,'' and it was cancelled. Critics panned it, and some viewers, unable to appreciate the show's subtle satire or even recognize it as a spoof, thought ''America 2-Night'' a poor attempt at a legitimate talk-show.

Despite his numerous television appearances and several motion picture roles (as a deejay in ''FM'' and as the father in ''My Bodyguard''), Mull is best known for his songs, which he writes and performs, accompanying himself with an electric guitar. (He told the *Detroit Free Press,* ''If God had meant for us to play acoustically, he never would have given us amps.'') His musical styles include bossa novas, blues, jazz, disco, and country, and his lyrics are dadaistic, often focusing on midgets, amputees, and other usually ''unsung heroes.'' Among his songs are ''Margie the Midget,'' who with her husband goes ''walking hand and ankle,'' ''Ventriloquist Love,'' about a man who can kiss without moving his lips, and ''Humming Song,'' a tune about sado-masochism, in which Mull hums all the implied nasty words.

Mull uses many props when performing his songs on stage or television. For instance, when he sings ''Hors D'Oeuvre'' (''It's so hard to say *au revoir* / So let's just say hors d'oeuvre''), he sports a black beret, hangs plastic grapes from the neck of his guitar, and places a checkered tablecloth and a loaf of French bread across his lap. Noting that much of Mull's comedy depends on such visual aids, Rob Patterson of *Creem* opined: ''Bringing Martin Mull . . . right into your living room is a task for video discs, not records, and it's a testament to his insanity that he comes across on vinyl so well anyway. Anyone with an interest in pop music will find Martin Mull's irreverence refreshingly funny.''

Mull's music, despite its humorous intent, is taken seriously by music critics. Robert E.A.P. Ritholz of *New Guard* noted: ''[Martin Mull] has made some of the funniest, but most neglected records around. . . . Satirists like Mull help to define and clarify musical styles by condensing and exaggerating them through the very act of parody.'' *Rolling Stone*'s Stephen Holden remarked: ''Mull is clearly capable of bridging the distance between light comic entertainment and comic art.''

Commenting on Mull's compositions, Patrick Snyder-Scumpy of *Crawdaddy* wrote: ''The depth of significance in those wincingly clever puns starts to reveal itself, the economy and smoothness of exposition becomes apparent, and the intelligence and complexity of the arrangements and production begins to tantalize your ear. . . . Like all excellent records, you find something new in it with each listening, a new connection, a further revelation of Mull's talent and craftsmanship. . . . Martin Mull joins the small, select group of wry, fragile observers whose music keeps us sane . . . and smiling.''

Making people smile is not Mull's only talent. He is also an accomplished artist, having earned his Master of Fine Arts degree in painting at the Rhode Island School of Design. He has exhibited his paintings in the Boston Institute of Contemporary Art and at the Red Piano Gallery in Hilton Head, S.C. His most notable display, however, was in the men's room of the Boston Museum of Fine Arts. Titled ''Flush with the Walls'' (or ''I'll Be Art in a Minute''), the exhibit was advertised on pieces of toilet paper. Mull told William S. Welt of the *Detroit Free Press:* ''About 300 people showed up, including some who came for the reasons God intended.'' Mull has also toured Boston and Cincinnati with an exhibit called ''Eat Art,'' composed of edible reproductions of great art works. Included were a Matisse nude made of pickles and matzo and a Brancusi of sausages. Evidently the artist, comedian, actor, and singer is, as he often reminds his audience, ''*Mull*ti-talented.''

BIOGRAPHICAL/CRITICAL SOURCES: Crawdaddy, January, 1973, March, 1973; *Newsweek,* August 6, 1973; *Rolling Stone,* August 16, 1973, September 27, 1973; *Detroit Free Press,* December 2, 1973; *New Guard,* December, 1976; *Creem,* May, 1977; *Contemporary Literary Criticism,* Volume 17, Gale, 1981.*

—*Sketch by Nancy S. Gearhart*

*   *   *

MURPHY, C. L.
See MURPHY, Charlotte A(lice)

*   *   *

MURPHY, Charlotte A(lice) 1924-
(C. L. Murphy, a joint pseudonym)

PERSONAL: Born November 15, 1924, in New York, N.Y.; daughter of Henry (an accountant) and Alice (Loewe) Heusser; married Lawrence A. Murphy (a writer), January 14, 1950; children: Steven Lawrence. *Education:* Attended Green Mountain College for Women, 1942-44. *Home and office:* 30 Mercedes Rd., Brockton, Mass. 02401.

CAREER: Bethlehem Steel Corp., Hingham Shipyard, Hingham, Mass., accountant, 1944-45; Columbia Broadcasting System, WEEI-Radio, Boston, Mass., worked in sales, sales promotion, traffic department, and program promotion, 1945-51; writer, 1966—. Associated with New England Home for Little Wanderers and Cardinal Cushing School and Training Center. *Member:* American Heart Association, American Cancer Society. *Awards, honors:* Scroll Award from Western Writers of America, 1967, for *Buffalo Grass.*

WRITINGS: (With husband, Lawrence A. Murphy, under joint pseudonym C. L. Murphy) *Buffalo Grass* (juvenile), Dial, 1967; (illustrator) Steven C. Lawrence, *A Northern Saga,* Playboy Press, 1976. Also author of ''Buffalo Grass,'' a screenplay based on her novel.

WORK IN PROGRESS: The Day Is New, The Tree, and *Thank You, God,* three self-illustrated children's books in poetry form; *In Which We Serve,* with husband, Lawrence A. Murphy, a young readers' novel about World War II; *Malpais Treasure,* with L. A. Murphy, a young readers' novel about the ''Lost Dutchman'' mine; ''Survival,'' a screenplay.

SIDELIGHTS: Charlotte Murphy wrote: ''Since before our marriage, my husband and I have worked together as a team, he the author, I the critic, editor, typist, 'Jill-of-all-writing-trades.' *Buffalo Grass* was my first actual collaboration with him in the writing of a book. Since then, we have together completed *Malpais Treasure* and a screenplay of *Buffalo Grass;* we are working on another screenplay, ''Survival,'' which is almost complete. I want to continue working closely with him on all forms of writing, and I hope also to put more time into my original writing for young children, most of which is and will be in poetry form and self-illustrated.

''Through my poetry I hope to help youngsters become more aware of the people, sounds, things in their world which may be taken for granted or overlooked because they are so commonplace. *The Day Is New* is a dawn-to-dusk description of everyday sights and sounds in which I hope to awaken a child to the sound of a frog or the rumble of thunder or the feel of a blade of grass. *Thank You, God* is intended to make real to the child the senses that are his and to be grateful for each one. *The Tree* tells the story of a sapling as it struggles through hot, dry summer, fall, and the chill and storms of winter to become a young tree. It continues growing and spreading its limbs to enclose a family of birds and other living things, each year braving the problems to grow larger and stronger and more beautiful. My effort is to do this type of book without preaching but to reach the child's enthusiasm through recognition of the simple but important things in his or her everyday.''

BIOGRAPHICAL/CRITICAL SOURCES: Brockton Enterprise-Times (Brockton, Mass.), August 3, 1966; *New York Times Book Review*, September 6, 1966; *Massachusetts Teacher Magazine*, November, 1966.

* * *

MURPHY, Jill 1949-

PERSONAL: Born July 5, 1949, in London, England; daughter of Eric Edwin (an engineer) and Irene (Lewis) Murphy. *Education:* Attended Chelsea, Croydon, and Camberwell art schools. *Religion:* None. *Agent:* A. P. Watt Ltd., 26/28 Bedford Row, London WC1R 4HL, England.

CAREER: Writer and illustrator, 1977—. *Awards, honors:* Nominated for Kate Greenaway Award from The British Library Association, 1981, for *Peace at Last.*

WRITINGS—All self-illustrated: The Worst Witch (juvenile), Puffin Books, 1975; *The Worst Witch Strikes Again* (juvenile), Puffin Books, 1979; *Peace at Last,* Macmillan, 1980; *A Bad Spell for the Worst Witch* (juvenile), Puffin Books, 1982. Also author of a picture book, *On the Way Home,* 1982.

SIDELIGHTS: Jill Murphy told *CA:* ''I was lucky; I inherited the ability to draw from my father and had a mother who *liked* being a mother. She encouraged me to be observant and to write from the age of three. I always had a difficult time at school because I never wanted to do anything except write stories and draw pictures, which drove my teachers to distraction. Now I write and draw because I always have. It was a choice of making a success of it or working in a shop. I can't think of a more satisfying career and feel very fortunate that I am able to do it. In my opinion, T. H. White was the best storyteller ever born; and I suspect my writing is heavily influenced by his style.

''I get on very well with kids. I worked in a children's home, off and on, for five years; I also worked as a nanny for a little boy. Being with children and listening to them keeps me in touch with what they like and what their problems are.

''I have an amazing dog who is used in television commercials. We have great fun together, and last year she earned enough money to buy us a car! I have lived in small villages in Ghana and Togo, and have traveled all over Europe.''

BIOGRAPHICAL/CRITICAL SOURCES: Washington Post Book World, February 14, 1982.

* * *

MURPHY, Larry
See MURPHY, Lawrence R(ichard)

* * *

MURPHY, Lawrence R(ichard) 1942-
(Larry Murphy)

PERSONAL: Born October 4, 1942, in Sacramento, Calif.; son of William R. (a physician) and Frances (Smith) Murphy. *Education:* University of Arizona, B.A., 1964, M.A., 1965; Texas Christian University, Ph.D., 1968. *Home:* 1821 West Alpine, Stockton, Calif. 95211. *Office:* Institute for Personal and Career Development, Central Michigan University, Mount Pleasant, Mich. 48859.

CAREER: Western Illinois University, Macomb, assistant professor, 1968-73, associate professor of history, 1973-79; University of the Pacific, Stockton, Calif., professor of history and dean of continuing education, 1979-81; Central Michigan University, Institute for Personal and Career Development, Mount Pleasant, director, 1981—. Visiting assistant professor at American University, Cairo, Egypt, 1971-73. Co-director of project to evaluate non-traditional programs, Board of Governors of State Colleges and Universities, Springfield, Ill. *Member:* Philmont Staff Association, Phi Delta Kappa, Phi Kappa Phi. *Awards, honors:* Best articles award from University of New Mexico, 1968, for ''The Beaubien and Miranda Land Grant, 1841-1846''; best biography award from Southwestern Library Association, 1973, for *Frontier Crusader: William F. M. Arny;* creative programming award from North American Association of Summer Sessions, 1980, for *Migrantes Envueltos en Nuevas.*

WRITINGS: (Editor) *Indian Agent in New Mexico, 1870,* Stagecoach Press, 1967; (under name Larry Murphy) *Out in God's Country: Colfax County, New Mexico,* Tribune Press, 1968; *Philmont: A History of New Mexico's Cimarron Country,* University of New Mexico Press, 1972; *Frontier Crusader: W.F.M. Arny,* University of Arizona Press, 1972; (with Ron C. Tyler) *The Slave Narratives of Texas,* Encino Press, 1974; *Lucien B. Maxwell: Napoleon of the Southwest,* University of Oklahoma Press, 1981. Editor of *Pacific Historian,* 1980-81.

WORK IN PROGRESS: Entrapped: Samuel Kent Neal Versus the United States Navy, publication expected in 1982.

SIDELIGHTS: Murphy told *CA:* ''A native Californian, I have devoted my attention to the history of the Southwest of New Mexico and Arizona, in which I developed an interest while studying and serving on the staff for many years at Philmont Scout Ranch. I also served in many university positions devoted to providing added educational opportunities for adults studying on a part-time basis.''

* * *

MURPHY, Patrick V(incent) 1920-

PERSONAL: Born May 15, 1920, in Brooklyn, N.Y.; son of Patrick A. (a policeman) and Ellen (Jones) Murphy; married Martha Elizabeth Cameron, June 2, 1945; children: Betty (Mrs. Thomas Kelley), Eileen (Mrs. Bernard Karam), Patrick, Anne T. (Mrs. Drew Zabriskie), Kevin, Gerard, Paul, Mark.

Education: St. John's University, B.A., 1954; graduated from Federal Bureau of Investigation National Law Enforcement Academy, 1957; City College (now of the City University of New York), M.P.A., 1960. *Politics:* Democrat. *Religion:* Roman Catholic. *Agent:* Theron Raines, Raines & Raines, 475 Fifth Ave., New York, N.Y. 10017. *Office:* Police Foundation, 1909 K St. N.W., Washington, D.C. 20006.

CAREER: New York Police Department, New York, N.Y., patrolman, 1945, patrol sergeant with emergency service division, 1948-51, lieutenant, 1951-54, instructor and training officer at police academy, 1954-61, captain with police commissioner's inspection squad, 1961-63, deputy inspector, 1963, deputy chief inspector and commanding officer of police academy, 1964, police commissioner, 1970-73; Syracuse Police Department, Syracuse, N.Y., police chief, 1963; U.S. Department of Justice, Washington, D.C., assistant director of Office of Law Enforcement, 1965-67, administrator of Law Enforcement Assistance Administration, 1968; District of Columbia, public safety director, 1967-68; Urban Institute, Washington, D.C., member of senior staff, 1969; Detroit Police Department, Detroit, Mich., police commissioner, 1970; Police Foundation (independent research group), Washington, D.C., president, 1973—. City College of New York (now City College of the City University of New York), lecturer in police science, 1954, dean of administration and police science department, 1964-65; instructor in law enforcement at the New School for Social Research, 1971-72. Adviser to National Crime Commission, 1965-67, and National Advisory Commission on Civil Disorders and Violence, 1967-68. Board member and co-chairman of Manhattan National Conference of Christians and Jews, 1973-81. *Military service:* U.S. Naval Reserve, served in World War II.

MEMBER: International Association of Chiefs of Police (chairman of education and training committee, 1970-71; chairman of organized crime committee, 1971-72), Beta Gamma Sigma. *Awards, honors:* Commendation for bravery from New York Police Department, 1962.

WRITINGS: Social Change and the Police, C. C Thomas, 1971; (with Thomas Plate) *Commissioner: A View From the Top of American Law Enforcement,* Simon & Schuster, 1977. Author of pamphlets and magazine articles on law enforcement.

SIDELIGHTS: Murphy is a former New York Police Department (NYPD) patrolman who moved up through the ranks to become the police commissioner of two major cities. As a patrolman, Murphy became aware that there was a high incidence of corruption within the police department. His distaste for this situation prompted his subsequent efforts toward police reform.

During the course of Murphy's career, he was offered a number of important posts as a direct consequence of his reputation as a reformer. In 1963, for example, Governor Nelson Rockefeller's special counsel on law enforcement, Eliot Lumbard, personally requested that Murphy take a leave of absence from the NYPD in order that he might accept the position of reform chief of the scandal-ridden police department in Syracuse, N.Y. A reporter for *Time* noted that Murphy also had been hired as New York City's police commissioner in order to "clean up the mess" that resulted from the disclosures of police pay-offs made by sergeant David Durk and patrolman Frank Serpico. As commissioner, "Murphy sought to instill honesty and physical restraint among the troops, and discipline and a sense of accountability up through the chain of command," said *Washington Post Book World* critic James Lardner.

Murphy's book *Commissioner: A View From the Top of American Law Enforcement* is an account of his career as a police official. Ralph G. Murdy of *America* called the book "an exciting blend of inside stories and highly unconventional opinions about what is wrong with our law-enforcement agencies and what can be done to improve them." Hindy Lauer Schacter, however, complained that Murphy relied too heavily on "personal reminiscence" and thereby lost the opportunity to present "an insider's broad-based analysis of police management practices, policy development, and reactions to mayoral guidance and control." Critic Lardner said that *Commissioner* "is an odd but agreeable blend of autobiography, sociology, and nuts-and-bolts analysis of police traditions, which offers many fascinating glimpses into the somewhat exclusive world of the big-city police chief."

AVOCATIONAL INTERESTS: Bicycling, swimming, sailing.

BIOGRAPHICAL/CRITICAL SOURCES: Time, June 19, 1968, September 13, 1971; *Newsweek,* September 21, 1970, September 6, 1971, February 6, 1978; *New Republic,* June 19, 1971; *America,* September 18, 1971, May 13, 1978; *New York Times Magazine,* December 19, 1971; *Saturday Review,* February 4, 1978; *New York Times Book Review,* February 5, 1978; *Washington Post Book World,* February 12, 1978; *New Leader,* February 13, 1978; *New York Times,* April 17, 1978.

*   *   *

MYDANS, Shelley Smith   1915-

BRIEF ENTRY: Born May 20, 1915, in Palo Alto, Calif. American journalist. Mydans became a reporter for *Life* in 1938. She has been a correspondent from Manila, Europe, and the Far East, including China, and was a prisoner of war of the Japanese during World War II. She wrote *Thomas* (Doubleday, 1965), *Violent Peace: A Report on Wars in the Postwar World* (Atheneum, 1968), and a historical novel, *The Vermillion Bridge* (Doubleday, 1980). *Address:* 212 Hommocki Rd., Larchmont, N.Y. 10538. *Biographical/critical sources: Current Biography,* Wilson, 1945; *New York Times,* July 15, 1980; *New York Times Book Review,* July 27, 1980; *Los Angeles Times,* August 21, 1980.

*   *   *

MYERS, Neil   1930-

PERSONAL: Born October 31, 1930, in Philadelphia, Pa.; son of Bernard H. (a dentist) and Anne (Sheinbaum) Myers; married Lorna Gordon (an arts administrator), June 24, 1962; children: Rachel, Julie. *Education:* University of Wisconsin (now Univeristy of Wisconsin—Madison), A.B., 1952; Harvard University, M.A., 1954, Ph.D., 1959. *Home:* 901 North Chauncey, West Lafayette, Ind. 47906. *Office:* Department of English, Purdue University, Heavilon Hall, West Lafayette, Ind. 47907.

CAREER: University of Minnesota, Minneapolis, instructor in English, 1958-61; Purdue University, West Lafayette, Ind., assistant professor, 1962-67, associate professor, 1967-81, professor of English, 1981—.

WRITINGS—Poetry: (With Tony Vevers) *Tippecanoe,* Zig/Zag, 1972; *All That, So Simple,* Purdue University Press, 1980. Contributor of poems to magazines, including *Massachusetts Review, Antioch Review, Esquire, Mademoiselle, Chariton Review,* and *Poetry Now,* and to newspapers.

WORK IN PROGRESS: More poetry and criticism.

MYHERS, John 1921-

PERSONAL: Born December 18, 1921, in Eau Claire, Wis.; son of Ole and Mabel (Borreson) Myhers; married Joan Benedict (an actress), July 12, 1962; children: Claudia. *Education:* University of Rome, Ph.D., 1950; attended Mac Phail School of Music and Drama; studied directing and film writing at Experimental Center of Cinematography. *Politics:* Democrat-Fundamentalist. *Religion:* Christian. *Agent:* International Creative Management, 8899 Beverly Blvd., Los Angeles, Calif. 90048.

CAREER: Actor, singer, director, and writer; appeared in numerous stageplays in Italy, including "Biography," "Androcles and the Lion," "Canada," "Boy Meets Girl," and "Hamlet"; toured in "Kiss Me, Kate," 1952-54; appeared in Broadway shows including "Chic," 1959, "The Golden Fleecing," 1959, and "The Good Soup," 1960; performed at the American Shakespeare Festival at Stratford, Conn., 1960; toured with the national company of "The Sound of Music," 1961-63; performed in numerous plays in Los Angeles, Calif., including "A Man for All Seasons," "Camelot," and "Idiot's Delight"; starred in motion pictures, including "How to Succeed in Business Without Really Trying," 1966, "The Private Army of Sgt. O'Farrell," 1968, "Willard," 1971, "1776," 1972, "Train Ride to Hollywood," 1975, "The Shaggy D.A.," 1976, "The Private Eyes," 1978, and "The History of the World—Part 1," 1981; director of motion pictures, including "Weddings and Babies," 1959, and "Saturday Night in Apple Valley," 1965; director of stageplays, including "The Sound of Music," "South Pacific," "Music Man," "Promises, Promises," "Last of the Red Hot Lovers," "Born Yesterday," "The Owl and The Pussycat," and "The Table"; adapted and directed "Pericles, Prince of Tyre," for "Theatre 40." Co-founder of Rome Theatre Guild and Rome Playhouse. Artistic director of the Shakespeare Repertory Co. *Military service:* U.S. Army, 1943-46; became captain. *Member:* American Film Institute.

AWARDS, HONORS: Cross of Merit, 1945; Prix de Rome, 1946; Clay Mask award from the Rome Theatre Guild, 1950, for acting in and directing "Androcles and the Lion"; International Critics Award from the Venice Film Festival, 1952, for "Weddings and Babies."

WRITINGS: (With Tim Conway) "The Private Eyes" (screenplay), New World Pictures, 1979. Also author of "Saturday Night in Apple Valley" (screenplay), 1965; (with Conway) "The Prizefighter" (screenplay), 1978; "The Pregnant Librarian" (stageplay; first produced in 1982), 1980; (with Conway) "The Brother Monks" (screenplay), 1981; (with Conway) "The Circus Murders" (screenplay). Also contributor of articles to magazines, including *American Cinema.*

WORK IN PROGRESS: "Plymouth on the Rocks," "a comedy of miracles that combines historical events with current problems, attitudes, and present-day leaders. Tim Conway will play William Bradford, the leader of the Pilgrims, and I will direct"; "Costumes," a play; "The Decision," a film based on the life of Robert E. Lee.

SIDELIGHTS: Before becoming primarily a screenwriter and director, Myhers was an actor, his most notable role being Captain von Trapp in "The Sound of Music." Of the more than seventeen hundred performances of that musical, Myhers never missed a show. As a screenwriter, he often collaborates with comedian and actor Tim Conway, writing what Myhers calls "good over evil."

Myhers told *CA:* "I have found satire to be an allegory which expresses comedic affirmation by negation of the contrary. You can't put your heart into religion without sufficient weapons."

N

NACHTIGALL, Lila Ehrenstein 1934-

BRIEF ENTRY: Born February 23, 1934, in New York, N.Y. American physician. Nachtigall has taught obstetrics and gynecology at New York University since 1964, and became director of the university's Gynecology-Endocrinology Out-Patient Department in 1973. She wrote *The Lila Nachtigall Report: The Intelligent Woman's Guide to Menopause, Estrogen, and Her Body* (Putnam, 1977). *Address:* 355 Riverside Dr., New York, N.Y. 10025; and Department of Obstetrics and Gynecology, New York University, Washington Sq., New York, N.Y. 10003. *Biographical/critical sources: Who's Who in the East,* 17th edition, Marquis, 1979.

* * *

NASSAUER, Rudolf 1924-

PERSONAL: Born November 8, 1924, in Frankfort, Germany (now West Germany); son of Franz (a wine merchant) and Hedwig Johanna (Weill) Nassauer; married Bernice Reubens (a novelist), December 29, 1947 (divorced); children: Sharon, Rebecca, Adam. *Education:* Attended University of Reading, 1943-45. *Religion:* Jewish. *Home:* 51 St. James's Gardens, London W.11, England. *Agent:* Ed Victor Ltd., 27 Soho Sq., London W1V 6AY, England. *Office:* Ehrmanns, 24/25 Scala St., London WC1 1LPU, England.

CAREER: Writer, 1947—.

WRITINGS: Poems, Methuen, 1947.

Novels; published by J. Cape, except as noted: *The Hooligan,* P. Owen, 1960; *The Cuckoo,* 1962; *The Examination,* 1973; *The Unveiling,* 1975; *The Agents of Love,* 1976; *Midlife Feasts,* 1977; *Reparations,* 1981.

WORK IN PROGRESS: Stories, tentatively titled *Gemma's Voyage of Discovery.*

SIDELIGHTS: Nassauer commented: "In *The Hooligan* I wanted to write a 'rational' book about Nazism. Since Nazi crimes were so irrational from the victims' side, I wrote the book from the Nazi angle and created Andreas, a 'rational' Nazi, the anti-hero hero. In literature the rational can be understood, whereas the irrational cannot. Good novels dictate themselves to the novelist, so much so that he is almost out of control."

He added: "I am a wine expert who was born into a dynasty of wine shippers."

AVOCATIONAL INTERESTS: Collecting pictures, especially English art.

BIOGRAPHICAL/CRITICAL SOURCES: Times Literary Supplement, March 6, 1981.

* * *

NAUER, Barbara Joan 1932-

BRIEF ENTRY: Born June 18, 1932, in Peoria, Ill. American magazine editor. Nauer has taught English and religion at high schools and universities and has worked as a librarian. Since 1978 she has edited *Jazz Arts/New Orleans.* She wrote *Rise Up and Remember* (Doubleday, 1977). *Address:* 834 St. Ann St., The Old Quarter, New Orleans, La. 70116. *Biographical/critical sources: Directory of American Scholars,* Volume IV: *Philosophy, Religion, and Law,* 7th edition, Bowker, 1978.

* * *

NAUGHTON, Bill 1910-

PERSONAL: Born June 12, 1910, in Ballyhaunis, County Mayo, Ireland; son of Thomas (a coal miner) and Maria (Fleming) Naughton; married Ernestine Pirolt. *Education:* Educated in England. *Home:* Kempis, Orrisdale Rd., Ballasalla, Isle of Man, England. *Agent:* Dr. Jan Van Loewen Ltd., 81-83 Shaftesburg Ave., London W1V 8BX, England.

CAREER: Writer and playwright. Worked as laborer, lorry driver, weaver, coalbagger, and bleacher. *Wartime service:* Civil Defense driver in London, England. *Awards, honors:* Screenwriters Guild Awards, 1967 and 1968; Prix Italia, 1974, for radio play; Other Award from Children's Rights Workshop, 1978, for *The Goalkeeper's Revenge.*

WRITINGS: A Roof Over Your Head (autobiography), Pilot Press, 1945, revised edition edited by Vincent Whitcombe, Blackie & Son, 1967; *Pony Boy* (juvenile novel), Pilot Press, 1946, revised edition, Harrap, 1966; *Rafe Granite* (novel), Pilot Press, 1947; *One Small Boy* (novel), MacKibbon & Kee, 1957, revised edition edited by David Grant, Harrap, 1970; *Late Night on Watling Street, and Other Stories,* MacGibbon & Kee, 1959, Ballantine, 1967, revised edition, Longmans, Green, 1969 (also see below); *The Goalkeeper's Revenge* (short stories), Harrap, 1961 (also see below); *Alfie* (novel), Ballantine, 1966 (also see below); *Alfie Darling* (novel), Simon & Schuster, 1970; *The Goalkeeper's Revenge* [and] *Spit Nolan,*

Macmillan, 1974; *The Bees Have Stopped Working, and Other Stories,* Wheaton & Co., 1976; *A Dog Called Nelson* (juvenile), Dent, 1976; *My Pal Spadger* (juvenile), Dent, 1977.

Plays: *My Flesh, My Blood* (two-act comedy; first broadcast in 1957), 1959, published as *Spring and Port Wine* (first produced on the West End, 1965), Samuel French, 1967 (also produced as "Keep It in the Family" on Broadway at Plymouth Theatre, September 27, 1967); *Alfie* (three-act; first broadcast as "Alfie Elkins and His Little Life," 1962; produced as "Alfie" in London, 1963), Samuel French, 1963; *All in Good Time* (comedy; first produced in London, 1963; produced in New York, N.Y., 1965), Samuel French, 1964; "He Was Gone When We Got There," first produced in London, 1966; "Annie and Fanny," first produced in Bolton, Lancashire, England, at Octagon Theatre, 1967; *June Evening* (first broadcast in 1958; produced in Birmingham, England, 1966), Samuel French, 1973; "Lighthearted Intercourse," first produced in Liverpool, England, at Liverpool Playhouse, December 1, 1971.

Radio plays: "Timothy," 1956; "She'll Make Trouble," 1958; "Late Night on Watling Street," 1959; "The Long Carry," 1959; "Seeing a Beauty Queen Home," 1960; "On the Run," 1960; "Wigan to Rome," 1960; "'30-'60," 1960; "Jackie Crowe," 1962; "November Day," 1963; "The Mystery," 1973.

Television plays: "Nathaniel Titlark" series, 1957; "Jim Batty," 1957; "Starr and Company" series, 1958; (with Alan Prior) "Yorky" series, 1960; "Somewhere for the Night," 1962; "Looking for Frankie," 1963; "It's Your Move," 1967.

SIDELIGHTS: A prolific writer of books and plays for the stage, radio, and television, Bill Naughton grew up in the coal-mining county of Lancashire, England. His first book, *A Roof Over Your Head,* is a semi-autobiographical volume that describes the typical life of poverty and hardship in Lancashire during the twenties. Lancashire is also the setting for many of Naughton's subsequent books and plays, including two of his most successful scripts, *Spring and Port Wine* and *All in Good Time.*

As in a number of Naughton's writings, family life is the subject of *Spring and Port Wine.* In this critically acclaimed play, Naughton relates a series of episodes that take place in a household during a spring weekend, with special attention paid to a young daughter who overindulges in port wine. *All in Good Time* deals with newlywed couples of Lancashire as they nervously face their wedding nights. Both of these works were later adapted for the screen: *All in Good Time* was released as "The Family Way" by Warner Bros. in 1967, and *Spring and Port Wine* was released by Warner-Pathe in 1970.

Naughton's radio play "Alfie Elkins and His Little Life" later became a stage play, a novel, and a motion picture called "Alfie." The 1966 Paramount film, a comedy-drama starring Shelley Winters and Michael Caine, portrayed a Londoner and his exploitation of women for pleasure.

BIOGRAPHICAL/CRITICAL SOURCES: Time, December 25, 1964; *New Yorker,* January 2, 1965; *Newsweek,* January 4, 1965, March 1, 1965, October 9, 1967.

*   *   *

NEAGOE, Peter   1881-1960

PERSONAL: Born November 7, 1881, in Transylvania (now Romania); came to United States in 1901; naturalized U.S. citizen; died October 28, 1960, in Woodstock, N.Y.; son of a notary; married Anna Frankeul (an artist), July 31, 1911.

Education: Attended University of Bucharest, Romanian Academy of Fine Arts, and National Academy of Design (New York). *Residence:* Woodstock, N.Y.; and Sarasota, Fla.

CAREER: Worked as translator and illustrator for mail-order catalogue, c. 1911-c.1919; artist, c. 1919-1928; writer, 1928-1960; *New Review* (literary journal), Paris, France, assistant editor, 1931; owner and co-editor, 1932. *Wartime service:* Prepared radio broadcasts for the Romanian people during World War II for the U.S. Office of War Information.

WRITINGS: (Editor and author of foreword) *Americans Abroad: An Anthology,* Service Press, 1932; *What Is Surrealism?,* New Review Press, 1932; *Storm: A Book of Short Stories,* New Review Press, 1932, enlarged edition, Obelisk Press, 1932; *Easter Sun* (novel), Coward, 1934, 1963; *Winning a Wife and Other Stories* (contains "Storm" [also see above], "Gavrila's Confession," "Kaleidoscope" [also see below], "Winning a Wife," "The Village Saint" [also see below], "A Pattern," "A Fact" [also see below] "A Segment of the Whole" [also see below], "The Holy Remedy" [also see below], "Susan and the Three Old Men," "The Shepherd of the Lord" [also see below], "Dreams" [also see below], "The Golden Path" [also see below], "Moonlit River," "Eyes," "The Watchmaker of Irmande," "A Simple Case," "The Greenhorn" [also see below], and "Contentment Is Silent" [also see below], introduction by Edward J. O'Brien, Coward, 1935, 1963; *There Is My Heart* (novel), Coward, 1936, 1963; *A Time to Keep* (memoirs), Coward, 1949, 1963; *No Time for Tears,* Kamin, 1958; *The Saint of Montparnasse: A Novel Based on the Life of Constantin Brancusi,* Chilton, 1965; *A Selection of Stories,* edited by John S. Mayfield, Syracuse University, 1969.

Contributor; short stories: "Kaleidoscope," published in *transition,* March, 1928; "A Segment of the Whole," *transition,* summer, 1928; "A Fact," *transition,* February, 1929; "Dreams," *transition,* November, 1929; "Shepherd of the Lord," *Story,* November-December, 1931; "It Dawned," *Readies for Bob Brown's Machine,* edited by Bob Brown, Roving Eye Press, 1931; "The Village Saint," *transition,* March, 1932; "The Greenhorn," *New Review,* April, 1932; "Holy Remedy," *Pagany,* July-September, 1932; "The Golden Path," *Contact,* October, 1932; "Contentment Is Silent," *Story,* February, 1934; "Then Was Hey-Day," *Story,* April, 1936; "A Drum Beat in Harvest Time," *Esquire,* February, 1938; "Ill Winds From the Wide World," *Story,* July-August, 1940; "The Lamb and the Wolves," *Story,* July-August, 1941.

SIDELIGHTS: Neagoe, a Romanian-born American who settled in Paris following World War I, abandoned a promising career as an artist to become a writer. Though best known as the author of short stories and novels about Romanian peasant life, Neagoe also edited the periodical *New Review* and an anthology of stories and poems by many of Neagoe's fellow expatriates entitled *Americans Abroad.* The volume includes works by Conrad Aiken, E. E. Cummings, John Dos Passos, Ernest Hemingway, Henry Miller, Ezra Pound, Gertrude Stein, and William Carlos Williams. Many of these literary figures, argued Neagoe in the foreword of *Americans Abroad,* fled the United States because they feared that America's trend toward uniformity would ultimately lead them to compromise their art. His own move to Paris had been motivated by the lower cost of living in France.

While residing in Paris, Neagoe wrote numerous short stories, many appearing in the periodicals *New Review, transition,* and *Story. Storm,* a collection of Neagoe's stories, was also published during this period. Set in the countryside of Romania, the tales were mildly erotic, causing customs officials to ban importation of the book into the United States. The prohibition merely served to intensify interest in the volume, and, as a result, *Storm* was reprinted several times.

Though life in rural Romania is also featured in Neagoe's *Winning a Wife, and Other Stories,* the collection also contains several stories with American settings. *New York Times* reporter Harold Strauss observed that in the American stories "Neagoe is curiously uneasy, puzzled, [and] unwilling to bring his narrative to a definite climax." The Romanian stories, though, were praised by several critics, including a *Saturday Review of Literature* reporter who said, "The strong and simple rhythms of [Neagoe's] prose are well suited to the evocation of Romanian peasant life which constitute the greater part of [*Winning a Wife*]. In describing Neagoe's stories, a *Boston Transcript* reporter remarked that "as examples of modern realism nothing better has been done."

Critics similarly praised the characterizations and style of Neagoe's novels. In reviewing *Easter Sun,* for example, a *Times Literary Supplement* reporter wrote, "Mr. Neagoe writes with an unaffected simplicity perfectly adapted to his subject . . . and one feels that his peasant characters are created out of an intimate understanding, not merely observed." Whit Burnett concurred, writing in *Books* that "Neagoe is a patient and almost prayerful evoker of natural sights and sounds and his style brings them forth so freshly, simply and precisely that the pages move with the wind in the wheatfields." Neagoe's second novel, *There Is My Heart,* about a Romanian peasant's attempt to emigrate to the United States, also was praised for its simplicity of style, which, said R. C. Wilson in *Books,* "is wholly without affectation."

Neagoe also wrote a book of childhood reminiscences entitled *Time to Keep,* in which he describes his boyhood in Romania. Again the simplicity of the author's style impressed critics. The book, said David Tilden in the *New York Herald Tribune Weekly Book Review,* is "written with the naturalness, freshness and gentle beauty of [Neagoe's] earlier stories." According to I. T. Sanders of the *Saturday Review of Literature,* "This is not a run-of-the mill autobiography: childhood is seen as an end in itself and not as some grim preparation for a successful career."

Neagoe's *The Saint of Montparnasse: A Novel Based on the Life of Constantin Brancusi,* and *Peter Neagoe: A Selection of His Stories* were published posthumously.

BIOGRAPHICAL/CRITICAL SOURCES—Books: Samuel Putnam, *Paris Was Our Mistress: Memoirs of a Lost and Found Generation,* Viking, 1947; Peter Neagoe, *A Time to Keep,* Coward, 1949; Hugh Ford, *Published in Paris: American and British Writers, Printers, and Publishers in Paris, 1920-1939,* Macmillan, 1975.

Periodicals: *Saturday Review of Literature,* March 24, 1934, December 10, 1949; *New York Times,* March 25, 1934, April 14, 1935, December 4, 1949; *Books,* March 25, 1934, April 21, 1935; *Nation,* May 29, 1935; *Boston Transcript,* June 5, 1935, April 25, 1936; *Time,* April 13, 1936; October 12, 1949; *New York Herald Tribune Weekly Book Review,* October 23, 1949; *Miorita: A Journal of Romanian Studies,* July, 1978.*

* * *

NEATE, Frank Anthony 1928-

PERSONAL: Born April 11, 1928, in Plympton, England; son of Ronald (a carpenter) and May Ethel (a draper's assistant; maiden name, Lowden) Neate; married Noia Moana (a nurse), 1956; children: Iwingaro Margaret, Tina Moana, Stephen Anthony. *Education:* Attended high school in Hutt Valley, New

Zealand. *Residence:* Greymouth, New Zealand. *Office:* Greymouth Evening Star, Greymouth, New Zealand.

CAREER: Journalist, 1945—. Associated with *Southern Cross,* Wellington, New Zealand, *Dominion,* Wellington, *Examiner,* Launceston, Tasmania, Australia, *Adelaide News,* Adelaide, Australia, *Canowindra Star,* New South Wales, Australia, and *Grey River Argus,* Greymouth, New Zealand; *Greymouth Evening Star,* Greymouth, New Zealand, sub-editor, 1959—. Member of Greymouth borough council, 1968—, justice of the peace, 1978—. Greymouth town planning commissioner, 1981—. Member of executive board of West Coast Theatre Trust. *Member:* P.E.N. International, New Zealand Journalists' Union, Greymouth Club, Greymouth Workingmen's Club, Greymouth Aero Club, Christchurch Media Club.

WRITINGS: The Hour Glass Girl (novel), Blackwood & Janet Paul, 1966; (editor with others) *The Shell Guide to New Zealand,* Whitcombe & Tombs, 1968; *Miss Fletcher's Plum Tree* (horror story), Pan Books, 1971.

WORK IN PROGRESS: "A whimsical series on white cats."

SIDELIGHTS: Neate commented: "I am consistently outraged by a seemingly unbreakable syndrome in which the gap between rich and poor widens, and in which inequity, injustice, inhumanity, and cruelty continue unceasingly. I remain optimistic, but the world seems to be taking a bloody long time to get better."

* * *

NELSON, Jane Armstrong 1927-

BRIEF ENTRY: Born March 25, 1927, in New York, N.Y. American educator and author. Nelson began teaching English at Northeastern University in 1969. She wrote *Form and Image in the Fiction of Henry Miller* (Wayne State University Press, 1970). *Address:* Department of English, Northeastern University, Boston, Mass. 02115. *Biographical/critical sources: Directory of American Scholars,* Volume II: *English, Speech, and Drama,* 7th edition, Bowker, 1978.

* * *

NELSON, Joseph Bryan 1932-

PERSONAL: Born March 14, 1932, in Shipley, England; son of Thomas William and Ida Nelson; married June Davison, December 31, 1960; children: Simon Philip and Rebecca Sarah (twins). *Education:* University of St. Andrews, B.Sc. (with first class honors), 1959; St. Catherine's College, Oxford, D.Phil., 1963. *Politics:* "Liberal Conservative." *Religion:* None. *Home:* Quilquox Croft, Ythanbank, Ellon, Aberdeen, Scotland. *Office:* Department of Zoology, University of Aberdeen, Tillydrone Ave., Aberdeen, Scotland.

CAREER: University of Aberdeen, Aberdeen, Scotland, lecturer, 1966-72, senior lecturer, 1972-79, reader in zoology, 1980—. Director of Azraq International Biological Station, Jordan, 1968-69. Radio broadcaster for British Broadcasting Corp. (BBC). *Member:* British Ornithologists Union, British Trust for Ornithology, Royal Society for the Protection of Birds, Royal Society (Edinburgh; fellow). *Awards, honors:* D'Arcy Thompson Medal from St. Andrew's University, 1959.

WRITINGS: Galapagos: Islands of Birds, Longmans, Green, 1968; *Azraq: Desert Oasis,* Allen Lane, 1973; *The Sulidae: Gannets and Boobies,* Oxford University Press, 1978; *The Gannet,* T. & A. D. Poyser, 1978; *Seabirds: Their Biology and Ecology,* Hamlyn, 1980. Contributor of about fifty articles and reviews to scientific journals and popular magazines, including *Field, Natural History,* and *Countryman.*

WORK IN PROGRESS: International research on the behavior and ecology of seabirds, especially sulids.

SIDELIGHTS: Nelson wrote: "I have strong conservation interests. I deplore ad hoc and indiscriminate use of advanced technology and adhere strongly to attitudes which are socially valuable and responsible. I dislike rabid consumerism and unthinking conformity."

AVOCATIONAL INTERESTS: Wilderness and wildlife, photography, tennis, sunbathing, rambling.

* * *

NELSON, Rowland Whiteway 1902-1979

OBITUARY NOTICE: Born May 17, 1902, in Brooklyn, N.Y.; died January 18, 1979. Educator and author. From 1938 until 1967 Nelson was a faculty member of Washington and Lee University, serving as professor of English beginning in 1956. He also founded the Lexington, Va., branch of the English-Speaking Union of the United States. Nelson's writings include *The Life of Lord Chesterfield,* which was published in 1926. Obituaries and other sources: *Blue Book: Leaders of the English-Speaking World,* St. Martin's, 1976. (Date of death provided by daughter, Joan Bargamin.)

* * *

NENNI, Pietro 1891-1980

OBITUARY NOTICE: Born February 9, 1981, in Faenza, Emilia-Romagna, Italy; died of a heart attack, January 1, 1980, in Rome, Italy. Statesman, politician, and author. Nenni joined the Partito Socialista Italiano (PSI) in 1921, becoming managing editor of the party's newspaper *Avanti!* until 1925 when the party rejected Nenni's suggestion of a leftist movement against the anti-proletarian platform of the Fascists. Nenni then began publishing *Il quarto stato,* a resistance journal, until its production was halted by the Fascists. Exiled in Paris, Nenni published *Nuovo Avanti* and wrote for French leftist publications. At the onset of World War II, Nenni's attempts to establish a Free Italian Legion failed. He was subsequently imprisoned by France's Vichy Government, and later by the Germans. Released in 1943, Nenni became secretary-general of the PSI, holding that position for nineteen years. As Deputy for Rome from 1948 to 1963, Nenni received the Stalin Peace Prize for opposing Italy's joining NATO, but returned the prize in 1956 when he began favoring a break with the Communists and supporting European unity. Nenni served as president of the PSI from 1963 until 1969. A contributor to *Avanti!* until his death, Nenni wrote numerous books, including *Lo spettro del comunismo, Pace e guerra nel Parlamento italiano, Garibaldi,* and *Intervista sul socialismo italiano.* Obituaries and other sources: *Current Biography,* Wilson, 1947, 1980; *The International Who's Who,* Europa, 1979; *The Annual Obituary 1980,* St. Martin's, 1981.

* * *

NEUMANN, Emanuel 1893-1980

OBITUARY NOTICE: Born July 2, 1893, in Liepaja, Russia (now Latvian Soviet Socialist Republic, U.S.S.R.); died October 26, 1980, in Tel Aviv, Israel. Lawyer, statesman, and author. Neumann was considered a key figure in the Zionist movement, which sought to restore the ancient Jewish homeland in Palestine. He co-founded Young Judea, a Zionist youth movement, served as educational director of the World Zionist Organization, and was a member of numerous groups, including the World Zionist Executive, Jewish Agency for Palestine in Jerusalem, and the American Palestine Committee. One Zionist desire was to acquire land in Israel and encourage Jews to settle there. Neumann ardently sought to promote land purchase, aiding the Jewish Agency for Palestine in directing Jewish immigration and settlement. In 1943 Neumann organized a group of engineers to provide the Jordan Valley with modern irrigation and hydroelectricity, and in 1944 he addressed the U.S. House of Representatives Foreign Affairs Committee, which later resolved that Palestine was open to Jews for colonization. Subsequent years found Neumann as president of the Zionist Organization in America and chairman for the U.S. branch of the World Zionist Organization, working to gain American political sympathy towards Israel. In addition to pursuing his Zionist activities, Neumann practiced law in New York City. A contributor to numerous Zionist publications, Neumann wrote an autobiography, *In The Arena.* Obituaries and other sources: *Current Biography,* Wilson, 1967; *Who's Who in America,* 40th edition, Marquis, 1978; *The Annual Obituary 1980,* St. Martin's, 1981.

* * *

NEUSE, Erna Kritsch 1923-

PERSONAL: Born August 7, 1923, in Austria; naturalized U.S. citizen; daughter of Frany and Julie (Jakupec) Kritsch; married Werner Neuse (a professor), August 14, 1965. *Education:* University of Vienna, Ph.D., 1947. *Home:* 7 Cobb Rd., New Brunswick, N.J. 08901. *Office:* Department of German, Rutgers University, New Brunswick, N.J. 08901.

CAREER: Rutgers University, New Brunswick, N.J., professor of German, 1954—. *Member:* Modern Language Association of America, American Association of Teachers of German, American Association of University Professors, ACSL.

WRITINGS: (Editor) *Neue deutsche Prosa,* Appleton, 1968; *Modernes Deutsch,* Prentice-Hall, 1970; *Deutsch fuer Anfaenger,* Prentice-Hall, 1971; *Die Deutsche Kurzgeschichte: Das Formexperiment der Moderne,* Bouvier, 1980. Contributor to language journals.

WORK IN PROGRESS: Studying the narrator in modern German prose fiction.

* * *

NEVINS, Deborah 1947-

PERSONAL: Born May 5, 1947, in New York, N.Y.; daughter of Irvin (an engineer) and Sarah (a teacher; maiden name, Winnick) Nevins. *Education:* Boston University, B.A., 1968; Columbia University, M.A., 1969, M.Phil., 1976. *Residence:* New York, N.Y.

CAREER: Architectural League of New York, New York City, program director, 1974-78; free-lance art historian, curator, and writer, 1978—. Also worked as a teacher. *Member:* Society of Architectural Historians, Gallery Association of New York, New York State Committee for the Preservation of Architectural Records. *Awards, honors:* Carey-Thomas Award, 1979, and TABA from the Association of American Publishers, 1980, both for *The Architect's Eye.*

WRITINGS: (With David Gebhard) *Two Hundred Years of American Architectural Drawing,* Whitney Library of Design, 1977; (with Robert Stern) *The Architect's Eye,* Pantheon, 1979.

WORK IN PROGRESS: Research on popular attitudes on gardening from 1600 to 1900.

* * *

NEWFELD, Frank 1928-

PERSONAL: Born May 1, 1928, in Brno, Czechoslovakia; came to Canada in 1947; son of Arnold and Rose (Deutsch) Newfeld; married Joan Barrie Hart, August 25, 1958; children: Philip Laurence, David Stefan. *Education:* Attended Brighton College of Art; Central School of Arts and Crafts, London, England, diploma, 1952. *Home:* 34 Palmdale Dr., Agincourt, Ontario, Canada M1T 3M7. *Office:* 111 Queen St. E., Toronto, Ontario, Canada M5C 1S2.

CAREER: Central Technical School, Toronto, Ontario, teacher, 1955-56; teacher at Ryerson Institute of Technology, 1956-57; Ontario College of Art, Toronto, teacher, 1958-65; McClelland & Stewart Ltd. (publisher), Toronto, art director and member of board of directors, 1963, director of design and production, 1964, creative director, 1965-69, vice-president of publishing, 1969-74, director, 1974-76, consultant, 1976-78; MacPherson Newfeld Ltd., Toronto, president, 1970—. Publishing consultant, 1973-75; lecturer and member of advisory council for Sheridan College. Work represented in exhibitions in Canada, Czechoslovakia, Germany, Holland, Israel, Japan, Spain, the United Kingdom and the United States. *Member:* Royal Canadian Academy (member of council), American Institute of Graphic Art.

AWARDS, HONORS: Award from annual book jacket competition in Scotland, 1960; Hans Christian Andersen Award honorable mentions, 1962, for *The Princess of Tombose*, and 1975; award from Annual Book Exhibition in Leipzig, East Germany, 1963; awards from International Book Exhibition in Leipzig, 1965 and 1977; Canadian Centennial Medal, 1967; awards from Printing Industries of America, 1968 and 1971; award from Society of Illustrators, 1968; Look of Books Awards, 1970, 1972, 1974, and 1976; Queen's Silver Jubilee Medal, 1977; Ruth Schwartz/CBA Award for best children's book, 1978.

WRITINGS: (Contributor) *Great Canadian Painting: A Century of Art,* Canadian Centennial Publishing, 1966; (with William Toye; self-illustrated) *Simon and the Golden Sword,* Oxford University Press, 1976.

Illustrator: Charles Marius Barbeau, editor, *The Princess of Tomboso: A Fairy-Tale in Pictures,* Oxford University Press, 1960; Dennis Lee, *Alligator Pie* (poems), Macmillan (Toronto), 1974, Houghton, 1975; Lee, *Nicholas Knock and Other People* (poems) Macmillan (Toronto), 1974, Houghton, 1976; Lee, *Garbage Delight* (poems), Houghton, 1977; Peter Desbarats, *The Night the City Sang,* McClelland, 1977, also published as *Halibut York and More.* Contributor of illustrations to numerous periodicals.

SIDELIGHTS: Frank Newfeld is one of the leading illustrators in Canada and is prominent in the field of book design. During his career he has designed nearly five hundred books for publishing firms in Canada, the United States, the United Kingdom, and for museums and galleries, including the Art Gallery of Ontario, the Museum of Modern Art in New York, and the National Gallery of Canada.

One of Newfeld's criteria in illustrating children's books is to avoid violence in any form. Humor rests just beneath the surface of his whimsical drawings, which are regarded for their sense of warmth and color.

AVOCATIONAL INTERESTS: Horses, theatre.*

NEWLAND, T. Ernest 1903-

PERSONAL: Born June 3, 1903, in Cincinnati, Ohio; son of Frank C. (a railroad fireman) and Rolana (Kyle) Newland; married Frances Schneider (divorced); married Mary C. Jarrett (a secretary), November 23, 1945; children: Dorothy Newland Potts, Theryl E. *Education:* Wittenberg College, A.B., 1925; Ohio State University, A.M., 1929, Ph.D., 1931. *Religion:* Unitarian-Universalist. *Home:* 1004 Ross Dr., Champaign, Ill. 61820.

CAREER: Teacher of math and geography at public junior high school in Springfield, Ohio, 1925; Emporia State College, Emporia, Kan., assistant professor of psychology, 1927-29; Bucknell University, Lewisburg, Pa., assistant professor of education, 1931-37; Pennsylvania Department of Public Instruction, Harrisburg, chief of special education, 1938-42; University of Tennessee, Knoxville, associate professor of psychology and director of Psychology Clinic, 1948-51; University of Illinois, Urbana, professor of educational psychology, 1951-71; writer, 1971—. Field selection officer for U.S. Peace Corps; evaluation officer for Teacher Corps; clinical psychologist at Veterans Administration Hospital, Acuff, Knoxville, Tenn.; member of medical staff at Veterans Administration Office, Knoxville. *Military service:* U.S. Navy, in communications, 1942-46; became lieutenant commander. U.S. Naval Reserve, 1948-50; became commander. U.S. Army, assistant director of military leadership at U.S. Military Academy, West Point, 1946-48. U.S. Army Reserve, 1946-48; became lieutenant colonel. *Member:* American Psychological Association, American Association for the Advancement of Science, Council for Exceptional Children.

WRITINGS: The Blind Learning Aptitude Test, University of Illinois Press, 1971; *The Gifted in Socioeducational Perspective,* Prentice-Hall, 1976; (contributor) Robert T. Brown and Cecil R. Reynolds, *Psychological Perspectives of Exceptional Children,* Wiley, 1981. Also contributor of about one hundred seventy-five articles to psychology and education journals.

WORK IN PROGRESS: Research on intellectual processing of information by children.

SIDELIGHTS: Newland told *CA:* "I'm quite interested in conceptual development of children, especially the younger ones. I'm repeatedly irked at the incessant rediscovery of the wheel. I'm disappointed that so many basically good psychological and educational ideas are overgeneralized into absurdities. However, I've reached the stage where I'm enjoying the good work of many of my graduate students, whom I seem not to have impeded too much in their progress toward fuller intellectual maturing."

* * *

NEWLEY, Anthony (George) 1931-

PERSONAL: Born September 24, 1931, in Hackney, London, England; son of George Anthony Newley (a shipping clerk) and Frances Grace Newley Gardiner; married Anne E. Lynn (an actress), August 30, 1956 (divorced, 1963); married Joan Collins (an actress), May 27, 1963 (divorced August 13, 1971); children: Tara Cynara, Alexander Anthony. *Education:* Studied with Dewsbury Repertory Co., England; trained for stage with Italia Conti. *Religion:* Jewish.

CAREER: Worked in insurance office and as office boy, c. 1945. Actor, director, playwright, composer, lyricist, and singer, 1946—. Actor in plays, including "Winds of Heaven," 1946, repertory productions of Dewsbury Co., 1950, "Lady of the House," 1953, "Cranks," 1955, (and director) "Stop the World—I Want to Get Off," 1961, (and director) "The Roar of the Greasepaint—The Smell of the Crowd," 1965, "The Good Old Bad Old Days," 1972, "Royalty Follies," 1974. Also starred in "It's a Funny Old World We Live In" and "The World's Not Entirely to Blame." Director of motion picture "Summertree," 1971.

Actor in films, including "The Adventures of Dusty Bates," 1946, "Little Ballerina," 1947, "Vice Versa," 1948, "Oliver Twist," 1948, "The Guinea Pig," 1948, "Vote for Huggett," 1949, "Don't Ever Leave Me," 1949, "A Boy, a Girl, and a Bike," 1949, "Golden Salamander," 1950, "Madeleine," 1950, "Highly Dangerous," 1950, "Those People Next Door," 1952, "Top of the Form," 1953, "The Weak and the Wicked," 1954, "Up to His Neck," 1954, "Above Us the Waves," 1955, "Cockleshell Heroes," 1955, "Blue Peter," 1955.

"Port Afrique," 1956, "Last Man to Hang," 1956, "X, the Unknown," 1956, "Battle of the River Plate," 1956, "The Good Companions," 1957, "Fire Down Below," 1957, "How to Murder a Rich Uncle," 1957, "High Flight," 1957, "No Time to Die," 1958, "Task Force," 1958, "The Man Inside," 1958, "The Bandit of Zhobe," 1959, "The Lady Is a Square," 1959, "Idle on Parade," 1959, "The Heart of a Man," 1959, "Killers of Kilimanjaro," 1959, "Jazz Boat," 1959, "In the Nick," 1960, "Let's Get Married," 1960, "Play It Cool," 1961, "The Small World of Sammy Lee," 1963, "Doctor Doolittle," 1967, (and producer) "Sweet November," 1968, (director and producer) "Can Heironymus Merkin Ever Forget Mercy Humppe and Find True Happiness?," 1969, "Mr. Quilp," 1975, "A Good Idea at the Time," 1976.

Actor in television series, including "Sammy," 1958, and "The Strange World of Gurney Glade," 1960-61. Also appeared on television programs, including "The Vic Oliver Show," "The Alfred Marks Show," "The Wharf Road Mob," "Picture Parade," "Focus on Youth," "The Shirley Bassey Show," "Music Shop," "The Tonight Show," "The Merv Griffin Show," "Hollywood Squares," "Sunday Night Palladium," "Saturday Spectaculars," "The Johnny Darling Show," 1962, "Lucky in London," 1966, "The Anthony Newley Show," 1972, and "Burt Bacharach!," 1972.

Performer in night clubs and concert theatres, including Caesar's Palace, Las Vegas, Nev., 1969; Empire Room of the Waldorf-Astoria, New York City, 1969; Harrah's, Lake Tahoe, Calif., 1970; (with Buddy Hackett) Fisher Theatre, Detroit, Mich., 1971; (with Henry Mancini) Uris Theatre, New York City, 1974; (with Burt Bacharach) Westbury Music Fair, New York, 1976.

MEMBER: American Federation of Television and Radio Artists, Actor's Equity Association, British Actor's Equity Association. Awards, honors: Ivor Novello award and Broadcast Music Inc. (BMI) award, both 1962, both for song "What Kind of Fool Am I?"; British Writers Guild Award for best original screenplay, 1969, for "Can Heironymus Merkin Ever Forget Mercy Humppe and Find True Happiness?"

WRITINGS—Librettist and composer and lyricist of songs for plays; all with Leslie Bricusse, except as noted: "ABC," "I Wanna Be Rich," "Typically English," "A Special Announcement," "Lumbered," "Welcome to Sludgepool," "Gonna Build a Mountain," "Glorious Russia," "Meilinki Meilchick," "Family Fugue," "Typische Deutsche," "Nag! Nag! Nag!," "All-American," "Once in a Lifetime" "Mumbo Jumbo," "Welcome to Sunvale," "Someone Nice Like You," and "What Kind of Fool Am I?" from Stop the World—I Want

to Get Off (first produced on the West End at Queen's Theatre, July 20, 1961, produced on Broadway at Shubert Theatre, October 3, 1962, and at Ambassador Theatre, September, 1963), A. Meyerson, 1962; "The Beautiful Land," "A Wonderful Day Like Today," "It Isn't Enough," "Things to Remember," "Put It in the Book," "This Dream," "Where Would You Be Without Me?," "Look at that Face," "My First Love Song," "The Joker," "Who Can I Turn to (When Nobody Needs Me)," "Funny Funeral," "That's What It Is to Be Young," "What a Man!," "Feeling Good," "Nothing Can Stop Me Now," "My Way," and "Sweet Beginning" from "The Roar of the Greasepaint—The Smell of the Crowd," first produced on West End at Royalty Theatre, August, 1964, produced on Broadway at Shubert Theatre, May 16, 1965.

"The Good Old Bad Old Days," "The Fool Who Dared to Dream," "The Wisdom of the World," "Thanksgiving Day," "Today," "Tomorrow," "Yesterday," "It's a Musical World," "I Do Not Love You," "A Cotton Pickin' Moon," "The Good Things in Life," "The People Tree," and "We've a Cure for Everything on Broadway" from "The Good Old Bad Old Days," first produced on West End at Prince of Wales' Theatre, December 20, 1972. Also librettist, composer, and lyricist with John Taylor of "The Royalty Follies," first produced on West End at Royalty Theatre, March, 1974.

Composer and lyricist of songs for films; all with Bricusse, except as noted: "Goldfinger," United Artists, 1964; "Willy Wonka and the Chocolate Factory," Paramount, 1971; (sole composer) "Mr. Quilp," Avco Embassy, 1975.

Recordings: "Stop the World—I Want to Get Off," London, c. 1962; "In My Solitude," RCA, 1964; "The Roar of the Greasepaint—The Smell of the Crowd," RCA, 1965; "Doctor Doolittle," RCA, 1967; "Ain't It Funny," GM-Verve, 1973. Also original cast albums of "Cranks" and "The Good Old Bad Old Days."

Screenplay: (With Herman Raucher) "Can Heironymus Merkin Ever Forget Mercy Humppe and Find True Happiness?," Regional, 1969.

SIDELIGHTS: During the bombing of London in World War II, Anthony Newley was sent from his city school to foster parents in the English countryside. Under the care of George Pecud, a retired entertainer, the youth was introduced to a new world that included painting, sketching, and singing. With this background, Newley began to study acting seriously after the war. Shortly after he began his professional education, the young actor made his debut as the child star of "The Adventures of Dusty Bates." From this beginning, Newley moved on to more challenging acting assignments until he expanded into every aspect of the entertainment industry. Known for his versatility, he revealed to a Guardian reporter that his drive was a "mad search for respect and admiration," an impulsion reflected in his work.

As the librettist, composer, lyricist, director, and star of two musicals, Newley concentrated on the theme of the individual fighting the big system. Called "a notable theatrical achievement" by Richard Watts, Jr., of the New York Post, Newley's first production, "Stop the World—I Want to Get Off," is a simple, satirical fantasy which symbolically traces the seven ages of man through the life and death of the character Littlechap. Seeking fame and fortune at the play's opening, Littlechap battles his way to the top only to realize the foolishness of his pursuit.

Popular with audiences, "Stop the World" ran for two years in London and for 556 Broadway performances. "The secret of the show's popularity," said Mel Gussow in the New York

Times, "is, of course, the score." The reviewer singled out three "powerhouse" numbers in the production: "Gonna Build a Mountain," "Once in a Lifetime," and "What Kind of Fool Am I?" These he labeled "inspirational standards." The last song, sung by Littlechap when he sees the folly of his struggles, has been recorded in over seventy versions and has grossed enough profits for Newley to have retired in 1962. Besides "What Kind of Fool Am I?," Newley's "hallmark" in "Stop the World" was his ability to pantomime. Though he never studied mime, his performance was compared by some critics to the art of Marcel Marceau.

"Stop the World" has twice been adapted for the screen. The first version, which Newley was originally scheduled to direct and star in, was released by Warner Brothers in 1966, filmed by another director and featuring Tony Tanner. The second picture, starring Sammy Davis, Jr., was the screen adaptation of Davis's Americanized version of Newley's play. "Sammy Stops the World" was released by Special Event Entertainment in 1979.

"The Roar of the Greasepaint—The Smell of the Crowd," Newley's second musical, carried on his theme of the working class against the establishment. Although the play only ran for seven months on Broadway, its original cast album sold over one hundred thousand copies. In 1969 the play was filmed by Jack Haley, Jr.'s production company. Newley and Bricusse wrote several new songs for the movie, and Newley played the lead.

"The Roar of the Greasepaint" preceded two more musicals, though Newley expected it to be his last endeavor in the genre. "I want to direct movies," he remarked shortly after "The Roar of the Greasepaint" opened. "I want to perform in movies. I'm too old for this sort of thing."

In 1975 Newley wrote the music and lyrics for as well as starred in the motion picture "Mr. Quilp." Hailing Newley as "magnificent," David A. Tyler found the entertainer to be "the best part of *Mr. Quilp*."

Based on Dickens's *The Old Curiosity Shop,* the film tells the story of a misanthropic moneylender's ruination of Little Nell, one of Dickens's more pathetic children, and her grandfather. Called a "one-man show," "Mr. Quilp" centers on the villain, Newley's character. The actor's performance, wrote David Sterritt of the *Christian Science Monitor,* "is more realistic—and more extravagantly Dickensian—than I dreamed it could be." The scope of Newley's portrayal looms over the other characters, who, noted *Newsweek*'s Bruce Cook, "fade into the wallpaper whenever Newley appears." "He plays the grasping moneylender with such manic ferocity," Cook continued, "that whenever he is off-screen for an instant the picture goes flat." "Thank heaven, in fact, for large villains," Charles Champlin agreed. "For so long as he is making his mugging way across the screen, leering and loping and abusing everyone in sight, Newley gives *Mr. Quilp* the air of fabulous make believe it so desperately requires."

More recently, Newley, a British tax-exile living in the United States, was one of the headline entertainers at President Ronald Reagan's 1981 inaugural celebration. Considered "the largest entertainment project ever," the inaugural balls featured shows in the night club tradition. The gala's coordinators, Robert K. Gray and Charles Z. Wick, promised that "there is no precedent in either inaugural history or entertainment history for such a show of performing talent."

AVOCATIONAL INTERESTS: Photography, painting, fishing.

BIOGRAPHICAL/CRITICAL SOURCES: New York Times, May 2, 1949, February 28, 1951, July 31, 1951, May 14, 1956,

June 4, 1956, November 3, 1956, November 27, 1956, August 9, 1957, October 26, 1957, February 5, 1959, April 7, 1960, September 17, 1962, September 30, 1962, October 4, 1962, August 14, 1963, May 17, 1965, June 15, 1965, May 12, 1966, December 20, 1967, February 9, 1968, March 20, 1969, June 17, 1971, July 1, 1971, August 4, 1978, May 8, 1979, September 21, 1979, January 8, 1981; *Guardian,* June 12, 1961; *London Times,* July 1, 1961, June 23, 1964, August 7, 1964, December 9, 1972, December 21, 1972, February 24, 1974, March 24, 1974, March 26, 1974, March 31, 1974, November 21, 1975.

New York Herald Tribune, September 30, 1962; *New York Post,* October 4, 1962, November 8, 1975; *New York Times Magazine,* October 7, 1962; *Time,* October 12, 1962, May 28, 1965, March 28, 1969, December 8, 1975; *New Yorker,* October 13, 1962, May 29, 1965; *Newsweek,* October 15, 1962, May 31, 1965, April 7, 1969, November 24, 1975; *Vogue,* October 15, 1962; *Nation,* October 20, 1962; *Saturday Review,* October 20, 1962, June 5, 1965, April 5, 1969; *New York Post Magazine,* October 21, 1962; *Theatre Arts,* November, 1962; *Commonweal,* November 16, 1962, April 18, 1969; *New York Sunday News,* November 25, 1962, May 23, 1965; *Life,* November 30, 1962, November 29, 1963; *Catholic World,* December, 1962, May, 1965; *Dance Magazine,* December, 1962, July, 1965; *America,* December 8, 1962, June 12, 1965; *Reporter,* December 20, 1962, April 8, 1965.

New York Herald Tribune Magazine, May 16, 1965; *Seventeen,* October, 1967; *Variety,* December 24, 1969, March 18, 1970; *Christian Century,* January 7, 1970; *Show Business,* January 24, 1970; *Look,* August 24, 1971; Richard Lewine and Alfred Simon, *Songs of the American Theatre,* Dodd, 1973; *Film Information,* November, 1975; *Women's Wear Daily,* November 7, 1975; *New York Magazine,* November 17, 1975; *Los Angeles Times,* November 19, 1975; *Senior Scholastic,* December 16, 1975; *Christian Science Monitor,* December 5, 1975; Brian Rust and Rex Bunnett, *London Musical Shows on Record, 1897-1976,* Gramophone, 1977.*

—*Sketch by Charity Anne Dorgan*

* * *

NEWMAN, Ruth (May) G(allert) 1914-

PERSONAL: Born June 16, 1914, in New York, N.Y.; daughter of Ernest Ezra and Belle (Cohen) Gallert; married James R. Newman (a writer), July 27, 1940 (died July, 1966); children: Jeffrey Frederick, Brooke Anne Newman Carlson. *Education:* Douglass College, Rutgers University, B.A., 1937; George Washington University, M.A., 1950; University of Maryland, Ph.D., 1956. *Politics:* Democrat. *Religion:* Jewish. *Home and office:* 2761 Brandywine St. N.W., Washington, D.C. 20008. *Agent:* Virginia Pryor Gould, Literistic Ltd., 32 West 40th St., New York, N.Y.

CAREER: Private practice of psychotherapy in Washington, D.C. Georgetown Day School, Washington, D.C., psychologist, 1949-52; National Institutes of Health, director of education in child research branch, 1954-60; Washington School of Psychiatry, Washington, D.C., director of school research program, 1960-66; director of Institute for Educational Service, 1966-67; Children's Hospital, Washington, D.C., director of group and family therapy at Hillcrest Children's Center, 1967—. Associate professor at University of Maryland, 1969—; guest professor at American University; member of executive committee of Washington School of Psychiatry. Consultant to District of Columbia School-Pupil Personnel Service, 1967—. Member of Castle Hill Center for the Arts. *Member:* American

Orthopsychiatric Association (fellow; executive vice-president), American Psychological Association, American Association of University Professors, Group Therapy Association (fellow), A. K. Rice Institute of Group Relations (fellow). *Awards, honors:* Poetry award from New Jersey College for Women, 1937; National Institutes of Health research grant, 1960-63 and 1971-72; Meyer Foundation grant, 1963-66.

WRITINGS: Psychological Consultation in the Schools, Basic Books, 1967; *Groups and Schools,* Simon & Schuster, 1974; (with Nicholas J. Long and William C. Morse), *Conflict in the Classroom,* edited by Long, Wadsworth, 1976, 4th edition, 1980. Also contributor to *Women and Anger* for Menninger. Contributor of articles and poems to education and psychology journals and newspapers.

WORK IN PROGRESS: A book on aging; a book expressing Newman's personal philosophy and reminiscences; research on charismatic leadership.

SIDELIGHTS: Ruth Newman commented that her interests include "emotional disturbances affecting behavior and learning, group forces (conscious and unconscious) affecting personal and political behavior, human development, the process of aging, and women and aging."

* * *

NEWSOME, Walter L(ee) 1941-

PERSONAL: Born October 11, 1941, in Panama City, Fla.; son of John Clinton and Hilda Elaine (Blackburn) Newsome; married Carolyn Helen Wegner; children: Cynthia Marie, Donna Carol. *Education:* Pensacola Junior College, A.A., 1961; Florida State University, B.S., 1963, M.S.L.S., 1965. *Home:* 1407 Baker St., Charlottesville, Va. 22903. *Office:* Public Documents, Alderman Library, University of Virginia, Charlottesville, Va. 22901.

CAREER: Pensacola Junior College, Pensacola, Fla., adult programs librarian, 1965-67; Florida Atlantic University, Boca Raton, documents and reference librarian, 1967-70; University of Virginia, Charlottesville, public documents librarian, 1970—.

WRITINGS: New Guide to Popular Government Publications for Libraries and Home Reference, Libraries Unlimited, 1978; *Government Reference Books, 1978-79: A Biennial Guide to U.S. Government Publications, Sixth Biennial Volume,* Libraries Unlimited, 1980. Contributor to *American Reference Books Annual* and to library journals.

WORK IN PROGRESS: Government Reference Books, 1980-81: A Biennial Guide to U.S. Government Publications, publication expected circa 1982.

* * *

NIAS, D(avid) K(enneth) B(oydell) 1940-

PERSONAL: Born November 4, 1940, in Westmorland, England; son of John F.S. (in British Army) and M.H. Joy (Ponsford) Nias. *Education:* University of Leicester, B.A. (with honors), 1964; University of London, M.Phil., 1968, Ph.D., 1975. *Home:* Shirley House, Upper Beeding, Steyning, Sussex, England. *Agent:* Andrew Best, Curtis Brown Academic Ltd., 1 Craven Hill, London W2 SE5, England. *Office:* Department of Psychology, Institute of Psychiatry, University of London, London SE5, England.

CAREER: University of London, Institute of Psychiatry, London, England, clinical psychologist, 1964-70, researcher, 1970—. Researcher at Loughborough University, Loughbor-

ough, England, 1966-68. *Member:* British Psychological Society (associate).

WRITINGS: (With Glenn Wilson) *The Mystery of Love,* Quadrangle, 1976; (with H. J. Eysenck) *Sex, Violence, and the Media,* Harper, 1979; (with Eysenck) *Astrology: Science or Superstition?,* Maurice Temple Smith, 1981.

WORK IN PROGRESS: An evaluation of sports psychology, publication in *Advances in Behavior Research and Therapy* expected in 1982.

SIDELIGHTS: Nias told *CA:* "Our work is based on testing theories against facts. Too often people attempt to elaborate and apply theories without first checking that they are consistent with known facts. A rational approach is particularly important in psychology, which is only at an early stage of scientific development.

"Our work in astrology and sports psychology has indicated that most, but not all, of the existing theories and practices are without validity. This is a pity since new and potentially valuable theories can readily be developed using research material that is already available."

* * *

NICHOLL, Louise Townsend 1890(?)-1981

OBITUARY NOTICE—See index for *CA* sketch: Born c. 1890 in Scotch Plains, N.J.; died November 10, 1981, in Plainfield, N.J. Editor, poet, and author. In 1954 Nicholl won the $5000 fellowship of the Academy of American Poets and in so doing became the first woman to secure that award. She was described by reviewers as a religious poet and a poet of revelation. Nicholl wrote eight books of poetry, including *Water and Light, Life Is the Flesh, The Explicit Flower,* and *The World's One Clock,* and one novel, *The Blossom-Print.* Obituaries and other sources: *Publishers Weekly,* January 29, 1982.

* * *

NICHOLLS, Peter (Douglas) 1939-

PERSONAL: Born March 8, 1939, in Melbourne, Australia; son of Alan Whyte (a journalist) and Shirley Alice (a teacher of classics; maiden name, Campbell) Nicholls; married Sari Elizabeth Wawn (a teacher), February 2, 1963 (divorced July, 1971); children: Sophia Alice, Saul Alan. *Education:* University of Melbourne, B.A. (with first class honors), 1961; attended Boston University, 1968-69. *Politics:* "Center left." *Religion:* None. *Home and office:* 23 Laurier Rd., London NW5 1SH, England. *Agent:* A. D. Peters & Co. Ltd., 10 Buckingham St., London WC2N 6BU, England.

CAREER: University of Melbourne, Parkville, Australia, tutor in English literature, 1962-64; University of Sydney, Sydney, Australia, senior tutor in English literature, 1964-68; Boston University, Boston, Mass., Harkness fellow, 1968-69; Universal Studios, Hollywood, Calif., worked on film "The Andromeda Strain," 1970; North East London Polytechnic, London, England, senior lecturer in English literature and administrator of Science Fiction Foundation, 1971-77; freelance writer, 1978—. Radio broadcaster; television scriptwriter. *Member:* Science Fiction Research Association, National Film Theatre, British Science Fiction Association. *Awards, honors:* Harkness fellowship for the United States, 1968; Hugo Science Fiction Achievement Award from Noreascon World Science Fiction Convention and Locus Award from *Locus* magazine, both 1980, both for *The Science Fiction Encyclopedia;* Pilgrim Award from Science Fiction Research Association, 1980.

WRITINGS: (Editor and contributor) *Science Fiction at Large,* Gollancz, 1977, Harper, 1978, reprinted as *Exploration of the Marvellous,* Fontana, 1978; (editor and contributor) *Foundations: Numbers 1 to 8,* Gregg, 1978; (editor and contributor) *The Science Fiction Encyclopedia,* Doubleday, 1979 (published in England as *The Encyclopedia of Science Fiction,* Granada, 1979); *The Science in Science Fiction,* M. Joseph, 1982.

Contributor: Christopher Carrell, editor, *Beyond This Horizon,* Ceolfrith Press, 1973; Frank N. Magill, editor, *Survey of Science Fiction Literature,* Salem Press, 1979; (author of introduction) Frank Herbert, *The Dragon in the Sea,* Gregg, 1980; (author of introduction) Philip Jose Farmer, *To Your Scattered Bodies Go,* Gregg, 1980; (author of introduction) Brian W. Aldiss, *The Saliva Tree,* Gregg, 1981; Everett F. Bleiler, editor, *Science Fiction Writers,* Scribner, 1982; Magill, editor, *Survey of Modern Fantasy Literature,* Salem Press, 1982.

Work represented in anthologies, including *Nebula Award Stories Eleven,* edited by Ursula K. Le Guin, 1976. Contributor to magazines and newspapers, including *Guardian* and *Washington Post.* Editor of *Foundation: The Review of Science Fiction,* 1974-78; deputy editor of *The Omni Book of the Future,* 1981.

WORK IN PROGRESS: The Encyclopedia of Fantasy; editing and writing part of *Revolutions in Ideas,* including ideas in law, economics, religion, science, medicine, the arts, politics, and philosophy, "concentrating on periods where new paradigms of thought are set up"; research on science fiction and fantasy in literature and in film and illustration; research on recent scientific developments.

SIDELIGHTS: Nicholls wrote: "At university I changed to arts after two years studying science and medicine, and ever since I have found my intellectual life hovering somewhere between the two cultures; hence, in part, the interest in science fiction, which was much developed when I worked as a student of Robert Wise on the science fiction film 'The Andromeda Strain' in 1970 in Hollywood. I have never been wholly happy with academic work, enjoying the teaching, but disliking the rat race. I took no further degrees after my B.A.

"My father was a journalist, and I have always felt close to the media—newspapers, television, and film. I have free lanced in all three fields, and did so even when I was an academic.

"I believe, rather strongly and angrily, that the versions of intellectual history (especially the history of literature) as taught in most universities are disgracefully narrow and elitist; in particular the genres are very nearly ignored (adventure fiction, romances, gothics, thrillers, westerns, detective stories, fantasy and science fiction, and so on). As a result, many students graduate with very little notion of what, at any given period of history, the ordinary person believed and thought about. Even second-rate genre literature (and illustration, theater, music, et cetera) is valuable for the sociological and historical insights it affords us. Furthermore, the genres have produced a great deal of excellent work in themselves.

"This situation continues. Film now has a good coverage, but the literary genres continue to be ignored, even though they are what most people read. In other words, literary studies have become increasingly divorced from reality.

"Even the history of ideas, as taught academically, is rather skewed toward 'respectability.' I especially enjoy science fiction, fantasy, and the cinema, because each medium gives us a kind of access into the unconscious desires and fears of the populace at large. They are popular art forms."

Nicholls added a personal note: "I am an Australian in exile in London, and have been since 1970. I am also a renegade academic. All of this, plus the nature of my professional interests, leads to a certain rootlessness which is probably useful when thinking about science fiction and fantasy. I am divorced, wine-drinking, unathletic (I fall over when I ski), ill-tempered, and sociable. Thinly disguised portraits of me, as a villain, appear in several novels. I am scornful to the point of arrogance about the standard of much published criticism. I own five thousand books, of which over half are science fiction."

* * *

NICHOLS, James R(ichard)   1938-

PERSONAL: Born June 29, 1938, in Troy, N.Y.; son of Elmer James (a sales manager) and Mary (a seamstress; maiden name, Crandell) Nichols; married Adelaide Corbin, July 3, 1963 (divorced, 1977); married Carla Hutchens (a librarian), April 5, 1980; children: James Harrison, Jonothan Carver. *Education:* Union College, Schenectady, N.Y., B.A., 1961; University of North Carolina, M.A., 1966, Ph.D., 1969. *Home:* 172 Highland Dr., New Concord, Ohio 43762. *Office:* Department of English, Muskingum College, New Concord, Ohio 43762.

CAREER: Sales clerk at department store in Albany, N.Y., 1954-55; in sales for bakery in Green Island, N.Y., 1955-57; Muskingum College, New Concord, Ohio, assistant professor, 1969-75, professor of English, 1975—, chairman of department, 1978—. Member of Ohio English Association. Gives readings from his work. *Military service:* U.S. Marine Corps, 1961-65; became captain. *Member:* Modern Language Association of America, American Association of University Professors (president, 1971, 1973), National Council of College Publications Advisers, Lawrence Durrell Society. *Awards, honors:* Grants from Mack Foundation, 1972, 1975, and 1981, and from National Endowment for the Humanities, 1972.

WRITINGS: Children of the Sea (novel), Blair, 1977; *Art and Irony: The Tragic Vision of H. H. Richardson,* University Publications of America, 1981. Contributor to magazines, including *Literary Review* and *Encore.* Associate editor of *Ohio English Bulletin,* 1972-75.

WORK IN PROGRESS: A Discrete Passion, a novel, publication expected in 1982; *All My Young Sons,* a novel, publication expected in 1983.

SIDELIGHTS: Nichols commented: "I write to learn about language and how it may discover people. I'm interested in the continuity of human experience, where people come from and where they're going. My academic interests are in the novel and Commonwealth novelists such as Patrick White, Janet Frame, and Doris Lessing."

* * *

NICOLAYSEN, Bruce   1934-

PERSONAL: Born November 14, 1934, in New Jersey; son of Frederick (in insurance) and Joan (Musgrave) Nicolaysen; married, 1962 (divorced, 1970); married Deirdre Marynissen (a television producer), July 4, 1978; children (first marriage) Kjirsti, Inger. *Education:* Fordham College (now University), A.B., 1958. *Residence:* Bennington, Vt. 05201. *Agent:* Nat Sobel, 128 East 56th St., New York, N.Y. 10022.

CAREER: Free-lance television writer, producer, and director, 1965-70; creative director of Ogilvy & Mather (advertising agency), 1970-74; writer, 1974—. Consultant to Shell Co. *Military service:* U.S. Marine Corps, 1954-56. *Member:* Writers Guild of America (West).

WRITINGS: Perilous Passage, Playboy Press, 1977; From Distant Shores, Avon, 1980; On Maiden Lane: The Novel of New York, Avon, 1981.

Films: "The Innocents," Twentieth Century-Fox, 1961; "The Passage" (based on own book Perilous Passage), United Artists, 1979. Also author of "Big Stickup at Brinks."

WORK IN PROGRESS: Three novels, for Avon.

MEDIA ADAPTATIONS: "The Passage," the United Artists 1979 film adaptation of Nicolaysen's book Perilous Passage, starred Anthony Quinn, James Mason, and Patricia Neal.

BIOGRAPHICAL/CRITICAL SOURCES: New York Times Book Review, January 16, 1977; New York Times, March 9, 1979.

* * *

NIELSEN, Margaret A(nne)

PERSONAL: Born in Omaha, Neb.; daughter of Carl C. and Christine M. Nielsen. Education: Attended University of California, Berkeley, 1924-25; University of Nebraska, A.B., 1928; Northwestern University, M.A., 1931. Home: 12665 Southwest Prince Edward Court, Tigard, Ore. 97223.

CAREER: High school and junior college teacher in Iowa and Nebraska, 1928-37; high school speech and drama teacher in Omaha, Neb., 1937-65; University of Oregon, Eugene, writer, editor, and research assistant in education, 1965-72; writer, 1972—. Member: Altrusa Club, Business and Professional Women, Phi Beta Kappa, Phi Beta, Delta Kappa Gamma (state president, 1975-77; member of executive board).

WRITINGS: (Contributor) Paul B. Jacobson, editor, The Principalship: New Perspectives, Prentice-Hall, 1973; (with Ingeborg MacHaffie) Of Danish Ways, Dillon, 1976. Contributor to education journals; feature writer for Tigard Courier.

WORK IN PROGRESS: Free-lance articles.

SIDELIGHTS: Margaret Nielsen commented: "I have done publicity work for projects designed to improve the image of education in America and to restore public confidence in the efficacy of the schools. My interest was challenged by the statement recently made by Fred Hechinger, distinguished former editor of the New York Times, 'America is in headlong retreat from its commitment to its schools.' I believe our system of public education is absolutely basic to our democracy. We must make it our top priority in quality and support."

AVOCATIONAL INTERESTS: Scandinavian travel.

* * *

NIETZKE, Ann 1945-

PERSONAL: Name legally changed, 1966; born September 16, 1945, in Alton, Ill.; daughter of William Chester (a tool and die maker) and Lottie (Joyner) Tidwell. Education: University of Illinois, B.S. (with honors), 1967; Illinois State University, M.A., 1969. Residence: Venice, Calif. Agent: Sandra Goldbeck, Sanford J. Greenburger Associates, Inc., 825 Third Ave., New York, N.Y. 10022.

CAREER: High school English teacher in Normal, Ill., 1967; St. Joseph's Hospital, Bloomington, Ill., radiology transcriber, 1970-71; Mennonite Hospital, Bloomington, medical transcriber, 1972-76; University of California, Los Angeles, secretary and staff writer in department of psychiatry, 1977-79; Social and Public Art Resource Center, Los Angeles, secretary and grant writer, 1979-80; Light Publishing Associates, Los Angeles, editorial consultant, 1980—.

WRITINGS: Windowlight: A Woman's Journal From the Edge of America (novel), Capra, 1981.

Contributor: J. H. Brennecke and R. G. Amick, editors, Readings in Psychology and Human Experience, Glencoe, 1974, 2nd edition, 1978; Joan Valdes and Jeanne Crow, editors, The Media Reader, Pflaum Press, 1975; Glen Gaviglio and David E. Raye, editors, Society As It Is: A Reader, 2nd edition, Macmillan, 1976; William Rivers and Leonard Sellers, editors, Mass Media Issues: Articles and Commentaries, Prentice-Hall, 1977; W. A. Ferrell and N. A. Salerno, editors, Strategies in Prose, 4th edition, Holt, 1978; Alan Wells, editor, Mass Media and Society, Mayfield, 1979; Death and Dying, Social Resources Series, 1979; Joel M. Charon, editor, The Meaning of Sociology: A Reader, Alfred Publishing, 1980. Contributor to popular magazines and newspapers, including Woman's World, Village Voice, Playgirl, Saturday Review, Society, and Cosmopolitan. Contributing editor of Human Behavior, 1974-79.

SIDELIGHTS: Ann Nietzke wrote: "Windowlight is a work of autobiographical fiction. Its narrator is a recently divorced woman in her thirties who comes to Venice, California, from the Midwest and experiences all the culture shock attendant in such a move. Her close observations of life on the boardwalk are paralleled by and interwoven with an inner dialogue with her past and with herself as a woman newly alone, coming to terms with things and beginning a journey as writer and artist. The six chapters are structured thematically, and the book progresses more through character and theme than through any traditional sort of plot line."

* * *

NIHILO, Arthur X. 1938-

PERSONAL: Surname is pronounced Nee-a-lo; born February 29, 1938, in Utopia, Kan.; son of Neil X. (a vacuum cleaner salesman) and Nadia (deNada) Nihilo; married Alice S. Nix (a prostheticist), June, 1965; children: Nils, Rienne. Education: Utopia State College, B.A., 1960; Balsamo University, Ph.D., 1964. Religion: Mithraist. Politics: Nihilist. Home: 221 Lewiston Rd., Grosse Pointe Farms, Mich. 48236.

CAREER: Catawba College, Black Hollow, N.C., assistant professor, 1964-68, associate professor, 1968-75; Midwest Institute of Philosophical Studies, Wyandotte, Mich., head of ontology department, 1975—. Military service: U.S. Coast Guard Reserve, 1961-67. Member: American Philosophical Association, Midwestern Society for Being, Ontological Society, Philosophers Outing Club. Awards, honors: Bronze Medal from Midwestern Society for Being, 1971, for The Reality of Nonexistence; Pinocchio Award from Quarterly Review of Ontology and Metaphysics, 1978, for Being for Beginners.

WRITINGS: A Predominance of Vacancy: A Critique of Sartre's "Being and Nothingness," Platonic Press, 1966; Zero-Sum Metaphysics: A Philosophical Dilemma, Platonic Press, 1969; The Reality of Nonexistence, LaBlanc Books, 1971; To Be or Not to Be (novel), Crater, 1976; Being for Beginners: A Layman's Guide to Ontology, Platonic Press 1978; The Quest for Personality (autobiography), Basten, 1981.

WORK IN PROGRESS: Slings and Arrows, another novel; a monograph on the question of virtual existence; a book on metaphysics, for general readers.

SIDELIGHTS: Nihilo's first book, A Predominance of Vacancy, won a cult following on college campuses in the late 1960's, though it was ignored by most serious scholars at the time. Nihilo examined Sartre's existentialism and offered a highly modified version of it, arguing that existence neither precedes nor follows essence, but that they are different aspects of what Nihilo called "parareality." Nihilo based his thesis on the discoveries of quantum physics and on the work of psychologist Timothy Leary. It was in *A Predominance of Vacancy* that Nihilo coined the now-familiar phrase "reality is a crutch ."

Reese Peaco, book reviewer for the *Grinnell College Scarlet & Black,* wrote: "The book's complex arguments are explained in a lively, aphoristic style that in no way detracts from the substance. While the philosophical establishment will no doubt sneer at a book so accessible, others will welcome the opportunity to hitch-hike on Nihilo's trip. This is a very heavy book." R. D. Aldrich of *Applied Metaphysics* however, found the book's "few worthwhile insights . . . buried beneath epistomological confusion and terminological obfuscation. Nihilo may have something to offer philosophy, but it won't be found in this jargon-ridden exercise."

The Reality of Nonexistence won the approval of reviewers such as Aldo Anselmo of *Existentialism Journal,* who remarked, "Nihilo's ideas have been refined over the past five years, though the assumptions on which they are based have remained constant. While many will dispute his conclusions, few will deny that Nihilo has written an immensely important book which indisputably demonstrates the relevance of philosophy to the real—or as Nihilo would say, 'parareal'—world." A reviewer for the *Kansas Philosophical Quarterly* called the book "a lucid and profound analysis of the fundamental problems of ontology." But *The Reality of Nonexistence* was not without detractors. Aldrich, in *Hermes,* wrote: "Former guru and philosophical con-man Nihilo, sensing the imminent demise of the hippie movement, has obviously decided to try working the other side of the street. While his new book is free from the ostentatious 'with-itness' of his early work, its content is the same: puerile, meandering speculation, soft-headed analogical arguments, and astounding illiteracy. That Nihilo can devote 358 pages to the problem of nonexistence without once considering (or mentioning, even in a footnote) the work of Porterfield or any other linguistic philosophers, points up the pointlessness of this silly volume."

Nihilo's novel *To Be or Not to Be* is the story of a young philosophy professor and his wife, who scandalize the faculty of a small southern college with their sexual and other escapades but manage to blackmail several powerful individuals into promoting the professor. Aldrich, in *Piedmont Review,* remarked, "Nihilo proves that he can't write fiction either." But *To Be or Not to Be* was generally well received, Webster R. Swenson of the *Downriver Quarterly* calling it "a picaresque delight, a dashing, splashing, erotic romp of a novel. . . . Nihilo's antiheroes and antivillains careen madly through a world where not only goodness, truth and beauty, but existence itself seems to be in doubt—and they (and the reader) love every minute of it."

"The novel's philosophical concerns sometimes threaten to overwhelm the story," noted Peaco in the *Springfield Review of Books,* "but the characters are enthralling, dialogue sharp and on target, and Nihilo's comic touch is sure. Especially funny is the scene in which the protagonist seduces the wife of the head of the philosophy department in the back of a classroom while her husband is attempting to deliver a lecture and avoid being stung by a bee. In scenes like this one senses the full range of Nihilo's power as a novelist: humor, ideas, and a sure grasp of the emotional meaning of twentieth century life."

Nihilo's introduction to ontological thought, *Being for Beginners,* has become a standard textbook at many community colleges, and has been praised by Suzanne D. Monke of *Philosophy Teachers Journal* as "the best book of its kind."

BIOGRAPHICAL/CRITICAL SOURCES: Grinnell College Scarlet & Black, November 12, 1966; *Applied Metaphysics,* January, 1967; *Existentialism Journal,* August, 1971; *Kansas Philosophical Quarterly,* fall, 1971; *Hermes,* January, 1972; *Piedmont Review,* spring, 1976; *Downriver Quarterly,* summer, 1976; *Springfield Review of Books,* July 7, 1976; *Philosophy Teachers Journal,* March, 1979; Arthur X. Nihilo, *The Quest for Personality,* Basten, 1981.

*   *   *

NOBLE, Marguerite (Buchanan)   1910-

PERSONAL: Born January 29, 1910, in Roosevelt, Ariz.; daughter of Daniel Webster (a cattle rancher) and Arminda Jane (a cattle rancher; maiden name, Solomon) Parker; married Harry R. Buchanan, June, 1936 (died, 1963); married Charles Noble (a florist), June 16, 1974; children: (first marriage) Roger, Cynthia. *Education:* Arizona State University, B.A., 1931, M.A., 1950; graduate study at University of Arizona, Northern Arizona University, Memphis College, Phoenix College, and University of California, Los Angeles. *Politics:* Republican. *Religion:* Protestant. *Home:* 908 South Mud Springs Rd., Payson, Ariz. 85541. *Agent:* Lynn Nesbit, International Creative Management, 40 West 57th St., New York, N.Y. 10019. *Office:* P.O. Box 1324, Payson, Ariz.

CAREER: Teacher of language arts in a junior high school in Phoenix, Ariz., 1943-73; Gila Pueblo College, Payson, Ariz., instructor in writing, 1980—. Cafe owner in Phoenix, 1945-47; owner of guest ranch in Arizona, 1952-60. Public speaker and lecturer on writing and Southwestern history.

MEMBER: American Association of University Women, National League of American Pen Women, Authors Guild, American National Cowbelles, Society of Southwestern Authors, Arizona Authors Association, Arizona Historical Society, Arizona State Cowbelles, Northern Gila County Historical Society (secretary), Verde Valley Horseman's Council, Phoenix Writers Club, Payson Hospital Association, Payson's Woman's Club, Payson Chamber of Commerce Chamberettes, Pine-Strawberry Archaeological and Historical Society, Creighton District Teachers Association (secretary), Creighton Teachers Association (president). *Awards, honors:* Freedoms Foundation award, 1961, for article on freedom; National Educational Association press award, 1969, for best feature story; honored by governor of Arizona on "Marguerite Noble Day," 1979.

WRITINGS: Filaree: A Novel of an American Life, Random House, 1979. Also author of television script "Filaree" for Columbia Broadcasting System. Contributor of articles and stories to magazines and newspapers, including *New York Times, Arizona, Western Horseman, Arizona Education, Tonto Trails,* and *White Mountains.*

WORK IN PROGRESS: Working on a novel with a Southwestern pioneer background.

SIDELIGHTS: Born in the territory of Arizona, Noble grew up on a cattle ranch in an isolated frontier community. Her novel, *Filareee,* is based upon her recollections about life on the Arizona frontier. It is about a turn-of-the-century pioneer woman whose hardiness matches that of the nearly indestructible range forage, filaree, which becomes a metaphor for her life. A *New York Times* critic remarked that the book "has some of the authentic quality of a reminiscence."

Noble wrote *Filaree* to emphasize that, although most accounts of the American pioneering effort focus on the role played by men, women also made substantial contributions to the "winning of the West."

Noble told *CA:* "I am especially interested in Southwestern history as it pertains to the settlers in this area during the late 1800's and early 1900's. I have deep empathy with the women pioneers as I feel history has not given them full credit for their contributions to the colonization of the country.

"Many years ago I was impressed by the 'earthiness,' the 'gut-writing on the emotions,' as portrayed by Steinbeck in *The Grapes of Wrath*—especially the primitive-simple style of his writing in this particular novel. I have also been greatly influenced by my parents' philosophy on living and standards: (1) We do not accept 'charity' per se; (2) we work as work is honorable; (3) our word is good; (4) we do not cheat; and (5) we are democratic to all persons. I have also been greatly influenced in my writing by my daughter, Cynthia, who is a novelist, playwright, poet, and writer of comedy acts for television."

AVOCATIONAL INTERESTS: "Good food" preparation, bridge, golf, horseback riding, wildlife enjoyment.

BIOGRAPHICAL/CRITICAL SOURCES: Arizona Statesman, winter, 1979; *Northlander,* July 5, 1979; *New York Times,* September 2, 1979.

* * *

NORDLICHT, Lillian

PERSONAL: Born in New York, N.Y.; daughter of Jack and Rose Keiman; married Myron Nordlicht; children: Scott, Jonathan, Robert. *Education:* Attended Queen's College of the City University of New York and Bank Street College of Education. *Residence:* La Jolla, Calif. *Address:* c/o Raintree Publishers, Inc., 205 West Highland Ave., Milwaukee, Wis. 53203.

CAREER: Free-lance writer, 1968—. *Member:* National League of American Pen Women, Society of Children's Book Writers. *Awards, honors:* Awarded second prize for light verse in National League of American Pen Women competition, 1979.

WRITINGS—Juvenile: A Medal for Mike (illustrated by Sylvia Stone), Scholastic Book Services, 1979; (adapter) Jack London, *The Call of the Wild* (illustrated by Juan Barberis), Raintree Publishers, 1980; *I Love to Laugh* (illustrated by Allen Davis), Raintree Publishers, 1980; (adapter) Jules Verne, *20,000 Leagues Under the Sea* (illustrated by Steve Butz), Raintree Publishers, 1980. Contributor of stories to school textbooks and anthologies and to periodicals such as *Highlights for Children.*

WORK IN PROGRESS: Suigene and Chinese Chamber of Commerce, "a story of the conflicts between first-generation parents with a fierce devotion to old-world Chinese customs and second-generation American children who are trying to define their place in both these worlds."

SIDELIGHTS: Nordlicht told *CA:* "Words, precisely tooled and tuned, are exciting instruments to work with. Using a minimum amount of words to get a maximum amount of action and feeling into a story is what makes writing for children so exhilirating.

"*A Medal for Mike* concerns the ability of a boy to deal with what he considers an injustice to his father, and his father's refusal to 'set the record straight' for a deserved but withheld medal."

* * *

NORMAN, Marsha 1947-

PERSONAL: Born September 21, 1947, in Louisville, Ky.;

married Michael Norman (a teacher; divorced, 1974); married Dann C. Byck, Jr. (a theatrical producer), November, 1978. *Education:* Agnes Scott College, B.A., 1969; University of Louisville, M.A.T., 1971. *Residence:* New York, N.Y. *Agent:* Samuel Liff, William Morris Agency, 1350 Avenue of the Americas, New York, N.Y. 10019.

CAREER: Teacher for Kentucky Arts Commission; teacher of gifted children; book reviewer and editor for *Louisville Times;* worked with disturbed children at Kentucky Central State Hospital. *Awards, honors:* American Theatre Critics Association named "Getting Out" the best play produced in regional theatre during 1977-78; National Endowment for the Arts playwright-in-residence grant, 1978-79, at Actors Theatre of Louisville; John Gassner New Playwrights Medallion from Outer Critics Circle and George Oppenheimer-Newsday Award, both 1979, both for "Getting Out"; Rockefeller playwright-in-residence grant, 1979-80, at the Mark Taper Forum.

WRITINGS—Plays: Getting Out (two-act; first produced in Louisville, Ky., at Actors Theatre of Louisville, 1977; produced Off-Broadway at Phoenix Theatre, 1978), Avon, 1977; *Third and Oak: The Laundromat* [and] *The Pool Hall* (two one-act plays; first produced in Louisville, at Actors Theatre of Louisville, 1978), Dramatists Play Service, 1978; "It's the Willingness" (teleplay), first broadcast by Public Broadcasting Service (PBS), 1978; "Circus Valentine" (two-act), first produced in Louisville at Actors Theatre of Louisville, 1979; "The Holdup" (two-act), first produced in workshop at Actors Theatre of Louisville, 1980; "In Trouble at Fifteen," first broadcast on television program "Skag," Lorimar Productions, 1980. Also author of unproduced screenplays "The Children With Emerald Eyes," for Columbia, "The Bridge," for Joseph E. Levine, and "Thy Neighbor's Wife," for United Artists.

Work represented in anthology *The Best Plays of 1978-1979: The Burns Mantle Yearbook of the Theatre,* edited by Otis L. Guernsey, Jr., Dodd, 1980.

WORK IN PROGRESS: A two-character, no-intermission ordeal play.

SIDELIGHTS: Norman told *CA:* "I always write about the same thing: people having the nerve to go on. The people I care about are those folks you wouldn't even notice in life—two women in a laundromat late at night as you drive by, a thin woman in an ugly scarf standing over the luncheon meat at the grocery, a tiny gray lady buying a big sack of chocolate-covered raisins and a carton of Kools. Someday I'd love to write a piece about people who can talk. The problem is I know so few of them."

Marsha Norman astounded the theatre community with her stage-writing debut "Getting Out." Richard Eder of the *New York Times* called the play "a triumph of the [1979 theatre] season." A drama about a woman released from prison after eight years, the play explores the psychological changes she underwent, transforming her from a hate-filled child named Arlie into the rehabilitated woman Arlene. "The emotional impact of 'Getting Out,'" Eder continued, "is so honest and direct and the performances are so incandescent that it all seems very simple: just a blaze of theatrical energy that lights up the Off Broadway scene as nothing else has done this season." First produced in Louisville, Kentucky, the play ran in Los Angeles, California, and Off-Broadway at the Phoenix Theatre before again playing Off-Broadway at the Theatre De Lys in 1979. The play did not advance to Broadway, "to which it is preeminently suited," claimed John Simon in *New York,* because of the "bungling" of producers. Even so, "Getting Out" made Norman "an impressive addition to the list of good young American playwrights," stated *Commonweal*'s Gerald Weales.

Norman's entry into the field was fortuitous. At the age of twenty-nine, she decided to take on a "project." She visited Jon Jory, the producing director of the Actors Theatre of Louisville, and he suggested she write a play on "a painful subject" such as busing. Norman explained her reaction in the *New York Times*: "I went home and thought about it for a week, then came back and said no. I expected him to say, 'Well, goodbye,' but we sat down and began to talk, and we finally settled on the subject of 'Getting Out,' simply because it was the thing I was so excited about."

For the play, she drew on her experiences with disturbed children at Kentucky Central State Hospital. "What we had there were children who never talked at all, as well as ones who would just as soon stab you in the back as talk to you," Norman disclosed. "There were lots of violent kids there, lots of Arlies there. But there was one girl in particular, a 13-year-old, who was absolutely terrifying. She's the kind of kid you would not for your life be locked up in a room with for 10 minutes. People got bruises when this kid walked in the room, she was so vicious. . . . Eight years later, when I began to think about writing my first play, I thought back to that experience, because it was so terrifying to me."

A month after her conversation with Jory, Norman had completed the first draft of "Getting Out." The finished product contrasted two sides of a woman's personality. To accomplish this, Norman used two actresses on stage simultaneously. The story is told through the interaction between the selves Arlie and Arlene. Weales explained that the "characters interpenetrate, Arlie's scenes sparking off Arlene's, working alongside without intruding on them." Arlie is a victim of parental abuse whose hate and rage spur her to commit acts of violence. She eventually murders a taxi driver during a robbery attempt and is sent to prison. There she hurls obscenities at guards and throws her food. Because of her truculent behavior, Arlie is locked up in solitary confinement, where she suffers a nervous breakdown. When allowed out, Arlene "tries to carve her evil self out of her body with a fork," described Weales. "Once she is physically well," Weales noted, "Arlene dwindles into a model prisoner and a parolee." On the outside as a parolee, Arlene hesitantly attempts to go straight. She lives in a run-down apartment, and although "the violence [is] burned out of her," revealed *Newsweek*'s Jack Kroll, "it is replaced by a pervasive terror at facing life without training, without prospects, without love." Arlene is successful, however, overcoming the influences of her mother, her former pimp, and a smothering prison guard suitor.

Critics raved about "Getting Out." Kroll asserted that in this "superb first play . . . we see one of those before-and-after diptychs living right before our eyes, but this one blazes in the uncompromising light of truth." Simon declared, "the marvelous balance of *Getting Out* is such that the play neither preaches nor sentimentalizes; least of all does it offer easy solutions for problems that seem all but insoluble. Keeping its sense of horror and sense of humor equally to the fore, it points no accusing fingers and hands out no facile accolades." Simon continued: "No gesture is arbitrary, no syllable rings false. The language is the play's greatest asset: coarse-grained, unvarnished, often hateful, sometimes fumbling for tenderness, funny yet beyond laughter (except the hysterical kind), heartbreaking yet a stranger to tears. And always frighteningly true."

BIOGRAPHICAL/CRITICAL SOURCES: New York Times, May 17, 1979, May 27, 1979, June 8, 1979, September 15, 1979;

New York, November 13, 1978, May 28, 1979; *Time*, May 28, 1979; *Newsweek*, May 28, 1979; *New Republic*, July 7, 1979; *Commonweal*, October 12, 1979.

—*Sketch by Anne M. Guerrini*

* * *

NORTHEN, Rebecca Tyson 1910-

PERSONAL: Born August 24, 1910, in Detroit, Mich.; daughter of William Elicott (a physician) and Elizabeth (Weems) Tyson; married Henry Theodore Northen (a professor of botany), August 9, 1937 (deceased); children: Elizabeth Northen Lyons, Philip Tyson, Thomas Henry. *Education:* Attended Radcliffe College, 1930-33; Wayne State University, A.B., 1935; Mount Holyoke College, M.A., 1937. *Home:* 1215 Drake Circle, San Luis Obispo, Calif. 93401.

CAREER: Writer and horticulturalist. *Member:* American Orchid Society (member of board of trustees, 1972-77), New Zealand Orchid Society, Australian Native Orchid Society, Illinois Orchid Society, Utah Orchid Society, Sacramento Orchid Society, Cabrillo Orchid Society, Denver Orchid Society, Sigma Xi. *Awards, honors:* Gold medal from American Orchid Society, 1979, for outstanding contributions to horticultural literature.

WRITINGS: Home Orchid Growing, Van Nostrand, 1950, 4th edition, 1982; (with husband, Henry T. Northen) *The Secret of the Green Thumb*, Ronald, 1954; (with H. T. Northen) *Greenhouse Gardening*, Ronald, 1955, 2nd edition, Wiley, 1973; *Orchids as House Plants*, Van Nostrand, 1955, 2nd edition, Dover, 1976; (with H. T. Northen) *Ingenious Kingdom: The Remarkable World of Plants*, Prentice-Hall, 1970; *Miniature Orchids*, Van Nostrand, 1980. Contributor to magazines, including orchid journals.

SIDELIGHTS: Rebecca Northen commented: "I have traveled and collected orchids in many tropical countries, from Mexico to Peru and from Jamaica to South Africa. I have participated in a number of World Orchid Conferences held in the United States and foreign countries. I give talks to orchid societies around the country and also to non-orchid groups. I am especially interested in saving orchid species threatened by development and other causes, actually saving the fast-disappearing forests in which they live and the wildlife that surrounds them. *Home Orchid Growing*, which is sold around the world, is credited with doing more to spread orchid growing than any other factor."

* * *

NOURSE, James G(regory) 1947-

PERSONAL: Born December 14, 1947, in Buffalo, N.Y., son of Thomas Miller (a writer and consultant) and Dorothy (Beale) Nourse; married Cynthia Bishop (a neurophysiologist), July 11, 1981. *Education:* Columbia University, B.S., 1969; California Institute of Technology, Ph.D., 1974. *Home:* 408 Metzgar St., Half Moon Bay, Calif. 94109. *Office:* Department of Chemistry, Stanford University, Stanford, Calif. 94305.

CAREER: Stanford University, Stanford, Calif., research affiliate in computer science, 1976-79, research associate in chemistry, 1979—. Consultant for government agencies and industrial corporations. *Member:* American Chemical Society, American Association for the Advancement of Science, Sigma Xi.

WRITINGS: The Simple Solution to Rubik's Cube (nonfiction), Bantam, 1981. Contributor to *Journal of American Chemical Society* and *Journal of Organic Chemistry*.

WORK IN PROGRESS: "Research on computer applications to chemistry; puzzles and games (particularly Rubik's cube and similar puzzles)."

SIDELIGHTS: Nourse told *CA:* "The Rubik's cube puzzle phenomenon (or perhaps plague) provided an ideal opportunity for a scientist specializing in chemical applications of group theory and computer algorithms to contribute in the mass market. A treatise entitled 'An Efficient Canonicalization Algorithm' would have seen limited demand. The same treatise retitled *The Simple Solution to Rubik's Cube* proved more popular. Opportunities are where you find them."

BIOGRAPHICAL/CRITICAL SOURCES: San Francisco Chronicle and Examiner, July 26, 1981; *Atlanta Journal and Constitution,* August 1, 1981.

*   *   *

NOVAK, Jane Dailey   1917-

PERSONAL: Born August 27, 1917, in Omaha, Neb.; daughter of Charles Edward (in sales) and Alice (a volunteer worker; maiden name, Atkinson) Dailey; married Tabor Robert Novak, March 30, 1940; children: Nana Alice Novak Freret, Tabor Robert, Jr., Kay Douglass, Clare Novak Renaud. *Education:* Carleton College, B.A. (summa cum laude), 1938; University of Miami, Coral Gables, Fla., M.A., 1964; University of Chicago, Ph.D., 1970. *Office:* Department of English, University of Queensland, St. Lucia, Brisbane, Queensland 4067, Australia.

CAREER: Batten, Barton, Durstine & Osborne, Inc. (advertising agency), Chicago, Ill., interviewer and supervisor of market research, 1938-40; *Millar's Chicago Letter,* Chicago, assistant editor, 1940-41; Commercial Services (market research firm), Detroit, Mich., manager, 1941-42; free-lance writer, 1942-62; University of Illinois at Chicago Circle, Chicago, instructor, 1965-70, assistant professor of English, 1970-73; University of East Anglia, Norwich, England, Leverhulme visiting fellow in English and American studies, 1973-74; University of Queensland, Brisbane, Australia, senior lecturer in English, 1974—. Visiting associate professor at University of Texas, 1981. *Member:* Australia and New Zealand American Studies Association, Modern Language Association of America, South Pacific and Commonwealth Literature and Language Association, Phi Beta Kappa. *Awards, honors:* Woodrow Wilson grant, 1967.

WRITINGS: The Razor Edge of Balance: A Study of Virginia Woolf, University of Miami Press, 1975. Contributor to literature journals.

WORK IN PROGRESS: A critical biography of Rose Macaulay, publication by University of Texas Press expected in 1983.

SIDELIGHTS: Jane Novak wrote: "I am characteristic of many American women who begin or return to careers in middle life, and the opportunities of study, travel, teaching, and writing on three continents have given me the sense of having lived several lives. Outside America I have come to understand the power and uniqueness of its belief in human resilience. American women have benefited from this common faith.

"I'm working on a book about Rose Macaulay, who wrote her best novel at the age of seventy-five, and it was not only *her* best out of twenty-three, but a human flourish of wit, vitality, and verbal delight that rouses the spirit, a 'best' by any standard and at any authorial age."

*   *   *

NOVAK, Rose   1940-
(Marcia Rose, a joint pseudonym)

PERSONAL: Born September 18, 1940, in Atlanta, Ga.; daughter of Gad (a retail merchant) and Leah (Dreeker) Jacobson; married Ronald Novak (a civil engineer), July 1, 1962; children: Mara, Leila. *Education:* Simmons College, B.S., 1962. *Home and office:* 38 Orange St., Brooklyn Heights, N.Y. 11201. *Agent:* Goodman Associates, 500 West End Ave., New York, N.Y. 10024.

CAREER: Free-lance writer, 1964—.

WRITINGS—With Marcia Kamien, under joint pseudonym Marcia Rose: *Prince of Ice,* Avon, 1979; *Music of Love,* Ballantine, 1980; *Second Chances,* Ballantine, 1981; *Choices,* Ballantine, 1982.

WORK IN PROGRESS: Connections, a contemporary romantic novel written under the Marcia Rose pseudonym, completion expected in 1982.

SIDELIGHTS: Rose Novak and her co-author, Marcia Kamien, jointly wrote Sidelights, describing their particular writing method. Please refer to Marcia Kamien's sketch in this volume for the text of these Sidelights.

BIOGRAPHICAL/CRITICAL SOURCES: West Coast Review of Books, September, 1979; *Pittsburgh Courier,* August 29, 1981; *Chicago Tribune,* August 30, 1981; *Willoughby News-Herald* (Ohio), August 30, 1981; *Bradenton Herald* (Fla.), September, 1981; *Kingsport Times-News* (Tenn.), September 6, 1981; *Warren Tribune Chronicle* (Ohio), September 6, 1981.

*   *   *

NOWLAN, James Dunlap   1941-

BRIEF ENTRY: Born September 8, 1941, in Kewanee, Ill. American political scientist, educator, and author. Nowlan has taught political science at Black Hawk College since 1969 and at Western Illinois University since 1973. He wrote *Illinois Major Party Platforms, 1900-1964* (Institute of Government and Public Affairs, University of Illinois, 1966) and *The Politics of Higher Education: Lawmakers and the Academy in Illinois* (University of Illinois Press, 1976). *Address:* 209 South Miller, Toulon, Ill. 61483. *Biographical/critical sources: Who's Who in American Politics,* 5th edition, Bowker, 1975.

*   *   *

NUETZEL, Charles (Alexander)   1934-
(Albert Augustus, Jr., Charles English, Alec Rivere)

PERSONAL: Surname pronounced *New*-zel; born November 10, 1934, in San Francisco, Calif.; son of Albert Augustus (a commercial artist) and Betty (Stockberger) Nuetzel; married Brigitte Marianne Winter (a banker), October 13, 1962. *Education:* Attended Valley Community College (San Fernando, Calif.), 1954-55, Palmer Institute of Authorship, 1956-59, and Moorpark Community College (Moorpark, Calif.), 1978. *Residence:* Thousand Oaks, Calif. *Agent:* Forrest J Ackerman, 2495 Glendower Ave., Hollywood, Calif. 90027.

CAREER: Writer, 1960—. Also worked as film technician, cook, pop music singer, and real estate salesman, 1964-65; *Military service:* Air National Guard, 1952-58; became staff sergeant.

WRITINGS: (Under pseudonym Alec Rivere) *Lost City of the Damned* (novel), Pike, 1961 (also see below); (under pseudonym Charles English) *Lovers: 2075* (novel), Scorpion, 1964; (editor) *If This Goes On* (anthology), Book Company of America, 1965; *Whodunit? Hollywood Style,* Book Company of America, 1965; *Queen of Blood* (novelization of screenplay by Curtis Harrington), Greenleaf Classics, 1966; *Images of Tomorrow* (short stories), Powell, 1969; *Jungle Jungle* (collection; part one contains abridged version of *Lost City of the Damned),* Powell, 1969; *Raiders of Noomas* (novel), Powell, 1969; *Warriors of Noomas* (novel), Powell, 1969; *Swordmen of Vistar* (novel), Powell, 1969; *Murder Times Four* (novel), Powell, 1969; *Softly as I Kill You* (novel), Powell, 1969; (under pseudonym Albert Augustus, Jr.) *The Slaves of Lomooro* (novel), Powell, 1969; *Last Call for the Stars* (novel), Lenox Hill Press, 1971; (with George P. Bendall) *Now the Time* (novel), Martin Press, 1981.

Author of more than one hundred books under dozens of pseudonyms. Publisher/packager of more than forty-five books. Contributor of short stories and articles to numerous magazines, including *Jade, Cocktail, Vertex, If Worlds of Science Fiction, Spaceway, Famous Monsters of Filmland,* and *Knight.* Editor of Powell Sci-Fi series (pocket books), 1969-70. Also copywriter for books and magazines.

WORK IN PROGRESS: Science fiction short stories.

SIDELIGHTS: Charles Nuetzel wrote: "I started writing in 1960, willing to do whatever was necessary to get published in the commercial marketplace. That first year I wrote some one hundred short manuscripts, selling about two a month. In 1961 my agent, Forrest J Ackerman, called and asked if I could give him some twenty thousand words in one week (half a short 'novel') for a possible pocket book sale. I started writing almost immediately upon hanging up the phone, developing an approach to novel-plotting that I used many times since: a novel is a series of incidents leading up to a short story. I did from thirty to forty pages a day and finished the first draft in one week. I ran the novel through the typewriter one more time at the editor's request, though only after his acceptance of the book. That was my first novel sale.

"The above is not to suggest I deserve gold stars; only that writing, at least for people like myself, must be entered into as a hard-nosed business. I learned about plotting, sub-plotting, character development, etc., with the help of some writer friends and by reading a few books and taking the Palmer Institute of Authorship course, then by writing a lot of words. I was told that quality came with quantity. Writing is a business; it must be approached as such. This is hardly a romantic concept of writing, but it is basic fact for writers like myself. I'm still learning my craft and will continue to learn every time I put a piece of paper in the typewriter.

"I believe that it would be dishonest of me to avoid this chance to say a few things about writing as a career. As a career it is a combination of ecstasy and hell—demanding, difficult, pestering, brain-bashing, and at times very exciting. The number one trap to avoid is the Number Game. Oh, how easy it is to fall into the trap of saying, 'My, I did X number of words today, now if I can do that many each and every day. . . .' It takes years of writing to discover through painful experience just how many words per page it is possible to rush through the typewriter per day, week, year. Only then is it possible to set realistic goals and to approach deadlines in a manner that is not destined to totally ruin one's health and nerves. You learn to accept the daily payoffs of writing to offset the negatives. 'You don't gotta work eight hours a day'; you can spend more time in activities that are of interest to you (don't feel guilty about that, because even these activities are of value to your professional output).

"I would do everything I could to talk beginning writers out of trying to become professional, full-time authors. I would suggest they learn all they can concerning grammar and English and about writing itself. Then if they have not been turned away from the insane idea of writing, I would tell them to buy ten reams of paper with the idea of filling them with words.

"The harsh, personal reality of writing is that we do create for the pure pleasure it can bring to us at times and for the hoped for pleasure it may give some others—and maybe with the wish we have said something moving or instructive or inspirational. We hope we have communicated a part of ourselves to some other person out there and touched him."

AVOCATIONAL INTERESTS: Ancient history, science, cooking, travel.

BIOGRAPHICAL/CRITICAL SOURCES: R. Reginald, editor, *Science Fiction and Fantasy Literature,* Gale, Volume I: *Indexes to the Literature,* 1979, Volume II: *Contemporary Science Fiction Authors II,* 1979.

*   *   *

NYERERE, Julius Kambarage   1922-

BRIEF ENTRY: Born in April, 1922, in Butiama-Musoma, Tanganyika (now Tanzania). Tanzanian statesman and author. Nyerere founded and became president of the Tanganyika African National Union in 1954. He served as chief minister and prime minister of the Republic of Tanganyika from 1961 to 1962 and became president of the republic in 1964. He has retained his presidency since Tanganyika united with Zanzibar under the name Tanzania in 1964. Nyerere's writings include *Freedom and Socialism: Uhuru na Ujamaa* (Oxford University Press, 1968), *Ujamaa: Essays on Socialism* (Oxford University Press, 1968), *Freedom and Development: Uhuru na Maendelo* (Oxford University Press, 1973), and *Crusade for Liberation* (Oxford University Press, 1978). *Address:* P.O. Box 9120, Dar es Salaam, Tanzania; and State House and Cabinet Secretariat, Dar es Salaam, Tanzania. *Biographical/critical sources: Africa South of the Sahara,* 1980-81, Europa, 1980.

O

OAKSEY, John 1929-
(Audax, Marlborough)

PERSONAL: Born March 21, 1929, in London, England; son of Lord Geoffrey Lawrence (a judge) and Marjorie (Robinson) Oaksey; married Victoria Dennistoun; children: Patrick Lawrence, Sara Lawrence. *Education:* Oxford University, B.A., 1954; attended Yale University, 1954. *Home:* Hill Farm, Oaksey, Malmesbury, Wiltshire, England. *Agent:* Bagenal Harvey, London, England. *Office:* Daily Telegraph, Fleet St., London, England.

CAREER: Daily Telegraph, London, England, racing correspondent (under pseudonym Marlborough), 1956—. Commentator for ITV, 1970—. Justice of the peace. *Military service:* Royal Air Force Volunteer Reserve, pilot in Queen's Royal Lancers, 1951-54; became second lieutenant. *Member:* Brooks's Club.

WRITINGS: (With Michael Seth-Smith, Peter Willett, and Roger Mortimer) *History of Steeplechasing,* M. Joseph, 1966; *The Story of Mill Reef,* M. Joseph, 1974; *Pride of the Shires: Story of the Whitbread Horses,* Hutchinson, 1979. Correspondent for *Sunday Telegraph,* 1956—, and *Horse and Hound* (under pseudonym Audax), 1959—.

WORK IN PROGRESS: Memoirs, publication by M. Joseph expected in 1982.

SIDELIGHTS: Oaksey told *CA:* "I started writing because I got hooked on raceriding over fences and hurdles as an amateur, and could only go on doing it if I found a job that paid me to go on racing. It worked pretty well for twenty years; I rode in just over two hundred races and earned a living-of-sorts in the process. I rode in eleven Grand Nationals and described all of them in the next day's *Sunday Telegraph*—rather a tight assignment with the race usually off at 3:30 P.M. and my deadline to start dictating at 6:20 P.M."

*   *   *

OBOLER, Arch 1909-

BRIEF ENTRY: Born December 6, 1909 (some sources say 1907), in Chicago, Ill. American playwright, director, and producer. Oboler began writing for radio in the mid-1930's. In the 1940's he began writing, directing, and producing screenplays, including the first three-dimensional film, "Bwana Devil" (United Artists, 1952). He has more than four hundred plays as well as a 1945 Peabody Broadcasting Award for radio drama to his credit. Oboler's writings include a collection of plays, *Night of the Auk* (Horizon Press, 1958), a novel, *House on Fire* (Bartholomew, 1969), and two filmscripts, "The Bubble" (1966) and "Domo Arigato" (Sharpix, 1973). *Address:* Route 4, Malibu, Calif. 90265; and 4119 St. Clair Ave., Studio City, Calif. *Biographical/critical sources: Current Biography,* H. W. Wilson, 1940; *Twentieth Century Authors: A Biographical Dictionary of Modern Literature,* H. W. Wilson, 1st supplement, 1955.

*   *   *

O'BRIEN, Jacqueline Robin 1949-

PERSONAL: Born November 18, 1949, in Brooklyn, N.Y.; daughter of Paul (a professor) and Clara (Sadacca) Wasserman; married John Michael O'Brien (a musician), June 6, 1979; children: Jennie Rebecca. *Education:* Attended California State University, Fullerton, 1970-72. *Home:* 13-A Laurel Hill Rd., Greenbelt, Md. 20770.

CAREER: P. W. Associates, College Park, Md., editor, 1972—.

WRITINGS: (With father, Paul Wasserman) *Speakers and Lecturers: How to Find Them,* Gale, 1979, revised edition, 1981; (with Wasserman) *Statistics Sources,* Gale, 1980, revised edition, 1982.

AVOCATIONAL INTERESTS: Interior decorating, antiques, music, the arts, genealogy.

*   *   *

OCAMPO, Victoria 1891-1979

PERSONAL: Original name, Victoria Ocampo de Estrada; born in 1891 in Argentina; died January 27, 1979, in San Isidro, Argentina; married, c. 1912 (separated, c. 1923). *Residence:* San Isidro, Argentina.

CAREER: Author, editor, and publisher. Founding editor of *Sur,* beginning 1931. Head of management of Teatro Colon, Buenos Aires, Argentina, 1933; co-founder of Argentine Women's Union, 1936 (president, 1936, 1938); president of Commission of Letters of National Foundation for the Arts in Argentina. *Member:* International P.E.N., Argentine Academy of Letters. *Awards, honors:* Grand prize of honor from Argentine Society of Writers, 1950; Premio Alberti y Sarmiento,

1967; decorated Palmes Academiques; officer of French Legion of Honor; Commander of Order of the British Empire.

WRITINGS—In English: *338171 T.E.* (biography of T. E. Lawrence), Sur, 1942, translation by David Garnett published under same title, Dutton, 1963; (contributor) Doris Meyer, *Victoria Ocampo: Against the Wind and the Tide* (includes fifteen essays by Ocampo), Braziller, 1980.

Other: *De Francesca a Beatrice: A Traves de La Divina Comedia*, 1924, Revista de Occidente (Madrid), 1928, Sur, 1963; *La mujer y su expresion*, Sur, 1936; *Domingos en Hyde Park*, Sur, 1936; *Emily Bronte*, Sur, 1938; *Virginia Woolf: Orlando y cia*, Sur, 1938; *San Isidro: Con un poema de Silvina Ocampo y 68 fotos de Gustav Thorlichen*, Sur, 1941; *Henry V y Laurence Olivier, con los principales pasajes de la obra*, Sur, 1947; *Lawrence de Arabia, y otros ensayos*, Aguilar, 1951; *Habla el algarrobo*, Sur, 1959; *Tagore en las barrancas de San Isidro*, Sur, 1961; *Victoria Ocampo por Fryda Schultz de Mantovani*, Ediciones Culturales Argentinas, 1963; *La belle y sus enamorados*, Sur, 1964.

Also author of *La laguna de los nenufares*, 1926; *Testimonios* (memoirs, personal essays, and criticism), ten volumes, c. 1935-75; *Soledad sonora*, 1950; *El viajero y una de sus sumbras*, 1951; *Antologia de Jawaharlal Nehru: Seleccion y prologo*, 1966; *Dialogos con Borges*, 1969; *Dialogos con Mallea*, 1969.

Translator of works by various authors, including William Faulkner, Graham Greene, D. H. Lawrence, Albert Camus, Collette, Dylan Thomas, John Osborne, and Lanza del Vasto.

SIDELIGHTS: Though Victoria Ocampo's writings are extensive, they stand in the background of her work as editor of the Argentine literary magazine *Sur.* For more than forty years the magazine served as a forum for both Latin and North American authors and earned Ocampo the distinction as the "grande dame" of Argentine letters.

Ocampo was born into a family that stood "at the center of artistic, financial, and social aristocracy" in her country, reported Eleanor Munro in her feature article for *Ms.* At the age of six Ocampo lived in London and Paris, and she learned English, French, and Italian as a child. Her first literary interests were the works of French and English authors; it was not until she was in her thirties, when she read the writings of Jose Ortego y Gasset, that she developed an appreciation of her native Spanish language.

The same aristocratic upbringing that provided her an education also restricted her. Women were not expected to achieve outside the home, and her father reinforced that notion: he once lamented that Victoria was born a girl, for she would otherwise have been a brilliant student. The limits of her class also confined Ocampo, whose love of Shakespeare and Racine had made her want to pursue an acting career. As Munro noted, the possibility of becoming an actress "was out of the question for a girl of her class." Ocampo would likely have taken up writing sooner, too, if it were not for her society's belief that "women didn't write."

Despite familial and cultural restrictions, Ocampo managed to establish herself in the Buenos Aires literary world. She befriended Indian poet Rabindranath Tagore on his visit to Argentina in 1923, and a year later her first book, a guide to Dante's *Divine Comedy,* was published. In 1929 novelist and critic Waldo Frank urged Ocampo to begin an avant-garde literary magazine of her own. With that advice and the additional encouragement from Ortega y Gasset, Ocampo published the first edition of *Sur* in 1931.

According to Munro, *Sur* was Ocampo's "bridge of human understanding between artists of the world." The magazine held a dual function for its readers: it introduced new Latin American talent while offering in Spanish the works of North American and European artists. Ocampo is credited with being the first to publish a number of Argentine writers, most notably Jorge Luis Borges. At the same time she brought the works of D. H. Lawrence, William Faulkner, Richard Wright, James Joyce, Carl Jung, and Virginia Woolf, among others, to Latin American readers. Through her efforts with *Sur,* Ocampo "put her personal and financial resources at the disposition of Argentine letters," observed H. Ernest Lewald of *Books Abroad* in 1968. "*Sur* has been the finest literary outlet in Latin America for almost forty years."

Ocampo's only book to appear in English was her 1963 biography of T. E. Lawrence (Lawrence of Arabia), *338171 T.E.* The bulk of her effort went towards *Sur,* and because of it, declared Munro, Ocampo "is still a legend in the international literary world."

BIOGRAPHICAL/CRITICAL SOURCES: Time, April 8, 1946; *Books Abroad,* spring, 1969; *Ms.,* January, 1975; *Americas,* May, 1976; *UNESCO Courier,* August, 1977; Doris Meyer, *Victoria Ocampo: Against the Wind and the Tide,* Braziller, 1980.

OBITUARIES: Time, February 12, 1979; *Publishers Weekly,* February 26, 1979.*

*   *   *

OCHSNER, (Edward William) Alton   1896-1981

OBITUARY NOTICE—See index for *CA* sketch: Born May 4, 1896, in Kimball, S.D.; died September 24, 1981, in New Orleans, La. Cardiologist, educator, editor, and author best known as one of the first doctors to suspect a link between cigarette smoking and cancer. In 1927, less than two years after completing his medical training, Ochsner was appointed professor of surgery and chairman of the department of surgery at Tulane University. In 1936 he began to note and call attention to the connection between the number of Americans smoking and the number of cases of lung cancer reported in the United States. Ochsner and four other doctors opened, in 1941, the Ochsner Medical Institutions, to the bitter opposition of some New Orleans doctors. The center quickly became recognized as one of the country's leading medical centers. The complex has grown to include a 530-bed hospital, a clinic, a clinical research center, and a hotel, all of which handle about one hundred thousand persons each year. Ochsner performed nearly twenty thousand operations during his career, and included among his patients were Argentine dictator Juan Peron and film star Gary Cooper. He taught an estimated three thousand medical students and more than two hundred surgeons, including Michael DeBakey. Ochsner was the author of books on medical topics, including *Varicose Veins, Smoking and Cancer: A Doctor's Report, Smoking and Your Life,* and *Smoking: Your Choice Between Life and Death.* Obituaries and other sources: *New York Times,* September 25, 1981.

*   *   *

O'DAY, Rey   1947-

PERSONAL: Born June 23, 1947, in Honolulu, Hawaii; daughter of Jon and Nancy O'Day; married Edward A. Powers. *Education:* Attended University of California, Los Angeles, 1969, and Citrus College, 1971-73. *Home:* 215 East 24th St., New York, N.Y. 10010; and 900 Sierra Madre Ave., Azusa, Calif. 91702.

CAREER: Singer and dancer on stage and television, including ''The Young Americans'' and ''The Kids Next Door'', 1962-68; Doodletown Pipers, assistant to producer, 1968-69; choreographer for Centaur Artists and New Establishment, 1969-72; Diamond Bar Children's Theatre, Diamond Bar, Calif., founder and executive director, 1972-74; City of Glendora, Calif., cultural arts coordinator, 1974; Busch Gardens, Los Angeles, Calif., entertainment manager, 1975-77; Citrus College, Azusa, Calif., member of dance faculty, 1975—. Partner of Wings of Fame Productions, 1977—. Member of board of directors of Sierra Village Homeowners Association. *Member:* International Association of Amusement Parks and Attractions, American Theatre Association.

WRITINGS: (With husband, Edward A. Powers) *Theatre of the Spirit: A Worship Handbook,* Pilgrim Press, 1980.

WORK IN PROGRESS: A book about teaching fine arts to children.

SIDELIGHTS: ''I have always been an avid reader,'' Rey O'Day wrote. ''I enjoy good writing. My writing began when I gave a speech on 'Why All the Fuss About Language?,' which addressed the problem of stereotyping and restricting human potential. It was eventually published. I learned I had a lot to say and have come to enjoy writing immensely.''

*   *   *

O'DOHERTY, Brian   1934-
(Patrick Ireland)

PERSONAL: Born in 1934 in Ballaghaderrin, Ireland; son of Michael and Martha O'Doherty; married Barbara Novak (an art historian). *Home:* 15 West 67th St., New York, N.Y. 10023.

CAREER: Director of visual arts programs of National Endowment for the Arts, 1969—. Solo shows (under pseudonym Patrick Ireland), including Corcoran Gallery of Art, Hirshhorn Museum, and Los Angeles County Museum of Art. *Awards, honors:* Gold medal from Eire Society, 1963; Mather Award from College Art Association of America, 1964.

WRITINGS: Maxim Karolik, Museum of Fine Arts (Boston, Mass.), 1963; *Object and Idea,* Simon & Schuster, 1967; *Museums in Crisis,* Braziller, 1972; *American Masters: The Voice and the Myth,* Random House, 1973. Editor of *Art in America,* 1970-73.

*   *   *

OGILVIE, Robert Maxwell   1932-1981

OBITUARY NOTICE—See index for *CA* sketch: Born June 5, 1932, in Edinburgh, Scotland; died November 7, 1981, in St. Andrews, Scotland. Educator, editor, and author. Ogilvie was a Harmsworth Senior Scholar at Merton College, Oxford, and was elected to the British Academy while headmaster at Tonbridge School in 1972. He was the author of *Latin and Greek, Commentary on Livy Books 1-5,* and *The Library Lactantius.* He was co-editor of *Classical Quarterly* in 1977. Obituaries and other sources: *London Times,* November 13, 1981.

*   *   *

OGILVY, David Mackenzie   1911-

BRIEF ENTRY: Born June 23, 1911, in West Horsley, England. British advertising executive and author. The founder of the advertising agency Ogilvy & Mather International (formerly Ogilvy, Benson & Mather), Ogilvy has served as its president and creative director since 1948. He was also a U.S.

diplomat in the 1940's. He wrote *Confessions of an Advertising Man* (Atheneum, 1963) and *Blood, Brains and Beer: An Autobiography* (Atheneum, 1978). *Address:* Chateau de Touffou, 86300 Bonnes, France. *Biographical/critical sources: Who's Who in Advertising,* 3rd edition, Redfield, 1980.

*   *   *

OHIRA, Masayoshi   1910-1980

OBITUARY NOTICE: Born March 12, 1910, in Toyohama, Shikoku Island, Kagawa Prefecture, Japan; died June 12, 1980, in Tokyo, Japan. Politician and author. Ohira was associated with Japan's Ministry of Finance from 1936 until 1952 when he was elected to the House of Representatives as a member of the Liberal Democratic Party. In 1960 he was named chief cabinet secretary and in 1962 was promoted to minister of foreign affairs. Japan's economic growth while Ohira held the latter post is credited to Ohira's establishment of close ties with the United States. Ohira enjoyed another diplomatic victory when as foreign minister in the cabinet of Kakuei Tanaka he arranged a friendship treaty with the People's Republic of China, resulting in an increase of trade between the two countries. Ohira was elected prime minister in 1978, but his popularity with the Japanese people waned when several members of his administration were accused of participating in a series of scandals. Although Ohira was not implicated, the scandal, coupled with Japan's double-digit inflation, prompted a no-confidence motion in the Japanese Diet. Ohira died soon after, shortly before the general elections in which Liberal Democratic Party candidate Zenko Suzuki was elected to replace Ohira. Among Ohira's writings are *Sugao no Daigishi* (''A Parliamentarian As He Is'') and *Random Thoughts on Public Finance.* Obituaries and other sources: *Current Biography,* Wilson, 1964, 1980; *New York Times,* November 28, 1978, June 12, 1980; *The International Who's Who,* Europa, 1980; *The Annual Obituary 1980,* St. Martin's, 1981.

*   *   *

OKARA, Gabriel Imomotimi Gbaingbain   1921-

PERSONAL: Born April 24, 1921, in Bumoundi, Nigeria; son of Samson G. (in business) and Martha (Olodiama) Okara; married and divorced three times; children: Timi Okara-Schiller, Ebi Daniel. *Education:* Attended Government College, 1935-41. *Religion:* Christian Scientist. *Home:* 24 Nembe Rd., Port Harcourt, Rivers, Nigeria. *Office:* Council for Arts and Culture, 74/76 Bonny St., Port Harcourt, Rivers, Nigeria.

CAREER: Printer and bookbinder for Government Press, 1945-54; principal for Government Information Office, 1964-70; general manager of Rivers State Newspaper and Television Corps, Nigeria, 1971-75; currently associated with Council for Arts and Culture, Port Harcourt, Nigeria. Commissioner for information and broadcasting for government of state of Rivers, Nigeria, 1971-76. *Member:* Society of Nigerian Artists. *Awards, honors:* ''Best all-round'' award from Nigerian Festival of the Arts, 1953, for poem ''Call of the Nun''; Commonwealth Joint Poetry Award, 1979, for *The Fisherman's Invocation.*

WRITINGS: The Voice (novel), F. Watts, 1964; *The Fisherman's Invocation* (poems), Heinemann, 1978. Author of a column in *Tide.* Contributor to journals, including *Transition.*

WORK IN PROGRESS: A series of supplementary reading textbooks for Rivers state schools.

SIDELIGHTS: Okara commented: ''I wrote *The Voice* because of the inconsistencies of our rulers after the British had left Nigeria. In the fight for independence our politicians denounced certain measures and attitudes of the colonial government, only to perpetrate the same ones when they took over. To protest openly was to invite political and economic suicide or ostracism by sycophants and camp followers, or even physical harassment. So *The Voice* was my counter oblique harassment!''

* * *

OKRENT, Daniel 1948-

PERSONAL: Born April 2, 1948, in Detroit, Mich.; son of Harry (an attorney) and Gizella (a social worker; maiden name, Adler) Okrent; married Cynthia Boyer, June 23, 1969 (divorced, August 3, 1977); married Rebecca Kathryn Lazear (a landscape designer), August 28, 1977; children: John Lazear. *Education:* University of Michigan, B.A., 1969. *Home and office address:* P.O. Box 417, Worthington, Mass. 01098. *Agent:* John Cushman, JCA Literary Agency, 242 West 27th St., New York, N.Y. 10001.

CAREER: Alfred A. Knopf, Inc., New York City, editor, 1969-72; Viking Press, Inc., New York City, editor, 1973-76; Harcourt Brace Jovanovich, Inc., New York City, editor-in-chief, 1976-77; Texas Monthly Press, Inc., Austin, president, 1979—. President of Hilltown Press, Inc., Worthington, Mass., 1978—; secretary of Worthington Health Association, 1978-79; commissioner of Rotisserie Baseball League, 1980—. Lecturer in publishing at Radcliffe College, 1977—, and Rice University, 1979—.

WRITINGS: (Editor with Harris Lewine) David Nemec, *The Ultimate Baseball Book,* Houghton, 1979, revised edition, 1981. Contributor to periodicals, including *Sports Illustrated, Esquire,* and *Inside Sports.*

WORK IN PROGRESS: A behind-the-scenes book focusing on one baseball game, publication by Viking expected in 1983.

SIDELIGHTS: Okrent is best known as the editor of *The Ultimate Baseball Book,* a history of the game loaded with photographs, anecdotes, and statistics. Christopher Lehmann-Haupt called it ''a wonderful potpourri composed of a long historical text, a collection of first-class essays and enough illustrations of players, teams, bubble-gum cards and other memorabilia to stuff the attics of the Hall of Fame at Cooperstown, N.Y.'' He added that ''one could go on and on extolling the surprises and pleasures'' the illustrations provide. Bill Brashler agreed. ''Besides giving us the facts . . . ,'' he declared, ''the book is full of delicious anecdotes, one-liners, and offhand information.''

Okrent told *CA:* ''I began to write by accident—I had always loved baseball, and devoted rather more time to it than was reasonable for a grown man. Editor friends, bemused by my passion, threw a little money at me to share it with a magazine public. Soon, I had talked myself into believing their entreaties were wise, and my first book was the result. I still don't consider myself a writer—I'm someone who just happens to be practicing in the public prints. I was an editor for too many years to believe that one is a writer simply by claiming to be one. The act of writing, itself, I find as pleasant as walking on hot coals. Having written, on the other hand, is unalloyed joy.''

BIOGRAPHICAL/CRITICAL SOURCES: New York Times, September 18, 1979; *New York Times Book Review,* October 7, 1979.

* * *

OLDENBURG, E(gbert) William 1936-1974

PERSONAL: Born April 4, 1936, in Muskegon, Mich.; died from injuries sustained in an automobile accident, September 7, 1974, in Muskegon, Mich.; buried in Restlawn Cemetery, Muskegon, Mich.; son of William (in maintenance) and Tressa (Kroes) Oldenburg; married Jean Dyk (a microbiologist), August 13, 1963; children: Jennifer, Ryan. *Education:* Calvin College, B.A., 1958; University of Michigan, Ann Arbor, M.A., 1959, Ph.D., 1966. *Religion:* Protestant. *Agent:* Jean Oldenburg Yonker, 2935 Princeton Ct., Muskegon, Mich. 49441.

CAREER: Calvin College, Grand Rapids, Mich., teaching assistant, 1960-61; Grand Valley State College, Allendale, Mich., assistant professor, 1965-68, associate professor of English, 1968-74, chairman and co-chairman of department of English, 1973-74. Active in civic theatre, including Port City Playhouse, Central Park Players, Hope College Summer Theatre, and Grand Valley State College Theatre. *Awards, honors:* Award for short story from *Banner,* 1963, for ''With Liberty and Adjustment for All.''

WRITINGS: Potawatomi Indian Summer (novel), illustrations by Betty Beeby, Eerdmans, 1975; (contributor) Merle Meeter, compiler, *The Country of the Risen King: An Anthology of Christian Poetry,* Baker Book, 1978. Contributor of poems, short stories, and plays to periodicals. Editor and founder, *For the Time Being,* 1970-74.

WORK IN PROGRESS: At the time of his death Oldenberg was in the process of taping oral history from elderly Grand Haven, Mich., residents in order to write a history of Grand Haven.

SIDELIGHTS: Oldenburg's wife, Jean Oldenburg Yonker, told *CA:* ''Oldenburg was a poet, playwright, fiction writer, and actor. His Christian background shows throughout his works. The conflict of good and evil is strongly sensed in his literary themes.''

[Sketch verified by wife, Jean Oldenburg Yonker]

* * *

OLDFIELD, A(rthur) Barney 1909-

PERSONAL: Born December 18, 1909, in Tecumseh, Neb.; son of Adam William (a police officer) and Anna Ota (Fink) Oldfield; married Vada Margaret Kinman, May 6, 1935. *Education:* University of Nebraska, A.B., 1933; attended Army Command and General Staff College, 1948-49. *Politics:* Republican. *Religion:* Protestant. *Home:* 10650 Holman Ave., No. 301, Los Angeles, Calif. 90024. *Office:* Litton Industries, Inc., 360 North Crescent Dr., Beverly Hills, Calif. 90210.

CAREER: U.S. Army, career officer in public relations, stationed in United States and Europe, 1932-49, leaving service as lieutenant colonel; U.S. Air Force, career officer in public relations, stationed in United States and Europe, 1949-62, retiring as colonel; Litton Industries, Inc., Beverly Hills, Calif., vice-president of Litton International Development Corp., 1963—. Former host of nightly radio show ''Here's Hollywood'' on KFOR-Radio in Lincoln, Neb. Founder of Radio and Television News Directors Foundation, Luftwaffe/U.S. Air Force International Friendship Foundation, and Aviation/Space Writers Foundation; member of board of trustees of University of Nebraska Foundation and Edward R. Murrow Symposium at Washington State University.

MEMBER: Overseas Press Club of America, Radio and Television News Directors Association, Aviation/Space Writers Association, Writers Guild of America (West), Greater Los Angeles Press Club. *Awards, honors—Military:* Legion of Merit, Bronze Star, five battle stars. *Other:* Colonel Barney Oldfield

Humanitarian Award was named in his honor by American Research and Medical Services Foundation, 1978, as was Colonel Barney Oldfield Scholarship by University of Nebraska, 1979.

WRITINGS: Never a Shot in Anger (nonfiction), Duell, Sloan & Pearce, 1956; *Those Wonderful Men in the Cactus Starfighter Squadron,* Anderson, 1976; *Operation Narcissus* (novel), Pandick, 1978; (contributor) J. Mel Hickerson, editor, *The Sale I Made Which Meant the Most to Me,* Wiley, 1981. Author of script "The Road to Berlin," produced by Columbia Broadcasting System (CBS).

Reporter for *Lincoln Journal* (Lincoln, Neb.), 1930-40, editor of motion picture section, 1933-40, author of column "Theatre Topics," 1938-40. Contributor to magazines.

WORK IN PROGRESS: A book about Litton Industries.

SIDELIGHTS: Oldfield commented: "I have lived, worked, and done assignments in sixty-nine countries and continue to interest myself in foreign affairs and their implications.

"I was public relations man for Errol Flynn, Ann Sheridan, Elizabeth Taylor, Janis Paige, and Ronald Reagan (I wrote four gags a day for seven months for his 1980 Presidential campaign). I perpetrated the longest running publicity gag of all time, the Valentine made of ice for Sonja Henie, which still exists and is stored in Omaha, Nebraska.

"Reflectively, I try to use writing as a means of accomplishing other things. *Never a Shot in Anger* (about World War II correspondents) was instrumental in setting up the endowment base for an annually–awarded pair of R.O.T.C. scholarships. *Those Wonderful Men* set up the endowment for the Luftwaffe/ U.S. Air Force International Friendship Foundation, which gives annual awards to boys' and girls' clubs and other charities in Arizona. The first edition of *Operation Narcissus* gives support to the American Research and Medical Services Foundation, the Edward R. Murrow Endownment Fund at Washington State University, the School of Journalism at the University of Nebraska, and the Aviation/Space Writers Foundation, which makes grants to students who write or do documentaries on aerospace subjects. I believe it is far more dramatic, more attention getting, to give something of one's self and what he does than merely to give money, transferring it from one account to another. Recipients tend to be more moved and interested when they have evidence that somebody gave a damn and did his giving in a special way."

* * *

OLEA, Maria Florencia Varas 1938-
(Florencia Varas)

PERSONAL: Born February 23, 1938, in Santiago, Chile; daughter of Eduardo Varas Videla (a judge of the Supreme Court of Justice) and Maria Olea Salinas; divorced; children: three sons (one deceased). *Education:* University of Chile, B.A., 1962, M.A., 1966. *Home:* Nueva Costanera 4233 Santiago, Chile.

CAREER: Worked as a political interviewer on television programs, 1966-73; *The Times* and *Sunday Times,* London, England, correspondent in Chile, 1973—; *O Globo,* Rio de Janeiro, Brazil, correspondent in Chile, 1979—. Elections correspondent in Sweden for *O Estado,* Sao Paulo, Brazil, 1976.

WRITINGS—Under name Florencia Varas: Conversaciones con Viaux (title means "Conversations with Viaux"), [Chile], 1972; (with Jose Manuel Vegara) *Operacion Chile* (title means "Op-

eration Chile"), Editorial Pomaire, 1973; *Coup,* Stein & Day, 1974; *El caso Letelier* (title means "The Letelier Case"), Editorial Aconcagua, 1979; *Gustavo Leigh, el general disidente* (title means "Gustavo Leigh, the Dissenting General"), Editorial Aconcagua, 1979.

WORK IN PROGRESS: A collection of interviews with five world leaders, publication expected in 1983.

SIDELIGHTS: Varas told *CA:* "I have expressed myself through writing since I was a child. I did my first interview at the age of seventeen with Salvador Dali. I remember the emotion I felt as I walked through the New York streets on my way to the Saint Regis Hotel where the meeting took place.

"The books I have written have been based on my interviews with people who have held power and subsequently lost it. My first book, *Conversaciones con Viaux,* is based on several interviews with General Roberto Viaux. I carried these out while he was serving a sentence in the public jail in Santiago for his participation in the assassination attempt on Commander Rene Schneider, an attempt which was intended as a way to prevent the elected socialist president Salvador Allende from taking office. The second book, *Coup,* describes the events of September 11, 1973, when a military coup in Chile ended the government of President Allende.

"*El caso Letelier* reports on the assassination of Orlando Letelier, Allende's former minister of defense and foreign affairs. According to the version given in 1975 by the main witness, the American Michael Townley, the assassination was carried out by agents of the Chilean Secret Police. *Gustavo Leigh, el general disidente* is based on interviews with General Leigh, the former commander of the Chilean Air Force and a member of the Chilean military junta which overthrew Allende. General Pinochet, the current president of Chile and a member of the junta, expelled him from the group in 1978.

"Between 1966 and 1973 I had my own television program, which also was based on interviews with those personalities of the day who were making news. In 1965 I was awarded a scholarship from the Thompson Foundation, and I have been invited to visit most of the European and Latin American countries. Currently I am preparing a book based on interviews with five world leaders and a narration of my experiences as a journalist.

"I enjoy walking and swimming; I admire Graham Greene. I like British journalism because it comes closest to reflecting a fair balance between objectivity in its account of events and the subjective feelings of the author. I also enjoy Brazilian music, the south of Chile, English pubs, walking through the streets of London, and Rio de Janeiro.

"To be a journalist gives me a great sense of freedom; it enables me to look at the world from a theatre box while influencing the action on the stage."

* * *

OLIVER, Andrew 1906-1981

OBITUARY NOTICE: Born March 14, 1906, in Morristown, N.J.; died October 20, 1981, in Boston, Mass. Lawyer, historian, and author. A specialist in corporate, trust, and estate law, Oliver was also an avid historian, serving as the first vice-president of the New York Historical Society, president of the Essex Institute in Salem, Mass., and a commissioner of the National Portrait Gallery in Washington, D.C. Oliver wrote several books, including *Faces of a Family, Portraits of John and Abigail Adams,* and *The Portrait of John Marshall.* Obituaries and other sources: *Directory of American Scholars,* Volume I: *History,* 7th edition, Bowker, 1978; *Who's Who in America,* 40th edition, Marquis, 1978; *New York Times,* October 22, 1981; *AB Bookman's Weekly,* December 7, 1981.

* * *

OLIVER, Robert (Shelton)   1934-

PERSONAL: Born August 4, 1934, in Mount Vernon, N.Y.; son of Shelton H. (in sales) and Mary (a librarian; maiden name, Chamberlain) Oliver; married Virginia Mussin (a nutrition consultant), March 14, 1959; children: Richard, John. *Education:* Cornell University, B.S., 1956. *Home:* 964 Forest Ave., Pacific Grove, Calif. 93950. *Office:* Farmers Insurance, 505 Lighthouse Ave., Pacific Grove, Calif. 93950.

CAREER: Insurance Co. of North America, Denver, Colo., underwriter, 1961-66; Royal Globe Insurance Co., San Francisco, Calif., underwriter, 1966-70; Alexander & Alexander, San Francisco, underwriter, 1970-74; Farmers Insurance, Pacific Grove, Calif., agent, 1974—. *Military service:* U.S. Army, 1957-60.

WRITINGS: Cornucopia (poetry for children), Atheneum, 1978. Musical composer. Contributor of poems and stories to *Poetry Shell* magazine.

WORK IN PROGRESS: Poems.

SIDELIGHTS: Oliver told *CA:* "I hope my poems help children (and their elders) capture a sense of wonder and delight in the natural world around us."

AVOCATIONAL INTERESTS: Composing music for piano.

* * *

OLSON, Lois Ellen   1941-

PERSONAL: Born August 2, 1941, in Kokomo, Ind.; daughter of Earl Milton (a builder) and Mildred (Hinds) Rayl; married Thomas Cheuvront Olson (a minister), August 26, 1962; children: Sally Ann, Amy Cheuvront. *Education:* Attended Ohio State University; Miami University, Oxford, Ohio; University of Dayton; University of Denver; Fort Wright College; and Emory University. *Religion:* United Methodist. *Home and office:* 235 Third St. S., Okanogan, Wash. 98840.

CAREER: Worked as secretary and teacher, 1962—. Speaker and leader of retreats on spiritual growth, self-acceptance, and marriage enrichment.

WRITINGS: Meeting Him in the Wilderness, Doubleday, 1980.

WORK IN PROGRESS: A New Song in My Mouth, a book on marriage; a historical novel.

SIDELIGHTS: Lois Olson wrote: "My motivation is to share what God impresses upon me to relate about His work in and through us. My joy is in knowing that my obedience is pleasing to God and a source of blessings to others."

* * *

OLSON, Sigurd F(erdinand)   1899-1982

OBITUARY NOTICE—See index for *CA* sketch: Born April 4, 1899, in Chicago, Ill.; died of a heart attack, January 13, 1982, in Ely, Minn. Biologist, zoologist, educator, conservationist, and author. Olson spent most of his life trying to preserve the wilderness areas along the U.S.-Canadian border. He was president of the National Parks Association from 1954 to 1960 and had been a consultant to the U.S. Department of the Interior since 1962. During the 1957 Minnesota Centennial,

Olson's book *The Singing Wilderness* was chosen as one of ten best books of the century written by a native Minnesotan. He was the author of other books on conservation, including *Runes of the North, The Hidden Forest,* and an autobiography, *Open Horizons.* Olson suffered a fatal heart attack after snowshoeing in northern Minnesota. Obituaries and other sources: *New York Times,* January 15, 1982; *Time,* January 25, 1982; *AB Bookman's Weekly,* February 22, 1982.

* * *

OMAN, Charles Chichele   1901-1982

OBITUARY NOTICE—See index for *CA* sketch: Born June 5, 1901, in Oxford, England; died after a brief illness, January 26, 1982, in England. Curator and author. Oman was keeper of metalwork at the Victoria and Albert Museum from 1945 to 1966. He had joined the museum in 1924 as assistant keeper in the department of engravings and moved to the department of metalwork the following year. Oman's specialty was British silver, and his writings on the subject are regarded as the basic textbooks for its study. They include *English Domestic Silver, English Church Plate, The English Silver in the Kremlin 1557-1663,* and *English Engraved Silver 1150-1900.* Obituaries and other sources: *London Times,* January 29, 1982.

* * *

O'NEIL, Isabel MacDonald   1908(?)-1981

OBITUARY NOTICE: Born c. 1908; died after a long illness, November 19, 1981. Furniture expert and author. A specialist in furniture painting and restoration, O'Neil founded the Studio/Workshop for the Art of the Painted Finish, where she taught her techniques. O'Neil's book, *The Art of the Painted Finish,* is based on her craft. Obituaries and other sources: *New York Times,* November 25, 1981.

* * *

ORIGO, Iris (Margaret Cutting)   1902-

PERSONAL: Born August 15, 1902, in Birdlip, Gloucestershire, England; daughter of William Bayard (a diplomat) and Sybil Marjorie (Cuffe) Cutting; married Antonio Origo (an agriculturist), 1924; children: Gian Clemente Bayard (deceased), Benedetta, Donata. *Education:* Educated privately in Florence, Italy. *Home:* La Foce, Chianciano Terme 53042, Siena, Italy.

CAREER: Biographer. Lecturer in medieval history at Harvard University, Cambridge, Mass., 1958; vice-president of International Social Service. *Member:* Royal Society of Literature (fellow). *Awards, honors:* Isabella d'Este Medal, 1966; honorary doctorate from Wheaton College, 1960, and Smith College, 1964.

WRITINGS—All biographies, except as noted: *Gianni,* privately printed, 1933; *Leopardi: A Biography,* foreword by George Santayana, Oxford University Press, 1935, revised edition published as *Leopardi: A Study in Solitude,* Hamish Hamilton, 1953; *Allegra,* Hogarth, 1935; *Tribune of Rome: A Biography of Cola de Rienzo,* Hogarth, 1938; *War in Val d'Orcia: A Diary* (autobiography), J. Cape, 1947; *The Last Attachment: The Story of Byron and Teresa Guccioli as Told in Their Unpublished Letters and Other Family Papers,* Scribner, 1949, revised edition, Collins, 1962; *Giovanna and Jane,* J. Cape, 1950.

A Measure of Love, J. Cape, 1957, Pantheon, 1958; *The Merchant of Prato: Francesco di Marco Datini,* J. Cape, 1956,

Knopf, 1957, revised edition, Penguin, 1963; *The World of San Bernardino,* Harcourt, 1962; (author of introduction) Bernhard Berenson, *Sunset and Twilight,* Hamish Hamilton, 1964; (editor and translator, with John Heath-Stubbs) Giacomo Leopardi, *Selected Prose and Poetry,* Oxford University Press, 1966, New American Library, 1967; *Images and Shadows: Part of a Life* (autobiography), J. Murray, 1970, Harcourt, 1971; (compiler) *The Vagabond Path* (poems and prose), Scribner, 1972. Contributor of articles to *Atlantic Monthly, Times Literary Supplement, History Today, Speculum,* and other periodicals.

WORK IN PROGRESS: A Need to Testify, a collection of essays, for Harcourt.

SIDELIGHTS: Iris Origo has been called "the best writer in English about things Italian." Born of Anglo-Irish and American parents, she was raised in Italy and tutored by a noted classical scholar, Solone Monti. She traveled widely in her youth, and made Italy her permanent home when she married an Italian marchese in 1924. Her books reflect this background: the subjects of her biographies have been Italians of the Middle Ages and the nineteenth century.

Origo's first published biography was a life of the melancholy nineteenth-century poet Giacomo Leopardi. On *Leopardi*'s publication, the *Times Literary Supplement* pronounced it "wise and illuminating," and Stark Young of the *New Republic* called it "excellent . . . balanced, sane and on the whole distinguished." Some critics faulted Origo for restricting herself to Leopardi's life and attempting no thorough critical assessment of his work. "The literary aspect of the biography is not its strongest claim to our admiration," wrote Peter Quennell of *New Statesman and Nation,* who nonetheless called the book "well written, nicely balanced, carefully documented." When a new edition was published eighteen years later, Forscarina Alexander wrote of Origo in the *Spectator:* "Sympathetic and discerning, devoted to her subject yet recognizing his considerable faults of character, expert at sifting evidence and settling old controversies, she is the ideal biographer."

Leopardi was followed by a study of Allegra Clairmont, Lord Byron's illegitimate daughter. Following one more book, a biography of fourteenth-century Roman patriot Cola di Rienzo, World War II brought a hiatus in Origo's writing. The author devoted herself to work with the Red Cross and established a home for refugee children on her estate, La Foce. She and her husband also aided the anti-Fascist resistance, hiding partisans and escaped prisoners of war in La Foce's woods. La Foce was bombed and shelled, and the Origos were turned out of their home by German soldiers and forced to walk, with twenty-three small children, twelve miles to the nearest village. Iris Origo's diary of those years was published in 1947 as *War in Val d'Orcia.*

Returning to biography in 1949, Origo examined, in *The Last Attachment,* Byron's love affair with Contessa Teresa Guccioli. Origo persuaded Teresa's great-nephew to grant her access to Byron's love letters and many other documents, access he had denied to several would-be biographers. This was a challenge since he was quite deaf and, Origo remarked, "it is difficult to be persuasive or reassuring at the top of one's voice." The book was hailed as a "first-rate biography with a dash of mystery" by Clive Bell of the *Spectator,* and the *San Francisco Chronicle* said, "no previous biographer . . . has probed so deeply into the period of . . . [Byron's] Italian residence." The *Times Literary Supplement* found the new material, which included the complete Italian text of 149 of Byron's letters, "overcrowded" by Origo's retelling of previously known facts. "A briefer view of the known story," it was suggested, "would

have left more room for the author's fine imaginative and interpretative talent." When the book was reissued in 1971, the *Times Literary Supplement* called it "still our fullest, most balanced, and most perceptive account of the relationship."

Origo's books continued to win critical acclaim. *A Measure of Love,* comprising five biographical essays on British and Italian figures of the nineteenth century, was applauded by the *Manchester Guardian* as "a fascinating expose of nineteenth century attitudes," and Quennell wrote in the *New York Times:* "Marchesa Origo is a biographer who understands the heart. Her personages move and speak." In *The Merchant of Prato,* Origo drew on the many documents left by Francesco di Marco Datini, reconstructing his domestic, social, and business life. Sidney Painter of the *New York Times* observed that the biography is "both a scholarly monograph . . . and a literary work of art. . . . Origo's characters live and breathe, hate, love and believe." Her biography of San Bernardino was also well received. The Tuscan saint, who was canonized only six years after his death in 1444, was one of the most popular preachers of his time. Origo's book quotes many of his sermons. As the *Critic* noted, "They are filled with the life of his day and often, judged by the standards of our day, have the abrasive quality of sandpaper." The *Economist* called *The World of San Bernardino* "a vivid and lively picture not only of the saint and his work, but also of the world in which he lived and the people to whom he preached. . . . It is a brilliant idea, brilliantly carried out; it combines scholarship with fine writing and vivid narrative."

Origo also won praise when she wrote of her own life in *Images and Shadows.* That book tells of her childhood in Italy, Ireland, and America; of her studies with Monti, who provided an education in the fifteenth-century humanist tradition; and of her and her husband's work in reclaiming the eroded, exhausted farmland of their estate in Tuscany. Critics found Origo's portraits of her parents especially memorable. Her father, "an intense, many-sided, and sane young man," who encouraged her to read and to exercise her intellect, died before she was eight; nevertheless, he "casts the longest shadow across this book," William Archer of *Best Sellers* remarked. Origo writes of her three years in "society"—which she considered a waste of time—with "refreshing wit and merciless precision," the *Listener* observed. She writes also of the gardens she created at La Foce and of the problems of biography, concluding that "only by discovering what life 'felt like,' to our subject . . . can we become aware of him as a *person* at all." *Images and Shadows,* wrote Anne Fremantle in the *New York Times Book Review,* is "a book nourishing from every point of view, filled with relations, friends, family, travel, work and war, but, above all, with love and learning."

BIOGRAPHICAL/CRITICAL SOURCES: Times Literary Supplement, June 20, 1935, September 16, 1949, October 2, 1953, November 13, 1970, July 16, 1971; *New Statesman and Nation,* July 6, 1935; *New Republic,* August 21, 1935, May 8, 1971; Iris Origo, *War in Val d'Orcia: A Diary,* J. Cape, 1947; *Spectator,* September 16, 1949, November 27, 1953; *San Francisco Chronicle,* November 20, 1949; *New York Times,* April 28, 1957, November 10, 1957; *Manchester Guardian,* October 22, 1957; *Critic,* December 1962-January 1963; *Commonweal,* March 15, 1963; *Economist,* April 6, 1963; *Listener,* December 24, 1970; Origo, *Images and Shadows: Part of a Life,* Harcourt, 1971; *Saturday Review,* May 8, 1971; *Best Sellers,* May 15, 1971; *New York Times Book Review,* May 23, 1971; *Atlantic Monthly,* July, 1971.

—*Sketch by Tim Connor*

ORR, Gregory 1947-

PERSONAL: Born February 3, 1947, in Albany, N.Y.; son of James Wendell (a physician) and Barbara (Howe) Orr; married Trisha Winer (a painter), March 3, 1973. *Education:* Attended Hamilton College, 1964-66; Antioch College, B.A., 1969; Columbia University, M.F.A., 1972. *Residence:* Earlysville, Va. *Office:* Department of English, University of Virginia, Charlottesville, Va. 22903.

CAREER: University of Virginia, Charlottesville, 1975—, began as assistant professor, became associate professor of English. Gives readings at colleges, universities, and Library of Congress, and for British Broadcasting Corp. *Member:* International P.E.N., Poetry Society of America. *Awards, honors:* Discovery Award from Poetry Center of Young Men's-Young Women's Hebrew Association, New York, N.Y., 1970; poets' prize from Academy of American Poets, 1970; junior member of Society of Fellows at University of Michigan, 1972-75; fellow of *Transatlantic Review* at Bread Loaf Writers Conference, 1976; Guggenheim fellow, 1977-78; National Endowment for the Arts fellow, 1978-79; sesquicentennial associate of Center for Advanced Studies, 1981-82.

WRITINGS—Books of poems: *Burning the Empty Nests,* Harper, 1973; *Gathering the Bones Together,* Harper, 1975; *Salt Wings* (chapbook), Poetry East, 1980; *The Red House,* Harper, 1980.

Work represented in anthologies, including *The American Poetry Anthology,* edited by Halpern, Avon, 1975; *The Poet's Choice,* Tendril Press, 1981; *Young American Poets,* edited by Roger Gaess, International Publishers, 1981. Contributor of poems and translations to literary journals and popular magazines, including *Harper's, New Yorker, Atlantic Monthly, Nation, Paris Review, Poetry Now,* and *Antioch Review.*

WORK IN PROGRESS: A criticism of poetry by Stanley Kunitz, for Columbia University Press.

*   *   *

OWEN, Marsha
See STANFORD, Sally

P

PA CHIN
See LI Fei-kan

*   *   *

PAGE, Drew 1905-

PERSONAL: Born January 5, 1905, in Mineral Wells, Tex.; son of Ben Richer (a carpenter) and Lillian (Hendricks) Page; married Margaret Fay McClure, April 4, 1930; children: Margie Drew Page Regenhardt, Netta Fay Page Carver. *Education:* Attended Phoenix Music Conservatory, 1924-25, and East Central Teachers College (now East Central University), 1925-26. *Home:* 1412 Cottonwood Pl., Las Vegas, Nev. 89104.

CAREER: Professional musician. *Military service:* Oklahoma National Guard, 1921-24. *Member:* American Society of Composers, Authors, and Publishers, American Association of Retired Persons, Musicians Union, East Central University Alumni Association, Las Vegas Press Club. *Awards, honors:* Honorary teaching certificate from University of Oklahoma, 1948; "Lonesome Horn" was named album of the week by Channel 11, Los Angeles, Calif., 1956; Deems Taylor Award from American Society of Composers, Authors, and Publishers, 1981, for *Drew's Blues.*

WRITINGS: Drew's Blues: A Sideman's Life With the Big Bands, Louisiana State University Press, 1980.

WORK IN PROGRESS: A complete method for the clarinet, Page's main instrument, for Golden West.

SIDELIGHTS: Page commented: "I had wanted to try for a career in music ever since I heard at the age of fifteen that one could get paid for playing it, and never considered doing anything else. I had hopes of getting out and seeing some of the world and earning my way by doing something I liked.

"My career started in 1924 with a traveling carnival band. I entered the field of jazz in 1926 with Johnny McFall in Texas and Mexico. In 1927 I went with Ted FioRito in New York, and in 1929 with Jack Crawford on a tour of forty-two states. Back to Texas, then to Chicago in 1934, where I worked with Paul Ash, Bob Crosby, local bands, and the NBC-Radio staff orchestra. In 1939 and 1940 I toured with Harry James. I went to Hollywood in 1941, where I worked with Ben Pollack, Horace Heidt, Phil Harris, Wingy Manone, Red Nichols, and Freddy Martin. In 1948 I toured with Jack Fina, and in 1950 with Will Osborne. I went with the Billy Roe Trio in 1951,

stayed in Bakersfield for six years, then in Las Vegas in 1958 for five years, working with Charlie Ventura, lounge groups, and show bands. From 1965 to 1968 I toured the United States, Canada, Greenland, and the West Indies with Freddie Masters out of New York, in 1968 with 'Hello, Dolly!,' and from 1969 to 1970 with 'Cabaret.' I joined the Russ Morgan Orchestra under the direction of Jack Morgan in 1970 for six years, playing two four-month periods a year at the Dunes Hotel in Las Vegas and making two tours a year.

"A music historian and writer in New York heard about my career and wrote to me for information about some musicians of the early days. After I had been supplying him with information and corrections of misinformation he had received from other contributors for a couple of years, he remarked that, because of my 'fabulous memory' for names, places, and details, I should write my own book. I had been urged to do so by a few bandmates along the way and had had the idea for some time myself, so in 1976, at the age of seventy-one, I retired from full-time performing to devote my time to writing.

"I had only a smattering of knowledge of the craft, but I had read so much affectatious, highfalutin, literary gobbledygook about mostly unliterary people that I was determined to write my story in plain words that they and everybody else could understand without feeling 'written down to.' I read a little Mencken, Alexander King, and Ben Hecht to try to get the hang of informal diction. Fortunately, according to critics, the informal style was acceptable.

"Besides telling a story about musicians and the music business in the informal language of musicians, I was careful to avoid writing untruths, half-truths, hearsay, and fiction. Inadvertently I placed a town in the wrong state and misspelled a couple of names, and this has been corrected for future printings, but I did not go beyond the actual facts of the events that took place in my story. Researchers can feel confident that they are not being misinformed. Everything that happened was told by me as a participant or from firsthand observation. Nothing is from research."

BIOGRAPHICAL/CRITICAL SOURCES: Ada News, October 14, 1979; *International Musician,* April, 1980; *Sunday Oklahoman,* January 11, 1981; *Desert Aria,* July, 1981; *Allen Advocate,* August 13, 1981.

*   *   *

PALAMAS, Kostes 1859-1943

BRIEF ENTRY: Born January 13, 1859, in Patras, Greece; died

February 27, 1943, in Athens, Greece. Greek playwright, poet, and critic. As founder of the "new school of Athens," Palamas led the renaissance that ushered Greek literature into the twentieth century. With such poetry collections as *Tragedy of My Country* (1886), he convinced Greek writers and critics that the future of Greek literature depended on demotic speech, the "living language" of the people. His victory came when demotic Greek was made the official language of the land. His early work was in the Orphic (classical) tradition. But after the debacle of Greece's war with Turkey in 1897, Palamas dedicated himself to the Greek land, the Greek people, and the Greek soul, working to rebuild national pride and create hope for the future. Critics believe the best of his writing occurred immediately after the war. *Life Immovable* (1904) captured the versatility of his resources, including his vast knowledge of the European intellectual world and the wide variety of his own interests. *The Twelve Lays of the Gypsy* (1907), an exuberant, lyrical blend of an Orphic story with the imagery and lively language of modern-day Greece, has been hailed as his masterpiece. His later work was less influential on the international scene, but with his autobiography and his criticism, Palamas remained a force in the revival of Greek letters. *Biographical/critical sources: Columbia Dictionary of Modern European Literature,* Columbia University Press, 1947; *Prairie Schooner,* spring, 1967; Thanasis Maskaleris, *Kostis Palamas,* Twayne, 1972; *World Authors, 1950-1970,* H. W. Wilson, 1975.

* * *

PALECKIS, Justas (Ignovich) 1899-1980

OBITUARY NOTICE: Born January 10, 1899 (some sources list January 22), in Telsiai, Lithuania; died February 21, 1980, in Verkovny, Soviet Lithuania. Statesman, journalist, and author. After serving as director of the Lithuanian Wire and Telegraph Agency, Paleckis worked as a journalist from 1927 until 1939. While writing for newspapers and magazines, Paleckis became interested in Communist doctrines and began writing pamphlets for the Baltic Communist movement. He was imprisoned for his activities by the Lithuanian nationalists with the onset of World War II, but was released and appointed premier of that country when the Soviets occupied it. Paleckis organized resistance forces against the Germans in 1941 and aided the Soviets in capturing Lithuania in 1944. He was later designated Chairman of the Presidium of the Supreme Soviet of Lithuania, and in 1952 was elected a candidate member of the Central Committee of the Soviet Union. Paleckis's writings include *The Last Tsar, 1937-38.* Obituaries and other sources: *The International Who's Who,* Europa, 1977; *The Annual Obituary 1980,* St. Martin's, 1981.

* * *

PAPE, Gordon 1936-

PERSONAL: Born March 16, 1936, in San Francisco, Calif.; son of Clifford Baume (a researcher and manager) and Lethe Mary (a secretary; maiden name, Chenevert) Pape; married Shirley Ann Cloutier, May 5, 1962; children: Kimberley Anne, Kendrew Gordon, Deborah Margaret. *Education:* Carleton University, B.A., 1959; graduate study at University of Toulouse, 1960-61. *Politics:* Independent. *Religion:* Protestant. *Home:* 372 Woodsworth Rd., Willowdale, Ontario, Canada M2L 2T6. *Agent:* John Cushman Associates, Inc., 242 West 27th St., New York, N.Y. 10001. *Office: Today,* 2180 Yonge St., Toronto, Ontario, Canada.

CAREER: Montreal Gazette, Montreal, Quebec, education editor, 1962-63, chief of bureau in Quebec, Quebec, 1963-66, parliamentary correspondent from Ottawa, Ontario, 1966-70; Southam News Services, London, England, bureau chief, 1970-73; *Montreal Gazette,* associate editor, 1973-74; *Financial Times of Canada,* Toronto, Ontario, assistant to publisher, 1974-75; *Canadian,* Toronto, publisher, 1975-79; *Today,* Toronto, president, publisher, and director, 1979—. Publisher of *Canadian Homes,* 1976-79; president and publisher of *Canadian Weekend,* 1979-80. Vice-president and member of board of directors of National Magazine Awards Foundation, 1980, president, 1981; vice-chairman and member of board of directors of Magazines Canada, 1981. Host of "Capital Report," on CBC-Radio, 1968-70; guest on television programs, including "Viewpoint" and "Twenty Million Questions." *Member:* Magazine Association of Canada (member of board of directors, 1981), Donelda Club, Wig and Pen Club, Rockingham Fish and Game Club. *Awards, honors:* Named Canadian wine taster of the year by Opimian Society, 1975; communications award from Heritage Canada, 1976, for *Montreal at the Crossroads.*

WRITINGS: (With Donna Gabeline and Dane Lanken) *Montreal at the Crossroads,* Harvest House, 1975; (with Tony Aspler) *Chain Reaction* (novel; Book-of-the-Month Club alternate selection), Viking, 1978; (with Aspler) *The Scorpion Sanction* (novel), Viking, 1980. Founder of *Perspective on Money,* 1974. Contributor to magazines, including *Reader's Digest.*

WORK IN PROGRESS: The Music Wars, a novel, with Aspler, publication expected in 1982.

SIDELIGHTS: Pape commented: "I covered education in Quebec during the period of that province's changeover from a basically church-run education system to a public education system. I covered Quebec City during the Lesage years. Major events during this period included the Queen's visit of 1964, the rise of separatism, the decline of the role of the church in Quebec, the federal-provincial confrontations, and the growing social consciousness on all levels in Quebec society. I covered Ottawa during the period of transition from the Pearson years to the Trudeau years. I wrote extensively about the Conservative and Liberal leadership campaigns which brought Stanfield and Trudeau to power, and covered the 1968 general election in depth.

"As bureau chief in London, I covered such stories as the civil war in Northern Ireland (and made numerous trips to Ulster during a three-year period), Britain's entry into the European Common Market, the collapse of the Heath government, and the growing strains on the British economy. I traveled extensively in Africa and the Middle East, writing articles for newspapers across Canada on topics ranging from the weakness in foreign aid programs in Africa to Israeli occupation of the Golan Heights and the Sinai Peninsula. Countries visited on assignment included Ireland, Nigeria, South Africa, Rhodesia, Tanzania, Zanzibar, Kenya, Libya, Egypt, Israel, Jordan, Lebanon, Cyprus, Malta, Luxembourg, Sweden, Greece, and Turkey.

"The novels I wrote with Tony Aspler all deal with major contemporary issues set against a background of tension and intrigue. *Chain Reaction* focuses on the separatist movement in the province of Quebec. *The Scorpion Sanction* deals with the pressures of Islamic fundamentalism in modern Egypt. *The Music Wars* explores the plight of dissidents in the Soviet Union. In my view, a novel should hold the reader's interest and attention from start to finish. It should also leave the reader more knowledgeable than when he began it."

AVOCATIONAL INTERESTS: Reading, chess, wine, golf, snorkeling.

* * *

PARAKH, Jal Sohrab 1932-

BRIEF ENTRY: Born February 2, 1932, in Secunderabad, India. American biologist, educator, and author. Parakh has been a professor of biology and science education at Western Washington State College since 1966. He wrote *Teaching Children Science: Why, What, How, and How Well* (Wadsworth, 1972). *Address:* 3923 Cliffside Dr., Bellingham, Wash. 98225; and Department of Biology, Western Washington State College, Bellingham, Wash. 98225. *Biographical/critical sources: Who's Who in the West,* 15th edition, Marquis, 1976.

* * *

PARIS, Erna 1938-

PERSONAL: Born May 6, 1938, in Toronto, Ontario, Canada; daughter of Jules (a chartered accountant) and Christine (Lipkin) Newman; married Jacques Paris, December 28, 1961 (divorced, 1973); married Thomas M. Robinson (a professor of philosophy), April 26, 1981; children: (first marriage) Michelle Anne, Roland Charles. *Education:* University of Toronto, B.A. (with honors), 1960; Sorbonne, University of Paris, Diplome Superieur, Civilisation Francaise, 1961; attended Ontario College of Education, 1964. *Home:* 173 Strathearn Rd., Toronto, Ontario, Canada, M6C 1S3.

CAREER: Teacher of English in Scarborough, Ontario, 1964-66; free-lance writer and broadcaster, 1968—. Host of "In Touch," on Canadian Broadcasting Corp. (CBC-TV), 1974; associate producer of "Seeing for Ourselves," on CBC-TV, 1978; host of "Roll Call," on OECA Television, 1978. *Member:* Association of Canadian Television and Radio Artists, Periodical Writers' Association of Canada (co-founder; president, 1978-79), Canadian Civil Liberties Association. *Awards, honors:* Awards from Media Club of Canada, 1970, for article "Sometimes Being an Ex-Priest Is Even Harder Than Being a Priest," 1973, for radio documentary "Why Italian Women Wear Black," 1973, for article "Why Secretaries Get Mad," and 1974, for radio documentary "Paul Smithers, a Case of Race and Death."

WRITINGS: (With Myrna Kostash and others) *Her Own Woman: Profiles of Canadian Women,* Macmillan of Canada, 1975; *Jews: An Account of Their Experience in Canada,* Macmillan of Canada, 1980. Radio writer. Co-author with David Lewis Stein of "A Man and a Woman," a monthly column in *Chatelaine,* 1977-80. Contributor to magazines. Assistant editor of *Maclean's,* 1972.

SIDELIGHTS: Erna Paris wrote: "My writing career began in an unconventional way. In 1968 I was called to jury duty, the only woman on a rape trial. The experience so disturbed me that I felt a need to write about it, and to my surprise I managed to sell the piece to a national magazine. If I can write and sell a piece once, I thought, I can do it twice.

"My recent book on the political and social experience of Canadian Jews began as an attempt to understand the evolution of values and attitudes in three generations of several representative families. But the historical events of their times began to loom larger in my mind than the lives of particular individuals, and I realized that I as well as other Canadian Jews were largely unaware of our own history. Traditionally it had been confused with, and wrongly thought to be the same as, the history of Jews in the U.S.A. I shifted my focus and wrote a different book, the first of its kind in Canada, I believe.

"Sometimes I think I continue to write free lance because I'm a masochist, and I actually enjoy wondering when I'll see the next paycheck. However, it is more likely that the pleasure of struggling to find the right language to express my own thoughts, perceptions, judgments, and observations is simply unequalled."

* * *

PARK, David 1919-

PERSONAL: Born October 13, 1919, in New York, N.Y.; son of Edwin Avery (an architect and painter) and Frances (a writer) Park; married Clara Claiborne (a teacher and writer), August 19, 1945; children: Katharine Park Dyer, Rachel Park Failes, Paul Claiborne, Jessica Hilary. *Education:* Harvard University, A.B., 1941; University of Michigan, Ph.D., 1951. *Home:* 29 Hoxsey St., Williamstown, Mass. 01267. *Office:* Department of Physics, Williams College, Williamstown, Mass. 01267.

CAREER: Williams College, Williamstown, Mass., assistant professor, 1951-56, associate professor, 1956-60, professor of physics, 1960—. Member of visiting faculty at University of Ceylon (now Sri Lanka), 1955-56, 1972, Cambridge University, 1962-63, and University of North Carolina, 1964. Member of Institute for Advanced Study, Princeton, N.J., 1950-51. *Member:* International Society for the Study of Time (president, 1973-76), American Physical Society, National Society for Autistic Children (member of board of directors, 1976—; third vice-president), Sigma Xi. *Awards, honors:* Science book award from Phi Beta Kappa, 1980, for *The Image of Eternity.*

WRITINGS: Introduction to the Quantum Theory, McGraw, 1964, 2nd edition, 1974; *Contemporary Physics,* Harcourt, 1964; *Classical Dynamics and Its Quantum Analogues,* Springer-Verlag, 1979; *The Image of Eternity: Roots of Time in the Physical World,* University of Massachusetts Press, 1980. Contributor of about seventy-five articles and reviews to scientific journals and newspapers.

WORK IN PROGRESS: A book on the relation of scientific theory to experience; scientific research.

SIDELIGHTS: Park wrote: "It seems to me that the aim of fundamental science is the same as that of the arts: to give meaning to our experience of the world and move our emotions. I am aware that some people would put other considerations in front of these, but I do not think that either science or art would have very much life in it if I were wrong. It is the pleasure of sharing these meanings and emotions that leads people to become teachers of the arts and sciences, and to become writers. The great thing is to have these experiences, to feel them deeply, and to help lead others to have them, too. I think this is what my life has been about.

"I have explored several areas of science: pure and applied physics, physiology of the nervous system, cosmology, even written a paper on population statistics. I have traveled, reasonably slowly and thoughtfully, in forty-eight countries. I can get around in several languages, including, among others less obvious, Indonesian and Melanesian Pidgin. I have slept on the stones of Easter Island and traveled the Sepik River in a dugout canoe, and walked up eighteen thousand feet to be in the middle of the mountains around Everest. I don't distinguish between this kind of exploration and the kind one does in a quiet office with pencil and paper. Perhaps some day I'll write about the world."

PARK, Jordan
See KORNBLUTH, C(yril) M.

*   *   *

PARK, (Rosina) Ruth

PERSONAL: Born in Auckland, New Zealand; married D'Arcy Niland (a journalist, playwright, and author), 1942 (died March 29, 1967); children: Anne, Rory, Patrick, Deborah, Kilmeny. *Education:* Attended St. Benedict's College, Auckland University, and New Zealand University. *Religion:* Roman Catholic. *Residence:* Norfolk Island, Australia. *Address:* c/o Angus & Robertson, 102 Glover St., Cremorne Junction, New South Wales 2090, Australia.

CAREER: Proofreader and editor of children's pages for *Auckland Star,* Auckland, New Zealand; editor of children's page for *Zealandia,* Auckland; welfare worker in Auckland; *Sydney Mirror,* Sydney, Australia, reporter, beginning 1941; scriptwriter for Twentieth Century-Fox, London, England; free-lance writer and journalist. *Awards, honors: Sydney Morning Herald* prize, 1948, for *The Harp in the South;* runner-up in Australian Book of the Year Award, 1975, for *Callie's Castle;* Miles Franklin Award, 1978; Children's Book of the Year Award, 1980, for *Playing Beatie Bow.*

WRITINGS—Novels; all published by Angus & Robertson, except as noted: *The Harp in the South,* Houghton, 1948; *Poor Man's Orange,* 1949, published as *12½ Plymouth Street,* Houghton, 1951; *The Witch's Thorn,* 1951, Houghton, 1952; *A Power of Roses,* 1953; *Pink Flannel,* illustrations by Phil Taylor, 1955; *One-a-Pecker, Two-a-Pecker,* 1957, published as *The Frost and the Fire,* Houghton, 1958; *The Good-Looking Women,* 1961; *Serpent's Delight,* Doubleday, 1968.

"The Muddle-Headed Wombat" series; for children; all published by Educational Press, except as noted: *The Muddle-Headed Wombat,* 1962; *The Muddle-Headed Wombat on Holiday,* 1964; *. . . in the Treetops,* 1965; *. . . at School,* 1966; *. . . in the Snow,* 1966; *. . . on a Rainy Day,* 1969; *. . . in the Springtime,* 1970; *. . . on the River,* 1970; *. . . and the Bush Band,* Angus & Robertson, 1973; *. . . on Clean-Up Day,* Angus & Robertson, 1976; *. . . and the Invention,* Angus & Robertson, 1976.

Other children's books: *The Hole in the Hill,* illustrations by Jennifer Murray, Ure Smith, 1961, published as *The Secret of Maori Cave,* Doubleday, 1964; *The Ship's Cat,* illustrations by Richard Kennedy, St. Martin's, 1961; *Uncle Matt's Mountain,* illustrations by Laurence Broderick, St. Martin's 1962; *The Road to Christmas,* St. Martin's, 1962; *The Road Under the Sea,* illustrations by Murray, Ure Smith, 1962, Doubleday, 1966; *Shaky Island,* illustrations by Iris Millington, McKay, 1962; *Airlift for Grandee,* illustrations by Sheila Hawkins, St. Martin's, 1964; *Ring for the Sorcerer,* illustrations by William Stobbs, Hurwitz Martin, 1967; *The Sixpenny Island,* illustrations by David Cox, Ure Smith, 1968, published as *Ten-Cent Island,* illustrations by Robert Frankenberg, Doubleday, 1968; *Nuki and the Sea Serpent,* illustrations by Zelma Blakely, Longmans, Green, 1969; *Callie's Castle,* illustrations by daughter, Kilmeny Niland, Angus & Robertson, 1974; *The Gigantic Balloon,* illustrations by daughters K. Niland and Deborah Niland, Collins, 1975, Parents Magazine Press, 1976; *Merchant Campbell,* illustrations by Edwin Bell, Collins, 1976; *Roger Bandy,* illustrations by K. Niland and D. Niland, Rigby, 1977.

Plays: *The Uninvited Guest,* Angus & Robertson, 1948. "The Muddle-Headed Wombat" radio play series.

Other: (With husband, D'Arcy Niland) *The Drums Go Bang* (autobiography), illustrations by Phil Taylor, Angus & Robertson, 1956; *Tales of the South,* Macmillan, 1961; *The Companion Guide to Sydney,* Collins, 1973; *Swords and Crowns and Rings,* Thomas Nelson, 1977, St. Martin's, 1978; *Come Danger, Come Darkness,* Hodder & Stoughton, 1978; *Flights of Angels,* Thomas Nelson, 1981; *When the Wind Changed,* Coward, 1981.

SIDELIGHTS: When Seymour Krim described Ruth Park's first novel, *Harp in the South,* he compared the book to "an old-fashioned stove." "It is a little squat and homely," said the reviewer, "but it gives out enough heat to warm the chill print of half a dozen of our streamlined models." Indeed, most critics agree that, though unprentious, Park's works are engaging.

While Park's plots have been called commonplace, "she is a master of the episode," stated Bradford Smith of the *New York Herald Tribune Book Review.* Some scenes in *The Witch's Thorn* reflected, in the opinion of the *San Francisco Chronicle's* J. H. Jackson, "such horrifying cruelty that the reader's hair will stand on end." Park's characters, too, have been praised. "Her bad people," commented C. H. Grattan, "are never lacking in humanity," while "her good people are of humanity all compound." Park's works are set in her homeland, helping make the environment and the story equally interesting to readers.

Park told *CA:* "Although I am mostly known as an adult novelist, I have always written for children. I come of an isolated, storytelling family. Before my marriage I spent several years editing a large children's newspaper, and there learned that what adults would like children to read, they simply don't. For this reason I have no interest in book awards, critiques, or scholarly dissertations from people who have never had any children and have never spent any time with them. My one criterion is whether children like to read my books; if they didn't, I'd stop writing them. Aside from having five children of my own, I always try out a children's story on a group, usually kindergarten.

"I have been published in the United States for many years. I have also written dozens of storybook texts for German, Nigerian, and Scandinavian books. For the ABC Children's session I have written for close on twenty-five years. The best known of these many series is *The Muddle-Headed Wombat.* About Wombat there are eleven books available. I also do educational books about some industry or aspect of Australian life. Lately, I have done several adventure books for older age groups. They are all set in and around the Pacific, with which I am very familiar. *The Hole in the Hill, The Road Under the Sea,* and *Ten-Cent Island* are some of these.

"I like children enormously and have spent much of my life with them, as a teacher, a children's editor, and finally a mother. I like interesting and amusing children, and this is why I wrote children's books. Being a severely practical writer, I write for children only, not publishers, adult buyers, or adult critics. My idea of a successful children's book is not one that wins a prize but one that gets worn out in all the libraries. Writing for children is different from writing for adults and much more difficult. Most adult writing is designed to expand the inner world of the reader. Children's writing is the reverse. For a child all the doors of his imaginative vision open outwards; the content of the story is the marvelous world beyond these doors, the style is what opens them for boys and girls too small to reach the knobs."

BIOGRAPHICAL/CRITICAL SOURCES: New York Times, February 22, 1948, January 28, 1951, April 13, 1958; *New*

York Herald Tribune Book Review, February 22, 1948, January 28, 1951, December 7, 1952, April 6, 1958; *Saturday Review of Literature,* February 28, 1948; *Atlantic,* April, 1948; *New Statesman and Nation,* May 1, 1948; *Commonweal,* May 14, 1948, February 13, 1953; *Chicago Sunday Tribune,* February 11, 1951, December 28, 1952; *Catholic World,* April, 1951; *San Francisco Chronicle,* December 18, 1952; *Observer,* September 24, 1978; *New Yorker,* January 15, 1979.

* * *

PARKE, Herbert William   1903-

PERSONAL: Born September 7, 1903, in Moneymore, Northern Ireland; son of William and Bertha (Blair) Parke; married Nancy Bankart Gurney, 1930; children: one daughter. *Education:* Wadham College, Oxford, M.A. (with first class honors), 1924, graduated (with first class honors), 1926. *Home:* 8 Christchurch Pl., Christchurch Mount, Epsom, Surrey KT19 8RS, England.

CAREER: Trinity College, Dublin, Ireland, fellow, 1929-73, professor of ancient history, 1934-73, librarian, 1949-65, vice-provost, 1952-73, curator, 1965-73, fellow emeritus, 1973—. L. C. Purser Lecturer in archaeology, 1934. Temporary principal of Irish Board of Trade, 1942-44. Member of Institute for Advanced Study, Princeton, N.J., 1960. *Member:* Royal Irish Academy, Royal Numismatic Society (fellow), Kildare Street Club, University Club (Dublin). *Awards, honors:* D.Lit. from Queen's University, Belfast, 1974.

WRITINGS: A History of the Delphic Oracle, Basil Blackwell, 1939, revised edition (with Donald Ernest Wilson Wormell) published as *The Delphic Oracle,* Volume I: *The History,* Volume II: *The Oracular Responses,* 1956; *The Oracles of Zeus: Dodona, Olympia, Ammon,* Harvard University Press, 1967; *Greek Oracles,* Humanities, 1967; *Festivals of the Athenians,* Cornell University Press, 1977. Contributor to *Encyclopaedia Britannica, Chambers's Encyclopaedia,* and *Oxford Classical Dictionary.* Contributor to classical journals.

BIOGRAPHICAL/CRITICAL SOURCES: Times Literary Supplement, April 8, 1977.*

* * *

PARKER, John
See WYATT, John

* * *

PARSEGHIAN, Ara (Raoul)   1923-

BRIEF ENTRY: Born May 21, 1923, in Akron, Ohio. American college football coach and sports commentator. Parseghian was a football coach at University of Notre Dame from 1964 to 1975. He is a sports commentator for American Broadcasting Company (ABC) and host of the television series "Ara's Sports World." He was named coach of the year in 1964. Parseghian wrote *Parseghian and Notre Dame Football* (Doubleday, 1973). *Address:* American Broadcasting Co., Inc., 1330 Avenue of the Americas, New York, N.Y. 10019; and St. Joseph Bank Building, South Bend, Ind. 46601. *Biographical/critical sources: Chicago Daily News,* December 31, 1973; *Biography News,* Gale, Volume I, 1974, Volume II, 1975; *Sport,* September, 1975.

* * *

PARSONS, Geoffrey   1908-1981

OBITUARY NOTICE: Born July 3, 1908, in New York, N.Y.; died September 17, 1981, in Benisa, Alicante Province, Spain. Editor and journalist. Parsons began his journalism career with the *Boston Globe* before becoming the Chicago correspondent for the *New York Herald Tribune,* where he covered the rash of strikes that sparked the labor movement in the thirties. In 1940 he became London correspondent for the *Herald Tribune.* When Paris was liberated from German occupation in 1944, Parsons went there to begin printing the *Herald Tribune's* European edition, which had been banned during the war. He remained editor of the paper until 1950 when he was named chief press officer and director of information of the North Atlantic Treaty Organization (NATO), serving until 1957. In addition, he was a vice-president of the Northrop Corporation. Obituaries and other sources: *Who's Who in the World,* 2nd edition, Marquis, 1973; *New York Times,* September 18, 1981.

* * *

PASK, Raymond (Frank)   1944-

PERSONAL: Born May 27, 1944, in Melbourne, Australia; son of Frank and May (Sturgess) Pask. *Education:* Monash University, B.A., 1964, Diploma in Education, 1965. *Office address:* c/o 4/91 Albion Rd., Melbourne 3128, Australia.

CAREER: Teacher at public schools in Melbourne, Australia, 1966-69; Inner London Education Authority, London, England, teacher, 1969—.

WRITINGS: People and Places, Cassell, 1970, 2nd edition, 1974; (with Joseph Hajdu and Bill Stringer) *The Global Systems Levels: Space in Change,* Jacaranda Press, 1973, 2nd edition, 1978; *Develop the Pilbara,* Sorrett Publishing, 1974; (with Lee Bryant) *A Teacher's Kit on Australia and New Zealand,* Heinemann, 1976; (with Bryant) *Australia and New Zealand: A New Geography,* Heinemann, 1976, 2nd edition, 1980; *China's Changing Landscapes,* Heinemann, 1979; (with Gina Corrigan) *China,* Heinemann, 1982; (with Bryant) *Using the Earth,* Heinemann, 1982; (with Bert Sandford) *Mapwork One, Two, Three,* Ginn, 1982. Contributor of articles and photographs to magazines, including *Geographical* and *Geo.* Geography review editor of *Contact,* 1974—.

WORK IN PROGRESS: Research on China.

SIDELIGHTS: Pask commented: "I have a passionate belief in my subject and try to develop its understanding by others through my textbooks, articles, lectures, classes, and photographs. The photography has developed as a successful commercial sideline. Most of my recent books are illustrated with my own photographs. These photographs now form the basis of a picture library which operates on a commercial level. At the same time my research on China continues to not only satisfy my own curiosity but provides ammunition in my crusade for having that country dealt with in education syllabuses and texts."

* * *

PASTOR, Robert (Alan)   1947-

PERSONAL: Born April 10, 1947, in Newark, N.J.; son of Norman and Ruth (Kagan) Pastor; married Margaret McNamara (a consultant), June 16, 1979; children: Tiffin Margaret. *Education:* Attended University of Birmingham, England, 1967-68; Lafayette College, B.A., 1969; Harvard University, M.P.A., 1974, Ph.D., 1977. *Home:* 3101 Worthington St. N.W., Washington, D.C. 20015. *Office:* Brookings Institution, 1775 Massachusetts Ave. N.W., Washington, D.C. 20036.

CAREER: Library of Congress, Washington, D.C., research assistant in Foreign Affairs Division of Congressional Research Service, 1969; U.S. Peace Corps, Washington, D.C., volunteer adviser to Malaysian Department of Agriculture in Sarawak, 1970-72; Harvard University, Cambridge, lecturer at Institute of Politics, 1974; Commission on the Organization of the Government for the Conduct of Foreign Policy (Murphy Commission), Washington, D.C., consultant, 1974-75; Commission on U.S.-Latin American Relations (Linowitz Commission), Washington, D.C., executive director, 1975-77; National Security Council, Washington, D.C., White House staff coordinator for Latin American and Caribbean affairs, 1977-81; Brookings Institution, Washington, D.C., guest scholar in foreign policy studies, 1981—. Member of President Carter's foreign policy and defense task force, 1976. *Member:* Phi Beta Kappa, Phi Alpha Theta.

WRITINGS: (Contributor) Abraham F. Lowenthal, editor, *The Conduct of Routine Economic Relations: U.S. Foreign Policy-Making to Latin America,* U.S. Government Printing Office, 1975; *Congress and the Politics of U.S. Foreign Economic Policy, 1929-1976,* University of California Press, 1980. Contributor to economic and foreign affairs journals, to popular magazines, including *New Republic,* and to newspapers.

WORK IN PROGRESS: A book on U.S. policy toward Latin America, publication expected in 1982 or 1983.

*　　*　　*

PAUL, Charles B. 1931-

PERSONAL: Born June 24, 1931, in Antwerp, Belgium; came to the United States in 1946, naturalized in 1954; son of Maurice and Paula (Wenig) Paul; married Janina O'Hanrahan (a librarian), March 3, 1967. *Education:* Antioch College, B.A., 1957; Case Western Reserve University, M.A., 1959; University of California, Berkeley, Ph.D., 1966. *Office:* Department of Humanities, San Jose State University, San Jose, Calif. 95192.

CAREER: Antioch College, Yellow Springs, Ohio, instructor in history and French, 1957-58; San Jose State University, San Jose, Calif., assistant professor, 1964-70, associate professor, 1970-75, professor of humanities, 1975—. *Military service:* U.S. Marine Corps, 1951-53; became sergeant. *Member:* American Historical Association, American Society for French Historical Studies, American Association for Eighteenth-Century Studies, Western Society for Eighteenth-Century Studies, Western Society for French Historical Studies.

WRITINGS: Student Workbook: Modern Europe, St. Martin's, 1964; *Science and Immortality,* University of California Press, 1980. Contributor to musicology and comparative literature journals.

WORK IN PROGRESS: An *Anthology of French Romantic Travel Literature, 1790-1870;* a bibliography of Jean-Philippe Rameau, 1683-1983; *The New Scientist in Eighteenth-Century French Drama,* completion expected in 1984.

SIDELIGHTS: Paul told *CA:* "In my writing and teaching I aim to breach the barriers separating the standard academic disciplines and move beyond the provincial limits of the here and now. Accordingly, I have published material on the politics of music and on the aesthetics of scientific eulogy, and have given courses on travel literature and foreign perspectives of America as well as interdisciplinary studies of European history. I cannot remember any time in my life in Belgium, France, Switzerland, and the United States when I have not tried to see the world from a wider-than-usual perspective. My var-

iegated residential experience, joined to a very diverse occupational history (I have held over thirty jobs in manufacturing, commerce, and academia to pay my way through college), has proved to be extremely valuable (and sometimes disconcerting) background for my teaching and writing."

AVOCATIONAL INTERESTS: Baking bread, "caring for an assortment of small and large animals," horseback riding.

*　　*　　*

PAWLEY, Bernard C(linton) 1911-1981

OBITUARY NOTICE—See index for *CA* sketch: Born January 24, 1911, in Portsmouth, England; died November 15, 1981. Clergyman and author. Pawley was Archdeacon of Canterbury from 1972 until shortly before his death. He was ordained an Anglican priest in 1936 and later served as an army chaplain with the British Army in Africa during World War II. He was captured by the Nazis in the Western Desert and was interned for the duration of the war. In 1960 he became the Archbishop of Canterbury's first representative to the Vatican since the Reformation, serving in that role until 1965. He also represented the Archbishop of Canterbury at Vatican Council II. In 1975 Pawley and his wife, Margaret, wrote *Rome and Canterbury Through Four Centuries.* He was also the author of *Looking at the Vatican Council* and *The Second Vatican Council.* Obituaries and other sources: *London Times,* November 17, 1981.

*　　*　　*

PAXTON, Thomas R. 1937-
(Tom Paxton)

PERSONAL: Born October 31, 1937, in Chicago, Ill.; son of George Burton (a chemist) and Esther (Peterson) Paxton; married Margaret Cummings, August 5, 1963; children: Jennifer Ann, Katy. *Education:* University of Oklahoma, B.F.A., 1959. *Address:* c/o RD III Ventures, 20 Welwyn Place, Great Neck, N.Y. 11021. *Office:* Deep Fork Music, Inc., 1942 East 34th St., New York, N.Y. 10016.

CAREER: Singer and songwriter. *Military service:* U.S. Army, 1960. *Member:* American Society of Composers, Authors, and Publishers; Masons.

WRITINGS—Under name Tom Paxton: *Ramblin' Boy and Other Songs,* illustrations by Agnes Friesen, Oak Publications, 1965; *Jennifer's Rabbit* (juvenile), illustrations by Wallace Tripp, Putnam, 1970.

Composer of numerous songs, including "The Last Thing on My Mind," "Bottle of Wine," "Goin' to the Zoo," "Talking Vietnam Potluck Blues," "Whose Garden Was This," "Jesus Christ, S.R.O.," and "Wasn't That a Party?"

Recordings: "Ramblin' Boy," Elektra, 1964; "Ain't That News," Elektra; "Outward Bound," Elektra, 1966; "Morning Again," Elektra, 1968; "The Things I Notice Now," Elektra, 1969; "Tom Paxton No. 6," Elektra, 1970; "The Compleat Tom Paxton," Elektra, 1971; "How Come the Sun," Reprise, 1971; "Peace Will Come," Reprise, 1972; "New Songs for Old Friends," Reprise, 1973; "Something in My Life," Private Stock, 1975; "Saturday Night," MAM; "New Songs From the Briarpatch," Vanguard, 1977; "Heroes," Vanguard; "The Paxton Report," Flying Fish, 1981.

SIDELIGHTS: Tom Paxton was among the performers who led the contemporary folk music movement of the early 1960's. "I didn't burst upon the folk scene like a young Homer; to be more accurate, I snuck in, but here I am," he remarked in the liner notes on his album "Outward Bound." Paxton began playing the guitar when he was sixteen, and wrote his first songs during Shakespeare lectures in college. While he was in the army in 1960, he wrote his first published song, "The Marvelous Toy," and began appearing in Greenwich Village clubs. He soon earned a reputation as one of the best of the generation of songwriters that also included Bob Dylan and Phil Ochs.

Like Dylan and Ochs, Paxton wrote many topical and protest songs, such as "Lyndon Johnson Told the Nation" and "A Rumblin' in the Land." Unlike many folksingers, Paxton has remained resolutely political in his work, with songs like "The White Bones of Allende" and "You Can Eat Dog Food." The latter, a satirical attack on Republican welfare policies, was written—tongue in cheek—as a theme song for Gerald Ford's 1976 presidential campaign. But Paxton is probably best known for love songs like "The Last Thing on My Mind," humorous songs like "Talking Vietnam Potluck Blues" and "Not Tonight, Marie," and children's songs like "Goin' to the Zoo" and "Jennifer's Rabbit." His songs have been recorded by many singers, including Pete Seeger, Judy Collins, Peter, Paul, and Mary, Perry Como, and John Denver.

BIOGRAPHICAL/CRITICAL SOURCES: Milton Okun, editor, *Something to Sing About,* Macmillan, 1968; *Vogue,* April 1, 1970; *Crawdaddy,* November, 1973; *Esquire,* June, 1974.

*   *   *

PAXTON, Tom
See PAXTON, Thomas

*   *   *

PAYNE, Ernest A(lexander)   1902-1980

OBITUARY NOTICE—See index for *CA* sketch: Born February 19, 1902, in London, England; died January 14, 1980, in Oxford, England. Clergyman, educator, historian, editor, and author. In 1968 Payne became president of the World Council of Churches, the first English Freechurchman to do so. Payne was ordained a Baptist minister in 1928 and spent four years as a pastor at a village church before devoting eight years of work to the Baptist Missionary Society. From 1940 to 1946 he taught church history at Regent's Park College, followed by five years on the faculty of the University of Oxford. In 1951 Payne was named general secretary of the Baptist Union of Great Britain and Ireland, and in 1954 he was elected vice-chairman of the Central Committee of the World Council of Churches. He became president of that organization in 1968 and served until 1975, when he became vice-president, and later, president of the Baptist Union of Great Britain and Ireland. Payne was the author of dozens of books on religion, including *The Free Churches and the State* and *Baptists and Church Relations.* He was the editor of *Baptist Quarterly* from 1944 to 1950. Obituaries and other sources: *The Annual Obituary 1980,* St. Martin's, 1981.

*   *   *

PEAIRS, Richard Hope   1929-

BRIEF ENTRY: Born February 15, 1929, in Normal, Ill. American psychologist, educator, and author. Peairs taught psychology at California State University, Northridge, until 1966. Since 1967 he has directed the western regional office of the American Association of University Professors. He edited the journal *New Directions for Higher Education.* His writings include *What Every Child Needs* (Harper, 1974) and *Avoiding*

Conflict in Faculty Personnel Practices (Jossey-Bass, 1974). *Address:* 370 Loyola Dr., Millbrae, Calif. 94030; and Western Regional Office, American Association of University Professors, 582 Market St., Suite 1406, San Francisco, Calif. 94104. *Biographical/critical sources: Who's Who in America,* 40th edition, Marquis, 1978.

*   *   *

PEARSON, Diane
See McCLELLAND, Diane Margaret

*   *   *

PEARSON, Diane Margaret   1931-

PERSONAL: Born November 5, 1931, in Croydon, England; daughter of William Holker and Miriam (Pearson) Youde; married Richard Leeper McClelland (a physician and actor). *Education:* Attended secondary school in Croydon, England. *Agent:* Curtis Brown Ltd., 1 Craven Hill, London W2 3EP, England.

CAREER: Jonathan Cape Ltd., London, England, in production department, 1948-52; County Hall, London, government official, 1952-60; Purnells Publishing, London, in advertising department, 1962-63; Transworld Publishers Ltd., London, managing editor, 1963—.

WRITINGS—Novels: *Bride of Tancred,* Bantam, 1967; *The Marigold Field,* Lippincott, 1969; *Sarah Whitman,* Lippincott, 1971; *Csardas,* Lippincott, 1975.

WORK IN PROGRESS: Another novel.

SIDELIGHTS: Pearson told *CA:* "I really don't know why I write—I just do. If I have any motive, other than wanting to tell a tale, it is to represent 'little people'—those whose lives are just as complicated, tragic, funny, and dramatic as those of the giants, but who are inarticulate."

*   *   *

PEEK, Merle   1938-

PERSONAL: Born May 23, 1938, in Denver, Colo.; son of Jesse B. (a tire builder) and Queenie (Ridge) Peek. *Education:* Attended University of Colorado, 1956; California College of Arts and Crafts, B.F.A., 1960. *Home:* 2329 South Ogden St., Denver, Colo. 80210.

CAREER: Time, New York City, layout artist, 1960-67; free-lance illustrator, 1967-69; *New York* (magazine), New York City, designer, 1969-71; free-lance illustrator, 1971-80; *Denver* (magazine), Denver, Colo., art director, 1980-81; free-lance illustrator, 1981—.

WRITINGS—Self-illustrated: *Cricket's Tangrams* (juvenile), Random House, 1977; *Roll Over!: A Counting Song* (juvenile), Houghton, 1981.

Illustrator of books, including: Donald Nelson, *The Spotted Cow,* Parents' Magazine Press, 1973; Stephen Manes, *Hooples on the Highway,* Coward, 1978; Michael O'Donoghue, *Bears* (poems), Ghost Fox, 1979.

WORK IN PROGRESS: A juvenile fantasy, *Waterlily Lodge;* two illustrated songs for children, *The Farmer in the Dell* and *Animal Song.*

SIDELIGHTS: Peek told *CA:* "I am satisfying a longtime ambition by adding to the not-very-old (about one hundred fifty years) tradition of children's literature. I especially enjoy illustrating classic texts. I illustrated a story about Paul Revere by Stephen Vincent Benet for a school textbook for Houghton, and I've illustrated a number of Bible stories for Winston Press. I had been wishing to illustrate something classic, but little did I think that my wish would be granted with Bible stories, which, of course, are about as classic as one can get.

"My favorite compliment is having my work described as having a timeless quality. As much as I enjoy illustrating the words of others, the ultimate pleasure comes from conceiving the entire book myself—words and pictures. Though the bulk of my work has been for children, it also has a whimsical appeal to adults. I like it when I see an adult smiling with pleasure while viewing my work.

"Since I'm an animal lover, my visual iconography is loaded with animals. I like slipping animals into unexpected places such as architectural detail or as a part of furniture carving. Invariably children spot these details before adults do.

"Communication has become a key word for me. While in college studying fine arts, I felt self-expression was the end-all as far as art is concerned. But now I feel (and this is the point of illustration) that communication is the point of artistic endeavor. I want the child and the adult to understand my work, not to be mystified by it.

"In 1967 I made a trip around the world. Since then I have traveled to Europe several times. After about ten years in New York City, I moved to the Catskills, where I spent about ten idyllic years being close to nature and the garden. Now I have returned to the house I grew up in."

AVOCATIONAL INTERESTS: Playing the piano, riding roller coasters, ice-dancing.

* * *

PELTZ, Mary Ellis 1896-1981

OBITUARY NOTICE—See index for *CA* sketch: Born May 4, 1896, in New York, N.Y.; died October 24, 1981, in New York, N.Y. Music critic, archivist, editor, and author. Peltz was music critic of the *New York Evening Sun* for three years following her graduation from Barnard College in 1920. In 1936 she was invited by Metropolitan Opera Guild founder Eleanor Robson Belmont to become the first editor of the guild's publication, the *Opera News.* Peltz served in that position until 1957, during which time the publication's circulation grew to sixty thousand. Peltz became the Metropolitan Opera's archivist after her retirement as editor and worked in that post until shortly before her death. She was the author of numerous books about the Metropolitan Opera, including *Metropolitan Opera Milestones, Behind the Gold Curtain: The Story of the Metropolitan Opera, 1883-1950,* and *The Magic of Opera: A Picture Memoir of the Metropolitan.* Obituaries and other sources: *New York Times,* October 27, 1981.

* * *

PENN, Margaret ?-1981

OBITUARY NOTICE: Died December 29, 1981, in Exmouth, England. Author. Penn wrote of life in Lancashire, a working-class English village, in her three autobiographical novels. The trilogy contains *Manchester XIV Miles, The Foolish Virgin,* and *Young Mrs. Burton.* Obituaries and other sources: *London Times,* January 11, 1982; *AB Bookman's Weekly,* February 22, 1982.

* * *

PERRY, Wilma I. 1912-

PERSONAL: Born July 28, 1912, in Elk City, Okla.; daughter of William Parry (a builder) and Susan (Elliott) Snyder; married Clarence C. Perry (in sales), July 10, 1928. *Education:* Attended Southwestern Oklahoma State University; Anderson College, B.S., 1945; University of Oregon, M.Ed., 1954, D.Ed., 1965; postdoctoral study at University of Portland and University of Southern California. *Home:* 233 North Val Vista Dr. Sp. 196, Mesa, Ariz. 85203.

CAREER: Warner Press, Anderson, Ind., staff writer for *Christian Education,* 1943-54, and *Pathways,* 1954-78; free-lance writer, 1979—. Member of faculty at Warner Pacific College, 1954-79, director of Center for Human Services, 1977-79. Chairperson of National Council of Churches state committee on religion and public education, 1960; president of Northwestern Readers Conference, 1965-70. Pastor at Protestant church in Eugene, Ore., 1948-54; speaker at religious conventions and on world tour of missions in Japan, Africa, India, the Middle East, and Western Europe; seminar leader. *Member:* Oregon Society of Individual Psychology (president, 1965). *Awards, honors:* Named outstanding woman of Oregon by *Oregonian,* 1978.

WRITINGS: Awake the Sleeping Giant Within You, Revell, 1979. Contributor of articles and reviews to magazines, including *Vital Christianity* and *Reach.*

SIDELIGHTS: Wilma Perry wrote: "My interests are contemporary Christian issues and apologetics, psychology, youth and marriage problems and challenges. I have also done some feature writing in gerontology."

AVOCATIONAL INTERESTS: Travel, horseback riding, fishing, reading, foreign languages.

* * *

PESHKOV, Alexei Maximovich 1868-1936 (Jehudil Chlamyda, Maxim Gorky)

BRIEF ENTRY: Born March 28, 1868, in Nizhny-Novgorod, Russia (now Gorky, U.S.S.R.); died June 18, 1936, in Moscow, U.S.S.R. Russian author. Gorky was one of the most prominent writers in Russia in the early twentieth century. He was successful in czarist Russia and the new-born Soviet Union, providing a strong bridge between the old life and the new. His autobiographies, *My Childhood* (1915), *In the World* (1917), and *My University Days* (1923), were probably his most respected contributions to Soviet literature. They reveal a sharp eye for observation and a gift for colloquial speech, and they reflect vividly the changing times in which Gorky lived. His early stories, plays, and novels show, in almost sordid detail, the squalor and brutality of his own youth, marking him as the first truly proletarian writer of the Soviet Union. His play "The Lower Depths" (1902) and his novel *Mother* (1907) are among the first works of socialist realism. All his writings are set before the 1917 revolution and express his contempt for mankind and for the society that permits such degradation. Nevertheless, he maintained a romantic awe of man's potential. Gorky was a friend of Lenin and a heavy contributor of money to the socialist cause, but there is doubt about the depth of his political convictions. His insistence on independence as a writer annoyed the Soviet bureaucracy, just as his radical writings had irritated the czarist regime. After the revolution, Gorky worked to discover and nurture young writers, interceding with Lenin to keep many from prison and starvation. *Biographical/critical sources: Twentieth Century Authors: A Biographical Dictionary of Modern Literature,* H. W. Wilson, 1942; *The Concise Encyclopedia of Modern World Literature,* Hutchinson, 1963.

PETERSON, Nancy L(ee) 1939-

PERSONAL: Born September 15, 1939, in Des Moines, Iowa; daughter of Leonard E. (a railroad executive) and Arlene M. (a teacher; maiden name, Brubaker) Peterson; children: Ted Paul. Education: DePauw University, A.B., 1961; University of California, Los Angeles, M.A., 1965. Religion: Lutheran. Home: 839 Washington Ave., Albany, Calif. Agent: Susan P. Urstadt, Inc., 125 East 84th St., New York, N.Y. 10028. Office: U.S. Department of Health and Human Services, 50 United Nations Plaza, Room 403, San Francisco, Calif. 94102.

CAREER: U.S. Bureau of Indian Affairs, Washington, D.C., elementary school teacher in Crownpoint, N.M., 1961-63, employment assistance specialist in Los Angeles, Calif., 1964-72, special assistant to commissioner of Indian Affairs in Washington, 1972-73; U.S. Department of Health, Education and Welfare, San Francisco, Calif., manager of Federal Women's Program, 1974-80; U.S. Department of Health and Human Services, San Francisco, manager of Equal Employment Opportunity, 1980—. Program director of San Francisco conference of International Women's Year, 1975; California delegate to National Women's Conference, 1977. Member of board of directors of Oakland Young Women's Christian Association and Planned Parenthood. Member: American Women for International Understanding, Association of Federal Women Executives and Advocates for Non-Veterans Employment Rights (founder), American Civil Liberties Union (member of northern California board of directors). Awards, honors: Carl XVI Medal from Swedish Consulate, 1977, for promoting Swedish-American understanding.

WRITINGS: Our Lives for Ourselves: Women Who Have Never Married, Putnam, 1981.

SIDELIGHTS: Nancy Peterson wrote: "I am interested in the lives of contemporary women, with a special emphasis on marital status, childrearing, and the resolution of conflicting values and emphases for contemporary American women. My own life includes single motherhood, and balancing the conflicting demands of career and achievement-oriented things with personal needs. Our Lives for Ourselves is related to these, as well as to my desire to redefine never-married women as a group who leads lives of positive autonomy."

BIOGRAPHICAL/CRITICAL SOURCES: Los Angeles Times, June 26, 1981; San Francisco Chronicle/Examiner, July 12, 1981.

*　　*　　*

PETIEVICH, Gerald 1944-

PERSONAL: Born October 15, 1944, in Los Angeles, Calif.; son of Zarko (a policeman) and Dorothy (an artist; maiden name, Hibbert) Petievich; married Pamela Lentz (a teacher), December 23, 1968; children: Emma. Education: California State University, Los Angeles, B.A., 1966. Agent: Knox Burger, 39 Washington Sq., New York, N.Y. 10012. Office: U.S. Secret Service, 300 North Los Angeles St., Room 4324, Los Angeles, Calif. 90012.

CAREER: Associated with U.S. Secret Service, 1970—. Military service: U.S. Army, 1967-70; in intelligence corps; became sergeant. Member: Society for Investigative and Forensic Hypnosis, Mystery Writers of America, Authors Guild.

WRITINGS: Money Men/One Shot Deal (two novellas), Harcourt, 1981. Contributor to Writer.

WORK IN PROGRESS: The Quality of the Informant, a mystery novel to be published in 1982.

SIDELIGHTS: Petievich's Money Men/One Shot Deal contains two mystery novellas centering on a United States Treasury agent named Charles Carr. In both tales, Carr hunts counterfeiters, though in the second story there is also an element of swindling. A reviewer in New York Times Book Review called the tales "unusually good," and noted that "nothing about the writing suggests that they are first novellettes." The reviewer also declared that "Petievich goes about it all with a good deal of confidence, a sure hand, a fine ear for dialogue and canny feel for plot."

Petievich told CA: "In my novellas, I've tried to draw the milieu in which cops and crooks thrash about as I have seen it—from street level. I have always been fascinated by the atmosphere of violence and self interest which governs the underworld. There, the extreme is normal. Perfidy is custom. A touch of bad luck means time in the penitentiary or perhaps death. Success is measured by the yardstick of evil. It's society's distorted reflection in a fun house mirror."

BIOGRAPHICAL/CRITICAL SOURCES: New York Times Book Review, July 12, 1981; Los Angeles Times, July 23, 1981.

*　　*　　*

PHARR, Susan J(ane) 1944-

PERSONAL: Born March 16, 1944, in Atlanta, Ga.; daughter of Marion T. (a lawyer) and Gladys (a secretary; maiden name, Chappelear) Pharr. Education: Emory University, B.A. (with high honors), 1966; Columbia University, M.A., 1970, Ph.D., 1975. Home: 2204 Eton Ridge, Madison, Wis. 53705. Office: Department of Political Science, University of Wisconsin—Madison, Madison, Wis. 53706.

CAREER: Social Science Research Council, New York, N.Y., staff associate, 1974-76; University of Wisconsin—Madison, assistant professor, 1977-80, associate professor of political science, 1980—, associate chairman of department, 1979-81. Lecturer on WHA-Radio, 1978. Visiting foreign research scholar at Sophia University, 1971-72, and University of Tokyo, 1978. Editorial associate for Encyclopaedia Britannica, 1971. Member of board of directors of Midwest Regional Seminar on Japan, 1978-81; member of American Council of Learned Societies-Social Science Research Council committee on Japanese studies, 1980—.

MEMBER: International Political Science Association, International Society of Political Psychology (founding member), Association for Asian Studies (member of Northeast Asia council, 1976-79), American Political Science Association, Phi Beta Kappa. Awards, honors: Woodrow Wilson fellowship, 1966-67; grants from Yoshida Foundation, 1971-72, National Endowment for the Humanities, 1976-78, and Japan Foundation, 1978.

WRITINGS: Political Women in Japan, University of California Press, 1981.

Contributor: Lewis Austin, editor, Japan: The Paradox of Progress, Yale University Press, 1976; Janet Z. Giele and Audrey C. Smock, editors, Women: Role and Status in Eight Countries, Wiley, 1977; Kokusai Josei Gakkai 78 Tokyo Kaigi Hokokusho (title means "Transactions of the International Women's Studies Conference, Tokyo, 1978"), International Christian University Press, 1978; L. H. Redford, editor, The Occupation of Japan: Impact of Legal Reform, MacArthur Memorial, 1978; Distinguished Lecturer Series of Political Science Faculty of Meiji University, Meiji University Press, 1978;

Merry I. White and Barbara Molony, editors, *Proceedings of the Tokyo Symposium on Women,* International Group for the Study of Women, 1979.

Contributor: Takenaka Kazuro, editor, *Gendai Shakai Ron* (title means "Essays on Contemporary Society"), Hyoronsha, 1980; Bradley Richardson, editor, *Business and Society in Japan,* Praeger, 1981; Robert E. Ward and Sakamoto Yoshikazu, editors, *Policy and Planning During the Allied Occupation of Japan,* University of Tokyo Press, 1982; L. H. Redford, editor, *The Occupation of Japan: Impact of Social Reform,* MacArthur Memorial, 1982; Terry E. MacDougall, editor, *Political Leadership in Modern Japan* (monograph), University of Michigan Press, 1982. Contributor to *Encyclopedia of Japan.* Contributor to academic journals.

WORK IN PROGRESS: Status Politics in Japan, completion expected in 1982; *State and Opposition in Japan,* with Ellis S. Krauss, completion expected in 1983; *Conflict in Japan,* edited with Krauss, Patricia Steinhoff, and Thomas Rohlen, publication expected in 1983.

SIDELIGHTS: Susan Pharr wrote: "I have a long-standing interest, developed over numerous trips to Japan since 1970, in contemporary Japanese society and politics. As one who came to adulthood in New York City at the height of the feminist movement, I am also interested in the problems of women in the United States and worldwide. I have attempted to illuminate those problems in much of my writing to date."

*　　*　　*

PICKERING, Frederick Pickering 1909-

PERSONAL: Born March 10, 1909, in Bradford, England; son of F. W. and Martha (Pickering) Pickering; married Florence Joan Anderson, 1939. *Education:* University of Leeds, B.A.; University of Breslau, Ph.D. *Home address:* Arborfield Court, Arborfield Cross, Berkshire, England.

CAREER: Lecturer in English, 1931-32; Victoria University of Manchester, Manchester, England, 1932-41, began as assistant lecturer, became lecturer in German; worked for British Foreign Office, 1941-45; University of Sheffield, Sheffield, England, head of department of German, 1945-53; University of Reading, Reading, England, professor of German, 1953-74, dean of faculty of letters, 1957-60; writer, 1974—.

WRITINGS: Literatur und darstellende Kunst im Mittelalter, E. Schmidt, 1966, translation published as *Literature and Art in the Middle Ages,* University of Miami Press, 1970; (editor) *University German: A Reader for Arts Students,* Clarendon Press, 1968; (editor) *The Anglo-Norman Text of the Holkham Bible Picture Book,* Basil Blackwell, 1971; *Essays on Medieval German Literature and Iconography,* Cambridge University Press, 1980.

In German: (Editor) *Christi Leiden in einer Vision geschaut,* Manchester University Press, 1952; *Augustinius oder Boethius?: Geschichtsschreibung und epische Dichtung im Mittelalter und in der Neuzeit,* E. Schmidt, Volume I: *Einfuehrender Teil,* 1967, Volume II: *Darstellender Teil,* 1976. Contributor of articles and reviews to learned journals.

*　　*　　*

PICKERING, George (White) 1904-1980

OBITUARY NOTICE—See index for *CA* sketch: Born June 26, 1904, in Whalton, Northumberland, England; died September 3, 1980, in Oxford, England. Physician, educator, and author best known for his research into the causes and treatment of

hypertension. In 1955, after twenty-five years of vascular study, Pickering published *High Blood Pressure,* which is regarded as an important work on the subject. His continued research produced results that were controversial; he concluded that heredity and stress rather than salt in the diet were responsible for essential hypertension. Pickering was knighted for his work in 1957. He was also the author of other books on the subject of high blood pressure, including *The Nature of Essential Hypertension* and *Hypertension: Causes, Consequences, and Management.* Obituaries and other sources: *The Annual Obituary 1980,* St. Martin's, 1981.

*　　*　　*

PILCHER, George William 1935-

PERSONAL: Born September 30, 1935, in Chillicothe, Ohio; son of George William (a machinist) and Elia (Huizinga) Pilcher; married Jean Rickstrew (a teacher), May 23, 1959; children: Ian, Crystal. *Education:* University of Dayton, B.A., 1957; Oklahoma State University, M.A., 1959; University of Illinois, Ph.D., 1963. *Home:* 16 Pine Brook Rd., Boulder, Colo. 80302. *Office:* Department of History, University of Colorado, Box 234, Boulder, Colo. 80309.

CAREER: Oklahoma State University, Stillwater, assistant professor of history, 1963-65; University of Colorado, Boulder, assistant professor, 1965-69, associate professor, 1969-73, professor of history, 1973—, chairman of department, 1975-81. Fulbright professor at University of Bordeaux, 1973-74. *Member:* American Historical Association, Organization of American Historians, Institute of Early American History and Culture, Sierra Club, Colorado Mountain Club, Phi Alpha Theta, Omicron Delta Kappa, Phi Kappa Phi.

WRITINGS: (Editor) *The Reverend Samuel Davies Abroad,* University of Illinois Press, 1967; *Samuel Davies: Apostle of Dissent in Colonial Virginia,* University of Tennessee Press, 1971. Contributor of articles and reviews to scholarly journals.

WORK IN PROGRESS: A study of the revivals of religion in the eighteenth-century English-speaking world, publication expected in 1985.

SIDELIGHTS: Pilcher commented: "I am interested in the reasons for personal and societal action in the past as an explanation for contemporary affairs and conditions. Avocationally, I extend this to the study of such diverse topics as the Native American, political terrorism and violence, irregular warfare, the American Revolution, western American exploration, and contemporary Native American art."

*　　*　　*

PINCUS, Lily 1898-1981

OBITUARY NOTICE—See index for *CA* sketch: Born March 13, 1898, in Karlovy Vary, Czechoslovakia; died October 22, 1981, in London, England. Family-relations counselor and author. Pincus fled Nazi Germany in 1939 and became a British citizen after World War II. In 1948 she helped found the Family Discussion Bureau (now Institute of Marital Studies) which, through its psychodynamic approach to interactive processes, greatly influenced British social work. The group's success was so great that many other social work agencies began to seek its training. Two books described the group's work, *Social Casework and Marital Problems* and *Marriage: Studies in Emotional Conflict and Growth.* After the death of her husband in 1963, Pincus began to phase out her active participation in the Institute of Marital Studies in order to devote more of her time to writing. Her later books include *Death and the Family,*

Secrets in the Family, and her final book, published just prior to her death, *The Challenge of a Long Life.* Obituaries and other sources: *London Times,* October 27, 1981.

* * *

PITCAIRN, Frank
See COCKBURN, (Francis) Claud

* * *

PLAINE, Alfred R.   1898(?)-1981

OBITUARY NOTICE: Born c. 1898; died after a long illness, December 19, 1981, in New York, N.Y. Publisher. Plaine co-founded Almat Publishing Corporation in 1949 and published paperback fiction and nonfiction under such imprints as Pyramid Books, Little Paperback Classics, and Hi-Lo Books. Obituaries and other sources: *Publishers Weekly,* January 29, 1982.

* * *

PLUMB, Charles P.   1900(?)-1982

OBITUARY NOTICE: Born c. 1900; died of complications from a heart condition, January 19, 1982, in Ashland, Ore.; buried in Port Charlotte, Fla. Cartoonist and author best known as the creator of the comic strip "Ella Cinders." Published in both newspapers and comic books from 1924 to 1951, it was the first comic strip to be made into a full-length motion picture. Plumb also wrote three books, *Tin Can Island, The Tattooed Gun Hand,* and *The Murderous Move.* Obituaries and other sources: *Chicago Tribune,* January 22, 1982.

* * *

POLK, James   1939-

PERSONAL: Born September 1, 1939, in Fort Madison, Iowa; son of Raymond W. (a physician) and Lucille (a teacher and library consultant; maiden name, Carroll) Polk. *Education:* University of Montana, B.A., 1961; Harvard University, M.A., 1962, Ph.D., 1968. *Religion:* "Lapsed Catholic." *Agent:* Elaine Markson, 44 Greenwich Ave., New York, N.Y. 10011. *Office:* House of Anansi Press, 35 Britain St., Toronto, Ontario, Canada M5A 1R7.

CAREER: Idaho State University, Pocatello, instructor in English, 1964-65; University of Alberta, Edmonton, assistant professor of English, 1968-70; House of Anansi Press, Toronto, Ontario, editor, 1971-73, editorial director, 1973—. *Awards, honors:* Woodrow Wilson fellowship, 1961-62; first prize for best first story in *Atlantic Monthly,* 1973, for "The Phrenology of Love."

WRITINGS: Wilderness Writers (biographies of Canadian writers), Clarke Irwin, 1972; (editor, and author of introduction) A. S. Holmes, *Belinda; or, the Rivals,* Anansi, 1975; *The Passion of Loreen Bright Weasel* (novel), Houghton, 1981. Contributor of stories and articles to periodicals, including *Atlantic Monthly, Oui, Mademoiselle, University of Toronto Quarterly, Canadian Literature,* and *Alphabet.*

WORK IN PROGRESS: Two novels.

SIDELIGHTS: "*The Passion of Loreen Bright Weasel* is so rich in comic situations, quirky characters, and down-home talk that it is a good bet . . . for funniest novel of the year," said Canadian novelist David Williamson. At the heart of Polk's comic satire is a young Indian woman, Loreen Bright Weasel, who zealously converts to Catholicism and sets out to redeem

the town of Hebb, Montana. Among those Loreen targets for 'Corporate Works of Mercy' are Sheep Triumph, who wants to run for mayor and rid the town of his ex-wife's bordello, and Winn Triumph, Sheep's long-suffering wife and the only one in town "who knows anything about Caesar salads and smoked oysters."

Reviews included this response from Cathleen Hoskins, published in the *Toronto Star:* "Polk . . . obviously had great fun writing this book. The good-natured humor flows like a virtuoso performance of one-liners. Though his subjects are all easy marks—religion, small town death-in-life, the appalling botch-up of Indian-white relations, politics, marriage, midlife crisis—there's no denying he's bitten off quite a chunk to satirize and, for the most part, done a clever job of chewing." B. Derek Johnson, writing in the *Toronto Globe and Mail,* commented: "Myopic religious zeal and small-town Western kitsch are an unlikely pair of targets for a single satire, yet James Polk . . . has successfully braided them into one hilarious short novel."

Reviewers also discussed the particular strengths of Polk's writing and the nature of his comedy. Johnson observed: "Polk writes like a lean, low-cholesterol version of Tom Robbins. He has a ball with hyperbole and will often chase a good joke at the risk of losing credibility. . . . His crisp, neatly-folded sentences reveal the sensibility of an editor rather than a writer. He lines up his words with a pool cue." Williamson, whose review appeared in the *Winnipeg Free Press,* stated that "Mr. Polk's comedy has all the richness and humanity of Roch Carrier's novels. His ability to pump new life into old cliches smacks of Peter De Vries, and his raunchy treatment of the contemporary American West brings to mind such fine writers as Larry McMurtry and John Nichols. But his style is distinctly his own; his comedy is never black, always compassionate, and all his characters are lovable."

Polk told *CA:* "*The Passion of Loreen Bright Weasel* took five years to write, coming together after my first published short stories in *Atlantic Monthly, Oui,* and *Mademoiselle* in the mid-1970's. I have been busy editing other writers for Anansi Press in Canada, but also I write very slowly, typing the paragraphs and sentences over and over, continually struggling with the octopus of plot. Since comedy depends so much on style and plot complications, it seems absolutely necessary to dawdle over words the way I do, but I hope my next novel won't take as long. I don't see how it can. I've been writing it concurrently with *Loreen* since I've found it healthier to be writing several things at once: When that black despair hits you over one project, there's always another palpitating in the wings.

"The critical response to *Loreen Bright Weasel* has been heart warming. All have said (so far) that the book is funny—even 'great fun' (*Publishers Weekly*), 'hilarious' (*Toronto Globe*), and 'a ferociously funny first novel' (*New Yorker*). I hope some Catholic readers will also see that the book is cast in the traditional form of a saint's life, with the protagonist having visions, undergoing trials, and changing society through love. Of course, Loreen's energetic march to canonization brings total chaos in its wake, but she really does 'save' the other characters in that they are happier emotionally after she gets through with her Corporate Works of Mercy. Loreen herself suffers a 'passion' in the religious sense, too, since she experiences great anguish for the love of mankind, who doesn't ask for salvation to begin with and scarcely knows what to do with it.

"One review from the Virginia Kirkus Service accused Loreen's ministrations as being 'a dumb Indian act' and discerned a tinge of racism overall. This charge is so upsetting and so far from my purpose that it's worth emphasizing the obvious: Loreen is morally and spiritually good. She is not dumb: far from it. She's a bright student with her own eccentric ideas of the universe, and if anybody is dumb in the book it is the white society which expects her to mix martinis and understand the garbage disposal unit and which fills her mind with Catholic mythology. My book pokes fun at racist attitudes, yes, but my heroine is lovable and a kind of genius in her way; the whites really aren't so bad either. It's a plot where the Indian triumphs and prevails, and everybody is happy at the end. Oh, Virginia Kirkus, why can't you understand this?!

"After some ten years in publishing, I especially wanted to write a book that was enjoyable, and I think *Loreen* is, if nothing else, a 'good read.' It's toying with fate to discuss future books, but I'll risk saying that I have two novels mapped out, both comedies along the *Loreen* line, one about parents, the other about old friends, with my stomping grounds, southeastern Montana, featured in one way or another.

"I've been a lucky writer so far. I have done another nonfiction book, on Canadian animal-story writers, which was a lot of fun to research and put together. The reviews for my first novel have been good, and my publisher, Houghton Mifflin, is exemplary, with some of the editors referring to Loreen as if she were a real live person—the ultimate compliment. Also, my family and friends back in Miles City see *Loreen*'s satire on small-town life for what it is: not a put-down but a tongue-in-cheek celebration. Short of seeing *The Passion of Loreen Bright Weasel* opening in selected drive-ins across America as a major motion picture with Robert Redford and Barbara Streisand, what more could I ask?"

BIOGRAPHICAL/CRITICAL SOURCES: Toronto Star, April 18, 1981; *Macleans,* May 11, 1981; *Toronto Globe and Mail,* May 16, 1981; *Winnipeg Free Press,* May 23, 1981.

* * *

POMFRET, John Edwin 1898-1981

OBITUARY NOTICE—See index for *CA* sketch: Born September 21, 1898, in Philadelphia, Pa.; died after a brief illness, November 26, 1981, in Camden, S.C. Historian, educator, editor, and author. Pomfret was the president of the College of William and Mary from 1941 to 1951, when he resigned after a dispute with the college's directing board. Pomfret then accepted the directorship of the H. E. Huntington Library and Art Gallery in San Marino, California, and remained in that post until his retirement in 1966. As a historian, Pomfret was interested in Colonial America, especially New Jersey. His book titles include *The Struggle for Land in Ireland, The Geographic Pattern of Mankind, The Province of West New Jersey,* and *Founding the American Colonies.* Obituaries and other sources: *New York Times,* November 27, 1981.

* * *

PONTIFLET, Ted 1932-

PERSONAL: Surname is pronounced Pon-ti-flay; born June 19, 1932, in Oakland, Calif.; son of John W. (a legal recorder) and Victoria E. Pontiflet; married Addie Roberson (a hospital administrator), November 17, 1966; children: Pamela Denise. *Education:* California College of Arts and Crafts, B.F.A., 1962; Yale University, M.F.A. (with honors), 1971. *Home and office:* 1050 7th St. N. 1205, Oakland, Calif. 94607.

CAREER: Nungua Secondary School, Nungua, Ghana, teacher of art, 1963-66; Medgar Evers College of the City University of New York, Brooklyn, N.Y., consultant and teacher of literature and art, 1971-76; Contra Costa College, San Pablo, Calif., teacher of Afro-American humanities and history, 1979—. Photographs exhibited on the East Coast, including a showing at the Smithsonian Institution. *Military service:* U.S. Army 82nd Airborne Division, Paratroops, 1952-55. *Member:* International Black Photographers, National Conference of Artists, West Oakland Writers Workshop (director and founder). *Awards, honors:* Travel grant from Yale University, 1970, for research of Afro-American art in Ghana.

WRITINGS: Poochie (juvenile; illustrated by Mahiri Fufuka), Dial, 1978.

WORK IN PROGRESS: Other Poochie-related stories; "When Violence Dies,"a one-act play exploring physical and emotional violence by blacks from 1940 to 1970; "The Preacher's Son," a two-act play about a talented son with a drug problem; *Home and Back,* a novel dealing with the emotional and psychological metamorphosis of blacks in Africa.

SIDELIGHTS: Ted Pontiflet told *CA:* "More important than the work of art produced is the statement of the human condition that it must express." His concern for the problems of blacks led Pontiflet to Ghana, where he lived and taught for three years. Recalling the experience, Pontiflet told the Oakland Public Library Association: "I'm not sure if I was running to Africa or from America. . . . While there, I saw and lived an alternative to this country. By having the experience of seeing black men as doctors, lawyers, judges, policemen, clerks in stores, civil servants, in control of their own environment, I developed a belief in an alternative destiny."

Pontiflet's self-expression has taken many forms. "I have always been motivated to create something or other," he told *CA.* "I have gone from a deep passion for sculpture, to painting, to photography, to writing. I find writing to be the greater challenge because of the language factor. But the graphic and literary canvas (audience) seems to be shrinking; sooner or later I will be working mostly in video and film."

A short film about Pontiflet's life and work, entitled "Ponti," was produced in 1980 by Nebby Crawford Bello.

BIOGRAPHICAL/CRITICAL SOURCES: Oakland Public Library Association Newsletter, June, 1980.

* * *

POPOV, Dusko 1912(?)-1981

OBITUARY NOTICE: Born c. 1912, in Dubrovnik, Yugoslavia; died after a long illness, August 21, 1981, in Opio, France. Government agent and author. A double agent for Britain in World War II, Popov was the model for Ian Fleming's fictional character, James Bond. Although all of the Bond experiences do not directly parallel those of Popov, many are based upon his exploits as agent Tricycle. Fleming met the ruggedly handsome playboy early in the war, and witnessed as Popov placed a $50,000 bet in a Portuguese casino in an attempt to eliminate a Russian spy. The scene was transferred, along with the Popov personality, to the baccarat tables of the first James Bond novel, *Casino Royale.* Popov's spying activities bore great importance for the war; he was responsible for diverting the Germans while Allied troops invaded on D day, and made more trips to maintain German ties than any other British spy. Popov wrote a book about his experiences, *Spy, Counter Spy,* in 1974. Obituaries and other sources: *Biography News,* Volume I, Gale, 1974; *Miami Herald,* June 23, 1974; *New York Times,* August 24, 1981; *Time,* September 7, 1981.

PORTER, Michael E. 1947-

PERSONAL: Born May 23, 1947, in Ann Arbor, Mich.; son of Howard Eugene (an army officer) and Stana (in retail sales; maiden name, von Werner) Porter. *Education:* Princeton University, B.S.E. (with high honors), 1969; Harvard University, M.B.A. (with high distinction), 1971, Ph.D., 1973. *Home:* 22 Agassiz St., Cambridge, Mass. 02140. *Office:* School of Business, Harvard University, 210 Morgan Hall, Boston, Mass. 02163.

CAREER: Harvard University, School of Business, Boston, Mass., assistant professor of business administration and lecturer in economics, 1973-77, associate professor of business, 1977—. Member of board of directors of Alpine, Inc., Anatar Investments, and Harvard Cooperative Society; consultant on competitive strategy to U.S. and overseas firms and to government agencies. *Military service:* U.S. Army Reserve, 1969-77; became captain. *Member:* American Economic Association, American Marketing Association, Phi Beta Kappa, Sigma Xi, Tau Beta Pi.

AWARDS, HONORS: Member of National Collegiate Athletic Association Golf All-American Team, 1968; David A. Wells Prize in Economics from Harvard University, 1973-74, for outstanding doctoral research; McKinsey Foundation Award, 1979, for year's best *Harvard Business Review* article; Graham and Dodd Award from Financial Analysts Federation, 1980, for outstanding research; George F. Baker Scholar at Harvard Business School; *Competitive Strategy* was named an outstanding academic book of 1980-81 by *Choice.*

WRITINGS: Interbrand Choice, Strategy, and Bilateral Market Power, Harvard University Press, 1976; (with A. M. Spence, R. E. Caves, and J. M. Scott) *Studies in Canadian Industrial Organization,* Canadian Royal Commission on Corporate Concentration, 1978; *Competitive Strategy,* Free Press, 1980; (with Spence and Caves) *Competition in the Open Economy,* Harvard University Press, 1980; *Cases in Competitive Strategy,* Free Press, 1982; (with C. R. Christensen, K. R. Andrews, R. L. Hammermesch, and J. L. Bower) *Business Policy: Text and Cases,* fifth edition, Irwin, 1982 (Porter not associated with earlier editions); *Competitive Strategy in Global Industries,* Free Press, 1983; *Advanced Topics in Competitive Strategy,* Free Press, 1983.

Contributor to economic journals, popular magazines, and newspapers, including *Fortune* and *Wall Street Journal.* Contributing editor of *Journal of Business Strategy;* associate editor of *Review of Economics and Statistics.*

SIDELIGHTS: Porter wrote: "My long-term research thrust has been to build a conceptual bridge between the business strategy field and applied microeconomics, two areas that had been largely independent. This broad intersection is the subject of the great majority of my writings. *Competitive Strategy* is the first comprehensive statement of this research in a form accessible to the practicing manager. This has opened up a whole new area in the business strategy field. Increasingly, both the study of business administration and the study of economics can benefit from each other's perspective. Modern research on business strategy can aid in helping U.S. companies become more competitive in world markets. My recent work, on worldwide competition, is addressed to this subject."

AVOCATIONAL INTERESTS: Athletics, the music industry (as manager of aspiring recording artists).

BIOGRAPHICAL/CRITICAL SOURCES: Boston Globe, May 11, 1980; *New York Times,* January 2, 1981; *Fortune,* October 19, 1981.

*   *   *

POSTAN, Michael Moissey 1899-1981

OBITUARY NOTICE: Born in September, 1899, in Tighina, Bessarabia; died December 12, 1981. Educator, essayist, editor, and author. An economic historian at the University of London and Cambridge University, Postan was influential in the field of medieval studies. Much of his writing was in the form of essays, including the philosophical essays consolidated in his book *Fact and Relevance.* His other publications include *Studies in English Trade in the Fifteenth Century, The Medieval Economy and Society,* and chapters of *The Cambridge Economic History.* Postan was also an accomplished editor, and under his direction the *Economic History Review* at Cambridge became the international forerunner of journals of its kind. After retirement Postan continued to edit new volumes of the *Cambridge Economic History of Europe.* Obituaries and other sources: *Who's Who,* 131st edition, St. Martin's, 1979; *London Times,* December 16, 1981.

*   *   *

POTTER, Eloise Fretz 1931-

PERSONAL: Born February 17, 1931, in Norfolk, Va.; daughter of James B. and Lillian Doreatha (Rackley) Fretz; married James McConnell Potter, Jr., June 12, 1950 (divorced February, 1976); children: James Brian, David Theodore, Crystal Lillian (Mrs. Brian Douglas Horsley), Patricia Eileen (Mrs. Thomas W. Morgan). *Education:* Attended Meredith College, 1949-50. *Religion:* Methodist. *Home address:* Route 3, Box 114AA, Zebulon, N.C. 27597.

CAREER: Chat, Raleigh, N.C., editor, 1963—. Worked as linotype operator and proofreader. Volunteer associate curator of birds at North Carolina State Museum, 1977—. *Member:* American Ornithologists Union, Northeastern Bird-Banding Association, Association of Southeastern Biologists, Carolina Bird Club, North Carolina Society of County and Local Historians, Sampson County Historical Society, Little River Historical Society (president, 1981).

WRITINGS: (With James F. Parnell and Robert P. Teulings) *Birds of the Carolinas,* University of North Carolina Press, 1980. Author of "Potter Patter," a column in *Zebulon Record,* 1957-59. Contributor to biology journals, including *Auk, Journal of Field Ornithology,* and *Chat.*

WORK IN PROGRESS: A bio-geography of North Carolina birds, with David S. Lee, publication in *Chat* expected in 1983; a genealogical study of the descendants of Edward Rackley of colonial Virginia, publication expected in 1983; research on grooming behaviors of wild birds.

SIDELIGHTS: "My life has been blessed by gifted teachers," Eloise Potter told *CA,* "beginning with parents who took time to help me reason out or look up the answers to my own questions. The dictionary, atlas, and encyclopedia were as much the toys of my childhood as the dolls, coloring books, and tricycles. In the public schools I found teachers who emphasized understanding basic concepts rather than rote memorization. At Meredith College I found a faculty dedicated to preparing young women for a lifetime of independent learning. When I left Meredith to get married, I knew my education would continue whether I returned to the classroom or not; but

I certainly had no intention of becoming an ornithologist, amateur or otherwise.

"Gladys Baker, a Zebulon school teacher who shares my interest in wild flowers, introduced me to bird study by suggesting that a feeder would help my children learn about nature. The children mostly ignored the birds, but my husband and I became fascinated by them. Soon we were involved in bird banding, bird photography, and the Carolina Bird Club. When the editor of *Chat* resigned, I was asked to edit the journal, even though I had been watching birds only five years and lacked formal training in ornithology. Soon I found myself consulting many of the outstanding zoologists and biological editors of my time. Their generous sharing of knowledge with an unknown amateur touched me deeply.

"In writing *Birds of the Carolinas,* we tried to communicate effectively with the general reader without neglecting the professional biologist's need for accurate data on the distribution of birds in the region. The three of us talked about our writing problems in terms of an eighth grader who might use our book as well as an adult whose high school or college biology course scarcely mentioned birds. We deliberately kept the vocabulary simple and free from jargon. We feel that we accomplished our original goal, which was to write an introduction to bird study in the Carolinas that would prepare the general reader to approach the advanced literature with understanding and confidence.

"By the time the bird book was off the press, I had been researching Rackley genealogy for three years. The project began as a casual search for the full name of my great-grandfather, V. V. Rackley. It has led me to a new interest in regional, state, and local history as well as into fascinating correspondence with Rackleys all over the country. Working with a team of about one hundred fifty cooperators, I hope to complete the research, type camera-ready copy, and have a book on the Rackleys in America in print soon.

"As a generalist in a world of specialists, I have no idea where my curiosity will lead me once the Rackley book is finished. All I know is that research, writing, and editing are my favorite forms of recreation. There is no sport more exciting than gathering and analyzing data, formulating a logical question, and finding a satisfactorily documented answer to that question. If a publishable manuscript results from the research, so much the better."

*　　*　　*

POTTS, Charles 1943-

PERSONAL: Born August 28, 1943, in Idaho Falls, Idaho; son of Verl and Sarah (Gray) Potts; married Judith Silverman; children: Emily Karen. *Education:* Idaho State University, B.A., 1965. *Home:* 525 Bryant, Walla Walla, Wash. 99362.

CAREER: Litmus, Inc. (nonprofit literary service), founder and director, 1966—; producer of festivals, 1966—; poet. Gives readings throughout the United States; host of "Oasis" on KUER-Radio, 1976—; guest on television and radio programs. Member of faculty at Free University of Seattle, 1966-67.

WRITINGS—Books of poems, except as noted: *Blues From Thurston County,* Grade Ronde, 1966; *Burning Snake,* Presna de Lagar-Wine Press, 1967; *Little Lord Shiva,* Noh Directions-Aldebaran Review, 1969; *The Litmus Papers,* Gunrunner, 1969; *Blue up the Nile,* Quixote, 1972; *Waiting in Blood,* Rainbow Resin, 1973; *The Trancemigracion of Menzu,* Empty Elevator Shaft, 1973; *The Golden Calf,* Litmus, 1975; *Charle Kiot,* Folk Frog Press, 1976; *The Opium Must Go Thru* (prose),

Litmus, 1976; *Valga Krusa: Psychological Autobiography* (prose), Litmus, 1977; *Rocky Mountain Man,* Smith, 1978.

Work represented in anthologies, including *The Smith/17: Eleven Young Poets,* Smith, 1975; *The Far Side of the Storm,* San Marcos, 1975; *The Face of Poetry,* Gallimaufry, 1977. Contributor of articles, poems, and reviews to more than one hundred magazines, including *Wild Dog, West Coast Review, Aldebaran Review, New: American and Canadian Poetry, Kalaidescope,* and *Berkeley Barb.* Co-editor of *Margins.*

WORK IN PROGRESS: A book of poems, *A Rite to the Body;* two books or prose, *Lake Earth* and *The Farmer's Daughter.*

SIDELIGHTS: Potts told *CA:* "I used to be politically motivated in my writing, but have ceased to have any real interest in politics. I am now more interested in psychology and in cultural and natural history. I read many books on various aspects of psychology.

"I call my writing style reductivism—I seek to reduce things to their most essential elements. I think of this as the opposite of minimalism.

"I also play the guitar and write songs, and I'm beginning to try to have them published. I believe strongly in the importance of the musical element in poetry."

BIOGRAPHICAL/CRITICAL SOURCES: Hugh Fox, *The Poetry of Charles Potts,* Dust, 1980.

*　　*　　*

POWERS, Doris Cooper 1918-

PERSONAL: Born February 25, 1918, in Englewood, N.J.; daughter of Edwin I. (an electrical engineer) and Edith M. (Richter) Cooper; married David Bruce Powers (an army officer), October 21, 1936. *Education:* Wellesley College, A.B., 1945, M.A., 1950; University of California, Berkeley, Ph.D., 1966. *Home:* 339 East Concorda Dr., Tempe, Ariz. 85282.

CAREER: Arizona State University, Tempe, associate professor of English, 1960-80; writer, 1980—. *Member:* Modern Language Association of America, Phi Kappa Phi.

WRITINGS: English Formal Satire: Elizabethan to Augustan, Mouton, 1971. Contributor to English studies and folklore journals.

WORK IN PROGRESS: Research on Elizabethan prose humor and on linguistic awareness in late Elizabethan and early seventeenth-century English writers.

*　　*　　*

PRAGER, Jonas 1938-

PERSONAL: Born November 5, 1938, in Bronx, N.Y.; son of Julius (a baker) and Bella (Tannenberg) Prager; married Helen May, June 9, 1963; children: Joel, Sharon. *Education:* Yeshiva College (now University), A.B. (magna cum laude), 1959; Columbia University, Ph.D., 1964. *Home:* 76-19 174th St., Flushing, N.Y. 11366. *Office:* Department of Economics, New York University, 269 Mercer St., New York, N.Y. 10003.

CAREER: New York University, New York, N.Y., instructor, 1962-64, assistant professor, 1964-69, associate professor of economics, 1969—, director of graduate studies in economics, 1977—. Visiting senior economist at Bank of Israel, 1965-67; lecturer at National Strategy Information Center. *Member:* American Economic Association, American Finance Association, Eastern Economic Association. *Awards, honors:* Fulbright fellow, 1971; grants from American Philosophical Society, 1974-75, 1975-76.

WRITINGS: (Author of instructor's manual) E. Shapiro, E. Solomon, and W. L. White, *Money and Banking,* Holt, 1968; (editor) *Monetary Economics: Controversies in Theory and Policy,* Random House, 1971; *Fundamentals of Money, Banking, and Financial Institutions,* Harper, 1982. Contributor to *Funk & Wagnall's Encyclopedia.* Contributor of about fifteen articles to economic journals, international studies journals, and newspapers.

WORK IN PROGRESS: Study on galloping inflation.

* * *

PRATT, Willis Winslow 1908-

BRIEF ENTRY: Born August 20, 1908, in Los Angeles, Calif. American educator and author. Pratt has been a professor of English at University of Texas since 1950. He joined the faculty in 1936. Pratt edited *Modern Drama: An Anthology of Nine Plays* (Ginn, 1963) and wrote *Byron at Southwell: The Making of a Poet* (University of Texas, 1948). *Address:* 3001 West 35th St., Austin, Tex. 78703; and Department of English, University of Texas, Austin, Tex. 78712. *Biographical/critical sources: Directory of American Scholars,* Volume II: *English, Speech, and Drama,* 7th edition, Bowker, 1978.

* * *

PRESTON, William L(ee) 1949-

PERSONAL: Born September 14, 1949, in Tulare, Calif.; son of Norman G. (a poultry processor) and Lucilda (a billing clerk; maiden name, Neves) Preston. *Education:* College of the Sequoias, A.A., 1969; California State University, Fresno, B.A., 1971, M.A., 1973; University of Oregon, Ph.D., 1979. *Home:* 529 High St., San Luis Obispo, Calif. 93401. *Office:* Department of Geography, California Polytechnic University, San Luis Obispo, Calif. 93407.

CAREER: California State University, Sacramento, lecturer in geography, 1979; California Department of Parks and Recreation, Sacramento, interpretive specialist, 1980; California Polytechnic University, San Luis Obispo, assistant professor of geography, 1980—. *Member:* Association of Pacific Coast Geographers, California Council for Geographic Education, San Luis Obispo County Archaeological Society, Tulare County Historical Society, California Native Plant Society.

WRITINGS: Vanishing Landscapes: Land and Life in the Tulare Lake Basin, University of California Press, 1981.

WORK IN PROGRESS: Compiling and analyzing literary observations of environmental change in the Tulare Valley of California, and attempting to elucidate contemporary witnesses' reactions to the remaking of the landscapes of that region.

SIDELIGHTS: Preston wrote: "I am deeply concerned with people's role in changing the face of the earth, especially over the course of the past century, and believe that by gaining a better understanding of the impacts of past environmental alterations we become better equipped to deal with the world as we remake it today. I have traveled extensively in the American West, Peru, and Baja California to acquaint myself with different cultural landscapes, and plan to continue teaching and writing about man's impacts on the Americas, especially on California."

PRICE, Raymond (Kissam, Jr.) 1930-

PERSONAL: Born May 6, 1930, in New York, N.Y.; son of Raymond Kissam (an investment banker) and Beth (Porter) Price. *Education:* Yale University, B.A., 1951. *Politics:* Republican. *Home and office:* 372½ Pacific St., Brooklyn, N.Y. 11217.

CAREER: Collier's, New York City, assistant to editor, 1955-57; *Life,* New York City, reporter, 1957; *New York Herald Tribune,* New York City, member of editorial staff, 1957-64, editor of editorial page, 1964-66; assistant to Richard M. Nixon, 1967-69, special assistant, 1969-73, special consultant, 1973-74, 1980. Writer. Chief speechwriter for President Nixon. Fellow at John F. Kennedy Institute of Politics, Harvard University, and visiting fellow at American Enterprise Institute, both 1977; Nixon Professor at Whittier College, Whittier, Calif., 1978. *Military service:* U.S. Naval Reserve, active duty, 1952-55; became lieutenant junior grade. *Member:* Overseas Press Club of America, Aurelian Honor Society, Federal City Club, Metropolitan Club, Yale Club, Skull and Bones Club.

WRITINGS: With Nixon, Viking, 1977. Contributor of columns to *Now* magazine (London), 1981—.

WORK IN PROGRESS: Working with former President Nixon in the preparation of his forthcoming book.

SIDELIGHTS: Price's *With Nixon* is one of the few memoirs to come out of the Nixon administration that attempts to absolve the former president of guilt for the Watergate crimes. "'With Nixon' is the most persuasive attempt to date to argue that he [Nixon] was not guilty, or at least that he should not have been forced from office," commented Godfrey Hodgson of the *New York Times Book Review.* Hodgson went on to summarize several points of Price's thesis: (1) Watergate was contrived by Democratic congressmen and press enemies to remove Nixon from office; (2) any "dirty tricks" that members of Nixon's staff were guilty of were no worse than the indiscretions of other administrations; (3) accomplishments Nixon made while in office compensate for any negative aspects of his presidency; and (4) Nixon was guilty only of inattention and of trusting his subordinates too much.

In the end, however, Price's arguments "won't wash," declared Hodgson. "The fundamental reason for believing that Richard Nixon was unfit to be President always was precisely the suspicion that he thought truth and the law trivial in comparison with his own ambitions and convictions." Hodgson added that Price "was deluded . . . by his affection for and loyalty to Richard Nixon."

Newsweek's Richard Boeth also questioned some of Price's premises, but he maintained: "Still, there are some valuable balancing insights in the disarray. The author knew Nixon well and liked him and offers a friend's view of this knotty man's many personal graces and kindnesses, his not infrequent wisdom, selflessness and breadth of spirit, his unfailing passion to serve America as he understood that calling."

BIOGRAPHICAL/CRITICAL SOURCES: New York Times Book Review, November 20, 1977; *Newsweek,* November 28, 1977; *New York Review of Books,* April 6, 1978.

* * *

PRICE, Richard 1941-

PERSONAL: Born November 30, 1941, in New York, N.Y. *Education:* Harvard University, A.B. (magna cum laude), 1963,

Ph.D., 1970; attended Ecole Pratique des Hautes Etudes, 1963-64. *Home:* 215 Overhill Rd., Baltimore, Md. 21218. *Office:* Department of Anthropology, Johns Hopkins University, Baltimore, Md. 21218.

CAREER: Yale University, New Haven, Conn., lecturer, 1969, assistant professor, 1970-73, associate professor of anthropology, 1973-74; Johns Hopkins University, Baltimore, Md., professor of anthropology, 1974—, chairman of department, 1974-77, 1979—. Guest curator of Museum of Cultural History at University of California, Los Angeles, and of Walters Art Gallery, Baltimore, 1978-81. Conducted field research in Peru, 1961, Martinique, 1962-63, Andalusia, 1964, Mexico, 1965-66, and Surinam, 1966—. *Member:* Phi Beta Kappa.

AWARDS, HONORS: Fellowship from Social Science Research Council and American Council of Learned Societies for Latin America, 1972-73; National Science Foundation grant, 1976-78; fellowship-in-residence at Netherlands Institute for Advanced Study, 1977-78; American Council of Learned Societies fellowship, 1978; senior Fulbright fellowship for University of Leiden and University of Utrecht, 1981-82; National Endowment for the Humanities research grant, 1981-83.

WRITINGS: (Editor and author of introduction) *Maroon Societies: Rebel Slave Communities in the Americas,* Doubleday, 1973, revised edition, Johns Hopkins Press, 1979; *Saramaka Social Structure: Analysis of a Maroon Society in Surinam* (monograph), Institute of Caribbean Studies, University of Puerto Rico, 1975; (with Sidney W. Mintz) *An Anthropological Approach to the Afro-American Past,* ISHI Publications, 1976; *The Guiana Maroons: A Historical and Bibliographical Introduction,* Johns Hopkins University Press, 1976; (with Sally Price) *Afro-American Arts of the Suriname Rain Forest,* University of California Press, 1980; (editor and author of introduction and notes) *Captain Stedman's Original Narrative of a Five Years' Expedition,* University of Minnesota Press, 1983; *The Making of an Afro-American People: Saramaka Culture and Society in the Eighteenth Century,* in press; *First-Time: An Afro-American Vision of the Formative Years,* in press.

Contributor: Evon Z. Vogt, editor, *Aerial Photography in Anthropological Field Work,* Harvard University Press, 1974; Barbara Kirshenblatt-Gimblett, editor, *Speech Play,* University of Pennsylvania Press, 1976; (author of foreword) Roger Bastide, *The African Religions of Brazil,* Johns Hopkins Press, 1978; S. W. Mintz, editor, *Esclave—facteur de production,* Dunod, 1981.

Editor of "Studies in Atlantic History and Culture," a series, Johns Hopkins Press, 1974—; general editor of "Studies on the Non-Western Arts," G. K. Hall, 1980—. Contributor of about sixty articles and reviews to scholarly journals.

SIDELIGHTS: Price made a sound recording with Sally Price entitled "Music From Saramaka: A Dynamic Afro-American Tradition," released by Folkways Records in 1977.

*   *   *

PRICE, Susan 1955-

PERSONAL: Born July 8, 1955, in Brades Row, England; daughter of Alan (an electrical motor technician) and Jessy (a laborer; maiden name, Hanley) Price. *Education:* Educated in Tividale, England. *Politics:* Socialist. *Religion:* Atheist. *Residence:* Tividale, Warley, Worcestershire, England. *Agent:* Osyth Leeston, A. M. Heath & Co., 40-42 William IV St., London WC2N 4DD, England.

CAREER: Worked variously in a bakery, supermarket, warehouse, museum, and hotel, 1973-79; North Riding College of Education, Scarborough, England, resident creative writer, 1980. *Awards, honors:* Other Award from Children's Rights Workshop, 1975, for *Twopence a Tub.*

WRITINGS—Juvenile: *The Devil's Piper,* Faber, 1973, Greenwillow Books, 1976; *Twopence a Tub,* Faber, 1975, Merrimack, 1978; *Sticks and Stones,* Faber, 1976, Merrimack, 1978; *Home From Home,* Faber, 1977, Merrimack, 1978; *Christopher Uptake,* Faber, 1981; *The Carpenter, and Other Stories,* Faber, 1981.

SIDELIGHTS: The Devil's Piper, written when Price was sixteen, is a fantasy tale involving an evil "luchorpan" named Toole O'Dyna. Toole mesmerizes and kidnaps children with the beautiful music he produces on his pipe. He also changes the seasons, readjusts time to his liking, and raises a man from the dead. All of these activities, which are forbidden to luchorpans, get Toole in trouble with his master, the Devil.

Price's next book, *Twopence a Tub,* explores, through the eyes of youngster Jek Davies, the plight of colliers in Nottingham in the mid-1800's. The miners go on strike for higher wages with a disastrous result. Instead of receiving a raise, their pay is reduced. Price contrasts the miners' struggle against hunger with the affluence enjoyed by the mine owners.

In *Sticks and Stones* the author chronicles the efforts of sixteen-year-old Graeme to choose his own profession in the face of parental opposition. Graeme's father wants him to stay at a supermarket where there is a chance of being promoted to a managerial position. The boy, however, wishes to become a park gardener. Conflicts result, but, unlike his older brother, Graeme does not run away from home. In remaining at home Graeme reaches an understanding with his father.

Home From Home is about young Paul Mentor's relationship with an old woman. Coming from a troubled home, Paul has difficulty in getting along with his parents and schoolmates. His concerned teacher involves Paul in a charitable group devoted to helping elderly people. The adolescent begins to care for Mrs. Maxwell and a special friendship develops between the two. Cecilia Gordon of the *Times Literary Supplement* noted that "once again Susan Price has turned her discerning eye on the confused emotions and communication problems of adolescent boys." A *Growing Point* reviewer added that "this observant, quirky tale of everyday life keeps a delicate balance between comedy and pathos."

Price told *CA:* "I was born and raised in a heavy industrial town, now severely hit by unemployment. My family is working class, with intelligence and talent but no property and no savings. If it had not been for the election of the Labour party (socialist) in 1948, I would never have received the education permitting me to be a writer.

"I write for working-class kids. Their parents have been conned and the kids will be, so they'd better start thinking for themselves. Socialism and atheism are tools towards that; cynicism is a better one."

BIOGRAPHICAL/CRITICAL SOURCES: Times Literary Supplement, April 4, 1975, July 16, 1976, March 25, 1977, July 24, 1981; *Growing Point,* April, 1977.

*   *   *

PUTNAM, Michael Courtney Jenkins 1933-

PERSONAL: Born September 20, 1933, in Springfield, Mass.; son of Roger Lowell and Caroline (Jenkins) Putnam. *Education:* Harvard University, A.B., 1954, A.M., 1956, Ph.D., 1959. *Politics:* Democrat. *Religion:* Roman Catholic. *Home:*

77 Williams St., Providence, R.I. 02906. *Office:* Department of Classics, Brown University, Providence, R.I. 02912.

CAREER: Smith College, Northampton, Mass., instructor in classics, 1959-60; Brown University, Providence, R.I., 1960-67, began as instructor, became assistant professor, then associate professor, professor of classics, 1967—, chairman of department, 1968, 1970-72, 1977-78, acting director of Center for Hellenic Studies, 1961-62. Scholar-in-residence at American Academy in Rome, 1969-70; sole trustee of Lowell Observatory, 1967—; senior fellow at Center for Hellenic Studies, Washington, D.C., 1971—; associate of Columbia University seminar on classical civilization, 1972—. Member of Catholic Commission on Intellectual and Cultural Affairs, 1969—. Member of board of trustees of Bay Chamber Concerts, Camden, Maine, 1972—.

MEMBER: American Philological Association (member of board of directors, 1972-75; chairman of committee on award of merit, 1978—), Archaeological Institute of America, Mediaeval Academy of America, Virgilian Society of America (member of board of trustees, 1969-73; vice-president, 1974-76), Classical Association of New England, Providence Art Club, Boston Tavern Club. *Awards, honors:* Rome Prize from American Academy in Rome, 1963-64; Guggenheim fellow, 1966-67; Charles J. Goodwin Award of Merit from American Philological Association, 1971; senior fellow of National Endowment for the Humanities, 1973-74.

WRITINGS: The Poetry of the Aeneid: Four Studies in Imaginative Unity and Design, Harvard University Press, 1965; *Virgil's Pastoral Art: Studies in the Eclogues,* Princeton University Press, 1970; *Tibullus: A Commentary,* University of Oklahoma Press, 1973; *Virgil's Poem of the Earth: Studies in the Georgics,* Princeton University Press, 1979. Contributor to classical studies journals.*

Q

QUIGLESS, Helen Gordon 1944-

BRIEF ENTRY: Born July 16, 1944, in Washington, D.C. American librarian and poet. Quigless worked as a media specialist at Federal City College in 1968. Her poems have been anthologized in *For Malcolm* (Broadside Press, 1967), *The New Black Poetry* (International Publishing, 1968), *Today's Negro Voices* (Messner, 1970), and *New Negro Poets* (1970). *Address:* 1884 Columbia Rd., Washington, D.C. 20009. *Biographical/critical sources: Living Black American Authors: A Biographical Dictionary*, Bowker, 1973; *Black American Writers Past and Present: A Biographical and Bibliographical Dictionary*, Scarecrow, 1975.

* * *

QUILICI, Folco 1930-

PERSONAL: Born April 9, 1930, in Ferrara, Italy; son of Nello (a writer) and Mimi (a painter; maiden name, Buzzacchi) Quilici; children: Brando. *Politics:* Liberal. *Religion:* Roman Catholic. *Home:* 96 Viale Vaticano, Rome, Italy. *Office:* 3 Via Gomenizza, Rome Italy.

CAREER: Journalist, film director, writer, 1952—. Director of television series and programs; instructor at University of Bologna. *Military service:* Italian Army, 1965. *Awards, honors:* First prize from Mar della Plata Film Festival for "Sesto Continente," 1955; Silver Bear from Berlin Film Festival for "Ultimo Paradiso," 1957; UNESCO Award for "Tikoyo e il suo Pescecane," 1964; International Prize from Taormina Film Festival for "Oceano," 1971; first prize from International Festival of Cartagena for "Fratello Mare," 1975; Premio Ravenna for *Mediterraneo,* 1980.

WRITINGS—Illustrated with own photographs, except as noted: *Avventura nel sesto continente* (adapted from own film), with photographs by Quilici and Giorgio Ravelli, Leonardo da Vinci, 1953, also published in *Sesto continente e altre avventure* (see below), translation published as *The Blue Continent,* Rinehart, 1954; *Mala Kebir: L'avventura dei subacquei di sesto continente alla conquista di un primato mondiale,* with photographs by Quilici and Ravelli, G. Casini, 1955, also published in *Sesto continente e altre avventure* (see below); *Ultimo paradiso* (adapted from own film), Leonardo da Vinci, 1960; *Mezzomondo,* Editrice Italiana, 1964; *I mille fuochi,* second edition, Leonardo da Vinci, 1965; *Sesto continente e altre avventure,* with photographs by Quilici and Ravelli, Leonardo da Vinci, 1965.

Alla scoperta dell'Africa (adapted from own television documentary), Vallecchi, 1966; *Giramare,* Casini, 1966; *Giraterra,* Casini, 1966; *Malimba: La nuova Africa al Festival di Dakar,* De Donato, 1967; *Safari attorno al mondo,* De Agostini, 1967; *Sui mari del Capitano Cook* (adapted from own television documentary), Vallecchi, 1968; *Nelle isole del Sud-Pacifico,* Edizioni "Reporter," 1968; *I grandi deserti,* Rizzoli, 1968, adaptation and translation by Margaret Oldroyd Hyde published as *The Great Deserts,* McGraw-Hill, 1969; *Viaggio nel primitivo,* Immordino, 1969; *L'Africa,* CEI, 1969.

(With Maria Quilici) *Esploratori e esplorazioni,* Societa Editrice Internazionale, 1970; *Oceano,* (adapted from own film), De Donato, 1972; *Gli ultimi primitivi,* Rizzoli, 1972, translation published as *Primitive Societies,* F. Watts, 1972; (with Carlo Alberto Pinelli and Bruno Modugno) *Il Dio sotto la pelle,* introduction by A. Tocisco, Minerva Italica, 1974; (with Pinelli) *L'Alba dell'uomo,* De Donato, 1974; *Le isole di corallo,* Istituto Giografico De Agostini, 1975; *I mari del mondo,* Edizioni del Sole, 1975.

India, un pianeta, Societa Editrice Internazionale, 1976; *Natura chiama uomo,* Minerva Italica, 1976; *Uomini e mare,* preface by P. G. D'Ayala, A. Mondadori, 1976; *Io Africa,* De Donato, 1977; *Magia,* A. Curcio, 1977; *Il libro del sub,* Mondadori, 1977; *Le frontiere di Allah,* introduction by Andre Miquel, A. Monadori, 1978; *Mediterraneo,* Rusconi, 1980; *Lungo le rotte del Capitano Cook,* Rizzoli, 1980.

Author of series, "Italia vista dal cielo" (Italy Seen From the Sky), adapted from own film series, including: *Basilicata e Calabria,* introduction by Giuseppe Berto, Esso Standard Italiana, 1967; *Abruzzo e Molise,* introduction by Ignazio Silone, Canesi, 1970; (with Mario Praz) *Toscana,* A. Pizzi, 1972; *Campania,* Esso Standard Italiana, 1972; (with Italo Calvino) *Liguria,* Ufficio Publiche Relazioni della Esso Italiana, 1973; (with Praz) *Puglia,* Ufficio Publiche Relazioni della Esso Italiana, 1974; (with Praz) *Lazio,* Ufficio Pubbliche Relazioni della Esso Italiana, 1975; (with Leonardo Sciascia) *Sicilia,* Silvana, 1977; (with Cesare Brandi) *Umbria,* Silvana, 1977; (with Mario Soldati) *Piemonte e Valle d'Aosta,* Silvana, 1978; (with Guido Lopez) *Lombardia,* Silvana, 1979; *Veneto,* Esso Italiana, 1980.

Feature films and full-length documentaries: "Blue Continent," 1954; "Last Paradise," 1957; "From the Appennines to the Andes," 1959; "Tiko and the Shark," 1961; "The Voyage of Tanai," 1970; "Brother Sea," 1975.

Television documentaries: "Captain Cook," five-part series, 1964; "In Search of Africa," seven-part series, 1965; "Malimba," six-part series, 1966; "Black Theatre Today," four-part series, 1967; "India," nine-part series, 1968; "The Primitives," ten-part series, 1969; "Islam," eight-part series, 1970; "The Dawn of Man," eight-part series, 1975; "Mysteries of the Sea," seven-part series, 1977; "The Mediterranean," thirteen-part series, 1978; "European Man," nine-part series, 1980.

Creator of more than one hundred short and medium-length films, including a fourteen-part series, "Italy Seen From the Sky."

WORK IN PROGRESS: Children of Allah, editing an eight-volume work, *The Great Encyclopoedia of the Sea.*

SIDELIGHTS: Quilici's work explores diverse peoples and cultures, and demonstrates his commitment to preserving images of disappearing civilizations.

*   *   *

QUINN, (Mary) Bernetta   1915-
(Sister Bernetta Quinn)

PERSONAL: Birth-given name Roselyn Viola Quinn; born September 15, 1915, in Lake Geneva, Wis.; daughter of Bernard Franklin (a miller) and Ellen (Foran) Quinn. *Education:* College of St. Teresa, B.A., 1942; Catholic University of America, M.A., 1944; University of Wisconsin (now University of Wisconsin—Madison), Ph.D., 1952. *Politics:* Democrat. *Residence:* Assisi Heights, Rochester, Minn. 55901. *Office:* Department of English, St. Andrew's Presbyterian College, Laurenburg, N.C. 28352.

CAREER: Entered Order of St. Francis (Franciscans; O.S.F.), 1934; name in religion, Sister Bernetta Quinn; teacher at Catholic high schools in Winona, Minn., 1942-43, and Austin, Minn., 1944-46; College of St. Teresa, Winona, member of faculty, 1946-69; Allen University, Columbia, S.C., visiting professor of English, 1969-72. Visiting professor at Norfolk State University, 1972-81, and St. Andrew's Presbyterian College, 1981—. Involved in prison rehabilitation work.

MEMBER: American Association of University Professors, PEN American Center, WCW Society, Urban League, South Atlantic Modern Language Association, Poetry Society of Virginia. *Awards, honors:* Fellow of National Endowment for the Humanities, 1967-68, MacDowell Colony, Yaddo Colony, Ossabaw, Virginia Center for the Creative Arts, and Weymouth Place; Rockefeller Foundation fellow in Bellagio, Italy. ·

WRITINGS: The Metamorphic Tradition in Modern Poetry: Essays on the Work of Ezra Pound, Wallace Stevens, William Carlos Williams, T. S. Eliot, Hart Crane, Randall Jarrell, and William Butler Yeats, Rutgers University Press, 1955, revised edition, Gordian, 1966; *Give Me Souls: A Life of Raphael Cardinal Merry del Val,* Newman Press, 1958; *To God Alone the Glory: A Life of St. Bonaventure,* Newman Press, 1962; *Ezra Pound: An Introduction to the Poetry,* Columbia University Press, 1972; *Randall Jarrell,* G. K. Hall, 1981; *Dancing in Stillness* (poems), St. Andrew's Press, 1982. Contributor of poems to literary journals, including *Literary Review, Sewanee Review, Yale Review,* and *Southern Review.*

WORK IN PROGRESS: A literary biography of Dr. John Stone.

SIDELIGHTS: Quinn made a two-cassette sound recording, "Ezra Pound," released by Everett/Edwards in 1976.

She told *CA:* "From my early research in metamorphosis as a literary device, I have been concerned with the changes whereby life (inner and outer) becomes a 'new creation.' As a Franciscan, I regard art, as well as its inspiration (the world and 'the world within the world'), as cause for celebration. At the same time, like my favorite composer, Mozart, I recognize the writer's role as one in which the joy and pain of being human are inextricably entwined. The good fortune of several trips to European countries and to Japan (on research or university teaching ventures) has afforded me deepened insight into cultures other than my own, as have my years as visiting professor at two predominantly black universities.

"At the moment, my chief attraction, except for an occasional critical piece in the spirit of 'love, so that you may understand,' is to poetry. An accident in June, 1981, led to the sequence 'Journey of a Pilgrim on Crutches.' I love this concept of each of us, here on this amazing planet, as 'pilgrims,' and in my own case consider it 'a vocation within a vocation.'"

*   *   *

QUINN, Sister Bernetta
See QUINN, (Mary) Bernetta

R

RABIN, Chaim 1915-

PERSONAL: Born November 22, 1915, in Giessen, Germany (now West Germany); son of Israel (a teacher) and Matel (Wolodarsky) Rabin; married Betty Batya Emanuel (a translator and writer), December 21, 1951; children: Yemima. *Education:* Attended Hebrew University of Jerusalem, 1933-34; London School of Oriental and African Studies, London, B.A. (with honors), 1937, Ph.D., 1939; Oxford University, D.Phil., 1943. *Religion:* Jewish. *Home address:* P.O. Box 7158, Jerusalem, Israel 91071. *Office:* Department of Hebrew Language, Hebrew University of Jerusalem, Jerusalem, Israel.

CAREER: Oxford University, Oxford, England, Cowley Lecturer in Post-Biblical Hebrew, 1941-56; Hebrew University of Jerusalem, Jerusalem, Israel, professor of Hebrew language, 1956—. Member of Hebrew Language Academy, 1958—. *Member:* Israel Association for Applied Linguistics (president, 1974—), Israel Translators Association.

WRITINGS: Everyday Hebrew, Dent, 1943, McKay, 1944; (with Charles Singer) *A Prelude to Modern Science . . . Vesalius,* Cambridge University Press, 1946; *Arabic,* Lund, Humphries, 1947, revised edition, 1962, published as *Arabic Reader,* Harvard University Press, 1963; *Hebrew,* Lund, Humphries, 1949; *Ancient West-Arabian,* Taylor's Foreign Press, 1951; *Qumran Studies,* Oxford University Press, 1957, Greenwood Press, 1976; (contributor) *Aspects of Translation,* Secker & Warburg, 1958; *Mehkarim be-keter Aram-Tsovah, bearikhat,* Magnes Press, 1960; *The Influence of Different Systems of Hebrew Orthography in Reading Efficiency,* Israel Institute of Applied Social Research, 1968; *A Short History of the Hebrew Language,* Jewish Agency, 1974; (with Frank Talmage and Libby Garshowitz) *Study Guide for Sifron-la Student,* University of Toronto Press, 1971; (contributor) *Language and Texts,* University of Michigan Press, 1975.

Editor: (With Yigael Yadin) *Aspects of the Dead Sea Scrolls,* Magnes Press, 1958, second edition, 1965; *'Iyienim be-sefer Yehoshu'a,* Israel Society for Biblical Research, 1960; *Studies in the Bible,* Magnes Press, 1961; Shalom Rabinowitz, *Shalom Aleichem Reader in Easy Hebrew,* World Zionist Organization, 1962; Eliezer Ben-Yehudah, *The Dream and Its Realisation* (autobiography), World Zionist Organization, 1963; Solomon Lavi, *Shalom Laish's Aliyar,* World Zionist Organization, 1964; Aharon Megged, *Four Stories,* World Zionist Organization, 1966; Megged, *Hannah Szenes* (play), World Zionist Organization, 1969.

Translator: Moses ben Maimon, *The Guide of the Perplexed,* introduction and commentary by Julius Guttman, East and West Library, 1952; (and editor) *The Zadokite Documents,* Claridon Press, 1954, revised edition, 1958, Volume I: *The Admonition,* Volume II: *The Laws.*

Also author of *ha-Adam melikh ha-hayot,* 1954; *Tahbir leshon ha-mikra,* 1963; *Yesodot ha-dikduk ha-mashuen shel ha-lashon ha-'writ,* 1966; *Toldot ha-lashon,* 1968; *Otsar ha-millim* (title means "Thesaurus of the Hebrew Language in Dictionary Form"), 1970; *Torat ha-hegen shel ha-'Ivrit ha-mikra'it,* 1970; *Mashma'uyotehem shel ha-tsurot ha-dikdukeyot,* 1971; *'Ikre toldot ha-lashon ha-'ivrit,* 1972; *'Ivrit be-siman-tov,* 1974; *Kileshon'amo,* 1976; and *Sefir me'ir Valenshtain* (title means "Studies in the Bible and the Hebrew Language").

Contributor to *Encyclopaedia Britannica, Hebrew Encyclopedia,* and *Encyclopedia Judaica.* Contributor of more than three hundred fifty articles to scholarly journals. Editor of *Sifrut: Journal for Hebrew Literature,* 1954-55.

WORK IN PROGRESS: Research on historical sociolinguistics, history of the Hebrew language, comparative Semitics, etymology, discourse analysis, and linguistics and sociolinguistics of translation.

SIDELIGHTS: Rabin wrote: "Many of my interests derive from my involvement with the revival of the Hebrew language and with the linguistic situation of a language revived within the last one hundred years, as does my scientific interest (rare among linguists) in the phenomenon of normativism in the life of a language."

*   *   *

RABINOWITZ, Howard Neil 1942-

PERSONAL: Born June 19, 1942, in Brooklyn, N.Y.; son of Abe (in small business) and Gertrude (Finkleman) Rabinowitz; married Anita Blau, August 28, 1966 (divorced March 20, 1981); children: Lori, Deborah. *Education:* Swarthmore College, B.A. (with high honors), 1964; University of Chicago, M.A., 1967, Ph.D., 1973. *Residence:* Albuquerque, N.M. *Office:* Department of History, University of New Mexico, Albuquerque, N.M. 87131.

CAREER: Grinnell College, Grinnell, Iowa, visiting instructor in American history, 1970-71; University of New Mexico, Albuquerque, instructor, 1971-73, assistant professor, 1973-

77, associate professor of American history, 1977—. Vice-chairman of Albuquerque Landmarks and Urban Conservation Commission, 1978—; consultant to Museum of Albuquerque. *Member:* Organization of American Historians, Southern Historical Association. *Awards, honors:* Fellow of National Endowment for the Humanities, 1978-79; Pulitzer Prize nomination, 1978, for *Race Relations in the Urban South.*

WRITINGS: Race Relations in the Urban South, 1865-1890, Oxford University Press, 1978; (editor and contributor) *Southern Black Leaders in the Reconstruction Era,* University of Illinois Press, 1982.

Contributor: Blaine Brownell and David Goldfield, editors, *The City in Southern History,* Kennikat, 1977; Ray Browne and Marshall Fishwick, editors, *Icons of America,* Popular Press, 1978; Gerald Nash, editor, *The Urban West,* Sunflower Press, 1979; Jeffrey Crow, editor, *Blacks in North Carolina and the South,* University of North Carolina Press, 1982. James D. Gardiner and George R. Adams, editors, *Ordinary People and Everyday Life: Perspectives on the New Social History,* Association for State and Local History, 1982. Contributor to history journals. Member of board of editors of *Journal of Southern History,* 1980—.

WORK IN PROGRESS: The First New South, 1877-1920, publication by AHM Press expected in 1984; *Albuquerque, New Mexico, 1940-1974,* completion expected in 1985; research on southern race relations, 1890-1920.

SIDELIGHTS: Rabinowitz commented: "My choice of an academic career was in large measure due to the example of my uncle, Arthur Mann, now a professor of history at University of Chicago. Along with my major professors, my uncle has had the greatest impact on how I teach and write history. As a southern historian I have been most influenced by the issues raised in C. Vann Woodward's *Origins of the New South,* perhaps one of the two or three greatest works in American history. There has been no equivalent book in my work as a black and urban historian.

"In studying black history I try to treat blacks as subjects rather than as mere objects of history who are acted upon by others with little to say about their fate. My work in urban history focuses on two regions of the country—the South and the West—neglected by most urban historians. In all three fields I've been governed by a desire to recreate the past rather than to dole out praise or blame. It is all too easy to damn the dead. The more difficult task is to try to *understand* people and events. To do otherwise is to fall into the trap of ascribing simplistic motives to what are usually complex attitudes and forms of behavior. I seek to avoid the lure of presentism, that is, reading into history trends and beliefs common today. I am especially wary of overemphasizing the force of racism *per se* in American history and the homogenizing effects of urbanization."

BIOGRAPHICAL/CRITICAL SOURCES: Albuquerque News, March 8, 1978; *Albuquerque Tribune,* April 1, 1978.

*   *   *

RABKIN, Gerald Edward   1930-

BRIEF ENTRY: Born January 4, 1930, in Brooklyn, N.Y. American educator and author. Rabkin has been a professor of theatre at Rutgers University since 1970. He has written *Drama and Commitment: Politics in the American Theatre of the Thirties* (Indiana University Press, 1964) and *Dirty Movies: An Illustrated History of the Stag Film, 1915-1970* (Chelsea House, 1976). *Address:* Department of Theatre Arts, Living-

ston College, Rutgers University, New Brunswick, N.J. 08903. *Biographical/critical sources: Times Literary Supplement,* August 6, 1964.

*   *   *

RADO, James   1939-

PERSONAL: Original surname, Radomski; born January 23, 1939, in Los Angeles, Calif.; son of Alexander (a professor and sociologist) Radomski. *Education:* Studied acting with Lee Strasberg in New York, N.Y.

CAREER: Librettist, lyricist, and composer. Actor in plays, including "Marathon '33," 1963, "Hang Down Your Head and Die," 1964, "She Loves Me," 1964, "Quality Street," 1965, "The Knack," 1965, "The Lion in Winter," 1966, "The Infantry," 1966, "Hair," 1968, and "The Rainbow, Rainbeam, Radio, Roadshow," 1974. Producer of play "Rainbow," 1972.

AWARDS, HONORS: Named best lyricist by *Variety* New York Drama Critics' Poll, 1967, for "Hair"; Best Broadway Show Album award, 1968, for "Hair"; Grammy Award from National Academy of Recording Arts and Sciences, 1968, for best score from original cast show album for "Hair," and 1969, for record of the year for single "Aquarius/Let the Sunshine In"; gold record award from Recording Industry Association of America, Inc., for album "Hair," and for singles "Aquarius/Let the Sunshine In," and "Hair," all 1969; "Hair" named best-selling original cast album, 1969, 1970, and 1971.

WRITINGS—Librettist and lyricist of songs for plays: (With Gerome Ragni; music by Galt MacDermot) "Aquarius," "Donna," "Hashish," "Sodomy," "Colored Spade," "Manchester," "Ain't Got No," "I Believe in Love," "Air," "Initials," "I Got Life," "Going Down," "Hair," "My Conviction," "Easy to Be Hard," "Hung," "Don't Put It Down," "Frank Mills," "Hare Krishna," "Where Do I Go?," "Electric Blues," "Black Boys," "White Boys," "Walking in Space," "Abie Baby," "Prisoners in Niggertown," "What a Piece of Work Is Man," "Good Morning Starshine," "The Bed," and "Let the Sunshine In" (also called "Flesh Failures") from *Hair: The American Tribal Love-Rock Musical* (two-act; first produced in New York City at Joseph Papp's New York Shakespeare Festival Theatre, October 17, 1967; produced Off-Broadway at Anspacher Theatre, October 29, 1967; rewritten and produced on Broadway at Biltmore Theatre, April 29, 1968; revival produced on Broadway at Biltmore Theatre, October 5, 1977), Pocket Books, 1969.

(Written with brother Ted Rado, and composer) "Who Are We?" "Love Me, Love Me, Dorothy Lamour, La Sarong," "Fruits and Vegetables," "Welcome Banana," "Questions, Questions," "Song to Sing," "My Lungs," "You Got to Be Clever," "Tangled Tangents," "What Can I Do For You?" "Oh, I Am a Fork," "People Stink," "Guinea Pig," "Give Your Heart to Jesus," "Joke a Cola," "Mama Loves You," "I Want to Make You Cry," "I Am a Cloud," "A Garden for Two," "Starry Old Night," "Bathroom," "O.K., Goodbye," "Deep in the Dark," "You Live in Flowers," "I Don't Hope for Great Things," "Globligated," "Be Not Afraid," "Obedience," "Ten Days Ago," "Oh, Oh, Oh," "Moosh, Moosh," "The Man," "The World Is Round," "Stars and Bars," "Cacophony," "Groovy, Green Man, Groovy," "Heliopolis," "I Am Not Free," "We Are the Clouds," "How Dreamlike," "Somewhere Under the Rainbow," and "Star Song" from "Rainbow" (two-act), first produced Off-Broadway at Orpheum Theatre, December 18, 1972, rewritten play first produced as "The Rainbow, Rainbeam, Radio, Roadshow,'' in Washington, D.C., at American Theatre, January 22, 1974.

Recordings: ''Hair,'' original cast album, RCA, 1968.

SIDELIGHTS: In 1970 Richard Crinkley declared in the *National Review* that the first pop-rock musical, ''Hair,'' had developed into ''an institution.'' In the three years since its first production in 1967, the almost plotless paean to youth, exuberance, and rebellion had become, according to *Newsweek*'s Jack Kroll, ''the greatest global cultural event of the '60's.'' ''Hair'' companies had sprouted up all over the world. In addition to its Broadway run, the musical simultaneously played in Los Angeles, Boston, Chicago, San Francisco, London, England, Paris, France, Dusseldorf, West Germany, Belgrade, Yugoslavia, Finland, Spain, Italy, Israel, Czechoslovakia, and Japan.

''Hair'' was a project long in the making for its creators James Rado and Gerome Ragni. For two years, the men jotted down various thoughts and ideas about the turbulent 1960's. Their numerous notes covered topics ranging from the hippie movement, drugs, sex, racism, and be-ins to the Vietnam war and the draft. The accumulation of these scraps of paper became ''Hair.'' David Ewen remarked in the *New Complete Book of the American Musical Theatre* that ''one suspects . . . the authors . . . threw all the slips of paper high in the air, let them fall pell-mell, and then proceeded to write their text by picking up the pieces of paper at random and following the chain of thought in the same sequence in which those papers were so haphazardly picked up.'' Ewen described the result as ''an explosion.''

The montage-like play did incorporate a story line, however nominal. The musical's protagonist, Claude, a long-haired hippie from Flatbush masquerading as an import from Manchester, England, travels to New York City, befriends a group of hippies, and establishes himself in a menage a trois with their leader Berger and his girlfriend Sheila. Together they engage in all the activities that have come to represent the youth-culture phenomenon of the 1960's. When Claude is drafted into the army, the hippies mourn the demise of his soul. At the end of the play, after he presents Berger with his shorn hair, Claude is killed in Vietnam.

The musical's debut at Joseph Papp's New York Shakespeare Festival Theatre was greeted with guarded enthusiasm. Kroll praised the show, proclaiming that it ''ignites the key images and issues of the lost-and-found generation . . . into a vivid uproar that has more wit, feeling and musicality than anything since 'West Side Story.''' Other reviewers maintained their reservations while commenting favorably on the production's youthful vitality. Some felt the subject matter of ''Hair'' had already become passe. Harold Clurman asserted in *Nation,* ''The protest theatre of 1967 has already become a stereotype,'' and intimated that ''the 'hippie movement' . . . is . . . showing decrepitude, no doubt petrified by publicity.'' *New Republic*'s Robert Brustein agreed: ''Since the hippies have recently become the victims of a vast publicity network, there is also something intrinsically voguish about their scene, and this gives one the recurrent feeling that *Hair* is going out of fashion even as it is being performed.'' Brustein and Clurman also noted the absence of serious reflection in the play. The former averred that ''Hair'' ''is entertaining, but in none of it do we sense that the authors have thought about or felt their material very deeply, and they are too mindless in their acceptance of the teenage version of reality.'' The latter pointed out that ''the trouble is that on the stage we tend to use every new social phenomenon as grist to the amusement industry, rather than as a subject for study and thought.''

Another prevalent opinion among critics branded the play's plot insufficient. A writer for *Time* stated that ''Hair'' ''is crippled by being a bookless musical and, like a boneless fish, it drifts when it should swim.'' Nonetheless, after the production's run at the New York Shakespeare Festival Theatre and at the discotheque Cheetah, Rado and Ragni rewrote the play, deleting much of the already scant plot and adding new scenes and songs. The finished product, claimed Ewen, ''was an almost entirely new stage adventure.'' A collection of views showing the hippies smoking marijuana, participating in protests against the establishment, and indulging in free love, ''Hair'' also sported more four-letter words and a nude sequence. This version first appeared on Broadway in 1968, and continued to run for a total of 1,742 performances.

The production's return to the stage met with a mixed critical reception. Many writers expressed, like Kroll, that ''something had been lost'' in the transition. The play had lost its former spontaneity. John Simon explained in *Commonweal* that though the first version had been ''youthful, zestful, tuneful, and brimful of life,'' the second ''is merely fulsome.'' The reviewer added that the original ''story with its anti-war but also anti-bourgeois bias was either soft-pedaled or transmogrified into stingless farce.'' Crinkley observed that ''the show is embalmed, a bourgeois-ossification of hippiedom.''

In spite of the less than favorable reviews, ''Hair'' became very popular. In 1969 one of the musical's principal investors, Michael Butler, speculated: ''I think 'Hair' will go on for ten years. . . . Maybe it will become a kind of permanent celebration.'' The show earned for its backers more than $2 million profit by 1970. ''Hair'' began to play around the world, and its authors, Rado and Ragni, who both acted in the Broadway version, traveled to watch and sometimes participate in the foreign productions.

Since the format of ''Hair'' allowed for improvisation, the play was often altered to appeal to its various audiences. A *Newsweek* reporter clarified: ''On foreign soil 'Hair' takes on the character of the cultural transplant that it is. The Paris version, for example, has been changed to include topical political humor. When a hippie distributes LSD sugar cubes, he says, 'Here's one for Francois Mauriac, one for Tante Yvonne [the nickname of Charles de Gaulle's spouse] and one for Madame Pompidou.''' Extremely successful in the French capital, the play had advance ticket sales of eighty thousand dollars, the highest of any show in history. The correspondent further related that in Belgrade ''Hair'' was known as ''Kosa.'' As in France, political jokes were changed for the Yugoslavian viewers: Pot-shots were taken at Mao Tse-tung and Albania.

Ten years after its debut, ''Hair'' was revived on Broadway in 1977. *New Yorker*'s Brendan Gill wondered, ''Why on earth should anyone have wished to bring back 'Hair'?'' A *Time* critic concurred: ''Hair is deader than King Tut and the relics that were buried with him.'' Many cited the change in the social atmosphere as the reason ''Hair'' seemed so ''bald,'' as one reviewer quipped. Kroll elucidated that ''a lot has happened in the decade since 'Hair' first blew in our eyes, and the Revelation According to St. Hippie is both too close chronologically and too distant emotionally to work now.'' The *Time* writer disclosed that ''the show's major bolstering prop was always offstage—the Viet Nam War—and its only emotional cohesion was the passions that the war aroused. Those passions are spent, the war has ended and, even more pertinently, it was lost.''

Nevertheless, ''Hair'' was not forgotten. In 1979 the play was made into a motion picture. To effect the change of medium, the screenplay gave a story line to the plotless play. Claude becomes an Oklahoma farm boy who travels to New York City to enlist in the army. On his last day of freedom, he joins a group of hippies in Central Park and meets Sheila, a debutante. As he discovers psychedelic drugs and anti-American criticism, Claude also tries to woo Sheila over to a more hip way of life. Eventually, Claude must report for duty, but in a last-minute twist, the hippie leader Berger exchanges places with him. The film ends with the death of Berger in Vietnam.

For the most part, reviewers conceded that the picture was good. Many thought it would fall prey to the same defects the 1977 stage revival had. The motion picture, however, avoided appearing out of date and self-conscious. "The film version of *Hair* is proof that real miracles can happen in show business," related *Time*'s T. E. Kalem. "If ever a project looked doomed, it was this one." Kalem continued: "There are no false moves. *Hair* succeeds at all levels—as lowdown fun, as affecting drama, as exhilarating spectacle and as provocative social observation." Kroll placed credit for the film's success on its spontaneity, which harkened back to the original Papp production. "[Motion picture] scenarist Michael Weller has made some changes that make this 'Hair' less like . . . [the] Broadway version and more like the original Joseph Papp's Public Theatre." Kroll concluded that "'Hair' is for everyone, a loving, knowing tribute to an amazing moment when American innocence tried to cleanse itself of corruption with the ancient energies of music and dance."

Rado continued the story begun in the stage version of "Hair" (in which Claude, not Berger, is killed in Vietnam) in his play "Rainbow." "Rainbow" begins with Claude, now re-named Man, going to the otherworld, into Rainbow land. Rainbow land literally turns out to be "just that great big radio station in the sky," as Clive Barnes described it in the *New York Times*. The inhabitants of this world are "obsessed, but not too intently, with preparing commercials for such soap products as Oxydol." Barnes commented upon the play's similarity to "Hair": "It has the style, manner and energy of 'Hair,' as well as its chaotic organization and its simplistic view of a far from simple world." The critic was impressed with Rado's score. "The musical is joyous and life-assertive. It is the first musical to derive from 'Hair' that really seems to have the confidence of a new creation about it, largely derived from James Rado's sweet and fresh music and lyrics."

MEDIA ADAPTATIONS: In 1979 director Milos Forman adapted "Hair" into a motion picture, starring John Savage, Treat Williams, and Beverly D'Angelo, for United Artists.

BIOGRAPHICAL/CRITICAL SOURCES: New York Times, October 30, 1967, November 14, 1967, November 19, 1967, December 22, 1967, April 30, 1968, May 19, 1968, September 29, 1968, February 5, 1969, June 2, 1969, June 7, 1969, September 13, 1969, January 13, 1970, September 5, 1970, September 27, 1970, October 10, 1972, October 22, 1972, December 19, 1972, October 6, 1977, March 25, 1979; *New Yorker,* November 11, 1967, May 11, 1968, June 14, 1969, October 17, 1977, April 16, 1979; *Newsweek,* November 13, 1967, May 13, 1968, July 7, 1969, October 17, 1977, March 19, 1979; *New Republic,* November 18, 1967, April 14, 1979; *Nation,* November 20, 1967; *Dance,* December, 1967, July, 1968.

Saturday Review, January 13, 1968, May 11, 1968; *Reporter,* April 4, 1968; *Time,* May 10, 1968, December 12, 1969, October 17, 1977, March 19, 1979; *Commonweal,* May 17, 1968, May 25, 1979; *National Review,* May 21, 1968, March 24, 1970, May 11, 1979; *America,* June 8, 1968, April 7, 1979; *Saturday Evening Post,* August 10, 1968; *Harper,* September, 1968; *L'Express,* June 9-15, 1969; *Wall Street Journal,*

June 11, 1969; *Hi Fi,* July, 1969; *Theology Today,* July, 1969; *Opera News,* December 20, 1969; David Ewen, *New Complete Book of the American Musical Theatre,* Holt, 1970; *Life,* April 17, 1970; *Ebony,* May, 1970; *English Journal,* May, 1971; *New York Post,* October 6, 1977; *New York,* October 24, 1977, March 19, 1979; *New York Theatre Annual, 1977-78,* Volume 2, Gale, 1978; Stanley Richards, *Great Rock Musicals,* Stein & Day, 1979; *Macleans,* March 26, 1979; *New Leader,* April 9, 1979; *Encore,* April 16, 1979; *Esquire,* May 8, 1979; *USA Today,* July, 1979; *Contemporary Literary Criticism,* Volume 17, Gale, 1981.*

—*Sketch by Anne M. Guerrini*

* * *

RADO, Sandar   1900-1981

OBITUARY NOTICE: Born in 1900 in Hungary; died August 19, 1981, in Budapest, Hungary. Cartographer, journalist, educator, intelligence agent, and author. While working at his map news service, Geopress, Rado was recruited by Soviet military intelligence in 1935. During World War II Rado filed reports from Geneva under the code name Dora. Upon his return to Stalinist Russia in 1945, he was arrested along with many others who had served abroad. He was sentenced to death but the judgment was commuted, and he instead spent ten years at hard labor. He was released upon Stalin's death and settled in Hungary where he was head of the Government Mapping Service in Budapest and founder of Cartactual, a news service for mapmakers. His publications include a tourist guide to the Soviet Union; his memoirs, *Code Name Dora;* and *The Atlas of Today and Tomorrow.* Obituaries and other sources: *Who's Who in the Socialist Countries,* K. G. Saur, 1978; *New York Times,* August 21, 1981.

* * *

RAESCHILD, Sheila   1936-
(Sheila Grawoig, Sheila Jurnak)

PERSONAL: Birth-given name, Sheila Miller; born November 4, 1936, in Pittsburgh, Pa.; daughter of David Earl (in shoe sales) and Rae (Seewald) Miller; children: (from previous marriages) Betsy Grawoig, Susan Grawoig, Paul Grawoig, Seth Jurnak. *Education:* Georgia State University, B.A. (summa cum laude), 1967; Tulane University, M.A., 1970, Ph.D., 1971. *Religion:* Jewish. *Home address:* R.D. 4, Box 4141, Stroudsburg, Pa. 18360. *Agent:* Liz Trupin, Jet Literary Associates, Inc., 124 East 84th St., Suite 4A, New York, N.Y. 10028. *Office:* Department of English, East Stroudsburg State College, East Stroudsburg, Pa. 18301.

CAREER: Ex-Addict Rehabilitation Manpower Training Center, New Orleans, La., planner and reports specialist, 1972; Information Dynamics, Inc., Reading, Mass., consultant systems analyst, 1973; Clarkson College of Technology, Potsdam, N.Y., assistant professor of humanities, 1974-78; Pennsylvania State University, Capitol Campus, Middletown, visiting assistant professor of humanities, 1978-80; East Stroudsburg State College, East Stroudsburg, Pa., assistant professor of English, 1980—. Gives poetry and fiction readings, including one at University of the West Indies.

MEMBER: Modern Language Association of America, Poetry Society of America, Mensa, Sigma Tau Delta (president), Crimson Key. *Awards, honors:* Woodrow Wilson fellowship, 1967-68; award from Phi Beta Kappa, 1967, for "best graduate at Georgia State University"; fellowship from English-Speaking Union for University of London, 1968; first prize from

Academy of American Poets, 1970, for "untitled collection of poems"; attended Bread Loaf Writers' Conference, 1975; National Endowment for the Humanities fellowship, 1976.

WRITINGS: (Under name Sheila Jurnak; with R. Dunn and R. Ansell) *Analysis and Preliminary Design of the Northern Virginia Community College Learning Resource System,* Information Dynamics, 1973; *Lessons in Leaving* (poems), Know, Inc., 1974; *Trolleysong* (novel), Zebra Books, 1981. Also author of *The Making of Australia,* Volume IX.

Work represented in anthologies, including (under name Sheila Grawoig) *Best College Verse of 1970; National Anthology of College Poetry;* (under name Sheila Jurnak) *New Orleans Poets: An Anthology.* Contributor of articles, poems, and stories, some under names Sheila Grawoig and Sheila Jurnak, to literary journals and popular magazines, including *For Women Only, Cavalier, Redbook, Andover Review, New York Quarterly,* and *Women Together.*

WORK IN PROGRESS: Haitian Scenes, a novel of a woman's self-discovery; *Runaround,* a novel dealing with marathons, murder, and toxic wastes; a novel.

SIDELIGHTS: Sheila Raeschild wrote: "I write to create a world, not necessarily to create order out of chaos, just to create—godlike. What a life! I see in the progression of my writing forms a constant movement in the direction of greater audience. Somehow a writer without readers is a contradiction in terms, yet that is exactly the position many writers find themselves in. I moved from poetry to short fiction to novels. I hope to be able to write them all simultaneously someday, although it does seem that whatever mental mode establishes itself when I'm writing poetry disappears when I'm working in prose. They seem to come from different places within me, and I can't keep the faucet open to both taps at once.

"Themes that particularly interest me are two: (1) Some problems (or life situations) are unresolvable; no way is a best way, and it's even hard to figure out which way might be the 'better' one. (2) Evil exists and has as much energy and power as good."

* * *

RAGNI, Gerome 1942-

PERSONAL: Born September 11, 1942, in Pittsburgh, Pa.; married wife, Stephanie, May 18, 1963; children: Eric. *Education:* Attended Georgetown University and Catholic University, Washington, D.C.; studied acting with Philip Burton.

CAREER: Actor, 1954—; librettist and lyricist, 1967—. Actor in stage plays, including "Shadows and Substances," 1954, "Legend of Lovers," 1959, "War," 1963, "Hamlet," 1964, "Hang Down Your Head and Die," 1964, "The Knack," 1964, "Viet Rock," 1966, and "Hair," 1967. Actor in films, including "Hamlet," Warner Bros., 1964, and "Lions in Love," Raab, 1969. Also appeared at Village Gate night club, New York City, February 4, 1971.

AWARDS, HONORS: Barter Theatre award, 1963, for outstanding actor; named best lyricist by *Variety* New York Critics Poll, 1967-68, for "Hair"; "Hair" named best Broadway show album, 1968; Grammy Awards from National Academy of Recording Arts and Sciences, 1968, for best score from original cast show album for "Hair" and, 1969, for record of the year for "Aquarius/Let the Sun Shine In"; gold record awards from Recording Industry Association of America, Inc. (RIAA), for original cast album "Hair," for single "Aquarius/Let the Sun Shine In," and for single "Hair," all 1969; "Hair" named

best-selling original cast album by National Association of Recording Merchandisers, Inc. (NARM), 1969, 1970, and 1971.

WRITINGS—Librettist and lyricist of songs for plays: (With James Rado; music by Galt MacDermot) "Aquarius," "Donna," "Hashish," "Sodomy," "Colored Spade," "Manchester," "Ain't Got No," "Dead End," "I Believe in Love," "Air," "Initials," "I Got Life," "Going Down," "Hair," "My Conviction," "Easy to Be Hard," "Hung," "Don't Put It Down," "Frank Mills," "Be-In," "Hare Krishna," "Where Do I Go?," "Electric Blues," "Black Boys," "White Boys," "Walking in Space," "Abie Baby," "Three-Five-Zero-Zero," "Prisoners in Niggertown," "What a Piece of Work Is Man," "Good Morning Starshine," "The Bed," and "Flesh Failures" (or "Let the Sun Shine In") from *Hair: A Tribal Love-Rock Musical* (two-act; first produced in New York at Joseph Papp's New York Shakespeare Festival Theatre, October 17, 1967; produced Off-Broadway at Florence Sutro Anspacher Theatre, October 29, 1967; rewritten and produced on Broadway at Biltmore Theatre, April 29, 1968; revival produced on Broadway at Biltmore Theatre, October 5, 1977), Pocket Books, 1969.

(Music by MacDermot) "Overture," "Theatre/Theatre," "A-Stage," "The Mountains," "Pears and Peaches," "Eat It," "Suzi Moon," "Y. O. U.," "I Love My Boo Boo," "Hum Drum Life," "Who's It?," "Talk to Me About Love," "Goodbyes," "I'm Small," "You Can Do Nothing About It," "The Handsomest Man," "Electric Prophet," "No-One," "Who Will Be the Children," "Go Holy Ghost," "A Song to Sing," "A Dawn," "The Days of This Life," "I Never Knew," "Air Male," "Undo," "The Earth," "My Darling I Love You March," "So Long Dude," "Peace Peace," "Jesus Hi," "Baby Breath," and "Sweet Dreams" from "Dude, the Highway Life," first produced on Broadway at Broadway Theatre, October 9, 1972.

Recordings: "Hair" (original cast album), RCA, 1968; "Dude, the Highway Life" (original cast album), Columbia, 1972.

SIDELIGHTS: When Gerome Ragni was five years old he would paint pictures on the walls of his family's home, and no one could deter this practice. "Even then he believed he was a genius," said Adela Holzer, the backer of Ragni's second musical. "That belief has made him tireless."

Twenty years after his wall painting efforts, Ragni's creative talents received recognition with the production of his first libretto. His masterpiece, "Hair" was first produced for Joseph Papp's New York Shakespeare Festival Theatre's 1967 fall season. For the musical, Ragni and his writing partner James Rado jotted notes and collected ideas from the phenomena around them. Once assembled, these random clippings of popular culture and politics became the framework for the revolutionary musical. In the *New Complete Book of the American Musical Theatre,* David Ewen suggested that the librettists wrote their observations on strips of scrap paper and "then threw all the slips of paper high in the air, let them fall pell-mell, and then proceeded to write their text by picking up the pieces of paper at random and following the chain of thought in the same sequence in which those papers were so haphazardly picked up (very much in the same way some aleatory composers write their music)."

With no actual plot or central focus, "Hair" was seen as a vehicle through which to understand the youth of the 1960's. The production revealed what the world looked like to young adults, and, said Henry Hewes in an issue of *Saturday Review,* "it seems to be a truer and fairer representation of hippiedom than anything the theatre has offered so far." Called a "psychedelic picaresque'' by Richard Brustein, ''Hair'' traced the joint exploits of Berger, a drop-out and a member of the lower class, and of Claude, a member of the middle class. Together with the rest of the cast these characters rebelled against the Establishment and delighted in liberty. Attacking middle America's values, not to mention middle Americans, as well as war in Vietnam, the cast of ''Hair'' addressed and embraced promiscuity, drugs, and love.

What the production ''quite properly tries to do,'' observed *Newsweek*'s Jack Kroll, ''is present the hippie phenomenon as the mixed-up but inescapably alive eruption of energy that it is.'' And Harold Clurman noted in *Nation* that ''Hair,'' while it is a celebration of youth, also ''kids them.'' Another critic, however, wrote that Ragni and Rado's study of youth was an investigation without analysis. The authors, a *New Republic* reviewer stated, were ''too mindless in their acceptance of the teenage version of reality.''

Nevertheless, ''Hair'' did have an impact on musicals as a genre. Because of Ragni's production, ''it will be very hard, in future,'' said Brustein, ''to compose a Richard Rodgers-type work with quite the same confidence and equanimity as before.''

After its premier at Papp's theatre, ''Hair'' was rewritten and taken to Broadway. Though it remained a ''wonderful'' and innovative production, the play lost something when it was revised, most notably its plot. A *Time* reviewer, though he conceded that the play ''thrums with vitality,'' noticed that the production ''is crippled by being a bookless musical and, like a boneless fish, it drifts when it should swim.'' Without the plot, Hewes stated, ''Hair'' became ''a documentary collage of hippie behavior.'' John Simon submitted that some of the musical's original zestfulness and youthfulness were missing from the Broadway version, which magnified the profanity and perversions while adding nudity. ''It is a *Hair* both overgrown and shorn,'' he said, yet he still recommended seeing it.

Breaking with Broadway convention, ''Hair'''s nude scene and profanity exemplified the theatre's movement into the ''freedom of expression'' already adapted by filmmakers and accepted by modern audiences. Those appalled by the adult nature of the production, believed Hewes, ''if they make the effort to stay with the impulses of the show's creativeness, . . . will be rewarded with a remarkable experience.'' ''One sits and gapes and listens and consents,'' commented Brendan Gill of the *New Yorker,* ''and the fact is that one can't not consent to this merry mind-blowing exercise in holy gibberish.''

While the musical was enjoying its long run on Broadway (1,742 performances), ''Hair'' was presented by various theatre companies throughout the United States, Canada, and Europe. The beauty of the international interpretations of ''Hair'' came from the fact that directors could add local humor, issues, and personalities, namely, Charles de Gaulle's wife and Mao Tse-tung, to their productions, endearing the play to individual nationalities without changing its intent. As Gerald Freedman, ''Hair'''s director when it first appeared at the New York Shakespeare Festival Theatre, explained: ''The hippies in Tokyo look exactly like the hippies in Rome and St. Mark's Place. And in every country you can find the immediate conditions that motivate unrest and dissatisfaction with the Establishment.''

On the international market, the musical grossed $350,000 per week and broke theatre sales records. For example, in Paris ''Hair'' was the first American musical presented in French to be a box office sellout. With $80,000 in advance sales, it surpassed the records of any other show.

Meanwhile in ''Hair'''s native country, critics were agreeing with an *America* reviewer's statement that the musical was ''novel and highly diverting'' until, as one *Time* critic noted in 1968, the social issues became dated. By its 1977 revival, the production's novelty wore off, and T. E. Kalem of *Time* remarked that ''a decade of history . . . [wrote] good night to *Hair.*''

The musical was no longer timely; it was neither history nor nostalgia. As Richard Eder said, ''its message—liberation, joy, pot and multiform sex, the vision of youth as a social class of its own and, in short, the notion that there can be flowers without stalks, roots or muck to grow in—has faded.'' Cultural, psychological, and intellectual changes since 1967 removed the play from the audience. The passion aroused by the Vietnam War in the 1960's had cooled ten years later, so viewers in 1977 found the topic emotionally distant. ''O for a depilatory,'' wrote Simon, ''to rid us of this unwanted (worse than face or body) *Hair*!''

After seeing the 1979 film adaptation of ''Hair,'' Jack Kroll advised audiences to ''forget about *Hair* being dated.'' ''Milos Forman's new film,'' he said, ''treats the 'American Tribal Love-Rock Musical' exactly as it should be treated—as a myth of our popular consciousness, no more dated than your last dream of happiness after a bad day in the real world.'' Forman, the movie's director, added a plot focusing on the character of Claude, a chronological structure, and dialogue to his version of the musical. Working on the premise that ''Hair'' itself was a cultural event of the sixties, the film examined the mood that permeated America during that period of history, and it put the social and cultural issues of that time, such as Vietnam, in historical perspective. Instead of just nostalgia, '' 'Hair' is . . . a loving, knowing tribute,'' wrote Kroll, ''to an amazing moment when American innocence tried to cleanse itself of corruption with the ancient energies of music and dance.''

In 1972, Ragni introduced ''Dude, the Highway Life'' to Broadway audiences. This musical, labeled ''the son of 'Hair,''' was similar to its predecessor in form and plotlessness. The theme of ''Dude,'' critics assumed, exemplified the loss of innocence. A god-like creature named #33 and his entourage of three goddesses confronted the devil-like Zero and his two cohorts, proving to Clive Barnes that ''all the world's a stage and the actors [are] Jesus-people at their symbolic heart.'' Apparently a variation of the Genesis story, ''Dude'' represented Adam and Eve through the characters of Harold and Reba, two actors who believed they had landed roles in ''Richard III.'' Tempted by Zero, Adam and Eve became the parents of Dude, who grew into a lascivious drug addict. Downhearted, Dude's mother wondered where her husband failed her son while Dude's father questioned where his wife went wrong. At the production's end, #33 comforted Harold and Reba, explaining that life is just a stage play, and defeated Zero.

A familiar story line, but the play was still unintelligible. ''I'm very fond of Ragni but the truth must be told,'' said the musical's star William Redfield. ''The songs were great but the script remained a mass of undoable nonsense.'' No element in ''Dude'' tied it together. The bits of content that were apparent were compared by a *New York Times* critic to ''carelessly scrawled telephone messages'' strewn about for anybody that could find them to pick up. The play's music, heralded by some critics, functioned ''to mask the absence of anything strong enough to offer frame or excuse for the evening,'' noted Walter Kerr. Even the humor in ''Dude'' was too typical to save it. Lines like ''get down there off your asteroid'' prompted Kerr to say that none of the humor in the musical ''would have been considered good enough, or even bad enough, to have done duty at Minsky's in the twilight of burlesque.''

Besides the shortcomings of its plot, "Dude" met with many production problems, the first of which was finding a theatre. Initially, Ragni wanted to reconstruct the Shubert Theatre for his production. Though the negotiations were lengthy and expensive, his backers, Peter and Adela Holzer, arranged for the Shubert to be taken apart for the musical, but restored when the play closed. Nevertheless, by the time the negotiations were completed, Ragni had changed his mind and rejected the Shubert. "Dude" was finally booked for the Broadway Theatre, which is known as the "death house" to show people since so many unsuccessful works open there. Then the project faced delays in obtaining the building permits required to carry out the extensive reconstruction to the interior of the Broadway.

Ragni planned to refurbish the Broadway Theatre so that a closer relationship between the players and the spectators could be established. He moved the stage over the conventional orchestra pit and banked seats all around it, making the stage an arena surrounded by the audience. He suspended cupids, trapezes, and vines from the ceiling of the theatre as well as a rock group from a theatre box. Compared to a circus ring, the stage was supplemented with runways and rostrums.

Hoping to create the illusion of heaven and hell in "Dude," Ragni had the stage covered with two tons of earth. But the clouds of dirt and dust that resulted impeded the actors' performances, so the soil was watered down to eliminate the dust storms. This left the cast standing in mud. Eventually the stage was covered with synthetic dirt made of plastic.

In addition to its setting problems, the stage itself proved too small. "An amphitheatre without elbow room," as Kerr called it, the stage was crowded with actors who appeared to the critic to be in a situation analogous to a traffic jam. Plus the stage had insufficient access to electrical outlets, leaving wires lying in aisles, between audience members, and on stairs. Such wiring difficulties, one *New York Times* reviewer thought, would have "disturbed an alert Fire Commissioner."

Many of the other innovations Ragni devised for "Dude" required modification, too. For example, the librettist considered releasing live butterflies in the audience or allowing pigs and chickens to run through the theatre during intermission. Ragni's script also needed revision. Originally two thousand pages long, the manuscript was pared down to one-tenth that size, but the story made no sense. ". . . [I]t had no plot line," Adela Holzer told the *New York Times.* "That worried me a little. I see now it should have worried me more."

Ragni refused to rewrite "Dude" until the producers threatened to close the show. So the actors in the starring roles became their own writers. "We had to," said Rae Allen and Redfield. "It was either write it or stand mute in the confusion." In fact, the script changed so drastically and so often that producing an accurate program was impossible.

The cast, too, underwent variations. Kevin Geer, a twenty-three-year-old white man, was originally hired to play the title role. To Ragni's dismay, his producers felt that Geer was "probably a talented actor but this was a major singing role," and the backers did not think Geer could sing. A black eleven-year-old took over the role of Dude, necessitating the script's revision to allow for "big Dude," played by Nat Morris, and "little Dude" roles. Geer, however, was featured on the promotional material.

The rest of the company became disgruntled. A meeting to discuss the play's situation was held, and, reported Redfield, "we became hysterical and released all our hostilities about the show, our fears. 'When was Gerry going to write some new dialogue?' we screamed. Later we began yelling about

our careers and what the theatre meant to us and what life on earth meant to us. . . ." Ragni's sister recorded the proceedings of the meeting; she gave them to her brother; and he incorporated the statements into the dialogue of the play along with autobiographical comments referring to "Hair." Ragni's brother, a Catholic priest, also contributed to the musical. According to the *New York Times,* he barraged "the production staff with religious ideas" until "he was finally barred from the theatre."

Initially, "Dude" met with unfavorable audience reactions. "The audience wanted to kill," Redfield remembered. "They kept yelling 'rip-off!'" After opening night reviews, "Dude"'s box office sales only amounted to $500. In total, the play cost its backers close to $1 million.

Critically, the play commanded attention because it claimed that it would restructure modern theatre. The staging met with some acceptance since, as Barnes observed, "it does have a freshness for Broadway and seems a real attempt to involve the entire audience for a big musical in a closer relationship with the cast than is customary." But the musical still did not revolutionize the theatre, said Kerr, although the critic explained that "Dude" did have a mission. "Dude" served as an example to other rock musicals, illustrating the plight of a plotless show whose music alone is appealing. "It may have become an inadvertent function of 'Dude,'" Kerr noted, "to expose that weakness so blatantly that all future rock musicals will have to face up to it before they dare take guitar or saw in hand." When rock musicals refuse to adopt plot foundations, Kerr concluded, they become concerts instead of theatrical productions.

"Dude"'s director Tom O'Horgan disagreed: "When an innovative musical like 'Dude' fails, it makes it 95 per cent more difficult to get fresh experimental stuff on. 'Dude' was different—but it was a good show."

MEDIA ADAPTATIONS: In 1979, director Milos Forman adapted "Hair" into a United Artists motion picture, starring John Savage, Treat Williams, and Beverly D'Angelo.

BIOGRAPHICAL/CRITICAL SOURCES: New York Times, October 28, 1959, October 19, 1964, November 11, 1966, October 30, 1967, November 14, 1967, November 19, 1967, December 22, 1967, April 30, 1968, May 19, 1968, September 29, 1968, February 5, 1969, June 2, 1969, September 13, 1969, January 13, 1970, September 5, 1970, September 27, 1970, October 10, 1972, October 22, 1972, October 6, 1977, March 25, 1979; *New Yorker,* November 11, 1967, May 11, 1968, June 14, 1969, September 23, 1972, October 21, 1972, October 17, 1977, April 16, 1979; *Newsweek,* November 13, 1967, May 13, 1968, July 7, 1969, October 30, 1972, October 17, 1977, March 19, 1979; *New Republic,* November 18, 1967, April 14, 1979; *Nation,* November 20, 1967, October 30, 1972; *Dance Magazine,* December, 1967, July, 1968.

Saturday Review, January 13, 1968, May 11, 1968; *Reporter,* April 4, 1968; *Time,* May 10, 1968, December 12, 1969, October 23, 1972, October 17, 1977, March 19, 1979; *Commonweal,* May 17, 1968, May 25, 1979; *National Review,* May 21, 1968, March 24, 1970, May 11, 1979; *America,* June 8, 1968, April 7, 1979; *Saturday Evening Post,* August 10, 1968; *Harper,* September, 1968; *L'Express,* June 9-15, 1969; *Wall Street Journal,* June 11, 1969; *Hi Fi,* July, 1969; *Theology Today,* July, 1969; *Opera News,* December 20, 1969; David Ewen, *New Complete Book of the American Musical Theatre,* Holt, 1970; *Life,* April 17, 1970; *Ebony,* May, 1970; *English Journal,* May, 1971; *Vogue,* October 15, 1972; *New York Post,* October 6, 1977; *New York,* October 24, 1977, March 19,

1979; Stanley Richards, *Great Rock Musicals,* Stein & Day, 1979; *Maclean's,* March 26, 1979; *New Leader,* April 9, 1979; *Encore,* April 16, 1979; *Esquire,* May 8, 1979; *USA Today,* July, 1979; *Contemporary Literary Criticism,* Volume 17, Gale, 1981.*

—*Sketch by Charity Anne Dorgan*

* * *

RAHV, Betty T(homas) 1931-

PERSONAL: Born March 30, 1931, in Charleston, W.Va.; daughter of Andrew S. and Marion (Pope) Thomas; children: William L.S. McIlvain. *Education:* Sweet Briar College, B.A., 1953; Middlebury College, M.A., 1955; Indiana University, Ph.D., 1968. *Home:* 67 Dedham St., Newton, Mass. 02161. *Office:* Boston College, Chestnut Hill, Mass. 02167.

CAREER: Brandeis University, Waltham, Mass., instructor in French literature, 1961-64; University of Massachusetts, Boston, assistant professor, 1965-70; Boston College, Chestnut Hill, Mass., associate professor, 1970—. *Member:* Modern Language Association of America, American Association of Teachers of French, Renaissance Society of America. *Awards, honors:* Fulbright scholarship for France; grant from Government of West Germany.

WRITINGS: From Sartre to the New Novel, Kennikat, 1972.

WORK IN PROGRESS: Nietzsche's Notion of Decadence; The Marais Recaptured.

* * *

RAI, Kul B(husan) 1937-

PERSONAL: Born May 4, 1937, in India; came to the United States in 1965, naturalized citizen, 1976; son of Laj Pat and Prakash Rai; married Priya Muhar (a librarian), June 12, 1962. *Education:* Patna University, B.A. (with honors), 1958, M.A., 1960; University of Rochester, Ph.D., 1970. *Home:* 10 Charles Court, North Haven, Conn. 06473. *Office:* Department of Political Science, Southern Connecticut State College, New Haven, Conn. 06515.

CAREER: Denison University, Granville, Ohio, assistant professor of political science, 1968-69; Southern Connecticut State College, New Haven, assistant professor, 1969-73, associate professor, 1973-77, professor of political science, 1977—. Visiting fellow at Yale University, 1975, 1979, visiting lecturer, 1976, 1979. *Member:* American Political Science Association.

WRITINGS: (With John Blydenburgh) *Political Science Statistics,* Hollbrook Press, 1973. Contributor to political science journals.

WORK IN PROGRESS: American Aid Repayments; Power and Conflict in Three Worlds.

* * *

RAKOWSKI, James Peter 1945-

PERSONAL: Born September 5, 1945, in Philadelphia, Pa.; son of Alexander and Mary (Mocrytzki) Rakowski; married Daphne M. Evans, September 2, 1972; children: David, Susan. *Education:* Princeton University, B.A. (cum laude), 1967; Columbia University, Ph.D., 1971; postdoctoral study at University of British Columbia, 1971-72. *Home:* 2934 Cross Village Cove, Germantown, Tenn. 38138. *Office:* Department of Marketing, Memphis State University, Memphis, Tenn. 38152.

CAREER: University of Minnesota, Minneapolis, assistant professor of management, 1972-78; Memphis State University, Memphis, Tenn., associate professor, 1978-81, professor of marketing, 1981—. *Member:* American Economic Association, American Society of Traffic and Transportation, Western Economic Association, Southwestern Marketing Association, Southern Marketing Association.

WRITINGS: Transportation Economics, Gale, 1976; (contributor) Grant Davis, editor, *Collective Ratemaking in the Motor Carrier Industry,* Interstate, 1980. Contributor of more than twenty articles and reviews to business and economic journals.

WORK IN PROGRESS: Research on business logistics management, transportation system analysis, and industrial development.

SIDELIGHTS: Rakowski told *CA:* "For anyone writing on business-related topics, the last few years have brought momentous change. The consumer movement of the seventies and the recent move to lessen government regulation have changed the business environment in many ways. The challenge of business over the next decade will be to achieve societal economic goals and productive efficiency with minimal negative impact on any specific subgroups."

* * *

RAMRUS, Al 1930-

PERSONAL: Born November 19, 1930, in Brooklyn, N.Y.; son of Max (a postal supervisor) and Miriam (Cooper) Ramrus; married Alleen Morris (a clothing designer), June 2, 1973; children: Tracey. *Education:* Attended City College of New York (now of the City University of New York), 1948-52. *Politics:* Libertarian. *Religion:* None. *Home:* 15254 Earlham St., Pacific Palisades, Calif. 90272. *Agent:* William Morris Agency, 151 El Camino Dr., Beverly Hills, Calif. 90212.

CAREER: CHML-Radio, Hamilton, Ontario, Canada, newsman, 1954-56; "Mike Wallace Interview," New York, N.Y., writer and reporter, 1956-61; Wolper Productions, Los Angeles, Calif., writer and producer of television documentaries, 1961-63; writer. *Awards, honors:* Christopher Award from Film Council of Greater Columbus, 1963, for "George Bernard Shaw," and 1973, for "The World Turned Upside Down"; George Foster Peabody Award from University of Georgia, 1963, for "Biography" series; award from Venice Film Festival, 1964, for "How to Succeed as a Gangster"; Gold Medal from Atlanta Film Festival, Silver Award from New York Film Festival, and President's Award from Columbus Film Festival, all 1972, all for "Surrender at Appomatox."

WRITINGS: (With John Herman Shaner) *The Ludendorff Pirates* (novel), Doubleday, 1978.

Screenplays; with Shaner, except as noted: (With James Schmerer) "World Without Sun" (documentary), Columbia, 1964; "Halls of Anger," United Artists, 1971; "Island of Dr. Moreau," American International, 1978; "Goin' South," Paramount, 1979.

Teleplays: "George Bernard Shaw" (documentary), National Broadcasting Co. (NBC), 1963; "How to Succeed as a Gangster" (documentary), NBC, 1964; "Surrender at Appomatox" (documentary), Columbia Broadcasting System (CBS), 1972; "The World Turned Upside Down" (documentary), CBS, 1973; (with Shaner) "My Husband Is Missing," NBC, 1980; (with Shaner) "The Darker Side of Terror," CBS, 1980.

WORK IN PROGRESS: The Final Conspiracy, a novel.

SIDELIGHTS: Ramrus told *CA:* "Somerset Maugham once described the writer's chief job as making the reader want to turn the page and find out what happens next. That just about sums it up for either fiction or nonfiction, print or film. A writer's characters, subject matter, themes, etc., frequently just drop into his lap, born more often than not in his subconscious. The hard part is putting them together so they grab the reader or audience by the mind or by the emotions (both at the same time is best) and refuse to let go. The finished product should look inspired, as natural as a rushing river or a soaring eagle. But it's about as natural, or easy, as laying hexagonal eggs."

*   *   *

RAND, Ayn 1905-1982

OBITUARY NOTICE—See index for *CA* sketch: Born February 2, 1905, in St. Petersburg, Russia (now Leningrad, U.S.S.R.); died March 6, 1982, in New York, N.Y. Philosopher, playwright, screenwriter, and author who developed the pro-capitalist philosophy of objectivism and the concept of rational selfishness through her four novels, *We the Living, Anthem, The Fountainhead,* and *Atlas Shrugged.* Rand graduated from the University of Leningrad in 1924 at the age of nineteen, and two years later immigrated to the United States, where she worked in Hollywood as a movie extra and a junior scriptwriter. In 1937 she took a job, without pay, as a typist for architect Eli Jacques Kahn in order to do research work for *The Fountainhead.* Rand worked for various motion picture studios in a variety of jobs during the 1930's and 1940's, eventually writing the screenplay for *The Fountainhead* in 1949. After 1951 she devoted all her time to writing and lecturing. Following the publication of *Atlas Shrugged* in 1957, Rand abandoned the novel in favor of more direct exposition of her views, as in *For the New Intellectual: The Philosophy of Ayn Rand.* Rand's concept of rational selfishness is based on her belief that human survival is dependent upon the objective contributions of rational persons; that a system of laissez-faire capitalism rewards and promotes these contributions whereas collectivism demands the abdication of self, reinforces conformity, and thus stifles objective truth. She drew a distinction between rational selfishness and hedonism, in which pleasure is regarded as the only standard of morality. Rand's basic political principle was that no person or group had the right to initiate the use of physical force against others. Obituaries and other sources: *New York Times,* March 7, 1982, March 9, 1982; *Los Angeles Times,* March 7, 1982; *Detroit Free Press,* March 7, 1982; *London Times,* March 8, 1982.

*   *   *

RANDOLPH, Vance 1892-
(Anton S. Booker)

PERSONAL: Born February 23, 1892, in Pittsburg, Kan.; son of John and Theresa (Gould) Randolph; married Marie Wardlaw Wilbur, March 27, 1930 (deceased). *Education:* Kansas State Teachers College, A.B., 1914; Clark University, M.A., 1915; further graduate study at University of Kansas, 1922-24. *Politics:* Democrat. *Religion:* Episcopalian. *Home:* 900 North Leverett St., Apt. 206, Fayetteville, Ark. 72701.

CAREER: Staff writer for *Appeal to Reason,* 1917; University of Kansas, Lawrence, assistant instructor in psychology, 1924; Metro-Goldwyn-Mayer Studios, Culver City, Calif., scenario writer, 1933-34; assistant state supervisor of Federal Writers Project, 1936-37; free-lance writer, 1937—. Field worker for Archive of American Folklore, Library of Congress, 1941-43. *Military service:* Served in infantry of U.S. Army. *Member:*

American Folklore Society, American Dialect Society, Arkansas Folklore Society (past president), Sigma Xi, Beta Chi Sigma, Psi Chi, Elks, American Legion, Disabled American Veterans. *Awards, honors:* Litt.D. from University of Arkansas, 1951.

WRITINGS—Folklore: *The Ozarks: An American Survival of Primitive Society,* Vanguard, 1931; *Ozark Mountain Folks,* Vanguard, 1932; *From an Ozark Mountain Holler: Stories of Ozark Mountain Folk,* illustrated by Richard Loederer, Vanguard, 1933; (with Guy W. Von Schriltz) *Ozark Outdoors: Hunting and Fishing Stories of the Ozarks,* Vanguard, 1934.

(Editor and author of introduction) *An Ozark Anthology,* Caxton, 1940; (editor) *Ozark Folksongs,* State Historical Society of Missouri, 1946-50, Volume I: *British Ballads and Songs,* Volume II: *Songs of the South and West,* Volume III: *Humorous and Play-Party Songs,* Volume IV: *Religious Songs and Other Items; Ozark Superstitions,* Columbia University Press, 1947, later published as *Ozark Magic and Folklore,* Dover, 1964.

We Always Lie to Strangers: Tall Tales From the Ozarks, illustrated by Glen Rounds, Columbia University Press, 1951, reprinted Greenwood Press, 1974; *Who Blowed Up the Church House? and Other Ozark Folk Tales,* illustrated by Rounds, Columbia University Press, 1952, reprinted, Greenwood Press, 1975; (with George P. Wilson) *Down in the Holler: A Gallery of Ozark Folk Speech,* University of Oklahoma Press, 1953; *The Devil's Pretty Daughter and Other Ozark Folk Tales,* illustrated by Rounds, Columbia University Press, 1955; *The Talking Turtle and Other Ozark Folk Tales,* illustrated by Rounds, Columbia University Press, 1957; *Sticks in the Knapsack and Other Ozark Folk Tales,* illustrated by Rounds, Columbia University, 1958.

(Editor) *Hot Springs and Hell; and Other Folk Jests and Anecdotes From the Ozarks,* illustrated by William Cechak, Folklore Associates, 1965; *Ozark Folklore: A Bibliography,* Indiana University Research Center for the Language Sciences, 1972; *Pissing in the Snow and Other Ozark Folktales,* University of Illinois Press, 1976. Also editor of *"Unprintable" Songs From the Ozarks,* 1949.

Little Blue Books; published by Haldeman-Julius Co.: *Ancient Philosophers,* 1924; *Modern Philosophers,* 1924; *Religious Philosophers,* 1924; *Physiology Self Taught,* 1924; *How to Know the Song Birds,* 1925; (under pseudonym Anton S. Booker) *Freud on Sleep and Sexual Dreams,* 1925; *Beekeeping for Profit,* 1925; *Our Insect Enemies,* illustrated by Peter Quinn, 1925. Also author of *How to Know the Spiders,* illustrated by Quinn; *German Self Taught; Pocket Dictionary: English-French, French-English; Pocket Dictionary: English-German, German-English; The Psychology of Affections;* and *A History of the Mediaeval Christian Church.*

Little Blue Book "Life Among . . ." series: *Life Among the Bees,* 1924; . . . *Ants,* 1925; . . . *Butterflies,* 1925; . . . *Dragonflies,* 1925.

"The ABC of . . ." series; published by Vanguard: *The ABC of Evolution,* 1926; . . . *Biology,* 1927; . . . *Physiology,* 1927; . . . *Psychology,* 1927.

Other: *The Camp on Wildcat Creek,* illustrated by Howard Simon, Knopf, 1934; *Hedwig* (novel), Vanguard, 1935; (with Nancy Clemens) *The Camp-Meeting Murders,* Vanguard, 1936. Contributor to magazines, including *Journal of Contemporary Psychology* and *Esquire,* to anthropology journals, and to newspapers.

SIDELIGHTS: In his book *Pissing in the Snow,* Vance Randolph, a noted folklorist renowned for his study of the Ozarks, has compiled over one hundred examples of that region's ribald folk literature. Because of their bawdy nature, these anecdotes and folktales are usually avoided by compilers. But Randolph has succeeded in providing a scholarly volume that "gives a sensitive portrayal of a fast-vanishing breed of people, a vastly amusing insight to a way of life that is rapidly passing," remarked a *Choice* reviewer. Though some critics warn that readers may find the material offensive or in poor taste, many agree with the *BooksWest* reviewer who said: "Still, these tales represent a genuine thread of American culture, and have been collected and presented with great care."

BIOGRAPHICAL/CRITICAL SOURCES: Journal of American Folklore, July, 1954, October, 1973, January, 1979; *Choice,* June, 1973, April, 1977; *Bibliographical Society of America—Papers,* January, 1974; *BooksWest,* April, 1977; *New York Times Book Review,* November 27, 1977; *American Anthropologist,* March, 1978; *Changing Times,* April, 1978; *Modern Philology,* May, 1979.*

* * *

RANGELL, Leo 1913-

PERSONAL: Born October 1, 1913, in New York, N.Y.; son of Morris and Pauline (Kaiser) Rangell; married Anita J. Buchwald, February 22, 1939; children: Judith Ellen, Susan Roberta, Richard Neal, Paul Charles. *Education:* Columbia University, A.B., 1933; University of Chicago, M.D., 1937; psychoanalytic training at New York Psychoanalytic Institute, 1941-43, and Los Angeles Psychoanalytic Institute, 1946-50. *Home:* 456 North Carmelina Ave., Los Angeles, Calif. 90049.

CAREER: Licensed to practice medicine in New York, 1937, and California; diplomate of American Board of Neurology and Psychiatry; Brooklyn Jewish Hospital, Brooklyn, N.Y., intern, 1937-39; Montefiore Hospital, New York City, resident in neurology, 1939, research fellow in neuropsychiatry, 1942-43; Grasslands Hospital, Valhalla, N.Y., resident in psychiatry, 1940; New York State Psychiatric Institute and Hospital, New York City, resident in psychiatry, 1941; private practice of neurology and psychiatry, New York City, 1942-43; Columbia University College of Physicians and Surgeons, New York City, instructor in neurology, 1942-46; private practice of psychoanalysis and neuropsychiatry, Beverly Hills and Los Angeles, Calif., 1946—; University of California, Los Angeles School of Medicine, associate clinical professor of psychiatry, 1953-57, clinical professor of psychiatry, 1957—; Los Angeles Psychoanalytic Institute, Los Angeles, training analyst, 1956—, director of extension division, 1956-57; University of California, San Francisco, clinical professor of psychiatry, 1976—. John B. Turner Visiting Professor of Psychiatry at Columbia University Psychoanalytic Clinic for Training and Research, 1971-72. Fellow of Center for Advanced Study of Behavioral Sciences, 1962-63. Consultant to Reiss-Davis Clinic for Child Guidance, 1953-65. Member of board of trustees of Los Angeles Psychoanalytic Institute, 1958—; president of board of directors, Westwood Hospital, 1959-60. *Military service:* U.S. Army Air Forces, 1943-46, served in medical corps; became major.

MEMBER: International Psychoanalytic Association (vice-president, 1967-69; president, 1969-73), American Psychoanalytic Association (president, 1961-62, 1966-67), American Psychiatric Association, American Medical Association, Southern California Psychiatric Association (president, 1955-56), Los Angeles Psychoanalytic Society (president, 1956-58 and 1964-65). *Awards, honors:* International Clinical Essay prize from British Institute of Psychoanalysis, 1951 and 1953; Guggenheim fellow, 1971-72.

WRITINGS: The Mind of Watergate: An Exploration of the Compromise of Integrity, Norton, 1980. Contributor of articles to medical journals. Member of editorial boards of *Journal of the Philadelphia Association for Psychoanalysis, Imago, Israel Annals of Psychiatry and Related Disciplines,* and *Hillside Journal of Clinical Psychiatry.*

SIDELIGHTS: Rangell's book, *The Mind of Watergate,* is a psychoanalytical study of the political career of former U.S. President Richard M. Nixon and of the psychological relationship that existed between Nixon, his staff, and the American public through the course of the Watergate scandal. In the book Rangell contends that a parent-child relationship developed between a president and the public and that the initial reluctance of the public to believe that Nixon was involved in any wrongdoing in the Watergate affair was an extension of the psychological forces that cause children to resist the notion that their parents can do wrong.

BIOGRAPHICAL/CRITICAL SOURCES: New York Times, July 26, 1971; *New Republic,* March 29, 1980; *New York Times Book Review,* April 6, 1980; *Best Sellers,* June, 1980.*

* * *

RASCH, Sunna Cooper 1925-

PERSONAL: Born March 21, 1925, in Greenwich, N.Y.; daughter of Morris and Mary (Abrahams) Cooper; married Donald B. Rasch, October 26, 1947; children: Nancy Jo, Alfred Cooper. *Education:* New York College for Teachers (now State University of New York at Albany), B.A., 1945; graduate study at Columbia University, 1947, and New York University, 1958, 1964. *Home and office:* 19 Clinton Ave., Monticello, N.Y. 12701.

CAREER: Periwinkle Productions, Monticello, N.Y., founder, 1963, executive producer and president, 1964—. Co-founder of Dramatic Workshop in Sullivan County, N.Y., 1950; lecturer in poetry at State University of New York, 1966, Hofstra University, 1967, and St. Mary's College, 1967; regional director of Children's Theatre Conference, 1966-70. *Member:* International Association Theatre for Children and Youth, American Theatre Association, Actors' Equity Association.

WRITINGS: (Compiler with Lee Bennett Hopkins) *I Really Want to Feel Good About Myself: Poems by Former Drug Addicts,* Thomas Nelson, 1974.

Plays; all for children: "Poetry in 3-D," first produced in Middletown, N.Y., 1964; "The Magic Word," first produced in New York City, 1968. Also author of "Which Way, America," first produced in Chicago, Ill., and "Brumm, Brumm, Zip," first produced in New York City.

WORK IN PROGRESS: How to Start a Children's Theatre; compiling a collection of children's writings, *Merry Little Souls.*

SIDELIGHTS: Rasch told *CA:* "I grew up loving theatre. Acting was what I wanted most out of life, career-wise, but the practical instincts of my father directed me into getting a teaching certificate. In all my life I have taught only three years in a school system—but somewhere along the way I saw the magic that could be created if you merged theatre and education. It was a new concept then; now it is firmly established and referred to as 'the arts in education.'

"When I look back, I see how natural this was for me. I acted in summer stock, I did professional radio, I founded a community theatre group, I taught school, I had children. The latter is the most important thing that ever happened to me. I wanted to expose my own children to good children's theatre at the same time I wanted to share my own concepts of educational theatre with everybody else's children. That's how Periwinkle Productions was born. I do not really believe there is a difference between children's theatre and adult theatre. It is either *good* theatre or it is not. If it is good, one can appreciate it no matter the age.

"The characteristic element in my work is a core of *feeling* that makes a child respond, while he or she is simultaneously expanding his own/her own thinking, creativity, imagination. In addition, the actors must believe and respect the integrity of the work.

"In 1973, we toured Brooklyn with a poetry show. It was surprisingly successful and included some contemporary poetry, some original poetry, along with the classics. The original poetry dealt mostly with identity. This struck home and the principal asked me to research more on the subject to see if I could come back with another program that would reach those junior high students who were reaching out for the wrong things, like drugs. I volunteered my services at Samaritan Halfway Society and conducted poetry workshops. A two-time thing turned into a year's happiness for me as I met weekly and did creative writing with troubled young people. The end result, most inadvertently, is *I Really Want to Feel Good About Myself.* I still hear from some of these kids and number some among my closest friends. They are grown up, out in the world, beautiful people. Not everybody made it back, but most did.

"My personal/professional goals? I want to get back into acting, either on the stage or in commercials and documentaries."

*   *   *

RASKIN, Joseph 1897-1982

OBITUARY NOTICE—See index for *CA* sketch: Born April 14, 1897, in Russia (now U.S.S.R.); died January 26, 1982, in Manhattan, N.Y. Artist and author. Raskin's paintings and etchings have been widely exhibited in galleries in the United States, France, Germany, and Israel. Raskin and his wife, Edith Raskin, wrote several books for young adults about early American life, including *Indian Tales, Tales Our Settlers Told, Tales of Justice in Early America,* and *Indentured Servants.* Obituaries and other sources: *New York Times,* January 28, 1982; *AB Bookman's Weekly,* February 15, 1982.

*   *   *

RASKY, Harry 1928-

PERSONAL: Born September 5, 1928, in Toronto, Ontario, Canada; son of Leib (a teacher) and Perl (Krazner) Rasky; married Ruth Arlene Werkhoven (a researcher), March 20, 1965; children: Holly Laura, Adam Louis. *Education:* University of Toronto, B.A., 1949. *Residence:* Toronto, Ontario, Canada. *Agent:* Lucinda Vardey, 97 Maitland, Toronto, Ontario, Canada M4Y 1E3. *Office:* Canadian Broadcasting Corp., Box 500, Terminal A, Toronto, Ontario, Canada.

CAREER: Canadian Broadcasting Corp., Toronto, Ontario, producer, director, and writer, 1952-55; Columbia Broadcasting System, New York City, producer, director, and writer, 1955-60; National Broadcasting Co., New York City, producer, director, and writer, 1961; American Broadcasting Companies, Inc., New York City, producer, director, and writer, 1961-71; Canadian Broadcasting Corp., producer, director, and writer, 1971—. President of Harry Rasky Productions, Inc. Lecturer at universities, including Columbia University, Ohio State University, and New School for Social Research. *Member:* Directors Guild of America (member of board of direc-

tors), Writers Guild of America (East), National Academy of Television Arts and Sciences, Association of Canadian Television and Radio Artists.

AWARDS, HONORS: Emmy Award from Academy of Television Arts and Sciences, 1966, for "Hall of Kings"; award from Venice Film Festival, 1970, for "Upon This Rock"; awards from Association of Canadian Television and Radio Artists, 1973, for "Tennessee Williams' South," 1974, for "Next Year in Jerusalem," and 1981, for "Africa Week"; International Emmy Award from Academy of Television Arts and Sciences, 1975, for "Travels Through Life With Leacock," and 1978, for "Homage to Chagall: The Colours of Love"; nominations for Oscar from Motion Picture Academy of Arts and Sciences, 1978, for "Homage to Chagall: The Colours of Love"; Minneapolis Film Festival Award, 1980; grand prize from New York International Film and Television Festival; silver prize from Festival of Americas; New York Mayor's Citation; special jury prize from San Francisco International Film Festival; awards from American Council for Better Broadcasters, Writer's Guild of America, Freedom Foundation, Montreal World Film Festival, Toronto Festival of Festivals, Ohio State University, Overseas Press Club, and Australian National Advisory Board; other awards include Peabody Award, Sylvania Award, Jerusalem Medal, Hollywood International Television Award, Canadian Wilderness Award, Actra Prize, and International Golden Eagle Award.

WRITINGS: Nobody Swings on Sunday: The Many Lives and Films of Harry Rasky, (autobiography), P. Collier, 1980.

Television scripts: "Hall of Kings," American Broadcasting Co. (ABC-TV), 1966; "The Legend of Silent Night," ABC-TV, 1968-69; "Upon This Rock," National Broadcasting Co. (NBC-TV), 1971; "The Wit and World of George Bernard Shaw," Canadian Broadcasting Corp. (CBC-TV), 1971; "Tennessee Williams' South," CBC-TV, 1972; "Homage to Chagall: The Colours of Love," CBC-TV, 1977; "Arthur Miller on Home Ground," CBC-TV, 1979; "The Song of Leonard Cohen," CBC-TV, November 5, 1980; "The Man Who Hid Anne Frank," CBC-TV, December 17, 1980; "The Spies Who Never Were," CBC-TV, 1981. Also author of "An Invitation to the Wedding," 1972; "Next Year in Jerusalem," 1974; "Baryshnikov," 1974; "The Peking Man Mystery," 1977; "The Lessons of History," 1978; "Being Different," 1981; "Thorn of Plenty," ABC-TV; "This Proud Land," ABC-TV; "The Lion and the Cross," Columbia Broadcasting System (CBS-TV); "The African Revolution" series, CBS-TV; "Panama: Danger Zone," NBC-TV; "Cuba and Castro Today," ABC-TV; "The Forty-ninth State," CBS-TV; "A Child Is to Love"; and "The Twentieth Century." Contributor to "CBC Newsmagazine" series, CBC-TV.

Author of radio scripts for Canadian radio, including "George the Good." Contributor to United Features and to magazines and newspapers, including *Nation, Saturday Night,* and *Toronto Telegram.*

SIDELIGHTS: Rasky told *CA:* "I make literary films of compassion, a mixture of drama and documentary that the *Los Angeles Times* called 'Raskymentary.' I also broadcast and write works of love."

Rasky received international recognition in 1978 as author of "Homage to Chagall," a documentary on the ninety-year-old creator of numerous works celebrating Jewish traditions. For more than two years, Rasky conducted interviews with Chagall and studied the artist's writings as well as his work in painting, stained glass, tapestries, and other media. A *Saturday Review* critic called the film "a paean to life and the glories of living" and praised its "spiritual refreshment."

BIOGRAPHICAL/CRITICAL SOURCES: *Saturday Review,* June 25, 1977.

*   *   *

RASS, Rebecca   1936-

PERSONAL: Born December 9, 1936, in Israel; daughter of Meir (associated with a driving school) and Rachel (Berger) Wilcher; married Izzy Abrahami (a writer; marriage ended); children: Enid. *Education:* Attended University of Tel Aviv, 1955-57; State University of New York Empire State College, B.A., 1977; Brooklyn College of the City University of New York, M.F.A., 1979. *Home:* 319 Broadway, New York, N.Y. 10007.

CAREER: City College of the City University of New York, New York, N.Y., adjunct lecturer in English, 1971-78; Hofstra University, Long Island, N.Y., lecturer in writing, 1979—. Adjunct lecturer at Queens College of the City University of New York, 1978—, and Pace University, 1979—; member of faculty at University of Oslo, 1964, and University of Groningen, 1965-71. Gives poetry readings. *Member:* Poets and Writers, New York Press Club. *Awards, honors:* Fiction award from Creative Artists Public Service, 1981, for *Gemini People.*

WRITINGS: From A to Z (prose poem), Thomas Rap Publishers, 1969; *From Moscow to Jerusalem* (nonfiction), Shengold, 1976; *The Fairy Tales of My Mind* (novel), Lintel, 1978; *The Mountain* (novel), Lintel, 1982. Also author of *Word War I and Word War II* (poems), 1974.

Translator from English into Hebrew, including works by Graham Greene, James Michener, Willis Lindquist, and Izzy Abrahami.

Translator from French into Hebrew, including works by Guy de Maupassant and Sara Bernhardt.

Work represented in anthologies, including *Solo: Women on Woman Alone,* Dell, 1977; *New Writing From the Middle East,* New American Library, 1978. Cultural correspondent for *Yedioth Ahronoth,* 1965—. Author of a monthly column in *Zero.* Contributor to newspapers.

WORK IN PROGRESS: Gemini People, nonfiction; *On the Road,* a novel.

SIDELIGHTS: Rebecca Rass told *CA:* "From 1959 to 1971 I traveled throughout Europe. I spent a year in Paris, 1961, nine months in Ireland, two years in England, and a year in Norway, 1964. I spent a few months in Sweden, Denmark, and five years in Amsterdam, 1965-71, where I published my first book. It was done into a television show in Amsterdam and a multimedia opera in Germany.

"In my writing I venture beyond reality into the limitless world of the imagination, exploring different realities and alternative life styles. Realistic writing bores me. Writing devoid of poetic and philosophical levels does not excite me. In my own writing I try to merge fiction and nonfiction, prose and poetry, searching for unity. More than a vocation, writing is my life-style, my vision of the world, a total experience."

*   *   *

RAVIN, Neil   1947-

PERSONAL: Born May 13, 1947, in Washington, D.C.; son of Louis (a gerontologist) and Jean (a teacher; maiden name, Ziman) Ravin; married Claudia Reid (a nurse and midwife), May 13, 1979. *Education:* Brown University, A.B., 1969; Cornell University, M.D., 1973. *Residence:* Washington, D.C.

Office: Foxhall Square, Suite 212, 3301 New Mexico Ave. N.W., Washington, D.C. 20016.

CAREER: Cornell Medical Center, Ithaca, N.Y., 1973-76, began as intern, became junior resident, then senior resident; Cornell-New York Hospital, New York, N.Y., fellow in department of medicine, 1976-77; University of Rhode Island Health Services, Kingston, physician, 1977-78; Brown University, Providence, R.I., clinical instructor in medicine, 1977-79, instructor in community health and head of second medical service in medicine program, 1978-79; Yale University, New Haven, Conn., endocrinology fellow in department of medicine, 1979-81; in private practice, 1981—. Participant in Clinico-Pathological Conference in Rhode Island, 1979, and Society of Bone and Mineral Metabolism Meeting, 1981.

WRITINGS: M.D. (novel), Delacorte, 1981. Contributor to *New England Journal of Medicine* and *American Journal of Cardiology.*

WORK IN PROGRESS: An article to appear in a journal.

SIDELIGHTS: Ravin told *CA:* "People keep asking whether I'm a writer or a doctor, as if the two were mutually exclusive. I suppose I can see the point. I used to feel guilty reading a novel or taking the time to type up another crank letter to *Time.* Now I've got a financial excuse: I made more money this year from *M.D.* than I did from being an endocrine fellow. Not that that says a whole lot. Fellows aren't really supposed to make ends meet on their stipends. Moonlighting is built into the plan for postgraduate fellowships.

"My moonlighting was done in advance: two years before I headed for Yale I 'dropped out' for a year. I became a doctor at a college infirmary after all that highpowered training in New York. All my friends were horrified. People had stopped dropping out by the early 1970's and this was 1977. I was never one to be trendy: years after everyone else had stopped being disaffected, hippy, anti-establishment, and truculent I decided the straight and narrow path was a treadmill of little real value. So I took a chance and jumped off the academic carousel, went to Rhode Island, and wrote what became *M.D.* It didn't start out as *M.D.*

"It started out as *The Great White Tower* and was conceived as the *Catch-22* of medical novels. But I couldn't bring myself to do it. It turned out, as I entered the trance-like sessions of memory in which the book was written, that the hospital experience was not, after all, as absurd as the war experience. The absurd voice worked well enough, but was essentially a lie. The more I remembered the more it all made sense. There was plenty of craziness, of course, but basically the hospital is the polar opposite of war; it is man's last best work. Often it doesn't work, of course, but the whole idea springs from the noble side. So it changed from a farce, a depiction of absurdity, to a defense.

"It got finished, copied, and mailed off (unsolicited) to about seven publishers. Then I started getting the manuscripts back with nice, signed, encouraging letters from editors, but no takers. And walking past a bookstore, I caught sight of *House of God.* Shem did what I couldn't believe in—he indicted the whole effort of physician training in academic settings. And he got published.

"Oh well—people will hear what they want to hear. One of the editors suggested I get an agent, recommending Scott Meredith, who read it for a fee. It didn't fit his formula: reject. But ultimately, Sam Lawrence sent me a letter. He wanted me to work with Brendan Boyd, his editor. Brendan had pulled it out of the slush pile and was pushing Sam to take it on.

"Here I am in Washington, D.C., trying to get a practice in internal medicine underway and working on a book about medical researchers. And it won't be an indictment.

"Influences? Everyone always wants to know about influences. I read a lot of Hemingway, Heller, and Muriel Spark while I was writing *M.D.* Now I can't seem to put down Joseph Wambaugh, especially *The Choirboys.* Policemen and doctors see the raw side of people. I guess there are fewer misanthropes among the docs, but Wambaugh speaks clearly to me."

BIOGRAPHICAL/CRITICAL SOURCES: Washington Post Book World, March 8, 1981; *Philadelphia Inquirer,* April 4, 1981; *Anniston Star* (Ala.), April 5, 1981; *St. Paul Pioneer Press,* April 18, 1981.

*   *   *

RAWLINS, Clive Leonard 1940-

PERSONAL: Born July 20, 1940, in Birmingham, England; son of Leonard William and Mary Rawlins; married Veronica Ann Green (a pharmacist), March 13, 1964; children: Stephen-John, Philip Bruce. *Education:* Moorlands Bible College, diploma in theology, 1963; graduated (with distinction) from Victoria University of Manchester, 1968. *Home:* 1 Bridge St., East Linton, East Lothian, Scotland.

CAREER: Assistant financial accountant; ordained to Baptist ministry, 1968; worked in publishing, 1971-78; writer.

WRITINGS: (Editor) F. F. Bruce, *Answers to Questions,* Paternoster Press, 1972; (editor) William Barclay, *Men and Affairs,* Mowbray, 1978; (editor) *Index to Daily Study of the Bible,* University of St. Andrews Press, 1978; (contributor) *Plain Uncommon Man,* Hodder & Stoughton, 1980.

WORK IN PROGRESS: An authorized biography of William Barclay; a book on Old Testament theology.

AVOCATIONAL INTERESTS: Sport, driving fast cars, "do-it-yourself" work, photography, reading.

*   *   *

RAYMOND, James Crossley 1917-1981

OBITUARY NOTICE: Born February 25, 1917, in Riverside, Conn.; died of cancer, October 14, 1981, in Boynton Beach, Fla. Cartoon illustrator known for drawing the cartoon strip "Blondie." Raymond drew the immensely popular cartoon, which runs in more than eighteen hundred newspapers in fifty-five countries, for more than forty years. Obituaries and other sources: *New York Times,* October 15, 1981; *Chicago Tribune,* October 16, 1981; *Time,* October 26, 1981.

*   *   *

REED, Alison Touster 1952-
(Alison Touster)

PERSONAL: Surname is pronounced *Tau*-ster; born January 29, 1952, in Nashville, Tenn.; daughter of Oscar (a professor of biochemistry) and Eva Katherine (a professor of English) Touster; married Robert Murphy Reed (a psychiatrist). *Education:* Vanderbilt University, B.A. (summa cum laude), 1976, M.A., 1977. *Home:* 5303 Lancelot Rd., Nashville, Tenn. 37027.

CAREER: Vanderbilt University, Nashville, Tenn., teaching fellow in English, 1976—. *Member:* Academy of American Poets, Phi Beta Kappa. *Awards, honors:* First prize from Academy of American Poets, 1971, for "Neshoba County, Mississippi"; Merrill Moore Award for literary promise from Van-

derbilt University, 1976; Indiana University Foundation Award in Poetry from Indiana Writers Conference, 1976, for "The Act of Creation, or the Poet at His Desk."

WRITINGS—Under name Alison Touster: *The First Movement* (poetry), Dragon's Teeth Press, 1976; *Bid Me Welcome* (poetry), Golden Quill Press, 1978. Contributor to literary journals, including *Nimrod, Southern Poetry Review, DeKalb Literary Arts Journal, Hollins Critic, Poem, Huron Review,* and *Mississippi Valley Review.* Poetry editor of *Front Street Trolley.*

WORK IN PROGRESS: A Skein of Wild Ones, a volume of poetry.

*   *   *

REES, David Bartlett 1936-

PERSONAL: Born in 1936 in London, England; son of Gerald (a civil servant) and Margaret (Healy) Rees; married Jenny Lee Watkins (a teacher), July 23, 1966 (divorced); children: Stephen, Adam. *Education:* Queen's College, Cambridge, B.A., 1958. *Home:* Pilgrim Cottage, Crockernwell, Exeter, Devonshire, England. *Office:* School of Education, St. Luke's College, University of Exeter, Exeter EX1 2LU, England.

CAREER: Schoolmaster at secondary schools in London, England, 1960-65, and in Ickenham, England, 1965-68; St. Luke's College, Exeter, England, lecturer, 1968-73, senior lecturer, 1973-77; University of Exeter, Exeter, lecturer in education, 1977—. *Awards, honors:* Carnegie Medal from Library Association, 1978, for *The Exeter Blitz;* Other Award from Children's Rights Workshop, 1980, for *The Green Bough of Liberty.*

WRITINGS—Novels, except as noted: *Storm Surge,* Lutterworth, 1975; *Quinton's Man,* Dobson, 1976, Elsevier Nelson, 1979; *The Missing German,* Dobson, 1976; *Landslip* (juvenile), Hamish Hamilton, 1977; *The Ferryman,* Dobson, 1977; *The Spectrum,* Dobson, 1977; *Risks,* Heinemann, 1977, Thomas Nelson, 1978; *The Exeter Blitz,* Hamish Hamilton, 1978, Elsevier Nelson, 1980; *The House That Moved* (juvenile), Hamish Hamilton, 1978; *In the Tent,* Dobson, 1979; *Silence,* Dobson, 1979, Elsevier Nelson, 1981; *The Green Bough of Liberty,* Dobson, 1980; *The Lighthouse,* Dobson, 1980; *The Marble in the Water* (essays on children's writers), Horn Book, 1980; *The Night Before Christmas Eve* (juvenile), Wheaton, 1980; *Miss Duffy Is Still With Us,* Dobson, 1980; *A Beacon for the Romans* (juvenile), Wheaton, 1981; *Holly, Mud, and Whisky* (juvenile), Dobson, 1981; *The Milkman's on His Way,* Gay Men's Press, 1982; *The Flying Island* (juvenile), Dobson, 1982; *Beach Boy, Gipsy Girl,* Longman, in press.

Work represented in anthologies, including *Remember Last Summer?,* edited by John Foster, Heinemann, 1980; *Cracks in the Image,* Gay Men's Press, 1981. Author of column in *Gay News.* Regular contributor of book reviews to *Times Literary Supplement* and contributor to literature and library journals.

SIDELIGHTS: Rees commented: "I'm not sure why I write, but I hope my books will make teenagers and children happier than I was. I see connections between bits of my life and other people's lives and try to work them into a coherent, meaningful shape. I write a lot about disasters, ancestors, and landscape—place is *very* important to me—particularly Devonshire and Exeter, but also London, Greece, America, and Ireland."

AVOCATIONAL INTERESTS: Travel, classical music, attending concerts, surfing, tracing his family tree.

REESE, Algernon B(everly) 1896-1981

OBITUARY NOTICE: Born July 28, 1896, in Charlotte, N.C.; died after a long illness, October 19, 1981, in Bedford Hills, N.Y. Physician, educator, and author. Reese was internationally renowned for his contributions to ophthalmological medicine, particularly the diagnosis and treatment of retinoblastoma, a disease of malignant eye tumors in children. A leader in ophthalmic oncology and pathology, Reese treated many political figures and celebrities, including Madame Chiang Kaishek, the Duke and Duchess of Windsor, Babe Ruth, Bob Hope, and Ernest Hemingway. The majority of his professional career was spent in association with Columbia University, but he was a consultant to many medical institutions. Reese contributed numerous articles to scientific journals and wrote the leading textbook *Tumors of the Eye.* Obituaries and other sources: *Who's Who in America,* 41st edition, Marquis, 1980; *New York Times,* October 20, 1981.

* * *

REEVES, Amber
See BLANCO WHITE, Amber

* * *

REEVES, (Richard) Ambrose 1899-1980

OBITUARY NOTICE: Born December 6, 1899, in Norwich, Norfolk, England; died December 23, 1980, in England. Clergyman, anti-apartheid crusader, and author. From 1949 to 1961 Reeves was the Anglican bishop of Johannesburg, South Africa. As an opponent of the government policy of apartheid, he was deported in 1961. He then conducted his opposition as president of the British Anti-Apartheid Movement from 1970 until his death. Reeves also continued his crusade against apartheid in his writings, including *The Shooting at Sharpeville: The Agony of South Africa* and *South Africa, Yesterday and Tomorrow: A Challenge to Christians.* Obituaries and other sources: *Who's Who,* 132nd edition, St. Martin's, 1980; *The International Who's Who,* Europa, 1980; *The Annual Obituary 1980,* St. Martin's, 1981; *The Writers Directory, 1982-84,* Gale, 1981.

* * *

REEVES, Lawrence F. 1926-
(Warren Lyfick, R. Seever)

PERSONAL: Born June 2, 1926, in Belmont, Mass.; son of Ralph F. (a printer) and Lillian (a nurse; maiden name, Brandon) Reeves; married wife, Thetis Powers (a publisher), March 1, 1972; children: (first marriage) Kristin and Michael (twins). *Education:* Syracuse University, B.A., 1951, M.S.L.S., 1952. *Politics:* Liberal ("discouraged"). *Religion:* None. *Home:* Creamery Rd., Stanfordville, N.Y. *Office:* Harvey House Publishers, 20 Waterside Plaza, New York, N.Y. 10010.

CAREER: Associated with State University of New York at New Paltz, 1952-54; Dedham Public Library, Dedham, Mass., director, 1954-56; associated with State University of New York at New Paltz, 1956-59; Harper & Brothers, New York City, sales representative, 1956-59; Golden Press, New York City, sales manager, 1959-65; Grosset & Dunlap, Inc., New York City, vice-president, 1965-73; Harvey House Publishers, New York City, president, 1973—. *Member:* American Library Association, Syracuse University Library Associates (board of trustees). *Military service:* U.S. Navy, 1944-46.

WRITINGS—For children: (Compiler; under pseudonym Warren Lyfick) *The Little Book of Limericks* (illustrated by Chris Cummings), Harvey House, 1978; (under pseudonym R. Seever) *Mopeds,* Harvey House, 1979; (compiler; under pseudonym Warren Lyfick) *The Punny Pages* (illustrated by Cummings), Riverhouse, 1979; (under pseudonym Warren Lyfick) *Animal Tales* (illustrated by Joe Kohl), Riverhouse, 1980; (under pseudonym Warren Lyfick) *Little Book of Fowl Jokes* (illustrated by Cummings), Harvey House, 1980.

WORK IN PROGRESS: A book of fish stories, to be published under the pseudonym Warren Lyfick, and a Boston coloring book, to be published under the pseudonym R. Seever.

SIDELIGHTS: Lawrence Reeves commented: "I started doing a few books for kids for a number of reasons. One reason is that I am a poor sleeper and spend hours in the middle of the night reading. It seemed wise to try to do something more productive with that time. As a publisher I've discovered that it is often difficult to find an author who can write a simple declarative sentence. Once I learned how to do that I decided to try to write a book for kids. I did. It sold well. I'm not sure how I got started on joke books but I rather enjoy them. They are fun to do, although keeping the card index up is about as exciting as watching grass grow. Getting a good illustrator is important in joke books. I like to develop a good team effort. We sometimes take turns being the straight man.

"Do I think there is a place in children's literature for serious work? Of course. I may even try my pen at it sometime. One of the problems of writing for children is that kids don't get much chance to choose what they get to read. There seems always to be an adult standing between the author and the kid. The problem with adults is that they seem to lose their sense of 'wonderment' and excitement. They are often very much out of touch with the kids' world.

"Being the son of a printer I was early on instilled with a sense of the wonder of the printed word. There were always books in our house. There were three newspapers a day and who knows how many magazines. So I grew up to be a compulsive reader, even to the label on the ketchup bottle if there was nothing else. I guess publishing and now writing are logical extensions of that early environment. My goodness!"

* * *

REIG, June 1933-

PERSONAL: Born June 1, 1933, in Schenectady, N.Y.; daughter of Wallace J. (a business administrator) and Lillian (a pianist; maiden name, Gay) Wilson; married Robert Maxwell (a composer), November 26, 1969. *Education:* State University of New York at Albany, B.A. (summa cum laude), 1954; New York University, M.A., 1962, further graduate study, 1962-1967. *Home:* New York, N.Y. *Office:* Bunny/Chord Productions, Inc., 119 West 57th St., Suite 1106, New York, N.Y. 10019.

CAREER: New York University, New York City, university theatre producer and director, and instructor in dramatic arts, 1962-1967; National Broadcasting Co. (NBC-TV), New York City, writer, producer, and director, 1963-1976; Bunny/Chord Productions, Inc., New York City, president, 1972—. *Member:* National Academy of Television Arts and Sciences, Directors Guild of America, Writers Guild, National Audubon Society, National Wildlife Federation, Friends of Animals, Society for Animal Rights. *Awards, honors:* Prix Jeunesse for best children's program in the world, 1965, for "The World of Stuart Little"; Brotherhood Award from National Council of Christians and Jews, 1968, for "The Reluctant Dragon With Burr Tillstrom"; Christopher Award, 1971, for "As I See It"; Action for Children's Television award, 1973, for "Watch Your Child—The Me Too Show."

WRITINGS: Diary of the Boy King, Tutankhamen (juvenile; self-illustrated), Scribner, 1978.

Teleplays; first broadcast by National Broadcasting Co. (NBC-TV): "The World of Stuart Little," 1965; "The Heart of Christmas," 1965; "An Afternoon at Tanglewood," 1966; "Rabbit Hill," 1967; "The Enormous Egg," 1968; "The Reluctant Dragon With Burr Tillstrom," 1968; "Pets Allowed," 1970; "As I See It," 1971; "A Day With Bill Cosby," 1971; "Watch Your Child—The Me Too Show," 1972-73.

WORK IN PROGRESS: Two novels, entitled *My Sister's Keeper* and *The Boy Who Dared to Be Himself;* "Play With Me," a television series.

SIDELIGHTS: June Reig told *CA:* "Whether I am working on a teleplay or book, I write about things I believe children are interested in: feelings, animals, loving, and caring. As I see it, too much of the fare for young people gives them a distorted view of how much violence there is in the world, and I want to counteract that impression. I want to write about things that create a sense of warm comfort and an absence of anxiety. When I write about the darker things that do happen in life, it is *only* to help the young person understand the situation, himself, and others. But most important, as that *soupcon* of shallot to the salad, so is gentle humor to my writing, humor in the everyday things we do or don't do."

*　　　*　　　*

REINACH, Jacquelyn (Krasne) 1930-

PERSONAL: Born September 17, 1930, in Omaha, Neb.; daughter of Clyde and Dorothy (Reuben) Krasne; married Anthony M. Reinach, 1953 (divorced, 1961); married Harry Wolff, 1969 (divorced, 1972); married Paul B. Morofsky, 1973 (divorced, 1979); children: (first marriage) Barron Anthony, Alan Jay. *Education:* Attended Stanford University, 1947-48; University of California, Los Angeles, B.A., 1951. *Politics:* Libertarian. *Religion:* Jewish. *Home and office:* 1 Lincoln Plaza, New York, N.Y. 10023.

CAREER: Goodson-Todman Co., New York City, in television production, 1952-53; music therapist in Westchester County, N.Y., 1953-60; scriptwriter for Tottle (CBS-TV) and Fran Allison's "Learn at Home," 1960-64; Disco-book, Inc., New York City, co-founder and vice-president, 1970-75; writer. Designer of games. Co-founder and president of Childways, Inc.; director of Euphrosyne, Inc.; founder of Operation Saturday; president of Reinach Productions. Member of National Committee for Excellence in Children's Television programming. *Member:* American Society of Composers, Authors and Publishers (ASCAP), Child Study Association of America, Dramatists Guild, National Academy of Recording Arts and Sciences, Council for Basic Education. *Awards, honors:* American Society of Composers, Authors and Publishers award, 1970, for song "Liberation Now."

WRITINGS: Carefree Cooking, Hearthside, 1970; *Reading Awareness Program: My Book Book,* with teacher's manual and tape cassettes, Lippincott, 1971; (with Charles Walcutt) *The Reading Works* (with own musical compositions), New Dimensions in Education, 1975.

"Headstart" series; with Shari Lewis; published by McGraw: *The Headstart Book of Knowing and Naming,* 1966; . . . *Look-*

ing and Listening, 1966; . . . *Thinking and Imagining,* 1966; . . . *Be Nimble and Be Quick,* 1968.

"Sweet Pickle" series; edited by Ruth Lerner Perle; illustrated by Richard Hefter; published by Holt: *Who Stole Alligator's Shoe?,* 1977; *Fixed by Camel,* 1977; *Elephant Eats the Profits,* 1977; *Goose Goofs Off,* 1977; *Me Too Iguana,* 1977; *Quail Can't Decide,* 1977; *Fish and Flips,* 1978; *Jackal Wants Everything,* 1978; *Nuts to Nightingale,* 1978; *Octopus Protests,* 1978; *Rest Rabbit Rest,* 1978; *Happy Birthday, Unicorn,* 1979. Also author of *Scaredy Bear.*

"Sweet Pickle" series; published by Euphrosyne: *Rainy Day Parade,* 1981; *Wait Wait Wait,* 1981; *What a Mess,* 1981; *A Bad Break,* 1981; *What's So Great About Nice?,* 1981; *Wet Paint,* 1981; *Ice Cream Dreams,* 1981.

Other "Sweet Pickle" materials: "Early Childhood Filmstrip Programs," Phoenix Films/BFA, 1978; "Reading Readiness" (multi-media program), BFA/Holt Education, 1978; "Sweet Pickles Double Record Album," Euphrosyne Music, 1979; "Sweet Pickle Activity Records," Disc Incentive, 1981.

Other recordings: "A Child's Introduction to Reading, Writing, and Arithmetic," Golden Records, 1963; "Music to Read the Pretenders By," Mercury Records, 1969; "Liberation Now," Decca Records, 1970.

WORK IN PROGRESS: "Play Along Stories," a new version of the "Headstart" series, publication by Scholastic, Inc., expected in 1982; more "Sweet Pickles" books, for Random House; an adult love story for musical theatre.

SIDELIGHTS: Reinach told *CA:* "In the Midwest, where I spent my first seven years, there was very little joy. It was the Depression, and daily life concentrated on where the next meal was coming from. I always thought there was more to life than that—and found my answers in the library. I must have read my way through every children's book and begun on quite unsuitable adult books before I was nine. The greatest punishment for me was not to be able to go to the library. (I read *Les Miserables* about the age of nine because my father thought I was staying indoors too much and told me I could only take *one* book out of the library that week. So I chose the fattest, biggest, thickest book I could!)

"I knew I wanted to be a writer by the time I was ten, but of what? I wrote stories, poetry, and songs constantly and had some poems published in the *Oakland Tribune.* At Stanford University I had my own radio show, making up silly stories on the origin of pop songs; at U.C.L.A. I wrote the campus musical in my senior year while completing my degree in psychology. At that time, I had no idea where my interests in both psychology and writing were going. Over the years, as I began to develop multi-media programs, always writing music and using music to communicate ideas, I realized that there is a common theme behind everything I've written—a desire to communicate feelings, even to translate hard facts into a feeling state to make them relevant. I see literary form as the means of communication. So, some ideas seem better in story form, some in song, some in graphics. The 'Sweet Pickles' series is a synthesis of everything I believe in."

Books in the "Sweet Pickles" series have been published in England, Australia, New Zealand, Israel, France, Germany, Switzerland, Spain, Latin America, Italy, Scandinavia, Belgium, Holland, and Luxembourg. Selected books have been sold through the Sweet Pickles Book Club, the Better Homes and Gardens Book Club, and the Book-of-the-Month Club. Captain Kangaroo has devoted parts of his CBS-TV shows to the adventures of the A-to-Z animals in the town of Sweet Pickles.

REKAI, Kati 1921-
(Kati)

PERSONAL: Born October 20, 1921, in Budapest, Hungary; married John Rekai (a surgeon and hospital administrator); children: Julie Rekai Rickerd, Judyth Rekai Nuttall. *Education:* Attended high school in Budapest, Hungary. *Home:* 45 Nanton Ave., Toronto, Ontario, Canada M4W 2Y8.

CAREER: Writer. Vice-president of women's committee of Crest Theatre and board of directors of Podium Literary Cabaret; chairman of public relations for Theatre Toronto Guild and Guild of St. Lawrence Centre for the Arts; executive member of Toronto Welcoming Board. *Member:* Writers Union of Canada.

WRITINGS—Under name Kati; juveniles: "The Adventures of Mickey, Taggy, Puppo and Cica, and How They Discover . . ." series; published by Canadian Stage & Arts Publications: *The Adventures of Mickey, Taggy, Puppo and Cica, and How They Discover Toronto,* 1976, 3rd edition, 1979; . . . *Ottawa,* 1976; . . . *Montreal,* 1979; . . . *Budapest,* 1979; . . . *Kingston and the Thousand Islands,* 1979; . . . *Vienna,* 1980; . . . *Amsterdam,* in press; . . . *Zurich, Geneva, Davos and Crans-Montana,* in press.

Also author of puppet plays, including "The Great Totem Pole Caper," "The Tale of Tutankhamun," and "The Boy Who Forgot."

Contributor to magazines.

SIDELIGHTS: Kati Rekai's books and stories have been adapted for the puppet stage and translated into French.

In *Spark,* the in-house publication of Toronto's Central Hospital, she wrote: "My realization of the need of a children's guide book to Toronto (and to other cities in Canada) dates back to 1967, Canada's Centennial Year. This was the year when Canada was truly 'put on the map' and the whole world started to discover that, apart from the cold, Eskimos, Indians and hockey, Canada also had beauty, history, culture and modern, dynamic cities, but alas, visitors could not find any guidebooks for their children about Toronto.

"Only after I started to show the manuscripts for approval, however, did I realize how great an impact my idea for a children's guide book would have on the community.

"My favorite subjects were always history, geography and the arts, and in the *Adventures of Mickey, Taggy, Puppo and Cica and How They Discover Toronto* I not only wanted to describe the landmarks, but also convey my love of them. The mixture of learning with pleasure, and showing Toronto's international side in its people, buildings, arts, foods, merchandise and medical services and the accessibility to all this by public transportation was my objective."

BIOGRAPHICAL/CRITICAL SOURCES: Spark, Fall, 1974; *Toronto,* October 31, 1979.

* * *

REVES, Emery 1904-1981

OBITUARY NOTICE: Born February 16, 1904, in Bacsfoldvar, Hungary; died in 1981 in Switzerland. Publisher and author. In 1930 Reves founded the Cooperation Press Service and Cooperation Publishing Co., an international syndicate for publication of the views of leading statesmen. Before communications were curtailed by World War II, his syndicate was publishing in four hundred newspapers almost every day. Antagonistic toward Nazis and Fascists, he refused to allow his syndicate to become a Nazi propaganda machine, and in 1935 he was forced to leave his headquarters in Rome after printing an anti-Fascist article. In the early stages of World War II he provided a valuable service for democratic leaders, printing testimonials of German and Italian nationals opposed to Nazi and Fascist doctrines. In February, 1941, Reves came to the United States and established his firm in New York City. The books he commissioned included *I Paid Hitler* by Fritz Thyssen and *Conversations With Hitler* by Herman Rauschning. His firsthand observations of the war inspired his own political theories, which are expressed, in part, in his own books *The Anatomy of Peace* and *A Democratic Manifesto.* Obituaries and other sources: *Current Biography,* Wilson, 1946; *AB Bookman's Weekly,* November 2, 1981.

* * *

REY, Margret (Elisabeth) 1906-

PERSONAL: Born in May, 1906, in Hamburg, Germany (now West Germany); came to the United States in 1940, naturalized citizen, 1946; married H(ans) A(ugusto) Rey (a writer and illustrator), 1935 (died, 1977). *Education:* Attended Bauhaus, 1927, Dusseldorf Academy of Art, 1928-29, and University of Munich, 1930-31. *Home and office:* 14 Hilliard St., Cambridge, Mass. 02138. *Agent:* A. P. Watt & Son, 26-28 Bedford Row, London WC1R 4HL, England.

CAREER: Reporter and advertising copywriter in Berlin, Germany, 1928-29; held one-woman shows of watercolors in Berlin, 1929-34; photographer in London, England, Hamburg, Germany, and Rio de Janeiro, Brazil, 1930-35; free-lance writer in Paris, France, 1936-40, and in New York, N.Y., 1940-63; writer of children's books, 1937—; Brandeis University, Waltham, Mass., instructor in creative writing, 1978—. *Awards, honors:* Children's Book Award from the Child Study Association of America, 1966, for *Curious George Goes to the Hospital.*

WRITINGS—All illustrated by husband, H. A. Rey: *Pretzel,* Harper, 1944; *Spotty,* Harper, 1945; *Pretzel and the Puppies,* Harper, 1946; *Billy's Picture,* Harper, 1948.

With H. A. Rey: *How the Flying Fishes Came Into Being,* Chatto & Windus, 1938; *Raffy and the Nine Monkeys,* Chatto & Windus, 1939, reprinted, 1960, published as *Cecily G. and the Nine Monkeys,* Houghton, 1942; *How Do You Get There?,* Houghton, 1941; *Elizabite: The Adventures of a Carnivorous Plant,* Harper, 1942; *Anybody at Home?* (verse), Chatto & Windus, 1939, reprinted, 1951; *Tit for Tat* (verse), Harper, 1942; *Where's My Baby?* (verse), Houghton, 1943; *Feed the Animals* (verse), Houghton, 1944; *Mary Had a Little Lamb,* Penguin, 1951; *See the Circus* (verse), Houghton, 1956.

"Curious George" series; published by Houghton (all titles published in England as "Zozo" series by Chatto & Windus): *Curious George,* 1941; *Curious George Takes a Job,* 1947; *Curious George Rides a Bike,* 1952; *Curious George Gets a Medal,* 1957; *Curious George Flies a Kite,* 1958; *Curious George Learns the Alphabet,* 1963; *Curious George Goes to the Hospital,* 1966.

WORK IN PROGRESS: Curious George films for television.

SIDELIGHTS: Born and educated in Germany, Margret Rey studied art at various German schools before moving to Brazil in 1935. While working as a photographer there, she met H.A. Rey, with whom she founded Rio de Janeiro's first advertising agency. The couple subsequently married and moved to Paris, where Margret worked as a free-lance writer while H.A. sold sketches to numerous French publications.

In Paris the Reys began collaborating on children's books, with Margret providing the text for H.A.'s illustrations. Their book *Raffy and the Nine Monkeys* inspired their popular "Curious George" series, written in the United States after the Reys fled Paris during World War II.

The "Curious George" books, about the antics of a mischievous monkey named George, were highly praised by critics and are now regarded as classics. Translated into twelve different languages and published as the "Zozo" series in England, the humorous, colorful volumes are still enjoyed by countless children.

Margret Rey told *CA:* "I now am involved in supervising the production of Curious George films for television and am teaching a course on the craft of writing. I enjoy teaching enormously."

*   *   *

REYNOLDS, Malvina   1900-1978

OBITUARY NOTICE: Born August 23, 1900, in San Francisco, Calif.; died March 17, 1978, in Berkeley, Calif. Singer, guitarist, composer, and lyricist. Reynolds began her music career in the 1950's as a writer of protest songs. Her many popular songs include "Little Boxes," "What Have They Done to the Rain?," and "Turn Around." Also a writer of children's music, she was a frequent guest on the children's television show "Sesame Street." Her songs were popular with other recording artists and have been recorded by Harry Belafonte, Joan Baez, and Pete Seeger. Obituaries and other sources: *Biographical Dictionary of American Music,* Parker Publishing, 1973; *Who's Who in America,* 40th edition, Marquis, 1978; *Time,* April 3, 1978; *Rolling Stone,* May 18, 1978.

*   *   *

REYNOLDS, (Marjorie) Moira Davison   1915-
(Marna Moore)

PERSONAL: Born June 22, 1915, in Bangor, Northern Ireland; American citizen born abroad; daughter of Asa Francis (a master mariner) and Marjorie (a music teacher; maiden name, Bolton) Davison; married Orland Bruce Reynolds (a college professor), September 4, 1954; children: Ronald Davison. *Education:* Dalhousie University, B.A., 1937; Boston University, A.M., 1949, Ph.D., 1952. *Politics:* Independent. *Religion:* "Free thinker." *Home:* 225 East Michigan, Marquette, Mich. 49855.

CAREER: Quincy City Hospital, Quincy, Mass., medical technologist, 1939-42; Faulker Hospital, Boston, Mass., medical technologist, 1942-46; Wayne University (now Wayne State University), Detroit, Mich., medical technologist, 1946-48; Boston University, Boston, Mass., member of cancer research team, 1952-62; Porter Hospital, Middlebury, Vt., head of laboratory department, 1963-68; free-lance writer, 1968—. Charter member of Marquette-Alger Planned Parenthood, 1971—, member of board of directors, 1980—; member of Marquette Transit Authority, 1976—; member of Michigan Health Facilities and Agencies Advisory Committee, 1980—. *Member:* American Association for Clinical Chemistry (president of northeast section, 1957-58), American Association for Cancer Research, American Association of University Women (president of Marquette, Mich., branch, 1977-79), American Cancer Society (president of Marquette County chapter, 1975-79; member of state board of directors, 1978—), Zonta Interna-

tional (president of Marquette area club, 1978-79). *Awards, honors:* President's award for distinguished citizenship from Northern Michigan University, 1979.

WRITINGS: Clinical Chemistry for the Small Hospital Laboratory, C. C Thomas, 1969; *Aim for a Job in the Medical Laboratory,* Richards Rosen, 1972; *The Outstretched Hand: Modern Medical Discoveries,* Richards Rosen, 1980; *Margaret Sanger* (biography), Story House, 1981. Contributor to magazines (sometimes under pseudonym Marna Moore), including *Great Lakes Gazette, Maine Life, Cadence, Atlantic Advocate, South Jersey Living,* and *Lutheran Journal.*

WORK IN PROGRESS: Research for a book on the reception of *Uncle Tom's Cabin* before the Civil War.

SIDELIGHTS: "My strongest point," Moira Reynolds commented, "is the ability to put complex ideas into simple language. For this reason, I write nonfiction, rather than fiction. I write short humor as a hobby and have some success in publication; however, the market for my type of humor is so tight that I consider this writing secondary to more serious nonfiction. With regard to my current work in progress, my motivation came from my grandmother, a great admirer of the works of Charles Dickens. By the time I was in high school, I realized that she was as much interested in Dickens's attempts to expose social evils as she was in his plots and characters. Until then, I had thought that the writer's mission was solely to entertain. Gradually I began to look for a message in the books I read. *Uncle Tom's Cabin,* is, of course, a prime example of a novel that changed attitudes. I have been fascinated by this book for years, but it is only now that I have an opportunity to study it thoroughly in the light of its time. I hope that I can show contemporary readers the great significance of this novel written by Harriet Beecher Stowe more than one hundred years ago."

*   *   *

REYNOLDS, Peter C(arlton)   1943-

PERSONAL: Born November 13, 1943, in New York, N.Y.; son of Walter Carlton and Maria (King) Reynolds. *Education:* University of California, Berkeley, A.B., 1965; Yale University, Ph.D., 1972. *Residence:* Chicago, Ill. *Office:* BIPED, Inc., 7514 North East Lake Terrace, Chicago, Ill. 60626.

CAREER: Stanford University, Stanford, Calif., research scientist, 1972-74; Australian National University, Canberra, research scientist, 1974-80. *Member:* Friends of Midland Authors (president, 1981). *Awards, honors:* Guggenheim fellowship, 1980-81.

WRITINGS: On the Evolution of Human Behavior, University of California Press, 1981.

WORK IN PROGRESS: Technology: The Social Control of Matter.

SIDELIGHTS: Reynolds told *CA:* "I am an officer of BIPED, Inc., a nonprofit corporation that undertakes scientific research in the Indo-Pacific region relevant to economic development, social change, and resource management. Also, I am completing work on a book that examines in detail the differences between ape and man in the use of tools and the basic cognitive operations that must be postulated to account for a human level of technology. I give public lectures on the subject of behavioral evolution in primatives."

*   *   *

RHODES, James Allen   1909-

BRIEF ENTRY: Born September 13, 1909, in Coalton, Ohio.

American politician and author. Rhodes has been governor of Ohio since 1975, a post he also held from 1963 to 1970. He was an official of the Amateur Athletic Association during the late 1940's. He wrote *The Court-Martial of Commodore Perry* (Bobbs-Merrill, 1961), *Alternative to a Decadent Society* (Sams, 1969), and *Vocational Education and Guidance* (C. E. Merrill, 1970). *Address:* 358 North Parkview, Bexley, Ohio 43209. *Biographical/critical sources: Current Biography,* Wilson, 1949.

* * *

RICH, Gerry
See BRANDON, Johnny

* * *

RICHARD, Lucien J(oseph)   1931-

PERSONAL: Born December 20, 1931, in Berlin, N.H.; son of Leopold J. (a mill worker) and Albertine (Godbout) Richard. *Education:* University of St. Thomas Aquinas, Rome, Italy, B.A., 1954, B.S., 1955, Ph.L., 1956, S.T.L., 1960; Harvard University, Ph.D., 1971. *Office:* Department of Theology, Weston School of Theology, 3 Phillips Pl., Cambridge, Mass. 02138.

CAREER: Entered Oblate of Mary Immaculate; ordained Roman Catholic priest, 1959; Oblate Seminary, Natick, Mass., associate professor of systematic theology, 1960-64, dean of School of Theology, 1962-64 and 1967-68; Weston School of Theology, Cambridge, Mass., associate professor of systematic and historical theology, 1968—, chairperson of department of theology, 1969-72. Visiting professor at Oblate College of the Southwest, 1972—, Pastoral Institute of Archdiocese of Boston, Mass., 1973, Pastoral Institute of Diocese of Manchester, N.H., 1974-75, Salve Regina College, 1976-77, and Notre Dame Institute for Clergy, 1979. *Member:* American Academy of Religion, North American Ecumenists, Catholic Theological Society, Institute on Religion in an Age of Science, Karl Barth Society, Boston Theological Society. *Awards, honors:* Grants from American Theological Society, 1977 and 1978.

WRITINGS: (Contributor) Jasper Hopkins, editor, *Anselm of Canterbury,* Harper, 1970; *The Spirituality of John Calvin,* John Knox, 1974; *What Are They Saying About Christ and World Religions?,* Paulist/Newman, 1981; *A New Approach to Kenotic Christology,* University Press of America, 1981. Contributor to *New Catholic Encyclopedia.* Contributor to theology journals.

WORK IN PROGRESS: Ministry to and With the Elderly.

SIDELIGHTS: In addition to his formal teaching positions, Richard has organized and directed a center for adult Christian education, worked as a career counselor for an ecumenical counseling agency, and worked toward continuing education for ministers. He also organized an advocacy group for elderly people and participated in a counseling program for delinquent youngsters.

His varied research interests include the interaction of culture and religion, the relation of Christianity to world religions, the nature and dynamics of faith, and the theology and spirituality of John Calvin. He is concerned about religion and the situation of the elderly in the United States, the question of death and dying, Jung and the nature of symbolism, and feminism and Christianity.

* * *

RICHARDS, Kay
See BAKER, Susan (Catherine)

RICHARDSON, Dorsey   1896-1981

OBITUARY NOTICE: Born June 20, 1896, in Dorchester County, Md.; died November 8, 1981, in Princeton, N.J. Investment banker, U.S. State Department official, presidential economic adviser, and author. Following military service in World War I, Richardson received his doctorate and then joined the State Department in Washington. He entered investment banking in 1927 as European representative of the firm of Lehman Brothers, for which he served as vice-president from 1940 to 1958. He also served as president of the Investment Company Institute and of the One William Street Fund, Inc. In 1963 Richardson was appointed by President John F. Kennedy to a government-industry task force and was reappointed by President Lyndon B. Johnson. As presidential economic adviser Richardson promoted foreign investment in the United States. He wrote fiction and feature articles, which appeared in various magazines, and books, including *The Constitutional Doctrines of Justice Oliver Wendell Holmes* and *Will They Pay? A Primer of the War Debts.* Obituaries and other sources: *Who Was Who Among North American Authors, 1921-1939,* Gale, 1976; *New York Times,* November 11, 1981; *Time,* November 23, 1981.

* * *

RICHARDSON, Ethel Florence (Lindesay)   1870-1946
(Henrietta Richardson, Henry Handel Richardson)

BRIEF ENTRY: Born January 3, 1870, in East Melbourne, Victoria, Australia; died March 20, 1946, in Fairlight, Sussex, England; cremated, with ashes scattered on English Channel. Australian novelist, translator, and short story writer. Hailed as one of the best naturalistic novelists and the greatest Australian novelist, Richardson based most of her writing on personal experiences. For example, her first novel, *Maurice Guest* (1908), explores the life and love affair of a music student in Leipzig, where the author herself had studied music and met her husband. In *The Getting of Wisdom,* Richardson tells the story of life at a girls' boarding school similar to the Presbyterian Ladies' College which she had attended. Her most famous work, the *Fortunes of Richard Mahoney* trilogy, which contains *Australia Felix* (1917), *The Way Home* (1925), and *Ultima Thule* (1929), recounts the tragic life of the author's father. Some hold this trilogy to be the first large-scale Australian classic. Richardson said that Flaubert was her mentor, but Stendhal, Tolstoy, Bjornson, and Dostoyevsky were also influential. Her other works include *The End of Childhood and Other Stories* (1934), *Young Cosimo* (1939), and *Myself When Young* (1948). *Residence:* Sussex, England. *Biographical/critical sources:* Nettie Palmer, *Henry Handel Richardson: A Study,* Richard West, 1950; *Encyclopedia of World Literature in the Twentieth Century,* updated edition, Ungar, 1967; Vincent Buckley, *Henry Handel Richardson,* Folcroft, 1973; William D. Elliot, *Henry Handel Richardson,* Twayne, 1975; *Twentieth-Century Literary Criticism,* Volume 4, Gale, 1981.

* * *

RICHARDSON, Henrietta
See RICHARDSON, Ethel Florence (Lindesay)

* * *

RICHARDSON, Henry Handel
See RICHARDSON, Ethel Florence (Lindesay)

RICHTER, Alice 1941-

PERSONAL: Born October 19, 1941, in Brooklyn, N.Y.; daughter of William (an artist) and Florence (a home economics teacher; maiden name, Joffe) Numeroff; married Gerald Richter (a real estate broker), October 10, 1965; children: Douglas, Nancy. *Education:* New York University, B.S., 1962.

CAREER: Feature writer for newspaper in central New Jersey, 1975-76; English teacher at middle school in New Jersey, 1977—.

WRITINGS: (With sister, Laura Numeroff) *Emily's Bunch* (juvenile), Macmillan, 1978; (with L. Numeroff) *You Can't Put Braces on Spaces* (juvenile), Greenwillow, 1979.

WORK IN PROGRESS: A novel for children and a novel for young adults.

SIDELIGHTS: Alice Richter commented: "I particularly enjoy writing stories which are liberally sprinkled with humor. Although the characters in my books deal with real-life problems, they hopefully provide the readers with an opportunity to stand back, look at themselves, and laugh!"

* * *

RIEGERT, Ray 1947-

PERSONAL: Born March 11, 1947, in New York. *Education:* University of New Mexico, B.A., 1970. *Agent:* Maria Theresa Caen, 2459 Pacific Ave., San Francisco, Calif. *Office address:* And/Or Press, P.O. Box 2246, Berkeley, Calif. 94702.

CAREER: Daily Californian, Berkeley, staff writer, 1973-75; *Berkeley Barb,* Berkeley, editor-in-chief, 1976-78; currently associated with And/Or Press, Berkeley. *Member:* Pacific Area Travel Association.

WRITINGS: Hidden Hawaii (travel book), And/Or Press, 1979. West Coast correspondent for *New Times,* 1977-78. Contributor to journals including *New West* and *Travel and Leisure.* Editor of *Grassroots,* 1974.

WORK IN PROGRESS: American Heroes, an oral history.

SIDELIGHTS: Riegert wrote: "My professional interests are twofold: writing on contemporary history and travel writing."

* * *

RIOS, Francisco Giner de los
See GINER de los RIOS, Francisco

* * *

RITCHIE-CALDER, Peter Ritchie 1906-1982
(Ritchie Calder)

OBITUARY NOTICE—See index for *CA* sketch: Born January 7, 1906, in Forfar, Scotland; died January 31, 1982. Educator, explorer, lecturer, consultant, journalist, and author of more than thirty books on political and scientific subjects. Following his long career as a journalist, Ritchie-Calder became a professor of international relations at Edinburgh University. He also served as an adviser to the United Nations and to various government and research groups. Ritchie-Calder's books, which have been translated into nineteen languages, include *Science in Our Lives, Living With the Atom,* and *Agony of the Congo.* Obituaries and other sources: *London Times,* February 2, 1982; *Chicago Tribune,* February 2, 1982; *New York Times,* February 3, 1982.

RIVERE, Alec
See NUETZEL, Charles (Alexander)

* * *

ROBERTS, Charles G(eorge) D(ouglas) 1860-1943

BRIEF ENTRY: Born January 10, 1860, in Douglas, New Brunswick, Canada; died November 26, 1943, in Toronto, Ontario, Canada; buried in Fredericton, New Brunswick, Canada. Canadian author. Many critics regard Roberts as the father of modern Canadian literature, dating the modern era from the publication of his *Orion and Other Poems* (1880). Roberts was the first poet to bolster Canadian nationalism with his writing. His best lyric poems describe rural life in Nova Scotia and New Brunswick. Some of his most acclaimed work was collected in *In Divers Tones* (1887) and *The Vagrant of Time* (1927). Among his prominent works in prose are *Earth's Enigmas* (1896) and *A History of Canada* (1897). Roberts also wrote historical novels for children. *Biographical/critical sources: Twentieth Century Authors: A Biographical Dictionary of Modern Literature,* H. W. Wilson, 1942.

* * *

ROBERTSON, Alec
See ROBERTSON, Alexander Thomas Parke Anthony Cecil

* * *

ROBERTSON, Alexander Thomas Parke Anthony Cecil 1892-1982
(Alec Robertson)

OBITUARY NOTICE—See index for *CA* sketch: Born June 3, 1892, in Southsea, Portsmouth, England; died January 18, 1982. Clergyman, broadcaster, and author of more than twenty books on music. Robertson, a convert to Catholicism, left his position as head of the educational department of the Gramaphone Company to become a priest. Discovering that he lacked a vocation for the priesthood, Robertson began a new career as a broadcaster for the British Broadcasting Company (BBC-Radio), but he returned to the priesthood during the 1960's. Robertson's knowledge of church liturgy enabled him to write several reliable volumes on religious music, including *The Interpretation of Plainchant, Music of the Catholic Church,* and *Requiem.* Other works by Robertson include *How to Listen to Music, The Pelican History of Music,* and his autobiography, *More Than Music.* Obituaries and other sources: *London Times,* January 20, 1982, January 26, 1982.

* * *

ROBINSON, Ras 1935-

PERSONAL: Born March 20, 1935, in Ovett, Miss.; son of Ras B., Jr. (a farmer) and Irah Robinson; married wife, Beverly, June 15, 1957; children: Robin Robinson Bohlin, Kevin. *Education:* Louisiana State University, B.S., 1960, M.B.A., 1961. *Religion:* Baptist. *Residence:* Fort Worth, Tex. *Office:* Fulness House, Inc., P.O. Box 79350, Fort Worth, Tex. 76179.

CAREER: Baptist Sunday School Board, Nashville, Tenn., marketing coordinator, 1961-70, manager of Boardman products department, 1970-75; Pathway, Inc., Fort Worth, Tex., president, 1975-77; currently associated with Fulness House,

Inc., Fort Worth. *Military service:* U.S. Air Force, 1953-57. *Member:* Delta Sigma Pi, Pi Tau Pi.

WRITINGS: Before the Sun Goes Down, Broadman, 1975. Editor of *Fulness,* 1977-81.

WORK IN PROGRESS: You Are a New Creation (tentative title), dealing with ''the believer in Jesus Christ who has been made to be a new creation and has the rights and privileges of a child of the King of Kings and Lord of Lords.''

* * *

ROBINSON, (Wanda) Veronica   1926-

PERSONAL: Born February 21, 1926, in Jersey, Channel Islands, United Kingdom; daughter of Arthur James (a teacher) and Wanda Casimir (Mrowczynska) Robinson. *Education:* Attended Jersey College for Girls, 1935-45. *Residence:* London, England. *Office:* Swiss Cottage Library, Camden, London NW3, England.

CAREER: Jersey Public Libraries, Jersey, Channel Islands, United Kingdom, assistant, 1946-50; Margate Public Libraries, Margate, Kent, England, children's librarian, 1950-52; Dudley Public Libraries, Dudley, Worcestershire, England, children's librarian, 1952-57; Holborn Public Libraries, Holborn, England, children's librarian, 1957-70; Camden Public Libraries, Swiss Cottage Library, London, senior children's librarian, 1970-81. Sculptor, 1968—; has exhibited work at Mall Gallery, London, and Hampstead Artists Council annual exhibition, Hampstead, England.

*WRITINGS—*All for children: *The Captive Isle,* illustrations by Geraldine Spence, Dent, 1960; *The Willow Pattern Story,* illustrations by W. F. Phillipps, Oliver & Boyd, 1964; *David in Silence,* illustrations by Victor Ambrus, Deutsch, 1965, Lippincott, 1966; *Delos,* Deutsch, 1980.

SIDELIGHTS: Veronica Robinson told *CA:* ''The unconscious motive, only realized much later, for writing *David in Silence* was my own inability to express myself when I was young. I was so reserved I could more easily understand the predicament and frustrations of the deaf. *Delos* is the escape from a trap, any trap, again based on my experience. Similarly, my first book, *The Captive Isle,* was based on my experience of the German occupation of the Channel Islands, the only bits of British land that Hitler succeeded in capturing.''

AVOCATIONAL INTERESTS: Travel, archaeology, reading, art, psychology.

* * *

ROBINSON, W(alter) Stitt   1917-

BRIEF ENTRY: Born August 28, 1917, in Matthews, N.C. American historian, educator, and author. Robinson joined the faculty at University of Kansas in 1950 and became a professor of history in 1959. He edited *Richard Oswald's Memorandum on the Folly of Invading Virginia* (University Press of Virginia, 1953) and wrote *Mother Earth: Land Grants in Virginia, 1607-1699* (Virginia Three Hundred Fiftieth Anniversary Celebration Corp., 1957) and *The Southern Colonial Frontier, 1607-1763* (University of New Mexico Press, 1979). *Address:* Department of History, University of Kansas, Lawrence, Kan. 66044. *Biographical/critical sources: Directory of American Scholars,* Volume I: *History,* 7th edition, Bowker, 1978.

* * *

ROCHESTER, Devereaux   1917-

PERSONAL: Born December 20, 1917, in New York, N.Y.; daughter of Richard and Aimee (Gunning) Rochester. *Education:* Attended school in St. Albans, England, and in Salzburg and Vienna, Austria. *Religion:* Roman Catholic. *Home:* 89 Rue du Marechal Leclerc, Dinard, France 35800. *Agent:* Roberta Pryor, International Creative Management, 40 West 57th St., New York, N.Y. 10019.

CAREER: Time, Life, Inc., Paris, France, librarian, 1949; freelance writer, 1950-53; Palais des Sports, advertising agent, 1953-64; writer, 1964—. *Wartime service:* French Resistance Movement, 1942-45; received Croix de Guerre and Legion d'Honneur.

WRITINGS: Full Moon to France (memoirs), Harper, 1977; *Crinolines and Canons* (novel), R. Hale, 1980.

WORK IN PROGRESS: Another volume of memoirs, expected in 1982; translation into French of *Crinolines and Cannons;* Christmas short stories in French and some children's stories in English.

SIDELIGHTS: Rochester told *CA:* ''*Full Moon to France* is a personal account of how I got involved in the Resistance, entangled in a mesh of intrigue and adventure. My unfinished second book of memoirs is a continuation of my adventures, with fear walking perpetually at my side. It also contains flashbacks to my rather varied education that certainly left me unprepared for such things as blowing up trains and training youths in the use of firearms and silent killing.

''In contrast, my children's and Christmas stories are romantic and imaginative fantasies, far removed from a world of violence. I always write them with pleasure.''

* * *

ROEBUCK, Carl Angus   1914-

BRIEF ENTRY: Born February 23, 1914, in Toronto, Ontario, Canada. American classicist, educator, and author. Roebuck has been a professor at Northwestern University since 1957 and was named John Evans Professor of Classics in 1962. His field experience includes archaeological work in Turkey. Roebuck's writings include *Ionian Trade and Colonization* (Archaeological Institute of America, 1959), *The World of Ancient Times* (Scribner, 1966), and *The Muses at Work: Arts, Crafts, and Professions in Ancient Greece and Rome* (M.I.T. Press, 1969). *Address:* 1527 Washington Ave., Wilmette, Ill. 60091. *Biographical/critical sources: Who's Who in America,* 41st edition, Marquis, 1980.

* * *

ROEVER, J(oan) M(arilyn)   1935-

PERSONAL: Born December 13, 1935, in Philadelphia, Pa.; married Wilfried Roever (a systems test engineer). *Education:* Attended Drexel University and Philadelphia Museum College of Art. *Home:* 251 14th St. S., Cocoa Beach, Fla. 32931.

CAREER: Author and illustrator of children's books. Artist with works represented in Mississippi State Museum, Jackson, and Cameron County Library, Cameron County, La. *Member:* Society of Animal Artists.

*WRITINGS—*Juvenile; self-illustrated; published by Steck, except as noted: *The Rascally Ringtails,* 1970; (with husband, Wilfried Roever) *The Mustangs,* 1971; *The Whooping Crane,* 1971; *The Black-Footed Ferret,* 1972; (with W. Roever) *The North American Eagles,* 1973; *The Brown Pelican,* 1974; *Wolves,* 1974; *Whales in Danger,* 1975; *Snake Secrets,* Walker & Co., 1979.

Illustrator; published by Steck: Iona Seibert Hiser, *The Coyote*, 1968; Evelyn Brown and M. Vere DeVault, *The Western Diamondback Rattlesnake*, 1969; Hiser, *The Mountain Lion*, 1970; Hiser, *The Gila Monster*, 1972; Ernie M. Holyer, *The Southern Sea Otter*, 1975.

SIDELIGHTS: In her many books about wildlife, Roever presents general information about the habits, history, and biology of certain animals. Focusing on endangered species, such as the whale, North American eagle, and brown pelican, she stresses the need for conservation and suggests ways by which children and adults can help protect animals from extinction.

AVOCATIONAL INTERESTS: Conservation, fishing, camping, nature study.*

* * *

ROGERS, Will(iam Penn Adair) 1879-1935

BRIEF ENTRY: Born November 4, 1879, in Oologah, Indian Territory (now Oklahoma); died in a plane crash, August 15, 1935, near Point Barrow, Alaska. American humorist and author. Rogers began as a rancher and rodeo cowboy, then graduated to vaudeville. His rope tricks put him on the stage with Ziegfeld's Follies, where his drawling, homespun philosophy won him much attention. He became a regular performer with the Follies and began to make appearances in feature films. About 1926 he began writing a syndicated newspaper column through which he disseminated his good-natured but sharp commentary on American politics and society. Rogers was universally admired for his perception, wit, and kindly down-home charm. His newspaper columns were eventually collected in *Sanity Is Where You Find It* (1955). Earlier books included *The Cowboy Philosopher on Prohibition* (1919), *The Illiterate Digest* (1924), *There's Not a Bathing Suit in Russia* (1927), and *The Autobiography of Will Rogers* (1949). *Biographical/critical sources: Twentieth Century Authors: A Biographical Dictionary of Modern Literature*, H. W. Wilson, 1942, 1st supplement, 1955; *The Reader's Encyclopedia of American Literature*, Crowell, 1962; *Webster's American Biographies*, Merriam, 1974.

* * *

ROGLIERI, John Louis 1939-

PERSONAL: Born June 24, 1939, in Plainfield, N.J.; son of Vito (a turret lathe operator) and Grace Mary (DeCristofaro) Roglieri; married Geraldine Piller (an English teacher), 1963; children: Maria, Ann, John. *Education:* Lehigh University, A.B. and B.S., both 1960; Harvard University, M.D., 1966; Columbia University, M.S., 1978. *Religion:* Roman Catholic. *Home:* 16 Park St., Tenafly, N.J. 07670. *Agent:* Diana Price, Frommer-Price Agency, 185 East 85th St., New York, N.Y. 10028. *Office:* Presbyterian Hospital, PH-134, 622 West 68th St., New York, N.Y. 10032.

CAREER: Bellevue Hospital, New York City, medical intern, 1966-67; Presbyterian Hospital, New York City, medical resident, 1969-71; Columbia University, New York City, research assistant, 1970-71, director of Division of Ambulatory Care in department of medicine, 1973-75, assistant professor of clinical medicine, 1973—, director of Robert Wood Johnson Clinical Scholars Program, 1974-76; Presbyterian Hospital, director of ambulatory and emergency medical services, 1973-75, vice-president of ambulatory services, 1975-80. Research fellow at Harvard University, 1971-72, instructor in medicine, 1972-73; clinical and research fellow at Massachusetts General Hospital, 1971-73, assistant director of computer science lab-

oratory, director of ambulatory screening clinic, and member of executive committee of clinics, all 1972-73; special fellow of National Center for Health Services Research and Development, 1971-73. Member of board of directors of Amarco International, Inc. *Military service:* U.S. Public Health Service, 1967-69; became lieutenant commander. *Member:* American Society of Internal Medicine, American Public Health Association, American Federation for Clinical Research, American Association for the Advancement of Science, Society for Prospective Medicine.

WRITINGS: Odds on Your Life, Seaview, 1980. Contributor to *Good Housekeeping Family Medical Guide* and *Health Care Year Book*. Contributor to medical journals.

SIDELIGHTS: Roglieri told *CA:* "Americans no longer die from diseases doctors can cure. They die now from diseases that patients can prevent or postpone. The written word is the most efficient medium for conveying life-style related health-risk data and schemes for personalized decision-making to the information-poor, intelligence-rich reader."

BIOGRAPHICAL/CRITICAL SOURCES: Time, November 3, 1980.

* * *

ROLEDER, George 1928-

PERSONAL: Born October 27, 1928, in Beaverhills, Alberta, Canada; came to the United States in 1935, naturalized citizen, 1943; son of Emil J. (a minister) and Selma (Schmidt) Roleder; married Elizabeth Ann Boebel (a reference librarian), August 17, 1952; children: Cynthia Beth Roleder Kasten, Nancy Diane Roleder Carter, Amy. *Education:* Wartburg College, B.A., 1950; Wartburg Theological Seminary, M.Div., 1954; Claremont Graduate School, M.A., 1962; University of Southern California, Ph.D., 1976. *Home:* 2499 Mesa Ter., Upland, Calif. 91786. *Office:* Department of Psychology, Mount San Antonio College, Walnut, Calif. 91789.

CAREER: Ordained American Lutheran minister, 1953; associate pastor in Compton, Calif., 1953-55; pastor in Yucaipa, Calif., 1955-58; Mount San Antonio College, Walnut, Calif., professor of psychology, 1960—. Counselor at Voorman Psychiatric Clinic, 1968-69, and Affiliated Center for Self-Actualization, 1979. Visiting professor at University of Southern California graduate program in Germany, 1978-79. Member of board of convocators of California Lutheran College. *Member:* National Audubon Society, California Council on Family Relations, California Teachers Association, Faculty Association of California Community College.

WRITINGS: (Contributor) E. A. Powers and M.W. Lees, editors, *Process in Relationship*, West Publishing, 1976; (editor) *Marriage Means Encounter*, W. C. Brown, 1973, 2nd edition, 1979; *Famlab: Family Laboratory*, Kendall/Hunt, 1970, 4th edition, 1981. Contributor to *Journal of Counseling Psychology*.

WORK IN PROGRESS: Research on predictive testing of community college dropouts.

SIDELIGHTS: Roleder told *CA:* "*Marriage Means Encounter* was edited to include a much wider range of attitudes and values in the approach to marriage and family literature. This is especially vital in teaching students at the community college level. I have a very positive attitude toward marriage. The basic functions of marriage still provide the most important aspects of personal fulfillment and are the basis for our Western culture. What changes constantly is the way in which the functions are carried out by the members of the family. My classes give small groups the opportunity to learn the art of communication and the expression of affection as vital tools for maintaining the marriage relationship.''

* * *

ROOKS, George 1951-

PERSONAL: Born March 5, 1951, in Anderson, S.C.; son of G. M. (in business) and Miriam (Bailey) Rooks; married Linda Callis (a lecturer); children: George, Brendan. *Education:* University of Georgia, B.A., 1973; University of California, Davis, M.A., 1975. *Residence:* Davis, Calif. *Office:* Department of English for Students, University of California, 4465 Chem Annex, Davis, Calif. 95616.

CAREER: University of California, Davis, lecturer in English as a second language, 1976—.

WRITINGS: The Book of Losers, St. Martin's, 1980; *Nonstop Discussion Workbook,* Newbury House, 1981; (with Ken Scholberg and Diana Scholberg) *Conversar sin parar* (title means "Limitless Conversation"), Newbury House, 1981. Contributor to *Arizona Quarterly* and *Paideuma.*

WORK IN PROGRESS: Academic textbooks.

SIDELIGHTS: Rooks wrote: "At present I'm working exclusively on academic textbooks, particularly ones related to English and English as a second language. I love to write, and I look forward to returning to general trade books. I want to try historical novels, but like to experiment with all types of writing. I adhere to Gertrude Stein's dictum, 'If you can do something well, why do it?'"

AVOCATIONAL INTERESTS: Travel (Mexico, Canada, Scandinavia, central and southern Europe), marathoning, tennis.

* * *

ROOSEVELT, Elliott 1910-

PERSONAL: Born September 23, 1910, in New York, N.Y.; son of Franklin Delano (president of the United States) and Anna Eleanor (Roosevelt) Roosevelt; married Elizabeth Donner, 1931 (divorced, 1933); married Ruth Josephine Googins, July 22, 1933 (divorced); married Faye Emerson, 1944 (divorced, 1950); married Minnewa Bell, 1951 (divorced); married Patricia Whitehead, 1960; children: (first marriage) William Donner; (second marriage) Ruth Chandler, Elliott, David Boynton. *Education:* Attended private secondary school in Groton, Mass., 1923-29. *Home:* Establishment VIC, 6 rue Bellot, Geneva, Switzerland. *Agent:* Rosalind Cole, Waldorf Towers, 100 East 50th St., New York, N.Y. 10022.

CAREER: Worked in advertising, editing, and broadcasting, 1929-41; president and director of Dalco Uranium, Inc., 1957—. Writer and rancher. Vice-president of Aeronautical Chamber of Commerce of America, 1934-35; mayor of Miami Beach, Fla., 1965-69. Member of board of Texas Agricultural and Mechanical College (now Texas A & M University), 1937-39. *Military service:* U.S. Army Air Forces, 1940-45; became brigadier general; received Legion of Merit, Distinguished Flying Cross with one Oak Leaf Cluster, Air Medal with one Oak Leaf Cluster, and Croix de Guerre with Palm. *Member:* Masons, Denver Country Club, Phoenix Country Club, Paradise Valley Racquet Club (Scottsdale, Ariz.). *Awards, honors:* Chevalier of French Legion of Honor; commander of the Order Assoum Alacuite; commander of the Order of the British Empire.

WRITINGS: As He Saw It, foreword by Eleanor Roosevelt, Duell, Sloan & Pearce, 1946, reprinted, Greenwood Press, 1974; (editor) *F.D.R.: His Personal Letters,* Duell, Sloan & Pearce, 1947-50, Volume I: *The Early Years,* Volume II: *1905-1928,* Volumes III-IV: *1928-1945;* (with James Brough) *An Untold Story: The Roosevelts of Hyde Park,* Putnam, 1973; (with Brough) *A Rendezvous With Destiny: The Roosevelts of the White House,* Putnam, 1975; (with Brough) *Mother R.: Eleanor Roosevelt's Untold Story,* Putnam, 1977. Also editor with Brough of *The Way It Really Was,* 1973.

SIDELIGHTS: Elliott Roosevelt accompanied his father to several international conferences during World War II, and his first book was based on those experiences. His account of those conferences and Franklin D. Roosevelt's view of them was controversial. Some critics, including Arthur Schlesinger, Jr., Harold Laski, and Henry Steele Commager, questioned the accuracy of the facts and interpretations put forward in *As He Saw It* and criticized Roosevelt's vagueness about the sources of some of his information. Schlesinger, in the *Nation,* described some portions as "inherently implausible" and said that, if inaccurate, it was "an infinitely mischievous book." But he added, "one must caution against an *a priori* acceptance or rejection of the thesis of *As He Saw It* simply because it coincides with or contradicts current political interests." Amid questions of authenticity, the book's significance was recognized. "Politicians and historians may violently quarrel over [*As He Saw It*]," wrote Jonathan Daniels of the *Saturday Review of Literature,* "but neither politicians nor historians will ever be able to disregard it."

Three decades later, Roosevelt's trilogy recounting his family's history aroused controversy. The first volume, *An Untold Story,* tells of the Roosevelts' life before 1932 and attracted attention largely because of its revelations about Franklin Roosevelt's sex life. Elliott tells of his father's affairs with Lucy Mercer, Eleanor's social secretary, and with Franklin's personal secretary, Missy LeHand. The relationship with Lucy Mercer was well known before; that with Missy LeHand was not, and some critics expressed skepticism. Kenneth Davis of the *New York Times Book Review* called the case "unproved," and he criticized Elliott's use of what Davis called "innuendo and unsupported (and untrue) assertions." Elliott's own siblings publicly disassociated themselves from the book.

In response, Elliott pointed out that the sexual aspects of his parents' lives made up only a small part of the book and asserted that his purpose in writing it was to correct impressions created by other books about his parents, especially Joseph Lash's *Eleanor and Franklin.* According to Elliott, Lash's book "had a completely inaccurate depiction of my parents. . . . It painted Father as a crippled, weak person completely dominated by his wife and mother. That just wasn't true." Elliott saw his father as "a very dominant figure indeed," and his mother, at that point in her life, as a "shy, chronic introvert."

A Rendezvous With Destiny told of the Roosevelts' years in the White House, through the Depression and World War II. Several of Franklin Roosevelt's associates were portrayed in the book and, as Esmond Wright of the *Times Literary Supplement* observed, "some reputations suffer savagely," Joseph Kennedy's and Dwight D. Eisenhower's among them. But Wright noted: "For the central figure there are no reservations: 'History must record that he led the greatest social revolution the free world has ever known. . . . There have been differences in the characters of Presidents and the Presidency in recent years, but few improvements.'" *A Rendezvous With Destiny* was dismissed by Michael Howard of *Books and Bookmen* and Charles L. Mee of the *New York Times Book Review,* respectively, as "trivial" and "superficial," but Wright found it "moving and vivid."

In the final volume of the trilogy, *Mother R.*, Elliott told of Eleanor Roosevelt's life after 1945, when she became a public figure in her own right. As a delegate to the United Nations and a leader of the Democratic party she campaigned for peace and equality and became known as "The First Lady of the Western World." The book received mixed reviews, but Marlene Veach of *Best Sellers* praised "the charm of candid sketchings . . . of a truly great woman."

BIOGRAPHICAL/CRITICAL SOURCES: Saturday Review of Literature, October 5, 1946; *New York Times*, October 6, 1946; *New Republic*, October 7, 1946; *Nation*, November 2, 1946; *Washington Star-News*, April 20, 1973; *New York Times Book Review*, May 20, 1973, October 19, 1975; *Authors in the News*, Volume 2, Gale, 1976; *Books and Bookmen*, October, 1977; *Times Literary Supplement*, October 21, 1977; *Best Sellers*, January, 1978.*

*   *   *

ROSE, Lynn Edmondson 1934-

BRIEF ENTRY: Born January 28, 1934, in Columbus, Ohio. American philosopher, educator, and author. Rose began teaching at the State University of New York at Buffalo in 1961 and became a professor of philosophy in 1969. She wrote *Aristotle's Syllogistic* (C. C Thomas, 1968). *Address:* Department of Philosophy, State University of New York at Buffalo, Buffalo, N.Y. 14214. *Biographical/critical sources: Directory of American Scholars*, Volume IV: *Philosophy, Religion, and Law*, 7th edition, Bowker, 1978.

*   *   *

ROSE, Marcia
See KAMIEN, Marcia
and NOVAK, Rose

*   *   *

ROSEN, Shirley 1933-

PERSONAL: Born July 26, 1933, in Walla Walla, Wash.; daughter of David Walter (in sheet metal) and Esther (an office worker; maiden name, Lund) Lapham; married Enard LeRoy Rosen (a truck driver), February 11, 1956; children: Keith L., Teresa L., Christopher. *Education:* Attended Shoreline Community College, 1979-81. *Politics:* Democrat. *Religion:* Lutheran. *Home:* 19202 38th Place N.E., Seattle, Wash. 98155.

CAREER: Olympic Steamship Co., Seattle, Wash., secretary-accountant, 1951-52; Blocks Shoe Stores, Seattle, secretary, 1952-54; Ford Motor Co., Seattle, executive secretary of Lincoln-Mercury division, 1954-59; Providence Hospital, Seattle, in public relations, 1963; Shoreline School District, Seattle, information specialist, 1976-79; writer. Member of Shoreline PTSA Council, Washington State Committee for Full Funding of Common Schools, and Lewis and Clark College Greater Seattle Parent Committee. *Member:* Pacific Northwest Writers Conference, Seattle Free Lances. *Awards, honors:* Community Service Award from Lake Forest Park, 1975; Golden Acorn Award from Shoreline School District PTSA Council, 1976.

WRITINGS: Truman of St. Helens: The Man and His Mountain, Madrona and Longview Publishing, 1981.

WORK IN PROGRESS: Texts for collections of Josef Scaylea's photography on rowing and the Skagit River Valley; "an article on my daughter's recent six-month trip of living with the Sherpas in Nepal, near Mount Everest."

SIDELIGHTS: Rosen told *CA:* "In May of 1980, when much of America was fascinated with the eruption of Mount St. Helens, I was devastated. What was being shown on TV was the destruction of an area I had loved since I was fourteen and, along with it, my uncle, Harry Truman, who steadfastly refused to leave his mountain resort despite the pending eruption.

"As therapy I retreated to my room and started typing. I also wanted my three children to have a permanent record about that area and what my irascible uncle was like. What fun it was to write about Truman clad only in his jocky shorts, chasing bears out of garbage cans on moonlit nights at Spirit Lake. Other vignettes about Truman's World War I experiences, flying and his prohibition rum-running, tumbled into the typewriter.

"I shared my stories with my English teacher at Shoreline Community College in Seattle. He said, 'Shirley, these are good—write a book.' With that, plus the encouragement of my children, I was off. The result was over one hundred ten taped interviews with people who had known Truman.

"Parenting had always been fun for me and an important full-time job. But writing about Truman's life became an obsession. I had to tell the world that he was not only a colorful character, but a complicated man who had many reasons for not leaving his mountain.

"I had always enjoyed writing, but a book—under a very tight deadline—was not part of my background. The interviewing and writing took nine months of excruciating work. When it was done I felt I had given birth to my fourth child—only this time it was a book. And what a rewarding experience. When I finished I wondered what the critics would say. And what fun that is—especially when the reviews are good. It seems a little like a dream now. When I was flown to New York for the 'Today' show and Tom Brokaw said to me, on the air 'it's a wonderful book,' I felt like pinching myself.

"I think the greatest reward of writing this particular book were all the people I met. So many people so willing to share a part of themselves with me. I couldn't have done it without them. I wasn't quite prepared for the promotional aspect of publishing. My first experience—being interviewed by Brokaw on 'Today.' And all those radio talk shows and newspaper interviews. I must admit, I loved every minute of it.

"Writing may be lonely at times and not particularly lucrative, but it sure is fun! I think I am most proud of the fact that my book has been judged so accurate in its detailing of places and events that it has been accepted and is on the approved list of the U.S. Forest Service and is available in their official information centers in this area."

Skip Johnson of the *Charleston Gazette* wrote: "Ms. Rosen . . . has done a remarkable job in her first attempt at writing a book. . . . It is lively, entertaining, humorous and sad. . . . Ms. Rosen has woven [a tale] with style and pathos."

BIOGRAPHICAL/CRITICAL SOURCES: Bellevue Journal American, March 19, 1981; *Longview Daily News*, March 19, 1981; *Seattle Post-Intelligencer*, May 10, 1981; *Northgate Journal*, May 13, 1981; *Shoreline Journal*, May 13, 1981; *Lake City Journal*, May 13, 1981; *Seattle Times*, July 5, 1981 August 28, 1981; *Vancouver Columbian*, July 17, 1981; *Charleston Gazette*, August 6, 1981.

*   *   *

ROSENBAUM, Patricia L(eib) 1932-

PERSONAL: Born July 11, 1932, in Harrisburg, Pa.; daughter of Frank R. (in insurance sales) and Ruth (in banking; maiden name, Esbenshade) Leib; married Robert C. Rosenbaum (a manager), March 7, 1959; children: Ann Katherine. *Education:* Wilson College, B.A., 1954; Washington University, St. Louis, Mo., M.A., 1978, Ph.D., 1980. *Politics:* Democrat. *Home:* 444 Iowa St., Oak Park, Ill. 60302. *Office:* Human Resources Center, University of Pennsylvania, 3611 Locust St., Philadelphia, Pa. 19174.

CAREER: University of Pennsylvania, Philadelphia, research assistant at Human Resources Center, 1969-75, program coordinator, 1980—. Vice-president of Citizens Information Service; member of Oak Park Community Relations Commission; consultant to League of Women Voters of Illinois. *Member:* American Sociological Association.

WRITINGS: (With Sandra Schoenberg) *Neighborhoods That Work,* Rutgers University Press, 1980. Contributor to education journals.

WORK IN PROGRESS: Research on citizen participation in urban policy and on management of public transportation systems.

SIDELIGHTS: Patricia Rosenbaum wrote: "I lean toward practical application and action rather than writing, most of which is done in service to some action goal.

"My major interests are in developing channels through which average citizens can take part in the lives of their communities and exert some influence on the making of public policy that affects them. The feeling that you can exercise some measure of control over what happens in the place where you live is key to the creation of neighborhoods that work, no matter who you are."

*   *   *

ROSENFIELD, Leonora Cohen   1909-1982

OBITUARY NOTICE—See index for *CA* sketch: Born February 14, 1909, in New York, N.Y.; died of sepsis, January 15, 1982, in Washington, D.C. Educator and author. In 1980 Rosenfield was named professor emeritus at the University of Maryland, where she taught French literature, civilization, and culture for more than thirty years. Her books include *From Beast-Machine to Man-Machine* and *Portrait of a Philosopher: Morris R. Cohen in Life and Letters.* Obituaries and other sources: *Washington Post,* January 18, 1982.

*   *   *

ROSENTHAL, Alan   1936-
(Gil Talkin)

PERSONAL: Born February 5, 1936, in London, England; son of Lewis and Sarah Rosenthal; married Miriam (a psychologist); children: Gril, Tal. *Education:* Oxford University, B.A., M.A.; Stanford University, M.A. *Office:* Araness Communications, 1619 Broadway, Suite 812, New York, N.Y. 10019.

CAREER: Associated with Hebrew University, York University, and Mexican National Film School; currently film director and producer for Araness Communications, New York, N.Y. *Awards, honors:* Gold medals from New York International Film and Television Festival, 1976, 1977, and 1978, and from Miami International Film Festival, 1978.

WRITINGS: The New Documentary in Action, University of California Press, 1971; *The Documentary Conscience,* University of California Press, 1980. Also author of stories, under pseudonym Gil Talkin.

ROSOVSKY, Henry   1927-

BRIEF ENTRY: Born September 1, 1927, in Danzig (now Gdansk), Poland. American economist, educator, and author. Rosovsky has been a professor at Harvard University since 1965. He was named Walter S. Barker Professor of Economics in 1975 and dean of the faculty of arts and sciences in 1973. His writings include *Discord in the Pacific: Challenges to the Japanese-American Alliance* (Columbia Books, 1972), *Japanese Economic Growth: Trend Acceleration in the Twentieth Century* (Stanford University Press, 1973), and *Asia's New Giant: How the Japanese Economy Works* (Brookings Institution, 1976). *Address:* 37 Beechcroft Rd., Newton, Mass. 02158; and University Hall, Harvard University, Cambridge, Mass. 02138. *Biographical/critical sources: Who's Who in America,* 40th edition, Marquis, 1978.

*   *   *

ROSSEL, Sven H(akon)   1943-

PERSONAL: Born October 25, 1943, in Bangkok, Thailand; came to the United States in 1974, naturalized citizen, 1976; son of Leo Hancke (a managing director) and Maria (Mueller) Rossel; children: Eva Maria Katharina. *Education:* University of Copenhagen, Ph.D., 1968. *Home:* 18725 65th Pl. N.E., Seattle, Wash. 98155. *Office:* Department of Scandinavian Languages Literature, University of Washington, Seattle, Wash. 98195.

CAREER: University of Hamburg, Hamburg, West Germany, assistant professor of Danish language and literature, 1968-69; University of Kiel, Kiel, West Germany, assistant professor of Danish language and literature, 1969-71; University of Copenhagen, Copenhagen, Denmark, researcher on Scandinavian balladry, 1971-74; University of Washington, Seattle, associate professor, 1974-80, professor of Scandinavian languages and literature and comparative literature, 1980—, chairman of department of Scandinavian languages literature, 1981—. Member of board of directors of Nordic Heritage Museum, 1980—.

MEMBER: International Association of Scandinavian Studies, Danish Folklore Society, Society for the Advancement of Scandinavian Studies, Arbeitsgemeinschaft Norden-Deutschland, Medieval Association of the Pacific, Seattle Danish Club (vice-president, 1976-77). *Awards, honors:* Grant from University of Copenhagen, 1971; Grundtvig-Olrik Award from University of Copenhagen, 1976, 1980, for ballad research; award from Denmark-America Foundation, 1980, for research on Johannes V. Jensen and America; special award from the state of Washington, 1981, for translating work of Hans Christian Andersen.

WRITINGS: (Editor and translator, with Patricia L. Conroy, and author of introduction and notes) *Hans Christian Andersen's Tales and Stories,* University of Washington Press, 1980; *A History of Scandinavian Literature, 1870-1980,* University of Minnesota Press, 1981.

Other: *Den literare vise i folketraditionen* (title means "The Literary Ballad in Folk Tradition"), two volumes, Akademisk Forlag, 1971; *Danske digtere i folketraditionen: En materialesamling* (title means "Danish Writers in Folk Tradition: A Collection of Materials"), Universitetsforlaget, 1971; *Skandinavische literatur, 1870-1970* (title means "Scandinavian Literature, 1870-1970"), Verlag W. Kohlhammer, 1973; *Dansk litterature mellem Holberg og Ewald, 1730-1766* (title means

"Danish Literature Between Holberg and Ewald, 1730-1766"), Gyldendal, 1975; (with Richard Hornby and Erik Soenderholm) *Danmarks gamle folkeviser* (title means "Denmark's Ancient Ballads"), Volume XII, Akademisk Forlag, 1975.

Contributor to *Ungar's Encyclopedia of World Literature, Columbia Dictionary of World Literature,* and *Dansk Biografisk Leksikon.* Contributor to scholarly journals and Danish newspapers.

WORK IN PROGRESS: Johannes V. Jensen: Criticism and Interpretation, for Twayne; research on Scandinavian balladry and folklore, modern European literature, the work of Hans Christian Andersen, Scandinavian romanticism, and Danish broadsides.

SIDELIGHTS: Rossel told *CA:* "Since all valuable literature deals with the three enternal subjects (God, love, and death), I have always attempted to trace these subjects in world literature and for the same reason selected the medieval and baroque periods as my favorite ones.

"Through the inspiration of my outstanding teachers at the University of Copenhagen I have employed a historical-biographical and comparative view, focusing on the relationship between national literatures and between literature and history, culture and the arts.

"Within the performing arts I have found the above-mentioned subjects most fascinatingly expressed in music—the cantatas by Bach, the chamber music by Beethoven, and the operas by Wagner. Music has also offered me consolation in this vale of tears.

"I could (and probably should) spend my life listening to these composers, visiting baroque churches in southern Europe and English pubs, reading poetry—and traveling: 'To travel is to live,' as my favorite author, Hans Christian Andersen, wrote.

"However, since one has to make a living, teaching literature, doing research, and writing are the second-best choices. As a teacher and scholar I favor as wide a perspective as possible, making literature available also to a noninitiated audience."

*   *   *

RUBIN, Vitalii 1923-1981

OBITUARY NOTICE—See index for *CA* sketch: Born September 14, 1923, in Moscow, U.S.S.R.; died in an automobile accident, October 18, 1981, near Beersheba, Israel. Educator and author of *Individual and State in Ancient China.* Rubin, who contracted tuberculosis of the spine while confined in a Soviet concentration camp, became an aggressive advocate of such issues as human rights and free emigration. Dismissed from his position at Moscow's Institute of Oriental Studies in 1972, Rubin requested, but was denied, permission to leave the country. After American scholars began an active campaign in his behalf, however, Rubin was issued an exit visa. He immigrated to Israel where he became a professor of Chinese philosophy at Hebrew University. Obituaries and other sources: *New York Times,* October 21, 1981; *Newsweek,* November 2, 1981.

*   *   *

RUDENSTINE, Neil Leon 1935-

BRIEF ENTRY: Born January 21, 1935, in Ossining, N.Y. American educator and author. Rudenstine began teaching at Princeton University in 1966; he has been a professor of English since 1968 and provost since 1977. He wrote *Sidney's Poetic*

Development (Harvard University Press, 1967) and edited *English Prose Satire: Wyatt to Byron* (Holt, 1972). *Address:* 139 Broadmead, Princeton, N.J. 08540; and Department of English, Princeton University, Princeton, N.J. 08540. *Biographical/critical sources: Who's Who in America,* 40th edition, Marquis, 1978.

*   *   *

RUEHLMANN, William 1946-

PERSONAL: Born April 27, 1946, in Cincinnati, Ohio; son of William Edward (a colonel in U.S. Air Force) and Margaret Thelma (a nurse; maiden name, Smith) Ruehlmann; married Lynn Elise Klausli (an actress), September 6, 1969. *Education:* American University, B.A., 1968; University of Arizona, M.A., 1970; University of Cincinnati, Ph.D., 1974. *Politics:* Independent. *Religion:* Presbyterian. *Home:* 1609 Colonial Ave., Norfolk, Va. 23517. *Office: Norfolk Ledger-Star,* 150 West Brambleton Ave., Norfolk, Va. 23501.

CAREER: High school English teacher in Cincinnati, Ohio, 1970-71; *Kentucky Post,* Covington, reporter, 1974-75; Suffolk University, Boston, Mass., assistant professor of journalism, 1975-77; *Norfolk Ledger-Star,* Norfolk, Va., feature writer and critic, 1977—. Lecturer for schools, colleges, and professional groups. *Military service:* U.S. Marine Corps, 1968-69. Army National Guard, engineer, 1970-74; became platoon sergeant. *Member:* Investigative Reporters and Editors, Virginia Writers Club, Sigma Delta Chi. *Awards, honors:* Slover Award from *Norfolk Ledger-Star,* 1977, for excellence in reporting; named to honor roll of National Council of College Publications Advisers, 1977, for professional excellence in advising student journalists.

WRITINGS: Saint With a Gun: The Unlawful American Private Eye (criticism), New York University Press, 1974; *Stalking the Feature Story,* Writer's Digest, 1978. Contributor to magazines.

WORK IN PROGRESS: A novel.

SIDELIGHTS: Ruehlmann told *CA:* "Writing is a narcotic, addictive pleasure-pain, but it has led me into a lot of situations that would have been closed to me without it. I've been up in hot-air balloons and open-cockpit planes, ridden Brahma bulls and circus elephants, wrestled bears, fought fires, shot rapids— all in search of a subject. Without the necessity for something to write about, I should have been quite content to sit in my room and dream."

*   *   *

RUSSELL, Howard S(ymmes) 1887-1980

PERSONAL: Born July 28, 1887, in Arlington, Mass. died April 8, 1980; son of Ira L. (a market gardener) and Louisa (Locke) Russell; married Mabel Briggs Coolidge, December 29, 1913; children: Constance Symmes. *Education:* Attended high school in Arlington, Mass. *Politics:* Republican. *Religion:* Baptist.

CAREER: Market gardener in Arlington, Mass., 1908-20, and Wayland, Mass., 1920-25; Howard S. Russell Insurance Agency, Waltham, Mass., owner, 1925-55; *Wayland Town Crier,* Wayland, columnist, 1957-80. President of Massachusetts Farm Bureau Federation, 1920-21, executive secretary, 1921-45. Executive manager of Mutual Farm Underwriters, 1925-57; partner of Goodnow & Russell Insurance Agency, 1934-55. Member of Wayland Planning Board, 1926-50, and past chairman; town moderator of Wayland, 1939-59; member of Massachusetts House of Representatives, 1948-54. Past member of board of trustees of Massachusetts State College.

WRITINGS: A Long Deep Furrow (history), University Press of New England, 1976; *Indian New England Before the Mayflower,* University Press of New England, 1980. Contributor to magazines, including *New England Galaxy* and *New England Homestead.* Past editor of *Farm Bureau in Massachusetts* and *Massachusetts Baptist.*

SIDELIGHTS: Russell's wife, Mabel, provided background information: "On the death of his father in 1908, Howard took over the market garden begun by his grandfather. His agricultural interests lasted throughout his lifetime, first with his own farms, then with his business of selling farm fire insurance and inspecting farms for fire prevention purposes. His research on the Indians was a lifelong hobby."

*   *   *

RUSSELL, (Henry) Ken(neth Alfred)   1927-

PERSONAL: Born July 3, 1927, in Southampton, England; son of Henry (an owner of shoe stores) and Ethel (Smith) Russell; married Shirley Ann Kingdon (a costume designer), 1957 (divorced, 1979); children: Alex, James, Victoria, Xavier, Toby. *Education:* Attended Walthamstow Art School, 1949, and International Ballet School (London), 1950. *Religion:* Roman Catholic.

CAREER: Screenwriter and director of motion pictures and television productions. Worked as member of Norwegian ballet company, 1950, and as actor with Garrick Players, 1951; free-lance photographer, 1952-57; director of thirty-five television productions for British Broadcasting Corp. (BBC-TV), including "Elgar," 1962, "Bartok," 1964, "Isadora Duncan: The Biggest Dancer in the World," 1966, "Dante's Inferno," 1967, "A Song of Summer," 1968, "The Dance of the Seven Veils: A Comic Strip in Seven Episodes on the Life of Richard Strauss," 1970, and "Clouds of Glory," 1978; director of motion pictures, including "French Dressing," Associated British, 1963, "Billion Dollar Brain," United Artists, 1970, "Savage Messiah," Metro-Goldwyn-Mayer (MGM)/EMI, 1972, and "Altered States," Warner Bros., 1980. *Military service:* Royal Air Force, 1946-49. *Awards, honors:* Nomination for Academy Award for best director from Academy of Motion Picture Arts and Sciences, 1969, for "Women in Love."

WRITINGS—Screenplays; also director: (With Larry Kramer) "Women in Love" (adapted from the novel by D. H. Lawrence), United Artists, 1969; "The Devils" (adapted from the play by Aldous Huxley, "The Devils of Loudon," and the play by John Whiting), Warner Bros., 1971; "The Boy Friend" (adapted from the stage musical by Sandy Wilson), Metro-Goldwyn-Mayer (MGM)/EMI, 1972; "Mahler," Goodtimes Enterprises, 1974; "Tommy" (adapted from the rock opera by Peter Townshend), Columbia, 1975; "Lisztomania," Goodtimes Enterprises, 1975; (with Mardick Martin) "Valentino" (adapted from the biography by Brad Steiger and Chaw Monk, *Valentino: An Intimate Expose of the Sheik*), United Artists, 1977.

Television scripts; also director: (With Melvyn Bragg) "The Debussy Film" (biography of Claude Debussy), British Broadcasting Corp. (BBC-TV), 1966; "Always on Sunday" (biography of Henri Rousseau), BBC-TV, 1969.

Also author and director of independently produced films, including "Peepshow," 1956, "Amelia and the Angel," 1957, and "Lourdes," 1958, and an unfinished film, "Knights on Bikes," 1957.

Contributor to periodicals, including *Film* and *Books and Bookmen.*

WORK IN PROGRESS: Directing the motion picture "The Beethoven Secret."

SIDELIGHTS: Russell is generally considered Britain's most eccentric filmmaker. He is the director of deliberate and understated works such as "A Song of Summer" and "Clouds of Glory"; but he is also director of several fantastical biographies, including "Lisztomania" and "Valentino," that have been called "half-baked" and "relentlessly outrageous." He has succeeded critically and commercially with such diverse works as "Women in Love" and "Tommy," and failed as drastically with their respective counterparts, "The Music Lovers" and "Lisztomania." He has been condemned by his detractors as a "vulgarian," and praised by his supporters as a "genius." But throughout his erratic career, Russell has pursued his own vision, rarely compromising to critical or public expectations. "It is a pity," he notes, "when one, either through force of circumstance or because one is afraid of being ridiculed by others, won't produce and expose to everyone that little spark of something special which is unique to him alone."

Russell commenced filmmaking after failing as a dancer and actor. He used his earnings as a free-lance photographer to finance three amateur films in the late 1950's. Executives at the British Broadcasting Corporation were considerably impressed with Russell's work, and in 1960 they offered him directorial duties on films concerning coal mining and dancing. His first important work as a director, however, was "Elgar," a documentary on the celebrated composer of "Pomp and Circumstance." Prevented from using actors and dialogue, Russell relied on breathtaking images of nature to accompany the generous selections from Elgar's canon. The result, according to Gene D. Phillips, was "one of the most popular single TV programs ever screened in Britain."

After the success of "Elgar," Russell began altering the limited documentary format employed by the BBC. In "Bartok," a biography of the twentieth-century Hungarian composer, Russell introduced close-ups, and in his 1965 biography of French composer Claude Debussy, Russell used his own script as the basis for the first British documentary to feature dialogue. The same year Russell also wrote and directed "Always on Sunday," a biography of French painter Henri Rousseau that was the first completely dramatic biography presented by the BBC.

Russell continued with the dramatic format as director of biographies of Isadora Duncan, Dante Gabriel Rossetti, and Frederick Delius. The latter work, entitled "A Song of Summer," is generally considered Russell's best-directed biography. The film details the final days of the British composer who was crippled and blinded by syphilis. *New York Times* reviewer Peter G. Davis wrote that Russell's "images are of such evocative power that one feels instinctively how the profound mystery of natural forces came to pervade all of Delius's music."

In addition to the BBC films, Russell had already directed two motion pictures by 1969. "French Dressing," a farce about two men attempting to lure vacationers to a seaside resort by starting a nudist colony and hosting an international film festival, failed at box offices in 1963. "Billion Dollar Brain," Russell's 1967 contribution to the "Harry Palmer" espionage series, was similarly neglected by moviegoers. Studio officials at United Artists, however, were impressed with the second film, and in 1969 they asked Russell to direct Larry Kramer's adaptation of D. H. Lawrence's *Women in Love.*

Russell took the job, but after reading both the novel and Kramer's script, he decided that the latter needed rewriting.

"I would go around to Larry's flat in the afternoons and say 'These are the bits I like in the book,'" Russell recalled. "He'd say 'Well, just read it out.' I read it out and he typed it." After the rewrite was completed, Russell was surprised to see Kramer receiving sole credit for their work. "By the time we got back to London the script had been printed," Russell told John Baxter, "and when I opened it up there was 'Screenplay by Larry Kramer.' I immediately rang him up and said 'What's this? We wrote the script together.' (Actually Lawrence wrote 90% of it and we did the rest.) 'But I wrote it down' Larry said. 'I regard myself as your pencil, Ken.'" Russell then asked Kramer, "Whoever heard of giving a pencil full screen credit?" Kramer eventually asked Russell to grant him the entire credit, whereupon Russell "just gritted my teeth and got on with it."

Kramer and Russell remained faithful to Lawrence's story of two sisters, Ursula and Gudrun Brangwen, and their respective relationships with writer Rupert Birkin and mine-owner Gerald Crich. The film's first half focuses on Birkin's efforts to establish ideal bonds with his eventual wife, Ursula, and his friend Gerald. The second half details the combative relationship between Gerald and Gudrun. She confronts Gerald with the revelation that his possessive notion of love is destructive, then spurns his company for that of Loerke, a homosexual sculptor. Gerald then walks into the Alps and freezes to death. The film, like the novel, concludes with Ursula challenging Birkin's belief that Gerald's friendship offered a male counterpart to their own relationship.

"Women in Love" proved immensely successful for Russell. Critics such as the *New York Times*'s Vincent Canby hailed it as "a loving, intelligent, faithful adaptation" and praised its portrayal of nature and physical intimacy as "about as sensuous as anything . . . probably ever seen in a film." Canby was also impressed with Russell's handling of nudity, particularly during a wrestling match between Gerald and Birkin set before a glowing fireplace. Canby deemed this scene "the movie's loveliest sequence—there is a sense of positive grace in the eroticism."

After "Women in Love," Russell was besieged with offers to direct adaptations of other British classics. He declined them all, however, to direct "The Music Lovers," a study of Russian composer Peter Tchaikovsky. Russell contended that Tchaikovsky's music prospered at the expense of those who inspired it, and he wanted to present the personal tragedies as consequences of the selfishness and insecurity that spurred Tchaikovsky's creativity. "Instead of facing even a vestige of reality," Russell claimed, "Tchaikovsky put all his problems into his music and thought that they would disappear and everything would be solved. This merely made him more mixed up than ever and so he destroyed the people he came up against . . . , because they were real and their problems were real." Russell called "The Music Lovers" "a black comedy about the decadence of romanticism" and warned that the film should not be construed as a factual biography of Tchaikovsky. "I'm not too interested in the external trappings of a person's life," he said. "The music speaks far more eloquently and truthfully than all the dry everyday facts that have been written about him ever can do."

In "The Music Lovers," Tchaikovsky is depicted as an insecure artist tormented by his own homosexuality, his wife's nymphomania, and memories of his mother's death from cholera. His marriage collapses after he rejects his wife's sexual advances. He is then torn by the desire to succumb to Count Chivulsky's sexual overtures and the necessity of preserving his reputation to retain the patronage of the prudish Madame von Mecke. Pressures in both his public and private life finally prove too much for Tchaikovsky, and he willingly drinks contaminated water that will cause his own death from cholera. The film ends with Tchaikovsky's wife mentally ravaged by the realization that her life was destroyed by her husband.

Several reviewers objected to Russell's interpretation of Tchaikovsky's life and music. *New Yorker*'s Pauline Kael accused Russell of possessing "a profusion of bad ideas," and Gary Arnold charged that "Russell is such an enthusiast and unscrupulous reveller that he fabricates scandals and traumas and neuroses and psychoses on the flimsiest historical rumors in order to keep the cinematic orgy rolling." Similarly, Canby found Russell's style both excessive and inconsequential. "Never, perhaps, has one movie contained so many smashed champagne glasses," he declared, "so many lyrical fantasies . . . , so many sordid confrontations, so many clothes torn off in twisted passion, so many references to the joys and terrors of artistic creation, even so much music—but all to such little ultimate effect."

Although "The Music Lovers" was also a box-office disappointment, it was not unanimously rejected. Stephen Farber praised it as both "a pointed study of the decay of the nineteenth-century romanticism" and "a harsh nihilistic vision of the triumph of chaos." Michael Dempsey agreed, writing that "the film speaks for an age that can no longer believe so deeply in art or stand in such awe before the artist-as-priest." Other defenders argued that disenchanted reviewers denied Russell the same creative flexibility granted artists in other media. "It would seem that the same kind of poetic license that the old Hollywood biographies enjoyed should be extended Russell in order to allow him to illuminate the personalities as well as the lives of the subjects of his biopics," Phillips asserted in his *Ken Russell*. "After all, his highly imaginative approach to his material is a clear tip-off that he is presenting his own interpretation of an artist's private life and public accomplishments, an interpretation which the viewer is free to accept or reject." Similarly, Joseph Gomez wrote in his *Ken Russell: The Adapter as Creator* that "The Music Lovers" "seems excessive only to those who have failed to see that [it] is a radical critique of romantic self-indulgence and romantic evasions."

In 1970 Russell also returned to television to direct "The Dance of the Seven Veils," a film on composer Richard Strauss. Russell, however, was dissatisfied with the dramatic, but solemn, style he'd introduced in his previous biographies. "The whole idea had degenerated into a series of third-rate cliches," he commented. "I wanted to dress people in old clothes and do it in a totally *unreal* way, and thus make it more real than ever, and in the process send up this new civil service/academic way of doing films." He presented Strauss as an overrated and egomaniacal artist. "He was a Fascist," Russell insisted. "Everything he did, I think, was a glorification of the Master Race, just as bombastic and just as sham and hollow." To emphasize the bombastic aspects of Strauss's life and music, Russell elevated the story to the level of fantasy. Strauss is seen making love while an orchestra performs in his bedroom; conducting another orchestra while Nazis carve the Star of David into the chest of a Jew; and hanging from a cross after experiencing sexual relations with several nuns. These images provoked extremely negative reactions from some viewers. The British Parliament condemned the film as "vicious, savage, and brutal"; Strauss's son threatened the BBC with a lawsuit. Russell, however, contended that "The Dance of the Seven Veils" derived from Strauss's own work. "Most people objected to the violence, but it's all there in his sick operas," he claimed. "I was also blamed for putting comic dialogue in the mouth of the great man, even though it was all originally said by the man himself. And if the film was highly coloured, schmaltzy and crude, it was simply because I wished to reflect those elements in his music.''

Russell next directed the equally controversial motion picture ''The Devils,'' which he adapted from works by Aldous Huxley and John Whiting. The film details events leading to the public burning of Urbain Grandier, a priest in seventeenth-century France whose resistance to the ambitious Cardinal Richelieu leads to his own persecution. The self-destructive Grandier adheres to an unorthodox conception of sexual morality; when he clashes with Richelieu's henchmen, they pervert his beliefs into proof of his heresy. Grandier is then tortured, publicly denounced as a heretic, and burned.

For Russell, Grandier is a reluctant martyr, victimized by the false testimony of Richelieu's vindictive minions, and his death typifies the absurdity inherent in Christianity. ''What the film is saying,'' Russell explained, ''is that this would be a terrible joke if it weren't all so horrible and hadn't actually happened. I found it extraordinary that Grandier was convicted and burnt on the strength of ludicrous statements which even a child would find implausible.'' ''The Devils'' is rife with images of violence and suffering. The film begins with a glimpse of maggots feasting on a rotted corpse, continues with scenes of crucifixions and an orgy involving bald nuns, and concludes with the sight of Grandier's body swelling and blistering within the flames. Many reviewers responded to ''The Devils'' with disgust, calling it ''a truly degenerate and despicable piece of art'' and ''a farrago of witless exhibitionism.'' Stephen Farber, however, justified the violence as Russell's attempt to ''underscore the harshness of life, a vision of agony which any creative or spiritual quest must acknowledge.'' He added that ''the terrifying, fantastical nightmare images have astonishing psychological power.'' And Russell defended the film as a realistic reenactment of actual events. ''*The Devils* is a harsh film,'' he admitted, ''but it's a harsh subject. I wish the people who were horrified and appalled by it had read the book, because the facts are more horrible than anything in the film.''

After completing ''The Devils,'' Russell sought a whimsical topic. He settled on ''The Boy Friend,'' a successful stage musical. After adapting the script, Russell anticipated a relaxed and enjoyable filming experience. Unfortunately, technical and financial limitations quickly turned Russell's enthusiasm into frustration. ''I thought I would try making a musical film just for the fun,'' he acknowledged. ''But *The Boy Friend* turned out to be the most complicated project that I had ever attempted, given the time and money I had to work with.'' Dance sequences were rechoreographed to accommodate diminutive sets, and special effects were redesigned to conform to budgeting necessities. The close-knit environment Russell hoped to create among the cast and crew was also undermined by animosity and occasional violence. ''A great deal of bitterness and jealousy also spilled over into life outside the theatre,'' he revealed, ''with hotel doors being kicked down in the middle of the night, punch-ups in bedrooms and on one occasion the old dramatic overdose of sleeping pills.''

Russell's disappointment continued after ''The Boy Friend'' was released. Professing boredom with the ''cardboard characters'' of the original play, Russell had rewritten the original story—a musical salute to the Roaring Twenties—as a ''show within a show'' focusing on an understudy's sudden opportunity for stardom. But audiences failed to support the film, and Russell sympathized with them. ''In view of the public reaction to the film—I think it was too insipid for modern tastes—I'm not sure I did the right thing,'' he conceded. Rus-

sell added that ''the film should have been called *The Devils Take a Holiday.*''

In 1972 Russell directed ''Savage Messiah,'' a biography of sculptor Henri Gaudier who was killed in World War I. Gaudier typifies creative struggle for Russell, and the film is intended to erase ''the notion that most artists live in an ivory tower.'' Russell charged that ''Gaudier's life was a good example to show that art, which is simply exploiting to the full one's natural gifts, is really bloody hard work, misery, momentary defeat,'' and he contended that Gaudier would ''push a pen, wield a pick, pick fights, make enemies, contradict himself and work twenty hours a day to fulfill his vision.'' But the film also dealt considerably with Gaudier's platonic love for Sophie Brzeska. ''Of course it's a very romantic film,'' Russell said, ''but not at all sensual; very austere actually.'' Robert Phillip Kolker agreed. ''Gaudier succumbs to the world's demands, as do all of Russell's artists,'' he observed. ''But he does it with a grace and vitality and sanity that Russell heretofore has never permitted his subjects.''

Despite Russell's restrained approach, ''Savage Messiah'' was poorly received. ''Russell takes the mystique away from art,'' Canby granted, ''but supplies nothing much in its place.'' By film's end, contended Canby, ''we haven't a clue as to what Gaudier-Brzeska was up to.'' Pauline Kael asserted that the film ''is very poor technically; but that's not all that makes it bad.'' She charged Russell with replacing compassion with ''bravura splashiness'' at Gaudier's expense. ''One can't dismiss Russell's movies, because they have an influence,'' she concluded. ''They cheapen everything they touch—not consciously, I think, but instinctively.''

Russell followed ''Savage Messiah'' with another biography, ''Mahler,'' which heavily fantasized on the life of the turn-of-the-twentieth-century composer. Like Tchaikovsky in ''The Music Lovers,'' Mahler is depicted as an insecure and selfish artist willing to sacrifice his marriage for his work. ''Russell places Mahler more or less in the same category with Tchaikovsky as a man who had no qualms about subordinating his wife's life and personal interests to his own,'' Phillips noted. ''Russell implies Mahler was responsible for the atrophy of his wife's own admittedly lesser potential for musical composition because he demanded that she devote herself entirely to helping him further his career.'' Russell also criticizes Mahler's conversion from Judaism to Catholicism as a calculated business maneuver. In a symbolic sequence, Mahler appears as a rabbi clutching a Star of David. He is then transformed into an armored knight holding a cross. He presents the cross to Richard Wagner's widow, Cossima, an anti-Semite with considerable influence in German art circles. Mahler is later seen defying Jewish kosher customs by consuming pork and milk.

Russell believed that ''Mahler'' had ''the best examples of the mingling of reality and fantasy of any film that I have made.'' Audiences, however, were not lured by Russell's newest work. After playing briefly in Britain, ''Mahler'' was screened with disastrous repercussions in Los Angeles and was never commercially released across America. In *New Yorker*, Penelope Gilliatt declared that the film contained ''absolutely nothing that is serious'' and ''no insight into the tensity of Mahler's music.'' Tom Allen cited ''Mahler'' for ''juvenile excesses.''

But Russell rebounded in 1975 with ''Tommy,'' his adaptation of the rock opera by The Who's Peter Townshend. Featuring several rock performers, including The Who's vocalist Roger Daltrey as Tommy, the film succeeded at box offices in America and Europe. The story concerns a deaf, mute, and blind adolescent's rise to fame as a champion pinball player. Tommy's scheming parents parlay his popularity into a highly profitable network of summer camps, where Tommy's followers are encouraged to stifle their own senses of sight, sound, and speech. Upon discovering that Tommy's parents are exploiting them for their money, Tommy's followers rebel and destroy the camp. The film ends with Tommy's escape to an island, where he jubilantly celebrates his new life.

Critics found "Tommy" uniquely suited to Russell's skills as a director. Comparing "Tommy" to other Russell films, David Wilson wrote, "Where previously the garish, only superficially outrageous display has obstinately remained just that, there is evidence here of subject and author making a genuine, if often troubled, marriage of like minds." And Gomez acknowledged that "*Tommy,* perhaps, more than any other of his film adaptations, allowed Russell to be totally free in creating visuals from his own personal vision to match the songs and music."

"Tommy" was followed later that year by "Lisztomania," a fantasy-biography of composer Franz Liszt. The largely symbolic film focuses initially on Liszt's life as lover, composer, and performer. Harrassed by zealous fans and his lover's irate husband, Liszt moves to a winter house, where he imagines his former lovers collaborating in an attempt to dismember him. The second half dwells on Liszt's relationship with Richard Wagner, whom Russell characterizes as a Nietzschean madman bent on creating a race of Aryan "supermen." Liszt discovers Wagner's plot and uses the power of music to convert a piano into a flamethrower with which he kills Wagner. Later, in heaven, Liszt learns that Wagner's ghost has returned to earth as an enormous robot murdering European Jews with a machine-gun guitar. Liszt charges to earth in a rocket and destroys Wagner once again, then flies back to heaven celebrating his triumph.

"Lisztomania" was poorly received by viewers. Tony Raynes called it "perversely self-indulgent," while John Simon deemed it "a completely unmitigated catastrophe." Davis implied that Russell used rock performers and a rearranged score to court the lucrative rock audience—the same act of pandering that Russell criticized in Tchaikovsky and Mahler. "It's difficult to regard the director's recent efforts as other than a simple case of selling out," claimed Davis, "especially since Russell himself . . . confesses that he actually detests rock music." Farber called the situation a "double irony" and warned that "an artist who begins with a healthy desire to violate fastidious standards of good taste and shock the philistines may before long be playing to the gallery, going for broad, splashy effects that delight his less demanding fans." Russell conceded that "Lisztomania" was his worst biographical film. "The symbolism . . . is a bit too relentless and the fantasy sequences tend to submerge the reality of the characters," he noted. "I think I had exhausted the vein of biographies of composers at the time I made *Lisztomania,* at least for a while."

Russell's next film, "Valentino," failed as severely as "Lisztomania", both with critics and with the public. Although the biography of the infamous silent-film actor was considerably more realistic than "Mahler" and "Lisztomania," few viewers accepted Russell's depiction of sex-symbol Valentino as a reluctant celebrity yearning to become an orange grower. "If anything can be stated with certainty in this life," declared Kael, "it is that *nobody* becomes a movie star who wants only to grow oranges." Kael also contested Russell's broad characterizations of real individuals. "Russell takes people we're already interested in and makes them homosexual, grossly perverse, and rotten," she stated.

In 1977, the broadcast of "Clouds of Glory" marked Russell's return to British television after a seven-year absence. The film

is actually two one-hour biographies of poets William Wordsworth and Samuel Taylor Coleridge. The biography of Wordsworth, subtitled "William and Dorothy," was especially noteworthy for its subtle portrayal of the poet's intense bond with his sister. "'William and Dorothy' is the most subdued film I have done since *Delius* and *Savage Messiah,*" Russell observed. Phillips agreed, noting that "William and Dorothy's unresolved emotional conflict is beautifully understated in the film." The Coleridge biography, subtitled "The Rime of the Ancient Mariner," relies more on Russell's usual brand of fantasy, particularly in the scenes involving the poet's obsession with opium. Tony Palmer was especially impressed with a fantasy sequence in which Coleridge, under the influence of opium, sinks an anchor into his wife's chest. Palmer claimed that the scene "dwarfs almost everything else seen on television in the last decade." He added that Russell was "just the best English film director we have."

The following year Russell tried to interest studios in producing biographies of composers Ralph Vaughan Williams and Ludwig Beethoven. Producers, however, were reluctant to support Russell after the commercial failure of "Lisztomania" and "Valentino." "After VALENTINO, I was sort of dead as a director," Russell said. "When friends said they were afraid I wouldn't work again after it, I told them, 'You're not the only one!'" But that winter Russell was asked to replace Arthur Penn as director of "Altered States," a stalled project plagued by special-effects problems and creative differences between Penn and screenwriter Paddy Chayefsky. With only two months to prepare for filming, Russell nonetheless accepted the position. "I was impressed with Paddy's script," he related. "I thought there was too much dialogue, but the ideas behind it were good."

"Altered States" is Chayefsky's story of Dr. Eddie Jessup, a Harvard professor obsessed with discovering his primal self. Through sensory deprivation and hallucinogenic drugs, Jessup regresses to a simian, and eventually cellular, state, in which he discovers that the universe is a vast emptiness. The film ends with Jessup's realization that his love for his wife is all that prevents him from succumbing to the despair of his discovery.

During filming, Russell and Chayefsky disagreed on the visual interpretations. "I didn't change any of the dialogue—that was part of the deal, and Paddy wouldn't have allowed it," Russell noted, "but I was insistent upon doing the hallucinations my way." Chayefsky was displeased with Russell's overtly symbolic visuals, and argued that Russell was violating the screenwriter's intentions. Chayefsky also objected to Russell's view of the characters, and the writer began counseling actors on the set. Russell then demanded that Chayefsky be barred from the set. The producers complied, and Chayefsky, charging that "the difference between my script and what Russell did with it is the difference between art and hyperbole," removed his name from the credits.

"Altered States" proved to be Russell's most successful film since "Tommy." Andrew Sarris praised his handling of the material, and *Cinefantastique* called the film "a work of art." Among the most enthusiastic reviewers was *Time*'s Richard Corliss, who deemed "Altered States" one of 1980's ten best films. "It opens at fever pitch and then starts soaring," Corliss declared. "Russell's direction of actors and camera has never been so cagey, so controlled, so alive to the nuances of language and personality. Orchestrating the efforts of a superb production team—and of the reluctant Mr. Chayefsky—Russell has devised a film experience that will astound some viewers, outrage others and bore nobody."

Throughout his career, Russell has persisted in trying to hold the audience's interest. "I want to entertain people rather than ram ideas down their throats," he told Phillips. "I follow this code: entertain first, instruct second. I've got lots of films inside me. Some of them will be good, some will be bad. But I'll go on, whatever the critics say about me." He spoke similarly to *People*. "A critic's typical praise is 'Beautifully understated,'" Russell said. "That means beautifully false. . . . I'd rather go the other way—to gamble rather than play it safe. If I err it's by overstating, but I try to get it right."

AVOCATIONAL INTERESTS: Classical music.

BIOGRAPHICAL/CRITICAL SOURCES—Books: John Baxter, *An Appalling Talent/Ken Russell*, Michael Joseph, 1973; Colin Wilson, *Ken Russell: A Director in Search of a Hero*, Intergroup Publishers, 1974; Thomas R. Atkins, editor, *Ken Russell*, Simon & Schuster, 1976; Joseph Gomez, *Ken Russell: The Adapter as Creator*, Frederick Muller Ltd., 1977; Diane Rosenfeldt, *The Film Career of Ken Russell*, G.K. Hall, 1978; Gene D. Phillips, *Ken Russell*, Twayne, 1979; *Contemporary Literary Criticism*, Volume 16, Gale, 1981.

Periodicals: *Films and Filming*, July, 1964, January, 1968, March, 1971, August, 1971, April, 1972, January, 1976; *Manchester Guardian*, November 26, 1966; *Sight and Sound*, winter, 1969-70, autumn, 1972, summer, 1975; *New York Times*, March 26, 1970, March 29, 1970, January 17, 1971, January 25, 1971, February 21, 1971, July 17, 1971, August 15, 1971, August 29, 1971, December 17, 1971, October 15, 1972, November 9, 1972, January 7, 1973, June 23, 1974, October 19, 1975; *New Yorker*, March 28, 1970, October 30, 1971, January 8, 1972, November 18, 1972, November 7, 1977; *Film Comment*, fall, 1970, May-June, 1973, November-December, 1975; *Film Quarterly*, fall, 1970, spring, 1972, spring, 1978; *Movie Maker*, May, 1971, October, 1971, April, 1972; *Film Heritage*, summer, 1971, winter, 1973-74; *Film Journal*, September, 1972; *New Republic*, September 11, 1971, April 26, 1975; *Interview*, November, 1972; *Newsweek*, November 20, 1972, October 20, 1975; *Esquire*, May, 1973; *Oui*, June, 1973; *Observer*, September 8, 1974; *Literature/Film Quarterly*, winter, 1973; *Times Literary Supplement*, November 8, 1974; *Saturday Review*, February 8, 1975, May, 1981; *New York*, May 7,

1975, October 27, 1975; *Christian Science Monitor*, June 2, 1975, October 31, 1975; *Playboy*, October, 1975; *New York Post*, October 11, 1975; *Los Angeles Times*, October 17, 1975; *Monthly Film Bulletin*, November, 1975; *London Times*, November 15, 1975, November 16, 1975; *Rolling Stone*, December 18, 1975; *America*, May 8, 1976; *Films in Review*, June-July, 1976; *London Telegraph Sunday Magazine*, July 16, 1978; *People*, March 30, 1981; *Cinefantastique*, fall, 1981.*

—*Sketch by Les Stone*

* * *

RUSSELL, Sarah
 See LASKI, Marghanita

* * *

RUSSON, Allien R. 1905-

PERSONAL: Born December 31, 1905, in Moab, Utah; daughter of C. A. (a lawyer) and Eva (Taylor) Robertson; married Stanley Russon (an actor and jeweler), May 28, 1928; children: Shirley Russon Ririe, Diane Russon Chatwin, Robb S. *Education:* University of Utah, B.A., 1927, M.A., 1946; University of California, Los Angeles, Ed.D., 1954. *Home:* 1145 East 400 S., Salt Lake City, Utah 84102. *Office:* Department of Business, University of Utah, 1071 Annex, Salt Lake City, Utah 84112.

CAREER: University of Utah, Salt Lake City, professor of management, 1943-74. Visiting professor for U.S. Air Force in Mildenhall, England, 1970, 1971, 1973. *Member:* American Association of University Professors, UEA, Alpha Kappa Phi, Phi Kappa Phi, Beta Gamma Sigma (president, 1965, 1967), Delta Pi Sigma, Phi Chi Theta, Theta Alpha Phi, Pi Beta Phi.

WRITINGS: Business Behavior, South-Western, 1964; *Philosophy and Psychology of Teaching Typewriting*, South-Western, 2nd edition, 1972; *Personality Development for Business*, South-Western, 1973; *Personality Development for Work*, South-Western, 1981.

Author of "Your People and My People" (two-act play), anthologized in *MIA Book of Plays*.

S

SACH, Nathan
See ZACH, Nathan

* * *

SADOCK, Benjamin James 1933-

BRIEF ENTRY: Born December 22, 1933, in New York, N.Y. American psychiatrist, educator, and author. Sadock joined the faculty of New York Medical College in 1965 and became a professor of psychiatry in 1975. He also was named co-director of the Sexual Therapy Center in 1972 and director of continuing education in psychiatry in 1975. His books include *Comprehensive Group Psychotherapy* (Williams & Wilkins, 1971), *Group Treatment of Mental Illness and New Models for Group Therapy* (Dutton, 1972), *The Sexual Experience* (Williams & Wilkins, 1975), and *Modern Synopsis of Comprehensive Textbook of Psychiatry* (Williams & Wilkins, 1976). *Address:* 4 East 89th St., New York, N.Y. 10021; and Department of Psychology, New York Medical College, New York, N.Y. 10029. *Biographical/critical sources: Biographical Directory of the Fellows and Members of the American Psychiatric Association,* Bowker, 1977.

* * *

SAFARIAN, Albert Edward 1924-

PERSONAL: Born April 19, 1924, in Hamilton, Ontario, Canada; son of Israel and Annie (Simonian) Safarian; married Joan Elizabeth Shivvers, January, 1950; children: Mark, David, Laura, Paul. *Education:* University of Toronto, B.A., 1946; University of California, Berkeley, Ph.D., 1956. *Home:* 58 St. Andrews Gardens, Toronto, Ontario, Canada M4W 2E1. *Office:* Department of Political Economy, University of Toronto, 100 St. George St., Toronto, Ontario, Canada.

CAREER: Dominion Bureau of Statistics, Ottawa, Ontario, statistician in balance of payments, 1950-55; Royal Commission on Canada's Economic Prospects, Ottawa, member of research staff, 1956; University of Saskatchewan, Saskatoon, associate professor, 1956-61, professor of economics and head of department of economics and political science, 1962-66; University of Toronto, Toronto, Ontario, professor of economics, 1966—, dean of School of Graduate Studies, 1971-76. Member of faculty at Banff School of Advanced Management. Member of Task Force on the Structure of Industry, 1967. *Member:* Canadian Economic Association (president, 1976-

77), Royal Society of Canada (fellow), American Economic Association, Royal Economic Society, Ontario Economic Council.

WRITINGS: *The Canadian Economy in the Great Depression,* University of Toronto Press, 1959; *Foreign Ownership of Canadian Industry,* McGraw, 1966, 2nd edition, University of Toronto Press, 1973; *The Performance of Foreign-Owned Firms in Canada,* Canadian-American Committee, 1969; *Canadian Federalism and Economic Integration,* Privy Council Office, Government of Canada, 1974. Contributor to finance journals.*

* * *

SAGSTETTER, Karen 1941-

PERSONAL: Born August 25, 1941, in Memphis, Tenn.; daughter of William J. (an advertising manager) and Margaret (in public relations; maiden name, Young) Sagstetter; married Peter R. Lloyd-Davies, May 24, 1969 (divorced May, 1980). *Education:* Rice University, B.A., 1969, M.A. (English), 1970; State University of New York College at Buffalo, M.A. (humanities and creative writing), 1977. *Office:* Department of Foreign Area Studies, American University, 5010 Wisconsin Ave. N.W., Washington, D.C. 20016.

CAREER: Scholastic Magazines, New York City, editorial assistant, 1970-72; high school English teacher in Webster, N.Y., 1973-75; Franklin Watts, Inc., New York City, writer, 1975-76; Nero & Associates, Roslyn, Va., state coordinator, 1976-77; JWK International Corp., Annandale, Va., research analyst, 1978-80; American University, Washington, D.C., chief editor in department of foreign area studies, 1980—, teacher of creative writing, 1981—. Member of faculty at Glen Echo Writer's Center, 1977—. *Member:* Associated Writing Programs.

WRITINGS: *Lobbying* (juvenile), F. Watts, 1978; *Scholastic Composition Six* (Juvenile), Scholastic Book Services, 1980; *Half the Story* (poems), Charles Street Press, 1981; *Ceremony* (poems), State Street Press, 1982.

Work represented in anthologies, including *The Poet Upstairs,* edited by Octave Stevenson, Washington Writers Publishing House, 1979; *Takoma Park Writers,* edited by Suzanne Rodenbaugh, Down County Press, 1981. Contributor of poems to magazines, including *Shenandoah, Bits,* and *Miscellany.*

WORK IN PROGRESS: *Any Belief.*

SIDELIGHTS: Karen Sagstetter wrote: "I came to poetry only in my late twenties while I was teaching writing courses. Teaching writing is very stimulating for my own work, as is the comradeship and criticism of other writers. Writing poems is a way of cherishing experience for me." *Avocational interests:* Travel (Greece, Italy, Peru, Mexico, Ecuador).

*   *   *

St. JOHN, Nicole
See JOHNSTON, Norma

*   *   *

SAKHAROV, Andrei Dimitrievich 1921-

BRIEF ENTRY: Born May 21, 1921, in Moscow, U.S.S.R. Russian nuclear physicist and author. In 1945 Sakharov became a physicist at Moscow's Academy of Sciences, attached to the P.N. Lebedov Physics Institute. His research on nuclear fusion led to the development of the Soviet Union's hydrogen bomb, and he was subsequently awarded the Order of Lenin. As early as 1958 Sakharov was advocating educational reform in the Soviet Union; eventually his views expanded to include strenuous appeals for intellectual and political freedom for the Russian scientific community. He wrote of his visions for human development in *Progress, Coexistence, and Intellectual Freedom* (Norton, 1968). In 1970 he became a co-founder of the Human Rights Commission. Sakharov's social philosophy soon embraced freedom for all oppressed people, including Russian Jews, and he was awarded the Nobel Peace Prize in 1975. Other writings include *Sakharov Speaks* (Knopf, 1974), *My Country and the World* (Knopf, 1975), and *Alarm and Hope* (Knopf, 1978). *Address:* c/o U.S.S.R. Academy of Sciences, Leninsky Prospekt 14, Moscow, U.S.S.R. *Biographical/critical sources: Current Biography,* Wilson, 1971; *New York Times,* November 4, 1973, October 10, 1975, December 4, 1981; *Washington Post,* December 6, 1981.

*   *   *

SALPER, Roberta Linda 1940-

PERSONAL: Born September 16, 1940, in Boston, Mass. *Education:* Boston University, B.A., 1959; Harvard University, M.A., 1961, Ph.D., 1967. *Office:* Department of Communicative and Creative Arts, State University of New York College at Old Westbury, Old Westbury, N.Y. 11568.

CAREER: Milton College, Milton, Wis., instructor in Spanish literature, 1965-66; University of Pittsburgh, Pittsburgh, Pa., assistant professor of Hispanic literature, 1968-70, director of comparative literature program, 1970; State University of New York College at Old Westbury, visiting associate professor, 1970-71, associate professor of humanities, 1971—, chairperson of department of communicative and creative arts, 1973—. Fellow at Institute International, Madrid, 1961-62; guest lecturer at Sorbonne, University of Paris, 1970; visiting distinguished professor at San Diego State College, 1970-71; lecturer at Harvard University, 1972. *Member:* Modern Language Association of America. *Awards, honors:* Fellow of Harvard University in Spain, 1966-68; grant from University of Pittsburgh for Cuba, 1969; National Endowment for the Humanities younger humanist fellow, 1972-73.

WRITINGS: (Contributor) *Female Studies,* Volume I, Volume II, Volume V, Know Inc., 1970-72; (editor and author of introduction) *Female Liberation: History and Current Politics,* Knopf, 1972. Contributor to magazines, including *Ramparts* and *Ms.* Member of editorial board of *Journal of Women's Studies.**

SALTER, Elizabeth 1925-1980

PERSONAL: Born in 1925 in Bream, Gloucestershire, England; died May 7, 1980; married David Salter; children: one son, one daughter. *Education:* Attended Bedford College, University of London.

CAREER: Cambridge University, Cambridge, England, lecturer in English, 1952-63; University of York, Heslington, England, professor of English, beginning in 1963. Distinguished member of faculty at University of Connecticut.

WRITINGS: Piers Plowman: An Introduction, Harvard University Press, 1962, 2nd edition, 1969; *Chaucer: The Knight's Tale and The Clerk's Tale,* Barron's, 1962; *Chaucer,* Edward Arnold, 1962; (editor) William Langland, *Piers Plowman,* Northwestern University Press, 1967; *Piers Plowman: The C Text,* Edward Arnold, 1968; (with Derek Albert Pearsall) *Landscapes and Seasons of the Medieval World,* Elek, 1973; *Nicholas Love's "Myrrour of the Blessed Lyf of Jesu Christ,"* Institut fuer Englische Sprache und Literatur, University of Salzburg, 1974. Also author of *The Mediaeval Landscape,* 1971. Contributor to scholarly journals.

OBITUARIES: London Times, May 15, 1980.*

*   *   *

SALTUS, Edgar (Everton) 1855-1921

BRIEF ENTRY: Born October 8, 1855, in New York, N.Y.; died July 31, 1921; buried at Sleepy Hollow Cemetery, Tarrytown, N.Y. American novelist. Saltus's novels, beginning with *Mr. Incoul's Adventure* (1887), were sensational melodramas, erotic tales of murder and violence in exotic settings. His popular writings, including such historical fiction as *The Imperial Orgy* (1920), were attacked by some critics for their cynicism, eroticism, and hedonistic philosophies. Saltus's keen wit was revealed in the epigrams that ran through his fiction. His other writings include books about Balzac, Schopenhauer, and Wilde. The significance of Saltus to modern critics lies in his role as an innovator who broke the literary conventions of his time. *Biographical/critical sources: Twentieth Century Authors: A Biographical Dictionary of Modern Literature,* H.W. Wilson, 1942; *The Oxford Companion to American Literature,* 4th edition, Oxford University Press, 1965.

*   *   *

SALZER, L. E.
See WILSON, Lionel

*   *   *

SAMLI, A. Coskun 1931-

PERSONAL: Born July 21, 1931, in Istanbul, Turkey; son of S. Seref (a merchant) and Guzin (Tuncer) Samli; married Marcqueta Hill, June 19, 1959 (divorced May, 1973); married Jane H. Walter (a professor), July 12, 1976; children: (first marriage) Evan K.; (second marriage) Gena, Susan, Ayla. *Education:* Istanbul Academy of Communication Sciences, B.A., M.A., 1953; University of Detroit, M.B.A., 1956; Michigan State University, Ph.D., 1961. *Politics:* Democrat. *Religion:* Unitarian-Universalist. *Home:* 334 Loudon, Blacksburg, Va. 24060. *Office:* Department of Marketing, Virginia Polytechnic Institute and State University, Blacksburg, Va. 24061.

CAREER: California State University, Sacramento, assistant professor of marketing, 1961-65; Southern Illinois University,

Carbondale, associate professor of marketing, 1965-66; University of Southern California, Los Angeles, associate professor of marketing, 1966-68; Virginia Polytechnic Institute and State University, Blacksburg, professor of marketing, 1968—. Vice-president and member of board of directors of Sacramento Consumers Cooperative; member of board of directors of Nu-Mac Corp. *Member:* Academy of Marketing Sciences (chairman of board of governors), American Marketing Association, Academy of International Business, Southern Marketing Association, Torch International.

WRITINGS: Marketing and Distributions in Eastern Europe, Praeger, 1978.

Contributor of numerous chapters to books in his field. Contributor to marketing journals. Member of editorial review board of *Journal of Academy of Marketing Science* and *Journal of Macro Marketing.*

WORK IN PROGRESS: Utilizing Marketing Research for Marketing Strategy Decisions; Retail Marketing Strategy Development.

SIDELIGHTS: Samili commented: "I am interested in marketing, international marketing, retailing, and quality of life. As an academician I am involved in constant research. The availability of good colleagues and a reward system that considers scholarly activity to be of utmost importance are necessary ingredients of my writing."

*   *   *

SAMPLEY, J(ohn) Paul 1935-

PERSONAL: Born March 5, 1935, in Lumpkin, Ga.; married, 1956. *Education:* Duke University, B.A., 1956; Southern Methodist University, B.D., 1959, S.T.M., 1960; Yale University, B.A., 1960, Ph.D., 1966. *Office:* Department of Religious Studies, Indiana University, Bloomington, Ind. 47401.

CAREER: Clergyman of Methodist church; Drew University, Madison, N.J., instructor, 1965-66, assistant professor of religion, 1966-69, chairman of department, 1967-69; Indiana University, Bloomington, associate professor of religion, 1969—. *Member:* Society of Biblical Literature, American Academy of Religion.

WRITINGS: "And the Two Shall Become One Flesh": A Study of Traditions in Ephesians 5:21-33, Cambridge University Press, 1971; (editor with Fred O. Francis) *Pauline Parallels,* Fortress, 1975; (co-author) *Ephesians, Colossians, II Thessalonians: The Pastoral Epistles,* Fortress, 1978; *Pauline Partnership in Christ: Christian Community and Commitment in Light of Roman Law,* Fortress, 1980.*

*   *   *

SAMWAY, Patrick H(enry) 1939-

PERSONAL: Born May 12, 1939, in New York, N.Y.; son of Henry (in book sales) and Mary (Mahan) Samway. *Education:* Fordham University, B.A., 1963, Ph.L., 1964, M.A., 1965; Woodstock College, M.Div., 1969; University of North Carolina, Ph.D., 1974. *Residence:* Syracuse, N.Y. *Office:* Department of English, LeMoyne College, Syracuse, N.Y. 13214.

CAREER: Entered Society of Jesus (Jesuits), 1957, ordained Roman Catholic priest, 1969; teacher of English at Roman Catholic high school in Rochester, N.Y., 1964-66; Georgetown University, Washington, D.C., instructor in theology, 1968; LeMoyne College, Syracuse, N.Y., assistant professor, 1973-77, associate professor of English, 1973—, chairman of

department, 1977-81, chairman of Forum on Religion and Literature, 1978—. Fulbright lecturer at University of Nantes, 1975-76, and University of Paris, 1979-80; lecturer at State University of Congo, State University of Gabon, State University of Togo, State University of the Ivory Coast, State University of Morocco, University of Louvain, and University of Liege, all 1980; conducted seminars at American Cultural Center, Rome, Italy, 1980; speaker at colleges and universities in Europe. Co-sponsor of First International Faulkner Colloquium, Paris, France, 1980. *Member:* Modern Language Association of America, Association of Departments of English.

WRITINGS: (Editor with Raymond Schroth and others) *Jesuit Spirit in a Time of Change,* Newman, 1968; (contributor) James Meriwether, editor, *A Faulkner Miscellany,* University Press of Mississippi, 1974; (editor with Benjamin Forkner) *Stories of the Modern South,* Bantam, 1978, revised edition, Penguin, 1980; *Faulkner's "Intruder in the Dust": A Critical Study of the Typescripts,* Whitston Publishing, 1980; (contributor) Glenn Carey, editor, *Faulkner: The Unappeased Imagination,* Whitston Publishing, 1980. Contributor of articles and reviews to literature journals and popular magazines, including *Commonweal.*

WORK IN PROGRESS: A book on the notion of repetition in Faulkner's works, completion expected in 1982-83; "The Intertextuality of Faulkner's 'Mistral,'" to be included in a book of essays on Faulkner's short stories, edited by Maxine Rose, Louisiana State University Press, 1982; "Faulkner's Poetic Vision," to be included in a book on the Southern renaissance, edited by Ann Abadie and Doreen Fowler, University Press of Mississippi, 1982.

SIDELIGHTS: Samway wrote: "As a Jesuit priest, I am interested in the field of theology and literature, as well as the art of storytelling. Scripture scholars and poets, theologians and novelists have always had a profound reverence for both the spoken and the written word. What I find is that language helps us to understand what C. S. Lewis calls 'the pang and tether of the particular' as it leads us to more and more horizons of the mysterious. My interest in Faulkner and Southern literature is rooted in a desire to explore the American dimensions of such mystery."

*   *   *

SANDERS, Ed Parish 1937-

PERSONAL: Born April 18, 1937, in Grand Prairie, Tex.; married, 1963. *Education:* Texas Wesleyan College, B.A., 1959; Southern Methodist University, B.D., 1962; Union Theological Seminary, Th.D., 1966. *Office:* Department of Religion, McMaster University, Hamilton, Ontario, Canada L8S 4K1.

CAREER: McMaster University, Hamilton, Ontario, 1966-74, began as assistant professor, became associate professor, professor of religion, 1974—, chairman of department, 1969-71, associate dean of graduate studies, 1971-74. *Member:* Society of Biblical Literature, Society for Studies in the New Testament. *Awards, honors:* Canada Council fellowship and grant, 1968-69, grant, 1976-81; American Council of Learned Societies fellow, 1974-75; Killam senior research scholar, 1975-76; National Religious Book Award from *Religious Media Today,* 1978; National Religious Book Award from *Religious Book Review,* 1978.

WRITINGS: The Tendencies of the Synoptic Tradition, Cambridge University Press, 1969; *Paul and Palestinian Judaism: A Comparison of Patterns of Religion,* Fortress, 1977; (editor)

Jewish and Christian Self-Definition: The Shaping of Christianity in the Second and Third Centuries, Volume I, Fortress, 1980. Contributor to theology journals.

BIOGRAPHICAL/CRITICAL SOURCES: Christian Century, May 10, 1978; *Commonweal,* October 13, 1978.*

*   *   *

SANDERS, Joseph Lee   1940-

PERSONAL: Born June 29, 1940, in Crawfordsville, Ind.; son of Deryl Lee (a farmer) and Mary Frances (a teacher; maiden name, Joseph) Sanders; married Mary Sutter (a social worker), September 10, 1966; children: Benjamin, Christopher, Gregory. *Education:* DePauw University, B.A., 1962; Claremont Graduate School, M.A., 1964; Indiana University, Ph.D., 1972. *Religion:* Presbyterian. *Home:* 6354 Brooks Blvd., Mentor, Ohio 44060. *Office:* Department of English, Lakeland Community College, Mentor, Ohio 44060.

CAREER: Indiana University, Indianapolis, part-time instructor in English, 1966-68; Moorhead State College, Moorhead, Minn., assistant professor of English, 1968-72; Lakeland Community College, Mentor, Ohio, associate professor of English, 1972-73, professor of English, 1973—. *Member:* Modern Language Association of America, Science Fiction Research Association, National Education Association, Midwest Conference on English in the Two-Year College, Lakeland Faculty Association.

WRITINGS: (Contributor) Thomas D. Clareson, editor, *Voices for the Future,* Volume II, Bowling Green University, 1979; *Roger Zelazny: A Primary and Secondary Bibliography,* G. K. Hall, 1980; *A Reader's Guide to E. E. Smith,* Starmont, in press. Contributor of articles and reviews to magazines, including *Progressive, Science Fiction Studies, Science Fiction Commentary, College Press Review,* and *Lake County Historical Society Quarterly.*

WORK IN PROGRESS: "Academic Periodicals and Selected Fanzines," to be included in *Science Fiction and Fantasy Magazines,* edited by Marshall B. Tymn, Greenwood Press, 1984; a chapter on Mervyn Peake, to be included in *Voices for the Future,* Volume III, edited by Thomas D. Clareson, publication by Bowling Green University expected in 1984.

SIDELIGHTS: Sanders told *CA:* "I grew up in relative isolation, an only child raised on a farm. As a result, I read everything I could find, becoming especially interested in science fiction and fantasy. As I read, I began to analyze the things I enjoyed. My work as a critic emerged naturally from that interest in literary values—and in the whole process of communication. My purpose in writing about a piece of literature is to open it up so that readers can have a fuller, more complete experience of reading, and so that they can read more fully the next time for themselves.

"I have been very lucky in being able to do things I've enjoyed about people whose work I've liked for one reason or another. Writing a historical society article about the last real blacksmith in this area and writing a critical essay about a science fiction writer I admire have both helped me extend my skills as a writer and have brought me closer in touch with humanity. I value this as a reader, writer, and teacher. Thus, I can't help being frightened that such growth is less and less valued. Going into elementary classrooms to teach poetry writing, I'm saddened to see kids already oblivious to the pleasures of reading or writing; they are sure they have no need to—or no personal substance to—communicate. Many of the college students I see have sunk even deeper into this attitude. They are as isolated in their way as I was when I was a child, but they are doing nothing that will ever get them out of their trap. Sometimes I wonder whether it is possible to help them see and/or change. But, I keep trying."

*   *   *

SANDERS, Peter B(asil)   1938-

PERSONAL: Born in 1938, in London, England; son of Basil Alfred (a trade union official) and Ellen May (a machinist; maiden name, Cockrell) Sanders; married Janet Valerie Child (a teacher), June 30, 1961; children: Claire, Richard, Philip. *Education:* Wadham College, Oxford, M.A., 1960, D. Phil., 1970. *Politics:* Labour. *Home:* 34 Highfield Ave., Headington, Oxfordshire, England. *Office:* Commission for Racial Equality, Elliot House, Allington St., London S.W.1, England.

CAREER: Administrative officer in Lesotho, Africa, 1961-66; Ministry of Defence, London, England, officer, 1971-73; Race Relations Board, London, principal conciliation officer, 1973-74, deputy chief officer, 1974-77; Commission for Racial Equality, London, director of Equal Opportunities Division, 1977—.

WRITINGS: Moshweshwe of Lesotho, Heinemann, 1971; (editor and translator, with M. Damane) *Lithoko: Sotho Praise-Poems,* Clarendon Press, 1974; *Moshoeshoe: Chief of the Sotho,* Heinemann, 1975, Holmes & Meier, 1976. Contributor to *Journal of African History.*

WORK IN PROGRESS: Essex and the East End of London.

*   *   *

SANDERSON, Warren   1931-

PERSONAL: Born February 9, 1931, in Boston, Mass.; son of Harry (in sales) and Getrude (Marcks) Sanderson; married Edith Sylvia Lamm (a writer and editor), July 3, 1952; children: Douglas Jay, Lisa Jeanette Sanderson Haney. *Education:* Boston University, B.A., 1954, M.A., 1956; Universtiy of the Saarland, Certificate in Art History, 1960; New York University, Ph.D., 1965. *Politics:* Independent. *Home address:* P.O. Box 509, Champlain, N.Y., 12919. *Office:* Department of Art History, Concordia University, 1455 deMaisonneuve Blvd. W., Montreal, Quebec, Canada H3G 1M8.

CAREER: Southern Illinois University, Carbondale, assistant professor of art history, 1960-62; Boston University, Boston, Mass., instructor in fine arts, 1963-64; State University of New York College at Buffalo, associate professor of art history, 1964-66; University of Illinois at Chicago Circle, Chicago, associate professor, 1966-68, professor of history of art and architecture, 1968-70; Florida State University, Tallahassee, professor of art history, 1970-76, member of monograph advisory committee of Florida State University Press; Concordia University, Montreal, Quebec, associate professor, 1976-79, professor of art history, 1979—, director of graduate division of faculty of fine arts, 1979-81, fellow in fine arts, 1978—. Visiting associate professor at University of Notre Dame, summer, 1966; visiting adjunct professor at Rosary College, 1968-69; Deutsche Forschungsgemeinschaft Professor at University of Trier, 1977-78. Principal planner of excavation of the former monastery of St. Maximin at Trier, 1978. Member of Montreal's Center for Medieval Art, New York, N.Y.; senior Canadian member of International Committee for History of Art, 1980—, President of Canadian National Committee for History of Art, 1980; chairman of symposia; director of forums. Member of Oak Park Citizen's Action Committee, 1969-70.

MEMBER: Society for the Study of Architecture in Canada, Universities Arts Association of Canada, Society of Architectural Historians, College Art Association of America, Mediaeval Academy of America, Archaeological Institute of America (member of executive board of Montreal chapter, 1978—), Oak Park Historical Society (charter member). *Awards, honors:* Fulbright grants for Europe, 1959-60, 1966; Fritz Thyssen Foundation grant, 1965-68; American Philosophical Society grant (from Penrose Fund) for Belgium, 1969; Canada Council grant, 1980.

WRITINGS: (Contributor) Reinhard Schindler and Heinz Cueppers, editors, *Hundertjahresfestschrift: Rheinisches Landesmuseum Trier* (title means "Centennial Commemorative Publication of the Rheinisches Landesmuseum at Trier"), Philip von Zabern Press, 1980; (editor, translator, and contributor) *The International Handbook of Contemproary Developments in Architecture,* Greenwood Press, 1981; (contributor) Alfred Schmid, editor, *Religious Reform and the Arts During the Carolingian Era,* International Congress of History of Art, 1982; (contributor) Friedhelm Lach, editor, *The Avant-Garde and Semiotics,* Indiana University Press, 1982. Contributor of articles and reviews to arts history journals in the United States, Canada, and abroad. Member of advisory board of *Archaeological News,* 1972—.

WORK IN PROGRESS: A book tentatively titled *Innovation and Tradition in Contemporary Global Architecture Since 1960,* publication expected in 1984; *Modern Architecture in Mexico, 1930-1982,* publication expected in 1985; a monograph on the architecture of Agustin Hernandez in Mexico, completion expected in 1986; *The Architecture of St. Maximin at Trier, 350-1250,* a monograph, publication by Zabern Press expected in 1988; research on ideas in twentieth-century architecture and on the development of ivory carving from about 870 through 970 in western Europe.

SIDELIGHTS: Sanderson wrote: "My entire life has been involved with art and its histories, from a summer moment when, at the age of nine, I was introduced to the collections of the Boston Museum of Fine Arts. When I was a young man, only the precision of the hard sciences vied with my fascination with art. I taught high school sciences for two years in a small village in upstate New York, and considered attending medical school, but chose instead to go to graduate school in art history. Above all else, I have given myself to teaching.

"Throughout my career I have sustained a great interest in and enthusiasm for architecture, its history and technology. I had taught architectural history and had written on medieval art and architecture when I was invited to conceive a plan for an international handbook of contemporary architecture. Since then a great deal of my thinking has been about modern architecture, and it will continue to occupy the greater portion of my time. For me architecture (and art) provides insights into the ways in which people think, if not into the thoughts themselves.

"Vital to me, aside from architecture and art, and in order of importance are international politics, international economics, and the scanning of foreign newspapers whenever time permits (particularly *Die Zeit* from Hamburg and *Corriera della Sera* from Milan). In the realm of politics I am most particularly concerned about the coincidence of, and possible causal interrelationships between, on the one hand, the leveling, homogenizing, and artificial effects of television (such as news that editorializes unannouncedly by visual imagery alone) and, on the other, the broadly based conditions that have tended to obstruct development of an enlightened, responsible, and effective leadership in most of the world during the last score of years. I am more than slightly concerned at the drastically decreasing awareness of individual, personal, and public responsibilities that I have observed on the part of so many during the last decade and more, since this bodes badly for the future of both tolerance and liberty. There seems to have arisen a sardonic misunderstanding of the differences between liberty and libertarianism in North America and Europe, but also elsewhere. Though it is certainly no longer in vogue, a measure of the puritanism about which I learned as a boy in Boston might be useful today in that city, as in others, to help tip the scales of moral and ethical values toward a better balance, a balance upon which personal and national prides may rest in realistic and humane relationships with the necessarily pragmatic requirements of daily life."

AVOCATIONAL INTERESTS: Politics, music (classical, jazz, and bluegrass), ice hockey, football, travel.

*   *   *

SANGSTER, Margaret E(lizabeth)   1894-1981

OBITUARY NOTICE: Born in 1894 in Brooklyn, N.Y.; died in 1981 in Valatie, N.Y. Poet, editor, scriptwriter, journalist, and novelist. Sangster served variously as contributor, war correspondent, and columnist for the *Christian Herald* magazine. She also wrote poems, short stories, novels, and radio and television scripts. Among her published works are *Cross Roads, The Island of Faith, The Stars Come Close,* and *Singing on the Road.* Obituaries and other sources: *American Authors and Books, 1640 to the Present Day,* 3rd revised edition, Crown, 1972; *AB Bookman's Weekly,* December 7, 1981.

*   *   *

SANTOLI, Al   1949-

PERSONAL: Born June 20, 1949, in Cleveland, Ohio; son of Albert A. (employed by National Aeronautics and Space Administration) and Faye (Ambrogio) Santoli. *Education:* Attended Ohio State University; College of Marin, A.A., 1975; Naropa Institute, B.A., 1977. *Residence:* New York, N.Y. *Agent:* John Thaxton, 212 East 18th St., New York, N.Y. 10018.

CAREER: Free-lance writer, 1972—. Playwright, actor, and director in New York, N.Y., 1978—. *Military service:* U.S. Army, 1967-70; served in Vietnam; became sergeant; received Bronze Star and three Purple Hearts. *Member:* Dramatists Guild. *Awards, honors:* Rockefeller Foundation fellowship, 1977; Muriel Rukeyser Award for poetry from New York Quarterly Poetry Foundation, 1980, for "R and R."

WRITINGS: Everything We Had: An Oral History of the Vietnam War by Thirty-Three American Soldiers Who Fought It (selection of Book-of-the-Month Club, History Book Club, and Adventure Book Club), Random House, 1981.

Plays: "Ashes to Ashes" (one-act), first produced in Boulder, Colo., at 1111 Pearl St., 1976; "The Screaming Eagles" (one-act), first produced in New York, N.Y., at American Theatre of Actors, 1980.

Contributor of poems and articles to *New York Quarterly* and *Family Weekly.*

WORK IN PROGRESS: Another book, completion expected in 1983; research for a play about Robert Kennedy.

SIDELIGHTS: Everything We Had, Santoli's oral history of the Vietnam War, was praised by Ron Kovic of the *Washington Post Book World* as "a magnificent achievement. One of the most powerful and truthful documents to come out of the Vietnam war, it should be read by every American, every representative and senator, and the president of the United States. It is personal, it is authentic, it has great dignity, and it will last.'' Santoli interviewed thirty-three Vietnam veterans and transcribed their stories of the war. ''These voices,'' wrote Jack Fuller of the *Chicago Tribune,* ''are treated with a kind of care that gives them a legitimacy they never had before, an authenticity. . . . As the anecdotes mount—from the first shocks of basic training through the ordeal of first fire and the wounds and deaths until the soldiers come home to the final shock of indifference—the complex sadness is hard to bear. . . . Santoli . . . [has] done us all a great service.''

Marc Leepson of the *New York Times Book Review* found portions of the book unsatisfying. ''Too many of these first-person accounts are pointlessly anecdotal, and a few are barely intelligible. And yet there are some gems. . . . One section is truly brilliant: a 13-page juxtaposition of the reminiscences of a lieutenant with a cushy job near Saigon and of a Marine stuck in the hell of Khe Sanh. This deft opposition of stories provides an inspired metaphor for the surrealistic craziness of the war.''

Santoli wrote: ''When I got out of the army, I almost became a physical therapist, but an English teacher at Ohio State realized that my urge to communicate as a writer, especially after my Vietnam experience as a teenage infantry sergeant, was much more vital, even though I could not write about it at that time.

''It took me ten years to begin to recount my war experiences. The most important element of *Everything We Had* is the human quality of the perceptions and feelings of each soldier: understanding the vulnerability that is inherent in courage and the acknowledgment of fear in bravery. This was my reality as a combat soldier and through my background in poetry and the theatre. The emotional content of each person's memory is what makes the stories in the book unforgettable.

''As with the ancient Greek poets and historians whose epics were passed on in oral tradition, and with the way Shakespeare's works are widely remembered accounts of the historical periods his characters represent, the thirty-three people in *Everything We Had* are very real ordinary Americans who became extraordinary by overcoming the horrors of war and the postwar stigma imposed on Vietnam veterans. Through inner strength they had the courage not to give up on the country that sent them to war and then betrayed their sacrifice. Most important, looking at war as the most dramatic and condensed epitome of the human condition, after all we've been through, we still have the hope that future generations may learn the advantages of peace through our accounts.''

BIOGRAPHICAL/CRITICAL SOURCES: Films in Review, November, 1979; *Book Digest,* April, 1981; *Time,* April 20, 1981; *Washington Post Book World,* April 26, 1981; *Washington Star,* April 29, 1981; *Cleveland Press,* May 7, 1981, May 14, 1981; *Chicago Tribune,* May 17, 1981; *New York Times Book Review,* May 17, 1981; *Los Angeles Times,* June 5, 1981; *New York Times,* June 10, 1981; *Cleveland,* July, 1981; *Boston Globe,* July 13, 1981.

*   *   *

SARJEANT, William A(ntony) S(within)   1935-

PERSONAL: Born July 15, 1935, in Sheffield, England; son of Harold (a steelworks storekeeper) and Margaret (a legal executive) Sarjeant; married Jacqueline Patricia Scott (a teacher), 1960 (divorced, 1964); married Anne Margaret Crowe (a librarian), 1966; children: (second marriage) Nicola Rosalind,

Rachel Penelope, Juliet Katharine. *Education:* University of Sheffield, B.Sc. (with honors), 1956, Ph.D., 1959; University of Nottingham, D.Sc., 1972. *Politics:* ''No party allegiance.'' *Religion:* United Church of Canada. *Home:* 674 University Dr., Saskatoon, Saskatchewan, Canada S7N 0J2. *Office:* Room 108/2, Department of Geological Science, General Purpose Building, University of Saskatchewan, Saskatoon, Saskatchewan, Canada S7N 0W0.

CAREER: University of Reading, Reading, England, research fellow, 1961-62; University of Nottingham, Nottingham, England, assistant lecturer, 1963-65, lecturer in geology, 1965-72; University of Saskatchewan, Saskatoon, associate professor, 1972-75, professor of geological science, 1975—. Visiting professor at University of Oklahoma, 1968-69. Chairman of Saskatoon Special Committee on Historic Buildings, 1974-80; member of Saskatchewan Heritage Advisory Board, 1977—; consultant to oil companies and commercial research organizations.

MEMBER: Geological Association of Canada, Society of Economic Paleontologists and Mineralogists (chairman of trace fossil research group, 1976-77), American Association of Stratigraphical Palynologists, Geological Society (fellow), Linnean Society (fellow), Geological Society of France, Paleontological Association, Saskatoon Environmental Society (chairman, 1974-75), Explorers Club.

WRITINGS: (With Charles Downie) *Bibliography and Index of Fossil Dinoflagellates and Acritarchs,* Geological Society of America, 1964; (with Geoffrey Norris) *A Descriptive Index of Genera of Fossil Dinophyceae and Acritarcha,* New Zealand Geological Survey, 1965; (with Sally P. Clubb) *Saskatoon's Historic Buildings and Sites,* Saskatoon Environmental Society, 1973, 3rd edition, 1980; (with Graham L. Williams and Evan J. Kidson) *A Glossary of the Terminology Applied to Dinoflagellate Amphiesmae and Cysts and Acritarchs,* American Association of Stratigraphic Palynologists, 1973, 2nd edition, 1978; *Fossil and Living Dinoflagellates,* Academic Press, 1974; (with William P. Delainey) *Saskatoon: The Growth of a City,* Part I: *The Formative Years,* Saskatoon Environmental Society, 1975, 2nd edition, 1976; (editor with Marjorie D. Muir) *Palynology,* two volumes, Dowden, 1977; *An Identification Guide to Jurassic Dinoflagellate Cysts,* Department of Geology and Geophysics, Louisiana State University, 1978; (editor with Walter O. Kupsch) *History of Concepts in Precambrian Geology,* Geological Association of Canada, 1979; *Geologists and the History of Geology,* five volumes, Arno, 1980; (editor) *Terrestrial Trace-Fossils,* Hutchinson & Ross, 1982.

Translator and editor; published by National Lending Library: T. F. Vozzhennikova, *Type Pyrrophyta Pyrrophytic Algae,* 1966; Vozzhennikova, *Introduction to the Study of Fossilised Peridinid Algae,* 1967; *Papers Presented to the Palaeontological Congress, Novobirsk, 1965,* 1967; Vozzhennikova, editor, *Fossil Algae of the U.S.S.R.,* 1969; Vozzhennikova, *Fossilised Peridinid Algae in the Jurassic, Cretaceous and Palaeogene Deposits of the U.S.S.R.,* two volumes, 1971; B. V. Timofeev, *Micropalaeophytological Research Into Ancient Strata,* 1974.

Contributor of more than one hundred sixty articles to scientific journals; contributor of articles on local history, folksong, and detective fiction to newspapers and periodicals, including *Urban History Review, Folk Review, Canada Folk Bulletin, The Armchair Detective,* and *The Poisoned Pen.* Editor of *Sorby Record,* Sheffield, England, 1958-59, and *Mercian Geologist,* 1964-70.

WORK IN PROGRESS: Editing *Treatise on Invertebrate Paleontology,* volumes on dinoflagellates and acritarchs, publication by Geological Society of America expected in 1984; a supplement to *Geologists and the History of Geology,* publication by Arno expected in 1984; fiction.

SIDELIGHTS: Sarjeant commented: ''My parents' interest in archaeology stimulated an interest in the past, which in my case focused on fossils and led to a career in geology. A passion for reading and a liking for the organizing of data (and material objects!) made me a collector and ultimately a bibliographer.

''Geological research has taken me to Sicily, Algeria, Tunisia, Iran, Australia, and to many parts of the United States; private travels have taken me to most countries of western Europe.

''Wide-ranging interests in natural history, travel, and—perhaps more unexpectedly—folksong, blues, and jazz have enriched and added variety to what might otherwise have been a dull life. I ran a folksong club in Nottingham and currently sing in a group called the Prairie Higglers. I have also produced and introduced three series of folksong programs for CJUS-FM Radio in Saskatoon, using my large record collection as a basis.

''Because of a quirk of eyesight, I cannot watch television; instead, I read voraciously and have a book collection of some fifty thousand volumes, in particular on geology, mystery fiction, the history of archaeology (and history generally), English humor (mostly twentieth century), folk music and jazz, and fantasy. My taste in fiction is decidedly escapist; too much realism, in mysteries or novels, is unwelcome, and a good imagination and storytelling ability generally means more to me than fine writing.''

BIOGRAPHICAL/CRITICAL SOURCES: Geoscience Canada, May, 1976; *Geology,* March, 1981.

*   *   *

SARNDAL, Carl Erik   1937-

PERSONAL: Born July 17, 1937, in Herrljunga, Sweden; son of Carl O. F. and Signe M. (Andersson) Sarndal. *Education:* University of Lund, Ph.D., 1962. *Home:* 223 Willowdale, Montreal, Quebec, Canada. *Office:* Department of Mathematics and Statistics, University of Montreal, Montreal, Quebec, Canada H3C 3J7.

CAREER: University of British Columbia, Vancouver, professor of statistics, 1970-80; University of Montreal, Montreal, Quebec, professor of statistics, 1980—. Member of National Central Bureau of Statistics, Stockholm, Sweden. *Member:* International Statistical Institute, Canadian Statistical Association, American Statistical Association (fellow), Institute of Mathematical Statistics (fellow), Swedish Association of Statisticians (president, 1970).

WRITINGS: Information From Censored Samples (monograph), Almqvist & Wiksell, 1962; *Foundations of Inference in Survey Sampling,* Wiley, 1977. Editor of *Journal of the American Statistical Association* and *Canadian Journal of Statistics.*

WORK IN PROGRESS: Research on survey sampling and analysis of data.

*   *   *

SASLOW, Helen   1926-

PERSONAL: Born March 20, 1926, in Brooklyn, N.Y.; daughter of Isidore (a decorator) and Sadie (in business) Loss; married George Saslow (an educator), April 6, 1952; children: Elizabeth, Claudia. *Education:* Brooklyn College (now of City University of New York), B.A., 1948. *Home:* 3626 Kings Highway, Brooklyn, N.Y. 11234.

CAREER: Board of Education, New York, N.Y., substitute teacher, 1951-65; writer, 1965—.

WRITINGS: Arctic Summer (poems), Barlenmir, 1974.

Work represented in anthologies, including *Hellcoal Annual,* 1978. Contributor to magazines, including *New York Quarterly, Hanging Loose, Glassworks, Confrontation, Phoenix,* and *Moonlight Review.*

WORK IN PROGRESS: November Passage, poems; a novel; short stories.

SIDELIGHTS: Helen Saslow commented: ''All my life I have found great pleasure in writing; I began composing short stories at the age of ten and poetry as a freshman in high school. The poetry readings I've given at Brown University, churches, playhouses, and to poetry workshops have proved to be meaningful experiences as well. As a young teacher in the 1950's I was encouraged by my supervisors to offer creative writing workshops, and I have compiled a book of lesson plans for teachers on my methods.''

*   *   *

SAUL, Mary

CAREER: Author.

WRITINGS: (With Arthur Peter Hoblyn Oliver) *Collecting Tropical Marine Molluscs,* Conchological Society of Great Britain and Ireland, 1972; *Shells: An Illustrated Guide to a Timeless and Fascinating World,* Country Life Books, 1974.*

*   *   *

SAUNDERS, Richard   1947-

PERSONAL: Born August 26, 1947, in Chattanooga, Tenn.; son of Herbert (in sales) and Gretchen (a dancer; maiden name, De Haven) Saunders; married Paula Olsson (a florist), June 27, 1970. *Education:* Monterey Peninsula College, A.A., 1971; Sonoma State College, B.A., 1975. *Home:* 228 Wood St., Pacific Grove, Calif. 93950. *Agent:* Harvey Klinger, Inc., 301 West 53rd St., New York, N.Y. 10019.

CAREER: House painter, 1969-72; furniture repairer, 1972—. Antiques dealer, 1976—. *Member:* Authors Guild, Authors League of America.

WRITINGS: Collecting and Restoring Wicker Furniture, Crown, 1976; *The World's Greatest Hoaxes,* Playboy Press, 1980; (author of introduction) *The 1898 Heywood Brothers and Wakefield Company Catalogue,* Dover, 1982; *The Official Price Guide to Wicker Furniture,* House of Collectibles Press, 1982.

WORK IN PROGRESS: Smile, My Ass! (tentative title), the autobiography of Allen Funt, with Funt, publication expected in 1983; *The Fallen Eagle,* a book about the ill-fated 1897 Swedish balloon expedition to the North Pole, 1983.

SIDELIGHTS: Saunders wrote: ''I feel the balance created by writing *and* working with my hands is a most productive and enjoyable one.''

*   *   *

SAUSSURE, Eric de
See de SAUSSURE, Eric

SAXTON, Alexander P(laisted) 1919-

PERSONAL: Born July 16, 1919, in Great Barrington, Mass.; married, 1941; children: two. *Education:* University of Chicago, A.B., 1940; University of California, Berkeley, M.A., 1962, Ph.D., 1967. *Office:* Department of History, University of California, Los Angeles, Calif. 90024.

CAREER: University of California, Berkeley, instructor in American history, 1966-67; Wayne State University, Detroit, Mich., assistant professor of American history, 1967-68; University of California, Los Angeles, associate professor, 1968-76, professor of American history, 1976—. *Military service:* U.S. Merchant Marine, 1943-46. *Member:* American Historical Association, American Studies Association.

WRITINGS: Grand Crossing, Harper, 1943; *The Great Midland,* Appleton, 1948; *Bright Web in the Darkness,* St. Martin's, 1958; *The Great Fear,* Holt, 1970; *The Indispensable Enemy: Labor and the Anti-Chinese Movement in California,* University of California Press, 1971; (contributor) *As It Happened: A History of the United States,* McGraw, 1975. Contributor to history journals.*

*　　　*　　　*

SAXTON, Judith 1936-
(Judy Turner)

PERSONAL: Born March 5, 1936, in Norwich, England. *Home:* 110 Park Ave., Wrexham, Denbighshire, Wales. *Agent:* Murray Pollinger, 11 Long Acre, London WC2E 9LH, England.

CAREER: Writer.

WRITINGS—All historical novels: *The Bright Day Is Done: The Story of Amy Robsart,* Constable, 1974; *Princess in Waiting,* Constable, 1976; *Winter Queen,* Constable, 1977.

Under name Judy Turner: *Ralegh's Fair Bess,* St. Martin's, 1974; *Cousin to the Queen: The Story of Lettice Knollys,* Constable, 1974. Also author of *Feather Light, Diamond Bright,* 1974, *My Master Mariner,* 1974, and *The Queen's Corsair,* 1976.*

*　　　*　　　*

SCHAFFER, Jeff(rey P.) 1943-

PERSONAL: Born April 2, 1943, in Glendale, Calif.; son of Francis M. (a postmaster) and Lorraine M. (a library clerk; maiden name, Mollner) Schaffer. *Education:* Attended Massachusetts Institute of Technology, 1961-62; University of California, Berkeley, B.A., 1965, M.A., 1969, doctoral study, 1971-72. *Politics:* "Liberal philosophy, but economic responsibility." *Religion:* "None—ex-Catholic." *Office:* Wilderness Press, 2440 Bancroft Way, Berkeley, Calif. 94704.

CAREER: Wilderness Press, Berkeley, Calif., principal author and mapper of Pacific Crest Trail mapping project, 1972, assistant publisher, 1973—. Photographer, cartographer, and naturalist. *Member:* American Civil Liberties Union, Common Cause, Zero Population Growth.

WRITINGS—Published by Wilderness Press: *The Pacific Crest Trail* (self-illustrated), Volume I (with Thomas Winnett, Jim Jenkins, Andy Husari, and John W. Robinson): *California,* 1973, revised edition, 1975, 3rd revised edition, 1982, Volume II (with Beverly Hartline and Fred Hartline): *Oregon and Washington,* 1974, revised edition, 1976, 3rd revised edition, 1979;

The Tahoe Sierra: A Natural History Guide to One Hundred Hikes in the Northern Sierra, 1975, fourth revised edition, 1979; *Sonora Pass High Sierra Hiking Guide,* 1976, revised edition, 1978; *Yosemite National Park,* 1978; *Desolation Wilderness and the South Lake Tahoe Basin,* 1980; *Lassen Volcanic National Park and Vicinity,* 1981.

SIDELIGHTS: Schaffer commented: "I never planned to be a writer. In college I dreaded term papers, even though I did well on them. However, I liked nature and took one or more courses in virtually every field of natural science; this background, coupled with my mountaineering and photographic experience, led me quite naturally to Wilderness Press. I am a fanatic on accuracy and detail. My main goal is to produce outdoor books of exceptional quality. I attempt to convey to the public the most up-to-date natural history information on the areas I cover, even if I have to do the scientific field work (usually geology) myself. I see to it that my maps surpass the toughest standards of accuracy. The public deserves the very best."

*　　　*　　　*

SCHAMA, Simon Michael 1945-

PERSONAL: Surname is pronounced Sha-ma; born February 13, 1945, in London, England; came to the United States in 1980; son of Arthur Osias and Gertrude Clare (Steinberg) Schama. *Education:* Christ's College, Cambridge, B.A., 1966, M.A., 1969. *Home:* 49 Hancock St., Boston, Mass. 02114. *Agent:* A . D. Peters & Co. Ltd., 10 Buckingham St., London WC2N 6BU, England. *Office:* 5 Bryant St., Cambridge, Mass. 02138.

CAREER: Cambridge University, Cambridge, England, fellow of Christ's College and director of studies in history, 1966-76; Oxford University, Oxford, England, fellow of Brasenose College and tutor in history, 1976-80; Harvard University, Cambridge, Mass., professor of history, 1980—. *Awards, honors:* Wolfson Prize for History from Wolfson Foundation, 1977, and Leo Gersoy Memorial Prize from American Historical Association, 1978, both for *Patriots and Liberators.*

WRITINGS: (Editor with Eric Homberger and William Janeway) *The Cambridge Mind,* Little, Brown, 1970; *Patriots and Liberators: Revolution in the Netherlands, 1780-1813,* Knopf, 1977; *Two Rothschilds and the Land of Israel,* Knopf, 1979; *Affluence and Anxiety: A Social Interpretation of Dutch Culture in Its Golden Age,* Knopf, 1983. Contributor to magazines and newspapers.

WORK IN PROGRESS: Waltzes: Europe 1800-1870, a history of nineteenth-century Europe; a book on the sociology of culture and the history of the art market in the seventeenth century.

SIDELIGHTS: Schama wrote: "My interests have moved from eighteenth-century politics via Jewish history, back to the culture of early modern Europe, especially with respect to the relation between money, guilt, and art. I am plundering unscrupulously the techniques of art history and anthropology."

AVOCATIONAL INTERESTS: 1966 claret, Schubert.

*　　　*　　　*

SCHAUB, Thomas Hill 1947-

PERSONAL: Born January 17, 1947, in Aurora, Ill.; son of Louis E. (a teacher) and Orise (a teacher; maiden name, Hill) Schaub. *Education:* Cornell College, Mount Vernon, Iowa, B.A., 1969; attended Yale University, 1969; University of

Iowa, Ph.D., 1976. *Office:* Department of English, University of California, Berkeley, Calif. 94720.

CAREER: University of California, Berkeley, assistant professor of English, 1980—. *Member:* Modern Language Association of America. *Awards, honors:* Danforth fellowship, 1969-76; Rockefeller Brothers fellowship, 1969.

WRITINGS: Pynchon: The Voice of Ambiguity, University of Illinois Press, 1981.

WORK IN PROGRESS; Research on American fiction and criticism, especially since World War II.

SIDELIGHTS: Schaub told *CA:* "Writing about fiction is a consequence both of my training and of my engagement with writing and ideas. I feel lucky to have a job that requires and allows this writing. A growing sidelight is my interest in the personal essay. I spent three years in Maine, where I bought land and built a house, and while there began to write about what I'd been doing in the years prior. This led to an interest in the personal-essay genre, which I now teach in my composition classes. Writing is itself always an immediate experience and exciting on that account; and I find the personal essay doubly so because of the imagination required to bring sense and coherence to one's own life. I hope to find time to develop the work I began in Maine.

"Criticism of American fiction written since World War II often seems entirely at odds with the spirit and intent of the writing. Thus far there are no satisfactory overviews of these thrity-five years, and criticism has tended to identify schools of writers (Beats, New Yorker writers, Jewish writers, meta-fictionists). None of this analysis has been very compelling, and much of it unsympathetic because the critics have brought to this postwar writing the expectations and predilections formed in the twenty years before World War II. In particular, many critics have objected to a perceived abdication of the writer's obligation to address social issues. This indictment has always puzzled me, though the claims made against such books as *Invisible Man, Naked Lunch,* and *The Crying of Lot 49* suggest that the real issue for these critics is one of deportment and manner, rather than social conscience. More understanding and sympathetic accounts of this writing have appeared, of course, and these will increase, especially as time gives us the aid of perspective."

*   *   *

SCHEFF, Thomas Joel   1929-

PERSONAL: Born August 1, 1929, in Wewoka, Okla.; son of Arthur (a merchant) and Sarah (Goldman) Scheff; married Elin Pratt, April 17, 1953 (divorced, 1972); married Jane Hewitt (a marriage counselor), July 14, 1975; children: Karl Jacob, Robin Ann, Julie Susan. *Education:* University of Arizona, B.S., 1950; University of California, Berkeley, M.A., 1958, Ph. D., 1960. *Home:* 2607 Puesta del Sol, Santa Barbara, Calif. 93105. *Office:* Department of Sociology, University of California, Santa Barbara, Calif. 93106.

CAREER: University of Wisconsin (now University of Wisconsin—Madison), assistant professor of sociology, 1959-63; University of California, Santa Barbara, visiting assistant professor, 1963-64, associate professor, 1964-67, professor of sociology, 1967—. *Military service:* U.S. Army, 1953-55. *Member:* American Sociological Association, American Psychological Assocation. *Awards, honors:* Social Science Research Council fellow, 1963-64.

WRITINGS: Being Mentally Ill, Aldine, 1966; *Mental Illness and Social Process,* Harper, 1970; *Labeling Madness,* Pren-

tice-Hall, 1972; *Catharsis in Healing, Ritual, and Drama,* University of California Press, 1980. Contributor to journals in the social and behavioral sciences.

WORK IN PROGRESS: Good Grief!; research on video tape studies of emotional processes.

*   *   *

SCHEFFER, Nathalie P.   1890(?)-1981

OBITUARY NOTICE: Born c. 1890 in St. Petersburg (now Leningrad), Russia (now U.S.S.R.); died of cardiac arrest, December 11, 1981, in Washington, D.C. Librarian and author. Scheffer came to the United States in 1930 and settled in the Washington, D.C., area. In 1945 she joined the staff of the Dumbarton Oaks Research Library and Collection, where she headed the Slavic division until her retirement in 1965. Scheffer's articles and books, which discuss the Russian Revolution and Russian iconography, include *Russian Icon.* Her memoirs, *Twice Born in Russia,* appeared in the 1920's. Obituaries and other sources: *Washington Post,* December 23, 1981.

*   *   *

SCHERR, Max   1916(?)-1981

OBITUARY NOTICE: Born c. 1916; died of cancer, c. November, 1981, in Berkeley, Calif. Founder and publisher of the *Berkeley Barb.* Scherr founded the underground newspaper in 1965 during Berkeley's free speech movement. The *Barb* promoted drugs, "free" sex, and revolution, expressing ideas of the student activism of the 1960's. Scherr's newspaper peaked in popularity in 1969; it closed in 1980. Obituaries and other sources: *Time,* November 16, 1981.

*   *   *

SCHIVELBUSCH, Wolfgang   1941-

PERSONAL: Born November 26, 1941, in Berlin, Germany; came to the United States in 1975; son of Kurt (a merchant) and Waltraud (Dannenberg) Schivelbusch. *Education:* Attended Goethe Universitaet, Frankfurt, 1964-72; Freie Universitaet, Berlin, Ph.D., 1972. *Home:* 310 Greenwich St., New York, N.Y. 10013.

CAREER: Writer. *Awards, honors:* Deutscher Sachbuchpreis (German nonfiction award), 1978; fellowship from New York Institute for the Humanities, 1980-81.

WRITINGS: Sozialistisches Drama nach Brecht (title means "Socialist Drama After Brecht"), Luchterhand, 1974; *Geschichte der Eisenbahnreise,* Hanser, 1977, translation by Anselm Hollo published as *The Railway Journey,* Urizen, 1980; *Das Paradies, der Geschmack und die Vernunft* (title means "Paradise, Taste, and Reason"), Hanser, 1980.

WORK IN PROGRESS: A study of intellectual life in Frankfurt during the Weimar Republic, publication by Insel Verlag expected in 1982; a cultural history of lighting during the nineteenth century, publication by Hanser Verlag expected in 1983.

SIDELIGHTS: Schivelbusch told *CA:* "My main interest is in the cultural history and anthropology of the industrial revolution, particularly in relation to the cultural and psychological effects of certain technological innovations, such as railways, gas-light, and drugs."

BIOGRAPHICAL/CRITICAL SOURCES: New York Times Book Review, January 11, 1981.

SCHLABRENDORFF, Fabian von
See von SCHLABRENDORFF, Fabian

*   *   *

SCHMID, Carol L(ouise) 1946-

PERSONAL: Born December 11, 1946, in Santa Barbara, Calif.; daughter of William E. (a teacher) and Martha (Smith) Thomas; married Peter Schmid (a chemist), December 6, 1969. *Education:* University of California, Santa Cruz, B.A., 1969; McMaster University, M.A., 1974, Ph.D., 1978. *Home address:* Route 2, Box 118-B, Julian, N.C. 27283. *Office:* Department of Sociology, Guilford College, Greensboro, N.C. 27410.

CAREER: Kuoni Travel Ltd., Zurich, Switzerland, travel consultant, 1970-71; University of Oregon, Eugene, visiting assistant professor of sociology, 1977-79; Guilford College, Greensboro, N.C., assistant professor of sociology, 1979—. *Member:* American Sociological Association, Society for the Study of Social Problems, Sociologists for Women in Society, Southern Sociological Society. *Awards, honors:* Travel grant from Social Science and Humanities Council of Canada, 1976-77.

WRITINGS: Conflict and Consensus in Switzerland, University of California Press, 1981. Contributor to sociology journals in the United States and abroad.

WORK IN PROGRESS: Research on citizenship and race relations, minority women, and social policy and planning.

AVOCATIONAL INTERESTS: Travel, music, gardening.

*   *   *

SCHNABEL, Truman Gross, Jr. 1919-

PERSONAL: Born January 5, 1919, in Philadelphia, Pa.; son of Truman Gross and Hildegard (Rohner) Schnabel; married Mary Hyatt, September 13, 1947; children: Ann, Daniel, Paul, Brooke. *Education:* Attended Bowdoin College, 1936-37; Yale University, B.S., 1940; University of Pennsylvania, M.D., 1943. *Home:* 306 South Roberts Rd., Rosemont, Pa. 19010. *Office:* Philadelphia General Hospital, 34th St. and Civic Center Blvd., Philadelphia, Pa. 19104.

CAREER: University of Pennsylvania Hospital, Philadelphia, intern, 1944; assistant resident in medicine at Massachusetts General Hospital, 1947-48; University of Pennsylvania, resident in medicine at hospital, 1948-49, instructor in physiology, 1949-50, assistant instructor, 1949-50, instructor, 1950-51, research associate, 1951-54, assistant professor, 1954-56, associate professor, 1956-63, professor of medicine, 1963—, C. Mahlon Professor of Medicine, 1977—, member of hospital staff, 1952—, in cardiovascular service, 1977—. Diplomate of American Board of Internal Medicine; worked at St. Erick's Hospital, Stockholm, Sweden, 1955-56; attending physician at Veterans Administration Hospital, Philadelphia, 1956—; ward chief at University of Pennsylvania division of Philadelphia General Hospital, 1959-73, coordinator of University of Pennsylvania Medical Service, 1965-71, chief of service, 1966-72, chairman of department of medicine and department coordinator, 1967—. D. V. Mattia Lecturer at Rutgers University, 1975; Neuton Stern Lecturer and visiting professor at University of Tennessee, 1977. Member of medical education advisory committee of Rehabilitation Service Administration of U.S. Department of Health, Education and Welfare (now Department of Health and Human Services), 1968-71. *Military service:* U.S. Army, 1944-46; became captain.

MEMBER: American College of Physicians (member of board of regents, 1967-71; president-elect, 1973-74; president, 1974-75), Association of American Physicians, American Clinical and Climatological Association (vice-president, 1968-69, 1976-77), American Society for Clinical Investigation, American Physiological Society, American Medical Association. *Awards, honors:* Markle scholar at University of Pennsylvania, 1952-57; Alfred E. Stengel Memorial Award from American College of Physicians, 1978.

WRITINGS: (With Marion Laffey Fox) *A Patient's Guide to Medical Testing,* Charles Press, 1979, also published as *It's Your Body, Know What the Doctor Ordered!: Your Complete Guide to Medical Testing,* Charles Press, 1979.

BIOGRAPHICAL/CRITICAL SOURCES: Good Housekeeping, November, 1979.*

*   *   *

SCHOR, Amy 1954-

PERSONAL: Born December 4, 1954, in New York, N.Y.; daughter of Sam J. (a business owner) and Bea (Dorfman) Schor. *Education:* Royal Holloway College, London, Certificate of Honor, 1972. *Religion:* Buddhist. *Home:* 320 West 90th St., New York, N.Y. 10024. *Agent:* William Morris Agency, 1350 Avenue of the Americas, New York, N.Y. 10019.

CAREER: Writer. Worked in sales and as receptionist.

WRITINGS: Line by Line (novel), Richard Marek, 1981. Also author of screenplay "Line by Line."

WORK IN PROGRESS: A novel based on an incident that happened to an Oklahoma family in the early 1950's.

*   *   *

SCHRAG, Adele Frisbie 1921-

PERSONAL: Born May 7, 1921, in Cynthiana, N.Y.; daughter of Shirley and Edna Kate (Ford) Ledyard; married William Albert Schrag, April 6, 1963; children: Marie Carol (stepdaughter). *Education:* Temple University, B.A., 1942; New York University, M.A., 1944, Ph.D., 1961. *Religion:* Presbyterian. *Home:* 305 Longfield Rd., Philadelphia, Pa. 19118. *Office:* Department of Vocational Education, Temple University, Ritter Hall Annex 207, Philadelphia, Pa. 19122.

CAREER: Teacher of business at high schools in Millersville, Pa., 1942-43, and Downingtown, Pa., 1943-50; Temple University, Philadelphia, Pa., instructor, 1950-54, assistant professor, 1954-60, professor of business and vocational education, 1960—. Visiting lecturer at New York University and University of Wisconsin. Director of Delta Pi Epsilon Research Foundation; trustee of Methodist Hospital, Philadelphia, Pa.; member of Business Education Certification Council. *Member:* Society for Automation in Business Education (president, 1969-73; member of board of directors, 1974), Phi Gamma Nu (national treasurer and secretary), Delta Pi Epsilon. *Awards, honors:* Panhellenic Award from National Panhellenic Association, 1963.

WRITINGS: (Editor) *Business Education for the Automated Office,* Somerset Press, 1964; (with Estelle L. Popham and Wanda Blockhus) *A Teaching-Learning System for Business Education,* McGraw, 1975; *How to Dictate,* McGraw, 1981; *The Returning Office Worker: Update,* McGraw, 1982. Contributor to business and education journals.

WORK IN PROGRESS: Revising *A Teaching-Learning System for Business Education,* publication by McGraw expected in 1984.

SIDELIGHTS: Adele Schrag is a specialist in office systems and performance evaluations. *Avocational interests:* Travel (Asia and Europe).

* * *

SCHRAMM, Wilbur (Lang) 1907-

PERSONAL: Born August 5, 1907, in Marietta, Ohio; son of A. A. and Louise Schramm; married Elizabeth Donaldson, 1934; children: one son, one daughter. *Education:* Marietta College, B.A., 1928; Harvard University, M.A., 1930; University of Iowa, Ph.D., 1932. *Home:* 1650 Ala Moana, Apt. 3009, Honolulu, Hawaii 96815. *Office:* East-West Center, 1777 East-West Rd., Honolulu, Hawaii 96822.

CAREER: Worked for *Boston Herald,* Boston, Mass.; Associated Press, 1924-30, began as reporter, became desk editor, then correspondent; University of Iowa, Iowa City, 1935-41, began as assistant professor, became associate professor, then professor of English; Harcourt Brace & Co. (now Harcourt Brace Jovanovich, Inc.), New York, N.Y., editor, 1941; U.S. Office of War Information, Washington, D.C., director of educational services in Office of Facts and Figures, 1942-43; University of Iowa, professor of journalism and director of School of Journalism, 1943-47; University of Illinois, Champaign-Urbana, professor of journalism, assistant to president of university, and director of Institute of Communications Research, 1947-55, dean of Division of Communications, 1950-55; Stanford University, Stanford, Calif., professor of communications, 1955-73, Janet M. Peck Professor of International Communications, 1962, professor of education, 1967-73, professor emeritus, 1973—, director of Institute for Communication Research, 1958-73; East-West Center, Honolulu, Hawaii, director of East-West Communication Institute, 1973-76, distinguished researcher, 1976—, senior fellow, 1979—.

Fellow of Center for Advanced Study in the Behavioral Sciences, Palo Alto, Calif., 1959-60; Aw Boon Haw Professor of Communication at Chinese University of Hong Kong, 1977-78; Howard R. Marsh Visiting Professor of Communication at University of Michigan, 1978-79. Founder of Iowa Writers Workshop, 1937. Past professional baseball player and member of New England Symphony Orchestra. Director of University of Illinois Press, 1947-55. Chairman of U.S. National Council on Research in Journalism; founder of Iowa Bureau of Audience Research, 1946; chairman of U.S. Secretary of Defense's Technical Advisory Panel on Special Operations, 1956; member of Defense Science Board, 1956-59; chairman of U.S. Office of Education's advisory committee on educational media, 1963-66; delegate to United Nations Conference on Peaceful Uses of Outer Space, 1968; educational adviser to U.S. Department of War, 1943-46; consultant to U.S. Department of the Navy.

MEMBER: International Association for Mass Communication Research (chairman of social psychology section, 1959-65), American Association for the Advancement of Science, American Sociological Association, American Association for Education in Journalism, American Association for Public Opinion Research, American Psychological Association. *Awards, honors:* Litt.D. from Marietta College, 1945.

WRITINGS: Approaches to a Science of English Verse, University of Iowa, 1935, reprinted, Folcroft, 1969; *The Story Workshop* (stories), Little, Brown, 1938, reprinted, Norwood, 1978; *Windwagon Smith and Other Yarns,* Harcourt, 1947; (with John W. Riley, Jr.) *The Reds Take a City: The Communist Occupation of Seoul, With Eyewitness Accounts,* 1951, reprinted, Greenwood Press, 1973; (contributor) *Four Working*

Papers on Propaganda Theory, Institute of Communications Research, University of Illinois, 1955; (with Fred S. Siebert and Theodore Peterson) *Four Theories of the Press: The Authoritarian, Libertarian, Social Responsibility, and Soviet Communist Concepts of What the Press Should Be and Do,* 1956, reprinted, Books for Libraries, 1973; *Responsibility in Mass Communication,* Harper, 1957, revised edition (with William L. Rivers), 1969.

(With Ruth T. Storey) *Little House: A Study of Senior Citizens,* Peninsula Volunteers, 1961; (with Jack Lyle and Edwin B. Parker) *Television in the Lives of Our Children,* Stanford University Press, 1961; *Programmed Instruction: Today and Tomorrow,* Fund for the Advancement of Education, 1962; *The Research on Programmed Instruction: An Annotated Bibliography,* Institute for Communication Research, Stanford University, 1962; (with Herbert Potell and George D. Spache) *Steps to Better Reading* (programmed textbook), Harcourt, 1963; (with Lyle de Sola Pool and Ithiel de Sola Pool) *The People Look at Educational Television: A Report of Nine Representative ETV Stations,* Stanford University Press, 1963; *Mass Media and National Development: The Role of Information in the Developing Countries,* Stanford University Press, 1964, abridged edition published as *The Role of Information in National Development,* UNESCO, 1964; (with Godwin C. Chu) *Learning From Television: What the Research Says,* Institute for Communication Research, Stanford University, 1967; *The New Media: Memo to Educational Planners,* UNESCO, 1967; *Classroom Out-of-Doors: Education Through School Camping,* Sequoia Press, 1969; *Instructional Television in the Educational Reform of El Salvador,* Information Center on Instructional Technology, 1973; *Men, Messages, and Media: A Look at Human Communication,* Harper, 1973; (contributor) *Proceedings of the National Academy of Education,* Volume III, National Academy of Education, 1976; *Big Media, Little Media: Tools and Technologies for Instruction,* Sage Publications, 1977.

Editor: (With Seymour M. Pitcher and Joseph E. Baker) *Two Creative Traditions in English Poetry,* 1939, reprinted, Books for Libraries, 1972; *Communications in Modern Society: Fifteen Studies of the Mass Media,* University of Illinois Press, 1948; *Mass Communications: A Book of Readings Selected and Edited for the Institute of Communications Research in the University of Illinois,* University of Illinois Press, 1949, 2nd edition, 1960; *Great Short Stories,* Harcourt, 1950; *The Process and Effects of Mass Communication,* University of Illinois Press, 1954, revised edition (with Donald F. Roberts), 1971; (also contributor) *Adventures for Americans,* Harcourt, 1956, 2nd edition, 1963; *One Day in the World's Press: Fourteen Great Newspapers on a Day of Crisis, November 2, 1956,* Stanford University Press, 1959.

The Impact of Educational Television: Selected Studies, University of Illinois Press, 1960; *The Science of Human Communication: New Directions and New Findings in Communication Research,* Basic Books, 1963; (with Daniel Lerner) *Communication and Change in the Developing Countries,* foreword by Lyndon B. Johnson, East-West Center Press, 1967; *Quality in Instructional Television,* University Press of Hawaii, 1972; (with I. de Sola Pool) *Handbook of Communication,* Rand McNally, 1973; (with Lerner) *Communication and Change: The Last Ten Years—and the Next,* University Press of Hawaii, 1976; (with Lerner and Lyle M. Nelson) *Communication Research: A Half-Century Appraisal,* University Press of Hawaii, 1977.

Also author of *American Medley* (stories), 1937, *Francis Parkman,* 1938, *Literary Scholarship,* 1941, *The Lost Train,* 1948, and *An Introduction to Communication Research for Developing Countries*. Also editor of *American Literature*, 1946. Editor of ''Iowa Studies in Newspaper Reading,'' University of Iowa, 1946-47. Member of editorial board of *Public Opinion Quarterly, Journalism Quarterly*, and *Communication Review*.

BIOGRAPHICAL/CRITICAL SOURCES: Saturday Evening Post, May, 1979.*

* * *

SCHREINER, Olive (Emilie Albertina)   1855-1920
(Ralph Iron)

BRIEF ENTRY: Born March 24, 1855, in Wittebergen, Basutoland (now Lesotho); died December 12, 1920, in Cape Town, South Africa; buried at the summit of Buffels Kop, South Africa. South African author. Olive Schreiner created a sensation in Victorian England with her semi-autobiographical novel, *The Story of an African Farm* (1883), published under the pseudonym Ralph Iron. This original story, which she began writing in her teenyears, was an instant success. Critics regarded it as a powerful evocation of African life and a detailed, imaginative study of psychology and the natural world. Schreiner gained further notoriety when the public realized that the novel's true author was a woman. In that book, as in all her later writings, Schreiner left no doubt about her ardent feminism, radically liberal views, and antipathy to Christianity. A later effort, *Woman and Labour* (1911), was praised by feminists and critics as a passionate demand for the social and economic liberation of women. *Biographical/critical sources: Twentieth Century Authors: A Biographical Dictionary of Modern Literature*, H.W. Wilson, 1942; *Cyclopedia of World Authors*, Harper, 1958.

* * *

SCHUBART, Mark Allen   1918-

PERSONAL: Born May 24, 1918, in New York, N.Y.; son of Henry Allen and Pauline (Werner) Schubart. *Education:* Studied music privately, including composition with Roger Sessions. *Home:* 134 East 93rd St., New York, N.Y. 10028. *Office:* 140 West 65th St., New York, N.Y. 10023.

CAREER: Worked as associate editor for Eton Publishing Corp., 1937-40; assistant music editor of *PM*, 1940-44; *New York Times*, New York City, music editor, 1944-46; Juilliard School of Music, New York City, director of public activities, 1946-49, dean and vice-president of school, 1949-62; Lincoln Center Performing Arts, Inc., New York City, executive director of Lincoln Center Fund, 1963-66, director of education at center, 1966-75, director of Lincoln Center Institute, 1975—, also chairman of council on educational programs. Member of board of directors of Young Audiences, Inc.; member of music advisory committee of Institute for International Education. *Member:* Society for Strings (member of board of directors), Metropolitan Opera Association, Century Association.

WRITINGS: The Hunting of the Squiggle: A Study of a Performing Arts Institution and Young People, Lincoln Center, 1972, reprinted as *Performing Arts Institutions and Young People: Lincoln Center's Study, ''The Hunting of the Squiggle,''* Praeger, 1972. Composer of song cycles, opera, overtures, and songs. Contributor to music journals.*

* * *

SCHUESSLER, Karl F(rederick) 1915-

PERSONAL: Born February 15, 1915, in Quincy, Ill.; son of

Hugo and Elsa (Westerbeck) Schuessler; married Lucille Smith, June 27, 1946; children: Thomas Brian. *Education:* Evansville College (now University of Evansville), B.A., 1936; University of Chicago, M.A., 1939; Indiana University, Ph.D., 1947. *Home:* 1820 East Hunter St., Bloomington, Ind. 47401. *Office:* Department of Sociology, Indiana University, Bloomington, Ind. 47401.

CAREER: Sociology research intern at Illinois State Penitentiary, 1938; high school history teacher in Highland Park, Ill., 1939-1940; Vanderbilt University, Nashville, Tenn., instructor, 1946-47; Indiana University, Bloomington, faculty member; 1947—, professor of sociology, 1960-76, distinguished professor of sociology, 1976—, chairman of department, 1961-69. Visiting professor at University of California, Los Angeles, 1957; University of California, Berkeley, 1965-66, University of Washington, 1967. Guest scholar at Center for Survey Research, Mannheim, West Germany, 1979-80. Member of Indiana governor's Commission on Mental Health; past chairman of research advisory committee of Indiana Department of Corrections; past member of population statistics advisory committee of Indiana Department of Public Health; consultant to National Science Foundation, National Institute of Mental Health, and National Research Council. *Military service:* U.S. Navy, 1942-46; became lieutenant. *Member:* American Sociological Association (member of council), American Statistical Association.

WRITINGS: (With John Henry Mueller) *Statistical Reasoning in Sociology*, Houghton, 1961, 3rd edition, 1977; *Social Research Methods*, Institute of Public Administration, Thammasat University, 1963; *Analyzing Social Data: A Statistical Orientation*, Houghton, 1971; (editor of revision) Edwin Hardin Sutherland, *On Analyzing Crime*, 2nd edition, University of Chicago Press, 1973; (editor) *Social Policy and Sociology*, Academic Press, 1975; (editor) *Sociological Methodology*, Jossey-Bass, 1978; *Musical Taste and Socio-Economic Background*, Arno, 1980. Also editor, with Jay Demerath and Otto Larsen, of *Public Policy and Sociology*, 1975. Editor of *American Sociological Review*, 1969-71, and *Sociological Methodology*, 1977—.

WORK IN PROGRESS: A nontechnical book on time series methods for studying social change.

SIDELIGHTS: During the 1950's, Schuessler conducted research on social psychology, criminology, and social anthropology, carrying out studies on the process by which children learn about money, doing research on capital punishment and on crime rates of large cities, and using factor analysis to classify territorial populations on the basis of their cultural trait distributions. He also studied social aspects of mental health in Indiana.

His 1971 book, *Analyzing Social Data,* is an attempt to make intermediate topics in statistical methods (such as factor analysis and co-variance analysis) readily accessible to statistically-minded sociologists.

More recently he has been working on a battery of tests for measuring attitudes toward self and others in society (including pessimism, cynicism, and fatalism), and on a weighting system for removing statistically the effect of response biases.

* * *

SCHULKE, Flip Phelps Graeme   1930-

PERSONAL: Born June 24, 1930, in St. Paul, Minn.; son of Walter Edward and Elizabeth (Kalman) Schulke; married Marlene Phyllis Wallner, August 7, 1950 (divorced); married Pauline Kay Gillham; children: (first marriage) Robin, Paul, Lisa, Maria. *Education:* Macalester College, B.A., 1953. *Home:* 8305 Southwest 72nd Ave., Miami, Fla. 33143; and 12 Enderley House, Sylvan Rd., Upper Norwood, London S.E.19, England.

CAREER: University of Miami, Coral Gables, Fla., photographer, 1953-57; Black Star Publishing Co., New York, N.Y., staff photographer, 1957—. Owner of Flip Schulke Enterprises, Inc., 1950-51; contract photographer for *Life* magazine, 1965-69. *Military service:* U.S. Army, 1950-51. *Member:* National Press Photographers Association, American Society of Magazine Photographers, Academy of Underwater Photographers.

WRITINGS: (Editor) *Martin Luther King, Jr.: A Documentary, Montgomery to Memphis,* Norton, 1976; *Underwater Photography for Everyone,* Prentice-Hall, 1978.

BIOGRAPHICAL/CRITICAL SOURCES: Popular Photography, September 1980.*

* * *

SCHULTS, Raymond L. 1926-

PERSONAL: Born July 5, 1926, in Hillside, N.J.; son of Leslie Taylor and Hettie (Williams) Schults; married Virginia Bish, September 9, 1949 (divorced, 1973); married Ninon King (a librarian), May 19, 1973; children: (first marriage) Leslie Barbara. *Education:* University of California, Los Angeles, B.A., 1949, M.A., 1950, Ph.D., 1957. *Politics:* Liberal Democrat. *Religion:* "Tasmanian devil worshiper." *Home address:* Route 3, Box 634, Spokane, Wash. 99203. *Office:* Department of History, Eastern Washington University, Cheney, Wash. 99004.

CAREER: Ranch hand in Pear Blossom, Wyo., 1948-50; truck driver in Santa Monica, Calif., 1951-52; manager of pool hall in Los Angeles, Calif., 1953-54; associated with Eastern Washington University, Cheney. *Military service:* U.S. Navy, 1943-45; became seaman first class. *Member:* American Federation of Teachers, Conference of British Studies.

WRITINGS: Crusader in Babylon, University of Nebraska Press, 1972. Contributor to history journals.

WORK IN PROGRESS: The Wounded Lion, on England's Labour governments since World War II; a survey of English history since World War II.

AVOCATIONAL INTERESTS: Drinking beer, camping.

* * *

SCHUTZ, Susan Polis 1944-

PERSONAL: Born May 23, 1944, in New York, N.Y.; daughter of David and June (Keller) Polis; married Stephen Schutz (an artist), April 13, 1970; children: one son. *Education:* Rider College, B.A., 1966; attended Long Island University, 1967-69. *Office:* Blue Mountain Press, Inc., P.O. Box 4549, Boulder, Colo. 80302.

CAREER: Worked as elementary school teacher in New York, N.Y., 1967-69; social worker, public relations writer, and reporter; associated with Blue Mountain Press, Inc., Boulder, Colo., 1971—. Guest on television programs. *Member:* National Organization for Women.

WRITINGS—Published by Blue Mountain Press (Boulder, Colo.); poems: *Come Into the Mountains, Dear Friend,* 1972; *I Want to Laugh, I Want to Cry,* 1973; *Peace Flows From the Sky,* 1974; *Someone Else to Love,* 1976; *I'm Not That Kind of*

Girl, 1976; *Yours If You Ask,* 1978; *Love, Live, and Share,* 1980.

Contributor to numerous magazines, including *Saturday Evening Post.*

SIDELIGHTS: Susan Schutz's first poems were published in greeting cards and poster-sized prints, illustrated by her artist husband. She has sold more than eighty million cards and four million books. In all their ventures, the Schutzes have worked together, whether they were making silk-screened posters, running a publishing company, or writing or illustrating a book.

Schutz describes her writing as a simple expression of her thoughts. *Someone Else to Love,* for example, contains the poems she wrote before and during her pregnancy and after the birth of her son.

BIOGRAPHICAL/CRITICAL SOURCES: Woman's Day, February 12, 1980; *Woman's Sports,* November, 1980; *New Woman,* February, 1981; *L.A. Times,* February 12, 1981; *Lady's Circle* March, 1981.

* * *

SCHWARZ, Jordan A(braham) 1937-

PERSONAL: Born September 13, 1937, in Chicago, Ill.; son of Oscar (in business) and Helen (Karp) Schwarz; married Linda Leibowitz (a director of research services), May 26, 1963; children: Orrin, Jessica. *Education:* City College (now of the City University of New York), B.A., 1959; Columbia University, M.A., 1960, Ph.D., 1967. *Religion:* Jewish. *Home:* 1601 Mayflower, DeKalb, Ill. 60115. *Office:* Department of History, Northern Illinois University, DeKalb, Ill. 60115.

CAREER: Cedar Crest College, Allentown, Pa., instructor in history, 1964-65; Northern Illinois University, DeKalb, instructor, 1965-67, assistant professor, 1967-70, associate professor, 1970-80, professor of history, 1980—. President of Northern Illinois Jewish Community Center, 1975-77, 1979-81. *Member:* American Historical Association, Organization of American Historians, Economic History Association. *Awards, honors:* American Philosophical Society grant, 1970-71.

WRITINGS: (Editor) *1933, Roosevelt's Decision: The United States Leaves the Gold Standard,* Chelsea House, 1969; *The Interregnum of Despair: Hoover, Congress, and the Depression,* University of Illinois Press, 1970; (editor) *The Ordeal of Twentieth-Century America: Interpretive Readings,* Houghton, 1973; (co-author) *Generations of Americans: A History of the United States,* St. Martin's, 1976; *The Speculator: Bernard M. Baruch in Washington,* University of North Carolina Press, 1981. Contributor to history journals.

WORK IN PROGRESS: Inflation in Twentieth-Century America: A Political History, completion expected in 1985.

BIOGRAPHICAL/CRITICAL SOURCES: New York Times Book Review, August 30, 1981; *Fortune,* September 21, 1981.

* * *

SCOTT, Alexander 1920-

PERSONAL: Born November 28, 1920, in Aberdeen, Scotland; married Catherine Goodall, 1944; children: two sons. *Education:* University of Aberdeen, M.A. (with honors), 1947. *Home:* 5 Doune Gardens, Glasgow G20 6DJ, Scotland. *Agent:* SCO, 2 Clifton St., Glasgow G.3, Scotland.

CAREER: University of Edinburgh, Edinburgh, Scotland, assistant lecturer, 1947-48, lecturer, 1948-63, senior lecturer,

1963-71, professor of Scottish literature, 1971—, head of department, 1971—. Member of Universities Committee on Scottish Literature. *Military service:* British Army, 1941-45; received Military Cross. *Member:* Association for Scottish Literature Studies (member of council). *Awards, honors:* Poetry awards from Festival of Britain, 1951; drama award from Arts Council, 1952; award from Scottish Community Drama Association, 1954; award from Scottish Arts Council, 1969.

WRITINGS: Still Life: William Soutar, 1898-1943, W. & R. Chambers, 1958; *The MacDiarmid Makars, 1923-1972*, Akros Publications, 1973.

Poems: *The Latest in Elegies*, Caledonian Press, 1949; *Selected Poems*, Oliver & Boyd, 1950; *Mouth Music: Poems and Diversions*, M. Macdonald, 1954; *Cantrips*, Akros Publications, 1968; *Greek Fire: A Sequence of Poems*, Akros Publications, 1971; *Double Agent: Poems in English and Scots*, Akros Publications, 1973; *Selected Poems, 1943-1974*, Akros Publications, 1975.

Editor: *The Poems of Alexander Scott, 1530-1584*, Oliver & Boyd, 1952; William Jeffrey, *Selected Poems*, Serif Books, 1952; William Soutar, *Diaries of a Dying Man*, W. & R. Chambers, 1955; (with Norman MacCaig) *Contemporary Scottish Verse, 1959-1969*, Calder & Boyars, 1970; (with Michael Grieve) *The Hugh MacDiarmid Anthology: Poems in Scots and English*, Routledge & Kegan Paul, 1972; (with Douglas Gifford) *Neil M. Gunn: The Man and the Writer*, Barnes & Noble, 1973; *Scottish Poetry Seven*, University of Glasgow Press, 1974; (with Maurice Lindsay and Roderick Watson) *Scottish Poetry Eight: An Anthology*, Carcanet Press, 1975; *Scottish Poetry Nine*, Carcanet Press, 1976; *Modern Scots Verse, 1922-1977*, Akros Publications, 1978.

Plays: *Prometheus 48* (first produced in Aberdeen, Scotland), SRC, 1948; *Untrue Thomas*, Caledonian Press, 1952; "Right Royal," first produced in Glasgow, Scotland, 1954; *Shetland Yarn*, Evans Brothers, 1954; "Tam O'Shanter's Tryst," first produced in Glasgow, 1955; "The Last Time I Saw Paris," published in *Saltire Review*, 1957; "Truth to Tell," first produced in Glasgow, 1958.

Work represented in anthologies. General editor of "The Scottish Library," Calder & Boyars, 1968-71, and "The Scottish Series," Routledge & Kegan Paul, 1972—. Contributor to magazines and newspapers, including *Lines Review, Scottish Poetry, Scotsman, Akros, Scotia,* and *Catalyst.* Editor of *Northeast Review*, 1945-46, and *Scots Review*, 1950-51; founding editor of *Saltire Review*, 1954-57.

BIOGRAPHICAL/CRITICAL SOURCES: Akros Nine, 1969; *Akros Nineteen*, 1972; *Akros Twenty-Five*, 1974.*

*   *   *

SCOTT, Elaine   1940-

PERSONAL: Born June 20, 1940, in Philadelphia, Pa.; daughter of George Jobling (a banker) and Ethel (Smith) Watts; married Parker Scott (a geophysical engineer), May 16, 1959; children: Cynthia Ellen, Susan Elizabeth. *Education:* Attended Southern Methodist University, 1957-59, and Southern Methodist University and University of Houston, 1979-81. *Religion:* Methodist. *Home:* 13042 Taylorcrest, Houston, Tex. 77079. *Agent:* Jean V. Naggar, 336 East 73rd St., New York, N.Y. 10021.

CAREER: Writer, 1975—. Teacher of leadership workshops for Texas Conference of the United Methodist Church, 1978; teacher of writing workshops at Southwest Writer's Conference, Houston, Tex., 1979, and at Trinity University, San Antonio, Tex., 1980. Volunteer teacher of leadership workshops at United Methodist Church, Houston, 1959-77; volunteer publicity director for Camp Fire Girls of America, 1973-74. *Member:* Society of Children's Book Writers, Associated Authors of Children's Literature (president, 1979-80).

WRITINGS—Juvenile nonfiction: *Adoption*, F. Watts, 1980; *The Banking Book*, Warne, 1981; *Doodlebugging for Oil: The Biggest Treasure Hunt of All*, Warne, 1982.

Contributor of articles to periodicals, including *Houston Home and Garden*. Contributing editor to *Houston City Magazine* and *Houston Town and Country*.

WORK IN PROGRESS: The Ice Cream Book, a juvenile nonfiction book on the history of ice cream from ancient days to the present; *The Birth of a Book From Author's Idea to Publisher's Product*, a juvenile nonfiction book; a young adult novel dealing with an adolescent's pain as she struggles to regain a popularity she once had and lost, tentatively titled *The Worst of Friends; Doggonit, Delilah!*, an easy-to-read book about "the misadventures of a mischievous black labrador pup and the family she owns"; *Painted Sepulchres*, an adult novel dealing with hypocrisy, power, and the corruption of power.

SIDELIGHTS: Scott told *CA:* "I'm not certain when someone decides that he might want to become an author. I suppose that some people are always aware that they have something to say and are always searching for a way to say it. That has not been the case with me. Oh, I have always loved to read, and I realize that that is the first prerequisite in becoming an author, but my love of reading merely led to long letters to my grandmother while she vacationed winters in Florida. The thought that I might someday join the list of persons who had their words printed on paper for others to read never entered my mind until I was ten.

"I was in the sixth grade when I was ten, and our teacher decided on a dreary, early March afternoon that the entire class would write a poem during recess instead of sliding around the frozen turf of the school yard. Along with the rest of the class, I agonized as I stared at the blank piece of paper that lay in front of me on the desk. What to write about? What did I have to say about anything? Any writer, no matter how young, writes about what he knows, and I was no exception. That very morning as I left for school, I noticed the sorry state of the snowman I had built the week before. The thirty-two-degrees-plus temperature was playing havoc with his physique, pulling him steadily toward his demise, so I wrote my poem called 'A Tale of Woe,' about three snowmen whose fate it was to melt with the coming of spring. I got an 'A' for my efforts and that grade thrilled me, but not nearly as much as the thrill I received when I heard that my teacher had entered my poem in a state-wide contest in Pennsylvania, and it won second prize. After I won the prize, I enjoyed a certain modest notoriety, and I began to whip off poems and articles for the school paper at the drop of a pencil. I was in real danger of becoming a hack at the ripe old age of ten.

"Fortunately, the Fates intervened, and within a few months my family moved to Texas. No one was clamoring for my talents there, and for the next twenty-five years I wrote nothing creative other than term papers and letters home.

"Even though I majored in English during my college years and had always read everything I could get my hands on—from *Peter Rabbit* to *Hamlet, Jack and Jill* to the *New Yorker*—it never occurred to me during those days of career choices that I might want to become a writer. I suppose it seemed to me to be as remote a possibility as becoming an astronaut. And so I surprised myself years later when the opportunity to write an essay for a literary journal came my way, and I accepted the challenge. The journal was called *Touchstone,* and its editor, Gudia Jackson, wanted to zero in on the theme of the world's overpopulation. She wanted to publish a point of view that affirmed parenthood through adoption. Since my husband and I had adopted one daughter and had the other by the conventional method, she thought I might be a good candidate to write the piece. After it was published, the editor of the *Houston Town and Country* saw it and asked me to contribute occasionally to that magazine. Eventually, I became a contributing editor there and began to write for other regional publications, too.

"Up to this point, everything I wrote was article-length and was for adults. I never really thought about writing for children until I went to the Southwest Writer's Conference at the University of Houston. Because of a lull in my schedule, I dropped into a workshop on writing nonfiction for children. As I listened to an editor speak about the need for good philosophical books for children, the idea for my book *Adoption* began to form in my subconsicous. By the end of the day, the idea had forced itself into my conscious thought and was no longer merely an idea, but a tangible form—a rough outline of the book. I plucked up the courage to approach Jean Naggar, a literary agent who was appearing at the university, and asked her what she thought of my book proposal. Jean was enthusiastic and agreed to represent me. She quickly sold that book proposal and has sold all my other books as well. Jean continues to represent me now.

"As I think about the books I have written up to now, I realize I haven't traveled too far from the child of ten who wrote about her melting snowmen. I still write about subjects I know and care about. I believe that without caring (and caring can mean hating, as well as loving) about his subject, the writer is in real danger of becoming nothing but a flesh and blood word processor—spitting out facts and nothing more. I think a writer should share himself, as well as his information, with his reader. It should be his voice that says to the reader, 'Come with me and together we'll explore sensitive issues like adoption, or complicated subjects like banking. Together, you and I will visit the remote corners of the world, searching for oil with the doodlebuggers.' For me that is the essence of writing—it's really a dialogue between me and my reader. I am grateful for the reader, and out of that gratitude comes a willingness to share myself and my experience of life with him."

BIOGRAPHICAL/CRITICAL SOURCES: Houston Chronicle, November 30, 1980, January 8, 1981; *Texas Association for Childhood Education News,* fall, 1981.

*　　*　　*

SCOTT, J(ames) M(aurice) 1906-

PERSONAL: Born December 13, 1906, in Egypt; married Pamela Watkins; children: two sons. *Education:* Clare College, Cambridge, M.A. *Home:* Thatched Cottage, Yelling, Huntingdon, Cambridgeshire, England.

CAREER: Member of H. G. Watkins's expedition to Labrador, 1928-29; writer. British Council representative in Yugoslavia. *Member:* Royal Geographical Society (fellow). *Awards, honors:* Officer of Order of the British Empire, 1945.

WRITINGS: The Land That God Gave Cain: An Account of H. G. Watkins' Expedition to Labrador, 1928-1929, Chatto & Windus, 1933; *Gino Watkins,* Hodder & Stoughton, 1935, 4th edition, 1937; (editor and author of introduction) *The Polar Regions: An Anthology of Arctic and Antarctic Photographs,*

Oxford University Press, 1935; *The Silver Land* (novel), Hodder & Stoughton, 1937; *Unknown River,* Hodder & Stoughton, 1939; *The Cold Lands,* Methuen, 1939; *The Pole of Inaccessibility,* Hodder & Stoughton, 1947; *The Will and the Way,* Dutton, 1949.

(Editor of abridgement) *Snowstone,* University of London Press, 1950; *Vineyards of France,* Hodder & Stoughton, 1950; *Hudson of Hudson's Bay,* H. Schuman, 1951, reprinted, Chivers, 1973; *The Touch of the Nettle* (novel), Hodder & Stoughton, 1951; *Heather Mary,* Dutton, 1953; *The Man Who Made Wine,* Hodder & Stoughton, 1953, Dutton, 1954; *Portrait of an Ice Cap, With Human Figures: An Account of the Experiences of the British Arctic Air Route Expedition on a Greenland Ice-Cap, 1930-1931,* Chatto & Windus, 1953; *White Magic,* Holt, 1955; *The Other Half of the Orange,* Dutton, 1955; *Sea-Wyf and Biscuit* (novel), Heinemann, 1955, reprinted, Ian Henry Publications, 1976, published in the United States as *Sea-Wyf,* Dutton, 1956; *I Keep My Word,* Heinemann, 1957; *The Lady and the Corsair,* Dutton, 1958; *A Choice of Heaven,* Heinemann, 1959, Dutton, 1960.

Where the River Bends, Heinemann, 1962; *The Tea Story,* Heinemann, 1964, published in the United States as *The Great Tea Venture,* Dutton, 1965; *The Book of Pall Mall,* Heinemann, 1965; *Dingo* (science fiction novel), Heinemann, 1966, Chilton, 1967; *The Devil You Don't,* Heinemann, 1967, Chilton, 1969; *Italy,* Benn, 1967; *In a Beautiful Pea-Green Boat,* Bles, 1968, Chilton, 1969; *The White Poppy: A History of Opium,* Funk, 1969; *From Sea to Ocean: Walking Along the Pyrenees,* Bles, 1969; *George Sand,* Edito-Service, 1969.

Fridtjof Nansen, Heron Books, 1971; *Michael Anonymous,* Chilton, 1971; *Extel 100: The Centenary History of the Exchange Telegraph Company,* Benn, 1972; *A Walk Along the Apennines,* Bles, 1973; *Boadicea,* Constable, 1975; *A Journey of Many Sleeps,* Chatto & Windus, 1976, reprinted as *Desperate Journey,* Beaver Books, 1978; *Icebound: Journeys to the Northwest Sea,* Gordon & Cremonesi, 1977.

Also author of *Land of Seals,* 1949, *Bright Eyes of Danger,* 1950, *The Other Side of the Moon,* 1950, *Captain Smith and Pocahontas,* 1953, and (with Robert Theobold) *Teg's 1994: An Anticipation of the Near Future,* 1972. Work represented in anthologies, including *Reader's Digest Anthology of Mystery and Suspense,* 1961; *The Masterpieces,* 1965.

MEDIA ADAPTATIONS: Sea-Wyf was made into "Sea Wife," a film released in 1957, starring Richard Burton and Joan Collins.

BIOGRAPHICAL/CRITICAL SOURCES: Times Literary Supplement, December 21, 1967, January 13, 1978; *Best Sellers,* February 15, 1969; *Books and Bookmen,* July, 1969.*

*　　*　　*

SCOTT-JAMES, Anne Eleanor 1913-

PERSONAL: Born April 5, 1913. *Education:* Attended Somerville College, Oxford. *Home:* Rose Cottage, Aldworth, Reading, Berkshire, England.

CAREER: Worked as member of editorial staff of *Vogue,* 1934-41; woman's editor of *Picture Post,* 1941-45; editor of *Harper's Bazaar,* 1945-51; woman's editor of *Sunday Express,* 1953-57, woman's adviser for Beaverbrook Newspapers in England, 1959-60; columnist for *Daily Mail* in England, 1960-68; writer. Member of council of Royal College of Art, 1948-51.

WRITINGS: In the Mink, M. Joseph, 1952; *Down to Earth* (gardening book), M. Joseph, 1971; *Sissinghurst: The Making of a Garden,* M. Joseph, 1975; (with Osbert Lancaster) *The Pleasure Garden: An Illustrated History of British Gardening,* J. Murray, 1977; *A Gardener's Dozen,* BBC Publications, 1980. Contributor to magazines.

BIOGRAPHICAL/CRITICAL SOURCES: Times Literary Supplement, December 16, 1977, May 8, 1981; *Los Angeles Times Book Review,* February 22, 1981; *Washington Post Book World,* May 17, 1981.

*   *   *

SEATON, George   1911-1979

PERSONAL: Original name, George Stenius; named legally changed August 19, 1937; born April 17, 1911, in South Bend, Ind.; died of cancer, July 28, 1979, in Beverly Hills, Calif.; son of Carl A. (a chef) and Olga (Berglund) Stenius; married Phyllis Laughton (an actress, drama coach, and former mayor of Beverly Hills), February 22, 1936; children: Mary Seaton Henderson, Marc Laughton (deceased). *Education:* Attended Exeter Academy. *Home:* 813 Monte Leon Dr., Beverly Hills, Calif. 90210. *Office:* Universal City Studios, Inc., Universal City, Calif. 90210.

CAREER: Jessie Bonstelle Stock Co., Detroit, Mich., actor, 1929-31; actor and playwright in New York City, 1931-33; actor in radio program "The Lone Ranger," Detroit, 1933; Metro-Goldwyn-Mayer, Inc. (MGM), Culver City, Calif., writer, 1933-37; Columbia Pictures Industries, Inc., Hollywood, Calif., writer, 1940-41; Twentieth Century-Fox Film Corp., Los Angeles, Calif., writer, 1942-44, director, 1944-52; Paramount Pictures Corp., Hollywood, Calif., writer and director, 1952-61; Metro-Goldwyn-Mayer, Inc. (MGM), writer and director, 1963-67; Universal Pictures, Universal City, Calif., writer, producer, and director, 1967-72.

Producer of motion pictures, including "Rhubarb," 1951, "Aaron Slick From Pumkin Crick," 1952, "Somebody Loves Me," 1952, (with William Perlberg) "The Bridges at Toko-Ri," Paramount, 1953, (with Perlberg) "The Tin Star," Paramount, 1957, "But Not for Me," 1959, (with Perlberg) "The Rat Race," Paramount, 1960, "Twilight of Honor," 1963, (and director) "Showdown," Universal, 1972.

Director of motion pictures, including "Williamsburg—The Story of a Patriot," Paramount, 1956, "Teacher's Pet," Paramount, 1957, "The Pleasure of His Company," Paramount, 1960, "The Hook," MGM, 1962. Director of stage productions, including "Juno and the Paycock," 1974.

Formed Perlberg-Seaton Company, 1952. Faculty member of University of California, Los Angeles, 1952-62. Served as music and theatre commissioner for Los Angeles County. Member of board of trustees of American Film Institute, 1968-73, Colonial Williamsburg Foundation, and Motion Picture and Television Fund. Member of advisory council of district attorney of Los Angeles, 1965, of advisory committee on the arts for State Department's Cultural Exchange Program, 1966-68, and of volunteer advisory council of attorney general of California, 1971. Co-founder of Beverly Hills Municipal League; founding member of Watts Writers' Workshop.

MEMBER: Screen Writers Guild (now Writers Guild of America [West]; president, 1947-48), Screen Directors Guild (vice-president, 1950-51), Academy of Motion Picture Arts and Sciences (president, 1955-58), Motion Picture and Television Fund (board member and officer), Center Theatre Group (vice-president), All Saints Episcopal Church Vestry, Hawthorne P.T.A. (life member). *Awards, honors:* Academy Award nomination for best screenplay from Academy of Motion Picture Arts and Sciences, 1943, for "The Song of Bernadette"; Academy Award for best screenplay from Academy of Motion Picture Arts and Sciences, 1947, for "Miracle on 34th Street"; Academy Award for best screenplay and nomination for best director from Academy of Motion Picture Arts and Sciences, 1954, both for "The Country Girl"; Cavaliere Ordine Al Merito, 1957, and Commendatore Ordine Al Merito, 1961, both from Italian Government; Laurel Award from Writers Guild of America (West), 1961; Jean Hersholt Humanitarian Award from Academy of Motion Picture Arts and Sciences, 1962; Valentine Davies Award from Writer Guild of America (West), 1968; Academy Award nomination for best screenplay—based on another medium from Academy of Motion Picture Arts and Sciences, 1970, for "Airport"; Medallion for Humanitarian Service from Motion Picture Television Fund, 1971; named writer-director of the year by National Association of Theatre Owners, 1972; Will Rogers Memorial Award from Beverly Hills Chamber of Commerce, 1973; Morgan Cox Award from Writers Guild of America (West), 1979.

WRITINGS—Screenplays; all produced by Metro-Goldwyn-Mayer (MGM): "Student Tour," 1934, "Winning Ticket," 1935, (with Robert Pirosh and George Oppenheimer) *A Day at the Races* (produced in 1937), Viking, 1972; (and director) "36 Hours," 1965.

All produced by Columbia: (With Ken Englund) "The Doctor Takes a Wife," 1940; (with Englund and P. J. Wolfson) "This Thing Called Love," 1941; (contributor to treatment) "Bedtime Story," 1941.

All produced by Twentieth Century-Fox: "Charley's Aunt," 1941; (adapter; with Lynn Starling) "Three Blind Mice," 1941; (with Bess Meredith and Hal Long) "That Night in Rio," 1941; (additional dialogue) "Ten Gentlemen From West Point," 1942; "The Magnificent Dope," 1942; (with Allan House) "The Meanest Man in the World," 1942; "Coney Island," 1943; "The Song of Bernadette," 1943; "The Eve of St. Mark," 1944; (and director) "Billy Rose's Diamond Horseshoe," 1945; (and director) "Junior Miss," 1945; (and director; with Karl Tunberg and Darrell Ware) "The Shocking Miss Pilgrim," 1946; (and director) "Miracle on 34th Street," 1947; (and director; with Valentine Davies) "Chicken Every Sunday," 1947; (and director) "Apartment for Peggy," 1948; (and director) "The Big Lift," 1949; (and director) "For Heaven's Sake," 1950.

All produced by Paramount; all directed by Seaton: (Written with Oppenheimer) "Anything Can Happen," 1951; "Little Boy Lost," 1952; "The Country Girl," 1954; "The Proud and the Profane," 1956; "Counterfeit Traitor," 1961.

All produced by Universal; all directed by Seaton: (Written with Pirosh) "What's So Bad About Feeling Good?," 1968; "Airport," 1970.

Other: *But Not Goodbye* (three-act comedy; first produced as motion picture "The Cockeyed Miracle," MGM, 1946), Samuel French, 1944.

SIDELIGHTS: George Seaton was both an honored creative talent and a respected businessman in the film industry. "Song of Bernadette," the motion picture about the French peasant girl who received visions of the Virgin Mary at Lourdes, became the model for religious epics such as "Going My Way," "The Bells of St. Mary's," and "The Miracle of the Bells." Grossing $45 million, Seaton's "Airport," Universal's largest moneymaker until "Jaws"'s release in 1975, became the prototype for Hollywood disaster movies. Seaton was also credited with recognizing and developing the acting abilities of Natalie Wood and Grace Kelly.

At the business end of the industry, the filmmaker held several executive positions for professional organizations, including a three-year presidency of the Academy of Motion Picture Arts and Sciences. One of Seaton's more notable accomplishments occurred in 1958. He was instrumental in instigating the repeal of an Academy rule, enacted during the blacklisting of the fifties, that rendered any person suspected of affiliating with the Communist party ineligible for receiving an Academy Award.

CA INTERVIEW

In a telephone interview on July 1, 1980, Phyllis Seaton talked to *CA* about her husband's life and work.

CA: Mr. Seaton felt that one of his greatest strengths as a writer was character construction. Was that directly inspired by people he knew, by actors he envisioned in certain roles?

SEATON: No. I would say it was always from the character he was writing. If you look over his list of credits, you'll see that his very best job—with the exception perhaps of "Miracle on 34th Street," written in conjunction with Valentine Davies—was "The Country Girl," based on the play. The characters were there. "Song of Bernadette" is another good example. I think he honestly enjoyed translating from another medium. In all of the screenplays written from another medium, such as a book or a play or an original idea, and then directed by him, his forte was the development of character. You know that in many books and many plays the main characters are fine, but where are the lesser ones? He always knew who they were, and he always felt that in direction and in writing something must happen to the characters in the course of the play or the picture. They shouldn't be the same at the beginning as they are at the end, most particularly the leading character. In *Airport,* all those people on the airplane were not extras, but actors. He wrote a life story for all of them so that they knew who they were sitting on that airplane. So when anything happened in the airplane, although they may not have had one word to say, their reactions were what those persons would have reacted to. You can only get an actor to do that, and of course they saved a fortune that way. On the airplane's blowup, if you remember, when everything fell apart in the back cabin, that was one take. And that was because each actor knew how he would react as that character when that happened.

Sometimes there's a good line that may prompt an actor to say to a director, "I don't really feel that I can say that or do that." George was capable of saying, "Well, either I've written it incorrectly, or you're not being that character. Because as I saw it, he would be doing that, and one or the other would be true." Either it was not well written, or the actor was not living that character.

CA: That's very different from some of the movies being made now in which actors are given some degree of freedom to develop a part.

SEATON: No, he could never work that way, and I think that's one reason actors always wanted to work with him, and many of them gave their best performances for him. He knew the characters, and he could, with the actor, delineate what he felt that character was living through, thinking about, and feeling. Bing Crosby, of course, adored him because, although he was more popular in other things, he gave two of his finest performances in "Little Boy Lost" and "Country Girl." And Bill Holden worked with him I don't know how many times. All actors wanted to work with him. After filming "Airport," he received a gift from Helen Hayes, a silver cigarette box with a picture of herself and George on location laminated into the top of the box. It was signed, "To the best director I ever had." He cherished it, and now I do. Helen Hayes adored him. And who doesn't adore her! She was marvelous in that picture. But she loves direction—most good actors do.

CA: He was also good at many kinds of writing and was never stereotyped.

SEATON: That's correct. This is what differentiated him from directors like Hitchcock, for instance, who were one-picture men in terms of the kind of story they did. If you look at George's, you see that he was interested in all kinds of situations, except he did not believe that the screen or the stage was the place for violence or pornography. He saw it really as a delineation of people, growing or deteriorating, one or the other; but he always had hope in his pictures.

CA: Did he enjoy one particular kind of writing more than the others, or were they all fun?

SEATON: No, I think the span of the kinds of writing will show that it was always the people or the situations and what they did that interested him. I think the thing that runs through all his pictures is humor. He felt there was no life without humor, and from where I sit now, it's very difficult living without that man in the house. He always found the opposite point of view, which was humorous. It was a tremendous gift.

CA: You had theatrical experience also and sometimes worked as a drama coach. How often did you and Mr. Seaton work together on films?

SEATON: Just once, by force of circumstance—when he did "The Big Lift" in Berlin. This was with the airlift, and there were no actors in it except the two from America, Paul Douglas and Montgomery Clift. The girls were all from Germany and were a little bit deficient in English. And of course the pilots and all those other people were all Air Force boys, so they had no theatrical experience. I was able to help some. But I said when we came home on the airplane, "That's the end of that, George; I'll never work with you again. I'd rather live with you." He didn't need a dialogue director; he needed me there because most of them were not actors.

As far as his writing was concerned, I think I was a good sounding board. I never wrote one word of George's dialogue, and I don't think I gave him very many ideas. I sometimes would question a situation. We were both very good at acting, so we sometimes would play a scene; once you play the character, you know if something's not right. But we did that very seldom. He was so good. I was a good sounding board. He would come in from the office, while perhaps I was in the kitchen, and say, "Would you listen to this?" I learned very early in my married life to turn off all the gas jets and sit down and listen.

CA: You mentioned "The Big Lift." How did you and the two children happen to go to Berlin for the making of that movie?

SEATON: George wouldn't go without me, and I wouldn't go without the children, and so we were a family there. It was a very interesting experience.

CA: The circumstances you had to live under must have been harrowing.

SEATON: No, it really wasn't bad, to tell you the truth. I think it did the children an enormous amount of good. They learned what was essential in life and what was not. We were there in all climates, no heat; you learned that wood was very valuable and that it wasn't important that everybody had their own rooms because you only had enough wood for one fireplace and that's where you were. If you were cold you put on long underwear and four sweaters. As far as food was concerned, we were rationed not only in terms of what was available, but in terms even of how much money one could spend per person. Milk and sugar and things like that were strictly rationed. Nobody had milk except the children. The amazing thing was, because the strict rationing was based primarily on calorie intake plus money, the people who came over a little overweight became thin, and those who were thin became normal. It was quite interesting.

The children did just fine and learned a great deal of the essentials of life. They didn't even know it was hard. We had a house that was requisitioned by the army. It was a large house, and it belonged to a member of the SS [the Schutzstaffel elite guard]. There was practically no furniture in it; there were no curtains on the windows; and the chandeliers were gone. There was one 125-watt bulb hanging down from the ceiling and no rugs on the floor. The first morning that we got up, having had a traumatic experience getting into Berlin the night before, Marc, who was then only three-and-a-half years old, ran downstairs first into the dining room. I had looked at the room the night before and said, "We can't eat here; there's nothing here, just a round Grand Rapids table and chairs that don't do anything." It was a great, empty hall almost. Instead it became a tremendously wonderful thing. The little boy, Marc, ran down and went around the dining room with his sister and called upstairs to me, "Mom! Mom! There's an echo in the dining room!" So you see, through the eyes of a child. We have so many things we don't need.

CA: Vincent Canby attacked "Airport" in the New York Times, *implying in part that mass appeal and quality couldn't go together. Mr. Seaton responded with a letter to the editor. Was he very sensitive to criticism?*

SEATON: He never minded being criticized. He always said, even to the crew, "If you see something that doesn't strike you as real, tell me." Not that he would take it, always, but he was always open to listening. I never knew a man who listened better—and never with hostility.

CA: Did he feel most newspaper critics were fair and capable?

SEATON: One of his main thoughts about criticism was that very few critics knew how pictures were shot and the difficulty in making them. He did a picture using critics ("Teacher's Pet" with Clark Gable) in which a lot of action took place in the city room of a newspaper. He used critics from all over the country. They were delighted to come to Hollywood. Many of them became better critics thereby and so stated in articles in their columns. It's so easy to criticize when we don't know what's going on, right?

CA: Mr. Seaton also worked with early psychodrama. What were his reactions to that experience?

SEATON: I think it was the Williamsburg film, "The Patriot," when he wanted people to be actors without knowing it. He took some of the disturbed people from the mental hospital and gave them parts to play, and there they are in the film. He didn't know he was working psychodrama at all.

CA: And he felt that some of those people were actually helped through the experience?

SEATON: Oh, there's no question about it. [The *Richmond-Times Dispatch* reported that Seaton "found out that the temporary 'new identities' in many cases relieved personal pressures, and several of the extras were released from the hospital months sooner than had been predicted."]

CA: He also was involved in a great many civic and humanitarian activities. Was there a single one that was most important to him?

SEATON: I would say that one of the greatest joys of his life was working on the board of trustees for the Colonial Williamsburg Foundation. He served on that board for twenty-two years. His lifelong interest was working on the board of the Motion Picture and Television Fund, which he did for about forty years, I think. He also served the local community: He served the county as music and theatre commissioner, and he was on the founding board of the Center Theatre Group downtown. He was president of the Writers Guild; vice-president of the Screen Directors Guild; and a member of the founding board of the American Film Institute; and a founding member of the Watts Writers' Workshop. He and Bill Perlberg instituted the apprentice program at UCLA's theatre arts department. His services were endless. Were I ever to try and write anything about my husband, I think I would barely mention the pictures, except the names of them, because it really was the man who was the important person. I think it's one reason he was such a good director and such a good writer. He was very, very interested in human beings. I don't know how he found the time to do what he did.

CA: He brought some of his UCLA theatre students home occasionally, didn't he, to continue discussions they were having in class?

SEATON: Oh, yes. And bring up questions and all that kind of thing. The way it used to be in college—the professor cared. It wasn't out of a textbook; it was from experience.

CA: He won a number of awards. Which of them do you think meant the most to him?

SEATON: Of the Academy Awards, I think probably the Humanitarian Award in 1962 meant the most to him. He was as interested in the nominations he received for his pictures as he was in the awards he won for them. He felt that you were nominated by your peers and that being one of the five that are nominated is the honor because choosing a winner from the five can have to do with many more things that what is the best. Who knows what best is? If you took one picture and had five different actors play the lead, you'd know which one was the best. If you took one picture and had five different directors direct it, then you might know. But it's difficult, isn't it? So nominations are generally the most important thing, although, of course, it's lovely to get the award itself.

I think the one he treasured was the Humanitarian Award, which was a tremendous surprise to him. He didn't think he had done nearly enough. I remember, and Bill Holden used it in his eulogy, that when he got the Humanitarian Award at the Academy, he was overwhelmed. He said, "Thank you. All this makes me know is that I will try very hard for the rest of my life to deserve it."

And he was also pleased with the Laurel Award, which he won in 1961. He won all the awards that the Writers Guild can give, and there's a fascinating little story about that, too. He was very ill when he got the last award [the Morgan Cox Award] from the Writers Guild, and they had sent him a notice saying he'd been unanimously chosen for it. He read the letter—this was at the end of his life and he really was quite ill—and he just looked at me and said, "I can't accept that kind of award. They're just doing it because I'm ill and they know I don't have much longer to go. I really think I must say no. It's a very kind gesture, but not deserved." And so I said to him, "You want me to call a member of the board and tell him that?," and he said, "Yes, I really think you should." So I called Bill Ludwig, who had been on the board and was a very close friend. Bill came right over and said to George, "Phyllis tells me that you don't think you can accept this." And George said, "No, I can't." Bill took out of his pocket two typewritten pages of what George had done for the Writers Guild, and George read the first page, turned it over, and at the very top of the second page he smiled, he looked at Bill, and he said, "Yes, I think this man really deserves it." That's what I mean by living with humor.

CA: The movie industry went through many changes during Mr. Seaton's career. Were there any he felt strongly about?

SEATON: He was no longer going to write or direct. He felt that he had done the best he knew how to do, and he could not and would not do violence, the kind of violence they have in movies today. He could not do a story in which the characters were unimportant as people. George couldn't possibly have done "Star Wars," as great a success as it was, or anything like it. He couldn't have done "Apocalypse Now." He could have done "Kramer vs. Kramer." He felt that he had done what he was to do, and he was going to write a book—not a book about himself, but of a life. We lived forty-three years together, and I wasn't all that young when I married him. We had seen even the electric light come in. The book would have been very interesting. I'm sorry he didn't get to it.

CA: How did you and Mr. Seaton meet?

SEATON: We both came from Detroit, Michigan, and we both worked with the Jessie Bonstelle Stock Company. That is where we met. We had worked together for two or three years in different situations, and after that we had only corresponded a few times, and then with Christmas cards. We met again when I was leaving New York to come and be the head of the talent department at Paramount, and George was coming out to work at MGM as a junior writer for Thalberg. We were both in love with other people, but three years later, we decided we didn't love them. It was nice. It was wonderful to have a marriage which was lucky enough to be based on friendship.

CA: What did Mr. Seaton feel was his greatest contribution to the movies?

SEATON: I don't think we ever discussed it. He was so modest he wouldn't dream of discussing it. He was happy if he had a good story with people—I'm not talking about a moral, just a good story that people love to go and see, laugh a little, cry a little, be moved a little, maybe come out and want to talk about it. Look what "Miracle" did to this country for a little while, and nobody really wanted to make it. He spanned a lot of interests.

BIOGRAPHICAL/CRITICAL SOURCES: New York Times, October 31, 1934, February 11, 1935, June 18, 1937, June 15, 1940, February 14, 1941, March 10, 1941, July 5, 1941, August 2, 1941, June 5, 1942, July 3, 1942, February 25, 1943, June 17, 1943, January 27, 1944, May 31, 1944, May 3, 1945, October 25, 1946, February 12, 1947, June 5, 1947, October 16, 1948, January 19, 1949, April 27, 1950, December 16,

1950, August 31, 1951, April 4, 1952, April 19, 1952, September 25, 1952, September 22, 1953, December 16, 1954, January 21, 1955, June 14, 1956, April 1, 1957, October 24, 1957, March 20, 1958, October 3, 1959, May 26, 1960, June 2, 1961, April 18, 1962, February 16, 1963, November 14, 1963, January 29, 1965, May 25, 1968, March 6, 1970, June 7, 1970, January 3, 1971, November 22, 1973; *Films in Review,* May/June, 1950, August/September, 1953, March/April, 1955, March, 1958, April, 1970, November, 1971.

Films and Filming, May, 1955, June, 1958, April, 1961, August, 1961, March, 1963, February, 1965, October, 1966, June, 1970; *Filmfacts,* Volume I, 1958, Volume IV, 1961, Volume V, 1962, Volume VI, 1963, Volume VIII, 1965, Volume XI, 1968; *Writer,* August, 1958; *Sight and Sound,* winter, 1964-65; *Film Quarterly,* spring, 1965; *Action,* July/August, 1970, November/December, 1970; *Newsweek,* March 16, 1970; *Time,* March 23, 1971; *Richmond Times-Dispatch,* November 21, 1971; *Variety,* January 15, 1972; *Dialogue on Film,* Volume II, 1972; *Choice,* March, 1973; Richard Koszarski, *Hollywood Directors, 1941-1976,* Oxford, 1977; *George Seaton: An American Film Institute Seminar on His Work,* Microfilming Corp. of America, 1977.

OBITUARIES: New York Times, July 29, 1979; *Washington Post,* July 30, 1979; *Newsweek,* August 13, 1979; *Time,* August 13, 1979.

—*Interview by Jean W. Ross*

*   *   *

SEEVER, R.
     See REEVES, Lawrence F.

*   *   *

SEIFERT, Anne   1943-

PERSONAL: Born January 1, 1943, in Long Island, N.Y.; daughter of H. William and Anne (Varnes) Seifert; married Fred W. Hoyt IV (a manufacturer and inventor), September 17, 1969. *Education:* Hofstra University, B.A., 1963; Smith College, M.A., 1964; University of California, Berkeley, M.P.H, 1970, Ph.D., 1972. *Agent:* Linda Chester, 265 Coast, La Jolla, Calif. 92037. *Office:* 1818 Country Club Lane, Escondido, Calif. 92026.

CAREER: Harvard University School of Public Health, Boston, Mass., researcher in department of nutrition, 1964-66; Foote, Cone & Belding, New York City, special assistant to technical director of research development, 1967; Columbia University College of Physicians and Surgeons, New York City, research associate at International Institute for the Study of Human Reproduction, 1967-68; University of California School of Public Health, Berkeley, researcher in department of maternal and child care, 1968-69; Cowell Hospital, Berkeley, Calif., chairman of student health services advisory committee, 1967-70; Department of Health Services of County of Marin, San Rafael, Calif., evaluation analyst, 1972-74; Bay Area Comprehensive Health Planning Council, San Francisco, Calif., data manager of regional office, 1974; Institute of Health Research, San Francisco, Calif., co-principal investigator for health profile program, 1976-78.

Consultant to agencies and organizations, including American Society of Internal Medicine, Institute for Scientific Analysis, West Coast Cancer Foundation, Department of Health and Human Services of County of Marin, Stanford University Department of Engineering-Economic Systems, National Center for Health Statistics, and University of California School of

Public Health, 1974-78; writer, 1979—. Case-aide worker at Northampton State Hospital. Chairperson of Bay Area Mental Health Program Evaluation Group, 1973-74. Lecturer in epidemiology at San Francisco State University, 1974; lecturer on psychological and physical well being for institutions and organizations. Guest on radio and television programs.

MEMBER: American Public Health Association, American Federation of Television and Radio Artists, Association for Women in Science, Society for Epidemological Research, Smith Club of San Francisco (president, 1975-76), Consultant's Committee of One Hundred (appointed member). *Awards, honors:* Smith College fellowship, 1963; named Outstanding Young Woman of America, 1968.

WRITINGS: His, Mine, and Ours: A Guide to Keeping Marriage From Ruining a Perfectly Good Relationship, Macmillan, 1979. Contributor to professional journals, including *Journal of General Psychology* and *Experientia.*

WORK IN PROGRESS: A book on holistic health, publication expected in 1982; research on physical and psychological well being.

SIDELIGHTS: According to Jim Sanderson of the *Los Angeles Times,* Anne Seifert is one of those women who view marriage "as a trap designed to keep her forever subordinate." So when Seifert married, she "decided that separate was the only way a wife ever was going to get equal." With this in mind, Seifert made her marriage a fifty-fifty relationship. She and her husband, Fred W. Hoyt, have their own identities; they maintain separate names, separate possessions, and separate bedrooms. They each have their own careers and bank accounts, and both parties are responsible for their designated household chores and laundry duties. Absolutely equal partners, they record their expenses and settle up their IOUs like college roommates. When they go out to dinner, Seifert pays for what she ate, and Hoyt picks up only his share of the tab. Fifty-fifty, suggests Seifert, keeps marriage "from ruining a perfectly good relationship."

Seifert reveals her formula for a happy marriage in *His, Mine, and Ours,* which she wrote because "all my friends viewed our marriage as one of the kookiest relationships ever, [but] we seemed to be getting happier while they were splitting up. I felt I had a social message to convey." The crux of her philosophy is expressed in her four major marital stressors: identity, money, housework, and space. Seifert feels a good marriage preserves the independence and individuality of both people. By retaining her maiden name, by cultivating her career, and by owning her own possessions, a wife, says Seifert, sustains her identity. Financially, a couple should split expenses equally, though either the husband or the wife may acquire private, personal luxury items. If one party contributes more for an item of mutual use, then that party owns a greater percentage of the item.

"The disharmonious aspects of our life," commented Seifert, "are discussed and a settlement is reached to prevent future bickering." For example, the couple has assigned household chores. It is a rule: If Hoyt takes the garbage cans out, Seifert retrieves them. The couple finds it more functional to sleep in separate bedrooms. Otherwise, when one wants the lights off while the other wants them on, Seifert asserts, resentment builds and quarrels develop. Nor is it "sexually exciting to sleep with someone who snores, who tosses and turns, who likes the room cool when you like it warm, or who wakes you when you want to sleep," she explained in the *Los Angeles Times.* Seifert and Hoyt do, however, "visit" each other nightly to talk about their days, and "before we part we hug and kiss."

Critically, *His, Mine, and Ours* has been labeled "well organized and easy to read." And the book was well received by the public, probably, as Seifert told Kathlyn Russell of the *Times-Advocate,* because "I was only confirming what people intuitively knew to be a logical alternative."

Like *His, Mine, and Ours,* Seifert's second book, which concentrates on approaches to fitness, comes from her own experience. The author, by nature sedentary, searched three years to find a fitness program to suit her personal needs. So, Russell observed, Seifert wrote a book that would "share what she has learned with others who have no taste for the up-and-at-'em fitness formulas."

Seifert told *CA:* "I believe that freedom, independence, and autonomy are essential to happiness. Marriage can compromise our freedom by making us economically dependent or liable; it threatens our autonomy by usurping or blending individual identities. Marriage should be the structure that serves our hearts, not the master that enslaves our bodies.

"In my writing I convey to people that they are in control of their own destiny. I can tell them how to achieve greater fulfillment in life, but they must be willing to give themselves permission to throw away old notions that no longer serve them."

BIOGRAPHICAL/CRITICAL SOURCES: Times-Advocate, October 2, 1979; *Los Angeles Times,* May 25, 1980.

*   *   *

SELIGMAN, Susan Meilach   1950-

PERSONAL: Born November 3, 1950, in Chicago, Ill.; daughter of Melvin Meyer (an orthodontist) and Dona Z. (an author) Meilach; married Richard Howard Seligman (a physician), April 15, 1973; children: Jordan Michael, Adam Mark. *Education:* University of Illinois, B.S., 1971. *Office:* 7514 El Morro N.E., Albuquerque, N.M. 87109.

CAREER: Helene Curtis Industries, Chicago, Ill., copywriter, 1971-72; LaSalle Extension University, Chicago, sales promotion manager, 1972-73; Kennedy & Green Advertising, Richmond, Va., copywriter, 1974-75; writer, 1978—. *Member:* Authors Guild.

WRITINGS: Now That I'm a Mother, What Do I Do for Me?, Contemporary Books, 1980; (with mother, Dona Z. Meilach) *Power Packed Play* (creative ideas for small children), Contemporary Books, 1982.

SIDELIGHTS: Susan Seligman wrote: "A good way to find subject material is to research information that you need to know for yourself. *Now That I'm a Mother* was written in response to the questions I had as a new mother. *Power Packed Play* grew out of a lack of resources suggesting easy and fun things to do around the house with children three years old and younger."

BIOGRAPHICAL/CRITICAL SOURCES: Albuquerque Tribune, November 18, 1980, May 19, 1981; *Carlsbad Journal,* December 31, 1980; *Blade Tribune,* February 18, 1981; *American Baby,* April, 1981.

*   *   *

SELTZER, Richard (Warren, Jr.)   1946-

PERSONAL: Born February 23, 1946, in Clarksville, Tenn.; son of Richard Warren (an educator) and Helen (a writer; maiden name, Estes) Seltzer; married Barbara Hartley (a writer and publisher), July 28, 1973; children: Robert Richard Hartley,

Heather Katherine Hartley, Michael Richard Hartley. *Education:* Yale University, B.A., 1969, graduate study, 1969-70; University of Massachusetts, M.A., 1973. *Home:* 33 Gould St., West Roxbury, Mass. 02132. *Agent:* Ashley Darlington Grayson, 1342 18th St., San Pedro, Calif. 90732. *Office:* B & R Samizdat Express, West Roxbury, Mass. 02132.

CAREER: University of Massachusetts, Amherst, Mass., instructor, 1973; Benwill Publishing, Boston, Mass., editor of *Electronics Test* and *Circuits Manufacturing* magazines, 1973-79; B & R Samizdat Express, West Roxbury, Mass., publisher, 1974—; *Word Guild* magazine, Cambridge, Mass., editor, 1977; Digital Equipment Corp., Maynard, Mass., editor of employee newspaper, 1979—. Free-lance translator of Russian. *Military service:* U.S. Army Reserve, 1969-75; became specialist, fifth class.

WRITINGS: The Lizard of Oz (fiction), B & R Samizdat Express, 1974; *Now and Then and Other Tales from Ome* (juvenile), B & R Samizdat Express, 1976; "Rights Crossing" (two-act play; first produced in Columbia, Pa., 1977), Lancaster Historical Society, 1979; *The Name of Hero* (novel; first volume of trilogy), J. P. Tarcher, 1981. Also author of plays "Amythos" (three-act) and "Mercy" (two-act).

WORK IN PROGRESS: The second and third volumes of a trilogy of historical novels based on the life of Russian cavalry officer, explorer, and monk Anthony Bulatovich, *The Name of Man* and *The Name of God,* publication by J. P. Tarcher expected in 1982 or 1983.

SIDELIGHTS: Seltzer told *CA:* "I suppose I use my writings as a tool for discovery. I want to know what motivates people to act as they do, how people find or create meaning for their lives, often making their limitations the source of their strength, and how they sometimes seem to undermine their own efforts, putting themselves in self-limiting, self-blinding boxes. I'm fascinated by paradoxes of human behavior. *The Lizard* playfully explores paradoxes of the human mind, the implications of language, and the difficulties encountered in dealing with a multiform and changing world.

"My historical plays were a warm-up for the historical novel *The Name of Hero,* which is based on an episode in the life of Anthony Bulatovich. I suppose it was the odd shifts in the career of Bulatovich that first drew me to him as a subject for a historical novel. I came across him in the *London Times* of 1913 while doing research for another book. He was presented as a Russian officer of the guard, who had been an explorer in Ethiopia, had fought in China, and then had become a monk at Mount Athos in Greece, where he became involved in a heresy battle. I was interested in the man himself—his evident energy and enthusiasm and his sudden shifts. I was also drawn to what was, for me, a strange world and psychology—a heresy battle in the twentieth century, on the eve of World War I. It seemed so anachronistic and yet so characteristic of Russia at that time. I wanted to understand the man and the time; I wanted to get some insight into what motivated this man so different in background and viewpoint from myself, what motivated those around him, how the people and circumstances interacted to produce this peculiar set of events. I sensed that this work could help me better understand myself and human behavior in general, in particular our need and quest for meaning and understanding.

"In my fiction, I'm primarily interested in character—the plot grows out of my understanding of the characters. I often use dialogue and would probably write more plays if I had an outlet for them. Of what I've written, the parts I like best are the dream sequences, the little parables, and the word play.

"Concerned about the decreasing publishing opportunities for original fiction, my wife and I started our own publishing company, B & R Samizdat Express, in 1974. Increasingly, I've come to realize that publishing and writing are two interdependent aspects of the same impulse, that without publishing opportunities writing atrophies. In the best of all possible worlds, with easily accessible channels for distribution and publicity, self-publishing would be the rule rather than the exception."

BIOGRAPHICAL/CRITICAL SOURCES: The Self-Publishing Writer, Spring, 1976.

*   *   *

SENDER, Ramon (Jose)   1902-1982

OBITUARY NOTICE—See index for *CA* sketch: Born February 3, 1902, in Alcolea de Cinca, Spain; died of emphysema, January 15, 1982, in San Diego, Calif. Educator and author of many books about the Spanish civil war and Spanish military campaigns in Morocco. Sender, who supported the republican cause during the civil war in Spain, was forced to leave that country in 1937. He eventually settled in the United States where he became a professor of Spanish literature. Though Sender was best known for his nine-volume collection of novels, *Chronicle of the Dawn,* some critics consider *Mr. Witt Among the Rebels,* a story of the Murcian rebellion of 1873, to be the author's most effective single work. Sender's novels were originally published in Spanish, but many, including *Pro Patria* and *Seven Red Sundays,* are available in English translation. In 1969 Sender received Spain's most prestigious literary award, the Planeta Prize. Obituaries and other sources: *London Times,* January 19, 1982; *Chicago Tribune,* January 19, 1982.

*   *   *

SENN, Steve   1950-

PERSONAL: Born August 4, 1950, in Americus, Ga.; son of Homer Will (a grocer) and Angelyn (a nurse; maiden name, Gay) Senn; married Linda Harris (a teacher), September 18, 1978; children: David. *Education:* Attended Ringling School of Art, 1968-71. *Home:* 2875 Sydney St., Jacksonville, Fla. 32205. *Agent:* Dorothy Markinko, McIntosh & Otis, Inc., 475 Fifth Ave., New York, N.Y. 10017. *Office:* William Cook Advertising, American Heritage Building, Jacksonville, Fla. 32202.

CAREER: Miami Herald, Miami, Fla., editorial artist, 1978; *Florida Times-Union,* Jacksonville, editorial artist and illustrator, 1978-81; William Cook Advertising, Jacksonville, staff writer, 1981—.

WRITINGS—Juveniles: *The Double Disappearance of Walter Fozbek,* Hastings House, 1980; *Spacebread,* Atheneum, 1981; *A Circle in the Sea,* Atheneum, 1981; *Born of Flame,* Atheneum, 1982.

WORK IN PROGRESS: Odin's Hostage, a historical novel about Vikings, gods, and hostage princes; *Three Hungers Touch the Moon,* a contemporary juvenile book about deformity; adult stories of horror and fantasy.

SIDELIGHTS: Senn told *CA:* "Storytelling is the parent of civilization, and imagination is the reason we do not live in trees. That sounds grandiose, perhaps because we are usually dwarfed uncomfortably by anything that is distinctly true, but it may help explain why so many people, including me, write. Creating fiction is like calling God on the telephone. When I first tried constructing sentences, around age ten, it amazed me that another world could be created so instantly and so completely by written language. It is still exhilarating.

"All I want to do is tell good stories that bring new feelings, fears, loves, ideas, and insights to the reader. It would be nice to be paid for them. My success so far has been with children's stories, which are really stories made up by an adult and then streamlined to the limit of leanness, with a kid as protagonist. I like having my protagonist be able to react to things from a totally fresh viewpoint. Besides, children will go places with you that adults will not. I feel very lucky in finding editors, chiefly Jean Karl, who will let me take them where I want to go (usually).

"Eventually, I would like to draw on my childhood in small-town Georgia for some children's books. Perhaps it was the place itself that made me want to invent other places and people. The place I came from was haunted. The lives of the people were bent in odd, Southern ways. Life there was contorted around several blatant but invisible lies, and in such an atmosphere it is easy to believe in witches and vampires and serpents and gods, and vital to believe in good and evil. There was an old colonial mansion on my street, and two of its columns were gone and had been replaced by timber frames. An aging heiress, in an alcoholic fog, lived inside with millions of old magazines. Never coming outside, she was companioned only by a black maid who brought boxes of groceries and booze balanced on her head back to the mansion. Chandeliers watched this woman die. Perhaps that sounds like a cliche from a Williams play, but it is a part of my personal myth. There are stories inside me which draw on that myth and whisper secrets about the land, about chains of both steel and of lies, and some beauty that is tied up in all of it. Someday I will tell them."

* * *

SETON, Marie 1910-

PERSONAL: Born in 1910 in Walton-on-Thames, England; married Donald L. Hesson (divorced). *Education:* Attended private girls' school in London, England. *Home:* 8b Albert Pl., London W.8, England.

CAREER: Writer and film producer.

WRITINGS: Sergei M. Eisenstein: A Biography, A. A. Wyn, 1952, revised edition, Dobson, 1979; *Paul Robeson,* Dobson, 1958; *Film as an Art and Film Appreciation,* National Institute of Audio Visual Education, National Council of Educational Research and Training (New Delhi, India), 1964; *Panditji: A Portrait of Jawaharlal Nehru,* Taplinger, 1967. Also author of *Film Appreciation: The Art of Five Directors,* National Institute of Audio Visual Education, National Council of Educational Research and Training (New Delhi, India).

Contributor to magazines, including *Sight and Sound, Soviet Studies,* and *Painter and Sculptor,* and newspapers.

BIOGRAPHICAL/CRITICAL SOURCES: Times Literary Supplement, April 6, 1967; *Listener,* May 4, 1967; *New York Times Book Review,* October 22, 1967.*

* * *

SEYMOUR, Henry
See HARTMANN, Helmut Henry

* * *

SHACKELFORD, Jean 1946-

PERSONAL: Born March 11, 1946, in Lexington, Ky.; daugh-

ter of Thomas B. (a landscape architect) and Delmyre (a teacher; maiden name, Cable) Shackelford; married Ronald J. Brinkman (a computer scientist), June 1, 1975; children: Brian Geoffrey. *Education:* Kansas State University, B.A., 1967; University of Kentucky, M.A., 1968, Ph.D., 1974. *Office:* Department of Economics, Bucknell University, Lewisburg, Pa. 17837.

CAREER: University of Alabama, Huntsville, instructor in economics, 1971-73; State University of New York College at Geneseo, assistant professor of economics, 1973-75; Bucknell University, Lewisburg, Pa., 1975—, began as assistant professor, became associate professor of economics. Founder, incorporator, and president of Lewisburg Area Child Care Center, Inc. *Member:* International Studies Association, American Economic Association (member of executive committee and Eastern chairperson of Committee on the Status of Women in the Economic Profession), Eastern Economic Association.

WRITINGS: (With Tom Riddell and Steve Stamos) *Economics: A Tool for Understanding Society,* Addison-Wesley, 1979; *Urban and Regional Economics,* Gale, 1980.

WORK IN PROGRESS: Research on labor force participation rates of women.

* * *

SHADILY, Hassan 1920-

PERSONAL: Born May 19, 1920, in Pamekasan, Indonesia; son of Kusumanegara (a merchant) and Halimah (a merchant) Abdurachman; married wife, Julia, May 19, 1953; children: Fatimah, Farida, Amalia, Arlan. *Education:* Attended Mosvia, Magelang, Indonesia, 1938-41, and International School, Tokyo, Japan, 1944-47; Cornell University, M.A., 1955. *Religion:* Islam. *Home and office:* 35 Jalan Maluku, Jakarta, Indonesia.

CAREER: Government of the Netherlands Indies, Pamekasan, Indonesia, officer, 1941-44; Franklin Book Programs, Inc., New York, N.Y., manager in Jakarta, Indonesia, 1955; C. V. Antarkarya Book Publishers, Jakarta, director, 1972—. Jakarta manager for Elsevier Publishing Co., 1972-80. Lecturer at University of Indonesia. Consultant. *Member:* Jakarta Golf Club, Rotary.

WRITINGS: (With John Echols) *Indonesian-English Dictionary,* Cornell University Press, 1963; (with Echols) *An English-Indonesian Dictionary,* Cornell University Press, 1975.

Other: *Sosiology untuk Masyarakat Indonesia* (title means "Sociology for the Indonesian Community"), P. T. Pembangunan, 1952, 8th edition, 1967; (co-editor) *Ensiklopedi Umum* (title means "Encyclopedia in One Volume"), Kanisius, 1972; *Ensiklopedi Indonesia,* six volumes, Ichtiar Baruvan Hoeve, 1980.

WORK IN PROGRESS: Editing a six-volume children's encyclopedia, for publication by P. T. Balai Pustaka.

BIOGRAPHICAL/CRITICAL SOURCES: Tempo, November 22, 1980.

* * *

SHADOIAN, Jack 1940-

PERSONAL: Born August 7, 1940, in New York, N.Y.; son of Vartan and Margaret (Baronian) Shadoian; married Carol Fossett (a teacher), June 12, 1964; children: Christopher, Jessica. *Education:* City College (now of City University of New York), B.A., 1963; University of Connecticut, M.A. and Ph.D. *Home address:* R.F.D.3, Leverett, Mass. 01002.

CAREER: Pennsylvania State University, University Park, assistant professor of English, 1967-70; University of Massachusetts, Amherst, assistant professor, 1970-76, associate professor of English, 1976—.

WRITINGS: *Dreams and Dead Ends: The American Gangster/Crime Film,* M.I.T. Press, 1977. Contributor of articles, poems, and reviews to journals and magazines, including *Rolling Stone* and *Fusion.*

SIDELIGHTS: Shadoian wrote: ''I grew up in the great baseball town of New York City—movies three or four times a week, radio and television, street sports, comic books, all kinds of music, and Armenian culture at home. I would live it all over again, except for one serious mistake—a lifelong devotion to the Chicago Cubs which has produced, I can say without exaggeration, some three decades of embarrassment and torment, but also a compensating compassion for all underdogs.

''In college I learned what could be done with language. However, I write, think, behave, and understand, not only out of big writers like Shakespeare, Pope, Tennyson, and the Greeks and Latins, but also Bud Powell, Charlie Parker, Lester Young, James Cagney, Buster Keaton, E. C. Comics, and Sandy Koufax. Of present writers I like R. Meltzer—for his fearlessness. Now I am thinking and writing about popular culture.''

AVOCATIONAL INTERESTS: Playing saxophone, softball, stickball, Scrabble, and poker.

*   *   *

SHAFAREVICH, Igor Rostislavovich 1923-

PERSONAL—Education: Attended Moscow M. V. Lomonosov State University, 1940. Office: Mathematics Institute, U.S.S.R. Academy of Sciences, Ul. Vavilova 42, Moscow 117333, Soviet Union.

CAREER: U.S.S.R. Academy of Sciences, Moscow, research associate at Mathematics Institute, 1943—, instructor in mathematics, 1944—, member of bureau of department of physics and mathematics, 1960-63. Member of Committee for Defense of Human Rights in the U.S.S.R. Member: American Academy of Sciences (honorary member). Awards, honors: Mathematics prize from German Academy of Sciences; Lenin Prize, 1959.

WRITINGS: (With S. P. Demushkin) *The Embedding Problem for Local Fields* (not originally in English), American Mathematical Society, 1963; (contributor) Ichiro Satake, editor, *Theory of Spherical Functions on Reductive Algebraic Groups,* Institut des hautes etudes scientifiques, 1963; (with Zenon Ivanovich Borevich) *Teoriia chisel,* Nauka, 1964, 2nd edition, 1972, translation by Newcomb Greenleaf published as *Number Theory,* Academic Press, 1966; (editor) *Algebraicheskie poverkhnosti,* Nauka, 1965, translation by Suzan Walker published as *Algebraic Surfaces,* American Mathematical Society, 1967; *Lectures on Minimal Models and Birational Transformations of Two Dimensional Schemes* (not originally in English), Tata Institute of Fundamental Research, 1966; *Osnovy algebraicheskoi geometrii,* Nauka, 1972, translation by K. A. Hirsch published as *Basic Algebraic Geometry,* Springer-Verlag, 1974, revised edition, 1977; *The Socialist Phenomenon,* translated by William Tjalsma, Harper, 1980. Also author of other works.

BIOGRAPHICAL/CRITICAL SOURCES: *New York Times Book Review,* November 16, 1980; *Los Angeles Times Book Review,* November 30, 1980.*

SHAKESPEARE, Geoffrey (Hithersay) 1893-1980

OBITUARY NOTICE: Born September 23, 1893, in Norwich, Norfolk, England; died September 8, 1980, in Chislehurst, Kent, England. Politician, journalist, businessman, and author. Educated at Cambridge, Shakespeare pursued a career in law before becoming, in 1921, private secretary to England's Prime Minister David Lloyd George. In this capacity Shakespeare participated in the settlement of disputes between Britain and the Southern Irish Governments. He was elected to the House of Commons and served there from 1922 to 1923. After six years as political correspondent for the *Daily Chronicle* Shakespeare was again elected to Parliament in 1929, where he held a seat for sixteen years. During this time he served variously as junior lord of the treasury, parliamentary secretary at the Ministry of Health, parliamentary under-secretary of state at the Dominions Office, and chairman of the Children's Overseas Reception Board. Shakespeare received a baronetcy in 1942 and became a privy councillor in 1945. Beginning in the mid-1940's he turned to industry and held several business posts. His memoirs, *Let Candles Be Brought In,* appeared in 1949. Shakespeare also wrote plays, including ''A Midsummer Morn's Awakening,'' which was broadcast on American television, and ''The Amorous Ghost.'' Obituaries and other sources: Geoffrey Shakespeare, *Let Candles Be Brought In,* MacDonald, 1949; *The International Year Book and Statesman's Who's Who,* Kelly's Directories, 1980; *The Annual Obituary 1980,* St. Martin's, 1981.

*   *   *

SHALAMOV, Varlam (Tikhonovich) 1907(?)-1982

OBITUARY NOTICE: Born c. 1907; died of heart failure, January 17, 1982, in Moscow, U.S.S.R. Political prisoner, poet, and author. Shalamov was arrested in 1937 during the Communist party purges ordered by Soviet leader Joseph Stalin. Shalamov had aroused suspicion by praising Russian emigre writer Ivan Bunin, winner of the 1933 Nobel Prize for literature. Sentenced to seventeen years of forced labor in Siberia, Shalamov was sent to the Kolyma labor camps, where prisoners were employed mining gold and where an estimated three million prisoners have died. He was released in the 1950's and permitted to publish poetry. His account of life in the labor camps was secretly circulated in Moscow and published outside the Soviet Union in emigre journals. A French version of the stories was published in 1969. The English-language translation, *Kolyma Tales,* appeared in 1980. Shalamov was forced to publicly denounce the stories' publication. Obituaries and other sources: *Survey,* spring, 1979; *New York Times Book Review,* March 9, 1980, May 4, 1980; *New York Review of Books,* August 14, 1980; *Contemporary Literary Criticism,* Volume 18, Gale, 1981; *Chicago Tribune,* January 20, 1982; *London Times,* January 20, 1982; *Newsweek,* February 1, 1982.

*   *   *

SHALVEY, Thomas (Joseph) 1937-

PERSONAL: Born July 3, 1937, in New York, N.Y. Education: Fordham University, B.A., 1961, M.A., 1964; Georgetown University, Ph.D., 1970. Office: Department of Philosophy, Southern Connecticut State College, New Haven, Conn. 06515.

CAREER: Fordham University, Bronx, N.Y., instructor in classical languages at preparatory school, 1962-65; Southern Connecticut State College, New Haven, 1968-74, began as assistant professor, became associate professor, professor of philosophy, 1974—, chairman of department, 1973-75. *Member:* American Association of University Professors, American Philosophical Association, Metaphysical Society of America, American Catholic Philosophical Association, Society for Phenomenology and Existential Philosophy.

WRITINGS: Claude Levi-Strauss: Social Psychotherapy and the Collective Unconscious, University of Massachusetts Press, 1979.*

* * *

SHANDS, Harley C. 1916-1981

OBITUARY NOTICE: Born September 10, 1916, in Jackson, Miss.; died of a ruptured aortic aneurysm, December 4, 1981, in New York, N.Y. Psychiatrist, educator, and author. Shands was a resident at the Mayo Clinic from 1941 to 1945 and then served until 1953 as a research fellow in psychiatry at Massachusetts General Hospital in Boston. While in Boston he also taught at Harvard University. From 1967 until his death he served as department of psychiatry chairman at St. Lukes-Roosevelt Hospital Center and as professor of psychiatry at Columbia University College of Physicians and Surgeons. Shands wrote several books, including *Thinking and Psychotherapy, The War With Words, Language and Psychiatry,* and *Speech as Instruction.* Obituaries and other sources: *Who's Who in America,* 40th edition, Marquis, 1978; *American Men and Women of Science: The Physical and Biological Sciences,* 14th edition, Bowker, 1979; *New York Times,* December 7, 1981.

* * *

SHAPIRO, Max 1912(?)-1981
(Monroe Stuart)

OBITUARY NOTICE: Born c. 1912; died October 26, 1981, in St. Louis, Mo. Publisher, editor, and author. Shapiro was founder and president of Cadillac Publishing Co., publishers of encyclopedias, self-help books, and reference works, and co-founder of Made Simple Books, Inc. He co-wrote, under the pseudonym Monroe Stuart, the popular text *Mathematics Made Simple,* and served as editor-in-chief of the *Cadillac Modern Encyclopedia.* Obituaries and other sources: *Publishers Weekly,* November 20, 1981.

* * *

SHARP, Buchanan 1942-

PERSONAL: Born September 25, 1942, in Dumbarton, Scotland; married, 1964; children: two. *Education:* University of California, Berkeley, A.B., 1964, Ph.D., 1971; University of Illinois, M.A., 1965. *Office:* Department of History, College V, University of California, Santa Cruz, Calif. 95064.

CAREER: University of California, Santa Cruz, assistant professor, 1970-77, associate professor of history, 1977—. *Member:* American Historical Association, Economic History Society, Past and Present Society, Scottish Historical Society.

WRITINGS: In Contempt of All Authority: Rural Artisans and Riot in the West of England, University of California Press, 1980.

BIOGRAPHICAL/CRITICAL SOURCES: Times Literary Supplement, December 26, 1980.*

* * *

SHAWCROSS, William 1946-

PERSONAL: Born in 1946 in Sussex, England; son of Hart-ley W. Shawcross (a prosecutor); married Marina Warner (a writer), January 31, 1972. *Education:* Received B.A. from University College, Oxford. *Residence:* London, England. *Agent:* Roberta Pryor, International Creative Management, 40 West 57th St., New York, N.Y. 10019. *Office:* c/o *London Sunday Times,* 200 Grays Inn Rd., London W.C.1, England.

CAREER: Free-lance journalist in Czechoslovakia, 1968-69; *London Sunday Times,* London, England, writer on Eastern European affairs, beginning in 1969, war correspondent in Indochina, 1970-72; correspondent in Washington, D.C., for *New Statesman* (London) and *Far Eastern Economic Review* (Hong Kong). War correspondent in Indochina for newspapers. Visiting research fellow at Merton College, Oxford. *Member:* American Political Science Association (congressional fellow). *Awards, honors:* Grants from Harkness Foundation and from Field Foundation (through Center for National Security Studies); Sidney Hillman Foundation Award; George Polk Award in journalism.

WRITINGS: Dubcek, Weidenfeld & Nicholson, 1970, Simon & Schuster, 1971; (with Lewis Chester and others) *Watergate: The Full Inside Story,* Ballantine, 1973; *Crime and Compromise: Janos Kadar and the Politics of Hungary Since Revolution,* Dutton, 1974; *Sideshow: Kissinger, Nixon, and the Destruction of Cambodia,* Simon & Schuster, 1979. Contributor of articles to periodicals, including *Guardian, New Statesman, New York Review of Books,* and *New Republic.*

WORK IN PROGRESS: A book about responses to international catastrophes.

SIDELIGHTS: In *Sideshow: Kissinger, Nixon, and the Destruction of Cambodia,* William Shawcross documents America's involvement in Cambodia, beginning immediately after President Richard Nixon's inauguration in 1969 and ending six years later. After examining numerous declassified U.S. government documents and interviewing hundreds of people, including American and foreign cabinet ministers, members of the military, civil servants, journalists, and refugees, Shawcross concluded that, from the first invasion of U.S. troops into Cambodia, Nixon and Secretary of State Henry Kissinger did everything they could to conceal U.S. involvement in Cambodia from the American public, from manipulating the press to falsifying Pentagon records.

According to Shawcross, Nixon ordered the illegal bombing of Cambodian border areas as early as March, 1969, hoping to destroy the North Vietnamese headquarters that were reported to be in sanctuary there. The attack, contrary to Nixon's goal, merely forced the North Vietnamese troops to move farther into the supposedly neutral country, and into areas of increasingly dense population. The initial bombing—code-named "Breakfast"—was followed by invasions called "Lunch," "Snack," "Dinner," "Dessert," and "Supper." The Nixon administration later defended "Operation Menu" by saying that it had been instituted in order to expedite removal of U.S. troops from Vietnam. If that was the purpose of the operation, then why, Shawcross asks, did the United States engage in its heaviest bombing during 1973, when there were no U.S. troops left in Vietnam? That year, he notes, the tonnage of bombs dropped on Cambodia was greater than that dropped by the United States on Japan during all of World War II.

Shawcross divides America's Cambodian involvement into four stages. The first stage, the 1969 bombing of Cambodian border areas, pushed the North Vietnamese into increasing conflict with the forces of Cambodia's ruler, Prince Norodom Sihanouk. Stage two came in 1970, when Sihanouk was overthrown in a coup led by Cambodia's prime minister, General Lon Nol.

Shawcross suggests that Kissinger (then assistant to the president for national security affairs) encouraged—perhaps even aided—Lon Nol in his effort to oust Sihanouk. Whether Kissinger was involved or not, Lon Nol and his co-conspirators "clearly acted in the expectation of American support, which they promptly got," noted *New Republic*'s Michael Walzer. *Saturday Review*'s Fredric M. Kaplan observed that "immediately upon Lon Nol's successful deposition of Sihanouk in 1970, Nixon and Kissinger rushed U.S. support to the new government despite direct warnings . . . that such actions would compromise Cambodia's neutrality and thus invite a dangerous broadening of the war."

Stage three followed immediately, beginning with the April, 1970, invasion of Cambodia by U.S. and South Vietnamese troops. The invasion, like previous attacks, did more damage to Cambodian civilians than to the Communist forces it was allegedly designed to destroy. As the North Vietnamese moved farther into the Cambodian countryside, the United States responded by helping Lon Nol build his army. Lon Nol knew, however, that Cambodia was incapable of defending itself, and it was at this point, says Shawcross, that Lon Nol realized exactly what U.S. support meant. According to David Butler of *Newsweek,* Lon Nol came to believe that the U.S. invasion was designed not to destroy the sanctuaries of the North Vietnamese and the Vietcong (North Vietnamese guerrillas), but to drive them farther from South Vietnam and deeper into Cambodia.

Stage four marked the rising of the Khmer Rouge, a band of Communist terrorists that had grown steadily in number since the days of Prince Norodom Sihanouk. In 1975 the Khmer Rouge seized Phnom Penh, Cambodia's capital city. Between bombings by the United States and continuous terrorist attacks by the Khmer Rouge, Cambodia was transformed into a nation of refugees. "Moreover," commented Butler, "the South Vietnamese [who were] sent in as 'allies' of Lon Nol displayed an aptitude for killing Cambodians—and looting their villages and raping their women—that they had rarely shown against the Vietcong." Millions of Cambodians were driven from their homes in the country into the cities during the course of the war, Shawcross writes. After the Khmer Rouge's victory, they were driven back to the countryside, where, noted Walzer, "there was, after the years of war, neither food nor shelter nor medical supplies available." "Through all the suffering," a *Time* writer said, "Washington continued to support the 'bankrupt' and 'corrupt' regime of Lon Nol because he was willing, if far from able, to go on fighting the Communists."

"What was the strategic purpose of all this?," wondered Walzer. "Ostensibly, we fought in Cambodia in order to facilitate our withdrawal from Vietnam, 'to save American lives'—at a cost in Cambodian lives so incredible as to overwhelm the calculation, except that there is no evidence that American policy-makers counted Cambodians when they did their calculating. Nor is there much evidence that American lives were saved: it probably wasn't in the interests of the Communists to kill a lot of Americans in 1970 and 1971, when the withdrawal was proceeding rapidly."

The motive for U.S. interference in Cambodia is difficult to discern, Shawcross acknowledges in *Sideshow*. He postulates that the entire Cambodian affair was engineered and executed under direct order from Nixon and Kissinger, and he reasons that nothing short of a mad hunger for power and a paranoia about the spread of Communism could have prompted them to act as they did. Shawcross's point, deduced Fredric M. Kaplan, is that "the workings of Kissinger's ego—coupled with Nixon's self-described 'madman' policy-making—were more di-

rectly responsible for the devastation in Cambodia than were geopolitical necessities."

Though *Sideshow* was characterized by John Leonard of the *New York Times* as having "the sweep and the shadows of a spy novel" and was written, according to the *Washington Post Book World*'s Jean Lacouture, with "admirable competence, precision, factual richness and talent for description," a writer for the *National Review* found Shawcross's analysis of the Cambodian situation and his explanation of Nixon's motive simplistic and farfetched. The mistake was not, as Shawcross argues, in attacking Cambodia, but in attacking too late to avert the spread of Communism, contended the *National Review* writer. He was also critical of Shawcross's condemnation of Nixon, and he insisted that Nixon's fear of Communism was justified, saying that "the diminution caused by the American incursion [into Cambodia] was small potatoes alongside the diminution suffered [under Communist rule]."

While the destruction and suffering that took place in Cambodia under the rule of Pol Pot (Communist leader of the 1975 revolution who later became prime minister of Cambodia) may well have been greater than that which occurred during the years of American involvement there, Shawcross asserts that the Communist takeover was a direct result of U.S. involvement. American intervention created an ideal climate for the growth of Communism, said Leonard, for "by abetting Lon Nol's overthrow of the man in the middle, Prince Sihanouk, in March 1970, we managed to give the Khmer Rouge a popular target to attack and made Pol Pot, or someone like him, inevitable." (According to a 1979 *New Yorker* article, after Pol Pot's 1975 victory he established "one of the most ferocious totalitarian regimes ever known," and, under his leadership, "the population was reduced, through execution, disease, and malnutrition, from some seven million to some four and a half million.")

Harrison E. Salisbury, writing for the *Chicago Tribune Book World,* praised Shawcross for providing his study at "a moment when some have begun to long nostalgically for the 'professional' diplomacy of the Nixon-Kissinger team." Though he found *Sideshow* a brilliant and timely work, Salisbury felt that Shawcross evaded the issue of motive in his discussion of Nixon's actions. "This is the only important fact that eludes Shawcross in his devastating expose," he wrote. "Why did the United States deliberately exterminate a small neutral Asian country with which it was not at war; why the secret bombing; why the crushing invasion in search of the illusory 'Communist Pentagon East' in whose existence only visionary military word-painters could have any belief? Was it simply to demonstrate to the Communist world that Nixon was prepared to follow his Madman Theory to the limit? Or was the irrationality genuine? Was it, in fact, madness?"

Michael Walzer declared that U.S. participation in Cambodia demonstrated "our capacity for destruction." Both the Vietnamese and the Khmer Rouge, he reflected, had discernible motives for their actions in Cambodia. "The Vietnamese aimed ultimately at the subordination of Cambodia within an Indochinese federation. The Khmer Rouge aimed at the creation of a primitive, ascetic and autarchic communism. But the Americans never seem to have had a clear local purpose." The United States had to reassert, Walzer inferred from *Sideshow,* "an imperial 'will' which might otherwise have been thought to have faltered in the long course of the Vietnam war."

When the American public responded indignantly to news of U.S. involvement in Cambodia, Nixon countered by resolving to take strong measures to resist domestic dissent, Shawcross maintains. The implication in *Sideshow,* wrote Walzer, is "that

Cambodia was the real Watergate . . . and the real corruption of democratic processes, and it led to evils that make the harassments of the Democrats [during the 1972 presidential campaign] seem petty indeed.''

In the end, Shawcross passes judgment on Nixon and Kissinger by naming the Cambodian tragedy a crime for which both are responsible. Salisbury agreed with his conclusion, calling American involvement in Cambodia a "crime which no number of presidential pardons can wash off his [Nixon's] record and that of his collaborator, Henry Kissinger. The spot will not out.''

AVOCATIONAL INTERESTS: Sailing.

BIOGRAPHICAL/CRITICAL SOURCES: Observer Review, August 16, 1970; *Times Literary Supplement,* August 21, 1970; *Saturday Review,* June 26, 1971, June 9, 1979; *New York Review of Books,* September 2, 1971, February 22, 1979; *America,* June 29, 1974; *New Yorker,* September 16, 1974, November 5, 1979; *New Republic,* March 24, 1979, May 26, 1979; *Chicago Tribune Book World,* April 22, 1979; *New York Times Book Review,* April 22, 1979; *New York Times,* April 24, 1979, May 13, 1979; *Washington Post Book World,* April 29, 1979; *Newsweek,* April 30, 1979; *Harper's,* May, 1979; *Time,* May 7, 1979; *National Review,* May 25, 1979; *London Times,* April 5, 1980.*

—*Sketch by Mary Sullivan*

*   *   *

SHEDLEY, Ethan I.
    See BEIZER, Boris

*   *   *

SHEED, Francis Joseph   1897-1981
    (Frank Sheed)

OBITUARY NOTICE: Born March 20, 1897, in Sydney, Australia; died November 20, 1981, in Jersey City, N.J. Roman Catholic lay theologian, lecturer, publisher, and author. Sheed left law studies in Australia to travel in Europe and England. In London he joined the Catholic Evidence Guild, a group of Roman Catholic street speakers, and soon became one of the Guild's most effective speakers. In all, he delivered more than seven thousand open-air lectures in his lifetime. Sheed married fellow Guild member Maisie Ward in 1926, and together they established in England the firm of Sheed & Ward to publish English Catholic Revival authors, historians, philosophers, and church defenders. The New York branch of Sheed & Ward was founded in 1933. Among Sheed & Ward's writers were Hilaire Belloc, G. K. Chesterton, Sigrid Undset, and Francois Mauriac. Sheed's own publications include *Nullity of Marriage, Communism and Man, Theology and Sanity, Society and Sanity,* and a translation of St. Augustine's *Confessions.* Sheed's son is the celebrated American novelist Wilfred Sheed. Obituaries and other sources: *Catholic Authors: Contemporary Biographical Sketches,* Volume I: *1930-1947,* St. Mary's Abbey, 1948; *The Author's and Writer's Who's Who,* 6th edition, Burke's Peerage, 1971; *New York Times Book Review,* April 2, 1972; Frank Sheed, *The Church and I,* Doubleday, 1974; *Current Biography,* Wilson, 1981; *New York Times,* November 21, 1981; *Chicago Tribune,* November 22, 1981; *London Times,* November 24, 1981; *Newsweek,* November 30, 1981; *Publishers Weekly,* December 4, 1981.

SHEED, Frank
    See SHEED, Francis Joseph

*   *   *

SHELDON, Charles S(tuart) II   1917-1981

OBITUARY NOTICE: Born May 18, 1917, in Shanghai, China; died of cancer, September 11, 1981, in Arlington, Va. Adviser to U.S. Congress, educator, and author. An expert on the Soviet space program, Sheldon became in 1955 a member of the Science Policy Research Division of the Congressional Research Service at the Library of Congress, where he served as chief from 1966 to his retirement in 1981. Sheldon, who received his doctorate in economics from Harvard University in 1942, was a naval officer in World War II and the Korean War before becoming an instructor at the University of Washington. As a member of the Congressional Research Service he helped draft both the National Aeronautics and Space Act of 1958 and the Communications Satellite Act of 1962. His research was considered invaluable to the study of Soviet space activities. Many of Sheldon's studies pieced together details of the Soviet space program's development. In addition to Congressional reports and journal articles, Sheldon's writings include such books as *Soviet Economic Growth, Review of the Soviet Space Program,* and *The Soviet Space Program.* Obituaries and other sources: *American Men and Women of Science: The Social and Behavioral Sciences,* 12th edition, Bowker, 1973; *Who's Who in Government,* Marquis, 1975; *New York Times,* September 12, 1981; *Time,* September 21, 1981.

*   *   *

SHEPARD, Thomas Rockwell, Jr.   1918-

PERSONAL: Born August 22, 1918, in New York, N.Y.; son of Thomas Rockwell and Marie (Dickinson) Shepard; married Nancy Kruidenier, September 20, 1941; children: Sue (Mrs. R. Gerald Mould), Molly (Mrs. Karl K. Lunkenheimer), Amy K., Thomas Rockwell III. *Education:* Amherst College, B.A., 1940. *Politics:* Republican. *Home:* 44 Lismore Lane, Greenwich, Conn. 06830.

CAREER: Assistant promotion manager of Vick Chemical Co., 1942; *Look,* New York City, West Coast manager, 1947-49, assistant to publisher in charge of promotion, 1955-56, New York manager and eastern advertising manager, 1956-57, assistant advertising manager, 1957-62, advertising sales manager of Cowles magazines and broadcasting, and vice-president, 1961-64, advertising director, 1964-67, publisher, 1967-72; consultant, 1972-74; Institute of Outdoor Advertising, New York City, president, 1974-77; consultant, 1977—. President of Rehabilitation International and Greenwich Community Chest, 1964-65; chairman of Robert A. Taft Institute of Government, 1978—; vice-president of Cowles Communications, Inc., 1958-71 (member of board of directors, 1968-71), and National Institute of Social Sciences; director of Greenwich Boys Club, 1960-66; member of board of directors of Advertising Council (past president). *Military service:* U.S. Naval Reserve, active duty, 1941-45; became lieutenant commander.

MEMBER: Children's Aid Society (member of board of directors), Delta Upsilon (member of board of directors), Field Club, Belle Haven Beach Club, Round Hill Club, Circumnavigators Club. *Awards, honors:* George Washington Honor Medal from Freedoms Foundation, 1970 and 1973.

WRITINGS: (With Melvin J. Grayson) *The Disaster Lobby: Prophets of Ecological Doom and Other Absurdities,* Follett,

1973. Contributor to magazines, including *Reader's Digest* and *National Observer*, and newspapers.*

* * *

SHEPHERD, Nan 1893-

PERSONAL: Born February 11, 1893, in Cults, Scotland; daughter of John (an engineer) and Jean (Kelly) Shepherd. *Education:* University of Aberdeen, M.A., 1945. *Home:* 503 North Deeside Rd., Cults, Aberdeen AB1 9ES, Scotland.

CAREER: Aberdeen College of Education, Aberdeen, Scotland, lecturer in English literature, 1915-56; *Aberdeen University Review,* Aberdeen, editor, 1956-63; writer and editor, 1963—. *Awards, honors:* LL.D. from University of Aberdeen, 1964.

WRITINGS: The Quarry Wood (novel), Dutton, 1928; *The Weatherhouse* (novel), Dutton, 1930; *A Pass in the Grampions* (novel), Dutton, 1933; *In the Cairngorms* (poems), Moray Press, 1934; (contributor) Charles Murray, *The Last Poems,* Aberdeen University Press, 1969; *Living Mountain: Celebration of the Cairngorm Mountains of Scotland,* Aberdeen University Press, 1977. Also co-editor of *The Fusion of 1860,* Aberdeen University Press, and editor of *Hamewith: The Complete Poems of Charles Murray,* Pergamon, and *Poems of J. C. Milne,* 1964.

SIDELIGHTS: Shepherd told *CA:* "My chief interests are Scottish literature, particularly of the northeast, and hills and hill-walking."

* * *

SHEPHERD, Walter Bradley 1904-

PERSONAL: Born in 1904 in Southampton, England; married Joan Hester Angus; children: one son.

CAREER: Worked as features editor in Press Office of Ministry of Supply, England, 1942-43; assistant feature editor for Allied Newspapers, 1943; assistant editor in book department of Odhams Press, 1944-47; Working Men's College, London, England, lecturer in physical geography; schoolmaster, survey and research geologist; editor for George Newnes; Hutchinson Publishing Group Ltd., London, began as manager of scientific technology department, became manager and director of medical publications; writer and illustrator. *Member:* Geographical Society (fellow).

WRITINGS: Science Marches On: The Origins, Progress, and Significance of Scientific Knowledge (self-illustrated juvenile), Harcourt, 1939, revised edition published as *A New Survey of Science,* Harrap, 1949, Harcourt, 1950; *For Amazement Only* (maze puzzles), Penguin, 1942, 2nd edition published as *Mazes and Labyrinths: A Book of Puzzles,* Dover, 1961; *The Living Landscape of Britain,* Faber, 1952, new edition, 1963; revised edition published as *The Wonder Book of Science,* Ward, Lock, 1953, new edition, 1962; *The Countryside Round the Year* (self-illustrated juvenile), Jenkins, 1953; (with Wilfred G. Moore and Peter Hood) *The World We Live In: The Geography of Our Earth and Its Peoples* (juvenile), New Educational Press, 1958.

The Universe, Messner, 1960; (editor with Gerald E. Speck and J. E. Radford) *Junior Pictorial Encyclopaedia of Science,* Ward, Lock, 1961; *Our Universe,* Ward, Lock, 1961; *Wealth From the Ground* (juvenile), John Day, 1962; *Rocks, Minerals, and Fossils* (self-illustrated juvenile), Weidenfeld & Nicolson, 1962; *Looking at the Landscape* (self-illustrated juvenile), Phoenix House, 1963; (with Maurice Burton) *The Wonder Book*

of Our Earth, Ward, Lock, 1963; *How to Use a Microscope* (self-illustrated), Weidenfeld & Nicolson, 1964, New American Library, 1966; *Great Pioneers of Science,* Ward, Lock, 1964; *Electricity* (juvenile), John Day, 1964; *Let's Look at Trees* (juvenile), Muller, 1964; *Archaeology* (self-illustrated juvenile), Weidenfeld & Nicolson, 1965, New American Library, 1966; *Let's Look at Insects,* Muller, 1965; *Outline History of Science,* Ward, Lock, 1966, Philosophical Library, 1968; *The Earth's Surface,* Golden Press, 1968; *The Story of Man* (juvenile), Golden Press, 1968; *Geophysics* (self-illustrated juvenile), Hart-Davis, 1969, Putnam, 1970.

How Airplanes Fly, John Day, 1971 (published in England as *How Aeroplanes Fly,* Hart-Davis, 1971); *The Puzzle Book,* F. Watts, 1971; *Jungles,* John Day, 1971; *Shepherd's Glossary of Graphic Signs and Symbols,* Dent, 1971, Dover, 1972; *Textiles,* Hart-Davis, 1971, John Day, 1972, revised edition, Hart-Davis, 1976; *Flint: Its Origin, Properties, and Uses,* Transatlantic, 1972; *The Big Book of Mazes and Labyrinths,* Dover, 1973; *Our Landscape: Discovering How It Was Made,* Arrow Books, 1977; *Picture Puzzles,* Beaver Books, 1977; *On the Scent With Sherlock Holmes: Some Old Problems Resolved,* Arthur Barker, 1978.

Also author of (with W. M. Franklin, D. R. Smith, and J. A. Hetherington) *The Wonder Book of Why and What,* 1961, and *Heroes of Science,* 1964. Also editor of *Pictorial Knowledge,* George Newnes. Contributor to geography journals and popular magazines, including *Sphere, Country Life,* and *Schoolmaster,* and newspapers.*

* * *

SHEPPARD, Stephen 1945-

PERSONAL: Born in 1945 in Bristol, England. *Education:* Studied art at Dartington Hall in England; attended Royal Academy of Dramatic Art, London. *Address:* c/o Summit Books, Simon & Schuster, Inc., 1230 Avenue of the Americas, New York, N.Y. 10020.

CAREER: Actor; appeared in British Broadcasting Corp. (BBC) productions and motion pictures, including "Villain," 1971, and "Lady Caroline Lamb," 1972; writer, 1979—. Painter.

WRITINGS: The Four Hundred, Summit Books, 1979. Also author of screenplays.

WORK IN PROGRESS: The Frozen Horsemen.

SIDELIGHTS: Sheppard was inspired to write *The Four Hundred* upon reading of a crime committed more than one hundred years ago when four American men defrauded the Bank of England of $2 million. Fascinated by the incident, Sheppard spent eighteen months researching the history and events of nineteenth-century England, then began writing what he originally intended to be a screenplay. He told Robert Dahlin of *Publishers Weekly:* "At first I thought it would be a good film idea, but the more I researched the time, the richer and richer it became, and I couldn't bring myself to leave anything out." Thus, the project resulted in a four-hundred-page novel.

The Four Hundred was, nevertheless, destined for the screen. When literary agent Ed Victor read and loved the book, he called producer Daniel Melnick, who flew to London to read the manuscript. Within several days, Melnick and Warner Brothers had purchased the film rights of the then-unpublished book for $1 million.

Sheppard told the *Los Angeles Times* that desperation motivated him to write *The Four Hundred.* "Let's just say that during the three years it took me to write it, I felt like a gambler who just had to win.'' Evidently Sheppard's work was not in vain. Aside from the immediate sale of its film rights, the book was applauded by critics. The *Chicago Tribune Book World* noted: ''Sheppard's style is lean, his sensitivity to the subtleties of human emotion uncanny, his timing superb.'' Charles Nicol of the *Washington Post Book World* remarked: ''Sheppard has given us a skilled and rather elegant caper, cheerfully written and attractively printed.''

BIOGRAPHICAL/CRITICAL SOURCES: New York Times, February 18, 1979; *Publishers Weekly,* July 30, 1979; *Washington Post,* October 20, 1979; *New York Times Book Review,* November 11, 1979; *Chicago Tribune Book World,* November 25, 1979.*

*   *   *

SHERMAN, William David   1940-

PERSONAL: Born December 24, 1940, in Philadelphia, Pa.; son of Louis (an attorney) and Gertrude (Benn) Sherman; married Barbara Beaumont, July 22, 1970 (divorced, 1978). *Education:* Temple University, A.B. (cum laude), 1962; State University of New York at Buffalo, M.A., 1964, Ph.D., 1968; attended Dickinson School of Law, 1974-75. *Home address:* c/o 4805 B St., Philadelphia, Pa. 19120.

CAREER: Teacher at high school in London, England, 1964; University of Maryland, European Division, United Kingdom Office, London, instructor in English, 1965; State University of New York at Buffalo, lecturer in cinema, 1967; University of Hull, Hull, England, lecturer in American studies, 1967-68; teacher of humanities at high school in London, 1969; University of Wales, University College of Wales, Aberystwyth, lecturer in American literature, 1969-72; writer, 1972-76; Open University, London, part-time tutor and counselor in the arts, 1976-79; Samuel Pepys High School, London, teacher of physical education, 1979-80; University of Maryland, European Division, United Kingdom Office, part-time instructor in literary criticism, 1980—. Founder, editor, and publisher of Branch Redd Publications, 1976-79. Giver of poetry readings.

WRITINGS: (With Leon Lewis) *The Landscape of Contemporary Cinema,* Buffalo Spectrum Press, 1967; *The Cinema of Orson Welles,* State University of New York at Buffalo Publications, 1967; ''The Case of Ezra Pound'' (one-act play in six scenes), published in *Anglo-Welsh Review,* autumn, 1970; *The Springbok* (poetry chapbook), Aloes Books, 1973; *Hydra* (poem), Poets and Painters Press, 1973; *The Hard Sidewalk* (poetry chapbook), privately printed, 1974, revised edition, Spanner, 1975; *The Horses of Gwyddno Garanhir* (poems), New London Pride Editions, 1976; *Mermaids: Part One* (poems), X Press, 1977; *Heart Attack and Spanish Songs in Mandaine Land* (poems), Dream Tree Press, 1981; *The Time the A's Went West* (poems), New London Pride Editions, 1982.

Screenplays: (With Theodora Cichy) ''On Maximus to Himself,'' Library of British Film Institute, 1967.

Work represented in anthologies, including *Spanner Six,* 1976; *New Poetry Three,* Arts Council of Great Britain, 1977; *Nouvelle Poetry Anglaise,* edited by Pierre Joris and Paul Buck, Christian Bourgois Editions.

London correspondent for *Take One,* 1968-70, correspondent-at-large, 1970-75. Contributor of more than one hundred articles, poems, and reviews to journals, including *Atlantic Review, Journal of American Studies, Cold Mountain Review, Sight and Sound, Poetry Wales,* and *Intrepid.* Guest editor of

Sixpack, 1973; founder, editor, and publisher of *Branch Redd Review,* 1976-79.

WORK IN PROGRESS: The Pageant, a novel.

SIDELIGHTS: Sherman wrote: ''I first left America in the summer of 1962, and returned to Europe in the summer of 1964. I remained for one year, mostly in London, where a significant friendship began with the English poet Kate Glason (nee Ruse). I taught in England in 1967, and at the close of that academic year journeyed to Greece, where I worked as a writer for a time, with the encouragement of poet Leonard Cohen. After that, I went to Israel, but found myself alienated there. I was more attracted to the Arab way of life than the sabra one, and the Chassidic world was closed to me.

''Although I had lived and traveled abroad, I date my expatriation, which is a psychological and not a geographical condition, from 1968, when I returned to the United States with no plans to leave, and felt myself a tourist in my own country.

''For the past ten years, I have helped to build a community of poets in London. I have been closely associated since 1975 with poets Allen Fisher, Pierre Joris, and Eric Mottram.''

*   *   *

SHERMAN, William Lewis   1927-

PERSONAL: Born April 9, 1927, in Pasadena, Calif.; married, 1960; children: three. *Education:* Woodbury College, B.B.A., 1949; American Institute for Trade, B.F.T., 1940; University of the Americas, M.A., 1958; University of New Mexico, Ph.D., 1967. *Office:* Department of History, University of Nebraska, Lincoln, Neb. 68508.

CAREER: U.S. Department of State, Washington, D.C., foreign service officer in Germany, 1951-53; Mexico City College, Mexico City, Mexico, assistant to president, 1959-60; University of New Mexico, Albuquerque, coordinator of U.S. Peace Corps Latin American area studies, 1963-65; West Coast University, Los Angeles, Calif., assistant professor of history, 1965-66; Colorado State University, Fort Collins, assistant professor of history, 1966-68; University of Nebraska, Lincoln, assistant professor, 1968-70, associate professor, 1970-75, professor of history, 1975—. *Military service:* U.S. Navy, Air Corps, 1944-46. *Member:* Conference on Latin American History, Sociedad de Geografia e Historia de Guatemala (corresponding member). *Awards, honors: Forced Native Labor in Sixteenth-Century Central America* and *The Course of Mexican History* were both named outstanding academic books of 1979 by *Choice.*

WRITINGS: (Co-author) *Victoriano Huerta: A Reappraisal,* Mexico City College, 1960; *Forced Native Labor in Sixteenth-Century Central America,* University of Nebraska Press, 1979; (with M. Meyer) *The Course of Mexican History,* Oxford University Press, 1979. Contributor to scholarly journals in the United States and abroad.

WORK IN PROGRESS: Research on the conquest and settlement of Nicaragua.

*   *   *

SHERO, Fred (Alexander)   1925-

PERSONAL: Original name Fred Alexander Schirock, name legally changed; born October 23, 1925, in Winnipeg, Manitoba, Canada; married wife, Mariette; children: Jean-Paul, Rejean. *Residence:* Cherry Hill, N.J.

CAREER: Professional hockey player, 1943-57; New York Rangers, New York, N.Y., played defense and coached farm clubs, 1957-58; Buffalo Sabres, Buffalo, N.Y., coach, 1968-70; coach in Omaha, Neb., 1970-71; Philadelphia Flyers, Philadelphia, Pa., coach, 1971-78; New York Rangers, general manager and coach, 1978-80.

WRITINGS: (With Vijay S. Kothare) *Shero: The Man Behind the System,* Chilton, 1975; (with Andre Beaulieu) *Hockey for the Coach, the Player, and the Fan,* Simon & Schuster, 1979.

SIDELIGHTS: Shero coached the Philadelphia Flyers to Stanley Cup victories in 1974 and 1975.

BIOGRAPHICAL/CRITICAL SOURCES: Time, January 6, 1975; *Sports Illustrated,* May 26, 1975; *Biography News,* Gale, September-October, 1975; *Esquire,* January, 1976; Rhoda Rappeport, *Fred Shero: A Kaleidoscopic View of the Philadelphia Flyers' Coach,* St. Martin's, 1977; *New York Times,* June 3, 1978, November 22, 1980.*

* * *

SHIMAZAKI, Haruki 1872-1943
(Toson Shimazaki)

BRIEF ENTRY: Born February 17, 1872, in Kamisaka, Japan; died August 22, 1943. Japanese poet and novelist. Shimazaki, considered by his critics to be one of the world's major modern novelists, has not been widely translated. His early work *Collection of Young Leaves* (1907) attracted critical attention for its combination of idealistic and sentimental lyrics with a verse form new to Japanese poetry. Shimazaki's first novel, *The Broken Promise* (1906), is a naturalist work that broke Japanese tradition by dealing with the problem of the *eta,* the outcast members of society. The major events of his life were described in detail in his autobiographical novels, *Spring* (1908), *The Destiny of Two Households* (1911), and *A New Life* (1919). His greatest critical success was the historical novel *Before the Dawn* (1935), set in his native Nagano district before and during the restoration of the Meiji period. While Shimazaki's writing shows the strong influence of Western civilization and culture, this last novel illustrates the anti-foreign attitudes prevalent during the growth of Japanese nationalism. *Biographical/critical sources:* Edwin McClellan, *Two Japanese Novelists: Soseki and Toson,* University of Chicago Press, 1969; *Cassell's Encyclopaedia of World Literature,* revised edition, Morrow, 1973; *Who's Who in Twentieth Century Literature,* Holt, 1976; Janet A. Walker, *The Japanese Novel of the Meiji Period and the Ideal of Individualism,* Princeton University Press, 1979.

* * *

SHIMAZAKI, Toson
See SHIMAZAKI, Haruki

* * *

SHONFIELD, Andrew (Akiba) 1917-1981

PERSONAL: Born August 10, 1917, in Tadworth, England; died January 23, 1981, in Tooting, England; son of Victor and Rachel Lea (Sternberg) Shonfield; married Zuzanna Maria Przeworska, 1942; children: David, Katherine. *Education:* Magdalen College, Oxford, B.A., (with honors), 1939. *Home:* 21 Paultons Sq., London S.W. 3, England.

CAREER: Financial Times, London, England, member of staff, 1945-50, foreign editor, 1950-57; *Observer,* London, economic editor,1958-61; Royal Institute of International Affairs, London, director of studies, 1961-68, research fellow, 1969-71, director, 1977; European University Institute, Florence, Italy, professor of economics, beginning in 1978. Fellow of

Imperial College of Science and Technology, London, 1970; Reith Lecturer for British Broadcasting Corp., 1972. Chairman of Social Science Research Council, 1969-71; member of International Social Science Council; member of Royal Commission on Trade Unions and Employers' Associations, 1965-67, Duncan Committee on British Overseas Representation, 1968-69, and European Commission's Vedel Committee on European Economic Community Interests, 1971-72. Economic affairs commentator on radio and television. *Military service:* British Army, Artillery, 1940-46; served in Italy; became major; mentioned in dispatches. *Awards, honors:* D.Lit. from Loughborough University of Technology, 1972; Cortina Ulisse Literary Prize, 1974, for *Europe: Journey to an Unknown Destination;* knighted, 1978.

WRITINGS: (Editor) *Chambers of Commerce Manual: 1958,* United Trade Press, 1957; *British Economic Policy Since the War,* Penguin, 1958, revised edition, 1959; *The Attack on World Poverty,* Random House, 1960; *A Man Beside Himself* (novel), Deutsch, 1964; *Modern Capitalism: The Changing Balance of Public and Private Power,* Oxford University Press, 1965; (contributor) Anthony Moncrieff, editor, *Second Thoughts in Aid: The Theory, Problems, Practice, and Future of Aid to Under-Developed Countries,* BBC Publications, 1965.

(With Albert B. Cherns) *Social Science Research in India: A Report Submitted to the Indian Council of Social Science Research* (monograph), Indian Council of Social Science Research, 1971; (editor with Charles P. Kindleberger) *North American and Western European Economic Policies: Proceedings of a Conference Held by the International Economic Association,* Heinemann, 1972; *Europe: Journey to an Unknown Destination—An Expanded Version of the BBC Reith Lectures, 1972,* Allen Lane, 1973, International Arts and Sciences Press, 1974; *International Economic Relations: The Western System in the 1960's and 1970's,* Sage Publications, 1976; (editor) *International Economic Relations of the Western World, 1959-71,* Volume I: *Politics and Trade,* Volume II: *International Monetary Relations,* Oxford University Press, 1976. Contributor to magazines, including *Encounter* and *Listener.*

SIDELIGHTS: Shonfield made a phonodisc, with Nicholas Kaldor, "The Common Market," released by Holt Information Systems in 1972.

BIOGRAPHICAL/CRITICAL SOURCES: New York Times, December 2, 1965.

OBITUARIES: London Times, January 24, 1981; *New York Times,* January 28, 1981; *AB Bookman's Weekly,* March 9, 1981.

* * *

SHORE, June Lewis

PERSONAL: Born in Louisville, Ky.; daughter of Rue Lewis; married Ken Shore (a psychologist), 1953; children: Stephen Wakefield, Melissa, Alison, Becky, Susan. *Education:* Western Kentucky University, B.A., 1952. *Residence:* Jeffersontown, Ky.

CAREER: Worked as an art and English teacher in public schools in Battle Creek, Mich., and Jefferson County, Ky., and as a special education teacher in Victoria, British Columbia. *Member:* Mansfield Players (president). *Awards, honors:* Ellen Wilson Prize from Indiana University Writers' Conference, 1971; Abingdon Award from Abingdon Press, 1973, for *What's the Matter With Wakefield?*

WRITINGS: What's the Matter With Wakefield? (Junior Literary Guild selection; illustrated by David K. Stone), Abingdon, 1974; *Summer Storm* (juvenile; illustrated by Charles Mikolaycak), Abingdon, 1977. Contributor of stories and articles to periodicals, including *Look, Good Housekeeping,* and *North American Review.*

SIDELIGHTS: June Shore began her writing career after she had read "a spate of novels without any plot" and felt she could do better. She told the *Louisville Courier-Journal and Times,* "I like a story with a beginning, middle, and ending." Though Shore likes writing short humorous pieces the most, she's had her greatest success with children's literature. "There's a lot of freedom in writing for children," Shore commented. "If you write for adults, you almost have to tailor it to the market or to what the publishers think the market is."

AVOCATIONAL INTERESTS: Reading, baking, travel.

BIOGRAPHICAL/CRITICAL SOURCES: Louisville Courier-Journal and Times, February 3, 1974; *Authors in the News,* Volume I, Gale, 1976.*

*   *   *

SHORT, Philip   1945-

PERSONAL: Born April 17, 1945, in Bristol, England; son of Wilfred (a teacher) and Marion (Edgar) Short; married Christine Victoria Baring-Gould, August 9, 1968; children: Sengan. *Education:* Queen's College, Cambridge, B.A., 1966, M.A., 1968. *Agent:* David Higham Associates Ltd., 5/8 Lower John St., Golden Sq., London W1R 4HA, England. *Office:* c/o Lloyds Bank, 20 Badminton Rd., Dowend, Bristol, England.

CAREER: Free-lance correspondent from Malawi, 1967-70, and Uganda, 1971-73; British Broadcasting Corp., London, correspondent from Moscow, Soviet Union, 1974-76, and Peking, China, 1977—.

WRITINGS: Banda, Routledge & Kegan Paul, 1974; *The Dragon, the Bear, and the Future of the West,* Hodder & Stoughton, 1981.

*   *   *

SHTAINMETS, Leon

PERSONAL: Born in Siberia, U.S.S.R. *Education:* Attended Moscow Academy of Art. *Residence:* Philadelphia, Pa.

CAREER: Author and illustrator of books for young people; artist, with one-man shows in Moscow, U.S.S.R., Rome, Italy, and New York, N.Y. *Member:* Artists Guild of the U.S.S.R. *Awards, honors:* Award for best designed art book of the year in U.S.S.R., 1968; Biennale of European Artists and Sculptors prize, 1973; Children's Reading Round Table Award, 1975; Breadloaf Writers' Conference fellow, 1976.

WRITINGS—Self-illustrated: (Reteller) Hans Christian Andersen, *Hans Clodhooper,* Lippincott, 1975; *The Story of Ricky the Royal Dwarf,* Harper, 1976.

Illustrator: Ruth Manning-Sanders, *Old Dog Sirko: A Ukrainian Tale,* Methuen, 1974; Manning-Sanders, *Stumpy: A Russian Tale,* Methuen, 1974; Gaile Bodwell, *The Long Day of the Giants,* McGraw, 1975; I. L. Peretz, *The Case Against the Wind, and Other Stories,* translated and adapted by Esther Hautzig, Macmillan, 1975.*

*   *   *

SHTERNFELD, Ari A(bramovich)   1905-1980

OBITUARY NOTICE: Born in 1905 in Sieradz, Poland; died July 5, 1980, in Moscow, U.S.S.R. Rocket expert and author. In the 1920's, as one of the early rocket researchers promoting astronautics, Shternfeld calculated space flight paths. He published *An Introduction to Astronautics* in 1933 and was subsequently awarded the Hirsch Prize for Astronautics in Paris. Shternfeld's early years were spent in Poland and France; he moved to the Soviet Union in 1935, where he continued to write about space exploration. His publications include *Artificial Satellites of the Earth* and *Soviet Space Flight.* Because he was a Jew, Shternfeld was never admitted to the upper echelon of Soviet space science. Obituaries and other sources: *Who's Who in the Socialist Countries,* K. G. Saur, 1978; *New York Times,* July 19, 1980; *The Annual Obituary 1980,* St. Martin's, 1981.

*   *   *

SHUTE, Wilfred Eugene   1907-

PERSONAL: Born October 21, 1907, in Berkeley, Ontario, Canada; son of Richard James (a physician) and Elizabeth Jane (Treadgold) Shute. *Education:* University of Toronto, B.A., 1929, M.D., 1933. *Religion:* Reorganized Church of Jesus Christ of Latter-Day Saints (Mormons).

CAREER: Clinical investigator of the functions of vitamin E, 1937—; co-founder of Evan Shute Foundation for Medical Research. Keeper of prints of art gallery at Hart House, official photographer for Hart House Theatre. *Member:* Canadian Medical Association, Ontario Medical Association.

WRITINGS: (With Evan V. Shute) *Your Heart and Vitamin E,* Devin-Adair, 1956; (with E. V. Shute) *Alpha Tocopherol (Vitamin E) in Cardiovascular Disease,* Ryerson, 1956; (with Harald J. Taub) *Vitamin E for Ailing and Healthy Hearts,* Pyramid House, 1969; (with H. Rudolph Alsleben) *How to Survive the New Health Catastrophes,* Survival Publications, 1973; *Dr. Wilfred E. Shute's Complete Updated Vitamin E Book,* Keats Publishing, 1975; (with Karen Shute Berry and Barbara Shute Carnahan) *Health Preserver: Defining the Versatility of Vitamin E,* Rodale Press, 1977; *Your Child and Vitamin E,* Keats Publishing, 1979. Contributor to medical journals.

AVOCATIONAL INTERESTS: Breeding Doberman pinschers, judging dog shows, photography.*

*   *   *

SIEGAL, Sanford (Sherwin)   1928-

PERSONAL: Born December 28, 1928, in Pittsburgh, Pa.; son of George Harry and Esther Gertrude (Goodman) Siegal; married Lyndol Diane Touchton (in personnel work), December 10, 1970; children: Melissa (Mrs. Geoffrey Bestor), Marc, Matthew, Jason. *Education:* University of Pittsburgh, B.S., 1950; graduate study at Duquesne University, 1950-52; Des Moines Still College, D.O., 1956; California College of Medicine, M.D., 1962. *Home:* 7720 Southwest 102nd Pl., Miami, Fla. 33173. *Agent:* Lisa Collier, Collier Associates, 280 Madison Ave., New York, N.Y. 10016. *Office:* 8045 Northwest 36th St., Suite 549, Miami, Fla. 33133.

CAREER: Siegal Medical Group Professional Associates, Miami, Fla., medical director; writer. Consultant to Centro Medical Siegal, Mexico and Colombia. *Member:* American Osteopathic Association.

WRITINGS: Dr. Siegal's Natural Fiber Permanent Weight Loss Diet, Dial, 1975; *Dr. Siegal's Natural Fiber Cookbook,* Dial, 1976; *Dr. Siegal's Hunger Book,* Macmillan, 1982.

SILBERGER, Julius, Jr. 1929-

PERSONAL: Born July 25, 1929, in Cleveland, Ohio; son of Julius (a plumber) and Sarah (Leb) Silberger; married Rae Fishman (a psychiatric social worker), February 26, 1961; children: Julie, Katherine, Peter. *Education:* Harvard University, A.B., 1951; University of Wisconsin, Madison, M.A., 1953; University of Chicago, M.D., 1957. *Politics:* Liberal. *Religion:* Jewish. *Home and office:* 172 Buckminster Rd., Brookline, Mass. 02146.

CAREER: Philadelphia General Hospital, Philadelphia, Pa., intern, 1957-58; Massachusetts Mental Health Center, Boston, private practice of psychiatry and psychoanalysis in Brookline, Mass., 1963—. Harvard University, Cambridge, Mass., assistant psychiatrist, 1964-66, instructor in psychiatry, 1966-69, assistant clinical professor of psychiatry, 1980—; psychiatrist at Harvard University's Medical Area Health Service, 1979—. Instructor at Boston Psychoanalytic Society and Institute. *Military service:* U.S. Army Reserve, active duty, 1961-63; became captain. *Member:* American Psychoanalytic Association, American Psychiatric Association, Massachusetts Medical Society.

WRITINGS: (With E. V. Semrad, D. Buie, J. T. Maltsheiser, and D. VanBuskirk) *Mary Baker Eddy: An Interpretive Biography of the Founder of Christian Science*, Little, Brown, 1980.

WORK IN PROGRESS: A Psychoanalytic Approach to the Novel.

SIDELIGHTS: Silberger wrote: "Books are often somewhat transformed reflections on the personal experiences of their authors, who are writing for a reader characterized by Nathaniel Hawthorne as 'a kind and apprehensive, though not the closest friend.' That's how it is with me, too.

"My biography of Mary Eddy was conceived from my perspective as a psychoanalyst and psychiatrist. I wanted to show how one could understand and even admire a difficult but determined and imaginative person who was, in her own peculiar way, a native genius."

*   *   *

SILLMAN, Leonard (Dexter) 1908-1982

OBITUARY NOTICE: Born May 9, 1908, in Detroit, Mich.; died after a long illness, January 23, 1982, in New York, N.Y. Theatrical and motion picture producer and director, and author of autobiography, *Here Lies Leonard Sillman, Straightened Out at Last.* Sillman performed in vaudeville and Broadway productions as a singer, dancer, and actor before producing his first New York show, "New Faces of 1934." He then focused mainly on producing, while occasionally directing and performing. Sillman's productions included thirteen "New Faces" revues, introducing such stars as Henry Fonda, Imogene Coca, Eartha Kitt, Tyrone Power, and Alice Ghostly. In 1970 Sillman produced a revival of Noel Coward's "Hay Fever." Sillman's autobiography appeared in 1961. Obituaries and other sources: *The Biographical Encyclopaedia and Who's Who of the American Theatre*, James Heineman, 1966; *Encyclopaedia of the Musical Theatre*, Dodd, 1976; *Notable Names in the American Theatre*, James T. White, 1976; *Who's Who in the Theatre: A Biographical Record of the Contemporary Stage*, 17th edition, Gale, 1981; *Time*, February 8, 1982; *Newsweek*, February 8, 1982.

SIMMONS, James (Stewart Alexander) 1933-

PERSONAL: Born February 14, 1933, in Londonderry, Northern Ireland; married Laura Stinson; children: four daughters, one son. *Education:* University of Leeds, B.A. (with honors), 1958. *Home:* 15 Kerr St., Portrush, Northern Ireland.

CAREER: Teacher at Quaker school in Lisburn, Northern Ireland; associated with Ahmadu Bello University, Zaria, Nigeria; associated with New University of Ulster, Coleraine, Northern Ireland, 1968—. *Awards, honors:* Eric Gregory Award, 1962; Cholmondeley Award, 1976.

WRITINGS—Poetry; except as noted: (Editor) *Out on the Edge*, University of Leeds, 1958; *Thoughts From the Mind*, Exposition Press, 1962; (with T. W. Harrison) *Aikin Mata: The Lysistrata of Aristophanes (play)*, Oxford University Press, 1966; *Ballad of a Marriage*, Queen's University, Belfast, 1966; *Late But in Earnest*, Bodley Head, 1967; *Ten Poems*, Festival Publications, 1968; *In the Wilderness, and Other Poems*, Bodley Head, 1969; *Songs for Derry* (songs, with lyrics), Ulsterman Publications, 1969; *No Ties*, Ulsterman Publications, 1970; *Energy to Burn*, Bodley Head, 1971; *No Land Is Waste, Dr. Eliot*, Keepsake Press, 1973; *The Long Summer Still to Come*, Blackstaff Press, 1973; (editor and contributor) *Ten Irish Poets: An Anthology of Poems*, Dufour, 1974; *West Strand Visions*, Blackstaff Press, 1975; *Memorials of a Tour in Yorkshire*, Ulsterman Publications, 1976; *The Selected James Simmons*, Blackstaff Press, 1978; *Constantly Singing*, Blackstaff Press, 1980.

Also author of *Judy Garland and the Cold War*, 1976. Work represented in anthologies, including *Soundings: An Annual Anthology of New Irish Writing*, Blackstaff Press, 1976. Contributor to magazines, including *Encounter*, *Paris Review*, *Spectator*, *Counter Measures*, and *Atlantis*, and newspapers. Editor of *Poetry and Audience*, 1957-58; founder of *Honest Ulsterman*.

SIDELIGHTS: Simmons made a sound recording, "City and Western," released by Outlets Records, and another, "Pubs," released by British Broadcasting Corp.

BIOGRAPHICAL/CRITICAL SOURCES: Confrontations, spring, 1975; *Literary Review*, winter, 1979.*

*   *   *

SIMON, Anne W(ertheim) 1914-

PERSONAL: Born November 20, 1914, in Greenwich, Conn.; daughter of Maurice (a banker) and Alma (Morgenthau) Wertheim; married Walter Werner (a professor of law), May 26, 1974; children: Thomas Haufman, Betsy L. Schulberg, Lynn L. Lilienthal, Deborah L. Lesser. *Education:* Received B.A. from Smith College and M.S. from Columbia University. *Home:* 1 West 81st St., New York, N.Y. 10024. *Agent:* Harold Ober Associates, Inc., 40 East 49th St., New York, N.Y. 10017.

CAREER: Writer. Worked as television editor for *Nation* and *McCall's*. *Awards, honors:* American Book Award nomination for science, 1980, for *The Thin Edge: Coast and Man in Crisis*.

WRITINGS: Stepchild in the Family: A View of Children in Remarriage, Odyssey, 1964; *The New Years: A New Middle Age*, Knopf, 1968; *No Island Is an Island: The Ordeal Of Martha's Vineyard*, Doubleday, 1973; *The Thin Edge: Coast and Man in Crisis*, Harper, 1978.

WORK IN PROGRESS: Sea Change, a book about changing the oceans and how it may effect the globe for centuries, publication expected in 1983.

SIDELIGHTS: In *No Island Is an Island* Anne Simon delivered a plea for the preservation of Martha's Vineyard; in her next book, *The Thin Edge*, she appealed for the protection of the world's coastlines. According to Simon, one of the major threats to coastlines is the oil industry. In its zealous search for new energy sources, Simon argues, the industry threatens the ocean with oil spills and other "nickel-and-dime" disasters. "The trade-off," she says, "is almost made—a viable coast for the plunge off-shore, for a few more moments of twilight before the oil lamp goes out."

Coastline damage is also caused by the dense concentration of people and industries along land boundaries. The excessive amounts of human and industrial waste, Simon maintains, disrupt the coasts' natural checks and balances, and erosion results.

Simon praises preservation projects that have already been undertaken, but she cautions that much more must be done. The survival of the world's coastlines, she insists, is dependent upon man's willingness to sacrifice: "We may have to give up some pleasure, renounce some opportunities, if we want to have coasts we can walk on and swim from."

Simon's unbelligerent approach to her cause has drawn comments from reviewers of *The Thin Edge*. Anatole Broyard of the *New York Times* wrote, "Some of her answers have an uncomfortable austerity about them, but she believes that partial renunciation now is preferable to further deprivation in the foreseeable future." And *Time*'s Peter Stoler remarked that Simon's arguments were "quiet and less acrimonious" than the "environmental polemics" of the 1960's. But, Stoler added, "she makes it clear that the seas and coastlines need not die. Hers is a tocsin that cannot be sounded enough."

Simon told *CA:* "The changes we are realizing in the state of the coast and ocean may soon bring about huge disasters, such as the disappearance of fish safe for eating, pollution of ocean and coastal waters, and the decline of ocean flora and fauna. We need to see what we are doing and correct it, *soon.*"

BIOGRAPHICAL/CRITICAL SOURCES: *Time*, January 30, 1978; *New York Times*, March 4, 1978.

*　　*　　*

SIMON, Carly 1945-

PERSONAL: Born June 25, 1945, in New York, N.Y.; daughter of Richard (a publisher) and Andrea Simon; married James Taylor (a singer and composer), November 3, 1972 (marriage ended, 1981); children: Sarah Maria, Benjamin Simon. *Education:* Attended Sarah Lawrence College; studied with Pete Seeger. *Residence:* Martha's Vineyard, Mass.; and New York, N.Y. *Agent:* Arlyne Rothberg, Inc., 145 Central Park W., New York, N.Y. 10023.

CAREER: Worked at various media jobs, including writer of commercial jingles; also worked as secretary and teacher of guitar. Singer, composer, and recording artist, 1964—. Singer with the Simon Sisters and Elephant's Memory. Appeared in motion picture "Taking Off," Universal, 1971. Owner of club Hot Tin Roof, Martha's Vineyard, Mass.

AWARDS, HONORS: Grammy Award from National Academy of Recording Arts and Sciences, 1971, for best new artist; National Association of Recording Merchandisers, Inc. (NARM) award, 1972, for most promising female vocalist/ best selling female artist; gold record awards for albums "No Secrets," 1973, "Anticipation," 1974, "Hotcakes," 1974, "The Best of Carly Simon," 1975, and "Boys in the Trees," 1978; gold record awards for singles "You're So Vain," 1973, "Mockingbird," 1975, and "Nobody Does It Better," 1977; "Hotcakes" named top pop album of the year, 1974, by *Cue;* platinum record award for album "Boys in the Trees," 1978.

WRITINGS: *The Carly Simon Complete: Songs, Pictures, Words,* Knopf, 1975.

Recordings; released by Elektra, except as noted: *Carly Simon* (includes "That's the Way I've Always Heard It Should Be"), 1971; *Anticipation* (contains "Anticipation," "Legend in Your Own Time," "Our First Day Together," "The Girl You Think You See," "Summer's Coming Around Again," "Share the End," "The Garden," "Three Days," "Julie Through the Glass," and "I've Got to Have You"), 1971; *No Secrets* (contains "The Right Thing to Do," "The Carter Family," "You're So Vain," "His Friends Are More Than Fond of Robin," "[We Have] No Secrets," "Embrace Me, You Child," "Waited So Long," "It Was So Easy," "Night Owl," and "When You Close Your Eyes"), 1972; *Hotcakes* (contains "Safe and Sound," "Mind on My Man," "Think I'm Gonna Have a Baby," "Older Sister," "Just Not True," "Hotcakes," "Misfit," "Forever My Love," "Mockingbird," "Grownup," and "Haven't Got Time for the Pain"), 1974.

Playing Possum (contains "Attitude Dancing," "Slave," "After the Storm," "Love Out in the Street," "Look Me in the Eyes," "More and More," "Sons of Summer," "Waterfall," "Are You Ticklish," and "Playing Possum"), 1975; *The Best of Carly Simon* (contains "That's the Way I've Always Heard It Should Be," "The Right Thing to Do," "Mockingbird," "Legend in Your Own Time," "Haven't Got Time for the Pain," "You're So Vain," "[We Have] No Secrets," "Night Owl," "Anticipation," and "Attitude Dancing"), 1975; *Another Passenger* (contains "Half a Chance," "He Likes to Roll," "In Times When My Head," "One Love Stand," "Riverboat Gambler," "Darkness 'Til Dawn," "Dishonest Modesty," "Libby," and "Be With Me"), 1976.

The Spy Who Loved Me (original motion picture score; includes "Nobody Does It Better"), United Artists Records, 1977; *Boys in the Trees* (contains "You Belong to Me," "Boys in the Trees," "Back Down to Earth," "Devoted to You," "De Bat [Fly in Me Face]," "Haunting," "Tranquillo [Melt My Heart]," "You're the One," "In a Small Moment," "One Man Woman," and "For Old Time's Sake"), 1978; *Spy* (contains "Vengeance," "We're So Close," "Just Like You Do," "Coming to Get You," "Never Been Gone," "Pure Sin," "Love You by Heart," "Spy," and "Memorial Day"), 1979; *Come Upstairs* (contains "Jesse," "James," "Take Me as I Am," "Stardust," "Come Upstairs," "Then," "In Pain," "Three of Us in the Dark," and "The Desert"), Warner Bros., 1980; *Torch* (contains "I'll Be Around," "I Got It Bad [and That Ain't Good]," "Spring Is Here," "I Get Along Without You Very Well," "Body and Soul," "From the Heart," "What Shall We Do With the Child," "Pretty Strange," "Hurt," "Blue of Blue," and "Not a Day Goes By"), Warner Bros., 1981.

Recorded albums with sister, Lucy Simon, as Simon Sisters, including "Cuddlebug" and "The Simon Sisters," which featured song "Winkin, Blinkin, and Nod," both released by Kapp, c. 1964.

SIDELIGHTS: Carly Simon was born into a family of achievers, a birthright that she found not entirely advantageous. An insecure child, she had difficulty deciding who Carly Simon, the third daughter of the publishing magnate Richard Simon, should be. "See, my older sister [Joanna] was definitely one way," she remarked to Jane Shapiro of *Ms.* magazine. "She was born that way and she was allowed to be that way—always sophisticated, always very poised and theatrical. And Lucy [Simon's second sister] was another way, shy and angelic and sweet and soft and adorable. I remember thinking, literally, that I had to make a conscious decision about it: to decide who I had to be.''

With little sense of herself, Simon, as she told a *Rolling Stone* interviewer, felt that her beautiful and talented sisters were favored by her parents, especially her father. She did not know how to compete for his attention; he seemed involved in his work and unexcited by his third child. To win his attention, Simon followed her mother's instructions. She remembered: ''I think my mother knew early on that I wasn't terribly interesting to him; she used to give me *tips on how to win him.* She'd say, 'Go into his room, honey, and make a funny face!' I developed a repertoire of faces . . . I guess he laughed, he thought I was funny. I know he did react.''

Simon began to feel that the only way to receive love and attention was to perform for it, and because of this attitude she found her nook in the family. Recalling the day a nurse arrived for her younger brother Peter, Simon illustrated the life-shaping scene for Stuart Werbin of *Rolling Stone:* ''I remember Joey [Joanna] in a very dignified voice said 'How do you do?' and then Lucy just kind of stood back and she said 'howdoyoudo?' and I thought, my God, here I have two sisters who seem to have taken up the whole road. You know they've got all the corners. Where do I stand in order to be different from them? . . . I jumped up on the coffee table and spread out my arms and said 'Hi!''' ''From then on,'' she continued, as she reiterated the story for *Newsweek,* ''I became sort of the family clown. It was the only way I could think of to get any attention.''

Manifesting and compounding her insecurity, Simon stuttered badly as a child. So Simon's mother told her when she could not speak up to sing out, and this moved her to develop her musical talents. Having had no formal training in music, Simon allowed the classical tastes of her parents to influence her musically, though she studied indirectly with her idol, the folksinger Odetta. ''I used to stand outside Carly's room,'' her mother told Shapiro, ''crying with joy, as she sang with [records by] Odetta.'' Another folksinger, Pete Seeger, was Simon's first music teacher when she attended a school in Greenwich Village. While in college, she began to study this genre seriously.

Around the same time, she sang professionally with her sister Lucy as the Simon Sisters. They both appeared on the television program ''Houtenanny,'' and together they recorded three albums. In 1964 the Simon Sisters released the single ''Winkin, Blinkin, and Nod,'' which ranked seventy-eighth among that year's popular music releases. The group dissolved when Lucy Simon married, and Simon continued as a solo artist.

Originally, Simon's manager Albert Grossman packaged her as a ''female Dylan,'' a distinction Simon deemed inappropriate, since ''I couldn't sing like Dylan.'' So she dismissed Grossman and worked at various media jobs until 1970. At this time, Simon began composing much of her own material, and she accepted a recording contract with Elektra Records. Simon's first album for the company proved that she was ''an adept composer in a fair range of styles,'' a *Time* reviewer noted. Named after its artist, ''Carly Simon'' sold 400,000 copies, and reviewers proclaimed the singer ''poised and dusky.'' One song from the album attracted great critical and popular attention: ''That's the Way I've Always Heard It Should Be,'' a ''haunting,'' ''ambivalent,'' and ''cynical'' ballad about marriage. The single appeared as a top-ten hit on *Billboard* magazine's music popularity chart in April, 1971, and it re-

mained there for seventeen weeks. For her performance on ''That's the Way I've Always Heard It Should Be,'' Simon received a Grammy Award as the best new artist of 1971.

The following year, Simon introduced her second album, ''Anticipation.'' Eventually selling over 610,000 copies, the album sold 400,000 copies in four months. ''Anticipation'' reached the thirteenth position on the *Billboard* chart, and the title song appeared on the charts for thirteen weeks beginning in December, 1971. Later the song was featured as the jingle for a Heinz catsup commercial.

In 1973 Elektra released ''No Secrets,'' the album that contained the single ''You're So Vain,'' probably Simon's most famous work. ''I love 'You're So Vain,''' said Ellen Willis of the *New Yorker.* ''It's great rock and roll; the inspired sloppiness of its language is positively Dylanesque; and it has a lot more verve than Helen Reddy's manifesto. It's not so much the words that carry the message—although 'You're so vain, you prob'ly think this song is about you' is one of the all-time great lines—as the good-humored nastiness in Carly's voice.''

Shortly after the song's release, fans initiated contests in an attempt to discover the identity of the song's subject. The possibilities included Kris Kristofferson, about whom Simon had supposedly written two other songs, ''Anticipation'' and ''Three Days.'' Mick Jagger, who was responsible for some of the back-up vocals on the recording, held the lead in several contests; many suggested that he had been duped into singing on a record that bantered about himself. Others speculated that the vain individual was either Warren Beatty or Simon's husband, James Taylor. Simon would not reveal the man's name ''because it wouldn't be fair,'' but Taylor told a *Rolling Stone* interviewer that the person in question was not Jagger, Kristofferson, or himself. Regardless, the mystery and the melody took ''You're So Vain'' to the top of *Billboard*'s chart. Reaching the number one spot, the song appeared on the chart in December, 1972, and remained there for seventeen weeks.

''Hotcakes,'' the album which followed ''No Secrets,'' turned gold (sold 500,000 copies) one week after its release in 1974, a statistic which reinforced critics' beliefs that Simon surpassed her peers as an entertainer and as a songwriter. ''Her skill with verse and melody,'' observed *Newsweek*'s Charles Michener, ''lifts her well above the run of current songwriters; her animal vitality and wide-ranging vocalism rivet audiences in a way few of her contemporaries can match.'' Comparing Simon with other contemporary female performers, such as Janice Ian, Carole King, and Phoebe Snow, Stephen E. Rubin added that Simon was ''probably the most slickly facile and surely the most accessible to a broad audience.'' As a performer, Simon has been called ''spontaneous,'' ''real,'' and ''direct.'' Her voice, commented Loraine Alterman of the *New York Times,* is ''rich,'' ''expressive,'' and energy-charged. She ''is gifted,'' noted *People*'s Jim Jerome, ''with one of the most powerfully affecting voices in pop-rock.''

Subject to severe anxiety attacks, Simon is often overcome by stage fright. ''Every time I go onstage,'' she said, ''I go back to that feeling of it being a primal fact of life and death whether my parents loved me or not. In order to get my parents' love at a certain point, I felt that it was necessary that I perform for them. Their love meant survival, so sometimes I transfer that to an audience, and if they don't love me, it's my death.'' More than anything else, she fears the expectations and energy of audiences. She loves their enthusiasm, ''but if there's too much of it, it scares me.'' Unlike many other victims of stage fright, Simon does not feel isolated from her audiences, nor does she find them hostile. ''Her stage fright is something that escalated as she became a hit,'' explained her writing partner

Jacob Brackman. "As people's expectations of her grew, so did her fear of not living up to them."

Simon avoids touring, yet she wants to perform. She likes small concerts during which she can make eye contact and talk to the audience; and Simon once commented in *Maclean's Magazine* that if she could meet everyone in the audience before a show, she could cope better during a performance. She later found that "the main thing is that I must give myself room to let anything happen. Even if I fall over the edge, it's going to be all right. Also, I really feel like a star now." "Getting out there and jumping through the hoop has lessened my fear," Simon said in 1978 after her first concert tour in six years. "I'm anxious to do it again."

As a composer Simon has distinguished herself, prompting *Cue* magazine to suggest that "no one writes songs quite like Carly Simon." The strongest element in her compositions is her ability to create "melodies that catch the ear easily," wrote Alterman. Rooted in her classical background, melodies are what Simon holds most dear. "I am obsessed and intrigued and moved by melody more than I am by anything else in a song—even though I am sort of moved viscerally by tempo and rhythm, too," she related in an issue of *Saturday Review*. Melody comes naturally to the writer, though she occasionally struggles with lyrics.

Lyrically, Simon communicates basic human experiences, another factor contributing to her wide appeal. Through her songs, she expresses many universal feelings that the average individual experiences but cannot describe or define. As writer and comedian Mel Brooks once told the composer: "That's what your talent is, you say things that are obvious but nobody else thinks to say them."

From the beginning, Simon wrote out of a need to hear "people from the outside saying 'Carly Simon, you're all right.'" Thematically, she concentrated on autobiographical songs or on compositions exploring the relationship between men and women. Until the mid-seventies, she had been producing complex, intellectual songs because she felt that she "should include at least one song on each record about the political situation in Albania or something." At this time, she started writing more love songs as well as simplifying her works. For example, "Playing Possum," which Simon called a "body album," contained earthy songs that dealt almost exclusively with sex and the relationship between the sexes.

According to Timothy Crouse of *Rolling Stone,* Simon's autobiographical songs illustrate that "the rich, the well-known, and the college-educated often find themselves in the highest dues paying bracket." She writes songs detailing her childhood, especially her insecurities and fears. For instance, during a childhood illness, Simon had a fever-induced dream about menacing teddy bears. Since that dream the composer has disliked the creatures; she even remembers fearing her own teddy bear so much that she pulled out his eyes in a sort of exorcism. Many of her songs then, such as "It Was So Easy" or "Grownup," contain allusions based on her fear of bears.

"Embrace Me, You Child," on the other hand, deals more specifically with Simon's relationship with her father. It expresses the anger and the fear that she faced as a teenager whose father was dying. "I felt abandoned," she revealed. "And I was angry at the thought of being abandoned by him. At the same time I was abandoned by Daddy, I was abandoned by God, because losing my father also meant losing my faith in God who I had prayed to every night that I wouldn't lose my father. From the time that he had his first heart attack to the time that he died I used to knock on wood 500 times every night, thinking that my magic was gonna keep him away from death. I feared his death incredibly, and in fearing his death, moved away from him, fearing that I might die." Songs like "Embrace Me, You Child" prove to Simon herself that nothing in her songs is incidental. Rather every allusion is part of her. "I don't think any lyric is by accident," she maintained. "The things that you dream aren't by accident either, and the things that come out, even though they might be a stream of consciousness, are there for some reason."

The fact that Simon and husband James Taylor both write autobiographical songs contributed to public perception of the couple's married life. Anticipating that the couple's life would be reflected in their works, fans attempted to patch together snatches of songs, such as Taylor's "B.S.U.R." or Simon's "Fairweather Father" and "James," to imagine what the Simon-Taylor household was like. Though she was unaffected by the public's fabrications, Simon often shuffled the circumstances in songs "so they won't look like an expose."

From the start of their marriage in 1972, when Taylor was a heroin addict just beginning to detoxify, Simon and Taylor were the subject of rumors that they would be divorcing soon. In a *Rolling Stone* interview, Taylor suggested that a source of tension in his marriage was his history of drug addiction and drinking, the possibility of hurting himself and Simon. "I think that sometimes my behavior threatens her, 'cause she feels I might really harm myself," he said. "And it's hard to commit yourself emotionally to someone who could do damage to you through your commitment to them. It's this business of whether or not you can afford to really put your life in the hands of someone who may not be in enough control of themselves to keep themselves alive. And I think there have been times when Carly worried about that with me. It's not that she was trying to control me; she was trying to decide whether or not she was gonna be able to stand to love me if she might have to lose me. And there were years and there have been instances when that was possible."

Simon told *People* magazine that her mood swings and Taylor's inaccessibility caused some conflict, too, as did a struggle with conventional male and female roles. "James doesn't like the fact that I am so financially independent," she commented, "and, as for me, I wish he would participate more in day-to-day household responsibilities."

Taylor's absence as a husband and a father became what Timothy White of *Rolling Stone* called "the basic bone of contention" that resulted in the couple's separation toward the end of 1981. Speaking of her marriage's dissolution, Simon said: "There are good reasons for the decision. Our needs are different; it seemed impossible to stay together. James needs a lot more space around him—aloneness, remoteness, more privacy. I need more closeness, more communication. He's more abstract in our relationship. I'm more concrete. He's more of a . . . poet, and I'm more of a . . . reporter."

White, too, pointed out basic differences in Simon's and Taylor's lifestyles. "He does drugs," the reporter noted. "She *hates* them. He drinks and parties with abandon. She is embarassed for both of them. He roams where he pleases, slipping away on the Vineyard to carouse for days with his brothers, or flying off to St. Maartens and St. Bart's to go on benders with singer Jimmy Buffet. She also follows her own impulses, but they always lead her straight home to her children and her wifely responsibilities, i.e., away from him." But the crux of the matter seemed to be that Taylor did not do as much fathering as Simon did mothering.

Simon's children, Sarah and Ben, have been her top priority since their arrivals. So she balances her career to meet their needs, scheduling recording dates, rehearsals, and even tours in order to be at home at night with the children. Though she sometimes misses the night life, Simon is willing to forgo impromptu trips and watching sunrises so that she will be able to start the day at six in the morning with Ben and Sarah. This makes her, said Simon's sister Lucy, "one of the most devoted parents a kid could hope to have." Lucy also suggested that Simon is a good mother because of her sensitivity to the events of her own childhood. "Recalling the pain of her own childhood in minute detail," the elder Simon remarked, "she has a wellspring of empathy and compassion for her own children." Simon, on the other hand, feels that mothering has allowed her to discover "a new dimension to love—cherishing this little person without any barriers."

Almost single-handedly, Simon organizes her home, plans meals, runs errands, and the like. She goes "through 10 checklists a day—'Where are the kids now? Are they home from the picnic? Have I bought the meat for dinner?' I cannot be totally without a consciousness of where the kids are. I have almost all the responsibilities of running the household and pulling the whole thing together. It's hard.''

Still Simon and Taylor are dedicated to raising their children together, even though their marriage has ended. "We failed in the context of marriage, but not as people," Simon assessed. "James taught me what I needed to know about myself *and* him and made me a better person for the next person I'll want to love. Funny thing is, if I met James now, I would know much more and be a better partner, but that sounds a bit unrealistic, huh?"

AVOCATIONAL INTERESTS: Boating.

BIOGRAPHICAL/CRITICAL SOURCES—Books: Mike Jahn, *Rock: From Elvis Presley to the Rolling Stones,* Time Books, 1973; Katherine Orloff, *Rock 'n Roll Woman,* Nash Publishing, 1974; Carly Simon, *Carly Simon Complete: Songs, Pictures, Words,* Knopf, 1975; Charles Morse and Ann Morse, *Carly Simon,* Creative Education, 1975.

Periodicals: *Rolling Stone,* April 29, 1971, December 23, 1971, January 4, 1973, May 22, 1975, June 1, 1978, September 6, 1979, June 11, 1981, December 10, 1981; *Time,* July 12, 1971, May 5, 1975; *Newsweek,* March 12, 1972, November 13, 1972; *Redbook,* September, 1972; *Newsday,* September 3, 1972; *Harper's Bazaar,* November, 1972; *Circus,* February, 1973, May, 1974; *Let It Rock,* February, 1973; *Sound,* February, 1973; *Records and Reviews,* February, 1973; *Creem,* March, 1973; *Words and Music,* March, 1973; *Stereo Review,* March, 1973; *New Yorker,* March 3, 1973; *Crawdaddy,* April, 1973; *High Fidelity,* April, 1973; *Previews,* November, 1973; *Popular Music and Society,* winter, 1973.

New York Times, April 12, 1974, June 12, 1977; *Cue,* December 9, 1974, December 27, 1975; *Biography News,* July, 1975; *Toronto Globe and Mail,* September 17, 1975; *School Library Journal,* January, 1976; *Saturday Review,* October 16, 1976; *Ms.,* February, 1977; *Maclean's Magazine,* May 29, 1978; *People,* July 17, 1978, August 18, 1980, October 6, 1980, November 9, 1981; *Chicago Tribune,* March 7, 1982.*

—*Sketch by Charity Anne Dorgan*

*   *   *

SIMON, (Edward) Ted   1931-

PERSONAL: Born May 1, 1931, in Hamburg, Germany (now West Germany); British subject born abroad; son of Henry (a linguist) and Auguste (a teacher; maiden name, Fluegge) Simon; married Teresa Francesca King (a weaver), March 9,

1979. *Education:* Attended Imperial College of Science and Technology, London, 1949-51. *Home:* East Lane, Covelo, Calif. 95428. *Agent:* A. D. Peters, 10 Buckingham St., London W.C.2, England.

CAREER: Continental Daily Mail, Paris, France, copytaster, 1952, subeditor in Barrow-in-Furness, England, 1954; *Daily Express,* London, England, subeditor, reporter, and feature writer, 1957-58; *Daily Sketch,* London, features editor, 1959-63, magazine editor, 1964-67; free-lance writer and restorer of ancient ruins, 1968-73; columnist, 1973-77. *Military service:* Royal Air Force National Service, 1954-57; served as editor.

WRITINGS: The Chequered Year, Cassell, 1971, published as *The Grand Prix Year,* Coward, 1972; *Jupiter's Travels,* Hamish Hamilton, 1979, Doubleday, 1980.

WORK IN PROGRESS: "A voluminous and somewhat baffling work of semi-autobiographical fiction"; a sequel to *Jupiter's Travels,* for Penguin.

SIDELIGHTS: Simon told *CA:* "Both books of mine involved travel, though, in the first case, fortuitously. Travel is a simple device for enabling one to shift mental perspectives, which is why I value it so much, though the same result can undoubtedly be achieved in a cell.

"None of my work so far is fictional, though I am feeling my way there and imagine I will fall over the brink at any moment. One of my principal concerns is a particular honesty and accuracy that is my main defense in a society that seems as superficial and empty as a balloon. In part, I write for the same reason that a good housekeeper keeps accounts, but it is such a laborious and painful business that I must hope it also serves some greater purpose."

Simon speaks French, German, Spanish, "and smatterings of non-European languages."

AVOCATIONAL INTERESTS: "Traveling, farming, indulging myself, and doing without."

*   *   *

SIMONS, Elwyn LaVerne   1930-

PERSONAL: Born July 14, 1930, in Lawrence, Kan.; son of Verne Franklin and Verna (Cuddleback) Simons; married Mary Fitch, June, 1964 (divorced); married Friderun Annurselankel (a primatologist), December 2, 1972; children: (first marriage) David D. B.; (second marriage) Cornelia V. M., Verne F. H. *Education:* Rice University, A.B., 1953; Princeton University, M.A., 1955, Ph.D., 1956; University College, Oxford, D. Phil., 1959. *Office:* Director, Duke Primate Center, 3705 Erwin Rd., Durham, N.C. 27705.

CAREER: Oxford University, Oxford, England, demonstrator and exhibitor in anthropology, 1956-58; Princeton University, Princeton, N.J., lecturer in geology, 1958-59; University of Pennsylvania, Philadelphia, assistant professor of zoology, 1959-61; Yale University, New Haven, Conn., visiting associate professor, 1960-61, associate professor, beginning in 1961, professor of geology and paleontology, 1967-77, curator of vertebrate paleontology, 1960-61, associate curator of Peabody Museum of Natural History, 1961-64, curator in charge of Division of Vertebrate Paleontology, 1967-77; Duke University, Durham, N.C., professor of anthropology and anatomy and director of Duke Primate Center, 1977—. Barbour-Schramm Memorial Lecturer at University of Nebraska, 1974; David French Lecturer at Claremont Colleges, 1974; distinguished lecturer in anthropology at University of Pittsburgh, 1976; traveling lecturer for French Bureau of Foreign Affairs, 1976; lecturer at symposiums and conferences. Research associate at American Museum of Natural History; director of paleontological expeditions to Fayum Badlands, Egypt, 1961-67, 1977-80, northern India, 1968-69, Iran, 1970-71, Spain, 1971, and Bighorn Basin, Wyoming, 1961-64, 1967-68, 1970-75, 1979-80. *Military service:* U.S. Naval Reserve, Officer Training Corps, college program, 1951-52.

MEMBER: International Association of Human Biologists, International Primatological Society, American Association for the Advancement of Science, American Association of Physical Anthropology, Geological Society of America, American Society of Zoologists, American Society of Naturalists, Institute of Human Paleontology, Society of Vertebrate Paleontology, Society for the Study of Human Biology, Society for the Study of Evolution, British Society for the Study of Human Biology, Sigma Xi. *Awards, honors:* Fulbright fellowship from Utrecht Univeristy, Holland, 1956 (declined); General George Marshall Scholar at Oxford Univeristy, 1956-59; Boise Fund fellow at Oxford University, 1958-59; M.A. from Yale University, 1965; Richard C. Hunt Memorial Fellow of Wenner-Gren Foundation for Anthropological Research, 1965; Anadale Memorial Medal from Asiatic Society of Calcutta, 1973, for contributions to the understanding of human evolution in Asia; Alexander von Humboldt Senior Scientists' Award from the Federal Republic of Germany, 1975-76.

WRITINGS: The Paleocene Pantodonta, American Philosophical Society, 1960; *Primate Evolution: An Introduction to Man's Place in Nature,* Macmillan, 1972; *A Simons Family History: In England and America,* Macmillan, 1975; (with Philip D. Gingerich) *Systemics, Phylogeny, and Evolution of Early Eocene Adapidae (Mammalia, Primates) in North America,* Museum of Paleontology, University of Michigan, 1977. Co-editor of "Series in Physical Anthropology," Macmillan.

Contributor: J. Buettner-Janusch, editor, *Genetic and Evolutionary Biology of the Primates,* Academic Press, 1963; P. L. De Vore, editor, *The Origin of Man: A Symposium,* Wenner-Gren Foundation for Anthropological Research, 1965; D. Starck, R. Schneider, and H. J. Kuhn, editors, *Neue Ergebnisse der Primatologie,* Fischer, 1967; G. Kurth, editor, *Evolution and Hominization,* 2nd edition, Fischer, 1968; *Early Cenozoic Mammalian Faunas, Fayum Province, Egypt,* Peabody Museum of Natural History, Yale University, 1968; J. F. Napier and R. P. Napier, editors, *Old World Monkeys: Evolution, Systemics, and Behavior,* Academic Press, 1970; (with David Pilbeam) R. Tuttle, editor, *The Functional and Evolutionary Biology of Primates,* Aldine, 1972; (with John Fleagle) Duane M. Rumbaugh and S. Karger, editors, *Gibbon and Siamang,* Volume II, Basel, 1973; R. D. Martin, G. A. Doyle, and A. Walker, editors, *Prosimian Biology,* Duckworth, 1974; R. B. Masterson, editor, *Evolution of the Nervous System and Behavior,* V. H. Winston, 1976; M. Goodman and R. Tashian, *Molecular Anthropology,* Plenum, 1977; (with Pilbeam) V. J. Maglio and H.B.S. Cooke, editors, *Evolution of African Mammals,* Harvard University Press, 1978; C. J. Jolly, *Early Hominids of Africa,* St. Martin's, 1978; (with R. F. Kay) *New Interpretations of Ape and Human Ancestry,* Plenum, 1981. Also contributor to *McGraw-Hill Yearbook of Science and Technology,* 1971 and 1980. Contributor of numerous articles to scientific journals.

SIDELIGHTS: Simons made a sound recording, "Evolution and the Descent of Man," with Theodosius Dobzhansky. It was released by American Association for the Advancement of Science in 1972.

Simons told *CA:* "I have always considered it important to be in direct contact with scientific research sources. To this end, I have studied directly all of the world's major collections of fossil primates and conducted direct investigations on about two-thirds of the species of living lower primates. I have been director of two expeditions in search of fossil primates to India, two to Iran, and twenty-one to the Paleocene and Eocene rocks of the Bighorn Basin, Wyoming. My investigations of human origins in Africa have led to many trips to Kenya and to my direction of a dozen field sessions in the Oligocene Badlands of the Fayum, Egypt. In order to better understand prosimian biology, I have made three expeditions to Madagascar.

"Besides my personal interests in tracing the course of evolution of man's ancestors from the earliest primates up to man, I have always been broadly interested in living primates, other living mammals and birds, and in natural history, generally. These interests were stimulated by my parents and grandparents. As I was the oldest grandchild in both families, I have in effect six parents. Early experiences include collecting marine fossils with one of my grandmothers in Kansas and membership in an ornithological and tropical fish club. I studied at the Houston Museum of Fine Arts on an art scholarship from 1939 to 1947 and have been involved in creative painting, portraiture, and scientific illustration, having done the illustrations for my Princeton doctoral dissertation as well as for several other papers. I have collected folk songs for the Library of Congress folklore collection and am avidly interested in geneology and folksinging. My geneological research has contributed to several different published family histories, and I have myself authored a geneology of the Simons family."

BIOGRAPHICAL/CRITICAL SOURCES: Science News, February 16, 1980.

*   *   *

SIMPSON, William Kelly   1928-

PERSONAL: Born January 3, 1928, in New York, N.Y.; son of Kenneth Farrand and Helen L.K. (Porter) Simpson; married Marilyn E. Milton, June 19, 1953; children: Laura Knickerbacker (Mrs. Grover O'Neill III), Abby Rockefeller. *Education:* Yale University, B.A., 1947, M.A., 1948, Ph.D., 1954; also attended Ecole Practique Hautes Etudes. *Home address:* R.D. 1, Box 327, Katonah, N.Y. 10536.

CAREER: Metropolitan Museum of Art, New York City, museum assistant in Egyptian art, 1948-54; Harvard University, Cambridge, Mass., research fellow at Center for Middle East Studies, 1957-58; Yale University, New Haven, Conn., began as assistant professor, 1958, became professor of Egyptology, 1965—, chairman of department of Near Eastern languages, 1966-69, director and editor of papers of Penn-Yale Archaeological Expedition to Egypt, 1960—. Visiting professor at University of Pennsylvania; president and member of board of trustees of American School of Classical Studies, Athens, Greece, 1970—. Curator of Egyptian and ancient Near Eastern art at Museum of Fine Arts, Boston, Mass., 1970—. Partner of Kin & Co., 1967-69, Pocantino Fund, 1969—, and Venrock, 1970—. President of Wrexham Foundation, 1965-67; member of advisory council of foreign currency program at Smithsonian Institution, 1966-69; member of international council of Museum of Modern Art, New York City; member of board of trustees of Museum of Primitive Art, 1956—, American Research Center in Egypt, 1960-68, Sleepy Hollow Restorations, 1963, American University in Cairo, Rockefeller Family Fund, and French Institute. *Military service:* New York National Guard, 1948-54; became first lieutenant.

MEMBER: American Oriental Society, Archaeological Institute of America, Society for Coptic Archaeology, Egypt Exploration Society, Societe francaise d'egyptologie, German Archaeological Institute, Foundation egyptologique Reine Elisabeth, Century Club, Metropolitan Opera Club, University Club, Union Club (New York, N.Y.), Union Boat Club (Boston, Mass.), Bedford Golf and Tennis Club, Graduates Club. *Awards, honors:* Fulbright fellow in Egypt, 1955-57; Guggenheim fellow, 1965.

WRITINGS: (With Nicholas B. Millet and others) *Heka-Nefer and the Dynastic Material From Tashka and Arminna,* Peabody Museum of Natural History, Yale University, 1963; *Papyrus Reisner,* Museum of Fine Arts (Boston, Mass.), Volume I: *The Records of a Building Project in the Reign of Sesostris I,* 1963, Volume II: *Accounts of the Dockyard Workshop at This in the Reign of Sesostris I,* 1965, Volume III: *Records of a Building Project in the Early Twelfth Dynasty,* 1969; (with William W. Hallo) *The Ancient Near East: A History,* Harcourt, 1971; (editor, translator with R. O. Faulkner and Edward F. Wente, Jr., and author of introduction) *The Literature of Ancient Egypt: An Anthology of Stories, Instructions, and Poetry,* Yale University Press, 1972, 3rd edition, 1977; *The Offering Chapel of Sekhem-ankh-ptah,* Museum of Fine Arts (Boston, Mass.), 1976; *The Face of Egypt: Permanence and Change in Egyptian Art, From the Museum and Private Collections,* Katonah Gallery, 1977; (co-author) *Ancient Egypt: Discovering Its Splendors,* National Geographic Society, 1978. Also author of *Mastabas of the Western Cemetery,* 1980.*

*　　*　　*

SIMS, Phillip L(eon) 1940-

PERSONAL: Born April 7, 1940, in Mountain View, Okla.; married Connie R. Saunders, June 20, 1962; children: Amy, Aaron. *Education:* Oklahoma State University, B.S., 1962, M.S., 1964; Utah State University, Ph.D., 1967. *Religion:* Church of Christ. *Home:* 2712 Oak Hollow St., Woodward, Okla. 73801. *Office:* U.S. Department of Agriculture, 2000 18th St., Woodward, Okla. 73801.

CAREER: Colorado State University, Fort Collins, assistant professor, 1967-72, associate professor of range science, 1972-77; associated with the U.S. Department of Agriculture, Woodward, Okla., 1977—. *Member:* American Society for Range Management (state president, 1975; chairman of advisory council), American Society of Animal Science, American Soil Conservation Society, British Ecological Society, Sigma Xi, Phi Sigma, Xi Sigma Pi, Alpha Zeta. *Awards, honors:* Named outstanding range science professor, 1974.

WRITINGS: (Editor with John F. Vallentine) *Range Science: A Guide to Information Sources,* Gale, 1980.

*　　*　　*

SINCLAIR, John L(eslie) 1902-

PERSONAL: Born December 6, 1902, in New York, N.Y.; son of John Leslie (a sea captain) and Gertrude (Corbin) Sinclair; married Evelyn Fox (a writer for children), May 9, 1947. *Education:* Attended private schools in England; studied agriculture in Scotland. *Home and office address:* P.O. Box 668, Bernalillo, N.M. 87004.

CAREER: Agricultural apprentice, Drumlanrig Castle, Scotland, 1919-23; cowboy in southern New Mexico, 1923-37; Museum of New Mexico, Santa Fe, research assistant, 1938-40; Lincoln County Museum, Lincoln, N.M., curator, 1940-42; free-lance writer, 1942-44; Coronado State Monument,

Bernalillo, N.M., superintendent, 1944-46; conducted research in Mexico, 1946-47; Coronado State Monument, superintendent, 1947-62; writer, 1962—. *Member:* Western Writers of America, Rio Grande Writers Association. *Awards, honors:* Golden Spur Award from Western Writers of America and Western Heritage Wrangler Award from National Cowboy Hall of Fame, both 1978, both for article "Where the Cowboys Hunkered Down"; honorary life member of National Cowboy Hall of Fame and Western Heritage Center, 1978.

WRITINGS: In Time of Harvest (novel), Macmillan, 1943, reprinted, University of New Mexico Press, 1979; *Death in the Claimshack* (novel), Sage Books (Denver, Colo.), 1947; (with George Fitzpatrick) *Profile of a State: New Mexico,* N.M. Horn & Wallace, 1964; *Cousin Drewey and the Holy Twister* (novel), Columbia Publishing, 1980; *New Mexico: The Shining Land* (nonfiction), University of New Mexico Press, 1980; *Cowboy Riding Country* (nonfiction), University of New Mexico Press, 1982; *Cabin on the Sandy Land* (two short novels), Columbia Publishing, 1982. Contributor of more than two hundred articles, stories, and novelettes to magazines, including *Saturday Evening Post, Collier's, Argosy, American Heritage, Southwest Review,* and *Westways.*

SIDELIGHTS: "My father was born in Glasgow, Scotland," Sinclair commented, "and he attended school in France and Germany until he was sixteen; then, threatened with further education in England, he rebelled by going to sea as a deckhand on a sailing vessel to Nova Scotia. He had adventure in his blood and wanted nothing of upper-class family structure. On his return to Scotland my grandfather had him apprenticed on vessels of the British Indian Steam Navigation Company. A born mariner, he earned his master certificate in 1888 at the age of twenty-five. His home port was Melbourne, Australia, and from there he sailed on voyages to ports all over the world. He married an Australian and had a child (or children) who died very young in Calcutta. In 1887 he served as mate on the *Loch Vennachar,* the famous clipper ship that raced with others around Cape Horn to London River with the Australian wool clip, the winner receiving a bounty. His first wife died in London before the turn of the century. He was appointed marine superintendent for the Bucknell Steamship Lines, a British company in New York, remarried, and I was born in 1902.

"I was an only child, and my father died in New York in 1906. I was sent to Scotland at an early age for upbringing in the Scottish tradition by my grandfather and his family, as I was the last of the family line. I studied agriculture in Scotland, specializing in cattle breeding, preparatory for ranching in Canada. I left Scotland in 1923, Canada-bound, but stopped in New Mexico on the way west. I decided to stay there and was disowned by my family in Scotland.

"Left to make my own way, I took a job as a cowboy in southern New Mexico, in the days when the cowboy life was the cowboy life indeed. I started writing in 1936, and gave up that cowboy life after fourteen years of it to settle in Santa Fe and other parts of northern New Mexico, working for the Museum of New Mexico.

"The museum is located in the Palace of the Governors in Santa Fe, the oldest public building in the United States, dating back to 1610. The Lincoln County Museum is in the village of Lincoln, and concerned chiefly with the Lincoln County War of 1878-1881, and with the outlaw, Billy the Kid. The museum is located in the old courthouse where Billy the Kid was jailed in 1881 and from where he made his famous escape. The Coronado State Monument is near Bernalillo and comprises an ancient Indian ruin (1300-1680 A.D.) believed to be the site of the camp of the Coronado Expedition of 1540-1542.''

"For the last fifteen years I have been living and writing in the lava rock mesa country of the Santa Ana Indian Reservation, northwest of Albuquerque, among Indian people I have known for over forty years.''

BIOGRAPHICAL/CRITICAL SOURCES: Los Angeles Times Book Review, January 18, 1981.

* * *

SINCLAIR, Lister (Shedden) 1921-

PERSONAL: Born January 9, 1921, in Bombay, India; son of W. Shedden (a chemical engineer) and Lillie Agnes Sinclair; married Alice Mather, December 24, 1942 (marriage ended); married Margaret Eileen Jennifer Watchman, June 2, 1965; children: (first marriage) Peter Elliot; (second marriage), William Andrew Alexander. *Education:* University of British Columbia, B.A., 1942; University of Toronto, M.A., 1945. *Religion:* Unitarian-Universalist. *Office:* Canadian Broadcasting Corp., 790 Bay St., Toronto, Ontario, Canada.

CAREER: University of Toronto, Toronto, Ontario, lecturer in mathematics, 1945-48; Canadian Broadcasting Corp., Toronto, music critic, 1947, executive producer, 1967—, executive vice-president, 1972-75, vice-president in program policy and development, 1975—. Actor, including performances in "The Inner Man" and "Comparisons"; producer of shortwave radio broadcasts to Europe. Member of faculty at Academy of Radio Arts and Royal Conservatory of Music, Toronto, 1952; instructor at University of British Columbia, summers, 1946-47. Member of Canadian Theatre Centre.

MEMBER: Association of Canadian Television and Radio Artists. *Awards, honors:* First prizes from Ohio State University, 1945, for "A Play on Words," 1948, for "The Case Against Cancer," and 1948, for adaptation of "Murder in the Cathedral"; Canada Council senior arts fellowship, 1960; LL.D. from Mount Allison University, 1970, and University of British Columbia, 1972; D.Litt. from Waterloo Lutheran College, 1970; Litt.D. from Memorial University of Newfoundland, 1971; ten Ohio Radio Awards, including one for a reading, "The Poetry of T.S. Eliot"; Edison Award; Emmy Award.

WRITINGS: A Play on Words and Other Radio Plays (contains "A Play on Words," first broadcast November 12, 1944), Dent, 1948; (contributor) Walter Goldschmidt, editor, *Ways of Mankind: Thirteen Dramas of Peoples of the World and How They Live,* Beacon Press, 1954; (with Goldschmidt) *Ways to Justice: An Adult Discussion Program* (to accompany radio program "Ways to Justice"), Fund for Adult Education, 1955; *The Blood Is Strong: A Drama of Early Scottish Settlement in Cape Breton* (play; first produced in Toronto, Ontario, at Jupiter Theatre), Book Society of Canada, 1956; *Socrates* (three-act play; first produced in Toronto at Jupiter Theatre, February, 1952), Book Society of Canada, 1957; (with George E. Probst), *Democracy in America: Scripts of Fourteen Dramatizations by Lister Sinclair and George E. Probst Based on the Classic Work by Alexis de Tocqueville,* National Educational Television and Radio Center, 1962; (with John A. Livingston) *Darwin and the Galapagos* (first broadcast by CBC-TV), Canadian Broadcasting Corp., 1966; (with Jack Pollock) *The Art of Norval Morrisseau,* Methuen, 1979.

Work represented in anthologies, including *Canadian Anthology,* edited by C. F. Klinck and R. E. Watters, Gage, 1955.

Unpublished scripts: "Encounter by Moonlight," first broadcast by CBC-Radio, March 3, 1948; "The Empty Frame," first produced in 1955; (author of adaptation) Christopher Marlowe, "Dr. Faustus," first broadcast May 1, 1964; (author of adaptation) T. S. Eliot, "Murder in the Cathedral," first broadcast February 5, 1965; "One John Smith," first produced in Toronto, Ontario; "Man in the Moon," first produced in Toronto. Also author of "We All Hate Toronto."

Television scripts for Canadian Broadcasting Corp. include work on series "Horizon" and "The Nature of Things." Author of documentary programs for Ford Foundation. Contributor to magazines, including *Canadian Forum, Saturday Night, Maclean's, Here and Now, Canadian Poetry,* and *Performing Arts in Canada.**

* * *

SINGER, Milton Borah 1912-

PERSONAL: Born July 5, 1912, in Poland; came to the United States in 1920, naturalized citizen, 1921; son of Julius M. and Esther (Greenberg) Singer; married Helen Goldbaum, October 1, 1935. *Education:* University of Texas, B.A., 1934, M.A., 1936; University of Chicago, Ph.D., 1940. *Home:* 5550 Dorchester Ave., Chicago, Ill. 60637. *Office:* Department of Anthropology, University of Chicago, Chicago, Ill. 60637.

CAREER: University of Chicago, Chicago, Ill., member of faculty, beginning in 1941, professor of social science, 1950—, Paul Klapper Professor of Social Science, 1952—, professor of anthropology, 1954—, chairman of social sciences staff, 1947-53, executive secretary of committee on Asian studies, 1955-67, chairman of committee, 1967-70, chairman of civilization studies and member of governing board of Collegiate Division, 1966-71, associate director of Redfield project on comparative civilizations, 1958-61, co-director of Southern Asia Language and Area Center, 1959-63. Senior anthropologist at Institute of International Studies, University of California, Berkeley, 1956; fellow of Center for Advanced Studies in the Behavioral Sciences, Palo Alto, Calif., 1957-58; fellow of American Institute of Indian Studies, 1964; visiting professor at University of Hawaii, 1966-67, and University of California, San Diego, 1971.

MEMBER: International Society for the Comparative Study of Civilization (honorary member), American Academy of Arts and Sciences (fellow), American Anthropological Association (fellow), American Institute of Indian Studies (vice-president, 1961-64), Association for Asian Studies, Phi Beta Kappa.

WRITINGS: (Translator with wife, Helen Singer) A. Gratry, *Logic,* Open Court, 1944; (with Gerhart Piers) *Shame and Guilt: A Psychoanalytic and a Cultural Study,* C. C Thomas, 1953, 2nd edition, 1973; (editor) *Introducing India in Liberal Education: Proceedings of a Conference Held at University of Chicago, May 17, 18, 1957,* University of Chicago, 1957; (editor and contributor) *Traditional India: Structure and Change,* American Folklore Society, 1959; (editor and contributor) *Krishna: Myths, Rites, and Attitudes,* East-West Center Press, 1966; (editor with Bernard S. Cohn, and contributor) *Structure and Change in Indian Society,* Wenner-Gren Foundation for Anthropological Research, 1968; *When a Great Tradition Modernizes: An Anthropological Approach to Indian Civilization,* Praeger, 1972; (editor and contributor) *Entrepreneurship and Modernization of Occupational Cultures in South Asia,* Duke University, 1973. Editor and contributor to *A Conversation of Cultures: The United States and Southern Asia,* 1977. Co-editor of "Comparative Studies of Culture and Civilization," a series, 1953-58. Contributor to scholarly journals.*

SINGER, Ray 1916-

PERSONAL: Born October 24, 1916, in New York, N.Y.; son of William Z. (a salesman) and Esther (Sadolsky) Singer; married Monia Abrahamson, October 13, 1940; children: Laurie Russ, John. *Education:* Attended City College of the City University of New York. *Religion:* Jewish. *Residence:* Beverly Hills, Calif.

CAREER/WRITINGS: Writer of radio shows for Milton Berle, Fred Allen, Phil Baker, Kate Smith, and Henny Youngman, 1938-41; writer for "Milton Berle Radio Show," 1941, and for "Sealtest Village Store" radio show, 1942-47; contributor to screenplays for motion pictures, including "She Gets Her Man," Universal, 1945, "Neptune's Daughter," Metro-Goldwyn-Mayer (MGM), 1950, and "A Woman of Distinction," Columbia, 1950; co-author of "Phil Harris-Alice Faye" radio show, 1947-53; writer, producer, and creator of motion pictures for MGM and of television programs for National Broadcasting Co. (NBC), including "It's a Great Life," 1953-62; head writer of "The Frank Sinatra Show," 1962-63; producer and head writer of "The Jim Bakus Show" (NBC), 1963-64.

Producer and head writer of "The Donna Reed Show," 1965-66; writer of television scripts for "My Three Sons," "Family Affair," "The Doris Day Show," and "The Danny Thomas Show," 1965-69; creator and head writer of "The Danny Thomas Special" and "Block Party," 1966; writer of scripts for television programs, including (co-creator) "Here's Lucy," 1966-71, "Love American Style," 1972, and "All in the Family," 1972; screenwriter, with Everett Freeman, of motion picture "The Maltese Bippy," MGM, 1969; co-author of television special "Jack Benny's Bag," 1969; free-lance writer, 1973-74. Collaborator with Dick Chevillar, 1942-65. Associate professor of screen and television writing at California State University, Northridge, 1974—, and at University of California, Los Angeles, 1975—. Member of board of governors of Hollywood branch of Television Academy, 1956-58 and 1971-73; member of board of national trustees of American Academy of Television Arts and Sciences, 1971-73.

Also author of plays, including "The Forties Fling" and "But Mother, Everybody Does It."

WORK IN PROGRESS: A musical, "Maharajah."

SIDELIGHTS: Ray Singer and Everett Freeman wrote the screenplay for "The Maltese Bippy," a movie starring the comedy team of Dan Rowan and Dick Martin from the "Laugh-In" television series. The movie, said Vincent Canby of the *New York Times,* "concerns two aging roues who make poor exploitation films and live in a haunted house in Flushing." Critically, the film's success was attributed to its screenwriters. Rowan and Martin, wrote Archer Winsten of the *New York Post,* are "extremely funny because they've got such good satiric material from writers Everett Freeman and Ray Singer." Written for fans of satire, "The Maltese Bippy," noted Winsten, is a "special picture" for "special taste."

One of Singer's most notable television achievements was a script for the Lucille Ball show which called for the "classic confrontation" between Ball and Jack Benny. The script, written with Milt Josefsberg, transported many of Benny's famous trademarks of his radio days to television, including his reputation as a tightwad, his old car, and the fabled vault located underneath his home.

Singer told *CA:* "I have been a writer since the age of ten. Writing to me is like the breath of life. I can't imagine my life without it. It gives me the opportunity to express my innermost thoughts to the world. I believe that all writers who reach the public have a responsibility to that public: because with our writings we can sway people and help form opinions and lifestyles. Ours is a God-given talent which should not be abused, but should be used to help make a better life for our fellow man."

BIOGRAPHICAL/CRITICAL SOURCES: New York Post, June 19, 1969; *New York Times,* June 19, 1969; John Dunning, *Tune in Yesterday: The Ultimate Encyclopedia of Old-Time Radio, 1925-76,* Prentice-Hall, 1976; Milt Josefsberg, *The Jack Benny Show,* Arlington House, 1977.

*   *   *

SINGH, St. Nihal 1884-

PERSONAL: Born in 1884 in Rawalpindi, Pakistan; married Kate Kinsey (deceased).

CAREER: Journalist and author.

WRITINGS: India's Fighters: Their Mettle, History, and Services to Britain, Low, 1914; *The King's Indian Allies: The Rajas and Their India,* Low, 1915; *"Dry" America: An Object-Lesson to India,* Ganesh & Co., 1921, reprinted as *"Dry" America: Its Significance to Ceylon,* 1921; *Shree Bhagvat Sinhjee: The Maker of Modern Gondal,* Golden Jubilee Committee, 1934; (contributor) *Maharaja Ranjit Singh: First Death Centenary Memorial,* 1939, reprinted, Languages Department of Punjab, 1970; *The Secretary of State for India and His Council,* Munshi Ram Manohar Lal, 1962; (with W. K. Ho) *English Practice for School Certificate,* Oxford University Press, 1969; *Malaysia: A Commentary,* International Book Distributors, 1972; *From the Jhelum to the Volga,* Nachiketa Publications, 1973.

Also author of *Essays on India,* 1907; *Messages of Uplift of India,* 1909; *Japan's Modernization,* 1913; *Progressive British India,* 1913; *India: New and Old,* 1924; *Ceylon: New and Old,* 1928; *Ceylon's Scenic Splendour,* 1929; *Hyderabad Today,* 1947; *Dharmapala: The Man and the Missioner,* 1958. Contributor to newspapers and magazines, including *London Quarterly Review* and *Wireless.*

BIOGRAPHICAL/CRITICAL SOURCES: World Press Review, September, 1980.*

*   *   *

SKLAR, Lawrence 1938-

PERSONAL: Born June 25, 1938, in Baltimore, Md.; son of Herman J. (an engineer) and Anne (Schoenberg) Sklar; married Elizabeth Sherr (a professor), June 24, 1962; children: Jessica K. *Education:* Oberlin College, B.A., 1958; Princeton University, M.A., 1960, Ph.D., 1964. *Office:* Department of Philosophy, University of Michigan, Ann Arbor, Mich. 48109.

CAREER: Swarthmore College, Swarthmore, Pa., assistant professor of philosophy, 1962-66; Princeton University, Princeton, N.J., assistant professor of philosophy, 1966-68; University of Michigan, Ann Arbor, associate professor, 1968-74, professor of philosophy, 1974—.

WRITINGS: Space, Time, and Spacetime, University of California Press, 1974.

*   *   *

SKOCPOL, Theda Ruth 1947-

BRIEF ENTRY: Born May 4, 1947, in Detroit, Mich. American

sociologist, educator, and author. Skocpol has taught sociology at Harvard University since 1975. She wrote *States and Social Revolutions: A Comparative Analysis of France, Russia, and China* (Cambridge University Press, 1979). *Address:* 36 Carver St., Cambridge, Mass. 02138; and Department of Sociology, Harvard University, 680 William James Hall, Cambridge, Mass. 02138. *Biographical/critical sources: Who's Who of American Women*, 11th edition, Marquis, 1979.

*   *   *

SKUTCH, Margaret F. 1932-

PERSONAL: Born May 24, 1932, in Richmond, Va.; married Lawrence Skutch (divorced); children: David, Christopher. *Education:* Attended Longwood State Teachers College (now Longwood College), Whitman School of Art, and Fairleigh Dickinson University; Goddard College, B.A.; Antioch College, M.A. *Office:* Early Learning Center, Inc., 12 Gary Rd., Stamford, Conn. 06903.

CAREER: Teacher at schools in Darien, Conn., and Greenwich, Conn., 1963-64; Early Learning Center, Inc. (Montessori school), Stamford, Conn., founder and teacher, 1964—. Adjunct professor at Antioch College; field professor at Goddard College. Co-director of "I'll Do It," a children's program first broadcast in September, 1979. Director of education at Community Learning Centers, Inc., Washington, D.C.; designed Learning Place, for Electric Energy Association of America; consultant to Far West Laboratories and Educational Facilities Laboratories of the City of New York.

WRITINGS: To Start a School, Little, Brown, 1971.

SIDELIGHTS: After a lengthy search to find a suitable nursery school for her son, Margaret Skutch discovered a Montessori school an hour's drive from her home. Prompted by the scarcity of such schools, she decided to open her own Montessori school, which she called the Early Learning Center, Inc. According to Lisa Hammel of the *New York Times*, "the school, which has moved away from its original Montessori beginnings and incorporated other educational ideas as well, is host to scores of visitors, among them prominent names in education, who come to observe and learn from Margaret Skutch's unusual and highly effective experiment."

Margaret Skutch commented that her objectives are "to provide superior pre-school education for local children; to establish a teacher training program that would, through the medium of teacher workshops, help to disseminate the theories and methods of the Early Learning Center, Inc.; and to serve as a prototype and aid in the development of similar schools."

BIOGRAPHICAL/CRITICAL SOURCES: New York Times, March 30, 1972.

*   *   *

SMALLEY, Barbara Martin 1926-

PERSONAL: Born in 1926 in Everton, Ind.; married, 1952. *Education:* Indiana University, B.S., 1954; University of Illinois, M.A., 1965, Ph.D., 1968. *Home:* 1006 South Busey, Urbana, Ill. 61801.

CAREER: University of Illinois, Urbana, assistant professor of English and comparative literature, 1968—. *Member:* International Comparative Literature Association, Modern Language Association of America, American Comparative Literature Association, American Association of University Professors.

WRITINGS: George Eliot and Flaubert: Pioneers of the Modern Novel, Ohio University Press, 1974; (editor) George H. Lewes, *Ranthorpe*, Ohio University Press, 1974. Contributor to literature journals.*

*   *   *

SMALLWOOD, Joseph R(oberts) 1900-

PERSONAL: Born December 24, 1900, in Gambo, Newfoundland, Canada; son of Charles W. (a woodsman) and Minnie (Devannah) Smallwood; married Clara Isobel Oates, November 25, 1925; children: Ramsay, William, Clara. *Education:* Attended Rand School of Social Science. *Religion:* United Church of Canada. *Home:* 119 Portugal Cove Rd., St. John's, Newfoundland, Canada A1B 2N1; and Box 1, Site 4, R.R.1, Roaches Line, Newfoundland, Canada.

CAREER: Apprentice to printer in St. John's, Newfoundland; reporter and editor for *St. John's Evening Telegram;* associated with the *Herald,* Halifax, Nova Scotia; reporter for the Boston Herald-Traveler, Boston, Mass.; free-lance writer in New York, N.Y.; free-lance writer in England, 1926-27; broadcasted weekly radio show in Newfoundland, 1932-39; operator of hog farm in Newfoundland; interim prime minister of province of Newfoundland, 1949, premier and minister of economic development, 1949-72; leader of Liberal Reform party, 1975-77. Leader of Newfoundland's and Labrador's "Confederation With Canada" movement; member of National Convention of Newfoundland; organizer of Newfoundland trade unions and cooperatives until 1946; founder and leader of Newfoundland Liberal party, 1949-72; member of Privy Council of Canada, 1967.

MEMBER: Liberal Club, St. John's Club, Masons (York rite, Scottish rite, Shrine; past master). *Awards, honors:* D.C.L. from Acadia University, University of Victoria, McGill University, and University of Windsor; LL.D. from University of British Columbia, Dalhousie University, University of New Brunswick, St. Dunstan's University, and Waterloo Lutheran University; D.Litt. from Memorial University of Newfoundland.

WRITINGS: The New Newfoundland: An Account of the Revolutionary Developments Which Are Transforming Britain's Oldest Colony From the "Cinderella of the Empire" Into One of the Great Small Nations of the World, Macmillan, 1931; (editor) *The Book of Newfoundland*, Newfoundland Book Publishers, Volume I-II, 1937, Volumes III-IV, 1967, Volumes V-VI, 1975; *Dr. William Carson, the Great Newfoundland Reformer: His Life, Letters, and Speeches—Raw Material for a Biography*, 1940, reprinted, Newfoundland Book Publishers, 1978; *Our Case: Premier Smallwood's Statement of Policy* (bound with *Newfoundland, the Fortress Isle*, by James Wentworth Day), Brunswick Press, 1960; *Peril and Glory*, High Hill Publishing House, 1966; *To You With Affection From Joey: A Short Message From Your Premier*, Action for Joey Committee, 1969; *I Chose Canada: The Memoirs of the Honourable Joseph R. "Joey" Smallwood*, Macmillan of Canada, 1973, published in the United States in two volumes, New American Library, 1975; (editor) *Newfoundland Miscellany*, Volume I, Newfoundland Book Publishers, 1978; (editor) *No Apology From Me: A Book of Startling Surprises About Confederation*, Newfoundland Book Publishers, 1979.

Also author of *Coaker of Newfoundland: The Man Who Led the Deep-Sea Fishermen to Political Power*, 1926, *The New Newfoundlander*, 1932, *Newfoundland Hand Book, Gazetteer, and Almanac*, 1940, *Surrogate Robert Carter*, 1940, and *The Face of Newfoundland*, 1967. Contributor to magazines, including *Saturday Night*.

BIOGRAPHICAL/CRITICAL SOURCES: Standard, August 27, 1948; Pathfinder, March 23, 1949; Maclean's, August 15, 1949, July 2, 1979; Ewart Young, editor, This Is Newfoundland, Ryerson, 1949; New Liberty, July, 1951; Time, September 22, 1952, February 14, 1972; New York Times: Men in the News, Volume II, Lippincott, 1960; Richard J. Gwyn, Smallwood: The Unlikely Revolutionary, McClelland & Stewart, revised edition, 1972; Yousuf Karsh, Karsh Canadians, University of Toronto Press, 1978.*

*   *   *

SMART, James Dick   1906-1982

OBITUARY NOTICE—See index for CA sketch: Born March 1, 1906, in Alton, Ontario, Canada; died January 23, 1982, in Rosedale, Ontario, Canada. Educator, clergyman, and author of more than thirty books on the Bible and Christian education. Smart served as pastor of several churches in Ontario, Canada, including Toronto's Rosedale Presbyterian Church. He was also a professor of biblical interpretation at the Union Theological Seminary in New York, N.Y. Smart's books include The Interpretation of Scripture, History and Theology in Second Isiah, and Doorway to a New Age: A Study of Paul's Letter to the Romans. Obituaries and other sources: New York Times, January 27, 1982.

*   *   *

SMILEY, Sam Max   1931-

PERSONAL: Born February 15, 1931, in Columbus, Ind.; married, 1952; children: three. Education: Illinois Wesleyan University, B.F.A., 1952; University of Iowa, M.F.A., 1955; Indiana University, Ph.D., 1967. Office: Department of Theatre and Drama, Theatre Building, Indiana University, Bloomington, Ind. 47401.

CAREER: Georgia State College for Women (now Georgia College at Milledgeville), instructor in drama, 1956-57; University of Evansville, Evansville, Ind., 1967-69, began as assistant professor, became professor of drama; University of Missouri, Columbia, professor of drama, 1969-73; Indiana University, Bloomington, professor of theatre and drama, 1973—. Visiting instructor at University of Idaho, summer, 1959; member of Indiana governor's Commission on the Arts, 1962 and 1963; chairman of playwriting awards at American College Theatre Festival, 1973. Member: American Theatre Association, Speech Communication Association.

WRITINGS: Playwriting: The Structure of Action, Prentice-Hall, 1971; The Drama of Attack: Didactic Plays of the American Depression, University of Missouri Press, 1972; (contributor) Studies in Theater and Drama, Mouton, 1972; Date (one-act play), Samuel French, 1976. Contributor to theatre and literature journals. Associate editor of Quarterly Journal of Speech, 1970-71.*

*   *   *

SMITH, Anthony Peter   1912-1980
(Tony Smith)

OBITUARY NOTICE: Born in 1912 in South Orange, N.J.; died of heart failure, December 26, 1980, in New York, N.Y. Architect, sculptor, educator, and author of articles on art and sculpture. Smith studied architecture at the New Bauhaus in Chicago, then worked as assistant to Frank Lloyd Wright from 1938 to 1940. He maintained a private practice in architecture from 1940 to 1960 and began teaching architecture and design in 1946. Smith began sculpting in 1960, creating his first steel

piece in 1962. From his first exhibition in 1964 Smith was critically acclaimed and his work was in great demand. Many of his large, polyhedral structures are displayed on the grounds of major modern-art museums. Obituaries and other sources: Time, September 14, 1970; Art News, April, 1971; Lucy T. Lippard, Tony Smith, Abrams, 1972; Dictionary of American Art, Harper, 1979; The Annual Obituary 1980, St. Martin's, 1981.

*   *   *

SMITH, Dick King
See KING-SMITH, Dick

*   *   *

SMITH, Eliot Fremont
See FREMONT-SMITH, Eliot

*   *   *

SMITH, Jackson Algernon   1917-

BRIEF ENTRY: Born October 21, 1917, in Oklahoma City, Okla. American psychiatrist, educator, and author. Smith has been a professor of psychiatry and department chairman at Loyola University of Chicago since 1964. He wrote Psychiatry: Descriptive and Dynamic (Williams & Wilkins, 1959), Difficult Patients (Year Book Medical Publishers, 1963), The Paranoid (Little, Brown, 1970), and Up Your Spirit! (Atheneum, 1978). Address: Stritch School of Medicine, Loyola University, 2160 South First Ave., Maywood, Ill. 60153. Biographical/critical sources: American Men and Women of Science: The Physical and Biological Sciences, 14th edition, Bowker, 1979.

*   *   *

SMITH, Joseph H(enry)   1913-1981

OBITUARY NOTICE: Born September 4, 1913, in New York, N.Y.; died November 25, 1981, in Norwalk, Conn. Lawyer, educator, historian, editor, and author. Smith received his law degree from Columbia University in 1938 and then conducted research in legal history there until 1942. He attained the rank of lieutenant while serving in U.S. Navy intelligence from 1942 to 1945. Smith served in private law practice beginning in 1946; in addition, he taught at the New York Law School from 1951 to 1961, when he joined the faculty at Columbia University School of Law. While at Columbia he co-edited the legal papers of Alexander Hamilton, which were published in a five-volume study. Among Smith's books are Appeals to the Privy Council From the American Plantations and Cases and Materials on the Development of Legal Institutions. Obituaries and other sources: Directory of American Scholars, Volume I: History, 7th edition, Bowker, 1978; Who's Who in America, 40th edition, Marquis, 1978; New York Times, November 28, 1981.

*   *   *

SMITH, Manuel (Juan)   1934-

PERSONAL: Born January 27, 1934, in New York, N.Y. Education: San Diego State College, B.A., 1959, M.S., 1960; University of California, Los Angeles, Ph.D., 1966. Office: Psychology Clinic, University of California, 405 Hilgard Ave., Los Angeles, Calif. 90024.

CAREER: U.S. Navy Electronics Laboratories, psychologist, 1958-60; University of California, Los Angeles, assistant research psychologist, 1960-64, research psychologist, 1964-66, assistant professor, 1967-69, clinical professor of psychology, 1970—, clinical scholar, 1968-70, clinical training fellow, 1969-70. Clinical psychologist at Los Angeles County Mental Health Department, 1970—. *Member:* American Psychological Association.

WRITINGS: (Contributor) *Methods and Instrumentation in Experimental Psychology*, McGraw, 1966; *When I Say No, I Feel Guilty: How to Cope, Using the Skills of Systematic Assertive Therapy*, Dial, 1975; *Kicking the Fear Habit: Using Your Automatic Orienting Reflex to Unlearn Your Anxieties, Fears, and Phobias*, Dial, 1977. Contributor to psychology journals.

WORK IN PROGRESS: Research into the theory and practice of systematic assertive therapy in desensitization of anxiety to criticism, guilt induction, and manipulation.

BIOGRAPHICAL/CRITICAL SOURCES: New York Times Book Review, April 13, 1975.*

*   *   *

SMITH, Patricia Jean Adam
See ADAM-SMITH, Patricia Jean

*   *   *

SMITH, Red
See SMITH, Walter W(ellesley)

*   *   *

SMITH, Robert Allan   1909-1980

OBITUARY NOTICE: Born May 14 (some sources say May 15), 1909, in Kelso, Scotland; died May 16, 1980, in Kelso, Scotland. Physicist, educator, and author. Smith received his doctorate in mathematics at Cambridge University in 1936. During World War II he participated in research resulting in the installation of radar. His further work in radio communications contributed significantly to improved navigational accuracy. After the war Smith worked for England's Royal Radar Establishment as senior staff member and, from 1946 to 1961, as head of the physics department. He served as professor of physics and director of the Center for Materials Science and Engineering at Massachusetts Institute of Technology from 1962 to 1968. He returned to England in 1968 as principal and vice-chancellor of Heriot-Watt University, where he was instrumental in developing the university's science, engineering, and research departments. He was decorated Commander of the Order of the British Empire in 1960. Among his publications are *Radio Aids to Navigation, The Physical Principles of Thermodynamics,* and *Semiconductors.* Obituaries and other sources: *The Author's and Writer's Who's Who,* 6th edition, Burke's Peerage, 1971; *The International Who's Who,* Europa, 1978; *Who's Who in the World,* 4th edition, Marquis, 1978; *The Annual Obituary 1980,* St. Martin's, 1981.

*   *   *

SMITH, Robert Houston   1931-

PERSONAL: Born February 13, 1931, in McAlester, Okla.; son of Vaughn Hubert (an abstractor of land titles) and Bobbie L. (Nelson) Smith; married Geraldine Warshaw, January 26, 1969; children: Vanessa Eleanor. *Education:* University of Tulsa, B.A., 1952; Yale University, B.D., 1955, Ph.D., 1960. *Religion:* Presbyterian. *Home:* 1117 Quinby Ave., Wooster, Ohio 44691. *Office:* College of Wooster, Wooster, Ohio 44691.

CAREER: College of Wooster, Wooster, Ohio, instructor, 1960-62, assistant professor, 1962-65, associate professor, 1965-70, professor of religion, 1970—, Fox Professor of Religion, 1972—, chairman of department, 1981—, director of archaeological expedition to Pella, Jordan, 1966—, curator of the college's Near East Collection, 1966—. Director of excavations at Khirbet Kufin, Jordan, 1958; plot supervisor for University of Pennsylvania's archaeological expedition to El Jib, Gibeon, Jordan (now occupied by Israel), 1959, area supervisor of excavation at Tell es-Saidiyeh, Jordan, 1964. Lecturer on "Digging up the Past," a series on NBC-TV, 1968. Member of board of trustees of American Center of Oriental Research, Amman, Jordan. *Member:* Society of Professional Archaeologists, American Schools of Oriental Research, Archaeological Institute of America, Society of Biblical Literature, American Oriental Society. *Awards, honors:* Two Brothers fellow of Yale University at American Schools of Oriental Research, Jerusalem, 1958-59; grants from National Endowment for the Humanities, 1979-81, and National Geographic Society, 1979-81, for archaeological work at Pella, Jordan.

WRITINGS: Excavations in the Cemetery at Khirbet Kufin, Palestine (monograph), Colt Archaeological Institute, 1962; *Pella of the Decapolis,* Volume I: *The 1967 Season of the Wooster Expedition to Pella,* College of Wooster, 1973; *Patches of Godlight: The Pattern of Thought of C. S. Lewis,* University of Georgia Press, 1981. Contributor to *One-Volume Interpreter's Commentary.* Contributor to learned journals.

WORK IN PROGRESS: Research on archaeology of the Middle East and the classical world, on religion and literature, and on American business ethics.

SIDELIGHTS: Smith commented: "I wear several hats, some of them quite different from each other. I am, among other things, a professor of religion, a field archaeological director, a historian of American business ethics, and a specialist in the thought of C. S. Lewis. I enjoy detail and like working with my hands, whether I am using a word processor, making measured drawings, or remodeling a house. If I were to have a second career, it might well be as a museum director. My next venture may be in the writing of fiction, to fulfill an interest of long standing."

BIOGRAPHICAL/CRITICAL SOURCES: University of Tulsa Alumni, October, 1964.

*   *   *

SMITH, Tony
See SMITH, Anthony Peter

*   *   *

SMITH, Walter W(ellesley)   1905-1982
(Red Smith)

OBITUARY NOTICE—See index for *CA* sketch: Born September 25, 1905, in Green Bay, Wis.; died of vascular complications, January 15, 1982, in Stamford, Conn. Columnist and author of books on sports. Smith, a syndicated columnist for the *New York Times,* was described in *Time* as "the most influential and admired sportswriter of our time." His column, "Sports of the Times," known for its witty, informative style, appeared in about five hundred newspapers throughout the world. In 1976 it earned Smith the Pulitzer Prize for commentary. Smith's books include *Out of the Red, Views of Sports,* and *The Sporting World of Red Smith.* Obituaries and other sources: *New York Times,* January 16, 1982; *Time,* January 25, 1982.

SMITH, William Martin 1911-

PERSONAL: Born November 24, 1911, in Flint, Mich.; son of William Martin (a farmer) and Mertie (Holiday) Smith; married Ruth E. Henderson, September 3, 1938; children: Colborn W., Elaine Smith Hawkins, Maureen Smith Hoffert, Deborah Smith Randzio. *Education:* Ohio State University, B.Sc., 1935; Cornell University, M.S., 1937, Ph.D., 1942. *Politics:* Democrat. *Religion:* Episcopal. *Home:* 428 East Hamilton Ave., State College, Pa. 16801. *Office:* Department of Agricultural Economics and Rural Sociology, Pennsylvania State University, Weaver Building, University Park, Pa. 16802.

CAREER: Cornell University, Ithaca, N.Y., extension specialist and assistant instructor in rural sociology, 1935-37, 1937-43; farmer in Norwalk, Ohio, 1943-45; University of Illinois, Champaign, assistant professor of rural sociology and specialist at rural youth extension, 1945-47; Pennsylvania State University, University Park, associate professor of home economics, 1947-50, professor of family relations, 1950-59, state 4-H Club leader, 1959-63, assistant director of extension, 1963-69, professor of rural sociology, 1969-76, professor emeritus, 1976—. Fulbright professor at Agricultural University of the Netherlands, 1964-65, distinguished foreign professor, 1973-74; visiting professor at University of Arkansas, Columbia University, and University of California, Davis. Member of governor's committee on children and youth and Central Pennsylvania Family Planning Council (president, 1976-77).

MEMBER: National Council on Family Relations (president, 1966-67), American Sociological Association, Rural Sociological Society, American Education Association, American Association of Marriage and Family Therapists, American Association of University Professors, University Club (vice-president), Phi Kappa Phi, Alpha Zeta, Gamma Xi Delta, Phi Delta Kappa, Epsilon Sigma Phi, Alpha Kappa Delta, Phi Gamma Mu. *Awards, honors:* Grant Foundation fellow at Merrill-Palmer Institute, 1954-55; Fulbright fellow, 1964-65; service to families award from Pennsylvania Association of Extension Home Economists, 1979.

WRITINGS: (With Jessie Bernard and Helen E. Buchanan) *Dating, Mating, and Marriage,* Howard Allen, 1958; (with Ray Coward) *The Family in Rural Society,* Westview, 1981; (with Ray Coward) *Rural Family Services: Status and Needs,* University of Nebraska Press, 1982.

Co-author of films "Directing Your Dollars," released by Institute of Life Insurance, 1956, and "The Dating Scene," released by Coronet Instructional Films, 1972.

Editor of "Teacher Exchange for High School Family Life Educators," a column in *Marriage and Family Living,* 1958-60. Contributor to *Encyclopedia of Education.* Contributor to academic journals and popular magazines. Editor of *Family Coordinator: A Journal of Education, Counseling, and Services,* 1967-69, associate editor, 1971; associate editor of *Forum,* 1971.

SIDELIGHTS: Smith told *CA:* "I believe that the most significant relationships in life are developed and maintained within families. The person who never stops growing—from birth to death—has the greatest opportunities for creative, open, positive living and loving. Society—the public—works against the nourishing function of families, trying to evaluate them in production terms rather than as the seed-beds of personality and personal fulfillment. In the traditional rural family, values were supported which need to be rediscovered: responsibility

for oneself and others; pride in excellence; concern for the well-being of all; cooperation before competition; the integration of person, group, and the natural world; and freedom with one's past. In teaching and research I have tried to help others see that each of us can influence the course of social action—developing leadership, fighting crime and poverty, exposing bigotry and prejudice, and respecting the integrity of personality."

*   *   *

SMITTEN, Jeffrey Roger 1941-

PERSONAL: Born July 8, 1941, in Oakland, Calif.; son of Roger Macalpine (an insurance executive) and Faye (Strickland) Smitten; married Lizabeth Wallace Anderson (a medical administrator), September 24, 1966. *Education:* University of California, Berkeley, B.A., 1963, M.A., 1966; University of Wisconsin—Madison, Ph.D., 1972. *Office:* Department of English, Texas Tech University, Lubbock, Tex. 79409.

CAREER: Humboldt State College (now University), Arcata, Calif., lecturer in English, 1966-67; Texas Tech University, Lubbock, assistant professor, 1972-78, associate professor of English, 1978—. *Member:* Modern Language Association of America, American Society for Eighteenth-Century Studies, South Central Society for Eighteenth-Century Studies (founder; acting president, 1975-76). *Awards, honors:* Grant from University of Wisconsin, for Linacre College, Oxford, 1970-71; fellow of National Endowment for the Humanities at University of California, Irvine, 1978.

WRITINGS: (Contributor) Wolodymyr T. Zyla and Wendell M. Aycock, editors, *Joseph Conrad: Theory and World Fiction,* Texas Tech Press, 1974; (editor with Peter L. Abernethy and Christian J. W. Kloesel) *English Novel Explication: Supplement I Through 1975,* Shoe String, 1976; (editor with Kloesel) *English Novel Explication: Supplement II Through 1979,* Shoe String, 1981; (editor with Ann Daghistany) *Spatial Form in Narrative,* Cornell University Press, 1981. Contributor to language and literature journals.

WORK IN PROGRESS: A book on the relationship of narrative structure to historical explanation in the work of Gibbon, Hume, Robertson, and Ferguson.

SIDELIGHTS: Smitten told *CA:* "One of the guiding principles in my work on narrative form has been an interdisciplinary approach. This approach has consisted of two aspects: the examination of a given narrative in light of its immediate aesthetic context in its historical period and in light of its place in the entire genre of narrative. No literary work can be adequately understood when it is separated from its historical milieu, nor can it be adequately understood if it is isolated from works written in other periods. The fullest comprehension comes when these two aspects of literary study are combined into a genuine interdisciplinary study."

*   *   *

SNELL, Tee Loftin 1922-

PERSONAL: Born January 27, 1922, in Kinston, N.C.; daughter of Kirby William and Tiffany West (Whaley) Loftin; married Edwin M. Snell, March 4, 1942; children: Suzanne (Mrs. Stephen Henneman), James L. *Education:* University of Missouri, B.J., 1942; American University, M.A., 1965. *Home:* 3100 R St. N.W., Washington, D.C. 20007. *Office:* National Geographic Society, Washington, D.C. 20036.

CAREER: Writer and announcer for KFRU-Radio, Columbia, Mo., KBWD-Radio, Brownwood, Tex., and KMOX-Radio,

St. Louis, Mo., 1942-44; *Daily Free Press,* Kinston, N.C., special writer, 1948-58; editorial assistant to U.S. congressman, 1953-54 and 1956; television writer, 1955-65; National Geographic Society, Washington, D.C., writer and researcher, 1967—. *Member:* Theta Sigma Phi.

WRITINGS: The Wild Shores: America's Beginnings, photographs by Walter Meayers Edwards, paintings by Louis S. Glanzman, foreword by David Mark Griffiths, National Geographic Society, 1974. Author of *1865 Stranger's Guide.* Editor for publication of National Academy of Engineering, 1966.*

*   *   *

SNEPP, Frank (Warren III) 1943-

PERSONAL: Born May 3, 1943, in Kinston, N.C.; son of Frank Warren (a judge) and Nancy (Goodwin) Snepp. *Education:* Columbia University, B.A., 1965, M.I.A., 1968; graduate study at New School for Social Research, 1965-66. *Residence:* Arlington, Va. *Agent:* Lyn Nesbit, International Creative Management, 40 West 57th St., New York, N.Y. 10019. *Office:* c/o Random House, 201 East 50th St., New York, N.Y. 10022.

CAREER: Columbia Broadcasting System, New York, N.Y., news researcher, 1966; Central Intelligence Agency, Washington, D.C., officer, 1968-76; writer, 1977—. *Awards, honors:* Medal of Merit from Central Intelligence Agency, 1975.

WRITINGS: Decent Interval (nonfiction), Random House, 1977; *Convergence of Interest* (novel), Random House, 1982; *Irreparable Harm* (nonfiction), Random House, 1982.

WORK IN PROGRESS: "In the Name of National Security," a screenplay about an ex-CIA agent's struggle to expose wrongdoing by his former employer.

SIDELIGHTS: Frank Snepp served in Vietnam as the chief strategic analyst for the Central Intelligence Agency (CIA) station in Saigon. He was present for the fall of South Vietnam in 1975, and drove Vietnamese president Thieu to his getaway plane. Appalled by the chaos of the American evacuation, in which thousands of Vietnamese who had worked for the CIA were left in Saigon along with many secret documents on U.S. intelligence activities, Snepp pressed his superiors to undertake a study of the mistakes made at the war's end. When it became clear that the agency preferred to cover up its own failures and those of the State Department, Snepp resigned and wrote his own analysis, *Decent Interval.*

Though the CIA was aware of Snepp's intention to publish his expose and twice sought an injunction to stop him, the book was completed and shipped to bookstores before the Justice Department could act. Upon its appearance, the book was denounced by former Secretary of State Henry Kissinger, former U.S. ambassador to Saigon Graham Martin, and others whom Snepp had criticized. Though Snepp insisted that he had been careful not to reveal any classified information, *Decent Interval* was called a threat to national security by many, including President Jimmy Carter, and the CIA announced its intention to prosecute Snepp. But Laurence Stern of the *Washington Post Book World* observed, "*Decent Interval* raises a security issue only to those who cannot draw the distinction between national security and their own political reputations." And William F. Buckley of the *National Review,* while reluctant to condone Snepp's refusal to submit the manuscript to CIA review, concluded, "the justification for this book is its contents."

Among those Snepp blamed for the disaster were Kissinger, Martin, and the former CIA station chief in Saigon, Thomas Polgar. Kissinger was criticized for failing to negotiate a North Vietnamese withdrawal from South Vietnam as part of the Paris peace agreement, and for pursuing the illusory goal of a coalition government in the final weeks of the war, in the face of mounting evidence that the North Vietnamese were intent on military conquest. Polgar refused to believe his own intelligence reports, distorting them to support his own policy recommendations for a negotiated settlement in April, 1975. And Martin flatly refused, until a few days before Saigon fell, to consider even the possibility of an evacuation or to allow effective preparations for one to be made. Snepp also acknowledged his own mistakes in interpreting intelligence. He described the panic that spread through Saigon when it became clear that the city would be taken and that the Americans were leaving, and he concluded, "In terms of squandered lives, blown secrets and the betrayal of agents, friends and collaborators, our handling of the evacuation was an institutional disgrace."

Kevin Buckley of the *New York Times Book Review* described *Decent Interval* as "rich in detail, vivid, filled with appalling scenery and accusations." He called Snepp's case "intriguing and convincingly argued." Stern wrote that the book "is by far the richest document yet produced on the American and South Vietnamese endgame" and pointed out that "no after-battle report of comparable quality has been compiled within the government and placed in the public domain."

Some other reviewers found the book flawed by a lack of historical and political perspective. Wilfred Burchett, in *Harper's,* noted that "readers will seek in vain for any analysis of why America was in Vietnam or of what the real reasons were for defeat." Norman Hannah of the *National Review* observed that Snepp "seems uninterested in the relationship between his own experiences and the event that occurred before 1968, when he first arrived in Vietnam—as if the shape and direction of the war had not been set long before the Tet offensive." And John Leonard of the *New York Times* wrote, "There isn't a gleam of political intelligence anywhere in *Decent Interval,* a grain of historical sense, any feeling at all for the larger moral failure of which the fall of Saigon was merely a symptom." Snepp, however, had disavowed any intention of considering the conduct or propriety of the war as a whole. "By now," he wrote in the book's foreword, "most Americans have made up their minds about the rightness or wrongness of the Vietnam war, and the aptness of its ending." As William F. Buckley noted, Snepp's anger was directed at the handling of the evacuation: "Concerning the war itself, Snepp is detached. He sees reasons for prosecuting the war, and he sees reasons for never having gone into it. He sees no excuses for doing what we did on our way out, which was in effect to betray about thirty thousand . . . of our most valiant South Vietnamese friends."

In 1978 the government filed a civil suit against Snepp, charging him with breach of contract for violating the secrecy agreement he signed when he joined the CIA and seeking as damages all his profits from *Decent Interval.* Snepp contended that, since the book contained no classified information that had not already been publicized, he was not obliged to submit it to CIA screening. He argued that since the CIA's censorship authority extends only to classified material, the agency would have had to approve the entire manuscript anyway and so had suffered no damage through its unapproved publication. In addition, Snepp claimed that the secrecy agreement itself was an unconstitutional prior restraint on his freedom of speech. The government argued that Snepp had freely and legally waived his First Amendment rights by signing the agreement, and that, even though he had revealed no secrets, the CIA could not rely on its former employees to protect classified information, unless it could screen their manuscripts before publication. After a series of appeals, the Supreme Court found in the government's favor, in a controversial 6-3 ruling.

CA INTERVIEW

CA interviewed Frank Snepp by phone on November 25, 1980, at work in Arlington, Virginia.

CA: Did you anticipate the severity of the legal consequences when you decided not to submit the Decent Interval *manuscript to the CIA before publication?*

SNEPP: No, because I felt I was operating inside the law. Admittedly, I was fearful the CIA might trump up a case against, me, but I thought it would be something along the lines of the suit brought against Victor Marchetti, who was sued and gagged in the early 1970's when it was discovered he was preparing to publish secrets in his book, *The CIA and the Cult of Intelligence,* as in fact he had already done in a magazine article. I thought the agency might allege there was something classified in my book and proceed from there. And I was prepared to argue that whatever sensitive material there was had already been inadvertently "blown" by the agency through carelessness and mismanagement. I was not prepared for a suit that had nothing to do with the release of secrets.

CA: One of the unusual aspects of the United States Supreme Court's treatment of the case is that it received no briefs and allowed no oral arguments. Why do you think the court in effect failed to consider the important legal issues involved in the case?

SNEPP: Most speculation has it that the six justices in the majority were operating out of the misguided notion that I was like one of the Court clerks who had leaked privileged information to Bob Woodward and Scott Armstrong for their highly critical book on the Court, *The Brethren.* The majority apparently was looking to develop some standard by which they could punish such leakers; my case happened to be the first one on the docket that could be bent to that purpose. Also, there had been a great deal of controversy about my case from the start. The CIA had gone to great lengths to discredit and ridicule me, and I think that influenced the outcome.

Interestingly, the justices in the majority did not appear really to understand the case. For instance, though the government had never accused me of publishing even nonclassified secrets—that is, confidential material—the Court intimated that I had. It also accepted as fact that my unclassified writings had frightened off intelligence sources by undermining *their* confidence in the CIA's ability to protect secrets. The Court may have believed this, but no one in the CIA had ever been able to prove it. So the Court posited facts where there weren't any. It also posited *law* where there wasn't any. There is nothing in the National Security Acts which would allow the director of the CIA to curb *unclassified* writings. The Court, however, ignored this inconvenient reality and proclaimed the CIA director free to do what he did to me. All of which led the dissenting justices—Stevens, Marshall, and Brennan—to lambaste their colleagues for engaging in an "unprecedented exercise" in lawmaking. In short, they felt the Court was acting as a legislature, and thus flouting the Separation of Powers doctrine which is central to our Constitution.

CA: What about the fact that the majority opinion was unsigned?

SNEPP: My lawyers think that either Rehnquist or White wrote it, probably White. Yet whoever wrote it paid due attention to a lot of different prejudices on the Court. For instance, the right of the Court to fashion judicial restraints on free speech—without the help of Congress—was a principle articulated by Chief Justice Burger in his dissenting opinion in the great Pentagon Papers case. There, his view was in the minority. In my case, the Court adopted it as the consensus.

CA: Were many friends or former co-workers in sympathy with your writing of the book? Did you get active encouragement from people?

SNEPP: Yes. That's one of the reasons the book is so long. People started coming to me and volunteering anecdotes and information as word got around that I was writing. As a result, I was constantly stitching in new material. After the case broke, in February, 1978, I was out at the CIA for pretrial question-and-answer sessions; as I was walking down the halls, many of my former colleagues came running up to pass me notes praising the book. But since the Supreme Court decision, such support has dropped off, partly because the decision was so harsh, and partly because the atmosphere at the CIA has changed to one of uncertainty and fear as a result of an ongoing bureaucratic housecleaning. People out at Langley [CIA headquarters] are afraid of associating with "undersirable elements" like myself, lest they get themselves fired.

CA: Thomas Powers wrote in Commonweal *that the CIA feared the breakdown of the American good-soldier system by which people do as they are told by higher authority and keep quiet about it. In the last months of the American presence in Vietnam, did you see many signs that the good-soldier system might break down?*

SNEPP: During the last days of the war it broke down entirely—and thank goodness! Many young CIA and State Department officers seized the initiative and arranged for the evacuation, on U.S. cargo planes, of thousands of Vietnamese friends and colleagues when there was no guidance from the top. Had they not done so, those Vietnamese would have been left behind, as so many others were. But mind you, it is a token of how strong the good-soldier system was that such acts of initiative and heroism were so late in coming. In fact it's amazing so many young CIA officers managed to break lock-step. You see, you're indoctrinated as a "good soldier" from the very start of your career. It's as if your're joining a sort of mystic sect. And to turn against the sect, or "cult," as Victor Marchetti has called it, takes a great deal of soul-wrenching. Few of my older colleagues were up to it. They seethed in silence and left their Vietnamese friends on the tarmac.

The fall of Vietnam, and the betrayal of so many of our allies, taught these "good soldiers" nothing. They continue to toe the company line, even though many of them have a lot of complaints with it. Oh sure, morale in the CIA has declined in the past two or three years, but not because discipline is slipping or because a couple of "good soliders" like myself kicked the traces, or even because Congress has become too inquisitive of CIA activities (which it hasn't). If there's been demoralization, the chief cause is poor management, starting with Admiral Stansfield Turner's decision in late 1977 to fire surplus personnel peremptorily without taking into consideration personal factors. He computerized the process, as no one before him had—and made a lot of veterans mad. Some of the eccentric ones, who didn't measure up to his ideal-employee profile, were summarily booted out. The number of such unfortunates now stands between eight hundred and a thousand.

My book came out just as Turner was starting this purge, and given the resentments it generated, he had to reckon with the possibility that there might be eight hundred to a thousand potential authors out there writing away out of spite. With that prospect to plague him, he had to make an example of me, which is another reason the suit was brought.

CA: Do you mean that he literally programmed into a computer the profile of the ideal CIA employee?

SNEPP: Of course it was a little more complicated than that. You had to meet various criteria if you were to stay on the payroll. Even so, the selection process was misconceived. In the CIA you can't draw fine lines. Someone may be a very good linguist, for instance, and a failure at recruiting agents. Turner didn't appreciate this—perhaps understandably, since he had had no experience in intelligence. Traditionally, outsiders have never done very well in the director's chair. The one possible exception is John McCone, but he had a very strong infrastructure in the form of Richard Helms and his coterie, men like former counterintelligence chief James Angelton.

CA: Did you do your graduate work with the intention of joining the CIA?

SNEPP: No. I went to graduate school to prepare for a career in journalism. But then, as the Vietnam War started heating up, one of my professors, who was spotting for the CIA, came to me and said, "Undoubtedly you're facing the draft. Why don't you join the CIA? You can stay out of Vietnam." That seemed like an eminently sensible idea. It was a way of disposing of my obligation for public service—with honor. So I signed up, only to get myself assigned to Vietnam by accident. And the irony is, I spent more years there—nearly five of them—than most foot soldiers did in their careers.

CA: You were awarded the CIA's Medal of Merit for your performance in Vietnam. Is it true that you did not want to accept that award?

SNEPP: No, it is not true. My feeling was: why grandstand here? Many of my colleagues had performed heroically during the evacuation of Vietnam. It would have been a disservice to them to disrupt the awards ceremony. Besides, I was still trying, at that point, to nudge the CIA into doing a postmortem on Saigon's end game. I didn't realize that it was futile—that my superiors were out to protect their flanks by whitewashing the truth.

CA: And there was total resistance to that?

SNEPP: To writing a postmortem?—yes, indeed. Trying to get one done was like trying to nail Jello to the wall. In late 1975 the agency was going through the trauma of congressional investigations. The last thing my colleagues wanted was to open another Pandora's box. And it appeared to some that I was threatening to do just that. Oh, how I tried! I would go about asking, "Are we going to do an after-action report?" But no one would answer directly. Finally I was called in by a representative of the CIA's inspector general. He asked if I would discuss the intelligence reporting from Vietnam. I said yes, and I did. Then toward the end of the interview I said, "Now let's discuss the evacuation, the real tragedy." He said something like, "We can't tolerate anything so controversial; the only thing I'm interested in is arming William Colby [former CIA director] with ammunition to fend off Congress." It was as if he had struck a match to my conscience. I realized

the agency was not going to do an after-action report; it was not going to exorcise our ghosts or try to learn from its mistakes.

That's when I began seriously contemplating writing a book. And contrary to the popular misconception, I made no secret of it. I told my superiors immediately I was thinking about writing a postmortem of my own. The only thing I didn't tell them was the name of the publisher I had approached. Why? Because I was fearful they would intervene to frighten Random House off, or might even steal the manuscript. Oh yes, that *was* a possibility. In 1964, the CIA actually stole the manuscript of an "objectionable" book—*The Invisible Government* by David Wise and Thomas B. Ross—from Random House. Later the agency absconded with Victor Marchetti's manuscript. And in editing it—or I should say in *censoring* it—CIA officials demanded far more deletions than were justified under any kind of national security standard. So, in light of all this, I decided to keep the name of my publisher secret. But it wasn't kept secret. A friend in the CIA, who knew it, identified Random House to my superiors. Ironically, they chose not to credit this "intelligence" because they couldn't accept that such a neophyte as I could have attracted so prestigious a publisher as Random House.

All of which, by the way, belies the Supreme Court's finding that I wrote the book "surreptitiously." After I left the CIA in January, 1976, my (former) superiors circulated memos to all staff chiefs indicating that I had resigned rather than agree to submit my manuscript for review. So for the agency and the Supreme Court to suggest that I wrote the book secretly is simply at odds with the record.

CA: Is there any chance for an appeal?

SNEPP: No. The Supreme Court has refused my request for a rehearing. So the case is closed, and the Court's ruling is the law of the land. What that means, in the broadest possible terms, is that the government can subject any "responsible" official, or ex-official, of any agency to censorship. For instance, if I worked for the National Parks Service, I would, under the *Snepp* ruling, be obliged to clear anything I might write for review, whether or not it was classified, whether or not I'd signed a secrecy agreement. That's because the Court endorsed the government's view that "position" alone carries with it certain obligations. If you're in a "position of trust" in the government—anywhere in government—you're now implicitly obligated to submit to "Big Brotherism," censorship of anything you might write or say publicly, as a result of your government experience. Also, the ruling limits the prerogatives of publishers or anyone who might collaborate with an official in a position of responsibility, because under the legal principle upheld in my case, not only is the primary party, the culprit, culpable for "breaching a trust," so is anybody who helps him do it. Attorneys for the Justic Department actually considered suing Random House, my publisher, and "60 Minutes," which did an interview with me. They decided not to do so because they realized that would stir up all the legal experts in the country. Instead, they chose to keep the lawsuit narrowly focused on me, so there wouldn't be a public outcry.

CA: Have the book and the lawsuit brought a great deal of response from the general public?

SNEPP: The book has been picked up abroad, translated into Japanese and French, and reprinted by Penguin-Viking in the United Kingdom and Australia. Here at home the sales were quite substantial for this kind of book. So was public reaction. I got a lot of letters, and small checks from people—from strangers—which helped to sustain me. Recently a letter showed up from a member of the family who figured in C. D. Bryan's *Friendly Fire.* She was simply expressing her sympathy. It was indicative of the kind of letter I've been getting.

CA: You've mentioned that one of the problems arising from the Supreme Court's ruling is that it has forced you to do speaking engagements without notes or outlines.

SNEPP: The latest CIA guidelines on the subject say explicitly that any kind of speech or public pronouncement on intelligence or related matters must be cleared; and if you're speaking extemporaneously, you must give the agency the topic in advance so its censors can decide whether or not you have to prepare a text for clearance. It's a real Catch-22. Which, incidentally, brings up a very important point. George Bush has recently done a lot of speaking based on his government experience, and has been cashing in on it; so have Kissinger and a number of other former "trustees" of the government. None of them, however, has been forced to clear what he's saying or writing, or has been sued and impoverished for failing to do so.

That really is the most pernicious aspect of my case. To put it bluntly, the government has enforced its secrecy strictures only against critics. It has sued John Stockwell, the former CIA operative who wrote *In Search of Enemies,* an indictment of CIA performance in Angola. (He settled out of court and was allowed to keep the money he had already earned from the book.) It also sued Philip Agee, author of *Inside the Company: CIA Diary,* who's made a career of leaking all sorts of classified names and secrets. Now I don't approve of Agee, but because his suit came on the heels of those brought against me and Stockwell, the presiding judge felt there was *prima facie* evidence that the government was prosecuting only people it didn't like while letting more friendly scofflaws get off scot-free (For example, ex-CIA men Tom Braden, William Buckley, Miles Copeland, Joseph Smith, David Phillips, and James Angleton have all written articles and books on intelligence without CIA approval—and without sanction.)

Such discriminatory law enforcement amounts, in effect, to an informal licensing system aimed at stopping unpopular speech—and that's something the courts have long considered unconstitutional. That's why Agee was allowed to keep his profits. Of course, the irony of this cannot be lost on anyone with a sense of fair play. On the one hand, a man who revels in jeopardizing the lives of CIA agents—Agee—walks off with his pockets full; on the other hand I have been ruined financially for publishing nonsecrets.

CA: How are works in progress and future writing plans affected by your legal situation?

SNEPP: The agency's censorship authority now extends to almost any form of expression which bears on my experience with the CIA. In fact, the Court's injunction says that I have to clear any written or oral presentation based on what I've learned simply *as a result* of my CIA experience. Well, I've learned a great deal about the law by virtue of my agency career and the legal fallout from it. I'm writing a book on the law and on my case for Random House, and that will have to be cleared. I've written a novel, which I am in the process of revising. The initial draft had to be cleared; so will the final draft and the galleys.

CA: It sounds something like the censorship in South Africa.

SNEPP: As a matter of fact, the *New Statesman* in Britain compared my situation to that of a dissident in South Africa.

When one becomes a "banned person" there, everything he writes has to be submitted to the censors.

CA: Are there other comments you'd like to make about your case?

SNEPP: I think it is important to emphasize that—contrary to the popular view—the case brought against me was not a simple contract case. The agency has constantly portrayed it as such in hopes of defusing public concern over it. But the agency is fudging. It isn't a contract case. If it were, I would have all of my money, because under contract law you can't collect for damages without proving damages before a jury. Never once in the litigation against me was the government obliged to *prove* it had suffered damage because of my book. Never once was I given a jury trial. In other words, the government and the courts took every possible shortcut in order to punish me—so many, in fact, they literally had to make up law as they went along.

BIOGRAPHICAL/CRITICAL SOURCES: Frank Snepp, *Decent Interval,* Random House, 1977; *Newsweek,* November 28, 1977; *New York Times,* December 20, 1977, February 15, 1978, June 19, 1978, July 8, 1978, February 20, 1980; *New York Times Book Review,* January 8, 1978; *Washington Post Book World,* January 8, 1978; *Harper's,* March, 1978; *National Review,* March 3, 1978, May 26, 1978; *Nation,* April 29, 1978; *New Statesman,* July 14, 1978; *First Principles,* May, 1980.

—*Sketch by Tim Connor*
—*Interview by Jean W. Ross*

* * *

SNYDER, Charles Royce 1924-

PERSONAL: Born December 28, 1924, in Haverford, Pa.; son of Edward D. and Edith (Royce) Snyder; married Patricia Hanson, June 30, 1951; children: Stephen Hoyt, Christiana Marie, Constance Patricia, Daniel Edward. *Education:* Yale University, B.A., 1944, M.A., 1949, Ph.D., 1954. *Home:* 705 Taylor Dr., Carbondale, Ill. 62901. *Office:* Department of Sociology, Southern Illinois University, Carbondale, Ill. 62901.

CAREER: Yale University, New Haven, Conn., member of staff of Yale Center for Alcohol Studies, 1950-60, assistant professor of sociology, 1956-60; Southern Illinois University, Carbondale, professor of sociology, 1960—, chairman of department, 1964-75. Member of theology committee of United Church of Christ, 1964—; consultant to National Institute of General Medical Sciences. *Military service:* U.S. Naval Reserve, active duty, World War II. *Member:* American Sociological Association (fellow), American Association of University Professors, Midwest Sociological Society (member of board of directors, 1970—), Society for the Study of Social Problems (vice-president, 1963-64).

WRITINGS: Alcohol and the Jews: A Cultural Study of Drinking and Sobriety, Free Press, 1958; (editor with David Joshua Pittman) *Society, Culture, and Drinking Patterns,* Southern Illinois University Press, 1962; (editor) *Proceedings of Research Sociologists' Conference on Alcohol Problems,* Southern Illinois University Press, 1964; (with Gunnar Boalt) *Alkohol och alienation,* Almqvist & Wiksell, 1968. Member of editorial board of *Quarterly Journal of Studies on Alcohol,* 1957—; associate editor of *Sociological Quarterly,* 1960-63.*

* * *

SOMERLOTT, Robert 1928-

PERSONAL: Born September 17, 1928, in Huntington, Ind.;

son of Vera Somerlott. *Education:* Attended Northwestern University, 1946, Michigan State University, 1947, and University of Michigan, 1948. *Home:* Apdo. 288, San Miguel de Allende, Mexico. *Agent:* McIntosh & Otis, Inc., 475 Fifth Ave., New York, N.Y. 10017.

CAREER: Professional actor and stage director, 1948-63; freelance writer in San Miguel de Allende, Mexico, 1963—. Lecturer on Mexican studies. *Member:* International P.E.N. *Awards, honors:* Short story prize from *Atlantic Monthly,* 1964, for "Eskimo Pies."

WRITINGS: Introduction to the Maya Epic (nonfiction), University of Wisconsin Press, 1974; *The Flamingos* (fiction), Little, Brown, 1967; *The Inquisitor's House* (fiction), Viking, 1968; *Here, Mr. Splitfoot* (nonfiction), Viking, 1971; *The Writing of Modern Fiction* (essays), Writer, 1972.

Work represented in anthologies, including *Best American Short Stories,* 1965, *Stories That Scared Even Me,* edited by Alfred Hitchcock, 1972, and *The Twelve Crimes of Christmas,* edited by Isaac Asimov, 1981.

Contributor to magazines, including *Cosmopolitan, Ms., Mademoiselle, American Heritage, Ellery Queen's Mystery Magazine, Good Housekeeping,* and *Atlantic.*

WORK IN PROGRESS: A novel, publication by Viking expected in 1983.

SIDELIGHTS: Somerlott commented: "I moved to Mexico in hope of a career as a free-lance writer. Almost immediately I began to publish short stories, then novels and other works. Most of my work is set in Mexico and I draw heavily from Mexican archaeology and history."

Somerlott's books have been translated into most European languages.

AVOCATIONAL INTERESTS: Mexican archaeology, German shepherd dogs.

* * *

SOMMERFELD, Ray(nard) M(athias) 1933-

PERSONAL: Born August 10, 1933, in Sibley, Iowa; son of Ernest Robert (a minister) and Lillian (a nurse; maiden name, Matthias) Sommerfeld; married Barbara Ann Spear, June 9, 1956; children: Andrea Joan, Kristin Elaine. *Education:* Attended University of Miami, Coral Gables, Fla., 1952; University of Iowa, B.S.C., 1956, M.A., 1957, Ph.D., 1963. *Politics:* Independent. *Religion:* Lutheran. *Home:* 6018 Mount Bonnell Hollow, Austin, Tex. 78731. *Office:* BEB 203, Graduate School of Business, University of Texas, Austin, Tex. 78712.

CAREER: University of Texas, Austin, assistant professor, 1963-66, associate professor, 1966-68, professor, 1968-72, Arthur Young Professor of Accounting, 1963-76; Arthur Young & Co. (certified public accountants), Reston, Va., director of tax education, 1976-78. *Military service:* U.S. Air Force, 1957-60. U.S. Air Force Reserve, 1960-65; became captain. *Member:* American Institute of Certified Public Accountants, American Accounting Association, American Taxation Association (president, 1975-76), National Tax Association, Texas Society of Certified Public Accountants (member of board of directors, 1967-69).

WRITINGS: Tax Reform and the Alliance for Progress, University of Texas Press, 1965; (with Hershel M. Anderson and Horace R. Brock) *An Introduction to Taxation,* Harcourt, 1969, 8th edition, 1982; *Federal Taxes and Management Decisions,*

Irwin, 1974, revised edition, 1978; *The Dow Jones-Irwin Guide to Tax Planning,* Dow Jones-Irwin, 1974, revised edition, 1978; (with G. Fred Streuling) *Tax Research Techniques,* American Institute of Certified Public Accountants, 1976; (with others) *An Introduction to Taxation,* Harcourt, 1980. Contributor to journals. Member of editorial advisory board of *Tax Adviser,* 1974-76, and *Accounting Review,* 1975-81.

SIDELIGHTS: Sommerfeld commented: "Most of my books have grown from my dissatisfaction with otherwise available educational materials. I specialize in federal taxation."

* * *

SOMORJAI, Gabor Arpad 1935-

PERSONAL: Born May 4, 1935, in Budapest, Hungary; came to the United States in 1957, naturalized citizen, 1962; son of Charles and Livia (Ormos) Somorjai; married Judith Kaldor (a financial analyst), September 2, 1957; children: Nicole, John. *Education:* Budapest Technical University, Ch.E., 1956; University of California, Berkeley, Ph.D., 1960. *Office:* Department of Chemistry, University of California, Berkeley, Calif. 94720.

CAREER: International Business Machines Corp., Yorktown, N.Y., member of research staff at Research Center, 1960-64; University of California, Berkeley, assistant professor, 1964-67, associate professor, 1967-72, professor of chemistry, 1972—, Miller Professor of Chemistry, 1977-78. Principal investigator in Materials and Molecular Research Division of Lawrence Berkeley Laboratory, 1964—. Visiting fellow at Emmanuel College, Cambridge, 1969; Unilever Visiting Professor at University of Bristol, 1971-72; Baker Lecturer at Cornell University, 1977. Chairman of International Conference on Structure and Chemistry of Solid Surfaces, 1968.

MEMBER: American Chemical Society, American Physical Society (fellow), National Academy of Sciences. *Awards, honors:* Guggenheim fellow, 1969-70; Kokes Award from Johns Hopkins University, 1976, for research in surface science; Emmett Award from American Catalysis Society, 1977, for fundamental catalysis; award in surface chemistry from American Chemical Society, 1981, for frontier research in surface chemistry.

WRITINGS: Principles of Surface Chemistry, Prentice-Hall, 1972; *Chemistry in Two Dimensions,* Cornell University Press, 1981. Contributor of more than two hundred fifty articles to scientific journals.

WORK IN PROGRESS: "Continued research in surface science and heterogeneous catalysis."

SIDELIGHTS: Somarjai told *CA:* "The history of the twentieth century should be told by exposing the lives of scientists and by describing the new technologies created by them. Physical scientists are the unsung heroes of our struggles for higher living standards, longer and healthier life and the energy war. I would love to write a history book of this slant but I am much too busy with research and teaching for the time being."

* * *

SOPER, Alexander Coburn 1904-

PERSONAL: Born February 18, 1904, in Chicago, Ill.; son of Alexander Coburn and Bertha (Dunlop) Soper; married Suzanne Townley Smyth, June 15, 1929; children: Suzanne Soper Clohesy, John Dunlop. *Education:* Hamilton College, B.A., 1925; Princeton University, M.F.A., 1929, Ph.D., 1944. *Home:* 1441 Orchard Way, Rosemont, Pa. 19010. *Office:* Institute of

Fine Arts, New York University, 1 East 78th St., New York, N.Y. 10021.

CAREER: Princeton University, Princeton, N.J., instructor in architecture, 1929-30, instructor in art and archaeology, 1935-38; Bryn Mawr College, Bryn Mawr, Pa., associate professor, 1939-48, professor of art history, 1948-62; New York University, New York, N.Y., professor of fine art, 1960—, Jayne Wrightsman Professor, 1971-73. Patten Foundation lecturer at Indiana University, 1968. *Military service:* U.S. Marine Corps Reserve, active duty, 1942-46; became major.

MEMBER: College Art Association of America, American Oriental Society, Association for Asian Studies, Asia Society (member of board of trustees, 1967-73), Japan Society. *Awards, honors:* Rockefeller Foundation fellow in Japan, 1935-38; distinguished humanistic scholar award from American Council of Learned Societies, 1962; L.H.D. from Hamilton College, 1963; distinguished teacher of art history award from College Art Association of America, 1977.

WRITINGS: The Evolution of Buddhist Architecture in Japan, Princeton University Press, 1942, reprinted, Hacker, 1979; (translator) Jo-hsu Kuo, *Experiences in Painting: An Eleventh-Century History of Chinese Painting,* American Council of Learned Societies, 1951; (with Robert Treat Paine) *The Art and Architecture of Japan,* Penguin, 1955, revised edition, 1975; (with Laurence C. Sickman) *The Art and Architecture of China,* Penguin, 1956, 3rd edition, 1968; *Literary Evidence for Early Buddhist Art in China,* Artibus Asiae, 1959.

(Translator) Ch'eng-shih Tuan, *A Vacation Glimpse of the T'ang Temples of Ch'ang-an,* Artibus Asiae, 1960; *Chinese, Korean, and Japanese Bronzes: A Catalogue of the Auriti Collection Donated to Istituto Italiano per il Medio ed Estremo Oriente and Preserved in the Museo nazionale d'arte orientale in Rome,* Istituto Italiano per il Medio ed Estremo Oriente, 1966; *Textual Evidence for the Secular Arts of China in the Period From Liu Sung Through Sui (A.D. 420-618),* Artibus Asiae, 1967; *The ''Jen Shou'' Mirrors* (bound with *The Evolution of the T'ang Lion and Grapevine Mirror,* by Nancy Thompson), Artibus Asiae, 1967; (translator) Terukaza Akiyama and Saburo Matsubara, *Arts of China,* Volume II: *Buddhist Cave Temples,* Kodansha, 1969; (editor of revision and author of foreword) Helen Burwell Chapin, *A Long Roll of Buddhist Images,* Artibus Asiae, 1972; (contributor) Diana Turner, editor, *Chinese, Korean, and Japanese Sculpture: The Avery Brundage Collection, Asian Art Museum of San Francisco,* Kodansha, 1974. Contributor to *Pelican History of Art.* Contributor to art journals. Editor of *Artibus Asiae,* 1958.*

* * *

SOPER, Tony 1939-

PERSONAL: Born January 10, 1939, in Southampton, England; son of Albert E. and Ellaline May (Lythgoe) Soper; married Hilary Brooke (a writer), 1971; children: Timothy, Jack. *Education:* Attended secondary school in Plymouth, England. *Home and office:* 1 Above Town, Dartmouth, Devonshire TQ6 9RG, England.

CAREER: British Broadcasting Corp., Natural History Unit, Bristol, England, film producer, 1960-65. Free-lance writer, filmmaker, and presenter of television programs on natural history. Past chairman of Devonshire Trust for Nature Conservation. *Member:* Royal Society for the Protection of Birds (member of council).

WRITINGS: The Bird Table Book, David & Charles, 1965; (with John Sparks) *Penguins,* Taplinger, 1967; (with Sparks)

Owls, Taplinger, 1970; *The Hungry Bird Book,* Taplinger, 1971 (published in England as *The New Bird Table Book,* David & Charles, 1973); *The Shell Book of Beachcombing,* David & Charles, 1972; *Wildlife Begins at Home,* David & Charles, 1975; *Everyday Birds,* David & Charles, 1976; *Beside the Sea,* BBC Publications, 1979; *Birdwatch,* Webb & Bower, 1982.

Author of film scripts for BBC-TV, including ''The Fulmar,'' ''Shelducks,'' ''Animal Design,'' ''Animal Marvels,'' ''Beside the Sea,'' and ''Wildtrack.''

WORK IN PROGRESS: A film series, ''Birds and Birdwatching,'' with an accompanying book; books on the coast; a bird-watcher's diary.

SIDELIGHTS: Soper commented: ''My main interest is marine natural history, especially coast and estuarine, from the point of view of a filmmaker. As a keen sailor, I also organize bird-watching cruises.'' *Avocational interests:* Books, cooking sausages on driftwood fires, islands.

* * *

SORINE, Stephanie Riva 1954-

PERSONAL: Born March 9, 1954, in Brooklyn, N.Y.; daughter of Alfred Bernard (a corporation president) and Shirley (a fashion coordinator; in showroom sales; maiden name, Bassoff) Silverman; married Daniel S. Sorine (a photographer), July 1, 1977. *Education:* Attended Hunter College of the City University of New York, 1973; studied at School of American Ballet, 1964-70, and Royal Ballet School, 1970-72. *Residence:* New York, N.Y. *Agent:* Carol Masius, 355 East 72nd St., New York, N.Y. 10021.

CAREER: Professional ballet dancer, 1968-75; Royal Opera Company, London, England, dancer, 1970-72; Harkness Ballet, New York City, apprentice, 1973-74; Austrian Ballet, Klagenfurt, Austria, solo dancer, 1974-75; Henry Le Tang's Dance School, New York City, ballet teacher, 1977—; Manya Kahn's Health Salon, New York City, exercise instructor, 1975-78; Anatomy Asylum, Beverly Hills, Calif., teacher of ballet and exercise, 1976-77; Farnworth & Hauer School of Dance, New York City, exercise instructor, 1978; Dance Movement, New York City, teacher of ballet technique, pointe, and exercise, 1978-81; Harkness Ballet School, New York City, teacher of ballet, 1981—. Opera singer; photographers' model; workshop instructor; guest on radio programs.

WRITINGS—With photographs by husband, Daniel S. Sorine: *Dancershoes* (adult), Knopf, 1979; *Imagine That!: It's Ballet* (juvenile), Knopf, 1981; *Our Ballet Class* (juvenile), Knopf, 1981. Author of text for desk diaries and ballet poster.

WORK IN PROGRESS: A jazz dance book, publication by Knopf expected in 1982; a book for young people, tentatively titled *Dollfriends,* publication by Random House expected in 1982.

SIDELIGHTS: In addition to ballet, Stephanie Sorine has studied piano, violin, and eurythmics. She performed as a child dancer in Rudolph Nureyev's choreography of ''The Nutcracker'' and has performed as both singer and dancer in such operas as ''The Bishop of Brindisi'' and ''Falstaff.''

Sorine told *CA:* ''Through my dance books and the classes I teach, I try to make dance less intimidating and more accessible so it can be, as it should, a part of everyone's life. To dance is a glorious way of releasing energy, expressing feelings and moods and communicating stories. Watching dance inspires creativity and expands the imagination.''

BIOGRAPHICAL/CRITICAL SOURCES: Life, November, 1979; New York Times, January 20, 1980; Toronto Star, February 2, 1980; Footwear News, February 11, 1980; Anniston Star, March 29, 1981; Independent Press, September 17, 1980.

*   *   *

SPENCER MEEK, Margaret (Diston) 1925- (Margaret Meek)

PERSONAL: Born January 14, 1925, in Leven, Scotland; daughter of Robert John and Elizabeth Blyth (Ballingall) Meek; married Patrick Downing Spencer (a banker), October 1, 1960; children: Sophie Eleanor, Jonathan Edmund. Education: University of Edinburgh, M.A., 1947; also attended University of Paris. Politics: Liberal. Religion: Anglican. Home: 15 Denbigh Close, London W11 2QH, England. Office: Institute of Education, University of London, London, England.

CAREER: Senior lecturer at University of London, Institute of Education, London, England. Member: International Board on Books for the Young, London Association for the Teaching of English. Awards, honors: Eleanor Farjeon Award for services to women's literature.

WRITINGS—Under name Margaret Meek: Geoffrey Treese, Bodley Head, 1958; Rosemary Sutcliffe, Bodley Head, 1960; (editor with A. Warlow and G. Barlan) The Cool Web: The Pattern of Children's Reading, Bodley Head, 1977; Coming to Know (edited by P. Salman), Routledge & Kegan Paul, 1980; Learning to Read, Bodley Head, 1981. Contributor to newspapers. Review editor of School Librarian.

WORK IN PROGRESS: Longitudinal studies of children with reading difficulties.

SIDELIGHTS: Margaret Spencer Meek wrote: "I am interested in modern studies of literacy, reading, and the relationship of literature to literacy."

*   *   *

SPIEGEL, Ted 1934-

BRIEF ENTRY: Born June 15, 1934, in Newark, N.J. American photojournalist. Spiegel has been a free-lance photojournalist since 1961, with work exhibited at Expo '67. He also worked for Columbia Pictures and Avco Embassy Pictures. He wrote Golden Islands of the Caribbean (Crown, 1972) and Western Shores: Canada's Pacific Coast (McClelland & Stewart, 1975). Address: Laurie Lane, South Salem, N.Y. 10590. Biographical/critical sources: Who's Who in the East, 17th edition, Marquis, 1979.

*   *   *

SPIVAK, John L(ouis) 1897-1981

OBITUARY NOTICE: Born June 13, 1897, in New Haven, Conn.; died September 30, 1981, in Philadelphia, Pa. Journalist and author. Spivak first worked for various New York newspapers as head of news bureaus in Moscow and Berlin. In the 1920's he returned to the United States as an investigative reporter. Spivak exposed underground Nazi groups, the Ku Klux Klan, corrupt mental hospitals and prisons, and robber barons of the steel and coal industries. Spivak's books, such as Georgia Nigger, Plotting American's Pogroms, and A Pattern for American Fascism, examine the bigotry and corruption he uncovered in his reporting. He retired to write his autobiography, A Man in His Time, but after the book's publication in 1967 he abandoned retirement to return to journalism. Among his other books are America Faces the Barricades, Europe Under the Terror, and Honorable Spy. Obituaries and other sources: John L. Spivak, A Man in His Time, Horizon, 1967; American Authors and Books, 1640 to the Present Day, 3rd revised edition, Crown, 1972; Who's Who in America, 39th edition, Marquis, 1976; Chicago Tribune, October 4, 1981.

*   *   *

SPIVEY, Ted R(ay) 1927-

PERSONAL: Born July 1, 1927, in Fort Pierce, Fla.; son of Theodore Roosevelt (a merchant) and Pearl (Sumner) Spivey; married Julia Douglass (a teacher), June 30, 1962; children: Mary Leta, John Andrew. Education: Emory University, A.B., 1949; University of Minnesota, M.A., 1951, Ph.D., 1954. Politics: Democrat. Religion: Episcopalian. Home: 3181 Frontenac Court N.E., Atlanta, Ga. 30319. Office: Department of English, Georgia State University, University Plaza, Atlanta, Ga. 30303.

CAREER: Emory University, Atlanta, Ga., instructor in English, 1954-56; Georgia State University, Atlanta, 1956—, began as instructor, became professor of modern British literature. Military service: U.S. Navy, 1945-46; became seaman first class. Member: Modern Language Association of America, American Association of University Professors, Society for the Study of Southern Literature, South Atlantic Modern Language Association.

WRITINGS: (With Kenneth M. England) A Manual of Style, Foote & Davies, 1961, revised edition, 1964; Religious Themes in Two Modern Novelists, Georgia State University, 1965; The Humanities in the Contemporary South, Georgia State University, 1968; The Renewed Quest, Foote & Davies, 1969; The Coming of the New Man, Vantage, 1971; Journey Beyond Tragedy: A Study of Modern Myth and Literature, University Presses of Florida, 1980; Southern Writers in the Modern City, University Presses of Florida, 1982. Contributor to literature journals. Contributing editor of Studies in the Literary Imagination and International Journal of Symbology.

WORK IN PROGRESS: A City Observed, a collection of poems; Conrad Aiken and Walker Percy.

SIDELIGHTS: Spivey commented: "The chief motivation for my writing, which is mainly about literature, is the search for the underlying basis of all literature, which can be located in the realm of symbol, myth, and ritual. The subject of the hero is vital in any study of literature and in its various connections with lived experience. In my later studies I have tried to take the study of myth and ritual and apply it to studies of man in the modern urban scene in order to make the study of literature more vital and to try to find ways of improving the cultural basis of the modern city. My travels have been very important to me, particularly a trip around the world in 1963, when I studied myth and ritual in many cultures."

*   *   *

SPRINGFIELD, David
See LEWIS, (John) Roy(ston)

*   *   *

SPRINGSTUBB, Tricia 1950-

PERSONAL: Born September 15, 1950, in New York, N.Y.; daughter of Kenneth J. (an insurance manager) and Katherine (Hagerty) Carroll; married Paul Springstubb (a teacher), August 18, 1973; children: Zoe. Education: State University of

New York at Albany, B.A., 1972. *Residence:* Pine Plains, N.Y. 12567. *Address:* c/o Little, Brown & Co., 34 Beacon St., Boston, Mass. 02114.

CAREER: Writer. *Member:* Authors Guild.

WRITINGS: My Minnie Is a Jewel (juvenile), Carolrhoda, 1980; *Give and Take* (young adult novel), Little, Brown, 1981; *The Blueberry Troll* (juvenile), Carolrhoda, 1981; *The Magic Guinea Pig* (juvenile), Morrow, 1982; *Her Own Sweet Own* (young adult novel), Little, Brown, 1982. Contributor of articles and stories to magazines, including *Redbook, McCall's, Woman's Day, Ohio Review,* and *Writer.*

WORK IN PROGRESS: An adult novel.

SIDELIGHTS: Tricia Springstubb commented: "I am still pleased to find myself a writer except, of course, when the work isn't going well. I didn't begin writing until I was twenty-six; until then I'd expected to be a social worker. In a different way than I had imagined, it's what I've become. The 'moral' of all my work so far seems to be the necessity of extending ourselves. Taking risks, letting life surprise you: these seem to me key ingredients of happiness and, happily, of my craft."

*　　*　　*

SPROUL, Barbara Chamberlain 1945-

PERSONAL: Born June 18, 1945, in New York, N.Y.; daughter of Albert Eugene Sproul, Jr., and Dorothy Noyes Kane Evans; married Herb Gardner (a playwright). *Education:* Sarah Lawrence College, B.A., 1966; Columbia University, M.A., 1968, Ph.D., 1972. *Politics:* "Human rights; peace." *Religion:* "Non-affiliated." *Office:* Department of Religion, Hunter College of the City University of New York, 695 Park Ave., New York, N.Y. 10021.

CAREER: Hunter College of the City University of New York, New York, N.Y., assistant professor, 1972-77, associate professor of religion, 1977—, chairman of program in religion, 1973—. *Member:* Amnesty International (member of board of directors, 1971—), American Academy of Religion.

WRITINGS: (Editor) *Primal Myths,* Harper, 1979.

*　　*　　*

SQUIRE, Robin 1937-

PERSONAL: Born April 18, 1937, in Kingston-upon-Thames, England; son of Walter William (a sales director) and Mabel (Floyd) Squire; married Anneliese Bohner, May 5, 1967 (divorced, 1972); children: Natalie Brigitte, Kerry Melanie. *Education:* Attended grammar school in Sale County, England. *Politics:* "Few." *Religion:* Church of England. *Home:* 4 Vernon Dr., Stanmore, Middlesex, England. *Agent:* London Management, 235 Regent St., London W1A 2JT, England.

CAREER: Sales representative in London, England, 1959-67; writer, 1967—. *Military service:* British Army, 1955-59.

WRITINGS: Square One, W. H. Allen, 1968; *A Portrait of Barbara,* St. Martin's, 1978. Author of film scripts, including "The Lion's Share," "And Soon the Rains," "String Horses," and "Gramps." Also author of "Housey-Housey," a play. Writer for television series, including "Kim and Company." Contributor to *She.*

WORK IN PROGRESS: "Hyde," a screenplay of *Dr. Jekyll and Mr. Hyde;* a feature film and subsequent television series; westerns.

SIDELIGHTS: Squire commented: "I was motivated to pursue a writing career because it held a promise of adventure, and I was even less competent and far more unhappy doing anything else. Essentially a 'loner' (as they say), I regard what I do in much the same light as a man setting out on foot across the desert with no water but hoping there might be some oases along the way to keep him going.

"A nonintellectual, un-put-together man, then—easily dominated by weaklings and fools, dismissive of sane advice—I radiated for many years an aura of futility, failure, and insane optimism in the face of seemingly hopeless odds (such as my apparent lack of any talent or flair in the trade that had 'chosen' me). Because of my square-peg mentality, ludicrous shyness, and terror of anyone who represented authority in any form—such as book and script editors—I alienated many such excellent citizens by having no qualities whatever that they could admire or respond to positively. I would send them abusive letters when they rejected my work (always), because I actually really did believe they'd made a terrible mistake in passing me over—denying me, by such blind crassness, access to the public out there hungering to be entertained by me.

"Yet during those destructive times I learned, very slowly, about this loonie whose skin I inhabited—and began to look at other people in more than a superficial way; and was enchanted, awed and aghast to find they were just as baffled, frustrated, vulnerable, and daft as me. This wonderful discovery marked a turning point in my writing, and the characters and worlds that I rather pompously like to create fictionally, because that's the only way I'll ever be boss, took on strange new colors and realities and identities.

"The years of toil across my 'desert,' then—with its paucity of oases—have brought me a profound compassion for fellow beings, because we're all idiots together, really. This naive view is another reason why I'm not famous, but I keep learning and keep trying, so I'll wind up with a ripple of cliches of the kind that have given me such a bad time: 'hang in there,' 'keep moving forward, however tired,' 'for God's sake recognize when you *haven't* got it right,' and 'don't be afraid to be humble and poor, even at the risk of being pitied or despised.'"

*　　*　　*

STAMPFLE, Felice 1912-

PERSONAL: Born July 25, 1912, in Kansas City, Mo.; daughter of Harry J. and Grace (Suiter) Stampfle. *Education:* Washington University, St. Louis, Mo., A.B., 1934, A.M., 1942; further graduate study at Radcliffe College, 1943-45. *Home:* 450 East 63rd St., New York, N.Y. 10021. *Office:* Pierpont Morgan Library, 29 East 36th St., New York, N.Y. 10016.

CAREER: Legal secretary and teacher, 1934-40; City Art Museum, St. Louis, Mo., research assistant, 1942-43; Pierpont Morgan Library, New York, N.Y., curator of drawings and prints, 1945—. *Member:* College Art Association of America, Museums Council of New York, Phi Beta Kappa, Cosmopolitan Club.

WRITINGS: (With Jacob Bean) *The Italian Renaissance,* Metropolitan Museum of Art and Pierpont Morgan Library, 1965; (with Bean) *The Seventeenth Century in Italy,* Metropolitan Museum of Art and Pierpont Morgan Library, 1967; (with others) *Rembrandt: Experimental Etcher,* Museum of Fine Arts (Boston, Mass.), 1969; (with Cara Dufour) *Artists and Writers: Nineteenth and Twentieth Century Portrait Drawings From the Collection of Benjamin Sonnenberg,* Pierpont Morgan Library, 1971; (with Bean) *The Eighteenth Century in Italy,* Metropolitan Museum of Art and Pierpont Morgan Library, 1971; (with Cara D. Denison) *Drawings From the Collection of Lore and Rudolf Heinemann,* Pierpont Morgan Library, 1973; (with Denison) *Drawings From the Collection of Mr. and Mrs. Eugene V. Thaw: Catalogue,* Pierpont Morgan Library, 1975; *Giovanni Battista Piranesi: Drawings in the Pierpont Morgan Library,* Dover, 1978; *Rubens and Rembrandt in Their Century: Flemish and Dutch Drawings of the Seventeenth Century From the Pierpont Morgan Library,* Pierpont Morgan Library, 1979; *Piranesi: Drawings and Etchings at the Avery Architectural Library, Columbia University, New York,* Arthur M. Sacklen Foundation, 1979. Contributor of articles and reviews to art journals. Editor of *Master Drawings,* 1963—.

BIOGRAPHICAL/CRITICAL SOURCES: New York Review of Books, August 16, 1979.*

* * *

STANDISH, Robert 1898(?)-1981

OBITUARY NOTICE: Born c. 1898; died in 1981 in Valbonne, France. Novelist. Standish wrote more than sixty books, including *Singapore Kate, The Story of Mary Lee, The Three Bamboos, Elephant Walk, The Cruise of the Three Brothers,* and *The Silk Tontine.* Obituaries and other sources: *The Author's and Writer's Who's Who,* 6th edition, Burke's Peerage, 1971; *AB Bookman's Weekly,* December 7, 1981.

* * *

STANFORD, Sally 1903-1982
(Mabel Janice Busby, Sally Gump, Marsha Owen)

OBITUARY NOTICE: Born in 1903 in Baker City, Ore.; died of heart failure, February 1, 1982, in Greenbrae, Calif. Madam, politician, and author of her memoirs. Stanford began her career as madam of a San Francisco house of prostitution and hosted such celebrity clientele as Errol Flynn and Humphrey Bogart. In 1949, after police raided her establishment, she opened a restaurant in Sausalito. She ran unsuccessfully for the Sausalito city council five times under the name Marsha Owen, then was elected in 1972 as Sally Stanford. She became Sausalito's mayor in 1976 and served as the city's vice-mayor from 1978 until her death. Her memoirs of life as a madam, *Lady of the House,* appeared in 1966 and became the basis for a television drama of the same title starring Dyan Cannon as Stanford. Obituaries and other sources: *Life,* May 7, 1951; Sally Stanford, *Lady of the House,* Putnam, 1966; *Time,* March 22, 1976; *Women in Public Office: A Biographical Directory and Statistical Analysis,* 2nd edition, Scarecrow, 1978; *Newsweek,* June 19, 1978; *New York Times,* February 2, 1982.

* * *

STANTON, Dorothy
See KAUMEYER, Dorothy

* * *

STANWOOD, Brooks
See KAMINSKY, Howard

* * *

STARK, Gary Duane 1948-

PERSONAL: Born June 27, 1948, in St. Paul, Minn.; son of Albert Carl and Clara (Swanson) Stark; married Mary Galen Thomas (a journalist; in public relations), February 23, 1978.

Education: Hamline University, B.A., 1970; Johns Hopkins University, M.A., 1972, Ph.D., 1974. *Office:* Department of History, University of Texas, Arlington, Tex. 76019.

CAREER: Dalhousie University, Halifax, Nova Scotia, visiting assistant professor of history, 1974-75; University of Texas, Arlington, assistant professor, 1975-81, associate professor of history, 1981—. *Member:* American Historical Association, Conference Group on Central European History, Western Association for German Studies, Southern Historical Association.

WRITINGS: Entrepreneurs of Ideology, University of North Carolina Press, 1981. Contributor to history and German studies journals.

WORK IN PROGRESS: Research on cultural censorship in imperial Germany.

* * *

STEELE, Gordon (Charles) 1892-1981

PERSONAL: Born November 1, 1892, in Exeter, England; died January 4, 1981, in England; son of H. W. (a captain in the Royal Navy) and Selina May (Symonds) Steele. *Education:* Attended secondary school in Ramsgate, England.

CAREER: Royal Navy, career officer, 1909-57, served on submarines, including *Iron Duke,* during World War I, commander of H.M.S. *P63* and *Cornflower,* 1917-18, motor boat commander in coastal raid on Kronstadt Harbor, 1919, captain superintendent of Thames Nautical Training College on H.M.S. *Worcester,* off Greenhithe, 1929-57, naval interpreter of Russian, anti-submarine commander of H.M.S. *Osprey,* and inspector of anti-submarine equipment, 1939-45, retiring as commander. Cadet with Peninsular & Oriental Steamship Navigation Co. Younger brother of Trinity House; freeman of City of London. *Awards, honors*—Military: Mentioned in dispatches, 1915; Victoria Cross, 1919; named honorary captain of Royal Naval Reserve, 1949; fellow of Institute of Navigation, 1951.

WRITINGS: (Editor of revision, with David Wilson-Barker) Wilson-Barker and W. Allingham, *Navigation,* 4th edition (Steele was not associated with earlier editions), 1938; *Electrical Knowledge for the Merchant Navy Officer,* Brown, Son & Ferguson, 1950, 2nd edition published as *Electrical Knowledge for Ship's Officers,* 1954; *The Story of the Worcester,* Harrap, 1962; *To Me God Is Real,* Stockwell, 1974; *About My Father's Business,* Stockwell, 1975; *In My Father's House,* Stockwell, 1976; *Where God Steps In,* privately printed, 1976; *One in All and All in One,* Stockwell, 1977.

OBITUARIES: London Times, January 7, 1981.*

* * *

STEESE, Edward 1902-1981

OBITUARY NOTICE: Born October 2, 1902, in Scarsdale, N.Y.; died August 8, 1981, in Scarsdale, N.Y. Architect, architectural historian, artist, editor, and poet. Steese received his master's degree in architecture from Princeton University in 1927 and established a private architectural practice in 1933. He was influential in the efforts to preserve New York City's historic sites and architecture and compiled *New York Landmarks 1957,* listing and documenting New York's historic structures. Editor of *A Princeton Anthology,* Steese composed several volumes of verse, including *Storm in Harvest and Other Poems, Spring Night,* and *First Snow.* Obituaries and other sources: *Anthology of Magazine Verse for 1926 and Yearbook of American Poetry,* Books for Libraries, 1972; *International Who's Who in Poetry,* 5th edition, 1977; *Who's Who in Amer-*

ica, 40th edition, Marquis, 1978; New York Times, August 12, 1981.

*   *   *

STENIUS, George
See SEATON, George

*   *   *

STEPHEN, Sid   1942-

PERSONAL: Born July 28, 1942, in Halifax, Nova Scotia, Canada; son of Alan and Nora (MacDonald) Stephen; married wife, Carol; children: Brandy Lee, Jillian. Education: University of Alberta, B.A. (magna cum laude), 1972; Royal Military College of Canada, M.A., 1980; Canadian Land Forces Command and Staff College, graduated, 1980. Residence: London, Ontario, Canada.

CAREER: Career officer in Royal Canadian Air Force, worked as based supply officer in London, Ontario, present rank, major. Member: League of Canadian Poets (president, 1979-80). Awards, honors: Poetry prize from Canadian Authors Association, 1977.

WRITINGS: Air One, Bryte Raven, 1971; Beothuck Poems, Oberon Press, 1976; Waiting for the Stones, Oberon Press, 1981.

WORK IN PROGRESS: A collection of short stories; poems.

SIDELIGHTS: Stephen commented: "A poet who is also a military officer is as much of a contradiction as a military officer who is also a poet. I do both to the best of my ability."

*   *   *

STERN, Curt   1902-1981

OBITUARY NOTICE: Born August 30, 1902, in Hamburg, Germany (now West Germany); died after a long illness, October, 1981, in Sacramento, Calif. Geneticist, educator, and author. Stern received a Ph.D. in zoology at the age of twenty-one from the University of Berlin. He then studied at Columbia University, where he made significant contributions to the field of genetics through the study of fruit flies. After teaching at the University of Rochester from 1933 to 1947, Stern became a faculty member of the University of California at Berkeley. He was named professor emeritus at Berkeley in 1970. Influential in his work on the basic mechanisms of heredity, Stern promoted genetics curricula in medical schools. His publications include Principles of Human Genetics and Genetic Mosaics and Other Essays. Obituaries and other sources: Nature, May 11, 1963; Who's Who in America, 39th edition, Marquis, 1976; American Men and Women of Science: The Physical and Biological Sciences, 14th edition, Bowker, 1979; The International Who's Who, Europa, 1980; New York Times, October 31, 1981.

*   *   *

STERNHEIM, (William Adolf) Carl   1878-1942

BRIEF ENTRY: Born April 1, 1878, in Leipzig, Germany (now East Germany); died November 3, 1942, in Brussels, Belgium. German playwright and novelist. Sternheim's ruthless satirization of early twentieth-century German society made him a popular dramatist in his day and marked him as one of modern Germany's leading writers. In his play "Die Hosen" (1910) Sternheim began his attack on the German bourgeoisie, castigating the part of society he saw as smug, materialistic, greedy,

and malicious. He was fearful of the combination of bourgeois traits that he considered a danger to German freedom, but he chose ridicule, rather than outspoken criticism, as his major literary weapon. When Hitler came into power Sternheim's perception was proved accurate. He exiled himself from his homeland in the 1930's, and his work was later banned in Germany. Altogether he wrote a series of eleven social satires, collected in Aus dem buergerlichen Heldenleben (1922). This body of work is characterized by a cynical, expressionistic brevity of speech and puppet-like characters whose grotesque appearances accentuated their ugly behavior and shallow values. He has often been compared to the French playwright Moliere. Biographical/critical sources: Encyclopedia of World Literature in the Twentieth Century, updated edition, Ungar, 1967; McGraw-Hill Encyclopedia of World Drama, McGraw, 1972.

*   *   *

STEVENS, Roger (Bentham)   1906-1980

OBITUARY NOTICE: Born June 8, 1906, in Lewes, Sussex, England; died February 20, 1980, in Thursley, Surrey, England. Diplomat, educator, and author. During his first ten years in British consular service, Stevens served in Argentina, the United States, and Belgium. He distinguished himself in the Foreign Office and assumed various key posts. He was Britain's assistant under-secretary of state in London from 1948 to 1951, ambassador to Sweden from 1951 to 1954, and ambassador to Iran from 1954 to 1958. When promoted to deputy under-secretary in Britain's Foreign Office, Stevens was responsible for diplomatic activity in the Middle East and Africa, devoting much attention to the developing Third World governments. Entering the academic arena in 1963, Stevens became vice-chancellor of Leeds University. He worked successfully with student political activists to draft a new constitution for the university, then retired from his post there in 1970. Stevens was named Knight Commander of St. Michael and St. George in 1954 and Knight Grand Cross of the order in 1964. His book, The Land of the Great Sophy, recognized as a standard work on Iranian history and British diplomatic history, first appeared in 1962; a new edition was published in 1971. Obituaries and other sources: Who's Who in the United Nations and Related Agencies, Arno, 1975; The International Who's Who, Europa, 1978; The International Year Book and Statesmen's Who's Who, Kelly's Directories, 1980; The Annual Obituary 1980, St. Martin's, 1981.

*   *   *

STINCHCOMBE, William   1937-

PERSONAL: Born May 30, 1937, in Farwell, Mich.; son of Homer (a teacher and guidance counselor) and Christine Stinchcombe; married Jean Lovelace (a writer), August 17, 1963; children: Thomas, Marjorie, John. Education: San Francisco State College, B.A., 1960; University of Michigan, M.A., 1962, Ph.D., 1967. Home: 110 Poole Rd., Dewitt, N.Y. 13214. Office: Department of History, 311 Maxwell Hall, Syracuse University, Syracuse, N.Y. 13210.

CAREER: Syracuse University, Syracuse, N.Y., assistant professor, 1967-70, associate professor, 1970-78, professor of history, 1978—, diplomatic editor of "The Papers of John Marshall," 1972-79. Member: American Historical Association, Organization of American Historians. Awards, honors: Grant from American Philosophical Society, 1968-71; fellow of American Council of Learned Societies, 1978-79.

WRITINGS: Revolutionary Politics and Foreign Policy: The French Alliance in the American Revolution, Syracuse University Press, 1969; (editor) *The Papers of John Marshall,* Volume III, University of North Carolina Press, 1979; *The XYZ Affair,* Greenwood Press, 1981. Contributor to history and philosophy journals.

WORK IN PROGRESS: A book dealing with conceptions of American foreign policy in the eighteenth century and how they influenced the writing of the Constitution.

* * *

STINE, Jovial Bob
See STINE, Robert Lawrence

* * *

STINE, Robert Lawrence 1943-
(Jovial Bob Stine)

PERSONAL: Born October 8, 1943, in Columbus, Ohio; son of Lewis (a shipping manager) and Anne (Feinstein) Stine; married Jane Waldhorn (an editorial director of a children's magazine), June 22, 1969; children: Matthew Daniel. *Education:* Ohio State University, B.A., 1965; graduate study at New York University, 1966-67. *Religion:* Jewish. *Home:* 225 West 71st St., New York, N.Y. 10023. *Office:* Scholastic Magazines, 50 West 44th St., New York, N.Y. 10036.

CAREER: Social Studies teacher at junior high schools in Columbus, Ohio, 1967-68; *Junior Scholastic* (magazine), New York City, associate editor, 1969-71; *Search* (magazine), New York City, editor, 1972-75; *Bananas* (magazine), New York City, editor, 1972—.

WRITINGS:—All juveniles; all under name Jovial Bob Stine: *The Absurdly Silly Encyclopedia and Flyswatter,* illustrations by Bob Taylor, Scholastic Book Services, 1978; *How to Be Funny: An Extremely Silly Guidebook,* illustrations by Carol Nicklaus, Dutton, 1978; *The Complete Book of Nerds,* illustrations by Sam Viviano, Scholastic Book Services, 1979; *The Dynamite Do-It-Yourself Pen Pal Kit,* illustrations by Jared Lee, Scholastic Book Services, 1980; *Dynamite's Funny Book of the Sad Facts of Life,* illustrations by Lee, Scholastic Book Services, 1980; *Going Out! Going Steady! Going Bananas!,* photographs by Dan Nelken, Scholastic Book Services, 1980; *The Pigs' Book of World Records,* illustrations by Peter Lippman, Random House, 1980; (with wife, Jane Stine) *The Sick of Being Sick Book,* edited by Ann Durrell, illustrations by Nicklaus, Dutton, 1980; *Bananas Looks at TV,* Scholastic Book Services, 1981; *The Beast Handbook,* illustrations by Taylor, Scholastic Book Services, 1981; (with Jane Stine) *The Cool Kids' Guide to Summer Camp,* illustrations by Jerry Zimmerman, Scholastic Book Services, 1981; *Gnasty Gnomes,* illustrations by Lippman, Random House, 1981; *How to Wash a Duck,* illustrations by Larry Rose, Wanderer Books, 1982; *Don't Stand in the Soup,* illustrations by Nicklaus, Bantam Books, 1982; (with Jane Stine) *Great Boredom Beater Book,* illustrations by Zimmerman, Four Winds Press, 1982.

SIDELIGHTS: Stine told *CA:* "I believe that kids as well as adults are entitled to books of no socially redeeming value. I try to write children's books that are only funny and not helpful in any way. Although my wife and I are not known to very many adults, we most likely have more readers under the age of sixteen than anyone!"

* * *

STOKER, Abraham 1847-1912
(Bram Stoker)

BRIEF ENTRY: Born in 1847 in Dublin, Ireland; died April 20, 1912, in London, England. Irish critic, lecturer, and author. Stoker achieved fame as a writer with the horror novel *Dracula* (1897). His success stemmed from the novelty of his compelling tale of vampires and werewolves, a tale which has remained popular ever since its original publication. Stoker worked as a civil servant, as a drama critic, and later as a lecturer on American life. He also served for many years as manager to actor Sir Henry Irving, an experience that Stoker described in *Personal Reminiscences of Henry Irving* (1906-07). Though he wrote other novels and some nonfiction, it was *Dracula* that brought Stoker lasting recognition. The novel has been adapted for the screen several times; notable among these films is a 1931 production starring Bela Lugosi. *Biographical/critical sources: Cyclopedia of World Authors,* Harper, 1958.

* * *

STOKER, Bram
See STOKER, Abraham

* * *

STONE, Doris (Zemurray) 1909-

PERSONAL: Born November 19, 1909, in New Orleans, La.; daughter of Samuel and Sarah Zemurray; married Roger Thayer Stone, November 22, 1930; children: Samuel, Alison B. (deceased). *Education:* Radcliffe College, A.B., 1930. *Home address:* P.O. Box 295, Madisonville, La. 70447. *Office:* Peabody Museum, Harvard University, Cambridge, Mass. 02138.

CAREER: Tulane University, New Orleans, La., associate archaeologist at Middle American Research Institute, 1930—. Peabody Museum of Archaeology and Ethnology, Harvard University, Cambridge, Mass., research associate, 1954-66, associate in Central American archaeology and ethnology, 1966-71, honorary associate, 1971—. President of board of directors of Escuela Agricola Panamericana, Tegucigalpa, Honduras, 1942-63, honorary chairwoman emeritus, 1980—; president of Committee of Indian Protection, Costa Rica, 1945-66, and board of the National Museum of Costa Rica, 1949-66; president of thirty-third International Congress of Americanists, San Jose, Costa Rica, 1958, member of permanent council, 1958—, chief of Costa Rican Delegation, Vienna, Austria, 1960, Mexico, 1962, Spain, 1964, Argentina, 1966, and Germany, 1968. Vice-president of Academia Costarricense de la Historia, 1956-57. Member of Andean Institute, 1958, board of visitors of Tulane University, 1976—, national council of Museum of the American Indian, New York, N.Y., 1978, board of managers of School of American Research, 1978—, and advisory committee of the Bunting Institute of Radcliffe College, 1978—. Trustee of Radcliffe College, 1941-53, 1968-80, and New Orleans Museum of Art, 1969-74, honorary life trustee, 1976—. Adviser to the Universidad de San Pedro Sula, Honduras, 1980—.

MEMBER: American Anthropological Association (fellow), American Ethnographical Society, American Geographical Society, Society for American Archaeology (fellow), American Ethnological Society (fellow), Sociedad Mexicana de Antropologia, Royal Anthropological Institute of Great Britain and Ireland (fellow), Society of Women Geographers, Societe des Americanistes, Sociedad de Geografia e Historia de Honduras.

AWARDS, HONORS: Citation from Radcliffe College, 1954; comendador of Order of Ruben Dario of Nicaragua, 1955, and Order of Francisco Morazan of Honduras, 1957; named honorary citizen of Honduras, 1956; caballero of Order of Vasco Nunez de Balboa of Panama, 1957; LL.D. from Tulane University, 1957; chevalier of French Legion of Honor, 1958; D.Litt. from Union College, Schenectady, N.Y., 1973.

WRITINGS: Some Spanish Entradas (monograph), Middle American Research Institute, Tulane University, 1932; *Masters in Marble* (monograph), Middle American Research Institute, Tulane University, 1932; *Archaeology of the North Coast of Honduras,* Peabody Museum of Archaeology and Ethnology, Harvard University, 1941, reprinted, Kraus Reprint, 1978; *The Boruca of Costa Rica,* Peabody Museum of Archaeology and Ethnology, Harvard University, 1949, reprinted, Kraus Reprint, 1957; *The Archaeology of Central and Southern Honduras,* Peabody Museum of Archaeology and Ethnology, Harvard University, 1958; *Introduction to the Archaeology of Costa Rica,* Museo Nacional (San Jose, Costa Rica), 1958, revised edition, 1966; *The Talamancan Tribes of Costa Rica,* Peabody Museum of Archaeology and Ethnology, Harvard University, 1962; (editor of reprint) Maria Soltera, *A Lady's Ride Across Spanish Honduras,* University Presses of Florida, 1964; *Pre-Columbian Man Finds Central America: The Archaeological Bridge* (edited by Emily Flint), Peabody Museum of Archaeology and Ethnology, Harvard University, 1972; (editor and contributor with Frederick W. Lange) *Lower Central American Archaeology: Past, Present, and Future,* University of New Mexico Press, 1982.

In Spanish: *Estampas de Honduras* (title means "Pictures of Honduras"), Impresora Galve, 1954; *Biografia de Anastasio Alfaro Gonzalez* (title means "Biography of Anastasio Alfaro Gonzalez"), Junio (San Jose, Costa Rica), 1956; (with Carlos Balser) *Arte precolombino de Costa Rica* (title means "Pre-Columbian Art of Costa Rica"), Museo Nacional (San Jose), 1964, 2nd edition, Ministerio de Cultura Juventud y Deportes, 1973.

Contributor to *Handbook of South American Indians.*

WORK IN PROGRESS: Pre-Columbian Man in Honduras.

BIOGRAPHICAL/CRITICAL SOURCES: Americas, January, 1953.

*   *   *

STONE, Ellery W(heeler)   1894-1981

OBITUARY NOTICE: Born January 14, 1894, in Oakland, Calif.; died September 18, 1981, in Montclair, N.J. Naval officer, communications executive, and author. A lieutenant in the U.S. Navy during World War I, Stone remained in the Naval reserve during the 1920's and 1930's as he pursued a career in communications. He served as president of the Federal Telegraph Corporation from 1924 until 1931 when the company became part of the International Telephone and Telegraph Corporation (ITT). He held various posts within ITT and was a vice-president and director of the corporation from 1947 to 1969. Returning to active naval duty in 1943, Stone was promoted to rear admiral in 1944 and served on the Allied Control Commission in Italy. He received distinguished service medals from the U.S. Navy and U.S. Army, was named Knight Commander of the British Empire and Officer in the French Legion of Honor, and was awarded Italy's Grand Cross of St. Maurice and St. Lazarus, among other honors. His book, *Elements of Radio Communication,* appeared in 1926. Obituaries and other sources: *Who's Who in America,* 39th edition, Marquis, 1976; *The International Who's Who,* Europa, 1980; *New York Times,* September 20, 1981.

*   *   *

STONE, Josephine Rector
See DIXON, Jeanne

STOTT, Raymond Toole
See TOOLE STOTT, Raymond

*   *   *

STRAUCH, Katina (Parthemos)   1946-
(Katina Alexis)

PERSONAL: Surname is pronounced Strauck; born December 24, 1946, in Columbia, S.C.; daughter of James (an economist) and Helen (Sterghos) Parthemos; married John Raymond Walser, June 21, 1969 (divorced, 1976); married Arnold Bruce Strauch (a lawyer and professor), September 10, 1977; children: (first marriage) Raymond. *Education:* Attended University of North Carolina, Greensboro, 1965-67; University of North Carolina, Chapel Hill, A.B., 1969, M.S., 1972. *Religion:* Greek Orthodox. *Home:* C-9 Hagood Ave., Citadel, Charleston, S.C. 29409. *Office:* Library, College of Charleston, Charleston, S.C. 29424.

CAREER: Duke University, Durham, N.C., head librarian at school of nursing, 1972-76, reference and audiovisual librarian at medical library, 1976-77; Trident Technical College, Palmer Campus, Charleston, S.C., head librarian, 1977–78; Low Country Rural Health Education Consortium, Charleston, coordinator of library resources, 1978-79; College of Charleston, Charleston, head of collection development at library, 1979—. *Member:* American Library Association, Medical Library Association, Southeastern Library Association, South Carolina Library Association, Metropolitan Opera Guild. *Awards, honors: Guide to Library Resources for Nursing* was named outstanding academic book by *Choice,* 1980.

WRITINGS: (With Dorothy J. Brundage) *Guide to Library Resources for Nursing,* Appleton, 1980; *Introduction to Bibliography and Research Methods Handbook,* Contemporary Publishing, 1981; *Theory and Design for Bibliographic Education,* Bowker, 1982; (under pseudonym Katina Alexis) *Young Blood* (novel), Pinnacle Books, 1982. Contributor to library journals.

AVOCATIONAL INTERESTS: Travel (England, France, Greece), reading, music, piano.

*   *   *

STRAUS, Dennis
(Ascher/Straus, a joint pseudonym)

PERSONAL: Born in New York, N.Y.; son of Frank and Roslyn (Bassin) Straus. *Education:* Received B.A. from Brooklyn College and M.A. from Columbia University. *Home:* 176 B. 123rd St., Rockaway, N.Y. 11694.

CAREER: Writer, 1973—. *Awards, honors:* Experimental fiction prize from *Panache* magazine, 1973, for story "City/Edge"; Pushcart Prize from Pushcart Press, 1978-79, for excerpt from novel, titled "Even After a Machine Is Dismantled, It Continues to Operate, With or Without Purpose."

WRITINGS—With Sheila Ascher, under joint pseudonym Ascher/Straus: *Letter to an Unknown Woman* (story), Treacle Press, 1980; *The Menaced Assassin* (novel), Treacle Press, 1982; *Woman's Nightmare "A"* (novella), Sun & Moon Press, 1982; *Double/Profile* (story collection), Annex Press, 1982.

Space novels; with Ascher, under joint pseudonym Ascher/Straus: "As It Returns," first presented in New York at Contemporary Arts Gallery of New York University, May, 1975, presented in Philadelphia, Pa., at Y Poetry Center, October 6-31, 1976, presented in Reno at University of Nevada, April, 1977, presented in Kansas City, Mo., at TELIC Exhibition of Art Research Center, May-July, 1977, published in *Seventh Assembling,* 1977, and in *Intermedia,* for forthcoming issue; "The Blue Hangar," first presented in New York at Gateway National Recreation Area, August 2-3, 1975, presented in New York at Twelfth Annual New York Avant Garde Festival, September 27, 1975, published in *Coda,* April/May, 1976, in *Queen Stree T Magazine,* Spring, 1977; and in *Interstate,* 1979; "Twelve Simultaneous Sundays," first presented in New York at Gegenschein Vaudeville Placenter, September 19-December 5, 1976. Also co-publisher with Straus of "Green Inventory," partially published by Ghost Dance Press, winter, 1975-76, and spring, 1977.

Creator of language art gallery installations, including "Language and Structure in North America," Toronto, "Beyond the Page," Philadelphia, "Last Correspondence Show," Sacramento, "First New York Post Card Show," New York, "International Mail Art Exhibition," Northampton, Mass., "TELIC Exhibition," Kansas City, Mo., and "Assembling Exhibition," New York.

Contributor to anthologies, including *Pushcart Prize Anthology III,* Pushcart Press, 1978-79; *Likely Stories,* Treacle Press, 1981.

Contributor to journals, including *Chicago Review, Interstate, Exile, Chouteau Review, Sun and Moon, Chelsea, Paris Review, Beyond Baroque, Gallimafry, Panache, Aspen Anthology, Aphra, Intermedia, Tamarisk, Zone, Annex, Benzene, Fifth Assembling, Ghost Dance, Neoneo Do-Do, Telephone, Sixth Assembling, Gegenschein Quarterly, Source, Eighth Assembling, Margins,* and *Precisely.*

WORK IN PROGRESS: "Several projects are in the works, the most immediate and important of which is a long novel to be published jointly with Sheila Ascher. I'm also working on a volume of 'chamber' texts, minimal narratives that test the essential properties of fiction as well as the deployment of language on the page."

SIDELIGHTS: "There is no question when you read what they write, you're in the presence of Genius," said Hugh Fox of Sheila Ascher and Dennis Straus, the people behind the Ascher/Straus pseudonym. Though they sign both names on their writings, Ascher and Straus do not work together, and they write for different reasons.

In order to produce a work, the authors avoid collaborating in the conventional manner. They share experiences, material, and observations, but one writes while the other criticizes and edits. "We're a Collective," Ascher told the *Cumberland Journal.* "We POOL everything. We don't work together. I don't know what he's doing, he doesn't know what I'm doing, then we put it all together It's very strange." According to Straus, Ascher writes to discover life's guiding principles while he identifies writing with dreaming. "For me reading and writing were like always forms of a dream, a waking dream," he explained. Writing, he continued, is "a matter of finding a way of dreaming—on paper."

Ascher and Straus produce very experimental literature. Perhaps the most conventional in appearance, *The Menaced Assassin,* their first novel in book form, takes place on the plane of magic and dreams. In the novel, a woman tries to make herself into the person she wants to be, an individual who reflects the cultural obsessions generated by contemporary media.

Unlike *The Menaced Assassin,* Ascher and Straus's other creations are space novels, works that use non-written components like photographs or airfields as well as the written word. Using architecture, "public spaces," or huge edifices to structure these "environmental narratives," the authors bring physical and material elements to the works, so reading the novel becomes an active, public experience instead of a private pastime. For instance, "Twelve Simultaneous Sundays" is a space novel written publicly on twelve consecutive Sundays. "Each week a new element was installed," explained Ascher, "and there was no way to read the whole book at any one time, you had to keep coming back." Such an innovation, the authors suggested, could change the style of the novel as a genre. "The space novel," they remarked, "might at some point signal the end of the novel as a bastion of art privacy, of private consumerism, of product purchase, relaxation, nest building, and interior decoration."

Straus told *CA:* "Hannah Arendt wrote that the greatest threat to the continued development of the novel as a high art form is not the popular novel, but the serious, middlebrow novel, novels of big ideas or rhetorical playfulness that don't continue the major adventure of the novel as the ultimate art form. Artificial, philosophical, musical, painterly, architectural, poetic, cinematic—within a ground of storytelling, the novel can be anything, discontinuous and inclusive, not without governing principles, but generating new ones.

"The culture's strictures against adventurous fiction are severe, oddly more severe in regard to the homegrown product than the imported. And nothing less than total commitment, writing as *first* profession no matter what the risks and sacrificies, is sufficient to accomplish anything under such cultural conditions.

"More than anything, I suppose, the literary alliance with Sheila Ascher has been a way (pooling materials, resources, survival techniques as well as more narrowly technical services, editing and the like, though rarely collaborating in the ordinary sense of the word) of maintaining an uncompromising commitment. The only area where Sheila and I are co-authors in anything approaching the traditional sense is in a series of 'environmental' narratives: 'As It Returns,' 'The Blue Hangar,' and 'Twelve Simultaneous Sundays.'

"Along the same lines, a writer should never lose his youthful anger. A certain revulsion for what exists is what makes things new. And this anger or revulsion, beyond any particular theory (all theories advance sets of conventions), the anger and revulsion of the author for what exists and for what is merely assumed in language, structure, and general approach to the reader is what gives moral and aesthetic energy to writing."

BIOGRAPHICAL/CRITICAL SOURCES: Cumberland Journal, spring, 1981; *Zone,* spring/summer, 1981; *Library Journal,* October, 1981; *Chelsea #36,* 1977, *Interstate 12,* 1979.

*   *   *

STRONG, Kenneth William Dobson   1900-1982

OBITUARY NOTICE—See index for *CA* sketch: Born September 9, 1900; died of bronchial failure, January 11, 1982, in Eastbourne, England. Military officer and author of *Intelligence at the Top* and *Men of Intelligence.* Strong, an authority on Germany's war potential, held the post of chief of intelligence on the staff of General Dwight Eisenhower during World War II. As the war ended, Strong served as a British representative during the peace negotiations with Italy and Germany. He later established the Joint Intelligence Bureau, becoming its first director. He also acted as the director of the Defence Intelligence Staff until his retirement in 1966. Strong's services to the British Government were rewarded with a knighthood in 1952. Obituaries and other sources: *London Times*, January 13, 1982; *Newsweek*, January 25, 1982.

* * *

STROOP, Helen E.
See WITTY, Helen E. S(troop)

* * *

STRUNK, (William) Oliver   1901-1980

PERSONAL: Born March 22, 1901, in Ithaca, N.Y.; died February 24, 1980, in Grottaferrata, Italy; son of William, Jr. (a professor of English) and Olivia Emilie (Locke) Strunk; married Mildred Altemose, June 23, 1930 (died, 1973). *Education:* Attended Cornell University, 1917-19, 1927, and University of Berlin, 1927-28.

CAREER: Library of Congress, Washington, D.C., member of staff of music division, 1928-37, chief of music staff, 1934-37; Princeton University, Princeton, N.J., member of faculty, 1937-50, professor of music, 1950-66, professor emeritus, 1966-80. Lecturer at Catholic University of America, 1934-37, Columbia University, summers, 1948, 1952, University of Michigan, summer, 1952, and Harvard University, autumn, 1974-75. Traveling fellow of American Council of Learned Societies, 1934. Member of Institute for Advanced Study, Princeton, 1944, and International Congress for Sacred Music, Rome, Italy, 1950. Member of editorial board of Monumenta Musicae Byzantinae, Copenhagen, Denmark, 1958-60, director, 1961-71.

MEMBER: International Musicological Society, American Academy of Arts and Sciences, American Musicological Society (founder; president, 1959-60; honorary member), Medieval Academy of America (fellow), Royal Musical Association (honorary foreign member), British Academy (corresponding fellow), Royal Danish Academy, Dansk Selskab for Musikforskning, Gesellschaft fuer Musikforschung, Societa Italiana di Musicologia, Vereniging voor Nederlandse Muziekgeschiedenis, Music Library Association (president, 1935-37).

AWARDS, HONORS: Litt.D. from University of Rochester, 1936; Guggenheim fellow, 1951; award from American Council of Learned Societies, 1961, for distinguished scholarship in humanities; Fulbright scholar, 1961-62; L.H.D. from University of Chicago, 1970; National Book Award nomination for *Essays on Music in the Western World*, 1975; Derek Allen Prize from British Academy, 1977.

WRITINGS: The State and Resources of Musicology in the United States: A Survey Made for the American Council of Learned Societies, American Council of Learned Societies, 1932; (translator) Alfred Einstein, *The Italian Madrigal*, Princeton University Press, 1949, reprinted, 1971; (editor) *Source Readings in Music History From Classical Antiquity Through the Romantic Era*, Norton, 1950, reprinted as *Source Readings in Music History*, Volume I: *Antiquity and the Middle Ages*, Volume II: *The Renaissance*, Volume III: *The Baroque Era*, Volume IV: *The Classical Era*, Volume V: *The Romantic Era*, 1965; (editor with Harold Powers) *Studies in Music History*, Princeton University Press, 1968; (editor) Carl Engel, *Music From the Days of George Washington*, AMS Press, 1970; *Essays on Music in the Western World*, Norton, 1974; (with Enrica Follieri) *Triodium Athoum*, 1975; *Essays on Music in*

the Byzantine World, Norton, 1977. Also author of *Specimina notationum antiquorum*, 1966. Contributor to music journals. Editor of journal of American Musicological Society, 1947-48.

SIDELIGHTS: An authority on early Christian music, Strunk helped to establish musicology as a discipline in American universities. He attended Cornell University, where his father, William Strunk, Jr., author of *Elements of Style*, was a professor of English.

OBITUARIES: New York Times, February 26, 1980.*

* * *

STUART, Monroe
See SHAPIRO, Max

* * *

STUEART, Robert D.   1935-

PERSONAL: Born June 1, 1935, in Monticello, Ark.; son of Ira and Lois (Roberts) Stueart; married Marie-Louise Hille; children: Christian, Sabine. *Education:* Southern Arkansas University, B.A.; Louisiana State University, M.S.L.; University of Pittsburgh, Ph.D. *Home:* 43 Avon Rd., Wellesley, Mass. 02181. *Office:* School of Library Science, Simmons College, 300 The Fenway, Boston, Mass. 02115.

CAREER: Employed at University of Colorado, Boulder, 1962-66; Pennsylvania State University, University Park, assistant director for systems and processes at library, 1966-68; University of Pittsburgh, Pittsburgh, Pa., visiting lecturer in library science, 1968-71; College of Librarianship, Wales, visiting lecturer in library science, 1971-72; University of Denver, Denver, Colo., assistant dean of Graduate School of Librarianship, 1972-74; Simmons College, Boston, Mass., dean of School of Library Science, 1975—. *Awards, honors:* Received Melville Dewey Medal, 1980, and Whiting Foundation research grant, 1981.

WRITINGS: The Area Specialist Bibliographer: An Inquiry Into His Role, Scarecrow, 1972; (contributor) *Studies in Library Management*, Volume II, Bengley, 1974; (with John T. Eastlick) *Library Management*, Libraries Unlimited, 1977, 2nd edition, 1980; (with Richard Johnson) *New Horizons for Academic Libraries*, K. G. Saur, 1979; (with George Miller) *Collection Development in Libraries*, Parts A and B, JAI Press, 1980.

Editor: Betty Jo Mitchell, *Cost Analysis of Library Functions: A Total System Approach*, JAI Press, 1978; Lynn S. Smith, *A Practical Approach to Serials Cataloging*, JAI Press, 1978; Norman E. Tanis and David L. Perkins, *China in Books: A Basic Bibliography in Western Language*, JAI Press, 1979; Harold R. Jenkins, *The Management of a Public Library*, JAI Press, 1980; Michael Gabriel and Dorothy Ladd, *The Microfilm Revolution in Libraries*, JAI Press, 1980; Barbara J. Robinson and J. Cordell Robinson, *The Mexican American: A Critical Guide to Research Aids*, JAI Press, 1980; *Academic Librarianship—Yesterday, Today and Tomorrow*, Neal-Schuman, 1982; *Information Services in the 80's*, JAI Press, 1982.

Contributor to *Encyclopedia of Library and Information Sciences*. Contributor to library journals.

SIDELIGHTS: Stueart told *CA:* "Management of information is a primary challenge facing society as it moves into the twenty-first century. For librarians/information scientists that is a unique challenge since our profession plays a key role in the information transfer process. Two important areas are: (1) collection development, including in-house development and cooperation with other units through mechanical and other processes; and (2) management of all resources, both material and personnel, to achieve the primary goals. Those areas are of greatest interest to me as an educator charged with preparing future professionals to address those issues.''

*   *   *

STUECK, William Whitney, Jr. 1945-

PERSONAL: Born May 10, 1945, in New London, Conn.; son of William Whitney (in small business; an engineer) and Philena (a musician; maiden name, Knox) Stueck; married Patricia O'Connell (a teacher), June 17, 1967; children: Whitney Todd, Kendra Sanderson. *Education:* Springfield College, B.S., 1967; Queens College of the City University of New York, M.A., 1971; Brown University, Ph.D., 1977. *Office:* Department of History, Purdue University, West Lafayette, Ind. 47906.

CAREER: New College of the University of South Florida, Sarasota, visiting assistant professor of history, 1977-78; Syracuse University, Syracuse, N.Y., postdoctoral fellow, 1978-79; University of Georgia, Athens, lecturer in history, 1979-81; Purdue University, West Lafayette, Ind., assistant professor of history, 1981—. *Member:* American Historical Association, Society for Historians of American Foreign Relations.

WRITINGS: The Road to Confrontation: American Policy Towards China and Korea, 1947-1950, University of North Carolina Press, 1981.

WORK IN PROGRESS: The Diplomacy of the Korean War, for University of North Carolina Press; research for *Richard Russell, the Senate, and American National Security Policy.*

*   *   *

SUMMERS, Ian 1939-

PERSONAL: Born September 29, 1939, in Paterson, N.Y.; son of Morris (a textile jobber) and Muriel (Popkins) Summers; married Rochelle Osur (a psychotherapist), July 8, 1963; children: Shaun (daughter), Amy. *Education:* University of Bridgeport, B.S., 1961; also attended Montclair State College, 1962-63, and New York University, 1969. *Home:* 297 Warwick Ave., Teaneck, N.J. 07666. *Office:* Summers Productions, Inc., 595 Madison Ave., New York, N.Y. 10022.

CAREER: Art teacher at public schools in Wayne, N.J., 1961-63; American School in London, London, England, art teacher, 1963-64; Lightolier (lighting fixtures company), Jersey City, N.J., in merchandising, 1964-65; associated with Applied Concepts (producers of industrial films), New York City, 1965-66; associated with Gordon Crowe Productions (film producers), New York City, 1967-68; associated with Farsight Group (research and development firm), New York City, 1968-69; Beaumont-Bennett (advertising agency), New York City, creative director, 1969-70; Waring & La Rosa (advertising agency), New York City, art director, 1970-72; Leber Katz Partners (advertising agency), creative director, 1972-74; Ballantine Books, Inc., New York City, vice-president and art director, 1974-78; Summers Productions (book packagers), New York City, president, 1978—. Member of faculty at Fashion Institute of Technology, 1973, Parsons School of Design, 1977-78, and School of Visual Arts; editorial consultant to Bantam Books, Inc., 1979-81.

MEMBER: Society of Illustrators. *Awards, honors:* Art direction awards include gold medal from Society of Illustrators; book award from American Institute of Graphic Arts; nomi-

nated for American Book Award, 1979, for *Barlowe's Guide to Extraterrestrials.*

WRITINGS: Yearbook Book, Ballantine, 1976; *Nosemasks,* Workman Publishing, 1977; (editor) *Tomorrow and Beyond,* Workman Publishing, 1978; *The Art of the Brothers Hildebrandt,* Ballantine, 1979; (with Barlowe) *Barlowe's Guide to Extraterrestrials,* Workman Publishing, 1979; (with Difate) *Difate's Catalog of Science Fiction Hardware,* Workman Publishing, 1980; *Cattle Mutilations: The Anatomy of a Phenomenon,* Bantam, 1981; *The Book of Knights,* Bantam, 1981.

WORK IN PROGRESS: Sportsman, a novel; *The Joy of Depression,* a parody.

SIDELIGHTS: Summers wrote: "I have designed over two thousand books, and the books and calendars I have produced include *The Muppet Movie Book, The Dallas Family Album,* and 'The Dallas Cowboy Cheerleaders Calendar.'

"I left Ballantine to start Summers Productions, a book packaging company. We think up book concepts and develop them. Or someone brings us an idea and we develop it together. Or someone brings us a complete manuscripts and we function as agents. Or a publisher has an idea and presents it to us to develop.

"Many of our projects are visually oriented and we are starting to get involved in investigative journalism and film production. We represent about thirty writers and artists.

"I have lived and traveled in Europe. I continue to paint. I was involved in men's consciousness-raising groups for several years. I have appeared on more than seventy-five television and radio shows throughout the United States and lecture at college on subjects that include art careers and creative problem-solving.''

*   *   *

SUSLOV, Alexander 1950-

PERSONAL: Born April 18, 1950, in Moscow, U.S.S.R.; came to United States, 1976; son of Vasiliy Ivanovich (a radio technician) and Eleanora Mikhailovna (a laboratory assistant; maiden name, Znutas) Suslov; married Eugenia Dyrda (a language instructor), June 17, 1971; children: Philip, Katherine, Alexandra. *Education:* Attended Moscow Literary Institute, 1972-75, and Georgetown University, 1979-81. *Religion:* Russian Orthodox. *Home:* 3535 Cornell Rd., Fairfax, Va. 22030. *Agent:* Ardis Publishers, 2901 Heatherway, Ann Arbor, Mich. 48104.

CAREER: Moscow Teacher's Institute, Moscow, U.S.S.R., editor, 1973-74; Writer's Union, Moscow, literary secretary, 1975; worked as clerk, carpenter, and electrician in Sea Cliff, N.Y., 1976-79; Transemantics, Inc., Washington, D.C., translator, 1979-81; Department of State, Washington, D.C., language instructor, 1980-81; writer.

WRITINGS: Loosestrife City (novel), translated by David Lapeza, Ardis, 1980; *Swarm of Memory* (novel), Ardis, 1982.

WORK IN PROGRESS: Two screenplays, "Leonid" and "Siberian Plot"; a dissertation, *Crisis of Socialist Realism in Soviet Literature,* completion expected in 1982.

SIDELIGHTS: Suslov's novel *Loosestrife City* has been described by critics as "fantastical" and "frightening." The *Los Angeles Times*'s Edward Condren wrote that "a specific story does not interest the author as much as the death toward which everything presses." He added: "Eventually the distinction between life and death vanishes completely, as corpses come and go. Finally, no one really cares, for the effort needed to make Russia's social experiment succeed has made life itself harder to endure than any loss of life.'' In *World Literature Today,* Jo Ann Bailey wrote that *Loosestrife City* "indicts in particular unexposed or unpunished cruelty, whether mass executions directed from above, or the comparatively mundane persecution of one's neighbor in order to obtain his apartment.'' She declared, ''In probing the monumental, quasi-religious symbols through which Soviet authorities portray both themselves and their vision of the world, Suslov has often found a deeper, more authentic resonance that turns these symbols against their creators.'' Bailey called Suslov's vision ''pessimistic.''

Suslov told *CA:* ''All my works have been written on a theme extremely disadvantageous for any Russian emigre writer—Russia. Not containing sensational documents smuggled across the border, they blend invisibly among hundreds of other works with the same theme. My first two novels were not intended to become entertaining best-sellers, nor could they ever be considered a rekindling of a great classical tradition. I write about strange misfortunes in the central 'zone' (polosa) of Russia, and just as this same word also means 'period' in my native tongue, my writings draw deeply from the Russian period of my life.

''My second novel explores the conclusion that a great deal of these misfortunes were born of the slogan 'equality'—and philosophy that idealized equality of welfare turned out to be less significant for real life than its neglected part, equality of misfortune.

''Indeed, such a theme is not very pleasant and I am not planning to let it haunt me forever. New plots already beckon me through my American window. Someday I shall lay my Russian theme to rest in a heavy book, like a coffin, and bury it. I shall try to forget it like an old shrew and fall in love with a new passion, prettier, and, hopefully, much less painful.''

BIOGRAPHICAL/CRITICAL SOURCES: Los Angeles Times, August 31, 1980; *Saturday Review,* September, 1980; *Washington Star,* October 19, 1980; *World Literature Today,* spring, 1981.

* * *

SUSLOV, Mikhail Andreyevich 1902-1982

OBITUARY NOTICE: Born November 21, 1902, in Shakhovskol, Simbirsk (now Ulyanovsk), Russia (now U.S.S.R.); died of a stroke, January 25, 1982; buried next to Joseph Stalin, beside the Kremlin Wall. Soviet Communist party leader and editor of *Pravda* from 1949 to 1950. Mikhail Suslov, protege of Joseph Stalin, rose swiftly in the ranks of the Soviet Communist party hierarchy to become its chief ideologue. Under Stalin, Suslov served as chairman of the Central Committee Bureau for Lithuania, ''a job he carried out with complete ruthlessness involving the deportation and death of thousands of Lithuanians,'' said the *London Times.* Suslov held major roles in other Stalin-directed purges that led to the deaths of some 20 million people between 1931 and 1953. After Stalin died in 1953, Suslov retained his membership in the ruling elite under Stalin's successor, Nikita Khrushchev, and later under Leonid Brezhnev. Though he opposed many of Khrushchev's policies, Suslov supported Brezhnev's and, according to *Time,* he ''could also be counted upon to supply the ideological rationale for such demonstrations of force as the Soviet invasion of Czechoslovakia in 1968 and the military occupation of Afghanistan in 1979.'' Suslov was active in the suppression of Poland's Solidarity movement, denouncing Western interference in Poland and encouraging Polish authorities to establish martial law in their country, which they

did in December of 1981. Had he outlived Brezhnev, Suslov was expected to oversee the transition of power from Brezhnev to Brezhnev's successor. Suslov's death left the smoothness of that eventual transition less certain. *On the Roads of the Construction of Communism,* a two-volume collection of Suslov's speeches, appeared in 1977. Obituaries and other sources: *Current Biography,* Wilson, 1957; *International Who's Who,* Europa, 1978; *London Times,* January 27, 1982; *New York Times,* January 27, 1982; *Time,* February 8, 1982.

* * *

SUTHERLAND, Efua (Theodora Morgue) 1924-

PERSONAL: Born June 27, 1924, in Cape Coast, Ghana; married William Sutherland (an educator), 1954; children: three. *Education:* Earned B.A. from Homerton College, Cambridge; attended School of Oriental and African Studies, London, and University of Cape Coast, Ghana. *Residence:* Legon, Ghana. *Agent:* c/o Longman Group, Longman House, Burnt Mill, Harlow, Essex CM20 2JE, England. *Office:* c/o Institute of African Studies, University of Ghana, Legon.

CAREER: Playwright, producer, director, and writer of children's stories. Teacher in Ghana, 1951-54. Founding director of Experimental Theatre Players (now Ghana Drama Studio), Accra, 1958—. Co-founder (with husband, William Sutherland) of school in Trans-Volta region of upper Ghana. Founder of Ghana Society of Writers (now University of Ghana Writers Workshop), Legon. Founding director of Kusum Agoromba (children's touring theatre group) at University of Ghana School of Drama, Legon.

WRITINGS—Plays: *Edufa* based on the play *Alcestis,* by Euripedes; produced in Accra at Ghana Drama Studio, 1962), Longmans, Green, 1967, published in *Plays From Black Africa,* edited by Fredric M. Litto, Hill & Wang, 1968; *Foriwa* (three-act; produced in Accra at Ghana Drama Studio, 1962), Ghana State Publishing Corporation, 1962, Panther House, 1970; *Vulture! Vulture! and Tahinta: Two Rhythm Plays* (juvenile), Ghana Publishing House, 1968, Panther House, 1970; *The Marriage of Anasewa: A Storytelling Drama* (one-act; first produced in Accra, Ghana, September, 1971), Longman, 1975; ''Anase and the Dwarf Brigade'' (juvenile; based on *Alice and Wonderland,*) first produced in Cleveland at Karamu House Theatre, February 5, 1971.

Other: *Playtime in Africa* (poems for children; photographs by Willis E. Bell), Brown, Knight, & Truscott, 1960, Atheneum, 1962; *The Roadmakers* (travel; photographs by Bell), Ghana Information Services, 1961; *The Original Bob: The Story of Bob Johnson, Ghana's Ace Comedian* (photographs by Bell), Educational Publications, 1970.

Also author of radio plays, including ''Odasani'' (based on *Everyman*), ''The Pineapple Child'' (a fantasy), ''Nyamekye'' (music and dance), and ''Anansegoro: You Swore an Oath'' (one-act). Contributor of poems and plays to various periodicals. Co-founder of *Okyeame* magazine, Accra.

SIDELIGHTS: Brought up in the Ghanaian city of Cape Coast, Sutherland was isolated from the traditional folk culture of her country's rural areas. Her goal has since been to discover that which is uniquely Ghanaian and to convey these traditional elements through her writing, uniting them with modern themes and techniques.

In addition, Sutherland has sought to unify Ghana through the preservation of national art forms. To this end, she has designed open-air theatres that are well suited for the performance of traditional story-telling and of contemporary drama as well.

Sutherland's own writing helps to preserve national art forms by incorporating traditional Ghanaian dramatic techniques such as story-telling and audience participation into her poems and plays.

Sutherland's plays, often based on traditional African folklore, are heavily sight-and sound-oriented. They emphasize rhyme, rhythm, music, dance, and spectator response, and best achieve their effect in live or broadcast performance. Consequently, much of Sutherland's work is not represented in print.

Sutherland writes for children in both English and Akan, a native Ghanaian language, as part of her efforts to promote a bilingual society in Ghana. Fearing that the language problem in Ghana will eventually result in the adoption of English as the official national language, Sutherland urges bilingual education for all children in both elementary and secondary schools.*

*   *   *

SUTHERLAND, Lucy Stuart   1903-1980

OBITUARY NOTICE—See index for *CA* sketch: Born June 21, 1903, in Geelong, Victoria, Australia; died August 20, 1980, in Oxford, England. Historian, educator, and author. Sutherland was affiliated with Oxford University for most of her career, serving as principal of Lady Margaret Hall for more than twenty-five years. During World War II she also held a post with the Board of Trade and later served on the United Nations Relief and Rehabilitation Administration. Sutherland's books, which explore the economics and politics of the eighteenth century, include *A London Merchant, 1695-1776, The East India Company in Eighteenth Century Politics,* and *The Correspondence of Edmund Burke.* She also wrote *The University at Oxford in the Eighteenth Century.* Obituaries and other sources: *The Annual Obituary 1980,* St. Martin's, 1981.

*   *   *

SUTRO, Alfred   1863-1933

BRIEF ENTRY: Born August 7, 1863, in London, England; died September 11, 1933, in Surrey, England. British translator and playwright. One of the most popular writers of Edwardian England, Sutro excelled at drama and light comedy. His most popular play, ''The Walls of Jericho'' (1904), was characteristic of his talent for structure, plot, narrative, and the creation of realistic characters. His career proceeded in an unusually businesslike and premeditated manner. Sutro devoted his youthful energies to amassing enough of an industrial fortune to retire at the age of thirty to write plays. He turned out one slick, popular work after another, averaging at least one a year. His play ''The Perplexed Husband'' (1911) dealt with the contemporary feminist movement. He ended his career with an autobiography, *Celebrities and Simple Souls* (1933). Though his plays remained fashionable throughout his life and could not be attacked for any fault of structure or style, critics were often unable to find a message in his work or any motivation beyond a desire for financial success. Sutro's critical reputation was cemented, instead, by his translations of virtually all the work of his friend Maurice Maeterlinck. *Biographical/critical sources: Twentieth Century Authors: A Biographical Dictionary of Modern Literature,* H. W. Wilson, 1942.

*   *   *

SUTTON, John L(awrence)   1917-

PERSONAL: Born June 20, 1917, in Zanesville, Ohio; son of James C. (in business) and Louise (Derwacter) Sutton; married

Theresa Brunner, October, 1950; children: John Lawrence, Jr., Thomas J., Anne L. *Education:* University of Notre Dame, B.A., 1939, M.A., 1940; University of Geneva, Dr. es Sciences Politiques, 1949. *Home:* 10255 North Morrison Rd., Dresden, Ohio. 43821.

CAREER: U.S. Air Force, 1944-71, combat fighter pilot and staff officer in European theater, 1944-46, assistant professor of history at Minot State College in Minot, N.D., 1946-47, intelligence staff officer in Washington, D.C., and Wiesbaden, West Germany, 1949-55, assistant air attache at U.S. embassy in Bonn, West Germany, 1955-57, associate professor of history at U.S. Air Force Academy in Colorado, 1957-61, staff officer in Washington, D.C., 1961-65, research associate at Institute for Strategic Studies in London, England, 1965-66, U.S. national military representative at Supreme Headquarters, Allied Power Europe (SHAPE) in Paris, France, and Casteau, Belgium, 1966-68, Reserve Officers Training Corps (ROTC) professor at University of Kentucky, Lexington, 1968-71, retiring as colonel, 1971; University of Pittsburgh at Johnstown, Johnstown, Pa., associate professor of history, 1971-81. Writer. *Member:* International Institute for Stategic Studies, American Historical Association.

WRITINGS: The King's Honor and the King's Cardinal, University Press of Kentucky, 1980. Contributor to European studies and military affairs journals.

*   *   *

SWAYBILL, Roger E(lliot)   1943-

PERSONAL: Born March 3, 1943, in New York, N.Y.; son of Bertram (a dress manufacturer) and Florence (an apparel buyer; maiden name, Temmler) Swaybill; married Marion Lear (a writer and television news producer), December 18, 1966; *Education:* Yale University, B.A. (cum laude), 1964; *Politics:* ''Liberal Democrat (still).'' *Religion:* Jewish. *Residence:* New York, N.Y. *Agent:* Jonathan Dolger, 49 East 96th St., New York, N.Y. 10028; and Harold Cohen, 9200 Sunset Blvd., Los Angeles, Calif. 90069.

CAREER: United Artists Pictures, New York, N.Y., executive trainee and assistant story editor, 1964-66; writer. *Member:* Writers Guild of America (East), Yale Club, East Hampton Tennis Club. *Awards, honors:* Writers Guild award nomination for best adaptation of a dramatic feature film for television, 1980, for ''The Lathe of Heaven.''

WRITINGS: ''Breaking Point'' (screenplay), Twentieth Century-Fox, 1976; *Threads* (novel), Delacorte, 1980; ''The Lathe of Heaven'' (teleplay; adapted from the novel by Ursula Le Guin), Public Broadcasting Service, 1980; ''Porky's'' (screenplay), Twentieth Century-Fox, 1981. Also author of unproduced screenplays, including ''The Bartender,'' ''The Shrink,'' ''The Fuzz and the Fence,'' and ''Meet Me at Bloomie's.''

WORK IN PROGRESS: A political novel about a Justice Department coverup of the assassination of America's foremost consumer advocate, publication by Avon expected in 1982; a ''highly secret novel,'' publication by Bantam expected in 1983; two screenplays.

SIDELIGHTS: Swaybill told *CA:* ''I am not conscious of possessing a personal cosmology. If there is a view of the world in my writing, it's spontaneous, inadvertent, and not perceptible to me. I don't approach the writing of a novel or screenplay by digging within myself. Rather, I respond to an external stimulus—something I've read about, heard about, or best of all, observed firsthand. I'm drawn to stories situated in the present or recent past, or stories that can be projected into the near future. I'm also more interested in people and their relationships with one another than I am with events, though when I write for the screen I'm obliged to remember that film requires personal relationships to be expressed visually and, to a substantial degree, through action.

"At this point in my career, I see myself as part sponge, part filter. I absorb everything I can about individuals and circumstances which compel me, and then I pass my observations along to the reader or viewer. I'm essentially a storyteller.

"I haven't confined my writing to a genre, and I never intend to. I want to feel unencumbered to react to whatever around me may capture my interest. Even if my political thriller should be a huge success, I would be disinclined to repeat that mode in the near future. The novel for Bantam and two screenplays are already on my agenda, and they have little in common with things I've written recently and nothing in common with one another. (It's curious that as a screenwriter my disposition toward diversity is seen as a virtue, while as a novelist my unpredictability is perceived as a debit.)"

AVOCATIONAL INTERESTS: "The preeminent one is lending my wholehearted support to my wife as she pursues her own career endeavors. Second is my obsessive love of tennis, and my pursuit of the perfect topspin forehand (after which will come the perfect topspin backhand, followed by the perfect serve and the, at least, mediocre volley). As for travel, my only interest is the 105 miles between Manhattan and East Hampton, the one place in the world which—at least for this time in my life—provides me with a sense of serenity."

BIOGRAPHICAL/CRITICAL SOURCES: Los Angeles Times Book Review, January 1, 1981.

*   *   *

SWEENEY, Amin   1938-

PERSONAL: Born December 13, 1938, in London, England; came to the United States in 1977; son of Louis Michael (in business) and Mary Patricia (a customs officer; maiden name, Howard) Sweeney; separated; children: Mubin (son), Maria. *Education:* London School of Oriental and African Studies, Ph.D., 1970. *Residence:* Richmond, Calif. *Office:* Department of South and Southeast Asian Studies, University of California, Berkeley, Calif. 94720.

CAREER: Teacher of literature at a private school in Kelantan, Malaysia, 1960-64; tutor to the crown prince of Kelantan in Malaysia, 1963-64; National University of Malaysia, Kuala Lumpur, assistant professor, 1970-73, associate professor of Malay, 1973-77; University of California, Berkeley, professor of South and Southeast Asian studies, 1977—. Conducted research in Southeast Asia, 1968-70; visiting professor at Universiti Sains Malaysia, 1980. *Military service:* British Army, Royal Army Educational Corps, 1958-60; became sergeant. *Member:* Royal Asiatic Society, Royal Institute of Linguistics and Anthropology (Netherlands). *Awards, honors:* Grant from Japan Foundation, 1976-77.

WRITINGS: Malay Shadow-Puppets, British Museum, 1972; *The Ramayana and the Malay Shadow-Play,* National University of Malaysia, 1972; (with William P. Malm) *Studies in Malaysian Oral and Musical Traditions,* University of Michigan Press, 1974; (with Nigel Phillips) *The Voyages of Mohamed Ibrahim Munshi,* Oxford University Press, 1975; (editor) *The Tarikh Datuk Bentara Luar Johor,* Center for South and Southeast Asia Studies, University of California, Berkeley, 1980; *Authors and Audiences in Traditional Malay Literature* (monograph), Center for South and Southeast Asia Studies,

University of California, Berkeley, 1980; *Reputations Live On An Early Malay Autobiography,* University of California Press, 1980.

Co-author of "The Malay Shadow Play," a film released by Centre for East Asian Cultural Studies and United Nations Educational, Scientific & Cultural Organization, 1976. Contributor to literature and folklore journals.

WORK IN PROGRESS: A book on orality and literacy in Southeast Asia, publication expected in 1982.

SIDELIGHTS: Sweeney wrote: "I first went to Southeast Asia when I was in the army. I then lived in Malay society for over twenty years and I am now a citizen of Malaysia. I am particularly interested in the interaction between Malay-Indonesian and Western cultures and in observing how Western perceptions of Southeast Asian cultures have influenced the ways in which Southeast Asians look at themselves. My own experiences have caused me to become something of a cultural schizophrenic."

*   *   *

SWERDLOW, Amy (Miriam) G(alstuck)   1923-

PERSONAL: Born January 20, 1923, in New York, N.Y.; daughter of Joseph J. and Esther (Rodner) Galstuck; married Stanley H. Swerdlow, November 27, 1949; children: Joan, Ezra, Lisa, Thomas. *Education:* New York University, B.A., 1963; Sarah Lawrence College, M.A., 1973. *Home:* 7 West 81st St., New York, N.Y. 10024. *Office:* Department of History, Sarah Lawrence College, Bronxville, N.Y. 10708.

CAREER: University of Wisconsin Press, Madison, editorial assistant, 1947-48; A. A. Wynn Publications, New York, N.Y., book production designer and manager, 1948-49; Sarah Lawrence College, Bronxville, N.Y., professor of women's and American history, 1981—, associate director of women's studies program, 1973-76, director of summer institute for integration of women's history into the high school curriculum, 1976. Director of American Historical Association's Institutes for Women's History in Secondary Schools, 1976-79. Member of reprints advisory committee and board of directors of Feminist Press. Founder of Women Strike for Peace; member of executive committee of Jeanette Rankin Brigade, 1968, and Columbia University seminar on women and society, 1980-81; chairperson of Women's Emergency Coalition, 1969; delegate to National Women's Conference, 1977. *Member:* American Historical Association, Organization of American Historians, Institute for Research in History, Berkshire Conference of Women Historians.

WRITINGS: (Editor and contributor) *Household and Kin: Families in Flux,* Feminist Press, 1980; (editor) *Sex, Race, Class, and the Dynamics of Social Control,* G. K. Hall, 1982. Contributor to journals, including *Women's Studies.* Editor of *Memo* of Women Strike for Peace, 1969-72.

WORK IN PROGRESS: History of Women Strike for Peace.

SIDELIGHTS: Swerdlow told *CA:* "My major interest as a teacher, scholar, writer, and social activist is in the history of women in movements against war and social injustice. I focus particularly on how participation in such movements leads women to take stock of their own status and their own powerlessness to influence human destiny. How this leads to a new consciousness and a political program aimed at bringing about the emancipation of women is an important area of study for those who want to learn from the past to understand the present and improve the future."

SWINBURNE, Algernon Charles   1837-1909

BRIEF ENTRY: Born April 5, 1837, in London, England; died of pneumonia, April 10, 1909, in Putney, England; buried in Bonchurch, Isle of Wight. British poet and critic. Swinburne's success as a lyrical poet came with the dramatic work *Atalanta in Calydon* (1865). Its recreation of the form of Greek tragedy and the musical power of its verse made it an immediate and lasting success. Swinburne's attacks on Christianity and conventional morality shocked the sensibilities of Victorian England, as did his masochistic and carefree life-style. Such books of verse as *Poems and Ballads* (1866) were vilified by readers of the day as little more than an affront to morality and good taste. But critics have agreed that his strongest and most appealing poems were written in his frenzied early years; he lived a much more subdued life after a near-fatal collapse in 1879. The relaxed morality of later years lessened the shock of his work, and at the same time more critics began to appreciate his extraordinary lyrical power, nearly hypnotic at times, his vigorous rhyme, and his unbridled imagination. *Biographical/critical sources: Cyclopedia of World Authors,* Harper, 1958; Robert L. Peters, *The Crowns of Apollo, Swinburne's Principles of Literature and Art: A Study in Victorian Criticism and Aesthetics,* Wayne State University Press, 1965; *The McGraw-Hill Encyclopedia of World Biography,* McGraw, 1973.

*   *   *

SYMONDS, John

PERSONAL—Agent: c/o Gerald Duckworth Ltd., The Old Piano Factory, 43 Gloucester Crescent, London NW1 7DY England. *Awards, honors: The Magic Currant Bun* was chosen as one of the best illustrated children's books of 1952 by the *New York Times.*

WRITINGS—Novels: *The Lady in the Tower,* Chapman & Hall, 1955; *The Bright Blue Sky,* Chapman & Hall, 1956; *A Girl Among Poets,* Chapman & Hall, 1957; *The Only Thing That Matters,* Unicorn Press, 1960, Horizon, 1961; *Bezill: A Novel,* Unicorn Press, 1962; *Light Over Water,* Unicorn Press, 1963; *With a View on the Palace,* Baker, 1966; *The Hurt Runner,* Baker, 1968, John Day, 1969; *Prophecy and the Parasites: A Novel,* Duckworth, 1973, Braziller, 1975; *The Shaven Head: A Novel,* Duckworth, 1974; *Letters From England,* Duckworth, 1975; *The Child: Prologue to an Earthquake,* Duckworth, 1976.

Plays: "Sheila," first produced in London, England, 1953; *The Bicycle Play* [and] *The Winter Forest,* Duckworth, 1976. Also author of "The Other House," and "I, Having Dreamt, Awake."

Juveniles: *William Waste,* Sampson, Low, Marston & Co., 1947; *The Magic Currant Bun,* Lippincott, 1952; *Travellers*

Three, Lippincott, 1953; (with Gerard Hoffnung) *The Isle of Cats,* Dobson, 1955; *Away to the Moon,* Lippincott, 1956; *Lottie,* Bodley Head, 1957; *Elfrida and the Pig,* Harrap, 1959, Watts, 1960; *Dapple Gray: The Story of a Rocking-Horse,* Harrap, 1962; *The Story George Told Me,* Harrap, 1963, Pantheon, 1964; *Tom and Tabby,* Universe Books, 1964; *Grodge-Cat and the Window Cleaner,* Pantheon, 1965; *The Stuffed Dog,* Dent, 1967; *Harold: The Story of a Friendship,* Dent, 1973.

Other: *The Great Beast: The Life of Aleister Crowley,* Rider, 1951, Roy, 1952, revised edition published as *The Great Beast: The Life and Magick of Aleister Crowley,* Macdonald, 1971; *The Magic of Aleister Crowley,* Muller, 1958; *Madame Blavatsky, Medium and Magician,* Odhams, 1959, published as *The Lady With the Magic Eyes: Madame Blavatsky, Medium and Magician,* Yoseloff, 1960; *Thomas Brown and the Angels: A Study in Enthusiasm,* Hutchinson, 1961; (editor with Kenneth Grant) *The Confessions of Aleister Crowley: An Autohagiography,* abridged edition, Cape, 1969, Bantam, 1971; (editor with Grant) *The Magical Record of the Beast 666: The Diaries of Aleister Crowley, 1914-1920,* Duckworth, 1972; (editor with Grant) *Magick,* Routledge & Kegan Paul, 1973; (editor with Grant) Aleister Crowley, *White Stains,* Duckworth, 1973; *Conversations With Gerald,* Duckworth, 1974; (editor with Grant) Crowley *Magical and Philosophical Commentaries on The Book of the Law,* 93 Publishing, 1974; (editor with Grant) Crowley, *Moonchild,* Sphere, 1974; (editor with Grant) *The Complete Astrological Writings of Aleister Crowley,* Duckworth, 1975.

SIDELIGHTS: Symonds's novels are often touched with mystery and a sense of the bizarre. Some are humorous and have been called outrageous. *The Hurt Runner,* for example, centers around Feliks, the illegitimate, drug-abusing, dwarf son of a promiscuous woman. Feliks aspires to be a photographer and is surrounded by such eccentrics as a catatonic grandmother who fears her house slippers will bite her.

No less eccentric are his tales for children. The characters fantasize freely about off-beat treats such as lemonade rain and doughnut trees. They take trips to the moon, babble blithely about death, are befriended by animals, and perform daring rescue and escape missions. Andre Francois's illustrations, which most often accompany Symonds's texts, have been characterized as both amusing and grotesque.

Symonds is noted in the field of parapsychology for his biography of British mystic Aleister Crowley. He was appointed Crowley's literary executor and, together with Kenneth Grant, edited several of Crowley's works.

BIOGRAPHICAL/CRITICAL SOURCES: Times Literary Supplement, July 18, 1975, June 4, 1976; *New York Times Book Review,* November 16, 1975; Leslie A. Shepard, editor, *Encyclopedia of Occultism and Parapsychology,* Gale, 1978.*

T

TABAK, Israel 1904-

BRIEF ENTRY: Born December 7, 1904, in Bucovina, Rumania. Rabbi and author. Tabak has been a rabbi since 1923 and has led the congregation of Shaarei Zion in Baltimore, Maryland, since 1931. He was named honorary president of the Rabbinical Council of America in 1951 and chairman of the executive board of the Religious Zionist Organization of America in 1957. Tabak's writings include *The Function of the Synagogue During the Second Temple in Jerusalem* (1966), *Separation of Religion and State in Jewish History* (1967), *The Lloyd Street Synagogue of Baltimore: A National Shrine* (1973), and *Rabbi Moshe Leib of Sassoy: Nineteenth Century Pioneer of Hasidism* (1975). *Address:* 6804 Cross Country Blvd., Baltimore, Md. 21215; and 6602 Park Heights Ave., Baltimore, Md. 21215.

* * *

TABER, Anthony Scott 1944-
(Anthony)

PERSONAL: Born September 5, 1944, in New York, N.Y.; son of Scott Wilbur (a cartoonist) and Nancy (Jones) Taber; married Mariann Carpenter (a computer consultant), December 31, 1977; children: Julian Scott, Anna Rose Emily. *Education:* Philadelphia College of Art, B.F.A., 1971. *Home and office:* 153 Enfield Main Rd., Box A, Ithaca, N.Y. 14850.

CAREER: Free-lance graphic artist and cartoonist, 1963—.

WRITINGS: Cats' Eyes (self-illustrated), Dutton, 1978; *Nightcats,* Congdon, 1982. Contributor of cartoons and graphic narratives, under name Anthony, to *New Yorker* and *Audubon;* art and cartoon work has also appeared in *Better Homes and Gardens, Saturday Review, New York Times, Esquire,* and *National Demographics.*

AVOCATIONAL INTERESTS: "I and my wife share a strong interest in transcendental meditation. We have been practicing for seven years and devote much of our spare time to the local program in Ithaca. Other interests include gardening, fine art, reading, woodworking, hiking, and weightlifting."

* * *

TAFT, Charles Phelps 1897-

BRIEF ENTRY: Born September 20, 1897, in Cincinnati, Ohio. American lawyer, politician, and author. Taft has been an attorney in Cincinnati since 1922, and served as the city's mayor from 1955 to 1957. The son of President William Howard Taft, he wrote *You and I—and Roosevelt* (Farrar & Rinehart, 1936). Other books include *City Management: The Cincinnati Experience* (1933), *Why I Am for the Church* (1947), *Democracy in Politics and Economics* (Farrar & Strauss, 1950), and *Trade Barriers and the National Interest* (Southern Methodist University Press, 1955). *Address:* 1071 Celestial St., Cincinnati, Ohio 45202; and Highland Towers, Cincinnati, Ohio 45202. *Biographical/critical sources: Who's Who in America,* 40th edition, Marquis, 1978; *Who's Who,* 131st edition, St. Martin's, 1979.

* * *

TALKIN, Gil
See ROSENTHAL, Alan

* * *

TALL, Deborah 1951-

PERSONAL: Born March 16, 1951, in Washington, D.C.; daughter of Max M. (an engineer) and Selma (Donnerstein) Tall; married David Weiss (a writer), September 9, 1979. *Education:* University of Michigan, B.A., 1972; Goddard College, M.F.A., 1979. *Residence:* Baltimore, Md. *Agent:* Sterling Lord Agency, Inc., 660 Madison Ave., New York, N.Y. 10021.

CAREER: Free-lance writer in Ireland, 1972-77; CK Studios, New York, N.Y., typographical designer, 1978-80; University of Baltimore, Baltimore, Md., assistant professor of English, 1980—. Director of Inishbofin Arts Week, 1977. *Member:* Associated Writing Programs. *Awards, honors:* Hopwood Award for poetry, 1972, and Michael R. Gutterman Award for poetry, both from University of Michigan, both 1972.

WRITINGS: Eight Colors Wide (poems), London Magazine Editions, 1974; *Ninth Life,* Ithaca House, 1982. Contributor of poems to magazines, including *Poetry, Nation, Iowa Review, Yale Review, Ploughshares,* and *Ironwood.*

WORK IN PROGRESS: The Island of the White Cow, memoirs of her years in rural Ireland.

* * *

TANCOCK, John (Leon) 1942-

PERSONAL: Born June 11, 1942, in London, England; son of

Arthur Joseph and Lilian Maud Tancock. *Education:* Downing College, Cambridge, M.A., 1963; Courtauld Institute of Art, London, Ph.D., 1978. *Home:* 425 East 86th St., New York, N.Y. 10028. *Office:* Sotheby Parke Bernet, 980 Madison Ave., New York, N.Y. 10028.

CAREER: Philadelphia Museum of Art, Philadelphia, Pa., associate curator, 1967-72; Sotheby Parke Bernet, New York, N.Y., head of department of impressionist and modern paintings, 1972—.

WRITINGS: Multiples: The First Decade, Philadelphia Museum of Art, 1971; *The Sculpture of Auguste Rodin,* David R. Godine, 1976.

SIDELIGHTS: Tancock commented: "My published works were the outcome of professional assignments at the Philadelphia Museum of Art. Since then my writing has only been occasional. Writing, in my experience, is not something to be fitted into one's spare time. For the moment my role in the art world keeps me fully occupied."

* * *

TANNEN, Mary 1943-

PERSONAL: Born June 2, 1943, in New London, Conn.; daughter of Matthew W. (an educator) and Doris (Beal) Gaffney; married Michael Tannen (a lawyer), June 25, 1965; children: Catherine, Noah. *Education:* Attended William Smith College, 1961-63; Barnard College, B.A., 1965. *Home and office:* 90 Riverside Dr., New York, N.Y. 10024.

CAREER: Men's Wear, New York City, copy writer, 1965; *Popular Mechanics,* New York City, in promotion, 1965-66; *Show,* New York City, copy writer, 1966-67; Avon Products, New York City, copy writer, 1967-70.

WRITINGS: The Wizard Children of Finn (juvenile), Knopf, 1981; *The Lost Legend of Finn* (juvenile), Knopf, 1982.

WORK IN PROGRESS: A contemporary novel.

SIDELIGHTS: Mary Tannen told *CA:* "My work habits are probably as bad as anyone's. I'm at the typewriter whenever I have time, usually a few hours every day. Most of what I put down is between me and the wastebasket, as I do countless numbers of drafts.

"I think anyone who wants to write should go ahead and do it. It's a way of responding to life, like dancing, or throwing pots, or spinning deals. I wasted many years not daring to write because I was afraid I wouldn't like what I wrote. Finally, the urge to join my voice to the great babble of humanity overcame my fear or modesty. Now I'm so happy at my work that I think only old age and debilitating infirmities will stop me.

"I do have strong beliefs, but I'm not given to aphorisms. I guess that's why I enjoy writing fiction, because the ideas I hold most sacred can seep up out of the story, to be recognized, or not, by the reader. In fact, I'm often surprised myself by what comes to the surface.

"*The Wizard Children of Finn* and *The Lost Legend of Finn* were written purely to entertain children. It was only after I had finished them that I realized the books had to do with a family: the relationships of the members to each other, and the ties that bind them to their ancestors."

* * *

TATE, Eleanora E(laine) 1948-

PERSONAL: Born April 16, 1948, in Canton, Mo.; daughter of Clifford and Lillie (Douglas) Tate; married Zack E. Hamlett III (a photographer), August 19, 1972; children: Gretchen. *Education:* Drake University, B.A., 1973. *Home:* 1203 Carver St., Myrtle Beach, S.C. 29577. *Agent:* Charlotte Sheedy, Charlotte Sheedy Literary Agency, 145 West 86th Street, New York City, N.Y. 10024.

CAREER: Iowa Bystander, West Des Moines, news editor, 1966-68; *Des Moines Register* and *Des Moines Tribune,* Des Moines, Iowa, staff writer, 1968-76; *Jackson Sun,* Jackson, Tenn., staff writer, 1976-77; Kreative Koncepts, Inc., Myrtle Beach, S.C., writer and researcher, 1979—. Free-lance writer for *Memphis Tri-State Defender,* 1977. Contributor to black history and culture workshops in Des Moines, 1968-76; giver of poetry presentations at Iowa Arts Council Writers in the Schools program, 1969-76, Rust College, 1973, and Grinnell College, 1975. *Awards, honors:* Fifth Annual Third World Writing Contest finalist, 1973; Unity Award from Lincoln University, 1974, for educational reporting; Community Lifestyles award from Tennessee Press Association, 1977; fellowship in children's fiction for Bread Loaf Writers' Conference, 1981.

WRITINGS: (Editor with husband, Zack E. Hamlett III, and contributor) *Eclipsed* (poetry), privately printed, 1975; (editor and contributor) *Wanjiru: A Collection of Blackwomanworth,* privately printed, 1976; *Just an Overnight Guest* (juvenile novel), Dial, 1980.

Contributor: Rosa Guy, editor, *Children of Longing,* Bantam, 1970; *Impossible?* (juvenile), Houghton, 1972; *Broadside Annual 1972,* Broadside Press, 1972; *Communications* (juvenile), Heath, 1973; *Off-Beat* (juvenile), Macmillan, 1974; *Sprays of Rubies* (anthology of poetic prose), Ragnarok, 1975; *Valhalla Four,* Ragnarok, 1977. Contributor of poetry and fiction to periodicals, including *Journal of Black Poetry* and *Des Moines Register Picture Magazine.*

WORK IN PROGRESS: A Woman for the People, for adults; *Raisin,* for juveniles.

SIDELIGHTS: Set in a small Missouri town, *Just an Overnight Guest* details nine-year-old Margie Carson's gradual acceptance of her half-white cousin Ethel. As a member of a close and loving family, Margie does not understand Ethel, an abused and abandoned child. When Ethel moves into the Carson home, first as an overnight guest and later as a permanent occupant, Margie feels angry and threatened. She regards Ethel as an intruder vying for her parents' love and attention. With her father's help, however, Margie comes to understand her cousin. "In this first novel," commented Merri Rosenberg in the *New York Times Book Review,* "Eleanora Tate does a fine job presenting the emotional complexities of Margie's initiation into adult life's moral ambiguities. She does so with sympathy and sensitivity." The critic continued that "if she [Tate] drives home her point with a slightly heavy hand . . . [she] has imbued the situation with enough realism to make it plausible." Sue Ellen Bridgers observed in the *Washington Post Book World,* "Tate's language is true, and she has an easy, natural style . . . [she] is just beginning to shine."

Tate told *CA:* "Growing out of some deep yearning, I suppose, for a return to girlhood, I have gotten a thrill out of writing about children. Part of it—my intent from now on is to write more in the children's field than for adults—stems from my belief that I had a very happy childhood, with a certain richness to it that I want today's children to share. Certainly today's children, many of them, have happy childhoods, and for that I am grateful. I would like to add my voice in print, as well as my emotions, to the thought that children's childhoods can be happy if they can learn that they can do anything they set their minds to, if they try.

"This is what motivated me to write the book, *Just an Overnight Guest*. The theme was different, but the motivation was still there. And because of that motivation, I set aside a woman's 'liberation' book, *A Woman for the People*, to do it. For a number of years, in fact, all through the writing of *Just an Overnight Guest*, I struggled with *A Woman for the People*, which started out as a twenty-seven-page short that people wanted to see as a book."

BIOGRAPHICAL/CRITICAL SOURCES: Myrtle Beach Sun News, November 23, 1980; *New York Times Book Review*, February 8, 1981; *Des Moines Register*, March 1, 1981; *Washington Post Book World*, May 10, 1981.

*   *   *

TAUBER, Maurice F(alcolm) 1908-1980

PERSONAL: Born February 14, 1908, in Norfolk, Va.; died after a short illness, September 21, 1980, in New York, N.Y.; son of A. Albert and Leona (Miller) Tauber; married Rose Anne Begner, May 15, 1932 (died May, 1964); children: Robert M., Frederic J. *Education:* Temple University, B.S. (English and sociology), 1930, Ed.M., 1939; Columbia University, B.S. (library service), 1934; University of Chicago, Ph.D., 1941.

CAREER: Temple University, Philadelphia, Pa., library assistant, 1927-35, head of catalog department, 1935-38, librarian at teachers college, 1934-35; University of Chicago, Chicago, Ill., chief of libraries' catalog department, 1941-42, and Preparations Division, 1942-44, instructor, 1942-44, assistant professor of library science, 1944; Columbia University, New York, N.Y., assistant director of libraries, 1944-47, assistant professor, 1944-46, associate professor, 1946-49, professor, 1949-54, Melvil Dewey Professor of Library Science, 1954-76, Dewey professor emeritus, 1976-80. Member of Librarian of Congress's advisory committee, 1946-47; committee member of American Documentation Institute, 1948-58; member of board of advisers of Naval War College; member of library advisory board of Air University; consultant to Canadian Department of Agriculture, National Science Foundation, and Pace Institute. *Awards, honors:* Margaret Mann Award, 1953; Melvil Dewey Medal, 1955; Fulbright scholar in Australia, 1961; award from New York Technical Services Librarians, 1973.

WRITINGS: (With William H. Jesse) *Report of a Survey of the Libraries of the Virginia Polytechnic Institute*, Virginia Polytechnic Institute, 1949; (with Eugene H. Wilson) *Report of a Survey of the Library of Montana State University*, American Library Association, 1951; (editor with Ralph U. Blasingame and others) *Technical Services in Libraries: Acquisitions, Cataloging, Classification, Binding, Photographic Reproduction, and Circulation Operations*, Columbia University Press, 1953; (with Louis Round Wilson) *The University Library*, Columbia University Press, 2nd edition, 1956; *The Hampton Institute Library: Report of a Survey Made at the Request of the President of Hampton Institute*, 1958.

Cataloging and Classification, Graduate School of Library Science, Rutgers University, 1960; (with Edith Wise) *Classification Systems* (bound with *Gifts* by Donald E. Thompson and *Exchanges* by Thompson), Graduate School of Library Science, Rutgers University, 1961; (with Robert Ernest Kingery) *The Central Technical Processing of the Nassau Library System: A Report on the Organization, Facilities, Operations, and Problems*, Nassau Library System (Hempstead, N.Y.), 1962; (editor with Helen M. Welch) *Current Trends in U.S. Periodical Publishing*, Graduate School of Library Science, University of Illinois, 1962; *Resources of Australian Libraries*,

three volumes, Australian Advisory Council on Bibliographical Services, 1962; (editor with Kingery and Hilda Feinberg) *Book Catalogs*, Scarecrow, 1963; *Book Catalogs for Smaller Libraries*, New Jersey Library Association, 1964; *Technical Services in the Libraries of the University of New Mexico*, University of New Mexico, 1964.

(With Felix Reichmann and Joanne Rein) *Library Resources in the Mid-Hudson Valley: Columbia, Duchess, Greene, Orange, Putnam, Rockland, Sullivan, Ulster*, [Poughkeepsie, N.Y.], 1965; *Conference on the Use of Printed and Audio-Visual Materials for Instructional Purposes, Columbia University, 1965: Final Report*, School of Library Service, Columbia University, 1966; (editor with Jerrold Orne) *Louis Round Wilson, Education and Libraries: Selected Papers*, Shoe String, 1966; *Louis Round Wilson: Librarian and Administrator*, Columbia University Press, 1967; (editor with Irlene R. Stephens) *Library Surveys*, Columbia University Press, 1967; (editor) *The Dewey Decimal Classification*, Columbia University Press, 1968.

(With Stephens) *The Naval War College Libraries: A Survey*, Naval War College, 1971; (editor of revision) L. N. Feipel and E. W. Browning, *Library Binding Manual: A Handbook of Useful Procedures for the Maintenance of Library Volumes*, Library Binding Institute, 1972.

Contributor to library journals. Editor and managing editor of *College and Research Libraries*, 1948-62; editor of *Library Trends;* member of editorial board of *Library Resources and Technical Services, American Documentation, Journal of Higher Education*, and *College and Research Libraries*.

BIOGRAPHICAL/CRITICAL SOURCES: College and Research Libraries, October, 1947, April, 1954, May, 1962; *American Libraries*, December, 1976.

OBITUARIES: New York Times, September 26, 1980; *AB Bookman's Weekly*, December 15, 1980.*

*   *   *

TAYLOR, Alfred 1896-1973

PERSONAL: Born January 11, 1896, in Pawtucket, R.I.; died August 6, 1973; son of Peter and Esther (Schofield) Taylor; married Nell Carmichael. *Education:* University of Oregon, B.A., 1932; Oregon State College (now University), M.A., 1933, Ph.D., 1935.

CAREER: Oregon State College (now University), Corvallis, instructor in animal biology, 1935-40; University of Texas, Austin, research scientist, 1940-65; Krotona School of Theosophy, Ojai, Calif., instructor, 1965-67, director and instructor, 1967-72. *Military service:* Royal Air Force, 1917-19.

WRITINGS: Understanding Through the Ancient Wisdom and Modern Science, Theosophical Publishing, 1959; *The Secret Doctrine: Commentaries and Analogies*, Krotona School of Theosophy, Series I, 1970, Series II, 1971; *A Human Heritage: The Wisdom in Science and Experience*, Theosophical Publishing, 1975. Contributor to science and philosophy journals, including *Main Currents in Modern Thought, Theosophist*, and *American Theosophist*.

[Sketch verified by wife, Nell C. Taylor]

*   *   *

TAYLOR, Cecil Philip 1929-1981

OBITUARY NOTICE—See index for *CA* sketch: Born November 6, 1929, in Glasgow, Scotland; died December 9, 1981. Author of numerous plays for the stage and television. Taylor, whose career was centered in Edinburgh, Scotland, was described in the *London Times* as "a regional writer with an international viewpoint." Taylor's most recent works, "Good" and "Happy Lies," utilized a stream-of-consciousness form that was derived from the playwright's experimental adaptations of works by Ibsen, Sternheim, and Brecht. He also wrote television documentaries. Obituaries and other sources: *Christian Science Monitor*, May 24, 1969; *Stage and Television Today*, December 3, 1970; *Stage*, April 22, 1971; *London Times*, December 15, 1981.

* * *

TAYLOR, David (Conrad) 1934-

PERSONAL: Born February 11, 1934, in Rochdale, England; son of Frank (a clothier) and Marian (Fielding) Taylor; married Shelagh M. Ford, September, 1956 (divorced, 1976); married Hannelore Lonkwitz, October, 1976; children: Stephanie, Lindsey. *Education:* University of Glasgow, B.V.M.S., 1956. *Home:* 2 Withy Close, Lightwater, Surrey, England.

CAREER: Partner and veterinarian of Whittle & Taylor, 1955-68; and Taylor & Greenwood (zoo veterinary consultants), 1968—. Consultant to zoos, aquariums, marine lands, and safari parks all over the world. *Member:* Royal College of Veterinary Surgeons (fellow).

WRITINGS: Zoo Vet, Lippincott, 1976; *Is There a Doctor in the Zoo?*, Lippincott, 1978; *Going Wild: Aventures of a Zoo Vet*, Stein & Day, 1980; *Next Panda Please*, Allen & Unwin, 1982.

SIDELIGHTS: Taylor commented: "As an exotic animal doctor, I have treated animals ranging from pandas to pangolins to porpoises, in places from Greenland to Arabia to the Far East."

* * *

TAYLOR, Gordon Rattray 1911-1981

OBITUARY NOTICE—See index for *CA* sketch: Born January 11, 1911, in Eastbourne, England; died December 7, 1981. Journalist, free-lance writer, and author of books on science and social change. Taylor's best known works, *The Biological Time Bomb* and *The Doomsday Book*, discuss ways in which man is destroying himself and his environment. Both books became best sellers and were translated into about twenty languages. The author's most recent work, *The Great Evolution Mystery*, which reexamines the work of Darwin and Lamarck, will be published posthumously. Taylor served as editor of the British Broadcasting Corporation's "Horizon" series. Obituaries and other sources: *London Times*, December 12, 1981.

* * *

TAYLOR, Jenny 1910-

PERSONAL: Born May 10, 1910, in Waterfoot, Lancashire, England; daughter of Albert and Alice (Greenoff) Taylor. *Education:* Edgehill Training College, Teacher's Certificate, 1930. *Home and office:* 32 Norwich Rd., Chichester, Sussex PO19 4DG, England.

CAREER: Teacher at schools in Manchester, Lancashire, England, 1930-49; Mulberry Street Infants School, Manchester, headmistress, 1949-66; free-lance writer, 1966—. Lecturer on the teaching of reading at Victoria University of Manchester, variously between 1949 and 1968.

WRITINGS—Juveniles: "Ann's Toys" series, four books, Oliver & Boyd, 1953; "John's Toys" series, four books, Oliver & Boyd, 1953; "Squirrel Books" series, six books, Oliver & Boyd, 1955.

With Terry Ingleby; juveniles: "Round and About Books" series, four books, Oliver & Boyd, 1958; "Town Books" series, four books, Oliver & Boyd, 1958; "Let's Learn to Read" series, eight books, Blackie & Son, 1960; "Reading with Rhythm" series (illustrated by Derek Crowe), five books, Longmans, Green, 1961; "Infant Book Shelf" series, four books, Blackie & Son, 1962, reprinted as *Blackie's Infant Bookshelf*, 1967; "What Would You Like to Be?" series (illustrated by Sam Fair), Blackie & Son, 1962, Book I: *Kennel Maid?*, Book II: *Air Stewardess?*, Book III: *Postman?*, Book IV: *Policeman?*, Book V: *Footballer?*, Book VI: *Nurse?;* "A Lot of Things" series, four books, Oliver & Boyd, 1963; *Measuring and Recording* (illustrated by Alan Jessett), Longmans, Green, 1963; *Number Words* (illustrated by Jessett), Longmans, Green, 1963; "Read by Reading" series, three books, Longmans, Green, 1964; "Stories Around Us" series, eight books, Longmans, Green, 1964;

"The Baxter Family" series (illustrated by Will Nickless), six books, Blackie & Son, 1965; "Numbers" series (illustrated by Jessett), two books, Longmans, Green, 1965; "Shapes" series, six books, Longmans, Green, 1965; "This Is the Way I Go" series (illustrated by Jessett), six books, Longmans, Green, 1965; *Picture Dictionary*, Longmans, Green, 1969; "A Set of Things to See" series, four books, Oliver & Boyd, 1970; *Messy Malcolm*, World's Work, 1972; *Maps for Mandy and Mark*, Longman, 1974; *The Scope Storybook* (illustrated by Andrew Sier, Joanna Troughton, and Barry Wilkinson), Longman, 1974; "Seven Silly Stories" series, Longman, 1974, Book I: *The Fox and Stork*, Book II: *Brer Rabbit and the Honey Pot*, Book III: *Noisy Neville*, Book IV: *Mr. Stupid*, Book V: *The Foolish Tortoise*, Book VI: *The Well Diggers*, Book VII: *The Miller and His Donkey;* "Whizz Bang" series, two books, Longman, 1976; "Can You Do This?" series (illustrated by David Frankland), Longman, 1978, Set I: four books, Set II: four books; *Messy Malcolm's Birthday* (illustrated by Lynette Hemmant), World's Work, 1978; *Messy Malcolm's Dream*, World's Work, 1982.

WORK IN PROGRESS: The Talking Cat.

SIDELIGHTS: Jenny Taylor told *CA* her enthusiasm for writing books especially suited to children from deprived homes began soon after she was appointed headmistress at Mulberry Street Infants School. "It proved to be a highly infectious enthusiasm for Terry Ingleby," she said, and thus began their writing partnership which still continues.

"While at school," Taylor commented, "we were able to try out our ideas. The children were a constant stimulus and help.

"My work with children from deprived areas made me appreciate more than ever that school should be a lively, stimulating place; a place full of opportunities for first-hand discoveries experiences, and enjoyment, where children are encouraged to talk and to listen to others talking. It also made me realize that getting on good terms with the parents is half of the battle.

"I feel that storytime should be an exciting time for both the teacher and the children, a time when you provide language for your class to savor: Words—accurate, precise, repetitive; nonsense words, rhythmic and musical words. Speech is the chief tool of all social communication and understanding.

"Next to the spoken word in importance is the written word, so it is books, books, and more books, to be valued and treated with respect—books with varied subjects and good illustrations to rouse the interest, and stories of life, fantasy, and humor to sustain and sharpen that interest. In all my writing I have tried to keep these thoughts in mind, so that reading will be not only educational but also give enjoyment.''

Two Taylor and Ingleby series, ''This Is the Way I Go'' and ''Can You Do This?,'' have been adopted for use by Developmental Learning Material. *The Picture Dictionary* is used by Time-Life, and cassettes of the book in English and in Mandarin Chinese have been made for use in China.

AVOCATIONAL INTERESTS: Amateur dramatics, acting and producing, travel, music.

*   *   *

TAYLOR, Lawrence   1942-

PERSONAL: Born April 1, 1942, in Los Angeles, Calif.; son of Forrest Everett (a fireman and naval officer) and Lyla (a travel agent; maiden name, Sherwood) Taylor; married Linda Sue Collelo (a court clerk), June 4, 1978; children: Christopher Scott. *Education:* University of California, Berkeley, B.A., 1966; University of California, Los Angeles, J.D., 1969. *Home:* 5 Oakmont Dr., Los Angeles, Calif. 90049. *Agent:* George Diskant, 9255 West Sunset Blvd., No. 1122, Los Angeles, Calif. 90069. *Office:* School of Law, Pepperdine University, Malibu, Calif. 90265.

CAREER: Admitted to the Bar of California State, 1970, and the Bar of the U.S. Supreme Court, 1979; Los Angeles County, Los Angeles, Calif., deputy county counsel, 1969-70, deputy public defender, 1970-71, deputy district attorney, 1971-72; private practice of law in Los Angeles, 1972—. Judge pro tem of Santa Monica Municipal Court, 1977-78, and Los Angeles Municipal Court, 1978-80; judge of Moot Court at University of California, Los Angeles, School of Law, 1977 and 1980. Special independent prosecutor for attorney general of Montana, 1975-76. Guest lecturer in criminal law and the constitution, 1973, and visiting associate professor of law, 1981-82, at Pepperdine University; adjunct associate professor of law at California State University, fall, 1977 and 1979. *Military service:* U.S. Marine Corps, 1960-63.

MEMBER: American Bar Association, American Board of Criminal Lawyers, Author's Guild of America, Santa Monica Bay District Bar Association. *Awards, honors:* Selected for Moot Court honors by University of California, Los Angeles, 1967.

WRITINGS: Handling Criminal Appeals (law text), Bancroft-Whitney, 1980; *Trail of the Fox* (nonfiction), Simon & Schuster, 1980; *A Trial of Generals* (nonfiction), Icarus, 1981; *Drunk Driving Defense* (law text), Little, Brown, 1981; *Setting Sail* (nonfiction), Icarus, 1981; *Eyewitness Identification* (law and police text), Bobbs-Merrill, 1982; *Witness Immunity,* C. C Thomas, inpress; *Scientific Truth Detection,* Bobbs-Merrill, in press. Contributor of eleven articles to law journals and newspapers, including *Case and Comment, Judicature, California State Bar Journal,* Los Angeles Daily Journal Report, and *Cincinnati Post.*

WORK IN PROGRESS: A novel about a Los Angeles district attorney investigation; a novel about World War II horse soldiers in Tibet.

SIDELIGHTS: Taylor told *CA:* ''Why do I write? Understand that there are those who call themselves 'writer,' and there are those who write. They are not the same for a very simple reason. Behind the romance of the image are, as must so often be the case, toil and loneliness. Writing is, after all, a miserable existence. Who in his right mind would voluntarily isolate himself from family, friends, and a fascinating world to do

battle for endless days and red-eyed nights with but a cold, hostile sheet of very blank paper for company?

''And for what? The pitiful chances of even modest sucess are well known, the financial rewards laughable; the vagaries of publishers and the ravages of the critics' talons await the hardy survivor. Then why? Because for a writer there is no alternative: He must write! Much as a woman swelling with a child, there is a growing thing inside which must come out, which will come out. Yet, once out, the joy and satisfaction is all too short-lived. There is the next book to begin, and then the next. . . . It is, at once, a blessed gift and a terrible curse.

''I write because that is who I am.''

MEDIA ADAPTATIONS: A motion picture based on *Trail of the Fox* is scheduled by Quinn-Martin Productions.

BIOGRAPHICAL/CRITICAL SOURCES: Los Angeles Times, October, 1980, June 25, 1981; *Times Literary Supplement,* October 30, 1981.

*   *   *

TEILHARD de CHARDIN, (Marie Joseph) Pierre   1881-1955

BRIEF ENTRY: Born May 1, 1881, in Sarcenat, France; died April 10, 1955, in New York, N.Y. French philosopher. Teilhard de Chardin is now regarded as a major voice in twentieth-century Christianity, though in his lifetime he was known mainly for his studies of paleontology and geology. He became a Jesuit priest in 1911 and began a university career. As early as 1924 he alarmed his superiors with some unorthodox views. Restrictions were placed on his activities, and finally he was banned from teaching. Teilhard proceeded to China, where he conducted anthropological research for several years and participated in the discovery of "Peking Man" in 1929. The Society of Jesus had forbidden him to publish his philosophical theories during his lifetime, but their posthumous publication gained international attention. His *Phenomenon of Man* (1955) combined his greatest loves—science and Christianity—into a unified philosophy. He interpreted matter (science) and spirit (Christianity) as two different aspects of one reality. He saw biological evolution as a concurrent event with God's creation; the end-point of organic evolution would coincide with the second coming of Christ. The necessary catalyst, he postulated, was human consciousness, which placed man at the very center of the universe. The only inhibitor was the devil, or sin, which Teilhard correlated with entropy. His later publications *The Future of Man* (1964) and *Man's Place in Nature* (1966) serve as introductions to his basic philosophy. *Biographical/critical sources: Columbia Dictionary of Modern European Literature,* Columbia University Press, 1947; *The McGraw-Hill Encyclopedia of World Biography,* McGraw, 1973.

*   *   *

TESICH, Steve   1943(?)-

PERSONAL: Birth-given name Stoyan Tesich; born c. 1943, in Uzice, Yugoslavia; son of a steel mill worker; married wife, Becky. *Education:* Attended Indiana University, c. 1964; Columbia University, M.A., 1967.

CAREER: Writer. Worked as a caseworker for Brooklyn Department of Welfare, N.Y., c. 1968. *Member:* Phi Beta Kappa. *Awards, honors:* Award for best original screenplay from Academy of Motion Picture Arts and Sciences, 1979, for "Breaking Away."

WRITINGS—Published plays: *The Carpenters* (one-act; first produced in New York City at St. Clement's Church, December, 1970), Dramatists Play Service, c. 1971; *Nourish the Beast* (two-act; first produced in New York City as "Baba Goya" at American Place Theatre, June, 1973), Samuel French, 1974; *Passing Game* (two-act; first produced in New York City at American Place Theatre, December 1, 1977), Samuel French, c. 1978.

Unpublished plays: "Touching Bottom" (three one-acts; contains "The Road," "A Life," and "Baptismal"), first produced in New York City at American Place Theatre, December 17, 1978; "Division Street," first produced in Los Angeles, Calif., at Ahmanson Theatre, 1980. Also author of "Lake of the Woods," first produced in New York City at American Place Theatre, and "Gorky," first produced in New York City at American Place Theatre.

Screenplays: "Breaking Away," Twentieth Century-Fox, 1979; "Eyewitness," Twentieth Century-Fox, 1981; "Four Friends," Filmways, 1981. Also author of "The World According to Garp" (adapted from the novel by John Irving).

SIDELIGHTS: Tesich is best known as the screenwriter of the popular motion picture "Breaking Away." The film concerns a group of high school graduates coping with the responsibilities of working and planning for college in a campus town where "townees" are slighted by the university students. The four youths have distinct personalities: one is athletic and headstrong; another prematurely embraces adulthood through marriage; one seeks self-satisfaction from the others with his humorous comments and pranks; and the fourth member dreams of becoming a great bicyclist like the Italians he admires. Particular emphasis is given to the bicyclist, Dave, as he weighs his parents' insistence on a college education against his friends' disdain for the university. After a heartfelt exchange with his father, Dave seems willing to attend college and overcome his feelings of inferiority and hostility towards the college students. The film culminates in a thrilling bicycle race in which Dave leads his friends to victory over a team of campus heroes.

"Breaking Away" proved an immense success with critics and the public. Reviewers for both *Rolling Stone* and *New York Times* called it "wonderful," and *Los Angeles Times*'s Wayne Warga praised its "grasp of our mores and attitudes—both of which it examines warmly." "Breaking Away" eventually garnered an Academy Award and was deemed the best film of 1979 by the National Society of Film Critics.

After the success of "Breaking Away" was assured, Tesich revealed his own reservations about the film in an interview. "I feel that anything I love, people will hate," he told *Rolling Stone*. "When I really got to like the film, I figured that was it. Everyone would hate it." His doubts were also partially founded by the fact that "Breaking Away" was actually a combination of two scripts that Tesich had seen rejected by film studios. He merged the two stories at the suggestion of director Peter Yates, who then produced and directed the film. "Ours was a total collaboration," Tesich observed. "I was certain it would never work until we started filming."

In 1981 Tesich and Yates attempted to repeat their film success with "Eyewitness," an offbeat urban thriller about a janitor, Daryll Deever, whose obsession with a newswoman leads to danger. When a murder occurs in the building where Daryll works, he misleads the reporter into believing that he has witnessed the murder. Daryll's best friend becomes the prime suspect in the killings, but after several harrowing plot twists, the killer is exposed as the newswoman's fiance, an Israeli agent whose job entailed taking any precautions necessary to ensure the safety of Jews defecting from Communist countries. Korean occupants of Daryll's building were involved in an attempt to interfere with a defection, so the fiance murdered their boss.

Many critics contended that the numerous plot contrivances flawed "Eyewitness." "The sympathetic viewer will want to rescue [the characters], not from the bad guys," charged *Time*'s reviewer, "but from the mechanism of this eyewitless plot." Similarly, *Newsweek*'s David Ansen noted that "'Eyewitness' is least satisfying as a mystery; the plot doesn't do justice to the characters." Vincent Canby agreed, declaring that the plot involving the Israeli agent "is something less than totally convincing or even absorbing" and concluding that "'Eyewitness' is not terrifically strong on logic."

But "Eyewitness" lured favorable responses with its wealth of eccentric characters. Ansen acknowledged that "Tesich has crammed his twist-filled script with juicy characters, none of whom is quite what he or she appears to be." Canby contended that the film "runs on the energy generated by its appealing oddball characters" and dubbed it "an eccentric treat."

Tesich's skill at characterization was evident in his screenplay "Four Friends," which concerns the adventures of three young men and the woman they all loved during the 1960's. The film focuses on the experiences of Danilo, the son of Slavic immigrants. His struggles as a worker and as a student whose ideals clash with those of his parents provide unique insight into second-generation immigrants and the 1960's. Although "Four Friends" met with an uneven critical reception, it was praised by *Chicago Tribune*'s Gene Siskel as "a very good American movie" and considered by *New York Times*'s Canby as one of 1981's best films.

Creating eccentric characters has also been Tesich's strength as a playwright. His first major production, "The Carpenters," dealt with a family forced into subservience by their bomb-wielding son. Another play, "Baba Goya," concerned "an indomitable figure who guides, coaxes, wisecracks and bullies those around her into solving their existential problems," according to John Simon. He summed up the characters as a "loveable set of oddballs."

Some of Tesich's plays recall the works of absurdist Samuel Beckett. Each of the three one-act dramas comprising "Touching Bottom" has its roots in Beckett's theatre: "The Road" echoes Beckett's "Waiting for Godot" in its depiction of two characters passing on a highway; "A Life," noted Mel Gussow, "takes its cue from 'Krapp's Last Tape,'" another play by Beckett; and "Baptismal," the third play, also reminded Gussow of "Waiting for Godot." Simon suggested that Tesich's similarities to Beckett derived from naivety, not intention. "Unless you are to be a primitive playwright," Simon counseled, "for which Tesich is really too sophisticated, you have to read a little more. Otherwise you risk reinventing plays already extant."

Tesich seemed to deviate from absurdism in both "The Passing Game" and "Division Street." The former concerns two husbands plotting to murder their wives during a vacation. Both men see their wives as reminders of the youthful ambitions they've compromised. The play concludes with the husbands abandoning their plan as pathetically as they once abandoned their goals in life. Gussow deemed "The Passing Game" "far less interesting than [Tesich's] earlier work." Marilyn Stasio observed that "the heavy atmospheric pressures are okay for inducing thrills and chills, but they can't replace such technical niceties as characterization and plotting."

Tesich defined his first play of the 1980's, "Division Street," as the closest "I can come to a classic farce." He added: "It deals with a look at what happens to several '60's radicals today. What interests me is ideals. Can they survive? Does the time come when dreamers say that's enough? My answer is no—they don't die. . . . I think of this play as a comedy of ideas."

Despite success as both a playwright and screenwriter, Tesich expressed his discontent with his hectic work schedule during 1980. "I don't like the image of myself as a busy writer," he told the *Los Angeles Times,* "and in some ways I wish all of these things weren't happening at once. I like to immerse myself in my work. I like to have hours to think and I wish things had spaced themselves out more. Still, it is wrong to complain."

MEDIA ADAPTATIONS: In 1980, the American Broadcasting Company (ABC-TV) adapted "Breaking Away" into a television series starring Shaun Cassidy.

BIOGRAPHICAL/CRITICAL SOURCES: New York Times, December 18, 1970, December 22, 1970, December 27, 1970, July 15, 1979, July 18, 1979, August 14, 1979, April 12, 1980, February 27, 1981; *Nation,* January 11, 1971; *New Leader,* January 11, 1971; *Cue,* June 2, 1973, December 24, 1977; *New York,* June 11, 1973; *Los Angeles Times,* March 26, 1980; *Rolling Stone,* April 17, 1980; *Newsweek,* March 2, 1981; *Time,* March 2, 1981; *Chicago Tribune,* January 10, 1982.*

—Sketch by Les Stone

*　　*　　*

THEALL, Donald Francis   1928-

PERSONAL: Born October 13, 1928, in Mount Vernon, N.Y.; son of Harold A. and Helen A. (Donaldson) Theall; married Joan Ada Benedict, June 14, 1950; children: Thomas, Margaret, John, Harold, Lawrence, Michael. *Education:* Yale University, B.A., 1950; University of Toronto, M.A., 1951, Ph.D., 1954. *Home:* 1604 Champlain Dr., Peterborough, Ontario, Canada K9L 1N6. *Office:* Office of the President, Trent University, Peterborough, Ontario, Canada.

CAREER: University of Toronto, Toronto, Ontario, teaching fellow, 1950-52, assistant instructor, 1952-53, lecturer, 1953-56, assistant professor, 1956-58, member of graduate faculty, 1958-60, associate professor, 1960-64, professor of English and chairman of department, 1964-65; York University, Toronto, professor of English, chairman of department, and director of communications, 1965-66; McGill University, Montreal, Quebec, professor of English and chairman of department, 1966-74, Molson Professor of English, 1972-80, director of graduate program in communications, 1976-79; Trent University, Peterborough, Ontario, president and vice-chancellor, 1980—. Cultural exchange professor in People's Republic of China, 1974-75; seminar director. Member of Cooperative Educational Television Board of Canada and the United States. Canadian representative to UNESCO's conference on student participation in university government.

MEMBER: International Communications Association (member of board of directors, 1978—), International Institute of Communications (member of board of directors, 1978-81), Canadian Communications Association (president, 1979—), Canadian Association of University Teachers, Canadian Association of Chairmen of English (founding chairman, 1971-74), Modern Language Association of America, Linguistic Society of America, Science Fiction Research Association, Philosophical Society of Great Britain, Cinematique Canadienne,

Arts Canada, Society of Arts Publishers (past vice-president), Ontario Council of Teachers (past member of board of directors), Association of Teachers of English (Quebec), Academy of Medicine of Toronto (corresponding fellow), Baie D'Urfe Club, Curling Club, Yale Club, Southwest One Racquet Club. *Awards, honors:* Grant from Department of Citizenship and Immigration, 1956-59; senior fellowship from Canada Council, 1975.

WRITINGS: (With Richard H. Robinson and John W. Wevers) *Let's Speak English,* four volumes, Gage, 1960-62; (contributor) N. Frye, editor, *Design for Learning,* University of Toronto Press, 1962; (contributor) J. Orrell, editor, *Studies of Major Works in English,* Oxford University Press, 1970; *The Medium Is the Rear View Mirror: Understanding McLuhan,* McGill-Queen's University Press, 1971; (editor with Gertrude Joch Robinson) *Studies in Canadian Communications,* McGill University, 1975. Contributor to speech journals. Member of editorial board of *Science Fiction Studies,* 1976—, *Journal of Canadian Communications,* 1979—, and *Culture and Context,* 1979—.

*　　*　　*

THEODORAKIS, Michalis   1925-
(Mikis Theodorakis)

BRIEF ENTRY: Born July 29, 1925, in Chios, Greece. Greek composer and musician. Theodorakis composed the theme music for feature films "Zorba the Greek" (1964), "Z" (1969), and "State of Siege" (1973). He was a popular figure in Greece by the early 1960's, but when his music became associated with the resistance movement against military rule, following the coup of 1967, Theodorakis received even more popular support. At that time his work was banned and he was imprisoned several times from 1967 to 1970. In 1970 he was permitted to leave Greece for Western Europe and the United States. He wrote *Journal of Resistance* (Coward, 1973). *Biographical/critical sources: Current Biography,* Wilson, 1973.

*　　*　　*

THEODORAKIS, Mikis
See THEODORAKIS, Michalis

*　　*　　*

THOMAS, Art(hur Lawrence)   1952-

PERSONAL: Born July 8, 1952, in Cleveland, Ohio; son of Anthony L. (an electrician) and Anne L. (Rinkus) Thomas. *Education:* Baldwin-Wallace College, B.A., 1974; graduate study at Kent State University, 1981—. *Politics:* Independent. *Religion:* Roman Catholic. *Home:* 12500 Edgewater Dr., Lakewood, Ohio 44107.

CAREER: Teacher of English, writing, and drama at public schools in Cleveland, Ohio, 1975-80; Brooklyn City Schools, Brooklyn, Ohio, teacher of English, writing, and drama, 1980—. Business manager of New Mayfield Repertory Cinema, 1975—; member of advisory board of Pioneer Drama Service, Denver, Colo., and board of directors of Ohio City Players Theater. *Member:* International Thespian Society, Mensa, National Council of Teachers of English, U.S. Institute of Theater Technology, Music Box Society, Cleveland Critics Circle.

WRITINGS—Juveniles: Recreational Wrestling, A.S. Barnes, 1976; *Wrestling Is for Me,* Lerner, 1979; *Bicycling Is for Me,* Lerner, 1979; *Volleyball Is for Me,* Lerner, 1979; *Theater Publicity Handbook,* Pioneer Drama Service, 1979; *Back-*

packing Is for Me, Lerner, 1980; *Fishing Is for Me,* Lerner, 1980; *Merry-Go-Rounds,* Carolrhoda, 1981; *Horseback Riding Is for Me,* Lerner, 1981; *Archery Is for Me,* Lerner, 1982; *Boxing Is for Me,* Lerner, 1982.

Author of "Theater in Review," a column in *West Life.* Contributor to magazines and newspapers. Entertainment editor of *West Life.*

WORK IN PROGRESS: A series of theater books for elementary, junior, and senior high school students, publication expected in 1984.

SIDELIGHTS: Thomas commented: "My first experience with writing came when I was in college and forced into the position of entertainment editor of our newspaper. I had no previous experience, but this broke the barrier of 'mysticism' associated with writers.

"I was prepared to teach at the high school level, and in an education course found a statement to the effect that 'anyone who thinks that he knows something about a topic should be forced to write a book on it.' Because I was an entertainment editor, I selected a field far removed from my specialty, and my first book was a sports book. That seemed to put me in a 'rut' of writing sports books.

"Like most writers, I find it difficult to force myself to sit at the typewriter for the length of time it takes to get started. For me, almost an hour passes before I actually start writing. I try to keep in shape by writing shorter articles for newspapers.

"I suppose that one of my reasons for writing is to achieve a kind of immortality. Someone once said, 'if you can't be immortal, why bother?' Like an actor, I enjoy the audience response. It's nice to receive letters from children who have read one of my books.

"I enjoy travel and try to fill every day, especially when on vacation. Because I am single, it is sometimes difficult to find a traveling companion who is willing to share a frantic vacation schedule. I like to visit amusement parks and am a real fan of roller coasters. I also try to see what's happening with live theatre whenever I travel.

"We all seem to respect those who do things that we don't and I have a special regard for playwrights and novelists. Although I teach creative writing, I seem to lack the patience and skill to create in these forms."

AVOCATIONAL INTERESTS: "My spare time is spent bicycling through the summer months, and acting in and directing for community and semi-professional theatres in the Cleveland area, and in magic, juggling, and the occult."

*   *   *

THOMAS, (William) Miles (Webster)   1897-1980
(Baron of Remenham, Lord Thomas)

OBITUARY NOTICE: Born March 2, 1897, in Ruabon, Wales; died February 8, 1980, in Slough, Berkshire, England. Aviator, airline administrator, industrialist, and author. During World War I, Miles Thomas served in the Royal Flying Corps and later in the Royal Air Force. Following the war, he worked as a reporter and editor for motoring journals. In 1924 he began working for Morris Motors Ltd., an automobile manufacturing company, as an adviser on sales promotion. He remained with that company for the next twenty-three years, becoming, in 1940, managing director and vice-chairman in charge of all sixty-three of its factories. During World War II the company converted to production of munitions and aircraft repair. For

his efforts during the war, Thomas was knighted. In 1948 he became deputy chairman of British Overseas Airways Corp. An early believer in the potential for growth in commercial civil aviation, Thomas directed his efforts toward attracting passengers to jet travel. He later served as chairman of Britannia Airways Ltd. and in 1965 became chairman of the National Savings Committee of Great Britain. Thomas's autobiography, *Out on a Wing,* was published in 1964. He also wrote *Development and Use of Multi-Wheel Vehicles for Cross-Country and Military Purposes.* Obituaries and other sources: *Current Biography,* Wilson, 1952; *The International Who's Who,* Europa, 1978; *The Annual Obituary 1980,* St. Martin's, 1981.

*   *   *

THOMPSON, Edward Thorwald   1928-

PERSONAL: Born February 13, 1928, in Milwaukee, Wis.; son of Edward Kramer (an editor) and Marguerite Minerva (Maxam) Thompson; married Margaret Kessler, July, 1949 (divorced, 1964); married Nancy Cale, May 28, 1966 (divorced, 1981); children: (first marriage) Edward T., Anne B., Evan K., David S.; (second marriage) Julie H. *Education:* Massachusetts Institute of Technology, S.B., 1949. *Politics:* Independent. *Residence:* Guard Hill Rd., Bedford, N.Y. 10506. *Office: Reader's Digest,* Pleasantville, N.Y. 10570.

CAREER/WRITINGS: Mobil Oil Co., Beaumont, Tex., engineer, 1949-52; *Chemical Engineering* magazine, New York City, associate editor, 1952-55; *Chemical Week* magazine, New York City, managing editor, 1955-56; *Fortune* magazine, New York City, writer, associate editor, 1956-60; *Reader's Digest,* Pleasantville, N.Y., 1960—, began as associate editor, 1960, managing editor, 1973-76, editor-in-chief, 1976—. Director and executive committee member of Reader's Digest Association; director of Reader's Digest Foundation. Chairman of Westchester County United Way Leadership Campaign, 1980—. *Military service:* U.S. Naval Reserve, 1952-60; became lieutenant. *Member:* American Society of Magazine Editors, River Club (New York City), Bedford Golf and Tennis Club, Jupiter Hills Country Club. *Awards, honors:* Golden Plate Award from American Academy of Achievement, 1976.

SIDELIGHTS: Thompson told *CA:* "My transition from chemical engineer to editor of the world's biggest magazine always fascinated people. Actually, the progression was much more logical than the end points make it seem. From a working engineer I moved to being a junior editor of a technical magazine, *Chemical Engineering,* in hopes that this might give me an overview of opportunities in the industry. But I found I liked the editing—not a total surprise, since my father was a prominent editor. So I 'progressed' from an engineering journal to an industry technical news weekly, to a general business magazine (*Fortune*), to the *Reader's Digest.* And I was glad for each change.

"Although at various points in my career I've been basically a writer, writing is not something I enjoy. Perhaps, as one of my editors used to say, *no* writer likes to write; but all writers like to have written. Not in my case. I get much more enjoyment out of working with writers and writings, to be in contact with a vast array of people around the world. From this international vantage point one learns vividly the differences among people and, more importantly, the similarities.

"We now publish in seventeen languages; our world readership is more than 110 million each month. I'm sure that when our internationalization began in the late 1930's that our founder, DeWitt Wallace, had no idea that we would spread our wings so wide. But, then, who could know that his philosophies, derived out of the American Dream, would prove so universal in nature.

"How do we judge what to publish? Is the article useful; does it touch the reader's own concerns; is it talkable, quotable; and, most important, is it of *lasting* interest? If so, we perform an important service simply by bringing it to our readers, but we perform a second service by presenting it in condensed form, staying true to the original's style and intent but allowing readers to get the essence, with flourishes, in far less time."

AVOCATIONAL INTERESTS: Stamps, skiing, boating.

*   *   *

THOMPSON, James W.   1935-
(Abba Elethea)

PERSONAL: Born December 21, 1935, in Detroit, Mich. *Education:* Attended University of Detroit, 1959-60, Wayne State University, 1960-62, and New School for Social Research, 1965. *Home address:* P.O. Box 07243, Detroit, Mich. 48207.

CAREER: Worked as copywriter in New York City; professional dancer in Fairbanks and Anchorage, Alaska, 1955; professional dancer, 1956; member of staff of Boone House Poets, 1959-61; *Umbra,* New York City, member of staff, 1962-65, editor, 1965-66; Clifford Fears Dance Company, Stockholm, Sweden, dancer, 1967; Harlem Cultural Council, New York City, artistic consultant, 1968-71; Antioch College, Yellow Springs, Ohio, poet-in-residence, 1971-72; Clark College, Springfield, Ohio, seminar consultant, 1972-73; Clifford Fears Dance Theatre, featured artist and instructor in dance, 1975-76; writer. Assistant director of One Act Theatre, 1962-66; lecturer and workshop leader; gives readings from his works at colleges, museums, galleries, theatres, and churches. *Awards, honors:* Grant from Detroit Council for the Arts.

WRITINGS: First Fire: Poems, 1957-1960, Paul Bremen, 1970; *The Antioch Suite-Jazz* (poems), Lotus Press, 1980; *Fire in the Flesh* (poems), Fire Publications, 1981.

Work represented in anthologies, including *Sixes and Sevens; Deep Rivers; Exploring Life Through Literature.* Author of "Elethea's Journal," a column in *Detroit Sun* (under pseudonym Abba Elethea), 1975-76. Contributor of poems to magazines, including *Essence, Antioch Review, Black World, Transatlantic Review, Negro History Bulletin,* and *Obsidian.* Poetry editor of *Rights and Reviews,* 1962-66; dance editor and critic of *Feet,* 1968-71.

SIDELIGHTS: Thompson has described himself as a professor of the streets. He teaches Afro-American history and culture through poetry, music, and song. As an educator and consultant, he has created teaching materials for preschool through high school, and has devised courses for college students and adult education programs. His own work has been read at festivals all over the world.

BIOGRAPHICAL/CRITICAL SOURCES: Eccentric, April 14, 1977; *Detroit News,* June 29, 1979.

*   *   *

THORMAN, Richard   1924-

PERSONAL: Born November 21, 1924, in New York, N.Y.; son of Lester K. (an importer) and Helen (Tillis) Thorman; married Margaret Spencer, December 28, 1950 (divorced November, 1981); Robin Hall (an education executive), April, 1982; children: Adam, Thomas, H. Barrett Pottle. *Education:*

Williams College, A.B., 1946; Columbia University, A.M., 1948. *Religion:* "Born-again agnostic." *Address:* P.O. Box 173, Raphine, Va. 24472. *Agent:* Paul R. Reynolds, 12 East 41st St., New York, N.Y. 10017.

CAREER: City College (now of the City University of New York), New York, N.Y., instructor in English, 1948-49; instructor in English at private high school in Paris, France, 1949-50; Central Intelligence Agency (CIA), Washington, D.C., 1951-56; National Academy of Sciences, Washington, D.C., information officer, 1956-59; radio station operator in Herkimer, N.Y., 1959-66; writer. Member of numerous community organizations in Herkimer. *Military service:* U.S. Naval Reserve during World War II.

WRITINGS: Bachman's Law (novel), Norton, 1981.

WORK IN PROGRESS: Three novels, *The Best People,* publication expected by Mohawk Valley Novels, *Some Saints and Others,* and *Come to the Fair.*

SIDELIGHTS: Thorman's *Bachman's Law* was praised by Newgate Callendar for its "interesting twists." Callendar described Thorman as "a skilled and sensitive writer" and applauded the book's twin interest in father-son relations and mystery.

Thorman told *CA:* "My motivation is to make enough money to meet my obligations and to give me enough time to make a craft into art. That sounds pretentious, but I gather it is what other writers are about, too. That is, the honest ones."

Thorman speaks French, German, Italian, and some Latin and Greek.

BIOGRAPHICAL/CRITICAL SOURCES: New York Times Book Review, April 26, 1981; *Herkimer Evening Telegram,* May 7, 1981; *Roanoke Times and World News,* May 11, 1981; *Utica Observer-Dispatch,* June 14, 1981.

*   *   *

THORNTON, Michael   1941-

PERSONAL: Born January 6, 1941, in Pinkney's Green, Berkshire, England; son of Reginald Leonard (an army officer) and Anne Maria (Roberts) Thornton. *Education:* Attended King's College, London University, 1960-63. *Politics:* Conservative. *Religion:* Church of England. *Home:* La Cumbre, Es Mila, Lista de Correos, Mahon, Menorca, Islas Baleares, Spain. *Agent:* Curtis Brown Ltd., 1 Craven Hill, London W2 3EP, England. *Office:* Vincent Shaw Associates, 75 Hammersmith Rd., London W14 8UZ, England.

CAREER: Sunday Express, London, England, film and drama critic, 1964-67, special features, 1969—. Charity work includes Committee for Writing and Reading Aids for the Paralyzed. *Member:* Arts Theatre Club (London), The Mousetrap Club (London).

WRITINGS: (Contributor) Stephen Grenfell, editor, *Gilbert Harding by His Friends,* Deutsch, 1961; *Jessie Matthews,* Hart-Davis, MacGibbon, 1974; *Forget Not,* W. H. Allen, 1975; "Elizabeth of Glamis" (two-act play), first produced in London, 1982; "Sex Symbol" (two-act play), first produced in London, 1982. Contributor of reviews and feature articles to periodicals, including *London Times, The Stage, London Daily Express,* and *Overtures.* Editor of *The Trumpet,* 1962-63; show business editor of *What's on in London,* London, 1976-77.

WORK IN PROGRESS: Editing *The Theatregoer's Companion.*

SIDELIGHTS: Thornton's 1974 biography of British actress Jessie Matthews became the center of a controversy between Thornton and his publisher over sales of the book in South Africa. Thornton, who opposes South Africa's officially-promoted policies of racism and apartheid, had specified that *Jessie Matthews* not be offered for sale in that country. When he discovered that copies of his book had indeed been sold in South Africa, Thornton halted further sales and donated the royalties resulting from his publisher's mistake to the Anti-Apartheid Movement.

Thornton told *CA:* "I never thought of myself as an author or any kind of a writer. I came into that profession almost by accident, straight from university, at the age of twenty-three, when the *Sunday Express* asked me to replace their resident film critic. My 1974 biography of the British actress Jessie Matthews was an immense job of research, but it got me hooked on the fascination and excitement of sleuthing out facts, dates, and details like a detective. I am now engaged on a gigantic job of research with twelve thousand entries to write for *The Theatregoer's Companion.* I have started to write plays, and I would now like to write fiction as a relief from the strain and exhaustion that this sort of research entails."

AVOCATIONAL INTERESTS: Watching old movies on television, collecting nostalgic albums of film and stage musicals.

BIOGRAPHICAL/CRITICAL SOURCES: The Stage, September 5, 1974; *Times Literary Supplement,* October 25, 1974, December 19, 1975; *Drama,* January, 1975; *London Sunday Times,* July 27, 1975; *London Times,* September 21, 1981.

*   *   *

(al-)TIBAWI, A(bdul-)L(atif)   1910-1981

OBITUARY NOTICE—See index for *CA* sketch: Born April 29, 1910, in Taibeh, Palestine (now Israel); died in an accident, October 16, 1981, in London, England. Historian, educator, and author of books and articles on the Middle East. Tibawi was known for his advocacy of the Palestinian Arab cause and for his detailed knowledge of Islamic law. His books include *British Interests in Palestine, A Modern History of Syria Including Lebanon and Palestine,* and *Anglo-Arab Relations and the Question of Palestine, 1914-1921.* Obituaries and other sources: *London Times,* October 29, 1981.

*   *   *

TOOKE, Louise Mathews   1950-
(Louise Mathews)

PERSONAL: Born June 15, 1950, in New York, N.Y.; daughter of William Cooper (an educator) and Edith (Combes) Mathews; married November 28, 1980. *Education:* Attended School of Visual Arts, 1970-72. *Address:* c/o Dodd, Mead & Co., 79 Madison Ave., New York, N.Y. 10016.

CAREER: Private art teacher and free-lance designer in Winter Park, Fla., 1970-78; writer, 1978—.

WRITINGS—Juveniles; under name Louise Mathews: *Bunches and Bunches of Bunnies,* Dodd, 1978; *Gator Pie,* Dodd, 1979; *The Great Take-Away,* Dodd, 1980.

SIDELIGHTS: Louise Tooke wrote: "My picture books revolve around a mathematical or other educational concept." *Avocational interests:* Dancing, puppet design, toy design.

*   *   *

TOOLE STOTT, Raymond   1910-1982

OBITUARY NOTICE: Born in 1910 in London, England; died

January 10, 1982, in Westminster, London, England. Circus historian, bibliographer, and journalist. Best known for his four-volume bibliography of publications concerning the circus, Raymond Toole Stott also published a series of bibliographies on the writings of novelist W. Somerset Maugham. Included among Toole Stott's works are *Circus and Allied Arts: A World Bibliography, The Writings of W. Somerset Maugham: A Bibliography,* and *Supplement to the Writings of W. Somerset Maugham.* Obituaries and other sources: *The Author's and Writer's Who's Who,* 6th edition, Burke's Peerage, 1971; *London Times,* January 23, 1982.

*   *   *

TOPOR, Tom   1938-

PERSONAL: Born in 1938 in Vienna, Austria. *Education:* Attended Brooklyn College (now of the City University of New York). *Office: New York Post,* 210 South St., New York, N.Y. 10002. *Address:* c/o W. W. Norton & Co., Inc., 500 Fifth Ave., New York, N.Y. 10036.

CAREER: Journalist and playwright. Worked for *New York Daily News* and *New York Times;* currently associated with *New York Post.*

WRITINGS—Novels: *Tightrope Minor,* Doubleday, 1971; *Bloodstar,* Norton, 1978.

Plays: "The Playpen" (one-act), first produced Off-Off Broadway at Extension Theatre, June, 1969; "Up the Hill" (one-act), first produced Off-Off Broadway at Extension Theatre, June, 1969; *Answers,* Dramatists Play Service, 1973 (also published in *Best Short Plays of 1972,* edited by Stanley Richards, Chilton, 1972); "Nuts" (three-act), first produced on Broadway at Biltmore Theatre, April 29, 1980.

SIDELIGHTS: Topor's dramas have been produced at a number of Off-Off Broadway theatres, including Cafe Cino, Cafe La Mama, Extension, and Playwright's Unit. His plays often feature characters whose off-beat actions are contrary to expected behavior. For example, Topor's courtroom melodrama "Nuts" focuses on Claudia, a young woman who has been placed under psychiatric observation in a mental hospital following her indictment for manslaughter. Claudia, unlike those who plead insanity in order to avoid prison sentences, requests a hearing in order to prove that she is indeed competent enough to stand trial.

Saturday Review's Stanley Kauffmann maintained that Topor uses Claudia's unusual behavior as a gimmick that allows a conventional courtroom drama to "masquerade as a daring probe" and dismissed the play as "an old dish" with "new sauce." A *New York Times* critic disagreed with Kauffmann and argued that "it's in an old form that a playwright finds it easiest to get something new said." Topor's "Nuts," he maintained, is a novel commentary on a recent trend in which individuals are demanding the right to accept personal responsibility for their own actions.

BIOGRAPHICAL/CRITICAL SOURCES: Show Business, June 21, 1969; *New York Times,* April 29, 1980, June 8, 1980; *New York Post,* April 29, 1980; *New Yorker,* May 12, 1980; *Saturday Review,* August, 1980.*

*   *   *

TOPSFIELD, L(eslie) T(homas)   1920-1981

OBITUARY NOTICE—See index for *CA* sketch: Born January 6, 1920, in Westcliff-on-Sea, Essex, England; died November 3, 1981. Educator and author of scholarly works on medieval topics. Topsfield acquired a reputation for distinguished scholarship following the publication of *Les Poesies du troubadour Raimon de Miravel,* a critical study of the works of de Miravel, and *Troubadours and Love,* a discourse on courtly love. Shortly before his death, Topsfield completed a major study of the Arthurian legends entitled *Chretien de Troyes.* Obituaries and other sources: *London Times,* November 12, 1981.

*   *   *

TORBERT, Floyd James   1922-

PERSONAL: Born February 7, 1922, in Jacksonville, Fla.; son of James Knox and Gertrude (Voss) Torbert; married Margaret Fryer (deceased); children: Bruce (deceased). *Education:* Attended Philadelphia College of Art. *Religion:* Baptist. *Home and office:* 73 Chapel Rd., New Hope, Pa. 18938.

CAREER: Free-lance illustrator for magazines, books, comic books, newspapers, and advertising agencies. Portrait painter and art teacher. Work exhibited at several one-man shows in Pennsylvania and New Jersey. *Military service:* U.S. Army Air Forces, special services, illustrator for *Daily Okinawan,* 1942-45; became sergeant. *Member:* New Hope Art League (president, 1974-79), Doylestown Art League, Hunterdon Art Center.

WRITINGS—Self-illustrated; all published by Hastings House: *Policemen the World Over,* 1965; *Postmen the World Over,* 1966; *Firefighters the World Over,* 1967; *Park Rangers and Game Wardens the World Over,* 1968.

Illustrator; all published by Hastings House, except as noted: Cornelius McGillicuddy, *Connie Mack's Baseball Book,* Knopf, 1950; Ada Claire Barby, *Brave Venture,* Winston, 1951; Joseph H. Gage, *The Beckoning Hills,* Winston, 1951; Mark Twain, *Tom Sawyer,* Winston, 1952; Shepherd Knapp, *Rope 'Em Cowboy,* Knapp, 1954; Robert Ashley, *Rebel Raiders,* Winston, 1956; C. Paul Jackson, *Tommy: Soap Box Derby Champion,* 1963; Helen D. Francis, *Martha Norton: Operation U.S.A.,* 1963; Anne Molloy, *Mystery of the Pilgrim Trading Post,* 1964; Jackson, *Super Modified Driver,* 1964; Donald E. Cooke, *Presidents in Uniform,* 1969; Dorothy Shuttlesworth, *The Tower of London: Grim and Glamorous,* 1970; Jackson, *Fifth Inning Fade-Out,* 1972.

WORK IN PROGRESS: A book tentatively titled *To Be an Artist.*

SIDELIGHTS: Torbert commented: "I work in all media. I love animals and people—they are my favorite subjects to paint and illustrate. I also like sports of all kinds.

"I was strongly influenced by Henry Pitz and Thorton Oakley as teachers. Norman Rockwell was my idol."

BIOGRAPHICAL/CRITICAL SOURCES: Daily Intellegencia, January 30, 1979.

*   *   *

TORRENS, Robert George   ?-1981

OBITUARY NOTICE: Dental surgeon and author. Robert Torrens wrote books on dentistry and the occult, including *Dental Disease: Its Chemical Causation and Cure, The Golden Dawn: Its Inner Teachings,* and *The Secret Rituals of the Golden Dawn.* Obituaries and other sources: *The Author's and Writer's Who's Who,* 6th edition, Burke's Peerage, 1971; *The Writers Directory, 1976-1978,* St. Martin's, 1976. (Date of death provided by son Hugh Torrens.)

TOSON, Shimazaki
See SHIMAZAKI, Haruki

*   *   *

TOTH, Susan Erickson Allen   1940-

PERSONAL: Born June 24, 1940, in Ames, Iowa; daughter of Edward Douglas (a professor of economics) and Hazel (a professor of English; maiden name, Erickson) Allen; married Louis E. Toth, 1963 (divorced, 1974); children: Jennifer Lee. *Education:* Smith College, B.A., 1961; University of California, Berkeley, M.A., 1963; University of Minnesota, Ph.D., 1969. *Home:* 1648 Eleanor Ave., St. Paul, Minn. 55116. *Agent:* Molly Friedrich, Aaron M. Priest Literary Agency, Inc., 150 East 35th St., New York, N.Y. 10016. *Office:* Department of English, Macalester College, St. Paul, Minn. 55105.

CAREER: San Francisco State College, San Francisco, Calif., instructor in English, 1963-64; Macalester College, St. Paul, Minn., assistant professor, 1969-75, associate professor of English, 1975—. *Awards, honors:* Fellow of Minnesota State Arts Board, 1980.

WRITINGS: Blooming: A Small Town Girlhood (memoirs), Little, Brown, 1981. Contributor of articles and stories to literature and geography journals, magazines, including *Harper's, Redbook, Ms., Cosmopolitan, McCall's,* and *Great River Review,* and newspapers.

WORK IN PROGRESS: Another memoir; a novel; a short novel for young adults; a book of short stories.

SIDELIGHTS: Susan Toth told *CA:* "I'd like to think it might be encouraging for other writers who started late to know that I didn't begin to write fiction and other pieces (aside from scholarly work) until I was in my mid-thirties. Then I began absolutely cold, without knowing anyone in the publishing world to whom I could show my stories. Through an over-the-transom submission, I found one editor who encouraged me; she in turn introduced my work to someone else. One *can* start writing in the middle years in a small upstairs room in Minnesota!"

BIOGRAPHICAL/CRITICAL SOURCES: New York Times Book Review, May 23, 1981; *St. Paul Pioneer Press,* May 23, 1981; *Minneapolis Tribune,* May 29, 1981; *Des Moines Register,* June 4, 1981; *Cedar Rapids Gazette,* July 5, 1981.

*   *   *

TOUSTER, Alison
See REED, Alison Touster

*   *   *

TOWERS, Ivar
See KORNBLUTH, C(yril) M.

*   *   *

TRACY, Jack W.   1945-

PERSONAL: Born February 13, 1945, in Albuquerque, N.M. *Education:* Attended Indiana University, 1963-67. *Politics:* Republican. *Home and office:* 112 East Second, Bloomington, Ind. 47401.

CAREER: Worked as a producer of radio programs; worked as a television program executive and producer of television programs; Gaslight Publications, Bloomington, Ind., publisher, 1979—. *Member:* Baker Street Irregulars. *Awards, hon-*

ors: Feldman-Morley-Montgomery Award for Sherlockian writing from Baker Street Irregulars, 1978; special Edgar Allan Poe Award from Mystery Writers of America for *Encyclopaedia Sherlockiana,* 1978.

WRITINGS: The Encyclopaedia Sherlockiana; or, A Universal Dictionary of the State of Knowledge of Sherlock Holmes and His Biographer John H. Watson, M.D., Doubleday, 1977; (with Jim Berkey) *Subcutaneously, My Dear Watson: Sherlock Holmes and the Cocaine Habit,* James A. Rock, 1978; *Conan Doyle and the Latter Day Saints,* Gaslight, 1979; (editor) Sir Arthur Conan Doyle, *Sherlock Holmes: The Published Apocrypha,* Houghton, 1980; (editor) Doyle, *Brigadier Gerard,* Jove, 1982; (editor) Doyle, *The Return of Gerard,* Jove, 1982.

Calendars: (With Philip C. Thompson and Ned Shaw) "Sherlock Holmes Calendar, 1978," Doubleday, 1977; (with Thompson and Paul M. McCall) "Sherlock Holmes Calendar, 1979," Doubleday, 1978; (with Anneke Campbell) "Your Pregnancy Year," Doubleday, 1979.

WORK IN PROGRESS: A novel about Sir Arthur Conan Doyle's 1922 American lecture tour promoting spiritualism, for publication by Avon.

SIDELIGHTS: Tracy's *Encyclopaedia Sherlockiana* is a dictionary of phrases, terms, and customs used by Sir Arthur Conan Doyle in the Sherlock Holmes tales. Although these terms were understood by readers in Victorian England, they are unfamiliar to modern American readers. Tracy spent six years compiling and researching the book, which contains 3500 entries complete with citations and cross-references. *Chronicle of Higher Education* critic Howard Lachtman praised *Encyclopaedia Sherlockiana* for its usefulness, calling the book "a browser's delight, a student's resource, and a scholar's aid." Newgate Callendar said "Tracy has done much more than compile a series of index cards. He has written a thoughtful introduction about Holmes and the Victorian period, has found some lovely illustrations, and has worked up a book that will answer any conceivable factual question about any of the Holmes exploits."

Sherlock Holmes: The Published Apocrypha is a collection of eleven stories either written or sanctioned by Doyle, but never included in the "official" tally of the fifty-six short stories and four novels which comprise the Holmes series. Tracy included in the book "The Speckled Band" and "The Crown Diamond," which are the only two stories Doyle adapted into plays, as well as two stories in which Doyle teases the reader with a parody of the Holmes and Watson characters. Doyle, who reportedly had grown to dislike the Holmes character, was able to exact some revenge by having the master sleuth arrive at an incorrect solution to a case. Lachtman, reviewing for the *Los Angeles Times,* wrote that "these apocryphal adventures have a peculiar fascination. While they may not reveal anything new or startling about the private life or public career of Sherlock Holmes, they do shed light on Doyle's own personal and professional attitudes toward his most celebrated literary creation."

Tracy told *CA:* "The publicity blurb for one of my books called me a 'popularizer' of serious Sherlockian studies. That's a good description. Most Sherlockians, like scholars everywhere, tend to write for one another, but I've never seen the attraction of addressing a limited audience, and so I find myself in the uncommon, lucrative, and occasionally maligned role of popularizer. It suits my nature.

"It means, too, that I am among the 15 percent or so of Holmes scholars who choose not to play the 'game'—that Holmes was a real person, that the cases actually happened, that Watson actually wrote them up, and Sir Arthur Conan Doyle acted only as Watson's 'literary agent.' Having out of professional necessity looked upon the Holmes saga as a work of fiction created by one of the Victorian era's most resourceful authors, I find myself a greater admirer of Conan Doyle than I ever was of Sherlock Holmes. The creator is naturally superior to the creation, and Doyle's real-life character and accomplishments are far more interesting—and admirable—than the fictional adventures of Sherlock Holmes. That is why my novel is about Conan Doyle, and that is why I've established Gaslight Publications, to celebrate this unique Victorian romanticist."

BIOGRAPHICAL/CRITICAL SOURCES: New York Times Book Review, January 1, 1978, December 16, 1979, November 9, 1980; *Best Sellers,* March, 1978; *New Republic,* March 4, 1978; *Chronicle of Higher Education,* June 26, 1978; *Books and Bookmen,* July, 1979; *Changing Times,* February, 1980; *Los Angeles Times,* December 16, 1980.

*   *   *

TREDENNICK, (George) Hugh (Percival Phair) 1899-1981

OBITUARY NOTICE: Born June 30, 1899, in Birmingham, England; died December 31, 1981. Educator, translator, editor, and author. Hugh Tredennick, former professor of classics at Royal Holloway College, London, was a highly respected translator of the works of the Greek philosophers Aristotle and Plato and the Greek historian Xenophon. Included among those translations are *Metaphysics, Posterior Analytics, The Last Days of Socrates,* and *Symposium.* From 1961 to 1967, Tredennick served as co-editor of the *Classical Review.* He also contributed numerous articles on literature and philosophy to classical journals. Obituaries and other sources: *Who's Who,* 126th edition, St. Martin's, 1974; *Who Was Who Among English and European Authors, 1931-1949,* Gale, 1978; *London Times,* January 11, 1982.

*   *   *

TREGIDGO, Philip Sillince 1926-

PERSONAL: Surname is pronounced Tre-*gidge*-o; born March 3, 1926, in Portsmouth, England; son of Percy James (a shop assistant) and Daisy (Sillince) Tregidgo; married Vera Williams, August 19, 1950; children: Stephen, Mark, Jane Ann. *Education:* Oriel College, Oxford, B.A., 1949, diploma in education, 1950; University of Reading, M.A., 1971. *Home:* Winneba, 11 The Avenue, Petersfield, Hampshire, England.

CAREER: Coal miner, 1944-48; teacher of French, English, and religion at boys' junior technical school in Wimbledon, England, 1951-53; British Colonial Service and Ghana Ministry of Education, Accra, Ghana, senior education officer and English teaching organizer, 1954-63; writer, 1963—. *Member:* International Association of Teachers of English as a Foreign Language, Linguistic Association of Great Britain, Society of Authors.

WRITINGS—For non-English-speaking students: *Practical English Usage,* Longmans, Green, 1959, 2nd edition, 1962; *A Background to English,* Longmans, Green, 1962, 2nd edition, 1971; (with P. A. Ogundipe) *Practical English,* Books 1-5, Longmans, Green, 1965-66, 2nd edition, 1972-75; *Building Our English,* Books 1-2, Longmans, Green, reprinted as *English for Tanzanian Schools,* Standards 6-7, 1967-70; (with J.A.F. Sokoya) *Day-by-Day English Course for Western Nigeria,* Longmans, Green, 1967; *The Story of the Aeroplane,* Longmans, Green, 1969; *The Magic Rocks,* Longmans, Green, 1969.

(With I. K. Hoh) *Longman New Ghana English Course,* Books 1-3, Longman, 1970-78; *The Story of the Motor-Car,* Longman, 1971; *The Story of Trains,* Oxford University Press, 1975; (with Ogundipe) *Practical English Workbooks,* Books 1-3, Longman, 1976-78; *English Grammar in Practice,* Longman, 1979; (with A. L. Mawasha) *Advance With English,* Standards 6-8, Longman, 1979-81.

Contributor to education journals.

WORK IN PROGRESS: Research on English grammar from the point of view of the foreign learner.

SIDELIGHTS: Tregidgo told *CA:* "Having studied linguistics at Reading in 1970-71, I retain a general interest in the subject but find much of it, especially transformational-generative grammars, overly theoretical and of no practical use. English language teaching is subject to pseudoscientific fashions, such as 'communicative' teaching. Each fashion has something useful in it, but language teaching is fundamentally a craft and a natural human exercise rather than a science, and it is not capable of scientific development. There is no reason to suppose that we moderns teach foreign languages any better than the ancient Romans taught Greek."

AVOCATIONAL INTERESTS: Choral singing.

*   *   *

TREPPER, Leopold Leib   1904-1982(?)

OBITUARY NOTICE: Born in 1904 in Poland; died c. January, 1982, in Jerusalem, Israel. During World War II, Leopold Trepper served as resident director of the Soviet spy network in Belgium. German troops raided the network's headquarters on December 13, 1941, but Trepper managed to elude them. The German's second attempt to arrest him, on November 16, 1942, was successful. Trepper cooperated with his captors until his escape in June of 1943. When the war ended, he was recalled to Moscow and was sentenced to serve ten years in prison. Trepper's book *Le Grand Jeu* was published in 1977 as *The Great Game: Memoirs of the Spy Hitler Couldn't Silence.* Obituaries and other sources: *Who Was Who in World War II,* Arms & Armour Press, 1978; *Time,* February 1, 1982.

*   *   *

TRICKETT, Joyce   1915-

PERSONAL: Born November 21, 1915, in Uralla, Australia; daughter of Frederick Emmanuel (in business) and Louisa Carver (Felton) Trickett. *Education:* Attended secondary school in Armidale, New South Wales, Australia; studied singing and speech privately in Sydney, Australia. *Politics:* Liberal. *Religion:* Uniting Church. *Home:* Quibree, 23 Lavender Cres., Lavender Bay, North Sydney 2060, Australia.

CAREER: Women's and children's session announcer with 2NZ Commercial Radio, 1946-50; 2CH Commercial Radio, Sydney, Australia, narrator and performer on "Treasury of Song" and "The Poetry of the People" and special feature writer, 1951-53; free-lance broadcaster and scriptwriter with Australian Broadcasting Commission, 1953-78; teacher at Tudor House (boys' preparatory school), 1958—. Teacher at private girls' school, 1958-70; singer, 1964-77; adjudicator in speech and drama; artist, with exhibitions for charity, 1971—. *Member:* Australian Authors Society, New South Wales Musical Association, 2NZ Radio Service Club, 2CH Radio Service Club. *Awards, honors:* Search for Australian musical award from General Motors Holden, 1965, for "Jenolan Adventure."

WRITINGS: The Light Shines (stories and poems), privately printed, 1964, 2nd edition, 1975; *Pool of Quiet* (poems and broadcasts), privately printed, 1965; "Jenolan Adventure" (three-act musical play for young people), first produced in Bowral, New South Wales, Australia, 1966; *Bless This House* (poems and broadcasts), privately printed, 1970, 4th edition, 1975; *An Australian Vision* (spiritual stage concept), Epworth, 1972; *Christmas Is Forever* (poems and prayers), privately printed, 1975; (with Annette Kosseris, Catherine Blowen, and Dora Friendship) *Seven to Ten and Back Again* (poems for children), Hutchens, 1975, 2nd edition, 1978; (with Kosseris) *Up to Six and Over* (poems for children), Hutchens, 1980.

Television scripts: "I Found Driftwood," first broadcast by Australian Broadcasting Commission, 1965; "Let Christmas In," first broadcast by Australian Broadcasting Commission, 1968; "The Great Meeting of Children," first broadcast by Australian Broadcasting Commission, 1972.

Composer and lyricist of songs, including "The Wooden Madonna," Southern Music, 1961; "Bridges Blues," Southern Music, 1962; "Dearer Than Yesterday," Southern Music, 1964; "City in Cellophane," Southern Music, 1965.

WORK IN PROGRESS: The Catitudes of Chairman Meow, on the wisdom of a cat, with oil-chalk illustrations, publication expected in 1983; *Teens and Upward,* poems for speaking.

SIDELIGHTS: Joyce Trickett told *CA:* "I've written since the age of ten, finding deepest satisfaction in painting with words the scene, happening, aspiration, or longing I hope to perpetuate. A poem is born, not made. I abhor awkwardness in writing and cut up prose called poetry. I loathe ugliness in the human voice. My greatest response to a spoken poem was to 'Driftwood,' a poem I presented on Australian Broadcasting Commission television, with accompanying driftwood visuals. Filmed on Whale Beach, it is a poem on man's progressing faith. My supreme joy on radio was to devise and present 'The Poetry of the People.' A humbling moment came when I was interviewing the great Helen Keller on stage in Sydney's Town Hall.

"Poetry, I believe, is spoken song, and for me the words must be easy on the tongue and rememberable. Broken up prose on a page is not true poetry unless the poetic pulse throbs there. The computer can never supply the inspiration that motivates the creative soul of mankind.

"To survive as creative beings we must turn to the creative worth within people, educate and value this above all so that this age withstands the terrible takeover. So shall we leave to posterity the art, music, and word beauty of our day.

"As a poet I smile to think that it was a protest poem against developer devastation of Sydney Harbor's foreshores that people most remember and quote."

*   *   *

TRUMAN, (Mary) Margaret   1924-

PERSONAL: Born February 17, 1924, in Independence, Mo.; daughter of Harry S. (a U.S. president) and Elizabeth Virginia (Wallace) Truman; married E. Clifton Daniel, Jr. (a newspaper editor), April 21, 1956; children: Clifton, William, Harrison, Thomas. *Education:* George Washington University, A.B., 1946. *Politics:* Democrat. *Religion:* Episcopalian. *Residence:* New York, N.Y. *Agent:* Scott Meredith, Scott Meredith Literary Agency, Inc., 845 Third Ave., New York, N.Y. 10022.

CAREER: Writer. Worked as opera coloratura, 1947-54; summer stock actress; host of radio program "Weekday," 1955, and host of television program. Director of Riggs National Bank, Washington, D.C., and of Seabury Press, New York, N.Y.; trustee of Harry S. Truman Institute and of Church Pension Fund Board. *Awards, honors:* L.H.D. from Wake Forest University, 1972; Litt.D. from George Washington University, 1975; H.H.D. from Rockhurst College, 1976.

WRITINGS: Souvenir, McGraw, 1956; *White House Pets,* McKay, 1969; *Harry S. Truman* (biography), Morrow, 1973; *Women of Courage,* Morrow, 1976; *Murder in the White House* (mystery novel), Arbor House, 1980; *Murder on Capitol Hill* (mystery novel), Arbor House, 1981.

SIDELIGHTS: Margaret Truman lived in the White House for more than seven years and later employed her knowledge of life at 1600 Pennsylvania Avenue to write her first novel, *Murder in the White House.* She insists, however, that the book is "pure fiction" and that none of the characters are based on real people. The daughter of former President Harry Truman "has been so circumspect in her narrative that there would be no reason to suspect she had been any closer to the inner circle of the White House than a Sunday afternoon tour," commented Peter Andrews of the *New York Times Book Review.*

Murder in the White House concerns the death of Lansard Blaine, a corrupt secretary of state. Because Blaine was a reputed womanizer and had been involved in illegal business deals, there are numerous suspects in the case. "Blaine may have been put out of business by one of these females," theorized Chris Chase of the *Chicago Tribune,* "or he may have been killed by the agent of a foreign power . . . , or he may have been killed by 'someone fairly highly placed in the White House.'" The ensuing investigation exposes personal and political scandals that plague the White House and the first family.

Reviewers noted that *Murder in the White House* contains the makings of a fine mystery novel but suffers from a lack of polish. Edwin J. Miller of *Best Sellers* maintained that the idea of "the murder of the Secretary of State in the family quarters in the White House . . . could have made a first-rate book." He noted, however, that Truman's final product was only an "excellent outline." Andrews similarly pointed out that "the author has most of the elements in place, but she never sets them in motion in an arresting manner." Truman "shows herself to be a writer with a clear, straightforward style," added Andrews. "A bit more thought and some rudimentary editing might have turned her book into a really interesting story. . . . All the evidence indicates that Margaret Truman is capable of doing much more interesting work than this."

Truman also called on her knowledge of life in the nation's capital to write her second novel. In *Murder on Capitol Hill* it is the slaying of the Senate majority leader that begins the action. Among the suspects are members of the senator's family, including his wife, a talk show host, and a political rival in the Senate. The involvement of the slain senator's son in a religious cult and a long-unsolved crime—the murder of the senator's adopted niece—add further twists to Truman's detailed plot.

As in her first novel, critics found flaws in *Murder on Capitol Hill* as well as signs of promise. Jean M. White of the *Washington Post Book World* criticized Truman's "uninspired" prose style and said the author "clutters her plot and cast of characters." Still, White noted, Truman "writes entertainingly about the Washington scene and not without a touch of gentle amusement." Alice Cromie also praised the "expertly detailed" Washington milieu of the novel. "The opening is far better than the wind-up," remarked the *Chicago Tribune Book World* critic, "but it looks as if Truman is serious about the genre."

Truman told *CA:* "I am always glad when a book or a magazine article is finished. I promise myself never to write another one, but I shall probably do one. Writing is the hardest and most exacting career I've ever had."

The movie rights for *Murder in the White House* have been purchased by Dick Clark Cinema Productions.

BIOGRAPHICAL/CRITICAL SOURCES: New York Times, April 24, 1980; *People,* June 16, 1980; *Chicago Tribune,* July 6, 1980; *New York Times Book Review,* July 20, 1980; *Best Sellers,* July, 1980; *Chicago Tribune Book World,* June 21, 1981; *Washington Post Book World,* July 19, 1981.

*   *   *

TRUPP, Beverly Ann 1937-

PERSONAL: Born June 19, 1937, in Santa Monica, Calif.; daughter of Everett Arthur and Betty Elaine (Anderson) Graves. *Education:* Recieved B.A. and M.A. from University of Southern California. *Religion:* "Born-again Christian." *Home:* 701 North Bundy Dr., Los Angeles, Calif. 90049. *Office:* Color Design Art, 1823 Stanford St., Santa Monica, Calif. 90404.

CAREER: Color Design Art, Santa Monica, Calif., president, 1970—.

WRITINGS: Color It Home, CBI Publishing, 1981. Contributing editor of *Professional Builder.*

SIDELIGHTS: Beverly Trupp told *CA:* "I am a person who loves to grow, and becoming a businesswoman afforded me the greatest opportunity to do that. Writing my book stirred up a sense of responsibility in me to my profession and a respect for the unending amount there is to learn! Being a permanent student of life, I am grateful to be part of a dynamic profession. Taking business into team efforts with clients, where we work together toward a common goal, is truly rewarding.

"Travel to many parts of the country to serve the markets in the housing field has allowed me to understand and observe life-styles from coast to coast, which enables me to be more sensitive to the many markets in which I am actively involved."

AVOCATIONAL INTERESTS: Skiing, tennis, enjoying the sunshine, "conversations over dinner."

*   *   *

TRUSE, Kenneth (Philip) 1946-

PERSONAL: Born March 8, 1946, in Chicago, Ill. *Education:* De Paul University, B.A. (summa cum laude), 1968; University of Wisconsin—Madison, M.A. (English), 1969; University of Iowa, M.A. (film and broadcasting), 1974. *Home and office:* 1950 Osage Lane, Santa Fe, N.M. 87501.

CAREER: Chemical company representative; former professor of communications; free-lance author, 1977—. *Awards, honors:* National Endowment for the Humanities fellowship, 1976-77.

WRITINGS: Benny's Magic Baking Pan (juvenile; illustrated by Bill Morrison), Garrard, 1974.

WORK IN PROGRESS: A contemporary novel; several children's stories.

SIDELIGHTS: Truse told *CA:* "I am particularly interested in blending comedy with tragedy to examine social and psychological currents in contemporary American culture. In my recent work for adults and children, I try to deal with the intense emotional problems created by such changes as new jobs, new hopes, and shattered dreams."

TUCKER, Irwin St. John   1886-1982
(Friar Tuck)

OBITUARY NOTICE: Born in 1886 in Mobile, Ala.; died January 8, 1982, in Evanston, Ill. Clergyman, journalist, poet, and author. A journalist on the staff of the *Chicago Herald-American* for thirty years, Irwin Tucker was the paper's religion editor at the time of his retirement in 1954. The former literature director for the American Socialist party, he also contributed poetry, under the pseudonym Friar Tuck, to the *Chicago Tribune*. In addition to his journalistic activities, Tucker served as an Episcopal minister for nearly forty years until resigning in 1950 after converting to Catholicism. He wrote numerous books, including *A History of Imperialism, Out of the Hellbox, A Minstrel Friar,* and *Geography of the Gods.* Obituaries and other sources: *Chicago Tribune,* January 10, 1982.

* * *

TULLY, Mary Jo   1937-

PERSONAL: Born December 25, 1937, in Chicago, Ill.; daughter of Martin Joseph (in police work) and Mary (Kenney) Tully. *Education:* De Paul University, Ph.B., 1963; Loyola University, Chicago, Ill., M.R.E., 1969. *Home:* 3950 Lake Shore Dr., No. 1119 D, Chicago, Ill. 60613. *Office:* Archdiocesan Center of Confraternity of Christian Doctrine, 1025 West Fry St., Chicago, Ill. 60622.

CAREER: Worked as elementary school teacher, 1958-63, and high school teacher, 1963-67; Archdiocesan Center of Confraternity of Christian Doctrine, Chicago, Ill., youth consultant, 1967-69, executive assistant, 1969-77, director, 1977—. Part-time catechetics lecturer and professor at St. Mary of the Lake Seminary, Institute of Pastoral Studies of Loyola University, and St. Thomas University, 1967-81; adjunct professor of theology at Loyola University, 1970-75. *Member:* National Catholic Education Association, National Conference of Diocesan Directors, Religious Education Association. *Awards, honors:* Best regular column award from National Catholic Press Association, 1981.

WRITINGS: A Family Book of Praise; or, Would You Rather Be a Hippopotamus?, Sadlier, 1981; (with Sandra Hirstein) *Light of Faith* (textbook), six volumes, W.C. Brown, 1981; *Blessed Be. . .* (adult religious education program), W.C. Brown, 1981. Author of a column in *Chicago Catholic.*

WORK IN PROGRESS: Four books for the series in adult religious education, publication by W.C. Brown expected in 1982.

SIDELIGHTS: Mary Tully commented: "My main areas are the communication of the Roman Catholic faith as well as the joys and delights of Christianity and the challenge of relating that message to the human experience."

In his review of *A Family Book of Praise,* John Shea wrote in the *Chicago Catholic:* "The theme of this book is celebration. Celebration is understood as a resounding 'Yes!' to the Mystery of life, even though that Mystery contains ambiguity and pain. Through Miss Tully's evocative language, we are taken on a tour of the life stages. We enter into the wonder of creation itself, the fun of the early years, the playfulness of childhood, the clumsiness and romance of adolescence, the ennui and search for meaning of young adulthood, and the memory, reconciliation, and hope of the mature years. There is also a chapter on Eucharistic celebration which spells out clearly and concretely the overriding vision of the book."

BIOGRAPHICAL/CRITICAL SOURCES: Chicago Catholic, October 3, 1980.

* * *

TURLEY, William S(tephen)   1943-

PERSONAL: Born April 6, 1943, in Wallace, Idaho; son of Abel G. and Gertrude (Gnaedinger) Turley; married Clarisse Zimra (a professor), November 23, 1971; children: Olivia. *Education:* Whitman College, A.B., 1965; University of Washington, Seattle, M.A., 1967, Ph.D., 1972. *Home:* 300 Friedline Dr., Carbondale, Ill. 62901. *Office:* Department of Political Science, Southern Illinois University, Carbondale, Ill. 62901.

CAREER: Southern Illinois University, Carbondale, instructor, 1971-72, assistant professor, 1972-76, associate professor of political science, 1976—. Visiting professor at University of Saigon, 1972-73. *Member:* International Studies Association, American Political Science Association, Association for Asian Studies (member of executive committee of Vietnam studies group, 1975-80), Inter-University Seminar on the Armed Forces and Society. *Awards, honors:* U.S. Department of State fellow in Vietnam, 1967-68; Ford Foundation fellow in Vietnam, 1972-73; grants from Inter-University Seminar on the Armed Forces and Society, 1977, and Association for Asian Studies, 1979.

WRITINGS: (Contributor) Joseph Zasloff and Allan E. Goodman, editors, *Indochina in Conflict: A Political Assessment,* Heath, 1972; (contributor) Zasloff and MacAlister Brown, editors, *Communism in Indochina: New Perspectives,* Heath, 1975; (editor and contributor) *Vietnamese Communism in Comparative Perspective,* Westview Press, 1980; (contributor) Jonathan R. Adelman, editor, *Communist Armies in Politics,* Westview Press, 1981. Contributor of more than fifteen articles and reviews to political science and international studies journals.

WORK IN PROGRESS: "North Vietnam at War," an article to be included in a history of the Vietnam War, edited by Herbert Golden and others, for U.S. News and World Report.

* * *

TURNBULL, Agnes Sligh   1888-1982

OBITUARY NOTICE—See index for *CA* sketch: Born October 14, 1888, in New Alexandria, Pa.; died January 31, 1982, in Livingston, N.J. Author. After twelve years of writing short stories, Turnbull began her career as a novelist with an epic work entitled *The Rolling Years.* It was followed by other works about the inhabitants of rural Pennsylvania, including *Remember the End, The Day Must Dawn,* and *The Bishop's Mantle.* Espousing the "old-fashioned" virtues and optimistic about humanity, Turnbull's novels have been regarded by some critics as anachronistic. All of her works, however, have been widely read and have appeared in paperback editions and in foreign translations. Turnbull's most recent novel was *The Two Bishops.* Obituaries and other sources: *Booklist,* November 1, 1968; *Publishers Weekly,* August 10, 1970, June 26, 1972; *New York Times,* November 26, 1972, February 2, 1982; *Books and Bookmen,* October, 1973; *AB Bookman's Weekly,* February 22, 1982.

* * *

TURNER, Judy
See SAXTON, Judith

TURNER, Paul Digby Lowry 1917-

PERSONAL: Born May 11, 1917, in West Hartlepool, England; son of Percy Reginald (a minister) and Sarah Violet (a missionary; maiden name, Gourley) Turner; married Jane Enid Mary Fossey (a British Red Cross worker), May 11, 1967. *Education:* King's College, Cambridge, degree, 1939, M.A., 1944. *Home:* 17 Walton St., Oxford, England. *Office:* Linacre College, Oxford University, Oxford, England.

CAREER: Ministry of Health, London, England, assistant principal, 1939-45; University of London, King's College, London, England, assistant lecturer in English, 1946-48; Cambridge University, Cambridge, England, assistant lecturer in English, 1948-53; St. Marylebone Grammar School, London, teacher of classics, 1953-55; University of London, lecturer in English, 1955-61; University of Ankara, Ankara, Turkey, professor of English, 1961-62; University of London, lecturer in English, 1962-63; University of Ankara, professor of English, 1963-64; Oxford University, Oxford, England, lecturer in English literature and fellow of Linacre College, 1964—. Chairman of Oxfordshire Council for Voluntary Service, 1978-81. *Military service:* Royal Naval Volunteer Reserve, Fleet Air Arm, 1939-45; became lieutenant commander. *Member:* Association of University Teachers, Society of Authors, Tennyson Society, Classical Society, Joint Association of Classical Teachers.

WRITINGS: Tennyson, Routledge & Kegan Paul, 1976.

Editor: (And author of introduction) Caius Plinius Secundus, *Selections From the History of the World,* translated by Philemon Holland, Centaur Press, 1962; (and author of introduction) Plutarch, *Selected Lives From the Lives of the Noble Grecians and Romans,* two volumes, translated from the Greek into French by James Amyot and from the French into English by Thomas North, Centaur Press, 1963; (and author of introduction) Thomas More, *Utopia,* Penguin, 1965; Jonathan Swift, *Gulliver's Travels,* Oxford University Press, 1971; Robert Browning, *Men and Women,* Oxford University Press, 1972.

Translator: John Barclay, *Euphormio's Satyricon,* Golden Cockerel, 1954; (and author of introduction) Longus, *Daphnis and Chloe,* Penguin, 1956, revised edition, 1968; Tyrius Apollonius, *Apollonius of Tyre: Histoiria Apollonii Regis Tyri,* Golden Cockerel, 1956; Xenophon, *The Ephesian Story,* Golden Cockerel, 1957; Lucian, *True History* [and] *Lucius; or, The Ass,*

illustrated by Hellmuth Weissenborn, J. Calder, 1958; Ernst Theodor Wilhelm Hoffmann, *The King's Bride,* J. Calder, 1959; Friedrich Heinrich Carl de La Motte Fouque, *Undine,* J. Calder, 1960; (and author of introduction) Lucian, *Satirical Sketches,* Penguin, 1961; (and author of introduction) Publius Ovidius Naso, *The Techniques of Love* [and] *Remedies for Love,* translation by Jack Shapiro, Panther, 1968.

WORK IN PROGRESS: Oxford History of English Literature: 1830-1890, publication by Oxford University Press expected in 1986.

AVOCATIONAL INTERESTS: Music (violin and piano), languages (Greek, Latin, French, German, Italian, Turkish), travel (especially Greece and France), dogs, cats, walking.

* * *

TUSAN, Stan 1936-

PERSONAL: Born August 6, 1936, in Fresno, Calif.; son of Leo and Anna (Dalalian) Tusan; married Barbara Gould, August 15, 1969; children: Cary, Ali. *Education:* Fresno City College, A.A., 1956; Art Instruction School, Minneapolis, Minn., diploma in correspondence course, 1958; Chouinard Art Institute, Los Angeles, Calif., B.F.A., 1960. *Residence:* Walnut Creek, Calif.

CAREER: UPA Animated Film Studio, Los Angeles, Calif., storyboard artist, 1960; N.W. Ayer Advertising Agency, Chicago, Ill., art director, 1962-63; *Children's Digest* (magazine), New York, N.Y., art director, 1970-75.

WRITINGS: (Self illustrated) *Write-a-Letter Book,* Grosset, 1971.

Illustrator: Christopher Davis, *Sad Adam—Glad Adam,* Crowell, 1966; Barbro Lindgren, *Hilding's Summer,* Macmillan, 1967; Ann Wainwright, *Girls and Boys Easy-to-Cook Book,* edited by Barbara Zeitz, Grosset, 1967; Zeitz, *Make-a-Sweet Cookbook,* Grosset, 1969; Robyn Supraner, *Giggly-Wiggly, Snickety-Snick,* Parents Magazine Press, 1978; Joan Eckstein and Joyce Gleit, *Fun With Making Things,* Avon, 1979. Author and illustrator of works for Hallmark cards, educational books and materials, and magazines.

SIDELIGHTS: Tusan commented: "Working with or for children is a most satisfying pleasure. The usual research involved with each different assignment is an enlightening sidelight. I have found that one can never grow 'too young!'"

U

UDOVITCH, Abraham Labe   1933-

BRIEF ENTRY: Born May 31, 1933, in Winnipeg, Manitoba, Canada. Historian, educator, and author. Udovitch joined the faculty at Princeton University in 1967; he has been a professor of Islamic history since 1971. His writings include *Partnership and Profit in Medieval Islam* (Princeton University Press, 1970), *Studia Islamica* (1975), *The Middle East: Oil, Conflict, and Hope* (Lexington Books, 1976), and *The Islamic Middle East, 700-1900: Studies in Economic and Social History* (Darwin Press, 1981). *Address:* 247 Hartley Ave., Princeton, N.J. 08540; and Department of Near Eastern Studies, 110 Jones Hall, Princeton University, Princeton, N.J. 08540. *Biographical/ critical sources: Who's Who in America,* 40th edition, Marquis, 1978; *Directory of American Scholars,* Volume I: *History,* 7th edition, Bowker, 1978.

* * *

UHLMAN, Fred   1901-

PERSONAL: Born January 19, 1901, in Stuttgart, Germany (now West Germany); son of Ludwig and Johanna Uhlman; married Diana Croft, November 4, 1936; children: Francis, Caroline Uhlman Compton. *Education:* Received D.J. from University of Tuebingen. *Home:* Croft Castle, near Leominster, England.

CAREER: Attorney and writer. *Member:* Royal Society of Arts (fellow).

WRITINGS: Captivity, J. Cape, 1946; *The Making of an Englishman* (autobiography), Gollancz, 1960; *Reunion,* introduction by Arthur Koestler, Adam Books, 1971.

BIOGRAPHICAL/CRITICAL SOURCES: Studio, December 5, 1949.

* * *

ULIBARRI, Sabine Reyes   1919-

BRIEF ENTRY: Born September 21, 1919, in Santa Fe, N.M. American educator and author. Ulibarri has been teaching at the University of New Mexico since 1947. He became a professor of Spanish in 1968 and was named chairperson of the department of modern and classical languages in 1973. His writings include *Amor y Ecuador* (Ediciones Jose Porrua Turanzas, 1966), an edition and translation of *La fruga a sin fuego/ No Fire for the Forge: Stories and Poems in New Mexican*

Spanish and English Translation (San Marcos Press, 1971), *El alma de la raza* (Minority Group Cultural Awareness Center, University of New Mexico, 1971), and *Tierra Amarilla: Stories of New Mexico* (University of New Mexico Press, 1971). *Address:* Department of Modern and Classical Languages, University of New Mexico, Albuquerque, N.M. 87106. *Biographical/critical sources: Directory of American Scholars,* Volume III: *Foreign Languages, Linguistics, and Philosophy,* 7th edition, Bowker, 1978.

* * *

UNDERWOOD, Tim   1948-

PERSONAL: Born January 12, 1948, in Sault Sainte Marie, Mich.; son of John Norman (a chemist) and Johanna Wilma (a teacher; maiden name, Able) Underwood. *Education;* Attended Michigan State University, 1965-67, and College of Marin, 1973. *Home address:* P.O. Box 5402, San Francisco, Calif. 94101. *Office:* Underwood/Miller, 239 North Fourth St., Columbia, Pa. 17512.

CAREER: East-West Musical Instrument Co., San Francisco, Calif., assistant production manager, 1972-76; Underwood/ Miller (publishers), Columbia, Pa., and San Francisco, vice-president, 1976—; Prana Yoga Ashram, Berkeley, Calif., publications manager and yoga instructor, 1980—.

WRITINGS: (With Daniel J.H. Levack) *Fantasms,* Underwood/Miller, 1979; (editor with Chuck Miller) *Jack Vance,* Taplinger, 1980; (editor with Miller) *The Book of the Sixth World Fantasy Convention,* Underwood/Miller, 1980; (editor with Miller) *Fear Itself: The Horror Fiction of Stephen King,* Underwood/Miller, 1982.

WORK IN PROGRESS: The Worlds of James Clavell, publication expected in 1983.

SIDELIGHTS: Underwood told *CA:* "Moral fantasy is the most important and significant genre of fiction today. So I enjoy publishing it as well as writing about it. Since I also teach and study yoga, I'm always affected by honest books that show some spiritual emphasis and understanding."

* * *

UNRUH, John D., Jr.   1938(?)-1976

OBITUARY NOTICE: Educator and author. At the time of his death, John Unruh was an associate professor of history at

Bluffton College. His book *The Plains Across: The Overland Emigrants and the Trans-Mississippi West, 1840-1860* was posthumously published in 1979. Obituaries and other sources: *Chicago Tribune Book World,* November 11, 1979.

*   *   *

URQUHART, Brian Edward   1919-

PERSONAL: Born February 28, 1919, in Bridport, England; son of Murray and Bertha (Rendall) Urquhart; married Alfreda Huntington, March 31, 1944 (marriage ended, 1963); married Sidney Damrosch Howard, April 29, 1963; children: (first marriage) Thomas, Katharine, Robert; (second marriage) Rachel, Charles. *Education:* Attended Christ Church, Oxford, 1937-39. *Home:* 131 East 66th St., New York, N.Y. 10021. *Office:* United Nations, New York, N.Y. 10017.

CAREER: United Nations, New York, N.Y., personal assistant to executive secretary of Preparatory Commission in London, England, 1945-46, personal assistant to secretary-general, 1946-49, secretary of collective measures committee, 1951-53, member of Office of Undersecretary for special political affairs, 1954-71, assistant secretary-general, 1972-74, under-secretary-general for special political affairs, 1974—, executive secretary of conferences on peaceful uses of atomic energy, 1955 and 1958, worked with emergency force in the Middle East, 1956, deputy executive secretary of Preparatory Commission of International Atomic Energy Agency, 1957, assistant to special representative in the Congo, 1960, representative in Katanga, Congo, 1961-62. *Military service:* British Army, Dorset Regiment and Airborne Forces, 1939-45; served in North Africa, Sicily, and Europe; became major; mentioned in dispatches. *Member:* Century Association. *Awards, honors:* Member of Order of the British Empire, 1945.

WRITINGS: Hammarskjold, Knopf, 1972. Contributor of articles and reviews to magazines.

V

VAILLANCOURT, Jean-Guy 1937-

PERSONAL: Born May 24, 1937, in Chelmsford, Ontario, Canada; son of R. A. (in business) and Marie (Lavallee) Vaillancourt; married Pauline Marie Hansen (a professor of political science); children: Veronique. *Education:* Laurentian University, B.A., 1957; Faculte de Philosophie des Jesuites (Montreal, Quebec), Licentiate in Philosophy, 1961; Gregorian University, Licentiate in Sociology, 1964; University of California, Berkeley, Ph.D., 1975. *Office:* Department of Sociology, University of Montreal, C.P. 6128, Succursale A, Montreal, Quebec, Canada H3C 3J7.

CAREER: College de Saint-Boniface, Winnipeg, Manitoba, lecturer in sociology, 1964-65; University of Montreal, Montreal, Quebec, assistant professor, 1969-76, associate professor of sociology, 1976—. Lecturer at University of Manitoba, summer, 1965; visiting professor, Bishop's University, 1975-76, and Universite du Quebec a Chicoutimi, 1980-81. Member of Dunham city council, 1976-80. *Member:* International Sociological Association, Association of French-Speaking Canadian Sociologists and Anthropologists, American Sociological Association.

WRITINGS: (With Reinhard Bendix and others) *State and Society,* University of California Press, 1973; (with Daniel Latouche and Guy Lord) *Le Processus electoral au Quebec: Les Elections de 1970 et 1973* (title means "The Electoral Process in Quebec: The Elections of 1970 and 1973"), HMH, 1976; *Papal Power: A Study of Vatican Control Over Lay Catholic Elites,* University of California Press, 1980. Contributor of articles and reviews to journals, including *Our Generation* and *Synthesis.* Editor in chief of *Sociologie et Societes.*

WORK IN PROGRESS: Research on religious, ecological, and cooperative organizations.

SIDELIGHTS: Vaillancourt told *CA:* "I am basically a teacher (of sociology of religion, of organizations, of the environment) and a researcher. I love to write and publish, especially shorter, more polemical articles and reviews. My next book will probably be a translation into French of C. Wright Mills's essays, if I can iron out a series of problems concerning translation and rights.

"I am presently very involved in energy issues. I have written half a dozen shorter pieces in various Quebec publications in the past year on such topics, sometimes in collaboration with other people preoccupied with the questions of conservation and of nuclear energy.

"Also, with ninety-nine other Quebeckers from universities, unions, and community groups, I have participated recently in the publication of a socialist manifesto for Quebec. Our aim is to launch a Quebec socialist movement (not a party, at least for the time being) to promote the goals of socialism, democracy, independence, and the equality of men and women in Quebec. We are neither social-democrats nor Marxist-Leninists, but rather democratic socialists like those who recently [1981] won elections in France and in Greece."

*   *   *

VALDES, Ivy 1921-

PERSONAL: Born in 1921 in London, England. *Education:* Attended convent school in Essex, England. *Home:* 6 Lorraine Court, Osborne Villas, Hove, Sussex, England.

CAREER: Writer. *Member:* Society of Authors, Romantic Novelists Association.

WRITINGS—Novels: *Nicola,* Hurst & Blackett, 1964; *Gift From a Stranger,* Hurst & Blackett, 1965, New American Library, 1978; *Man of the Sea,* Hurst & Blackett, 1966; *It Happened in Spain,* Hurst & Blackett, 1967, U.S. edition (bound with *Christina's Fantasy*), New American Library, 1978; *Over My Shoulder,* Hurst & Blackett, 1968; *Brighton Fantasy,* Hurst & Blackett, 1969; *The House by the Lake,* Hurst & Blackett, 1970; *Chase a Dark Shadow,* Hurst & Blackett, 1971; *Sylvia's Daughter,* Hurst & Blackett, 1972; *The Drury Affair,* Hurst & Blackett, 1974; *The Devil's Rock,* Hurst & Blackett, 1975; *Emmy,* R. Hale, 1980.*

*   *   *

VALIN, Martial (Henry) 1898-1980

OBITUARY NOTICE: Born May 14, 1898, in Limoges, Haute-Vienne, France; died September 19, 1980, in Paris, France. Military officer and author. Martial Valin, who won his first Croix de Guerre as an infantryman in World War I, joined the French Air Force in 1927 and began training as a night bomber pilot. He became a squadron leader and in 1939, after the outbreak of war in Europe, commanded the first reconnaissance mission over German lines. In 1940, when the French Government signed an armistice with Nazi Germany, Valin went to England, where he joined Charles de Gaulle's Free French forces. He became minister of war in de Gaulle's National Committee and also served as general of the air force. He ignored the death sentence that the Vichy Government, which was collaborating with Germany, had passed against him in absentia. Valin received a second Croix de Guerre after World War II and wrote a history of the Free French Air Force entitled *Les Sans-culottes de l'air*. Obituaries and other sources: *New York Times,* September 20, 1980; *The Annual Obituary 1980,* St. Martin's, 1981.

* * *

VALLEJO, Cesar (Abraham) 1892-1938

BRIEF ENTRY: Born March 16, 1892, in Santiago de Chuco, Peru; died of tuberculosis, April 15, 1938, in Paris, France. Peruvian poet. Vallejo's surrealistic and satirical verse earned him a reputation as one of the greatest modern South American poets. Born of poor parents in a remote Andean village, Vallejo attended the University of Trujillo where he became involved in political activity, for which he was imprisoned in 1920. His prison experiences and his homesickness are major themes of his second book of poems, *Trilce* (1922). These poems anticipated surrealism with their dreamlike imagery, distorted syntax, and preoccupation with absurdity. In 1923 Vallejo left Peru to spend the rest of his life in Europe, supporting himself meagerly in Paris by writing articles and books. He joined the Communist party and traveled to the U.S.S.R. and to Spain during its civil war; the latter trip inspired the poems that were published after his death in *Spain, Let This Cup Pass From Me* (1940). That and Vallejo's other posthumous collection, *Human Poems* (1939), are considered more accessible than *Trilce,* yet their imagery is also surreal and their view of life based on absurdity. In his later poems Vallejo looked to revolution as the answer to absurdity, but this poetry avoids narrow, propagandistic politics. "Although unfailingly on the side of the fallen peasant," wrote Candace Salter, "he is never shrill nor doctrinaire, and his hatred of the oppressor is virtually nonexistent when compared with his love for the oppressed." Vallejo's other works include *Los heraldos negros* (1918), *El Tungsteno* (1931), and *Rusia en 1931: Reflexiones al pie del Kremlin* (1931). *Residence:* Paris, France. *Biographical/critical sources: Encyclopedia of World Literature in the Twentieth Century,* Ungar, 1967; *Americas,* November-December, 1968; *Times Literary Supplement,* September 29, 1969; *World Authors, 1950-1970,* H. W. Wilson, 1975; *Review,* spring, 1976; *Twentieth-Century Literary Criticism,* Volume 3, Gale, 1981.

* * *

VANCE, William E. 1911-

PERSONAL: Born June 21, 1911, in Alabama; son of William O. (a veterinarian) and Dez (Hopkins) Vance; married Lucile Gibbs, March 28, 1932 (marriage ended); married Elsie Lewis (an accountant), February 18, 1948; children: Bruce, Elva, Kathleen, Scott, Suzanne. *Home and office:* 2519 14th Ave. S., No. 427, Seattle, Wash. 98144.

CAREER: Federal Aviation Agency, Albuquerque, N.M., flight specialist, 1940-54; U.S. Army, Fort Rucker, Ala., civilian editor of *U.S. Army Aviation Digest,* 1955-60; free-lance writer in Centralia, Wash., 1960-67; public relations information officer in Seattle, Wash., 1967-71; Social and Health Services, Olympia, Wash., work specialist, 1971-76; free-lance writer, 1976—. *Military service:* U.S. Navy, 1928-35. *Member:* Western Writers of America, Mystery Writers of America, Authors Guild.

WRITINGS: The Branded Lawman (western novel; bound with *Plunder Valley,* by N. C. Nye), Ace Books, 1952; *Apache War Cry* (western novel), Popular Library, 1955; *Way Station West* (western novel; bound with *High Saddle,* by W. L. Hopson), Ace Books, 1955; *Outlaw Brand* (western novel), Bouregy, 1964; *Tracker,* Bouregy, 1964; *Homicide Lost* (mystery novel), Graphic Books, 1967; *Drifter's Gold,* Doubleday, 1979; *Death Stalks the Cheyenne Trail* (western novel), Doubleday, 1980; *Law and Outlaw* (western novel), Doubleday, 1981.

Editor of *Lewis County Labor News,* 1948-50.

* * *

VANDERBURGH, R(osamond) M(oate) 1926-

PERSONAL: Born October 2, 1926, in Arlington, Mass.; daughter of Herbert A. and Katharine (Eberhardt) Moate; married Albert Henry Vanderburgh (an engineer), September 11, 1954; children: Matthew, Katharine. *Education:* Radcliffe College, B.A. (cum laude), 1948; Northwestern University, M.A., 1951; attended University of Pennsylvania, 1951-54. *Residence:* Mississauga, Ontario, Canada. *Office:* Erindale College, University of Toronto, Mississauga, Ontario, Canada L5L 1C6.

CAREER: Royal Ontario Museum, Toronto, curatorial assistant in department of ethnology, 1954-56; University of Toronto, Toronto, special lecturer, 1967-71, assistant professor, 1971-77, associate professor of anthropology, 1977—. Member of board of directors of Mississauga Historical Foundation, 1962—, and Mississauga Visual Arts, 1979—. *Member:* American Anthropological Association, American Ethnological Society, Current Anthropology (fellow), Canadian Ethnology Society.

WRITINGS: I Am Nokomis, Too (biography), General Publishing, 1977; (with Nan F. Salerno) *Shaman's Daughter* (novel), Prentice-Hall, 1980. Contributor to anthropology journals.

WORK IN PROGRESS: Tomorrow's Elders; a biography of Ojibwa artist Daphne Odjig; research on life histories of southern Ojibwa women, urbanization of native Canadians, the art of Manitoulin Island and the elders' role there, and the role of Indian women in reserve and urban politics.

SIDELIGHTS: Rosamond Vanderburgh commented: "All my writing is based on my professional research. *Shaman's Daughter* was an experiment to see if anthropological data could be presented in popular form to reach a wider audience."

* * *

VanDEVENTER, Robert

PERSONAL: Born in Indiana. *Education:* Duke University, A.B. *Home:* 2004 Yardley Rd., Yardley, Pa. 19067.

CAREER: Writer.

WRITINGS: Mr. and Mrs. Markham, New American Library, 1974. Contributor to newspapers.

WORK IN PROGRESS: A novel of boyhood humor; a novel of contemporary conflict.

* * *

VANGEN, Roland Dean 1935-

PERSONAL: Born August 8, 1935, in Waukon, Iowa; son of Edgar Ludvig and Mildred Irene Vangen; married Dorothy Jean Kotouc, May 20, 1960; children: Felicia, Alison. *Religion:* Lutheran. *Home:* 612 35th St. N.E., Cedar Rapids, Iowa 52402.

CAREER: Writer. Factory worker. *Military service:* U.S. Navy.

WRITINGS: Indian Weapons, Filter Press, 1972.

SIDELIGHTS: Vangen commented: "My goal is to someday have one of my unpublished novels published and made into a movie."

* * *

VAN HATTUM, Rolland J(ames) 1924-

PERSONAL: Born July 14, 1924, in Grand Rapids, Mich.; son of Peter W. (an accountant) and Mabel (Mol) Van Hattum; married Joyce Hocker (a nurse), March 15, 1948; children: Steven, Shari Van Hattum Schmidt, Susan, Sally Van Hattum Kelley, Sandra Van Hattum McDonnell. *Education:* Western Michigan University, B.S., 1950; Pennsylvania State University, M.S., 1952, Ph.D., 1954. *Religion:* Episcopalian. *Home:* 181 Hennepin Rd., Grand Island, N.Y. 14072. *Office:* Department of Communication Disorders, State University of New York College at Buffalo, 1300 Elmwood, Buffalo, N.Y. 14222.

CAREER: Pennslyvania State University, University Park, Pa., instructor in speech pathology, 1950-54; Board of Education, Rochester, N.Y., consultant in special education, 1954-58; Kent County Intermediate School District, Grand Rapids, Mich., director of special education, 1958-63; State University of New York College at Buffalo, professor of communication disorders, 1963—. Lecturer at Michigan State University, University of Michigan, Western Michigan University, Nazareth College, and University of Rochester. President of Kent County Council for Retarded Children, 1961; president and member of board of directors of Grand Rapids Hearing and Speech Center, 1961-63; consultant to Eastman Dental Center, 1963-67, and Buffalo Children's Hospital, 1969-78. *Military service:* U.S. Army, 1943-46; became sergeant; received five battle stars.

MEMBER: Council for Exceptional Children (president of Division for Children With Communication Disorders, 1968), American Speech-Language-Hearing Association (fellow; president, 1977), Smithsonian Institution, New York State Speech and Hearing Association (president, 1969), Grand Rapids Area Psychological Association (president, 1960), Sigma Xi, Delta Sigma Phi, Psi Chi, Buffalo Launch Club.

WRITINGS: Clinical Speech in the Schools, C. C Thomas, 1969; *Developmental Programming for the Retarded,* Allyn & Bacon, 1979; *Communication Disorders,* Macmillan, 1980; *Taped Articulation Therapy,* Developmental Learning Materials, 1981; *Speech-Language Programming in Schools,* C. C Thomas, 1981. Contributor to scholarly and medical journals.

WORK IN PROGRESS: Netherlands Cook Book.

SIDELIGHTS: Van Hattum commented: "People assume that persons who write do so because it comes easily to them. For me, at least, this is completely untrue. I was born and raised (for my first few years) in a foreign-language environment, and writing is the most difficult of my professional tasks. I write to share, to stimulate, to invite improvement, but mostly to try to help others. I doubt that my writing has earned a nickel an hour, but my feelings of contribution and involvement are worth more than a million dollars to me.

"Writing is communication and communication is the essence of being human. The difference between authors and many persons who *should* write is effort—perseverance. There must be a terrible lack of the feeling of fulfillment in people who have ideas that are unique, original, interesting, entertaining, informative, or persuasive, and do not share them."

* * *

VAN WERT, William F(rancis) 1945-

PERSONAL: Born August 25, 1945, in Midland, Mich.; son of James F. (in business) and Dolores (Leonard) Van Wert; married Johanna Rucker (a teacher), August 7, 1971; children: Ian, David, Daniel. *Education:* Attended University of Aix-en Provence, 1965-66, and University of Madrid, 1967-68; University of Michigan, B.A., 1967; Indiana University, M.A. (comparative literature), 1970, M.A. (English and creative writing), 1972, Ph.D., 1975. *Home:* 7200 Cresheim, Apt. C-1, Philadelphia, Pa. 19119. *Office:* Department of English, Temple University, Philadelphia, Pa. 19122.

CAREER: Indiana University, Bloomington, lecturer in comparative literature, 1969-70; University of Maryland, Far East Division, Southeast Asia, lecturer in English, 1970-72; Indiana University, lecturer, 1973-74, instructor in comparative literature, 1974; Temple University, Philadelphia, Pa., assistant professor, 1974-78, associate professor of English, 1979—. Public speaker on film subjects; gives readings of fiction; film reviewer for WHYY-Radio. *Member:* International P.E.N. (Poets and Writers), Modern Language Association of America, Society for Cinema Studies, Phi Beta Kappa. *Awards, honors:* Fulbright-Hays fellow, 1967-68; Woodrow Wilson fellow, 1967.

WRITINGS: Hot Candy (poetry chapbook), Raintree, 1977; *The Film Career of Alain Robbe-Grillet,* G. K. Hall, 1977; (contributor) Karyn Kay and Gerald Peary, editors, *Women and the Cinema,* Dutton, 1977; *The Theory and Practice of the Cine-Roman,* Arno, 1978; *The Laying on of Hands* (poetry), Raintree, in press; *Dime Stories,* Moonlight Express Press, in press.

Contributor to *Guidebook to Film.* Contributor of nearly one hundred articles, stories, poems, and reviews to magazines, including *New England Review, Poet Lore, North American Review, Miscellany, Film Quarterly,* and *Western Humanities Review.* Editor of *Jump Cut,* 1975—, and *Tracks,* 1976—.

WORK IN PROGRESS: Tales for Expectant Fathers, stories; *Missing in Action,* stories; *From Dylan to Dr. Strangelove,* stories; *Spectator Sports,* stories; *Family Poses,* stories; *The Mere Property Shop of Illusion,* stories; *The Third Eye: Essays on Film Form; Jump Cuts: The Age of Editing,* film essays; *The Age of Spectator Sports,* a novel; *The French Experimental Avant-Garde Film,* for Twayne; *Game Structures in Modern Fiction; Pieces of Eight,* a novel; *The Lowest E.R.A.,* a novel; *The Book of Job,* a combination of fact and fiction.

* * *

VARAS, Florencia
See OLEA, Maria Florencia Varas

* * *

VENDLER, Zeno 1921-

BRIEF ENTRY: Born December 22, 1921, in Devecser, Hungary. American philosopher, educator, and author. Vendler has been a professor of philosophy at the University of California, San Diego, since 1975. His writings include *Linguistics in Philosophy* (Cornell University Press, 1967), *Adjectives and Nominalizations* (Mouton, 1968), and *"Res Cognitas": An Essay in Rational Psychology* (Cornell University Press, 1972). *Address:* Department of Philosophy, University of California, San Diego, Box 109, La Jolla, Calif. 92037. *Biographical/critical sources: Directory of American Scholars,* Volume IV: *Philosophy, Religion, and Law,* 7th edition, Bowker, 1978.

* * *

VERVAL, Alain
See LANDE, Lawrence (Montague)

VESEY-FitzGERALD, Brian Seymour   1900-1981

OBITUARY NOTICE—See index for *CA* sketch: Born July 5, 1900, in Wrexham, Wales; died October 23, 1981. Naturalist, journalist, and author of almost fifty books. Vesey-FitzGerald, the son of a civil servant, spent his childhood in India where he became conversant in Hindustani. He also became fluent in Romany as a result of his association with gypsies whom he met while on walking tours through the English countryside. His book, *Gypsies of Britain,* grew out of his regard for the gypsy tradition. Most of Vesey-FitzGerald's books, however, reflect the author's interest in naturalism. The best known of these are "The Country Books" series, which he edited for Robert Hale, and *It's My Delight.* Vesey-FitzGerald also was the editor of *The Gamekeeper* and *The Field.* Obituaries and other sources: *London Times,* November 4, 1981.

*   *   *

VICTOR, Joan Berg   1942-
(Joan Berg)

PERSONAL: Born July 11, 1942, in Chicago, Ill.; daughter of Sam L. and Roselyn M. Berg; married; children: Daniel, Elizabeth. *Education:* Received B.F.A. (with honors) from Tulane University and M.F.A. (with honors) from Yale University. *Home and office:* 863 Park Ave., New York, N.Y. 10021.

CAREER: Artist and writer. Work displayed in exhibitions throughout the United States, including Delgado Museum, New Orleans, La., and Art Institute of Chicago, Chicago, Ill. *Awards, honors:* Grant from National Endowment for the Arts.

WRITINGS—Self-illustrated: (Under name Joan Berg) *The Bunny Who Wanted a Friend,* Golden Press, 1966; (under name Joan Berg) *My Friend the Squirrel,* Bobbs-Merrill, 1966; *Bigger Than an Elephant,* Crown, 1968; *Sh-h! Listen Again! Sounds of the Season,* World, 1969; (editor) *To Remember Is to Love: A Birthday Book,* C. R. Gibson, 1971; (editor) *A Time to Love: Love Poems for Today,* Crown, 1971; *Where Is My Monster?* (juvenile), Crown, 1971; *Do You Really Love Me?,* Grosset, 1973; *To Be Alone: The Sweet and Bittersweet* (poems), Crown, 1974; *The World Is Round* (nonfiction), Grosset, 1974; *Shells Are Skeletons* (nonfiction), Crowell, 1977; (with Joelle Sander) *The Family: The Evolution of Our Oldest Human Institution* (nonfiction), Bobbs-Merrill, 1978; *Tarantulas* (juvenile), Dodd, 1979.

Illustrator under name Joan Berg: Roma Gans, *The Wonder of Stones,* Crowell, 1963; Elizabeth Jamison Hodges, *The Three Princes of Serendip,* Atheneum, 1964; Alice Virginia Wright, *The Seed Is Blown,* Rand McNally, 1965; Hertha Ernestine Pauli, *The First Christmas Gifts,* Washburn, 1965; Wendell V. Tangborn, *Glaciers* (juvenile), Crowell, 1965; Louis Untermeyer, *Thanks: A Poem,* Odyssey, 1965; Charlotte Zolotow, *Flocks of Birds,* Abelard, 1966.

Illustrator under name Joan Berg Victor: William Julius Lederer, *The Story of Pink Jade,* Norton, 1966; Untermeyer, *Merry Christmas,* Golden Press, 1967; Untermeyer, editor, *Songs of Joy From the Book of Psalms,* World, 1967; Untermeyer, editor, *A Time for Peace: Verses From the Bible,* World, 1969; Walter Dumaux Edmonds, *Time to Go House,* Little, Brown, 1969; *Poems of Childhood,* C. R. Gibson, 1969.

WORK IN PROGRESS: Poems.

VIER, Gene   1926-

PERSONAL: Born June 10, 1926, in Detroit, Mich.; son of Edmund Patrick (a professor) and Maude (Foley) Vier. *Education:* Attended University of Western Ontario. *Politics:* Democrat. *Home:* 11213/4 West Kensington Rd., Los Angeles, Calif. 90026. *Agent:* Peter Sabiston, 10840 Lindbrook Dr., Los Angeles, Calif. 90024. *Office: Van Nuys Daily News,* 14539 Sylvan St., Van Nuys, Calif. 91411.

CAREER: Worked as film critic for *Americans Abroad,* London, England; *Van Nuys Daily News,* Van Nuys, Calif., began as copy editor, currently author of film column. *Member:* Wig and Pen Club.

WRITINGS: Tennis: Myth and Method, Viking, 1979. Editor of *El Segundo Herald.*

WORK IN PROGRESS: Press Lord of the West: Otis Chandler and His Times.

*   *   *

VIKSNINS, George J(uris)   1937-
(G. J. Kennecott)

PERSONAL: Born August 17, 1937, in Riga, Latvia; came to the United States in 1950, naturalized citizen, 1958; son of Nicholas and Helen (Ansons) Viksnins; married Mara Karulis, January 31, 1961; children: Helen, Ingrid, Peter, Brigit. *Education:* Temple University, B.A., 1959; University of Pennsylvania, M.A., 1960; Georgetown University, Ph.D., 1964. *Politics:* Republican. *Religion:* Lutheran. *Home:* 3731 T St. N.W., Washington, D.C. 20007. *Office:* Department of Economics, Georgetown University, 37th & O Sts. N.W., Washington, D.C. 20057.

CAREER: Georgetown University, Washington, D.C., instructor, 1963-64, assistant professor, 1964-68, associate professor, 1968-77, professor of economics, 1978—. With U.S. Agency for International Development in Bangkok, Thailand, 1968-70. Member of board of directors of FMI Financial Corp., 1976-81; consultant to L. F. Rothschild. *Member:* American Economic Association, American Association of University Professors, National Association of Business Economists, Society for International Development, Royal Economic Society.

WRITINGS: Economies of Southeast Asia in the 1980's, Center for Strategic and International Studies, Georgetown University, 1975; (editor with L. R. Vasey) *The Emerging Economic and Political Growth Pattern of Asia and the Pacific,* Pacific Forum, 1976; *Financial Deepening in the Asian Countries,* University Press of Hawaii, 1980. Contributor to economic and foreign studies journals, sometimes under pseudonym G. J. Kennecott.

WORK IN PROGRESS: Research on housing finance and financial institutions.

*   *   *

VILLADA, Gene Harold Bell
See BELL-VILLADA, Gene Harold

*   *   *

VIVIENNE
See ENTWISTLE, Florence Vivienne

von HABSBURG-LOTHRINGEN, Geza Louis Eusebius Gebhard Ralphael Albert Maria 1940-

PERSONAL: Born November 14, 1940, in Budapest, Hungary; son of Joseph Francis and Anna Monica Habsburg-Lothringen; married Monica Hildegart Decker, July 17, 1965; children: Francis, Ferdinand, Maximilian. *Education:* University of Fribourg, Ph.D., 1965. *Home:* 10 chemin des Corneilles Thonex, Geneva 1226, Switzerland. *Office:* 8 place de la Taconnerie, Geneva 1204, Switzerland.

CAREER: Christie's, Geneva, Switzerland, co-founder and specialist in paintings of old masters and Russian art, 1967; Christie's, Duesseldorf, West Germany, co-founder, 1971; Christie's, London, England, director, 1973—.

WRITINGS: (With A. von Solodkoff) *Faberge: Court Jeweler to the Tsars,* translated by J. A. Underwood, Rizzoli International, 1979.

In German: *Vom goldenen Ueberfluss der Welt: Bilder und Skizzen,* Salzer, 1978.

BIOGRAPHICAL/CRITICAL SOURCES: New York Times Book Review, November 25, 1979; *Economist,* January 12, 1980.*

*　　*　　*

VON HAGEN, Victor Wolfgang 1908-

PERSONAL: Born February 29, 1908, in St. Louis, Mo.; son of Henry (a chemist) and Eleanor Josephine (Stippe-Hornbach) Von Hagen; married Christine Brown, May 29, 1933 (divorced); married Silvia Hofmann-Edzard, 1951 (divorced, 1962); children: (first marriage) Victoria (Mrs. Jacques Bordaz); (second marriage) Adriana, Bettina. *Education:* Attended Morgan Park Military Academy, New York University, University of Quito, and University of Gottingen. *Home:* Trevignano Romano, Rome, Italy 00069. *Agent:* John McLaughlin, c/o Campbell, Thompson, McLaughlin Ltd., 31 Newington Green, London N169PU, England.

CAREER: Author, explorer, naturalist. Embarked upon exploratory expedition to Africa, 1927; completed expeditions to Mexico, 1931-33, 1957, and to Galapagos Islands, Ecuador, the Upper Amazon, and Peru, 1934-36; conducted additional research in the regions of the Mosquito Coast of Honduras and Guatemala to find and capture the quetzal bird, 1937-38; explored Panama and Costa Rica, 1940; toured Colombia and Peru, 1947-48; resided in the British West Indies, 1949-50; director of the Inca Highway Expedition to Peru, Bolivia, and Ecuador for the American Geographic Society, 1953-55; studied Roman roads from the Rhine to Africa, 1955; further exploration of the Yucatan Peninsula, 1958-59; organizer and leader of the Roman Road expeditions throughout Europe and North Africa, 1961-70; organizer and leader of the American Geographic Society Expedition through Iran, Iraq, and Turkey mapping the Royal Persian Road, 1973-75. Research associate at Museum of the American Indian, New York, N.Y.; adviser on Latin America to *Encyclopedia Americana;* consultant to the United Nations; founder and organizer of a project to establish a Charles Darwin Residence Station in the Galapagos Islands, 1936-63. *Military service:* U.S. Army, 13th Infantry, served in World War II. *Member:* American Geographical Society (director), Royal Geographic Society, Academia de Historia de Bogota (Colombia), Centro de Historia de Pasto (Colombia), Instituto Investigaciones Historicas del Puna (Peru), Zoological Society of London. *Awards, honors:* Orden de Merito (Ecuador); Comander, Orden de Merito (Peru); Guggen-

heim fellowship for creative writing, 1949, 1950; American Philosophical Society research fellow.

WRITINGS: Off With Their Heads, Macmillan, 1937; (with Quail Hawkins) *Quetzal Quest: The Story of the Capture of the Quetzal, the Sacred Bird of the Aztecs and the Mayas,* Harcourt, 1939; *The Tsatchela Indians of Western Ecuador,* Museum of the American Indian, 1939; (author of preface) M. Maeterlinck, *Life of the White Ant,* McClelland, 1939; *Ecuador the Unknown: Two and a Half Years Travels in the Republic of Ecuador and Galapagos Islands,* Jarrolds, 1939, Oxford University Press, 1940.

Jungle in the Clouds, Duell, Sloan, 1940; (author of epilogue and bibliographic notes) Herman Melville, *Las Encantadas,* W. P. Wreden, 1940; *Riches of South America,* Heath, 1941; *Riches of Central America,* Heath, 1942; *The Aztec and Maya Papermakers,* J. J. Augustin, 1943, reprinted, Hacker Art Books, 1977; *The Jicaque (Torrupan) Indians of Honduras,* Museum of the American Indian, 1943, reprinted, AMS Press, 1980; *South America Called Them: Explorations of the Great Naturalists, La Condamine, Humboldt, Darwin, Spruce,* Knopf, 1945; *South American Zoo,* Messner, 1946; *Maya Explorer: John Lloyd Stephens and the Lost Cities,* University of Oklahoma Press, 1947; (editor) *The Green World of the Naturalists: A Treasury of Five Centuries of Natural History in South America,* Greenberg, 1948; *Ecuador and the Galapagos Islands,* University of Oklahoma Press, 1949.

Frederick Catherwood, Architect, introduction by Aldous Huxley, Oxford University Press, 1950, published as *Frederick Catherwood, Architect-Explorer of Two Worlds,* Barre Publishers, 1968; (with wife, Christine Von Hagen) *The Four Seasons of Manuela, a Biography: The Love Story of Manuela Saenz and Simon Bolivar,* Duell, Sloan, 1952 (published in England *The Love Story of Manuela Saenz and Simon Bolivar,* Dent, 1952); *Highway of the Sun,* Little, Brown, 1955; *Realm of the Incas,* New American Library, 1957, revised edition, 1961; *The Aztec: Man and Tribe,* New American Library, 1958, revised edition, 1962; (editor) Pedro de Cieza de Leon, *The Incas,* University of Oklahoma Press, 1959.

World of the Maya, New American Library, 1960; *The Ancient Sun Kingdoms of the Americas: Aztec, Maya, Inca,* World Publishing, 1961; (editor) William H. Prescott, *History of the Conquest of Peru,* Muller, 1961; (editor) John Lloyd Stephens, *Incidents of Travel in Yucatan,* University of Oklahoma Press, 1962; *The Desert Kingdoms of Peru,* New American Library, 1964; *The Roads That Led to Rome,* World Publishing, 1967.

(Editor) John Lloyd Stephens, *Incidents of Travel in Egypt, Arabia Petraea, and the Holy Land,* University of Oklahoma Press, 1970; *Der Ruf der Neuen Welt: Deutsche Bauen Amerika,* Droemer Knaur, 1970, translation published as *The Germanic People in America,* University of Oklahoma Press, 1976; *Search for the Maya: The Story of Stephens and Catherwood,* Saxon House, 1973; *The Golden Man: A Quest for El Dorado,* Saxon House, 1974; *Ecuador: A Journey in Time,* Plata Verlag (Switzerland), 1976; *The Royal Road of the Inca,* Gordon & Cremonesi, 1976; *Alexander Von Humboldt's America,* Plata Verlag, 1977; *The Persian Realms,* New American Library, 1977.

For children: (With Quail Hawkins) *Treasure of the Tortoise Islands,* Harcourt, 1940; *Miskito Boy,* Collins, 1943; *The Sun Kingdom of the Aztecs,* World Publishing, 1958; *Maya: Land of the Turkey and the Deer,* World Publishing, 1960; *The Incas: People of the Sun,* World Publishing, 1961; *Roman Roads,* World Publishing, 1966.

"A Guide to" series: *A Guide to Cusco,* Guide Books, 1949; *. . . Lima, the Capital of Peru,* Farnam, 1949; *. . . Machu Picchu,* Farnam, 1949; *. . . Sacsahuaman, the Fortress of Cusco,* Guide Books, 1949; *. . . Guayaquil,* Farnum, 1950.

Also author of *El Dorado: The Golden Kingdoms of Colombia,* 1951; *The Life of E. George Squier,* 1951; *The High Voyage,* 1956; (translator) *The Journals of J. B. Boussingault,* 1957; *People's War, People's Army,* 1962; *The Mochicas and the Chimus,* 1963; *The Road Runner* (autobiography), 1970; *I, Bernal Diaz, Conus Conquistador* (for children), 1977.

Contributor to the *Encyclopaedia Britannica* as well as various periodicals, including *Travel, Science Digest, Nature Magazine, Natural History,* and *Scientific Monthly.*

SIDELIGHTS: On an early expedition to Ecuador, Von Hagen and his first wife lived for about eight months with the Jivaros Indians, a tribe of headhunters. The Von Hagens observed the culture and customs of the Jivaros and published their findings in *Off With Their Heads.* Von Hagen became so engrossed in his study that he accompanied some of the war parties on their excursions and witnessed the ancient art and ritual of shrinking heads.

A few years later, on an expedition to Honduras and Guatemala, Von Hagen located and captured specimens of the quetzal, a bird revered by the Aztecs and Mayas. With the aid of a twelve-year-old boy, Dr. Von Hagen was able to overcome the superstitions of the natives and secure quetzals to be shipped to the London Zoo and the Bronx Zoo. During this same expedition Von Hagen discovered a tribe of Jicaque Indians, descendants of the Mayas, formerly believed to be extinct.

The explorer-naturalist is credited with compiling the first complete study of the Great Tortoise of the Galapagos Islands. He is also an authority on the ecology of plant life in the archipelago. For his work in fostering the preservation of plant and animal life in the area, Von Hagen was awarded the Orden de Merito by the Republic of Ecuador. Von Hagen is also responsible for the erection of a monument to Charles Darwin and for the establishment of the Charles Darwin Residence Station in the Galapagos.

Von Hagen applied his interest in papermaking to *The Aztec and Maya Papermakers.* In the book he corrected the misapprehension that Mexican paper was made from the agave plant. He found that Aztecs and Mayas made paper by preparing the inner bark of the fig tree and that of trees in the mulberry family.

In 1961 the American Broadcasting Company televised the documentary motion picture "Weavers of Death." This film records one of Von Hagen's Peruvian expeditions, exploring the ruins of the ancient Nazca, Ica, and Inca civilizations. The explorers explain how the discovery of treasures and artifacts have enabled archaeologists to reconstruct the history and culture of these civilizations.

Collections of Von Hagen's artifacts are on display at the British Museum and the American Museum of Natural History.

BIOGRAPHICAL/CRITICAL SOURCES: New Yorker, January 3, 1953; *Cosmopolitan,* January, 1960.*

*   *   *

VON ROSENSTIEL, Helene   1944-

PERSONAL: Born January 14, 1944, in Cincinnati, Ohio; daughter of Werner H. (a lawyer) and Marion (a professor of English; maiden name, Ahrens) Von Rosenstiel. *Education:*

Ohio Wesleyan University, B.F.A., 1966; Drexel Institute of Technology, M.S., 1970; also attended Fashion Institute of Technology, 1970-73. *Home and office:* Restorations, 382 11th St., Brooklyn, N.Y. 11215. *Agent:* Susan Ann Protter, 156 East 52nd St., New York, N.Y. 10022.

CAREER: Lord & Taylor, Jenkintown, Pa., in sales, 1967-70; Brooklyn Museum, Brooklyn, N.Y., textile and costume restorer, 1970-77; private textile conservator, 1977—. Workshop instructor at American Institute of Textile Arts, 1972, 1978, 1979, and 1980; member of Park Slope Civic Council, 1977; consultant to New York State Council on the Arts. *Member:* Costume Society of America (member of board of directors, 1978—), Society of Architectural Historians, Textile Conservation Group, Costume Society (England), Women's City Club of New York.

WRITINGS: (With Pamela Clabburn) *The Needleworker's Dictionary,* Morrow, 1976; *American Rugs and Carpets: From the Seventeenth Century to Modern Times,* Morrow, 1978. Contributor to textile journals.

WORK IN PROGRESS: An article on rugs.

*   *   *

von SCHLABRENDORFF, Fabian   1907-1980

OBITUARY NOTICE: Born July 1, 1907, in Halle, Saxony, Germany (now East Germany); died September 4, 1980, in Wiesbaden, Hesse, West Germany. Jurist, anti-Nazi, and author. As a German army officer in World War II, von Schlabrendorff was involved in plots to assassinate Adolf Hitler. In March, 1943, von Schlabrendorff removed from Hitler's plane a disguised bomb that had failed to detonate, thereby concealing the assassination plot. At a conference in East Prussia on July 20, 1944, another assassination attempt was made on Hitler, also involving von Schlabrendorff. For his role in this attempt he was arrested, tortured by the Gestapo, and tried in a Nazi court. He was held for execution at Flossenburg Concentration Camp but was eventually liberated by Allied troops. After the war he practiced law in Frankfurt and Wiesbaden, becoming a constitutional court judge in 1967. He wrote several books about the military plots against Hitler, including a 1966 work, *The Secret War Against Hitler.* Obituaries and other sources: *Saturday Evening Post,* July 20, 1946, July 27, 1946; Gero v.S. Gaevernitz, editor, *They Almost Killed Hitler,* Macmillan, 1947; *New York Times,* September 5, 1980; *Newsweek,* September 15, 1980; *The Annual Obituary 1980,* St. Martin's, 1981.

*   *   *

von WEIZSAECKER, Carl Friedrich   1912-

PERSONAL: Surname is pronounced "Vite-secker;" born June 28, 1912, in Kiel, Germany (now West Germany); son of Ernst (a diplomat) and Marianne (von Graevenitz) von Weizsaecker; married Gundalena Wille, March 30, 1937; children: Carl-Christian, Ernest-Ulrich, Elisabeth von Weizsaecker Raiser, Heinrich. *Education:* Attended University of Berlin, 1929; attended University of Goettingen and University of Copenhagen; University of Leipzig, D. Phil., 1933. *Home:* Alpenstrasse 15, D-8135 Soecking, West Germany.

CAREER: University of Leipzig, Leipzig, Germany, assistant at Institute of Theoretical Physics, 1934-36; Kaiser Wilhelm Institute, Berlin, Germany, lecturer, 1936-42; University of Strasbourg, Strasbourg, France, associate professor, 1942-44; Max Planck Institute for Physics, Goettingen, West Germany, head of department, 1946-57; University of Hamburg, Hamburg, West Germany, professor of philosophy, 1957-69; Max Planck Institute on the Preconditions of Human Life in the Modern World, Starnberg, West Germany, director, 1970-1980. Honorary professor of theoretical physics at University of Goettingen, 1946-57; Gifford lecturer at University of Glasgow, Glasgow, Scotland, 1959-61; honorary professor of philosophy at University of Munich, Munich, West Germany, 1970—.

MEMBER: Deutsche Akademie Naturforscher Leopoldina, Deutsche Akademie fuer Sprache und Dichtung, Oesterreichische Akademie der Wissenschaften, Bayerische Akademie der Wissenschaften, Saechsische Akademie der Wissenschaften, Goettinger Akademie der Wissenschaften, Max-Planck-Gesellschaft, Joachim-Jungius-Gesellschaft der Wissenschaften. *Awards, honors:* Max Planck Medal, 1957 and 1966; Goethe Prize from the city of Frankfurt am Main, 1958; Order of Merit of the Federal Republic of Germany, 1959-73; Order of Merit for Sciences and Arts, 1961; Peace Prize of the German Book Trade, 1963; Arnold Reymont Prize for Physics and Wilhelm Boelsche Gold Medal, both 1965; Erasmus Prize, 1969.

WRITINGS—In English: *Die Geschichte der Natur*, 1943, translation by Fred D. Wieck published as *The History of Nature*, University of Chicago Press, 1949, reprinted, 1976; (with Johannes Juilfs) *Physik der Gegenwart*, 1952, translation by Arnold J. Pomerans published as *The Rise of Modern Physics*, Braziller, 1957; *The Relevance of Science: Creation and Cosmogony* (lectures), Harper, 1964; *The Spectrum of Turbulence With Large Reynolds Numbers*, translation by Barbara Dickson, British Ministry of Technology, 1966; (author of introduction) Gopi Krishna, *Biologische Basis religioser Ehrfahrung*, O. W. Barth, 1971, translation published as *The Biological Basis of Religion and Genius*, NC Press, 1971; *Die Einheit der Natur* (essays), C. Hanser, 1977, translation by Francis J. Zucker published as *The Unity of Nature*, Farrar, Straus 1980; *Wege in der Gefahr: Eine Studie ueber Wirtschaft, Gesellschaft, und Kriegsverhuetung*, C. Hanser, 1977, translation by Michael Shaw published as *The Politics of Peril: Economics, Society, and the Prevention of War*, Seabury Press, 1978.

Other writings: *Bedingungen des Friedens*, Vandenhoeck & Ruprecht, 1964; *Dialog des Abendlandes: Physik und Philosophie*, List, 1966; *Gedanken ueber unsere Zukunft*, Vandenhoeck & Ruprecht, 1967; *Das Problem der Zeit als Philosophische Problem*, Wichern-Verl, 1967; (contributor) *Ist der Weltfriede unvermeidlich?*, von Decker, 1967; (contributor) *Freiheit als Stoerfaktor in einer programmierten Gesellschaft?*, Bergedorfer Gespraechskreis zu Fragen der Freien Industriellen Gesellschaft, 1968; (contributor) *Hundret Jahre Philosophische Bibliothek 1868-1968*, Meiner, 1968; *Saekularisierung und Saekularismus*, Jugenddienst-Verlag, 1968; *Der ungesicherte Friede*, Vandenhoeck & Ruprecht, 1969; *Das Philosophische Problem der Kybernetik*, illustrations by Heinz Troekes, Belser, 1969.

(With Manfred Kulessa and Juergen Heinrichs) *Indiengespraeche: Indien als Modelfall der Entwicklungspolitik*, Bruck-

mann, 1970; *Kriegsfolgen und Kriegsverhuetung* C. Hanser, 1971; *Platonische Naturwissenschaft im Laufe der Geshichte*, Vandenhoeck & Ruprecht, 1971; *Deutlichkeit: Beitraege zu politischen und religioesen Gegenwartsfragen*, C. Hanser, 1978; (with Helmut Hirsch and Walter Schueller) *Kernenergie: Lebensnotwendige Kraft oder toedlich Gefahr?*, Niedersaechsische Landzentrale fuer Politische Bildung, 1979.

Also author of *Die Atomkerne*, 1937; *Zum Weltbild der Physik*, 1943; *Atomenergie und Atomzeitalter*, 1957; *Christliche Glaube und Naturwissenschaft*, 1959; *Die Verantwortung der Wissenschaft im Atonzeitalter*, 1963; *Voraussetzung der Naturwissenschaftlichen Denkens*, 1972; *Fragen zur Weltpolitik*, 1975; *Der Garten des Menschlichen: Beitraege zur geschichtlichen Anthropologie*, 1977.

SIDELIGHTS: Weizsaecker is known as both a physicist and a philosopher. During World War II he worked on the German atomic bomb project and developed his ideas about the origin of the solar system. His version of the nebular hypothesis (which suggests that the sun and planets were formed from a cloud of dust and gas) led scientific opinion to shift away from catastrophe theories. After the war, much of Weizsaecker's writing was focused on philosophical problems, especially the relationships among science, philosophy, and religion. He also studied and wrote on the problems of world peace and nuclear arms control.

BIOGRAPHICAL/CRITICAL SOURCES: Christian Century, February 1, 1950; *Times Literary Supplement*, December 10, 1964; *Science*, March 19, 1965; *New York Review of Books*, April 22, 1965; *Christian Science Monitor*, March 12, 1980.

*   *   *

VOSS, Thomas M(ichael) 1945-

PERSONAL: Born January 5, 1945, in Chicago, Ill.; son of Myron I. (in business) and Blanche (Kahn) Voss; married Betsy Moore, December 20, 1968. *Education:* Northwestern University, B.A., 1966; attended Johns Hopkins University, 1966-67, and Brown University, 1970. *Agent:* Virginia Barber, 353 West 21st St., New York, N.Y. 10011.

CAREER: Brown University Press, Providence, R.I., editor, 1971-72; Temple University Press, Philadelphia, Pa., editor, 1973-74; J. B. Lippincott Co., Philadelphia, copywriter, 1974-76; free-lance writer, 1976-80; Rodale Press, Inc., Emmaus, Pa., editor, 1980—.

WRITINGS: Antique American Country Furniture, Lippincott, 1978; (with Samuel Pennington and Lita Solis-Cohen) *Americana at Auction*, Dutton, 1979; *The Bargain Hunter's Guide to Used Furniture*, Dell, 1980; (with Charles Santore) *The Windsor Style in America*, Running Press, 1981. Contributor to magazines, including *McCall's, Country Journal, Maine Antique Digest*, and *Prevention*.

WORK IN PROGRESS: A novel, publication expected in 1983.

W

WACHER, John Stewart 1927-

BRIEF ENTRY: Born August 12, 1927, in Canterbury, England. British archaeologist and author. Wacher is a member of the faculty of archaeology at the University of Leicester. His books include *The Towns of Roman Britain* (Batsford, 1975), *Roman Britain* (Dent, 1978), and *The Coming of Rome* (Routledge & Kegan Paul, 1979). *Address:* 29 Bell Lane, Husbands Bosworth, Lutterworth, Leicestershire, England.

*   *   *

WAGNER, Eliot 1917-

PERSONAL: Born December 19, 1917, in New York, N.Y.; son of Fred and Fay (Rappaport) Wagner; children: Miriam (Mrs. Paul E. Rice). *Education:* City College (now of the City University of New York), B.A., 1937. *Religion:* Jewish. *Home:* 140 West End Ave., New York, N.Y. 10023. *Agent:* Joan Raines, Raines & Raines, 475 Fifth Ave., New York, N.Y. 10017.

CAREER: City College of the City University of New York, New York, N.Y., teacher of writing and administrator, 1953-73; writer, 1973—. *Member:* Authors Guild.

WRITINGS: Grand Concourse (novel), Bobbs-Merrill, 1954; *Better Occasions* (novel), Crowell, 1974; *My America!* (novel), Kenan Press, 1980. Contributor of stories to magazines, including *Commentary.*

WORK IN PROGRESS: Two novels, one "about office life in the fifties in New York, with the local collegiate basketball bribing scandals somewhere in the background."

SIDELIGHTS: Wagner wrote: "All I can do at this point is to continue to deploy my native talent against the literary tides by unforced organization (in fiction) of assimilated experience of reality."

BIOGRAPHICAL/CRITICAL SOURCES: Los Angeles Times Book Review, December 7, 1980.

*   *   *

WAGNER, Richard Vansant 1935-

BRIEF ENTRY: Born November 19, 1935, in Baltimore, Md. American psychologist, educator, and author. Wagner has taught psychology at Bates College since 1970. His writings include *The Study of Attitude Change* (Brooks/Cole, 1969) and *A Study of Systematic Resistance to Utilization of ITV in Public School Systems* (Bureau of Research, U.S. Office of Education, 1969). *Address:* Department of Psychology, Bates College, Lewiston, Maine 04240. *Biographical/critical sources: American Men and Women of Science: The Social and Behavioral Sciences,* 13th edition, Bowker, 1978.

*   *   *

WAIDE, Jan 1952-

PERSONAL: Born June 7, 1952, in Wichita Falls, Tex.; daughter of Elmer A. (a petroleum engineer) and Margaret (an artist; maiden name, Jones) Milz; married John Waide (a professor of philosophy), January 5, 1974. *Education:* Attended University of Texas at Austin, 1970-72; Harris School of Art, Franklin, Tenn., certificate in illustration, 1975. *Home and office:* 1750 Crump Ave., Memphis, Tenn, 38107.

CAREER: Free-lance artist and illustrator, 1975—; United Methodist Publishing House, Nashville, Tenn., artist and designer, 1978-79. Speaker at illustration and writing demonstrations. Teacher of art at elementary schools. Work exhibited in one-woman shows in Georgetown, Tex., and Austin, Tex., both in 1977; work included in group exhibitions at the Watercolor Art Society, Houston, Tex., 1976, and the Southwestern Watercolor Society, 1977. *Member:* Society of Children's Book Writers, Gray Panthers, Watercolor Art Society, Germantown Art League.

WRITINGS: Jennifer (juvenile), self-illustrated, Shoal Creek Publishers, 1978; *Weed* (juvenile), self-illustrated, Shoal Creek Publishers, 1980.

Illustrator: Vivan Montgomery, *Mr. Jellybean* (juvenile), Shoal Creek Publishers, 1980.

WORK IN PROGRESS: Four picture books—two based on childhood memories, one fantasy, and one folktale; a nonfiction book about blackbirds.

SIDELIGHTS: Jan Waide told *CA:* "Having grown up with an artistic mother, I have had painting and drawing for my companions for most of my life. Writing is new to me. I first became interested in writing as well as illustrating books for children when I heard an interview with Leo Lionni in 1975. He described the joy and the challenge of creating a book whose design, words, and pictures work together as a whole. Since then, *Jennifer* and *Weed* have been published.

"I've read what many illustrators and writers have written about picture books, and I have experimented with their advice. I do aspire to making books that adults consider well-designed works of art. My fondest hope, though, is someday to take a book I've written and illustrated from a library shelf and find its pages scribbled on, smudged, and dog-eared. Then I'd know that children loved it.''

*   *   *

WALCH, Timothy (George) 1947-

PERSONAL: Born December 6, 1947, in Detroit, Mich.; son of George L. (an accountant) and Margaret M. (a teacher; maiden name, DeSchryver) Walch; married Victoria Irons (an archivist), June 24, 1978. *Education:* University of Notre Dame, B.A., 1970; Northwestern University, Ph.D., 1975. *Home:* 9927 Capperton Dr., Oakton, Va. 22124. *Office:* National Archives and Records Service, Washington, D.C. 20408.

CAREER: Northwestern University, Evanston, Ill., research associate in university archives, 1974-75; Society of American Archivists, Chicago, Ill., director of special programs, 1975-79; National Historical Publications and Records Commission, Washington, D.C., program analyst, 1979-81; National Archives and Records Service, Washington, D.C., archivist, 1981—. *Member:* Society of American Archivists, Organization of American Historians.

WRITINGS: (With Harold F. Williamson and others) *Northwestern University: A History, 1851-1975*, Northwestern University Press, 1976; *Archives and Manuscripts: Security*, Society of American Archivists, 1977; (editor with Michael W. Sedlak) *American Educational History*, Gale, 1981. Contributor of more than twenty articles to scholarly journals and popular magazines.

WORK IN PROGRESS: A brief history of Roman Catholic schools in the United States, publication by Nelson-Hall expected in 1984.

SIDELIGHTS: Walch told *CA:* "The recent news has not been good for contemporary writers. Illiteracy has increased dramatically in recent years, undercutting the demand for books and magazines. The average income from writing has dropped below $5,000 per year, forcing even the nation's best writers to seek additional employment to sustain themselves and their families. But contemporary writers can and will surmount these challenges, sustained, to a large extent, by the personal satisfaction and sense of achievement that comes from producing a high-quality product. In short, contemporary writers will continue to write and publish first-rate books and articles in spite of all disincentives. It is my hope that American society will eventually come to recognize the value of this contribution to the intellectual life of the nation.''

*   *   *

WALDMAN, Max 1919-1981

PERSONAL: Born June 2, 1919, in New York, N.Y.; died of cancer, March 1, 1981, in New York, N.Y.; son of Alex and Molly (Lobel) Waldman. *Education:* State University of New York at Buffalo, B.S.F.A., 1944; Columbia University, M.A.F.A., 1947. *Home:* 21 West 17th St., New York, N.Y. 10011. *Agent:* Bertha Klausner International Literary Agency, Inc., 71 Park Ave., New York, N.Y. 10016.

CAREER: Free-lance photographer, 1947-81. Photographs have been exhibited in solo and group shows all over the world and are represented in collections, including New York Cultural Center, Metropolitan Opera House, Museum of Modern Art, George Eastman House, and Library of Congress. *Member:* Brooklyn Society of Artists. *Awards, honors:* Creative Artists Public Service grants from New York State Council on the Arts, 1971, 1976; National Endowment for the Arts grant, 1972.

WRITINGS—With own photographs: *Zero on Mostel*, Horizon Press, 1965; *Waldman on Theater* (introduction by Clive Barnes), Doubleday, 1971; *Waldman on Dance* (introduction by Barnes), Morrow, 1977.

Contributor of articles and photographs to magazines, including *Life, Playboy, Popular Photography, Aperture, Drama Review,* and *After Dark.*

SIDELIGHTS: Waldman began his career as an advertising photographer, but after 1966 he devoted himself to artistic photography. His specialty was photographing theater and dance; his subjects included such performers as Mikhail Baryshnikov, Marcel Marceau, and Lawrence Olivier. Waldman rarely photographed actual performances on stage, preferring to recreate scenes in his studio. Gene Thornton of the *New York Times* wrote of Waldman's photographs: "They are not mere records of theatrical performances, and they are far too theatrical themselves to recreate the effects of real performances. . . . Instead they seem to be celebrations of theatricality itself by someone who clearly loves it and expects that we will love it too." In the introduction to *Waldman on Theater* Clive Barnes wrote, "Waldman makes the image of the theater live on the insides of our brains.''

BIOGRAPHICAL/CRITICAL SOURCES: Aperture, Volume XIII, number 2, 1967; *Popular Photography*, January, 1970, March, 1973; Max Waldman, *Waldman on Theater*, introduction by Clive Barnes, Doubleday, 1971; *New York Times*, October 29, 1972; *Boston Phoenix*, July 31, 1973.

[Information provided by executrix, Carol Greunke]

*   *   *

WALKER, Earl Thomas 1891-

PERSONAL: Born July 31, 1891, in Horton, Kan.; son of Frank and Anna (McDermott) Walker; married Velma Alice Howard, 1917; children: Eva Mae Walker Martin. *Education:* Attended college. *Home:* 712 Aspen, Dalhart, Tex. 79022.

CAREER: Rock Island Railroad, helping machinist, 1911-13, fireman, 1913-17, engineer, 1917-61; writer, 1961—. Member of city council of Liberal, Kan., 1925-31, mayor, 1931 and 1935.

WRITINGS: The Fighting Railroad Mayor (autobiography), Johnson Publishing (Boulder, Colo.), 1968.

WORK IN PROGRESS: Another book on railroading, publication expected in 1983. "If I am tagged by the Grim Reaper, my daughter will complete the manuscript.''

SIDELIGHTS: Walker was elected mayor of Liberal, somewhat unexpectedly, in 1931. He wrote: "I was fired for refusing to sell out the poor, and had fight after fight. I withstood six attempted frame-ups that flopped, and finally was reinstated and paid. I earned the name 'The Fighting Railroad Mayor.'

"To stay out of trouble let it be known you have the ability and willingness to break a pick handle over an obstructionist's head; it's unlikely you'll ever have to do it, a fact our foreign policy makers should keep in mind.''

AVOCATIONAL INTERESTS: Travel (Mexico, Surinam, Brazil).

WALKER, William Otis   1896-1981

OBITUARY NOTICE: Born September 19, 1896, in Selma, Ala.; died of a heart attack, October 29, 1981, in Cleveland, Ohio. Publisher and journalist. During the nearly half a century that William Walker served as publisher of the *Cleveland Call and Post,* circulation of the black weekly newspaper rose from one thousand to forty thousand. Walker's column, "Down the Big Road," appeared regularly in the paper. In 1963, when Governor James A. Rhodes appointed him director of state industrial relations, Walker became the first black ever to serve on the cabinet of an Ohio governor. He also acted as national chairman of Black Republicans for Ronald Reagan and George Bush during the 1980 presidential campaign. Obituaries and other sources: *New York Times,* October 30, 1981.

*   *   *

WALLACE, Henry A(gard)   1888-1965

PERSONAL: Born October 7, 1888, in Adair County, Iowa; died November 18, 1965, in Danbury, Conn.; buried in Des Moines, Iowa; son of Henry Cantwell (a magazine editor) and Carrie May (Brodhead) Wallace; married Ilo Browne, May 20, 1914; children: Henry Browne, Robert Browne, Jean Browne. *Education:* Iowa State College (now University), B.S., 1910.

CAREER: Wallace's Farmer, Iowa, associate editor, 1910-24, editor, 1924-29; *Iowa Homestead and Wallace's Farmer,* editor, 1929-33; U.S. secretary of agriculture, 1933-40; vice-president of the United States, 1941-45; U.S. secretary of commerce, 1945-46; *New Republic,* editor, 1946-48, contributing editor, beginning in 1948; writer, 1948-65. Broadcast "The Farm and Home Hour" on radio. Progressive party candidate for U.S. president, 1948. *Awards, honors:* M.S. in Agriculture from Iowa State College, 1920; award from *Churchman,* 1945.

WRITINGS: Agricultural Prices, Wallace Publishing, 1920; (with Earl N. Bressman) *Corn and Corn-Growing,* Wallace Publishing, 1923, 5th edition, Wiley, 1949; *Our Debt and Duty to the Farmer,* Century Co., 1925; *New Frontiers,* Reynal, 1934, reprinted, Greenwood Press, 1969; *Statesmanship and Religion,* Round Table Press, 1934; *America Must Choose: The Advantages and Disadvantages of Nationalism, of World Trade, and of a Planned Middle Course,* World Peace Foundation, 1934; *Whose Constitution?: An Inquiry Into the General Welfare,* Reynal, 1936, reprinted, 1964; *Paths to Plenty,* National Home Library Foundation, 1938, reprinted as *The Price of Freedom,* 1940.

(Co-author) *Christian Bases of World Order,* Abingdon-Cokesbury, 1943, reprinted, Books for Libraries, 1971; *The Century of the Common Man,* edited by Russell Lord, Reynal, 1943; *Democracy Reborn: Selected From Public Papers,* edited by Lord, Reynal, 1944; *Our Job in the Pacific,* American Council, Institute of Pacific Relations, 1944; *Sixty Million Jobs,* Simon & Schuster, 1945; (with Andrew J. Steiger) *Soviet Asia Mission,* Reynal, 1946; *Toward World Peace,* Reynal, 1948, reprinted, Greenwood Press, 1970; (with William L. Brown) *Corn and Its Early Fathers,* Michigan State University Press, 1956; *The Price of Vision: The Diary of Henry A. Wallace, 1942-46,* edited by John Morton Blum, Houghton, 1973. Also author of *Corn and the Midwestern Farmer,* 1956, and *The Long Look Ahead,* 1960.

SIDELIGHTS: A *Time* reporter related that "at an age when most moppets hope to grow up to be President, Henry Wallace once answered a kindly visitor who asked what his ambition was: 'To make the world safe for corn breeders.' " It was an ambition that Wallace pursued throughout his life, first as a student, journalist, and editor, and then as secretary of agriculture, vice-president of the United States, secretary of commerce, and presidential candidate.

A third generation agrarian, Henry Agard Wallace was the son of Henry Cantwell Wallace, an agricultural leader and secretary of agriculture under President Warren G. Harding, and the grandson of Henry Wallace I, founder of *Wallace's Farmer,* an influential agricultural periodical. After graduating from Iowa State College, where he majored in agriculture, Wallace joined the family magazine as an associate editor in 1910. While employed by the journal, he conducted research that established his reputation as a leading agronomist. Among Wallace's contributions to farming were his experiments in plant genetics that resulted in high-yielding strains of corn and which enabled him to forecast corn yields on the basis of temperature and rainfall records. In addition, Wallace's price and price-trend studies produced the first corn-hog ratio charts from which he was able to predict the likely course of future markets. His prognostications were so accurate that in 1919 he correctly foretold the agricultural crash of 1920. His price-trend studies also led to the publication in 1920 of the first of his many books, *Agricultural Prices.*

In 1921, when his father went to Washington as secretary of agriculture, Wallace assumed leadership of *Wallace's Farmer.* He officially became the magazine's editor in 1924, following the death of Henry Cantwell Wallace, and he remained with the publication after its merger in 1929 with the *Iowa Homestead,* retaining the position of editor until he himself left for Washington in 1933.

Like his father and grandfather before him, Wallace was a Republican editor. However, in 1928 he crossed party lines and publicly supported Democrat Al Smith's presidential candidacy, because he believed that Smith had "social vision." It was for this same reason that Wallace backed Franklin Delano Roosevelt's presidential bid in 1932, and it was Wallace's support that was credited with swinging the usually Republican Iowa vote in Roosevelt's favor. After the election Wallace was the new president's choice for secretary of agriculture, a position that he assumed in 1933. In spite of the fact that Wallace served as a cabinet member in a Democratic administration, it was not until 1936 that he actually registered as a Democrat.

Among Wallace's first official acts as secretary of agriculture was the formulation of the controversial Agricultural Adjustment Act, a program aimed at raising plummeting farm prices through crop control. Under the act's directives, corn and cotton were plowed under and six million young pigs were slaughtered. After all of his years of research on how to produce higher crop yields, Wallace was telling farmers they must now grow less. The enormous waste dictated by the act was untenable to millions of Americans trying to survive the Depression. Thus, after the first Agricultural Adjustment Act was declared unconstitutional, Wallace rewrote the act, carefully avoiding future agricultural waste by establishing a food stamp plan that provided for distribution of food surplus to the needy.

Instrumental in reorganizing the Department of Agriculture, Wallace traveled, spoke, and wrote countless articles defending and explaining the department's activities; in the process he also became an active spokesman for other administration policies. In 1934 he published two books which established him as a major proponent of the New Deal. *America Must Choose* was regarded by many, according to the *Springfield Republican,* "as the most important statement of issues that has emanated from the present administration." In the same year

Wallace's *New Frontiers,* an exposition and defense of the New Deal, including a history and defense of the Agricultural Adjustment Act, was labeled "a veritable gospel of the new deal" by *Christian Science Monitor* critic W. J. Bailey. H. E. Barnes of *Nation* called the book "the finest sermon which has emerged from the Roosevelt Administration, not even excepting the best speeches of the President himself." Nettleton suggested: "To those who disagree with the New Deal no better recommendation can be made than that they read Mr. Wallace's book in order at least to know what to attack. They may find more to agree with than they expect."

Whose Constitution?: An Inquiry Into the General Welfare, considered a sequel to *New Frontiers,* was published in 1936, an election year. Alluding to speculation that the book was "campaign literature," Herschel Brickell of *Review of Reviews* noted the work's "importance in a red-hot political campaign." The existing political climate was reflected in the wide range of reviews. Walter Millis, reviewing for *Books,* wrote, "Here is the basic philosophy of the New Deal as refined and rationalized against the backgrounds of constitutional history . . . set forth with the quiet vividness of statement, the moderation and the homespun integrity which have made Secretary Wallace by far the most effective voice in the New Deal hierarchy." At the same time a *Christian Science Monitor* critic stated: "Mr. Wallace, as a writer and thinker, barely escapes the pitfalls of pedagogism. He assumes as existing a more or less hypothetical problem or condition, and then proceeds to build around it or eliminate by means and theories of his own devising."

When Roosevelt was elected for a second term of office, Wallace once again served as his secretary of agriculture. His ardent support of New Deal programs led, in 1940, to his selection as the Democratic party's vice-presidential candidate. Elected to the vice-presidency on November 5, 1940, Wallace traveled extensively as an ambassador of goodwill. *Century of the Common Man,* an outgrowth of the vice-president's speaking and writing activities, was published in 1943. John MacCormac of the *New York Times* noted: "Somebody said the chief duty of a Vice President is to make speeches. Henry Wallace has taken his duty so seriously that [editor] Russell Lord was able to find fifteen of them, delivered in the course of the last two and a half years, to make up this little volume. . . . It seems safe to say that no other Vice President, in so short a space of time, ever said so much that mattered."

After the United States entered World War II, Wallace assumed many emergency responsibilities in addition to the usual duties of the vice-presidency, including leadership of the Board of Economic Warfare (BEW). A primary function of the BEW was acquisition of strategic materials, specifically scarce minerals and other commodities available only from foreign sources. However, all of the board's foreign purchases were financed by an agency under the jurisdiction of the Department of Commerce, the Reconstruction Finance Corporation (RFC), which at the time was headed by the staunchly conservative secretary of commerce, Jesse Jones. Following several bitter disputes between the two groups, Roosevelt took disciplinary action against the participants by abolishing the BEW in favor of a new agency, the Office of Economic Warfare, and by assigning the new agency some of the power formerly held by the RFC. This incident, along with the State Department's accusations that Wallace had overstepped his authority by mixing diplomacy with business in the purchase of strategic materials, resulted in his failure to receive the 1944 Democratic vice-presidental nomination. Reputedly offered any post in the cabinet except that of secretary of state, Wallace chose the position of secretary of commerce, necessitating Jesse Jones's removal

from the post as well as Jones's replacement as head of the RFC. A Senate battle over Wallace's appointment was resolved only after the RFC, along with its $32 billion budget, was separated by a "bill of divorcement" from the Department of Commerce.

As secretary of commerce, Wallace undertook the reorganization and revitalization of the department. Among his projected programs was a plan for a full-employment, high-income level economy. His book *Sixty Million Jobs* outlined his intentions. Calling the work "an enormous blueprint for sixty million jobs by 1950," Les Barnes of *Saturday Review of Literature* stated, "It is also a passionate statement of a remarkable American's basic political, social, and personal philosophy." Precisely because of his "passionate" beliefs, Wallace never had the opportunity to implement his plans for the Department of Commerce. In September of 1946 he was forced to resign because of his outspoken opposition to President Harry Truman's foreign policy.

The Price of Vision: The Diary of Henry A. Wallace, 1942-46, published posthumously in 1973, covers the years during which Wallace evolved the thinking that ultimately led to his dismissal by Truman. Reviewing the book for the *New York Times Book Review,* Cabell Phillips remarked, "Wallace longed for a close cultural and political alliance with all the nations of the Western hemisphere, and for a strong United Nations whose beneficent reign would shelter all mankind for all time against want and adversity." Also, Phillips explained, Wallace was committed to the belief that the Russians could and would be substantial peacetime allies provided that efforts to win their confidence were not continually undermined "by reactionaries and militarists who could envision the Communists only as mortal enemies." In July, 1946, Wallace wrote a four thousand-word memorandum to Truman urging a change in policy regarding Russia. In the seventeen-page document Wallace warned against an atomic arms race with the Soviets and called for measures to counteract the escalating fear of Russia, which he charged was being systematically built up in the minds of the American people. Then, two months later, while Secretary of State James Byrnes was at the Paris Peace Conference, Wallace, in a speech at Madison Square Garden, repeated his views and publicly attacked the administration's policy of "getting tough" with the Russians. Angered by Wallace's ill-timed remarks, Truman demanded his resignation from the cabinet, effective September 20, 1946. Thus, after thirteen years as a public servant, Wallace, the last of the New Dealers to leave the administration, resigned his government post and returned to journalism as the editor of the *New Republic,* a liberal weekly periodical.

Throughout 1947 there was considerable talk about the possibility of forming a third political party for the 1948 presidential election. Questioning the effectiveness of such a move, Wallace voiced his intentions to continue working within the Democratic party. However, by late 1947 Wallace, unable to reconcile his differences with the foreign policies of both major parties, announced his candidacy for the U.S. presidency on the Progressive Party of America's ticket.

Toward World Peace, Wallace's statement of his political views on peace, world politics, and U.S. foreign policy, was published in 1948. Generally regarded as campaign literature, the book elicited widely divergent reviews. The *Saturday Review of Literature* ran two contrary reviews of the book in a single issue. In one of the reviews Frank Altschul stated: "It is a matter of regret, though it has long since ceased to be a matter of surprise, to find Henry Wallace echoing so faithfully the editorial column of the Daily Worker. He represents a totally distorted picture of the American scene.'' On the next page, S. K. Padover opined: ''I have rarely read a book that is so quotable, so glowing with righteous cause. It is packed with true observations and frequently rises to heights of eloquence.''

In the 1948 presidential election Wallace tallied just over 1,150,000 votes, half of which were from the state of New York. He received no electoral votes. His ''quixotic campaign for the Presidency,'' remarked Cabell Phillips, was a ticket to ''political oblivion.'' Wallace retired from politics, leaving the Progressive party in 1950 after it repudiated his endorsement of U.S. intervention in Korea. He had become disenchanted with the Soviets after learning in 1949 that they had engineered the Czechoslovakian coup that had installed a totalitarian government in place of the existing democratic regime. Years later Wallace told Phillips, ''I was mistaken in my estimation of the Russians' intentions. . . . I believed that if we could overcome the Russians' centuries-old distrust of Western imperialism and their later fear of Western capitalism, they would collaborate in the building of a truly democratic world.''

In his introduction to *The Price of Vision*, editor John Morton Blum referred to Wallace as ''a good man'' of occasionally ''cloudy vision.'' And it is difficult, if at all possible, to find sources that dispute Wallace's basic sincerity and integrity. ''What he was,'' assessed Phillips, ''was an idealogue, a man so possessed by ideals, and humanitarian impulses that his capacity for practical rationalization was nearly always hampered. Even in the heyday of his career as Secretary of Agriculture . . . he was the consummate paradox of the Washington scene—the shy, moody, introverted loner whom, it was said, no one ever really got to know, but who won and held the respect of a great President, of many liberal intellectuals, and even of a few workaday politicians.''

BIOGRAPHICAL/CRITICAL SOURCES—Books: Paul Henry DeKruif, *Hunger Fighters*, Harcourt, 1928; Roger Ward Babson, *Washington and the Revolutionists*, Harper, 1934; Robert Merrill Bartlett, *They Work for Tomorrow*, Association Press, 1943; Frank Kingdon, *An Uncommon Man*, Readers Press, 1945; Russell Lord, *The Wallaces of Iowa*, Houghton, 1947; K. M. Schmidt, *Henry Wallace: Quixotic Crusade, 1948*, Syracuse University Press, 1960; Henry A. Wallace, *The Price of Vision: The Diary of Henry A. Wallace, 1942-1946*, edited by John Morton Blum, Houghton, 1973.

Periodicals: *Collier's*, April 1, 1933, September 9, 1933; *Literary Digest*, March 3, 1934, May 26, 1934; *Springfield Republican*, May 3, 1934, May 9, 1934, July 5, 1936, April 25, 1948; *New York Herald Tribune*, May 9, 1934, October 4, 1934; *Books*, May 27, 1934, June 5, 1936; *New York Times*, June 10, 1934, October 7, 1934, July 11, 1943, September 9, 1945, April 18, 1948; *America*, July, 1934, June, 1941; *Christian Science Monitor*, October 4, 1934, September 7, 1945; *Saturday Review of Literature*, October 6, 1934, July 11, 1936, March 30, 1940, September 8, 1945, April 17, 1948; *Nation*, December 5, 1934, May 8, 1935, August 1, 1936, September 29, 1945, June 26, 1948, November 19, 1973; *American Mercury*, March, 1935; *Review of Reviews*, August, 1936; *Saturday Evening Post*, July 3, 1937, November 24, 1940; *North American Review*, December, 1937, March, 1939; *Time*, December 19, 1938, July 29, 1940, August 5, 1940, September 23, 1940, October 7, 1940, November 25, 1940; *Life*, September 2, 1940, December 16, 1940; *Current History and Forum*, December 24, 1940; *Fortune*, November, 1942; *Look*, November 3, 1942; *Free World*, April, 1945; *New Republic*, September 17, 1945, November 3, 1973; *PM*, October 26, 1947, November 9, 1947; *Liberty*, December, 1947; *New York Herald Tribune Weekly Book Review*, April 18, 1948; *San Francisco Chronicle*, April 25, 1948; *New York Times Book Review*, October 14, 1973.

OBITUARIES: New York Times, November 19, 1965; *Time*, November 26, 1965; *New Republic*, December 4, 1965.*

—*Sketch by Lillian S. Sims*

*　　　*　　　*

WALLACE, Lila Bell Acheson 1889-

BRIEF ENTRY: Born December 25, 1889, in Virden, Manitoba, Canada. American editor and publisher. Wallace cofounded *Reader's Digest* in 1921. She edited the magazine until 1965, at which time she became chairman of the board of directors. She received a Medal of Freedom from the president of the United States in 1972. *Address:* High Winds, Mount Kisco, N.Y. 10549. *Biographical/critical sources: Current Biography*, Wilson, 1956.

*　　　*　　　*

WALLACE, Pamela 1949-

PERSONAL: Born May 28, 1949, in Exeter, Calif.; daughter of Ray M. and Yvonne (Haines) Bradley; married Earl W. Wallace (a writer), April 27, 1974; children: Christopher E. *Education:* University of California, Los Angeles, B.A., 1971. *Politics:* Democrat. *Agent:* Harold Greene, Eisenbach-Greene-Duchow, Inc., 760 North La Cienega Blvd., Los Angeles, Calif. 90069.

CAREER: Member of editorial staffs of several magazines, including *Playgirl*, 1971—.

WRITINGS—Novels: *The Fires of Beltane*, Pinnacle Books, 1978; *Caresse*, Pinnacle Books, 1979; *Love Again*, Pinnacle Books, 1981. Writer for television series, ''Serpico.''

WORK IN PROGRESS: A ''generational novel'' set in California's San Joaquin Valley; a novel for Silhouette's new ''Rendezvous'' line, publication expected in 1982.

*　　　*　　　*

WALLACE, Phyllis Ann

PERSONAL: Born in Baltimore, Md.; daughter of John L. and Stevella (Parker) Wallace. *Education:* New York University, B.A., 1943; Yale University, M.A., 1944, Ph.D., 1948. *Home:* 780 Boylston St., Boston, Mass. 02199. *Office:* Sloan School of Management, Massachusetts Institute of Technology, Cambridge, Mass. 02139.

CAREER: National Bureau of Economic Research, economist and statistician, 1948-52; Atlanta University, Atlanta, Ga., associate professor of economics, 1953-57; U.S. Government, economic analyst, 1957-65; U.S. Equal Employment Opportunity Commission, Washington, D.C., chief of technical studies, 1966-69; Metropolitan Applied Research Center, New York, N.Y., vice-president for research, 1969-72; Massachusetts Institute of Technology, Cambridge, visiting professor, 1972-75, professor of management, 1975—. Lecturer at City College (now of City Univeristy of New York), 1948-51. Member of board of directors of State Street Bank and Trust Co., Stop and Shop Companies, Manpower Demonstration Research Corp., and Boston Museum of Fine Arts; member of board of trustees of Brookings Institution; member of Minimum Wage Study Commission and President's Pay Advisory Committee. *Member:* American Economic Association, Industrial Relations Research Association. *Awards, honors:* LL.D. from Valparaiso University, 1977; Wilbur Lucius Cross Medal from Yale University, 1980.

WRITINGS: Pathways to Work, Lexington Books, 1974; (editor) *Equal Employment Opportunity and the AT&T Case*, M.I.T.

Press, 1976; (editor with Annette LaMond) *Women, Minorities, and Employment Discrimination,* Lexington Books, 1977; *Black Women in the Labor Force,* M.I.T. Press, 1980; *Women in the Workplace,* Auburn Publishing, 1981.

WORK IN PROGRESS: Upward Mobility of Young Managers.

* * *

WALLERSTEIN, Judith Hannah Saretsky 1921-

BRIEF ENTRY: Born December 27, 1921, in New York, N.Y. American social worker and author. Wallerstein was a psychiatric social worker and child therapist at the Menninger Foundation from 1949 to 1957. Since 1966 she has been a lecturer at the University of California, Berkeley. She wrote *Surviving the Breakup: How Children and Parents Cope With Divorce* (Basic Books, 1980). *Address:* 290 Beach Rd., Belvedere, Calif. 94920; and School of Social Welfare, University of California, Berkeley, Calif. 94920. *Biographical/critical sources: Who's Who of American Women,* 10th edition, Marquis, 1977.

* * *

WALLERSTEIN, Mitchel B(ruce) 1949-

PERSONAL: Born March 8, 1949, in New York, N.Y.; son of Melvin J. (an attorney) and Rita (a teacher; maiden name, Nomburg) Wallerstein; married Susan E. Perlik (a social program administrator), June 29, 1974; children: Matthew P. *Education:* Dartmouth College, A.B., 1971; Syracuse University, M.P.A., 1972; Massachusetts Institute of Technology, M.S., 1976, Ph.D., 1978. *Office:* Department of Nutrition and Food Science, Massachusetts Institute of Technology, 20A-202, 18 Vassar St., Cambridge, Mass. 02139.

CAREER: Dartmouth College, Hanover, N.H., associate director of Public Affairs Center, 1972-74; Holy Cross College, Worcester, Mass., assistant professor of political science, 1979-81; Massachusetts Institute of Technology, Cambridge, associate director of International Food and Nutrition Policy Program, 1978—, assistant professor, 1978—. Consultant to Ford Foundation, Executive Office of the President, and U.S. Department of State. *Member:* International Studies Association, World Future Society, American Political Science Association, American Association for the Advancement of Science. *Awards, honors:* Fellow at Institute for the Study of World Politics, 1976-78.

WRITINGS: (With E. R. Pariser, C. J. Corkery, and N. L. Brown) *Fish Protein Concentrate: Panacea for Protein Malnutrition?,* M.I.T. Press, 1978; *Food for War—Food for Peace: U.S. Food Aid in a Global Context,* M.I.T. Press, 1980; (contributor) Philip White and Nancy Selvey, editors, *Nutrition in the 1980's: Constraints on Our Knowledge,* Alan R. Liss, 1981; (editor with Nevin S. Scrimshaw) *Nutrition Policy Implementation: Issues and Experience,* Plenum, 1982; (with Raymond F. Hopkins and Robert L. Paarlberg) *Food in the Global Arena,* Holt, 1982; (contributor) *Proceeding of the Twelfth International Congress on Nutrition,* Alan R. Liss, 1982.

SIDELIGHTS: Wallerstein told *CA:* "I am a food policy analyst writing about the delicate and complex interface between the science of nutrition and the real world impact on those who are hungry and malnourished. I am also concerned greatly with issues of international development and the impact of institutions and government policies on closing the gap between the rich and the poor. The problem of hunger has proven among the most intractable of all the issues facing the global village;

it represents one of the most profound challenges in the remainder of this century."

* * *

WALTERS, John Bennett, Jr. 1912-

PERSONAL: Born May 13, 1912, in Cordele, Ga.; son of John Bennett Walters; married, 1938; children: two. *Education:* Vanderbilt University, Ph.D., 1947. *Home:* 277 Cardinal Crest Rd., Montevallo, Ala. 35115. *Office:* Department of Social Science, University of Montevallo, Montevallo, Ala. 35115.

CAREER: Vanderbilt University, Nashville, Tenn., member of faculty of political science, 1945-47; Emory and Henry College, Emory, Va., member of faculty of history and political science, 1947-56; University of Montevallo, Montevallo, Ala., professor of history and political science and chairman of department of social science, 1956—, dean of men, 1959—. Member of faculty at University of Virginia, 1950-66; chairman of board of directors of Shelby Memorial Hospital, 1975-79. *Member:* Southern Historical Association.

WRITINGS: Merchant of Terror: General Sherman and Total War, Bobbs-Merrill, 1973.

BIOGRAPHICAL/CRITICAL SOURCES: Journal of American History, December, 1974.*

* * *

WALTON, Ed(ward Hazen) 1931-

PERSONAL: Born April 21, 1931, in Easton, Pa.; son of Edward Hazen (an engineer) and Nina Virginia (a secretary; maiden name, Kellam) Walton; married Ruth E. Dow (a teacher), April 23, 1955; children: William Edward, Susan Louise (Mrs. Harold Peck III). *Education:* Attended Lebanon Valley College, 1949-50, and University of Connecticut, 1950-53. *Religion:* Congregationalist. *Home:* 492 Winnepoge Dr., Fairchild, Conn. 06430. *Office:* Department of Administrative Services, University of Bridgeport, 380 University Ave., Bridgeport, Conn. 06601.

CAREER: Bridgeport Brass Co., Bridgeport, Conn., manager of office services, 1955-60; Columbia Broadcasting System (CBS), Bridgeport, director of office services of Columbia Records division, 1960-64; University of Bridgeport, Bridgeport, director of administrative services, 1964—. Member of Bridgeport Postal Council, 1962—. Loan officer of University of Bridgeport Credit Union; member of board of directors of Fairfield Junior Pro Basketball and Fairfield Little League Baseball; chairman of American Red Cross's Home Service to Veterans, Bridgeport, 1969-70. *Military service:* U.S. Army, Finance Corps, 1953-55; served in Korea. *Member:* Administrative Management Society (president, 1964), Society for American Baseball Research. *Awards, honors:* Merit award, 1968, diamond merit award, 1972, and "300" Club award, 1981, all from Administrative Management Society, all for service to the society.

WRITINGS: This Date in Boston Red Sox History, Stein & Day, 1977, 3rd edition, 1978; *Red Sox Triumphs and Tragedies,* Stein & Day, 1980; *The Rookies,* Stein & Day, 1981. Contributor to magazines, including *Connecticut Circle.*

WORK IN PROGRESS: Two general interest books on baseball, publication expected in 1982.

SIDELIGHTS: Walton commented: "Having been a baseball fan for forty years and having done a number of research projects in that field, I find that writing books about baseball has been a most rewarding endeavor for me. In the course of research, I have made many enduring friendships among players, front-office personnel, and fellow researchers. The travel, experiences, and stories uncovered about this part of Americana have also been rewarding. Speaking engagements and radio and television appearances have provided an education in themselves, and I have had letters and phone calls from around the world.

"*This Date in Boston Red Sox History* is a totally new approach to the history of a professional baseball team and is the first in what has developed into a series of histories of baseball teams using my format. All three of my baseball books have been very well accepted, a fact that has pleased me personally. It was my hope that the facts in these works would be set down once and for all for the enjoyment of baseball fans. Some of my research has caused certain baseball records to be changed, corrected really, and this has been rewarding for me and has stimulated research by others.

"My books represent a lifetime of collecting baseball facts. My motivation was simply love of the subject. I suppose the memories they bring up are the real secret of my success. Baseball is a vital part of everyday life in the United States, and who among us doesn't like to revert to those days of our youth that are related to certain events or players who were heroes?"

* * *

WANDERER, Zev W(illiam) 1932-

PERSONAL: Born April 4, 1932, in New York, N.Y.; son of Jacob and Annie Wanderer. *Education:* City University of New York, M.S.Ed., 1956; Columbia University, M.A., 1958, Ph.D., 1964. *Home:* 30004 Zenith Point Rd., Malibu, Calif. 90265.

CAREER: Institute for Juvenile Research, Chicago, Ill., research director of William Healy School; University of California, Los Angeles, clinical professor of psychology; Center for Behavior Therapy, Beverly Hills, Calif., founder and director. Diplomate of American Board of Professional Psychology; assistant professor at University of Illinois. Conducts therapeutic workshops; guest on television and radio programs. *Member:* Behavior Therapy and Research Society (clinical fellow), Columbia University Graduate Faculties Alumni Association (member of board of directors).

WRITINGS: (With Tracy Cabot) *Letting Go: A Twelve-Week Personal Action Program to Overcome a Broken Heart,* Putnam, 1978; (with Erika Fabian) *Making Love Work,* Putnam, 1979; (with David Radell) *How Big Is Big?,* Warner Books, 1981. Also author of "Letting Go: The Movie." Contributor of about one dozen articles to professional journals.

* * *

WANTLING, William 1933-1974

PERSONAL: Born November 7, 1933, in Peoria, Ill.; died May 4, 1974; married; children: two. *Education:* Illinois State University, B.S.Ed., 1969.

CAREER: Poet and novelist. Also worked as factory worker, zoo keeper, and teacher. Inmate at San Quentin State Penitentiary, convicted on forgery and narcotics charges, 1958-63. *Military service:* U.S. Marine Corps; served in Korea; became sergeant.

WRITINGS: The Search (poems; edited by Kirby Congdon), Hors Commerce Press, 1964; *Machine and Destiny: A Dirge for Three Artists* (poems), Hors Commerce Press, 1964; *Head*

First: Poems, Erick Kiviat, 1964; *Heroin Haikus* (poems), Fenian Head Center Press, 1965; *Five Poem Songs,* Hors Commerce Press, 1965; *Down, Off, and Out: A Selection of Some Real Down, Some Half Off, and Some Way Out Work* (poems), Mimeo Press, 1966; *The Source* (poems), Dustbooks, 1966; *The Awakening* (poems), Turret Books, 1967, revised edition, Rapp & Whiting, 1968; (with Alan Jackson and Jeff Nuttall) *Penguin Modern Poets Twelve,* Penguin, 1968; *Young and Tender* (novel), Bee Line Books, 1969; *Sick Fly* (novel; edited by Peter Finch), Second Aeon, 1970; *Ten Thousand R.P.M. and Diggin It, Yeah* (poems), Second Aeon, 1973; *San Quentin's Stranger,* Second Aeon, 1973.*

* * *

WARBURG, Fredric (John) 1898-1981

PERSONAL: Born November 27, 1898, in London, England; died May 27, 1981, in London, England; son of John Cimon and Violet Amalia (Sichel) Warburg; married May Nellie Holt, 1924 (divorced); married Pamela de Bayou de Brinvilliers (a printer and designer), 1931 (died, 1978); children: David John, Hew Francis, Jeremy Fredric. *Education:* Christ Church, Oxford, M.A., 1922. *Politics:* Liberal. *Religion:* "Good will." *Home:* 29 St. Edmunds Court, St. Edmunds Ter., London N.W.3, England. *Office:* Martin Secker & Warburg, 54 Poland St., London W1V 3DF, England.

CAREER: George Routledge & Sons Ltd. (publisher), London, England, began as apprentice, 1922, became joint managing director, 1931-35; Martin Secker & Warburg, London, owner, publisher, and chairman, 1936-81. Joined Heinemann Group of Publishers, 1951, served as director, 1961-71. Tried at Central Criminal Court for publishing allegedly obscene novel, and acquitted, 1954. *Military service:* British Army, Royal Garrison Artillery, 1917-19; became lieutenant.

WRITINGS: An Occupation for Gentlemen, Hutchinson, 1959, Houghton, 1960; *All Authors Are Equal: The Publishing Life of Fredric Warburg, 1936-1971,* St. Martin's, 1973. Also author of "A Slight Case of Obscenity," published in *New Yorker,* April 20, 1957.

WORK IN PROGRESS: Obituary, his autobiography.

SIDELIGHTS: Fredric Warburg gained notoriety with the 1944 publication of George Orwell's satirical work *Animal Farm.* The satire was aimed at the Soviet Union, then a British ally, and as the book's publisher Warburg was criticized for making the work available. Several years later, after publishing Stanley Kaufmann's *The Philanderer,* Warburg was tried, but later acquitted, on charges of publishing an obscene work.

Shortly before his death, Warburg told *CA:* "My intention was to publish only books of literary merit, mainly novels, and nonfiction books of substantial interest in a very wide field (but not technical books). I was prosecuted for publishing an allegedly obscene American book, *The Philanderer.* This now famous case led to drastic changes in the law and is described in *All Authors Are Equal.*"

BIOGRAPHICAL/CRITICAL SOURCES: Fredric Warburg, *All Authors Are Equal: The Publishing Life of Fredric Warburg,* St. Martin's, 1973; *Observer,* October 28, 1973; *Listener,* November 22, 1973; *Times Literary Supplement,* November 23, 1973.

OBITUARIES: Publishers Weekly, June 12, 1981.

* * *

WARCH, Richard 1939-

PERSONAL: Born August 4, 1939, in Hackensack, N.J.; son

of George William (an insurance agent and broker) and Helen (Hansen) Warch; married Margot Lynn Moses (a special education teacher), September 8, 1962; children: Stephen Knud, David Preston, Karin. *Education:* Williams College, B.A., 1961; attended University of Edinburgh, 1962-63; Yale University, B.D., 1964, Ph.D., 1968. *Home:* 229 North Park Ave., Appleton, Wis. 54911. *Office:* Office of the President, Lawrence University, Appleton, Wis. 54912.

CAREER: Yale University, New Haven, Conn., lecturer, 1968-69, assistant professor, 1969-73, associate professor of American studies and history, 1973-77, director of history of education project, 1970-72, Morse fellow, 1972-73; Lawrence University, Appleton, Wis., professor of history and vice-president for academic affairs, 1977-79; president of university, 1979—. Ordained minister of United Presbyterian Church in the U.S.A., 1968; member of Winnebago Presbytery. *Member:* American Studies Association, Society for Values in Higher Education (fellow). *Awards, honors:* D.H., Ripon College, 1980.

WRITINGS: School of the Prophets: Yale College, 1701-1740, Yale University Press, 1973; (editor with Jonathan F. Fanton) *John Brown,* Prentice-Hall, 1973; (with M. Antier, B. Laffay, and A. James) *US/GB/la vie d' aujourd' hui de A a Z* (title means "United States, Great Britain, and Life Today From A to Z"), Hachette, 1973.

* * *

WARE, W. Porter 1904-

PERSONAL: Born November 27, 1904, in Baltimore, Md.; son of Sedley Lynch (a university professor) and Alice (Porter) Ware; married Emma Kelly, December 28, 1928 (died, 1930); married Louise Thornton, January 2, 1936; children: Barbara Porter Ware (died, 1960), Mary Dabney Moore. *Education:* Attended University of the South, 1922-23, University of Tennessee, 1923-25, and University of Virginia, 1925-26. *Politics:* Democrat. *Religion:* Episcopalian. *Home:* Plum Tree Cottage, Sewanee, Tenn. 37375.

CAREER: University of the South, Sewanee, Tenn., public relations representative, 1928-62, registrar, 1962-71; writer, 1949—. Member of Faculty Club and *Manuscripts. Wartime service:* American Red Cross, 1945-46; served in Pacific. *Awards, honors:* Received medal from Jenny Lind Society in Stockholm, Sweden, 1981.

WRITINGS: Occupational Shaving Mugs, Lightner Publishing Corp., 1949; *Cigar Store Figures in American Folk Art,* Lightner Publishing Corp., 1955; (with Thaddeus C. Lockard, Jr.) *The Lost Letters of Jenny Lind,* Gollancz, 1966; (with Lockard) *P. T. Barnum Presents Jenny Lind: The American Tour of the Swedish Nightingale,* Louisiana State University Press, 1981.

WORK IN PROGRESS: "Editing a manuscript by Mrs. Charles Higgins on her experiences during the Japanese occupation of China in World War II."

SIDELIGHTS: W. Porter Ware's second book on Jenny Lind is a chronicle of her 1850 American tour. The soprano, who proved to be one of America's greatest adopted sweethearts, landed in New York from her home in Sweden on September 1, 1850, to begin perhaps the most consequential tour in her career. With the showman P. T. Barnum as her promoter, Lind earned $176,000 in eight months plus one husband, her accompanist Otto Goldschmidt, while Barnum grossed over $200,000. Enraptured by the "Swedish nightingale," Americans stampeded box offices to buy tickets for her concerts, rioted when they could not see her, and serenaded her through-

out her travels. Though her concerts were short by contemporary standards, Lind still enchanted her audiences with her mastery of the coloratura. Her voice, a nineteenth-century critic wrote, was "as near perfection as anything human can be," and as a person Lind was known for her endearing qualities.

Though they traveled together to backward villages in addition to cities such as New York, Boston, Philadelphia, and New Orleans, Barnum and Lind, as Ware illustrated in *P. T. Barnum Presents Jenny Lind,* were polarities. Lind, with a reputation for virtue and altruism, worked tirelessly in order to earn money for charities, most notably for a girl's school she established in Sweden. Barnum, on the other hand, was looking to turn a profit—as part of his campaign slogan suggested; "And you will touch their hearts, and I will tap their pockets;/And if between us the public isn't skinned,/Why my name isn't Barnum, nor your name Jenny Lind!"

Undaunted by the expense, American audiences apparently felt they got their money's worth. "But not [*sic*] matter how costly the tickets," Joseph Leach observed in the *Journal of American History,* "Lind's charm, her warmth, and her high regard for her audiences as human beings celebrating with her the blessings of music always seemed to justify the high prices." Americans bought just about anything associated with the singer, so the mania of the tour resulted in Jenny Lind bonnets, Jenny Lind cooking stoves, even Jenny Lind horse blinders.

Using newspaper clippings, letters, diaries, programs, and general memorabilia, Ware and his co-author Thaddeus C. Lockard construct a "brief, scholarly and diverting volume" on Lind, commented a *New Yorker* reviewer. *P. T. Barnum Presents Jenny Lind,* Hugh Walker said, "caught my fancy, banished cynicism and reduced me pretty nearly to a state of sentimental burbling." According to Patrick O'Connor of the *New York Times,* "Professors Lockard and Ware are to be congratulated on writing a book which adds considerably to our knowledge not only of the main participants but of music making and showmanship in America before the Civil War."

BIOGRAPHICAL/CRITICAL SOURCES: Los Angeles Times, December 14, 1980; *Tennessean,* December 14, 1980; *New Yorker,* February 2, 1981; *Times Literary Supplement,* February 20, 1981; *Journal of American History,* June, 1981.

* * *

WARREN, Harry
See GUARAGNA, Salvatore

* * *

WASHBURN, Sherwood L(arned) 1911-

BRIEF ENTRY: Born November 26, 1911, in Cambridge, Mass. American anthropologist, educator, and author. Washburn was a professor of anthropology at University of California, Berkeley, from 1958 to 1979. He received a Viking Fund medal in 1960, a medal from CIBA Foundation in 1965, and the Huxley Medal in 1967. His books include *Human Evolution: Biosocial Perspectives* (Benjamin-Cummings, 1978) and *Ape Into Human: A Study of Human Evolution,* 2nd edition (Little, Brown, 1980). *Address:* 2797 Shasta Rd., Berkeley, Calif. 94708. *Biographical/critical sources: Who's Who in America,* 41st edition, Marquis, 1980.

* * *

WATHERN, Peter 1947-

PERSONAL: Born April 12, 1947, in Stroud, England; son of

William Percy (an engineer) and Winifred Daisy (Shipton) Wathern; married Julie Caroline Brown, September 17, 1966; children: Andrea, Matthew. *Education:* Sheffield City College of Education, Certificate of Education, 1968; Bedford College, London, B.S. (with honors), 1971; University of Sheffield, D.Phil., 1976. *Home:* Erwau Glas, Talybont, Dyfed, Wales. *Office:* Department of Botany and Microbiology, University College of Wales, University of Wales, Aberystwyth, Dyfed, Wales.

CAREER: University of Aberdeen, Aberdeen, Scotland, research fellow in environmental planning, 1974-78; University of Wales, University College of Wales, Aberystwyth, lecturer in applied ecology, 1978—. *Member:* British Ecological Society, Institute of Biology.

WRITINGS: Assessment of Major Industrial Applications: A Manual, H.M.S.O., 1976, 2nd edition, 1981; *Environmental Impact Assessment,* Bowker, 1980. Contributor to scientific journals.

WORK IN PROGRESS: Research on the role of ecology in environmental management and planning.

SIDELIGHTS: Wathern told *CA:* "I am interested in international solutions to environmental problems. Therefore I enjoy traveling to look at both the problems and their solutions. My writing on environmental issues is particularly concerned with the revegetation of derelict and despoiled land."

*   *   *

WATSON, Francis M(arion)   1921-

PERSONAL: Born August 23, 1921, in Griffin, Ga.; son of Francis M., Sr. (in insurance) and Lillian (Peacock) Watson; married Virginia Scott, October 16, 1941; children: Carol (Mrs. Hendree Harrison), Laura (Mrs. John Keys), Scott, John. *Education:* University of Georgia, B.S., 1958, M.A., 1959. *Religion:* Episcopal. *Home:* 8301 Winder St., Vienna, Va. 22180. *Office address:* P.O. Box 125, Dunn Loring, Va. 22027.

CAREER: U.S. Army, career officer, 1942-66, served as infantry combat engineer and public information officer, retiring as lieutenant colonel; American University, Washington, D.C., research scientist, 1966-69; American Institute for Research, Washington, D.C., information system manager, 1969-70; National Media Analysis, Inc., Washington, D.C., research director, 1970-71; private consultant to government, educational institutions, and industry, 1971—. *Awards, honors:* Legion of Merit.

WRITINGS: Political Terrorism: The Threat and the Response, Luce, 1976; *The Alternate Media,* Rockford Institute, 1979.

WORK IN PROGRESS: A study of the potential for terrorism affecting the United States in the immediate future.

SIDELIGHTS: Watson wrote: "I have lived or traveled in Europe, Asia, and the Pacific for about twelve years of my life, and lived in several sections of the United States. My continuing major interests are social systems, how they work, how they fail to work, the impacts of communications and violence on them, information and propaganda, cross-cultural communications, and human relations."

AVOCATIONAL INTERESTS: Public speaking, reading aloud to groups (especially children and older people).

*   *   *

WATT, Frank Hedden   1889-1981

OBITUARY NOTICE: Born in 1889; died in 1981 in Waco, Tex. Archaeologist and author. Of the six Ice Age skeletons discovered in the Western Hemisphere, two were found in central Texas during archaeological excavations in which Frank Watt participated. Watt was the author of *John Watt, Pioneer: A Genealogical Collection.* Obituaries and other sources: *AB Bookman's Weekly,* December 21, 1981.

*   *   *

WAYNE, (Anne) Jenifer   1917-

PERSONAL: Born in 1917 in London, England; married C. Rolph Hewitt in 1948; children: two daughters, one son. *Education:* Somerville College, Oxford, B.A. (with honors), 1939. *Home:* Rushett Egde, Bramley, Guildford, Surrey GU5 0LH, England.

CAREER: Associated with London Ambulance Service, London, England, 1939; teacher of English in Nottinghamshire, England, 1940-41; British Broadcasting Corp. (BBC), London, scriptwriter and producer in radio features department, 1941-48; writer, 1948—.

WRITINGS: This Is the Law: Stories of Wrongdoers by Fault or Folly, Sylvan Press, 1948; *The Shadows and Other Poems,* Secker & Warburg, 1959; *Brown Bread and Butter in the Basement: A Twenties Childhood,* Gollancz, 1973; *The Purple Dress: Growing Up in the Thirties,* Gollancz, 1979.

For children; published by Heinemann, except as noted: *Clemence and Ginger,* 1960; *The Day the Ceiling Fell Down,* 1961, Puffin, 1978; *Kitchen People,* 1963; Bobbs-Merrill, 1964; *The Night the Rain Came In, Merry by Name,* 1964; *The Ghost Next Door,* 1965; *Saturday and the Irish Aunt,* 1966; *Someone in the Attic,* 1967; *Ollie,* 1969; *Sprout,* 1970, McGraw, 1976; *Something in the Barn,* 1971; *Sprout's Window-Cleaner,* 1971, McGraw, 1976; *Sprout and the Dogsitter,* 1972, McGraw, 1977; *The Smoke in Albert's Garden,* 1974; *Sprout and the Helicopter,* 1974, McGraw, 1977; *Sprout and the Conjuror,* 1976, published as *Sprout and the Magician,* McGraw, 1977.

SIDELIGHTS: Jenifer Wayne, best known for her children's stories, is the creator of Sprout, an irrepressible youngster with a voracious appetite and a penchant for mischef. There are six books in the *Sprout* series; in each, the well-intentioned but headstrong Sprout becomes ensnarled in some misadventure, and his efforts to extricate himself only result in greater confusion. Sprout's particular weaknesses for food and animals—especially elephants—are his downfall. His pursuit of those passions lures him into various complicated situations, but ultimately he always manages to disentangle himself, and the stories end happily.

AVOCATIONAL INTERESTS: Music, collage, old china.*

*   *   *

WEBB, Clifford (Cyril)   1895-1972

PERSONAL: Born February 14, 1895, in London, England: died July 29, 1972; married Ella Monckton, 1924; children: two sons, one daughter. *Education:* Attended Westminster School of Art. *Residence:* Abinger Hammer, Surrey, England.

CAREER: Artist, illustrator, engraver, and author. Worked as apprentice to a lithographer; Birmingham School of Art, Birmingham, England, teacher of drawing, 1922-26; Westminster School of Art, London, England, lecturer, c. 1927-1940; St. Martin's School of Art, London, teacher of engraving, beginning 1945. Work represented in permanent collections of British Museum, Royal Academy of Arts, and Victoria and Albert Museum, all in London. *Military service:* British Army, 1914-

1918; mentioned in dispatches. Worked for the Ministry of Fuel and Power during World War II. *Member:* Royal Society of British Artists, Royal Society of Painter-Etchers and Engravers, National Society of Painters, Sculptors and Gravers, Society of Wood Engravers (founding member).

WRITINGS—For young people; self-illustrated: *The Story of Noah,* F. J. Ward, 1931, Warne, 1932; *Butterwick Farm,* Warne, 1933; *A Jungle Picnic,* Warne, 1934; *The North Pole Before Lunch,* Warne, 1936, reprinted, 1968; *Animals From Everywhere,* Warne, 1938, revised edition, 1950; *Magic Island,* Warne, 1956; *More Animals From Everywhere.* Warne, 1959; *The Friendly Place,* Warne, 1962; *Strange Creatures,* Warne, 1963; *The Thirteenth Pig,* 1965; *All Kinds of Animals,* Warne, 1970.

Illustrator: Arthur Ransome, *Swallowdale,* J. Cape, 1931; Ransome, *Swallows and Amazons,* J. Cape, 1931; Marmaduke Dixey, *Words, Beasts, and Fishes* (poems), Faber, 1936; Patrick Miller, *Ana the Runner,* Golden Cockerel, 1937; Ernest Blakeman Vesey, *The Hill Fox,* Constable, 1937; Ventura Garcia Calderon, *The White Llama,* Golden Cockerel, 1938; Somerset De Chair, translator, *The First Crusades: The Deeds of the Franks and Other Jerusalemites,* Golden Cockerel, 1945; Kathleen Joan Burrell, *The Pig Who Was Too Thin,* Warne, 1947; Ralph Wightman, *Moss Green Days,* Westhouse, 1947; Ivor Bannet, *The Amazons,* Golden Cockerel, 1948; Julius Caesar, *Commentaries: A Modern Rendering,* edited by De Chair, Golden Cockerel, 1951; De Chair, *The Story of a Lifetime,* Golden Cockerel, 1954; Ella Monckton, *The Boy and the Mountain,* 1961.

OBITUARIES: London Times, August 12, 1972.

*   *   *

WEBB, Karl (Eugene) 1938-

PERSONAL: Born March 12, 1938, in Lehi, Utah; son of Karl and Josephine (Muhlestein) Webb; married Deanna Gerber; children: Erik, Phillip, Christopher, Anne. *Education:* Brigham Young University, B.A., 1962; University of Pennsylvania, M.A., 1965, Ph.D., 1969. *Residence:* Orono, Me. 04473. *Office:* Department of Foreign Languages and Classics, University of Maine at Orono, Orono, Me. 04469.

CAREER: University of Houston, Houston, Tex., instructor, 1965-69, assistant professor, 1963-73, associate professor, 1973-78, professor of German, 1978-79, associate dean of College of Humanities and Fine Arts, 1976-79, acting dean of College of Humanities and Fine Arts, 1978-79; University of Maine at Orono, professor of German, 1979—, dean of College of Arts and Sciences, 1979—. *Member:* Modern Language Association of America, Northeast Modern Language Association, Southwest Modern Language Association, Phi Beta Kappa.

WRITINGS: Rainer Maria Rilke and Jugendstil: Affinities, Influences, Adaptations, University of North Carolina Press, 1978; (editor with Gertrud Pickar) *German Expressionism: Literature and the Arts—The Procedings of the University of Houston Symposium on German Expressions,* Fink Verlag, 1979. Contributor to literature and German studies journals.

WORK IN PROGRESS: A book on artist Egon Schiele and poet Georg Trakl.

*   *   *

WEBSTER, Thomas Bertram Lonsdale 1905-

PERSONAL: Born in July, 1905; son of T. Lonsdale and Esther (Dalton) Webster; married Amy Marjorie Dale, 1944 (died,

1967). *Education:* Attended Christ Church, Oxford, and University of Leipzig. *Office:* Department of Classics, Stanford University, Stanford, Calif. 94305.

CAREER: Oxford University, Christ Church, Oxford, England, tutor, 1927-31; Victoria University of Manchester, Manchester, England, Hulme Professor of Greek, 1931-48; University of London, London, England, professor of Greek, 1948-68, professor emeritus, 1968—, honorary fellow, 1969; Stanford University, Stanford, Calif., professor of classics, 1968-70, professor emeritus, 1970—. Professor at Royal Academy of Arts, 1955. Chairman of Gilbert Murray Trust, 1959.

MEMBER: Society of Antiquaries (fellow), British Academy (fellow), Hellenic Society (president, 1950), Classical Association (vice-president, 1948; president, 1959), Joint Association of Classical Teachers (president, 1965), Royal Society of Arts and Sciences (Sweden), Royal Danish Academy of Sciences and Letters (foreign member), Royal Society of Humane Letters (Sweden; corresponding member), Austrian Academy of Sciences (corresponding member), Norwegian Academy of Science and Letters, German Archaeological Institute (corresponding member), Athenaeum Club. *Awards, honors:* D.Litt. from Victoria University of Manchester, 1965.

WRITINGS: An Introduction to Sophocles, Clarendon Press, 1936, reprinted, Methuen, 1969; *Greek Art and Literature, 500-400 B.C.,* Clarendon Press, 1939; *Greek Interpretations,* Manchester University Press, 1942; *Political Interpretations in Greek Literature,* Manchester University Press, 1948.

Studies in Menander, Manchester University Press, 1950, 2nd edition, 1960; *Studies in Later Greek Comedy,* Manchester University Press, 1953, 2nd edition, Barnes & Noble, 1970; *Art and Literature in Fourth-Century Athens,* Athlone Press, 1956, Greenwood Press, 1969; *Greek Theatre Production* Methuen, 1956, 2nd edition, 1970; *From Mycenae to Homer,* Barnes & Noble, 1958, 2nd edition, Norton, 1964; *Greek Art and Literature, 700-530 B.C.: The Beginnings of Modern Civilization,* Methuen, 1959, Praeger, 1961.

Monuments Illustrating Old and Middle Comedy, Institute of Classical Studies, University of London, 1960, 3rd edition, 1978; *Monuments Illustrating New Comedy,* Institute of Classical Studies, University of London, 1961, 2nd edition, 1969; *Die Nachfahren Nestors: Mykene und die Anfaenge griechischer Kultur* (translated by Ernst Doblhofer), Oldenbourg, 1961; *Monuments Illustrating Tragedy and Satyr Play,* Institute of Classical Studies, University of London, 1962, 2nd edition, 1967; *Griechische Buehnenaltertuemer,* Vandenhoeck & Ruprecht, 1963; *Hellenistic Poetry and Art,* Methuen, 1964, Barnes & Noble, 1965; (with John Rogers Davis) *Cesnola Terracottas in the Stanford University Museum,* Humanities, 1964; *Hellenismus* (translated by Ulrike Thimme), Holle, 1966; *The Art of Greece: The Age of Hellenism,* Crown, 1966, revised edition, Greystone Press, 1967; *The Tragedies of Euripides,* Methuen, 1967; *Hellenistic Art,* Methuen, 1967; (editor with E. G. Turner) Amy Marjorie Dale, *Collected Papers of A. M. Dale,* Cambridge University Press, 1969; *Everyday Life in Classical Athens,* Putnam, 1969.

The Greek Chorus, Methuen, 1970; (editor) Sophocles, *Philoctetes,* Cambridge University Press, 1970; (with Arthur Dale Trendall) *Illustrations of Greek Drama,* Praeger, 1971; *Potter and Patron in Classical Athens,* Barnes & Noble, 1972; *Athenian Culture and Society,* University of California Press, 1973; *An Introduction to Menander,* Barnes & Noble, 1974. Also author of (with A. S. Owen) *Forum Romanum,* 1930; *Cicero: Pro Flacco,* 1931; (with E. Vinaver) *Renan: Priere sur l'Acropole,* 1934. Also editor of (with E. S. Forster) *An*

Anthology of Greek Prose, 1933, and (with Forster) *An Anthology of Greek Verse,* 1935. Editor of revision of *Dithyramb: Tragedy and Comedy,* by A. W. Pickard-Cambridge, 1962. Contributor to classical journals.

BIOGRAPHICAL/CRITICAL SOURCES: *Times Literary Supplement,* July 11, 1975.*

*   *   *

WECHSBERG, Joseph   1907-

PERSONAL: Born August 29, 1907, in Moravska-Ostrava (now Ostrava), Austria (now Czechoslovakia); came to United States in 1938, naturalized citizen, 1944; son of Siegfried (a banker) and Hermine (Kreiger) Wechsburg; married Jo-Ann Novak (a designer), March 24, 1934; children: Josephine Hermine. *Education:* Attended Vienna State Academy of Music, 1925-30, and Sorbonne, University of Paris, 1926-29; University of Prague Law School, LL.D. (summa cum laude), 1930. *Home:* Sunset Hill, Redding, Conn. *Agent:* Paul R. Reynolds & Son, Inc. 12 East 41st St., New York, N.Y. 10017.

CAREER: Worked as a photographer and malt salesman in Europe; worked as a violinist and orchestra leader on ocean liners and in cabarets and nightclubs in Paris; worked as a attorney in Prague, Czechoslovakia, beginning 1930; secretary to member of Czechoslovakian Chamber of Deputies, 1935; free-lance journalist and writer,1938—; *New Yorker* (magazine), New York, N.Y., writer, 1943—, foreign correspondent, 1949—. *Military service:* Czechoslovakian Army, 1939; became lieutenant. U.S. Army, served during World War II, technical sergeant in psychological warfare division. *Awards, honors:* Literary fellowship from Houghton-Mifflin, 1944; Order of the White Lion from Czechoslovakian Government; Sidney Hillman Foundation magazine award, 1953, for article "Reporter in Germany."

WRITINGS: *Die grosse Mauer, das Buch einer Weltreise* (travelogue), J. Kittls Nachfolger, 1938; *Visum fur Amerika,* J. Kittls Nachfolger, 1939; *Looking for a Bluebird* (correspondence), Houghton, 1945, reprinted, Greenwood Press, 1974; *Homecoming,* Knopf, 1946; *The Continental Touch* (novel), Houghton, 1948; *Sweet and Sour* (autobiographical), Houghton, 1948; *Blue Trout and Black Truffles: The Peregrinations of an Epicure,* Knopf, 1953; *The Self-Betrayed* (novel), Knopf, 1954; *Avalanche!,* Knopf, 1958.

Red Plush and Black Velvet: The Story of Melba and Her Times, Little, Brown, 1961; *Dining at the Pavillion,* Little, Brown, 1962; *Lebenskunst und andere Kunste,* Rowohlt, 1963, translation published as *The Best Things in Life,* Little, Brown, 1964; *Journey Through the Land of Eloquent Silence: East Germany Revisited,* Little, Brown, 1964; *The Merchant Bankers* (nonfiction), Little, Brown, 1966; (editor and author of introduction) Simon Wiesenthal, *The Murderers Among Us: The Simon Wiesenthal Memoirs,* McGraw, 1967; *A Walk Through the Garden of Science: A Profile of the Weizmann Institute,* Weidenfeld & Nicholson, 1967; *Vienna, My Vienna,* Macmillan, 1968; (co-author) *The Cooking of Vienna's Empire,* Time-Life, 1968; *Sounds of Vienna,* Weidenfeld & Nicolson, 1968; *The Pantheon Story of Music for Young People,* Pantheon, 1968; *The Voices,* Doubleday, 1969.

The First Time Around: Some Irreverent Recollections, Little, Brown, 1970; *Prague, the Mystical City,* Macmillan, 1971; *The Opera,* Macmillan, 1972; *The Violin,* Calder & Boyars, 1973; *The Waltz Emperors: The Life and Times and Music of the Strauss Family,* Putnam, 1973; *The Glory of the Violin,* Viking, 1973; *Verdi,* Putnam, 1974; *Dream Towns of Europe,*

Putnam, 1976; *In Leningrad,* Doubleday, 1977; *Schubert: His Life, His Work, His Time,* Rizzoli, 1977; *The Danube,* Newsweek, 1979; *The Vienna I Knew: Memories of a European Childhood,* Doubleday, 1979; *The Lost World of the Great Spas,* Harper, 1979.

Contributor of articles to magazines, including *Atlantic Monthly, Esquire, Saturday Evening Post, Horizon, Town and Country,* and *Travel.*

SIDELIGHTS: In several of Joseph Wechsberg's books, including *The Vienna I Knew: Memories of a European Childhood* and *Sweet and Sour,* he reminisces about his idyllic childhood in prewar Europe. The product of affluent, loving parents, Wechsberg recalls the period preceding World War I as carefree and relaxed. Life changed drastically with the onset of the war. Wechsberg's father was killed in action on the Russian front, and his mother, who invested her inheritance in government bonds, soon lost everything. *The Vienna I Knew* contains Wechsberg's recollections of his youth, but it "is in no way a mournful book: young Wechsberg found the prewar years entertaining, and his inquiring, wry mind makes the postwar years equally so," commented a *New Yorker* critic.

In *Sweet and Sour,* Wechsberg recalls having an early affinity for music; he learned to play the violin under the tutelage of his uncle. In later years, he worked as a violinist and orchestra leader on ocean liners, as well as in nightclubs and cabarets in Paris. His interest in music is reflected in such writings as *The Glory of the Violin, Verdi,* and *Schubert: His Life, His Work, His Time.*

In addition to writing about music, Wechsberg has written books on history, travel, and international cuisine. He also edited and wrote the introduction for Simon Weisenthal's *The Murderers Among Us,* which contains Wiesenthal's account of his efforts to bring to justice the more than twenty thousand Nazi war criminals who are still at large. "It is a widely held belief, not only in Germany and Austria, that the whole Nazi episode should now be buried and forgotten. Mr. Wiesenthal feels that reconciliation is only possible on the basis of knowledge of what happened," observed a *Times Literary Supplement* reviewer. "At a time when neo-Nazism in Germany shows signs of revival," wrote Louis Harap of *Nation,* "the memoirs of this dedicated humanist sound a strong note of warning." Harap also noted that Wechsberg's introductory profile of Weisenthal "reveals an incorruptible, selfless, deeply humane man," and he praised Wechsberg's "superbly edited volume."

BIOGRAPHICAL/CRITICAL SOURCES: *Time,* March 31, 1967; *Saturday Review,* April 15, 1967; *Time Literary Supplement,* June 8, 1967; *Nation,* July 3, 1967; *New Yorker,* July 30, 1979; *Chicago Tribune Book World,* August 12, 1979; *New York Times Book Review,* November 18, 1979.*

*   *   *

WEDEL, Waldo Rudolph   1908-

BRIEF ENTRY: Born September 10, 1908, in North Newton, Kan. American archaeologist and author. Wedel worked at the U.S. National Museum from 1936 to 1978; he was head curator of anthropology, 1962-65, senior archaeologist, 1965-76, and was named emeritus archaeologist in 1978. He wrote *An Introduction to Kansas Archeology* (U.S. Government Printing Office, 1959), *Prehistoric Man on the Great Plains* (University of Oklahoma Press, 1961), and *The Prehistoric and Historic Habitat of the Kansa Indians* (Garland Publishing, 1974). *Address:* Office of Anthropology, Smithsonian Institution, Washington, D.C. 20560. *Biographical/critical sources: Directory of American Scholars,* Volume I: *History,* 7th edition, Bowker, 1978.

*   *   *

WEDGWOOD, C(icely) V(eronica)   1910-

PERSONAL: Born July 20, 1910, in Stocksfield, Northumberland, England; daughter of Ralph Lewis (a railway chairman) and Iris (Pawson) Wedgwood. *Education:* Received degree with first class honors from Lady Margaret Hall, Oxford, 1931. *Office:* c/o William Collins, Sons & Co. Ltd., 14 St. James's Place, London SW1A 1PS, England.

CAREER: Historian, translator, and writer. Literary adviser at Jonathan Cape Ltd. (publishers), 1941-44; literary editor of *Time and Tide* (weekly newspaper), 1944-50, and director, 1948-58. Member of Royal Commission on Historical Manuscripts, 1952-78, Institute for Advanced Study, Princeton, N.J., 1953-68, advisory council of Victoria and Albert Museum, 1959-69, and Arts Council Literature Panel, 1965-67. Clark Lecturer at Cambridge University, 1957-58; Northcliffe Lecturer at University of London, 1959; special lecturer at University College, London, 1962-70, and honorary fellow, 1965; honorary fellow of Lady Margaret Hall, Oxford University, 1962. Trustee of National Gallery, London, England, 1960-76. Honorary bencher, Middle Temple, London, 1978.

MEMBER: International P.E.N. (president of English center, 1951-57), British Academy (fellow), Royal Historical Society (fellow), English Association (president, 1955-56), Society of Authors (president, 1972-77), Royal Society of Literature of the United Kingdom (fellow), Scottish Historical Society, American Academy of Arts and Letters (honorary member), American Academy of Arts and Sciences (honorary member).

AWARDS, HONORS: James Tait Black Memorial Prize, 1944, for *William the Silent;* Officer, Order of Orange-Nassau, 1946; LL.D. from University of Glasgow, 1955; Member of the Order of the British Empire, 1956, Dame, 1968; Goethe Medal from Goethe Institute for the Cultivation of the German Language and Culture in Foreign Lands, 1958; D.Litt. from Glasgow University, 1956, University of Sheffield, 1958, University of Keele, 1959, Smith College, 1960, Harvard University, 1964, Oxford University, 1965, University of Sussex, 1974, and University of Liverpool, 1975; Order of Merit (British), 1969.

WRITINGS: Strafford, 1593-1641, J. Cape, 1935, reprinted, Greenwood Press, 1970, revised edition published as *Thomas Wentworth: First Earl of Strafford, 1593-1641; A Revaluation,* J. Cape, 1961, Macmillan, 1962; *The Thirty Years War,* J. Cape, 1938, Yale University Press, 1939, reprinted, Methuen, 1981; *Oliver Cromwell,* Duckworth, 1939, Macmillan, 1956, revised edition, Duckworth, 1973, original edition also published as *The Life of Cromwell,* Collier, 1966.

William the Silent: William of Nassau, Prince of Orange, 1533-1584, Yale University Press, 1944; *Velvet Studies* (essays), J. Cape, 1946, reprinted, Folcroft, 1973; *Richelieu and the French Monarchy,* Hodder & Stoughton, 1949, Macmillan, 1950, reprinted, 1974; *Seventeenth-Century English Literature,* Oxford University Press, 1950, revised edition, 1977; *The Last of the Radicals: Josiah Wedgwood, M.P.,* J. Cape, 1951, reprinted, 1974; *Montrose,* Collins, 1952, Anchor Books, 1966; *The Great Rebellion,* Volume I: *The King's Peace, 1637-1641,* Macmillan, 1955, Volume II: *The King's War, 1641-1647,* Collins, 1958, Macmillan, 1959.

Truth and Opinion: Historical Essays, Macmillan, 1960, published as *The Sense of the Past: Thirteen Studies in the Theory and Practice of History,* Collier, 1967; *Poetry and Politics Under the Stuarts,* Cambridge University Press, 1960, University of Michigan Press, 1964; *A Coffin for King Charles: The Trial and Execution of Charles I,* Macmillan, 1964 (published in England as *The Trial of Charles I,* Collins, 1964); (with the editors of Time-Life Books) *The World of Rubens, 1577-1640,* Time-Life, 1967; *Milton and His World,* Lutterworth, 1969; *Oliver Cromwell and the Elizabethan Inheritance,* J. Cape, 1970; *The Political Career of Peter Paul Rubens,* Thames & Hudson, 1975.

Other: (Translator) Carl Brandi, *The Emperor Charles V: The Growth and Destiny of a Man and of a World-Empire,* J. Cape, 1939; *Battlefields in Britain* (photographs, with commentary by Wedgwood), Hastings House, 1945; (translator) Elias Canetti, *Auto da fe,* J. Cape, 1946, reprinted, Pan Books, 1978; (editor) *New Poems, 1965: A P.E.N. Anthology of Contemporary Poetry,* Nelson, Foster & Scott, 1966; (author of foreword) Violet A. Rowe, *Sir Henry Vane the Younger: A Study in Political and Administrative History,* University of London Press, 1970. Contributor of articles and reviews to newspapers, magazines, and journals, including *Saturday Review, Daily Telegraph, Times Literary Supplement, History Today,* and *Horizon.*

WORK IN PROGRESS: A world history in two volumes, completion of first volume expected in 1982.

SIDELIGHTS: Distinguished British historian C. V. Wedgwood has earned acclaim for her entertaining and lucidly written histories and biographies. Her subjects have ranged from the Thirty Years War to her ancestor Josiah Wedgwood, while her specialty has been seventeenth-century British history.

Wedgwood's methods as a historian have been compared to those of her contemporaries G. M. Trevelyan and A. L. Rowse. Their "narrative" approach tells how events occurred instead of analyzing why, and Wedgwood has defended her method by insisting one must know how things happened before they can be understood. "I have tried," she wrote in *The King's Peace,* "to describe the variety, vitality and imperfections as well as the religion and government of the British Isles in the seventeenth century, deliberately avoiding analysis and seeking rather to give an impression of its vigorous and vivid confusion." Commenting on this statement, Rowse wrote in *Time and Tide:* "How right she is, as against the fashionable analytical historians who are so determined to show how clever they are at the expense of history. Her beguilingly modest attitude is really cleverer and more subtle."

Wedgwood's historical narratives are spiced by a writing style that has been praised throughout her career. Her second book, *The Thirty Years War,* was written with "a clarity and vividness of style," remarked W. K. Ferguson of *Books.* Similar attention came with *William the Silent* (1944), which has, as *Commonweal*'s H.G.J. Beck pointed out, "an English style that is crystal clear and a scholarship beyond reproach." Fifteen years later Leo Gerchoy of the *New York Herald Tribune Book Review* said that if *The King's War* were "fiction, no reader could fail to admire the masterly skill, the symphonic sense with which she brings together the actors and the events." Wedgwood's reputation as a gifted writer was reinforced again when in 1964 Lawrence Stone of the *New York Review of Books* declared her "the best narrative historian writing in the English language. She is a superb stylist."

Within Wedgwood's specialty, seventeenth-century Britain, it is the English civil war that has captured most of her attention. She has written biographies of the premier political figures of the era, King Charles I and Oliver Cromwell, as well as a two-volume history of the war, *The Great Rebellion.* The *Spectator*'s W. K. Hancock remarked upon reading the first volume, *The King's Peace,* that "there is no more exciting period in the history of the British Isles. The time is ripe for telling the story again and Miss Wedgwood is the perfect storyteller."

Some of the objections to the second volume, *The King's War,* centered on Wedgwood's use of narrative over interpretative history. "We are left with a masterful political and military narrative," commented George Dangerfield of the *Nation,* "in which we flounder helplessly in search of the 'underlying causes' which set it in motion." The *Spectator*'s Christopher Hill reflected this attitude when he said that "Wedgwood does extract explanation from narrative. But the trick is not always successful. . . . We badly need a new synthesis which will bring home to us why our seventeenth-century forefathers fought and killed and died. Granted her limited aim in telling us merely how they did these things, Miss Wedgwood's book could hardly be better."

Wedgwood told *CA:* "I am by nature an optimist. I continue stubbornly to believe that if an intelligent reader is given all the facts (or should I say all the available facts), he should be able to work out his own conclusions about the underlying causes. There is after all an organic relation between what happened (the facts) and why it happened (the causes). I have a very deep suspicion of the modern habit of analyzing causes without a close attention to facts. Our twentieth-century minds inevitably introduce ideas and theories belonging to the twentieth century which may be either irrelevant or misleading when applied to the remoter past."

BIOGRAPHICAL/CRITICAL SOURCES: Spectator, October 28, 1938, May 26, 1944, October 6, 1950, January 14, 1955, December 12, 1958, February 19, 1960; *Times Literary Supplement,* November 19, 1938, May 6, 1944, February 3, 1945, October 6, 1950, January 7, 1955, November 28, 1958, January 29, 1960, November 17, 1961, August 27, 1964; *Saturday Review,* May 6, 1939, December 9, 1944, September 24, 1955, April 4, 1959, May 28, 1960, September 19, 1964; *Books,* June 11, 1939; *Commonweal,* December 15, 1944.

Time and Tide, January 8, 1955; *New York Herald Tribune Book Review,* September 25, 1955, April 5, 1959, August 28, 1960, October 28, 1962; *New York Times,* October 2, 1955, April 19, 1959; *Nation,* December 10, 1955, June 20, 1959; *Time,* April 13, 1959, September 4, 1964; *American Historical Review,* October, 1959, July, 1963; *Christian Science Monitor,* May 19, 1960; *New Statesman,* December 16, 1961, August 28, 1964; *New York Review of Books,* September 10, 1964; *New York Times Book Review,* September 20, 1964.

*   *   *

WEESNER, Theodore

PERSONAL: Born in Flint, Mich.

CAREER: Novelist and author of short stories.

WRITINGS: "Irene, Goodnight" (short story), published in *Atlantic,* January, 1970; "Hearing" (short story), published in *New Yorker,* April 10, 1971; *The Car Thief* (novel), Random House, 1972; *A German Affair* (novel), Random House, 1976.

SIDELIGHTS: Theodore Weesner's *The Car Thief* is the story of Alex, a delinquent youth growing up in Michigan in the 1950's. Depressed, lonely, and confused, sixteen-year-old Alex is sent to a detention home after stealing his fourteenth car. "It's a stereotype situation," reported Armand Gebert of the *Detroit News.* "There are hundreds of real life Alex Housmans. . . . Social workers have bulging files of almost iden-

tical or even worse cases." But, continued Gebert, Weesner capitalizes on the commonplace and "develops it into a penetrating probe of an adolescent's thoughts, feelings and self-conscious reactions."

Through a "hard active engagement" with life in the detention home, Alex begins "an uncertain new gathering of self," commented Joseph McElroy of the *New York Times Book Review.* "Weesner conveys in a factual rhythm so natural one sees only later that he has evoked the continuum of human growth." Alex eventually moves out of the detention home and back to his father, a defeated man dependent on Alex. The book concludes with Alex visiting his brother, who still lives with his mother and her second husband. There, through his brother, Alex "comprehends the tragedy of . . . [his] father and the happiness of his mother," noted McElroy. "Alex has found a way home to himself."

Praise for *The Car Thief* centered on Weesner's portrayal of character. "In deceptively simple language he has revealed the loneliness and the frustrations of his characters without in any way becoming morbid, depressing, or maudlin," observed C. P. Collier of *Best Sellers. Time*'s Lance Morrow, meanwhile, called *The Car Thief* "an achievement of almost perfect sympathy. One begins caring about Alex." Gebert, too, commented on the sympathetic portrayal of Alex, adding, "It's a story told so honestly that it leaves the reader at times not knowing whether to laugh or cry."

Weesner's second novel, *A German Affair,* also focuses on a troubled youth. The hero is Billy, a U.S. Army private stationed in Germany in 1952. There, reported Christopher Lehmann-Haupt, "he finds himself 'alone with the mere flesh and shell of himself' and desperate to make some sort of connection. The connection," added the *New York Times* critic, "proves to be sex." According to Martin Levin of the *New York Times Book Review,* Weesner "makes such familiar materials as these shine with a fresh brilliance. He captures the scene and the moment of a deprived youth from Detroit suddenly tuned into the 'magic' of life."

"But *A German Affair* isn't about his sharp sexual hungers (and their satisfactions) as much as it is a portrayal of a developing sensibility," argued the *Sewanee Review*'s Bruce Allen. The novel is "an almost completely internalized character study," continued Allen. "Weesner has an enviable ability to concentrate so intensely on his hero that we perceive his 'sentimental affection' exactly as he himself does." Lehmann-Haupt, however, felt that the "extreme absorption" in Billy's "somewhat murky sensibilities" flawed the book; but "when Mr. Weesner steps outside his protagonist and gives us prostitutes, or beerhall Bavarians, or Army routine, or the pinched soul of Billy's seamstress girlfriend, he writes sharply and entertainingly."

BIOGRAPHICAL/CRITICAL SOURCES: New York Times Book Review, June 18, 1972, March 13, 1977; *Best Sellers,* July 15, 1972; *Time,* July 24, 1972; *New York Review of Books,* October 5, 1972; *Commonweal,* October 27, 1972; *New York Times,* January 28, 1977; *Saturday Review,* October, 1977.*

*   *   *

WEINER, Marcella Bakur 1925-

BRIEF ENTRY: Born September 13, 1925, in New York, N.Y. American psychologist, gerontologist, and author. Weiner has been a psychotherapist and an adjunct assistant professor at Columbia University since 1972. She wrote *Working With the Aged: Practical Approaches in the Institution and Community*

(Prentice-Hall, 1978) and *The Starr and Weiner Report on Sex and Sexuality in the Mature Years* (Paddington, 1980). *Address:* Department of Psychology, Kingsbrook Jewish Medical Center, Brooklyn, N.Y. 11203. *Biographical/critical sources: Who's Who of American Women,* 10th edition, Marquis, 1977; *New York Times,* August 24, 1981.

* * *

WEIS, Jack 1932-

PERSONAL: Born October 1, 1932, in Tampa, Fla.; son of George Weis and Anne Catherine Stimac; married Pamela Anne Dallas, April 15, 1961; children: Alexandrea. *Education:* Notre Dame University, B.S., 1948; University of Chicago, M.S., 1950. *Home:* 6771 Marshal Foch, New Orleans, La. 70124. *Office:* Associated Productions, Inc., 627 Dumaine, New Orleans, La. 70116.

CAREER: Account executive at D.B.D. & O., New York City, 1953-56; cameraman, film editor, producer, writer, and director of motion pictures. *Military service:* U.S. Air Force, 1953; became major. *Member:* Directors Guild of America, Producers Guild of America, Writers Guild of America, Friars Club.

WRITINGS—Screenplays; also director and producer: "Storyville," 1972; "Damballa," 1973; "Crypt of Darkness," 1975; "Lelia," 1979; "Mardi Gras Massacre," 1979; "You Never Gave Me Roses," 1981; "The Perfect Circle," 1981-82. Author, director, and producer of other screenplays.

Also author of scripts for television series, including "Highway Patrol," United Artists, "Car 54, Where Are You?," National Broadcasting Co. (NBC-TV), "The Rat Patrol," Mirish-Rich TV Productions, and "Mission Impossible," Paramount.

WORK IN PROGRESS: Two films, "Snow on the Bayou" and "The Vicky Daniels Story."

SIDELIGHTS: Weis told *CA:* "I was taught screenwriting on the job, more or less. While working as an assistant director or sometimes as a cameraman, I watched and got the feel of writing for quicky TV series like 'Rat Patrol' and 'Highway Patrol.' I watched the process of the writing coming alive to the screen via the camera. In so learning, I got the quick feel of the screen in relation to the written word."

* * *

WEISS, Thomas J(oseph) 1942-

PERSONAL: Born July 21, 1942, in Kingston, N.Y.; son of Jacob J. and Harriet (Wojdan) Weiss; married Patricia Tario (an administrative assistant), July 30, 1966; children: Joan P. *Education:* Holy Cross College, B.S., 1964; University of North Carolina, Ph.D., 1967. *Home:* 3128 Campfire Court, Lawrence, Kan. 66044. *Office:* Department of Economics, University of Kansas, Lawrence, Kan. 66045.

CAREER: University of North Carolina, Chapel Hill, part-time instructor in economics, 1965-66; University of Kansas, Lawrence, assistant professor, 1967-71, associate professor, 1971-75, professor of economics, 1975—, chairman of department, 1980—. Member of Conference on Research in Income and Wealth, National Bureau of Economic Research; consultant to Midwest Research Institute. *Member:* Economic History Association, Business and Industrial History Association, Economic and Business Historical Society, Southern Economic Association, Midwest Economic Association. *Awards, honors:* National Science Foundation grants, 1969, 1971, and 1975.

WRITINGS: The Service Sector in the United States: 1839 Through 1899, Arno, 1975; *A Deplorable Scarcity: The Failure of Industrialization in the Antebellum South,* University of North Carolina Press, 1981. Contributor to *Dictionary of American History.* Contributor of about twenty-five articles and reviews to economic and history journals.

WORK IN PROGRESS: Estimating the U.S. Labor Force by State for the Nineteenth Century; a short story.

SIDELIGHTS: Weiss told *CA:* "I write in order to illuminate the past, but suspect I only muddy the water further. My goal is to be the Graham Greene or Eric Ambler of historical tomes." *Avocational interests:* Photography, golf, watching and playing most sports, travel (especially Europe and the Rocky Mountains).

* * *

WEIZSAECKER, Carl Friedrich von
See von WEIZSAECKER, Carl Friedrich

* * *

WELCH, Kenneth Frederick 1917-

PERSONAL: Born in 1917 in Birmingham, England; son of Frank (a pathology technician) and Caroline Welch; married Joan Audrey Tyrrell (a lecturer), November 21, 1953; children: Hilary Anne; Judith R. Wrigley (stepdaughter). *Education:* Open University, B.A., 1979. *Politics:* Conservative. *Religion:* Church of England. *Home:* Third Acre, Watling Lane, Dorchester-on-Thames, Oxfordshire OX9 8JQ, England.

CAREER: Town Clerk's Department, Portsmouth, England, clerk, 1935-39, committee clerk, 1946-47; temporary high school teacher of English, art, and music history in Portsmouth, Hampshire, England, 1947-48; Teacher Training College, Swindon, Wiltshire, England, lecturer in art and educational principles of music history, mathematics, science, and English, 1948-49; high school teacher of history, art, and English in Dorchester-on-Thames, Oxfordshire, England, 1949-56; teacher at primary schools in Didcot, Berkshire, England, 1957-62; Oxford College of Further Education, Oxford, England, lecturer in English and general studies, 1962-77; writer, 1977—. Member of local parish council, 1955-65. *Military service:* British Army, Radar, 1939-46, in Territorial Army's Royal Intelligence Corps, 1949-51; became staff sergeant. *Member:* Society of Authors, Oxfordshire Record Society.

WRITINGS: North of the Line (novel), Brown & Watson, 1959; *They Shall Be Remembered* (novel), Brown & Watson, 1959; *We the Dying* (novel), Brown & Watson, 1960; *The Sound of Death* (novel), Brown & Watson, 1961; *Animal, Vegetable, or Mineral* (quiz book), Blandford, 1961; *The Spy Among Them* (novel), Brown & Watson, 1962; *Metric Mathematics,* J. Brodie, 1968; *Decimal Currency for Junior and Middle Schools,* three volumes, J. Brodie, 1970; *The History of Clocks and Watches,* Drake, 1972 (published in England as *Time Measurement: An Introductory History,* David & Charles, 1972); *World of Time Map,* Bartholomew & Son, 1978; (with P. Allison) *General and Communications Studies Manual for TEC,* Longman, 1979.

Author of educational filmstrips. Contributor to *Junior Encyclopaedia Britannica, World Book Encyclopedia,* and *Academic American Encyclopedia.* Contributor of articles and reviews to magazines.

WORK IN PROGRESS: How to Carry Out a Local History Survey; a short guide to Dorchester-on-Thames; a science fiction novel.

SIDELIGHTS: Welch wrote: "In the United Kingdom I am especially interested in archaeology and writing. Local histories are important in view of the destruction of so much of our small country by 'progress.'

"During the mid-1960's I was offered two weeks in Romania to write a composite work on the country for foreigners. 'How much do people know about Romania?' is an interesting question with a depressing answer . . . nothing. But I could not obtain a publishing contract or a grant. In 1978 the Egyptian embassy in London offered a free two weeks' vacation in that country for any United Kingdom undergraduate who could write an acceptable article on any aspect of Egypt. Among the ten winners was my article, 'What Happened to Egyptian Art?,' and I had a most enjoyable two weeks. Incidentally, few people know anything of Egyptian art beyond what they know of wall paintings, yet there is a modern and flourishing school. The travel itinerary was heavy and I had no time to collect all the material for a book I wish to write on modern Egyptian art. Nothing has been published here in England since a poor book in French, dated about 1953, and that only in the Oriental Library of the Ashmolean Museum, Oxford.

"The more I write, the more I learn about writing—one of the most difficult of crafts. I write for two reasons—the pleasure in creating something, and for the money—in that order."

AVOCATIONAL INTERESTS: Archaeology, art, travel, history.

* * *

WELK, Lawrence 1903-

BRIEF ENTRY: Born March 11, 1903, in Strasburg, N.D. American orchestra leader and author. Welk has been a professional accordionist since 1920 and an orchestra leader since 1927. His television program was broadcast nationally by ABC-TV from 1955 to 1971 and has been in syndication since 1971. His many awards include a Horatio Alger Award in 1967, Freedom Awards in 1968 and 1969, and a Brotherhood Award from the National Council of Christians and Jews in 1969. He wrote *My America, Your America* (G. K. Hall, 1977), *This I Believe* (Prentice-Hall, 1979), and *You're Never Too Young* (Prentice-Hall, 1981). *Address:* 100 Wilshire Blvd., Santa Monica, Calif. 90401. *Biographical/critical sources: Who's Who in America,* 41st edition, Marquis, 1980.

* * *

WELLES, Samuel Gardner 1913(?)-1981

OBITUARY NOTICE: Born c. 1913; died of heart failure, November 30, 1981, in Charlotte, N.C. Journalist, editor, and author. In his thirty-year career with Time-Life, Inc., Samuel Welles served variously as a correspondent for *Fortune* magazine, *Time* bureau chief in Ottawa, Ontario, and Chicago, Ill., and senior editor of *Life* magazine. During World War II Welles was assistant to the U.S. ambassador in London, England. Following the war he returned to *Time* and established the magazine's Russian desk. Welles's book, *Profile of Europe,* appeared in 1948. Obituaries and other sources: *New York Times,* December 2, 1981; *Chicago Tribune,* December 3, 1981.

* * *

WELTNER, Linda R(iverly) 1938-

PERSONAL: Born October 13, 1938, in Worcester, Mass.; daughter of William (a wool dealer) and Dorothy (Rosenberg) Holbert; married John Sigmund Weltner (a child psychiatrist), June 7, 1959; children: Laura Marjorie, Julia Hesse. *Education:* Wellesley College, B.A. (with honors), 1960; attended University of Michigan, 1960, Maine Photographic Institute, 1974, and Harvard Divinity School, 1977. *Home:* Crown Way, Marblehead, Mass. 01945.

CAREER: Elementary school teacher in Chelsea, Mich., 1960-61; Boston Lying-In Hospital, Maternal-Infant Health Program, Boston, Mass., research assistant, 1962; Ginn & Co. (publishers), Boston, assistant editor, 1962-64; *Marblehead Messenger,* Marblehead, Mass., staff reporter and photographer, 1969-73; free-lance writer and photographer, 1974—. Co-founder of Periwinkle Cooperative Nursery School, 1969, and Marblehead Alternative Religious Community, 1974. Member of board of directors of Municipal Power Advocacy Coalition, 1981, advisory committee of Harvard Divinity School Theological Opportunities Program, 1977, and Wellesley College Communications Board, 1979—. Teacher of mini-course in marine biology, 1974, and six-week course "Surviving the 1980's Together," for the Marblehead Community Counseling Center, 1980. Public speaker.

WRITINGS: (Contributor) Sharon Strassfeld and Michael Strassfeld, editors, *The Third Jewish Catalog,* Jewish Publication Society, 1980; *Beginning to Feel the Magic* (young adult), Little, Brown, 1981; *The New Voice* (young adult; based on the television series "The New Voice"), Beacon Press, 1981.

Author of plays, including "As Lonely as American Pie," 1977, "Love for Sale," 1978, "Are You Ready for a New Me?," 1979, and "A Pox on Your Lips Now," 1980. Author of weekly column "Ever So Humble," for *Boston Globe.* Contributor of articles to periodicals and newspapers, including *Marblehead Magazine, Wellesley, New York Times,* and *Boston Globe.*

SIDELIGHTS: A free-lance writer, Weltner wrote her first novel, *Beginning to Feel the Magic,* as an expansion of an autobiographical piece she did for the *Boston Globe.* The article, a first-person account of a hospital patient recalling a childhood tonsillectomy, caught the attention of an editor at Little, Brown, who then wrote the author offering her a chance to turn the essay into a book for teenagers. Although her entrance into the world of young-adult literature was sudden, Weltner was ready for it. The mother of two high-school-age daughters, she had been reading teen books for years. "Everything they read, I read," she told Peggy Shehan McLean in an interview for the *Salem Evening News.* "It was like eating candy. I couldn't stop. You can read those books in about an hour and a half. So when John Keller (Little, Brown editor) called, I was prepared. I'd probably read 100 of those teen books."

An admirer of young-adult-author Judy Blume, Weltner felt that many of Blume's copiers were stooping to sensationalism, titillation, and what she calls "child porn" in their work. Believing that a simple story about a family could still be powerful, Weltner determined to "write a book that wasn't sensational. That had no drugs, no alcohol and no divorce." *Beginning to Feel the Magic* is the result of her efforts.

Set in the early 1960's, the book is about a young girl, Julie Langer, who lives in a working-class neighborhood and attends a racially-mixed school.

Dealing with many of the classic problems and experiences that confront adolescents, such as sibling rivalry and first boy-girl relationships, the novel aims to portray the highs and lows felt so acutely during the teen years. In the novel, Julie wins the lead in the school play opposite the boy of her dreams and then loses the part because she is hospitalized with pneumonia. Weltner, however, was particularly careful about providing a realistic outcome to the situation. In order to insure the story's credibility, the author engaged the services of her own daughter Julie, then fourteen years old, as an editorial assistant. "After I had finished the first 40 pages of 'Beginning to Feel the Magic' I showed the pages to Julie,'' Robert Taylor quoted Weltner in the *Boston Globe*. "Julie hated it. She wanted more dialogue and shorter chapters. Together we went over all of the manuscript, and she even made me rewrite the last chapter. She was right about the changes, too—I knew I had missed. Julie's was the natural ending.''

Julie also served as a consultant on her mother's second novel, *The New Voice*. Based on a PBS television series about an interracial group of high school students running a school newspaper, the book explores social problems, such as alcoholism, teenage pregnancy, and suicide, from a teenage perspective. A reviewer for *Seventeen* magazine noted: "Ms. Weltner's strong characterizations give the reader an appreciation of each student's strengths and goals. While seriously questioning current attitudes, her characters gradually come to an understanding of themselves. . . . Ms. Weltner creates a fresh approach to the high school scene. Her intelligence, warmth, and humor make *The New Voice* and unusual and enjoyable read.''

Weltner told *CA:* "The task of writing weekly about home, viewing it as a metaphor for life in the twentieth century, is one of the most challenging tasks I've ever undertaken. I'm hoping these essays will eventually appear in book form.

"My writing has never been an act separate from my life. I write to communicate what I have learned from intense attention to the details of daily living. I take the same care with family and friends that I do with a recalcitrant paragraph, and I am proudest of the fact that I have not sacrificed time with the first in pursuit of success with the last.''

BIOGRAPHICAL/CRITICAL SOURCES: Boston Globe, May 3, 1981; *Salem Evening News* (Mass.), July 22, 1981; *Seventeen,* October, 1981.

*   *   *

WENDEL, Tim 1956-

PERSONAL: Born January 25, 1956, in Philadelphia, Pa.; son of Peter Kent (an engineer) and Jane Margorie (an artist; maiden name, Harry) Wendel. *Education:* Syracuse University, B.A., 1978. *Home:* 7400 Canal Rd., Lockport, N.Y. 14094. *Agent:* George Wieser, Wieser & Wieser, Inc., 60 East 42nd St., Suite 902, New York, N.Y. 10017. *Office:* 613 Richmond Ave., Apt. 2, Buffalo, N.Y. 14222.

CAREER: Free-lance writer, 1978—; 13-30 Corp., Knoxville, Tenn., assistant editor, 1979-80; *Buffalo Courier Express,* Buffalo, N.Y., rewrite editor, 1981—. *Member:* Authors Guild.

WRITINGS: Going for the Gold; or, How the Americans Won at Lake Placid, Lawrence Hill, 1981. Contributing editor of *Hockey,* 1978-81. Also, contributor to *Women's Sports.*

WORK IN PROGRESS: Fire on the Mountain, publication expected in 1983.

SIDELIGHTS: Wendel told *CA:* "The major thing I've learned about writing, especially books, is not to be afraid of failing. If some idea or concept seems like a winner, forget about the editors, advertising men, and even friends who disagree with you, and go for it. Don't be afraid to commit yourself to a dream.

"*Fire on the Mountain* is a nonfiction effort and it will focus on forest fires and the people who fight them. Firefighters are a colorful lot—a throwback to yesterday's heroes. For the next year, I'm traveling the country, talking with firefighters and fighting fires alongside them.''

*   *   *

WENTINK, Andrew Mark 1948-

PERSONAL: Born October 18, 1948, in Paterson, N.J.; son of Andrew (a foreman) and Margaret (MacKenzie) Wentink. *Education:* Middlebury College, A.B., 1970; Columbia University, M.L.S., 1972. *Politics:* Independent. *Religion:* Roman Catholic. *Home:* 70 West 71st St., Apt. 3E, New York, N.Y. 10023.

CAREER: New York Public Library at Lincoln Center, New York City, manuscript analyst, 1972-77; New York City Ballet, New York City, press assistant, 1977-78; writer, 1978—. *Awards, honors:* Blue ribbon from American Film Festival and Golden Hugo from Chicago Film Festival, both for "Ruth Page.''

WRITINGS: (Editor) *Page by Page,* Dance Horizons, 1978; (editor) Walter Terry, *I Was There,* Dekker, 1978; (editor) Sono Osato, *Distant Dances,* Knopf, 1980; *Balletomania,* Doubleday, 1980.

Films: "Ruth Page: An American Original'' (television documentary).

Contributor to *Dance* and *Dance Chronicle.*

WORK IN PROGRESS: A dance dictionary; a book of photographs on George Balanchine's ballet, "The Steadfast Tin Soldier,'' publication expected by Dance Horizons; a novel set in seventeenth-century England; a contemporary novel; a documentary film on American choreography; a screenplay about the Yukon gold rush.

SIDELIGHTS: Wentink told *CA:* "I am particularly concerned with making a successful transition from the specialized area of dance into fiction and screenwriting. In my creative writing, I would like to develop a style which investigates the psychological responses of the individual to the cultural milieu in which he exists, at any given point in history, including the present.''

AVOCATIONAL INTERESTS: Travel, reading, music, dance, theatre, art, photography.

*   *   *

WERNER, Vivian 1921-
(Stephanie Jackson, John Lester)

PERSONAL: Born September 5, 1921, in Bellingham, Wash.; daughter of Elias E. (a court reporter) and Daisy (Fleishman) Lescher; married Steven L. Werner, June 13, 1943 (divorced, 1951); children: Jan S.L., Paul T. *Education:* Bennington College, B.A., 1943; Alliance Francaise, Diplome, 1958. *Home:* 95 Thankful Stow Rd., Guilford, Conn. 06437. *Agent:* Carole Abel, 160 West 87th St., New York, N.Y. 10024. *Office address:* P.O. Box 111, Guilford, Conn. 06437.

CAREER: Pathfinder (magazine), Washington, D.C., music editor, 1943-46; *New Haven Register,* New Haven, Conn., feature writer and book critic, 1948-53; Volitant Publishing Corp., New York, N.Y., correspondent in Paris, 1956-72; writer, 1960—. Writer in charge of music programming for WELI-Radio and WBIB-FM Radio, 1952-53; staff writer for Industrial Relations, Inc., 1956-57; correspondent in Paris for

Overseas Weekly and *Overseas Family,* 1957-61; associate editor for *Pharmaceutical News* in Paris, 1958-60. *Member:* Authors Guild, Word Guild. *Awards, honors:* Nominated for Prix Formentor by International Formentor Committee, 1962, for *The Breaking Wave.*

WRITINGS: *The Breaking Wave* (novel), Hart-Davis, 1963; (under pseudonym Stephanie Jackson) *Washington Slept Here* (novel), Manor Books, 1975; *Passion's Splendid Wings* (novel), Fawcett, 1977.

For young adults: (Under pseudonym John Lester) *DeGaulle: King Without a Crown* (biography), Hawthorn, 1968; *Scientist Versus Society* (nonfiction), Hawthorn, 1976.

For children: *Timmie in Paris,* Doubleday, 1965; *Timmie in London,* Doubleday, 1966; *Margaret Sanger: Woman Rebel,* Hawthorn, 1970; *Our World: France,* Messner, 1972; *Ballet: How It All Began,* Atheneum, 1982.

Translator: Giorgio de Chirico, *Hebdomeros,* Four Seasons Foundation, 1966.

WORK IN PROGRESS: A children's book, tracing the evolution of music.

SIDELIGHTS: Vivian Werner told *CA:* "I have been writing for as long as I can remember. My first poems were published in newspapers when I was eleven.

"My major in college was music. My first job after college was as music editor on a now-defunct national magazine. I have written music for plays produced by semi-professional theatre groups, and music is still one of my major interests.

"Dance has also been important to me, and I have written music for it. I am not a dancer myself, but have worked with Martha Graham and Jose Limon in modern dance, and had ballet training as a small child. Ballet was the subject of the novel called, alas, *Passion's Splendid Wings* (my own title was *Pas de Deux*). I have also written a book on the evolution—as distinct from the history—of ballet, for children. It traces the development of ballet from the beginning of the fifteenth century, and of dance from the medieval period, relating each innovation to its social context.

"My background in music and dance has played an important part in my approach to writing. I rely on words—*le mot juste*—to express my ideas. But I rely on sound, rhythm, and form to express—or evoke—emotion. And possibly the greatest single influence on my writing is Martha Graham's concept of movement and dance, which I believe is applicable to any art form."

AVOCATIONAL INTERESTS: European travel, classical music and jazz, dance, literature.

*   *   *

WERTHAM, Fredric   1895-1981

OBITUARY NOTICE—See index for *CA* sketch: Born in 1895 in Munich, Germany (now West Germany); died November 18, 1981, in Kempton, Pa. Psychiatrist and author. An authority on criminal psychology, Wertham wrote that violent behavior is a "non-instinctual" trait that is acquired from such cultural influences as comic books, movies, and television. He blamed the mass media, for example, for juvenile delinquency, arguing that television has become "a school for violence." *The Show of Violence, Seduction of the Innocent,* and *A Sign for Cain: An Exploration of Human Violence* are among Wertham's books. Obituaries and other sources: *American Dialog,*

spring, 1967; *New Statesman,* November 17, 1967; *Time,* December 14, 1981.

*   *   *

WERTHER, William B(lanchfield), Jr.   1947-

PERSONAL: Born April 11, 1947, in New York, N.Y.; son of William B. (in U.S. Air Force) and Thea (a manager; maiden name, Corbean) Werther; divorced; children: William B. III. *Education:* University of Florida, B.S.B.A. (with high honors), 1968, M.A., 1969, Ph.D., 1971. *Office:* Department of Management, College of Business Administration, Arizona State University, Tempe, Ariz. 85287.

CAREER: Arizona State University, Tempe, assistant professor, 1971-75, associate professor, 1975-78, professor of management, 1978—. Arbitrator for Federal Mediation and Conciliation Service, 1973—; consultant to Federal Judicial Center, American Productivity Center, and American Express; Chairman of Public Employment Relations Board, 1980—. *Member:* American Arbitration Association (arbitrator, 1973—), Academy of Management, American Society for Personnel Administrators, Industrial Relations Research Association, Arizona Industrial Relations Association, East Valley Personnel Management Association (president, 1980-81), Phi Beta Kappa.

WRITINGS: (With Carol A. Lockhart) *Labor Relations in the Health Professions,* Little, Brown, 1976; *Labor Relations for Nursing,* Nursing Resources, 1980; (with Keith Davis) *Personnel Management and Human Resources,* McGraw, 1981. Contributor of more than forty articles to management and business journals.

WORK IN PROGRESS: *Organizational Politics,* publication expected in 1985; a textbook on business policy, publication expected in 1987.

SIDELIGHTS: Werther told *CA:* "My interest in writing is to explore pathways for organizations to achieve higher levels of productivity. This adds to the wealth of society and indirectly reduces the disturbing side effects of poverty, while concurrently improving the quality of work life for those who are members of organizations. It is the organizations of society that create society's wealth. The two pressing questions facing society seem to be how do we increase the well-being of society and the well-being of the lives of those who make our organizations work?"

AVOCATIONAL INTERESTS: Travel (England, France, Mexico, the Bahamas), music, sailing, theatre.

*   *   *

WESTERN, John (Charles)   1947-

PERSONAL: Born April 14, 1947, in Margate, England; came to United States, 1972; son of Charles Henry (a printer) and Marion (a teacher; maiden name, Christal) Western; married Wendy Woodward, July 24, 1976. *Education:* Jesus College, Oxford, B.A. (with honors), 1968; University of Western Ontario, M.A., 1972; University of California, Los Angeles, Ph.D., 1978. *Residence:* Philadelphia, Pa. *Office:* Department of Geography, Temple University, Philadelphia, Pa. 19122.

CAREER: Voluntary Service Overseas, London, England, volunteer high school teacher of geography and history in Burundi, 1968-70; University of Cape Town, Cape Town, South Africa, research scholar, 1974-76; Ohio State University, Columbus, visiting assistant professor of geography, 1977-78; Temple University, Philadelphia, Pa., assistant professor of geography, 1978—. *Member:* Amnesty International, Association of

American Geographers, African Studies Association, South African Institute of Race Relations, American Geographical Society of New York.

WRITINGS: Outcast Cape Town, University of Minnesota Press, 1981.

Contributor: David Ley and Marwyn Samuels, editors, *Humanistic Geography,* Maaroufa Press, 1978, Methuen, 1980; Carolyn Adams, editor, *Self-Help in Housing: An International Survey,* Temple University Press, 1982; John Agnew, John Mercer, and David Sopher, editors, *The City in Cultural Context,* Syracuse Geographical Series, 1982; D. T. Herbert and R. J. Johnston, editors, *Geography and the Urban Environment,* Volume 5, Wiley, 1982. Also contributor to *Funk and Wagnall's New Encyclopedia* and contributor of articles and reviews to geography journals.

SIDELIGHTS: Western wrote: "Since I was a child I have been intrigued by the beauty and intricacy of maps and their sleeve-tugging promise of unknown territory on the far side of the hill. As a child, also, I was fascinated by steam railroads (and still am) and the locomotives with freight bound for distant parts that switched the yard at the rear of our home in England. These two holds on my imagination must have combined to make me an avid traveler and explorer from adolescence onward. Add to this two excellent high school teachers of political history and geography, plus a developing interest in the variations of cultural patterns and social organization across the earth, and I find that my post as a university teacher of human geography offers me a job that I really enjoy. Also, the long period of 'perpetual studenthood' before finally getting my doctorate permitted, with minimal responsibilities, much low-budget travel; for example, hitchhiking from Cape Town via Victoria Falls up to Tanzania and Burundi and back in 1975 or bicycling around Finland in 1966 or hitching rides all over North America from Quebec to Mississippi to California in the early 1970's.

"A formative experience was certainly the two years' teaching (in French) on an isolated mission-station in the materially poor but beautiful hill country of Burundi, where I had my English upbringing forced into a world perspective by the peasant life with which I was surrounded. My French subsequently was instrumental when an imaginative master's thesis supervisor at University of Western Ontario directed me to the bayous of southern Louisiana, where I researched and lived with the Cajuns for a summer—a tremendously interesting time.

"Not surprisingly, when my wife and I read Paul Theroux's *The Great Railway Bazaar,* we decided we had to do that, and for three months in 1979 we traveled overland (mostly by train) through Sri Lanka, India, Nepal, Kashmir, to Pakistan, Afghanistan, Uzbekistan, Armenia, Georgia, Russia, the Ukraine, and Czechoslovakia, to Poland (to stay with friends, who taught us a great deal about the realities of life in Gdansk, that we met hitchhiking in East Africa.) Such expeditions—despite travelers' joys like food poisoning in India—seem to serve only to whet one's appetite for more. One hopes that perhaps mainland China might be next. . . .

"Out of all these places the most beloved country for me remains South Africa, and the most poignant place of all—both because of its unmatched spectacular beauty and because of the courage of some of its inhabitants—has to be Cape Town. It is a great and tragic evil that man is doing to man there, a conscious act of anti-humanity, and the pity of it is that the bitter racial struggles that are surely coming are by no means inevitable."

BIOGRAPHICAL/CRITICAL SOURCES: New York Times Book Review, January 24, 1982.

*   *   *

WESTMAN, Barbara

PERSONAL: Born in Boston, Mass.; daughter of Frederick Waldemar (an architect) and Eleanor Proctor (a concert pianist; maiden name, Furminger) Westman; married Arthur C. Danto (a professor of philosophy), February 15, 1980. *Education:* Goucher College, A.B., 1950; attended Malschule Die Form, Munich, West Germany, 1953-56; Museum of Fine Arts School, Boston, Mass., special artists' diploma (with highest honors), 1961. *Home:* 420 Riverside Dr., Apt. 1-C, New York, N.Y. 10025.

CAREER: Museum of Fine Arts School, Boston, Mass., teacher of painting, drawing, and design, 1963-67; Museum of Fine Arts, Boston, teacher of painting and drawing, 1963-65; art teacher at country day school in Brookline, Mass., 1963-65; Harvard University, Cambridge, Mass., archaeological draftsman and designer at Peabody Museum of Archaeology and Ethnology, 1967-77; *Harvard Gazette,* Cambridge, staff artist, 1977-80; artist, 1980—. Work has been exhibited in the Boston area and is represented in collections, including Boston Athenaeum, Busch-Reisinger Museum, Wiggin Collection of Prints and Drawings (Boston Public Library), Harvard's Peabody Museum, and Museum of Fine Arts, Boston. *Awards, honors:* Ruth Sturdivant travel scholarship from Museum of Fine Arts, Boston, Mass., for Europe, 1962.

WRITINGS—Self-illustrated: The Bean and the Scene: Drawings of Boston and Cambridge, Barre Publishers, 1969; *The Beard and the Braid: Drawings of Cambridge by Barbara Westman, With Her Own Observations,* Barre, 1970; (with Herbert A. Kenny) *A Boston Picture Book,* Houghton, 1974; *A Beacon Hill Christmas,* Houghton, 1976; *Anna's Magic Broom* (juvenile), Houghton, 1977.

Illustrator: Philip Phillips and James A. Brown, *Spiro Pre-Columbian Shell Engravings,* Peabody Museum Press (Harvard), 1975; Jeffrey P. Brain, *Tunica Treasures,* Peabody Museum Press (Harvard), 1979. Contributor of illustrations to magazines and newspapers, including *Harvard, Travel and Leisure, New Yorker,* and *Cricket.*

WORK IN PROGRESS: Drawings of New York City, specifically people in relation to the city; a children's book.

SIDELIGHTS: Barbara Westman commented: "I am specifically interested in drawing people in places; that is, a family at the breakfast table, a group of fancy people at an exhibition opening, clowns performing in a circus, or people in a marketplace. My four years of travel and observation in Europe have heightened my sense of observation, and I draw with great detail and sometimes comedy. My work has been described as both lovely and rowdy."

*   *   *

WETTSTEIN, Howard K(enneth) 1943-

PERSONAL: Born August 11, 1943, in Richmond, Va.; son of Hyman S. (a university professor) and Rosalie (Saks) Wettstein; married Barbara Lipner (a teacher), 1969; children: Jonathan, Eve. *Education:* Yeshiva College (now University), B.A., 1965; City University of New York, M.A., 1974, Ph.D., 1976. *Office:* Department of Philosophy, University of Minnesota, Morris, Minn. 56267.

CAREER: University of Minnesota, Morris, instructor, 1974-76, assistant professor, 1976-79, associate professor of philosophy, 1979—. Visiting associate professor at University of Iowa, 1980; visiting scholar at Stanford University, 1981-82; consultant to Minnesota Humanities Commission. *Member:* American Philosophical Association, American Association of University Professors. *Awards, honors:* Grant from American Council of Learned Societies, 1977; fellow of National Endowment for the Humanities, 1981-82.

WRITINGS: (Editor with P. A. French and T. E. Uehling) *Midwest Studies in Philosophy,* University of Minnesota Press, Volume I: *Studies in the History of Philosophy,* 1976, Volume II: *Studies in the Philosophy of Language,* 1977, Volume III: *Studies in Ethical Theory,* 1978, Volume IV: *Studies in Metaphysics,* 1979, Volume V: *Studies in Epistemology,* 1980, Volume VI: *Foundations of Analytic Philosophy,* 1981, Volume VII: *Social and Political Philosophy,* 1982; (editor with French and Uehling) *Contemporary Perspectives in the Philosophy of Language,* University of Minnesota Press, 1978. Contributor to philosophy journals.

WORK IN PROGRESS: Reference and Propositional Thought.

* * *

WHALEN, Charles William, Jr. 1920-

PERSONAL: Born July 31, 1920, in Dayton, Ohio; son of Charles William and Colette E. (Kelleher) Whalen; married Mary Barbara Gleason, December 27, 1958; children: Charles E., Daniel D., Edward J., Joseph M., Anne Elizabeth, Mary Barbara. *Education:* University of Dayton, B.S., 1942; Harvard University, M.B.A., 1946; further graduate study at Ohio State University, 1959-60. *Religion:* Roman Catholic. *Office:* New Directions, 305 Massachusetts Ave. N.E., Washington, D.C. 20002.

CAREER: Dayton Dress Co., Dayton, Ohio, vice-president, 1946-52; University of Dayton, Dayton, began as assistant professor, 1952, professor of retailing and chairman of department, 1954-63, professor of economics and chairman of department, 1963-66; U.S. House of Representatives, Washington, D.C., Republican representative, 1966-78, member of Foreign Affairs Committee; New Directions, Washington, D.C., president, 1978—. Member of Ohio House of Representatives, 1954-60, and Ohio Senate, 1960-66; U.S. delegate to the United Nations, 1977. Vice-president of Whalen Investment Co., 1954—; past member of board of trustees of Dayton Child Guidance Center, Aviation Hall of Fame, Grandview Hospital, Dayton Council on World Affairs, Dayton Urban League, and Laretto. *Military service:* U.S. Army, 1943-46; served in India-Burma theater; became first lieutenant.

MEMBER: University of Dayton Alumni Association, Harvard Business School Association, American Legion (past member of board of directors), Dayton Agonis Club, Dayton Nomad Club, Dayton Bicycle Club, Eta Mu Pi. *Awards, honors:* Named outstanding member of Ohio Senate, 1963; LL.D. from Central State University, 1966.

WRITINGS: Your Right to Know: How the Free Flow of News Depends on the Journalist's Right to Protect His Sources, Random House, 1973. Also co-author of *How to End the Draft: The Case for an All-Volunteer Army,* National Press.*

* * *

WHEDON, Margaret B(runssen) 1926-
(Peggy Whedon)

PERSONAL: Born January 6, 1926, in New York, N.Y.; daughter of Henry and Anna Margaret (Nickel) Brunssen; married G. Donald Whedon (a physician), May 12, 1948; children: Karen Ann Green, David Marshall. *Home:* 702E, 4201 Cathedral Ave., N.W., Washington, D.C. 20036. *Office:* ABC-News, 1717 Desales St., N.W., Washington, D.C. 20036.

CAREER: National Broadcasting Co. (NBC)-News, New York City, writer and assistant producer of "The Kate Smith Show," 1949-52; American Broadcasting Co. (ABC)-News, Washington, D.C., associate producer of "College News Conference," 1952-1960, producer of "Issues and Answers," 1960—, correspondent, 1960—, radio commentator, 1962-64, producer of radio program "From the Capital," 1962—. *Member:* American Academy of Television Arts and Sciences, American Federation of Television and Radio Artists (AFTRA), American Newspaper Women's Club, American Women in Radio and Television, National Press Club, Women's National Press Club, State Department Corespondents Association, White House Correspondents Association, Radio and Television Correspondents Association, Overseas Press Club. *Awards, honors:* Special award from National Conference of Christians and Jews, 1968.

WRITINGS—Under name Peggy Whedon: *Always on Sunday,* Norton, 1980.

SIDELIGHTS: The first woman producer of a major network news panel program, Whedon has produced "Issues and Answers" since its debut in November, 1960. Whedon's first book, *Always on Sunday,* records the highlights of the author's twenty years with the show which is broadcast each Sunday at noon, Eastern time, on the ABC-TV Network. The program is carried by more than two hundred affiliates of the American Information Radio Service and since its inception Whedon has traveled worldwide to interview heads-of-state and foreign dignitaries. Guests of the program who have granted exclusive interviews to Whedon include President Jimmy Carter, Senator Edward Kennedy, Egyptian President Anwar el-Sadat, Palestine Liberation Organization leader Yassar Arafat, Prime Minister Indira Gandhi of India, Israeli Prime Minister Menachem Begin, and Prince Philip of Great Britian.

AVOCATIONAL INTERESTS: Painting in oils, violin.

BIOGRAPHICAL/CRITICAL SOURCES: Washington Post, November 3, 1980, January 22, 1982; *Oregon Journal,* April 24, 1981.

* * *

WHEDON, Peggy
See WHEDON, Margaret B(runssen)

* * *

WHITAKER, Haddon 1908(?)-1982

OBITUARY NOTICE: Born c. 1908; died January 5, 1982. Publisher. For forty years, Haddon Whitaker served as managing director of Whitaker & Sons Ltd., publishers of the *Bookseller,* a weekly book-trade magazine, and *Whitaker's Almanack.* Obituaries and other sources: *London Times,* January 12, 1982.

* * *

WHITAKER, John O(gden), Jr. 1935-

PERSONAL: Born April 22, 1935, in Oneonta, N.Y.; son of John O. (a dentist) and Ruth (Teal) Whitaker; married Royce Bagg, June 9, 1957; children: John, Lynne, Bill. *Education:*

Cornell University, B.S., 1957, Ph.D., 1962. *Home:* 3513 Marquette, Terre Haute, Ind. 47809. *Office:* Department of Life Science, Indiana State University, Terre Haute, Ind. 47809.

CAREER: Indiana State University, Terre Haute, assistant professor, 1962-66, associate professor, 1966-71, professor of life science, 1971—. President of board of directors of Terre Haute Recycling Center. *Member:* American Association for the Advancement of Science (fellow), American Society of Mammalogists, Ecological Society of America, Society for the Study of Amphibians and Reptiles, American Institute of Biological Sciences, Indiana Academy of Science (fellow).

WRITINGS: Keys to Vertebrates of the Eastern United States, Burgess, 1968; (with W. J. Hamilton, Jr.) *Mammals of the Eastern United States,* Cornell University Press, 1979; *The Audubon Society Field Guide to North American Mammals,* Knopf, 1980; (with R. E. Mumford) *Mammals of Indiana,* Indiana University Press, 1981; *Ectoparasites of Mammals of Indiana* (monograph), Indiana Academy of Science, 1982.

SIDELIGHTS: Whitaker commented: "I conduct research on food habits and ectoparasites of North American mammals. I believe that the world's main problems are in the areas of ecology, conservation, overpopulation, and energy depletion. Attempts to help solve these problems include my teaching and my work with a recycling center."

* * *

WHITE, Amber Blanco
See BLANCO WHITE, Amber

* * *

WHITE, Brian Terence   1927-

PERSONAL: Born in 1927 in Luton, England; married Janis Christine Ongley; children: two sons, one daughter. *Home:* 14 North Way, Uxbridge, Middlesex, England.

CAREER: Writer. Associated with Imperial War Museum, 1948-56; associated with airline, 1956—.

WRITINGS: British Tanks, 1915-1945, Ian Allan, 1963; *British Armoured Cars, 1914-1945,* Ian Allan, 1964; *German Tanks and Armoured Vehicles, 1914-1945,* Ian Allan, 1966, Arco, 1968; *British Tanks and Fighting Vehicles, 1941-1945,* Ian Allan, 1970; *British Tanks and Fighting Vehicles, 1914-1915,* Ian Allan, 1970; *Tanks and Other Armoured Fighting Vehicles, 1900 to 1918,* Macmillan, 1970; *Tanks and Other A.F.V.'s of the Blitzkrieg Era, 1939 to 1941,* Blandford, 1972; *Tanks and Other Armoured Fighting Vehicles, 1942-45,* Blandford, 1975, Macmillan, 1976; *British Tank Markings and Names: The Unit Markings, Individual Names and Paint Colours of British Armoured Fighting Vehicles, 1914-1945,* Arms and Armour Press, 1978; *Tanks and Other Tracked Vehicles in Service,* Blandford, 1978. Also author of *Churchill: British Infantry Tank Mark IV, Valentine: Infantry Tank Mark III,* and *Armoured Cars: Guy, Humber, Daimler,* all published by Profile Publications. Contributor to magazines, including *Elevenses.**

* * *

WHITE, Osmar Egmont Dorkin   1909-
(Robert Dentry)

BRIEF ENTRY: Born April 2, 1909. Journalist. White's books include *Australia for Everyone: A Modern Guide* (Wren, 1974), *Australia Illustrated* (Lansdowne, 1974), *Melbourne for Everyone* (Wren, 1974), and *Silent Reach* (Scribner, 1980). His

fiction appears under the pseudonym Robert Dentry. *Address:* 35 John St., Lower Templestowe, Victoria, Australia.

* * *

WHITE, Sheldon Harold   1928-

PERSONAL: Born November 30, 1928, in New York, N.Y.; son of Edward and Edith (Boorstein) White; married Barbara Elizabeth Notkin, June 29, 1958; children: Andrew Seth, Gregory Samuel. *Education:* Harvard University, A.B., 1951; Boston University, M.A., 1952; Iowa State University, Ph.D., 1957. *Home:* 214 Upland Rd., Newtonville, Mass. 02160. *Office:* Department of Psychology and Social Relations, Harvard University, Cambridge, Mass. 02138.

CAREER: University of Chicago, Chicago, Ill., instructor, 1957-59, assistant professor of psychology, 1959-63; Harvard University, Cambridge, Mass., lecturer in psychology, 1963-64; University of Chicago, assistant professor of psychology, 1964-65; Harvard University, associate professor, 1965-67, professor, 1967-68, Roy E. Larsen Professor of Educational Psychology, 1968—. Consultant to Rand Corp., Huron Institute, and Educational Testing Service. *Military service:* U.S. Army, 1952-54. *Member:* American Psychological Association, American Association for the Advancement of Science, Society for Research in Child Development, Association for the Advancement of Child Psychology and Psychiatry, Society for Psychophysiological Research, British Association for Child Psychology and Psychiatry, Sigma Xi.

WRITINGS: (Co-author) *Federal Programs for Young Children: Review and Recommendations,* Volume I: *Goals and Standards of Public Programs for Children,* Volume II: *Review of Evaluation Data for Federally Sponsored Projects for Children,* Volume III: *Recommendations for Federal Program Planning,* Volume IV: *Summary,* U.S. Department of Health, Education and Welfare, 1973; (editor with Barbara Welsh) *Human Development in Today's World,* Educational Associates, 1976; *To End a Silence—Or Begin One,* Vantage, 1979; (with wife, Barbara N. White) *Childhood: Pathways of Discovery,* Harper, 1979.

Contributor to psychology journals. Corresponding editor of *Journal of Child Psychology and Psychiatry,* 1964—.*

* * *

WHITEHEAD, James D(ouglas)   1939-

PERSONAL: Born February 25, 1939, in Fargo, N.D.; son of James Edwin and Aurea (Barrett) Whitehead; married Evelyn Eaton (a writer), 1970. *Education:* St. Louis University, B.A., 1963, M.A. (philosophy), 1964, M.A. (theology), 1970; Harvard University, Ph.D., 1976. *Home and office:* 19120 Oakmont South Dr., South Bend, Ind. 46637.

CAREER: Daegun Pontifical Seminary, Kwangju, Korea, assistant professor of theology, 1964-67; Loyola University, Chicago, Ill., lecturer in pastoral studies, 1970-73; University of Notre Dame, Notre Dame, Ind., assistant professor of theology, 1973-78; Whitehead Associates, South Bend, Ind., consultant in education and ministry, 1978—. Co-director of Office of Field Education in Ministry, 1973-78; member of associate faculty at Loyola University, Chicago, 1978—; research fellow at Center for the Advanced Study of Religion, Divinity School, University of Chicago, 1981.

MEMBER: American Academy of Religion, Catholic Theological Society of America, Association for Asian Studies, Society for the Study of Chinese Religions. *Awards, honors:*

Grant from American Council of Learned Societies, 1977; *China and Christianity* was named outstanding book on China and Christianity by *International Bulletin of Missionary Research*, 1979.

WRITINGS: (Editor with Yy-ming Shaw and N. J. Girardot) *China and Christianity: Historical and Future Encounters*, Notre Dame Press, 1979; (contributor) Donald Beisswenger and others, editors, *Resources in Theological Field Education*, Volume I, Association of Theological Field Education, 1977; (with wife, Evelyn Eaton Whitehead) *Christian Life Patterns: The Psychological Challenges and Religious Invitations to Adult Life* (Catholic Book Club selection), Doubleday, 1979; (contributor) *Paths of Life: Parenting*, Paulist/Newman, 1979; (with E. E. Whitehead) *Method in Ministry: Theological Reflection and Christian Ministry*, Seabury, 1980; (with E. E. Whitehead) *Marrying Well: Possibilities in Christian Marriage Today*, Doubleday, 1981; (contributor) William Clements, editor, *Ministry With the Aging*, Harper, 1981; (with E. E. Whitehead) *Community of Faith*, Seabury, 1982; (with E. E. Whitehead) *Christians Gather in Community*, Seabury, 1982; (contributor) Kendall W. Folkert, editor, *Wilfred Cantwell Smith Festschrift*, Center for the Study of World Religions, in press.

Audio-tape series for N.C.R. Cassettes: "Ministering to the Sense of the Faithful"; (co-author) "Sexuality and Christian Intimacy"; (co-author) "Adulthood: The Context of Religious Development"; (co-author) "Forming a Community of Faith"; (co-author) "The Emerging Parish: An Adult Community of Faith."

Contributor to *Abingdon Dictionary of Living Religions*. Contributor to theology journals and religious magazines, including *Bible Today*.

WORK IN PROGRESS: With wife, Evelyn Eaton Whitehead, *Personal Power: Psychological Maturity and Religious Experience* (tentative title).

*   *   *

WHITING, Allen S. 1926-

BRIEF ENTRY: Born October 27, 1926, in Perth Amboy, N.J. American political scientist, educator, and author. Whiting has worked as a social scientist for Rand Corporation and as an international relations assistant for the U.S. Department of State's Bureau of Intelligence and Research. He was deputy U.S. consul in Hong Kong from 1966 to 1968. Since 1968 he has been a professor of political science at University of Michigan and research associate at the university's Center for Chinese Studies. Whiting's books include *China and the United States: What Next?* (Foreign Policy Association, 1976), *China's Future* (McGraw, 1977), *Chinese Domestic Politics and Foreign Policy in the 1970's* (Center for Chinese Studies, University of Michigan, 1979), and *Siberian Development and East Asia* (Association of American Geographers, 1980). *Address:* 1700 Hermitage, Ann Arbor, Mich. 48104; and Department of Political Science, University of Michigan, Ann Arbor, Mich. 48104. *Biographical/critical sources: American Men and Women of Science: The Social and Behavioral Sciences*, 14th edition, Bowker, 1979.

*   *   *

WHITNEY, John Raymond 1920-

PERSONAL: Born January 28, 1920; married, 1943; children: one. *Education:* Brown University, A.B., 1948; Alfred University, M.Ed., 1950; Virginia Theological Seminary, B.D., 1953; Pennsylvania State University, Ph.D., 1967. *Office:* De-

partment of Religious Studies, Pennsylvania State University, University Park, Pa. 16802.

CAREER: Ordained Episcopal minister; social studies teacher at private school, 1949-50; Pennsylvania State University, University Park, Episcopal chaplain, 1953-57; rector of Episcopal church in State College, Pa., 1957-64; Pennsylvania State University, instructor, 1965-66, assistant professor of religious studies, 1966—. Director of state course development project, 1967-68. *Military service:* U.S. Army Air Forces, 1941-46; became captain.

WRITINGS: (With Susan W. Howe) *Student's Guide to Religious Literature of the West*, Department of Public Instruction (Harrisburg, Pa.), 1968, reprinted as *Religious Literature of the West*, Augsburg, 1971, revised edition published as *Comparative Religious Literature: Tanach, Apocrypha, Pirke Avot, Midrash, New Testament, Koran*, Ktav, 1977; (contributor) *The Religious Situation, 1968*, Beacon Press, 1968. Contributor to theology journals.*

*   *   *

WHITTAKER, Robert Harding 1920-

PERSONAL: Born December 27, 1920, in Wichita, Kan.; son of Clive Charles and Adeline (Harding) Whittaker; married Clara Caroline Buehl, January 1, 1953 (died December, 1976); married Linda Susan Olsvig, December 12, 1979; children: (first marriage) John Charles, Paul Louis, Carl Robert. *Education:* Washburn Municipal University, A.B., 1942; University of Illinois, Ph.D., 1948. *Home:* 318 Winthrop Dr., Ithaca, N.Y. 14850.

CAREER: Washington State College, Pullman, instructor, 1948-50, assistant professor of zoology, 1950-51; General Electric Co., Hanford Atomic Products Operations, Hanford, Wash., senior scientist in biology, 1951-54; Brooklyn College (now of the City University of New York), Brooklyn, N.Y., instructor, 1954-58, assistant professor, 1958-62, associate professor of biology, 1962-64; Brookhaven National Laboratory, Upton, N.Y., visiting scientist in biology department, 1964-66; University of California, Irvine, professor of biology, 1966-68; Cornell University, Ithaca, N.Y., professor of biology, ecology, and systematics, 1968-76, Charles A. Alexander Professor of Biology, 1976—. *Military service:* U.S. Army Air Forces, 1942-46.

MEMBER: International Society of Tropical Ecology, International Association of Phytosociology, Ecological Society of America, American Institute of Biological Sciences, American Society of Limnology and Oceanography, American Society of Naturalists (president, 1980), American Association for the Advancement of Science, American Society of Zoologists, National Academy of Sciences, American Academy of Arts and Sciences, Swedish Plant Geographic Society (honorary member), British Ecological Society (honorary member), Torrey Botanical Club, Phi Beta Kappa, Sigma Xi. *Awards, honors:* Mercer Award from Ecological Society of America, 1966.

WRITINGS: Classification of Natural Communities, New York Botanical Garden, 1962, 3rd edition (with Frank N. Egerton), Arno, 1978; *Communities and Ecosystems*, Macmillan, 1970, 2nd edition, 1975; (editor) *Ordination and Classification of Communities*, Junk, 1973; (editor with Simon A. Levin) *Niche: Theory and Application*, Dowden, 1975; (editor with H. Leith) *Primary Productivity of the Biosphere*, Springer-Verlag, 1975; (editor) *Classification of Plant Communities*, Kluwer Boston, 1978; (editor) *Ordination of Plant Communities*, Kluwer Boston, 1978. Also author of *Handbook of Vegetarian Science*, Part V. Contributor to scientific journals.*

WHYTE, (Harry Archibald) Maxwell 1908-

PERSONAL: Born May 3, 1908, in London, England; son of Archibald J. and Ethel (Telling) Whyte; married Olive McGregor Hughes (a secretary), June 8, 1934 (marriage ended); children: David John, Michael Gordon, Stephen Timothy, John Philip. *Education:* Studied at Bible school of Apostolic Faith Church. *Politics:* Conservative. *Home:* 2 Delbert Dr., Scarborough, Ontario, Canada M1P 1X1.

CAREER: Ordained minister, 1946; pastor of a church in Toronto, Ontario, 1947-78. *Military service:* Royal Air Force, signals officer, 1939-45; became squadron leader. *Member:* Full Gospel Ministers Fellowship (vice-president).

WRITINGS: The Power of the Blood, privately printed, 1952, revised edition, Whitaker House, 1973; *Dominion Over Demons,* privately printed, 1958, revised edition, Whitaker House, 1973; *Charismatic Gifts,* seventh edition, privately printed, 1976; *Hidden Spirits,* privately printed, 1962, fifth edition, 1976; *Pulling Down Strongholds,* privately printed, 1964, fifth edition, 1976; *The Prophetic Word,* privately printed, 1964, fourth edition, 1973; *Divine Health,* privately printed, 1965, fifth edition, 1974; *Return to the Pattern,* privately printed, 1965, third edition, 1973; *Bible Baptisms,* privately printed, 1967, third edition, 1973; *The Body for the Lord,* privately printed, 1969, third edition, 1974; *The Emerging Church,* privately printed, 1971; *Two Together* (autobiography), privately printed, 1971; *Is Mark 16 True?,* privately printed, 1972; *The Kiss of Satan,* Whitaker House, 1972; *Manual on Exorcism,* Whitaker House, 1974; *The Working of Miracles,* privately printed, 1979. Also author of *Fear Destroys* and *Where Is the Antichrist?*

SIDELIGHTS: Whyte commented: "I write on matters concerning the present charismatic renewal of the whole church and am probably the original writer in this field. The *New York Times* has stated I am the father of the deliverance ministry in North America, which is probably true." Some of Whyte's books have appeared in translation.

* * *

WICKERSHAM, Joan Barrett 1957-

PERSONAL: Born March 20, 1957, in New York, N.Y.; daughter of I. John (in business) and Rowena (a real estate broker; maiden name, Faber) Barrett; married James H. Wickersham III (an architect), September 30, 1978. *Education:* Yale University, B.A., 1978. *Home:* 2 Ware St., Cambridge, Mass. 02138.

CAREER: Marvin & Leonard Advertising Agency, Boston, Mass., copywriter, 1980—.

WRITINGS: (With Sally Goldfarb) *The Insider's Guide to Prep Schools,* Dutton, 1979.

* * *

WIGODER, Geoffrey Bernard 1922-

PERSONAL: Born August 3, 1922, in Leeds, England; son of Louis and Paula (Lubelski) Wigoder; married Deborah MacDwyer, 1949; children: Shimson, Meir. *Education:* Trinity College, Dublin, M.A., 1944; Oriel College, Oxford, Ph.D.; attended Jews' College and Jewish Theological Seminary of America. *Home:* 11 Hameyasedim St., Bet haKarem, Jerusalem, Israel.

CAREER: Radio Kol Zion Lagodah, director of English broadcasts, 1950-60; Radio Kol Israel, director of foreign broadcasts, 1960-67; *Encyclopedia Judaica,* began as deputy editor-in-chief, 1967, currently editor-in-chief. Director of audio-visual department at Institute of Contemporary Jewry, Hebrew University of Jerusalem, 1959—. Worked as correspondent for British Broadcasting Corp.

WRITINGS: (Editor with Raphael Jehudah Zwi Werblowsky) *The Encyclopedia of the Jewish Religion,* Massada-P.E.C. Press, 1965, Holt, 1966; (editor with Cecil Roth) *Entsiklopedyah shel ha-Yahadut,* 1969, translation published as *The Standard Jewish Encyclopedia,* 1960, revised edition (by Wigoder only) published as *The New Standard Jewish Encyclopedia,* W. H. Allen, 1975, 5th edition (with Itzhak Karpman), Doubleday, 1977; (editor and author of introduction) Abraham bar Hiyya, *Hegyon ha-nefesh ha-atsuvah,* 1971, translation by Wigoder published as *The Meditation of the Sad Soul,* Routledge & Kegan Paul, 1969; (editor) *Jewish Art and Civilization,* two volumes, Walker & Co., 1972; (editor) *Everyman's Judaica: An Encyclopedia Dictionary,* W. H. Allen, 1974; (editor) *Encyclopedic Dictionary of Judaica,* Leon Amiel, 1974. Also editor of *Letters of Chaim Weizmann; Jewish Lexicon,* 1969; *Israel Pocket Library,* 1974; *Bet ha-tefutsot: Museum of the Jewish Diaspora* (in Hebrew and English), 1978. Contributor to magazines and newspapers, including *Davar.*

BIOGRAPHICAL/CRITICAL SOURCES: Booklist, November 15, 1978.*

* * *

WILDMAN, Allan K. 1927-

PERSONAL: Born November 16, 1927, in Wooster, Ohio; married, 1957; children: three. *Education:* University of Michigan, B.A., 1950; University of Chicago, B.D., 1955, Ph.D., 1961. *Office:* Department of History, Ohio State University, Columbus, Ohio 43210.

CAREER: State University of New York at Stony Brook, began as instructor, became professor of history, 1961-78; Ohio State University, Columbus, professor of history, 1978—. *Member:* American Historical Association, American Association for the Advancement of Slavic Studies. *Awards, honors:* Fellowship from American Council of Learned Societies and Social Science Research Council, 1969-70; senior scholarship from American Council of Learned Societies and U.S.-U.S.S.R. Exchange Program, 1970.

WRITINGS: The Making of a Workers' Revolution: Russian Social Democracy, 1891-1903, University of Chicago Press, 1967; *The End of the Russian Imperial Army: The Old Army and the Soldiers' Revolt (March-April 1917),* Princeton University Press, 1980.

Contributor: *Communism and Western Society: A Comparative Encyclopedia,* Herder, 1972; *Storia del Marxisma Contemporanea* (title means "The History of Contemporary Marxism"), Istituto Giangiacomo Feltrinelli, 1973. Also contributor to *Revolution and Politics in Russia: Essays in Memory of B. I. Nicolaevsky.* Contributor to Slavic studies journals.

BIOGRAPHICAL/CRITICAL SOURCES: South Atlantic Quarterly, winter, 1969.*

* * *

WILKINS, Burleigh Taylor 1932-

PERSONAL: Born July 1, 1932, in Bridgetown, Va.; son of Burleigh and Marie (Taylor) Wilkins; married Mary Fisher

Cowgill, August 16, 1958; children: Brita Taylor, Carla Cowgill. *Education:* Duke University, B.A. (summa cum laude), 1952; Harvard University, M.A., 1954; Princeton University, M.A., 1963, Ph.D., 1965. *Office:* Department of Philosophy, University of California, Santa Barbara, Calif. 93106.

CAREER: Shorter College, Rome, Ga., assistant professor of history, 1956-57; Massachusetts Institute of Technology, Cambridge, instructor in humanities, 1957-60; Princeton University, Princeton, N.J., instructor in philosophy, 1960-61, 1963; Rice University, Houston, Tex., assistant professor, 1965-66, associate professor of philosophy, 1966-67; University of California, Santa Barbara, associate professor, 1967-68, professor of philosophy, 1968—. *Member:* Phi Beta Kappa.

WRITINGS: Carl Becker: A Biographical Study in American Intellectual History, M.I.T. Press, 1961; *The Problem of Burke's Political Philosophy,* Clarendon Press, 1967; *Hegel's Philosophy of History,* Cornell University Press, 1974; *Has History Any Meaning?: A Critique of Popper's Philosophy of History,* Cornell University Press, 1978.

BIOGRAPHICAL/CRITICAL SOURCES: Encounter, April, 1979.*

* * *

WILKINS, Marilyn (Ruth) 1926-
(Marne Wilkins)

PERSONAL: Born August 23, 1926, in Elkhorn, Wis.; daughter of Harold F. (in business) and Helen E. (Reed) Opitz; married Alfred Springborg Wilkins (an attorney), June 27, 1950; children: Marilyn Elizabeth (Mrs. Charles A. Johnson), Emily Ann (Mrs. Walter Eagleson Robb IV). *Education:* University of Wisconsin (now University of Wisconsin—Madison), B.S., 1949; further study at University of California, La Jolla Art Center, 1963-65. *Politics:* Independent. *Religion:* Congregational. *Home address:* P.O. Box 932, Weaverville, Calif. 96093.

CAREER: Flight instructor in Columbia, Mo., Elkhorn, Wis., Madison, Wis., and Palo Alto, Calif., 1944-51; free-lance interior designer in San Diego, Calif., 1952-65; Shasta Community College, Weaverville, Calif., adult education instructor in drawing and textile arts, 1966-76; Trinity High School, Weaverville, librarian, 1968-69. Writer, 1943—. Drawing instructor and charter member of board of directors of Highland Art Center, 1968-79; member of Trinity County Board of Education, 1972—, president, 1976, 1980; member of board of directors of Northern California Girl Scout Council, 1967; member of numerous civic committees, including Citizens Committee for Architecture in San Diego, 1962, Junior League Community Service Board, 1963-64, State Art Advisory Committee, 1980—, and County Art Advisory Board, 1981—. *Member:* American Craft Council, Handweavers Guild of America, Association of Junior Leagues, Audubon Society, California Crafts Museum, League of Women Voters.

WRITINGS: California Dye Plants, Thresh Publications, 1976; (under name Marne Wilkins) *Long Ago Lake: A Child's Book of Nature Lore and Crafts,* Scribner, 1978.

WORK IN PROGRESS: A book of loom patterns for home craftsmen; a book about women; a history of red dye; Forty Acres, a history of a settler's ranch in the San Joaquin Valley, California.

SIDELIGHTS: "I have been writing and drawing all of my life," Wilkins told *CA,* "but I considered these activities to be forums rather than vocations. I never seem to stop research-ing and one thing leads to others—often into print. Publishing is fun, but only certain parts of it.

"I feel both my husband and I write because it is a way of 'passing the baton.' This, we feel, is a difficulty unique perhaps to our generation. We find it most difficult in America today to find recipients for verities learned in one's lifetime. Because our feelings are strong about the need for cultural continuity, we have found writing and teaching to be important to our lives.

"My husband and I have had a wonderful life and rewarding family, and believe deeply about many things. A search for truth and knowledge has led us to a commitment to the environment. We are devoted to Albert Schweitzer's philosophy of reverence for life, and so our animals are a special part of our family and home."

In addition to her work in the field of crafts and nature lore, Wilkins has the distinction of having been the first woman flight instructor in the state of Wisconsin.

* * *

WILKINS, Marne
See WILKINS, Marilyn (Ruth)

* * *

WILKINSON, Bud
See WILKINSON, Charles B(urnham)

* * *

WILKINSON, Charles B(urnham) 1916-
(Bud Wilkinson)

PERSONAL: Born April 23, 1916, in Minneapolis, Minn.; son of Charles Patton and Edith (Lindbloom) Wilkinson; married Mary Shifflett, August 29, 1939 (divorced August, 1974); married Donna O'Donnohue, November 18, 1977; children: Charles P., James G. *Education:* University of Minnesota, B.A., 1937; Syracuse University, M.A., 1940. *Religion:* Episcopal. *Home:* 4516 Pershing Pl., St. Louis, Mo. 63108. *Office:* Public Employees Benefit Services Corp., 400 Mansion House Center, St. Louis, Mo. 63102.

CAREER: Syracuse University, Syracuse, N.Y., assistant coach, 1937-40; University of Minnesota, Minneapolis, assistant coach, 1941; University of Oklahoma, Norman, assistant football coach, 1946, head football coach, 1947-64, athletic director, 1947-64; analyst and commentator for National Collegiate Athletic Association "College Game of the Week," 1965-77; St. Louis Cardinals (professional football team), St. Louis, Mo., coach, 1979-80; currently chairman of board of directors of Public Employees Benefit Service Corp., St. Louis. Sports announcer for Entertainment Sports Program Network. Chairman of board of directors of Planned Marketing Associates, 1971-75; member of board of directors of St. Louis Zoo, St. Louis Young Men's Christian Association, and St. Louis Family and Children's Services Agency. Co-director of Coach of the Year Football Clinics. Republican candidate for U.S. Senate, 1964; member of Republican National Committee, 1966-72; chairman of citizens action program of National Council on Crime and Delinquency; White House liaison with President's Council on Employment of the Handicapped, American Red Cross, and Advertising Council; president of National Center for Voluntary Action; consultant to Presidents Kennedy and Nixon. *Military service:* U.S. Navy, hanger deck officer on aircraft carrier, 1942-45; served in Pacific theater; became lieutenant commander. *Member:* Rotary International, American Football Coaches Association.

AWARDS, HONORS: Named coach of the year by American Football Coaches Association, 1949, and Associated Press, 1951; named one of ten outstanding young men by Chamber of Commerce of the United States, 1950; award from B'nai B'rith, 1957; National Brotherhood Citation from National Council of Christians and Jews, 1959; Silver Anniversary All-American Award from *Sports Illustrated,* 1962; member of College Football Hall of Fame; D.Hum. from Oklahoma Christian College, 1973.

WRITINGS: Oklahoma Split-T Football, Prentice-Hall, 1950; (with Gomer Jones) *Modern Defensive Football,* Prentice-Hall, 1952.

Under name Bud Wilkinson: *Bud Wilkinson's Guide to Modern Physical Fitness,* Viking, 1972; *Sports Illustrated Football: Offense,* Sports Illustrated, 1973; *Sports Illustrated Football: Defense,* Sports Illustrated, 1974; *Sports Illustrated Football: Quarterback,* Sports Illustrated, 1975.

*　　*　　*

WILKINSON, J(oseph) F. 1925-

PERSONAL: Born April 1, 1925, in Fort Wayne, Ind.; son of Joseph F. and Veronica (Miller) Wilkinson; married Priscilla MacKenzie, July 12, 1952; children: Laura, Sarah. *Education:* Indiana Institute of Technology, B.C., 1946; Indiana University, A.B., 1949. *Home:* 161 Henry St., Brooklyn, N.Y. 11201. *Office:* McGraw-Hill, Inc., 1221 Sixth Ave., New York, N.Y. 10020.

CAREER: Brooklyn Eagle, Brooklyn, N.Y., reporter, 1950-55; U.S. Information Agency, Washington, D.C., press officer in Bombay, India, 1955-57; *Engineering News-Record,* New York City, managing editor, 1958-76; McGraw-Hill, Inc., New York City, editor of *Coal Age,* 1976—. Member of U.S. Committee on Large Dams. *Military service:* U.S. Army, 1944-46; became sergeant. *Member:* American Institute of Mining Engineers, Mining Club, New York Road Runners Club.

WRITINGS: Don't Raise Your Child to Be a Fat Adult, Bobbs-Merrill, 1980. Contributor to magazines, including *Sports Illustrated, True, Parents' Magazine, Popular Science, Today's Health,* and *Family Circle.*

AVOCATIONAL INTERESTS: Travel (Antarctica, Vietnam, China, Siberia, Saudi Arabia).

*　　*　　*

WILLEMS, Emilio 1905-

PERSONAL: Born August 18, 1905, in Cologne, Germany (now West Germany); married, 1932; children: three. *Education:* University of Berlin, M.A., 1928, Ph.D., 1930. *Office:* Department of Anthropology, Vanderbilt University, Nashville, Tenn. 37203.

CAREER: University of Sao Paulo, Sao Paulo, Brazil, assistant professor of sociology, 1937-41, professor of anthropology, 1941-49; Vanderbilt University, Nashville, Tenn., professor of anthropology, 1949—. Visiting professor at Michigan State University, 1952, University of Michigan, 1952-53, and National University of Colombia, 1962-63; consultant to United Nations Educational, Scientific and Cultural Organization. *Member:* American Anthropological Association, American Studies Association. *Awards, honors:* Guggenheim fellowship, 1951; Social Science Research Council grant, 1954.

WRITINGS: (With Gioconda Mussolini) *Buzios Island: A Caicara Community in Southern Brazil* (monograph), J. J. Augustin, 1952; *Followers of the New Faith: Culture Change and the Rise of Protestantism in Brazil and Chile,* Vanderbilt University Press, 1967; *Latin American Culture: An Anthropological Synthesis,* Harper, 1975.

Other writings: *Assimilacao e populacoes marginais no Brasil: Estudo sociologico dos imigrantes germanicos e seus descendentes,* Companhia Editora Nacional, 1940; *A aculturacao dos alamaes no Brasil: Estudo antropologico des imigrantes alemaes e seus descendentes no Brasil,* Companhia Editora Nacional, 1946; *Aspectos da aculturacao dos Japoneses no estado de Sao Paulo,* Faculdade de Filosofia, Ciencias e Letras, Universidade de Sao Paulo, 1948; (with Ettore Biocca) *Contribuicao para o estudo anthropometrica dos Indios Tukano, Tariana, e Maku, da regiao do alto Rio Negro (Amazonas),* [Brazil], 1947; (contributor) Carlos M. Delgado de Carvalho, editor, *Didatica das ciencias sociais: Observacoes criticas acerca do ensino de sociologia,* Impr. Oficial, 1949; *Dicionario de sociologia,* Editora Globo, 1950; *Brasil: Periodo indigena,* Instituto Panamericano de Geografia e Historia, 1953; *A familia portuguesa contemporanea,* [Brazil], 1955; *Uma vila brasiliera: Tradicao e transicao,* Difusao Europeia do Livro, 1961; *Antropologia social* (translated by Yolanda Leite), Difusao Europeia do Livro, 1962, 2nd edition, 1966; *El cambio cultural dirigido,* Impr. Nacional, 1963.*

*　　*　　*

WILLIAMS, Ferelith Eccles 1920-

PERSONAL: Born August 12, 1920, in Oxford, England; daughter of C. A. Eccles (a schoolmaster) and Hermone a Beckett (Terrell) Williams. *Education:* Attended Central School of Arts and Crafts, London, England, 1945-47. *Home:* Flat 8, 65/67 Longridge Rd., London SW5, England.

CAREER: Design Research Unit, London, England, junior designer, 1947; Colman Prentis & Varley, London, designer, 1947-48; Kemsley Newspapers, London, illustrator, 1948-51; Associated Newspapers, London, illustrator, 1951-53; Brighton Polytechnic, Brighton, England, instructor, 1964-71; Leicester Polytechnic, Leicester, England, instructor, 1971-73. Work Exhibited at A.I.A. Gallery, London, and London Group, Nash House. *Wartime service:* Red Cross ambulance driver, 1940-45. *Member:* Society of Industrial Artists and Designers, Association of Illustrators.

WRITINGS—Self-illustrated; published by World's Work, except as noted: *Dame Wiggins of Lee,* 1975; *One Old Oxford Ox,* 1976; *My Book About Forgiveness: The Sacrament of Penance for Children,* Collins, 1976; *The Oxford Ox's Alphabet,* 1977; *The Oxford Ox's Calendar,* 1980.

Illustrator: Juhn Pudney, *The Hartwarp Light Railway,* Hamish Hamilton, 1962; Pudney, *The Hartwarp Dump,* Hamish Hamilton, 1962; Pudney, *The Hartwarp Circus,* Hamish Hamilton, 1963; Pudney, *The Hartwarp Balloon,* Hamish Hamilton, 1963; Pudney, *The Hartwarp Bakehouse,* Hamish Hamilton, 1964; Susan Hale, *Painters Mate,* Methuen, 1964; Hale, *Mystery Boxes,* Methuen, 1964; Hale, *Mystery Boxes,* Methuen, 1965; Pudney, *The Hartwarp Jets,* Hamish Hamilton, 1967; Denise Hill, *Helicopter Children,* Methuen, 1967; Phyllis Arkle, *Magic at Midnight,* Brockhampton, 1967, Funk, 1968; Arkle, *The Village Dinosaur,* Brockhampton, 1968; Arkle, *Two Village Dinosaurs,* Brockhampton, 1969.

P. W. Cordin, *Number in Mathematics,* Books 1 and 2, Macmillan, 1970; Joan Cass, *The Witch of Withery Wood,*

Brockhampton, 1973; Pamela Oldfield, *The Halloween Pumpkin,* Brockhampton, 1974, Childrens Press, 1976; Cass, *The Witch and the Naughty Princesses,* Brockhampton, 1976; A. J. McCallen, *Listen!: Themes From the Bible Retold for Children,* Collins, 1976; Keith Snow, *I Am a Squirrel,* World's Work, 1978; Snow, *I Am a Hedgehog,* World's Work, 1979; Snow, *I Am a Badger,* World's Work, 1979; McCallen, *Praise,* Collins, 1979.

Illustrator of reading series "One Two Three and Away," by Sheila McCullagh, includes more than forty titles, Hart-Davis, 1964-79. Contributor of illustrations to magazines, including *Homes and Gardens.*

SIDELIGHTS: Williams commented: "My first venture into illustration came in 1949 when I went to work for the *London Daily Graphic;* until then I had been more concerned with typography and general designing. On the paper I did layouts for the feature pages and any drawings that were needed, always in a mad rush to catch the evening deadline. After three years the paper was sold to another press and it became the *London Daily Sketch.* As the *Sketch,* the pace was hotter, and at the end of another two years I felt like a one-woman factory turning out five pages and several drawings a day, always with one eye on the clock.

"I decided to get out and try free lancing as an illustrator. At this time (1955) there was a great deal of illustration in advertising and most of my work was in that field—working for J. Walter Thompson and other agencies. At the same time I started to work for several magazines, including *Homes and Gardens.* As the field of advertising changed, I gradually moved into publishing and started to illustrate more children's books. Today most of my work is in this field.

"In the sixties there was an expansion of art and design education in this country and a need for experienced professionals to bring their practical knowledge to the students. I thought this would be an interesting experience, and I spent the next nine years teaching. I enjoyed teaching, found the students stimulating and the work an interesting contrast to full-time illustrating.

"Usually I like to illustrate stories where I can have some fun and make people laugh. The more ridiculous the situation, the more I enjoy it. It is always exciting and sometimes surprising to see what emerges on the page."

*   *   *

WILLIAMS, John Henry   1887-1980

OBITUARY NOTICE: Born June 21, 1887, in Ystrad, Wales; died December 24, 1980. Educator, economist, and author. Professor emeritus of political economy at Harvard University, John Williams taught at a number of other universities during his career, including Princeton University, Brown University, and Northwestern University. He also served as consultant to the U.S. Treasury and State Departments from 1930 to 1940. Williams wrote *Argentine International Trade Under Inconvertible Paper Money* and *Post-War Monetary Plans and Other Essays.* He co-wrote *Financing American Prosperity* and *Economic Stability in a Changing World.* Obituaries and other sources: *The International Who's Who,* Europa, 1978; *New York Times,* December 26, 1980. (Exact date of death provided by wife, Katherine M. Williams.)

*   *   *

WILLIAMS, Wallace Edward   1926-

BRIEF ENTRY: Born July 18, 1926, in Corona, Calif. American educator and editor. Williams began teaching at Indiana University in 1959 and became a professor of English in 1970. He edited *Early Lectures of Ralph Waldo Emerson,* Volumes II-III (Harvard University Press, 1964, 1972) and *The Current Voice: Readings in Contemporary Prose* (Prentice-Hall, 1971). *Address:* Department of English, Indiana University, Elisha Ballantine Hall, Bloomington, Ind. 47401. *Biographical/critical sources: Directory of American Scholars,* Volume II: *English, Speech, and Drama,* 7th edition, Bowker, 1978.

*   *   *

WILLIAMS-ELLIS, (Mary) Amabel (Nassau Strachey)   1894-

PERSONAL: Born May 10, 1894, in Newlands Corner, near Guildford, England; daughter of John St. Loe (a journalist and editor) and Ann (an author; maiden name, Simpson) Strachey; married Bertram Clough Williams-Ellis (an architect and author), 1915 (died, 1978); children: Christopher (died, 1944), Susan, Charlotte. *Education:* Educated at home. *Home:* Plas Brondanw, Llanfrothen, North Wales.

CAREER: Writer. Literary editor of *Spectator* magazine, 1922-23.

WRITINGS—Novels: *Noah's Ark; or, The Love Story of a Respectable Young Couple,* J. Cape, 1925, George H. Doran, c. 1926; *The Wall of Glass,* George H. Doran, 1927; *To Tell the Truth,* J. Cape, 1933; *The Big Firm,* Houghton, 1938; *Learn to Love First,* Gollancz, 1939.

Other: *The Sea-Power of England* (play), Humphrey Milford, 1913; (with husband, Clough Williams-Ellis) *The Tank Corps,* George Newnes, 1919; *An Anatomy of Poetry,* Basil Blackwell, 1922, reprinted, Folcroft, 1973; (with C. Williams-Ellis) *The Pleasures of Architecture,* J. Cape, 1924, revised edition, 1954; *Good Citizens* (short stories), Gerald Howe, 1928, published as *Courageous Lives: Stories of Nine Good Citizens,* Coward, 1939; *The Tragedy of John Ruskin* (biography), J. Cape, 1928, published as *The Exquisite Tragedy: An Intimate Life of John Ruskin,* Doubleday, 1929, reprinted, Richard West, 1973; (with L. A. Plummer) *Why Should I Vote?: A Handbook for Voters,* Gerald Howe, 1929.

H.M.S. Beagle in South America (adapted from the narratives and letters of Charles Darwin and Captain Fitz Roy), C. A. Watts, 1930, published as *The Voyage of the Beagle,* Lippincott, 1931; (author of introduction) *The Modern Schools Handbook,* edited by Trevor Eaton Blewitt, Gollancz, 1934; (translator, editor, and author of introduction) *The White Sea Canal,* John Lane, 1935; (with Frederick Jack Fisher) *The Story of English Life,* Coward, 1936, revised edition, 1947 (published in England as *A History of English Life, Political and Social,* Methuen, 1936, third edition, 1953).

Women in War Factories, Gollancz, 1943; (editor with C. Williams-Ellis) *Vision of England,* Elek, 1946; (with C. Williams-Ellis and with children, Susan, Charlotte, and Christopher Williams-Ellis) *In and Out of Doors,* Routledge & Kegan Paul, 1937; (editor with C. Williams-Ellis) *Vision of Wales,* Elek, 1949.

The Art of Being a Woman, Longmans, Green, 1951; (with C. Williams-Ellis) *Headlong Down the Years: A Tale of Today,* University of Liverpool Press, 1951; (with Euan Stewart Cooper Willis) *Laughing Gas and Safety Lamp: The Story of Sir Humphry Davy,* Methuen, 1951, revised edition, Abelard, 1954; *The Art of Being a Parent,* Bodley Head, 1952; *Changing the World: Further Stories of Great Scientific Discoveries,* Bodley

Head, 1956; *Darwin's Moon: A Biography of Alfred Russel Wallace*, Blackie & Son, 1966.

Juveniles: *But We Know Better*, illustrated by C. Williams-Ellis, J. Cape, 1929; *How You Began: A Child's Introduction to Biology*, Gerald Howe, 1928, revised edition, Coward, 1929, reprinted, Transworld, 1975; *Men Who Found Out: Stories of Great Scientific Discoverers*, Gerald Howe, 1929, Coward, 1930, reprinted, Bodley Head, 1952; *How You Are Made*, A. & C. Black, 1932; *What Shall I Be?*, Heinemann, 1933; *Ottik's Book of Stories*, Methuen, 1939; *The Puzzle of Food and People: A Geography Reader*, Manhattan Publishing, 1951; *Engines, Atoms, and Power*, Putnam, 1958; *They Wanted the Real Answers*, Putnam, 1958, revised edition, 1959 (original edition published in England as *Seekers and Finders*, Blackie & Son, 1958); *The Unknown Ocean*, Putnam, 1959; *Princesses and Witches*, Blackie & Son, 1966; (contributor) *Monkeys and Magicians: A Collection of Modern and Traditional Stories*, Blackie & Son, 1967; (with William Stobbs) *Life in England*, Blackie & Son, Volume I: *Early and Medieval Times*, 1968, Volume II: *Tudor England*, 1968, Volume III: *Seventeenth-Century England*, 1968, Volume IV: *Georgian England*, 1969, Volume V: *Victorian England*, 1969, Volume VI: *Modern Times*, 1970; *Wonder Why Book of Your Body: What You Eat and Where It Goes*, Transworld, 1978.

Fairytales and folktales retold: *Fairies and Enchanters*, Thomas Nelson, 1933; *Princesses and Trolls*, Barrie & Rockliff, 1950; *The Arabian Nights*, Blackie & Son, 1957, Criterion, 1958, published in two volumes as *Ali Babba and the Forty Thieves From the Thousand and One Nights* and *Aladdin and Other Stories From the Thousand and One Nights*, Carousel, 1973; Jacob Ludwig Karl Grimm and Wilhelm Karl Grimm, *Fairy Tales*, Blackie & Son, 1959, revised edition published as *Fairy Tales From Grimm*, 1968, published as *Grimm's Fairy Tales*, Pan Books, 1964; *Fairy Tales From the British Isles*, Blackie & Son, 1960, Warner, 1964, published in two volumes as *British Fairy Tales* and *More British Fairy Tales*, Blackie & Son, 1965; *Round the World Fairy Tales*, Blackie & Son, 1963, Warner, 1966; (compiler and translator with Moura Budberg) *Russian Fairy Tales*, Blackie & Son, 1965; *Dragons and Princes: Fairy Tales From Round the World*, Blackie & Son, 1966; *Old World and New World Fairy Tales*, Warner, 1966; (editor) J.L.K. Grimm and W. K. Grimm, *More Fairy Tales*, Blackie & Son, 1968, published as *More Fairy Tales From Grimm*, 1978; *Gypsy Folk Tales*, Pan Books, 1971; *Fairy Tales From East and West*, Blackie & Son, 1977; *Fairy Tales From Everywhere*, Blackie & Son, 1977; *Fairy Tales From Here and There*, Blackie & Son, 1977; *Fairy Tales From Near and Far*, Blackie & Son, 1977; *The Rain-God's Daughter, and Other African Fairy Tales*, Blackie & Son, 1977; *The Story Spirits*, Heinemann, 1980.

Editor; all with Mably Owen, except as noted: *Out of This World: An Anthology of Science Fiction*, Blackie & Son, Volume I, 1960, Volume II, 1961, Volume III, 1962, Volume IV, 1964, Volume V, 1965, Volume VI, 1967, Volume VII, 1968, Volume VIII, 1970, Volume IX (with Michael Pearson), 1972, Volume X (with Pearson), 1973; *Worlds Apart: An Anthology of Science Fiction*, Blackie & Son, 1966; *Out of This World* (contains Volumes III and IV of *Out of This World: An Anthology of Science Fiction*), Blackie & Son, 1971; *Out of This World Choice* (contains Volumes II and V of *Out of This World: An Anthology of Science Fiction*), Blackie & Son, 1972; (with Pearson) *Tales From the Galaxies*, Pan Books, 1973, White Lion Publishers, 1976; (with Pearson) *Strange Universe: An Anthology of Science Fiction*, Blackie & Son, 1974; (with Owen and Pearson) *Strange Orbits: An Anthology of Science Fiction*, Blackie & Son, 1976; (with Owen and Pearson) *Strange*

Planets: An Anthology of Science Fiction, Blackie & Son, 1977.

Contributor to periodicals, including *Saturday Review of Literature*, *Fortune*, and *Living Age*.

BIOGRAPHICAL/CRITICAL SOURCES: Spectator, April 13, 1951; Charles Richard Sanders, *The Strachey Family 1588-1932: Their Writings and Literary Associations*, Duke University Press, 1953.

*   *   *

WILLISON, Marilyn Murray   1948-

PERSONAL: Born November 13, 1948, in Portland, Ore.; daughter of James Edward (in real estate) and Onie Augusta (Willis) Murray; married Bruce Gray Willison, 1968 (divorced, 1978); children: B(ruce) G(ray), Geoffrey. *Education:* University of California, Los Angeles, B.A., 1970. *Residence:* Glendale, Calif. *Agent:* George Diskant, 9255 Sunset Blvd., Beverly Hills, Calif. 90210. *Office:* Times Mirror Co., Times Mirror Sq., Los Angeles, Calif. 90053.

CAREER: Los Angeles Times, Los Angeles, Calif., book reviewer and general contributor, 1973—. Book reviewer for *Wall Street Journal*, 1974—; reporter for *Family Weekly*, 1978—. Member of board of directors of California Chamber Symphony Society.

WRITINGS: The Great Restaurants of California, Camaro, 1975; *Diary of a Divorced Mother*, Wyden Books, 1980; *Love Songs and Little Boys*, Bantam, 1982. Author of column "A Woman's Place," for *Los Angeles Herald Examiner*, 1978-79. Contributor to magazines and newspapers, including *Ladies' Home Journal*, *Family Circle*, *Cosmopolitan*, *Seattle Times*, and *Newsday*.

WORK IN PROGRESS: A sequel to *Love Songs and Little Boys*, tentatively titled *Kismet*.

SIDELIGHTS: When her husband of ten years divorced her to marry her best friend, Willison was emotionally and financially devastated. Left with two young sons to rear, a heavily mortgaged home in suburbia, and a badly damaged sense of self-esteem, Willison found herself with no place to turn for help. An only child whose parents were deceased, she had no family to rely on and was unable to afford counseling or therapy. "When it all happened, I went to the bookstore, searching . . . [for] something that would help me cope. There was nothing," she told *Houston Chronicle* reporter Gay Elliott McFarland. "Everything had to do with being a swinging single," Willison recalled in an interview with Mary Rue Smith in the *Glendale News-Press*. "I couldn't help but feel there were a lot more women like me who were more involved with the PTA than with disco dancing." *Diary of a Divorced Mother*, a journal written partially to salve her own wounds, is the author's gift to other women who, like herself, are struggling to build new lives after divorce.

Composed of fifty-two chapters that Willison refers to as "different essays about my life," *Diary* is a record of the experiences and feelings of a divorced mother of the 1970's. In the book, the author reveals how she learned to cope with problems involving father's visits, former in-laws, baby sitters, broken appliances, dating, too little time, too little money, bitterness, and loneliness. "I wrote it to help other women," Willison was quoted by Mary Every in the *Santa Barbara News-Press*. "I hope the book will help women to realize that they're not the only persons going through a marriage crumbling. I also want to remind them that feeling good about themselves should be a natural part of their life."

The book was well received by critics. "It's the story of a survivor. Yes, even a winner," commented Mary Rue Smith. "'Diary' mirrors a woman rebuilding her life, sometimes desperately, but always constructively." And, noted Doreen Fitzgerald of the *Bakersfield Californian,* Willison "tells her story with both humor and compassion." According to Every, "'Diary of a Divorced Mother,' [is] a touching, poignant book with patches of humor. There are episodes in the sensitively written account that could moisten the eyes of readers who don't even identify with Marilyn's plight." *Los Angeles Times* critic Jim Sanderson labeled the book "a lifeline for divorced moms," and he recommended the book as a gift for the divorced woman struggling to raise her children alone. "The one thing she can find in this book is reassurance, in a hundred different ways, that she can recover her life and make it something good," opined Sanderson. "You and I, as friends or relatives may try to tell her this, but maybe—as in Alcoholics Anonymous—she needs to hear it from somebody who's been there."

Diary has been serialized in *McCall's Working Mother* and *Cosmopolitan,* paperback rights have been sold, and a movie based on the book is being planned.

Willison told *CA:* "Although I've always thought of myself as a writer, it wasn't until I had to deal with the personal shock of being betrayed by both my husband and my friend that I had the strength to write of my own experiences. That pain led to *Diary,* which opened up a whole new world for me. Women responded from all over the country, and I answered every fan letter I received. I've expanded on my daily diary activities and my future books will probably call on those volumes for inspiration."

AVOCATIONAL INTERESTS: "I love English riding (jumping in particular)."

BIOGRAPHICAL/CRITICAL SOURCES: Montrose Ledger (Calif.), February 16, 1980; *Los Angeles Times,* March 28, 1980; *Los Angeles Herald Examiner,* April 1, 1980; *Bakersfield Californian,* April 6, 1980; *Santa Barbara News-Press* (Calif.), June 19, 1980; *Glendale News-Press* (Calif.), October 10, 1980; *Houston Chronicle,* February 17, 1981.

*   *   *

WILLS, Jean 1929-

PERSONAL: Born February 10, 1929, in London, England; daughter of Leonard (an optician) and Jane (Waller) Wilson; married Graham Boyce Wills (a physicist), November 15, 1952; children: Peter, Paula, Robert. *Education:* Attended Pitman's Secretarial College, 1945-46. *Home:* 70 Highview Rd., Ealing, London W13 0HW, England. *Office:* Garden House, 57-59 Long Acre, London WC2E 9JZ, England.

CAREER: Author of books for young people; British Broadcasting Corp. (BBC), London, England, secretary, 1947-48; British Insulated Callender's Cables, London, secretary, 1949-54. *Member:* Society of Authors.

WRITINGS—For young people; published by Hamish Hamilton: *The Sawdust Secret,* 1973; *The Sugar Trail,* 1974; *Who Wants a Job?,* 1976; *The Hope and Glory Band,* 1978; *Round the Twist,* 1979; *Sandy's Gargoyle,* 1979; *Nicky and the Genius,* 1980; *May Day Hullabaloo,* 1981; *Stargazer's Folly,* 1982.

Contributor of articles and short stories for adults and children to periodicals, and author of short stories for radio presentation.

SIDELIGHTS: Jean Wills writes: "The major discovery of my childhood was the public library, after which I never stopped reading. I had no definite idea of being a writer, however, until my first child was born. Teaching myself to write—a long, arduous process—I gradually realized my true interest lay in the field of children's books. My children's stories mostly reflect the suburban environment in which I have spent the major part of my life. I have often poached on my children's activities for 'copy' but now find myself using principally events in my own childhood."

AVOCATIONAL INTERESTS: Music, art, birdwatching.

*   *   *

WILLS, Maurice Morning 1932-
(Maury Wills)

BRIEF ENTRY: Born October 2, 1932, in Washington, D.C. American professional baseball player. Wills played for the Los Angeles Dodgers from 1959 to 1966, and during six of those years led the National League in stolen bases. He joined the Pittsburgh Pirates in 1966. In 1962 he was the National League's Most Valuable Player, Associated Press Athlete of the Year, and winner of the S. Rae Hickok Professional Athlete of the Year Award. Wills managed the Seattle Mariners from 1980 to 1981. He has written *It Pays to Steal* (Prentice-Hall, 1963) and *How to Steal a Pennant* (Putnam, 1976). *Biographical/critical sources: Current Biography,* Wilson, 1966.

*   *   *

WILLS, Maury
See WILLS, Maurice Morning

*   *   *

WILSON, Charles Reagan 1948-

PERSONAL: Born February 2, 1948, in Nashville, Tenn.; son of Clifford Martin, Jr. (a civil servant) and Maxine (in real estate; maiden name, Ward) Wilson. *Education:* University of Texas, El Paso, B.A., 1970, M.A., 1972; University of Texas, Austin, Ph.D., 1977. *Home address:* P.O. Box 6640, University, Miss. 38677. *Office:* Center for the Study of Southern Culture, University of Mississippi, University, Miss. 38677.

CAREER: University of Wuerzburg, Wuerzburg, West Germany, visiting professor of American Studies at Institute for English Philology, 1977-78; University of Texas, El Paso, instructor in history, 1978-80; Texas Tech University, Lubbock, visiting professor of history, 1980-81; University of Mississippi, Center for the Study of Southern Culture, University, editor of *Encyclopedia of Southern Culture,* 1981—. *Member:* American Studies Association, Southern Historical Association.

WRITINGS: Baptized in Blood: The Religion of the Lost Cause, 1865-1920, University of Georgia Press, 1980. Contributor to history journals.

WORK IN PROGRESS: Encyclopedia of Southern Culture, co-editor with William Ferris, publication expected in 1985; *The Southern Way of Death.*

SIDELIGHTS: "Born and reared in the South," Wilson wrote, "I became a historian of the region after my exposure to its literary and historical works. In college in the mid-1960's, I rebelled against interest or pride in the region, but after reading Faulkner, C. Vann Woodward, and others I became fascinated with the complexity and spiritual qualities of Dixie."

WILSON, Helen Van Pelt 1901-

PERSONAL: Born in 1901, in Collingswood, N.J.; daughter of John Oliver and Orella Eliza (Mowday) Wilson; married Arthur J. Collins, Jr., June 10, 1924; children: Cynthia Emily Collins Luden. *Education* Bryn Mawr College, A.B. (cum laude), 1923; graduate study at University of Pennsylvania. *Religion:* Episcopalian. *Home:* 65 Center St., Westport, Conn. 06880.

CAREER: Teacher of English and Latin at high school in Mount Holly, N.J., 1923-24; free-lance writer, 1927-38; garden editor of *Philadelphia Record*, Philadelphia, Pa., and *Camden Courier Post*, Camden, N.J., 1938-43; Barrows & Co., Inc., New York City, executive editor, 1943-51; William Morrow & Co., Inc., New York City, executive editor of Barrows Division, 1952-55; D. Van Nostrand Co., Princeton, N.J., home and garden editor, 1956-65; Barrows & Co., Inc., garden editor, 1965-68; Hawthorn Books, Inc., New York City, home and garden editor, beginning in 1969; writer.

MEMBER: International Geranium Society, Garden Writers of America, American Horticultural Society, African Violet Society of America, New York Horticultural Society, Pennsylvania Horticultural Society, Art Alliance of Philadelphia, Bryn Mawr Club, Federated Garden Club, Westport Garden Club. *Awards, honors:* Bronze medal from African Violet Society of America, 1954.

WRITINGS: A Garden in the House: The Culture of Bulbs, House Plants, and Terrariums, Leisure League of America, 1934; *Perennials Preferred*, Barrows, 1945, reprinted as *Perennials for Every Garden*, 1953, reprinted as *The New Perennials Preferred*, 1961; *Geraniums, Pelargoniums: For Windows and Gardens*, illustrations by Natalie Harlan Davis, Barrows, 1946, 3rd edition, 1957, reprinted as *The Joy of Geraniums: The Standard Guide to the Selection, Culture, and Use of the Pelargonium*, 1965; *The African Violet: Saintpaulia*, illustrations by Leonie Hagerty, Barrows, 1948, revised edition, 1949; (with Dorothy Helen Jenkins) *Enjoy Your House Plants*, Barrows, 1949, revised edition published as *House Plants for Every Window*, 1954.

The Complete Book of African Violets, Barrows, 1951, 2nd edition published as *The New Complete Book of African Violets*, 1963, reprinted as *Helen Van Pelt Wilson's African-Violet Book*, Hawthorn, 1970; (editor) *The Joy of Flower Arranging*, Barrows, 1951; *Climbing Roses*, illustrations by Leonie Bell, Barrows, 1955; (with Richard Thomson) *Roses for Pleasure*, D. Van Nostrand, 1957; (editor) *One Thousand One African Violet Questions Answered by Twelve Experts*, D. Van Nostrand, 1958, revised edition published as *African Violet and Gesneriad Questions Answered by Twenty Experts*, 1966; (editor) *Flower Arrangement: Designs for Today*, D. Van Nostrand, 1962; (editor) *The Gardener's Book of Verse*, Barrows, 1966; (with Bell) *The Fragrant Year: Scented Plants for Your Garden and Your House*, illustrations by Bell, Barrows, 1967.

Flowers, Space, and Motion: New Designs in Hanging Flower Arrangements, Simon & Schuster, 1971; (editor) *Joyful Thoughts for Five Seasons*, Hawthorn, 1971; *Helen Van Pelt Wilson's Own Garden and Landscape Book*, photographs by George Taloumis, Doubleday, 1973; *Houseplants Are for Pleasure: How to Grow Healthy Plants for Home Decoration*, Doubleday, 1973; *Successful Gardening in the Shade*, Doubleday, 1975; *Successful Gardening With Perennials: How to Select and Grow More Than Five Hundred Kinds for Today's Yard and Garden*, Doubleday, 1976; (editor) Elaine Davenport, *Ferns for Modern Living*, Merchants, 1977; *Color for Your Winter Yard and Garden, With Flowers, Berries, Birds, and Trees*, Scribner, 1978; (editor) M. Jane Coleman Helmer and Bonnie E. Stewart, *African Violets and Other Gesneriads for Modern Living*, illustrations by Dean Vavak, Merchants, 1978; (editor) Stewart, *One Hundred One Trouble Free Houseplants for Modern Living*, Merchants, 1978; *Color Me With Flowers, Berries, Birds, and Trees*, Scribner, 1978. Contributor to magazines. Editor of *Garden Calendar*, 1947-49, and *Flower Arrangement Calendar*, 1958—.

BIOGRAPHICAL/CRITICAL SOURCES: Publishers Weekly, March 13, 1954, August 18, 1969.*

*   *   *

WILSON, Joan Hoff 1937-

BRIEF ENTRY: Born June 27, 1937, in Butte, Mont. American historian, educator, and author. Wilson has been a professor of history since 1976. She received the Stuart L. Bernath Book Prize from the Society of Historians of American Foreign Relations in 1972 and the Berkshire Article Award from the Berkshire Conference of Women Historians in 1977. Her books include *Herbert Hoover, Forgotten Progressive* (Little, Brown, 1975), *Sexism and the Law: A Study of Male Beliefs and Legal Bias in Britain and the United States* (Free Press, 1978), and *Herbert Hoover as Secretary of Commerce: Studies in New Era Thought and Practice* (University of Iowa Press, 1981). *Address:* Department of History, Arizona State University, Tempe, Ariz. 85281. *Biographical/critical sources: Directory of American Scholars*, Volume I: *History*, 7th edition, Bowker, 1978.

*   *   *

WILSON, Lionel 1924-
(Peter Blackton, Herbert Ellis, L. E. Salzer)

PERSONAL: Born March 22, 1924, in New York, N.Y.; son of Jonas Antzel (a chemist) and Sylvia (a pianist; maiden name, Zeitlin) Salzer. *Education:* Attended New York University, 1941-42. *Politics:* Democrat. *Religion:* Jewish. *Home:* 308 East 79th St., New York, N.Y. 10021.

CAREER: Actor, 1942—. Has appeared on Broadway in seven plays, and on television in plays and commercials; other work includes touring in winter and summer stock productions and doing voice-overs for commercial television and audiovisual materials. *Awards, honors:* Barter Award, 1942.

WRITINGS—All juveniles: The Cat Who Never Enjoyed Himself, Guidance Associates, 1975; *The Mule Who Refused to Budge*, Crown, 1975; *The First Stunt Stars of Hollywood*, C.P.I., 1978; (under pseudonym L. E. Salzer) *Haunted House Mysteries*, C.P.I., 1979; (under pseudonym Herbert Ellis) *The Magic of Madame Tussaud*, C.P.I., 1979; *The Mystery of Dracula: Fact or Fiction?*, C.P.I., 1979; *The Mystery of the Human Wolves*, C.P.I., 1979; (under pseudonym Peter Blackton) *The Mysterious Strangers Within Us*, C.P.I., 1979; *Attack of the Killer Grizzly*, Raintree Publishers, 1980.

Plays: "Come and Be Killed" (adapted from the novel of the same title by Shelley Smith), first produced at Berkshire Drama Festival, Stockbridge, Mass., July, 1976.

Contributor to television serial, "Secret Storm," CBS-TV; author of audiovisual programs for Guidance Associates, Walt Disney Educational Media, C.P.I., and Board of Jewish Education.

WORK IN PROGRESS: More books for young people, including *The Mystery of the King Who Never Was: Louis XVII, They Refused to Say Die,* and *Run for Your Life,* all for C.P.I.; an adult novel tentatively entitled *The Deadly Grief;* also a series of filmstrips entitled "The Holidays," for the Board of Jewish Education.

SIDELIGHTS: Wilson told *CA:* "With the exception of *The Mule Who Refused to Budge,* all of my work has been nonfiction and has required a great deal of research—fascinating research. There are no two accounts of Madame Tussaud's story that are alike, so I have chosen, of course, the material that seemed to hold up best under scrutiny. *The First Stunt Stars of Hollywood* afforded me the opportunity of speaking with some of the pioneer daredevils who thrilled us so in the days of the movie serials and silent films. It was a particularly enjoyable experience for me to speak with Mr. Yakima Canutt, who thrilled us all with his 'transfer' work in 'Stagecoach' as John Wayne's double and as Rhett Butler, driving through the flames of Atlanta in 'Gone With the Wind.' Mr. Canutt, who became a stunt director (called second unit directors), staged the chariot races in 'Ben Hur.'

"The subject of *The Mystery of the King Who Never Was: Louis XVII* will always intrigue me, even though I do not believe that anyone will ever present any conclusive evidence as to his fate. But the accounts and theories concerning the survival of Marie Antoinette's son could easily fill a small library.

"I enjoy writing for young people and am particularly partial to nonfiction. Biographies attract me the most. There is always the possibility that they may stimulate a young person, perhaps even move him toward a vocation. But at the very least I think they are inspiring. I also am fascinated by the sources of classic legends and folktales, in the truths behind the fiction. Gloria Skurzynski's researched account of the legend of the Pied Piper is one of the most interesting and absorbing books I have ever come across. Her book, *What Happened in Hamlin,* is terrifying, touching, and beautifully written and should be filmed.

"At the moment I am almost half finished with an adult suspense novel, tentatively titled *The Deadly Grief.* My children's books seemed to have impressed a very fine literary agent, who has been insisting that I take a stab at maturer stuff. He has been supportive in the extreme, and also has approved the pages I gave him to look at."

AVOCATIONAL INTERESTS: "I am avid collector of books on Daumier and also have a fairly decent collection of his theatrical etchings"; teaching character-voice classes.

*   *   *

WILSON, Ronald E(merson) 1932-

PERSONAL: Born January 21, 1932, in Cambridge, Mass.; son of Paul E. (a chemist) and Cleora (Russell) Wilson; married Carole Dennis (a designer), November 13, 1959; children: Kenneth, Heather, Todd. *Education:* Gordon College, B.A., 1956; attended Syracuse University, 1957-59. *Politics:* Independent. *Home and office:* 470 Willwood, Earlysville, Va. 22936.

CAREER: Moody Monthly Magazine, Chicago, Ill., editor, 1959-61; Youth for Christ International, editor of *Campus Life,* 1962-65, vice-president for literature, 1965-70; COMPRO, Inc. (consulting firm), Glen Ellyn, Ill., management consultant, 1971-72; David C. Cook Publishing Co., Elgin, Ill., public relations director, 1973-76, acquisitions editor, 1976-78; free-lance writer, 1979—. Consultant to International Marketing Group.

WRITINGS: Multimedia Handbook for the Church, David Cook, 1975; *A Flower Grows in Ireland* (nonfiction), David Cook, 1976; *Adventure of the Iron Camels* (nonfiction), Tyndale, 1979; *Breaker, Breaker* (fiction), David Cook, 1980; *Lost in the Shenandoahs* (juvenile), David Cook, 1981. Editor of *Today's Christian Woman,* 1979—.

SIDELIGHTS: Wilson told *CA:* "I provide complete editorial services for business, government, and social, educational, and religious agencies. Communication begins with understanding your audience and knowing what response you want, and it includes choosing the right media and preparing messages suited to them."

*   *   *

WILSON, William A(lbert) 1933-

PERSONAL: Born September 23, 1933, in Tremonton, Utah; son of William LeRoy (a railroad worker) and Lucille (Green) Wilson; married Hannele Blomquist, May 31, 1957; children: Laila Maarit, Denise Ann, Sven Eric, Karl William. *Education:* Brigham Young University, B.A., 1958, M.A., 1962; Indiana University, Ph.D., 1974. *Politics:* Democrat. *Religion:* Church of Jesus Christ of Latter-day Saints (Mormons). *Home:* 1140 East 50th S., Logan, Utah 84321. *Office:* Department of English, Utah State University, Logan, Utah 84322.

CAREER: High school teacher of English in Bountiful, Utah, 1958-60; Brigham Young University, Provo, Utah, professor of English, 1960-78; Utah State University, Logan, professor of English and history, 1978—. Past member of board of directors of Utah Heritage Foundation; chairman of board of trustees of Utah Folklife Center, 1980—; member of folk arts panel of National Endowment for the Arts, 1981—. Folklife presenter at Smithsonian Institution's Festival of American Folklife, 1976; field worker for American Folklife Center, 1978. Radio broadcaster.

MEMBER: American Folklore Society, Association for Mormon Letters (member of executive board), Mormon History Association, Finnish Literature Society (corresponding member), California Folklore Society, Folklore Society of Utah (past president), Utah Historical Society.

AWARDS, HONORS: Fulbright fellow at University of Helsinki, 1965-66; Morris S. Rosenblatt Award from *Utah Historical Quarterly,* 1973, for article "Folklore and History: Facts Amid the Legends," and 1979, for article "Folklore of Utah's Little Scandinavia"; Gustave O. Arlt Humanities Award from Council of Graduate Schools in the United States, 1977, for *Folklore and Nationalism in Modern Finland;* grants from National Endowment for the Arts, 1979 and 1980.

WRITINGS: "Tarkea ja arvokas kirja" (radio script), Finnish National Radio, 1966; "Folklore and Finnish Independence" (radio script), KBYU-Radio, 1974; *Folklore and Nationalism in Modern Finland,* Indiana University Press, 1976; (contributor) Thomas G. Alexander, editor, *Essays on the American West,* Brigham Young University Press, 1976; (contributor) Edward B. Hart, editor, *Instruction and Delight,* Brigham Young University Press, 1976; (contributor) Felix J. Oinas, editor, *Folklore, Nationalism, and Politics,* Clavica Publishers, 1978; (contributor) Jan Harold Brunvand, editor, *Readings in American Folklore,* Norton, 1979. Contributor of articles, translations, and reviews to history and folklore journals. Book review editor of *Western Folklore,* 1972-78, editor, 1979—.

WORK IN PROGRESS: Research on Western customs and Mormon folklore.

SIDELIGHTS: Wilson told *CA:* "Through the study of folklore, I am interested in discovering more about what it means to be human—what it means to be human in different times, places, and circumstances."

*   *   *

WILTSE, David   1940-

PERSONAL: Born June 6, 1940, in Lincoln, Neb.; son of Homer George (an attorney) and Gretchen (in advertising; maiden name, Schrag) Wiltse; married Nancy Carlin, May 11, 1945; children: Laura Joan, Lisa Alexandra. *Education:* University of Nebraska, B.A., 1963. *Home:* 6 Nordholm Dr., Weston, Conn. 06883. *Agent:* International Creative Management, 40 West 57th St., New York, N.Y. 10019. *Office:* Saugatuck Productions, 6 Nordholm Dr., Weston, Conn. 06883.

CAREER: Writer. *Military service:* U.S. Army, 1963-66. *Awards, honors:* Drama Desk Award for most promising playwright, 1972, for "Suggs"; Edgar Allen Poe Award from Mystery Writers of America, 1981, for teleplay "Revenge of the Stepford Wives."

WRITINGS: (Editor) *It Only Hurts When I Serve*, Simon & Schuster, 1980; (contributor) Irving T. Marsh, editor, *Best Sport Stories, 1980,* Dutton, 1980; *The Wedding Guest* (novel), Delacorte, 1982; *The Serpent* (novel), Delacorte, in press.

Plays: "Tall and Rex" (one-act), first produced in New York City at Brooklyn Academy of Music, 1971; "Suggs" (two-act), first produced in New York City at Lincoln Center, 1972.

Screenplays: "Hurry Up or I'll Be Thirty," Avco-Embassy, 1973.

Teleplays: "Nightmare," 1974; "Revenge of the Stepford Wives," 1980.

Also, creator of television series "Ladies Man," Columbia Broadcasting System, Inc. (CBS-TV), 1980. Contributing editor of *Tennis.*

WORK IN PROGRESS: A play about patterns of behavior through generations.

SIDELIGHTS: Wiltse told *CA:* "A major source of pride for me in my writing is my versatility. I have worked successfully in plays, television, films, novels, and magazines and in the full range of genre from farcical situation comedies through melodramatic adventure to drama. Some of this I do for love and some for money, and I am striving to reach the day when the two are the same."

*   *   *

WINN, Janet Bruce   1928-

PERSONAL: Born May 21, 1928, in Orange, N.J.; daughter of A. Bruce (an executive) and Katherine (Baldwin) Boehm; married O. Howard Winn (a poet and teacher), July 15, 1950; children: Martin, Bruce, Kate, Martha. *Education:* Vassar College, B.A., 1950; Stanford University, M.A., 1951; doctoral study at State University of New York at Albany, 1979-81. *Politics:* "Independent (left)." *Home address:* Sheldon Dr., Poughkeepsie, N.Y. 12603. *Agent:* Heinle & Heinle, 29 Lexington Rd., Concord, Mass. 01742. *Office:* Department of Behavioral Science, Dutchess Community College, Poughkeepsie, N.Y. 12601.

CAREER: Ulster County Community College, Stone Ridge, N.Y., part-time instructor in philosophy, 1969-79; Dutchess Community College, Poughkeepsie, N.Y., part-time instructor

in sociology, 1973—. Member of board of directors and director of public relations of Hudson Valley Philharmonic Society, 1960-70. *Member:* Phi Beta Kappa.

WRITINGS: Home in Flames (young-adult novel), Follett, 1972; *Connecticut Low* (young-adult novel), Houghton, 1980.

Work represented in anthologies, including *Best Short Stories of 1968,* Houghton, 1968. Contributor of stories to magazines, including *Evidence, Husk, Prairie Schooner,* and *Cimmaron Review.*

WORK IN PROGRESS: Blue Hills (tentative title), a historical novel for young adults; research on the rationality of social science.

SIDELIGHTS: Janet Winn told *CA:* "What seems to motivate my fiction, my teaching, and my research in sociology and philosophy is a sense that much is askew ethically with the world. Nothing works the way it did in the children's books of the past: through Alice's looking glass is an uglier sight than Carroll knew. So into what I write seep ethical and political concerns, fed long ago by socially-concerned parents, by some extraordinary teachers, by a number of thinking, ethically-aware friends. These social concerns seem to have rung bells at a distance: a story of mine (concerning race relations, in part) has been translated and published in a Hungarian anthology."

*   *   *

WINTER, Colin O'Brien   1928-1981

OBITUARY NOTICE: Born in 1928; died November 17, 1981, in London, England. Church official and author. Colin Winter, bishop of Damaraland, South-West Africa, from 1968 to 1981, was an outspoken opponent of apartheid. He was the author of *Just People, For George and John,* and *Namibia.* Obituaries and other sources: *London Times,* November 18, 1981.

*   *   *

WINTERS, Jon
See CROSS, Gilbert B.

*   *   *

WINWARD, (Richard) Walter   1938-

PERSONAL: Born December 4, 1938, in York, England. *Agent:* London Management Ltd., 235-241 Regent St., London W1A 2JT, England.

CAREER: Writer.

WRITINGS—Novels: The Success, Delacorte, 1967; *A Cat With Cream,* Pan Books, 1972; *And Cry for the Moon,* Cassell, 1974; *Fives Wild,* Atheneum, 1976; *Rough Deal,* Weidenfeld & Nicolson, 1977; *The Conscripts,* Futura, 1977; *Hammerstrike,* Hamish Hamilton, 1978, Simon & Schuster, 1979; *Seven Minutes Past Midnight,* Hamish Hamilton, 1979. Also author of *Say Goodbye Forever,* 1977.

Contributor to magazines and newspapers, including *Penthouse* and *Books and Bookmen.**

*   *   *

WIRTH, Nicklaus   1934-

PERSONAL: Born February 15, 1934, in Winterthur, Switzerland; son of Walter (a professor of geography) and Hedwig (Keller) Wirth; married Nani Tucker; children: Carolyn, Christian, Tina. *Education:* Federal Institute of Technology, Zurich, Switzerland, E.E., 1958; Universite Laval, M.Sc., 1960; University of California, Berkeley, Ph.D., 1963. *Residence:* Gockhausen, Switzerland. *Office:* Institut fuer Informatik, Federal Institute of Technology, 8092 Zurich, Switzerland.

CAREER: Stanford University, Stanford, Calif., assistant professor of computer science, 1963-67; University of Zurich, Zurich, Switzerland, assistant professor, 1967-68, professor of computer science, 1968-75; Federal Institute of Technology, Zurich, professor of computer science, 1968—. *Member:* Association for Computing Machinery. *Awards, honors:* Honorary doctorates from University of York and Institute of Technology, Lausanne, Switzerland, both 1978.

WRITINGS: Systematic Programming, Prentice-Hall, 1973; (with Kathleen Jensen) *Pascal: User Manual and Report,* Springer-Verlag, 1974; *Algorithms and Data Structures: Programs,* Prentice-Hall, 1975.

SIDELIGHTS: Wirth is the designer of the computer programming languages Euler, Algol-W, PL 360, Pascal, and Modula.

* * *

WITCHEL, Dinah B(rown)   1936-

PERSONAL: Born October 9, 1936, in Schofield Barracks, Hawaii; daughter of John Maurice (in U.S. Army) and Alice (a social worker; maiden name, Wiley) Brown; married Lawrence Witchel (a publishing executive), March 2, 1962; children: John, Elisabeth. *Education:* University of Maryland, B.S., 1958. *Home:* 132 West 75th St., New York, N.Y. 10023. *Agent:* John Brockman Associates, Inc., 200 West 57th St., New York, N.Y. 10019. *Office:* Ziff-Davis Publishing Co., 1 Park Ave., New York, N.Y. 10016.

CAREER: Worked as editor, reporter, and writer for newspapers and magazines, 1953-71; free-lance writer, 1971-80; Ziff-Davis Publishing Co., New York, N.Y., executive editor of *Skiing,* 1980—.

WRITINGS: (With Elissa Slanger) *Ski Woman's Way,* Summit Books, 1979.

* * *

WITHAM, (Phillip) Ross   1917-

PERSONAL: Born April 11, 1917, in Stuart, Fla.; son of Paul N. (in U.S. Navy) and Lucille (Ross) Witham; married Mabel Josephine Blasko (a teacher of the handicapped), May 27, 1945; children: Chester Randolph, Steven Paul, Timothy Dean, Julie Ann Witham Hartwigger. *Education:* University of South Florida, B.I.S., 1973; University of Oklahoma, M.L.S., 1976. *Home:* 1457 Northwest Lake Point, Stuart, Fla. 33494. *Office:* Florida Department of Natural Resources, P.O. Box 941, Jensen Beach, Fla. 33457-0941.

CAREER: U.S. Navy, Jacksonville, Fla., civilian aircraft mechanic, 1949-52; Public Health Foundation for Cancer and Blood Pressure Research, Inc., Stuart, Fla., supervisor of hydroponics, 1959-66; Florida Department of Natural Resources, St. Petersburg, biologist, researcher on sea turtles, and supervisor of field station in Jensen Beach, 1965—. Curator of marine activities for Martin County Historical Society, 1955-65; biological aide with Florida Board of Conservation, 1963-65. Member of Southeast Region Marine Turtle Recovery Team, of National Marine Fisheries Service and U.S. Fish and Wildlife Service, and U.S. Army Corps of Engineers task force on sea turtles and dredging. *Military service:* U.S. Navy, aviation machinist's mate, 1934-44; served in Pacific theater.

MEMBER: American Institute of Biological Sciences, American Society of Zoologists, American Society of Ichthyologists and Herpetologists, American Institute of Fishery Research Biologists, Ecological Society of America, Izaak Walton League of America (past president of Martin County chapter), Explorers Club (fellow), Pearl Harbor Survivors Association (life member), Florida Academy of Sciences, Gulf and Caribbean Fisheries Institute.

WRITINGS: (With Sarah R. Riedman) *Turtles: Extinction or Survival?* (juvenile), Abelard, 1974. Contributor of more than fifteen articles to scientific journals, including *Sea Frontiers.*

WORK IN PROGRESS: Continuing research on sea turtles.

SIDELIGHTS: Witham told *CA:* "I became interested in sea turtles following the discovery of a nearly dead hatchling on Hutchinson Island, Martin County, Florida; I had been walking along the beach as rehabilitation therapy following knee surgery. I became interested in sea turtles and spiny lobsters, and these interests led to employment by the state of Florida, first to research spiny lobsters and later sea turtles. Authorship followed as a matter of course because of the need to publish research findings. My sea turtle research was featured on television programs, including 'Animals, Animals, Animals' and 'Those Amazing Animals.'"

* * *

WITKACY
See WITKIEWICZ, Stanislaw Ignacy

* * *

WITKIEWICZ, Stanislaw Ignacy   1885-1939
(Witkacy)

BRIEF ENTRY: Born February 24, 1885, in Krakow (some sources say Warsaw), Poland; committed suicide, September 18, 1939, in Jeziora, Poland. Polish painter and playwright. Witkiewicz earned his living as a portrait painter and developed a formal theory of art, but he used the stage as a medium for his formist philosophical views. In some thirty experimental plays, from "The New Deliverance" (1922) to "The Shoemakers" (1948), he expressed his fear of dehumanization and imminent disaster. Witkiewicz saw himself surrounded by insanity, isolated from society, and in danger of losing his individuality because of modern technology. As a result, the characters in his plays are intensely individualistic, their speech is rapid, and the prevailing mood is one of fear. His distortions were intended to accent his formist views, to elevate drama to the formal level of music and art; but the result was to underscore the rapidity of change in early twentieth-century Europe and the urgency of saving mankind from conformity. Witkiewicz used theatrical effects to such extremes that he was attacked by critics and regarded as a madman by his colleagues. He committed suicide in despair after Poland's invasion by Germany and Russia. It was only after surrealism and theatre of the absurd had gained popularity after World War II that Witkiewicz was recognized as a major influence on modern European literature. In 1956 his works were revived and formed an important foundation for avant-garde theatre in Poland. *Biographical/critical sources: Columbia Dictionary of Modern European Literature,* Columbia University Press, 1947; *McGraw-Hill Encyclopedia of World Drama,* McGraw, 1972.

* * *

WITTY, Helen E. S(troop)   1921-
(Helen E. Stroop)

PERSONAL: Born October 4, 1921, in Seattle, Wash.; daughter of George W. (a metallurgist) and Nellie B. (an educator; maiden name, Smith) Stroop; married Richard Lee Witty (a publishing consultant), 1957; children: Anne E., George Richard. *Education:* Attended University of California, Los Angeles, 1940-42; Columbia University, B.S., 1948. *Religion:* Protestant. *Home:* 240 West 98th St., New York, N.Y. 10025.

CAREER: Columbia University Press, New York City, senior editor, 1946-55; Dryden Press, New York City, editor and advertising director, 1955-57; senior editor of *International Review of Food and Wine*, 1977—. *Military service:* U.S. Army, Women's Army Corps, 1942-45; served in Pacific theater; became warrant officer; received battle stars. *Member:* Les Dames d'Escoffier. *Awards, honors:* Tastemaker Award Specialty from R. T. French Co., for *Better Than Store-Bought.*

WRITINGS: (Senior editor) *The Cooks' Catalogue*, Harper, 1975; (editor with B. J. Tatum, and contributor) *B. J. Tatum's Wild Foods Cookbook*, Workman Publishing, 1976; (editor with L. Kan, and contributor) *Chinese Casserole Cookery*, Workman Publishing, 1978; (with Elizabeth Schneider Colchie) *Better Than Store-Bought*, Harper, 1979. Author of "The Season's Fare," a column in *Home Garden*, 1965-68, and "One's Company," a monthly column in *International Review of Food and Wine*, 1978—. Also author of a column in *Bon Appetit*, 1976-77. Contributor to magazines (sometimes under name Helen E. Stroop), including *Gourmet*.

*   *   *

WOFSEY, Marvin M(ilton) 1913-

PERSONAL: Surname is pronounced Wahf-see; born June 1, 1913, in Connecticut; son of Herman A. (a news dealer) and Mary C. (Wofsy) Wofsey; married Erna Fuhrer, February 25, 1949; children: Avrom H. *Education:* New York University, B.S., 1935; American University, M.A., 1942, Ph.D., 1967. *Politics:* Democrat. *Religion:* Jewish. *Home:* 15311 Pine Orchard Dr., Silver Spring, Md. 20906.

CAREER: American University, Washington, D.C., head of computer laboratory, 1961-64; U.S. Department of Defense, Computer Institute, head of systems branch, 1964-67; George Washington University, Washington, D.C., professor of management emeritus, 1967—. Consultant to Chase-Manhattan Bank, International Monetary Fund, and Pan-American Health Organization. *Military service:* U.S. Navy, storekeeper, 1943-46. *Member:* Data Processing Management Association (life member; member of international board of directors, 1967-71). *Awards, honors:* President's award from Data Processing Management Association, 1975.

WRITINGS: Conversion to Automatic Data Processing: A Practical Primer, American University, 1962; *Management of Automatic Data Processing Systems*, Thompson Book Co., 1968, enlarged edition, Auerbach Publishers, 1973. Editor of "Administrative Seminar Series," Pan-American Health Organization, 1968. Contributor of articles to data processing and management journals.

WORK IN PROGRESS: Computer Security.

SIDELIGHTS: Wofsey commented: "My current avocation is helping (without pay) developing nations in their use of the computer. Countries so far include Taiwan, the Philippines, Japan, Canada, Mexico, Brazil, England, France, Switzerland, Israel, and Iran."

*   *   *

WOLD, Allen L. 1943-

PERSONAL: Born December 8, 1943, in Benton Harbor, Mich.;

son of Chester Ray (an advertising executive) and Eva Kathleen (an elementary school teacher; maiden name, Hall) Wold; married Diane Easterling (a statistician), June 24, 1972. *Education:* Pomona College, B.A., 1967. *Home and office address:* Route 5, Spring Hill, No. 5, Chapel Hill, N.C. 27514. *Agent:* Lea C. Braff, Jarvis, Braff Ltd., 90 Seventh Ave., Brooklyn, N.Y. 11215.

CAREER: Claremont Colleges, Claremont, Calif., assistant bibliographer at Honnold Library, 1968-72; writer, 1972—. *Member:* Science Fiction Writers of America.

WRITINGS: The Planet Masters (science fiction novel), St. Martin's, 1979; *Star God* (science fiction novel), St. Martin's, 1980.

WORK IN PROGRESS: Three science fiction novels, *Zhanae' Degau, The Eye in the Stone*, and *The Jewels of the Dragon; The Limitless Dream: Computer Assisted Role Playing Games.*

*   *   *

WOLFE, Rinna (Evelyn) 1925-

PERSONAL: Born May 2, 1925, in Brooklyn, N.Y.; daughter of Henry (an engineer) and Pauline (a bookkeeper; maiden name, Tabachnik) Wolfe. *Education:* Attended Brooklyn College (now of the City University of New York), 1942-44; City College (now of the City University of New York), B.B.A., 1957; San Francisco State University, M.A., 1966. *Religion:* Jewish. *Home and office:* 256 Fairlawn Dr., Berkeley, Calif. 94708.

CAREER: Charles Stores, New York City, buyer, 1946-55; Raylass Stores, New York City, buyer, 1955-59; teacher at public schools in Lompoc, Calif., 1959-60, Pleasant Hill, Calif., 1960-65, and Danville, Calif., 1965-67; teacher in Berkeley, Calif., 1967-80. Member of faculty at University of California extensions in Santa Cruz, Berkeley, Davis, and Merced, 1966-77. Volunteer worker for Shanti. *Member:* Women's National Book Association, California Writers Club. *Awards, honors:* Grant from FACE, 1972; Point Foundation fellowship, 1973.

WRITINGS: (Editor) *From Children With Love* (poems by children), Seabury, 1970; *The Singing Pope*, Seabury, 1980. Contributor of more than one dozen articles to education journals and popular magazines, including *Croft Nei, California Living, Civil Rights Digest*, and *Urban West.*

WORK IN PROGRESS: When Parents Become Our Children; plays based on folktales; scripts for children's television programs; *Joan Miro: Magician of Color*, a biography for children.

SIDELIGHTS: From Children With Love was based on Rinna Wolfe's public school teaching in the area of black studies. About the same time, she co-produced a filmstrip on black American artists. In 1972 she conducted a children's bus tour to Ensenada, Mexico, as part of a multiethnic school program. In 1974 she taught children's classes in the history of childhood and children's legal rights.

Wolfe wrote: "*When Parents Become Our Children*, my work in progress, is based on my personal experience of closing two parents' lives. If it can offer hints to others on how to avoid my pitfalls when faced with a similar situation, the painful writing will have a satisfying conclusion. If one wants to avoid a nursing-home ending, being alert, active, and involved is crucial to anyone fifty years or older in the 1980's. And if generations can re-bond and nourish each other, greater mental health among us all may abound."

AVOCATIONAL INTERESTS: Travel (Europe, Israel).

WOLFE, Winifred   1929-1981

OBITUARY NOTICE—See index for *CA* sketch: Born May 23, 1929, in Boston, Mass.; died October 27, 1981, in Manhattan, N.Y. Novelist and author of radio and television scripts for daytime serials, including "As the World Turns," "Somerset," and "High Hopes." Wolfe's novels *Ask Any Girl* and *If a Man Answers* were adapted as motion pictures. Obituaries and other sources: *New York Times,* October 29, 1981.

*   *   *

WOODHOUSE, Charles Platten   1915-

PERSONAL: Born in 1915 in Luton, England; son of Josiah John (a soldier) and Ethel (a tailoress; maiden name, Woodhouse) Woodhouse. *Education:* Educated privately. *Politics:* "Not a party man, but open-minded." *Religion:* "Basically Christian." *Home:* 157 Cowper St., Luton, Bedfordshire, England.

CAREER: Writer, 1947—. Worked in art and antiques trades, beginning 1936; dealer in fine art until 1960. *Member:* Royal Society of Arts (life fellow).

WRITINGS: Old English Toby Jugs, Mountrose Press, 1949; *Investment in Antiques and Art,* G. Bell, 1969; *The Victoriana Collector's Handbook,* G. Bell, 1970; *The World's Master Potters,* David & Charles, 1974; *Ivories,* David & Charles, 1976. Contributor to *Academic American Encyclopedia* and to *Antique Collector's and Dealer's Guide.*

WORK IN PROGRESS: Research for a book on the art and stylistic trends of the Victorian age in England and Europe.

SIDELIGHTS: Woodhouse told *CA:* "Through writing and lecturing I have tried to diminish the 'mystique' attached to art and antiques, to awaken the interest of 'ordinary' less-informed people about their natural heritage of beauty, craftsmanship, and art. To collect is to preserve, and so much may thus be saved for posterity which might otherwise be lost or destroyed. 'Art for money's sake' may be the current slogan among stamp dealers and investors, but with the less avaricious—and there *are* some even yet—it is still art for art's sake, or maybe beauty's sake."

*   *   *

WOOD-LEGH, Kathleen Louise   1901-1981

OBITUARY NOTICE: Born in 1901 in Ontario, Canada; died October 26, 1981, in Cambridge, England. Historian and author. The Lucy Cavendish Collegiate Society, Cambridge, grew out of a small group of academic women that Kathleen Wood-Legh helped organize in 1951. Wood-Legh served for many years as the group's steward, and after the group was recognized as a college of Cambridge University, she held such posts as founder fellow, pro-president, and fellow emeritus. A specialist in medieval history, Wood-Legh was the author of numerous works, including *Life Under Edward III* and *Principal Chantries in Britain.* Obituaries and other sources: *London Times,* October 27, 1981.

*   *   *

WOODRUFF, Archibald Mulford, Jr.   1912-

PERSONAL: Born July 30, 1912, in Newark, N.J.; son of Archibald Mulford and Eleanor B. (Van Etten) Woodruff; married Barbara Jane Bestor, July 13, 1940; children: Archibald Mulford III, Paul B., Nathan V.E., Timothy R. *Education:* Williams College, B.A., 1933; Princeton University, Ph.D., 1936; also attended University of Berlin, 1935. *Home address:* P.O. Box 582, Simsbury, Conn. 06070. *Office:* c/o Office of the President Emeritus, University of Hartford, 1040 Prospect St., West Hartford, Conn. 06117.

CAREER: Prudential Insurance Co., in mortgage department in Newark, N.J., 1936-44, 1947-50, and in Boston, Mass., 1944-47; University of Pittsburgh, Pittsburgh, Pa., Kelly Memorial Professor of Insurance and Urban Land Studies, 1950-59; George Washington University, Washington, D.C., dean of School of Government (now School of Government, Business, and International Affairs), 1959-64; University of Hartford, Hartford, Conn., provost, 1964-67, chancellor, 1967-70, president, 1970-77. Visiting lecturer at Claremont Men's College, 1962-63. Director of Bureau of Business Research, 1954-59; chairman of National Capital Planning Commission, 1960-61, vice-chairman, 1961-65; chairman of research committee of Urban Land Institute, 1966-71. Member of faculty and board of directors of Land Reform Training Institute, Tao-Yuan, Taiwan; member of board of directors of Society for Savings, C. G. Fund, Inc., Lincoln Foundation (also vice-president), Lincoln Institute of Land Policy, Wadsworth Athenaeum, and E. B. Foundation; member of board of trustees of Mark Twain Memorial and Young Men's Christian Association; past member of board of trustees of Tarkio College; chairman of board of directors of Watkinson School; past advisory director of Western Pennsylvania National Bank; past president of Connecticut Conference of Independent Colleges.

MEMBER: American Economic Association (past president), National Council for Development of Small Business Management, Phi Beta Kappa, Hartford Golf Club, Hartford Club, Princeton Club, Cosmos Club. *Awards, honors:* L.H.D. from Trinity College, 1972; LL.D. from Tarkio College, 1973, Williams College, 1978, University of Hartford, 1979, and Annhurst College, 1979; medal of Chinese culture from Ministry of Education, Republic of China (Taiwan).

WRITINGS: Farm Mortgage Loans of Life Insurance Companies, Yale University Press, 1937; (with T. G. Alexander) *Success and Failure in Small Manufacturing,* University of Pittsburgh Press, 1958; *The Frazzled Urban Fringe,* Land Reform Training Institute (Tao-Yuan, Taiwan), 1979; *The Farm and the City: Rivals or Allies?,* Prentice-Hall, 1980. Contributor of about one hundred articles to professional journals.

WORK IN PROGRESS: History of German Property Taxation, 1880-1914, With Relation to Asian Tax Systems, publication expected in 1982; *History and Theory of the German Rentenmark,* publication expected in 1982; *Food, Filth, and People: Feeding a World With Twelve Billion Inhabitants,* publication expected in 1983.

SIDELIGHTS: Woodruff told *CA:* "Aside from running the university, my chief interest of the last twenty years has been the uneven distribution of land ownership in developing countries along with the disposition of rack-rent tenants and the landless to rise in revolution. Land reform has proven to be possible in countries as diverse as Japan, South Korea, and Taiwan, without physical damage to life or property, and in Taiwan with virtually full monetary compensation to the former landlords. This has led to my involvement with the Land Reform Training Institute of Tao-Yuan, Taiwan, where I taught land-use officials from some thirty-five countries of the Third World who came to observe, firsthand, the Chinese model."

WOOLLCOTT, Alexander (Humphreys) 1887-1943

BRIEF ENTRY: Born January 19, 1887, in Phalanx, N.J.; died of a heart attack, January 23, 1943, in New York, N.Y.; buried in Hamilton College Cemetery, Clinton, N.Y. American journalist, critic, radio broadcaster, and essayist. Woollcott was best known as a theatre critic for various New York newspapers, in which capacity he had the power to make or break a play. Through his *New Yorker* column "Shouts and Murmurs" and his radio show "The Town Crier" he became noted for his witty, gossipy reportorial style, which was alternately sentimental and malicious. Woollcott's criticism, both dramatic and literary, is usually considered mediocre, but his ability as a reporter and a raconteur is still highly regarded. His criticism, essays, and sketches are collected in several books, including *Shouts and Murmurs* (1922), *Going to Pieces* (1928), and *While Rome Burns* (1934). He edited several anthologies of short fiction and collaborated with George S. Kaufman on two plays, "The Channel Road" (1930) and "The Dark Tower" (1933). He was the model for the character Sheridan Whiteside in Kaufman and Moss Hart's play "The Man Who Came to Dinner," and he performed the role in the West Coast and touring productions of that play. *Residence:* Lake Bomoseen, Vermont. *Biographical/critical sources: Twentieth Century Authors: A Biographical Dictionary of Modern Literature,* H. W. Wilson, 1942, 1st supplement, 1955; Samuel Hopkins Adams, *A. Woollcott: His Life and World,* Reynal & Hitchcock, 1945; Edwin Palmer Hoyt, *Alexander Woollcott: The Man Who Came to Dinner,* Abelard, 1968; Wayne Chatterton, *Alexander Woollcott,* Twayne, 1978.

*   *   *

WRIGHT, Basil Charles 1907-

PERSONAL: Born June 12, 1907, in London, England; son of Lawrence (a military officer) and Gladys (Marsden) Wright. *Education:* Corpus Christi College, Cambridge, B.A. (with honors). *Home:* Little Adam Farm, Frieth, Henley-on-Thames, Oxfordshire, England.

CAREER: Film producer and director, 1929—. Director of films, including "Windmill in Barbados," Empire Marketing Board, 1930; "O'er Hill and Dale," Empire Marketing Board, 1931; "The Country Comes to Town," Empire Marketing Board, 1932; "Cargo From Jamaica," Empire Marketing Board, 1933; "Liner Cruising South," Empire Marketing Board, 1933; "Song of Ceylon," 1935; "Night Mail," GPO Film Unit, 1936; "6:30 Collection," 1936; "Children at School," Realist Film Unit, 1937; "The Face of Scotland," 1938; "Evacuation," 1939; "The Battle for Freedom," 1942; "This Was Japan," 1945; "Southern Rhodesia," 1945; "The Story of Omolo," 1946; "Bernard Miles on Gun Dogs," 1948; "Waters of Time," 1951; "World Without End," UNESCO, 1953; "The Stained Glass at Fairford," 1956; "The Immortal Land," 1957; "Greek Sculpture," 1959; "A Place for Gold," 1960. Producer of films, including "The Immortal Land," "Greek Sculpture," "Waters of Time," "A Place for Gold," "Song of Ceylon," "This Was Japan," "The Story of Omolo," and "The Stained Glass at Fairford." Visiting lecturer at University of California, Los Angeles, 1962, 1968; senior lecturer at National Film School, 1971-73; visiting professor at Temple University, 1977-78. Worked with Empire Marketing Board Film Unit, 1929-31; founder of Realist Film Unit, 1937, and International Realist Ltd., 1953; executive producer of Film Centre Ltd., 1939-44; producer in charge of Crown Film Unit, 1945. Adviser to director of Ministry of Information, 1946. Member

of board of governors of Bryanston School, 1949—, and British Film Institute, 1953; member of council of Royal College of Art, 1954-57. Consultant to Canadian Government.

MEMBER: Savile Club. *Awards, honors:* Gold medal and government prize from Brussels Film Festival, 1935, for "Song of Ceylon"; fellow of British Film Academy, 1955; award from Council of Europe, 1959, for "The Immortal Land"; gold cross of Royal Order of King George I (Greece), 1963; guest of honor at Melbourne Film Festival, 1975-76.

WRITINGS: The Use of the Film, Bodley Head, 1948, Arno, 1972; (contributor) Arthur Calder-Marshall, *The Innocent Eye: The Life of Robert J. Flaherty,* W. H. Allen, 1963, Harcourt, 1966; *The Long View,* Knopf, 1974, new edition, Paladin, 1976.

BIOGRAPHICAL/CRITICAL SOURCES: G. Roy Levin, *Documentary Explorers,* Doubleday, 1971.*

*   *   *

WRIGHT, Herbert Curtis 1928-

PERSONAL: Born February 16, 1928, in Salt Lake City, Utah; son of Herbert Emil and Frances Minerva (Curtis) Wright; married Jeannene Dowding (a medical business manager), June 28, 1957; children: David, Newell, Tracy, Gordon, Bryan. *Education:* Brigham Young University, earned B.A., M.A., 1955; University of Southern California, M.S. in L.S., 1959; Case Western Reserve University, earned M.A., Ph.D., 1969. *Politics:* Conservative. *Religion:* Church of Jesus Christ of Latter-day Saints (Mormons). *Home:* 936 North 800 E., Orem, Utah 84057.

CAREER: Brigham Young University, Provo, Utah, cataloger, 1959-65, professor of library and information science, 1969—. *Military service:* U.S. Navy, 1946-48; became airman first class. *Member:* Association of American Library Schools, Society of Educators and Scholars, Utah Library Association.

WRITINGS: (Contributor) Conrad H. Rawski, editor, *Toward a Theory of Librarianship: Papers in Honor of Jesse Hauk Shera,* Scarecrow, 1973; *The Oral Antecedents of Greek Librarianship,* Brigham Young University Press, 1978. Contributor to *American Library Association World Encyclopedia of Library and Information Services.* Contributor of more than twenty articles to library and education journals.

WORK IN PROGRESS: A book on metallic epigraphy.

SIDELIGHTS: Wright told *CA:* "I am interested in developing the humanistic approach to librarianship and information science in order to propose an alternative to systems theory, which currently dominates both of these fields."

*   *   *

WRIGHT, Rebecca 1942-

PERSONAL: Born August 25, 1942, in Chicago, Ill.; daughter of Charles Milton (a plant pathologist) and Jeannette (a microbiologist; maiden name, Burns) Wright; children: Turan. *Education:* Attended Drury College, 1960-61, and University of Missouri, 1962-63. *Home address:* Route 1, Bald Hill Rd., Jefferson City, Mo. 65101.

CAREER: University of Missouri, Columbia, laboratory assistant in plant microbiology, 1961-63; Clinical Laboratories, St. Louis, Mo., laboratory assistant, 1963-65; Analysts, Inc., Oakland, Calif., laboratory assistant, 1966-67; Merck Institute for Therapeutic Research, Rahway, N.J., research technician, 1967-69; New York Blood Center, New York, N.Y., research assistant, 1973-74; University of Missouri Medical Center, research technician in physiology, 1974-76; Missouri Department of Agriculture, Jefferson City, microbiologist, 1976—.

WRITINGS—Poetry: *Elusive Continent,* Telephone Books, 1972; *Brief Lives,* Ants Forefoot, 1974; *Ciao, Manhattan,* Telephone Books, 1977.

WORK IN PROGRESS: Poems.

* * *

WUERPEL, Charles E(dward) 1906-

PERSONAL—Home: Quinta de Palmeira Encantada, Vale de Eguas, Almansil, Argarve, Portugal.

CAREER: New York University, New York City, adjunct professor at graduate school, 1945-47, technical director, 1948-56; Marquette Cement Manufacturing Co., Nashville, Tenn., vice-president, 1956-59, administrative vice-president, 1959-64, vice-president for operations and engineering, beginning in 1964; writer. Visiting lecturer at Harvard University, 1944-47.

WRITINGS: *The Algarve, Province of Portugal: Europe's South-West Corner,* David & Charles, 1974.*

* * *

WYATT, John 1925-
(John Parker)

PERSONAL: Born January 16, 1925, in England; son of Charles (a factory overlooker) and Grace Alexandra (Parker) Wyatt; married wife, Jose Mary (divorced); married Anne Rosemary Lowings, July, 1975; children: (first marriage) Martin, June Wyatt Lamb. *Education:* Attended Ruskin College, Oxford. *Home:* Eelhouse Cottage, Graythwaite, via Ulverston, Cumbria LA12 8BE, England. *Office:* Ranger's Office, Lake District National Park, Bank House, High St., Windermere, Cumbria, England.

CAREER: Lake District National Park, Windermere, England, chief ranger, 1960—. *Military service:* Royal Navy, 1942-46. *Member:* Society of Authors.

WRITINGS—All under pseudonym John Parker, except as noted: *Lake District Walks,* three volumes, F. Warne, 1971-73; (under name John Wyatt) *The Shining Levels,* Bles, 1973, Lippincott, 1974; *Cumbria,* John Bartholomew & Son, 1977; *The Observer's Book of the Lake District,* F. Warne, 1978; *Reflections on the Lakes,* W. H. Allen, 1980. Author of radio and television scripts. Contributor to national magazines and newspapers.

SIDELIGHTS: Wyatt told CA: "I have an obsessive but unsentimental and professional interest in trees, landscapes, wilderness, wild creatures, and conservation. I am worried about technology running wild, the craving of the Western world for better and better standards of living, and cynical utilitarian thinking. I like the simple life with no complications.

"Lecturing comes easy, particularly when I can promote immediate audience response. Writing often comes hard."

* * *

WYDEN, Peter H. 1923-

PERSONAL: Born October 2, 1923, in Berlin, Germany; came to the United States in 1937, naturalized citizen, 1943; son of Erich W. and Helen (Silberstein) Weidenreich; married Edith Rosenow, May 10, 1947 (divorced, 1961); married Barbara Woodman (a writer), July 6, 1961; children: (first marriage) Ronald Lee, Jeffrey Alan. *Home:* 17 East 89th St., New York, N.Y. 10028. *Office:* 747 Third Ave., New York, N.Y. 10017.

CAREER: *Daily Metal Reporter,* New York City, reporter, 1942-43; *Wichita Eagle,* Wichita, Kan., reporter, 1947-49; *St. Louis Post-Dispatch,* St. Louis, Mo., feature writer, 1949-54; *Newsweek,* New York City, correspondent in Washington, D.C., 1954-59; *Saturday Evening Post,* Indianapolis, Ind., served as associate editor, contributing editor, and correspondent in Chicago, Ill., and San Francisco, Calif., 1959-62; *McCall's,* New York City, senior editor, 1962-65; *Ladies' Home Journal,* New York City, executive editor, 1965-69; Peter H. Wyden, Inc. (book publisher), New York City, president, 1969—. Lecturer. *Military service:* U.S. Army; served in European theater.

WRITINGS: *Suburbia's Coddled Kids,* Doubleday, 1962; *The Hired Killers* (introductions by Karl Menninger and Estes Kefauver), Morrow, 1963; *The Overweight Society: An Authoritative, Entertaining Investigation Into the Facts and Follies of Girth Control,* Morrow, 1965; (with wife, Barbara Wyden) *Growing up Straight: What Every Thoughtful Parent Should Know About Homosexuality* (Literary Guild alternate selection), Stein & Day, 1968; (with B. Wyden) *How the Doctors Diet,* Trident, 1968; (with George Robert Bach) *The Intimate Enemy: How to Fight Fair in Love and Marriage,* Morrow, 1969; (with Lois Libien) *The All-in-One Diet Manual,* Bantam, 1970; (with B. Wyden) *Inside the Sex Clinic,* World Publishing, 1971; *Bay of Pigs: The Untold Story,* Simon & Schuster, 1979. Contributor to magazines.

BIOGRAPHICAL/CRITICAL SOURCES: *New York Times Book Review,* April 11, 1965, September 22, 1968, June 10, 1969; *Book World,* August 18, 1968, February 16, 1969; *Publishers' Weekly,* February 10, 1969; *Christian Science Monitor,* July 9, 1979; *Time,* July 9, 1979; *New Yorker,* August 20, 1979; *Saturday Review,* September 1, 1979.*

* * *

WYLIE, Betty Jane

PERSONAL: Born in Winnipeg, Manitoba, Canada; daughter of Jack (a physician) and Inga (Tergesen) McKenty; married William Tennent Wylie, June 7, 1952 (deceased); children: Elizabeth, Catherine, John, Matthew. *Education:* University of Manitoba, B.A. (with honors), 1951, M.A., 1952. *Politics:* Conservative. *Religion:* United Church of Canada. *Residence:* Toronto, Ontario, Canada. *Agent:* Nancy Colbert, 303 Davenport Rd., Toronto, Ontario, Canada M5R 1K5.

CAREER: Free-lance writer, 1952—. Presented "Betty Jane's Diary," a daily radio program, syndicated by Berkeley Studio of United Church of Canada. Member of board of directors of Junior League of Winnipeg, Art Gallery of Stratford, and Community Contacts for the Widowed; consultant to Puppeteers of America. *Member:* Canadian Association of Publishers, Authors, and Composers, Periodical Writers Association, Playwrights Canada, Guild of Canadian Playwrights (chairman of Ontario region, 1979-81), Association of Canadian Television and Radio Artists, Heliconian Society, Dramatists Guild. *Awards, honors:* Icelandic Canadian Poetry Prize from Icelandic Canadian Poetry Association, 1974.

WRITINGS: *The Clear Spirit* (biography), University of Toronto Press, 1966; *Beginnings: A Book for Widows,* McClelland & Stewart, 1977, 4th edition, 1980; *Encore: The Leftovers Cookbook,* McClelland & Stewart, 1979; *No Two Alike* (a collection of interviews), Image Press, 1981; *Betty Jane's Diary: Lessons Children Taught Me,* Image Press, 1981.

Published plays: *The Old Woman and the Pedlar/Kingsayer* (contains "Kingsayer," a one-act play for children, first produced in Winnipeg, Manitoba, at Manitoba Theatre Centre, November, 1967, and "The Old Woman and the Pedlar," a one-act play for children, first produced in Toronto, Ontario, at Young People's Theatre, September, 1977), Playwrights Canada, 1978; *Mark* (two-act; first produced in Stratford, Ontario, at Stratford Festival Theatre, July, 1972), Playwrights Canada, 1979; *Don't Just Stand There—Jiggle!* (puppet plays), Black Moss Press, 1980; *The Horsburgh Scandal: The Man and the Play,* Black Press, 1981.

Plays: "An Enemy of the People" (three-act adaptation of play by Ibsen), first produced in Winnipeg at Manitoba Theatre Centre, December, 1962; "George Dandin" (two-act musical adaptation of play by Moliere), first produced at Manitoba Theatre Centre, May, 1964; "I See You, I See You" (one-act), first produced at Stratford Festival Theatre, August, 1970; "The Horsburgh Scandal" (two-act), first produced in Toronto at Theatre Passe Muraille, March, 1976; "Size Ten" (two-act), first produced in Waterloo, Iowa, at Waterloo Playhouse, May, 1976; "Beowulf" (two-act rock opera), first produced in New York, N.Y., at AMAS Repertory Theater, December, 1977; "Soap Bubbles" (two-act musical, based on her newspaper soap opera serial), first produced in Gravenhurst, Ontario, at Muskoka Summer Theatre, August, 1979; (co-author) "Double Swap" (two-act comedy), first produced in Gravenhurst at Gravenhurst Opera House, March, 1979; "Blind Spot" (one-act), first produced in Vancouver, British Columbia, at New Play Centre, August, 1979.

Unproduced plays: "A Place on Earth" (one-act); "Second Shepherd's Play" (one-act musical adaptation).

Author of "Summer Soap," a daily column on soap operas in *Toronto Star,* 1979. Contributor of articles and poems to magazines, including *Maclean's, Canadian Forum, Fiddlehead, Westworld, Performing Arts,* and *Quest,* and newspapers.

WORK IN PROGRESS: "Boy in a Cage," an opera, for Co-Opera Theatre; "A Very Special Person," with Beth Palmer, a play based on the life of Emily Murphy, for Alberta Theatre Projects workshop at New Play Centre, Vancouver, British Columbia.

SIDELIGHTS: Betty Wylie commented: "I consider myself primarily a playwright, and do all my other writing to support my habit. I am what you might call eclectic. I have had a modest success in a number of different media, but with a low profile, such that I call myself a very prolific unknown. Just as well—I'm afraid of typecasting. The idea comes first, then the form. There is a through-line, of course. I am my common denominator. The book *Beginnings,* about widowhood, and my children's play, 'The Old Woman and the Pedlar,' both ask the same question, in different forms: 'Who am I?' and 'Where am I going?'"

*　　*　　*

WYLIE, Elinor (Morton Hoyt)　1885-1928

BRIEF ENTRY: Born September 7, 1885, in Somerville, N.J.; died of a stroke, December 16, 1928, in New York, N.Y.; buried at Woodlawn Cemetery. American poet and novelist. In her first major book of poems, *Nets to Catch the Wind* (1921), Wylie impressed critics with her technical skill and attracted many readers with her delicate verse. Her popularity was enhanced by poems of satire or fantasy appearing in *Saturday Review of Literature.* She also wrote novels, including *The Orphan Angel* (1926), most of which were colorful fan-

tasies. Several of her other novels such as *The Venetian Glass Nephew* (1925) and *Mr. Hodge and Mr. Hazard* (1928) required extensive historical research. Wylie married three times, and although her actions were viewed as public scandals by upper-class society, she was much admired for her well-crafted writings. Wylie's last works include the acclaimed sonnet sequence "One Person" (1928). *Biographical/critical sources: Twentieth Century Authors: A Biographical Dictionary of Modern Literature,* H. W. Wilson, 1942; *Cyclopedia of World Authors,* Harper, 1958; *Notable American Women, 1607-1950: A Biographical Dictionary,* Belknap Press, 1971.

*　　*　　*

WYMER, Thomas L(ee)　1938-

PERSONAL: Born November 25, 1938, in Columbus, Ohio; son of Robert Lee and Edna (Wesley) Wymer; married Penny Ray Anthis (in sales), September 8, 1962; children: Elizabeth Ray, William Lee. *Education:* Rice University, B.A., 1960; University of Oklahoma, Ph.D., 1968. *Home:* 732 Jefferson, Bowling Green, Ohio 43402. *Office:* Department of English, Bowling Green University, Bowling Green, Ohio 43403.

CAREER: Bowling Green University, Bowling Green, Ohio, instructor, 1966-68, assistant professor, 1968-72, associate professor, 1972-80, professor of English, 1980—. *Member:* Popular Culture Association, Science Fiction Research Association, Society for Technical Communicators.

WRITINGS: (With Alice Calderonello, Lowell P. Leland, Sara Jayne Steen, and R. Michael Evers) *Intersections: The Elements of Fiction in Science Fiction,* Bowling Green Popular Press, 1978; (contributor) Thom Dunn and Richard D. Erlich, editors, *The Mechanical God: Machines in Science Fiction,* Greenwood Press, 1981; (editor with David Cowart) *Dictionary of Literary Biography,* Volume 8: *Twentieth-Century American Science Fiction Writers,* two volumes, Gale, 1981; (contributor and editor with Thomas D. Clareson) *Voices for the Future: Essays on Major Science Fiction Writers,* Volume 3, Bowling Green Popular Press, 1982. Member of editorial board of *Extrapolation,* 1976—, and *Journal of Popular Culture,* 1977—. Contributor to journals, including *Extrapolation* and *Victorian Poetry.*

SIDELIGHTS: Wymer told *CA:* "My areas of scholarly concentration include nineteenth-century British literature with special interest in the relation between poetry and painting; science fiction and other forms of popular literature, such as fantasy, the detective, and the gothic; and technical writing. Although my scholarly productivity has not been terribly high, at least compared to some, I am proud of its quality. The piece on Swinburne appeared as the lead article in a special Swinburne issue of *Victorian Poetry* and was referred to a few years later as having since become 'the most common reading of *Atalanta*' by David G. Riede in *Swinburne: A Study of Romantic Mythmaking.*

"My work in science fiction has been consistently singled out by reviewers for special praise. The Vonnegut essay was one of three articles in the collection described by *Science-Fiction Studies* as 'outstanding contributions.'

"I think a strong undergraduate preparation in philosophy, history of art, and foreign languages (French and German), in addition to the English major, has had much to do with what scholarly success I have had. A good background in math and the physical sciences also helped maintain an interest that seemed to flower when the opportunity to teach science fiction emerged in 1971. There I seem to have found the ideal vehicle in which to combine my interests in symbolic art forms, the history of ideas, and the sciences.''

AVOCATIONAL INTERESTS: Running, tennis.

BIOGRAPHICAL/CRITICAL SOURCES: David G. Riede, *Swinburne: A Study of Romantic Mythmaking,* University of Virginia Press, 1978; *Choice,* March, 1979; *Washington Post Book World,* November 29, 1981.

*   *   *

WYNNE-JONES, Tim(othy)   1948-

PERSONAL: Born August 12, 1948, in Cheshire, England; son of Sydney Thomas (an engineer) and Sheila B. (Hodgson) Wynne-Jones; married Amanda West Lewis (a director, actress, and calligrapher), September 12, 1980; children: Virgil Alexander. *Education:* University of Waterloo, B.A., 1974; York University, M.F.A., 1979. *Religion:* Anglican. *Home:* 142 Winona Dr., Toronto, Ontario M6G 3S9, Canada.

CAREER: PMA Books, Toronto, Ontario, Canada, designer, 1974-76; University of Waterloo, Walterloo, Ontario, instructor in visual arts, 1976-78; Solomon & Wynne-Jones, Toronto, graphic designer, 1976-79; York University, Downsview, Ontario, instructor in visual arts, 1978-80; writer. *Awards, honors:* First novel award from Seal Books, 1980, for *Odds End.*

WRITINGS: Odds End (novel), Little, Brown, 1980; *A Case of Bad Memories* (novel), McClelland & Stewart, 1982; *Zoom at Sea* (juvenile), PMA Books, 1982.

Radio play: ''Thinking Room,'' first broadcast by Canadian Broadcasting Corp. (CBC-Radio), 1982.

SIDELIGHTS: Wynne-Jones's novel *Odd's End* is a thriller concerning a professor and his artist wife who find themselves the target of a psychotic intruder bent on possessing their home. A reviewer for the *Detroit News* wrote, ''The prof is almost insufferably stuffy, the painter is a high-strung charmer, and the psychotic invader's monologs, heavy with baroque elegance and monstrous egoism, are vastly entertaining.''

Wynne-Jones told *CA:* ''I like to tell stories—to entertain and instruct—about ordinary people in extraordinary circumstances or extraordinary people in very ordinary circumstances. Who else is worth hearing about? As an artist I was concerned with narrative art in an age which scarcely recognizes such a retrograde animal. I turned to performing and then writing. I still paint scenes or set the stage in my writing.''

BIOGRAPHICAL/CRITICAL SOURCES: Chicago Tribune Book World, December 28, 1980; *Detroit News,* January 4, 1981.

*   *   *

WYNOT, Edward D(avis), Jr.   1943-

PERSONAL: Born May 5, 1943, in New York, N.Y.; son of Edward Davis Wynot; married, 1968; children: one. *Education:* Dartmouth College, B.A., 1965; Indiana University, M.A., 1967, Certificate in East European Studies and Ph.D., both 1970. *Office:* Department of History, Florida State University, Tallahassee, Fla. 32306.

CAREER: Florida State University, Tallahassee, began as assistant professor, 1970, became professor of history, 1978—. Project director for National Endowment for the Humanities, 1975-77. *Member:* American Historical Association, American Association for the Advancement of Slavic Studies, American Association for the Advancement of Hungarian Studies, Polish American Historical Association, Association for the Advancement of Polish Studies, Association for the Study of Nationalities (vice-president, 1977—). *Awards, honors:* Fellow of International Research and Exchanges Board, 1972-73; Fulbright-Hays grant for Poland, 1972-73.

WRITINGS: Polish Politics in Transition: The Camp of National Unity and the Struggle for Power, 1935-1939, University of Georgia Press, 1974; (co-editor) *Poland and the Coming of the Second World War,* Ohio State University Press, 1976. Contributor to history journals.*

X-Y

XAVERIA, M. Barton
See BARTON, M. Xaveria

*　　*　　*

XAVERIA, Sister
See BARTON, M. Xaveria

*　　*　　*

YAKUMO KOIZUMI
See HEARN, (Patricio) Lafcadio (Tessima Carlos)

*　　*　　*

YAN, Chiou-Shuang Jou 1934-

BRIEF ENTRY: Born October 7, 1934, in T'ai-nan, Taiwan. Economist, educator, and author. Yan has taught economics at Drexel University since 1967. His writings include *Technical Change and Investment* (Institute for Research in the Behavioral Economics and Management Sciences, Purdue University, 1966), and *Introduction to Input-Output Economics* (Holt, 1969). *Address:* Department of Economics, Drexel University, 32nd and Chestnut Sts., Philadelphia, Pa. 19104. *Biographical/critical sources: Who's Who in Consulting,* 2nd edition, Gale, 1973.

*　　*　　*

YANKELOVICH, Daniel 1924-

PERSONAL: Born December 29, 1924, in Boston, Mass.; son of Frederick and Sadie (Mostow) Yankelovich; married Hasmieg Kaboolian; children: Nicole. *Education:* Harvard University, B.A., 1946, M.A., 1950; graduate study at Sorbonne, University of Paris, 1952. *Home:* 14 East 75th St., New York, N.Y. 10022. *Agent:* International Creative Management, 40 West 57th St., New York, N.Y. 10019. *Office:* Yankelovich, Skelly, & White, Inc., 575 Madison Ave., New York, N.Y. 10021.

CAREER: Nowland & Co., New York City, vice-president and director of research, 1952-58; Yankelovich, Skelly, & White, (business and social research), New York City, president, 1958-81, chairman, 1981—. Research professor at New York University; visiting professor at New School for Social Research; member of visiting committee at Harvard University; member of board of trustees of Brown University. Co-founder and president of Public Agenda Foundation; member of board of directors of Reliance Group, Inc., Meredith Corp., Reliance Insurance Co., Work in America, Inc., Harper's Magazine Foundation, Jerusalem Committee, Roper Center, and Institute for World Order; special adviser to Aspen Institute for Humanistic Studies; member of Sloan Commission. *Member:* Council on Foreign Relations, Economic Forum.

WRITINGS: (With William Barrett) *Ego and Instinct: Psychoanalysis and the Science of Man,* Random House, 1970; *Changing Values on Campus,* Simon & Schuster, 1972; *The New Morality: A Profile of American Youth in the Seventies,* McGraw, 1974; (with Raymond Katzell) *Work, Productivity, and Job Satisfaction,* Harcourt, 1975; *New Rules: Searching for Self-Fulfillment in a World Turned Upside Down,* Random House, 1981.

SIDELIGHTS: Yankelovich is renowned for his analysis of contemporary American culture. In *Ego and Instinct,* co-written with William Barrett, Yankelovich called for a merging of psychoanalysis with modern philosophy that would redeem humanity's quest for self-identity. The authors contended that a revision in the sciences would enable humanity to overcome the metaphysical dilemma of qualifying its own existance. *Nation's* Ronald Sampson objected to the new role for science proposed in *Ego and Instinct.* "The book is a brave and welcome expose of the fallacies of scientific materialism," he acknowledged; "it is important too for its sympathetic insight into the process of human psychic change. But the authors fail to see that the enterprise of a 'science' of man as a basis for successful social engineering is misconceived." A reviewer for *Choice* noted, "Some basic problems in both the philosophy of science and in psychoanalysis are brought out uniquely, as are some intriguing concepts about an approach to a revised metapsychology for psychoanalysis."

In *New Rules: Searching for Self-Fulfillment in a World Turned Upside Down,* Yankelovich deals with the evolution of American values in the 1970's. Using information culled from polls and interviews, Yankelovich charges that the "priority of the self" is shifting from self-satisfaction towards self-expression. He calls the new value an "ethic of commitment" and indicates that the evolving change in values may result in Americans accomplishing "what no other society has done: create a civilization that is economically viable, politically stable, sociologically integrated, and also open to the full promise of individual life."

The *New York Times*'s Christopher Lehmann-Haupt declared that "'New Rules' provides a lucid overview of what has been happening in this country during the last few decades. And just to understand Mr. Yankelovich's perspective is bound to produce some small measure of change in our search to fulfill the ever-elusive self.''

BIOGRAPHICAL/CRITICAL SOURCES: Nation, May 11, 1970; *Choice*, October, 1970; *Saturday Review*, June, 1981; *Washington Post Book World*, July 5, 1981; *New York Times Book Review*, July 12, 1981; *New York Times*, July 15, 1981; *Time*, August 3, 1981; *Newsweek*, August 10, 1981.

*   *   *

YARBROUGH, Camille

BRIEF ENTRY: Born in Chicago, Ill. American actress, singer, and poet. Yarbrough's acting credits include the national tour of "To Be Young, Gifted, and Black," the film, "Shaft," and the television program, "Caught in the Middle." She taught dancing at Southern Illinois's Performing Arts Training Center and has toured South America as a singer. Yarbrough wrote a nonfiction work for children, *Cornrows* (Coward, 1979), and recorded "The Iron Pot Cooker" (Vanguard Records, 1975). *Address:* c/o Moat Co., 163 West 79th St., New York, N.Y. 10024.

*   *   *

YARDE, Jeanne Betty Frances Treasure 1925- (Joan Hunter, Jeanne Montague)

PERSONAL: Born October 17, 1925, in Bath, England; daughter of Louis (a musician) and Winifred (a musician; maiden name, Smaggasgale) Field; married Graham Herbert Treasure (a studio manager), August 14, 1943 (divorced July, 1976); married Hank Yarde, December 23, 1981; children: (first marriage) Anthony, Vanessa Treasure Gordan, Louise, Bruce. *Education:* Attended Bath College of Art. *Politics:* Conservative. *Religion:* "Christened Church of England but follow the Old Religion." *Home and office:* 23 Vicarage St., Warminster, Wiltshire, England. *Agent:* David Higham Associates Ltd., 5-8 Lower John St., Golden Sq., London W1R 4HA, England.

CAREER: Associated with Citizen House (theatrical costumers), Bath, England, 1941-42 and 1945-47; writer, 1970—.

WRITINGS—All historical romances; under pseudonym Joan Hunter; *Courtney's Wench*, R. Hale, 1973, published as *Roxanna*, Pocket Books, 1975; *The Falcon and the Dove*, R. Hale, 1974, published as *Under the Raging Moon*, Pocket Books, 1975; *Rupert the Devil*, R. Hale, 1976, published as *Cavalier's Woman* (bound with *Cavalier*), Pocket Books, 1977; *Cavalier*, R. Hale, 1977; *The Lord of Kestle Mount*, Pocket Books, 1979.

Under pseudonym Jeanne Montague: *Touch Me With Fire*, Macdonald Futura, 1981; *Flower of My Heart*, Macdonald Futura, 1981; *So Cruel My Love*, Macdonald Futura, 1982.

WORK IN PROGRESS: Slave of My Desire, under pseudonym Jeanne Montague, for Macdonald Futura; another modern romance.

SIDELIGHTS: Jeanne Treasure Yarde wrote: "I was born of musical parents and, being the only child, had much care and attention lavished on me. I wanted to be an opera singer, but World War II prevented this.

"The atmosphere of the beautiful old city of Bath and the fact that both my parents loved historical novels and read them to me, developed my taste for this form of literature. I started

writing as early as ten years old, but was torn between my love of painting and my desires to sing and write.

"Being a highly romantic and somewhat solitary child, I fell in love early—too early, in fact, and was married by the time I was seventeen. My husband was an artist, but trouble soon started as he is a Virgo of a very conventional, Methodist background, whereas I am a Libra from a liberal, musical, theatrical family. The two just did not jell.

"I had never entirely given up writing and, in 1970, I sold my first romantic historical novel. I carried on against many difficulties. When I left my husband I lived for a year with my widowed mother in Bath. I was joined by my daughter Vanessa and her small daughter. She too had just finished a relationship. Together we bought our present home in Warminster. This is an eighteenth-century house, very old and interesting.

"I write all the time to make a living and it is very hard going. I did reasonably well from my early books, then wrote two which I cannot sell: *The Hour of the Wolf*, a long historical novel which I know is the best thing I have yet done, and a horror/ghost story set in modern times called *Hellspawn*. Unfortunately these do not conform to the genre demanded by today's publishers, so for two years we have been living in very straitened circumstances, literally starving at times. There is no money, and recession has not helped.

"Finally in 1980 I landed a contract from Macdonald Futura for their new series, 'Minstrel,' all highly romantic, sexy, historical romances.

"We live in a somewhat chaotic and unconventional way here, with many friends calling in, lots of music, and a great deal of fun despite the creditors at the door. We have no cars or transport. We struggle, but I'm sure we shall get there in the end."

AVOCATIONAL INTERESTS: Watching television, plays and films, operas and concerts, the occult (astrology, the tarot, ghosts, unidentified flying objects), music (the romantic composers).

*   *   *

YARROW, Marian J(eanette Radke) 1918-

BRIEF ENTRY: Born in 1918 in Horicon, Wis. American psychologist, educator, and author. Since 1953 Yarrow has been a research psychologist at the National Institute of Mental Health. She has also taught psychology at Massachusetts Institute of Technology, Queens College of the City University of New York, and University of Denver. Her books include *The Relation of Parental Authority to Children's Behavior and Attitudes* (University of Minnesota Press, 1946), *Human Aging: Biological and Behavioral Aspects* (U.S. Government Printing Office, 1963), *Child Rearing: An Inquiry Into Research and Methods* (Jossey-Bass, 1968), and *Recollections of Childhood: A Study of the Retrospective Method* (University of Chicago Press, 1970). *Address:* 7401 Nevis Rd., Bethesda, Md. 20014; and National Institute of Mental Health, 9000 Rockville Pike, Bethesda, Md. 20014. *Biographical/critical sources: American Men and Women of Science*, 14th edition, Bowker, 1979.

*   *   *

YATES, Frances A(melia) 1899-1981

OBITUARY NOTICE—See index for *CA* sketch: Born November 28, 1899, in Portsmouth, England; died in 1981 in England. Historian, educator, and author of books on the Renaissance, including *Theatre of the World* and *The Rosicrucian Enlight-*

enment. Yates was awarded the Wolfson Prize for historical writing in 1973. Obituaries and other sources: *Listener,* January 18, 1973; *AB Bookman's Weekly,* November 2, 1981.

* * *

YOUNG, Bertram Alfred 1912-

PERSONAL: Born January 20, 1912, in London, England; son of Bertram William and Dora Elizabeth (Knight) Young. *Education:* Attended private boys' school in London, England. *Politics:* "Neutral." *Religion:* Church of England. *Home:* Clyde House, Station St., Cheltenham GL50 3LX, England. *Agent:* John Farquharson Ltd., Bell House, 8 Bell Yard, London WC2A 2JU, England.

CAREER: Free-lance writer, 1930-39; *Punch,* London, England, assistant editor, 1949-63, drama critic, 1963-64; *Financial Times,* London, arts editor, 1964-77, drama critic, 1964—, radio critic, 1981—. Member of British Council drama advisory committee. *Military service:* British Army, 1939-48. *Member:* Garrick Club. *Awards, honors:* Officer of Order of the British Empire, 1980.

WRITINGS: Tooth and Claw (humor), Elek, 1958; *How to Avoid People* (humor), Muller, 1963; *Bechuanaland,* H.M.S.O., 1966; *Cabinet Pudding* (novel), Hamish Hamilton, 1967; *The Colonists From Space* (novel), William Kimber, 1979.

Radio plays; all first broadcast by British Broadcasting Corp. in London, England: "Death of Uncle George," 1939; "The Last Dart," 1939; "Birthday Present for Connie," 1939; "The Pistol," 1947; "The Happy Hostage," 1947; "Actaeon," 1948; "The Background," 1948; "Black Magic," 1948; "The Wide Boys," 1948; "A Present From Grandpa," 1949; "Pictures," 1949; "Ragnhild," 1949; "An Act of God," 1949; "Come to the Stolen Waters," 1949; "Cloud of Witnesses," 1950; "Repent at Leisure," 1951; "Pride," 1952; "Why Do the Nations?," 1952.

SIDELIGHTS: Bertram Young commented: "I began work originally for a magazine publisher, the Amalgamated Press, London, but left owing to illness. This is when I first began creative writing, both prose (journalism and an unpublished novel) and light verse. Writing was halted by the war after 1939 but began again about 1947, beginning with radio drama, which I had started in 1939. I found humorous writing for *Punch* easy and was invited to join the staff. Theatre criticism came later. I have a strong belief that the ability to write Latin prose at school was the chief influence on my English style."

* * *

YOUNG, Delbert Alton 1907-1975

PERSONAL: Born November 26, 1907, in Chalk River, Ontario, Canada; died January, 1975; married Phyllis Collier, 1946. *Education:* Received teaching certificate from normal school.

CAREER: Writer. Worked as a teacher for one year, as a farmer for seventeen years, and as a carpenter and builder, 1949-56. Also held numerous other jobs, including miner, railroad worker, and construction worker. *Military service:* Served in the Canadian Militia during World War II.

WRITINGS: Mutiny on Hudson: A Story About the Last Voyage of Henry Hudson (juvenile; illustrated by Doug Sneyd), Gage, 1963; *The Mounties* (nonfiction), Hodder & Stoughton, 1968; *Last Voyage of the Unicorn* (juvenile; illustrated by Mary Cserepy), Clarke, Irwin, 1969; *The Ghost Ship* (juvenile; illustrated

by William Taylor), Clarke, Irwin, 1972; *According to Hakluyt: Tales of Adventure and Exploration,* Clarke, Irwin, 1973.

SIDELIGHTS: Delbert Young was particularly interested in seafaring in the sixteenth century, and nearly all his books are set during this period. His novels are noted for their historical accuracy and deft characterizations.*

* * *

YOUNG, Mary Elizabeth Reardon 1901(?)-1981 (Mary Haworth)

OBITUARY NOTICE: Born c. 1901 in Riverside, Ohio; died of cancer, November 1, 1981, in Alexandria, Va. Journalist. Under the pseudonym Mary Haworth, Mary Elizabeth Young wrote a popular advice column for the *Washington Post* for more than thirty years. The column, which was originally entitled "This Business of Living," became "Mary Haworth's Mail" in 1936. Its author enjoyed national syndication in hundreds of newspapers. Obituaries and other sources: *Who's Who in America,* 40th edition, Marquis, 1978; *Washington Post,* November 2, 1981; *Chicago Tribune,* November 3, 1981.

* * *

YOUNG, Stark 1881-1963

PERSONAL: Born October 11, 1881, in Como, Miss.; died January 6, 1963, in New York, N.Y.; son of Alfred Alexander and Mary (Stark) Young. *Education:* University of Mississippi, B.A., 1901; Columbia University, M.A., 1902. *Residence:* New York, N.Y.

CAREER: University of Mississippi, University, instructor in English, 1904-07; University of Texas, Main University (now University of Texas at Austin), instructor, 1907-10, professor of English, 1910-15; Amherst College, Amherst, Mass., professor of English, 1915-21; *New Republic,* Washington, D.C., member of editorial staff and drama critic, 1921-24; *Theatre Arts Monthly,* New York City, associate editor, 1921-40; *New York Times,* New York City, drama critic, 1924-25; *New Republic,* Washington, D.C., member of editorial staff and drama critic, 1925-47. Director of plays, including Henri Rene Lenormand's "The Failures" and Eugene O'Neill's "Welded," in New York City, 1923-24. George Westinghouse Foundation Lecturer in Italy, 1931. Exhibited paintings in New York City art galleries. *Member:* Phi Beta Kappa, Sigma Chi, Sigma Upsilon, Curtain Club of the University of Texas (founder). *Awards, honors—*Military: Commander, Order of the Crown of Italy.

*WRITINGS—*Plays: *Guenevere* (five-act), Grafton Press, 1906; *Addio, Madretta, and Other Plays* (contains "Addio," "Madretta," "The Dead Poet," "The Star in the Trees," "The Seven Kings and the Wind," "The Queen of Sheba" [also see below], "The Twilight Saint" [also see below]), C. S. Sergel, 1912, Core Collection, 1976; *At the Shrine* (one-act; also see below), Theatre Arts, 1919; *Three One-Act Plays* (contains "Addio," "Madretta," and "At the Shrine"), Stewart Kidd, 1921; *The Queen of Sheba* (one-act; also see below), Theatre Arts, 1922; *The Colonnade,* Theatre Arts, 1924; *The Saint* (four-act), Boni & Liveright, 1925; *The Twilight Saint* (one-act), Samuel French, 1925; *Sweet Times and the Blue Policeman* (juvenile) Holt, 1925; "The King With the Iron Heart," published in *Another Treasury of Plays for Children,* edited by Montrose J. Moses, Little, Brown, 1926; "Rose Windows" and "The Queen of Sheba," published in *Plays of American Life and Fantasy,* edited by Edith J. Isaacs, Coward, 1929; *Artemis* (three-act), Von Boeckmann-Jones, 1942.

Criticism: *The Flower in Drama: A Book of Papers on the Theatre,* Scribner, 1923, also published with *Glamour: Essays on the Art of the Theatre* (also see below); *Glamour: Essays on the Art of the Theatre,* Scribner, 1925, Books for Libraries, 1971, facsimile edition, Arno, 1974, also published with *The Flower in Drama: A Book of Papers on the Theatre* (also see below); *Theatre Practice,* Scribner, 1926; *Encuastics,* New Republic Books, 1926, facsimile edition, Arno, 1975; *The Theatre,* Doran, 1927, Hill & Wang, 1954, Octagon, 1980; *Maurice Sterne, Retrospective Exhibition,* New Republic Books, 1933; *Immortal Shadows: A Book of Dramatic Criticism,* Scribner, 1948, Hill & Wang, 1959, Octagon, 1973; *The Flower in Drama and Glamour: Theatre Essays and Criticism,* Scribner, 1955, revised edition, Octagon, 1973.

Novels: *Heaven Trees,* Scribner, 1926; *The Torches Flare,* Scribner, 1928; *The River House,* Scribner, 1929; *So Red the Rose,* Scribner, 1934, revised edition, with introduction by Donald Davidson, 1953, Popular Library, 1963, Mockingbird Books, 1975, Larlin, 1978.

Other: *The Blind Man at the Window and Other Poems,* Grafton Press, 1906; *The Three Fountains* (travel sketches), Scribner, 1924; *The Street of the Islands* (short stories), Scribner, 1930; (contributor) *I'll Take My Stand: The South and the Agrarian Tradition; by Twelve Southerners,* Harper, 1930; *Feliciana* (short stories), Scribner, 1935; *The Pavilion: Of People and Times Remembered, of Stories and Places* (memoirs), Scribner, 1951, Augustus Kelley, 1974.

Translator: Jean Francois Regnard, *The Sole Heir,* University of Texas, Main University, 1912; Moliere, *George Dandin,* Theatre Arts, 1925; Machiavelli, *Mandragola,* Macaulay, 1927; Anton Chekhov, *The Sea Gull,* Scribner, 1939; Chekhov, *The Three Sisters,* Samuel French, 1941; Chekhov, *The Cherry Orchard,* Samuel French, 1947.

Editor: *The English Humorists of the Eighteenth Century,* Ginn, 1911; (with Rollo L. Lyman, Nell E. Moore, and Howard C. Hill) *A Southern Treasury of Life and Literature,* Scribner, 1937; (and author of preface) Sidney Lanier, *Selected Poems,* Scribner, 1947. Also editor of *The Best Plays by Chevkov,* 1956.

Contributor to magazines and periodicals, including the *Fugitive.*

SIDELIGHTS: Stark Young is best remembered for his Civil War novel *So Red the Rose,* and for his theatrical criticism, which appeared in the *New Republic* for twenty-six years. But his earliest literary ties were with a group of Southerners known as the Agrarians or the Fugitives. Consisting mainly of teachers and students devoted to writing and discussing poetry, the group formed shortly after World War I and included such notable figures as John Crowe Ransom, Allen Tate, and Robert Penn Warren. The Fugitives espoused both political and aesthetic theories that emphasized the preservation of tradition, particularly southern tradition, within modern society. The group's members contributed articles to magazines, including the *Fugitive, Southern Review, Kenyon Review,* and *Sewanee Review.* They also produced an anthology, *I'll Take My Stand: The South and the Agrarian Tradition.*

Young wrote frequently for the *Fugitive* and he contributed an essay, "Not in Memoriam but in Defense," to *I'll Take My Stand.* "Young is aware," commented Abbott Martin in 1930, "that the ideals and tendencies of our time seem to move in opposition to certain instincts or principles that are deeply rooted in the southern character." He sought to reconcile the Old South with the New, and he advocated, especially in his poetry and his fiction, "a clearer understanding of the Old South, a fairer evaluation of the forces at work, a truer perception of what was good in it, and a perpetuation of this good in the New."

Much of Young's fiction is set in the South, including his novel *River House,* which, according to Stringfellow Barr of the *Virginia Quarterly Review,* "is a backward glance at a dying culture submerged and overwhelmed not merely by America but by its own Americanized youth." The stories in Young's *Feliciana* and his *So Red the Rose,* which concerns the effects of the Civil War on a small group of Southerners, are similarly set in the South. *So Red the Rose* is, wrote Mary McCarthy in the *Nation,* "not truly a history or a novel, but a poem of glorification."

Stark Young wrote realistically of the Old South, commented Emily Clark in the *Virginia Quarterly Review.* In *Feliciana,* for example, he recreated "the dialect that all Southerners have known." By reproducing the flavor of southern conversation, he captured "the emotional capacity, the gift for feeling . . . , which the people beyond the Far South do not often share in a like degree." Though Young has been occasionally criticized for romanticizing the South, Clark maintained that "Young is the more realistic because he admits romance as an essential element of life."

Among those who have written about Young's critical work is Eric Bentley, who noted that "Young is not an aggressive critic. The most exciting passages in his work are passages of sheer appreciation." According to Bentley, Young's criticism displays an "unusual capacity for joy, a capacity that has its source in love. I do not mean Love as a Solvent, or anything religious, and certainly not sex. I mean a passionate, spontaneous 'being taken with' whatever deserves to be loved in nature and art and people, a spiritual eagerness, and receptiveness, and fullness." Also, Bentley wrote, "he *reads* plays, and can thus, unlike his Broadway colleagues, distinguish between play and performance. When the effort seems justified, he reads also the source of a play."

Montrose J. Moses, reviewing *The Flower in Drama* for *Outlook,* called the work a "creative criticism" marked by "calmness of judgment." In her review of *Theatre Practice* for *Theatre Arts,* Rosamond Gilder found that in Young's discussions of such aspects of the theatre as acting, directing, and costuming, "not only does he see the point, but he makes it luminously clear and inevitable." John Mason Brown, reviewing *Glamour* for *Theatre Arts,* explained Young's ability to seize upon the essentials of acting "with such an uncanny comprehension of the actor's problems and the actor's art, and . . . [to write] of them in a style at once so glamourous, revealing and precise, that the volume is lifted to that lean shelf reserved for the few permanently contributive books on the theatre."

The precision of Young's theatrical criticism, his discussion of the details of a play and of those elements that lead to artistic success or failure, are what connect him to the New Criticism, a school of thought that dominated American literary criticism during the 1930's and 1940's. The New Critics, who included such Agrarians as Tate and Ransom as well as influential writers like Kenneth Burke, R. P. Blackmur, and Edmund Wilson, sought an aesthetic approach to literature. They developed modes of formal analysis for evaluating literary quality that focused on elements such as style, form, and structure. Their purpose, derived from the work of poet T. S. Eliot, was to free literary appreciation from the limitations of such approaches as sociological and biographical criticism and, in so doing, make the experience of literature at once intellectual and emotional.

Young's critical writing is an attempt "to come closer than criticism usually does to the definition of our responses to works of art,'' observed Bentley. In each review, Young describes the particular theatrical event ''simply, yet as one civilized person to another, what it looked like, how it unfolded, what is essential to it, what considerations it leads to outside itself, what its achievement is as a script, a stage design, as acting, as a whole.'' The *New Republic* credited Young with initiating, ''almost singlehandedly, a tradition of serious American theater journalism which set the highest standards of style, sensibility and judgment for contemporaries and for those who were to follow. Young's writings were animated by a fierce, uncompromising love of art. Confronting a fundamentally impure medium still in its puling infancy in America, he continually elbowed aside the artless and the false, to seek the shimmering and the true.''

AVOCATIONAL INTERESTS: Painting.

BIOGRAPHICAL/CRITICAL SOURCES: Outlook, May 9, 1923; *Theatre Arts Monthly,* June, 1925, September, 1926, November, 1947; *Sewanee Review,* January-March, 1930; *Southern Review,* September 7, 1930; *Virginia Quarterly Review,* volume 6, 1930, volume 10, 1934, volume 11, 1935; *Nation,* August 8, 1934; *Time,* June 14, 1943, December 13, 1948; *Nineteenth Century,* November, 1949; *Kenyon Review,* winter, 1950; *New York Herald Tribune Book Review,* September 30, 1951; *Publishers Weekly,* January 21, 1963; *New Republic,* January 26, 1963; *The Pavilion: Of People and Times Remembered, of Stories and Places,* Scribner, 1951; Louis D. Rubin, Jr., editor, *Bibliographical Guide to the Study of Southern Literature,* Louisiana State University Press, 1969; John Pilkington, editor, *Stark Young: A Life in the Arts: Letters, 1900-1962,* Louisiana State University Press, 1975.*

—*Sketch by Andrea Geffner*

Z

ZABANEH, Natalia (Shefka)   1946-

PERSONAL: Surname is accented on second syllable; born August 12, 1946, in Palestine (now Israel); daughter of Jubrail Salim and Jana (Janowska) Zabaneh; married Martin Power (a civil servant), January 23, 1975; children: Eloise Jane, John Clement. *Education:* Westfield College, London, B.A. (with honors), 1967, M.Phil., 1972, Ph.D., 1975. *Home:* 60 Revell Rd., Kingston-on-Thames, Surrey, England.

CAREER: Teacher at Tiffin Girls' School, 1972-78; writer, 1971—.

WRITINGS: Backlash (novel), W. H. Allen, 1971.

SIDELIGHTS: Natalia Zabaneh commented: "I have decided that my previous literary interest—the love between adults—is an overplowed field, and I am now more interested in the love between adults and children—their own or, to be more precise, the love I have for my children. I wander about morosely, full of prose and poetry but unable to express it until the time of feeds and happy changes is over."

*   *   *

ZACH, Nathan   1930-

BRIEF ENTRY: Born in 1930 in Berlin, Germany. Israeli poet. Zach has lived in Israel since 1935. He has been a poet since 1950 and a translator from German into Hebrew. He wrote *Against Parting* (Royal Press, 1967), *Dekalim u-temarim* (title means "Palms and Dates: Arab Folksongs"; 1967), *Shirim Shonim* (1967?), and co-edited *The Burning Bush: Poems From Modern Israel* (Allen, 1977). *Address:* c/o Institute for Translation of Hebrew Literature, 66 Shlomo Melech St., Tel Aviv, Israel.

*   *   *

ZACHER, Christian Keeler   1941-

PERSONAL: Born March 6, 1941, in St. Louis, Mo.; married, 1967; children: one. *Education:* College of the Holy Cross, B.A., 1963; University of California, Riverside, M.A., 1965, Ph.D., 1969. *Office:* Department of English, Ohio State University, Columbus, Ohio 43210.

CAREER: Ohio State University, Columbus, assistant professor, 1968-74, associate professor of English, 1974—. *Member:* Modern Language Association of America, Mediaeval Academy of America, Society for the History of Discoveries, American Association of University Professors.

WRITINGS: (Editor with Donald Roy Howard) *Critical Studies of Sir Gawain and the Green Knight,* University of Notre Dame Press, 1968; *Curiosity and Pilgrimage: The Literature of Discovery in Fourteenth-Century England,* Johns Hopkins Press, 1976.

BIOGRAPHICAL/CRITICAL SOURCES: Times Literary Supplement, March 11, 1977.*

*   *   *

ZAMIATIN, Yevgenii
See ZAMYATIN, Evgeny Ivanovich

*   *   *

ZAMYATIN, Evgeny Ivanovich   1884-1937

BRIEF ENTRY: Born February 1, 1884, in Lebedyan, Russia (now U.S.S.R.); died March 10, 1937, in Paris, France. Russian author. Zamyatin anticipated the speculative fiction of H. G. Wells and Aldous Huxley in his novel *We* (1920), which described a totalitarian future in a dehumanized society. The book was also a transparent metaphor depicting Zamyatin's disenchantment with the new Soviet state. Throughout his career Zamyatin was recognized as a master of the written word and a daring expert in the use of metaphor. In his unflattering descriptions of England, he satirized middle-class conformity. His target in "A Provincial Tale" (1911) was man's inhumanity to man. His novellas parodied the transitional period in Russian life between the czarist regime and the new Soviet one. Though he was originally a Bolshevik, Zamyatin's later writings were openly critical of Soviet excess and repression. As a result, his work was banned and his reputation attacked by the government. Through the intercession of Russian writer Maxim Gorky, Zamyatin was permitted to immigrate to France. *Biographical/critical sources: Columbia Dictionary of Modern European Literature,* Columbia University Press, 1947; *Encyclopedia of World Literature in the Twentieth Century,* updated edition, Ungar, 1967.

*   *   *

ZATURENSKA, Marya   1902-1982

OBITUARY NOTICE—See index for *CA* sketch: Born September 12, 1902, in Kiev, Russia (now U.S.S.R.); died of heart failure, January 19, 1982, in Shelburne Falls, Mass. Poet. Zaturenska, who came to the United States at the age of eight, received a Pulitzer Prize in 1938 for her volume of poetry *Cold Morning Sky*. Zaturenska wrote seven other volumes of poetry and a biography of Christina Rossetti. She also edited six anthologies, some with her husband, the poet Horace Gregory. Obituaries and other sources: *New York Times,* January 21, 1982; *AB Bookman's Weekly,* February 22, 1982.

*   *   *

ZEMANSKY, Mark W(aldo)   1900-1981

OBITUARY NOTICE: Born May 5, 1900, in New York, N.Y.; died December 29, 1981, in Teaneck, N.J. Educator and author. Mark Zemansky, professor emeritus of physics at the City College of the City University of New York, received the Oersted Medal from the American Association of Physics Teachers in 1956 for his "outstanding contributions to the teaching of physics." He was the co-author of physics textbooks, including *University Physics* and *College Physics.* Obituaries and other sources: *American Men and Women of Science,* 13th edition, Bowker, 1976; *The Writers Directory, 1976-1978,* St. Martin's, 1976; *New York Times,* January 6, 1982.

*   *   *

ZIMMER, A(rno) B.   1945-

PERSONAL: Born December 10, 1945, in Rochester, N.Y.; son of Robert Norman and Frances (Bosworth) Zimmer; children: Arno II, Bridget. *Education:* University of Connecticut, B.A. (cum laude), 1968; Georgetown University, M.A., 1976. *Home and office address:* P.O. Box 1204, Alexandria, Va. 22313.

CAREER: University of Washington, Seattle, instructor in English composition, 1968; National Resource Development Associates, Inc. (management consultants), Silver Spring, Md., president, 1969-77; Eliot-Yeats, Inc. (management consultants), Alexandria, Va., president, 1978—. *Military service:* U.S. Army, 1969.

WRITINGS: Employing the Handicapped, American Management Association, 1981; *The Aging Factor,* American Management Association, 1982. Editor of management guides. Contributor to management journals.

SIDELIGHTS: Zimmer wrote: "The modern novelist Mark Harris once commented that he had learned to write, and it was up to the reader to learn to read. This had a profound effect on me, because it suggests the difficulty of the writer's craft. Like long-distance runners, we train constantly. Great writers have both inspired and humbled me; among these, Yeats and Henry James, and Samuel Johnson, who said, 'Anyone who writes for other than money is a damn fool.' Yes, it's a great feeling to know that someone walked into a bookstore and paid to read something I wrote! Equally important, it is gratifying and fulfilling to know that you have produced something which is of value to other persons."

*   *   *

ZINDEL, Bonnie   1943-

PERSONAL: Born May 3, 1943, in New York, N.Y.; daughter of Jack C. (a certified public accountant) and Claire (Bromberg) Hildebrand; married Paul Zindel (a writer), October 25, 1973; children: David, Lizabeth. *Education:* Hofstra University, B.A., 1964. *Residence:* Beverly Hills, Calif. *Agent:* Curtis Brown, Ltd., 575 Madison Ave., New York, N.Y. 10022.

CAREER: Clairol, New York City, in public relations, 1964; Cleveland Playhouse, Cleveland, Ohio, director of public relations and audience development, 1969-71; WCLV-Radio, Cleveland, producer and interviewer for intermission feature of Boston Symphony programs, 1970-72; Henry Street Settlement Urban Life Center, New York City, in public relations, 1971-72; writer, 1972—.

WRITINGS: "I Am a Zoo" (two-act play), first produced in New York City at Jewish Repertory Theatre, 1978; (with husband, Paul Zindel) *A Star for the Latecomer* (for young adults), Harper, 1980.

WORK IN PROGRESS: Coming of Age in a Dunne Buggy, a novel; "The Latecomer," a stage adaptation of her novel, *A Star for the Latecomer,* with P. Zindel.

SIDELIGHTS: In *A Star for the Latecomer,* the character Mrs. Hillary is determined that her daughter Brooke should have the theatrical career she had once envisioned for herself. Stardom, however, is not Brooke's ambition; she would rather marry and pursue her talents for homemaking. But Mrs. Hillary is dying, and Brooke is torn between her own wishes for marriage and a family and a desire to at least partly fulfill her mother's dream. "The authors have addressed themselves to an important aspect of life with a less than heavy hand and a brisk, readable and unsentimental style," wrote Jennifer Moody of the *Times Literary Supplement.* "The character of Mrs. Hillary is not that of [a] monster. . . . It is simply that she has the willpower for two, and she compels increasing respect as she braves pain and weakness for what she sees as her daughter's good." *Publishers Weekly* added, "The Zindels deserve honors for creating a touching, compassionate and illuminating story of two loving people in conflict."

Bonnie Zindel wrote: "There's a little voice inside each of us that tells us the truth. One has to just learn how to listen to it, interpret it. It's a kind of wonderful language hidden in our nerves, in our heartbeat, in our emotions. It tells us who we are. I try to interpret mine and write about it."

BIOGRAPHICAL/CRITICAL SOURCES: Scholastic, April 3, 1980; *Publishers Weekly,* April 18, 1980; *Times Literary Supplement,* July 18, 1980.

*   *   *

ZOLYNAS, Al(girdas Richard)   1945-

PERSONAL: Born June 1, 1945, in Dornbirn, Austria; came to the United States in 1960, naturalized citizen, 1965; son of Konstantine (an accountant) and Ona (an office worker; maiden name, Smilgevicius) Zolynas; married Arlen Williams, June 24, 1967. *Education:* University of Illinois, B.A., 1966; University of Utah, M.A., 1969, Ph.D., 1973. *Home:* 11356 Trebol, San Diego, Calif. 92126.

CAREER: Westminster College, Salt Lake City, Utah, instructor in English, 1969-71; Southwest State University, Marshall, Minn., instructor, 1971-72, assistant professor of English, 1972-75, writer-in-residence, 1974-75; Weber State College, Ogden, Utah, lecturer, 1976-77; United States International University, San Diego, Calif., associate professor of English, 1978—. Member of Minnesota Poetry Outloud; member of humanities panel of Southwest Minnesota Arts and Humanities Council, 1974-75; gives poetry readings. *Member:* Poets and Writers, World Runners, San Diego Zen Center. *Awards, honors:* Cortez Award from Weber State College.

WRITINGS: The New Physics (poems), Wesleyan University Press, 1979.

Work represented in anthologies, including *The Sensuous President; Eating the Menu: American Poetry, 1963-73; The Great Oasis*. Contributor of poems and reviews to magazines, including *Poetry Australia, Western Review, Dakotah Territory, Poet and Critic, Aspen Leaves,* and *Crazy Horse,* and newspapers. Poetry editor of *Appalachian Journal*, 1974-78.

WORK IN PROGRESS: A collection of poems, tentatively titled *Unfathomable Excellence Penetrating Everywhere.*

SIDELIGHTS: Zolynas commented: "While it is difficult for me to 'abstract' what I do as a poet, or to describe what motivates me to write, I think I can sum up my attitude by borrowing a phrase from Kenneth Rexroth. He says a poet is one who 'creates sacramental relationships.' At my best, I would like to think that I do that—sacramental relationships between people, between 'things,' and between the processes we are all apart of."

AVOCATIONAL INTERESTS: "Running long-distance road races for World Runners, an organization committed to communicating the message that world hunger can be ended in this century."

*   *   *

ZUCKERMAN, Alan S(aul)   1945-

PERSONAL: Born February 16, 1945, in Brooklyn, N.Y.; son of Udah Jacob (a truck driver; in sales) and Edith (Rochwarger) Zuckerman; married Roberta Susan Brenner (in insurance sales), October 21, 1965; children: Gregory, Ezra, Shara. *Education:* Brooklyn College of the City University of New York, B.A., 1966; Princeton University, M.A., 1968, Ph.D., 1971. *Religion:* Jewish. *Home:* 177 Morris Ave., Providence, R.I. 02906. *Office:* Department of Political Science, Brown University, Providence, R.I. 02912.

CAREER: Brown University, Providence, R.I., assistant professor, 1970-77, associate professor of political science, 1977—. Visiting associate professor at Tel-Aviv University, 1977-78; vice-president of Providence Hebrew Day School; member of Rhode Island Bureau of Jewish Education. *Member:* International Political Science Association, American Political Science Association, Association for the Sociological Study of Jewry. *Awards, honors:* Fellow of Social Science Research Council at University of Essex; fellow of Memorial Foundation for Jewish Culture.

WRITINGS: Political Clienteles in Power, Sage Publications, 1975; *Politics of Faction: Christian Democratic Rule in Italy,* Yale University Press, 1979.

WORK IN PROGRESS: Strategies of Survival: Modern Jewish Society and Politics, with Calvin Goldscherder.

SIDELIGHTS: Zuckerman has conducted field research in Italy and Israel.

*   *   *

ZUESSE, Evan M.   1940-

PERSONAL: Born October 20, 1940, in Washington, D.C.; son of Marin L. and Marcia (Jacobson) Zuesse; married Ingrid M. Kronberg, June 28, 1962; children: Rebecca M., Jonathan G., Emily A. *Education:* Dartmouth College, B.A. (cum laude), 1962; University of Chicago, M.A., 1964, Ph.D., 1971.

CAREER: Ministry of Education and Culture, Haifa, Israel, instructor, 1964; Beth Hasefer Hatichon, Kiryat Chaim, Israel, teacher, 1964-66; Allegheny College, Meadville, Pa., assistant professor of history of religion, 1969-75; Case Western Reserve University, Cleveland, Ohio, assistant professor of religion, 1975—. Director of Allegheny Jewish Community College, 1969—. *Member:* American Academy of Religion, African Studies Association.

WRITINGS: Ritual and World View: A Study of Ritual Symbolism in Some Traditional African Societies, E. J. Brill, 1975; *Ritual Cosmos: The Sanctification of Life in African Religions,* Ohio University Press, 1979. Contributor to scholarly journals.*

*   *   *

ZWAANSTRA, Henry   1936-

BRIEF ENTRY: Born January 1, 1936, in Grangeville, Idaho. American historian, educator, and author. Zwaanstra began teaching at Calvin Theological Seminary in 1963. He has been a professor of church history since 1973. He wrote *Reformed Thought and Experience in a New World: A Study of the Christian Reformed Church and Its American Environment, 1890-1918* (J. K. Kok, 1973). *Address:* Calvin Theological Seminary, 3233 Burton St. S.E., Grand Rapids, Mich. 49506. *Biographical/critical sources: Directory of American Scholars,* Volume IV: *Philosophy, Religion, and Law,* 7th edition, Bowker, 1978.